Chambers
pocket
dictionary

Chambers

CHAMBERS
An imprint of Chambers Harrap Publishers Ltd
7 Hopetoun Crescent
Edinburgh, EH7 4AY

Previous edition published 2001
This edition published by Chambers Harrap Publishers Ltd 2006

A CIP catalogue record for this book is available from the British
Library.

ISBN-13: 978 0550 10254 6
ISBN-10: 0550 10254 X

Designed and typeset by Chambers Harrap Publishers Ltd,
Edinburgh
Printed in Great Britain by Clays Ltd, St Ives plc

Contents

Contributors

Project Editor
Ian Brookes

Editors
Pat Bulhosen
Dana Darby Johnson
Andrew Holmes

Editorial Assistance
Vicky Aldus
Rosalind Fergusson
Alice Grandison
Mary O'Neill

Publishing Manager
Patrick White

Data Management
Gerry Breslin
Patrick Gaherty
Siri Hansen

Prepress
Susan Lawrie
Clair Simpson

Preface

Chambers Pocket Dictionary is derived from *Chambers Compact Dictionary* and provides up-to-date, straightforward and jargon-free definitions of words commonly used in contemporary English.

Entries show the spelling and meaning of words as well as giving help with irregular verbs, nouns and adjectives. Pronunciation guidance is given for words that may cause difficulty; the sounds of words are shown using the International Phonetic Alphabet, a key to which is provided below. Words derived from the main entry word, idioms and phrasal verbs are grouped alphabetically at the end of entries. A further feature of the dictionary is the presence of numerous notes on usage; these are scattered through the book offering practical help on areas of language where there is frequent uncertainty. Users who seek more detailed information about how the dictionary is arranged should look at the model of dictionary layout on pages vi-vii.

The compilers of this dictionary have tried to keep in mind the needs of the dictionary user and provide the answers to probable queries without omitting important information. We hope this makes *Chambers Pocket Dictionary* a reliable companion.

Pronunciation guide

English sounds

a	h<u>a</u>t	iː	m<u>e</u>	aɪ	b<u>y</u>	ɛə	h<u>air</u>	ʃ	<u>sh</u>e
ɑː	b<u>aa</u>	ɒ	l<u>o</u>t	eɪ	b<u>ay</u>	ʊə	p<u>oor</u>	ʒ	vi<u>s</u>ion
ɛ	b<u>e</u>t	ɔː	r<u>aw</u>	ɔɪ	b<u>oy</u>	θ	<u>th</u>in		
ə	<u>a</u>go	ʌ	c<u>u</u>p	aʊ	n<u>ow</u>	ð	<u>th</u>e		
ɜː	f<u>ur</u>	ʊ	p<u>u</u>t	oʊ	g<u>o</u>	j	<u>y</u>ou		
ɪ	f<u>i</u>t	uː	t<u>oo</u>	ɪə	h<u>ere</u>	ŋ	ri<u>ng</u>		

Common sounds in foreign words

French						Other languages	
ã	gr<u>an</u>d	œ̃	<u>un</u>	y	s<u>u</u>r	ç	German i<u>ch</u>
ɛ̃	v<u>in</u>	ø	p<u>eu</u>	ɥ	h<u>ui</u>t	x	Scottish lo<u>ch</u>
ɔ̃	b<u>on</u>	œ	c<u>oeu</u>r	ʀ	<u>r</u>ue	ł	Welsh L<u>l</u>an

Model of dictionary layout

Main headwords are shown in bold type.

Example phrases in italics illustrate meanings where this is helpful.

Entries may contain:
o Words derived from the headword
+ Idioms
◊ Phrasal verbs

Pronunciation guidance is given using the International Phonetic Alphabet (see page v).

Plural forms of nouns, past-tense and present-participle forms of verbs, and comparative and superlative forms of adjectives are shown in bold italic type where there could be doubt about them.

Parts of speech are marked with traditional labels, eg *n*, *vb*, *adj*, *adv*. A change within an entry to a new part of speech is indicated by an arrow.

Compounds formed from a main headword are listed as separate entries.

patch *n* **1** a piece of material sewn on or applied, eg to a garment or piece of fabric, etc, so as to cover a hole or reinforce a worn area. **2** a plot of earth: *a vegetable patch*. **3** a pad or cover worn as protection over an injured eye. **4** a small expanse contrasting with its surroundings: *patches of ice*. **5** a scrap or shred. **6** *colloq* a phase or period of time: *We went through a bad patch*. **7** *slang* the area patrolled by a police officer or covered by a particular police station. **8** *comput* a set of instructions added to a program to correct an error. ➤ *vb* **1** to mend (a hole or garment) by sewing a patch or patches on or over it. **2** (*also* **patch sth up**) to repair it hastily and temporarily. **3** *comput* to make a temporary correction in (a program).
o **patchy** *adj*. ◆ **not a patch on sb** or **sth** *colloq* not nearly as good as them. ◊ **patch sth up** *colloq* to settle (a quarrel), etc.

patchwork *n* **1** needlework done by sewing together small pieces of contrasting patterned fabric. **2** a piece of work produced in this way. **3** a variegated expanse: *a patchwork of fields*.

pate *n, old use or facetious* the head or skull.

pâté /ˈpateɪ/ *n* a spread made from minced meat, fish or vegetables blended with herbs, spices, etc.

pâté de foie gras see under FOIE GRAS

patella /pəˈtɛlə/ *n* (*patellae* /-ˈtɛliː/ *or* *patellas*) *anat* the KNEECAP.

paten /ˈpatən/ *n, relig* a circular metal plate on which the bread is placed in the celebration of the Eucharist.

patent /ˈpeɪtənt, ˈpatənt/ *n* **1** an official licence from the government granting a person or business the sole right, for a certain period, to make and sell a particular article. **2** the right so granted. **3** the invention so protected. ➤ *vb* to obtain a patent for (an invention, design, etc). ➤ *adj* **1** very evident: *a patent lie*. **2** concerned with the granting of, or protection by, patents. **3** of a product: made or protected under patent. **4** open for inspection: *letters patent*.
o **patentable** *adj*. o **patently** *adv* openly; clearly: *patently obvious*.

patent leather *n* leather made glossy by varnishing.

patent medicine *n, technical* a patented medicine which is available without prescription.

pater *n, old use or facetious* father.

prank *n* a playful trick; a practical joke.
○ **prankster** *n*.

praseodymium *n*, *chem* a soft silvery metallic element.

prat *n*, *slang* **1** *offensive* a fool; an ineffectual person. **2** the buttocks.

Labels indicate when the use of a word is restricted to a particular region, subject or style of language.

prate *vb*, *tr & intr* to talk or utter foolishly. ➤ *n* idle chatter.

prattle *vb*, *tr & intr* to chatter or utter childishly or foolishly. ➤ *n* childish or foolish chatter.
○ **prattler** *n*.

We regard it as normal for verbs to be used transitively (ie with an object). We indicate when a verb can be used intransitively (ie without an object).

prawn *n* a small edible shrimp-like marine crustacean.

pray *vb* (*often* **pray for sth** or **sb**) **1** *now usu intr* to address one's god, making earnest requests or giving thanks. **2** *old use*, *tr & intr* to entreat or implore: *Stop, I pray you!* **3** *tr & intr* to hope desperately. ➤ *exclam*, *old use* (now often uttered with quaint politeness or cold irony) please, or may I ask: *Pray come in* • *Who asked you, pray?*

pray A word often confused with this one is **prey**.

Usage notes give further information on aspects of English where there is frequent uncertainty.

prayer[1] /preə(r)/ *n* **1** an address to one's god, making a request or giving thanks. **2** the activity of praying. **3** an earnest hope, desire or entreaty.

prayer[2] /preɪə(r)/ *n* someone who prays.

Superscript numbers distinguish between identically spelt words.

prayerful *adj* **1** of someone: devout; tending to pray a lot or often. **2** said of a speech, etc: imploring.

praying mantis see under MANTIS

preach *vb* **1** *tr & intr* to deliver (a sermon) as part of a religious service. **2** (*often* **preach at sb**) to give them advice in a tedious or obtrusive manner. **3** to advise or advocate something. ○ **preacher** *n* someone who preaches, esp a minister of religion.

Small capital letters indicate a cross-reference to an entry in another part of the dictionary.

preamble *n* an introduction or preface, eg to a speech or document.

prearrange *vb* to arrange something in advance. ○ **prearrangement** *n*.

prebend /'prebənd/ *n* **1** an allowance paid out of the revenues of a cathedral or collegiate church to its canons or chapter members. **2** the piece of land, etc which is the source of such revenue. **3** a prebendary. ○ **prebendal** /prɪ'bendəl/ *adj*.

Abbreviations

abbrev	abbreviation	med	medicine
adj	adjective	meteorol	meteorology
adv	adverb	mil	military
agric	agriculture	mus	music
alt	alternative	myth	mythology
anat	anatomy	N	North
archit	architecture	n	noun
astrol	astrology	N Am	North American
astron	astronomy	naut	nautical
Aust	Australian	NZ	New Zealand
bacteriol	bacteriology	orig	originally
biochem	biochemistry	ornithol	ornithology
biol	biology	pathol	pathology
bot	botany	pfx	prefix
Brit	British	pharmacol	pharmacology
c	century (eg 15c)	philos	philosophy
c.	circa (ie	photog	photography
	approximately)	physiol	physiology
Can	Canadian	pl	plural
chem	chemistry	pol	politics
cinematog	cinematography	prep	preposition
C of E	Church of England	psychoanal	psychoanalysis
colloq	colloquial	psychol	psychology
comb	combining	RC	Roman Catholic
conj	conjunction	relig	religion
derog	derogatory	S	South
E	East	S Afr	South African
ecol	ecology	sb	somebody
econ	economy	Scot	Scottish
educ	education	sfx	suffix
elec	electricity	sing	singular
Eng	English	sociol	sociology
eng	engineering	sth	something
esp	especially	telecomm	telecommunications
EU	European Union	theat	theatre
euphem	euphemistic	tr	transitive
exclam	exclamation	trig	trigonometry
geog	geography	TV	television
geol	geology	US	United States
geom	geometry	USA	United States of
gram	grammar		America
hist	history, historical	usu	usually
hortic	horticulture	vb	verb
intr	intransitive	vet	veterinary
ling	linguistics	W	West
maths	mathematics	zool	zoology
mech	mechanics		

Aa

A¹ or **a** *n* (**As**, **A's** or **a's**) **1** the first letter of the English alphabet. **2** (*usu* **A**) the highest grade or quality. **3** (**A**) *mus* the sixth note in the scale of C major. **4** (*usu* **A**) someone or something that is first in a sequence, or belonging to a class arbitrarily designated A. ♦ **from A to B** from one place or point to another. **from A to Z** from beginning to end.

A² *abbrev* ampere.

a (used before a consonant or consonant sound, eg *a boy, a one*) or (used before a vowel or vowel sound, eg *an egg, an hour*) **an** *indefinite article* **1** used chiefly with a singular noun, usu where the thing referred to has not been mentioned before, or where it is not a specific example known to the speaker or listener. **2** used before a word describing quantity: *a dozen eggs*. **3 a** any or every: *A fire is hot*; **b** (used after *not* or *never*): any at all: *not a chance*. **4** each or every; per: *once a day*. **5** one of a specified type: *He's a real Romeo*.

> **a** Some people use **an** before words beginning with a weakly sounded *h*, eg *an hotel, an historic occasion*. This use of **an** is no more nor less correct than **a**; however, it is sometimes regarded as old-fashioned.

a-¹ *pfx*, signifying **1** to or towards: *ashore*. **2** in the process or state of something: *abuzz* ● *aroving*. **3** on: *afire*. **4** in: *asleep*.

a-² or (*before a vowel, and in scientific compounds before* **h**) **an-** *pfx*, signifying not; without; opposite to: *amoral* ● *anaemia*.

Å *symbol* Ångström or angstrom.

AA *abbrev* **1** Alcoholics Anonymous. **2** anti-aircraft. **3** *Brit* Automobile Association.

A & R *abbrev* artists and repertoire.

aardvark /ˈɑːdvɑːk/ *n* a nocturnal African mammal with a large snout and long ears.

AB *abbrev, Brit* able seaman.

ab- *pfx*, signifying opposite to; from; away from: *abnormal*.

aback *adv* (*always* **taken aback**) surprised or shocked.

abacus *n* an arithmetical calculating device consisting of several rows of beads strung on horizontal rods mounted in a frame.

abaft *naut, adv* in or towards the stern of a ship. ➢ *prep* behind.

abalone /æbəˈloʊnɪ/ *n* a marine gastropod mollusc with an oval shell lined with MOTHER-OF-PEARL.

abandon *vb* **1** to give something up completely: *I abandoned all hope of winning*. **2** to leave or desert (a person, post of responsibility, etc): *He abandoned his wife and children*. **3** (*usu* **abandon oneself to sth**) to let oneself be overcome by (strong emotion, passion, etc) ➢ *n* uncontrolled or uninhibited behaviour. ○ **abandonment** *n*.

abandoned *adj* **1** deserted. **2** having, or behaving as if one has, no sense of shame or morality.

abase *vb* to humiliate or degrade (someone or oneself). ○ **abasement** *n*.

abashed *adj* embarrassed, esp because of shyness.

abate *vb, tr & intr* to become or make less strong or severe. ○ **abatement** *n*.

abattoir /ˈæbətwɑː(r)/ *n* a slaughterhouse.

abbess *n* a woman in charge of a group of nuns living in an abbey.

abbey /ˈæbɪ/ *n* **1** a group of nuns or monks living as a community. **2** the buildings occupied by such a community. **3** a church associated with such a community.

abbot *n* the man in charge of a group of monks living in an abbey.

abbreviate *vb* to shorten, esp to represent (a long word) by a shortened form. ○ **abbreviation** *n*.

ABC *n* (**ABCs** or **ABC's**) **1** the alphabet. **2** the basic facts about a subject. **3** an alphabetical guide.

abdicate *vb* **1** *tr & intr* to give up one's right to (the throne). **2** to refuse or fail to carry out (one's responsibilities). ○ **abdication** *n*.

abdomen *n, zool, anat* **1** in vertebrates: the lower part of the main body cavity, containing the stomach, bowels and reproductive organs. **2** in arthropods, eg insects: the rear part of the body. ○ **abdominal** /æbˈdɒmɪnəl/ *adj*.

abduct *vb* to take someone away illegally. ○ **abduction** *n*. ○ **abductor** *n*.

abeam *adv* in a line at right angles to the length of a ship or aircraft.

aberrant *adj* differing or departing from what is normal or accepted as standard.

aberration *n* a temporary and usu brief change from what is normal or accepted as standard.

abet *vb* (**abetted, abetting**) to help or encourage someone to do something wrong. See also AID AND ABET at AID.

abeyance *n* of laws, customs, etc: the condition of not being used or followed, usu only temporarily: *fall into abeyance.*

abhor *vb* to hate

abhorrent *adj* hated or horrible. ○ **abhorrence** *n.*

abide *vb* (**abided** or **abode**) **1** (*esp with negatives and in questions*) to put up with or tolerate someone or something: *We cannot abide dishonesty.* **2** *intr* (**abide by sth**) to follow or obey (a decision, rule, etc). **3** *intr, old use* to remain.

abiding *adj* permanent or continuing for a long time.

ability *n* (**-ies**) **1** the power, skill or knowledge to do something. **2** great skill or intelligence.

abject *adj* **1** of living conditions, etc: extremely sad or miserable. **2** complete and total: *an abject apology.* ○ **abjectly** *adv.*

abjure *vb, formal* to promise solemnly, esp under oath, to stop believing or doing something.

ablative *gram, n* **1** in eg Latin: the form or CASE² (sense 7) of a noun, pronoun or adjective which expresses the place, means, manner or instrument of an action. **2** a noun, etc in this case.

ablaze *adj* **1** burning. **2** brightly lit. **3** (*usu* **ablaze with sth**) feeling (an emotion) with great passion.

able *adj* **1** having the necessary knowledge, power, time, opportunity, etc to do something. **2** clever or skilful. ○ **ably** *adv.*

able-bodied *adj* fit and healthy.

able seaman *n* a sailor able to perform all duties, with more training and a higher rating than an ORDINARY SEAMAN.

ablution *n* (*usu* **ablutions**) **1** the washing of the body, the hands or ritual vessels as part of a religious ceremony. **2** *colloq or facetious* the ordinary washing of oneself.

ABM *abbrev* anti-ballistic missile, a type of rocket which can destroy an enemy's ballistic missile in the air.

abnegation *n, formal* **1** the act of giving up something one wants. **2** the act of renouncing a doctrine, etc.

abnormal *adj* not normal or usual. ○ **abnormality** *n* (**-ies**). ○ **abnormally** *adv.*

Abo or **abo** *n, offensive, slang* an Australian aborigine.

aboard *adv, prep* **1** on, on to, in or into (a ship, train, aircraft, etc). **2** *naut* alongside.

abode *n, formal* the house or place where one lives.

abolish *vb* to stop or put an end to (customs, laws, etc).

abolition *n* the act of abolishing something; the state of being abolished.

A-bomb short for ATOM BOMB

abominable *adj* **1** greatly disliked or found loathsome, usu because morally bad. **2** *colloq* very bad. ○ **abominably** *adv.*

abominable snowman *n* a YETI.

abominate *vb* to hate something greatly. ○ **abomination** *n.*

aboriginal /abəˈrɪdʒɪnəl/ *adj* **1** of inhabitants: earliest known; indigenous. **2** referring to the Aboriginals of Australia or one of their languages. ➤ *n* (**Aboriginal**) a member of a people who were the original inhabitants of Australia.

aborigine /abəˈrɪdʒɪnɪ/ *n* **1** (*also* **Aborigine**) an Aboriginal. **2** a member of any people who were the first to live in a country or region.

abort *vb* **1** *intr* to expel (an embryo or fetus) spontaneously from the uterus before it is capable of surviving independently. **2** *intr* of a baby: to be lost in this way. **3** to induce termination of pregnancy before the embryo or fetus is capable of surviving independently. **4** *tr & intr* to stop (a plan, etc), or to be stopped, before reaching a successful conclusion.

abortion *n* **1** the removal of an embryo or fetus from the uterus before it is sufficiently developed to survive independently. Also called **termination, induced abortion. 2** the spontaneous expulsion of an embryo or fetus from the uterus before it is sufficiently developed to survive independently. Also called **miscarriage, spontaneous abortion. 3** the failure of a plan, project, etc. ○ **abortionist** *n.*

abortive *adj* unsuccessful.

abound *vb, intr* to exist in large numbers.

about *prep* **1** concerning someone or something; on the subject of them or it. **2** near to something. **3** centring on something. **4** in or at points throughout something. **5** all around or surrounding someone or something. ➤ *adv* **1** nearly or approximately. **2** nearby: *Is there anyone about?* **3** scattered here and there. **4** all around; in all directions. **5** in or to the opposite direction: *turn about.* **6** on the move; in action: *up and again after an illness.* ◆ **about to do sth** on the point of doing it.

about turn or **about face** *n* **1** a turn made so that one is facing in the opposite direction. **2** a complete change of plan or behaviour.

above *prep* **1** higher than or over something. **2** more or greater than something in quantity or degree. **3** higher or superior to someone in rank, importance, ability, etc. **4** too good for a specified thing: *above petty quarrels.* **5** beyond the understanding or abilities of someone. ➤ *adv* **1** at, in or to a higher position, place, rank, etc. **2** in an earlier passage of text. ➤ *n* (**the above**) something already mentioned.

above-board *adj* honest; not secret.

abracadabra *exclam* a word which supposedly has magic power, used by people when doing magic tricks.

abrasion *n* **1** a damaged area of skin, rock, etc which has been worn away by scraping or rubbing. **2** the act of scraping or rubbing away.

abrasive *adj* **1** of a material: capable of wearing something away by rubbing. **2** of a material: used to polish another surface by rubbing. **3** of people or their actions: likely to offend others by being harsh and rude. ➤ *n* any hard material that is used to wear away the surface of other materials.

abreast *adv* side by side and facing in the

same direction. ♦ **abreast of sth** up to date concerning it.

abridge vb to make (a book, etc) shorter. ○ **abridged** adj. ○ **abridgement** or **abridgment** n.

abroad adv **1** in or to a foreign country or countries. **2** in circulation; at large. **3** over a wide area.

abrogate vb to cancel (a law, agreement, etc) formally or officially. ○ **abrogation** n.

abrupt adj **1** sudden and unexpected. **2** esp of speech, etc: rather sharp and rude. ○ **abruptly** adv. ○ **abruptness** n.

abscess /'absɛs/ n, pathol a collection of pus in a cavity surrounded by inflamed tissue.

abscissa /ab'sɪsə/ n (**abscissas** or **abscissae** /-'sɪsiː/) maths on a graph: the first of a pair of numbers x and y, known as the x-coordinate, which specifies the distance of a point from the vertical or y-axis. Compare **ORDINATE**.

abscond vb, intr to depart or leave quickly and usu secretly.

abseil /'abseɪl/ vb, intr to go down a steep drop using a double rope wound round the body and fixed to a point higher up. ➢ n an act of abseiling. ○ **abseiling** n.

absence n **1** the state of being away. **2** the time when a person is away. **3** the state of not existing or of being lacking.

absent adj /'absənt/ **1** not in its or one's expected place; not present. **2** not existing, esp where normally to be expected. **3** not paying attention. ➢ vb /ab'sɛnt/ (now always **absent oneself**) to stay away from a meeting, gathering, etc. ○ **absently** adv.

absentee n someone who is not present at a particular time. ○ **absenteeism** n continual absence from work, school, etc.

absent-minded adj forgetting or not noticing things, esp because of thinking about something else. ○ **absent-mindedly** adv. ○ **absent-mindedness** n.

absinthe or **absinth** n a strong green alcoholic drink flavoured with plants such as aniseed and wormwood.

absolute adj **1** complete; total; perfect. **2** without limits; not controlled by anything or anyone else. **3** certain; undoubted. **4** not relative: an absolute standard. **5** pure. **6** gram **a** of a clause or phrase: standing alone, ie not dependent on the rest of the sentence. Compare **RELATIVE** (adj sense 5b); **b** of an adjective or a transitive verb: standing alone, ie without a noun or an object respectively. ➢ n a rule, standard, etc thought to be right in all situations.

absolutely adv **1** completely. **2** independently of anything else. **3** colloq really; very much. **4** with negatives at all: absolutely nothing. ➢ interj yes; certainly.

absolute majority n in an election: a number of votes for a candidate which is greater than the number of votes received by all the other candidates put together.

absolute zero n, physics the lowest temperature theoretically possible, 0 K on the **KELVIN SCALE**, equivalent to $-273.15°C$ or $-459.67°F$.

absolution n the formal forgiving of a person's sins by a priest.

absolutism n government by a person who has total power. ○ **absolutist** n, adj.

absolve vb **1** (usu **absolve sb from** or **of sth**) to release them or pronounce them free from a promise, duty, blame, etc. **2** of a priest: to forgive someone formally for their sins.

absorb vb **1** to take in (water, knowledge, energy, etc). **2** to receive or take something in as part of oneself or itself. **3** to engage all of (someone's attention). **4** to reduce or lessen (the shock or force of something). **5** physics to take up (energy) without emitting it. ○ **absorbent** adj.

absorption n **1** the act of absorbing, or the process of being absorbed. **2** the state of having all one's attention occupied by something.

abstain vb, intr (usu **abstain from sth** or **from doing sth**) **1** to choose not to take, have or do it. **2** to formally record one's intention not to vote in an election.

abstemious adj of people, habits, etc: taking food, alcohol, etc in very limited amounts.

abstention n **1** the act of choosing not to do something. **2** an instance of abstaining from voting.

abstinence n the practice or state of choosing not to do, have, or take something, esp sex or alcohol. ○ **abstinent** adj.

abstract adj /'abstrakt/ **1** referring to something which exists only as an idea or quality. **2** concerned with ideas and theory rather than with things which really exist or could exist. **3** of an art form, esp painting: that represents the subject by shapes and patterns, etc rather than in the shape or form it actually has. **4** gram of a noun: denoting a quality, condition or action rather than a physical thing. ➢ n /'abstrakt/ **1** a brief statement of the main points (of a book, speech, etc). **2** an abstract idea, theory, etc. **3** an example of abstract painting, etc. ➢ vb /ab'strakt/ **1** to take out or remove something. **2** to summarize (a book, speech, etc).

abstracted adj of a person: thinking about something so much that they do not notice what is happening around them. ○ **abstractedly** adv.

abstraction n **1** the act, or an example, of abstracting something. **2** something which exists as a general idea rather than as an actual example. **3** the state of thinking about something so much that one does not notice what is happening around one.

abstruse adj hard to understand.

absurd adj **1** not at all suitable or appropriate. **2** ridiculous; silly. ○ **absurdity** n (-ies). ○ **absurdly** adv.

abundance n **1** a large amount, sometimes more than is needed. **2** wealth. ○ **abundant** adj. ○ **abundantly** adv.

abuse vb /ə'bjuːz/ **1** to use (power, a system, etc) wrongly. **2** to treat someone or something cruelly or wrongly. **3** to betray (a confidence). **4** to speak rudely or insultingly to or about someone. ➢ n /ə'bjuːs/ **1** wrong use of power, a system, etc. **2** the physical, sexual, mental, or emotional maltreatment of someone, esp a child or spouse. **3** a bad or harmful use of something: *drug and alcohol abuse*. **4** rude or insulting words said to or about someone.

abusive adj insulting or rude; using insulting or rude language. ○ **abusively** adv.

abut vb (**abutted, abutting**) (usu **abut against** or **on sth**) of countries, areas of land, buildings, etc: to join, touch or lean against another.

abutment n, archit, eng the support at the end of an arch, bridge, etc.

abysmal adj, colloq extremely bad. ○ **abysmally** adv.

abyss /ə'bɪs/ n **1** a very large and deep chasm. **2** anything that seems to be bottomless or unfathomable.

AC abbrev ALTERNATING CURRENT. Compare DC.

Ac symbol, chem actinium.

a/c abbrev **1** account. **2** account current.

acacia /ə'keɪʃə/ n a tree or shrub which bears clusters of small yellow flowers.

academia n the scholarly world or life.

academic adj **1** to do with education. **2** to do with a university or college. **3** theoretical rather than practical. **4** of no practical importance, eg because impossible or unreal: *What we would do with a car is academic, since we can't afford one.* **5** of a person: fond of or having an aptitude for intellectual pursuits. ➢ n a member of the teaching or research staff at a university or college. ○ **academically** adv.

academy n (-ies) **1** a school or college that gives training in a particular subject or skill. **2** a society which encourages the study of science, literature, art or music. **3** in Scotland: a secondary school.

acanthus n **1** a plant with spiny leaves and bracts, and white, pink or purple flowers. **2** archit a conventionalized carving of an acanthus leaf used as a decoration, eg on columns.

ACAS /'eɪkæs/ abbrev, Brit Advisory, Conciliation and Arbitration Service.

accede vb, intr (often **accede to sth**) **1** to take office, esp (as **accede to the throne**) to become king or queen. **2** to agree. **3** to join with others in a formal agreement.

accelerando adv, adj, mus increasingly faster.

accelerate vb **1** tr & intr to increase the speed of something. **2** to make something happen sooner. ○ **acceleration** n.

accelerator n **1** a pedal or lever designed to control the speed of an electric motor or engine. **2** physics a piece of apparatus designed to increase the velocity of charged atomic particles.

accent n /'æksənt/ **1** the particular way words are pronounced by people who live in a parti-

cular place, belong to a particular social group, etc. **2** emphasis or stress put on a particular syllable in speaking. **3** a mark put over a vowel to show how it is pronounced. Compare DIACRITIC. **4** a feature, mark or characteristic which makes something distinct or special. **5** mus emphasis or stress placed on certain notes or chords. ➢ vb /ək'sɛnt/ **1** to mark an accent on (a written letter or syllable). **2** to emphasize or stress.

accentuate vb to emphasize, stress, or make something more evident or prominent. ○ **accentuation** n.

accept vb **1** to agree to receive (something offered). **2** tr & intr to agree to (a suggestion, proposal, etc). **3** to agree to do (a job, etc) or take on (a responsibility, etc). **4** to believe something to be true or correct. **5** to be willing to listen to and follow (advice, etc). **6** to be willing to suffer or take (blame, etc). **7** to allow someone into a group, treat them as a colleague, etc. **8** to tolerate something calmly.

acceptable adj **1** welcome or pleasing; suitable. **2** good enough, but usu only just; tolerable. ○ **acceptability** n. ○ **acceptably** adv.

acceptance n **1** the act or state of accepting something. **2** favourable reception of something. **3** a written or formal answer to an invitation, etc accepting it.

access n **1** a means of approaching or entering a place. **2** the right, opportunity or ability to use, approach, meet with or enter something. **3** comput the right and opportunity to log on to a computer system, and to read and edit its files. **4** comput the possibility of transferring data to and from a memory device. ➢ vb to locate or retrieve (information stored in the memory of a computer).

accessible adj **1** able to be reached easily. **2** willing to talk to or have friendly discussions with other people. **3** easy to understand and enjoy or get some benefit from. ○ **accessibility** n.

accession n the act or process of taking up a new office or responsibility, or of becoming a king or queen.

accessory n (-ies) **1** something additional to, but less important than, something else. **2** an item of dress, such as a bag, hat, etc which goes with a dress, coat, etc. **3** law someone who helps a criminal do something wrong.

accident n **1** an unexpected event which causes damage or harm. **2** something which happens without planning or intention: *I found it by accident.*

accidental adj **1** happening or done by accident; not planned. **2** incidental; not essential. ➢ n **1** in written music: a sign, such as a sharp or flat, put in front of a note to show that it is to be played higher or lower than the key signature indicates. **2** something which is not a necessary feature of something. ○ **accidentally** adv.

accident-prone adj of a person: frequently

causing or involved in accidents, usu minor ones.

acclaim vb **1** (usu **acclaim sb as sth**) to declare them to be a specified thing, with noisy enthusiasm. **2** to receive or welcome someone or something with noisy enthusiasm. ➢ n enthusiastic approval.

acclamation n approval or agreement demonstrated by applause or shouting.

acclimatize or **-ise** /ə'klaɪmətaɪz/ vb, tr & intr to make or become accustomed to a new place, situation, climate, etc. US equivalent **acclimate** /'akləmeɪt, ə'klaɪmət/. ○ **acclimatization** n.

accolade n **1** a sign or expression of great praise. **2** a touch on the shoulder with a sword when giving a person a knighthood.

accommodate vb **1** to provide someone with a place to stay. **2** to be large enough to hold something. **3** to oblige someone; to do them a favour. **4** to adapt or adjust something in order to make it more acceptable to or appropriate for something else.

accommodating adj helpful; willing to do what another person wants.

accommodation n **1** (also N Am **accommodations**) a room or rooms in a house or hotel in which to live. **2** willingness to accept other people's wishes, etc. **3** adaptation or adjustment.

> **accommodation** This word is often misspelt as **accomodation**: there should be two m's as well as two c's.

accompaniment n **1** something that happens or exists at the same time as something else, or which comes with something else. **2** music played to accompany a singer or another instrument.

accompanist n someone who plays a musical instrument to accompany a singer or another player.

accompany vb (**-ies, -ied**) **1** to come or go with someone. **2** to be done or found with something: The series is accompanied by a workbook. **3** to play a musical instrument to support someone who is playing another instrument or singing.

accomplice n someone who helps another commit a crime.

accomplish vb to manage to do something.

accomplished adj **1** expert or skilled. **2** completed or finished.

accomplishment n **1** a social or other skill developed through practice. **2** something special or remarkable which has been done; an achievement. **3** the finishing or completing of something.

accord vb **1** rather formal to give someone (a welcome, etc) or grant them (permission, a request, etc). **2** intr (usu **accord with sb** or **sth**) to agree or be in harmony with them. ➢ n agreement or harmony. ◆ **of one's own accord** willingly; without being told to or forced to. **with one accord** with everyone in agreement and acting at the same time.

accordance n agreement or harmony: in accordance with the law.

according adv **1** (usu **according to sb**) as said or told by them: According to my doctor I am getting better. **2** (usu **according to sth**) **a** in agreement with it: living according to your principles; **b** in proportion to it: Give to each according to his need.

accordingly adv **1** in an appropriate way: act accordingly. **2** therefore; for that reason.

accordion n a musical instrument with metal reeds blown by bellows, the melody being produced by means of buttons or a keyboard. ○ **accordionist** n.

accost vb to approach someone and speak to them, esp boldly or in a threatening way.

account n **1** a description or report. **2** an explanation, esp of one's behaviour. **3 a** an arrangement by which a bank or building society allows a person to have banking or credit facilities; **b** a deposit of money in a bank or building society. **4** a statement of the money owed to a person or company for goods or services. **5** (usu **accounts**) a record of money received and spent. **6** an arrangement by which a shop allows a person to buy goods on credit and pay for them later. ➢ vb, formal to consider someone or something to be as specified: accounted them all fools. ◆ **bring sb to account** to punish them for something wrong that has been done. **by all accounts** according to general opinion. **call sb to account** to demand an explanation from them for their action or behaviour. **hold sb to account** to consider them responsible. **on account of sth** because of it. **on no account** not for any reason. **take sth into account** or **take account of sth** to make allowances for or consider (a problem, opinion or other factor) when making a decision or assessment. ◇ **account for sth 1** to give a reason or explanation for it. **2** to make or give a reckoning of (money spent, etc). **account for sb** or **sth** to succeed in destroying or disposing of it or them.

accountable adj responsible; having to explain or defend one's actions or conduct. ○ **accountability** n.

accountant n a person whose profession is to prepare, keep or audit the financial records of a business, etc. ○ **accountancy** n.

accounting n the skill or practice of preparing or keeping the financial records of a company, etc.

accoutrements /ə'ku:trəmənts/ pl n **1** equipment. **2** a soldier's equipment apart from clothing and weapons.

accredit vb (**accredited, accrediting**) **1** (usu **accredit sth to sb** or **accredit sb with sth**) to attribute (a saying, action, etc) to them. **2** (usu **accredit sb to** or **at a place**) to send (an ambassador or diplomat) to (a foreign country) with official authority. **3** to state officially that something is of a satisfactory standard. ○ **accreditation** n.

accretion n, formal or technical **1** an extra layer of material which has formed on something else. **2** the process of separate things growing into one.

accrue vb **1** intr **a** to come in addition, as a product, result or development; **b** to be added as interest. **2** (often **accrue to sb** or **sth**) to fall to them or it naturally. **3** to collect: accrued a collection of antique vases. ○ **accrual** n.

accumulate vb **1** to collect or gather something in an increasing quantity. **2** intr to grow greater in number or quantity. ○ **accumulative** adj.

accumulation n **1** the activity or process of accumulating. **2** a heap or mass.

accumulator n **1** elec eng a storage battery that can be recharged by passing a current through it from an external direct current supply. **2** horse-racing (also **accumulator bet**) Brit a bet on four or more races, where the original money bet and any money won are bet on the next race.

accuracy n the state of being absolutely correct, esp through careful effort.

accurate adj **1** absolutely correct. **2** agreeing exactly with the truth or a standard. ○ **accurately** adv.

accursed /ə'kɜːsɪd, ə'kɜːst/ adj **1** colloq disliked or hated. **2** having been cursed.

accusation n **1** the act of accusing someone of having done something wrong. **2** law a statement charging a person with a crime. ○ **accusatory** adj.

accusative n, gram **1** in certain languages: the form or CASE² (sense 7b) of a noun, pronoun or adjective when it is the object of an action. **2** a noun, etc in this case.

accuse vb (usu **accuse sb of sth**) to charge them with (an offence). ○ **accuser** n. ○ **accusing** adj. ○ **accusingly** adv.

accustom vb (usu **accustom sb** or **oneself to sth**) to make them or oneself familiar with it.

accustomed adj usual; customary. ♦ **accustomed to sb** used to them. **accustomed to sth** familiar with or experienced in it.

ace n **1** cards the card in each of the four suits with a single symbol on it. **2** colloq someone who is extremely good at something. **3** a fighter pilot who has shot down many enemy aircraft. **4** tennis a serve that is so fast and cleverly placed that the opposing player cannot hit the ball back. ➤ adj, colloq excellent. ♦ **an ace up one's sleeve** a secret advantage, argument, etc. **within an ace of sth** or **of doing sth** very close to it: She came within an ace of winning.

acerbic /ə'sɜːbɪk/ adj **1** bitter and sour in taste. **2** bitter and harsh in manner, speech, etc.

acetate /'asəteɪt/ n **1** a salt or ester of acetic acid. **2** any of various synthetic fibres that are made from cellulose acetate.

acetic /ə'siːtɪk, ə'sɛtɪk/ adj consisting of or like vinegar.

acetic acid n a clear colourless pungent liquid present in vinegar.

acetone /'asətoʊn/ n, chem a colourless flammable volatile liquid with a characteristic pungent odour, widely used as a solvent for paints and varnishes, and as a raw material in the manufacture of plastics.

acetylene /ə'sɛtɪliːn/ n, chem a colourless highly flammable gas, used in chemical processes and in welding.

ache vb, intr **1** to feel a dull continuous pain. **2** to be the source of a dull continuous pain. **3** to want very much: I'm aching to tell him my news. ➤ n a dull continuous pain. ○ **aching** or **achy** adj (**-ier, -iest**).

achieve vb to reach, realize or attain (a goal, ambition, etc), esp through hard work. ○ **achievable** adj. ○ **achiever** n.

achievement n **1** the gaining of something, usu after working hard for it. **2** something that has been done or gained by effort.

Achilles' heel /ə'kɪliːz/ n a person's weak or vulnerable point.

Achilles' tendon n, anat the tendon situated at the back of the ankle, that connects the muscles in the calf to the heelbone.

achromatic adj **1** without colour. **2** of a lens: capable of transmitting light without separating it into colours.

acid n **1** chem any of a group of compounds that have a sour or sharp taste and react with bases to form salts. **2** slang LSD. ➤ adj **1** sour to taste. **2** of remarks, etc: expressing bitterness or anger. **3** chem containing or having the properties of an acid. ○ **acidic** adj. ○ **acidly** adv.

acid house or **Acid House** n a type of electronically produced disco music with a repetitive hypnotic beat, often associated with the use of certain drugs (esp Ecstasy), and usu played at large all-night parties.

acidify vb (**-ies, -ied**) tr & intr to make or become acid. ○ **acidification** n.

acidity n (**-ies**) **1** the quality of being acid or sour. **2** chem the extent to which something is acid, as indicated by its pH value.

acid rain n, ecol rain containing dissolved pollutants that have been released into the atmosphere as a result of the burning of fossil fuels.

the acid test n a decisive test to determine whether something is genuine or valid.

acknowledge vb **1** to admit or accept the truth of (a fact or situation). **2** to report that one has received (what has been sent). **3** to express thanks for something. **4** to show that one has noticed or recognized someone, by greeting them, nodding one's head, etc.

acknowledgement or **acknowledgment** n **1** the act of acknowledging someone or something. **2** something done, given or said to acknowledge something.

acme /'akmɪ/ n the highest point of achievement, success, etc.

acne /'aknɪ/ n a common skin disorder esp on the face, chest and back.

acolyte *n* 1 *Christianity* someone who assists a priest. 2 an assistant or attendant.

aconite *n* 1 a plant which has hooded bluish-purple flowers. 2 the narcotic analgesic drug obtained from the roots of this plant.

acorn *n* the nut-like fruit of the oak tree, which has a cup-shaped outer case.

acoustic or (*esp in senses 1 and 3*) **acoustical** *adj* 1 relating to, producing or operated by sound. 2 relating to the sense of hearing. 3 of a musical instrument, eg a guitar or piano: amplifying the sound by means of its body, not using an electrical amplifier. 4 of building materials, etc: designed so as to reduce noise. ○ **acoustically** *adv.*

acoustics *pl n* the characteristics of a room, theatre, etc that determine the nature and quality of sounds heard within it. ➣ *sing n* the scientific study of the production and properties of sound waves.

acquaint *vb* (*usu* **acquaint sb with sth**) to make them aware of or familiar with it. ◆ **be acquainted with sb** to know them personally but only slightly.

acquaintance *n* 1 slight knowledge of something or someone. 2 someone whom one knows slightly. ◆ **make sb's acquaintance** to meet someone for the first time.

acquiesce /akwɪ'ɛs/ *vb, intr* (*usu* **acquiesce in** or **to sth**) to accept it or agree to it without objection. ○ **acquiescence** *n.* ○ **acquiescent** *adj.*

acquire *vb* to get or develop something.

acquired taste *n* 1 a liking for something that develops as one has more experience of it. 2 a thing liked in this way.

acquisition *n* 1 something obtained or acquired. 2 a valuable addition to a collection, etc. 3 the act of obtaining, developing or acquiring a skill, etc.

acquisitive *adj* very eager to obtain and possess things.

acquit *vb* (**acquitted, acquitting**) (*often* **acquit sb of sth**) of a court or jury, etc: to declare a person accused of a crime to be innocent. ○ **acquittal** *n.* ◆ **acquit oneself** to behave or perform in a specified way: *They acquitted themselves with distinction.*

acre /'eɪkə(r)/ *n* 1 a measure of land area equal to 4840 square yards (4047 sq m). 2 (*usu* **acres**) *colloq* a large area. ○ **acreage** *n* the number of acres in a piece of land.

acrid *adj* 1 having a very bitter and pungent smell or taste. 2 of speech, manner, etc: sharp or bitter.

acrimony *n* bitterness in feeling, temper or speech. ○ **acrimonious** *adj.*

acrobat *n* an entertainer, eg in a circus, who performs skilful balancing acts and other athletic tricks. ○ **acrobatic** *adj.* ○ **acrobatically** *adv.*

acrobatics *sing n* the art or skill of an acrobat. ➣ *pl n* acrobatic movements.

acronym /'akrənɪm/ *n* a word made from the first letters or syllables of other words, and usu pronounced as a word in its own right, eg *NATO.*

acropolis /ə'krɒpəlɪs/ *n* the upper fortified part or citadel of an ancient Greek city.

across *prep* 1 to, at or on the other side of something. 2 from one side of something to the other. 3 so as to cross something: *arms folded across the chest.* ➣ *adv* 1 to, at or on the other side. 2 from one side to the other. 3 in a crossword: in the horizontal direction: *6 across.* Compare DOWN¹ (*adv* sense 10). ◆ **across the board** in all cases.

acrostic *n* a poem or puzzle in which the first, last or middle letters in each line, or a combination of these, form a word or proverb.

acrylic *n* any of various synthetic products derived from acrylic acid.

act *n* 1 a thing done; a deed. 2 the process of doing something: *caught in the act.* 3 behaviour that is not a sincere expression of feeling: *Her shyness is just an act.* 4 a a short piece of entertainment, usu one of a series in a variety show; **b** the person or people performing this. 5 a major division of a play, opera, etc. ➣ *vb* 1 *intr* to behave or function in a specified way: *act tough.* 2 *intr* to do something: *We need to act fast.* 3 *intr* to perform in a play or film. 4 a to perform (a part) in a play or film; **b** to perform (a play). 5 to play the part of someone or something: *to act the fool.* 6 *intr* (**act as sb** or **sth**) to perform the actions or functions of (a specified person or thing): *He acted as caretaker until an appointment was made.* 7 *intr* (**act for sb**) to stand in as substitute for them. 8 *intr* to show feelings one does not really have. ◆ **get in on the act** *colloq* to start taking part in some profitable activity, plan, etc in order to share in the benefits. **get one's act together** *colloq* to become organized and ready for action. ◇ **act on** or **upon sth** to follow (advice, instructions, etc).

acting *n* the profession or art of performing in a play or film. ➣ *adj* temporarily doing someone else's job or duties: *the acting headmaster.*

actinium *n, chem* a radioactive metal found in uranium ores.

action *n* 1 the process of doing something: *to put ideas into action.* 2 something done. 3 activity, force or energy: *a woman of action.* 4 a movement or gesture. 5 the working part of a machine, instrument, etc; a mechanism. 6 a battle; fighting: *He saw action in Iraq.* 7 (**the action**) the events of a play, film, etc. 8 *colloq* (**the action**) exciting activity or events going on around one. 9 a legal case. ◆ **out of action** not working.

actionable *adj* giving reasonable grounds for legal action.

action-packed *adj, colloq* filled with exciting activity.

action replay *n* on television: the repeating of a piece of recorded action, eg the scoring of a goal in football, usu in slow motion or from another angle.

action stations pl n **1** positions taken by soldiers ready for battle. **2** colloq posts assumed in readiness for any special combined task or action.

activate vb **1** to make something start working or go into operation. **2** to make (a material) radioactive. **3** to increase the speed of or to cause (a chemical reaction). ○ **activation** n.

active adj **1** of a person, etc: full of energy. **2** of a machine, etc: operating; working. **3** having an effect: the active ingredients. **4** of a volcano: liable to erupt; not extinct. **5** physics radioactive. **6** gram **a** relating to a verbal construction in which the subject performs the action or has the state described by the verb, as in the man fell, smoking kills you and God exists. Compare PASSIVE (sense 3a); **b** relating to the verb in such a construction. ➣ n, gram **1** (also **active voice**) the form or forms that an active verb takes. **2** an active verb or construction. ○ **actively** adv.

active service n military service in the battle area.

activist n someone who works for political or social change. ○ **activism** n.

activity n (-ies) **1** the state of being active or busy. **2** (often **activities**) something that people do, esp for pleasure, interest, exercise, etc.

actor n a person who performs in plays or films, esp as their profession.

actress n a female actor.

actual adj **1** existing as fact; real. **2** not imagined, estimated or guessed. **3** current; present.

actuality n (-ies) fact; reality.

actually adv **1** really; in fact. **2** usu said in surprise or disagreement: as a matter of fact.

actuary n (-ies) someone who calculates insurance risks, and gives advice to insurance companies, etc on what premiums to set. ○ **actuarial** /-'ɛərɪəl/ adj.

actuate vb to make (a mechanism, etc) go into action.

acuity /ə'kjuːɪtɪ/ n sharpness or acuteness, eg of the mind or vision.

acumen /'akjʊmən/ n the ability to judge quickly and well.

acupressure n, alt med pressure instead of needles applied at specified points.

acupuncture n, alt med a traditional Chinese method of healing by the insertion of thin needles at specified points. ○ **acupuncturist** n.

acute adj **1** of the senses: keen or sharp. **2** of mental powers, etc: quick and very good. **3** of a disease or symptoms: arising suddenly and often severe: acute pain • acute bronchitis. Compare CHRONIC (sense 1). **4** of any bad condition or situation: extremely severe: acute drought. **5** of hospital accommodation: intended for patients with acute illnesses. **6** geom of an angle: less than 90°. Compare OBTUSE (sense 3). ➣ n (also **acute accent**) a sign placed above a vowel to indicate a particular

pronunciation, as with é in French, or, as in Spanish, to indicate that the vowel is to be stressed. ○ **acutely** adv. ○ **acuteness** n.

AD abbrev in dates: Anno Domini (Latin), in the year of our Lord, used together with a figure to indicate a specified number of years after that in which Christ was once thought to have been born. Compare BC.

> **AD** **AD** is used with dates to denote the current era. It should, strictly speaking, precede the year number, as AD 2000, but 2000 AD is now common and acceptable. It is also legitimate to write eg the 6th century AD.

ad n, colloq an ADVERTISEMENT.

adage /'adɪdʒ/ n a proverb or maxim.

adagio /ə'dɑːdʒɪoʊ/ mus, adv slowly. ➣ n a piece of music to be played slowly.

adamant adj determined not to change one's mind or opinion.

Adam's apple n, anat the projection of the THYROID cartilage, lying just beneath the skin at the front of the throat.

adapt vb **1** tr & intr to change something, oneself, etc so as to fit new circumstances. **2** to alter or modify something. ○ **adaptable** adj. ○ **adaptation** n.

adaptor or **adapter** n **1** a device designed to connect two parts of different sizes. **2** a device that enables a plug and socket with incompatible terminals to be connected, or that allows more than one electrical appliance to be powered from a single socket.

add vb **1** (also **add sth together** or **add sth to sth else**) to put together or combine (two or more things). **2** (also **add sth up**) **a** to calculate the sum of two or more numbers or quantities in order to obtain their total value; **b** intr (also **add up**) to carry out the process of addition. **3** (**add sth on**) to attach it to something else. **4** (**add sth in**) to include it. **5** to say or write something further: They added a remark about the bad weather. ◊ **add up** colloq to make sense. See also verb (sense 2b) above.

addendum n (**addenda**) **1** an addition. **2** (usu **addenda**) an extra piece of text added to the end of a book.

adder n the common European VIPER, a poisonous snake with a dark zigzag line running down its back.

addict n **1** someone who is dependent on the habitual intake of a drug. **2** colloq someone who is extremely fond of a hobby, etc: a chess addict. ○ **addiction** n. ○ **addictive** adj.

addicted adj (esp **addicted to sth**) physically or emotionally dependent on it (esp a drug or a habit) and unable to give it up.

addition n **1** the act or operation of adding. **2** someone or something that is added. **3** maths the combination of two or more numbers to obtain their sum. ○ **additional** adj. ♦ **in addition (to)** as well as (as).

additive *n* any chemical substance that is deliberately added to another substance, usu in small quantities, for a specific purpose, eg a food flavouring or colouring.

addle *vb* **1** to confuse or muddle. **2** *intr* of an egg: to go bad. ○ **addled** *adj*.

add-on *n* anything added to supplement something else.

address *n* /ə'drɛs; *chiefly US* 'adrɛs/ **1** the number or name of the house or building, and the name of the street and town, where a person lives or works. **2** *rather formal* a speech or lecture. **3** *comput* a series of characters that identifies a place to which electronic mail can be sent. **4** *comput* a number giving the place in a computer memory where a particular piece of information is stored. ➤ *vb* /ə'drɛs/ **1** to put the name and address on (an envelope, etc). **2** to make a speech, give a lecture, etc to (a group of people). **3** to speak to someone. **4** (**address oneself to sb**) to speak or write to them. **5** (*also* **address oneself to sth**) to give one's attention to (a problem, etc).

addressee *n* the person to whom a letter, etc is addressed.

adduce *vb* to mention (a fact) as a supporting reason, piece of evidence, etc.

adenoids *pl n, anat* a pair of lymph glands located in the upper part of the throat at the back of the nasal cavity. ○ **adenoidal** *adj*.

adept *adj* (*often* **adept at sth**) skilful at doing it; proficient. ➤ *n* an expert at something.

adequate *adj* **1** enough; sufficient. **2** only just satisfactory. ○ **adequacy** *n*. ○ **adequately** *adv*.

adhere *vb, intr* (*often* **adhere to sth**) **1** to stick or remain fixed to something. **2** to remain loyal to (a religion, etc). **3** to follow (a plan, rule, etc) exactly.

adherent *n* a follower; a supporter. ➤ *adj* sticking or adhering. ○ **adherence** *n*.

adhesion *n* **1** the process of sticking. **2** the sticking together of two surfaces, esp by means of an adhesive. **3** *pathol* (*often* **adhesions**) a mass or band of fibrous connective tissue that develops, esp after surgery or injury, between membranes or other structures which are normally separate.

adhesive *adj* able to make things stick together. ➤ *n* any substance that is used to bond two surfaces together.

ad hoc *adj, adv* for one particular purpose, situation, etc only: *employed on an ad hoc basis*.

adieu /ə'djuː/ *n* (**adieus** or **adieux** /-z/) a goodbye. ➤ *exclam* goodbye.

ad infinitum /ad ɪnfɪ'naɪtəm/ *adv* without limit.

adipose *adj, technical* relating to, containing or consisting of fat; fatty.

adjacent *adj* (*often* **adjacent to sth**) lying beside or next to it.

adjective *gram, n* a word that describes or modifies a noun or pronoun, as *dark* describes *hair* in *She has dark hair*. ○ **adjectival** /-'taɪvəl/ *adj*.

adjoin *vb* to be next to and joined to something. ○ **adjoining** *adj*.

adjourn *vb* **1** to put off (a meeting, etc) to another time. **2** to finish (a meeting, etc), intending to continue it at another time or place. **3** *intr* to move to another place, usu for refreshment or rest. ○ **adjournment** *n*.

adjudge *vb* to declare or judge officially.

adjudicate *vb* **1** *intr* to act as judge. **2** to give a decision on (a disagreement between two parties, etc). ○ **adjudication** *n*. ○ **adjudicator** *n*.

adjunct *n* **1** something attached or added to something else but not an essential part of it. **2** a person who is below someone else in rank.

adjure *vb, formal* to request, beg or command someone formally or solemnly.

adjust *vb* **1** to change something or oneself, etc slightly so as to be more suitable for a situation, etc. **2** to change or alter something, esp only slightly, to make it more correct or accurate. **3** to calculate or assess (the amount of money payable in an insurance claim, etc). **4** *intr* (*often* **adjust to sth**) to change so that one fits in with it or becomes suited to it. ○ **adjustable** *adj*. ○ **adjuster** *n*. ○ **adjustment** *n*.

adjutant /'adʒʊtənt/ *n* an army officer who does administrative work.

ad-lib *vb* (**ad-libbed, ad-libbing**) *tr & intr* **1** to say something without preparation, esp as a departure from a prepared text or to fill time. **2** to improvise (music, etc). ➤ *adj* of speeches, etc: improvised. ➤ *adv* (**ad lib**) **1** without preparation. **2** *colloq* without limit; freely. ○ **ad-libbing** *n*.

admin *n, colloq* ADMINISTRATION (sense I).

administer *vb* **1** to manage, govern or direct (one's affairs, an organization, etc). **2** to give out something formally: *administer justice*. **3** to supervise a person taking (an oath). **4** to apply or provide (medicine).

administrate *vb, tr & intr* to administer.

administration *n* **1** the directing, managing or governing of a company's affairs, etc. **2** a period of government by a particular party or leader. **3** the group of people who manage a company's affairs or run the business of government. ○ **administrative** *adj*.

administrator *n* someone who manages, governs, directs, etc the affairs of an organization, estate, etc.

admirable *adj* worthy of being admired; excellent. ○ **admirably** *adv*.

admiral *n* a high-ranking officer in the navy.

admire *vb* to regard with respect or approval. ○ **admiration** /admɪ'reɪʃən/ *n*. ○ **admirer** *n*. ○ **admiring** *adj*.

admissible *adj* that can be allowed or accepted, esp as proof in a court of law. ○ **admissibility** *n*.

admission *n* **1** the act of allowing someone or something to enter or join. **2** the cost of entry. **3** **a** an act of admitting the truth of something; **b** something admitted or conceded.

admit *vb* (**admitted, admitting**) **1** *tr & intr* to confess the truth of something. **2** (*also* **admit to sth**) to agree that one is responsible for (an offence, etc). **3** *intr* (**admit of sth**) *formal* to allow it as possible or valid. **4** to allow someone to enter. **5** (*also* **admit sb to sth**) to allow them to enter or join it.

admittance *n* **1** the right or permission to enter. **2** the act of entering; entry.

admittedly *adv* as one must admit.

admixture *n*, *chiefly technical* **1** anything that is added to the main ingredient of a mixture. **2** the mixture itself.

admonish *vb* to scold or tell someone off firmly but mildly. ○ **admonition** *n*.

ad nauseam /ad 'nɔːzɪam/ *adv* **1** to a disgusting or objectionable extent. **2** excessively.

ado *n* difficulty or trouble. ♦ **without more or further ado** without any more delay.

adobe /ə'dəʊbɪ/ *n* a building material made of clay and straw, and dried in the sun.

adolescent *adj* **1** of a young person: between the beginning of puberty and adulthood. **2** relating to or typical of this state. **3** *colloq* of behaviour: silly and immature. ➤ *n* a young person between puberty and adulthood. ○ **adolescence** *n* this stage of development.

Adonis *n* a handsome young man.

adopt *vb* **1** *tr & intr* to take (a child of other parents) into one's own family, becoming its legal parent. **2** to take up (a habit, position, policy, etc). **3** to take (an idea, etc) over from someone else. ○ **adoption** *n*.

adoptive *adj* that adopts or is adopted.

adorable *adj*, *colloq* very charming and attractive.

adore *vb* **1** to love someone deeply. **2** *colloq* to like something very much. **3** to worship (a god). ○ **adoration** *n*. ○ **adoring** *adj*. ○ **adoringly** *adv*.

adorn *vb* **1** to decorate. **2** to add beauty to something. ○ **adornment** *n*.

adrenal /ə'driːnəl/ *adj*, *anat* **1** relating to or situated near the kidneys. **2** referring or relating to the adrenal glands.

adrenal gland *n*, *zool*, *anat* in mammals: either of a pair of glands, situated one above each kidney, that secrete adrenalin.

adrenalin or **adrenaline** *n*, *biol* a hormone secreted by the adrenal glands in response to fear, excitement or anger, which causes an increase in heartbeat and blood pressure.

adrift *adj*, *adv* **1** of a boat: not tied up. **2** without help or guidance. **3** *colloq* off course.

adroit *adj* quick and clever in action or thought. ○ **adroitly** *adv*. ○ **adroitness** *n*.

adsorb *vb*, *technical* of a solid: to accumulate a thin layer of atoms or molecules of (a solid, liquid, or gas) on its surface. ○ **adsorbent** *adj*. ○ **adsorption** *n*.

adulation *n* excessive praise or flattery.

adult *adj* **1** fully grown; mature. **2** typical of, or suitable for, a fully grown person. ➤ *n* a fully grown person, animal, bird or plant. ○ **adulthood** *n*.

adulterate *vb* to debase something by mixing it with something inferior or harmful. ○ **adulteration** *n*.

adultery *n* sexual relations willingly undertaken between a married person and a person who is not their spouse. ○ **adulterer** *n*. ○ **adulteress** *n*. ○ **adulterous** *adj*.

adumbrate *vb*, *formal* to indicate or describe in a general way.

advance *vb* **1** *tr & intr* to put, move or go forward. **2** *intr* to make progress. **3** to help the progress of something. **4** to propose or suggest (an idea, etc). **5** to put something at an earlier time or date than that previously planned. **6** *tr & intr* of a value, price or rate: to increase. ➤ *n* **1** progress. **2** a payment made before it is due. **3** money lent to someone. **4** an increase, esp in price. **5** (*esp* **advances**) a friendly or sexual approach to a person. ➤ *adj* done, made or given beforehand. ♦ **in advance** ahead in time, place or development.

advanced *adj* **1** having progressed or developed well or far. **2** modern; new or revolutionary.

Advanced level see A LEVEL

advancement *n* promotion in rank or improvement in status.

advantage *n* **1** a favourable circumstance; benefit. **2** a circumstance that may help one to succeed, win, etc. **3** superiority over another. **4** *tennis* the point scored after DEUCE. ➤ *vb* to benefit someone or improve their position. ○ **advantageous** *adj*. ♦ **take advantage of sb** or **sth 1** to make use of a situation, a person's good nature, etc in such a way as to benefit oneself. **2** *old use* to seduce someone.

advent *n* **1** coming or arrival; first appearance. **2** (**Advent**) *Christianity* the period which includes the four Sundays before Christmas. **3** (**Advent**) *Christianity* the first or second coming of Christ.

Adventist *n*, *Christianity* a member of a group which believes in the imminent second coming of Christ.

adventitious *adj* happening by chance.

adventure *n* **1** an exciting and often dangerous experience. **2** the excitement of risk or danger: *a sense of adventure*.

adventure playground *n* a playground with things for children to climb on and equipment for them to build with.

adventurer or **adventuress** *n* **1** a person who is willing to use any means, dishonest, immoral or dangerous, to make money, obtain power, etc. **2** someone who is eager for adventure.

adventurous *adj* **1** enjoying adventure; daring. **2** full of excitement, danger, etc.

adverb *n*, *gram* a word which describes or adds to the meaning of a verb, adjective or another adverb, such as *very* and *quietly* in *They were talking very quietly*. ○ **adverbial** /əd'vɜːbɪəl/ *adj*.

adversary /'advəsərɪ/ *n* (*-ies*) **1** an opponent in a competition, etc. **2** an enemy. ○ **adversarial** *adj*.

adverse *adj* **1** unfavourable to one's interests. **2** disapproving. **3** hurtful. ○ **adversely** *adv.*

> **adverse** A word sometimes confused with this one is **averse**.

adversity *n* (*-ies*) **1** circumstances that cause trouble or sorrow. **2** a misfortune.

advert *n, colloq* an ADVERTISEMENT.

advertise /'ædvətaɪz/ *vb* **1** to draw attention to or describe (goods for sale, services offered, etc) to encourage people to buy or use them. **2** (*usu* **advertise for sth** or **sb**) to ask for or seek it or them by putting a notice in a newspaper, shop window, etc. **3** to make something known publicly or generally. ○ **advertiser** *n.* ○ **advertising** *n.*

advertisement *n* a public notice, announcement, or short television film which advertises something. Often shortened to **ad**, **advert**.

advice *n* **1** suggestions or opinions given to someone about what they should do in a particular situation. **2** *business* an official note about a transaction, etc.

advisable *adj* of action to be taken, etc: to be recommended; sensible. ○ **advisability** *n.*

advise *vb* **1** to give advice to someone. **2** to recommend something. **3** (*usu* **advise sb of sth**) to inform them about it. ○ **adviser** or **advisor** *n.*

advisedly *adv* after careful thought.

advisory *adj* appointed in order to give advice.

advocaat /'ædvəʊkɑː, -kɑːt/ *n* a liqueur made from raw eggs, sugar and brandy.

advocacy *n* (*-ies*) recommendation or active support of an idea, etc.

advocate *n* /'ædvəkət/ **1** esp in Scotland: a lawyer who speaks for the defence or prosecution in a trial. **2** someone who supports or recommends an idea, proposal, etc. ➤ *vb* /'ædvəkeɪt/ to recommend or support (an idea, proposal, etc), esp in public.

adze *n* a tool with an arched blade set at right angles to its handle, used for cutting and shaping wood.

aegis /'iːdʒɪs/ *n* protection or patronage. ♦ **under the aegis of sb** or **sth** under their supervision, support or patronage.

aeolian harp /ɪ'əʊlɪən/ *n* a box-like musical instrument which has strings stretched across a hole, and which makes musical sounds when the wind passes through it.

aeon see EON

aerate *vb* to charge (a liquid) with carbon dioxide or some other gas, eg when making fizzy drinks. ○ **aeration** *n.*

aerial *n* a wire, rod or other device, esp on a radio or television, used to receive or transmit signals. ➤ *adj* **1** relating to the air or aircraft. **2** like air.

aero- *comb form, signifying* **1** air: *aerodynamics.* **2** aircraft: *aerodrome.*

aerobatics *pl n* spectacular or dangerous manoeuvres in an aircraft or glider. ➤ *sing n* the art of performing such manoeuvres in the air. ○ **aerobatic** *adj.*

aerobics *sing n* a system of physical exercise aimed at increasing the supply of oxygen in the blood and strengthening the heart and lungs. ➤ *pl n* energetic exercises. ○ **aerobic** *adj.*

aerodrome *n, Brit* a small area of land and its associated buildings, used by private and military aircraft.

aerodynamics *sing n* the study of the movement of air relative to moving objects, eg aircraft, cars, etc. ➤ *pl n* the qualities required for fast and efficient movement through the air. ○ **aerodynamic** *adj.*

aerofoil *n* any body or part shaped so as to provide lift or thrust when it is moving through the air, eg the wings of an aeroplane.

aeronautics *sing n* the scientific study of travel through the Earth's atmosphere. ○ **aeronautic** or **aeronautical** *adj.*

aeroplane *n* a powered machine used for travelling in the air, that is heavier than air and supported in its flight by fixed wings.

aerosol *n* **1** a suspension of fine particles of a solid or liquid suspended in a gas. **2** a can containing a product, eg paint, polish or insecticide mixed with a PROPELLANT, that can be sprayed to produce such a suspension.

aerospace *n* the Earth's atmosphere and the space beyond it. ➤ *adj* referring to the design and development of aircraft and spacecraft: *the aerospace industry.*

aesthete /'iːsθiːt/ or (*US*) **esthete** /'ɛsθiːt/ *n* someone who has or claims to have a special appreciation of art and beauty.

aesthetic or (*US*) **esthetic** /ɪs'θɛtɪk, ɛs-/ *adj* **1** able to appreciate beauty. **2** artistic; tasteful. ○ **aesthetically** *adv.*

aesthetics *sing n* **1** the branch of philosophy concerned with the study of the principles of beauty, esp in art. **2** the principles of good taste and the appreciation of beauty.

aetiology or (*US*) **etiology** /iːtɪ'ɒlədʒɪ/ *n* (*-ies*) **1** the science or philosophy of causes. **2** the scientific study of the causes or origins of disease. **3** the cause of a specific disease. ○ **aetiological** *adj.*

AF *abbrev* audio frequency.

afar *adv* at a distance. ♦ **from afar** from a great distance.

affable *adj* pleasant and friendly in manner. ○ **affability** *n.* ○ **affably** *adv.*

affair *n* **1** a concern, matter or thing to be done. **2** an event or connected series of events. **3** a sexual relationship between two people, usu when at least one of them is married to someone else. **4** (**affairs**) matters of importance and public interest: *current affairs.* **5** (**affairs**) private or public business matters: *I put my affairs in order.*

affect¹ *vb* **1** to have an effect on someone or something. **2** to cause someone to feel strong emotions, esp sadness or pity. **3** of diseases: to attack or infect. ○ **affecting** adj.

> **affect** A word often confused with this one is **effect**.

affect² vb **1** to pretend to feel or have (eg an illness or emotion). **2** to use, wear, etc something in a way that is intended to attract attention: *to affect an accent.*

affectation n unnatural behaviour or pretence which is intended to impress people.

affected adj **1** not genuine; pretended. **2** of a manner of speaking or behaving: put on to impress people.

affection n **1** a feeling of love or strong liking. **2** (**affections**) feelings.

affectionate adj showing love or fondness.

affidavit /afə'deɪvɪt/ n, law a written statement, sworn to be true by the person who makes it, for use as evidence in a court of law.

affiliate vb /ə'fɪlɪeɪt/ tr & intr (usu **be affiliated with** or **to sth**) to connect or associate a person or organization with a group or a larger organization. ➤ n /-ɪət/ a person or organization, etc that has an association with a group or larger body. ○ **affiliation** n.

affiliation order n, law a court order to a father to pay child support, used when the father is not married to the mother.

affinity n (**-ies**) **1** a strong natural liking for or feeling of attraction or closeness towards someone or something. **2** (usu **affinity with sb**) relationship to them, esp by marriage. **3** similarity in appearance, structure, etc, esp one that suggests relatedness. **4** (usu **affinity for sth**) chemical attraction between substances.

affirm vb **1** to state something as a fact. **2** to uphold or confirm (an idea, belief, etc). ○ **affirmation** n.

affirmative adj expressing agreement; giving the answer 'yes'. Opposite of NEGATIVE. ➤ n an affirmative word or phrase.

affix vb /ə'fɪks/ to attach or fasten. ➤ n /'afɪks/ gram a word-forming element which can be added to a word to form another word, eg un- in *unhappy* or -ness in *sadness*; a PREFIX or SUFFIX.

afflict vb to cause someone physical or mental suffering.

affliction n **1** distress or suffering. **2** a cause of this.

affluent adj having more than enough money; rich. ○ **affluence** n.

afford vb **1** (used with can, could, be able to) **a** to have enough money, time, etc to spend on something; **b** to be able to do something, or allow it to happen, without risk. **2** to give; to provide: *a room affording a view of the sea.* ○ **affordability** n. ○ **affordable** adj.

afforest vb to establish a forest on bare or cultivated land. ○ **afforestation** n.

affray n a fight in a public place.

affront n an insult, esp one delivered in public. ➤ vb **1** to insult someone, esp in public. **2** to

offend the pride of someone.

Afghan adj belonging or relating to Afghanistan, its inhabitants or their language. ➤ n **1** (also **Afghani**) a citizen or inhabitant of, or person born in, Afghanistan. **2** (also **Afghan hound**) a type of tall thin dog with long silky hair.

aficionado /əfɪʃɪə'nɑːdoʊ/ n someone who takes an enthusiastic interest in a particular sport or pastime.

afield adv to or at a distance; away from home: *far afield.*

aflame adj in flames; burning. **2** very excited.

afloat adj, adv **1** floating. **2** at sea; aboard ship. **3** out of debt; financially secure.

afoot adj, adv being prepared or already in progress or operation: *There is trouble afoot.*

afore adv, prep, old use or dialect before.

afore- comb form, signifying before; previously.

aforethought adj premeditated. ♦ **with malice aforethought** law of a criminal act: planned beforehand.

afraid adj **1** (often **afraid of sb** or **sth**) frightened of them or it. **2** (usu **afraid to do sth**) reluctant to do it out of fear or concern for the consequences. **3** as a polite formula of regret: sorry: *I'm afraid we're going to be late.*

afresh adv again, esp from the start.

African adj belonging or relating to the continent of Africa, its inhabitants, or their languages. ➤ n a citizen or inhabitant of, or person born in, Africa.

African-American n an American whose ancestors came from Africa. ➤ adj belonging or relating to African-Americans, their culture, etc.

African violet n a house plant with rounded hairy leaves and violet, bluish-purple, pink or white flowers.

Afrikaans n one of the official languages of S Africa, developed from Dutch.

Afrikaner n a white inhabitant of S Africa, esp one of Dutch descent, whose native language is Afrikaans.

Afro n a hairstyle consisting of thick bushy curls standing out from the head.

Afro- comb form, signifying African.

Afro-Caribbean n a native of the Caribbean whose ancestors came from Africa. ➤ adj relating to Afro-Caribbeans, their culture, etc.

aft /ɑːft/ adv, adj, chiefly naut at or towards the stern, rear or tail.

after prep **1** coming later in time than something. **2** following someone or something in position. **3** next to and following something in importance, order, etc. **4** because of something: *You can't expect to be promoted after that mistake.* **5** in spite of something: *He's still no better after all that medicine.* **6** about someone or something: *He asked after you.* **7** in pursuit of someone or something: *Run after him!* **8** of a painting or other work of art: in the style or manner of (someone else). **9** with a name derived from that of (someone else): *She's called Mary after her aunt.* **10** *N Am* past (an hour): *It's twenty after six.* ➤ *adv* **1** later in time. **2** behind in place. ➤ *conj* after the time when. ➤ *adj* **1** later: *in after years.* **2** *naut* further towards the stern of a ship: *the after deck.*

afterbirth *n, zool, med* the placenta, blood and ruptured membranes expelled from the uterus after the birth of a mammal.

aftercare *n* care and support given to someone after a surgical operation, a prison sentence, etc.

after-effect *n* a circumstance or event, usu an unpleasant one, that follows as the result of something.

afterglow *n* **1** a glow remaining in the sky after the sun has set. **2** a pleasant impression or feeling that remains when the experience, etc that caused it is over.

afterlife *n* the continued existence of one's spirit or soul after death.

aftermath *n* circumstances that follow and are a result of something, esp a great and terrible event.

afternoon *n* the period of the day between noon and the evening.

afters *sing n, Brit colloq* dessert; pudding.

aftershave *n* a perfumed lotion for a man to put on his face after shaving.

aftershock *n* a small earthquake that follows a large earthquake.

aftertaste *n* the taste that remains in the mouth or comes into it after one has eaten or drunk something.

afterthought *n* an idea thought of after the main plan, etc has been formed.

afterwards or (*esp US*) **afterward** *adv* later.

Ag *symbol, chem* silver.

again *adv* **1** once more; another time. **2** back to (a previous condition): *to get well again.* **3** in addition: *twice as much again.* **4** however; on the other hand: *He might come, but then again he might not.*

against *prep* **1** close to or leaning on something. **2** into collision with something or someone. **3** in opposition to something. **4** in contrast to something: *against a dark background.* **5** with a bad or unfavourable effect on someone or something: *His age counts against him.* **6** as a protection from someone or something. **7** in return for something: *the exchange rate against the euro.*

agape *adj* **1** of the mouth: gaping; open wide. **2** of a person: very surprised.

agaric *n, bot* any of various fungi that produce an umbrella-shaped spore-bearing structure with a central vertical stem supporting a circular cap.

agate /'agət/ *n, mineralogy* a variety of chalcedony consisting of concentrically arranged bands of two or more colours.

agave /ə'geɪvɪ/ *n, bot* a succulent plant, native esp to Central America, used to make tequila.

age *n* **1** the number of years, months, etc during which a person, animal or thing has lived or existed. **2** a particular stage in life: *old age.* **3** the fact or time of being old. **4** in the Earth's history: an interval of time during which specific life forms, physical conditions, geological events, etc were dominant: *the Ice Age.* **5** (*usu* **ages**) *colloq* a very long time. ➤ *vb* (**ageing** or **aging**) **1** *intr* to show signs of growing old. **2** *intr* to grow old. **3** *intr* to mature. **4** to make someone older or look old. ○ **ageing** or **aging** *n, adj.* ♦ **come of age** to become legally old enough to have an adult's rights and duties. **under age** too young to be legally allowed to do something.

aged /eɪdʒd/ *adj* **1** having a specified age. **2** /'eɪdʒɪd/ very old.

ageism or **agism** *n* the practice of treating people differently, and usu unfairly, on the grounds of age only. ○ **ageist** or **agist** *n, adj.*

ageless *adj* never growing old or fading; never looking older.

agency *n* (*-ies*) **1** an office or business that provides a particular service. **2** an active part played by someone or something in bringing something about. **3** *N Am* a government department.

agenda *sing n* a list of things to be done or discussed.

agent *n* **1 a** someone who represents an organization and acts on its behalf; **b** someone who deals with someone else's business matters, etc. **2** (*also* **secret agent**) a spy. **3** a substance that produces a particular effect. **4** someone who is the cause of something.

agent provocateur /French aʒɑ̃pʀɔvɔkatœʀ/ *n* (**agents provocateurs** /French aʒɑ̃pʀɔvɔkatœʀ/) someone employed to lead others in illegal acts for which they will be punished.

age-old *adj* done, known, etc for a very long time.

agglomerate *vb, tr & intr* to make into or become a mass. ➤ *n* **1** a mass or collection of things. **2** *geol* a type of volcanic rock consisting of a mass of coarse angular fragments of solidified lava. ○ **agglomeration** *n.*

agglutinate *vb* to stick or glue together. ○ **agglutination** *n.*

aggrandize or **-ise** *vb* to make someone or something seem greater than they really are. ○ **aggrandizement** *n.*

aggravate *vb* **1** to make (a bad situation, an illness, etc) worse. **2** *colloq* to make someone angry; to annoy them. ○ **aggravating** *adj.* ○ **aggravation** *n.*

aggravate Sense 2 is well established, especially in spoken English, although it is sometimes regarded as incorrect.

aggregate *n* /'agrəgət/ **1** a collection of separate units brought together; a total. **2** *civil eng, building* any material, esp sand, gravel or crushed stone, that is mixed with cement to form concrete. **3** *geol* a mass of soil grains or rock particles, or a mixture of both. ➤ *adj*

/ˈagrəgət/ formed of separate units combined together. ➤ *vb* /-geɪt/ **1** *tr & intr* to combine or be combined into a single unit or whole. **2** *colloq* to amount in total to something. ○ **aggregation** *n*.

aggression *n* **1** the act of attacking another person or country without being provoked. **2** an instance of hostile behaviour towards someone. **3** the tendency to make unprovoked attacks. **4** hostile feelings or behaviour.

aggressive *adj* **1** always ready to attack; hostile. **2** strong and determined. **3** of an action: hostile.

aggressor *n* the person, group or country that attacks first in a fight, war, etc.

aggrieved *adj* angry, hurt or upset.

aggro *n*, *Brit slang* **1** violent or threatening behaviour. **2** problems or difficulties.

aghast *adj* filled with fear or horror.

agile /ˈadʒaɪl or (*US*) ˈadʒəl/ *adj* able to move, change direction, etc quickly and easily; nimble. ○ **agilely** *adv*. ○ **agility** *n*.

agitate *vb* **1** to excite or trouble (a person, their feelings, etc). **2** *intr* to stir up public opinion for or against an issue. **3** to stir or shake (a liquid) vigorously. ○ **agitated** *adj*. ○ **agitatedly** *adv*. ○ **agitation** *n*. ○ **agitator** *n*.

aglow *adj* shining with colour or warmth; glowing.

AGM *abbrev* ANNUAL GENERAL MEETING.

agnostic *n* someone who believes that one can know only about material things and so believes that nothing can be known about the existence of God. ➤ *adj* relating to this view. ○ **agnosticism** *n*.

ago *adv* in the past; earlier.

agog *adj* very interested and excited; eager to know more. ➤ *adv* eagerly; expectantly.

agonize or **-ise** *vb*, *intr* (*esp* **agonize about** or **over sth**) to worry intensely or suffer great anxiety about it. ○ **agonized** *adj*. ○ **agonizing** *adj*.

agony *n* (*-ies*) severe bodily or mental pain.

agony aunt *n*, *colloq* a person who answers letters sent in to an agony column, or who gives similar advice on radio or television.

agony column *n* part of a newspaper or magazine where advice is offered to readers who write in with their problems.

agoraphobia *n*, *psychol* an irrational fear of open spaces or public places. ○ **agoraphobic** *adj*, *n*.

agrarian *adj* relating to land or agriculture.

agree *vb* (**agreed**, **agreeing**) *usu intr* (*often* **agree with sb** or **sth** or **about sth**) to be of the same opinion as them about it. **2** (*usu* **agree to sth**) to say yes to (a suggestion, request or instruction). **3** (*usu* **agree on** or **upon sth**) to reach a joint decision about it after discussion. **4** (*often* **agree with sth**) *gram* to have the same number, person, gender or case.

agreeable *adj* **1** of things: pleasant. **2** of people: friendly. **3** (*usu* **agreeable to sth**) of people: willing to accept (a suggestion, etc). ○ **agreeably** *adv*.

agreement *n* **1** a contract or promise. **2** a joint decision made after discussion. **3** the state of holding the same opinion. **4** *gram* the state of having the same number, person, gender or case.

agriculture *n* the cultivation of the land in order to grow crops or raise animal livestock as a source of food or other useful products. ○ **agricultural** *adj*. ○ **agriculturalist** or **agriculturist** *n*.

agrimony *n* (*-ies*) an erect plant with small yellow flowers in long terminal spikes.

agronomy *n* the scientific study of the cultivation of crops and soil management. ○ **agronomist** *n*.

aground *adj*, *adv* of ships: stuck on the bottom of the sea or rocks, usu in shallow water.

ague /ˈeɪgju:/ *n* **1** a fit of shivering. **2** malaria.

AH *abbrev* used in the Islamic dating system: *anno Hegirae* (Latin), in the year of the Hegira, ie counting from AD 622.

ah *exclam* expressing surprise, sympathy, admiration, pleasure, etc.

aha *exclam* expressing pleasure, satisfaction, triumph, surprise, etc.

ahead *adv* **1** at or in the front; forwards. **2** earlier in time; before: *She arrived ahead of me.* **3** in the lead: *ahead on points.* ♦ **get ahead** to make progress.

ahem *exclam* a sound made in the back of the throat, used to gain people's attention or to express doubt or disapproval.

ahoy *exclam*, *naut* a shout to greet or attract the attention of another ship.

AI *abbrev* **1** artificial insemination. **2** artificial intelligence.

aid *n* **1** help. **2** help or support in the form of money, supplies or services given to people who need it. **3** *often in compounds* a person or thing that helps do something: *a hearing-aid.* ➤ *vb* to help or support someone. ♦ **aid and abet** *law* to help and encourage someone to do something illegal. **in aid of sb** or **sth** in support of them or it.

aide *n* a confidential assistant or adviser.

aide-de-camp /ˌeɪddəˈkã/ *n* (**aides-de-camp** /ˌeɪddəˈkã/) an officer in the armed forces who acts as assistant to a senior officer.

AIDS or **Aids** *abbrev* acquired immune deficiency (or immunodeficiency) syndrome, a disease which destroys the immune system.

ail *vb* **1** *intr* to be ill and weak. **2** *old use* to cause pain or trouble to someone. ○ **ailing** *adj* ill.

aileron *n*, *aeronautics* one of a pair of hinged flaps at the rear edge of each wing of an aircraft, used to control roll.

ailment *n* an illness, esp a minor one.

aim *vb* **1** *tr & intr* (*usu* **aim at** or **for sb** or **sth**) to point or direct a weapon, remark, etc at them or it. **2** *intr* to plan, intend or try. ➤ *n* **1** what a person, etc intends to do. **2** the ability to hit what is aimed at: *good aim.*

aimless *adj* without any purpose. ○ **aimlessly** *adv*.

ain't *contraction, colloq* **1** am not; is not; are not. **2** has not; have not.

air *n* **1** the invisible odourless tasteless mixture of gases that forms the atmosphere surrounding the Earth, consisting mainly of nitrogen and oxygen. **2** the space above and around the Earth, where birds and aircraft fly. **3** moving air; a light breeze. **4** an appearance, look or manner: *a nonchalant air.* **5** (**airs**) behaviour intended to impress others, to show off, etc: *put on airs.* **6** a tune. ➤ *vb* **1** *tr & intr* to hang (laundry) to dry it or to remove unpleasant smells. **2** *tr & intr* **a** to let fresh air into (a room, etc); **b** of a room, etc: to become cooler or fresher in this way. **3** to make (one's thoughts, opinions, etc) known publicly. **4** *tr & intr, N Am* to broadcast something, or be broadcast, on radio or television. ♦ **into thin air** mysteriously and leaving no trace. **off the air** no longer or not yet being broadcast on radio or TV. **on the air** being broadcast on radio or TV.

air bag *n* in a vehicle: a bag that inflates automatically in a collision to protect the occupants.

air base *n* an operational centre for military aircraft.

airborne *adj* **1** flying in the air. **2** transported by air.

airbrush *n* **1** a device for painting which uses compressed air to form a spray. **2** in computer graphics: a similar effect. ➤ *vb* **1** to paint something using an airbrush. **2** to improve (the image of someone or something) by masking defects.

air chief marshal *n* a high-ranking officer in the Royal Air Force.

air commodore *n* an officer in the Royal Air Force.

air-conditioning *n* **1** any system used to control the temperature, humidity or purity of air, and to circulate it in a room, building or motor vehicle. **2** the control of room temperature, etc using such a system. ○ **air-conditioned** *adj.* ○ **air-conditioner** *n.*

aircraft *sing or pl n* any machine that is designed for travelling through air, eg an aeroplane or helicopter.

aircraft carrier *n* a large naval warship with a flat deck which aircraft can take off from and land on.

aircraftman or **aircraftwoman** *n, Brit* a person of the lowest rank in the air force.

air cushion *n* **1** a cushion that can be filled with air. **2** a pocket of down-driven air used for supporting a hovercraft, etc.

air-drop *n* a delivery of supplies, etc by parachute. ➤ *vb* to deliver (supplies, etc) by parachute.

airfield *n* an open expanse that is used by aircraft for landing and take-off. Compare AIRSTRIP.

air force *n* that part of a country's military forces which uses aircraft for fighting.

airgun *n* a gun that uses air under pressure to fire small pellets.

airhead *n, slang* an idiot.

air hostess *n, Brit* a female FLIGHT ATTENDANT.

airless *adj* **1** of the weather: unpleasantly warm, with no wind. **2** of a room: lacking fresh air; stuffy.

airlift *n* the transporting of people or goods in aircraft, esp in an emergency. ➤ *vb* to transport (people, goods, etc) in this way.

airline *n* a company or organization which provides a regular transport service for passengers or cargo by aircraft.

airliner *n* a large passenger aircraft.

airlock *n* **1** a bubble of air or gas that obstructs or blocks the flow of liquid through a pipe. **2** an airtight chamber with two entrances, on either side of which are different air pressures, eg between a space vehicle and outer space, or a submarine and the sea.

airmail *n* **1** the system of carrying mail by air. **2** mail carried by air. ➤ *vb* to send something by airmail.

airman or **airwoman** *n* a pilot or member of the crew of an aeroplane, esp in an air force.

air marshal *n* an officer in the air force of certain countries.

air miles or **Air Miles** *pl n* credits which are saved up to be redeemed for free air travel.

airplane *n, N Am* an aeroplane.

airplay *n* the broadcasting of recorded music on the radio.

air pocket *n* an area of reduced pressure in the air, or a downward current, which can cause an aircraft to lose height suddenly.

airport *n* a place where civil aircraft arrive and depart, with facilities for passengers and cargo, etc.

air raid *n* an attack by enemy aircraft.

air-rifle *n* a rifle that is fired by air under pressure.

airship *n* a power-driven aircraft that consists of a streamlined envelope containing helium gas, with an engine and a GONDOLA (sense 2) suspended from it.

airspace *n* the part of the atmosphere directly above a country, considered as part of that country.

airspeed *n* the speed of an aircraft, missile, etc in relation to the air through which it is moving.

airstrip *n* a strip of ground where aircraft can land and take off but which has no facilities. Compare AIRFIELD.

airtight *adj* **1** of a container, etc: which air cannot get into, out of, or through. **2** of an opinion, argument, etc: having no weak points.

airtime *n* on TV or radio: the length of time given to a particular item, programme or topic.

air vice-marshal *n* an officer in the air force of certain countries.

airwaves *pl n* **1** *colloq* the RADIO WAVES used for radio and television broadcasting. **2** the particular frequencies used for such broadcasting.

airway *n* **1** in the body: the route by which oxygen reaches the lungs, from the nose or mouth via the windpipe. **2** a route regularly followed by aircraft.

airwoman see AIRMAN

airy /ˈɛərɪ/ adj (**airier**, **airiest**) **1** with plenty of fresh cool air. **2** unconcerned. **3** light-hearted. ○ **airily** adv. ○ **airiness** n.

airy-fairy adj, colloq not based on facts or on awareness of real situations.

aisle /aɪl/ n a passage between rows of seats, eg in a church, aircraft, theatre, etc.

| **aisle** There is sometimes a spelling confusion between **aisle** and **isle**. |

aitch n the letter H or h.

aitchbone n **1** the rump bone in cattle. **2** a cut of beef from this.

ajar adj, adv partly open.

AKA or **aka** abbrev also known as.

akimbo /əˈkɪmbəʊ/ adj, adv with hands on hips and elbows bent outward.

akin adj **1** similar; being of the same kind. **2** related by blood.

Al symbol, chem aluminium.

à la prep in the manner or style of someone or something specified: mushrooms à la Grecque.

alabaster n a type of white stone used for ornaments, etc.

à la carte adv, adj of a meal in a restaurant: with each dish priced and ordered separately.

alacrity n quick and cheerful enthusiasm.

à la mode adj, adv according to current fashion.

alarm n **1** sudden fear produced by awareness of danger. **2** a noise warning of danger. **3** a bell, etc which sounds to wake a person from sleep. **4** an alarm clock. ➤ vb **1** to frighten. **2** to warn someone of danger. **3** to fit or switch on an alarm on (a house, car, etc). ○ **alarming** adj.

alarm clock n a clock that can be set to make a noise at a particular time, usu to wake someone up.

alarmist n someone who spreads unnecessary alarm.

alas exclam, old or literary expressing grief or misfortune.

albatross n **1** a large seabird with very long wings. **2** golf a score of three under par. Compare BIRDIE (sense 2), EAGLE (sense 2).

albeit /ɔːlˈbiːɪt/ conj even if; although.

albino /alˈbiːnəʊ or (US) alˈbaɪnəʊ/ n, biol an animal or person with an abnormal lack of pigmentation in the hair, skin and eyes.

album n **1** a book with blank pages for holding photographs, stamps, autographs, etc. **2** a record, CD, etc which contains multiple tracks.

albumen n, zool in the eggs of birds and some reptiles: the nutritive material surrounding the yolk; the white of an egg.

albumin n, biochem any of various water-soluble globular proteins that coagulate when heated, found in egg white, milk, blood serum, etc.

alchemy n the forerunner of modern chemistry, which centred around attempts to convert ordinary metals into gold, and to discover a universal remedy for illness, known as the elixir of life. ○ **alchemist** n.

alcohol n **1** chem any of numerous organic chemical compounds containing hydrogen and oxygen bound in groups, used as solvents for dyes, resins, varnishes, perfume oils, etc, and as fuels. **2** ETHANOL, esp when used as an intoxicant in alcoholic beverages. **3** any drink containing this liquid, such as wine or beer.

alcoholic adj **1** relating to, containing or having the properties of alcohol. **2** relating to alcoholism. ➤ n a person who suffers from alcoholism.

alcoholism n, pathol a condition caused by physical dependence on alcohol, habitual and extensive consumption of which impairs physical and mental health.

alcopop n an alcoholic drink bought ready-mixed with lemonade, etc.

alcove n a recess in the wall of a room or garden.

aldehyde n any of numerous organic chemical compounds formed by the oxidation of alcohols.

al dente /al ˈdɛntɪ/ adj, cookery of pasta and vegetables: cooked so as to remain firm when bitten.

alder n any of various deciduous trees and shrubs with oval or rounded toothed leaves, and CATKINS.

alderman n **1** in England and Wales until 1974: a member of a town, county or borough council elected by fellow councillors, below the rank of mayor. **2** in the US and Canada: a member of the governing body of a city.

ale n **1** a light-coloured beer flavoured with hops. **2** beer.

aleatory or **aleatoric** adj, technical depending on chance.

alehouse n, old use an inn or public house.

alert adj thinking and acting quickly. **2** (esp **alert to sth**) watchful and aware of (a danger, etc). ➤ n **1** a warning of danger. **2** the period of time covered by such a warning. ➤ vb (usu **alert sb to sth**) to warn them of (a danger); to make them aware of (a fact or circumstance). ○ **alertness** n. ♦ **on the alert** watchful.

A level (in full **Advanced level**) n **1** in England, Wales and N Ireland: an advanced examination in a single subject, usually taken about the age of 18. **2** a pass in such an examination.

alfalfa n a plant of the pulse family with purple flowers and spirally twisted pods, widely cultivated as a forage crop. Also called **lucerne**.

alfresco adv, adj in the open air.

algae /ˈalgiː, ˈaldʒiː/ pl n (sing **alga** /ˈalgə/) a large and very diverse group of mainly aquatic organisms.

algebra n the branch of mathematics that uses letters and symbols to represent variable quantities and numbers, and to express generalizations about them. ○ **algebraic** /-ˈbreɪk/ adj.

ALGOL or **Algol** n, comput a high-level programming language, formerly widely used for scientific problem solving.

algorithm n any procedure involving a series of steps that is used to find the solution to a specific problem, eg to solve a mathematical equation.

alias /ˈeɪlɪəs/ n a false or assumed name. ➣ adv also known as: John Smith, alias Mr X.

alibi /ˈalɪbaɪ/ n (**alibis**) **1** a plea of being somewhere else when a crime was committed. **2** colloq an excuse.

Alice band n a wide hair-band of coloured ribbon or other material, worn flat round the head.

alien n **1** a foreign-born resident of a country who has not adopted that country's nationality. **2** esp sci fi an inhabitant of another planet. ➣ adj **1** foreign. **2** (usu alien to sb or sth) not in keeping with them or it; unfamiliar.

alienable adj, law of property: able to be transferred to another owner.

alienate vb **1** to make someone become unfriendly or estranged. **2** to make someone feel unwelcome or isolated. **3** law to transfer ownership of (property) to another person. ○ **alienation** n.

alight[1] adj **1** on fire. **2** lighted up; excited.

alight[2] vb (**alighted** or **alit**) intr **1** (often alight from sth) to get down from or out of (a vehicle). **2** of a bird, etc: to land.

align vb **1** to put something in a straight line or bring it into line. **2** to bring (someone, a country, etc) into agreement with others, or with a political belief, cause, etc. ○ **alignment** n.

alike adj, adv like one another; similar.

alimentary adj relating to digestion, food, diet or nutrition.

alimentary canal n, anat a tubular organ extending from the mouth to the anus, along which food passes, and in which it is digested.

alimony n, law money for support paid by a man to his ex-wife or by a woman to her ex-husband, when they are legally separated or divorced.

aliphatic adj, chem of an organic compound: having carbon atoms arranged in chains rather than in rings. Compare AROMATIC (sense 2).

alive adj **1** living. **2** lively. **3** (usu alive to sth) aware of it. **4** (usu alive with sth) abounding in it.

alkali /ˈalkəlaɪ/ n (**alkalis** or **alkalies**) chem a hydroxide of any of various metallic elements that dissolves in water to produce an alkaline solution, and neutralizes acids to form salts. ○ **alkaline** adj. ○ **alkalinity** n.

alkaloid n, biochem any of numerous organic compounds that contain nitrogen, and which have toxic or medicinal properties.

all adj **1** the whole amount, number or extent of something; every. **2** the greatest possible: run

with all speed. **3** any whatever: beyond all doubt. ➣ n **1** every one of the things or persons concerned; the whole of something. **2** one's whole strength, resources, etc: give one's all. ➣ adv **1** entirely; quite. **2** colloq very: go all shy. **3** used in giving the score in various games: on each side: 30 all. ♦ **all along** the whole time. **all but** very nearly: He all but drowned. **all for sth** extremely enthusiastic about it. **all in all** considering everything. **at all** with negatives and in questions **1** in the least. **2** in any way. **in all** all together.

allay vb to make (pain, fear, suspicion, etc) less intense.

all clear n a signal or statement that the threat of danger is over.

allegation n an unsupported claim, statement or assertion.

allege vb to claim or declare something to be the case, usu without proof. ○ **alleged** adj presumed and claimed, but not proved, to be as stated. ○ **allegedly** /əˈlɛdʒɪdlɪ/ adv.

allegiance n commitment and duty to obey and be loyal to a government, sovereign, etc.

allegory /ˈaləgərɪ/ n (**-ies**) a story, play, poem, picture, etc in which the characters represent moral or spiritual ideas or messages. ○ **allegorical** adj.

allegretto mus, adv, adj played in a fairly quick and lively manner (less brisk than ALLEGRO). ➣ n a piece of music to be played in this way.

allegro mus, adv, adj played in a quick lively manner. ➣ n a piece of music to be played in this way.

alleluia see HALLELUJAH

allergen /ˈalədʒən/ n, med any foreign substance that induces an allergic reaction in someone.

allergic /əˈlɜːdʒɪk/ adj **1** (allergic to sth) having an allergy to it. **2** caused by an allergy: an allergic reaction.

allergy n (**-ies**) **1** pathol a hypersensitive reaction of the body to certain foreign substances known as ALLERGENS, eg specific foods, dust or pollen. **2** colloq a dislike.

alleviate vb to make (pain, a problem, suffering, etc) less severe. ○ **alleviation** n.

alley n **1** (also alleyway) a narrow passage behind or between buildings. **2** a long narrow channel used for bowling or skittles. **3** a path through a garden or park.

alliance n **1** the state of being allied. **2** an agreement or treaty by which people, countries, etc ally themselves with one another.

allied adj **1 a** joined by political agreement or treaty; **b** (Allied) belonging or referring to Britain and her allies in World Wars I and II: Allied troops. **2** similar; related.

alligator n a large reptile similar to a crocodile but with a broader head and blunter snout, and teeth that do not protrude over its jaws.

all-in wrestling n a style of wrestling with few rules or restrictions.

alliteration *n* the repetition of the same sound at the beginning of each word or each stressed word in a phrase, as in *sing a song of sixpence*. Compare ASSONANCE. ○ **alliterative** *adj*.

allocate *vb* to give, set apart or assign something to someone or for some particular purpose. ○ **allocation** *n*.

allot *vb* (*allotted, allotting*) **1** to give (a share of or place in something) to each member of a group. **2** to assign something to a specific purpose.

allotment *n* **1** *Brit* one of the subdivisions of a larger piece of public ground rented to individuals to grow vegetables, etc. **2** the act of allotting. **3** an amount allotted.

allotrope *n, chem* any of the two or more structural forms in which some elements can exist, eg graphite and diamond (allotropes of carbon). ○ **allotropic** *adj*. ○ **allotropy** *n*.

all-out *adj* using all one's strength, powers, etc.

allow *vb* **1** to permit (someone to do something, something to happen, etc). **2** to assign or allocate: *allow £10 for food*. **3** to admit or agree to (a point, claim, etc). **4** *intr* (**allow for sth**) to take it into consideration when judging or deciding something. ○ **allowable** *adj*.

allowance *n* **1** a fixed sum of money, amount of something, etc given regularly. **2** money given for expenses. **3** something allowed. ◆ **make allowances for sb** to judge them less severely, or expect less of them, because of particular circumstances applying to them. **make allowances for sth** to take it into consideration in one's plans.

alloy *n* /'alɔɪ/ a material consisting of a mixture of two or more metals, or a metal and a non-metal. ➤ *vb* /ə'lɔɪ/ to mix (one metal with another).

all-purpose *adj* useful for many different purposes.

all right or *sometimes* **alright** *adj* **1** unhurt; safe. **2** past about adequate, satisfactory, etc. ➤ *exclam* **1** used simply as a greeting: *All right? How's it going?* **2** used to signal agreement or approval. ➤ *adv* **1** satisfactorily; properly. **2** *colloq* used to reinforce what has just been said: *It's broken all right*.

all-round *adj* **1** having many different skills: *an all-round player*. **2** including everyone or everything: *an all-round education*. ➤ *adv* (**all round**) everywhere; in every respect: *All round, the situation of the refugees looks desperate*.

all-rounder *n* someone who has a lot of different skills.

All Saints' Day *n* a Christian festival held on 1 November to commemorate all church saints collectively.

All Souls' Day *n, RC Church* the day, 2 November, set aside for praying for souls in purgatory.

allspice *n* an aromatic spice; the dried unripe berries of the pimento tree.

all-time *adj, colloq* **1** of a record, esp a sporting one: best to date; unsurpassed. **2** of great and

permanent importance: *one of the all-time greats of jazz*.

allude *vb, intr* (*usu* **allude to sth**) to mention it indirectly or speak about it in passing.

allure *n* attractiveness, appeal or charm. ➤ *vb* to attract, charm or fascinate.

allusion *n* any indirect reference to something else. ○ **allusive** *adj*.

> **allusion** A word often confused with this one is **illusion**.

alluvium *n* (**alluvia**) fine particles of silt, clay, mud and sand that are carried and deposited by rivers. ○ **alluvial** *adj*.

ally *n* /'alaɪ/ (*-ies*) a country, state, etc that has formally agreed to help and support another. ➤ *vb* /ə'laɪ/ (*-ies, -ied*) **1** of a country, state, etc: to join or become joined politically or militarily with another, esp with a formal agreement. **2** of an individual or group: to join or become joined with someone else or another group.

alma mater *n* the school, college or university that someone used to attend.

almanac *n* a book, published yearly, with a calendar, information about the phases of the Moon and stars, dates of religious festivals, public holidays, etc.

almighty *adj* **1** having complete power: *an almighty god*. **2** *colloq* very great: *an almighty crash*. ➤ *n* (**the Almighty**) *Christianity* God.

almond /'ɑːmənd/ *n* **1** a kind of small tree related to the peach. **2** the nut-like seed from the fruit of this tree.

almoner *n, hist, Brit* a medical social worker.

almost *adv* nearly but not quite.

alms /ɑːmz/ *pl n, hist* donations of money, food, etc to the poor.

almshouse *n, Brit, hist* a place where the aged, poor, etc were supported by charity.

aloe *n* **1** a plant with long fleshy leaves with spiny edges. **2** (*usu* **aloes**) the dried juice of the leaves of this plant, formerly used as a purgative drug known as **bitter aloes**.

aloe vera /'aloʊ 'veɪrə/ *n* a species of ALOE plant, the leaves of which contain a juice that is said to have healing properties.

aloft *adv* **1** in the air; overhead: *I held the trophy aloft*. **2** *naut* in a ship's rigging.

alone *adj, adv* **1** by oneself. **2** without anyone or anything else: *The idea was mine alone*. **3** lonely. ◆ **go it alone** *colloq* to act on one's own and without help.

along *adv* **1** in some direction: *Her old banger just chugs along*. **2** in the company of someone else or with others: *I went along with him to the gig*. **3** into a more advanced state: *coming along nicely*. ➤ *prep* **1** by the side of something or near something. **2** down the length of or down part of the length of something: *The shops are just along that street*. ◆ **along with sth** or **sb 1** in addition to it or them. **2** in conjunction with it or them.

alongside *prep* close to the side of something. ➤ *adv* to or at the side.

aloof *adj* unfriendly and distant.

alopecia /ələ'piːʃə/ *n, pathol* baldness, either hereditary, such as the gradual loss of hair in men, or of the type caused by disease or old age.

aloud *adv* loud enough to be able to be heard: *reading aloud*.

alp *n* **1** a high mountain. **2** in Switzerland: pasture land on a mountainside.

alpaca *n* a S American mammal, closely related to the LLAMA, reared mainly for its long silky fleece.

alpha *n* **1** the first letter of the Greek alphabet. **2** *Brit* a mark indicating the highest grade.

alphabet *n* a set of letters, characters, symbols, etc, usu arranged in a fixed order that, by convention, are used to represent the spoken form of a language in writing and printing. ○ **alphabetical** *adj*. ○ **alphabetize** or **-ise** *vb*.

alphanumeric or **alphanumerical** *adj, comput* denoting characters, codes or data that consist of letters of the alphabet and numerals.

alpha particle *n, physics* a positively charged particle with a low energy content, produced by radioactive decay.

alpha ray *n, physics* a stream of ALPHA PARTICLES.

alpine *adj* **1** belonging or relating to alps or high mountains. **2** (**Alpine**) belonging or relating to the Alps. ➤ *n* a plant that grows in high mountain areas.

already *adv* **1** before the present time or the time in question: *We've already paid*. **2** so soon or so early: *It's already lunchtime*.

alright *adj* an alternative spelling of ALL RIGHT.

Alsatian *n* a German shepherd dog.

also *adv* in addition; as well as; besides.

also-ran *n* **1** a horse, dog, person, etc not finishing in one of the top three places in a race. **2** someone who is considered to be unimportant.

altar *n* **1** a table, raised structure, etc where sacrifices are made to a god. **2** *Christianity* the table at the front of a church, consecrated for use during communion.

altarpiece *n* a religious picture or carving, often in either two or three parts, that is placed above and behind an altar.

alter *vb, tr & intr* to change. ○ **alterable** *adj*. ○ **alteration** *n*.

altercate *vb, intr* to argue or dispute, esp angrily, heatedly, etc. ○ **altercation** *n*.

alter ego *n* **1** someone's second or alternative character: *Her aggressive alter ego surfaces when she drinks too much*. **2** a close and trusted friend.

alternate *adj* /ɒl'tɜːnət/ **1** of two feelings, states, conditions, etc: arranged or coming one after the other in turn: *alternate layers of pasta and sauce*. **2** every other; one out of two. ➤ *vb* /'ɔːltəneɪt/ **1** *tr & intr* of two things: to succeed or make them succeed each other by turns: *They alternate their days off*. **2** *intr* (**alternate between sth and sth else**) to change from one thing to another by turns. ➤ *n* /'ɔːltəneɪt; also (orig US)* 'ɒːltəneɪt/ a substitute, esp a person who covers in someone's absence. ○ **alternately** *adv*. ○ **alternation** *n*.

> **alternate, alternative** These words are often confused with each other.

alternate angles *pl n, geom* a pair of angles that lie on opposite sides and at opposite ends of a line that cuts two other lines.

alternating current *n* an electric current that reverses its direction of flow with a constant frequency, and is therefore continuously varying. Compare DIRECT CURRENT.

alternative *adj* **1** of two or more possibilities: secondary or different, esp in terms of being less favourable as a choice: *I had to make alternative travel plans*. **2** of a lifestyle, etc: outside the conventionally accepted ways of doing something. ➤ *n* **1** the possibility of having the option to choose, strictly speaking, between two things (but often used of more than two or of an unknown number): *We had no alternative but to take the train*. **2** something that represents another possible option. ○ **alternatively** *adv*.

alternative energy *n, ecol* energy derived from sources other than nuclear power or the burning of fossil fuels, eg SOLAR ENERGY.

alternative medicine or **complementary medicine** *n* the treatment of diseases and disorders using procedures other than those traditionally practised in orthodox medicine, eg ACUPUNCTURE, HOMEOPATHY.

alternator *n, elec eng* an electricity generator that produces ALTERNATING CURRENT by means of one or more coils rotating in a magnetic field.

although *conj* in spite of the fact that; though.

altimeter *n, aeronautics* a device used in aircraft for measuring height above sea or ground level.

altitude *n* height, esp above sea level, of a mountain, aircraft, etc.

alto *n* **1** the lowest female singing voice. Also called **contralto**. **2** the singing voice of a COUNTER-TENOR. **3** someone with either of these types of singing voice. **4** a part or piece of music written for a voice or instrument at this pitch. ➤ *adj* of a musical instrument, etc: having a high pitch: *alto sax*.

altogether *adv* **1** completely. **2 a** on the whole: *Altogether it was a wonderful holiday*; **b** taking everything into consideration: *Altogether the holiday cost £500*. ♦ **in the altogether** *colloq* naked.

altruism *n* an unselfish concern for the welfare of others. ○ **altruist** *n*. ○ **altruistic** *adj*.

alum *n, chem* aluminium potassium sulphate, a white crystalline compound used in dyeing and tanning, and as a medical astringent to stop bleeding.

aluminium or (*N Am*) **aluminum** /ə'luː-mɪnəm/ *n, chem* a silvery-white light metallic element that forms strong alloys which are used in the construction of aircraft and other vehicles, door and window frames, household utensils, drink cans, etc.

aluminize or **-ise** *vb* to coat (a mirror or other surface) with aluminium.

alumna /ə'lʌmnə/ *n* (*alumnae* /-niː/) a female ALUMNUS.

alumnus /ə'lʌmnəs/ *n* (*alumni* /-naɪ/) a former pupil or student of a school, college or university.

always *adv* **1** on every occasion. **2** continually; time and time again. **3** whatever happens; if necessary: *You can always take a taxi.*

alyssum *n* a bushy plant with white, yellow or purple cross-shaped flowers.

Alzheimer's disease /'æltshaɪməz/ *n, pathol* a disease in which degeneration of the brain cells results in gradual loss of memory, confusion, etc, eventually leading to total disintegration of the personality.

AM *abbrev* AMPLITUDE MODULATION.

Am *symbol, chem* americium.

am *vb* (used with *I*): the 1st person singular of the present tense of BE.

a.m., am, A.M. or **AM** *abbrev* ANTE MERIDIEM.

amalgam *n* **1** a mixture or blend. **2** *chem* an alloy of mercury with one or more other metals, which forms a soft paste on mixing but later hardens, used in dentistry to fill holes in drilled teeth.

amalgamate *vb* **1** *tr & intr* to join together or unite to form a single unit, etc. **2** *intr* of metals: to form an alloy with mercury. ○ **amalgamation** *n*.

amanuensis /əmanjʊ'ɛnsɪs/ *n* (*-ses* /-siːz/) a literary assistant or secretary, esp one who writes from dictation or copies from manuscripts.

amaranth *n* **1** any of various species of plant that produce spikes of small brightly coloured flowers. **2** *poetic* a fabled flower that never fades.

amaryllis *n* any of various plants, esp a S African species with strap-shaped leaves and large pink or white trumpet-shaped scented flowers.

amass *vb* to gather or collect (money, possessions, etc), esp in great quantity.

amateur *n* **1** someone who takes part in a sport, pastime, etc as a hobby and without being paid for it. **2** someone who is not very skilled in an activity, etc. ➤ *adj* **1** unskilled or non-professional: *playing the amateur detective.* **2** for, relating to or done by those who are not professional: *amateur dramatics.* ○ **amateurish** *adj.* ○ **amateurism** *n*.

amatory *adj* belonging or relating to, or showing, sexual love or desire.

amaze *vb* to surprise someone greatly; to astonish them. ○ **amazement** *n*. ○ **amazing** *adj.* ○ **amazingly** *adv*.

Amazon *n* **1** a member of a legendary nation of women warriors, eg from S America. **2** (*usu* **amazon**) any tall, well-built, strong woman.

ambassador *n* **1** a diplomat of the highest rank permanently appointed by a government, head of state, sovereign, etc to act on their behalf or to be their official representative in some foreign country, state, etc. **2** a representative, messenger or agent. ○ **ambassadorial** /ambasə'dɔːrɪəl/ *adj.* ○ **ambassadorship** *n*.

amber *n* **1** *geol* a transparent yellow or reddish fossilized resin, often carved and polished and used to make jewellery. **2** a yellow or yellow-brown colour. **3** a traffic light that serves as a means of delaying the change-over in traffic flow, in the UK appearing on its own between green for 'go' and red for 'stop' but appearing simultaneously with red to mark the transition the other way between red and green.

ambergris *n* a pale-grey waxy substance with a strong smell, produced in the intestines of sperm whales, and widely used until recently in the perfume industry.

ambidextrous *adj* able to use both hands equally well.

ambience or **ambiance** *n* the surroundings or atmosphere of a place. ○ **ambient** *adj*.

ambiguity *n* (*-ies*) **1** uncertainty of meaning. **2** a word or statement that can be interpreted in more than one way.

ambiguous *adj* having more than one possible meaning. ○ **ambiguously** *adv*.

ambit *n* **1** range or extent. **2** circumference or boundary.

ambition *n* **1** a strong desire for success, fame or power. **2** a thing someone wants to do or achieve.

ambitious *adj* **1** having a strong desire for success, etc. **2** enterprising or daring, but requiring hard work and skill: *an ambitious plan.*

ambivalence or **ambivalency** *n* the concurrent adherence to two opposite or conflicting views, feelings, etc about someone or something. ○ **ambivalent** *adj*.

amble *vb, intr* **1** to walk without hurrying; to stroll. **2** of a horse, etc: to walk by lifting the two feet on the same side together and then lifting the two feet on the other side together and so move in a smooth, flowing way. ➤ *n* **1** a leisurely walk. **2** a horse's ambling walk.

ambrosia *n* **1** *Greek myth* the food of the gods, believed to give them eternal youth and beauty. **2** something with a delicious taste or smell.

ambulance *n* a specially equipped vehicle for carrying sick or injured people to hospital.

ambulatory *adj* **1** belonging or relating to or designed for walking. **2** moving from place to place.

ambush *n* **1** the act of lying in wait to attack someone by surprise. **2** an attack made in this way. ➤ *vb* to lie in wait for someone or attack them in this way.

ameba an alternative *US* spelling of AMOEBA.

ameliorate /ə'miːlɪəreɪt/ *vb, tr & intr* to make or become better. ○ **amelioration** *n*.

amen *exclam* usu said at the end of a prayer, hymn, etc: so be it.

amenable /ə'miːnəbəl/ *adj* (*esp* **amenable to sth**) ready to accept (someone else's idea, advice, etc). ○ **amenably** *adv*.

amend *vb* to correct, improve or make minor changes to (esp a book, document, etc). ○ **amendable** *adj*. ♦ **make amends for sth** to make up for or compensate for (some injury, insult, etc).

amendment *n* **1** an addition or alteration, esp to a motion, official document, etc. **2** an act of correcting or improving something.

amenity *n* (*-ies*) **1** a valued public facility. **2** anything that makes life more comfortable and pleasant.

American *adj* **1** belonging or relating to the United States of America or its inhabitants. **2** belonging or relating to the continent of America, including North, South and Central America. ➢ *n* a citizen or inhabitant of, or person born in, the United States of America, or the American continent. ○ **Americanize** or **-ise** *vb*.

American football *n* a team game with 11 players on both sides, similar to RUGBY.

Americanism *n* a word, phrase, custom, etc that is characteristic of Americans.

americium *n, chem* a silvery-white radioactive metallic element that is produced artificially, used as a source of ALPHA PARTICLES.

amethyst *n* **1** a pale- to deep-purple transparent or translucent variety of the mineral QUARTZ used as a gemstone. **2** the purple or violet colour of this gemstone.

amiable *adj* friendly, pleasant and good-tempered. ○ **amiability** *n*. ○ **amiably** *adv*.

amicable *adj* **1** friendly. **2** done in a reasonably friendly manner: *an amicable parting*. ○ **amicably** *adv*.

amid or **amidst** *prep* in the middle of something; among.

amidships *adv* in, into or near the middle of a ship.

amine /'amiːn/ *n, chem* any member of a class of organic compounds, produced by decomposing organic matter, in which one or more of the hydrogen atoms of ammonia has been replaced by an organic group.

amino acid /ə'miːnəʊ/ *n* any of a group of water-soluble organic compounds that form the individual subunits of proteins.

amiss *adj* wrong; out of order. ➢ *adv* wrongly. ♦ **take sth amiss** to be upset or offended by it.

amity *n* friendship; friendliness.

ammeter *n, elec eng* a device used for measuring electric current in a circuit, usu in amperes.

ammo *n, colloq* short form of AMMUNITION.

ammonia *n, chem* **1** a colourless pungent gas formed naturally by the bacterial decomposition of proteins, etc. **2** an alkaline solution of ammonia in water, used as a bleach and cleaning agent.

ammonite *n, geol* the fossilized shell of an extinct marine cephalopod mollusc.

ammonium *n, chem* an ION formed by the reaction of ammonia with acid, found in many salts.

ammunition *n* **1** bullets, shells, bombs, etc made to be fired from a weapon. **2** anything that can be used against someone in an argument.

amnesia *n, pathol* the loss or impairment of memory. ○ **amnesiac** *n* someone suffering from amnesia.

amnesty *n* (*-ies*) **1** a general pardon, esp for people convicted or accused of political crimes. **2** a period of time when people can admit to crimes, hand in weapons, etc in the knowledge that they will not be prosecuted.

amniocentesis *n* (*-ses*) *obstetrics* a procedure that involves the insertion of a hollow needle through the abdominal wall into the uterus of a pregnant woman, enabling a small quantity of AMNIOTIC FLUID to be drawn off in order to test for fetal abnormalities.

amnion *n* (*amnia*) *anat* the innermost membrane that surrounds the embryo.

amniotic fluid *n, zool* the clear fluid that surrounds and protects the embryo.

amoeba or (*N Am*) **ameba** /ə'miːbə/ *n* (*amoebae* /ə'miːbiː/ or *amoebas*) *zool* a microscopic PROTOZOAN animal that inhabits water or damp soil and has no fixed shape. ○ **amoebic** or **amebic** *adj*.

amok or **amuck** *adv* (*usu* **run amok** or **amuck**) to rush about violently and out of control.

among or **amongst** *prep* used of more than two things, people, etc: **1** in the middle of them: *among friends*. **2** between them: *divide it among them*. **3** in the group or number of them: *among his best plays*. **4** with one another: *decide among yourselves*.

> **among** See note at **between**.

amoral /eɪ'mɒrəl/ *adj* having no moral standards or principles. ○ **amorality** *n*.

> **amoral, immoral** **Amoral** means 'having no morality', whereas **immoral** means 'violating a morality'.

amorous *adj* showing, feeling or relating to love, esp sexual love.

amorphous *adj* **1** without definite shape or structure. **2** without any clearly defined or thought-out purpose, identity, etc.

amortize or **-ise** *vb* **1** to gradually pay off (a debt) by regular payments of money. **2** to gradually write off (the initial cost of an asset) over a period. ○ **amortization** *n*.

amount *n* a quantity; a total or extent: *a large amount of money*. ➢ *vb* (*always* **amount to sth**) to be equal to it or add up to it in size, number, significance, etc.

amour *n, old use* a love affair.

amour-propre /*French* amurprɔpr/ *n* self-esteem.

amp *n* **1** an AMPERE. **2** *colloq* an AMPLIFIER.

amperage *n* the magnitude or strength of an electric current expressed in AMPERES.

ampere /'ampeə(r)/ *n* the SI unit of electric current.

ampersand *n* the symbol &, which means 'and'.

amphetamine /am'fɛtəmi:n, -mm/ *n, med* a potentially addictive synthetic drug, often used illegally as a stimulant.

amphibian *n* **1** *zool* a cold-blooded animal, eg a frog, toad or newt, which lives partly on or entirely on land but returns to water to lay its eggs. **2** a vehicle that can operate both on land and in water.

amphibious *adj* **1** *zool* of a living organism: capable of living both on land and in water. **2** of vehicles, equipment, etc: designed to be operated or used both on land, and on or in water. **3** of a military operation: using troops that have been conveyed across the sea.

amphitheatre *n* an oval or round building without a roof, with tiers of seats built around a central open area.

amphora /'amfərə/ *n* (*amphoras* or *amphorae* /'amfɔ:ri:/) *archaeol, etc* a large narrow-necked Greek or Roman jar with a handle on either side, used for storing liquids such as wine or oil.

ample *adj* **1** more than enough. **2** abundant. ○ **amply** *adv.*

amplifier *n* an electronic device that amplifies the strength of an electrical or radio signal, used in audio equipment, radio and television sets, etc.

amplify *vb* (*-ies, -ied*) **1** to increase the strength of (an electrical or radio signal) by transferring power from an external energy source. **2** *tr & intr* to add details or further explanation to an account, story, etc. ○ **amplification** *n.*

amplitude *n* **1** spaciousness, wide range or extent. **2** abundance. **3** *physics* in any quantity that varies in periodic cycles, such as a wave or vibration: the maximum displacement from its mean position, eg the angle between the vertical and the peak position in the swing of a pendulum.

amplitude modulation *n, telecomm* in radio transmission: the process whereby the amplitude of the CARRIER WAVE is made to increase or decrease instantaneously in response to variations in the characteristics of the signal being transmitted.

ampoule or (*US sometimes*) **ampule** *n, med* a small sealed container, usu of glass or plastic, containing one sterile dose of a drug for injection.

ampulla *n* (*ampullae* /am'puli:/) **1** *anat* the dilated end of a duct or canal. **2** a small container for oil, water or wine used in religious ceremonies.

amputate *vb, surgery* to remove (all or part of a limb). ○ **amputation** *n.* ○ **amputee** *n.*

amuck see AMOK

amulet *n* a small object, charm or jewel worn to protect the wearer from witchcraft, evil, disease, etc.

amuse *vb* **1** to make someone laugh. **2** to keep someone entertained and interested. ○ **amusing** *adj.*

amusement *n* **1** the state of being amused. **2** something that amuses. **3** a machine for riding on or playing games of chance.

amusement arcade *n, Brit* a place where people can play fruit machines, video games, etc.

an see A

> **an** See note at **a**.

an- see A-²

Anabaptist *n, Christianity* a member of various groups of believers advocating the baptism of believing adults only.

anabolic steroid *n, biochem* a synthetic hormone that increases muscle bulk and strength.

anabolism *n, biochem* in the cells of living organisms: the process whereby complex molecules are manufactured from smaller molecules. Compare CATABOLISM. ○ **anabolic** /anə'bɒlɪk/ *adj.*

anachronism *n* **1** the attribution of something to a historical period in which it did not exist. **2** a person, thing or attitude that is or appears to be out of date and old-fashioned. ○ **anachronistic** *adj.*

anaconda *n* a large S American snake that kills by strangulation.

anaemia or **anemia** *n, pathol* an abnormal reduction in the amount of HAEMOGLOBIN in the red blood cells, characterized by pallid skin, fatigue and breathlessness.

anaemic *adj* **1** suffering from anaemia. **2** pale or weak. **3** spiritless; lacking in energy.

anaesthesia or (*US*) **anesthesia** /anɪs'θi:zɪə/ *n* a reversible loss of sensation in all or part of the body, usu induced by drugs.

anaesthetic or (*US*) **anesthetic** /anəs'θɛtɪk/ *n* any agent, esp a drug, capable of producing anaesthesia.

anaesthetist /ən'i:sθətɪst/ or (*US*) **anesthetist** /ə'nɛs-/ *n* someone who has been specifically trained in the administration of anaesthetics to patients.

anaesthetize, -ise /ə'ni:sθətaɪz/ or (*US*) **anesthetize** /ə'nɛs-/ *vb* to give an anaesthetic to someone.

anagram *n* a word, phrase or sentence that is formed by changing the order of the letters of another word, phrase or sentence.

analgesia /anəl'dʒi:zɪə/ *n, physiol* a reduction in or loss of the ability to feel pain.

analgesic *n* a drug or other agent that relieves pain.

analog an alternative *US* spelling of ANALOGUE.

analogize or **-ise** *vb* to use analogy, esp in order to clarify a point or for rhetorical effect.

analogous adj similar or alike in some way.

analogue or (US) **analog** n something regarded in terms of its similarity or parallelism to something else. ➤ adj of a device or physical quantity: changing continuously rather than in a series of discrete steps, and therefore capable of being represented by an electric voltage: an analogue computer. Compare DIGITAL.

analogy n (-ies) 1 a similarity in some ways. 2 a way of reasoning which makes it possible to explain one thing or event by comparing it with something else. ○ **analogical** adj.

analyse or (US) **analyze** /'anəlaɪz/ vb 1 to examine the structure or content of something in detail. 2 to resolve or separate something into its component parts. 3 to detect and identify the different chemical compounds present in (a mixture). 4 to psychoanalyse someone.

analysis /ə'nalɪsɪs/ n (-ses /-siːz/) 1 a detailed examination of the structure and content of something. 2 a statement of the results of such an examination. 3 short for PSYCHOANALYSIS.

analyst /'anəlɪst/ n someone who is skilled in analysis.

analytic or **analytical** adj concerning or involving analysis. ○ **analytically** adv.

anaphylaxis /anafɪ'laksɪs/ n, med a sudden severe hypersensitive reaction to a particular foreign substance or antigen. ○ **anaphylactic** adj.

anarchist n 1 someone who believes that governments and laws are unnecessary and should be abolished. 2 someone who tries to overthrow the government by violence. 3 someone who tries to cause disorder of any kind. ○ **anarchism** n. ○ **anarchistic** adj.

anarchy n 1 confusion and lack of order, esp because of the failure or breakdown of law and government. 2 the absence of law and government. ○ **anarchic** /an'ɑːkɪk/ adj.

anathema /ə'naθəmə/ n 1 someone or something that is detested or abhorred. 2 a curse.

anathematize or **-ise** vb to curse or denounce.

anatomy n (-ies) 1 the scientific study of the structure of plants and animals. 2 the physical structure of a plant or animal, esp the internal structure. 3 any close examination, analysis or study of something. 4 non-technical someone's body. ○ **anatomical** /anə'tɒmɪkəl/ adj. ○ **anatomist** or n.

ANC abbrev African National Congress.

ancestor n 1 someone, usu more distant than a grandparent, from whom a person is descended. 2 a plant or animal that another type of plant or animal has evolved from.

ancestral adj belonging to or inherited from one's ancestors: the ancestral home.

ancestry n (-ies) lineage or family descent, esp when it can be traced back over many generations.

anchor n 1 a heavy piece of metal attached by a cable to a ship to restrict the ship's movement, often with barbs that catch in the seabed or riverbed. 2 anything that acts as a weight to secure something else. 3 anything that gives security or stability. ➤ vb 1 to fasten (a ship) using an anchor. 2 to fasten anything securely. 3 intr to drop an anchor and become moored by it; to be moored by an anchor.

anchorage n a place where a ship may anchor.

anchorite n someone who lives alone or separate from other people, usu for religious reasons.

anchorman n 1 TV, radio the person in the studio who provides the links with outside broadcast reporters, between commercial breaks, etc. 2 athletics the last person to run in a relay race.

anchovy /'antʃəvɪ/ n (-ies) a small fish related to the herring, with a pungent flavour.

ancien régime /French ɑ̃sjɛ̃ reʒim/ n (**anciens régimes** /ɑ̃sjɛ̃ reʒim/) 1 the French political, social and royal systems that were in place before the Revolution of 1789. 2 any outmoded system.

ancient adj 1 dating from very long ago. 2 very old. 3 dating from before the end of the Western Roman Empire in AD 476.

ancillary /an'sɪlərɪ/ adj 1 helping or giving support to something else, eg medical services. 2 being used as an extra. ➤ n (-ies) someone or something used as support or backup.

and conj 1 a used to show addition: dogs and cats; b used in sums of addition: two and two make four. 2 a used to connect an action that follows as a result or reason of a previous one: I fell and banged my head; b used to connect an action that follows on sequentially from another: Boil the kettle and make the tea. 3 used to show repetition or duration: She cried and cried. 4 used to show progression: The crowd got bigger and bigger. 5 used to show variety or contrast: We discussed the ins and outs of it. 6 used after some verbs instead of to: come and try • go and get it.

andante /an'dantɪ, -teɪ/ mus, adv, adj in a slow, steady manner. ➤ n a piece of music to be played in this way.

andiron /'andaɪən/ n a decorated iron bar, usu one of a pair, for supporting logs and coal in a big fireplace.

and/or conj either or both of two possibilities stated: cakes and/or biscuits.

androgynous adj 1 biol denoting an animal or plant that shows both male and female characteristics, esp both male and female sex organs. 2 showing both male and female traits, eg someone who could be mistaken for either sex.

android n a robot that resembles a human being in form or feature.

anecdote n a short entertaining account of an incident. ○ **anecdotal** adj.

anemia an alternative N Am spelling of ANAEMIA.

anemometer n a device for measuring wind speed.

anemone /ə'nɛmənɪ/ n 1 bot any of several

plants of the buttercup family, esp with red, purple, blue or white cup-shaped flowers. **2** *zool* short form of SEA ANEMONE.

aneroid barometer *n, meteorol* a type of barometer used to measure atmospheric pressure and to estimate altitude.

anesthesia an alternative *N Am* spelling of ANAESTHESIA.

anesthesiologist *n, US* an ANAESTHETIST.

aneurysm or **aneurism** /ˈanjərɪzəm/ *n, pathol* a balloon-like swelling in the wall of an artery.

anew *adv* **1** once more, again. **2** in a different way.

angel *n* **1** a messenger or attendant of God. **2** a representation of this in the form of a human being with a halo and wings. **3** *colloq* a good, helpful, pure or beautiful person. **4** *colloq* someone who puts money into an enterprise, particularly a theatrical production.

angelfish *n* a S American freshwater fish with a very deep body, flattened from side to side and covered with dark vertical stripes, and elongated pectoral fins.

angel food cake or **angel cake** *n, US* a light sponge cake.

angelic *adj* of someone's face, expression, behaviour, etc: like that of an angel, esp in being innocent, beautiful, etc. ○ **angelically** *adv*.

angelica *n* a tall plant whose stem and leaf stalks are crystallized in sugar and used as a food flavouring and cake decoration.

angelus /ˈandʒələs/ *n, Christianity* **1** a Roman Catholic prayer said in the morning, at noon and at sunset. **2** a bell rung to announce these prayers.

anger *n* a feeling of great displeasure or annoyance. ➤ *vb* to cause this kind of feeling in someone; to displease.

angina /anˈdʒaɪnə/ *n, pathol* severe pain behind the chest-bone, usu induced by insufficient blood supply to the heart muscle during exertion.

angiogram /ˈandʒɪoʊɡram/ *n, med* a type of X-ray photograph to record the condition of blood vessels.

Angle *n* a member of a N German tribe who settled in N and E England in the 5c, forming the kingdoms of Northumbria, Mercia and East Anglia.

angle[1] *n* **1** *maths* a measure of the rotation of a line about a point, usu measured in degrees, radians or revolutions. **2** the point where two lines or planes intersect. **3** the extent to which one line slopes away from another. **4** a corner. **5** a point of view. ➤ *vb* **1** *tr & intr* to move in or place at an angle. **2** to present a news story, information, etc from a particular point of view.

angle[2] *vb* **1** to use a rod and line for catching fish. **2** (**angle for sth**) to try to get it in a devious or indirect way. ○ **angler** *n*. ○ **angling** *n*.

Anglican *adj* relating to the Church of England or another Church in communion with it. ➤ *n* a member of an Anglican Church. ○ **Anglicanism** *n*.

Anglicism *n* **1** a specifically English word, phrase or idiom. **2** a custom or characteristic that is peculiar to the English.

anglicize or **-ise** *vb* to make something English in form or character.

Anglo- *comb form, denoting* **1** English: *Anglophobic*. **2** British: *Anglo-American*.

Anglo-Catholic *n* a member of an Anglican Church which emphasizes the Church's Catholic traditions. ○ **Anglo-Catholicism** *n*.

Anglo-Indian *n* **1** someone of British descent who has lived in India for a long time. **2** someone of mixed English and Indian descent.

anglophile or **Anglophile** *n* someone who admires England and the English.

anglophobe or **Anglophobe** *n* someone who hates or fears England and the English.

anglophone or **Anglophone** *n* someone who speaks English. ➤ *adj* belonging or relating to English-speaking people, countries, etc.

Anglo-Saxon *n* **1** a member of any of the Germanic tribes who settled in England in the 5c. **2** the English language before about 1150. **3** English as thought of in terms of its plain, usu monosyllabic, words including most of the taboo ones. **4** any English-speaking White person, usu one of Germanic descent. ➤ *adj* **1 a** belonging or relating to the Germanic peoples who settled in England; **b** belonging or relating to the early form of the English language. **2** of any English speech or writing: blunt and to the point. **3** belonging or relating to the shared cultural, legal, political, etc aspects of British and American life: *traditional Anglo-Saxon values*.

angora or **Angora** *n* the wool or cloth made from the soft silky wool of the Angora goat or rabbit. ➤ *adj* denoting a breed of domestic goat, rabbit or domestic cat with long white silky hair.

angry *adj* (**-ier, -iest**) **1** feeling or showing annoyance, resentment, wrath, disapproval, etc. **2** irritable, cross, etc: *an angry expression*. **3** of a wound, rash, etc: red and sore. ○ **angrily** *adv*.

angst *n* a feeling of apprehension or anxiety.

angstrom or **ångström** /ˈaŋstrəm/ *n* a unit of length equal to 10^{-10}m, but in the SI system now replaced by the NANOMETRE.

anguish *n* severe mental distress or torture. ➤ *vb, tr & intr* to suffer or cause to suffer severe mental distress or torture.

angular *adj* **1** of someone or part of someone's body, etc: thin and bony. **2** of actions, movement, etc: awkward or ungainly. **3** having sharp edges or corners. **4** measured by an angle: *angular distance*. ○ **angularity** *n*.

anhydrous *adj* denoting a chemical compound that contains no water.

aniline *n* a colourless oily highly toxic liquid organic compound, used in the manufacture of rubber, plastics, drugs and dyes.

animal *n* **1 a** *zool* any member of the kingdom of organisms that are capable of voluntary movement, and have specialized sense organs that allow rapid response to stimuli; **b** any of these excluding human beings. **2** someone who behaves in a rough uncivilized way. **3** colloq a person or thing: *This new multimedia PC is an altogether different animal.* ➤ adj **1** belonging or relating to, from or like, an animal: *animal fat.* **2** relating to physical desires; brutal; sensual: *animal passions.*

animalism n **1** an obsession with anything that is physical as opposed to the spiritual or intellectual. **2** the belief that humans are no better than other animals.

animality n **1** someone's animal nature or behaviour. **2** the state of being an animal.

animalize or **-ise** vb to make someone brutal or sensual.

animal magnetism n, often facetious the capacity to appear attractive, esp in a sexual way.

animal rights pl n the rights of animals to exist without being exploited by humans.

animate vb /'anɪmeɪt/ **1** to give life to someone or something. **2** to make something lively. **3** to record (drawings) on film in such a way as to make the images seem to move. ➤ adj /'anɪmət/ alive.

animated adj **1** lively; spirited: *an animated discussion.* **2** living. **3** moving as if alive: *animated cartoons.* ○ **animatedly** adv.

animation n **1** liveliness; vivacity. **2 a** the techniques used to record still drawings on film in such a way as to make the images seem to move; **b** any sequence of these images.

animator n someone who makes animated films or cartoons.

animism n the belief that plants and natural phenomena such as rivers, mountains, etc have souls. ○ **animist** n. ○ **animistic** adj.

animosity n (**-ies**) a strong dislike or hatred.

animus n a feeling of strong dislike or hatred.

anion /'anaɪən/ n, chem any negatively charged ION. Compare CATION. ○ **anionic** /anaɪ'ɒnɪk/ adj.

anise /'anɪs/ n an annual plant with small greyish-brown aromatic fruits containing liquorice-flavoured seeds.

aniseed n the liquorice-flavoured seeds of the anise plant, used as a flavouring.

ankh n the ancient Egyptian symbol of life in the form of a T-shaped cross with a loop above the horizontal bar.

ankle n **1** the joint that connects the leg and the foot. **2** the part of the leg just above the foot.

anklet n a chain or ring worn around the ankle.

ankylosis /aŋkɪ'ləʊsɪs/ n a disorder characterized by immobility or stiffening of a joint, the bones of which often become fixed in an abnormal position, as a result of injury, disease, surgery, etc.

annals pl n **1 a** yearly historical records of events; **b** recorded history in general. **2** regular reports of the work of an organization.

anneal vb, eng to heat (a material such as metal or glass) and then slowly cool it in order to make it softer, less brittle and easier to work.

annelid n, zool a worm with a long soft cylindrical body composed of many ring-shaped segments, eg the earthworm.

annex vb **1** to take possession of land or territory, esp by conquest or occupation. **2** to add or attach something to something larger. **3** colloq to take without permission. ➤ n an alternative US spelling of ANNEXE. ○ **annexation** n.

annexe or (US) **annex** n **1** an additional room, building, area, etc. **2** anything that has been added to something else, esp an extra clause, appendix, etc in a document.

annihilate vb **1** to destroy something completely. **2** to defeat, crush or humiliate someone, esp in an argument, sporting contest, etc. ○ **annihilation** n.

anniversary n (**-ies**) **1** a date on which some event took place in a previous year. **2** the celebration of this event on the same date each year.

Anno Domini see AD

annotate vb to add notes and explanations to (a book, article, etc). ○ **annotation** n.

announce vb **1** to make something known publicly. **2** to make (an arrival, esp of a guest or some form of transport) known. **3** to declare in advance: *The sign announced next week's sale.* **4** to be a sign of something: *dark clouds announcing a storm.* ○ **announcement** n.

announcer n someone who introduces programmes or reads the news on radio or television.

annoy vb **1** to anger or distress. **2** to harass or pester. ○ **annoyance** n. ○ **annoying** adj. ○ **annoyingly** adv.

annual adj **1** done or happening once a year or every year. **2** lasting for a year. ➤ n **1** bot a plant that germinates, flowers, produces seed, and dies within a period of one year. **2** a book published every year. ○ **annually** adv.

annual general meeting n a meeting of a public company, society, etc held once a year.

annualize or **-ise** vb to calculate (rates of interest, inflation, etc) for a year based on the figures for only part of it.

annuity /ə'njuːɪtɪ/ n (**-ies**) **1** a yearly grant or allowance. **2** money that has been invested to provide a fixed amount of interest every year.

annul vb (**annulled, annulling**) to declare publicly that a marriage, legal contract, etc is no longer valid. ○ **annulment** n.

annular adj ring-shaped.

annular eclipse n, astron an eclipse in which a thin ring of sunlight remains visible around the Moon's shadow.

annulate adj formed from or marked with rings.

the Annunciation n, Christianity **1** the announcement by the Angel Gabriel to Mary that she would be the mother of Christ (Luke 1.26–38). **2** the festival, held on 25 March, celebrating this.

anode n **1** in an electrolytic cell: the positive electrode, towards which negatively charged ions, usu in solution, are attracted. **2** the negative terminal of a battery. Compare CATHODE.

anodize or **-ise** *vb* to coat (an object made of metal, esp aluminium) with a thin protective oxide film by making that object the ANODE in a cell to which an electric current is applied.

anodyne *n* **1** a medicine or drug that relieves or alleviates pain. **2** anything that has a palliative effect, esp to hurt feelings, mental distress, etc. ➤ *adj* able to relieve physical pain or mental distress.

anoint *vb* to put oil or ointment on (someone's head, feet, etc), usu as part of a religious ceremony, eg baptism. ○ **anointment** *n*.

anomalous *adj* different from the usual; irregular; peculiar.

anomaly /ə'nɒmǝlɪ/ *n* (**-ies**) **1** something that is unusual or different from what is usual. **2** divergence from what is usual or expected.

anon[1] *abbrev* anonymous.

anon[2] *adv, old use* some time soon.

anonymous /ə'nɒnɪmǝs/ *adj* **1** having no name. **2** of a piece of writing, an action, etc: from or by someone whose name is not known or not given. **3** without character; nondescript. ○ **anonymity** /anǝ'nɪmɪtɪ/ *n*.

anorak *n* **1** a hooded waterproof jacket. **2** *slang* someone who is obsessively involved in something that is generally regarded as boring or unfashionable.

anorexia *n* **1** loss of appetite. **2** the common name for ANOREXIA NERVOSA.

anorexia nervosa *n* a psychological disorder characterized by a significant decrease in body weight, deliberately induced by refusal to eat because of an obsessive desire to lose weight. ○ **anorexic** *n, adj*.

another *adj, pron* **1** one more. **2** one of a different kind.

answer *n* **1** something said or done in response to a question, request, letter, particular situation, etc. **2** (**the answer**) **a** the solution: *Winning the lottery would be the answer to all our problems*; **b** the solution to a mathematical problem. ➤ *vb* **1** *tr & intr* to make a spoken or written reply to something or someone. **2** to react or respond to something (esp a doorbell, the telephone, someone calling one's name, etc). **3** to solve (esp a maths problem), write in response to (an exam question), etc. **4** *intr* (**answer to sb**) to have to account to them. **5** to put up a defence to or offer an explanation for something. ◊ **answer back** to reply rudely.

answerable *adj* (*usu* **answerable to sb for sth**) accountable to them for it.

answering machine, **answerphone** or **ansaphone** *n* a recording device attached to a telephone, which automatically answers incoming calls by playing a pre-recorded message to the caller and recording the caller's message for subsequent playback.

ant *n* a small social insect that lives in colonies.

antacid *n, med* an alkaline substance that neutralizes acidity in the stomach.

antagonism *n* openly expressed dislike or opposition.

antagonist *n* an opponent or enemy. ○ **antagonistic** *adj*.

antagonize or **-ise** *vb* **1** to make someone feel anger or hostility. **2** to irritate.

Antarctic *n* (**the Antarctic**) the area round the South Pole. ➤ *adj* relating to this area.

ante *n* **1** a stake put up by a player, usu in poker, but also in other card games, before receiving any cards. **2** an advance payment. ➤ *vb* **1** (**anted, anteing**) to put up as a stake. **2** *tr & intr* (*usu* **ante up**) *colloq, esp US* to pay. ♦ **raise** or **up the ante 1** to increase the stakes in a card game. **2** to elevate the importance of something.

ante- *pfx* before in place or time: *anteroom* • *antenatal*.

anteater *n* a mammal that has a long cylindrical snout and a bushy tail.

antecedent /antɪ'siːdǝnt/ *n* **1** an event or circumstance which precedes another. **2** *gram* a word or phrase that some other word, usu a RELATIVE pronoun, relates to, eg in *the man who came to dinner, who* is a relative pronoun and its antecedent is *the man*. **3** (*usu* **antecedents**) **a** someone's past history; **b** someone's ancestry. ➤ *adj* going before in time.

antechamber *n* an ANTEROOM.

antedate *vb* **1** to belong to an earlier period than (some other date). **2** to put a date (on a document, letter, etc) that is earlier than the actual date.

antediluvian *adj* **1** belonging to the time before the flood as described in the Bible. **2** *facetious* very old or old-fashioned.

antelope *n* (**antelope** or **antelopes**) any of various species of hoofed mammal, usu with paired horns, found mainly in Africa.

ante meridiem *adj* indicating the time from midnight to midday. Compare POST MERIDIEM.

antenatal *adj* **1** formed or occurring before birth. **2** relating to the health and care of women during pregnancy.

antenna *n* **1** (**antennae** /an'tɛni:/) in esp insects and crustaceans: one of a pair of long slender jointed structures on the head which act as feelers but are also concerned with the sense of smell. **2** (**antennas**) an AERIAL.

antepenultimate *adj* third from last. ➤ *n* anything that is in third last position.

anterior *adj* **1** earlier in time. **2** at or nearer the front. Compare POSTERIOR.

anteroom *n* a small room which opens into another, more important, room.

anthem *n* **1** a song of praise or celebration, esp a NATIONAL ANTHEM. **2** a piece of music for a church choir, usu set to a Biblical text.

anther *n, bot* the structure at the tip of the stamen which contains the pollen sacs within which the pollen grains are produced.

ant hill *n* a heap of earth, leaves, twigs, etc that ants pile up over their nest.

anthology n (-ies) a collection of poems, usu by different authors but with some kind of thematic link. ○ **anthologist** n.

anthracite n a hard shiny black coal that burns with a short blue flame, generating much heat but little or no smoke.

anthrax n, pathol an acute infectious disease, mainly affecting sheep and cattle, which can be transmitted to humans and is often fatal if left untreated.

anthropoid adj belonging or relating to, or like, a human being in form. ➢ n (also **anthropoid ape**) any of the apes that shows a relatively close resemblance to a human, eg a chimpanzee or gorilla.

anthropology n the study and analysis of the origins and characteristics of human beings and their societies, customs and beliefs. ○ **anthropological** adj. ○ **anthropologist** n.

anthropomorphism n the ascribing of a human form or human characteristics or attributes such as behaviour, feelings, etc to animals, gods, objects, etc. ○ **anthropomorphic** adj.

anti adj, colloq opposed to (a particular policy, party, ideology, etc). ➢ n someone who is opposed to something, esp a particular policy, party, ideology, etc. Compare PRO¹.

anti- pfx, signifying **1** opposed to: anti-war. Compare PRO- (sense 1). **2** opposite to: anticlockwise • anticlimax. **3** mainly of drugs, remedies, etc: having the effect of counteracting, resisting or reversing: antidepressant • antibiotic. **4** of a device, product, etc: preventing; having a counteracting effect: antifreeze • anti-lock braking system. **5** set up as a rival or alternative: Antichrist • antipope.

anti-aircraft adj of a gun or missile: designed for use against enemy aircraft.

antibiotic n a substance that can selectively destroy or inhibit bacteria or fungi.

antibody n (-ies) a protein that is produced in the blood and forms an important part of the body's immune response.

antic n (often **antics**) a playful caper or trick.

Antichrist n **1** an enemy of Christ. **2** Christianity the great enemy of Christ, expected by the early Church to appear and reign over the world before Christ's second coming.

anticipate vb **1** to see what will be needed or wanted in the future and do what is necessary in advance. **2** to predict something and then act as though it is bound to happen. **3** to expect something. **4** to look forward to something. **5** to know beforehand: I could anticipate his every move. **6** tr & intr to mention or think something before the proper time. ○ **anticipation** n. ○ **anticipatory** adj.

anticlimax n a dull or disappointing end to a series of events, a film, etc. ○ **anticlimactic** adj.

anticlockwise adv, adj in the opposite direction to the direction that the hands of a clock move.

anticyclone n, meteorol an area of relatively high atmospheric pressure from which light winds spiral outward in the opposite direction to that of the Earth's rotation. Compare CYCLONE (sense 1).

antidepressant n, med any drug that prevents or relieves the symptoms of depression.

antidote n **1** any agent, eg a drug, that counteracts or prevents the action of a poison. **2** anything that prevents or counteracts something bad.

antifreeze n any substance that is added to water or some other liquid in order to lower its freezing point, used eg in the radiators of motor vehicles.

antigen /'antɪdʒən/ n, biol any foreign substance that stimulates the body's immune system to produce antibodies.

antihero n (**antiheroes**) a principal character in a novel, play, film, etc who lacks the conventional qualities of a hero.

antihistamine n, med a drug that counteracts the effects of histamines produced in allergic reactions such as hay fever.

antiknock n any substance that is added to petrol in order to reduce KNOCK (noun sense 5), esp in the engines of motor vehicles.

anti-lock or **anti-locking** adj of a braking system: fitted with a special sensor that prevents the wheels of a vehicle locking when the brakes are applied vigorously.

antilogarithm n, maths the number whose logarithm to a specified base is a given number.

antimatter n a substance that is composed entirely of ANTIPARTICLES.

antimony /'antɪmənɪ/ n, chem a brittle bluishwhite metallic element used to increase the hardness of lead alloys.

antinomy /an'tɪnəmɪ/ n (-ies) **1** a contradiction between two laws or beliefs that are reasonable in themselves. **2** a conflict of authority.

antinuclear adj opposed to the use of nuclear weapons or nuclear power.

antiparticle n, physics a subatomic particle which has the opposite electrical charge, magnetic moment and spin from other subatomic particles of the same mass.

antipasto n (**antipasti** /antɪ'pastiː/) a starter of a meal.

antipathy /an'tɪpəθɪ/ n (-ies) a feeling of strong dislike or hostility.

anti-personnel adj of weapons and bombs: designed to attack and kill people rather than destroy buildings, other weapons, etc.

antiperspirant n a substance applied to the skin, esp the armpits, in order to reduce perspiration.

antiphon n a hymn or psalm sung alternately by two groups of singers.

antipodes /an'tɪpədiːz/ pl n (usu the **Antipodes**) two points on the Earth's surface that are diametrically opposite each other, esp Australia and New Zealand as being opposite Europe. ○ **antipodean** /-'dɪən/ adj, n.

antipope *n* a pope elected in opposition to one already chosen.

antipyretic /antɪpaɪə'rɛtɪk/ *n* a drug that reduces or prevents fever.

antiquarian /antɪ'kwɛərɪən/ *adj* referring or relating to, or dealing in, antiques and/or rare books. ➤ *n* an antiquary.

antiquary /'antɪkwərɪ/ *n* (**-ies**) someone who collects, studies or deals in antiques or antiquities.

antiquated *adj* old and out of date; old-fashioned.

antique *n* a piece of furniture, china, etc which is old and often valuable. ➤ *adj* 1 old and often valuable. 2 *colloq* old-fashioned.

antiquity *n* (*pl* in sense 3 only **-ies**) 1 ancient times, esp before the end of the Roman Empire in AD 476. 2 great age. 3 (**antiquities**) works of art or buildings surviving from ancient times.

antirrhinum *n* a bushy plant with large brightly coloured two-lipped flowers. Also called **snapdragon**.

anti-Semite *n* someone who is hostile to or prejudiced against Jews. ○ **anti-Semitic** *adj*. ○ **anti-Semitism** *n*.

antiseptic *n* a medicine or substance that kills or inhibits the growth of bacteria and other micro-organisms.

antiserum *n* (**antisera**) a blood serum containing antibodies that are specific for, and neutralize the effects of, a particular antigen, used in vaccines.

antisocial *adj* 1 reluctant to mix socially with other people. 2 of behaviour: harmful or annoying to the community in general. ○ **antisocially** *adv*.

antistatic *adj* preventing the accumulation of static electric charges.

antithesis /an'tɪθəsɪs/ *n* (**-ses**) 1 a direct opposite of something. 2 the placing together of contrasting ideas, words or themes in any oral or written argument, esp to produce an effect. ○ **antithetic** /antɪ'θɛtɪk/ or **antithetical** *adj*.

antitoxin *n*, *med* an antibody which neutralizes a toxin.

antitrades *pl n* winds that blow above and in the opposite direction to TRADE WINDS.

antler *n* either of a pair of usu branched solid bony outgrowths on the head of an animal belonging to the deer family. ○ **antlered** *adj*.

antonym *n* a word that is the opposite in meaning to another word.

antrum *n* (**antra**) *anat* a cavity or sinus, esp in a bone.

anus /'eɪnəs/ *n* the opening at the end of the alimentary canal, through which the faeces are expelled from the body. ○ **anal** *adj*.

anvil *n* a heavy iron block on which metal objects can be hammered into shape.

anxiety *n* (**-ies**) 1 a strong feeling of fear or distress. 2 *colloq* a worry.

anxious *adj* 1 worried, nervous or fearful. 2 causing worry, fear or uncertainty: *an anxious moment*. 3 very eager: *anxious to do well*. ○ **anxiously** *adv*.

any *adj* 1 one, no matter which: *I can't find any answer.* 2 some, no matter which: *Have you any apples?* 3 *with negatives and in questions* even a very small amount of something: *He won't tolerate any nonsense.* 4 indefinitely large: *You have any number of dresses.* 5 every, no matter which: *Any child could tell you.* ➤ *pron* any one or any amount. ➤ *adv*, *with negatives and in questions* in any way whatever: *It isn't any better.*

anybody *pron* 1 any person, no matter which: *There wasn't anybody home.* 2 an important person: *Everybody who is anybody will be invited.* 3 some ordinary person: *She's not just anybody, you know.*

anyhow *adv* 1 anyway. 2 carelessly; in an untidy state.

anyone *pron* anybody.

anything *pron* a thing of any kind; a thing, no matter which. ➤ *adv* in any way; to any extent: *She isn't anything like her sister.* ♦ **anything but** not at all: *It was anything but straightforward.*

anyway *conj* used as a sentence connector or when resuming an interrupted piece of dialogue: and so: *Anyway, you'll never guess what he did next.* ➤ *adv* 1 nevertheless; in spite of what has been said, done, etc. 2 *old use* in any way or manner: *Do it anyway you can.*

anywhere *adv* in, at or to any place. ➤ *pron* any place.

AOB or **a.o.b.** *abbrev* any other business, the last item on the agenda for a meeting, when any matter not already dealt with may be raised.

A1 *adj* first-rate or excellent.

aorta /eɪ'ɔːtə/ *n*, *anat* the main artery in the body, which carries oxygenated blood from the heart to the smaller arteries. ○ **aortic** *adj*.

apace *adv*, *literary* quickly.

Apache /ə'pætʃɪ/ *n* a member of a Native American people who formerly lived nomadically in New Mexico and Arizona.

apart *adv* 1 in or into pieces: *come apart.* 2 separated by a certain distance or time: *The villages are about 6 miles apart.* 3 to or on one side: *set apart for special occasions.* 4 disregarded, not considered, taken account of, etc: *joking apart.* 5 distinguished by some unique quality: *a breed apart.* ♦ **apart from sb** or **sth** not including them or it.

apartheid /ə'pɑːtheɪt, -haɪt/ *n* an official state policy, esp that operating in South Africa until 1992, of racial segregation.

apartment *n* 1 a single room in a house or flat. 2 (**apartments**) a set of rooms used for accommodation, usu in a large building. 3 *N Am* a self-contained set of rooms for living in, usu all on one floor, in a large building that is divided into a number of similar units. *Brit equivalent* **flat**.

apathy *n* 1 lack of interest or enthusiasm. 2 lack of emotion. ○ **apathetic** *adj*.

ape *n* 1 any of several species of primate that

differ from most monkeys, and resemble humans in that they have a highly developed brain, lack a tail and are capable of walking upright. **2** an ugly, stupid or clumsy person. ➤ *vb* to imitate (someone's behaviour, speech, habits, etc). ◆ **go ape** *slang* to go completely crazy.

apeman *n* any of various extinct primates thought to have been intermediate in development between humans and the higher apes.

aperient /ə'pɪərɪənt/ *n* a drug or other remedy that has a mild laxative effect.

aperitif /əpɛrɪ'tiːf/ *n* an alcoholic drink taken before a meal to stimulate the appetite.

aperture *n* **1** a small hole or opening. **2** the opening through which light enters an optical instrument such as a camera or telescope.

APEX *abbrev* Advance Purchase Excursion, a reduced fare for travel tickets booked a certain period in advance.

apex *n* (*apexes* or *apices* /'eɪpɪsiːz/) the highest point or tip.

aphasia *n, psychol* loss or impairment of the ability to speak or write, or to understand the meaning of spoken or written language.

aphelion /ap'hiːlɪən/ *n* (*aphelia*) the point in a planet's orbit when it is farthest from the Sun. Compare PERIHELION.

aphid /'eɪfɪd/ or **aphis** *n* (*aphids* or *aphides* /-diːz/) a small insect which feeds by piercing plant tissues and sucking the sap.

aphorism *n* a short and often clever or humorous saying expressing some well-known truth.

aphrodisiac /afrə'dɪzɪak/ *n* a food, drink or drug that is said to stimulate sexual desire. ➤ *adj* sexually exciting or arousing.

apiary /'eɪpɪərɪ/ *n* (*-ies*) a place where honey bees are kept.

apical /'apɪkəl, 'eɪ-/ *adj* belonging to, at or forming an apex.

apiculture *n* the rearing and breeding of honey bees.

apiece *adv* to, for, by or from each one: *They chipped in £5 apiece.*

apish *adj* **1** like an ape. **2** affected; silly.

aplenty *adv* in great numbers or abundance.

aplomb /ə'plɒm/ *n* calm self-assurance and poise.

apocalypse /ə'pɒkəlɪps/ *n* **1** (**Apocalypse**) the last book of the New Testament, also called the REVELATION of St John, which describes the end of the world. **2** any revelation of the future, esp future destruction or violence. ○ **apocalyptic** *adj*.

Apocrypha /ə'pɒkrɪfə/ *pl n* those books of the Bible included in the ancient Greek and Latin versions of the Old Testament but not in the Hebrew version, and which are excluded from modern Protestant Bibles but included in Roman Catholic and Orthodox Bibles.

apocryphal *adj* **1** being of doubtful authenticity. **2** of a story, etc: unlikely to be true; mythical. **3** (**Apocryphal**) of the Apocrypha.

apogee /'apoʊdʒiː/ *n, astron* the point in the orbit of the Moon or a satellite around the Earth when it is at its greatest distance from the Earth. Compare PERIGEE.

apolitical *adj* not interested or active in politics.

apologetic *adj* showing or expressing regret for a mistake or offence. ○ **apologetically** *adv*.

apologia *n* (*apologias*) a formal statement in defence of a belief, cause, etc.

apologist *n* someone who formally defends a belief or cause.

apologize or **-ise** *vb, intr* to acknowledge a mistake or offence and express regret for it.

apology *n* (*-ies*) **1** an expression of regret for a mistake or offence. **2** a formal defence of a belief or cause. ◆ **an apology for sth** a poor example of it.

apophthegm or **apothegm** /'apəθɛm/ *n* a short saying expressing some general truth.

apoplectic *adj* **1** suffering from, causing or relating to apoplexy. **2** *colloq* red-faced and seething with anger.

apoplexy *n* (*-ies*) the former name for a STROKE (sense 9) caused by a cerebral haemorrhage.

apostasy /ə'pɒstəsɪ/ *n* (*-ies*) the rejection of one's religion or principles or of one's affiliation to a political party, etc.

apostate *n* someone who rejects a religion, belief, political affiliation, etc that they previously held.

a posteriori /eɪ pɒstɛrɪ'ɔːraɪ/ *adj, adv* of an argument or reasoning: working from effect to cause or from particular cases to general principles. Compare A PRIORI.

apostle *n* **1** *Christianity* (often **Apostle**) someone sent out to preach about Christ in the early Church, esp one of the twelve DISCIPLES. **2** any enthusiastic supporter of a cause, belief, etc. ○ **apostolic** *adj*.

apostrophe[1] /ə'pɒstrəfɪ/ *n* a punctuation mark (') that in English is used to show that there has been an omission of a letter or letters, eg in a contraction such as *I'm* for *I am*, or as a signal for the possessive such as *Ann's book*.

apostrophe[2] /ə'pɒstrəfɪ/ *n, rhetoric* a passage in a speech, poem, etc which digresses to pointedly address a person or thing.

apothecary *n* (*-ies*) *old use* a chemist.

apotheosis /əpɒθɪ'əʊsɪs/ *n* (*-ses* /-siːz/) **1** the action of raising someone to the rank of a god. **2** a glorification or idealization of someone or something; **b** an ideal embodiment.

appal or (*N Am*) **appall** *vb* (*appals* or *appalls, appalled, appalling*) to shock, dismay or horrify.

appalling *adj* **1** causing feelings of shock or horror. **2** *colloq* extremely bad. ○ **appallingly** *adv*.

apparatchik *n* (*apparatchiks* or *apparatchiki*) an active member of an organization, esp a political party.

apparatus *n* (*apparatuses* or *apparatus*) **1** the

equipment needed for a specified purpose, esp in a laboratory, hospital, gym, etc. **2** an organization or system made up of many different parts.

apparel /ə'parəl/ *n, formal* clothing.

apparent *adj* **1** easy to see or understand; obvious. **2** seeming to be real but perhaps not actually so. ○ **apparently** *adv*.

apparition *n* **1** a sudden unexpected appearance, esp of a ghost. **2** a ghost.

appeal *n* **1 a** an urgent or formal request for help, money, medical aid, etc; **b** a request made in a pleading or heartfelt way. **2** *law* **a** an application or petition to a higher authority or law court to carry out a review of a decision taken by a lower one; **b** a review and its outcome as carried out by such an authority or court. **3** the quality of being attractive, interesting, pleasing, etc. **4** *cricket* a request made to the umpire from the fielding side to declare that a batsman is out. ➢ *vb, intr* **1** to make an urgent or formal request: *appealed for calm*. **2** *law* to request a higher authority or law court to review a decision given by a lower one. **3** *cricket* to ask the umpire to call a batsman out. **4** to be attractive, interesting, pleasing, etc. ○ **appealing** *adj* attractive.

appear *vb, intr* **1** to become visible or come into sight. **2** to develop: *Flaws in his design soon appeared*. **3** to seem. **4** to present oneself formally or in public, eg on stage. **5** to be present in a law court as either accused or counsel. **6** to be published.

appearance *n* **1** an act or instance of appearing. **2** the outward or superficial look of someone or something. **3** illusion; pretence: *the appearance of being a reasonable person*. **4** (**appearances**) the outward show or signs by which someone or something is judged or assessed: *Appearances can be deceptive*. ♦ **keep up appearances** to put on an outward public show that things are normal, stable, etc when they are not. **put in** or **make an appearance** to attend a meeting, party, etc only briefly.

appease *vb* **1** to calm, quieten, pacify, etc, esp by making some kind of concession. **2** to satisfy or allay (a thirst, appetite, doubt, etc). ○ **appeasement** *n*.

appellant *n* someone who makes an appeal to a higher court to review the decision of a lower one. ➢ *adj* of an appeal or appellant.

appellate /ə'pɛlɪt/ *adj, law* **1** concerned with appeals. **2** of a court, tribunal, etc: having the authority to review and, if necessary, overturn the earlier decision of another court.

appellation *n, formal* a name or title.

append *vb* to add or attach something to a document, esp as a supplement, footnote, etc.

appendage *n* **1** anything added or attached to a larger or more important part. **2** *zool* a part or organ, eg a leg, antenna, etc, that extends from the main body.

appendectomy or **appendicectomy** *n* (*-ies*)

surgery an operation to remove the appendix.

appendicitis *n, pathol* inflammation of the appendix.

appendix *n* (**appendixes** or **appendices** /ə'pɛn-dɪsiːz/) **1** a section containing extra information, notes, etc at the end of a book or document. **2** *anat* a short tube-like sac at the junction of the small and large intestines.

appertain *vb, intr* (*usu* **appertain to sth**) to belong or relate to it.

appetite *n* **1** a natural physical desire, esp for food. **2** the extent to which someone enjoys their food: *He has a very poor appetite*.

appetizer or **-iser** *n* a small amount of food or drink taken before a meal to stimulate the appetite.

appetizing or **-ising** *adj* stimulating the appetite, esp by looking or smelling delicious; tasty.

applaud *vb* **1** *intr* to show approval by clapping. **2** to express approval of something: *He applauded her brave decision*.

applause *n* approval or appreciation shown by clapping.

apple *n* **1** a small deciduous tree with pink or white flowers and edible fruit. **2** the firm round edible fruit of this tree, which has a green, red or yellow skin and white flesh. ♦ **in apple-pie order** neat and tidy. **the apple of one's eye** someone's favourite person. **upset the apple cart** to disrupt carefully made plans.

appliance *n* any electrical device, usu a tool or machine, that is used to perform a specific task, esp in the home.

applicable *adj* relevant; appropriate.

applicant *n* someone who has applied for a job, a university place, a grant, etc.

application *n* **1** a formal written or verbal request, proposal or submission, eg for a job. **2 a** the act of putting something on (something else); **b** something put on (something else): *an application of oil*. **3** the act of using something for a particular purpose: *the application of statistics to interpret the data*.

applicator *n* a device, eg on a tube of cream, etc, designed for putting something on to or into something else.

applied *adj* of a skill, theory, etc: put to practical use: *applied linguistics*. Compare PURE (sense 5).

appliqué /ə'pliːkeɪ/ *n* a decorative technique whereby fabrics are cut into various shapes and stitched onto each other. ➢ *vb* (**appliquéd, appliquéing**) to use this technique to create (a decorative article).

apply *vb* (*-ies, -ied*) **1** *intr* to make a formal request, proposal or submission, eg for a job. **2** to put something on to something else. **3** to spread something on a surface: *applied three coats of paint*. **4** *intr* to be relevant or suitable: *She thinks the rules don't apply to her*. **5** to put (a skill, rule, theory, etc) to practical use. **6** (*usu* **apply oneself to sth**) to give one's full attention or energy to (a task, etc).

appoint vb 1 tr & intr to give someone a job or position. 2 to fix or agree on (a date, time or place). 3 to equip or furnish. ○ **appointee** n.

appointment n 1 an arrangement to meet someone. 2 **a** the act of giving someone a job or position; **b** the job or position someone is given; **c** the person who is given a job or position. 3 (**appointments**) formal equipment and furnishings.

apportion vb to share out fairly or equally.

apposite adj suitable; well chosen; appropriate.

apposition n, gram a construction in which a series of nouns or noun phrases have the same grammatical status and refer to the same person or thing and give further information about them or it, eg Poppy, the cat.

appraisal n evaluation; an estimation of value.

appraise vb to decide the value or quality of (someone's skills, ability, etc).

appreciable adj significant; able to be measured or noticed: an appreciable difference.

appreciate vb 1 to be grateful or thankful for something. 2 to be aware of the value, quality, etc of something. 3 to understand or be aware of something. 4 usu intr to increase in value. ○ **appreciative** adj. ○ **appreciatively** adv.

appreciation n 1 gratitude or thanks. 2 sensitive understanding and enjoyment of the value or quality of something. 3 the state of knowing or being aware of something. 4 an increase in value.

apprehend vb 1 to arrest. 2 to understand.

apprehension n 1 fear or anxiety. 2 the act of capturing and arresting someone or something: They called for the immediate apprehension of the fugitive. 3 understanding.

apprehensive adj anxious or worried. ○ **apprehensively** adv.

apprentice n 1 someone, usu a young person, who works for an agreed period of time in order to learn a craft or trade. 2 anyone who is just beginning to learn something. ➢ vb to be or take someone on as an apprentice. ○ **apprenticeship** n.

apprise vb (usu **apprise sb of sth**) to give them information about it.

approach vb 1 tr & intr to come near or nearer in space, time, etc. 2 to begin to deal with, think about, etc (a problem, subject, etc): They approached the project from a new angle. 3 to contact someone, esp when wanting to suggest, propose, etc something. ➢ n 1 the act of coming near. 2 a way to, or means of reaching, a place. 3 a suggestion or proposal. 4 a way of considering or dealing with a problem, etc. 5 the course that an aircraft follows as it comes in to land. ○ **approachable** adj.

approbation n approval; consent.

appropriate adj /ə'prəʊprɪət/ suitable or proper. ➢ vb /-eɪt/ 1 to take something as one's own, esp without permission. 2 to put (money) aside for a particular purpose. ○ **appropriately** adv.

approval n 1 a favourable opinion. 2 official permission. ◆ **on approval** of goods for sale: able to be returned if not satisfactory.

approve vb 1 to agree to or permit. 2 intr (**approve of sb or sth**) to be pleased with or think well of them or it. ○ **approving** adj. ○ **approvingly** adv.

approx. abbrev approximate, approximately.

approximate adj /ə'prɒksɪmət/ almost exact or accurate. ➢ vb /-meɪt/ tr & intr to come close to something in value, quality, accuracy, etc. ○ **approximately** adv. ○ **approximation** n.

appurtenance n (usu **appurtenances**) an accessory to, or minor detail of, something larger, esp in reference to property-owning rights.

après-ski /ˌapreɪ'skiː/ n relaxation and entertainment after skiing.

apricot n 1 a small deciduous tree with oval toothed leaves and white or pale pink flowers. 2 the small edible fruit of this plant, which has yellow flesh and a soft furry yellowish-orange skin. 3 the colour of this fruit.

April n the fourth month of the year.

April fool n 1 someone who has had a practical joke played on them on 1 April. 2 a practical joke played on this date.

a priori /eɪ praɪ'ɔːraɪ/ adj, adv of an argument or reasoning: working from cause to effect or from general principles to particular cases. Compare A POSTERIORI.

apron n 1 a piece of cloth, plastic, etc tied around the waist and worn over the front of clothes to protect them. 2 a hard-surface area at an airport where aircraft are loaded. 3 theat the part of the stage that can still be seen when the curtain is closed. ◆ **tied to sb's apron strings** usu of a boy or man: completely dominated by and dependent on them, esp a mother or wife.

apropos /ˌaprə'pəʊ/ adj of remarks: suitable or to the point. ➢ adv by the way; appropriately. ◆ **apropos of sth** with reference to it.

apse n a semicircular recess, esp when arched and domed and at the east end of a church.

apt adj 1 suitable. 2 clever or quick to learn. ○ **aptly** adv. ○ **aptness** n. ◆ **apt to do sth** inclined or likely to do it.

aptitude n 1 (usu **aptitude for sth**) a natural skill or talent. 2 intelligence; speed in learning or understanding.

aqualung n a device that enables a diver to breathe under water, consisting of a mouth tube connected to cylinders of compressed air.

aquamarine n 1 geol a transparent bluish-green gemstone. 2 a bluish-green colour.

aquaplane n a board, similar to a water ski, on which the rider is towed along at high speed by a motor boat. ➢ vb, intr 1 to ride on an aquaplane. 2 of a vehicle: to slide along out of control on a thin film of water, the tyres having lost contact with the road surface.

aquarium n (**aquariums** or **aquaria**) 1 a glass tank that fish, other water animals and water plants are kept in so that they can be observed or displayed. **2** a building in a zoo, etc with several of these tanks.

Aquarius *n, astrol* **a** the eleventh sign of the zodiac; **b** a person born between 21 January and 19 February, under this sign.

aquatic *adj* **1** living or growing in, on or near water. **2** of sports: taking place in water. ➤ *n* **1** an aquatic animal or plant. **2** (**aquatics**) water sports.

aquatint *n* **1** a method of INTAGLIO etching that gives a transparent granular effect similar to that of watercolour. **2** a picture produced using this method of etching. ➤ *vb, tr & intr* to etch using this technique.

aqua vitae /ˈakwə ˈviːtaɪ/ *n* a strong alcoholic drink, esp brandy.

aqueduct *n* a channel or canal that carries water, esp one that is in the form of a tall bridge across a valley, river, etc.

aqueous *adj* **1** relating to water. **2** denoting a solution that contains water, or in which water is the solvent.

aqueous humour *n, anat* the clear liquid between the lens and the cornea of the eye.

aquiline *adj* **1** referring or relating to, or like, an eagle. **2** of someone's nose: curved like an eagle's beak.

Ar *symbol, chem* argon.

Arab *n* a member of a people living in the Middle East and N Africa. ➤ *adj* referring or relating to the Arabs.

arabesque *n* **1** *ballet* a position in which the dancer stands with one leg stretched out backwards and the body bent forwards from the hips. **2** a complex flowing design of leaves, flowers, etc woven together. **3** a short ornate piece of music.

Arabian *adj* belonging, referring or relating to Arabia or the Arabic language. ➤ *n* a person from Arabia.

Arabic *n* the language of the Arabs. ➤ *adj* belonging, relating or referring to Arabs, their language or culture.

Arabic numeral *n* any of the symbols 0, 1, 2, 3, 4, 5, 6, 7, 8 and 9, which are based on Arabic characters. Compare ROMAN NUMERALS.

arable *adj, agric* of land: suitable or used for ploughing and growing crops.

arachnid *n* any eight-legged invertebrate animal belonging to the class which includes spiders, scorpions and ticks.

arak see under ARRACK

Aramaic *n* any of a group of ancient languages, including the language spoken by Jesus Christ.

arbiter *n* **1** someone who has the authority or influence to settle arguments or disputes between other people. **2** someone who has great influence in matters of style, taste, etc.

arbitrary *adj* **1** capricious; whimsical. **2** based on subjective factors or random choice and not on objective principles. ○ **arbitrarily** *adv.*

arbitrate *vb, intr* to submit to or settle by arbitration. ○ **arbitrator** *n.*

arbitration *n* the settling of a dispute between two or more groups by some neutral person who is acceptable to all concerned.

arbor *n* **1** an axle or spindle. **2** an alternative *N Am* spelling of ARBOUR.

arboreal *adj* **1** relating to or resembling a tree. **2** denoting an animal that lives mainly in trees.

arboretum /ɑːbəˈriːtəm/ *n* (**arboreta** /-tə/) *bot* a botanical garden where trees and shrubs are grown.

arboriculture *n* the cultivation of trees and shrubs.

arbour or (*N Am*) **arbor** *n* a shady area in a garden formed by trees or climbing plants, usu with a seat.

arc *n* **1** a continuous section of a circle or other curve. **2** a continuous electric discharge, giving out heat and light, that is maintained across the space between two electrodes, used in welding, etc. ➤ *vb* **1** to form an arc. **2** to move in an apparent arc.

arcade *n* **1** a covered walk or passage, usu lined with shops. **2** a row of arches supporting a roof, wall, etc. **3** an AMUSEMENT ARCADE.

Arcadian *adj* characterized by simple rural pleasures.

arcane *adj* mysterious, secret or obscure.

arch¹ *n* **1** a curved structure forming an opening, used to sustain an overlying weight such as a roof or bridge, or for ornament. **2** anything shaped like an arch. **3** the bony structure of the foot between the heel and the toes, normally having an upward curve. ➤ *vb* **1** to form an arch. **2** to span something like an arch.

arch² *adj* **1** *usu in compounds* chief; principal: *arch enemy.* **2** cunning; knowing: *an arch look.* **3** self-consciously playful or coy. ○ **archly** cleverly; slyly.

arch- or **archi-** *comb form* **1** chief; most important: *archduke.* **2** most esteemed, feared, extreme, etc of its kind: *arch-criminal.*

archaeology or (*US*) **archeology** *n* the study of the physical remains of earlier civilizations, esp buildings and artefacts. ○ **archaeological** or **archeological** *adj.* ○ **archaeologist** or **archeologist** *n.*

archaeopteryx /ɑːkɪˈɒptərɪks/ *n* the oldest fossil bird, which differed from modern birds in having a long bony tail supported by vertebrae, and sharp teeth on both jaws.

archaic /ɑːˈkeɪɪk/ *adj* **1** from a much earlier period. **2** out of date; old-fashioned. **3** of a word, phrase, etc: no longer in general use.

archaism *n* an archaic word, expression or style.

archangel *n* an angel of the highest rank.

archbishop *n* a chief BISHOP who is in charge of all the other bishops, clergy and churches in a particular area.

archbishopric *n* **1** the office of an archbishop. **2** the area that is governed by an archbishop.

archdeacon *n, C of E* a member of the clergy who ranks just below a bishop. ○ **archdeaconry** *n.*

archdiocese *n*, *C of E* the area under the control of an archbishop.

archduchess *n* 1 *hist* a princess in the Austrian royal family. 2 the wife of an archduke.

archduchy *n* (*-ies*) the area ruled by an archduke.

archduke *n* the title of some princes, esp formerly the son of the Emperor of Austria.

archeology an alternative *US* spelling of ARCHAEOLOGY.

archer *n* someone who uses a bow and arrow.

archery *n* the art or sport of shooting with a bow and arrow.

archetype /ˈɑːkɪtaɪp/ *n* 1 an original model; a prototype. 2 a perfect example. ○ **archetypal** *adj*.

archi- see ARCH-

archidiaconal /ɑːkɪdaɪˈakənəl/ *adj* referring or relating to an archdeacon or archdeaconry.

archiepiscopal *adj* relating or referring to an archbishop.

archipelago /ɑːkɪˈpɛləɡoʊ/ *n*, *geog* a group or chain of islands separated from each other by narrow bodies of water.

architect *n* 1 someone who is professionally qualified to design buildings and other large structures and supervise their construction. 2 someone who is responsible for creating or initiating something: *the architect of modern Europe*.

architecture *n* 1 the art, science and profession of designing and constructing buildings, ships and other large structures. 2 **a** a specified historical, regional, etc style of building design: *Victorian architecture*; **b** the buildings built in any particular style. 3 the way in which anything is physically constructed. 4 *comput* the general specification and internal configuration of a computer. ○ **architectural** *adj*.

architrave /ˈɑːkɪtreɪv/ *n* 1 *archit* a beam that forms the bottom part of an ENTABLATURE and which rests across the top of a row of columns. 2 a moulded frame around a door or window.

archive /ˈɑːkaɪv/ *n* 1 (*usu* **archives**) **a** a collection of old public documents, records, etc; **b** a place where such documents are kept. 2 *comput* a place for keeping files which are seldom used. ➢ *vb* to store (documents, etc) in an archive.

archivist /ˈɑːkɪvɪst/ *n* someone who keeps and catalogues archives.

archway *n* a passage or entrance under an arch or arches.

Arctic *n* (**the Arctic**) the area round the North Pole. ➢ *adj* 1 belonging or relating to this area. 2 (**arctic**) *colloq* extremely cold: *arctic conditions*.

arc welding *n*, *eng* a form of welding in which two pieces of metal are joined by means of a continuous electric arc.

ardent *adj* 1 enthusiastic; eager. 2 passionate. ○ **ardently** *adv*.

ardour or (*US*) **ardor** *n* a great enthusiasm or passion.

arduous *adj* 1 difficult; needing a lot of work, effort or energy. 2 steep.

are[1] *vb* used with *you*, *we* and *they*: the 2nd person singular and 1st, 2nd and 3rd person plural of the present tense of BE: *You are here* • *We are alive* • *Here they are.*

are[2] *n* a unit of land measure equal to $100m^2$.

area *n* 1 a measure of the size of any surface, measured in square units. 2 a region or part. 3 any space set aside for a particular purpose. 4 the range of a subject, activity or topic. 5 an open space in front of a building's basement.

arena *n* 1 an area surrounded by seats, for public shows, sports contests, etc. 2 a place of great activity, esp conflict: *the political arena.*

aren't *contraction* 1 are not: *They aren't coming.* 2 *in questions* am not: *Aren't I lucky?*

areola *n* (**areolae** /əˈrɪəliː/ or **areolas**) *anat* the ring of pigmented tissue surrounding a nipple.

arête *n*, *mountaineering* a sharp ridge or mountain ledge.

argon *n*, *chem* a colourless odourless inert gas, one of the noble gases.

argot /ˈɑːɡoʊ/ *n* slang that is only used and understood by a particular group of people.

argue *vb* 1 *tr & intr* to put forward one's case, esp in a clear and well-ordered manner. 2 *intr* to quarrel or disagree. 3 to show or be evidence for something: *It argues a degree of enthusiasm on their part.* ○ **arguable** *adj*. ○ **arguably** *adv*.

argument *n* 1 a quarrel or unfriendly discussion. 2 a reason for or against an idea, etc.

argumentation *n* sensible and methodical reasoning.

argumentative *adj* fond of arguing; always ready to quarrel.

argy-bargy *n* a dispute. ➢ *vb* (*-ies, -ied*) *intr* to dispute or disagree.

aria /ˈɑːrɪə/ *n*, *mus* a long accompanied song for one voice, esp in an opera or oratorio.

arid *adj* 1 of a region or climate: characterized by very low rainfall. 2 lacking interest; dull. ○ **aridity** /əˈrɪdɪtɪ/ *n*.

Aries *n*, *astrol* **a** the first sign of the zodiac; **b** a person born between 21 March and 20 April, under this sign.

aright *adv*, *old use* correctly.

arise *vb* (**arose** /əˈrooz/, **arisen** /əˈrɪzən/) *intr* 1 to come into being. 2 (*usu* **arise from** or **out of sth**) to result from it. 3 to stand up. 4 to come to notice.

aristocracy *n* (*-ies*) 1 the highest social class. 2 **a** this class as a ruling body; **b** government by this class. 3 people considered to be the best representatives of something.

aristocrat *n* a member of the aristocracy.

aristocratic *adj* 1 referring or relating to the aristocracy. 2 proud and noble-looking.

arithmetic *n* /əˈrɪθmətɪk/ 1 the branch of mathematics that uses numbers to solve theoretical or practical problems, mainly by the processes of addition, subtraction, multiplication and division. **2** any calculation that involves the use of numbers. **3** skill, knowledge or understanding in this field. ➢ *adj* /ˌærɪθ-ˈmetɪk/ (*also* **arithmetical**) relating to arithmetic. ○ **arithmetically** *adv*. ○ **arithmetician** /ˌərɪθməˈtɪʃən/ *n*.

arithmetic progression *n* a sequence of numbers such that each number differs from the preceding and following ones by a constant amount, eg 4, 10, 16, 22.

ark *n, Bible* the vessel built by Noah in which his family and animals survived the Flood.

arm¹ *n* **1 a** in humans: either of the two upper limbs of the body, from the shoulders to the hands; **b** a limb of an octopus, squid, etc. **2** anything shaped like or similar to this: *an arm of the sea*. **3** the sleeve of a garment. **4** the part of a chair, etc that supports a person's arm. **5** a section or division of a larger group, eg of the army, etc. **6** power and influence: *the long arm of the law*. ♦ **at arm's length** at a distance, esp to avoid becoming too friendly. **with open arms** wholeheartedly.

arm² *n* (*usu* **arms**) **1** a weapon: *nuclear arms*. **2** fighting; soldiering. **3** a heraldic design that, along with others, makes up the symbol of a family, school, country, etc. ➢ *vb* **1** to equip (with weapons). **2** to prepare (a bomb) for use. ♦ **up in arms** openly angry and protesting.

armada *n* **1** a fleet of ships. **2** (**the Armada**) *hist* the fleet of Spanish ships sent to attack England in 1588.

armadillo *n* a small nocturnal burrowing American mammal, the head and body of which are covered with horny plates.

Armageddon *n* **1** a large-scale and bloody battle, esp the final battle between good and evil, as described in the New Testament (Revelation 16.16). **2** any war or conflict.

armament *n* **1** (**armaments**) weapons or military equipment. **2** preparation for war.

armature *n* **1** *eng* the moving part of an electromagnetic device in which a voltage is induced by a magnetic field. **2** a wire or wooden framework that forms the support for a sculpture as it is being modelled.

armband *n* a band of cloth or plastic worn round the arm.

armchair *n* a chair with arms at each side. ➢ *adj* taking no active part; taking an interest in the theory of something rather than its practice: *an armchair detective*.

armed forces *pl n* the military forces of a country, such as the army, air force and navy, thought of collectively.

armful *n* an amount that can be held in someone's arms.

armhole *n* the opening at the shoulder of a garment where the arm goes through.

armistice *n* an agreement between warring factions to suspend all fighting so that they can discuss peace terms; a truce.

Armistice Day *n* the anniversary of the day (11 Nov 1918) when fighting in World War I ended

and which, since the end of World War II, has been combined with Remembrance Day.

armlet *n* a band or bracelet worn round the arm.

armorial *adj* relating to heraldry or coats of arms.

armour or (*US*) **armor** *n* **1** *hist* a suit or covering of metal, chain-mail, etc, worn by men or horses to protect them against injury in battle. **2** metal covering to protect ships, tanks, etc against damage from weapons. **3** armoured fighting vehicles as a group. **4** a protective covering on some animals and plants. ○ **armoured** *adj*.

armourer *n* **1** someone whose job is to make or repair suits of armour, weapons, etc. **2** someone in charge of a regiment's arms.

armour-plate *n* strong metal or steel for protecting ships, tanks, etc. ○ **armour-plated** *adj*. ○ **armour-plating** *n*.

armoury *n* (-*ies*) **1** a place where arms are kept. **2** a collection of arms and weapons. **3** *US* a place where arms are manufactured.

armpit *n* the hollow under the arm at the shoulder.

army *n* (-*ies*) **1** a large number of people armed and organized for fighting on land. **2** the military profession. **3** a large number: *an army of Rangers supporters*.

arnica *n* **1** a composite plant with yellow flowers, valued for its medicinal properties. **2** a remedy made from the flowers of this plant.

A-road *n* in the UK: a main or principal road that can either be a dual or a single carriageway. Compare B-ROAD.

aroma *n* **1** a distinctive, usu pleasant, smell. **2** a subtle quality or charm.

aromatherapy *n* a form of therapy involving the use of essential plant oils, generally in combination with massage. ○ **aromatherapist** *n*.

aromatic *adj* **1** having a strong, but sweet or pleasant smell. **2** *chem* of an organic compound: having carbon atoms arranged in one or more rings rather than in chains. Compare ALIPHATIC. ➢ *n* anything, such as a herb, drug, etc, that gives off a strong fragrant smell. ○ **aromatically** *adv*.

around *adv* **1** on every side; in every direction: *throwing his money around*. **2** here and there; in different directions; in or to different places; with or to different people, etc: *You can see for miles around* • *It's best to shop around*. **3** approximately: *This cinema seats around 100*. **4** somewhere in the vicinity: *waiting around*. ➢ *prep* **1** on all sides of something. **2** in all directions from (a specified point): *The land around here is very fertile*. **3** over; in all directions: *Toys were scattered around the floor*. **4** so as to surround or encircle. **5** reached by making a turn or partial turn about: *The shop is around the corner*. **6** somewhere in or near. **7** approximately in or at; about. ♦ **get around to sth** or **to doing sth** to do it, esp eventually or reluctantly. **have been around** *colloq* to have had a great deal of experience of life.

arouse *vb* **1** to cause or produce (an emotion, reaction, response, etc). **2** to cause to become awake or active. ○ **arousal** *n*.

arpeggio /ɑːˈpɛdʒɪoʊ/ *n* a chord whose notes are played one at a time in rapid succession rather than simultaneously.

arrack or **arak** *n* an alcoholic drink made in Eastern and Middle Eastern countries from grain or rice.

arraign /əˈreɪn/ *vb* **1** to bring someone (usu someone who is already in custody) to a court of law to answer a criminal charge or charges. **2** to accuse someone. ○ **arraignment** *n*.

arrange *vb* **1** to put into the proper or desired order. **2** to settle the plans for something. **3** to make a mutual agreement. **4** to make (a piece of music) suitable for particular voices or instruments.

arrangement *n* **1** a plan or preparation for some future event. **2** the act of putting things into a proper order. **3** an agreement. **4** a piece of music which has been made suitable for particular voices or instruments.

arrant *adj* out-and-out; notorious: *an arrant liar.*

arras *n* a colourful woven tapestry often used as a wall hanging.

array *n* **1** a large and impressive number, display or collection. **2** a well-ordered arrangement, esp a military one: *troops in battle array.* **3** *comput* an arrangement of individual elements of data in such a way that any element can be located and retrieved. ➤ *vb* to put in order; to display.

arrears *pl n* an amount or quantity which still needs to be done or paid back. ◆ **in arrears** late in paying money that is owed.

arrest *vb* **1** to take someone into custody. **2** to stop or slow down the progress of (growth, development, decision, etc). **3** to catch or attract (someone's attention). **4** to seize (assets, property, freight, etc) by legal warrant. ➤ *n* **1** the act of taking, or state of being taken, into custody, esp by the police. **2** a stopping. **3** a halting or slowing down in the progress, development or growth of something. ◆ **under arrest** taken into police custody.

arresting *adj* strikingly individual or attractive.

arrival *n* **1** the act of coming to a destination. **2** someone or something that has arrived.

arrive *vb, intr* **1** to reach a place during a journey or come to a destination at the end of a journey. **2** (**arrive at sth**) to come to (a conclusion, decision, etc). **3** *colloq* to be successful or to attain recognition. **4** of a baby: to be born. **5** of a thing: to be brought, delivered, etc. **6** to come about or occur at last: *The day arrived when a decision had to be made.*

arrogant *adj* having or showing too high an opinion of one's own abilities or importance. ○ **arrogance** *n*.

arrogate *vb* to claim a responsibility, power, etc without having any legal right to do so.

arrow *n* **1** a thin straight stick with a sharp point at one end and feathers at the other, which is fired from a bow. **2** any arrow-shaped symbol or sign, esp one showing the way to go or the position of something.

arrowhead *n* the pointed tip of an arrow.

arrowroot *n* a fine-grained starch obtained from the tubers of a tropical plant, used as a food thickener.

arse or (*N Am*) **ass** *slang, n* the buttocks. ➤ *vb* (*also* **arse about** or **around**) to behave in a stupid, irritating way.

arsehole or (*N Am*) **asshole** *n, slang* **1** the anus. **2** someone whose behaviour, opinion, etc is not highly regarded.

arsenal *n* **1** a store for weapons, explosives, etc. **2** a factory or workshop where weapons are made, repaired or serviced. **3** the weapons, etc available to a country or group.

arsenic *n, chem* **1** a metalloid chemical element. **2** a powerful poison, an oxide of arsenic, used in insecticides, rodent poisons, etc. ○ **arsenical** /ɑːˈsɛnɪkəl/ *adj, n.*

arson *n* the crime of deliberately setting fire to a building, etc. ○ **arsonist** *n.*

art *n* **1 a** the creation of works of beauty, esp visual ones; **b** such creations thought of collectively. **2** human skill and work as opposed to nature. **3** a skill, esp one gained through practice: *the lost art of conversation.* **4** *colloq* cunning schemes.

art deco or **Art Deco** *n* a style of interior design, orig of the 1920s and 1930s, characterized by highly angular geometric shapes and strong colours.

artefact or **artifact** *n* a handcrafted object, eg a tool, esp one that is historically or archaeologically interesting.

arterial *adj* **1** affecting, relating to or like an artery or arteries. **2** of a road, etc: connecting large towns or cities; main, esp with lots of minor branches.

arteriosclerosis /ɑːtɪərɪoʊskləˈroʊsɪs, -sklɪə-/ *n* (*-ses* /-siːz/) *pathol* a disease of the arteries characterized by thickening of the artery walls, loss of elasticity and eventual obstruction of blood flow.

artery *n* (*-ies*) **1** *anat* a blood vessel that carries oxygenated blood from the heart to the body tissues. **2** a main road, railway or shipping lane.

artesian well *n, geol* a deep well in which the water is under pressure and so is forced to flow upward.

artful *adj* **1** cunning, esp in being able to achieve what one wants. **2** skilful. ○ **artfully** *adv.*

arthritis /ɑːˈθraɪtɪs/ *n, pathol* inflammation of one or more joints, characterized by swelling, pain and often restricted movement of the affected part. ○ **arthritic** /ɑːˈθrɪtɪk/ *adj.*

arthropod *n, zool* any invertebrate animal

such as an insect, crustacean, ARACHNID and MYRIAPOD.

artichoke *n* **1** a GLOBE ARTICHOKE. **2** a JERUSALEM ARTICHOKE.

article *n* **1** a thing or object. **2** a short written composition in a newspaper, magazine, etc. **3** a clause or paragraph in a document, legal agreement, etc. **4** *gram* the definite article 'the' or the indefinite article 'a' or 'an'.

articled *adj* of a trainee lawyer, accountant, etc: bound by a legal contract while working in an office to learn the job.

articular *adj* relating to or associated with a joint of the body.

articulate *vb* /ɑːˈtɪkjʊleɪt/ **1** *tr & intr* to pronounce (words) or speak clearly and distinctly. **2** to express (thoughts, feelings, ideas, etc) clearly. **3** *intr, physiol* to be attached by way of a joint: *The carpals articulate with the metacarpals.* ➢ *adj* /ɑːˈtɪkjʊlət/ **1 a** skilled at expressing one's thoughts clearly; **b** of a speech or a piece of writing: clearly presented, well-argued and to the point. **2** having joints. ○ **articulately** *adv.*

articulated lorry *n* a large lorry consisting of two or more separate parts, joined by a pivot.

articulation *n* **1** the act of speaking or expressing an idea in words. **2** *phonetics* **a** the process involved in uttering separate speech sounds; **b** the speech sound produced. **3** a joint.

artifact see ARTEFACT

artifice *n* **1** a clever trick or plan. **2** clever trickery; cunning.

artificer /ɑːˈtɪfɪsə(r)/ *n* **1** a skilled craftsman. **2** a mechanic in the army or navy.

artificial *adj* **1** made by human effort; not occurring naturally. **2** imitating something natural, esp in order to become a cheaper substitute for the natural product. **3** of someone, their behaviour, etc: not genuine or sincere. ○ **artificiality** *n.* ○ **artificially** *adv.*

artificial insemination *n, med* the introduction of semen into the vagina of a woman or female animal by artificial means in order to facilitate conception.

artificial intelligence *n* the development and use of computer systems that can perform some of the functions normally associated with human intelligence, such as learning and problem-solving.

artificial respiration *n* respiration that is stimulated and maintained manually or mechanically, by forcing air in and out of the lungs when normal spontaneous breathing has stopped.

artillery *n* (*-ies*) **1** large guns for use on land. **2** the part of an army equipped with such guns.

artisan *n* someone who does skilled work with their hands.

artist *n* **1** someone who produces works of art, esp paintings. **2** someone who is skilled at some particular thing. **3** an artiste. ○ **artistic** *adj.* ○ **artistically** *adv.*

artiste *n* a professional performer, esp a singer or dancer, in a theatre, circus, etc.

artistry *n* artistic skill and imagination.

artless *adj* **1** simple and natural in manner. **2** honest, not deceitful. ○ **artlessly** *adv.*

art nouveau /ɑː nuːˈvoʊ/ *n* a style of art, architecture and interior design that flourished towards the end of the 19c, characterized by the use of flowing curved lines that resemble plant stems interlaced with highly stylized flowers and leaves.

artwork *n* any illustrations, drawings, designs, etc in a book, magazine or other printed medium.

arty *adj* (**-ier, -iest**) *colloq* affectedly or ostentatiously artistic.

arum lily *n* a plant with large leaves shaped like arrow-heads and a yellow cylindrical SPADIX surrounded by a white, yellow or pink petal-like SPATHE.

Aryan *n* **1** *hist* in Nazi ideology: a European not of Jewish descent, esp someone of the northern European type with blonde hair and blue eyes. **2** a member of the peoples speaking any of the Indo-European languages, now esp the Indo-Iranian languages.

As *symbol, chem* arsenic.

as *conj* **1** when; while; during: *I met him as I was leaving the shop.* **2** because; since: *We didn't go as it was raining.* **3** in the manner that: *She was fussing as only a mother can.* **4** that which; what: *Do as you're told.* **5** to the extent that: *Try as he might, he still couldn't reach.* **6** for instance: *large books, as this one for example.* **7** in the same way that: *He married late in life, as his father had done.* **8** used to refer to something previously said, done, etc: like; just like: *As Frank says, the job won't be easy.* ➢ *prep* in the role of something: *speaking as her friend.* ➢ *adv* equally: *It was really hot yesterday, but I don't think today is as hot.* ◆ **as … as …** used in similes and for comparison: denoting that the things compared are the same or share the expected quality or characteristic: *as sly as a fox.* **as for** or **to sth** or **sb** with regard to it or them. **as if** or **as though** as he, she, etc would if: *We behaved as if nothing had happened.* **as well** also. **as yet** until now.

ASAP or **asap** *abbrev* as soon as possible.

asbestos *n* a fibrous mineral that is highly resistant to heat.

ASBO *abbrev* antisocial behaviour order, a court order forbidding unruly behaviour.

ascend *vb* **1** *tr & intr* to climb, go or rise up. **2** *intr* to slope upwards. **3** *intr* to rise to a higher level, rank, etc.

ascendancy or **ascendency** *n* controlling or dominating power.

ascendant or **ascendent** *adj* **1** having more influence or power. **2** *astrol* rising over the eastern horizon. ➢ *n, astrol* the sign of the zodiac rising over the eastern horizon at the time of an event, esp birth. ◆ **in the ascendant** showing an increase in power, wealth, etc.

ascension *n* **1** an act of climbing or moving upwards. **2** (**the Ascension**) Christ's believed passing into heaven. ♦ **Ascension Day** the fortieth day after Easter Sunday, when Christ's Ascension is celebrated.

ascent n **1** the act of climbing, ascending or rising. **2** an upward slope.

ascertain vb to find out; to discover (the truth, etc). ○ **ascertainment** n.

ascetic n someone who abstains from all physical comfort and pleasure, esp in solitude and for religious reasons. ➣ adj characterized by the abstinence from physical pleasure and comfort; self-denying.

ASCII /ˈaski:/ n, comput in digital computing systems: a code used for storage of text and for transmission of data between computers.

ascribe vb to attribute; assign. ○ **ascribable** adj.

asepsis /eɪˈsɛpsɪs/ n (-ses /-siːz/) the condition of being free from germs or other infection-causing micro-organisms. ○ **aseptic** adj, n.

asexual adj **1** denoting reproduction that does not involve sexual processes. **2** without functional sexual organs. ○ **asexuality** n. ○ **asexually** adv.

ash¹ n **1** the dusty residue that remains after something has been burnt. **2** the powdery dust that is put out by an erupting volcano. **3** (**ashes**) the remains of a body after cremation. ○ **ashy** adj (-ier, -iest).

ash² n **1** a deciduous tree or shrub with strong grey bark, small clusters of greenish flowers and winged fruits. **2** the timber of this tree.

ashamed adj **1** troubled by feelings of guilt, embarrassment, etc. **2** (usu **ashamed of sb** or **sth**) embarrassed or humiliated by them or it. **3** hesitant or reluctant (to do something) because of embarrassment, guilt, fear of disapproval, etc. ○ **ashamedly** /əˈʃeɪmɪdlɪ/ adv.

ashen adj of a face: very pale, usu from shock.

ashlar or **ashler** n **1** a large square-cut stone that is used for building or facing walls. **2** masonry made of ashlars.

ashore adv to, towards or onto the shore or land.

ashram n a place of retreat, esp in India, for a holy man or for a religious community.

ashtray n a dish or other container for the ash, butts, etc from cigarettes, etc.

Ash Wednesday n, Christianity the first day of LENT, so called because of the practice of sprinkling ashes on the heads of penitents.

Asian adj belonging or relating to the continent of Asia, its inhabitants or its languages. ➣ n **1** an inhabitant of, or person born in, Asia. **2** someone of Asian descent.

Asiatic adj belonging or relating to Asia or Asians. ➣ n, offensive an Asian.

aside adv **1** on, to, towards or over to one side. **2** away from everyone else: I took him aside to give him the news. **3** in a direction away from oneself: She tossed the magazine aside in disgust. **4** out of mind, consideration, etc, esp temporarily: He put his worries aside. ➣ n **1**

words said by a character in a play which the audience can hear, but which the other characters cannot. **2** a remark that is not related to the main subject of a conversation. ♦ **aside from sth** not including it.

asinine adj **1** relating to or resembling an ass. **2** stupid; idiotic; stubborn.

ask vb **1** tr & intr to question someone about something: I asked her name. **2** to call for an answer to (a question): We asked what qualifications she had. **3** to inquire about: You need to ask the way. **4** to invite. **5** to expect: I don't ask a lot of him. ◊ **ask after sb** to show concern about their health. **ask sb out** to invite them on a date.

askance adv sideways. ♦ **look askance at sb** or **sth** to consider them or it with suspicion or disapproval.

askew adv, adj squint; not properly straight or level.

asking price n the proposed selling price of something, set by the seller.

asleep adj **1** in a sleeping state. **2** colloq not paying attention. **3** of limbs, hands, feet, etc: numb. ➣ adv into a sleeping state: fall asleep.

AS level or **Advanced Subsidiary level** n **1** an examination taken by sixth-form students after one year of study, either for its own sake or as a preliminary to the A-level examination. **2** a pass in such an examination.

asp n **1** a small venomous S European snake. **2** the Egyptian cobra.

asparagus n **1** a plant with cylindrical green shoots or 'spears' that function as leaves. **2** the harvested shoots of this plant, eaten as a vegetable.

aspartame n an artificial sweetener, widely used in the food industry and by diabetics and dieters.

aspect /ˈaspɛkt/ n **1** a particular or distinct part or element of a problem, subject, etc. **2** a particular way of considering a matter: It's a very serious matter from all aspects. **3 a** the appearance something has to the eye: a lush green aspect; **b** a look or appearance, esp of a face: a worried aspect. **4** the direction something faces: a southern aspect.

aspen n a deciduous tree of the poplar family, with smooth grey bark and leaves that tremble in the slightest breeze.

asperity n (-ies) roughness, bitterness or harshness, esp of temper.

aspersion n. ♦ **cast aspersions on sb** or **sth** to make a damaging or spiteful remark.

asphalt n a brown or black semi-solid bituminous material used in the construction industry for roofing, or mixed with rock chips or gravel to make paving and road-surfacing materials. ➣ vb to cover with asphalt.

asphodel n a plant of the lily family with long narrow leaves and yellow or white star-shaped flowers.

asphyxia /asˈfɪksɪə/ n suffocation caused by any factor that interferes with respiration and prevents oxygen from reaching the body tissues, such as choking, drowning or inhaling poisonous gases.

asphyxiate vb, tr & intr **1** to stop or cause to stop breathing. **2** to suffocate. ◦ **asphyxiation** n.

aspic n a savoury jelly made from meat or fish stock, used as a mould for terrines, fish, eggs, etc.

aspidistra n an evergreen house plant with broad leathery leaves, and dull-purple bell-shaped flowers.

aspirate n /ˈaspɪrət/ phonetics the sound represented in English and several other languages by the letter h. ➤ vb /ˈaspɪreɪt/ **1** phonetics to pronounce the h sound in a word, or pronounce a word giving this sound its full phonetic value. **2** to withdraw (liquid, gas or solid debris) from a cavity by suction.

aspiration n **1** eager desire; ambition. **2** the removal of fluid from a cavity in the body by suction using an aspirator.

aspirator n a device used to withdraw liquid, gas or solid debris from a cavity of the body.

aspire vb (usu **aspire to** or **after sth**) to have a strong desire to achieve or reach (an objective or ambition): aspired to greatness.

aspirin n **1** an analgesic drug that is widely used to relieve pain and to reduce inflammation and fever. **2** a tablet of this drug.

ass¹ n **1** a hoofed mammal resembling, but smaller than, a horse, with longer ears. **2** colloq a stupid person.

ass² n, N Am slang ARSE.

assail vb **1** to make a strong physical attack. **2** to criticize fiercely. **3** to agitate, esp mentally. **4** to face up to something with the intention of mastering it. ◦ **assailant** n.

assassin n someone who kills someone else, esp for political or religious reasons.

assassinate vb to murder, esp for political or religious reasons. ◦ **assassination** n.

assault n **1** a violent physical or verbal attack. **2** law any act that causes someone to feel physically threatened. **3** euphem rape or attempted rape. ➤ vb to make an assault on someone or something.

assault and battery n, law the act of threatening to physically attack someone which is then followed by an actual physical attack.

assault course n an obstacle course used esp for training soldiers.

assay n, metallurgy the analysis of the composition and purity of a metal in an ore or mineral, or of a chemical compound in a mixture of compounds. ➤ vb to perform such an analysis on, or to determine the commercial value of (an ore or mineral) on the basis of such an analysis.

assegai or **assagai** n a thin light iron-tipped wooden spear used in southern Africa.

assemblage n **1** a collection of people or things. **2** the act of gathering together.

assemble vb **1** tr & intr to gather or collect together. **2** to put together (the parts of something, such as a machine).

assembler n, comput a computer program designed to convert assembly language into machine code.

assembly n (**-ies**) **1** a group of people gathered together, esp for a meeting. **2 a** the act of assembling; **b** the state of being assembled. **3** the procedure of putting together the parts of something, such as a machine.

assembly line n a continuous series of machines and workers that an article, product, etc passes along in the stages of its manufacture.

assent n consent or approval, esp official. ➤ vb (often **assent to sth**) to agree to it.

assert vb **1** to state firmly. **2** to insist on or defend (one's rights, opinions, etc). ◆ **assert oneself** to state one's wishes, defend one's opinions, etc confidently and vigorously.

assertion n **1** a positive or strong statement or claim. **2** the act of making such a claim or statement.

assertive adj of someone or their attitude: inclined to expressing wishes and opinions in a firm and confident manner. ◦ **assertively** adv. ◦ **assertiveness** n.

assess vb **1** to judge the quality or importance of something. **2** to estimate the cost, value, etc of something. **3** to fix the amount of (a fine or tax). ◦ **assessment** n.

assessor n **1** someone who assesses the importance or quality of something. **2** someone who assesses the value of property, etc for taxation. **3** someone who advises a judge, etc on technical matters.

asset n anything that is considered valuable or useful, such as a skill, quality, person, etc.

assets pl n, accounting the total value of the property and possessions of a person or company, esp when thought of in terms of whether or not it is enough to cover any debts.

asset-stripping n the practice of buying an unsuccessful company at a low price and selling off its assets separately for a profit.

asseverate vb to state solemnly.

asshole see ARSEHOLE

assiduous adj **1** hard-working. **2** done carefully and exactly. ◦ **assiduity** /əsɪˈdjuːɪtɪ/ n.

assign vb **1** to give (a task, etc) to someone. **2** to appoint someone to a position or task. **3** to fix (a time, place, etc) for a purpose. **4** to attribute or ascribe. **5** law, formerly to transfer (a title, property, interest, etc) to someone else.

assignation n a secret appointment to meet, esp between lovers.

assignee n, law someone to whom property, interest, etc is given by contract.

assignment n **1 a** a task or duty that has been selected for someone to do; **b** an exercise that is set for students, etc. **2** the act of assigning. **3** law a transfer of property, interest, etc to someone else.

assimilate vb **1** to become familiar with and

understand (information, etc) completely. **2** *tr & intr* to become part of, or make (people) part of, a larger group, esp when they are of a different race, etc. **3** to cause something to become similar to something else. ○ **assimilation** *n*.

assist *vb, tr & intr* to help. ○ **assistance** *n*.

assistant *n* **1** a person whose job is to help someone of higher rank, position, etc. **2** a person whose job is to serve customers in a shop: *sales assistant*.

assizes /ə'saɪziz/ *pl n, formerly* in England and Wales: court sittings which used to be held at regular intervals in each county.

assoc. *abbrev* **1** associated. **2** association.

associate *vb* /ə'səʊʃɪət, -sɪ-/ **1** to connect in the mind: *I associate lambs with spring.* **2** *intr* to mix socially: *Don't associate with him.* **3** to involve (oneself) in a group because of shared views or aims. **4** *intr* to join with people for a common purpose. ➤ *n* /-ət/ **1** a business partner or colleague. **2** a companion or friend. **3** someone who is admitted to a society, institution, etc without full membership. ➤ *adj* /-ət/ **1** joined with another, esp in a business: *an associate director.* **2** not having full membership of a society, institution, etc.

association *n* **1** an organization or club. **2** a friendship or partnership. **3** a connection in the mind. **4** the act of associating.

Association Football *n* the most common form of football, in which players are not allowed to use their hands.

associative *adj, maths* of an arithmetical process: resulting in the same answer, no matter which way the elements are grouped together.

assonance *n, prosody* a correspondence or resemblance in the sounds of words or syllables, either between their vowels, eg in *meet* and *bean*, or between all their consonants, eg in *keep* and *cape*. Compare ALLITERATION, RHYME.

assorted *adj* **1** mixed; consisting of various different kinds: *assorted chocolates.* **2** arranged in sorts; classified.

assortment *n* a mixed collection.

assuage /ə'sweɪdʒ/ *vb* to make (a pain, sorrow, hunger, etc) less severe.

assume *vb* **1** to accept something without proof; to take for granted. **2** to take on (a responsibility, duty, etc). **3** to take on or adopt (an appearance, quality, etc): *an issue assuming immense importance.* **4** to pretend to have or feel.

assumed *adj* false; not genuine: *an assumed name.*

assuming *adj* of someone or their attitude: arrogant; presumptuous. ➤ *conj* if it is taken as a fact: *Assuming that the meal won't cost too much, we should have enough money left.*

assumption *n* **1** something that is accepted as true without proof. **2** the act of accepting something as true without proof. **3** the act of assuming in other senses.

assurance *n* **1** a promise, guarantee or statement that something is true. **2** confidence and poise. **3** *Brit* insurance, esp life insurance.

assurance, insurance There is often confusion between **assurance** and **insurance**: with **assurance**, you have a guarantee of payment of a fixed sum at an agreed time, whereas with **insurance**, a variable sum is payable only if certain circumstances occur, eg fire or theft.

assure *vb* **1** to state positively and confidently; to guarantee. **2** to make (an event, etc) certain: *Her hard work assured her success.* **3** *Brit* to insure something (esp one's life). ○ **assurer** *n*.

assured *adj* **1** of someone or their attitude, behaviour, etc: confident and poised. **2** certain to happen. ○ **assuredly** /ə'ʃɔːrɪdlɪ/ *adv*.

AST *abbrev* Atlantic Standard Time.

astatine /'astətiːn/ *n, chem* a radioactive chemical element that occurs naturally in trace amounts and is produced artificially by bombarding bismuth with alpha particles.

aster *n* a plant with blue, purple, pink or white daisy-like flowers.

asterisk *n* a star-shaped symbol (*) used in printing and writing to mark a cross-reference to a footnote, an omission, etc. ➤ *vb* to mark with an asterisk.

astern *adv, adj* **1** in or towards the stern. **2** backwards. **3** behind.

asteroid *n* any of thousands of small rocky objects that orbit around the Sun, mainly between the orbits of Mars and Jupiter.

asthma /'asmə or (*US*) 'azmə/ *n* a respiratory disorder in which breathlessness and wheezing occur, caused by excessive contraction of muscles in the walls of the air passages. ○ **asthmatic** *n, adj*.

astigmatism /ə'stɪgmətɪzəm/ *n* a defect in a lens, esp abnormal curvature of the lens or cornea of the eye, causing distortion of the image of an object. ○ **astigmatic** *n, adj*.

astir *adj, adv* **1** awake and out of bed. **2** in a state of motion or excitement.

astonish *vb* to surprise greatly. ○ **astonishing** *adj*. ○ **astonishment** *n*.

astound *vb* to amaze or shock. ○ **astounding** *adj*.

astral *adj* of, or like, the stars.

astray *adj, adv* out of the right or expected way.

astride *adv* **1** with a leg on each side. **2** with legs apart. ➤ *prep* **1** with a leg on each side of something. **2** stretching across.

astringent *adj* **1** severe and harsh. **2** of a substance: causing cells to shrink. ➤ *n* an astringent substance. ○ **astringency** *n*.

astro- *comb form, denoting* stars or space.

astrolabe *n, astron, formerly* a navigational instrument used to observe the positions of the Sun and bright stars, and to estimate the local time by determining the altitude of the Sun or specific stars above the horizon.

astrology *n* the study of the movements of the

stars and planets, and of how they are thought to exert influences on people's lives, character traits, etc. ○ **astrologer** *n*. ○ **astrological** *adj*.

astronaut *n* someone who is trained to travel in space.

astronautics *sing n* the science of travel in space.

astronomical or **astronomic** *adj* **1** very large; vast. **2** relating to astronomy. ○ **astronomically** *adv*.

astronomy *n* the scientific study of celestial bodies, including the planets, stars and galaxies, and the universe as a whole.

astrophysics *sing n* the application of physical laws and theories to astronomical objects and phenomena. ○ **astrophysical** *adj*. ○ **astrophysicist** *n*.

astute *adj* mentally perceptive; shrewd. ○ **astutely** *adv*. ○ **astuteness** *n*.

asunder *adv* apart or into pieces.

asylum *n* **1** a place of safety or protection. **2** *hist* a mental hospital.

asymmetry *n* a lack of symmetry. ○ **asymmetric** and **asymmetrical** *adj*.

At *symbol, chem* astatine.

at *prep* **1** used to indicate position or place: in, within, on, near, etc: *She worked at a local factory*. **2** towards, in the direction of something: *working at getting fit*. **3** used to indicate a position in time: **a** around; on the stroke of: *The train arrives at six*; **b** having reached the age of: *At 17 you can start to drive*. **4** with, by, beside, next to, etc: *annoyed at her*. **5** engaged in; occupied with: *children at play*. **6** for; in exchange for: *I sold it at a profit*. **7** in a state of: *at liberty*.

atavism /ˈatəvɪzəm/ *n* **1** a resemblance to ancestors rather than immediate parents. **2** reversion to an earlier type. ○ **atavistic** *adj*.

ataxia /əˈtaksɪə/ or **ataxy** /əˈtaksɪ/ *n, pathol* inability of the brain to co-ordinate voluntary movements of the limbs.

ate *past tense of* EAT

atelier /əˈtɛlɪər; *French* atəlje/ *n* a workshop or artist's studio.

atheism *n* the belief that there is no god. ○ **atheist** *n*.

atherosclerosis *n* (*-ses*) *pathol* a form of ARTERIOSCLEROSIS in which fatty substances are deposited on the inner walls of arteries, eventually obstructing the flow of blood. ○ **atherosclerotic** /-ˈrɒtɪk/ *adj*.

athlete *n* **1** someone who trains for and competes in field and track events. **2** someone who is good at sports.

athlete's foot *n, colloq* a fungal infection of the foot.

athletic *adj* **1** of someone or their build: physically fit and strong. **2** relating to athletics. **3** of a physical type: distinguished by having well-developed muscles and a body that is in proportion. ○ **athletically** *adv*. ○ **athleticism** *n*.

athletics *sing n* competitive track and field sports such as running, jumping and throwing events.

Atlantic *n* (**the Atlantic**) the Atlantic Ocean, an ocean bounded by Europe and Africa to the East, and by N and S America to the West.

atlas *n* a book of maps and geographical charts.

ATM *abbrev* automated or automatic telling machine, a CASH MACHINE.

atmosphere *n* **1** the layer of gas surrounding a planet, esp the Earth, and held to it by gravity. **2** the air in a particular place. **3** the mood of a book, film, painting, piece of music, etc or the general impression that it gives. **4** the general or prevailing climate or mood: *an atmosphere of jubilation*. **5** a unit of pressure equal to normal air pressure at sea level. ○ **atmospheric** *adj*. ○ **atmospherically** *adv*.

atmospherics *pl n* radio-frequency electromagnetic radiation, produced by natural electrical disturbances in the Earth's atmosphere.

atoll *n* a circle of coral reef that surrounds a lagoon, and is itself surrounded by open sea.

atom *n* **1** the smallest unit of a chemical element that can display the properties of that element, and which is capable of combining with other atoms to form molecules. **2** *non-technical* a very small amount.

atom bomb or **atomic bomb** *n* a powerful explosive device that derives its force from the sudden release of enormous amounts of nuclear energy during nuclear fission.

atomic *adj* **1** relating to atoms. **2** obtained by atomic phenomena, esp nuclear fission: *atomic weapons*. ○ **atomically** *adv*.

atomic energy see NUCLEAR ENERGY

atomic mass unit *n, chem* a unit of mass which is equal to one twelfth of the mass of an atom of the carbon-12 isotope of carbon.

atomic number *n, chem* the number of protons in the nucleus of an atom of an element.

atomic theory *n, chem* the hypothesis that all atoms of the same element are alike and that a compound can be formed by the union of atoms of different elements in some simple ratio.

atomize or **-ise** *vb* **1** to reduce to atoms or small particles. **2** to reduce (a liquid) to a spray or mist of fine droplets by passage through a nozzle or jet under pressure. **3** to destroy by means of atomic weapons.

atomizer or **-iser** *n* a container that releases liquid, eg perfume, as a fine spray.

atonal *adj, mus* lacking tonality; not written in a particular key. ○ **atonality** *n*.

atone *vb* (*also* **atone for sth**) to make amends for (a wrongdoing, crime, sin, etc).

atonement *n* **1** an act of making amends for or paying for a wrongdoing, etc. **2** (**Atonement**) *Christianity* the reconciliation of God and man through the sufferings and death of Christ.

atop *adv* on top; at the top. ➤ *prep* on top of, or at the top of.

atrium *n* (**atria** /ˈeɪtrɪə, ˈɑːtrɪə/ or **atriums**) **1** a central court or entrance hall in an ancient Roman house. **2** a court in a public space, such as an office block, hotel, etc, that has galleries around it, and is often several storeys high. **3** *anat* either of the two upper chambers of the heart that receive blood from the veins. ○ **atrial** *adj*.

atrocious *adj* **1** *colloq* very bad. **2** extremely cruel or wicked. ○ **atrociously** *adv*.

atrocity *n* (**-ies**) **1** wicked or cruel behaviour. **2** an act of wickedness or cruelty.

atrophy /ˈatrəfɪ/ *vb* (**-ies, -ied**) *tr & intr* to diminish or die away; to cause to diminish or die away. ➢ *n* the process of atrophying.

atropine or **atropin** *n, med* a poisonous alkaloid drug, obtained from DEADLY NIGHT-SHADE.

attach *vb* **1** to fasten or join. **2** to associate (oneself) with or join. **3** to attribute or assign: *They attach great importance to detail.* ◊ **be attached to sb** or **sth** to be fond of them or it.

attaché /əˈtaʃeɪ/ *n* someone who is connected to a diplomatic department, etc because they have some specialized knowledge.

attaché-case *n* a small rigid leather case for holding documents, etc.

attached *adj* of someone: in a sexual relationship.

attachment *n* **1 a** an act or means of fastening; **b** the state of being fastened. **2** liking or affection. **3** an extra part that can be fitted to a machine, often used for changing its function slightly.

attack *vb* **1** to make a sudden violent attempt to hurt, damage or capture. **2** to criticize strongly in speech or writing. **3** to begin to do something with enthusiasm or determination. **4** *intr* to take the initiative in a game, contest, etc to attempt to score a goal, points, etc. ➢ *n* **1** an act or the action of attacking. **2** a sudden spell of illness: *an attack of flu.* **3** (**the attack**) the players, eg the strikers, forwards, etc in a team sport whose job is to score goals, points, etc. ○ **attacker** *n* someone who makes a physical, verbal, sporting, etc attack.

attain *vb* **1** to complete successfully; to achieve. **2** to reach (in space or time): *attained the summit.* ○ **attainable** *adj*.

attainment *n* **1** achievement, esp after some effort. **2** the act of achieving something. **3** something that is achieved.

attar *n* a fragrant essential oil that is distilled from rose petals, esp of the damask rose.

attempt *vb* **1** to try. **2** to try to master, tackle, answer, etc (a problem, etc). ➢ *n* an effort; an endeavour.

attend *vb* **1** *tr & intr* to be present at something. **2** to go regularly to (eg school, church, etc). **3** *intr* (**attend to sb** or **sth**) to take care of them or it or to take action over them or it. ○ **attender** *n*.

attendance *n* **1** the act of attending. **2** the number of people attending. **3** regularity of attending.

attendant *n* someone whose job is to help, guide or give some other service, esp to the public: *a museum attendant.* ➢ *adj* **1** being in or giving attendance. **2** accompanying: *attendant responsibilities.*

attention *n* **1** the act of concentrating or directing the mind. **2** notice; awareness: *The problem has recently come to my attention.* **3** special care and consideration: *attention to detail.* **4** (**attentions**) *old use* an act of politeness or courtship. ♦ **pay attention to sth 1** to listen to or concentrate on it closely. **2** to take care or heed of it.

attentive *adj* **1** showing close concentration; alert. **2** considerate. ○ **attentively** *adv*. ○ **attentiveness** *n*.

attenuated *adj* **1** thin. **2** diluted. **3** tapering.

attest *vb* **1** to be proof of the truth or validity of something. **2** *intr* (**attest to sth**) to certify that it is so, esp by giving a sworn statement. **3** to be evidence of something.

attic *n* a space or room at the top of a house under the roof.

attire *n* clothes, esp formal or elegant ones.

attitude *n* **1** a way of thinking or behaving. **2** a hostile or resentful manner. **3** a position of the body. **4** a pose, esp adopted for dramatic effect.

attitudinize or **-ise** *vb* to adopt an opinion or position for effect.

attorney /əˈtɜːnɪ/ *n* **1** someone able to act for another in legal or business matters. **2** *N Am* a lawyer.

Attorney General *n* (**Attorneys General** or **Attorney Generals**) in the UK, the US, Australia, New Zealand, etc: the chief law officer or chief government law officer.

attract *vb* **1** to cause (attention, notice, a crowd, interest, etc) to be directed towards oneself, itself, etc. **2** of a magnet: to pull (towards itself). **3** to arouse liking or admiration in someone; to be attractive to them.

attraction *n* **1** the act or power of attracting. **2** someone or something that attracts. **3** *physics* a force that tends to pull two objects closer together, such as that between opposite electric charges or opposite magnetic poles. Opposite of REPULSION.

attractive *adj* **1** appealing; enticing: *an attractive salary.* **2** appealing in looks or character. ○ **attractively** *adv*. ○ **attractiveness** *n*.

attribute *vb* /əˈtrɪbjuːt/ (*always* **attribute sth to sb** or **sth**) to think of it as being written, said, or caused by them or it; to ascribe: *We attributed the accident to human error.* ➢ *n* /ˈatrɪbjuːt/ a quality, characteristic, feature, etc, usu one that has positive or favourable connotations. ○ **attributable** *adj*. ○ **attribution** *n*.

attributive /əˈtrɪbjʊtɪv/ *adj, gram* of an adjective or noun in a noun phrase: placed before the noun it modifies, eg the adjective 'young' in *young girl*.

attrition *n* **1** a rubbing together; friction. **2** *mil* a relentless wearing down of an enemy's strength, morale, etc, esp by continual attacks: *war of attrition*.

attune *vb* (*often* **attune to** or **become attuned**

to sth) to adjust to or prepare for (a situation, etc). ○ **attunement** n.

atypical adj not typical, representative, usual, etc. ○ **atypically** adv.

Au symbol, chem gold.

aubergine n **1** a bushy plant that is cultivated for its edible fruit. **2** the large egg-shaped fruit of this plant, with a smooth skin that is usu deep purple in colour, eaten as a vegetable. N Am & Aust equivalent **eggplant**. **3** a deep purple colour. ➤ adj deep purple in colour.

aubrietia /ɔːˈbriːʃə/ n a dwarf plant with greyish leaves and purple, lilac, blue or pink cross-shaped flowers, widely cultivated as an ornamental plant in rock gardens.

auburn adj of hair: reddish-brown.

auction n a public sale in which each item is sold to the person who offers the most money. ➤ vb (often **auction sth off**) to sell something in an auction.

auctioneer n a person whose job is to conduct an auction by cataloguing and announcing the LOTS (sense 6) and presiding over the bids.

audacious adj **1** bold and daring. **2** disrespectful; impudent. ○ **audaciously** adv. ○ **audacity** n.

audible adj loud enough to be heard. ○ **audibly** adv.

audience n **1** a group of people watching a performance, eg of a play, concert, etc. **2** the people reached by a film, TV or radio broadcast, book, magazine, etc. **3** a formal interview with an important person.

audio adj **1** relating to hearing or sound. **2** relating to the recording and broadcasting of sound.

audio- comb form, denoting **1** sound, esp broadcast sound. **2** hearing.

audio frequency n any frequency that can be detected by the human ear, in the range 20 to 20,000Hz for normal hearing.

audiovisual adj of a device or teaching method: using both sound and vision.

audit n an official inspection of an organization's accounts by an accountant. ➤ vb (**audited, auditing**) to examine (accounts) officially.

audition n a test of the suitability of an actor, singer, musician, etc for a particular part or role, by way of a short performance. ➤ vb, tr & intr to test or be tested by means of an audition.

auditor n a person who is professionally qualified to audit accounts.

auditorium n (**auditoriums** or **auditoria**) the part of a theatre, hall, etc where the audience sits.

auditory adj belonging, relating or referring to hearing or the organs involved in hearing.

au fait /oʊ ˈfeɪ/ adj (usu **au fait with sth**) well informed about or familiar with it.

auger n a hand-tool with a corkscrew-like point for boring holes.

augment vb, tr & intr to make or become

greater in size, number, strength, amount, etc. ○ **augmentation** n.

au gratin /oʊ ˈɡratɛ̃/ adj, cookery of a dish: covered with breadcrumbs, or grated cheese, or a combination of both.

augur /ˈɔːɡə(r), ˈɔːɡjə(r)/ vb, intr (usu **augur well** or **ill**) to be a good or bad sign for the future.

augury n (**-ies**) **1** a sign or omen. **2** the practice of predicting the future.

August n the eighth month of the year.

august /ɔːˈɡʌst/ adj noble; imposing.

auk n a species of small diving seabird with a heavy body, black and white plumage, and short wings.

auld lang syne n, Scot days of long ago, esp those remembered nostalgically.

aunt n **1** the sister of one's father or mother. **2** the wife of one's uncle. **3** a close female friend of a child's parents.

auntie or **aunty** n (**-ies**) colloq an aunt.

Aunt Sally n (**Aunt Sallies**) **1** a game in which sticks or balls are thrown at a dummy. **2** any target of abuse.

au pair n a young person from abroad, usu female, who, in order to learn the language, helps with housework, looking after children, etc in return for board and lodging.

aura n (**auras** or **aurae** /ˈɔːriː/) **1** a distinctive character or quality around a person or in a place. **2** a fine substance coming out of something, esp that supposedly coming from and surrounding the body, which many mystics claim is visible as a faint light.

aural adj relating to the sense of hearing or to the ears. ○ **aurally** adv.

> **aural** A word often confused with this one is **oral**.

aureate adj **1 a** made of or covered in gold; gilded; **b** golden in colour. **2** of a speech, someone's writing style, etc: elaborate.

aureole or **aureola** n **1** a bright disc of light that surrounds the head of a holy figure in Christian art. **2** astron a hazy bluish-white halo surrounding the Sun or Moon.

au revoir /oʊ rəvˈwɑː(r)/ exclam goodbye.

auricle n, anat **1** the outer part of the ear. **2** the ear-shaped tip of the ATRIUM of the heart. ○ **auricular** adj.

auriferous adj of a substance: containing or yielding gold.

aurochs /ˈɔːrɒks, ˈaʊərɒks/ n (pl **aurochs**) an extinct wild ox.

aurora n (**auroras** or **aurorae** /əˈrɔːriː/) **1** astron the appearance of bands of coloured lights in the night sky, most often observed from the Arctic and Antarctic regions. **2** poetic the dawn.

auscultation n, med the practice of listening, esp with a stethoscope, to the sounds produced by the movement of blood or air within the heart, lungs, etc, in order to diagnose any abnormalities. ○ **auscultate** vb.

auspice n (usu **auspices**) protection; patronage. ♦ **under the auspices of sb** or **sth** with their or its help, support or guidance.

auspicious adj promising future success.

Aussie n, adj, colloq Australian.

austere adj **1** severely simple and plain. **2** severe; stern. **3** severe in self-discipline. ○ **austerely** adv.

austerity n **1** the state of being austere; strictness or harshness. **2** severe simplicity of dress, lifestyle, etc.

austral adj southern.

Australasian adj belonging or relating to Australia, New Zealand and the nearby Pacific islands, their inhabitants, or their language. ➤ n a citizen or inhabitant of, or person born in, Australia, New Zealand or the nearby Pacific islands.

Australian adj belonging or relating to Australia, a continent and country in the southern hemisphere, or its inhabitants. ➤ n a citizen or inhabitant of, or person born in, Australia.

Austrian adj belonging or relating to Austria or its inhabitants. ➤ n a citizen or inhabitant of, or person born in, Austria.

autarchy n (**-ies**) government of a country by a ruler who has absolute power.

autarky n (**-ies**) a system or policy of economic self-sufficiency in a country, state, etc.

authentic adj **1** genuine. **2** true to the original. ○ **authentically** adv. ○ **authenticity** n.

authenticate vb to prove something to be true or genuine. ○ **authentication** n.

author n **1** the writer of a book, article, play, etc. **2** the creator or originator of an idea, event, etc: the author of the peace plan. ➤ vb to be the author of (a book, article, play, etc).

authoring n an act or the process of composing, writing, compiling, etc using information technology, esp in the production of multimedia documents: a course in web authoring.

authoritarian adj in favour of, insisting on, characterized by, etc strict authority. ➤ n an authoritarian person. ○ **authoritarianism** n.

authoritarian, authoritative These words are often confused with each other.

authoritative adj **1** accepted as a reliable source of knowledge. **2** having authority; official. ○ **authoritatively** adv.

authority n (**-ies**) **1** the power or right to control or judge others, or to have the final say in something. **2** a position which has such a power or right. **3** (sometimes **authorities**) the person or people who have power, esp political or administrative: She reported them to the authorities. **4** the ability to influence others, usu as a result of knowledge or expertise. **5** well-informed confidence: She delivered her lecture with authority. **6** an expert.

authorize or **-ise** vb **1** to give someone the power or right to do something. **2** to give permission for something. ○ **authorization** n.

Authorized Version n the English translation of the Bible that was first published in 1611 under the direction of King James VI and I.

authorship n **1** the origin or originator of a particular piece of writing. **2** the profession of writing.

autism n, psychol a mental disorder that develops in early childhood and is characterized by learning difficulties, inability to relate to other people and the outside world, and repetitive body movements. ○ **autistic** adj.

auto n, N Am a motor car.

auto- or (before a vowel) **aut-** comb form **1** self; same; by or of the same person or thing: autobiography. **2** self-acting: automatic. **3** self-induced.

autobahn /ˈɔːtoʊbɑːn; German ˈaʊtobaːn/ n a motorway in Austria, Switzerland or Germany.

autobiography n (**-ies**) someone's own account of their life. ○ **autobiographical** adj.

autoclave n a strong steel container that can be made airtight and filled with pressurized steam in order to sterilize equipment, eg surgical instruments.

autocracy n (**-ies**) **1** absolute government by one person; dictatorship. **2** the rule of such a person. **3** a country, state, society, etc that is governed by one person.

autocrat n **1** a ruler with absolute power. **2** an authoritarian person. ○ **autocratic** adj. ○ **autocratically** adv.

autocross n a motor-racing sport for cars that takes place over a rough grass track.

Autocue n, trademark, TV a screen hidden from the camera which slowly displays a script line by line, so that the newscaster or speaker can read the script.

auto-da-fé /ˌɔːtoʊdɑːˈfeɪ/ n (**autos-da-fé**) hist **1** the ceremonial passing of sentence on heretics by the Spanish Inquisition. **2** the public burning of a heretic who had been sentenced by the Inquisition.

autogiro or **autogyro** n a type of aircraft with a propeller and rotor blades which are not mechanically powered but produce lift through being turned by the air when the aircraft is moving forwards.

autograph n someone's signature, esp that of a famous person. ➤ vb to sign (a photograph, book, poster, etc).

autoimmunity n, physiol the production by the body of antibodies that attack constituents of its own tissues, treating them as foreign material. ○ **autoimmune** adj.

automate vb to apply automation to (a technical process).

automatic adj **1** of a machine or device: capable of operating on its own and requiring little human control once it has been activated. **2** of an action: done without thinking; unconscious. **3** happening as a necessary result: The gravity of the offence meant an automatic driving ban. **4** of a firearm: able to reload itself and so fire continuously. **5** of a motor vehicle: having automatic transmission. ➤ *n* **1** an automatic firearm. **2** a vehicle with automatic transmission. **3** any machine that operates automatically. ○ **automatically** *adv.*

automatic pilot or **autopilot** *n* an electronic control device that automatically steers a vehicle, esp an aircraft, space vehicle or ship.

automation *n* the use of automatic machinery in manufacturing and data-processing, so that entire procedures can be automatically controlled with minimal or no human intervention.

automaton *n* (*automatons* or *automata*) **1** a machine or robot that has been programmed to perform specific actions in a manner imitative of a human or animal. **2** someone who acts like a machine, according to routine and without thinking.

automobile *n*, *N Am* a motor car.

automotive *adj* **1** relating to motor vehicles. **2** self-propelling.

autonomous *adj* **1** of a country, state, etc: self-governing. **2** independent of others. ○ **autonomously** *adv.*

autonomy *n* (*-ies*) **1** the power or right of self-government. **2** freedom from the intervention of others.

autopilot see AUTOMATIC PILOT

autopsy *n* (*-ies*) a POST MORTEM.

autoroute *n* in France and other French-speaking countries: a motorway.

autosave *n*, *comput* a computer program that causes newly recorded data to be automatically saved at regular intervals.

autostrada *n* in Italy: a motorway.

auto-suggestion *n*, *psychol* a form of psychotherapy that involves repeating ideas to oneself in order to change attitudes or habits, eg to reduce anxiety.

autumn *n* **1** (*also* **Autumn**) the season of the year between summer and winter, when leaves change colour and fall, and harvests ripen. *N Am equivalent* **fall**. **2** a period of maturity before decay. ○ **autumnal** /ɔːˈtʌmnəl/ *adj.*

auxiliary *adj* **1** helping or supporting. **2** additional or extra. ➤ *n* (*-ies*) **1** a helper. **2** (**auxiliaries**) foreign troops that help another nation that is engaged in a war. **3** *gram* an AUXILIARY VERB.

auxiliary verb *n*, *gram* a verb, such as *be*, *do*, *have*, *can*, *shall*, *may* or *must*, used with other verbs (such as *come*, *eat*, *sing* or *use*), to indicate TENSE[1], MOOD[2], VOICE (*noun* sense 9), etc, as in *I must go*, *you will go*, *they are going*, *they have been sent*, *I do not know*.

AV *abbrev* **1** audiovisual. **2** Authorized Version (of the Bible).

avail *vb* **1** *tr & intr* to help or be of use. **2** (**avail oneself of sth**) to make use of it or take advantage of it. ➤ *n* use; advantage.

available *adj* able or ready to be obtained or used. ○ **availability** *n.* ○ **availably** *adv.*

avalanche *n* **1** the rapid movement of a large mass of snow or ice down a mountain slope. **2** a sudden appearance or a large amount of something: *His book met with an avalanche of criticism.*

avant-garde /avãˈɡɑːd/ *n* the writers, painters, musicians, etc whose ideas and techniques are considered the most modern or advanced of their time, regarded collectively. ➤ *adj* of a work of art, a piece of literature, a film, idea, movement, etc: characterized by daring modernity.

avarice /ˈavərɪs/ *n* excessive desire for money, possessions, etc; greed. ○ **avaricious** /avəˈrɪʃəs/ *adj.*

avatar *n* **1** *Hinduism* the appearance of a god in human or animal form. **2** the visual manifestation of something abstract.

Ave[1] *abbrev* used in addresses: Avenue.

Ave[2] /ˈɑːvɪ/ or **Ave Maria** /məˈriːə/ *n* (*Aves* or *Ave Marias*) a prayer to the Virgin Mary.

avenge *vb* to carry out some form of retribution for (some previous wrongdoing). ○ **avenger** *n.*

avenue *n* **1** a a broad road or street, often with trees along the sides; b (**Avenue**) a street title in an address. **2** a tree-lined approach to a house. **3** a means, way or approach.

aver *vb* (*averred, averring*) to state firmly and positively.

average *n* **1** the usual or typical amount, extent, quality, number, etc. **2** *stats* any number that is representative of a group of numbers or other data, esp the arithmetic mean, which is equal to the sum of a set of *n* numbers, divided by *n.* ➤ *adj* **1** usual or ordinary. **2** estimated by taking an average. **3** mediocre: *He gave a pretty average performance.* ➤ *vb* **1** to obtain the numerical average of (several numbers). **2** to amount to on average: *Her speed averaged 90mph on the motorway.* ◆ **on average** usually; typically. ◊ **average out** to result in an average or balance.

averse *adj* (*always* **averse to sth**) reluctant about or opposed to it.

> **averse** A word sometimes confused with this one is **adverse**.

aversion *n* **1** a strong dislike. **2** something or someone that is the object of strong dislike.

avert *vb* **1** to turn away: *avert one's eyes.* **2** to prevent (esp danger): *Quick reactions averted the accident.*

avian /ˈeɪvɪən/ *adj* belonging, relating or referring to birds.

aviary *n* (*-ies*) a large enclosed area where birds are kept.

aviation *n* **1** the science or practice of mechanical flight through the air, esp by powered aircraft. **2** the production, design and operation of aircraft. **3** the aircraft industry.

aviator *n*, *old use* an aircraft pilot.

avid *adj* very enthusiastic: *an avid filmgoer.* ○ **avidly** *adv.*

avocado *n* **1** a tropical evergreen tree of the

laurel family. **2** the edible pear-shaped fruit of this tree, which has a rough thick greenish-brown skin and creamy flesh.

avocet /ˈavəsɛt/ *n* any of various large wading birds with long legs and a long slender upward curving bill.

avoid *vb* **1** to keep away from (a place, person, action, etc). **2** to stop, prevent, manage not to do, or escape something. ○ **avoidable** *adj*. ○ **avoidably** *adv*. ○ **avoidance** *n*.

avoirdupois /ˌavwɑːdjʊˈpwɑː, ˌavədəˈpɔɪz/ *n* a system of units of mass based on a pound (0.45kg) consisting of 16 ounces, formerly widely used in English-speaking countries, but now increasingly replaced by SI units.

avow *vb* to state openly; to declare or admit. ○ **avowal** *n*. ○ **avowed** /əˈvaʊd/ *adj*. ○ **avowedly** /əˈvaʊɪdlɪ/ *adv*.

avuncular *adj* relating to or like an uncle, esp in being kind and caring.

await *vb* **1** *formal* to wait for something. **2** to be in store for someone.

awake *vb* (*awoke, awoken*) *tr & intr* **1** to stop sleeping or cause to stop sleeping. **2** to become active or cause to become active. ➤ *adj* **1** not sleeping. **2** alert or aware.

awake, awaken	See note at **wake**.

awaken *vb, tr & intr* **1** to wake up. **2** to arouse or evoke (feelings, etc): *The photo awakened happy memories.*

award *vb* (*always* **award sth to sb** *or* **award sb sth**) **1** to present or grant them it, esp in recognition of some achievement. **2** *law* to decide and declare (a right or claim to something): *The judge awarded custody to the father.* ➤ *n* **1** a payment, prize, etc, esp one given in recognition of an achievement, etc. **2** a legal judgement granting something.

aware *adj* **1** (*often* **aware of sth** *or* **sb**) acquainted with or mindful of it or them. **2** (**aware that**) conscious that. **3** well informed: *ecologically aware.* ○ **awareness** *n*.

awash *adj, adv, colloq* covered or flooded with water.

away *adv* **1** from one place, position, person or time towards another. **2** in or to the usual or proper place: *put the books away.* **3** into the distance; into extinction: *fade away.* **4** apart; remote: *away from the city.* **5** continuously; repeatedly; relentlessly: *talking away.* **6** aside; in another direction: *I looked away.* **7** of a sporting event: on the opponent's ground. ➤ *adj* **1** not present; not at home. **2** distant: *not far away.* **3** of a sporting event: played on the opponent's ground: *an away game.* ➤ *n* a match played or won by a team playing on their opponent's ground. ♦ **right** *or* **straight away** immediately.

awe *n* admiration, fear and wonder. ➤ *vb* to fill with awe. ♦ **in awe of sb** *or* **sth** filled with admiration for, but also intimidated by, them or it.

aweigh *adv, naut* of an anchor: in the process of being raised from the bottom of the sea.

awe-inspiring *adj* **1** causing or deserving awe. **2** *colloq* wonderful.

awesome *adj* **1** causing awe; dreaded. **2** *colloq* completely and utterly wonderful.

awful *adj* **1** *colloq* very bad. **2** *colloq* very great: *an awful shame.* **3** terrible or shocking. ➤ *adv, non-standard* very: *I'm awful busy.* ○ **awfully** *adv* **1** very badly. **2** very: *awfully nice.* ○ **awfulness** *n*.

awhile *adv* for a short time.

awkward *adj* **1** clumsy and ungraceful. **2** embarrassed or embarrassing: *an awkward moment.* **3** difficult and dangerous: *Careful, it's an awkward turning.* **4** difficult or inconvenient to deal with. ○ **awkwardly** *adv*. ○ **awkwardness** *n*.

awl *n* a pointed tool used for boring small holes, esp in leather.

awn *n, bot* in some grasses, eg barley: a small stiff bristle projecting from the head.

awning *n* a plastic or canvas covering over the entrance or window of a shop, etc, that can be extended to give shelter from the sun or rain.

awoke, awoken see under AWAKE

AWOL *abbrev* absent without leave: absent from one's place of duty, esp in the armed forces, without permission.

awry *adj, adv* **1** twisted to one side. **2** wrong; amiss.

axe *or* (*US*) **ax** *n* a hand-tool with a long handle and a heavy metal blade, used for cutting down trees, chopping wood, etc. ➤ *vb* **1** to get rid of, dismiss or put a stop to something: *30 jobs were axed.* **2** to reduce (costs, services, etc). ♦ **have an axe to grind** to have a personal, often selfish, reason for being involved in something.

axes *pl of* AXE, AXIS

axial *adj* relating to, forming or placed along an axis. ○ **axially** *adv*.

axil *n, bot* the angle between the upper surface of a leaf or stem and the stem or branch from which it grows.

axiom *n* **1** a proposition, fact, principle, etc which, because it is long-established, is generally accepted as true. **2** a self-evident statement. ○ **axiomatic** *adj*.

axis *n* (*axes* /ˈaksiːz/) **1** an imaginary straight line around which an object, eg a planet, rotates. **2** an imaginary straight line around which an object is symmetrical. **3** *geom* one of the lines of reference used to specify the position of points on a graph, eg the horizontal x-axis and vertical y-axis in COORDINATES (see under CO-ORDINATE). ○ **axial** *adj*. ○ **axially** *adv*.

axle *n* a fixed or rotating rod designed to carry a wheel or one or more pairs of wheels which may be attached to it, driven by it, or rotate freely on it.

axolotl /ˈaksəˌlɒtl/ *n* a rare salamander, found in certain Mexican lakes.

ayatollah *or* **Ayatollah** *n* **1** in the hierarchy of Shiite religious leaders in Iran: someone who can demonstrate a highly advanced knowledge of the Islamic religion and laws. **2** any dictatorial or influential person.

aye or **ay** *adv, chiefly dialect* yes. ➤ *n* **1** a vote in favour of something, esp in the House of Commons. **2** someone who votes in favour of something. Opposite of NAY.

azalea /əˈzeɪlɪə/ *n* a deciduous shrub with large clusters of funnel-shaped flowers.

azimuth *n* in astronomy and surveying: the bearing of an object, eg a planet or star, measured in degrees as the angle around the observer's horizon clockwise from north, which is the zero point.

AZT *abbrev* azidothymidine, a drug that is used in the treatment of AIDS.

Aztec *n* **1** a group of Mexican Indian peoples whose great empire was overthrown by the Spanish in the 16c. **2** an individual belonging to this group of peoples. **3** their language. Also called **Nahuatl**. ➤ *adj* belonging or referring to this group or their language. ○ **Aztecan** *adj*.

azure *adj* deep sky-blue in colour. ➤ *n* **1** a deep sky-blue colour. **2** *poetic* the sky.

Bb

B¹ or **b** *n* (**Bs, B's** or **b's**) **1** the second letter of the English alphabet. **2** (*usu* **B**) the second highest grade or quality, or a mark indicating this. **3** (**B**) *mus* the seventh note in the scale of C major.

B² *abbrev* on pencils: black.

B³ *symbol* **1** *chess* bishop. **2** *chem* boron. **3** *physics* bel.

b. *abbrev* **1** born. **2** *cricket* bowled.

BA *abbrev* Bachelor of Arts.

Ba *symbol, chem* barium.

baa *n* the cry of a sheep or lamb. ➤ *vb, intr* to make this cry.

babble *vb* **1** *tr & intr* to talk or say something quickly, esp in a way that is hard to understand. **2** *intr, colloq* to talk foolishly. **3** *intr, literary* of a stream, etc: to make a low murmuring sound. **4** to give away (a secret) carelessly. ○ **babbling** *adj*.

babe *n* **1** *colloq* (often used as a term of affection) a girl or young woman. **2** *literary & old use* a baby.

babel /ˈbeɪbəl/ *n* **1** a confused sound of voices. **2** a scene of noise and confusion.

baboon *n* a large monkey, with a long muzzle, large teeth and a long tail.

baby *n* (*-ies*) **1** a newborn or very young child or animal. **2** an unborn child. **3** the youngest member of a group. **4** *derog* a childish person. **5** *colloq* a person's own particular project, etc. **6** *colloq, esp N Am* a term of affection for a girl or woman. ➤ *vb* (*-ies, -ied*) to treat someone as a baby. ○ **babyish** *adj*. ♦ **be left holding the baby** *colloq* to be left with the responsibility for something.

baby-sit *vb, tr & intr* to look after a child, usu in its own home, while the parents are out. ○ **baby-sitter** *n*. ○ **baby-sitting** *n*.

baccalaureate /bakəˈlɔːrɪət/ *n* **1** *formal* a Bachelor's degree (see BACHELOR sense 2). **2** a diploma of a lower status than a degree.

baccarat /ˈbakəraː/ *n* a card game in which players bet money against the banker.

bacchanalia /bakəˈneɪlɪə/ *pl n* drunken celebrations; orgies. ○ **bacchanalian** *adj*.

baccy *n, colloq* tobacco.

bachelor *n* **1** an unmarried man. **2** (**Bachelor**) a person who has taken a first university degree: *Bachelor of Arts/Science*. ○ **bachelorhood** *n*.

bacillus /bəˈsɪləs/ *n* (**bacilli** /-laɪ/) *biol* any of a large group of rod-shaped bacteria including many species that cause food spoilage and serious diseases.

back *n* **1 a** the rear part of the human body from the neck to the base of the spine; **b** the spinal column itself. **2** the upper part of an animal's body. **3** the part of an object that is opposite to or furthest from the front. **4** the side of an object that is not normally seen or used. **5** the upright part of a chair. **6** *sport* a player whose usual position is behind the forwards, and who in most sports is a defender, but who (eg in rugby) may also attack. Compare FORWARD (*noun*). ➤ *adj* **1** located or situated behind or at the back: *the back door*. **2** concerning, belonging to or from an earlier date: *back pay*. **3** away from or behind something, esp something more important: *back roads*. ➤ *adv* **1** to or towards the rear; away from the front. **2** in or into an original position or condition: *when I get back from holiday*. **3** in return or in response: *They hit back*. **4** in or into the past: *Let's look back to happier days*. ➤ *vb* **1** to help or support someone or something, usu with money. **2** *tr & intr* (usu **back away**, **out** or **out of sth**, or **back up**) to move or cause something to move backwards, away from or out of something. **3** to bet on the success of (a horse, etc). **4** (sometimes **back sb** or **sth up**) to provide a back or support for them. **5** to accompany (a singer) with music. **6** to lie at the back of something. **7** *intr, naut* of the wind: to change direction anticlockwise. Compare VEER (sense 2). ♦ **back to front 1** with the back where the front should be. **2** in the wrong order. **have one's back to the wall**

colloq to be in a very difficult situation. **put sb's back up** *colloq* to make them annoyed. ◊ **back down** to concede an argument or claim, esp under pressure. **back off 1** to move backwards or retreat. **2** to back down. **back onto sth** of a building, etc: to have its back next to or facing it. **back out of sth** to withdraw from (a promise or agreement, etc). **back sb up** to support or assist them. **back sth up** to copy (computer data) onto a disk or tape.

backbench *n* a seat in the House of Commons for members who do not hold an official position either in the government or in the opposition. ◦ **backbencher** *n*. Compare CROSS BENCH, FRONT BENCH.

backbite *vb, intr, colloq* to speak unkindly about someone who is absent. ◦ **backbiting** *n*.

backbone *n* **1** the spine. **2** in both physical and abstract senses: the main support of something: *the backbone of a company.* **3** strength of character.

backbreaking *adj* of a task, etc: extremely hard or tiring.

back burner *n* the rear burner on a stove. ♦ **keep** or **put sth on the back burner** to set it aside or keep it in reserve for later consideration or action.

backchat *n, Brit* impertinent replies, esp to a superior.

backcloth or **backdrop** *n* the painted cloth at the back of a stage, forming part of the scenery.

backcomb *vb* to comb (the hair) towards the roots to make it look thicker.

backdate *vb* to make something effective from a date in the past.

backdoor *adj* applied to an activity done secretly and often dishonestly: *a backdoor deal.* ➤ *n* (*usu* **the back door**) a clandestine or illicit means of achieving an objective: *He got into power by the back door.*

backer *n* a person who gives financial support to a project, etc.

backfire *vb, intr* **1** of an engine or vehicle: to make a loud bang as the result of an explosion of unburnt gases in the exhaust system. **2** of a plan, etc: to go wrong and have a bad effect on the person who originated it.

backgammon *n* a board game for two people, with pieces moved according to the throws of a dice.

background *n* **1** the space behind the main figures of a picture. **2** the events or circumstances that precede and help to explain an event, etc. **3** a person's social origins or education, etc. **4** a less noticeable or less public position: *She prefers to stay in the background.*

backhand *n, tennis, squash, etc* a stroke made with the back of the hand turned towards the ball.

backhanded *adj* **1** *tennis* of a stroke: made with or as a backhand. **2** of a compliment: ambiguous or doubtful in effect.

backhander *n* **1** *tennis* a backhand stroke of a ball. **2** *colloq* a bribe.

backing *n* **1** support, esp financial support. **2** material, etc that supports the back of something. **3** music accompanying a singer.

backlash *n* a sudden violent reaction to an action or situation, etc.

backlog *n* a pile or amount of uncompleted work, etc.

backpack *n* a rucksack. ➤ *vb, intr* to travel about carrying one's belongings in a pack on one's back. ◦ **backpacker** *n*.

back-pedal *vb, intr* **1** to turn the pedals on a bicycle backwards. **2** to withdraw rapidly from one's previous opinion or course of action.

back room *n* a place where secret work or activity takes place. ➤ *adj* (*usu* **backroom**) applied to important work done secretly behind the scenes: *backroom boys.*

back seat *n* a less important position.

back-seat driver *n, derog* a person, esp a passenger in a car, who gives unwanted advice.

backside *n, colloq* the buttocks.

backslide *vb, intr* to relapse into former bad behaviour, habits, etc. ◦ **backslider** *n*.

backspace *vb, intr* to move a computer cursor back one or more spaces.

backspin *n, sport* the spinning of a ball in the opposite direction to the way it is travelling, which reduces its speed when it hits a surface.

backstage *adv* behind a theatre stage. ➤ *adj* not seen by the public.

backstreet *n* a street away from a town's main streets. ➤ *adj* secret or illicit.

backstroke *n* a swimming stroke performed on the back, with the arms raised alternately in a backward circular motion.

backtrack *vb, intr* **1** to return in the direction from which one came. **2** to reverse one's previous opinion or course of action.

backup *n* **1** support. **2** *comput* **a** a procedure for copying data onto a disk or tape for security purposes; **b** a copy made by this procedure.

backward *adj* **1** directed behind or towards the back. **2** less advanced than normal in mental, physical or intellectual development. **3** reluctant or shy. ➤ *adv* backwards.

backwards or *sometimes* **backward** *adv* **1** towards the back or rear. **2** with one's back facing the direction of movement. **3** in reverse order: *counting backwards.* **4** in or into a worse state: *She felt her career going backwards.* ♦ **bend over backwards** *colloq* to try extremely hard to please someone.

backwater *n* **1** a pool of stagnant water connected to a river. **2** *derog* an isolated place, not affected by what is happening elsewhere.

backyard *n* **1** *Brit* a yard at the back of a house. **2** *N Am* a garden at the rear of a house.

bacon *n* meat from the back and sides of a pig, usu salted or smoked. ♦ **bring home the bacon** *colloq* **1** to earn enough money to support a household. **2** to accomplish a task successfully. **save sb's bacon** *colloq* to rescue them from a difficult situation.

bacteria *pl n* (*sing* **bacterium**) *biol* a diverse

group of microscopic organisms, including many that cause infectious diseases. ○ **bacterial** adj.

bacteriology n the scientific study of bacteria. ○ **bacteriologist** n.

bad adj (**worse, worst**) **1** not good. **2** wicked. **3** naughty. **4** (**bad at sth**) not skilled or clever (at some activity). **5** (**bad for sb**) harmful to them. **6** unpleasant; unwelcome. **7** decayed. **8** serious; severe: a bad cold. **9** unhealthy; injured; painful: a bad leg. **10** sorry, upset or ashamed. **11** not valid: a bad cheque. **12** US (**badder, baddest**) slang very good. ➢ adv, N Am colloq badly; greatly; hard: He needs the money bad. ➢ n **1** evil. **2** unpleasant events. ○ **badness** n. ◆ **not bad** colloq quite good. **too bad** colloq unfortunate (often used dismissively): She's still not happy with it, but that's just too bad.

bad blood or **bad feeling** n angry or bitter feelings.

badge n **1** a small emblem worn to show rank, membership of a society, etc. **2** any distinguishing feature.

badger n a stocky burrowing mammal with black and white stripes on its head. ➢ vb to pester someone.

badinage /ˈbadɪnɑːʒ/ n playful bantering talk.

bad language n coarse words and swearing.

badly adv (**worse, worst**) **1** poorly; inefficiently. **2** unfavourably: They came off badly in the review. **3** extremely; severely: I'm badly in arrears with the rent. ◆ **badly off** poor; hard up.

badminton n a game played with rackets and a SHUTTLECOCK which is hit across a high net.

bad-tempered adj easily annoyed or made angry.

baffle vb to confuse or puzzle. ➢ n a device for controlling the flow of gas, liquid or sound through an opening. ○ **bafflement** n. ○ **baffling** adj.

bag n **1** a container made of a soft material with an opening at the top, for carrying things. **2** the amount a bag holds. **3** a HANDBAG. **4** (**bags**, esp **bags of sth**) colloq a large amount of it. **5** offensive colloq an unpleasant or ugly woman. ➢ vb (**bagged, bagging**) **1** tr & intr (also **bag sth up**) to put into a bag. **2** to kill (game): They bagged six pheasants. **3** colloq to obtain or reserve (a seat, etc). ◆ **bags I** or **bags** or **bagsy** children's slang I want to do or have, etc (the thing specified): Bags I sit in the front. **in the bag** colloq as good as secured or done.

bagatelle n **1** a game played on a board with holes into which balls are rolled. **2** an unimportant thing. **3** a short piece of light music.

bagel /ˈbeɪgl/ n a hard, ring-shaped bread roll.

baggage n **1** a traveller's luggage. **2** the portable equipment of an army.

baggy adj (**-ier, -iest**) hanging loose or bulging.

bagpipes pl n a wind instrument consisting of a bag into which air is blown through a reed pipe (the CHANTER) by means of which the

melody is also created.

baguette /baˈgɛt/ n a long narrow French loaf.

bah exclam expressing displeasure, scorn or disgust.

bail¹ n **1** the temporary release of a person awaiting trial, secured by the payment of money and/or the imposition of special conditions. **2** money required as security for such a release. ➢ vb (usu **bail sb out**) **1** to provide bail for them. **2** colloq to help them out of difficulties, esp by lending them money. ◆ **jump bail** colloq to fail to return for trial after being released on bail.

bail² or **bale** vb (usu **bail out** or **bale out**) **1** tr & intr to remove (water) from a boat with a bucket. **2** intr to escape from an aeroplane by jumping out.

bail³ n (usu **bails**) cricket one of the cross-pieces laid on top of the stumps.

bail⁴ n on a typewriter or printer, etc: a hinged bar that holds the paper against the PLATEN.

bailey n (**-eys**) the courtyard or outer wall of a castle.

bailiff n **1** an officer of a lawcourt, esp one with the power to seize the property of a person who has not paid money owed to the court. **2** a person who looks after property for its owner.

bailiwick n, now often slightly facetious one's area of jurisdiction.

bain-marie /French bɛ̃mari/ n (**bain-maries**) cookery a pan filled with hot water in which a container of food can be cooked gently.

bairn n, dialect a child.

bait n **1** food put on a hook or in a trap to attract fish or animals. **2** anything intended to attract or tempt. ➢ vb **1** to put food on or in (a hook or trap). **2** to harass or tease (a person or animal). **3** to set dogs on (another animal, eg a badger). ○ **baiting** n, esp in compounds: bear-baiting.

baize n a woollen cloth, usu green and used as a covering on snooker and card tables, etc.

bake vb **1** tr & intr to cook (cakes, bread, vegetables, etc) using dry heat in an oven. **2** tr & intr to dry or harden by heat from the sun or a fire. **3** intr, colloq to be extremely hot.

baked beans pl n haricot beans baked in tomato sauce and usu tinned.

Bakelite /ˈbeɪkəlaɪt/ n, trademark a type of hard plastic formerly used to make dishes, buttons, etc.

baker n a person who bakes or sells bread and cakes, etc, esp as their profession.

baker's dozen n thirteen.

bakery n (**-ies**) a place where bread, cakes, etc are made or sold.

baking powder or **baking soda** see under BICARBONATE OF SODA.

baksheesh n in some Eastern countries: money given as a tip or present.

balaclava n a knitted hat that covers the head and neck, with an opening for the face.

balalaika /baləˈlaɪkə/ n a Russian musical instrument with a triangular body and normally three strings.

balance n 1 a state of physical stability in which the weight of a body is evenly distributed. 2 an instrument for weighing. 3 the amount by which the two sides of a financial account (money spent and money received) differ. 4 an amount left over. 5 a state of mental or emotional stability. 6 a state existing when two opposite forces are equal. 7 something that is needed to create such equality. 8 a device which regulates the speed of a clock or watch. ➤ vb 1 tr & intr to be in, or put into, a state of physical balance. 2 (often **balance sth against sth else**) to compare two or more things in one's mind; to compare their respective advantages and disadvantages. 3 to find the difference between money put into an account and money taken out of it, and to make them equal. 4 intr (also **balance out**) to be or become equal in amount. ○ **balanced** adj. ♦ **in the balance** not yet decided. **on balance** having taken all the advantages and disadvantages into consideration.

balance of payments n, econ the difference in value between the amount of money coming into a country and the amount going out of it.

balance of trade n, econ the difference in value of a country's imports and exports.

balance sheet n a summary and balance of financial accounts.

balcony n (-ies) 1 a platform surrounded by a wall or railing, projecting from the wall of a building. 2 an upper tier in a theatre or cinema.

bald adj 1 of a person: having little or no hair on their head. 2 of birds or animals: not having any feathers or fur. 3 bare or plain: the bald truth. ○ **balding** adj becoming bald. ○ **baldly** adv. ○ **baldness** n.

balderdash n, dated nonsense.

bale¹ n a large tied bundle of a commodity such as hay. ➤ vb to make (hay, etc) into bales.

bale² see BAIL²

baleen n whalebone.

baleful adj 1 evil; harmful. 2 threatening; gloomy. ○ **balefully** adv.

balk or **baulk** vb 1 intr (usu **balk at sth**) to hesitate, or refuse to go on, because of some obstacle. 2 to check or block. ➤ n, snooker, etc the part of the table behind a line (called the **balk line**) near one end, from within which the start and restarts are made.

Balkan adj belonging or relating to the peninsula in SE Europe (called the **Balkans**) which is surrounded by the Adriatic, Aegean and Black seas, or to its peoples or its countries.

ball¹ n 1 a round or roundish object used in some sports. 2 anything round or nearly round in shape: a ball of wool. 3 the act of throwing a ball, or the way a ball is thrown. 4 a rounded fleshy part of the body: the ball of the foot. 5 (usu **balls**) coarse slang a testicle. ➤ vb, tr & intr to form or gather into a ball. ♦ **have the ball at one's feet** to have the opportunity to do something. **on the ball** colloq well-informed; alert. **play ball** colloq to co-operate. **start** or **set or**

keep the ball rolling to begin or continue an activity, conversation, etc.

ball² n 1 a formal social meeting for dancing. 2 colloq an enjoyable time.

ballad n 1 a slow, usu romantic song. 2 a poem or song with short verses, which tells a popular story.

ballade /ba'lɑːd/ n 1 a poem consisting of verses grouped in threes, with a repeated refrain and a short concluding verse. 2 mus a short lyrical piece for piano.

ballast n 1 heavy material used to keep a ship steady or to weigh down and stabilize a hot-air balloon. 2 broken rocks used as a base for roads and railway lines. 3 anything used to give a steadying influence or lend weight or stability.

ball-bearing n 1 an arrangement of small steel balls between the moving parts of some machines, to help reduce friction. 2 one of these balls.

ballcock n a floating ball that rises and falls with the water level in a tank or cistern and, by means of a hinged rod to which it is attached, operates a valve controlling the inflow of water.

ballerina n a female ballet-dancer.

ballet n 1 a classical style of dancing, using set steps and movements. 2 a single performance or work in this style. ○ **balletic** adj.

ball game n 1 a game played with a ball; b N Am a baseball game. 2 colloq a situation or state of affairs: a whole new ball game.

ballistic adj 1 referring or relating to projectiles. 2 operating under the force of gravity. ○ **ballistics** sing n. ♦ **go ballistic** slang of a person: to fly into a rage.

ballistic missile n a type of missile which is initially guided but drops on its target under the force of gravity.

balloon n 1 a small rubber pouch with a neck, that can be inflated and used as a toy or decoration. 2 a large bag made of light material and filled with a light gas or hot air, designed to float in the air carrying people, etc in a basket underneath. 3 a balloon-shaped outline containing the words or thoughts of a character in a cartoon. ➤ vb 1 intr to travel by balloon. 2 intr to increase dramatically. ○ **balloonist** n.

ballot n a method or system of voting, usu in secret, by putting a marked paper into a box. ➤ vb (**balloted, balloting**) 1 to take the vote or ballot of (a group of people). 2 intr (esp **ballot for sth**) to vote by ballot (in favour of it).

ball park n, orig US 1 a baseball field. 2 a sphere of activity. ➤ adj (usu **ballpark**) approximate: ballpark figures.

ballpoint or **ballpoint pen** n a pen which has a tiny ball as the writing point.

ballroom n a large room with a spacious dance floor, in which balls (see BALL²) are held.

ballroom dancing n a formal kind of social dancing for couples.

balls *sing n, coarse slang* **1** N Am courage. **2** nonsense. ➤ *exclam* nonsense!

balls-up *n, Brit, coarse slang* something confused or bungled.

ballsy *adj (-ier, -iest) slang, esp US* tough and courageous.

bally *adj, adv, dated Brit colloq* a mild form of BLOODY.

ballyhoo *n, colloq* **1** a noisy confused situation. **2** noisy or sensational publicity.

balm *n* **1** an oil obtained from certain types of trees, having a pleasant smell and used in healing or reducing pain. **2** a fragrant and healing ointment. **3 a** an aromatic plant, esp one of the mint family; **b** (*also* **lemon balm**) a plant with an aroma similar to that of lemon. **4** something comforting to either the body or the spirit.

balmy *adj (-ier, -iest)* of the air: warm and soft.

baloney or **boloney** *n, slang* nonsense. ➤ *exclam* nonsense!

balsa /ˈbɔːlsə/ *n* **1** a tropical American tree. **2** (*also* **balsa-wood**) the very lightweight wood of this tree.

balsam *n* **1** a pleasant-smelling thick sticky substance obtained from some trees and plants, used to make medicines and perfumes. **2** a tree or plant from which this substance is obtained. **3** an aromatic, sticky or oily ointment, or similar healing and soothing preparation made from this substance. ○ **balsamic** *adj*.

balti /ˈbɔːltɪ/ *n* in Indian cookery: a style of curry in which the food is cooked in a two-handled wok-like pan.

Baltic *adj* belonging or relating to the sea between Scandinavia and the rest of NE Europe, or the states bordering it.

baluster *n* any one of a series of posts supporting a rail.

balustrade *n* a row of posts, joined by a rail, on the edge of a balcony, staircase, bridge, etc.

bamboo *n (pl* in sense 1 only *bamboos)* **1** a tall tropical grass with hollow stems. **2** the stems of this grass, used in furniture-making, etc and as a garden cane.

bamboozle *vb, colloq* **1** to cheat. **2** to confuse.

ban *n* an official order stating that something is not allowed. ➤ *vb (banned, banning)* **1** to forbid. **2** to forbid someone from going somewhere or doing something, esp officially.

banal /bəˈnɑːl/ *adj* lacking in interest or originality. ○ **banality** /bəˈnalɪtɪ/ *n*.

banana *n* **1** a large tree-like plant, that is cultivated throughout the tropics as a staple food crop. **2** the long curved fruit of this plant.

band¹ *n* **1** a flat narrow strip of cloth, metal, paper, etc used to hold things together or as a decoration. **2** a stripe of colour or strip of material differing from its background or surroundings. **3** a belt for driving machinery. **4** a group or range of radio frequencies between two limits. **5** a range of values between two limits. ➤ *vb* to fasten or mark with a band.

band² *n* **1** a group of people with a common purpose. **2** a group of musicians who play music other than classical music. ➤ *vb (usu* **band** (**sb**) **together**) to act as a group, or to organize (people) to act as a group or to work for a common purpose.

bandage *n* a strip of cloth for winding round a wound or an injured limb. ➤ *vb* to wrap (esp a wound or an injured limb) in a bandage.

Band-aid *n, trademark, esp N Am* a type of sticking-plaster with attached dressing, for covering minor wounds.

bandana or **bandanna** *n* a large brightly-coloured cotton or silk square, folded and worn around the neck or head.

B and B or **B & B** or **b & b** *n (pl* **B and B's**, **B & B's** or **b & b's**) a BED AND BREAKFAST.

bandbox *n* a light round box for holding hats.

bandeau /ˈbandoʊ/ *n (bandeaux* /-doʊz/) a narrow band of material worn around the head.

bandicoot *n* an Australian MARSUPIAL, with elongated hindlegs and a long flexible snout.

bandit *n* an armed robber, esp a member of a gang.

bandoleer or **bandolier** /bandəˈlɪə(r)/ *n* a leather shoulder belt, esp one for carrying bullets.

band-saw *n* a saw consisting of a blade with teeth attached to a metal band which moves around two wheels.

bandstand *n* a platform with a roof, often in a park, where bands play music.

bandwagon *n, hist* a wagon carrying a musical band in a procession. ♦ **jump** or **climb on the bandwagon** to join, or show interest in, an activity or movement only after it becomes fashionable or likely to succeed.

bandwidth *n* **1** the width or spread of the range of frequencies used for transmitting TV or radio signals. **2** the capacity for transmitting information over a link between computers.

bandy¹ *vb (-ies, -ied) (usu* **bandy about** or **around**) **1** to pass (a story, etc) from one person to another. **2** to mention (someone's name) in rumour. ♦ **bandy words with sb** to exchange angry words with them.

bandy² *adj (-ier, -iest)* of a person's or animal's legs: curved or bending wide apart at the knees.

bane *n* the cause of trouble or evil: *the bane of my life.* ○ **baneful** *adj*.

bang *n* **1** a sudden loud explosive noise. **2** a heavy blow. ➤ *vb, tr & intr* **1** to make, or cause (something) to make, a loud noise by hitting, dropping or closing (it) violently, etc. **2** to hit something sharply, esp by accident. **3** to make, or cause to make, the sound of an explosion. ➤ *adv, colloq* **1** exactly: *bang on time.* **2** suddenly.

banger *n* **1** *colloq* a sausage. **2** *colloq* an old car in poor condition. **3** a loud firework.

bangle *n* a piece of jewellery in the form of a solid band, worn round the arm or leg.

banish *vb* **1** to send someone away from a place. **2** to put (thoughts, etc) out of one's mind. ○ **banishment** *n*.

banister or **bannister** n (usu **banisters**) a row of posts and the hand-rail they support, running up the side of a staircase.

banjo n (**banjos** or **banjoes**) a guitar-like stringed musical instrument with a long neck and a round body. ○ **banjoist** n.

bank¹ n **1** a financial organization which keeps money in accounts for its clients, lends money, etc. **2** also in compounds a place where something is stored for later use: databank. **3** in some games: a stock of money controlled by one of the players. ➤ vb **1** to put (money) into a bank. **2** intr to have a bank account: We bank with Lloyds. ○ **banking** n. ◊ **bank on sth** to rely on it.

bank² n **1** the side or slope of a hill. **2** also in compounds the ground at the edge of a river or lake, etc. **3** a long raised pile of earth or snow, etc. ➤ vb **1** to enclose something with a bank, or form a bank to it. **2** tr & intr of an aircraft: to change direction, with one wing higher than the other.

bank³ n a collection of similar things arranged in rows.

bankable adj (used esp in the film industry) likely to ensure profitability.

bank account n an arrangement by which a person or company keeps money in a bank and takes it out when needed.

bank card or **banker's card** n a CHEQUE CARD or DEBIT CARD.

bank draft n a written order sent from one bank to another bank for paying money to a customer.

banker¹ n **1** a person who owns or manages a bank. **2** in some games: a person in charge of the bank (see BANK¹ noun sense 3).

banker² n, Aust, NZ a river that has risen up to, or is overflowing, its banks.

banker's order n a STANDING ORDER (sense 1).

bank holiday n in the UK: any one of several days in the year on which banks are closed, usu observed as a public holiday.

banknote n a special piece of paper, issued by a bank, which serves as money.

bankroll n financial resources. ➤ vb, colloq to provide financial resources for someone or something.

bankrupt n **1** someone who is legally recognized as not being able to pay their debts. **2** someone whose character is completely lacking in a specified respect: a moral bankrupt. ➤ adj **1** not having money to pay one's debts. **2** exhausted of or lacking (some quality, etc): bankrupt of ideas. ➤ vb (**bankrupted, past participle bankrupt**) to make someone bankrupt. ○ **bankruptcy** n (-ies).

banner n a large piece of cloth or cardboard, with a design or slogan, etc, carried or displayed at public meetings and parades.

banner headline n a newspaper headline written in large letters across the width of the page.

banns pl n the public announcement of an intended marriage.

banquet n a sumptuous formal dinner. ➤ vb, intr (**banqueted, banqueting**) to take part in a banquet.

banshee n, esp Irish & Scot folklore a female spirit whose wailing warns of a death in a house.

bantam n a small breed of farm chicken.

bantamweight n **1** a class for boxers, wrestlers and weightlifters of not more than a specified weight, for example 53.5kg (118 lb) in professional boxing. **2** a boxer, wrestler, etc of this weight.

banter n light-hearted friendly talk. ➤ vb, intr to engage in banter.

Bantu n (pl **Bantu**) **1** a group of languages spoken in southern and central Africa. **2** pl the group of peoples who speak these languages. **3** offensive a Black speaker of one of these languages. ➤ adj belonging or relating to the Bantu languages or Bantu-speaking people.

banyan or **banian** n an Indian fruit tree with branches from which shoots grow down into the ground and take root.

baobab / 'beɪoʊbab/ n a large deciduous African tree with a massive soft trunk.

bap n, Scot & N Eng dialect a large flat bread roll.

baptism n the religious ceremony of baptizing a person by immersion in, or sprinkling with, water. ○ **baptismal** adj.

Baptist n a member of a Christian group which believes that only adults should be baptized into the Church, and that this should be by complete immersion in water.

baptize or **-ise** vb **1** to immerse someone in, or sprinkle them with, water as a sign of them having become a member of the Christian Church. **2** to give a name to someone. Compare CHRISTEN (sense 1).

bar¹ n **1** a block of some solid substance. **2** a long piece of a strong rigid material used as a weapon, an obstruction, etc. **3** anything that prevents or hinders, such as a non-physical barrier: a bar on alcohol. **4** a band of colour or light, etc, esp a stripe on a heraldic shield. **5** a room or counter in a restaurant or hotel, etc, or a separate establishment, where alcoholic drinks are sold and drunk. **6** in compounds a small café serving drinks and snacks: a coffee bar. **7 a** (also **bar-line**) a vertical line marked on music, dividing it into sections of equal value; **b** one of these sections. **8** the rail in a law court where the accused person stands. **9** (**the Bar**) the profession of barristers. ➤ vb (**barred, barring**) **1** to fasten with a bar. **2** (often **bar sb from sth**) to forbid them from entering, eg a place or event, doing something, etc. **3** to hinder or prevent (someone's progress). ➤ prep except; except for: every suspect, bar one. ♦ **be called to the Bar** in the UK: to be admitted as a barrister. **behind bars** in prison.

bar² n, physics, meteorol, etc in the metric system: a unit of pressure equal to 10^5 newtons per square metre.

barb *n* **1** a point on a hook facing in the opposite direction to the main point. **2** a humorous but hurtful remark. ➤ *vb* to provide something with barbs or a barb. ○ **barbed** *adj*.

barbarian *n* **1** someone who is cruel and wild in behaviour. **2** an uncivilized and uncultured person. ➤ *adj* cruel and wild; uncivilized. ○ **barbaric** *adj*.

barbarism *n* **1** the state of being uncivilized, coarse, etc. **2** a cruel, coarse or ignorant act. **3** a word or expression which is considered ungrammatical.

barbarity *n* (*-ies*) BARBARISM (in senses 1 and 2).

barbarous *adj* **1** uncultured and uncivilized. **2** extremely cruel or brutal.

barbecue *n* **1** a frame on which food is grilled over hot charcoal. **2** food cooked in this way. **3** a party held out of doors at which food is cooked on a barbecue. ➤ *vb* to cook (food) on a barbecue.

barbed wire *n* wire with short sharp points twisted on at intervals, used for making fences, etc.

barbel *n* **1** a freshwater fish of the carp family, which has four long sensory feelers or **barbels** around its mouth. **2** a whisker-like outgrowth found around the mouth of some fishes, esp catfish and barbels.

barbell *n* a bar with heavy metal weights at each end, used for weightlifting exercises.

barber *n* someone who cuts and styles men's hair and shaves their beards.

barbican *n* a tower over the outer gate of a castle or town, for the purpose of defending the gate.

barbie *n*, *Aust colloq* a barbecue.

barbiturate *n*, *med* a salt or ester of a crystalline acid, used as a source of sedative drugs.

bar chart or **bar graph** *n* a graph which shows amounts by means of vertical bars. Compare PIE CHART.

bar code *n* a series of numbers and parallel lines used on product labels, that represents information about the product for sales checkouts, etc.

bard *n* **1** *literary* a poet. **2** a poet who has won a prize at the Eisteddfod in Wales.

bare *adj* **1** not covered by clothes. **2** without the usual or natural covering: *bare trees*. **3** empty. **4** plain: *the bare facts*. **5** essential: *the bare necessities*. ➤ *vb* to uncover. ○ **bareness** *n*.

bareback *adv, adj* on a horse without a saddle.

bare bones *pl n* the essential facts of a situation.

barefaced *adj* having no shame or regret: *a barefaced lie*.

barefoot or **barefooted** *adj, adv* not wearing shoes or socks.

barely *adv* **1** scarcely or only just: *barely enough food*. **2** plainly or simply: *barely furnished*.

bargain *n* **1** an agreement made between people buying and selling things, offering and accepting services, etc. **2** something offered for sale, or bought, at a low price. ➤ *vb, intr* (*often* **bargain with sb**) to discuss the terms for buying or selling, etc. ♦ **into the bargain** in addition; besides. ◊ **bargain for** or **on sth** to expect it.

barge *n* **1** a long flat-bottomed boat used on rivers and canals. **2** a large boat, often decorated, used in ceremonies, celebrations, etc. ➤ *vb, intr* (*esp* **barge about** or **around**) to move in a clumsy way. ◊ **barge in** to interrupt, esp rudely or abruptly.

bargee *n* a person in charge of a barge.

bargepole *n* a long pole used to move a barge. ♦ **not touch sth** or **sb with a bargepole** *colloq* to refuse to have anything to do with it or them.

barite /ˈbɛəraɪt/ *n*, *geol* BARYTES.

baritone *mus, n* **1** the second lowest male singing voice. **2** a singer with such a voice. ➤ *adj* referring to the pitch and compass of a baritone.

barium *n*, *chem* a soft silvery-white metallic element.

bark¹ *n* the short sharp cry of a dog, fox, etc. ➤ *vb* **1** *intr* to make this sound. **2** *tr & intr* to speak loudly and sharply. ♦ **bark up the wrong tree** *colloq* to have the wrong idea, follow a mistaken course of action or investigation, etc.

bark² *n*, *bot* the tough protective outer layer consisting mainly of dead cells, that covers the stems and roots of woody plants, eg trees. ➤ *vb* **1** to scrape or rub off the skin from (one's leg, etc). **2** to strip or remove the bark from (a tree, etc).

barley *n* **1** a cereal of the grass family which bears a dense head of grains. **2** (*also* **barleycorn**) the grain of this plant, used as feed for animal livestock and in the production of beer and whisky.

barley sugar *n* a kind of hard orange-coloured sweet.

barley water *n* a drink made from water in which barley has been boiled, usu with fruit juice added.

barm *n* the froth formed on fermenting liquor.

barmaid or **barman** *n* a woman or man who serves drinks in a bar.

bar mitzvah *n* a Jewish ceremony in which a boy (usu aged 13) formally accepts full religious responsibilities.

barmy *adj* (*-ier, -iest*) *colloq* crazy.

barn *n* a building in which grain or hay, etc is stored, or for housing cattle, etc.

barnacle *n* a marine CRUSTACEAN which clings to rocks, hulls of boats, etc.

barn dance *n* **1** a kind of party at which there is country dancing. **2** a particular kind of country dance, esp SQUARE DANCE.

barney *n* (*-eys*) *colloq* a rough noisy quarrel.

barnstorm *vb, intr* **1** to tour a district, stopping briefly in each town to give theatrical performances. **2** *N Am* to travel about the country making political speeches just before an election. ○ **barnstorming** *adj* impressively flamboyant.

barnyard *n* the area around or adjoining a barn.

barometer *n, meteorol* an instrument which measures atmospheric pressure, esp in order to predict changes in the weather or to estimate height above sea level. ○ **barometric** *adj*.

baron *n* **1** a man holding the lowest rank of the British nobility. **2** a powerful businessman: *oil baron*. ○ **baronial** *adj*.

baroness *n* **1** a baron's wife. **2** a woman holding the title of baron in her own right.

baronet *n* in the UK: **a** a hereditary title ranking below that of baron, not part of the PEERAGE; **b** a man holding such a title. ○ **baronetcy** *n* (*-ies*).

baroque *n* (*also* **Baroque**) a complex decorative style of architecture, art and music, popular in Europe from the late 16c to the early 18c. ➤ *adj* **1** (*also* **Baroque**) built, designed or written, etc in such a style. **2** of ornamentation, etc: extravagant.

barque *n* **1** a small sailing ship with three masts. **2** *literary* any boat.

barrack¹ *n* (*usu* **barracks**) a building or group of buildings for housing soldiers. ➤ *vb* to house (soldiers) in barracks.

barrack² *vb, tr & intr, chiefly Brit* to shout and laugh rudely or hostilely at (a speaker, sports team, etc).

barracuda *n* (*barracuda* or *barracudas*) a large tropical sea fish which feeds on other fish.

barrage *n* **1** *mil* a long burst of gunfire over a wide area. **2** a large number of things, esp questions or criticisms, etc, coming in quickly one after the other. **3** an artificial barrier across a river.

barrage balloon *n* a large balloon attached to the ground by a cable and often with a net hanging from it, formerly used to prevent attack by low-flying aircraft.

barre /bɑː(r)/ *n, ballet* a rail fixed to a wall at waist level, which dancers use to balance themselves while exercising.

barrel *n* **1** a large round container with a flat top and bottom and curving out in the middle, usu made of planks of wood held together with metal bands. **2** the amount a barrel holds. **3** a measure of capacity, esp of industrial oil. **4** the long hollow tube-shaped part of a gun or pen, etc. ♦ **over a barrel** at a great disadvantage.

barrel organ *n* a large mechanical instrument which plays music when a handle is turned.

barren *adj* **1** of a woman or female animal: not able to bear offspring. **2** of land or soil, etc: not able to produce crops or fruit, etc. **3** not producing results. **4** dull; unresponsive. ○ **barrenness** *n*.

barricade /ˈbarɪkeɪd/ *n* a barrier, esp one erected hastily. ➤ *vb* to block or defend something with a barricade.

barrier *n* **1** a fence, gate or bar, etc put up to defend, protect, separate, etc. **2** something

that separates people, items, etc.

barring *prep* except for.

barrister *n* in England and Wales: a lawyer qualified to act for someone in the higher law courts.

barrow¹ *n* **1** a small one-wheeled cart used to carry tools, earth, etc. **2** a larger cart, with two or four wheels, from which goods are often sold in the street.

barrow² *n, archaeol* a pile of earth over an ancient grave.

barrow boy *n* a boy or man who sells goods from a barrow.

bartender *n, N Am* someone who serves drinks in a bar.

barter *vb, tr & intr* to trade or exchange (goods or services) without using money. ➤ *n* trade by exchanging goods rather than by selling them for money.

baryon /ˈbarɪɒn/ *n, physics* a heavy subatomic particle whose mass is greater than or equal to that of the proton.

barytes /baˈraɪtiːz/ *n, geol* the mineral form of barium sulphate, the chief ore of barium.

basal /ˈbeɪsl/ *adj* **1** at, referring to or forming a base. **2** at the lowest level.

basalt /ˈbasɔlt/ *n, geol* a fine-grained dark volcanic rock. ○ **basaltic** *adj*.

base¹ *n* **1** the lowest part or bottom; the part which supports something or on which something stands. **2** the origin, root or foundation of something. **3** the headquarters or centre of activity or operations. **4** a starting point. **5** the main part of a mixture. **6** *chem* any of a group of chemical compounds that can neutralize an acid to form a salt and water. **7** *baseball* any one of four fixed points on the pitch which players must run around to score. **8** *maths* in a numerical system: the number of different symbols used, eg in the BINARY number system the base is two, because only the symbols 0 and 1 are used. **9** *maths* in logarithms: the number that, when raised to a certain power (see POWER *noun* sense 12), has a logarithm equal in value to that power. **10** *geom* the line or surface, usu horizontal, on which a geometric figure rests. ➤ *vb* to use as a base or basis.

base² *adj* **1** lacking morals; wicked. **2** not pure. **3** low in value.

baseball *n* **1** a team game using a truncheon-shaped bat and a ball, in which the person batting attempts to run as far as possible round a diamond-shaped pitch formed by four bases (see BASE¹ *noun* sense 7), aiming to get back to the home plate to score a run. **2** the ball used in this game.

baseless *adj* having no cause or foundation.

baseline *n* **1** one of the two lines which mark the ends of a tennis court. **2** an amount or value taken as a basis for comparison.

basement *n* the lowest floor of a building, usu below ground level.

base metal *n* any metal that readily corrodes, tarnishes or oxidizes on exposure to air, moist-

ure or heat, eg zinc, copper, lead. Compare
NOBLE METAL.

base rate n, finance the rate used by a bank as
the base or starting point in fixing the rate of
interest offered to customers.

bash vb, colloq **1** to strike or smash something
bluntly. **2** to attack something or someone
harshly with words. ➤ n **1** a heavy blow. **2** a
mark made by a heavy blow. **3** slang a noisy
party. ♦ **have a bash (at sth)** colloq to have a try.

bashful adj shy; self-conscious. ○ **bashfully**
adv. ○ **bashfulness** n.

BASIC or **Basic** n a high-level computer programming language.

basic adj **1** referring to or forming the base or
basis of something. **2** belonging to, or at, a very
simple or low level: Her grasp of French is basic.
3 without additions: basic salary. **4** chem referring or relating to, or forming, a base or bases.
➤ n (usu **the basics**) the essential facts or principles. ○ **basically** adv.

basil n an aromatic plant widely cultivated as a
culinary herb.

basilica n **1** an ancient Roman public hall, with
a rounded wall at one end and a row of stone
pillars along each side. **2** a church shaped like
this.

basilisk n, myth a snake which can kill people
by breathing on them or looking at them.

basin n **1** a wide open dish, esp one for holding
water. **2** a bowl or sink in a bathroom, etc for
washing oneself in. **3** (also **basinful**) the
amount a basin holds. **4** a valley or area of land
drained by a river, or by the streams running
into a river. **5** the deep part of a harbour; a
dock. **6** geol a large depression into which sedi-
ments deposit.

basis n (pl **-ses** /-siːz/) **1** a principle on which
an idea or theory, etc is based. **2** a foundation
or starting point: a basis for discussion.

bask vb, intr **1** to lie in comfort, esp in warmth or
sunshine. **2** to enjoy and take great pleasure:
basking in her success.

basket n **1** a container made of interwoven
twigs, canes, etc, often with a handle across
the top. **2** (also **basketful**) the amount a basket
holds. **3** basketball **a** either of the nets into
which the ball is thrown to score a goal; **b** a
goal scored.

basketball n **1** a team game in which players
score by throwing a ball into a net fixed high
up at each end of the court. **2** the ball used in
this game.

basketwork sing n articles made of strips of
wood, cane, twigs, etc, woven together.

basmati rice n a type of long-grain rice, eaten
esp with Indian food.

Basque n **1** a member of a people living in the
western Pyrenees, in Spain and France. **2** the
language spoken by these people. ➤ adj belonging or relating to the Basque people or
their language.

basque n a tight-fitting bodice for women.

bas-relief /ba:rɪˈliːf/ n, art sculpture in which

the relief figures are only slightly raised.

bass[1] /beɪs/ mus, n **1** the lowest male singing
voice. **2** a singer with such a voice. **3** a musical
part written for such a voice or for an instrument of the lowest range. **4** colloq a bass instrument, esp a bass guitar or a double-bass. **5** a
low frequency sound as output from an amplifier, etc; **b** a dial that adjusts this sound. ➤ adj
of a musical instrument, voice or sound: low in
pitch and range. ○ **bassist** n.

bass[2] /bas/ n (**bass** or **basses**) **1** an edible marine fish. **2** a similar freshwater fish.

bass clef n, mus a sign (𝄢) placed at the beginning of a piece of written music, which fixes the
note F below middle C on the fourth line of the
stave which follows.

basset or **basset hound** n a breed of dog with
a long body, smooth hair, short legs and long
drooping ears.

bassinet n a baby's basket-like bed or pram,
usu hooded.

bassoon n a large woodwind instrument
which produces a very low sound.
○ **bassoonist** n.

bastard n **1** dated, often offensive a child born
of parents not married to each other. **2** coarse
slang **a** a term of abuse or sympathy for a person: poor bastard; **b** a person generally: lucky
bastard. **3** coarse slang something annoying or
difficult. ➤ adj **1** of a person: ILLEGITIMATE. **2**
not genuine or pure.

bastardize or **-ise** vb to make something less
genuine or pure. ○ **bastardization** n.

baste[1] vb to pour hot fat or juices over (esp
roasting meat) during cooking.

baste[2] vb to sew (eg a seam) with temporary
loose stitches.

bastion n **1** a kind of tower which sticks out at
an angle from a castle wall. **2** a person, place or
thing regarded as a defender of a principle, etc:
a bastion of freedom.

bat[1] n **1** a shaped piece of wood, with a flat or
curved surface, for hitting the ball in cricket,
baseball, etc. **2** chiefly cricket a batsman or
batswoman. ➤ vb (**batted, batting**) **1** intr,
cricket, baseball, etc to take a turn at hitting a
ball with a bat. **2** to hit with, or as if with, a
bat. ♦ **off one's own bat** without prompting or
help.

bat[2] n any of various small nocturnal flying
mammals.

bat[3] vb (**batted, batting**) to open and close
(one's eyelids) very quickly. ♦ **not bat an eye**
or **eyelid** colloq to show no surprise.

batch n a number of things or people dealt with
at the same time. ➤ vb to arrange or treat in
batches.

batch file n, comput a text file containing a series of commands which are executed in order
when the name of the file is called.

bated adj, archaic diminished; restrained.
♦ **with bated breath** hushed and tense with
excitement or anxiety.

bath n **1** a large open container for water, in

which to wash the whole body while sitting in it. **2** an act of washing the body in a bath. **3** the water filling a bath. **4** (**the baths**) a public swimming pool. **5** a liquid with or in which something is washed, heated or steeped, etc, as a medicinal or cleansing treatment, etc or as part of a process such as developing photographs. ➢ *vb* to wash in a bath.

Bath chair *n, esp formerly* a wheeled and usu hooded chair in which an invalid can be pushed.

bathe *vb* **1** *intr* to swim in the sea, etc for pleasure. **2** *intr, chiefly N Am* to wash (oneself) in a bath. **3** to wash or treat (part of the body, etc) with water, or with a liquid, etc to clean it or to lessen pain. **4** of light, etc: to cover and surround: *Sunlight bathed the room.* ○ **bather** *n*.

bathos /ˈbeɪθɒs/ *n* in speech or writing: a sudden descent from serious or beautiful ideas to very ordinary or trivial ones. ○ **bathetic** *adj*.

> **bathos** A word sometimes confused with this one is **pathos**.

bathrobe *n* a loose towelling coat used esp before and after taking a bath.

bathroom *n* **1** a room containing a bath and other washing facilities, a lavatory, etc. **2** *esp N Am* a room with a lavatory.

bathyscaphe or **bathyscape** /ˈbæθɪskeɪf/ *n* a crewed underwater vessel, used for exploring the ocean depths.

bathysphere *n* a deep-sea observation chamber, consisting of a watertight steel sphere that is lowered and raised from a surface vessel.

batik /bəˈtiːk/ *n* **1** a technique of printing cloth in which those parts not to be coloured are covered with wax. **2** cloth coloured by this method.

batman *n* an officer's personal servant in the armed forces.

baton /ˈbatən, -tɒn; *US* bəˈtɑːn/ *n* **1** a thin stick used by the conductor of an orchestra or choir, etc to direct them. **2** a short heavy stick carried by a policeman as a weapon. **3** a short stick passed from one runner to another in a relay race. **4** a stick tossed and twirled by a person at the head of a marching band.

> **baton, batten** There is sometimes a spelling confusion between **baton** and **batten**.

baton round *n, formal* a plastic or rubber bullet.

bats *adj, colloq* crazy; BATTY.

batsman *n, chiefly cricket* (*also* **batswoman**) a person who bats or is batting.

battalion *n* an army unit made up of several smaller companies (see COMPANY *noun* sense 6), and forming part of a larger BRIGADE.

batten *n* **1** a long flat piece of wood used for keeping other pieces in place. **2** a strip of wood used to fasten the covers over the hatches in a

ship's deck, etc. ➢ *vb* to fasten, strengthen or shut (eg a door) with battens. ◆ **batten down the hatches** *colloq* to prepare for a danger or crisis.

batter[1] *vb* **1** *tr & intr* to hit something or someone hard and often. **2** to damage or wear out through continual use. ○ **battering** *n*.

batter[2] *n* a mixture of eggs, flour and either milk or water, used in cooking.

batter[3] *n, esp baseball* a person who bats or is batting.

battering-ram *n* a large wooden beam, formerly used in war for breaking down walls or gates.

battery *n* (*-ies*) **1** a device that converts chemical energy into electrical energy in the form of direct current. **2** a number of similar things: *a battery of photographers.* **3** a long line of small cages in which hens are kept. **4** *law* intentional physical attack on a person, including touching the clothes or body in a threatening manner. **5** a group of heavy guns.

battle *n* **1** a fight between opposing armies, etc or people. **2** a competition between opposing groups: *a battle of wits.* **3** a long or difficult struggle: *a battle for equality.* ➢ *vb, intr* **1** to fight. **2** to campaign vigorously.

battle-axe *n* **1** *colloq* a domineering older woman. **2** *hist* a large broad-bladed axe.

battle-cruiser *n* a large warship, faster than a battleship but with fewer guns.

battle-cry *n* **1** a shout given by soldiers charging into battle. **2** a slogan used to arouse support for a cause, etc.

battledress *n* a soldier's ordinary uniform.

battlefield or **battleground** *n* the place at which a battle is or was fought.

battlement *n* a low wall around the top of a castle, etc with gaps for shooting through.

battle royal *n* (*battles royal*) **1** a large brawl. **2** a long heated argument.

battleship *n* the largest type of warship.

batty *adj* (*-ier, -iest*) *colloq* crazy; eccentric.

bauble *n* **1** a small cheap trinket. **2** a round coloured decoration hung on Christmas trees.

baulk *see* BALK.

bauxite *n, geol* a clay-like substance which is the main ore of aluminium.

bawdy *adj* (*-ier, -iest*) of language or writing, etc: containing coarsely humorous references to sex. ○ **bawdily** *adv.* ○ **bawdiness** *n*.

bawl *vb, intr* **1** to cry loudly in distress, pain, etc. **2** (*also* **bawl out**) to shout loudly. ➢ *n* a loud shout.

bay[1] *n* a body of water that forms a widemouthed indentation in the coastline.

bay[2] *n* **1** an enclosed or partly enclosed area within a building, vessel, etc for storage or some other purpose. **2** *in compounds* a compartment for storing or carrying, eg in an aircraft: *bomb bay.* **3 a** a parking bay; **b** a loading bay. **4** a small area of a room set back into a wall.

bay[3] *adj* of a horse: reddish-brown in colour,

usu with black mane and tail. ➤ *n* a bay-coloured horse.

bay⁴ *n* **1** any of various evergreen trees of the LAUREL family with shiny dark-green leaves. **2** (*usu* **bays**) a wreath of bay leaves, traditionally worn on the head by champions in some competitions, etc.

bay⁵ *vb* **1** *intr* esp of large dogs: to make a deep howling cry. **2** *intr* of a crowd, etc: to howl or shout loudly. ➤ *n* the baying sound of a dog, etc. ♦ **keep sth** or **sb at bay** to fight it or them off. **2** to keep it or them at a distance.

bayonet *n* **1** a steel knife that fixes to the muzzle of a rifle. **2** (*also* **bayonet fitting**) a type of fitting for a light bulb, etc in which prongs on its side fit into slots to hold it in place. ➤ *vb* (**bayoneted, bayoneting**) to stab with a bayonet.

bay window *n* a three-sided or rounded window that juts out from the wall of a building.

bazaar *n* **1** a sale of goods in aid of charity. **2** in Eastern countries: a market place or exchange.

bazooka *n* a portable anti-tank gun which fires small rockets.

BBC *abbrev* British Broadcasting Corporation.

BC *abbrev* in dates: before Christ, used together with a figure to indicate a specified number of years before that in which Christ was once thought to have been born. Compare AD.

> **BC** BC follows the year number: *753 BC*. Compare note at AD.

BCG or **bcg** *abbrev* bacillus Calmette-Guérin, a vaccine given to a person to prevent tuberculosis.

Be *symbol, chem* beryllium.

be *vb* (*past participle* **been**; *present participle* **being**; *present tense* **am, are, is**; *past tense* **was, were**) *intr* **1** to exist or live: *I think, therefore I am.* **2** to occur or take place: *Lunch is in an hour.* **3** to occupy a position in space: *She is at home.* **4** *in past tense* to go: *He's never been to Italy.* **5** to remain or continue without change: *Let it be.* **6** used to link a subject and what is said about it: *She is a doctor.* **7** used with the INFINITIVE form of a verb to express a possibility, command, intention, outcome, etc: *if it were to rain • We are to come tomorrow • It was not to be.* ➤ *auxiliary vb* **1** used with a past PARTICIPLE to form a PASSIVE construction: *The film was shown last night.* **2** used with a present PARTICIPLE to form the PROGRESSIVE tenses: *He was running.*

beach *n* the sandy or stony shore of a sea or lake. ➤ *vb* to push, pull or drive (esp a boat) onto a beach.

beachcomber /'biːtʃkoʊmə(r)/ *n* someone who searches beaches for things of value.

beachhead *n, mil* an area of shore captured from the enemy, on which an army can land men and equipment.

beacon *n* **1** a warning or guiding device for aircraft or ships, eg a lighthouse or (*in full* **radio beacon**) a radio transmitter that broadcasts signals. **2** a fire on high ground, lit as a signal.

bead *n* **1** a small and usu round ball made of glass or stone, etc strung with others, eg in a necklace. **2** (**beads**) a string of beads worn as jewellery, or one used when praying (a ROSARY). **3** a small drop of liquid. **4** BEADING. ➤ *vb* to decorate with beads or beading. ○ **beaded** *adj*.

beading *n* thin strips of patterned wood used to decorate the edges of furniture, etc.

beadle *n, Brit* **1** a person who leads formal processions in church or in some old universities and institutions. **2** in Scotland: a church officer who attends the minister. **3** *formerly* in England: a minor parish official who had the power to punish minor offences.

beady *adj* (**-ier, -iest**) *usu derog* of a person's eyes: small, round and bright.

beagle *n* a breed of small hunting-dog with a short-haired coat.

beak *n* **1** the horny projecting jaws of a bird. **2** *Brit, slang* a headmaster, judge or magistrate.

beaker *n* **1** a large drinking-glass. **2** a glass container used in laboratory work.

beam *n* **1** a long thick piece of wood, used eg as a main structural component in a building. **2** a ray of light. **3** the widest part of a ship. **4** a raised narrow horizontal wooden bar on which gymnasts perform balancing exercises. **5** *physics* a directed flow of electromagnetic radiation or of particles. ➤ *vb* **1** *intr* to smile broadly with pleasure; a tiny amount of money: **2** *intr* (*often* **beam down** or **out**) to shine. **3** to send out or transmit (eg rays of light, radio waves, etc). ♦ **off beam** *colloq* wrong; misguided.

bean *n* **1** a general name applied to the edible seed of plants belonging to the pea family. **2** any plant belonging to the pea family that bears such seeds, such as the BROAD BEAN or RUNNER BEAN. **3** (*usu* **beans**) *cookery* a seed or young pod of such a plant, used as food. **4** any other seed that superficially resembles those of the pea family: *coffee bean.* **5** *colloq, with negatives* a small coin; a tiny amount of money: *I haven't got a bean.* ♦ **full of beans** *colloq* full of energy; very lively and cheerful.

bean bag *n* **1** a small cloth bag filled with dried beans used like a ball in children's games. **2** a very large cushion filled with polystyrene chips, etc, kept on the floor as seating.

beanfeast *n, Brit colloq* a party.

beano *n, Brit colloq* a beanfeast.

beanpole *n, colloq* a tall thin person.

beansprout or **beanshoot** *n* a young shoot of a bean plant eaten as a vegetable, esp in Chinese food.

bear¹ *vb* (*past tense* **bore**, *past participle* **borne** or (*in sense 7b*) **born**, *present participle* **bearing**) **1** to support or sustain (a weight or load). **2** to take or accept: *I'll bear the blame.* **3** to put up with or tolerate. **4 a** to allow; to be fit or suitable for something: *It doesn't bear thinking about;* **b** to stand up to or be capable of withstanding something: *It will not bear close scrutiny.* **5** to bring or take something with one; to carry: *bearing gifts.* **6** to produce. **7 a** to give birth to (a child or offspring); **b** in the passive using past participle *born*: *He was born in 1990*; **c** in the past tense using past participle *borne*: *Has she borne children?* **8** to carry something in one's thought or memory: *I don't bear grudges.* **9** to have: *He bears no resemblance to his father.* **10** to show or be marked by something: *Her cheeks bore the traces of tears.* **11** *intr* to turn slightly in a given direction: *Let's bear left.* ○ **bearable** *adj.* ◆ **bring sth to bear** to apply or exert esp pressure or influence, or bring something into operation. ◊ **bear down on sb** or **sth** to move threateningly towards them or it. **bear on sth** to affect, concern or relate to it. **bear sb** or **sth out** to support or confirm them or it. **bear up** to remain strong or brave, etc under strain. **bear with sb** to be patient with them.

bear² *n* (*bears* or *bear*) **1** any of various large carnivorous animals with a heavily built body, covered with thick fur. **2** a rough ill-mannered person. **3** a teddy bear. **4** *stock exchange* someone who sells shares, hoping to buy them back later at a much lower price. Compare BULL¹ (*noun* sense 3). ○ **bearish** *adj.* ◆ **like a bear with a sore head** *colloq* of a person: exceptionally bad-tempered.

beard *n* **1** the hair that grows on a man's chin and neck. **2** a beard-like growth on the lower jaw of some animals, esp goats. ➤ *vb* to face or oppose somebody boldly or impudently. ○ **bearded** *adj.*

bearer *n* **1** a person or thing that bears, carries or brings something. **2** a person who holds a banknote, cheque or other money order which can be exchanged for money.

bear hug *n*, *colloq* a rough tight embrace.

bearing /ˈbɛərɪŋ/ *n* **1** the way a person stands, walks, behaves, etc: *a proud bearing.* **2** relevance. **3 a** the horizontal direction of a fixed point, or the path of a moving object, measured from a reference point on the Earth's surface, and normally expressed as an angle measured in degrees clockwise from the north; **b** (*usu* **bearings**) position or a calculation of position: *compass bearing.* **4** (**bearings**) *colloq* a sense or awareness of one's own position or surroundings. **5** any part of a machine or device that supports another part, and allows free movement between the two parts, eg a BALL-BEARING.

bearskin *n* **1** the skin of a bear. **2** a tall fur cap worn as part of some military uniforms.

beast *n* **1** any large animal, esp a wild one. **2** *colloq* a cruel brutal person. **3** *colloq* a difficult or unpleasant person or thing.

beastly *adj* (*-ier*, *-iest*) *colloq* unpleasant; disagreeable.

beat *vb* (*past tense* **beat**, *past participle* **beaten** or (*now rare*) **beat**, *present participle* **beating**) **1** to hit (a person, animal, etc) violently and repeatedly. **2** to strike something repeatedly, eg

to remove dust or make a sound. **3** *intr* (*usu* **beat against** or **at** or **on sth**) to knock or strike repeatedly: *rain beating against the window.* **4** to defeat; to do something better, sooner or quicker than (someone else): *Dad always beats me at chess.* **5** to be too difficult to be solved or understood by someone. **6** (*sometimes* **beat sth up**) to mix or stir thoroughly: *Beat two eggs in a bowl.* **7** (*also* **beat out**) **a** to make or shape something by repeatedly striking the raw material: *beating out horseshoes*; **b** to flatten or reduce the thickness of something by beating. **8** *intr* to move in a regular pattern of strokes, etc: *I heard my heart beating.* **9** *tr & intr* to move rhythmically up and down: *tent-flaps beating in the wind.* **10** (*usu* **beat time** or **beat out time**) to mark or show (musical time or rhythm) with the hand or a baton, etc. **11** (**beat sb** or **sth back** or **down** or **off**) to drive or force them or it away. **12** (*also* **beat up**) *tr & intr* to strike (bushes or trees, etc) to force birds or animals into the open for shooting. ➤ *n* **1** a regular recurrent stroke, or its sound: *the beat of my heart.* **2 a** in music and poetry, etc: the basic pulse, unit of rhythm or accent: *two beats to the bar*; **b** the conductor's stroke of the hand or baton indicating such a pulse: *Watch the beat*; **c** in popular music: rhythm; a strong rhythmic pulse. **3** a regular or usual course or journey: *a policeman's beat.* ➤ *adj*, *colloq*, *esp US* exhausted. ○ **beater** *n* a person or thing that beats, eg a person who rouses game for shooting, an electric or hand-operated device for beating, etc. ○ **beating** *n.* ◆ **beat about the bush** to talk tediously about a subject without coming to the main point. **beat it** *slang* to go away immediately and quickly. **off the beaten track** away from main roads and towns; isolated. ◊ **beat down 1** of the sun: to give out great heat. **2** of rain: to fall heavily. **beat sb down** to force them to reduce the price of something by bargaining. **beat sb up** or (*US*) **beat up on sb** to hit them severely and repeatedly.

beaten *adj* **1** defeated or outmanoeuvred. **2** *colloq*, *esp Aust & NZ* exhausted or worn out. **3** made smooth or hard by beating or treading: *beaten path.* **4** shaped and made thin by beating: *beaten gold.*

beatific *adj* expressing or revealing supreme peaceful happiness.

beatify *vb* (*-ies*, *-ied*) *RC Church* to declare the blessed status of (someone who has died), usu as the first step towards full canonization. ○ **beatification** *n.*

beatitude /bɪˈatɪtjuːd/ *n* **1** (**the Beatitudes**) *Bible* the group of statements made by Christ during the Sermon on the Mount about the kinds of people who receive God's blessing. **2** a state of blessedness or of extreme happiness.

beatnik *n* in the 1950s and 60s: a young person who rejected the accepted social and political ideas, etc of the time.

beat-up *adj*, *colloq* in a dilapidated condition.

beau /bou/ *n* (**beaux** or **beaus** /bouz/) **1** *US* or *dated Brit* a boyfriend or male lover. **2** *old use* a DANDY.

Beaufort scale /ˈbəʊfət/ *n, meteorol* a system for estimating wind speeds without using instruments.

beauteous *adj, poetic* beautiful.

beautician *n* a person who gives hair and skin treatments, etc to women, esp in a beauty parlour.

beautiful *adj* **1** having an appearance or qualities which please the senses or give rise to admiration in the mind. **2** *colloq* very enjoyable; excellent. ○ **beautifully** *adv*.

beautify *vb* (*-ies, -ied*) to make beautiful.

beauty *n* (*-ies*) **1** a quality pleasing to the senses, esp to the eye. **2** *colloq* an excellent example of something: *a beauty of a black eye.* **3** a benefit or particular strength or quality: *The beauty of the plan is its flexibility.* **4** a beautiful woman.

beauty parlour or **beauty salon** *n* a place where people go for beauty treatments such as hairdressing, facials, manicure, etc.

beauty spot *n* **1** a place of great natural beauty. **2** a small dark natural or artificial mark on the face, believed to enhance beauty.

beaver *n* **1** a large semi-aquatic rodent with soft dark-brown fur, large incisor teeth, webbed hind feet and a broad flat tail. **2** its valuable fur. **3** a hat made of beaver fur. ➤ *vb, intr* (*esp* **beaver away at sth**) *colloq, chiefly Brit* to work very hard at something.

bebop *n* (*often shortened to* **bop**) a variety of jazz music with complex rhythms and harmonies.

becalmed *adj* of a sailing ship: unable to move because of lack of wind.

because *conj* for the reason that. ♦ **because of sth** or **sb** by reason of, or on account of, it or them.

because See note at **due**.

béchamel /ˈbeɪʃəmɛl/ or **béchamel sauce** *n, cookery* a white sauce flavoured with onion and herbs.

beck[1] *n, archaic* a beckoning gesture. ♦ **at sb's beck and call** having to be always ready to carry out their orders.

beck[2] *n, N Eng dialect* a stream.

beckon *vb, tr & intr* to summon with a gesture.

become *vb* (*past tense* **became**, *past participle* **become**, *present participle* **becoming**) **1** *intr* to come or grow to be something. **2** *formal* esp of clothing: to suit, look good on or befit someone: *That hat becomes you.*

becoming *adj* **1** attractive. **2** of behaviour, etc: suitable or proper.

becquerel /ˈbɛkərɛl/ *n, physics* in the SI system: the unit of activity of a radioactive source per second.

BEd *abbrev* Bachelor of Education.

bed *n* **1** a piece of furniture for sleeping on. **2** a place in which anything (eg an animal) sleeps or rests. **3** *colloq* sleep or rest: *ready for bed.* **4** the bottom of a river, lake or sea. **5** an area of ground in a garden, for growing plants. **6** a flat surface, esp one made of slate or tile, on which something can be supported or laid down. **7** a layer, eg of oysters, sedimentary rock, etc. **8** a place available for occupancy in a residential home, nursing home or hospital. ➤ *vb* (**bedded, bedding**) **1** *tr & intr* (*usu* **bed down**) to go to bed, or put someone in bed or in a place to sleep. **2** (*usu* **bed out**) to plant something in the soil, in a garden, etc. **3** to place or fix something firmly: *bedded in concrete.* **4** *colloq* to have sex with someone. **5** *tr & intr* to arrange in or to form, layers. ♦ **get out of bed on the wrong side** *colloq* to start the day in a bad mood. **go to bed with sb** *colloq* to have sexual intercourse with them.

bed and breakfast *n* (**bed and breakfasts**) **1** at a guest-house, etc: overnight accommodation with breakfast included in the price. **2** a guest-house, etc that provides accommodation and breakfast.

bedbug *n* any of various species of household pest that infest bedding and feed on human blood.

bedclothes *pl n* sheets, blankets, etc for a bed.

bedding *n* **1** bedclothes, and sometimes also a mattress and pillows, etc. **2** straw or hay, etc for animals to sleep on. **3** *geol* stratification.

bedeck *vb* to cover with decorations.

bedevil *vb* (**bedevilled, bedevilling;** *US* **bedeviled, bedeviling**) **1** to cause continual difficulties to. **2** to throw into confusion.

bedfellow *n* **1** a partner or associate. **2** a person with whom one shares a bed.

bedlam *n, colloq* a very noisy confused place or situation.

bed linen *n* sheets and pillowcases for a bed.

bed of roses *n* an easy or comfortable place or situation: *Her life is no bed of roses.*

Bedouin *n* (**Bedouin** or **Bedouins**) a member of a nomadic tent-dwelling Arab tribe.

bedpan *n* a shallow pan used as a toilet by someone who is unable to get out of bed.

bedraggled *adj* of a person or animal: very wet and untidy.

bedridden *adj* not able to get out of bed, esp because of old age or sickness.

bedrock *n* **1** the solid rock forming the lowest layer under soil and rock fragments. **2** the basic principle or idea, etc on which something rests.

bedroom *n* a room for sleeping in. ➤ *adj* **1** for a bedroom: *bedroom furniture.* **2** esp of a comedy: including references to sexual activity.

bedside manner *n* a doctor's way of dealing with a patient.

bedsitting-room *formal,* **bedsit** or **bedsitter** *n, Brit* a single room used as a combined bedroom and sitting-room.

bedsore *n* an ulcer on a person's skin, caused by lying in bed for long periods.

bedspread or **bedcover** *n* a top cover for a bed.

bedstead *n* the frame of a bed.

bed-wetting *n* accidental urination in bed at night.

bee[1] *n* a four-winged insect, some species of which live in colonies and are often kept for their honey. ♦ **a bee in one's bonnet** an idea which has become an obsession.

bee[2] *n* (**bees**) *N Am* a meeting of friends to work on a particular task together (eg a **quilting bee**) or in competition (eg a **spelling bee**).

beech *n* 1 (*also* **beech tree**) a deciduous tree or shrub with smooth grey bark. 2 (*also* **beechwood**) the hard wood of this tree, widely used for furniture making.

beef *n* (*pl* in sense 3 only **beefs**) 1 the flesh of a bull, cow or ox, used as food. 2 *colloq* muscle; muscular force or strength. 3 *slang* a complaint. ➤ *vb, intr, slang* to complain, esp vigorously or at length. ◊ **beef sth up** *colloq* to make it stronger, more interesting or exciting.

beefburger *n* a piece of minced beef made into a flat round shape and grilled or fried.

beefeater or **Beefeater** *n, Brit* a Yeoman Warder at the Tower of London.

beef tea *n* a drink made from beef stock.

beefy *adj* (*-ier, -iest*) 1 made of or like beef. 2 *colloq* eg of a person: fleshy or muscular. ◊ **beefiness** *n*.

beehive *n* a box in which bees are kept.

beekeeper *n* a person who keeps bees for their honey, as a hobby, etc. ◊ **beekeeping** *n*.

beeline *n* a straight line between two places. ♦ **make a beeline for sth** or **sb** to go directly or purposefully to it or them.

beep *n* a short high-pitched sound, like that made by a car horn.

beer *n* 1 an alcoholic drink brewed by the slow fermentation of malted cereal grains, usu barley, flavoured with hops, eg ALE, LAGER and STOUT. 2 a glass, can or bottle of this drink.

beeswax *n* 1 a solid yellowish substance produced by bees for making the cells in which they live. 2 this substance in a refined form, used esp as a wood-polish.

beet *n* any of several types of plant with large roots which are cooked and used as food, or for making sugar (called **beet sugar**).

beetle[1] *n* an insect with thickened forewings that are not used for flight but modified to form rigid horny cases which cover the hindwings. ➤ *vb, intr* (*usu* **beetle about, around** or **away**) *Brit* to move quickly or as if in a hurry to get away.

beetle[2] *vb, intr* to project or jut out. ◊ **beetling** *adj*.

beetroot *n* a type of plant with a round dark-red root which is cooked and used as a vegetable.

befall *vb* (**befell, befallen**) *old or literary* 1 *intr* to happen. 2 to happen to: *I alone knew what had befallen him.*

befit *vb* (**befitted, befitting**) *formal* to be suitable or right for. ◊ **befitting** *adj*.

before *prep* 1 earlier than something: *before noon.* 2 ahead of or in front of someone or something. 3 in the presence of, or for the attention of, someone: *The question before us is a complex one.* 4 rather than or in preference to someone or something: *Never put money before friendship.* ➤ *conj* 1 earlier than the time when something occurs: *Tidy up before Mum gets back.* 2 rather than or in preference to doing something: *I'd die before I'd surrender.* ➤ *adv* previously.

beforehand *adv* 1 in advance. 2 in preparation or anticipation.

befriend *vb* to become the friend of or start a friendship with someone.

befuddle *vb* (*used esp in the passive*) to confuse someone, eg with the effects of alcohol.

beg *vb* (**begged, begging**) *tr & intr* 1 to ask for (money or food, etc). 2 to ask earnestly or humbly: *Give me one chance, I beg you.* ♦ **beg the question** in an argument: to assume the truth of something which is in fact a part of what is still to be proved. **go begging** *colloq* to be unused or unwanted.

beget *vb* (*past tense* **begot** or **begat,** *past participle* **begotten,** *present participle* **begetting**) 1 *rather formal* to cause; to give rise to something: *Envy begets strife.* 2 esp in the Authorized Version of the Bible: to be the father of someone: *Abraham begat Isaac.*

beggar *n* 1 a person who lives by begging. 2 *colloq, chiefly Brit* a gently reproachful term for a person: *cheeky beggar.* ◊ **beggarly** *adj*. ♦ **beggar description** or **belief** to be impossible to describe or believe: *That story beggars belief.*

begin *vb* (*past tense* **began,** *past participle* **begun,** *present participle* **beginning**) 1 *tr & intr* to start. 2 *tr & intr* to bring or come into being: *Our story begins in 1970.* 3 *intr* to start speaking. 4 *intr* to be the first or to take the first step: *Vernon, will you begin?* 5 *intr, colloq* to have the ability or possibility to do something: *I can't even begin to understand.*

beginner *n* someone who is just starting to learn, or is still learning, how to do something.

beginning *n* 1 the point or occasion at which something begins. 2 an opening or first part of something.

begone *exclam, poetic or old use* go away!

begonia *n* a tropical plant with brightly coloured waxy flowers.

begrudge *vb* 1 to do, give or allow something unwillingly or with regret. 2 (**begrudge sb sth**) to envy or resent them for it. ◊ **begrudgingly** *adv*.

beguile /bɪ'gaɪl/ *vb* to charm or captivate. ◊ **beguiling** *adj*.

behalf *n* interest, part or benefit. ♦ **on** or (*N Am*) **in behalf of sb** or **sth** and **on** or (*N Am*) **in sb's** or **sth's behalf** 1 as a representative of them or it. 2 in the interest of them or it.

behave *vb* 1 *intr* to act in a specified way. 2 *tr &*

intr (**behave oneself**) to conduct oneself in an orderly way.

behaviour or (*US*) **behavior** *n* **1** way of behaving; manners. **2** *psychol* a response to a stimulus. ○ **behavioural** *adj*.

behaviourism or (*US*) **behaviorism** *n*, *psychol* the psychological theory that aims to interpret behaviour as being governed by conditioning (see CONDITION *verb* sense 2) as opposed to internal processes (eg thoughts). ○ **behaviourist** *n*.

behead *vb* to cut off the head of someone, esp as a form of capital punishment.

behemoth /bɪˈhiːmɒθ/ *n* something huge or monstrous.

behind *prep* **1** at or towards the back or the far side of something or someone. **2** later or slower than something; after in time: *behind schedule*. **3** supporting: *We're all behind you.* **4** in the past with respect to someone or something: *Those problems are all behind me now.* **5** not as far advanced as someone or something: *Technologically, they are way behind the Japanese.* **6** being the cause or precursor of something: *reasons behind the decision.* ➢ *adv* **1** in or to the back or far side of something or someone. **2** remaining; in a place, etc that is or was being left or departed from: *Wait behind after class.* **3** following: *The dog was running behind.* **4** in or into arrears: *They fell behind with the rent.* ➢ *adj* **1** not up to date; late: *I'm behind with the payments.* **2** not having progressed enough: *I got behind with my work.* ➢ *n*, *colloq* the buttocks. ◆ **behind sb's back** without their knowledge.

behindhand *adj* (following a verb) *dated* **1** not up to date with regard to something; in arrears; behind. **2** late; occurring later or progressing more slowly than expected.

behold *literary or old use, vb (past tense & past participle **beheld**)* to see; to look at. ➢ *exclam* see!; look! See also LO. ○ **beholder** *n*.

beholden *adj* (**beholden to**) *formal* owing a debt or favour to someone or something.

behove or (*chiefly US*) **behoove** *vb* (**behove, behoving; behooved, behooving**) *old use or formal* to be necessary or fitting: *It behoves me to tell you the truth.*

beige *n* a pale yellowish-brown colour. ➢ *adj* having, referring to, made in, etc this colour.

being *n* **1** existence; life: *come into being.* **2** a living person or thing. **3** essential nature, esp that of a person: *She was like part of my very being.*

bejewelled *adj* wearing or decorated with jewels.

bel *n*, *physics* a unit used to represent the ratio of two different power levels, eg of sound, equal to 10 decibels.

belabour or (*US*) **belabor** *vb* (**belaboured, belabouring;** (*US*) **belabored, belaboring**) **1** to argue about or discuss at excessive length. **2** to attack or batter someone or something thoroughly, either physically or with words.

belated *adj* happening or coming late, or too late: *belated birthday greetings.* ○ **belatedly** *adv*.

belay *vb* **1** *mountaineering* to make (a climber) safe by tying their rope to a rock or a wooden or metal pin. **2** *naut* to make (a rope) secure by winding it round a hook or peg, etc.

belch *vb* **1** *intr* to give out air noisily from the stomach through the mouth; to burp. **2** (*also* **belch out**) of a chimney, etc: to send out (eg smoke) forcefully or in quantity. ➢ *n* an act of belching.

beleaguer *vb* **1** to cause someone bother or worry: *She beleaguered her parents with constant demands.* **2** to surround (eg a city) with an army and lay siege to it. ○ **beleaguered** *adj*.

belfry *n* (*-ies*) **1** the upper part of a tower or steeple, where the bells are hung. **2** a tower for bells, usu attached to a church.

Belgian *adj* belonging or relating to Belgium or its inhabitants. ➢ *n* a citizen or inhabitant of, or person born in, Belgium.

belie /bɪˈlaɪ/ *vb* (**belying**) **1** to show something to be untrue or false: *The new figures belied previous impressive reports.* **2** to give a false idea or impression of something: *Her cheerful face belied the seriousness of the situation.* **3** to fail to fulfil or justify (a hope, etc).

belief *n* **1** a principle or idea, etc accepted as true, esp without proof. **2** trust or confidence: *He has no belief in people.* **3** a person's religious faith. **4** a firm opinion.

believe *vb* **1** to accept something as true. **2** (**believe sth of sb**) to accept what is said or proposed, eg about someone, as true. **3** *intr* to have trust or confidence. **4** *intr* (**believe in sth**) to be convinced of the existence of: *Do you believe in ghosts?* **5** *intr* to have religious faith. ○ **believable** *adj*. ○ **believer** *n*.

belittle *vb* to treat something or someone as unimportant.

bell *n* **1** a deep hollow object, usu one made of metal, rounded at one end and wide and open at the other, which makes a ringing sound when struck by the small CLAPPER fixed inside it. **2** any other device which makes a ringing or buzzing sound, eg an electric doorbell. **3** the sound made by such an object or device. **4** *Brit colloq* a telephone call.

belladonna *n* **1** DEADLY NIGHTSHADE. **2** a compound, used medicinally, obtained from the deadly nightshade plant.

bell-bottoms *pl n* trousers which are much wider at the bottom of the leg than at the knee.

belle *n*, *dated* a beautiful woman.

belles-lettres /bɛlˈlɛtrə/ *pl n* works of literature, esp poetry and essays, valued for their elegant style.

bellicose *adj* likely to, or seeking to, cause an argument or war; aggressive; warlike.

belligerent *adj* **1** aggressive and unfriendly; ready to argue. **2** fighting a war. ➢ *n* a person, faction or country fighting a war. ○ **belligerence** *n*.

bell jar *n* a bell-shaped glass cover put over apparatus, experiments, etc in a laboratory, to stop gases escaping, etc, or used to protect a delicate object.

bellow vb **1** intr to make a loud deep cry like that of a bull. **2** tr & intr (often **bellow out**) to shout out loudly. ➢ n **1** the loud roar of a bull. **2** a deep loud sound or cry.

bellows sing or pl n **1** (also **a pair of bellows**) a device consisting of a bag-like part with folds in it, which is squeezed to create a current of air, used eg to fan a fire. **2** on some cameras: a sleeve with bellows-like folds connecting the body of the camera to the lens.

bellringer n a person who rings a bell, esp at a church. ○ **bellringing** n.

belly n (-ies) **1** the part of the human body below the chest, containing the organs used for digesting food. **2** the stomach. **3** the lower or under part of an animal's body, which contains the stomach and other organs. **4** the deep interior of something. **5** a swelling exterior part of something, eg the underside of a plane, etc. ➢ vb (-ies, -ied) tr & intr (usu **belly out**) to bulge out, or make something bulge or swell out.

bellyache n, colloq a pain in the belly. ➢ vb, intr, slang to complain repeatedly.

belly button n, colloq the navel.

belly dance n a sensual dance performed by women, in which the belly and hips are moved around in a circling motion. ➢ vb (**belly-dance**) intr to perform a belly dance. ○ **belly-dancer** n.

belly flop n a dive into water in which the body hits the surface flat, instead of at an angle. ➢ vb (**belly-flop**) intr to perform a belly flop.

bellyful n **1** enough to eat. **2** slang (**a bellyful of sth or sb**) more than enough, or more than one can bear of it, them, or their behaviour, etc.

belly laugh n a deep unrestrained laugh.

belong vb, intr **1** (**belong to sb** or **sth**) to be the right or property of. **2** (**belong to sth**) to be a member of (a group, club, etc) or a native of (a place). **3 a** to have a proper place, or have the right qualities to fit (esp with or in something or someone); to go along or together (with something or someone); **b** to be properly classified (in a class, section, under a heading, etc). **4** to be at home, or to fit in: It's a nice place, but somehow I just don't belong. ○ **belonging** n (esp in **a sense of belonging**) fitting in within a group.

belongings pl n personal possessions.

beloved /bɪˈlʌvd, bɪˈlʌvɪd/ adj, often in compounds much loved: my beloved wife. ➢ n, chiefly literary or old use a person who is much loved.

below prep **1** lower in position, rank, amount, degree, number or status, etc than a specified thing: 40 degrees below zero. **2** not worthy of someone. **3** under the surface of something: below deck. ➢ adv **1** at, to or in a lower place, point or level. **2** further on in a book, etc: See paragraph below.

belt n **1** a long narrow piece of leather or cloth

worn around the waist. **2** a SEAT BELT. **3** an area or zone, usu a long and narrow one: a belt of rain. **4** often in compounds a band of rubber, etc moving the wheels, or round the wheels, of a machine: fan belt. **5** slang a hard blow. ➢ vb **1** to put a belt around. **2** to beat with a belt. **3** tr & intr (often **belt into**) colloq to hit someone repeatedly. **4** intr (esp **belt along**) colloq to move very fast, esp in a specified direction. **5** (also **belt sth on**) to fasten it with, or on with, a belt. ♦ **below the belt** colloq not following the accepted rules of behaviour. **under one's belt** colloq of an achievement, qualification, valuable experience, etc: firmly secured and in one's possession. ◊ **belt sth out** colloq to sing or say it very loudly. **belt up** colloq **1** to be quiet. **2** to fasten one's seat-belt.

beluga /bəˈluːgə/ n **1** a kind of large sturgeon. **2** caviar from this type of sturgeon. **3** a white whale.

belvedere n, archit **1** a turret, lantern or room built on the top of a house, with open or glazed sides to provide a view. **2** a SUMMERHOUSE on high ground.

bemoan vb to express great sadness or regret about something.

bemused adj bewildered; confused.

ben n, Scot esp in place names: a mountain or mountain peak: Ben Nevis.

bench n **1** a long seat for seating several people. **2** a work-table for a carpenter, scientist, etc. **3** (**the bench** or **the Bench**) **a** the place where the judge or magistrate sits in court; **b** judges and magistrates as a group or profession.

benchmark n **1** anything used as a standard or point of reference. **2** surveying a permanent mark cut on a post, building, etc giving the height above sea level of the land at that exact spot.

bend vb (**bent**) **1** tr & intr to make or become angled or curved. **2** intr to move or stretch in a curve. **3** intr (usu **bend down** or **over**) to move the top part of the body forward and down towards the ground. **4** tr & intr to submit or force to submit: He bent them to his will. **5** to aim or direct (one's attention, etc) towards something. ➢ n **1** a curve or bent part. **2** the act of curving or bending. ○ **bendy** adj (-ier, -iest). ♦ **bend the rules** to interpret the rules in one's favour, without actually breaking them. **round the bend** colloq mad.

bender n, slang a drunken spree.

the bends sing or pl n a non-technical name for DECOMPRESSION SICKNESS.

beneath prep **1** under; below. **2** not worthy of someone or something: He thinks the job is beneath him. ➢ adv, rather formal or archaic below; underneath.

Benedictine n **1** a member of the Christian religious order (the **Order of St Benedict**) that follows the teachings of St Benedict. **2** a liqueur first made by Benedictine monks.

benediction n, Christianity **1** a prayer giving

blessing, esp at the end of a religious service. **2** *RC Church* a service in which the congregation is blessed. ○ **benedictory** *adj*.

benefaction *n* **1** a gift or donation from a benefactor. **2** an act of doing good; help or charity given.

benefactor *n* a person who gives help, esp financial help, to an institution, cause or person. Also (if a female benefactor) **benefactress**.

benefice *n* a position as a priest or minister, or other church office, and the income which goes with it.

beneficent /bɪˈnɛfɪsənt/ *adj* kind and generous. ○ **beneficence** *n*.

beneficial *adj* having good results or benefits.

beneficiary *n* (*-ies*) **1** a person who benefits from something. **2** *law* **a** a person who is entitled to estate or interest held for them by trustees; **b** a person who receives property or money, etc in a will, or benefits under an insurance policy, etc.

benefit *n* **1** something good gained or received. **2** advantage or sake. **3** (*often* **benefits**) a payment made by a government or company insurance scheme, usu to someone who is ill or out of work. **4** a concert, football match, etc from which the profits are given to a particular person or group in need. ➤ *vb* (**benefited, benefiting;** *US also* **benefitted, benefitting**) **1** *intr* (*esp* **benefit from** or **by**) to gain an advantage from something. **2** to do good to someone.

benevolence *n* **1** the desire to do good. **2** an act of kindness. ○ **benevolent** *adj*.

Bengali *adj* belonging or relating to Bangladesh and the state of W Bengal, their inhabitants, or their language. ➤ *n* **1** a citizen or inhabitant of, or person born in, Bangladesh or W Bengal. **2** (*also* **Bangla**) the official language of Bangladesh and the chief language of W Bengal.

benign /bɪˈnaɪn/ *adj* **1** kind; gentle. **2** *med* **a** of a disorder: not having harmful effects; of a mild form; **b** specifically of a cancerous tumour: of a type that does not invade and destroy the surrounding tissue. Compare MALIGNANT. **3** favourable. ○ **benignly** *adv*.

benignant *adj* **1** *med* of a disease or growth, etc: not fatal; a later and less common word for BENIGN. **2** kind. **3** favourable. ○ **benignancy** *n* (*-ies*).

bent *adj* **1** curved or having a bend. **2** *Brit slang* **a** corrupt; **b** obtained dishonestly; stolen: *selling bent videos.* **3** *Brit, derog slang* homosexual. **4** (*usu* **bent on** or **upon sth**) having all one's attention or energy directed on it, or on doing it: *He's bent on revenge.* ➤ *n* a natural inclination, liking or aptitude: *a bent for music.* ➤ *vb, past tense, past participle of* BEND.

benumb *vb* **1** to make numb. **2** to stupefy (esp the senses or the mind).

Benzedrine *n, trademark* an AMPHETAMINE drug.

benzene *n, chem* an inflammable colourless liquid HYDROCARBON, mainly obtained from petroleum, that is widely used as a solvent.

benzine or **benzin** *n* a volatile mixture of HYDROCARBONS distilled from petroleum, used as a motor fuel and solvent, etc.

bequeath *vb* **1** to leave (personal property) in a will (to someone). **2** to pass on or give to posterity.

bequest *n* **1** an act of leaving personal property in a will. **2** anything left in someone's will.

berate *vb* to scold someone severely.

Berber *n* **1** any of several native Muslim tribes of N Africa. **2** an individual belonging to any of these tribes. **3** any of a group of Afro-Asiatic languages spoken by these people. ➤ *adj* belonging or relating to this group or their language.

bereaved *adj* deprived of a close relative or friend by death. ○ **bereavement** *n*.

bereft *adj* (*usu* **bereft of sth**) deprived of it.

beret /ˈbɛreɪ, *N Am* bəˈreɪ/ *n* a round flat cap made of soft material.

bergamot *n* **1** a small citrus tree that produces acidic pear-shaped fruits. **2** (*also* **bergamot oil**) the oil extracted from the rind of the fruit of this tree, used in perfumery.

beriberi *n, pathol, med* a deficiency disease caused by lack of vitamin B_1.

berk or **burk** *n, Brit slang* a fool.

berkelium *n, chem* a radioactive metallic element manufactured artificially.

Bermuda shorts or **Bermudas** *pl n* knee-length shorts.

berry *n* (*-ies*) **1** *bot* an INDEHISCENT fleshy fruit that contains seeds which are not surrounded by a stony protective layer, eg grape, cucumber, tomato. **2** *loosely* any of the various small fleshy edible fruits that are not true berries, eg strawberry.

berserk *adj* (*esp* **go berserk**) **1** violently angry; wild and destructive. **2** *colloq & facetious* furious; crazy.

berth *n* **1** a sleeping-place in a ship or train, etc. **2** a place in a port where a ship or boat can be tied up. **3** enough room for a ship to be able to turn round in. ➤ *vb* **1** to tie up (a ship) in its berth. **2** *intr* of a ship: to arrive at its berth; to moor. **3** to provide a sleeping-place for someone. ♦ **give sb** or **sth a wide berth** to stay well away from them or it.

> **berth** There is sometimes a spelling confusion between **berth** and **birth**.

beryl *n, geol* a hard mineral, used as a source of BERYLLIUM and as a gemstone, the most valuable varieties being AQUAMARINE and EMERALD.

beryllium *n, chem* a silvery-grey metal, obtained from the mineral BERYL.

beseech *vb* (**besought** or **beseeched**) *formal or literary* to ask someone earnestly.

beset *vb* (**beset, besetting**) *now chiefly literary or formal* **1** to worry someone, or to hamper something. **2** to surround or attack (a person or people) on every side.

beside *prep* **1** next to, by the side of or near something or someone. **2** not relevant to something: *beside the point.* **3** as compared with something or someone: *All beauty pales beside hers.* ◆ **beside oneself** in a state of uncontrollable anger, excitement or other emotion.

> **beside, besides** There is often confusion between **beside** and **besides**: **beside** means 'next to, at the side of', whereas **besides** means 'in addition to, other than'.

besides *prep* in addition to, as well as or apart from something or someone. ➤ *adv* **1** also; as well. **2** (often as a sentence connector) moreover; in any case: *I don't want to go; besides, I'm not dressed.*

besiege *vb* **1** to surround (a town or stronghold) with an army in order to force it to surrender. **2** to gather round something or someone in a crowd: *besieged by excited fans.* **3** to annoy someone constantly: *She besieged me with questions.* **4** to inundate someone: *We're besieged with offers of help.*

besmirch *vb, formal* to spoil or stain (the reputation, name, etc of someone).

besom *n* a large brush made from sticks tied to a long wooden handle.

besotted *adj* foolishly infatuated (with or by someone or something).

bespatter *vb* to cover something or someone with splashes, esp of a dirty liquid.

bespeak *vb, formal* **1** to claim, engage or order something in advance. **2** to show or be evidence of something.

bespectacled *adj* wearing spectacles.

bespoke *adj, now rather formal* **1** of clothes: made to fit a particular person. **2** of a tailor: making clothes to order, to fit individual customers and their requirements.

best *adj* (*superlative of* GOOD) **1** most excellent, suitable or desirable. **2** most successful, clever, able or skilled, etc. **3** the greatest or most: *the best part of an hour.* ➤ *adv* (*superlative of* WELL[1]) **1** most successfully or skilfully, etc: *Who did best in the test?* **2** more than, or better than, all others: *Which hat looks best?* ➤ *n* **1** (**the best**) the most excellent or suitable person or thing; the most desirable quality or result, etc: *the best of the bunch.* **2** the greatest effort; one's utmost: *Do your best.* **3** (**the best**) victory or success: *He got the best of the argument.* **4** (*usu* **the best of sth**) a winning majority from (a given number, etc): *the best of three.* ➤ *vb, colloq* to defeat someone.

bestial *adj* **1** *derog* cruel; savage; brutish. **2** rude; unrefined; uncivilized. **3** sexually depraved. **4** like or referring to an animal in character, behaviour, etc.

bestiality *n* **1** disgusting or cruel behaviour. **2** sexual intercourse between a human and an animal.

bestiary *n* (*-ies*) a book containing pictures and descriptions of animals.

bestir *vb* (**bestir oneself**) to make an effort to become active.

best man *n* a bridegroom's chief attendant at a wedding.

bestow *vb* (**bestow on** or **upon**) *formal* to give or present (a title, award, etc) to someone. ○ **bestowal** *n*.

bestride *vb* (**bestrode, bestridden**) *formal or literary* to sit or stand across (eg a horse) with one leg on each side.

bestseller *n* a book or other item which sells in large numbers. ○ **bestselling** *adj*.

bet *vb* (**bet** or **betted, betting**) **1** *tr & intr* to risk (a sum of money or other asset) on predicting the outcome or result of a future event, esp a race or other sporting event. **2** (*usu* **bet sb sth**) to make a bet (with someone) of (a specified amount). **3** *colloq* to feel sure or confident: *I bet they've forgotten.* ➤ *n* **1** an act of betting. **2** a sum of money, or other asset, betted. **3** *colloq* an opinion or guess: *My bet is that he's bluffing.* **4** *colloq* a choice of action or way ahead: *Our best bet is to postpone the trip.*

beta *n* **1** the second letter of the Greek alphabet. **2** a mark indicating the second highest grade. **3** the second in a series, or the second of two categories or types.

beta-blocker *n, med* a drug that slows the heartbeat, used to treat high blood pressure, angina and abnormal heart rhythms.

betacarotene *n, biochem* a form of the pigment CAROTENE, found in yellow and orange fruits and vegetables, that is converted to vitamin A in the body.

beta particle *n, physics* an ELECTRON or POSITRON produced when a neutron inside an unstable radioactive nucleus turns into a proton, or a proton turns into a neutron.

betatron *n, physics* a device that is used to accelerate charged subatomic particles, used in medicine and industry, which continuously increases the magnetic FLUX within the orbit of a charged particle.

betel /ˈbiːtəl/ *n* an Asian palm, the fruit of which (the **betel nut**) is mixed with lime and chewed as a mild stimulant.

bête noire /bɛt nwɑː(r)/ *n* (**bêtes noires**) a person or thing that esp bothers or frightens someone.

betide *vb* (now limited to this form, as infinitive and 3rd person subjunctive) *literary or archaic* **1** *intr* to happen; to come to pass: *whate'er may betide.* **2** to happen to someone; to befall: *Woe betide you.*

betoken *vb, formal* to be evidence of something.

betray *vb* **1** to hand over or expose (a friend or one's country, etc) to an enemy. **2** to give away or disclose (a secret, etc). **3** to break (a promise, etc) or to be unfaithful to someone. **4** to be evidence of (something, esp something intended to be hidden): *Her face betrayed her un-*

happiness. ○ **betrayal** *n.* ○ **betrayer** *n.*

betrothal *n, formal* engagement to be married.

betrothed *formal or facetious, adj* of a person: engaged to marry someone. ➤ *n* a person to whom someone is betrothed.

better *adj* (*comparative of* GOOD) **1** more excellent, suitable or desirable, etc. **2** (*usu* **better at sth**) more successful, skilful, etc in doing it. **3** (*comparative of* WELL¹) (*esp* **be** or **feel** or **get better**) improved in health or recovered from illness. **4** greater: *the better part of a day.* ➤ *adv* (*comparative of* WELL¹) **1** more excellently, successfully or fully, etc. **2** in or to a greater degree. ➤ *n* **1** (*esp* **betters**) a person superior in quality or status, etc. **2** (**the better**) the thing or person that is the more excellent or suitable, etc of two comparable things or people. ➤ *vb* (**bettered, bettering**) **1** to beat or improve on something. **2** to make something more suitable, desirable or excellent, etc. ♦ **get the better of sb** to gain the advantage over them; to outwit them. **had better do sth** ought to do it, esp to avoid some undesirable outcome.

betterment *n* improvement or advancement.

betting *n* gambling by predicting the outcome of some future event, esp a sporting event.

betting-shop *n, Brit* a licensed establishment where the public can place bets.

between *prep* **1** in, to, through or across the space dividing (two people, places, times, etc). **2** to and from: *I'm travelling between Leeds and Bradford.* **3** in combination; acting together: *They bought the house between them.* **4** shared out among: *Divide the money between you.* **5** involving a choice between alternatives: *choose between right and wrong.* **6** including; involving: *a fight between rivals.* ➤ *adv* (*also* **in between**) in or into the middle of (two points in space or time, etc): *I eat a light breakfast and lunch with nothing between.*

> **between, among** It is acceptable to use **between** with reference to more than two people or things: *Viewers tend to switch between channels.* However, **among** is sometimes more appropriate when there is a distinct notion of sharing or distributing: *Hand these out among all of you.* **Between** is more usual when individual people or things are named: *Duties are divided between John, Margaret and Catherine.*

betwixt *prep, adv, old use* between. ♦ **betwixt and between** undecided; in a middle position.

bevel *n* a sloping edge to a surface, meeting another surface at an angle between the horizontal and the vertical. ➤ *vb* (**bevelled, bevelling;** *US* **beveled, beveling**) **1** to give a bevel to (eg a piece of wood). **2** *intr* to slope at an angle.

beverage *n, formal* a prepared drink.

bevvy or **bevy** *n* (*-ies*) *colloq* **1** alcoholic drink, or an individual alcoholic drink. **2** a drinking session.

bevy *n* (*-ies*) **1** a group, orig a group of women or girls. **2** a flock of larks, quails or swans.

bewail *vb, chiefly literary* to express great sorrow about something, or to lament over it.

beware *vb* (not inflected in modern use, but used as an imperative or infinitive) **1** *intr* (*usu* **beware of**) to be careful of something. **2** *old use or literary* to be on one's guard against something or someone.

bewilder *vb* to confuse, disorientate or puzzle thoroughly. ○ **bewildering** *adj.* ○ **bewilderment** *n.*

bewitch *vb* **1** to charm, fascinate or enchant. **2** to cast a spell on someone or something. ○ **bewitching** *adj.*

beyond *prep* **1** on the far side of something: *beyond the hills.* **2** farther on than something in time or place. **3** out of the range, reach, power, understanding, possibility, etc of someone or something. **4** greater or better than something in amount, size, or level: *beyond all our expectations.* **5** other than, or apart from, something: *unable to help beyond giving money.* ➤ *adv* farther away; to or on the far side of something.

bezel *n* **1** the sloped surface of a cutting tool. **2** a grooved rim which holds a watch-glass, precious gem, etc in its setting. **3** an oblique side or face of a cut gem.

bhaji / 'bɑːdʒiː/ *n* (**bhajis**) *cookery* an Indian appetizer consisting of vegetables in a batter of flour and spices, formed into a ball and deep-fried.

bhang *n* the leaves and shoots of the CANNABIS plant, used as a narcotic and intoxicant.

bhangra *n* a style of pop music created from a mix of traditional Punjabi and Western pop.

bhp *abbrev* brake horsepower.

Bi *symbol, chem* bismuth.

biannual *adj* occurring or produced, etc twice a year. ○ **biannually** *adv.*

bias *n* **1** an inclination to favour or disfavour one side against another in a dispute, competition, etc; a prejudice. **2** a tendency or principal quality in a person's character. **3** *bowls, etc* a weight on or in an object (eg a bowl) which makes it move in a particular direction. ➤ *vb* (**biased, biasing;** *also* **biassed, biassing**) **1** to influence or prejudice, esp unfairly or without objective grounds. **2** to give a bias to something. ○ **biased** or **biassed** *adj.*

bias binding *n, dressmaking, etc* a long narrow folded strip of cloth cut on the bias, used to bind hems.

biathlon *n* an outdoor sporting event involving skiing and shooting.

biaxial *adj* esp of a crystal: having two axes (see AXIS sense 2).

bib *n* **1** a piece of cloth or plastic fastened under a child's chin to protect its clothes while eating or drinking. **2** the top part of an apron or overalls.

Bible *n* **1 a** (**the Bible**) the sacred writings of the Christian Church, consisting of the Old and New Testaments; **b** (*sometimes* **bible**) a copy of these writings. **2 a** (**the Bible**) the Jewish Scriptures; the Old Testament or Hebrew Bible; **b** (*sometimes* **bible**) a copy of these. **3** (*usu* **bible**) an authoritative book on a particular subject. ○ **biblical** *adj*.

bibliography *n* (*-ies*) **1** a list of books by one author or on one subject. **2** a list of the books used as sources during the writing of a book or other written work, usu printed at the end of it. **3** the study, description or knowledge of books, in terms of their subjects, authors, editions, history, format, etc. ○ **bibliographer** *n*.

bibliophile *n* an admirer or collector of books.

bibulous *adj, humorous* liking alcohol too much.

bicameral *adj* of a legislative body: made up of two chambers.

bicarbonate *n, chem* an acid salt of carbonic acid.

bicarbonate of soda *n, colloq* (often shortened to **bicarb**) sodium bicarbonate, a white powder used in baking to make cakes, etc rise (as **baking soda** and **baking powder**), and as an indigestion remedy.

bicentenary *n* (*-ies*) *esp Brit* **1** a two-hundredth anniversary of an event. **2** a celebration held in honour of such an anniversary. ➤ *adj* marking, belonging to, referring to or in honour of a bicentenary.

bicentennial *n, adj, chiefly N Am* bicentenary.

biceps *n* (*pl* **biceps**) *anat* any muscle that has two points of origin, esp the muscle at the front of the upper arm.

bicker *vb, intr, colloq* to quarrel in a petty way (esp about or over something trivial).

bicuspid /barˈkʌspɪd/ *adj* esp of a tooth: having two cusps or points. ➤ *n, N Am* a PREMOLAR tooth.

bicycle *n* a vehicle consisting of a metal frame with two wheels one behind the other, and a saddle between and above them, which is driven by turning pedals with the feet and steered by handlebars attached to the front wheel. ➤ *vb, intr, rather formal* to ride a bicycle.

bid[1] *vb* (**bid, bidding**) **1** *tr & intr* to offer (an amount of money) when trying to buy something, esp at an auction. **2** *tr & intr, cards* to state in advance (the number of tricks one will try to win). **3** *intr* (*esp* **bid for sth**) to state a price one will charge for work to be done. ➤ *n* **1** an offer of an amount of money in payment for something, esp at an auction. **2** *cards* a statement of how many tricks one proposes to win. **3** *colloq* an attempt to obtain or achieve something: *a bid for freedom*. ○ **bidder** *n*.

bid[2] *vb* (*past tense* **bade** /bad, beɪd/, *past participle* **bidden,** *present participle* **bidding**) *formal, archaic or literary* **1** to express (a wish or greeting, etc) (to someone): *We bid you welcome*. **2** (with an imperative) to command someone (to do a specified thing): *The king bade him kneel*. **3** (*often* **bid sb to sth** or **to do sth**) to invite them to it, or to do it.

biddable *adj* obedient; docile.

bidding *n* **1** a command, request or invitation. **2** the offers at an auction. **3** *cards* the act of making bids.

biddy *n* (*-ies*) *slang, chiefly derog* (*esp* **old biddy**) a woman, esp an old, doddery, fussy or cantankerous one.

bide *vb* (*past tense* **bided** or **bode,** *past participle* **bided,** *present participle* **biding**) *intr, Scot or old use* to wait or stay. ◆ **bide one's time** to wait patiently for a good opportunity or for the right moment.

bidet /ˈbiːdeɪ/ *n* a small low basin with taps, for washing the genital and anal areas.

biennial *adj* **1** of an event: occurring once in every two years. **2** esp of a plant: lasting two years. ➤ *n* **1** *bot* a plant which takes two years to complete its life cycle. **2** an event which takes place, or is celebrated, every two years.

bier *n* a movable stand on which a coffin rests or is transported.

biff *slang, esp Brit, vb* to hit very hard, usu with the fist. ➤ *n* a hard sharp blow.

bifid *adj, biol* divided into two parts by a deep split.

bifocal *adj* of a lens: **1** having two different focal lengths. **2** of spectacle or contact lenses: having two separate sections with different focal lengths, one for near vision, and one for viewing distant objects.

bifocals *pl n* a pair of glasses with BIFOCAL lenses.

bifurcate /ˈbaɪfəkeɪt/ *vb, intr, formal* of roads, etc: to divide into two parts or branches; to fork. ➤ *adj* forked or branched into two parts. ○ **bifurcation** *n*.

big *adj* **1** large or largest in size, amount, weight, number, power, etc. **2** significant or important to someone. **3** important, powerful or successful. **4** elder: *my big sister*. **5** grown-up: *You're not big enough to go on your own*. **6** *often ironic* generous or magnanimous: *That was big of him*. **7** boastful; extravagant; ambitious: *big ideas*. **8** (*usu* **big on sth**) *colloq, esp US* fond of or enthusiastic (about it). ➤ *adv, colloq* **1** in a boastful, extravagant or ambitious way: *He likes to act big*. **2** greatly or impressively: *Your idea went over big with the boss*.

bigamy *n* (*-ies*) the crime of being married to two wives or husbands at the same time. ○ **bigamist** *n*. ○ **bigamous** *adj*.

Big Bang *n* a hypothetical model of the origin of the universe which postulates that all matter and energy were once concentrated into an unimaginably dense state, which underwent a gigantic explosion between 13 and 20 billion years ago.

Big Brother *n* an all-powerful government or organization, etc, or its leader, keeping complete control over, and a continual watch on, its citizens.

big business *n* powerful commercial and industrial organizations, esp considered as a group.

big end *n*, *Brit* in an internal-combustion engine: the larger end of the main connecting rod.

big game *n* large animals, such as lions, tigers and elephants, etc hunted for sport.

bighead *n*, *colloq*, *derog* a conceited or arrogant person. ○ **bigheaded** *adj*.

bight /baɪt/ *n* 1 a stretch of gently curving coastline. 2 a loose curve or loop in a rope.

bigot *n* someone who is persistently prejudiced, esp about religion, politics or race, and refuses to tolerate the opinions of others. ○ **bigoted** *adj*. ○ **bigotry** *n* (*-ies*).

big time *n*, *colloq* success in an activity or profession, esp in show business.

big top *n* the main tent of a circus.

bigwig *n*, *colloq* an important person.

bijou /ˈbiːʒuː/ *n* (**bijoux** or **bijous**) a small delicate jewel or trinket. ➤ *adj* small and elegant.

bike *n*, *colloq* 1 a bicycle. 2 a motorcycle. ➤ *vb*, *intr* to ride a bicycle or motorcycle. ○ **biker** *n*.

bikini *n* a small two-piece swimming costume for women.

bilateral *adj* 1 of a treaty, agreement, talks, etc: involving the participation of, affecting, or signed or agreed by, two countries, parties or groups, etc. 2 having, belonging or referring to, or on, two sides. ○ **bilaterally** *adv*.

bilberry *n* (*-ies*) 1 a small deciduous shrub which has bright green oval leaves and pink globular flowers. 2 its edible round black berry.

bile *n* 1 *biol* a thick yellowish-green alkaline liquid produced by the liver to aid the digestion of fats. 2 *literary* irritability or bad temper.

bilge *n* 1 a the broadest part of a ship's bottom; b (*usu* **bilges**) the lowest parts on the inside of a ship's hull. 2 (*also* **bilge-water**) the dirty water that collects in a ship's bilge. 3 *dated colloq* nonsense.

bilharzia /bɪlˈhɑːtsɪə/ *n*, *pathol* another name for the parasitic disease SCHISTOSOMIASIS.

biliary *adj* concerned with, relating or belonging to bile, the bile ducts or the gall bladder.

bilingual *adj* 1 written or spoken in two languages. 2 of a person: able to speak two languages. ○ **bilingualism** *n*.

bilious *adj* 1 affected by a disorder relating to the secretion of BILE. 2 of a colour: unpleasant and sickly. 3 bad-tempered.

bilk *vb* 1 to avoid paying someone money owed. 2 (**bilk sb out of sth**) to make them lose something by dishonest means.

bill¹ *n* 1 a a statement of the amount of money owed for goods or services received; b such a statement for food and drink received in a restaurant or hotel; c the amount of money owed. 2 a written plan or draft for a proposed law. 3 *N Am* a BANKNOTE. 4 an advertising poster. 5 a list of items, events or performers, etc. ➤ *vb* 1 to send or give a bill to someone, requesting payment for goods, etc. 2 to advertise (a person or event) in a poster, etc: *They were billed as Britain's best new comedy act.* ♦ **fit** or **fill the bill** *colloq* to be what is required.

bill² *n* 1 the beak of a bird. 2 any structure which resembles this.

billabong *n*, *Aust* 1 a pool of water left when most of a stream has become dry. 2 a branch of a river which comes to an end without flowing into a sea, lake, or another river.

billboard *n*, *esp N Am* a HOARDING.

billet¹ *n* 1 a house, often a private home, where soldiers are given food and lodging temporarily. 2 *colloq, chiefly Brit* a job or occupation. ➤ *vb* to give or assign lodging to, or to accommodate (soldiers, etc).

billet² *n* 1 a chunk of wood, eg for firewood. 2 a small bar of metal.

billet-doux /ˌbɪliˈduː, ˌbɪleɪˈduː/ *n* (**billets-doux** /-ˈduː, -ˈduːz/) *old use, literary* or *humorous* a love-letter.

billhook *n* a cutting tool with a long curved blade, used for pruning, etc.

billiards *sing n* a game played with a CUE² and coloured balls on a cloth-covered table, which has pockets at the sides and corners into which the balls can be struck to score points.

billion *n* (**billions** or after a number **billion**) 1 a the cardinal number 10^9; b the quantity that this represents, being a thousand million. 2 *formerly* in the UK and France, etc: a million million (ie unit and twelve zeros). 3 a set of a billion people or things: *one billion pounds.* 4 (*usu* a **billion** or **billions of sth**) *colloq* a great number. ○ **billionth** *adj*, *n*.

billionaire or **billionairess** *n* a person who owns money and property worth over a billion pounds, dollars, etc.

bill of exchange *n* (**bills of exchange**) *finance* esp in international trade: a document promising payment of a specified sum of money to a certain person on a certain date or when payment is asked for.

bill of fare *n* (**bills of fare**) a menu.

bill of lading *n* (**bills of lading**) an official receipt detailing a ship's cargo.

billow *vb*, *intr* 1 eg of smoke: to move in large waves or clouds. 2 (*usu* **billow out**) to swell or bulge. ➤ *n* 1 a rolling upward-moving mass of smoke or mist, etc. 2 *literary* a large wave. ○ **billowing** or **billowy** *adj*.

billy or **billycan** *n* (**billies**; **billycans**) *Brit* & *esp Aust* a metal cooking pot with a lid and wire handle used esp when camping.

billy goat *n* an adult male goat.

bimbo *n*, *derog slang* a young woman who is attractive, but empty-headed.

bimetallic *adj* made of or using two metals.

bin *n* 1 a container for rubbish. 2 a container for storing some kinds of food: *bread bin.* 3 a large industrial container for storing goods in large quantities. 4 a stand or case for storing bottles of wine. ➤ *vb* (**binned, binning**) to put (eg rubbish) into a bin.

binary /ˈbaɪnərɪ/ *adj* 1 consisting of or containing two parts or elements. 2 *comput, maths* denoting a system that consists of two components, esp a number system which uses the digits 0 and 1. ➤ *n* (*-ies*) a thing made up of two parts.

binary code *n, comput* a code of numbers that involves only two digits, 0 and 1.

binary star *n, astron* (also **binary**) a system of two stars that share and orbit around the same centre of mass.

binary system *n, maths & esp comput* a number system to the base 2 that uses only the binary digits 0 and 1, and that forms the basis of the internal coding of information in electronics and computers.

bind *vb* (**bound**) **1** to tie or fasten tightly. **2** (*often* **bind up**) to tie or pass strips of cloth or bandage, etc around something. **3** to control or prevent someone or something from moving. **4** to make someone promise to do something. **5** to require or oblige someone to do something: *He is legally bound to reply.* **6** to fasten together and put a cover on (the separate pages of a book). **7** to put a strip of cloth on the edge of something to strengthen it. **8** to cause (dry ingredients) to stick together. **9** *intr* to stick together. ➤ *n, colloq* **1** a difficult, tedious or annoying situation: *What a bind! The train's late again.* **2** a restriction; something that limits or hampers one: *What a bind!* ◊ **bind sb over** *Brit law* to make them legally obliged to do a particular thing.

binder *n* **1** a hard book-like cover in which loose pieces of paper can be kept in order. **2** a person or business that binds books. **3** a reaping machine which ties cut grain into bundles. ◦ **bindery** *n* (*-ies*) a place where books are bound.

binding *n* **1** the part of a book cover onto which the pages are stuck. **2** cloth or tape, etc used to bind something. ➤ *adj* legally obliging someone to do something: *a binding contract.*

bindweed *n* any of numerous plants with funnel-shaped flowers, including many climbing species which twine around the stems of other plants.

binge *n, colloq* a bout of over-indulgence, usu in eating and drinking. ➤ *vb* (**bingeing** or **binging**) *intr* to indulge in a binge.

bingo *n* a game in which each player has a card with a set of numbers on it, and may cover a number if it is called out at random by the **bingo-caller**, the winner being the first player with a card on which all or a certain sequence of the numbers have been called.

binnacle *n, naut* a case for a ship's compass.

binocular *adj* relating to the use of both eyes simultaneously.

binoculars *pl n* an optical instrument designed for viewing distant objects, consisting of two small telescopes arranged side by side.

binomial *n* **1** *maths* an algebraic expression that contains two VARIABLES, eg 6x−3y. **2** *biol* in the taxonomic system (known as **binomial nomenclature**): a two-part name for an animal or plant, made up of two Latin words, first the genus name and then the species name,

eg *Homo sapiens.* ➤ *adj* **1** *maths* containing two variables. **2** consisting of two names or terms.

binomial theorem *n, maths* a formula for finding any power of a BINOMIAL without lengthy multiplication, eg $(a+b)^2 = (a^2 + 2ab + b^2)$.

biochemistry *n* the study of the chemical compounds and chemical reactions that occur within the cells of living organisms. ◦ **biochemical** *adj.* ◦ **biochemist** *n.*

biodegradable *adj* of a substance or waste product, etc: capable of being broken down by bacteria, fungi or other living organisms.

biodiversity *n, biol* a measure of the number of different species of living organism that are present within a given area.

bioengineering or **biological engineering** *n* **1** *med* the application of engineering methods and technology to biology and medicine, esp in the field of designing and manufacturing artificial limbs, heart pacemakers, etc. **2** *biol* the application of engineering methods and technology to the biosynthesis of plant and animal products.

biofuel *n* any fuel produced from organic matter.

biography *n* (*-ies*) **1** an account of a person's life, written by someone else and published or intended for publication. **2** biographies as a genre. ◦ **biographer** *n.* ◦ **biographical** *adj.*

biological *adj* **1** relating to biology. **2** physiological. **3** of a detergent: containing enzymes that remove dirt of organic origin, eg blood or grass. ◦ **biologically** *adv.*

biological clock *n* a supposed natural mechanism of the body which controls the rhythm of its functions.

biological control *n, biol* the control of plant or animal pests by the introduction of natural predators or parasites, etc.

biological warfare *n* the use of toxins and micro-organisms as weapons of war, to kill or incapacitate the enemy.

biology *n* the scientific study of living organisms. ◦ **biologist** *n.*

biomass *n, biol, ecol* **1** the total mass of living organisms in an ecosystem, population or designated area at a given time. **2** vegetation that can be converted into useful fuel.

biomechanics *sing n* the mechanics of movement in living things.

bionic *adj* **1** using, or belonging or relating to, BIONICS. **2** *colloq, sci fi* having extraordinary superhuman powers of speed or strength, etc.

bionics *sing n* **1** the study of how organisms function, and the application of the principles observed to develop computers and other machines which work in similar ways. **2** the replacement of damaged parts of the body, such as limbs and heart valves, by electronic devices.

biophysics *sing n* the application of the ideas and methods of physics to the study of biological processes. ○ **biophysical** adj. ○ **biophysicist** n.

biopic n a film telling the life-story of a famous person.

biopsy n (-ies) pathol the removal and examination of a small piece of living tissue from an organ or part of the body in order to determine the nature of any suspected disease.

biorhythm n, biol 1 a periodic change in the behaviour or physiology of many animals and plants (eg hibernation and migration). **2** a CIRCADIAN rhythm associated eg with sleep, and independent of day-length. **3** any of three cyclical patterns which have been suggested as influencing physical, intellectual and emotional aspects of human behaviour.

biosphere n that part of the Earth's surface and its atmosphere in which living organisms are known to exist.

biosynthesis n the manufacture by living organisms of complex organic compounds such as proteins and fats, etc from simpler molecules. ○ **biosynthetic** adj.

biotechnology n, biol the use of living organisms (eg bacteria), or the enzymes produced by them, in the industrial manufacture of useful products, or the development of useful processes.

bipartisan adj belonging to, involving, supported by or consisting of two groups or political parties.

bipartite adj **1** consisting of or divided into two parts. **2** of an agreement, etc: involving, affecting or agreed by two parties.

biped /ˈbaɪpɛd/ n an animal with two feet, eg man. ➤ adj (also **bipedal**) /baɪˈpiːdəl/ of an animal: having two feet; walking on two feet.

biplane n a type of aeroplane with two sets of wings, one above the other.

bipolar adj having two poles or extremes. ○ **bipolarity** n.

birch n **1** a slender deciduous tree or shrub with silvery-white bark that often peels off in long papery strips. **2** (also **birchwood**) the strong fine-textured wood of this tree. **3** (**the birch**) **a** a bundle of birch branches, formerly used to inflict physical punishment; **b** the punishment of being beaten with the birch. ➤ adj made of birch wood. ➤ vb to flog someone with a birch.

bird n **1** any member of a class of warm-blooded vertebrate animals that have feathers, front limbs modified to form wings, and projecting jaws modified to form a beak. **2** Brit slang, often considered offensive a girl or woman. **3** colloq, old use a person, esp a strange or unusual one: He's a funny old bird. ◆ **birds of a feather** Brit colloq people who are like each other, who share the same ideas, lifestyle, etc.

birdie n **1** colloq used by or to a child: a little bird. **2** golf a score of one stroke under PAR for a particular hole on a course. Compare ALBATROSS (sense 2), EAGLE (sense 2). ➤ vb (**birdying**) tr & intr, golf to complete (a hole) with a birdie score.

bird-lime n a sticky substance put on the branches of trees to catch small birds.

bird of paradise n (**birds of paradise**) any of various brilliantly coloured birds, native to New Guinea and Australia.

bird of prey n (**birds of prey**) any of several types of bird that kill other birds and small mammals for food, eg the owl, hawk and eagle.

bird's-eye view n **1** a wide general overall view from above. **2** a general impression.

birdwatcher n a person who studies wild birds in their natural habitat, esp as a hobby.

biretta n a stiff square cap worn by Roman Catholic clergy.

biriani or **biryani** n, cookery a type of spicy Indian dish consisting mainly of rice, with meat or fish and vegetables, etc.

Biro n, Brit trademark a type of BALLPOINT pen.

birth n **1** the act or process of bearing offspring. **2** the act or process of being born. **3** ancestry: of humble birth. **4** beginning; origins: the birth of socialism. ◆ **give birth** to bear or produce (offspring). **give birth to sth** to produce or be the cause or origin of it.

> **birth** There is often a spelling confusion between **birth** and **berth**.

birth certificate n an official document that records a person's birth, stating the date and place, the parents, etc.

birth control n the prevention of pregnancy, esp by means of CONTRACEPTION.

birthday n **1** the anniversary of the day on which a person was born. **2** (also **birth day**) the day on which a person was born.

birthmark n a blemish or mark that is present on the skin at birth.

birthplace n the place where a person was born or where something began.

birth rate n the ratio of the number of live births occurring over a period of a year in a given area per thousand inhabitants.

birthright n the rights a person may claim by being born into a particular family or social class, etc.

birth sign n, astrol the SIGN OF THE ZODIAC under which a person was born.

biscuit n **1** esp Brit **a** a small sweet cake, in any of numerous varieties or flavours, etc; **b** a small thin crisp plain or savoury cake. **2** objects made from baked clay that have not been glazed. **3** a pale golden brown colour. ➤ adj pale golden brown or pale tan in colour.

bisect maths, etc, vb to divide something into two equal parts. ○ **bisection** n.

bisexual adj **1** sexually attracted to both males and females. **2** having the sexual organs of both sexes. ➤ n a bisexual person or organism, etc. ○ **bisexuality** n.

bishop n **1** (often **Bishop**) Christianity a senior priest or minister in the Roman Catholic, Anglican and Orthodox Churches, in charge of a group of churches in an area or a DIOCESE. **2** *chess* a piece shaped like a bishop's mitre at the top, which may only be moved diagonally across the board.

bishopric *n, Christianity* **1** the post or position of bishop. **2** the area under the charge of a bishop.

bismuth *n, chem* a hard silvery-white metallic element with a pinkish tinge, used to make lead alloys and the insoluble compounds of which are used in medicine.

bison *n (pl bison)* either of two species of large hoofed mammal with a dark-brown coat, broad humped shoulders and long shaggy hair on its head, neck, shoulders and forelegs.

bisque¹ *n, cookery* a thick rich shellfish soup.

bisque² *n* a type of baked clay or china, which has not been glazed. ➤ *adj* pale golden-brown or pale tan in colour, like unglazed pottery.

bistro *n* a small bar or informal restaurant.

bit¹ *n* a small piece or amount of something.
♦ **a bit** *colloq* **1** a short time or distance: *Wait a bit.* **2** a little: *I feel a bit of a fool.* **3** a lot: *It takes a bit of doing.*

bit² *n* **1** a small metal bar which a horse holds in its mouth as part of the bridle with which it is controlled. **2** *(also drill bit)* a tool with a cutting edge, which can be fitted into a drill and turned at high speed.

bit³ *n, comput* a binary digit with a value of either 0 or 1, representing the smallest piece of information that can be dealt with by a computer.

bit⁴ *past tense of* BITE

bitch *n* **1** a female of the dog family. **2** *offensive or derog slang* an unpleasant or spiteful woman. **3** *slang* a difficult or unpleasant thing: *Life's a bitch.* ➤ *vb, intr (also bitch about)* to complain or talk maliciously (about someone or something).

bitchy *adj (-ier, -iest) colloq* petulantly bad-tempered or malicious. ○ **bitchiness** *n.*

bite *vb (bit, bitten, biting)* **1** *tr & intr (sometimes bite sth away or off or out)* to grasp, seize or tear with the teeth. **2** *tr & intr* of snakes and insects: to puncture (a victim's skin) with the fangs, mouthparts, etc. **3** *tr & intr* to smart or sting, or to make something do so. **4** *colloq* to annoy or worry: *What's biting him?* **5** of acid, etc: to eat into something chemically. **6** *intr* to start to have an effect, usu an adverse one: *The spending cuts are beginning to bite.* **7** *intr, angling* of fish: to be caught on the hook on a fishing line, by taking the bait into the mouth. **8** *intr* of a wheel or screw, etc: to grip firmly. ➤ *n* **1** an act or an instance of biting. **2** a wound or sting caused by biting. **3** a piece of something removed or taken, etc by biting. **4** *colloq* a small amount of food. **5** strength, sharpness or bitterness of taste. **6** *angling* of a fish: an act or an instance of biting or nibbling at the bait.
♦ **bite the dust** *colloq* **1** of a plan or project, etc: to fail or come to nothing. **2** of a person: to fall down dead.

biting *adj* **1** bitterly and painfully cold. **2** of a remark: sharp and hurtful.

bit-mapping *n, comput* a method of organizing the display on a computer screen so that each PIXEL is assigned to one or more bits (see BIT³) of memory, depending on the shading or number of colours required. ○ **bit map** *n.*

bit-part *n* a small acting part in a play or film.

bitter *adj* **1** having a sharp, acid and often unpleasant taste. **2** feeling or causing sadness or pain: *bitter memories.* **3** difficult to accept: *a bitter disappointment.* **4** showing an intense persistent feeling of dislike, hatred or opposition: *bitter resentment.* **5** of the weather, etc: painfully cold. ➤ *n, Brit* a type of beer with a slightly bitter taste. Compare MILD *(noun).* ○ **bitterly** *adv.* ○ **bitterness** *n.*

bittern *n* a long-legged marsh bird, the male of which has a distinctive booming call.

bitters *pl n* a liquid made from bitter herbs or roots, used to flavour certain alcoholic drinks.

bittersweet *adj* pleasant and unpleasant, or bitter and sweet, at the same time: *a bittersweet love story.*

bitty *adj (-ier, -iest) colloq* consisting of small unrelated bits or parts, esp when put together awkwardly or untidily. ○ **bittiness** *n.*

bitumen *n* any of various black solid or tarry flammable substances composed of an impure mixture of hydrocarbons and which is used for surfacing roads and pavements, etc. ○ **bituminous** *adj.*

bivalve *zool, adj* of a mollusc: having a shell composed of two valves hinged together. ➤ *n* any of numerous mainly marine species of mollusc with a shell composed of two valves hinged together, eg clam and scallop.

bivouac *n* a temporary camp or camping place without tents. ➤ *vb (bivouacked, bivouacking) intr* to camp out temporarily at night without a tent.

bizarre *adj* weirdly odd or strange. ○ **bizarrely** *adv.*

Bk *symbol, chem* berkelium.

blab *vb (blabbed, blabbing)* **1** *tr & intr (usu blab sth out)* to tell or divulge (a secret, etc). **2** *intr* to chatter foolishly or indiscreetly.

blabber *vb, intr* to talk nonsense, esp without stopping or without being understood. ➤ *n* a blabbermouth.

blabbermouth *n, slang, orig US* a person who talks foolishly and indiscreetly.

black *adj* **1** having the darkest colour, the same colour as coal. **2** without any light. **3** *(now usu Black)* used of people: dark-skinned, esp of African, West Indian or Australian Aboriginal origin. **4** *(usu Black)* belonging or relating to Black people. **5** of coffee or tea: without added milk. **6** angry; threatening. **7** of hands, clothes etc: dirty. **8** sad, gloomy or depressed. **9** promising trouble: *The future looks black.* **10** wicked or sinister; grim or macabre: *black comedy.* ➤ *n* **1** the colour of coal, etc, the darkest colour, or absence of colour. **2** anything which is black in colour, eg a black chess piece. **3** (*usu* **Black**) a dark-skinned person, esp one of African, West Indian or Australian Aboriginal origin. **4** black clothes worn when in mourning. **5** a black pigment or dye. **6** the credit side of an account; the state of not being in debt, eg to a bank. Compare RED (*noun* sense 5). ➤ *vb* **1** to BLACKEN. **2** to clean (shoes, etc) with black polish. **3** of a trade union: to forbid work to be done on or with (certain goods). ○ **blackness** *n*. ◇ **black out 1** of a person: to lose consciousness. **2** to deprive something of light; to extinguish or cover (lights), or all lights in (a place). **3** to prevent (information) from being broadcast or published.

black and blue *adj, colloq* of a person or of a person's skin: covered in bruises.

black and white *adj* **1** used of photographs or TV images: having no colours except black, white, and shades of grey. **2** either good or bad, right or wrong, etc, with no compromise.

blackball *vb* **1** to vote against (a candidate for membership of something), orig by putting a black ball in the ballot box. **2** to refuse to see or speak to someone.

black belt *n, judo, karate, etc* **1** a belt indicating that the wearer has reached the highest possible level of skill. **2** a person who is entitled to wear a black belt.

blackberry *n* (*-ies*) a thorny shrub or one of the dark purple-coloured berries it produces.

blackbird *n* a small European bird, the male of which is black with a yellow beak.

blackboard *n* a black or dark-coloured board for writing on with chalk.

black box *n* a FLIGHT RECORDER in an aircraft.

blackcurrant *n* a widely cultivated shrub or one of the small round black fruits it produces.

the Black Death *n, hist* a virulent plague which spread across Europe from Asia in the 14c.

black economy *n* unofficial business or trade not declared for tax purposes.

blacken *vb* **1** *tr & intr* (also **black**) to become or cause something to become black or very dark in colour. **2** to damage (someone's reputation).

black eye *n* an eye with darkened bruised swollen skin around it, usu caused by a blow.

blackguard /ˈblagɑːd/ *n, dated or facetious* a rogue or villain.

blackhead *n* a small black spot on the skin caused by sweat blocking one of the skin's tiny pores.

black hole *n, astron* a region in space, believed to be formed when a large star has collapsed in on itself at the end of its life, with such a strong gravitational pull that not even light waves can escape from it.

black ice *n* a thin transparent layer of ice that forms on road surfaces, making driving hazardous.

blacking *n, dated* black polish, esp for shining

shoes or fireplaces, etc.

blackjack *n* **1** *cards* PONTOON² or a similar game. **2** *N Am* a length of hard flexible leather, esp one used for hitting people.

black lead *n* GRAPHITE.

blackleg *n, chiefly Brit derog* a person who refuses to take part in a strike, or who works in a striker's place during a strike. ➤ *vb* (*black-legged, blacklegging*) *intr* to refuse to take part in a strike.

blacklist *n* a list of people convicted or suspected of something, or not approved of, to be boycotted or excluded, etc. ➤ *vb* to put (someone or someone's name) on such a list.

black magic *n* magic which supposedly invokes the power of the devil to perform evil.

blackmail *vb* **1** to extort money, etc illegally from someone by threatening to reveal harmful information about them. **2** to try to influence someone by using unfair pressure or threats. ➤ *n* an act of blackmailing someone. ○ **blackmailer** *n*.

Black Maria /məˈraɪə/ *n, colloq* a police van for transporting prisoners.

black mark *n* a sign or demonstration, etc of disapproval towards someone, or of a failure on their part.

black market *n* the illegal buying and selling of goods which are scarce, strictly regulated or in great demand. ○ **black-marketeer** *n*.

black mass *n* a blasphemous parody of the Christian mass, in which Satan is worshipped rather than God.

blackout *n* **1** an enforced period during which all the lights in an area are turned out, eg during World War II as a precaution during an air raid at night. **2** an electrical power-failure or power-cut. **3** a sudden loss of memory or of consciousness. **4** a suppression or stoppage of news, information, communications, etc.

black pepper *n* pepper produced by grinding the dried fruits of the pepper plant without removing their dark outer covering.

black pudding *n* a dark sausage made from pig's blood and fat, cereal, etc.

black sheep *n* a member of a family or group who is disapproved of in some way.

blacksmith *n* a person who makes and repairs by hand things made of iron, such as horseshoes.

black spot *n, chiefly Brit* **1** a dangerous stretch of road where accidents often occur. **2** an area where an adverse social condition is prevalent: *an unemployment black spot.*

blackthorn *n* a thorny shrub or small tree, with conspicuous black twigs, white flowers and rounded bluish-black fruits known as SLOEs.

black tie *n* a black BOW TIE, esp one worn with a dinner jacket. ➤ *adj* (*usu* **black-tie**) of a celebration or function: at which guests are expected to wear evening dress.

black widow *n* any of various venomous spiders, esp a N American species, the female of which commonly eats the male after mating.

bladder *n* **1** *anat* in all mammals, and some fish, amphibians and reptiles: a hollow sac-shaped organ in which urine is stored before it is discharged. **2** any of various similar hollow organs in which liquid or gas is stored, eg the gall bladder of animals, or the swim bladder of bony fish. **3** a hollow bag made eg of leather, which can be stretched by filling it with air or liquid. **4** in certain plants: a hollow sac-like structure.

blade *n* **1** the cutting part of a knife or sword, etc. **2** the flat, usu long and narrow, part of a leaf, petal or sepal. **3** the wide flat part of an oar, bat or propeller, or of certain tools and devices. **4** a broad flat bone, eg the SHOULDER BLADE. **5** the runner of an ice-skate, that slides on the surface of the ice.

blag *vb* (**blagged, blagging**) *slang* to scrounge something; to get something for nothing: *He blagged his way into the club.*

blame *vb* **1** to consider someone as responsible for something bad, wrong or undesirable. **2** to find fault with someone. ➤ *n* (*esp* **the blame**) responsibility for something bad, wrong or undesirable. ○ **blameless** *adj.*

blameworthy *adj* deserving blame.

blanch *vb* **1** to make something white by removing the colour. **2** *usu intr* to become pale or white, esp out of fear. **3** *cookery* to prepare (vegetables or meat) by boiling in water for a few seconds.

blancmange /bləˈmɒndʒ/ *n* a cold sweet jelly-like pudding made with milk.

bland *adj, derog* **1** of food: having a very mild taste. **2** lacking interest. **3** of a person or their actions: showing no strong emotion.

blandish *vb* to persuade someone by gentle flattery.

blandishments *pl n* flattery intended to persuade.

blank *adj* **1** of paper: not written or printed on. **2** of magnetic tape, etc: with no sound or pictures yet recorded on it. **3** with spaces left for details, information, a signature, etc. **4** not filled in. **5** showing no expression or interest. **6** having no thoughts or ideas: *My mind went blank.* **7** without a break or relieving feature: *a blank wall.* **8** sheer; absolute: *blank refusal.* ➤ *n* **1** an empty space. **2** an empty space left (on forms, etc) to be filled in with particular information. **3** a printed form with blank spaces left for filling in. **4** a state of having no thoughts or ideas: *My mind went a complete blank.* **5** a dash written in place of a word or letter. **6** a cartridge containing an explosive but no bullet. ➤ *vb* **1** to ignore someone. **2** to obscure or hide something: *I tried to blank the incident from my mind.* **3** (*usu* **blank out**) to blot or cross something out. ○ **blankly** *adv.* ♦ **draw a blank** *colloq* to get no results; to fail.

blank cheque *n* **1** a cheque which has been signed but on which the amount to be paid has been left blank. **2** complete freedom or authority.

blanket *n* **1** a thick covering of material, used to cover beds or for wrapping a person in for warmth. **2** a thick layer or mass which covers or obscures: *a blanket of fog.* ➤ *adj* (*used before the noun it describes*) applying to or covering all cases, people, etc: *blanket coverage.* ➤ *vb* (**blanketed, blanketing**) **1** to cover something with, or as if with, a blanket. **2** to cover or apply something in a general, comprehensive or indiscriminate way.

blanket stitch *n* a type of stitch used to strengthen and bind the edge of thick fabric, esp a blanket.

blank verse *n, prosody* poetry which does not rhyme.

blare *vb* (*often* **blare out**) **1** *intr* to make a sound like a trumpet. **2** *tr & intr* to sound or say something loudly and harshly. ➤ *n* a loud harsh sound.

blarney *n* flattering words used to persuade, deceive or cajole.

blasé /ˈblɑːzeɪ/ *adj* lacking enthusiasm or interest, or unconcerned, esp as a result of over-familiarity.

blaspheme *vb* **1** *tr & intr* to show disrespect for (God or sacred things) in speech. **2** *intr* to swear or curse using the name of God or referring to sacred things. ○ **blasphemer** *n.*

blasphemy *n* (**-ies**) **a** speaking about God or sacred matters in a disrespectful or rude way; **b** an action, word or sign that intentionally insults God, or something held sacred, in such a way. ○ **blasphemous** *adj.*

blast *n* **1** an explosion, or the strong shock waves spreading out from it. **2** a strong sudden stream or gust (of air or wind, etc). **3** a sudden loud sound of a trumpet or car horn, etc. **4** a sudden and violent outburst of anger or criticism. **5** *colloq* a highly enjoyable or exciting event, occasion or activity, esp a party. ➤ *vb* **1** to blow up (a tunnel or rock, etc) with explosives. **2** *tr & intr* (*esp* **blast out**) to make or cause something to make a loud or harsh sound. **3** to criticize someone severely. ➤ *exclam* (*also* **blast it!**) *colloq* expressing annoyance or exasperation, etc. ♦ **at full blast** at full power or speed, etc; with maximum effort or energy. ◊ **blast off** of a spacecraft: to take off from its launching pad.

blasted *adj, colloq* (often used as an intensifier) annoying; damned; stupid; infuriating.

blast furnace *n* a tall furnace that is used to extract iron from iron ores.

blast-off *n* **1** the moment at which a spacecraft or rocket-propelled missile is launched. **2** the launching of a spacecraft or rocket-propelled missile.

blatant *adj* **1** very obvious and without shame. **2** very noticeable and obtrusive. ○ **blatantly** *adv.*

blaze¹ *n* **1** a bright strong fire or flame. **2** a brilliant display. **3** a sudden and sharp bursting out of feeling or emotion. **4** an intense burst or spate: *a blaze of publicity.* ➤ *vb, intr* **1** to burn or shine brightly. **2** *colloq* to show great emotion, esp to be furious. **3** (*often* **blaze away**) *intr* **a** of a person: to fire a gun rapidly and without stopping; **b** of a gun: to fire rapidly and without stopping.

blaze² *n* **1** a white mark or band on an animal's face. **2** a mark made on the bark of a tree, esp to show a route or path. ➤ *vb* to mark (a tree or path, etc) with blazes. ♦ **blaze a trail** to be the first to do, study or discover something, etc.

blaze³ *vb* (*esp* **blaze abroad**) to make (news or information) widely known.

blazer *n* a light jacket, often in the colours of a school or club.

blazon *vb* **1** (*often* **blazon abroad**) to make something public. **2** *heraldry* to describe (a coat of arms) in technical terms. **3** *heraldry* to paint (names, designs, etc) on (a coat of arms). ➤ *n, heraldry* a shield or coat of arms.

bleach *vb, tr & intr* to whiten or remove colour from (a substance) by exposure to sunlight or certain chemicals. ➤ *n* a liquid chemical used to bleach clothes, etc.

bleak *adj* **1** exposed and desolate. **2** cold and unwelcoming. **3** offering little hope. ○ **bleakly** *adv.* ○ **bleakness** *n.*

bleary *adj* (**-ier, -iest**) **1** of a person's eyes: red and dim, usu from tiredness or through crying. **2** blurred, indistinct and unclear. ○ **blearily** *adv.*

bleat *vb* **1** *intr* to cry like a sheep, goat or calf. **2** *intr, colloq* to complain whiningly (about something).

bleed *vb* (**bled**) **1** *intr* to lose or let out blood. **2** to remove or take blood from. **3** *intr* of plants, etc: to lose juice or sap. **4** to empty liquid or air from (a radiator, hydraulic brakes, etc). **5** *colloq* to obtain money from someone, usu illegally. **6** *intr* of dye or paint: to come out of the material when wet. ♦ **one's heart bleeds for sb** *usu ironic* one feels great pity for them.

bleeding *adj, adv, Brit slang* (used as an intensifier) expressing anger or disgust: *a bleeding idiot.*

bleep *n* **1** a short high-pitched burst of sound, usu made by an electronic machine. **2** a BLEEPER. ➤ *vb* **1** *intr* of an electronic machine, etc: to give out a short high-pitched sound. **2** to call someone using a bleeper.

bleeper *n* a portable radio receiver that emits a bleeping sound, used esp to call a doctor or police officer carrying such a device.

blemish *n* a stain, mark or fault. ➤ *vb* to stain or spoil the beauty of something.

blench *vb, intr* to start back or move away, esp in fear.

blend *vb* **1** to mix (different sorts or varieties) into one. **2** *intr* (*often* **blend in**, *also* **blend with**) to form a mixture or harmonious combination; to go well together. **3** to mix together, esp harmoniously. **4** *intr* esp of colours: to shade gradually into another. ➤ *n* a mixture or combination.

blende *n* any naturally occurring metal sul-phide, eg zinc blende.

blender *n* a machine for mixing food or esp for making it into a liquid or purée.

blenny *n* (**-ies**) any of various small fishes which have a long tapering scaleless body and long fins.

bless *vb* (*past tense* **blessed**, *past participle* **blessed** or **blest**, *present participle* **blessing**) **1** to ask for divine favour or protection for someone or something. **2 a** to make or pronounce someone or something holy; **b** to make the sign of the cross over someone or something or to cross oneself. **3** to praise; to give honour or glory to (a deity). **4** to thank or be thankful for something: *I bless the day I met him.* ♦ **be blessed with** to have the benefit or advantage of (some attribute). **bless me** or **bless my soul** an expression of surprise, pleasure or dismay, etc. **bless you!** said to a person who has just sneezed.

blessed /ˈblɛsɪd, blɛst/ *adj* **1 a** (*also* **blest**) holy; **b** consecrated. **2** /ˈblɛsɪd/ *RC Church* of a dead person, and used as a title: pronounced holy by the Pope, usu as the first stage towards becoming a saint. **3** *euphem, colloq* (pronounced /ˈblɛsɪd/ when preceding its noun) damned: *This blessed zip's stuck.* **4** very fortunate or happy.

blessing *n* **1** a wish or prayer for happiness or success. **2** *relig* **a** an act which invites the goodness of God to rest upon someone; **b** a short prayer said before or after a meal or church service, etc. **3** a cause of happiness, or sometimes of relief or comfort; a benefit or advantage. **4** approval or good wishes.

blether or **blather** *chiefly Scot, vb, intr* **1** to talk foolishly and long-windedly. **2** to chat or gossip idly. ➤ *n* **1** long-winded nonsense. **2** a chat or gossip.

blight *n* **1** a fungal disease of plants that usu attacks an entire crop, or (*in compounds*) one specific crop throughout a particular region: *potato blight.* **2** a fungus that causes blight. **3** (*esp* **cast a blight on sth**) something or someone that has a distressing or destructive effect on something, or that spoils it. **4** *often in compounds* an ugly or neglected state or condition: *urban blight.* ➤ *vb* **1** to affect with blight. **2** to harm or destroy. **3** to disappoint or frustrate: *Our hopes were blighted.*

blighter *n, colloq, old use* (often used as a term of mild abuse) a contemptible person, usu a man.

blimey *exclam, Brit slang* expressing surprise or amazement.

blimp *n* **1** a type of nonrigid airship. **2** a sound-proof cover for a film camera.

blind *adj* **1** not able to see. **2** (*always* **blind to sth**) unable or unwilling to understand or appreciate something: *She's blind to his faults.* **3** without reason or purpose: *blind hatred.* **4** hidden from sight: *blind entrance.* **5** not allowing sight of what is beyond: *blind summit.* **6** of flying, navigating, etc: relying completely on instruments inside the craft. **7 a** having no openings or windows, etc: *blind wall*; **b** blocked or walled up: *blind arch*. **8** closed at one end: *blind alley*. ➤ *adv* **1** without being able to see. **2** without having gained proper knowledge of the item concerned: *I bought the car blind*. ➤ *n* **1** (**the blind**) blind people as a group. **2** a screen to stop light coming through a window. **3** a person, action or thing which hides the truth or deceives. **4** anything which prevents sight or blocks out light. ➤ *vb* **1** to make someone blind. **2** to make someone unreasonable or foolish, etc. **3** (*usu* **blind sb with sth**) to confuse or dazzle them with it: *He tried to blind me with legal jargon.* ○ **blinding** *adj*. ○ **blindly** *adv*. ○ **blindness** *n*. ◆ **blind drunk** *colloq* helplessly drunk. **turn a blind eye to sth** to pretend not to notice it.

blind date *n* **1** a date with a person whom one has not met before. **2** the person met on such a date.

blinder *n*, *colloq* a spectacular performance, esp in a sporting contest.

blindfold *n* a piece of cloth used to cover the eyes to prevent a person from seeing. ➤ *adj*, *adv* with one's eyes covered with a blindfold. ➤ *vb* to cover the eyes of someone to prevent them from seeing.

blind spot *n* **1** on the retina of the eye: a small area from which no visual images can be transmitted. **2** a place where vision is obscured. **3** any subject which a person either cannot understand, or refuses even to try to understand.

blindworm *n* a SLOWWORM.

blink *vb* **1** *intr* to shut and open the eyes again quickly, esp involuntarily. **2** to shut and open (an eyelid or an eye) very quickly. **3** *intr* of a light: to flash on and off; to shine unsteadily. ➤ *n* **1** an act of blinking. **2** a quick glimmer of light, such as a brief moment of sunshine. ◆ **on the blink** *colloq* not working properly.

blinker *n* (*usu* **blinkers**) one of two small flat pieces of leather attached to a horse's bridle to prevent it from seeing sideways. ➤ *vb* **1** to put blinkers on (a horse). **2** to limit or obscure the vision or awareness of (a person, etc).

blinking *adj*, *adv*, *slang* used to express mild annoyance: *a blinking idiot.*

blip *n* **1** a sudden sharp sound produced by a machine such as a radar screen. **2** a spot of light on a radar screen, showing the position of an object. **3** a short interruption, pause or irregularity in the expected pattern or course of something.

bliss *n* **1** very great happiness. **2** the special happiness of heaven. ○ **blissful** *adj*. ○ **blissfully** *adv*.

blister *n* **1** a small swelling on or just beneath the surface of the skin, containing watery fluid. **2** a bubble in a thin surface coating of paint, etc. ➤ *vb* **1** to make a blister or blisters occur on something. **2** *intr* of hands or feet, etc: to come up in blisters. **3** to criticize or attack someone with scathing language. ○ **blistering** *adj*.

blithe *adj* **1** without worries or cares. **2** heedless or thoughtless. ○ **blithely** *adv*.

blithering *adj*, *derog colloq* stupid; jabbering.

blitz *n* **1** a sudden strong attack, or period of such attacks, esp from the air. **2** (*esp* **have a blitz on sth**) *colloq* a period of hard work, etc to get something done quickly. ➤ *vb* **1** to attack, damage or destroy something as if by an air raid. **2** *colloq* to work hard at something for a short period.

blitzkrieg /ˈblɪtskriːɡ/ *n* a sudden and intensive attack to win a quick victory in war.

blizzard *n* a severe snowstorm with strong winds.

bloat *vb* **1** *tr & intr* to swell or make something swell or puff out with air, pride, food, etc, esp unpleasantly or uncomfortably. **2** to prepare (fish, esp herring) by salting and half-drying in smoke. ○ **bloated** *adj*.

blob *n* **1** a small soft round mass of something. **2** a small drop of liquid.

bloc *n* a group of countries or people, etc that have a common interest, purpose or policy.

block *n* **1** a mass of hard material, usu with flat sides. **2** a piece of wood or stone, etc used for chopping and cutting on. **3** a wooden or plastic cube, used as a child's toy. **4** *slang* a person's head. **5** a large building containing offices, flats, etc. **6 a** a group of buildings with roads on all four sides; **b** the distance from one end of such a group of buildings to the other. **7** *Aust, NZ* an extensive area of land for settlement or farming, etc. **8** a compact mass, group or set. **9** a group of seats, votes, shares, etc thought of as a single unit. **10** something which causes or acts as a stopping of movement or progress, etc. **11** *athletics, often in pl* a starting-block. **12** a piece of wood or metal which has been cut to be used in printing. **13** *eng* a pulley or set of pulleys mounted in a case. ➤ *vb* **1** (*often* **block sb** or **sth in** or **out**) to obstruct or impede. **2** to print (a design, title, etc) on (the cover of a book, etc). **3** (*usu* **block sth out** or **in**) to draw or sketch roughly.

blockade *n* the closing off of a port or region, etc by surrounding it with troops, ships and/or air-power, in order to prevent people or goods, etc from passing in and out. ➤ *vb* to impose a blockade on (a port or country, etc).

blockage *n* **1** anything that causes a pipe or roadway, etc to be blocked. **2** the state of being blocked or the act of blocking.

block and tackle *n*, *mech*, *eng* a device used for lifting heavy objects, consisting of a case or housing (the BLOCK) containing a pulley or system of pulleys and a rope or chain passed over it (the TACKLE).

blockbuster *n*, *colloq* a highly popular and successful film, book, etc.

block capital or **block letter** *n* a plain capital letter written in imitation of printed type.

blockhead *n*, *derog colloq* a stupid person.

blog or (*in full*) **weblog** *n* a personal journal that is published on the Internet. ➤ *vb* to write a blog. ○ **blogger** n.

bloke n, Brit colloq a man. ○ **blokeish** or **blokey** adj.

blond or (the feminine form) **blonde** adj **1** of a person: having light-coloured hair and usu fair skin and blue or grey eyes. **2** of a person's hair: fair. ➤ n a person with fair hair.

blood n **1** a fluid tissue that circulates in the arteries veins, and capillaries of the body as a result of muscular contractions of the heart. **2** relationship through belonging to the same family or race, etc: royal blood. **3** near family: my own flesh and blood. **4** bloodshed or murder. **5** a life or vitality; **b** (esp **new blood** and **young blood**) a group of people seen as adding new strength, youth, ideas, etc to an existing group. ➤ vb **1** hunting to give (a young hound) its first taste of a freshly killed animal. **2** to give someone the first experience of (war, etc). ◆ **in cold blood** deliberately or cruelly; showing no concern. **in sb's blood** in their character. **make sb's blood boil** to make them extremely angry. **make sb's blood run cold** to horrify them.

blood bank n a place where blood collected from donors is stored.

bloodbath n a massacre.

blood brother n **1** a man or boy who has promised to treat another as his brother, usu in a ceremony in which some of their blood has been mixed. **2** a true brother, by birth.

blood count n, med a numerical calculation to determine the number of red or white blood cells in a known volume of blood.

bloodcurdling adj causing a chilling fear.

blood donor n a person who donates blood to be used for transfusion.

blood group or **blood type** n, med any one of the various types into which human blood is classified.

bloodhound n a large breed of dog, known for its keen sense of smell.

bloodless adj **1** without violence or killing. **2** pale, lifeless or sickly. **3** dull, tedious or without emotion.

bloodletting n **1** killing; bloodshed. **2** the removal of blood, formerly used to treat numerous disorders.

blood money n money gained at the cost of someone's life: **a** money paid for committing murder; **b** money earned by supplying information that will cause someone to be convicted on a charge punishable by death; **c** money paid in compensation to the relatives of a murdered person.

blood poisoning n a serious condition caused by the presence of either bacterial toxins or large numbers of bacteria in the bloodstream.

blood pressure n the pressure of the blood within the blood vessels, esp the pressure within the arteries.

blood relation or **blood relative** n a person related to one by birth, rather than by marriage.

bloodshed n the shedding of blood or killing of people.

bloodshot adj of the eyes: red and irritated.

blood sports pl n sports that involve the killing of animals.

bloodstock n pedigree horses.

bloodstream n the flow of blood through the arteries, veins and capillaries of an animal's body.

bloodsucker n **1** an animal that sucks blood, eg the leech. **2** colloq a person who extorts money from another, or who persistently sponges off them.

bloodthirsty adj eager for or fond of killing or violence.

blood transfusion n, med the introduction of a volume of donated blood directly into a person's bloodstream.

blood type see BLOOD GROUP

blood vessel n in the body of an animal: any tubular structure through which blood flows.

bloody adj (-ier, -iest) **1** stained or covered with blood. **2** involving or including much killing. **3** slang used as an intensifier expressing annoyance, etc. **4** murderous or cruel. ➤ adv, slang used as an intensifier: in the BLOODY bloom of youth. ➤ vb (-ies, -ied) to stain or cover with blood. ○ **bloodiness** n.

bloody-minded adj, derog of a person: deliberately unco-operative.

bloom n **1** a a flower, esp one on a plant valued for its flowers; **b** such flowers or blossoms collectively. **2** the state of being in flower. **3** a state of perfection or great beauty: in the full bloom of youth. **4** a glow on the skin. **5** a powdery or waxy coating on the surface of certain fruits (eg grapes) or leaves. ➤ vb, intr **1** of a plant: to be in or come into flower. **2** to be in or achieve a state of great beauty or perfection. **3** of a person, eg an expectant mother: to be healthy; to flourish.

bloomer[1] n, Brit colloq an embarrassing mistake.

bloomer[2] n, Brit a crusty loaf of white bread.

bloomers pl n **1** colloq, facetious or old use women's baggy knickers. **2** (also **bloomer trousers**) hist loose trousers for women, gathered at the knee or ankle.

blooming adj **1** of a plant: flowering. **2** of someone or something: flourishing. **3** slang used as an intensifier: **a** expressing annoyance, etc; a euphemism for BLOODY (adj sense 3); **b** complete and utter: a blooming idiot. ➤ adv, slang used as an intensifier: **a** expressing annoyance, etc; **b** very or completely.

blossom n **1** a flower or mass of flowers, esp on a fruit tree. **2** the state of being in flower. ➤ vb, intr **1** of a plant, esp a fruit tree: to produce blossom or flowers. **2** (sometimes **blossom out**) to develop successfully.

blot n **1** a stain, esp of ink. **2** a blemish which spoils the beauty of something. **3** a stain on a

person's good reputation. ➤ *vb* (**blotted, blotting**) **1** to make a stain on something, esp with ink. **2 a** to dry something with blotting paper; **b** (*sometimes* **blot up**) to soak up (excess liquid) by pressing eg a cloth or tissue against it.
♦ **blot one's copybook** to spoil one's good reputation. ◊ **blot out 1** to hide something from sight. **2** to refuse to think about or remember (a painful memory).

blotch *n* a large irregular-shaped coloured patch on the skin, etc. ➤ *vb* to mark something with blotches. ○ **blotchy** *adj* (**-ier, -iest**).

blotter *n* a sheet of blotting paper.

blotting paper *n* soft thick unsized paper for absorbing excess ink.

blotto *adj, dated Brit slang* helplessly drunk.

blouse *n* **1** a woman's garment very similar to a shirt. **2** *esp formerly* a loose jacket belted in at the waist, forming part of a soldier's or airman's uniform.

blouson *n* a loose jacket gathered in tightly at the waist.

blow¹ *vb* (*past tense* **blew**, *past participle* **blown**, *present participle* **blowing**) **1** *intr* of a current of air or wind, etc: to be moving, esp rapidly. **2** *tr & intr* to move or cause something to move by a current of air or wind, etc. **3** to send (a current of air) from the mouth. **4** to form or shape (eg bubbles, glass) by blowing air from the mouth. **5** to shatter something by an explosion. **6** to produce a sound from (an instrument, etc) by blowing into it. **7** to clear something by blowing through it: *I blew my nose.* **8** *colloq* **a** to make (an electric fuse) melt and so interrupt the circuit; **b** (*also* **blow out**) *intr* of an electric fuse: to melt, causing an interruption in the flow of current. **9** to break into (a safe, etc) using explosives. **10** *slang* to spoil or bungle (an opportunity, etc): *He had his chance, and he blew it.* **11** *slang* to spend (a large amount of money), esp quickly or recklessly. **12** *slang* to disclose or give away (something secret or confidential). **13** *intr* to breathe heavily. ➤ *n* **1** an act or example of blowing. **2** a spell of exposure to fresh air. ➤ *exclam* (*also* **blow it!**) expressing annoyance; damn! ♦ **blow hot and cold** *colloq* to keep changing one's mind. **blow sb's mind** *slang* to make someone become intoxicated or ecstatic under the influence of a drug or of some exhilarating experience. **blow one's own trumpet** *colloq* to praise oneself or one's own abilities and achievements. **blow one's top** *colloq* to explode in anger. ◊ **blow sb away** *N Am slang* **1** to murder them with a gun. **2** to surprise and excite them. **blow out 1** to put out (a flame, etc) by blowing. **2** of a tyre: to burst. **3** of an electric fuse: to melt or blow (see *verb* sense 8b above). **blow over** of a quarrel, threat, storm, etc: to pass by, esp without having any harmful or lasting effect. **blow up 1** *colloq* of a person: to explode in anger. **2** to fill up or swell up with air or gas. **3** to explode. **4** to inflate (eg a balloon). **5** to produce a larger version of (a photograph, etc). **6** *colloq* to make

something seem more important than it really is. **7** to destroy something by way of an explosion.

blow² *n* **1** a forceful knock with the hand or with a weapon. **2** a sudden shock or misfortune.

blow-by-blow *adj* of a description, etc: giving all the details precisely.

blow-dry *vb* to dry (hair) in a particular style using a hand-held hairdrier. ➤ *n* an act or process of blow-drying. ○ **blow-drier** *n*.

blower *n* **1** a device or machine that blows out a current of air. **2** (**the blower**) *Brit colloq* the telephone.

blowfly *n* any of various flies whose eggs are laid in rotting flesh.

blowhole *n* **1** a hole in an area of surface ice, where seals, etc can go to breathe. **2** a modified nostril on top of a whale's head. **3** *geol* a natural vent from the roof of a sea cave up to the ground surface.

blowlamp or (*esp N Am*) **blowtorch** *n* a small portable burner, that produces an intense hot flame, used for paint-stripping, etc.

blow-out *n* **1** *colloq* a tyre-burst. **2** *oil industry* a violent escape of gas and oil from a well or on a rig, etc. **3** *colloq* a large filling meal. **4** *elec eng* **a** an incident in which a circuit is broken by a fuse blowing; **b** a blown fuse.

blowpipe *n* **1** in glass-blowing: an iron tube used to blow air into molten glass which can then be shaped as it cools. **2** a small tube that carries a stream of air into a flame in order to concentrate and direct it. **3** a long tube from which someone blows a dart, etc.

blow-up *n, colloq* an enlargement of a photograph.

blowy *adj* (**-ier, -iest**) windy.

blowzy or **blowsy** /'blaʊzɪ/ *adj* (**-ier, -iest**) *derog, colloq* of a woman: **1** fat and red-faced. **2** dirty and dishevelled.

blubber *n* **1** the fat of sea animals such as the whale. **2** *colloq* excessive body fat. ➤ *vb, intr, derog colloq* to weep, esp unrestrainedly.

bludgeon *n* a club with a heavy end. ➤ *vb* **1** to hit someone or something with or as if with a bludgeon. **2** (*usu* **bludgeon sb into sth**) to force them into doing it.

blue *adj* **1** with the colour of a clear cloudless sky. **2** sad or depressed. **3** of a film or joke etc: pornographic or indecent. ➤ *n* **1** the colour of a clear cloudless sky; any blue shade or hue. **2** blue paint or dye. **3** blue material or clothes. **4** a person who has been chosen to represent a college or university at sport, esp at Oxford or Cambridge. **5** *Aust & NZ slang* an argument or fight. **6** *Aust & NZ colloq* a mistake. ○ **blueness** *n*. ♦ **out of the blue** unexpectedly.

blue baby *n* a newborn baby suffering from congenital heart disease which leads to lack of oxygen in the blood, giving the skin and lips a bluish tinge.

bluebell *n* **1** a spring-flowering plant with clusters of bell-shaped flowers that are usu blue (also called **wild hyacinth**). **2** *Scot, N Eng* the HAREBELL.

blueberry *n* (*-ies*) **1** any of various deciduous shrubs, native to N America, with white or pinkish flowers and edible berries. **2** the bluish-black edible berry produced by this plant.

bluebird *n* any of various birds of the thrush family, the male of which has bright blue plumage on its back.

blue blood *n* royal or aristocratic ancestry.

bluebottle *n* a large blowfly, so called because its abdomen has a blue sheen.

blue cheese *n* cheese with veins of blue mould running through it.

blue-chip *adj* **1** *stock exchange* of stocks and shares: considered reliable and secure, though less secure than GILT-EDGED ones. **2** *loosely* prestigious and valuable. ➤ *n* a blue-chip stock.

blue-collar *adj* of workers: doing manual work.

blue-pencil *vb* to correct, edit or cut parts out of (a piece of writing).

blueprint *n* **1 a** a pattern, model or prototype; **b** a detailed original plan of work to be done to develop an idea, scheme, etc. **2** *technical* a photographic print of plans, engineering or architectural designs, etc consisting of white lines on a blue background.

blue ribbon or **blue riband** *n* **1** a first prize awarded in a competition, or some other very high distinction. **2** *Brit* the blue silk ribbon of the Order of the Garter.

blues *sing* or *pl n* (*usu* **the blues**) **1** a feeling of sadness or depression. **2** slow melancholy jazz music of Black American origin. ○ **bluesy** *adj* (*-ier, -iest*).

bluestocking *n, often derog* a highly educated woman who is interested in serious academic subjects.

blue tit *n* a small bird, which has a bright blue crown, wings and tail, and yellow underparts.

blue whale *n* a rare type of whale, the largest living animal, which has a bluish body with pale spots.

bluff[1] *vb, tr & intr* to deceive or try to deceive someone by pretending to be stronger, cleverer, etc than one really is. ➤ *n* an act of bluffing. ♦ **call sb's bluff** to challenge them by making them prove the genuineness of their claim, threat, etc.

bluff[2] *adj* **1** of a person, character, manner, etc: rough, cheerful and honest. **2** usu of a cliff or of the bow of a ship: broad, steep and upright. ➤ *n* a steep cliff or high bank of ground.

blunder *n* a foolish or thoughtless mistake. ➤ *vb* **1** *intr* to make a blunder. **2** *intr* to act or move about awkwardly and clumsily. ○ **blundering** *adj*.

blunderbuss *n, hist* a type of musket with a wide barrel and a flared muzzle.

blunt *adj* **1** of a pencil, knife or blade, etc: having no point or sharp edge. **2** of a person, char-

acter or manner, etc: honest and direct in a rough way. ➤ *vb* to make something blunt or less sharp. ○ **bluntly** *adv*. ○ **bluntness** *n*.

blur *n* **1** a thing not clearly seen or heard, or happening too fast or too distantly, etc to be clearly seen, comprehended or recognized. **2** a smear or smudge. ➤ *vb* (**blurred, blurring**) **1** *tr & intr* to become or cause something to become less clear or distinct. **2** to rub over and smudge something. **3** to make (one's memory or judgement, etc) less clear. ○ **blurred** or **blurry** *adj* (*-ier, -iest*).

blurb *n* a brief description of a book, usu printed on the jacket in order to promote it.

blurt *vb* (*usu* **blurt out**) to say something suddenly or without thinking.

blush *vb, intr* to become red or pink in the face because of shame, excitement, joy, etc. ➤ *n* (**blushes**) **1** a red or pink glow on the skin of the face, caused by shame, excitement, etc. **2** *esp literary* a pink rosy glow.

blusher *n* a cosmetic cream used to give colour to the cheeks.

bluster *vb, intr* **1** to speak in a boasting or threatening way. **2** of the wind or waves, etc: to blow or move roughly. ➤ *n* speech that is ostentatiously boasting or threatening. ○ **blustery** *adj*.

B-movie *n, dated* a film, usu cheaply produced, made to support the main film in a cinema programme.

b.o. *abbrev* (*also* **BO**) body odour.

boa *n* **1 a boa constrictor**, or any similar snake of the mainly S American type that kill by winding themselves round their prey and crushing it. **2** a woman's long thin scarf, usu made of feathers or fur.

boar *n* (**boars** or **boar**) **1** a wild ancestor of the domestic pig. **2** a mature uncastrated male pig.

> **boar** There is sometimes a spelling confusion between **boar** and **boor**.

board *n* **1** a long flat strip of wood. **2** *often in compounds* a piece of material resembling this, made from fibres compressed together: *chipboard*. **3** *often in compounds* **a** a flat piece of wood or other hard solid material, used for a specified purpose or of a specified kind: *ironing board*; **b** a slab, table or other flat surface prepared for playing a game on: *chessboard*. **4** thick stiff card used eg for binding books. **5** a person's meals, provided in return for money: *bed and board*. **6 a** an official group of people controlling or managing an organization, etc, or examining or interviewing candidates: *a board of examiners*; **b** (*also* **board of directors**) a group of individual directors appointed by a company, who are collectively responsible for its management. **7** (**the boards**) a theatre stage: *tread the boards*. **8** *naut* the side of a ship. ➤ *vb* **1** to enter or get onto (a ship, aeroplane, bus, etc). **2** (*usu* **board up**) to cover (a gap or entrance) with boards. **3** *intr* **a** to receive accommodation and meals in someone else's house, in return for payment; **b** to receive accommodation and meals at school; to attend school as a BOARDER. **4** to provide someone with accommodation and meals in return for payment. **5** (*also* **board sb out**) to arrange for them to receive accommodation and meals away from home. ♦ **go by the board** *colloq* to be given up or ignored. **on board** on or into a ship or aeroplane, etc.

boarder *n* a pupil who lives at school during term time.

board game *n* a game (such as chess or draughts) played with pieces or counters that are moved on a specially designed board.

boarding house *n* a house in which people live and take meals as paying guests.

boarding school *n* a school at which all or most of the pupils live during term time.

boardroom *n* a room in which the directors of a company meet.

boardwalk *n*, *N Am* a footpath made of boards, esp on the seafront.

boast *vb* **1** *intr* (*often* **boast about** or **of**) to talk with excessive pride about (one's own abilities or achievements, etc). **2** to have (something it is right to be proud of): *The hotel boasts magnificent views.* ➤ *n* **1** an act of boasting. **2** a thing one is proud of. ○ **boastful** *adj.* ○ **boasting** *n*, *adj.*

boat *n* **1** a small vessel for travelling over water. **2** *colloq*, *loosely* a larger vessel. **3** *in compounds* a boat-shaped dish for serving sauce, etc: *gravy boat.* ➤ *vb, intr* to sail or travel in a boat, esp for pleasure. ♦ **in the same boat** of people: finding themselves in the same difficult circumstances. **miss the boat** to lose an opportunity. **rock the boat** to disturb the balance of a situation.

boater *n* a straw hat with a flat top and a brim.

boathouse *n* a building in which boats are stored, esp by a lake or river.

boating *n* the sailing or rowing, etc of boats for pleasure.

boatman *n* a man who is in charge of, or hires out, etc a small boat or boats.

boatswain or **bosun** /'bəʊsən/ *n* the officer who is in charge of a ship's equipment.

bob[1] *vb* (**bobbed, bobbing**) *intr* **1** (*sometimes* **bob along** or **past**, *etc*) to move up and down quickly. **2** (*usu* **bob up**) to appear or reappear suddenly. ➤ *n* a quick up-and-down bouncing movement.

bob[2] *n* **1** a short hairstyle with the hair cut evenly all round the head. **2** a hanging weight on a clock's pendulum or plumbline, etc. ➤ *vb* (**bobbed, bobbing**) to cut (hair) in a bob.

bob[3] *n* (*pl* **bob**) *Brit colloq*, *old use* a shilling.

bobbin *n* a small cylindrical object on which thread, etc is wound.

bobble *n* **1** a small ball, often fluffy or made of tufted wool, used to decorate clothes, etc, esp on the top of a knitted **bobble-hat**. **2** a little ball formed on the surface of a fabric during use, through rubbing, etc. ○ **bobbly** *adj.*

bobby *n* (**-ies**) *Brit colloq* a policeman.

bobcat *n* a solitary nocturnal member of the cat family.

bobsleigh or (*esp US*) **bobsled** *n*, *sport* a sledge for two or more people, for racing on an ice-covered track. ➤ *vb, intr* to ride on a bobsleigh.

bod *n*, *colloq* **1** a person. **2** a body.

bode *vb* to be a sign of something.

bodge *colloq*, *vb, tr & intr* to make a mess of something.

bodhran /'bɔːrɑːn/ *n* a shallow one-sided drum played in Scottish and Irish folk-music.

bodice *n* **1** the close-fitting upper part of a woman's dress, from shoulder to waist. **2** a woman's close-fitting waistcoat, worn over a blouse. **3** *formerly* a similar tight-fitting stiffened undergarment for women.

bodily *adj* belonging or relating to, or performed by, the body. ➤ *adv* **1** taking the whole body: *He carried me bodily to the car.* **2** in person.

bodkin *n* a large blunt needle.

body *n* (**-ies**) **1** the whole physical structure of a person or animal. **2** the physical structure of a person or animal excluding the head and limbs. **3** a corpse. **4** the main or central part of anything, such as the main or central part of a vehicle. **5** a person's physical needs and desires as opposed to spiritual concerns. **6** a substantial section or group: *a body of opinion.* **7** a group of people regarded as a single unit. **8** a quantity or mass: *a body of water.* **9** a distinct mass or object: *a foreign body.* **10** applied to wine, music, etc: a full or strong quality or tone. **11** thickness. **12** a legless tight-fitting one-piece garment for women. **13** *colloq* a person.

body bag *n* a bag in which a dead body, esp that of a war casualty or accident victim, is transported.

body blow *n* **1** *boxing* a blow to the torso. **2** a serious setback.

body-building *n* physical exercise designed to develop the muscles. ○ **bodybuilder** *n.*

bodyguard *n* a person or group of people whose job is to give protection to an important person, etc.

body language *n* the communication of information by means of conscious or unconscious gestures, attitudes, facial expressions, etc, rather than by words.

body politic *n* (*usu* **the body politic**) all the people of a nation in their political capacity.

body snatcher *n*, *hist* a person who steals dead bodies from their graves, usu to sell them for dissection.

body stocking *n* a tight-fitting one-piece garment worn next to the skin, covering all of the body and often the arms and legs.

body warmer *n* a padded sleeveless jacket.

bodywork *n* the outer shell of a motor vehicle.

Boer *n* a descendant of the early Dutch settlers in S Africa. ➤ *adj* belonging or relating to the Boers.

boffin n, Brit colloq a scientist.

bog n 1 ecol an area of wet spongy poorly-drained ground, composed of acid peat and slowly decaying plant material. 2 Brit slang a toilet. ➤ vb (**bogged, bogging**) (usu **bog down**) 1 to become or cause someone or something to become stuck. 2 to hinder or hold up the progress of. ○ **bogginess** n. ○ **boggy** adj (-ier, -iest).

bogey¹ or **bogy** n (**bogeys** or **bogies**) 1 an evil or mischievous spirit. 2 something feared or dreaded. 3 slang a piece of nasal mucus.

bogey² golf, n (**bogeys**) a score of one over PAR on a specific hole. ➤ vb to complete a (specified hole) in one over par.

bogeyman or **bogyman** n a frightening person or creature, existing or imaginary, used to threaten or frighten children.

boggle vb, intr, colloq 1 to be amazed or unable to understand or imagine: the mind boggles. 2 (usu **boggle at**) to hesitate over something, out of surprise or fright, etc.

bogie or **bogey** n, mainly Brit a frame with four or six wheels used as part of a pivoting undercarriage, supporting a railway carriage.

bog-standard adj, colloq ordinary.

bogus adj not genuine.

bohemian n someone who lives in a way which ignores standard customs and rules of social behaviour. ➤ adj ignoring standard customs and rules of social behaviour. ○ **bohemianism** n.

boil¹ vb 1 intr of a liquid: to change rapidly to a vapour on reaching a certain temperature. 2 intr of a container, eg a kettle: to have contents that are boiling. 3 a to make (a liquid) reach its boiling point rapidly; b to boil the contents of (a container). 4 tr to cook (food) by heating in boiling liquid. 5 (sometimes **boil up**) to bring (a container or its contents) to boiling point. 6 (usu **be boiling**) colloq a to be very hot: It's boiling in the car; b to be extremely angry. 7 intr of the sea, etc: to move and bubble violently as if boiling. ➤ n (usu **a boil** or **the boil**) the act or point of boiling. ◊ **boil down to** colloq to have something as the most important part or factor. **boil over** 1 of a liquid: to boil and flow over the edge of its container. 2 colloq to speak out angrily.

boil² n a reddened pus-filled swelling in the skin, caused by bacterial infection of a hair follicle.

boiler n 1 any closed vessel that is used to convert water into steam, in order to drive machinery. 2 an apparatus for heating a building's hot water supply.

boilersuit n a one-piece suit worn over normal clothes to protect them while doing manual work.

boiling point n 1 the temperature at which a particular substance changes from a liquid to a vapour. 2 a point of great anger or high excitement.

boisterous adj 1 of people, behaviour, etc: very lively, noisy and cheerful. 2 of the sea,

etc: rough and stormy.

bold adj 1 daring and brave. 2 not showing respect. 3 striking and clearly marked. ○ **boldly** adv. ○ **boldness** n.

bole n the trunk of a tree.

bolero n 1 /bəˈlɛərəʊ/ **a** a traditional Spanish dance; **b** the music for this dance, usu in triple time. 2 /ˈbɒlərəʊ/ a short open jacket reaching not quite to the waist.

boll n a rounded capsule containing seeds, esp of a cotton or flax plant.

bollard n 1 Brit a small post used to mark a traffic island or to keep traffic away from a certain area. 2 a short but strong post on a ship or quay, etc around which ropes are fastened.

bollocks or **ballocks** coarse slang, pl n 1 the testicles. 2 (functions as sing n) rubbish; nonsense. ➤ exclam! rubbish! nonsense!

boloney see BALONEY

bolshie or **bolshy** Brit derog colloq, adj (-ier, -iest) 1 bad-tempered and unco-operative. 2 left-wing. ➤ n a Bolshevik.

bolster vb (often **bolster sth up**) to support it, make it stronger or hold it up. ➤ n 1 a long narrow pillow. 2 any pad or support.

bolt¹ n 1 a rod that slides into a hole or socket to fasten a door, etc. 2 a small thick round bar of metal, with a screw thread, used with a NUT to fasten things together. 3 a sudden movement away, esp to escape from someone or something: Let's make a bolt for it. 4 a flash of lightning. 5 a short arrow fired from a crossbow. ➤ vb 1 to fasten (a door, etc) with a bolt. 2 to fasten (two or more things) together with bolts. 3 to eat (a meal, etc) very quickly. 4 intr to run away suddenly and quickly. 5 intr of a horse: to run away out of control. 6 intr of a plant: to flower and produce seeds too early. ◆ **a bolt from the blue** a sudden, completely unexpected event. **bolt upright** absolutely straight and stiff.

bolt² or **boult** vb 1 to pass (flour, etc) through a sieve. 2 to examine, sift or investigate (information, etc).

bolthole n, Brit colloq a secluded private place to hide away in.

bomb n 1 a hollow device containing a substance capable of causing an explosion, fire or smoke, etc. 2 (**the bomb**) the atomic bomb, or nuclear weapons collectively. 3 (**a bomb**) Brit colloq a lot of money. ➤ vb 1 to attack or damage something with a bomb or bombs. 2 (esp **bomb along** or **off**, etc) intr, colloq to move or drive quickly. 3 intr, N Am colloq to fail badly. ○ **bombing** n. ◆ **go like a bomb** colloq, chiefly Brit 1 to move very quickly. 2 to go or sell, be extremely well.

bombard vb 1 to attack (a place, target, etc) with large, heavy guns or bombs. 2 to direct questions or abuse at someone very quickly and without stopping. 3 to batter or pelt something or someone heavily and persistently. 4 physics to subject (a target, esp an atom) to a stream of high-energy particles. ○ **bombardment** n.

bombardier /bɒmbə'dɪə(r)/ n 1 Brit a non-commissioned officer in the Royal Artillery. 2 the member of a bomber's crew who aims and releases the bombs.

bombast n pretentious, boastful or insincere words having little real meaning. ○ **bombastic** adj.

bomber n 1 an aeroplane designed for carrying and dropping bombs. 2 a person who bombs something or who plants bombs.

bombshell n a piece of surprising and usu devastating news.

bona fide /'boʊnə 'faɪdɪ/ adj genuine or sincere; done or carried out in good faith: a bona fide offer. ➤ adv genuinely or sincerely.

bonanza n 1 an unexpected and sudden source of good luck or wealth. 2 a large amount of something desirable. 3 N Am a rich mine or vein of precious ore such as gold or silver.

bond n 1 something used for tying, binding or holding. 2 (usu bonds) something which restrains or imprisons someone. 3 something that joins people together: a bond of friendship. 4 a binding agreement. 5 finance a DEBENTURE. 6 law a written agreement to pay money or carry out the terms of a contract. 7 chem the strong force of attraction that holds together two atoms in a molecule or a crystalline salt. ➤ vb 1 to join, secure or tie (two or more things) together. 2 intr to hold or stick together securely.

bondage n 1 slavery. 2 the state of being confined or imprisoned, etc. 3 a sexual practice in which one partner is tied up.

bonded warehouse n a building in which goods are kept until customs or other duty on them is paid.

bond paper n very good quality writing paper.

bone n 1 the hard dense tissue that forms the skeleton of vertebrates. 2 any of the components of the skeleton, made of this material. 3 (bones) the skeleton. 4 (chiefly one's bones) the body as the place where feelings or instincts come from. 5 a substance similar to human bone, such as ivory and whalebone, etc. 6 (bones) the basic or essential part. ➤ vb 1 to take bone out of (meat, etc). 2 to make (a piece of clothing, eg a corset) stiff by adding strips of bone or some other hard substance. ◆ **have a bone to pick with sb** to have something to disagree about with them. **make no bones about sth** 1 to admit or allow it without any fuss or hesitation. 2 to be quite willing to say or do it openly. **near** or **close to the bone** colloq of speech, etc: 1 referring too closely to a subject which it would have been tactful to avoid. 2 rather risqué. ◊ **bone up on** colloq to learn about (a subject).

bone china n a type of fine china or PORCELAIN made from clay mixed with ash from bones.

bone-dry adj completely dry.

bone-idle adj, colloq utterly lazy.

bone marrow see MARROW (sense I)

bone meal n dried and ground bones, used as a fertilizer and in animal feed.

boneshaker n, colloq an old uncomfortable and unsteady vehicle.

bonfire n a large outdoor fire.

bongo n (**bongos** or **bongoes**) each of a pair of small drums held between the knees and played with the hands.

bonhomie /'bɒnɒmiː/ n cheerful friendliness.

bonk vb, tr & intr 1 to hit. 2 coarse slang to have sexual intercourse with someone. ➤ n 1 a blow. 2 coarse slang an act of sexual intercourse.

bonkers adj, chiefly Brit slang mad.

bon mot /bɛ̃'moʊ/ n (**bons mots** /bɛ̃'moʊ/) a short clever remark.

bonnet n 1 a type of hat fastened under the chin with ribbon. 2 Brit the hinged cover over a motor vehicle's engine. 3 Scot a soft brimless cap.

bonny adj (**-ier, -iest**) 1 chiefly Scot & N Eng attractive. 2 looking very healthy.

bonsai n (pl **bonsai**) a miniature tree cultivated in a small container.

bonus n 1 an extra sum of money given on top of what is due as wages, interest or dividend, etc. 2 an unexpected extra benefit given with something else. 3 insurance an additional sum of money payable to the holder of a policy when it matures.

bony adj (**-ier, -iest**) 1 consisting of, made of or like bone. 2 full of bones. 3 of a person or animal: thin, so that the bones are very noticeable.

boo exclam, n a sound expressing disapproval, or made when trying to frighten or surprise someone. ➤ vb (**booed, booing**) tr & intr to shout 'boo' to express disapproval (of someone or something).

boob[1] n, colloq (also **booboo**) a stupid or foolish mistake. ➤ vb, intr, colloq to make a stupid or foolish mistake.

boob[2] n, slang a woman's breast.

booby n (**-ies**) 1 any of various seabirds of the gannet family. 2 old use, colloq a foolish person.

booby prize n a prize (usu a joke prize) for the lowest score in a competition.

booby trap n 1 a bomb which is disguised so that it is set off by the victim. 2 a trap, esp one intended as a practical joke. ➤ vb (**boobytrap**) to put a booby trap in or on (a place).

boogie colloq, vb (**boogieing** or **boogying**) intr to dance to pop music. ➤ n 1 a trap, or dancing, to pop music. 2 BOOGIE-WOOGIE.

boogie-woogie n, mus a style of jazz piano music with a constantly repeated, strongly rhythmic bass.

boo-hoo exclam, n the sound of noisy weeping. ➤ vb (**boo-hooed**) intr to weep noisily.

book n 1 a number of printed pages bound together along one edge and protected by covers. 2 a piece of written work intended for publication, eg a novel, etc. **3** a number of sheets of blank paper bound together. **4** (*usu* **the books**) a record or formal accounts of the business done by a company, society, etc. **5** a record of bets made. **6** (*usu* **Book**) a major division of a long literary work. **7** a number of stamps, matches or cheques, etc bound together. **8** the words of an opera or musical. ➤ *vb* **1** *tr & intr* to reserve (a ticket, seat, etc), or engage (a person's services) in advance. **2** of a police officer, traffic warden, etc: to record the details of (a person who is being charged with an offence). **3** *football* of a referee: to enter (a player's name) in a notebook as a record of an offence. ○ **bookable** *adj*. ◆ **be in sb's good** or **bad books** to be in or out of favour with them. **bring sb to book** to punish them or make them account for their behaviour. **by the book** strictly according to the rules. **take a leaf out of sb's book** to benefit from their example. ◇ **book in** *esp Brit* **1** to sign one's name on the list of guests at a hotel. **2** to report one's arrival at a hotel, etc. **book sb in** to reserve a place or room for them in a hotel, etc. **book up** to reserve in advance the tickets and other arrangements for (a holiday, show, etc).

bookcase *n* a piece of furniture with shelves for books.

book club *n* a club which sells books to its members at reduced prices and generally by mail order.

book end *n* each of a pair of supports used to keep a row of books standing upright.

bookie *n*, *mainly Brit colloq* a bookmaker.

booking *n* **1** a reservation of a theatre seat, hotel room, etc. **2** esp in sport: the recording of an offence. **3** an engagement for the services of a person or company, esp for a theatrical or musical performance, etc.

bookish *adj*, *often derog* **1** extremely fond of reading. **2** having knowledge based on books rather than practical experience.

bookkeeper *n* a person who keeps a record of the financial transactions of a business or organization, etc. ○ **bookkeeping** *n*.

booklet *n* a small book with a paper cover.

bookmaker *n*, *mainly Brit* a person whose job is to take bets on horse races, etc and pay out winnings. ○ **bookmaking** *n*.

bookmark or *sometimes* **bookmarker** *n* a strip of leather, card, etc put in a book, esp to mark one's place.

bookstall *n* a small shop in a station, etc where books, newspapers, magazines, etc are sold.

bookworm *n* **1** *colloq* a person who is extremely fond of reading. **2** a small insect which feeds on the paper and glue used in books.

boom¹ *n* a deep resounding sound. ➤ *vb*, *intr* to make a deep resounding sound.

boom² *n* **1** a sudden growth in business, prosperity, activity, etc. **2** a period of such rapid growth or activity, etc. ➤ *vb*, *intr* **1** esp of a business: to become rapidly and suddenly prosperous. **2** of a commodity, etc: to increase sharply in value.

boom³ *n* **1** *naut* a pole to which the bottom of a ship's sail is attached, keeping the sail stretched tight. **2** a heavy pole or chain, or a barrier of floating logs, etc across the entrance to a harbour or across a river. **3** *cinema, TV, etc* a long pole with a microphone, camera or light attached to one end, held above the heads of people being filmed.

boomerang *n* **1** a piece of flat curved wood used by Australian Aborigines for hunting, often so balanced that, when thrown to a distance, it returns towards the person who threw it. **2** a malicious act or statement which harms the perpetrator rather than the intended victim. ➤ *vb*, *intr* of an act or statement: to go wrong and harm the perpetrator rather than the intended victim.

boon¹ *n* an advantage, benefit or blessing.

boon² *adj* close, convivial, intimate or favourite: *a boon companion*.

boor *n*, *derog* a coarse person with bad manners. ○ **boorish** *adj*.

> **boor** There is sometimes a spelling confusion between **boor** and **boar**.

boost *vb* **1** to improve or encourage something or someone. **2** to make something greater or increase it: *boost profits*. **3** to promote something by advertising. ➤ *n* **1** a piece of help or encouragement, etc. **2** a push upwards. **3** a rise or increase: *a boost in sales*.

booster *n* **1** (*also* **booster shot**) a dose of vaccine that is given in order to renew or increase the immune response to a previous dose of the same vaccine. **2** *aerospace* an engine in a rocket that provides additional thrust at some stage of the vehicle's flight. **3** (*also* **booster rocket**) a rocket that is used to launch a space vehicle, before another engine takes over. **4** *electronics* a radio-frequency amplifier that is used to amplify a weak TV or radio signal.

boot¹ *n* **1** an outer covering, made of leather or rubber, etc, for the foot and lower part of the leg. **2** *Brit* a compartment for luggage in a car, usu at the back. **3** *colloq* a hard kick. **4** (**the boot**) *colloq* dismissal from a job. ➤ *vb* **1** to kick. **2** (*usu* **boot sb** or **sth out**) to throw them or it out, or remove them or it by force. **3** (*often* **boot up**) *comput* to start or restart (a computer) by loading the programs which control its basic functions. ◆ **put the boot in** *colloq* **1** to kick viciously. **2** to deliver further hurt, torment, etc.

boot² *n*, *archaic* an advantage. ◆ **to boot** as well.

bootee *n* a soft knitted boot for a baby.

booth *n* **1** a small temporary roofed structure, esp a covered stall at a fair or market. **2** a small partly-enclosed compartment, eg one in a restaurant containing a table and seating, or one intended for a specific purpose.

bootleg *vb* (**bootlegged, bootlegging**) **1** to make, sell or transport (alcoholic drink) illegally, esp in a time of prohibition. **2** to make or deal in (illicit goods such as unofficial recordings of copyright music, videos, etc). ➤ *n* illegally produced, sold or transported goods. ○ **bootlegger** *n*.

bootlicker *n, colloq* a person who tries to gain the favour of someone in authority by flattery, excessive obedience, etc.

booty *n (-ies)* valuable goods taken in wartime or by force.

booze *slang, n* alcoholic drink. ➤ *vb, intr* to drink a lot of alcohol, or too much of it. ○ **boozy** *adj (-ier, -iest)*.

boozer *n, slang, Brit, Aust & NZ* **1** a public house or bar. **2** a person who drinks alcohol excessively.

bop[1] *colloq, vb (bopped, bopping) intr* to dance to popular music. ➤ *n* **1** a dance to popular music. **2** BEBOP.

bop[2] *colloq, often humorous, vb (bopped, bopping)* to hit. ➤ *n* a blow or knock.

borage *n* a plant with oval hairy leaves widely cultivated as a herb for use in salads and medicinally.

borax *n* a colourless crystalline salt, found in saline lake deposits, used in the manufacture of glass, and as a mild antiseptic.

border *n* **1** a band or margin along the edge of something. **2** the boundary of a country or political region, etc. **3** the land on either side of a country's border. **4** a narrow strip of ground planted with flowers, surrounding an area of grass. **5** any decorated or ornamental edge or trimming. ➤ *adj* belonging or referring to the border, or on the border. ➤ *vb* **1** to be a border to, adjacent to, or on the border of something. **2** to provide something with a border.

borderland *n* **1** land at or near a country's border. **2** the undefined margin or condition between two states, eg between sleeping and waking.

borderline *n* **1** the border between one thing, country, etc and another. **2** a line dividing two things: *the borderline between passing and failing.* ➤ *adj* on the border between one thing, state, etc and another: *a borderline result.*

bore[1] *vb* **1** to make a hole in something by drilling. **2** to produce (a borehole, tunnel or mine, etc) by drilling. ➤ *n* **1** the hollow barrel of a gun, or the cavity inside any such tube. **2 a** *in compounds* the diameter of the hollow barrel of a gun, esp to show which size bullets the gun requires: *12-bore shotgun;* **b** the diameter of the cavity inside any such tube or pipe. **3** a BOREHOLE.

bore[2] *vb* to make someone feel tired and uninterested, by being dull, tedious, etc. ➤ *n* a dull or tedious person or thing. ○ **boredom** *n*. ○ **boring** *adj*.

bore[3] *n* a solitary high wave of water caused by constriction of the spring tide as it enters a narrow estuary.

bore[4] see under BEAR[1]

borehole *n* a deep narrow hole made by bor-

ing, esp one made in the ground to find oil or water, etc.

boric or **boracic** *adj* relating to or containing BORON.

born *adj* **1** brought into being by birth. **2** having a specified quality or ability as a natural attribute: *a born leader.* **3 (born to sth)** destined to do it: *born to lead men.* ➤ *vb, past participle of* BEAR[1]. ◆ **not born yesterday** not naive or foolish.

born-again *adj* converted or re-converted, esp to a fundamentalist or evangelical Christian faith.

boron *n, chem* a non-metallic element found only in compounds, eg BORAX, and used in hardening steel.

borough *n* **1** (*also* **parliamentary borough**) in England: a town or urban area represented by at least one member of Parliament. **2** *hist* in England: a town with its own municipal council and special privileges granted by royal charter. **3** a division of a large town, esp of London or New York, for local-government purposes.

borrow *vb* **1** to take something temporarily, usu with permission and with the intention of returning it. **2** *intr* to get (money) in this way, from a bank, etc. **3** to take, adopt or copy (words or ideas, etc) from another language or person, etc. ○ **borrower** *n*. ○ **borrowing** *n*.

borscht, **bortsch** or **borsh** *n* a Russian and Polish beetroot soup.

borstal *n, Brit, formerly* an institution to which young criminals were sent.

borzoi *n* a large breed of dog with a tall slender body, a long thin muzzle, a long tail and a long soft coat.

bosh *n, exclam, colloq* foolish talk.

bosom *n* **1** a person's chest or breast, now esp that of a woman. **2** (*sometimes* **bosoms**) *colloq* a woman's breasts. **3** a loving or protective centre: *the bosom of one's family.* **4** *chiefly literary* the seat of emotions and feelings; the heart.

bosom friend or **bosom buddy** *n* a close or intimate friend.

boss[1] *colloq, n* a person who employs others, or who is in charge of others. ➤ *vb* **1** (*esp* **boss sb about** or **around**) to give them orders in a domineering way. **2** to manage or control someone.

boss[2] *n* **1** a round raised stud on a shield, etc, usu for decoration. **2** *archit* a round raised decorative knob found where the ribs meet in a vaulted ceiling.

bossy *adj (-ier, -iest) colloq* inclined to give orders like a BOSS[1]; disagreeably domineering. ○ **bossiness** *n*.

bosun see BOATSWAIN

bot *n, comput* a computer program designed to perform certain routine tasks without being prompted by the user.

botany *n* the branch of biology concerned with the scientific study of plants. ○ **botanic** or **botanical** *adj*. ○ **botanist** *n*.

botch *colloq, vb (esp* **botch up**) **1** to do something badly and unskilfully. **2** to repair something carelessly or badly. ➢ *n* (also **botch-up**) a badly or carelessly done piece of work, repair, etc.

both *adj, pron* (*sometimes* **both of sth**) the two; the one and the other: *I'd like you both to help.* ➢ *adv* as well. ♦ **both … and …** not only … but also …

bother *vb* **1** to annoy, worry or trouble someone or something. **2** *tr & intr* (*usu* **bother about sth**) to worry about it. **3** *intr* (*esp* **bother about** or **with sth**) to take the time or trouble to do it or consider it, etc: *We never bother with convention here.* ➢ *n* **1** a minor trouble or worry. **2** a person or thing that causes bother. ➢ *exclam, mainly Brit* expressing slight annoyance. ♦ **be bothered** to take the trouble (to do something).

bothersome *adj* causing bother.

bothy *n* (**-ies**) *chiefly Scot* **1** a simple cottage or hut used as temporary shelter. **2** a basically furnished dwelling for farm workers, etc.

Botox treatment *n, trademark* a treatment in which a substance is injected into the skin to make wrinkles less apparent.

bottle *n* **1** a hollow glass or plastic container with a narrow neck, for holding liquids. **2** (also **bottleful**) the amount a bottle holds. **3** a baby's feeding bottle or the liquid in it. **4** *Brit, slang* courage, nerve or confidence. **5** (*usu* **the bottle**) *slang* drinking of alcohol, esp to excess (*esp* **hit** or **take to the bottle**). ➢ *vb* to put something into a bottle. ◊ **bottle up** to suppress (one's feelings about something).

bottle bank *n* a large container into which people can put empty glass bottles and jars, etc to be collected and recycled.

bottle-feed *vb* to feed (a baby) with milk from a bottle rather than the breast.

bottle green *n* a dark-green colour. ➢ *adj* (**bottle-green**) dark green.

bottleneck *n* **1** a place or thing which impedes or is liable to impede the movement of traffic, esp a narrow or partly-blocked part of a road. **2** something that holds up progress.

bottom *n* **1** the lowest position or part. **2** the point farthest away from the front, top, most important or most successful part: *the bottom of the garden* • *bottom of the class.* **3** the buttocks. **4** the base on which something stands or rests. **5** the ground underneath a sea, river or lake. ➢ *adj* lowest or last. ♦ **at bottom** in reality; fundamentally. **be at the bottom of sth** to be the basic cause of it. **get to the bottom of sth** to discover the real cause of (a mystery or difficulty, etc). ◊ **bottom out** of prices, etc: to reach and settle at the lowest point, esp before beginning to rise again.

bottomless *adj* extremely deep or plentiful.

bottom line *n* **1** *colloq* the essential or most important factor or truth in a situation. **2** the last line of a financial statement, showing profit or loss.

botulism *n, pathol* a severe form of food poisoning, caused by a bacterial toxin that is found in poorly preserved foods.

bouclé /'buːkleɪ/ *n* **1** a type of wool with curled or looped threads. **2** a material made from this.

boudoir /'buːdwɑː(r)/ *n, dated* a woman's private sitting-room or bedroom.

bouffant /'buːfɒnt; *French* bufɑ̃/ *adj* of a hairstyle, or a skirt, sleeve, dress, etc: very full and puffed out.

bougainvillea /buːgən'vɪliə/ *n* a S American climbing shrub.

bough /baʊ/ *n* a branch of a tree.

bouillon /'buːjɒ̃/ *n* a thin clear soup or stock.

boulder *n* a large piece of rock that has been rounded and worn smooth by weathering.

boules /buːl/ *sing n* a form of BOWLS popular in France, played on rough ground, in which players throw metal bowls to land as close as possible to a target bowl (the JACK).

boulevard *n* a broad street in a town or city, esp one lined with trees.

boult see BOLT².

bounce *vb* **1** *intr* of a ball, etc: to spring or jump back from a solid surface. **2** to make (a ball, etc) spring or jump back from a solid surface. **3** *intr* (*often* **bounce about** or **up**) to move or spring suddenly: *The dog bounced about the room excitedly.* **4** (*often* **bounce in** or **out**) to rush noisily, angrily or with a lot of energy, etc, in the specified direction: *He bounced out in a temper.* **5** *colloq* **a** of a bank, etc: to return (a cheque) to the payee because of insufficient funds in the drawer's account; **b** *intr* of a cheque: to be returned to the payee in this way. ➢ *n* **1** the ability to spring back or bounce well. **2** *colloq* energy and liveliness. **3** a jump or leap. **4** the act of springing back from a solid surface. ○ **bouncy** *adj* (**-ier, -iest**) ◊ **bounce back** to recover one's health or good fortune after a difficult or adverse period.

bouncer *n* **1** *colloq, orig US* a person employed by a club, etc to stop unwanted guests entering, and to throw out troublemakers. **2** *cricket* a ball bowled so as to rise sharply off the ground.

bouncing *adj* esp of a baby: strong, healthy and lively.

bound¹ *adj* **1** tied with or as if with a rope or other binding. **2** *in compounds* restricted to or by the specified thing: *housebound* • *snowbound.* **3** obliged. **4** of a book: fastened with a permanent cover. ➢ *vb*, past participle of BIND. ♦ **bound to do sth** certain or obliged to do it. **bound up with sth** closely linked with it.

bound² *adj* **1 a** (*usu* **bound for somewhere** or **sth**) on the way to or going towards it; **b** *following an adv*: *homeward bound.* **2** *in compounds* going in a specified direction: *southbound* • *Manchester-bound.*

bound³ *n* **1** (*usu* **bounds**) a limit or boundary, eg of that which is reasonable or permitted: *His arrogance knows no bounds.* **2** (*usu* **bounds**) a limitation or restriction. **3** (**bounds**) land generally within certain understood limits; the district. ➢ *vb* **1** to form a boundary to or of something; to surround. **2** to set limits or bounds to something; to restrict. ○ **boundless** *adj.* ♦ **out of bounds** usu of a place: not to be visited or entered, etc; outside the permitted limits.

bound⁴ *n* **1** a jump or leap upwards. **2** a bounce (eg of a ball). ➤ *vb, intr* **1** (*often* **bound across, in, out, over** or **up**, *etc*) to spring in the specified direction; to move energetically. **2** to move or run with leaps. **3** of a ball: to bounce back.

boundary *n* (*-ies*) **1** a line or border marking the farthest limit of an area, etc. **2** a final or outer limit to anything: *the boundary of good taste*. **3** the marked limits of a cricket field. **4** *cricket* a stroke that hits the ball across the boundary line, scoring four or six runs.

bounder *n, colloq* a person who behaves dishonourably.

bounteous *adj, literary* **1** generous. **2** of things: freely given; plentiful.

bountiful *adj, now chiefly literary* **1** of a person, etc: generous. **2** ample; plentiful.

bounty *n* (*-ies*) **1** a reward or premium given, esp by a government. **2** *chiefly literary* generosity. **3** a generous gift.

bouquet *n* **1** a bunch of flowers arranged in an artistic way. **2** the delicate smell of wine, etc.

bouquet garni /ˈbuːkeɪ ˈɡɑːniː/ *n* (*bouquets garnis* /ˈbuːkeɪ ˈɡɑːniː/) *cookery* a bunch of mixed herbs used eg in stews to add flavour during cooking.

bourbon /ˈbɜːbən/ *n* a type of whisky made from maize and rye.

bourgeois /ˈbɔːʒwɑː/ *n* (*pl* **bourgeois**) *usu derog* **1** a member of the middle class (**the bourgeoisie**), esp someone regarded as politically conservative and socially self-interested. **2** a person with capitalist, materialistic or conventional values. ➤ *adj* **1** of the middle class or bourgeoisie. **2** in Marxist use: exploiting the working classes.

bourn or **bourne** *n, chiefly Southern Eng* a small stream, esp one that only flows after heavy rains.

bourse /bɔːs/ *n* (*usu* **Bourse**) a European stock exchange, esp that in Paris.

bout *n* **1** a period or turn of some activity. **2** an attack or period of illness. **3** a boxing or wrestling match.

boutique *n* a small shop, esp one selling fashionable clothes.

bouzouki *n* a Greek musical instrument with a long neck and metal strings, related to the mandolin.

bovine *adj* **1** belonging or relating to, or characteristic of, cattle. **2** *derog* of people: dull or stupid.

bovine spongiform encephalopathy /ˈbəʊvaɪn ˈspʌndʒɪfɔːm ɛnkɛfəˈlɒpəθɪ/ *n* a notifiable and fatal brain disease of cattle.

bow¹ /baʊ/ *vb* **1** (*also* **bow down**) to bend (the head or the upper part of the body) forwards and downwards. **2** (*also* **bow down before sb** or **sth**) *intr* to bend the head or the upper part of the body forwards and downwards, usu as a sign of greeting, respect, shame, etc or to acknowledge applause. **3** (*usu* **bow to**) to accept or submit to something, usu unwillingly. ➤ *n* an act of bowing. ♦ **bow and scrape** *derog* to behave with excessive politeness or deference. **take a bow** to acknowledge applause or recognition. ◊ **bow out** to stop taking part; to retire or withdraw.

bow² /bəʊ/ *n* **1 a** a knot made with a double loop, to fasten the two ends of a lace or string, etc; **b** a lace or string, etc tied in such a knot; **c** a looped knot of ribbons, etc used to decorate anything. **2** a weapon made of a piece of flexible wood or other material, bent by a string stretched between its two ends, for shooting arrows. **3** a long, thin piece of wood with horsehair stretched along its length, for playing the violin, etc. **4** anything which is curved in shape, eg a rainbow. ➤ *vb, tr & intr* to bend or make something bend into a curved shape.

bow³ /baʊ/ *naut, n* **1** (*often* **bows**) the front part of a ship or boat. **2** *rowing* the rower nearest the bow.

bowdlerize or **-ise** /ˈbaʊdləraɪz/ *vb* to remove passages or words from (a book or play, etc), esp on moral rather than aesthetic grounds. ○ **bowdlerization** *n.*

bowel *n* **1** an intestine, esp the large intestine in humans. **2** (*usu* **bowels**) the depths or innermost part of something: *the bowels of the earth*.

bower *n* a place in a garden, etc which is enclosed and shaded from the sun by plants and trees.

bowie knife *n* a strong single-edged curved sheath-knife.

bowl¹ *n* **1** a round deep dish for mixing or serving food, or for holding liquids or flowers, etc. **2** (*also* **bowlful**) the amount a bowl holds. **3** the round hollow part of an object, eg of a spoon, pipe, lavatory, etc.

bowl² *n a* a heavy wooden ball for rolling, esp one for use in the game of BOWLS; **b** a similar metal ball used in tenpin bowling. ➤ *vb* **1** to roll (a ball or hoop, etc) smoothly along the ground. **2** *intr* to play bowls, or tenpin bowling, etc. **3** *tr & intr, cricket* to throw (the ball) towards the person batting at the wicket. **4** (*often* **bowl sb out**) *cricket* to put (the batsman) out by hitting the wicket with the ball. **5** (*sometimes* **bowl along** or **on**, *etc*) *intr* to roll or trundle along the ground. **6** (*usu* **bowl along**) to move smoothly and quickly. ◊ **bowl sb over** **1** *colloq* to surprise, delight or impress them thoroughly. **2** to knock them over.

bow legs /baʊ/ *pl n* legs which curve out at the knees. ○ **bow-legged** *adj* of a person: having bow legs.

bowler¹ *n* **1** a person who bowls the ball in cricket, etc. **2** a person who plays bowls.

bowler² *n* (*also* **bowler hat**) a hard, usu black, felt hat, with a rounded crown and a narrow curved brim.

bowline /ˈbaʊlɪn/ *n, naut* **1** a rope used to keep

a sail taut against the wind. **2** (*also* **bowline knot**) a knot which makes a loop that will not slip at the end of a piece of rope.

bowling *n* **1** the game of BOWLS. **2** a game (eg esp TENPIN BOWLING) played indoors, in which a ball is rolled along an alley at a group of skittles. **3** *cricket* the act, practice or a turn or spell of throwing the ball towards the person batting at the wicket.

bowls *sing n* a game played on smooth grass with bowls (see BOWL²), the object being to roll these as close as possible to a smaller ball called the JACK.

bowsprit /ˈbaʊsprɪt/ *n, naut* a spar projecting from the front of a ship, often with ropes from the sails fastened to it.

bowstring *n, archery* the string on a bow.

bow tie /boʊ/ *n* a necktie which is tied in a double loop to form a horizontal bow at the collar.

bow window /boʊ/ *n* a window which projects towards the centre, forming a curved shape.

box¹ *n* **1** a container made from wood, cardboard or plastic, etc, usu square or rectangular and with a lid. **2** (*also* **boxful**) the amount a box holds. **3** *a in compounds* a small enclosed area, shelter or kiosk, etc for a specified purpose: *telephone box • witness box*; **b** in a theatre, etc: a separate compartment for a group of people, containing several seats; **c** (*often* **horse box**) an enclosed area for a horse in a stable or vehicle. **4** an area in a field, pitch, road, printed page, etc marked out by straight lines. **5** (**the box**) *Brit colloq* **a** the television; **b** *football* the penalty box. **6** an individually allocated pigeonhole at a newspaper office or other agency, in which mail is collected to be sent on to, or collected by, the person it is intended for: *Reply to box number 318.* ➤ *vb* **1** (*also* **box up**) to put something into a box or boxes. **2** (**box sb** or **sth in** or **up**) to confine or enclose them or it. ○ **boxlike** *adj*.

box² *vb* **1** *tr & intr* to fight someone with the hands formed into fists and protected by thick leather gloves, esp as a sport. **2** *colloq* to hit (esp someone's ears) with the fist, or sometimes the hand. ➤ *n, colloq* (usu **a box on the ears**) a punch with the fist, or sometimes a cuff or slap, esp on the ears.

box³ *n* **1** (*also* **boxtree**) an evergreen shrub or small tree with small leathery paired leaves. **2** (*also* **boxwood**) the hard durable fine-grained yellow wood of this tree.

boxer *n* **1** a person who boxes, esp as a sport. **2** a breed of dog with a muscular body and a short broad muzzle with pronounced jowls.

boxer shorts *pl n* (*also* **boxers**) underpants resembling shorts, with a front opening.

box girder *n, eng* a hollow girder made of steel, timber or concrete.

boxing *n* the sport of fighting with the fists.

Boxing Day *n* in the UK and the Commonwealth: the first weekday after Christmas, ob-

served as a public holiday.

box number *n* a box, or the number of a box (see BOX¹ *noun* sense 6) at a newspaper office or post office, etc to which mail, eg replies to advertisements, may be sent.

box office *n* **1** an office at which theatre, cinema or concert tickets, etc are sold. **2** **a** theatrical entertainment seen in terms of its commercial value: *The new show is wonderful box office*; **b** theatrical entertainment seen in terms of its popular appeal, ie its ability to attract an audience.

box pleat *n* on a skirt or dress: a large double pleat formed by folding the material in two pleats facing in opposite directions.

boxroom *n, chiefly Brit* a small room, usu without a window, used esp for storage.

boy *n* **1** a male child. **2** a son: *He's our youngest boy.* **3** a young man, esp one regarded as still immature. ○ **boyhood** *n.* ○ **boyish** *adj*.

boycott *vb* **1** to refuse to have any business or social dealings with (a company or a country, etc), usu as a form of disapproval or coercion. **2** to refuse to handle or buy (goods), as a way of showing disapproval or of exerting pressure, etc. ➤ *n* an act or instance of boycotting.

boyfriend *n* a regular male friend and companion, esp as a partner in a romantic or sexual relationship.

bp *abbrev* (*also* **BP**) blood pressure.

Bq *symbol* becquerel.

Br¹ *abbrev* **1** Britain. **2** British.

Br² *symbol, chem* bromine.

bra *n* a woman's undergarment which supports and covers the breasts.

brace *n* **1** a device, usu made from metal, which supports, strengthens or holds two things together. **2** (**braces**) *Brit* straps worn over the shoulders, for holding trousers up. **3** a wire device worn on the teeth to straighten them. **4** *building, etc* a tool used by carpenters and metalworkers to hold a BIT² and enable it to be rotated (see also BRACE AND BIT). **5** *printing* either of two symbols, { and }, used to connect lines, figures, staves of music, parts of text, etc. **6** (*in pl also* **brace**) a pair or couple, esp of game birds. **7** *naut* a rope attached to a ship's YARD¹ (sense 2), used for adjusting the sails. ➤ *vb* **1** to make something tight or stronger, usu by supporting it in some way. **2** (**brace oneself**) to prepare oneself for a blow or shock, etc.

brace and bit *n* a hand tool for drilling holes, consisting of a BRACE with the drilling BIT² in place.

bracelet *n* a band or chain worn as a piece of jewellery round the arm or wrist.

brachiopod /ˈbreɪkɪəpɒd/ *n* (**brachiopods** or **brachiopoda** /-ˈɒpədə/) *zool* an invertebrate marine animal with a shell consisting of two unequal valves.

bracing *adj* of the wind, air, etc: stimulatingly cold and fresh.

bracken *n* the commonest fern in the UK,

which has tall fronds, and spreads rapidly.

bracket *n* **1** *non-technical* either member of several pairs of symbols, ( ), [ ], { }, < > , used to group together or enclose words, figures, etc. **2** *usu in compounds* a group or category falling within a certain range: *It's out of my price bracket.* **3** an L-shaped piece of metal or strong plastic, used for attaching shelves, etc to walls. ➤ *vb* **1** to enclose or group (words, etc) together in brackets. **2** (*usu* **bracket sb** or **sth together**) to put them or it into the same group or category.

brackish *adj* of water: slightly salty.

bract *n, bot* a modified leaf, usu smaller than a true leaf and green in colour, in whose AXIL or INFLORESCENCE develops.

brae / breɪ/ *n, Scot* a slope or a hill.

brag *vb* (**bragged, bragging**) *intr, derog* to talk boastfully about oneself. ➤ *n* **1** a boastful statement or boastful talk. **2** a card game similar to poker.

braggart *n* someone who brags a lot.

Brahman or (*esp formerly*) **Brahmin** *n* a Hindu who belongs to the highest of the four major CASTES, traditionally the priestly order.

braid *n* **1** a band or tape, often made from threads of gold and silver twisted together, used as a decoration on uniforms, etc. **2** *now chiefly N Am* a length of interwoven hair. ➤ *vb* **1** to interweave (several lengths of thread or hair, etc) together. **2** to decorate something with braid. ○ **braiding** *n*.

Braille or **braille** *n* a system of printing for the blind, consisting of dots which can be read by touch.

brain *n* **1** the highly developed mass of nervous tissue that co-ordinates and controls the activities of the central nervous system of animals. **2** (*esp* **brains**) *colloq* cleverness; intelligence. **3** (*esp* **brains** or **the brains**) *colloq* a very clever person. **4** (*usu* **the brains**) *colloq* a person who thinks up and controls a plan, etc. ➤ *vb, colloq* to hit someone hard on the head. ○ **brainless** *adj*. ♦ **have sth on the brain** *colloq* to be unable to stop thinking about it.

brainchild *n* a person's particular and original theory, idea or plan.

brain death *n* the functional death of the parts of the brain that control breathing and other vital reflexes, so that the affected person is incapable of surviving without the aid of a ventilator. ○ **brain-dead** *adj*.

brain drain *n, colloq* the steady loss of scientists, academics, professionals, etc to another country.

brainstorm *n, colloq* a sudden loss of the ability to think clearly and act properly or sensibly.

brainstorming *n* the practice of trying to solve problems by group discussion in which suggestions are made spontaneously.

brainteaser *n* a difficult exercise or puzzle.

brainwash *vb* to force someone to change their beliefs, etc by applying continual and prolonged mental pressure. ○ **brainwashing** *n*.

brainwave *n* **1** *colloq* a sudden, bright or clever idea. **2** a wave representing the pattern of electrical activity in the brain.

brainy *adj* (**-ier, -iest**) *colloq* intelligent.

braise *vb* to cook (meat, vegetables, etc) slowly with a small amount of liquid in a closed dish.

brake¹ *n* **1** a device used to slow down or stop a moving vehicle or machine, or to prevent the movement of a parked vehicle. **2** anything which makes something stop or prevents or slows down progress, etc: *a brake on public spending.* ➤ *vb* **1** *intr* to apply or use a brake. **2** to use a brake to make (a vehicle) slow down or stop.

brake² *n* an area of wild rough ground covered with low bushes, etc.

bramble *n* **1** (*also* **bramble-bush**) a blackberry bush. **2** any other wild prickly shrub. **3** *esp Scot* a blackberry. ○ **brambly** *adj*.

bran *n* the outer covering of cereal grain, removed during the preparation of white flour.

branch *n* **1** an offshoot arising from the trunk of a tree or the main stem of a shrub. **2** a main division of a railway line, river, road or mountain range. **3** a local office of a large company or organization. **4** a subdivision or section in a family, subject, group of languages, etc. ➤ *vb, intr* (*esp* **branch off**) **1** to divide from the main part: *a road branching off to the left.* **2** (*sometimes* **branch out** or **branch out from sth**) to send out branches, or spread out from it as a branch or branches. ◊ **branch out** to develop different interests or projects, etc.

brand *n* **1** a distinctive maker's name or trademark, symbol or design, etc used to identify a product or group of products. **2** a variety or type. **3** an identifying mark on cattle, etc, usu burned on with a hot iron. **4** (*also* **branding-iron**) a metal instrument used for branding animals. **5** a sign or mark of disgrace or shame. ➤ *vb* **1** to mark (cattle, etc) with a hot iron. **2** to give someone a bad reputation. **3** to fix a brand or trademark, etc upon (a product or group of products).

brandish *vb* to flourish (a weapon, etc) as a threat or display.

brand-new *adj* completely new.

brandy *n* (**-ies**) a strong alcoholic drink distilled from grape wine.

brash *adj* **1** very loud, flashy or showy. **2** impudent, overbearingly forward. ○ **brashness** *n*.

brass *n* (*pl* **brasses** or when treated as pl in collective senses 3 and 5 **brass**) **1** an alloy of copper and zinc. **2** an ornament, tool or other object made of brass, or such objects collectively. **3** (*sing or pl noun*) **a** wind instruments made of brass, such as the trumpet and horn; **b** the people who play brass instruments in an orchestra. **4** a piece of flat engraved brass in a church, in memory of someone who has died. **5** (*usu* **top brass** or **the brass**) *colloq* people in authority or of high military rank collectively. **6** *colloq, esp N Eng* money. ➤ *adj* made of brass. ♦ **brassed off** *Brit slang* fed up.

brass band n a band consisting mainly of brass instruments.

brasserie n a small and usu inexpensive restaurant, serving food, and orig beer.

brassica n any member of a genus of plants that includes cabbage, cauliflower, broccoli, brussels sprout, turnip, swede.

brassière /'brazɪə(r)/ n the full name for BRA.

brass rubbing n 1 a copy of the design on a BRASS (sense 4) made by putting paper on top of it and rubbing with coloured wax or charcoal. 2 the process of making such a copy.

brass tacks pl n, colloq the essential details; the basic principles or practicalities.

brassy adj (-ier, -iest) 1 esp of colour: like brass in appearance. 2 of sound: similar to a brass musical instrument; hard, sharp or strident. 3 colloq of a person: loudly confident and rude. 4 flashy or showy.

brat n, derog a child, esp a badly-behaved one.

bravado n (bravados or bravadoes) a display of confidence or daring, often a boastful one.

brave adj 1 of a person, or their character, actions, etc: having or showing courage in facing danger or pain, etc. 2 chiefly literary or old use fine or excellent, esp in appearance. ➤ n, formerly a warrior, esp one from a Native American tribe. ➤ vb to meet or face up to (danger, pain, etc) boldly. ○ **bravery** n.

bravo exclam shouted to express one's appreciation at the end of a performance, etc: well done! excellent! ➤ n a cry of 'bravo'.

bravura n 1 a display of great spirit, dash or daring. 2 mus esp in vocal music: virtuosity, spirit or brilliance in performance.

brawl n a noisy quarrel or fight, esp in public. ➤ vb, intr to quarrel or fight noisily.

brawn n 1 muscle; muscular or physical strength. 2 jellied meat made from pig's head and ox-feet. ○ **brawny** adj (-ier, -iest).

bray vb 1 intr of a donkey: to make its characteristic loud harsh cry. 2 intr of a person: to make a loud harsh sound. 3 to say something in a loud harsh voice. ➤ n 1 the loud harsh braying sound made by a donkey. 2 any loud harsh grating cry or sound.

braze vb, eng to join (two pieces of metal) by melting an alloy with a lower melting point than either of the metals to be joined, and applying it to the joint.

brazen adj 1 (also **brazen-faced**) bold; impudent; shameless. 2 made of brass or like brass. ○ **brazenly** adv. ◇ **brazen out** to face (an embarrassing or difficult situation) boldly and shamelessly.

brazier[1] /'breɪzɪə(r)/ n a portable metal container for holding burning coal or charcoal.

brazier[2] /'breɪzɪə(r)/ n a person who works in brass.

Brazilian adj belonging or relating to the country of Brazil or its inhabitants. ➤ n a citizen or inhabitant of, or person born in, Brazil.

brazil nut n an edible long white nut from a S American tree.

breach n 1 an act of breaking, esp breaking of a law or promise, etc. 2 a serious disagreement. 3 a gap, break or hole. ➤ vb 1 to break (a promise, etc). 2 to make an opening or hole in something.

bread n 1 a staple food prepared from flour mixed with water or milk, kneaded into a dough with a leavening agent, eg yeast, and baked. 2 (often **daily bread**) food and the other things one needs to live. 3 slang money. ➤ vb to cover (a piece of food) with breadcrumbs before cooking.

bread and butter n a means of earning a living.

breadfruit n (breadfruit or breadfruits) 1 a SE Asian tree. 2 the large oval edible fruit of this tree, which can be baked whole and eaten.

breadline n a queue of poor people waiting for handouts of food. ◆ **on the breadline** of a person or people: having hardly enough food and money to live on.

breadth n 1 the measurement from one side of something to the other. Compare LENGTH. 2 an area, section or extent (eg of cloth) taken as the full or standard width. 3 openness and willingness to understand and respect other people's opinions and beliefs, etc. 4 extent, size.

breadwinner n the person who earns money to support a family.

break vb (past tense **broke**, past participle **broken**, present participle **breaking**) 1 tr & intr to divide or cause something to become divided into two or more parts as a result of stress or a blow. 2 a intr of a machine or tool, etc: to become damaged, so as to stop working and be in need of repair; b to damage (a machine or tool, etc) in such a way. 3 to fracture a bone in (a limb, etc). 4 to burst or cut (the skin, etc). 5 to do something not allowed by (a law, agreement, promise, etc). 6 to exceed or improve upon (a sporting record, etc). 7 intr to stop work, etc for a short period of time. 8 to interrupt (a journey, one's concentration, etc). 9 intr of a boy's voice: to become lower in tone on reaching puberty. 10 to defeat or destroy something: They finally broke the strike. 11 to force something open with explosives. 12 intr of a storm: to begin violently. 13 tr & intr of news, etc: to make or cause something to become known: He was away when the story broke. 14 intr (also **break up**) to disperse or scatter: The crowd broke up. 15 to reduce the force of (a fall or a blow, etc). 16 intr of waves, etc: to collapse into foam. 17 to lose or disrupt the order or form of something: Don't break ranks. 18 intr of the weather: to change suddenly, esp after a fine spell. 19 tr & intr to cut or burst through: The sun was breaking through the clouds. 20 intr to come into being: Day broke. 21 tr & intr to make or become weaker. 22 to make someone bankrupt. 23 to decipher (a code, cipher). 24 to prove (an alibi, etc). 25 to interrupt the flow of electricity in (a circuit). 26 intr, snooker to take

the first shot at the beginning of a game. **27** *tr &
intr, tennis* to win a game when one's opponent
is serving. **28** *intr, boxing* to come out of a
clinch. **29** to make someone give up (a bad
habit, etc). ➢ ➢ **1** an act or result of breaking.
2 a a pause, interval or interruption in some
ongoing activity or situation; **b** (*also* **break-
time**) a short interval in work or lessons, etc. **3**
a change or shift from the usual or overall
trend: *a break in the weather*. **4** a sudden rush,
esp to escape: *Let's make a break for it.* **5** *colloq*
a chance or opportunity to show one's ability,
etc, often a sudden or unexpected one. **6** *colloq* a piece of luck: *lucky break*. **7** *snooker, billiards, etc* a series of successful shots played
one after the other. **8** *snooker, billiards, etc* the
opening shot of a game. **9** *tennis* an instance of
winning a game when one's opponent is serving. **10** an interruption in the electricity flowing
through a circuit. **11** *mus* in jazz, etc: a short
improvised solo passage. ○ **breakable** *adj*.
♦ **break camp** to pack up the equipment after
camping. **break even** to make neither a profit
nor a loss in a transaction. **break the ice** *colloq*
to overcome the awkwardness on a first meeting. **break wind** to expel gas from the body
through the anus. ◊ **break away 1** to escape
from control, esp suddenly or forcibly. **2** to put
an end to one's connection with a group or custom, etc, esp suddenly. **break down 1** of a machine, etc: to stop working properly. **2** to
collapse, disintegrate or decompose. **3** of a
person: to give way to emotions. **4** of human
relationships: to be unsuccessful and so come
to an end. **5** of a person: to suffer a nervous
breakdown. **break sth down 1** to use force to
crush or knock it down. **2** to divide it into separate parts and analyse it. **break in 1** to enter a
building by force, esp to steal things inside. **2**
(*also* **break in on sth**) to interrupt (a conversation, etc). **break sb in** to train or familiarize
them in a new job or role. **break sth in 1** to use
or wear (new shoes, etc) so that they lose their
stiffness, etc. **2** to train (a horse) to carry a saddle and a rider. **break off 1** to become detached
by breaking. **2** to come to an end abruptly. **3** to
stop talking. **break sth off 1** to detach it by
breaking. **2** to end a relationship, etc abruptly.
break out 1 to escape from a prison, etc using
force. **2** to begin suddenly: *War broke out.* **3** (*esp*
break out in sth) to become suddenly covered
in (spots or a rash, etc). **break through 1** to
force a way through. **2** to make a new discovery or be successful, esp after an unsuccessful
period. **break up 1** to break into pieces. **2** to
come to an end. **3** of people: to end a relationship or marriage. **4** of a school or a pupil: to end
term and begin the holidays. **break sth up 1** to
divide it into pieces. **2** to make it finish or come
to an end.

breakage *n* **1** the act of breaking. **2** a broken
object; damage caused by breaking.

breakaway *n* an act of breaking away or escaping. ➢ *adj, always before its noun* that has
broken away: *a breakaway republic*.

breakdown *n* **1** a failure in a machine or device. **2** a failure or collapse of a process: *a
breakdown in communications.* **3** a process or
act of dividing something into separate parts
for analysis. **4** (*also* **nervous breakdown**) a failure or collapse in a person's mental health.

breaker *n* a large wave which breaks on rocks
or on the beach.

breakfast *n* the first meal of the day. ➢ *vb, intr*
to have breakfast.

break-in *n* an illegal entry by force into a building, esp to steal property inside.

breaking point *n* the point at which something, esp a person or relationship, can no
longer stand up to a stress or strain, and breaks
down.

breakneck *adj* of speed: dangerously, fast.

breakout *n* an act or instance of breaking out,
esp an escape by force: *a mass breakout from
the city jail.*

breakthrough *n* a decisive advance or discovery.

break-up *n* **1** the ending of a relationship or situation. **2** the scattering or dividing up of
something.

breakwater *n* a strong barrier built out from a
beach to break the force of the waves.

bream *n* (*pl* **bream**) **1** any of various freshwater
fish of the carp family which have a deep body
covered with silvery scales. **2** (*usu* **sea bream**)
an unrelated deep-bodied marine fish.

breast *n* **1** *anat* in women: each of the two
mammary glands, which form soft protuber-
ances on the chest. **2** the front part of the body
between the neck and the belly. **3** the part of a
garment covering the breast. ➢ *vb* **1** to face, or
fight against something. **2** to come to the top of
(a hill, etc).

breastbone *n, non-technical* the STERNUM.

breastfeed *vb, tr & intr* to feed (a baby) with
milk from the breast.

breastplate *n* a piece of armour which protects the chest.

breaststroke *n* a style of swimming breast-
downwards in the water, in which the arms
are pushed out in front and then pulled outward and backward together.

breastwork *n, fortification* a temporary defensive wall, reaching to about chest-height.

breath *n* **1** *physiol* the air drawn into, and then
expelled from, the lungs. **2** exhaled air as
odour, vapour or heat. **3** a single inhalation of
air: *a deep breath.* **4** a faint breeze. **5** a slight
hint or rumour. **6** a slight trace of perfume,
etc. **7** life: *not while I have breath in my body.*
♦ **catch one's breath 1** to stop breathing for a
moment, from fear, amazement or pain, etc. **2**
to stop doing something until one's normal
breathing rate returns. **out of** or **short of
breath** breathless, esp after strenuous exercise. **take one's** or **sb's breath away** *colloq* to
astound or amaze one or them. **under one's
breath** in a whisper.

Breathalyser *n, trademark* a device used to

test the amount of alcohol on a driver's breath. ○ **breathalyse** vb.

breathe vb **1** tr & intr to respire by alternately drawing air into and expelling it from the lungs. **2** tr & intr to say, speak or sound quietly. **3** intr to take breath; to rest or pause: *I haven't had a moment to breathe*. **4** intr of fabric, etc: to allow air and moisture, etc to pass through. **5** intr of wine: to develop flavour when exposed to the air. **6** to live; to continue to draw breath. **7** intr to blow softly. ♦ **breathe again** or **easily** or **easy** or **freely** colloq to feel relieved after a period of anxiety or fear. **breathe one's last** euphem to die.

breather n, colloq a short break from work or exercise.

breathing-space n a short time allowed for rest.

breathless adj **1** having difficulty in breathing normally, because of illness or from hurrying, etc. **2** very eager or excited. **3** with no wind or fresh air. ○ **breathlessly** adv. ○ **breathlessness** n.

breathtaking adj very surprising, exciting or impressive.

breathy adj (-ier, -iest) of a voice: accompanied by a sound of unvocalized breathing.

breech n **1** the back part of a gun barrel, where it is loaded. **2** old use the buttocks.

breeches or (chiefly N Am) **britches** pl n short trousers fastened usu just below the knee: *riding breeches*.

breed vb (**bred**) **1** intr of animals and plants: to reproduce sexually. **2** to make (animals or plants) reproduce sexually. **3** to make or produce: *Dirt breeds disease*. **4** to train, bring up or educate (children, etc) in a specified way. ➤ n **1** an artificially maintained subdivision within an animal species, produced by domestication and selective breeding, eg Friesian cattle. **2** a race or lineage. **3** a kind or type. ○ **breeder** n.

breeding n **1** biol the process of controlling the manner in which plants or animals reproduce. **2** the result of a good education and training, social skills, manners, etc. **3** the act of producing offspring.

breeze¹ n **1** a gentle wind. **2** colloq a pleasantly simple task. ➤ vb, intr, colloq to move briskly, in a confident manner.

breeze² n ashes from coal, coke or charcoal.

breezeblock n a type of brick made from BREEZE² and cement, used for building houses, etc.

breezy adj (-ier, -iest) **1** rather windy. **2** of a person: lively, confident and casual: *You're bright and breezy today.*

brent goose or (esp N Am) **brant goose** n the smallest and darkest of the black geese, which has a white marking on each side of the neck.

brethren see under BROTHER

breve n **1** a mark (˘) sometimes put over a vowel to show that it is short or unstressed. **2** mus a note twice as long as a SEMIBREVE

(now only rarely used).

breviary n (-ies) RC Church a book containing the hymns, prayers and psalms which form the daily service.

brevity n **1** the use of few words. **2** shortness of time.

brew vb **1** to make (eg beer) by mixing, boiling and fermenting. **2** (also **brew up**) tr & intr to make (tea, etc) by mixing the leaves, etc with boiling water. **3** intr to be in the process of brewing. **4** (also **brew up**) intr to get stronger and threaten: *There's a storm brewing.* ➤ n **1** a drink produced by brewing, esp tea or beer. **2** a concoction or mixture: *a heady brew of passion and intrigue.* ○ **brewer** n. ○ **brewery** n (-ies).

briar¹ or **brier** n any of various prickly shrubs, esp a wild rose bush.

briar² or **brier** n **1** a shrub or small tree, native to S Europe, with a woody root. **2** a tobacco pipe made from this root.

bribe n **1** a gift, usu of money, offered to someone to persuade them to do something illegal or improper. **2** something offered to someone in order to persuade them to behave in a certain way. ➤ vb **1** usu tr to offer or promise a bribe, etc to someone. **2** to gain influence over someone, by offering a bribe. ○ **bribery** n.

bric-à-brac n small ornamental objects of little financial value kept as decorations.

brick n **1** a rectangular block of baked clay used for building. **2** the material used for making bricks. **3** a child's plastic or wooden building block. **4** something in the shape of a brick: *a brick of ice cream.* ➤ adj **1** made of brick or of bricks. **2** (also **brick-red**) having the dull brownish-red colour of ordinary bricks. ➤ vb (usu **brick in** or **over** or **up**) to close, cover, fill in or wall up (eg a window) with bricks.

brickbat n an insult.

bricklayer n in the building trade: a person who builds with bricks.

bridal adj belonging or relating to a bride or a wedding.

bride n a woman who has just been married, or is about to be married.

bridegroom n a man who has just been married, or is about to be married.

bridesmaid n a girl or woman who attends the bride at a wedding.

bridge¹ n **1** a structure that spans a river, road, railway, etc, providing a continuous route across it for pedestrians, vehicles or trains. **2** anything that joins or connects two separate things or parts of something, or that connects across a gap. **3** on a ship: the narrow raised platform from which the officers direct its course. **4** the hard bony upper part of the nose. **5** in a pair of spectacles: the part of the frame that rests on the bridge of the nose, connecting the two lenses. **6** on a violin or guitar, etc: a thin, upright piece of wood, which supports the strings and keeps them stretched tight. **7** dentistry a fixed replacement for one or more missing teeth, consisting of a partial denture that is secured to adjacent natural teeth. ➤ *vb* **1** to form or build a bridge over (eg a river or railway). **2** to make a connection across something, or close the two sides of (a gap, etc): *We bridged our differences.*

bridge² *n, cards* a game which developed from WHIST, for four people playing in pairs.

bridgehead *n, mil* a fortified position held at the end of a bridge which is nearest to the enemy.

bridle *n* **1** the leather straps put on a horse's head which help the rider to control the horse. **2** anything used to control or restrain. ➤ *vb* **1** to put a bridle on (a horse). **2** to bring something under control. **3** (*esp* **bridle at sth** or *sometimes* **bridle up**) *intr* to show anger or resentment, esp by moving the head upwards proudly or indignantly.

bridle path or **bridle way** *n* a path for riding or leading horses along.

brief *adj* **1** lasting only a short time. **2** short or small: *a brief pair of shorts.* **3** of writing or speech: using few words. ➤ *n* **1** *law* **a** a summary of the facts and legal points of a case, prepared for the barrister who will be dealing with the case in court; **b** a case taken by a barrister; **c** *colloq* a barrister. **2** (*also* **briefing**) instructions given for a task. **3** (**briefs**) a woman's or man's close-fitting underpants without legs. **4** (*also* **papal brief**) *RC Church* a letter from the Pope written on a matter of discipline. ➤ *vb* **1** to prepare someone by giving them instructions in advance. **2** *law* **a** to inform (a barrister) about the facts of a case; **b** to retain (a barrister) as counsel. ○ **briefly** *adv.* ♦ **in brief** in few words.

briefcase *n* a light, usu flat, case for carrying papers, etc.

brier see BRIAR¹, BRIAR²

brig *n* a type of sailing ship with two masts and square sails.

brigade *n* **1** one of the subdivisions in the army, consisting eg of a group of regiments, usu commanded by a BRIGADIER. **2** *esp in compounds* a group of people organized for a specified purpose: *the fire brigade.*

brigadier *n* **a** an officer commanding a brigade; **b** a senior officer in the British Army and Royal Marines.

brigand *n* a member of a band of robbers, esp one operating in a mountain area.

brigantine *n* a two-masted sailing ship.

bright *adj* **1** giving out or shining with much light. **2** of a colour: strong, light and clear. **3** lively; cheerful. **4** *colloq* clever and quick to learn. **5** full of hope or promise: *a bright future.* ➤ *adv* brightly. ○ **brightly** *adv.* ○ **brightness** *n.*

brighten *vb, tr & intr* (*often* **brighten up**) **1** to become, or make, bright or brighter. **2** to become or make someone become happier or more cheerful.

brill *n* (**brills** or **brill**) a large flatfish which has a freckled sandy brown body.

brilliant *adj* **1** very bright and sparkling. **2** of a

colour: bright and vivid. **3** of a person: showing outstanding intelligence or talent. **4** *colloq* exceptionally good. **5** (*usu* **brilliant-cut**) *technical* of a gem, esp a diamond: cut so as to have a lot of facets, so that it sparkles brightly. ➤ *n* a diamond or other gem. ○ **brilliance** *n.*

brim *n* **1** the top edge or lip of a cup, bowl, etc. **2** the projecting edge of a hat. ➤ *vb* (**brimmed**, **brimming**) *intr* to be, or become, full to the brim. ○ **brimful** *adj.* ○ **brimless** *adj.*

brimstone *n, old use* sulphur.

brindled *adj* of animals: brown or grey, and marked with streaks of a darker colour.

brine *n* **1** very salty water, used for preserving food. **2** *literary* the sea.

bring *vb* (**brought**) **1** to carry or take something or someone to a stated or implied place or person. **2** to make someone or something be in, or reach, a certain state: *It brought him to his senses.* **3** to make or result in something: *War brings misery.* **4** (*esp* **bring oneself**) *usu with negatives* to persuade, make or force oneself (to do something unpleasant). **5** (*esp* **bring in**) to be sold for (a stated price); to produce (a stated amount) as income. **6** to make (a charge or action, etc) against someone. ◊ **bring about** to make something happen; to cause it. **bring back** to make (a thought or memory) return. **bring sb down 1** to make them sad or disappointed, etc. **2** to demean them. **bring sth down** to make it fall or collapse. **bring forward 1** to move (an arrangement, etc) to an earlier date or time. **2** *bookkeeping* to transfer (a partial sum) to the head of the next column. **bring in 1** to introduce something or make it effective, etc. **2** to produce (income or profit). **bring off** *colloq* to succeed in doing (something difficult). **bring sb over** or **round** or **around** to convince them that one's own opinions, etc are right. **bring sb round** to cause them to recover consciousness. **bring sb to** to make (someone who is asleep or unconscious) wake up. **bring sb up** to care for and educate them when young. **bring up 1** to introduce (a subject) for discussion. **2** to vomit (something eaten).

brink *n* **1** the edge or border of a steep dangerous place or of a river. **2** the point immediately before something dangerous, unknown or exciting, etc starts or occurs: *the brink of disaster.* ♦ **on the brink of sth** at the very point or moment when it might start or occur, etc.

brinkmanship or **brinksmanship** *n* esp in politics: the practice of going to the very edge of a dangerous situation (eg war) before withdrawing.

briny *adj* (**-ier, -iest**) of water: very salty. ➤ *n* (**the briny**) *colloq* the sea.

briquette or **briquet** *n* a block made of compressed coal-dust or charcoal, etc, used for fuel.

brisk *adj* **1** lively, active or quick: *a brisk walk.* **2** of the weather: pleasantly cold and fresh. ○ **briskly** *adv.*

brisket *n* meat from the breast of a bull or cow.

brisling *n* a small marine fish of the herring family.

bristle *n* **1** a short stiff hair on an animal or plant. **2** something similar to this but artificial, used eg for brushes. ➤ *vb* **1** *tr & intr* of an animal's or a person's hair: to stand upright and stiff. **2** (*usu* **bristle with sth**) *intr* to show obvious anger or rage, etc: *bristling with resentment*. **3** (*usu* **bristle with sth**) *intr* to be covered or closely-packed with (upright objects). ○ **bristly** *adj*.

Brit *n, colloq* a British person.

Brit. *abbrev* **1** Britain. **2** British.

Britannic *adj, formal* in some official titles: belonging or relating to Britain: *His Britannic Majesty.*

britches see BREECHES

British *adj* **1** belonging or relating to Great Britain or its inhabitants. **2** belonging or relating to the British Empire or to the Commonwealth. **3** belonging or relating to the variety of English used in Britain. ➤ *n* (**the British**) the people of Great Britain.

British Summer Time *n* the system of time (one hour ahead of GREENWICH MEAN TIME) used in Britain during the summer to give extra daylight in the evenings.

Briton *n* **1** a British person. **2** (*also* **ancient Briton**) *hist* one of the Celtic people living in Southern Britain before the Roman conquest.

brittle *adj* **1** of a substance: hard but easily broken or likely to break. **2** sharp or hard in quality: *a brittle laugh.* **3** of a condition or state, etc: difficult to keep stable or controlled.

broach *vb* **1** to raise (a subject) for discussion. **2** to open (a bottle, barrel, etc) to remove liquid. **3** to open (a bottle or other container) and start using its contents. ➤ *n* **1** a long tapering pointed tool for making and rounding out holes. **2** a roasting-spit.

> **broach** There is sometimes a spelling confusion between **broach** and **brooch**.

B-road *n* in the UK: a secondary road. Compare A-ROAD.

broad *adj* **1** large in extent from one side to the other. **2** wide and open; spacious. **3** general, not detailed: *a broad inquiry.* **4** clear; full: *in broad daylight.* **5** strong; obvious: *a broad hint.* **6** concentrating on the main elements rather than on detail: *the broad facts of the case.* **7** tolerant or liberal: *I'm taking a broad view.* **8** of an accent or speech: strongly marked by local dialect or features: *broad Scots.* **9** usu of a joke, etc: rather rude. ➤ *n* **1** *US offensive slang* a woman. **2** (**the Broads**) a series of low-lying shallow lakes connected by rivers in E Anglia. ○ **broadly** *adv* widely; generally.

broadband *adj* **1** *telecomm* across, involving or designed to operate across a wide range of frequencies. **2** *comput* capable of accommodating data from a variety of input sources, such as voice, telephone, TV, etc.

broad bean *n* **1** an annual plant of the bean family. **2** one of the large flattened pale green edible seeds growing in pods on this plant.

broadcast *vb* **1** *tr & intr* to transmit (a radio or TV programme, speech, etc) for reception by the public. **2** *intr* to take part in a radio or TV broadcast. **3** to make something widely known. **4** to sow (seeds) by scattering them. ➤ *n* a radio or TV programme. ○ **broadcaster** *n*. ○ **broadcasting** *n*.

broaden *vb* (*also* **broaden out**) *tr & intr* to become or make something broad or broader.

broadloom *adj* esp of a carpet: woven on a wide loom to give broad widths.

broad-minded *adj* tolerant of other people's opinions, preferences, habits, etc.

broadsheet *n* a newspaper printed on large sheets of paper. Compare TABLOID.

broadside *n* **1** a strongly critical verbal attack. **2** *navy* **a** all of the guns on one side of a warship; **b** the firing of all of these guns simultaneously.

broadsword *n, old use* a heavy sword with a broad blade, used for cutting with a two-handed swinging action.

brocade *n* a heavy silk fabric with a raised design on it, often using one silver or silver threads.

broccoli *n* (**broccolis**) a type of cultivated cabbage or its immature flower buds eaten as a vegetable.

brochure *n* a booklet or pamphlet, esp one giving information about holidays, products, etc.

broderie anglaise *n* open embroidery used for decorating cotton and linen.

brogue[1] *n*, (*usu* **brogues**) a type of strong heavy-soled leather shoe, with decorative punched holes.

brogue[2] *n* a strong but gentle accent, esp the type of English spoken by an Irish person.

broil *vb* **1** *chiefly N Am* to grill (food). **2** *intr* to be extremely hot.

broiler *n* **1** a small chicken suitable for broiling. **2** esp *N Am* a grill.

broke *adj, colloq* **1** bankrupt. **2** short of money.

broken *adj* **1** smashed; fractured. **2** disturbed or interrupted. **3** not working properly. **4** of a promise, agreement or law, etc: not kept. **5** of a marriage or family, etc: split apart by divorce. **6** of language, esp speech: not perfect or fluent. **7** usu of a person: brought down, weakened and tired out.

broken chord *n, mus* an ARPEGGIO.

broken-down *adj* **1** of a machine, etc: not in working order. **2** of an animal or person: not in good condition.

broken-hearted *adj* overwhelmed with sadness or grief.

broker *n* **1** a person employed to buy and sell stocks and shares. **2** *in compounds* a person who acts as an agent for other people in buying and selling goods or property: *insurance broker.* **3** a negotiator or middleman.

brokerage *n* the profit taken by, or fee charged by, a broker for transacting business for other people.

brolly n (*-ies*) *chiefly Brit colloq* an UMBRELLA (*noun* sense 1).

bromide n *chem* a compound of bromine, esp one used medicinally as a sedative.

bromine n, *chem* a non-metallic element consisting of a dark-red highly-corrosive liquid with a pungent smell, used in photographic film.

bronchial *adj, anat* relating to either of the bronchi.

bronchitis n, *pathol* inflammation of the mucous membrane of the bronchi.

bronchus /ˈbrɒŋkəs/ n (*bronchi* /-kaɪ/) either of the two main airways to the lungs that branch off the lower end of the TRACHEA.

bronco n a wild or half-tamed horse from the western US.

brontosaurus /brɒntəˈsɔːrəs/ n (*brontosauri* /-raɪ/) a herbivorous dinosaur with a long neck and small head.

bronze n 1 an alloy of copper and tin. 2 the dark orangey-brown colour of bronze. 3 a BRONZE MEDAL. 4 a work of art made of bronze. ➤ *adj* 1 made of bronze. 2 having the colour of bronze. ➤ *vb, intr* to become the colour of bronze.

Bronze Age n (*usu* the Bronze Age) the period in the history of humankind, between about 3000 and 1000 BC, when tools, weapons, etc were made out of bronze.

bronze medal n in athletics, etc: a medal given to the competitor who comes third.

brooch n a piece of jewellery with a hinged pin at the back for fastening it to clothes.

> **brooch** There is sometimes a spelling confusion between **brooch** and **broach**.

brood n 1 a number of young animals, esp birds, that are produced or hatched at the same time. 2 *colloq, usu humorous* all the children in a family. 3 a kind, breed or race of something. ➤ *vb, intr* 1 of a bird: to sit on (eggs) in order to hatch them. 2 (*often* **brood about, on** or **over**) to think anxiously or resentfully about something for a period of time. ○ **brooding** *adj*.

broody *adj* (*-ier, -iest*) 1 of a bird: ready and wanting to brood. 2 of a person: introspective. 3 *colloq* of a woman: eager to have a baby.

brook[1] n a small stream.

brook[2] *vb, formal, usu with negatives* to tolerate or accept: *I shall brook no criticism.*

broom n 1 a a long-handled sweeping brush, formerly made from the stems of the broom plant; b a BESOM. 2 any of various deciduous shrubby plants of the pea family.

broomstick n the long handle of a BROOM (sense 1).

Bros *abbrev* (*used esp in the name of a company*) Brothers.

broth n a thin clear soup made by boiling meat, fish or vegetables, etc in water.

brothel n a house where men can go to have sexual intercourse with prostitutes for money.

brother n (*brothers* or (*archaic or formal except in sense 3*) *brethren*) 1 a boy or man with the same natural parents as another person or people. 2 a man belonging to the same group, trade union, etc as another or others. 3 (*pl brethren*) a man who is a member of a religious group, esp a monk. ○ **brotherly** *adj*.

brotherhood n 1 an association of men formed for a particular purpose, esp a religious purpose. 2 a sense of companionship or unity, etc felt towards people one has something in common with. 3 the state of being a brother.

brother-in-law n (*brothers-in-law*) 1 the brother of one's husband or wife. 2 the husband of one's sister. 3 the husband of the sister of one's own wife or husband.

brouhaha /ˈbruːhɑːhɑː/ n noisy, excited and confused activity.

brow n 1 (*usu* brows) short form of EYEBROW. 2 the forehead. 3 the top of a hill, road or pass, etc. 4 the edge of a cliff, etc.

browbeat *vb* to intimidate someone by speaking angrily or by looking fierce.

brown *adj* 1 having the colour of dark soil or wood. 2 of bread, etc: made from wholemeal flour. 3 having a dark skin. 4 having a skin tanned from being in the sun. ➤ *n* 1 any of various dark earthy colours, like those of bark, coffee, etc. 2 brown paint, dye, pigment, material or clothes. ➤ *vb, tr & intr* to become or cause to become brown by cooking, tanning in the sun, etc.

browned off *adj, colloq* bored or discouraged.

brownie n 1 *folklore* a friendly goblin, traditionally said to help with domestic chores. 2 a small square piece of chewy chocolate cake containing nuts.

Brownie Guide or **Brownie** n a girl belonging to the junior section of the Guides Association in Britain (see GUIDE *noun* sense 4). Compare CUB (*noun* sense 2).

brownie point or **Brownie point** n, *colloq, usu ironic or facetious* an imaginary mark of approval awarded for doing something helpful, etc.

browning n, *cookery, chiefly Brit* a substance used to turn gravy a rich brown colour.

brown rice n unpolished rice from which only the fibrous husk has been removed, leaving the yellowish-brown bran layer intact.

browse *vb, tr & intr* 1 to look through a book, etc, or look around a shop, etc in a relaxed or haphazard way. 2 of certain animals, eg deer: to feed by continually nibbling on young buds, shoots, leaves, etc as opposed to grazing. 3 *comput* to examine information stored in (a database, etc). ➤ *n* an act of browsing.

brucellosis n, *vet med* an infectious disease, mainly affecting cattle.

bruise n 1 an area of skin discoloration and swelling caused by the leakage of blood from damaged blood vessels following injury. 2 a similar injury to a fruit or plant, shown as a soft discoloured area. ➤ *vb* **1** to mark and discolour (the surface of the skin or of a fruit, etc) in this way. **2** *intr* to develop bruises. **3** *tr & intr* to hurt (someone's feelings, pride, etc) or be hurt emotionally.

bruiser *n, colloq* a big strong person, esp one who likes fighting or who looks aggressive.

brunch *n, colloq* a meal that combines breakfast and lunch, eaten late in the morning.

brunette or (*US*) **brunet** *n* a woman or girl with brown or dark hair. ➤ *adj* of hair colour: brown, usu dark brown.

brunt *n* (*esp* **the brunt of**) the main force or shock of (a blow, attack, etc).

brush¹ *n* **1** a tool with lengths of stiff nylon, wire, hair, bristles or something similar set into it, used for tidying the hair, cleaning, painting, etc. **2** an act of brushing. **3** a light grazing contact. **4** a short encounter, esp a fight or disagreement: *a brush with the law*. **5** a fox's bushy tail. **6** *elec* a metal or carbon conductor that maintains sliding contact between the stationary and moving parts of an electric motor or generator. ➤ *vb* **1** to sweep, groom or clean (the hair, teeth, a floor, etc) with a brush. **2** (*also* **brush against**) *tr & intr* to touch lightly in passing. ◊ **brush sth** or **sb aside** to pay no attention to it or them. **brush sth** or **sb off** to refuse to listen to it or them. **brush up** to tidy one's appearance, etc. **brush up (on)** to refresh one's knowledge of (a language or subject, etc).

brush² *n* BRUSHWOOD.

brushed *adj* of a fabric: treated by a brushing process so that it feels soft and warm.

brush-off *n* (*usu* **the brush-off**) *colloq* an act of ignoring, rebuffing or dismissing someone in an offhand manner.

brushwood *n* **1** dead, broken or lopped-off branches and twigs, etc from trees and bushes. **2** small trees and bushes on rough land. **3** rough land covered by such trees and bushes.

brushwork *n* a particular technique a painter uses to apply the paint to a canvas, etc.

brusque *adj* of a person or their manner, etc: blunt and often impolite. ○ **brusquely** *adv*. ○ **brusqueness** *n*.

Brussels sprout or **brussels sprout** *n* (*usu as pl* **Brussels sprouts** or (*colloq*) **sprouts**) a type of cabbage or one of its swollen edible buds cooked and eaten as a vegetable.

brut *adj* of sparkling wines, esp champagne: very dry.

brutal *adj* **1** savagely cruel or violent. **2** ruthlessly harsh or unfeeling. ○ **brutality** *n* (*-ies*). ○ **brutally** *adv*.

brutalism *n* applied to art, architecture, etc: deliberate crudeness or harshness of style.

brutalize or **-ise** *vb* **1** to make someone or something brutal. **2** to treat someone or something brutally. ○ **brutalization** *n*.

brute *n* **1** a cruel, brutal or violent person. **2** an animal other than a human. ➤ *adj* **1** instinctive, not involving rational thought: *brute force*. **2** coarse, crudely sensual or animal-like. **3** in its natural or raw state: *brute nature*. ○ **brutish** *adj*.

bryony *n* (*-ies*) a climbing plant which has tiny yellowish-green flowers followed by highly poisonous red berries.

BSc *abbrev* Bachelor of Science.

BSE *abbrev* bovine spongiform encephalopathy.

BST *abbrev* British Summer Time.

Bt *abbrev* Baronet.

bubble *n* **1** a thin film of liquid forming a hollow sphere filled with air or gas. **2** a ball of air or gas which has formed in a solid or liquid. **3** a dome made of clear plastic or glass. **4** a sound of or like bubbling liquid. ➤ *vb, intr* **1** to form or give off bubbles, or to rise in bubbles. **2** (*often* **bubble away**) to make the sound of bubbling liquid. **3** (*often* **bubble over with sth**) to be full of or bursting with (happiness, excitement, enthusiasm, good ideas, etc).

bubble and squeak *n, cookery, chiefly Brit* cooked cabbage and potatoes fried together.

bubble gum *n* a type of chewing gum which can be blown into bubbles.

bubbly *adj* (*-ier, -iest*) **1** having bubbles, or being like bubbles. **2** of a person or their character: lively and cheerful. ➤ *n, colloq* champagne.

bubo /ˈbjuːboʊ/ *n* (**buboes**) *pathol* a swollen tender lymph node, esp in the armpit or groin. ○ **bubonic** *adj*.

bubonic plague *n, pathol* the commonest form of plague, characterized by the development of buboes, and known in the Middle Ages as the Black Death.

buccaneer *n, hist & literary* a pirate, esp in the Caribbean during the 17c.

buck¹ *n* **1** a male animal, esp a male deer, goat, antelope, rabbit, hare or kangaroo. **2** an act of bucking. ➤ *vb* **1** *intr* of a horse, etc: to make a series of rapid jumps into the air, with the back arched and legs held stiff. **2** of a horse, etc: to throw (a rider) from its back in this way. **3** *colloq* to oppose or resist (an idea or trend, etc). ◊ **buck up** *colloq* **1** to become more cheerful. **2** to hurry up. **3** *colloq* to make someone more cheerful. **4** *colloq* to improve or liven up (one's ways or ideas, etc).

buck² *n, colloq* **1** *N Am, Aust, NZ, etc* a dollar. **2** *S Afr* a rand.

buck³ *n, cards* in the game of poker: a token object placed before the person who is to deal the next hand. ♦ **pass the buck** *colloq* to shift the responsibility for something onto someone else.

bucket *n* **1** a round open-topped container for holding liquids and solids such as sand, etc. **2** (*also* **bucketful**) the amount a bucket holds. **3** *colloq* a rubbish-bin. **4** the scoop of a dredging machine. ➤ *vb, colloq* (*also* **bucket down**) *intr* of rain: to pour down heavily.

bucket shop *n, derog colloq chiefly Brit* a travel agent that sells cheap airline tickets.

buckle *n* a flat piece of metal or plastic, etc usu

attached to one end of a strap or belt, with a pin in the middle which goes through a hole in the other end of the strap or belt to fasten it. ➤ *vb, tr & intr* **1** to fasten with a buckle. **2** to bend (metal, etc) out of shape, using or as a result of great heat or force. ◊ **buckle down to sth** *colloq* to begin working seriously on it.

buckler *n, hist* a small round shield, usu with a raised centre.

buckram *n* cotton or linen stiffened with SIZE², used to line clothes or cover books, etc.

buckshee *adj, adv, slang* free of charge.

buckshot *n* a large type of lead shot used in hunting.

buckskin *n* **1** a strong greyish-yellow leather made from the skin of deer. **2** a strong smooth twilled woollen fabric.

buckthorn *n* any of various shrubs or small trees, esp a thorny deciduous shrub with black berries.

bucktooth *n* a large front tooth which sticks out. ◊ **bucktoothed** *adj*.

buckwheat *n* **1** a fast-growing plant with leathery leaves and clusters of tiny pink or white flowers. **2** the greyish-brown triangular seeds of this plant, which can be cooked whole, or ground into flour.

bucolic / bjʊˈkɒlɪk/ *adj* concerned with the countryside or people living there.

bud *n* **1** in a plant: an immature knob-like shoot that will eventually develop into a leaf or flower. **2** a flower or leaf that is not yet fully open. **3** *biol* in yeasts and simple animals: a small outgrowth from the body of the parent that becomes detached and develops into a new individual. ➤ *vb* (**budded, budding**) **1** *intr* of a plant, etc: to develop buds. **2** *biol* of a yeast or a simple animal: to reproduce asexually by the production of buds (*noun* sense 3). ◆ **nip sth in the bud** to put a stop to it at a very early stage.

Buddhism *n* a religion that originated in India, founded by the Buddha, Siddhartha Gautama, in the 6c BC, and based on his teachings regarding freedom from human concerns and desires. ◊ **Buddhist** *n, adj*.

budding *adj* of a person: developing; beginning to show talent in a specified area: *a budding pianist*.

buddleia / ˈbʌdlɪə/ *n* any of various deciduous shrubs or small trees with long pointed fragrant flower heads which attract butterflies.

buddy *n* (*-ies*) *colloq, esp N Am* (sometimes shortened to **bud**, when used as a term of address in these senses) **a** a friend; **b** a term of address used to a man, often expressing a degree of annoyance or aggression, etc.

budge *vb, tr & intr* **1** to move, or to make something or someone move. **2** to change one's mind, or make someone change their mind.

budgerigar *n* (*also colloq* **budgie**) a type of small parrot native to Australia.

budget *n* **1** a plan, esp one covering a particular period of time, specifying how money

coming in will be spent and allocated. **2** (**the Budget**) *Brit* a periodic assessment of and programme for national revenue and expenditure, proposed by the government. **3** the amount of money set aside for a particular purpose. ➤ *adj* low in cost: *budget holidays*. ➤ *vb* **1** *intr* to calculate how much money one is earning and spending, so that one does not spend more than one has. **2** (*usu* **budget for**) *intr* to plan, arrange or allow for (a specific expense) in a budget. **3** to provide (an amount of money, or sometimes time, etc) in a budget. ◊ **budgetary** *adj*.

buff¹ *n, colloq, usu in compounds* a person who is enthusiastic about and knows a lot about a specified subject: *an opera buff*.

buff² *n* **1** a dull-yellowish colour. **2** a soft undyed leather. **3** (*sometimes* **buffer**) a cloth or pad of buff (*noun* sense 2) or other material, used for polishing. ➤ *adj* **1** dull yellow in colour. **2** made of buff (*noun* sense 2): *a military buff coat*. ➤ *vb* **1** (*also* **buff up**) to polish something with a buff or a piece of soft material. **2** to make (leather) soft like buff. ◆ **in the buff** *Brit colloq* naked.

buffalo *n* (**buffalo** or **buffaloes**) **1** (*also* **African buffalo**) a member of the cattle family, native to S and E Africa, which has a heavy black or brown body and thick upward-curving horns. **2** (*also* **Indian buffalo**) a member of the cattle family, native to SE Asia, the wild form of which has a black coat. **3** sometimes used generally to refer to the American BISON.

buffer¹ *n* **1** an apparatus designed to take the shock when an object such as a railway carriage hits something. **2** a person or thing which protects from harm or shock, etc, or makes its impact less damaging or severe. **3** *comput* a temporary storage area for data that is being transmitted from the central processing unit to an output device such as a printer. **4** *chem* a chemical solution that maintains its pH at a constant level when an acid or alkali is added to it.

buffer² *n, Brit colloq* a rather foolish or dull person, esp a man.

buffer state or **buffer zone** *n* a neutral country or zone situated between two rival powers.

buffet¹ / ˈbʊfeɪ; *US* bəˈfeɪ/ *n* **1** a meal set out on tables from which people help themselves. **2** a place, room or counter, etc where light meals and drinks may be bought.

buffet² / ˈbʌfɪt/ *n* **1** a blow with the hand or fist. **2** a stroke or blow, esp a heavy or repeated one: *a sudden buffet of wind*. ➤ *vb* (**buffeted, buffeting**) **1** to strike or knock with the hand or fist. **2** to batter repeatedly: *a ship buffeted by the waves*.

buffoon *n* **1** a person who sets out to amuse people with comic behaviour. **2** someone who does foolish things. ◊ **buffoonery** *n*.

bug *n* **1** the common name for any of thousands of insects with a flattened oval body and mouthparts modified to form a beak for piercing and sucking. **2** *N Am* a popular name for any kind of insect. **3** *colloq* a popular name for a bacterium or virus that causes infection or illness. **4** *colloq* a small hidden microphone. **5** *colloq* a fault in a machine or computer program which stops it from working properly. **6** *colloq* an obsession or craze: *the skiing bug.* ➤ *vb* (**bugged, bugging**) **1** *colloq* to hide a microphone in (a room, telephone, etc) so as to be able to listen in to any conversations carried on there. **2** *slang* to annoy someone.

bugbear *n* an object of fear or annoyance.

bugger *coarse slang, n* **1** a person who practises anal sex. **2** a person or thing considered to be difficult or awkward. **3** a person one feels affection or pity for: *poor bugger.* ➤ *vb* **1** to practise anal sex with someone. **2** to exhaust someone. **3** (*also* **bugger up**) to ruin something. ➤ *exclam* (*also* **bugger it!**) expressing annoyance or frustration. ◊ **bugger about** or **around** to waste time. **bugger sb about** to mislead them or cause them problems. **bugger off** to go away.

buggery *n* anal sex.

buggy *n* (**-ies**) **1** a light open carriage pulled by one horse. **2** a light folding pushchair for a small child. **3** (*also* **baby buggy**) *N Am* a pram. **4** *often in compounds* a small motorized vehicle, used for a specified purpose: *beach buggy.*

bugle *n* a brass instrument similar to a small trumpet, used mainly for sounding military calls. ➤ *vb, intr* to sound a bugle. ○ **bugler** *n*.

build *vb* (**built**) **1** to make or construct something from parts. **2** (*also* **build up**) *intr* to increase gradually in size, strength, amount, intensity, etc: *Outside the excitement was building.* **3** to make something in a specified way or for a specified purpose: *built to last.* **4** to control the building of something; to have something built: *The government built two new housing schemes.* ➤ *n* physical form, esp that of the human body. ◊ **build sb** or **sth up** to speak with great enthusiasm about them or it. **build sth up** to build or amass it in stages or gradually.

builder *n* a person who builds, or organizes and supervises the building of, houses, etc.

building *n* **1** the business, process, art or occupation of constructing houses, etc. **2** a structure with walls and a roof, such as a house.

building society *n, Brit* a finance company that lends money to its members for buying or improving houses, and in which customers can invest money in accounts to earn interest.

build-up *n* **1** a gradual increase. **2** a gradual approach to a conclusion or climax. **3** publicity or praise of something or someone given in advance of its or their appearance.

built-in *adj* **1** built to form part of the main structure or design of something, and not as a separate object: *built-in wardrobes.* **2** included as, forming or designed as an integral part of something: *built-in insurance cover.* **3** present naturally, by genetic inheritance, etc.

built-up *adj* **1** of land, etc: covered with build-

ings. **2** increased in height by additions to the underside: *built-up shoes.* **3** made up of separate parts.

bulb *n* **1** in certain plants, eg tulip and onion: a swollen underground organ that functions as a food store and consists of a modified shoot and roots growing from its lower surface. **2** a flower grown from a bulb. **3** a light-bulb.

bulbous *adj* **1** fat, bulging or swollen. **2** having or growing from a bulb.

bulge *n* **1** a swelling, esp where one would expect to see something flat. **2** a sudden and usu temporary increase, eg in population. ➤ *vb, intr* (*often* **bulge out** or **bulge with sth**) to swell outwards: *a sack bulging with presents.*

bulghur or **bulgur** *n* wheat that has been boiled, dried, lightly milled and cracked.

bulimia /bʊ'lɪmɪə/ *n, med, psychol* a disorder in which bouts of excessive eating are followed by self-induced vomiting or laxative abuse. ○ **bulimic** *adj.*

bulk *n* **1** size, esp when large and awkward. **2** the greater or main part of something. **3** a large body, shape, structure or person. **4** a large quantity: *buy in bulk.* **5** dietary fibre. ○ **bulky** *adj.* ◆ **bulk large** to be or seem important: *an issue which bulks large in his mind.*

bulkhead *n* a wall in a ship or aircraft, etc which separates one section from another.

bull¹ *n* **1** the uncastrated male of animals in the cattle family. **2** the male of the elephant, whale and some other large animals. **3** *stock exchange* someone who buys shares hoping to sell them at a higher price at a later date. Compare BEAR² (*noun sense 4*). **4** *colloq* a BULL'S-EYE (*sense I*). ➤ *adj* **1** male: *a bull walrus.* **2** *stock exchange* of a market: rising. **3** massive; coarse; strong. ◆ **take the bull by the horns** to deal boldly with a challenge.

bull² *n* **1** *slang* meaningless, pretentious talk. **2** an illogical nonsensical statement.

bull³ *n* an official letter or written instruction from the Pope.

bulldog *n* a breed of dog with a heavy body and a large square head with a flat upturned muzzle.

bulldoze *vb* **1** to use a bulldozer to move, flatten or demolish something. **2** (**bulldoze sb into sth**) to force them to do something they do not want to do. **3** to force something through against all opposition: *He bulldozed his scheme through the Council.*

bulldozer *n* a large, powerful, heavy tractor with a vertical blade at the front, for pushing heavy objects, clearing the ground or making it level.

bullet *n* a small metal cylinder for firing from a gun.

bulletin *n* **1** a short official statement of news issued as soon as the news is known. **2** a short printed newspaper or leaflet, esp one produced regularly by a group or organization.

bulletin board *n* **1** *N Am* a noticeboard. **2** *comput* an electronic data system containing messages and programs accessible to a number of users.

bullet-proof *adj* of a material, etc: strong enough to prevent bullets passing through.

bullfight *n* a public show, esp in Spain and Portugal, etc in which people bait, and usu ultimately kill, a bull. ○ **bullfighter** *n*. ○ **bullfighting** *n*.

bullfinch *n* a small bird of the finch family, the male of which has a conspicuous red breast.

bullfrog *n* any of various large frogs with a loud call.

bullion *n* gold or silver that has not been coined, esp in large bars, or in mass.

bullish *adj* aggressively confident.

bullock *n* a castrated bull.

bullring *n* an arena where bullfights take place.

bull's-eye *n* 1 the small circular centre of a target used in shooting or darts, etc. 2 *darts, etc* a shot which hits this. 3 *colloq* anything which hits its target or achieves its aim, etc.

bullshit *coarse slang, n* 1 nonsense. 2 deceptive, insincere or pretentious talk. ➤ *vb* 1 to talk bullshit to someone, esp in order to deceive them. 2 *intr* to talk bullshit. ○ **bullshitter** *n*.

bull terrier *n* a breed of dog with a heavy body and a short smooth coat.

bully¹ *n* (*-ies*) a person who hurts, frightens or torments weaker or smaller people. ➤ *vb* (*bullies, bullied*) 1 to threaten or persecute (them). 2 (*bully sb into sth*) to force them to do something they do not want to do. ○ **bullying** *n*. ♦ **bully for you!** *colloq, ironic* good for you!

bully² or **bully beef** *n* esp in the armed services: corned beef; tinned or pickled beef.

bully³ *vb* (*bullies, bullied*) *intr* (*usu bully off*) *hockey, formerly* to begin or re-start a game by performing a **bully** or **bully-off**, a move involving hitting one's stick three times against an opponent's before going for the ball.

bulrush *n* 1 a tall waterside plant with one or two spikes of tightly packed dark-brown flowers. 2 *Bible* a papyrus plant.

bulwark *n* 1 a wall built as a defence, often one made of earth; a rampart. 2 a BREAKWATER or sea-wall. 3 someone or something that defends a cause. 4 (*esp bulwarks*) *naut* the side of a ship projecting above the deck.

bum¹ *n, Brit colloq* 1 the buttocks. 2 *coarse* the anus.

bum² *colloq, esp N Am & Aust, n* 1 someone who lives by begging. 2 someone who is lazy and shows no sense of responsibility. ➤ *adj* dud or useless. ➤ *vb* (*bummed, bumming*) 1 to get something by begging, borrowing or cadging: *He bummed a lift.* 2 (*usu bum around* or *about*) *intr* to spend one's time doing nothing in particular. ○ **bummer** *n*.

bum bag *n, Brit colloq* a small bag on a belt, worn round the waist.

bumble *vb, intr* 1 (*often bumble about*) to move or do something in a clumsy way. 2 to speak in

a confused or confusing way. ○ **bumbling** *adj*.

bumble-bee *n* a large hairy black and yellow bee.

bumf or **bumph** *n, Brit colloq* miscellaneous useless leaflets, official papers and documents, etc.

bump *vb* 1 *tr & intr* to knock or hit someone or something, esp heavily or with a jolt. 2 to hurt or damage (eg one's head) by hitting or knocking it. 3 (*usu bump together*) *intr* of two moving objects: to collide. 4 (*also bump along*) *intr* to move or travel with jerky or bumpy movements. ➤ *n* 1 a knock, jolt or collision. 2 a dull sound caused by a knock or collision, etc. 3 a lump or swelling on the body, esp one caused by a blow. 4 a lump on a road surface. ○ **bumpy** *adj* (*-ier, -iest*). ◊ **bump into sb** *colloq* to meet them by chance. **bump sb off** *slang* to kill them. **bump up** *colloq* to increase or raise (eg production or prices).

bumper *n, Brit* a bar on the front or back of a motor vehicle which lessens the shock or damage if it hits anything. ➤ *adj* exceptionally good or large: *a bumper edition.*

bumpkin *n, colloq, usu derog* an awkward or simple person from the countryside.

bump-start *vb* to start (a car) by pushing it and engaging the gears while it is moving. ➤ *n* (**bump start**) an act or instance of bump-starting a car.

bumptious *adj* irritatingly conceited or self-important.

bun *n* 1 *esp Brit* **a** a small, round, usu sweetened, roll, often containing currants, etc; **b** a small round cake of various types, eg an individual sponge cake. 2 a mass of hair fastened in a round shape on the back of the head.

bunch *n* 1 a number of things fastened or growing together. 2 (*usu bunches*) long hair divided into two sections and tied separately at each side or the back of the head. 3 *colloq* a group or collection. 4 *colloq* a group of people: *The drama students are a strange bunch.* ➤ *vb, tr & intr* (*sometimes bunch up*) to group (people or things) together in, or to form a bunch or bunches.

bundle *n* 1 a number of things loosely fastened or tied together. 2 a loose parcel, esp one contained in a cloth. 3 (*also vascular bundle*) *bot* one of many strands of conducting vessels or fibres in the stems and leaves of plants. 4 *slang* a large amount of money. ➤ *vb* 1 (*often bundle up*) to make something into a bundle or bundles. 2 to put quickly and unceremoniously, roughly or untidily: *They bundled him into a taxi.* 3 (**bundle with**) *marketing* to sell (a product) along with (another related product) as a single package.

bun fight *n, Brit colloq* a noisy occasion or function.

bung *n* a small round piece of wood, rubber or cork, etc used to close a hole eg in the top of a jar. ➤ *vb* 1 (*esp bung up*) **a** to block (a hole) with a bung; **b** *colloq, esp in passive* to block, plug or clog something: *My nose is bunged up.* **2** *slang* to throw or put something somewhere in a careless way: *Just bung my coat in there.*

bungalow *n* a single-storey house.

bungee jumping *n* a pastime in which a person jumps from a height with strong rubber cables attached to their ankles to ensure that they bounce up before they reach the ground.

bungle *vb, tr & intr* to do (something) carelessly or badly. ➤ *n* carelessly or badly done work; a foul-up. ○ **bungler** *n.* ○ **bungling** *n, adj.*

bunion *n* a painful swelling on the first joint of the big toe.

bunk¹ *n* **1** a narrow bed attached to the wall in a cabin in a ship, caravan, etc. **2** a BUNK BED. ➤ *vb, intr, colloq* (*esp* **bunk down**) to lie down and go to sleep, esp in some improvised place.

bunk² *n, Brit slang* (*usu* **do a bunk**) leaving the place where one ought to be, usu furtively: *He did a bunk from gym.* ◊ **bunk off** to stay away from school or work, etc when one ought to be there.

bunk bed *n* each of a pair of single beds fixed one on top of the other.

bunker *n* **1** an obstacle on a golf course consisting of a hollow area containing sand. **2** a large container for storing fuel. **3** an underground shelter.

bunkum or (*chiefly US*) **buncombe** *n, colloq* nonsense.

bunny *n* (*-ies*) (*also* **bunny rabbit**) a child's word for a RABBIT.

Bunsen burner /ˈbʌnsən/ *n* a gas burner, used mainly in laboratories, with an adjustable inlet hole which allows the gas-air mixture to be controlled so as to produce a very hot flame with no smoke.

bunting¹ *n* a row of small flags on a string.

bunting² *n* any of various small finch-like birds with a short stout bill.

buoy /bɔɪ; *N Am* ˈbuːɪ/ *n* a brightly-coloured floating object fastened to the bottom of the sea by an anchor, to warn ships of rocks, etc or to mark channels, etc. ➤ *vb* **1** to mark (eg an obstruction or a channel) with a buoy or buoys. **2** (*usu* **buoy up**) to keep something afloat. **3** (*usu* **buoy up**) to lift the spirits of someone. **4** (*often* **buoy up**) to sustain, support or boost something: *Profits were buoyed by the new economic confidence.* **5** *intr* to rise or float to the surface.

buoyant /ˈbɔɪənt; *N Am* ˈbuːjənt/ *adj* **1** of an object: able to float in or on the surface of a liquid. **2** of a liquid or gas: able to keep an object afloat. **3** of a person: cheerful; resilient. ○ **buoyancy** *n* (*-ies*).

bur or **burr** *n* **1** any seed or fruit with numerous hooks or prickles. **2** any plant that produces such seeds or fruits.

burble *vb* **1** (*often* **burble on** or **away**) *intr* to speak at length but with little meaning or purpose. **2** *intr* of a stream, etc: to make a bubbling murmuring sound. **3** to say something in a way

that is hard to understand, esp very quickly or incoherently. ➤ *n* a bubbling murmuring sound.

burbot *n* (*burbot* or *burbots*) a large fish, the only freshwater species in the cod family.

burden¹ *n* **1** something to be carried. **2** a duty or obligation, etc which is time-consuming, costly, or hard to endure. **3** the carrying of a load or loads: *a beast of burden.* ➤ *vb* to weigh someone down (with a burden, difficulty, problem, etc). ○ **burdensome** *adj.*

burden² *n* **1** the main theme, esp of a book or speech, etc. **2** a line repeated at the end of each verse of a song.

burdock *n* any of various plants, with heart-shaped lower leaves and spiny fruits or burrs.

bureau /ˈbjʊroʊ/ *n* (**bureaux** or **bureaus** /-roʊz/) **1** *Brit* a desk for writing at, with drawers and usu a front flap which opens downwards to provide the writing surface. **2** *N Am* a chest of drawers. **3** an office for business, esp for collecting and supplying information. **4** *N Am* a government or newspaper department.

bureaucracy *n* (*-ies*) **1** a system of government by officials who are responsible to their department heads and are not elected. **2** these officials as a group, esp when regarded as oppressive. **3** any system of administration in which matters are complicated by complex procedures and trivial rules.

bureaucrat *n* **1** a government official. **2** an official who follows rules rigidly, so creating delays and difficulties. ○ **bureaucratic** *adj.*

burette *n, chem* a long vertical glass tube marked with a scale and having a tap at the bottom, used to deliver controlled volumes of liquid.

burgeon *vb, intr* (*sometimes* **burgeon forth**) to grow or develop quickly; to flourish.

burger *n* **1** a hamburger. **2** *esp in compounds* a hamburger covered with something: *cheeseburger.* **3** *esp in compounds* an item of food shaped like a hamburger but made of something different: *nutburger.*

burgh /ˈbʌrə/ *n* in Scotland until 1975: an incorporated town or borough, with a certain amount of self-government under a town council.

burgher *n, dated or facetious* a citizen of a town, esp a town on the Continent, or of a borough.

burglar *n, law* a person who commits the crime of BURGLARY.

burglary *n* (*-ies*) *law* the crime of entering a building illegally in order to steal, or to commit another crime. Compare ROBBERY.

burgle *vb* **1** to enter (a building, etc) illegally and steal from it. **2** *intr* to commit burglary.

burgundy *n* (*-ies*) **1** a wine made in the Burgundy region of France, esp a red wine. **2** a deep or purplish-red colour. ➤ *adj* deep or purplish-red in colour.

burial *n* the burying of a dead body in a grave.

burk see BERK

burlesque *n* **1** a piece of literature, acting or some other presentation which exaggerates or mocks a serious subject or art form. **2** *N Am* a type of theatrical entertainment involving humorous sketches, songs and usu striptease. ➤ *adj* belonging to or like a burlesque.

burly *adj* (**-ier, -iest**) of a person: strong and heavy in build.

Burmese *adj* belonging or relating to Burma (since 1989 officially called Myanmar), its inhabitants or their language. ➤ *n* **1** a citizen or inhabitant of, or person born in, Burma. **2** the official language of Burma.

burn¹ *vb* (**burned** or **burnt**) **1** *tr & intr* to be on fire or set something on fire. **2** *tr & intr* to damage or injure someone or something, or be damaged or injured, by fire or heat. **3** to use something as fuel. **4** *tr & intr* to char or scorch someone or something, or become charred or scorched. **5** to make (a hole, etc) by or as if by fire or heat, etc: *Acid can burn holes in material.* **6** *intr* to be or feel hot. **7** *tr & intr* to feel or make something feel a hot or stinging pain: *Vodka burns my throat.* **8** (*usu* **be burning to do sth**) *intr, colloq* to want to do it very much: *He's burning to get his revenge.* **9** (*esp* **be burning with sth**) *intr* to feel strong emotion: *I was burning with shame.* **10** to use (coal, oil, etc) as fuel. **11** *tr & intr* to kill someone or die by fire. ➤ *n* **1** an injury or mark caused by fire, heat, acid, friction, etc. **2** an act of firing the engines of a space rocket so as to produce thrust. ◆ **burn one's boats** or **bridges** *colloq* to do something which makes it impossible for one to return to one's former situation or way of life, etc. **burn one's fingers** or **get one's fingers burnt** *colloq* to suffer as a result of getting involved in something foolish, dangerous, etc. **burn the candle at both ends** to exhaust oneself by trying to do too much, usu by starting work early in the morning and staying up late at night. **burn the midnight oil** to work late into the night. ◊ **burn sb** or **oneself out** to exhaust them or oneself by too much work or exercise. **burn sth out** to make it stop working from overuse or overheating.

burn² *n, chiefly Scot* a small stream.

burner *n* **1** the part of a gas lamp or stove, etc which produces the flame. **2** a piece of equipment, etc for burning something.

burning *adj* **1** on fire. **2** feeling extremely hot. **3** very strong or intense. **4** very important or urgent: *the burning question.*

burnish *vb* to make (metal) bright and shiny by polishing. ➤ *n* polish; lustre.

burnous *n* (**burnouses** or **burnous**) a long cloak with a hood, worn by Arabs.

burn-out *n* physical or emotional exhaustion caused by overwork or stress.

burp *colloq, vb* **1** *intr* to let air escape noisily from one's stomach through one's mouth. **2** to rub or pat (a baby) on the back to help get rid of air in its stomach. ➤ *n* a belch.

burr¹ *n* **1** in some accents of English: a rough 'r'

sound pronounced at the back of the throat. **2** a continual humming sound made eg by a machine. **3** a rough edge on metal or paper. **4** a small rotary drill used by a dentist or surgeon.

burr² see BUR

burrito *n* (**burritos**) a Mexican dish consisting of a TORTILLA folded around a filling.

burrow *n* a hole in the ground, esp one dug by a rabbit or other small animal for shelter. ➤ *vb* **1** (*esp* **burrow in** or **into** or **through** or **under sth**) *tr & intr* to make (a hole) or tunnel in or under it. **2** *intr* of an animal: to make burrows or live in a burrow. **3** (*esp* **burrow away, down, in** or **into sth**) *tr & intr* of a person: to keep (oneself, or something belonging to oneself, etc) cosy, protected or hidden away. **4** *intr* (*usu* **burrow into sth**) to search deeply into it.

bursar *n* **1** a treasurer in a school, college or university. **2** in Scotland and New Zealand: a student or pupil who has a bursary.

bursary *n* (**-ies**) **1** esp in Scotland and New Zealand: a grant of money made to a student. **2** the bursar's room in a school, college, etc.

burst *vb* (**burst**) **1** *tr & intr* to break or fly open or into pieces, usu suddenly and violently, or cause something to do this. **2** (*esp* **burst in, into** or **out of somewhere** or **sth**) *intr* to make one's way suddenly or violently into or out of it, etc. **3** (*usu* **burst onto**) *intr* to appear suddenly in (a specified circle or area) and be immediately important or noteworthy: *She burst onto the political scene.* **4** *intr* **a** to be completely full; **b** to break open; to overflow, etc: *My suitcase is bursting*; **c** to be overflowing with or unable to contain (one's excitement, anger or other emotion). ➤ *n* **1** an instance of bursting or breaking open. **2** the place where something has burst or broken open, or the hole or break, etc made by it bursting. **3** a sudden, brief or violent period of some activity, eg speed, gunfire, applause.

burton *n, Brit slang* now only in the phrase **gone for a burton** meaning: **1** lost for good. **2** dead, killed or drowned. **3** broken or destroyed.

bury *vb* (**buries, buried**) **1** to place (a dead body) in a grave, the sea, etc. **2** to hide something in the ground. **3** to put something out of sight; to cover: *He buried his face in his hands.* **4** to put something out of one's mind or memory: *Let's bury our differences.* **5** to occupy (oneself) completely with something: *She buried herself in her work.* ◆ **bury the hatchet** to stop quarrelling and become friends again.

bus *n* (**buses** or (*chiefly US*) **busses**) **1** a large road vehicle which carries passengers to and from established stopping points along a fixed route for payment. **2** *comput* a set of electrical conductors that form a channel along which data or power may be transmitted to and from all the main components of a computer. ➤ *vb* (**buses** or **busses, bused** or **bussed, busing** or **bussing**) **1** (*also* **bus it**) *intr* to go by bus. **2** *esp US* to transport (children) by bus to a school in a different area, as a way of promoting racial integration.

busby n (-ies) 1 a tall fur hat worn as part of some military uniforms. 2 colloq a BEARSKIN (sense 2).

bush¹ n 1 a low woody perennial plant, esp one having many separate branches originating at or near ground level. 2 (usu the bush) wild uncultivated land covered with shrubs or small trees, esp in Africa, Australia or New Zealand. 3 something like a bush, esp in thickness, shape or density. ○ **bushy** adj.

bush² n a sheet of thin metal lining a cylinder in which an axle revolves. ➤ vb to provide (eg a bearing) with a bush.

bushbaby n an agile nocturnal African primate with large eyes and a long tail.

bushed adj, colloq extremely tired.

bushel n in the imperial system: a unit for measuring dry or liquid goods by volume, equal to 8 gallons or 36.4 litres in the UK (35.2 litres in the USA). ♦ **hide one's light under a bushel** to keep one's talents hidden from other people.

bushman n 1 Aust, NZ someone who lives or travels in the bush. 2 (**Bushman**) a member of an aboriginal race of nomadic hunters in S Africa.

bushranger n 1 Aust, hist an outlaw living in the bush. 2 N Am someone who lives far from civilization.

bush telegraph n, chiefly Brit, humorous the rapid spreading of information, rumours, etc, usu by word of mouth.

business n 1 the buying and selling of goods and services. 2 a shop, firm or commercial company, etc. 3 a regular occupation, trade or profession. 4 the things that are one's proper or rightful concern: mind your own business. 5 serious work or activity: Let's get down to business. 6 an affair or matter: a nasty business. 7 colloq a difficult or complicated problem. 8 commercial practice or policy: Prompt invoicing is good business. 9 commercial dealings, activity, custom or contact: I have some business with his company.

businesslike adj practical and efficient.

businessman or **businesswoman** n a man or woman working in commerce, esp at quite a senior level.

business park n an area designed to accommodate business offices and light industry.

busk vb, intr, chiefly Brit to sing, play music, etc in the street for money. ○ **busker** n.

busman's holiday n leisure time spent doing what one normally does at work.

bus stop n a stopping place for a bus.

bust¹ n 1 a woman's bosom. 2 a sculpture of a person's head, shoulders and upper chest.

bust² colloq, vb (**bust** or **busted**) 1 tr & intr to break or burst something. 2 of the police: to arrest someone. 3 to raid or search. 4 N Am, usu mil to demote (someone). ➤ adj 1 broken or burst. 2 having no money left; bankrupt.

bustard n a large ground-dwelling bird with speckled grey or brown plumage and long powerful legs.

bustier n, fashion a short tight-fitting strapless bodice for women.

bustle¹ vb 1 (usu bustle about) intr to busy oneself in a brisk, energetic and/or noisy manner. 2 to make someone hurry or work hard, etc: She bustled her out of the room. ➤ n hurried, noisy and excited activity. ○ **bustling** adj.

bustle² n, hist a frame or pad for holding a skirt out from the back of the waist.

bust-up n, colloq a quarrel; the ending of a relationship or partnership.

busty adj (-ier, -iest) colloq of a woman: having large breasts.

busy adj (-ier, -iest) 1 fully occupied; having much work to do. 2 full of activity: a busy street. 3 of a telephone line, etc: in use. 4 constantly working or occupied. ➤ vb (-ies, -ied) to occupy (someone or oneself) with a task, etc. ○ **busily** adv.

busybody n (-ies) someone who is always interfering in other people's affairs.

but conj 1 contrary to expectation: She fell down but didn't hurt herself. 2 in contrast: You've been to Spain but I haven't. 3 other than: You can't do anything but wait. 4 used to emphasize the word that follows it: Nobody, but nobody, must go in there. ➤ prep except: They are all here but him. ➤ adv only: I can but try. ➤ n an objection: no buts about it.

butane n a colourless highly flammable gas used in the manufacture of synthetic rubber, and in liquid form as a fuel.

butch /butʃ/ adj, slang of a person: aggressively masculine in manner or looks, etc.

butcher n 1 a person or shop that sells meat. 2 someone whose job is slaughtering animals and preparing the carcasses for use as food. 3 a person who kills people needlessly and savagely. ➤ vb 1 to kill and prepare (an animal) for sale as food. 2 to kill (esp a large number of people or animals) cruelly or indiscriminately. 3 colloq to ruin or make a botch of something: He completely butchered his solo.

butchery n 1 the preparing of meat for sale as food; the trade of a butcher. 2 senseless, cruel or wholesale killing.

butler n the chief male servant in a house.

butt¹ vb, tr & intr 1 to push or hit hard or roughly with the head, in the way a ram or goat might. 2 (esp butt against or on sth) to join or be joined end to end with it. ➤ n 1 a blow with the head or horns. 2 the place where two edges join. ◊ **butt in** colloq to interrupt or interfere. **butt into** to interrupt (eg a conversation).

butt² n 1 the unused end of a finished cigar or cigarette, etc. 2 the thick, heavy or bottom end of a tool or weapon. 3 chiefly N Am colloq the buttocks.

butt³ n 1 a person who is often a target of ridicule or criticism, etc. 2 a mound of earth behind a target on a shooting range.

butt⁴ *n* a large barrel for beer or rainwater, etc.

butte /bjuːt/ *n, geol* an isolated flat-topped hill with steep sides.

butter *n* **1** a solid yellowish edible food, made from the fats in milk by churning, and used for spreading on bread, and in cooking. **2** *in compounds* any of various substances that resemble this food in appearance or texture: *peanut butter*. ➤ *vb* to put butter on or in something. ○ **buttery** *adj*. ◇ **butter sb up** *colloq* to flatter them, usu in order to gain a favour.

butter bean *n* any of several varieties of bean plants or one of their large edible seeds.

buttercup *n* any of various plants with bright yellow cup-shaped flowers.

butterfingers *sing n, colloq* a person who often drops things, or who fails to catch things.

butterfly *n* (*-ies*) **1** an insect which has four broad, often brightly coloured wings, and a long proboscis for sucking nectar from flowers. **2** a person who is not very serious, but is only interested in enjoying themselves: *a social butterfly*. **3** (**butterflies**) *colloq* a nervous or fluttering feeling in the stomach. **4** BUTTERFLY STROKE.

butterfly nut or **butterfly screw** *n* a screw or nut with two flat projections which allow it to be turned with the fingers.

butterfly stroke *n* a swimming stroke in which both arms are brought out of the water and over the head at the same time.

buttermilk *n* the slightly sharp-tasting liquid left after all the butter has been removed from milk after churning.

butterscotch *n* a kind of hard toffee made from butter and sugar.

buttery *n* (*-ies*) *Brit* a room, esp in a university, where food is kept and supplied to students.

buttock *n* (*usu* **buttocks**) each of the fleshy parts of the body between the base of the back and the top of the legs.

button *n* **1** a small round piece of metal or plastic, etc sewn onto a piece of clothing, which fastens by being passed through a buttonhole. **2** (*sometimes* **push button**) a small round disc pressed to operate a door, bell, electrical appliance, etc. **3** a small round object worn as decoration or a badge. ➤ *vb* **1** (*also* **button up**) to fasten or close something using a button or buttons. **2** *intr* to be capable of being fastened with buttons or a button: *This dress buttons at the back*.

buttonhole *n* **1** a small slit or hole through which a button is passed to fasten a garment. **2** a flower or flowers worn in a buttonhole or pinned to a lapel. ➤ *vb* to stop someone, and force conversation on them.

buttress *n* **1** *archit, civil eng* a projecting support made of brick or masonry, etc built onto the outside of a wall. **2** any support or prop. ➤ *vb* **1** to support (a wall, etc) with buttresses. **2** to support or encourage (an argument, etc).

butty *n* (*-ies*) *Brit, esp N Eng, colloq* a sandwich.

buxom *adj* of a woman: attractively plump and full-bosomed.

buy *vb* (**bought**) **1** to obtain something by paying a sum of money for it. **2** to be a means of obtaining something: *There are some things money can't buy*. **3** to obtain something by giving up or sacrificing something else: *success bought at the expense of happiness*. **4** *colloq* to believe something: *I didn't buy his story*. **5** (*also* **buy off**) to bribe somebody: *He can't be bought, he's thoroughly honest*. ➤ *n* (*usu* in **a good buy** or **a bad buy**) a thing bought. ◇ **buy sth in 1** to buy a stock of it. **2** at an auction: to buy it back for the owner when the RESERVE PRICE is not reached. **buy into** to buy shares or an interest in (a company, etc). **buy off** to get rid of (a threatening person, etc) by paying them money. **buy sb out** to pay to take over possession of something from them, esp to buy all the shares that they hold in a company. **buy sth up** to buy the whole stock of it.

buyer *n* **1** a person who buys; a customer. **2** a person employed by a large shop or firm to buy goods on its behalf.

buy-out *n, commerce* the purchase of all the shares in a company in order to get control of it.

buzz *vb* **1** *intr* to make a continuous, humming or rapidly vibrating sound, like that made by the wings of a bee. **2** *intr* to be filled with activity or excitement. **3** (*often* **buzz about** or **around**) *intr* to move quickly or excitedly. **4** *colloq* to call someone using a BUZZER. **5** *colloq* to call someone on the telephone. **6** *colloq* of an aircraft: to fly very low over or very close to (another aircraft or a building, etc). ➤ *n* (**buzzes**) **1** a humming or rapidly vibrating sound, such as that made by a bee. **2** *colloq* a telephone call. **3** *colloq* a very pleasant, excited, or exhilarated feeling: *Joy-riding gives him a real buzz*. **4** a low murmuring sound such as that made by many people talking. ◇ **buzz off** *colloq* to go away.

buzzard *n* **1** any of several large hawks that resemble eagles in their effortless gliding flight. **2** *N Am* a vulture.

buzzer *n* an electrical device which makes a buzzing sound, used as a signal or for summoning someone.

buzz word *n, colloq* a fashionable new word or expression, usu in a particular subject, social group, or profession.

by *prep* **1** next to, beside or near: *standing by the door*. **2** past: *I'll drive by the house*. **3** through, along or across: *He entered by the window*. **4** (esp after a passive verb) used to indicate the person or thing that does, causes or produces, etc something: *The shed was destroyed by fire*. **5** used to show method or means: *I sent it by registered post*. **6** not later than: *I'll be home by 10pm*. **7** during: *We'll escape by night*. **8** used to show extent or amount: *It was worse by far*. **9** used in stating rates of payment, etc: *He's paid by the hour*. **10** according to: *It's 8.15 by my watch*. **11** used to show the part of someone or something held, taken or used, etc: *She was pulling me by the hand.* **12** used to show the number which must perform a mathematical operation on another: *multiply three by four.* **13** used in giving measurements and compass directions, etc: *a room measuring six feet by ten.* **14** used to show a specific quantity or unit, etc that follows another to bring about an increase or progression: *two by two.* **15** with regard to someone or something: *He'll do his duty by them.* **16** in oaths, etc: in the name of, or strictly 'with the witness of' or 'in the presence of' (a specified deity, thing or person): *By God, you're right!* **17** fathered by: *two children by her first husband.* ➤ *adv* **1** near: *I live close by.* **2** past: *They drive by without stopping.* **3** aside; away; in reserve: *I've got some money by.* ➤ *n* (**byes**) same as BYE¹. ◆ **by and by** *rather literary or old use* after a short time; at some time in the not-too-distant future. ◆ **by and large** all things considered. **by the by** or **by the bye** or **by the way** *colloq* incidentally.

bye¹ *n* **1** *sport, etc* a pass into the next round of a competition, given to a competitor or team that has not been given an opponent in the current round. **2** *cricket* a run scored from a ball which the batsman has not hit or touched. ◆ **by the bye** see BY THE BY at BY.

bye² or **bye-bye** *exclam, colloq* goodbye.

by-election *n* an election held during the sitting of parliament, in order to fill a seat which has become empty because the member has died or resigned.

bygone *adj* former: *in bygone days.* ➤ *n* (**bygones**) events, troubles or arguments which occurred in the past. ◆ **let bygones be bygones** to agree to forget past disagreements.

by-law or **bye-law** *n, Brit* a law or rule made by a local authority.

byline *n* **1** *journalism* a line under the title of a newspaper or magazine article which gives the name of the author. **2** *football* the touchline.

bypass *n* **1** a major road which carries traffic on a route that avoids a city centre, town or congested area. **2** *med* the redirection of blood flow so as to avoid a blocked or diseased blood vessel, esp a coronary artery. **3** a channel or pipe, etc which carries gas or electricity, etc when the main channel is blocked. ➤ *vb* **1** to avoid (a congested or blocked place) by taking a route which goes round or beyond it. **2** to leave out or avoid (a step in a process), or ignore and not discuss something with (a person): *I managed to bypass the usual selection procedure.*

by-product *n* **1** a secondary product that is formed at the same time as the main product during a chemical reaction or manufacturing process. **2** an unexpected or extra result. Compare END PRODUCT.

byre *n, mainly Scot* a cowshed.

byroad or **byway** *n* a minor or secondary road.

bystander *n* a person who happens to be standing by, who sees but does not take part in what is happening.

byte *n, comput* **1** a group of adjacent bits (see BIT³) that are handled as a single unit, esp a group of eight. **2** the amount of storage space occupied by such a group.

byword *n* **1** a person or thing that is well known as an example of something: *a byword for luxury.* **2** a common saying.

Byzantine *adj* **1** *hist* relating to Byzantium or the eastern part of the Roman Empire from AD 395 to 1453. **2** belonging or relating to the style of architecture and painting, etc developed in the Byzantine Empire, with domes, arches, stylized mosaics and icons, etc. **3** belonging or relating to the **Byzantine Church**, ie the Eastern or Orthodox Church. **4** secret, difficult to understand, and extremely intricate and complex. **5** eg of attitudes or policies: rigidly hierarchic; inflexible. ➤ *n, hist* an inhabitant of Byzantium.

Cc

C¹ or **c** *n* (**Cs**, **C's** or **c's**) **1** the third letter of the English alphabet. **2** (*usu* **C**) the third highest grade or quality, or a mark indicating this. **3** (**C**) *mus* a musical key with the note C as its base. **4** (**C**) *comput* a high-level programming language.

C² *abbrev* **1** Celsius. **2** centigrade. **3** century: *C19.*

C³ *symbol* **1** the Roman numeral for 100. **2** *chem* carbon.

c. *abbrev* **1** *cricket* caught. **2** cent. **3** century. **4** chapter. **5** (*also* **ca**) *circa* (Latin), approximately.

Ca *symbol, chem* calcium.

cab *n* **1** a taxi. **2** the driver's compartment in a lorry, railway engine, etc.

cabal /kə'bal/ *n* **1** a small group formed within a larger body, for secret, esp political, discussion, etc. **2** a political plot or conspiracy.

cabaret /'kabəreɪ/ *n* entertainment with songs, dancing, etc at a restaurant or nightclub.

cabbage *n* **1** a vegetable with a compact head of green, white or red leaves. **2** *derog* a dull inactive person.

cabby or **cabbie** n (*-ies*) colloq a taxi-driver.

caber n, Scot athletics a heavy wooden pole of c. 3–4m in length, that must be carried upright and then tipped end over end, during a contest called **tossing the caber**.

cabin n 1 a small house, esp one made of wood. 2 a small room on a ship for living, sleeping or working in. 3 the section of a plane for passengers or crew. 4 the driving compartment of a large commercial vehicle.

cabinet n 1 a piece of furniture with shelves and doors, for storing or displaying items. 2 a body of senior ministers in charge of the various departments of government.

cabinet-maker n a skilled craftsman who makes and repairs fine furniture. ○ **cabinet-making** n.

cable n 1 a strong wire cord or rope. 2 two or more electrical wires bound together but separated from each other by insulating material, and covered by a protective sheath, used to carry electricity, television signals, etc. 3 (*also* **cablegram**) a telegram sent by cable. 4 short for CABLE TELEVISION. ➤ vb 1 to tie up or provide with a cable or cables. 2 tr & intr to send a cable, or send (a message) to someone by cable.

cable car n a small carriage suspended from a continuous moving cable, for carrying passengers up or down a steep mountain, across a valley, etc.

cable television, **cable TV** or **cablevision** n a television broadcasting system in which television signals are relayed directly to individual subscribers by means of cables. Often shortened to **cable**.

caboodle n, colloq (esp **the whole caboodle**) the whole lot; everything.

caboose n, N Am a guard's van on a railway train.

cabriolet /kabrıou'leı/ n 1 hist a light two-wheeled carriage drawn by one horse. 2 a car with a folding roof.

cacao /kə'kɑːou/ n the edible seed of a small evergreen tree, used to make chocolate, cocoa and cocoa butter.

cache /kaʃ/ n 1 a hiding place, eg for weapons. 2 a collection of hidden things. ➤ vb to put or collect in a cache.

cache memory n, comput an extremely fast part of the main store of computer memory.

cachet /'kaʃeı/ n 1 something which brings one respect or admiration. 2 a distinguishing mark.

cack-handed adj, colloq clumsy; awkward.

cackle n 1 the sound made by a hen or a goose. 2 derog a raucous laugh like this. 3 shrill, silly chatter. ➤ vb, intr 1 to laugh raucously. 2 to chatter noisily. 3 to utter as a cackle.

cacophony /kə'kɒfənı/ n (*-ies*) a disagreeable combination of loud noises. ○ **cacophonous** adj.

cactus n (*cacti* /'kaktaı/ or *cactuses*) any of numerous plants with sharp spines, which usu store water in fleshy stems.

CAD abbrev computer-aided design.

cad n, Brit colloq a man who behaves discourteously or dishonourably.

cadaver /kə'dɑːvə(r)/ n, med a human corpse, esp one used for dissection.

cadaverous adj corpse-like in appearance; pale and gaunt.

caddie or **caddy** n (*-ies*) someone whose job is to carry the golf clubs around the course for a golf-player. ➤ vb (*caddies, caddied, caddying*) intr to act as a caddie.

caddy n (*-ies*) 1 a small container for loose tea. 2 US any storage container.

cadence /'keıdəns/ n 1 the rising and falling of the voice in speaking. 2 rhythm or beat. 3 mus a succession of notes that closes a musical passage.

cadenza n, mus an elaborate virtuoso passage given by a solo performer towards the end of a movement.

cadet n 1 a trainee for the armed forces or police. 2 a school pupil undergoing simple military training.

cadge vb, tr & intr, colloq (also **cadge sth from** or **off sb**) to get (something, esp money or food) by scrounging or begging. ○ **cadger** n.

cadi, **kadi** or **qadi** n in Muslim countries: a judge or magistrate.

cadmium n, chem a soft bluish-white toxic metallic element.

cadre /'kadə(r)/ n 1 mil a permanent core unit which can be expanded when required, eg by conscription. 2 an inner group of activists in a revolutionary party, esp a Communist one.

caecum or (esp US) **cecum** /'siːkəm/ n (*caeca* /-kə/) anat a blind-ended pouch at the junction of the small and large intestines.

Caenozoic see CENOZOIC

caesarean section or (US) **cesarean section** n a surgical operation in which a baby is delivered through an incision in the lower abdomen.

caesium or (US) **cesium** /'siːzıəm/ n, chem a soft silvery-white metallic element.

caesura or **cesura** /sı'zjʊərə/ n (*caesuras* or *caesurae* /-riː/) a pause near the middle of a line of verse.

café or **cafe** n a usu small restaurant that serves light meals or snacks.

cafeteria n a self-service restaurant.

cafetière /kafə'tjɛə(r)/ n a coffee-pot with a plunger for separating the grounds from the liquid.

caffeine n a bitter-tasting alkaloid, found in coffee beans, tea leaves and cola nuts, a stimulant of the central nervous system. ○ **caffeinated** adj.

caftan or **kaftan** n a long loose-fitting robe.

cage n an enclosure, usu with bars, in which birds and animals are kept. ➤ vb (also **cage sb in**) to put them in a cage or confine them. ○ **caged** adj.

cagey or **cagy** adj (*cagier, cagiest*) colloq secretive and cautious; not forthcoming. ○ **cagily** adv.

cagoule or **kagoule** *n* a lightweight water-proof hooded anorak.

cahoots *pl n.* ♦ **in cahoots with sb** *usu derog, colloq* working in close partnership with them, esp in the planning of something unlawful.

cairn[1] *n* a heap of stones piled up to mark something, eg a grave or pathway.

cairn[2] or **cairn terrier** *n* a small breed of dog with short legs, a thick shaggy brown coat and erect ears.

cairngorm *n, geol* a yellow or smoky-brown variety of the mineral quartz, often used as a gemstone.

caisson /ˈkeɪsən/ *n* **1** a watertight chamber used to protect construction workers doing underwater work. **2** the pontoon or floating gate used to close a dry dock.

cajole *vb* (*usu* **cajole sb into sth**) to persuade them using flattery, promises, etc. ○ **cajolery** *n*.

Cajun *n* a member of a group of people of French descent living in Louisiana. ➤ *adj* of or relating to the Cajuns or their culture.

cake *n* **1** a solid food made by baking a mixture of flour, fat, eggs, sugar, etc. **2** a portion of some other food pressed into a particular shape: *fish cake*. **3** a solid block of a particular substance, eg soap. ➤ *vb* **1** *intr* to dry as a thick hard crust. **2** to cover in a thick crust: *skin caked with blood*. ♦ **a piece of cake** *colloq* a very easy task. **have one's cake and eat it** *colloq* to enjoy the advantages of two alternative courses of action. **sell** or **go like hot cakes** to be bought enthusiastically in large numbers.

cal. *abbrev* calorie.

calabash *n* the dried shell of the flask-shaped fruit of the **calabash tree**, used as a bowl or water container.

calabrese /ˌkaləˈbreɪzeɪ/ *n* a type of green sprouting broccoli.

calamari *pl n* in Mediterranean cookery: squid.

calamine *n* a fine pink powder containing zinc oxide and small amounts of ferric oxide, used in a lotion or ointment.

calamity *n* (**-ies**) a catastrophe, disaster or serious misfortune. ○ **calamitous** *adj*.

calcareous /kalˈkeərɪəs/ *adj* containing or resembling calcium carbonate.

calciferous *adj* **1** *chem* containing lime. **2** *biol* containing or producing calcium or calcium salts.

calcify *vb* (**-ies, -ied**) *tr & intr* **1** to harden as a result of the deposit of calcium salts. **2** to change or be changed into lime. ○ **calcification** *n*.

calcite *n, geol* a white or colourless mineral, composed of crystalline calcium carbonate.

calcium *n, chem* a soft, silvery-white metallic element which occurs mainly in the form of calcium carbonate minerals such as chalk, limestone and marble.

calcium carbonate *n, chem* a white powder or colourless crystals, occurring naturally as limestone, marble, chalk, etc, which is used in the manufacture of glass, cement, etc.

calculate *vb* **1** to work out, find out or estimate, esp by mathematical means. **2** (*often* **calculate on sth**) *intr* to make plans that depend on or take into consideration some probability or possibility. **3** to intend or aim: *The measures were calculated to avoid mass redundancy.*

calculated *adj* intentional; deliberate: *a calculated insult.*

calculating *adj, derog* deliberately shrewd and selfish.

calculation *n* **1** the act, process or result of calculating. **2** *derog* the cold and deliberate use of people or situations.

calculator *n* a small *usu* hand-held electronic device that is used to perform numerical calculations.

calculus *n* (**calculuses** or **calculi** /ˈkalkjʊlaɪ, -liː/) **1** the branch of mathematics concerned with the differentiation and integration of functions. **2** *med* a stone-like mass that forms within body structures such as the kidney, urinary bladder, gall bladder or bile ducts.

Caledonian *adj, esp formerly* belonging or relating to Scotland or its inhabitants.

calendar *n* **1** any system by which the beginning, length and divisions of the year are fixed. **2** a booklet, chart, etc that shows such an arrangement. **3** a timetable or list of important dates, events, appointments, etc.

calendar month see under MONTH

calender *n* a machine through which paper or cloth is passed in order to give it a smooth shiny finish. ➤ *vb* to give a smooth finish to (paper or cloth) by passing it through such a machine.

calends or **kalends** *pl n* in the ancient Roman calendar: the first day of each month.

calf[1] *n* (**calves**) **1** the young of any bovine animal, esp domestic cattle. **2** the young of certain other mammals, eg the elephant and whale.

calf[2] *n* (**calves**) the thick fleshy part of the back of the leg, below the knee.

calf love see PUPPY LOVE

calibrate *vb* to mark a scale on (a measuring instrument) so that it can be used to take readings in suitable units. ○ **calibration** *n*.

calibre /ˈkalɪbə(r)/ *n* **1** the internal diameter of a gun barrel or tube. **2** the outer diameter of a bullet, shell or other projectile. **3** quality; standard; ability.

calico *n* (**calicoes**) a kind of cotton cloth, usu plain white or in its natural unbleached state.

californium *n, chem* a synthetic radioactive metallic element.

caliph, calif, kalif or **khalif** *n* the chief Muslim civil and religious leader.

call *vb* **1** *tr & intr* (*also* **call out**) to shout or speak loudly in order to attract attention. **2** to ask someone to come, esp with a shout. **3** to summon or invite someone. **4** *tr & intr* to telephone. **5** *intr* to make a visit: *I'll call at the grocer's.* **6** to give a name to someone or something. **7** to consider something as something specified: *I* *call that strange.* **8** to summon or assemble people for (a meeting). **9** (*often* **call for sth**) *tr & intr* to make a demand or appeal for it: *call a strike.* **10** *intr* to predict which way a coin will land when tossed. **11** *intr* of a bird, etc: to make its typical or characteristic sound. ➤ *n* **1** a shout or cry. **2** the cry of a bird or animal. **3** an invitation or summons. **4** a demand, request or appeal. **5** (*usu* **call on sth**) a claim or demand for it: *too many calls on my time.* **6** a brief visit. **7** an act of contacting someone by telephone; a telephone conversation. **8** a need or reason: *There's not much call for Latin teachers.* **9** a player's turn to bid or choose trumps in a card game. ○ **caller** *n*. ◆ **on call** eg of a doctor: available if needed, eg to deal with an emergency. ◊ **call for sth** *or* **sb 1** to require it or them. **2** to collect or fetch it or them. **call sth off 1** to cancel a meeting, arrangement, etc. **2** to give orders for something to be stopped. **call sb up 1** to conscript them into the armed forces. **2** *colloq* to telephone them. **call sth up 1** to cause (memories, etc) to come into the mind. **2** to retrieve (data) from a computer.

call box *n* a public telephone box.

call girl *n* a prostitute with whom appointments are made by telephone.

calligraphy *n* **1** handwriting as an art. **2** beautiful decorative handwriting. ○ **calligrapher** *n*.

calling *n* **1** a trade or profession. **2** an urge to follow a particular profession, esp the ministry or one involving the care of other people.

calliper *n* **1** a measuring device, consisting of two hinged prongs attached to a scale, which is used to measure the linear distance between the prongs. **2** a splint for supporting a leg.

callisthenics *pl n* a system of physical exercises to increase the strength and grace of the body.

callous *adj* unconcerned for the feelings of others; deliberately cruel. ○ **callously** *adv*. ○ **callousness** *n*.

callow *adj* young and inexperienced.

callus *n* **1** a thickened hardened pad of skin. **2** a mass of tissue that forms around a wound on a plant or around the exposed ends of a fractured bone.

calm *adj* **1** relaxed and in control; not anxious, upset, angry, etc. **2** of the weather, etc: still, quiet or peaceful. ➤ *n* **1** peace, quiet and tranquillity. **2** stillness of weather. ➤ *vb, tr & intr* (*usu* **calm down**) to become calmer. **2** (*usu* **calm sb** *or* **sth down**) to make them calmer. ○ **calmly** *adv*. ○ **calmness** *n*.

Calor gas *n, trademark* a mixture of liquefied butane and propane gases used as fuel.

calorie *n* a metric unit denoting the amount of heat required to raise the temperature of one gram of water by 1 °C.

calorific *adj* referring or relating to heat or calories.

calumet / ˈkaljʊmɛt/ *n* a tobacco-pipe, smoked as a token of peace by Native Americans.

calumniate *vb* to accuse someone falsely; to slander.

calumny *n* (*-ies*) **1** an untrue and malicious spoken statement about a person. **2** the act of uttering such a statement.

calve *vb, intr* **1** to give birth to (a calf). **2** of a glacier or iceberg: to release (masses of ice) on breaking up.

calypso *n* a type of popular song originating in the West Indies.

calyx / ˈkeɪlɪks/ *n* (*calyces* /-lɪsiːz/, *calyxes* /-lɪksiːz/) *bot* the outermost whorl of a flower, that protects the developing flower bud.

CAM *abbrev, comput* computer-aided manufacture.

cam *n, eng* an irregular projection on a wheel or rotating shaft, shaped so as to transmit regular movement to another part in contact with it.

camaraderie *n* a feeling of friendship and cheerful support between friends.

camber *n* a slight convexity on the upper surface of a road.

Cambrian *geol, adj* relating to the earliest period of the PALAEOZOIC era. ➤ *n* the Cambrian period.

cambric *n* a fine white cotton or linen fabric.

camcorder *n* a portable video camera that is used to record images and sound.

camel *n* **1** a large mammal with a long neck and legs, and one or two humps on its back. **2** the pale brown colour of this animal.

camellia / kəˈmiːlɪə/ *n* an evergreen shrub with attractive white, pink or crimson flowers and glossy leaves.

cameo *n* **1** a rounded gemstone with a raised design of a head in profile carved on it. **2** (*also* **cameo role**) a small part in a play or film performed by a well-known actor.

camera *n* **1** an optical device that records images as photographs. **2** a device in a television broadcasting system that converts visual images into electrical signals for transmission.

cameraman *n* in TV or film-making: someone who operates a camera.

camiknickers *pl n* a woman's undergarment consisting of a camisole and knickers combined.

camisole *n* a woman's loose vest-like undergarment, with narrow shoulder straps.

camomile or **chamomile** *n* **1** a strongly scented plant which has finely divided leaves, and white and yellow daisy-like flower heads. **2** the dried crushed flowers or leaves of this plant, used for their soothing medicinal properties, esp in the form of a herbal tea.

camouflage *n* **1** any device or means of disguising or concealing a person or animal, or of deceiving an adversary, esp by adopting the colour, texture, etc, of natural surroundings or backgrounds. **2** the use of such methods to conceal or disguise the presence of military troops, equipment, vehicles or buildings, by imitating the colours of nature. **3** the colour pattern or other physical features that enable an animal to blend with its natural environment and so avoid detection by predators. ➤ *vb* to disguise or conceal with some kind of camouflage.

camp[1] *n* **1** a piece of ground on which tents have been erected. **2** a collection of buildings, huts, tents, etc used as temporary accommodation or for short stays for a particular purpose. **3** a permanent site where troops are housed or trained. **4** a group having a particular set of opinions, beliefs, etc. ➤ *vb, intr* to stay in a tent or tents. ○ **camping** *n*.

camp[2] *adj, colloq, sometimes derog* **1** of a man or his behaviour: effeminate, esp in an exaggerated way. **2** of a man: homosexual. ♦ **camp it up** to behave in an exaggerated theatrical way; to overact.

campaign *n* **1** an organized series of actions intended to gain support for or build up opposition to a particular practice, group, etc. **2** the operations of an army while fighting in a particular area or to achieve a particular goal. ➤ *vb, intr* (*usu* **campaign for** or **against sth**) to organize or take part in a campaign. ○ **campaigner** *n*.

campanile /kampə'ni:li/ *n* esp in Italy: a bell tower that is free-standing.

campanology *n* the art of bell-ringing.

camp bed *n* a light portable folding bed.

camper *n* **1** someone who camps. **2** a motor vehicle equipped for sleeping in.

camphor *n* a white or colourless crystalline compound with a strong aromatic odour, used as a medicinal liniment and inhalant, and to make Celluloid.

campion *n* a plant which has bright pink or white flowers.

campsite *n* a piece of land on which people are allowed to camp.

campus *n* the grounds of a college or university.

camshaft *n, eng* a shaft to which one or more CAMS are attached.

can[1] *vb* (*past tense* **could**) **1** to be able to: *Can you lift that?* **2** to know how to: *He can play the guitar.* **3** to feel it right to: *How can you believe that?* **4** to have permission to: *Can I take an apple?* **5** used when asking for help, etc: *Can you give me the time?*

can, may Essentially, **can** denotes capability or capacity, and **may** denotes permission or opportunity. Because these two sets of meaning constantly overlap, the two words have become highly interchangeable, with **can** more versatile than **may**:

Hospital trusts attract more staff and can determine their own pay rates.
You can do it when you come home from work.
In both these examples, **may** is also poss-

ible. Both **can** and **may** are used to denote what is probable or habitual:
A quiet river on a summer's day may be a raging torrent in February.
Things can go dreadfully wrong at this stage.
When capability or capacity is predominant, **can** is used:
I can't cope with life at the moment.
Can you see the point I am trying to make?

can[2] *n* **1** a sealed container, usu of tin plate or aluminium, used to contain food and esp fizzy drinks. **2** a large container made of metal or another material, for holding liquids, eg oil or paint. **3** (**the can**) *slang* prison. **4** *N Am, slang* (*usu* **the can**) a lavatory. ➤ *vb* (**canned, canning**) to seal (food or drink) in metal containers in order to preserve it.

canal *n* **1** an artificial channel or waterway, usu constructed for navigation or irrigation. **2** *anat* any tubular channel or passage that conveys food, air or fluids from one part of the body to another: *alimentary canal.*

canalize or **-ise** *vb* **1** to make or convert into a canal or system of canals. **2** to guide or direct into a useful, practical or profitable course.

canapé /'kanəpeɪ/ *n* a small piece of bread or toast spread or topped with something savoury.

canard *n* a false report or piece of news.

canary *n* (**-ies**) a small finch with bright yellow plumage, very popular as a caged bird.

canasta *n* a card game similar to rummy played with two packs of cards.

cancan *n* a lively dance usu performed by dancing girls, who execute high kicks, raising their skirts to reveal their petticoats.

cancel *vb* (**cancelled, cancelling**) **1** to stop (something already arranged) from taking place. **2** to stop (something in progress) from continuing. **3** *intr* to tell a supplier that one no longer wants something. **4** to delete or cross out something. **5** to put an official stamp on (eg a cheque or postage stamp) so that it cannot be re-used. **6** *maths* to strike out (equal quantities) from opposite sides of an equation, or (common factors) from the NUMERATOR and DENOMINATOR of a fraction. **7** (*usu* **cancel sth out**) to remove the effect of it, by having an exactly opposite effect; to counterbalance. ○ **cancellation** *n*.

Cancer *n, astrol* **a** the fourth sign of the zodiac; **b** a person born between 22 June and 23 July, under this sign.

cancer *n* **1** *pathol* any form of malignant tumour or disease that develops when the cells of a tissue or organ multiply in an uncontrolled manner. **2** an evil within an organization, community, etc that is gradually destroying it. ○ **cancerous** *adj.*

candela /kan'di:lə/ *n* the SI unit of luminous intensity.

candelabrum or (*sometimes used wrongly as*

sing) **candelabra** *n* (*candelabrums, candelabra* or *candelabras*) a candle-holder with branches for several candles, or a light-fitting for overhead lights designed in the same way.

candid *adj* **1** honest and open about what one thinks; outspoken. **2** *colloq* of a photograph: taken without the subject's knowledge so as to catch them unawares.

candidate *n* **1** someone who is competing with others for a job, prize, parliamentary seat, etc. **2** someone taking an examination. **3** a person or thing considered suitable for a particular purpose or likely to suffer a particular fate. ○ **candidacy** or **candidature** *n*.

candle *n* a piece of wax or (esp formerly) tallow, formed around a wick, which is burnt to provide light.

candlelight *n* the light given by a candle or candles. ○ **candlelit** *adj*.

candlestick *n* a holder, usu portable, for a candle.

candlewick *n* a cotton fabric with a tufted surface formed by cut loops of thread, used for bedcovers, etc.

candour or (*US*) **candor** *n* the quality of being candid; frankness and honesty.

candy *n* (*-ies*) *N Am* **1** a sweet. **2** sweets or confectionery. ➤ *vb* (*-ies, -ied*) to preserve (fruit, peel, etc) by boiling in sugar or syrup. ○ **candied** *adj*.

candy floss *n* a fluffy mass of coloured spun sugar served on a stick.

candy stripe *n* a textile fabric patterned with narrow stripes, usu pink or red, on a white background.

cane *n* **1** the long jointed hollow or pithy stem of certain plants, esp various small palms (eg rattan) and larger grasses (eg bamboo and sugar cane). **2** SUGAR CANE. **3** thin stems or strips cut from stems, eg of rattan, for weaving into baskets, etc. **4** a walking-stick. **5** a long slim stick for beating people as a punishment. ➤ *vb* to beat someone with a cane as a punishment. ○ **caning** *n*.

canine *adj* of or like a dog; the dog family. ➤ *n* **1** any animal belonging to the dog family, esp a domestic dog. **2** CANINE TOOTH.

canine tooth *n* in most mammals: any of the long sharp pointed teeth, two in each jaw, located between the incisors and premolars.

canister *n* a container for storing tea or other dry foods.

canker *n* **1** a fungal, bacterial or viral disease of trees and woody shrubs, eg fruit trees. **2** an ulcerous disease of animals that causes eg inflammation of the ears of cats and dogs. **3** an evil, destructive influence, etc.

cannabis *n* a narcotic drug, prepared from the leaves and flowers of a plant in the hemp family.

canned *adj* **1** contained or preserved in cans. **2** *slang* drunk. **3** *colloq* previously recorded: *canned laughter.*

cannelloni *pl n* a kind of pasta in the form of large tubes, served with a filling of meat, cheese, etc.

cannery *n* (*-ies*) a factory where goods are canned.

cannibal *n* **1** someone who eats human flesh. **2** an animal that eats others of its own kind. ○ **cannibalism** *n*.

cannibalize or **-ise** *vb, colloq* to take parts from (a machine, vehicle, etc) for use in repairing another.

cannon *n* (*cannons* or in senses 1 and 2 *cannon*) **1** *hist* a large gun mounted on wheels. **2** a rapid-firing gun fitted to an aircraft or ship. **3** in billiards, pool and snooker: a shot in which the cue ball strikes one object ball and then strikes another. ➤ *vb, intr* in billiards, pool and snooker: to play a cannon shot.

cannonade *n* a continuous bombardment of heavy guns.

cannonball *n, hist* a ball, usu of iron, for shooting from a cannon.

cannon fodder *n, colloq* soldiers regarded merely as material to be sacrificed in war.

cannot *vb* can not. See also CAN'T.

canny *adj* (*-ier, -iest*) **1** wise and alert; shrewd. **2** careful; cautious. ○ **cannily** *adv*.

canoe *n* a light narrow boat propelled manually by one or more paddles. ➤ *vb* (*canoeing*) *intr* to travel by canoe. ○ **canoeing** *n*. ○ **canoeist** *n*.

canon *n* **1** a basic law, rule or principle. **2** **a** a member of the clergy attached to a cathedral; **b** *C of E* a member of the clergy who has special rights with regard to the election of bishops. **3** an officially accepted collection of writing, or work considered to be by a particular writer. **4** in the Christian Church: a list of saints. **5** a piece of music, similar to a round, in which a particular sequence is repeated with a regular overlapping pattern.

canonical *adj* **1** according to, of the nature of or included in a canon. **2** orthodox or accepted.

canonical hours *pl n, now esp RC Church* **a** the hours appointed for prayer and devotion; **b** the services prescribed for these times.

canonize or **-ise** *vb* **1** to officially declare someone to be a saint. **2** to treat someone as a saint. ○ **canonization** *n*.

canon law *n* the law of the Christian Church.

canoodle *vb, intr, colloq* to hug and kiss; to cuddle.

canopy *n* (*-ies*) **1** an ornamental covering hung over a bed, throne, etc. **2** a covering hung or held up over something or someone, usu for shelter. **3** *archit* a roof-like structure over an altar, recess, etc. **4** *bot* the topmost layer of a wood or forest.

cant¹ *n* **1** *derog* insincere talk, esp with a false display of moral or religious principles. **2** the special slang or jargon of a particular group of people, eg lawyers, etc. ➤ *vb, intr* to talk using cant.

cant² *n* a slope. ➤ *vb, tr & intr* to tilt, slope or tip up.

can't *contraction* cannot.

cantabile /kan'tɑːbɪleɪ/ *mus, adv* in a flowing and melodious manner. ➤ *adj* flowing and melodious.

cantaloup or **cantaloupe** *n* a type of melon with a thick ridged skin and orange-coloured flesh.

cantankerous *adj* bad-tempered.

cantata /kan'tɑːtə/ *n* a musical work which is sung, with parts for chorus and soloists.

canteen *n* **1** a restaurant attached to a factory, office, etc for the use of employees. **2 a** a case containing cutlery; **b** the full set of cutlery contained in the case.

canter *n* a horse-riding pace between trotting and galloping. ➤ *vb, tr & intr* to move or cause to move at this pace.

canticle *n* a non-metrical hymn or chant with a text taken from the Bible.

cantilever *n* a beam or other support that projects from a wall to support a balcony, staircase, etc.

cantilever bridge *n* a fixed bridge consisting of two outer spans that project towards one another and support a suspended central span.

canto *n* a section of a long poem.

canton *n* a division of a country, esp one of the separately governed regions of Switzerland.

cantor *n* **1** *Judaism* a man who chants the liturgy and leads the congregation in prayer. **2** *Christianity* someone who leads the choir in a church service.

canvas *n* **1** a thick heavy coarse cloth, made from cotton, hemp or flax, used to make sails, tents, etc and for painting pictures on. **2** a painting done on a piece of canvas. ✦ **under canvas 1** in tents. **2** *naut* with sails spread.

canvass *vb* **1** *tr & intr* to ask for votes or support from someone. **2** to find out the opinions of (voters, etc). ➤ *n* a solicitation of information, votes, opinions, etc. ○ **canvasser** *n*.

canyon *n* a deep gorge or ravine with steep sides.

cap *n* **1** any of various types of hat, eg with a flat or rounded crown and a peak. **2** a small hat often worn as an indication of occupation, rank, etc. **3** a lid, cover or top, eg for a bottle or pen. **4** (*also* **percussion cap**) a little metal or paper case containing a small amount of gunpowder that explodes when struck, used eg to make a noise in toy guns. **5** a protective or cosmetic covering fitted over a damaged or decayed tooth. **6** the top or top part. **7** (**the cap** or **Dutch cap**) a contraceptive device used by a woman, consisting of a rubber cover that fits over the CERVIX (sense I) and prevents the sperm entering. ➤ *vb* (**capped, capping**) **1** to put a cap on, or cover the top or end of, something with a cap. **2** to be or form the top of. **3** to do better than, improve on or outdo someone or something. **4** to set an upper limit to (a tax), or to the tax-gathering powers of (a local authority).

cap. *abbrev* **1** capacity. **2** capital.

capability *n* (*-ies*) **1** ability or efficiency. **2 a** power or ability, often one that has not yet been made full use of: *The USA has a strong nuclear capability.*

capable *adj* **1** clever; able; efficient. **2** (**capable of sth**) having the ability or disposition to do it. ○ **capably** *adv*.

capacious *adj, formal* having plenty of room for holding things; roomy.

capacitance *n, elec* the ability of the conductors in a capacitor to store electric charge.

capacitor *n, elec* a device consisting of two conducting surfaces separated by a dielectric material, that can store energy in the form of electric charge.

capacity *n* (*-ies*) **1** the amount that something can hold. **2** the amount that a factory, etc can produce. **3** (**capacity for sth**) the ability or power to achieve it: *capacity for change*. **4** function; role. **5** mental ability or talent.

cape¹ *n* **1** a short cloak. **2** an extra layer of cloth attached to the shoulders of a coat, etc.

cape² *n* a part of the coast that projects into the sea.

caper¹ *vb, intr* to jump or dance about playfully. ➤ *n* a playful jump.

caper² *n* a young flower bud of a small deciduous shrub, pickled in vinegar and used as a condiment.

capercaillie or **capercailzie** /kapə'keɪlɪ/ *n* a large game bird.

capillarity *n* the phenomenon, caused by surface tension effects, whereby a liquid such as water rises up a narrow tube placed in the liquid.

capillary /kə'pɪlərɪ; *US* 'kapɪlərɪ/ *n* (*-ies*) **1** a tube, usu made of glass, which has a very small diameter. **2** in vertebrates: the narrowest type of blood vessel.

capital¹ *n* **1** the chief city of a country, usu where the government is based. **2** a capital letter (see *adj* sense 2 below). **3** the total amount of money or wealth possessed by a person or business, etc, esp when used to produce more wealth. ➤ *adj* **1** principal; chief. **2** of a letter of the alphabet: in its large form, as used eg at the beginnings of names and sentences. Also called **upper-case**. **3** of a crime: punishable by death. ✦ **make capital out of sth** to use a situation or circumstance to one's advantage.

capital² *n, archit* the slab of stone, etc that forms the top section of a column or pillar.

capital gains tax *n, commerce* a tax on the profit obtained by selling assets.

capitalism *n* an economic system based on private, rather than state, ownership of businesses, services, etc, with free competition and profit-making.

capitalist *n* **1** someone who believes in capitalism. **2** *derog* a wealthy person, esp one who is obviously making a great deal of personal profit from business, etc. ○ **capitalistic** *adj*.

capitalize or **-ise** *vb* **1** *intr* (*esp* **capitalize on sth**) to exploit (an asset, achievement, etc) to one's advantage. **2** to write with a capital letter or in capital letters. **3** to sell (property, etc) in order to raise money. **4** to supply (a business, etc) with needed capital. ○ **capitalization** n.

capital punishment n punishment of a crime by death.

capitation n a tax of so much paid per person.

capitulate vb, intr **1** to surrender formally, usu on agreed conditions. **2** to give in to argument or persuasion. ○ **capitulation** n.

capon /ˈkeɪpən, -pɒn/ n a castrated male chicken fattened for eating.

cappuccino /kapʊˈtʃiːnoʊ/ n espresso coffee made with frothy hot milk and usu dusted with chocolate powder on top.

caprice /kəˈpriːs/ n **1** a sudden change of mind for no good or obvious reason. **2** the tendency to have caprices. ○ **capricious** adj.

Capricorn n, astrol **a** the tenth sign of the zodiac; **b** a person born between 23 December and 20 January, under this sign.

caprine adj belonging or relating to, or characteristic of, a goat.

capsicum n **1** a tropical shrub belonging to the potato family. **2** the red, green or yellow fruit of this plant, eaten raw in salads or cooked as a vegetable.

capsize vb **1** intr usu of a boat: to tip over completely; to overturn. **2** to cause (a boat) to capsize.

capstan n **1** a cylinder-shaped apparatus that is turned to wind a heavy rope or cable, eg that of a ship's anchor. **2** in a tape recorder: either of the shafts or spindles round which the tape winds.

capsule n **1** a hard or soft soluble case, usu made of gelatine, containing a single dose of a powdered drug to be taken orally. **2** (also **space capsule**) a small spacecraft or a compartment within a spacecraft that contains the instruments and crew. **3** anat a membranous sheath, sac or other structure that surrounds an organ or tissue. **4** bot in some flowering plants: a dry fruit, formed by the fusion of two or more carpels, that splits open to release its many seeds.

Capt. abbrev Captain.

captain n **1** a leader or chief. **2** the commander of a ship. **3** the commander of a company of troops. **4** a naval officer of the rank below commodore. **5** an army officer of the rank below major. **6** the chief pilot of a civil aircraft. **7** the leader of a team or side, or chief member of a club. ➤ vb to be captain of something. ○ **captaincy** n (-ies).

caption n **1** the words that accompany a photograph, cartoon, etc to explain it. **2** a heading given to a chapter, article, etc. **3** wording appearing on a television or cinema screen as part of a film or broadcast. ➤ vb to provide a caption or captions for something.

captious adj inclined to criticize and find fault. ○ **captivating** adj. ○ **captivation** n.

captivate vb to delight, charm or fascinate. ○ **captivating** adj. ○ **captivation** n.

captive n a person or animal that has been caught or taken prisoner. ➤ adj **1** kept prisoner. **2** held so as to be unable to get away. ○ **captivity** n (-ies) the condition or period of being captive or imprisoned.

captor n someone who takes a person or animal captive.

capture vb **1** to catch; to take prisoner; to gain control of someone or something. **2** to succeed in recording (a subtle quality, etc): The novel accurately captured the mood. ➤ n **1** the capturing of someone or something. **2** the person or thing captured.

capybara /kapɪˈbɑːrə/ n the largest living rodent, native to S America, which has partially webbed toes and no tail.

car n **1** a self-propelled four-wheeled road vehicle designed to carry passengers and powered by an internal-combustion engine. **2** N Am a railway carriage or van: dining car. **3** a passenger compartment in eg a balloon, airship, lift or cable railway.

carafe /kəˈraf/ n a wide-necked bottle or flask for wine, etc, for use on the table.

caramel n **1** a brown substance produced by heating sugar solution until it darkens, used as a food colouring and flavouring. **2** a toffeelike sweet made from sugar, animal fat and milk or cream. **3** the pale yellowish brown colour of this.

caramelize or **-ise** vb **1** to change (sugar) into caramel. **2** intr to turn into caramel.

carapace n, zool the hard thick shell that covers the upper part of the body of some tortoises, turtles and crustaceans.

carat n **1** a unit of mass, equal to 0.2g, used to measure the mass of gemstones, esp diamonds. **2** a unit used to express the purity of gold in an alloy with another metal (usu copper), equal to the number of parts of gold in 24 parts of the alloy.

caravan n **1** a vehicle fitted for living in, designed for towing by a motor vehicle. **2** a large covered van, formerly pulled by horses, used as a travelling home by Romanies, etc. **3** hist a group of travellers, merchants, etc, usu with camels, crossing the desert as a large company for safety. ➤ vb (**caravanned, caravanning**) intr to go travelling with or stay in a caravan. ○ **caravanning** n.

caravanserai n (**caravanserais** or **caravanseries**) in some Eastern countries: an inn with a central courtyard for receiving caravans crossing the desert, etc.

caraway seed n the dried ripe fruit of the caraway plant which contains an aromatic oil and is widely used as a flavouring.

carb n, colloq short for CARBOHYDRATE.

carbide n, chem any chemical compound consisting of carbon and another element (except for hydrogen), usu a metallic one.

carbine n a short light rifle.

carbohydrate n any of a group of organic compounds, present in the cells of all living organisms, which consist of carbon, hydrogen and oxygen and are formed in green plants during photosynthesis.

carbolic acid *n* PHENOL (sense 1).

carbon *n* **1** a non-metallic element that occurs in all organic compounds, and as two crystalline ALLOTROPES, namely DIAMOND and GRAPHITE. **2** a sheet of carbon paper. **3** a carbon copy.

carbonaceous *adj* containing large amounts of, or resembling, carbon.

carbonate *n, chem* any salt of carbonic acid. ➤ *vb* to combine or treat (a liquid) with carbon dioxide, to make it fizzy. ○ **carbonated** *adj*.

carbon copy *n* an exact duplicate.

carbon dating *n, archaeol* a method of estimating the age of archaeological specimens, by measuring the amount of the radioactive ISOTOPE carbon-14 they contain.

carbon dioxide *n, chem* a colourless odourless tasteless gas, present in the atmosphere and formed during respiration.

carbonic *adj* of a compound: containing carbon, esp carbon with a valency of four.

carboniferous *adj* **1** producing carbon or coal. **2** (**Carboniferous**) *geol* relating to the fifth geological period of the PALAEOZOIC era, characterized by extensive swampy forests which subsequently formed coal deposits. ➤ *n, geol* the Carboniferous period.

carbonize or **-ise** *vb* **1** *tr & intr* to convert or reduce (a substance containing carbon) into carbon, either by heating or by natural methods such as fossilization. **2** to coat (a substance) with a layer of carbon. ○ **carbonization** *n*.

carbon monoxide *n, chem* a poisonous colourless odourless gas formed by the incomplete combustion of carbon, eg in car-exhaust gases.

carbon paper *n* paper coated on one side with an ink-like substance containing carbon, which is placed between two or more sheets of paper so that a copy of what is on the top sheet is made on the lower sheets.

carboy *n* a large glass or plastic bottle, usu protected by a basketwork casing.

carbuncle *n* **1** a boil on the skin. **2** a rounded red gemstone, esp a garnet in uncut form.

carburettor *n* the part of an internal-combustion engine in which the liquid fuel and air are mixed in the correct proportions and vaporized before being sucked into the cylinders.

carcass or **carcase** *n* **1** the dead body of an animal. **2** *colloq* the body of a living person.

carcinogen /ˈkɑːˈsɪnədʒən/ *n, pathol* any substance capable of causing cancer. ○ **carcinogenic** /ˌkɑːsɪnəˈdʒɛnɪk/ *adj*.

carcinoma *n, pathol* any cancer that occurs in the skin or in the tissue that lines the internal organs of the body.

card[1] *n* **1** a kind of thick, stiff paper or thin cardboard. **2** (*also* **playing card**) a rectangular piece of card bearing a design, usu one of a set, used eg for playing games, fortune-telling, etc. **3** a small rectangular piece of card or plastic, showing eg one's identity, job, membership of an organization, etc. **4** a CREDIT CARD or DEBIT CARD. **5** *comput* a piece of card on which information is stored in the form of punched holes or magnetic codes. **6** a piece of card, usu folded double and bearing a design and message, sent to someone on a special occasion. ♦ **on the cards** *colloq* likely to happen.

card[2] *n* a comb-like device with sharp teeth for removing knots and tangles from sheep's wool, etc before spinning, or for pulling across the surface of cloth to make it fluffy. ➤ *vb* to treat (wool, fabric) with a card. ○ **carding** *n*.

cardamom or **cardamon** *n* the dried aromatic seeds of a tropical shrub, which are used as a spice.

cardboard *n* a stiff material manufactured from pulped waste paper, used for making boxes, card, etc.

card-carrying *adj* officially registered as a member of a political party, etc and openly supporting it.

cardiac *adj* relating to or affecting the heart.

cardiac arrest *n, pathol* the stopping of the heartbeat and therefore the pumping action of the heart.

cardigan *n* a long-sleeved knitted jacket that fastens down the front.

cardinal *n, RC Church* one of a group of leading clergy, who elect and advise the pope. ➤ *adj* highly important; principal.

cardinal number *n* one of a series of numbers expressing quantity (eg 1, 2, 3, …). Compare ORDINAL NUMBER.

cardinal virtue *n* any of the most important virtues, usu listed as justice, prudence, temperance, fortitude, faith, hope and charity.

cardiography *n* the branch of medicine concerned with the recording of the movements of the heart.

cardiology *n* the branch of medicine concerned with the study of the structure, function and diseases of the heart. ○ **cardiologist** *n*.

cardiopulmonary *adj, anat* relating to the heart and lungs.

cardiovascular *adj, anat* relating to the heart and blood vessels.

care *n* **1** attention and thoroughness. **2** caution; gentleness; regard for safety. **3** the activity of looking after someone or something, or the state of being looked after. **4** worry or anxiety. **5** a cause for worry; a responsibility. ➤ *vb, intr* **1** to mind or to be upset by something, or the possibility of something. **2** (*usu* **care about** or **for sb** or **sth**) to concern oneself about them or be interested in them. **3** (*always* **care for sth**) to have a wish or desire for it: *Would you care for a drink?* **4** to wish or be willing: *Would you care to come?* **5** (*always* **care for sth**) to like or approve of it. **6** (*always* **care for sb** or **sth**) to look after them or it. ♦ **care of** (abbrev **c/o**) written on letters, etc addressed to a person at someone else's address. **take care** to be cautious, watchful or thorough. **take care of sb** or **sth 1** to look after them or it. **2** to attend to or organize them or it.

careen *vb, intr* of a ship: to lean over to one side; to keel over.

career *n* **1** one's professional life; one's progress in one's job. **2** a job, occupation or profession. **3** one's progress through life generally. ➤ *vb, intr* to rush in an uncontrolled or headlong way.

careerist *n, sometimes derog* someone who is chiefly interested in the advancement of their career. ○ **careerism** *n*.

carefree *adj* having few worries; cheerful.

careful *adj* **1** giving or showing care and attention. **2** taking care to avoid harm or damage.

careless *adj* **1** not careful or thorough enough; inattentive. **2** lacking or showing a lack of a sense of responsibility.

carer *n* the person who has the responsibility for looking after an ill, disabled or dependent person.

caress *vb* to touch or stroke gently and lovingly. ➤ *n* a gentle loving touch or embrace.

caret *n* a mark (∧) made on written or printed material to show where a missing word, letter, etc should be inserted.

caretaker *n* a person whose job is to look after a house or a public building, eg a school, esp at times when the building would otherwise be unoccupied. ➤ *adj* temporary; stopgap: *caretaker president*.

careworn *adj* worn out with or marked by worry and anxiety.

carfuffle, **kefuffle** or **kerfuffle** *n, colloq* a commotion; agitation.

cargo *n* (*cargoes*) the goods carried by a ship, aircraft or other vehicle.

Caribbean *adj* belonging or relating to **the Caribbean**, the part of the Atlantic and its islands between the West Indies and Central and S America, or its inhabitants.

caribou *n* (*caribous* or *caribou*) a large deer belonging to the same species as the reindeer, found in N America and Siberia.

caricature *n* **1** a representation, esp a drawing, of someone with their most noticeable and distinctive features exaggerated for comic effect. **2** a ridiculously poor attempt at something. ➤ *vb* to make or give a caricature of someone.

caries /ˈkɛəriːz/ *n* (*pl caries*) the progressive decomposition and decay of a tooth or bone.

carillon /kəˈrɪljən/ *n* **1** a set of bells hung usu in a tower. **2** a tune played on such bells.

caring *adj* **1** showing concern for others; sympathetic and helpful. **2** professionally concerned with social, medical, etc welfare.

carmine *n* a deep red colour; crimson.

carnage *n* great slaughter.

carnal *adj* **1** belonging to the body or the flesh, as opposed to the spirit or intellect. **2** sexual.

carnation *n* a plant with scented pink, white, red, yellow, orange or multicoloured flowers.

carnelian see CORNELIAN

carnival *n* **1** a period of public festivity with eg street processions, colourful costumes, singing and dancing. **2** a circus or fair.

carnivore *n* an animal that feeds mainly on the flesh of other animals. ○ **carnivorous** *adj*.

carol *n* a religious song, esp one sung at Christmas. ➤ *vb* (**carolled, carolling**) **1** *intr* to sing carols. **2** to sing joyfully.

carotene or **carotin** *n, biochem* any of a number of reddish-yellow pigments, widely distributed in plants, that are converted to vitamin A in the body.

carotid /kəˈrɒtɪd/ *n* (*also* **carotid artery**) either of the two major arteries that supply blood to the head and neck.

carousal *n* a drinking bout or party; a noisy revel.

carouse /kəˈraʊz/ *vb, intr* to take part in a noisy drinking party. ➤ *n* CAROUSAL.

carousel /karəˈsɛl/ *n* **1** a revolving belt in an airport, etc onto which luggage is unloaded for passengers to collect. **2** *N Am* a merry-go-round.

carp[1] *n* (*carps* or *carp*) a deep-bodied freshwater fish.

carp[2] *vb, intr* (*often* **carp at sb** or **sth**) to complain, find fault or criticize, esp unnecessarily.

carpal *adj, anat* relating to the CARPUS. ➤ *n* in terrestrial vertebrates: any of the bones that form the carpus.

carpel *n, bot* the female reproductive part of a flowering plant, consisting of a STIGMA (sense 2), STYLE (sense 6) and OVARY (sense 2).

carpenter *n* someone skilled in working with wood, eg in building houses, etc or in making and repairing fine furniture. ○ **carpentry** *n*.

carpet *n* **1** a covering for floors and stairs, made of heavy fabric. **2** something that covers a surface like a carpet does: *a carpet of rose petals*. ➤ *vb* (**carpeted, carpeting**) **1** to cover something with or as if with a carpet. **2** *colloq* to reprimand or scold. ♦ **on the carpet** *colloq* scolded or reprimanded by someone in authority.

carpetbagger *n, derog* a politician seeking election in a place where he or she is a stranger, with no local connections.

carpus *n* (*carpi* /ˈkɑːpaɪ, -piː/) *anat* the eight small bones that form the wrist.

carrageen or **carragheen** /ˈkarəgiːn/ *n* a type of purplish-red, edible seaweed found in the N Atlantic.

carriage *n* **1** a four-wheeled horse-drawn passenger vehicle. **2** a railway coach for carrying passengers. **3** a moving section of a machine, eg a typewriter, that carries some part into the required position. **4** the way one holds oneself when standing or walking.

carriageway *n* the part of a road used by vehicles, or a part used by vehicles travelling in one direction.

carrier *n* **1** a person or thing that carries. **2** a person or firm that transports goods. **3** an individual who may transmit a disease or hereditary disorder to other individuals or to his or her offspring, but who may remain without symptoms. **4** a carrier bag.

carrier bag *n* a plastic or paper bag with handles.

carrier wave *n, physics* a continuously transmitted radio wave whose amplitude or frequency is made to increase or decrease instantaneously, in response to variations in the signal being transmitted.

carrion *n* dead and rotting animal flesh.

carrot *n* **1** a plant with a large orange root eaten as a vegetable. **2** *colloq* something offered as an incentive. ○ **carroty** *adj* of hair: having a strong reddish colour.

carry *vb* (*-ies, -ied*) **1** to hold something in one's hands, have it in a pocket, bag etc, or support its weight on one's body, while moving from one place to another. **2** to bring, take or convey something. **3** to have on one's person: *He always carried a credit card.* **4** to be the means of spreading (a disease, etc): *Mosquitos carry malaria.* **5** to be pregnant with (a baby or babies). **6** to hold (oneself or a part of one's body) in a specified way: *She really carries herself well.* **7** to bear the burden or expense of something. **8** to do the work of (someone who is not doing enough) in addition to one's own. **9** to print or broadcast: *The story was first carried by the tabloids.* **10** *intr* of a sound or the source of a sound: to be able to be heard a distance away. **11** to take to a certain point: *carry politeness too far.* **12** *maths* to transfer (a figure) in a calculation from one column to the next. ➣ *n* (*-ies*) **1** an act of carrying. **2** *N Am* the land across which a vessel has to be transported between one navigable stretch and another. ♦ **be** or **get carried away** *colloq* to become over-excited or over-enthusiastic. ◊ **carry sth forward** to transfer (a number, amount, etc) to the next column, page or financial period. **carry sth off 1** to manage (an awkward situation, etc) well. **2** to win (a prize, etc). **3** to take something away by force. **carry on 1** to continue; to keep going. **2** *colloq* to make a noisy or unnecessary fuss. **carry sth out** to accomplish it successfully. **carry sth through** to complete or accomplish it.

carrycot *n* a light box-like cot with handles, for carrying a baby.

carry-on *n* an excitement or fuss.

cart *n* **1** a two- or four-wheeled horse-drawn vehicle for carrying goods or passengers. **2** a light vehicle pushed or pulled by hand. ➣ *vb* **1** to carry in a cart. **2** (*often* **cart sth around** or **off**, *etc*) *colloq* to carry or convey it.

carte blanche *n* complete freedom of action or discretion.

cartel *n* a group of firms that agree, esp illegally, on similar fixed prices for their products, so as to reduce competition and keep profits high.

carthorse *n* a large strong horse bred for pulling heavy loads on farms, etc.

cartilage *n* in humans: a tough flexible materi-

al that forms the skeleton of the embryo, but is converted into bone before adulthood, persisting in the adults in structures such as the larynx and trachea.

cartography *n* the art or technique of making or drawing maps. ○ **cartographer** *n*.

carton *n* **1** a plastic or cardboard container in which certain foods or drinks are packaged for sale. **2** a cardboard box.

cartoon *n* **1** a humorous drawing in a newspaper, etc, often ridiculing someone or something. **2** (*also* **animated cartoon**) a film made by photographing a series of drawings, each showing the subjects in a slightly altered position, giving the impression of movement when the film is run at high speed. **3** (*also* **strip cartoon**) a strip of drawings in a newspaper, etc showing a sequence of events. ○ **cartoonist** *n*.

cartouche *n* **1** *archit* a scroll-like ornament or decorative border with rolled ends. **2** in Egyptian hieroglyphics: an oval figure enclosing a royal or divine name.

cartridge *n* **1** a metal case containing the propellant charge for a gun. **2** the part of the pickup arm of a record player that contains the stylus. **3** a small plastic tube containing ink for loading into a fountain pen. **4** a plastic container holding a continuous loop of magnetic tape for playing on a tape deck, video recorder, etc. **5** a plastic container holding photographic film for use in a camera.

cartridge paper *n* a type of thick roughsurfaced paper for drawing or printing on.

cartwheel *n* **1** the wheel of a cart. **2** an acrobatic movement in which one throws one's body sideways with the turning action of a wheel, supporting one's body weight on each hand and foot in turn. ➣ *vb, intr* to perform a cartwheel.

carve *vb* **1** to cut (wood, stone, etc) into a shape. **2** to make something from wood, stone, etc by cutting into it. **3** *tr & intr* to cut (meat) into slices; to cut (a slice) of meat. ○ **carver** *n*. ◊ **carve sth up 1** to cut it up into pieces. **2** *colloq* to divide (territory, spoils, etc), esp in a crude or wholesale manner.

carvery *n* (*-ies*) a restaurant where meat is carved from a joint for customers on request.

carve-up *n* a wholesale division, often dishonest, of territory or spoils.

carving *n* a figure or pattern, etc produced by carving wood, stone, etc.

carving-knife *n* a long sharp knife for carving meat.

caryatid /kærɪˈatɪd/ *n* (**caryatids** or **caryatides** /kærɪˈatɪdiːz/) *archit* a carved female figure used as a support for a roof, etc, instead of a column or pillar.

cascade *n* **1** a waterfall or series of waterfalls. **2** something resembling a waterfall in appearance or manner of falling: *a cascade of hair.* **3** a large number of things arriving or to be dealt with suddenly. ➣ *vb, intr* to fall like a waterfall.

case¹ *n* **1** *often in compounds* a box, container or cover, used for storage, transportation, etc: *suitcase*. **2** an outer covering, esp a protective one. ➤ *vb* to put something in a case.

case² *n* **1** a particular occasion, situation or set of circumstances. **2** an example, instance or occurrence. **3** someone receiving some sort of treatment or care. **4** a matter requiring investigation. **5** a matter to be decided in a law court. **6** (*sometimes* **case for** or **against sth**) the set of argument, statements, etc, for or against something. **7** *gram* **a** the relationship of a noun, pronoun or adjective to other words in a sentence; **b** one of the forms or categories indicating the relationship: *nominative case*. ♦ **in any case** no matter what happens. **in case** so as to be prepared or safe (if a certain thing should happen).

case history *n* a record of relevant details from someone's past kept by a doctor, social worker, etc.

casein /ˈkeɪsiːn/ *n* a milk protein that is the main constituent of cheese.

case law *n* law based on decisions made about similar cases in the past, as distinct from STATUTE LAW.

casement or **casement window** *n* a window with vertical hinges that opens outwards like a door.

casework *n* social work concerned with the close study of the background and environment of individuals and families.

cash *n* **1** coins or paper money, as distinct from cheques, credit cards, etc. **2** *colloq* money in any form. ➤ *vb* to obtain or give cash in return for (a cheque, traveller's cheque, postal order, etc). ◊ **cash in on sth** *colloq* to make money by exploiting a situation, etc.

cash-and-carry *n* (*-ies*) a large, often wholesale, shop where customers pay for goods in cash and take them away immediately.

cash book *n* a written record of all money paid out and received by a business, etc.

cash crop *n* a crop that is grown for sale rather than for consumption by the farmer's household.

cash desk *n* a desk in a shop, etc at which one pays for goods.

cashew *n* (*also* **cashew nut**) the curved edible seed of a small evergreen tree.

cash flow *n* the amount of money coming into and going out of a business, etc.

cashier¹ *n* in a business firm, bank, etc: any person who receives, pays out and generally deals with the cash.

cashier² *vb* to dismiss (an officer) from the armed forces in disgrace.

cash machine or **cash dispenser** *n* an electronic machine, often in the outside wall of a bank, from which one can obtain cash using a cash card.

cashmere *n* a type of very fine soft wool from a longhaired Asian goat.

cash point *n* **1** the place in a shop, etc where money is taken for goods purchased. **2** a CASH MACHINE.

cash register *n* a machine in a shop, etc that calculates and records the amount of each sale and from which change and a receipt are usu given.

casing *n* a protective covering.

casino *n* a public building or room for gambling.

cask *n* a barrel for holding liquids, esp alcoholic liquids.

casket *n* **1** a small case for holding jewels, etc. **2** *N Am* a coffin.

cassava *n* **1** a shrubby plant cultivated throughout the tropics for its fleshy tuberous edible roots. **2** a starchy substance obtained from the root of this plant.

casserole *n* **1** an ovenproof dish with a lid, in which meat, vegetables, etc can be cooked and served. **2** the food cooked and served in this kind of dish. ➤ *vb* to cook in a casserole.

cassette *n* **1** a plastic case containing a long ribbon of magnetic tape wound around two reels, that can be inserted into an audio or video tape recorder. **2** a small lightproof plastic cartridge containing photographic film for a camera.

cassette recorder or **cassette player** *n* a machine that records or plays material on audio cassette.

cassock *n* a long black or red garment worn in church by clergymen and male members of a church choir.

cast *vb* (*past tense & past participle* **cast**) **1** to throw. **2** to direct (one's eyes, a glance, etc) on or over something. **3** to throw off or shed something: *She cast her clothes in a heap*. **4** to project; to cause to appear: *cast a shadow*. **5** *tr & intr* to throw (a fishing line) out into the water. **6** to let down (an anchor). **7** (*usu* **cast sth off**, **aside** or **out**) to throw it off or away; to get rid of it. **8** to give (an actor) a part in a play or film; to distribute the parts in a film, play, etc. **9** to shape (molten metal, plastic, etc) by pouring it into a mould and allowing it to set. **10** to give or record (one's vote). ➤ *n* **1** a throw; an act of throwing (eg dice, a fishing line). **2** an object shaped by pouring metal, plastic, etc, into a mould and allowing it to set. **3** (*also* **plaster cast**) a rigid casing, usu of plaster of Paris, moulded round a broken limb or other body part while the plaster is still wet, and then allowed to set in order to hold the broken bone in place while it heals. **4** the set of actors or performers in a play, opera, etc. **5** *formal* type, form, shape or appearance. **6** a slight tinge; a faint colour. ◊ **cast about** or **around for sth** **1** to look about for it. **2** to try to think of it: *cast about for ideas*. **cast off 1** to untie a boat ready to sail away. **2** to finish off and remove knitting from the needles. **cast on** to form (stitches or knitting) by looping and securing wool, etc over the needles.

---

cast, caste These words are sometimes confused with each other.

---

castanets pl n a musical instrument used by Spanish dancers, consisting of two hollow pieces of wood or plastic attached to each other by string, which are held in the palm and struck together rhythmically.

castaway n someone who has been shipwrecked.

caste n 1 a any of the four hereditary social classes into which Hindu society is divided; b this system of social class division. 2 any system of social division based on inherited rank or wealth.

castellated adj of a building: having turrets and battlements like those of a castle.

caster see CASTOR

caster sugar n finely crushed white sugar used in baking, etc.

castigate vb to criticize or punish severely.

casting vote n the deciding vote, used by a chairperson when the votes taken at a meeting, etc are equally divided.

cast iron n any of a group of hard heavy alloys of iron, containing more carbon than steels, and cast into a specific shape when molten. ➤ adj (**cast-iron**) 1 made of cast iron. 2 of a rule or decision: firm; not to be altered.

castle n 1 a large, fortified building with battlements and towers. 2 a large mansion. 3 chess a piece that can be moved any number of empty squares forwards or backwards, but not diagonally. Also called **rook**.

cast-off n something, esp a garment, discarded or no longer wanted. ➤ adj no longer needed; discarded.

castor or **caster** n a small swivelling wheel fitted to the legs or underside of a piece of furniture so that it can be moved easily.

castor oil n a yellow or brown non-drying oil obtained from the seeds of a tropical African plant, used as a lubricant and a strong laxative.

castrate vb 1 to remove the testicles of a male person or animal. 2 to deprive of vigour or strength. ○ **castrated** adj. ○ **castration** n.

castrato n (**castrati** or **castratos**) in 17c and 18c opera: a male singer castrated before puberty to preserve his soprano or contralto voice.

casual adj 1 happening by chance. 2 careless; showing no particular interest or concern. 3 without serious intention or commitment: casual sex. 4 of clothes: informal. ➤ n 1 an occasional worker. 2 (usu **casuals**) clothes suitable for informal wear. ○ **casually** adv. ○ **casualness** n.

casualty n (**-ies**) 1 someone killed or hurt in an accident or war. 2 the casualty department of a hospital. 3 something that is lost, destroyed, sacrificed, etc as a result of some event.

cat n 1 any of a wide range of carnivorous mammals, including the lion, leopard and tiger, as well as the domestic cat. 2 the domesticated member of this family, which has soft fur and

whiskers. 3 CAT-O'-NINE-TAILS. ♦ **let the cat out of the bag** colloq to give away a secret unintentionally. **put** or **set the cat among the pigeons** to cause trouble or upset.

catabolism n, biochem the metabolic process whereby complex organic compounds in living organisms are broken down into simple molecules. Compare ANABOLISM.

cataclysm n 1 an event, esp a political or social one, causing tremendous change or upheaval. 2 a terrible flood or other disaster. ○ **cataclysmic** adj.

catacomb /ˈkatəkuːm, ˈkatəkoʊm/ n (usu **catacombs**) an underground burial place, esp one consisting of a system of tunnels with recesses dug out for the tombs.

catafalque /ˈkatəfalk/ n a temporary platform on which the body of an important person lies in state, before or during the funeral.

catalepsy n (**-ies**) a trance-like state characterized by the abnormal maintenance of rigid body postures. ○ **cataleptic** adj, n.

catalogue n 1 a list of items arranged in a systematic order, esp alphabetically. 2 a brochure, booklet, etc containing a list of goods for sale. 3 a list or index of all the books in a library. ➤ vb (**cataloguing**) 1 to make a catalogue of (a library, books, etc). 2 to enter (an item) in a catalogue. 3 to list or mention one by one: He catalogued her virtues.

catalyse or (US) **-lyze** vb, chem of a CATALYST: to alter the rate of (a chemical reaction) without itself undergoing any permanent chemical change.

catalysis n (**-ses**) chem the process effected by a catalyst. ○ **catalytic** /katəˈlɪtɪk/ adj.

catalyst n 1 chem any substance that accelerates a chemical reaction. 2 something or someone that speeds up the pace of something, or causes change.

catalytic converter n a device fitted to the exhaust system of a motor vehicle that is designed to reduce toxic and polluting emissions from the engine.

catamaran n a sailing-boat with two hulls parallel to each other.

catapult n 1 a Y-shaped stick with an elastic or rubber band fitted between its prongs, used esp by children for firing stones, etc. 2 hist a weapon of war designed to fire boulders. ➤ vb 1 to fire or send flying with, or as if with, a catapult. 2 intr to be sent flying as if from a catapult.

cataract n 1 pathol an opaque area within the lens of the eye that produces blurring of vision. 2 an immense rush of water, eg from a large waterfall that consists of a single vertical drop.

catarrh /kəˈtɑː(r)/ n inflammation of the mucous membranes lining the nose and throat, causing an excessive discharge of thick mucus.

catastrophe /kəˈtastrəfɪ/ n a terrible blow, calamity or disaster. ○ **catastrophic** /katəˈstrɒfɪk/ adj. ○ **catastrophically** adv.

catatonia *n, pathol* an abnormal mental state characterized either by stupor or by excessive excitement and violent activity. ○ **catatonic** *adj, n.*

cat burglar *n* a burglar who breaks into buildings by climbing walls, water pipes, etc.

catcall *n* a long shrill whistle expressing disagreement or disapproval.

catch *vb (past tense, past participle* **caught***)* **1** to stop (a moving object) and hold it. **2** to manage to get hold of or trap, esp after a hunt or chase. **3** to be in time to get, reach, see, etc something: *catch the last post.* **4** to overtake or draw level with someone or something. **5** to discover someone or something in time to prevent, or encourage, the development of something: *The disease can be cured if caught early.* **6** to surprise someone doing something wrong or embarrassing. **7** to trick or trap. **8** to become infected with (a disease, etc). **9** *tr & intr* to become or cause to become accidentally attached or held: *My dress caught on a nail.* **10** to manage to hear, see or understand something: *I didn't quite catch your third point.* **11** *cricket* to put (a batsman) out by gathering the ball he has struck before it touches the ground. ➢ *n* **1** an act of catching. **2** a small device for keeping a lid, door, etc closed. **3** something caught. **4** the total amount of eg fish caught. **5** a hidden problem or disadvantage; a snag. **6** someone or something that it would be advantageous to get hold of, eg a certain person as a husband or wife. **7** a children's game of throwing and catching a ball. ○ **catcher** *n.* ♦ **catch fire** to start burning. **catch sight of** or **catch a glimpse of sb** or **sth** to see them only for a brief moment. ◊ **catch on** *colloq* **1** to become popular. **2** (*sometimes* **catch on to sth**) to understand it. **catch sb out 1** to trick them into making a mistake. **2** to discover them or take them unawares in embarrassing circumstances. **catch up 1** (*often* **catch up with sb**) to draw level with someone ahead. **2** (*sometimes* **catch up on sth**) to bring oneself up to date with one's work, the latest news, etc. **3** to immerse or occupy: *caught up in her studies.*

catching *adj* **1** infectious. **2** captivating.

catchment *n* **1** the area of land that is drained by a particular river system or lake. **2** the population within the catchment area of a school, hospital, etc.

catchment area *n* **1** the area served by a particular school, hospital, etc, encompassing those people who are expected to make use of the facilities within it. **2** (*also* **drainage basin**) the area of land whose rainfall feeds a particular river, lake or reservoir.

catchpenny *adj* of a product: poor in quality but designed to appeal to the eye and sell quickly.

catchphrase *n* a well-known phrase or slogan, esp one associated with a particular celebrity.

catch-22 *n* a situation in which one is frustrated and from which one cannot escape, since all possible courses of action either have undesirable consequences or lead inevitably to further frustration of one's aims.

catchword *n* a much-repeated well-known word or phrase.

catchy *adj (***-ier, -iest***)* of a song, etc: tuneful and easily remembered.

catechism *n* a series of questions and answers about the Christian religion, or a book containing this, used for instruction. ○ **catechist** *n.*

catechize or **-ise** *vb* to instruct someone in the ways of the Christian faith, esp by means of a catechism.

categorical or **categoric** *adj* **1** of a statement, denial, etc: absolute or definite. **2** relating or belonging to a category. ○ **categorically** *adv.*

categorize or **-ise** *vb* to put something into a category or categories. ○ **categorization** *n.*

category *n (***-ies***)* a group of things, people or concepts classed together because of qualities they have in common.

cater *vb, intr* to supply food for an event. ◊ **cater for sb** or **sth** to make provision for them; to take them into account. **cater to sth** to indulge or pander to (unworthy desires, etc).

caterer *n* a person whose professional occupation is to provide food, etc for social occasions. ○ **catering** *n.*

caterpillar *n* **1** the larva of a butterfly or moth. **2** (*usu* **Caterpillar**) *trademark* **a** a continuous band or track made up of metal plates driven by cogs, used instead of wheels on heavy vehicles for travelling over rough surfaces; **b** a vehicle fitted with such tracks.

caterwaul *vb, intr* esp of a cat: to make a loud high wailing noise. ➢ *n* a loud high wail.

catfish *n* a freshwater fish with long whiskerlike sensory barbels around the mouth.

catgut *n* a strong cord made from the dried intestines of sheep and other animals, used in surgery for making stitches, and also used for stringing violins, etc.

catharsis /kə'θɑːsɪs/ *n (***-ses** /-siːz/*)* **1** the emotional relief that results either from allowing repressed thoughts and feelings to surface, as in psychoanalysis, or from an intensely dramatic experience. **2** *med* the process of clearing out or purging the bowels. ○ **cathartic** *adj.*

cathedral *n* the principal church of a DIOCESE.

catheter *n, med* a slender flexible tube that can be introduced into a narrow opening or body cavity, usu in order to drain a liquid, esp urine.

cathode *n* **1** in an electrolytic cell: the negative electrode, towards which positively charged ions, usu in solution, are attracted. **2** the positive terminal of a battery. Compare ANODE.

cathode rays *pl n* a stream of electrons emitted from the surface of a cathode in a vacuum tube.

cathode-ray tube *n* an evacuated glass tube in which streams of CATHODE RAYS are produced, used to display images in television sets, visual display units, etc.

catholic adj 1 (**Catholic**) relating or belonging to the Roman Catholic Church. 2 esp of a person's interests and tastes: broad; wide-ranging. ➢ n (**Catholic**) a member of the Roman Catholic Church.

Catholicism n the teachings of the ROMAN CATHOLIC church.

cation /'katəɪən/ n, chem any positively charged ion, which moves towards the CATHODE during ELECTROLYSIS. Compare ANION.

catkin n, bot in certain tree species, eg birch, hazel: a flowering shoot that bears many small unisexual flowers, adapted for wind pollination.

catmint or **catnip** n, bot a plant in the mint family whose smell excites cats.

catnap n a short sleep. ➢ vb, intr to doze; to sleep briefly.

cat-o'-nine-tails n (pl **cat-o'-nine-tails**) hist a whip with nine knotted rope lashes.

Cat's-eye n, trademark a small glass reflecting device, set in the road to guide drivers in the dark.

cat's paw n a person used by someone else to perform an unpleasant job.

catsuit n a close-fitting one-piece garment, combining trousers and top, usu worn by women.

catsup another spelling of KETCHUP

cattery n (-ies) a place where cats are bred or looked after in their owner's absence.

cattle pl n large heavily built grass-eating mammals, including wild species and the domestic varieties which are farmed for their milk, meat and hides.

cattle grid n a grid of parallel metal bars that covers a trench in a road where it passes through a fence, designed to allow pedestrians and wheeled vehicles to pass while preventing the passage of animal livestock.

catty adj (-ier, -iest) colloq malicious; spiteful. ○ **cattily** adv. ○ **cattiness** n.

catwalk n the narrow raised stage along which models walk at a fashion show.

Caucasian n 1 an inhabitant or native of the Caucasus, a mountain range between the Black Sea and the Caspian Sea. 2 a a member of one of the light- or white-skinned races of mankind; b loosely a white-skinned person.

caucus n 1 a small dominant group of people taking independent decisions within a larger organization. 2 N Am a group of members of a political party, or a meeting of such a group.

caudal adj, anat 1 relating to, resembling or in the position of a tail. 2 relating to the tail end of the body.

caudate or **caudated** adj, zool having a tail or a tail-like appendage.

caul n, anat a membrane that sometimes surrounds an infant's head at birth.

cauldron n a very large metal pot, often with handles, for boiling or heating liquids, esp over a fire.

cauliflower n the firm head of a type of cabbage, made up of white florets and eaten as a vegetable.

cauliflower ear n an ear permanently swollen and misshapen by injury, esp from repeated blows.

caulk vb to fill up (seams or cracks) with OAKUM.

causal adj relating to or being a cause. ○ **causally** adv.

causality n (-ies) 1 the relationship between cause and effect. 2 the principle that everything has a cause.

causation n 1 causality. 2 the process of causing.

causative adj 1 producing an effect. 2 gram expressing the action of causing.

cause n 1 someone or something that produces an effect. 2 a reason or justification: no cause for concern. 3 an ideal, principle, aim, etc that people support and work for. ➢ vb to produce as an effect; to bring about something.

cause célèbre /kouz sə'lɛb, kɔːz sɛ'lɛbrə/ n (**causes célèbres** /kouz sə'lɛb, kɔːz sɛ'lɛbrə/) a legal case, or some other matter, that attracts much attention and causes controversy.

causeway n 1 a raised roadway crossing lowlying marshy ground or shallow water. 2 a stone-paved pathway.

caustic adj 1 chem of a chemical substance, eg sodium hydroxide: strongly alkaline and corrosive to living tissue. 2 of remarks, etc: sarcastic; cutting; bitter. ➢ n a caustic substance. ○ **caustically** adv.

caustic soda see SODIUM HYDROXIDE

cauterize or **-ise** vb to destroy (tissue) by the direct application of a heated instrument or a caustic chemical. ○ **cauterization** n.

caution n 1 care in avoiding danger. 2 a warning. 3 a formal reprimand for an offence, accompanied by a warning not to repeat it. ➢ vb 1 tr & intr to warn or admonish someone. 2 to give someone a legal caution. ○ **cautionary** adj.

cautious adj having or showing caution; careful; wary. ○ **cautiously** adv. ○ **cautiousness** n.

cavalcade n 1 a ceremonial procession of cars, horseback riders, etc. 2 any procession or parade.

cavalier n 1 a courtly gentleman. 2 (**Cavalier**) hist a supporter of Charles I during the 17c English Civil War. ➢ adj, derog of a person's behaviour, attitude, etc: thoughtless, offhand, or disrespectful.

cavalry n (-ies) 1 usu hist the part of an army consisting of soldiers on horseback. 2 the part of an army consisting of soldiers in armoured vehicles. ○ **cavalryman** n.

cave n a large natural hollow chamber either underground or in the side of a mountain, hillside or cliff. ◊ **cave in 1** of walls, a roof, etc: to collapse inwards. 2 colloq of a person: to give way to persuasion.

caveat n 1 a warning. 2 law an official request that a court should not take some particular action without warning the person who is making the request.

cave-in n 1 a collapse. 2 a submission or surrender.

caveman n 1 (*also* **cave-dweller**) a person of prehistoric times, who lived in caves, etc. 2 *derog* a man who behaves in a crude, brutish way.

cavern n a large cave or an underground chamber.

cavernous adj of a hole or space: deep and vast.

caviar or **caviare** n the salted hard roe of the sturgeon, used as food and considered a delicacy.

cavil vb (**cavilled, cavilling**) intr (*usu* **cavil at** or **about sth**) to make trivial objections to something. ➢ n a trivial objection.

caving n the sport of exploring caves.

cavity n (*-ies*) 1 a hollow or hole. 2 a hole in a tooth, caused by decay.

cavort vb, intr to jump or caper about.

caw n the loud harsh cry of a crow or rook. ➢ vb, intr to make such a cry.

cay see KEY²

cayenne /ˈkeɪˈɛn/ or **cayenne pepper** n a hot spice made from the seeds of various types of CAPSICUM.

cayman or **caiman** n a S American reptile closely related to the alligator.

cc abbrev 1 carbon copy. 2 cubic centimetre.

CCTV abbrev closed-circuit television.

CD abbrev compact disc.

Cd symbol, chem cadmium.

cd abbrev candela.

CD-i or **CDI** abbrev compact disc interactive, a type of CD-ROM that responds intelligently to instructions given by the user.

CD-ROM abbrev, comput compact disc read-only memory, a compact disc allowing examination, but not alteration, of text.

CE or **C.E.** abbrev 1 Church of England. 2 Common Era.

Ce symbol, chem cerium.

cease vb, tr & intr to bring or come to an end.

ceasefire n 1 a break in the fighting during a war, agreed to by all sides. 2 the order to stop firing.

ceaseless adj continuous; going on without a pause or break. ○ **ceaselessly** adv.

cedar n 1 a tall coniferous tree with widely spreading branches, cones, needle-like leaves and reddish-brown bark. 2 (*also* **cedarwood**) the hard yellow sweet-smelling wood of this tree.

cede vb to hand over or give up something formally.

cedilla /səˈdɪlə/ n 1 in French and Portuguese: a DIACRITIC put under c in some words, eg *façade*, to show that it is to be pronounced like s, not like k. 2 the same mark used under other letters in other languages to indicate various sounds.

ceilidh /ˈkeɪlɪ/ n in Scotland and Ireland: an informal social gathering, with traditional music and dancing.

ceiling n 1 the inner roof of a room, etc. 2 an upper limit.

celandine n a plant with heart-shaped dark-green leaves, and flowers with glossy golden-yellow petals.

celebrant n someone who performs a religious ceremony.

celebrate vb 1 to mark (an occasion, esp a birthday or anniversary) with festivities. 2 *intr* to do something enjoyable to mark a happy occasion, anniversary, etc. 3 to give public praise or recognition to someone or something, eg in the form of a poem. 4 to conduct (a religious ceremony, eg a marriage or mass). ○ **celebration** n. ○ **celebratory** adj.

celebrated adj famous; renowned.

celebrity n (*-ies*) 1 a famous person. 2 fame or renown.

celeriac /səˈlɛrɪak/ n a variety of celery, cultivated for the swollen edible base of its stem, which is eaten as a vegetable.

celerity /səˈlɛrɪtɪ/ n, formal quickness; rapidity of motion or thought.

celery n (*-ies*) a plant with deeply grooved leaf stalks that are eaten as a vegetable.

celesta n a keyboard instrument from which soft bell-like sounds are produced by hammers striking steel plates suspended over wooden resonators.

celestial adj 1 belonging or relating to the sky: *celestial bodies*. 2 heavenly; divine: *celestial voices*.

celibate adj 1 unmarried, esp in obedience to a religious vow. 2 having no sexual relations with anyone. ➢ n someone who is unmarried, esp because of a religious vow. ○ **celibacy** n.

cell n 1 a small room occupied by an inmate in a prison or monastery. 2 *biol* the basic structural unit of all living organisms, consisting of a mass of protein material which is composed of the CYTOPLASM and usu a NUCLEUS (sense 2). 3 *elec* a device consisting of two ELECTRODES immersed in an ELECTROLYTE, for converting electrical energy into chemical energy. 4 one of the compartments in a honeycomb or in a similarly divided structure. 5 *comput* a unit or area of storage.

cellar n 1 a room, usu underground, for storage. 2 a stock of wines.

cello n a large stringed musical instrument of the violin family, which is played held between the knees of a seated player. ○ **cellist** n.

Cellophane n, trademark a thin transparent wrapping material.

cellphone n a MOBILE PHONE.

cellular adj 1 composed of cells or divided into cell-like compartments. 2 relating to mobile phones.

cellular radio n a system of radio communication used esp for mobile phones, based on a network of small geographical areas called cells, each of which is served by a transmitter.

cellulite *n* deposits of fat cells said to be resistant to changes in diet or exercise regime, and which give the skin a dimpled, pitted appearance.

Celluloid *n, trademark* a transparent plastic.

cellulose *n* a complex carbohydrate that is the main constituent of plant cell walls, and is used in the manufacture of paper, rope, textiles and plastics.

Celsius scale *n* a scale of temperature in which the freezing point of water is 0°C and its boiling point is 100°C.

Celt *n* a member of one of the ancient peoples that inhabited most parts of Europe in pre-Roman and Roman times, or of the peoples descended from them, eg in Scotland, Wales and Ireland.

Celtic or **Keltic** *adj* relating to the Celts or their languages. ➤ *n* a branch of the Indo-European family of languages, including Gaelic, Welsh, and Breton.

cement *n* **1** a fine powder, composed of a mixture of clay and limestone, that hardens when mixed with water, and is used to make mortar and concrete. **2** any of various substances used as adhesives for bonding to a hard material. **3** *dentistry* any of various substances used to fill cavities in teeth. ➤ *vb* **1** to stick together with cement. **2** to apply cement. **3** to bind or make firm (eg a friendship).

cemetery *n* (*-ies*) a burial ground.

cenotaph *n* a tomb-like monument in honour of a person or persons buried elsewhere, esp soldiers killed in war.

Cenozoic or **Caenozoic** /si:nou'zouɪk/ or **Cainozoic** /kaɪnou'zouɪk/ *geol, adj* denoting the most recent era of the Phanerozoic eon. ➤ *n* the Cenozoic era.

censer *n* a container in which incense is burnt, used eg in some churches.

censor *n* an official who examines books, films, newspaper articles, etc, with the power to cut out any parts thought politically sensitive or offensive, or to forbid showing altogether. ➤ *vb* **1** to alter or cut out parts of something, or forbid its publication, showing or delivery. **2** to act as a censor. ○ **censorship** *n*.

censorious *adj* inclined to find fault; severely critical.

censure *n* severe criticism or disapproval. ➤ *vb* to criticize severely or express strong disapproval.

census *n* an official count of a population, carried out at periodic intervals, which covers information such as sex, age, job, etc.

cent *n* a unit of currency of various countries, worth one hundredth of the standard unit, eg of the EURO or the US dollar.

centaur *n, Greek myth* a creature with a man's head, arms and trunk, joined to the body and legs of a horse.

centenarian *n* someone who is 100 years old or more.

centenary *n* (*-ies*) the one-hundredth anniversary of some event, or the celebration of it.

centennial *n, N Am* a centenary. ➤ *adj* **1** relating to a period of 100 years. **2** occurring every 100 years. **3** lasting 100 years.

centi- *pfx, denoting* one-hundredth: *centilitre*.

centigrade *n* the former name for the CELSIUS SCALE of temperature.

centilitre or (*US*) **centiliter** *n* one hundredth of a litre.

centime /'sɒnti:m/ *n* a currency unit of several countries, worth one hundredth of the standard unit, eg of the Swiss franc.

centimetre or (*US*) **centimeter** *n* in the metric system: a basic unit of length equal to 0.01m (one hundredth of a metre).

centipede *n* any of numerous species of terrestrial arthropod which have a long rather flat segmented body and usu a pair of legs for each body segment.

central *adj* **1** at or forming the centre of something. **2** near the centre of a city, etc; easy to reach. **3** principal or most important. ○ **centrality** *n*. ○ **centrally** *adv*.

central bank *n* a national bank acting as banker to the government, issuing currency, controlling the amount of credit in the country and having control over interest rates.

central government *n* the government that has power over a whole country, as distinct from local government.

central heating *n* a system for heating a whole building, by means of pipes, radiators, etc connected to a central source of heat.

centralism *n* the policy of bringing the administration of a country under central control, with a decrease in local administrative power. ○ **centralist** *n, adj*.

centralize or **-ise** *vb, tr & intr* to bring under central control. ○ **centralization** *n*.

central nervous system *n* in vertebrates: the part of the nervous system that is responsible for the co-ordination and control of the various body functions; it consists of the brain and spinal cord.

central processing unit *n, comput* the part of a computer that controls and co-ordinates the operation of all the other parts.

central reservation *n, Brit* a narrow strip of grass, concrete, etc dividing the two sides of a dual carriageway or motorway.

centre or (*US*) **center** *n* **1** a part at the middle of something. **2** a point inside a circle or sphere that is an equal distance from all points on the circumference or surface, or a point on a line at an equal distance from either end. **3** a point or axis round which a body revolves or rotates. **4** a central area. **5** *chiefly in compounds* a place where a specified activity is concentrated or specified facilities, information, etc are available: *a sports centre*. **6** something that acts as a focus: *the centre of attraction*. **7** a point or place from which activities are controlled: *the centre of operations*. **8** a position that is at neither extreme, esp in politics. **9** in some field sports, eg football: **a** a position in the middle of the field; **b** a player in this position. ➤ *adj* at the centre; central. ➤ *vb* **1** to place in or at the centre. **2** *tr & intr* (*often* **centre on** *or* **upon sth**) to concentrate on it.

centreboard *n* in a sailing boat or dinghy: a movable plate which can be let down through the keel to prevent sideways drift.

centrefold *n* **1** the sheet that forms the two central facing pages of a magazine, etc. **2** a photograph of a naked or nearly naked person on such pages.

centrepiece *n* **1** a central or most important item. **2** an ornament or decoration for the centre of a table.

centrifugal force *n* an apparent force that seems to exert an outward pull on an object that is moving in a circular path. Compare CENTRIPETAL FORCE.

centrifuge *n* a device containing a rotating device that is used to separate solid or liquid particles of different densities. ➤ *vb* to subject something to centrifugal action.

centripetal force *n* the force that is required to keep an object moving in a circular path. Compare CENTRIFUGAL FORCE.

centurion *n*, *hist* in the army of ancient Rome: an officer in charge of a CENTURY (*noun sense* 3).

century *n* (*-ies*) **1** a period of 100 years. **2** *cricket* a score of 100 runs made by a batsman in a single innings. **3** *hist* in the army of ancient Rome: a company of (orig) 100 foot soldiers.

cephalic /sɪˈfalɪk/ *adj* relating to the head or the head region.

cephalopod /ˈsɛfələpɒd/ *n* any invertebrate animal with a head and many tentacles surrounding its mouth, eg squid, octopus, cuttlefish.

ceramic *n* **1** any of a number of hard brittle materials produced by baking or firing clays at high temperatures. **2** an object made from such a material. ➤ *adj* relating to or made of such a material.

ceramics *sing n* the art and technique of making pottery.

cereal *n* **1** a grass that is cultivated as a food crop for its nutritious edible seeds, ie grains, eg barley, wheat, rice, etc. **2** the grain produced. **3** a breakfast food prepared from this grain.

cerebellum /sɛrəˈbɛləm/ *n* (**cerebella** /-lə/) *anat* in vertebrates: the main part of the hindbrain, concerned primarily with the co-ordination of movement. ○ **cerebellar** *adj*.

cerebral /ˈsɛrəbrəl, səˈriːbrəl/ *adj* **1** relating to the brain, esp the front of the brain. **2** intellectual rather than emotional: *a cerebral argument*.

cerebral palsy *n*, *pathol* a failure of the brain to develop normally due to brain damage before or around the time of birth, resulting in weakness and lack of co-ordination of the limbs.

cerebrate *vb*, *intr*, *facetious* to think; to use one's brain.

cerebrospinal *adj* relating to the brain and spinal cord together: *cerebrospinal fluid*.

cerebrum /ˈsɛrəbrəm, səˈriːbrəm/ *n* (**cerebrums** or **cerebra** /-brə/) *anat* in higher vertebrates: the larger part of the brain, situated at the front, which controls thinking, emotions and personality.

ceremonial *adj* relating to, used for or involving a ceremony. ➤ *n* a system of rituals. ○ **ceremonially** *adv*.

ceremonious *adj* excessively formal. ○ **ceremoniously** *adv*.

ceremony *n* (*-ies*) **1** a ritual performed to mark a particular, esp public or religious, occasion. **2** formal politeness. ◆ **stand on ceremony** to insist on behaving formally.

cerise /səˈriːz, səˈriːs/ *n* a bright cherry-red colour.

cerium *n*, *chem* a soft silvery-grey metallic element used in catalytic converters, alloys, etc.

cert *n*, *colloq* (*usu* **dead cert**) a certainty, esp a horse that is bound to win a race.

certain *adj* **1** proved or known beyond doubt. **2** (*sometimes* **certain about** *or* **of sth**) having no doubt about it; absolutely sure. **3** used with reference to the future: definitely going to happen, etc; able to rely on or be relied on. **4** particular and, though known, not named or specified: *a certain friend of yours*. **5** of a quality: undeniably present without being clearly definable: *The beard gave his face a certain authority*. **6** some, though not much: *That's true to a certain extent*. ◆ **for certain** definitely; without doubt.

certainly *adv* **1** without any doubt. **2** definitely. **3** in giving permission: of course.

certainty *n* (*-ies*) **1** something that cannot be doubted or is bound to happen. **2** the state of being sure.

certifiable *adj* **1** capable of or suitable for being certified. **2** *colloq* of a person: mad; crazy.

certificate /səˈtɪfɪkət/ *n* an official document that formally acknowledges or witnesses a fact, an achievement or qualification, or one's condition: *marriage certificate*. ➤ *vb* /səˈtɪfɪkeɪt/ to provide with a certificate.

certificated *adj* qualified by a particular course of training.

certified *adj* **1** possessing a certificate. **2** endorsed or guaranteed. **3** of a person: insane.

certify *vb* (*-ies, -ied*) **1** *tr & intr* to declare or confirm officially. **2** to declare someone legally insane. **3** to declare to have reached a required standard, passed certain tests, etc.

certitude *n* a feeling of certainty.

cervical *adj* relating to the cervix.

cervix *n*, *anat* (**cervixes** or **cervices** /sɜːˈvaɪsiːz/) **1** the neck of the uterus. **2** the neck.

cessation *n* a stopping or ceasing; a pause.

cession *n* the giving up or yielding of territories, rights, etc to someone else.

cesspit *n* **1** a pit for the collection and storage of sewage. **2** a foul and squalid place.

cesspool *n* a tank, well, etc for the collection and storage of sewage and waste water.

cetacean /sɪˈteɪʃən/ *n* any animal belonging to the order which includes dolphins, porpoises and whales.

cetane /ˈsiːteɪn/ *n* a colourless liquid hydrocarbon found in petroleum, used as a solvent.

cetane number *n* a measure of the ignition quality of diesel fuel when it is burnt in a standard diesel engine.

Cf *symbol, chem* californium.

cf *abbrev: confer* (Latin), compare.

CFC *abbrev* chlorofluorocarbon.

ch *abbrev* **1** chapter. **2** church.

cha-cha or **cha-cha-cha** *n* **1** a Latin American dance. **2** a piece of music for it. ➤ *vb, intr* to perform this dance.

chador, **chadar** or **chuddar** /ˈtʃʌdə(r)/ *n* a thick veil worn by some Muslim women that covers the head and body.

chafe *vb* **1** *tr & intr* to make or become sore or worn by rubbing. **2** *intr* (also **chafe at** or **under sth**) to become angry or impatient: *chafe at the rules*.

chafer *n* any of various species of large slow-moving nocturnal beetle, found mainly in the tropics.

chaff¹ *n* **1** the husks that form the outer covering of cereal grain, and are separated from the seeds during threshing. **2** chopped hay or straw used as animal feed or bedding. **3** worthless material.

chaff² *n* light-hearted joking or teasing. ➤ *vb* to tease or make fun of someone in a good-natured way.

chaffinch *n* a finch with a blue crown, reddish body, stout bill and conspicuous white wing bars.

chagrin *n* acute annoyance or disappointment. ➤ *vb* to annoy or embarrass someone.

chain *n* **1** a series of interconnecting links or rings, esp of metal, used for fastening, binding or holding, or, eg in jewellery, for ornament. **2** a series or progression: *a chain of events*. **3** a number of shops, hotels, etc under common ownership or management. **4** (**chains**) something that restricts or frustrates. **5** *chem* a number of atoms of the same type that are joined in a line to form a molecule. ➤ *vb* (*often* **chain sb** or **sth up** or **down**) to fasten, bind or restrict with, or as if with, chains.

chain gang *n* a group of prisoners chained together for working outside the prison.

chain reaction *n* **1** a nuclear or chemical reaction that is self-sustaining. **2** a series of events, each causing the next.

chainsaw *n* a portable power-driven saw with cutting teeth linked together in a continuous chain.

chain-smoke *vb, tr & intr* to smoke (cigarettes, etc) continuously, esp lighting each one from its predecessor. ◊ **chain-smoker** *n*.

chair *n* **1** a seat for one person, with a back-support and usu four legs. **2** the office of chairman or chairwoman at a meeting, etc, or the person holding this office. **3** a professorship. **4** (**the chair**) *colloq N Am, esp US* the electric chair as a means of capital punishment. ➤ *vb* to control or conduct (a meeting) as chairman or chairwoman. ◆ **in the chair** acting as chairman or chairwoman. **take the chair** to be chairman or chairwoman.

chairlift *n* a series of seats suspended from a moving cable, for carrying skiers, etc up a mountain.

chairman, **chairwoman** or **chairperson** *n* **1** someone who conducts or controls a meeting or debate. **2** someone who presides over a committee, board of directors, etc.

chaise /ʃeɪz/ *n, hist* a light open two-wheeled horse-drawn carriage, for one or more persons.

chaise longue /ʃeɪzˈlɒŋ/ *n* (**chaises longues** /ʃeɪzˈlɒŋ, -lɒŋz/) a long seat with a back and one armrest, on which one can recline at full length.

chalcedony /kalˈsɛdənɪ/ *n* (*-ies*) *geol* a fine-grained variety of the mineral quartz, which occurs in various forms, eg agate, jasper, onyx.

chalet /ˈʃaleɪ/ *n* **1** a style of house typical of Alpine regions, built of wood, with window-shutters and a heavy sloping roof. **2** a small cabin for holiday accommodation.

chalice *n* **1** *poetic* a wine cup; a goblet. **2** in the Christian Church: the cup used for serving the wine at Communion or Mass.

chalk *n* **1** a soft fine-grained porous rock, composed of calcium carbonate. **2** a material similar to this, usu calcium sulphate, in stick form, used for writing and drawing, esp on a blackboard. ➤ *vb* to write or mark in chalk. ◊ **chalky** *adj*. ◆ **as different** or **as like as chalk and cheese** *colloq* completely different. **not by a long chalk** *colloq* not at all. ◊ **chalk sth up to sb** to add it to the account of money owed by or to them.

chalkboard *n, N Am* a blackboard.

challenge *vb* **1** to call on someone to settle a matter by any sort of contest. **2** to cast doubt on something or call it in question. **3** to test, esp in a stimulating way: *a task that challenges you*. **4** of a guard or sentry: to order someone to stop and show official proof of identity, etc. **5** *law* to object to the inclusion of someone on a jury. ➤ *n* **1** an invitation to a contest. **2** the questioning or doubting of something. **3** a problem or task that stimulates effort and interest. **4** an order from a guard or sentry to stop and prove identity. **5** *law* an objection to the inclusion of someone on a jury. ◊ **challenger** *n*. ◊ **challenging** *adj*.

challenged *adj, usu in compounds* a supposedly neutral term, denoting some kind of handicap, impairment or disability: *physically challenged*.

chamber *n* **1** *old use* a room, esp a bedroom. **2**

a hall for the meeting of an assembly, esp a legislative or judicial body. **3** one of the houses of which a parliament consists. **4** (**chambers**) a suite of rooms used by eg a judge or lawyer. **5** an enclosed space or hollow; a cavity. **6** the compartment in a gun into which the bullet or cartridge is loaded. **7** a room or compartment with a particular function: *a decompression chamber*.

chamberlain *n* someone who manages a royal or noble household. Sometimes given the title **Lord Chamberlain**.

chambermaid *n* a woman who cleans bedrooms in a hotel, etc.

chamber of commerce *n* an association of business people formed to promote local trade.

chamberpot *n* a receptacle for urine, etc for use in a bedroom.

chameleon /kə'miːlɪən/ *n* **1** lizard whose granular skin changes colour rapidly in response to changes in its environment. **2** *derog* a changeable unreliable person.

chamfer *vb* to give a smooth rounded shape to (an edge or corner). ➤ *n* a rounded or bevelled edge.

chamois *n* (*pl chamois*) **1** *sing and pl* /'ʃæmwɑː/ an agile antelope, native to S Europe and Asia. **2** /'ʃæmɪ/ soft suede leather, formerly made from the skin of this animal, but now usu made from the hides of sheep, lambs or goats. **3** /'ʃæmɪ/ (*pl* /-mɪz/) a piece of this used as a polishing cloth for glass, etc. Also written **shammy**.

chamomile see CAMOMILE

champ[1] *vb, tr & intr* to munch noisily. ➤ *n* the sound of munching. ♦ **champ at the bit** to be impatient to act.

champ[2] *n, colloq* a champion.

champagne *n* **1** *strictly* a sparkling white wine made in the Champagne district of France. **2** *loosely* any sparkling white wine. **3** a pale pinkish-yellow colour. ➤ *adj* **1** champagne-coloured. **2** relating to champagne: *champagne bottle*. **3** denoting an extravagant way of life: *champagne lifestyle*.

champion *n* **1** in games, competitions, etc: a competitor that has defeated all others. **2** the supporter or defender of a person or cause. ➤ *vb* to strongly support or defend (a person or cause). ➤ *adj, N Eng dialect* excellent. ○ **championship** *n*.

chance *n* **1** the way that things happen unplanned and unforeseen. **2** fate or luck; fortune. **3** an unforeseen and unexpected occurrence. **4** a possibility or probability. **5** a possible or probable success. **6** an opportunity: *your big chance*. **7** risk; a gamble: *take a chance*. ➤ *vb* **1** to risk something. **2** *intr* to do or happen by chance: *I chanced to meet her*. ♦ **on the off chance** in hope rather than expectation. **take one's chance** or **chances** to risk an undertaking; to accept whatever happens. ◇ **chance on** or **upon sb** or **sth** to meet or find them or it by accident.

chancel *n* the eastern part of a church containing the altar, usu separated from the nave by a screen or steps.

chancellery or **chancellory** *n* (**-ies**) **1** the rank of chancellor. **2** a chancellor's department or staff. **3** (*also* **chancery**) **a** the offices or residence of a chancellor; **b** the office of an embassy or consulate.

chancellor *n* **1** the head of the government in certain European countries. **2** a state or legal official of various kinds. **3** in the UK: the honorary head of a university. **4** in the US: the president of a university or college. ○ **chancellorship** *n*.

chancer *n, colloq, derog* someone inclined to take any opportunity to profit, whether honestly or dishonestly.

chancery *n* (**-ies**) **1** (*also* **Chancery**) a division of the High Court of Justice. **2** a record office containing public archives. **3** a CHANCELLERY.

chancre /'ʃæŋkə(r)/ *n, pathol* a small hard growth that develops in the primary stages of syphilis and certain other diseases.

chancy *adj* (**-ier, -iest**) risky; uncertain.

chandelier /ʃændə'lɪə(r)/ *n* an ornamental light-fitting hanging from the ceiling, with branching holders for candles or light-bulbs.

chandler *n* a dealer in candles, oil, groceries, etc. ○ **chandlery** *n* (**-ies**) goods sold by a chandler.

change *vb* **1** *tr & intr* to make or become different. **2** to give, leave or substitute one thing for another. **3** to exchange (usu one's position) with another person, etc. **4** *tr & intr* to remove (clothes, sheets, a baby's nappy, etc) and replace them with clean or different ones. **5** *tr & intr* (*sometimes* **change into sth**) to make into or become something different. **6** to obtain or supply another kind of money: *change pounds into euros*. **7** *tr & intr* to put a vehicle engine into (another gear). ➤ *n* **1** the process of changing or an instance of it. **2** the replacement of one thing with another. **3** a variation, esp a welcome one, from one's regular habit, etc: *Let's eat out for a change*. **4** the leaving of (one vehicle) for another during a journey. **5** a fresh set (of clothes) for changing into. **6** (*also* **small** or **loose change**) coins as distinct from notes. **7** coins or notes given in exchange for ones of higher value. **8** money left over or returned from the amount given in payment. **9** (**the change**) *colloq* the menopause. ○ **changeable** *adj*. ○ **changeless** *adj*. ♦ **change hands** to pass into different ownership. **change one's mind** or **tune** to adopt a different intention or opinion. ◇ **change over** to change from one preference or situation to another.

changeling *n, folklore* a child substituted by the fairies for an unbaptized human baby.

change of heart *n* a change of attitude often resulting in the reversal of a decision.

change of life *n* the menopause.

changing room *n* a room in a sports centre, etc where one can change one's clothes.

channel n 1 any natural or artificially constructed water course. 2 the part of a river, waterway, etc, that is deep enough for navigation by ships. 3 a wide stretch of water, esp between an island and a continent, eg the English Channel. 4 *electronics* a the frequency band that is assigned for sending or receiving a clear radio or television signal; b a path along which electrical signals flow. 5 a groove, furrow or any long narrow cut, esp one along which something moves. 6 *comput* the path along which electrical signals representing data flow. 7 (*often* channels) a means by which information, etc is communicated, obtained or received. 8 a course, project, etc into which some resource may be directed: *a channel for one's energies.* 9 (**the Channel**) the English Channel, the stretch of sea between England and France. ➤ vb (**channelled, channelling**) 1 to make an island or channels in something. 2 to convey (a liquid, information, etc) through a channel. 3 to direct (eg talent, energy, money) into a course, project, etc.

chant vb, tr & intr 1 to recite in a singing voice. 2 to keep repeating, esp loudly and rhythmically. ➤ n 1 a type of singing used in religious services for passages in prose, with a simple melody and several words sung on one note. 2 a phrase or slogan constantly repeated, esp loudly and rhythmically. ○ **chanting** n, adj.

chanter n on a set of bagpipes: the pipe on which the melody is played.

chanty another spelling of SHANTY²

chaos n complete confusion or disorder. ○ **chaotic** adj. ○ **chaotically** adv.

chap¹ n, colloq (also **chappie**) a man or boy; a fellow.

chap² vb (**chapped, chapping**) tr & intr of the skin: to make or become cracked, roughened and red as a result of rubbing or exposure to cold. ➤ n a cracked roughened red patch on the skin, formed in this way.

chap. abbrev chapter.

chaparajos or **chaparejos** see under CHAPS

chapati or **chapatti** /tʃə'pɑːtɪ/ n (chapati, chapatis or chapaties) in Indian cooking: a thin flat portion of unleavened bread.

chapel n 1 a recess within a church or cathedral, with its own altar. 2 a place of worship attached to a house, school, etc. 3 in England and Wales: a place of Nonconformist worship. 4 in Scotland and N Ireland: the place of worship for Roman Catholics or Episcopalians. 5 an association of workers in a newspaper office, or a printing- or publishing-house.

chaperone or **chaperon** /'ʃapəroʊn/ n 1 formerly an older woman accompanying a younger unmarried one on social occasions. 2 an older person accompanying and supervising a young person or group of young people. ➤ vb to act as chaperone to someone.

chaplain n a member of the clergy attached to a school, hospital or other institution, sometimes having a chapel, or to the armed forces.

○ **chaplaincy** n (-ies) the position or office of chaplain.

chaplet n a wreath of flowers or a band of gold, etc worn on the head.

chapman n, hist a travelling dealer; a pedlar.

chapped adj of the skin and lips: dry and cracked.

chappie see CHAP¹

chaps, chaparajos or **chaparejos** /ʃapə'reɪoʊs/ pl n protective leather riding leggings, worn over the trousers.

chapter n 1 one of the numbered or titled sections into which a book is divided. 2 a period associated with certain happenings: *University was an exciting chapter in my life.* 3 a sequence or series: *a chapter of accidents.* 4 N Am a branch of a society. 5 the body of canons of a cathedral, or of the members of a religious order. ◆ **chapter and verse** an exact reference, description of circumstances, etc.

char¹ vb (**charred, charring**) tr & intr to blacken or be blackened by burning; to scorch.

char² vb (**charred, charring**) intr to do paid cleaning work in someone's house, an office, etc. ➤ n, colloq a charwoman.

char³ n, slang tea.

char⁴ or **charr** n (char, charr, chars or charrs) a fish related to and resembling the salmon, native to cool northern lakes and rivers.

charabanc /'ʃarəbaŋ/ n, dated a single-decker coach for tours, sightseeing, etc.

character n 1 the combination of qualities that makes up a person's nature or personality. 2 the combination of qualities that typifies anything. 3 type or kind. 4 strong admirable qualities such as determination, courage, honesty, etc. 5 interesting qualities that make for individuality: *a house with character.* 6 someone in a story or play. 7 an odd or amusing person. 8 reputation: *blacken someone's character.* 9 a letter, number or other written or printed symbol. 10 *comput* a symbol represented by a unique finite length bit pattern. ○ **characterless** adj. ◆ **in** or **out of character** typical or untypical of a person's nature.

characteristic n 1 a distinctive quality or feature. 2 *maths* the integral part of a logarithm. ➤ adj indicative of a distinctive quality or feature; typical: *a characteristic feature.* ○ **characteristically** adv.

characterize or **-ise** vb to describe, be or give the chief or distinctive qualities of someone or something. ○ **characterization** n.

charade /ʃə'rɑːd, ʃə'reɪd/ n 1 derog a ridiculous pretence; a farce. 2 (**charades**) a party game in which players mime each syllable of a word, or each word of a book title, etc, while the watching players try to guess the complete word or title.

charcoal n 1 a black form of carbon produced by heating organic material, esp wood, in the absence of air. 2 a stick of this used for drawing. 3 a drawing done in charcoal. 4 (also **charcoal grey**) a dark grey colour.

charge vb **1** to ask for an amount as the price of something. **2** to ask someone to pay an amount for something. **3** to accuse someone officially of a crime. **4** intr to rush at someone or something in attack. **5** to rush. **6** formal to officially order someone to do something: She was charged to appear in court. **7** to load (a gun, furnace, etc) with explosive, fuel, etc. **8** formal & old use to fill up: charge your glasses. **9** intr of a battery, capacitor, etc: to take up or store electricity. **10** to cause (a battery, capacitor, etc) to take up or store electricity. **11** to fill: The moment was charged with emotion. ➤ n **1** an amount of money charged. **2** control, care or responsibility: in charge of repairs. **3** supervision or guardianship: The police arrived and took charge. **4** something or someone, eg a child, that is in one's care. **5** something of which one is accused: a charge of murder. **6** a rushing attack. **7** (also **electrical charge**) a deficiency or excess of electrons on a particular object, giving rise to a positive or negative charge, respectively. **8** the total amount of electricity stored by an insulated object such as an accumulator or capacitor. **9** a quantity of material appropriate for filling something. **10** an amount of explosive, fuel, etc, for loading into a gun, furnace, etc. **11** an order. **12** a task, duty or burden. **13** a debt or financial liability. ○ **chargeable** adj. ◆ **press** or **prefer charges** to charge someone officially with a crime, etc.

charge card n a small card issued by a store, which entitles the holder to buy goods on credit.

charge hand n the deputy to a foreman in a factory, etc.

charge nurse n a nurse in charge of a hospital ward, esp if a male; the equivalent of a SISTER.

charger n, hist a strong horse used by a knight in battle, etc.

chariot n, hist a two-wheeled vehicle pulled by horses, used in ancient times for warfare or racing. ○ **charioteer** n a chariot-driver.

charisma /kəˈrɪzmə/ n a strong ability to attract people, and inspire loyalty and admiration. ○ **charismatic** /karɪzˈmatɪk/ adj.

charitable adj **1** having a kind and understanding attitude to others. **2** generous in assisting people in need. **3** relating to, belonging to, or in the nature of a charity: charitable institutions. ○ **charitably** adv.

charity n (-ies) **1** assistance given to those in need. **2** an organization established to provide such assistance. **3** a kind and understanding attitude towards, or judgement of, other people.

charlatan /ˈʃɑːlətən/ n, derog someone posing as an expert in some profession, esp medicine.

charm n **1** the power of delighting, attracting or fascinating. **2** (**charms**) delightful qualities possessed by a person, place, thing, etc. **3** an object believed to have magical powers. **4** a magical saying or spell. **5** a small ornament, esp of silver, worn on a bracelet. ➤ vb **1** to delight, attract or fascinate someone. **2** (usu

charm sb into or **out of sth**) to influence or persuade them by charm. ○ **charmer** n. ○ **charmless** adj.

charming adj delightful; attractive; enchanting. ○ **charmingly** adv.

charnel house n, hist a building where dead bodies or bones are stored.

chart n **1** a map, esp one designed as an aid to navigation by sea or air. **2** a sheet of information presented as a table, graph or diagram. **3** (**the charts**) colloq a weekly list of top-selling recordings, usu of pop music. ➤ vb **1** to make a chart of something, eg part of the sea. **2** to plot (the course or progress of something). **3** intr, colloq to appear in the recording charts.

charter n **1** a formal deed guaranteeing the rights and privileges of subjects, issued by a sovereign or government. **2** a document in which the constitution and principles of an organization are presented. **3** a document creating a borough or burgh. **4** the hire of aircraft or ships for private use, or a contract for this. ➤ vb **1** to hire (an aircraft, etc) for private use. **2** to grant a charter to someone.

chartered adj **1** qualified according to the rules of a professional body that has a royal charter: chartered accountant. **2** having been granted a CHARTER (noun sense 4): a chartered plane.

charter flight n a flight in a chartered aircraft.

chartreuse /ʃɑːˈtrɜːz/ n a green or yellow liqueur made from aromatic herbs and brandy.

charwoman or **charlady** n a woman employed to clean a house, office, etc.

chary /ˈtʃɛərɪ/ adj (-ier, -iest) (usu **chary of sth**) **1** cautious or wary. **2** sparing; rather mean: chary of praise.

chase[1] vb **1** (often **chase after sb**) to follow or go after them in an attempt to catch them. **2** (often **chase sb away** or **off**, etc) to drive or force them away, off, etc. **3** intr to rush; to hurry. **4** colloq to try to obtain or achieve something, esp with difficulty: too many applicants chasing too few jobs. **5** colloq to pursue a particular matter urgently with someone: chase the post office about the missing parcel. **6** colloq to pursue (a desired sexual partner) in an obvious way. ➤ n a pursuit.

chase[2] vb to decorate (metal) with engraved or embossed work.

chasm /ˈkazəm/ n **1** a deep crack or opening in the ground. **2** a very wide difference in opinion, feeling, etc.

chassis /ˈʃasɪ/ n (pl **chassis** /ˈʃasɪz/) the structural framework of a motor vehicle, to which the body and movable working parts are attached.

chaste adj **1** sexually virtuous or pure. **2** of behaviour, etc: modest; decent. **3** of clothes, jewellery, style, etc: simple; unadorned. ○ **chasteness** n.

chasten vb **1** to free someone from faults by punishing them. **2** to moderate or restrain something.

chastise vb 1 to scold someone. 2 to punish someone severely, esp by beating. ○ **chastisement** n.

chastity n 1 the state of being CHASTE. 2 simplicity or plainness of style.

chasuble /'tʃazjʊbəl/ n, Christianity a long sleeveless garment, worn by a priest when celebrating Mass or Communion.

chat vb (chatted, chatting) intr to talk or converse in a friendly informal way. ➤ n informal familiar talk; a friendly conversation. ◊ **chat sb up** colloq to speak to them flirtatiously, or with an ulterior motive.

château /'ʃatəʊ/ n (châteaux /-təʊz/) a French castle or country seat.

chat show n a TV or radio programme in which well-known people are interviewed informally.

chattel n any kind of MOVABLE (sense 2) property. ♦ **goods and chattels** all personal movable possessions.

chatter vb, intr 1 to talk rapidly and unceasingly, usu about trivial matters. 2 of the teeth: to keep clicking together as a result of cold or fear. 3 eg of monkeys or birds: to make rapid continuous high-pitched noises. ➤ n 1 a sound similar to this. 2 idle talk or gossip. ○ **chatterer** n.

chatterbox n, derog someone who is inclined to chatter.

chatty adj (-ier, -iest) colloq 1 given to amiable chatting. 2 of writing: friendly and informal in style. ○ **chattily** adv. ○ **chattiness** n.

chauffeur n someone employed to drive a car for someone else. ➤ vb, tr & intr to act as a driver for someone.

chauvinism /'ʃəʊvənɪzəm/ n, derog an unreasonable belief, esp if aggressively expressed, in the superiority of one's own nation, sex, etc. ○ **chauvinist** n, adj. ○ **chauvinistic** adj.

chav n, Brit slang a feckless member of the working class.

cheap adj 1 inexpensive. 2 being or charging less than the usual. 3 low in price but of poor quality. 4 having little worth. 5 vulgar or nasty. ➤ adv, colloq cheaply: Good houses don't come cheap. ○ **cheaply** adv. ○ **cheapness** n.

cheapen vb 1 to cause to appear cheap or not very respectable. 2 tr & intr to make or become cheaper.

cheapjack n, derog a seller of cheap poor-quality goods. ➤ adj of poor quality.

cheapskate n, derog colloq a mean, miserly person.

cheat vb 1 to trick, deceive or swindle. 2 (usu cheat sb of or out of sth) to deprive them of it by deceit or trickery. 3 intr to act dishonestly so as to gain an advantage: cheat at cards. 4 intr (often cheat on sb) colloq to be unfaithful to (one's spouse, lover etc), esp sexually. ➤ n 1 someone who cheats. 2 a dishonest trick. ○ **cheater** n.

check vb 1 tr & intr to establish that something is correct or satisfactory, esp by investigation or enquiry. 2 to hold back or restrain: He was

about to complain, but checked himself. 3 colloq to reproach or rebuke someone. 4 N Am to mark something correct, etc with a tick. ➤ n 1 an inspection or investigation. 2 a standard or test by means of which to check something. 3 a stoppage in, or control on, progress or development. 4 a pattern of squares: cotton with a purple check. 5 N Am, esp US a tick marked against something. 6 N Am, esp US a cheque. 7 N Am a restaurant bill. 8 chess the position of the king when directly threatened by an opposing piece. ○ **checker** n. ◊ **check in** to report one's arrival at an air terminal or a hotel. **check sb or sth in** 1 to register or report the arrival of someone, especially guests at a hotel or passengers at an air terminal. 2 to hand in (luggage for weighing and loading) at an air terminal. **check sth off** to mark (an item on a list) as dealt with. **check out** 1 to register one's departure, esp from a hotel on paying the bill. 2 chiefly N Am of information etc: to be satisfactory or consistent. **check sb or sth out** to investigate them or it thoroughly. **check up on sb or sth** to enquire into or examine them or it (eg evidence).

checked adj having a squared pattern: purple-checked cotton.

check-in n at an air terminal: the desk at which passengers' tickets are checked and luggage weighed and accepted for loading.

checklist n a list of things to be done or systematically checked.

checkmate chess, n a winning position, putting one's opponent's king under inescapable attack. ➤ vb to put the (opposing king) into checkmate.

checkout n the pay desk in a supermarket.

checkpoint n a place, eg at a frontier, where vehicles are stopped and travel documents checked.

check-up n a thorough examination, esp a medical one.

Cheddar n a hard cheese made from cow's milk.

cheek n 1 either side of the face below the eye; the fleshy wall of the mouth. 2 impudent speech or behaviour. 3 colloq either of the buttocks. ♦ **cheek by jowl** very close together. **turn the other cheek** to refuse to retaliate.

cheekbone n either of a pair of bones that lie beneath the prominent part of the cheeks.

cheeky adj (-ier, -iest) impudent or disrespectful. ○ **cheekily** adv. ○ **cheekiness** n.

cheep vb, intr esp of young birds: to make high-pitched noises; to chirp. ➤ n a sound of this sort.

cheer n 1 a shout of approval or encouragement. 2 old use disposition; frame of mind: be of good cheer. ➤ vb 1 intr to shout in approval or encouragement. 2 (sometimes cheer someone on) to encourage them by shouting. ◊ **cheer up** to become more cheerful. **cheer sb up** to make them more cheerful.

cheerful adj 1 happy; optimistic. 2 bright and cheering. 3 willing; ungrudging.

cheering *adj* bringing comfort; making one feel glad or happier.

cheerio *exclam, Brit colloq* goodbye.

cheerleader *n* esp in the US: someone who leads organized cheering, applause, etc, esp at sports events.

cheerless *adj* depressing, dreary or dull.

cheers *exclam, Brit colloq* **1** used as a toast before drinking. **2** thank you. **3** goodbye.

cheery *adj* (*-ier, -iest*) cheerful; lively; jovial. ○ **cheerily** *adv.* ○ **cheeriness** *n.*

cheese *n* **1** a solid or soft creamy food that is prepared from the curds of milk. **2** a wheel-shaped solid mass of this substance. ♦ **cheesed off** *Brit slang, dated* fed up or annoyed. **hard cheese!** *Brit slang* bad luck!

cheeseburger *n* a hamburger served with a slice of melted cheese.

cheesecake *n* a sweet cake with a pastry base, topped with cream cheese, sugar, eggs etc.

cheesecloth *n* **1** a type of thin cloth used for pressing cheese. **2** a loosely woven cloth used for shirts, etc.

cheeseparing *adj, derog* mean with money; miserly. ➤ *n* miserliness.

cheesy *adj* (*-ier, -iest*) **1** like cheese eg in smell, flavour, etc. **2** *colloq* cheap, inferior; hackneyed, trite. **3** of a smile: wide but insincere.

cheetah *n* a large member of the cat family and the fastest land mammal, found in Africa and Asia, which has a tawny or grey coat with black spots.

chef *n* a cook in a restaurant etc, esp the principal one.

chemical *adj* **1** relating to or used in the science of chemistry. **2** relating to a substance or substances that take part in or are formed by reactions in which atoms or molecules undergo changes. ➤ *n* a substance that has a specific molecular composition, and takes part in or is formed by reactions in which atoms or molecules undergo changes. ○ **chemically** *adv.*

chemical element *n* a substance which cannot be broken down into simpler substances by chemical means, and which is composed of similar atoms that all have the same ATOMIC NUMBER.

chemical warfare *n* warfare involving the use of toxic chemical substances as weapons.

chemise *n* a woman's shirt or loose-fitting dress.

chemist *n* **1** a scientist who specializes in chemistry. **2** someone qualified to dispense medicines; a pharmacist. **3** a shop dealing in medicines, toiletries, cosmetics, etc.

chemistry *n* the scientific study of the composition, properties and reactions of chemical elements and their compounds.

chemotherapy *n, med* the treatment of a disease or disorder by means of drugs or other chemical compounds. Compare RADIO-THERAPY.

chenille /ʃəˈniːl/ *n* a soft shiny velvety fabric.

cheque *n* a printed form on which to fill in instructions to one's bank to pay a specified sum of money from one's account to another account.

cheque card *n* a card issued to customers by a bank, guaranteeing payment of their cheques up to a stated amount.

chequered *adj* **1** patterned with squares or patches of alternating colour. **2** of a person's life, career, etc: eventful, with alternations of good and bad fortune.

chequers or (*US*) **checkers** *sing n* the game of draughts.

cherish *vb* **1** to care for lovingly. **2** to cling fondly to (a hope, belief or memory).

cheroot *n* a cigar that is cut square at both ends.

cherry *n* (*-ies*) **1** a small round red or purplish fruit containing a small stone surrounded by pulpy flesh. **2** any of various small deciduous trees which bear this fruit. **3** a bright red colour.

cherry-picking *n, colloq* the practice of choosing only the best among assets, staff members, etc, and discarding the rest.

cherub *n* **1** (*pl also* **cherubim** /ˈtʃɛrəbɪm/) **a** an angel, represented in painting and sculpture as a winged child; **b** in the traditional medieval hierarchy of angels: an angel of the second-highest rank. **2** a sweet, innocent and beautiful child. ○ **cherubic** /tʃəˈruːbɪk/ *adj.*

chervil *n* a plant that is widely cultivated for its aromatic leaves, which are used as a garnish and for flavouring salads, etc.

chess *n* a game of skill played on a chequered board, a **chessboard**, by two people, each with 16 playing-pieces, **chessmen**, the object of which is to trap the opponent's king.

chest *n* **1** the front part of the body between the neck and the waist; the non-technical name for the thorax. **2** a large strong box used for storage or transport. ♦ **get sth off one's chest** *colloq* to relieve one's anxiety about a problem, wrongdoing, etc by talking about it openly.

chesterfield *n* a heavily padded leather-covered sofa with arms and back of the same height.

chestnut *n* **1** (*also* **sweet chestnut**) a deciduous tree which has simple toothed glossy leaves, and prickly globular fruits containing large edible nuts. **2** the large reddish-brown edible nut produced by this tree. **3** (*also* **horse chestnut**) a large deciduous tree which has brown shiny inedible seeds, popularly known as **conkers**. **4** the hard timber of either of these trees. **5** a reddish-brown colour, esp of hair. **6** a reddish-brown horse.

chest of drawers *n* a piece of furniture fitted with drawers.

chesty *adj* (*-ier, -iest*) *colloq, Brit* liable to, suffering from or caused by illness affecting the lungs: *a chesty cough.* ○ **chestiness** *n.*

chevron *n* **1** a V-shaped mark or symbol, esp one worn on the sleeve of a uniform to indicate non-commissioned rank. **2** on a road sign: a horizontal row of black and white V-shapes indicating a sharp bend ahead.

chew *vb* **1** *tr & intr* to use the teeth to break up (food) inside the mouth before swallowing. **2** *tr & intr* (*sometimes* **chew at** or **on sth**) to keep biting or nibbling it. ➤ *n* **1** an act of chewing. **2** something for chewing, eg a sweet. ◊ **chew on sth** or **chew sth over** *colloq* to consider it or discuss it at length.

chewing gum *n* a sticky sweet-flavoured substance for chewing without swallowing.

chewy *adj* (*-ier, -iest*) *colloq* requiring a lot of chewing. ○ **chewiness** *n*.

chiaroscuro /kɪɑːrouˈskʊərou/ *n*, *art* the management of light and shade in a picture.

chic /ʃiːk/ *adj* of clothes, people, etc: appealingly elegant or fashionable. ➤ *n* stylishness; elegance.

chicane /ʃɪˈkeɪn/ *n*, *motor sport* on a motor-racing circuit: a series of sharp bends.

chicanery *n* **1** clever talk intended to mislead. **2** trickery.

chick *n* **1** the young of a bird, esp a domestic fowl. **2** *dated slang* a young woman.

chicken *n* **1** the domestic fowl, bred for its meat and eggs. **2** *derog slang* a cowardly person. ➤ *adj*, *derog colloq* cowardly. ◊ **chicken out of sth** to avoid or withdraw from (an activity or commitment) from lack of nerve or confidence.

chickenfeed *n* **1** food for poultry. **2** something small and insignificant, esp a paltry sum of money.

chicken-hearted or **chicken-livered** *adj*, *derog*, *colloq* cowardly.

chickenpox *n* an infectious viral disease which mainly affects children, characterized by a fever and an itchy rash.

chicken wire *n* wire netting.

chickpea *n* a large yellow pea-like edible seed used in Middle Eastern cooking.

chickweed *n* a sprawling plant with oval pointed leaves and tiny white flowers.

chicory *n* (*-ies*) **1** a plant with stalked lower leaves, stalkless upper leaves and a long stout tap root. **2** the dried root of this plant, which is often ground, roasted and blended with coffee. **3** the leaves of this plant, eaten raw as a vegetable.

chide *vb* (*past tense* **chided** or **chid**, *past participle* **chidden** or **chided**) *chiefly literary* to scold or rebuke. ○ **chiding** *n* a scolding or a rebuke.

chief *n* **1** the head of a tribe, clan, etc. **2** the person in charge of any group, organization, department, etc. ➤ *adj* **1** used in titles, etc: first in rank; leading: *chief inspector*. **2** main; most important.

chiefly *adv* **1** mainly. **2** especially.

chieftain *n* the head of a tribe or clan.

chiffchaff *n* an insect-eating warbler.

chiffon /ˈʃɪfɒn/ *n* a very fine transparent silk or nylon fabric.

chiffonier or **chiffonnier** /ʃɪfəˈnɪə(r)/ *n* **1** a tall elegant chest of drawers. **2** a low wide cabinet with an open or grille front.

chigger, **chigoe** /ˈtʃɪgoʊ/ or **jigger** *n* a tropical flea, the pregnant female of which burrows under the skin of the host.

chignon /ˈʃiːnjɒn/ *n* a soft bun or coil of hair worn at the back of the neck.

chihuahua /tʃɪˈwɑːwɑː/ *n* a tiny dog which has a disproportionately large head with large widely spaced eyes and large ears.

chilblain *n* a painful itchy swelling of the skin, esp on the fingers, toes or ears, caused by exposure to cold.

child *n* (*children*) **1** a boy or girl between birth and physical maturity. **2** one's son or daughter. **3** *derog* an innocent or naive person. **4** someone seen as a typical product of a particular historical period, etc: *He was a child of his time*. ○ **childless** *adj*. ○ **childlessness** *n*. ○ **childlike** *adj*. ◆ **with child** *old use* pregnant.

childbearing *n* the act of giving birth to a child. ➤ *adj* suitable for or relating to the bearing of children: *childbearing hips*.

childbirth *n* the process at the end of pregnancy whereby a mother gives birth to a child.

childhood *n* the state or time of being a child.

childish *adj* **1** *derog* silly; immature. **2** relating to children or childhood; like a child.

childminder *n* an officially registered person who looks after children in return for payment.

childproof or **child-resistant** *adj* designed so as not to be able to be opened, operated, etc by a child: *childproof lock*.

child's play *n*, *colloq* a basic or simple task.

chill *n* **1** a feeling of coldness. **2** a cold that causes shivering, chattering teeth, etc, commonly caused by exposure to a cold damp environment. **3** a feeling, esp sudden, of depression or fear. ➤ *vb* **1** *tr & intr* to make or become cold. **2** to cause to feel cold. **3** to scare, depress or discourage. ◊ **chill out** *slang* to relax or calm oneself.

chilled *adj* **1** made cold. **2** hardened by chilling. **3** preserved by chilling.

chilli or **chili** *n* (*chillis* or *chillies*) **1** the fruit or pod of one of the varieties of capsicum, which has a hot spicy flavour. **2** CHILLI CON CARNE.

chilli con carne *n* a spicy Mexican dish of minced meat and beans, flavoured with chilli.

chilling *adj* frightening. ○ **chillingly** *adv*.

chilly *adj* (*-ier, -iest*) **1** rather cold. **2** *colloq* unfriendly; hostile. ○ **chilliness** *n*.

chime *n* **1** the sound made by a clock, set of tuned bells, etc. **2** (*usu* **chimes**) a percussion instrument consisting of hanging metal tubes that are struck with a hammer. ➤ *vb* **1** *intr* of bells: to ring. **2** *tr & intr* of a clock: to indicate (the time) by chiming. ◊ **chime in 1** to interrupt or join in a conversation, esp to repeat or agree with something. **2** to agree with someone or to fit in with them.

chimera or **chimaera** /kaɪˈmɪərə/ *n* **1** a wild or impossible idea. **2** (**Chimera**) *Greek myth* a fire-breathing monster, with the head of a lion, the body of a goat and the tail of a serpent. **3** a beast made up from various different animals, esp in art.

chimney n 1 a vertical structure made of brick, stone or steel, that carries smoke, steam, fumes or heated air away from a fireplace, stove, furnace or engine. 2 the top part of this structure, rising from a roof.

chimney breast n a projecting part of a wall built round the base of a chimney.

chimneypot n a short hollow rounded fitting, usu made of pottery, that sits in the opening at the top of a chimney.

chimney-sweep n someone whose job is to clean soot out of chimneys.

chimp n, colloq a CHIMPANZEE.

chimpanzee n the most intelligent of the great apes, found in tropical rainforests of Africa.

chin n the front protruding part of the lower jaw. ♦ **keep one's chin up** colloq to stay cheerful in spite of misfortune or difficulty.

china sing n 1 articles made from a fine translucent earthenware, orig from China. 2 articles made from similar materials. ➢ adj made of china.

china clay n another name for KAOLIN.

chinchilla n a small S American mammal with a thick soft grey coat, a bushy tail and large round ears.

chine n 1 the backbone. 2 a cut, esp of pork, which consists of part of the backbone and adjoining parts.

Chinese adj belonging or relating to China, a state in central and E Asia, its inhabitants, or their language. ➢ n 1 a citizen or inhabitant of, or person born in, China. 2 any of the closely related languages of the main ethnic group of China.

Chinese gooseberry n another name for KIWI FRUIT.

chink[1] n 1 a small slit or crack. 2 a narrow beam of light shining through such a crack.

chink[2] n a faint short ringing noise; a clink: a chink of glasses. ➢ vb, tr & intr to make or cause to make this noise.

chinless adj, derog having a weak indecisive character.

chinoiserie /ʃɪnˈwɑːzəriː/ n a European style of design and decoration which imitates or uses Chinese motifs and methods.

chinos /ˈtʃiːnəʊz/ pl n trousers made from the material **chino**, a strong khaki-like twilled cotton.

chintz n a cotton fabric printed generally in bright colours on a light background, esp used for soft furnishings.

chintzy adj (-ier, -iest) derog sentimentally or quaintly showy.

chinwag n, colloq a chat.

chip vb (chipped, chipping) 1 (sometimes chip at sth) to knock or strike small pieces off (a hard object or material). 2 intr to be broken off in small pieces; to have small pieces broken off. 3 to shape by chipping. 4 tr & intr, golf, football to strike the ball so that it goes high up in the air over a short distance. ➢ n 1 a small piece chipped off. 2 a place from which a piece has been chipped off: a chip in the vase. 3 Brit (usu **chips**) strips of deep-fried potato. 4 N Am (also **potato chip**) a potato crisp. 5 in gambling: a plastic counter used as a money token. 6 comput a SILICON CHIP. 7 a small piece of stone. 8 golf, football a short high shot or kick. ○ **chipped** adj 1 shaped or damaged by chips. 2 shaped into chips: chipped potatoes. ♦ a **chip off the old block** colloq someone who strongly resembles one of their parents in personality or appearance. **have a chip on one's shoulder** colloq to feel resentful about something, esp unreasonably. **have had one's chips** colloq 1 to have failed or been beaten. 2 to have been killed. **when the chips are down** colloq at the moment of crisis. ◊ **chip in** colloq 1 to interrupt. 2 tr & intr to contribute (eg money): We all chipped in for the car.

chipboard n thin solid board made from compressed wood chips.

chipmunk n a small ground squirrel, found in N America and N Asia, which has reddish-brown fur.

chipolata n a small sausage.

chipper adj, N Am colloq of a person: cheerful and lively.

chippy n (-ies) Brit colloq 1 a chip shop, where take-away meals of chips and other fried foods are sold. 2 a carpenter or joiner.

chirography or **cheirography** n handwriting or penmanship.

chiropodist /kɪˈrɒpədɪst, ʃɪ-/ n someone who treats minor disorders of the feet, eg corns. ○ **chiropody** n.

chiropractic /kaɪrəʊˈpraktɪk/ n a method of treating pain by manual adjustment of the spinal column, etc, so as to release pressure on the nerves. ○ **chiropractor** n.

chirp vb 1 intr of birds, grasshoppers, etc: to produce a short high-pitched sound. 2 tr & intr to chatter or say something merrily. ➢ n a chirping sound.

chirpy adj (-ier, -iest) colloq lively and merry. ○ **chirpiness** n.

chirrup vb, intr of some birds and insects: to chirp, esp in little bursts. ➢ n a burst of chirping.

chisel n a hand tool which has a strong metal blade with a cutting edge at the tip, used for cutting and shaping wood or stone. ➢ vb (chiselled, chiselling) to cut or shape (wood or stone) with a chisel.

chit[1] n 1 a short note or voucher recording money owed or paid. 2 a note.

chit[2] n, derog a a cheeky young girl; b a mere child.

chitchat n, colloq 1 chatter. 2 gossip. ➢ vb, intr to gossip idly.

chitin /ˈkaɪtɪn/ n, zool, biol a carbohydrate substance that forms the tough outer covering of insects and crustaceans.

chitterlings or **chitlings** sing or pl n the intestines of a pig or another animal prepared as food.

chivalrous *adj* **1 a** brave or gallant; **b** courteous or noble. **2** relating to medieval chivalry.

chivalry *n* **1** courtesy and protectiveness, esp as shown by men towards women. **2** *hist* a code of moral and religious behaviour followed by medieval knights.

chive *n* a plant of the onion family with purple flowers and long thin hollow leaves used as a flavouring or garnish.

chivvy or **chivy** *vb* (*-ies, -ied*) to harass or pester someone.

chloride *n* **1** *chem* **a** a compound of chlorine with another element or RADICAL (*noun* sense 3); **b** a salt of hydrochloric acid. **2** chloride of lime, a bleaching agent.

chlorinate *vb* to treat (eg water) with, or cause (a substance) to combine with, chlorine. ○ **chlorination** *n*.

chlorine *n*, *chem* a greenish-yellow poisonous gas with a pungent smell, widely used as a disinfectant and bleach.

chlorofluorocarbon *n*, *chem* a compound composed of chlorine, fluorine and carbon, formerly used as an aerosol propellant and refrigerant, but now widely banned because of the damage such compounds cause to the ozone layer.

chloroform *n*, *chem* a sweet-smelling liquid, formerly used as an anaesthetic, and still used as a solvent.

chlorophyll *n*, *bot* the green pigment, found in all green plants, that absorbs light energy from the Sun during PHOTOSYNTHESIS.

chloroplast *n*, *bot* any structure containing chlorophyll in a plant cell.

chock *n* a heavy block or wedge used to prevent movement of a wheel, etc.

chock-a-block or **chock-full** *adj* tightly jammed; crammed full.

chocolate *n* **1** a food product made from CA-CAO beans. **2** an individual sweet made from or coated with this substance. **3** a drink made by dissolving a powder prepared from this substance in hot water or milk. **4** a dark-brown colour. ○ **chocolaty** or **chocolatey** *adj*.

choice *n* **1** the act or process of choosing. **2** the right, power or opportunity to choose. **3** something or someone chosen. **4** a variety of things available for choosing between: *a wide choice.* ➢ *adj* select; worthy of being chosen: *choice cuts of meat.*

choir *n* **1** an organized group of trained singers, esp one that performs in church. **2** the area, esp in a church, occupied by a choir.

choke *vb* **1** *tr & intr* to prevent or be prevented from breathing by an obstruction in the throat. **2** to stop or interfere with breathing in this way. **3** to fill up, block or restrict something. **4** (*often* **choke something up**) to fill up, block or restrict it. **5** to restrict the growth or development of: *plants choked by weeds.* ➢ *n* **1** the sound or act of choking. **2** *eng* a valve in the carburettor

of a petrol engine that reduces the air supply and so gives a richer fuel/air mixture while the engine is still cold. ◊ **choke sth back** to suppress something indicative of feelings, esp tears, laughter or anger.

choker *n* a close-fitting necklace or broad band of velvet, etc worn round the neck.

choler /ˈkɒlə(r)/ *n*, *dated* anger or irritability. ○ **choleric** *adj* irritable or bad-tempered.

cholera /ˈkɒlərə/ *n*, *pathol* an acute and potentially fatal bacterial infection of the small intestine.

cholesterol /kəˈlɛstərɒl/ *n*, *biochem* in animal cells: a STEROL present in all cell membranes, and associated with ATHEROSCLEROSIS when present at high levels in the blood.

chomp *vb*, *tr & intr* to munch noisily. ➢ *n* an act or sound of chomping.

choose *vb* (**chose, chosen**) **1** *tr & intr* to take or select (one or more things or persons) from a larger number. **2** to decide; to think fit. **3** *intr* to be inclined; to like: *I will leave when I choose.*

choosy *adj* (*-ier, -iest*) *colloq* difficult to please; fussy.

chop¹ *vb* (**chopped, chopping**) **1** to cut with a vigorous downward or sideways slicing action, with an axe, knife, etc. **2** to hit (a ball) with a sharp downwards stroke. ➢ *n* **1** a slice of pork, lamb or mutton containing a bone, esp a rib. **2** a chopping action or stroke. **3** a sharp downward stroke given to a ball. **4** in boxing, karate etc: a short sharp blow.

chop² *vb* (**chopped, chopping**) to change direction or have a change of mind. ◆ **chop and change** to keep changing one's mind, plans, etc. **chop logic** to use over-subtle or complicated and confusing arguments.

chopper *n* **1** *colloq* a helicopter. **2** *colloq* a motorcycle with high handlebars. **3** a short-handled axe. **4** (**choppers**) *colloq* the teeth.

choppy *adj* (*-ier, -iest*) of the sea, weather etc: rather rough. ○ **choppiness** *n*.

chops *pl n* the jaws or mouth, esp of an animal.

chopsticks *pl n* a pair of slender sticks made from wood, plastic or ivory, which are held in one hand and used for eating with, chiefly in Oriental countries.

chop suey *n* a Chinese-style dish of chopped meat and vegetables fried in a sauce, usu served with rice.

choral *adj* relating to, or to be sung by, a choir or chorus.

chorale or **choral** /kɒˈrɑːl/ *n* **1** a hymn tune with a slow dignified rhythm. **2** *N Am* a choir or choral society.

chord¹ *n*, *mus* a combination of musical notes played together. ○ **chordal** *adj*.

chord² *n* **1** *anat* another spelling of CORD. **2** *maths* a straight line joining two points on a curve.

chore *n* **1** a domestic task. **2** a boring or unenjoyable task.

chorea /kɔːˈrɪə/ *n*, *pathol* either of two disorders of the nervous system that cause rapid involuntary movements of the limbs and sometimes of the face.

choreograph *vb* to plan the choreography for (a dance, ballet, etc).

choreography *n* **1** the arrangement of the sequence and pattern of movements in dancing. **2** the steps of a dance or ballet. ○ **choreographer** *n*.

chorister *n* a singer in a choir.

chortle *vb, intr* to laugh joyfully. ➤ *n* a joyful laugh.

chorus *n* **1** a set of lines in a song, sung as a refrain after each verse. **2** a large choir. **3** a piece of music for such a choir. **4** the group of singers and dancers supporting the soloists in an opera or musical show. **5** something uttered by a number of people at the same time: *a chorus of 'No's'*. **6** *theat* an actor who delivers an introductory or concluding passage to a play. **7** *Gr theat* a group of actors, always on stage, who comment on developments in the plot. ➤ *vb* to say, sing or utter simultaneously.

choux pastry / ʃuː/ *n* a very light pastry made with eggs.

chow *n* a breed of dog with thick fur, a curled tail and a blue tongue.

chowder *n, chiefly N Am* a thick soup or stew usu made from clams or fish with vegetables.

chow mein *n* a Chinese-style dish of chopped meat and vegetables, served with fried noodles.

chrism or **chrisom** *n, relig* holy oil used for anointing in the Roman Catholic and Greek Orthodox Churches.

Christ *n* **1** the Messiah whose coming is prophesied in the Old Testament. **2** Jesus of Nazareth, or Jesus Christ, believed by Christians to be the Messiah. **3** a figure or picture of Jesus.

christen *vb* **1** to give a person, esp a baby, a name as part of the religious ceremony of receiving them into the Christian Church. Compare BAPTIZE. **2** to give a name or nickname to someone. **3** *humorous, colloq* to use something for the first time: *Shall we christen the new wine glasses?* ○ **christening** *n*.

Christendom *n* all Christian people and parts of the world.

Christian *n* **1** someone who believes in, and follows the teachings and example of, Jesus Christ. **2** *colloq* someone having Christian qualities. ➤ *adj* **1** relating to Jesus Christ, the Christian religion or Christians. **2** *colloq* showing virtues associated with Christians, such as kindness, patience, tolerance and generosity. ○ **Christianity** *n*.

Christian era *n* the period of time from the birth of Jesus Christ to the present.

christian name *n* **1** *loosely* anyone's first or given name. **2** the personal name given to a Christian at baptism.

Christmas *n* **1** the annual Christian festival held on 25 December, which commemorates the birth of Christ. **2** the period of, mostly non-

religious, celebration surrounding this date. ○ **Christmassy** *adj*.

chromatic *adj* **1** relating to colours; coloured. **2** *mus* relating to, or using notes from, the CHROMATIC SCALE.

chromatic scale *n, mus* a scale which proceeds by SEMITONES.

chromatin *n, biol* in a cell nucleus: the material, composed of DNA, RNA and proteins, which becomes organized into visible chromosomes at the time of cell division.

chromatography *n, chem* a technique for separating the components of a mixture of liquids or gases by allowing them to pass through a material through which different substances are adsorbed at different rates.

chrome *n, non-technical* chromium, esp when used as a silvery plating for other metals. ➤ *vb* **1** in dyeing: to treat with a chromium solution. **2** to plate with chrome.

chromite *n, geol* a mineral that is the main source of chromium.

chromium *n, chem* a hard silvery metallic element that is resistant to corrosion, used in electroplating and in alloys with iron and nickel to make stainless steel.

chromosome *n* in the nucleus of a cell: any of a number of thread-like structures which contain, in the form of DNA, all the genetic information needed for the development of the cell and the whole organism.

chromosphere or **chromatosphere** *n, astron* a layer of gas, mainly hydrogen, that lies above the Sun's PHOTOSPHERE.

chronic *adj* **1** of a disease or symptoms: longlasting, usu of gradual onset and often difficult to treat: *chronic pain*. Compare ACUTE (*adj* sense 3). **2** *Brit colloq* very bad; severe: *The film was chronic*. **3** *habitual*: *a chronic dieter*.

chronicle *n* (*often* **chronicles**) a record of historical events year by year in the order in which they occurred. ➤ *vb* to record (an event) in a chronicle.

chronological *adj* **1** according to the order of occurrence. **2** relating to chronology. ○ **chronologically** *adv*.

chronology *n* (*-ies*) **1** the study or science of determining the correct order of historical events. **2** the arrangement of events in order of occurrence. **3** a table or list showing events in order of occurrence.

chronometer *n* a type of watch or clock, used esp at sea, which is designed to keep accurate time in all conditions.

chrysalis / ˈkrɪsəlɪs/ or **chrysalid** *n* (*chrysalises* or **chrysalides** / -ˈsalɪdiːz/) **1** the pupa of insects that undergo METAMORPHOSIS, eg butterflies, moths. **2** the protective case that surrounds the pupa.

chrysanthemum *n* a garden plant of the daisy family, with large bushy flowers.

chub *n* a small fat river-fish of the carp family.

chubby *adj* (*-ier, -iest*) plump. ○ **chubbiness** *n*.

chuck[1] *vb* **1** *colloq* to throw or fling. **2** to give someone an affectionate tap under the chin. ➤ *n* **1** *colloq* a toss, fling or throw. **2** an affectionate tap under the chin. ◇ **chuck sth in** *colloq* to give it up or abandon it. **chuck sb or sth out** *colloq* to get rid of them or it.

chuck² *n* a device for holding a piece of work in a lathe, or for holding the blade or bit in a drill.

chuckle *vb, intr* to laugh quietly, esp in a half-suppressed private way. ➤ *n* an amused little laugh.

chuff *vb, intr* of a steam train: to progress with regular puffing noises.

chuffed *adj, Brit colloq* very pleased.

chug *vb* (**chugged, chugging**) *intr* of a motor boat, motor car, etc: to progress while making a quiet thudding noise.

chukker or chukka *n* any of the six periods of play in polo each of which normally lasts for seven and a half minutes.

chum *colloq, n* a close friend. ➤ *vb* (**chummed, chumming**) **1** *intr* (*usu* **chum up with sb**) to make friends with them. **2** to accompany someone: *She chummed me to the clinic.* ◦ **chummy** *adj* (**-ier, -iest**).

chump *n* **1** *colloq* an idiot; a fool. **2** the thick end of anything, esp of a loin cut of lamb or mutton: *a chump chop.* **3** a short thick heavy block of wood.

chunk *n* **1** a thick, esp irregularly shaped, piece. **2** *colloq* a large or considerable amount.

chunky *adj* (**-ier, -iest**) **1** stockily or strongly built. **2** of fabrics, etc: thick; bulky. **3** solid and strong.

church *n* **1** a building for public Christian worship. **2** the religious services held in a church. **3** (**the Church**) the clergy as a profession: *enter the Church.* **4** (*usu* **Church**) any of many branches of Christians with their own doctrines, style of worship, etc: *the Methodist Church.* **5** the whole Christian establishment.

churchgoer *n* someone who regularly attends church services.

churchman or churchwoman *n* a member of the clergy or of a church.

churchwarden *n* in the Church of England: either of two lay members of a congregation elected to look after the church's property, money, etc.

churchyard *n* the burial ground round a church.

churl *n* an ill-bred surly person. ◦ **churlish** *adj* ill-mannered or rude. ◦ **churlishly** *adv*.

churn *n* **1** a machine in which milk is vigorously shaken to make butter. **2** a large milk can. ➤ *vb* **1 a** to make (butter) in a churn; **b** to turn (milk) into butter in a churn. **2** (*often* **churn sth up**) to shake or agitate it violently. ◇ **churn out** to keep producing things of tedious similarity in large quantities.

chute¹ *n* **1** a sloping channel down which to send water, rubbish, etc. **2** a slide in a children's playground or swimming-pool. **3** a waterfall or rapid.

chute² *n, colloq* short for PARACHUTE.

chutney *n* a type of pickle, orig from India, made with fruit, vinegar, spices, sugar, etc.

chutzpah /ˈxʊtspə/ *n, chiefly N Am colloq* self-assurance bordering on impudence.

Ci *symbol, physics* curie.

ciabatta /tʃəˈbatə/ *n* (**ciabattas or ciabatte** /-teɪ/) **1** Italian bread with an open texture, made with olive oil. **2** a loaf of this bread.

ciao *exclam* an informal greeting used on meeting and parting.

cicada /sɪˈkɑːdə/ *or* **cicala** /sɪˈkɑːlə/ *n* (**cicadas** *or* **cicadae** /-diː/; **cicalas** *or* **cicale** /-leɪ/) a large insect of tropical regions, the male of which is noted for its high-pitched warbling sound.

cicatrice /ˈsɪkətrɪs/ *or* **cicatrix** /ˈsɪkətrɪks/ *n* (**cicatrices** /-trɪsiːz, -traɪsiːz/ *or* **cicatrixes**) *med* the scar tissue that lies over a healed wound.

cider or cyder *n* an alcoholic drink made from apples.

cigar *n* a long roll of tobacco leaves for smoking.

cigarette *n* a tube of finely cut tobacco rolled in thin paper, for smoking.

cigarillo *n* a small cigar.

cilium *n* (**cilia** /ˈsɪlɪə/) *biol* any of the short hair-like appendages that project from the surface of certain cells, and whose rhythmic movement aids cell movement.

cinch /sɪntʃ/ *n, colloq* **1** an easily accomplished task. **2** a certainty.

cinchona /sɪŋˈkoʊnə/ *n* any tree of the type yielding bark from which quinine and related by-products are obtained.

cincture *n, chiefly literary* a belt or girdle.

cinder *n* **1** a piece of burnt coal or wood. **2** (**cinders**) ashes.

Cinderella *n* someone or something whose charms or merits go unnoticed.

cinema *n* **1** a theatre in which motion pictures are shown. **2** (*usu* **the cinema**) **a** a motion pictures or films generally; **b** the art or business of making films. ◦ **cinematic** *adj*.

cinematography *n* the art of making motion pictures. ◦ **cinematographer** *n*.

cinerarium /sɪnəˈrɛərɪəm/ *n* (**cineraria** /-rɪə/) a place for keeping the ashes of the dead.

cinnabar *n* **1** *geol* a bright red mineral form of mercury sulphide. **2** a bright orange-red colour.

cinnamon *n* a spice obtained from the cured dried bark of a SE Asian tree.

cinquefoil *n* **1** a plant of the rose family with five-petalled flowers, and leaves divided into five sections. **2** *archit* a design composed of five petal-like arcs.

cipher or cypher *n* **1** a secret code. **2** something written in code. **3** the key to a code. **4** an interlaced set of initials; a monogram. **5** *maths, old use* the symbol 0, used to fill blanks in writing numbers, but of no value itself. **6** a person or thing of no importance. ➤ *vb* to write (a message, etc) in code.

circa *prep* used esp with dates: about; approximately: *circa 1250*.

circadian *adj, biol* relating to a biological

circle *n* **1** a perfectly round two-dimensional figure that is bordered by the CIRCUMFERENCE, every point of which is an equal distance from the CENTRE. **2** anything in the form of a circle. **3** a circular route. **4** in a theatre, auditorium etc: a gallery of seats above the main stalls. **5** a series or chain of events, steps or developments, ending at the point where it began. **6** a group of people associated in some way. ➤ *vb* **1** *tr & intr* **a** to move in a circle; **b** to move in a circle round something. **2** to draw a circle round something. ◆ **go round in circles** to be trapped in a frustrating cycle of repetitive discussion or activity.

circlet *n* **1** a simple band or hoop of gold, silver, etc worn on the head. **2** a small circle.

circuit *n* **1** a complete course, journey or route round something. **2** a race track, running-track, etc. **3** (*sometimes* **electric circuit**) a path consisting of various electrical devices joined together by wires, to allow an electric current to flow continuously through it. **4** a round of places made by a travelling judge. **5** *sport* the round of tournaments in which competitors take part. ➤ *vb* to go round.

circuitous /sə'kjuːɪtəs/ *adj* indirect; roundabout.

circuitry *n* (*-ies*) *elec* the components or system of electronic or electrical circuits in a particular device.

circular *adj* **1** having the form of a circle. **2** moving or going round in a circle, leading back to the starting point. **3** of reasoning, etc: illogical, since the truth of the premise cannot be proved without reference to the conclusion. **4** of a letter, etc: addressed and copied to a number of people. ➤ *n* a circular letter or notice. ○ **circularity** *n*.

circularize or **-ise** *vb* to send circulars to (people).

circulate *vb* **1** *tr & intr* to move or cause to move round freely, esp in a fixed route: *traffic circulating through the town.* **2** *tr & intr* to spread; to pass round: *circulate the report.* **3** *intr* to move around talking to different people, eg at a party. ○ **circulatory** *adj*.

circulation *n* **1** the act or process of circulating. **2** *anat* in most animals: the system of blood vessels that supplies oxygenated blood pumped by the heart to all parts of the body, and that transports deoxygenated blood to the lungs. **3 a** the distribution of a newspaper or magazine; **b** the number of copies of it that are sold. ◆ **in** or **out of circulation 1** of money: being, or not being, used by the public. **2** taking part, or not taking part, in one's usual social activities.

circumcise *vb* **1** to cut away all or part of the foreskin of the penis, as a religious rite or medical necessity. **2** to cut away the clitoris and sometimes the labia of (a woman). ○ **circumcision** *n*.

circumference *n* *geom* the length of the boundary of a circle. **2** the boundary of an area of any shape. **3** the distance represented by any of these.

circumflex *n* (*also* **circumflex accent**) in some languages, eg French: a mark placed over a vowel, eg ô, û, as an indication of pronunciation, length or the omission of a letter formerly pronounced.

circumlocution *n* an unnecessarily long or indirect way of saying something. ○ **circumlocutory** *adj*.

circumnavigate *vb* to sail or fly round, esp the world.

circumscribe *vb* **1** to put a boundary, or draw a line, round something. **2** to limit or restrict something. ○ **circumscription** *n*.

circumspect *adj* prudent; wary. ○ **circumspection** *n*.

circumstance *n* **1** (*usu* **circumstances**) a fact, occurrence or condition, esp when relating to an act or event: *She died in mysterious circumstances.* **2** (**circumstances**) one's financial situation. **3** events that one cannot control; fate. **4** ceremony: *pomp and circumstance.*

circumstantial *adj* **1** relating to or dependent on circumstance. **2** of an account of an event: full of detailed description, etc.

circumvent *vb* **1** to find a way of getting round or evading (a rule, law, etc). **2** to outwit or frustrate someone.

circus *n* **1 a** a travelling company of performers including acrobats, clowns and often trained animals, etc; **b** a performance by such a company. **2** *colloq* a scene of noisy confusion. **3** in ancient Rome: an oval or circular open-air stadium for chariot-racing, etc.

cirque /sɜːk/ *n, geog* a deep semicircular hollow with steep side and back walls, located high on a mountain slope.

cirrhosis /sə'rəʊsɪs/ *n, pathol* a progressive disease of the liver, esp alcohol related, which results in a wasting away of normal tissue.

cirrocumulus /sɪrəʊ'kjuːmjʊləs/ *n* (**cirrocumuli** /-laɪ/) *meteorol* a type of high cloud which consists of small masses of white clouds that form a rippled pattern.

cirrostratus /sɪrəʊ'strɑːtəs/ *n* (**cirrostrati** /-taɪ/) *meteorol* a type of high cloud which forms a thin whitish layer with a fibrous appearance.

cirrus /'sɪrəs/ *n* (**cirri** /-raɪ/) *meteorol* a common type of high cloud with a wispy appearance.

cissy see SISSY

cistern *n* **1** a tank for storing water. **2** *archaeol* a natural underground reservoir.

citadel *n* a fortress built close to or within a city, for its protection and as a place of refuge.

citation *n* **1** the quoting or citing of something as example or proof. **2** a passage quoted from a book, etc. **3 a** a special official commendation or award for merit, bravery, etc; **b** a list of the reasons for such an award.

cite *vb* **1** to quote or mention as an example, illustration, or proof. **2** *law* to summon someone to appear in court. **3** to mention someone in an official report by way of commendation: *cited for bravery.*

citizen *n* **1** an inhabitant of a city or town. **2** a native of a country or state, or a naturalized member of it.

citizenry *n* (*-ies*) the citizens of a town, country, etc.

citizenship *n* **1** the status or position of a citizen. **2** the rights and duties of a citizen. **3** a person's conduct in relation to such duties.

citrate *n, chem* a salt or ester of citric acid.

citric *adj* **1** derived from citric acid. **2** relating to or derived from citrus fruits.

citric acid *n, chem* an organic acid found in citrus fruit.

citron *n* **1** a fruit like a large lemon, with a thick sweet-smelling yellow rind. **2** the candied rind of this fruit, used for flavouring or decorating cakes, etc.

citrus *n* any of a group of edible fruits with a tough outer peel enclosing juicy flesh rich in vitamin C, citric acid and water.

city *n* (*-ies*) **1** any large town. **2** in the UK: a town with a royal charter and usu a cathedral. **3** the body of inhabitants of a city. **4** (**the City**) the business centre of a city, esp London.

city fathers *pl n* **a** the magistrates of a city; **b** the members of a city's council.

city hall *n* (often **City Hall**) **a** the local government of a city; **b** the building in which it is housed.

civet *n* **1** (*also* **civet cat**) a small spotted and striped carnivorous mammal found in Asia and Africa. **2** a strong-smelling fluid secreted by this animal, used in perfumes to make their scent last. **3** the fur of the animal.

civic *adj* relating to a city, citizen or citizenship. ○ **civically** *adv.*

civics *sing n* the study of local government and of the rights and duties of citizenship.

civil *adj* **1** relating to the community: *civil affairs.* **2** relating to or occurring between citizens: *civil disturbances.* **3 a** relating to ordinary citizens; **b** not military, legal or religious. **4** *law* relating to cases about individual rights, etc, not criminal cases. **5** polite. ○ **civilly** *adv.*

civil engineering *n* the branch of engineering concerned with the design, construction, and maintenance of roads, bridges, railways, tunnels, docks, etc as carried out by a **civil engineer.**

civilian *n* anyone who is not a member of the armed forces or the police force.

civility *n* (*-ies*) **1** politeness. **2 a** an act of politeness; **b** a polite remark or gesture.

civilization or **-isation** *n* **1** a stage of development in human society that is socially, politically, culturally and technologically advanced. **2** the parts of the world that have reached such a stage. **3** the state of having achieved or the process of achieving such a stage. **4** *usu hist* a people and their society and culture: *the Minoan civilization.* **5** built-up areas as opposed to wild, uncultivated or sparsely populated parts. **6** intellectual or spiritual enlightenment, as opposed to brutishness or coarseness.

civilize or **-ise** *vb* **1** to lead out of a state of barbarity to a more advanced stage of social development. **2** to educate and enlighten morally, intellectually and spiritually. ○ **civilized** *adj.*

civil service *n* the body of officials employed by a government to administer the affairs of a country, excluding the military, naval, legislative and judicial areas. ○ **civil servant** *n.*

civil war *n* a war between citizens of the same state.

civvy *n* (*-ies*) *colloq* **1** a civilian. **2** (**civvies**) ordinary civilian clothes as opposed to a military uniform.

CJD *abbrev* Creutzfeldt-Jakob disease.

Cl *symbol, chem* chlorine.

cl *abbrev* centilitre.

clack *n* a sharp noise made by one hard object striking another. ➤ *vb, tr & intr* to make or cause something to make this kind of noise.

clad *adj, literary* **1** clothed. **2** covered: *stone-clad.* ➤ *vb* (**cladded, cladding**) to cover one material, eg brick or stonework, with a different material, esp to form a protective layer.

cladistics *sing n, biol* a system of classification in which organisms are grouped together on the basis of similarities.

claim *vb* **1** to state something firmly, insisting on its truth. **2** to declare oneself (to be, to have done, etc). **3** to assert that one has something: *He claimed no knowledge of the crime.* **4** *tr & intr* to demand or assert as a right: *He claimed his prize.* **5** to take or use up something: *The hurricane claimed 300 lives.* **6 a** to need; **b** to have a right to something: *The baby claimed its mother's attention.* **7** to declare that one is the owner of something. ➤ *n* **1** a statement of something as a truth. **2** a demand, esp for something to which one has, or believes one has, a right: *lay claim to the throne.* **3** a right to or reason for something: *a claim to fame.* **4** something one has claimed, eg a piece of land or a sum of money. **5** a demand for compensation, in accordance with an insurance policy, etc. ○ **claimable** *adj.* ○ **claimant** *n.*

clairvoyance or **clairvoyancy** *n* the alleged ability to see into the future, or know things that cannot be discovered through the normal range of senses. ○ **clairvoyant** *n, adj.*

clam *n* **1 a** any of various BIVALVE shellfish; **b** their edible flesh. **2** *colloq* an uncommunicative person. ➤ *vb* (**dammed, clamming**) *intr, chiefly US* to gather clams. ◊ **clam up** *colloq* to stop talking suddenly.

clamber *vb, intr* to climb using one's hands as well as one's feet. ➤ *n* an act of clambering.

clammy *adj* (*-ier, -iest*) unpleasantly moist or damp.

clamour or (*US*) **clamor** *n* **1** a noise of shouting or loud talking. **2** loud protesting or demands. ➤ *vb, intr* to make a loud continuous outcry.

clamp *n* **1** a tool with adjustable jaws for gripping things firmly or pressing parts together. **2** (*usu* **wheel clamp**) a heavy metal device fitted to the wheels of an illegally parked car, to prevent it being moved. ➤ *vb* **1** to fasten together or hold with a clamp. **2** to fit a clamp to a wheel of (a parked car) to stop it being moved. **3** to hold, grip or shut tightly. ◊ **clamp down on sth** or **sb** to put a stop to or to control it or them strictly.

clampdown *n* a measure or action to suppress an activity: *a clampdown on drugs*.

clan *n* **1** in Scotland or among people of Scots origin: a group of families, generally with the same surname, and (esp formerly) led by a chief. **2** *humorous* one's family or relations. **3** a group of people who have similar interests, concerns, etc.

clandestine *adj* kept secret; surreptitious. ○ **clandestinely** *adv*.

clang *vb, tr & intr* to ring or make something ring loudly. ➤ *n* this ringing sound.

clanger *n, colloq* a tactless, embarrassing and obvious blunder. ♦ **drop a clanger** to make such a blunder.

clangour or (*US*) **clangor** *n, poetic* a loud resounding noise.

clank *n* a sharp metallic sound like pieces of metal striking together. ➤ *vb, tr & intr* to make or cause something to make such a sound.

clannish *adj, derog* of a group of people: closely united, with little interest in people not belonging to the group.

clap *vb* (**clapped, clapping**) **1** *tr & intr* to strike the palms of (one's hands) together with a loud noise, in order to mark (a rhythm), gain attention, etc. **2** *tr & intr* to applaud someone or something by clapping. **3** to strike someone softly with the palm of the hand, usu as a friendly gesture. **4** to place forcefully: *clapped the book on the table*. ➤ *n* **1** an act of clapping. **2** the sudden loud explosion of noise made by thunder.

clapped out *adj, colloq* **1** of a machine, etc: old, worn out and no longer working properly. **2** *Aust, NZ* of a person: exhausted.

clapper *n* the dangling piece of metal inside a bell that strikes against the sides to make it ring. ♦ **like the clappers** *colloq* very quickly.

clapperboard *n* a pair of hinged boards clapped together in front of the camera before and after shooting a piece of film, to help synchronize sound and vision.

claptrap *n* meaningless, insincere or pompous talk.

claque *n* **1** a group of people paid to applaud a speaker at a meeting or performer in a theatre, etc. **2** a circle of flatterers or admirers.

claret *n* **1** a French red wine, esp from the Bordeaux area in SW France. **2** the deep reddish-purple colour of this.

clarify *vb* (**-ies, -ied**) *tr & intr* **1** to make or become clearer or easier to understand. **2** of butter, fat, etc: to make or become clear by heating. ○ **clarification** *n*.

clarinet *n, mus* a woodwind instrument with a cylindrical tube and a single REED (sense 2). ○ **clarinettist** *n*.

clarion *n, chiefly poetic, hist* an old kind of trumpet with a shrill sound: *a clarion call*.

clarity *n* **1** the quality of being clear and pure. **2** the quality of being easy to see, hear or understand.

clash *n* **1** a loud noise, like that of metal objects striking each other. **2** a serious disagreement. **3** a fight, battle or match. ➤ *vb* **1** *tr & intr* of metal objects, etc: to strike against each other noisily. **2** *intr* to come into physical or verbal conflict. **3** *intr* of commitments, etc: to coincide, usu not fortuitously. **4** *intr* of colours, styles, etc: to be unpleasing or unharmonious together.

clasp *n* **1** a fastening on jewellery, a bag, etc made of two parts that link together. **2** a firm grip, or act of gripping. ➤ *vb* **1** to hold or take hold of someone or something firmly. **2** to fasten or secure something with a clasp.

class *n* **1** a lesson or lecture. **2** a number of pupils taught together. **3** *esp US* the body of students that begin or finish university or school in the same year: *the class of '94*. **4** a category, kind or type, members of which share common characteristics. **5** a grade or standard. **6** any of the social groupings into which people fall according to their job, wealth, etc. **7** the system by which society is divided into such groups. **8** *colloq* **a** stylishness in dress, behaviour, etc; **b** good quality. **9** *biol* in taxonomy: any of the groups into which a PHYLUM in the animal kingdom or a DIVISION (sense 7) in the plant kingdom is divided, and which is in turn subdivided into one or more orders. ➤ *vb* **a** to regard someone or something as belonging to a certain class; **b** to put into a category.

class-conscious *adj, derog* aware of one's own and other people's social class.

classic *adj* **1** made of or belonging to the highest quality; established as the best. **2** entirely typical. **3** simple, neat and elegant, esp in a traditional style. ➤ *n* **1** an established work of literature. **2** an outstanding example of its type. **3** something, eg an item of clothing, which will always last, irrespective of fashions and fads. ○ **classically** *adv*.

classical *adj* **1** of literature, art, etc: from or in the style of ancient Greece and Rome. **2** of architecture or the other arts: showing the influence of ancient Greece and Rome: *a classical façade*. **3** of music and arts related to this: having an established, traditional and somewhat formal style and form. **4** of a shape, design, etc: simple; pure; without complicated decoration. **5** of a language: being the older literary form. **6** of an education: concentrating on Latin, Greek and the humanities.

classicism n 1 in art and literature: a simple elegant style based on the Roman and Greek principles of beauty, good taste, restraint and clarity. 2 a Latin or Greek idiom or form.

classicist n someone who has studied classics, esp as a university subject.

classics sing n (often **the Classics**) a the study of Latin and Greek; b the study of the literature and history of ancient Greece and Rome.

classification n 1 the arrangement of things and people into classes. 2 a group or class into which a person or thing is put.

classified adj 1 arranged in groups or classes. 2 of information: kept secret or restricted by the government.

classify vb (-ies, -ied) 1 to put into a particular group or category. 2 of information: to declare it secret and not for publication. ○ **classifiable** adj.

classless adj 1 of a community, society etc: not divided into social classes. 2 not belonging to any particular social class.

classmate n a fellow student in one's class at school or college.

classroom n a room in a school or college where classes are taught.

classy adj (-ier, -iest) colloq a fashionable; b superior.

clatter n a loud noise made by hard objects striking each other, or falling onto a hard surface. ➤ vb, tr & intr to make or cause to make this noise.

clause n 1 gram a a group of words that includes a subject and its related finite verb, and which may or may not constitute a sentence (eg if time permits and we will come tomorrow). See MAIN CLAUSE, SUBORDINATE CLAUSE; b a group of words with a similar grammatical function, but which has no expressed subject (eg while running for the bus), no finite verb (eg time permitting), or neither a subject nor a verb (eg if possible). 2 law a paragraph or section in a contract, will or act of parliament. ○ **clausal** adj.

claustrophobia n an irrational fear of being in confined spaces. ○ **claustrophobic** adj.

clavichord n an early keyboard instrument with a soft tone.

clavicle n, anat in vertebrates: either of two short slender bones linking the shoulder-blades with the top of the breastbone.

claw n 1 a hard curved pointed nail on the end of each digit of the foot in birds, most reptiles and many mammals. 2 the foot of an animal or bird with a number of such nails. 3 something with the shape or action of a claw, eg part of a mechanical device. ➤ vb, tr & intr (often **claw at sth**) to tear or scratch it with claws, nails or fingers. ◊ **claw sth back 1** of a government: to recover money given away in benefits and allowances by imposing a new tax. 2 to regain something with difficulty (eg commercial advantage etc): She clawed her way back to solvency.

clay n 1 geol a poorly draining soil consisting mainly of aluminium SILICATES, which is pliable when wet and is used to make pottery, bricks, ceramics, etc. 2 earth or soil generally. 3 poetic the substance of which the human body is formed.

claymore n, hist a two-edged broadsword used by Scottish highlanders.

clean adj 1 free from dirt or contamination. 2 not containing anything harmful to health; pure. 3 pleasantly fresh: a clean taste. 4 recently washed. 5 hygienic in habits: a clean animal. 6 unused; unmarked. 7 neat and even: a clean cut. 8 simple and elegant: a ship with good clean lines. 9 clear of legal offences: a clean driving licence. 10 morally pure; innocent. 11 of humour, etc: not offensive or obscene. 12 fair: a clean fight. 13 slang not carrying drugs or offensive weapons. 14 absolute; complete: make a clean break. ➤ adv 1 colloq completely: I clean forgot. 2 straight or directly; encountering no obstruction: It sailed clean through the window. ➤ vb, tr & intr to make or become free from dirt. ➤ n an act of cleaning. ♦ **come clean** colloq to admit the truth about something that one has previously concealed or lied about. **make a clean breast of sth** to confess to having done it, esp through feelings of guilt. ◊ **clean sth out** to clean (a room or cupboard, etc) thoroughly. **clean up 1** to clean a place thoroughly. 2 slang to make a large profit.

clean-cut adj 1 pleasingly regular in outline or shape: clean-cut features. 2 neat; respectable.

cleaner n 1 someone employed to clean inside buildings, etc. 2 a machine or substance used for cleaning. 3 (usu **cleaners**) a shop where clothes, etc can be taken for cleaning. ♦ **take sb to the cleaners** colloq to take away, esp dishonestly, all of their money.

cleanly adv 1 in a clean way. 2 tidily; efficiently; easily. ○ **cleanliness** /'klɛnlɪnəs/ n.

cleanse vb 1 to clean someone or something. 2 to purify someone or something. ○ **cleanser** n.

clean-shaven adj of men: with facial hair shaved.

clean sheet n a record with no blemishes.

clean sweep n 1 a complete or overwhelming success. 2 a complete change or clear-out.

clear adj 1 transparent; easy to see through. 2 of weather, etc: not misty or cloudy. 3 of the skin: healthy; unblemished by spots, etc. 4 a easy to see, hear or understand; b lucid. 5 bright; sharp; well-defined: a clear photograph. 6 of vision: not obstructed. 7 certain; having no doubts or confusion. 8 free of doubt or confusion. 9 obvious. 10 free from obstruction: a clear path. 11 well away from something: well clear of the rocks. 12 free of it; no longer affected by it. 13 of the conscience, etc: free from guilt, etc. 14 free of appointments, etc. ➤ adv 1 in a clear manner. 2 completely: get clear away. 3 N Am all the way: see clear to the hills. 4 well away from something: steer clear of trouble. ➤ vb 1 tr & intr to make or become clear, free of obstruction, etc. **2** to remove or move out of the way. **3** to prove or declare to be innocent. **4** to get over or past something without touching: *clear the fence*. **5** to make as profit over expenses. **6** to pass inspection by (customs). **7** to give or get official permission for (a plan, etc). **8** to approve someone for a special assignment, etc. **9** *tr & intr* of a cheque: to pass from one bank to another through a clearing-house. **10** to pay a debt. **11** *tr & intr* to give or receive clearance: *The aeroplane was cleared for take-off.* ♦ **clear the air** *colloq* to get rid of bad feeling, esp by frank discussion. **in the clear** no longer under suspicion, in difficulties, etc. ◊ **clear sth away** to remove it. **clear off** *colloq* to go away. **clear out** *colloq* to go away. **clear sth out** to rid it of rubbish, etc. **clear up 1** of the weather: to brighten after rain, a storm, etc. **2** to get better. **clear sth up 1** to tidy up a mess, room, etc. **2** to solve a mystery, etc.

clearance *n* **1** the act of clearing. **2** the distance between one object and another passing beside or under it. **3** permission, or a certificate granting this: *The plane was given clearance to land.*

clear-cut *adj* clear.

clear-headed *adj* capable of, or showing, clear logical thought.

clearing *n* an area in a forest, etc that has been cleared of trees, etc.

clearing bank *n* a bank using the services of a central clearing-house.

clearing-house *n* **1** an establishment that deals with transactions between its member banks. **2** a central agency that collects, organizes and distributes information.

clearly *adv* **1** in a clear manner: *to speak clearly.* **2** obviously: *Clearly, he's wrong.*

clear-out *n* a clearing out of something, eg rubbish, possessions, etc.

clear-sighted *adj* capable of, or showing, accurate observation and good judgement.

clearstory see CLERESTORY

clearway *n* a stretch of road on which cars may not stop except in an emergency.

cleat *n* **1** a wedge. **2** a piece of wood attached to a structure to give it extra support.

cleavage *n* **1** *colloq* the hollow between a woman's breasts, esp as revealed by a top with a low neck. **2** *geol* **a** the splitting of rocks into thin parallel sheets; **b** the splitting of a crystal in one or more specific directions to give smooth surfaces.

cleave[1] *vb* (*past tense* **clove**, **cleft** or **cleaved**, *past participle* **cloven**, **cleft** or **cleaved**) *tr & intr, formal or literary* **1** to split or divide. **2** to cut or slice.

cleave[2] *vb, intr* to cling or stick.

cleaver *n* a knife with a large square blade, used esp by butchers for chopping meat.

clef *n, mus* a symbol placed on a STAVE to indicate the pitch of the notes written on it.

cleft[1] *n* a split, fissure, wide crack or deep indentation.

cleft[2] *adj* split; divided. ➤ *vb* see CLEAVE[1].
♦ **in a deft stick** in a difficult or awkward situation.

cleft palate *n, pathol* a split in the palate caused by the failure of the two sides of the mouth to meet and fuse together in the developing fetus.

clematis /ˈklɛmətɪs, kləˈmeɪtɪs/ *n* a garden climbing plant with purple, yellow or white flowers.

clemency *n* **1** the quality of being clement. **2** mercy.

clement *adj* of the weather: mild; not harsh or severe.

clementine *n* a citrus fruit which is a type of small tangerine or a hybrid of a tangerine and an orange.

clench *vb* **1** to close one's teeth or one's fists tightly, esp in anger. **2** to hold or grip firmly.

clerestory or **clearstory** /ˈklɪəstɔːrɪ/ *n* (*-ies*) *archit* in a church: a row of windows in the nave wall, above the roof of the aisle.

clergy *sing or pl n* (*-ies*) the ministers or priests of a religion. ○ **clergyman** or **clergywoman** *n*.

cleric *n* a clergyman or clergywoman.

clerical *adj* **1** relating to clerks or office work. **2** relating to the clergy.

clerihew /ˈklɛrɪhjuː/ *n* a humorous poem about a famous person, consisting of two short couplets.

clerk /klɑːk; *US* klɜːrk/ *n* **1** in an office or bank: someone who deals with accounts, records, files, etc. **2** in a law court: someone who keeps records or accounts. **3** a public official in charge of the records and business affairs of the town council. **4** an unordained or lay minister of the Church. **5** *N Am* a shop assistant or hotel receptionist.

clever *adj* **1** good or quick at learning and understanding. **2** skilful, dexterous, nimble or adroit. **3** well thought out; ingenious. ○ **cleverly** *adv.* ○ **cleverness** *n*.

cliché /ˈkliːʃeɪ/ *n, derog* a once striking and effective phrase or combination of words which has become stale and hackneyed through overuse.

click *n* a short sharp sound like that made by two parts of a mechanism locking into place. ➤ *vb* **1** *tr & intr* to make or cause to make a click. **2** *intr, colloq* to meet with approval. **3** *intr, colloq* to become clear or understood: *The meaning clicked after a while.* **4** *comput* to press and release one of the buttons on a MOUSE. **5** *intr* of two or more people: to instantly get along very well.

client *n* **1** someone using the services of a professional institution, eg a bank. **2** a customer.

clientele /kliːɒnˈtɛl/ *n* **1** the clients of a professional person, customers of a shopkeeper, etc. **2** people habitually attending a theatre, pub, etc.

cliff *n* a high steep rock face, esp on the coast or the side of a mountain.

cliffhanger *n* **1** a story that keeps one in suspense. **2** the ending of an episode of a serial story which leaves the audience in suspense.

climacteric n **1** biol in living organisms: a period of changes, eg those associated with the menopause in women. **2** a critical period.

climate n **1** the average weather conditions of a particular region of the world over a long period of time. **2** a part of the world considered from the point of view of its weather conditions: move to a warmer climate. **3** a current trend in general feeling, opinion, policies, etc. ○ **climatic** adj. ○ **climatically** adv.

climax n **1** the high point or culmination of a series of events or of an experience. **2** a sexual orgasm. **3** a rhetoric the arrangement of a series of sentences, etc, in order of increasing strength; **b** loosely the final term of the arrangement. ⟩ vb, tr & intr **1** to come or bring to a climax. **2** intr to experience sexual orgasm. ○ **climactic** or **climactical** adj.

climb vb **1** (often **climb up**) to mount or ascend (a hill, ladder, etc), often using hands and feet. **2** tr & intr to rise or go up. **3** intr to increase. **4** intr to slope upwards: The path started to climb suddenly. **5** of plants: to grow upwards using tendrils, etc. ⟩ n **1** an act of climbing. **2** a slope to be climbed. ○ **climbable** adj. ○ **climbing** n. ◊ **climb down 1** to descend. **2** to concede one's position on some issue, etc.

climb-down n a dramatic change of mind or concession, often humiliating.

climber n **1** a climbing plant. **2** a mountaineer. **3** derog a SOCIAL CLIMBER.

clime n, chiefly poetic or humorous a region of the world: foreign climes.

clinch vb **1** to settle something finally and decisively, eg an argument, deal, etc. **2** intr, boxing, wrestling of contestants: to hold each other in a firm grip. **3** intr, colloq to embrace. **4** to bend over and hammer down the projecting point of a nail, etc, so as to secure it. ⟩ n **1** an act of clinching. **2** boxing, wrestling an act of clinging to each other to prevent further blows, create a breathing space, etc. **3** colloq an embrace between lovers.

clincher n a point, argument or circumstance that finally settles or decides a matter.

cling vb (**clung**) intr **1** to hold firmly or tightly; to stick. **2** to be emotionally over-dependent. **3** to refuse to drop or let go.

clingfilm n a thin clear plastic material that adheres to itself, used for wrapping food.

clinic n **1** a private hospital or nursing home that specializes in the treatment of particular diseases or disorders. **2** a department of a hospital or a health centre which specializes in one particular area, eg a family planning clinic. **3** the instruction in examination and treatment of patients that is given to medical students, usu at the patient's bedside in a hospital ward. **4** a session in which an expert is available for consultation.

clinical adj **1** of a clinic or hospital. **2** of medical studies: based on, or relating to, direct obser-

vation and treatment of the patient. **3** of manner, behaviour, etc: cold; impersonal; unemotional or detached. **4** of surroundings, etc: severely plain and simple, with no personal touches. ○ **clinically** adv.

clink[1] n a short sharp ringing sound. ⟩ vb, tr & intr to make or cause to make such a sound.

clink[2] n, slang prison.

clinker n a mass of fused ash or slag left unburnt in a furnace.

clinker-built adj of the hull of a boat: built with planks, each of which overlaps the one below it on the outside.

clip[1] vb (**clipped, clipping**) **1** to cut (hair, wool, etc). **2** to trim or cut off the hair, wool or fur of (an animal). **3** to punch out a piece from (a ticket) to show that it has been used. **4** to cut (an article, etc) from a newspaper, etc. **5** colloq to hit or strike someone or something sharply. **6** to excerpt a section from (a film, etc). ⟩ n **1** an act of clipping. **2** a short sequence extracted from a film, recording, etc. **3** colloq a sharp blow: a clip round the ear. **4** colloq speed; rapid speed: going at a fair clip.

clip[2] n **1** any of various devices, usu small ones, for holding things together or in position. **2** (also **cartridge clip**) a container for bullets attached to a gun, that feeds bullets directly into it. **3** a piece of jewellery in the form of a clip which can be attached to clothing. ⟩ vb (**clipped, clipping**) to fasten something with a clip.

clipboard n a firm board with a clip at the top for holding paper, which can be used as a portable writing surface.

clipped adj **1** of the form of a word: shortened, eg deli from delicatessen. **2** of speaking style: **a** tending to shorten vowels, omit syllables, etc; **b** curt and distinct.

clipper n **1** hist a fast sailing ship with large sails. **2** someone or something which clips.

clippers pl n a clipping device: nail clippers.

clipping n a cutting from a newspaper, hair, etc.

clique /kli:k/ n, derog a group of friends, colleagues, etc who stick together and are unfriendly towards outsiders. ○ **cliquey** (**cliquier, cliquiest**) adj.

clitoris /ˈklɪtərɪs/ n, anat a small highly sensitive organ in front of the vaginal opening. ○ **clitoral** adj.

cloaca /kloʊˈeɪkə/ n (**cloacae** /-ˈeɪsiː, -ˈɑːkaɪ/) **1** zool in most vertebrates apart from mammals: the terminal region of the gut, into which the alimentary canal and the urinary and reproductive systems all open and discharge their contents. **2** a sewer.

cloak n **1** a loose outdoor garment, usu sleeveless, fastened at the neck so as to hang from the shoulders. **2** a covering: a cloak of mist. ⟩ vb to cover up or conceal something.

cloak-and-dagger adj of stories, situations, etc: full of adventure, mystery, spying, etc.

cloakroom n **a** a room where coats, hats, etc

may be left; **b** a room containing a WC.

clobber[1] *vb, colloq* **1** to beat or hit someone very hard. **2** to defeat someone completely. **3** to criticize someone severely.

clobber[2] *n, slang* clothing; personal belongings, equipment, etc.

cloche /klɒʃ/ *n* **1** a transparent glass or plastic covering for protecting young plants from frost, etc. **2** a woman's close-fitting dome-shaped hat.

clock *n* **1** a device for measuring and indicating time. **2** *comput* an electronic device that synchronizes processes within a computer system, by issuing signals at a constant rate. **3** a device that synchronizes the timing in switching circuits, transmission systems, etc. **4** (**the clock**) *colloq* **a** a MILEOMETER; **b** a SPEEDOMETER. **5** (in full **time clock**) a device for recording the arrival and departure times of employees. ➤ *vb* **1** to measure or record (time) using such a device. **2** to record with a stopwatch the time taken by (a racer, etc) to complete a distance, etc. **3** *colloq* to travel at (a speed as shown on a speedometer). **4** *slang* to hit someone. ♦ **round the clock** throughout the day and night. ◊ **clock in** or **on** to record one's time of arrival at a place of work. **clock out** or **off** to record one's time of departure from a place of work.

clockwise *adj, adv* moving, etc in the same direction as that in which the hands of a clock move.

clockwork *n* a mechanism like that of some clocks, working by means of gears and a spring that must be wound periodically. ➤ *adj* operated by clockwork: *a clockwork mouse*. ♦ **like clockwork** smoothly and with regularity.

clod *n* **1** a lump of earth, clay, etc. **2** *colloq* a stupid person.

clodhopper *n, colloq* **1** a clumsy person. **2** a large heavy boot or shoe.

clog *n* **1** a shoe carved entirely from wood, or having a thick wooden sole. **2** *Scot* a heavy block of wood. ➤ *vb* (**dogged, clogging**) *tr & intr* to obstruct or become obstructed so that movement is difficult or impossible. ♦ **pop one's clogs** *slang* to die. ◊ **clog up** to block or choke up.

cloister *n* **1** a covered walkway built around a garden or quadrangle. **2 a** a place of religious retreat, eg a monastery or convent; **b** the quiet secluded life of such a place. ➤ *vb* to keep someone away from the problems of normal life in the world. ◊ **cloistered** *adj* secluded.

clone *n* **1** *biol* a cell, gene or organism genetically identical to its parent, created either by genetic engineering or by asexual reproduction. **2** *colloq* a person or thing that looks like someone or something else, eg a product that is an imitation of a more expensive one. ➤ *vb* **1** to produce a set of identical cells or organisms from (a single parent cell or organism). **2** to produce many identical copies of (a gene) by genetic engineering. **3** to produce replicas of,

or to copy something: *cloned ideas*.

clonk *n* a noise of a heavy, esp metal, object striking something. ➤ *vb* **1** *intr* to make or cause to make this noise. **2** to hit.

close[1] /kloʊs/ *adj* **1** near in space or time; at a short distance. **2 a** near in relationship: *a close relation*; **b** intimate. **3** touching or almost touching. **4** tight; dense or compact; with little space between: *a close fit*. **5** near to the surface. **6** thorough; searching: *a close reading*. **7** of a contest, etc: with little difference between entrants, etc. **8** (*often* **close to sth**) about to happen, on the point of doing it, etc: *close to tears*. **9** similar to the original, or to something else: *a close resemblance*. **10** uncomfortably warm; stuffy. **11** secretive. **12** mean. **13** heavily guarded: *under close arrest*. **14** of an organization, etc: restricted in membership. ➤ *adv* **1** often in compounds in a close manner; closely: *follow close behind*. **2** at close range. ◊ **closely** *adv*. ◊ **closeness** *n*.

close[2] /kloʊz/ *vb* **1** *tr & intr* to shut. **2** (*sometimes* **close sth off**) to block (a road, etc) so as to prevent use. **3** *tr & intr* of shops, etc: to stop or cause to stop being open to the public for a period of time. **4** *tr & intr* of a factory, business, etc: to stop or cause to stop operating permanently. **5** *tr & intr* to conclude; to come or bring to an end: *He closed with a joke*. **6** *tr & intr* to join up or come together; to cause edges, etc, of something to come together. **7** to settle or agree on something: *close a deal*. **8** *fin, econ* of shares, etc: to be worth (a certain amount) at the end of a period of trading. ➤ *n* an end or conclusion. ◊ **close down** of a business: to close permanently. **close in on sb** to approach and surround them.

closed *adj* **1** shut; blocked. **2** of a community or society: exclusive; with membership restricted to a chosen few.

closed-circuit television *n* a TV system serving a limited number of receivers, eg within a building, the signal being transmitted by cables or telephone links.

closed shop *n* an establishment, eg a factory, which requires its employees to be members of a trade union.

close harmony *n, mus* harmony in which the notes of chords lie close together.

close-knit *adj* of a group: closely bound together.

close-range *adj* **1** in, at or within a short distance. **2** eg of a gun: fired from very close by.

close-run *adj* of a competition, election, etc: fiercely contested; having close results.

close season *n* the time of year when it is illegal to kill certain birds, animals or fish for sport.

close shave or **close call** *n* a narrow or lucky escape.

closet *n* **1** *chiefly N Am* a tall recessed space in a room or corridor, for clothing or storage. **2** *old use* a small private room. **3** *old use* a WATER CLOSET. ➤ *adj* not openly declared: *a closet gambler*. ➤ *vb* (**closeted, closeting**) to shut away in private, eg for confidential discussion.

close-up n 1 a photograph, television shot, etc taken at close range. 2 a detailed look at, or examination of, something.

closure n 1 the act of closing something, eg a business or a transport route. 2 a device for closing or sealing something. 3 a parliamentary procedure for cutting short a debate and taking an immediate vote.

clot n 1 a soft semi-solid mass, esp one formed during the coagulation of blood. 2 *Brit colloq* a fool. ➤ vb (**clotted, clotting**) tr & intr to form into clots.

cloth n 1 woven, knitted or felted material. 2 *often in compounds* a piece of fabric for a special use: *tablecloth*. 3 (**the cloth**) the clergy.

clothe vb (past tense, past participle **clothed** or **clad**) 1 to cover or provide someone with clothes. 2 to dress someone. 3 to cover, conceal or disguise someone or something: *hills clothed in mist*.

clothes pl n 1 articles of dress for covering the body, for warmth, decoration, etc. 2 BED-CLOTHES.

clothes horse n a hinged frame on which to dry or air clothes indoors.

clothesline n a rope, usu suspended outdoors, on which washed clothes, etc are hung to dry.

clothing n clothes collectively.

clotted cream n thick cream made by slowly heating milk and taking the cream from the top.

cloud n 1 *meteorol* a visible floating mass of small water droplets or ice crystals suspended in the atmosphere above the Earth's surface. 2 a visible mass of particles of dust or smoke in the atmosphere. 3 a circumstance that causes anxiety. 4 a state of gloom, depression or suspicion. ➤ vb 1 tr & intr (usu **cloud over** or **cloud sth over**) to make or become misty or cloudy. 2 intr (often **cloud over**) of the face: to develop a troubled expression. 3 to make dull or confused. 4 to spoil or mar. ○ **cloudless** adj. ♦ **on cloud nine** colloq extremely happy. **with one's head in the clouds** colloq preoccupied with one's own thoughts.

cloudburst n a sudden heavy downpour of rain.

cloud-cuckoo-land n the imaginary dwelling-place of over-optimistic unrealistic people.

cloudy adj (**-ier, -iest**) 1 full of clouds; overcast. 2 eg of a liquid: not clear. 3 confused; muddled.

clout n 1 colloq a blow or cuff. 2 colloq influence or power. ➤ vb, colloq to hit or cuff.

clove[1] n the strong-smelling dried flower-bud of a tropical evergreen tree, used as a spice.

clove[2] n one of the sections into which a compound bulb, esp of garlic, naturally splits.

clove[3] past tense of CLEAVE[1]

cloven hoof or **cloven foot** n the partially divided hoof of various mammals, including cattle, deer, sheep, goats and pigs.

clover n a small plant that grows wild in temperate regions and which has leaves divided into usu three leaflets and small dense red or white flowers. ♦ **in clover** colloq in great comfort and luxury.

clown n 1 in a circus or pantomime, etc: a comic performer, usu wearing ridiculous clothes and make-up. 2 someone who behaves comically. 3 derog a fool. ➤ vb, intr (often **clown about** or **around**) to play the clown.

cloy vb 1 intr to become distasteful through excess, esp of sweetness. 2 to satiate to the point of disgust. ○ **cloying** adj.

club n 1 a stick, usu thicker at one end, used as a weapon. 2 in various sports, esp golf: a stick with a specially shaped head, used to hit the ball. 3 an INDIAN CLUB. 4 a society or association. 5 the place where such a group meets. 6 a building with dining, reading and sleeping facilities for its members. 7 a NIGHTCLUB. 8 a (**clubs**) one of the four suits of playing-cards, with a black clover-leaf-shaped symbol (♣); b a playing-card of this suit. ➤ vb (**clubbed, clubbing**) to beat (a person, animal, etc) with a club. ○ **clubber** n. ○ **clubbing** n.

club foot n, *non-technical* a congenital deformity in which the foot is twisted down and turned inwards.

clubhouse n a building where a club meets.

club soda n, *chiefly US* soda water.

cluck n 1 the sound made by a hen. 2 any similar sound. ➤ vb, intr 1 of a hen: to make such a sound. 2 to express disapproval by making a similar sound with the tongue.

clue n 1 a fact or circumstance which helps towards the solution of a crime or a mystery. 2 in a crossword puzzle: a word or words representing, in a more or less disguised form, a problem to be solved. ♦ **not have a clue** colloq to be completely ignorant about something.

clued-up adj, colloq shrewd; knowledgeable.

clueless adj, derog stupid, incompetent or ignorant.

clump n 1 a group or cluster of something, eg trees or people standing close together. 2 a dull heavy sound, eg of treading feet. 3 a shapeless mass: *a clump of weeds*. ➤ vb 1 intr to walk with a heavy tread. 2 tr & intr to form into clumps.

clumpy adj (**-ier, -iest**) large and heavy: *clumpy shoes*.

clumsy adj (**-ier, -iest**) 1 unskilful with the hands or awkward and ungainly in movement. 2 badly or awkwardly made. ○ **clumsily** adv. ○ **clumsiness** n.

clunk n the sound of a heavy object, esp a metal one, striking something. ➤ vb, tr & intr to make or cause to make such a sound.

clunky adj (**-ier, -iest**) colloq clumsy and awkward.

cluster n 1 a small group or gathering. 2 a number of flowers growing together on one stem. ➤ vb, tr & intr to form into a cluster or clusters.

clutch[1] vb 1 to grasp something tightly. 2 (usu **clutch at sth**) to try to grasp it. ➤ n 1 (usu **clutches**) control or power. 2 the device in a motor vehicle that transmits the driving force from engine to gearbox. **3** in a motor vehicle: the pedal operating this device. **4** a grasp.

clutch² n **1** a number of eggs laid at the same time. **2** a brood of newly hatched birds, esp chickens.

clutter n an untidy accumulation of objects. ➤ vb (often **clutter sth up**) to overcrowd it or make it untidy with accumulated objects. ○ **cluttered** adj.

Cm symbol, chem curium.

cm abbrev centimetre.

Co symbol, chem cobalt.

c/o abbrev care of: see under CARE.

coach n **1** a railway carriage. **2** a bus designed for long-distance travel. **3** hist a closed horse-drawn carriage. **4** a trainer or instructor, esp in sport. **5** a private tutor, esp one for examinations. ➤ vb, tr & intr **a** to train in a sport, etc; **b** to teach privately. ○ **coaching** n.

coachman n, hist the driver of a horse-drawn coach.

coachwork n the painted outer bodywork of a motor or rail vehicle.

coagulate /kəʊˈagjʊleɪt/ vb, tr & intr of a liquid: to become clotted or curdled, or to form a soft semi-solid mass. ➤ n the soft semi-solid mass produced by this process. ○ **coagulation** n.

coal n **1** a hard brittle CARBONACEOUS rock, usu black or brown in colour, formed from partially decomposed plant material and used as a fuel. **2** a piece of this. ◆ **coals to Newcastle** something brought to a place where it is already plentiful. **haul sb over the coals** colloq to scold them severely.

coalesce /kəʊəˈlɛs/ vb, intr to come together to form a single mass.

coal gas n a flammable gas, mainly hydrogen and methane, obtained by the distillation of coal and formerly used as a fuel.

coalition /kəʊəˈlɪʃən/ n, pol a combination or temporary alliance, esp between political parties.

coal tar n a thick black liquid obtained as a by-product during the manufacture of coke, and used in drugs, dyes, etc.

coaming n, naut the raised edging round the hatches on a ship, to keep out water.

coarse adj **1** rough or open in texture. **2** rough or crude; not refined. **3** of behaviour, speech, etc: rude or offensive. ○ **coarsely** adv. ○ **coarseness** n.

coarse fish n a freshwater fish, other than trout and salmon.

coarsen vb, tr & intr to make or become coarse.

coast n the land that borders the sea. ➤ vb, intr **1** to travel downhill, eg on a bicycle, relying on gravity or momentum rather than power. **2** to progress smoothly and satisfactorily without much effort. ○ **coastal** adj. ◆ **the coast is clear** colloq there is no danger of being seen or caught.

coaster n **1** a vessel that sails along the coast

taking goods to coastal ports. **2** a small mat placed under a glass, etc to protect the table surface.

coastguard n **1** an official organization which rescues people at sea, prevents smuggling, etc. **2** a member of this organization.

coastline n the shape of the coast.

coat n **1** an outer garment with long sleeves, typically reaching below the waist. **2** any similar garment, eg a jacket. **3** the hair, fur or wool of an animal. **4** a covering or application of something eg paint, dust, sugar, etc. ➤ vb to cover with a layer of something. ○ **coating** n a covering or outer layer.

coat-hanger n a shaped piece of wood, plastic or metal with a hook, on which to hang clothes.

coat of arms n (**coats of arms**) a heraldic design consisting of a shield bearing the special insignia of a particular family, organization, etc.

coat-tails pl n the two long pieces of material which hang down at the back of a man's tailcoat.

coax vb **1** (often **coax sb into** or **out of sth**) to persuade them, using flattery, promises, etc. **2** to get something by coaxing. **3** to manipulate something patiently: *I coaxed the key into the lock.*

coaxial adj **1** having or mounted on a common axis. **2** elec of a cable: consisting of a conductor in the form of a metal tube surrounding and insulated from a second conductor.

cob n **1** a short-legged sturdy horse used for riding. **2** a male swan. **3** a hazelnut or hazel tree. **4** a CORNCOB. **5** Brit a loaf with a rounded top.

cobalt n, chem a hard silvery-white metallic element commonly used in ALLOYS to produce cutting tools and magnets.

cobber n, Aust & NZ colloq used as a form of address: a pal or mate.

cobble¹ n a rounded stone used esp formerly to surface streets. Also called **cobblestone**. ➤ vb to pave with cobblestones. ○ **cobbled** adj.

cobble² vb **1** to mend (shoes). **2** (often **cobble sth together** or **up**) to put it together roughly or hastily.

cobbler n someone who makes or mends shoes.

cobblers pl n, Brit slang nonsense.

cobra n any of various species of venomous snake found in Africa and Asia which, when threatened, rear up and spread the skin behind the head to form a flattened hood.

cobweb n **1** a web of fine sticky threads spun by a spider. **2** a single thread from this.

coca n **1** either of two S American shrubs whose leaves contain cocaine. **2** the leaves of this shrub chewed as a stimulant.

cocaine n, med an addictive narcotic drug, obtained from the leaves of the coca plant, used medicinally as a local anaesthetic and illegally as a stimulant.

coccus /ˈkɒkəs/ n (**cocci** /ˈkɒk(s)aɪ/) biol a spherical bacterium.

coccyx /'kɒksɪks/ n (**coccyges** /kɒk'saɪdʒiːz/) *anat* in humans and certain apes: a small triangular tail-like bone at the base of the spine.

cochineal n a bright red pigment widely used as a food colouring.

cochlea /'kɒklɪə/ n (**cochleae** /-iː/) *anat* in the inner ear of vertebrates: a hollow spirally coiled structure which converts the vibrations of sound waves into nerve impulses.

cock¹ n **1** a male bird, esp an adult male chicken. **2** a STOPCOCK. **3** the hammer of a gun which, when raised and let go by the trigger, produces the discharge. **4** *coarse slang* the penis. ➤ vb **1** to turn in a particular direction: *cock an ear towards the door.* **2** to draw back the hammer of a gun. **3** to set (one's hat) at an angle.

cock² n a small heap of hay, etc. ➤ vb to pile into such heaps.

cockade n, *hist* a feather or a rosette of ribbon worn on the hat as a badge.

cock-a-doodle-doo n an imitation of the sound of a cock crowing.

cock-a-hoop adj, *colloq* **1** jubilant; exultant. **2** boastful.

cock-a-leekie n soup made from chicken and leeks.

cockamamie adj, *US dated slang* ridiculous.

cock-and-bull story n, *colloq* an unlikely story.

cockatiel n a small, crested parrot of the cockatoo family.

cockatoo n a light-coloured parrot with an erectile crest on its head, native to Australasia.

cock-crow n dawn.

cocked hat n, *hist* a three-cornered hat with upturned brim.

cockerel n a young cock.

cock-eyed adj, *colloq* **1** crooked; lopsided. **2** senseless; crazy; impractical.

cockle n an edible BIVALVE shellfish with a rounded and ribbed shell. ♦ **warm the cockles of the heart** *colloq* to delight someone.

cockney n **1** (*often* Cockney) **a** *loosely* a native of London, esp of the East End; **b** *strictly* someone born within the sound of Bow Bells. **2** the dialect used by Cockneys. ➤ adj relating to Cockneys or their dialect.

cockpit n **1** in an aircraft: the compartment for the pilot and crew. **2** in a racing-car: the driver's seat. **3** *naut* the part of a small yacht, etc which contains the wheel and tiller. **4** *hist* a pit into which cocks were put to fight.

cockroach n an insect which infests houses, etc.

cockscomb or **coxcomb** n **1** the fleshy red crest on a cock's head. **2** (**coxcomb**) *old use, derog* a foolishly vain or conceited man.

cocksure adj foolishly over-confident.

cocktail n **1** a mixed drink of spirits and other liquors. **2** a mixed dish esp of seafood and mayonnaise. **3** a mixture of different things: *a cocktail of drink and drugs.*

cocktail stick n a short thin pointed stick on which small items of food are served at parties, etc.

cock-up n, *slang* a mess or muddle resulting from incompetence.

cocky adj (-**ier**, -**iest**) *derog* cheekily self-confident. ○ **cockily** adv. ○ **cockiness** n.

cocoa n **1** the seed of the CACAO tree. **2** a powder prepared from the seeds of this tree after they have been fermented, dried and roasted. **3** a drink prepared by mixing this powder with hot milk or water.

cocoa bean n one of the seeds from the CACAO tree.

cocoa butter n a pale yellow fat obtained from cocoa beans, which is used in the manufacture of chocolate, cosmetics, etc.

coconut n **1** (*also* **coconut palm**, **coco**) a tropical palm tree cultivated for its edible fruit. **2** the large single-seeded fruit of this tree, with a thick fibrous outer husk and a hard woody inner shell enclosing a layer of white edible flesh and a central cavity.

cocoon n **1** the protective silky covering that many animals, eg spiders, spin around their eggs. **2** a similar covering that a larva spins around itself before it develops into a pupa. ➤ vb **1** to wrap someone or something up as if in a cocoon. **2** to protect someone from the problems of everyday life.

cod¹ n (pl **cod**) a large food fish, found mainly in the N Atlantic Ocean.

cod² n, *slang* **1** a hoax. **2** a parody.

c.o.d. *abbrev* cash on delivery.

coda /'kəʊdə/ n, *mus* a passage added at the end of a movement or piece, to bring it to a satisfying conclusion.

coddle vb **1** to cook something (esp eggs) gently in hot, rather than boiling, water. **2** to pamper or over-protect someone or something.

code n **1** a system of words, letters or symbols, used in place of those really intended, for secrecy's or brevity's sake. **2** a set of signals for sending messages, etc. **3** *comput* the instructions that make up a computer program. **4** a set of principles of behaviour. **5** a set of laws. **6** *telecomm* the number dialled before a personal telephone number when making a non-local call. ➤ vb **1** to put something into a code. **2** *comput* to generate a set of instructions that make up a computer program.

codeine /'kəʊdiːn/ n, *med* a morphine derivative that relieves pain and has a sedative effect.

codex n (**codices** /kəʊdɪsiːz/) an ancient manuscript, bound in book form.

codger n, *colloq* a man, esp an old one.

codicil /'kəʊdɪsɪl, 'kɒdɪsɪl/ n, *law* a supplement to a will.

codify vb (-**ies**, -**ied**) to arrange something into a systematic code.

cod-liver oil n an oil obtained from the livers of cod, rich in vitamins A and D.

codpiece n, *hist* a pouch attached to the front of a man's breeches, covering his genitals.

codswallop n, Brit slang nonsense.

co-ed abbrev, colloq coeducation or co-educational.

coeducation n the teaching of pupils of both sexes in the same school or college. ○ **co-educational** adj.

coefficient n 1 algebra a number or other constant factor placed before a variable to signify that the variable is to be multiplied by that factor. 2 physics a number or parameter that is a measure of a specified property of a particular substance under certain conditions.

coelacanth /ˈsiːləkanθ/ n a primitive bony fish believed extinct until a live specimen was found in 1938.

coelenterate /siːˈlɛntəreɪt/ n, zool any member of the PHYLUM of invertebrate animals which have a single body cavity and usu show radial symmetry, eg jellyfish, sea anemones, etc.

coeliac or (esp US) **celiac** /ˈsiːlɪak/ adj relating to the abdomen.

coenobite /ˈsiːnəbaɪt/ n a member of a monastic community.

coerce /kəʊˈɜːs/ vb (often **coerce sb into sth**) to force or compel them to do it. ○ **coercion** /kəʊˈɜːʃən/ n. ○ **coercive** adj.

coeval /kəʊˈiːvəl/ adj, formal belonging to the same age or period of time.

co-exist vb, intr 1 to exist together, or simultaneously. 2 to live peacefully side by side in spite of differences, etc. ○ **co-existence** n. ○ **co-existent** adj.

coffee n 1 an evergreen tree or shrub which has red fleshy fruits. 2 the seeds, or beans, of this plant. 3 a drink, usu containing CAFFEINE, which is prepared from the roasted and ground beans of the coffee plant.

coffee table n a small low table.

coffer n 1 a large chest for holding valuables. 2 (**coffers**) a treasury or supply of funds.

cofferdam n a watertight chamber allowing construction workers to carry out building work underwater.

coffin n a box in which a corpse is cremated or buried.

cog n 1 one of a series of teeth on the edge of a wheel or bar which engage with another series of teeth to bring about motion. 2 a small gear wheel. 3 someone unimportant in, though necessary to, a process or organization.

cogent /ˈkəʊdʒənt/ adj of arguments, reasons, etc: strong; convincing. ○ **cogency** n.

cogitate /ˈkɒdʒɪteɪt/ vb, intr to think deeply; to ponder. ○ **cogitation** n. ○ **cogitative** adj.

cognac /ˈkɒnjak/ n a high-quality French brandy.

cognate adj 1 descended from or related to a common ancestor. 2 of words or languages: derived from the same original form. 3 related; akin. ➤ n something that is related to something else.

cognition n, psychol the mental processes, such as perception, reasoning, problem-solving, etc, which enable humans to experience and process knowledge and information. ○ **cognitive** adj.

cognizance or **cognisance** n 1 knowledge; understanding. 2 the range or scope of awareness or knowledge. ○ **cognizant** adj. ♦ take cognizance of sth to take it into consideration.

cognomen /kɒgˈnəʊmən/ n (**cognomens** or **cognomina** /-ˈnəʊmɪnə/) 1 Roman history a Roman's third name, often in origin an epithet or nickname, which became their family name. 2 a nickname or surname.

cognoscenti /kɒnjəʊˈʃɛntɪ/ pl n knowledgeable people.

cogwheel n a toothed wheel.

cohabit vb, intr to live together as husband and wife, usu without being married. ○ **cohabitation** n.

cohere vb, intr 1 to stick together. 2 to be consistent; to have a clear logical connection.

coherent adj 1 of a description or argument: logical and consistent. 2 speaking intelligibly. 3 sticking together; cohering. 4 physics of two or more radiating waves: having the same frequency, and either the same PHASE (noun sense 4) or a constant phase difference. ○ **coherence** n.

cohesion n 1 sticking together. 2 physics the attraction between atoms or molecules of the same substance, which produces SURFACE TENSION. ○ **cohesive** adj.

cohort n 1 hist in the ancient Roman army: one of the ten divisions of a legion. 2 a group of people sharing a common quality or belief.

coif[1] /kɔɪf/ n a close-fitting cap worn esp by women in medieval times.

coif[2] /kwɑːf/ n a hairstyle. ➤ vb (**coiffed, coiffing**) to dress (hair).

coiffeur /kwɑːˈfɜː(r)/ or **coiffeuse** /kwɑːˈfɜːz/ n a male and female hairdresser respectively.

coiffure /kwɑːˈfʊə(r)/ n a hairstyle.

coil[1] vb, tr & intr (sometimes **coil up**) to wind round and round in loops to form rings or a spiral. ➤ n 1 something looped into rings or a spiral: a coil of rope. 2 a single loop in such an arrangement. 3 elec a conducting wire wound into a spiral, used to provide a magnetic field, or to introduce inductance into an electrical circuit. 4 non-technical an IUD.

coil[2] n, old use trouble and tumult. ♦ this mortal coil the troubles of the world.

coin n 1 a small metal disc stamped for use as currency. 2 coins generally. ➤ vb 1 a to manufacture (coins) from metal; b to make (metal) into coins. 2 to invent (a new word or phrase).

coinage n 1 the process of coining. 2 coins.

coincide vb, intr 1 to happen at the same time. 2 to be the same. 3 to occupy the same position.

coincidence n 1 the striking occurrence of events together or in sequence, without any causal connection. 2 the fact of being the same.

coincident adj 1 coinciding in space or time. 2 in agreement.

coincidental *adj* happening by coincidence. ○ **coincidentally** *adv*.

coir /ˈkɔɪə(r)/ *n* fibre from coconut shells, used for making ropes, matting, etc.

coition /kəʊˈɪʃən/ or **coitus** /ˈkəʊɪtəs, kɔɪ-/ *n* sexual intercourse. ○ **coital** /ˈkəʊɪtəl, kɔɪ-/ *adj*.

coke¹ *n* a brittle greyish-black solid left after gases have been extracted from coal. ➤ *vb, tr & intr* to convert (coal) into this material.

coke² *n, colloq* cocaine.

Col. *abbrev* Colonel.

col *n, geol* in a mountain range: a pass between two adjacent peaks, or the lowest point in a ridge.

cola or **kola** *n* **1** a tree native to Africa, cultivated for its seeds called **cola nuts**. **2** a soft drink flavoured with the extract of the seeds of this tree.

colander *n* a perforated bowl used to drain the water from cooked vegetables, etc.

cold *adj* **1** low in temperature. **2** lower in temperature than is normal, comfortable or pleasant. **3** of food: cooked, but not eaten hot: *cold meat*. **4** unfriendly. **5** comfortless; depressing. **6** *colloq* unenthusiastic: *The suggestion left me cold*. **7** without warmth or emotion: *a cold calculating person*. **8** sexually unresponsive. **9** of colours: producing a feeling of coldness. **10** *colloq* unconscious: *out cold*. **11** dead. **12** of a trail or scent: not fresh. ➤ *adv* without preparation or rehearsal. ➤ *n* **1** lack of heat or warmth; cold weather. **2** a highly contagious viral infection whose symptoms include a sore throat, coughing and sneezing, and a congested nose. ○ **coldly** *adv*. ○ **coldness** *n*. ◆ **get cold feet** *colloq* **1** to lose courage. **2** to become reluctant to carry something out. **in cold blood** deliberately and unemotionally. **pour** or **throw cold water on sth** *colloq* to be discouraging or unenthusiastic about a plan, idea, etc.

cold-blooded *adj* **1** of all animals except mammals and birds: having a body temperature that varies with the temperature of the surrounding environment. **2 a** lacking emotion; **b** callous or cruel.

cold comfort *n* no comfort at all.

cold front *n, meteorol* the leading edge of an advancing mass of cold air moving under a retreating mass of warm air.

cold-hearted *adj* unkind.

cold sore *n* a patch of small blister-like spots on or near the lips, caused by the herpes simplex virus.

cold storage *n* **1** the storage of food, etc under refrigeration, in order to preserve it. **2** the state of being put aside till another time.

cold sweat *n* a chill caused by a feeling of fear or nervousness.

cold turkey *n, drug-taking slang* a way of curing drug addiction by suddenly and completely stopping the use of drugs.

cold war *n* a state of hostility and antagonism between nations, without actual warfare.

cole *n* any of various vegetables belonging to the cabbage family.

coleslaw *n* a salad made with raw cabbage, onion, carrots and mayonnaise.

coley *n* a large edible fish of the cod family.

colic *n, pathol* severe spasmodic abdominal pain. ○ **colicky** *adj*.

colitis *n* inflammation of the COLON².

collaborate *vb, intr* **1** to work together. **2** *derog* to co-operate with an enemy. ○ **collaboration** *n*. ○ **collaborative** *adj*. ○ **collaborator** *n*.

collage /kɒˈlɑːʒ, ˈkɒlɑːʒ/ *n* **1** a design or picture made up of pieces of paper, cloth, photographs, etc. **2** the art of producing such works.

collagen *n, biol* a tough fibrous protein of CONNECTIVE TISSUE found in skin, bones, teeth, cartilage, ligaments, etc.

collapse *vb* **1** *intr* of buildings, etc: to fall or cave in. **2** *intr* of people: **a** to drop into a state of unconsciousness; **b** to drop in a state of exhaustion or helplessness. **3** *intr* to break down emotionally. **4** *intr* to fail suddenly and completely: *Several firms collapsed*. **5** *tr & intr* to fold up compactly esp for storage. ➤ *n* **1** a process or act of collapsing. **2** a breakdown. ○ **collapsible** *adj*.

collar *n* **1 a** a band or flap round the neck of a garment; **b** the neck of a garment generally. **2** something worn round the neck. **3** a band of leather, etc worn round the neck by an animal. **4** a coloured ring around the neck of certain animals. **5** a cut of meat from the neck of an animal. **6** a ring-shaped fitting for joining two pipes, etc together. ➤ *vb, colloq* to catch or capture someone or something.

collarbone *n, non-technical* the CLAVICLE.

collate *vb* **1** to study and compare. **2** to check and arrange (sheets of paper) in order. ○ **collator** *n*.

collateral *adj* **1** descended from a common ancestor, but through a different branch of the family. **2** additional; secondary in importance. ➤ *n* **1** a collateral relative. **2** assets offered to a creditor as security for a loan.

collation *n* **1** the act of collating. **2** a light meal.

colleague *n* a fellow-worker, esp in a profession.

collect¹ *vb* **1** *tr & intr* to bring or be brought together. **2** to build up a collection of things of a particular type as a hobby: *collect stamps*. **3** to call for someone or something: *I'll collect you in the evening*. **4** *tr & intr* to get something from people, eg money owed or voluntary contributions, etc. **5** to calm oneself; to get one's thoughts, etc under control. ○ **collected** *adj*.

collect² *n, Christianity* a short prayer.

collectable *adj* desirable to a collector.

collection *n* **1** the act of collecting. **2** an accumulated assortment of things of a particular type: *a stamp collection*. **3** an amount of money collected. **4** the removal of mail from a postbox at scheduled times.

collective *adj* of, belonging to or involving all

the members of a group: *a collective effort.* ➤ *n* an organized group or unit who run some kind of business, etc.

collective noun *n* a singular noun which refers to a group of people, animals, things, etc, such as *cast, flock, gang*.

collectivism *n* the economic theory that industry should be carried on with collective capital.

collectivize or **-ise** *vb* to group (farms, factories, etc) into larger units and bring them under state control and ownership.

collector *n, often in compounds, denoting* someone who collects: *debt-collector* • *stamp-collector*.

collector's item or **collector's piece** *n* an object which would interest a collector.

colleen *n, Irish* a girl.

college *n* **1** an institution, either self-contained or part of a university, which provides higher education, further education or professional training. **2** the staff and students of a college. **3** the buildings which make up a college. **4** (*often* **College**) a name used by some larger secondary schools. **5** an official body of members of a profession, concerned with maintaining standards, etc.

collegiate *adj* **1** of, relating to or belonging to a college. **2** of a university: consisting of individual colleges.

collide *vb, intr* **1** to crash together or crash into someone or something. **2** of people: to disagree or clash.

collie *n* a longhaired dog, orig used for herding sheep.

collier *n* **1** a coal-miner. **2** a ship that transports coal.

colliery *n* (*-ies*) a coalmine with its surrounding buildings.

collision *n* **1** a violent meeting of objects; a crash. **2** a conflict.

collocate *vb* **1** to arrange or group together in some kind of order. **2** *gram* of a word: to occur frequently alongside another word.

colloid *n, chem* an intermediate state between a SUSPENSION (sense 5) and a true SOLUTION (sense 3), in which fine particles of one substance are spread evenly throughout another.

colloquial *adj* of language or vocabulary: **a** informal; **b** used in familiar conversation rather than in formal speech or writing. ○ **colloquially** *adv.*

colloquialism *n* a word or expression used in informal conversation.

colloquium /kə'loʊkwɪəm/ *n* (*colloquia* /-ə/ or *colloquiums*) an academic conference; a seminar.

colloquy *n* (*-quies*) a conversation; talk.

collude *vb, intr* to plot secretly with someone, esp with a view to committing fraud.

collusion *n* secret co-operation for the purpose of fraud or other criminal activity, etc. ○ **collusive** *adj.*

collywobbles *pl n* (*usu* **the collywobbles**) col-

loq **1** pain or discomfort in the abdomen. **2** nervousness.

cologne see EAU DE COLOGNE

Colombian *adj* belonging or relating to Colombia or its inhabitants. ➤ *n* a citizen or inhabitant of, or person born in, Colombia.

colon[1] *n* a punctuation mark (:), properly used to introduce a list, an example or an explanation.

colon[2] *n, anat* in vertebrates: the part of the large intestine lying between the CAECUM and RECTUM. ○ **colonic** *adj.*

colonel /'kɜːnəl/ *n* a senior army officer, in charge of a regiment.

colonial *adj* **1** relating to, belonging to or living in a colony or colonies. **2** possessing colonies. ➤ *n* an inhabitant of a colony.

colonialism *n, often derog* the policy of acquiring colonies, esp as a source of profit. ○ **colonialist** *n, adj.*

colonize or **-ise** *vb* **1** *tr & intr* to establish a colony in (an area or country). **2** to settle (people) in a colony. ○ **colonist** *n.* ○ **colonization** *n.*

colonnade *n, archit* a row of columns placed at regular intervals.

colony *n* (*-ies*) **1 a** a settlement abroad established and controlled by the founding country; **b** the settlers living there; **c** the territory they occupy. **2** a group of the same nationality or occupation forming a distinctive community within a city, etc: *writers' colony.* **3** *zool* a group of animals or plants of the same species living together in close proximity. **4** *bacteriol* an isolated group of bacteria or fungi growing on a solid medium, usu from the same single cell.

colophon *n* a publisher's ornamental mark or device.

colorant or **colourant** *n* a substance used for colouring.

coloration or **colouration** *n* arrangement or combination of colours.

coloratura /kɒlərə'tʊərə/ *n, mus* **1** an elaborate and intricate passage or singing style. **2** (*also* **coloratura soprano**) a soprano specializing in such singing.

colossal *adj* huge; vast.

colossus *n* (*colossi* /kə'lɒsaɪ/ or *colossuses*) **1** a gigantic statue. **2** an overwhelmingly powerful person or organization.

colostomy *n* (*-ies*) *surgery* an operation in which part of the colon is brought to the surface of the body through an incision in the abdomen, through which the colon can be emptied.

colour or (*US*) **color** *n* **1** the visual sensation, eg red, produced when light of different wavelengths is absorbed by the eye and relayed to the brain. **2** any of these colours, often with the addition of black and white. **3** *photog, art* the use of some or all colours, as distinct from black and white only: *in full colour.* **4** a colouring substance, esp paint. **5** the shade of a person's skin, as related to race. **6** pinkness of the face or cheeks, usu indicating healthiness. **7**

lively or convincing detail: *add local colour to the story.* ➤ *vb* **1 a** to put colour on to something; **b** to paint or dye. **2** (*often* **colour sth in**) to fill in (an outlined area) with colour. **3** to influence: *Personal feelings can colour one's judgement.* **4** *intr* to blush. ♦ **off colour** *colloq* unwell.

colour bar *n* social discrimination against people of different races.

colour-blind *adj* unable to distinguish between certain colours. ○ **colour-blindness** *n*.

coloured *adj* **1** *also in compounds* having colour, or a specified colour: *coloured paper.* **2 a** belonging to a dark-skinned race; **b** non-white. **3** (**Coloured**) *S Afr* being of mixed white and non-white descent. **4** distorted: *Her judgement was coloured because of past experiences.* ➤ *n* **1** *often offensive* someone of a dark-skinned race. **2** (**Coloured**) *S Afr* a person of mixed white and non-white descent.

colour-fast *adj* of fabrics: dyed with colours that will not run or fade when washed.

colourful *adj* **1** full of esp bright colour. **2** lively; full of interest or character. ○ **colourfully** *adv*.

colouring *n* **1** a substance used to give colour, eg to food. **2** the applying of colour. **3** arrangement or combination of colour. **4** facial complexion, or this in combination with eye and hair colour.

colourless *adj* **1** without or lacking colour. **2** uninteresting; lifeless: *a colourless existence.*

colours *pl n* **1** the flag of a nation, regiment or ship. **2** the coloured uniform or other distinguishing badge awarded to team-members in certain games. **3** a badge of ribbons in colours representing a particular party, etc, worn to show support for it. ♦ **in one's true colours** as one really is. **with flying colours** with great success.

colt *n* **1** a male horse or pony less than four years old. **2** *sport* an inexperienced young player.

columbine *n* a wild flower related to the buttercup.

column *n* **1** *archit* a vertical pillar, usu cylindrical, with a base and a CAPITAL². **2** something similarly shaped; a long and more or less cylindrical mass. **3** a vertical row of numbers. **4** a vertical strip of print on a newspaper page, etc. **5** a regular section in a newspaper concerned with a particular topic, or by a regular writer. **6** a troop of soldiers or vehicles standing or moving a few abreast.

columnist *n* someone who writes a regular section of a newspaper.

coma *n* a prolonged state of deep unconsciousness from which a person cannot be awakened, caused by head injury, etc.

comatose *adj* **1** in a coma. **2** *facetious* sound asleep.

comb *n* **1 a** a rigid toothed device for tidying and arranging the hair; **b** a similar device worn in the hair to keep it in place. **2** a toothed implement for disentangling and cleaning wool or cotton. **3** an act of combing. **4** a honeycomb. **5** the fleshy serrated crest on the head of a fowl. ➤ *vb* **1** to arrange, smooth or clean something with a comb. **2** to search (a place) thoroughly.

combat *n* a fight or contest. ➤ *vb* (**combated, combating**) to fight against someone or something.

combatant *n* someone involved in or ready for a fight.

combative *adj* inclined to fight or argue.

combination *n* **1** the process of combining or the state of being combined. **2 a** two or more things, people, etc combined; **b** the resulting mixture or union. **3** a sequence of numbers or letters for opening a combination lock. **4** *Brit* a motorcycle with sidecar.

combine /kəm'baɪn/ *vb, tr & intr* **1** to join together. **2** *chem* to coalesce or make things coalesce so as to form a new compound. ➤ *n* /'kɒmbaɪn/ **1** a group of people or businesses associated for a common purpose. **2** *colloq* a combine harvester.

combine harvester *n, agric* a machine used to both reap and thresh crops.

combo *n, colloq* a small jazz band.

combustible *adj* liable to catch fire and burn readily. ➤ *n* something that is liable to catch fire and burn readily.

combustion *n* **1** the process of catching fire and burning. **2** *chem* a chemical reaction in which a gas, liquid or solid is rapidly OXIDIZED, producing heat and light.

come *vb* (*past tense* **came**, *past participle* **come**) *intr in most senses* **1** to move in the direction of a speaker or hearer. **2** to reach a place; to arrive. **3** (*usu* **come to** or **into sth**) to reach (a certain stage or state). **4** to travel or traverse (a distance, etc). **5** to enter one's consciousness or perception: *come into view.* **6** to occupy a specific place in order, etc: *In 'ceiling', 'e' comes before 'i'.* **7** to be available; to exist: *Those purple jeans come in several sizes.* **8** to become: *come undone.* **9** *intr, colloq* to have a sexual orgasm. **10** on the arrival of (a particular point in time): *Come next Tuesday, I'll be free.* ➤ *exclam* used to reassure or admonish: *Oh, come now, don't exaggerate.* ♦ **come again?** *colloq* could you repeat that? ◊ **come about** to happen. **come across** to make a certain impression: *Her speech came across well.* **come across sth** or **sb** to discover them accidentally. **come at sth** or **sb** to attack them. **come back 1** to be recalled to mind. **2** to become fashionable again. **come between sb** or **sth and sb** or **sth else** to create a barrier or division between them. **come by sth** to obtain it, esp accidentally. **come down 1** to lose one's social position. **2** of an heirloom, etc: to be inherited. **3** to decide. **4** to descend. **come down on** or **upon sb** or **sth** to deal with them severely. **come down to sth** to be equivalent to it, in simple terms: *It comes down to this: we stay or we leave.* **come down with sth** to develop (an illness). **come in 1** to arrive; to be received. **2** to have a particular role, function or use: *This is where you come in*. **3** to become fashionable. **come in for sth** to deserve or incur it. **come off 1** to become detached. **2** to succeed. **3** *colloq* to take place. **come on 1** to start. **2** to prosper or make progress. **3** to appear or make an entrance on stage. **4** *colloq* to begin: *He could feel the flu coming on*. **come on to sb** *colloq* to flirt with them or make sexual advances towards them. **come out 1** to become known; to become public. **2** to be removed. **3** to be released or made available. **4** to go on strike. **5** to emerge in a specified position or state: *come out well from the affair*. **6** *colloq* to declare openly that one is a homosexual. Compare OUT (*verb* sense 2). **7** *old use* of a girl: to be launched in society. **come out in sth** to develop (a rash, etc). **come out with sth** to make a remark, etc. **come over 1** to change one's opinion or side. **2** to make a specified impression: *comes over well on television*. **3** *colloq* to feel or become: *come over a bit faint*. **come round 1** to regain consciousness. **2** to change one's opinion. **come through 1** to survive. **2** to emerge successfully. **come to** to regain consciousness. **come to sth** to reach or total (a sum of money). **come up 1** to occur; to happen. **2** to be considered or discussed: *The question didn't come up*. **come up against sb or sth** to be faced with them as an opponent, challenge, etc. **come up to sth** to extend to or reach (a level, standard, etc). **come up with sth** to offer it; to put it forward. **come upon sth or sb** to discover it or them by chance.

comeback *n* **1** a return to former success. **2** a retort.

comedian or **comedienne** *n* **1** a male or female entertainer who tells jokes, performs comic sketches, etc. **2** an actor in comedy.

comedown *n* **1** a decline in social status. **2** an anticlimax.

comedy *n* (*-ies*) **1** a light amusing play or film. **2** in earlier literature: a play with a fortunate outcome. **3** funny incidents.

come-hither *adj*, *colloq* seductive: *a come-hither look*.

comely *adj* (*-ier, -iest*) *dated* of a person: attractive in a wholesome way. ○ **comeliness** *n*.

come-on *n*, *colloq* sexual encouragement.

comestible *n* (*usu* **comestibles**) *affected* something to eat.

comet *n*, *astron* a small body which follows an elliptical orbit around the Sun, leaving a trail.

come-uppance *n*, *colloq* justified punishment or retribution.

comfit *n* a type of sweet, containing a sugar-coated nut, liquorice, etc.

comfort *n* **1** a state of contentedness or well-being. **2** relief from suffering, or consolation in grief. **3** a person or thing that provides such relief or consolation. **4** (*usu* **comforts**) something that makes for ease and physical wellbeing. ➣ *vb* to relieve from suffering; to console or soothe.

comfortable *adj* **1** in a state of wellbeing, esp physical. **2** at ease. **3** providing comfort. **4** *colloq* financially secure. **5** of a hospital patient, etc: in a stable condition. ○ **comfortably** *adv*.

comforter *n* **1** someone who comforts. **2** *old use* a warm scarf. **3** *old use* a baby's dummy.

comfrey *n* a bristly, robust plant with tubular white, pink or purple flowers, traditionally used medicinally.

comfy *adj* (*-ier, -iest*) *colloq* comfortable.

comic *adj* **1** characterized by or relating to comedy. **2** funny. ➣ *n* **1** a comedian. **2** a paper or magazine which includes strip cartoons, illustrated stories, etc.

comical *adj* funny; humorous; ludicrous. ○ **comically** *adv*.

comic strip *n* in a newspaper, magazine, etc: a brief story or episode told through a short series of cartoon drawings.

coming *n* an arrival or approach. ➣ *adj* **1** *colloq* likely to succeed: *the coming man*. **2** approaching: *in the coming months*. ◆ **have it coming to one** to deserve what is about to happen to one. **up and coming** promising; progressing well.

comity *n* (*-ies*) civility; politeness.

comma *n* a punctuation mark (,) indicating a slight pause made for the sake of clarity, to separate items in a list, etc.

command *vb* **1** to order formally. **2** to have authority over or be in control of someone or something. **3** to deserve or be entitled to something. **4** to look down over something: *The window commands a view of the bay*. ➣ *n* **1** an order. **2** control; charge. **3** knowledge of and ability to use something: *a good command of the English language*. **4** a military unit or a district under one's command. **5** *comput* an instruction to initiate a specific operation.

commandant / ˈkɒmǝndant / *n* a commanding officer, esp of a prisoner-of-war camp or a military training establishment.

commandeer *vb* **1** to seize (property) for military use. **2** to seize without justification.

commander *n* **1** a naval officer of the rank below captain. **2** a high-ranking police officer. **3** a senior member in some orders of knighthood.

commanding *adj* **1** powerful; leading. **2** in charge. **3** inspiring respect or awe. **4** giving good views all round: *a house with a commanding position*.

commandment *n* **a** a divine command; **b** (**Commandment**) one of the 10 rules given to Moses by God as the basis of a good life.

commando *n* **1** a unit of soldiers specially trained to carry out dangerous raids. **2** a member of such a unit.

commemorate *vb* **1** to honour the memory of (a person or event) with a ceremony, etc. **2** to be a memorial to someone or something. ○ **commemoration** *n*. ○ **commemorative** *adj*.

commence *vb*, *tr & intr* to begin. ○ **commencement** *n*.

commend *vb* **1** to praise. **2** to recommend. **3**

(*usu* **commend sth to sb**) to entrust it to them. ○ **commendable** *adj*. ○ **commendation** *n*.

commensurable *adj* **1** *maths* having a common factor. **2** denoting quantities whose ratio is a rational number. **3** denoting two or more quantities that can be measured in the same units.

commensurate *adj* **1** in equal proportion to something; appropriate to it. **2** equal in extent, quantity, etc to something.

comment *n* **1** a remark or observation, esp a critical one. **2** talk, discussion or gossip. **3** an explanatory or analytical note on a passage of text. ➤ *vb, tr & intr* (*often* **comment on sth**) to make observations, remarks, etc.

commentary *n* (*-ies*) **1** an ongoing description of an event, eg a football match, as it happens. **2** a set of notes explaining or interpreting points in a text, etc.

commentate *vb, intr* to act as a commentator.

commentator *n* **1** a broadcaster who gives a commentary on an event, etc. **2** the writer of a textual commentary.

commerce *n* the buying and selling of commodities and services.

commercial *adj* **1** relating to, engaged in or used for commerce. **2** profitable; having profit as the main goal. **3** paid for by advertising. ➤ *n* a radio or TV advertisement.

commercialism *n* **1** commercial attitudes and aims. **2** undue emphasis on profit-making.

commercialize or **-ise** *vb* **1** *derisive* to exploit for profit, esp by sacrificing quality. **2** to make commercial. ○ **commercialization** *n*.

commis or **commis chef** *n* (*pl* **commis** or **commis chefs**) a trainee waiter or chef.

commiserate *vb, tr & intr* (*often* **commiserate with sb**) to express one's sympathy for them. ○ **commiseration** *n*.

commissar *n* in the former Soviet Union: a Communist Party official responsible for the political education of military units.

commissariat *n* in the army: a department responsible for food supplies.

commissary *n* (*-ies*) **1** *US* a store supplying provisions and equipment to a military force. **2** a deputy, esp one representing a bishop.

commission *n* **1 a** a formal or official request to someone to perform a task or duty; **b** the authority to perform such a task or duty; **c** the task or duty performed. **2** a military rank above the level of officer. **3** an order for a piece of work, esp a work of art. **4** a board or committee entrusted with a particular task: *the equal rights commission*. **5** a fee or percentage given to an agent for arranging a sale, etc. ➤ *vb* **1** to give a commission or authority to someone. **2** to grant a military rank above a certain level to someone. **3** to request someone to do something. **4** to place an order for something, eg a work of art, etc. **5** to prepare (a ship) for active service. ♦ **in** or **out of commission** in or not in use or working condition.

commissionaire *n, chiefly Brit* a uniformed attendant at the door of a cinema, theatre, office or hotel.

commissioned officer *n* a military officer who holds a commission.

commissioner *n* **1** a representative of the government in a district, department, etc. **2** a member of a commission.

commit *vb* (**committed, committing**) **1** to carry out or perpetrate (a crime, offence, error, etc). **2** to have someone put in prison or a mental institution. **3** to promise or engage, esp oneself, for some undertaking, etc. **4** to dedicate oneself to a cause, etc from a sense of conviction: *She committed herself to Christ*. ○ **commitment** *n*. ♦ **commit oneself** to make an irrevocable undertaking. **commit sth to memory** to memorize it.

committal *n* the action of committing someone to a prison or mental institution.

committee *n* a group of people selected by and from a larger body to undertake certain duties on its behalf.

commode *n* **1** a chair with a hinged seat, designed to conceal a chamber pot. **2** an ornate chest of drawers.

commodious *adj* comfortably spacious.

commodity *n* (*-ies*) **1** something that is bought and sold, esp a manufactured product or raw material. **2** something, eg a quality, from the point of view of its value or importance in society: *Courtesy is a scarce commodity*.

commodore *n* **1** a naval officer of the rank below rear-admiral. **2** the president of a yacht club.

common *adj* **1** frequent; familiar: *a common mistake*. **2** shared by two or more people, things, etc: *characteristics common to both animals*. **3** publicly owned. **4** widespread: *common knowledge*. **5** *derog* lacking taste or refinement; vulgar. **6 a** of the ordinary type: *the common cold*; **b** esp of plants and animals: general or ordinary: *common toad*. **7** *maths* shared by two or more numbers: *highest common factor*. ➤ *n* a piece of land that is publicly owned or available for public use. ○ **commonly** *adv*. ♦ **in common 1** of two people with regard to their interests, etc: shared. **2** in joint use or ownership.

common denominator *n* **1** *maths* a whole number that is a multiple of each of the DENOMINATORs of two or more FRACTIONs, eg 15 is a common denominator of 1/3 and 3/5. **2** something that enables comparison, agreement, etc between people or things.

commoner *n* someone who is not a member of the nobility.

Common Era *n* a culturally neutral term for the era reckoned from the birth of Christ, sometimes used instead of ANNO DOMINI.

common law *n, law* law based on custom and decisions by judges, in contrast to STATUTE law. ➤ *adj* (**common-law**) denoting the relationship of two people who live together as man and wife but are not officially married.

common-or-garden *adj* ordinary; everyday.

commonplace *adj* **1** ordinary; everyday. **2** *derog* unoriginal; lacking individuality; trite. ➤ *n* **1** *derog* a trite comment; a cliché. **2** an everyday occurrence.

common room *n* in a college, school, etc: a sitting-room for general use by students or one used by staff.

commons *pl n* **1** *hist* (**the commons**) the ordinary people. **2** *old use, facetious* shared food rations. ➤ *sing n* (**the Commons**) the House of Commons.

common sense *n* practical wisdom. ○ **common-sense** *adj*.

commonwealth *n* **1** a country or state. **2** an association of states that have joined together for their common good. **3** a state in which the people hold power; a republic.

commotion *n* **1** a disturbance; an upheaval. **2** noisy confusion.

communal /'kɒmjʊnəl, kə'mjuːnəl/ *adj* **1** relating or belonging to a community. **2** relating to a commune or communes. ○ **communally** *adv*.

commune¹ /'kɒmjuːn/ *n* **1** a number of unrelated families and individuals living together as a mutually supportive community, with shared accommodation, responsibilities, etc. **2** in some European countries: the smallest administrative unit locally governed.

commune² /kə'mjuːn/ *vb, intr* **1** to communicate intimately. **2** to get close to or relate spiritually to (eg nature).

communicable *adj* **1** of a disease: easily transmitted from one organism to another. **2** capable of being communicated.

communicant *n, Christianity* someone who receives communion.

communicate *vb* **1** *tr & intr* **a** to impart (information, ideas, etc); to make something known or understood; **b** to get in touch. **2** to pass on or transmit (a feeling, etc). **3** *intr* to understand someone; to have a comfortable social relationship. ○ **communicative** *adj*.

communication *n* **1 a** the process or act of communicating; **b** the exchanging or imparting of ideas and information, etc. **2** a piece of information, a letter or a message. **3** social contact. **4** (**communications**) the various means by which information is conveyed from one person or place to another.

communion *n* **1** the sharing of thoughts, beliefs or feelings. **2** a group of people sharing the same religious beliefs. **3** (*also* **Holy Communion**) *Christianity* a church service at which bread and wine are taken as symbols of Christ's body and blood.

communiqué /kə'mjuːnɪkeɪ/ *n* an official announcement.

communism *n* **1** a political ideology advocating a classless society where all sources of wealth and production are collectively owned and controlled by the people. **2** (**Communism**) a political movement founded on the principles of communism set out by Karl Marx. **3** the political and social system established on these principles in the former Soviet Union and other countries. ○ **communist** and **Communist** *n*.

community *n* (*-ies*) **1** the group of people living in a particular place. **2** a group of people bonded together by a common religion, nationality or occupation: *the Asian community*. **3** a group of states with common interests. **4** the public; society in general. **5** *biol* a naturally occurring group of different plant or animal species that occupy the same habitat and interact with each other.

commute *vb* **1** *intr* to travel regularly between two places which are a significant distance apart, esp between home and work in a city, etc. **2** to alter (a criminal sentence) to one less severe. **3** to substitute; to convert. **4** to exchange (one type of payment) for another, eg a single payment for one made in instalments.

commuter *n* someone who regularly travels a significant distance to work.

compact¹ /kəm'pakt/ *adj* **1** firm and dense in form or texture. **2** small, but with all essentials neatly contained. **3** concise. ➤ *vb* /kəm'pakt/ to compress. ➤ *n* /'kɒmpakt/ a small case for women's face powder, usu including a mirror. ○ **compactly** *adv*. ○ **compactness** *n*.

compact² /'kɒmpakt/ *n* a contract or agreement.

compact disc *n* a small disc used to record audio and/or visual information in the form of digital data, which can be read by laser.

companion *n* **1** a friend or frequent associate. **2** *hist* a woman employed by another woman to live or travel with her and to keep her company. **3** esp as a title: a handbook or guide. **4** one of a pair. ○ **companionship** *n*.

companionable *adj* friendly; sociable; comfortable as a companion.

companionway *n* on a ship: a staircase from a deck to a cabin, or between decks.

company *n* (*-ies*) **1** the presence of another person or other people; companionship. **2** the presence of guests or visitors, or the people involved: *expecting company*. **3** one's friends or associates: *get into bad company*. **4** a business organization. **5** a troop of actors or entertainers. **6** a military unit of about 120 men. ◆ **keep sb company** to act as their companion. **part company with sb 1** to separate from them. **2** to disagree with them.

comparable *adj* **1** being of the same or equivalent kind. **2** able to be compared. ○ **comparability** *n*.

comparative *adj* **1** as compared with others. **2** relating to, or using the method of, comparison. **3** relative: *their comparative strengths*. **4** *gram* of adjectives and adverbs: in the form denoting a greater degree of the quality in question but not the greatest, formed either by using the suffix *-er* or the word *more*, eg *larger* or *more usual*. Compare POSITIVE, SUPERLATIVE. ➤ *n, gram* **1** a comparative adjective or adverb. **2** the comparative form of a word. ○ **comparatively** adv.

compare vb **1** to examine (items, etc) to see what differences or similarities they have. **2** intr (often **compare with sth** or **sb**) to be comparable with it or them: *He can't compare with his predecessor in ability.* **3** (often **compare sb** or **sth** to **sb** or **sth else**) to liken them to each other: *He compares her to an angel.* **4** intr to relate (well, badly, etc) when examined: *The two books compare well.* ◆ **beyond** or **without compare** formal without equal; incomparable. **compare notes** to exchange ideas and opinions.

comparison n **1** the process of, an act of or a reasonable basis for, comparing: *There can be no comparison between them.* **2** gram the POSITIVE (sense 13), COMPARATIVE (adj sense 4) and SUPERLATIVE (adj sense 1) forms of adjectives and adverbs.

compartment n a separated-off or enclosed section.

compartmentalize or **-ise** vb to divide, distribute or force into categories.

compass n **1** any device for finding direction, esp one consisting of a magnetized needle that points to magnetic north, from which true north can be calculated. **2** (usu **compasses**) a device consisting of two hinged legs, for drawing circles, measuring distances on maps, etc. Also called **pair of compasses**. **3** range or scope: *within the compass of philosophy.* ➢ vb **1** to pass or go round. **2** to surround or enclose. **3** to accomplish or obtain. **4** to comprehend.

compassion n a feeling of sorrow and pity for someone in trouble. ○ **compassionate** adj. ○ **compassionately** adv.

compatible adj (often **compatible with sth** or **sb**) **1** able to associate or exist together agreeably. **2** consistent or congruous: *His actions were not compatible with his beliefs.* **3** comput capable of being used with a particular computer system. ○ **compatibility** n.

compatriot n someone from one's own country.

compel vb (**compelled, compelling**) **1** to force; to drive. **2** to arouse; to elicit or evoke: *Their plight compels sympathy.*

compelling adj **1** powerful; forcing one to agree, etc. **2** irresistibly fascinating.

compendious adj concise but comprehensive.

compendium n (**compendiums** or **compendia** /kəmˈpɛndɪə/) **1** a concise summary; an abridgement. **2** a collection of boardgames, puzzles, etc in a single container.

compensate vb **1** to make amends to someone for loss, injury or wrong, esp by payment. **2** intr (often **compensate for sth**) to make up for (a disadvantage, loss, etc). ○ **compensatory** adj.

compensation n **1** the process of compensating. **2** something that compensates. **3** a sum of money awarded to make up for loss, injury, etc.

compere or **compère** n someone who hosts a radio or television show, introduces performers, etc. ➢ vb, tr & intr to act as compere for (a show).

compete vb, intr **1** to take part in a contest. **2** to strive to be best: *compete with other firms.* ○ **competitor** n.

competent adj **1** efficient. **2** having sufficient skill or training to do something. **3** legally capable. ○ **competence** n.

competition n **1** an event in which people compete. **2** the process or fact of competing. **3** rivals, eg in business, or their products.

competitive adj **1** involving rivalry. **2** characterized by competition; aggressive; ambitious. **3** of a price or product: reasonably cheap; comparing well with those of market rivals. ○ **competitiveness** n.

compile vb to collect and organize (information, etc) from different sources. ○ **compilation** n. ○ **compiler** n.

complacent adj **1** self-satisfied; smug. **2** too easily satisfied; disinclined to worry. ○ **complacence** or **complacency** n. ○ **complacently** adv.

complain vb, intr **1** to express dissatisfaction or displeasure. **2** (**complain of sth**) to say that one is suffering from (a pain, disease, etc).

complainant n, law a plaintiff.

complaint n **1** the act of complaining. **2** an expression of dissatisfaction. **3** a grievance. **4** a disorder, illness, etc.

complaisant /kəmˈpleɪzənt/ adj eager to please; obliging. ○ **complaisance** n.

complement n **1** something that completes; something that provides a needed balance or contrast. **2** (often **full complement**) the number or quantity required to make something complete, eg the crew of a ship. **3** gram a word or phrase added to a verb to complete the PREDICATE of a sentence, eg *dark* in It grew *dark*. **4** geom the amount by which an angle or arc falls short of a right angle or QUADRANT. ➢ vb to be a complement to something.

complement There is often a spelling confusion between **complement** and **compliment**.

complementary adj **1** serving as a complement to something. **2** of two or more things: complementing each other.

complete adj **1** whole; finished; with nothing missing. **2** thorough; absolute; total: *a complete triumph.* **3** perfect. ➢ vb **1 a** to finish; **b** to make complete or perfect. **2** to fill in (a form). ○ **completely** adv. ○ **completion** n.

complex adj **1** composed of many interrelated parts. **2** complicated; involved. ➢ n **1** something made of interrelating parts, eg a multi-purpose building: *a leisure complex.* **2** psychoanal a set of repressed thoughts and emotions that strongly influence an individual's behaviour and attitudes. **3** colloq an obsession or phobia.

complexion *n* **1** the colour or appearance of the skin, esp of the face. **2** character or appearance: *That puts a different complexion on the matter.*

complexity *n* (*-ies*) **1** the quality of being complex. **2** a complication; an intricacy.

compliance *n* **1** yielding. **2** agreement; assent. **3** submission. ○ **compliant** *adj*.

complicate *vb* to add difficulties to something; to make complex.

complicated *adj* **1** difficult to understand or deal with. **2** intricate; complex.

complication *n* **1** a circumstance that causes difficulties. **2** *pathol* a second and possibly worse disease or disorder that arises during the course of, and often as a result of, an existing one.

complicity *n* the state of being an accomplice in a crime or wrongdoing.

compliment *n* **1** an expression of praise, admiration or approval. **2** a gesture implying approval: *He paid her the compliment of dancing with her.* **3** (**compliments**) formal regards accompanying a gift, etc. ➤ *vb* (*often* **compliment sb on sth**) **1** to congratulate them for it. **2** to praise them; to pay them a compliment.

> **compliment** There is often a spelling confusion between **compliment** and **complement**.

complimentary *adj* **1** paying a compliment; admiring or approving. **2** given free.

comply *vb* (*-ies, -ied*) *intr* (*usu* **comply with sth**) to act in obedience to an order, request, etc.

component *n* any of the parts or elements that make up a machine, instrument, etc. ➤ *adj* functioning as one of the parts of something.

comport *vb* **1** (*always* **comport oneself**) to behave in a specified way. **2** *intr* (*always* **comport with sth**) to suit or be appropriate to it. ○ **comportment** *n* behaviour.

compose *vb* **1** *tr & intr* to create (music). **2** to write (a poem, letter, etc). **3** to make up or constitute something. **4** to arrange as a balanced, artistic whole. **5** to calm (oneself); to bring (thoughts, etc) under control. **6** to settle (differences between people in dispute). **7** *printing* to arrange (type) or set (a page, etc) in type ready for printing.

composed *adj* of a person: calm; controlled.

composer *n* someone who composes, esp music.

composite *adj* made up of different parts, materials or styles. ➤ *n* **1** something made up of different parts, materials or styles. **2** *bot* a member of the largest family of flowering plants (*Compositae*) with a flower head consisting of a crowd of tiny florets often surrounded by a circle of bracts, eg daisy.

composition *n* **1** something composed, esp a musical work. **2** the process of composing. **3** *art* arrangement, esp with regard to balance and visual effect: *photographic composition.* **4** *old use* a school essay. **5** the constitution of something. **6** a synthetic material of various kinds. **7** *printing* the arrangement of pages of type ready for printing.

compositor *n, printing* someone who sets or arranges pages of type ready for printing.

compos mentis *adj, law* sound in mind; perfectly rational.

compost *n* a mixture of decomposed organic substances such as rotting vegetable matter, etc, which is used to enrich soil and nourish plants. ➤ *vb* **1** to treat with compost. **2** to convert (decaying organic matter) into compost.

composure *n* mental and emotional calmness.

compound[1] /ˈkɒmpaʊnd/ *n* **1** (*in full* **chemical compound**) *chem* a substance composed of two or more elements combined in fixed proportions and held together by chemical bonds. **2** something composed of two or more ingredients or parts. ➤ *adj* composed of a number of parts or ingredients. ➤ *vb* /kəmˈpaʊnd/ **1 a** to make (esp something bad) much worse; **b** to complicate or add to (a difficulty, error, etc). **2** *law* to agree to overlook (an offence, etc) in return for payment.

compound[2] /ˈkɒmpaʊnd/ *n* an area enclosed by a wall or fence, containing eg buildings, a prison, etc.

compound fracture *n, med* a type of bone fracture in which the overlying skin is pierced by the broken bone. Compare SIMPLE FRACTURE.

compound interest *n* interest calculated on the original sum of money borrowed and on any interest already accumulated. Compare SIMPLE INTEREST.

comprehend *vb* **1** to understand. **2** to include. ○ **comprehensible** *adj*.

comprehension *n* **1 a** the process or power of understanding; **b** the scope or range of someone's knowledge or understanding. **2** a school exercise for testing understanding of a passage of text.

comprehensive *adj* **1** covering or including a large area or scope. **2** of a school or education: providing teaching for pupils of all abilities aged between 11 and 18. ➤ *n* a comprehensive school.

compress *vb* /kəmˈprɛs/ **1** to press, squeeze or squash together. **2** to reduce in bulk; to condense. ➤ *n* /ˈkɒmprɛs/ a cloth or pad soaked in water and pressed against a part of the body to reduce swelling, stop bleeding, etc. ○ **compressible** *adj*. ○ **compression** *n*.

compressor *n, eng* a device that compresses a gas.

comprise *vb* **1** to contain, include or consist of something specified. **2** to go together to make up something.

> **comprise** When you say that A comprises Bs, you mean that Bs are the parts or elements of A:

✓ *The village school comprises one old building dating back to 1868 and two modern buildings.*

Because it means the same as **consist of**, it is sometimes confused with this and followed by 'of', but this use is ungrammatical:

✗ *The instructions comprised of two sheets of A5 paper.*

compromise *n* **1** a settlement of differences agreed upon after concessions have been made on each side. **2** anything of an intermediate type which comes halfway between two opposing stages. ➤ *vb* **1** *intr* to make concessions; to reach a compromise. **2** to endanger or expose to scandal, by acting indiscreetly.

comptroller *n* a CONTROLLER (sense 2).

compulsion *n* **1** the act of compelling or condition of being compelled. **2** an irresistible urge to perform a certain action, esp an irrational one.

compulsive *adj* **1** having the power to compel. **2** of an action: resulting from a compulsion. **3** of a person: acting on a compulsion. **4** holding the attention; fascinating. ○ **compulsively** *adv*.

compulsory *adj* required by the rules, law, etc.

compunction *n* a feeling of guilt or regret.

computation *n* **1** the process or act of calculating or computing. **2** a result calculated or computed. ○ **computational** *adj*.

compute *vb, tr & intr* **1** to calculate or estimate, esp with the aid of a computer. **2** to carry out (a computer operation).

computer *n* an electronic device which processes data at great speed according to a PROGRAM (see under PROGRAMME) stored within the device.

computerize or **-ise** *vb* **a** to transfer (a procedure, system, etc) to control by computer; **b** to organize (information, data, etc) by computer; **c** to install (computers) for this purpose. ○ **computerization** *n*.

computing *n* the act or process of using a computer.

comrade *n* **1** a a friend or companion; **b** an associate, fellow worker, etc. **2** a fellow communist or socialist. ○ **comradeship** *n*.

con[1] *colloq, n* a CONFIDENCE TRICK. ➤ *vb* (**conned, conning**) to swindle or trick someone, esp after winning their trust.

con[2] *n* an argument against something. See also PROS AND CONS.

con[3] *n, prison slang* a prisoner or inmate.

concatenation *n, formal* a series of items linked together in a chain-like way. ○ **concatenate** *vb*.

concave *adj* of a surface or shape: inward-curving, like the inside of a bowl. Compare CONVEX. ○ **concavity** *n*.

conceal *vb* **1** to hide; to place out of sight. **2** to keep secret. ○ **concealer** *n*. ○ **concealment** *n*.

concede *vb* **1** to admit to be true or correct. **2** to

give or grant. **3** to yield or give up. **4** *intr* to admit defeat in (a contest, etc) often before the end.

conceit *n* **1** a an inflated opinion of oneself; **b** vanity. **2** *old use* a fanciful or ingenious thought or idea.

conceited *adj* **a** having too good an opinion of oneself; **b** vain.

conceivable *adj* imaginable; possible: *every conceivable method*. ○ **conceivably** *adv*.

conceive *vb* **1** *tr & intr* to become pregnant. **2** *tr & intr* (often **conceive of sth**) to think of or imagine (an idea, etc).

concentrate *vb* **1** *intr* (often **concentrate on sth** or **sb**) to give full attention and energy to them or it. **2** to focus: *concentrate our efforts*. **3** *chem* to increase the strength of (a dissolved substance in a solution), either by adding more of it or by evaporating the liquid in which it is dissolved. ➤ *n* a concentrated liquid or substance. ○ **concentrated** *adj*.

concentration *n* **1** intensive mental effort. **2** the act of concentrating or the state of being concentrated. **3** the number of molecules or ions of a substance present in a solution or mixture. **4** a concentrate.

concentration camp *n* a prison camp used to detain civilians, esp as in Nazi Germany.

concentric *adj, geom* of circles, spheres, etc: having a common centre.

concept *n* a notion; an abstract or general idea.

conception *n* **1** an idea or notion. **2** the origin or start of something, esp something intricate. **3** the act or an instance of conceiving. **4** *biol* the fertilization of an ovum by a sperm, representing the start of pregnancy.

conceptual *adj* relating to or existing as concepts or conceptions.

conceptualize or **-ise** *vb* to form a concept or idea of something. ○ **conceptualization** *n*.

concern *vb* **1** to have to do with someone or something: *It concerns your son*. **2** (often **be concerned about sth** or **sb**) to worry or interest. **3** to affect; to involve. ➤ *n* **1** a worry or a cause of worry; **b** interest or a subject of interest. **2** someone's business or responsibility: *That's my concern*. **3** an organization or company.

concerned *adj* worried. ♦ **concerned with sth** or **sb** having to do with it or them; involving it or them.

concerning *prep* regarding; relating to; about.

concert *n* /ˈkɒnsət/ **1** a musical performance given before an audience by singers or players. **2** agreement; harmony. ➤ *vb* /kənˈsɜːt/ to endeavour or plan by arrangement. ♦ **in concert 1** jointly; in co-operation. **2** of singers, musicians, etc: in a live performance.

concerted /kənˈsɜːtɪd/ *adj* planned and carried out jointly.

concertina *n* a musical instrument like a small accordion. ➤ *vb, tr & intr* to fold or collapse like a concertina.

concerto /kənˈtʃɛətəʊ/ *n* (**concertos** or **concerti** /-tiː/) *mus* a composition for an orchestra and one or more solo performers.

concession n 1 the act of conceding. 2 something conceded or allowed. 3 the right, granted under government licence, to extract minerals, etc in an area. 4 the right to conduct a business from within a larger concern. 5 a reduction in ticket prices, fares, etc for categories such as students, the elderly, etc. ○ **concessionary** adj.

concessionaire or (US) **concessioner** n the holder of a concession.

conch n (conchs or conches) 1 any of a family of large marine snails, native to warm shallow tropical waters. 2 the large, colourful shell of this animal often used as a trumpet.

concierge / 'kɒnsɪˌɛəʒ/ n a warden or caretaker of a block of flats, esp one who lives on the premises.

conciliate vb 1 to overcome the hostility of someone. 2 to reconcile (people in dispute, etc). ○ **conciliation** n. ○ **conciliatory** adj.

concise adj brief but comprehensive. ○ **concisely** adv. ○ **conciseness** n.

conclave n 1 a private or secret meeting. 2 RC Church the body of cardinals gathered to elect a new pope.

conclude vb 1 tr & intr to come or bring to an end. 2 to reach an opinion based on reasoning. 3 to settle or arrange: to conclude a treaty.

conclusion n 1 an end. 2 a judgement or opinion based on reasoning: to draw a conclusion. 3 logic a statement validly deduced from a previous PREMISE. 4 a result or outcome (of a discussion, event, etc). ♦ **in conclusion** finally. **jump to conclusions** to presume something without adequate evidence.

conclusive adj of evidence, proof, etc: convincing; leaving no room for doubt. ○ **conclusively** adv.

concoct vb 1 to make something, esp ingeniously from a variety of ingredients. 2 to invent (a story, excuse, etc). ○ **concoction** n.

concomitant adj accompanying because of or as a result of something else. ➤ n a concomitant thing, person, etc.

concord n 1 agreement; peace or harmony. 2 gram AGREEMENT (sense 4). 3 mus a combination of harmonious sounds. ○ **concordant** adj.

concordance n 1 a state of harmony. 2 a book containing an alphabetical index of principal words used in a major work, usu supplying citations and their meaning.

concordat n an agreement between church and state, esp the Roman Catholic Church and a secular government.

concourse n 1 in a railway station, airport, etc: a large open area where people can gather. 2 a throng; a gathering.

concrete n a building material consisting of a mixture of cement, sand, gravel and water, which forms a hard rock-like mass when dry. ➤ adj 1 relating to such a material. 2 relating to items which can be felt, touched, seen, etc:

concrete objects. 3 definite, as opposed to vague or general: concrete evidence. ➤ vb 1 to cover with or embed in concrete. 2 tr & intr to solidify.

concretion n, pathol a hard stony mass which forms in body tissues or natural cavities.

concubine n 1 hist a woman who lives with a man and has sex with him, without being married to him. 2 in polygamous societies: a secondary wife.

concupiscence / kən'kjuːpɪsəns/ n strong desire, esp sexual. ○ **concupiscent** adj.

concur vb (concurred, concurring) intr 1 to agree. 2 to happen at the same time; to coincide.

concurrent adj 1 happening or taking place simultaneously. 2 of lines: meeting or intersecting; having a common point. 3 in agreement. ○ **concurrence** n. ○ **concurrently** adv.

concuss vb to cause concussion in someone.

concussion n a violent shaking or jarring of the brain, caused by severe injury to the head, and usu resulting in temporary loss of consciousness.

condemn vb 1 to declare something to be wrong or evil. 2 to pronounce someone guilty; to convict someone. 3 (usu condemn sb to sth) a to sentence them to (a punishment, esp death); b to force into (a disagreeable fate). 4 to show the guilt of someone; to give away or betray someone: His obvious nervousness condemned him. 5 to declare (a building) unfit to be used or lived in. ○ **condemnation** n.

condensation n 1 chem the process whereby a gas or vapour turns into a liquid as a result of cooling. 2 meteorol the production of water droplets in the atmosphere.

condense vb 1 to decrease the volume, size or density of (a substance). 2 to concentrate something. 3 tr & intr to undergo or cause to undergo condensation. 4 to summarize.

condenser n 1 elec a CAPACITOR. 2 chem an apparatus for changing a vapour into a liquid by cooling it and allowing it to condense. 3 optics a lens or series of lenses that is used to concentrate a light source.

condescend vb, intr 1 to act in a gracious manner towards those one regards as inferior. 2 to be gracious enough to do something, esp as though it were a favour. ○ **condescending** adj. ○ **condescension** n.

condiment n any seasoning or sauce, eg salt, pepper, mustard, etc, added to food at the table.

condition n 1 a particular state of existence. 2 a state of health, fitness or suitability for use: out of condition. 3 an ailment or disorder: a heart condition. 4 (conditions) circumstances: poor working conditions. 5 a requirement or qualification. 6 a term of contract. ➤ vb 1 to accustom or train someone or something to react in a particular way. 2 to prepare or train (a person or animal) for certain activities or conditions of living. 3 to affect or control. 4 to improve (the physical state of hair, skin, fabrics, etc) by applying a particular substance. ○ **conditioning** n. ♦ **on condition that** only if: *I will go on condition that you come too.*

conditional *adj* **1** dependent on a particular condition, etc. **2** *gram* expressing a condition on which something else is dependent, as in the first clause in 'If it rains, I'll stay at home'.

conditioner *n, often in compounds* a substance which attempts to improve the condition of something, esp hair: *hair conditioner • fabric conditioner.*

condolence *n* (*usu* **condolences**) an expression of sympathy: *I offered my condolences.*

condom *n* a thin rubber sheath worn on the penis during sexual intercourse, to prevent pregnancy and the spread of sexually transmitted diseases.

condominium *n* **1** *N Am* **a** a building, eg an apartment block, in which each apartment is individually owned and any common areas are commonly owned; **b** an apartment in such a block. Often shortened to **condo**. **2** a country which is controlled by two or more other countries.

condone *vb* **1** to pardon or overlook (an offence or wrong). **2** *loosely* to tolerate.

condor *n* either of two species of large American vulture.

conducive *adj* (*often* **conducive to sth**) likely to achieve a desirable result; encouraging.

conduct *vb* /kənˈdʌkt/ **1** to lead or guide. **2** to manage; to control: *conduct the firm's business.* **3** *tr & intr* to direct the performance of an orchestra or choir by movements of the hands or a baton. **4** to transmit (heat or electricity) by CONDUCTION. **5** to behave (oneself) in a specified way: *One should always conduct oneself with dignity.* ➤ *n* /ˈkɒndʌkt/ **1** behaviour. **2** the managing or organizing of something.

conductance *n* **a** the ability of a material to conduct heat or electricity; **b** in a direct current circuit: the reciprocal of RESISTANCE.

conduction *n* **1** the transmission of heat through a material from a region of higher temperature to one of lower temperature, without any movement of the material itself. **2** the flow of electricity through a material under the influence of an electric field, without any movement of the material itself.

conductivity *n* **1** a measure of the ability of a material to conduct electricity. **2** the ability of a material to conduct heat.

conductor *n* **1** the person who conducts a choir or orchestra. **2** a material that conducts heat or electricity. **3** someone who collects fares from passengers on a bus, etc. **4** *N Am* the official in charge of a train.

conduit /ˈkɒndjʊɪt/ *n* a channel, pipe, tube or duct through which a fluid, a liquid or a gas, may pass.

cone *n* **1** *geom* a solid, three-dimensional figure with a flat base in the shape of a circle or ellipse, and a curved upper surface that tapers

to a fixed point. **2** something similar to this in shape, eg a hollow pointed wafer for holding ice cream. **3** *anat* in the retina: a type of light-sensitive receptor cell specialized for the detection of colour. **4** *bot* the woody fruit of a coniferous tree, consisting of overlapping scales. **5** a plastic cone-shaped bollard which is placed on the road temporarily, to divert traffic, etc.

confab *n, colloq* a conversation.

confabulate *vb, intr, formal* to talk, discuss or confer. ○ **confabulation** n.

confection *n* **1** any sweet food, eg a cake, sweet, biscuit or pudding. **2** *dated, facetious* a fancy or elaborate garment.

confectioner *n* someone who makes or sells sweets or cakes.

confectionery *n* (*-ies*) **1** sweets, biscuits and cakes. **2** the work or art of a confectioner.

confederacy *n* (*-ies*) a league or alliance of states.

confederate *n* /kənˈfɛdərət/ **1** a member of a confederacy. **2** a friend or an ally; an accomplice or a fellow conspirator. ➤ *vb* /-reɪt/ *tr & intr* to unite into or become part of a confederacy.

confederation *n* **1** the uniting of states into a league. **2** the league so formed.

confer *vb* (**conferred, conferring**) **1** *intr* to consult or discuss together. **2** (*usu* **confer sth on sb**) to grant them (an honour or distinction). ○ **conferment** n.

conference *n* **1** an organized gathering for a formal discussion. **2** consultation: *in conference with the Prime Minister.*

confess *vb* **1** *tr & intr* **a** to own up to (a fault, wrongdoing, etc); **b** to admit (a disagreeable fact, etc). **2** *tr & intr, Christianity* to declare (one's sins) to a priest or directly to God, in order to gain absolution.

confession *n* **1** the admission of a sin, fault, crime, distasteful or shocking fact, etc. **2** *Christianity* the formal act of confessing one's sins to a priest. **3** a declaration of one's religious faith or principles.

confessional *n* in a church: the small enclosed stall in a church where a priest sits when hearing confessions. ➤ *adj* relating to a confession.

confessor *n* **1** *Christianity* a priest who hears confessions. **2** a person who makes a confession.

confetti *n* tiny pieces of coloured paper traditionally thrown over the bride and groom by wedding guests.

confidant or **confidante** *n* a close friend (male or female, respectively) with whom one discusses personal matters.

confide *vb* **1** to tell (a secret, etc) to someone. **2** to entrust someone (to someone's care). **3** (*usu* **confide in sb**) to speak freely and confidentially with them about personal matters.

confidence *n* **1** trust or belief in a person or thing. **2** faith in one's own ability; self-assurance. **3** a secret, etc confided to someone. **4** a relationship of mutual trust. ◆ **in confidence** in secret.

confidence trick *n* a form of swindle in which the swindler first wins the trust of the victim. Often shortened to **con**[1].

confident *adj* **1** (*sometimes* **confident of sth**) certain; sure: *confident of success.* **2** self-assured.

confidential *adj* **1** secret; not to be divulged. **2** trusted with private matters. **3** indicating secrecy: *a confidential whisper.* ○ **confidentiality** *n.* ○ **confidentially** *adv.*

confiding *adj* trusting. ○ **confidingly** *adv.*

configuration *n* **1** the positioning or distribution of the parts of something, relative to each other. **2** an outline or external shape.

confine *vb* **1** to restrict or limit. **2** to keep prisoner. **3** eg of ill health: to restrict someone's movement.

confinement *n* **1** the state of being shut up or kept in an enclosed space. **2** *old use* the period surrounding childbirth.

confirm *vb* **1** to provide support for the truth or validity of something. **2** to finalize or make definite (a booking, etc). **3** of an opinion, etc: to strengthen it or become more convinced in it. **4** to give formal approval to something. **5** *Christianity* to accept someone formally into full membership of the Church. ○ **confirmation** *n.*

confirmed *adj* so firmly settled into a state, habit, etc as to be unlikely to change: *confirmed bachelor.*

confiscate *vb* to take away something from someone, usu as a penalty. ○ **confiscation** *n.*

conflagration *n* a large destructive blaze.

conflate *vb* to blend or combine (two things, esp two different versions of a text, story, etc) into a single whole.

conflict *n* / ˈkɒnflɪkt / **1** disagreement; fierce argument; a quarrel. **2** a clash between different interests, ideas, etc. **3** a struggle or battle. ➤ *vb* / kənˈflɪkt / *intr* to be incompatible or in opposition. ○ **conflicting** *adj.*

confluence or **conflux** *n* **1** the point where two rivers flow into one another. **2** an act of meeting together. ○ **confluent** *adj* flowing together.

conform *vb, intr* **1** (*often* **conform to** or **with sth**) to comply with (laws, standards, etc). **2** to behave, dress, etc in obedience to some standard considered normal by the majority. ○ **conformist** *n.* ○ **conformity** *n.*

conformation *n* a shape, structure or arrangement of something.

confound *vb* **1** to puzzle; to baffle. **2** to mix up or confuse (one thing with another). ◆ **confound it!** damn it!

confront *vb* **1** to face someone, esp defiantly or accusingly. **2** (*usu* **confront sb with sth**) to bring them face to face with it, esp when it is damning or revealing. **3** to prepare to deal firmly with something. **4** of an unpleasant prospect: to present itself to someone. ○ **confrontation** *n.*

confuse *vb* **1** to put into a muddle or mess. **2** to

mix up or fail to distinguish (things, ideas, people, etc): *Don't confuse 'ascetic' with 'aesthetic'.* **3** to puzzle, bewilder or muddle. **4** to complicate. ○ **confusing** *adj.* ○ **confusingly** *adv.* ○ **confusion** *n.*

confute *vb* to prove (a person, theory, etc) wrong or false.

conga *n* **1** an orig Cuban dance of three steps followed by a kick, performed by people moving in single file. **2** a tall narrow drum beaten with the fingers. ➤ *vb* (**congaed, congaing**) *intr* to dance the conga.

congeal *vb, tr & intr* of a liquid, eg blood: to thicken or coagulate, esp through cooling.

congenial *adj* **1** of people: compatible; having similar interests. **2** pleasant or agreeable. ○ **congeniality** *n.*

congenital *adj* **1** of a disease or deformity: present at or before birth, but not inherited. **2** complete, as if from birth: *a congenital liar.* ○ **congenitally** *adv.*

conger *n* a large marine eel.

congest *vb, tr & intr* **1** to excessively crowd or become excessively crowded. **2** of an organ: to accumulate or make something accumulate with blood, often causing inflammation. **3** of the nose or other air passages: to block up with mucus. ○ **congested** *adj.* ○ **congestion** *n.*

conglomerate *n* / kənˈɡlɒmərət / **1** a miscellaneous collection or mass. **2** *geol* a sedimentary rock consisting of small rounded pebbles embedded in a fine matrix of sand or silt. **3** a business group composed of a large number of firms with diverse and often unrelated interests. ➤ *vb* / -reɪt / *intr* to accumulate into a mass. ○ **conglomeration** *n.*

congratulate *vb* (*usu* **congratulate sb on sth**) **1** to express pleasure to someone at their success, good fortune, etc. **2** to consider (oneself) clever to have managed something. ○ **congratulatory** *adj.*

congratulations *pl n* often as an exclamation: an expression used to congratulate someone.

congregate *vb, tr & intr* to gather together into a crowd.

congregation *n* a gathering of people, esp for worship in church. ○ **congregational** *adj.*

congress *n* **1** a large, esp international, assembly of delegates. **2** in some countries: a name used for the law-making body. **3** (**Congress**) in the US: the federal legislature, consisting of the Senate and the House of Representatives. ○ **congressional** *adj.*

congressman or **congresswoman** *n* someone who is a member of a congress.

congruent *adj* **1** *geom* of two or more figures: identical in size and shape. **2** (*often* **congruent with sth**) suitable or appropriate to it. ○ **congruence** or **congruency** *n.*

congruous *adj* (*often* **congruous with sth**) **1** corresponding. **2** fitting; suitable.

conic or **conical** *adj, geom* **a** relating to a cone; **b** resembling a cone.

conic section *n, geom* the curved figure produced when a PLANE[2] (*noun* sense 1) intersects a cone.

conifer *n* an evergreen tree or shrub with needle-like leaves, which produce their pollen and seeds in cones, eg pine, spruce, etc. ○ **coniferous** *adj*.

conjecture *n* **1** an opinion based on incomplete evidence. **2** the process of forming such an opinion. ➢ *vb, intr* to make a conjecture. ○ **conjectural** *adj*.

conjoin *vb, tr & intr* to join together, combine or unite.

conjoined twins *pl n* twins who are physically joined to each other from birth. Also called **Siamese twins**.

conjugal *adj* relating to marriage, or to the relationship between husband and wife.

conjugate *vb* /ˈkɒndʒʊgeɪt/ **1** *gram* **a** to give the inflected parts of (a verb), indicating number, person, tense, MOOD[2] and VOICE (*noun* sense 9); **b** *intr* of a verb: to undergo inflection. **2** *intr, biol* to reproduce by conjugation.

conjugation *n* **1** *gram* **a** the inflection of a verb to indicate number, person, tense, VOICE (*noun* sense 9) and MOOD[2]; **b** a particular class of verbs having the same set of inflections. **2** a uniting, joining or fusing.

conjunction *n* **1** *gram* a word used to link sentences, clauses or other words, eg *and, but, if, or, because*, etc. **2** a joining together; combination. **3** the coinciding of two or more events. **4** *astron, astrol* the alignment of two or more heavenly bodies, as seen from Earth. ♦ **in conjunction with sth** together with it.

conjunctiva /ˈkɒndʒʌŋkˈtaɪvə/ *n* (*conjunctivas* or *conjunctivae* /-viː/) *anat* in the eye of vertebrates: the thin mucous membrane that lines the eyelids and covers the exposed surface of the cornea at the front of the eyeball. ○ **conjunctival** *adj*.

conjunctive *adj* **1** connecting; linking. **2** *gram* relating to conjunctions. ➢ *n, gram* a word or phrase used as a conjunction.

conjunctivitis *n* inflammation of the conjunctiva. Also called **pink eye**.

conjuncture *n* a combination of circumstances, esp one leading to a crisis.

conjure /ˈkʌndʒə(r)/ *vb* **1** *intr* to perform magic tricks. **2** to summon (a spirit, demon, etc) to appear. **3** /kənˈdʒʊə(r)/ *old use* to beg someone earnestly to do something. ○ **conjurer** or **conjuror** *n* someone who performs magic tricks, etc. ○ **conjuring** *n*. ◇ **conjure sth up 1** to produce it as though from nothing. **2** to call up, evoke or stir (images, memories, etc).

conk[1] *n, slang* **1** the nose. **2** the head. **3** a blow, esp on the head or nose. ➢ *vb* to hit someone on the nose or head.

conk[2] *vb, intr, slang* (*usu* **conk out**) **1** of a machine, etc: to break down. **2** of a person: to collapse with fatigue, etc.

conker *n, colloq* the brown shiny seed of the HORSE CHESTNUT tree.

conkers *sing n, Brit* a game played with con-

kers threaded onto strings, the aim being to shatter one's opponent's conker by hitting it with one's own.

con man *n, colloq* a swindler who uses a CONFIDENCE TRICK.

connect *vb* (*usu* **connect to** or **with sb** or **sth**) **1** *tr & intr* (*sometimes* **connect sth up** or **connect up**) to join; to link. **2** to associate or involve: *something connected with advertising*. **3** *tr & intr* to associate or relate mentally: *We connected immediately*. **4** to join by telephone. **5** *intr* of aeroplanes, trains, buses, etc: to be timed to allow transfer from one to another. ○ **connective** *adj*. ○ **connector** or **connecter** *n*.

connection or **connexion** *n* **1** the act of connecting or state of being connected. **2** something that connects; a link. **3** a relationship through marriage or birth. **4** an esp influential person whom one meets through one's job, etc; a contact. **5 a** a train, bus, etc timed so as to allow transfer to it from another passenger service; **b** the transfer from one vehicle to another. ♦ **in connection with sth** to do with it; concerning it.

connective tissue *n, anat* any of several widely differing tissues, usu containing COLLAGEN, that provide the animal body and its internal organs with structural support, eg bone, cartilage, tendons, ligaments.

conning tower *n* the raised part of a submarine containing the periscope.

connive *vb, intr* (*often* **connive with sb**) to conspire or plot. ○ **connivance** *n*.

connoisseur *n* someone who is knowledgeable about and a good judge of a particular subject, eg the arts, wine, food, etc.

connotation *n* an idea, association or implication additional to the main idea or object expressed. ○ **connote** *vb*.

connubial *adj* pertaining to marriage, or to relations between a husband and wife.

conquer *vb* **1** to gain possession or dominion over (territory) by force. **2** to defeat or overcome. **3** to overcome or put an end to (a failing, evil, etc). ○ **conquering** *adj*. ○ **conqueror** *n*.

conquest *n* **1** the act of conquering. **2** something won by effort or force. **3** someone whose affection or admiration has been won.

conquistador /kənˈkwɪstədɔː(r)/ *n* (*conquistadores* /kənkwɪstəˈdɔːreɪz/ or *conquistadors*) an adventurer or conqueror, esp one of the 16th-century Spanish conquerors of Peru and Mexico.

consanguinity *n* relationship by blood.

conscience *n* the moral sense of right and wrong that determines someone's thoughts and behaviour. ♦ **in all conscience** by any normal standard of fairness. **on one's conscience** making one feel guilty.

conscience-stricken *adj* feeling guilty over something one has done.

conscientious *adj* **1** careful; thorough; painstaking. **2** guided by conscience. ○ **conscientiously** *adv*. ○ **conscientiousness** *n*.

conscious adj 1 awake; aware of one's thoughts and surroundings. 2 aware; knowing: *She was conscious that someone was watching her.* 3 deliberate: *I made a conscious effort to be polite.* ➤ n the part of the human mind which is responsible for perception and reaction. ○ **consciously** adv. ○ **consciousness** n.

conscript vb /kən'skrɪpt/ to enlist for compulsory military service. ➤ n /'kɒnskrɪpt/ someone who has been conscripted. ○ **conscription** n.

consecrate vb 1 to set something apart for a holy use; to make sacred. 2 to devote something to a special use.

consecutive adj following one after the other; in sequence. ○ **consecutively** adv.

consensus n general feeling or agreement; the majority view.

consent vb, intr (often **consent to sth**) to agree to something or give one's permission for it. ➤ n agreement; permission.

consequence n 1 something that follows from, or is caused by, an action or set of circumstances. 2 importance or significance: *of no consequence.*

consequent adj following as a result or inference.

consequential adj 1 significant or important. 2 following as a result.

consequently adv as a result; therefore.

conservancy n (**-ies**) an area under special environmental protection.

conservation n 1 the act of conserving; the state of being conserved. 2 the protection and preservation of the environment, its wildlife and its natural resources. 3 the preservation of historical artefacts for future generations. ○ **conservationist** n.

conservative adj 1 favouring that which is established or traditional, with an opposition to change. 2 of an estimate or calculation: deliberately low, for the sake of caution. 3 of tastes, clothing, etc: restrained or modest. 4 (**Conservative**) relating to a Conservative Party. ➤ n 1 a traditionalist. 2 (**Conservative**) a member or supporter of a Conservative Party. ○ **conservatism** n.

conservatoire /kən'sɜːvətwɑː(r)/ n a school specializing in the teaching of music.

conservatory n (**-ies**) 1 a a greenhouse for plants; b a similar room used as a lounge, which is attached to and entered from, the house. 2 a conservatoire.

conserve vb /kən'sɜːv/ 1 to keep safe from damage, deterioration, loss or undesirable change. 2 to preserve (fruit, etc) with sugar. ➤ n /'kɒnsɜːv/ a type of jam, esp one containing chunks of fruit.

consider vb 1 to go over something in one's mind. 2 to look at someone or something thoughtfully. 3 to call to mind for comparison, etc. 4 to assess with regard to employing, using, etc: *consider someone for a job.* 5 to contemplate doing something. 6 to regard as

something specified: *He considered Neil to be his best friend.* 7 to think; to have as one's opinion.

considerable adj 1 large; great. 2 having many admirable qualities; worthy: *a considerable person.* ○ **considerably** adv largely; greatly.

considerate adj thoughtful regarding the feelings of others.

consideration n 1 thoughtfulness on behalf of others. 2 careful thought. 3 a fact, circumstance, etc to be taken into account. 4 a payment, reward or recompense. ♦ **take sth into consideration** to allow for it; to bear it in mind. **under consideration** being considered.

considered adj 1 carefully thought about: *my considered opinion.* 2 *with an adverb* thought of or valued in a specified way: *highly considered.*

considering prep in view of; when one considers. ➤ conj taking into account. ➤ adv taking the circumstances into account: *Her results were pretty good, considering.*

consign vb 1 to hand over; to entrust. 2 to send, commit or deliver formally. 3 to send (goods). ○ **consignee** n. ○ **consigner** or **consignor** n.

consignment n 1 a load of goods, etc sent or delivered. 2 the act of consigning.

consist vb, intr 1 (always **consist of sth**) to be composed or made up of several elements or ingredients. 2 (always **consist in** or **of sth**) to have it as an essential feature.

---

consist See note at **comprise**.

---

consistency or **consistence** n (**-ies**) 1 the texture or composition of something, with regard to thickness, firmness, etc. 2 agreement; harmony.

consistent adj 1 (usu **consistent with sth**) in agreement or in keeping with it. 2 reliable; regular; steady. ○ **consistently** adv.

console¹ /kən'səʊl/ vb to comfort in distress, grief or disappointment. ○ **consolation** n.

console² /'kɒnsəʊl/ n 1 mus the part of an organ with the keys, pedals and panels of stops. 2 a panel of dials, switches, etc for operating electronic equipment. 3 a freestanding cabinet for audio or video equipment.

consolidate vb, tr & intr 1 to make or become solid or strong. 2 of businesses, etc: to combine or merge into one. ○ **consolidation** n. ○ **consolidator** n.

consommé /kən'sɒmeɪ/ n a type of thin clear soup made usu from meat stock.

consonance n the state of agreement.

consonant n a any speech-sound produced by obstructing the passage of the breath in any of several ways; b a letter of the alphabet representing such a sound. Compare VOWEL. ➤ adj (**consonant with sth**) in harmony or suitable with it.

consort¹ /'kɒnsɔːt/ n a wife or husband, esp of a reigning sovereign. ➤ vb /kən'sɔːt/ (usu **consort with sb**) (usu with unfavourable implications) to associate with them.

consort² /'kɒnsɔːt/ n a group of musicians, esp

one playing early music.

consortium /kən'sɔ:tɪəm/ n (*consortia* /-ɪə/ or *consortiums*) an association of several banks, businesses, etc.

conspicuous adj **1** visibly noticeable or obvious. **2** notable; striking; glaring. ○ **conspicuously** adv.

conspiracy n (*-ies*) **1** the act of plotting in secret. **2** a plot.

conspire vb, intr **1** to plot secretly together, esp for an unlawful purpose. **2** of events: to seem to be working together to achieve a certain end: *Everything conspired to make me miss my train.* ○ **conspirator** n. ○ **conspiratorial** adj.

constable n a police officer of the most junior rank.

constabulary n (*-ies*) the police force of a district or county.

constant adj **1** never stopping. **2** frequently recurring. **3** unchanging. **4** faithful; loyal. ➤ n, maths a symbol representing an unspecified number, which remains unchanged, unlike a VARIABLE (*noun* sense 3). ○ **constancy** n. ○ **constantly** adv.

constellation n **1** astron a named group of stars seen as forming a recognizable pattern in the night sky. **2** a group of associated people or things.

consternation n anxiety, dismay or confusion.

constipation n a condition in which the faeces become hard, and bowel movements occur infrequently or with pain or difficulty.

constituency n (*-ies*) **1** the district represented by a member of parliament or other representative in a legislative body. **2** the voters in that district.

constituent adj **1** forming part of a whole. **2** having the power to create or alter a constitution: *a constituent assembly.* **3** having the power to elect. ➤ n **1** a necessary part; a component. **2** a resident in a constituency.

constitute vb **1** to be; to make up. **2** to establish formally.

constitution n **1** a set of rules. **2** the supreme laws and rights upon which a country is founded. **3** one's physical make-up, health, etc.

constitutional adj **1** legal according to a given constitution. **2** relating to, or controlled by, a constitution. **3** relating to one's physical make-up, health, etc. ➤ n, dated a regular walk taken for health.

constrain vb **1** to force; to compel. **2** to limit the freedom, scope or range of someone.

constrained adj awkward; embarrassed; forced.

constraint n **1** a limit or restriction. **2** force; compulsion. **3** awkwardness, embarrassment or inhibition.

constrict vb **1 a** to squeeze or compress; **b** to enclose tightly, esp too tightly. **2** to inhibit. ○ **constriction** n. ○ **constrictive** adj.

constrictor n **1** a snake that kills by coiling

around its prey and squeezing it until it suffocates. **2** anat any muscle that compresses an organ or narrows an opening.

construct vb /kən'strʌkt/ **1** to build. **2** to form, compose or put together. **3** geom to draw (a figure). ➤ n /'kɒnstrʌkt/ **1** something constructed, esp in the mind. **2** psychol a complex idea or thought constructed from a number of simpler ones.

construction n **1** the process of building or constructing. **2** something built or constructed. **3** gram the arrangement of words in a particular grammatical relationship. **4** interpretation. ○ **constructional** adj.

constructive adj **1** helping towards progress or development; useful. **2** law of facts: inferred rather than directly expressed.

construe vb **1** to interpret or explain. **2** gram to analyse the grammatical structure of (a sentence, etc). **3** gram (often **construe with**) to combine words grammatically.

consul n **1** an official representative of a state, stationed in a foreign country. **2** hist in ancient Rome: either of the two joint chief magistrates. ○ **consular** adj. ○ **consulship** n.

consulate n the post or official residence of a consul.

consult vb **1** to ask the advice of. **2** to refer to (a map, book, etc). **3** intr (often **consult with sb**) to have discussions with them.

consultant n **1** someone who gives professional advice. **2** a doctor or surgeon holding the most senior post in a particular field of medicine. ○ **consultancy** n (*-ies*).

consultation n **1** the act or process of consulting. **2** a meeting for the obtaining of advice or for discussion. ○ **consultative** adj.

consume vb **1** to eat or drink. **2** to use up. **3** to destroy. **4** to devour or overcome completely. ○ **consumable** adj. ○ **consuming** adj overwhelming.

consumer n someone who buys goods and services for personal use or need.

consumer durables pl n goods that are designed to last for a relatively long time, eg furniture, television sets, etc.

consumerism n **1** the protection of the interests of consumers. **2** econ the theory that steady growth in the consumption of goods is necessary for a sound economy.

consummate vb /'kɒnsəmeɪt, 'kɒnsjʊmeɪt/ **1** to finish, perfect or complete something. **2** to complete (a marriage) in its full legal sense through the act of sexual intercourse. ➤ adj /kən'sʌmɪt/ **1** supreme; very skilled. **2** complete; utter: *a consummate idiot.* ○ **consummately** adv. ○ **consummation** n.

consumption n **1** the act or process of consuming. **2** the amount consumed. **3** the buying and using of goods. **4** dated another name for TUBERCULOSIS of the lungs.

consumptive adj **1** relating to consumption; wasteful or destructive. **2** suffering from TUBERCULOSIS of the lungs. ➤ n someone suffering from tuberculosis of the lungs.

cont. or **contd.** *abbrev* continued.

contact *n* **1** the condition of touching physically. **2** communication or a means of communication. **3** an acquaintance whose influence or knowledge may prove useful, esp in business. **4** in an electrical device: a connection made of a conducting material that allows the passage of a current by forming a junction with another conducting part. **5** someone who has been exposed to an infectious disease. **6** a contact lens. ➤ *vb* to get in touch with someone. ○ **contactable** *adj*.

contact lens *n* a small lens which is placed in direct contact with the eyeball to correct vision.

contagion *n* **1** the transmission of a disease by direct physical contact with an infected person. **2** *dated* a disease that is transmitted in this way.

contagious *adj* **1** of a disease: only able to be transmitted by direct contact with or close proximity to an infected individual, eg the common cold. **2** of a mood, laughter, etc: spreading easily from person to person.

> **contagious** See note at **infectious**.

contain *vb* **1** to hold. **2** to consist of something specified. **3** to control, limit, check or prevent the spread of something: *They were eventually able to contain the riot.* **4** to control (oneself or one's feelings). **5** to enclose or surround. ○ **containable** *adj*.

container *n* **1** an object designed for holding or storing, such as a box, tin, carton, etc. **2** a huge sealed metal box of standard size and design for carrying goods by lorry or ship.

containerize or **-ise** *vb* **1** to put (cargo) into containers. **2** to convert so as to be able to handle containers.

containment *n* the action of preventing the expansion of a hostile power, etc.

contaminate *vb* **1** to pollute or infect (a substance). **2** to make something radioactive. ○ **contaminant** *n*. ○ **contamination** *n*.

contemplate *vb* **1** *tr & intr* to think about; to meditate. **2** to look thoughtfully at something. **3** to consider something as a possibility. ○ **contemplation** *n*.

contemplative *adj* thoughtful; meditative. ➤ *n* someone whose life is spent in religious contemplation.

contemporaneous *adj* (*often* **contemporaneous with sth**) existing or happening at the same time.

contemporary *adj* **1** (*often* **contemporary with sth**) belonging to the same period or time as something. **2** (*often* **contemporary with sb**) around the same age as them. **3** modern. ➤ *n* (*-ies*) **1** someone who lives or lived at the same time as another. **2** someone of about the same age as another.

contempt *n* **1** scorn. **2** *law* disregard of or disobedience to the rules of a court of law. ◆ **hold**

sb in contempt to despise them.

contemptible *adj* despicable; disgusting; vile.

contemptuous *adj* (*often* **contemptuous of sb** or **sth**) showing contempt or scorn.

contend *vb* **1** *intr* (*often* **contend with sb or sth**) to deal with, fight, or compete. **2** *intr* to argue earnestly. **3** to say, maintain or assert something. ○ **contender** *n*.

content[1] /kən'tɛnt/ *adj* (*often* **content with sth**) satisfied; happy. ➤ *vb* to satisfy or make (oneself or another) satisfied. ➤ *n* peaceful satisfaction. ○ **contented** *adj*. ○ **contentment** *n*.

content[2] /'kɒntɛnt/ *n* **1** the subject-matter of a book, speech, etc. **2** the proportion in which a particular ingredient is present in something: *a diet with a high starch content.* **3** (**contents**) **a** the text of a book, divided into chapters; **b** a list of these chapters at the beginning of the book.

contention *n* a point that one asserts or maintains in an argument.

contentious *adj* **1** likely to cause argument. **2** quarrelsome or argumentative.

contest *n* /'kɒntɛst/ **1** a competition. **2** a struggle. ➤ *vb* /kən'tɛst/ **1** to enter the competition or struggle for something. **2** *tr & intr* to dispute (a claim, a will, etc). ○ **contestable** *adj*.

contestant *n* someone who takes part in a contest; a competitor.

context *n* **1** the pieces of writing in a passage which surround a particular word, phrase, etc and which contribute to the full meaning of the word, phrase, etc in question. **2** circumstances, background or setting. ○ **contextual** *adj*.

contiguous *adj* (*often* **contiguous with** or **to sth**) touching.

continent[1] *n* **1 a** any of the seven main land masses of the world (Europe, Asia, N America, S America, Africa, Australia and Antarctica); **b** the mainland portion of one of these land masses. **2** (**the Continent**) the mainland of Europe, as regarded from the British Isles. ○ **continental** *adj*.

continent[2] *adj* **1** able to control one's bowels and bladder. **2** self-controlled, esp with regard to one's passions. ○ **continence** *n*.

continental breakfast *n* a light breakfast of rolls and coffee.

continental drift *n, geol* the theory that the continents were formed by the break-up of a single land mass.

continental quilt *n* a DUVET.

continental shelf *n, geol* the part of a continent that is submerged in an area of relatively shallow sea.

contingency *n* (*-ies*) **1** something liable, but not certain, to occur. **2** something dependent on a chance future happening.

contingent *n* **1** a body of troops. **2** any identifiable body of people: *There were boos from the Welsh contingent.* ➤ *adj* **1** (*usu* **contingent on** or **upon sth**) dependent on some uncertain circumstance. **2** liable but not certain to occur. **3** accidental.

continual adj **1** constantly happening or done; frequent. **2** constant; never ceasing. ○ **continually** adv.

continual See note at **continuous**.

continuance n **1** the act or state of continuing. **2** duration.

continue vb **1** tr & intr to go on without stopping. **2** tr & intr to last or cause to last. **3** tr & intr or start again after a break. **4** intr to keep moving in the same direction. ○ **continuation** n.

continuity n the state of being continuous, unbroken or consistent.

continuous adj **1** incessant. **2** unbroken; uninterrupted. ○ **continuously** adv.

continuous, continual Note that something that is **continuous** exists or happens for a period without a break, whereas something that is **continual** exists or happens repeatedly over a period, so that a continuous disturbance goes on for a time without a break, whereas continual disturbances are several occurrences with gaps between them.

continuum /kɒnˈtɪnjʊʌm/ n (**continua** /-jʊə/ or **continuums**) a continuous sequence; an unbroken progression.

contort vb, tr & intr to twist violently out of shape. ○ **contorted** adj. ○ **contortion** n.

contortionist n an entertainer who is able to twist their body into spectacularly unnatural positions.

contour n **1** (often **contours**) the distinctive outline of something. **2** a line on a map joining points of the same height or depth. ➤ vb **1** to shape the contour of, or shape so as to fit a contour. **2** to mark the contour lines on (a map).

contraband n smuggled goods. ➤ adj **1** prohibited from being imported or exported. **2** smuggled.

contraception n the deliberate prevention of pregnancy by artificial or natural means.

contraceptive n a drug or device that prevents pregnancy.

contract n /ˈkɒntrakt/ **1** an agreement, esp a legally binding one. **2** a document setting out the terms of such an agreement. ➤ vb /kənˈtrakt/ **1** tr & intr to make or become smaller. **2** tr & intr of muscles: to make or become shorter, esp in order to bend a joint, etc. **3** to catch (a disease). **4** to enter into (an alliance or marriage). **5** tr & intr of a word, phrase, etc: to reduce to a short form: 'Are not' is contracted to 'aren't'. **6** tr & intr (often **contract with sb**) to enter a legal contract concerning them. ○ **contractable** adj of a disease, etc: likely to be contracted. ○ **contractible** adj of a muscle, word, etc: capable of being contracted. ◊ **contract in** or **out** to arrange to participate, or not to participate, eg in a pension scheme. **contract sth out** of a company, etc: to arrange for part of a job to be done by another company.

contraction n **1** the process of contracting or state of being contracted. **2** a decrease in length, size or volume. **3** a tightening of the muscles caused by a shortening in length of the muscle fibres. **4** one of the regular painful spasms of the uterus that occur during labour. **5** a shortened form of a word or phrase which includes at least the last letter of the word or phrase: 'Aren't' is a contraction of 'are not'.

contractor n a person or firm that undertakes work on contract.

contractual adj relating to a contract or binding agreement.

contradict vb **1** to assert the opposite of or deny (a statement, etc) made by (a person). **2** of a statement, action, etc: to disagree or be inconsistent with another. ○ **contradiction** n. ○ **contradictory** adj.

contradistinction n a distinction made in terms of a contrast between qualities, properties, etc.

contraflow n a form of traffic diversion whereby streams of traffic moving in opposite directions share the same carriageway of a motorway, dual carriageway, etc.

contralto /kənˈtraltəʊ/ n (**contraltos** or **contralti** /-tiː/) **a** the female singing voice that is lowest in pitch; **b** a singer with this voice; **c** a part to be sung by this voice.

contraption n, colloq a machine or apparatus which is usu ingenious rather than effective.

contrapuntal adj, mus relating to or arranged as COUNTERPOINT.

contrariwise adv **1** on the other hand. **2** the opposite way round. **3** in the opposite direction.

contrary adj **1** /ˈkɒntrərɪ/ (often **contrary to sth**) opposite; quite different; opposed. **2** /ˈkɒntrərɪ/ of a wind: blowing against one; unfavourable. **3** /kənˈtrɛərɪ/ obstinate, perverse, or wayward. ➤ n /ˈkɒntrərɪ/ (**-ies**) **1** an extreme opposite. **2** either of a pair of opposites. ○ **contrariness** n. ◆ **on the contrary** in opposition to what has just been said. **to the contrary** giving the contrasting position.

contrast n /ˈkɒntrɑːst/ **1** dissimilarity between things or people that are being compared. **2** a person or thing that is strikingly different from another. **3** the degree of difference in tone between the colours, or the light and dark parts, of a photograph or television picture. ➤ vb /kənˈtrɑːst/ **1** to compare so as to reveal differences. **2** (often **contrast with sth**) to show the difference.

contravene vb to break or disobey (a law or rule, etc). ○ **contravention** n (often **in contravention of sth**) infringement of a law, etc.

contretemps /ˈkɒntrətɑ̃/ n (pl **contretemps** /-tɑ̃z/) **1** an awkward or embarrassing moment, situation, etc. **2** a slight disagreement.

contribute vb (usu **contribute to sth**) **1** tr & intr to give (money, time, etc) for some joint purpose. **2** intr to be one of the causes of something. **3** to supply (an article, etc) for publication in a magazine, etc. ○ **contribution** *n*. ○ **contributor** *n*. ○ **contributory** *adj*.

con trick *n*, *colloq* short for a CONFIDENCE TRICK.

contrite *adj* **1** sorry for something one has done. **2** resulting from a feeling of guilt: *a contrite apology*.

contrivance *n* **1** the act or power of contriving. **2** a device or apparatus, esp an ingenious one. **3** a scheme; a piece of cunning.

contrive *vb* **1** to manage or succeed. **2** to bring about something: *contrive one's escape*. **3** to make or construct something, esp with difficulty.

contrived *adj* forced or artificial.

control *n* **1** authority or charge; power to influence or guide: *take control*. **2** a means of limitation. **3** (**controls**) a device for operating, regulating, or testing (a machine, system, etc). **4** the people in control of some operation: *mission control*. **5** the place where something is checked: *passport control*. **6** (*in full* **control experiment**) a scientific experiment that attempts to validate the results of a parallel experiment, eg by studying patients who have not received a drug being tested in the parallel experiment. ➤ *vb* (**controlled, controlling**) **1** to have or exercise power over someone or something. **2** to regulate. **3** to limit. **4** to operate, regulate or test (a machine, system, etc). ○ **controllable** *adj*.

controller *n* **1** a person or thing that controls. **2** someone in charge of the finances of an enterprise, etc. **3** an official in charge of public finance.

control tower *n* a tall building at an airport from which take-off and landing instructions are given to aircraft pilots by air-traffic controllers.

controversy *n* (*-ies*) a usu long-standing dispute or argument, esp one where there is a strong difference of opinion. ○ **controversial** *adj*.

controvert *vb* **1** to oppose or contradict. **2** to argue against something.

contumacy /ˈkɒntjʊməsɪ/ *n*, *formal* obstinate refusal to obey.

contumely /ˈkɒntjuːmlɪ/ *n* (*-ies*) *formal* **1** scornful or insulting treatment or words. **2** a contemptuous insult.

contusion *n*, *technical* a bruise.

conundrum *n* **1** a confusing problem. **2** a riddle, esp one involving a pun.

conurbation *n* an extensive cluster of towns, the outskirts of which have merged resulting in the formation of one huge urban development.

convalesce *vb*, *intr* to recover one's strength after an illness, operation or injury, esp by resting. ○ **convalescence** *n* the gradual recovery of health and strength. ○ **convalescent** *n*, *adj*.

convection *n* the process by which heat is transferred through a liquid or gas as a result of movement of their molecules.

convector *n* an electrical device used to heat

the surrounding air in rooms, etc, by convection.

convene *vb*, *tr & intr* to assemble or summon to assemble.

convener *or* **convenor** *n* someone who convenes or chairs a meeting.

convenience *n* **1** the quality of being convenient. **2** something useful or advantageous. **3** *Brit euphem* a lavatory, esp a public one. ♦ **at one's convenience** when and where it suits one.

convenience food *n* any food which has been partially or entirely prepared by the manufacturer.

convenience store *n* a small grocery shop that stays open after normal hours.

convenient *adj* **1** fitting in with one's plans, etc; not causing trouble or difficulty. **2** useful; handy; saving time and trouble. **3** available; at hand. ○ **conveniently** *adv*.

convent *n* **a** a community of nuns; **b** the building they occupy.

conventicle *n*, *hist* a secret, esp unlawful, religious meeting.

convention *n* **1** a large and formal conference or assembly. **2** a formal treaty or agreement. **3** a custom or generally accepted practice, esp in social behaviour. **4** *US pol* a meeting of delegates from one party to nominate a candidate for office.

conventional *adj* **1** traditional; normal; customary. **2** conservative or unoriginal. **3** of weapons or warfare: non-nuclear. ○ **conventionality** *n*. ○ **conventionally** *adv*.

converge *vb*, *intr* **1** (*often* **converge on** *or* **upon** *sb or* sth) to move towards or meet at one point. **2** eg of opinions: to tend towards one another; to coincide. ○ **convergence** *n*. ○ **convergent** *adj*.

conversant *adj* (*usu* **conversant with** sth) having a thorough knowledge of it.

conversation *n* informal talk between people; communication.

conversational *adj* **1** relating to conversation. **2** used in conversation rather than formal language. ○ **conversationalist** *n*.

converse[1] /kənˈvɜːs/ *vb*, *intr* (*often* **converse with** sb) *formal* **1** to hold a conversation; to talk. **2** to commune spiritually.

converse[2] /ˈkɒnvɜːs/ *adj* reverse; opposite. ➤ *n* opposite. ○ **conversely** *adv*.

conversion *n* **1** the act of converting. **2** something converted to another use. **3** *rugby, American football* the scoring of further points after a TRY *or* TOUCHDOWN by kicking the ball over the goal.

convert *vb* /kənˈvɜːt/ **1** *tr & intr* to change the form or function of one thing into another. **2** *tr & intr* to win over, or be won over, to another religion, opinion, etc. **3** to change into another measuring system or currency. **4** *rugby, American football* to achieve a conversion after (a try or touchdown). ➤ *n* /ˈkɒnvɜːt/ someone who has been converted to a new religion, practice, etc.

converter or **convertor** *n* 1 a person or thing that converts. 2 a device for converting, eg a signal from one frequency to another.

convertible *adj* 1 capable of being converted. 2 of a currency: capable of being freely converted into other currencies. ➤ *n* a car with a fold-down top.

convex *adj* of a surface or shape: outward-curving, like the surface of the eye. Compare CONCAVE. ○ **convexity** *n*.

convey *vb* 1 to carry; to transport. 2 to communicate. 3 *law* to transfer the ownership of (property). ○ **conveyable** *adj*. ○ **conveyor** *n*.

conveyance *n* 1 the process of conveying. 2 a vehicle of any kind. 3 *law* a the transfer of the ownership of property; b the document setting out such a transfer. ○ **conveyancer** *n*.

conveyor belt *n* an endless moving rubber or metal belt for the continuous transporting of articles, eg in a factory.

convict *vb* /kən'vɪkt/ to prove or declare someone guilty (of a crime). ➤ *n* /'kɒnvɪkt/ 1 someone serving a prison sentence. 2 someone found guilty of a crime.

conviction *n* 1 the act of convicting; an instance of being convicted. 2 the state of being convinced; a strong belief.

convince *vb* to persuade someone of something; to make or cause to make them believe it. ○ **convinced** *adj*. ○ **convincing** *adj*. ○ **convincingly** *adv*.

convivial *adj* 1 lively; jovial, sociable and cheerful. 2 festive. ○ **conviviality** *n*.

convocation *n* 1 the act of summoning together. 2 an assembly, esp of graduates of a university.

convoke *vb* to call together; to assemble.

convoluted *adj* 1 coiled and twisted. 2 complicated; difficult to understand.

convolution *n* 1 a twist or coil. 2 *anat* any of the sinuous folds of the brain. 3 a complication.

convolvulus /kən'vɒlvjʊləs/ *n* (**convolvuluses** or **convolvuli** /-laɪ/) a trailing or twining plant native to temperate regions, with funnel-shaped flowers.

convoy *n* a group of vehicles or merchant ships travelling together, or under escort.

convulse *vb, tr & intr* to jerk or distort violently by or as if by a powerful spasm. ○ **convulsive** *adj*.

convulsion *n* 1 (*often* **convulsions**) a violent involuntary contraction of the muscles of the body, or a series of such contractions, resulting in contortion of the limbs and face. 2 (**convulsions**) *colloq* spasms of uncontrollable laughter.

cony or **coney** *n* (**conies** or **coneys**) 1 *dialect* a rabbit. 2 rabbit fur.

coo[1] *n* the soft murmuring call of a dove. ➤ *vb* (**cooed, cooing**) 1 *intr* to make this sound. 2 *tr & intr* to murmur affectionately.

coo[2] *exclam, Brit colloq* used to express amazement.

cooee *exclam* a usu high-pitched call used to attract attention.

cook *vb* 1 *tr & intr* to prepare (food) or be prepared by heating. 2 *colloq* to alter (accounts, etc) dishonestly. ➤ *n* someone who cooks or prepares food. ◆ **cook the books** *colloq* to falsify accounts, records, etc. ◊ **cook sth up** *colloq* to concoct or invent it.

cooker *n* 1 an apparatus for cooking food; a stove. 2 *Brit colloq* a COOKING APPLE.

cookery *n* (*pl* in sense 2 only **-ies**) 1 the art or practice of cooking food. 2 *US* a place equipped for cooking.

cookie *n* 1 *chiefly N Am* a biscuit. 2 *colloq* a person: *a smart cookie*. ◆ **that's the way the cookie crumbles** *N Am colloq* that's the way it goes.

cooking apple or **cooker** *n* an apple sour in taste, which is used for cooking rather than eating raw. Compare EATING APPLE.

cool *adj* 1 between cold and warm; fairly cold. 2 pleasantly fresh; free of heat: *a cool breeze*. 3 calm; laid-back: *He was very cool under pressure*. 4 lacking enthusiasm; unfriendly: *a cool response*. 5 of a large sum: exact; at least: *made a cool million*. 6 *colloq* admirable; excellent. 7 of colours: suggestive of coolness, typically pale and containing blue. 8 sophisticated. ➤ *n* 1 a cool part or period; coolness: *the cool of the evening*. 2 *colloq* self-control; composure: *keep your cool*. ➤ *vb, tr & intr* (*often* **cool down** or **off**) 1 to become cool. 2 to become less interested or enthusiastic. ○ **coolly** *adv*. ○ **coolness** *n*.

coolant *n* a liquid or gas used as a cooling agent, esp to absorb and remove heat from its source in a system such as a car radiator, nuclear reactor, etc.

cooler *n* 1 a container or device for cooling things. 2 *slang* prison.

coolie *n, offensive* 1 an unskilled native labourer in Eastern countries. 2 *S Afr* an Indian.

coomb, coombe, comb or **combe** /ku:m/ *n* 1 in S England: a short deep valley. 2 a deep hollow in a hillside.

coop *n* 1 a cage for hens. 2 any confined or restricted space. ➤ *vb* (*usu* **coop sb** or **sth up**) to confine in a small space.

co-op *n, colloq* a co-operative society or a shop run by one.

cooper *n* someone who makes or repairs barrels.

co-operate *vb, intr* 1 (*often* **co-operate with sb**) to work together with them. 2 to be helpful, or willing to fit in with the plans of others. ○ **co-operation** *n*.

co-operative *adj* 1 relating to or giving co-operation. 2 helpful; willing to fit in with others' plans, etc. 3 of a business or farm: jointly owned by workers, with profits shared equally. ➤ *n* a co-operative business or farm.

co-operative society *n* a profit-sharing association for the cheaper purchase of goods.

co-opt *vb* of the members of a body, etc: to elect an additional member, by the votes of the existing ones.

co-ordinate *vb* 1 to integrate and adjust (a

number of different parts or processes) so as to relate smoothly one to another. **2** to bring (one's limbs or bodily movements) into a smoothly functioning relationship. ➤ *adj* relating to or involving co-ordination or co-ordinates. ➤ *n* **1** (*usu* **coordinate**) *maths, geog* either of a pair of numbers taken from a vertical and horizontal axis which together establish the position of a fixed point on a map. **2** *geom* any of a set of numbers, esp either of a pair, that are used to define the position of a point, line or surface by reference to a system of axes that are usu drawn through a fixed point at right angles to each other. ○ **co-ordination** *n*. ○ **co-ordinator** *n*.

coot *n* **1** an aquatic bird with dark plumage, a characteristic white shield above the bill and large feet with lobed toes. **2** *dated, colloq* a fool.

cop *n, slang* **1** a policeman. **2** an arrest: *a fair cop*. ➤ *vb* (**copped, copping**) **1** to catch. **2** to grab; to seize. **3** to suffer (a punishment, etc). ◆ **cop it** *slang* to be punished. ◊ **cop out** *colloq* to avoid a responsibility; to escape. See also COP-OUT.

cope[1] *vb, intr* to manage; to deal with (a problem, etc) successfully: *She coped well with the difficulties.*

cope[2] *n* a long sleeveless cape worn by clergy on ceremonial occasions.

cope[3] *vb, building* to cut (a piece of moulding) so that it fits over another piece.

copier see under COPY.

co-pilot *n* the assistant pilot of an aircraft.

coping *n* a capping along the top row of stones in a wall, designed to protect it from the weather.

coping saw *n* a small saw used for cutting curves in relatively thick wood or metal. Compare FRETSAW.

copious *adj* plentiful. ○ **copiously** *adv*.

cop-out *n, colloq* an avoidance of a responsibility; an escape or withdrawal.

copper[1] *n* **1** *chem* a soft reddish-brown metallic element, which is an excellent conductor of heat and electricity. **2** (*usu* **coppers**) any coin of low value made of copper or bronze. **3** a large metal vessel for boiling water in. **4** a reddish-brown colour. ➤ *adj* **1** made from copper. **2** copper-coloured.

copper[2] *n, slang, chiefly Brit* a policeman. Often shortened to **cop**.

copper-bottomed *adj* **1** eg of ships or pans: having the bottom protected by a layer of copper. **2** *colloq* reliable, esp financially.

copperplate *n* **1** *printing* **a** a copper plate used for engraving or etching; **b** a print made from it. **2** fine regular handwriting of the style formerly used on copperplates.

coppice *n, bot* an area of woodland in which trees are regularly cut back to ground level to encourage the growth of side shoots.

copra *n* the dried kernel of the coconut, rich in coconut oil.

copse *n* a COPPICE.

Coptic *n* the language of the Copts, now used only in the Coptic Church. ➤ *adj* relating to the Copts or their language.

copula /ˈkɒpjʊlə/ *n* (**copulas** or **copulae** /-liː/) *gram* a verb that links the subject and COMPLEMENT of a sentence, eg *is* in *She is a doctor* or *grew* in *It grew dark*.

copulate *vb, intr* to have sexual intercourse. ○ **copulation** *n*.

copy *n* (**-ies**) **1** an imitation or reproduction. **2** one of the many specimens of a book or of a particular issue of a magazine, newspaper, etc. **3** written material for printing, esp as distinct from illustrations, etc. **4** the wording of an advertisement. **5** *colloq* material suitable for a newspaper article. ➤ *vb* (**-ies, -ied**) **1** to imitate. **2** to make a copy of something; to transcribe. ○ **copier** *n* a person or machine that makes copies.

copybook *n* a book of handwriting examples for copying. ➤ *adj* **1** *derog* unoriginal. **2** faultless; perfect. ◆ **blot one's copybook** to spoil one's good record by misbehaviour or error.

copycat *n, colloq derisive* an imitator or person who copies the work of another.

copyist *n* **1** someone who copies (documents, etc) in writing, esp as an occupation. **2** an imitator.

copyright *n* the sole right, granted by law, to print, publish, translate, perform, film or record an original literary, dramatic, musical or artistic work. ➤ *adj* protected by copyright. ➤ *vb* to secure the copyright of something.

copywriter *n* someone who writes advertising copy.

coquette *n* a flirtatious woman. ○ **coquettish** *adj*.

cor *exclam, colloq* expressing surprise or pleasure.

coracle *n* a small oval rowing-boat made of wickerwork covered with hides or other waterproof material.

coral *n* **1** a tiny invertebrate marine animal, consisting of a hollow tube with a mouth surrounded by tentacles at the top, which is found mainly in tropical seas. **2** a hard chalky substance of various colours, formed from the skeletons of this animal. **3** a pinkish-orange colour. ➤ *adj* pinkish-orange in colour.

cor anglais /ˈkɔːrˈɒŋɡleɪ/ (**cors anglais** /ˈkɔːzˈɒŋɡleɪ/) *n, mus* a woodwind instrument similar to, but lower in pitch than, the oboe.

corbel *n, archit* a projecting piece of stone or timber, coming out from a wall and taking the weight of (eg a parapet, arch or bracket).

corbie *n, Scot* a crow or raven.

cord *n* **1** a thin rope or string consisting of several separate strands twisted together. **2** *anat* any long flexible structure resembling this: *umbilical cord*. **3** *N Am* the cable of an electrical appliance. **4** a ribbed fabric, esp corduroy. **5** (**cords**) corduroy trousers. **6** a unit for measuring the volume of cut wood, equal to 128 cubic ft. (3.63 m³). ➤ *vb* to bind with a cord.

cordate *adj* heart-shaped.

corded *adj* **1** fastened with cords. **2** of fabric: ribbed.

cordial *adj* **1** warm and affectionate. **2** heartfelt; profound. ➤ *n* a concentrated fruit-flavoured drink, which is usu diluted before being drunk. ○ **cordially** *adv.*

cordite *n* any of various smokeless explosive materials used as a propellant for guns, etc.

cordless *adj* of an electrical appliance: operating without a flex connecting it to the mains, powered instead by an internal battery: *cordless phone.*

cordon *n* **1** a line of police or soldiers, or a system of road blocks, encircling an area so as to prevent or control passage into or out of it. **2** a ribbon bestowed as a mark of honour. **3** *hortic* a fruit tree trained to grow as a single stem. ➤ *vb* (*often* **cordon sth off**) to close off (an area) with a cordon.

cordon bleu *adj* of a cook or cookery: being of the highest standard.

corduroy *n* **1** a thick ribbed cotton fabric. **2** (**corduroys**) trousers made of corduroy.

core *n* **1** the fibrous case at the centre of some fruits, eg apples and pears, containing the seeds. **2** the innermost, central, essential or unchanging part. **3** the central region of a star or planet, or of a nuclear reactor. **4** the main memory of a computer. **5** a cylindrical sample of rock, soil, etc. ➤ *vb* to remove the core of (an apple, etc).

co-respondent *n, law* in divorce cases: someone supposed to have committed adultery with the RESPONDENT (*noun* sense 2).

corgi *n* a sturdy short-legged breed of dog with a thick coat and fox-like head.

coriander *n* **1** a plant with narrowly lobed leaves and globular aromatic fruits. **2** the leaves and dried ripe fruit of this plant, widely used as a flavouring in cooking.

cork *n* **1** *bot* a layer of tissue that forms below the epidermis in the stems and roots of woody plants, eg trees, which is often cultivated for commercial use. **2** a piece of this used as a stopper for a bottle, etc. ➤ *vb* (*often* **cork up** or **cork sth up**) to stop up (a bottle, etc) with a cork.

corkage *n* the fee charged by a restaurant for serving customers wine, etc that they have bought off the premises.

corked *adj* of wine: spoiled as a result of having a faulty cork.

corkscrew *n* a tool with a spiral spike for screwing into bottle corks to remove them. ➤ *vb, tr & intr* to move spirally.

corm *n, bot* in certain plants, eg crocus: a swollen underground stem.

cormorant *n* a seabird with dark brown or black plumage, webbed feet, a long neck and a slender bill.

corn¹ *n* **1** in the UK: the most important cereal crop of a particular region, esp wheat in England, and oats in Scotland and Ireland. **2** in N America, Australia and New Zealand: MAIZE. **3** the harvested seed of cereal plants; grain. **4** *slang* a song, film, etc, that is trite and sentimental.

corn² *n* a small painful area of hard thickened skin, usu on or between the toes, which is caused by pressure or friction.

corncob *n* the woody core of an ear of maize, to which the rows of kernels are attached. See also CORN ON THE COB.

corncrake *n* a bird of the rail family with a rasping cry.

corn dolly *n* a decorative figure made of plaited straw.

cornea /'kɔːnɪə/ *n* (**corneas** or **corneae** /-iː/) in vertebrates: the convex transparent membrane that covers the front of the eyeball. ○ **corneal** *adj.*

corned beef *n* beef that has been cooked, salted and then canned.

cornelian /kɔː'niːlɪən/ or **carnelian** /kɑː-/ *n, geol* a red and white form of agate, used as a semi-precious stone.

corner *n* **1 a** a point or place where lines or surface-edges meet; **b** the inside or outside of the angle so formed. **2** an intersection between roads. **3** a quiet or remote place. **4** an awkward situation: *in a tight corner.* **5** *boxing* either of the angles of the ring used as a base between bouts by contestants. **6** in some sports, esp football: a free kick from a corner of the field. ➤ *vb* **1** to force into a place or position from which escape is difficult. **2** to gain control of (a market) by obtaining a monopoly of a certain commodity or service. **3** *intr* of a driver or vehicle: to turn a corner. ♦ **cut corners** to spend less money, effort, etc on something than one should.

cornerstone *n* **1** a stone built into the corner of the foundation of a building. **2** a crucial or indispensable part; a basis.

cornet *n* **1** a brass musical instrument similar to the trumpet. **2** an edible cone-shaped holder for ice cream. ○ **cornetist** or **cornettist** *n* someone who plays the cornet.

cornflakes *pl n* toasted maize flakes, usu eaten as a breakfast cereal.

cornflour *n, cookery* a finely ground flour, usu made from maize, which is used for thickening sauces, etc. *N Am equivalent* **cornstarch.**

cornflower *n* a plant with narrow hairy leaves and deep blue flowers.

cornice *n* **1** a decorative border of moulded plaster round a ceiling. **2** *archit* the projecting section of an ENTABLATURE.

Cornish *adj* belonging to Cornwall, a county in SW England, its people or language. ➤ *n* the Celtic language once spoken in Cornwall, related to Welsh.

corn on the cob *n* a CORNCOB cooked and served as a vegetable.

cornstarch see under CORNFLOUR

cornucopia *n* **1** *art* in painting, sculpture, etc:

a horn full to overflowing with fruit and other produce, used as a symbol of abundance. Also called **horn of plenty**. **2** an abundant supply.

corny adj (**-ier, -iest**) colloq **1** of a joke: old and stale. **2** embarrassingly old-fashioned or sentimental.

corolla n, bot the collective name for the petals of a flower.

corollary /kə'rɒlərɪ/ n (**-ies**) **1** something that directly follows from another thing that has been proved. **2** a natural or obvious consequence.

corona /kə'roʊnə/ n (**coronae** /-iː/ or **coronas**) **1** astron the outer atmosphere of the Sun, consisting of a halo of hot luminous gases, visible during a total solar eclipse. **2** astron a circle of light which appears around the Sun or the Moon. **3** bot in certain plants, eg the daffodil: a trumpet-like outgrowth from the petals. **4** physics the glowing region produced by ionization of the air surrounding a high-voltage conductor.

coronary /'kɒrənərɪ/ adj, physiol denoting vessels, nerves, etc which encircle a part or organ, esp the arteries which supply blood to the heart muscle. ➤ n (**-ies**) pathol a CORONARY THROMBOSIS.

coronary thrombosis n, pathol the formation of a blood clot in one of the two coronary arteries, which blocks the flow of blood to the heart and usu gives rise to a heart attack.

coronation n the ceremony of crowning a monarch or CONSORT[1] (noun).

coroner n a public official whose chief responsibility is the investigation of sudden, suspicious or accidental deaths.

coronet n **1** a small crown. **2** a circlet of jewels for the head.

corporal[1] n a non-commissioned officer in the army or air force.

corporal[2] adj relating or belonging to the body.

corporal punishment n physical punishment such as beating or caning.

corporate adj **1** shared by members of a group; joint: corporate membership. **2** belonging or relating to a corporation: corporate finance. **3** formed into a corporation: a corporate body.

corporation n **1** a body of people acting jointly, eg for administration or business purposes. **2** the council of a town or city.

corporatism or **corporativism** n, pol the control of a country's economy by groups of producers who have the authority to implement social and economic policies.

corporeal adj **1** relating to the body as distinct from the soul; physical. **2** relating to things of a material nature.

corps /kɔː(r)/ n (pl **corps**) **1** a military body or division forming a tactical unit: the intelligence corps. **2** a body of people engaged in particular work: the diplomatic corps.

corps de ballet /French kɔːdəbalɛ/ n a company of ballet dancers, eg at a theatre.

corpse /kɔːps/ n the dead body of a human being.

corpulent adj fat; fleshy; obese. ○ **corpulence** or **corpulency** n.

corpus n (**corpora** /'kɔːpərə/) **1** a body of writings, eg by a particular author, on a particular topic, etc. **2** a body of written and/or spoken material for language research.

corpuscle /'kɔːpʌsəl/ n, anat any small particle or cell within a tissue or organ, esp a red or white blood cell. ○ **corpuscular** adj.

corral /kə'rɑːl/ chiefly N Am, n **1** an enclosure for driving horses or cattle into. **2** a defensive ring of wagons. ➤ vb (**corralled, corralling**) to herd or pen into a corral.

correct vb **1** to set or put right; to remove errors from something. **2** to mark the errors in. **3** to adjust or make better. **4** old use to rebuke or punish. ➤ adj **1** free from error; accurate. **2** appropriate; conforming to accepted standards: very correct in his behaviour. ○ **correctly** adv. ○ **correctness** n. ♦ **stand corrected** to acknowledge one's mistake.

correction n **1** the act of correcting. **2** an alteration that improves something. **3** old use punishment. ○ **correctional** adj.

corrective adj having the effect of correcting or adjusting. ➤ n something that has this effect.

correlate vb **1** tr & intr of two or more things: to have a connection or correspondence. **2** to combine, compare or show relationships between (information, reports, etc.) ➤ n either of two things which are related to each other. ○ **correlation** n.

correlative adj **1** mutually linked. **2** gram of words: used as an interrelated pair, although not necessarily together, eg like either and or. ➤ n a correlative word or thing.

correspond vb, intr **1** (usu **correspond to sth**) to be similar or equivalent. **2** (usu **correspond with** or **to sth** or **sb**) to be compatible or in agreement; to match. **3** (usu **correspond with sb**) to communicate, esp by letter. ○ **corresponding** adj. ○ **correspondingly** adv.

correspondence n **1** similarity; equivalence. **2** agreement. **3 a** communication by letters; **b** the letters received or sent.

correspondent n **1** someone with whom one exchanges letters. **2** someone employed by a newspaper, radio station, etc to send reports from a particular part of the world or on a particular topic: political correspondent.

corridor n a passageway in a building or on a train.

corrie n in the Scottish Highlands: **1** a semicircular hollow on a hillside. **2** a CIRQUE.

corroborate vb to confirm (eg someone's statement), esp by providing evidence. ○ **corroboration** n. ○ **corroborative** adj.

corrode vb **1** tr & intr of a material or object: to eat or be eaten away, esp by rust or chemicals. **2** to destroy gradually. ○ **corrosion** n. ○ **corrosive** adj.

corrugate *vb* to fold into parallel ridges, so as to make stronger. ○ **corrugated** *adj.* ○ **corrugation** *n.*

corrupt *vb* **1** *tr & intr* to change for the worse, esp morally. **2** to spoil, deform or make impure. ➤ *adj* **1** morally evil. **2** involving bribery. **3** of a text: so full of errors and alterations as to be unreliable. **4** *comput* of a program or data: containing errors and therefore no longer reliable. ○ **corruptive** *adj.* ○ **corruptly** *adv.*

corruptible *adj* capable of being or liable to be corrupted.

corruption *n* **1** the process of corrupting or condition of being corrupt. **2** a corrupted or altered form of a word or phrase: 'Santa Claus' is a corruption of 'Saint Nicholas'.

corsage /kɔːˈsɑːʒ/ *n* a small spray of flowers for pinning to the bodice of a dress.

corsair /ˈkɔːseə(r)/ *n, old use* **1** a pirate or pirate ship. **2** a privately owned warship.

corselet *n* **1** *hist* a protective garment or piece of armour for the upper part of the body. **2** (*usu* **corselette**) a woman's undergarment combining girdle and bra.

corset *n* **1** a tightly fitting women's undergarment used for shaping or controlling the figure. **2** a similar garment worn to support an injured back.

cortège /kɔːˈteʒ/ *n* a procession, esp at a funeral.

cortex /ˈkɔːrtɛks/ *n* (**cortices** /-tɪsiːz/) *anat* the outer layer of an organ or tissue, when this differs in structure or function from the inner region.

cortisone /ˈkɔːtɪzəʊn/ *n, biochem* a naturally occurring steroid hormone which, in synthetic form, is used to treat rheumatoid arthritis, certain eye and skin disorders, etc.

corundum *n, geol* a hard aluminium oxide mineral, used as an abrasive. Its crystalline forms include ruby and sapphire.

coruscate *vb, intr* to sparkle; to give off flashes of light.

corvette *n* a small warship for escorting larger vessels.

cos¹ or **cos lettuce** *n* a type of lettuce with crisp slim leaves.

cos² *abbrev* cosine.

cosecant /kəʊˈsiːkənt/ *n, trig* for a given angle in a right-angled triangle: a FUNCTION (*noun* sense 4) that is the ratio of the length of the HYPOTENUSE to the length of the side opposite the angle under consideration; the reciprocal of the sine of an angle.

cosh *n* a club, esp a rubber one filled with metal, used as a weapon. ➤ *vb, colloq* to hit with a cosh or something heavy.

cosine /ˈkəʊsaɪn/ *n, trig* in a right-angled triangle: a FUNCTION (*noun* sense 4), that is the ratio of the length of the side adjacent to the angle to the length of the HYPOTENUSE.

cosmetic *n* (*often* **cosmetics**) any application intended to improve the appearance of the body, esp the face. ➤ *adj* **1** used to beautify the face, body or hair. **2** improving superficially, for the sake of appearance only. ○ **cosmetically** *adv.*

cosmic *adj* **1** relating to the Universe. **2** coming from outer space: cosmic rays.

cosmology *n* (**-ies**) **1** the scientific study of the origin, nature, structure and evolution of the Universe. **2** a particular theory or model of the origin and structure of the Universe. ○ **cosmological** *adj.* ○ **cosmologist** *n.*

cosmonaut *n* an astronaut from Russia or the former Soviet Union.

cosmopolitan *adj* **1** belonging to or representative of all parts of the world. **2** free of national prejudices; international in experience and outlook. **3** composed of people from all different parts of the world. ➤ *n* someone of this type; a citizen of the world.

cosmos *n* the Universe seen as an ordered system.

cosset *vb* (**cosseted, cosseting**) to pamper.

cost *vb* (in senses 1 and 2 *past tense, past participle* **cost**) **1** to be obtainable at a certain price. **2** *tr & intr* to involve the loss or sacrifice of someone or something. **3** (*past tense, past participle* **costed**) to estimate or decide the cost of something. ➤ *n* **1** what something costs. **2** loss or sacrifice: The war was won but the cost of human life was great. **3** (**costs**) *law* the expenses of a case, generally paid by the unsuccessful party. ♦ **at all costs** no matter what the risk or effort may be. **count the cost 1** to consider all the risks before taking action. **2** to realize the bad effects of something done.

co-star *n* a fellow star in a film, play, etc. ➤ *vb* **1** *intr* of an actor: to appear alongside another star. **2** of a production: to feature as fellow stars: The play co-starred Gielgud and Olivier.

cost-effective *adj* giving acceptable financial return in relation to initial outlay.

costermonger *n, Brit* someone who sells fruit and vegetables from a barrow. Also called **coster**.

costive *adj, old use* **1** constipated. **2** mean; stingy.

costly *adj* (**-ier, -iest**) **1** involving much cost; expensive. **2** involving major losses or sacrifices. ○ **costliness** *n.*

cost of living *n* the expense to the individual of the ordinary necessities such as food, clothing, fuel, etc.

costume *n* **1** a set of clothing of a special kind, esp of a particular historical period or country. **2** a garment or outfit for a special activity: a swimming-costume. ➤ *vb* to provide a costume or costumes for a person, play, etc.

costume jewellery *n* inexpensive jewellery made from artificial materials.

costumier *n* someone who makes or supplies costumes.

cosy *adj* (**-ier, -iest**) **1** warm and comfortable. **2** friendly, intimate and confidential: a cosy chat. ➤ *n* (**-ies**) a cover to keep something warm, esp a teapot or boiled egg. ○ **cosily** *adv.* ○ **cosiness** *n.*

cot[1] *n* **1** a small bed with high, barred sides for a child. **2** a portable bed.

cot[2] *n* **1** *poetic* a cottage. **2** *usu in compounds* a shortened form of COTE: *dovecot*.

cotangent *n, trig* for a given angle in a right-angled triangle: a FUNCTION (*noun* sense 4) that is the ratio of the length of the side adjacent to the angle under consideration, to the length of the side opposite it; the reciprocal of the tangent of an angle.

cot death *n* a non-technical name for SUDDEN INFANT DEATH SYNDROME.

cote *n, usu in compounds* a small shelter for birds or animals: *dovecote*.

coterie /'kəʊtərɪ/ *n* a small exclusive group of people who have the same interests.

cotoneaster /kətəʊnɪ'astə(r)/ *n* a shrub or small tree with clusters of white or pink flowers, followed by red or orange berries.

cottage *n* a small house, esp one in a village or the countryside. ○ **cottager** *n.*

cottage cheese *n* a type of soft white cheese made from the curds of skimmed milk.

cottage industry *n* a craft industry such as knitting or weaving, employing workers in their own homes.

cottar or **cotter** *n, Scot hist* a farm labourer occupying a cottage rent-free, in return for working on the farm.

cotton *n* **1** a shrubby plant cultivated for the creamy-white downy fibres which surround its seeds. **2** the soft white fibre obtained from this plant, used in the production of textiles. **3** the cloth or yarn that is woven from these fibres. ➢ *adj* made from cotton. ➢ *vb* (*often* **cotton on to sth**) *colloq* to begin to understand it. ○ **cottony** *adj.*

cotton candy *n, US* CANDY FLOSS.

cotton wool *n* soft fluffy wadding made from cotton fibre, which is used in the treatment of injuries, application of cosmetics, etc.

cotyledon /kɒtɪ'liːdən/ *n, bot* in flowering plants: one of the leaves produced by the embryo.

couch[1] /kaʊtʃ/ *n* **1** a sofa or settee. **2** a bed-like seat with a headrest, eg for patients to lie on when being examined or treated by a doctor or psychiatrist. ➢ *vb* to express in words of a certain kind.

couch[2] /kaʊtʃ, kuːtʃ/ or **couch grass** *n* a grass with rough dull green or bluish-green leaves.

couch potato *n, colloq* someone who spends their leisure time watching television or videos.

cougar /'kuːgə(r)/ *n, N Am* a PUMA.

cough *vb* **1** *intr* to expel air, mucus, etc from the throat or lungs with a rough sharp noise. **2** *intr* of an engine, etc: to make a similar noise. **3** to express with a cough. ➢ *n* **1** an act or sound of coughing. **2** a condition of lungs or throat causing coughing. ◊ **cough sth up** to bring up mucus, phlegm, blood, etc by coughing. **cough up**

slang to provide (money, information, etc), esp reluctantly.

could *vb* **1** *past tense of* CAN: *I found I could lift it*. **2** used to express a possibility: *You could be right*. **3** used to express a possible course of action: *You could try telephoning her*. **4** used in making requests: *Could you help me?* **5** to feel like doing something or able to do something: *I could have strangled him*.

couldn't *contraction* could not.

coulis /'kuːliː/ *n* (*pl* **coulis** /-liːz/) a purée of fruit, vegetables, etc often served as a sauce.

coulomb /'kuːlɒm/ *n* the SI unit of electric charge.

council *n* a body of people whose function is to advise, administer, organize, or legislate, esp an elected body that directs the affairs of a town, district, etc.

council house *n* a house built, owned and rented out by a local council.

councillor *n* an elected member of a council.

> **councillor, counsellor** These words are often confused with each other.

counsel *n* **1** advice. **2** consultation, discussion or deliberation. **3** a lawyer or group of lawyers that gives legal advice and fights cases in court. ➢ *vb* (**counselled, counselling**) to advise.

counsellor or (*N Am*) **counselor** *n* **1** an adviser. **2** *N Am* a lawyer.

count[1] *vb* **1** *intr* to recite numbers in ascending order. **2** to find the total amount of (items), by adding up item by item. **3** to include: *Did you remember to count Iain?* **4** *intr* to be important: *Good contacts count in the music business*. **5** to consider: *He counted himself lucky that he still had a job*. ➢ *n* **1** an act of counting. **2** the number counted. **3** a charge brought against an accused person. ○ **countable** *adj.* ♦ **keep** or **lose count** to keep, or fail to keep, a note of the running total. **out for the count 1** *boxing* of a floored boxer: unable to rise to his feet within a count of ten. **2** unconscious. **3** *facetious* fast asleep. ◊ **count against sb** to be a disadvantage to them. **count on sb** or **sth** to rely on them or it. **count sb out 1** *boxing* to declare (a floored boxer) to have lost the match if they are unable to get up within ten seconds. **2** to exclude them from consideration.

count[2] *n* a European nobleman, equal in rank to a British earl.

countdown *n* a count backwards from a certain number, with zero as the moment for action, used eg in launching a rocket.

countenance *n* face; expression or appearance. ➢ *vb* **1** to favour or support. **2** to allow; to tolerate.

counter[1] *n* **1** a long flat-topped fitting in a shop, cafeteria, bank, etc over which goods are sold, food is served or business is transacted. **2** in various board games: a small flat disc used as a playing-piece. **3** a disc-shaped token used as a substitute coin. ♦ **under the counter** by secret illegal sale, or by unlawful means.

counter² *vb, tr & intr* to oppose, act against or hit back. ➤ *adv* (*often* **counter to sth**) in the opposite direction to it; in contradiction of it. ➤ *adj* contrary; opposing. ➤ *n* **1** a return blow; an opposing move. **2** an opposite or contrary. **3** something that can be used to one's advantage in negotiating or bargaining. **4** *naut* the curved, overhanging part of a ship's stern. ◆ **run counter to sth** to act in a way contrary to it.

counteract *vb* to reduce or prevent the effect of something. ○ **counteraction** *n*. ○ **counteractive** *adj*.

counter-attack *n* an attack in reply to an attack. ➤ *vb, tr & intr* to attack in return.

counterbalance *n* a weight, force or circumstance that balances another or cancels it out. ➤ *vb* to act as a counterbalance to; to neutralize or cancel out.

counter-clockwise *adj, adv, esp N Am* anticlockwise.

counter-espionage *n* activities undertaken to frustrate spying by an enemy or rival. Also called **counter-intelligence**.

counterfeit /ˈkaʊntəfɪt/ *adj* **1** made in imitation of a genuine article, esp with the purpose of deceiving; forged. **2** not genuine; insincere. ➤ *n* an imitation, esp one designed to deceive; a forgery. ➤ *vb* **1** to copy for a dishonest purpose; to forge. **2** to pretend.

counterfoil *n* the section of a cheque, ticket, etc retained as a record by the person who issues it.

counter-intelligence *n* another name for COUNTER-ESPIONAGE.

countermand *vb* to cancel or revoke (an order or command). ➤ *n* a command which cancels a previous one.

counter-measure *n* an action taken to counteract a threat, dangerous development or move.

counterpane *n, dated* a bedspread.

counterpart *n* **1** one of two parts which form a corresponding pair. **2** a person or thing which is not exactly the same as another, but which is equivalent to it in a different place or context.

counterpoint *n, mus* **1** the combining of two or more melodies sung or played simultaneously into a harmonious whole. **2** a part or melody combined with another. ➤ *vb* to set in contrast to.

counterpoise *n* **1** a weight which balances another weight. **2** a state of equilibrium. ➤ *vb* to balance with something of equal weight.

counter-productive *adj* tending to undermine productivity and efficiency; having the opposite effect to that intended.

counter-revolution *n* a revolution to overthrow a system of government established by a previous revolution. ○ **counter-revolutionary** *adj, n*.

countersign *vb* to sign (a document, etc already signed by someone else) by way of confirmation. ➤ *n* a password or signal used in response to a sentry's challenge; a sign or signal given in response to another sign or signal.

countersink *vb* to widen the upper part of (a screw hole) so that the top of the screw will be level with the surrounding surface.

counter-tenor *n, mus* an adult male voice, higher than the TENOR.

counterweight *n* a counterbalancing weight.

countess *n* **1** the wife or widow of an earl or count. **2** a woman with the rank of earl or count.

countless *adj* numerous; so many as to be impossible to count.

count noun *n, gram* a noun which can be qualified in the singular by the indefinite article and can also be used in the plural, eg *car* (as in *a car* or *cars*) but not *furniture*. Compare MASS NOUN.

countrified *adj* rural; rustic in appearance or style.

country *n* (*-ies*) **1** an area of land distinguished from other areas by its culture, inhabitants, political boundary, etc. **2** the population of such an area of land. **3** a nation or state. **4** one's native land. **5** (*often* **the country**) open land, away from the towns and cities, usu characterized by moors, woods, hills, fields, etc. ◆ **across country** not keeping to roads. **go to the country** *Brit* of a government in power: to dissolve parliament and hold a general election.

country and western *n* a style of popular music, based on the white folk music of the Southern USA.

country club *n* a club in a rural area with facilities for sport and recreation.

country dance *n* any one of many traditional British dances in which partners face each other in lines or sometimes form circles. ○ **country dancing** *n*.

country house or **country seat** *n* a large house in the country, esp one belonging to a wealthy landowner.

countryman or **countrywoman** *n* **1** someone who lives in a rural area. **2** someone belonging to a particular country, esp the same country as oneself.

country music *n* a category of popular music, including COUNTRY and WESTERN.

countryside *n* rural land situated outside or away from towns.

county *n* (*-ies*) **1** any of the geographical divisions within England, Wales and Ireland that form the larger units of local government. **2** in the USA: the main administrative subdivision within a state.

coup /kuː/ *n* **1** a brilliantly successful move. **2** (*also* **coup d'état**) the sudden, usu violent, overthrow of a government.

coupé /ˈkuːpeɪ/ *n* a car with four seats, two doors and a sloping rear.

couple *n* **1** a pair of people attached in some way, often romantically. **2** a pair of partners, eg for dancing. **3** (*usu* **a couple of**) two, or a few: *I'll call you in a couple of weeks.* ➤ *vb* **1** to associate; to link. **2** to connect (two things). **3** *intr* to have sexual intercourse.

couplet *n* a pair of consecutive lines of verse, esp ones which rhyme and have the same metre.

coupling *n* a link for joining things together.

coupon *n* a form or slip of paper entitling one to something, eg a discount.

courage *n* **1** bravery. **2** cheerfulness or resolution in coping with setbacks.

courageous *adj* having or showing courage. ○ **courageously** *adv.*

courgette /kɔːˈʒet/ *n* a variety of small marrow. Also called **zucchini**.

courier *n* **1** a guide who travels with and looks after, parties of tourists. **2** a messenger, esp one paid to deliver special or urgent messages or items.

course *n* **1** the path in which anyone or anything moves. **2** a direction taken or planned: *go off course.* **3** the channel of a river, etc. **4** the normal progress of something. **5** the passage of a period of time: *in the course of the next year.* **6** a line of action: *Your best course is to wait.* **7 a** a series of lessons, etc; a curriculum; **b** the work covered in such a series. **8** a prescribed treatment, eg medicine to be taken, over a period. **9** any of the successive parts of a meal. **10** *often in compounds* the ground over which a game is played or a race run: *golf course.* **11** *building* a single row of bricks or stones in a wall, etc. ➤ *vb* **1** *intr* to move or flow. **2** to hunt (hares, etc) using dogs. ✦ **a matter of course** a natural or expected action or result. **in due course** at the appropriate or expected time. **in the course of sth** while doing it; during it. **of course 1** as expected. **2** naturally; certainly; without doubt. **stay the course** to endure to the end.

courser *n* **1** a person or hound who courses (hares, etc). **2** *poetic* a swift horse.

court *n* **1** the judge, law officials and members of the jury gathered to hear and decide on a legal case. **2** the room or building used for this. **3** an area marked out for a particular game or sport: *a basketball court.* **4** an open space or square surrounded by houses or by sections of a building. **5** (*often* **Court**) used in names: **a** a group of houses arranged around an open space; **b** a block of flats; **c** a country mansion. **6** the palace, household, attendants, and advisers of a sovereign. ➤ *vb* **1** *tr & intr, old use* to try to win the love of someone. **2** to try to win the favour of someone. **3** to risk or invite: *court danger.* ✦ **go to court** to take legal action. **hold court** to be surrounded by a circle of admirers. **out of court** without legal action being taken. **pay court to sb** to pay them flattering attention. **take sb to court** to bring a legal case against them.

court card *n* in a pack of playing cards: the king, queen or jack.

courteous *adj* polite; considerate; respectful. ○ **courteously** *adv.*

courtesan /ˈkɔːtɪzan/ *n, hist* a prostitute with wealthy or noble clients.

courtesy *n* (*-ies*) **1** courteous behaviour; politeness. **2** a courteous act. ✦ **by courtesy of sb** permitted or given by them.

courthouse *n* a building in which the lawcourts are held.

courtier *n* **1** someone in attendance at a royal court. **2** an elegant flatterer.

courtly *adj* **1** having fine manners. **2** flattering.

court-martial *n* (**courts-martial** or **court-martials**) a military court which tries members of the armed forces for breaches of military law. ➤ *vb* (**court-martialled, court-martialling**) to try by court-martial.

court of law see LAWCOURT

court order *n* a direction or command of a judiciary court which, if not complied with, may lead to criminal proceedings against the offender or offenders.

courtroom *n* a room in which a lawcourt is held.

courtship *n, dated* **1** the courting or wooing of an intended spouse. **2** the period for which this lasts.

courtyard *n* an open space surrounded by buildings or walls.

couscous /ˈkʊskʊs/ *n* a N African dish of crushed semolina, which is steamed and served with eg vegetables, chicken, fish, etc.

cousin *n* a son or daughter (**first cousin**) or grandson or granddaughter (**second cousin**) of one's uncle or aunt.

couture /kuːˈtʊə(r)/ *n* the designing, making and selling of fashionable clothes.

couturier /kuːˈtʊərɪeɪ/ or **couturière** /-rɪeə(r)/ *n* a male, or female, fashion designer.

cove¹ *n* a small and usu sheltered bay or inlet on a rocky coast.

cove² *n, Brit & Aust, dated, colloq* a fellow.

coven /ˈkʌvən/ *n* a gathering of witches.

covenant /ˈkʌvənənt/ *n* **1** *law* a formal sealed agreement to do something, eg pay a sum of money regularly to a charity. **2** a formal binding agreement. **3** *Bible* an agreement made between God and some person or people. ➤ *vb, tr & intr* to agree by covenant to do something.

cover *vb* **1** to form a layer over someone or something. **2** to protect or conceal someone or something by putting something over them or it. **3** to clothe. **4** to extend over something. **5** to strew, sprinkle, spatter, mark all over, etc. **6** to deal with (a subject). **7** of a reporter, etc: to investigate or report on (a story). **8** to have as one's area of responsibility. **9** to travel (a distance). **10** to be adequate to pay: *He had enough money to cover the meal.* **11** to insure; to insure against something. **12** to shield with a firearm at the ready or with actual fire. **13** *sport* to protect (a fellow team-member) or obstruct (an opponent). **14** to record a cover version of (a song, etc). **15** *intr* (*usu* **cover for sb**) to take over the duties of an absent colleague, etc. ➤ *n* **1** something that covers. **2** a lid, top, protective casing, etc. **3** the covering of something. **4** (**covers**) the sheets and blankets on a bed. **5** the paper or board binding of a book, magazine, etc; one side of this. **6** an envelope: *a first-day cover*. **7** shelter or protection. **8** insurance. **9** service: *emergency cover*. **10** a pretence; a screen; a false identity: *His cover as a salesman was blown*. **11** armed protection; protective fire. **12** *cricket* see COVER POINT. **13** a COVER VERSION. ♦ **under cover 1** in secret. **2** within shelter. ◊ **cover sth up 1** to cover it entirely. **2** to conceal (a dishonest act, a mistake, etc).

coverage *n* **1** an amount covered. **2** the extent to which a news item is reported in any of the media, etc.

cover charge *n* in a restaurant, café, etc: a service charge made per person.

cover girl *n* a girl or woman whose photograph is shown on a magazine cover.

covering *n* something that covers, eg a blanket, protective casing, etc.

covering letter *n* a letter explaining the documents or goods it accompanies.

coverlet *n* a thin top cover for a bed; a bedspread.

cover note *n* a temporary certificate of insurance, giving cover until the issue of the actual policy.

cover point *n*, *cricket* the fielding position forward and to the right of the batsman.

covert *adj* /ˈkʌvət, ˈkəʊvɜːt/ secret; concealed. ➤ *n* /ˈkʌvət/ **1** a thicket or woodland providing cover for game. **2** a shelter for animals. ○ **covertly** *adv*.

cover-up *n* an act of concealing or withholding information about something suspect or illicit.

cover version *n* a recording of a song, which has already been recorded by another artist.

covet *vb* (**coveted, coveting**) to long to possess something (esp something belonging to someone else).

covetous *adj* envious; greedy. ○ **covetously** *adv*.

covey /ˈkʌvɪ/ *n* **1** a small flock of game birds of one type, esp partridge or grouse. **2** a small group of people.

cow[1] *n* **1** the mature female of any bovine animal, esp domesticated cattle. **2** the mature female of certain other mammals, eg the elephant, whale and seal. **3** loosely used to refer to any domestic breed of cattle. **4** *derog slang* a woman. ♦ **till the cows come home** *colloq* for an unforeseeably long time.

cow[2] *vb* to frighten something into submission.

coward *n* someone easily frightened, or lacking courage to face danger or difficulty. ○ **cowardice** *n*. ○ **cowardly** *adv*.

cowboy *n* **1** in the US: a man who tends cattle on horseback, esp formerly in the Wild West. **2** *slang, derog* someone who undertakes building or other work without proper training or qualifications; a dishonest businessman.

cowcatcher *n*, *US* a concave metal fender

fixed onto the front of a railway engine for clearing cattle and other obstacles from the line.

cower *vb*, *intr* to shrink away in fear.

cowhide *n* the leather made from the hide of a cow.

cowl *n* **1** a monk's large loose hood or hooded habit. **2** any large loose hood. **3** a revolving cover for a chimney-pot for improving ventilation.

cowlick *n* a tuft of hair that grows in a different direction from the rest, usu hanging over the forehead.

cowling *n* the streamlined metal casing, usu having hinged or removable panels, that houses the engine of an aircraft or other vehicle.

co-worker *n* a fellow worker; a colleague.

cowpat *n* a flat deposit of cow dung.

cowpox *n*, *med* a viral infection of cows that can be transmitted to humans by direct contact, and used to formulate a vaccine against smallpox.

cowrie or **cowry** *n* (**-ries**) **1** a marine snail, found mainly in tropical waters. **2** the brightly coloured glossy egg-shaped shell of this animal.

cowslip *n* a plant with a cluster of yellow sweet-smelling flowers.

cox *n* short for COXSWAIN. ➤ *vb*, *tr & intr* to act as cox of (a boat).

coxcomb see COCKSCOMB

coxswain or **cockswain** /ˈkɒksən/ *n* someone who steers a small boat.

coy *adj* **1** shy; modest; affectedly bashful. **2** irritatingly uncommunicative about something. ○ **coyly** *adv*. ○ **coyness** *n*.

coyote /ˈkɔɪəʊtiː/ *n* (**coyotes** or **coyote**) a wild animal of the dog family that lives in N America, found mainly in deserts, prairies and open woodland.

coypu *n* (**coypus** or **coypu**) a large rat-like aquatic rodent which has a broad blunt muzzle and webbed hind feet.

CPR *abbrev* cardiopulmonary resuscitation, an emergency life-saving technique.

CPU *abbrev*, *comput* central processing unit.

Cr *abbrev* Councillor.

Cr *symbol*, *chem* chromium.

crab[1] *n* **1** a marine crustacean with a hard flattened shell and five pairs of jointed legs, the front pair being developed into pincers. **2** (**crabs**) infestation by the CRAB LOUSE.

crab[2] *n* **1** short for CRAB APPLE. **2** a grumpy or irritable person.

crab apple *n* **1** a large deciduous shrub or small tree with thorny branches, oval toothed leaves and white flowers. **2** the small hard round sour fruit of this tree.

crabbed /ˈkrabɪd, krabd/ *adj* **1** bad-tempered; grouchy. **2** of handwriting: cramped and hard to decipher.

crabby *adj* (**-ier, -iest**) *colloq* bad-tempered.

crab louse *n* a crab-shaped parasitic louse

which infests the hair of the human pubic area.

crack vb **1** tr & intr to fracture or cause to fracture without breaking into pieces. **2** tr & intr to split or make something split. **3** tr & intr to make or cause to make a sudden sharp noise. **4** to strike sharply. **5** tr & intr to give way or make someone or something give way: *He finally cracked under the pressure.* **6** to force open (a safe). **7** to solve (a code or problem). **8** to tell (a joke). **9** intr of the voice: to change pitch or tone suddenly and unintentionally. **10** chem, tr & intr to break down long-chain hydrocarbons produced during petroleum refining into lighter more useful short-chain products. ➤ n **1** a sudden sharp sound. **2** a partial fracture in a material. **3** a narrow opening. **4** a resounding blow. **5** a highly addictive derivative of cocaine, consisting of hard crystalline lumps that are heated and smoked. **6** (*usu* **the crack** or **the craic**) the latest news or gossip. **7** *Irish* (*also* **craic**) fun, enjoyable activity and conversation: *We had some good crack at the races.* ➤ adj, colloq expert: *a crack shot.* ♦ **a fair crack of the whip** a fair opportunity. **at the crack of dawn** colloq at daybreak. **get cracking** colloq to make a prompt start with something. **have a crack at sth** colloq to attempt it. ◊ **crack down on sb or sth** colloq to take firm action against them or it. **crack up** colloq **1** to suffer an emotional breakdown. **2** to collapse with laughter.

crackbrained adj, colloq mad; crazy.

crackdown n a firm action taken against someone or something.

cracked adj **1** colloq crazy; mad. **2** of a voice: harsh; uneven in tone. **3** damaged by splitting.

cracker n **1** a thin crisp unsweetened biscuit. **2** a party toy in the form of a paper tube usu containing a paper hat, gift and motto, that pulls apart with an explosive bang. **3** a small, noisy firework. **4** colloq an exceptional person or thing.

crackers adj, colloq mad.

cracking adj, colloq **1** very good: *a cracking story.* **2** very fast: *a cracking pace.*

crackle vb, intr to make a faint continuous cracking or popping sound. ➤ n this kind of sound. ◊ **crackly** adj (-**ier, -iest**).

crackling n the crisp skin of roast pork.

cracknel n **1** a light brittle biscuit. **2** a hard nutty filling for chocolates.

crackpot colloq, adj crazy. ➤ n a crazy person.

cradle n **1** a cot for a small baby, esp one that can be rocked. **2** a place of origin; the home or source of something: *the cradle of civilization.* **3** a suspended platform or cage for workmen engaged in the construction, repair or painting of a ship or building. ➤ vb **1** to rock or hold gently. **2** to nurture. ♦ **from the cradle to the grave** throughout the whole of one's life.

cradle-snatcher n, derog someone who chooses a much younger person as a lover or spouse.

craft n **1** a skill, trade or occupation, esp one requiring the use of the hands. **2** skilled ability.

3 cunning. ➤ pl n, often in compounds boats, ships, air or space vehicles collectively. ➤ vb to make something skilfully.

craftsman or **craftswoman** n someone skilled at a craft.

craftsmanship n the skill of a craftsman or craftswoman.

crafty adj (-**ier, -iest**) clever, shrewd, cunning or sly. ◊ **craftily** adv. ◊ **craftiness** n.

crag n a rocky peak or jagged outcrop of rock. ◊ **craggy** adj. (-**ier, -est**).

cram vb (**crammed, cramming**) **1** to stuff full. **2** (*sometimes* **cram sth in** or **together**) to push or pack it tightly. **3** tr & intr to study intensively, or prepare someone rapidly, for an examination.

crammer n a person or school that prepares pupils for examinations by rapid or intensive study.

cramp¹ n **1** a painful involuntary prolonged contraction of a muscle or group of muscles. **2** (**cramps**) severe abdominal pain. ➤ vb to restrict with or as with a cramp. ♦ **cramp sb's style** to restrict or prevent them from acting freely or creatively.

cramp² n a piece of metal bent at both ends, used for holding stone or timbers together.

cramped adj **1** overcrowded; closed in. **2** of handwriting: small and closely written.

crampon n a spiked iron attachment for climbing boots, to improve grip on ice or rock.

cranberry n (-**ies**) **1** a shrub with oval pointed leaves, pink flowers and red berries. **2** the sour-tasting fruit of this plant.

crane n **1** a machine with a long pivoted arm from which lifting gear is suspended, allowing heavy weights to be moved both horizontally and vertically. **2** a large wading bird with a long neck and long legs. ➤ vb, tr & intr to stretch (one's neck), or lean forward, in order to see better.

cranefly n (-**ies**) a long-legged, two-winged insect.

cranesbill n a plant with white, purple or blue flowers and slender beaked fruits.

cranial adj relating to or in the region of the skull.

cranium /ˈkreɪnɪəm/ n (**crania** /-nɪə/ or **craniums**) **1** the dome-shaped part of the skull, consisting of several fused bones, that encloses and protects the brain. **2** the skull.

crank n **1** a device consisting of an arm connected to and projecting at right angles from the shaft of an engine or motor. **2** a handle bent at right angles and incorporating such a device, used to start an engine or motor by hand. Also called **crank handle, starting handle. 3** derog an eccentric person. **4** N Am derog a bad-tempered person. ➤ vb **1** to rotate (a shaft) using a crank. **2** (*sometimes* **crank sth up**) to start (an engine, a machine, etc) using a crank. ◊ **crank sth up** to increase its volume, intensity, etc.

crankshaft n the main shaft of an engine or other machine, bearing one or more cranks, used to transmit power from the cranks to the connecting rods.

cranky adj (**-ier, -iest**) **1** colloq eccentric or faddy. **2** N Am bad-tempered.

cranny n (**-ies**) a narrow opening; a cleft or crevice.

crap[1] coarse slang, n **1** faeces. **2** nonsense; rubbish. ➤ vb (**crapped, crapping**) intr to defecate. ○ **crappy** adj (**-ier, -iest**) rubbishy; inferior.

crap[2] n **1** (usu **craps**) a gambling game in which the player rolls two dice. **2** a losing throw in this game. ♦ **shoot craps** to play craps.

crape see CRÊPE (noun sense 1)

crapulent or **crapulous** adj **1** suffering from sickness caused by overdrinking. **2** relating to or resulting from intemperance.

crash vb **1** tr & intr to fall or strike with a banging or smashing noise. **2** tr & intr (often **crash into sth**) of a vehicle: to collide or cause it to collide with something. **3** intr to make a deafening noise. **4** intr to move noisily. **5** intr of a business or stock exchange: to collapse. **6** intr of a computer or program: to fail completely, because of a malfunction, fluctuation in the power supply, etc. **7** to cause a computer system or program to break down completely. **8** slang to gatecrash (a party, etc). **9** (often **crash out**) slang to fall asleep. ➤ n **1** a violent impact or breakage, or the sound of it. **2** a deafening noise. **3** a traffic or aircraft accident. **4** the collapse of a business or the stock exchange. **5** the failure of a computer or program.

crash barrier n a protective metal barrier along the edge of a road, carriageway, the front of a stage, etc.

crash dive n **1** a rapid emergency dive by a submarine. **2** a sudden dive by an aircraft, ending in a crash.

crash helmet n a protective helmet worn eg by motorcyclists, motor-racing drivers, etc.

crashing adj, colloq utter; extreme: a crashing bore.

crash-land vb, tr & intr of an aircraft or pilot: to land or cause (an aircraft) to land, usu without lowering the undercarriage and with the risk of crashing. ○ **crash-landing** n.

crass adj **1** gross; vulgar. **2** colossally stupid. **3** utterly tactless or insensitive. ○ **crassly** adv. ○ **crassness** n.

crate n **1** a strong wooden, plastic or metal case with partitions, for storing or carrying breakable or perishable goods. **2** derog slang a decrepit vehicle or aircraft. ➤ vb to pack in a crate.

crater n **1** the bowl-shaped mouth of a volcano or geyser. **2** a hole left in the ground where a meteorite has landed, or a bomb or mine has exploded. **3** astron a circular, rimmed depression in the surface of the Moon. ➤ vb, tr & intr to form craters in (a road, a surface, etc). ○ **cratered** adj.

cravat /krə'vat/ n a formal style of neckerchief worn instead of a tie.

crave vb **1** (often **crave for** or **after sth**) to long

for it; to desire it overwhelmingly. **2** old use, formal to ask for politely; to beg. ○ **craving** n.

craven adj cowardly; cringing.

craw n the CROP (noun sense 6) of a bird. ♦ **stick in one's craw** colloq to be difficult for one to swallow or accept.

crawl vb, intr **1** of insects, worms, etc: to move along the ground slowly. **2** of a human: to move along on hands and knees. **3** eg of traffic: to progress very slowly. **4** to be, or feel as if, covered or overrun with something: The place was crawling with police. **5** (often **crawl to sb**) derog colloq to behave in a fawning way, often to someone in a senior position. ➤ n **1** a crawling motion. **2** a very slow pace. **3** swimming a stroke with an alternate overarm action together with a kicking leg action.

crawler n **1** someone or something that crawls. **2** derog colloq someone who behaves in a fawning and ingratiating way, esp to those in senior positions.

crayfish or **crawfish** n an edible, freshwater crustacean, similar to a small lobster.

crayon n **1** a pencil or stick made from coloured wax, chalk or charcoal and used for drawing. **2** a drawing made using crayons. ➤ vb, tr & intr to draw or colour with a crayon.

craze n an intense but passing enthusiasm or fashion. ➤ vb **1** to make crazy. **2** tr & intr eg of a glazed or varnished surface: to develop or cause to develop a network of fine cracks.

crazy adj (**-ier, -iest**) **1** mad; insane. **2** foolish; absurd; foolhardy. ○ **crazily** adv. ○ **craziness** n. ♦ **be crazy about sb** or **sth** to be madly enthusiastic about them or it. **like crazy** colloq keenly; fast and furious.

crazy paving n a type of paving made up of irregularly shaped slabs of stone or concrete.

creak n a shrill squeaking noise made typically by an unoiled hinge or loose floorboard. ➤ vb, intr to make or seem to make this noise. ○ **creakily** adv. ○ **creakiness** n. ○ **creaky** adj (**-ier, -iest**).

cream n **1** the yellowish fatty substance that rises to the surface of milk, and yields fat when churned. **2** any food that resembles this substance in consistency or appearance. **3** any cosmetic substance that resembles cream in texture or consistency. **4** the best part of something; the pick. **5** a yellowish-white colour. ➤ vb **1** to beat (eg butter and sugar) till creamy. **2** to remove the cream from (milk). **3** (often **cream sth off**) to select or take away (the best part). ○ **creamy** adj (**-ier, -iest**).

cream cheese n a soft cheese made from soured milk or cream.

creamery n (**-ies**) a place where dairy products are made or sold.

cream of tartar n a white crystalline powder, soluble in water, which is used in baking powder, soft drinks, laxatives, etc.

crease n **1** a line made by folding, pressing or crushing. **2** a wrinkle, esp on the face. **3** cricket a line marking the position of batsman or bowler. ➢ *vb, tr & intr* **1** to make a crease or creases in (paper, fabric, etc); to develop creases. **2** to graze with a bullet. ◊ **crease up** or **crease sb up** *colloq* to be or make helpless or incapable with laughter.

create *vb* **1** to form or produce from nothing: *create the universe.* **2** to bring into existence: *create a system.* **3** to cause. **4** to produce or contrive. **5** *tr & intr* said of an artist, etc: to use one's imagination to make something. **6** *intr, Brit colloq* to make a fuss.

creation *n* **1** the act of creating. **2** something created, particularly something special or striking. **3** the universe. **4** (*often* **the Creation**) *Christianity* God's act of creating the universe.

creative *adj* **1** having or showing the ability to create. **2** inventive or imaginative. ○ **creativity** *n.*

creator *n* **1** someone who creates. **2** (**the Creator**) *Christianity* God.

creature *n* **1** a bird, beast or fish. **2** a person: *a wretched creature.* **3** the slavish underling or puppet of someone.

creature comforts *pl n* material comforts or luxuries such as food, clothes, warmth, etc which add to one's physical comfort.

crèche /krɛʃ/ *n* **1** a nursery where babies can be left and cared for while their parents are at work, shopping, exercising, etc. **2** a model representing the scene of Christ's nativity.

cred *n, slang* credibility: *street cred.*

credence *n* faith or belief placed in something: *give their claims no credence.*

credentials *pl n* **1** personal qualifications and achievements that can be quoted as evidence of one's trustworthiness, competence, etc. **2** documents or other evidence of these.

credible *adj* **1** capable of being believed. **2** reliable; trustworthy. ○ **credibility** *n.*

credit *n* **1** faith placed in something. **2** honour or a cause of honour: *To her credit, she didn't say anything.* **3** acknowledgement, recognition or praise. **4** (**credits**) a list of acknowledgements to those who have helped in the preparation of a book, film, etc. **5** trust given to someone promising to pay later for goods already supplied: *buy goods on credit.* **6** one's financial reliability, esp as a basis for such trust. **7** the amount of money available to one at one's bank. **8 a** an entry in a bank account acknowledging a payment; **b** the side of an account on which such entries are made. Compare DEBIT. **9 a** a certificate of completion of a course of instruction; **b** a distinction awarded for performance on such a course. ➢ *vb* **1** to believe; to place faith in someone or something. **2** (*often* **credit sth to sb** or **sb with sth**) to enter a sum as a credit on someone's account, or allow someone a sum as credit. **3** (*often* **credit sb with sth**) to attribute a quality or achievement to someone.

creditable *adj* praiseworthy; laudable.

credit card *n* a card issued by a bank, finance company, etc authorizing the holder to purchase goods or services on credit. Compare DEBIT CARD.

creditor *n* a person or company to whom one owes money. Compare DEBTOR.

creditworthy *adj* judged as deserving financial credit on the basis of earning ability, previous promptness in repaying debts, etc. ○ **creditworthiness** *n.*

credo /'kriːdoʊ/ *n* a belief or set of beliefs.

credulity *n* a tendency to believe something without proper proof.

credulous *adj* apt to be too ready to believe something, without sufficient evidence. ○ **credulously** *adv.*

creed *n* **1** (*often* **Creed**) a statement of the main points of Christian belief. **2** (**the Creed**) the statement of the main principles and ideology of the Christian faith. **3** any set of beliefs or principles, either personal or religious.

creek *n* **1** a small narrow inlet or bay in the shore of a lake, river or sea. **2** *N Am, Aust, NZ* a small natural stream or tributary, larger than a brook and smaller than a river. ♦ **up the creek** *colloq* in desperate difficulties.

creel *n* a large wicker basket for carrying fish.

creep *vb* (**crept**) *intr* **1** to move slowly, with stealth or caution. **2** to move with the body close to the ground. **3** of a plant: to grow along the ground, up a wall, etc. **4** to enter slowly and almost imperceptibly: *Anxiety crept into her voice.* **5** esp of the flesh: to have a strong tingling sensation as a response to fear or disgust. **6** to act in a fawning way. ➢ *n* **1** an act of creeping. **2** *derog* an unpleasant person. ○ **creeping** *adj.* ♦ **give sb the creeps** *colloq* to disgust or frighten them.

creeper *n* a creeping plant.

creepy *adj* (*-ier, -iest*) *colloq* slightly scary; spooky.

creepy-crawly *n* (*-ies*) *colloq* a small creeping insect.

cremate *vb* to burn (a corpse) to ashes. ○ **cremation** *n* the act or process of cremating a corpse, as an alternative to burial.

crematorium /krɛmə'tɔːrɪəm/ *n* (*crematoria* /-rɪə/ or *crematoriums*) a place where corpses are cremated.

crème de la crème /krɛm də la 'krɛm/ *n* the very best; the elite.

crème de menthe /krɛm də 'mɒnθ/ *n* (*crème de menthes*) a green peppermint-flavoured liqueur.

crème fraîche /krɛm 'frɛʃ/ *n* cream thickened with a culture of bacteria, used in cooking.

crenellate *vb, archit* to furnish with battlements.

creole *n* **1** a PIDGIN language that has become the accepted language of a community or region. **2** (**Creole**) the French-based creole spoken in the US states of the Caribbean Gulf. **3** (**Creole**) a native-born West Indian or Latin American of mixed European and Negro blood. **4** (**Creole**) a French or Spanish native of the US Gulf states.

creosote n 1 a thick dark oily liquid, obtained by distilling coal tar, used as a wood preservative. 2 a colourless or pale yellow oily liquid with a penetrating odour, obtained by distilling wood tar, used as an antiseptic. ➢ vb to treat (wood) with creosote.

crêpe or **crepe** /kreɪp, krɛp/ n 1 (also **crape** /kreɪp/) a thin finely-wrinkled silk fabric. 2 rubber with a wrinkled surface, used for shoe soles. 3 a thin pancake, often containing a filling.

crêpe paper n a type of thin paper with a wrinkled elastic texture, used for making decorations, etc.

crepuscular adj 1 relating to or like twilight; dim. 2 denoting animals that are active before sunrise or at dusk.

crescendo /krɛ'ʃɛndəʊ/ n 1 a gradual increase in loudness. 2 a musical passage of increasing loudness. 3 a high point or climax. ➢ adv, mus played with increasing loudness. Compare DIMINUENDO.

crescent n 1 the curved shape of the Moon during its first or last quarter, when it appears less than half illuminated. 2 something similar in shape to this, eg a semicircular row of houses. 3 (often **Crescent**) chiefly Brit used in names: a street of houses arranged in a crescent shape.

cress n a plant cultivated for its edible seed leaves which are eaten raw in salads, sandwiches, etc and used as a garnish.

crest n 1 a comb or a tuft of feathers or fur on top of the head of certain birds and mammals. 2 a ridge of skin along the top of the head of certain reptiles and amphibians. 3 a plume on a helmet. 4 the topmost part of something, esp a hill, mountain or wave. ➢ vb 1 to reach the top of (a hill, mountain, etc). 2 to crown; to cap. 3 intr of a wave: to rise or foam up into a crest. ○ **crested** adj.

crestfallen adj dejected as a result of a blow to one's pride or ambitions.

cretaceous geol, adj 1 (**Cretaceous**) relating to the last period of the MESOZOIC era, or the rocks formed during this period. 2 composed of or resembling chalk. ➢ n (usu the **Cretaceous**) the Cretaceous age or rock system.

cretin n 1 someone suffering from cretinism. 2 offensive, loosely an idiot.

cretinism n a chronic condition caused by a congenital deficiency of thyroid hormone resulting in retarded physical and mental development.

cretonne n a strong cotton material, usu with a printed design, used for curtains, chair-covers, etc.

Creutzfeldt-Jakob disease /'krɔɪtsfɛlt 'jakɒb/ n, pathol a rare degenerative brain disease, characterized by dementia, wasting of muscle tissue and various neurological abnormalities.

crevasse /krə'vas/ n 1 geol a deep vertical crack in a glacier. 2 US a breach in the bank of the river. ➢ vb to make a fissure in (a wall, a dyke, etc).

crevice /'krɛvɪs/ n 1 a narrow crack or fissure, esp in a rock. 2 a narrow opening.

crew¹ n 1 the team of people manning a ship, aircraft, train, bus, etc. 2 a ship's company excluding the officers. 3 a team engaged in some operation: camera crew. 4 colloq, usu derog a group of people: a strange crew. ➢ vb, intr to serve as a crew member on a yacht, etc.

crew² past tense of CROW

crewcut n a closely cropped hairstyle.

crewel n thin loosely twisted yarn for tapestry or embroidery. ○ **crewelwork** n.

crew neck n a firm round neckline on a sweater.

crib n 1 a baby's cot or cradle. 2 a manger. 3 a model of the nativity, with the infant Christ in a manger. 4 a literal translation of a text, used as an aid by students. 5 something copied or plagiarized from another's work. 6 short for CRIBBAGE. ➢ vb (**cribbed, cribbing**) 1 tr & intr to copy or plagiarize. 2 to put in or as if in a crib.

cribbage n a card game for two to four players, who each try to be first to score a certain number of points.

crick colloq, n a painful spasm or stiffness of the muscles, esp in the neck. ➢ vb to wrench (eg one's neck or back).

cricket¹ n an outdoor game played using a ball, bats and wickets, between two sides of eleven players. ○ **cricketer** n. ♦ **not cricket** colloq unfair; unsporting.

cricket² n a species of mainly nocturnal insect related to the grasshopper, which has long slender antennae and whose males can produce a distinctive chirping sound by rubbing their forewings together.

crier n, hist an official who announces news by shouting it out in public.

crikey exclam, dated slang an expression of astonishment.

crime n 1 an illegal act; an act punishable by law. 2 such acts collectively. 3 an act which is gravely wrong in a moral sense. 4 colloq a deplorable act; a shame.

criminal n someone guilty of a crime or crimes. ➢ adj 1 against the law. 2 relating to crime or criminals, or their punishment. 3 colloq very wrong; wicked. ○ **criminalize** or **-ise** vb. ○ **criminally** adv.

criminology n the scientific study of crime and criminals. ○ **criminologist** n.

crimp vb 1 to press into small regular ridges; to corrugate. 2 to wave or curl (hair) with crimping-irons. 3 US to thwart or hinder. ➢ n a curl or wave in the hair. ○ **crimped** adj.

crimping irons or **crimpers** pl n a tong-like device with two metal plates each with a series of ridges, which are used to form waves in hair that is pressed between the heated plates.

Crimplene n, trademark a crease-resistant clothing fabric made from a thick polyester yarn.

crimson *n* a deep purplish red colour.

cringe *vb, intr* **1** to cower away in fear. **2** *derog* to behave in a submissive, over-humble way. **3** *loosely* to wince in embarrassment, etc. ➤ *n* an act of cringing.

crinkle *vb, tr & intr* to wrinkle or crease. ➤ *n* a wrinkle or crease; a wave. ○ **crinkly** *adj* (*-ier, -iest*).

crinoline *n, hist* a petticoat fitted with hoops to make the skirts stick out.

cripple *vb* **1** to make lame; to disable. **2** to damage, weaken or undermine: *policies which crippled the economy*. ➤ *n* **1** *offensive* someone who is lame or badly disabled. **2** someone who is damaged psychologically: *an emotional cripple*.

crisis *n* (*-ses* /'kraɪsiːz/) **1** a crucial or decisive moment. **2** a turning-point, eg in a disease. **3** a time of difficulty or distress. **4** an emergency.

crisp *adj* **1** dry and brittle. **2** of vegetables or fruit: firm and fresh. **3** of weather: fresh; bracing. **4** of a person's manner or speech: firm; decisive; brisk. **5** of fabric, etc: clean; starched. ➤ *n, Brit* (*usu* **crisps**) thin deep-fried slices of potato, usu flavoured and sold in packets as a snack. Also called **potato crisps**. ➤ *vb, tr & intr* to make or become crisp. ○ **crisply** *adv.* ○ **crispness** *n.* ○ **crispy** *adj* (*-ier, -iest*).

crispbread *n* a brittle unsweetened biscuit made from wheat or rye.

criss-cross *adj* **1** of lines: crossing one another in different directions. **2** of a pattern, etc: consisting of criss-cross lines. ➤ *adv* in a criss-cross way or pattern. ➤ *'n* a pattern of criss-cross lines. ➤ *vb, tr & intr* to form, mark with or move in a criss-cross pattern.

criterion /kraɪ'tɪərɪən/ *n* (*criteria* /-rɪə/) a standard or principle on which to base a judgement.

> **criterion** Note that **criteria** is plural. 'A criteria' is often heard, but is not correct.

critic *n* **1** a professional reviewer of literature, art, drama, music, etc. **2** someone who finds fault with or disapproves of something.

critical *adj* **1** fault-finding; disapproving. **2** relating to a critic or criticism. **3** involving analysis and assessment. **4** relating to a crisis; decisive; crucial. **5** urgent; vital. **6** of a patient: so ill or seriously injured as to be at risk of dying. **7** *physics* denoting a state, level or value at which there is a significant change in the properties of a system: *critical mass*. **8** *nuclear physics* of a fissionable material, a nuclear reactor, etc: having reached the point at which a nuclear chain reaction is self-sustaining. ○ **critically** *adv.*

criticism *n* **1** fault-finding. **2** reasoned analysis and assessment, esp of art, literature, music, drama, etc. **3** the art of such assessment. **4** a critical comment or piece of writing.

criticize or **-ise** *vb, tr & intr* **1** to find fault; to express disapproval of someone or something. **2** to analyse and assess.

critique *n* **1** a critical analysis. **2** the art of criticism.

croak *n* the harsh throaty noise typically made by a frog or crow. ➤ *vb* **1** intr to make this sound. **2** to utter with a croak. **3** *intr* to grumble or moan. **4** *intr, slang* to die.

crochet /'krəʊʃeɪ/ *n* decorative work consisting of intertwined loops, made with wool or thread and a hooked needle. ➤ *vb* (**crocheted, crocheting**) *tr & intr* to make this kind of work.

crock¹ *n, colloq* a decrepit person or an old vehicle, etc.

crock² *n* an earthenware pot.

crockery *n* earthenware or china dishes collectively.

crocodile *n* **1** a large amphibious reptile. **2** *colloq* a line of schoolchildren walking in twos.

crocodile tears *n* a show of pretended grief.

crocus *n* a small plant with yellow, purple or white flowers and an underground CORM.

croft *n* esp in the Scottish Highlands: a small piece of enclosed farmland attached to a house.

croissant /'krwasã/ *n* a flaky crescent-shaped bread roll, made from puff pastry or leavened dough.

cromlech /'krɒmlɛk/ *n, archaeol* **1** a prehistoric stone circle. **2** *loosely* a DOLMEN.

crone *n, derog* an old woman.

crony *n* (*-ies*) a close friend.

crook *n* **1** a bend or curve. **2** a shepherd's or bishop's hooked staff. **3** *colloq* a thief or swindler; a professional criminal. ➤ *adj, Aust & NZ colloq* **1** ill. **2** not working properly. **3** nasty; unpleasant. ➤ *vb* to bend or curve.

crooked *adj* **1** bent, curved, angled or twisted. **2** not straight; tipped at an angle. **3** *colloq* dishonest. ○ **crookedly** *adv.* ○ **crookedness** *n.*

croon *vb, tr & intr* to sing in a subdued tone and sentimental style. ➤ *n* this style of singing. ○ **crooner** *n.*

crop *n* **1** *agric* a plant grown for food, fodder, or raw materials. **2** *agric* the total yield harvested from such a plant, or from a field. **3** a batch: *this year's crop of graduates*. **4** a very short style of haircut. **5 a** a whip handle; **b** a horserider's short whip. **6** *zool* in the gullet of birds: the pouch where food is stored before it is digested. ➤ *vb* (**cropped, cropping**) **1** to trim; to cut short. **2** of animals: to feed on grass, etc. **3** to harvest a cultivated crop. **4** *intr* of land: to produce a crop. ◊ **crop up** *colloq* to occur or appear unexpectedly.

cropper *n* a person or thing that crops. ♦ **come a cropper** *colloq* **1** to fall heavily. **2** to fail disastrously.

croquet /'krəʊkeɪ/ *n* a game played on a lawn, in which the players use mallets to drive wooden balls through a sequence of hoops.

croquette /krəʊ'kɛt/ *n* a ball or round cake made from eg minced meat, fish, potato, etc which is coated in breadcrumbs and fried.

crosier or **crozier** *n* a bishop's hooked staff, carried as a symbol of office.

cross n **1 a** a mark, structure or symbol composed of two lines, one crossing the other in the form + or ×; **b** the mark × indicating a mistake or cancellation. Compare TICK[1] (noun sense 3); **c** the mark × used to symbolize a kiss. **2** a vertical post with a shorter horizontal bar fixed to it, on which criminals were crucified in antiquity. **3** (**the Cross**) Christianity **a** the cross on which Christ was crucified, or a representation of it; **b** this as a symbol of Christianity. **4** a variation of this symbol, eg the MALTESE CROSS. **5** a burden or affliction: have one's own cross to bear. **6 a** a monument in the form of a cross; **b** as a place name: the site of such a monument. **7** a medal in the form of a cross. **8** a plant or animal produced by interbreeding. **9** a mixture or compromise: a cross between a bedroom and a living room. **10** sport, esp football a pass of (a ball, etc) from the wing to the centre. ➤ vb **1** tr & intr (often **cross over**) to get across (a road, a path, etc). **2** to place one across the other: cross one's legs. **3** intr to intersect. **4** intr of letters between two correspondents: to be in transit simultaneously. **5** to make the sign of the Cross. **6** to make (a cheque) payable only through a bank by drawing two parallel lines across it. **7** (usu **cross out, off** or **through**) to delete or cancel something by drawing a line through it. **8** to interbreed species, etc: cross a labrador with a collie. **9** to frustrate or thwart. **10** to cause unwanted connections between (telephone lines). **11** sport, esp football to pass (the ball, etc) from the wing to the centre. ➤ adj **1** angry; in a bad temper. **2** in compounds **a** across: cross-country; **b** intersecting or at right angles: crossbar; **c** contrary: cross purposes; **d** intermingling: cross-breeding. ◆ **cross one's heart** to make a crossing gesture over one's heart as an indication of good faith. **cross sb's mind** to occur to them.

crossbar n **1** a horizontal bar, esp between two upright posts. **2** the horizontal bar on a man's bicycle.

crossbeam n a beam which stretches across from one support to another.

cross bench n a seat in the House of Commons for members not belonging to the government or opposition. ○ **cross bencher** n. Compare BACKBENCH, FRONT BENCH.

crossbill n a finch with a beak in which the points cross instead of meeting.

crossbones pl n see under SKULL AND CROSSBONES

crossbow n a bow placed crosswise on a STOCK (noun sense 5), with a crank to pull back the bow and a trigger to release arrows.

cross-breed biol, vb to mate (two animals or plants of different pure breeds) in order to produce offspring in which the best characteristics of both parents are combined. ➤ n an animal or plant that has been bred from two different pure breeds.

crosscheck vb to verify (information) from an independent source. ➤ n a check of this kind.

cross-country adj, adv across fields, etc rather than on roads.

cross-dress vb, intr esp of men: to dress in the clothes of the opposite sex. ○ **cross-dressing** n.

crosse n a long stick with a netted pocket at one end, used in playing lacrosse.

cross-examine vb **1** law to question (esp a witness for the opposing side) so as to develop or throw doubt on his or her statement. **2** to question very closely. ○ **cross-examination** n. ○ **cross-examiner** n.

cross-eyed adj **1** squinting. **2** having an abnormal condition in which one or both eyes turn inwards towards the nose.

cross-fertilization or **-isation** n **1** in animals: the fusion of male and female GAMETES from different individuals to produce an offspring. **2** in plants: another name for CROSS-POLLINATION. **3** the fruitful interaction of ideas from different cultures, etc. ○ **cross-fertilize** vb.

crossfire n **1** gunfire coming from different directions. **2** a bitter or excited exchange of opinions, arguments, etc.

crossing n **1** the place where two or more things cross each other. **2** a place for crossing a river, road, etc. **3** a journey across something, esp the sea: a rough crossing.

cross-legged adj, adv sitting, usu on the floor, with the ankles crossed and knees wide apart.

crosspatch n, colloq a grumpy or bad-tempered person.

cross-ply adj of a tyre: having fabric cords in the outer casing that run diagonally to stiffen and strengthen the side walls.

cross-pollination n, bot the transfer of pollen from the ANTHER of one flower to the STIGMA of another flower of the same species.

cross-purposes pl n confusion in a conversation or action by misunderstanding. ◆ **be at cross purposes** to misunderstand or clash with one another.

cross-refer vb, tr & intr to direct (the reader) from one part of a text to another. ○ **cross-reference** n.

crossroads sing n **1** the point where two or more roads cross or meet. **2** a point at which an important choice has to be made.

cross section n **1** the surface revealed when a solid object is sliced through, esp at right angles to its length. **2** a representative sample.

crosswise or **crossways** adj, adv **1** lying or moving across, or so as to cross. **2** in the shape of a cross.

crossword or **crossword puzzle** n a puzzle in which numbered clues are solved and their answers in words inserted into their correct places in a grid of squares that cross vertically and horizontally.

crotch n **1** (also **crutch**) **a** the place where the body or a pair of trousers forks into the two legs; **b** the human genital area. **2** the fork of a tree.

crotchet n, mus a note equal to two QUAVERS

or half a MINIM (sense I) in length.

crotchety *adj, colloq* irritable; peevish.

crouch *vb, intr* (*sometimes* **crouch down**) **1** to bend low or squat with one's knees and thighs against one's chest and often also with one's hands on the ground. **2** of animals: to lie close to the ground ready to spring up. ➤ *n* a crouching position or action.

croup¹ /kruːp/ *n* a condition, esp in young children, characterized by inflammation and consequent narrowing of the larynx, resulting in a hoarse cough, difficulty in breathing and fever.

croup² /kruːp/ *n* the rump or hindquarters of a horse.

croupier /'kruːpɪeɪ/ *n* in a casino: someone who presides over a gaming-table, collecting the stakes, dealing the cards, paying the winners, etc.

croûton *n* a small cube of fried or toasted bread, served in soup, etc.

crow *n* **1** a large black bird, usu with a powerful black beak and shiny feathers. **2** the shrill drawn-out cry of a cock. ➤ *vb* (*past tense* **crowed** or **crew**) *intr* **1** of a cock: to cry shrilly. **2** of a baby: to make happy inarticulate sounds. **3** (*usu* **crow over** sb or sth) to triumph gleefully over them; to gloat. ◆ **as the crow flies** in a straight line.

crowbar *n* a heavy iron bar with a bent flattened end, used as a lever.

crowd *n* **1** a large number of people gathered together. **2** the spectators or audience at an event. **3** (*usu* **crowds**) *colloq* a large number of people. **4** (**the crowd**) the general mass of people. ➤ *vb* **1** *intr* to gather or move in a large, usu tightly-packed, group. **2** to fill. **3** to pack; to cram. **4** to press round, or supervise someone too closely. ◇ **crowded** *adj*. ◇ **crowd** sb or sth **out** to overwhelm and force them out.

crown *n* **1** the circular, usu jewelled, gold head-dress of a sovereign. **2** (**the Crown**) **a** the sovereign as head of state; **b** the authority or jurisdiction of a sovereign or of the government representing a sovereign. **3** a wreath for the head or other honour, awarded for victory or success. **4** a highest point of achievement: *the crown of one's career*. **5** the top, esp of something rounded. **6 a** the part of a tooth projecting from the gum; **b** an artificial replacement for this. **7** a representation of a royal crown used as an emblem, symbol, etc. **8** an old British coin worth 25 pence (formerly 5 shillings). ➤ *vb* **1** to place a crown ceremonially on the head of someone, thus making them a monarch. **2** to be on or round the top of someone or something. **3** to reward; to make complete or perfect: *efforts crowned with success*. **4** to put an artificial crown on (a tooth). **5** *colloq* to hit on the head. **6** *draughts* to give (a piece) the status of king, by placing another piece on top of it. ◆ **to crown it all** *colloq* as the finishing touch to a series of esp unfortunate events.

crown colony *n* a colony under the direct con-

trol of the British government.

crown jewels *pl n* the crown, sceptre and other ceremonial regalia of a sovereign.

crown prince *n* the male heir to a throne.

crown princess *n* **1** the wife of a crown prince. **2** the female heir to a throne.

crow's feet *pl n* the wrinkles at the outer corner of the eye.

crow's nest *n* at the top of a ship's mast: a look-out platform.

crozier see CROSIER

crucial *adj* **1** decisive; critical. **2** very important; essential. **3** *slang* very good; great. ◇ **crucially** *adv*.

crucible *n* **1** an earthenware pot in which to heat metals or other substances. **2** a severe test or trial.

crucifix *n* a representation, esp a model, of Christ on the cross.

crucifixion *n* **1** execution by crucifying. **2** (**Crucifixion**) *Christianity* the crucifying of Christ, or a representation of this.

cruciform *adj* cross-shaped.

crucify *vb* (*-ies, -ied*) **1** to put to death by fastening or nailing to a cross by the hands and feet. **2** *slang* to persecute or humiliate.

crud *n, slang* dirt or filth, esp if sticky. ◇ **cruddy** *adj* (*-ier, -iest*).

crude *adj* **1** in its natural unrefined state. **2** rough or undeveloped: *a crude sketch*. **3** vulgar; tasteless. ➤ *n* short for CRUDE OIL. ◇ **crudely** *adv*.

crude oil *n* petroleum in its unrefined state. Often shortened to **crude**.

cruel *adj* (**crueller, cruellest**) **1** deliberately and pitilessly causing pain or suffering. **2** painful; distressing: *a cruel blow*. ◇ **cruelly** *adv*. ◇ **cruelty** *n*.

cruet *n* **1** a small container which holds salt, pepper, mustard, vinegar, etc, for use at table. **2** a stand for a set of such jars.

cruise *vb* **1** *tr & intr* to sail about for pleasure, calling at a succession of places. **2** *intr* eg of a vehicle or aircraft: to go at a steady comfortable speed. ➤ *n* an instance of cruising, esp an ocean voyage for pleasure.

cruiser *n* **1** a large fast warship. **2** (*also* **cabin-cruiser**) a large motor boat with living quarters.

crumb *n* **1** a particle of dry food, esp bread. **2** a small amount: *a crumb of comfort*.

crumble *vb* **1** *tr & intr* to break into crumbs or powdery fragments. **2** *intr* to collapse, decay or disintegrate. ➤ *n* a baked dessert of stewed fruit covered with a crumbled mixture of sugar, butter and flour. ◇ **crumbly** *adj* (*-ier, -iest*).

crumby *adj* (*-ier, -iest*) full of, like, or in crumbs.

crummy *adj* (*-ier, -iest*) *colloq, derog* shoddy, dingy, dirty or generally inferior.

crumpet *n* **1** a thick round cake made of soft light dough, eaten toasted and buttered. **2** *offensive slang* **a** a woman; **b** female company generally.

crumple *vb* **1** *tr & intr* to make or become creased or crushed. **2** *intr* of a face or features:

to pucker in distress. **3** *intr* to collapse; to give away.

crunch *vb* **1** *tr & intr* to crush or grind noisily between the teeth or under the foot. **2** *intr* to produce a crunching sound. **3** *tr & intr, comput, colloq* to process (large quantities of data, numbers, etc) at speed. ➤ *n* **1** a crunching action or sound. **2** (**the crunch**) *colloq* the moment of decision or crisis. ➤ *adj* crucial or decisive: *crunch talks*.

crunchy *adj* (**-ier, -iest**) able to be crunched; crisp. ○ **crunchiness** *n*.

crusade *n* **1** a strenuous campaign in aid of a cause. **2** (**Crusades**) *hist* any of the eight Holy Wars from 1096 onwards, which were fought to recover the Holy Land from the Muslims. ➤ *vb, intr* to engage in a crusade; to campaign. ○ **crusader** *n*.

crush *vb* **1** to break, damage, bruise, injure or distort by compressing violently. **2** to grind or pound into powder, crumbs, etc. **3** *tr & intr* to crumple or crease. **4** to defeat, subdue or humiliate. ➤ *n* **1** violent compression. **2** a dense crowd. **3** a drink made from the juice of crushed fruit: *orange crush.* **4** *colloq* **a** an amorous passion, usu an unsuitable one; an infatuation; **b** the object of such an infatuation. ○ **crushing** *adj*.

crust *n* **1 a** the hard outer surface of a loaf of bread; **b** a piece of this or a dried-up piece of bread. **2** the pastry covering a pie, etc. **3** a crisp or brittle covering. ➤ *vb, tr & intr* to cover with or form a crust.

crustacean *zool, n* any invertebrate animal which typically possesses two pairs of antennae and a segmented body covered in a chalky CARAPACE, eg crabs, lobsters, woodlice, etc. ➤ *adj* relating to these creatures.

crusty *adj* (**-ier, -iest**) **1** having a crisp crust. **2** irritable, snappy or cantankerous. ○ **crustiness** *n*.

crutch *n* **1** a stick, usu one of a pair, used as a support by a lame person, with a bar fitting under the armpit or a grip for the elbow. **2** a support, help or aid. **3** *Brit* another word for CROTCH (sense 1). ➤ *vb, Aust, NZ* to cut off wool from the hindquarters of a sheep.

crux *n* (*cruces* /ˈkruːsiːz/ or *cruxes*) a decisive, essential or crucial point.

cry *vb* (**cries, cried**) **1** *intr* to shed tears; to weep. **2** *intr* (often **cry out**) to shout or shriek, eg in pain or fear, or to get attention or help. **3** (often **cry out**) to exclaim (words, news, etc). **4** *intr* of an animal or bird: to utter its characteristic noise. ➤ *n* (**cries**) **1** a shout or shriek. **2** an excited utterance or exclamation. **3** an appeal or demand. **4** a bout of weeping. **5** the characteristic utterance of an animal or bird. ◆ **a far cry** **1** a great distance. **2** very different. **cry one's eyes** or **heart out** to weep long and bitterly. **cry over spilt milk** to cry over something which cannot be changed. ◇ **cry off** *colloq* to cancel an engagement or agreement. **cry out for sth** to be in obvious need of it.

crybaby *n, derog, colloq* a person, esp a child, who weeps at the slightest upset.

crying *adj* demanding urgent attention: *a crying need.*

cryogenics *sing n* the branch of physics concerned with very low temperatures, and of the phenomena that occur at such temperatures.

crypt *n* an underground chamber or vault, esp one beneath a church, often used for burials.

cryptic *adj* **1** puzzling, mysterious, obscure or enigmatic. **2** secret or hidden. **3** of a crossword puzzle: with clues in the form of riddles, puns, anagrams, etc. ○ **cryptically** *adv*.

cryptogram *n* something written in a code or cipher.

cryptography *n* the study of writing in and deciphering codes. ○ **cryptographer** *n*.

crystal *n* **1** (*also* **rock crystal**) colourless transparent quartz. **2 a** a brilliant, highly transparent glass used for cut glass; **b** cut-glass articles. **3** *chem* any solid substance consisting of a regularly repeating arrangement of atoms, ions or molecules. **4** *elec* a crystalline element, made of piezoelectric or semiconductor material, that functions as a transducer, oscillator, etc in an electronic device. ➤ *adj* belonging or relating to, or made of, crystal. ◆ **crystal clear** as clear or obvious as can be.

crystal ball *n* a globe of rock crystal or glass into which a fortune-teller or clairvoyant gazes, apparently seeing visions of the future.

crystal-gazing *n* **1** a fortune-teller's practice of gazing into a crystal ball long and hard enough to apparently conjure up a vision of the future. **2** *derog* guesswork about the future.

crystalline *adj* **1** composed of or having the clarity and transparency of crystal. **2** *chem* displaying the properties or structure of crystals, eg with regard to the regular internal arrangement of atoms, ions or molecules.

crystallize or **-ise** *vb* **1** *tr & intr* to form crystals. **2** to coat or preserve (fruit) in sugar. **3** *tr & intr* of plans, ideas, etc: to make or become clear and definite. ○ **crystallization** *n*.

crystallography *n* the scientific study of the structure, forms and properties of crystals.

Cs *symbol, chem* caesium.

CS gas *n* an irritant vapour which causes a burning sensation in the eyes, choking, nausea and vomiting, used in riot control.

ct *abbrev* **1** carat. **2** cent. **3** court.

Cu *symbol, chem* copper.

cu *abbrev* cubic.

cub *n* **1** the young of certain carnivorous mammals, such as the fox, wolf, lion and bear. **2** (**Cub**) a member of the junior branch of the Scout Association. Also called **Cub Scout**. ➤ *vb* (**cubbed, cubbing**) *tr & intr* to give birth to cubs.

cubbyhole *n, colloq* **1** a tiny room. **2** a cupboard, nook or recess in which to accumulate miscellaneous objects.

cube *n* **1** *maths* a solid figure having six square faces of equal area. **2** a block of this shape. **3**

maths the product of any number or quantity multiplied by its square, ie the third power of a number or quantity. ➤ *vb* **1** to raise (a number or quantity) to the third power. **2** to form or cut into cubes.

cube root *n, maths* the number or quantity of which a given number or quantity is the cube, eg 3 is the cube root of 27 since $3 \times 3 \times 3 = 27$.

cubic *adj* **1** relating to or resembling a cube. **2** having three dimensions. **3** *maths* of or involving a number or quantity that is raised to the third power, eg a cubic equation (in which the highest power of the unknown variable is three). **4** *maths* of a unit of volume: equal to that contained in a cube of specified dimensions.

cubicle *n* a small compartment for sleeping or undressing in, screened for privacy.

Cubism *n, art* an early-20c movement in painting which represented natural objects as geometrical shapes. ○ **Cubist** *n, adj.*

cubit *n* an old unit of measurement equal to the length of the forearm.

cuboid *adj* (*also* **cuboidal**) resembling a cube in shape. ➤ *n, maths* a solid body having six rectangular faces, the opposite faces of which are equal.

Cub Scout see CUB (*noun* sense 2)

cuckold *old use, derisive, n* a man whose wife is unfaithful. ➤ *vb* to make a cuckold of (a man).

cuckoo *n* an insectivorous bird which lays its eggs in the nests of other birds. ➤ *adj, colloq* insane; crazy.

cuckoo clock *n* a clock from which a model cuckoo springs on the hour, uttering the appropriate number of cries.

cuckoo-pint *n* a European plant with large leaves shaped like arrow-heads, and a pale-green SPATHE partially surrounding a club-shaped SPADIX.

cuckoo spit *n* a white frothy mass found on the leaves and stems of plants, surrounding and secreted by the larvae of some insects.

cucumber *n* **1** a creeping plant cultivated for its edible fruit. **2** a long green fruit of this plant, containing juicy white flesh, which is often used raw in salads, etc. ♦ **cool as a cucumber** *colloq* calm and composed.

cud *n* in ruminant animals: partially digested food that is regurgitated from the first stomach into the mouth to be chewed again. ♦ **chew the cud** *colloq* to meditate, ponder or reflect.

cuddle *vb* **1** *tr & intr* to hug or embrace affectionately. **2** (*usu* **cuddle in** or **up**) to lie close and snug; to nestle. ➤ *n* an affectionate hug. ○ **cuddly** *adj* (**-ier, -iest**) pleasant to cuddle.

cudgel *n* a heavy stick or club used as a weapon. ➤ *vb* (**cudgelled, cudgelling**) to beat with a cudgel.

cue¹ *n* **1** the end of an actor's speech, or something else said or done by a performer, that serves as a prompt for another to say or do something. **2** anything that serves as a signal

or hint to do something. ➤ *vb* (**cueing**) to give a cue to someone. ♦ **on cue** at precisely the right moment.

cue² *n* in billiards, snooker and pool: a stick tapering almost to a point, used to strike the ball. ➤ *vb* (**cueing**) *tr & intr* to strike (a ball) with the cue.

cue ball *n* in billiards, snooker and pool: the ball which is struck by the cue.

cuff¹ *n* **1** a band or folded-back part at the lower end of a sleeve, usu at the wrist. **2** *N Am* the turned-up part of a trouser leg. **3** (**cuffs**) *slang* handcuffs. ♦ **off the cuff** *colloq* without preparation or previous thought.

cuff² *n* a blow with the open hand. ➤ *vb* to hit with an open hand.

cufflink *n* one of a pair of decorative fasteners for shirt cuffs, used in place of buttons.

cuisine /kwɪˈziːn/ *n* **1** a style of cooking. **2** the range of food prepared and served at a restaurant, etc.

cul-de-sac /ˈkʌldəsak/ *n* (**culs-de-sac** /ˈkʌldəsak/ or **cul-de-sacs**) a street closed at one end; a blind alley.

culinary *adj* relating to cookery or the kitchen.

cull *vb* **1** to gather or pick up (information or ideas). **2** to select and kill (weak or surplus animals) from a group, eg seals or deer, in order to keep the population under control. ➤ *n* **1** an act of culling. **2** an inferior animal eliminated from the herd, flock, etc.

culminate *vb, tr & intr* (*often* **culminate in** or **with sth**) to reach the highest point or climax. ○ **culmination** *n.*

culottes *pl n* wide-legged trousers for women, intended to look like a skirt.

culpable *adj* deserving blame. ○ **culpability** *n.*

culprit *n* someone guilty of a misdeed or offence.

cult *n* **1 a** a system of religious belief; **b** the sect following such a system. **2** an esp extravagant admiration for a person, idea, etc.

cultivate *vb* **1** to prepare and use (land or soil) for growing crops. **2** to grow (a crop, plant, etc). **3** to develop or improve: *cultivate a taste for literature*. **4** to try to develop a friendship, a relationship, etc with someone, esp for personal advantage.

cultivated *adj* well bred and knowledgeable.

cultivation *n* **1** the act of cultivating. **2** education, breeding and culture.

cultivator *n* **1** a tool for breaking up the surface of the ground. **2** someone or something which cultivates.

cultural *adj* **1** relating to a culture. **2** relating to the arts. ○ **culturally** *adv.*

culture *n* **1** the customs, ideas, values, etc of a particular civilization, society or social group. **2** appreciation of art, music, literature, etc. **3** improvement and development through care and training: *beauty culture*. **4** *biol* a population of micro-organisms, cells or tissues grown in a CULTURE MEDIUM usu for scientific study or medical diagnosis. ➤ *vb* to grow (micro-organisms, cells, etc) in a CULTURE MEDIUM for study.

cultured adj 1 well-educated; having refined tastes and manners. 2 of micro-organisms, cells or tissues: grown in a CULTURE MEDIUM.

culture medium n, biol a solid or liquid nutrient medium in which micro-organisms, cells or tissues can be grown under controlled conditions in a laboratory.

culture shock n, sociol disorientation caused by a change from a familiar environment, culture, ideology, etc, to another that is radically different or alien.

culvert n a covered drain or channel carrying water or electric cables underground, eg under a road or railway.

cumbersome adj awkward, unwieldy or unmanageable.

cumin or **cummin** /'kʌmɪn/ n a Mediterranean plant whose seeds are used as a spice.

cummerbund n a wide sash worn around the waist, esp with a dinner jacket.

cumulative /'kju:mjʊlətɪv/ adj increasing in amount, effect or strength with each successive addition.

cumulonimbus /kju:mjʊloʊ'nɪmbəs/ n, meteorol a type of cumulus cloud, with a dark and threatening appearance, and associated with thunderstorms.

cumulus /'kju:mjʊləs/ n (**cumuli** /-laɪ/) meteorol a fluffy heaped cloud with a rounded white upper surface and a flat horizontal base, which usu develops over a heat source, eg a volcano or hot land surface.

cuneiform /'kju:nɪfɔ:m/ adj 1 relating to any of several ancient Middle-Eastern scripts with impressed wedge-shaped characters. 2 wedge-shaped. ➤ n cuneiform writing.

cunnilingus n oral stimulation of a woman's genitals.

cunning adj 1 clever, sly or crafty. 2 ingenious, skilful or subtle. ➤ n 1 slyness; craftiness. 2 skill; expertise.

cunt n 1 taboo the female genitals. 2 offensive slang an abusive term for an unpleasant person.

cup n 1 a small, round, open container, usu with a handle, used to drink from. 2 the amount a cup will hold, used as a measure in cookery. 3 a container or something else shaped like a cup: egg cup. 4 an ornamental trophy awarded as a prize in sports competitions, etc. 5 a competition in which the prize is a cup. 6 a wine-based drink, with added fruit juice, etc: claret cup. 7 literary something that one undergoes or experiences: one's own cup of woe. ➤ vb (**cupped, cupping**) 1 to form (one's hands) into a cup shape. 2 to hold something in one's cupped hands. ♦ **one's cup of tea** colloq one's personal preference.

cupboard n a piece of furniture or a recess, fitted with doors, shelves, etc, for storing provisions, etc.

cupboard love n an insincere show of affec-

tion towards someone or something in return for some kind of material gain.

cupid n a figure of Cupid, the Roman god of love, represented in art or sculpture.

cupidity n greed for wealth and possessions.

cupola /'kju:pələ/ n 1 a small dome or turret on a roof. 2 a domed roof or ceiling.

cuppa n, Brit colloq a cup of tea.

cupric /'kju:prɪk/ adj, chem denoting any compound of copper in which the element has a VALENCY of two, eg cupric chloride. Compare CUPROUS.

cupro-nickel /kju:proʊ'nɪkəl/ n an alloy of copper and nickel that is resistant to corrosion, used to make silver-coloured coins in the UK.

cuprous /'kju:prəs/ adj, chem denoting any compound of copper in which the element has a VALENCY of one, eg cuprous chloride. Compare CUPRIC.

cur n, derog, old use 1 a surly mongrel dog. 2 a scoundrel.

curable adj capable of being cured.

curacy /'kjʊərəsɪ/ n (**-ies**) the office or benefice of a curate.

curare /kjʊ'rɑ:rɪ/ n 1 a poisonous black resin obtained from certain tropical plants in South America, which has medicinal uses as a muscle relaxant. 2 any of the plants from which this resin is obtained.

curate n 1 C of E a clergyman who acts as assistant to a vicar or rector. 2 in Ireland: an assistant barman.

curate's egg n anything of which some parts are excellent and some parts are bad.

curative adj able or tending to cure. ➤ n a substance that cures.

curator n the custodian of a museum or other collection.

curb n 1 something that restrains or controls. 2 a a chain or strap passing under a horse's jaw, attached at the sides to the bit; b a bit with such a fitting. 3 a raised edge or border. 4 N Am a kerb. ➤ vb 1 to restrain or control. 2 to put a curb on (a horse).

curd n 1 (often **curds**) the clotted protein substance, as opposed to the liquid component, formed when fresh milk is curdled, and used to make cheese, etc. Compare WHEY. 2 any of several substances of similar consistency. ➤ vb, tr & intr to make or turn into curd.

curdle vb, tr & intr to turn into curd; to coagulate. ♦ **curdle sb's blood** to horrify or petrify them.

cure vb 1 to restore someone to health or normality; to heal them. 2 to get rid of (an illness, harmful habit or other evil). 3 to preserve (food, eg meat, fish, etc) by salting, smoking, etc. 4 to preserve (leather, tobacco, etc) by drying. 5 to vulcanize (rubber). ➤ n 1 something that cures or remedies. 2 restoration to health. 3 a course of healing or remedial treatment. 4 relig the responsibility of a minister for the souls of the parishioners.

cure-all n a universal remedy.

curettage *n* the process of using a curette.

curette or **curet** *n, surgery* a spoon-shaped device used to scrape tissue from the inner surface of an organ or body cavity. ➤ *vb* to scrape with a curette.

curfew *n* **1 a** an official order restricting people's movements, esp after a certain hour at night; **b** this hour. **2** *hist* the ringing of a bell as a signal to put out fires and lights.

curie *n, physics* the former unit of radioactivity, now replaced by the BECQUEREL.

curio / ˈkjʊərɪəʊ/ *n* an article valued for its rarity or unusualness.

curiosity *n* (*-ies*) **1** eagerness to know. **2** something strange, rare or unusual.

curious *adj* **1** strange; odd. **2** eager or interested. **3** inquisitive (often in an uncomplimentary sense). ○ **curiously** *adv*.

curium / ˈkjʊərɪəm/ *n, chem* a radioactive element formed by bombarding plutonium-239 with alpha particles.

curl *vb* **1** to twist, roll or wind (hair) into coils or ringlets. **2** *intr* to grow in coils or ringlets. **3** *tr & intr* to move in or form into a spiral, coil or curve. **4** *intr* to take part in the game of curling. ➤ *n* **1** a small coil or ringlet of hair. **2** a twist, spiral, coil or curve. ♦ **curl one's lip** to sneer. ◊ **curl up 1** to sit or lie with the legs tucked up. **2** *colloq* to writhe in embarrassment, etc.

curler *n* **1** a type of roller for curling the hair. **2** someone who takes part in the sport of curling.

curlew *n* a large wading bird, with a slender down-curved bill and long legs.

curlicue *n* **a** a fancy twist or curl; **b** a flourish made with a pen.

curling *n* a team game played on ice with smooth heavy stones with handles, that are slid towards a circular target marked on the ice.

curly *adj* (*-ier, -iest*) **1** having curls; full of curls. **2** tending to curl.

curmudgeon / kəˈmʌdʒən/ *n* a bad-tempered or mean person. ○ **curmudgeonly** *adj*.

currant *n* a small dried seedless grape.

currency *n* (*-ies*) **1** the system of money, or the coins and notes, in a country. **2** general acceptance or popularity, esp of an idea, theory, etc.

current *adj* **1** generally accepted. **2** belonging to the present: *current affairs*. **3** in circulation; valid. ➤ *n* **1** the continuous steady flow of a body of water, air, heat, etc, in a particular direction. **2** the rate of flow of electric charge through a conductor per unit time. **3** an ELECTRIC CURRENT. **4** a popular trend or tendency. ○ **currently** *adv* at the present time.

current account *n* a bank account from which money or cheques can be drawn without notice, and on which little or no interest is paid.

curriculum / kəˈrɪkjʊləm/ *n* (**curricula** /-lə/ or **curriculums**) **1** a course of study. **2** a list of all the courses available at a school, university, etc. ○ **curricular** *adj*.

curriculum vitae / kəˈrɪkjələm ˈviːtaɪ, ˈvaɪtiː/ *n* (**curricula vitae**) a written summary of one's personal details, education and career, produced to accompany job applications, etc.

curry¹ *n* (*-ies*) a dish, orig Indian, of meat, fish, or vegetables usu cooked with hot spices. ➤ *vb* (*-ies, -ied*) to prepare (food) using curry powder.

curry² *vb* **1** to groom (a horse). **2** to treat (tanned leather) so as to improve its flexibility, strength and waterproof quality. ♦ **curry favour with sb** to use flattery to gain their approval.

curry powder *n* a preparation of various spices used to give curry its hot flavour.

curse *n* **1** a blasphemous or obscene expression, usu of anger; an oath. **2** an appeal to God or some other divine power to harm someone. **3** the resulting harm suffered by someone: *under a curse*. **4** a cause of harm or trouble. **5** *colloq* (**the curse**) menstruation. ➤ *vb* **1** to utter a curse against. **2** *intr* to use violent language; to swear. ♦ **be cursed with sth** to be burdened or afflicted with it.

cursed / ˈkɜːsɪd, kɜːst/ *adj* **1** under a curse. **2** damnable; hateful.

cursive *adj* of handwriting: having letters which are joined up rather than printed separately.

cursor *n* **1** on a computer screen: a mark that indicates where the next character to be entered will appear. **2** the transparent movable part of a measuring device, esp a slide rule.

cursory *adj* hasty; not thorough. ○ **cursorily** *adv*.

curt *adj* rudely brief; dismissive; abrupt. ○ **curtly** *adv*.

curtail *vb* to reduce; to cut short. ○ **curtailment** *n*.

curtain *n* **1** a hanging cloth over a window, round a bed, etc for privacy or to exclude light. **2** *theat* a hanging cloth in front of the stage to screen it from the auditorium. **3** *theat* (*often* **the curtain**) the rise of the curtain at the beginning, or fall of the curtain at the end, of a stage performance, act, scene, etc. **4** something resembling a curtain: *a curtain of thick dark hair*. **5** (**curtains**) *colloq* the end; death. ➤ *vb* **1** (*often* **curtain sth off**) to surround or enclose it with a curtain. **2** to supply (windows, etc) with curtains.

curtain call *n* an audience's demand for performers to appear in front of the curtain after it has fallen, to receive further applause.

curtain-raiser *n* **1** *theat* a short play, etc before the main performance. **2** any introductory event.

curtsy or **curtsey** *n* (**curtsies** or **curtseys**) a slight bend of the knees with one leg behind the other, performed as a formal gesture of respect by women. ➤ *vb* (*-ies, -ied*) *intr* to perform a curtsy.

curvaceous *adj, colloq* of a woman: having a shapely figure.

curvature *n* **a** the condition of being curved; **b** the degree of curvedness.

curve *n* **1** a line no part of which is straight, or a surface no part of which is flat. **2** any smoothly arched line or shape, like part of a circle or sphere. **3** (**curves**) *colloq* the rounded contours and shapes of a woman's body. **4** any line (including a straight line) representing data or an equation on a graph. ➤ *vb, tr & intr* to form a curve. ○ **curvy** *adj* (*-ier, -iest*).

curvilinear *adj* consisting of or bounded by a curved line.

cushion *n* **1** a fabric case stuffed with soft material, for sitting on, etc. **2** something that softens an impact, unpleasant effects, etc. **3** the resilient inner rim of a billiard table. ➤ *vb* to soften the unpleasant or violent effect of something.

cushy *adj* (*-ier, -iest*) *colloq* comfortable; easy; undemanding.

cusp *n* **1** *geom* a point formed by the meeting of two curves, corresponding to the point where the two tangents coincide. **2** *astron* either point of a crescent Moon. **3** *anat* a sharp raised point on the grinding surface of a molar tooth. **4** *astrol* the point of transition between one sign of the zodiac and the next.

cuss *old use, colloq, n* **1** a curse. **2** a person or animal, esp if stubborn. ➤ *vb, tr & intr* to curse or swear.

cussed /ˈkʌsɪd/ *adj* **1** obstinate, stubborn, awkward or perverse. **2** cursed.

custard *n* **1** a sauce made with sugar, milk and cornflour. **2** (*also* **egg custard**) a baked dish or sauce of eggs and sweetened milk.

custodian *n* someone who has care of something, eg a public building. ○ **custodianship** *n*.

custody *n* **1** protective care, esp the guardianship of a child, awarded to someone by a court of law. **2** the condition of being held by the police; arrest or imprisonment. ○ **custodial** *adj*.

custom *n* **1** a traditional activity or practice. **2** a personal habit. **3** the body of established practices of a community; convention. **4** an established practice having the force of a law. **5** the business that one gives to a shop, etc by regular purchases. ➤ *adj* made to order.

customary *adj* usual; traditional; according to custom. ○ **customarily** *adv*.

custom-built or **custom-made** *adj* built or made to an individual customer's requirements: *custom-built car*.

customer *n* **1** someone who purchases goods from a shop, uses the services of a business, etc. **2** *colloq* someone with whom one has to deal: *an awkward customer*.

custom house *n* the office at a port, etc where customs duties are paid or collected.

customs *pl n* taxes or duties paid on imports. ➤ *sing n* **1** the government department that collects these taxes. **2** the place at a port, airport or frontier where baggage is inspected for goods on which duty must be paid and illegal goods.

cut *vb* (**cut, cutting**) **1** *tr & intr* (*also* **cut sth off** or **out**) to slit, pierce, slice or sever (a person or thing) using a sharp instrument. **2** (*often* **cut sth up**) to divide something by cutting. **3** to trim (hair, nails, etc). **4** to reap, prune, or mow (crops or plants). **5** (*sometimes* **cut sth out**) to form it by cutting. **6** to shape the surface of (a gem) into facets, or decorate (glass) by cutting. **7** to shape the pieces of (a garment): *He cuts clothes so that they hang perfectly.* **8** to make (a sound recording). **9** to hurt: *cut someone to the heart.* **10** to reduce. **11** to delete, edit, shorten, or omit. **12** *intr* to stop filming. **13** *intr, cinema* of a film or camera: to change directly to another shot, etc. **14** *maths* to cross or intersect. **15** to reject or renounce: *cut one's links with one's family.* **16** *colloq* to ignore or pretend not to recognize someone. **17** to stop: *He cut his drinking.* **18** *colloq* to absent oneself from something: *cut classes.* **19** to switch off (an engine, etc). **20** to grow (teeth). **21** *intr* (*usu* **cut across** or **through**) to take a short route. **22** to dilute (eg an alcoholic drink) or adulterate (a drug). ➤ *n* **1** an act of cutting; a cutting movement or stroke. **2** a slit, incision or injury made by cutting. **3** a reduction. **4** a deleted passage in a play, etc. **5** the stoppage of an electricity supply, etc. **6** *slang* one's share of the profits. **7** a piece of meat cut from an animal. **8** the style in which clothes or hair are cut. ♦ **a cut above sth** *colloq* superior to it. **cut and dried** decided; definite; settled beforehand. **cut and run** *colloq* to escape smartly. **cut both ways** to have advantages and disadvantages; to bear out both sides of an argument. **cut sb dead** to ignore them completely. **cut it fine** *colloq* to leave barely enough time, etc for something. **cut it out** *slang* to stop doing something bad or undesirable. **cut out for** or **to be sth** having the qualities needed for it. **cut sb short** to silence them by interrupting. **cut up** *colloq* distressed; upset. **to cut a long story short** to come straight to the point. ◊ **cut across sth 1** to go against (normal procedure, etc). **2** to take a short cut through it. **cut back on sth** to reduce spending, etc. **cut down on sth** to reduce one's use of it. **cut in 1** to interrupt. **2** of a vehicle: to move suddenly in front of another vehicle. **cut sth off 1** to separate or isolate it. **2** to stop (the supply of gas, electricity, etc). **3** to stop it or cut it short. **cut sb off** to disconnect them during a telephone call. **cut out** of an engine or electrical device: to stop or switch off. **cut sth out 1** to remove or delete it. **2** to clip pictures, etc out of a magazine, etc. **3** *colloq* to stop doing it. **4** to exclude it from consideration. **5** to block out the light or view.

cutaway *adj* of a diagram, etc: having outer parts omitted so as to show the interior.

cutback *n* a reduction in spending, use of resources, etc.

cute *adj, colloq* **1** attractive; pretty. **2** clever; cunning; shrewd. ○ **cuteness** *n*.

cut glass *n* glassware decorated with patterns cut into its surface.

cuticle /'kjuːtɪkəl/ *n, anat* the outer layer of cells in hair, and the dead hardened skin at the base of fingernails and toenails.

cutis /'kjuːtɪs/ *n* the anatomical name for the skin.

cutlass *n, hist* a short, broad, slightly curved sword with one cutting edge.

cutler *n* someone who manufactures and sells cutlery.

cutlery *n* knives, forks and spoons used to eat food.

cutlet *n* **1 a** a small piece of meat with a bone attached, usu cut from a rib or the neck; **b** a piece of food in this shape: *nut cutlet*. **2** a slice of veal. **3** a rissole of minced meat or flaked fish.

cut-off *n* **1** the point at which something is cut off or separated. **2** a stopping of a flow or supply. **3** (**cutoffs**) *colloq* shorts which have been made by cutting jeans to above the knee.

cut-out *n* **1** something which has been cut out of something else, eg a newspaper clipping. **2** a safety device for breaking an electrical circuit.

cutter *n* **1** a person or thing that cuts. **2** a small single-masted sailing ship.

cut-throat *adj* **1** of competition, etc: very keen and aggressive. **2** of a card game: played by three people. ➤ *n* **1** a murderer. **2** (*also* **cut-throat razor**) a long-bladed razor that folds into its handle.

cutting *n* **1** an extract, article or picture cut from a newspaper, etc. **2** *hortic* a piece cut from a plant for rooting or grafting. **3** a narrow excavation made through high ground for a road or railway. ➤ *adj* **1** hurtful; sarcastic: *a cutting comment*. **2** of wind: penetrating.

cutting edge *n* a part or area (of an organization, branch of study, etc) that breaks new ground, effects change and development, etc.

cuttlefish *n* a mollusc related to the squid and octopus, which has a shield-shaped body containing an inner chalky plate, and a small head bearing eight arms and two long tentacles.

CV or **cv** *abbrev* (**CVs, cvs**) curriculum vitae.

cwm /kuːm/ *n* in Wales: a valley.

cwt. *abbrev* hundredweight.

cyan *n* **1** a greenish blue colour. **2** *printing* a blue ink used as a primary colour.

cyanide *n* any of the poisonous salts of hydrocyanic acid, esp potassium cyanide, which is extremely toxic.

cyanosis *n, pathol* a bluish discoloration of the skin usu caused by lack of oxygen in the blood.

cybernetics *sing n* the comparative study of communication and automatic control processes in mechanical, electronic or biological systems. ○ **cybernetic** *adj*.

cyberspace *n* the three-dimensional artificial environment of VIRTUAL REALITY.

cyclamen /'sɪkləmən/ *n* a plant with heart-shaped leaves and white, pink or red flowers with turned-back petals. ➤ *adj* coloured like a pink cyclamen.

cycle *n* **1** a constantly repeating series of events or processes. **2** a recurring period of years; an age. **3** *physics* one of a regularly repeated set of similar changes, eg in the movement of a wave. **4** a series of poems, songs, plays, etc centred on a particular person or happening. **5** short for: **a** BICYCLE; **b** MOTORCYCLE; **c** TRICYCLE. ➤ *vb, tr & intr* to ride a bicycle.

cyclic or **cyclical** *adj* **1** relating to, containing, or moving in a cycle. **2** recurring in cycles. **3** *chem* an organic chemical compound whose molecules contain one or more closed rings of atoms, eg benzene.

cyclist *n* the rider of a bicycle, motorcycle, etc.

cyclone *n* **1** *meteorol* (*also* **depression** or **low**) an area of low atmospheric pressure, often associated with stormy weather, in which winds spiral inward towards the centre. Compare ANTICYCLONE. **2** a violent, often highly destructive, tropical storm with torrential rain and extremely strong winds. ○ **cyclonic** /saɪ-'klɒnɪk/ *adj*.

cygnet *n* a young swan.

cylinder *n* **1** *geom* a solid figure of uniform circular cross-section, in which the curved surface is at right angles to the base. **2** a container, machine part or other object of this shape, eg a storage container for compressed gas. **3** *eng* in an internal-combustion engine: the tubular cylinder within which the chemical energy of the burning fuel is converted to the mechanical energy of a moving piston. ○ **cylindrical** *adj*.

cymbal *n* a thin plate-like brass percussion instrument, either beaten with a drumstick, or used as one of a pair that are struck together to produce a ringing clash.

cyme *n, bot* an INFLORESCENCE in which the main stem and each of its branches ends in a flower, and all subsequent flowers develop from lateral buds arising below the apical flowers.

Cymric /'kʌmrɪk, 'kɪmrɪk/ *adj* Welsh.

cynic *n* **1** someone who takes a pessimistic view of human goodness or sincerity. **2** (**Cynic**) *philos* a member of a sect of ancient Greek philosophers who scorned wealth and enjoyment of life.

cynical *adj* disinclined to believe in the goodness or sincerity of others. ○ **cynically** *adv*.

cynicism *n* **1** the attitude, beliefs or behaviour of a cynic. **2** a cynical act, remark, etc.

cynosure /'saɪnəʃʊə(r)/ *n* the focus of attention; the centre of attraction.

cypher see CIPHER

cypress *n* any of a family of dark-green coniferous trees, or their wood.

Cyrillic *adj* belonging or relating to the alphabet used for Russian, Bulgarian and other Slavonic languages.

cyst /sɪst/ *n* **1** *pathol* an abnormal sac that contains fluid, semi-solid material or gas. **2** *anat* any normal sac or closed cavity.

cystic fibrosis *n, pathol* a serious hereditary

disease causing digestive and respiratory problems.

cystitis *n*, *pathol* inflammation of the urinary bladder, characterized by a desire to pass urine frequently, accompanied by a burning sensation.

cytology *n* the study of the structure and function of individual cells in plants and animals.

cytoplasm *n*, *biol* the part of a living cell, excluding the NUCLEUS (sense 2), enclosed by the cell membrane. ◦ **cytoplasmic** *adj*.

cytosine *n*, *biochem* one of the four bases found in NUCLEIC ACID.

czar see TSAR

Czech /tʃɛk/ *adj* belonging or relating to the Czech Republic or to its inhabitants or their language. ➤ *n* **1 a** a citizen or native of the Czech Republic; **b** *formerly, from 1918 to 1993* a citizen or native of Czechoslovakia. **2** the official language of the Czech Republic.

Dd

D¹ or **d** *n* (*Ds, D's* or *d's*) **1** the fourth letter of the English alphabet. **2** (**D**) *mus* the second note in the scale of C major. **3** (*usu* **D**) the fourth highest grade.

D² *symbol* **1** the Roman numeral for 500. **2** *chem* deuterium.

d *abbrev* **1** daughter. **2** day. **3** deci-. **4** *denarius* (Latin), (in the UK before 1971) a penny, or pence. **5** died.

'd *contraction* **1** would: *I'd go*. **2** had: *He'd gone*. **3** *colloq* did: *Where'd they go?*

dab¹ *vb* (*dabbed, dabbing*) *tr & intr* (*often* **dab at sth**) to touch something lightly with a cloth, etc. ➤ *n* **1** a small amount of something creamy or liquid. **2** a light touch. **3** (**dabs**) *slang* fingerprints.

dab² *n* a small brown flatfish.

dabble *vb* **1** *tr & intr* to move or shake (a hand, foot, etc) about in water. **2** *intr* (*often* **dabble at, in** or **with sth**) to do something without serious effort. ◦ **dabbler** *n*.

dab hand *n* an expert.

dace *n* (*dace* or *daces*) a small European river fish.

dachshund /ˈdaksənd/ *n* a small dog with a long body and short legs.

dactyl *n*, *poetry* a foot consisting of a long or stressed syllable followed by two short or unstressed ones. ◦ **dactylic** *adj*.

dad or **daddy** *n* (*-ies*) *colloq* father.

daddy-long-legs *n* (*pl* **daddy-long-legs**) *Brit, Austral, NZ colloq* a CRANEFLY.

dado /ˈdeɪdoʊ/ *n* (*dadoes* or *dados*) **1** the lower part of an indoor wall when different from the upper part. **2** *archit* the plain square part of the base of a column or pedestal.

daemon /ˈdiːmən/ *n* a spirit, often a guardian spirit. ◦ **daemonic** /diːˈmɒnɪk/ *adj*.

daffodil *n* a plant with yellow trumpet-shaped flowers.

daft *adj*, *colloq* **1** silly; foolish. **2** mad. **3** (**daft about** or **on sth**) enthusiastic about it.

dag *n*, *Aust colloq* a scruffy, untidy person. ◦ **daggy** *adj*.

dagger *n* **1** a pointed knife for stabbing. **2** *printing* the symbol †. ◆ **at daggers drawn** openly showing hostility. **look daggers at sb** to give them a hostile look.

dahlia /ˈdeɪlɪə/ *n*, *bot* a garden plant with large, brightly coloured flowers.

daily *adj* **1** happening, appearing, etc every day, or every day except Sunday, or except Saturday and Sunday. **2** relating to a single day. ➤ *adv* every day, or every weekday. ➤ *n* (*-ies*) **1** a newspaper published every day except Sunday. **2** *colloq* a person who comes in to clean a house.

dainty *adj* (*-ier, -iest*) small, pretty or delicate. ➤ *n* (*-ies*) something small and nice to eat. ◦ **daintily** *adv*. ◦ **daintiness** *n*.

daiquiri /ˈdakəri/ *n* a drink made with rum, lime juice and sugar.

dairy *n* (*-ies*) **1** a farm building where milk is stored or where butter and cheese are made. **2** a business or factory that bottles and distributes milk and manufactures dairy products. **3** a shop that sells milk, butter, etc. ➤ *adj* relating to milk production or milk products: *a dairy farm*.

dais /ˈdeɪɪs/ *n* a raised platform in a hall, eg for speakers.

daisy *n* (*-ies*) a small flower with heads consisting of a yellow centre surrounded by white petals.

daisy-wheel *n* a rotating metal disc in a typewriter, etc consisting of spokes with letters at the end which print when the keys are struck.

dal, **dahl** or **dhal** /dɑːl/ *n* **1** any of various edible dried split pea-like seeds. **2** a cooked dish made of these.

dale *n* a valley.

dally *vb* (*-ies, -ied*) *intr* **1** to waste time idly or frivolously. **2** (*often* **dally with sb**) *old use* to flirt with them. ◦ **dalliance** *n*.

dam¹ *n* **1** a barrier built to hold back water. **2** the water confined behind such a structure. ➤ *vb* (*dammed, damming*) to hold back (water, etc) with a dam.

dam² n of horses, cattle and sheep: a female parent.

damage n 1 harm or injury, or loss caused by injury. 2 (**damages**) law payment due for loss or injury. 3 colloq amount owed: What's the damage? ➤ vb to cause harm, injury or loss to someone or something. ○ **damaging** adj.

damask n a patterned silk or linen cloth, used for tablecloths, curtains, etc.

dame n 1 a woman who has been honoured by the Queen or the Government for service or merit. 2 NAm slang a woman. 3 a comic female character in a pantomime, usu played by a man.

damn vb 1 relig to sentence someone to punishment in hell. 2 to declare someone or something to be useless or worthless. 3 to prove someone's guilt. ➤ exclam (often **damn it**) expressing annoyance. ➤ adj, colloq annoying; hateful: the damn cold. ➤ adv, colloq used for emphasis: It's damn cold. ○ **damning** adj. ♦ **damn sb** or **sth with faint praise** to praise them or it so unenthusiastically as to seem disapproving. **not give a damn** colloq not to care at all.

damnable adj 1 awful. 2 annoying.

damnation n, relig punishment in hell. ➤ exclam expressing annoyance.

damned adj 1 relig sentenced to damnation. 2 colloq annoying, hateful, etc. ➤ n (**the damned**) those sentenced to punishment in hell. ➤ adv, colloq extremely: damned cold. ♦ **do one's damnedest** colloq to try as hard as possible.

damp adj slightly wet. ➤ n slight wetness, esp if cold and unpleasant. ➤ vb 1 to wet something slightly. 2 (often **damp down**) to make (emotions, interest, etc) less strong. 3 (often **damp down**) to make (a fire) burn more slowly. ○ **damply** adv. ○ **dampness** n.

damp-course or **damp-proof course** n a layer of material in a wall of a building which stops damp rising up through the wall.

dampen vb 1 to make something slightly wet. 2 tr & intr (usu **dampen down** or **dampen down**) **a** of emotions, interest, etc: to make or become less strong; **b** to make (a fire) burn more slowly. ○ **dampener** n.

damper n 1 something which lessens enthusiasm, interest, etc. 2 a movable plate controlling air flow to a fire, etc. 3 mus in a piano, etc: a pad which silences a note after it has been played. ♦ **put a damper on sth** to lessen enthusiasm for it.

damsel n, old use or literary a young woman.

damson n 1 a small purple plum. 2 the tree it grows on.

dan n 1 any of the ten grades of BLACK BELT in judo, karate, etc. 2 someone who has such a grade.

dance vb 1 intr & tr to make rhythmic steps or movements (usu in time to music). 2 intr (usu **dance about** or **around**) to move or jump about quickly. ➤ n 1 a pattern of rhythmic steps, usu

in time to music. 2 a social gathering for dancing. 3 music played for dancing. ○ **dancer** n. ○ **dancing** n. ♦ **dance attendance on sb** derog to follow them closely and do whatever they want.

D and C abbrev, med DILATATION AND CURETTAGE.

dandelion n a plant with notched leaves and yellow flowerheads on hollow stems.

dander n. ♦ **get one's** or **sb's dander up** colloq to become angry, or make someone angry.

dandle vb to bounce (usu a small child) on one's knee.

dandruff n whitish flakes of dead skin shed from the scalp.

dandy n (**-ies**) a man who is concerned to dress very fashionably or elegantly. ➤ adj, colloq (**-ier, -iest**) good; fine.

Dane n a citizen or inhabitant of, or person born in, Denmark.

danger n 1 a situation or state of possible harm, injury or loss. 2 a possible cause of harm, injury or loss.

danger money n extra money paid to a person doing a dangerous job.

dangerous adj likely or able to cause harm or injury. ○ **dangerously** adv. ○ **dangerousness** n.

dangle vb 1 tr & intr to hang loosely. 2 to offer (an idea, a possible reward, etc) to someone.

Danish adj belonging or relating to Denmark, its inhabitants or their language. ➤ n 1 the official language of Denmark. 2 (**the Danish**) the people of Denmark.

Danish blue n a strong-tasting white cheese with streaks of bluish mould through it.

Danish pastry n a flat cake of rich light pastry, with a sweet filling or topping.

dank adj unpleasantly wet and cold. ○ **dankness** n.

dapper adj smart in appearance and lively in movement.

dappled adj with spots or patches of a different, usu darker, colour.

dapple-grey adj of a horse: pale-grey with darker spots. ➤ n a dapple-grey horse.

dare vb 1 intr to be brave enough to do something. 2 to challenge someone to do something difficult, dangerous, etc. ➤ auxiliary vb used in questions and negative statements, as in Daren't he tell her? and I dared not look at him. ➤ n a challenge to do something dangerous, etc. ♦ **I dare say** or **daresay** probably; I suppose.

daredevil n a person who does dangerous things without worrying about the risks involved.

daring adj 1 courageous or adventurous. 2 intended to shock or surprise. ➤ n boldness.

dark adj 1 without light. 2 closer to black than to white. 3 of a person or skin or hair colour: not light or fair. 4 sad or gloomy. 5 evil or sinister: dark powers. 6 mysterious and unknown: a dark secret. ➤ n 1 (usu **the dark**) the absence of light. 2 the beginning of night-time. 3 a dark colour. ○ **darkly** adv. ○ **darkness** n. ♦ **in the dark** not knowing or not aware of something.

the Dark Ages pl n the period of European history from about the 5c to the 11c.

darken vb, tr & intr to make or become dark or darker.

dark horse n someone who keeps their past, life, abilities, etc secret.

darkroom n a room into which no ordinary light is allowed, used for developing photographs.

darling n **1** used esp as a form of address: a dearly loved person. **2** a lovable person or thing. ➤ adj **1** well loved. **2** colloq delightful.

darn¹ vb to mend (a hole, a garment, etc) by sewing with rows of stitches which cross each other. ➤ n a darned place.

darn² exclam a substitute for DAMN. ○ **darned** adj.

dart n **1** a narrow pointed weapon that can be thrown or fired. **2** a small sharp-pointed object thrown in the game of DARTS. **3** a sudden quick movement. **4** a fold sewn into a piece of clothing. ➤ vb **1** intr to move suddenly and quickly. **2** to send or give (a look or glance) quickly.

dartboard n a circular target at which darts are thrown in the game of DARTS.

darts sing n a game in which darts are thrown at a dartboard.

Darwinism n, biol the theory of evolution proposed by Charles Darwin (1809–82). ○ **Darwinian** and **Darwinist** adj, n.

dash vb **1** intr to run quickly. **2** intr to crash or smash. **3** (often **dash against sth**) to hit or smash into it violently. **4** to put an end to (hopes, etc). ➤ n **1** a quick run or sudden rush. **2** a small amount of something, esp a liquid. **3** a patch of colour. **4** a short line (–) used in writing to show a break in a sentence, etc. **5** in MORSE code: the longer of the two lengths of signal element. Compare DOT (sense 2). **6** confidence, enthusiasm and stylishness. **7** a DASH-BOARD. ◊ **dash sth off** to produce or write it hastily.

dashboard n a panel with dials, switches, etc in front of the driver's seat in a car, boat, etc.

dashing adj **1** smart; stylish. **2** lively and enthusiastic. ○ **dashingly** adv.

dastardly adj, old use cowardly, mean and cruel.

DAT abbrev digital audio tape.

data n (orig pl of DATUM but now generally treated as sing) **1** information or facts, esp if obtained by scientific observation or experiment. **2** information in the form of numbers, characters, electrical signals, etc that can be supplied to, stored in or processed by a computer.

database n, comput a collection of computer DATA.

data capture n, comput changing information into a form which can be fed into a computer.

data processing n, comput the processing of data by a computer system.

date¹ n **1** the day of the month and/or the year, given as a number or numbers. **2** the day on which a letter, etc was written, sent, etc, an event took place or is planned to take place, etc. **3** a particular period of time in history: tools of an earlier date. **4** colloq a planned meeting or social outing, usu with a person one is romantically attached to. **5** esp N Am, colloq a person whom one is meeting or going out with, esp romantically. **6** colloq an agreed time and place of performance. ➤ vb **1** to put a date on (a letter, etc). **2** to find, decide on or guess the date of something. **3** to show the age of someone or something; to make (esp a person) seem old. **4** intr to become old-fashioned. **5** intr (always **date from** or **back to**) to have begun or originated (at a specified time). **6** tr & intr, colloq to go out with someone, esp regularly for romantic reasons. ○ **datable** or **dateable** adj. ○ **dated** adj old-fashioned. ♦ **to date** up to the present time.

date² n the fruit of the DATE PALM.

dateline n a line, usu at the top of a newspaper article, which gives the date and place of writing.

date palm n a tall tree with a crown of leaves, cultivated for its edible fruit.

dative gram, n **1** in certain languages: the CASE² (noun sense 7) of a noun, pronoun or adjective which is used chiefly to show that the word is the indirect object of a verb. **2** a noun, etc in this case. ➤ adj belonging to or in this case.

datum n (data) a piece of information.

daub vb **1** to spread something roughly or unevenly onto a surface. **2** to cover (a surface) with a soft sticky substance or liquid. **3** tr & intr, derog to paint carelessly or without skill. ➤ n **1** soft, sticky material such as clay, often used as a covering for walls. **2** derog, colloq an unskilful or carelessly done painting.

daughter n **1** a female child. **2** a woman closely associated with, involved with or influenced by a person, thing or place: a faithful daughter of the Church. ➤ adj **1** biol of a cell: formed by division. **2** physics of an element: formed by nuclear fission. ○ **daughterly** adj.

daughter-in-law n (daughters-in-law) the wife of one's son.

daunt vb to frighten, worry or discourage someone. ○ **daunting** adj intimidating; discouraging.

davenport n **1** Brit a type of desk. **2** N Am a large sofa.

davit /'davɪt/ n either of a pair of crane-like devices on a ship on which a lifeboat is hung.

Davy Jones's locker n the bottom of the sea.

dawdle vb, intr **1** to walk unnecessarily slowly. **2** to waste time, esp by taking longer than necessary to do something.

dawn n **1** the time of day when light first appears. **2** the beginning of (a new period of time, etc). ➤ vb, intr **1** of the day: to begin. **2** (usu **dawn on sb**) to begin to be realized by them.

dawn chorus n the singing of birds at dawn.

day n 1 a period of 24 hours, esp from midnight to midnight. 2 the period from sunrise to sunset. 3 the period in any 24 hours normally spent doing something: *the working day*. 4 (**day** or **days**) a particular period of time, usu in the past: *childhood days*. 5 time of recognition, success, influence, power, etc: *Their day will come.* ♦ **all in a** or **the day's work** a normal or acceptable part of one's work or routine. **at the end of the day** when all is said and done. **call it a day** to leave off doing something. **day in, day out** continuously and tediously without change. **make sb's day** to satisfy or delight them. **that will be the day** *colloq* that is unlikely to happen.

daybreak n dawn.

day care n supervision and care given to young children, the elderly or handicapped people during the day.

day centre or **day care centre** n a place which provides day care and/or social activities for the elderly, the handicapped, etc.

daydream n pleasant thoughts which take one's attention away from what one is, or should be, doing. ➤ *vb, intr* to be engrossed in daydreams. ○ **daydreamer** n.

dayglo adj luminously brilliant green, yellow, pink or orange.

daylight n 1 the light given by the sun. 2 the time when light first appears in the sky. ♦ **in broad daylight 1** during the day. 2 openly. **scare** or **frighten the living daylights out of sb** *colloq* to frighten them greatly. **see daylight** to be close to completing a difficult or long task.

daylight robbery n, *colloq* greatly overcharging for something.

daylight-saving time n time, usu one hour ahead of standard time, adopted, usu in summer, to increase the hours of daylight at the end of the day.

day release n a system by which employees are given time off work (usu one day a week) to study at college, etc.

day return n a ticket at a reduced price for a journey to somewhere and back again on the same day.

day room n a room used as a communal living room in a school, hospital, hostel, etc.

day shift n 1 a period of working during the day. 2 the people who work during this period.

daytime n the time between sunrise and sunset.

day-to-day adj daily; routine.

daze vb to make someone confused or unable to think clearly (eg by a blow or shock). ➤ n a confused, forgetful or inattentive state of mind. ○ **dazed** adj.

dazzle vb 1 to make someone unable to see properly, with or because of a strong light. 2 to impress someone greatly by one's beauty, charm, skill, etc. ○ **dazzling** adj. ○ **dazzlingly** adv.

dB abbrev decibel.

DC abbrev direct current. Compare AC.

DCC abbrev digital compact cassette.

DD abbrev: *Divinitatis Doctor* (Latin), Doctor of Divinity.

D-Day n 1 the date of the Allied invasion of Europe in World War II, 6 June 1944. 2 any critical day of action.

DDT abbrev dichlorodiphenyltrichloroethane, a highly toxic insecticide, now restricted or banned in most countries.

de- pfx, signifying 1 down or away: *debase*. 2 reversal or removal: *decriminalize*.

deacon n 1 a member of the lowest rank of clergy in the Roman Catholic and Anglican churches. 2 in some other churches: a person with certain duties such as looking after the church's financial affairs.

deactivate vb to remove or lessen the capacity of (something such as a bomb) to function or work. ○ **deactivation** n.

dead adj 1 no longer living. 2 not alive. 3 no longer in existence. 4 with nothing living or growing in or on it. 5 not, or no longer, functioning; not connected to a source of power. 6 no longer burning. 7 no longer in everyday use: *a dead language*. 8 no longer of interest or importance: *a dead issue*. 9 having little or no excitement or activity. 10 without feeling; numb. 11 complete. 12 of a sound: dull. 13 *sport* of a ball: out of play. ➤ n (**the dead**) dead people. ➤ *adv, slang* absolutely; very: *dead drunk*. ♦ **dead on** exact; exactly. **the dead of night** the middle of the night, when it is darkest. **the dead of winter** the middle of winter, when it is coldest.

deadbeat n, *colloq* a useless person.

dead beat adj, *colloq* exhausted.

dead duck n, *colloq* someone or something with no chance of success or survival.

deaden vb 1 to lessen or weaken something or make it less sharp, strong, etc. 2 to make something soundproof.

dead end n 1 a passage, road, etc, closed at one end. 2 a situation or activity with no possibility of further progress. ➤ adj (**dead-end**) allowing no progress or improvement.

deadhead n, chiefly N Am 1 someone who enjoys free privileges. 2 an ineffective unproductive person. 3 a train, etc, travelling empty. 4 a sunken or semi-submerged log in a waterway. ➤ vb to remove withered or dead flowers from (plants).

dead heat n the result when two or more competitors produce equally good performances or finish a race in exactly the same time.

dead letter n 1 a rule or law no longer obeyed or in force. 2 a letter that can neither be delivered nor returned to the sender because it lacks the necessary address details.

deadline n a time by which something must be done.

deadlock n a situation in which no further progress towards an agreement is possible. ➤ vb, *tr & intr* to make or come to a deadlock.

dead loss *n, colloq* someone or something that is totally useless.

deadly *adj* (**-ier, -iest**) **1** causing or likely to cause death. **2** *colloq* very dull or uninteresting. **3** very great: *in deadly earnest.* ➤ *adv* very; absolutely.

deadly nightshade *n* a plant with bell-shaped purple flowers and poisonous black berries.

dead man's handle or **dead man's pedal** *n* a device on a machine, eg a railway engine, which stops the machine if pressure on it is released.

dead march *n, mus* a piece of solemn music played at funeral processions, esp those of soldiers.

dead-nettle *n* any of various plants superficially like a nettle but without a sting.

dead-on *adj, colloq* accurate; spot-on.

deadpan *adj* showing no emotion or feeling, esp when joking but pretending to be serious.

dead reckoning *n* estimating the position of a ship, etc from the distance and direction travelled, without looking at the position of the stars, Sun or Moon.

dead set *adj* determined.

dead weight *n* **1** a heavy load. **2** *technical* (*also* **deadweight**) the difference in the displacement of a ship when unloaded and loaded.

dead wood *n, colloq* someone or something that is no longer useful or needed.

deaf *adj* **1** unable to hear at all or to hear well. **2** (*usu* **deaf to sth**) not willing to listen to (advice, appeals, etc). ○ **deafness** *n.*

deafen *vb* to make someone deaf or temporarily unable to hear. ○ **deafening** *adj* **1** extremely loud. **2** causing deafness. ○ **deafeningly** *adv.*

deaf-mute *n, often considered offensive* someone who is both deaf and unable to speak. ➤ *adj* unable to hear or speak.

deal¹ *n* **1** a bargain, agreement or arrangement. **2** particular treatment of or behaviour towards someone: *a rough deal.* **3** the act or a player's turn of sharing out cards among the players in a card game. ➤ *vb* (*past tense & past participle* **dealt** /delt/) *tr & intr* **1** (*always* **deal in sth**) to buy and sell it. **2** (*also* **deal out**) to divide the cards among the players in a card game. **3** (*also* **deal out**) to give something out to a number of people, etc. ◆ **a good** or **great deal 1** a large quantity. **2** very much or often. **deal sb a blow** to hit or distress them. ◇ **deal with sth** or **sb 1** to take action regarding them. **2** to be concerned with them.

deal² *n* a plank or planks of fir or pine wood.

dealer *n* **1** a person or firm dealing in retail goods. **2** the player who deals in a card game. **3** someone who sells illegal drugs. ○ **dealership** *n* **1** a business which buys and sells things. **2** a business licensed to sell a particular product by its manufacturer.

dealings *pl n* **1** one's manner of acting towards others. **2** business, etc contacts and transactions.

dean *n* **1** a senior clergyman in an Anglican cathedral. **2** a senior official in a university or college. **3** the head of a university or college faculty.

deanery *n* (**-ies**) **1** the house of a dean. **2** a group of parishes for which a rural dean has responsibility.

dear *adj* **1** high in price; charging high prices. **2** lovable; attractive. **3** used in addressing someone at the start of a letter. **4** (*usu* **dear to sb**) greatly loved by, or very important or precious to, them. ➤ *n* (*also* **deary, dearie**) (**-ies**) **1** a charming or lovable person. **2** used esp as a form of address: *a person one loves or likes.* ➤ *exclam* (*also* **deary, dearie**) used as an expression of dismay, etc: *Dear me!* ○ **dearly** *adv.* ◆ **cost sb dear** to result in a lot of trouble or suffering.

dearth /dɜːθ/ *n* a scarceness or lack.

death *n* **1** the time, act or manner of dying; the state of being dead. **2** *often humorous* something which causes a person to die: *His antics will be the death of me.* **3** the end or destruction of something. **4** (**Death**) the figure of a skeleton, as a symbol of death. ○ **deathless** *adj, often ironic* immortal; unforgettable: *deathless prose.* ○ **deathly** *adj.* ◆ **at death's door** near death; gravely ill. **catch one's death (of cold)** *colloq* to catch a very bad cold. **do sth to death** to overuse it. **like death warmed up** *colloq* very unwell. **put sb to death** to kill them or have them killed. **to death** extremely: *bored to death.*

deathbed *n* the bed in which a person died or is about to die.

deathblow *n* **1** a blow which causes death. **2** an action, etc which puts an end to (hopes, plans, etc).

death certificate *n* a certificate stating the time and cause of someone's death.

death knell *n* **1** the ringing of a bell when someone has died. **2** an action, announcement, etc that heralds the end or destruction of (hopes, plans, etc).

death mask *n* a mask made from the cast of a person's face after they have died.

death penalty *n* punishment of a crime by death.

death row *n, esp US* the part of a prison where people who have been sentenced to death are kept.

deathtrap *n* a building, vehicle, place, etc which is very unsafe.

death warrant *n* an official order for a death sentence to be carried out.

deathwatch beetle *n* a beetle which makes a ticking sound once believed to herald a death in the building where it was heard.

death wish *n* a desire to die, or that someone else should die.

deb *n, colloq* a DEBUTANTE.

debacle or **débâcle** /deɪˈbɑːkəl/ *n* total disorder, defeat, collapse of organization, etc.

debar vb to stop someone from joining, taking part in, doing, etc something.

debase vb 1 to lower the value, quality, or status of something. 2 to lower the value of (a coin) by adding metal of a lower value. ○ **debasement** n.

debate n 1 a formal discussion. 2 a general discussion. ➤ vb, tr & intr 1 to hold or take part in a debate. 2 to consider the arguments for or against something. ○ **debatable** or **debateable** adj doubtful; not agreed.

debauch /dɪˈbɔːtʃ/ vb to cause or persuade someone to take part in immoral, esp sexual, activities or excessive drinking. ➤ n a period of debauched behaviour. ○ **debauched** adj corrupted; immoral. ○ **debauchery** n.

debenture n, finance a type of loan to a company or government agency which is usu made for a set period of time and carries a fixed rate of interest.

debilitate vb to make someone weak or weaker. ○ **debilitating** adj. ○ **debilitation** n. ○ **debility** n.

debit n 1 an entry in an account recording what is owed or has been spent. 2 a sum taken from a bank, etc account. 3 a deduction made from a bill or account. Compare CREDIT (noun sense 8). ➤ vb (**debited, debiting**) 1 to take from (an account, etc). 2 to record something in a debit entry.

debit card n a plastic card used by a purchaser to transfer money directly from their account to the retailer's. Compare CREDIT CARD.

debonair adj esp of a man: charming, elegant and well-mannered.

debouch vb, intr, technical of troops or a river, etc: to come out of a narrow place or opening into a wider or more open place. ○ **debouchment** n.

debrief vb to gather information from (a diplomat, astronaut, soldier, etc) after a battle, event, mission, etc. ○ **debriefing** n.

debris or **débris** /ˈdebriː/ n 1 what remains of something crushed, smashed, destroyed, etc. 2 rubbish. 3 small pieces of rock.

debt n 1 something owed. 2 the state of owing something. ♦ **in sb's debt** under an obligation to them.

debtor n someone owing money. Compare CREDITOR.

debug vb 1 to remove secret microphones from (a room, etc). 2 to remove faults in (a computer program).

debunk vb to show (a person's claims, good reputation, etc) to be false or unjustified.

debut or **début** /ˈdeɪbjuː/ n the first public appearance of a performer.

debutante or **débutante** /ˈdeɪbjʊtɒnt/ n a young woman making her first formal appearance as an adult in upper-class society, usu at a ball.

deca- or (before a vowel) **dec-** comb form, signifying ten: decagon • decalitre.

decade n 1 a period of 10 years. 2 a group or series of 10 things, etc.

decadence n 1 a falling to low standards in morals, art, etc. 2 the state of having low or immoral standards of behaviour, etc. ○ **decadent** adj. ○ **decadently** adv.

decaff or **decaf** colloq, adj decaffeinated. ➤ n decaffeinated coffee.

decaffeinate vb to remove all or part of the caffeine from (eg coffee). ○ **decaffeinated** adj.

decagon n, geom a polygon with 10 sides. ○ **decagonal** adj.

decahedron n a solid figure with 10 faces. ○ **decahedral** adj.

decamp vb, intr 1 to go away suddenly, esp secretly. 2 to break camp.

decant vb 1 to pour (wine, etc) from one container to another, leaving sediment behind. 2 to remove (people) from where they usu live to some other place.

decanter n an ornamental bottle with a stopper, used for decanted wine, sherry, etc.

decapitate vb to cut off the head of someone. ○ **decapitation** n.

decapod n, zool 1 a crustacean with 10 limbs. 2 a sea creature with 10 arms, eg a squid.

decarbonize or **-ise** or **decarburize** or **-ise** vb to remove carbon from (an internal-combustion engine).

decathlon n an athletic competition involving 10 events over two days. ○ **decathlete** n.

decay vb 1 tr & intr to make or become rotten, ruined, etc. 2 intr, physics of a radioactive substance: to break down into radioactive or non-radioactive ISOTOPEs. ➤ n 1 the natural breakdown of dead organic matter. 2 physics the breakdown of a radioactive substance into one or more ISOTOPEs. 3 a gradual decrease in health, power, quality, etc. 4 rotten matter in a tooth, etc.

decease n, formal, law death.

deceased adj, formal, law dead, esp recently dead.

deceit n 1 an act of deceiving or misleading. 2 dishonesty; willingness to deceive. ○ **deceitful** adj. ○ **deceitfully** adv. ○ **deceitfulness** n.

deceive vb 1 to mislead or lie to someone. 2 to convince (oneself) that something untrue is true.

decelerate vb, tr & intr to slow down, or make something slow down. ○ **deceleration** n.

December n the twelfth month of the year.

decennial adj 1 happening every 10 years. 2 consisting of 10 years.

decent adj 1 respectable; not vulgar or immoral. 2 kind, tolerant or likeable. 3 fairly good; adequate. ○ **decency** n (-ies) 1 decent behaviour or character. 2 (**decencies**) the generally accepted rules of respectable or moral behaviour. ○ **decently** adv.

decentralize or **-ise** vb, tr & intr to make or become less centralized. ○ **decentralist** or **decentralizer** n. ○ **decentralization** n.

deception n 1 deceiving or being deceived. 2

something which deceives. ○ **deceptive** adj. ○ **deceptiveness** n.

deci- pfx, denoting one-tenth: decilitre.

decibel n a unit equal to one-tenth of a BEL, used for comparing levels of power, esp sound.

decide vb 1 intr (sometimes **decide on** or **about sth**) to establish an intention or course of action regarding it. 2 (**decide to do sth**) to make up one's mind to do it. 3 to settle something, or make its final result certain. 4 to make someone decide in a certain way. 5 to make a formal judgement.

decided adj 1 clear and definite. 2 determined; showing no doubt. ○ **decidedly** adv.

decider n 1 someone or something that decides. 2 something that decides a result, eg a winning goal.

deciduous adj 1 bot shedding leaves once a year. Compare EVERGREEN. 2 biol shed after a period of growth, eg milk teeth.

decilitre n one-tenth of a litre.

decimal adj 1 based on the number 10 or powers of 10. 2 denoting a system of units related to each other by multiples of 10. ➤ n a decimal fraction.

decimal fraction n a fraction in which tenths, hundredths, etc are written in figures after a decimal point, eg $0.5 = \frac{5}{10}$ or $\frac{1}{2}$. Compare VULGAR FRACTION.

decimalize or **-ise** vb to convert (numbers, a currency, etc) to a decimal form. ○ **decimalization** n.

decimal point n the point which precedes the DECIMAL FRACTION.

decimal system n a system of units related by multiples of 10.

decimate vb to destroy a large part or number of something. ○ **decimation** n.

decimetre n one-tenth of a metre.

decipher vb 1 to translate (eg a message in code) into ordinary language. 2 to work out the meaning of something obscure or difficult to read. ○ **decipherable** adj. ○ **decipherment** n.

decision n 1 the act of deciding. 2 something decided. 3 the ability to make decisions and act on them firmly: act with decision in a crisis.

decisive adj 1 putting an end to doubt or dispute. 2 having or showing decision. ○ **decisively** adv. ○ **decisiveness** n.

deck[1] n 1 a platform forming a floor or covering across a ship. 2 a floor or platform in a bus, bridge, etc. 3 N Am a pack of playing-cards. 4 the part of a tape recorder, record player or computer which contains the mechanism for operation. ◆ **clear the decks** to clear away obstacles or deal with preliminary jobs in preparation for further activity.

deck[2] vb (usu **deck sth out**) to decorate or embellish it.

deck chair n a light folding chair made of wood and a length of heavy fabric.

decking n a wooden floor in a garden or the material used to make it.

deckle edge n the rough edge of handmade paper, or an imitation of this.

declaim vb 1 tr & intr to make (a speech) in an impressive and dramatic manner. 2 intr (usu **declaim against sth**) to protest about it loudly and passionately. ○ **declamation** n. ○ **declamatory** adj.

declare vb 1 to announce something publicly or formally. 2 to say something firmly or emphatically. 3 intr (often **declare for** or **against sth**) to state one's support or opposition regarding it. 4 to make known (goods on which duty must be paid, income on which tax should be paid, etc). 5 intr, cricket to end an innings voluntarily before 10 wickets have fallen. 6 tr & intr, cards to state or show that one is holding (certain cards). ○ **declaration** n. ○ **declaratory** adj.

declassify vb (-ies, -ied) to state that (an official document, etc) is no longer secret. ○ **declassification** n.

declension n, gram 1 in certain languages: any of various sets of forms taken by nouns, adjectives or pronouns to indicate case, number and gender. 2 the act of stating these forms.

declination n 1 technical the angle between TRUE NORTH and MAGNETIC NORTH. 2 astron the angular distance of a star or planet north or south of the celestial equator.

decline vb 1 to refuse (an invitation, etc), esp politely. 2 intr to become less, less strong, less healthy or less good. 3 gram to state the DECLENSION of (a word). ➤ n a lessening of strength, health, quality, quantity, etc.

declivity n (-ies) formal a downward slope. ○ **declivitous** adj.

declutch vb, intr to release the clutch of (a motor vehicle).

decoct vb to extract the essence, etc of (a substance) by boiling. ○ **decoction** n.

decode vb to translate (a coded message) into ordinary language. ○ **decoder** n.

decoke vb, colloq to DECARBONIZE.

décolletage /deɪkɒlˈtɑːʒ/ n 1 a low-cut neckline on a woman's dress, etc. 2 the resulting exposure of the neck and shoulders.

décolleté or **décolletée** /deɪˈkɒlət eɪ/ adj 1 of a dress, etc: low-cut. 2 of a woman: wearing such a dress, etc.

decommission vb to take (eg a warship or atomic reactor) out of use or operation.

decompose vb 1 intr of a dead organism: to rot. 2 tr & intr, technical to separate or break down into smaller or simpler elements. ○ **decomposition** n.

decompress vb, technical to decrease or stop the pressure on something. ○ **decompression** n. ○ **decompressor** n.

decompression sickness n a disorder suffered by a person who has been breathing air under high pressure returning too quickly to normal atmospheric pressure.

decongestant med, n a drug which reduces nasal congestion. ➤ adj relieving congestion.

decontaminate vb to remove poisons, radio-activity, etc from something. ○ **decontamination** n.

décor /'deɪkɔː(r)/ n **1** the style of decoration, furnishings, etc in a room or house. **2** a theatre set.

decorate vb **1** to beautify something with ornaments, etc. **2** to put paint or wallpaper on (a wall, etc). **3** to give a medal to someone as a mark of honour. ○ **decorative** adj. ○ **decorator** n.

decoration n **1** something used to decorate. **2** the act of decorating. **3** the state of being decorated. **4** a medal given as a mark of honour.

decorous adj socially correct or acceptable; showing proper respect. ○ **decorously** adv.

decorum /dɪ'kɔːrəm/ n correct or socially acceptable behaviour.

decoy vb to lead or lure into a trap. ➢ n someone or something used to lure (a person or animal) into a trap.

decrease vb /dɪ'kriːs/ tr & intr to make or become less. ➢ n /'diːkriːs/ a lessening or loss. ○ **decreasingly** adv.

decree n **1** a formal order or ruling. **2** law a ruling made in a law court. ➢ vb (**decreed, decreeing**) to order or decide something formally or officially.

decree absolute n, law a decree in divorce proceedings which officially ends a marriage.

decree nisi /'naɪsaɪ/ n, law a decree of divorce which will become a DECREE ABSOLUTE after a period of time unless some reason is shown why it should not.

decrepit adj **1** weak or worn out because of old age. **2** in a very poor state because of age or long use. ○ **decrepitude** n.

decretal n a papal decree.

decriminalize or **-ise** vb, law to make (something) no longer a criminal offence. ○ **decriminalization** n.

decry vb (**-ies, -ied**) to criticize or express disapproval of someone or something.

dedicate vb (usu **dedicate oneself** or **sth to sb** or **sth**) **1** to give or devote (oneself or one's time, money, etc) to some purpose, cause, etc. **2** to devote or address (a book, piece of music, etc) to someone as a token of affection or respect. **3** to set something apart for some sacred purpose.

dedicated adj **1** committing a great deal of time and effort to something. **2** committed to a cause, etc. **3** assigned to a particular purpose: *a dedicated phone line*. **4** technical of a computer: designed to carry out one function.

dedication n **1** the quality of being dedicated. **2** the act of dedicating. **3** the words dedicating a book, etc to someone.

deduce vb to think out or judge on the basis of what one knows or assumes to be fact. ○ **deducible** adj.

deduct vb to take away (a number, amount, etc). ○ **deductible** adj.

deduction n **1** the act or process of deducting

or deducing. **2** something, esp money, which has been or will be deducted. **3** something that has been deduced. Compare INDUCTION (sense 5). ○ **deductive** adj.

deed n **1** something done. **2** a brave action or notable achievement. **3** law a signed statement recording an agreement, esp about a change in ownership of property.

deed poll n, law a deed made and signed by one person only, esp when changing their name.

deejay n, colloq a DISC JOCKEY.

deem vb, formal, old use to judge, think or consider.

deep adj **1** far down from the top or surface; with a relatively great distance from the top or surface to the bottom. **2** far in from the outside surface or edge. **3** usu in compounds far down by a specified amount: *knee-deep in mud*. **4** in a specified number of rows or layers: *lined up four deep*. **5** coming from or going far down; long and full: *a deep sigh*. **6** very great: *deep trouble*. **7** of a colour: strong and relatively dark. **8** low in pitch: *deep-toned*. **9** of emotions, etc: strongly felt. **10** obscure; hard to understand: *deep thoughts*. **11** of a person: mysterious; keeping secret thoughts. **12** cricket not close to the wickets. **13** football well behind one's team's front line of players. ➢ adv **1** deeply. **2** far down or into. **3** late on in or well into (a period of time). ➢ n **1** (**the deep**) the ocean. **2** (also **deeps**) old use a place far below the surface of the ground or the sea. ○ **deeply** adv very greatly. ○ **deepness** n. ♦ **deep in sth** fully occupied or involved with it: *deep in thought*. **go off (at) the deep end** colloq to lose one's temper suddenly and violently. **in deep water** colloq in trouble or difficulties.

deepen vb, tr & intr to make or become deeper, greater, more intense, etc.

deep-freeze n a refrigeration unit, or a compartment in a refrigerator, designed for storing perishables below −18°C (0°F). ➢ vb to preserve perishable material, esp food, by storing it in a frozen state.

deep-fry vb to fry something by completely submerging it in hot fat or oil.

deep-laid adj secretly plotted or devised.

deep-rooted or **deep-seated** adj of ideas, habits, etc: deeply and firmly established.

deer n (pl **deer**) a RUMINANT mammal, the male of which has antlers.

deerstalker n a hat with peaks at the front and back and flaps at the side that can cover the ears.

deface vb to deliberately spoil the appearance of something (eg by marking or cutting). ○ **defacement** n.

de facto adj, adv actual or actually, though not necessarily legally so. Compare DE JURE.

defame vb to attack the good reputation of someone. ○ **defamation** n. ○ **defamatory** adj.

default vb, intr **1** (usu **default on sth**) to fail to do what one should do, esp to fail to pay what is due. **2** *law* to fail to appear in court when called upon. ➢ *n* **1** a failure to do or pay what one should. **2** *comput* a preset option which will always be followed unless the operator enters a command to the contrary. ○ **defaulter** *n*. ◆ **by default** because of someone's failure to do something. **in default of sth** in the absence of it.

defeat *vb* **1** to beat someone, eg in a war, competition, game or argument. **2** to make (plans, etc) fail. ➢ *n* defeating or being defeated.

defeatism *n* a state of mind in which one too readily expects or accepts defeat or failure. ○ **defeatist** *adj, n*.

defecate *vb* to empty the bowels of waste matter. ○ **defecation** *n*.

defect *n* /ˈdiːfɛkt/ a flaw or fault. ➢ *vb* / dɪˈfɛkt/ *intr* to leave one's country, political party, etc, esp to go to or join an opposing one. ○ **defection** *n*. ○ **defector** *n*.

defective *adj* having a defect or defects. ○ **defectively** *adv*. ○ **defectiveness** *n*.

> **defective** A word often confused with this one is **deficient**.

defence or (*US*) **defense** *n* **1** the act of defending against attack. **2** the method or equipment used to protect against attack or when attacked. **3** the armed forces of a country. **4** (**defences**) fortifications. **5** a person's answer to an accusation, justifying or denying what they have been accused of. **6** (**the defence**) *law* in a court: the person or people on trial and the lawyer or lawyers acting for them. **7** (**the defence**) *sport* the players in a team whose main task is to prevent their opponents from scoring. ○ **defenceless** *adj*.

defend *vb* **1** to guard or protect someone or something against attack or when attacked. **2** to explain, justify or argue in support of the actions of someone accused of doing wrong. **3** to be the lawyer acting on behalf of (the accused) in a trial. **4** *tr & intr, sport* to try to prevent one's opponents from scoring. **5** *sport* to take part in a contest against a challenger for (a title, etc one holds). ○ **defender** *n*.

defendant *n* someone against whom a charge is brought in a law-court.

defensible *adj* able to be defended or justified. ○ **defensibility** *n*.

defensive *adj* **1** defending or ready to defend. **2** attempting to justify one's actions when criticized or when expecting criticism. ○ **defensively** *adv*. ○ **defensiveness** *n*. ◆ **on the defensive** defending oneself or prepared to defend oneself against attack or criticism.

defer[1] *vb* (**deferred, deferring**) to put off something until a later time. ○ **deferment** or **deferral** *n*.

defer[2] *vb* (**deferred, deferring**) *intr* (*usu* **defer to sb**, *etc*) to yield to their wishes, opinions or orders.

deference *n* **1** willingness to consider or respect the wishes, etc of others. **2** the act of de-

ferring. ○ **deferential** *adj*. ○ **deferentially** *adv*.

defiance *n* open disobedience or opposition. ○ **defiant** *adj*. ○ **defiantly** *adv*.

deficiency *n* (*-ies*) **1** a shortage or lack in quality or amount. **2** the thing or amount lacking.

deficient *adj* not good enough; not having all that is needed.

> **deficient** A word often confused with this one is **defective**.

deficit *n* the difference between what is required and what is available.

defile[1] *vb* **1** to make something dirty or polluted. **2** to take away or spoil the goodness, purity, holiness, etc of something. ○ **defilement** *n*.

defile[2] *n* a narrow valley or passage between mountains. ➢ *vb, intr* to march in file.

define *vb* **1** to fix or state the exact meaning of (a word, etc). **2** to fix, describe or explain (opinions, duties, the qualities or limits of something, etc). **3** to make clear the outline or shape of something. ○ **definable** *adj*.

definite *adj* **1** fixed or firm; not liable to change. **2** sure. **3** clear and precise. **4** having clear outlines. ○ **definitely** *adv* **1** as a definite fact; certainly. **2** in a definite way.

definite article *n, gram* the word THE, or any equivalent word in other languages. Compare INDEFINITE ARTICLE.

definition *n* **1** a statement of the meaning of a word or phrase. **2** the act of defining a word or phrase. **3** the quality of having clear precise limits or form. **4** clearness and preciseness of limits or form.

definitive *adj* **1** settling a matter once and for all. **2** complete and authoritative. ○ **definitively** *adv*.

deflate *vb* **1** *tr & intr* to collapse or grow smaller by letting out gas. **2** to reduce or take away the hopes, excitement, etc of someone. **3** *tr & intr, econ* to undergo or make something undergo DEFLATION. Compare INFLATE (sense 2), REFLATE.

deflation *n* **1** deflating or being deflated. **2** the state of feeling deflated. **3** *econ* a reduction in the amount of available money in a country, lowering economic activity, industrial output, employment and wage rises. ○ **deflationary** *adj*.

deflect *vb, tr & intr* to turn aside from the correct or intended course. ○ **deflection** *n*. ○ **deflector** *n*.

deflower *vb, literary* to take away someone's virginity.

defoliant *n, technical* a herbicide that makes the leaves of plants fall off. ○ **defoliate** *vb*. ○ **defoliation** *n*.

deforest *vb, agric* to clear forested land. ○ **deforestation** *n*.

deform *vb* to change the shape of something, making it look ugly, unnatural or spoiled. ○ **deformed** *adj*.

deformity n (-*ies*) 1 being deformed or misshapen. 2 disfigurement; an ugly feature.

defraud vb (*usu* defraud sb of sth) to dishonestly prevent someone getting or keeping something which belongs to them or to which they have a right.

defray vb, *formal* to provide the money to pay (someone's costs or expenses). ○ **defrayal** or **defrayment** n.

defrock vb to remove (a priest) from office.

defrost vb, tr & intr 1 to remove ice from something. 2 to thaw.

deft adj skilful, quick and neat. ○ **deftly** adv. ○ **deftness** n.

defunct adj no longer living, existing, active, usable or in use.

defuse vb 1 to remove the fuse from (a bomb, etc). 2 to make (a situation, etc) harmless or less dangerous.

defy vb (-*ies*, -*ied*) 1 to resist or disobey someone boldly and openly. 2 to dare or challenge someone. 3 *formal* to make something impossible or unsuccessful: *defying explanation*.

degenerate adj /dɪˈdʒɛnərət/ physically, morally or intellectually worse than before. ➤ n /-rət/ a degenerate person or animal. ➤ vb /-reɪt/ intr to become degenerate. ○ **degeneracy** n. ○ **degeneration** n. ○ **degenerative** adj.

degrade vb 1 to disgrace or humiliate someone. 2 to reduce someone or something in rank, status, etc. 3 tr & intr, *chem* to change or be converted into a substance with a simpler structure. ○ **degradable** adj. ○ **degradation** n. ○ **degrading** adj humiliating; debasing.

degree n 1 an amount or extent. 2 *physics* (symbol °) a unit of temperature. 3 *geom* (symbol °) a unit by which angles are measured, equal to $\frac{1}{360}$ of a circle. 4 an award given by a university or college. 5 a comparative amount of severity or seriousness. ◆ **by degrees** gradually.

dehumanize or -**ise** vb to remove the human qualities from someone. ○ **dehumanization** n.

dehydrate vb 1 to remove water from (a substance or organism). 2 tr & intr to lose or make someone or something lose too much water from the body. ○ **dehydrated** adj. ○ **dehydration** n.

de-ice vb to make or keep something free of ice. ○ **de-icer** n.

deify /ˈdeɪfaɪ/ vb (-*ies*, -*ied*) to regard or worship someone or something as a god. ○ **deification** n.

deign /deɪn/ vb, intr to do something in a way that shows that one considers the matter unimportant or beneath one's dignity.

deindustrialize or -**ise** vb to reduce the industrial organization and potential of a nation, area, etc. ○ **deindustrialization** n.

deism /ˈdeɪzəm, ˈdiː-/ n belief in the existence of God without acceptance of any religion or message revealed by God to man. ○ **deist** n. ○ **deistic** or **deistical** adj.

deity /ˈdeɪtɪ, ˈdiː-/ n (-*ies*) *formal* 1 a god or goddess. 2 the state of being divine. 3 (**the Deity**) God.

déjà vu /deɪʒà ˈvuː/ n the feeling that one has experienced something before although one is actually experiencing it for the first time.

dejected adj miserable. ○ **dejectedly** adv. ○ **dejection** n.

de jure /diː ˈdʒʊərɪ/ adv, adj, *law* according to law; by right. Compare DE FACTO.

dekko or **decko** n (*usu* have or take a dekko) *slang* a look.

delay vb 1 to slow someone or something down or make them late. 2 to put off to a later time. 3 intr to be slow in doing something. ➤ n 1 delaying or being delayed. 2 the amount of time by which someone or something is delayed.

delectable adj delightful; delicious. ○ **delectably** adv.

delectation n, *formal* delight, enjoyment or amusement.

delegate vb /ˈdɛlɪgeɪt/ 1 to give (part of one's work, power, etc) to someone else. 2 to send or name someone as a representative, as the one to do a job, etc. ➤ n /ˈdɛlɪgət/ someone chosen to represent others, eg at a meeting.

delegation n 1 a group of delegates. 2 delegating or being delegated.

delete vb to rub out, score out or remove something, esp from something written or printed. ○ **deletion** n.

deleterious /dɛlɪˈtɪərɪəs/ adj, *formal* harmful or destructive.

deli n a DELICATESSEN.

deliberate adj /dɪˈlɪbərət/ 1 done on purpose. 2 slow and careful. ➤ vb /dɪˈlɪbəreɪt/ tr & intr to think about something carefully. ○ **deliberately** adv.

deliberation n 1 careful thought. 2 (**deliberations**) formal and thorough thought and discussion. 3 slowness and carefulness.

delicacy n (-*ies*) 1 the state or quality of being delicate. 2 something considered particularly delicious to eat.

delicate adj 1 easily damaged or broken. 2 not strong or healthy. 3 having fine texture or workmanship. 4 small and attractive. 5 small, neat and careful: *delicate movements*. 6 requiring tact and careful handling: *a delicate situation*. 7 careful not to offend others. 8 of colours, flavours, etc: light; not strong. ○ **delicately** adv. ○ **delicateness** n.

delicatessen n a shop or counter selling eg cheeses, cooked meats, and unusual or imported foods.

delicious adj 1 with a very pleasing taste or smell. 2 giving great pleasure. ○ **deliciously** adv.

delight vb 1 to please greatly. 2 intr (**delight in sth**) to take great pleasure from it. ➤ n 1 great pleasure. 2 something or someone that gives great pleasure. ○ **delighted** adj. ○ **delightedly** adv. ○ **delightful** adj.

delimit vb to mark or fix the limits of (powers, etc). ○ **delimitation** n.

delineate *vb* 1 to show something by drawing. 2 to describe something in words. ○ **delineation** *n*.

delinquent *n* someone, esp a young person, guilty of a minor crime. ➤ *adj* guilty of a minor crime or misdeed. ○ **delinquency** *n* (*-ies*) 1 minor crime, esp committed by young people. 2 delinquent nature or behaviour.

deliquesce *vb, intr, chem* esp of salts: to dissolve slowly in water absorbed from the air. ○ **deliquescence** *n*. ○ **deliquescent** *adj*.

delirious *adj* 1 affected by DELIRIUM. 2 very excited or happy. ○ **deliriously** *adv*.

delirium *n* 1 a state of madness or mental confusion and excitement, often caused by fever, drugs, etc. 2 extreme excitement or joy.

delirium tremens /ˈtrɛmɛnz/ *n* delirium caused by chronic alcoholism.

deliver *vb* 1 to carry (goods, letters, etc) to a person or place. 2 to give or make (a speech, etc). 3 to help (a woman) at the birth of (a child). 4 *tr & intr, colloq* to keep or fulfil (a promise or undertaking). 5 *formal* to aim or direct (a blow, criticism, etc). ◆ **deliver the goods** *colloq* to fulfil a promise or undertaking.

deliverance *n, formal* the act of rescuing, freeing or saving from danger or harm.

delivery *n* (*-ies*) 1 the carrying of (goods, letters, etc) to a person or place. 2 the thing or things being delivered. 3 the process or manner of giving birth to a child. 4 the act or manner of making a speech, etc. 5 the act or manner of throwing a ball.

dell *n* a small valley or hollow, usu wooded.

delphinium *n* (*delphiniums* or *delphinia* /dɛlˈfɪnɪə/) a garden plant with tall spikes of usu blue flowers.

delta *n* 1 the fourth letter of the Greek alphabet. 2 an area of silt, sand, gravel or clay, often roughly triangular, at a river mouth.

delude *vb* to deceive or mislead someone.

deluge /ˈdɛljuːdʒ/ *n* 1 a flood. 2 a downpour of rain. 3 a great quantity of anything pouring in. ➤ *vb, formal* to flood; to cover in water.

delusion *n* 1 the act of deluding or the state of being deluded. 2 *psychol* a false or mistaken belief. ○ **delusive** and **delusory** *adj*.

de luxe or **deluxe** *adj* 1 very luxurious or elegant. 2 with special features or qualities.

delve *vb, intr* 1 (*usu* **delve into sth**) to search it for information. 2 (*usu* **delve through sth**) to search through it.

demagnetize or **-ise** *vb* to remove the magnetic properties of something. ○ **demagnetization** *n*.

demagogue *n, derog* someone who tries to win power or support by appealing to people's emotions and prejudices. ○ **demagogic** *adj*. ○ **demagoguery** or **demagogy** *n*.

demand *vb* 1 to ask or ask for firmly, forcefully or urgently. 2 to require or need something. 3 to claim something as a right. ➤ *n* 1 a forceful request or order. 2 an urgent claim for action or attention: *demands on one's time*. 3 people's de-

sire or ability to buy or obtain goods, etc. 4 *econ* the amount of any article, commodity, etc which consumers will buy. Compare SUPPLY (*noun* sense 6). ◆ **in demand** popular; frequently asked for. **on demand** when asked for.

demanding *adj* 1 requiring a lot of effort, ability, etc. 2 needing or expecting a lot of attention.

demarcation *n* 1 the marking out of limits or boundaries. 2 the strict separation of the areas or types of work to be done by the members of the various trade unions in a factory, etc. ○ **demarcate** *vb*.

demean *vb* to lower the dignity of or lessen respect for (esp oneself).

demeanour or (*US*) **demeanor** *n* way of behaving.

demented *adj* mad. ○ **dementedly** *adv*.

dementia /dɪˈmɛnʃə/ *n, psychol* a loss or severe lessening of normal mental ability and functioning, esp in the elderly.

demerara or **demerara sugar** *n* a form of crystallized brown sugar.

demerit *n, formal* a fault or failing.

demi- *comb form, signifying* half or partly: *demigod*.

demigod or **demigoddess** *n* 1 *myth* someone part human and part god; a lesser god. 2 a person idolized as if they were a god.

demijohn *n* a large bottle with a short narrow neck and one or two small handles, used for storing eg wine.

demilitarize or **-ise** *vb* to remove armed forces from (an area) and/or not allow any military activity in it. ○ **demilitarization** *n*.

demi-monde *n* 1 women in an unrespectable social position. 2 any group considered not completely respectable.

demise *n* 1 *formal or euphem* death. 2 a failure or end.

demisemiquaver *n, mus* a note equal in time to half a SEMIQUAVER.

demist /diːˈmɪst/ *vb* to free (a vehicle's windscreen, etc) from condensation by blowing warm air over it. ○ **demister** *n*.

demo *n, colloq* 1 a public demonstration of opinion on a political or moral issue. 2 (*also* **demo tape**) a recording made usu by unsigned musicians to demonstrate their music to record companies.

demob *vb, Brit colloq* (*demobbed, demobbing*) to DEMOBILIZE.

demobilize or **-ise** *vb* to release someone from service in the armed forces, eg after a war. ○ **demobilization** *n*.

democracy *n* (*-ies*) 1 a form of government in which the people govern themselves or elect representatives to govern them. 2 a country, state or other body with such a form of government.

democrat *n* 1 someone who believes in DEMOCRACY. 2 (**Democrat**) a member or supporter of any political party with *Democratic* in its title. Compare REPUBLICAN.

democratic adj 1 concerned with or following the principles of democracy. 2 believing in or providing equal rights and privileges for all. 3 (**Democratic**) belonging or relating to the US Democratic Party. Compare REPUBLICAN. ○ **democratically** adv.

demodulation n, electronics the inverse of MODULATION, a process by which an output wave is obtained that has the characteristics of the original modulating wave.

demography n, technical the scientific study of population statistics. ○ **demographer** n. ○ **demographic** adj.

demolish vb 1 to pull down (a building, etc). 2 to destroy (an argument, etc). 3 facetious to eat up. ○ **demolition** n.

demon n 1 an evil spirit. 2 a cruel or evil person. 3 someone who has great energy, enthusiasm or skill: a demon at football. 4 a DAEMON. ○ **demonic** adj.

demoniac /dɪ'məʊnɪak/ or **demoniacal** /diːmə'naɪəkəl/ adj 1 of or like a demon or demons. 2 influenced by demons; frenzied or very energetic.

demonstrate vb 1 to show or prove something by reasoning or evidence. 2 tr & intr to show how something is done, operates, etc. 3 tr & intr to show (support, opposition, etc) by protesting, marching, etc in public. ○ **demonstrable** adj. ○ **demonstrably** adv. ○ **demonstration** n.

demonstrative adj 1 showing one's feelings openly. 2 (usu **demonstrative of sth**) showing evidence of it; proving it to be so. ○ **demonstratively** adv.

demonstrator n 1 someone who demonstrates equipment, etc. 2 someone who takes part in a public demonstration.

demoralize or **-ise** vb to take away the confidence, courage or enthusiasm of someone. ○ **demoralization** n.

demote vb to reduce someone to a lower rank or grade. ○ **demotion** n.

demotic adj of a language: popular, everyday. ➤ n colloquial language.

demur vb (**demurred, demurring**) intr to object or show reluctance. ○ **demurral** n. ◆ **without demur** without objecting.

demure adj quiet, modest and well-behaved. ○ **demurely** adv. ○ **demureness** n.

demystify vb (**-ies, -ied**) to remove the mystery from something. ○ **demystification** n.

den n 1 a wild animal's home. 2 a centre (often secret) of illegal or immoral activity. 3 colloq a room or hut used as a place to work or play.

denarius /dɪ'nɛərɪəs/ n (**denarii** /-rɪaɪ, -riː/) an ancient Roman silver coin.

denary /'diːnərɪ/ adj decimal.

denationalize or **-ise** vb to transfer (an industry) to private ownership from state ownership. ○ **denationalization** n.

denature or **denaturize** or **-ise** vb 1 to change the structure or composition of (something). 2 to add an unpalatable substance to (alcohol),

so that it is unfit for human consumption.

dendrology n the scientific study of trees. ○ **dendrological** adj. ○ **dendrologist** n.

dengue /'dɛŋgeɪ/ n an acute tropical viral fever transmitted by mosquitos.

denial n 1 denying something; declaring something not to be true. 2 an act of refusing something to someone. 3 a refusal to acknowledge connections with somebody or something.

denier /'dɛnɪə(r)/ n the unit of weight of silk, rayon or nylon thread, usu used as a measure of the fineness of stockings or tights.

denigrate vb to attack or belittle someone's reputation, character or worth. ○ **denigration** n. ○ **denigrator** n.

denim n 1 a hard-wearing twilled cotton cloth. 2 (**denims**) clothing, esp jeans, made of denim. ➤ adj made of denim.

denizen n 1 formal an inhabitant. 2 biol a species of animal or plant which has become well established in a place to which it is not native.

denominate vb, formal to give a specific name or title to something.

denomination n 1 a religious group with its own beliefs, organization and practices. 2 a particular unit of value of a postage stamp, coin or banknote, etc. ○ **denominational** adj.

denominator n, maths in a VULGAR FRACTION, the number below the line. Compare NUMERATOR.

denote vb 1 to mean; to be the name of or sign for something. 2 to be a sign, mark or indication of something. ○ **denotation** n.

denouement or **dénouement** /deɪ'nuːmã/ n the final part of a story or plot, in which uncertainties, problems and mysteries are resolved.

denounce vb 1 to inform against or accuse someone publicly. 2 to condemn (an action, proposal, etc) strongly and openly.

dense adj 1 closely packed or crowded together. 2 thick: dense fog. 3 colloq stupid; slow to understand. ○ **densely** adv.

density n (**-ies**) 1 the state of being dense; the degree of denseness. 2 the ratio of the mass of a substance to its volume. 3 the number of items within a specific area or volume. 4 comput the number of bits that can be stored on one track of a disk or within a specific area of magnetic tape, etc.

dent n 1 a hollow made by pressure or a blow. 2 a noticeable, usu bad, effect; a lessening (eg of resources, money, etc). ➤ vb 1 to make a dent in something. 2 intr to become dented. 3 to injure (someone's pride, etc).

dental adj 1 concerned with the teeth or dentistry. 2 phonetics of a sound: produced by putting the tongue to the teeth. ➤ n, phonetics a dental sound.

dental floss n a soft thread used for cleaning between the teeth.

dental surgeon n a dentist.

dentate adj, technical with tooth-like notches round the edge.

dentifrice /'dɛntɪfrɪs/ n paste or powder for cleaning the teeth.

dentine or **dentin** n, anat the hard material that forms the bulk of a tooth.

dentist n someone who diagnoses, treats and prevents diseases of the oral cavity and teeth. ○ **dentistry** n.

dentition n, technical the number, arrangement and type of teeth in a human or animal.

denture n a false tooth or (usu **dentures**) set of false teeth.

denude vb 1 to make someone or something completely bare. 2 to strip (land) through weathering and erosion. ○ **denudation** n.

denunciation n a public condemnation or accusation.

deny vb (-ies, -ied) 1 to declare something not to be true. 2 to refuse to give or allow something to someone. 3 to refuse to acknowledge. ○ **deniable** adj. ♦ **deny oneself sth** to do without (something that one wants or needs).

deodorant n a substance that prevents or conceals unpleasant smells, esp on the human body.

deodorize or **-ise** vb to remove, conceal or absorb the unpleasant smell of something.

deoxyribonucleic acid /di:ˈɒksɪraɪbəʊnjuː-ˈkleɪk/ n, biochem the nucleic acid that forms the material that chromosomes and genes are composed of.

depart vb, intr 1 to leave. 2 (usu **depart from sth**) to stop following or decline to follow a planned or usual course of action. ○ **departed** adj, formal dead.

department n 1 a section of an organization. 2 a subject or activity which is someone's special skill or responsibility. ○ **departmental** adj.

department store n a large shop with many departments selling a wide variety of goods.

departure n 1 an act of going away or leaving. 2 (often **departure from sth**) a change from a planned or usual course of action. 3 (often **new departure**) a new and different activity.

depend vb, intr (usu **depend on** or **upon sb** or **sth**) 1 to trust or rely on them or it. 2 to rely on financial or other support from someone. 3 to be decided by or vary according to something else.

dependable adj trustworthy; reliable. ○ **dependability** n. ○ **dependably** adv.

dependant n a person who is kept or supported financially by another.

dependence n (usu **dependence on sth** or **sb**) 1 the state of being dependent on it or them. 2 trust and reliance.

dependency n (-ies) 1 a country governed or controlled by another. 2 excessive dependence on someone or something, eg addiction to a drug.

dependent adj (often **dependent on sth** or **sb**) 1 relying on it or them for financial or other support. 2 to be decided or influenced by them or it: Success is dependent on all our efforts.

depict vb 1 to paint or draw something. 2 to describe something. ○ **depiction** n.

depilate vb to remove hair from (a part of the body). ○ **depilation** n. ○ **depilatory** /dɪˈpɪl-ətərɪ/ n, adj.

deplete vb to reduce greatly in number, quantity, etc; to use up (money, resources, etc). ○ **depletion** n.

deplorable adj very bad, shocking or regrettable. ○ **deplorably** adv.

deplore vb to feel or express great disapproval of or regret for something.

deploy vb 1 tr & intr to position (troops) ready for battle. 2 to organize and bring (resources, arguments, etc) into use. ○ **deployment** n.

deponent n, law someone who makes a deposition (see DEPOSITION sense 3), esp under oath.

depopulate vb to greatly reduce the number of people living in (an area, country, etc). ○ **depopulation** n.

deport¹ vb to legally remove or expel (a person) from a country. ○ **deportation** n. ○ **deportee** n.

deport² vb, formal to behave (oneself) in a particular way. ○ **deportment** n 1 one's bearing. 2 behaviour.

depose vb to remove (someone) from a high office or powerful position.

deposit vb (**deposited, depositing**) 1 to put down or leave something. 2 to put (money, etc) in a bank, etc. 3 to give (money) as the first part of the payment for something. 4 to pay (money) as a guarantee against loss or damage. ➤ n 1 money, etc deposited in a bank, etc. 2 money given as part payment for something or as a guarantee against loss or damage. 3 solid matter that has settled at the bottom of a liquid, or is left behind by a liquid. 4 geol a layer (of coal, oil, minerals, etc) occurring naturally in rock. ○ **depositor** n.

deposit account n a bank account in which money gains interest but which cannot be used for money transfers by eg cheque or standing order.

depositary n (-ies) 1 formal a person, etc to whom something is given for safekeeping. 2 a DEPOSITORY (sense l).

deposition n 1 deposing or being deposed. 2 the act of depositing or process of being deposited. 3 law a written statement made under oath and used as evidence in a court of law.

depository n (-ies) 1 a place where anything may be left for safe-keeping, eg a furniture store. 2 a DEPOSITARY (sense l).

depot /'dɛpəʊ; N Am 'diːpəʊ/ n 1 a storehouse or warehouse. 2 a place where buses, trains and other vehicles are kept and repaired. 3 N Am a bus or railway station.

depraved adj morally corrupted. ○ **depravity** n.

deprecate vb to express or feel disapproval of something. ○ **deprecatingly** adv. ○ **deprecation** n. ○ **deprecatory** adj 1 showing or expressing disapproval. **2** apologetic; trying to avoid disapproval.

depreciate *vb* **1** *tr & intr* to fall, or make something fall, in value. **2** to belittle someone or something. ○ **depreciatory** *adj.*

depreciation *n* **1** *econ* a fall in value of a currency against the value of other currencies. **2** the reduction in the value of assets through use or age. **3** the process of depreciating.

depredation *n* (*often* **depredations**) damage, destruction or violent robbery.

depress *vb* **1** to make someone sad and gloomy. **2** *formal* to make (prices, etc) lower. **3** *formal* to press down. **4** to weaken something. ○ **depressing** *adj.* ○ **depressingly** *adv.*

depressant *adj, med* of a drug: able to reduce mental or physical activity. ➤ *n* a depressant drug.

depressed *adj* **1** sad and gloomy. **2** *psychol* suffering from depression. **3** of a region, etc: suffering from high unemployment and low standards of living. **4** of trade, etc: not flourishing.

depression *n* **1** *psychol* a mental state characterized by prolonged and disproportionate feelings of sadness, apathy, low self-esteem and despair. **2** a period of low business and industrial activity accompanied by a rise in unemployment. **3** (**the Depression**) the period of worldwide economic depression from 1929 to 1934. **4** *meteorol* a CYCLONE. **5** a hollow, esp in the ground.

depressive *adj* **1** depressing. **2** suffering from frequent bouts of depression. ➤ *n* someone who suffers from depression.

deprive *vb* (*usu* **deprive sb of sth**) to prevent them from having or using it. ○ **deprivation** *n.*

deprived *adj* **1** lacking money, reasonable living conditions, etc. **2** of a district, etc: lacking good housing, schools, medical facilities, etc.

dept *abbrev* department.

depth *n* **1** the distance from the top downwards, from the front to the back or from the surface inwards. **2** intensity or strength. **3** extensiveness: *the depth of one's knowledge*. **4** (*usu* **the depths**) somewhere far from the surface or edge of somewhere: *the depths of the ocean*. **5** (*usu* **the depths**) an extreme feeling (of despair, sadness, etc) or great degree (of deprivation, etc). **6** (*often* **the depths**) the middle and severest or most intense part (of winter, etc). **7** (**depths**) serious aspects of a person's character that are not immediately obvious. **8** of sound: lowness of pitch. ◆ **in depth** deeply and thoroughly. **out of one's depth 1** in water deeper than one's height. **2** not able to understand information or an explanation; in a situation too difficult to deal with.

depth charge *n* a bomb which explodes underwater.

deputation *n* a group of people appointed to represent and speak on behalf of others.

depute /dɪ'pjuːt/ *vb, formal* to formally appoint someone to do something.

deputize or **-ise** *vb, intr* (*often* **deputize for sb**) to act as their deputy.

deputy *n* (*-ies*) **1** a person appointed to act on behalf of, or as an assistant to, someone else. **2** in certain countries: a person elected to the lower house of parliament. ➤ *adj* in some organizations: next in rank to the head.

derail *vb, tr & intr* to leave or make (a train, etc) leave the rails. ○ **derailment** *n.*

derange *vb* **1** to make someone insane. **2** to disrupt or throw into disorder or confusion. ○ **deranged** *adj.* ○ **derangement** *n.*

derby[1] /'dɑːbɪ/ *n* (*-ies*) **1** (**the Derby**) a horse race held annually at Epsom Downs. **2** a race or a sports event, esp a contest between teams from the same area.

derby[2] /'dɜːbɪ/ *n* (*-ies*) *N Am* a bowler hat.

deregulate *vb* to remove controls and regulations from (a business or business activity). ○ **deregulation** *n.*

derelict *adj* **1** abandoned. **2** of a building: in ruins. ➤ *n* a tramp with no home or money.

dereliction *n* **1** (*usu* **dereliction of duty**) neglect or failure. **2** the state of being abandoned.

derestrict *vb* to remove a restriction from (something), esp a speed limit from (a road). ○ **derestriction** *n.*

deride *vb* to laugh at or make fun of someone. ○ **derision** *n.*

de rigueur /də rɪ'gɜː(r)/ *adj* required by fashion, custom or the rules of politeness.

derisive *adj* scornful. ○ **derisively** *adv.*

derisory *adj* ridiculous and insulting, esp ridiculously small.

derivation *n* **1** deriving or being derived. **2** the source or origin (esp of a word).

derivative *adj* not original; derived from or copying something else. ➤ *n* **1** something which is derived from something else. **2** *gram* a word formed by adding one or more AFFIXes to another word. **3** *chem* a compound, usu organic, that is made from another compound. **4** *maths* the result of differentiation in calculating the changes in one variable produced by changes in another. **5** *stock exchange* (**derivatives**) FUTURES and OPTIONS.

derive *vb* **1** *intr* (*usu* **derive from sth**) to have it as a source or origin. **2** (*usu* **derive sth from sth else**) to obtain or produce one thing from another.

dermatitis *n, med* inflammation of the skin in the absence of infection, eg eczema and psoriasis.

dermatology *n* the study of the skin and treatment of its diseases. ○ **dermatologist** *n.*

derogate *vb, intr* (**derogate from sth**) *formal* to make it appear inferior; to show one's low opinion of it. ○ **derogation** *n.*

derogatory /dɪ'rɒgətərɪ/ *adj* showing dislike, scorn or lack of respect. ○ **derogatorily** *adv.* ○ **derogatoriness** *n.*

derrick *n* **1** a type of crane with a movable arm. **2** a framework built over an oil-well, for raising and lowering the drill.

derring-do *n, old use, literary* daring deeds.

derv *n, Brit* diesel oil used as a fuel for road vehicles.

dervish *n* a Muslim ascetic, noted for performing spinning dances as a religious ritual.

desalinate *vb, technical* to remove salt from (esp seawater). ○ **desalination** and **desalinization** or **-isation** *n*.

descale *vb* to remove encrusted deposits from (a pipe, kettle, etc).

descant /'dɛskant/ *mus, n* a melody played or harmony sung above the main tune. ➤ *adj* of a musical instrument: having a higher pitch and register than others of the same type.

descend *vb* 1 *tr & intr* to move from a higher to a lower place or position. 2 *intr* to lead or slope downwards. 3 *intr (often* **descend on sb** or **sth**) to invade or attack them or it. ◆ **be descended from sb** to have them as an ancestor.

descendant *adj (also* **descendent**) descending. ➤ *n* a person or animal, etc that is the child, grandchild, etc of another.

descent *n* 1 the act or process of coming or going down. 2 a slope downwards. 3 family origins or ancestry; being descended from someone. 4 a sudden invasion or attack.

describe *vb* 1 to say what someone or something is like. 2 *technical, geom* to draw or form (eg a circle).

description *n* 1 the act of describing. 2 a statement of what someone or something is like. 3 *colloq* a sort, type or kind: *toys of every description*.

descriptive *adj* describing, esp describing vividly. ○ **descriptively** *adv*.

descry /dɪ'skraɪ/ *vb (-ies, -ied) formal* 1 to see or catch sight of something. 2 to see or discover by looking carefully.

desecrate *vb* to treat or use (a sacred object) or behave in (a holy place) in a way that shows a lack of respect. ○ **desecration** *n*.

desegregate *vb* to end segregation, esp racial segregation in (public places, schools, etc). ○ **desegregation** *n*.

deselect *vb* not to reselect (eg a sitting MP or councillor). ○ **deselection** *n*.

desensitize or **-ise** *vb* to make someone or something less sensitive to light, pain, suffering, etc. ○ **desensitization** *n*.

desert[1] *vb* 1 to leave or abandon (a place or person). 2 *intr* to leave (esp a branch of the armed forces) without permission. 3 to take away support from (a person, cause, etc). ○ **deserter** *n*. ○ **desertion** *n*.

> **desert**   There is often a spelling confusion between **desert** and **dessert**.

desert[2] *n* an area of land with little rainfall and scarce vegetation.

desertification *n* the process by which new desert is formed.

deserts *pl n (usu* **just deserts**) what one deserves, usu something bad.

deserve *vb* to have earned or be worthy of (a reward or punishment, etc). ○ **deservedly** /dɪ-'zɜːvɪdlɪ/ *adv*.

deserving *adj (usu* **deserving of sth**) worthy of being given support, a reward, etc. ○ **deservingly** *adv*.

desiccate *vb* 1 to dry or remove the moisture from something, esp from food in order to preserve it. 2 *intr* to dry up. ○ **desiccated** *adj*. ○ **desiccation** *n*.

design *vb* 1 to make a preparatory plan, drawing or model of something. 2 *formal* to plan, intend or develop something for a particular purpose. ➤ *n* 1 a plan, drawing or model showing how something is to be made. 2 the art or job of making such drawings, plans, etc. 3 the way in which something has been made. 4 a decorative picture, pattern, etc. 5 a plan, purpose or intention. ○ **designedly** /dɪ'zaɪnɪdlɪ/ *adv* intentionally. ○ **designing** *adj, derog* using cunning and deceit to achieve a purpose. ○ **designingly** *adv*. ◆ **have designs on sb** or **sth** to have plans to appropriate them or it.

designate *vb* /'dɛzɪgneɪt/ 1 to choose or specify someone or something for a purpose or duty. 2 to mark or indicate something. 3 to be a name or label for someone or something. ➤ *adj* /-nət/ *usu following its noun* appointed to some official position but not yet holding it: *editor designate*. ○ **designation** *n*.

designer *n* someone who makes plans, patterns, drawings, etc. ➤ *adj* 1 designed by and bearing the name of a famous fashion designer: *designer dresses*. 2 *colloq, sometimes derog* following current fashion: *designer stubble*.

designer drug *n, med* a drug designed to differ slightly from an illegal drug (and so not be illegal) yet have similar effects.

desirable *adj* 1 pleasing; worth having. 2 sexually attractive. ○ **desirability** *n*. ○ **desirably** *adv*.

desire *n* 1 a longing or wish. 2 strong sexual interest and attraction. ➤ *vb* 1 *formal* to want. 2 to feel sexual desire for someone.

desirous *adj, formal (usu* **desirous of sth**) wanting it keenly.

desist *vb, intr, formal (often* **desist from sth**) to stop.

desk *n* 1 a table, often with drawers, for sitting at while writing, etc. 2 a service counter in a public building. 3 a section of a newspaper, etc office with responsibility for a particular subject: *news desk*.

deskilling *n* the process of removing the element of human skill from a job, process, etc through automation, computerization, etc.

desktop *adj* small enough to fit on the top of a desk. ➤ *n* a desktop computer.

desktop publishing *n* the preparation and production of typeset material using a desktop computer and printer.

desolate *adj* /'dɛsələt/ 1 barren and lonely. 2 very sad. 3 lacking pleasure or comfort: *a des-*

olate life. **4** lonely; alone. ➢ *vb* /-leɪt/ **1** to overwhelm someone with sadness or grief. **2** to lay waste (an area). ○ **desolately** *adv*. ○ **desolation** *n*.

despair *vb, intr* (*often* despair of sth *or* despair of doing sth) to lose or lack hope. ➢ *n* the state of having lost hope.

despatch see DISPATCH

desperado *n* (*desperados* or *desperadoes*) a bandit or outlaw.

desperate *adj* **1** extremely anxious, fearful or despairing. **2** willing to take risks because of hopelessness and despair. **3** very serious, difficult, dangerous and almost hopeless: *a desperate situation*. **4** dangerous and likely to be violent: *a desperate criminal*. **5** extreme and carried out as a last resort: *desperate measures*. **6** very great: *desperate need*. **7** extremely anxious or eager: *desperate to go to the concert*. ○ **desperately** *adv*. ○ **desperation** *n*.

despicable *adj* contemptible. ○ **despicably** *adv*.

despise *vb* to scorn or have contempt for someone or something.

despite *prep* in spite of.

despoil *vb, formal, literary* to steal everything valuable from (a place). ○ **despoliation** *n*.

despondent *adj* sad; dejected. ○ **despondency** *n*. ○ **despondently** *adv*.

despot *n* someone who has great or total power, esp if cruel or oppressive. ○ **despotic** *adj*. ○ **despotically** *adv*.

despotism *n* complete or absolute power.

dessert *n* a sweet food served after the main course of a meal.

dessert There is often a spelling confusion between **dessert** and **desert**.

dessertspoon *n* **1** a spoon about twice the size of a TEASPOON. **2** the amount a dessertspoon will hold.

destabilize or **-ise** *vb* to make (a country, an economy, etc) less stable. ○ **destabilization** *n*.

destination *n* the place to which someone or something is going.

destine *vb, formal* (*usu* be destined for sth *or* to do sth) to have it as one's fate.

destiny *n* (*-ies*) **1** the purpose or future as arranged by fate or God. **2** (*also* Destiny) fate.

destitute *adj* extremely poor. ○ **destitution** *n*.

destroy *vb* **1** to break something into pieces, completely ruin it, etc. **2** to put an end to something. **3** to defeat someone totally. **4** to ruin the reputation, health, financial position, etc of someone. **5** to kill (a dangerous, injured or unwanted animal).

destroyer *n* **1** someone or something that destroys. **2** a type of small fast warship.

destruction *n* **1** the act or process of destroying or being destroyed. **2** something that destroys. ○ **destructible** *adj*.

destructive *adj* **1** causing destruction or serious damage. **2** of criticism, etc: pointing out

faults, etc without suggesting improvements. ○ **destructively** *adv*.

desuetude /dɪˈsjuːɪtʃuːd/ *n* disuse; discontinuance.

desultory /ˈdɛzəltərɪ/ *adj* jumping from one thing to another with no plan, purpose or logical connection. ○ **desultorily** *adv*.

detach *vb* **1** *tr & intr* to unfasten or separate. **2** *mil* to select and separate (soldiers, etc) from a larger group, esp for a special task. ○ **detachable** *adj*.

detached *adj* **1** of a building: not joined to another on either side. **2** feeling no emotional involvement; showing no prejudice. ○ **detachedly** *adv*.

detachment *n* **1** the state of being emotionally detached or free from prejudice. **2** a group (eg of soldiers) detached for a purpose. **3** detaching or being detached.

detail *n* **1** a small feature, fact or item. **2** something considered unimportant. **3** all the small features and parts of something: *an eye for detail*. **4** a part of a painting, map, etc considered separately. **5** *mil* a group of eg soldiers given a special task. ➢ *vb* **1** to describe or list fully. **2** to appoint someone to do a particular task. ○ **detailed** *adj* **1** of a list, etc: itemized. **2** of a story, picture, etc: intricate. ♦ **in detail** giving or looking at all the details.

detain *vb* **1** to delay someone or something. **2** of the police, etc: to keep someone in a cell, prison, etc. ○ **detainee** *n*. ○ **detainment** *n*.

detect *vb* **1** to see or notice. **2** to discover, and usu indicate, the presence or existence of (something). ○ **detectable** or **detectible** *adj*. ○ **detector** *n*.

detection *n* **1** detecting or being detected. **2** investigating and solving crime.

detective *n* a police officer whose job is to solve crime by observation and gathering evidence.

détente /deɪˈtɑːt/ *n* a lessening of tension, esp between countries.

detention *n* **1** the act of detaining or the state of being detained, esp in prison or police custody. **2** a punishment in which a pupil is kept at school after the other pupils have gone home.

deter *vb* (*deterred, deterring*) to discourage or prevent something, or someone from doing something, because of possible unpleasant consequences.

detergent *n* a soap-like cleansing agent. ➢ *adj* having the power to clean.

deteriorate *vb, intr* to grow worse. ○ **deterioration** *n*.

determinant *n* **1** a determining factor or circumstance. **2** *maths* in a square matrix of elements, the difference between the multiplied diagonal terms. ➢ *adj* determining.

determinate *adj* having definite fixed limits, etc.

determination *n* **1** firmness or strength of will, purpose or character. **2** the act of determining or process of being determined.

determine *vb* **1** to fix or settle the exact limits or nature of something. **2** to find out or reach a conclusion about something by gathering facts, making measurements, etc. **3** *tr & intr* to decide or make someone decide. **4** to be the main or controlling influence on someone or something.

determined *adj* **1** (**determined to do sth**) firmly intending to do it. **2** having or showing a strong will. ○ **determinedly** *adv*.

determiner *n, gram* a word that precedes a noun and limits its meaning in some way, eg A¹, THE, THIS, EVERY, SOME.

determinism *n, philos* the theory that whatever happens has to happen and could not be otherwise. ○ **determinist** *n*.

deterrent *n* something which deters, eg a weapon that deters attack. ➤ *adj* capable of deterring. ○ **deterrence** *n*.

detest *vb* to dislike someone or something intensely. ○ **detestable** *adj* hateful.

dethrone *vb* **1** to remove (a monarch) from the throne. **2** to remove someone from a position of power or authority. ○ **dethronement** *n*.

detonate *vb, tr & intr* to explode or make something explode. ○ **detonation** *n*.

detonator *n* an explosive substance or a device used to make a bomb, etc explode.

detour *n* a route away from and longer than a planned or more direct route. ➤ *vb, intr* to make a detour.

detoxify *vb* (**-ies, -ied**) **1** to remove poison, drugs or harmful substances from (a person, etc). **2** to treat (a patient) for alcoholism or drug addiction. Often shortened to **detox**. ○ **detoxification** *n*.

detract *vb, intr* (*chiefly* **detract from sth**) to take away from it or lessen it. ○ **detraction** *n*. ○ **detractor** *n*.

detriment *n* harm or loss. ○ **detrimental** *adj* harmful; damaging. ○ **detrimentally** *adv*.

detritus /dɪˈtraɪtəs/ *n* bits of rubbish left over from something.

deuce /djuːs/ *n* **1** *tennis* a score of forty points each in a game or five games each in a match. **2** a card, dice throw, etc, of the value two.

deus ex machina /ˈdiːəs ɛks məˈʃiːnə, ˈdeɪʊs ɛks ˈmakɪnə/ *n* in literature: someone or something providing a contrived solution to a difficulty.

deuterium *n, chem* one of the three isotopes of hydrogen.

devalue or **devaluate** *vb* **1** *tr & intr* to reduce the value of (a currency) in relation to the values of other currencies. **2** to make (a person, action, etc) seem less valuable or important. ○ **devaluation** *n*.

devastate *vb* **1** to cause great destruction in or to something. **2** to overwhelm someone with grief or shock. ○ **devastated** *adj*. ○ **devastating** *adj*. ○ **devastation** *n*.

develop *vb* (**developed, developing**) **1** *tr & intr* to make or become more mature, advanced, detailed, etc. **2** to change to a more complex structure. **3** to begin to have, or to have more

of, something: *develop an interest in politics*. **4** *tr & intr* to appear and grow; to have or suffer from something which has appeared and grown: *She was developing a cold*. **5** to convert an invisible image on (exposed photographic film or paper) into a visible image. **6** to bring into fuller use (the natural resources, etc of a country or region). **7** to build on (land) or prepare (land) for being built on.

developer *n* **1** a chemical used to develop film. **2** someone who builds on land or improves and increases the value of buildings.

developing country *n, econ* a country with a low level of economic development which is trying to industrialize.

development *n* **1** the act of developing or the process of being developed. **2** a new stage, event or situation. **3** a result or consequence. **4** land which has been or is being developed, or the buildings built or being built on it. ○ **developmental** *adj*.

deviant *adj* not following the normal patterns, accepted standards, etc. ➤ *n* someone who behaves in a way not considered normal or acceptable, esp sexually. ○ **deviance** and **deviancy** *n*.

deviate /ˈdiːvɪeɪt/ *vb, intr* to move away from what is considered a correct or normal course, standard of behaviour, way of thinking, etc. ○ **deviation** *n*.

device *n* **1** a tool or instrument. **2** a plan or scheme, sometimes involving trickery or deceit. **3** *heraldry* a sign, pattern or symbol eg on a crest or shield. ◆ **be left to one's own devices** to be left alone and without help.

devil *n* **1** (**the Devil**) *relig* the most powerful evil spirit; Satan. **2** any evil spirit. **3** *colloq* a mischievous or bad person. **4** *colloq* a person: *lucky devil*. **5** someone or something difficult to deal with. **6** someone who excels at something. **7** (**the devil**) used for emphasis in mild oaths and exclamations: *What the devil is he doing?* ➤ *vb* (**devilled, devilling; US deviled, deviling**) **1** to prepare or cook (meat, etc) with a spicy seasoning. **2** *intr* to be a drudge. ◆ **between the devil and the deep blue sea** in a situation where the alternatives are equally undesirable. **speak** or **talk of the devil** said on the arrival of someone one has just been talking about.

devilish *adj* **1** characteristic of, like, or as if produced by a devil. **2** very wicked. ➤ *adv, old use* very.

devil-may-care *adj* cheerfully heedless of danger, etc.

devilment *n* mischievous fun.

devilry *n* (**-ies**) **1** mischievous fun. **2** wickedness or cruelty. **3** witchcraft.

devil's advocate *n* someone who argues for or against something simply to encourage discussion or argument.

devious *adj* **1** not totally open or honest. **2** cunning, often deceitfully. **3** not direct: *He came by a devious route*. ○ **deviously** *adv*.

devise *vb* to think up (a plan, etc).

devoid *adj* (*always* **devoid of sth**) free from it or lacking it.

devolution *n* the act of devolving, esp of giving certain powers to a regional government by a central government. ○ **devolutionary** *adj*. ○ **devolutionist** *n, adj*.

devolve *vb* (*usu* **devolve to** or **on** *upon sb*) **1** *tr & intr* of duties, power, etc: to be transferred or to transfer them to someone else. **2** *intr, law* to pass by succession.

Devonian *adj, geol* **1** relating to the fourth period of the PALAEOZOIC era. **2** relating to the rocks formed during this period.

devote *vb* to use or give up (eg time or money) to a purpose.

devoted *adj* **1** (*usu* **devoted to sb**) loving and loyal to them. **2** (*usu* **devoted to sth**) given up to it; totally occupied by it. ○ **devotedly** *adv*.

devotee /dɛvoʊˈtiː/ *n* **1** a keen follower or enthusiastic supporter. **2** a keen believer in a religion.

devotion *n* **1** great love or loyalty. **2** devoting or being devoted. **3** religious enthusiasm and piety. **4** (**devotions**) *relig* worship and prayers. ○ **devotional** *adj*.

devour *vb* **1** to eat up something greedily. **2** to completely destroy something. **3** to read (a book, etc) eagerly. **4** (*usu* **be devoured**) to be taken over totally: *devoured by guilt*.

devout *adj* **1** sincerely religious. **2** deeply felt; earnest. ○ **devoutly** *adv*.

dew *n* tiny droplets of water deposited on eg leaves close to the ground on cool clear nights. ○ **dewy** *adj* (*-ier, -iest*).

dewberry *n* (*-ies*) **1** a trailing type of BRAMBLE. **2** the fruit of this plant.

dewclaw *n* a small functionless toe or claw on the legs of some dogs and other animals.

dewlap *n* a flap of loose skin hanging down from the throat of certain animals.

dexter *adj, heraldry* on the side of the shield on the bearer's right-hand side. Compare SINISTER (sense 2).

dexterity *n* **1** skill in using one's hands. **2** quickness of mind.

dexterous or **dextrous** *adj* having, showing or done with dexterity. ○ **dexterously** or **dextrously** *adv*.

dextrin or **dextrine** *n, biochem* a substance produced during the breakdown of starch or glycogen, used as a thickener.

dextrose *n* a type of GLUCOSE.

dhal see DAL.

dharma /ˈdɑːmə/ *n* **1** *Buddhism* truth. **2** *Hinduism* the universal laws, esp the moral laws.

dhoti /ˈdoʊtɪ/ or **dhooti** /ˈduːtɪ/ *n* a long strip of cloth wrapped around the waist and between the legs, worn by some Hindu men.

di- *pfx* **1** two or double: *dicotyledon*. **2** *chem* containing two atoms of the same type: *dioxide*.

diabetes /daɪəˈbiːtiːz/ *n* a disorder characterized by thirst and excessive production of urine.

diabetic *n* someone suffering from diabetes. ➤ *adj* **1** relating to or suffering from diabetes. **2** for people who have diabetes.

diabolic *adj* **1** devilish. **2** very wicked or cruel.

diabolical *adj, Brit colloq* very shocking, annoying, bad, difficult, etc. ○ **diabolically** *adv*.

diabolism *n* satanism. ○ **diabolist** *n*.

diaconal *adj* relating to a deacon.

diaconate /daɪˈakəneɪt/ *n* **1** the position of deacon. **2** one's period of time as a deacon. **3** deacons as a group.

diacritic *n* a mark over, under or through a letter to show that it has a particular sound, as in é, è, ç, ñ. Compare ACCENT (*noun* sense 3).

diadem /ˈdaɪədɛm/ *n* a crown or jewelled headband.

diaeresis or (*N Am*) **dieresis** /daɪˈɛrəsɪs/ *n* (*-ses* /-siːz/) a mark (¨) placed over a vowel to show that it is to be pronounced separately, as in naïve.

diagnosis *n* (*-ses* /-siːz/) *med* the identification of a medical disorder on the basis of its symptoms. ○ **diagnose** *vb*. ○ **diagnostic** *adj*.

diagonal *adj* **1** *maths* of a straight line: joining non-adjacent corners of a POLYGON or vertices not on the same face in a POLYHEDRON. **2** sloping or slanting. ➤ *n* a diagonal line. ○ **diagonally** *adv*.

diagram *n* a drawing that shows something's structure or the way in which it functions. ○ **diagrammatic** *adj*.

dial *n* **1** a plate on a clock, radio, meter, etc with numbers on it and a movable indicator, used to indicate eg measurements or selected settings. **2** the round numbered plate on some telephones and the movable disc fitted over it. ➤ *vb* (**dialled, dialling;** *US* **dialed, dialing**) *tr & intr* to use a telephone dial or keypad to call (a number).

dialect *n* a form of a language spoken in a particular region or by a certain social group. ○ **dialectal** *adj*.

dialectic *n, philos* **1** (*also* **dialectics**) the establishing of truth by discussion. **2** (*also* **dialectics**) a debate which aims to resolve the conflict between two opposing theories rather than to disprove either of them. **3** the art of arguing logically. ○ **dialectical** *adj*.

dialling tone or (*N Am*) **dial tone** *n* the sound heard on picking up a telephone receiver which indicates that a number can be dialled.

dialogue or *sometimes* (*US*) **dialog** *n* **1** a conversation, esp a formal one. **2** the words spoken by the characters in a play, book, etc. **3** a discussion with a view to resolving conflict or achieving agreement.

dialogue box or **dialog box** *n, comput* a small on-screen box that prompts the user to give information or enter an option.

dialysis /daɪˈalɪsɪs/ *n* (*-ses* /-siːz/) **1** *chem* the separation of particles in a solution by diffusion through a semipermeable membrane. **2** *med* the removal of toxic substances from the blood by such a process in an artificial kidney

machine. ○ **dialyse** or (*chiefly N Am*) **dialyze** *vb.*
○ **dialyser** *n.*

diamanté /dɪəˈmɒnteɪ, -ˈmantɪ/ *adj* decorated with small sparkling ornaments.

diameter *n, geom* **1** a straight line drawn across a circle through its centre. **2** the length of this line.

diametric or **diametrical** *adj* **1** relating to or along a diameter. **2** of opinions, etc: directly opposed; very far apart. ○ **diametrically** *adv.*

diamond *n* **1** a colourless crystalline form of carbon, the hardest mineral and a gemstone. **2** a RHOMBUS. **3 a** (**diamonds**) one of the four suits of playing-cards, with a red rhombus-shaped symbol (♦); **b** a playing-card of this suit. **4** a baseball pitch, or the part of it between the bases. ➣ *adj* **1** resembling, made of or marked with diamonds. **2** rhombus-shaped.

diamond wedding *n* the sixtieth anniversary of a marriage.

diapason /daɪəˈpeɪzən/ *n, mus* **1** the whole range or compass of tones. **2** a standard of pitch. **3** a full volume of various sounds in concord. **4** an organ stop extending through its whole compass.

diaper *n, N Am* a baby's nappy.

diaphanous /daɪˈafənəs/ *adj* of cloth: light and fine, and almost transparent.

diaphragm /ˈdaɪəfram/ *n* **1** *anat* the sheet of muscle that separates the THORAX from the ABDOMEN. **2** *optics* an opaque disc with an adjustable aperture that is used to control the amount of light entering eg a camera or microscope. **3** a thin vibrating disc or cone that converts sound waves to electrical signals in a microphone, or electrical signals to sound waves in a loudspeaker. **4** a CAP (*noun* sense 7).

diapositive *n* a transparent photographic slide.

diarist *n* a person who writes a diary, esp one which is published.

diarrhoea or (*N Am*) **diarrhea** /daɪəˈrɪə/ *n, med* a condition in which the bowels are emptied frequently and the faeces are very soft or liquid.

diary *n* (**-ies**) **1 a** a written record of daily events in a person's life; **b** a book containing this. **2** *Brit* a book with separate spaces or pages for each day of the year in which appointments, daily notes and reminders may be written.

the Diaspora /daɪˈaspərə/ *n* **1** the scattering of the Jewish people to various countries following their exile in Babylon in the 6c BC. **2** (*also* **diaspora**) a dispersion of people of the same nation or culture.

diastole /daɪˈastəlɪ/ *n, med* the rhythmic expansion of the chambers of the heart during which they fill with blood. ○ **diastolic** /daɪə-ˈstɒlɪk/ *adj.*

diatom *n* a microscopic one-celled alga.

diatomic *adj, chem* denoting a molecule that consists of two identical atoms.

diatonic *adj, mus* relating to, or using notes from, the **diatonic scale**, a scale consisting of

only the basic notes proper to a particular key with no additional sharps, flats or naturals.

diatribe *n* a bitter or abusive critical attack.

diazepam /daɪˈazəpam, daɪˈeɪ-/ *n, med* a tranquillizing drug which relieves anxiety.

dibble *n* a short pointed hand-tool used for making holes in the ground for seeds, young plants, etc.

dice *n* (*pl* **dice**) **1** a small cube with 1 to 6 spots on each of its faces, used in games of chance. **2** a game of chance played with dice. ➣ *vb* **1** to cut (vegetables, etc) into small cubes. **2** *intr* to play or gamble with dice. ♦ **dice with death** to take a great risk.

dicey *adj* (**dicier, diciest**) *colloq* risky.

dichotomy /daɪˈkɒtəmɪ/ *n* (**-ies**) a division or separation into two groups or parts, esp when these are sharply opposed or contrasted. ○ **dichotomous** *adj.*

dichromatic *adj* **1** of eg animals: having two variant colours or colourings. **2** able to see only two colours and combinations of these.

dick *n* **1** *coarse slang* the penis. **2** *slang* a detective.

dickens *n, colloq* (*usu* **the dickens**) the devil, used esp for emphasis: *What the dickens are you doing?*

Dickensian *adj* **1** resembling the 19c English social life depicted in the novels of Charles Dickens, eg the poor living and working conditions. **2** characteristic of or relating to Charles Dickens or to his writings.

dickhead *n, coarse slang* a stupid person; an idiot.

dicky¹, **dickey** or **dickie** *n* (**-ies** or **-eys**) a false shirt front worn with evening dress.

dicky² *adj* (**-ier, -iest**) *colloq* **1** shaky; unsteady. **2** not in good condition.

dicky bow *n* a bow tie.

dicotyledon /daɪkɒtɪˈliːdən/ *n, bot* a flowering plant with an embryo that has two COTYLEDONS. Compare MONOCOTYLEDON.

dicta see DICTUM

Dictaphone *n, trademark* a small tape recorder for use esp when dictating letters.

dictate *vb* /dɪkˈteɪt/ **1** to say or read out something for someone else to write down. **2** to state or lay down (rules, terms, etc) forcefully or with authority. **3** *tr & intr, derog* to give orders to or try to impose one's wishes on someone. ➣ *n* /ˈdɪkteɪt/ (*usu* **dictates**) **1** an order or instruction. **2** a guiding principle. ○ **dictation** *n.*

dictator *n* **1** a ruler with total power. **2** someone who behaves in a dictatorial manner. ○ **dictatorial** *adj* fond of imposing one's wishes on or giving orders to other people. ○ **dictatorially** *adv.* ○ **dictatorship** *n.*

diction *n* the way in which one speaks.

dictionary *n* (**-ies**) **1** a book containing the words of a language arranged alphabetically with their meanings, etc, or with the equivalent words in another language. **2** an alphabetically arranged book of information.

dictum *n* (**dictums** or **dicta** /ˈdɪktə/) **1** a formal or authoritative statement of opinion. **2** a popular saying.

didactic /daɪˈdaktɪk/ *adj* intended to teach or instruct. ○ **didactically** *adv.* ○ **didacticism** *n.*

diddle *vb, colloq* to cheat or swindle.

didgeridoo *n, mus* a native Australian wind instrument, consisting of a long tube which, when blown into, produces a low droning sound.

didn't *contraction of* did not.

die¹ *vb* (**dies, died, dying**) *intr* **1** to stop living. **2** to come to an end or fade away. **3** of an engine, etc: to stop working suddenly and unexpectedly. **4** (*usu* **die of sth**) to suffer or be overcome by the effects of it: *die of laughter.* ♦ **be dying for sth** or **to do sth** *colloq* to have a strong desire or need for it or to do it. **die hard** to be difficult to change or remove. **to die for** *colloq* highly desirable: *a dress to die for.* ◊ **die away 1** to fade away from sight or hearing until gone. **2** to become steadily weaker and finally stop. **die back** *bot* of a plant's soft shoots: to die or wither from the tip back to the hard wood. **die down** to lose strength or force. **die off** to die one after another; to die in large numbers. **die out** to cease to exist anywhere.

die² *n* **1** (*pl* **dies**) **a** a metal tool or stamp for cutting or shaping metal or making designs on coins, etc; **b** a metal device for shaping or moulding a semisoft solid material. **2** (*pl* **dice**) a DICE. ♦ **straight as a die 1** completely straight. **2** completely honest. **the die is cast** an irreversible decision has been made or action taken.

diehard *n* a person who stubbornly refuses to accept new ideas or changes.

dielectric *physics, n* a non-conducting material whose molecules align or polarize under the influence of applied electric fields, used in capacitors. ➤ *adj* denoting such a material.

dieresis an alternative *N Am* spelling of DIAERESIS.

diesel *n* **1** DIESEL FUEL. **2** a DIESEL ENGINE. **3** a train, etc driven by a diesel engine.

diesel engine *n* a type of internal-combustion engine in which air in the cylinder is compressed until it reaches a sufficiently high temperature to ignite the fuel.

diesel fuel or **diesel oil** *n, eng* liquid fuel for use in a diesel engine.

diet¹ *n* **1** the food and drink habitually consumed by a person or animal. **2** a planned or prescribed selection of food and drink, eg for weight loss. ➤ *adj* containing less sugar than the standard version: *diet lemonade.* ➤ *vb* (**dieted, dieting**) *intr* to restrict the quantity or type of food that one eats, esp in order to lose weight. ○ **dietary** *adj.* ○ **dieter** *n.*

diet² *n* a legislative assembly.

dietetic *adj* **1** concerning or belonging to DIET¹. **2** for use in a special medical diet.

dietetics *sing n* the scientific study of DIET¹ and its relation to health. ○ **dietician** or **dietitian** *n.*

differ *vb, intr* **1** to be different or unlike in some way. **2** (*often* **differ with sb**) to disagree.

difference *n* **1** something that makes one thing or person unlike another. **2** the state of being unlike. **3** a change from an earlier state, etc. **4** the amount by which one quantity or number is greater or less than another. **5** a quarrel or disagreement.

different *adj* **1** (*usu* **different from** or **to sth** or **sb**) not the same; unlike. **2** separate; distinct; various. **3** *colloq* unusual. ○ **differently** *adv.*

differential *adj* constituting, showing, relating to or based on a difference. ➤ *n* **1** *maths* an infinitesimal change in the value of one or more variables as a result of a similarly small change in another variable or variables. **2** a difference in the rate of pay between one category of worker and another in the same industry or company. **3** a DIFFERENTIAL GEAR.

differential calculus *n, maths* a procedure for calculating the rate of change of one variable quantity produced by changes in another variable.

differential gear *n* an arrangement of gears that allows the wheels on either side of a vehicle to rotate at different speeds, eg when cornering.

differentiate *vb* **1** *tr & intr* (*usu* **differentiate between things**, or **one thing from another**) to establish a difference between them; to be able to distinguish one thing from another. **2** (*usu* **differentiate one thing from another**) to constitute a difference between things, or a difference in (one thing as against another). **3** to become different. ○ **differentiation** *n.*

difficult *adj* **1** requiring great skill, intelligence or effort. **2** not easy to please; unco-operative. **3** of a problem, situation, etc: potentially embarrassing; hard to resolve or get out of.

difficulty *n* (**-ies**) **1** the state or quality of being difficult. **2** a difficult thing to do or understand. **3** a problem, obstacle or objection. **4** (*usu* **difficulties**) trouble or embarrassment, esp financial trouble.

diffident *adj* lacking in confidence; too modest or shy. ○ **diffidence** *n.* ○ **diffidently** *adv.*

diffraction *n, physics* the spreading out of waves (eg light or sound waves) as they emerge from a small opening or slit. ○ **diffract** *vb.* ○ **diffractive** *adj.*

diffuse *vb* /dɪˈfjuːz/ *tr & intr* to spread or send out in all directions. ➤ *adj* /dɪˈfjuːs/ **1** widely spread. **2** using too many words. ○ **diffusely** *adv.* ○ **diffuseness** *n.* ○ **diffuser** *n.* ○ **diffusible** *adj.* ○ **diffusive** *adj.*

diffusion *n* **1** diffusing or being diffused. **2** *physics* the gradual and spontaneous dispersal of a fluid from a region of high concentration to one of low concentration. **3** *anthropol* the spread of cultural elements from one community, region, etc to another.

dig *vb* (**dug, digging**) **1** *tr & intr* to turn up or move (earth, etc) esp with a spade. **2** to make (a hole, etc) by digging. **3** *tr & intr* to poke. **4** *old slang* to appreciate. **5** *tr & intr, old slang* to understand. ➤ ➤ **1** a remark intended to irritate, criticize or make fun of someone. **2** a place where archaeologists are digging. **3** a poke. **4** an act of digging. ♦ **dig in one's heels** to refuse to change one's mind. ◊ **dig in 1** *colloq* to start to eat. **2** to work hard. **dig oneself in** to establish a firm or protected place for oneself. **dig into sth 1** *colloq* to start eating (a meal, etc). **2** to examine or search through it for information. **dig sth out** to find it by extensive searching. **dig sth up 1** to find or reveal something buried or hidden by digging. **2** *colloq* to search for and find (information, etc).

digest¹ /daɪˈdʒɛst/ *vb* **1** *tr & intr* to break down (food), or be broken down, in the stomach, intestine, etc into a form which the body can use. **2** to hear and consider the meaning and implications of (information). ○ **digestible** *adj.*

digest² /ˈdaɪdʒɛst/ *n* **1** a collection of summaries of news stories or current literature, etc. **2** a summary or shortened version.

digestion *n* **1** the process whereby food is broken down by enzymes in the ALIMENTARY CANAL. **2** the process of absorbing information, etc.

digestive *adj* concerned with or for digestion.

digger *n* **1** a machine for digging and excavating. **2** someone who digs. **3** *colloq* an Australian or New Zealander.

digit *n* **1** any of the figures 0 to 9. **2** *technical* a finger or toe.

digital *adj* **1** showing numerical information in the form of DIGITS, rather than by a pointer on a dial. **2** operating by processing information supplied and stored in the form of a series of binary digits: *digital recording.* **3** *electronics* denoting an electronic circuit that responds to and produces signals which at any given time are in one of two possible states. Compare ANALOGUE.

digital audio tape *n, electronics* a magnetic audio tape on which sound has been recorded after it has been converted into a binary code.

digital compact cassette *n* a DIGITAL AUDIO TAPE in standard cassette format.

digitalis /dɪdʒɪˈteɪlɪs/ *n* **1** *bot* any plant of the genus that includes the foxglove. **2** *med* a collective term for drugs that stimulate the heart muscle, orig obtained from foxglove leaves.

digitize or **-ise** *vb* to convert (data) into BINARY form. ○ **digitization** *n.* ○ **digitizer** *n.*

dignify *vb* (**-ies, -ied**) **1** to make something impressive or dignified. **2** to make something seem more important or impressive than it is. ○ **dignified** *adj* **1** showing or consistent with dignity. **2** stately; noble; serious.

dignitary *n* (**-ies**) someone of high rank or position.

dignity *n* **1** stateliness, seriousness and formality of manner and appearance. **2** goodness and nobility of character. **3** calmness and self-control. **4** high rank or position. ♦ **beneath one's dignity 1** not worthy of one's attention or time, etc. **2** degrading.

digraph *n* a pair of letters that represent a single sound, eg the *ph* of *digraph.*

digress *vb, intr* to wander from the point, or from the main subject in speaking or writing. ○ **digression** *n.*

digs *pl n, Brit colloq* lodgings.

dike see DYKE¹, DYKE²

dilapidated *adj* falling to pieces; in great need of repair. ○ **dilapidation** *n.*

dilatation and curettage *n, med* a gynaecological operation in which the CERVIX is dilated and a CURETTE is passed into the uterus to scrape the lining.

dilate *vb, tr & intr* to make or become larger, wider or further open. ○ **dilatation** or **dilation** *n.*

dilatory /ˈdɪlətərɪ/ *adj* slow in doing things; inclined to or causing delay. ○ **dilatorily** *adv.* ○ **dilatoriness** *n.*

dildo *n* an object shaped like an erect penis, used for sexual pleasure.

dilemma *n* a situation in which one must choose between two or more courses of action, both/all equally undesirable.

dilettante /dɪləˈtantɪ/ *n* (**dilettantes** or **dilettanti** /-tiː/) *often derog* someone interested in a subject but who does not study it in depth. ○ **dilettantism** *n.*

diligent *adj* **1** hard-working and careful. **2** showing or done with care and serious effort. ○ **diligence** *n.* ○ **diligently** *adv.*

dill *n* a herb used in flavouring.

dilly-dally *vb* (**-ies, -ied**) *intr, colloq* **1** to be slow or waste time. **2** to be unable to make up one's mind.

dilute *vb* **1** to decrease the concentration of a SOLUTE in a solution by adding more SOLVENT, eg water. **2** to reduce the strength, influence or effect of something. ➤ *adj, chem* of a solution: containing a relatively small amount of SOLUTE compared to the amount of SOLVENT present. ○ **dilution** *n.*

diluvial or **diluvian** *adj* concerning or pertaining to a flood, esp the Flood mentioned in the Book of Genesis.

dim *adj* **1** not bright or distinct. **2** lacking enough light to see clearly. **3** faint; not clearly remembered: *a dim memory.* **4** *colloq* not very intelligent. **5** of eyes: not able to see well. **6** *colloq* not good; not hopeful: *dim prospects.* ➤ *vb* (**dimmed, dimming**) *tr & intr* to make or become dim. ○ **dimly** *adv.* ○ **dimness** *n.* ♦ **take a dim view of sth** *colloq* to disapprove of it.

dime *n* **1** a coin of the US and Canada worth ten cents. **2** ten cents.

dimension *n* **1** a measurement of length, width or height. **2** a measurable quantity. **3** *geom* any of the parameters needed to specify the size of a geometrical figure and the location of points on it, eg a triangle has two dimensions and a pyramid has three. **4** (*often* **dimensions**) size or extent. **5** a particular aspect of a problem, situation, etc: *the religious dimension of the* *problem.* ○ **dimensional** *adj.*

dimer *n, chem* a chemical compound composed of two MONOMERS. ○ **dimeric** *adj.*

diminish *vb* **1** *tr & intr* to become or make something less or smaller. **2** to make someone or something seem less important, valuable or satisfactory.

diminuendo *mus, adj, adv* with gradually lessening sound. ➤ *n* **1** a gradual lessening of sound. **2** a musical passage with gradually lessening sound. Compare CRESCENDO.

diminution *n* a lessening or decrease.

diminutive *adj* very small. ➤ *n, gram* **1** an ending added to a word to indicate smallness, eg *-let* in *booklet*. **2** a word formed in this way.

dimmer or **dimmer switch** *n* a control used to modify the brightness of a light.

dimple *n* a small hollow, esp in the skin of the cheeks, chin or, esp in babies, at the knees and elbows. ➤ *vb* to show or form into dimples.

dim sum *n* a selection of Chinese foods, usu including steamed dumplings with various fillings.

dimwit *n, colloq* a stupid person. ○ **dimwitted** *adj.*

din *n* a loud, continuous and unpleasant noise. ➤ *vb* (**dinned, dinning**) (*usu* **din sth into sb**) to repeat something forcefully to someone over and over again so that it will be remembered.

dinar /ˈdiːnɑː(r)/ *n* the standard unit of currency in the Union of Serbia and Montenegro, Macedonia (usu in the form **denar**), and several Arab countries.

dine *vb, formal* **1** *intr* to eat dinner. **2** *intr* (*usu* **dine off, on** or **upon sth**) to eat it for one's dinner. **3** to give dinner to someone: *He's wining and dining his girlfriend.* ◇ **dine out** to have dinner somewhere when one's own house, eg in a restaurant. **dine out on sth** to be invited out to dinner so that others may hear one tell (an amusing story).

diner *n* **1** someone who dines. **2** a restaurant car on a train. **3** *N Am* a small cheap restaurant.

ding-dong *n* **1** the sound of bells ringing. **2** *colloq* a heated argument or fight.

dinghy /ˈdɪŋɡɪ, ˈdɪŋɪ/ *n* (*-ies*) **1** a small open boat. **2** a small collapsible rubber boat.

dingle *n* a deep wooded hollow.

dingo *n* (**dingoes**) an Australian wild dog.

dingy /ˈdɪndʒɪ/ *adj* (*-ier, -iest*) **1** faded and dirty-looking: *dingy clothes.* **2** dark and rather dirty: *a dingy room.* ○ **dinginess** *n.*

dinkum *adj, Aust & NZ colloq* genuine; honest. ➤ *adv* genuinely; honestly.

dinky *adj* (*-ier, -iest*) **1** *colloq* neat; dainty. **2** *N Am colloq* trivial; insignificant.

dinner *n* **1** the main meal of the day, eaten in the middle of the day or in the evening. **2** a formal meal, esp in the evening.

dinner jacket *n* a man's formal jacket for evening wear.

dinner service or **dinner set** *n* a complete set of plates and dishes for serving dinner to several people.

dinosaur *n* **1** a prehistoric reptile. **2** *often jocular* a chance survivor of a type characteristic of past times.

dint *n* a dent. ◆ **by dint of sth** by means of it.

diocese /ˈdaɪəsɪs/ *n* the district over which a bishop has authority. ○ **diocesan** /daɪˈɒsɪzən/ *adj.*

diode *n, electronics* an electronic device containing an ANODE and a CATHODE, allowing current to flow in one direction only.

dioptre or (*esp N Am*) **diopter** /daɪˈɒptə(r)/ *n, optics* a unit used to express the power of a lens.

dioxide *n, chem* a compound formed by combining two atoms of oxygen with one atom of another element.

dip *vb* (**dipped, dipping**) **1** to put something briefly into a liquid. **2** *intr* to go briefly under the surface of a liquid. **3** *intr* to drop below a surface or level. **4** *tr & intr* to go, or push something, down briefly and then up again. **5** *intr* to slope downwards. **6** *tr & intr* to put (one's hand, etc) into a dish, etc and take out some of the contents. **7** to immerse (an animal) in disinfectant that kills parasites. **8** *Brit* to lower the beam of (a vehicle's headlights). ➤ *n* **1** an act of dipping. **2** a downward slope or hollow (eg in a road). **3** a short swim or bathe. **4** a chemical liquid for dipping animals. **5** a type of thick sauce into which biscuits, raw vegetables, etc are dipped. ◇ **dip into sth 1** to take or use part of it. **2** to look briefly at a book or study a subject in a casual manner.

Dip Ed *abbrev* Diploma in Education.

diphtheria /dɪpˈθɪərɪə, dɪf-/ *n, med* a disease which affects the throat, causing difficulty in breathing and swallowing.

diphthong /ˈdɪpθɒŋ, ˈdɪf-/ *n* two vowel sounds pronounced as one syllable, such as the sound represented by the *ou* in *sounds.*

diploid *adj, genetics* having two sets of chromosomes, one from each parent.

diploma *n* a document certifying that one has passed an examination or completed a course of study.

diplomacy *n* **1** the art or profession of making agreements, treaties, etc between countries, or of representing and looking after the affairs of one's own country in a foreign country. **2** skill and tact in dealing with people. ○ **diplomatic** *adj.* ○ **diplomatically** *adv.*

diplomat *n* **1** a government representative engaged in diplomacy. **2** a very tactful person.

diplomatic immunity *n* the privilege granted to diplomats by which they may not be taxed, arrested, etc by the country in which they are working.

dipole *n, physics* a separation of electric charge, in which two equal and opposite charges are separated from each other by a small distance. ○ **dipolar** *adj.*

dipper *n* **1** a type of ladle. **2** a small songbird which can swim under water and feeds on river-beds.

dippy adj (-ier, -iest) colloq crazy; mad.

dipsomania n, med an insatiable craving for alcoholic drink. ○ **dipsomaniac** n.

dipstick n 1 a stick used to measure the level of a liquid in a container, esp the oil in a car engine. 2 slang a stupid person.

dipswitch n a switch used to dip the headlights of a motor vehicle.

diptych /'dɪptɪk/ n a work of art, esp on a church altar, consisting of a pair of pictures painted on hinged wooden panels which can be folded together like a book.

dire adj 1 dreadful. 2 extreme; very serious; very difficult. ○ **direly** adv.

direct adj 1 following the shortest path. 2 open, straightforward and honest; going straight to the point. 3 actual: the direct cause of the accident. 4 not working or communicating through other people, organizations, etc: a direct link with the chairman. 5 exact; complete: a direct opposite. 6 in an unbroken line of descent from parent to child to grandchild, etc: a direct descendant of Sir Walter Raleigh. ➤ vb 1 to point, aim or turn something in some direction. 2 to show the way to someone. 3 tr & intr (usu direct sb to do sth or that sth be done) to give orders or instructions. 4 to control, manage or be in charge of something. 5 tr & intr to supervise the production of (a play or film). 6 formal to put a name and address on (a letter, etc). ➤ adv by the quickest or shortest path. ○ **directness** n.

direct access n, comput the ability to access data directly without having to scan the storage file.

direct current n electric current which flows in one direction. Compare ALTERNATING CURRENT.

direct debit n, finance an order to one's bank which allows someone else to withdraw sums of money from one's account, esp in payment of bills. Compare STANDING ORDER.

direction n 1 the place or point towards which one is moving or facing. 2 the way in which someone or something is developing. 3 (usu directions) information, instructions or advice, eg on how to operate a piece of equipment. 4 (directions) instructions about the way to go to reach a place. 5 management or supervision. 6 the act, style, etc of directing a play or film.

directional adj relating to direction in space.

directive n an official instruction issued by a higher authority.

directly adv 1 in a direct manner. 2 by a direct path. 3 at once. 4 very soon. 5 exactly: directly opposite.

direct object n, gram the noun, phrase or pronoun which is directly affected by the action of a transitive verb, eg the dog in the boy kicked the dog. Compare INDIRECT OBJECT.

director n 1 a senior manager of a business firm. 2 the person in charge of an organization, institution or special activity. 3 the person directing a play, film, etc. 4 mus, esp N Am a

CONDUCTOR (sense 1). ○ **directorial** adj. ○ **directorship** n.

directorate n 1 the directors of a business firm. 2 the position or office of director.

director-general n (directors-general or director-generals) the chief administrator of an organization.

directory n (-ies) 1 a book with a (usu alphabetical) list of names and addresses. 2 comput a named grouping of files on a disk.

direct speech n, gram speech reported in the actual words of the speaker, eg "Hello" in the sentence "Hello," said Henry. Compare INDIRECT SPEECH.

direct tax n a tax paid directly to the government by a person or organization, eg INCOME TAX. Compare INDIRECT TAX.

dirge n 1 a funeral song or hymn. 2 sometimes derog a slow sad song or piece of music.

dirigible n, technical an AIRSHIP.

dirk n a small knife or dagger.

dirndl /'dɜːndəl/ n 1 a type of dress, with a tight-fitting bodice and a very full skirt, traditionally worn by peasant women in the Alps. 2 a skirt that is tight at the waist and wide at the lower edge.

dirt n 1 mud, dust, etc. 2 soil. 3 a mixture of earth and cinders used to make road surfaces. 4 euphem excrement. 5 colloq obscene speech or writing. 6 colloq scandal.

dirt-cheap adj, adv, colloq very cheap.

dirt track n 1 a rough unsurfaced track. 2 a motorcycle racing course made of cinders, etc.

dirty adj (-ier, -iest) 1 marked with dirt. 2 making one become soiled with dirt: a dirty job. 3 unfair; dishonest: dirty tricks. 4 obscene or pornographic: dirty films. 5 of weather: rainy or stormy. 6 of a colour: dull. 7 showing dislike or disapproval: a dirty look. 8 unsportingly rough or violent: a dirty tackle. ➤ vb (-ies, -ied) to make dirty. ➤ adv 1 dirtily: fight dirty. 2 very: dirty great stains. ○ **dirtiness** n. ♦ **do the dirty on sb** colloq to cheat or trick them.

dirty word n 1 a vulgar word. 2 colloq an unpopular concept: Ambition is a dirty word.

dirty work n 1 work that makes a person dirty. 2 colloq unpleasant or dishonourable tasks.

dis- pfx, forming words denoting 1 the opposite of the base word: disagree • dislike. 2 reversal of the action of the base word: disassemble. 3 removal or undoing: dismember • disrobe.

disability n (-ies) 1 the state of being disabled. 2 a physical or mental handicap.

disable vb 1 to deprive someone of a physical or mental ability. 2 to make (eg a machine) unable to work; to make something useless. ○ **disablement** n.

disabled adj 1 having a physical or mental handicap. 2 made unable to work. 3 designed or intended for people with physical disabilities.

disabuse vb (always disabuse sb of sth) to rid them of a mistaken idea or impression.

disadvantage *n* **1** a difficulty, drawback or weakness. **2** an unfavourable situation. ➤ *vb* to put someone at a disadvantage. ○ **disadvantaged** *adj* in an unfavourable position; deprived of normal social or economic benefits. ○ **disadvantageous** *adj.*

disaffected *adj* dissatisfied and no longer loyal or committed. ○ **disaffection** *n.*

disagree *vb, intr* **1** to have conflicting opinions. **2** (*often* **disagree with sth**) to be opposed to it. **3** (*always* **disagree with sb**) of food: to give them digestive problems. **4** *euphem* to quarrel.

disagreeable *adj* **1** unpleasant. **2** bad-tempered. ○ **disagreeably** *adv.*

disagreement *n* **1** the state of disagreeing. **2** *euphem* a quarrel.

disallow *vb* **1** to formally refuse to allow or accept something. **2** to judge something to be invalid. ○ **disallowance** *n.*

disappear *vb, intr* **1** to vanish. **2** to cease to exist. **3** to go missing. ○ **disappearance** *n.*

disappoint *vb* **1** to fail to fulfil the hopes or expectations of someone. **2** *formal* to prevent (eg a plan) from being carried out. ○ **disappointed** *adj.* ○ **disappointing** *adj.* ○ **disappointment** *n.*

disapprobation *n, formal* disapproval, esp on moral grounds.

disapprove *vb, intr* (*usu* **disapprove of sth** or **sb**) to think it or them bad or wrong. ○ **disapproval** *n.* ○ **disapproving** *adj.* ○ **disapprovingly** *adv.*

disarm *vb* **1** to take weapons away from someone. **2** *intr* to reduce or destroy one's own military capability. **3** to take the fuse out of (a bomb). **4** to take away the anger or suspicions of someone.

disarmament *n* the reduction or destruction by a nation of its own military forces.

disarming *adj* quickly winning confidence or affection. ○ **disarmingly** *adv.*

disarrange *vb* to make something untidy. ○ **disarrangement** *n.*

disarray *n* a state of disorder or confusion. ➤ *vb* to throw something into disorder.

disassociate *vb, tr & intr* to DISSOCIATE. ○ **disassociation** *n.*

disaster *n* **1** an event causing great damage, injury or loss of life. **2** a total failure. **3** extremely bad luck: *Disaster struck.* ○ **disastrous** *adj.* ○ **disastrously** *adv.*

disavow *vb, formal* to deny knowledge of, a connection with, or responsibility for something or someone. ○ **disavowal** *n.*

disband *vb, tr & intr* to stop operating as a group. ○ **disbandment** *n.*

disbar *vb* to expel (a barrister) from the Bar (see BAR[1] *noun* sense 9).

disbelieve *vb* **1** to believe something to be false or someone to be lying. **2** *intr* to have no religious faith. ○ **disbelief** *n.*

disburse *vb* to pay out (a sum of money). ○ **disbursement** *n.*

disc *n* **1** a flat thin circular object. **2** any disc-shaped recording medium, such as a RECORD

(*noun* sense 4) or COMPACT DISC. **3** *anat* a plate of fibrous tissue between two adjacent vertebrae in the spine. **4** *comput* see DISK.

discard *vb* **1** to get rid of something useless or unwanted. **2** *cards* to put down (a card of little value) eg when unable to follow suit.

disc brake *n* a brake in which pads are pressed against a metal disc attached to the wheel.

discern *vb* to perceive, notice or make out something. ○ **discernible** *adj.* ○ **discernibly** *adv.* ○ **discerning** *adj* having or showing good judgement. ○ **discernment** *n* good judgement.

discharge *vb* /dɪs'tʃɑːdʒ/ **1** to allow someone to leave; to dismiss or send away (a person). **2** to perform or carry out (eg duties). **3** *tr & intr* to flow out or make something flow out or be released. **4** *law* to release someone from custody. **5** *tr & intr* to fire (a gun). **6** *law* to pay off (a debt). **7** *tr & intr* to unload (a cargo). ➤ *n* /'dɪstʃɑːdʒ/ **1** the act of discharging. **2** something discharged. **3** *formal, law* release or dismissal. **4** *physics* the flow of electric current through a gas. **5** *elec* the release of stored electric charge from a capacitor, battery or accumulator. **6** *elec* a high-voltage spark of electricity. **7 a** an emission of a substance, liquid, etc; **b** the substance, etc emitted.

disciple /dɪ'saɪpl/ *n* **1** someone who believes in, and follows, the teachings of another. **2** one of the twelve close followers of Christ. ○ **discipleship** *n.*

discipline *n* **1 a** a strict training, or the enforcing of rules, intended to produce controlled behaviour; **b** the ordered behaviour resulting from this. **2** punishment designed to create obedience. **3** a branch of learning, study or a sport. ➤ *vb* **1** to train or force (oneself or others) to behave in an ordered and controlled way. **2** to punish someone. ○ **disciplinarian** *n* someone who enforces strict discipline on others. ○ **disciplinary** *adj* characteristic of, relating to or enforcing discipline; intended as punishment.

disc jockey *n* someone who presents recorded popular music on the radio, at a club, etc. Also called **DJ**.

disclaim *vb* **1** to deny (eg involvement with or knowledge of something). **2** to give up a legal claim to something. ○ **disclaimer** *n* **1** a written statement denying legal responsibility. **2** a denial.

disclose *vb* to make something known or visible. ○ **disclosure** *n.*

disco *n* **1** a night-club where people dance to recorded pop music. **2** a party with dancing to recorded music. **3** mobile hi-fi and lighting equipment. ➤ *adj* suitable for, or designed for, discos.

discolour or (*US*) **discolor** *vb, tr & intr* to stain or dirty something; to change in colour. ○ **discoloration** or **discolouration** *n.*

discomfit *vb* (*discomfited, discomfiting*) to make someone feel embarrassed, uneasy or perplexed. ○ **discomfiture** *n.*

discomfort n a slight physical pain or mental uneasiness.

discompose vb to upset or worry someone. ○ **discomposure** n.

disconcert vb to make someone feel anxious, uneasy or flustered. ○ **disconcerting** adj.

disconnect vb **1** to break the connection between (esp an electrical device and a power supply). **2** to stop the supply of (eg a public service such as the gas supply or the telephone) to (a building, etc). ○ **disconnection** n.

disconnected adj esp of speech: not correctly constructed, and often not making sense.

disconsolate adj deeply sad or disappointed. ○ **disconsolately** adv.

discontent n dissatisfaction. ○ **discontented** adj. ○ **discontentedly** adv.

discontinue vb **1** tr & intr to stop or cease. **2** to stop producing something. ○ **discontinuance** or **discontinuation** n.

discontinuous adj having breaks or interruptions. ○ **discontinuity** n (-ies).

discord n **1** disagreement; conflict. **2** mus an unpleasant combination of notes; lack of harmony. **3** uproarious noise. ○ **discordant** adj. ○ **discordantly** adv.

discotheque n, dated, formal a DISCO.

discount n /'dɪskaʊnt/ **1** an amount deducted from the normal price. **2** the rate or percentage of the deduction granted. ➤ vb /dɪs'kaʊnt/ **1** to disregard as unlikely, untrue or irrelevant. **2** to make a deduction from (a price).

discountenance vb **1** to refuse support to someone or something. **2** to show disapproval for someone or something. **3** to embarrass someone.

discourage vb **1** to deprive someone of confidence, hope or the will to continue. **2** to seek to prevent (a person or an action) with advice or persuasion. ○ **discouragement** n. ○ **discouraging** adj.

discourse n /'dɪskɔːs/ **1** a formal speech or essay on a particular subject. **2** serious conversation. ➤ vb /dɪs'kɔːs/ intr to speak or write at length, formally or with authority.

discourteous adj impolite. ○ **discourteously** adv. ○ **discourtesy** n (-ies).

discover vb **1** to be the first person to find something or someone. **2** to find by chance. **3** to learn of or become aware of for the first time. ○ **discoverer** n.

discovery n (-ies) **1** the act of discovering. **2** a person or thing discovered.

discredit n loss of good reputation, or the cause of it. ➤ vb **1** to make someone or something be disbelieved or regarded with suspicion. **2** to damage the reputation of someone. ○ **discreditable** adj.

discreet adj **1** careful to prevent suspicion or embarrassment, eg by keeping a secret. **2** avoiding notice. ○ **discreetly** adv.

| discreet, discrete | These words are sometimes confused with each other. |

discrepancy n (-ies) a failure (eg of sets of information) to correspond or be the same. ○ **discrepant** adj.

discrete adj separate; distinct. ○ **discretely** adv. ○ **discreteness** n.

discretion n **1** behaving discreetly. **2** the ability to make wise judgements. **3** the freedom or right to make decisions and do as one thinks best. ○ **discretional** or **discretionary** adj.

discriminate vb, intr **1** to see a difference between two people or things. **2** (usu **discriminate in favour of** or **against sb**) to give different treatment to different people or groups. ○ **discriminating** adj showing good judgement; seeing even slight differences. ○ **discrimination** n. ○ **discriminatory** adj displaying or representing unfairly different treatment.

discursive adj of spoken or written style: wandering from the main point; moving from point to point. ○ **discursively** adv. ○ **discursiveness** n.

discus n (**discuses** or **disci** /'dɪskaɪ/) **1** a heavy disc thrown in athletic competitions. **2** the competition itself.

discuss vb **1** to examine or consider something in speech or writing. **2** to talk or argue about something in conversation. ○ **discussion** n.

disdain n dislike due to a feeling that something is not worthy of attention; contempt. ➤ vb **1** to refuse or reject someone or something out of disdain. **2** to regard someone or something with disdain. ○ **disdainful** adj. ○ **disdainfully** adv.

disease n a disorder or illness caused by infection. ○ **diseased** adj.

diseconomy n (-ies) an economic drawback.

disembark vb, tr & intr to take or go from a ship on to land. ○ **disembarkation** n.

disembodied adj **1** separated from the body; having no physical existence. **2** seeming not to come from, or be connected to, a body.

disembowel vb (**disembowelled, disembowelling**) to remove the internal organs of someone or something. ○ **disembowelment** n.

disenchant vb to make someone dissatisfied or discontented. ○ **disenchanted** adj. ○ **disenchantment** n.

disenfranchise see DISFRANCHISE

disengage vb **1** to release or detach someone or something from a connection. **2** tr & intr to withdraw (troops) from combat. ○ **disengaged** adj. ○ **disengagement** n.

disentangle vb **1** to free something from complication, difficulty or confusion. **2** to take the knots or tangles out of (eg hair). ○ **disentanglement** n.

disestablish vb to take away the official status or authority of (an organization, etc), esp the national status of (a church). ○ **disestablishment** n.

disfavour or (N Am) **disfavor** n **1** a state of being disliked, unpopular or disapproved of. **2** dislike or disapproval.

disfigure vb to spoil the beauty or general appearance of something. ○ **disfigurement** *n*.

disfranchise or **disenfranchise** *vb* to deprive someone of the right to vote or other rights of a citizen. ○ **disfranchisement** *n*.

disgorge *vb* **1** *tr & intr* to vomit. **2** to discharge or pour out something.

disgrace *n* a shame or loss of favour or respect; **b** the cause of it; **c** an example of it. ➤ *vb* to bring shame upon someone. ○ **disgraceful** *adj*. ○ **disgracefully** *adv*. ♦ **in disgrace** out of favour.

disgruntled *adj* annoyed and dissatisfied.

disguise *vb* **1** to hide the identity of someone or something by a change of appearance. **2** to conceal the true nature of (eg intentions). ➤ *n* **1** a disguised state. **2** something, esp a combination of clothes and make-up, intended to disguise.

disgust *vb* to sicken; to provoke intense dislike or disapproval in someone. ➤ *n* intense dislike. ○ **disgusted** *adj*. ○ **disgusting** *adj*.

dish *n* **1** a shallow container in which food is served or cooked. **2** its contents, or the amount it can hold. **3** anything shaped like this. **4** a particular kind of food, esp food prepared for eating. **5** (**dishes**) the used plates and other utensils after the end of a meal. **6** a large dish-shaped aerial. **7** *colloq* a physically attractive person. ➤ *vb* to put (food) into a dish for serving at table. ◊ **dish sth out** *colloq* **1** to distribute it. **2** (*esp* **dish it out**) to give out punishment. **dish sth up** *colloq* **1** to serve (food). **2** to offer or present (eg information), esp if not for the first time.

disharmony *n* disagreement; lack of harmony. ○ **disharmonious** *adj*.

dishcloth *n* a cloth for washing or drying dishes.

dishearten *vb* to dampen the courage, hope or confidence of someone. ○ **disheartening** *adj*.

dishevelled *adj* of clothes or hair: untidy.

dishonest *adj* not honest; likely to deceive or cheat. ○ **dishonestly** *adv*. ○ **dishonesty** *n*.

dishonour or (*US*) **dishonor** *n* a shame or loss of honour; **b** the cause of it. ➤ *vb* **1** to bring dishonour on someone or something. **2** to treat someone or something with no respect. **3** *commerce* to refuse to honour (a cheque). ○ **dishonourable** *adj*.

dishwasher *n* **1** a machine that washes and dries dishes. **2** someone employed to wash dishes.

dishwater *n* **1** water in which dirty dishes have been washed. **2** any liquid like it.

dishy *adj* (**-ier, -iest**) *colloq* sexually attractive.

disillusion *vb* to correct the mistaken beliefs or illusions of someone. ➤ *n* (also **disillusionment**) a state of being disillusioned. ○ **disillusioned** *adj*.

disincentive *n* something that discourages or deters.

disinclined *adj* unwilling. ○ **disinclination** *n*.

disinfect *vb* to clean something with a sub-

stance that kills germs. ○ **disinfectant** *n, adj*.

disinformation *n* false information intended to deceive or mislead.

disingenuous *adj* not entirely sincere or open. ○ **disingenuously** *adv*.

disinherit *vb* to legally deprive someone of an inheritance. ○ **disinheritance** *n*.

disintegrate *vb, tr & intr* **1** to break into tiny pieces. **2** to break up. **3** to undergo or make a substance undergo nuclear fission. ○ **disintegration** *n*.

disinter *vb* **1** to dig up (esp a body from a grave). **2** to discover and make known (a fact, etc). ○ **disinterment** *n*.

disinterested *adj* **1** not having an interest in a particular matter; impartial. **2** *colloq* showing no interest; UNINTERESTED. ○ **disinterest** *n*.

---

disinterested, uninterested **Disinterested** used to mean the same as **uninterested**, but has developed the separate meaning given as sense 1, 'impartial'. The two words therefore relate to different senses of **interest**. The difference can be seen in the following examples:

He claimed that he had been a disinterested spectator in the affair (= not personally involved in it).

He left most of his meal, and seemed uninterested in any of the conversation she attempted (= not interested in it or concerned about it).

Disinterested is not usually followed by **in**, although **uninterested** often is.

---

disjointed *adj* esp of speech: not properly connected; incoherent.

disjunctive *adj* marked by breaks; discontinuous.

disk *n* **1** *comput* a MAGNETIC DISK. **2** *esp US* a DISC.

disk drive *n, comput* a part of a computer that can read and write data on a disk.

diskette *n, comput* a FLOPPY DISK.

dislike *vb* to consider someone or something unpleasant or unlikeable. ➤ *n* **1** mild hostility. **2** something disliked.

dislocate *vb* **1** to dislodge (a bone) from its normal position. **2** to disturb or disrupt something. ○ **dislocation** *n*.

dislodge *vb* to force something or someone out of a fixed position.

disloyal *adj* not loyal. ○ **disloyalty** *n*.

dismal *adj* **1** not cheerful; causing or suggesting sadness. **2** *colloq* third-rate; of poor quality. ○ **dismally** *adv*.

dismantle *vb* **1** to take something to pieces. **2** to abolish or close down something, esp bit by bit.

dismay *n* **1** a feeling of sadness arising from deep disappointment or discouragement. **2** alarm. ➤ *vb* to make someone discouraged, sad or alarmed.

dismember *vb* **1** to tear or cut the limbs from (the body). **2** to divide up (esp land). ○ **dismemberment** *n*.

dismiss *vb* **1** to refuse to consider or accept (an idea, claim, etc). **2** to put someone out of one's employment. **3** to send someone away. **4** to close (a court case). **5** *cricket* to bowl (a batsman) out. ○ **dismissal** *n*. ○ **dismissive** *adj*.

dismount *vb, intr* to get off a horse, bicycle, etc.

disobedient *adj* refusing or failing to obey. ○ **disobedience** *n*.

disobey *vb* to act contrary to the orders of someone; to refuse to obey (a person, a law, etc).

disobliging *adj* unwilling to help.

disorder *n* **1** lack of order; confusion. **2** unruly or riotous behaviour. **3** a disease or illness. ○ **disordered** *adj*.

disorderly *adj* **1** not neatly arranged. **2** causing trouble in public.

disorganize or **-ise** *vb* to disturb the order or arrangement of something; to throw someone into confusion. ○ **disorganization** *n*. ○ **disorganized** *adj*.

disorientate or **disorient** *vb* to make someone lose all sense of position, direction or time. ○ **disorientation** *n*.

disown *vb* to deny having any relationship to, or connection with, someone or something.

disparage *vb* to speak of someone or something with contempt. ○ **disparagement** *n*. ○ **disparaging** *adj*.

disparate /'dɪspərət/ *adj* completely different; too different to be compared. ○ **disparity** *n* (*-ies*).

dispassionate *adj* not influenced by personal feelings. ○ **dispassionately** *adv*.

dispatch or **despatch** *vb* **1** to send (mail, a person, etc) to a place. **2** to finish off or deal with something quickly: *dispatch a meal*. **3** *euphem* to kill. ➤ *n* **1** (*often* **dispatches**) an official (esp military) report. **2** a journalist's report sent to a newspaper. **3** the act of dispatching. **4** *old use* speed or haste.

dispatch rider *n* someone who delivers messages by motorcycle.

dispel *vb* (**dispelled, dispelling**) to drive away or banish (thoughts or feelings).

dispensable *adj* **1** able to be done without. **2** able to be dispensed.

dispensary *n* (*-ies*) a place where medicines are dispensed.

dispensation *n* **1** special exemption from a rule or obligation. **2** the act of dispensing. **3** *relig* God's management of human affairs.

dispense *vb* **1** to give out (eg advice). **2** to prepare and distribute (medicine). **3** to administer (eg the law). **4** (*always* **dispense with sth**) to do without it. ○ **dispenser** *n*.

dispensing optician see OPTICIAN

disperse *vb, tr & intr* **1** to spread out over a wide area. **2** to break up, or make (a crowd) break up, and leave. **3** to vanish or make something vanish. **4** *physics* of white light: to break up into the colours of the spectrum. **5** *physics* of particles: to become evenly distributed throughout a liquid or gas. ○ **dispersal** *n*. ○ **dispersion** *n*.

dispirit *vb* to dishearten or discourage someone. ○ **dispirited** *adj*.

displace *vb* **1** to put or take something or someone out of the usual place. **2** to remove someone from a post.

displaced person *n* someone forced to leave their home through war or persecution.

displacement *n* **1** the act of displacing. **2** *technical* the quantity of liquid, gas, etc displaced by an immersed object, eg of water by a floating ship.

display *vb* **1** to put someone or something on view. **2** to show or betray (eg feelings). ➤ *n* **1** the act of displaying. **2** an exhibition or show. **3** the showing of information on a screen, calculator, etc, or the information shown. **4** a pattern of animal behaviour involving stereotyped sounds, movements, etc, that produces a specific response in another individual.

displease *vb* to annoy or offend someone. ○ **displeasure** *n*.

disport *vb, tr & intr, literary* to indulge (oneself) in lively amusement.

disposable *adj* **1** intended to be thrown away or destroyed after one use. **2** of income or assets: remaining after tax and other commitments are paid, so available for use. ➤ *n* a product intended for disposal after one use.

disposal *n* getting rid of something. ♦ **at the disposal of sb** available for their use.

dispose *vb* **1** *intr* (*always* **dispose of sth**) to get rid of it. **2** *intr* (*always* **dispose of sth**) to deal with or settle it. **3** to place something in an arrangement or order. ♦ **be disposed to do sth** to be inclined or willing to do it: *I am not disposed to try.* **be disposed to** or **towards sb** or **sth** to have specified feelings about or towards them or it: *ill-disposed towards us*.

disposition *n* **1** temperament; tendency. **2** arrangement; distribution.

dispossess *vb* (*always* **dispossess sb of sth**) to take (esp property) away from them. ○ **dispossessed** *adj*. ○ **dispossession** *n*.

disproportion *n* lack of balance.

disproportionate *adj* unreasonably large or small in comparison with something else. ○ **disproportionately** *adv*.

disprove *vb* to prove something to be false or wrong.

dispute *vb* /dɪs'pjuːt/ **1** to question or deny the accuracy or validity of (a statement, etc). **2** to quarrel over rights to or possession of something. **3** *tr & intr* to argue about something. ➤ *n* /dɪs'pjuːt, 'dɪspjuːt/ an argument. ○ **disputable** *adj*. ○ **disputably** *adv*. ○ **disputation** *n*. ○ **disputatious** *adj*.

disqualify *vb* **1** to ban someone from doing something. **2** to make someone or something unsuitable or ineligible. ○ **disqualification** *n*.

disquiet n anxiety or uneasiness. ➤ vb to make someone anxious, uneasy, etc. ∘ **disquieting** adj. ∘ **disquietude** n.

disquisition n, formal a long and detailed discussion.

disregard vb 1 to pay no attention to someone or something. 2 to dismiss something as unworthy of consideration. ➤ n dismissive lack of attention or concern.

disrepair n bad condition or working order.

disreputable adj having a bad reputation. ∘ **disreputably** adv. ∘ **disrepute** n.

disrespect n lack of respect; impoliteness. ∘ **disrespectful** adj.

disrobe vb, tr & intr, literary to undress.

disrupt vb to disturb the order or peaceful progress of (an activity, process, etc). ∘ **disruption** n. ∘ **disruptive** adj.

dissatisfied adj feeling discontent. ∘ **dissatisfaction** n.

dissect /dɪˈsɛkt, daɪ-/ vb 1 to cut open (a plant or dead body) for scientific or medical examination. 2 to examine something in minute detail, esp critically. ∘ **dissection** n.

dissemble vb, tr & intr to conceal or disguise (true feelings or motives). ∘ **dissemblance** n.

disseminate vb to make (eg news or theories) widely known. ∘ **dissemination** n.

dissension n disagreement, esp if leading to strife.

dissent n 1 disagreement, esp open or hostile. 2 voluntary separation, esp from an established church. ➤ vb, intr (often **dissent from sb** or **sth**) 1 to disagree with them. 2 to break away, esp from an established church. ∘ **dissenter** n. ∘ **dissenting** adj.

dissentient /dɪˈsɛnʃənt/ adj, formal disagreeing with a majority or established view.

dissertation n 1 a long essay. 2 a formal lecture.

disservice n a wrong; a bad turn.

dissident n someone who disagrees publicly, esp with a government. ➤ adj dissenting. ∘ **dissidence** n.

dissimilar adj (often **dissimilar to sth**) different. ∘ **dissimilarity** n.

dissimulate vb, tr & intr to disguise (esp feelings). ∘ **dissimulation** n.

dissipate vb 1 tr & intr to separate and scatter. 2 to squander something. ∘ **dissipated** adj overindulging in pleasure and enjoyment. ∘ **dissipation** n.

dissociate vb 1 to regard something or someone as separate. 2 to declare someone or oneself to be unconnected with someone or something else. ∘ **dissociation** n.

dissoluble adj able to be dissolved.

dissolute adj indulging in pleasures considered immoral. ∘ **dissoluteness** n.

dissolution n 1 the breaking up of a meeting or assembly. 2 the ending of a formal or legal partnership. 3 abolition, eg of the monarchy. 4 breaking up into parts.

dissolve vb 1 tr & intr to merge with a liquid. 2 to

bring (an assembly) to a close. 3 to end (a legal partnership). 4 tr & intr to disappear or make something disappear. 5 intr (often **dissolve into laughter, tears,** etc) to be overcome emotionally. 6 intr, technical of a film or television image: to fade out as a second image fades in.

dissonance n 1 mus an unpleasant combination of sounds. 2 disagreement. ∘ **dissonant** adj.

dissuade vb (usu **dissuade sb from doing sth**) to deter them by advice or persuasion. ∘ **dissuasion** n.

dissyllable and **dissyllabic** see DISYLLABLE

distaff n the rod on which wool, etc is held ready for spinning. ♦ **the distaff side** old use the wife's or mother's side of the family.

distance n 1 the length between two points in space. 2 the fact of being apart. 3 any faraway point or place; the furthest visible area. 4 coldness of manner. ➤ vb 1 to put someone or something at a distance. 2 (usu **distance oneself from sb** or **sth**) to declare oneself to be unconnected or unsympathetic to them. ♦ **go the distance** colloq to last out until the end.

distant adj 1 far away or far apart in space or time. 2 not closely related. 3 cold and unfriendly. 4 appearing to be lost in thought. ∘ **distantly** adv.

distaste n dislike. ∘ **distasteful** adj.

distemper¹ n any of several infectious diseases of animals, esp **canine distemper**, an often fatal viral infection of dogs.

distemper² n a water-based paint, esp mixed with glue. ➤ vb to paint (eg a wall) with distemper.

distend vb, tr & intr to make or become swollen or stretched. ∘ **distensible** adj. ∘ **distension** n.

distil or (N Am) **distill** vb (**distilled, distilling**) 1 to purify a liquid by heating it to boiling point and condensing the vapour formed. 2 to produce alcoholic spirits in this way. 3 to create a shortened version of something. ∘ **distillate** n. ∘ **distillation** n.

distillery n (**-ies**) a place where alcoholic spirits are distilled. ∘ **distiller** n.

distinct adj 1 clear or obvious. 2 noticeably different or separate. ∘ **distinctly** adv.

distinction n 1 exceptional ability or achievement, or an honour awarded in recognition of it. 2 the act of differentiating. 3 the state of being noticeably different. 4 a distinguishing feature.

distinctive adj easily recognized because very individual. ∘ **distinctiveness** n.

distinguish vb 1 (often **distinguish one thing from another**) to mark or recognize them as different. 2 intr (often **distinguish between things** or **people**) to see the difference between them. 3 to make out or identify something. 4 (always **distinguish oneself**) often ironic to be outstanding because of some achievement. ∘ **distinguishable** adj. ∘ **distinguishing** adj.

distinguished adj 1 famous (and usu well respected). **2** with a noble or dignified appearance.

distort vb **1** to twist something out of shape. **2** to change the meaning or tone of (a statement, etc) by inaccurate retelling. **3** radio, telecomm to alter the quality of (a signal). ○ **distortion** n.

distract vb **1** (usu distract sb or sb's attention from sth) to divert their attention from it. **2** to entertain or amuse someone. ○ **distracted** adj.

distraction n **1** something that diverts the attention. **2** an amusement. **3** anxiety; anger. **4** madness.

distrain vb, law to seize (eg property) as, or in order to force, payment of a debt. ○ **distraint** n.

distrait /dɪ'streɪ/ adj, literary thinking of other things.

distraught adj in an extremely troubled state of mind.

distress n **1** mental or emotional pain. **2** financial difficulty. **3** great danger: a ship in distress. ➤ vb **1** to upset someone. **2** to give (fabric, furniture, etc) the appearance of being older than it is. ○ **distressing** adj.

distribute vb **1** to give out something. **2** to supply or deliver (goods). **3** to spread (something) widely.

distribution n **1** the process of distributing or being distributed. **2** the placing of things spread out. **3** stats a set of measurements or values, together with the observed or predicted frequencies with which they occur. ○ **distributive** adj.

distributor n **1** a person or company that distributes goods, esp between manufacturer and retailer. **2** a device in a vehicle ignition system that directs pulses of electricity to the spark plugs.

district n a region; an administrative or geographical unit.

district nurse n a nurse who treats patients in their homes.

distrust vb to have no trust in someone or something. ➤ n suspicion. ○ **distrustful** adj.

disturb vb **1** to interrupt someone. **2** to inconvenience someone. **3** to upset the arrangement or order of something. **4** to upset the peace of mind of someone. ○ **disturbed** adj, psychol emotionally upset or confused. ○ **disturbing** adj.

disturbance n **1** an outburst of noisy or violent behaviour. **2** an interruption.

disunite vb to cause disagreement or conflict between (people) or within (a group). ○ **disunity** n.

disuse n the state of no longer being used, practised or observed. ○ **disused** adj.

disyllable or **dissyllable** /'daɪsɪləbəl/ n a word of two syllables. ○ **disyllabic** or **dissyllabic** adj.

ditch n a narrow channel dug in the ground. ➤ vb **1** slang to get rid of or abandon someone or something. **2** tr & intr, colloq of an aircraft or a pilot: to bring or come down in the sea.

dither vb, intr to act in a nervously uncertain manner. ➤ n a state of nervous indecision.

○ **ditherer** n. ○ **dithery** adj.

ditto n the same thing; that which has just been said. ➤ adv likewise.

ditto marks n a symbol (″) written immediately below a word, etc in a list to mean 'same as above'.

ditty n (-ies) a short simple song or poem.

diuretic /daɪjʊ'rɛtɪk/ med, n a drug or other substance that increases the volume of urine produced and excreted. ➤ adj increasing the production and excretion of urine.

diurnal /daɪ'ɜːnəl/ adj, formal, technical **1** daily. **2** during the day. **3** active during the day.

diva /'diːvə/ n (divas or dive /'diːveɪ/) a great female singer.

divalent adj, chem of an atom: able to combine with two atoms of hydrogen or another atom.

divan n **1** a sofa with no back or sides. **2** a bed without a raised board at either end.

dive¹ vb (past tense & past participle dived or (N Am) dove) intr **1** to throw oneself into water, or plunge down through water. **2** of a submarine, etc: to become submerged. **3** to descend or fall steeply through the air. **4** to throw oneself to the side or to the ground. **5** to move quickly and suddenly out of sight: diving behind a tree. ➤ n **1** an act of diving. **2** slang any dirty or disreputable place, esp a bar or club. **3** boxing slang a faked knockout: He took a dive. ◊ **dive in** to help oneself to (food). **dive into sth 1** to plunge one's hands (eg into a bag). **2** to involve oneself enthusiastically in an undertaking.

dive² see DIVA

dive-bomber n an aeroplane that releases a bomb while diving. ○ **dive-bomb** vb.

diver n **1** someone who dives. **2** someone who works underwater. **3** a duck-like diving bird.

diverge vb, intr **1** to separate and go in different directions. **2** to differ. ○ **divergence** n. ○ **divergent** adj.

diverse adj **1** various; assorted. **2** different.

diversify vb (-ies, -ied) **1** tr & intr to become or make something diverse. **2** intr to engage in new and different activities. ○ **diversification** n.

diversion n **1** the act of diverting; the state of being diverted. **2** a detour from a usual route. **3** something intended to draw attention away. **4** amusement. ○ **diversionary** adj.

diversity n (-ies) variety; being varied or different.

divert vb **1** to make someone or something change direction. **2** to draw away (esp attention). **3** to amuse someone.

divertimento /dɪvɜːtɪ'mɛntəʊ/ n (divertimenti /-tiː/ or divertimentos) a light musical composition.

divest vb (usu divest sb of sth) **1** to take away or get rid of it. **2** rather formal to take something off: She divested herself of her jacket.

divide vb **1** tr & intr to split up or separate into parts. **2** (also divide sth up) to share. **3** maths a to determine how many times one number is contained in (another); **b** intr of a number: to be a number of times greater or smaller than another: *3 divides into 9.* **4** to bring about a disagreement among (people). **5** to serve as a boundary between something. **6** *intr* of an assembly, Parliament, etc: to form into groups voting for and against a motion. ➤ *n* **1** a disagreement. **2** a gap or split. **3** *esp US* a ridge of high land between two rivers.

dividend *n* **1** a portion of a company's profits paid to a shareholder. **2** a benefit: *Meeting her would pay dividends.* **3** *maths* a number divided by another number.

dividers *pl n* a V-shaped device with movable arms ending in points, used in geometry, etc for measuring.

divination *n* the practice of foretelling the future by, or as if by, supernatural means.

divine *adj* **1** belonging or relating to, or coming from, God or a god. **2** *colloq* extremely good, pleasant or beautiful. ➤ *vb* **1** to foretell something. **2** to realize something by intuition. **3** *tr & intr* to search for (underground water) with a divining rod. ➤ *n* a member of the clergy who is expert in theology. ○ **divinely** *adv.* ○ **diviner** *n.*

diving bell *n* a large hollow bottomless container which traps air, in which divers can work under water.

divining rod or **dowsing rod** *n* a stick held when divining for water, which moves when a discovery is made.

divinity *n* (*-ies*) **1** theology. **2** a god. **3** the state of being God or a god.

divisible *adj* able to be divided.

division *n* **1** dividing or being divided. **2** something that divides or separates. **3** one of the parts into which something is divided. **4** a major unit of an organization such as an army or police force. **5** *maths* the process of determining how many times one number is contained in another. **6** a formal vote in Parliament. **7** *bot* any of the major groups into which the plant kingdom is divided. ○ **divisional** *adj.*

division sign *n* the symbol ÷, representing division in calculations.

divisive *adj* tending to cause conflict.

divisor *n*, *maths* a number by which another number is divided.

divorce *n* **1** the legal ending of a marriage. **2** a complete separation. ➤ *vb* **1** *tr & intr* to legally end marriage to someone. **2** to separate.

divorcee *n* someone who has been divorced.

divot *n* a piece of grass and earth.

divulge *vb* to make something known. ○ **divulgence** *n.*

divvy[1] *slang*, *n* (*-ies*) a dividend or share. ➤ *vb* (*-ies, -ied*) (*also* **divvy up sth**) to divide or share it.

divvy[2] *n* (*-ies*) *colloq* a fool.

Diwali / diˈwɑːliː/ or **Divali** /-ˈvɑːliː/ *n* a Hindu festival held in honour of Lakshmi, goddess of wealth and good fortune.

DIY *abbrev* do-it-yourself.

dizzy *adj* (*-ier, -iest*) **1** experiencing or causing a

spinning sensation in the head. **2** *colloq* silly; not reliable or responsible. **3** *colloq* bewildered. ➤ *vb* (*-ies, -ied*) **1** to make someone dizzy. **2** to bewilder someone. ○ **dizziness** *n.*

DJ *abbrev* **1** *slang* dinner jacket. **2** disc jockey.

djinn or **djinni** see JINNI

dl *abbrev* decilitre.

DLitt *abbrev*: *Doctor Litterarum* (Latin), Doctor of Letters.

DNA *abbrev* DEOXYRIBONUCLEIC ACID.

DNA fingerprinting *n* GENETIC FINGER-PRINTING.

D-notice *n* a notice sent by the government to newspapers asking them not to publish certain security information.

do[1] *vb* (**does**, *past tense* **did**, *past participle* **done**, *present participle* **doing**) **1** to carry out, perform or commit something. **2** to finish or complete something. **3** *tr & intr* (*also* **do for sb**) to be enough or suitable. **4** to work at or study: *Are you doing maths?* **5** *intr* to be in a particular state: *Business is doing well.* **6** to put in order or arrange. **7** *intr* to act or behave. **8** to provide something as a service: *They do lunches.* **9** to bestow (honour, etc). **10** to cause or produce. **11** to travel (a distance). **12** to travel at (a speed). **13** *colloq* to improve or enhance something or someone: *This dress doesn't do much for me.* **14** *colloq* to cheat someone. **15** *colloq* to mimic someone. **16** to visit (a place, etc) as a tourist. **17** *colloq* to ruin something: *Now he's done it!* **18** *colloq* to assault or injure someone: *I'll do you.* **19** *colloq* to spend (time) in prison. **20** *colloq* to convict someone. **21** *intr*, *colloq* to happen: *There was nothing doing.* **22** *slang* to take (drugs). ➤ *auxiliary vb* **1** used in questions and negative statements or commands, as in *Do you smoke?*, *I don't like wine* and *Don't go!* **2** used to avoid repetition of a verb, as in *She eats as much as I do.* **3** used for emphasis, as in *She does know you've arrived.* ➤ *n* (**dos** or **do's**) *colloq* **1** a party or other gathering. **2** something done as a rule or custom: *dos and don'ts.* ♦ **could do with sth** or **sb** would benefit from having it or them. **have** or **be to do with sb** or **sth 1** to be related to or connected with someone or something: *What has that to do with me?* **2** to be partly or wholly responsible for something: *I had nothing to do with it.* ◊ **do away with sb** or **sth 1** to murder them. **2** to abolish it. **do sb** or **sth down** to speak of them or it disparagingly. **do for sb** *colloq* **1** to do household cleaning for them. **2** to defeat, ruin or kill them. **do sb in** *colloq* **1** to kill them. **2** to exhaust them. **do sb out of sth** to deprive them of it, esp by trickery. **do sb over** *slang* to rob, attack or injure them. **do oneself up** to dress up. **do sth up** *colloq* **1** to repair, clean or improve the decoration of (a building, etc). **2** to fasten it; to tie or wrap it up. **do without sth** to manage without it.

do[2] see DOH

Dobermann pinscher /ˈdəʊbəmən ˈpɪnʃə(r)/ or **Dobermann** *n* a large breed of dog with a smooth black-and-tan coat.

doc n, colloq a doctor.

docile adj easy to manage or control. ○ **docilely** adv. ○ **docility** n.

dock[1] n 1 a harbour where ships are loaded, unloaded and repaired. **2** (**docks**) the area surrounding this. ➤ vb, tr & intr **1** to bring or come into a dock. **2** of space vehicles: to link up in space.

dock[2] vb **1** to cut off all or part of (an animal's tail). **2** to make deductions from (eg someone's pay). **3** to deduct (an amount).

dock[3] n a weed with large broad leaves.

dock[4] n the enclosure in a court of law where the accused sits or stands.

docker n a labourer who loads and unloads ships.

docket n a note accompanying a package, eg detailing contents or recording receipt. ➤ vb (**docketed, docketing**) to fix a label to something.

dockyard n a shipyard, esp a naval one.

Doc Martens pl n, trademark a make of lace-up leather boots with thick soles.

doctor n **1** someone qualified to practise medicine. **2** N Am **a** a dentist; **b** a veterinary surgeon. **3** someone holding a DOCTORATE. ➤ vb **1** to falsify (eg information). **2** to tamper with something. **3** colloq to sterilize or castrate (an animal).

doctorate n a high academic degree, awarded esp for research.

doctrinaire adj, derog adhering rigidly to theories or principles, regardless of practicalities or appropriateness.

doctrine /'dɒktrɪn/ n a religious or political belief, or a set of such beliefs. ○ **doctrinal** /dɒk-'traɪnəl/ adj.

docudrama n a play or film based on real events and characters.

document n **1** any piece of writing of an official nature. **2** comput a text file. ➤ vb **1** to record something, esp in written form. **2** to provide written evidence to support or prove something.

documentary n (-ies) a film, etc presenting real people in real situations. ➤ adj **1** connected with, or consisting of, documents: documentary evidence. **2** of the nature of a documentary.

documentation n documents or documentary evidence.

dodder vb, intr to move in an unsteady trembling fashion, usu as a result of old age. ○ **dodderer** n. ○ **doddery** adj.

doddle n, colloq something easily done.

dodeca- comb form, signifying twelve.

dodecagon /doʊ'dɛkəɡɒn/ n a flat geometric figure with 12 sides and angles.

dodecahedron /doʊdɛkə'hiːdrən/ n a solid geometric figure with 12 faces.

dodge vb **1** to avoid (a blow, a person, etc) by moving quickly away, esp sideways. **2** to escape or avoid something by cleverness or deceit. ➤ n **1** a sudden movement aside. **2** a

trick to escape or avoid something. ○ **dodger** n.

Dodgems pl n, trademark a fairground amusement in which drivers of small electric cars try to bump each other.

dodgy adj (-ier, -iest) colloq **1** difficult or risky. **2** untrustworthy; dishonest, or dishonestly obtained.

dodo n (**dodos** or **dodoes**) a large extinct flightless bird.

doe n (**does** or **doe**) an adult female rabbit, hare or small deer.

doer n a busy active person.

does see under DO[1]

doesn't contraction of does not.

doff vb, old use, literary to lift (one's hat) in greeting.

dog n **1** a carnivorous mammal such as a wolf, jackal or fox. **2** a domestic species of this family. **3** the male of any such animal. **4** colloq a person. ➤ vb (**dogged, dogging**) **1** to follow someone very closely. **2** to trouble someone. ♦ **a dog's life** a life of misery.

dogcart n a two-wheeled horse-drawn passenger carriage with seats back-to-back.

dog collar n **1** a collar for a dog. **2** colloq a stiff collar worn by certain clergy.

dog days pl n the hottest period of the year.

doge /doʊdʒ/ n the chief magistrate of Venice or Genoa.

dog-eared adj of a book: with its pages turned down at the corners.

dog-end n, slang a cigarette end.

dogfight n **1** a battle at close quarters between two fighter aircraft. **2** any violent fight.

dogfish n any of various kinds of small shark.

dogged /'dɒɡɪd/ adj determined; resolute. ○ **doggedly** adv. ○ **doggedness** n.

doggerel n **1** badly written poetry. **2** poetry with an irregular rhyming pattern for comic effect. ➤ adj of poor quality.

doggo adv. ♦ **lie doggo** colloq to hide; to lie low.

doggy adj (-ier, -iest) colloq **1** belonging to, like or relating to dogs. **2** fond of dogs. ➤ n (-ies) a child's word for a dog.

doggy-bag n a bag in which a customer at a restaurant can take home uneaten food.

doggy-paddle or **doggie-paddle** or **dog-paddle** n a basic swimming stroke with short paddling movements. ➤ vb, intr to swim using this stroke.

doghouse n, now chiefly N Am a KENNEL. ♦ **in the doghouse** colloq out of favour.

dog in the manger n someone who has no need of something but refuses to let others use it.

dogleg n a sharp bend, esp on a golf course.

dogma n (**dogmas** or **dogmata** /'dɒɡmətə/) **1** a belief or principle laid down by an authority as unquestionably true. **2** such beliefs or principles in general.

dogmatic adj **1** of an opinion: forcefully and arrogantly stated as if unquestionable. **2** of a person: tending to make such statements of opinion. ○ **dogmatically** *adv*. ○ **dogmatism** *n*. ○ **dogmatist** *n*.

do-gooder *n, colloq* an enthusiastic helper of other people, esp one whose help is not appreciated.

dog-paddle see DOGGY-PADDLE

dogsbody *n (-ies) colloq* someone who does menial tasks.

dog's breakfast or **dinner** *n* anything very messy.

dog-tired *adj, colloq* extremely tired.

doh or **do** /dou/ *n, mus* in sol-fa notation: the first note of the major scale.

doily or **doyley** *n (-ies* or *-eys)* a small decorative napkin of lace-like paper laid on plates under sandwiches, cakes, etc.

doings *pl n* activities; behaviour.

do-it-yourself *n* the practice of doing one's own household repairs, etc without professional help. ➤ *adj* designed to be built, constructed, etc by an amateur rather than a fully trained professional.

Dolby or **Dolby system** *n, trademark* a system of noise reduction in audio tape-recording.

the doldrums *pl n* **1** a depressed mood. **2** a state of inactivity. **3** *(also* **the Doldrums)** *meteorol* a hot humid region on either side of the Equator where there is little wind.

dole *n, colloq* (**the dole**) unemployment benefit. ➤ *vb (always* **dole sth out)** to hand it out or give it out. ♦ **on the dole** *colloq* unemployed.

doleful *adj* sad; mournful. ○ **dolefully** *adv*. ○ **dolefulness** *n*.

doll *n* **1** a toy in the form of a small model of a human being. **2** *derog, colloq* a showy overdressed woman. **3** *slang, often offensive* any girl or woman, esp when considered pretty. **4** *colloq* a term of endearment, esp for a girl. ➤ *vb (always* **doll oneself up)** to dress smartly or showily.

dollar *n* (symbol $) the standard unit of currency in the US, Canada, Australia and other countries, divided into 100 CENTS.

dollop *n, colloq* a small shapeless mass.

dolly *n (-ies)* **1** *colloq* a doll. **2** *cinema, TV* a frame with wheels on which a film or television camera is mounted for moving shots.

dolman sleeve *n* a kind of sleeve that tapers from a very wide armhole to a tight wrist.

dolmen *n* a simple prehistoric monument consisting of a large flat stone supported by several vertical stones.

dolphin *n* a small toothed variety of whale.

dolphinarium *n (dolphinaria* or *dolphinariums)* a large open-air aquarium in which dolphins are kept.

dolt *n, derog* a stupid person. ○ **doltish** *adj*.

domain *n* **1** the scope of any subject or area of interest. **2** a territory owned or ruled by one person or government. **3** *maths* the set of values specified for a given mathematical function.

dome *n* **1** a hemispherical roof. **2** anything of

similar shape. ○ **domed** *adj*.

domestic *adj* **1** belonging or relating to the home, the family or private life. **2** kept as a pet or farm animal. **3** within or relating to one's country: *domestic sales*. **4** enjoying home life. ➤ *n* **1** *colloq* a fight, usu in the home, between members of a household. **2** a household servant. ○ **domestically** *adv*.

domesticate *vb* **1** to train (an animal) to live with people. **2** *often facetious* to train someone in cooking, housework, etc. ○ **domestication** *n*.

domesticity *n* home life, or a liking for it.

domestic science *n* training in household skills, esp cooking.

domicile /ˈdɒmɪsaɪl/ *n* a legally recognized place of permanent residence. ➤ *vb, law* to establish or be settled in a fixed residence.

dominant *adj* **1** most important, evident or active. **2** tending or seeking to command or influence others. **3** of a building, etc: overlooking others from an elevated position. **4** *biol* **a** denoting a gene whose characteristics are always fully expressed in an individual. Compare RECESSIVE; **b** denoting a characteristic determined by such a gene. ➤ *n* **1** *mus* the fifth note of a musical scale. **2** *biol* a dominant gene. ○ **dominance** *n*.

dominate *vb, tr & intr* **1** to have command or influence over someone. **2** to be the most important, evident or active of (a group). **3** to stand above (a place). ○ **dominating** *adj*. ○ **domination** *n*.

domineering *adj* overbearing; arrogant.

Dominican *n* a member of a Christian order of friars and nuns orig founded by St Dominic in 1215. ➤ *adj* belonging or relating to this order.

dominion *n* **1** rule; power. **2** a territory or country governed by a single ruler or government. **3** *formerly* a self-governing colony within the British Empire.

domino *n (dominoes)* **1** any of the small rectangular tiles marked, in two halves, with varying numbers of spots, used in the game of **dominoes**. **2** *(dominoes)* a game in which these tiles are laid down, with matching halves end to end. **3** a black cloak with a hood and mask.

don¹ *n* a university lecturer.

don² *vb (donned, donning)* to put on (clothing).

donate *vb* to give, esp to charity. ○ **donation** *n*.

done *vb, past participle of* DO¹. ➤ *adj* **1** finished; completed. **2** fully cooked. **3** socially acceptable. **4** used up. **5** *colloq* exhausted. ➤ *exclam* expressing agreement or completion of a deal. ♦ **done for** *colloq* facing ruin or death.

doner kebab /ˈdɒnə(r)/ *n* thin slices cut from a block of minced lamb grilled on a spit and eaten on unleavened bread.

Don Juan /dɒn ˈdʒuːən, dɒn ˈhwɑːn/ *n* a man who seduces women.

donkey *n* **1** a hoofed herbivorous mammal related to but smaller than the horse. **2** *colloq* a stupid person.

donkey jacket *n* a heavy jacket made of a thick woollen fabric, usu black or dark blue.

donkey's years *pl n, colloq* a very long time.

donkey-work *n* **1** heavy manual work. **2** preparation; groundwork.

donor *n* **1** someone who donates something, esp money. **2** a person or animal that provides blood, semen, living tissue or organs for medical use.

donor card *n* a card indicating that its carrier is willing, in the event of sudden death, to have their organs removed for transplantation.

don't *contraction of* do not. ➤ *n, colloq* something that must not be done: *dos and don'ts*.

doodle *vb, intr* to scrawl or scribble meaninglessly. ➤ *n* a meaningless scribble.

doolally *adj, slang* mentally unbalanced.

doom *n* inescapable death, ruin or other unpleasant fate. ➤ *vb* to condemn someone to death or some other dire fate.

doomsday *n* the last day of the world.

door *n* **1** a movable barrier opening and closing an entrance. **2** an entrance. **3** a house considered in relation to others: *three doors away*. **4** a means of entry: *The competition opened the door to stardom*. ♦ **close the door to sth** to make it impossible. **lay sth at sb's door** to blame them for it.

doorbell *n* a bell on or next to a door, rung by visitors as a sign of arrival.

doorjamb or **doorpost** *n* one of the two vertical side pieces of a door frame.

doorknocker see KNOCKER

doorman *n* a man employed to guard the entrance to a hotel, club, etc and assist guests or customers.

doormat *n* **1** a mat for wiping shoes on before entering. **2** *colloq* a person easily submitting to unfair treatment by others.

doorstep *n* **1** a step in front of a building's door. **2** *slang* a thick sandwich or slice of bread. ➤ *vb* **1** to go from door to door canvassing. **2** of journalists, etc: to pester someone by waiting at their door.

doorstop *n* **1** a device, eg a wedge, for holding a door open. **2** a device, eg a fixed knob, for preventing a door opening too far.

doorway *n* the space where there is or might be a door.

dope *n* **1** *colloq* a drug taken for pleasure, esp cannabis. **2** *colloq* a drug given to athletes, dogs or horses to affect performance. **3** *colloq* a stupid person. **4** (**the dope**) *slang* information, esp when confidential. ➤ *vb* to give or apply drugs to (a person or animal).

dopey or **dopy** *adj, colloq* (**dopier, dopiest**) **1** sleepy or inactive, as if drugged. **2** stupid.

doppelgänger /ˈdɒpəlgɛŋə(r)/ *n* a double of a person.

Doppler effect or **Doppler shift** *n, physics* the change in wavelength observed when the distance between a source of waves and the observer is changing.

Doric *adj, archit* denoting an order of classical architecture, characterized by thick fluted columns.

dormant *adj* **1** temporarily quiet, inactive or out of use. **2** *biol* in a resting state. ○ **dormancy** *n*.

dormer or **dormer window** *n* a window fitted vertically into an extension built out from a sloping roof.

dormitory *n* (*-ies*) **1** a large bedroom for several people. **2** *esp US* a hall of residence in a college or university. Often shortened to **dorm**.

dormitory town or **dormitory suburb** *n* a town or suburb from which most residents travel to work elsewhere.

Dormobile *n, trademark* a van equipped for living and sleeping in.

dormouse *n* a small nocturnal rodent with rounded ears, large eyes, velvety fur, and a bushy tail.

dorp *n, S Afr* a small town or village.

dorsal *adj, biol, physiol* belonging or relating to the back.

dory *n* (*-ies*) a golden-yellow fish of the mackerel family.

DOS /dɒs/ *abbrev, comput* disk-operating system, a program for handling information on a disk.

dos or **do's** see under DO[1]

dose *n* **1** *med* the measured quantity of medicine, etc that is prescribed by a doctor to be administered to a patient. **2** the amount of radiation a person is exposed to over a specified period of time. **3** *colloq* a bout, esp of an illness or something unpleasant. **4** *slang* a sexually transmitted disease, esp gonorrhoea. ➤ *vb* (*also* **dose sb up with sth**) to give them medicine, esp in large quantities. ○ **dosage** *n*. ♦ **like a dose of salts** *colloq* extremely quickly and effectively.

dosh *n, slang* money.

doss *vb, intr, slang* (*often* **doss down**) to settle down to sleep, esp on an improvised bed.

dosser *n, slang* **1** a homeless person sleeping on the street. **2** a lazy person.

dossier /ˈdɒsɪeɪ, ˈdɒsɪə(r)/ *n* a file of papers containing information on a person or subject.

dot *n* **1** a spot; a point. **2** in MORSE code: the shorter of the two lengths of signal element. Compare DASH (sense 5). ➤ *vb* (**dotted, dotting**) **1** to put a dot on something. **2** to scatter; to cover with a scattering: *a lawn dotted with daisies*. ♦ **dot the i's and cross the t's 1** to pay close attention to detail. **2** to finish the last few details of something. **on the dot** exactly on time.

dotage *n* feeble-mindedness owing to old age.

dotard *n* someone in their dotage.

dotcom *adj* of a company: trading through the Internet. ➤ *n* a company that trades through the Internet.

dote *vb, intr* **1** (*always* **dote on** or **upon sb** or **sth**) to show a foolishly excessive fondness for them. **2** to be foolish or weak-minded, esp because of old age. ○ **doting** adj excessively fond of someone.

dotty adj (**-ier, -iest**) colloq silly; crazy. ○ **dottiness** n.

double adj **1** made up of two similar parts; in pairs. **2** twice the weight, size, etc, or twice the usual weight, size, etc. **3** for two people: a double bed. **4** ambiguous: double meaning. **5** of a musical instrument: sounding an octave lower: double bass. ➤ adv **1** twice. **2** with one half over the other: folded double. ➤ n **1** a double quantity. **2** a duplicate or lookalike. **3** an actor's stand-in. **4** a double measure of alcoholic spirit. **5** a racing bet in which winnings from the first stake become a stake in a subsequent race. **6** a win in two events on the same racing programme. ➤ vb **1** tr & intr to make or become twice as large in size, number, etc. **2** (often **double sth over**) to fold one half of it over the other. **3** intr to have a second use or function: The spare bed doubles as a couch. **4** intr to turn round sharply. **5** intr (often **double for sb**) to act as their substitute. ◆ **at** or **on the double** very quickly. ◇ **double back** to turn and go back, often by a different route. **double up 1** to bend sharply at the waist, esp through pain. **2** (also **double up with sb**) to share a bedroom with another person.

double agent n a spy working for two opposing governments at the same time.

double-barrelled or (N Am) **double-barreled** adj **1** having two barrels. **2** of a surname: made up of two names.

double bass n the largest and lowest in pitch of the orchestral stringed instruments.

double bluff n an action or statement which is meant to be seen as a bluff, but which is in fact genuine.

double-breasted adj of a coat or jacket: having overlapping front flaps.

double-check vb to check twice or again.

double chin n a chin with an area of loose flesh underneath.

double cream n thick cream with a high fat content.

double-cross vb to cheat or deceive (esp an ally). ➤ n such a deceit.

double-dealing n cheating.

double-decker n **1** a bus with two decks. **2** colloq anything with two levels or layers.

double Dutch n, colloq nonsense.

double-edged adj **1** having two cutting edges. **2** having two possible meanings or purposes.

double entendre /ˈduːbəl ãˈtãdrə/ n a remark having two possible meanings, one of them usu sexually suggestive.

double-entry n, bookkeeping a method by which two entries are made of each transaction.

double figures pl n the numbers between 10 and 99 inclusive.

double-glazing n windows constructed with

two panes separated by a vacuum, providing added heat insulation.

double-jointed adj having extraordinarily flexible body joints.

double negative n an expression containing two negative words, esp where only one is logically needed: He hasn't never asked me.

double-park vb to park at the side of another vehicle parked alongside the kerb.

double-quick adj, adv very quick or quickly.

doubles sing n a competition in tennis, etc between two teams of two players each.

double standard n (often **double standards**) a principle or rule applied firmly to one person or group and loosely or not at all to another, esp oneself.

doublet n **1** hist a close-fitting man's jacket. **2** a pair of objects of any kind, or each of these.

double take n an initial inattentive reaction followed swiftly by a sudden full realization.

double-talk n talk that seems relevant but is really meaningless, esp as offered up by politicians.

doublethink n simultaneous belief in, or acceptance of, two opposing ideas or principles.

double time n **1** a rate of pay equal to double the basic rate. **2** mus a time twice as fast as the previous time. **3** mus DUPLE time.

doubloon n a gold coin formerly used in Spain and S America.

doubly adv **1** to twice the extent; very much more. **2** in two ways.

doubt vb **1** to feel uncertain about something; to be suspicious of it. **2** to be inclined to disbelieve something. ➤ n **1** a feeling of uncertainty, suspicion or mistrust. **2** an inclination to disbelieve. ○ **doubter** n.

doubtful adj **1** feeling doubt. **2** uncertain; able to be doubted. **3** likely not to be the case. ○ **doubtfully** adv.

doubtless adv probably; certainly. ○ **doubtlessly** adv.

douche /duːʃ/ n **1** a powerful jet of water that is used to clean a body orifice, esp the vagina. **2** an apparatus for producing such a jet. ➤ vb, tr & intr to apply or make use of a douche.

dough n **1** a mixture of flour, liquid and yeast, used in the preparation of bread, pastry, etc. **2** slang money.

doughnut or (esp US) **donut** n a portion of sweetened dough fried in deep fat, usu with a hole in the middle or with a filling.

doughty /ˈdaʊtɪ/ adj (**-ier, -iest**) literary brave.

dour /dʊə(r)/ adj stern; sullen. ○ **dourness** n.

douse or **dowse** /daʊs/ vb **1** to throw water over something; to plunge something into water. **2** to extinguish (a light or fire).

dove[1] N Am past tense of DIVE[1]

dove[2] /dʌv/ n **1** any of various pigeons. **2** pol a person favouring peace rather than hostility. Compare HAWK[1] (sense 2).

dovecote or **dovecot** n a building or shed in which domestic pigeons are kept.

dovetail n a joint, esp in wood, made by fitting

V-shaped parts into corresponding slots. ➢ *vb, tr & intr* **1** to fit using one or more dovetails. **2** to fit or combine neatly.

dowager *n* a title given to a nobleman's widow, to distinguish her from the wife of her late husband's heir.

dowdy *adj* (*-ier, -iest*) dull, plain and unfashionable. ○ **dowdily** *adv.* ○ **dowdiness** *n.*

dowel *n* a wooden peg, esp used to join two pieces by fitting into corresponding holes in each.

dower *n* a widow's share, for life, in her deceased husband's property.

dower house *n* a house smaller than, and within the grounds of, a large country house.

down[1] *adv* **1** towards or in a low or lower position, level or state; on or to the ground. **2** from a greater to a lesser size, amount or level: *scaled down.* **3** towards or in a more southerly place. **4** in writing; on paper: *take down notes.* **5** as a deposit: *put down five pounds.* **6** to an end stage or finished state: *hunt someone down.* **7** from earlier to later times: *handed down through generations.* **8** to a state of exhaustion, defeat, etc: *worn down by illness.* **9** not vomited up: *keep food down.* **10** in a crossword: in the vertical direction: *5 down.* Compare ACROSS (*adv* sense 3). ➢ *prep* **1** in a lower position on something. **2** along; at a further position on, by or through: *down the road.* **3** along in the direction of the current of a river. **4** from the top to or towards the bottom. **5** *dialect* to or in (a particular place): *going down the town.* ➢ *adj* **1** sad. **2** going towards or reaching a lower position: *a down pipe.* **3** made as a deposit: *a down payment.* **4** reduced in price. **5** of a computer, etc: out of action, esp temporarily. ➢ *vb* **1** to drink something quickly, esp in one gulp. **2** to force someone or something to the ground. ➢ *exclam* used as a command to animals, esp dogs: *get or stay down.* ➢ *n* **1** an unsuccessful or otherwise unpleasant period: *Life has its ups and downs.* **2** (**downs**) an area of rolling (esp treeless) hills. ◆ **down tools** *colloq* to stop working, as a protest. **down to the ground** *colloq* completely; perfectly. **down under** *colloq* in or to Australia and/or New Zealand. **down with …!** let's get rid of …! **have a down on sb** *colloq* to be ill-disposed towards them.

down[2] *n* soft fine feathers or hair. ○ **downy** *adj.*

down-and-out *adj* homeless and penniless. ➢ *n* a down-and-out person.

down-at-heel *adj* shabby.

downbeat *adj* **1** pessimistic. **2** relaxed. ➢ *n, mus* the first beat of a bar or the movement of the conductor's baton indicating this.

downcast *adj* **1** glum; dispirited. **2** of eyes: looking downwards.

downer *n* **1** *colloq* a state of depression. **2** *slang* a tranquillizing or depressant drug.

downfall *n* failure or ruin, or its cause.

downgrade *vb* to reduce to a lower grade.

downhearted *adj* dispirited; discouraged.

downhill *adv* **1** downwards. **2** to or towards a worse condition. ➢ *adj* downwardly sloping. ➢ *n* a ski race down a hillside. ◆ **go downhill** to deteriorate (in health, morality or prosperity).

down-in-the-mouth *adj* unhappy.

download *vb, comput* to transfer (data) from one computer to another or to a disk.

down-market *adj* cheap, of poor quality or lacking prestige.

down payment *n* a deposit.

downpour *n* a very heavy fall of rain.

downright *adj* utter: *downright lunacy.* ➢ *adv* utterly.

downside *n, colloq* a negative aspect; a disadvantage.

downsizing *n* reducing the size of a workforce, esp by redundancies.

Down's syndrome *n, pathol* a congenital disorder which results in learning disability, flattened facial features, and slight slanting of the eyes.

downstairs *adv* to or towards a lower floor; down the stairs. ➢ *adj* on a lower or ground floor. ➢ *n* a lower or ground floor.

downstream *adj, adv* further along a river towards the sea.

downtime *n* time during which work ceases because a machine is not working.

down-to-earth *adj* sensible and practical.

downtown *adj, adv* in or towards either the lower part of the city or the city centre. ➢ *n* this area of a city.

downtrodden *adj* ruled or controlled tyrannically.

downturn *n* a decline in economic activity.

downward *adj* leading or moving down; declining. ➢ *adv* (*usu* **downwards**) to or towards a lower place or a less important or junior position. ○ **downwardly** *adv.*

downwind *adv* **1** in or towards the direction in which the wind is blowing. **2** with the wind carrying one's scent away from (eg an animal one is stalking). ➢ *adj* moving with, or sheltered from, the wind.

dowry *n* (*-ies*) an amount of wealth handed over by a woman's family to her husband on marriage.

dowse[1] *vb, intr* to search for underground water with a DIVINING ROD. ○ **dowser** *n.*

dowse[2] see DOUSE

doxology *n* (*-ies*) a Christian hymn, verse or expression praising God.

doyen /ˈdɔɪən/ *n, literary* the most senior and most respected member of a group or profession.

doyenne /dɔɪˈɛn/ *n* a female DOYEN.

doyley see DOILY

doze *vb, intr* to sleep lightly. ➢ *n* a brief period of light sleep. ◊ **doze off** to fall into a light sleep.

dozen *n* (**dozens** or, following a number, *dozen*) **1** a set of twelve. **2** (*often* **dozens**) *colloq* very many. ○ **dozenth** *adj.*

dozy adj (**-ier, -iest**) 1 sleepy. 2 colloq stupid; slow to understand; not alert.

DPP abbrev Director of Public Prosecutions.

Dr abbrev Doctor.

Dr. abbrev in addresses: Drive.

drab adj (**drabber, drabbest**) 1 dull; dreary. 2 of a dull greenish-brown colour. ○ **drabness** n.

drachm /dram/ n a measure equal to ⅛ of an ounce or fluid ounce.

draconian or **draconic** adj of a law, etc: harsh.

draft n 1 a written plan; a preliminary sketch. 2 a written order requesting a bank to pay out money. 3 a group of people drafted. 4 esp US conscription. ➤ vb 1 to set something out in preliminary sketchy form. 2 to select and send off (personnel) to perform a specific task. 3 esp US to conscript.

> **draft** A word often confused with this one is **draught**.

drag vb (**dragged, dragging**) 1 to pull someone or something along roughly, slowly and with force. 2 tr & intr to move or make something move along scraping the ground. 3 colloq (usu **drag sb away**) to force or persuade them to come away. 4 to search (eg a lake) with a hook or dragnet. ➤ n 1 an act of dragging; a dragging effect. 2 a person or thing that makes progress slow. 3 colloq a draw on a cigarette. 4 colloq a dull or tedious person or thing. 5 colloq women's clothes worn by a man. 6 the resistance to motion encountered by an object travelling through a liquid or gas. ♦ **drag one's feet** or **heels** colloq to be deliberately slow to take action. ◊ **drag sth out** colloq to make it last as long as possible. **drag sth up** colloq to mention an unpleasant subject long forgotten or not usu introduced.

draggle vb, tr & intr to make or become wet and dirty eg through trailing on the ground.

dragnet n a heavy net pulled along the bottom of a river, lake, etc in a search for something.

dragon n 1 a mythical, fire-breathing, reptile-like creature with wings and a long tail. 2 colloq a frighteningly domineering woman.

dragonfly n (**-ies**) an insect with a long slender brightly coloured body and gauzy translucent wings.

dragoon n, hist but still used in regimental titles: a heavily armed mounted soldier. ➤ vb to force someone into doing something.

drag race n a contest in acceleration between specially designed cars or motorcycles over a short distance. ○ **drag-racing** n.

drain vb 1 to empty (a container) by causing or allowing liquid to escape. 2 (**drain sth of liquid**) to remove liquid from it. 3 (often **drain sth off** or **away**) to cause or allow (a liquid) to escape. 4 intr (often **drain off**) of liquid, etc: to flow away. 5 intr (often **drain away**) to disappear. 6 to drink the total contents of (a glass, etc). 7 to use up the strength, emotion or resources of (someone). 8 of a river: to carry away surface water from (land). ➤ n a device,

esp a pipe, for carrying away liquid. ♦ **a drain on sth** anything that exhausts or seriously depletes a supply. **down the drain** colloq wasted; lost.

drainage n the process or a system of draining.

draining board n a sloping, and often channelled, surface at the side of a sink allowing water from washed dishes, etc to drain away.

drainpipe n a pipe carrying waste water or rainwater.

drake n a male duck.

dram n 1 colloq a small amount of alcoholic spirit, esp whisky. 2 a measure of weight equal to 1/16 of an ounce.

drama n 1 a play. 2 plays in general. 3 the art of producing, directing and acting in plays. 4 excitement and emotion; an exciting situation.

dramatic adj 1 relating to plays, the theatre or acting in general. 2 exciting. 3 sudden and striking. 4 of a person or behaviour: flamboyantly emotional. ○ **dramatically** adv.

dramatics sing n or pl n activities associated with the staging and performing of plays. ➤ pl n exaggeratedly emotional behaviour.

dramatis personae /ˈdramətɪs pɜːˈsəʊnaɪ/ pl n (often functioning as sing n) 1 a list of the characters in a play. 2 these characters.

dramatist n a writer of plays.

dramatize or **-ise** vb 1 to make something into a work for public performance. 2 to treat something as, or make it seem, more exciting or important. ○ **dramatization** n.

drape vb 1 to hang cloth loosely over something. 2 to arrange or lay (cloth, etc) loosely. ➤ n, theat or (esp **drapes**) N Am a curtain or hanging.

draper n someone who sells fabric.

drapery n (**-ies**) 1 fabric. 2 curtains and other hanging fabrics. 3 a draper's business or shop.

drastic adj extreme; severe. ○ **drastically** adv.

drat exclam, colloq expressing anger or annoyance.

draught n 1 a current of air, esp indoors. 2 a quantity of liquid swallowed in one go. 3 any of the discs used in the game of DRAUGHTS. 4 colloq draught beer. 5 a dose of liquid medicine. ➤ adj 1 of beer: pumped direct from the cask to the glass. 2 esp in compounds of an animal: used for pulling loads.

> **draught** A word often confused with this one is **draft**.

draughts sing n a game for two people played with 24 discs on a chequered board (a **draughtboard**).

draughtsman n 1 someone skilled in drawing. 2 someone employed to produce accurate and detailed technical drawings. ○ **draughtsmanship** n.

draughty adj (**-ier, -iest**) prone to or suffering draughts of air.

draw vb (past tense **drew**, past participle **drawn**, present participle **drawing**) 1 tr & intr to make a picture of something or someone, esp with a pencil. **2** to pull out or take out something: *draw water from a well*. **3** *intr* to move or proceed steadily in a specified direction: *draw nearer*. **4** to pull someone along or into a particular position: *drawing her closer to him*. **5** to open or close (curtains). **6** to attract (eg attention or criticism). **7** *tr & intr* (*also* **draw with sb**) to end a game equal with an opponent. **8** to choose or be given as the result of random selection: *draw lots*. **9** to arrive at or infer (a conclusion). **10** *a intr* (*also* **draw on** (**a cigarette**)) to suck air (through a cigarette); *b* of a chimney: to make air flow through a fire, allowing burning. **11** *technical* of a ship: to require (a certain depth of water) to float. **12** *intr* of tea: to brew or infuse. **13** to disembowel: *hang, draw and quarter*. **14** to write (a cheque). ➤ *n* **1** a result in which neither side is the winner. **2** *a* the making of a random selection, eg of the winners of a competition; *b* a competition with winners chosen at random. **3** the potential to attract many people, or a person or thing having this. **4** the act of drawing a gun. ♦ **be drawn on sth** to be persuaded to talk about it: *He refused to be drawn on his plans*. **draw a blank** to get no result. **draw the line** to fix a limit, eg on one's actions or tolerance. ◊ **draw in** of nights: to start earlier, making days shorter. **draw on sth** to make use of assets: *draw on reserves of energy*. **draw sb out** to encourage them to be less shy. **draw up** to come to a halt. **draw sth up** to plan and write (a document).

drawback *n* a disadvantage.

drawbridge *n* a bridge that can be lifted to prevent access across or allow passage beneath.

drawer *n* **1** a sliding lidless storage box fitted as part of a desk or other piece of furniture. **2** someone who draws. **3** (**drawers**) *old use* knickers.

drawing *n* **1** a picture made up of lines. **2** the act or art of making such pictures.

drawing pin *n* a short pin with a broad flat head.

drawing room *n* a sitting room or living room.

drawl *vb, tr & intr* to speak or say in a slow lazy manner, esp with prolonged vowel sounds.

drawn[1] *adj* showing signs of mental strain or tiredness.

drawn[2] *vb, past participle of* DRAW. ➤ *adj, in compounds* pulled by: *horse-drawn*.

drawstring *n* a cord sewn inside a hem eg on a bag, closing up the hem when pulled.

dray[1] *n* a low horse-drawn cart.

dray[2] see DREY

dread *n* great fear or apprehension. ➤ *vb* to look ahead to something with dread.

dreadful *adj* **1** inspiring great fear. **2** *loosely* very bad, unpleasant or extreme. ○ **dreadfully** *adv* **1** terribly. **2** *colloq* very.

dreadlocks *pl n* thin braids of hair tied tightly all over the head.

dream *n* **1** thoughts and mental images experienced during sleep. **2** a state of being completely engrossed in one's own thoughts. **3** a distant ambition, esp if unattainable. **4** *colloq* an extremely pleasing person or thing: *He's a dream to work with*. ➤ *adj, colloq* luxurious, ideal. ➤ *vb* (*past tense & past participle* **dreamed** /driːmd, drɛmt/ *or* **dreamt** /drɛmt/) **1** *tr & intr* to have thoughts and visions during sleep. **2** (*usu* **dream of sth**) *a* to have a distant ambition or hope; *b* to imagine or conceive of something. **3** *intr* to have unrealistic thoughts or plans. **4** *intr* to be lost in thought. ○ **dreamer** *n*. ◊ **dream sth up** to devise or invent something unusual or absurd.

dream ticket *n, chiefly N Am* an ideal pair or list, esp of electoral candidates.

dreamy *adj* (*-ier, -iest*) **1** unreal, as if in a dream. **2** having or showing a wandering mind. **3** *colloq* lovely. ○ **dreamily** *adv*. ○ **dreaminess** *n*.

dreary *adj* (*-ier, -iest*) **1** dull and depressing. **2** uninteresting. ○ **drearily** *adv*. ○ **dreariness** *n*.

dredge[1] *vb, tr & intr* to clear the bottom of or deepen (the sea or a river) by bringing up mud and waste. ➤ *n* a machine for dredging. ○ **dredger** *n*. ◊ **dredge sth up** *colloq* to mention or bring up something long forgotten.

dredge[2] *vb* to sprinkle (food), eg with sugar. ○ **dredger** *n*.

dregs *pl n* **1** solid particles in a liquid that settle at the bottom. **2** worthless or contemptible elements.

drench *vb* **1** to make something or someone soaking wet. **2** to administer liquid medicine to (an animal). ➤ *n* a dose of liquid medicine for an animal.

dress *vb* **1** *tr & intr* to put clothes on; to wear, or make someone wear, clothes (of a certain kind). **2** to treat and bandage (wounds). **3** to prepare, or add seasoning or a sauce to (food). **4** to arrange a display in (a shop window). **5** to shape and smooth (esp stone). **6** *intr* to put on or have on formal evening wear. ➤ *n* **1** a woman's garment with top and skirt in one piece. **2** clothing: *in evening dress*. ➤ *adj* formal; for wear in the evenings: *dress jacket*. ◊ **dress sb down** to scold them. **dress up 1** to put on fancy dress. **2** to dress in smart or formal clothes. **dress sth up** to make it appear more pleasant or acceptable by making additions or alterations.

dressage /ˈdrɛsɑːʒ/ *n* the training of a horse in, or performance of, set manoeuvres signalled by the rider.

dress circle *n, theat* a balcony in a theatre, esp the first above the ground floor.

dresser *n* **1** a free-standing kitchen cupboard with shelves above. **2** *US* a chest of drawers or dressing table. **3** a theatre assistant employed to help actors with their costumes. **4** a person who dresses in a particular way.

dressing *n* **1** *cookery* any sauce added to food, esp salad. **2** *N Am, cookery* STUFFING. **3** a covering for a wound. **4** *agric* an application of fertilizer to the soil surface.

dressing gown *n* a loose robe worn informally indoors, esp over nightclothes.

dressing room *n* a room used for changing clothing, esp in a theatre.

dressing table *n* a piece of bedroom furniture with drawers and a large mirror.

dressmaking *n* the craft of making esp women's clothes. ○ **dressmaker** *n*.

dress rehearsal *n* 1 *theat* the last rehearsal of a performance, with full costumes, lighting and other effects. 2 a practice under real conditions.

dress shirt *n* a man's formal shirt worn with a dinner jacket.

dressy *adj* (*-ier, -iest*) 1 dressed or dressing stylishly. 2 of clothes: for formal wear. 3 *colloq* fancy. ○ **dressily** *adv*.

drey or **dray** *n* a squirrel's nest.

dribble *vb* 1 *intr* to fall or flow in drops. 2 *intr* to allow saliva to run slowly down from the mouth. 3 *tr & intr, football, hockey, etc* to move along keeping (a ball) in close control with frequent short strokes. ➤ *n* 1 a small quantity of liquid, esp saliva. 2 *football, hockey, etc* an act of dribbling a ball.

dribs and drabs *pl n* very small quantities at a time.

drier or **dryer** *n* 1 a device or substance that dries clothing, hair, paint, etc. 2 a person or thing that dries.

drift *n* 1 a general movement or tendency to move. 2 degree of movement off course caused by wind or a current. 3 the general meaning of something. ➤ *vb, intr* 1 to float or be blown along or into heaps. 2 to move aimlessly from one place or occupation to another. 3 to move off course.

drifter *n* 1 a fishing boat that uses a DRIFT NET. 2 someone who moves aimlessly from place to place.

drift net *n* a large fishing net allowed to drift with the tide.

driftwood *n* wood floating near, or washed up on, a shore.

drill[1] *n* 1 a tool for boring holes. 2 a training exercise or session. 3 *colloq* correct procedure. ➤ *vb* 1 to make (a hole) in something with a drill. 2 to exercise or teach through repeated practice.

drill[2] *n* thick strong cotton cloth.

drill[3] *n* 1 a shallow furrow in which seeds are sown. 2 the seeds sown or plants growing in such a row. 3 a machine for sowing seeds in rows. ➤ *vb* to sow (seeds) in rows.

drilling platform *n* a floating or fixed offshore structure supporting the apparatus required for drilling an oil well.

drink *vb* (*past tense* **drank**, *past participle* **drunk**) 1 *tr & intr* to take in (a liquid) by swallowing. 2 *intr* to drink alcohol; to drink alcohol to excess. 3 to get oneself into a certain state by drinking alcohol: *Joe drank himself into a stupor.* ➤ *n* 1 an act of drinking. 2 liquid for drinking. 3 alcohol of any kind; the habit of drinking

alcohol to excess. 4 a glass or amount of drink. 5 (**the drink**) *colloq* the sea. ○ **drinkable** *adj*. ○ **drinker** *n* someone who drinks, esp alcohol, and esp too much. ◆ **drink to** or **drink the health of sb** to drink a toast to them. ◊ **drink sth in** 1 to listen to it eagerly. 2 to absorb it.

drink-driving *n* the act or practice of driving while under the influence of alcohol. ○ **drink-driver** *n*.

drip *vb* (**dripped, dripping**) 1 *tr* to release or fall in drops. 2 *intr* to release a liquid in drops. 3 *tr & intr, colloq* to have a large amount of something: *a film dripping with sentimentality.* ➤ *n* 1 the action or noise of dripping. 2 a device for passing a liquid solution slowly and continuously into a vein. 3 *derog, colloq* someone who lacks spirit.

drip-dry *adj* requiring little or no ironing if hung up to dry. ➤ *vb, tr & intr* to dry in this way.

drip-feed *n* a DRIP (*noun* sense 2). ➤ *vb* to feed something or someone with a liquid using a drip.

dripping *n* fat from roasted meat.

drive *vb* (*past tense* **drove**, *past participle* **driven**) 1 a to control the movement of (a vehicle); b to be legally qualified to do so. 2 *intr* to travel in a vehicle. 3 to take or transport someone or something in a vehicle. 4 to urge or force someone or something to move: *boats driven on to the beach by the storm.* 5 to make someone or something get into a particular state or condition: *It drove me crazy.* 6 to force by striking: *He drove the nail into the wood.* 7 to produce motion in something; to make it operate: *machinery driven by steam.* 8 *sport* a in golf: to hit (a ball) from the tee; b in cricket: to hit (a ball) forward with an upright bat; c to hit or kick (a ball, etc) with great force. 9 to conduct or dictate: *You drive a hard bargain.* ➤ *n* 1 a trip in a vehicle by road. 2 a path for vehicles, leading from a private residence to the road outside. 3 (**Drive**) a street title in an address. 4 energy and enthusiasm. 5 an organized campaign; a group effort: *an economy drive.* 6 operating power, or a device supplying them. 7 a forceful strike of a ball in various sports. 8 a united movement forward, esp by a military force. 9 a meeting to play a game, esp cards. ○ **driver** *n*. ◆ **be driven by sth** to be motivated by it. **be driving at sth** to intend or imply it as a meaning or conclusion. **drive sth home** 1 to make it clearly understood. 2 to force (a bolt, nail, etc) completely in.

drive-in *adj* providing a service or facility for customers remaining seated in vehicles.

drivel *n* nonsense. ➤ *vb* (**drivelled, drivelling**) *intr* 1 to talk nonsense. 2 to dribble.

drive-through *n, esp N Am* a shop, restaurant, etc from a window of which drivers can be served without leaving their cars.

driveway *n* a DRIVE (*noun* sense 2).

drizzle *n* fine light rain. ➤ *vb, intr* to rain lightly. ○ **drizzly** *adj*.

droll *adj* oddly amusing. ○ **drollery** *n*. ○ **drolly** *adv*.

dromedary /ˈdrɒmədərɪ/ n (-ies) a single-humped camel.

drone vb, intr **1** to make a low humming noise. **2** (usu **drone on**) to talk at length in a monotonous voice. ➤ n **1** a deep humming sound. **2** a male bee whose sole function is to mate with the queen. Compare QUEEN (sense 3), WORKER (sense 4). **3** a lazy person, esp one living off others. **4 a** the bass-pipe of a set of bagpipes; **b** the low sustained note it produces.

drool vb, intr **1** to dribble or slaver. **2** (usu **drool over sth**) to show uncontrolled admiration for it or pleasure at the sight of it.

droop vb, intr **1** to hang loosely. **2** to be or grow weak with tiredness. ➤ n a drooping state. ○ **droopy** adj (-ier, -iest).

drop vb (**dropped, dropping**) **1** tr & intr to fall or allow to fall. **2** tr & intr to decline or make something decline; to lower or weaken. **3** to give up or abandon (eg a friend or a habit). **4** to stop discussing (a topic). **5** (also **drop sb** or **sth off**) to set them down from a vehicle; to deliver or hand them in. **6** to leave or take out someone or something. **7** to mention something casually: drop a hint. **8** to fail to pronounce (esp a consonant): drop one's h's. **9** colloq to write informally: Drop me a line. **10** rugby to score (a goal) by a DROP KICK. **11** coarse slang except when of an animal to give birth to (a baby). **12** slang to beat to the ground. ➤ n **1** a small round or pear-shaped mass of liquid; a small amount (of liquid). **2** a descent; a fall. **3** a vertical distance. **4** a decline or decrease. **5** any small round or pear-shaped object. **6** (**drops**) liquid medication administered in small amounts. **7** a delivery. ◆ **at the drop of a hat** colloq promptly; for the slightest reason. **let sth drop** to make it known inadvertently or as if inadvertently. ◇ **drop back** or **behind** to fall behind others in a group. **drop in** or **by** to pay a brief unexpected visit. **drop off 1** colloq to fall asleep. **2** to become less. **drop out 1** (often **drop out of sth**) to withdraw from an activity. **2** colloq to adopt an alternative lifestyle as a reaction against traditional social values.

drop-dead adv, slang stunningly or breathtakingly, particularly in a sexual way: drop-dead gorgeous.

drop goal n, rugby a goal scored by a DROP KICK.

drop-in adj of a café, day centre, clinic, etc: where clients are free to attend informally and casually.

drop kick rugby, n a kick in which the ball is released from the hands and struck as it hits the ground. ➤ vb (**drop-kick**) to kick (a ball) in this way.

droplet n a tiny drop.

dropout n **1** a student who quits before completing a course of study. **2** a person whose alternative lifestyle is a reaction against traditional social values.

dropper n a short narrow glass tube with a rubber bulb on one end, used in medicine, etc

for applying liquid in drops.

droppings pl n animal or bird faeces.

drop-shot n in tennis, badminton, etc: a shot hit so that it drops low and close to the net.

dropsy n the former name for OEDEMA. ○ **dropsical** adj.

dross n **1** waste coal. **2** scum that forms on molten metal. **3** derog colloq rubbish.

drought n a prolonged lack of rainfall.

drove¹ past tense of DRIVE

drove² n **1** a moving herd of animals, esp cattle. **2** a large moving crowd.

drover n, hist someone employed to drive farm animals to and from market.

drown vb **1** intr to die by suffocation as a result of inhaling liquid. **2** to kill by suffocation in this way. ◇ **drown sth out** to suppress the effect of one sound with a louder one.

drowse vb, intr to sleep lightly for a short while.

drowsy adj (-ier, -iest) **1** sleepy. **2** quiet and peaceful. ○ **drowsily** adv. ○ **drowsiness** n.

drub vb (**drubbed, drubbing**) **1** to defeat severely. **2** to beat; to thump. ○ **drubbing** n.

drudge vb, intr to do hard, tedious or menial work. ➤ n a servant; a labourer. ○ **drudgery** n.

drug n **1** a medicine. **2** an illegal addictive substance. **3** anything craved for. ➤ vb (**drugged, drugging**) **1** to administer a drug to (a person or animal). **2** to poison or stupefy with drugs. **3** to mix or season (food) with drugs.

drug addict n someone who has become dependent on drugs. ○ **drug addiction** n.

druggist n, now N Am a pharmacist.

drugstore n, N Am a chemist's shop, esp one also selling refreshments.

druid or **Druid** n **1** a Celtic priest in pre-Christian times. **2** an eisteddfod official. ○ **druidic** or **druidical** adj.

drum n **1** a percussion instrument consisting of a hollow frame with a membrane stretched tightly across it, sounding when struck. **2** a cylindrical container. **3** an eardrum. ➤ vb (**drummed, drumming**) **1** intr to beat a drum. **2** tr & intr to make or cause to make continuous thumping sounds. **3** (usu **drum sth into sb**) to force it into their mind through constant repetition. ○ **drummer** n. ◇ **drum sb out** to expel them. **drum sth up** colloq to achieve or attract it by energetic persuasion.

drumbeat n the sound made when a drum is hit.

drum machine n a SYNTHESIZER for simulating the sound of percussion instruments.

drum major n the leader of a marching (esp military) band.

drum majorette n another name for a MAJORETTE.

drumstick n **1** a stick used for beating a drum. **2** the lower leg of a cooked fowl, esp a chicken.

drunk vb, past participle of DRINK. ➤ adj lacking control in movement, speech, etc through having consumed too much alcohol. ➤ n a drunk person, esp one regularly so.

drunkard n someone who is often drunk.

drunken *adj* **1** drunk. **2** relating to, or brought on by, alcoholic intoxication. ○ **drunkenly** *adv*. ○ **drunkenness** *n*.

drupe *n, bot* a fleshy fruit with one or more seeds.

dry *adj* (**drier, driest**) **1** free from or lacking moisture or wetness. **2** with little or no rainfall. **3** from which all the water has evaporated or been taken: *a dry well*. **4** thirsty. **5** of an animal: no longer producing milk. **6** of wine, etc: not sweet. **7** not buttered: *dry toast*. **8** of humour: expressed in a quietly sarcastic or matter-of-fact way. **9** forbidding the sale and consumption of alcohol. **10** of eyes: without tears. **11** dull; uninteresting. **12** lacking warmth of character. **13** of a cough: not producing catarrh. ➤ *vb* (**dries, dried**) **1** *tr & intr* to make or become dry. **2** to preserve (food) by removing all moisture. ○ **drily** or **dryly** *adv*. ○ **dryness** *n*. ◊ **dry out 1** to become completely dry. **2** *colloq* to be cured of addiction to alcohol. **dry up 1** to dry dishes after they have been washed. **2** to dry thoroughly or completely. **3** to cease to produce or be produced. **4** *colloq* of a speaker or actor: to run out of words; to forget lines while on stage. **5** *slang* to be quiet.

dryad *n, Greek myth* a woodland nymph.

dry cell *n* a battery in which current is passed through an electrolyte consisting of a moist paste.

dry-clean *vb* to clean (esp clothes) with liquid chemicals, not water. ○ **dry-cleaner** *n*. ○ **dry-cleaning** *n*.

dry dock *n* a dock from which the water can be pumped out to allow work on a ship's lower parts.

dry ice *n* solid carbon dioxide used as a refrigerating agent and also (*theat*) for creating special effects.

dry rot *n, bot* a serious type of timber decay caused by a fungus common in damp buildings.

dry run *n* **1** a rehearsal, practice or test. **2** *mil* a practice exercise.

dry-stone *adj* of a wall: made of stones wedged together without mortar.

DSC *abbrev* Distinguished Service Cross.

DSc *abbrev* Doctor of Science.

DSM *abbrev* Distinguished Service Medal.

DSO *abbrev* Distinguished Service Order.

DT or **DTs** *abbrev* delirium tremens.

DTP *abbrev* desktop publishing.

dual *adj* **1** consisting of or representing two separate parts. **2** double; twofold. ○ **duality** *n*.

dual carriageway *n* a road on which traffic moving in opposite directions is separated by a central barrier or strip of land.

dual-purpose *adj* serving two purposes.

dub[1] *vb* (**dubbed, dubbing**) **1** to give a name, esp a nickname, to someone. **2** to smear (leather) with grease.

dub[2] *vb* (**dubbed, dubbing**) **1** to add a new soundtrack to (eg a film), esp in a different language. **2** to add sound effects or music to (eg a film). ➤ *n* a type of REGGAE music in which bass, drums and the artistic arrangement are given prominence over voice and other instruments.

dubbin *n* a wax-like mixture for softening and waterproofing leather.

dubiety /dʒuːˈbaɪɪtɪ/ *n, formal* dubiousness.

dubious /ˈdʒuːbɪəs/ *adj* **1** feeling doubt. **2** arousing suspicion; potentially dishonest or dishonestly obtained. ○ **dubiously** *adv*. ○ **dubiousness** *n*.

ducal /ˈdʒuːkəl/ *adj* belonging or relating to a duke.

ducat /ˈdʌkət/ *n* a former European gold or silver coin.

duchess *n* **1** the wife or widow of a duke. **2** a woman of the same rank as a duke in her own right.

duchy *n* (*-ies*) the territory owned or ruled by a duke or duchess.

duck[1] *n* **1** a water bird with short legs, webbed feet, and a large flattened beak. **2** the flesh of this bird used as food. **3** the female of such a bird, as opposed to the male DRAKE. **4** *colloq* **a** a likeable person; **b** (*also* **ducks**) a term of endearment. **5** *cricket* a batsman's score of zero. ♦ **like water off a duck's back** *colloq* having no effect at all.

duck[2] *vb* **1** *intr* to lower the head or body suddenly, esp to avoid notice or a blow. **2** to push someone or something briefly under water. ◊ **duck out of sth** *colloq* to avoid something unpleasant or unwelcome.

duck-billed platypus see PLATYPUS

duckling *n* a young duck.

duckweed *n* a plant with broad flat leaves that grows on the surface of water.

ducky *n* (*-ies*) *colloq* a term of endearment.

duct *n* **1** *anat* a tube in the body, esp one for carrying glandular secretions. **2** a casing for pipes or electrical cables, or a tube used for ventilation and air-conditioning.

ductile *adj* **1** denoting metals that can be drawn out into a thin wire without breaking. **2** easily influenced by others. ○ **ductility** *n*.

dud *colloq*, *n* **1** a counterfeit article. **2** a bomb, firework, etc that fails to go off. **3** any useless or ineffectual person or thing. **4** (**duds**) clothes. ➤ *adj* **1** useless. **2** counterfeit.

dude *n, colloq, orig N Am* **1** a man. **2** a city man, esp an Easterner holidaying in the West. **3** a man preoccupied with dressing smartly.

dudgeon *n* (*usu* **in high dudgeon**) the condition of being very angry or indignant.

due *adj* **1** owed; payable. **2** expected according to timetable or pre-arrangement. **3** proper. ➤ *n* **1** what is owed; something that can be rightfully claimed or expected. **2** (**dues**) subscription fees. ➤ *adv* directly: *due north*. ♦ **due to sth** or **them** caused by it or them. **2** because of it or them. **give sb their due** to acknowledge their qualities or achievements, esp when disapproving in other ways. **in due**

course in the ordinary way when the time comes.

duel n 1 a pre-arranged fight between two people to settle a matter of honour. 2 any serious conflict between two people or groups. ➤ vb (**duelled, duelling**) intr to fight a duel. ○ **duellist** or **dueller** n.

duet n 1 a piece of music for two singers or players. 2 a pair of musical performers. ○ **duettist** n.

duff¹ adj, colloq useless; broken.

duff² vb, colloq 1 to bungle something. 2 esp golf to mishit (a shot). ➤ adj bungled. ◊ **duff sb up** slang to treat them violently.

duffel or **duffle** n a thick coarse woollen fabric.

duffel bag n a cylindrical canvas shoulder bag with a drawstring fastening.

duffel coat n a heavy, esp hooded, coat made of DUFFEL.

duffer n, colloq a clumsy or incompetent person.

dug¹ past tense, past participle of DIG

dug² n an animal's udder or nipple.

dugong /'duːɡɒŋ/ n a seal-like tropical sea mammal.

dugout n 1 a canoe made from a hollowed-out log. 2 a soldier's rough shelter dug into a slope or in a trench. 3 a covered shelter at the side of a sports field, for the trainer, substitutes, etc.

duke n 1 a nobleman of the highest rank. 2 the ruler of a small state or principality. 3 old slang use (often **dukes**) a fist. ○ **dukedom** n the title or property of a duke.

dulcet /'dʌlsɪt/ adj, literary of sounds: sweet and pleasing to the ear.

dulcimer n, mus a percussion instrument consisting of a box with tuned strings stretched across, struck with small hammers.

dull adj 1 of colour or light: lacking brightness or clearness. 2 of sounds: deep and low; muffled. 3 of weather: cloudy. 4 of pain: not sharp. 5 of a person: slow to learn or understand. 6 uninteresting; lacking liveliness. 7 of a blade: blunt. ➤ vb, tr & intr to make or become dull. ○ **dullness** n. ○ **dully** adv.

dulse n an edible red seaweed.

duly adv 1 in the proper way. 2 at the proper time.

dumb adj 1 temporarily or permanently unable to speak. 2 of animals: not having human speech. 3 silent; not expressed in words. 4 colloq, esp US foolish; unintelligent. 5 performed without words: dumb show. ➤ vb, tr & intr (always **dumb down**) to present (information) in a less sophisticated form in order to appeal to a large number of people. ○ **dumbly** adv.

dumbbell n a short metal bar with a weight on each end, used in muscle-developing exercises.

dumbfound or **dumfound** vb to astonish someone; to leave someone speechless.

dumb show n miming.

dumbstruck adj silent with astonishment or shock.

dumb waiter n 1 a small lift for transporting laundry, dirty dishes, etc between floors in a restaurant or hotel. 2 a movable shelved stand for food. 3 a revolving food tray.

dumdum n a bullet that expands on impact, causing severe injury.

dummy /'dʌmɪ/ n (-**ies**) 1 a life-size model of the human body, eg used for displaying clothes. 2 a realistic copy. 3 a rubber teat sucked by a baby for comfort. 4 colloq, chiefly N Am a stupid person. 5 sport an act of dummying with the ball. 6 a person or company seemingly independent, but really the agent of another. 7 bridge an exposed hand of cards. ➤ adj false. ➤ vb (-**ies**, -**ied**) tr & intr, sport a to make as if to move one way before sharply moving the other, in order to deceive (an opponent); b to do so with (a ball).

dummy run n a practice.

dump vb 1 to put something down heavily or carelessly. 2 tr & intr to dispose of (rubbish), esp in an unauthorized place. 3 slang to break off a romantic relationship with someone. 4 econ to sell (goods not selling well on the domestic market) abroad at a much reduced price. 5 comput to transfer (computer data) from one program to another or onto disk or tape. ➤ n 1 a place where rubbish may be dumped. 2 a military store, eg of weapons or food. 3 comput a printed copy of the contents of a computer's memory. 4 colloq a dirty or dilapidated place.

dumper truck or **dumptruck** n a lorry which can be emptied by raising one end of the carrier to allow the contents to slide out.

dumpling n 1 a baked or boiled ball of dough served with meat. 2 a rich fruit pudding. 3 colloq a plump person.

dumps pl n. ◆ **down in the dumps** colloq in low spirits; depressed.

dumpy adj (-**ier**, -**iest**) short and plump.

dun¹ adj (**dunner, dunnest**) greyish-brown. ➤ n 1 a dun colour. 2 a horse of this colour.

dun² vb (**dunned, dunning**) to press someone for payment. ➤ n a demand for payment.

dunce n a stupid person.

dune n a ridge or hill of windblown sand.

dung n animal excrement.

dungarees pl n loose trousers with a bib and shoulder straps attached.

dungeon n a prison cell, esp underground.

dunghaap or **dunghill** n 1 a pile of dung. 2 any squalid situation or place.

dunk vb 1 to dip (eg a biscuit) into tea or a similar beverage. 2 to submerge or be submerged.

dunlin n a small brown wading bird.

dunno colloq, contraction of I do not know.

dunnock n the hedge sparrow.

duo n 1 a pair of musicians or other performers. 2 any two people considered a pair. 3 mus a duet.

duodecimal adj relating to or based on the

number twelve, or multiples of it.

duodenum /dʒu:ou'di:nəm/ n (**duodena** /-'di:nə/ or **duodenums**) anat the first part of the small intestine, into which food passes after leaving the stomach. ○ **duodenal** adj.

duologue or (sometimes US) **duolog** n 1 a dialogue between two actors. 2 a play for two actors.

dupe vb to trick or deceive. ➤ n a person who is deceived.

duple adj double; twofold. 2 mus having two beats in the bar.

duplex n, N Am 1 (also **duplex apartment**) a flat on two floors. 2 (also **duplex house**) a semi-detached house. ➤ adj 1 double; twofold. 2 of a computer circuit: allowing transmission of signals in both directions simultaneously.

duplicate adj /'dʒu:plɪkət/ identical to another. ➤ n /-kət/ 1 an exact copy. 2 another of the same kind. ➤ vb /-keɪt/ 1 to make or be an exact copy of something. 2 to repeat something. ○ **duplication** n. ○ **duplicator** n. ◆ **in duplicate** in two exact copies.

duplicity n (-**ies**) formal deception; trickery. ○ **duplicitous** adj.

durable adj 1 lasting a long time without breaking. 2 long-lasting. ➤ n a durable item. ○ **durability** n (-**ies**).

dura mater /'dʒuərə 'meɪtə(r)/ n, anat the outermost and thickest of the three membranes that surround the brain and spinal cord.

duration n the length of time that something lasts or continues.

duress n the influence of force or threats.

during prep 1 throughout the time of something. 2 in the course of something.

durum or **durum wheat** n a kind of wheat whose flour is used for making pasta.

dusk n the period of semi-darkness before night.

dusky adj (-**ier**, -**iest**) 1 dark; shadowy. 2 dark-coloured; dark-skinned. ○ **duskily** adv. ○ **duskiness** n.

dust n 1 earth, sand or household dirt in the form of fine powder. 2 a cloud of this. 3 any substance in powder form. ➤ vb 1 to remove dust from (furniture, etc). 2 to sprinkle something with powder. ◆ **let the dust settle** colloq to wait until calm is restored before acting. **not see sb for dust** not to see them again because they have gone away rapidly and suddenly. **throw dust in sb's eyes** colloq to deceive them.

dustbin n a large lidded container for household rubbish.

dust bowl n an area of land from which the topsoil has been removed by winds and drought.

dustcart n a vehicle in which household rubbish is collected.

dust cover n 1 a DUST JACKET. 2 a DUST SHEET.

duster n a cloth for removing household dust.

dust jacket or **dust cover** n a loose protective paper cover on a book.

dustman n someone employed to collect household rubbish.

dustpan n a handled container into which dust is swept.

dust sheet or **dust cover** n a cloth or plastic sheet used to protect furniture from dust or paint.

dust-up n, colloq a fight.

dusty adj (-**ier**, -**iest**) 1 covered with or containing dust. 2 of a colour: dull. 3 old-fashioned. ○ **dustily** adj. ○ **dustiness** n.

Dutch adj belonging or referring to the Netherlands, its inhabitants or their language. ➤ n 1 the official language of the Netherlands. 2 (the Dutch) the people of the Netherlands. ◆ **go Dutch** colloq to agree for each person to pay their own share of a meal, etc.

Dutch auction n an auction at which the price is gradually lowered until someone agrees to buy.

Dutch cap see CAP (noun sense 7)

Dutch courage n artificial courage gained by drinking alcohol.

Dutch elm disease n, bot a serious disease of elm trees, caused by a fungus and spread by a beetle.

Dutchman or **Dutchwoman** n a native or citizen of, or a person born in, the Netherlands.

Dutch uncle n someone who openly criticizes or reprimands where appropriate.

duteous adj, literary dutiful.

dutiable adj of goods: on which duty is payable.

duty n (-**ies**) 1 an obligation or responsibility, or the awareness of it. 2 a task, esp part of a job. 3 tax on goods, esp imports. 4 respect for elders, seniors or superiors. ○ **dutiful** adj. ○ **dutifully** adv. ◆ **off duty** not working. **on duty** working; liable to be called upon to go into action.

duty-bound adj obliged by one's sense of duty.

duty-free adj of goods, esp imports: non-taxable. ➤ n, colloq 1 a shop where duty-free goods are sold. 2 an article or goods for sale at such a shop.

duvet /'du:veɪ/ n a thick quilt for use on a bed instead of a sheet and blankets.

dwarf n (**dwarfs** or less often **dwarves**) 1 an abnormally small person. 2 an animal or plant that is much smaller or shorter than others of its species, usu as a result of selective breeding. 3 a mythical man-like creature with magic powers. ➤ vb to make something seem small or unimportant.

dwell vb (past tense & past participle **dwelt** or **dwelled**) intr, formal, literary to reside. ○ **dweller** n. ◊ **dwell on sth** to think or speak about it obsessively.

dwelling n, formal, literary a place of residence.

dwindle vb, intr to shrink in size, number or intensity.

Dy symbol, chem dysprosium.

dye vb (**dyeing**) tr & intr to colour or stain something, or undergo colouring or staining. ➤ *n* **1** a coloured substance that is used in solution to give colour to a material. **2** the solution used for dyeing. **3** the colour produced by dyeing. ○ **dyer** *n*.

dyed-in-the-wool *adj* of firmly fixed opinions.

dying *vb*, present participle of DIE¹. ➤ *adj* **1** expressed or occurring immediately before death: *her dying breath*. **2** final: *the dying seconds of the match*.

dyke¹ or **dike** *n* **1** a wall or embankment built to prevent flooding. **2** *esp Scot* a wall, eg surrounding a field.

dyke² or **dike** *n*, *offensive slang* a LESBIAN.

dynamic *adj* **1** full of energy, enthusiasm and new ideas. **2** relating to DYNAMICS. ○ **dynamically** *adv.*

dynamics *sing n* the branch of mechanics that deals with motion and the forces that produce motion. ➤ *pl n* **1 a** movement or change in any sphere; **b** the forces causing this: *political dynamics*. **2** *mus* the signs indicating varying levels of loudness.

dynamism *n* limitless energy and enthusiasm.

dynamite *n* **1** a powerful explosive. **2** *colloq* a thrilling or dangerous person or thing. ➤ *vb* to explode something with dynamite.

dynamo *n* **1** an electric generator that converts mechanical energy into electrical energy. **2** *colloq* a tirelessly active person.

dynasty *n* (*-ies*) **1** a succession of rulers from the same family. **2** their period of rule. **3** a succession of members of a powerful family or group. ○ **dynastic** *adj.*

dysentery *n*, *med* severe infection and inflammation of the intestines.

dysfunction *n* impairment or abnormality of functioning. ○ **dysfunctional** *adj.*

dyslexia *n*, *psychol*, *med* a disorder characterized by difficulty in reading, writing and spelling correctly. ○ **dyslexic** *adj*, *n*.

dysmenorrhoea or **dysmenorrhea** /dɪsmɛnəˈrɪə/ *n*, *med* pain in the lower abdomen, associated with menstruation.

dyspepsia *n*, *pathol* indigestion. ○ **dyspeptic** *adj.*

dysprosium *n* a soft, silvery-white magnetic metallic element.

dystrophy *n* (*-ies*) *med* a disorder of organs or tissues, esp muscle, arising from an inadequate supply of nutrients.

Ee

E¹ or **e** *n* (*E, E's* or *e's*) **1** the fifth letter of the English alphabet. **2** *mus* (E) the third note in the scale of C major.

E² *abbrev* **1** East. **2** Ecstasy. **3** *physics* electromotive force. **4** (*also* **e**) electronic: *E-mail*. **5** *physics* (*also* **E**) energy. **6** English. **7** *also in compounds* European: *E-number*.

each *adj* applied to every one of two or more people or items considered separately. ➤ *pron* every single one of two or more people, animals or things. ➤ *adv* to, for or from each one: *Give them one each.* ◆ **each other** used as the object of a verb or preposition when an action takes place between two (or more than two) people, etc: *They talked to each other.*

eager *adj* **1** (often **eager for sth** or **to do sth**) feeling or showing great desire or enthusiasm. **2** excited by desire or expectancy: *an eager glance*. ○ **eagerly** *adv.* ○ **eagerness** *n*.

eagle *n* **1** any of various kinds of large birds of prey. **2** *golf* a score of two under par.

eagle eye *n* **1** exceptionally good eyesight. **2** careful supervision, with an ability to notice small details. ○ **eagle-eyed** *adj.*

eaglet *n* a young eagle.

ear¹ *n* **1** the sense organ that is concerned with hearing. **2** the external part of the ear. **3** the ability to hear and appreciate the difference between sounds: *an ear for music*. ◆ **be all ears** *colloq* to listen attentively or with great interest. **fall on deaf ears** of a remark, etc: to be ignored. **in one ear and out the other** *colloq* listened to but immediately disregarded. **lend an ear to sb** or **sth** *colloq* to listen. **out on one's ear** *colloq* dismissed swiftly and without politeness. **play it by ear** *colloq* to act without a fixed plan, according to the situation that arises. **up to one's ears in sth** *colloq* deeply involved in it or occupied with it.

ear² *n* the part of a cereal plant, such as wheat, that contains the seeds.

earache *n* pain in the inner part of the ear.

eardrum *n* the small thin membrane inside the ear, which transmits vibrations made by sound waves to the inner ear.

earful *n*, *colloq* **1** a long complaint or telling-off. **2** as much talk or gossip as one can stand.

earl *n* a male member of the British nobility ranking below a marquess and above a viscount. ○ **earldom** *n*.

earlobe *n* the soft, loosely hanging piece of flesh which forms the lower part of the ear.

early *adv*, *adj* (*-ier*, *-iest*) **1** characteristic of or near the beginning of (a period of time, period of development, etc). **2** sooner than others, sooner than usual, or sooner than expected or intended. **3** in the near future. **4** in the distant past. ○ **earliness** n.

earmark vb to set aside something or someone for a particular purpose. ➤ n a distinctive mark.

earn vb **1** tr & intr to gain (money, wages, one's living, etc) by working. **2** to gain. **3** to deserve. ○ **earner** n.

earnest adj **1** serious or over-serious. **2** showing determination, sincerity or strong feeling. ○ **earnestness** n. ◆ **in earnest 1** serious or seriously. **2** sincere. **3** not as a joke; in reality.

earnings pl n money earned.

earphones pl n another name for HEADPHONES.

ear-piercing adj of a noise: loud and shrill.

earplug n a piece of wax or rubber, etc placed in the ear as a protection against noise, cold or water.

earring n a piece of jewellery worn attached to the ear, esp to the earlobe.

earshot n the distance at which sound can be heard: out of earshot.

ear-splitting adj of a noise: extremely loud.

earth n **1** (often **the Earth**) the planet on which we live, the third planet from the Sun. **2** the land and sea, as opposed to the sky. **3** dry land; the land surface; the ground. **4** soil. **5** a hole in which an animal lives, esp a badger or fox. **6 a** an electrical connection with the ground; **b** a wire that provides this. ➤ vb, electronics to connect to the ground. ◆ **come back** or **down to earth** to become aware of the realities of life. **on earth** used for emphasis: What on earth is that?

earthbound adj **1** attached or restricted to the earth. **2** moving towards the Earth.

earthen adj **1** of a floor, etc: made of earth. **2** of a pot, etc: made of baked clay.

earthenware n pottery made of a kind of baked clay.

earthly adj (-ier, -iest) **1** literary referring, relating or belonging to this world; not spiritual. **2** colloq, with negatives used for emphasis: We have no earthly chance.

earthquake n a succession of vibrations that shake the Earth's surface, caused by shifting movements in the Earth's crust, volcanic activity, etc.

earth science n any of the sciences broadly concerned with the Earth, eg geology and meteorology.

earth-shattering adj, colloq being of great importance.

earthwork n, technical excavation and embanking, eg as a process in road-building.

earthworm n any of several types of worm which live in and burrow through the soil.

earthy adj (-ier, -iest) **1** consisting of, relating to, or like earth or soil. **2** coarse or crude.

earwig n an insect with pincers at the end of its body.

ease n **1** freedom from pain, anxiety or embarrassment. **2** absence of difficulty or restriction. **3** leisure. ➤ vb **1** to free someone from pain, trouble or anxiety. **2** to make someone comfortable. **3** to relieve or calm something. **4** to loosen something. **5** to make something less difficult; to assist: ease his progress. **6** intr (often **ease off** or **up**) to become less intense. **7** intr to move gently or very gradually. ◆ **at ease** relaxed; free from anxiety or embarrassment.

easel n a stand for supporting a blackboard or an artist's canvas, etc.

east n (also **East** or **the East**) **1** the direction from which the Sun rises at the equinox. **2** any part of the earth, a country or a town, etc lying in that direction. **3** (**the East**) **a** the countries of Asia, east of Europe; **b** pol the former communist countries of eastern Europe. ➤ adj **1** situated in the east; on the side which is on or nearest the east. **2** facing or towards the east. **3** esp of wind: coming from the east. ➤ adv in, to or towards the east.

eastbound adj going or leading towards the east.

Easter n, Christianity a religious festival celebrating the resurrection of Christ, held on the Sunday after the first full moon in spring, called **Easter Day** or **Easter Sunday**.

easterly adj **1** of a wind, etc: coming from the east. **2** looking or lying, etc towards the east; situated in the east. ➤ adv to or towards the east. ➤ n (-ies) an easterly wind.

eastern or **Eastern** adj situated in, directed towards or belonging to the east or the East. ○ **easterner** or **Easterner** n. ○ **easternmost** adj.

eastward adv (also **eastwards**) towards the east. ➤ adj towards the east.

easy adj (-ier, -iest) **1** not difficult. **2** free from pain, trouble, anxiety, etc. **3** not stiff or formal. **4** tolerant. **5** not tense or strained. **6** colloq having no strong preference. **7** of financial circumstances: comfortable. ➤ adv, colloq in a slow, calm or relaxed way: take it easy. ○ **easily** adv. ○ **easiness** n. ◆ **go easy on** or **with sb** to deal with them gently or calmly. **go easy on** or **with sth** to use, take, etc not too much of it.

easy-going adj not strict; relaxed, tolerant or placid.

eat vb (past tense **ate** /ɛt, eɪt/, past participle **eaten**) **1** to bite, chew and swallow (food). **2** intr to take in food. **3** to eat into something. **4** colloq to trouble or worry someone: What's eating you? ○ **eater** n. ◆ **be eaten up by** or **with sth** to be greatly affected by it (usu a bad feeling): He's eaten up with jealousy. **eat one's heart out** to suffer, esp in silence, from some longing or anxiety, or from envy. **what's eating you, him, etc?** what's wrong with you, him, etc? ◊ **eat into** or **through sth 1** to use it up gradually. **2** to waste it. **3** to destroy its material, substance or form, etc, esp by chemical action. **eat out** to eat at a restaurant, cafe, etc rather than at home. **eat up** to finish one's food. **eat sth up 1** to finish (one's food). **2** to destroy it.

eatable *adj* fit to be eaten. ➣ *n* (*usu* **eatables**) an item of food. Compare EDIBLE.

eating apple *n* an apple for eating raw. Compare COOKING APPLE.

eau de Cologne /oʊ də ˈkəloʊn/ or **cologne** *n* a mild type of perfume, orig made in Cologne in Germany in 1709.

eaves *pl n* the part of a roof that sticks out beyond the wall, or the underside of it.

eavesdrop *vb, intr* (*also* **eavesdrop on sb**) to listen secretly to a private conversation. ○ **eavesdropper** *n*.

ebb *vb, intr* **1** of the tide: to move back from the land. Compare FLOW (*verb* sense 7). **2** (*also* **ebb away**) to grow smaller or weaker. ➣ *n* **1** the movement of the tide away from the land. **2** a decline. ♦ **at a low ebb** in a poor or weak state, mentally or physically. **on the ebb** in decline.

ebony *n* (*-ies*) a type of extremely hard, heavy and almost black wood. ➣ *adj* **1** made from this wood. **2** black.

ebullient *adj* very high-spirited. ○ **ebullience** *n*.

EC *abbrev* **1** European Commission. **2** European Community.

eccentric *adj* **1** of a person or behaviour, etc: odd or unconventional. **2** *technical* of a wheel, etc: not having the axis at the centre. **3** *geom* of circles: not having a common centre. **4** of an orbit: not circular. ➣ *n* an eccentric person. ○ **eccentricity** *n* (*-ies*).

ecclesiastic *n, formal* a clergyman or a member of a holy order. ➣ *adj* (*also* **ecclesiastical**) relating to the church or the clergy. ○ **ecclesiastically** *adv*.

ECG *abbrev* **1** electrocardiogram. **2** electrocardiograph.

echelon /ˈɛʃəlɒn/ *n, formal* a level or rank in an organization, etc.

echinoderm /ɪˈkaɪnoʊdɜːm/ *n* a sea animal noted for having tube feet and a plated body, eg starfish and sea urchins.

echo *n* (*echoes*) **1** the repeating of a sound caused by the sound waves striking a surface and coming back. **2** a sound repeated in this way. **3** an imitation or repetition, sometimes an accidental one. **4** (*often* **echoes**) a trace; something which brings to mind memories or thoughts of something else. **5** a reflected radio or radar beam, or the visual signal it produces on a screen. ➣ *vb* (**echoes, echoed**) **1** to send back an echo of something. **2** to repeat (a sound or a statement). **3** to imitate or in some way be similar to something. **4** *intr* to resound; to reverberate.

echo chamber *n* a room where the walls reflect sound.

echolocation *n* the determining of the position of objects by measuring the time taken for an echo to return from them, and the direction of the echo.

echo-sounding *n* a method used at sea, etc for determining the depth of water, locating

shoals of fish, etc, by measuring the time taken for a signal sent out from the ship, etc to return as an echo.

éclair *n* a long cake of choux pastry with a cream filling and chocolate icing.

eclampsia *n, pathol* a toxic condition which may develop during the last three months of pregnancy.

eclectic *adj* selecting material or ideas from a wide range of sources or authorities. ○ **eclectically** *adv*. ○ **eclecticism** *n*.

eclipse *n* **1** the total or partial obscuring of one planet or heavenly body by another, eg of the Sun when the Moon comes between it and the Earth (a **solar eclipse**) or of the Moon when the Earth's shadow falls across it (a **lunar eclipse**). **2** a loss of fame or importance. ➣ *vb* **1** to cause an eclipse of (a heavenly body). **2** to surpass or outshine.

ecliptic *n* (**the ecliptic**) the course which the Sun seems to follow in relation to the stars.

eco-friendly *adj* not harmful to the environment.

E. coli *abbrev* Escherichia coli.

ecology *n* **1** the relationship between living things and their surroundings. **2** the study of plants, animals, peoples and institutions in relation to the environment. ○ **ecological** *adj*. ○ **ecologist** *n*.

economic *adj* **1** relating to or concerned with economy or economics. **2** relating to industry or business. **3** of a business practice or industry, etc: operated at, or likely to bring, a profit. **4** economical.

---

economic, economical Although there is some overlap in meaning, **economic** is more closely associated with **economics**, and **economical** has a less specific sense related to the general sense of **economy** : *Consultation will focus on the economic and diplomatic issues.*
It may be economical to use a cheaper form of fuel.

---

economical *adj* not wasting money or resources. ○ **economically** *adv*.

economics *sing n* **1** the study of the production, distribution and consumption of money, goods and services. **2** the financial aspects of something. ○ **economist** *n* an expert in economics.

economize or **-ise** *vb, intr* to cut down on spending or waste.

economy *n* (*-ies*) **1** the organization of money and resources within a nation or community, etc, esp in terms of the production, distribution and consumption of goods and services. **2** a system in which these are organized in a specified way. **3** careful management of money or other resources. **4** (*usu* **economies**) an instance of economizing; a saving. **5** efficient or sparing use of something: *economy of movement*. ➣ *adj* **a** of a class of travel, esp air travel: of the cheapest kind; **b** (*also* **economy-size** or **economy-sized**) of a packet of food, etc: larger than the standard or basic size, and proportionally cheaper.

ecosystem *n* a community of living things and their relationships to their surroundings.

ecotourism *n* the careful management of tourism in areas of unspoiled natural beauty, so that the environment is preserved and the income from tourists contributes to its conservation.

ecru *adj* off-white or greyish-yellow in colour. ➤ *n* this colour.

ecstasy *n* (*-ies*) **1** a feeling of immense joy; rapture. **2** (**Ecstasy**) a powerful hallucinatory drug. ○ **ecstatic** *adj.*

ECT *abbrev* electroconvulsive therapy.

ectopic pregnancy *n, pathol* the development of a fetus outside the uterus, esp in a Fallopian tube.

ectoplasm *n* the substance thought by some people to be given off by the body of a medium during a trance.

ecumenical or **oecumenical** /iːkjʊˈmɛnɪkəl, ɛk-/ or **ecumenic** or **oecumenic** *adj* **1** bringing together different branches of the Christian Church. **2** working towards the unity of the Christian Church. **3** referring to or consisting of the whole Christian Church: *an ecumenical council.* ○ **ecumenicalism** or **ecumenicism** or **ecumenism** *n* the principles or practice of Christian unity.

eczema /ˈɛksɪmə/ *n, pathol* a skin disorder in which red blisters form on the skin, usu causing an itching or burning sensation.

ed. *abbrev* **1** (*eds*) edition. **2** (*also* **Ed.**) (*eds* or **Eds**) editor.

eddy *n* (*-ies*) **1** a current of water running back against the main stream or current, forming a small whirlpool. **2** a movement of air, smoke, fog, etc similar to this. ➤ *vb* (**eddies, eddied**) *tr & intr* to move or make something move in this way.

edelweiss /ˈeɪdəlvaɪs/ *n* (*pl* **edelweiss**) a small white mountain plant.

Eden *n* **1** (*also* **Garden of Eden**) the garden where, according to the Bible, the first man and woman lived after being created. **2** a beautiful region; a place of delight.

edentate /iːˈdɛnteɪt/ *biol, adj* having few or no teeth. ➤ *n* an animal belonging to a group of mammals which have few or no teeth, such as the anteater, armadillo and sloth.

edge *n* **1** the part farthest from the middle of something; a border or boundary; the rim. **2** the area beside a cliff or steep drop. **3** the cutting side of something sharp such as a knife. **4** *geom* the meeting point of two surfaces. **5** sharpness or severity: *bread to take the edge off his hunger.* **6** bitterness: *There was an edge to his criticism.* ➤ *vb* (**edged, edging**) **1** to form or make a border to something. **2** to shape the edge or border of something. **3** *tr & intr* to move gradually and carefully, esp sideways.

○ **edging** *n.* ♦ **have the edge on** or **over sb** or **sth 1** to have an advantage over them. **2** to be better than them. **on edge** uneasy; nervous and irritable. ◊ **edge out sth** or **sb 1** to remove or get rid of it or them gradually. **2** to defeat them by a small margin.

edgeways or **edgewise** *adv* **1** sideways. **2** with the edge uppermost or forwards. ♦ **not get a word in edgeways** to be unable to contribute to a conversation because the others are talking continuously.

edgy *adj* (*-ier, -iest*) *colloq* easily annoyed; anxious, nervous or tense. ○ **edgily** *adv.* ○ **edginess** *n.*

edible *adj* fit to be eaten; suitable to eat. ➤ *pl n* (**edibles**) food; things that are fit to be eaten. Compare EATABLE. ○ **edibility** *n.*

edict /ˈiːdɪkt/ *n* an order issued by any authority.

edifice *n, formal* a building, esp an impressive one.

edify *vb* (*-ies, -ied*) *formal* to improve the mind or morals of someone. ○ **edification** *n.* ○ **edifying** *adj.*

edit *vb* (**edited, editing**) **1** to prepare (a book, newspaper, film, etc) for publication or broadcasting, esp by making corrections or alterations. **2** to be in overall charge of the process of producing (a newspaper, etc). **3** to compile (a reference work). **4** (*usu* **edit out sth**) to remove (parts of a work) before printing, broadcasting, etc. **5** to prepare (a cinema film or a TV or radio programme) by putting together material previously photographed or recorded. **6** to prepare (data) for processing by a computer. ➤ *n* a period or instance of editing.

edition *n* **1** the total number of copies of a book, etc printed at one time. **2** one of a series of printings of a book, periodical, etc, produced with alterations and corrections made by the author or an editor. **3** the form in which a book, etc is published: *the paperback edition.*

editor *n* **1** a person who edits. **2** a person who is in charge of a newspaper, magazine, etc, or one section of it. **3** a person who is in charge of a radio or TV programme which is made up of different items. **4** a person who puts together the various sections of a film, etc. ○ **editorship** *n.*

editorial *adj* referring or relating to editors or editing. ➤ *n* an article written by or on behalf of the editor of a newspaper or magazine, usu one offering an opinion on a current topic. ○ **editorially** *adv.*

educate *vb* **1** to train and teach. **2** to provide school instruction for someone. ○ **educative** *adj.*

educated *adj* **1** having received an education, esp to a level higher than average. **2** produced by or suggesting an education, usu a good one. **3** based on experience or knowledge: *an educated guess.*

education *n* **1** the process of teaching. **2** the instruction received. ○ **educational** *adj.*

○ **educationalist** *n* an expert in methods of education. ○ **educationally** *adv.*

Edwardian *adj* belonging to or characteristic of Britain in the years 1901–10, the reign of King Edward VII.

EEG *abbrev* 1 electroencephalogram. 2 electroencephalograph.

eel *n* any of several kinds of fish with a long smooth snake-like body and very small fins.

EEPROM *abbrev, comput* electrically erasable programmable read-only memory. Compare EPROM.

eerie *adj* strange and disturbing or frightening. ○ **eerily** *adv.* ○ **eeriness** *n.*

efface *vb* 1 to rub or wipe out something. 2 to block out (a memory, etc). 3 to avoid drawing attention to (oneself). ○ **effacement** *n.*

effect *n* 1 a result. 2 an impression given or produced. 3 operation; a working state: *The ban comes into effect today.* 4 (*usu* **effects**) *formal* property. 5 (*usu* **effects**) devices, esp lighting and sound, used to create a particular impression in a film or on a stage, etc. ➤ *vb, formal* to do something; to make something happen, or to bring it about. ♦ **in effect** in reality. **take effect** to come into force.

> **effect** A word often confused with this one is **affect**.

effective *adj* 1 having the power to produce, or producing, a desired result. 2 producing a pleasing effect. 3 impressive; striking. 4 in, or coming into, operation. 5 actual, rather than theoretical. ○ **effectively** *adv.* ○ **effectiveness** *n.*

effectual *adj* 1 producing the intended result. 2 of a document, etc: valid. ○ **effectually** *adv.*

effeminate *adj, derog* of a man: having features of behaviour or appearance more typical of a woman; not manly. ○ **effeminacy** *n.* ○ **effeminately** *adv.*

effervesce /ɛfə'vɛs/ *vb, intr* 1 of a liquid: to give off bubbles of gas. 2 to behave in a lively or energetic way. ○ **effervescence** *n.* ○ **effervescent** *adj.*

effete /ɪ'fiːt/ *adj, derog* 1 lacking strength or energy. 2 made weak by too much protection or refinement.

efficacious *adj, formal* producing, or certain to produce, the intended result. ○ **efficacy** *n.*

efficient *adj* 1 producing satisfactory results with an economy of effort and a minimum of waste. 2 of a person: capable of competent work within a relatively short time. 3 *in compounds* economical in the use or consumption of a specified resource: *energy-efficient.* ○ **efficiency** *n (-ies).* ○ **efficiently** *adv.*

effigy *n (-ies)* 1 a crude doll or model representing a person, on which hatred of, or contempt for, the person can be expressed, eg by burning it. 2 *formal* a portrait or sculpture of a person used as an architectural ornament.

efflorescence *n* 1 a short period in which artistic activity flourishes. 2 *chem* a powdery substance formed as a result of crystallization or loss of water to the atmosphere. 3 *bot* the period during which a plant is producing flowers.

effluent *n* liquid industrial waste or sewage released into a river, the sea, etc.

effluvium *n (effluvia)* *formal* an unpleasant smell or vapour given off by something, eg decaying matter.

efflux *n* 1 the process of flowing out. 2 something that flows out.

effort *n* 1 hard mental or physical work, or something that requires it. 2 an act of trying hard. 3 the result of an attempt; an achievement. ○ **effortless** *adj.* ○ **effortlessly** *adv.*

effrontery *n (-ies)* shameless rudeness.

effusion *n* 1 the act or process of pouring or flowing out. 2 something that is poured out. 3 an uncontrolled flow of speech or writing.

effusive *adj, derog* expressing feelings, esp happiness or enthusiasm, in an excessive or very showy way. ○ **effusively** *adv.* ○ **effusiveness** *n.*

eg *abbrev: exempli gratia* (Latin), for example.

egalitarian *adj* relating to, promoting or believing in the principle that all human beings are equal and should enjoy the same rights. ➤ *n* a person who upholds this principle. ○ **egalitarianism** *n.*

egg *n* 1 the reproductive cell produced by a female animal, bird, etc, from which the young one develops. 2 a reproductive cell or developing embryo produced and deposited in a hard shell by female birds, reptiles, and certain animals. 3 a hen's egg, used as food. ♦ **have egg on one's face** *colloq* to be made to look foolish. **put all one's eggs in one basket** to depend entirely on one plan, action, etc.

egg *vb* (*usu* **egg sb on**) *colloq* to urge or encourage them.

eggcup *n* a small cup-shaped container for holding a boiled egg.

egghead *n, colloq, sometimes derog* a very clever person.

eggnog or **egg-flip** *n* a drink made from raw eggs, milk, sugar and rum or brandy.

eggplant *n, N Am* an AUBERGINE.

eggshell *n* the hard thin porous covering of an egg. ➤ *adj* 1 of paint or varnish: having a slightly glossy finish. 2 of articles of china: very thin and fragile.

ego *n* 1 personal pride. 2 *psychoanal* in Freudian theory: the part of a person that is conscious and thinks. Compare ID, SUPEREGO. 3 one's image of oneself. 4 egotism.

egocentric *adj, derog* interested in oneself only.

egoism *n* 1 selfishness. 2 egotism. ○ **egoist** *n.* ○ **egoistic** or **egoistical** *adj.*

egomania *n, psychol* extreme self-interest or egotism. ○ **egomaniac** *n.*

egotism *n, derog* the fact of having a very high opinion of oneself. ○ **egotist** *n.* ○ **egotistic** or **egotistical** *adj.*

ego trip *n, colloq* something carried out mainly to increase one's high opinion of oneself.

egregious /ɪˈgriːdʒəs/ *adj, formal* outrageous; shockingly bad.

egress /ˈiːgrɛs/ *n, formal or law* 1 the act of leaving a building or other enclosed place. 2 an exit. 3 the power or right to depart.

egret /ˈiːgrət/ *n* any of various white wading birds similar to herons.

Egyptian *adj* belonging or relating to Egypt, its inhabitants or their language. ➤ *n* a citizen or inhabitant of, or person born in, Egypt.

Egyptology *n* the study of the culture and history of ancient Egypt. ○ **Egyptologist** *n*.

eh *exclam* 1 used to request that a question, remark, etc be repeated. 2 added to a question, often with the implication that agreement is expected. 3 used to express surprise.

eider /ˈaɪdə(r)/ or **eider duck** *n* a large sea duck from northern countries.

eiderdown *n* 1 the down or soft feathers of the eider. 2 a quilt filled with this or some similar material.

eight *n* 1 a the cardinal number 8; b the quantity that this represents, being one more than seven. 2 any symbol for this, eg *8* or *VIII*. 3 the eighth hour after midnight or midday. 4 a set or group of eight people or things. ➤ *adj* 1 totalling eight. 2 aged eight. ○ **eighth** *adj, n, adv*.

eighteen *n* 1 a the cardinal number 18; b the quantity that this represents, being one more than seventeen, or the sum of ten and eight. 2 any symbol for this, eg *18* or *XVIII*. 3 (written 18) a film classified as suitable for people aged eighteen and over. ➤ *adj* 1 totalling eighteen. 2 aged eighteen. ○ **eighteenth** *adj, n, adv*.

eightfold *adj* 1 equal to eight times as much or many. 2 divided into, or consisting of, eight parts. ➤ *adv* by eight times as much.

eighties (often written **80s** or **80's**) *pl n* 1 (one's **eighties**) the period of time between one's eightieth and ninetieth birthdays. 2 (**the eighties**) the range of temperatures between eighty and ninety degrees. 3 (**the eighties**) the period of time between the eightieth and ninetieth years of a century: *born in the 80s*.

eightsome reel *n* a lively Scottish dance for eight people.

eighty *n* (*-ies*) 1 a the cardinal number 80; b the quantity that this represents, being one more than seventy-nine, or the product of ten and eight. 2 any symbol for this, eg *80* or *LXXX*. ➤ *adj* 1 totalling eighty. 2 aged eighty. ○ **eightieth** *adj, n, adv*.

einsteinium *n* an element produced artificially from plutonium.

eisteddfod /aɪˈstɛdfəd, -ˈstɛðvɒd/ *n* (**eisteddfods** or **eisteddfodau** /aɪˈstɛðvɒdaɪ/) a Welsh festival during which competitions are held to find the best poetry, drama, songs, etc.

either *adj* 1 any one of two. 2 each of two: *a garden with a fence on either side*. ➤ *pron* any one of two things, people, etc. ➤ *adv, with negatives* 1 also; as well: *I thought him rather unpleasant, and I didn't like his wife either.* 2 what is more; besides: *He plays golf, and he's not bad, either.* ♦ **either … or …** introducing two choices or possibilities: *I need either a pen or a pencil.*

ejaculate *vb* 1 *tr & intr* of a man or male animal: to discharge (semen). 2 to exclaim. ○ **ejaculation** *n*.

eject *vb* 1 to throw out someone or something with force. 2 to force someone to leave. 3 *intr* to leave a moving aircraft using an ejector seat. ○ **ejection** *n*. ○ **ejector** *n*.

ejector seat or (*US*) **ejection seat** *n* a type of seat fitted in an aircraft, etc, designed to propel the occupant out of the aircraft at speed in case of emergency.

eke /iːk/ *vb* (*always* **eke sth out**) 1 to make (a supply) last longer, eg by adding something else to it or by careful use. 2 to manage with difficulty to make (a living, etc).

elaborate *adj* /ɪˈlabərət/ 1 complicated in design; complex. 2 carefully planned or worked out. ➤ *vb* /-reɪt/ 1 *intr* (*usu* **elaborate on** or **upon sth**) to add detail to it. 2 to work out something in great detail. ○ **elaborately** *adv*. ○ **elaboration** *n*.

élan /eɪˈlan; *French* elɑ̃/ *n, literary* impressive and energetic style.

eland /ˈiːlənd/ *n* (**elands** or **eland**) a large African antelope with spiral horns.

elapse *vb, intr, formal* of time: to pass.

elastic *adj* 1 of a material or substance: able to return to its original shape or size after being pulled or pressed out of shape. 2 of a force: caused by, or causing, such an ability. 3 flexible. 4 made of elastic. ➤ *n* stretchable cord or fabric woven with strips of rubber. ○ **elastically** *adv*. ○ **elasticated** *adj*. ○ **elasticity** *n*.

elastic band *n* a thin loop of rubber for keeping papers, etc together.

elate *vb* to make someone intensely happy. ○ **elated** *adj*. ○ **elation** *n*.

elbow *n* 1 the joint where the human arm bends. 2 the part of a garment which covers this joint. 3 the corresponding joint in animals. ➤ *vb* 1 to push or strike something with the elbow. 2 to make (one's way through) by pushing with the elbows.

elbow room *n* enough space for moving or doing something.

elder[1] *adj* 1 older. 2 (**the elder**) used before or after a person's name to distinguish them from a younger person of the same name. ➤ *n* 1 a person who is older. 2 (*often* **elders**) an older person, esp someone regarded as having authority. 3 in some tribal societies: a senior member of a tribe, who is invested with authority. 4 in some Protestant Churches: a lay person who has some responsibility for pastoral care and decision-making.

elder, older **Older** is the more general adjective. **Elder** is restricted in use to people, and is generally only used as an adjective in the context of family relationships, as in *an elder brother/sister*. It is always used before a noun or pronoun, or in **the elder**. **Elder** is not used in comparisons with **than**:

She is older (not *elder*) *than me*.

elder² *n* a bush or small tree with white flowers and purple-black or red berries.

elderly *adj* **1** rather old. **2** bordering on old age.

eldest *adj* oldest. ➤ *n* someone who is the oldest of three or more.

El Dorado /ɛldə'rɑːdoʊ/ *n* a legendary place where wealth is easy to accumulate.

eldritch *adj, orig Scot* weird; uncanny.

elect *vb* **1** to choose someone to be an official or representative by voting. **2** to choose something by vote, in preference to other options. ➤ *adj following its noun* elected to a position, but not yet formally occupying it: *president elect*. ○ **electable** *adj*.

election *n* **1** the process or act of choosing people for office, esp political office, by taking a vote. **2** the act of electing or choosing.

electioneer *vb, intr* to work for the election of a candidate, esp in a political campaign. ○ **electioneering** *n, adj*.

elective *adj* **1** of a position or office, etc: to which someone is appointed by election. **2** optional.

elector *n* someone who has the right to vote at an election. ○ **electoral** *adj* concerning or relating to elections or electors. ○ **electorally** *adv*.

electorate *n* all the electors of a city, country, etc.

electric *adj* **1** (*also* **electrical**) relating to, produced by, worked by or generating electricity. **2** of a musical instrument: amplified electronically. **3** having or causing great excitement, tension or expectation. ➤ *pl n* (**electrics**) **1** electrical appliances. **2** *colloq* wiring. ○ **electrically** *adv*.

electrical engineering *n* the branch of engineering concerned with the practical applications of electricity and magnetism. ○ **electrical engineer** *n*.

electric blanket *n* a blanket incorporating an electric element, used for warming a bed.

electric chair *n, US* a chair used for executing criminals by sending a powerful electric current through them.

electric current *n* the flow of electric charge, in the form of ELECTRONs, in the same direction through a conductor.

electric eel *n* an eel-like fish which is able to deliver electric shocks by means of an organ in its tail.

electrician *n* a person whose job is to install, maintain and repair electrical equipment.

electricity *n* **1** the energy which exists in a negative form in electrons and in a positive form in protons, and also as a flowing current usu of electrons. **2** an electric charge or current. **3** a supply of this energy to a household, etc, eg for heating and lighting. **4** excitement, tension or expectation.

electrify *vb* (-*ies*, -*ied*) **1** to give an electric charge to something. **2** to equip (eg a railway system) for the use of electricity as a power supply. **3** to cause great excitement in (eg a crowd). ○ **electrification** *n*. ○ **electrifying** *adj* extremely exciting.

electrocardiogram *n, med* the diagram or tracing produced by an electrocardiograph.

electrocardiograph *n, med* an apparatus which registers the electrical variations of the beating heart, as a diagram or tracing.

electroconvulsive therapy *n, med* the treatment of mental illness by passing small electric currents through the brain.

electrocute *vb* **1** to kill someone or something by electric shock. **2** to carry out a death sentence on someone by means of electricity. ○ **electrocution** *n*.

electrode *n, technical* either of the two conducting points by which electric current enters or leaves a battery or other electrical apparatus.

electrodynamics *sing n* the study of electricity in motion.

electroencephalogram *n, med* a diagram or tracing produced by an electroencephalograph.

electroencephalograph *n, med* an apparatus which registers the electrical activity of the brain.

electrolysis /ɛlək'trɒlɪsɪs/ *n* **1** *chem* the decomposition of a chemical in the form of a liquid or solution by passing an electric current through it. **2** the removal of tumours or hair roots by means of an electric current. ○ **electrolytic** *adj*.

electrolyte *n, chem* a solution of chemical salts which can conduct electricity. ○ **electrolytic** *adj*.

electromagnet *n, physics* a piece of soft metal, usu iron, made magnetic by the passage of an electric current through a coil of wire wrapped around the metal. ○ **electromagnetic** *adj* having electrical and magnetic properties. ○ **electromagnetism** *n* magnetic forces produced by electricity.

electromotive *adj, physics* producing or tending to produce an electric current.

electron *n, physics* a particle, present in all atoms, which has a negative electric charge and is responsible for carrying electricity in solids.

electronegative *adj* carrying a negative charge, tending to form negative ions.

electronic *adj* **1** operated by means of electrical circuits, usu several very small ones, which handle very low levels of electric current. **2**

produced, operated, etc using electronic apparatus. **3** concerned with electronics. ○ **electronically** *adv.*

electronic mail see under E-MAIL

electronic publishing *n* the publishing of computer-readable texts on disk, CD-ROM, CD-I, etc.

electronics *sing n* the science that deals with electronic circuits and their applications in machines, etc. ➤ *pl n* the electronic parts of a machine or system.

electron microscope *n* a microscope which operates using a beam of electrons rather than a beam of light, and is capable of very high magnification.

electronvolt *n, nuclear physics* a unit of energy equal to that acquired by an electron when accelerated by a potential of one volt.

electroplate *vb* to coat (an object) with metal, esp silver, by electrolysis. ➤ *n* articles coated in this way.

electrostatics *sing n* the branch of science concerned with electricity at rest. ○ **electrostatic** *adj.*

elegant *adj* **1** having or showing good taste in dress or style, combined with dignity and gracefulness. **2** of a movement: graceful. **3** of apparatus, work in science, a plan, etc: simple and ingenious. ○ **elegance** *n*. ○ **elegantly** *adv.*

elegiac / ɛləˈdʒaɪək / *adj, formal, literary* mournful or thoughtful.

elegy / ˈɛlədʒɪ / *n* (*-ies*) a mournful or thoughtful song or poem, esp one whose subject is death or loss.

element *n* **1** a part of anything; a component or feature. **2** *chem, physics* any substance that cannot be split by chemical means into simpler substances. **3** a person or small group within a larger group. **4** a slight amount. **5** the wire coil through which an electric current is passed to produce heat in various electrical appliances. **6** any one of the four basic substances (earth, air, fire and water) from which, according to ancient philosophy, everything is formed. **7** (**the elements**) weather conditions, esp when severe. **8** (**the elements**) basic facts or skills. ○ **elemental** *adj* **1** basic or primitive. **2** referring or relating to the forces of nature, esp the four elements (earth, air, fire and water). **3** immense; referring to the power of a force of nature. ♦ **in one's element** in the surroundings that one finds most natural and enjoyable.

elementary *adj* **1** dealing with simple or basic facts; rudimentary. **2** belonging or relating to the elements or an element.

elementary particle *n, chem, physics* any of the twenty or more particles (eg ELECTRONS, PROTONS and NEUTRONS) which make up an atom.

elementary school *n, N Am* primary school.

elephant *n* (*elephants* or *elephant*) the largest living land animal, with thick greyish skin, a nose in the form of a long hanging trunk, and two curved tusks, surviving in two species, the larger **African elephant** and the **Indian elephant**.

elephantiasis / ɛlɪfənˈtaɪəsɪs / *n, pathol* a disease in which the skin becomes thicker and the limbs become greatly enlarged.

elephantine *adj* like an elephant, esp in being large or clumsy.

elevate *vb* **1** to raise or lift. **2** to give a higher rank or status to someone or something.

elevated *adj* **1** of a rank, position, etc: very high. **2** of thoughts, ideas, etc: intellectually advanced or very moral. **3** of land or buildings: raised above the level of their surroundings.

elevation *n* **1** the act of elevating or state of being elevated. **2** *technical* height, eg of a place above sea-level. **3** *technical* a drawing or diagram of one side of a building, machine, etc.

elevator *n* **1** *N Am* a LIFT (*noun* sense 4). **2** a lift or machine for transporting goods to a higher level.

eleven *n* **1 a** the cardinal number 11; **b** the quantity that this represents, being one more than ten. **2** any symbol for this, eg *11* or *XI*. **3** the eleventh hour after midnight or midday. **4 a** a set or group of eleven people or things; **b** *football, cricket, hockey, etc* a team of players. ➤ *adj* **1** totalling eleven. **2** aged eleven. ○ **eleventh** *adj, n, adv.*

elevenses *pl n* (*often used with sing verb*) *colloq* a mid-morning snack.

elf *n* (*elves*) *folklore* a tiny supernatural being with a human form. ○ **elfin** *adj.*

elicit *vb* to cause something to happen; to bring something out into the open.

elide *vb, gram* to omit (a vowel or syllable) at the beginning or end of a word. ○ **elision** *n.*

eligible *adj* **1** suitable, or deserving to be chosen (for a job, as a husband, etc). **2** having a right to something: *eligible for compensation*. ○ **eligibility** *n.*

eliminate *vb* **1** to get rid of or exclude. **2** to expel (waste matter) from the body. **3** to exclude someone or something from a competition by defeat. **4** *slang* to kill or murder someone. ○ **elimination** *n*. ○ **eliminator** *n.*

elite or **élite** / eˈliːt / *n* **1** the best, most important or most powerful people within society. **2** the best of a group or profession.

elitism *n* **1** the belief in the need for a powerful social elite. **2** the belief in the natural social superiority of some people. **3** *often derog* awareness of, or pride in, belonging to an elite group in society. ○ **elitist** *adj, n.*

elixir / ɪˈlɪksə(r) / *n* **1** in medieval times: a liquid chemical preparation believed to have the power to give people everlasting life or to turn base metals into gold. **2** *pharmacol* a liquid medicine mixed with honey or alcohol, to hide the unpleasant taste.

Elizabethan *adj* relating to or typical of the reign of Queen Elizabeth, esp Queen Elizabeth I of England (1558–1603).

elk *n* (*elks* or *elk*) **1** a large deer with flat rounded antlers, found in Europe and Asia, and in N America where it is called the MOOSE. **2** *N Am* the WAPITI.

ellipse *n, geom* a regular oval, as formed by a diagonal cut through a cone above the base.

ellipsis *n* (*-ses* /-siːz/) **1** *gram* a figure of speech in which a word or words needed for the sense or grammar are omitted but understood. **2** in text: a set of three dots (…) that indicate the omission of a word or words, eg in a lengthy quotation.

ellipsoid *n, geom* a surface or solid object of which every plane section is an ellipse or a circle.

elliptical or **elliptic** *adj* **1** *maths* relating to, or having the shape of, an ELLIPSE. **2** of speech or writing: **a** containing an ELLIPSIS; **b** so concise as to be unclear or ambiguous.

elm *n* **1** (*also* **elm tree**) a tall deciduous tree with broad leaves. **2** (*also* **elmwood**) the hard heavy wood of this tree.

elocution *n* the art of speaking clearly and effectively. ○ **elocutionist** *n*.

elongate *vb* to lengthen or stretch something out. ○ **elongation** *n*.

elope *vb, intr* to run away secretly in order to get married. ○ **elopement** *n*.

eloquence *n* **1** the art or power of using speech to impress, move or persuade. **2** persuasive and fluent language. ○ **eloquent** *adj*. ○ **eloquently** *adv*.

else *adv, adj* different from or in addition to something or someone known or already mentioned: *Where else can you buy it?* ♦ **or else 1** or if not … ; otherwise … : *Hurry up, or else we'll be late.* **2** *colloq* or there will be trouble: *Give me the money, or else!*

elsewhere *adv* somewhere else.

elucidate *vb* to make clear; to shed light on something. ○ **elucidation** *n*.

elude *vb* **1** to escape or avoid something by quickness or cleverness. **2** to fail to be understood, discovered or remembered by someone.

elusive *adj* **1** difficult to find or catch. **2** difficult to understand or remember. ○ **elusively** *adv*. ○ **elusiveness** *n*.

elver *n* a young eel.

Elysium /ɪˈlɪzɪəm/ *n* **1** *Greek myth* the place where the blessed were supposed to rest after death. **2** *poetic* a state or place of perfect happiness. ○ **Elysian** *adj*.

emaciated *adj* extremely thin, esp because of illness or starvation.

e-mail, **email** or **E-mail** *n* (*in full* **electronic mail**) **1** a system for transmitting messages and computer files electronically from one computer to another, eg within an office computer network, over the Internet, etc. **2** correspondence sent in this way. ➢ *vb* to send someone an electronic message.

emanate *vb, intr* **1** of an idea, etc: to emerge or originate. **2** of light, gas, etc: to flow. ○ **emanation** *n*.

emancipate *vb* to set someone free from slav-

ery, or from some other social or political restraint. ○ **emancipation** *n*.

emasculate *vb* to reduce the force, strength or effectiveness of someone or something. ○ **emasculation** *n*.

embalm *vb* **1** to preserve (a dead body) from decay. **2** to preserve something unchanged.

embankment *n* **1** a bank or wall of earth made to enclose a waterway. **2** a mound built to carry a road or railway over a low-lying place. **3** a slope of grass, earth, etc which rises from either side of a road or railway.

embargo *n* (*embargoes*) **1** an official order forbidding something, esp trade with another country. **2** any restriction or prohibition. ➢ *vb* (*embargoes, embargoed*) to place something under an embargo.

embark *vb* **1** *tr & intr* to go or put on board a ship or aircraft. **2** *intr* (*usu* **embark on** or **upon sth**) to begin (a task, esp a lengthy one). ○ **embarkation** *n*.

embarrass *vb* **1** *tr & intr* to make someone feel, or to become, anxious, self-conscious or ashamed. **2** to confuse or perplex. ○ **embarrassed** *adj*. ○ **embarrassing** *adj*. ○ **embarrassingly** *adv*. ○ **embarrassment** *n*.

embassy *n* (*-ies*) **1** the official residence of an ambassador. **2** an ambassador and his or her staff.

embattled *adj* **1** troubled by problems or difficulties. **2** surrounded by enemies.

embed *vb* (*embedded, embedding*) (*also* **imbed**) to set or fix something firmly and deeply.

embellish *vb* **1** to make (a story, etc) more interesting by adding details which may not be true. **2** to beautify something with decoration. ○ **embellishment** *n*.

ember *n* **1** a piece of glowing or smouldering coal or wood. **2** (*embers*) red-hot ash; the smouldering remains of a fire.

embezzle *vb* to take or use dishonestly (money or property with which one has been entrusted). ○ **embezzlement** *n*. ○ **embezzler** *n*.

embitter *vb* to make someone feel bitter. ○ **embittered** *adj*.

emblazon *vb* **1** to decorate with a coat of arms or some other bright design. **2** to display in a very obvious or striking way.

emblem *n* an object chosen to represent an idea, a quality, a country, etc. ○ **emblematic** *adj*.

embody *vb* (*-ies, -ied*) **1** to be an expression or a representation of something in words, actions or form. **2** to include or incorporate. ○ **embodiment** *n*.

embolden *vb* to make someone bold; to encourage.

embolism *n, pathol* the blocking of a blood vessel by an air bubble, a blood clot, etc.

embolus /ˈɛmbələs/ *n* (*emboli* /-laɪ/) *pathol* any obstruction in a blood vessel, esp a blood clot.

emboss *vb* to carve or mould a raised design on (a surface).

embrace *vb* 1 to hold someone closely in the arms, affectionately or as a greeting. 2 to take (eg an opportunity) eagerly, or accept (eg a religion) wholeheartedly. 3 to include. ➤ *n* an act of embracing.

embrasure *n* 1 an opening in the wall of a castle, etc for shooting through. 2 an opening in a thick wall for a door or window, with angled sides which make it narrower on the outside.

embrocation *n* a lotion for rubbing into the skin, eg as a treatment for sore or pulled muscles.

embroider *vb* 1 to decorate (cloth) with sewn designs. 2 to make (a story, etc) more interesting by adding details, usu untrue ones. ○ **embroidery** *n*.

embroil *vb* to involve in a dispute or argument.

embryo /'ɛmbrɪoʊ/ *n, biol* 1 in animals: the developing young organism until hatching or birth. 2 in humans: the developing young organism during the first seven weeks after conception (compare FETUS). 3 anything in its earliest stages. ○ **embryonic** *adj*.

embryology *n* the scientific study of embryos.

emend *vb* to edit (a text), removing errors and making improvements. ○ **emendation** *n*.

emerald *n* 1 a deep green variety of BERYL, highly valued as a gemstone. 2 (*also* **emerald green**) its colour.

emerge *vb, intr* 1 to come out from hiding or into view. 2 to become known or apparent. ○ **emergence** *n*. ○ **emergent** *adj*.

emergency *n* (*-ies*) 1 an unexpected and serious happening which calls for immediate action. 2 a a serious injury needing immediate medical treatment; b a patient suffering such an injury.

emeritus /ɪ'mɛrɪtəs/ *adj, often following its noun* retired or honourably discharged from office, but retaining a former title as an honour: *professor emeritus*.

emery *n* (*-ies*) a hard mineral, usu used in powder form, for polishing or abrading.

emery board *n* a strip of card coated with emery powder, for filing one's nails.

emetic *med, adj* making one vomit. ➤ *n* an emetic medicine.

EMF *abbrev* (*also* **emf**) electromotive force.

emigrate *vb, intr* to leave one's native country and settle in another. ○ **emigrant** *n, adj*. ○ **emigration** *n*.

> **emigrate** A related word often confused with this one is **immigrate**.

émigré /'ɛmɪɡreɪ/ *n* (*émigrés* /-ɡreɪz/) a person who has emigrated, usu for political reasons.

eminence *n* honour, distinction or prestige. ◆ **Your** or **His Eminence** (**Your** or **Their Eminences**) a title of honour used in speaking to or about a cardinal.

eminent *adj* 1 famous and admired. 2 distinguished. ○ **eminently** *adv* 1 very. 2 obviously.

emir /ɛ'mɪə(r)/ *n* a title given to various Muslim rulers. ○ **emirate** *n*.

emissary /'ɛmɪsərɪ/ *n* (*-ies*) a person sent on a mission, esp on behalf of a government.

emission *n* 1 the act of emitting. 2 something emitted.

emit *vb* (*emitted, emitting*) to give out (light, heat, a smell, etc).

emollient *adj* 1 *med* softening or soothing the skin. 2 *formal* advocating a calmer, more peaceful attitude. ➤ *n, med* a substance which softens or soothes the skin.

emolument *n, formal* (*often* **emoluments**) money earned or otherwise gained through a job or position, eg salary or fees.

emotion *n* a strong feeling. ○ **emotionless** *adj*.

emotional *adj* 1 referring or relating to the emotions. 2 causing or expressing emotion. 3 of a person: tending to express emotions easily or excessively. 4 *often derog* based on emotions, rather than rational thought: *an emotional response*. ○ **emotionally** *adv*.

emotive *adj* tending or designed to excite emotion.

empathize or **-ise** *vb, intr* (*usu* **empathize with sb**) to share their feelings; to feel empathy.

empathy *n* the ability to share, understand and feel another person's feelings. ○ **empathetic** or **empathic** *adj* able to share others' feelings.

emperor *n* the male ruler of an empire.

emphasis *n* (*-ses* /-siːz/) 1 (*usu* **emphasis on sth**) special importance or attention given to it. 2 greater force or loudness on certain words or parts of words to show that they are important or have a special meaning.

emphasize or **-ise** *vb* to put emphasis on something.

emphatic *adj* 1 expressed with or expressing emphasis. 2 of a person: speaking firmly and forcefully. ○ **emphatically** *adv*.

emphysema /ɛmfɪ'siːmə/ *n, pathol* the presence of air in the body tissues.

empire *n* 1 a group of nations or states under the control of a single ruler or ruling power. 2 a large commercial or industrial organization which controls many separate firms, esp one headed by one person.

empirical *adj* based on experiment, observation or experience, rather than on theory. ○ **empirically** *adv*.

empiricism *n, philos* the theory or philosophy stating that knowledge can only be gained through experiment and observation. ○ **empiricist** *n*.

emplacement *n, mil* a strongly defended position from which a large gun may be fired.

employ *vb* 1 to give work, usu paid work, to someone. 2 to use. ◆ **be in sb's employ** *formal* to be employed by them.

employee *n* a person who works for another in return for payment.

employer n a person or company that employs workers.

employment n 1 the act of employing or the state of being employed. 2 an occupation, esp regular paid work.

emporium n (*emporiums* or *emporia*) *formal* a shop, esp a large one that sells a wide variety of goods.

empower vb (*usu* **empower sb to do sth**) to give them authority or official permission to do it.

empress n 1 the female ruler of an empire. 2 the wife or widow of an emperor.

empty adj (*-ier, -iest*) 1 having nothing inside. 2 not occupied, inhabited or furnished. 3 not likely to be satisfied or carried out: *empty promises.* 4 (*usu* **empty of sth**) completely without it. ➤ vb (*-ies, -ied*) tr & intr 1 to make or become empty. 2 to tip, pour or fall out of a container. ➤ n (*-ies*) *colloq* an empty container, esp a bottle. ○ **emptiness** n.

empty-handed adj 1 carrying nothing. 2 having gained or achieved nothing.

empty-headed adj foolish or frivolous.

EMS abbrev European Monetary System.

EMU abbrev Economic and Monetary Union (between EU countries).

emu n a large flightless but swift-running Australian bird.

emulate vb 1 to try hard to equal or be better than someone or something. 2 to imitate. 3 tr & intr of a computer or a program: to imitate the internal design of another microprocessor-based device. ○ **emulation** n. ○ **emulator** n.

emulsifier or **emulsifying agent** n a chemical substance that coats the surface of droplets of one liquid so that they can remain dispersed throughout a second liquid (eg margarine or ice cream) forming a stable emulsion.

emulsify vb (*-ies, -ied*) tr & intr to make or become an emulsion. ○ **emulsification** n.

emulsion n 1 *chem* a COLLOID consisting of a stable mixture of two IMMISCIBLE liquids (such as oil and water), in which small droplets of one liquid are dispersed uniformly throughout the other, eg salad cream and low-fat spreads. 2 *photog* the light-sensitive material used to coat photographic film, paper, etc. 3 water-based paint. 4 a liquid mixture containing globules of fat or resinous or bituminous material.

enable vb 1 to make someone able; to give them the necessary means, power or authority (to do something). 2 to make something possible.

enact vb 1 to act or perform something on stage or in real life. 2 to establish by law. ○ **enactment** n.

enamel n 1 a hardened coloured glass-like substance applied as a decorative or protective covering to metal or glass. 2 any paint or varnish which gives a finish similar to this. 3 the hard white covering of the teeth. ➤ vb (**en-**

amelled, enamelling; US **enameled, enameling**) to cover or decorate something with enamel.

enamoured or (*US*) **enamored** adj 1 (*usu* **enamoured with sb**) *formal or literary* in love with them. 2 (*usu* **enamoured of sth**) very fond of it, pleased with it, or enthusiastic about it.

en bloc /ãblɔk/ adv all together; as one unit.

encamp vb, tr & intr to settle in a camp. ○ **encampment** n.

encapsulate or **incapsulate** vb 1 to express concisely the main points or ideas of something, or capture the essence of it. 2 to enclose something in, or as if in, a capsule. ○ **encapsulation** n.

encase vb 1 to enclose something in, or as if in, a case. 2 to surround or cover. ○ **encasement** n.

encephalitis /ɛnsɛfə'laɪtɪs, ɛŋkɛ-/ n, *pathol* inflammation of the brain.

enchant vb 1 to charm or delight. 2 to put a magic spell on someone or something. ○ **enchanted** adj. ○ **enchanting** adj. ○ **enchantment** n.

enchilada /ɛntʃɪ'lɑːdə/ n, *cookery* a Mexican dish consisting of a tortilla with a meat filling, served with chilli sauce.

encircle vb to surround, or form a circle round, something. ○ **encirclement** n.

enclave n 1 a small country or state entirely surrounded by foreign territory. 2 a distinct racial or cultural group isolated within a country.

enclose or **inclose** vb 1 to put something inside a letter or in its envelope. 2 to shut in or surround.

enclosure or **inclosure** n 1 the process of enclosing or being enclosed, esp with reference to common land. 2 land surrounded by a fence or wall. 3 an enclosed space at a sporting event. 4 an additional paper or other item included with a letter.

encode vb to express something in, or convert it into, code. ○ **encoder** n.

encomium n (*encomiums* or *encomia* /ɪŋ-'koʊmɪə/) a formal speech or piece of writing praising someone.

encompass vb 1 to include or contain something, esp to contain a wide range or coverage of something. 2 to surround something.

encore n a repetition of a performance, or an additional performed item, after the end of a concert, etc. ➤ *exclam* an enthusiastic call from the audience for such a performance.

encounter vb 1 to meet someone or something, esp unexpectedly. 2 to meet with (difficulties, etc). ➤ n a chance meeting.

encourage vb 1 to give support, confidence or hope to someone. 2 to urge someone to do something. ○ **encouragement** n.

encroach vb, intr (*usu* **encroach on sb or sth**) 1 to intrude or extend gradually (on someone else's land, etc). 2 to overstep proper or agreed limits. ○ **encroachment** n.

encrust or **incrust** vb to cover something with

a thick hard coating, eg of jewels or ice. ○ **encrustation** n.

encrypt vb to put information (eg computer data or TV signals) into a coded form.

encumber vb **1** to prevent the free and easy movement of someone or something; to hamper or impede. **2** to burden someone or something with a load or debt.

encumbrance or **incumbrance** n an impediment, hindrance or burden.

encyclical /ɛnˈsɪklɪkəl/ n, RC Church a letter sent by the Pope to all Roman Catholic bishops.

encyclopedia or **encyclopaedia** n a reference work containing information on every branch of knowledge, or on one particular branch, usu arranged in alphabetical order. ○ **encyclopedic** adj of knowledge: full and detailed.

end n **1** the point or part farthest from the beginning, or either of the points or parts farthest from the middle, where something stops. **2** a finish or conclusion. **3** (**the end**) colloq the last straw; the limit. **4** a piece left over: a cigarette end. **5** death or destruction: meet one's end. **6** an object or purpose: The end justifies the means. **7** sport one of the two halves of a pitch or court defended by a team or player. **8** the part of a project, etc for which one is responsible: They had a few problems at their end. ➢ vb **1** tr & intr to finish or cause something to finish. **2** intr to reach a conclusion or cease to exist. ✦ **at the end of one's tether** exasperated; at the limit of one's endurance. **in the end** finally; after much discussion or work, etc. **make ends meet** to live within one's income and avoid debts. **no end** colloq very much. **no end of people** or **things** very many; a lot. **on end 1** vertical; standing straight up. **2** continuously. ◇ **end up** colloq **1** to arrive or find oneself eventually or finally. **2** to finish.

endanger vb to put someone or something in danger; to expose them to possible loss or injury.

endangered species n any plant or animal species that is in danger of extinction.

endear vb (usu **endear sb to sb else**) to make them beloved or liked. ○ **endearing** adj.

endearment n **1** a word or phrase expressing affection. **2** affection or love.

endeavour or (US) **endeavor** vb (usu **endeavour to do sth**) to try to do it, esp seriously and with effort. ➢ n a determined attempt or effort.

endemic adj **1** of a disease, etc: regularly occurring in a particular area or among a particular group of people. **2** biol of a plant or animal: native to, or restricted to, a particular area.

ending n **1** the end, esp of a story, poem, etc. **2** gram the end part of a word, esp an INFLECTION.

endive /ˈɛndɪv/ n a plant whose crisp leaves are used in salads.

endless adj having no end, or seeming to have no end. ○ **endlessly** adv.

endmost adj farthest; nearest the end.

endocrine adj of a gland: ductless, and producing and secreting one or more hormones directly into the bloodstream.

endometrium /ɛndəʊˈmiːtrɪəm/ n, anat the mucous membrane which lines the UTERUS.

endorphin n, biochem any of a group of chemical compounds that occur naturally in the brain and have similar pain-relieving properties to morphine.

endorse or **indorse** vb **1** to sign the back of (a document, esp the back of a cheque) to specify oneself or another person as payee. **2** to make a note of an offence on (a driving licence). **3** to state one's approval of or support for something. ○ **endorsement** n.

endoscope n, med a long thin flexible instrument containing bundles of optical fibres and having a light at one end, used for viewing internal body cavities and organs. ○ **endoscopic** adj. ○ **endoscopy** n.

endoskeleton n, zool in vertebrates: an internal skeleton made of bone or cartilage.

endow vb **1** to provide a source of income for (a hospital or place of learning, etc), often by a bequest. **2** (**be endowed with sth**) to have a quality, ability, etc.

endowment n **1** a sum endowed. **2** a quality, skill, etc with which a person is endowed.

endpaper n, publishing, etc one of the two leaves at the front or back of a hardback book, fixed to the inside of the cover.

end product n the final product of a series of operations, esp industrial processes. Compare BY-PRODUCT.

endure vb **1** to bear something patiently; to put up with it. **2** intr, formal to continue to exist. ○ **endurance** n. ○ **enduring** adj.

endways or (esp N Am) **endwise** adv **1** with the end forward or upward. **2** end to end.

enema /ˈɛnəmə/ n (**enemas** or **enemata** /ɛˈnɛmətə/) med **1** the injection of a liquid into the rectum, eg to clean it out or to introduce medication. **2** the liquid injected.

enemy n (**-ies**) **1** a person who is actively opposed to someone else. **2** a hostile nation or force, or a member of it. **3** an opponent or adversary. **4** a person or thing that opposes or acts against someone or something: Cleanliness is the enemy of disease. ➢ adj hostile; belonging to a hostile nation or force.

energize or **-ise** vb **1** to stimulate, invigorate or enliven. **2** to provide energy for the operation of (a machine, etc). ○ **energizer** n.

energy n (**-ies**) **1** the capacity for vigorous activity; liveliness or vitality. **2** force or forcefulness. **3** physics the capacity to do work. ○ **energetic** adj.

enervate vb **1** to take energy or strength from something. **2** to deprive someone of moral or mental vigour. ○ **enervating** adj. ○ **enervation** n.

enfeeble vb, formal to make someone weak.

enfilade n, mil a continuous burst of gunfire

sweeping from end to end across a line of enemy soldiers.

enfold or **infold** vb 1 to wrap up or enclose. 2 to embrace.

enforce vb 1 to cause (a law or decision) to be carried out. 2 (usu enforce sth on sb) to impose (one's will, etc) on them. ∘ **enforceable** adj. ∘ **enforcement** n.

enfranchise vb, formal to give someone the right to vote in elections. ∘ **enfranchisement** n.

engage vb 1 to take someone on as a worker. 2 to book or reserve (eg a table or room). 3 to involve or occupy (a person or their attention). 4 tr & intr, mil to come or bring something into battle. 5 tr & intr to cause part of a machine (eg the gears) to fit into and lock with another part.

engaged adj 1 (usu engaged to sb) bound by a promise to marry them. 2 of a room, telephone line, etc: not free or vacant; occupied; in use. 3 geared together; interlocked.

engagement n 1 the act of engaging or state of being engaged. 2 a firm agreement between two people to marry. 3 an arrangement made in advance. 4 mil a battle.

engaging adj charming; attractive. ∘ **engagingly** adv.

engender vb to produce or cause (esp feelings or emotions).

engine n 1 a machine that is used to convert some form of energy into mechanical energy that can be used to perform useful work. 2 a railway locomotive.

engineer n 1 someone who designs, makes, or works with machinery, including electrical equipment. 2 an officer in charge of a ship's engines. 3 N Am the driver of a locomotive. 4 a person, esp a member of the armed forces, who designs and builds military apparatus and is trained in construction work. ➤ vb 1 often derog to arrange or bring something about by skill or deviousness. 2 to design or construct something as an engineer.

engineering n the application of scientific knowledge to the practical problems of design, construction, operation and maintenance of devices encountered in everyday life.

English adj 1 belonging or relating to England or its inhabitants. 2 relating to the English language. ➤ n 1 (the English) the people of England. 2 the native language of Britain, much of N America and the Commonwealth, and some other countries.

Englishman or **Englishwoman** n a male or female citizen of, or person born in, England.

engorged adj, pathol congested with blood. ∘ **engorgement** n.

engrave vb 1 to carve (letters or designs) on stone, metal, etc. 2 to decorate (stone, etc) in this way. 3 to fix or impress something deeply on the mind, etc. ∘ **engraver** n.

engraving n 1 the art or process of carving or incising designs on wood, metal, etc, esp for the purpose of printing impressions from them. 2 a print taken from an engraved metal plate, etc.

engross vb to take up someone's attention completely.

engulf vb 1 to swallow something up completely. 2 to overwhelm.

enhance vb to improve or increase the value, quality or intensity of something (esp something already good). ∘ **enhancement** n.

enigma n 1 a puzzle or riddle. 2 a mysterious person, thing or situation. ∘ **enigmatic** adj.

enjoin vb, formal to order or command someone to do something.

enjoy vb 1 to find pleasure in something. 2 to have, experience or have the benefit of something good: The room enjoys sunlight all day. ∘ **enjoyable** adj. ∘ **enjoyment** n.

enlarge vb 1 tr & intr to make or become larger. 2 to reproduce (a photograph, etc) in a larger form. 3 intr (usu enlarge on or upon sth) to speak or write about it at greater length or in greater detail. ∘ **enlargement** n. ∘ **enlarger** n.

enlighten vb 1 to give more information to someone. 2 to free someone from ignorance or superstition. 3 to make someone aware or uplift them by knowledge or religion. ∘ **enlightened** adj.

enlightenment n 1 the act of enlightening or the state of being enlightened. 2 freedom from ignorance or superstition. 3 (the Enlightenment) the philosophical movement originating in 18c Europe, with a belief in reason and human progress, and a questioning of tradition and authority.

enlist vb 1 intr & tr to join or be enrolled in one of the armed forces. 2 to obtain the support and help of someone; to obtain (support and help). ∘ **enlistment** n.

enliven vb (**enlivened, enlivening**) to make active or more active, lively or cheerful.

en masse /French āmas/ adv all together; as a mass or group.

enmesh vb to catch or trap something in a net, or as if in a net.

enmity n (**-ies**) 1 the state or quality of being an enemy. 2 ill will.

ennoble vb 1 to make something noble or dignified. 2 to make someone a member of the nobility.

ennui /ɒˈnwiː/ n, literary boredom or discontent caused by a lack of activity or excitement.

enormity n (**-ies**) 1 outrageousness or wickedness. 2 an outrageous or wicked act. 3 immenseness or vastness.

enormous adj extremely large; huge. ∘ **enormously** adv.

enough adj in the number or quantity needed; sufficient: enough food to eat. ➤ adv 1 to the necessary degree or extent. 2 fairly: She's pretty enough, I suppose. 3 quite: Oddly enough, I can't remember. ➤ pron the amount needed.

enquire, enquiring, enquiry see INQUIRE, etc.

enrage vb to make someone extremely angry.

enrapture vb to give intense pleasure or joy to someone. ○ **enraptured** adj.

enrich vb **1** to make something rich or richer, esp better or stronger in quality, value or flavour. **2** to make wealthy or wealthier. **3** to fertilize (soil, etc). ○ **enriched** adj. ○ **enrichment** n.

enrol or (US) **enroll** vb (**enrolled, enrolling**) **1** to add the name of (a person) to a list or roll, eg of members or pupils. **2** to secure the membership or participation of someone. **3** intr to add one's own name to such a list; to become a member. ○ **enrolment** n.

en route adv on the way: We'll stop en route for a meal.

ensconce vb, literary or humorous (often **be ensconced**) **1** to settle comfortably or safely. **2** to hide safely.

ensemble /ɒnˈsɒmbəl; French ɑ̃sɑ̃bl/ n **1** a small group of (usu classical) musicians who regularly perform together. **2** a passage in opera, ballet, etc performed by all the singers, musicians or dancers together. **3** a set of items of clothing worn together. **4** all the parts of a thing considered as a whole.

enshrine vb **1** to enter and protect (a right, an idea, etc) in the laws or constitution of a state, the constitution of an organization, etc. **2** to place something in a shrine.

enshroud vb **1** to cover something completely; to hide something by covering it up. **2** to cover something or someone in a shroud.

ensign /ˈɛnsaɪn, in senses 1 and 2 also ˈɛnsən/ n **1** the flag of a nation or regiment. **2** a coloured flag with a smaller Union flag in one corner. **3** hist the lowest rank of officer in the infantry, or an officer of this rank. **4** N Am a the lowest rank of officer in the navy; **b** an officer of this rank.

enslave vb to make someone into a slave. ○ **enslavement** n.

ensnare vb to catch something or someone in, or as if in, a trap; to trick or lead them dishonestly (into doing something).

ensue vb (usu **ensue from sth**) intr **1** to follow it; to happen after it. **2** to result from it. ○ **ensuing** adj.

en suite adv, adj forming, or attached as part of, a single unit or set. ➤ n, colloq an en suite bathroom.

ensure vb **1** to make something certain; to assure or guarantee it. **2** to make (a thing or person) safe and secure.

ENT abbrev, med ear, nose and throat.

entablature n, archit the part of a classical building directly supported by the columns.

entail vb **1** to have something as a necessary result or requirement. **2** (usu **entail sth on sb**) law to bequeath (property) to one's descendants, not allowing them the option to sell it. ○ **entailment** n.

entangle vb **1** to cause something to get caught in some obstacle, eg a net. **2** to involve someone or something in difficulties. **3** to make something complicated or confused. ○ **entanglement** n.

entente cordiale /ã'tãt kɔːdɪ'ɑːl/ n (**entente cordiales**) a friendly agreement or relationship between nations or states.

enter vb **1** tr & intr to go or come in or into (eg a room). **2** tr & intr to register (another person, oneself, one's work, etc) in a competition. **3** to record something in a book, diary, etc. **4** to join (a profession, society, etc). **5** to submit or present something: He entered a complaint. **6** intr, theat to come on to the stage. ◊ **enter into sth 1** to begin to take part in it. **2** to become involved in it; to participate actively or enthusiastically in it. **3** to agree to be associated in or bound by (eg an agreement).

enteric /ɛnˈtɛrɪk/ adj, anat intestinal.

enteritis /ɛntəˈraɪtɪs/ n, pathol inflammation of the intestines, esp the small intestine.

enterprise n **1** a project or undertaking, esp one that requires boldness and initiative. **2** boldness and initiative. **3** a business firm.

enterprising adj showing boldness and initiative.

entertain vb **1** to provide amusement or recreation for someone. **2** tr & intr to give hospitality to (a guest), esp in the form of a meal. **3** to consider or be willing to adopt (an idea, suggestion, etc). ○ **entertainer** n a person who provides amusement, esp one who does so as their profession.

entertaining adj interesting and amusing; giving entertainment. ➤ n provision of entertainment.

entertainment n **1** something that entertains, eg a theatrical show. **2** the act of entertaining. **3** amusement or recreation.

enthral or (esp US) **enthrall** vb (**enthralled, enthralling**) to fascinate.

enthrone vb to place someone on a throne. ○ **enthronement** n.

enthuse vb, tr & intr to be enthusiastic, or make someone enthusiastic.

enthusiasm n lively or passionate interest or eagerness.

enthusiast n someone filled with enthusiasm, esp for a particular subject; a fan or devotee. ○ **enthusiastic** adj. ○ **enthusiastically** adv.

entice vb to tempt or persuade, by arousing hopes or desires or by promising a reward. ○ **enticement** n. ○ **enticing** adj.

entire adj **1** whole or complete. **2** absolute or total. ○ **entirely** adv.

entirety n (-**ies**) completeness; wholeness; the whole.

entitle vb **1** to give (someone) a right to have or to do (something). **2** to give a title or name to (a book, etc). ○ **entitlement** n having a right to something.

entity n (-**ies**) something that has a real existence.

entomb vb **1** to put (a body) in a tomb. **2** to cover, bury or hide someone or something as if in a tomb.

entomology n the scientific study of insects. ○ **entomological** adj. ○ **entomologist** n.

entourage n a group of followers or assistants, esp one accompanying a famous or important person.

entrails pl n 1 the internal organs of a person or animal. 2 literary the inner parts of anything.

entrance¹ /'ɛntrəns/ n 1 a way in, eg a door. 2 formal the act of entering. 3 the right to enter.

entrance² /ɪn'trɑːns/ vb 1 to grip or captivate someone's attention and imagination. 2 to put someone into a trance. ○ **entrancement** n. ○ **entrancing** adj gripping the imagination; fascinating; delightful.

entrant n someone who enters something, esp an examination, a competition or a profession.

entrap vb 1 to catch something in a trap. 2 to trick someone into doing something. ○ **entrapment** n.

entreat vb, tr & intr to ask passionately or desperately; to beg. ○ **entreaty** n (-ies).

entrecôte /'ɒntrəkoʊt/ n, cookery a boneless steak cut from between two ribs.

entrée /'ɒntreɪ/ n 1 a small dish served after the fish course and before the main course at a formal dinner. 2 chiefly US a main course. 3 formal the right of admission or entry.

entrench or **intrench** vb 1 to fix or establish something firmly, often too firmly: deeply entrenched ideas. 2 to fortify something with trenches dug around. ○ **entrenchment** n.

entrepreneur n someone who engages in business enterprises, often with some personal financial risk. ○ **entrepreneurial** adj.

entropy /'ɛntrəpɪ/ n (-ies) physics a measure of the amount of disorder in a system, or of the unavailability of energy for doing work.

entrust or **intrust** vb (usu entrust sth to sb, or sb with sth) to give it to them to take care of or deal with.

entry n (-ies) 1 the act of coming or going in. 2 the right to enter. 3 a place of entering such as a door or doorway. 4 a person, or the total number of people, entered for a competition, etc. 5 an item written on a list or in a book, etc, or the act of recording an item or items in this way.

entwine vb to wind or twist (two or more things) together.

E-number n any of various identification codes, consisting of the letter E (for European) followed by a number, that are used to denote all food additives, except flavourings, that have been approved by the European Union.

enumerate vb 1 to list one by one. 2 to count. ○ **enumeration** n.

enumerator n someone who issues and then collects census forms.

enunciate vb 1 tr & intr to pronounce words clearly. 2 to state something formally. ○ **enunciation** n.

enure see INURE

enuresis /ɛnjʊˈriːsɪs/ n, pathol involuntary urination, esp during sleep.

envelop vb (enveloped, enveloping) 1 to cover or wrap something or someone completely. 2 to obscure or conceal: an event enveloped in mystery. ○ **envelopment** n.

envelope n 1 a thin flat sealable paper packet or cover, esp for a letter. 2 a cover or wrapper of any kind.

enviable adj likely to cause envy; highly desirable. ○ **enviably** adv.

envious adj feeling or showing envy. Compare JEALOUS. ○ **enviously** adv.

environment n 1 the surroundings or conditions within which something or someone exists. 2 (usu the environment) the combination of external conditions that surround and influence a living organism. ○ **environmental** adj.

environmentalist n someone who is concerned about the harmful effects of human activity on the environment. ○ **environmentalism** n.

environs pl n surrounding areas, esp the outskirts of a town or city.

envisage vb 1 to picture something in the mind. 2 to consider as likely in the future.

envoy n 1 a diplomat ranking next below an ambassador. 2 a messenger or agent, esp on a diplomatic mission.

envy n (-ies) 1 a feeling of resentment or regretful desire for another person's qualities, better fortune or success. 2 anything that arouses envy: She is the envy of his friends. ➤ vb (-ies, -ied) 1 to feel envy towards someone. 2 to covet; to wish to have something. 3 (envy sb sth) to feel envy towards them on account of (their success, etc).

enzyme n, biochem a specialized protein molecule that acts as a catalyst for the biochemical reactions that occur in living cells.

Eocene /'iːəʊsiːn/ geol, n the second epoch of the Tertiary period, lasting from about 54 million to 38 million years ago. ➤ adj relating to this epoch.

eolithic or **Eolithic** adj, archaeol belonging to the early part of the Stone Age, when crude stone tools were first used.

eon or **aeon** n 1 a long period of time; an endless or immeasurable period of time. 2 (usu eon) geol the largest unit of geological time, consisting of a number of ERAS. 3 astron a period of a thousand million years.

epaulette or (chiefly US) **epaulet** /ɛpə'lɛt/ n a decoration on the shoulder of a coat or jacket, esp of a military uniform.

épée /'eɪpeɪ/ n a sword with a narrow flexible blade, formerly used in duelling, now, with a blunted end, used in fencing.

ephemeral adj lasting a short time.

epic n 1 a long narrative poem telling of heroic acts, the birth and death of nations, etc. 2 a long adventure story or film, etc. ➤ adj referring to or like an epic.

epicene adj 1 having characteristics of both sexes, or of neither sex. 2 relating to, or for use by, both sexes.

epicentre or (US) **epicenter** n the point on the Earth's surface which is directly above the FOCUS (sense 4) of an earthquake, or directly above or below a nuclear explosion.

epicure *n* someone who has refined taste, esp one who enjoys good food and drink. ○ **epicurism** *n*.

epicurean /ɛpɪkjʊəˈrɪən/ *n* someone who likes pleasure and good living; an epicure. ➤ *adj* given to luxury or to the tastes of an epicure.

epidemic *n* **1** a sudden outbreak of infectious disease which spreads rapidly and widely in a particular area for a limited period of time. **2** a sudden and extensive spread of anything undesirable. ➤ *adj* referring to or like an epidemic: also used to describe a non-infectious condition such as malnutrition.

epidemiology /ɛpɪdiːmɪˈɒlədʒɪ/ *n, biol* the study of the distribution, effects and causes of diseases in populations. ○ **epidemiologist** *n*.

epidermis *n, biol* the outermost layer of a plant or animal, which serves to protect the underlying tissues from infection, injury and water loss. ○ **epidermal** *adj*.

epidural *med, adj* situated on, or administered into, the DURA MATER. ➤ *n* (*in full* **epidural anaesthetic**) the epidural injection of an anaesthetic to remove all sensation below the waist, used esp during childbirth.

epiglottis *n, anat* in mammals: a movable flap of cartilage hanging at the back of the tongue, which closes the opening of the larynx when food or drink is being swallowed.

epigram *n* **1** a witty or sarcastic saying. **2** a short poem with such an ending. ○ **epigrammatic** *adj*.

epigraph *n* **1** a quotation or motto at the beginning of a book or chapter. **2** an inscription on a building.

epilepsy *n, pathol* any of a group of disorders of the nervous system characterized by recurring attacks that involve impairment, or sudden loss, of consciousness.

epileptic *adj* **1** referring or relating to, or like, epilepsy. **2** suffering from epilepsy. ➤ *n* someone who suffers from epilepsy.

epilogue or (*US*) **epilog** *n* **1** the closing section of a book, programme, etc. **2 a** a speech addressed to the audience at the end of a play; **b** the actor making this speech.

Epiphany /ɪˈpɪfənɪ/ *n* (-*ies*) *Christianity* a festival on 6 January which commemorates, in the western Churches, the showing of Christ to the three wise men, and, in the Orthodox and other eastern Churches, the baptism of Christ.

episcopacy /ɪˈpɪskəpəsɪ/ *n* (-*ies*) **1** the government of the church by bishops. **2** bishops as a group.

episcopal *adj* **1** belonging or relating to bishops. **2** of a church: governed by bishops.

episcopalian *adj* **1** belonging or relating to an episcopal church. **2** advocating church government by bishops. ➤ *n* a member of an episcopal church, esp the Anglican Church. ○ **episcopalianism** *n*.

episcopate /ɪˈpɪskəpət/ *n* **1** the position or period of office of a bishop. **2** bishops as a group. **3** an area under the care of a bishop.

episiotomy /ɪpɪzɪˈɒtəmɪ/ *n* (-*ies*) *med* a surgical cut made at the opening of the vagina during childbirth, to assist the delivery of the baby.

episode *n* **1** one of several events or distinct periods making up a longer sequence. **2** one of the separate parts in which a radio or TV serial is broadcast, or a serialized novel is published. ○ **episodic** *adj* **1** consisting of several distinct periods. **2** occurring at intervals; sporadic.

epistemology /ɪpɪstəˈmɒlədʒɪ/ *n* the philosophical theory of knowledge. ○ **epistemological** *adj*. ○ **epistemologist** *n*.

epistle *n* **1** *literary* a letter, esp a long one, dealing with important matters. **2** (*usu* **Epistle**) *Christianity* each of the letters written by Christ's Apostles, which form part of the New Testament. ○ **epistolary** *adj, formal* relating to or consisting of letters.

epitaph *n* **1** an inscription on a gravestone. **2** a short commemorative speech or piece of writing in a similar style.

epithelium /ɛpɪˈθiːlɪəm/ *n* (**epithelia**) *anat* the layer of tissue that covers all external surfaces of a multicellular animal, and lines internal hollow structures. ○ **epithelial** *adj*.

epithet *n* an adjective or short descriptive phrase which captures the particular quality of the person or thing it describes.

epitome /ɪˈpɪtəmɪ/ *n* **1** a miniature representation of a larger or wider idea, issue, etc. **2** a person or thing that is the embodiment or a perfect example (of a quality, etc).

epitomize or **-ise** *vb* **1** to typify or personify. **2** to make an epitome of something; to shorten.

epoch /ˈiːpɒk/ *n* **1** a major division or period of history, or of a person's life, etc, usu marked by some important event. **2** *geol* an interval of geological time representing a subdivision of a period, and during which a particular series of rocks was formed. ○ **epochal** *adj*.

epoch-making *adj* highly significant or decisive.

eponymous /ɪˈpɒnɪməs/ *adj* of a character in a story, etc: having the name which is used as the title.

epoxy *chem, adj* consisting of an oxygen atom bonded to two carbon atoms. ➤ *n* (-*ies*) (*also* **epoxy resin**) any of a group of synthetic thermosetting resins that form strong adhesive bonds.

EPROM /ˈiːprɒm/ *abbrev, comput* erasable programmable read-only memory, a read-only memory in which stored data can be erased and reprogrammed. Compare EEPROM.

Epsom salts *sing or pl n* a preparation of magnesium sulphate, used as a medicine, eg for clearing the bowels.

equable /ˈɛkwəbəl/ *adj* **1** of a climate: never showing very great variations. **2** of a person: even-tempered. ○ **equably** *adv*.

equal *adj* **1** the same in size, amount, value, etc. **2** evenly balanced; displaying no advantage or bias. **3** having the same status; having or entitled to the same rights. ➤ *n* a person or thing of the same age, rank, ability, etc. ➤ *vb* (**equalled, equalling**) **1** to be the same in amount, value, size, etc as someone or something. **2** to be as good as someone or something. **3** to achieve something which matches (a previous achievement or achiever). ○ **equality** *n* (**-ies**). ○ **equally** *adv.* ♦ **equal to sth** having the necessary ability for it.

equalize or **-ise** *vb* **1** *tr & intr* to make or become equal. **2** *intr* to reach the same score as an opponent, after being behind. ○ **equalization** *n.* ○ **equalizer** *n.*

equal opportunities *pl n* the principle of equal treatment of all employees or candidates for employment, irrespective of race, religion, sex, etc.

equanimity *n* calmness of temper; composure.

equate *vb* **1** (*usu* **equate one thing to** or **with another**) to consider them as equivalent. **2** (*usu* **equate with sth**) to be equivalent to it.

equation *n* **1** *maths* a mathematical statement of the equality between two expressions involving constants and/or variables. **2** the act of equating.

equator *n* (*often* **the Equator**) *geog* the imaginary great circle that passes around the Earth at latitude 0 at an equal distance from the North and South Poles. ○ **equatorial** *adj.*

equerry /ˈɛkwərɪ/ *n* (**-ies**) an official who serves as a personal attendant to a member of a royal family.

equestrian *adj* **1** belonging or relating to horse-riding or horses. **2** on horseback. ○ **equestrianism** *n.*

equidistant *adj* equally distant.

equilateral *adj* having all sides of equal length.

equilibrium *n* (**equilibria** or **equilibriums**) **1** *physics* a state in which the various forces acting on an object or objects in a system balance each other. **2** a calm and composed state of mind. **3** a state of balance.

equine *adj, formal* belonging or relating to, or like, a horse or horses.

equinoctial *adj* happening on or near an equinox. ➤ *n* a storm occurring at an equinox.

equinox *n* either of the two occasions on which the Sun crosses the equator, making night and day equal in length, occurring about 21 March and 23 September.

equip *vb* (**equipped, equipping**) to fit out or provide someone or something with the necessary tools, supplies, abilities, etc. ○ **equipment** *n* **1** the clothes, machines, tools or instruments, etc necessary for a particular kind of work or activity. **2** *formal* the act of equipping.

equipoise *n, formal* a state of balance.

equitable /ˈɛkwɪtəbəl/ *adj* fair and just. ○ **equitably** *adv.*

equity *n* (**-ies**) **1** fair or just conditions or treatment. **2** *law* the concept of natural justice, as opposed to common law or statute law. **3** the excess in value of a property over the mortgage and other charges held on it. Compare NEGATIVE EQUITY. **4** (*usu* **equities**) an ordinary share in a company.

equivalent *adj* equal in value, power, meaning, etc. ➤ *n* an equivalent thing, amount, etc. ○ **equivalence** *n.*

equivocal /ɪˈkwɪvəkəl/ *adj* **1** ambiguous; of doubtful meaning. **2** of an uncertain nature. **3** questionable, suspicious or mysterious. ○ **equivocally** *adv.* ○ **equivocate** *vb, intr* to use ambiguous words in order to deceive or to avoid answering a question. ○ **equivocation** *n* evasive ambiguity.

Er *symbol, chem* erbium.

era *n* **1** a distinct period in history marked by or beginning at an important event. **2** *geol* the second largest unit of geological time, representing a subdivision of an EON.

eradicate *vb* to get rid of something completely. ○ **eradicable** *adj.* ○ **eradication** *n.* ○ **eradicator** *n.*

erase *vb* **1** to rub out (pencil marks, etc). **2** to remove all trace of something. **3** to destroy (a recording) on audio or video tape. ○ **erasable** *adj.* ○ **eraser** *n* something that erases, esp a rubber for removing pencil or ink marks. ○ **erasure** *n* **1** the act of rubbing out. **2** a place where something written has been erased.

erbium *n, chem* a soft silvery metallic element.

ere /ɛə(r)/ *prep, conj, now only poetic* before.

erect *adj* **1** upright; not bent or leaning. **2** *physiol* of the penis, clitoris or nipples: enlarged and rigid through being filled with blood, usu as a result of sexual excitement. ➤ *vb* **1** to put up or build something. **2** to set or put (a pole, flag, etc) in a vertical position. **3** to set up or establish something. ○ **erection** *n.*

erectile *adj, physiol* **1** of an organ, etc: capable of becoming erect. **2** capable of being erected.

ergo *adv, formal or logic* therefore.

ergonomics *sing n* the study of the relationship between people and their working environment. ○ **ergonomic** *adj.*

ergot *n* **1** a disease of rye and other cereals caused by a fungus. **2** this fungus, now an important source of alkaloid drugs.

ermine *n* (**ermine** or **ermines**) **1** the stoat in its winter phase, when its fur has turned white. **2** the fur of this animal.

erode *vb, tr & intr* to wear away, destroy or be destroyed gradually.

erogenous /ɪˈrɒdʒənəs/ *adj* of areas of the body, usu called **erogenous zones**: sensitive to sexual stimulation.

erosion *n* the loosening, fragmentation and transport from one place to another of rock material by water, wind, ice, gravity, or living organisms. ○ **erosive** *adj.*

erotic *adj* arousing; referring or relating to sexual desire, or giving sexual pleasure. ○ **erotically** *adv.*

erotica *pl n* erotic literature, pictures, etc.

eroticism *n* **1** the erotic quality of a piece of writing, a picture, etc. **2** interest in, or pursuit of, sexual sensations. **3** the use of erotic images and symbols in art, literature, etc.

err *vb, intr* **1** to make a mistake, be wrong or do wrong. **2** to sin.

errand *n* **1** a short journey made in order to get or do something, esp for someone else. **2** the purpose of such a journey. ♦ **run an errand** or **errands** to perform small pieces of business, deliver messages, etc.

errant *adj, literary* **1** doing wrong. **2** wandering in search of adventure: *a knight errant*.

erratic *adj* **1** irregular; having no fixed pattern or course. **2** unpredictable in behaviour. ○ **erratically** *adv.*

erratum *n* (**errata**) *formal* an error in writing or printing.

erroneous *adj* wrong or mistaken. ○ **erroneously** *adv.*

error *n* **1** a mistake, inaccuracy or misapprehension. **2** the state of being mistaken. **3** the possible discrepancy between an estimate and an actual value or amount.

ersatz /'ɜːzæts, 'eə-/ *adj, derog* substitute; imitation.

Erse *n* the name formerly used by lowland Scots for Scottish GAELIC; now also applied to Irish Gaelic.

erstwhile *adj, formal or archaic* former.

eructation *n, formal* a belch or the act of belching.

erudite /'erʊdaɪt/ *adj* showing or having a great deal of knowledge. ○ **erudition** *n.*

erupt *vb, intr* **1** of a volcano: to throw out lava, ash and gases. **2** to break out suddenly and violently. **3** of a skin blemish or rash: to appear suddenly and in a severe form. ○ **eruption** *n.* ○ **eruptive** *adj.*

erysipelas /ɛrɪ'sɪpɪləs/ *n, pathol* an infectious disease of the skin, esp of the face, which produces deep red sore patches, accompanied by fever.

erythrocyte *n* a red blood corpuscle.

Es *symbol, chem* einsteinium.

escalate *vb, tr & intr* to increase or be increased rapidly in scale, degree, etc. ○ **escalation** *n.* ○ **escalatory** *adj.*

escalator *n* a type of conveyor belt which forms a continuous moving staircase.

escalope /'eskəlɒp/ *n, cookery* a thin slice of boneless meat, esp veal.

escapade *n* a daring, adventurous or unlawful act.

escape *vb* **1** *intr* to gain freedom. **2** to manage to avoid (punishment, disease, etc). **3** not to be noticed or remembered by someone: *Nothing escapes his notice.* **4** *intr* of a gas, liquid, etc: to leak out or get out. **5** of words, etc: to be uttered unintentionally by someone. ➤ *n* **1** an act of escaping. **2** a means of escape. **3** the avoidance of danger or harm: *a narrow escape.* **4** a leak or release. **5** something providing a

break or distraction.

escapee *n* someone who has escaped, esp from prison.

escapement *n* the mechanism in a clock or watch which connects the moving parts to the balance.

escape velocity *n, physics* the minimum velocity required for an object to escape from the pull of the gravitational field of the Earth, or of another celestial body.

escapism *n* the means of escaping, or the tendency to escape, from unpleasant reality into daydreams or fantasy. ○ **escapist** *adj, n.*

escapology *n* the art or practice of freeing oneself from chains and other constraints as theatrical entertainment. ○ **escapologist** *n.*

escarpment *n, geol* a more or less continuous line of very steep slopes, formed by faulting or erosion, esp around the margins of a plateau.

eschatology /ɛskə'tɒlədʒɪ/ *n* the branch of theology dealing with final things, eg death, divine judgement and life after death. ○ **eschatological** *adj.*

escheat /ɪs'tʃiːt/ *law, n* **1** *formerly* the handing over of property to the state or a feudal lord in the absence of a legal heir. **2** property handed over in this way. ➤ *vb, intr* of property: to be handed over in this way.

Escherichia coli /eʃə'rɪkɪə 'kəʊlaɪ/ *n, biol* a species of bacterium that occurs naturally in the intestines of vertebrates including humans, and which sometimes causes disease.

eschew /ɪs'tʃuː/ *vb, formal* to avoid, keep away from or abstain from something. ○ **eschewal** *n.*

escort *n* /'eskɔːt/ **1** one or more people, vehicles, etc accompanying another or others for protection or guidance, or as a mark of honour. **2** someone of the opposite sex asked or hired to accompany another at a social event. ➤ *vb* /ɪ'skɔːt/ to accompany someone or something as an escort.

escudo /ɛ'skuːdəʊ/ *n* the former standard unit of currency of Portugal, replaced in 2002 by the euro.

esculent /'eskjʊlənt/ *formal, adj* edible. ➤ *n* any edible substance.

escutcheon *n* a shield decorated with a coat of arms. ♦ **a blot on the escutcheon** *facetious* a stain on one's good reputation.

Eskimo *now often offensive, n* (**Eskimos** or **Eskimo**) INUIT. ➤ *adj* INUIT.

esoteric /iːsəʊ'tɛrɪk/ *adj* understood only by those few people who have the necessary special knowledge; secret or mysterious. ○ **esoterically** *adv.*

ESP *abbrev* extrasensory perception, the ability to experience things using means other than sight, hearing, touch, taste and smell.

espadrille /'espədrɪl/ *n* a light canvas shoe with a sole made of rope or other plaited fibre.

espalier /ɪ'spælɪə(r)/ *n* **1** a trellis or arrangement of wires against which a shrub or fruit tree is trained to grow flat, eg against a wall. **2** such a shrub or tree.

especial *adj* special. ○ **especially** *adv* principally; more than in other cases.

especially See note at **special**.

Esperanto *n* a language invented for international use, based on European languages, and published in 1887. ○ **Esperantist** *n*.

espionage /'ɛspɪɒnɑːʒ/ *n* the activity of spying.

esplanade *n* **1** a long wide pavement next to a beach. **2** a level open area between a fortified place and the nearest houses.

espouse *vb* **1** *formal* to adopt or give one's support to (a cause, etc). **2** *old use* to marry, or to give (eg a daughter) in marriage. ○ **espousal** *n*.

espresso or **expresso** *n* coffee made by forcing steam or boiling water through ground coffee beans.

esprit de corps /ɛs'priː də kɔː(r)/ *n* loyalty to, or concern for the honour of, a group or body to which one belongs.

espy *vb* (**-ies, -ied**) *literary* to catch sight of someone or something; to observe. ◆

Esq. or **esq.** *abbrev* esquire.

esquire *n* **1** a title used after a man's name when no other form of address is used, esp when addressing letters. **2** *now chiefly hist* a squire.

essay *n* /'ɛseɪ/ **1** a short formal piece of writing, usu dealing with a single subject. **2** *formal* an attempt. ➣ *vb* /ɛ'seɪ/ *formal* to attempt. ○ **essayist** *n* a writer of literary essays.

essence *n* **1** the basic distinctive part or quality of something, which determines its nature or character. **2** a liquid obtained from a plant or drug, etc, which has its properties in concentrated form. ◆ **in essence** basically or fundamentally. ◆ **of the essence** absolutely necessary or extremely important.

essential *adj* **1** absolutely necessary. **2** relating to the basic or inner nature of something or its essence. ➣ *n* **1** something necessary. **2** (*often* **the essentials**) a basic or fundamental element, principle or piece of information. ○ **essentially** *adv*.

essential oil *n, bot* a mixture of volatile oils which have distinctive and characteristic odours, obtained from certain aromatic plants.

establish *vb* **1** to settle someone firmly in a position, place, job, etc. **2** to set up (eg a university or a business). **3** to find, show or prove something. **4** to cause people to accept (eg a custom or a claim).

establishment *n* **1** the act of establishing. **2** a business, its premises or its staff. **3** a public or government institution: *a research establishment*. **4** (**the Establishment**) the group of people in a country, society or community who hold power and exercise authority, and are regarded as being opposed to change.

estate *n* **1** a large piece of land owned by a person or group of people. **2** an area of land on which development of a particular kind has taken place, eg houses on a HOUSING ESTATE or factories on an INDUSTRIAL ESTATE. **3** *law* a

person's total possessions (property, money, etc), esp at death. **4** an ESTATE CAR. **5** *hist* any of various groups or classes within the social structure of society.

estate agent *n* a person whose job is the buying, selling, leasing and valuation of houses and other property.

estate car *n* a car with a large area behind the rear seats for luggage, etc, and a rear door. Often shortened to **estate**.

esteem *vb* **1** to value, respect or think highly of someone or something. **2** *formal* to consider someone to be a specified thing. ➣ *n* high regard or respect. ○ **esteemed** *adj*.

ester *n, chem* an organic chemical compound formed by the reaction of an alcohol with an organic acid, with the loss of a water molecule.

estimable *adj* highly respected; worthy of respect.

estimate *vb* /'ɛstɪmeɪt/ **1** to judge or calculate (size, amount, value, etc) roughly or without measuring. **2** to have or form an opinion. **3** to submit to a possible client a statement of (the likely cost) of carrying out a job. ➣ *n* /-mət/ **1** a rough assessment (of size, etc). **2** a calculation of the probable cost of a job. ○ **estimation** *n*. ○ **estimator** *n*.

estrange *vb* to cause someone to break away from a previously friendly state or relationship. ○ **estranged** *adj* no longer friendly or supportive; alienated: *his estranged wife*. ○ **estrangement** *n*.

estuary *n* (**-ies**) the broad mouth of a river that flows into the sea, where fresh water mixes with tidal sea water. ○ **estuarine** *adj*.

et al. /ɛt al/ *abbrev* **1** *et alia* (Latin), and other things. **2** *et alii* (Latin), and other people. **3** *et alibi* (Latin), and in other places.

et cetera or **etcetera** *adv* (abbrev **etc**) **1** and the rest; and so on. **2** and/or something similar.

etch *vb* **1** *tr & intr* to make designs on (metal, glass, etc) using an acid to eat out the lines. **2** to make a deep or irremovable impression. ○ **etcher** *n*. ○ **etching** *n*.

eternal *adj* **1** without beginning or end; everlasting. **2** unchanging; valid for all time. **3** *colloq* frequent or endless. ○ **eternally** *adv*.

eternity *n* (**-ies**) **1** time regarded as having no end. **2** the state of being eternal. **3** *relig* a timeless existence after death. **4** *colloq* an extremely long time.

ethane *n, chem* a colourless odourless flammable gas.

ethanol *n, chem* a colourless volatile flammable alcohol that is produced by fermentation of the sugar in fruit or cereals, constitutes the intoxicant in alcoholic beverages, and is used as a fuel.

ethene *n, chem* ETHYLENE.

ether *n* **1** any of a group of organic chemical compounds formed by the dehydration of alcohols, that are volatile and highly flammable and contain two hydrocarbon groups linked by an oxygen atom. **2** (*also* **diethyl ether**) the commonest ether, widely used as a solvent, and formerly employed as an anaesthetic. **3** (*also* **aether**) *physics* a substance formerly believed to be necessary for the transmission of electromagnetic radiation. **4** (*also* **aether**) *poetic* the clear upper air or a clear sky.

ethereal *adj* **1** having an unreal lightness or delicateness. **2** heavenly or spiritual. ○ **ethereally** *adv.*

ethic *n* the moral system or set of principles particular to a certain person, community or group. ○ **ethical** *adj* **1** relating to or concerning morals, justice or duty. **2** morally right. ○ **ethically** *adv.*

ethics *sing n* the study or the science of morals. ➤ *pl n* rules or principles of behaviour: *medical ethics.*

ethnic *adj* **1** relating to or having a common race or cultural tradition: *an ethnic group.* **2** associated with or resembling an exotic, esp non-European, racial or tribal group: *ethnic clothes.* **3** seen from the point of view of race, rather than nationality: *ethnic Asians.* **4** between or involving different racial groups: *ethnic violence.* ➤ *n, esp US* a member of a particular racial group or cult, esp a minority one. ○ **ethnically** *adv.*

ethnic cleansing *n* GENOCIDE or forced removal inflicted by one ethnic group on all others in a particular area.

ethnocentric *adj* relating to or holding the belief that one's own cultural tradition or racial group is superior to all others. ○ **ethnocentricity** *n.*

ethnology *n* the scientific study of different races and cultural traditions, and their relations with each other. ○ **ethnological** *adj.* ○ **ethnologist** *n.*

ethology *n, zool* the study of animal behaviour.

ethos *n* the typical spirit, character or attitudes (of a group or community).

ethyl /'ɛθɪl/ *n, chem* in organic chemical compounds: the (C_2H_5–) group, as for example in ethylamine ($C_2H_5NH_2$).

ethylene *n, chem* a colourless flammable gas with a sweet smell.

ethyne *n, chem* ACETYLENE.

etiolated /'iːtɪəʊleɪtɪd/ *adj bot* of a plant: having foliage that has become yellow through lack of sunlight. ○ **etiolation** *n.*

etiquette *n* **1** conventions of correct or polite social behaviour. **2** rules, usu unwritten ones, regarding the behaviour of members of a particular profession, etc towards each other.

étude /eɪ'tjuːd/ *n, mus* a short piece written for a single instrument, intended as an exercise or a means of showing talent.

etymology *n* (*-ies*) **1** the study of the origin and development of words and their meanings. **2** an explanation of the history of a particular word. ○ **etymological** *adj.* ○ **etymologist** *n.*

EU *abbrev* European Union.

Eu *symbol, chem* europium.

eucalyptus /juːkə'lɪptəs/ *n* (**eucalyptuses** or **eucalypti** /-taɪ/) **1** an evergreen tree, native to Australia, grown for timber, oil or ornamental appearance. **2** the hard durable wood of this tree. **3** eucalyptus oil.

Eucharist /'juːkərɪst/ *n, Christianity* **1** the sacrament celebrating Christ's Last Supper. **2** THE LORD'S SUPPER. **3** the elements of the sacrament, the bread and wine. ○ **Eucharistic** *adj.*

Euclidean or **Euclidian** /juː'klɪdɪən/ *adj* referring or relating to or based on the geometrical system devised by Euclid, a Greek mathematician who lived in c.300 BC.

eugenics /juː'dʒɛnɪks/ *sing n* the now largely discredited science of improving the human race by selective breeding. ○ **eugenic** *adj.* ○ **eugenically** *adv.*

eulogy *n* (*-ies*) **1** a speech or piece of writing in praise of someone or something. **2** high praise. ○ **eulogize** or **-ise** *vb.*

eunuch /'juːnək/ *n* **1** a man who has been castrated. **2** *esp formerly* such a man employed as a guard of a harem in Eastern countries.

euphemism *n* **1** a mild or inoffensive term used in place of one considered offensive or unpleasantly direct. **2** the use of such terms. ○ **euphemistic** *adj.* ○ **euphemistically** *adv.*

euphonium *n* a four-valved brass instrument of the tuba family.

euphony *n* (*-ies*) **1** a pleasing sound, esp in speech. **2** pleasantness of sound, esp of pronunciation. ○ **euphonious** or **euphonic** *adj* pleasing to the ear.

euphoria *n* a feeling of wild happiness and wellbeing. ○ **euphoric** *adj.*

eureka /jʊə'riːkə/ *exclam* expressing triumph at finding something or solving a problem, etc.

euro /'jʊərəʊ/ *n* (symbol €) (**euros** or **euro**) the basic monetary unit for most countries in the European Union, widely replacing former standard currencies in 2002, equal to 100 CENT.

Eurocentric *adj* centred, or concentrating, on Europe.

European *adj* belonging or relating to Europe. ➤ *n* a citizen or inhabitant of Europe.

europium *n, chem* a soft silvery metallic element belonging to the LANTHANIDE series.

Eurosceptic *n* someone who is not in favour of devolving powers from national government to the European Union.

Eustachian tube /juː'steɪʃən/ *n, anat* either of the two tubes which connect the MIDDLE EAR to the PHARYNX.

euthanasia *n* the act or practice of ending the life of a person who is suffering from an incurable illness.

evacuate *vb* **1** to leave (a place), esp because of danger. **2** to make (people) evacuate a place. **3** *technical* to empty (the bowels). **4** *physics* to create a vacuum in (a vessel). ○ **evacuation** *n.* ○ **evacuee** *n* an evacuated person.

evade *vb* **1** to escape or avoid something or someone by trickery or skill. **2** to avoid answering (a question).

evaluate *vb* **1** to form an idea or judgement about the worth of something. **2** *maths* to calculate the value of something. ○ **evaluation** *n*.

evanesce *vb, intr, literary* to disappear gradually; to fade from sight. ○ **evanescent** *adj* **1** quickly fading. **2** short-lived.

evangelical *adj* **1** based on the Gospels. **2** referring or relating to or denoting any of various groups within the Protestant Church stressing the authority of the Bible and claiming that personal acceptance of Christ as saviour is the only way to salvation. **3** enthusiastically advocating a particular cause, etc. ➤ *n* a member of an evangelical movement. ○ **evangelicalism** *n*. ○ **evangelically** *adv*.

evangelism *n* **1** the act or practice of evangelizing. **2** evangelicalism.

evangelist *n* **1** a person who preaches Christianity. **2** (*usu* **Evangelist**) any of the writers of the four biblical Gospels. ○ **evangelistic** *adj*.

evangelize or **-ise** *vb* **1** *tr & intr* to attempt to persuade someone to adopt Christianity. **2** *intr* to preach Christianity. ○ **evangelization** *n*.

evaporate *vb, tr & intr* **1** to change or cause something to change from a liquid into a vapour. **2** to disappear or make disappear. ○ **evaporation** *n* the process of evaporating; disappearance.

evaporated milk *n* unsweetened milk that has been concentrated by evaporation.

evasion *n* **1** the act of evading, esp evading a commitment or responsibility. **2** a trick or excuse used to evade (a question, etc).

evasive *adj* **1** intending or intended to evade something, esp trouble or danger. **2** not honest or open: *an evasive answer*. ○ **evasively** *adv*. ○ **evasiveness** *n*.

eve *n* **1** *esp in compounds* the evening or day before some notable event: *New Year's Eve*. **2** the period immediately before: *the eve of war*.

even¹ *adj* **1** smooth and flat. **2** constant or regular: *travelling at an even 50mph*. **3** *maths* of a number: divisible by two, with nothing left over. **4** designated or marked by an even number. **5** (*usu* **even with sth**) level, on the same plane or at the same height as it. **6** (*often* **even with sb**) having no advantage over or owing no debt to them. **7** of temper, character, etc: calm. **8** equal. ➤ *adv* **1** used with a comparative to emphasize a comparison with something else: *He's good, but she's even better.* **2** used with an expression stronger than a previous one: *He looked sad, even depressed.* **3** used to introduce a surprising piece of information: *Even John was there!* **4** used to indicate a lower extreme in an implied comparison: *Even a child would have known that!* ➤ *vb* (*often* **even sth up**) to make it equal. ➤ *n* **1** (*usu* **evens**) an even number, or something designated by one. **2** (**evens**) gambling odds offering the chance to win the amount staked. ○ **evenly** *adv*. ○ **evenness** *n*. ◆ **even if, even so** or **even though** used to emphasize that whether or not something is or might be true, the following or preceding state-

ment is or would remain true: *He got the job but, even so, he's still unhappy*. **get even with sb** to be revenged on them. ◊ **even out** to become level or regular. **even sth out** or **up** to make it smooth or level.

even² *n, old use or poetic* evening.

even-handed *adj* fair; impartial.

evening *n* **1** the last part of the day, usu from late afternoon until bedtime. **2** *often in compounds* a party or other social gathering held at this time: *a poetry evening*. ➤ *adj* referring to or during the evening.

evening dress *n* clothes worn on formal occasions in the evening.

evening primrose *n, bot* a plant with large scented yellow flowers that open at dusk.

evensong *n, C of E* the service of evening prayer.

event *n* **1** something that occurs or happens; an incident, esp a significant one. **2** an item in a programme of sports, etc. ◆ **at all events** or **in any event** in any case; whatever happens. **in the event** in the end; as it happened, happens or may happen. **in the event of** or **that sth** if it occurs: *in the event of a power cut*.

eventful *adj* full of or characterized by important or significant events. ○ **eventfully** *adv*.

eventide *n, poetic or old use* evening.

eventing *n* the practice of taking part in horse-riding events.

eventual *adj* happening after or at the end of a period of time, a process, etc. ○ **eventuality** *n* (*-ies*) a possible happening or result: *plan for every eventuality*. ○ **eventually** *adv* after an indefinite period of time; in the end.

ever *adv* **1 a** at any time. **b** *in compounds*: *ever-hopeful*. **3** *colloq* used for emphasis: *She's ever so beautiful!* ◆ **ever such a** ... *colloq* a very ... : *ever such a good boy*. **for ever 1** always. **2** *colloq* for a long time.

evergreen *bot, adj* denoting plants that bear leaves all the year round, eg pines or firs. ➤ *n* an evergreen tree or shrub. Compare DECIDUOUS.

everlasting *adj* **1** without end; continual. **2** lasting a long time, esp so long as to become tiresome. ➤ *n* **1** any of several kinds of flower that keep their shape and colour when dried. **2** eternity. ○ **everlastingly** *adv*.

evermore *adv* (*often* **for evermore**) for all time to come; eternally.

every *adj* **1** each one of a number or collection; omitting none. **2** the greatest or best possible: *making every effort.* ➤ *adv* at, in or at the end of each stated period of time or distance, etc: *every six inches.* ◆ **every bit** the whole; all of it; quite or entirely. **every last** (*used for emphasis*) every. **every now and then** or **every now and again** or **every so often** occasionally; from time to time. **every other** or **every second** one out of every two (things) repeatedly (the first, third, fifth, etc or second, fourth, sixth, etc): *comes every other day*.

everybody *pron* every person.

everyday *adj* **1** happening, done, used, etc daily, or on ordinary days, rather than on special occasions. **2** common or usual.

Everyman *n* (*also* **everyman**) the ordinary or common person; anybody; mankind.

everyone *pron* every person.

everything *pron* **1** all things; all. **2** the most important thing: *Fitness is everything in sport.*

everywhere *adv* in or to every place.

evict *vb* to put someone out of a house, etc or off land by force of law. ○ **eviction** *n*.

evidence *n* **1** information, etc that gives grounds for belief; that which points to, reveals or suggests something. **2** written or spoken testimony used in a court of law. ➢ *vb, formal* to be evidence of something; to prove. ○ **evidential** *adj*. ◆ **in evidence** easily seen; clearly displayed.

evident *adj* clear to see or understand; obvious or apparent. ○ **evidently** *adv* **1** obviously; apparently. **2** as it appears; so it seems: *Evidently they don't believe us.*

evil *adj* **1** morally bad or offensive. **2** harmful. **3** *colloq* very unpleasant: *an evil stench.* ➢ *n* **1** wickedness or moral offensiveness, or the source of it. **2** harm, or a cause of harm; a harmful influence. **3** anything bad or unpleasant, eg crime or disease. ○ **evilly** *adv*. ○ **evilness** *n*.

the evil eye *n* a glare, superstitiously thought to cause harm.

evince *vb, formal* to show or display something (usu a personal quality) clearly.

eviscerate /ɪˈvɪsəreɪt/ *vb, formal* to tear out the bowels of a person or animal; to gut. ○ **evisceration** *n, formal* disembowelling.

evoke *vb* **1** to cause or produce (a response, reaction, etc). **2** to bring (a memory, emotion, etc) into the mind. ○ **evocation** *n*. ○ **evocative** *adj*.

evolution *n* **1** the process of evolving. **2** a gradual development. **3** *biol* the cumulative changes in the characteristics of living organisms or populations of organisms from generation to generation. **4** *chem* the giving off of a gas. ○ **evolutionary** *adj* relating to, or part of, evolution. ○ **evolutionism** *n, anthropol, biol* the theory of evolution. ○ **evolutionist** *n* a person who believes in the theory of evolution.

evolve *vb* **1** *tr & intr* to develop or produce gradually. **2** *intr* to develop from a primitive into a more complex or advanced form. **3** *chem* to give off (heat, etc).

ewe *n* a female sheep.

ewer *n* a large water jug with a wide mouth.

ex¹ *n, colloq* a person who is no longer what he or she was, esp a former husband, wife or lover.

ex² *prep, commerce* **1** direct from somewhere: *ex warehouse.* **2** excluding something: *ex VAT.*

ex- *pfx, signifying* **1** former: *ex-wife.* **2** outside: *ex-directory.*

exacerbate /ɪgˈzæsəbeɪt/ *vb* to make (a bad situation, anger or pain, etc) worse or more se-

vere. ○ **exacerbation** *n*.

exact *adj* **1** absolutely accurate or correct. **2** insisting on accuracy or precision in even the smallest details. **3** dealing with measurable quantities or values: *Psychology is not an exact science.* ➢ *vb* **1** (*usu* **exact sth from** or **of sb**) to demand (payment, etc) from them. **2** to insist on (a right, etc). ○ **exacting** *adj* making difficult or excessive demands. ○ **exaction** *n, formal* **1** the act of demanding payment, or the payment demanded. **2** illegal demands for money; extortion. ○ **exactitude** *n, formal* accuracy or correctness. ○ **exactness** *n*.

exactly *adv* **1** just; quite, precisely or absolutely. **2** with accuracy; with attention to detail.

exaggerate *vb* **1** *tr & intr* to regard or describe something as being greater or better than it really is. **2** to emphasize something or make it more noticeable. **3** to do something in an excessive or affected way. ○ **exaggeration** *n*.

exalt *vb* **1** to praise (eg God) highly. **2** to fill someone with great joy. **3** to give a higher rank or position to someone or something. ○ **exaltation** *n*. ○ **exalted** *adj* **1** noble; very moral. **2** elevated; high. ○ **exaltedly** *adv*.

exam *n, colloq* an EXAMINATION (sense 1).

examination *n* **1** a set of tasks, esp in written form, designed to test knowledge or ability. **2** an inspection of a person's state of health, carried out by a doctor. **3** the act of examining or the process of being examined. **4** *law* formal questioning in a court of law.

examine *vb* **1** to inspect, consider or look into something closely. **2** to check the health of someone. **3** to test the knowledge or ability of (a person), esp in a formal examination. **4** *law* to question formally in a court of law. ○ **examinee** *n* a candidate in an examination. ○ **examiner** *n* someone who sets an examination.

example *n* **1** someone or something that is a typical specimen. **2** something that illustrates a fact or rule. **3** a person or pattern of behaviour, etc as a model to be, or not to be, copied: *He set a good example.* **4** a punishment given, or the person punished, as a warning to others: *I'm going to make an example of you.* ◆ **for example** as an example or illustration.

exasperate *vb* to make someone annoyed and frustrated; to anger them. ○ **exasperating** *adj*. ○ **exasperation** *n*.

excavate *vb* **1** to dig up or uncover something (esp historical remains). **2** to dig up (a piece of ground, etc); to make (a hole) by doing this. ○ **excavation** *n* **1** *esp archaeol* the process of excavating or digging up ground. **2** an excavated area or site. ○ **excavator** *n*.

exceed *vb* **1** to be greater than someone or something. **2** to go beyond; to do more than is required by something. ○ **exceedingly** *adv* very; extremely.

excel *vb* (**excelled, excelling**) **1** *intr* (*usu* **excel in** or **at sth**) to be exceptionally good at it. **2** to be better than someone or something. ◆ **excel**

oneself *often ironic* to do better than usual or previously.

excellence *n* great worth; very high or exceptional quality. ○ **excellent** *adj* of very high quality. ○ **excellently** *adv.*

Excellency *n* (*-ies*) (*usu* **His, Her** or **Your Excellency** or **Your** or **Their Excellencies**) a title of honour given to certain people of high rank, eg ambassadors.

except *prep* leaving out; not including. ➤ *vb* to leave out or exclude: *present company excepted.* ○ **excepting** *prep* leaving out; not including or counting.

exception *n* **1** someone or something not included. **2** someone or something that does not, or is allowed not to, follow a general rule: *make an exception.* **3** an act of excluding. ○ **exceptionable** *adj* **1** likely to cause disapproval, offence or dislike. **2** open to objection. ♦ **take exception to sth** to object to it; to be offended by it.

exceptional *adj* **1** remarkable or outstanding. **2** being or making an exception. ○ **exceptionally** *adv.*

excerpt *n* /ˈɛksɜːpt/ a short passage or part taken from a book, film, musical work, etc. ➤ *vb* /ɪkˈsɜːpt/ to select extracts from (a book, etc).

excess /ɪkˈsɛs/ *n* **1** the act of going, or the state of being, beyond normal or suitable limits. **2** an amount or extent greater than is usual, necessary or wise. **3** the amount by which one quantity, etc exceeds another; an amount left over. **4** (*usu* **excesses**) an outrageous or offensive act. ➤ *adj* /ˈɛksɛs/ **1** greater than is usual, necessary or permitted. **2** additional; required to make up for an amount lacking: *excess postage.* ○ **excessive** *adj* too great; beyond what is usual, right or appropriate. ○ **excessively** *adv* to an excessive degree. ♦ **in excess of sth** going beyond (a specified amount).

exchange *vb* **1** (*usu* **exchange one thing for another**) to give, or give up, something, in return for something else. **2** to give and receive in return. ➤ *n* **1** the giving and taking of one thing for another. **2** a thing exchanged. **3** a conversation or argument, esp a brief one. **4** the act of exchanging the currency of one country for that of another. **5** a place where shares are traded, or international financial deals carried out. **6** (*also* **telephone exchange**) a central telephone system where lines are connected, or the building housing this. ○ **exchangeable** *adj.* ♦ **in exchange for sth** in return for it.

exchange rate or **rate of exchange** *n* the value of the currency of one country in relation to that of another country or countries.

exchequer *n* (*often* **Exchequer**) the government department in charge of the financial affairs of a nation.

excise[1] *n* /ˈɛksaɪz/ the tax or duty payable on goods, etc produced and sold within a country, and on certain trading licences. ➤ *vb* /ɪkˈsaɪz/ **1** to charge excise on (goods, etc). **2** to force someone to pay excise. ○ **excisable** *adj.*

excise[2] /ɪkˈsaɪz/ *vb* **1** to remove (eg a passage from a text). **2** to cut something out or off by surgery. ○ **excision** *n.*

excite *vb* **1** to make someone feel lively expectation or a pleasant tension and thrill. **2** to arouse (feelings, emotions, sensations, etc). **3** to provoke (eg action). **4** to arouse someone sexually. **5** *physics* to raise (a nucleus, atom or molecule) from the GROUND STATE to a higher level. **6** *physics* to produce electric or magnetic activity in something. ○ **excitable** *adj.* ○ **excitation** *n.* ○ **excited** *adj.* ○ **excitedly** *adv.*

excitement *n* **1** the state of being excited. **2** objects and events which produce such a state, or the quality they have which produces it. **3** behaviour, a happening, etc which displays excitement.

exciting *adj* arousing a lively expectation or a pleasant tension and thrill. ○ **excitingly** *adv.*

exclaim *vb, tr & intr* to call or cry out suddenly and loudly, eg in surprise or anger.

exclamation *n* **1** a word or expression uttered suddenly and loudly. **2** the act of exclaiming. ○ **exclamatory** *adj.*

exclamation mark or (*US*) **exclamation point** *n* the punctuation mark (!), used to indicate an exclamation.

exclude *vb* **1** to prevent someone from sharing or taking part. **2** to shut someone or something out, or to keep them out. **3** to omit someone or something or leave them out of consideration. **4** to make something impossible. ○ **excluding** *prep* not counting.

exclusion *n* the act of excluding, or the state of being excluded.

exclusive *adj* **1** involving the rejection or denial of something else or everything else. **2** (**exclusive to sb** or **sth**) limited to, given to, found in, etc only that place, group or person. **3** (**exclusive of sb** or **sth**) not including a specified thing. **4** not readily accepting others into the group, esp because of a feeling of superiority: *an exclusive club.* **5** fashionable and expensive: *an exclusive restaurant.* ➤ *n* a report or story published or broadcast by only one newspaper, programme, etc. ○ **exclusively** *adv.* ○ **exclusiveness** or **exclusivity** *n.*

excommunicate *vb, Christianity* to exclude someone from membership of a church. ○ **excommunication** *n.*

excoriate /ɛksˈkɔːrɪeɪt/ *vb* **1** *technical* to strip the skin from (a person or animal). **2** to criticize someone severely. ○ **excoriation** *n.*

excrement *n* waste matter passed out of the body, esp faeces. ○ **excremental** *adj.*

excrescence *n* an abnormal, esp an ugly, growth on a part of the body or a plant. ○ **excrescent** *adj.*

excreta *pl n, formal* excreted matter; faeces or urine.

excrete *vb* of a plant or animal: to eliminate (waste products). ○ **excretion** *n.* ○ **excretive** or **excretory** *adj.*

excruciating *adj* **1** causing great physical or

mental pain. **2** *colloq* extremely bad or irritating. ○ **excruciatingly** *adv.*

exculpate /ˈɪksˈkʌlpeɪt/ *vb, formal* to free someone from guilt or blame. ○ **exculpation** *n.*

excursion /ɪksˈkɜːʒən/ *n* a short trip, usu one made for pleasure.

excuse *vb* /ɪkˈskjuːz/ **1** to pardon or forgive someone. **2** to offer justification for (a wrongdoing). **3** to free someone from (an obligation, duty, etc). **4** to allow someone to leave a room, etc, eg in order to go to the lavatory. ➤ *n* /ɪkˈskjuːs/ **1** an explanation for a wrongdoing, offered as an apology or justification. **2** *derog* a very poor example: *an excuse for a painting*. ○ **excusable** *adj.* ♦ **excuse me** an expression of apology, or one used to attract attention. **make one's excuses** to apologize for leaving or for not attending.

ex-directory *adj* of a telephone number: not included in the directory at the request of the subscriber.

execrable /ˈɛksəkrəbəl/ *adj* **1** detestable. **2** of very poor quality. ○ **execrably** *adv.*

execrate *vb, formal* **1** to feel or express hatred or loathing of something. **2** to curse. ○ **execration** *n.*

execute *vb* **1** to put someone to death by order of the law. **2** to perform or carry out something. **3** to produce something, esp according to a design. **4** *law* to make something valid by signing. **5** *law* to carry out instructions contained in (a will or contract). ○ **executer** *n* someone who carries out (a plan, etc) or puts (a law, etc) into effect.

execution *n* **1** the act, or an instance, of putting someone to death by law. **2** the act or skill of carrying something out; an instance or the process of carrying something out. ○ **executioner** *n* a person who carries out a sentence of death.

executive *adj* **1** in a business organization, etc: concerned with management or administration. **2** for the use of managers and senior staff. **3** *colloq* expensive and sophisticated: *executive cars*. **4** *law, pol* relating to the carrying out of laws: *executive powers*. ➤ *n* **1** someone in an organization, etc who has power to direct or manage. **2** (**the executive**) *law, politics* the branch of government that puts laws into effect.

executor *n, law* a male or female person appointed to carry out instructions stated in a will.

executrix /ɪɡˈzɛkjʊtrɪks/ *n* (**executrices** /-trɪsɪz/ or **executrixes**) *law* a female EXECUTOR.

exegesis /ɛksəˈdʒiːsɪs/ *n* (**-ses** /-siːz/) a critical explanation of a text, esp of the Bible.

exemplar *n* **1** a person or thing worth copying; a model. **2** a typical example.

exemplary *adj* **1** worth following as an example. **2** serving as an illustration or warning.

exemplify *vb* (**-ies, -ied**) **1** to be an example of something. **2** to show an example of something, or show it by means of an example. ○ **exemplification** *n.*

exempt *vb* to free someone from a duty or obligation that applies to others. ➤ *adj* free from some obligation. ○ **exemption** *n.*

exercise *n* **1** physical training or exertion for health or pleasure. **2** an activity intended to develop a skill. **3** a task designed to test ability. **4** a piece of written work intended as practice for learners. **5** *formal* the act of putting something into practice or carrying it out: *the exercise of one's duty*. **6** (*usu* **exercises**) *mil* training and practice for soldiers. ➤ *vb* **1** *tr & intr* to give exercise to (oneself, or someone or something else). **2** to use something or bring it into use: *He exercised his right to appeal*. **3** to trouble, concern, or occupy someone's thoughts. ○ **exercisable** *adj.* ○ **exerciser** *n.*

exert *vb* **1** to bring something into use or action forcefully: *She exerted her authority*. **2** (**exert oneself**) to force oneself to make a strenuous, esp physical, effort. ○ **exertion** *n.*

exeunt *vb, theat* as a stage direction: leave the stage; they leave the stage.

exfoliate *vb, tr & intr* of bark, rocks, skin, etc: to shed or peel off in flakes or layers. ○ **exfoliation** *n.*

ex gratia /ɛks ˈɡreɪʃɪə/ *adv, adj* given as a favour, not in recognition of any obligation, esp a legal one.

exhale *vb, tr & intr* **1** to breathe out. **2** to give off or be given off. ○ **exhalation** *n.*

exhaust *vb* **1** to make (a person or animal) very tired. **2** to use something up completely. **3** to say all that can be said about (a subject, etc). **4** *eng* to empty (a container) or draw off (gas). ➤ *n* **1** the escape of waste gases from an engine, etc. **2** the gases themselves. **3** the part or parts of an engine, etc through which the waste gases escape. ○ **exhausted** *adj.* ○ **exhaustible** *adj.* ○ **exhausting** *adj.* ○ **exhaustion** *n.*

exhaustive *adj* complete; comprehensive or very thorough. ○ **exhaustively** *adv.*

exhibit *vb* **1** to present or display something for public appreciation. **2** to show or manifest (a quality, etc). ➤ *n* **1** an object displayed publicly, eg in a museum. **2** *law* an object or article produced in court as part of the evidence. ○ **exhibitor** *n* a person who provides an exhibit for a public display.

exhibition *n* **1** a display, eg of works of art, to the public. **2** the act or an instance of showing something, eg a quality. ♦ **make an exhibition of oneself** to behave foolishly in public.

exhibitionism *n* **1** *derog* the tendency to behave so as to attract attention to oneself. **2** *psychol* the compulsive desire to expose one's sexual organs publicly. ○ **exhibitionist** *n.*

exhilarate *vb* to fill someone with a lively cheerfulness. ○ **exhilarating** *adj.* ○ **exhilaration** *n.*

exhort *vb* to urge or advise someone strongly and sincerely. ○ **exhortation** *n.*

exhume *vb, formal* **1** to dig up (a body) from a grave. **2** to reveal; to bring something up or mention it again. ○ **exhumation** *n* the digging up of a body from a grave.

exigency /ˈɛksɪdʒənsɪ/ *n* (*-ies*) *formal* **1** (*usu* **exigencies**) urgent need. **2** an emergency. ○ **exigent** *adj*.

exiguous /ɪgˈzɪgjʊəs/ *adj, formal* scarce or meagre. ○ **exiguity** /ɛksɪˈgjuːɪtɪ/ *n*.

exile *n* **1** enforced or regretted absence from one's country or town, esp for a long time and often as a punishment. **2** someone who suffers such absence. ➤ *vb* to send someone into exile.

exist *vb, intr* **1** to be, or to be present in the real world or universe rather than in story or imagination. **2** to occur or be found. **3** to manage to stay alive; to live with only the most basic necessities.

existence *n* **1** the state of existing. **2** a life, or a way of living. **3** everything that exists. ○ **existent** *adj*.

existential *adj* **1** relating to human existence. **2** *philos* relating to existentialism.

existentialism *n* a philosophy that emphasizes freedom of choice and personal responsibility for one's own actions. ○ **existentialist** *adj, n*.

exit *n* **1** a way out of a building, etc. **2** going out or departing. **3** an actor's departure from the stage. **4** a place where vehicles can leave a motorway or main road. ➤ *vb* (**exited, exiting**) *intr* **1** *formal* to go out, leave or depart. **2** *theat* **a** to leave the stage; **b** as a stage direction: (**exit**) he or she leaves the stage. **3** *comput* to leave (a program, system, etc).

exit poll *n* a poll of a sample of voters in an election, taken as they leave a polling station.

exocrine *adj, physiol* of a gland, such as the sweat gland or salivary gland: discharging its secretions through a duct.

exodus *n* a mass departure of people.

ex officio *adv, adj* by virtue of one's official position.

exonerate *vb* to free someone from blame, or acquit them of a criminal charge. ○ **exoneration** *n*.

exorbitant *adj* of prices or demands: very high, excessive or unfair. ○ **exorbitantly** *adv*.

exorcize or **-ise** *vb* in some beliefs: **1** to drive away (an evil spirit or influence) with prayer or holy words. **2** to free (a person or place) from the influence of an evil spirit in this way. ○ **exorcism** *n*. ○ **exorcist** *n*.

exoskeleton *n, zool* in some invertebrates: a skeleton forming a rigid covering on the outside of the body.

exotic *adj* **1** introduced from a foreign country, esp a distant and tropical country. **2** interestingly different or strange, esp colourful and rich, and suggestive of a distant land. ➤ *n* an exotic person or thing. ○ **exotically** *adv*. ○ **exoticism** *n*.

exotica *pl n* strange or rare objects.

expand *vb* **1** *tr & intr* to make or become greater in size, extent or importance. **2** *intr, formal* to become more at ease or more open and talkative. **3** *tr & intr* (*often* **expand on** or **upon sth**) to give additional information; to enlarge on (a description, etc). **4** *tr & intr, formal* to fold out flat or spread out. **5** to write something out in full. **6** *maths* to multiply out (terms in brackets). ○ **expandable** *adj*.

expanse *n* a wide area or space.

expansible *adj* able to expand or be expanded.

expansion *n* **1** the act or state of expanding. **2** the amount by which something expands. **3** *maths* the result of expanding terms in brackets.

expansionism *n* the act or practice of increasing territory or political influence or authority, usu at the expense of other nations or bodies. ○ **expansionist** *n, adj*.

expansive *adj* **1** ready or eager to talk. **2** wide-ranging. **3** able or tending to expand. ○ **expansiveness** *n*.

expat *n, colloq* an EXPATRIATE.

expatiate *vb, intr, formal* to talk or write at length or in detail. ○ **expatiation** *n*.

expatriate *adj* /ɛkˈspatrɪət/ **1** living abroad, esp for a long but limited period. **2** exiled. ➤ *n* a person living or working abroad. ➤ *vb* /-eɪt/ to banish or exile. ○ **expatriation** *n*.

expect *vb* **1** to think of something as likely to happen or come. **2** *colloq* to suppose: *I expect you're tired*. **3** (*usu* **expect sth from** or **of sb**) to require it of them; to regard it as normal or reasonable. ○ **expectable** *adj*. ♦ **be expecting** *colloq* to be pregnant.

expectancy *n* (*-ies*) **1** the act or state of expecting. **2** a future chance or probability.

expectant *adj* **1** eagerly waiting; hopeful. **2** not yet, but expecting to be something (esp a mother or father). ○ **expectantly** *adv*.

expectation *n* **1** the state, or an attitude, of expecting. **2** (*often* **expectations**) something expected, whether good or bad. **3** (*usu* **expectations**) money, property, etc that one expects to gain, esp by inheritance.

expectorant *med, adj* causing the coughing up of phlegm. ➤ *n* an expectorant medicine.

expectorate *vb, tr & intr, med* to cough up and spit out (phlegm). ○ **expectoration** *n*.

expedient *adj* **1** suitable or appropriate. **2** practical or advantageous, rather than morally correct. ➤ *n* a suitable method or solution, esp one quickly thought of to meet an urgent need. ○ **expediency** (*-ies*) or **expedience** *n* **1** suitability or convenience. **2** practical advantage or self-interest, esp as opposed to moral correctness. ○ **expediently** *adv*.

expedite *vb* **1** to speed up, or assist the progress of something. **2** to carry something out quickly.

expedition *n* **1** an organized journey with a specific purpose. **2** a group making such a journey. ○ **expeditionary** *adj*.

expeditious *adj, formal* carried out with speed and efficiency.

expel *vb* (**expelled, expelling**) **1** to dismiss from or deprive someone of membership of a club, school, etc, usu permanently as punishment for misconduct. **2** to get rid of something; to force it out.

expend *vb* to use or spend (time, supplies, effort, etc).

expendable *adj* **1** able to be given up or sacrificed for some purpose or cause. **2** not valuable enough to be worth preserving.

expenditure *n* **1** the act of expending. **2** an amount expended, esp of money.

expense *n* **1** the act of spending money, or the amount of money spent. **2** something on which money is spent. **3** (**expenses**) a sum of one's own money spent doing one's job, or this sum of money or an allowance paid by one's employer to make up for this. ✦ **at the expense of sth** or **sb 1** with the loss or sacrifice of them. **2** causing damage to their pride or reputation: *a joke at my expense.*

expensive *adj* involving much expense; costing a great deal. ○ **expensiveness** *n*.

experience *n* **1** practice in an activity. **2** knowledge or skill gained through practice. **3** wisdom gained through long and varied observation of life. **4** an event which affects or involves one. ➤ *vb* **1** to have practical acquaintance with someone or something. **2** to feel or undergo. ○ **experienced** *adj*.

experiential *adj*, *philos* of knowledge or learning: based on direct experience. ○ **experientially** *adv*.

experiment *n* **1** a trial carried out in order to test a theory, a machine's performance, etc or to discover something unknown. **2** the carrying out of such trials. **3** an attempt at something original. ➤ *vb, intr* (*usu* **experiment on** or **with sth**) to carry out an experiment. ○ **experimentation** *n*. ○ **experimenter** *n*.

experimental *adj* **1** consisting of or like an experiment. **2** relating to, or used in, experiments. **3** trying out new styles and techniques. ○ **experimentally** *adv*.

expert *n* someone with great skill in, or extensive knowledge of, a particular subject. ➤ *adj* **1** highly skilled or extremely knowledgeable. **2** relating to or done by an expert or experts. ○ **expertly** *adv*.

expertise *n* special skill or knowledge.

expiate *vb* to make amends for (a wrong). ○ **expiation** *n*.

expire *vb, intr* **1** to come to an end or cease to be valid. **2** to breathe out. **3** to die. ○ **expiration** *n*, *formal* **1** expiry. **2** the act or process of breathing out.

expiry *n* (*-ies*) the ending of the duration or validity of something.

explain *vb, tr & intr* **1** to make something clear or easy to understand. **2** to give, or be, a reason for. **3** (**explain oneself**) **a** to justify (oneself or one's actions); **b** to clarify one's meaning or intention. ○ **explainable** *adj*. ○ **explanation** *n*. ◊ **explain sth away** to dismiss it or lessen its importance by explanation.

explanatory *adj* serving to explain.

expletive *n* **1** a swear-word or curse. **2** a meaningless exclamation.

explicable *adj* able to be explained.

explicate *vb* **1** to explain (esp a literary work) in depth, with close analysis of particular points. **2** to unfold or develop (an idea, a theory, etc). ○ **explication** *n*.

explicit *adj* **1** stated or shown fully and clearly. **2** speaking plainly and openly. ○ **explicitly** *adv*.

explode *vb* **1** *intr* of a substance: to undergo an explosion. **2** to cause something to undergo an explosion. **3** *intr* to undergo a violent explosion as a result of a chemical or nuclear reaction. **4** *intr* to suddenly show a strong or violent emotion, esp anger. **5** to disprove (a theory, etc) with vigour. **6** *intr* esp of population: to increase rapidly.

exploded *adj* **1** blown up. **2** of a theory, etc: no longer accepted. **3** of a diagram: showing the different parts of something relative to, but slightly separated from, each other.

exploit *n* /ˈɛksplɔɪt/ (*usu* **exploits**) an act or feat, esp a bold or daring one. ➤ *vb* /ɪkˈsplɔɪt/ **1** to take unfair advantage of something or someone so as to achieve one's own aims. **2** to make good use of something. ○ **exploitable** *adj*. ○ **exploitation** *n*. ○ **exploitative** or **exploitive** *adj*. ○ **exploiter** *n*.

exploratory *adj* **1** of talks, etc: serving to establish procedures or ground rules. **2** of surgery: aiming to establish the nature of a complaint rather than treat it.

explore *vb* **1** to search or travel through (a place) for the purpose of discovery. **2** to examine something carefully. ○ **exploration** *n*. ○ **explorative** *adj*. ○ **explorer** *n*.

explosion *n* **1** *chem* a sudden and violent increase in pressure, which generates large amounts of heat and destructive shock waves. **2** the sudden loud noise that accompanies such a reaction. **3** a sudden display of strong feelings, etc. **4** a sudden great increase.

explosive *adj* **1** likely, tending or able to explode. **2** likely to become marked by physical violence or emotional outbursts. **3** likely to result in violence or an outburst of feeling. ➤ *n* any substance that is capable of producing an explosion. ○ **explosively** *adv*. ○ **explosiveness** *n*.

expo *n*, *colloq* a large public exhibition.

exponent *n* **1** someone able to perform some art or activity, esp skilfully. **2** someone who explains and promotes (a theory, belief, etc). **3** *maths* a number that indicates how many times a given quantity, called the **base**, is to be multiplied by itself, usu denoted by a superscript number or symbol immediately after the quantity concerned, eg $6^4 = 6 \times 6 \times 6 \times 6$. Also called **power, index**.

exponential *adj*, *maths* denoting a function that varies according to the power of another quantity, ie a function in which the variable quantity is an EXPONENT, eg if $y = a^x$, then y varies exponentially with x. ○ **exponentially** *adv* on an exponential basis; very rapidly.

export *vb* /ık'spɔːt/ to send or take (goods, etc) to another country, esp for sale. ➤ *n* /'ɛkspɔːt/ **1** the act or business of exporting. **2** something exported. ○ **exportation** *n*. ○ **exporter** *n*.

expose *vb* **1** to remove cover, protection or shelter from something, or to allow this to be the case: *exposed to the wind* • *exposed to criticism*. **2** to discover something (eg a criminal or crime) or make it known. **3** (*always* **expose sb to sth**) to cause or allow them to have experience of it. **4** to allow light to fall on (a photographic film or paper) when taking or printing a photograph. ♦ **expose oneself** to display one's sexual organs in public.

exposé /ɛk'spouzeı/ *n* **1** a formal statement of facts, esp one that introduces an argument. **2** an article or programme which exposes a public scandal or crime, etc.

exposition *n* **1** an in-depth explanation or account (of a subject). **2** the act of presenting such an explanation or a viewpoint. **3** a large public exhibition. **4** *mus* the part of a sonata, fugue, etc, in which themes are presented.

expository *adj* explanatory; serving as, or like, an explanation.

ex post facto *adj* retrospective. ➤ *adv* retrospectively.

expostulate *vb, intr* (*usu* **expostulate with sb about sth**) to argue or reason with them, esp in protest or so as to dissuade them. ○ **expostulation** *n*. ○ **expostulatory** *adj*.

exposure *n* **1** the act of exposing or the state of being exposed. **2** the harmful effects on the body of extreme cold. **3** the number or regularity of someone's appearances in public, eg on TV. **4** the act of exposing photographic film or paper to light. **5** the amount of light to which a film or paper is exposed, or the length of time for which it is exposed. **6** the amount of film exposed or to be exposed in order to produce one photograph.

expound *vb* **1** to explain something in depth. **2** (*often* **expound on sth**) *intr* to talk at length about it.

express *vb* **1** to put something into words. **2** to indicate or represent something with looks, actions, symbols, etc. **3** to show or reveal. **4** to press or squeeze out something. **5** to send something by fast delivery service. ➤ *adj* **1** of a train, etc: travelling fast, with few stops. **2** belonging or referring to, or sent by, a fast delivery service. **3** clearly stated: *his express wish*. **4** particular; clear: *with the express purpose of insulting him*. ➤ *n* **1** an express train. **2** an express delivery service. ➤ *adv* by express delivery service. ○ **expressible** *adj*. ○ **expressly** *adv* **1** clearly and definitely. **2** particularly or specifically. ♦ **express oneself** to put one's thoughts into words.

expression *n* **1** the act of expressing. **2** a look

on the face that displays feelings. **3** a word or phrase. **4** the indication of feeling, eg in a manner of speaking or a way of playing music. **5** *maths* a symbol or combination of symbols. ○ **expressionless** *adj* of a face or voice: showing no feeling.

Expressionism or **expressionism** *n* a movement in art, music and literature which aims to communicate the internal emotional realities of a situation, rather than its external 'realistic' aspect. ○ **Expressionist** *n, adj*.

expressive *adj* **1** showing meaning or feeling in a clear or lively way. **2** (*always* **expressive of sth**) expressing a feeling or emotion. ○ **expressiveness** *n*.

expresso see ESPRESSO

expressway *n, N Am* a motorway.

expropriate *vb, formal or law* esp of the state: to take (property, etc) from its owner for some special use. ○ **expropriation** *n*. ○ **expropriator** *n*.

expulsion *n* **1** the act of expelling from school or a club, etc. **2** the act of forcing or driving out. ○ **expulsive** *adj*.

expunge *vb* **1** to cross out or delete something (eg a passage from a book). **2** to cancel out or destroy something.

expurgate *vb* **1** to revise (a book) by removing objectionable or offensive words or passages. **2** to remove (such words or passages). ○ **expurgation** *n*. ○ **expurgator** *n*.

exquisite *adj* **1** extremely beautiful or skilfully produced. **2** able to exercise sensitive judgement; discriminating: *exquisite taste*. **3** of pain, pleasure, etc: extreme. ○ **exquisitely** *adv*.

ex-serviceman or **ex-servicewoman** *n* a former male or female member of the armed forces.

extant *adj* still existing; surviving.

extempore /ık'stɛmpərı/ *adv, adj* without planning or preparation. ○ **extemporaneous** or **extemporary** *adj* **1** spoken or done without preparation. **2** makeshift or improvised.

extemporize or **-ise** *vb, tr & intr* to speak or perform without preparation. ○ **extemporization** *n*.

extend *vb* **1** to make something longer or larger. **2** *tr & intr* to reach or stretch in space or time. **3** to hold out or stretch out (a hand, etc). **4** to offer (kindness, greetings, etc) to someone. **5** to increase something in scope. **6** (*always* **extend to sth**) *intr* to include or go as far as it: *Their kindness did not extend to lending money.* **7** to exert someone to their physical or mental limit: *extend oneself.* ○ **extendable**, **extendible**, **extensible** or **extensile** *adj*.

extended family *n* the family as a unit including all relatives. Compare NUCLEAR FAMILY.

extension *n* **1** the process of extending something, or the state of being extended. **2** an added part that makes the original larger or longer. **3** a subsidiary or extra telephone, connected to the main line. **4** an extra period beyond an original time limit. **5** range or extent.

extensive *adj* large in area, amount, range or effect. ○ **extensively** *adv* to an extensive degree; widely.

extensor *n, physiol* any of various muscles that straighten out parts of the body. Compare FLEXOR.

extent *n* **1** the area over which something extends. **2** amount, scope or degree.

extenuate *vb* to reduce the seriousness of (an offence) by giving an explanation that partly excuses it. ○ **extenuating** *adj* esp of a circumstance: reducing the seriousness of an offence by partly excusing it. ○ **extenuation** *n*.

exterior *adj* **1** on, from or for use on the outside. **2** foreign, or dealing with foreign nations. ➤ *n* **1** an outside part or surface. **2** an outward appearance, esp when intended to conceal or deceive.

exterminate *vb* to get rid of or completely destroy (something living). ○ **extermination** *n*. ○ **exterminator** *n*.

external *adj* **1** belonging to, for, from or on the outside. **2** being of the world, as opposed to the mind: *external realities*. **3** foreign; involving foreign nations: *external affairs*. **4** of a medicine: to be applied on the outside of the body. **5** taking place, or coming from, outside one's school, university, etc: *an external examination*. ○ **externally** *adv*.

externalize or **-ise** *vb* to express (thoughts, feelings, ideas, etc) in words.

extinct *adj* **1** of a species of animal, etc: no longer in existence. **2** of a volcano: no longer active. ○ **extinction** *n* **1** the process of making or becoming extinct; elimination or disappearance. **2** *biol* the total elimination or dying out of any species.

extinguish *vb* **1** to put out (a fire, etc). **2** *formal* to kill off or destroy (eg passion). **3** *law* to pay off (a debt). ○ **extinguishable** *adj*. ○ **extinguisher** *n*.

extirpate /'ɛkstəpeɪt/ *vb, formal* **1** to destroy completely. **2** to uproot. ○ **extirpation** *n*.

extol *vb* (**extolled, extolling**) *rather formal* to praise enthusiastically.

extort *vb* to obtain (money, information, etc) by threats or violence. ○ **extortion** *n*.

extortionate *adj* of a price, demand, etc: unreasonably high or great. ○ **extortionately** *adv*.

extra *adj* **1** additional; more than is usual, necessary or expected. **2** for which an additional charge is made. ➤ *n* **1** an additional or unexpected thing. **2 a** an extra charge; **b** an item for which this is made. **3** an actor employed for a small, usu non-speaking, part in a film. **4** a special edition of a newspaper containing later news. **5** *cricket* a run scored other than by hitting the ball with the bat. ➤ *adv* unusually or exceptionally.

extract *vb* /ɪk'strakt/ **1** to pull or draw something out, esp by force or with effort. **2** to separate (a substance) from a liquid or solid mixture. **3** to derive (pleasure, etc). **4** to obtain

(money, etc) by threats or violence. **5** to select (passages from a book, etc). ➤ *n* /'ɛkstrakt/ **1** a passage selected from a book, etc. **2** *chem* a substance that is separated from a liquid or solid mixture by using heat, solvents, distillation, etc. ○ **extractable** *adj*. ○ **extractor** *n* **1** a person or thing that extracts. **2** a fan for ventilating a room or building.

extraction *n* **1** the act of extracting. **2** the process whereby a metal is obtained from its ore. **3** the removal of a tooth from its socket. **4** family origin; descent: *of Dutch extraction*.

extra-curricular *adj* not belonging to, or offered in addition to, the subjects studied in the main teaching curriculum of a school, college, etc.

extradite *vb* to return (a person accused of a crime) for trial in the country where the crime was committed. ○ **extraditable** *adj*. ○ **extradition** *n*.

extramarital *adj* esp of sexual relations: taking place outside marriage.

extramural *adj* **1** of courses, etc: for people who are not full-time students at a college, etc. **2** outside the scope of normal studies.

extraneous /ɪk'streɪnɪəs/ *adj* **1** not belonging; not relevant or related. **2** coming from outside.

extraordinary *adj* **1** unusual; surprising or remarkable. **2** additional; not part of the regular pattern or routine: *extraordinary meeting*. **3** (*often following its noun*) *formal* employed to do additional work, or for a particular occasion: *ambassador extraordinary*. ○ **extraordinarily** *adv*.

extrapolate /ɪk'strapəleɪt/ *vb, tr & intr* **1** *maths* to estimate (a value that lies outside a known range of values), on the basis of those values and usu by means of a graph. **2** to make (estimates) or draw (conclusions) from known facts. ○ **extrapolation** *n*.

extrasensory *adj* achieved using means other than the ordinary senses of sight, hearing, touch, taste and smell: *extrasensory perception*.

extraterrestrial *adj* of a being, creature, etc: coming from outside the Earth or its atmosphere. ➤ *n* an extraterrestrial being.

extravagant *adj* **1** using, spending or costing too much. **2** unreasonably or unbelievably great: *extravagant praise*. ○ **extravagance** *n*. ○ **extravagantly** *adv*.

extravaganza *n* a spectacular display, performance or production.

extravert see EXTROVERT

extreme *adj* **1** very high, or highest, in degree or intensity. **2** very far, or furthest, in any direction, esp out from the centre. **3** very violent or strong. **4** not moderate; severe: *extreme measures*. ➤ *n* **1** either of two people or things as far, or as different, as possible from each other. **2** the highest limit; the greatest degree of any state or condition. ○ **extremely** *adv* to an extreme degree. ♦ **go to extremes** to take action beyond what is thought to be reasonable. **in the extreme** to the highest degree.

extreme unction *n, RC Church* former name for the sacrament of the sick.

extremist *n* someone who has extreme opinions, esp in politics. ➤ *adj* relating to, or favouring, extreme measures. ○ **extremism** *n*.

extremity *n* (*-ies*) **1** the furthest point. **2** an extreme degree; the quality of being extreme. **3** a situation of great danger. **4** (**extremities**) the hands and feet.

extricate *vb* to free someone or something from difficulties. ○ **extricable** *adj.* ○ **extrication** *n*.

extrinsic *adj* **1** external. **2** operating from outside. ○ **extrinsically** *adv.*

extrovert or **extravert** *n* **1** *psychol* someone who is more concerned with the outside world and social relationships than with their inner thoughts and feelings. **2** someone who is sociable, outgoing and talkative. ➤ *adj* having the temperament of an extrovert; sociable or outgoing. Compare INTROVERT. ○ **extroversion** *n*. ○ **extroverted** *adj.*

extrude *vb* **1** to squeeze something or force it out. **2** to force or press (a semisoft solid material) through a DIE² (sense 1b) in order to mould it into a continuous length of product. ○ **extrusion** *n*.

exuberant *adj* **1** in very high spirits. **2** enthusiastic and energetic. ○ **exuberance** *n*. ○ **exuberantly** *adv.*

exude *vb* **1** to give off or give out (an odour or sweat). **2** to show or convey (a quality, characteristic, etc) by one's behaviour. **3** *intr* to ooze out. ○ **exudation** *n*.

exult *vb, intr* **1** (*often* **exult in** or **at sth**) to be intensely joyful about it. **2** (*often* **exult over sth**) to show or enjoy a feeling of triumph. ○ **exultant** *adj.* ○ **exultation** *n*.

eye *n* **1** the organ of vision, usu one of a pair. **2** the area of the face around the eye. **3** (*often* **eyes**) sight; vision: *Surgeons need good eyes*. **4** attention, gaze or observation: *She caught my eye* ♦ *in the public eye*. **5** the ability to appreciate and judge: *an eye for beauty*. **6** a look or expression: *a hostile eye*. **7** *bot* the bud of a tuber such as a potato. **8** an area of calm and low pressure at the centre of a tornado, etc. **9** any rounded thing, esp when hollow, eg the hole in a needle or the small wire loop that a hook fits into. ➤ *vb* (**eyeing** or **eying**) to look at something carefully. ○ **eyeless** *adj.* ♦ **an eye for an eye** retaliation; justice enacted in the same way or to the same degree as the crime. **be all eyes** *colloq* to be vigilant. **clap, lay** or **set eyes on sb** or **sth** *colloq, usu with negatives* to see them or it: *I never want to set eyes on you again.* **have eyes for sb** to be interested in them. **have one's eye on sth** to be eager to acquire it. **in one's mind's eye** in one's imagination. **in the eyes of sb** in their estimation or opinion. **keep an eye on sb** or **sth** *colloq* to keep them or it under observation. **keep one's eyes skinned** or **peeled** *colloq* to watch or look out. **make eyes at sb** *colloq* to look at them with sexual interest

or admiration. **more than meets the eye** more complicated, difficult, etc than appearances suggest. **one in the eye for sb** *colloq* a harsh disappointment or rebuff for them. **see eye to eye with sb** to be in agreement with them. **up to the** or **one's eyes in sth** busy or deeply involved in (work, a commitment, etc). **with an eye to sth** having it as a purpose or intention. **with one's eyes open** with full awareness of what one is doing. ◊ **eye sb** or **sth up** *colloq* to assess their worth or attractiveness.

eyeball *n* the nearly spherical body of the eye. ➤ *vb, colloq* **1** to face someone; to confront them. **2** to examine something closely. ♦ **eyeball to eyeball** *colloq* of people: face to face and close together in a threatening confrontation.

eyebath or (*esp US*) **eyecup** *n* a small vessel for holding and applying medication, cleansing solution, etc to the eye.

eyebrow *n* the arch of hair on the bony ridge above each eye. ♦ **raise an eyebrow** or **one's eyebrows** to show surprise, interest or disbelief.

eyecatching *adj* drawing attention, esp by being strikingly attractive. ○ **eye-catcher** *n*.

eye contact *n* a direct look between two people.

eyeful *n, colloq* **1** an interesting or beautiful sight. **2** *slang* an attractive woman. **3** a look or view.

eyeglass *n* a single lens in a frame, to assist weak sight.

eyelash *n* any of the short protective hairs that grow from the edge of the upper and lower eyelids. Often shortened to **lash**.

eyelet *n* **1** a small hole in fabric, etc through which a lace, etc is passed. **2** the metal, etc ring reinforcing such a hole.

eyelid *n* a protective fold of skin and muscle that can be moved to cover or uncover the front of the eyeball.

eyeliner *n* a cosmetic used to outline the eye.

eye-opener *n, colloq* a surprising or revealing sight, experience, etc.

eyepiece *n, optics* the lens or group of lenses in an optical instrument that is nearest to the eye of the observer.

eyeshade *n* a VISOR.

eyeshadow *n* a coloured cosmetic for the eyelids.

eyesight *n* the ability to see.

eyesore *n, derog* an ugly thing, esp a building.

eyestrain *n* tiredness or irritation of the eyes.

eye tooth *n* a CANINE TOOTH. ♦ **give one's eye teeth for sth** to go to any lengths to obtain it.

eyewash *n* **1** liquid for soothing sore eyes. **2** *colloq, derog* nonsense; insincere or deceptive talk.

eyewitness *n* someone who sees something happen, esp a crime.

eyrie or **aerie** / ˈɪərɪ/ *n* **1** the nest of an eagle or other bird of prey, built in a high inaccessible place. **2** a building perched on high ground.

Ff

F¹ or **f** *n* (*Fs, F's* or *f's*) **1** the sixth letter of the English alphabet. **2** (**F**) *mus* the fourth note in the scale of C major.

F² *abbrev* **1** Fahrenheit. **2** farad. **3** Fellow (of a society, etc). **4** *physics* force.

F³ *symbol, chem* fluorine.

f *abbrev* **1** fathom. **2** female. **3** feminine. **4** (*pl* **ff.**) following (page).

fa see FAH.

fab *adj, colloq* fabulous.

fable *n* **1** a story with a moral, usu with animals as characters. **2** myths and legends generally. ○ **fabled** *adj*.

fabric *n* **1** woven, knitted or felted cloth. **2** the walls, floor and roof of a building. **3** orderly structure: *the fabric of society.*

fabricate *vb* **1** to invent or make up (a story, evidence, etc). **2** to make something, esp from whatever materials are available. ○ **fabrication** *n*.

fabulous *adj* **1 a** *colloq* wonderful; excellent; **b** immense; amazing. **2** legendary; mythical.

façade or **facade** /fə'sɑːd/ *n* **1** the front of a building. **2** a false appearance that hides the reality.

face *n* **1** the front part of the head, from forehead to chin. **2** the features or facial expression. **3** a surface or side, eg of a mountain, geometrical figure, etc. **4** the important or working side, eg of a golf-club head. **5 a** in a mine or quarry: the exposed surface from which coal, etc is mined; **b** on a cliff: the exposed surface, usu vertical. **6** the dial of a clock, watch, etc. **7** the side of a playing card that is marked with numbers, symbols, etc. **8** *printing* a typeface. ➤ *vb* **1** *tr & intr* to be opposite to something or someone; to look at or look in some direction. **2** to confront or cope with (problems, etc). **3** to accept (the unpleasant truth, etc). **4** to present itself to someone: *the scene that faced us.* **5** to cover with a surface: *The bricks were faced with plaster.* ♦ **face the music** *colloq* to accept unpleasant consequences at their worst; to brave a trying situation, etc. **face to face 1** in the presence of each other. **2** facing or confronting each other. **in the face of sth** in spite of a known circumstance, etc. **in your face 1** right in front of someone. **2** dealing with an issue in a direct and often provocative way. **on the face of sth** superficially; at first glance. **put a good** or **brave face on sth** to try to hide disappointment, fear, etc concerning it. **save face** to preserve one's reputation, while avoiding humiliation or the appearance of giving in or climbing down. **set one's face against sth** to oppose an idea, course of action, etc, firmly. **show one's face** *often with negatives* to make an appearance: *Ben didn't dare show his face.* **to sb's face** directly; openly, in someone's presence. ◇ **face up to sth** or **sb** to accept an unpleasant fact, etc; to deal with it or them bravely.

faceless *adj* **1** of a person: with identity concealed. **2** of bureaucrats, etc: impersonal.

facelift *n* **1** a surgical operation to remove facial wrinkles by tightening the skin. **2** any procedure for improving the external appearance of something.

facer *n colloq* a problem.

face-saving *adj* preserving a person's reputation, etc and avoiding humiliation or the appearance of climbing down. ○ **face-saver** *n*.

facet *n* **1** a face of a cut jewel. **2** an aspect, eg of a problem, topic or someone's personality.

facetious *adj* of a person or remark, etc: amusing or witty, esp unsuitably so.

face value *n* **1** the stated value on a coin, stamp, etc. **2** the apparent meaning or implication, eg of a statement, which may not be the same as its real meaning.

facial *adj* belonging or relating to the face: *facial hair.* ➤ *n* a beauty treatment for the face. ○ **facially** *adv*.

facile *adj* **1** of success, etc: too easily achieved. **2** of remarks, opinions, etc: over-simple; showing a lack of careful thought.

facilitate *vb* to make something easy or easier to do. ○ **facilitation** *n*.

facility *n* (*-ies*) **1** skill, talent or ability. **2** fluency; ease. **3** an arrangement, feature, etc that enables someone to do something. **4** (*chiefly* **facilities**) a building, service or piece of equipment for a particular activity.

facing *n* **1** an outer layer, eg of stone covering a brick wall. **2** a piece of material used to back and strengthen part of a garment.

facsimile /fak'sɪmɪlɪ/ *n* **1** an exact copy made, eg of a manuscript, picture, etc. **2** a FAX (*noun* sense 2).

fact *n* **1** a thing known to be true, to exist or to have happened. **2** truth or reality, as distinct from mere statement or belief. **3** a piece of information. ♦ **after** or **before the fact** after or before a crime is committed. **as a matter of fact** or **in actual fact** or **in fact** or **in point of fact** in reality; actually.

faction *n* **1** an active or trouble-making group

within a larger organization. **2** argument or dissent within a group. ○ **factional** adj.

factitious adj **1** deliberately contrived rather than developing naturally. **2** insincere; false.

fact of life n **1** an unavoidable truth, esp if unpleasant. **2** (**the facts of life**) basic information on sexual matters and reproduction.

factor n **1** a circumstance that contributes to a result. **2** maths one of two or more numbers that, when multiplied together, produce a given number: 4 is a factor of 12. **3** in Scotland: the manager of an estate.

factorial n, maths (symbol !) the number resulting when a whole number and all whole numbers below it are multiplied together eg, 5! is $5 \times 4 \times 3 \times 2 \times 1 = 120$.

factorize or **-ise** vb, maths to find the factors of (a number). ○ **factorization** n.

factory n (**-ies**) a building or buildings with equipment for the large-scale manufacture of goods.

factotum n a person employed to do a large number of different jobs.

factual adj **1** concerned with, or based on, facts. **2** actual. ○ **factually** adv.

faculty n (**-ies**) **1** a mental or physical power. **2** a particular talent or aptitude for something. **3** a section of a university, comprising a number of departments: the Faculty of Science; the professors and lecturers belonging to such a section. **4** N Am the staff of a college, school or university.

fad n, colloq **1** a shortlived fashion. **2** an odd idea, belief or practice. ○ **faddy** (**-ier, -iest**) adj.

fade vb **1** tr & intr to lose, or cause something to lose, strength, freshness, colour, etc. **2** intr of a sound, image, memory, etc: to disappear gradually. ◊ **fade sth in** or **out** cinematog, broadcasting to make (a sound or picture) become gradually louder and more distinct, or gradually fainter and disappear.

faeces or (N Am) **feces** /ˈfiːsiːz/ pl n waste matter discharged from the body through the anus. ○ **faecal** or **fecal** /ˈfiːkəl/ adj.

faff vb, intr, colloq (also **faff about**) to act in a fussy or dithering way.

fag¹ n **1** colloq a cigarette. **2** colloq a piece of drudgery; a bore. **3** dated a schoolboy who runs errands, etc for an older one. ➢ vb (**fagged, fagging**) **1** tr to tire out or exhaust. **2** intr, dated of a schoolboy: to act as fag. ◆ **fagged out** very tired.

fag² n, slang, derog a gay man.

faggot or (N Am) **fagot** n **1** a ball of chopped pork and liver mixed with breadcrumbs and herbs, and fried or baked. **2** a bundle of sticks, twigs, etc, used for fuel, etc. **3** slang, derog a gay man.

fah or **fa** n, mus in sol-fa notation: the fourth note of the major scale.

Fahrenheit scale /ˈfarənhaɪt/ n a scale of temperature on which water boils at 212° and freezes at 32° under standard atmospheric pressure.

faience or **faïence** /faɪˈɑːs/ n glazed decorated pottery.

fail vb **1** tr & intr (often **fail in sth**) not to succeed; to be unsuccessful in (an undertaking). **2** to judge (a candidate) not good enough to pass a test, etc. **3** intr of machinery, a bodily organ, etc: to stop working or functioning. **4** intr not to manage (to do something): Sue failed to pay the bill in time. **5** to let (someone) down; to disappoint. **6** of courage, strength, etc: to desert (one) at the time of need. **7** intr of a business, etc: to become insolvent or bankrupt. ➢ n a failure, esp in an exam. ◆ **without fail** for certain; with complete regularity and reliability.

failing n a fault; a weakness. ➢ prep in the absence of: Failing an agreement today, the issue will be referred for arbitration.

fail-safe adj of a machine, system, etc: designed to return to a safe condition if something goes wrong.

failure n **1** an act of failing; lack of success. **2** someone or something that is unsuccessful. **3** a stoppage in functioning, eg of a computer, machine, system, etc. **4** a poor result. **5** an instance or act of something not being done or not happening: failure to turn up.

fain adv, old use gladly; willingly.

faint adj **1** dim; slight. **2** on the verge of losing consciousness. **3** feeble; unenthusiastic. ➢ vb, intr to lose consciousness. ➢ n a sudden loss of consciousness.

faint-hearted adj timid; cowardly.

fair¹ adj **1** just; not using dishonest methods or discrimination. **2** in accordance with the rules. **3** a of hair and skin: light-coloured; **b** having light-coloured hair and skin. **4** old use beautiful. **5** quite good. **6** sizeable; considerable. **7** of weather: fine. **8** of the wind: favourable. ➢ adv in a fair way. ◆ **fairness** n. ◆ **fair-and-square** honest and open. **fair enough** all right.

fair² n **1** a collection of sideshows and amusements, often travelling from place to place. **2** hist a market for the sale of produce, livestock, etc, with or without sideshows. **3** an indoor exhibition of goods from different countries, firms, etc, held to promote trade.

fairground n the piece of land on which sideshows and amusements are set up for a fair.

fairing n an external structure fitted to an aircraft, vessel or other vehicle to reduce drag.

fairly adv **1** justly; honestly. **2** quite; rather.

fair play n honourable behaviour.

fairway n **1** golf a broad strip of short grass extending from the tee to the green. **2** a navigable deep-water channel.

fair-weather friend n someone who cannot be relied on in times of trouble.

fairy n (**-ies**) **1** myth a supernatural being, usu with magical powers and of diminutive and graceful human form. **2** slang, derog a gay man.

fairy godmother n someone who comes unexpectedly or magically to a person's aid.

fairy ring n a ring of darker grass marking the

outer edge of an underground growth of fungi.
fairy tale or **fairy story** n **1** a story about
fairies, magic and other supernatural things.
2 euphem, colloq a lie. ➢ adj (**fairy-tale**) beautiful, magical or marvellous.

fait accompli /feɪt ɔ'kɒmpliː/ n (**faits accom-
plis** /-pliː/) something done and unalterable.

faith n **1** trust or confidence. **2** strong belief, eg
in God. **3** a specified religion: the Jewish faith.

faithful adj **1** having or showing faith. **2** loyal
and true. **3** accurate. **4** loyal to a sexual partner. **5** reliable; constant. ○ **faithfully** adv.
○ **faithfulness** n.

faith healing n the curing of illness through
religious faith rather than medical treatment.
○ **faith healer** n.

faithless adj disloyal; treacherous.

fake n someone or something that is not genuine. ➢ adj not genuine; false. ➢ vb **1** tr to alter
something dishonestly; to falsify something. **2**
tr & intr to pretend to feel (an emotion) or have
(an illness).

fakir /'feɪkɪə(r)/ n a wandering Hindu or Muslim
holy man, depending on begging for survival.

falcon n a type of long-winged bird of prey that
can be trained to hunt small birds and animals.

falconry n **1** the breeding and training of falcons for hunting. **2** the sport of using falcons
to hunt prey. ○ **falconer** n.

fall vb (**fell, fallen**) intr **1** to descend or drop
freely and involuntarily, esp accidentally, by
force of gravity. **2** (also **fall over** or **down**) of
someone, or something upright: to drop to the
ground after losing balance. **3** of a building,
bridge, etc: to collapse. **4** of rain, snow, etc: to
come down from the sky. **5** of hair, etc: to hang
down. **6** to go naturally or easily into position. **7**
of a government, leader, etc: to lose power; to
be no longer able to govern. **8** of a stronghold:
to be captured. **9** of defences or barriers: to be
lowered or broken down. **10** to die or be badly
wounded in battle, etc. **11** of value, temperature, etc: to become less. **12** of sound: to diminish. **13** of silence: to intervene. **14** of darkness or
night: to arrive. **15** to pass into a certain state; to
begin to be in that state: fall asleep • fall in love.
16 to be grouped or classified in a certain way:
It falls into two categories. **17** to occur at a certain time or place: The accent falls on the first
syllable. **18** of someone's face: to show disappointment. ➢ n **1** an act or way of falling. **2**
something, or an amount, that falls. **3** (often
falls) a waterfall. **4** a drop in quality, quantity,
value, temperature, etc. **5** a defeat or collapse.
6 (also **Fall**) N Am autumn. **7** wrestling a manoeuvre by which one pins one's opponent's
shoulders to the ground. ◆ **fall foul of sb** or
sth to get into trouble or conflict with them or
it. **fall over oneself** or **fall over backwards** colloq to be strenuously or noticeably eager to
please or help. **fall short** or **fall short of sth 1**
to turn out not to be enough. **2** to fail to attain
or reach what is aimed at. **fall to pieces** or **bits 1**
of something: to break up; to disintegrate. **2** of

someone: to be unable to function normally.
◊ **fall about** colloq to be helpless with laughter.
fall apart 1 to break in pieces. **2** to fail; to collapse. **fall away 1** of land: to slope downwards.
2 to become fewer or less. **fall back on sth** to
make use of it in an emergency. **fall behind** or
fall behind with sth to fail to keep up with
someone, with one's work, with paying rent,
etc. **fall down** of an argument, etc: to be shown
to be invalid. **fall for sb** to fall in love with them.
fall for sth to be deceived or taken in by it. **fall
in 1** of a roof, etc: to collapse. **2** of a soldier, etc:
to take his or her place in a parade. **fall into sth**
to become involved in it, esp by chance or
without having put much effort into getting
there. **fall in with sb** to chance to meet or coincide with them. **fall in with sth** to agree to it; to
support it. **fall off** to decline in quality or quantity. **fall out** of a soldier: to come out of military
formation. **fall out with sb** to quarrel with
them, and then not have contact with them
for a period of time. **fall through** of a plan, etc:
to fail. **fall to sb** to become their job or duty.

fallacy n (**-ies**) **1** a mistaken notion. **2** a mistake
in reasoning that spoils a whole argument.
○ **fallacious** adj.

fallen adj **1** old use having lost one's virtue, honour or reputation: fallen woman. **2** killed in
battle.

fall guy n, colloq **1** someone who is easily
cheated. **2** someone who is left to take the
blame for something.

fallible adj capable of making mistakes.
○ **fallibility** n (**-ies**).

Fallopian tube n, anat, zool in female mammals: either of the two long slender tubes
through which the egg cells pass from the ovaries to the uterus.

fallout n **1** a cloud of radioactive dust caused
by a nuclear explosion. **2** the unpleasant results of a situation.

fallow adj of land: left unplanted after ploughing, to recover its natural fertility.

fallow deer n a small deer with a reddish-
brown coat that becomes spotted with white
in summer.

false adj **1** of a statement, etc: untrue. **2** of an
idea, etc: mistaken. **3** artificial; not genuine. **4**
of words, promises, etc: insincere. **5** treacherous; disloyal. ○ **falsely** adv. ○ **falseness** n.
○ **falsity** n (**-ies**). ◆ **under false pretences** by
giving a deliberately misleading impression.

false alarm n an alarm given unnecessarily.

falsehood n **1** dishonesty. **2** a lie.

false start n an invalid start to a race, in which
one or more competitors begin before the signal is given.

falsetto n an artificially high voice, esp produced by a tenor above his normal range.

falsify vb (**falsifies, falsified**) to alter (records,
accounts, etc) dishonestly, or make something
up, in order to deceive. ○ **falsification** n.

falter vb **1** intr to move unsteadily. **2** intr to start
functioning unreliably. **3** intr to lose strength or

conviction. **4** *tr & intr* to speak, or say something, hesitantly. ○ **faltering** *adj*.

fame *n* the condition of being famous; celebrity. ○ **famed** *adj* renowned.

familiar *adj* **1** well known or recognizable. **2** frequently met with. **3** (**familiar with**) well acquainted with or having a thorough knowledge of something. **4** friendly; close. **5** over-friendly. ➤ *n* a demon or spirit, esp one in the shape of an animal, that serves a witch. ○ **familiarity** *n*. ○ **familiarly** *adv*.

familiarize or **-ise** *vb* **1** (*usu* **familiarize with sth**) to make (someone or oneself) familiar with it. **2** to make something well known or familiar. ○ **familiarization** *n*.

family *n* (*-ies*) **1** a group consisting of a set of parents and children. **2** a group of people related to one another by blood or marriage. **3** a person's children. **4** a household of people. **5** all those descended from a common ancestor. **6** a related group, eg of languages, etc. **7** *biol* in taxonomy: a division of an ORDER (*noun sense 11*) which is subdivided into one or more genera. ➤ *adj* a belonging to or specially for a family: *family car*; **b** concerning the family: *family matters*; **c** suitable for the whole family: *family pub.* ○ **familial** *adj*.

family name *n* a surname.

family planning *n* BIRTH CONTROL.

family tree *n* the relationships within a family throughout the generations, or a diagram showing these.

famine *n* a severe, and often long-term, shortage, esp of food.

famished *adj* **1** starving. **2** (*also* **famishing**) *colloq* feeling very hungry.

famous *adj* **1** well known; renowned. **2** great; glorious: *a famous victory*. ○ **famously** *adv*.

fan¹ *n* **1** a hand-held device, usu made of silk or paper, for creating a cool current of air. **2** any mechanical or electrical device that creates air currents, esp for ventilation. **3** any structure that can be spread into the shape of a fan, eg a bird's tail. ➤ *vb* (**fanned, fanning**) **1** to cool or ventilate with a fan or similar device. **2** to kindle (flames, resentment, etc). **3** (*often* **fan out** or **fan sth out**) to spread out, or cause to spread out, in the shape of a fan.

fan² *n* an enthusiastic supporter or devoted admirer, esp of a pop group, a football team, a sport, etc.

fanatic *n* someone with an extreme or excessive enthusiasm for something, esp a religion or religious issues. ➤ *adj* (*also* **fanatical**) extremely or excessively enthusiastic about something. ○ **fanaticism** *n*.

fanciful *adj* **1** indulging in fancies. **2** existing in the imagination only. ○ **fancifully** *adv*.

fancy *n* (*-ies*) **1** the imagination. **2** an image, idea or whim. **3** a sudden liking or desire for something. ➤ *adj* (*-ier, -iest*) **1** elaborate. **2** *colloq* special, unusual or superior, esp in quality. **3** *colloq, facetious* of prices: too high. ➤ *vb* (**fancies, fancied**) **1** to think or believe some-

thing. **2** to have a desire for something. **3** *colloq* to be physically attracted to someone. **4** to consider likely to win or do well. **5** *tr & intr* to take in mentally; to imagine: *Fancy him getting married at last!* ➤ *exclam* (*also* **fancy that!**) expressing surprise. ○ **fanciable** *adj*. ○ **fancily** *adv*.

fancy dress *n* clothes for dressing up in, usu representing a historical, fictional, etc character.

fancy-free *adj* **1** not in love. **2** free to do as one pleases.

fandango *n* an energetic Spanish dance, or the music for it, in 3/4 time.

fanfare *n* a short piece of music played on trumpets to announce an important event or arrival.

fang *n* **1** a sharp pointed tooth, esp a large canine tooth of a carnivorous animal. **2** a tooth of a poisonous snake.

fanlight *n* a semicircular window over a door or window.

fanny *n* (*-ies*) **1** *Brit taboo slang* a woman's genitals. **2** *N Am slang* the buttocks.

fantasia *n* **1** a musical composition that is free and unconventional in form. **2** a piece of music based on a selection of popular tunes.

fantasize or **-ise** *vb, intr* (*often* **fantasize about sth**) to indulge in pleasurable fantasies or daydreams.

fantastic or **fantastical** *adj* **1** *colloq* splendid; excellent. **2** *colloq* enormous; amazing. **3** of a story, etc: unlikely; incredible. **4** fanciful; strange; unrealistic: *fantastic idea*. ○ **fantastically** *adv*.

fantasy *n* (*-ies*) **1** a pleasant daydream. **2** something longed-for but unlikely to happen. **3** a mistaken notion. **4** the activity of imagining. **5** a fanciful piece of writing, music, film-making, etc.

fanzine *n* a magazine written, published and distributed by and for a particular group of enthusiasts or fans.

FAQ *abbrev, comput* frequently asked questions.

far (**farther, farthest** or **further, furthest**) *adv* **1** at, to or from a great distance. **2** to or by a great extent: *My guess wasn't far out.* **3** at or to a distant time. ➤ *adj* **1** distant; remote. **2** the more distant of two things. **3** extreme: *the Far Right of the party.* ◆ **as far as** up to a certain place or point. **by far** or **far and away** by a considerable amount; very much. **far and wide** extensively; everywhere. **far from** the opposite of; not at all. **far gone** in an advanced state, eg of illness or drunkenness. **go far** to achieve great things. **go so far** or **as far as to do sth** to be prepared to do it; to go to the extent of doing it. **go too far** to behave, speak, etc unreasonably. **in so far as** to the extent that.

farad *n, electronics* the SI unit of electrical CAPACITANCE.

faraway *adj* **1** distant. **2** of a look or expression: dreamy; absent-minded.

farce n **1 a** a comedy involving a series of ridiculously unlikely turns of events; **b** comedies of this type. **2** an absurd situation; something ludicrously badly organized. ○ **farcical** adj. ○ **farcically** adv.

fare n **1** the price paid by a passenger to travel on a bus, train, etc. **2** a taxi passenger. **3** food or the provision of food. ➢ vb, intr, formal to get on (in a specified way): She fared well.

the Far East n a loosely-used term for the countries of E and SE Asia.

farewell exclam, old use goodbye! ➢ n an act of saying goodbye; an act of departure. ➢ adj parting; valedictory: a farewell party.

far-fetched adj of an idea, story, excuse, etc: unlikely; unconvincing.

far-flung adj **1** extensive. **2** distant: the far-flung corners of the world.

farm n **1** a piece of land with its buildings, used for growing crops, breeding livestock, etc. **2** a farmer's house and the buildings round it. **3** a place specializing in the rearing or growing of a specified type of livestock, crop, etc: dairy farm • fish farm. ➢ vb **1 a** tr to prepare and use (land) for crop-growing, animal-rearing, etc; **b** intr to be a farmer. **2** tr to collect and keep the proceeds from (taxes, etc) in return for a fixed sum. **3** tr (also **farm out**) **a** to hand over (a child, old person, etc) temporarily to a carer; **b** to hand over (work, etc) to another to do.

farmer n someone who earns a living by managing or operating a farm.

farming n the business of running a farm.

farmyard n an area surrounded by farm buildings.

far-off adj, adv distant.

far-out adj, colloq **1** strange; weird. **2** excellent.

farrago /fəˈrɑːgoʊ/ n (**farragos** or **farragoes**) a confused mixture.

far-reaching adj extensive in scope, influence, etc: far-reaching consequences.

farrier n a person who shoes horses.

farrow n a sow's litter of piglets. ➢ vb, tr & intr of a sow: to give birth to (piglets).

far-sighted adj **1** (also **far-seeing**) prudent; forward-looking. **2** long-sighted.

fart coarse slang, vb, intr to emit wind from the anus. ➢ n **1** an emission of this kind. **2** a term of abuse for a person: a boring old fart. ◊ **fart about** or **around** slang to fool about, waste time, etc.

farther adj, adv FURTHER (with reference to physical distance). See also FAR.

farthest adj, adv FURTHEST (with reference to physical distance).

farthing n, formerly **1** one quarter of an old British penny. **2** a coin of this value.

fascia /ˈfeɪʃə or ˈfaʃiə / n **1** the board above a shop entrance, bearing the shop name, etc. **2** Brit the dashboard of a motor vehicle. **3** archit a long flat band or surface.

fascinate vb **1** to interest strongly. **2** to hold spellbound. ○ **fascinating** adj. ○ **fascinatingly** adv. ○ **fascination** n.

fascism /ˈfaʃɪzəm/ n **1** a political movement or system characterized mainly by a belief in the supremacy of the chosen national group. **2** (**Fascism**) this system in force in Italy from 1922 to 1943. **3** any system or doctrine characterized by a belief in the supremacy of a particular way of viewing things. ○ **fascist** n, adj.

fashion n **1** style, esp the latest style, in clothes, music, lifestyle, etc. **2** a currently popular style or practice. **3** a manner of doing something: in a dramatic fashion. ➢ vb to form or make something into a particular shape, esp with the hands. ◆ **after a fashion** in a rather clumsy or inexpert way.

fashionable adj **1** of clothes, people, etc: following the latest fashion. **2** used by or popular with fashionable people. ○ **fashionably** adv.

fast¹ adj **1** moving, or able to move, quickly. **2** taking a relatively short time. **3** of a clock, etc: showing a time in advance of the correct time. **4** allowing or intended for rapid movement: the fast lane. **5** of a photographic film: requiring only brief exposure. **6** colloq seeking excitement; sexually promiscuous. **7** firmly fixed or caught; steadfast. **8** of friends: firm; close. **9** of fabric colours: not liable to run or fade. ➢ adv **1** quickly. **2** in quick succession: coming thick and fast. **3** firmly: The glue held fast. **4** completely; thoroughly: fast asleep. ◆ **play fast and loose** to behave irresponsibly or unreliably. **pull a fast one** colloq to cheat or deceive.

fast² vb, intr to go without food, or restrict one's diet, esp as a religious discipline. ➢ n a period of fasting. ○ **fast day** n. ○ **fasting** n.

fast-breeder reactor n a type of nuclear reactor in which the neutrons produced during nuclear fission are used to produce more of the same nuclear fuel, with as much fuel being produced as is consumed by the reactor.

fasten vb **1** (also **fasten up**) to make something firmly closed or fixed. **2** to attach something to something else. **3** intr to become fastened. **4** to be capable of being fastened. **5** intr (usu **fasten on** or **upon sth**) to concentrate on it eagerly. ○ **fastener** or **fastening** n a device that fastens something.

fast food n ready-prepared food, such as hamburgers, fried fish, chips, etc, either to be eaten in the restaurant or taken away.

fast-forward n a facility on a video player, cassette player, etc for advancing the tape quickly. ➢ vb to advance a tape quickly by this means.

fastidious adj particular in matters of taste and detail, esp excessively so.

fast-track colloq, n **1** a routine for accelerating a proposal, etc through its formalities. **2** a quick route to advancement. ➢ vb to process something or promote someone speedily.

fat n **1** any of a group of organic compounds that occur naturally in animals and plants, are solid at room temperature, and are insoluble in water. **2 a** in mammals: a layer of tissue that lies beneath the skin and between various organs, and which serves as a means of storing energy; **b** an excess of this. ➤ *adj* (**fatter, fattest**) **1** having too much fat on the body. **2** containing a lot of fat. **3** thick or wide. **4** *colloq* of a fee, profit, etc: large. ♦ **a fat chance** *slang* no chance at all.

fatal *adj* **1** causing death. **2** bringing ruin; disastrous: *a fatal mistake*. ○ **fatally** *adv.*

fatalism *n* **1** a belief or the philosophical doctrine that all events are predestined and humans cannot alter them. **2** a defeatist attitude or outlook. ○ **fatalist** *n.* ○ **fatalistic** *adj.*

fatality *n* (**-ies**) **1** an accidental or violent death. **2** a person who has been killed in an accident, etc.

fate *n* **1** (*also* **Fate**) the apparent power that determines the course of events, over which humans have no control. **2** the individual destiny of a person or thing. **3** death, downfall, destruction or doom.

fateful *adj* **1** decisive; critical; having significant results. **2** bringing calamity or disaster. ○ **fatefully** *adv.*

father *n* **1** a male parent. **2** (**fathers**) one's ancestors. **3** a founder, inventor, pioneer or early leader. **4** (**Father**) a title or form of address for a priest. **5** (**Father**) *Christianity* God. ➤ *vb* **1** to be the father of (a child). **2** to invent or originate (an idea, etc). ○ **fatherhood** *n.*

father figure *n* an older man who is respected and admired.

father-in-law *n* (**fathers-in-law**) the father of one's wife or husband.

fatherland *n* one's native country.

fatherly *adj* benevolent, protective and encouraging. ○ **fatherliness** *n.*

fathom *n* in the imperial system: a unit of measurement of the depth of water, equal to 6ft (1.8m). ➤ *vb* (*also* **fathom sth out**) to work out a problem; to get to the bottom of a mystery. ○ **fathomable** *adj.*

fatigue *n* **1** tiredness after work or effort, either mental or physical. **2** weakness, esp in metals, caused by variations in stress. **3** (**fatigues**) military clothing. ➤ *vb, tr & intr* to exhaust or become exhausted.

fatten *vb, tr & intr* (*also* **fatten up**) to make or become fat. ○ **fattening** *adj, n.*

fatty *adj* (**-ier, -iest**) **1** containing fat. **2** greasy; oily. **3** of an acid: occurring in, derived from or chemically related to animal or vegetable fats. ➤ *n* (**-ies**) *derog, colloq* a fat person.

fatuous *adj* foolish, esp in a self-satisfied way; empty-headed. ○ **fatuity** *n* (**-ies**) ○ **fatuously** *adv.*

fatwa or **fatwah** /ˈfatwɑ/ *n* a formal legal opinion or decree issued by a Muslim authority.

faucet /ˈfɔːsɪt/ *n* **1** a TAP² fitted to a barrel. **2** *N Am* a TAP² on a bath, etc.

fault *n* **1** a weakness or failing in character. **2** a flaw or defect in an object or structure. **3** a misdeed or slight offence. **4** responsibility for something wrong: *all my fault*. **5** *geol* a break

or crack in the Earth's crust. **6** *tennis, etc* an incorrectly placed or delivered serve. **7** *show-jumping* a penalty for refusing or failing to clear a fence. ➤ *vb* to blame someone. ○ **faultless** *adj.* ♦ **at fault** culpable; to blame. **find fault with sth** or **sb** to criticize it or them. **to a fault** to too great an extent.

faulty *adj* (**-ier, -iest**) **1** having a fault or faults. **2** particularly of a machine or instrument: not working correctly.

faun *n, Roman myth* a mythical creature with a man's head and body and a goat's horns, hind legs and tail.

fauna *n* (**faunas** or **faunae** /ˈfɔːniː/) the wild animals of a particular region, country, or time period. Compare FLORA. ○ **faunal** *adj.*

faux pas /foʊ pɑː/ *n* (*pl* **faux pas** /foʊ pɑːz/) an embarrassing blunder, esp a social one.

favour or (*N Am*) **favor** *n* **1** a kind or helpful action. **2** liking, approval or goodwill. **3** unfair preference. **4** *hist* something given or worn as a token of affection. ➤ *vb* **1** to treat someone or something with preference, or over-indulgently. **2** to prefer; to support. **3** of circumstances: to give an advantage to someone or something. **4** to look like (a relative, esp a mother or father). ○ **favoured** or (*N Am*) **favored** *adj.* ♦ **in favour of sth** or **sb 1** having a preference for it or them. **2** to their benefit. **3** in support of or approval of them. **in** or **out of favour with sb** having gained, or lost, their approval.

favourable or (*NAm*) **favorable** *adj* **1** showing or giving agreement or consent. **2** (**favourable to sb**) advantageous or helpful to them. **3** of a wind: following. ○ **favourably** *adv.*

favourite or (*N Am*) **favorite** *adj* best-liked; preferred. ➤ *n* **1** a favourite person or thing. **2** someone unfairly preferred or particularly indulged. **3** *sport* a horse or competitor expected to win.

favouritism or (*N Am*) **favoritism** *n* the practice of giving unfair preference, help or support to someone or something.

fawn¹ *n* **1** a young deer of either sex. **2** a yellowish-beige colour. ➤ *adj* of this colour.

fawn² *vb, intr* (*often* **fawn on** or **upon sb**) to flatter or behave over-humbly towards someone, in order to win approval.

fax *n* **1** a machine that scans documents electronically and transmits a photographic image of them to a receiving machine by telephone line. **2** a document sent or received by such a machine. **3** the process of copying and sending documents by such a machine. ➤ *vb* **1** to transmit (a document) by this means. **2** to send a communication (to someone) by fax.

faze *vb, colloq* to disturb, worry or fluster.

FBI *abbrev* Federal Bureau of Investigation.

Fe *symbol, chem* iron.

fealty /ˈfɪəltɪ/ *n* (**-ies**) *hist* the loyalty sworn by a vassal or tenant to a feudal lord.

fear *n* **1** anxiety and distress caused by the awareness of danger or expectation of pain. **2** a cause of this feeling. **3** *relig* reverence, awe or dread. ➤ *vb* **1** to be afraid of (someone or something). **2** to think or expect (something) with dread. **3** to regret; to be sorry to say something: *I fear you have misunderstood.* **4** *intr* (**fear for sth**) to be frightened or anxious about it: *The prisoners feared for their lives.* ○ **fearless** *adj.* ♦ **no fear** *colloq* no chance; definitely not.

fearful *adj* **1** afraid. **2** frightening. **3** *colloq* very bad: *a fearful mess.* ○ **fearfully** *adv.*

fearsome *adj* **1** causing fear. **2** frightening.

feasible *adj* **1** capable of being done or achieved. **2** *loosely* probable. ○ **feasibility** *n* (*-ies*). ○ **feasibly** *adv.*

feast *n* **1** a large rich meal, esp one prepared to celebrate something. **2** a pleasurable abundance of something. **3** *relig* a regularly occurring celebration commemorating a person or event. ➤ *vb* **1** *intr* to take part in a feast. **2** *old use* to provide a feast for someone; to entertain someone sumptuously. ○ **feasting** *n.* ♦ **feast one's eyes on** or **upon sth** to gaze at it with pleasure.

feat *n* a deed or achievement, esp one requiring extraordinary strength, skill or courage.

feather *n* **1** any of the light growths that form the soft covering of a bird. **2** something with a feather-like appearance. **3** plumage. ➤ *vb* **1** to provide, cover or line with feathers. **2** to turn (an oar, blade, etc) in order to lessen the resistance of the air or water. ○ **feathery** *adj.* ♦ **a feather in one's cap** something to be proud of. **feather one's own nest** to accumulate money for oneself, esp dishonestly.

feather bed *n* a mattress stuffed with feathers. ➤ *vb* (**featherbed**) **1** to spoil or pamper someone. **2** to protect (an industry, workers, etc) by practices such as overmanning in order to create or save jobs.

featherbrain *n* a silly, frivolous or empty-headed person. ○ **feather-brained** *adj.*

featherweight *n* **1** a class for boxers, wrestlers and weightlifters of not more than a specified weight, for example 57kg (126 lb) in professional boxing. **2** a boxer, wrestler, etc of this weight. **3** someone who is very light or unimportant.

feature *n* **1** any of the parts of the face, eg eyes, nose, mouth, etc. **2** (**features**) the face. **3** a characteristic. **4** a noticeable part or quality of something. **5** an extended article in a newspaper, discussing a particular issue. **6** an article or item appearing regularly in a newspaper. **7** (*also* **feature film**) a main film in a cinema programme. ➤ *vb* **1** to have as a feature or make a feature of something. **2** to give prominence to (an actor, a well-known event, etc) in a film. **3** *intr* (*usu* **feature in sth**) to play an important part or role in (a film, documentary, etc). ○ **featureless** *adj.*

febrile /ˈfiːbraɪl/ *adj* relating to fever; feverish.

February *n* the second month of the year, which has 28 days, except in LEAP YEARS when it has 29.

feckless *adj* **1** helpless; clueless. **2** irresponsible; aimless.

fecund *adj* fruitful; fertile; richly productive. ○ **fecundity** *n.*

federal *adj* **1** belonging or relating to a country consisting of a group of states independent in local matters but united under a central government for other purposes, eg defence, foreign policy: *the Federal Republic of Germany.* **2** relating to the central government of a group of federated states. ○ **federalism** *n.* ○ **federalist** *n.*

federate *vb* /ˈfɛdəreɪt/ *tr & intr* to unite to form a federation.

federation *n* **1** a FEDERAL union of states, ie a group of states united politically by a treaty. **2** a union of business organizations, institutions, etc. **3** the act of uniting in a league.

fed up *adj* (*also* **fed up with** or (*colloq*) **of sth**) bored; irritated.

fee *n* **1** a charge made for professional services. **2** a charge for eg membership of a society, sitting an examination, entrance to a museum, etc. **3** (*usu* **fees**) a payment for school or college education, or for a course of instruction. **4** a payment made to a football club for the transfer of one of its players. **5** *law* an estate in the form of land that is inheritable with either restricted rights (**fee tail**) or unrestricted rights (**fee simple**).

feeble *adj* **1** lacking strength; weak. **2** of a joke, an excuse, etc: lacking power, influence or effectiveness. ○ **feebly** *adv.*

feeble-minded *adj* **1** unable to make a decision. **2** stupid.

feed[1] *vb* (**fed**) **1** to give or supply food to (animals, etc). **2** to give something as food (to animals, etc). **3** to administer food (to an infant, young animal). **4** *in compounds* to administer food to someone in a specified way: *breast-feed.* **5** *intr* of animals: to eat food. **6** to supply a machine, etc with fuel or other material required for continued operation. **7** *theat* to provide (an actor, esp a comedian) with material or a cue. **8** *sport* to pass the ball to (a teammate). ➤ *n* **1** an act or session of feeding. **2** an allowance of food for animals, eg cattle or babies. **3** food for livestock, etc. **4** *colloq* a meal, esp a hearty one: *a good feed.* **5** the channel or mechanism by which a machine is supplied with fuel, etc. **6** *theat* an actor who feeds or cues another one. ○ **feeder** *n.* ◊ **feed sb up** to fatten them up with nourishing food.

feed[2] *past tense, past participle* of FEE

feedback *n* **1** responses and reactions to an inquiry or report, etc that provide guidelines for adjustment and development. **2** the process by which part of the output of a system or of a component of a living organism, is returned to the input, in order to regulate or modify subsequent output. **3** in a public-address system, etc: the partial return of the sound output to the microphone, producing a high-pitched whistle. **4** the whistling noise so produced.

feel vb (**felt**) **1** to become aware of something through the sense of touch. **2** tr & intr to have a physical or emotional sensation of something; to sense. **3** tr & intr to find out or investigate with the hands, etc. **4** tr & intr to have (an emotion). **5** tr & intr to react emotionally to something or be emotionally affected by something: Jo feels the loss very deeply. **6** intr (**feel for sb**) to have sympathy or compassion for them. **7** intr to give the impression of being (soft, hard, rough, etc) when touched. **8** intr to be or seem (well, ill, happy, etc). **9** to instinctively believe in something: She feels that this is a good idea. **10** tr & intr (also **feel like sth**) to seem to oneself to be: I feel a fool • I feel like an idiot. ➤ n **1** a sensation or impression produced by touching. **2** an impression or atmosphere created by something. **3** an act of feeling with the fingers, etc. **4** an instinct, touch or knack. ♦ **feel like sth** to have an inclination or desire for it. **feel oneself** to feel as well as normal: Katie felt herself again after a good sleep. **feel one's way** to make one's way cautiously. **feel up to sth** usu with negatives or in questions to feel fit enough for it. ◊ **feel sb up** slang to move one's hands over their body in a sexual way.

feeler n **1** a tentacle. **2** either of a pair of long slender jointed structures, sensitive to touch, on the head of certain invertebrate animals. ♦ **put out feelers** to sound out the opinion of others.

feelgood adj, colloq creating pleasant feelings of comfort, security, etc: the ultimate feelgood film.

feeling n **1** the sense of touch, a sensation or emotion. **2** emotion as distinct from reason. **3** strong emotion. **4** a belief or opinion. **5** (usu a **feeling for sth**) a natural ability for, or understanding of, an activity, etc. **6** affection. **7** mutual interactive emotion between two people, such as **bad feeling** (resentment), **good feeling** (friendliness), etc. **8** (often **feeling for sth**) an instinctive grasp or appreciation of it. **9** (**feelings**) one's attitude to something: mixed feelings. **10** (**feelings**) sensibilities: You've hurt his feelings.

feign /feɪn/ vb to pretend to have (eg an illness) or feel (an emotion), etc.

feint[1] n **1** in boxing, fencing, etc: a mock attack; a movement intended to deceive or distract one's opponent. **2** a misleading action or appearance. ➤ vb, intr to make a feint.

feint[2] adj of paper: ruled with pale horizontal lines to guide writing.

feisty /ˈfaɪstɪ/ adj (**-ier, -iest**) colloq **1** spirited. **2** irritable.

feldspar or **felspar** n, geol a rock-forming mineral found in most igneous and many metamorphic rocks. ◊ **feldspathic** or **felspathic** adj.

felicitous adj **1** of wording: elegantly apt; well-chosen. **2** pleasant; happy.

felicity n (**-ies**) **1** happiness. **2** a cause of happi-

ness. **3** elegance or aptness of wording.

feline adj **1** relating to the cat or cat family. **2** like a cat, esp in terms of stealth or elegance. ➤ n a member of the cat family.

fell[1] vb **1** to cut down (a tree). **2** to knock down someone or something.

fell[2] n (often **fells**) a hill, moor or upland tract of pasture or moorland.

fell[3] adj, old use destructive; deadly. ♦ **at** or **in one fell swoop** with a single deadly blow; in one quick operation.

fell[4] past tense of FALL

fellatio /fɛˈleɪʃɪəʊ/ n oral stimulation of the penis.

fellow n **1** a companion or equal. **2** (also colloq **fella, fellah** or **feller**) **a** a man or boy; **b** colloq a boyfriend. **3** a senior member of a college or university. **4** a postgraduate research student financed by a fellowship. **5** (**Fellow**) a member of a learned society. **6** one of a pair. ➤ adj relating to a person in the same situation as oneself, or having the same status, etc: a fellow worker.

fellowship n **1** friendly companionship. **2** commonness or similarity of interests between people, often common religious interests. **3** a society or association. **4** the status of a fellow of a college, society, etc. **5** a salary paid to a research fellow.

felon n, law a person guilty of FELONY.

felony n (**-ies**) law a serious crime. ◊ **felonious** adj.

felt[1] n a fabric formed by matting or pressing fibres, esp wool, together. ➤ vb **1** tr & intr to make into felt. **2** to cover with felt. **3** intr to become felted or matted.

felt[2] past tense, past participle of FEEL

felt pen, **felt-tip pen** or **felt tip** n a pen with a nib made of felt.

female adj **1** belonging or relating to the sex that gives birth to young, produces eggs, etc. **2** denoting the reproductive structure of a plant that contains an egg cell, such as the pistil of flowering plants. **3** belonging or relating to, or characteristic of, a woman. **4** eng of a piece of machinery, etc: having a hole or holes into which another part (the MALE adj sense 5) fits. ➤ n **1** a woman or girl. **2** a female animal or plant. ◊ **femaleness** n.

feminine adj **1** typically belonging or relating to, or characteristic of, a woman. **2** having or reflecting qualities considered typical of a woman. **3** gram in some languages: belonging or relating to the GENDER into which many nouns, including most words for animate females fall. Compare MASCULINE, NEUTER. ➤ n, gram **1** the feminine gender. **2** a word belonging to this gender. ◊ **femininity** n.

feminism n a belief or movement advocating women's rights and opportunities, particularly equal rights with men. ◊ **feminist** n.

femur /ˈfiːmə(r)/ n (**femurs** or **femora** /ˈfɛmərə/) **1** the longest bone of the human skeleton, from hip to knee. **2** the corresponding bone in the hind limb of four-limbed vertebrates.

○ **femoral** /'fɛmərəl/ adj.

fen n a wet area of lowland.

fence n **1** a barrier, eg of wood or wire, for enclosing or protecting land. **2** a barrier for a horse to jump. **3** slang someone who receives and disposes of stolen goods. **4** a guard or guide on a piece of machinery. ➤ vb **1** (also **fence sth in** or **off**) to enclose or separate with a fence, or as if with a fence. **2** intr to practise the art or sport of fencing. **3** to build fences. **4** intr, slang to be a receiver or purchaser of stolen goods. ♦ **sit on the fence** to be unable or unwilling to support either side in a dispute, etc.

fencing n **1** the art, act or sport of attack and defence with a foil, épée or sabre. **2** material used for constructing fences. **3** fences collectively.

fend vb **1** (usu **fend sth** or **sb off**) to defend oneself from (blows, questions, etc). **2** intr (esp **fend for sb**) to provide for, esp oneself.

fender n **1** a low guard fitted round a fireplace to keep coals, etc within the hearth. **2** N Am the wing or mudguard of a car. **3** a bundle of rope, tyres, etc hanging from a ship's side to protect it when docking, etc.

fenestration n, archit the arrangement of windows in a building.

feng shui /'fʌŋʃweɪ/ n the process of making the correct decisions about the location of a building or of furniture in a room, to ensure the optimum happiness for the occupants.

fennel n a strong-smelling plant, whose seeds and leaves are used in cooking.

fenugreek n a plant with strong-smelling seeds used in cooking.

feral adj of domesticated animals or cultivated plants: living or growing wild.

ferment n /'fɜːmɛnt/ **1** a substance, such as a yeast, that causes fermentation. **2** fermentation. **3** a state of agitation or excitement. ➤ vb /fə'mɛnt/ **1** intr to undergo fermentation. **2** to be, or make something be, in a state of excitement or instability.

fermentation n, chem a biochemical process in which micro-organisms break down an organic compound in the absence of oxygen.

fermium n, chem an artificially produced metallic radioactive element.

fern n a flowerless feathery-leaved plant that reproduces by spores. ○ **ferny** adj (**-ier, -iest**).

ferocious adj savagely fierce; cruel. ○ **ferociously** adv. ○ **ferocity** n.

ferret n a small, half-tame, albino type of polecat, used for driving rabbits and rats from their holes. ➤ vb (**ferreted, ferreting**) tr & intr to hunt (rabbits, etc) with a ferret. ◊ **ferret sth out 1** to drive (an animal, etc) out of a hiding place. **2** to find it out through persistent investigation.

ferric adj **1** referring or relating to iron. **2** chem denoting a compound that contains iron in its trivalent state.

ferrous adj **1** belonging or relating to iron. **2**

chem denoting a chemical compound that contains iron in its divalent state.

ferrule n **1** a metal ring or cap at the tip of a walking-stick or umbrella. **2** a cylindrical fitting, threaded internally like a screw, for joining pipes, etc together.

ferry n (**-ies**) **1** (also **ferryboat**) a boat that carries passengers and often cars across a strip of water, esp as a regular service. **2** the service thus provided. **3** the place or route where a ferryboat runs. ➤ vb (**ferries, ferried**) **1** tr & intr (sometimes **ferry across**) to transport or go by ferry. **2** to convey (passengers, goods, etc) in a vehicle: He ferried them to school each day.

fertile /'fɜːtaɪl, N Am 'fɜːtəl/ adj **1** of land, soil, etc: containing the nutrients required to support an abundant growth of crops, plants, etc. **2** producing or capable of producing babies, young or fruit. **3** of an egg or seed: capable of developing into a new individual. **4** of the mind: rich in ideas; very productive. **5** providing a wealth of possibilities. ○ **fertility** n.

fertilize or **-ise** vb **1** of a male gamete, esp a sperm cell: to fuse with (a female gamete, esp an egg cell) to form a ZYGOTE. **2** of a male animal: to inseminate or impregnate (a female animal). **3** of flowering/cone-bearing plants: to transfer (pollen) by the process of POLLINATION. **4** to supply (soil) with extra nutrients in order to increase its fertility. ○ **fertilization** n.

fertilizer or **fertiliser** n a natural or chemical substance added to soil to improve fertility.

fervent adj enthusiastic; ardent. ○ **fervently** adv.

fervid adj full of fiery passion or zeal. ○ **fervidly** adv.

fervour or (N Am) **fervor** n passionate enthusiasm; intense eagerness.

fescue n a tufted grass with bristle-like leaves, which forms much of the turf on chalk downs.

fest n, in compounds a gathering or festival for a specified activity: filmfest • thrill fest.

fester vb **1** intr of a wound: to form or discharge pus. **2** of an evil: to continue unchecked or get worse. **3** intr to rot or decay. **4** intr of resentment or anger: to become more bitter, usu over time.

festival n **1** a day or period of celebration, esp one kept traditionally. **2** relig a feast or saint's day. **3** a season or series of performances (of musical, theatrical or other cultural events).

festive adj **1** relating to a festival. **2** celebratory; joyous.

festivity n (**-ies**) **1** a lighthearted event; celebration. **2** (**festivities**) festive activities; celebrations.

festoon n **1** a decorative chain of flowers, ribbons, etc looped between two points. **2** archit a carved or moulded ornament representing this. ➤ vb to hang or decorate with festoons.

feta n a crumbly, white, ewe's- or goat's-milk cheese, orig made in Greece.

fetch vb **1** to go and get something, and bring it back. **2** to be sold for (a certain price). **3** colloq to deal someone (a blow, slap, etc). ◊ **fetch up** *colloq* to arrive; to end up.

fetching *adj, colloq* of appearance: attractive, charming.

fête or **fete** /feɪt, fɛt/ *n* an outdoor event with entertainment, competitions, stalls, etc, usu to raise money for a charity. ➤ *vb* to entertain or honour someone lavishly.

fetid or **foetid** *adj* having a strong disgusting smell.

fetish *n* **1** in some societies: an object worshipped for its perceived magical powers. **2** a procedure or ritual followed obsessively, or an object of obsessive devotion. **3** an object that is handled or visualized as an aid to sexual stimulation. ◦ **fetishism** *n*. ◦ **fetishist** *n*.

fetlock *n* the thick projection at the back of a horse's leg just above the hoof.

fetter *n* **1** (*usu* **fetters**) a chain or shackle fastened to a prisoner's ankle. Compare MANACLE. **2** (**fetters**) tiresome restrictions. ➤ *vb* **1** to put someone in fetters. **2** to restrict someone.

fettle *n* spirits; state of health.

fettuccine, **fettucine** or **fettucini** /fɛtu-'tʃiːnɪ/ *n* pasta made in long ribbons.

fetus or (*non-technical*) **foetus** /'fiːtəs/ *n* **1** the embryo of a VIVIPAROUS mammal during the later stages of development in the uterus. **2** a human embryo from the end of the eighth week after conception until birth. ◦ **fetal** or **foetal** /'fiːtəl/ *adj*.

feu /fjuː/ *n* **1** *often as adj* **a** a perpetual lease for a fixed rent: *feu-farm*; **b** a piece of land so held. **2** *Scots law* a right to the use of land, houses, etc in return for payment of **feu duty**, a fixed annual payment.

feud *n* a long-drawn-out bitter quarrel between families, individuals or clans. ➤ *vb, intr* (*often* **feud with sb**) to carry on a feud with them. ◦ **feuding** *n, adj*.

feudal *adj* relating to feudalism.

feudalism or **feudal system** *n* a system of social and political organization prevalent in W Europe in the Middle Ages, in which powerful land-owning lords granted degrees of privilege and protection to lesser subjects holding a range of positions within a rigid social hierarchy.

fever *n* **1** an abnormally high body temperature, often accompanied by shivering, thirst and headache. **2** a disease in which this is a marked symptom, eg scarlet fever, yellow fever. **3** an extreme state of agitation or excitement. ◦ **feverish** *adj*.

fever pitch *n* a state of high excitement.

few *adj* not many; a small number. ➤ *pron* (*used as a pl*) hardly any things, people, etc. ◆ **a few** a small number; some. **a good few** or **quite a few** *colloq* a fairly large number; several. **as few as** no more than (a stated number). **few and far between** *colloq* rare; scarce. **the few** the minority of discerning people.

fey /feɪ/ *adj* **1** strangely fanciful; whimsical. **2** able to foresee future events.

fez *n* (**fezzes** or **fezes**) a hat shaped like a flat-topped cone, with a tassel, worn by some Muslim men.

ff *abbrev* **1** *mus* fortissimo. **2** and the following (pages, etc).

fiancé or **fiancée** /fɪ'ɑ̃seɪ, fɪ'ɒnseɪ/ *n* respectively, a man or woman to whom one is engaged to be married.

fiasco *n* (**fiascos** or **fiascoes**) **1** a ludicrous or humiliating failure. **2** a bizarre or ludicrous happening: *What a fiasco!*

fiat /'faɪat/ *n* **1** an official command. **2** a formal authorization for some procedure.

fib *colloq, n* a trivial lie. ➤ *vb* (**fibbed, fibbing**) *intr* to tell fibs. ◦ **fibber** *n*.

fibre or (*NAm*) **fiber** *n* **1** a fine thread or thread-like cell of a natural or artificial substance, eg cellulose, nylon. **2** a material composed of fibres. **3** the indigestible parts of edible plants or seeds, that help to move food quickly through the body: *dietary fibre*. **4** strength of character; stamina: *moral fibre*.

fibreglass or (*N Am*) **fiberglass** *n* **1** a strong light plastic strengthened with glass fibres, which is used for boat-building, car bodies, etc. **2** material consisting of fine, tangled fibres of glass, used for insulation.

fibre optics or (*N Am*) **fiber optics** *sing n* the technique of using flexible strands of glass or plastic (OPTICAL FIBRES) to carry information in the form of light signals. ◦ **fibre-optic** *adj*.

fibril /'faɪbrɪl/ *n* **1** a small fibre or part of a fibre. **2** a hair on a plant's root.

fibrillate /'faɪbrɪleɪt/ *vb, intr, med* of the muscle fibres of the heart: to contract spontaneously, rapidly, and irregularly. ◦ **fibrillation** *n*.

fibroid *adj* fibrous. ➤ *n, pathol* a benign tumour, esp on the wall of the uterus.

fibrosis *n, pathol* the formation of an abnormal amount of fibrous connective tissue over or in place of normal tissue of an organ or body part.

fibrositis *n* inflammation of fibrous connective tissue, esp that sheathing the muscles of the back, causing pain and stiffness.

fibrous *adj* consisting of, containing or like fibre.

fibula *n* (**fibulae** /'fɪbjʊliː/ or **fibulas**) **1** the outer and narrower of the two bones in the lower leg, between the knee and the ankle. Compare TIBIA. **2** the corresponding bone in the hind limb of four-limbed vertebrates.

fickle *adj* changeable in affections, loyalties or intentions. ◦ **fickleness** *n*.

fiction *n* **1** literature concerning imaginary characters or events, eg a novel or story. **2** a pretence. **3** *law* a misrepresentation of the truth, accepted for convenience. ◦ **fictional** *adj*. ◦ **fictionalize** *vb*.

fictitious *adj* imagined; invented.

fiddle *n* **1** a violin, esp when used to play folk music or jazz. **2** *colloq* a dishonest arrangement; a fraud. **3** a manually delicate or tricky operation. ➤ *vb* **1** *intr* (*often* **fiddle with sth**) to play about aimlessly with it; to tinker or meddle with it. **2** *intr* (**fiddle around** or **about**) to waste time: *He kept fiddling about and got nothing done.* **3** *tr & intr* to falsify (accounts, etc); to manage or manipulate dishonestly. **4** *tr & intr* to play a violin or fiddle; to play (a tune) on one. ○ **fiddler** *n*. ♦ **as fit as a fiddle** in excellent health. **on the fiddle** *colloq* making money dishonestly. **play second fiddle to sb** to be subordinate to them.

fiddlesticks *exclam* expressing annoyance or disagreement.

fiddling *adj* unimportant; trifling.

fiddly *adj* (**-ier, -iest**) awkward to handle or do, esp if the task requires delicate finger movements.

fidelity *n* (**-ies**) **1** faithfulness; loyalty or devotion, esp to a sexual partner. **2** accuracy in reporting, describing or copying something. **3** precision in sound reproduction.

fidget *vb* (**fidgeted, fidgeting**) **1** *intr* to move about restlessly. **2** (*often* **fidget with sth**) to touch and handle it aimlessly. ➤ *n* **1** a person who fidgets. **2** (**the fidgets**) nervous restlessness. ○ **fidgety** *adj*.

fiduciary *law, n* (**-ies**) someone who holds something in trust. ➤ *adj* **1** held or given in trust. **2** relating to a trust or trustee.

fie *exclam, facetious or old use* expressing disapproval or disgust.

fief /fiːf/ *n, hist* land granted to a VASSAL by his lord, usu in return for military service.

field *n* **1** a piece of land enclosed for crop-growing or pasturing animals. **2** a piece of open grassland. **3** an area marked off as a ground for a sport, etc. **4** *in compounds* an area rich in a specified mineral, etc: *coalfield • oilfield.* **5** *in compounds* an expanse of something specified, usu from the natural world: *snowfields • poppy fields.* **6** an area of knowledge or study. **7** *physics* a region of space in which one object exerts force on another: *force field.* **8** the area included in something; the range over which a force, etc extends; the area visible to an observer at any one time: *field of vision.* **9 a** the contestants in a race, competition, etc; **b** all contestants except for the favourite. **10** a battlefield. **11** any place away from the classroom, office, etc where practical experience is gained. **12** the background to the design on a flag, coin, heraldic shield, etc. **13** *comput* a set of characters comprising a unit of information. ➤ *vb* **1** *tr & intr, sport, esp cricket* **a** of a team: to be the team whose turn it is to retrieve balls hit by the batting team; **b** *tr & intr* of a player: to retrieve the ball from the field; **c** *intr* of a player: to play in the field. **2** to put forward as (a team or player) for a match. **3** to enter someone in a competition: *Each group fielded a candidate.* **4** to deal with a succession of (inquiries, etc): *to field questions.* ♦ **lead the field** to be in the foremost or winning position. **play the field** *colloq*

to try out the range of possibilities before making a choice.

field day *n* **1** a day spent on some specific outdoor activity, such as nature study. **2** *colloq* any period of exciting activity.

fielder *n, sport, particularly cricket* a player in the field; a member of the fielding side.

field glasses *pl n* binoculars.

field hockey *n, N Am* hockey played on grass, as distinct from ice hockey.

field marshal *n, Brit* an army officer of the highest rank.

fieldmouse *n* any of various species of small mouse that live among dense vegetation.

field sports *pl n* sports carried out in the countryside, such as hunting, shooting, fishing, etc.

fieldwork *n* practical work or research done at a site away from the laboratory or place of study.

fiend *n* **1** a devil; an evil spirit. **2** *colloq* a spiteful person. **3** *colloq* an enthusiast for something specified: *sun fiend.*

fiendish *adj* **1** like a fiend. **2** devilishly cruel. **3** extremely difficult or unpleasant. ○ **fiendishly** *adv*.

fierce *adj* **1** violent and aggressive. **2** intense; strong: *fierce competition.* **3** severe; extreme: *a fierce storm.* ○ **fiercely** *adv*.

fiery *adj* (**-ier, -iest**) **1** of or like fire. **2** easily enraged: *a fiery temper.* **3** passionate; vigorous: *fiery oratory.* **4** of food: hot-tasting. ○ **fieriness** *n*.

fiesta *n* **1** esp in Spanish speaking communities: a religious festival with dancing, singing, etc. **2** any carnival, festivity or holiday.

fife *n* a small type of flute played in military bands.

fifteen *n* **1 a** the cardinal number 15; **b** the quantity that this represents, being one more than fourteen or the sum of ten and five. **2** any symbol for 15, eg *15* or *XV.* **3 a** a set or group of fifteen people or things; **b** *rugby union* a team of players. **4** (written **15**) *Brit* a film classified as suitable for people aged 15 and over. ➤ *adj* **1** totalling fifteen. **2** aged fifteen. ○ **fifteenth** *adj, n, adv*.

fifth (*often written* **5th**) *adj* **1** in counting: **a** next after fourth; **b** last of five. **2** in fifth position. **3** being one of five equal parts: *a fifth share.* ➤ *n* **1** one of five equal parts. **2** a FRACTION equal to one divided by five (usu written ⅕). **3** a person coming fifth, eg in a race or exam. **4** (**the fifth**) the fifth day of the month. **5** *mus* **a** an interval of four diatonic degrees; **b** a note at that interval from another, or a combination of two tones separated by that interval. ➤ *adv* fifthly. ○ **fifthly** *adv* used to introduce the fifth point in a list.

fifth column *n* a body of citizens prepared to co-operate with an invading enemy. ○ **fifth columnist** *n*.

fifties (*often written* **50s** or **50's**) *pl n* **1** (**one's fifties**) the period of time between one's fiftieth and sixtieth birthdays. **2** (**the fifties**) the range of temperatures between fifty and sixty degrees. **3** (**the fifties**) the period of time between the fiftieth and sixtieth years of a century: *She was born in the 50s.*

fifty *n* (*-ies*) **1 a** the cardinal number 50; **b** the quantity that this represents, being one more than forty-nine, or the product of ten and five. **2** any symbol for this, eg *50* or *L*. ➤ *adj* **1** totalling fifty. **2** aged fifty. ○ **fiftieth** *adj, n, adv.*

fifty-fifty *adj* **1** of a chance: equal either way. **2** half-and-half. ➤ *adv* divided equally between two; half-and-half.

fig *n* **1** a tropical and sub-tropical tree or shrub with a soft pear-shaped fruit full of tiny seeds. **2** its green, brown or purple fleshy fruit. ♦ **not give** or **care a fig** *colloq* not to care at all.

fight *vb* (**fought**) **1** *tr & intr* to attack or engage (an enemy, army, etc) in combat. **2** to take part in or conduct (a battle, campaign, etc). **3** *tr & intr* (*sometimes* **fight against**) to oppose (eg an enemy, a person, an illness, a cause, etc) vigorously. **4** *intr* to quarrel; to disagree, sometimes coming to blows. **5** *intr* (*often* **fight for sth** or **sb**) to struggle or campaign on their or its behalf. **6** *intr* to make (one's way) with a struggle. ➤ *n* **1** a battle; a physically violent struggle. **2** a quarrel; a dispute; a contest. **3** resistance. **4** the will or strength to resist. **5** a boxing match. **6** a campaign or crusade. ○ **fighter** *n*. ♦ **fight a losing battle** to continue trying for something even when there is little chance of succeeding. **fighting fit** *colloq* in vigorous health. ◊ **fight back** to resist an attacker; to counter an attack. **fight sth back** to try not to show (one's emotions, etc). **fight sb off** to repulse them (esp an attacker). **fight sth off** to get rid of or resist (an illness).

fighting chance *n* a chance to succeed dependent chiefly on determination.

fig leaf *n* **1** the leaf of a fig tree. **2** any device used to cover up something considered embarrassing.

figment *n* something imagined or invented.

figurative *adj* **1** metaphorical; not literal. **2** of writing, etc: full of figures of speech, esp metaphor. **3** representing a figure; representing using an emblem or symbol, etc. **4** of art: showing things as they actually look.

figure *n* **1** the form of anything in outline. **2** a symbol representing a number. **3** a number representing an amount; a cost. **4** an indistinctly seen or unidentified person. **5** a representation of the human form, esp in painting or sculpture. **6** (**figures**) arithmetical calculations. **7** a well-known person. **8** a diagram or illustration, esp in a text. **9** the shape of a person's body. **10** a geometrical shape. **11** *mus* a short distinctive series of notes in music. ➤ *vb* **1** *intr* (*usu* **figure in sth**) to play a part in it (eg a story, incident, etc). **2** *N Am* to think; to reckon. **3** to imagine. **4** *intr, colloq* to be probable or predictable; to make sense: *That figures!* ◊ **figure on sth** to count on, plan or expect it. **figure sb** or **sth**

out to come to understand them or it.

figurehead *n* **1** a leader in name only, without real power. **2** a carved wooden figure fixed to a ship's prow.

figure of speech *n* a device such as a META-PHOR, SIMILE, etc that enlivens language.

figure skating *n* skating where prescribed patterns are performed on the ice. ○ **figure skater** *n.*

figurine *n* a small carved or moulded figure, usu representing a human form.

filament *n* **1** a fine thread or fibre. **2** *elec* in electrical equipment: a fine wire with a high resistance that emits heat and light when an electric current is passed through it. **3** *bot* the stalk of a stamen, which bears the anther.

filbert *n* **1** the nut of the cultivated hazel. **2** (*also* **filbert tree**) the tree bearing the nut.

filch *vb* to steal something small or trivial.

file[1] *n* **1** a folder or box in which to keep loose papers. **2** a collection of papers so kept, esp dealing with a particular subject. **3** *comput* an organized collection of data that is stored in the memory of a computer as a single named unit. **4** a line of people or things positioned or moving one behind the other: *single file*. **5** *chess* any of the eight lines of squares extending across the chessboard from player to player. Compare RANK[1] (noun sense 8). ➤ *vb* **1** (*often* **file sth away**) to put (papers, etc) into a file. **2** (*often* **file for sth**) to make a formal application to a law court on (a specified matter): *to file a complaint • to file for divorce.* **3** to place (a document) on official or public record. **4** *intr* to march or move along one behind the other. **5** of a reporter: to submit (a story) to a newspaper. ♦ **on file** retained in a file (*noun* sense 1 or 3 above) for reference; on record.

file[2] *n* **1** a steel hand tool with a rough surface, used to smooth or rub away wood, metal, etc. **2** a small object of metal or emery board used for smoothing or shaping fingernails. ➤ *vb* to smooth or shape (a surface) using a file.

filename *n, comput* any name or reference used to specify a file stored in a computer.

filial *adj* belonging or relating to, or resembling, a son or daughter: *filial duties.*

filibuster *n* **a** the practice of making long speeches to delay the passing of laws; **b** a member of a law-making assembly who does this. ➤ *vb, intr* to obstruct legislation by making long speeches.

filigree *n* delicate work in gold or silver wire, twisted into convoluted forms and soldered together.

filing cabinet *n* a set of drawers, usu metal, for holding collections of papers and documents.

filings *pl n* particles rubbed off with a file.

fill *vb* **1** (*also* **fill sth up**) to make it full. **2** *intr* (*also* **fill up**) to become full. **3** to take up all the space in something. **4** to satisfy (a need); to perform (a role) satisfactorily. **5** (*sometimes* **fill up**) to occupy (time). **6** (*also* **fill sth in** or **up**) to put material into (a hole, cavity, etc) to level the surface. **7** to appoint someone to (a position or post of employment). **8 a** to take up (a position or post of employment); **b** to work in (a job), sometimes temporarily. ➤ *n* **1** anything used to fill something. **2** *sometimes in compounds* material used to fill a space to a required level: *rock-fill.* ○ **filler** *n*. ◆ **eat one's fill** to consume enough to satisfy. **to have had one's fill of sth** or **sb** to have reached the point of being able to tolerate no more of it or them. ◊ **fill sb in** to inform them fully; to brief them. **fill sth in 1** to write information as required on to (a form, etc). **2** to complete a drawing, etc, esp by shading. **fill in for sb** to take over their work temporarily. **fill out** to put on weight and become fatter. **fill sth out 1** to enlarge it satisfactorily. **2** *chiefly N Am* to fill in (a form, etc). **fill sth up** to fill in (a form, etc).

fillet *n* **1 a** a piece of meat without bone, taken as an undercut of the SIRLOIN, or the fleshy part of the thigh: *pork fillet*; **b** (*in full* **fillet steak**) the most highly valued cut of beef, cut from the lowest part of the LOIN. **2** a thin narrow strip of wood, metal or other material. **3** *archit* a narrow flat band, often between mouldings. ➤ *vb* (**filleted, filleting**) **a** to cut fillets from (meat or fish); **b** to remove the bones from (a fish).

filling *n* **1** *dentistry* a specially prepared substance, that is inserted into a cavity that has been drilled in a decaying tooth. **2** food put inside a pie, sandwich, etc. ➤ *adj* of food, a meal, etc: substantial and satisfying.

filling station *n* a place where motorists can buy petrol and other supplies.

fillip *n* **1** something that has a stimulating or brightening effect. **2** a movement of a finger when it is engaged under the thumb and then suddenly released away from the hand.

filly *n* (*-ies*) a young female horse or pony.

film *n* **1** a strip of thin flexible plastic, etc, coated so as to be light-sensitive and exposed inside a camera to produce still or moving pictures. **2** a series of images recorded and edited to tell a story, etc. **3** a fine skin, membrane or coating over something. **4** *sometimes in compounds* a thin sheet of plastic used for wrapping: *clingfilm.* ➤ *vb tr & intr* to record any series of images using a TV camera, video camera, etc.

filmy *adj* (*-ier, -iest*) of a fabric, etc: thin, light and transparent.

filo or **phyllo** /ˈfiːloʊ/ *n* (*in full* **filo pastry**) a type of Greek flaky pastry made in thin sheets.

filter *n* **1** a porous substance that allows liquid, gas, smoke, etc through, but traps solid matter, impurities, etc. **2** a device containing this. **3** a fibrous pad at the unlit end of a cigarette that traps some of the smoke's impurities. **4** a transparent tinted disc used to reduce the strength of certain colour frequencies in the light entering a camera or emitted by a lamp. **5** *elec, radio* a device for suppressing the waves of un-

wanted frequencies. **6** *Brit* a traffic signal at traffic lights that allows vehicles going in some directions to proceed while others are stopped. ➤ *vb* **1** *tr & intr* to pass something through a filter, often to remove impurities, particles, etc. **2** (*usu* **filter sth out**) to remove it (eg impurities from liquids, gases, etc) by filtering. **3** *intr* (*usu* **filter through** or **out**) of news: to leak out, often gradually.

filter paper *n* a porous paper through which a liquid can be passed in order to separate out any solid particles suspended in it.

filth *n* **1** repulsive dirt. **2** anything perceived as physically or morally obscene.

filthy *adj* (*-ier, -iest*) **1** extremely dirty. **2** obscenely vulgar: *filthy language.* **3** *colloq* or *dialect* extremely unpleasant: *filthy weather.* ➤ *vb* to make filthy. ➤ *adv, colloq* used for emphasis, esp showing disapproval: *filthy rich.* ○ **filthiness** *n*.

filtrate *chem, n* the clear liquid obtained after filtration. ➤ *vb, tr & intr* to filter. ○ **filtration** *n*.

fin *n* **1** a thin wing-like projection on a fish's body for propelling it through the water, balancing, steering, etc. **2** anything that resembles a fin in appearance or function, eg the vertical projection in the tail of an aircraft. ○ **finned** *adj*.

finagle /fɪˈneɪɡl/ *vb* **1** *tr & intr* to obtain by guile or swindling. **2** (*often* **finagle sb out of sth**) to cheat (them out of it).

final *adj* **1** occurring at the end; last in a series. **2** completed; finished. **3** of a decision, etc: definite; not to be altered. ➤ *n* **1 a** the last part of a competition at which the winner is decided; **b** (**finals**) the last round or group of contests resulting in a winner. **2** (**finals**) the examinations held at the end of a degree course, etc. ○ **finality** *n*. ○ **finally** *adv*.

finale /fɪˈnɑːlɪ/ *n* **1** the grand conclusion to a show, etc. **2** the last or closing movement of a symphony or other piece of music.

finalist *n* someone who reaches the final round in a competition.

finalize or **-ise** *vb* **1** to complete (an agreement or transaction). **2** to arrive at the final form of something.

finance *n* **1** money affairs and the management of them. **2** the money or funds needed or used to pay for something. **3** (**finances**) a person's financial state. ➤ *vb* to provide funds for something. ○ **financial** *adj*.

financier *n* someone engaged in large financial transactions.

finch *n* a small songbird, eg a canary, chaffinch, etc, with a short conical beak.

find *vb* (**found**) **1** to discover through search, enquiry, mental effort or chance. **2** to seek out and provide something. **3** to realize or discover something. **4** to experience something as being (easy, difficult, etc): *He finds it hard to express himself.* **5** to consider; to think. **6** to get or experience: *Many people find pleasure in reading.* **7** to become aware of something or someone: *The police found her beside him.* **8** to succeed in getting (time, courage, money, etc for something). **9** to see or come across. **10** to reach: *He has yet to find his best form.* **11** *tr & intr, law* of a jury or court, etc: to decide on and deliver a specified verdict (about an accused person): *They found her innocent.* ➤ *n* something or someone that is found; an important discovery. ◆ **find one's feet** to establish oneself confidently in a new situation. ◇ **find out about sth** to discover or get information about it. **find sb out** to discover the truth about them.

finder *n* **1** someone who finds something. **2** *astrol* a small telescope attached to a larger one for finding the required object and setting it in the centre of the field.

finding *n* **1** *law* a decision or verdict reached as the result of a judicial inquiry. **2** (*usu* **findings**) conclusions reached as the result of some research or investigation.

fine[1] *adj* **1** of high quality; excellent. **2** beautiful; handsome. **3** *facetious* grand; superior: *her fine relations.* **4** of weather: bright; not rainy. **5** well; healthy. **6** quite satisfactory: *That's fine by me.* **7** pure; refined. **8** thin; delicate. **9** close-set in texture or arrangement. **10** consisting of tiny particles. **11** intricately detailed: *fine embroidery.* **12** slight; subtle: *fine adjustments.* ➤ *adv* **1** *colloq* satisfactorily. **2** finely; into fine pieces. ○ **finely** *adv.* ○ **fineness** *n.* ◆ **cut or run it fine** *colloq* to leave barely enough time for something.

fine[2] *n* an amount of money to be paid as a penalty for breaking a regulation or law. ➤ *vb* to impose a fine on someone.

fine art *n* **1** art produced for its aesthetic value. **2** (*usu* **fine arts**) painting, drawing, sculpture and architecture.

finery *n* splendour; very ornate and showy clothes, jewellery, etc.

finespun *adj* delicate; over-subtle.

finesse /fiˈnɛs/ *n* **1** skilful elegance or expertise. **2** tact and poise in handling situations. **3** *cards* an attempt by a player holding a high card to win a trick with a lower one. ➤ *vb* to attempt to win a trick by finesse.

fine-tooth comb or fine-toothed comb *n* a comb with narrow close-set teeth. ◆ **go over or through sth with a fine-tooth comb** to search or examine it very thoroughly.

fine-tune *vb* to make slight adjustments to something to obtain optimum performance.

finger *n* **1** **a** one of the five jointed extremities of the hand; **b** any of the four of these other than the thumb; **c** *in compounds*: *fingerprint.* **2** the part of a glove that fits over a finger. **3** anything resembling or similar to a finger in shape. **4** a measure or quantity of alcoholic spirits in a glass, filling it to a depth which is equal to the width of a finger. ➤ *adj* relating to or suitable for fingers *finger buffet.* ➤ *vb* **1** to touch or feel something with the fingers, often affectionately or lovingly. **2** *mus* to indicate (on a part or composition) the choice and configuration

of fingers to be used for a piece of music. **3** *slang* to identify (a criminal) to the police, etc. **4** *colloq* to use the Internet or another network to obtain information about (another user). ◆ **get one's fingers burnt** *colloq* to suffer for one's over-boldness or mistakes. **have a finger in every pie** *colloq* to have an interest, or be involved, in many different things. **point the finger at sb** *colloq* to blame or accuse them. **slip through sb's fingers** to manage to escape from them. **wrap or twist sb round one's little finger** *colloq* to be able to get what one wants from them.

fingerboard *n* the part of a violin, guitar, etc against which the strings are pressed by the fingers.

fingering *n* **1** the correct positioning of the fingers for playing a particular musical instrument or piece of music. **2** the written or printed notation indicating this.

fingernail *n* the nail at the tip of one's finger.

fingerprint *n* **1** the inked impression made by the pattern of ridges on the surface of the ends of the fingers. **2** any accurate and unique identifying feature, esp that produced by analysis of a sample of a person's DNA, using **DNA fingerprinting** or **genetic fingerprinting**. ➤ *vb* to make an impression of the fingerprints of (someone).

fingertip *n* the end of one's finger. ◆ **have sth at one's fingertips** to know a subject thoroughly and have information readily available.

finicky or finickety *adj* **1** too concerned with detail. **2** of a task: intricate; tricky. **3** fussy.

finish *vb* (*often* **finish off** or **up**) **1** *tr & intr* to bring something to an end, or come to an end; to reach a natural conclusion. **2** to complete or perfect something. **3** to use, eat, drink, etc the last of something. **4** *intr* to reach or end up in a certain position or situation. **5** *intr* (*often* **finish with sb**) to end a relationship with them. **6** *intr* (**finish with sb or sth**) to stop dealing with or needing them or it. **7** to give a particular treatment to the surface of (cloth, wood, etc). ➤ *n* **1** the last stage; the end. **2** the last part of a race, etc. **3** perfecting touches put to a product. **4** the surface texture given to cloth, wood, etc. ◇ **finish sb or sth off 1** *colloq* to exhaust them emotionally or physically. **2** *colloq* to complete their defeat or killing.

finishing-school *n* a private school where girls are taught social skills and graces.

finishing touch *n* (*also* **finishing touches**) a last minor improvement or detail that makes something perfect.

finite *adj* **1** having an end or limit. **2** *maths* having a fixed, countable number of elements. **3** *gram* of a verb: being in a form that reflects person, number, tense, etc. Compare INFINITIVE.

fiord see FJORD

fir *n* **1** a coniferous evergreen tree, with leathery needle-like leaves. **2** any of various related trees, eg the Douglas fir. **3** the wood of any of these trees.

fire *n* **1** flames coming from something that is burning. **2** an occurrence of destructive burning of something: *a forest fire*. **3** mainly in homes: a mass of burning wood, coal or other fuel, usu in a grate, etc, used for warmth or cooking. **4** a gas or electric heater. **5** the discharge of firearms. **6** the launching of a missile. **7** heat and light produced by something burning or some other source. **8** enthusiasm; passion. **9** fever; a burning sensation from inflammation, etc. **10** sparkle; brilliance (eg of a gem). ➢ *vb* **1** *tr & intr* to discharge (a gun); to send off (a bullet or other missile) from a gun, bow, etc. **2** to launch (a rocket, missile, etc). **3** to detonate (an explosive). **4** of a gun, missile, etc: to be discharged, launched, etc: *The gun fired*. **5** to direct (eg questions) in quick succession at someone. **6** *colloq* to dismiss someone from employment. **7** *intr* of a vehicle engine, boiler, etc: to start working when a spark causes the fuel to burn: *The motor fired*. **8** to put fuel into (a furnace, etc). **9** (*also* **fire sb up**) to inspire or stimulate (someone). **10** *pottery* to bake (pottery, bricks, etc) in a kiln, usu at a very high temperature. ➢ *exclam* **1** a cry, warning others of a fire. **2** the order to start firing weapons, etc. ◆ **fire away** *colloq* an expression inviting someone to start saying what they have to say, esp to begin asking questions. **play with fire** *colloq* to take risks. **set fire to sth** or **set sth on fire** to make it burn. **under fire 1** being shot at. **2** being criticized or blamed.

firearm *n* (*often* **firearms**) a gun carried and used by an individual.

fireball *n* **1** a mass of hot gases at the centre of a nuclear explosion. **2** *colloq* a lively energetic person.

firebomb *n* an incendiary bomb. ➢ *vb* to attack or destroy something with firebombs.

firebrand *n* **1** a piece of burning wood. **2** someone who stirs up unrest.

fire brigade *n*, *chiefly Brit* an organized team of people trained and employed to prevent and extinguish fires. *N Am equivalent* **fire department**.

firecracker *n* a small firework that bangs repeatedly.

firedamp *n* an explosive mixture of methane gas and air, formed in coalmines by the decomposition of coal.

firedog *n* an ANDIRON.

fire door *n* **1** a fire-resistant door to prevent the spread of fire in a building. **2** a door leading out of a building which can be easily opened from the inside, used as an emergency exit.

fire-eater *n* a performer who pretends to swallow fire from flaming torches.

fire engine *n* a vehicle which carries firefighters and firefighting equipment to the scene of a fire.

fire escape *n* an external metal staircase by which people can escape from a burning building.

fire extinguisher *n* a portable device containing water, liquid carbon dioxide under pressure, foam, etc, for spraying on to a fire to put it out.

firefighter *n* a person who is trained to put out large fires and rescue those endangered by them. ○ **firefighting** *n*, *adj*.

firefly *n* (*-ies*) a small, winged, nocturnal beetle that emits light in a series of brief flashes.

fireguard *n* a metal or wire-mesh screen for putting round an open fire to protect against sparks or falling coal, logs, etc.

fire irons *pl n* a set of tools for looking after a coal or log fire, usu including a poker, tongs, brush and shovel.

firelighter *n* a block of flammable material placed underneath the fuel to help light a fire.

fireman *n* **1** a male member of a FIRE BRIGADE, officially called a FIREFIGHTER. **2** on steam trains or steamboats: a person who stokes the fire or furnace.

fireplace *n* mainly in homes: a recess for a fire or a tiled, marble, etc structure surrounding it.

firepower *n* the amount and effectiveness of the firearms possessed by a person, military unit, etc.

fire-raiser *n* someone who deliberately sets fire to buildings, etc. ○ **fire-raising** *n*.

firewall *n* **1** a fire-resistant wall in a building. **2** *comput* an item of software that protects a network against unauthorized users.

firewood *n* wood for burning as fuel.

firework *n* **1** a device that, when lit, produces coloured sparks, flares, etc, often with accompanying loud bangs. **2** (**fireworks** or **firework display**) a show at which such devices are let off for entertainment, usu to mark a special event. **3** (**fireworks**) *colloq* a show of anger or bad temper.

firing line *n* **1** the position from which gunfire, etc is delivered, esp the front line of battle. **2** the position at which criticisms, complaints, etc are directed.

firing squad *n* a detachment of soldiers with the job of shooting a condemned person.

firkin *n* **1** *brewing* a measure equal to 9 gallons (c. 40 litres). **2** a small container with a capacity equal to quarter of a barrel, varying in amount depending on the commodity.

firm¹ *adj* **1** strong; compact; steady. **2** solid; not soft or yielding. **3** definite: *a firm offer*. **4** of prices, markets, etc: steady or stable, with a slight upward trend. **5** determined. **6** of a mouth or chin: suggesting determination. ➢ *adv* in a determined and unyielding manner. ➢ *vb* to make something firm or secure. ○ **firmly** *adv*. ○ **firmness** *n*. ◊ **firm up** of prices, markets, etc: to become more stable, usu with a slight upward trend: *Prices were firming up*.

firm² *n* an organization or individual engaged in economic activity with the aim of producing goods or services for sale to others.

firmament *n*, *literary*, *old use* the sky; heaven.

firmware *n*, *comput* a software program which cannot be altered and is held in a computer's read-only memory, eg the operating system.

first (often written **1st**) *adj* **1** in counting: before all others; before the second and following ones. **2** earliest in time or order. **3** the most important: *first prize*. **4** basic: *first principles*. **5** *mus* **a** having the higher part: *the first violins*; **b** being the principal player: *the first clarinet*. ➤ *adv* **1** before anything or anyone else. **2** foremost: *Ted got in feet first*. **3** before doing anything else: *First make sure of the facts*. **4** for the first time: *since he first saw him*. **5** preferably; rather: *I'd die first*. **6** firstly. ➤ *n* **1** the starting object of a series of objects. **2** a person or thing coming first, eg in a race or exam. **3** *colloq* a first occurrence of something; something never done before: *That's a first for me!* **4** the beginning: *from first to last*. **5** (**the first**) the first day of the month. **6** (also **first gear**) the first or lowest forward gear in a gearbox. **7** *educ, chiefly Brit* first-class honours in a university degree. ○ **firstly** *adv* **1** used to introduce the first point in a list of things. **2** in the first place; to begin with. ♦ **at first** at the start of something; early on in the course of something. **at first hand** directly from the original source. **in the first place** from the start; to begin with. **not have the first idea** or **not know the first thing about sth** *colloq* to be completely ignorant about it.

first-born *literary or old use, n* the eldest child in a family. ➤ *adj* eldest.

first-class *adj* **1** referring to the best or highest grade in terms of value, performance or quality. **2** excellent. **3** referring to the most comfortable grade of accommodation in a train, plane, etc: *He took a first-class ticket from Edinburgh to Aberdeen*. **4** *chiefly Brit* the category of mail most speedily delivered. ➤ *n* (**first class**) first-class mail, transport, etc. ➤ *adv* (**first class**) by first-class mail, transport, etc.

first cousin see COUSIN

first-degree *adj* **1** *med* denoting the least severe type of burn in which only the outer layer of the skin is damaged. **2** *N Am law* denoting the most serious of the two levels of murder, ie unlawful killing with intent and premeditation.

first floor *n* **1** the floor directly above the ground floor. **2** *US* the ground floor.

first-hand *adj, adv* direct; from the original source.

first lieutenant *n* in the US army, air force and marine corps: an officer of the rank directly below captain.

first name *n* a personal name as distinct from a family name or surname.

first person see under PERSON

first-rate *adj* **1** being of the highest quality, as opposed to SECOND-RATE, etc. **2** excellent; fine.

firth *n esp in Scotland: a river estuary or an inlet.

fiscal *adj* **1** of or relating to government finances or revenue. **2** of or relating to financial matters generally. ➤ *n, Scot* a PROCURATOR FISCAL. ○ **fiscally** *adv*.

fish *n* (**fish** or **fishes**) **1** a cold-blooded aquatic vertebrate that breathes by means of gills, has a body covered with scales and swims using fins. **2** *in compounds* any of various water-inhabiting creatures: *shellfish • jellyfish*. **3** the flesh of fish used as food. ➤ *vb* **1** *intr* to catch or try to catch fish. **2** to catch or try to catch fish in (a river, lake, etc). **3** *intr* to search or grope: *Roy fished in his bag for a pen*. **4** *intr* to seek information, compliments, etc by indirect means. ♦ **a fish out of water** someone in an unaccustomed, unsuitable situation which makes them ill at ease. **have other fish to fry** *colloq* to have other, more important, things to do.

fisherman *n* a person who fishes as a job or hobby.

fishery *n* (**-ies**) **1** an area of water where fishing takes place, particularly sea waters. **2** the business or industry of catching, processing and selling fish.

fish finger *n* an oblong piece of filleted or minced fish coated in breadcrumbs.

fishing *n* the sport or business of catching fish.

fishmonger *n* a retailer of fish.

fishnet *n* a net for catching fish. ➤ *adj* of clothes: having an open mesh, like netting: *fishnet tights*.

fish slice *n* a kitchen utensil with a flat slotted head, for lifting and turning food in a frying pan, etc.

fishwife *n, derog* a loud-voiced, coarse woman.

fishy *adj* (**-ier, -iest**) **1** relating to fish, like or consisting of fish. **2** *colloq* dubious; questionable.

fissile *adj* **1** *geol* of certain rocks, eg shale: tending to split or capable of being split. **2** *nuclear physics* capable of undergoing nuclear fission.

fission *n* **1** a splitting or division into pieces. **2** *biol* the division of a cell or a single-celled organism into two or more new cells or organisms as a means of asexual reproduction. **3** *nuclear physics* see NUCLEAR FISSION. ○ **fissionable** *adj*.

fissure *n, geol* a long narrow crack or fracture esp in a body of rock, the Earth's surface or a volcano.

fist *n* a tightly closed hand with the fingers and thumb doubled back into the palm. ○ **fistful** *n*.

fisticuffs *pl n, humorous* fighting with fists.

fistula *n* (**fistulas** or **fistulae** /ˈfɪstjʊliː/) *pathol* an abnormal connection between two internal organs or body cavities.

fit¹ *vb* (**fitted** or (*N Am*) **fit**, **fitting**) **1** *tr & intr* to be the right shape or size for something or someone. **2** *intr* (*usu* **fit in** or **into sth**) to be small or few enough to be contained in it. **3** to be suitable or appropriate for something. **4** *tr & intr* to be consistent or compatible with something. **5** to install or put something new in place. **6** to equip. **7** *tr & intr* (*also* **fit together** or **fit sth together**) to join together to form a whole. **8** to make or be suitable. **9** to try clothes on someone to see where adjustment is needed. ➤ *n* the way something fits according to its shape or size: *a tight fit.* ➤ *adj* (**fitter, fittest**) **1 a** healthy; feeling good; **b** healthy, esp because of exercise. **2** about to do something, or apparently so: *Gretta looked fit to drop.* ➤ *adv* enough to do something: *He was laughing fit to burst.* ○ **fitly** *adv.* ○ **fitness** *n.* ♦ **fit for sth** suited to it; good enough for it. **fit like a glove** to fit perfectly. **fit the bill** to be perfectly suited to something; to be just right. **see** or **think fit** to choose to do something. ◊ **fit in 1** of someone in a social situation: to behave in a suitable or accepted way. **2** to be appropriate or to conform to certain arrangements. **fit sb** or **sth in** to find time to deal with them or it. **fit sth out** to furnish or equip it with all necessary things for its particular purpose: *fit out the ship.* **fit sb up** *colloq* to incriminate them.

fit² *n* **1** a sudden involuntary attack of convulsions, coughing, hysterics, etc. **2** a burst, spell or bout: *a fit of giggles.* ♦ **by** or **in fits and starts** in irregular spells. **have** or **throw a fit** to become very angry. **in fits** *colloq* laughing uncontrollably.

fitful *adj* irregular, spasmodic or intermittent. ○ **fitfully** *adv.*

fitment *n* a piece of equipment or furniture which is fixed to a wall, floor, etc.

fitted *adj* **1** made to fit closely: *fitted sheets.* **2** of a carpet: covering the floor entirely. **3** fixed; built-in: *fitted cupboards.* **4** of a kitchen, etc: with built-in cupboards, appliances, etc, usu of matching style.

fitter *n* a person who installs, adjusts or repairs machinery, equipment, etc.

fitting *adj* suitable; appropriate. ➤ *n* **1** an accessory or part: *a light fitting.* **2** (**fittings**) fitted furniture or equipment. **3** an act or an occasion of trying on a specially made piece of clothing, to see where adjustment is necessary. ○ **fittingly** *adv.*

five *n* **1 a** the cardinal number 5; **b** the quantity that this represents, being one more than four. **2** any symbol for this number, eg *5* or *V.* **3** the fifth hour after midnight or midday: *The meeting starts at five* • *5 o'clock* • *5am.* **4** a set or group of five people or things. ➤ *adj* **1** totalling five. **2** aged five.

fivefold *adj* **1** equal to five times as much or many. **2** divided into, or consisting of, five parts. ➤ *adv* by five times as much.

fiver *n,* *colloq* **a** *Brit* a five-pound note; **b** *N Am* a five-dollar bill.

fix *vb* **1** to attach or place something firmly. **2** to mend or repair something. **3** to direct; to concentrate: *Paul fixed his eyes on her.* **4** to arrange or agree (a time, etc). **5** *colloq* to arrange (the result of a race, trial, etc) dishonestly. **6** *colloq* to bribe or threaten someone into agreement. **7** *colloq* to thwart, punish or kill someone. **8** *photog* to make (the image in a photograph) permanent by the use of chemicals which dissolve unexposed silver halides. **9** *colloq* to prepare (a meal, etc): *I'll fix breakfast.* ➤ *n* **1** *colloq*

a situation which is difficult to escape from; a predicament. **2** *slang* **a** an act of injecting a narcotic drug, etc; **b** the quantity injected or to be injected in this way. **3** a calculation of the position of a ship, etc, by radar, etc. ◊ **fix sth up 1** to arrange a meeting, etc. **2** to get a place ready for some purpose. **3** to set it up, esp temporarily. **fix sb up (with sth)** to provide them with what is needed.

fixation *n* **1** (often abnormal) attachment, preoccupation or obsession. **2** *psychol* a strong attachment of a person to another person, an object or a particular means of gratification during childhood. **3** *chem* the conversion of a chemical substance into a form that does not evaporate, ie a non-volatile or solid form. **4** *psychol* inability to change a particular way of thinking or acting, which has become habitual as a result of repeated reinforcement or frustration. ○ **fixated** *adj.*

fixative *n* **1** a liquid sprayed on a drawing, painting or photograph to preserve and protect it. **2** a liquid used to hold eg dentures in place. **3** a substance added to perfume to stop it evaporating.

fixed *adj* **1** fastened; immovable. **2** unvarying; set or established: *fixed ideas.* **3** of a gaze or expression: steady; concentrated. **4** of a point: stationary. **5** permanent: *a fixed address.* ○ **fixedly** /ˈfɪksɪdlɪ/ *adv.*

fixer *n* **1** *photog* a chemical solution that FIXes photographic images. **2** *slang* a person who arranges things, esp illegally.

fixity *n* the quality of being fixed, unchanging, unmoving or immovable.

fixture *n* **1** a permanently fixed piece of furniture or equipment: *Fixtures and fittings are included in the house price.* **2 a** a match, horse race or other event in a sports calendar; **b** the date for such an event. **3** someone or something permanently established in a place or position.

fizz *vb, intr* **1** of a liquid: to give off bubbles of carbon dioxide with a hissing sound. **2** to hiss. ➤ *n* **1** a hiss or spluttering sound; fizziness. **2** vivacity; high spirits. **3** the bubbly quality of a drink. **4** any effervescent drink. ○ **fizziness** *n.* ○ **fizzy** *adj* (**-ier, -iest**).

fizzle *vb, intr* **1** to make a faint hiss. **2** (*usu* **fizzle out**) to come to nothing, esp after an enthusiastic start. ➤ *n* a faint hissing sound.

fjord or **fiord** /ˈfiːɔːd/ *n* a long narrow steep-sided inlet of the sea in a mountainous coast, formed by the flooding of a previously glaciated valley.

flab *n, colloq* excess flesh or fat on the body.

flabbergast *vb, colloq* to amaze.

flabby *adj* (**-ier, -iest**) *derog* **1 a** of flesh: sagging, not firm; **b** of a person: having excess or sagging flesh. **2** lacking vigour; feeble. ○ **flabbiness** *n.*

flaccid /ˈflasɪd, ˈflaksɪd/ *adj* limp and soft. ○ **flaccidity** *n.*

flag¹ *n* **1** a piece of cloth with a distinctive design, flown from a pole to represent a country, political party, etc, or used for signalling. **2** national identity represented by a flag. **3** any kind of marker used to indicate and draw special attention to something, eg a code placed at a particular position in a computer program, a paper marker pinned onto a map, etc. ➢ *vb* (*flagged, flagging*) to mark something with a flag, tag or symbol. ♦ **fly the flag** or **keep the flag flying** to maintain a show of support for or fight for something. ◊ **flag sb** or **sth down** to signal, usu with a hand, to a vehicle or driver to stop.

flag[2] *vb* (*flagged, flagging*) *intr* to grow weak or tired after a period of intense work or activity.

flag[3] *n* **1** (*also* **flagstone**) a large flat stone for paving. **2** a flat slab of any fine-grained rock which can be split into flagstones.

flagellate *vb* /ˈflædʒəˈleɪt/ to whip someone or oneself, for the purposes either of religious penance or for sexual stimulation. ➢ *adj* /ˈflædʒələt/ **1** *biol* having or relating to a flagellum or flagella. **2** whip-like. ➢ *n* a single-celled protozoan animal with one or more flagella.

flagellation *n* an act of whipping, for religious or sexual purposes.

flagellum /fləˈdʒɛləm/ *n* (*flagella* /-lə/) **1** *biol* a long whip-like structure that projects from the cell surface of sperm, certain bacteria, etc, used for propulsion. **2** *bot* a long thin runner or creeping shoot.

flageolet[1] /ˈflædʒoʊˈlɛt, -ˈleɪ/ *n* a small pale green kidney bean.

flageolet[2] /ˈflædʒoʊˈlɛt, -ˈleɪ/ *n* a high-pitched woodwind instrument similar to the recorder.

flagon *n* a large bottle or jug with a narrow neck, usu with a spout and handle.

flagpole or **flagstaff** *n* a pole from which a flag is flown.

flagrant *adj* of something or someone bad: undisguised; blatant: *a flagrant lie.* ◦ **flagrancy** *n.* ◦ **flagrantly** *adj.*

flagship *n* **1** the ship that carries and flies the flag of the fleet commander. **2** the leading ship in a shipping line. **3** a commercial company's leading product, model, etc.

flag-waving *n* an excessive demonstration of patriotic feeling.

flail *n* a threshing tool consisting of a long handle with a free-swinging wooden or metal bar attached to the end. ➢ *vb* to beat with or as if with a flail.

flair *n* **1** (*often* **flair for sth**) a natural ability or talent for something: *a flair for maths.* **2** stylishness; elegance: *She dresses with flair.*

flak *n* **1** anti-aircraft fire. **2** *colloq* unfriendly or adverse criticism.

flake *n*, *often in compounds* **1** a small flat particle which has broken away or is breaking away from a larger object: *flakes of plaster.* **2** a small piece or particle of: *snowflake* • *cornflake.* ➢ *vb* **1** *intr* to come off in flakes. **2** to break (eg cooked fish) into flakes. ◊ **flake out** *colloq* to collapse or fall asleep from exhaustion.

flaky *adj* (*-ier, -iest*) **1** made of flakes or tending to form flakes. **2** *chiefly US colloq* crazy; eccentric.

flambé /ˈflɒmbeɪ/ *adj* of food: soaked in a spirit, usu brandy, and set alight before serving. ➢ *vb* (*flambéed, flambéing*) to serve (food) in this way.

flamboyant *adj* **1** of a person or behaviour: colourful, exuberant, and showy. **2** of clothing or colouring: bright, bold and striking. ◦ **flamboyance** *n.*

flame *n* **1 a** a hot luminous flickering tongue shape of burning gases coming from something that is on fire; **b** (*often* **flames**) a mass of these: *The car burst into flames* • *to go up in flames.* **2** a strong passion or affection: *the flame of love.* **3** *comput, colloq* an abusive e-mail or message on a message board. ➢ *vb* **1** *intr* to burn with flames. **2** *intr* to shine brightly. **3** *intr* to explode with anger. **4** *intr* to get red and hot: *Her cheeks flamed with anger.* **5** *comput, colloq* to send an abusive e-mail or message to.

flamenco *n* **1** a rhythmical emotionally stirring type of Spanish Gypsy music, usu played on the guitar. **2** the dance performed to it.

flame-thrower *n* a device that discharges a stream of burning liquid, used as a weapon in war.

flaming *adj* **1** blazing. **2** bright; glowing, particularly a brilliant red. **3** *colloq* very angry; violent. **4** *colloq* damned: *That flaming dog!*

flamingo *n* (*flamingos* or *flamingoes*) a large wading bird with white or pinkish plumage, a long neck and long legs, webbed feet, and a broad down-curving bill.

flammable *adj* liable to catch fire. ◦ **flammability** *n.*

flammable, inflammable These mean the same thing; **inflammable** is not the opposite of **flammable**, it is simply a version of it preferred in everyday, non-technical contexts.

flan *n* an open pastry or sponge case with a savoury or fruit filling.

flange *n* a broad flat projecting rim, eg round a wheel, added for strength or for connecting with another object or part.

flank *n* **1 a** the side of an animal, between the ribs and hip; **b** the corresponding part of the human body. **2** a cut of beef from the flank. **3** the side of anything, eg a mountain, building, etc. **4** of a body of things, esp of troops in formation: the left or right extremities of that formation. ➢ *vb* **1 a** to be on the edge of (an object, a body of things, etc); **b** to move around the sides of a body of things. **2** *mil* **a** to guard on or beside the flank of a formation; **b** to move into a position in the flanks of a formation.

flannel *n* **1** soft woollen cloth with a slight nap used to make clothes. **2** (*also* **face flannel**) a small square of towelling for washing with. **3**

colloq flattery or meaningless talk intended to hide one's ignorance or true intentions. ➤ *vb* (**flannelled, flannelling;** *N Am* **flanneled, flanneling**) *tr & intr* to flatter or persuade by flattery, or to talk flannel.

flannelette *n* a cotton imitation of flannel, with a soft brushed surface.

flap *vb* (**flapped, flapping**) **1** *tr & intr* to wave something up and down, or backwards and forwards. **2** *tr & intr* of a bird: to move (the wings) up and down. **3** *intr, colloq* (often **flap about** or **around**) to get into or be in a flustered state. ➤ *n* **1** a broad piece or part of something attached along one edge and hanging loosely, usu as a cover to an opening: *pocket flaps.* **2** an act or sound of flapping. **3** *colloq* a flustered state. **4** a hinged section on an aircraft wing adjusted to control speed. ○ **flappy** *adj.*

flapjack *n* **1** a thick biscuit made with oats and syrup. **2** *N Am* a pancake.

flare *vb* **1** *intr* (*also* **flare up**) to burn with sudden brightness. **2** *intr* (*also* **flare up**) to explode into anger. **3** *tr & intr* to widen towards the edge. ➤ *n* **1** a sudden blaze of bright light. **2** a device composed of combustible material that produces a sudden blaze of intense light, and is activated to give warning, emergency illumination, or a distress signal. **3** in chemical plants and oil refineries: a device for burning off superfluous combustible gas or oil, in order to ensure its safe disposal. **4** a widening out towards the edges: *sleeves with a wide flare.*

flares *pl n, colloq* trousers with legs which widen greatly below the knee.

flare-up *n* **1** *colloq* a sudden explosion of emotion or violence. **2** a sudden burst into flames.

flash *n* **1** a sudden brief blaze of light. **2** an instant. **3** a brief but intense occurrence: *a flash of inspiration.* **4** a fleeting look on a face or in the eyes: *a flash of joy.* **5** *photog* **a** a bulb or electronic device attached to a camera which produces a momentary bright light as a picture is taken: *a camera with built-in flash;* **b** the bright light produced by it: *The flash made her blink.* **6** an emblem on a military uniform. ➤ *vb* **1** *tr & intr* to shine briefly or intermittently. **2** *tr & intr* to appear or cause to appear briefly; to move or pass quickly. **3** *intr* of the eyes: to brighten with anger, etc. **4** to give (a smile or look) briefly. **5** to display briefly; to flourish or flaunt. **6** *tr & intr* to send (a message) by radio, satellite, etc. **7** *tr & intr* to operate (a light) as a signal. **8** *intr, colloq* (*usu* **flash at sb**) of a man: to expose his genitals in a public place as an exhibitionist. ➤ *adj* **1** sudden and severe. **2** quick: *flash freezing.* **3** *colloq* smart and expensive. ◆ **a flash in the pan** *colloq* an impressive but untypical success, unlikely to be repeated.

flashback *n* esp in a film, novel, etc: a scene depicting events which happened before the current ones.

flashbulb *n* a small light bulb used to produce a brief bright light in photography.

flasher *n, colloq* a man who flashes (see FLASH *verb* sense 8).

flash flood *n* a sudden, severe and brief flood caused by a heavy rainstorm. ○ **flash flooding** *n.*

flashlight *n* **1** *N Am* a torch. **2** *photog* the momentary bright light emitted from an electronic flash or a flashbulb as a photograph is taken.

flash point *n* **1** a stage in a tense situation, etc where tempers flare and people may become angry or violent. **2** *chem* the temperature at which the vapour above a volatile liquid, eg petrol or oil, will ignite.

flashy *adj* (**-ier, -iest**) *colloq* ostentatiously smart and gaudy. ○ **flashily** *adv.* ○ **flashiness** *n.*

flask *n* **1** (*also* **hip flask**) a small flat pocket bottle for alcoholic spirits. **2** a VACUUM FLASK. **3** a narrow-necked bottle used in chemical experiments, etc.

flat[1] *adj* (**flatter, flattest**) **1** level; horizontal; even. **2** without hollows or prominences. **3** lacking the usual prominence: *a flat nose.* **4** not bent or crumpled. **5** of feet: having little or no arch to the instep. **6** of shoes: not having a raised heel. **7** bored; depressed. **8** dull; not lively. **9** toneless and expressionless. **10** *colloq* definite; emphatic: *a flat refusal.* **11** *mus* **a** of an instrument, voice, etc: lower than the correct PITCH[1] (*noun* sense 5); **b** *following its noun* lowering the specified note by a SEMITONE: *C flat.* Compare SHARP (*adj* sense 11). **12** of a tyre: having too little air in it. **13** of a drink: having lost its fizziness. **14** of a battery: having little or no electrical charge remaining. **15** of a price, rate, etc: fixed. **16** of a business, company, etc: commercially inactive. **17** of paint: matt. ➤ *adv* **1** stretched out rather than curled up, crumpled, etc. **2** into a flat compact shape: *It folds flat for storage.* **3** exactly: *in two minutes flat.* **4** bluntly and emphatically: *I can tell you flat.* **5** *mus* at lower than the correct pitch: *He sang flat.* ➤ *n* **1** something flat; a flat surface or part. **2** (**flats**) **a** an area of flat land; **b** a mud bank exposed at low tide. **3** *colloq* a punctured tyre on a vehicle. **4** *mus* **a** a sign (♭) that lowers a note by a SEMITONE from the note that it refers to; **b** a note lowered in this way. **5** a flat upright section of stage scenery slid or lowered onto the stage. **6** (**the flat**) *horse-racing* **a** FLAT RACING; **b** the season of flat racing, from March to November. ○ **flatly** *adv* emphatically: *She flatly refused to go.* ○ **flatness** *n.* ◆ **fall flat** *colloq* to fail to achieve the hoped-for effect: *The joke fell flat.* **flat broke** *colloq* completely without money. **flat out** *colloq* with maximum speed and energy.

flat[2] *n* a set of rooms for living in as a self-contained unit, in a building with a number of such units. *N Am equivalent* **apartment**.

flatfish *n* a horizontally flat-bodied fish, with both eyes on the upper surface, eg a sole.

flat-footed *adj* **1** having flat feet. **2** *derog* clumsy or tactless.

flatlet n a small FLAT².

flat racing n, horse-racing the sport of racing horses on courses with no obstacles for the horses to jump. ○ **flat race** n.

flat spin n 1 uncontrolled rotation of an aircraft in a horizontal plane around a vertical axis. 2 colloq a state of agitated confusion.

flatten vb 1 tr & intr to make or become flat or flatter. 2 colloq a to knock someone to the ground in a fight; b to overcome, crush or subdue someone utterly. 3 mus to lower the pitch of (a note) by one semitone.

flatter vb 1 to compliment someone excessively or insincerely, esp in order to win a favour from them. 2 of a picture or description: to represent someone or something overfavourably. 3 to show something off well: a dress that flatters the figure. 4 to make someone feel honoured. ○ **flatterer** n.

flattery n (-ies) 1 the act of flattering. 2 excessive or insincere praise.

flatulence n 1 an accumulation of gas formed during digestion in the stomach or intestines, causing discomfort. 2 pretentiousness. ○ **flatulent** adj.

flatworm n a type of worm with a flattened body, eg the TAPEWORM.

flaunt vb to display oneself or something in an ostentatious way, in the hope of being admired.

---

flaunt A word often confused with this one is **flout**.

---

flautist or (chiefly N Am) **flutist** n someone skilled in playing the flute.

flavour or (N Am) **flavor** n 1 a sensation perceived when eating or drinking which is a combination of taste and smell. 2 any substance added to food, etc to give it a particular taste. 3 a characteristic quality or atmosphere. ➤ vb to add something (usu to food) to give it a particular flavour or quality. ○ **flavourless** adj. ○ **flavoursome** adj.

flavouring or (N Am) **flavoring** n any substance added to food, etc to give it a particular taste.

flaw n 1 a fault, defect or blemish. 2 a mistake, eg in an argument. ○ **flawed** adj. ○ **flawless** adj.

flax n 1 a plant cultivated for the fibre of its stem and for its seeds. 2 the fibre of this plant, used to make thread and woven into LINEN.

flaxen adj 1 of hair: very fair. 2 made of or resembling flax.

flay vb 1 to strip the skin from (an animal or a person). 2 to whip or beat violently. 3 to criticize harshly.

flea n 1 a wingless blood-sucking jumping insect, that lives as a parasite on mammals (including humans) and some birds. 2 in compounds referring to small CRUSTACEANS which leap like fleas: sand flea • water flea. ♦ **a flea in one's ear** colloq a severe scolding.

flea market n, colloq a street market that sells second-hand goods.

flea-pit n, colloq a shabby cinema or other public building.

fleck n 1 a spot or marking: a white coat with flecks of gray. 2 a speck or small bit: a fleck of dirt. ➤ vb (also **flecker**) (**flecked, flecking; fleckered, fleckering**) to spot or speckle.

fledged adj 1 of a young bird: able to fly because the feathers are fully developed. 2 qualified; trained: a fully-fledged doctor.

fledgling or **fledgeling** n a young bird that has just grown its feathers and is still unable to fly.

flee vb 1 intr to run away quickly. 2 to hurriedly run away from or escape from (danger or a dangerous place).

fleece n 1 a sheep's woolly coat. 2 a sheep's wool cut from it at one shearing. 3 sheepskin or a fluffy fabric for lining garments, etc. 4 a garment made of fluffy acrylic thermal fabric and used like a jacket or pullover. ➤ vb 1 to shear (sheep). 2 slang to rob, swindle or overcharge. ○ **fleecy** adj (-ier, -iest).

fleet¹ n 1 a number of ships under one command and organized as a tactical unit. 2 all the ships of a nation. 3 a number of buses, aircraft, etc operating under the same ownership or management.

fleet² adj, poetic swift: fleet of foot.

fleeting adj brief; short-lived: a fleeting smile. ○ **fleetingly** adv.

Fleet Street n British newspapers or journalism collectively.

flesh n 1 in animals: the soft tissues covering the bones, consisting chiefly of muscle. 2 the meat of animals, as distinct from that of fish, used as food. 3 the pulp of a fruit or vegetable. 4 the body as distinct from the soul or spirit; bodily needs. 5 poetic humankind. 6 excess fat. 7 a yellowish-pink colour. ♦ **in the flesh** in person. **one's (own) flesh and blood** one's family or relations. ◊ **flesh sth out** to add descriptive detail to it.

fleshly adj relating to the body as distinct from the soul.

fleshpots pl n, facetious a place where bodily desires can be gratified.

flesh wound n a superficial wound, not deep enough to damage bone or a bodily organ.

fleshy adj (-ier, -iest) 1 plump. 2 relating to or like flesh. 3 of leaves, etc: thick and pulpy. ○ **fleshiness** n.

fleur-de-lis or **fleur-de-lys** /flɜːdə'li, flɜːdə'liːs/ n (**fleurs-de-lis, fleurs-de-lys** /flɜːdə'li, flɜːdə'liːs/) a stylized three-petal representation of a lily or iris, used as a heraldic design.

flex¹ vb 1 to bend (a limb or joint). 2 to contract or tighten (a muscle) so as to bend a joint.

flex² n flexible insulated electrical cable.

flexible adj 1 bending easily. 2 readily adaptable to suit circumstances. ○ **flexibility** n. ○ **flexibly** adv.

flexitime n a system of flexible working hours, allowing workers to choose when they put in their hours.

flexor *n, anat* any muscle that causes bending of a limb or other body part. Compare EXTENSOR.

flibbertigibbet *n* a frivolous or over-talkative person.

flick *vb* 1 to move or touch something with a quick light movement. 2 to move the hand or finger quickly and jerkily against something small in order to remove it. 3 *intr (usu* **flick through sth)** to glance quickly through it (eg a book, a video, etc), in order to get a rough impression of it. ➤ *n* 1 a flicking action. 2 *colloq (often pl)* a cinema film.

flicker *vb* 1 *intr* to burn or shine unsteadily by alternately flashing bright and dying away again. 2 *intr* to move lightly to and fro. ➤ *n* 1 a brief or unsteady light. 2 a fleeting appearance or occurrence: *a flicker of hope.*

flier or **flyer** *n* 1 a leaflet used to advertise a product, promote an organization, etc. 2 a pilot. 3 someone or something that flies or moves fast. 4 *colloq* a risky or speculative business transaction.

flight[1] *n* 1 the practice or an act of flying with wings or in an aircraft. 2 the movement of eg a vehicle, bird or projectile through the air. 3 a flock of birds flying together. 4 a regular air journey made by an aircraft. 5 a journey of a spacecraft. 6 a group of aircraft involved in a joint mission. 7 a set of steps or stairs. 8 a feather or something similar attached to the end of a dart or arrow. ◆ **a flight of fancy** *sometimes derog* a free use of the imagination. **in flight** flying.

flight[2] *n* the act of fleeing.

flight attendant *n* person who attends to the passengers on an aircraft.

flightless *adj* of certain birds or insects: unable to fly.

flight lieutenant *n* an officer in the Royal Air Force.

flight recorder *n* an electronic device fitted to an aircraft, recording information about its performance in flight, etc, often used in determining the cause of an air crash.

flighty *adj* (**-ier, -iest**) irresponsible; frivolous. ○ **flightiness** *n.*

flimsy *adj* (**-ier, -iest**) 1 of clothing, etc: light and thin. 2 of a structure: insubstantially made. 3 of an excuse, etc: inadequate or unconvincing. ○ **flimsily** *adv.* ○ **flimsiness** *n.*

flinch *vb, intr* 1 to start or jump in pain, fright, surprise, etc. 2 (*often* **flinch from sth**) to shrink back from or avoid something difficult such as a task, duty, etc.

fling *vb* (**flung**) 1 to throw something, esp violently or vigorously. 2 *sometimes intr* to throw oneself or one's body about. ➤ *n* 1 an act of flinging. 2 *colloq* a sexual relationship with someone for a short period of time. 3 *colloq* a spell of enjoyable self-indulgence. 4 a lively reel. ◇ **fling sb out** to get rid of them. **fling sth out** to throw it away or reject it.

flint *n* 1 *geol* a crystalline form of quartz consisting of hard dark-grey or black nodules. 2 *archaeol* a trimmed piece of this used as a tool. 3 a piece of a hard metal alloy from which a spark can be struck, eg in a cigarette lighter. ○ **flinty** *adj* (**-ier, -iest**).

flintlock *n, hist* a gun in which the powder was lit by a spark from a flint.

flip *vb* (**flipped, flipping**) 1 to toss (eg a coin) so that it turns over in mid-air. 2 *intr, colloq (also* **flip one's lid)** to lose one's temper. ➤ *n* 1 a flipping action. 2 a somersault, esp performed in mid-air. 3 an alcoholic drink made with beaten egg. ➤ *adj, colloq* flippant; over-smart.

flip-flop *n* 1 *colloq* a rubber or plastic sandal consisting of a sole held on to the foot by a thong that separates the big toe from the other toes. 2 *elec, comput* an electronic circuit that remains in one of two stable states until it receives a suitable electric pulse, which causes it to switch to the other state.

flippant *adj* not serious enough about grave matters; irreverent. ○ **flippancy** *n.* ○ **flippantly** *adv.*

flipper *n* 1 a limb adapted for swimming, eg in a whale, seal, etc. 2 a rubber foot-covering imitating an animal flipper, worn for underwater swimming.

flipping *adj, adv, colloq* used as an intensifier or to express annoyance: *He's flipping done it again!*

flip side *n, colloq* 1 of a coin: the reverse. 2 a different, and sometimes opposite, aspect or effect of something.

flirt *vb, intr* 1 (*usu* **flirt with sb**) to behave in a playful sexual manner (towards them). 2 (*usu* **flirt with sth**) to take a fleeting interest in it. 3 (*usu* **flirt with sth**) to treat it (eg death, danger, etc) lightly. ➤ *n* someone who flirts. ○ **flirtation** *n.* ○ **flirtatious** *adj.* ○ **flirty** *adj.*

flit *vb* (**flitted, flitting**) *intr* 1 **a** to move about lightly and quickly from place to place; **b** to fly silently or quickly from place to place. 2 *Scot & N Eng* to move house. 3 *Brit colloq* to move house stealthily to avoid paying debts, etc. ➤ *n* an act of flitting.

float *vb* 1 *tr & intr* to rest or move, or make something rest or move, on the surface of a liquid. 2 *intr* to drift about or hover in the air. 3 *intr* to move in an aimless or disorganized way. 4 to start up or launch (a company, scheme, etc). 5 to offer (stocks) for sale. 6 *finance* to allow (a currency) to vary in value in relation to other currencies. ➤ *n* 1 something that floats or is designed to keep something afloat. 2 *angling* a floating device fixed to a fishing-line, that moves to indicate a bite. 3 a low-powered delivery vehicle: *milk float*. 4 a vehicle decorated as an exhibit in a street parade. 5 an amount of money set aside each day for giving change, etc in a shop at the start of business. 6 a plasterer's trowel.

floating *adj* 1 not fixed; moving about: *a floating population*. 2 of a voter: not committed to supporting any one party. 3 of a currency: free to vary in value in relation to other currencies. **4** of a bodily organ, eg a kidney: moving about abnormally.

flocculent adj woolly; fleecy. ◇ **flocculence** n.

flock[1] n **1** a group of creatures, esp birds or sheep. **2** a crowd of people. **3** a body of people under the spiritual charge of a priest or minister. ➤ vb, intr to gather or move in a group or a crowd.

flock[2] n **1** (also **flocks**) waste wool or cotton used for stuffing mattresses, etc. **2** fine particles of wool or nylon fibre applied to paper, esp wallpaper, to give a raised velvety surface.

floe n a sheet of ice other than the edge of an ice shelf or glacier, floating in the sea.

flog vb (**flogged, flogging**) **1** to beat; to whip repeatedly, particularly as a form of punishment. **2** colloq to sell something. ♦ **flog a dead horse** colloq to waste time and energy trying to do something that is impossible.

flood n **1** an overflow of water from rivers, lakes or the sea on to dry land. **2** any overwhelming flow or quantity of something. **3** the rising of the tide. **4** colloq a floodlight. ➤ vb **1** to overflow or submerge (land) with water. **2** to fill something too full or to overflowing. **3** (usu **flood sb out**) to force them to leave a building, etc because of floods. **4** intr to become flooded, esp frequently. **5** intr to move in a great mass: Crowds flooded through the gates. **6** intr to flow or surge. **7** intr to bleed profusely from the uterus, eg after childbirth. **8** to supply (a market) with too much of a certain kind of commodity. **9** to supply (an engine) with too much petrol so that it cannot start.

floodgate n a gate for controlling the flow of a large amount of water. ♦ **open the floodgates** to remove all restraints.

floodlight n (also **floodlamp**) a powerful light used to illuminate extensive areas, esp sports grounds or the outside of buildings. ➤ vb (**floodlit**) to illuminate with floodlights.

floor n **1** the lower interior surface of a room or vehicle. **2** all the rooms, etc on the same level in a building; the storey of a building. **3** usu in compounds the lowest surface of some open areas, eg the ground in a forest or cave, the bed of the sea, etc. **4** the debating area in a parliamentary assembly or the open area of a stock exchange. **5** the right to speak in a parliamentary assembly: to have the floor. ➤ vb **1** to construct the floor of (a room, etc). **2** colloq to knock someone down. **3** colloq to baffle someone completely. ♦ **take the floor 1** to rise to speak in a debate, etc. **2** to start dancing.

flooring n **1** material for constructing floors. **2** a platform.

floor show n a series of performances such as singing and dancing at a nightclub or restaurant.

floosie, floozie or **floozy** n (**-sies** or **-zies**) colloq, often facetious a disreputable or immodest woman or girl.

flop vb (**flopped, flopping**) **1** intr to fall, drop, move or sit limply and heavily. **2** intr of eg hair: to hang or sway about loosely. **3** intr, colloq of a play, project, business, etc: to fail dismally. **4** intr, slang (usu **flop out**) to fall asleep, esp because of exhaustion. ➤ n **1** a flopping movement or sound. **2** colloq a complete failure. **3** N Am colloq a temporary place to sleep.

floppy adj (**-ier, -iest**) tending to flop; loose and insecure. ➤ n (**-ies**) comput a floppy disk.

floppy disk n, comput a small flexible magnetic disc, enclosed in a stiff plastic casing, used to store data. Compare HARD DISK.

flora n (**floras** or **florae** /ˈflɔːriː/) bot the wild plants of a particular region, country or time period. Compare FAUNA.

floral adj **1** consisting of or relating to flowers: a floral tribute. **2** patterned with flowers: floral curtains.

floret n, bot **1** a small flower; one of the single flowers in the head of a composite flower, such as a daisy or sunflower. **2** each of the branches in the head of a cauliflower or of broccoli.

florid adj **1** over-elaborate: a florid speech. **2** of a complexion: ruddy.

florin n a former British coin worth two shillings.

florist n someone who grows, sells or arranges flowers.

floss n **1** loose strands of fine silk which are not twisted together, used in embroidery, for tooth-cleaning (**dental floss**), etc. **2** the rough silk on the outside of a silkworm's cocoon. **3** any fine silky plant substance. ➤ vb, tr & intr to clean the teeth with dental floss. ◇ **flossy** adj.

flotation n **1** the launching of a commercial company with a sale of shares to raise money. **2** the act of floating.

flotilla n a small fleet, or a fleet of small ships.

flotsam n goods lost by shipwreck and found floating on the sea. Compare JETSAM. ♦ **flotsam and jetsam** odds and ends.

flounce[1] vb, intr to move in a way expressive of impatience or indignation. ➤ n a flouncing movement.

flounce[2] n a deep frill on a dress, etc.

flounder[1] vb, intr **1** to thrash about helplessly, as if caught in a bog. **2** to stumble helplessly in thinking or speaking, struggling to find the appropriate words, etc. ➤ n an act of floundering.

flounder[2] n a type of European FLATFISH, used as food.

flour n **1** the finely ground meal of wheat or other cereal grain. **2** a dried powdered form of any other vegetable material: potato flour. ➤ vb to coat, cover or sprinkle with flour. ◇ **floury** adj.

flourish vb **1** intr to be strong and healthy; to grow well. **2** intr to do well; to develop and prosper. **3** intr to be at one's most productive, or at one's peak. **4** to adorn with flourishes or ornaments. **5** to wave or brandish something. ➤ n **1** a decorative twirl in handwriting. **2** an elegant sweep of the hand. **3** a showy piece of music; a fanfare. **4** a piece of fancy language.

flout vb **1** to defy (an order, convention, etc) openly; to disrespect (authority, etc). **2** (usu **flout at**) intr to jeer.

> **flout** A word often confused with this one is **flaunt**.

flow vb, intr **1** to move along like water. **2** of blood or electricity: to circulate. **3** to keep moving steadily. **4** of hair: to hang or ripple in a loose shining mass. **5** of words or ideas: to come readily to mind or in speech or writing. **6** to be present in abundance. **7** of the tide: to advance or rise. Compare EBB (sense 1). ➤ n **1** the action of flowing. **2** the rate of flowing. **3** a continuous stream or outpouring. **4** the rising of the tide. ◆ **in full flow** speaking energetically.

flow chart n a diagram representing the nature and sequence of operations, esp in a computer program or an industrial process.

flower n **1** in a flowering plant: the structure that bears the reproductive organs. **2** a plant that bears flowers, esp if cultivated for them. **3** the best part. **4** the most distinguished person or thing. **5** a term of endearment. ➤ vb **1** intr to produce flowers. **2** intr to reach a peak; to develop to full maturity. ◆ **in flower** blooming or blossoming.

flowerpot n a clay or plastic container for growing plants in.

flowery adj **1** decorated or patterned with flowers. **2** of language or gestures: excessively elaborate. ○ **floweriness** n.

flowing adj **1** moving as a fluid. **2** smooth and continuous; fluent. **3** falling or hanging in folds or waves: a flowing dress.

fl. oz. abbrev fluid ounce.

flu n, colloq (often **the flu**) influenza.

fluctuate vb, intr of prices etc: to vary in amount, value, etc. ○ **fluctuation** n.

flue n **1** an outlet for smoke or gas, eg through a chimney. **2** a pipe or duct for conveying heat.

fluent adj **1** having full command of a foreign language: fluent in French. **2** spoken or written with ease: Della speaks fluent Russian. **3** speaking or writing in an easy flowing style. **4** of a movement: smooth, easy or graceful. ○ **fluency** n.

fluff n **1** small bits of soft woolly or downy material. **2** colloq a mistake, eg in speaking or hitting a ball. ➤ vb **1** (usu **fluff sth out** or **up**) to shake or arrange it into a soft mass. **2** tr & intr to make a mistake in (words, a shot, etc). ○ **fluffiness** n. ○ **fluffy** adj (-ier, -iest).

fluid n a substance, such as a liquid or gas, which can move about with freedom and has no fixed shape. ➤ adj **1** able to flow like a liquid. **2** of movements, etc: smooth and graceful. **3** altering easily; adaptable. ○ **fluidity** /floˈɪdɪtɪ/ or **fluidness** n.

fluid ounce n **1** in the UK: a unit of liquid measurement, equal to one twentieth of a British or imperial pint. **2** in the US: a unit of liquid

measurement, equal to one sixteenth of a US pint.

fluke¹ n a success achieved by accident or chance. ➤ vb to make, score or achieve something by a fluke. ○ **flukey** or **fluky** adj.

fluke² n **1** a parasitic flatworm. **2** a FLOUNDER².

fluke³ n **1** one of the triangular plates of iron on each arm of an anchor. **2** a barb, eg of an arrow, harpoon, etc. **3** a lobe of a whale's tail.

flume n **1 a** a chute with flowing water at a swimming pool, that people slide down, landing in the pool; **b** a ride at an amusement park with small boats which move through water-filled channels. **2** an artificial channel for water, used in industry.

flummery n (-ies) **1** a jelly made with oatmeal, milk, egg and honey. **2** pompous nonsense.

flummox vb, colloq to confuse someone.

flunk vb, esp N Am colloq **1** tr to fail (a test, examination, etc). **2** of an examiner: to fail (a candidate). ◊ **flunk out** intr to be dismissed from a school or university for failing examinations.

flunkey or **flunky** n (-eys or -ies) **1** a uniformed manservant, eg a footman. **2** derog a slavish follower. **3** N Am a person doing a humble or menial job.

fluor /ˈfluːɔː(r)/ n FLUORSPAR.

fluorescence n, physics **1** the emission of light and other radiation by an object after it has absorbed electrons or radiation of a different wavelength, esp ultraviolet light. **2** the radiation emitted as a result of fluorescence. ○ **fluoresce** vb. ○ **fluorescent** adj.

fluorescent light n, elec a type of electric light that emits visible light by the process of fluorescence.

fluoridate or **fluoridize** or **-ise** vb to add small amounts of fluoride salts to drinking water supplies to help prevent tooth decay.

fluoride n, chem any chemical compound consisting of fluorine and another element.

fluorine n, chem a highly corrosive poisonous yellow gas of the HALOGEN group.

fluorocarbon n, chem a compound of carbon and fluorine, formerly widely used as an aerosol propellant and refrigerant.

fluorspar, fluorite or **fluor** n, geol calcium fluoride, a mineral that is transparent when pure.

flurry n (-ies) **1** a sudden commotion or rush: a flurry of activity. **2** a sudden gust; a brief shower of rain, snow, etc: a flurry of snowflakes. ➤ vb (**flurries, flurried**) to agitate, confuse or bewilder someone.

flush¹ vb **1** usu intr to blush or make someone blush. **2** to clean out (esp a lavatory pan) with a rush of water. ➤ n **1** a redness or rosiness, esp of the cheeks or face. **2** a rush of water that cleans a lavatory pan, or the mechanism that controls it. **3** high spirits: in the first flush of enthusiasm. **4** freshness; vigour: the flush of youth.

flush² adj **1** (often **flush with sth**) level or even with an adjacent surface. **2** *colloq* having plenty of money. ➤ *adv* so as to be level with an adjacent surface: *She fixed it flush with the wall.*

flush³ *n, cards* a hand made up of cards from a single suit.

flush⁴ *vb, hunting* to startle (game birds) so that they rise from the ground. ◊ **flush sb** or **sth out** to drive them or it out of a hiding place.

fluster *vb* to agitate, confuse or upset. ➤ *n* a state of confused agitation.

flute *n* **1** a wind instrument consisting of a wooden or metal tube with holes stopped by the fingertips or by keys, which is held horizontally and played by directing the breath across the hole in the mouthpiece. See also FLAUTIST. **2** *archit* a rounded concave groove or furrow in wood or stone. **3** a tall narrow wineglass, used esp for champagne. ➤ *vb* to produce or utter (sounds) like the high shrill tones of a flute. ○ **fluty** *adj* like a flute in tone.

fluted *adj* ornamented with flutes (see FLUTE sense 2).

fluting *n* a series of parallel grooves cut into wood or stone.

flutist *n, N Am* a FLAUTIST.

flutter *vb* **1** *tr & intr* of a bird, etc: to flap (its wings) lightly and rapidly; to fly with a rapid wing movement. **2** *intr* of a flag, etc: to flap repeatedly in the air. **3** *intr* to drift with a twirling motion. **4** *intr* of the heart: to race, from excitement or some medical disorder. ➤ *n* **1** a quick flapping or vibrating motion. **2** agitation: *flutter of excitement.* **3** *colloq* a small bet.

fluvial *adj* relating to or found in rivers.

flux *n* **1** a flow of matter; a process or act of flowing. **2** constant change; instability. **3** any substance added to another in order to aid the process of melting. **4** in the smelting of metal ores: any substance that is added so that it will combine with impurities which can then be removed as a flowing mass of slag. **5** any substance that is used to remove oxides from the surfaces of metals that are to be soldered, welded or brazed. **6** *physics* the rate of flow of particles, energy, mass or some other quantity per unit cross-sectional area per unit time. ➤ *vb* **1** to apply flux to (a metal, etc) when soldering. **2** *tr & intr* to make or become fluid.

fly¹ *n* (*flies*) **1** a two-winged insect, esp the common housefly. **2** *in compounds* any of various other flying insects: *dragonfly.* **3** *angling* a fish hook tied with colourful feathers to look like a fly. ◆ **a fly in the ointment** a drawback to an otherwise satisfactory state of affairs. **a fly on the wall** the invisible observer, usu at a meeting or in a social situation, that one would like to be to find out what is happening without taking part. **no flies on sb** *colloq* the person specified is cunning and not easily fooled.

fly² *vb* (*3rd person present tense* **flies,** *past tense* **flew,** *past participle* **flown,** *present participle* **flying**) **1** *intr* a of birds, bats, insects and certain other animals: to move through the air using

wings or similar structures; **b** of an aircraft or spacecraft: to travel through the air or through space. **2** *tr & intr* to travel or convey in an aircraft: *They flew to Moscow* • *The company flew them to Moscow.* **3** to operate and control (an aircraft, kite, etc). **4** to cross (an area of land or water) in an aircraft: *They flew the Atlantic to New York.* **5 a** to raise (a flag); **b** *intr* of a flag: to blow in the wind. **6** *intr* to move or pass rapidly: *to fly into a temper* • *rumours flying around.* **7** *intr, colloq* to depart quickly: *I must fly.* **8** *tr & intr* to escape; to flee (a country, a war zone, etc). ➤ *n* (*flies*) **1** (*chiefly* **flies**) a zip or set of buttons fastening a trouser front, or the flap covering these. **2** a flap covering the entrance to a tent. **3** (*flies*) the space above a stage, concealed from the audience's view, from which scenery is lowered. ◆ **fly a kite** to release information about an idea, proposal, etc to find out what people's opinion might be about it. **fly in the face of sth** to oppose it; to be at variance with it.

fly³ *adj, colloq* cunning; smart.

flyblown *adj* **1** of food: covered with blowfly eggs. **2** shabby, dirty or dingy.

fly-by-night *adj, derog* of a person, business, etc: not reliable or trustworthy. ➤ *n* an unreliable person, esp one who avoids debts by disappearing overnight.

flyer see FLIER

fly-fish *vb, intr* to fish using artificial flies as bait. ○ **fly-fishing** *n.*

flying *adj* **1** hasty; brief: *a flying visit.* **2** designed or organized for fast movement. **3** able to fly or glide. **4** of hair, a flag, etc: streaming; fluttering. ➤ *n* **1** flight. **2** the activity of piloting, or travelling in, an aircraft.

flying colours *pl n* triumphant success: *She passed the exam with flying colours.*

flying fish *n* a fish with stiff, greatly enlarged pectoral fins that enable it to leap out of the water and glide for considerable distances.

flying officer *n* an officer in the Royal Air Force.

flying picket *n* a picket travelling from place to place to support local pickets during any strike.

flying saucer *n* an unidentified circular object reported in the sky, believed by some to be a craft from outer space.

flying squad *n* a body of police specially trained for quick response and available for duty wherever the need arises.

flying start *n* a very promising or advantageous beginning.

flyleaf *n* a blank page at the beginning or end of a book.

flyover *n* a bridge that takes a road or railway over another. *N Am equivalent* **overpass.**

flypaper *n* a strip of paper with a sticky poisonous coating that attracts, traps and kills flies.

flypast *n* a ceremonial flight of military aircraft.

flyposting *n* the putting up of advertising or political posters, etc illegally.

flysheet *n* a protective outer sheet for a tent which is fitted over the main body.

flyspray *n* a liquid poisonous to flies, sprayed from an aerosol can.

fly-tipping *n* unauthorized disposal of waste materials.

flytrap *n* 1 a device for catching flies. 2 *bot* a plant that traps flies and digests them.

flyweight *n* 1 a class of boxers, wrestlers and weightlifters of not more than a specified weight, for example 51kg (112 lb) in professional boxing. 2 a boxer, wrestler, etc of this weight.

flywheel *n* a heavy wheel that regulates the action of a machine.

FM *abbrev* frequency modulation.

Fm *symbol, chem* fermium.

foal *n* the young of a horse or of a related animal. ➤ *vb, intr* to give birth to a foal. ♦ **in foal** or **with foal** of a mare: pregnant.

foam *n* 1 a mass of tiny bubbles on the surface of liquids. 2 a substance composed of tiny bubbles formed by passing gas through it. 3 frothy saliva or perspiration. 4 a light cellular material used for packaging, insulation, etc. ➤ *vb, intr* (*sometimes* **foam up**) to produce or make something produce foam. ○ **foaming** *n, adj.* ○ **foamy** *adj.*

fob[1] *vb* (**fobbed, fobbing**) now only in phrases below. ◊ **fob sb off** to dismiss or ignore them: *He tried to fob off his critics.* **fob sb off with sth** to provide them with something inferior (eg a poor substitute, or an inadequate explanation), usu in the hope that they will be satisfied. **fob sth off on sb** to manage to sell or pass off something inferior to someone.

fob[2] *n* 1 a chain attached to a watch. 2 a decorative attachment to a key ring or watch chain.

focaccia /fə'katʃə/ *n* a flat round of Italian bread made with olive oil and herbs or spices.

focal point *n* 1 *optics* the point at which rays of light which are initially parallel to the axis of a lens or mirror converge. 2 a centre of attraction of some event or activity.

fo'c'sle /'fəʊksəl/ *n, naut* a spelling of FORE-CASTLE suggested by its pronunciation.

focus *n* (**focuses** or **foci** /'fəʊsaɪ/) 1 the point at which rays of light or sound waves converge or appear to diverge. 2 *optics* FOCAL POINT (sense 1). 3 a the condition in which an image is sharp; b the state of an instrument producing this image. 4 the location of the centre of an earthquake. 5 a centre of interest or attention. 6 special attention paid to something. ➤ *vb* (**focused, focusing**; *also* **focussed, focussing**) 1 *tr & intr* to bring or be brought into focus; to meet or make something meet or converge at a focus. 2 to adjust the thickness of the lens of (the eye) or to move the lens of (an optical instrument) so as to obtain the sharpest possible image. 3 (*often* **focus sth on sth**) *tr & intr* to con-

centrate attention, etc on it: *She focused her energies on the problem.* ○ **focal** *adj.*

fodder *n* 1 any bulk feed for cattle and other livestock. 2 *colloq* something that is constantly made use of: *fodder for the popular press.*

foe *n, literary, old use* an enemy.

foetid see FETID

foetus see FETUS

fog *n* 1 a suspension of tiny water droplets or ice crystals forming a cloud close to the ground surface. 2 *photog* an unwanted blurred patch on a negative, print or transparency, etc. 3 a blur; cloudiness. 4 a state of confusion or bewilderment. ➤ *vb* (**fogged, fogging**) *tr & intr* (*often* **fog over** or **up**) to obscure or become obscured with, or as if with, fog or condensation.

fogey or **fogy** *n* (**-eys** or **-ies**) someone with boring, old-fashioned and usu conservative ideas and attitudes. ○ **fogeyish** or **fogyish** *adj.*

foggy *adj* (**-ier, -iest**) 1 covered with or thick with fog. 2 not clear. ♦ **not have the foggiest** or **not have the foggiest idea** *colloq* not to know at all.

foghorn *n* a horn that sounds at regular intervals to ships in fog as a warning of some danger or obstruction.

foible *n* a slight personal weakness or eccentricity.

foie gras /fwɑː grɑː/ *n* a pâté made from specially fattened goose liver.

foil[1] *vb* to prevent, thwart or frustrate someone or something.

foil[2] *n* metal beaten or rolled out into thin sheets.

foil[3] *n, fencing* a long slender fencing sword with a blunt edge and a point protected by a button.

foist *vb* 1 (*usu* **foist sth on sb**) to inflict or impose something unwanted on them. 2 (*usu* **foist sth on sb**) to sell or pass on something inferior to them, while suggesting that it has value.

fold[1] *vb* 1 (*also* **fold over, back, up,** *etc*) to double (something) over so that one part lies on top of another. 2 *intr* (*also* **fold away**) to be able to be folded, or closed up so that it takes up less space, usu making it flat. 3 of an insect, etc: to bring in (wings) close to its body. 4 (*often* **fold up**) to arrange (clothes, etc) for storage by laying them flat and doubling each piece of clothing over on itself. 5 *intr* of flower petals: to close. 6 to clasp (someone) in one's arms, etc. 7 (*also* **fold up**) *colloq* of a business, etc: to fail. ➤ *n* 1 a doubling of one layer over another. 2 a rounded or sharp bend made by this, particularly the inside part of it. 3 a hollow in the landscape. 4 *geol* a buckling of stratified rocks as a result of movements of the Earth's crust.

fold[2] *n* 1 a walled or fenced enclosure or pen for sheep or cattle. 2 the body of believers within the protection of a church.

folder *n* a cardboard or plastic cover in which to keep loose papers.

foliage *n* the green leaves on a tree or plant.

folic acid /ˈfəʊlɪk, ˈfɒlɪk/ *n, biochem* a vitamin found in many foods, esp liver and green leafy vegetables, which is required for the formation of red blood cells.

folio *n* **1** a leaf of a manuscript, etc, numbered on one side. **2 a** a sheet of paper folded once to make two leaves for a book; **b** a book composed of such sheets. ➤ *adj* of a book: composed of folios: *a folio edition*.

folk *pl n* **1** people in general. **2** (*also colloq* **folks**) a person's family. **3** people belonging to a particular group, nation, etc: *country folk*. ➤ *sing n, colloq* folk music. ➤ *adj* traditional among, or originating from, a particular group of people or nation: *folk art*.

folklore *n* the customs, beliefs, stories, traditions, etc of a particular group of people, usu passed down through the oral tradition.

folk music *n* **1** traditional music handed down orally from generation to generation within a particular area or group of people. **2** contemporary music of a similar style.

folk song *n* any song or ballad originating among the people and traditionally handed down from generation to generation.

folksy *adj* (**-ier, -iest**) **1** simple and homely, esp in an over-sweet or twee way. **2** everyday; sociable; unpretentious.

folk tale or **folk story** *n* a popular story handed down by oral tradition from generation to generation.

follicle *n* a small cavity or sac within a tissue or organ: *hair follicle*. ○ **follicular** *adj*.

follow *vb* **1** *tr & intr* (*also* **follow after**) to go or come after (someone or something). **2** to secretly go after (someone or something). **3** to accept someone as leader or authority. **4** *intr* (*sometimes* **follow from**) to result from or be a consequence of (something). **5** to go along (a road, etc), alongside (a river, etc) or on the path marked by (signs). **6** to watch (someone or something moving): *His eyes followed her up the street*. **7** to do (something) in a particular way; to practise (something): *follow a life of self-denial*. ♦ *follow a trade*. **8** to conform to (something): *The novel follows a familiar pattern*. **9** to obey (advice, etc). **10** *tr & intr* to copy: *Try to follow her example*. **11** *tr & intr* to understand: *Do you follow me?* **12** to take a keen interest in (a sport, etc). ◆ **follow suit** to do what someone else has done without thinking much about it. ◊ **follow sth through** or **up** to pursue (an idea, a project, etc) beyond its early stages, and often to fruition. **follow sth up** to take the next step after a particular procedure.

follower *n* **1** someone or something that follows or comes after others. **2** an avid supporter or devotee, eg of a particular sport, celebrity, etc. **3** a disciple.

following *n* **1** a body of supporters, devotees, etc. **2** (**the following**) the thing or things, or the person or people, about to be mentioned or referred to: *I'll be discussing the following …* ➤ *adj* **1** coming after; next. **2** about to be mentioned: *I'll deal with the following points*. **3** of a wind, currents, etc: blowing in the direction in which a ship, etc is travelling. ➤ *prep* after.

follow-up *n* further action or investigation.

folly *n* (**-ies**) **1** foolishness; a foolish act. **2** a mock temple, castle, ruin, etc built eg as a romantic addition to a view.

foment /fəʊˈmɛnt/ *vb* to encourage or foster (ill-feeling, etc). ○ **fomentation** *n*.

fond *adj* **1** loving; tender: *fond glances*. **2** happy: *fond memories*. **3** of desire, hopes, etc: foolishly impractical: *a fond hope*. ○ **fondly** *adv*. ○ **fondness** *n*. ◆ **fond of sb** or **sth** liking them or it.

fondant *n* a soft sweet paste made with sugar and water, often flavoured and used in cake- and chocolate-making.

fondle *vb* to touch, stroke or caress someone or something lovingly, affectionately or lustfully.

fondue *n, cookery* a dish, orig Swiss, consisting of hot cheese sauce into which bits of bread are dipped.

font¹ *n* a basin in a church that holds water for baptisms.

font² *n* see FOUNT¹

fontanelle or (*chiefly US*) **fontanel** *n, anat* a soft membrane-covered gap between the bones of the skull of a young infant.

food *n* **1** a substance taken in by a living organism that provides it with energy and materials for growth and repair of tissues. **2** something that provides stimulation: *food for thought*.

food chain *n, ecol* a sequence of organisms each of which feeds on the organism below it in the chain and is a source of food for the organism above it.

foodie *n, colloq* a person employed by kings, nobles, etc to amuse them; a jester. ➤ *vb* **1** to deceive someone so that they appear foolish or ridiculous. **2** (**fool sb into** or **out of sth**) to persuade them by deception to do something or not to do it. **3** *intr* (*often* **fool about** or **around**) to behave stupidly or playfully. ◆ **make a fool of oneself** to act in a way that makes one appear foolish. **make a fool of sb** to trick them or make them appear ridiculous.

food poisoning *n* an illness caused by eating food or drinking water containing toxins or micro-organisms.

food processor *n* an electrical kitchen appliance for chopping, liquidizing, etc, food.

foodstuff *n* a substance used as food.

fool¹ *n* **1** someone who lacks common sense or intelligence. **2** someone made to appear ridiculous. **3** *hist* a person employed by kings, nobles, etc to amuse them; a jester. ➤ *vb* **1** to deceive someone so that they appear foolish or ridiculous. **2** (**fool sb into** or **out of sth**) to persuade them by deception to do something or not to do it. **3** *intr* (*often* **fool about** or **around**) to behave stupidly or playfully. ◆ **make a fool of oneself** to act in a way that makes one appear foolish. **make a fool of sb** to trick them or make them appear ridiculous.

fool² *n* a dessert of puréed fruit mixed with cream or custard.

foolery *n* (**-ies**) ridiculous behaviour.

foolhardy *adj* taking foolish risks; rash. ○ **foolhardiness** *n*.

foolish *adj* **1** unwise; senseless. **2** ridiculous; silly. ○ **foolishly** *adv*. ○ **foolishness** *n*.

foolproof *adj* of a plan, etc: designed so that it is easy to follow and very unlikely to go wrong.

foolscap *n* a large size of printing- or writing-paper, measuring 17 × 13½in (432 × 343mm).

fool's errand *n* a pointless or unprofitable task or venture; a futile journey.

fool's gold *n* another name for PYRITE.

fool's paradise *n* a state of happiness or confidence based on false expectations.

foot *n* (*pl usu* **feet**) **1** the part of the leg on which a human being or animal stands or walks. **2** in molluscs: a muscular organ used for locomotion, which can be retracted into the animal's shell. **3** the part of a sock, stocking, etc that fits over the foot. **4** the bottom or lower part of something: *the foot of a mountain.* **5** the part on which something stands; anything functioning as or resembling a foot. **6** the end of a bed where the feet go, as opposed to the head. **7** (*pl* **feet** or *often* **foot**) in the imperial system: a unit of length equal to 12 inches: *The room is sixteen foot by ten.* **8** prosody a unit of rhythm in verse containing any of various combinations of stressed and unstressed syllables. **9** a part of a sewing machine that holds the fabric in position. ♦ **foot the bill** to pay the bill. **have one foot in the grave** *colloq* to be very old or near death. **on foot** walking. **put one's best foot forward** to set off with determination. **put one's foot down** to be firm about something. **put one's foot in it** *colloq* to cause offence or embarrassment.

footage *n* **1** measurement or payment by the foot. **2 a** the length of film measured in feet; **b** a clip from a film, etc: *archive footage.*

football *n* **1** any of several team games played with a large ball that players try to kick or head into the opposing team's goal. **2** the ball used in the game. ○ **footballer** *n.*

footbridge *n* a bridge for pedestrians.

footed *adj*, in compounds **1** having a specified number or type of feet: *four-footed.* **2** having a specified manner of walking: *light-footed.*

footfall *n* the sound of a footstep.

foothill *n* (*usu* **foothills**) a lower hill on the approach to a high mountain or mountain range.

foothold *n* **1** a place to put one's foot when climbing. **2** a firm starting position.

footie or **footy** *n*, *colloq* football.

footing *n* **1** the stability of one's feet on the ground: *I lost my footing.* **2** basis or status. **3** relationship: *on a friendly footing.*

footlights *pl n*, *theat* **1** a row of lights set along the front edge of a stage to illuminate it. **2** the theatre in general, as a profession.

footloose *adj* free to go where, or do as, one likes.

footman *n* a uniformed male attendant.

footnote *n* a comment at the bottom of a page.

footpath *n* **1** a path or track for walkers, usu in the countryside: *public footpath.* **2** a pavement.

footplate *n* in a steam train: a platform for the driver and fireman.

footprint *n* **1** the mark or impression of a foot or shoe left eg in sand, in soft ground, etc. **2** *comput* the amount of space taken up by a computer and its hardware on a desk, etc.

footsore *adj* having sore and tired feet from prolonged walking.

footstep *n.* ♦ **follow in the footsteps of sb** to do the same as they did earlier; to succeed them.

footwear *sing n* shoes, boots, socks, etc.

footwork *n* the agile use of the feet in dancing or sport.

fop *n* a man who is very consciously elegant in his dress and manners. ○ **foppery** *n.* ○ **foppish** *adj.*

for *prep* **1** intended to be given or sent to someone: *This is for you.* **2** towards: *heading for home.* **3** throughout (a time or distance): *writing for half an hour.* **4** in order to have, get, etc: *to meet for a chat* ♦ *to fight for freedom.* **5** at a cost of something: *Adam said he'd do it for £10.* **6** as reward, payment or penalty appropriate to something: *He got six months for stealing* ♦ *to charge for one's work.* **7** with a view to something: *training for the race.* **8** representing; on behalf of someone: *the MP for Greenfield* ♦ *speaking for myself.* **9** to the benefit of someone or something: *What can I do for you?* **10** in favour of someone: *for or against the proposal.* **11** proposing to oneself: *I'm for bed.* **12** because of something: *Lucy couldn't see for tears.* **13** on account of something: *famous for its confectionery.* **14** suitable to the needs of something: *books for children.* **15** having as function or purpose: *scissors for cutting hair.* **16** on the occasion of something: *I got it for my birthday.* **17** meaning: *The German word for 'help' is 'helfen'.* **18** in place of; in exchange with something: *replacements for the breakages* ♦ *translated word for word.* **19** in proportion to something: *one woman for every five men.* **20** up to someone: *It's for him to decide.* **21** as being: *I took you for someone else* ♦ *I know for a fact.* **22** with regard to something: *You can't beat her for quality.* **23** considering what one would expect: *very serious for his age* ♦ *It's warm for winter.* **24** about; aimed at: *proposals for peace* ♦ *a desire for revenge.* **25** in spite of something: *He's quite nice for all his faults.* **26** available to be disposed of or dealt with by: *not for sale.* **27** with reference to time: **a** at or on: *an appointment for 12 noon on Friday;* **b** so as to be starting by: *7.30 for 8.00;* **c** throughout (a time): *in jail for 15 years.* ➤ *conj, archaic* because; as: *He left, for it was late.* ♦ **as for** as far as concerns. **be for it** or **be in for it** *colloq* to be about to receive a punishment, etc.

forage /ˈfɒrɪdʒ/ *n* **1** (*also* **forage crop**) a crop grown as feed for livestock. **2** the activity or an instance of searching around for food, provisions, etc. ➤ *v* **1** *intr* to search around, esp for food. **2** to rummage about (for something).

forasmuch as *conj, old use* since; seeing that.

foray /ˈfɒreɪ/ *n* **1** a raid or attack. **2** a venture; an attempt.

forbear¹ vb (past tense **forbore**, past participle **forborne**, present participle **forbearing**) **1** archaic to tolerate something. **2** intr (usu **forbear from** or **forbear to do**) to stop oneself going as far as; to refrain from: to forbear from answering • to forbear to mention it. ○ **forbearance** n.

forbear² see FOREBEAR

forbid vb (past tense **forbade** /fə'bad, -'beɪd/ or **forbad** /-'bad/, past participle **forbidden** or **forbid**, present participle **forbidding**) **1** to order not; to refuse to allow: I forbid you to go. **2** to prohibit: It is forbidden to smoke here.

forbidden adj prohibited; not allowed: forbidden acts.

forbidding adj **1** threatening; grim. **2** uninviting; sinister.

force n **1** strength; power; impact or impetus. **2** compulsion, esp with threats or violence. **3** military power. **4** passion or earnestness. **5** strength or validity. **6** meaning. **7** influence. **8** a person or thing seen as an influence. **9** physics **a** any external agent that produces a change in the speed or direction of a moving object, or that makes a stationary object move: the force of gravity; **b** any external agent that produces a strain on a static object. **10** any irresistible power or agency: the forces of nature. **11** the term used in specifying an index between 0 and 12 on the BEAUFORT SCALE, each of which corresponds to a different wind speed: a gale of force 8. **12 a** a military body; **b** (**the forces**) a nation's armed services. **13** any organized body of workers, etc. **14** (**the force**) the police force. ➤ vb **1** to make or compel (someone to do something). **2** to obtain (something) by effort, strength, threats, violence, etc. **3** to produce (something) with an effort. **4** to inflict (eg views, opinions etc) (on someone). **5** to make (a plant) grow or (fruit) ripen unnaturally quickly or early. **6** to strain. ♦ **force sb's hand** to compel them to act in a certain way. **in force 1** of a law, etc: valid; effective. **2** in large numbers: Protesters arrived in force. **join forces** to come together or unite for a purpose.

forced adj **1** of a smile, laugh, etc: unnatural. **2** done or provided under compulsion: forced labour. **3** carried out as an emergency: a forced landing.

force-feed vb to feed (a person or animal) forcibly, esp by passing liquid food through a soft rubber tube into the stomach via the mouth or nostril.

forceful adj powerful; effective. ○ **forcefully** adv. ○ **forcefulness** n.

forcemeat n a mixture of chopped ingredients, eg sausage meat, herbs, etc, used as stuffing.

forceps sing n (pl **forceps**) biol, med, etc an instrument like pincers, for gripping firmly, used in surgery, etc.

forcible adj **1** done by or involving force: forcible entry. **2** powerful: a forcible reminder. ○ **forcibly** adv.

ford n a place where a river or stream may be crossed by passing through shallow water. ➤ vb to ride, drive or wade across (a stream, river, etc) by passing through shallow water. ○ **fordable** adj.

fore¹ adj, usu in compounds towards the front. ➤ n **1** the front part. **2** naut the foremast. ♦ **to the fore** at or to the front; prominent.

fore² exclam, golf ball coming!; a warning shout to anybody who may be in the ball's path.

fore-and-aft adj, naut **1** at the front and rear of a vessel. **2** set lengthways, pointing to the bow and stern.

forearm n the lower part of the arm between wrist and elbow. ➤ vb to prepare someone or arm someone beforehand.

forebear or **forbear** n an ancestor, usu more remote than grandfather or grandmother.

foreboding n a feeling of impending doom.

forecast vb (**forecast** or sometimes **forecasted**, **forecasting**) tr & intr **1** to predict something. **2** to gauge or estimate (weather, statistics etc) in advance. ➤ n **1** a warning, prediction or advance estimate. **2** a weather forecast. ○ **forecaster** n.

forecastle /'fəʊksəl/ n a short raised deck at the front of a vessel.

foreclose vb of a mortgager, bank, etc: to repossess a property because of failure on the part of the mortgagee to repay agreed amounts of the loan. ○ **foreclosure** n.

forecourt n a courtyard or paved area in front of a building, eg a petrol station.

forefather n an ancestor.

forefinger n the INDEX FINGER.

forefront n **1** the very front. **2** the most prominent or active position.

forego¹ vb (**-goes**, **-went**, **-gone**, **-going**) tr & intr to precede.

forego² see FORGO

foregoing adj just mentioned. ➤ n the thing or person just mentioned.

foregone conclusion n an inevitable or predictable result.

foreground n **1** the part of a picture or view nearest to the observer. **2** a position where one is noticeable.

forehand tennis, squash, etc, adj of a stroke: with the palm in front. ➤ n **a** a stroke made with the palm facing forward; **b** the part of the court to the right of a right-handed player or to the left of a left-handed player.

forehead n the part of the face between the eyebrows and hairline.

foreign adj **1** concerned with or relating to, or coming from another country. **2** not belonging where found: a foreign body in my eye.

foreigner n a person from another country.

foreign minister or **foreign secretary** n the government minister responsible for a country's relationships with other countries. US equivalent **secretary of state**.

foreleg n either of the two front legs of a four-legged animal.

forelock n a lock of hair falling over the brow.

♦ **pull, touch** or **tug the forelock** to raise one's hand to the forehead as a sign of respect to someone.

foreman, **forewoman** or **foreperson** n 1 a worker who supervises other workers. 2 *law* the principal juror who presides over the deliberations of the jury and communicates their verdict to the court.

foremast n, *naut* the mast that is nearest to the bow of a ship. Compare MAINMAST.

foremost adj leading; best. ➢ adv leading.

forename n used on official forms, etc: one's personal name as distinct from one's family name or surname.

forenoon n the morning.

forensic adj 1 belonging or relating to courts of law, or to the work of a lawyer in court. 2 *colloq* concerned with the scientific side of legal investigations: *forensic laboratory*. ○ **forensically** adv.

foreordain vb to determine (events, etc) in advance.

foreplay n sexual stimulation, often leading up to sexual intercourse.

forerunner n 1 a person or thing that goes before; an earlier type or version. 2 a sign of what is to come.

foresee vb to see that something will happen in advance or know in advance. ○ **foreseeable** adj.

foreshadow vb to give or have some indication of something in advance.

foreshore n the area on the shore between the high and low water marks.

foreshorten vb to draw or paint something as if it is shortened.

foresight n 1 the ability to foresee. 2 wise forethought. 3 consideration taken or provision made for the future. ○ **foresighted** adj.

foreskin n, *anat* the retractable fold of skin that covers the tip of the penis. *Technical equivalent* **prepuce**.

forest n 1 a large area of land dominated by trees. 2 the trees growing on such an area. 3 a large number or dense arrangement of objects. ➢ vb to cover (an area) with trees. ○ **forested** adj.

forestall vb 1 to prevent something by acting in advance. 2 to anticipate (an event) or anticipate the action of (someone).

forester n a person whose job is to manage a forest.

forestry n the science or management of forests and woodlands.

foretaste n a brief experience of what is to come.

foretell vb to predict.

forethought n 1 consideration taken or provision made for the future. 2 deliberate or conscious intent.

forever adv (also **for ever**) 1 always; for all time. 2 continually: *forever whining*. 3 *colloq* for a very long time. ➢ n 1 an endless or indefinite length of time. 2 a very long time.

forewarn vb to warn beforehand; to give previous notice.

foreword n an introduction to a book, often by a writer other than the author.

forfeit n 1 something that is surrendered, usu as a penalty. 2 a penalty or fine imposed for a breach of regulations. ➢ vb to lose (the right to something), or to hand (something) over, as a penalty. ○ **forfeiture** n.

forge¹ n 1 a furnace for heating metal, esp iron, prior to shaping it. 2 the workshop of a blacksmith. ➢ vb 1 to shape metal by heating and hammering. 2 to make an imitation of (a signature, banknote, etc) for a dishonest or fraudulent purpose. ○ **forger** n.

forge² vb, *intr* 1 to progress swiftly and steadily. 2 (**forge ahead**) to progress or take the lead.

forgery n (-*ies*) 1 the act or an instance of making a copy of a picture, banknote, etc for a fraudulent purpose. 2 a copy of this kind.

forget vb (**forgot**, **forgotten**, **forgetting**) tr & intr 1 to fail to remember or be unable to remember (something). 2 to stop being aware of (something): *Alex forgot his headache in the excitement*. 3 to neglect or overlook (something). 4 to leave (something) behind accidentally. 5 *colloq* to dismiss something from one's mind. 6 to lose control over (oneself).

forgetful adj inclined to forget.

forget-me-not n a plant with small flowers, often pink in bud and turning blue as they open.

forgive vb (**forgave**, **forgiven**) 1 to stop being angry with (someone who has done something wrong) or about (an offence). 2 to pardon someone. 3 to spare (someone) the paying of (a debt). ○ **forgivable** adj. ○ **forgiving** adj.

forgiveness n 1 the act of forgiving or state of being forgiven. 2 readiness to forgive.

forgo or **forego** vb (-**goes**, -**went**, -**gone**, -**going**) to do or go without (something); to give (something) up.

fork n 1 an eating or cooking implement with prongs for spearing and lifting food. 2 a pronged digging or lifting tool. 3 a a division in a road, etc with two branches; b one such branch: *Take the left fork*. 4 something that divides similarly into two parts, eg the wheel support of a bicycle. ➢ vb 1 *intr* of a road, etc: to divide into two branches. 2 *intr* of a person or vehicle: to follow one such branch: *Fork left at the church*. 3 to dig, lift or move with a fork. ◇ **fork out for sth** *colloq* to pay (a specified amount) for it, usu unwillingly.

forked adj 1 dividing into two branches or parts. 2 of lightning: forming zigzagged lines.

fork-lift truck n a small vehicle equipped with two horizontal prongs that can be raised and lowered to move or stack goods.

forlorn adj 1 exceedingly unhappy. 2 deserted. 3 desperate. ○ **forlornly** adv.

form n 1 shape. 2 figure or outward appearance. 3 kind, type, variety or manifestation. 4 a document with printed text and spaces for the insertion of information. **5** a way, esp the correct way, of doing or saying something. **6** structure and organization in a piece of writing or work of art. **7** one's potential level of performance, eg in sport: *You'll soon find your form again.* **8** a way that a word can be spelt or grammatically inflected: *the past tense form.* **9** a school class. **10** a bench. **11** *slang* a criminal record. **12** a hare's burrow. ➤ *vb* **1** to organize or set something up. **2** *intr* to come into existence; to take shape. **3** to shape; to make (a shape). **4** to take on the shape or function of. **5** to make up; to constitute. **6** to develop: *to form a relationship.* **7** to influence or mould: *the environment that formed him.* ◆ **good** or **bad form** polite or impolite social behaviour. **in** or **on good form** in good spirits; acting or speaking in a particularly animated or entertaining way. **on** or **off form** performing well or badly. **true to form** in the usual, typical or characteristic way.

formal *adj* **1** relating to or involving etiquette, ceremony or conventional procedure generally: *formal dress.* **2** stiffly polite rather than relaxed and friendly. **3** valid; official: *a formal agreement.* **4** of language: strictly correct with regard to grammar, style and choice of words. **5** organized and methodical. **6** precise and symmetrical in design: *a formal garden.* **7** relating to outward form as distinct from content. ○ **formally** *adv.*

formaldehyde /fɔːˈmaldɪhaɪd/ *n, chem* a colourless pungent gas widely used as a disinfectant and preservative for biological specimens.

formality *n* (*-ies*) **1** a procedure gone through as a requirement of etiquette, ceremony, the law, etc. **2** a procedure gone through merely for the sake of correctness. **3** strict attention to the rules of social behaviour.

formalize or **-ise** *vb* **1** to make precise or give definite form to. **2** to make official. ○ **formalization** *n.*

format *n* **1** the size and shape of something, esp a book or magazine. **2** the style in which a television programme, radio programme, etc is organized and presented. **3** *comput* a specific arrangement of data in tracks and sectors on a disk. ➤ *vb* (**formatted, formatting**) **1** to design, shape or organize in a particular way. **2** to organize (data) for input into a particular computer. **3** to prepare (a new disk) for use by marking out the surface into tracks and sectors. ○ **formatter** *n, comput* a program for formatting a disk, tape, etc.

formation *n* **1** the process of forming, making, developing or establishing something. **2 a** a particular arrangement or order, particularly of troops, aircraft, players of a game, etc: *The planes flew in formation;* **b** a shape or structure. **3** *geol* a mass or area of rocks which have common characteristics.

formative *adj* **1** relating to development or growth: *the formative years.* **2** having an effect on development.

former *adj* **1** belonging to or occurring at an

earlier time. **2** of two people or things: mentioned, considered, etc first. **3** having once or previously been: *her former partner.* ◆ **the former** of two people or things: the first one mentioned, considered, etc. Compare LATTER.

formerly *adv* previously; at one time.

Formica *n, trademark* a hard, heat-resistant plastic.

formic acid *n, chem* a colourless, pungent, toxic liquid, present in ant bites and stinging nettles.

formidable *adj* **1** awesomely impressive. **2** of problems, etc: difficult to overcome. ○ **formidably** *adv.*

formless *adj* lacking a clear shape or structure.

formula *n* (**formulae** /ˈfɔːmjuliː, -laɪ/ or **formulas**) **1** the combination of ingredients used in manufacturing something. **2** a method or rule of procedure, esp a successful one. **3** *chem* a combination of chemical symbols that represents the chemical composition of a particular substance. **4** *maths, physics* a mathematical equation or expression, or a physical law, that represents the relationship between various quantities, etc. **5** an established piece of wording used by convention eg in religious ceremonies or legal proceedings. **6** a classification for racing cars according to design and engine size. **7** *N Am* powdered milk for babies. ○ **formulaic** *adj.*

formulate *vb* **1** to express something in terms of a formula. **2** to express something in systematic terms. **3** to express something precisely and clearly. ○ **formulation** *n.*

fornicate *vb, intr* to have sexual intercourse outside marriage. ○ **fornication** *n.* ○ **fornicator** *n.*

forsake *vb* (**forsook, forsaken**) **1** to desert; to abandon. **2** to renounce, or no longer follow or indulge in. ○ **forsaken** *adj.*

forsooth *adv, archaic* indeed.

forswear *vb* (**forswore, forsworn**) *old use* **1** to give up or renounce (one's foolish ways, etc). **2** to perjure (oneself).

fort *n* a fortified military building, enclosure or position. ◆ **hold the fort** to keep things running in the absence of the person normally in charge.

forte[1] /ˈfɔːteɪ/ *n* something one is good at.

forte[2] /ˈfɔːteɪ/ *mus, adv* in a loud manner. ➤ *adj* loud.

forth *adv, old use* except in certain set phrases **1** into existence or view: *to bring forth children.* **2** forwards: *to swing back and forth.* **3** out: *They set forth on a journey.* **4** onwards: *from this day forth.* ◆ **and so forth** and so on. **hold forth** to speak, esp at length.

forthcoming *adj* **1** happening or appearing soon. **2** of a person: willing to talk. **3** available.

forthright *adj* firm, frank and straightforward.

forthwith *adv* immediately.

forties (often written **40s** or **40's**) *pl n* **1** (**one's**

forties) the period of time between one's fortieth and fiftieth birthdays. **2** (**the forties**) the range of temperatures between forty and fifty degrees. **3** (**the forties**) the period of time between the fortieth and fiftieth years of a century: *She was born in the 40s.*

fortification *n* **1** the process of fortifying. **2** (**fortifications**) walls and other defensive structures built in preparation for an attack.

fortify *vb* (*-ies, -ied*) **1** to strengthen (a building, city, etc) in preparation for an attack. **2 a** to add extra alcohol to (wine) in the course of production, in order to produce sherry, port, etc; **b** to add extra vitamins, nutrients, etc to (food). **3** to strengthen or revive, either physically or mentally.

fortissimo *mus, adv* in a very loud manner. ➢ *adj* very loud.

fortitude *n* uncomplaining courage in pain or misfortune.

fortnight *n* a period of 14 days.

fortnightly *adj* occurring, appearing, etc once every fortnight. ➢ *adv* once a fortnight. ➢ *n* (*-ies*) a publication which comes out every two weeks.

fortress *n* a fortified town or large fort.

fortuitous *adj* happening by chance. ○ **fortuitously** *adv.*

fortunate *adj* **1** lucky; favoured by fate. **2** timely; opportune. ○ **fortunately** *adv.*

fortune *n* **1** chance as a force in human affairs. **2** luck. **3** (**fortunes**) unpredictable happenings that alter a situation: *the fortunes of war.* **4** (**fortunes**) the state of one's luck. **5** one's destiny. **6** a large sum of money.

fortune-teller *n* a person who claims to be able to tell people their destinies. ○ **fortune-telling** *n, adj.*

forty *n* (*-ies*) **1 a** the cardinal number 40; **b** the quantity that this represents, being one more than thirty-nine, or the product of ten and four. **2** any symbol for this, eg *40* or *XL.* ➢ *adj* **1** totalling forty. **2** aged forty. ○ **fortieth** *adj, n, adv.*

forty winks *pl n, colloq* a short sleep.

forum *n* (*fora*) **1** *hist* a public square or market place, esp that in ancient Rome where public business was conducted and law courts held. **2** a meeting to discuss topics of public concern. **3** a place, programme or publication where opinions can be expressed and openly discussed.

forward *adv* **1** (*also* **forwards**) in the direction in front or ahead of one. **2** (*also* **forwards**) progressing from first to last. **3** on or onward; to a later time. **4** to an earlier time. **5** into view or public attention. ➢ *adj* **1** in the direction in front or ahead. **2** at the front. **3** advanced in development. **4** concerning the future. **5** *derog* inclined to push oneself forward. ➢ *n, sport* a player whose task is to attack rather than defend. Compare BACK *noun* (sense 6). ➢ *vb* **1** to send (mail) on to another address from the one to which it arrived. **2** to help the progress of something.

fossil *n* **1** an impression or cast of an animal or plant preserved within a rock. **2** *colloq* a curiously antiquated person. ➢ *adj* **1** like or in the form of a fossil. **2** formed naturally through the decomposition of organic matter: *fossil fuels.*

fossil fuel *n* a fuel, such as coal, petroleum and natural gas, derived from fossilized remains.

fossilize or **-ise** *vb, tr & intr* **1** to change or be changed into a fossil. **2** to become or make old-fashioned, inflexible, etc. ○ **fossilization** *n.*

foster *vb* **1** *tr & intr* to bring up (a child that is not one's own). **2** to put (a child) into the care of someone who is not its parent, usu for a temporary period of time. **3** to encourage the development of (ideas, feelings, etc). ➢ *adj* **1** concerned with or offering fostering: *foster home.* **2** related through fostering rather than by birth: *foster mother.*

foul *adj* **1** disgusting: *a foul smell.* **2** soiled; filthy. **3** contaminated: *foul air.* **4** *colloq* very unkind or unpleasant. **5** of language: offensive or obscene. **6** unfair or treacherous: *by fair means or foul.* **7** of weather: stormy. ➢ *n, sport* a breach of the rules. ➢ *vb* **1** *tr & intr, sport* to commit a foul against (an opponent). **2** to make something dirty or polluted. **3** *tr & intr* (*sometimes* **foul up** or **foul sth up**) to become or cause it to become entangled. **4** *tr & intr* (*sometimes* **foul up** or **foul sth up**) to become or cause it to become clogged. ➢ *adv* in a foul manner; unfairly. ○ **foully** *adv.* ○ **foulness** *n.*

foul-mouthed or **foul-spoken** *adj* of a person: using offensive or obscene language.

foul play *n* **1** treachery or criminal violence, esp murder. **2** *sport* a breach of the rules.

found¹ *vb* **1** to start or establish (an organization, city, etc), often with a provision for future funding. **2** to lay the foundation of (a building). ○ **founder** *n.*

found² *vb* **1** to cast (metal or glass) by melting and pouring it into a mould. **2** to produce (articles) by this method.

found³ *past tense, past participle of* FIND

foundation *n* **1 a** an act or the process of establishing an institution, etc; **b** an institution, etc founded or the fund providing for it. **2** (*usu* **foundations**) the underground structure on which a building is supported and built. **3** the basis on which a theory, etc rests or depends.

foundation course *n* an introductory course, usu taken as a preparation for more advanced studies.

foundation stone *n* a stone laid ceremonially as part of the foundations of a new building.

founder *vb, intr* **1** of a ship: to sink. **2** of a vehicle, etc: to get stuck in mud, etc. **3** of a horse: to go lame. **4** of a business, scheme, etc: to fail.

foundling *n* an abandoned child of unknown parents.

foundry *n* (*-ies*) a place where metal or glass is melted and cast.

fount¹ or **font** *n, printing* a set of printing type of the same design and size.

fount² *n* **1** a spring or fountain. **2** a source of inspiration, etc.

fountain *n* **1 a** a jet or jets of water for ornamental effect; **b** an ornamental structure supporting this. **2** a structure housing a jet of drinking water, eg, in an office or public place. **3** a spring of water. **4** a source of wisdom, etc.

fountainhead *n* **1** a spring from which a stream flows. **2** the principal source of something.

fountain pen *n* a metal-nibbed pen equipped with a cartridge or reservoir of ink.

four *n* **1 a** the cardinal number 4; **b** the quantity that this represents, being one more than three. **2** any symbol for this, eg *4* or *IV*. **3** the fourth hour after midnight or midday: *Tea's at four • 4 o'clock • 4pm.* **4** a set or group of four people or things. **5 a** the crew of a rowing boat with four sweep oars; **b** such a boat. **6** *cricket* a score of four runs awarded if the ball reaches the boundary having hit the ground. ➤ *adj* **1** totalling four. **2** aged four. ◆ **on all fours** on hands and knees.

fourfold *adj* **1** equal to four times as much or many. **2** divided into, or consisting of, four parts. ➤ *adv* by four times as much.

four-letter word *n* a short obscene English word.

four-poster *n* a large bed with a post at each corner to support curtains and a canopy. Also called **four-poster bed**.

fourscore *adj, n, archaic* eighty.

foursome *n* **1** a set or group of four people. **2** *golf* a game between two pairs of players.

four-square *adj* **1** strong; steady; solidly based. **2** of a building: square and solid-looking. ➤ *adv* steadily; squarely.

fourteen *n* **1 a** the cardinal number 14; **b** the quantity that this represents, being one more than thirteen, or the sum of ten and four. **2** any symbol for this, eg *14* or *XIV*. ➤ *adj* **1** totalling fourteen. **2** aged fourteen. ○ **fourteenth** *adj, n, adv.*

fourth (often written **4th**) *adj* **1** in counting: **a** next after third; **b** last of four. **2** in fourth position. **3** being one of four equal parts. Usually called QUARTER: *a fourth share.* ➤ *n* **1** one of four equal parts. Usually called QUARTER. **2** a FRACTION equal to one divided by four (usu written ¼). Usually called QUARTER. **3** a person coming fourth, eg in a race or exam. **4** (**the fourth**) the fourth day of the month. **5** *mus* **a** an interval of three diatonic degrees; **b** a note at that interval from another, or a combination of two tones separated by that interval. ➤ *adv* fourthly. ○ **fourthly** *adv* used to introduce the fourth point in a list.

fourth dimension *n* **1** time regarded as a dimension complementing the three dimensions of space. **2** a dimension, such as a parallel universe, which may exist in addition to the three dimensions of space.

fowl *n* (**fowls** or **fowl**) **1** a farmyard bird, eg a chicken or turkey. **2** the flesh or meat of one of these birds used as food. ➤ *vb* (**fowled, fowling**) *intr* to hunt or trap wild birds.

fox *n* **1** a carnivorous mammal of the dog family, with a pointed muzzle, large pointed ears and a long bushy tail. **2** the fur of this animal. **3** *colloq* a cunning person. **4** *N Am* an attractive woman. ➤ *vb* **1** to puzzle, confuse or baffle. **2** to deceive, trick or outwit.

foxglove *n* a plant that produces tall spikes with many thimble-shaped purple or white flowers.

foxhole *n, mil* a hole dug in the ground by a soldier for protection from enemy fire.

foxhound *n* a breed of dog bred and trained to chase foxes.

fox hunt *n* **1** a hunt for a fox by people on horseback using hounds. **2** a group of people who meet to hunt foxes. ○ **foxhunting** *n.*

foxtrot *n* **1** a ballroom dance with gliding steps, alternating between quick and slow. **2** the music for this dance. ➤ *vb, intr* to perform this dance.

foxy *adj* (**-ier, -iest**) **1** referring to foxes. **2** cunning. **3** reddish brown in colour. **4** *slang* of a woman: sexually attractive. ○ **foxily** *adv.* ○ **foxiness** *n.*

foyer *n* an entrance hall of a theatre, hotel, etc.

Fr¹ *abbrev* Father, the title of a priest.

Fr² *symbol, chem* francium.

fracas /'fraka:/ *n* (**fracas**) a noisy quarrel or brawl.

fraction *n* **1** *maths* an expression that indicates one or more equal parts of a whole. **2** a portion; a small part of something. ○ **fractional** *adj.* ○ **fractionally** *adv.*

fractious *adj* cross and quarrelsome. ○ **fractiously** *adv.*

fracture *n* **1** the breaking or cracking of anything hard, esp bone, rock or mineral. **2** the medical condition resulting from this. ➤ *vb* **1** to break or crack something, esp a bone. **2** *intr* of a bone, etc: to break or crack.

fragile *adj* **1** easily broken. **2** easily damaged or destroyed. **3** delicate. **4** in a weakened state of health. ○ **fragility** *n.*

fragment *n* /'fragmant/ **1** a piece broken off; a small piece of something that has broken. **2** something incomplete; a small part remaining. ➤ *vb* /frag'mɛnt/ *tr & intr* to break into pieces. ○ **fragmentation** *n.*

fragmentary or **fragmented** *adj* consisting of small pieces.

fragrance *n* **1** sweetness of smell. **2** a sweet smell or odour. ○ **fragrant** *adj.*

frail *adj* **1** easily broken or destroyed. **2** in poor health; weak. **3** morally weak; easily tempted. ○ **frailness** *n.* ○ **frailty** *n* (**-ies**).

frame *n* **1** a hard main structure or basis to something, round which something is built or to which other parts are added. **2** a structure that surrounds and supports something. **3** something that surrounds. **4** a body, esp a human one, as a structure of a certain size and shape. **5** one of the pictures that make up a strip of film. **6** a single television picture, eg a still picture seen when the pause button on a video player is pressed. **7** one of the pictures in a comic strip. **8** a low glass or semi-glazed structure for protecting young plants growing out of doors. **9** a framework of bars, eg in a playground for children to play on. **10** *snooker, etc* **a** a triangular structure for confining the balls for a round; **b** each of the rounds of play, a predetermined number of which constitute the entire match. **11** the rigid part of a bicycle, usu made of metal tubes. ➢ *vb* **1** to put a frame round something. **b** to be a frame for something. **3** to compose or design something. **4** to shape or direct (one's thoughts, actions, etc) for a particular purpose. **5** *colloq* to dishonestly direct suspicion for a crime, etc at (an innocent person).

frame of mind *n* (*frames of mind*) a mood; state of mind.

frame of reference *n* (*frames of reference*) a set of facts, beliefs or principles that serves as the context within which specific actions, events or behaviour patterns can be analysed or described.

frame-up *n, colloq* a plot or arrangement to make an innocent person appear guilty.

framework *n* **1** a basic supporting structure. **2** a basic plan or system.

franc *n* **1** the standard unit of currency of various countries including Switzerland and Liechtenstein. **2** the former standard unit of currency of France, Belgium and Luxembourg, replaced in 2002 by the euro.

franchise *n* **1** the right to vote, esp in a parliamentary election. **2** a right, privilege, exemption from a duty, etc, granted to a person or organization. **3** an agreement by which a business company gives someone the right to market its products in an area. **4** a concession granted by a public authority to a TV, radio, etc company to broadcast in a certain area. ➢ *vb* to grant a franchise to (a person, a company, etc). ○ **franchisee** *n*. ○ **franchiser** or **franchisor** *n*.

francium *n, chem* a radioactive metallic element, the heaviest of the alkali metals, present in uranium ore.

francophone *n* a French-speaking person, esp in a country where other languages are spoken. ➢ *adj* **1** speaking French as a native language. **2** using French as a second mother-tongue or lingua franca.

frank *adj* **1** open and honest in speech or manner. **2** bluntly outspoken. **3** undisguised; openly visible. ➢ *vb* to mark (a letter), either cancelling the stamp or, in place of a stamp, to show that postage has been paid. ➢ *n* a franking mark on a letter. ○ **frankly** *adv*. ○ **frankness** *n*.

frankfurter *n* a type of spicy smoked sausage, orig made in Frankfurt am Main.

frankincense *n* an aromatic gum resin burnt

to produce a sweet smell, esp during religious ceremonies.

frantic *adj* **1** desperate, eg with fear or anxiety. **2** hurried. ○ **frantically** *adv*.

frappé /ˈfræpeɪ/ *adj* iced. ➢ *n* an iced drink.

fraternal *adj* **1** concerning a brother; brotherly. **2** of twins: developed from two ZYGOTES or fertilized eggs. Compare IDENTICAL (sense 3). ○ **fraternally** *adv*.

fraternity *n* (*-ies*) **1** a religious brotherhood. **2** a group of people with common interests. **3** the fact of being brothers; brotherly feeling. **4** *NAm* a social club for male students. Compare SORORITY.

fraternize or **-ise** *vb, intr* (*often* **fraternize with sb**) to meet or associate together as friends. ○ **fraternization** *n*.

fratricide *n* **1** the act of killing one's own brother. **2** someone who commits this act.

fraud *n* **1** an act or instance of deliberate deception, with the intention of gaining some benefit. **2** *colloq* someone who dishonestly pretends to be something they are not.

fraudster *n* a cheat; a swindler.

fraudulent *adj* involving deliberate deception; intended to deceive. ○ **fraudulence** or **fraudulency** *n*. ○ **fraudulently** *adv*.

fraught *adj, colloq* causing or feeling anxiety or worry. ♦ **fraught with danger,** *etc* full of danger, difficulties, etc.

fray¹ *vb, tr & intr* **1** of cloth or rope: to wear away along an edge or at a point of friction, so that individual threads come loose. **2** of tempers, nerves, etc: to make or become edgy and strained.

fray² *n* **1** a fight or quarrel. **2** any scene of lively action.

frazzle *n* **1** a state of nervous and physical exhaustion. **2** a scorched and brittle state: *burnt to a frazzle.* ➢ *vb* to tire out physically and emotionally.

freak *n* **1** a person, animal or plant of abnormal shape or form. **2** someone or something odd or unusual. **3** *esp in compounds* someone highly enthusiastic about the specified thing: *health freak • film freak.* **4** a drug addict: *an acid freak.* **5** a whim or caprice: *a freak of fancy.* ➢ *adj* abnormal: *a freak storm.* ➢ *vb, tr & intr* (*also* **freak out** or **freak sb out**) *colloq* **1 a** to become or make someone mentally or emotionally over-excited: *It really freaked him*; **b** to become frightened or paranoid, or make someone become so, esp through the use of hallucinatory drugs. **2** (*also* **freak out**) to become angry or make someone angry. ○ **freaky** *adj*.

freckle *n* a small yellowish-brown benign mark on the skin, usu becoming darker and more prominent with exposure to the sun. ➢ *vb, tr & intr* to mark, or become marked, with freckles. ○ **freckled** or **freckly** *adj*.

free *adj* **1** allowed to move as one pleases; not shut in. **2** not tied or fastened. **3** allowed to do as one pleases; not restricted, controlled or enslaved. **4** of a country: independent. **5** costing nothing. **6** open or available to all. **7** not working, busy, engaged or having another appointment. **8** not occupied; not being used. **9** of a translation: not precisely literal. **10** smooth and easy. **11** without obstruction. **12** *derog* of a person's manner: disrespectful, over-familiar or presumptuous. **13** *chem* not combined with another chemical element. **14** *in compounds* **a** not containing the specified ingredient, substance, factor, etc: *sugar-free*; **b** free from, or not affected or troubled by, the specified thing: *carefree*; **c** not paying or exempt from the specified thing: *tax-free*. ➤ *adv* **1** without payment: *free of charge*. **2** freely; without restriction: *to wander free*. ➤ *vb* **1** to allow someone to move without restriction after a period in captivity, prison, etc; to liberate someone. **2** (*usu* **free sb of** or **from sth**) to rid or relieve them of it. ○ **freely** *adv*. ○ **freeness** *n*. ◆ **feel free** *colloq* you have permission (to do something): *Feel free to borrow my bike*. **free and easy** cheerfully casual or tolerant. **a free hand** scope to choose how best to act. **free of** or **from sth** without; not or no longer having or suffering: *free from pain*. **free with sth** open, generous, lavish or liberal: *free with her money*.

freebie *n*, *colloq* something given or provided without charge, particularly as a sales promotion.

freeboard *n*, *naut* the distance between the top edge of the side of a boat and the surface of the water.

freebooter *n*, *hist* a pirate.

freeborn *adj* born as a free citizen, not a slave.

freedom *n* **1** the condition of being free to act, move, etc without restriction. **2** personal liberty or independence, eg from slavery, etc. **3** a right or liberty. **4** (*often* **freedom from sth**) the state of being without or exempt (from something). **5** autonomy, self-government or independence, eg of a state or republic. **6** unrestricted access to or use of something. **7** honorary citizenship of a place, entitling one to certain privileges: *She was granted the freedom of Aberdeen*. **8** frankness.

free enterprise *n* business carried out between companies, firms, etc without interference or control by the government.

free fall *n* **1** the fall of something acted on by gravity alone. **2** the part of a descent by parachute before the parachute opens.

free-for-all *n* a fight, argument, or discussion in which everybody present feels free to join.

free-form *adj* freely flowing; spontaneous.

freehand *adj*, *adv* of a drawing, etc: done without the help of a ruler, compass, etc.

free hand *n* complete freedom of action.

freehold *adj* of land, property, etc: belonging to the owner for life and without limitations. ➤ *n* ownership of such land, property, etc. Compare LEASEHOLD. ○ **freeholder** *n*.

free kick *n*, *football* a kick awarded to one side with no tackling from the other, following an infringement of the rules.

freelance *n* a self-employed person offering their services where needed, not under contract to any single employer. ➤ *adv* as a freelance: *She works freelance now*. ➤ *vb*, *intr* to work as a freelance.

freeload *vb*, *intr*, *colloq* to eat, live, enjoy oneself, etc at someone else's expense. ○ **freeloader** *n*.

Freemason or **Mason** *n* a member of an international secret male society, organized from LODGES, having among its purposes mutual help. ○ **Freemasonry** *n*.

free radical *n*, *chem* an uncharged atom or group of atoms containing at least one unpaired electron.

free-range *adj* **1** of animal livestock, esp poultry and pigs: allowed some freedom to move about and graze or feed naturally. **2** of eggs: laid by free-range poultry.

freesia *n* a plant of the iris family, widely cultivated for its fragrant trumpet-shaped flowers.

free speech *n* the right to express any opinion freely, particularly in public.

free-standing *adj* not attached to or supported by a wall or other structure.

freestyle *sport*, *adj* **1 a** denoting a competition or race in which competitors are allowed to choose their own style; **b** *swimming* denoting the front crawl stroke, most commonly chosen by swimmers in a freestyle event. **2** denoting ALL-IN WRESTLING. ➤ *n* a freestyle competition or race.

freethinker *n* someone who forms their own ideas, esp religious ones, rather than accepting the view of an authority. ○ **freethinking** *n*.

free trade *n* trade between or amongst countries without protective tariffs.

freeware *n*, *comput* software which is made available free of charge.

freeway *n*, *N Am* a toll-free highway.

freewheel *vb*, *intr* **1** to travel, usu downhill, on a bicycle, in a car, etc without using mechanical power. **2** to act or drift about unhampered by responsibilities.

free will *n* **1 a** the power of making choices without the constraint of fate, regarded as a human characteristic; **b** the philosophical doctrine that this human characteristic is not illusory. **2** a person's independent choice.

freeze *vb* (**freezes, froze, frozen, freezing**) **1** *tr & intr* to change (a liquid) into a solid by cooling it to below its freezing point. **2** of a liquid: to change into a solid when it is cooled to below its freezing point. **3** *tr & intr* (*often* **freeze together**) to stick or cause to stick together by frost. **4** *intr* of the weather, temperature, etc: to be at or below the freezing-point of water. **5** *tr & intr*, *colloq* to be or make very cold. **6** *intr* to die of cold. **7** *tr & intr* of food: to preserve, or be suitable for preserving, by refrigeration at or below freezing-point. **8** *tr & intr* to make or become motionless or unable to move, because of fear, etc. **9** to fix (prices, wages, etc) at a certain level. **10** to prevent (money, shares, assets, etc) from being used. **11** to stop (a video, a moving film, etc) at a certain frame. **12** to anaesthetize (a part of the body). ➤ *n* **1** a period of very cold weather with temperatures below freezing point. **2** a period during which wages, prices, etc are controlled. ➤ *exclam, chiefly US* a command to stop instantly or risk being shot. ○ **freezable** *adj*. ◊ **freeze sb out** to exclude them from an activity, conversation, etc by persistent unfriendliness.

freeze-dry *vb* to preserve (perishable material, esp food and medicines) by rapidly freezing it and then drying it under high-vacuum conditions.

freezer *n* a refrigerated cabinet or compartment in which to store or preserve food at a temperature below freezing point.

freezing point *n* **1** the temperature at which the liquid form of a particular substance turns into a solid. **2** (*also* **freezing**) the freezing point of water (0°C at sea level).

freight *n* **1** transport of goods by rail, road, sea or air. **2** the goods transported in this way. **3** the cost of such transport. ➤ *vb* **1** to transport (goods) by rail, road, sea or air. **2** to load (a vehicle, etc) with goods for transport.

freighter *n* a ship or aircraft that carries cargo rather than passengers.

French *adj* **1** belonging or relating to France or its inhabitants. **2** relating to the French language. ➤ *n* **1** (**the French**) the people of France. **2** the official language of France and various other countries.

French bean *n* a widely cultivated species of bean plant whose pods and unripe seeds are eaten together as a vegetable.

French bread, **French loaf** or **French stick** *n* white bread in the form of a long narrow loaf with tapered ends and a thick crisp crust.

French chalk *n* a form of the mineral talc used to mark cloth or remove grease marks.

French dressing *n* a salad dressing made from oil, spices, herbs, and lemon juice or vinegar.

French fries or **fries** *pl n, chiefly N Am colloq* long thin strips of potato deep-fried in oil, usu longer and thinner than chips.

French horn *n* an orchestral HORN.

French leave *n* leave taken without permission from work or duty.

French letter *n, slang* a condom.

French polish *n* a varnish for furniture, consisting of shellac dissolved in alcohol. ➤ *vb* (**French-polish**) to varnish (furniture, etc) with French polish.

French toast *n* slices of bread dipped in beaten egg and fried.

French windows or (*N Am*) **French doors** *pl n* a pair of glass doors that open on to a garden, etc.

frenetic or (*rare*) **phrenetic** *adj* frantic, distracted or wildly energetic. ○ **frenetically** or (*rare*) **phrenetically** *adv*.

frenzy *n* (*-ies*) **1** wild agitation or excitement. **2** a frantic burst of activity. **3** a state of violent mental disturbance. ○ **frenzied** *adj*.

frequency *n* (*-ies*) **1** the condition of happening often. **2** the rate at which a happening, phenomenon, etc, recurs. **3** *physics* a measure of the rate at which a complete cycle of wave motion is repeated per unit time. **4** *radio* the rate of sound waves per second at which a particular radio signal is sent out.

frequency modulation *n, radio* a method of radio transmission in which the frequency of the carrier wave increases or decreases in response to changes in the amplitude of the signal being transmitted.

frequent *adj* /ˈfriːkwənt/ **1** recurring at short intervals. **2** habitual. ➤ *vb* /frɪˈkwɛnt/ to visit or attend (a place, an event, etc) often. ○ **frequently** *adv*.

fresco *n* (**frescoes** or **frescos**) a picture painted on a wall, usu while the plaster is still damp. ○ **frescoed** *adj*.

fresh *adj* **1** newly made, gathered, etc. **2** having just arrived from somewhere, just finished doing something or just had some experience, etc: *fresh from university*. **3** other or another; clean: *a fresh sheet of paper*. **4** new; additional: *fresh supplies*. **5** original: *a fresh approach*. **6** of fruit or vegetables: not tinned, frozen, dried or otherwise preserved. **7** not tired; bright and alert. **8** cool; refreshing: *a fresh breeze*. **9** of water: not salty. **10** of air: cool and uncontaminated; invigorating. **11** of the face or complexion: youthfully healthy. **12** not worn or faded. **13** *colloq* of behaviour: offensively informal. ○ **freshly** *adv*. ○ **freshness** *n*.

freshen *vb* **1** to make something fresh or fresher. **2** *tr & intr* (*also* **freshen up** or **freshen oneself** or **sb up**) to get washed and tidy; to wash and tidy (oneself or someone). **3** *intr* of a wind: to become stronger.

fresher or (*N Am*) **freshman** *n* a student in their first year at university or college.

freshet *n* **1** a stream of fresh water flowing into the sea. **2** the sudden overflow of a river.

freshwater *adj* referring to, consisting of or living in fresh as opposed to salt water: *freshwater lake* • *freshwater fish*.

fret¹ *vb* (**fretted**, **fretting**) **1** *intr* (*also* **fret about** or **over sth**) to worry, esp unnecessarily. **2** to wear something away by rubbing or erosion.

fret² *n* any of the narrow metal ridges across the neck of a guitar or similar musical instrument, onto which the strings are pressed in producing the various notes.

fret³ *n* a type of decoration for a cornice, border, etc, consisting of a pattern of lines which form a continuous band. ➤ *vb* (**fretted**, **fretting**) to decorate something with a fret, or carve with fretwork.

fretful *adj* anxious and unhappy; tending to fret. ○ **fretfully** *adv*.

fretsaw *n* a narrow-bladed saw for cutting designs in wood or metal. Compare COPING SAW.

fretwork *n* fine decorative work in wood or metal including open spaces.

Freudian slip *n* an error or unintentional action, esp a slip of the tongue, taken as revealing an unexpressed or unconscious thought.

friable *adj* easily broken; easily reduced to powder. ○ **friability** *n*.

friar *n* a male member of any of various religious orders of the Roman Catholic Church.

friary *n* (-*ies*) **1** a building inhabited by a community of friars. **2** the community itself.

fricassee *n* a cooked dish, usu of pieces of meat or chicken served in a sauce. ➤ *vb* to prepare meat as a fricassee.

fricative *phonetics, adj* of a sound: produced partly by friction, the breath being forced through a narrowed opening. ➤ *n* a fricative consonant, eg *sh*, *f* and *th*.

friction *n* **1** the rubbing of one thing against another. **2** *physics* the force that opposes the relative motion of two bodies or surfaces that are in contact with each other. **3** quarrelling; conflict. ○ **frictional** *adj*.

Friday *n* the sixth day of the week.

fridge *n*, *colloq* a refrigerator.

friend *n* **1** someone whom one knows and likes, and to whom one shows loyalty and affection. **2** someone who gives support or help. **3** an ally. **4** someone or something already encountered or mentioned: *our old friend the woodworm*. **5** (**Friend**) a Quaker; a member of the Religious Society of Friends. **6** a member of an organization which gives voluntary financial or other support to an institution, etc: *Friends of the National Gallery*. ○ **friendless** *adj*. ○ **friendship** *n*.

friendly *adj* (-*ier*, -*iest*) **1** kind; behaving as a friend. **2** (**friendly with sb**) on close or affectionate terms with them. **3** relating to, or typical of, a friend. **4** being a colleague, partner, etc rather than an enemy: *friendly nations*. **5** *sport* of a match, etc: played for enjoyment or practice and not as part of a formal competition. **6** *in compounds, forming adjs* **a** denoting things that are made easy or convenient for those for whom they are intended: *user-friendly*; **b** indicating that something causes little harm to something: *dolphin-friendly*. ➤ *n* (-*ies*) *sport* a friendly match. ○ **friendliness** *n*.

frier see FRYER

fries¹ see under FRY¹

fries² see FRENCH FRIES

frieze *n* **1** a decorative strip running along a wall. **2** *archit* **a** a horizontal band between the cornice and capitals of a classical temple; **b** the sculpture which fills this space.

frigate *n* **1** a naval escort vessel, smaller than a destroyer. **2** *hist* a small fast-moving sailing warship.

fright *n* **1** sudden fear; a shock. **2** *colloq* a person or thing of ludicrous appearance. ♦ **take fright** to become scared.

frighten *vb* **1** to make someone afraid; to alarm them. **2** (*usu* **frighten sb away** or **off**) to drive them away by making them afraid. ○ **frightened** *adj*. ○ **frightening** *adj*.

frightful *adj* **1** frightening. **2** *colloq* bad; awful. **3** *colloq* great; extreme. ○ **frightfully** *adv*.

frigid *adj* **1** cold and unfriendly; without feeling. **2** of a woman: not sexually responsive. **3** *geog* intensely cold. ○ **frigidity** *n*.

frill *n* **1** a gathered or pleated strip of cloth attached along one edge to a garment, etc as a trimming. **2** (*usu* **frills**) something extra serving no useful purpose. ○ **frilled** *adj*. ○ **frilly** *adj* (-*ier*, -*iest*). ♦ **without frills** with no superfluous additions.

fringe *n* **1** a border of loose threads on a carpet, garment, etc. **2** hair cut to hang down over the forehead. **3** the part farthest from the main area or centre. ➤ *adj* **a** bordering, or just outside, the recognized or orthodox form, group, etc: *fringe medicine*; **b** unofficial, not part of the main event: *fringe meeting* • *fringe festival*; **c** less important or less popular: *fringe sports*. ➤ *vb* **1** to decorate something with a fringe. **2** to form a fringe round something.

fringe benefits *pl n* things that one gets from one's employer in addition to wages or salary, eg a cheap mortgage, a car, etc.

Frisbee *n*, *trademark* a light, plastic, saucer-shaped object that spins when thrown and is used in catching games.

frippery *n* (-*ies*) **1** showy but unnecessary adornment. **2** trifles; trivia.

frisk *vb* **1** *intr* (*also* **frisk about**) to jump or run about happily and playfully. **2** *slang* to search someone for concealed weapons, drugs, etc. ➤ *n* **1** a spell of prancing about. **2** an act of searching a person for weapons, etc.

frisky *adj* (-*ier*, -*iest*) lively; high-spirited. ○ **friskily** *adv*.

frisson /ˈfriːsɒn/ *n* a shiver of fear or excitement.

fritter¹ *n* a piece of meat, fruit, etc coated in batter and fried: *spam fritter* • *banana fritter*.

fritter² *vb* (*chiefly* **fritter sth away**) to waste (time, money, energy, etc) on unimportant things.

frivolous *adj* **1** silly; not sufficiently serious. **2** not useful and sensible. ○ **frivolity** *n* (-*ies*).

frizz *n* of hair: a mass of tight curls. ➤ *vb, tr & intr* (*also* **frizz sth up**) to form or make something form a frizz.

frizzle *vb, tr & intr* of food: to fry till scorched and brittle.

frizzy *adj* (-*ier*, -*iest*) tightly curled.

frock *n* **1** a woman's or girl's dress. **2** a priest's or monk's long garment, with large open sleeves. **3** a loose smock.

frog¹ *n* a tailless amphibian with a moist smooth skin and powerful hind legs for swimming and leaping. ♦ **a frog in one's throat** a throat irritation that temporarily interferes with one's speech.

frog² *n* a decorative looped fastener on a garment. ○ **frogging** *n* a set of such fasteners, esp on a military uniform.

frogman *n* an underwater swimmer wearing a protective rubber suit and using breathing equipment.

frogmarch *vb* to force someone forward, holding them firmly by the arms.

frogspawn *n* a mass of frogs' eggs encased in nutrient jelly.

frolic *vb* (**frolicked, frolicking**) *intr* to frisk or run about playfully. ➤ *n* a spell of happy playing or frisking. ○ **frolicsome** *adj*.

from *prep*, indicating **1** a starting-point in place or time: *from London to Glasgow* • *crippled from birth*. **2** a lower limit: *tickets from £12 upwards*. **3** repeated progression: *trailing from shop to shop*. **4** movement out of: *James took a letter from the drawer*. **5** distance away: *16 miles from Dover*. **6** a viewpoint: *You can see the house from here*. **7** separation; removal: *They took it away from her*. **8** point of attachment: *hanging from a nail*. **9** exclusion: *omitted from the sample*. **10** source or origin: *made from an old curtain*. **11** change of condition: *translate from French into English*. **12** cause: *ill from overwork*. **13** deduction as a result of observation: *You can see from her face she's angry*. **14** distinction: *I can't tell one twin from the other*. **15** prevention, protection, exemption, immunity, release, escape, etc: *safe from harm* • *excused from attending* • *released from prison*.

fromage frais /ˈfrɒmɑːʒ ˈfreɪ/ *n* a creamy low-fat cheese with the consistency of whipped cream.

frond *n, bot* a large compound leaf, esp of a fern or palm.

front *n* **1** the side or part of anything that is furthest forward or nearest to the viewer; the most important side or part. **2** any side of a large or historic building. **3** the part of a vehicle, etc that faces the direction in which it moves. **4** *theat* the auditorium of a theatre, etc. **5** the cover or first pages of a book. **6** a road or promenade in a town that runs beside the sea, or large lake, etc. **7** in war, particularly when fought on the ground: the area where the soldiers are nearest to the enemy: *eastern front*. **8** a matter of concern or interest: *no progress on the job front*. **9** *meteorol* the boundary between two air masses that have different temperatures. **10** an outward appearance. **11** (*usu* **Front**) a name given to some political movements, particularly when a number of organizations come together with a common goal. **12** *slang* an organization or job used to hide illegal or secret activity: *The corner shop was just a front for drug dealing*. ➤ *vb* **1** *tr & intr* of a building: to have its front facing or beside something designated: *The house fronts on to the main road*. **2** to be the leader or representative of (a group, etc). **3** to be the presenter of (a radio or television programme). **4** to cover the front of (a building, etc). **5** *intr* (*usu* **front for sth**) to provide a cover for it (eg an illegal activity, etc). ➤ *adj* **1** relating to, or situated at or in the front. **2** *phonetics* of a vowel: articulated

with the front of the tongue in a forward position. ♦ **in front 1** on the forward-facing side. **2** ahead. **in front of sb** or **sth 1** at or to a position in advance of them. **2** to a place towards which a vehicle, etc is moving: *Someone had run in front of a car*. **3** ahead of them: *He pushed in front of her*. **4** facing or confronting them: *I stood up in front of the audience*. **5** in their presence. **up front** *colloq* of money: paid before work is done or goods received, etc.

frontage *n* the front of a building.

frontal *adj* **1** relating to the front. **2** aimed at the front: *a frontal assault*. **3** *anat* relating to the forehead. **4** *meteorol* relating to the FRONT noun (sense 9): *frontal system*.

front bench *n* the seats in the House of Commons occupied on one side by Government ministers and on the other by leading members of the Opposition. ○ **frontbencher** *n*. Compare BACKBENCH, CROSS BENCH.

frontier *n* **1 a** the part of a country bordering onto another country; **b** a line, barrier, etc marking the boundary between two countries. **2** (**frontiers**) limits: *the frontiers of knowledge*. **3** *N Am hist* the furthest edge of civilization, habitation or cultivation.

frontiersman or **frontierswoman** *n* someone who lives on the frontier of a country, particularly on the outlying edges of a settled society.

frontispiece *n* a picture at the beginning of a book, facing the title page.

front line *n* **1** in a war: the area of a FRONT (*noun* sense 7) where soldiers are physically closest to the enemy. **2** that area in any concern where the important pioneering work is going on. ➤ *adj* (**front-line**) belonging or relating to the front line: *front-line soldiers*.

front-runner *n* the person most likely or most favoured to win a competition, election, etc.

frost *n* **1** a white deposit of ice crystals formed when water vapour comes into contact with a surface whose temperature is below freezing point. **2** an air temperature below freezing point: *12 degrees of frost*. ➤ *vb* **1** *tr & intr* (*also* **frost up** or **over**) to cover or become covered with frost. **2** to damage (plants) with frost.

frostbite *n* damage to the body tissues caused by exposure to very low temperatures. ○ **frostbitten** *adj*.

frosted *adj* **1** covered by frost. **2** damaged by frost. **3** of glass: patterned so as to be difficult to see through.

frosting *n, N Am* cake icing.

frosty *adj* (**-ier, -iest**) **1** covered with frost. **2** cold enough for frost to form. **3** of a person's behaviour or attitude: cold; unfriendly. ○ **frostily** *adv*.

froth *n* **1** a mass of tiny bubbles forming eg on the surface of a liquid, or round the mouth in certain diseases. **2** writing, talk, etc that has no serious point or purpose. **3** glamour; something frivolous or trivial. ➤ *vb, tr & intr* to produce or make something produce froth.

○ **frothy** adj (-**ier, -iest**).

frown vb, intr **1** to wrinkle one's forehead and draw one's eyebrows together in worry, disapproval, deep thought, etc. **2** (usu **frown at, on** or **upon** sth) to disapprove of it. ➤ n **1** the act of frowning. **2** a disapproving expression.

frowsty adj (-**ier, -iest**) stuffy; musty.

frowsy or **frowzy** adj (-**ier, -iest**) **1** of someone's appearance: untidy, dishevelled or slovenly. **2** of an atmosphere: stuffy.

frozen adj **1** preserved by keeping at a temperature below freezing point. **2** very cold. **3** stiff and unfriendly. ➤ vb past participle of FREEZE.

fructify vb (-**fies, -fied**) to produce fruit. ○ **fructification** n.

fructose n, biochem a sugar found in fruit and honey.

frugal adj **1** careful in financial matters; thrifty. **2** not large; costing little: a frugal meal. ○ **frugality** n. ○ **frugally** adv.

fruit n **1** the fully ripened ovary of a flowering plant, containing one or more seeds. **2** an edible part of a plant that is generally sweet and juicy, esp the ovary containing one or more seeds, but sometimes extended to include other parts, eg the leaf stalk in rhubarb. **3** plant products generally: the fruits of the land. **4** (also **fruits**) whatever is gained as a result of hard work, etc: the fruit of his labour. **5** derog slang, chiefly US a gay man. **6** old use, colloq a person: old fruit. **7** rare offspring: the fruit of her womb. ➤ vb, intr to produce fruit. ◆ **bear fruit 1** to produce fruit. **2** to produce good results. **in fruit** of a tree: bearing fruit.

fruitcake n **1** a cake containing dried fruit, nuts, etc. **2** colloq a slightly mad person.

fruiterer n a person who sells fruit.

fruitful adj producing useful results. ○ **fruitfully** adv. ○ **fruitfulness** n.

fruition n **1** the achievement of something that has been aimed at and worked for: The project finally came to fruition. **2** the bearing of fruit.

fruitless adj **1** useless; unsuccessful. **2** not producing fruit.

fruit machine n a coin-operated gambling machine with symbols in the form of fruits, that may be made to appear in winning combinations.

fruity adj (-**ier, -iest**) **1** full of fruit; having the taste or appearance of fruit. **2** of a voice: deep and rich in tone. **3** colloq of a story, etc: containing humorous and slightly risqué references to sexual matters.

frump n a woman who dresses in a dowdy way. ○ **frumpish** adj. ○ **frumpy** adj (-**ier, -iest**).

frustrate vb **1** to prevent (someone from doing something or from getting something); to thwart or foil (a plan, attempt, etc). **2** to make (someone) feel disappointed, useless, etc. ○ **frustrating** adj. ○ **frustratingly** adv. ○ **frustration** n.

fry[1] vb (**fries, fried**) tr & intr to cook (food) in hot oil or fat. ➤ n (**fries**) **1** a dish of anything fried. **2**

a FRY-UP. **3** (**fries**) FRENCH FRIES.

fry[2] pl n **1** young or newly spawned fish. **2** salmon in their second year.

fryer or **frier** n **1** a frying pan. **2** someone who fries something (esp fish).

frying pan n a shallow long-handled pan for frying food in.

fry-up n (**fry-ups**) a mixture of fried foods.

ft abbrev foot or feet.

FTP abbrev file-transfer protocol, a means of transferring data across a computer network.

fuchsia /ˈfjuːʃə/ n a shrub with purple, red or white hanging flowers.

fuck taboo slang, vb, tr & intr to have sex (with someone). ➤ n **1** an act of sexual intercourse. **2** a sexual partner. ➤ exclam an expression of anger, frustration, etc. ○ **fucking** adj, n, adv. ◊ **fuck off 1** to go away. **2** used in frustration or anger to demand someone leaves you alone. **fuck up** or **fuck sth up** to ruin or spoil it.

fuddle vb to confuse or stupefy. ➤ n a state of confusion or intoxication.

fuddy-duddy colloq, adj quaintly old-fashioned or prim. ➤ n (-**ies**) a fuddy-duddy person.

fudge[1] n a soft toffee made from butter, sugar and milk.

fudge[2] vb, colloq **1** to invent or concoct (an excuse, etc). **2** to distort or deliberately obscure (figures, an argument, etc), to cover up problems, mistakes, etc. **3** to dodge or evade something. **4** intr to avoid stating a clear opinion. ➤ n the action of obscuring, distorting an issue, etc.

fuel n **1** any material that releases energy when it is burned, which can be used as a source of heat or power. **2** fissile material that is used to release energy by nuclear fission in a nuclear reactor. **3** food, as a source of energy and a means of maintaining bodily processes. **4** something that feeds or inflames passions, etc. ➤ vb (**fuelled, fuelling**) **1** to fill or feed with fuel. **2** intr to take on or get fuel. **3** to inflame (anger or other passions).

fug n a hot, stuffy atmosphere. ○ **fuggy** (-**ier, -iest**) adj.

fugitive n a person who is fleeing someone or something, usu some kind of authority, such as the law, an army, etc. ➤ adj **1** fleeing away. **2** lasting only briefly.

fugue n, mus a style of composition in which a theme is introduced in one part and developed as successive parts take it up. ○ **fugal** adj.

fulcrum n (**fulcrums** or **fulcra** /ˈfʊlkrə/) technical the point on which a LEVER turns, balances or is supported.

fulfil or (N Am) **fulfill** vb (**fulfilled, fulfilling**) **1** to carry out or perform (a task, promise, etc). **2** to satisfy (requirements). **3** to achieve (an aim, ambition, etc). ○ **fulfilment** n.

full adj **1** (also **full of sth**) holding, containing or having as much as possible, or a large quantity. **2** complete: to do a full day's work. **3** detailed; thorough; including everything necessary: a *full report.* **4** occupied: *My hands are full.* **5** having eaten till one wants no more. **6** plump; fleshy: *the fuller figure* • *full lips.* **7** of clothes: made with a large amount of material: *a full skirt.* **8** rich and strong: *This wine is very full.* **9** rich and varied: *a full life.* **10** having all possible rights, privileges, etc: *a full member.* **11** of the Moon: at the stage when it is seen as a fully-illuminated disc. **12** of a brother or sister: having both the same parents as oneself. ➤ *adv* **1** completely; at maximum capacity: *Is the radiator full on?* **2** exactly; directly: *It hit him full on the nose.* ○ *fullness* or (*N Am or dated*) *fulness n.* ♦ **be full up 1** to be full to the limit. **2** to have had enough to eat. **full of oneself** having too good an opinion of oneself and one's importance. **in full 1** completely. **2** at length; in detail. **in full swing** at the height of activity. **to the full** to the greatest possible extent.

full-blast *adv* with maximum energy and fluency.

full-blooded *adj* **1** of pure breed; thoroughbred. **2** enthusiastic; whole-hearted.

full-blown *adj* having all the features of the specified thing: *a full-blown war.*

full board *n* accommodation at a hotel, guesthouse, etc including the provision of all meals, etc.

full-bodied *adj* having a rich flavour or quality.

full-circle *adv* **1** round in a complete revolution. **2** back to the original starting position.

full house *n* **1** a performance at a theatre, cinema, etc, at which every seat is taken. **2** *cards, esp poker* a set of five cards consisting of three cards of one kind and two of another. **3** in bingo: a card with all the winning numbers.

full-length *adj* **1** complete; of the usual or standard length. **2** showing the whole body: *a full-length mirror.* **3** of maximum length: *a full-length skirt.*

full moon *n* **1** one of the four phases of the Moon, when the whole of it is illuminated and it is seen as a complete disc. Compare NEW MOON. **2** the time when the Moon is full.

full-scale *adj* **1** of a drawing, etc: the same size as the subject. **2** using all possible resources, means, etc: *a full-scale search.*

full stop *n* a punctuation mark (.) used to indicate the end of a sentence or to mark an abbreviation.

full time *n* the end of the time normally allowed for a sports match, etc.

full-time *adj* occupied for or extending over the whole of the working week. ➤ *adv* (**full time**) for the whole of the working week. Compare PART-TIME. ○ **full-timer** *n.*

fully *adv* **1** to the greatest possible extent. **2** completely: *fully qualified.* **3** in detail: *We'll deal with it more fully next week.* **4** at least: *She stayed for fully one hour.*

fully-fledged *adj* **1** of a person: completely trained or qualified. **2** of a bird: old enough to have grown feathers.

fulminate *vb, intr* to utter angry criticism or condemnation. ○ **fulmination** *n.*

fulsome *adj* of praise, compliments, etc: so overdone as to be distasteful.

fumble *vb* **1** *intr* (*also* **fumble for sth**) to grope, clumsily. **2** to say or do awkwardly. **3** to fail to manage, because of clumsy handling: *The fielder fumbled the catch.* ➤ *n* an act of fumbling.

fume *n* **1** (*often* **fumes**) smoke, gases or vapour, esp if strong-smelling or toxic. **2** the pungent toxic vapours given off by solvents or concentrated acids. ➤ *vb* **1** *intr* to be furious. **2** *intr* to give off smoke, gases or vapours. **3** *intr* of gases or vapours: to come off in fumes, esp during a chemical reaction. **4** to treat (eg wood) with fumes.

fumigate *vb* to disinfect (a room, a building, etc) with fumes, in order to destroy pests. ○ **fumigation** *n.* ○ **fumigator** *n* an apparatus used to fumigate a place.

fun *n* **1** enjoyment; merriment. **2** a source of amusement or entertainment. ➤ *adj, colloq* for amusement, enjoyment, etc: *fun run.* ♦ **make fun of** or **poke fun at sb** or **sth** to tease or ridicule them or it.

function *n* **1** the special purpose or task of a machine, person, bodily part, etc. **2** an organized event such as a party, meeting, etc. **3** a duty particular to someone in a particular job. **4** *maths, logic* a mathematical procedure that relates one or more variables to one or more other variables. **5** *comput* any of the basic operations of a computer, usu corresponding to a single operation. ➤ *vb, intr* **1** to work; to operate. **2** to fulfil a duty or role. **3** to serve or act as something. ○ **functionality** *n.*

functional *adj* **1** of buildings, machines, etc: designed for efficiency rather than decorativeness. **2** in working order; operational. **3** referring to or performed by functions. ○ **functionally** *adv.*

functionalism *n* **1** the policy or practice of the practical application of ideas. **2** *art, archit* the theory that beauty is to be identified with functional efficiency. ○ **functionalist** *n.*

functionary *n* (*-ies*) *derog* someone who works as a minor official in the government, etc.

fund *n* **1** a sum of money on which some enterprise is founded or on which the expenses of a project are supported. **2** a large store or supply: *a fund of jokes.* **3** (**funds**) *colloq* money available for spending. ➤ *vb* **1** to provide money for a particular purpose: *funding the project.* **2** to make (a debt) permanent, with fixed interest. ♦ **in funds** *colloq* having plenty of cash.

fundament *n, euphem* the buttocks.

fundamental *adj* **1** basic; underlying: *fundamental rules of physics.* **2** large; important: *fundamental differences.* **3** essential; necessary. ➤ *n* **1** (*usu* **fundamentals**) a basic principle or rule. **2** *mus* the lowest note of a chord.

fundamentalism *n* in religion, politics, etc:

strict adherence to the traditional teachings of a particular doctrine. ○ **fundamentalist** n.

fundamental particle n, physics an elementary particle.

fundraiser n **1** someone engaged in raising funds for a charity, organization, etc. **2** an event held to raise money for a cause. ○ **fundraising** n, adj.

funeral n **1** the ceremonial burial or cremation of a dead person. **2** colloq one's own problem, affair, etc: That's his funeral. ➤ adj relating to funerals.

funeral director n an undertaker.

funeral parlour n **1** an undertaker's place of business. **2** a room that can be hired for funeral ceremonies.

funerary adj relating to or used for funerals.

funereal adj **1** associated with or suitable for funerals. **2** mournful; dismal. **3** extremely slow. ○ **funereally** adv.

funfair n a fair with sideshows, amusements, rides, etc.

fungicide n a chemical that kills or limits the growth of fungi. ○ **fungicidal** adj.

fungus n (**fungi** /'fʌngiː, -gaɪ, -dʒaɪ/ or **funguses**) an organism that superficially resembles a plant, but does not have leaves and roots, and lacks CHLOROPHYLL, so that it must obtain its nutrients from other organisms. ○ **fungal** adj. ○ **fungous** adj.

funicular /fjʊ'nɪkjʊlə(r)/ adj of a mountain railway: operating by a machine-driven cable, with two cars, one of which descends while the other ascends. ➤ n a funicular railway.

funk[1] n **1** colloq jazz or rock music with a strong rhythm and repeating bass pattern. **2** in compounds a mix of the specified types of music, containing elements from both traditions: jazz-funk • techno-funk.

funk[2] n, colloq **1 a** (also **blue funk**) a state of fear or panic; **b** shrinking back or shirking because of a loss of courage. **2** a coward. ➤ vb to avoid doing something from fear.

funky adj (**-ier, -iest**) colloq **1** of jazz or rock music: strongly rhythmical and emotionally stirring. **2** trendy.

funnel n **1** a tube with a cone-shaped opening through which liquid, etc can be poured into a narrow-necked container. **2** a vertical exhaust pipe on a steamship or steam engine through which smoke escapes. ➤ vb (**funnelled, funnelling**; (US) **funneled, funneling**) **1** intr to rush through a narrow space: wind funnelling through the streets. **2** to transfer (liquid, etc) from one container to another using a funnel.

funny adj (**-ier, -iest**) **1** amusing; causing laughter. **2** strange; mysterious. **3** colloq dishonest; shady. **4** colloq ill: feeling a bit funny. **5** colloq slightly crazy. ➤ n (**-ies**) colloq a joke. ○ **funnily** adv. ○ **funniness** n.

funny bone n a place in the elbow joint where the ulnar nerve passes close to the skin and, if accidentally struck, causes a tingling sensation.

fur n **1** the thick fine soft coat of a hairy animal. **2 a** the skin of such an animal with the hair attached, used to make, line or trim garments; **b** a synthetic imitation of this. **3** a coat, cape or jacket made of fur or an imitation of it. **4** a whitish coating on the tongue, generally a sign of illness. **5** a whitish coating that forms on the inside of water pipes and kettles in hard-water regions. ➤ vb (**furred, furring**) **1** tr & intr (often **fur up** or **fur sth up**) to coat or become coated with a fur-like deposit. **2** to cover, trim or line with fur. ○ **furry** adj (**-ier, -iest**).

furbelow n **1** a dress trimming in the form of a strip, ruffle or flounce. **2** (**furbelows**) fussy ornamentation.

furbish vb to restore, clean or renovate (something). ○ **furbishment** n.

furcate vb, intr to fork or divide. ➤ adj forked. ○ **furcation** n.

furious adj **1** violently or intensely angry. **2** raging; stormy: furious winds. **3** frenzied; frantic: furious activity. ○ **furiously** adv.

furl vb, tr & intr of flags, sails or umbrellas: to roll up.

furlong n a measure of distance now used mainly in horse-racing, equal to one eighth of a mile, or 220 yards (201.2m).

furlough /'fɜːloʊ/ n leave of absence, esp from military duty abroad.

furnace n **1** an enclosed chamber in which heat is produced, eg for smelting metal, heating water or burning rubbish. **2** colloq a very hot place.

furnish vb **1** to provide (a house, etc) with furniture. **2 a** to supply (what is necessary); **b** (**furnish sb with sth**) to supply them with what they require (eg information, documents). ○ **furnished** adj.

furnishings pl n articles of furniture, fittings, carpets, etc.

furniture n movable household equipment such as tables, chairs, beds, etc.

furore /fjʊ'rɔːrɪ/ or (esp N Am) **furor** /fʊə'rɔː(r)/ n a general outburst of excitement or indignation.

furrier n someone who makes or sells furs.

furrow n **1** a groove or trench cut into the earth by a plough. **2** a wrinkle, eg in the forehead. ➤ vb **1** to plough (land) into furrows. **2** intr to become wrinkled.

further adj **1** more distant or remote (than something else). **2** more extended than was orig expected: further delay. **3** additional: no further clues. ➤ adv **1** at or to a greater distance or more distant point. **2** to or at a more advanced point: further developed. **3** to a greater extent or degree: modified even further. **4** moreover. ➤ vb to help the progress of something. ○ **furtherance** n. ♦ **further to** following on from (our telephone conversation, your letter, etc).

further education n, Brit post-school education other than at a university. Compare HIGHER EDUCATION.

furthermore *adv* in addition to what has already been said.

furthermost *adj* most distant or remote.

furthest *adj* most distant or remote. ➤ *adv* **1** at or to the greatest distance or most distant point. **2** at or to the most advanced point; to the greatest extent or degree.

furtive *adj* secretive; stealthy. ○ **furtively** *adv*.

fury *n* (*-ies*) **1** (an outburst of) violent anger. **2** violence: *the fury of the wind.* **3** a frenzy: *a fury of activity.*

furze *n* GORSE.

fuse¹ *n, elec* a safety device consisting of a length of wire which melts when the current exceeds a certain value, thereby breaking the circuit. ➤ *vb, tr & intr* **1** to melt as a result of the application of heat. **2** (*also* **fuse together**) to join by, or as if by, melting together. **3** of an electric circuit or appliance: to cease to function as a result of the melting of a fuse. ♦ **blow a fuse** *colloq* to lose one's temper.

fuse² *or* (*US*) **fuze** *n* a cable containing combustible material, used for detonating an explosive. ➤ *vb* to fit with such a device. ♦ **have a short fuse** to be quick-tempered.

fuselage /'fjuːzəlɑːʒ/ *n* the main body of an aircraft, to which the wings and tail unit are attached.

fusilier /fjuːzɪ'lɪə(r)/ *n, hist* an infantryman armed with a light musket.

fusillade /fjuːsɪ'leɪd/ *n* **1** a simultaneous or continuous discharge of firearms. **2** an onslaught, eg of criticism.

fusion *n* **1** *chem* the process of melting, whereby a substance changes from a solid to a liquid. **2** the act of joining together. **3** NUCLEAR FUSION.

fuss *n* **1** agitation and excitement, esp over something trivial. **2** a commotion, disturbance or bustle. **3** a show of fond affection. ➤ *vb, intr* (*also* **fuss over** *or* **about sth**) **1** to worry needlessly. **2** to concern oneself too much with trivial matters. **3** to agitate. ♦ **make a fuss** *or* **make a fuss about sth** to complain about it. **make a fuss of sb** *colloq* to give them a lot of affectionate attention.

fusspot *n, colloq* someone who makes too much of trivial things.

fussy *adj* (*-ier, -iest*) **1** choosy; discriminating. **2** over-concerned with details or trifles. **3** bustling and officious. **4** of clothes, etc: overelaborate.

fustian *n* **1** a kind of coarse twilled cotton fabric with a nap. **2** a pompous and unnatural style of writing or speaking. ➤ *adj* made of fustian.

fusty *adj* (*-ier, -iest*) **1** stale-smelling; old and musty. **2** old-fashioned. ○ **fustiness** *n*.

futile *adj* unproductive, foolish, vain or pointless. ○ **futility** *n*.

futon /'fuːtɒn/ *n* a cloth-filled mattress used on the floor or on a wooden frame.

future *n* **1** the time to come; events that are still to occur. **2** *gram* **a** the future tense; **b** a verb in the future tense. **3** prospects: *He must think about his future.* **4** likelihood of success: *There's no future in that.* **5** (**futures**) *stock exchange* commodities bought or sold at an agreed price, to be delivered and paid for at a later date. ➤ *adj* **1** yet to come or happen. **2** about to become: *my future wife.* **3** *gram* of the tense of a verb: indicating actions or events yet to happen, in English formed with the auxiliary verb *will* and infinitive without *to*, as in *She will see him tomorrow.* ♦ **in future** from now on.

future perfect see under PERFECT

futurism *n* an artistic movement concerned with expressing the movement of machines in all art forms. ○ **futurist** *n*.

futuristic *adj* **1** of design, etc: so modern or original as to seem appropriate to the future, or considered likely to be fashionable in the future. **2** relating to futurism.

futurity *n* (*-ies*) **1** the future. **2** a future event.

fuzz *n* **1** a mass of fine fibres or hair, usu curly. **2** a blur. ➤ *vb* (*also* **fuzz sth up**) to make or become fuzzy.

the fuzz *n, slang* the police.

fuzzy *adj* (*-ier, -iest*) **1** covered with fuzz. **2** forming a mass of tight curls. **3** indistinct; blurred.

Gg

G *or* **g** *n* (*Gs, G's or g's*) **1** the seventh letter of the English alphabet. **2** (**G**) *mus* the fifth note in the scale of C major.

g *abbrev* **1** gallon. **2** gram or gramme. **3** gravity.

Ga *symbol, chem* gallium.

gab *colloq, n* idle talk; chat. ➤ *vb* (**gabbed, gabbing**) *intr* (*also* **gab on** *or* **away**) to talk idly, esp at length. ♦ **the gift of the gab** *colloq* the ability to speak with ease, esp persuasively.

gabble *vb, tr & intr* to talk or say something quickly and unclearly.

gaberdine *or* **gabardine** *n* **1** a closely woven twill fabric, esp of wool or cotton. **2** a coat or loose cloak made from this.

gable *n* **1** the triangular upper part of a side wall between the sloping parts of a roof. **2** a triangular canopy above a door or window. ○ **gabled** *adj* having a gable or gables.

gad *vb* (**gadded, gadding**) *intr, colloq* (*usu* **gad about** or **around**) to go from place to place busily, esp in the hope of finding amusement or pleasure.

gadabout *n, colloq, derog, often humorous* a person who gads about.

gadget *n* any small device, esp one more ingenious than necessary. ○ **gadgetry** *n*.

gadolinium *n, chem* a soft silvery-white metallic element, belonging to the LANTHANIDE series.

Gaelic *n* any of the closely related Celtic languages spoken in the Scottish Highlands and Islands /'gɑːlɪk/, or Ireland or the Isle of Man /'geɪlɪk/. ➤ *adj* relating to these languages or the people who speak them, or to their customs.

gaff[1] *n* **1** a long pole with a hook, for landing large fish. **2** *naut* a vertical spar to which the tops of certain types of sail are attached. ➤ *vb* to catch (a fish) with a gaff.

gaff[2] *n, slang* nonsense. ♦ **blow the gaff** *Brit* to give away a secret.

gaffe *n* a socially embarrassing action or remark.

gaffer *n* **1** *colloq* a boss or foreman. **2** *cinema & TV* the senior electrician in a production crew. **3** *dialect* an old man.

gag[1] *vb* (**gagged, gagging**) **1** to silence someone by putting something in or over their mouth. **2** to deprive someone of free speech. **3** *intr* to retch. **4** *intr* to choke. ➤ *n* **1** something put into or over a person's mouth to prevent them from speaking. **2** any suppression of free speech. **3** a CLOSURE (sense 3) applied to a parliamentary debate.

gag[2] *colloq, n* a joke or trick. ➤ *vb* (**gagged, gagging**) *intr* to tell jokes.

gaga *adj, colloq* **1** weak-minded through old age. **2** silly.

gage[1] *n* **1** an object given as security or a pledge. **2** *hist* something thrown down to signal a challenge, eg a glove.

gage[2] see GAUGE

gaggle *n* **1** a flock of geese. **2** *colloq* a group of noisy people.

gaiety *n* **1** the state of being merry or bright. **2** attractively bright appearance. **3** merry-making.

gaily *adv* **1** in a light-hearted, merry way. **2** brightly; colourfully.

gain *vb* **1** to get, obtain or earn (something desirable). **2** to win (esp a victory or prize). **3** to have or experience an increase in something: *to gain speed*. **4** *intr* (*usu* **gain on sb** or **sth**) to come closer to them or it. **5** *tr & intr* of a clock: to go too fast by (a specified amount of time). **6** to reach (a place). ➤ *n* **1** (*often* **gains**) something gained, eg profit. **2** an increase, eg in weight. **3** an instance of gaining.

gainful *adj* **1** profitable. **2** of employment: paid. ○ **gainfully** *adv*.

gainsay *vb* (**gainsaid**) *formal* to deny or contradict. ○ **gainsayer** *n*.

gait *n* **1** a way of walking. **2** the leg movements of an animal travelling at a specified speed, eg trotting.

gaiter *n* a leather or cloth covering for the lower leg and ankle.

gala /'gɑːlə/ *n* **1** an occasion of special entertainment or a public festivity. **2** a meeting for sports competitions, esp swimming.

galactic *adj* relating to a galaxy or the Galaxy.

galaxy *n* (*-ies*) **1** a huge collection of stars, dust and gas held together by mutual gravitational attraction. **2** (**the Galaxy**) the vast spiral arrangement of stars to which our solar system belongs, known as the Milky Way. **3** a fabulous gathering, eg of famous people.

gale *n* **1 a** *loosely* any very strong wind; **b** *technical* a wind that blows with a speed of 51.5 to 101.4km per hour, corresponding to force 7 to 10 on the BEAUFORT SCALE. **2** (*usu* **gales**) a sudden loud burst, eg of laughter.

galena *n* the most important ore of LEAD[2] (*noun sense* 1) which occurs as compact masses of very dense dark grey crystals consisting mainly of lead sulphide.

gall[1] *n* **1** *colloq* impudence. **2** bitterness or spitefulness. **3** something unpleasant. **4** *med, old use* bile.

gall[2] *n* a small round growth on the stem or leaf of a plant, usu caused by invading parasitic fungi, or by insects.

gall[3] *n* **1** a sore or painful swelling on the skin caused by chafing. **2** something annoying. **3** a state of being annoyed. ➤ *vb* **1** to annoy. **2** to chafe (skin).

gallant /'galənt, *also* gə'lant/ *adj* **1** brave. **2** *literary or old use* splendid, grand or fine. **3** /gə-'lant/ of a man: courteous and attentive to women.

gallantry *n* **1** bravery. **2** *old use* politeness and attentiveness to women.

gall bladder *n, anat* a small muscular pear-shaped sac lying beneath the liver that stores bile and releases it into the intestine.

galleon *n, hist* a large Spanish ship, usu with three masts, used for war or trade from 15c to 18c.

gallery *n* (*-ies*) **1** a room or building used to display works of art. **2** a balcony along an inside upper wall, eg of a church or hall, providing extra seating or reserved for musicians, etc. **3** a the upper floor in a theatre, usu containing the cheapest seats; **b** the part of the audience seated there. **4** a long narrow room or corridor. **5** an underground passage in a mine or cave. **6** a covered walkway open on one or both sides. **7** the spectators in the stand at a sports tournament.

galley *n* **1** *hist* a long single-deck ship propelled by sails and oars. **2** *hist* a Greek or Roman warship. **3** *naut* the kitchen on a ship.

galley slave *n* **1** *hist* a slave forced to row a galley. **2** *colloq* someone who is given menial tasks.

Gallic *adj* **1** typically or characteristically French. **2** *hist* relating to ancient Gaul or the Gauls.

gallinaceous *adj, biol* relating or referring to the order of birds that includes domestic fowl, turkeys, pheasants, grouse, etc.

galling *adj* irritating.

gallium *n, chem* a soft silvery metallic element found in zinc blende, bauxite and kaolin.

gallivant *vb, intr, humorous or derog, colloq* to go out looking for entertainment.

gallon *n* an imperial unit of liquid measurement equal to four quarts or eight pints, equivalent to 4.546 litres (an **imperial gallon**) in the UK, and 3.785 litres in the USA.

gallop *vb* **1** *intr* of a horse or similar animal: to move at a gallop. **2** *intr* to ride a horse, etc at a gallop. **3 a** to read, talk or do something quickly; **b** to make (a horse, etc) move at a gallop. **4** *intr, colloq* to move, progress or increase very quickly: *inflation is galloping out of control.* ➤ *n* **1** the fastest pace at which a horse or similar animal moves, during which all four legs are off the ground together. **2** a period of riding at this pace. **3** an unusually fast speed. ○ **galloping** *n, adj.*

gallows *sing n* a wooden frame on which criminals are put to death by hanging.

gallstone *n, pathol* a small hard mass that is formed in the gall bladder or one of its ducts.

galore *adv* (placed after the noun) in large amounts or numbers: *I read books galore.*

galosh or **golosh** *n, usu in pl* a waterproof overshoe.

galumph *vb, intr, colloq* **1** to stride along triumphantly. **2** to walk in a heavy ungainly manner.

galvanic *adj* **1** *physics* relating to or producing an electric current, esp a direct current, by chemical means. **2** of behaviour, etc: sudden, or startlingly energetic, as if the result of an electric shock.

galvanize or **-ise** *vb* **1** to stimulate or rouse to action. **2** *technical* to coat (a metallic surface, usu iron or steel) with a thin layer of zinc, in order to protect it from corrosion. **3** to stimulate by applying an electric current. ○ **galvanization** *n.*

gambit *n* **1** *chess* a chess move made early in a game, in which a pawn or other piece is sacrificed in order to gain an overall advantage. **2** an initial action or remark, esp one intended to gain an advantage.

gamble *vb* **1** *tr & intr* to bet (usu money) on the result of a card game, horse race, etc. **2** (*also* **gamble sth away**) to lose (money or other assets) through gambling. **3** *intr* (*often* **gamble on sth**) to take a chance or risk on it. ➤ *n* **1** an act of gambling. **2** a risk or a situation involving risk. ○ **gambler** *n.* **gambling** *n.*

gambol *vb* (**gambolled, gambolling;** *US also* **gamboled, gamboling**) *intr* to jump around playfully. ➤ *n* jumping around playfully.

game¹ *n* **1** an amusement or pastime. **2** the equipment used for this, eg a board, cards, dice, software, etc. **3** a competitive activity with rules, involving some form of skill. **4** an occasion on which individuals or teams compete at such an activity. **5** in some sports: a division of a match. **6** (**games**) an event consisting of competitions in various activities, esp sporting ones: *the Commonwealth games.* **7** *colloq, often derog* a type of activity, profession, or business. **8** playing ability or style: *Her game is very aggressive.* **9** *derog* an activity undertaken light-heartedly: *War is just a game to him.* **10** certain birds and animals which are killed for meat or sport. **11** *derog, colloq* a scheme, trick or intention: *Don't give the game away.* ➤ *adj, colloq* **1** (*also* **game for sth**) ready and willing to undertake it. **2** *old use* having plenty of fighting spirit; plucky. ➤ *vb, intr* to gamble. ○ **gamely** *adv* bravely, sportingly. ◆ **play the game** to behave fairly. **the game is up** the plan or trick has failed or has been found out.

game² *adj, old use* lame.

gamekeeper *n* a person employed to look after and manage GAME¹ (*noun sense 10*).

game show *n* a TV quiz.

gamesmanship *n, derog* the art, practice or process of winning games by trying to unsettle one's opponent or using unsporting tactics.

gamester *n* a gambler.

gamete *n, biol* in sexually reproducing organisms: a specialized sex cell, esp an OVUM or SPERM, which fuses with another gamete of the opposite type during fertilization.

gamine /ˈgamiːn/ *n* a girl or young woman with a mischievous, boyish appearance.

gaming *n* gambling.

gamma *n* **1** the third letter of the Greek alphabet. **2** the third element in a series.

gamma rays *pl n, physics* electromagnetic radiation of very high frequency, consisting of high-energy PHOTONs, often produced during radioactive decay. Also called **gamma radiation.**

gammon *n* **1** cured meat from the upper leg and hindquarters of a pig. **2** the back part of a side of bacon including the whole back leg and hindquarters.

gammy *adj* (**-ier, -iest**) *colloq, old use* lame with a permanent injury.

gamut /ˈgamət/ *n* **1** the whole range of anything, eg a person's emotions. **2** *mus, hist* a scale of notes.

gamy or **gamey** *adj* (**-ier, -iest**) of meat: having the strong taste or smell of game which has been kept for a long time.

gander *n* **1** a male goose. **2** *colloq* a look: *have a gander.*

gang *n* **1** a group, esp of criminals or troublemakers. **2** a group of friends, esp children. **3** an organized group of workers. ◇ **gang up on** or **against sb** to act as a group against them.

gangland *n* the world of organized crime.

gangling or **gangly** *adj* (**-ier, -iest**) tall and

thin, and usu awkward in movement.

ganglion *n* (*ganglia* or *ganglions*) **1** *anat* in the central nervous system: a group of nerve cell bodies, usu enclosed by a sheath or capsule. **2** *pathol* a cyst or swelling that forms on the tissue surrounding a tendon.

gangplank *n* a movable plank, usu with projecting crosspieces fixed to it, serving as a gangway for a ship.

gangrene *n*, *pathol* the death and subsequent decay of part of the body due to some failure of the blood supply to that region as a result of disease, injury, frostbite, etc. ○ **gangrenous** *adj*.

gangster *n* a member of a gang of violent criminals. ○ **gangsterism** *n*.

gangway *n* **1 a** a small movable bridge used for getting on and off a ship; **b** the opening on the side of a ship into which this fits. **2** a passage between rows of seats, eg on an aircraft or in a theatre. ➤ *exclam* make way!

ganja *n* marijuana.

gannet *n* **1** a large seabird which has a heavy body, white plumage with dark wing tips and webbed feet. **2** *colloq* a greedy person.

gantry *n* (*-ies*) a large metal supporting framework, eg for railway signals, serving as a bridge for a travelling crane, or used at the side of a rocket's launch pad.

gaol and **gaoler** see JAIL

gap *n* **1** a break or open space, eg in a fence, etc. **2** a break in time. **3** a difference or disparity: *the generation gap*. **4** a ravine or gorge. ○ **gappy** *adj* (*-ier, -iest*).

gape *vb, intr* **1** to stare with the mouth open, esp in surprise or wonder. **2** to be or become wide open. **3** to open the mouth wide. ➤ *n* **1** a wide opening. **2** an open-mouthed stare. **3** the extent to which the mouth can be opened. ○ **gaping** *adj*.

garage *n* **1** a building in which motor vehicles are kept. **2** an establishment where motor vehicles are bought, sold and repaired, often also selling petrol, etc. **3** a filling station. ➤ *vb* to put or keep (a car, etc) in a garage.

garb *literary, n* **1** clothing, esp as worn by people in a particular job or position. **2** outward appearance. ➤ *vb* to dress or clothe.

garbage *n* **1** *N Am, esp US* domestic waste. **2** worthless or poor quality articles or matter. **3** nonsense. **4** *comput* erroneous, irrelevant or meaningless data.

garble *vb* **1** to mix up the details of something unintentionally. **2** to deliberately distort the meaning of something, eg by making important omissions. ○ **garbled** *adj* of a report or account: muddled.

garden *n* **1** an area of land, usu one adjoining a house, where grass, trees, ornamental plants, fruit, vegetables, etc, are grown. **2** (*usu* **gardens**) such an area of land, usu of considerable size, with flower beds, lawns, trees, walks, etc, laid out for enjoyment by the public. ➤ *adj* **1** of a plant: cultivated, not wild. **2** belonging to or

for use in a garden. ➤ *vb, intr* to cultivate or take care of a garden. ○ **gardener** *n*. ○ **gardening** *n*. ✦ **lead sb up the garden path** *colloq* to mislead or deceive them deliberately.

garden centre *n* a place where plants, seeds, garden tools, etc are sold.

garden city *n* a spacious modern town designed with trees, private gardens and numerous public parks.

gardenia *n* **1** an evergreen shrub with glossy leaves and large, usu white, fragrant flowers. **2** the flower produced by this plant.

gargantuan or **Gargantuan** *adj* enormous.

gargle *vb, tr & intr* to cleanse, treat or freshen the mouth and throat by breathing out through (a medicinal liquid) that is held there for a while before spitting it out. ➤ *n* **1** gargling or the sound produced while gargling. **2** the liquid used.

gargoyle *n* a grotesque carved open-mouthed head or figure acting as a rainwater spout from a roof-gutter, esp on a church.

garish *adj, derog* unpleasantly bright or colourful. ○ **garishly** *adv*. ○ **garishness** *n*.

garland *n* a circular arrangement of flowers or leaves worn round the head or neck, or hung up as a decoration. ➤ *vb* to decorate something or someone with a garland.

garlic *n* **1** a plant of the onion family, widely cultivated for its underground bulb, which is divided into segments known as cloves. **2** the bulb of this plant, which is widely used as a flavouring in cooking.

garment *n*, *now rather formal* an article of clothing.

garner *vb, formal or literary* to collect and usu store (information, knowledge, etc).

garnet *n* any of various silicate minerals, esp a deep red variety used as a semi-precious stone.

garnish *vb* to decorate (esp food to be served). ➤ *n* a decoration, esp one added to food.

garret *n* an attic room, often a dingy one.

garrison *n* **1** a body of soldiers stationed in a town or fortress. **2** the building or fortress they occupy.

garrotte or **garotte** or (*US*) **garrote** / gəˈrɒt / *n* **1** a wire loop or metal collar that can be tightened around the neck to cause strangulation. **2** this method of execution. ➤ *vb* to execute or kill someone with a garrotte.

garrulous *adj* **1** of a person: tending to talk a lot, esp about trivial things. **2** *derog* of a speech, etc: long and wordy. ○ **garrulousness** *n*.

garter *n* **1** a band of tight material, usu elastic, worn on the leg to hold up a stocking or sock. **2** (**the Garter**) **a** the highest order of British knighthood; **b** membership of the order; **c** the emblem of the order, a blue garter.

gas *n* **1** a form of matter that has no fixed shape, is easily compressed, and which will expand to occupy all the space available. **2** a substance or mixture of substances which is in this state at ordinary temperatures, eg hydrogen, air. **3** NATURAL GAS used as a source of fuel for heating, lighting or cooking. **4** a gas, esp nitrous oxide, used as an anaesthetic. **5** FIRE-DAMP, explosive in contact with air. **6** a poisonous gas used as a weapon in war. **7** *colloq* gasoline; petrol. **8** *colloq* an amusing or entertaining event, situation or person: *The film was a real gas!* **9** *derog, colloq* foolish talk. ➤ *vb* (**gasses, gassed, gassing**) **1** to poison or kill (people or animals) with gas. **2** *intr, derog, colloq* to chat, esp at length, boastfully or about trivial things. ○ **gassy** *adj* (*-ier, -iest*).

gasbag *n, derog, colloq* someone who talks a lot.

gas chamber *n* a sealed room which is filled with poisonous gas and used for killing people or animals.

gaseous /'gasɪəs, 'geɪʃəs/ *adj* in the form of, or like, gas.

gash *n* a deep open cut or wound. ➤ *vb* to make a gash in something.

gasify *vb* (*-ies, -ied*) to convert something into gas.

gasket *n* a compressible ring or sheet made of rubber, paper or asbestos that fits tightly in the join between two metal surfaces to form an airtight seal. ♦ **blow a gasket** *colloq* to become extremely angry.

gaslight *n* **1** a lamp powered by gas. **2** the light from such a lamp.

gas mask *n* a type of mask that is used in warfare and certain industries to filter out any poisonous gases.

gasoline *n, N Am* petrol. Often shortened to **gas**.

gasometer *n* a large metal tank used for storing gas for use as fuel before it is distributed to customers.

gasp *vb* **1** *intr* to take a sharp breath in, through surprise, sudden pain, etc. **2** *intr* to breathe in with difficulty, eg because of illness, exhaustion, etc. **3** (*also* **gasp sth out**) to say it breathlessly. ➤ *n* a sharp intake of breath. ♦ **be gasping for sth** *colloq* to want or need it very much.

gas ring *n* a hollow ring with perforations that serve as gas JETs (see under JET²).

gastric *adj, med, etc* relating to or affecting the stomach.

gastritis *n, med* inflammation of the lining of the stomach.

gastroenteritis *n, med* inflammation of the lining of the stomach and intestine.

gastronome or **gastronomist** *n* a person who enjoys, and has developed a taste for, good food and wine.

gastronomy *n* the appreciation and enjoyment of good food and wine. ○ **gastronomic** *adj*.

gastropod or **gasteropod** *n, biol* a mollusc, eg snail, slug, whelk, winkle, which typically possesses a large flattened muscular foot and often has a single spirally coiled shell.

gasworks *sing n* a place where gas is manufactured.

gate *n* **1** a door or barrier, usu a hinged one, which is moved in order to open or close an entrance in a wall, fence, etc. **2** at an airport: any of the numbered exits from which passengers can board or leave a plane. **3** the total number of people attending a sports event or other entertainment. **4** (*also* **gate money**) the total money paid in admission fees to an entertainment. **5** *technical* an electronic circuit whose output is controlled by the combination of signals at the input terminals. ➤ *vb* to confine (pupils) to school after hours.

gateau or **gâteau** /'gatou/ *n* (**gateaux, gâteaux** or **gateaus** /-touz/) a large rich cake, esp one filled with cream.

gatecrash *vb, tr & intr, colloq* to join or attend (a party, meeting, etc) uninvited. ○ **gatecrasher** *n*.

gatehouse *n* a building at or above the gateway to a city, castle, etc.

gatepost *n* either of the posts on each side of a gate.

gateway *n* **1** an entrance with a gate across it. **2** a way in or to something: *the gateway to success*. **3** *comput, etc* a connection between computer networks, or between a computer network and a telephone line.

gather *vb* **1** *tr & intr* (*also* **gather together**) to bring or come together in one place. **2** (*also* **gather sth in**) to collect, pick or harvest it. **3** to increase in (speed or force). **4** to accumulate or become covered with (eg dust). **5** to learn or understand something from information received. **6** to pull (material) into small folds. **7** to pull someone or something close to oneself: *She gathered the child into her arms.* **8** to wrinkle (the brow). **9** to draw together or muster (strength, courage, etc) in preparation for something. ➤ *n* a small fold in material, often stitched.

gathering *n* a meeting or assembly.

gauche /gouʃ/ *adj* ill-at-ease, awkward in social situations.

gaucho /'gautʃou/ *n* a cowboy of the S American plains.

gaudy *adj* (*-ier, -iest*) *derog* coarsely and brightly coloured or decorated. ○ **gaudiness** *n*.

gauge or (*US*) **gage** /geɪdʒ/ *vb* **1** to measure something accurately. **2** to estimate or guess (a measurement, size, etc). **3** to judge or appraise. ➤ *n* **1** any of various instruments that are used to measure a quantity: *pressure gauge*. **2** each of the standard sizes used in measuring articles (esp by diameter) such as wire, bullets or knitting needles. **3** the distance between the rails on a railway. **4** the distance between wheels on an axle. **5** a standard against which other things are measured or judged.

Gaul *n, hist* an inhabitant of, or a person born in, ancient Gaul. See also GALLIC.

gaunt *adj* **1** thin or thin-faced; haggard. **2** of a place: barren and desolate.

gauntlet[1] n 1 hist a metal or metal-plated glove worn by medieval soldiers. 2 a heavy protective leather glove covering the wrist. ♦ **take up the gauntlet** to accept a challenge. **throw down the gauntlet** to make a challenge.

gauntlet[2] n. ♦ **run the gauntlet** to expose oneself to hostile treatment or criticism.

gauze n 1 thin transparent fabric, esp cotton muslin as used to dress wounds. 2 thin wire mesh. ○ **gauzy** adj (-ier, -iest).

gavel n a small hammer used by a judge, auctioneer, etc to call attention.

gawk colloq, vb, intr to stare blankly or stupidly. ➤ n, derog an awkward, clumsy or stupid person.

gawky adj (-ier, -iest) colloq, derog awkward-looking, ungainly, and usu tall and thin. ○ **gawkiness** n.

gawp vb, intr, colloq to stare stupidly, esp open-mouthed.

gay adj 1 homosexual. 2 happily carefree. 3 bright and attractive. 4 pleasure-seeking or fun-loving. ➤ n a homosexual.

gaze vb, intr (esp **gaze at sth** or **sb**) to stare fixedly. ➤ n a fixed stare.

gazebo /gə'ziːbəʊ/ n (gazebos or gazeboes) a small summerhouse usu situated in a place that offers pleasant views.

gazelle n (gazelles or gazelle) a fawn-coloured antelope with a white rump and belly found in Africa and Asia.

gazette n 1 an official newspaper giving lists of government, military and legal notices. 2 often facetious a newspaper.

gazetteer n a book or part of a book which lists place names and describes the places.

gazump vb, colloq to charge a prospective house buyer a higher price than has already been verbally agreed, usually because someone else has offered a higher price.

gazunder vb, colloq of a buyer: to lower the sum offered (to a seller of property) just before contracts are due to be signed.

GB abbrev Great Britain.

GBH or **gbh** abbrev grievous bodily harm.

GCSE (in full **General Certificate of Secondary Education**) n 1 in England, Wales and N Ireland: an examination in a single subject, usually taken about the age of 16. 2 a pass in such an examination.

Gd symbol, chem gadolinium.

Ge symbol, chem germanium.

gear n 1 (also **gearwheel**) a toothed wheel or disc that engages with another wheel or disc having a different number of teeth, and turns it, so transmitting motion from one rotating shaft to another. 2 the specific combination of such wheels or discs that is being used: second gear. 3 colloq the equipment or tools needed for a particular job, sport, etc. 4 aeronautics landing gear. 5 colloq personal belongings. 6 colloq clothes, esp young people's current fashion. 7 slang drugs. ➤ vb (usu **gear sth to**

or **towards sth else**) to adapt or design it to suit (a particular need). ◊ **gear oneself up** to become or make oneself ready or prepared.

gearbox n 1 esp in a motor vehicle: the set or system of gears that transmits power from the engine to the road wheels. 2 the metal casing that encloses this.

gearing n 1 a set of gearwheels as a means of transmission of motion. 2 finance the ratio of a company's equity to its debts.

gear lever or **gear stick** or (N Am) **gearshift** n a lever for engaging and disengaging gears, esp in a motor vehicle.

gecko n (geckos or geckoes) a nocturnal lizard found in warm countries.

gee[1] exclam (usu **gee up**) used to encourage a horse to move, or to go faster. ➤ vb (**geed, gee-ing**) to encourage (a horse, etc) to move or move faster.

gee[2] exclam, colloq expressing surprise, admiration or enthusiasm. Also **gee whiz**.

geek n, N Am slang 1 a strange, eccentric, or awkward person. 2 a person who is extremely and obsessively enthusiastic about a particular subject: a computer geek.

geese pl of GOOSE.

geezer n, colloq a man.

Geiger counter /'gaɪgə(r)/ n, physics an instrument that is used to detect and measure the intensity of radiation.

geisha /'geɪʃə/ n (geisha or geishas) a Japanese girl or woman who is trained to entertain men with music, dancing, conversation, etc.

gel n 1 a solid and a liquid that are dispersed evenly throughout a material and have set to form a jelly-like mass, eg gelatine. 2 (also **hair gel**) such a substance used in styling the hair or fixing it in place. ➤ vb (**gelled, gelling**) 1 tr & intr to become or cause something to become a gel. 2 to style (hair) using gel. 3 to JELL.

gelatine /'dʒelətiːn/ or **gelatin** /-tɪn/ n a clear tasteless protein extracted from animal bones and hides and used in food thickenings, photographic materials, etc.

gelatinous /dʒə'lætɪnəs/ adj like gelatine or jelly.

geld vb to castrate (a male animal, esp a horse) by removing its testicles. ○ **gelding** n a castrated male animal, esp a horse.

gelignite n a powerful explosive.

gem n 1 (also **gemstone**) a semi-precious or precious stone or crystal. 2 colloq someone or something that is valued, admired, etc.

Gemini sing n (pl in sense b **Geminis**) astrol a the third sign of the zodiac; b a person born between 21 May and 20 June, under this sign.

gemsbok /'gemzbɒk; S Afr 'xemz-/ n a large S African antelope with long straight horns and distinctive markings on its face and underparts.

gen n, colloq (esp **the gen**) the required or relevant information. ◊ **gen up on sth** (**genned up, genning up**) to obtain the relevant information about it.

gendarme /'ʒɒndɑːm/ *n* a member of an armed police force in France and other French-speaking countries.

gender *n* **1** the condition of being male or female; one's sex. **2** *gram* **a** in many languages: a system of dividing nouns and pronouns into different classes, often related to the sex of the persons and things denoted; **b** any of these classes, usu two or three in European languages (see FEMININE, MASCULINE and NEUTER).

gene *n* the basic unit of inheritance, consisting of a sequence of DNA that occupies a specific position on a CHROMOSOME. It is the means by which specific characteristics are passed on from parents to offspring.

genealogy *n* (*-ies*) **1 a** a person's direct line of descent from an ancestor; **b** a diagram or scheme showing this. **2** the study of the history and lineage of families. **3** the study of the development of plants and animals into present-day forms. ○ **genealogical** *adj.* ○ **genealogically** *adv.* ○ **genealogist** *n.*

genera *pl of* GENUS

general *adj* **1** relating to, involving or applying to all or most parts, people or things; widespread, not specific, limited, or localized: *as a general rule.* **2** not detailed or definite: *a general description.* **3** (esp before or after a job title) chief: *general manager.* ➢ *n* **1** an army officer of the rank below field marshal. **2** the commander of a whole army. ○ **generality** *n.* ♦ **in general** usually; mostly.

general anaesthetic *n, med* a drug that causes a complete loss of consciousness. Compare LOCAL ANAESTHETIC.

general election *n* a national election in which the voters of every constituency in the country elect a member of parliament.

generalissimo *n* a supreme commander of the combined armed forces in some countries, who often also has political power.

generalize or **-ise** *vb* **1** *intr* to speak in general terms or form general opinions, esp ones that are too general to be applied to all individual cases. **2** to make something more general, esp to make it applicable to a wider variety of cases. ○ **generalization** *n.*

generally *adv* **1** usually. **2** without considering details. **3** as a whole; collectively.

general practitioner *n* a community doctor who treats most illnesses and complaints, and refers appropriate cases to specialists.

general-purpose *adj* useful for a wide range of purposes.

general staff *n* military officers who advise senior officers on policy, administration, etc.

general strike *n* a strike by workers in all or most of the industries in a country at the same time.

generate *vb* to produce or create something. ○ **generative** *adj.*

generation *n* **1** the act or process of producing something, eg electricity or ideas. **2** *biol* of living organisms: the act or process of producing offspring. **3** all the individuals produced at a particular stage in the natural descent of humans or animals: *the younger generation.* **4** the average period between the birth of a person or animal and the birth of their offspring; in humans, about 30 years: *three generations ago.*

generation gap *n* the extent to which two, usu successive, generations differ, eg in lifestyles, ideas, values, etc and the lack of mutual understanding that results.

generator *n, elec* a machine that converts mechanical energy into electrical energy, eg a DYNAMO.

generic *adj* **1** belonging, referring or relating to any member of a general class or group. **2 a** esp of a drug: not protected by a trademark and sold as a specific brand; **b** applied to supermarket products: sold without a brand name. **3** applied to a product name that was originally a trademark: now used as the general name for the product.

generous *adj* **1** giving or willing to give or help unselfishly. **2** eg of a donation: large and given unselfishly. **3** large: *generous portions.* **4** kind; willing to forgive: *of generous spirit.* ○ **generosity** *n.* ○ **generously** *adv.*

genesis *n* (*-ses* /'dʒɛnəsiːz/) **1** a beginning or origin. **2** (**Genesis**) the title of the first book in the Old Testament which describes the creation of the world.

genetic *adj* **1** inherited: *a genetic defect.* **2** belonging or relating to origin. ○ **genetically** *adv.*

genetic engineering *n* a form of BIOTECHNOLOGY in which the genes of an organism are deliberately altered by a method other than conventional breeding in order to change the characteristics of the organism.

genetic fingerprinting *n* the process of analyzing samples of DNA from body tissues or fluids in order to establish a person's identity in criminal investigations, paternity disputes, etc.

genetics *sing n* the scientific study of heredity and of the mechanisms by which characteristics are transmitted from one generation to the next. ○ **geneticist** *n.*

genial *adj* **1** cheerful; friendly. **2** of climate: pleasantly warm or mild. ○ **geniality** *n.*

genie *n* (**genies** or **genii** /'dʒiːniɪaɪ/) in folk or fairy stories: a spirit with the power to grant wishes.

genitals or **genitalia** /dʒɛnɪ'teɪlɪə/ *pl n* the external sexual organs. ○ **genital** *adj.*

genitive *n, gram* in certain languages, eg Latin, Greek and German: the form or CASE² of a noun, pronoun or adjective which shows possession or association.

genius *n* **1** someone who has outstanding creative or intellectual ability. **2** such ability. **3** a person who exerts a powerful influence on another (whether good or bad).

genocide *n* the deliberate killing of a whole nation or people. ○ **genocidal** *adj.*

genome *n, genetics* the complete set of genetic material in the cell of a living organism.

genomics *sing n* the study of GENOMES.

genotype *n, genetics* the particular set of genes possessed by an organism.

genre /ˈʒɑ̃rə/ *n* **1** a particular type or kind of literature, music or other artistic work. **2** (*in full* **genre painting**) *art* a type of painting featuring scenes from everyday life.

genteel *adj* **1** *derog* polite or refined in an artificial, affected way approaching snobbishness. **2** well-mannered. **3** *old use, facetious* referring or suitable for the upper classes.

gentian /ˈdʒɛnʃən/ *n* a low-growing plant with funnel-shaped or bell-shaped flowers, often deep blue in colour.

gentile *n* (*often* **Gentile**) **a** used esp by Jews: a person who is not Jewish; **b** used esp by Mormons: a person who is not Mormon.

gentility *n* **1** good manners and respectability. **2** *old use* **a** a noble birth; **b** people of the upper classes.

gentle *adj* **1** mild-mannered, not stern, coarse or violent. **2** light and soft; not harsh, loud, strong, etc: *a gentle breeze*. **3** moderate; mild: *a gentle reprimand*. **4** of hills, etc: rising gradually. ○ **gentleness** *n*. ○ **gently** *adv*.

gentleman *n* **1** a polite name for a man: *Ask that gentleman*. **2** a polite, well-mannered, respectable man. **3** a man from the upper classes. ○ **gentlemanly** *adj*.

gentlewoman *n, dated* an upper-class woman.

gentrify *vb* (*-ies, -ied*) to make (an area) middle-class. ○ **gentrification** *n*.

gentry *pl n* (*esp* **the gentry**) people belonging to the class directly below the nobility: *the landed gentry*.

gents *sing n* (*often* **the gents**) a men's public toilet.

genuflect *vb, intr* to bend one's knee in worship or as a sign of respect. ○ **genuflection** or **genuflexion** *n*.

genuine *adj* **1** authentic, not artificial or fake. **2** honest; sincere.

genus /ˈdʒiːnəs, ˈdʒɛnəs/ *n* (**genera** /ˈdʒɛnərə/ or **genuses**) **1** *biol* in taxonomy: any of the groups into which a FAMILY (sense 7) is divided and which in turn is subdivided into one or more species. **2** a class divided into several subordinate classes.

geo- *comb form, signifying* **1** the Earth. **2** geography or geographical.

geocentric *adj* **1** of a system, esp the universe or the solar system: having the Earth as its centre. **2** measured from the centre of the Earth.

geodesic or **geodetic** *adj* denoting an artificial structure composed of a large number of identical components, esp a dome.

geography *n* (*-ies*) **1** the scientific study of the Earth's surface, esp its physical features, climate, resources, population, etc. **2** *colloq* the layout of a place. ○ **geographer** *n*. ○ **geographical** *adj*.

geological time *n* a time scale in which the Earth's history is subdivided into units known as EONS, which are further subdivided into ERAS, PERIODS, and EPOCHS.

geology *n* **1** the scientific study of the origins and structure, composition, etc of the Earth, esp its rocks. **2** the distinctive geological features of an area, country, etc. ○ **geological** *adj*. ○ **geologist** *n*.

geometric or **geometrical** *adj* **1** relating to or using the principles of GEOMETRY. **2** of a pattern, design, style of architecture, etc: using or consisting of lines, points, or simple geometrical figures such as circles or triangles.

geometry *n* the branch of mathematics dealing with lines, angles, shapes, etc and their relationships.

geophysics *sing n* the scientific study of the physical properties of the Earth. ○ **geophysical** *adj*. ○ **geophysicist** *n*.

georgette *n* a kind of thin silk material.

Georgian *adj* **1** belonging to or typical of the reigns of King George I, II, III and IV, ie the period 1714–1830. **2** of literature: typical of the kind that was written during the reign of King George V, especially the period 1910–20. **3** relating to the Caucasian republic of Georgia, its people or their language. **4** relating to the US state of Georgia or its people.

geostationary *adj, technical* of an artificial satellite above the Earth's equator: taking exactly 24 hours to complete one orbit and so appearing to remain stationary above a fixed point on the Earth's surface.

geothermal *adj, technical* **1** relating to the internal heat of the Earth. **2** relating to or using the energy that can be extracted from this heat.

geranium *n, bot* a plant or shrub with divided leaves and large flowers with five pink or purplish petals.

gerbil *n* a small burrowing rodent with long hind legs and a long furry tail.

geriatric *adj* **1** for or dealing with old people. **2** *derog, colloq* very old. ➤ *n* an old person.

geriatrics *sing n* the branch of medicine concerned with the health and care of the elderly.

germ *n* **1** a micro-organism, esp a bacterium or virus that causes disease. **2** the embryo of a plant, esp of wheat. **3** an origin or beginning.

German *adj* belonging or relating to Germany, its language, or its inhabitants. ➤ *n* **1** a native of Germany. **2** the official language of Germany.

Germanic *n* a branch of the Indo-European family of languages that includes both the modern and historical varieties. ➤ *adj* **1** relating to these languages or to the people speaking them. **2** typical of Germany or the Germans.

germanium *n, chem* a hard greyish-white metalloid element, widely used as a semiconductor.

German measles *sing n* RUBELLA.

germicide *n* any agent that destroys disease-causing micro-organisms such as bacteria and viruses. ○ **germicidal** *adj*.

germinate *vb* **1** *intr, biol* of a seed or spore: to show the first signs of development into a new individual. **2 a** to make (a seed, an idea, etc) begin to grow; **b** *intr* to come into being or existence. ○ **germination** *n*.

germ warfare *n* the use of bacteria to inflict disease on an enemy in war.

gerontology *n* the scientific study of old age, the ageing process and the problems of elderly people. ○ **gerontological** *adj*. ○ **gerontologist** *n*.

gerrymander *derog, vb* **1** to arrange or change the boundaries of (one or more electoral constituencies) so as to favour one political party. **2** to manipulate (eg data, a situation, etc) unfairly. ○ **gerrymandering** *n*.

gerund *n, gram* a noun formed from a verb and which refers to an action. In English gerunds end in -*ing*, eg 'the *baking* of bread' and '*Smoking* damages your health'.

gesso /'dʒesoʊ/ *n* (*gessoes*) plaster for sculpting with or painting on.

gestate *vb, tr & intr* **1** *zool* of a mammal: to carry (young) or be carried in the uterus, and to undergo physical development, in the period from fertilization to birth. **2** to develop (an idea, etc) slowly in the mind. ○ **gestation** *n*.

gesticulate *vb* **1** *intr* to make gestures, esp when speaking. **2** to express (eg feelings) by gestures. ○ **gesticulation** *n*.

gesture *n* **1 a** movement of a part of the body as an expression of meaning. **2** something done to communicate feelings or intentions, esp when these are friendly. **3** *derog* something done simply as a formality. ➤ *vb* **1** *intr* to make gestures. **2** to express (eg feelings) with gestures. ○ **gestural** *adj*.

get *vb* (**got**, *past participle* **got** or (*US*) **gotten**, **getting**) **1** to receive or obtain. **2** to have or possess. **3** *tr & intr* (*also* **get across** or **get sth across** or **away, to, through**, *etc*) to go or make them go, move, travel or arrive as specified: *I tried to get past him* • *Will you get him to bed at 8?* • *They got to Paris on Friday.* **4** (*often* **get sth down, in, out**, *etc*) to fetch, take, or bring it as specified: *Get it down from the shelf.* **5** to put into a particular state or condition: *Don't get it wet* • *The speech got him into trouble.* **6** *intr* to become: *I got angry.* **7** to catch (a disease, etc): *She got measles.* **8** to order or persuade: *Get him to help us.* **9** *colloq* to receive (a broadcast, etc): *We can't get the World Service.* **10** *colloq* to make contact with someone, esp by telephone: *I can never get him at home.* **11** *colloq* to arrive at (a number, etc) by calculation. **12** *intr, colloq* to receive permission (to do something): *Can you get to stay out late?* **13** *colloq* to buy or pay for something: *We got her some flowers.* **14** *colloq* to receive something as punishment: *They got ten years for armed robbery.* **15** (**get sb**) *colloq* to attack, punish, or otherwise cause harm to them: *I'll get you for that!* **16** *colloq* to annoy someone: *It really gets me.* **17** *colloq* to understand something. **18** *colloq* to hear something: *I didn't quite get his name.* **19** *colloq* to affect someone emotionally. **20** *colloq* to baffle someone: *You've got me there.* ➤ *n, derog slang* a stupid or contemptible person. ➤ *exclam* clear off! get lost! ◆ **be getting on 1** of a person: to grow old. **2** of time, etc: to grow late. **be getting on for** *colloq* to be approaching (a certain time or age). **get along with you!** *colloq* **1** go away! **2** an expression of disbelief. **get by** *colloq* **1** to manage to live. **2** to be just about acceptable. **get one's own back** *colloq* to have one's revenge. **get somewhere** *colloq* to make progress. **get there** *colloq* to make progress towards or achieve one's final aim. **have got to** to have to, to be required to do something. **◊ get about** or **around** *colloq* **1** to travel; to go from place to place. **2** of a rumour, etc: to circulate. **get sth across** to make it understood. **get along with sb** *colloq* to be on friendly terms with them. **get at sb** *colloq* **1** to criticize or victimize them persistently. **2** *colloq* to influence them by dishonest means. **get at sth 1** to reach or take hold of it. **2** *colloq* to suggest or imply it. **get away 1** to leave or be free to leave. **2** to escape. **3** *colloq* as an exclamation: used to express disbelief, shock, etc. **get away with sth** to commit (an offence or wrongdoing, etc) without being caught or punished. **get back at sb** or **get sb back** *colloq* to take revenge on them. **get sb down** *colloq* to make them sad or depressed. **get sth down 1** to manage to swallow it. **2** to write it down. **get down to sth** to apply oneself to (a task). **get in** of a political party: to be elected to power. **get into sth** *colloq* to develop a liking or enthusiasm for it. **get off** or **get sb off** *colloq* **1** to be released or to release someone without punishment or with only the stated punishment: *I was charged but got off* • *His lawyer managed to get him off with a warning.* **2** to fall asleep or send (eg a child) to sleep. **get on** *colloq* to make progress; to be successful. **get on with sb** to have a friendly relationship with them. **get on with sth** to continue working on it or dealing or progressing with it. **get over sb** or **sth** to be no longer emotionally affected by them or it. **get over sth** to recover from (an illness, disappointment, etc). **get sth over** to explain it successfully. **get over with** to deal with (something unpleasant) as quickly as possible. **get round** *colloq* of information, a rumour, etc: to become generally known. **get round sb** *colloq* to persuade them or win their approval or permission. **get round sth** to successfully pass by or negotiate (a problem, etc). **get round to sth** or **sb** to deal with it or them eventually. **get through sth 1** to complete (a task). **2** to use it steadily until it is finished. **3** *colloq* to pass (a test, etc). **get through to sb 1** to make contact with them by telephone. **2** to make them understand. **get to sb** *colloq* to annoy them. **get up 1** to get out of bed. **2** to stand up. **3** of the wind, etc: to become strong. **get up to sth** *colloq* to do or be involved in it, esp when it is something bad.

getaway *n* an escape.

get-out *n* a means or instance of escape.

get-together *n, colloq* an informal meeting.

get-up *n, colloq* an outfit or clothes, esp when considered strange or remarkable.

get-up-and-go *n, colloq* energy.

geyser /'gi:zə(r), 'gaɪzə(r)/ *n* 1 *geol* in an area of volcanic activity: a type of hot spring that intermittently spouts hot water and steam into the air. 2 a domestic appliance for heating water rapidly.

ghastly *adj* (**-ier, -iest**) 1 extremely frightening or horrific. 2 *colloq* very bad. 3 *colloq* very ill. ➤ *adv, colloq* extremely; unhealthily: *ghastly pale*. ○ **ghastliness** *n*.

ghee or **ghi** /gi:/ *n* in Indian cookery: clarified butter.

gherkin *n* 1 a variety of cucumber that bears very small fruits. 2 a small or immature fruit of a cucumber, used for pickling.

ghetto *n* (**ghettos** or **ghettoes**) 1 *derog* a poor area densely populated by people from a deprived social group, esp a racial minority. 2 *hist* a part of a city to which Jews were formerly restricted.

ghettoize or **-ise** *vb* to think of (a group of people or things) as being confined to a specific restricted function or area of activity. ○ **ghettoization** *n*.

ghost *n* 1 the spirit of a dead person when it is visible in some form to a living person. 2 a suggestion, hint or trace. ○ **ghostly** *adj*.

ghost town *n* a deserted town.

ghost writer *n* someone who writes books, speeches, etc on behalf of another person who is credited as their author.

ghoul *n* 1 someone who is interested in morbid or disgusting things. 2 a in Arab mythology: a demon that robs graves and eats dead bodies; b an evil spirit or presence. ○ **ghoulish** *adj*.

GI *n, colloq* a soldier in the US army, esp during World War II.

giant *n* 1 in stories: a huge, extremely strong creature of human form. 2 *colloq* an unusually large person or animal. 3 a person, group, etc of exceptional ability, importance or size. ➤ *adj* 1 *colloq* huge. 2 belonging to a particularly large species: *giant tortoise*.

gib /dʒɪb/ *n* a small metal or wooden wedge used for keeping a machine part in place. ➤ *vb* (**gibbed, gibbing**) *tr* to secure with a gib.

gibber *vb, intr* 1 to talk so fast that one cannot be understood. 2 *derog* to talk foolishly. ○ **gibbering** *adj*.

gibberish *n* 1 speech that is meaningless or difficult to understand. 2 utter nonsense.

gibbet *n, hist* 1 a gallows-like frame on which the bodies of executed criminals were hung as a public warning. 2 a gallows.

gibbon /'gɪbən/ *n* the smallest of the anthropoid apes, with very long arms.

gibe¹ or **jibe** /dʒaɪb/ *vb, intr* to mock, scoff or jeer. ➤ *n* a jeer.

gibe² see GYBE

giblets *pl n* the heart, liver and other internal organs of a chicken or other fowl.

giddy *adj* (**-ier, -iest**) 1 suffering an unbalancing spinning sensation. 2 causing such a sensation. 3 *literary* overwhelmed by feelings of excitement or pleasure. 4 light-hearted and carefree. ○ **giddily** *adv*. ○ **giddiness** *n*.

gift *n* 1 something given; a present. 2 a natural ability. 3 *colloq* something easily obtained, made easily available or simply easy. ➤ *vb, formal* to give something as a present to someone. ◆ **look a gift horse in the mouth** *usu with negatives* to find fault with a gift or unexpected opportunity.

gifted *adj* having a great natural ability.

gig¹ *n* 1 *hist* a small open two-wheeled horse-drawn carriage. 2 a small rowing boat carried on a ship.

gig² *colloq, n* 1 a pop, jazz or folk concert. 2 a musician's booking to perform. ➤ *vb* (**gigged, gigging**) *intr* to play a gig or gigs.

gig³ *n, colloq* a gigabyte.

giga- *pfx, denoting* 1 in the metric system: ten to the power of nine (10^9), ie one thousand million: *gigahertz*. 2 *comput* two to the power of thirty (2^{30}).

gigabyte *n, comput* a unit of storage capacity equal to 2^{30} bytes.

gigantic *adj* enormous. ○ **gigantically** *adv*.

gigantism *n, biol* 1 excessive overgrowth of the whole human body. 2 excessive size in plants.

giggle *vb, intr* to laugh quietly in short bursts or in a nervous or silly way. ➤ *n* 1 such a laugh. 2 (**the giggles**) a fit of giggling. 3 *colloq* a funny person, situation, thing, activity, etc. ○ **giggly** *adj* (**-ier, -iest**).

gigolo /'dʒɪgələʊ/ *n, derog* a young, and usu attractive, man who is paid by an older woman to be her companion, escort and/or lover.

gigot /'dʒɪgət/ *n* a leg of lamb or mutton.

gild¹ *vb* (**gilded** or **gilt**) 1 to cover something with a thin coating of gold or something similar. 2 to give something a falsely attractive or valuable appearance. ◆ **gild the lily** to try to improve something which is already beautiful enough.

gild² see GUILD

gill¹ /gɪl/ *n* 1 in all fishes and many other aquatic animals: a respiratory organ that extracts dissolved oxygen from the surrounding water. 2 (**gills**) *colloq* the flesh around the jaw.

gill² /dʒɪl/ *n* in the UK: a unit of liquid measure equal to 142.1ml or a quarter of a pint.

gillie or **ghillie** *n* a guide to a stalker or fisherman, esp in Scotland.

gilt¹ *adj* covered with a thin coating of gold or apparently so covered. ➤ *n* 1 gold or a gold-like substance used in gilding. 2 (**gilts**) gilt-edged securities. 3 superficial attractiveness. ➤ *vb, past tense, past participle of* GILD¹.

gilt² *n* a young female pig.

gilt-edged *adj* 1 of a book: having pages with

gilded edges. **2** of the highest quality. **3** of government securities with a fixed rate of interest: able to be sold at face value.

gimcrack /ˈdʒɪmkrak/ *derog, adj* cheap, showy and badly made. ➤ *n* a cheap and showy article.

gimlet *n* a T-shaped hand-tool for boring holes in wood.

gimmick *n, derog* a scheme or object used to attract attention, publicity or customers. ○ **gimmickry** *n*. ○ **gimmicky** *adj*.

gin[1] *n* an alcoholic spirit made from barley, rye or maize and flavoured with juniper berries.

gin[2] *n* (*also* **gin trap**) a wire noose laid as a snare or trap for catching game. ➤ *vb* (**ginned, ginning**) to snare or trap (game) in a gin.

gin[3] see GIN RUMMY

ginger *n* **1** an aromatic spicy swollen root, often dried and ground to a powder and widely used as a flavouring, or preserved in syrup. **2** the tropical plant from which this root is obtained. **3** a reddish-brown colour. ➤ *adj* **1** flavoured with ginger. **2** of hair: reddish-orange in colour; **b** reddish-brown in colour. ➤ *vb* (*usu* **ginger up**) *colloq* to urge, persuade or force someone or something to become more lively, active, interesting or efficient. ○ **gingery** *adj*.

gingerbread *n* a type of cake flavoured with treacle and ginger.

gingerly *adv* with delicate caution. ➤ *adj* very cautious or wary.

gingham /ˈgɪŋəm/ *n* striped or checked cotton cloth.

gingivitis /dʒɪndʒɪˈvaɪtɪs/ *n, med* inflammation of the gums.

ginormous *adj, colloq* exceptionally huge.

gin rummy or **gin** *n, cards* a type of RUMMY in which players have the option of ending the round at any time when their unmatched cards count ten or less.

ginseng /ˈdʒɪnsɛŋ/ *n* **1 a** a plant cultivated in E Asia for its roots; **b** a similar American species of this plant. **2** the aromatic root of either of these plants, prepared as a tonic, stimulant and aphrodisiac.

Gipsy see GYPSY

giraffe *n* (**giraffes** or **giraffe**) a very tall African mammal with an extremely long neck and legs, a small head, and large eyes.

gird *vb* (**girded** or **girt**) *literary* to encircle or fasten something (esp part of the body) with a belt or something similar. ◆ **gird** or **gird up one's loins** to prepare oneself for action.

girder *n* a large beam of wood, iron or steel used to support a floor, wall, road or bridge.

girdle[1] *n* **1** a woman's close-fitting elasticated undergarment that covers the area from waist to thigh. **2** *old use* a belt or cord worn round the waist. **3** a surrounding part. ➤ *vb* **1** to put a girdle on someone or something. **2** *literary* to surround something.

girdle[2] see GRIDDLE

girl *n* **1** a female child. **2** a daughter. **3** *often offensive* a young woman, esp an unmarried one.

4 *often offensive* a woman of any age. **5** *colloq* a sweetheart. ○ **girlhood** *n*. ○ **girlish** *adj*.

girlfriend *n* **1** a female sexual or romantic partner. **2** a female friend.

girlie or **girly** *adj, colloq* **1** of a magazine, picture, etc: featuring naked or nearly naked young women in erotic poses. **2** *derog* girlish, esp in being overly feminine.

giro /ˈdʒaɪrəʊ/ *n* **1** a banking system by which money can be transferred from one account directly to another. **2** *Brit colloq* a social security benefit received in the form of a cheque.

girth *n* **1** the distance round something such as a tree or a person's waist. **2** the strap round a horse's belly that holds a saddle in place. ➤ *vb* to put a girth on (a horse).

gismo or **gizmo** *n, colloq* a gadget.

gist /dʒɪst/ *n* the general meaning or main point of something said or written.

git *n, derog slang* a stupid or contemptible person.

give *vb* (**gave, given**) **1** to transfer possession of something permanently or temporarily: *I gave him my watch* • *Give me your bags.* **2** to provide or administer: *give advice* • *give medicine.* **3** to produce: *Cows give milk.* **4** to perform (an action, service, etc): *to give a smile* • *She gave a lecture.* **5** to pay: *She gave £20 for it.* **6** *intr* to make a donation: *Please give generously.* **7** (*also* **give sth up**) to sacrifice it: *to give one's life.* **8** to be the cause or source of something: *The whole situation gives me pain.* **9** *intr* to yield or break: *The bridge may give under pressure.* **10** to organize something at one's own expense: *to give a party.* **11** to have something as a result: *four into twenty gives five.* **12** to reward or punish with something: *He was given 20 years in prison.* **13** *colloq* to agree to or admit something: *I'll give you that.* **14** *sport* to declare someone to be a specified thing: *given offside.* ➤ *n* capacity to yield; flexibility: *a board with plenty of give.* ◆ **give and take** to make mutual concessions. **give as good as one gets** *colloq* to respond to an attack with equal energy, force and effect. **give or take sth** *colloq* allowing for a (specified) margin of error: *We have all the money, give or take a pound.* **give up the ghost** *colloq* to die. **give way 1** to allow priority. **2** to collapse under pressure. ◇ **give sb away 1** to betray them. **2** to present (the bride) to the bridegroom at a wedding ceremony. **give sth away 1** to hand it over as a gift. **2** to sell it at an incredibly low price. **3** to allow (a piece of information) to become known, usu by accident. **give in to sb** or **sth** to yield to them. **give sth off** to produce or emit (eg a smell). **give out** *colloq* to break down or come to an end. **give sth out 1** to announce or distribute it. **2** to emit (a sound, smell, etc). **give over!** *colloq* usually as a command: to stop (doing it): *Give over shouting!* **give sth over 1** to transfer it. **2** to set it aside or devote it to some purpose. **give up** to admit defeat. **give oneself up** to surrender. **give oneself up to sth** to devote oneself to (a cause, etc).

give sth up to renounce or quit (a habit, etc).

give-and-take n 1 mutual willingness to accept the other's point of view. 2 a useful exchange of views.

giveaway n, colloq 1 an act of accidentally revealing secrets, etc. 2 something obtained extremely easily or cheaply. 3 a free gift.

given adj 1 stated or specified. 2 admitted, assumed or accepted as true. ➤ prep, conj accepting (a specified thing) as a basis for discussion: given that she is a genius. ➤ n something that is admitted, assumed or accepted as true: Her genius is a given. ➤ vb, past participle of GIVE. ◆ **given to sth** having it as a habit.

gizzard n in birds, earthworms and certain other animals: a muscular chamber specialized for grinding up indigestible food.

glacé /'glaseɪ/ adj 1 coated with a sugary glaze. 2 applied esp to thin silk and kid leather: glossy, shiny.

glacial adj 1 geol, geog relating to or resembling a glacier. 2 referring or relating to ice.

glacier n a large slow-moving body of ice.

glad adj (gladder, gladdest) 1 (sometimes glad about sth) happy or pleased. 2 (glad of sth) grateful for it. 3 very willing: We are glad to help. 4 old use bringing happiness: glad tidings. ○ **gladly** adv. ○ **gladness** n.

gladden vb to make someone (or their heart, etc) happy or pleased.

glade n, literary an open space in a wood or forest.

gladiator n in ancient Rome: a man trained to fight against other men or animals in an arena. ○ **gladiatorial** adj.

glad rags pl n, colloq one's best clothes.

glam slang, adj glamorous. ➤ n glamour.

glamorize or **-ise** vb 1 to make someone or something glamorous. 2 to romanticize. ○ **glamorization** n.

glamorous adj full of glamour. ○ **glamorously** adv.

glamour n 1 the quality of being fascinatingly, if falsely, attractive. 2 great beauty or sexual charm, esp when created by make-up, clothes, etc.

glance vb, usu intr 1 (often glance at sth or sb) to look quickly or indirectly at it or them. 2 (often glance over or through sth) to read or look at it cursorily. 3 tr & intr (often glance off) a of a blow or weapon: to hit (a target) obliquely; b of light: to shine or reflect in flashes: The sunlight glanced off the table. ➤ n 1 a brief (and often indirect) look. 2 a deflection. 3 literary a brief flash of light.

gland n 1 zool in humans and animals: an organ that produces a specific chemical substance (eg a hormone) for use inside the body. 2 bot in plants: a specialized cell or group of cells involved in the secretion of plant products such as nectar, oils and resins.

glandular adj, zool, bot, etc relating to, containing or affecting a gland or glands.

glandular fever n infectious mononucleosis, a disease caused by the Epstein-Barr virus and with symptoms including swollen glands, sore throat, headache and fatigue.

glare vb 1 intr to stare angrily. 2 intr to be unpleasantly bright or shiny. 3 to express something with a glare. ➤ n 1 an angry stare. 2 dazzling light. 3 comput excessive brightness emitted from a VDU screen or from light reflecting off a terminal. 4 brash colour or decoration.

glaring adj 1 unpleasantly bright. 2 very obvious. ○ **glaringly** adv.

glasnost /'glaznɒst/ n a policy of openness and willingness to provide information on the part of governments, esp the Soviet government under Mikhail Gorbachev (President 1988–91).

glass n 1 a hard brittle non-crystalline material that is usu transparent or translucent. 2 an article made from this, eg a mirror, a lens or, esp, a drinking cup. 3 (also glassful) the amount held by a drinking glass. 4 (also glassware) articles made of glass: a collection of glass. 5 (glasses) spectacles. ➤ vb to supply or cover something with glass.

glass-blowing n the process of shaping molten glass by blowing air into it through a tube. ○ **glass-blower** n.

glass ceiling n an invisible but unmistakable barrier on the career ladder that certain categories of employees (esp women) find they cannot progress beyond.

glass fibre n glass that has been melted and then drawn out into extremely fine fibres, often set in plastic resin and used to make strong lightweight materials.

glasshouse n 1 a building constructed mainly or entirely of glass, esp a greenhouse. 2 slang a military prison.

glass wool n glass that has been spun into fine thread-like fibres, forming a wool-like mass, used in air filters, insulation, fibreglass, etc.

glassy adj (-ier, -iest) 1 like glass. 2 expressionless: glassy eyes.

glaucoma n, med, ophthalmol, etc an eye disease in which increased pressure within the eyeball causes impaired vision and which, if left untreated, can lead to blindness.

glaze vb 1 to fit glass panes into (a window, door, etc). 2 to achieve a glaze on or apply a glaze to (pottery, pastry, or painting). 3 intr (usu glaze over) of the eyes: to become fixed and expressionless. ➤ n 1 a hard glassy coating on pottery or the material for this coating before it is applied or fired. 2 in painting: a thin coat of semi-transparent colour. 3 a shiny coating of milk, eggs or sugar on food. ○ **glazed** adj. ○ **glazing** n.

glazier n someone whose job is to fit glass in windows, doors, etc.

gleam n 1 a gentle glow. 2 a brief flash of light. 3 a brief appearance or sign: a gleam of excitement in his eyes. ➤ vb, intr 1 to glow gently. 2 to shine with brief flashes of light. 3 of an emotion, etc: to be shown briefly.

glean vb **1** to collect (information, etc) bit by bit, often with difficulty. **2** tr & intr to collect (loose grain and other useful remnants of a crop left in a field) after harvesting.

glebe n **1** a piece of church-owned land providing income in rent, etc for the resident minister. **2** poetic land; a field.

glee n **1** joy. **2** a song with different parts for three or four unaccompanied voices, esp male voices.

gleeful adj joyful. ○ **gleefully** adv.

glen n esp in Scotland: a long narrow valley.

glib adj (**glibber, glibbest**) derog speaking or spoken readily and persuasively, but neither sincere nor reliable. ○ **glibly** adv. ○ **glibness** n.

glide vb, intr **1** to move smoothly and often without any visible effort: gliding along the ice. **2** of an aircraft: to travel through the air or to land without engine power. **3** to travel through the air by glider. ➤ n **1** a gliding movement. **2** the controlled descent of an aircraft without engine power. ○ **gliding** adj.

glider n an aircraft designed to glide and soar in air currents without using any form of engine power. ○ **gliding** n the sport of flying gliders.

glimmer vb, intr to glow faintly. ➤ n **1** a faint glow; a twinkle. **2** a hint or trace: a glimmer of hope. ○ **glimmering** n, adj.

glimpse n a very brief look. ➤ vb to see something or someone momentarily.

glint vb, intr to give off tiny flashes of bright light. ➤ n a brief flash of light.

glissando n (**glissandos** or **glissandi** /glɪˈsandiː/) mus **1** the effect produced by sliding the finger along a keyboard or a string. **2** a similar effect produced on the trombone.

glisten vb, intr often of something wet or icy: to shine or sparkle. ○ **glistening** adj.

glitch n, colloq a sudden brief irregularity or failure to function.

glitter vb, intr **1** to shine with bright flashes of light. **2** colloq to be sparklingly attractive. ➤ n **1** sparkle. **2** colloq bright attractiveness, often superficial. **3** tiny pieces of shiny material used for decoration. ○ **glittering** adj. ○ **glittery** adj.

glitterati /glɪtəˈrɑːtiː/ pl n, colloq famous, fashionable and beautiful people.

glitz n, colloq showiness; garishness.

glitzy adj (**-ier, -iest**) colloq extravagantly showy; flashy.

gloaming n, poetic or Scot dusk; twilight.

gloat vb, intr (often **gloat over sth**) to feel or show smug or vindictive satisfaction, esp in one's own success or in another's misfortune. ➤ n an act of gloating.

glob n, colloq a small amount of thick liquid.

global adj **1** affecting the whole world. **2** total. **3** comput affecting or applying to a whole program or file. ○ **globally** adv.

globalize or **-ise** vb, intr to extend commercial and cultural activities into all parts of the world. ○ **globalization** n.

global village n the world perceived as a single community.

global warming n, ecol a gradual increase in the average temperature of the Earth's surface and its atmosphere which has been attributed to the GREENHOUSE EFFECT.

globe n **1** (**the globe**) the Earth. **2** a sphere with a map of the world on it. **3** any approximately ball-shaped object.

globe artichoke n **1** a tall plant with deeply divided leaves and large purplish-blue flowers. **2** the fleshy base of the immature flower-head of this plant, eaten as a vegetable.

globetrotter n, colloq someone who travels all over the world. ○ **globetrotting** n.

globule n a small drop. ○ **globular** adj.

glockenspiel /ˈɡlɒkənspiːl, -ʃpiːl/ n a musical instrument consisting of tuned metal plates held in a frame, played with two small hammers.

gloom n **1** near-darkness. **2** sadness or despair. ➤ vb, intr **1** of the sky: to be dark and threatening. **2** to behave in a sad or depressed way.

gloomy adj (**-ier, -iest**) **1** dimly lit. **2** causing gloom. **3** sad or depressed. ○ **gloomily** adv. ○ **gloominess** n.

glorified adj, derog given a fancy name or appearance: a glorified servant.

glorify vb (**-ied**) **1** to exaggerate the beauty, importance, etc of something or someone. **2** to praise or worship (God). **3** to make someone or something glorious. ○ **glorification** n.

glorious adj **1** having or bringing glory. **2** splendidly beautiful. **3** colloq excellent. **4** humorous, colloq very bad: glorious mess.

glory n (**-ies**) **1** great honour and prestige. **2** great beauty or splendour. **3** praise and thanks given to God. ➤ vb (**-ies, -ied**) intr (usu **glory in sth**) to feel or show great delight or pride in it.

gloss¹ n **1** shiny brightness on a surface. **2** a superficial pleasantness or attractiveness. **3** (in full **gloss paint**) paint which produces a shiny finish. **4** a substance which adds shine: lip gloss. ➤ vb **1** to give a shiny finish to something. **2** to paint (a surface, etc) with gloss. ◊ **gloss over sth** to disguise or mask (a deficiency, mistake, etc), esp by treating a subject briefly and dismissively.

gloss² n **1** a short explanation of a difficult word, phrase, etc in a text, eg in the margin of a manuscript. **2** an intentionally misleading explanation. ➤ vb **1** to provide a gloss of (a word, etc) or add glosses to (a text). **2** (also **gloss sth over** or **away**) to explain it away with a false interpretation.

glossary n (**-ies**) a list of explanations of words, often at the end of a book.

glossy adj (**-ier, -iest**) **1** smooth and shiny. **2** superficially attractive. **3** of a magazine: printed on glossy paper. ➤ n (**-ies**) colloq such a magazine. ○ **glossily** adv. ○ **glossiness** n.

glottal stop n, ling a sound produced when the glottis is closed and then opened sharply.

glottis n (**glottises** or (anat) **glottides** /ˈɡlɒt-**

ɪdiːz/) the opening through which air passes from the pharynx to the trachea, including the space between the vocal cords.

glove *n* **1** a covering for the hand which usu has individual casings for each finger. **2** a similar padded hand covering used in sports such as boxing, baseball, etc. ➤ *vb* to cover something with a glove or gloves.

glove compartment *n* a small compartment in the dashboard of a car where small articles can be kept.

glow *vb*, *intr* **1** to give out a steady heat or light without flames. **2** to shine brightly, as if very hot. **3** to feel or communicate a sensation of intense contentment or well-being: *glowing with pride*. **4** of the complexion: to be well-coloured (ie rosy or tanned) and healthy-looking. ➤ *n* **1** a steady flameless heat or light. **2** bright, shiny appearance. **3** intensity of feeling, esp pleasant feeling. **4** a healthy colour of complexion.

glower *vb*, *intr* to stare angrily. ➤ *n* an angry stare.

glowing *adj* full of praise: *a glowing report.* ➤ *vb*, present participle of GLOW. ○ **glowingly** *adv.*

glow-worm *n* **1** a small nocturnal beetle, the wingless female of which attracts the male by giving out a bright greenish light from the underside of her abdomen. **2** *N Am* a luminous insect larva.

glucose *n*, *biochem* the most common form of naturally occurring sugar, in animals the main form in which energy derived from carbohydrates is transported around the bloodstream.

glue *n* **1** any adhesive obtained by extracting natural substances, esp from bone, in boiling water. **2** any adhesive made by dissolving synthetic substances such as rubber or plastic in a suitable solvent. ➤ *vb* (**glueing** or **gluing**) to use such an adhesive to stick (two materials or parts) together. ○ **gluey** *adj* (**gluier, gluiest**). ◆ **be glued to sth** *colloq* to have one's eyes fixed on it.

glum *adj* (**glummer, glummest**) in low spirits.

glut *n* an excessive supply of goods, etc. ➤ *vb* (**glutted, glutting**) **1** to feed or supply something to excess. **2** to block or choke up.

gluten *n*, *biochem* a mixture of two plant storage proteins occurring in the flour of wheat and other grains.

glutinous *adj* like glue; sticky. ○ **glutinously** *adv.* ○ **glutinousness** *n.*

glutton[1] *n* **1** *derog* someone who eats too much. **2** someone whose behaviour suggests an eagerness (for something unpleasant): *a glutton for hard work.* ○ **gluttonous** *adj.* ○ **gluttony** *n*, *derog* the habit or practice of eating too much.

glutton[2] *n* a WOLVERINE.

glycerine /ˈɡlɪsəriːn/ or **glycerin** /-rɪn/ *n*, *non-technical* GLYCEROL.

glycerol /ˈɡlɪsərɒl/ *n*, *chem* a colourless viscous sweet-tasting liquid that is a by-product in the manufacture of soap from naturally occurring fats and is widely used in various foodstuffs and medicines.

glycogen *n*, *biochem* a highly branched chain of glucose molecules, the main form in which carbohydrate is stored (esp in the liver and muscles) in vertebrates. ○ **glycogenic** *adj.*

gm *abbrev* gram or gramme.

GMT *abbrev* Greenwich Mean Time.

gnarled or **gnarly** *adj* (**-ier, -iest**) of tree trunks, branches, human hands, etc: twisted, with knotty swellings, usu as a result of age.

gnash *vb*, *tr & intr* to grind (the teeth) together, esp in anger or pain.

gnat *n* a small biting fly.

gnaw *vb* (*past participle* **gnawed** or **gnawn**) **1** (*also* **gnaw at** or **gnaw away at sth**) to bite it with a scraping action, causing a gradual wearing away. **2** to make (eg a hole) in this way. **3** *tr & intr* (*also* **gnaw at sb**) of pain, anxiety, etc: to trouble them persistently. ○ **gnawing** *adj.*

gnome *n* **1** a fairy-tale creature, usu in the form of a small misshapen old man, who lives underground, often guarding treasure. **2** a statue of such a creature used as a garden ornament.

gnomic *adj*, *formal* of speech or writing: **1** expressed in or containing short pithy aphorisms. **2** so terse or opaque as to be difficult to understand.

gnostic /ˈnɒstɪk/ *adj* **1** relating to knowledge, esp mystical or religious knowledge. **2** (**Gnostic**) relating to Gnosticism. ➤ *n* (**Gnostic**) an early Christian heretic believing in redemption of the soul through special religious knowledge.

gnu /nuː/ *n* (**gnus** or **gnu**) either of two species of large African antelope with horns, a long mane and tufts of hair growing from the muzzle, throat and chest. Also called **wildebeest**.

go *vb* (**goes, went, gone**) usu *intr* **1** (*often* **go about** or **by** or **down**, *etc*) to walk, move or travel in the direction specified. **2** to lead or extend: *The road goes to the farm.* **3** (*usu* **go to somewhere**) to visit or attend it, once or regularly: *to go to school.* **4** to leave or move away. **5** to be destroyed or taken away: *The old door had to go* • *The peaceful atmosphere has gone.* **6** to proceed or fare: *The scheme is going well.* **7** to be used up: *All his money went on drink.* **8** to be given or sold for a stated amount: *The desk went for £20.* **9** to leave or set out for a stated purpose: *to go on holiday* • *to go fishing.* **10** *tr & intr* to perform (an action) or produce (a sound): *Go like this.* **11** *colloq* to break, break down, or fail: *His eyes have gone.* **12** to work or be in working order: *See if you can make it go.* **13** to become: *to go mad.* **14** to belong; to be placed correctly: *Where does this go?* **15** to fit, or be contained: *Four into three won't go.* **16** to be or continue in a certain state: *to go hungry.* **17** of time: to pass. **18** of a story or tune: to run: *How does it go?* **19** (*often* **go for sb** or **sth**) to be valid or accepted for them: *The same goes for you* • *In this office, anything goes.* **20** *colloq* to carry authority: *What she says goes.* **21** (*often* **go**

with sth) of colours, etc: to match or blend. **22** to subject oneself: *Don't go to much trouble*. **23** to adopt a specified system: *to go metric*. **24** *tr* to bet (a specified amount), esp at cards: *She went five pounds*. **25** *colloq* to be in general, for the purpose of comparison: *As girls go, she's quite naughty*. **26** to exist or be on offer: *the best offer going at the moment*. **27** *very colloq* to say: *She goes, 'No, you didn't!' and I goes, 'Oh, yes I did!'* ➤ *n* **1** a turn: *It's my go*. **2** energy; liveliness: *She lacks go*. **3** *colloq* busy activity: *It's all go*. **4** *colloq* a success: *make a go of it*. ♦ **be going on for sth** *colloq* to be approaching (a specified age): *She's going on for 60*. **from the word go** from the very beginning. **give it a go** *colloq* to make an attempt at something. **go all out for sth** to make a great effort to obtain or achieve it. **go slow** to work slowly so as to encourage an employer to negotiate or meet a demand. See also GO-SLOW. **have a go** *colloq* to try; to make an attempt. **have a go at sb** *colloq* to attack them verbally. **have sth going for one** *colloq* to have it as an attribute or advantage. **no go** *colloq* not possible. **on the go** *colloq* busily active. **to be going on with** *colloq* for the immediate future: *enough to be going on with*. ◊ **go about 1** to circulate: *a rumour going about*. **2** *naut* to change course. **go about sth 1** to busy oneself with it. **2** to attempt or tackle it: *how to go about doing this*. **go against sb** to be decided unfavourably for them. **go against sth** to be contrary to it. **go ahead** to proceed. **go along with sb** or **sth** to agree with and support them or it. **go back on sth** to break (an agreement, etc). **go down 1** to decrease. **2** *colloq* to be accepted or received: *The joke went down well*. **go down with sth** to contract an illness. **go for sb** or **sth** *colloq* **1** to attack them. **2** to be attracted by them. **3** to choose them. **4** (*usu* **go for it**) *colloq* to try very hard to achieve something. **go in for sth** *colloq* **1** to take up (a profession). **2** to enter (a contest). **3** to be interested or attracted by something, as a rule: *I don't usually go in for films with subtitles*. **go into sth 1** to take up or join (a profession). **2** to discuss or investigate something. **go off 1** to explode. **2** *colloq* of perishables, eg food: to become rotten. **3** to proceed or pass off: *The party went off well*. **go off sb** or **sth** *colloq* to stop liking them or it. **go on 1** to continue or proceed. **2** *colloq* to talk too much. **3** (*only as exclam*) *colloq* expressing disbelief. **go out 1** of a fire or light: to become extinguished. **2** to be broadcast. **go out with sb** to spend time with someone socially or (esp) romantically. **go over** to pass off or be received: *The play went over well*. **go over sth 1** to examine it. **2** to revise or rehearse it. **go over to** to transfer support or allegiance: *to go over to the enemy*. **go round** to be enough for all. **go through** to be approved. **go through sth 1** to use it up. **2** to revise or rehearse it. **3** to examine it. **4** to suffer it: *I went through hell*. **5** to search it: *They went through our bags*. **go through with sth** to carry it out to the end. **go under** *colloq* to fail or be ruined. **go up 1** to in-

crease. **2** of a building, etc: to be erected. **go with sb** *colloq* to have a close romantic friendship with them. **go without sth** to suffer a lack of it.

goad *vb* (*usu* **goad sb into sth** or **to do sth**) to urge or provoke them to action. ➤ *n* **1** a sharp-pointed stick used for driving cattle, etc. **2** anything that provokes or incites.

go-ahead *colloq*, *adj* energetically ambitious and far-sighted. ➤ *n* (**the go-ahead**) permission to start.

goal *n* **1** in various sports, esp football: a set of posts with a crossbar, through which the ball is struck to score points. **2 a** an act of scoring in this way; **b** the point or points scored. **3** an aim or purpose: *a goal in life*. **4** a destination. ○ **goalless** *adj*.

goalie *n*, *colloq* a goalkeeper.

goalkeeper *n* in various sports: the player who guards the goal and tries to prevent the opposition from scoring.

goal line *n* in various sports: the line marking each end of the field of play.

goalpost *n* in various sports: each of two upright posts forming the goal. ♦ **move the goalposts** to change the accepted rules or aims of an activity during its course.

goat *n* **1** a herbivorous mammal, noted for its physical agility and sure-footedness, the males of which have tufty beards. **2** *derog colloq* a lecherous man, esp an old one. **3** *derog*, *colloq* a foolish person. ♦ **get sb's goat** *colloq* to annoy or irritate them.

goatee *n* a pointed beard growing only on the front of the chin.

goatherd *n* someone who looks after goats out in the pastures.

gob *n* **1** *coarse slang* the mouth. **2** a soft wet lump. **3** *coarse slang* spit. ➤ *vb* (**gobbed, gobbing**) *intr*, *coarse slang* to spit.

gobble[1] *vb*, *tr* & *intr* (*usu* **gobble sth up** or **down**) to eat hurriedly and noisily.

gobble[2] *vb*, *intr* of a male turkey: to make a loud gurgling sound in the throat. ➤ *n* the loud gurgling sound made by a male turkey.

gobbledygook or **gobbledegook** *n*, *colloq* **1** official jargon, meaningless to ordinary people. **2** nonsense.

go-between *n* a messenger between two people or sides.

goblet *n* a drinking-cup with a base and stem but no handles.

goblin *n* in folk-tales: an evil or mischievous spirit in the form of a small man.

gobsmacked *adj*, *colloq* astonished.

god *n* **1** (**God**) in monotheistic religions: the unique supreme being, creator and ruler of the universe. **2** in other religions: a superhuman male being with power over nature and humanity. Compare GODDESS. **3** a man greatly admired, esp for his fine physique or wide influence. **4** *often derog* an object of excessive influence: *He made money his god*. **5** (**the gods**) superhuman beings collectively, both male and female. **6** (**the gods**) the balcony or upper circle in a theatre. ➢ *exclam* (**God!** or **my God!**) expressing amazement, anger, etc. ○ **godlike** *adj*. ◆ **for God's sake 1** expressing pleading. **2** expressing irritation, disgust, etc.

godchild *n* a child that a godparent is responsible for.

goddaughter *n* a female godchild.

goddess *n* **1** a superhuman female being who has power over nature and humanity; a female object of worship. Compare GOD. **2** a woman greatly admired for her beauty.

godfather *n* **1** a male godparent. **2** the head of a criminal group, esp in the Mafia.

godforsaken (also **Godforsaken**) *adj, derog* of a place: remote and desolate.

godless *adj* **1** not believing in God. **2** having no god. **3** wicked; immoral. ○ **godlessness** *n*.

godly *adj* (**-ier, -iest**) pious. ○ **godliness** *n*.

godmother *n* a female godparent.

godparent *n* someone who, at baptism, guarantees a child's religious education and generally takes a personal interest in them.

godsend *n* someone or something whose arrival is unexpected but very welcome.

godson *n* a male godchild.

goer *n* **1** *in compounds* someone who makes visits, esp regular ones, to a specified place: *cinema-goer*. **2** *colloq* a sexually energetic person, esp a woman. **3** *colloq* something that travels fast or makes fast progress.

gofer *n, colloq* a junior employee who runs errands.

go-getter *n, colloq* an ambitious enterprising person.

goggle *vb* **1** *intr* to look with wide staring eyes. **2** to roll (the eyes). **3** *intr* of the eyes: to stick out. ➢ *n* a wide-eyed stare.

goggle-box *n* (*usu* **the goggle-box**) *colloq* the TV.

goggles *pl n* protective spectacles with edges that fit closely against the face.

go-go dancer *n* a female dancer, often scantily dressed, who performs to pop music, esp in a club or bar.

going *n* **1** leaving; a departure: *comings and goings of the lodgers*. **2** *horse-racing* the condition of the track. **3** progress: *We made good going*. **4** *colloq* general situation or conditions: *when the going gets tough*. **5** *in compounds* the act or practice of making visits, esp regular ones, to specified places: *theatre-going*. ➢ *vb, present participle of* GO about or intending (to do something). ➢ *adj* **1** flourishing, successful: *a going concern*. **2** usual or accepted: *the going rate*. **3** currently available: *These are the cheapest ones going*. ◆ **be tough** or **hard going** to be difficult to do. **going on** or **going on for sth** approaching (an age or time): *going on for sixteen*.

going-over *n* (**goings-over**) *colloq* **1** a beating. **2** a close inspection.

goings-on *pl n, colloq* events or happenings, esp if they are strange or disapproved of.

goitre or (*US*) **goiter** /ˈɡɔɪtə(r)/ *n, pathol* an abnormal enlargement of the THYROID gland which results in a large visible swelling in the neck.

go-kart or **go-cart** *n* a low racing vehicle consisting of a frame with wheels, engine and steering gear.

gold *n* **1** a soft yellow precious metallic element used for making jewellery, coins, etc. **2** articles made from it. **3** its value, used as a standard for the value of currency. **4** its deep yellow colour. **5** *colloq* a gold medal. **6** precious or noble quality: *heart of gold*. **7** monetary wealth. ➢ *adj* **1** made of gold. **2** gold-coloured.

golden *adj* **1** gold-coloured. **2** made of or containing gold. **3** happy; prosperous or thriving: *golden age*. **4** excellent; extremely valuable: *golden opportunity*. **5** greatly admired or favoured: *golden girl*. **6** denoting a 50th anniversary: *golden jubilee*.

golden age *n* **1** an imaginary past time of innocence and happiness. **2** the period of highest achievement in any sphere.

golden handshake *n, colloq* a large sum received from an employer on retirement or in compensation for compulsory redundancy.

golden mean *n* the midpoint between two extremes.

golden oldie *n, colloq* a song, recording, film, etc first issued years ago and still popular or well-known.

golden rule *n* any essential principle or rule.

goldfinch *n* a European finch which has a broad yellow bar across each wing.

goldfish *n* a yellow, orange or golden-red freshwater fish of the carp family.

goldfish bowl *n* **1** a spherical glass aquarium for fish. **2** a situation entirely lacking in privacy.

gold leaf *n* gold that is rolled or beaten into very thin sheets and used to decorate books, crockery, etc.

gold medal *n* a medal awarded to the winner of a sporting contest, or in recognition of excellence.

gold mine or **goldmine** *n* **1** a place where gold is mined. **2** *colloq* a source of great wealth.

gold plate *n* **1** a thin coating of gold, esp on silver. **2** articles such as spoons and dishes made of gold. ➢ *vb* (**gold-plate**) to coat (another metal) with gold. ○ **gold-plated** *adj*.

gold rush *n* a frantic scramble by large numbers of people to reach and exploit an area where gold has been discovered.

goldsmith *n* someone who makes articles out of gold.

gold standard *n* a monetary system in which the unit of currency is assigned a value relative to gold.

golf *n* a game played on a golf course, the object being to hit a small ball into each of a series of nine or eighteen holes using a set of clubs, taking as few strokes as possible. ➢ *vb, intr* to play this game. ○ **golfer** *n*.

golf club *n* **1** any of the set of long-handled

clubs used to play golf. **2 a** an association of players of golf; **b** its premises with a golf course attached.

golf course n an area of specially prepared ground on which golf is played.

golliwog or **gollywog** n an old-fashioned child's doll with a black face, bristling hair and bright clothes, now considered offensive.

golly[1] exclam, old use expressing surprise or admiration.

golly[2] n (-ies) colloq short form of GOLLIWOG.

gonad n, biol an organ in which eggs or sperm are produced, esp the OVARY or TESTIS.

gondola n **1** a long narrow flat-bottomed boat with pointed upturned ends, used to transport passengers on the canals of Venice. **2** the passenger cabin suspended from an airship, balloon or cable-railway. **3** a free-standing shelved unit for displaying goods in a supermarket. ○ **gondolier** n someone who propels a gondola in Venice.

gone vb, past participle of GO. ➢ adj **1** departed. **2** colloq of time: past: gone six. **3** used up. **4** lost. **5** dead. **6** colloq pregnant: four months gone. **7** colloq in an exalted state, eg from drugs.

goner n, colloq someone or something that is considered beyond hope of recovery.

gong n **1** a hanging metal plate that makes a resonant sound when struck, sometimes used as an orchestral percussion instrument. **2** slang a medal.

gonorrhoea or (N Am) **gonorrhea** /gɒnəˈrɪə/ n, pathol a sexually transmitted disease, infection of the genital tract by a bacterium.

goo n, colloq **1** any sticky substance. **2** derog excessive sentimentality.

good adj (**better, best**) **1 a** having desirable or necessary positive qualities; **b** patronizing used when addressing or referring to someone: my good man. **2** morally correct. **3** kind and generous. **4** bringing happiness or pleasure: good news. **5** well-behaved. **6** wise: a good buy. **7** thorough. **8** finest compared with others: my good china. **9** adequate: a good supply. **10** valid. **11** well-respected. **12** considerable; at least: We waited a good while • It lasted a good month. **13** certain to provide the desired result: good for a laugh. **14** used to introduce exclamations expressing surprise, dismay, or exasperation: good heavens • good grief. ➢ n **1** moral correctness; virtue. **2** benefit: It'll do you good • It turned out all to the good. ➢ exclam expressing approval or satisfaction. ➢ adv, colloq very well: The boy done good. ♦ **as good as ...** almost ... **as good as gold** esp of children: extremely well-behaved. **good and ...** colloq very ... : good and ready. **good for sb** or **sth** beneficial to them or it. **good for you,** etc! or (Aust & NZ colloq) **good on you,** etc! **1** an expression of approval or congratulation. **2** an expression of snide resentment. **good morning** or **good afternoon** or **good evening** traditional expressions used when either meeting or parting from someone at the specified time of day. **good night** a traditional expression used when parting from someone in the evening or at night. **in sb's good books** in favour with someone. **make good** to be successful. **make sth good 1** to repair it. **2** to carry it out or fulfil it. **to the good** on the credit side.

goodbye exclam used when parting from someone. ➢ n an act or instance of saying goodbye.

good-for-nothing adj lazy and irresponsible. ➢ n a lazy and irresponsible person.

Good Friday n a Christian festival on the Friday before Easter, in memory of Christ's crucifixion.

goodies pl n, colloq things considered pleasant or desirable: a table laden with goodies. See also GOODY.

goodly adj (-ier, -iest) old use or jocular **1** quite large: a goodly measure. **2** physically attractive.

good nature n natural goodness and mildness of disposition. ○ **good-natured** adj.

goodness n **1** the state or quality of being good. **2** euphem used in exclamations: God: goodness knows.

goods pl n **1** articles for sale. **2** colloq the required result: to deliver the goods.

goodwill n **1** a feeling of kindness towards others. **2** the good reputation of an established business, seen as having an actual value.

goody n (-ies) colloq a hero in a film, book, etc.

goody-goody n (-ies) colloq an ostentatiously virtuous person.

gooey adj (gooier, gooiest) colloq sticky.

goof chiefly N Am colloq, n **1** a silly or foolish person. **2** a stupid mistake. ➢ vb, intr **1** (sometimes **goof up**) to make a stupid mistake. **2** (often **goof about** or **around**) to mess about or behave in a silly way. **3** (**goof off**) to spend time idly when one should be working or doing something.

goofy adj (-ier, -iest) colloq **1** silly; crazy. **2** of teeth: protruding.

googly n (-ies) cricket a ball bowled so that it changes direction unexpectedly after bouncing.

goon n **1** colloq a silly person. **2** slang a hired thug.

goose n (**geese** in senses 1 to 4, **gooses** in sense 5) **1** any of numerous large wild or domesticated waterfowl, with a stout body, long neck, webbed feet and a broad flat bill. **2** the female of this, as opposed to the male (the GANDER). **3** the meat of this bird. **4** colloq, old use a silly person. **5** colloq a poke or pinch on the buttocks. ➢ vb, colloq to poke or pinch someone on the buttocks. ♦ **cook sb's goose** colloq to ruin their plans or chances.

gooseberry n (-ies) **1** a low-growing deciduous shrub with spiny stems and greenish flowers. **2** one of the small sour-tasting yellowish-green or reddish berries produced by this plant. ♦ **play gooseberry** colloq to be an unwanted third person, esp in the company of an amorous couple.

goose pimples or **goose bumps** *pl n* or **goose flesh** *sing n* a condition of the skin caused by cold or fear, in which the body hairs become erect, pimples appear and there is a bristling feeling.

goose-step *n* a military marching step in which the legs are kept rigid and swung very high. ➤ *vb, intr* to march with this step.

gopher *n* a small burrowing rodent with a stocky body, short legs and large chisel-like incisor teeth.

gore¹ *n* blood from a wound, esp when clotted.

gore² *vb* to pierce something or someone with a horn or tusk.

gore³ *n* a triangular piece of material, eg a section of an umbrella or a tapering piece in a garment, glove, etc. ➤ *vb* to construct something from, or shape it with, gores. ○ **gored** *adj* made with gores.

gorge *n* 1 a deep narrow valley, usu containing a river. 2 the contents of the stomach. 3 a spell of greedy eating. ➤ *vb* 1 *tr & intr* to eat or swallow greedily. 2 (*usu* gorge oneself) to stuff oneself with food. ◆ **make sb's gorge rise** to disgust or sicken them.

gorgeous *adj* 1 extremely beautiful or attractive. 2 *colloq* excellent; extremely pleasant.

gorgon *n* 1 (**Gorgon**) *myth* any of the three female monsters which had live snakes for hair and were capable of turning people to stone. 2 *derog, colloq* a fierce, frightening or very ugly woman.

gorilla *n* the largest of the apes, native to African rainforests, which has a heavily built body and jet black skin covered with dense fur.

gormless *adj, derog colloq* stupid; dim.

gorse *n* an evergreen shrub with leaves reduced to very sharp deeply furrowed spines and bright yellow flowers.

gory *adj* (**-ier, -iest**) 1 causing or involving bloodshed. 2 *colloq* unpleasant: *gory details.* 3 covered in GORE¹. ○ **goriness** *n*.

gosh *exclam, colloq* expressing mild surprise.

goshawk /ˈɡɒshɔːk/ *n* a large hawk with bluish-grey plumage, short rounded wings and a long tail.

gosling *n* a young goose.

go-slow *n* an instance or the process of deliberately working slowly so as to encourage an employer to negotiate.

gospel *n* 1 the life and teachings of Christ: *preach the gospel.* 2 (**Gospel**) each of the New Testament books ascribed to Matthew, Mark, Luke and John. 3 (*also* gospel truth) *colloq* the absolute truth. 4 a set of closely followed principles or rules. 5 (*also* gospel music) lively religious music of Black American origin.

gossamer *n* 1 fine filmy spider-woven threads seen on hedges or floating in the air. 2 any soft fine material.

gossip *n* 1 *derog* talk or writing about the private affairs of others, often spiteful and untrue. 2 *derog* someone who engages in or spreads such talk. 3 casual and friendly talk. ➤ *vb, intr* 1 to engage in, or pass on, malicious gossip. 2 to chat. ○ **gossiping** *n, adj.* ○ **gossipy** *adj.*

Goth *n* 1 a member of a Germanic people who invaded parts of the Roman Empire. 2 (*also* goth) someone who adopts a fashion style that involves dark clothing and stark black and white make-up.

Gothic *adj* 1 belonging or relating to the Goths or their language. 2 belonging or relating to a style of architecture featuring high pointed arches, popular in Europe between the 12c and 16c. 3 belonging or relating to a type of literature dealing with mysterious or supernatural events in an eerie setting, popular in the 18c. 4 (*also* gothick) belonging or relating to a modern style of literature, films, etc which imitates this. 5 *printing* relating to various styles of heavy type with elaborate angular features. ➤ *n* 1 Gothic architecture or literature. 2 Gothic lettering.

gouache /ɡʊˈɑːʃ/ *n* 1 a painting technique using a blend of watercolour and a glue-like substance, giving an opaque matt surface. 2 a painting done in this way.

gouge /ɡaʊdʒ/ *n* 1 a chisel with a rounded hollow blade, used for cutting grooves or holes in wood. 2 a groove or hole made using, or as if using, this. ➤ *vb* 1 to cut something out with or as if with a gouge. 2 (*usu* gouge sth out) to force or press it out of position.

goujons *pl n, cookery* strips of meat or fish coated in flour, batter or breadcrumbs and deep-fried.

goulash *n, cookery* a thick meat stew heavily seasoned with paprika, orig from Hungary.

gourd *n* 1 a a climbing plant that produces a large fruit with a hard woody outer shell; b the large fruit of this plant. 2 the hard durable shell of this fruit, often hollowed out, dried, and used as an ornament, cup, bowl, etc.

gourmand /ˈɡɔːmənd/ *n* 1 a greedy eater; a glutton. 2 a gourmet.

gourmet /ˈɡɔːmeɪ/ *n* someone who has expert knowledge of, and a passion for, good food and wine.

gout /ɡaʊt/ *n, med, pathol* a disease in which excess URIC ACID accumulates in the bloodstream and is deposited as crystals in the joints, causing acute ARTHRITIS, esp of the big toe.

govern *vb* 1 *tr & intr* to control and direct the affairs of (a country, state, or organization). 2 to guide or influence; to control or restrain: *unable to govern his temper.* ○ **governable** *adj.* ○ **governing** *adj.*

governance *n, formal* 1 the act or state of governing. 2 the system of government. 3 authority or control.

governess *n, chiefly formerly* a woman employed to teach, and perhaps look after, children, usu while living in their home.

government *n* 1 (*often* the Government) a

body of people, usu elected, with the power to control the affairs of a country or state. **2 a** the way in which this is done; **b** the particular system used. **3** the act or practice of ruling. **4** *gram* the power of one word to determine the form, CASE² (sense 7) or MOOD² (sense 1) of another. ○ **governmental** *adj*.

governor *n* 1 (*also* **Governor**) the elected head of a US state. **2** the head of an institution, eg a prison. **3** a member of a governing body of a school, hospital, college, etc. **4** (*also* **Governor**) the head of a colony or province, esp the monarch's representative. **5** *mech* a regulator or other device for maintaining uniform speed in an engine. **6** (*also* **guvnor** or **guv'nor**) *colloq* **a** (*often* **the governor**) a boss or father; **b** (*often* **guv**) a respectful, though now often ironical, form of address to a man. ○ **governorship** *n*.

gown *n* 1 a woman's long formal dress. **2** an official robe worn by clergymen, lawyers and academics. **3** a protective overall worn eg by surgeons, dentists, hairdressers' clients, etc.

grab *vb* (**grabbed, grabbing**) **1** *tr & intr* (*also* **grab at sth**) to seize suddenly: *grab a snack* • *grab an opportunity*. **2** *colloq* to impress or interest someone: *How does that grab you?* ➢ *n* **1** an act or an instance of grabbing something. **2** a mechanical device with scooping jaws, used eg for excavation. **♦ up for grabs** *colloq* available, esp easily or cheaply.

grace *n* 1 elegance and beauty of form or movement. **2** decency; politeness: *She had the grace to offer.* **3** a short prayer of thanks to God said before or after a meal. **4** a delay allowed, esp to a debtor, as a favour: *They gave us two days' grace.* **5** a pleasing or attractive characteristic: *a saving grace.* **6 a** *relig* the mercy and favour shown by God to mankind; **b** *relig* the condition of a person's soul when made free from sin and evil by God. **7** (**His** or **Her Grace** or **Your Grace**) a title used of or to a duke, duchess or archbishop. ➢ *vb* **1** often facetious to honour (an occasion, person, etc), eg with one's presence. **2** to add beauty or charm to something. **♦ with good** or **bad grace** willingly or unwillingly.

graceful *adj* having or showing elegance and beauty of form or movement. ○ **gracefully** *adv*. ○ **gracefulness** *n*.

graceless *adj* 1 awkward in form or movement. **2** bad-mannered. ○ **gracelessly** *adv*.

grace note *n, mus* a note introduced as an embellishment and not essential to the melody or harmony.

gracious *adj* 1 kind and polite. **2** of God: merciful. **3** having qualities of luxury, elegance, comfort and leisure: *gracious living.* **4** *formal* used out of polite custom to describe a royal person or their actions: *Her Gracious Majesty.* ➢ *exclam* (*also* **gracious me!**) expressing surprise. ○ **graciously** *adv*. ○ **graciousness** *n*.

gradation *n* 1 **a** a series of gradual and successive stages or degrees; **b** one step in this. **2** the act or process of forming grades or stages. **3** the gradual change or movement from one state, musical note, colour, etc to another.

grade *n* 1 a stage or level on a scale of quality, rank, size, etc. **2** a mark indicating this. **3** *N Am* **a** a particular class or year in school; **b** the level of work taught in it. **4** a slope or gradient. ➢ *vb* **1** to arrange (things or people) in different grades. **2** to award a mark indicating grade, eg on a piece of written work, essay, etc. **3** to adjust the gradients of (a road or railway). **♦ make the grade** *colloq* to reach the required or expected standard.

grade school *n, N Am* elementary or primary school.

gradient *n* 1 the steepness of a slope. **2** *formal* a slope. **3** *maths* the slope of a line or the slope of a tangent to a curve at a particular point. **4** *physics* the rate of change of a variable quantity over a specified distance.

gradual *adj* developing or happening slowly, by degrees. ○ **gradually** *adv*.

graduand *n* someone who is about to be awarded a higher-education degree.

graduate *vb* / ˈgradʒʊeɪt / **1** *intr* or (*N Am*) *sometimes* **be graduated** to receive an academic degree from a higher-education institution. **2** *intr, N Am* to receive a diploma at the end of a course of study at high school. **3** *intr* to move up from a lower to a higher level, often in stages. **4** to mark (eg a thermometer) with units of measurement or other divisions. **5** to arrange something into regular groups, according to size, type, etc. ➢ *n* / -ɪt/ someone who has a higher-education degree or (*N Am*) a high-school diploma. ○ **graduation** *n*.

graffiti *pl n*, sometimes used as *sing* (*sing also* **graffito**) words or drawings, usu humorous, political or rude, scratched, sprayed or painted on walls, etc in public places.

graft¹ *n* 1 *hortic* a piece of plant tissue that is inserted into a cut in the outer stem of another plant, resulting in fusion of the tissues and growth of a single plant. **2** *surgery* the transfer or transplantation of an organ or tissue from one individual to another, or to a different site within the same individual. **3** a transplanted organ. ➢ *vb* **1** (*also* **graft in** or **into** or **on** or **together**) **a** to attach a graft in something or someone; **b** to attach something as a graft. **2** *intr* to attach grafts.

graft² *n* 1 *colloq* hard work. **2** *slang* **a** the use of illegal or unfair means to gain profit or advantage, esp by politicians or officials; **b** the profit or advantage gained. ➢ *vb*, *colloq* **1** to work hard. **2** *slang* to practise graft. ○ **grafter** *n*.

grail or **Grail** *n* 1 (*in full* **Holy Grail**) the plate or cup used by Christ at the Last Supper, the object of quests by medieval knights. **2** a cherished ambition or goal.

grain *n* 1 a single small hard fruit, resembling a seed, produced by a cereal plant or other grass. **2** such fruits referred to collectively. **3** any of the cereal plants that produce such fruits, eg wheat, corn. **4** a small hard particle of anything. **5** a very small amount: *a grain of truth.* **6 a** the arrangement, size and direction of the fibres or layers in wood, leather, fabric, paper, etc; **b** the pattern formed as a result of this arrangement. **7** any of the small particles of metallic silver that form the dark areas of the image on a developed photograph. **8** in the avoirdupois system: the smallest unit of weight, equal to 0.065 grams, formerly said to be the average weight of a grain of wheat (7000 grains being equivalent to one pound avoirdupois). **9** in the troy system: a similar unit of weight (5760 grains being equivalent to one pound troy). ➤ *vb tr & intr* to form into grains or give the appearance of a grain. ○ **grained** *adj.* ○ **grainy** *adj* (*-ier, -iest*). ♦ **go against the grain** to be against someone's principles or natural character.

gram or **gramme** *n* in the metric system: the basic unit of mass, equal to one thousandth of a kilogram (0.035oz).

grammar *n* **1** the accepted rules by which words are formed and combined into sentences. **2** the use of these rules: *That's bad grammar.* ○ **grammatical** *adj* **1** relating to grammar. **2** correct according to the rules of grammar.

grammar school *n, Brit, esp formerly* a secondary school which emphasizes the study of academic rather than technical subjects.

gramophone *n, dated* a record player, esp an old-fashioned one.

gran *n, colloq* short form of GRANNY.

granary *n* (*-ies*) **1** a building where grain is stored. **2** a region that produces large quantities of grain. **3** (**Granary**) *trademark* a make of bread containing malted wheat flour. ➤ *adj,* *loosely* of bread: containing whole grains of wheat.

grand *adj* **1** large or impressive in size, appearance or style. **2** *sometimes derog* dignified; self-important. **3** intended to impress or gain attention: *a grand gesture.* **4** complete: *grand total.* **5** *colloq* excellent. **6** greatest; highest ranking: *Grand Master.* **7** highly respected: *grand old man.* **8** *in compounds* indicating a family relationship that is one generation more remote than that of the base word: *grandson.* See also GREAT *adj* sense 5. ➤ *n* (*pl* in sense 1 **grand**) **1** *slang* a thousand dollars or pounds. **2** *colloq* a grand piano. ○ **grandly** *adv.* ○ **grandness** *n.*

grandad or **granddad** *n, colloq* **1** a grandfather. **2** *offensive* an old man.

grandchild *n* a child of one's son or daughter.

granddaughter *n* a daughter of one's son or daughter.

grand duchy *n* a small European country or territory ruled by a grand duke or grand duchess.

grand duke *n* a high-ranking nobleman who rules a grand duchy. ○ **grand duchess** *n.*

grandee *n* **1** a Spanish or Portuguese nobleman of the highest rank. **2** any well-respected or high-ranking person.

grandeur / ˈgrandjə(r) / *n* **1** greatness of character, esp dignity or nobility. **2** impressive beauty; magnificence. **3** *derog* self-importance.

grandfather *n* the father of one's father or mother.

grandfather clock *n* a clock contained in a tall free-standing wooden case.

grandiloquent *adj, derog* spoken or written in a pompous style. ○ **grandiloquence** *n.*

grandiose *adj* **1** *derog* exaggeratedly impressive or imposing, esp on a ridiculously large scale. **2** magnificent.

grand jury *n* in the US: a jury which decides whether there is enough evidence for a person to be brought to trial.

grandma *colloq* or (*old use*) **grandmamma** *n* a grandmother.

grand mal / *French* grãmal / *n, med* a serious form of EPILEPSY in which there is sudden loss of consciousness followed by convulsions. Compare PETIT MAL.

grandmaster *n, chess* the title given to an extremely skilled player.

grandmother *n* the mother of one's father or mother.

grandpa *colloq* or (*old use*) **grandpapa** *n* a grandfather.

grandparent *n* either parent of one's father or mother.

grand piano *n* a large, harp-shaped piano that has its strings arranged horizontally.

grand prix / grã priː/ *n* (*pl* **grands prix** / grã priː/) **1** any of a series of races held annually in various countries to decide the motor racing championship of the world. **2** in other sports: any competition of similar importance.

grand slam *n* **1** *sport, eg tennis, rugby* the winning in one season of every part of a competition or of all major competitions. **2** *cards, esp bridge* the winning of all thirteen tricks by one player or side.

grandson *n* a son of one's son or daughter.

grandstand *n* a large covered sports-ground stand that has tiered seating and which provides a good view for spectators.

grange *n* a country house with attached farm buildings.

granite *n* a hard coarse-grained igneous rock, consisting mainly of quartz, feldspar and mica.

granny *n* (*-ies*) *colloq* a grandmother.

granny knot *n* a reef knot with the ends crossed the wrong way, allowing it to slip or undo easily.

grant *vb* **1** to give, allow or fulfil. **2** to admit something to be true. ➤ *n* **1** something granted, esp an amount of money from a public fund for a specific purpose. **2** *law* the transfer of property by deed.

granted *vb, past participle of* GRANT (*used as a sentence substitute*) an admission that something is true or valid: *She's a good writer. — Granted. But rather limited.* ➤ *conj* or *prep* though (a specific thing) is admitted: *granted you gave it back later* • *Granted his arrogance,* *still he gets results.* ◆ **take sb for granted** to treat them casually and without appreciation. **take sth for granted** to assume it to be true or valid.

granular *adj, technical* **1** made of or containing tiny particles or granules. **2** of appearance or texture: rough.

granulated sugar *n* white sugar in coarse grains.

granule *n* a small particle or grain.

grape *n* **1** a pale green or purplish-black juicy edible berry which may be eaten fresh, pressed to make wine or dried to form currants, raisins, etc. **2** any species of climbing vine that bears this fruit. **3** (**the grape**) *affected or literary* wine. ○ **grapey** or **grapy** *adj.*

grapefruit *n* (*grapefruit* or *grapefruits*) **1** an evergreen tree cultivated for its large edible fruits. **2** the round fruit produced by this tree which has acidic pale yellow or pink flesh.

grapeshot *n* ammunition in the form of small iron balls which scatter when fired in clusters from a cannon.

grapevine *n* **1** a vine on which grapes grow. **2** (**the grapevine**) *colloq* an informal means of spreading information through casual conversation.

graph *n* **1** a diagram that illustrates the way in which one quantity varies in relation to another, usu consisting of horizontal and vertical axes (see AXIS sense 3) which cross each other at a point called the ORIGIN. **2** a symbolic diagram. ➤ *vb* to represent something with or as a graph.

graphic or **graphical** *adj* **1** described or shown vividly and in detail. **2** referring to or composed in a written medium. **3** referring to the **graphic arts**, ie those concerned with drawing, printing and lettering. **4** relating to graphs; shown by means of a graph. ○ **graphically** *adv.*

graphics *sing n* the art or science of drawing according to mathematical principles. ➤ *pl n* **1** the photographs and illustrations used in a magazine. **2** the non-acted visual parts of a film or television programme, eg the credits. **3** *comput* a the use of computers to display and manipulate information in graphical or pictorial form, either on a visual-display unit or via a printer or plotter; **b** the images that are produced by this.

graphite *n* a soft black ALLOTROPE of carbon that is used as a lubricant and electrical contact, and is mixed with clay to form the 'lead' in pencils.

graphology *n* **1** the study of handwriting, esp as a way of analysing the writer's character. **2** *ling* the study of the systems and conventions of writing. ○ **graphologist** *n.*

graph paper *n* paper covered in small squares, used for drawing graphs.

grapnel *n* **1** a large multi-pointed hook on one end of a rope, used for securing a heavy object on the other end. **2** a light anchor for small boats.

grapple *vb* **1** struggle and fight, esp in hand-to-hand combat. **2** *intr* (**grapple with sth**) to struggle mentally with (a difficult problem). **3** to secure something with a hook, etc. ➤ *n* **1** a hook or other device for securing. **2** an act or way of gripping.

grasp *vb* **1** to take a firm hold of something or someone. **2** (*often* **grasp at** or **after sth**) to make a movement as if to seize it. **3** to understand. ➤ *n* **1** a grip or hold. **2** ability to reach, achieve or obtain: *The promotion was within his grasp.* **3** ability to understand: *beyond their grasp.*

grasping *adj, derog* greedy.

grass *n* **1** any of a family of plants (eg cereals, bamboos, etc) that typically have long narrow leaves, a jointed upright hollow stem and flowers with no petals. **2** such plants growing together as a lawn or meadow. **3** *slang* marijuana. **4** *slang* someone who betrays someone else, esp to the police. ➤ *vb* **1** to plant something with grass or turf. **2** to feed (animals) with grass. **3** *intr, slang* (*often* **grass on sb** or **grass sb up**) to inform on them, esp to the police. ○ **grassy** *adj.* ◆ **let the grass grow under one's feet** to delay or waste time. **put out to grass 1** to give a life of grazing to (eg an old racehorse). **2** *colloq* to put (eg a worker) into retirement.

grasshopper *n* a large brown or green jumping insect, the male of which produces a characteristic chirping sound.

grass roots *pl n* **1** *esp pol* ordinary people, as opposed to those in a position of power. **2** fundamental principles.

grass snake *n* a small non-venomous greenish-grey to olive-brown snake.

grass widow or **grass widower** *n* someone whose partner is absent from home for long periods.

grate¹ *vb* **1** to cut (eg vegetables or cheese) into shreds by rubbing them against a rough or perforated surface. **2** *tr & intr* to make, or cause something to make, a harsh grinding sound by rubbing. **3** *intr* (*usu* **grate on** or **upon sb**) to irritate or annoy them. ○ **grater** *n.*

grate² *n* **1** a framework of iron bars for holding coal, etc in a fireplace or furnace. **2** the fireplace or furnace itself.

grateful *adj* **1 a** feeling thankful; **b** showing or giving thanks. **2** *formal* pleasant and welcome: *grateful sleep.* ○ **gratefully** *adv.* ○ **gratefulness** *n.*

gratify *vb* (**-ied**) **1** to please someone. **2** to satisfy or indulge (eg a desire). ○ **gratification** *n.* ○ **gratifying** *adj.* ○ **gratifyingly** *adv.*

grating¹ *n* a framework of metal bars fixed into a wall (eg over a window) or into a pavement (eg over a drain).

grating² *adj* **1** of sounds, etc: harsh. **2** irritating. ➤ *n* a grating sound.

gratis *adv, adj* free; without charge.

gratitude *n* the state or feeling of being grateful; thankfulness.

gratuitous *adj* **1** done without good reason;

unjustified: *gratuitous violence*. **2** given or received without charge. ○ **gratuitously** *adv*.

gratuity *n* (*-ies*) a sum of money given as a reward for good service; a tip.

grave[1] / greɪv / *n* **1** a trench dug in the ground for burying a dead body. **2** the site of an individual burial. **3** (**the grave**) *literary* death.

grave[2] / greɪv / *adj* **1** giving cause for great concern. **2** solemn and serious in manner. ○ **gravely** *adv*. ○ **graveness** *n* (more commonly GRAVITY sense 3, 4).

grave[3] / grɑːv / or **grave accent** *n* a sign placed above a vowel in some languages, eg *à* and *è* in French, to indicate a particular pronunciation or extended length of the vowel.

gravel *n* **1** a mixture of small loose rock fragments and pebbles, coarser than sand. **2** *pathol* small stones formed in the kidney or bladder. ➢ *vb* (**gravelled, gravelling; US graveled, graveling**) **1** to cover (eg a path) with gravel. **2** to puzzle or perplex someone.

gravelly *adj* **1** full of, or containing, small stones. **2** of a voice: rough and deep.

graven image *n* a carved idol used in worship.

gravestone *n* a stone marking a grave, usu having the dead person's name and dates of birth and death engraved on it.

graveyard *n* a burial place.

gravid *adj, med* pregnant.

gravitas /ˈgravɪtɑːs/ *n* seriousness of manner; authoritativeness; weight.

gravitate *vb, intr* **1** to fall or be drawn under the force of gravity. **2** to move or be drawn gradually, as if attracted by some force: *He gravitated towards a life of crime*.

gravitation *n* **1** *physics* the force of attraction that exists between any two bodies on account of their mass. **2** the process of moving or being drawn, either by this force or some other attracting influence. ○ **gravitational** *adj*.

gravity *n* **1** the observed effect of the force of attraction that exists between two massive bodies. **2** the force of attraction between any object situated within the Earth's gravitational field, and the Earth itself, on account of which objects feel heavy and are pulled down towards the ground. **3** seriousness. **4** serious attitude.

gravy *n* (*-ies*) **1** the juices released by meat as it is cooking. **2** a sauce made by thickening and seasoning these juices.

gravy boat *n* a small boat-shaped container with a handle, for serving gravy and other sauces.

gravy train *n, slang* a job or scheme from which a lot of money is gained for little effort.

gray[1] *n* the SI unit of absorbed dose of ionizing radiation, equivalent to one joule per kilogram.

gray[2] see GREY

grayling (*grayling* or *graylings*) a freshwater fish that has silvery scales and a large purplish spiny dorsal fin.

graze[1] *vb* **1** *tr & intr* of animals: to eat grass. **2 a** to feed (animals) on grass; **b** to feed animals on

(an area of pasture). **3** *intr, colloq* to pilfer and eat food while shopping in a supermarket. **4** *tr & intr, colloq* to browse through TV channels, etc. ○ **grazer** *n*. ○ **grazing** *n* **1** the act or practice of grazing. **2** pasture.

graze[2] *vb* **1** to suffer a break in (the skin), through scraping against a hard rough surface. **2** to brush against something lightly in passing. ➢ *n* **1** an area of grazed skin. **2** the action of grazing skin.

grease *n* **1** animal fat softened by melting or cooking. **2** any thick oily substance, esp a lubricant for the moving parts of machinery. ➢ *vb* to lubricate or dirty something with grease. ◆ **grease sb's palm** or **hand** *colloq* to bribe them.

greasepaint *n* waxy make-up used by actors.

greaseproof *adj* resistant or impermeable to grease.

greasy *adj* (*-ier, -iest*) **1** containing, or covered in, grease. **2** having an oily appearance or slippery texture. **3** *colloq* insincerely friendly or flattering. ○ **greasiness** *n*.

great *adj* **1** outstandingly talented and much admired and respected. **2** very large in size, quantity, intensity or extent. **3** (**greater**) (added to the name of a large city) indicating the wider area surrounding the city, sometimes including other boroughs, etc, as well as the city itself: *Greater Manchester*. **4** (*also* **greater**) *biol* larger in size than others of the same kind, species, etc: *great tit*. **5** *in compounds* indicating a family relationship that is one generation more remote than that of the base word: *great-grandmother*. **6** *colloq* very enjoyable; excellent. **7** (*also* **great at sth**) *colloq* talented. **8** (*also* **great for sth**) *colloq* very suitable or useful. **9** most important: *the great thing about it*. **10** enthusiastic: *a great reader*. **11** *colloq* used to emphasize other adjectives describing size, esp big: *a great big dog*. **12** (**the Great**) in names and titles: indicating an importance or reputation of the highest degree: *Alexander the Great*. ➢ *n* a person who has achieved lasting fame: *one of the all-time greats*. ➢ *adv, colloq* very well. ○ **greatly** *adv*. ○ **greatness** *n*.

Great Britain *n* the largest island in Europe, containing England, Wales and Scotland.

greatcoat *n* a heavy overcoat.

greave *n* (*usu* **greaves**) armour for the legs below the knee.

grebe *n* any of various waterfowl with short wings, a pointed bill and almost no tail.

Grecian /ˈgriːʃən/ *adj* in the style of ancient Greece.

greed *n* **1** an excessive desire for, or consumption of, food. **2** selfish desire in general. ○ **greedy** *adj* (*-ier, -iest*).

Greek *adj* belonging or relating to Greece, its inhabitants or their language. ➢ *n* **1** a person from Greece. **2** the official language of Greece (**Modern Greek**) or the language of the ancient Greeks (**Ancient Greek**). **3** *colloq* any language, jargon or subject one cannot understand.

green adj **1** like the colour of the leaves of most plants. **2** covered with grass, bushes, etc. **3** consisting mainly of leaves: green salad. **4** of fruit: not yet ripe. **5** colloq of a person: young, inexperienced or easily fooled. **6** showing concern for, or designed to be harmless to, the environment. **7** of someone's face: showing signs of nausea. **8** not dried or dry: green timber. **9** extremely jealous or envious. **10** healthy, vigorous, or flourishing: green old age. ➤ n **1** the colour of the leaves of most plants. **2** something of this colour. **3** an area of grass, esp one in a public place: the village green. **4** an area of specially prepared turf: bowling green. **5** (greens) vegetables with edible green leaves and stems. **6** (sometimes Green) someone who supports actions or policies designed to protect or benefit the environment. ➤ vb, tr & intr to make or become green. ○ **greenness** n.

green bean n any variety of bean, such as the French bean, string bean, etc, of which the narrow green unripe pod and contents can be eaten whole.

green belt n open land surrounding a town or city, where building or development is strictly controlled.

green card n **1** an international motorists' insurance document. **2** an official US work and residence permit issued to foreign nationals.

greenery n green plants or their leaves.

greenfield site n a site which is to be developed for the first time.

green fingers pl n, colloq natural skill at growing plants.

greenfly n (**greenfly** or **greenflies**) any of various species of APHID.

greengage n **1** a cultivated variety of tree, sometimes regarded as a subspecies of the plum. **2** its small green plum-like edible fruit.

greengrocer n a person or shop that sells fruit and vegetables.

greenhorn n, colloq an inexperienced person.

greenhouse n a GLASSHOUSE, esp one with little or no artificial heating.

greenhouse effect n, meteorol, ecol, etc the warming of the Earth's surface as a result of the trapping of long-wave radiation by carbon dioxide, ozone, and certain other gases in the atmosphere.

greenhouse gas n any of various gases, eg carbon dioxide, which are present in the atmosphere and contribute to the greenhouse effect.

greenkeeper n someone who is responsible for the maintenance of a golf course or bowling green.

green light n **1** a signal to drivers of cars, trains, etc that they can move forward. **2** (**the green light**) colloq permission to proceed.

green paper n (often **Green Paper**) pol in the UK: a written statement of the Government's proposed policy on a particular issue.

green party or **Green Party** n a political party concerned with the protection and benefit of the environment.

green pepper n a green unripe sweet pepper, eaten as a vegetable.

green pound n the pound's value compared with that of the other European currencies used in trading EU farm produce.

greenroom n a backstage room in a theatre, etc where actors, musicians, etc can relax and receive visitors.

green tea n a sharp-tasting light-coloured tea made from leaves that have been dried quickly without fermenting.

Greenwich Mean Time /ˈɡrɛnɪtʃ/ n the local time at the line of 0° longitude, which passes through Greenwich in England, used to calculate times in most other parts of the world.

greet vb **1** to address or welcome someone, esp in a friendly way. **2** to receive or respond to something in a specified way: His remarks were greeted with dismay. **3** to be immediately noticeable to someone: smells of cooking greeted me.

greeting n **1** a friendly expression or gesture used on meeting or welcoming someone. **2** (**greetings**) a good wish; a friendly message.

gregarious adj **1** very sociable. **2** of animals: living in groups. ○ **gregariously** adv.

Gregorian chant n a type of PLAINSONG used in Roman Catholic religious ceremonies.

gremlin n an imaginary mischievous creature blamed for faults in machinery or electronic equipment.

grenade n a small bomb thrown by hand or fired from a rifle.

grenadier /ɡrɛnəˈdɪə(r)/ n a member of a regiment of soldiers formerly trained in the use of grenades.

grenadine n a syrup made from pomegranate juice, used to flavour drinks.

grey or (esp N Am) **gray** adj **1** of a colour between black and white, the colour of ash. **2** of the weather: dull and cloudy. **3 a** of someone's hair: turning white; **b** of a person: having grey hair. **4** derog anonymous or uninteresting; having no distinguishing features: a grey character. **5** colloq referring or relating to elderly or retired people: the grey population. ➤ n **1** a colour between black and white. **2** grey material or clothes: dressed in grey. **3** dull light. **4** an animal, esp a horse, that is grey or whitish in colour. ➤ vb, tr & intr to make or become grey. ○ **greyish** adj. ○ **greyness** n.

grey area n an unclear situation or subject, often with no distinct limits, guiding principles or identifiable characteristics.

greyhound n a tall dog with a slender body, renowned for its speed and raced for sport.

grey matter n **1** anat the tissue of the brain and spinal cord that appears grey in colour. Compare WHITE MATTER. **2** colloq intelligence.

grid n **1** a network of evenly spaced horizontal and vertical lines, such as one that can be superimposed on a map in order to locate specific points. **2** a network of power lines or pipes by which electricity, gas, water, etc is distributed across a region or country. **3** a framework of metal bars. **4** an arrangement of lines marking the starting-points on a motor-racing track.

griddle or (*Scot*) **girdle** *n* a flat iron plate that is heated for baking or frying.

gridiron *n* **1** a frame of iron bars used for grilling food over a fire. **2** *Amer football* the field of play.

gridlock *n* a situation in which no progress is possible, such as a traffic jam or a disagreement. ○ **gridlocked** *adj*.

grief *n* **1 a** great sorrow and unhappiness, esp at someone's death; **b** an event that is the source of this. **2** *colloq* trouble or bother: *I was getting grief from her parents for staying out late.* ◆ **come to grief** *colloq* to end in failure or disaster.

grief-stricken *adj* crushed with sorrow.

grievance *n* **1** a real or perceived cause for complaint. **2** a formal complaint.

grieve *vb* **1** *intr* to feel grief, esp at a death; **b** to mourn. **2** to upset or distress someone: *It still grieves me.*

grievous *adj* **1** very severe or painful. **2** causing or likely to cause grief. **3** showing grief. ○ **grievously** *adv*.

grievous bodily harm *n, law* **1** severe injury caused by a physical attack. **2** the criminal charge of causing such injury.

griffin or **gryphon** *n, myth* a winged monster with an eagle's head and a lion's body.

griffon *n* **1** a small dog with a coarse wiry blackish or black and tan coat. **2** a large vulture with a bald head.

grill *vb* **1** to cook over or, more usu, under radiated heat. **2** *colloq* to interrogate someone. **3** *intr* to suffer extreme heat. ➣ *n* **1** a device on a cooker which radiates heat downwards. **2** a metal frame for cooking food over a fire. **3** a dish of grilled food or a restaurant that specializes in this: *mixed grill.*

grille or **grill** *n* a protective framework of metal bars or wires, eg over a window.

grim *adj* (**grimmer, grimmest**) **1** stern and unsmiling. **2** terrible; horrifying. **3** resolute: *grim determination.* **4** depressing; gloomy. **5** *colloq* unpleasant. ○ **grimly** *adv*. ○ **grimness** *n*.

grimace *n* an ugly twisting of the face that expresses pain or disgust, or that is pulled for amusement. ➣ *vb, intr* to make a grimace.

grime *n* thick ingrained dirt. ➣ *vb* to make something filthy. ○ **grimy** *adj* (**-ier, -iest**).

grin *vb* (**grinned, grinning**) **1** *intr* to smile broadly, showing the teeth. **2** to express (eg pleasure) in this way. ➣ *n* a broad smile, showing the teeth. ○ **grinning** *adj, n*. ◆ **grin and bear it** *colloq* to endure something unpleasant without complaining.

grind *vb* (**ground**) **1** to crush something into small particles or powder by rubbing it between two hard surfaces. **2** to sharpen, smooth or polish something by rubbing against a hard

surface. **3** *tr & intr* to rub something together with a jarring noise. **4** to press something hard with a twisting action: *He ground his heel into the dirt.* **5** to operate something by turning a handle. ➣ *n* **1** *colloq* steady, dull and laborious routine. **2** the act or sound of grinding. **3** a specified size or texture of crushed particles: *fine grind.* ○ **grinder** *n*. ◆ **grind to a halt** to stop completely. ◊ **grind sb down** to crush their spirit.

grinding *adj* crushing; oppressive: *grinding poverty.*

grindstone *n* a revolving stone wheel used for sharpening and polishing. ◆ **have** or **keep one's nose to the grindstone** *colloq* to work hard and with perseverance.

grip *vb* (**gripped, gripping**) **1** to take or keep a firm hold of something. **2** to capture the imagination or attention of a person. ➣ *n* **1** a firm hold; the action of taking a firm hold. **2** a way of gripping. **3** a handle or part that can be gripped. **4** a U-shaped wire pin for keeping the hair in place. **5** a holdall. **6** *colloq* understanding. **7** *colloq* control: *to lose one's grip of the situation.* **8** *theat* a stagehand who moves scenery. **9** *cinema, TV* someone who manoeuvres a film camera. ○ **gripper** *n*. ◆ **get to grips with sth** to begin to deal with it.

gripe *vb* **1** *intr, colloq* to complain persistently. **2** *tr & intr* to feel, or cause someone to feel, intense stomach pain. ➣ *n* **1** *colloq* a complaint. **2** (*usu* **gripes**) *old use, colloq* a severe stomach pain.

gripping *adj* holding the attention; exciting.

grisly *adj* (**-ier, -iest**) horrible; ghastly.

grist *n* grain that is to be, or that has been, ground into flour. ◆ **grist to the mill** anything useful or profitable.

gristle *n* cartilage in meat. ○ **gristly** *adj* (**-ier, -iest**).

grit *n* **1** small particles of a hard material, esp of stone or sand. **2** *colloq* courage and determination. ➣ *vb* (**gritted, gritting**) **1** to spread grit on (icy roads, etc). **2** to clench (the teeth).

grits *pl n* coarsely ground grain with the husks removed. ➣ *sing n* a dish of this, boiled and eaten for breakfast in the southern US.

gritty *adj* (**-ier, -iest**) **1** full of or covered with grit. **2** like grit. **3** determined.

grizzle *vb, intr, colloq* **1** esp of a young child: to cry fretfully. **2** to sulk or complain.

grizzled *adj* **1** of the hair or a beard: grey or greying. **2** of a person: having such hair.

grizzly *adj* (**-ier, -iest**) grey or greying. ➣ *n* (**-ies**) *colloq* a grizzly bear.

grizzly bear *n* a large North American bear with brown fur.

groan *vb* **1** *intr* to make a long deep sound in the back of the throat, expressing distress, etc. **2** to utter or express something with or by means of a groan. **3** *intr* to creak loudly. **4** *intr* to be weighed down or almost breaking: *tables groaning with masses of food.* ➣ *n* an act, or the sound, of groaning.

groat *n* an obsolete British silver coin worth four old pennies.

groats *pl n* crushed grain, esp oats, with the husks removed.

grocer *n* a person or shop that sells food.

grocery *n* (*-ies*) 1 the trade or premises of a grocer. 2 (**groceries**) merchandise, esp food, sold in a grocer's shop.

grog *n* 1 a mixture of alcoholic spirit (esp rum) and water. 2 *Aust & NZ colloq* any alcoholic drink.

groggy *adj* (*-ier, -iest*) *colloq* weak, dizzy and unsteady on the feet, eg from the effects of illness or alcohol. ○ **groggily** *adv.*

groin *n* 1 the part of the human body where the lower abdomen joins the upper thigh. 2 *archit* the edge formed by the joining of two vaults in a roof; the rib covering the intersection. ➤ *vb, archit* to build (a vault, etc) with groins.

grommet or **grummet** *n* 1 a rubber or plastic ring around a hole in metal, to protect a tube or insulate a wire passing through. 2 a a metal ring lining an eyelet; b the eyelet itself. 3 *med* a small tube passed through the eardrum to drain the middle ear.

groom *n* 1 someone who looks after horses and cleans stables. 2 a bridegroom. 3 a title given to various officers in a royal household. ➤ *vb* 1 to clean, brush and generally smarten (animals, esp horses). 2 to keep (a person) clean and neat, esp regarding clothes and hair. 3 to train or prepare someone for a specified office, stardom or success in any sphere. 4 *colloq* to cultivate an apparently harmless friendship, eg on the Internet, with a child whom one intends to subject to sexual abuse.

groove *n* 1 a long narrow channel, esp one cut with a tool. 2 *colloq* a set routine, esp a monotonous one. 3 repetitive, rhythmic, musical patterns used in creating dance music for clubs. ➤ *vb* 1 to cut a groove in something. 2 *intr, dated slang* to enjoy oneself.

groovy *adj* (*-ier, -iest*) *dated slang* excellent, attractive or fashionable.

grope *vb* 1 *intr* to search by feeling about with the hands, eg in the dark. 2 *intr* to search uncertainly or with difficulty: *groping for answers*. 3 to find (one's way) by feeling. 4 *colloq* to touch or fondle someone sexually. ➤ *n, colloq* an act of sexual fondling. ○ **groping** *adj, n.*

gross *adj* (*-er, grossest*, except in sense 1) 1 total, with no deductions: *gross weight*. Opposite of NET². 2 very great; glaring: *gross negligence*. 3 *derog* vulgar. 4 *derog* unattractively fat. 5 *colloq, derog* very unpleasant. 6 dense; lush: *gross vegetation*. 7 *derog* lacking sensitivity or judgement. 8 solid; tangible; not abstract. ➤ *n* 1 (*pl* **gross**) twelve dozen, 144. 2 (*pl* **grosses**) the total amount or weight, without deductions. ➤ *vb* to earn (a specified sum) as a gross income or profit, before tax is deducted. ○ **grossly** *adv.* ◊ **gross sb out** *slang* to disgust or offend them.

grotesque *adj* 1 very unnatural or strange-looking, so as to cause fear or laughter. 2 exaggerated; ridiculous. ➤ *n* 1 (**the grotesque**) a 16c style in art which features animals, plants and people mixed together in a strange or fantastic manner. 2 a work of art in this style. ○ **grotesquely** *adv.*

grotto *n* (**grottos** or **grottoes**) 1 a cave, esp a small and picturesque one. 2 a man-made cave-like structure, esp in a garden or park.

grotty *adj* (*-ier, -iest*) *colloq* 1 *derog* unpleasantly dirty or shabby. 2 slightly ill. ○ **grottiness** *n.*

grouch *colloq, vb, intr* to grumble or complain. ➤ *n* 1 a complaining person. 2 a a bad-tempered complaint; b the cause of it.

grouchy *adj* (*-ier, -iest*) bad-tempered. ○ **grouchily** *adv.* ○ **grouchiness** *n.*

ground¹ *n* 1 the solid surface of the Earth, or any part of it; soil; land. 2 (*often* **grounds**) an area of land, usu extensive, attached to or surrounding a building. 3 an area of land used for a specified purpose: *football ground*. 4 distance covered or to be covered. 5 the substance of discussion: *to cover a lot of ground*. 6 a position or standpoint, eg in an argument: *stand or shift one's ground*. 7 progress relative to that made by an opponent: *lose or gain ground*. 8 (*usu* **grounds**) a reason or justification. 9 *N Am, elec* EARTH (*noun sense 6*). 10 (**grounds**) sediment or dregs, esp of coffee. ➤ *vb* 1 *tr & intr* to hit or cause (a ship) to hit the seabed or shore and remain stuck. 2 to refuse to allow (a pilot or aeroplane) to fly. 3 to forbid (eg teenagers) to go out socially as a punishment. 4 to lay (eg weapons) on the ground. 5 (*usu* **ground sb in sth**) to give them basic instructions in (a subject). 6 (*usu* **ground sth on sth else**) to base (an argument, a complaint, etc) on it: *an argument grounded on logic*. 7 *N Am, elec* to EARTH. ➤ *adj* on or relating to the ground: *ground forces*. ◆ **give ground** to give way. **go to ground** 1 of an animal: to go into a burrow to escape from hunters. 2 to go into hiding, eg from the police. **off the ground** started. **on the ground** amongst ordinary people.

ground² *past tense, past participle of* GRIND

groundbreaking *adj* innovative.

ground control *n* the control and monitoring from the ground of the flight of aircraft or spacecraft.

ground cover *n* low-growing plants that cover the surface of the ground.

ground crew *n* a team of mechanics whose job is to maintain aircraft.

ground floor *n* the floor of a building that is at street level.

grounding *n* a foundation of basic knowledge or instruction.

groundless *adj* having no reason or justification.

groundnut *n* 1 a a climbing plant of the pulse family that produces small edible underground tubers, seed pods, etc; b one of the tubers produced by such a plant. **2** *N Am* a peanut.

ground rule *n* a basic principle.

groundsheet *n* a waterproof sheet spread on the ground, eg in a tent.

groundsman *n* someone whose job is to maintain a sports field.

ground state *n, physics* the lowest energy state of an atom.

groundswell *n* **1** a broad high swell of the sea, often caused by a distant storm or earthquake. **2** a rapidly growing indication of public or political feeling.

groundwork *n* essential preparation.

group *n* **1** a number of people or things gathered, placed or classed together. **2** (*sometimes* **Group**) a number of business companies under single ownership and central control. **3** a band of musicians and singers, esp one that plays pop music. **4** a division of an air force. **5** *chem* in the periodic table: a vertical column representing a series of chemical elements with similar chemical properties. **6** *chem* a combination of two or more atoms that are bonded together and tend to act as a single unit in chemical reactions. ➤ *vb, tr & intr* to form (things or people) into a group.

group captain *n* an officer in the Royal Air Force.

groupie *n, colloq* **1** *often derog* an ardent follower of a touring pop star or group. **2** *loosely* someone who follows a specified activity, sport, pastime, etc. *a political groupie.*

groupware *n, comput* software that is designed for use on several computers at the same time.

grouse[1] *n* (*pl* **grouse**) a bird with a plump body, feathered legs and a short curved bill.

grouse[2] *colloq, vb, intr* to complain. ➤ *n* **1** a complaint or spell of complaining. **2** a querulous person; a moaner. ○ **grouser** *n.*

grout *n* thin mortar applied to the joints between bricks or esp ceramic tiles. ➤ *vb* to apply grout to the joints of something. ○ **grouting** *n.*

grove *n* **1** a small group of trees. **2** an area planted with fruit trees, esp citrus and olive.

grovel *vb* (**grovelled, grovelling;** (*US*) **groveled, groveling**) *intr* **1** to act with exaggerated respect or humility. **2** to lie or crawl face down, in fear or respect. ○ **groveller** *n.* ○ **grovelling** *adj.*

grow *vb* (**grew, grown**) **1** *intr* of a living thing: to develop into a larger more mature form. **2** *tr & intr* to increase, or allow (hair, nails, etc) to increase, in length. **3** *intr* to increase in size, intensity or extent. **4** to cultivate (plants). **5 a** to become ... gradually: *Over the years they grew very lazy;* **b** (*usu* **grow to ...**) to come gradually to (have a specified feeling): *She grew to hate him.* ◊ **grow into sth** to become big enough to wear (clothes that were orig too large). **grow on sb** to gradually come to be liked by them. **grow out of sth 1** to become too big to wear

(clothes that were orig the right size). **2** to lose a liking for it, with age. **grow up 1** to become, or be in the process of becoming, an adult. **2** to behave in an adult way. **3** to come into existence; to develop.

growing pains *pl n* **1** muscular pains sometimes experienced by growing children. **2** temporary difficulties in the early stages of a project.

growl *vb* **1** *intr* of animals: to make a deep rough sound in the throat, showing hostility. **2** *tr & intr* of people: to make a similar sound showing anger or displeasure; to speak or say something angrily. ➤ *n* an act of the sound of growling. ○ **growling** *adj, n.*

grown *adj* mature: *a grown woman.*

grown-up *colloq, adj* adult. ➤ *n* an adult.

growth *n* **1 a** the process or rate of growing; **b** the increase in size, weight and complexity of a living organism as it develops to maturity. **2** an increase. **3** *econ* an increase in economic activity or profitability. **4** *med* a tumour formed as a result of the uncontrolled multiplication of cells.

groyne *n* a BREAKWATER built to check land erosion.

grub *n* **1** the worm-like larva of an insect. **2** *colloq* food. ➤ *vb* (**grubbed, grubbing**) **1** *intr* (*usu* **grub about**) to dig or search in the soil. **2** *intr* (*usu* **grub around**) to search or rummage. **3** (*esp* **grub up**) to dig up (roots and stumps). **4** to clear (ground).

grubby *adj* (**-ier, -iest**) *colloq* dirty. ○ **grubbily** *adv.* ○ **grubbiness** *n.*

grudge *n* a long-standing feeling of resentment. ➤ *vb* **1** (*esp* **grudge doing sth**) to be unwilling to do it; to do it unwillingly. **2** (**to grudge sb sth**) **a** to be unwilling to give them it; to give them it unwillingly; **b** to feel envy or resentment at their good fortune.

grudging *adj* **1** resentful. **2** unwilling. ○ **grudgingly** *adv.*

gruel *n* thin porridge.

gruelling or (*US*) **grueling** *adj* exhausting; punishing.

gruesome *adj* inspiring horror or disgust.

gruff *adj* **1** of a voice: deep and rough. **2** rough, unfriendly or surly in manner. ○ **gruffly** *adv.*

grumble *vb, intr* **1** to complain in a bad-tempered way. **2** to make a low rumbling sound. ➤ *n* **1** a complaint. **2** a rumbling sound. ○ **grumbler** *n.* ○ **grumbling** *n, adj.*

grump *n, colloq* a grumpy person.

grumpy *adj* (**-ier, -iest**) bad-tempered. ○ **grumpily** *adv.* ○ **grumpiness** *n.*

grunge *n, slang, orig US* **1** dirt. **2** (*in full* **grunge rock**) a style of music with a discordant guitar-based sound. ○ **grungy** *adj* (**-ier, -iest**).

grunt *vb* **1** *intr* of animals, esp pigs: to make a low rough sound in the back of the throat. **2** *intr* of people: to make a similar sound. **3** to express or utter something with this sound. ➤ *n* an act or the sound of grunting.

gryphon see GRIFFIN

G-string n a garment which barely covers the pubic area, consisting of a strip of cloth attached to a narrow waistband.

guacamole / gwakə'mooli/ n a traditional Mexican dish of mashed avocado mixed with spicy seasoning.

guano / 'gwɑːnoʊ/ n the droppings of bats, seabirds or seals, used as a fertilizer.

guarantee n 1 a written statement that a product, service, etc will conform to specified standards for a particular period of time. 2 an assurance that something will have a specified outcome, condition, etc: *a guarantee that there wouldn't be more pay cuts.* 3 *law* an agreement under which one person, the GUARANTOR, becomes liable for the debt or default of another. 4 someone who agrees to give a guarantee. ➤ *vb* (**guaranteed, guaranteeing**) 1 to provide (eg a product, service, etc) with a guarantee. 2 to ensure or promise something. 3 to act as a GUARANTOR for something. ◦ **guaranteed** *adj.*

guarantor n someone who gives a guarantee.

guard vb 1 to protect someone or something from danger or attack. 2 to watch over someone in order to prevent their escape. 3 to control or check: *guard your tongue.* 4 to control passage through (eg a doorway). 5 *intr* (**guard against sth**) to take precautions to prevent it. ➤ n 1 a person or group whose job is to provide protection or to prevent escape. 2 *Brit* a person in charge of a railway train. 3 a state of readiness to give protection or prevent escape. 4 *boxing, cricket, etc* a defensive posture. 5 *esp in compounds* anything that gives protection from or to something: *shinguard.* 6 the act or duty of protecting. 7 (*often* **Guard**) a soldier in any of certain army regiments orig formed to protect the sovereign. ♦ **off guard** or **off one's guard** not on the alert. **on guard** 1 on sentry duty. 2 (*also* **on one's guard**) on the alert.

guarded *adj* cautious. ◦ **guardedly** *adv.*

guardian n 1 someone who is legally responsible for the care of another, esp an orphaned child. 2 a defender or protector. ◦ **guardianship** n.

guardian angel n an angel believed to watch over a particular person.

guardsman n 1 *Brit* a member of a regiment of Guards. 2 *US* a member of the National Guard.

guava / 'gwɑːvə/ n a small tropical tree or its edible yellow pear-shaped fruits.

gubernatorial / gʌbənə'tɔːrɪəl/ *adj, formal, esp US* referring or relating to a GOVERNOR (in senses 1–4, esp sense 1).

gudgeon[1] n 1 a small freshwater fish. 2 *colloq* a gullible person.

gudgeon[2] n 1 a pivot or pin of any kind. 2 the socket part of a hinge or rudder that the pin part fits into.

guernsey n 1 a hand-knitted woollen pullover, orig one worn by sailors. 2 *Aust* a sleeveless football jersey worn by Australian rules players.

guerrilla or **guerilla** n a member of a small,

independent armed force making surprise attacks, eg against government troops.

guess vb 1 *tr & intr* to make an estimate or form an opinion about something, based on little or no information. 2 to estimate something correctly. 3 to think or suppose: *I guess we could go.* ➤ n an estimate based on guessing.

guesstimate *colloq, n* a very rough estimate, based on guesswork. ➤ *vb* to estimate something using a rough guess.

guesswork n the process or result of guessing.

guest n 1 someone who receives hospitality in the home of, or at the expense of, another. 2 someone who stays at a hotel, boardinghouse, etc. 3 a person specially invited to take part in something. ➤ *vb, intr* to appear as a guest, eg on a television show.

guesthouse n a private home that offers accommodation to paying guests.

guff n, colloq, derog nonsense.

guffaw n a loud coarse laugh. ➤ *vb, intr* to laugh in this way.

guidance n 1 help, advice or counselling; the act or process of guiding. 2 direction or leadership.

guide vb 1 to lead, direct or show the way to someone. 2 to control or direct the movement or course of something. 3 to advise or influence. ➤ n 1 someone who leads the way for eg tourists or mountaineers. 2 any device used to direct movement. 3 a GUIDEBOOK. 4 (**Guide**) a member of a worldwide youth organization for girls. Also called **Girl Guide**. *US equivalent* **Girl Scout**. 5 someone or something, esp a quality, which influences another person's decisions or behaviour.

guidebook n a book containing information about a particular place or instructions for a practical activity.

guided missile n a jet- or rocket-propelled projectile that can be electronically directed to its target by remote control.

guide dog n a dog specially trained to guide a blind person safely.

guideline n (*often* **guidelines**) an indication of what future action is required or recommended.

guild or **gild** n 1 a medieval association of merchants or craftsmen for maintaining standards and providing mutual support. 2 a name used by various modern societies, clubs and associations.

guilder or **gilder** n (*pl* **guilder** or **guilders**) the former standard unit of currency of the Netherlands, replaced in 2002 by the euro.

guildhall n 1 a hall where members of a guild or other association meet. 2 a town hall.

guile / gaɪl/ n 1 the ability to deceive or trick. 2 craftiness or cunning. ◦ **guileful** *adj.* ◦ **guileless** *adj.*

guillemot / 'gɪlɪmɒt/ n a seabird with black and white plumage and a long narrow bill.

guillotine n 1 an instrument for beheading, consisting of a large heavy blade that slides rapidly down between two upright posts. **2** a device with a large blade moved by a lever, for cutting paper or metal. **3** *pol* a time limit set to speed up discussion of, and voting on, a parliamentary bill. ➤ *vb* to use a guillotine in any of the senses above.

guilt *n* **1** a feeling of shame or remorse resulting from a sense of having done wrong. **2** the state of having done wrong or having broken a law. **3** blame. **4** *law* liability to a penalty.

guiltless *adj* innocent. ○ **guiltlessly** *adv*.

guilty *adj* (*-ier, -iest*) (*often* guilty of sth) **1** responsible for a crime or wrongdoing, or judged to be so. **2** feeling, showing or involving guilt: *a guilty look*. **3** able to be justly accused of something: *guilty of working too hard*. ○ **guiltily** *adv*. ○ **guiltiness** *n*.

guinea *n* **1** an obsolete British gold coin worth 21 shillings (£1.05). **2** its value, still used as a monetary unit in some professions, esp horse-racing.

guinea fowl *n* (*pl* **guinea fowl**) a ground-living bird with a naked head and greyish plumage speckled with white.

guinea pig *n* **1** a tailless rodent, widely kept as a domestic pet and also used as a laboratory animal. **2** a person used as the subject of an experiment.

guise *n* **1** pretence: *under the guise of friendship*. **2** external appearance in general.

guitar *n* a musical instrument with a body generally shaped like a figure eight, a long fretted neck and usu six strings that are plucked or strummed. ○ **guitarist** *n*.

gulch *n*, *N Am* a narrow rocky ravine with a fast-flowing stream running through it.

gulf *n* **1** a very large and deeply indented inlet of the sea extending far into the land. **2** a vast difference or separation, eg between points of view, etc. **3** a deep hollow in the ground. **4** (**the Gulf**) **a** the region around the Persian Gulf in the Middle East; **b** the area around the Gulf of Mexico in North and Central America.

gull *n* an omnivorous seabird with a stout body and predominantly white or greyish plumage. Also called **seagull**.

gullet *n* the OESOPHAGUS or throat.

gullible *adj* easily tricked. ○ **gullibility** *n*.

gully or **gulley** *n* (**gullies** or **gulleys**) **1** a small channel or cutting with steep sides formed by running water. **2** *cricket* a fielding position between cover point and the slips.

gulp *vb* **1** *tr & intr* (*also* gulp down) to swallow (food, drink, etc) eagerly or in large mouthfuls. **2** (*usu* gulp sth back) to stifle (tears, etc). **3** *intr* to make a swallowing motion, eg because of fear. ➤ *n* **1** a swallowing motion. **2** an amount swallowed at once.

gum[1] *n* the firm fibrous flesh surrounding the roots of the teeth.

gum[2] *n* **1** a substance found in certain plants, esp trees, that produces a sticky solution or gel when added to water. **2** this or any similar substance used as glue. **3** *colloq* chewing gum.

➤ *vb* (**gummed, gumming**) to smear, glue or unite something with gum.

gum arabic *n* a thick sticky water-soluble gum exuded by certain acacia trees.

gumbo *n* a thick soup or stew thickened with okra.

gumboil *n* a small abscess on the gum.

gumboot *n* a WELLINGTON BOOT.

gummy[1] *adj* (*-ier, -iest*) toothless.

gummy[2] *adj* (*-ier, -iest*) **1** sticky. **2** producing gum.

gumption *n*, *colloq* **1** common sense; initiative. **2** courage.

gum tree *n*. ♦ **up a gum tree** *colloq* in a difficult position.

gun *n* **1** any weapon which fires bullets or shells from a metal tube. **2** any instrument which forces something out under pressure: *spray gun*. **3** *colloq* a gunman: *a hired gun*. **4** a member of a party of hunters. **5** the signal to start a race, etc. ➤ *vb* (**gunned, gunning**) *colloq* to rev up (a car engine) noisily. ♦ **be gunning for sb** to be searching determinedly for them, usu with hostile intent. **go great guns** *colloq* to function or be performed with great speed or success. ◊ **gun sb** or **sth down** to shoot them or it with a gun.

gunboat *n* a small warship with mounted guns.

gun cotton *n* a highly explosive material formed by treating cotton with nitric acid and sulphuric acid.

gun dog *n* a dog specially trained to FLUSH[4] birds or small mammals and to retrieve them when they have been shot.

gunfire *n* **1** the act of firing guns. **2** the bullets fired. **3** the sound of firing.

gunge *n*, *colloq* any messy, slimy or sticky substance.

gung-ho *adj*, *derog*, *colloq* excessively or foolishly eager.

gunk *n*, *colloq* any slimy or oily semi-solid substance.

gunman *n* **1** an armed criminal. **2** an assassin. **3** a terrorist.

gunmetal *n* **1** a dark-grey alloy, composed mainly of copper with small amounts of tin and zinc, formerly used to make cannons. **2** any of various other alloys that are used to make guns. **3** a dark-grey colour, esp if metallic.

gunner *n* **1** any member of an armed force who operates a heavy gun. **2** a soldier in an artillery regiment.

gunnery *n* **1** the use of guns. **2** the science of designing guns.

gunpoint *n* (*only* at gunpoint) threatening, or being threatened, with a gun.

gunpowder *n* the oldest known explosive, a mixture of potassium nitrate, sulphur and charcoal.

gunrunning *n* the act of smuggling arms into a country. ○ **gunrunner** *n*.

gunshot *n* **1** bullets fired from a gun. **2** the distance over which a gun can fire a bullet: *within gunshot*. **3** a sound of firing.

gunslinger *n, colloq* an armed fighter in the lawless days of the American West.

gunsmith *n* someone whose job is to make and/or repair firearms.

gunwale or **gunnel** /ˈgʌnəl/ *n* the upper edge of a ship's side.

guppy *n* (*-ies*) a small brightly coloured fresh-water fish that is a popular aquarium fish.

gurgle *vb* **1** *intr* of water: to make a bubbling noise when flowing. **2** *intr* to make a bubbling noise in the throat. **3** to utter something with a gurgle. ➤ *n* the sound of gurgling.

guru *n* **1** a Hindu or Sikh spiritual leader or teacher. **2** any greatly respected leader or adviser.

gush *vb* **1** *tr & intr* of a liquid: to flood out or make it flood out suddenly and violently. **2** *intr, derog, colloq* to speak or act with affected and exaggerated emotion or enthusiasm. ➤ *n* **1** a sudden violent flooding-out. **2** *derog, colloq* exaggerated emotion or enthusiasm. ○ **gushing** *adj, n.* ○ **gushingly** *adv.*

gusset *n, dressmaking* a piece of material sewn into a garment for added strength or to allow for freedom of movement, eg at the crotch.

gust *n* **1** a sudden blast or rush, eg of wind or smoke. **2** an emotional outburst. ➤ *vb, intr* of the wind: to blow in gusts.

gusto *n* enthusiastic enjoyment.

gusty *adj* (*-ier, -iest*) **1** blowing in gusts. **2** fitfully irritable or upset. ○ **gustily** *adv.*

gut *n* **1** *anat* the alimentary canal or part of it. **2** (**guts**) *colloq* the insides of a person or animal. **3** *colloq* the stomach or abdomen. **4** *colloq* a fat stomach. **5** (**guts**) *colloq* courage or determination. **6** (**guts**) *colloq* the inner or essential parts. **7** a CATGUT; **b** a fibre obtained from silkworms, used for fishing tackle. ➤ *vb* (**gutted, gutting**) **1** to take the guts out of (an animal, esp fish). **2** to destroy the insides of something: *Fire gutted the building*. ➤ *adj, colloq* based on instinct and emotion, not reason: *a gut reaction*. ◆ **work** or **sweat** or **slave one's guts out** *colloq* to work extremely hard.

gutless *adj, derog* cowardly.

gutsy *adj* (*-ier, -iest*) *colloq* **1** courageous and determined. **2** gluttonous.

gutta-percha *n* a whitish rubbery substance, obtained from the latex of certain Malaysian trees.

gutted *adj, colloq* extremely shocked or disappointed.

gutter *n* **1** a channel for carrying away rain-water, fixed to the edge of a roof or built between a pavement and a road. **2** *ten-pin bowling* either of the channels at the sides of a lane. **3** (**the gutter**) a state of poverty and social deprivation or of coarse and degraded living. **4** *printing* the inner margins between two facing pages. ➤ *vb* **1** *intr* of a candle: to have its melted wax suddenly pour down a channel on its side. **2** of a flame: to flicker and threaten to go out. ○ **guttering** *n.*

gutter press *n, derog* newspapers which deal largely with scandal and gossip.

guttersnipe *n, derog, old use* a raggedly dressed or ill-mannered person, esp a child.

guttural *adj* **1** *non-technical* of sounds: produced in the throat or the back of the mouth. **2** of a language or style of speech: having or using such sounds; harsh-sounding. ➤ *n, non-technical* a sound produced in the throat or the back of the mouth.

guy¹ *n* **1** *colloq* a man or boy. **2** *colloq, orig US* **a** a person; **b** (**guys**) used to address or refer to a group of people: *What do you guys think?* **3** a crude model of Guy Fawkes that is burnt on a bonfire on Guy Fawkes Night. ➤ *vb* to make fun of someone.

guy² *n* (*in full* **guy rope**) a rope or wire used to hold something, esp a tent, firm or steady. ➤ *vb* to secure something with guys.

guzzle *vb, tr & intr* to eat or drink greedily. ○ **guzzler** *n.*

gybe, gibe or **jibe** /dʒaɪb/ *vb, tr & intr, naut* **1** of a sail: to swing, or make it swing, over from one side of a boat to the other. **2** of a boat: to change or make it change course in this way.

gym *n, colloq* **1** GYMNASTICS. **2** GYMNASIUM.

gymkhana /dʒɪmˈkɑːnə/ *n* a local event consisting of competitions in sports, esp horse-riding.

gymnasium *n* (**gymnasiums** or **gymnasia** /dʒɪmˈneɪzɪə/) a building or room with equipment for physical exercise.

gymnast *n* someone who is skilled in gymnastics.

gymnastic *adj* **1** relating to gymnastics. **2** athletic; agile.

gymnastics *sing n* physical training designed to strengthen the body and improve agility, usu using special equipment. ➤ *pl n* **1** feats of agility. **2** difficult exercises that test or demonstrate ability of any kind: *mental gymnastics*.

gym shoe *n* a PLIMSOLL.

gym slip *n* a belted pinafore dress worn (*esp formerly*) by schoolgirls as part of their uniform.

gynaecology or (*US*) **gynecology** /gaɪnəˈkɒlədʒɪ/ *n* the branch of medicine concerned with the reproductive organs of the female body. ○ **gynaecological** *adj.* ○ **gynaecologist** *n.*

gyp or **gip** *n, colloq* pain or discomfort.

gypsum *n* a soft mineral composed of calcium sulphate, used to make plaster of Paris, cement, rubber and paper.

Gypsy or **Gipsy** *n* (*-ies*) **1** a member of a travelling people, orig from NW India, now scattered throughout Europe and N America. Also called **Romany**. **2** (*without capital*) someone who resembles or lives like a Gypsy.

gyrate *vb, intr* to move with a circular or spiralling motion. ○ **gyration** *n.*

gyroscope *n* a device consisting of a small flywheel with a heavy rim, mounted so that once in motion it resists any changes in the direction of axis, used in ship stabilizers and in automatic steering systems.

Hh

H¹ or **h** *n* (*Hs, H's* or *h's*) the eighth letter of the English alphabet.

H² *abbrev* 1 height. 2 hospital.

H³ *symbol* 1 *chem* hydrogen. 2 *physics* magnetic field strength. 3 *electronics* henry.

ha or **hah** *exclam* expressing surprise, happiness, triumph, etc.

ha *abbrev* hectare.

haar /hɑː(r)/ *n, Scot & NE Eng dialect* a cold mist or fog coming off the North Sea.

habeas corpus /ˈheɪbɪəs ˈkɔːpəs/ *n, law* a writ requiring a person to be brought into court for a judge to decide if their imprisonment is legal.

haberdasher *n, Brit* a person or shop that deals in sewing items, eg ribbons, needles, buttons, etc. ○ **haberdashery** *n* (*-ies*).

habit *n* 1 a tendency to behave, think, etc in a specific way. 2 a usual practice or custom. 3 an addiction. 4 a long loose garment worn by monks and nuns. 5 a characteristic form, type of development, growth or existence; general appearance. 6 (*in full* **riding habit**) a woman's riding dress.

habitable or **inhabitable** *adj* suitable or fit for living in.

habitat *n* the natural home of an animal or plant.

habitation *n* 1 the act of living in a particular dwelling place. 2 a house or home.

habit-forming *adj* likely to become a habit or addiction.

habitual *adj* 1 done regularly and repeatedly. 2 done, or doing something, by habit. 3 customary; usual. ○ **habitually** *adv*.

habituate *vb* to accustom. ○ **habituation** *n*.

habitué /həˈbɪtʃʊeɪ/ *n* a person who lives in or frequently visits a specified place.

háček /ˈhɑːtʃek/ *n* a diacritic (ˇ) placed over a letter in some Slavonic languages to modify the sound.

hachure /hæˈʃʊə(r)/ *n* 1 (**hachures**) parallel lines on a map where the closeness of the lines indicates the relative steepness of gradients. 2 one of these lines.

hacienda /hæsɪˈɛndə/ *n* in Spanish-speaking countries: 1 a ranch or large estate with a main dwelling-house on it. 2 this house.

hack¹ *vb* 1 to cut or chop roughly. 2 to cut a path, one's way, etc) through undergrowth, etc. 3 *intr, colloq* (*often* **hack into**) to use a computer to obtain unauthorized access to (computer files, etc). 4 *slang* to be able to bear, suffer, tolerate, etc. 5 *football, rugby* to kick the shin of (an opponent). ➤ *n* 1 a kick on the

shins. 2 a wound or rough cut. 3 a short dry cough. 4 a chop or blow.

hack² *n* 1 a horse kept for general riding, esp one for hire. 2 a ride on horseback. 3 an old or worn-out horse. 4 a writer who produces dull, mediocre or routine work. ➤ *vb* 1 *tr & intr* to ride a horse at a leisurely pace, usu for pleasure. 2 *intr* to work as a hack.

hacker *n* 1 someone or something that hacks. 2 *colloq* someone who uses computers to gain unauthorized access to data, other computers, etc.

hackles *pl n* the hairs or feathers on the back of the neck of some animals and birds, which are raised when they are angry. ◆ **make sb's hackles rise** to make them very angry.

hackney cab or **hackney carriage** *n* 1 *hist* a horse-drawn carriage for public hire. 2 *formal* a taxi.

hackneyed *adj* of a word, phrase, etc: meaningless and trite through too much use.

hacksaw *n* a saw for cutting metals.

haddock *n* (**haddock** or **haddocks**) a commercially important N Atlantic sea fish.

hadn't *contraction* had not.

haemal or **hemal** /ˈhiːməl/ *adj, med* relating to the blood or blood-vessels.

haematite or **hematite** /ˈhiːmətaɪt/ *n* a mineral containing ferric oxide, the most important ore of iron.

haematology or (*US*) **hematology** /hiːməˈtɒlədʒɪ/ *n* the branch of medicine concerned with the study of the blood and diseases of the blood. ○ **haematologic** or **haematological** *adj*. ○ **haematologist** *n*.

haemoglobin or **hemoglobin** *n, biochem* a protein in red blood cells that carries oxygen.

haemophilia or (*US*) **hemophilia** *n* a hereditary disease, usu only affecting males, in which the blood does not clot as it should. ○ **haemophiliac** or **haemophilic** *n, adj*.

haemorrhage or **hemorrhage** /ˈhɛmərɪdʒ/ *n* the escape of profuse amounts of blood, esp from a ruptured blood vessel. ➤ *vb, intr* to lose copious amounts of blood.

haemorrhoids or (*US*) **hemorrhoids** /ˈhɛmərɔɪdz/ *pl n, med* swollen veins in the anus.

hafnium *n, chem* a metallic element found mainly in zirconium minerals and used in electrodes.

haft *n* a handle of a knife, sword, axe, etc. ➤ *vb* to fit with a haft.

hag *n* 1 *offensive* an ugly old woman. 2 a witch. ○ **haggish** *adj*.

haggard adj looking very tired and upset, esp because of pain, worry, etc.

haggis n a Scottish dish made from sheep's or calf's offal mixed with suet, oatmeal and seasonings and then boiled in a bag traditionally made from the animal's stomach.

haggle vb, intr (often **haggle over** or **about**) to bargain over or argue about (a price, etc). ○ **haggler** n.

hagiography n (-ies) the writing of the lives of saints.

hag-ridden adj tormented; mentally oppressed.

hah see HA

ha-ha[1] or **haw-haw** exclam 1 a conventional way of representing the sound of laughter. 2 expressing triumph, mockery, scorn, etc.

ha-ha[2] or **haw-haw** n a wall or a fence separating areas of land in a large garden or park, but placed in a ditch to avoid interrupting the view.

haiku n (pl **haiku**) a Japanese poem which consists of three lines of five, seven and five syllables.

hail[1] n 1 grains of ice which fall from the clouds when there are strong rising air currents. 2 a large and forceful quantity (of words, questions, missiles, etc): a hail of criticism. ➢ vb, intr of hail: to fall from the clouds: It's hailing.

hail[2] vb 1 to attract attention by shouting or making gestures, eg to signal (esp a taxi) to stop. 2 to greet someone, esp enthusiastically. 3 to recognize or describe someone as being or representing something: He was hailed a hero. 4 intr (**hail from somewhere**) to come from or belong to (a place). ➢ exclam, old use an expression of greeting.

hail-fellow-well-met adj friendly and familiar, esp overly so.

hail Mary n (**hail Marys**) a prayer to the Virgin Mary, the English version of the Ave Maria (see AVE[2]).

hailstone n a single grain of hail.

hair n 1 a thread-like structure growing from the skin of animals. 2 a mass or growth of such strands, esp on a person's head. 3 an artificial strand similar to an animal's or person's hair. 4 bot a thread-like structure growing from the surface of a plant. 5 a hair's-breadth: She won by a hair. ♦ **get in sb's hair** colloq to annoy them incessantly. **keep your hair on!** colloq keep calm and don't get angry. **let one's hair down** colloq to enjoy oneself or behave without restraint. **make sb's hair curl** colloq to shock them. **make sb's hair stand on end** colloq to frighten them. **not turn a hair** to remain calm and show no surprise, anger, etc. **split hairs** to make unnecessary petty distinctions or quibbles. **tear one's hair out** to show extreme irritation or anxiety.

haircut n 1 the cutting of someone's hair. 2 the shape or style in which it is cut.

hairdo n, colloq a woman's haircut, esp after styling and setting.

hairdresser n 1 a person whose job is washing, cutting, styling, etc hair. 2 an establishment where this takes place. ○ **hairdressing** n.

hairdryer or **hairdrier** n an electrical device that dries hair by blowing hot air over it.

hairgrip n, chiefly Brit a small wire clasp for holding the hair in place.

hairline n 1 the line along the forehead where the hair begins to grow. 2 a very fine line.

hairnet n a fine-meshed net for keeping the hair in place.

hairpiece n 1 a wig or piece of false hair worn over a bald area on the head. 2 an attachment of hair added to a person's own hair to give extra length or volume.

hairpin n a thin flat U-shaped piece of wire for keeping the hair in place.

hair-raising adj extremely frightening or disturbing.

hair's-breadth n a very small distance or margin.

hair shirt n a shirt of coarse cloth made from horse hair, usu worn next to the skin as a religious penance.

hairspray n lacquer for holding the hair in place.

hairspring n a very small spiral spring which regulates a watch in conjunction with the balance wheel.

hairstyle n the way in which someone's hair is cut or shaped. ○ **hairstylist** n.

hair trigger n in a firearm: a trigger that responds to very light pressure.

hairy adj (-ier, -iest) 1 covered in hair. 2 colloq a dangerous, frightening or exciting; b difficult or tricky. ○ **hairiness** n.

hajj or **hadj** /hɑːdʒ, hadʒ/ n the Muslim pilgrimage to Mecca.

hake n (**hake** or **hakes**) an edible sea fish.

halal /ˈhalal/ n meat from an animal which has been killed according to Muslim holy law.

halberd or **halbert** n, hist a weapon of the Middle Ages that combines a spear with an axe blade.

halcyon /ˈhalsɪən/ adj peaceful, calm and happy: halcyon days.

hale adj strong and fit: hale and hearty. ○ **haleness** n.

half n (**halves**) 1 a one of two equal parts which together form a whole; b a quantity which equals such a part. 2 a FRACTION equal to one divided by two (usu written ½). 3 colloq a half pint, esp of beer. 4 Scot a measure of spirits, esp whisky. 5 one of two equal periods of play in a match. 6 football, hockey, etc the half of the pitch considered to belong to one team. 7 golf an equal score with an opponent. 8 a HALF-HOUR. 9 sport a HALFBACK. 10 a half-price ticket, esp for a child. ➢ adj 1 forming or equal to half of something: a half chicken. 2 not perfect or complete: We don't want any half measures. ➢ adv 1 to the extent or amount of one half: half finished. 2 almost; partly; to some extent: half dead with exhaustion. 3 thirty minutes past the hour stated: *half three.* ♦ **by half** *colloq* excessively: *He's too clever by half.* **by halves** without being thorough: *never do things by halves.* **go halves on sth** to share the cost of something. **not half** *colloq* **1** very: *It isn't half cold.* **2** not nearly: *I'm not half fit enough.* **3** yes, indeed. **one's other** or **better half** *colloq* one's husband, wife or partner.

half-and-half *adv, adj* in equal parts; in part one thing, in part another. ➤ *n* a mixture of two things in equal proportion.

halfback *n* **1** *football, hockey, etc* a player or position immediately behind the forwards and in front of the fullbacks. **2** *rugby* either the standoff half or the scrum half.

half-baked *adj* **1** *colloq* of an idea, scheme, etc: **a** not properly or completely thought out; **b** unrealistic or impractical. **2** foolish.

half-breed *n, dated, offensive* someone with parents of different races, esp one Caucasian and one Native American.

half-brother *n* a brother with whom one has only one parent in common.

half-caste *n, often offensive* a person who has parents of different races, esp an Indian mother and a European father.

half-cock *n* the position of a firearm's HAMMER when it cocks the trigger and therefore cannot reach the PRIMER[2] (sense 2) to fire the weapon. ♦ **to go off half-cocked** or **at half-cock** to fail due to insufficient preparation or premature starting.

half-cut *adj, slang* drunk.

half-day *n* a day on which someone only works, etc in the morning or in the afternoon.

half-hearted *adj* not eager; without enthusiasm. ○ **half-heartedly** *adv.* ○ **half-heartedness** *n.*

half-hitch *n* a simple knot or noose formed by passing the end of a piece of rope around the rope and through the loop made in the process.

half-hour *n* **1** a period of thirty minutes. **2** the moment that is thirty minutes after the start of an hour: *Buses run on the hour and on the half-hour.* ○ **half-hourly** *adj, adv.*

half-life *n, physics* the period of time required for half the original number of atoms of a radioactive substance to undergo spontaneous radioactive decay.

half-light *n* dull light, esp at dawn or dusk.

half mast *n* the lower-than-normal position at which a flag flies as a sign of mourning.

half-moon *n* the Moon when only half of it can be seen from the Earth.

half nelson *n, wrestling* a hold in which a wrestler puts an arm under one of their opponent's arms from behind, and pushes on the back of their neck.

halfpenny or **ha'penny** /ˈheɪpnɪ/ (**-ies** or **halfpence**) *n* **1** *formerly* a small British coin worth half a new penny. **2** *hist* an old British coin worth half an old penny.

half-sister *n* a sister with whom one only has

one parent in common.

half-term *n, Brit education* a short holiday halfway through an academic term.

half-timbered or **half-timber** *adj* of a building, esp one in Tudor style: having a visible timber framework filled with brick, stone or plaster. ○ **half-timbering** *n.*

half-time *n, sport* an interval between the two halves of a match.

half-title *n* a short title on the right-hand page of a book which precedes the title page.

half-tone *n* **1** a photographic process in which tones are broken up by a fine screen into dots of different sizes to produce varying shades. **2** the illustration obtained. **3** *N Am* a SEMITONE.

half-track *n* a vehicle, usu a military one, with wheels in front and caterpillar tracks behind.

half volley *n, sport* a stroke in which the ball is hit immediately after it bounces or as it bounces.

halfway *adj, adv* **1** at a point equally far from two others. **2** in an incomplete manner. ♦ **meet sb halfway** to come to a compromise with them.

halfway house *n* **1** *colloq* something which is between two extremes, and which has some features of each. **2** a home where former prisoners, psychiatric patients, etc stay temporarily to readjust to life outside prison, hospital, etc.

halfwit *n* a foolish or stupid person. ○ **halfwitted** *adj.* ○ **halfwittedly** *adv.*

halibut *n* (*halibut* or *halibuts*) a large edible flatfish found in the N Atlantic and N Pacific.

halite /ˈhalaɪt/ *n* a mineral consisting of sodium chloride in cubic crystalline form, a source of table salt.

halitosis *n* unpleasant-smelling breath.

hall *n* **1** a room or passage just inside the entrance to a house, which usu allows access to other rooms and the stairs. **2** a building or large room, used for concerts, public meetings, assemblies, etc. **3** (*usu* **Hall**) a large country house or manor. **4** *Brit* (*in full* **hall of residence**) a building where university or college students live. **5** *Brit* **a** the dining room in a college or university; **b** the dinner in such a room. **6** the main room of a great house, castle, etc. **7** *esp N Am* a corridor onto which rooms open.

hallelujah or **halleluia** /halɪˈluːjə/ or **alleluia** /alɪ-/ *exclam* expressing praise to God. ➤ *n* the exclamation of 'hallelujah'.

halliard see HALYARD

hallmark *n* **1** an official series of marks stamped on gold, silver and platinum articles to guarantee their authenticity. **2** any mark of genuineness or excellence. **3** a typical or distinctive feature, esp of quality. ➤ *vb* to stamp with a hallmark.

hallo see HELLO

halloo, hallo or **halloa** *n, exclam* **1** a cry to encourage hunting dogs or call for attention. **2** a shout of 'halloo'. ➤ *vb* (**hallooed**) *intr* to cry 'halloo', esp to dogs at a hunt.

hallow *vb* **1** to make or regard as holy. **2** to consecrate or set apart as being sacred. ○ **hallowed** *adj.*

Hallowe'en or **Halloween** *n* the evening of 31 October, the eve of All Saints Day.

hallucinate *vb, intr* to see something that is not actually present or which may not even exist. ○ **hallucination** *n.* ○ **hallucinatory** *adj.*

hallucinogen *n* a drug that causes hallucination. ○ **hallucinogenic** *adj.*

hallway *n* an entrance hall or corridor.

halo *n* (*halos* or *haloes*) **1** in paintings etc: a ring of light around the head of a saint, angel, etc. **2** the glory or glamour that is attached to a famous or admired person or thing. **3** a ring of light that can be seen around the sun or moon, caused by the refraction of light by ice crystals. ➤ *vb* (*haloes, haloed*) to put a halo round someone or something.

halogen /ˈhalədʒɛn/ *n, chem* any of the nonmetallic elements, fluorine, chlorine, bromine, iodine and astatine, which form salts when in union with metals.

halt *n* **1** an interruption or stop to movement, progression or growth. **2** *Brit* a small railway station without a building. ➤ *vb, tr & intr* to come or bring to a halt.

halter *n* **1** a rope or strap for holding and leading a horse by its head. **2** a HALTERNECK. ➤ *vb* to put a halter on (a horse, etc).

halterneck *n* a woman's top or dress held in place by a strap which goes round her neck, leaving the shoulders and back bare.

halting *adj* unsure; hesitant. ○ **haltingly** *adv.*

halve *vb* **1** to divide into two equal parts or halves. **2** to share equally. **3** *tr & intr* of costs, problems, etc: to reduce by half. **4** *golf* to take the same number of strokes as an opponent over (a hole or match).

halyard or **halliard** *n* a rope for raising or lowering a sail or flag on a ship.

ham¹ *n* **1** the top part of the back leg of a pig. **2** the meat from this part, salted and smoked. **3** *colloq* the back of the thigh.

ham² *n, colloq* **1** *theat* a bad actor, esp one who overacts or exaggerates. **2** an amateur radio operator. ➤ *vb* (*hammed, hamming*) *tr & intr* (*also* **ham up**) to overact or exaggerate. ○ **hammy** *adj* (*-ier, -iest*)

hamburger *n* a flat round cake of finely chopped beef, usu fried and served in a soft bread roll.

ham-fisted or **ham-handed** *adj, colloq* clumsy; lacking skill or grace.

hamlet *n* a small village.

hammer *n* **1** a tool with a heavy metal head on the end of a handle, used for driving nails into wood, breaking hard substances, etc. **2** the part of a bell, piano, clock, etc that hits against some other part, making a noise. **3** the part of a gun that strikes the PRIMER² or PERCUSSION CAP when the trigger is pulled and causes the bullet to be fired. **4** *sport* (the sport of throwing) a metal ball on a long flexible steel chain. **5** the

mallet with which an auctioneer announces that an article is sold. ➤ *vb* **1** *tr & intr* to strike or hit with or as if with a hammer. **2** *intr* to make a noise as of a hammer. **3** *colloq* to criticize, defeat or beat severely. ◆ **come** or **go under the hammer** to be sold at auction. **hammer and tongs** *colloq* with a lot of enthusiasm, effort or commotion. ◊ **hammer sth out** to reconcile or settle problems, differences, etc after a great deal of effort and discussion.

hammer and sickle *n* the sign of a hammer and a sickle laid across each other, symbolic of labour.

hammock *n* a piece of canvas or net hung by the corners, used as a bed.

hamper¹ *vb* to hinder the progress or movement of (someone or something).

hamper² *n* **1** a large basket with a lid, used esp for carrying food. **2** *Brit* the food and drink packed in such a basket.

hamster *n* a small nocturnal Eurasian rodent with a short tail and pouches in its mouth for storing food, often kept as a pet.

hamstring *n* **1** in humans: a tendon at the back of the knee attached to muscles in the thigh. **2** in horses: the large tendon at the back of the hind leg. ➤ *vb* (*hamstringed* or *hamstrung*) **1** to make powerless or hinder. **2** to lame by cutting the hamstring.

hand *n* **1** in humans: the extremity of the arm below the wrist. **2** a corresponding part in higher vertebrates. **3** something that resembles this in form or function. **4** *in compounds* made by hand rather than by a machine: *hand-knitted.* **5** control, agency or influence: *the hand of fate.* **6** (**a hand**) help; assistance: *He gave us a hand.* **7** a part or influence in an activity: *They had a hand in the victory.* **8** a needle or pointer on a clock, watch or gauge. **9** *colloq* a round of applause: *He got a big hand.* **10** a manual worker or assistant, esp in a factory, on a farm or on board ship: *All hands on deck!* **11** someone who is skilful at some specified activity: *a dab hand at baking.* **12** a specified way of doing something: *She has a light hand at pastry.* **13** *cards* **a** the cards dealt to a player in one round of a game; **b** one round of a card game. **14** a specified position in relation to an object or onlooker: *on the right hand.* **15** a source of information considered in terms of closeness to the original source: *I heard the news at first hand.* **16** an opposing aspect, point of view, etc: *on the other hand.* **17** someone's handwriting or style of handwriting. **18** a promise or acceptance of partnership, esp to marry: *He asked for her hand.* **19** in measuring the height of horses: a unit of measurement equal to 4in (about 10cm). ➤ *vb* **1** (*often* **hand sth back** or **in** or **out** or **round,** *etc*) to deliver or give it using the hand or hands. **2** to lead, help or escort in a specified direction with the hand or hands: *He handed her into the carriage.* ◆ **a free hand** freedom to do as desired. **a hand's turn** *usu with negatives* the least amount of work: *He* *didn't do a hand's turn all day.* **at first hand** directly from the source. **at hand** near by; about to happen. **by hand** using the hands or tools held in the hand rather than by mechanical means. **change hands** to pass to other ownership or custody. **come to hand** to arrive; to be received. **force sb's hand** to force them to act. **get one's hands on sb** or **sth** *colloq* to catch or find them or it. **hand and foot** completely; in every possible way: *Servants wait on him hand and foot.* **hand in glove** very closely associated. **hand in hand 1** with hands mutually clasped. **2** in close association. **hand it to sb** *colloq* to give them credit. **hand over fist** *colloq* in large amounts and very quickly: *making money hand over fist.* **hands down** without effort; easily: *We won hands down.* **hands off!** keep off!; do not touch! **hands up!** hold your hands up above your head. **have one's hands full** *colloq* **1** to be very busy. **2** to be plagued with problems. **have one's hands tied** to be unable to act, usu because of instructions from a higher authority. **in good hands** in good keeping; in the care of someone who may be trusted. **in hand 1** under control. **2** being done or prepared. **3** available in reserve: *with half an hour in hand.* **keep one's hand in** *colloq* to continue to have some involvement in an activity so as to remain proficient at it. **lend a hand** to give assistance. **lift a hand** *usu with negatives* to make the least effort: *He didn't lift a hand to help.* **live from hand to mouth 1** to live with only enough money and food for immediate needs. **2** to live without preparation or planning. **off one's hands** *colloq* no longer one's responsibility. **on hand** near; available if required. **on one's hands** *colloq* left over; not sold or used; to spare: *too much time on my hands.* **out of hand 1** beyond control. **2** immediately and without thinking: *to dismiss it out of hand.* **take sth off sb's hands** to relieve them of it. **the upper hand** power or advantage. **to hand** within reach. **try one's hand at sth** to attempt to do it. ◊ **hand sth down 1** to pass on (an heirloom, tradition, etc) to the next generation. **2** to pass on (an outgrown item of clothing) to a younger member of a family, etc. **3** *N Am, law* to pronounce (a verdict). **hand sth in** to return or submit (an examination paper, something found, etc). **hand sth out** to pass it by hand or distribute it to individuals. See also HANDOUT. **hand sth over** to transfer it or give possession of it to someone else. See also HANDOVER.

handbag *n* a small bag, often with a strap, for carrying personal articles.

handball *n* **1** a game in which two or four players hit a small ball against a wall with their hands. **2** the small hard rubber ball used in this game. **3** a game between goals in which the ball is struck with the palm of the hand. **4** *football* the offence a player other than a goalkeeper in their own penalty area commits if they touch the ball with their hand.

handbill *n* a small printed notice or advertisement distributed by hand.

handbook *n* **1** a manual that gives guidelines on maintenance or repair. **2** a guidebook that lists brief facts on a subject or place.

handbrake *n* **1** a brake on a motor vehicle, operated by a lever. **2** this lever.

h and c *abbrev* hot and cold (water).

handcart *n* a small light cart which can be pushed or pulled by hand.

handcuff *n* (**handcuffs**) a pair of steel rings, joined by a short chain, for locking round the wrists of prisoners, etc. ➤ *vb* to put handcuffs on someone.

handed *adj, in compounds* **1** using one hand in preference to the other: *left-handed.* **2** having or using a hand or hands as specified: *one-handed.* ○ **handedly** *adv.* ○ **handedness** *n.*

handful *n* **1** the amount or number that can be held in one hand. **2** a small amount or number. **3** *colloq* a difficult person or task.

handicap *n* **1** a physical or mental impairment. **2** something that impedes or hinders. **3 a** a disadvantage imposed on a superior competitor in a contest, race, etc, or an advantage given to an inferior one, so that everyone has an equal chance of winning; **b** a race or competition in which competitors are given a handicap. **4** the number of strokes by which a golfer's averaged score exceeds par for a course. ➤ *vb* (**handicapped, handicapping**) **1** to impede or hamper someone. **2** to impose special disadvantages or advantages on (a player, horse, etc) in order to make a better contest. ○ **handicapped** *adj.* ○ **handicapper** *n.*

handicraft *n* **1** an activity which requires skilful use of the hands, eg pottery. **2** (*usu* **handicrafts**) the work produced by this activity.

handiwork *n* **1** work, esp skilful work, produced by hand. **2** *often derog* the outcome of the action or efforts of someone or something.

handkerchief *n* (**handkerchiefs** or **handkerchieves**) a piece of cloth or soft paper used for wiping the nose, face, etc.

handle *n* **1** the part of a utensil, door, etc by which it is held. **2** an opportunity, excuse, etc for doing something: *Her shyness served as a handle for their bullying.* **3** *slang* a person's name or title. ➤ *vb* **1** to touch, hold, move or operate with the hands. **2** to deal with, control, manage, discuss, etc: *She handles all the accounts.* **3** to buy, sell or deal in (specific merchandise). **4** *intr* to respond in a specified way to being operated: *This car handles very smoothly.* ◆ **fly off the handle** *colloq* to become suddenly very angry.

handlebars *pl n, sometimes sing* a bar for steering a bicycle, motorcycle, etc.

handler *n* **1** someone who trains and controls an animal. **2** *in compounds* someone who handles something specified: *a baggage handler.*

handmade *adj* made by a person's hands or with hand-held tools.

handmaiden or **handmaid** *n, old use* a female servant.

hand-me-down *n, colloq* something, esp a

garment, passed down from one person to another.

handout n 1 money, food, etc given to people who need it. 2 a leaflet, free sample, etc, given out, eg as publicity for something.

handover n the transfer of power from one person or group to another.

hand-pick vb to choose carefully, esp for a particular purpose. ○ **hand-picked** adj.

handrail n a narrow rail running alongside a stairway, etc for support.

handset n the part of a telephone held in the hand while making a call.

handshake n an act of holding or shaking a person's hand, esp as a greeting or when concluding a deal.

hands-off adj 1 of a machine, etc: not touched or operated by the hands. 2 of a strategy, policy, etc: deliberately avoiding involvement.

handsome adj 1 of a man: good-looking. 2 of a woman: attractive in a strong, dignified, imposing way. 3 of a building, room, etc: well-proportioned; impressive. 4 substantial or generous: a handsome donation. 5 liberal or noble: a handsome gesture. ○ **handsomely** adv.

hands-on adj involving practical experience rather than just information or theory: hands-on training.

handspring n a somersault or cartwheel in which one lands first on one's hands and then on one's feet.

handstand n the act of balancing one's body on one's hands with one's legs in the air.

hand-to-hand adj of fighting: involving direct physical contact with the enemy.

hand-to-mouth adj, adv with just enough money or food for immediate needs only: We live hand-to-mouth.

handwriting n 1 writing with a pen or pencil rather than by typing or printing. 2 the characteristic way a person writes.

handy adj (-ier, -iest) 1 ready to use and conveniently placed. 2 easy to use or handle. 3 clever with one's hands. ○ **handily** adv. ○ **handiness** n.

handyman n a man skilled at, or employed to do, odd jobs around the house.

hang vb (**hung** or (in sense 3) **hanged**) 1 tr & intr to fasten or be fastened from above, esp with the lower part free. 2 tr & intr of a door, etc: to fasten or be fastened with hinges so that it can move freely. 3 tr & intr to suspend or be suspended by a rope around the neck until dead. 4 (sometimes **hang over**) to be suspended or hover, esp in the air or in a threatening way: The smell of paint hung in the air • The fear of redundancy hung over me. 5 tr & intr to droop or make something droop: to hang one's head in shame. 6 to fix (wallpaper) to a wall. 7 tr & intr of a painting, etc: to place or be placed in an exhibition. 8 to decorate (a room, wall, etc) with pictures or other hangings. 9 tr & intr, colloq to damn or be damned: Hang the expense. 10 intr of a piece of clothing: to sit in a specified

way when worn: a coat which hangs well. 11 to suspend game from a hook to allow it to decompose slightly and become more flavoursome. 12 comput of a computer or a program: to stop functioning. ➤ n 1 the way something hangs, falls or droops. 2 usu with negatives, colloq a damn: I couldn't give a hang. ♦ **get the hang of sth** colloq to learn or begin to understand how to do it. **hang fire 1** to delay taking action. 2 to cease to develop or progress. ◊ **hang about** or **around** colloq 1 to waste time; to stand around doing nothing. 2 to stay or remain. **hang back** to be unwilling or reluctant to do something. **hang on** colloq 1 to wait: I'll hang on for a bit. 2 to carry on bravely, in spite of problems or difficulties. **hang on sth** 1 to depend on it: It all hangs on the weather. 2 to listen closely to it: I was hanging on her every word. **hang on to sth** to keep a hold or control of it. **hang out 1** to lean or bend out (eg of a window, etc). 2 colloq to frequent a place: He hangs out in local bars. **hang together 1** of two people: to be united and support each other. 2 of ideas, etc: to be consistent. **hang up** to finish a telephone conversation by replacing the receiver.

---

hanged, hung The normal past tense and past participle of the verb **hang** is **hung**:
She hung the apron over the back of a chair.
Curtains could be hung from a pole.
When the verb refers to killing by hanging, the correct form of the past tense and past participle is **hanged**:
He was later hanged for his part in a bomb plot.
He hanged himself in his cell.
Hung is increasingly used in this sense also, but in formal English it is better to use **hanged**.

---

hangar n a large shed or building in which aircraft are kept.

hangdog adj of someone's appearance or manner: ashamed, guilty or downcast.

hanger n 1 (in full **coat-hanger**) a frame on which clothes are hung to keep their shape. 2 a someone who hangs something; b in compounds a person or contraption that hangs a specified thing: paper-hanger.

hanger-on n (**hangers-on**) a dependant or follower, esp one who is not wanted.

hang-glider n 1 a large light metal frame with cloth stretched across it and a harness hanging below it for the pilot, which flies using air currents. 2 the pilot of this. ○ **hang-gliding** n.

hanging n 1 the execution of someone by suspending their body by the neck. 2 (usu **hangings**) curtains, tapestries, etc hung on walls. ➤ adj 1 suspended; not fixed below. 2 undecided: a hanging question.

hangman n an official who carries out executions by hanging.

hangnail n a piece of loose skin that has been

partly torn away from the base or side of a fingernail.

hang-out *n, colloq* a place where one lives or spends much time.

hangover *n* **1** a collection of unpleasant physical symptoms that may follow a period of heavy drinking. **2** someone or something left over from or influenced by an earlier time.

hang-up *n, colloq* **1** an emotional or psychological problem or preoccupation. **2** a continual source of annoyance.

hank *n* a coil, loop or skein of wool, string, rope, etc.

hanker *vb, intr* (*usu* **hanker after** or **for sth**) to have a longing or craving for it. ○ **hankering** *n*.

hankie or **hanky** *n* (*-ies*) *colloq* a handkerchief.

hanky-panky *n, colloq* **1** slightly improper sexual behaviour. **2** dubious or foolish conduct.

hansom cab *n* a two-wheeled horse-drawn carriage with a driver's seat high up at the back, formerly used as a taxi.

ha'penny see HALFPENNY

haphazard *adj* **1** careless. **2** random. ➢ *adv* at random. ○ **haphazardly** *adv*. ○ **haphazardness** *n*.

hapless *adj* unlucky; unfortunate.

haploid *biol, adj* of a cell nucleus: having a single set of unpaired chromosomes. ➢ *n* a haploid cell or organism.

happen *vb, intr* **1** to take place or occur. **2** (**happen to sb**) of an unforeseen, esp unwelcome, event: to be done to them or experienced by them. **3** to have the good or bad luck (to do something): *I happened to meet him on the way.* ➢ *adv, N Eng dialect* perhaps. ◊ **happen on** or **upon sth** to discover or encounter it, esp by chance.

happening *n* **1** an event. **2** a performance, esp one which takes place in the street, which has not been fully planned, and in which the audience is invited to take part. ➢ *adj* fashionable and up to the minute.

happy *adj* (*-ier, -iest*) **1** feeling or showing pleasure or contentment: *a happy smile.* **2** causing pleasure: *a happy day for the company.* **3** suitable; fortunate: *a happy coincidence.* **4** suitably expressed; appropriate: *a happy reply.* **5** *colloq* slightly drunk. **6** *in compounds* overcome with the thing specified: *power-happy.* ○ **happily** *adv.* ○ **happiness** *n*.

happy-go-lucky *adj* carefree and easy-going.

hara-kiri /harə'kɪrɪ/ or **hari-kari** /harɪ'kɑːrɪ/ *n* ritual suicide by cutting one's belly open with a sword, formerly practised in Japan to avoid dishonour.

harangue /hə'raŋ/ *n* a loud forceful speech either to attack people or to try to persuade them to do something. ➢ *vb* to address such a speech to (someone or a crowd).

harass *vb* **1** to pester, torment or trouble (someone) by continually questioning or attacking them. **2** to make frequent sudden attacks on (an enemy). ○ **harassed** *adj*. ○ **harassment** *n*.

harbinger /'hɑːbɪndʒə(r)/ *n* a person or thing that announces or predicts something to come; a forerunner.

harbour or (*N Am*) **harbor** *n* **1** a place of shelter for ships. **2** a refuge or safe place. ➢ *vb* **1** to give shelter or protection to (someone, esp to a criminal). **2** to have (a feeling, etc) in one's head: *to harbour a grudge.*

hard *adj* **1** of a substance: resistant to scratching or indentation; firm; solid. **2** toughened; not soft or smooth: *hard skin.* **3** difficult to do, understand, solve or explain. **4** using, needing or done with a great deal of effort. **5** demanding: *a hard master.* **6** harsh; cruel. **7** tough or violent: *a hard man.* **8** of weather: severe. **9** forceful: *a hard knock.* **10** cool or uncompromising: *a long hard look.* **11** causing hardship, pain or sorrow: *hard times.* **12** harsh and unpleasant to the senses: *a hard light.* **13** of information, etc: proven and reliable: *hard facts.* **14** shrewd or calculating: *a hard businesswoman.* **15** of water: containing calcium or magnesium salts, and tending to produce an insoluble scum instead of a lather with soap. **16** of a drug: highly addictive. **17** of an alcoholic drink: very strong, esp one which is a spirit rather than a beer, wine, etc. **18** politically extreme: *the hard right.* **19** *phonetics, non-technical* of the sounds of certain consonants: produced as a stop rather than a fricative, as eg the *c* in *cat* and the *g* in *got.* **20** of currency: in strong demand due to having a stable value and exchange rate. **21** of credit: difficult to obtain. **22** of pornography: sexually explicit. **23** as a classification of pencil leads: indicating durable quality and faintness in use. ➢ *adv* **1** with great effort or energy: *She works hard.* **2** *in compounds* with difficulty or as a result of great effort: *a hard-won victory* • *hard-earned results.* **3** earnestly or intently: *He thought hard to find a solution.* **4** with great intensity: *The news hit us hard.* ○ **hardness** *n*. ♦ **be hard going** to be difficult to do. **be hard put to do sth** to have difficulty doing it. **hard at it** working hard. **hard by** close by. **hard done by** *colloq* unfairly treated. **hard of hearing** partially deaf. **hard up** *colloq* in need of money.

hard-and-fast *adj* of a rule or principle: permanent or absolute.

hardback *n* a book with a hard cover.

hardball *n* no-nonsense tough tactics, used esp for political gain.

hard-bitten *adj, colloq* of a person: tough and ruthless.

hardboard *n* light strong board made by compressing wood pulp.

hard-boiled *adj* **1** of eggs: boiled until the yolk is solid. **2** *colloq* of a person: tough; cynical.

hard case *n, colloq* a tough, often violent, person who is reluctant to reform.

hard cash *n* coins and banknotes, as opposed to cheques and credit cards.

hard copy *n* a printed version of information held in computer files.

hardcore n 1 pieces of broken brick, stone, etc used as a base for a road. 2 (also **hard core**) the central, most important group within an organization, resistant to change. ➤ adj (often **hard-core**) 1 of pornography: sexually explicit. 2 having long-lasting, strong and unchanging beliefs: *hard-core revolutionaries.*

hard disk or **hard disc** n, comput a rigid aluminium disk, normally permanently sealed within a disk drive, with a large capacity for storing data. Compare FLOPPY DISK.

hard-earned adj having taken a great deal of hard work to achieve or acquire.

harden vb 1 tr & intr to make or become hard or harder. 2 tr & intr to become or make less sympathetic or understanding. 3 to make or become stronger or firmer. 4 intr, commerce **a** of prices, a market, etc: to stop fluctuating; **b** of prices: to rise. ○ **hardened** adj 1 rigidly set. 2 toughened through experience and not likely to change: *a hardened criminal.* ○ **hardener** n. ◊ **harden sth off** to accustom (a plant) to cold, frost, etc by gradually exposing it to outdoor conditions.

hard-headed adj 1 tough, realistic or shrewd. 2 not influenced by emotion.

hard-hearted adj feeling no pity or kindness; intolerant.

hardihood n courage or daring.

hard labour n, law, formerly a punishment involving heavy physical work in addition to a sentence of imprisonment.

hard line n an uncompromising course, opinion, decision or policy. ○ **hardliner** n.

hardly adv 1 barely; scarcely: *I hardly knew the man.* 2 only just: *She could hardly keep her eyes open.* 3 often ironic certainly not: *They'll hardly come now.* 4 with difficulty: *I can hardly believe it.*

hard-nosed adj, colloq 1 tough and shrewd. 2 influenced by reason, not emotion.

hard-on n, coarse slang an erection of the penis.

hardpad n hardness of the pads of the feet, a symptom of DISTEMPER[1] in dogs.

hard palate n the bony front part of the palate, which separates the mouth from the nasal cavities.

hard-pressed or **hard-pushed** adj 1 having problems; in difficulties. 2 threatened by severe competition or attack. 3 closely pursued.

hardship n 1 living conditions that are difficult to endure. 2 severe suffering or pain, or a cause of this.

hard shoulder n, Brit a hard verge along the side of a motorway, on which vehicles can stop if in trouble.

hardtack n a kind of hard biscuit, formerly given to sailors as food on long journeys.

hardware n 1 metal goods such as pots, cutlery, tools, etc. 2 comput the electronic, electrical, magnetic and mechanical components of a computer system, as opposed to the programs that form the SOFTWARE. 3 heavy military equipment, eg tanks and missiles.

hard-wearing adj durable; designed to last a long time and stay in good condition despite regular use.

hard-wired adj of computers: having functions that are controlled by hardware and cannot be altered by software programmes.

hardwood n the wood of a slow-growing deciduous tree, such as the oak, mahogany or teak.

hardy adj (-ier, -iest) 1 tough; strong; able to bear difficult conditions. 2 of a plant: able to survive outdoors in winter. ○ **hardily** adv. ○ **hardiness** n.

hardy annual n a plant that lives for up to a year and which can withstand severe climatic conditions.

hare n a herbivorous mammal like a rabbit but slightly larger and with longer legs and ears. ➤ vb, intr colloq to run very fast or wildly.

harebell n a wild plant with violet-blue bell-shaped flowers.

hare-brained adj foolish; rash; heedless.

harelip n a deformity of the upper lip, present from birth, in which there is a cleft on one or both sides of the centre, often occurring with a CLEFT PALATE.

harem /'hɑːriːm, hɑː'riːm/ n 1 a separate part of a traditional Muslim house in which wives, concubines, etc live. 2 the women living in this.

haricot /'harıkoʊ/ or **haricot bean** n a small white dried bean, used as food.

hari-kari see HARA-KIRI

hark vb, intr, literary & dialect to listen attentively. ◊ **hark back to sth** to refer to or remind one of (past experience).

harken see HEARKEN

harlequin n (also **Harlequin**) theat a humorous character from traditional Italian plays who wears a black mask and a brightly coloured, diamond-patterned costume. ➤ adj in varied bright colours.

harlequinade /hɑːləkwɪ'neɪd/ n 1 (also **Harlequinade**) theat a play in which a harlequin has a leading role. 2 buffoonery.

harlot n, old use a prostitute.

harm n physical, emotional, etc injury or damage. ➤ vb to injure or damage. ○ **harmful** adj. ○ **harmless** adj.

harmonic adj relating or referring to, or producing, harmony; harmonious. ➤ n, mus an overtone of a fundamental note, produced on a stringed instrument by touching one of the strings lightly at one of the points which divide the string into exact fractions. ○ **harmonically** adv.

harmonica n a small wind instrument with metal reeds along one side, played by being held against the mouth, blown or sucked, and moved from side to side to change the notes.

harmonious adj 1 pleasant-sounding and tuneful. 2 forming a pleasing whole: *a harmonious arrangement of colours.* 3 without disagreement or bad feeling. ○ **harmoniously** adv.

harmonium n a musical instrument with a keyboard, in which air from bellows pumped by the feet makes the reeds vibrate to produce sound.

harmonize or **-ise** vb 1 tr & intr to be in or bring into musical harmony. 2 tr & intr to form or be made to form a pleasing whole. 3 to add notes to (a simple tune) to form harmonies. 4 intr to sing in harmony, eg with other singers. ○ **harmonization** n.

harmony n (-ies) 1 mus **a** a pleasing combination of notes or sounds produced simultaneously; **b** the whole chordal structure of a piece as distinguished from its MELODY or its RHYTHM; **c** the art or science concerned with combinations of chords. 2 a pleasing arrangement of parts or things: a harmony of colour. 3 agreement in opinions, actions, feelings, etc.

harness n 1 a set of leather straps used to attach a cart to a horse, and to control the horse's movements. 2 a similar set of straps for attaching to a person's body, eg to hold a child who is just learning to walk. ➣ vb 1 to put a harness on (a horse, person, etc). 2 to attach (a draught animal to a cart, etc). 3 to control (resources, esp natural ones) so as to make use of the potential energy or power they contain.

harp n a large upright musical instrument with a series of strings stretched vertically across it, played by plucking the strings. ➣ vb, intr 1 to play the harp. 2 colloq (**harp on about sth**) to talk or write repeatedly and tediously about it. ○ **harpist** n.

harpoon n a barbed spear fastened to a rope, used for catching whales, etc. ➣ vb to strike (a whale, etc) with a harpoon. ○ **harpooner** or **harpooner** n.

harpsichord n a triangular-shaped keyboard instrument in which the strings are plucked mechanically when the player presses the keys. ○ **harpsichordist** n.

harpy n (-ies) 1 Greek myth an evil creature with the head and body of a woman and the wings and feet of a bird. 2 a cruel, grasping woman.

harridan n a bad-tempered, scolding old woman; a nag.

harrier[1] n 1 a cross-country runner. 2 a hound used orig for hunting hares.

harrier[2] n 1 a diurnal bird of prey with broad wings and long legs. 2 any person or thing that harries.

harrow n a heavy metal framed farm implement with spikes or teeth, used to break up clods of soil and cover seed. ➣ vb 1 to pull a harrow over (land). 2 to distress greatly; to vex. **harrowing** adj extremely distressing.

harry vb (-ies, -ied) 1 to destroy (a town, etc). 2 to annoy or worry someone.

harsh adj 1 rough; grating; unpleasant to the senses. 2 strict, cruel or severe. ○ **harshly** adv. ○ **harshness** n.

hart n a male deer.

harum-scarum / ˈhɛərəmˈskɛərəm/ adj wild and thoughtless; reckless. ➣ adv recklessly.

➣ n someone who is wild, impetuous or rash.

harvest n 1 the gathering in of ripened crops, usu in late summer or early autumn. 2 the season when this takes place. 3 the crop or crops gathered. 4 the product or result of some action, effort, etc. ➣ vb 1 tr & intr to gather (a ripened crop). 2 to receive or reap (benefits, consequences, etc). ○ **harvester** n. ○ **harvesting** n.

harvest moon n the full moon nearest to the autumnal equinox.

has-been n, colloq someone or something that once was, but is no longer, successful, important or influential.

hash[1] n 1 a dish of cooked meat and vegetables chopped up together and recooked. 2 a re-using of old material. 3 colloq a mess: I made a hash of it. ➣ vb 1 to chop up into small pieces. 2 to mess up.

hash[2] n, slang hashish.

hashish or **hasheesh** / ˈhaʃiːʃ/ n CANNABIS.

hasn't contraction has not.

hasp n a hinged metal fastening for a door, box, etc, often secured by a padlock.

hassle colloq, n 1 trouble, annoyance or inconvenience, or a cause of this. 2 a fight or argument. ➣ vb 1 to annoy or bother someone, esp repeatedly; to harass. 2 intr to argue or fight.

hassock n 1 a firm cushion for kneeling on, esp in church. 2 a tuft of grass.

haste n 1 speed, esp in an action. 2 urgency of movement. ➣ vb to hasten. ♦ **in haste** in a hurry. **make haste** to hurry.

hasten vb 1 tr & intr to hurry or cause to hurry. 2 (always **hasten to do sth**) to do it eagerly and promptly: He hastened to admit we were right.

hasty adj (-ier, -iest) 1 hurried; swift; quick. 2 without enough thought or preparation; rash. 3 short-tempered. 4 conveying irritation or anger: hasty words. ○ **hastily** adv. ○ **hastiness** n.

hat n 1 a covering for the head, usu worn out of doors. 2 colloq a role or capacity: wearing her critic's hat. ♦ **keep sth under one's hat** colloq to keep it secret. **take one's hat off to sb** colloq to admire or praise them.

hatch[1] n 1 a door covering an opening in a ship's deck. 2 a hatchway. 3 a door in an aircraft or spacecraft. 4 an opening in a wall between a kitchen and dining room, used esp for serving food.

hatch[2] vb 1 intr (also **hatch out**) of an animal or bird: to break out of an egg. 2 intr of an egg: to break open, allowing young animals or birds to be born. 3 to produce (young animals or birds) from eggs. 4 (often **hatch up**) to plan or devise (a plot, scheme, etc), esp in secret.

hatch[3] vb to shade (the surface of a map, drawing, engraving, etc) with close parallel or crossed lines. ○ **hatching** n.

hatchback n 1 a sloping rear end of a car with a single door which opens upwards. 2 a car with such a rear end.

hatchery n (-ies) a place where eggs, esp fish

eggs, are hatched under artificial conditions.

hatchet *n* a small axe held in one hand.

hatchet man *n, colloq* a person employed to carry out illegal, unpleasant or destructive assignments.

hatchway *n* **1** an opening in a ship's deck for loading cargo through. **2** a similar opening in a wall, ceiling, floor, etc.

hate *vb* **1** to dislike intensely. **2** *colloq* to regret: *I hate to bother you.* ➤ *n* **1** an intense dislike. **2** (*esp* **pet hate**) *colloq* an intensely disliked person or thing. ○ **hatable** or **hateable** *adj*.

hateful *adj* causing or deserving great dislike; loathsome.

hatpin *n* a long metal pin, often decorated, pushed through a woman's hat and hair to keep the hat in place.

hatred *n* intense dislike; enmity; ill-will.

hatstand or (*esp US*) **hat tree** *n* a piece of furniture with pegs for hanging hats, coats, etc on.

hatter *n* someone who makes or sells hats.

◆ **mad as a hatter** extremely mad or eccentric.

hat trick *n* the scoring of three points, goals, victories, etc in a single period of time or match.

haughty *adj* (*-ier, -iest*) very proud; arrogant or contemptuous. ○ **haughtily** *adv*. ○ **haughtiness** *n*.

haul *vb* **1** *tr & intr* to pull with great effort or difficulty. **2** to transport by road, eg in a lorry. **3** *naut* to alter the course of a vessel, esp so as to sail closer to the wind. **4** (*usu* **haul up**) to bring (someone before some authority) for punishment, reprimand etc: *hauled up before the boss.* ➤ *n* **1** a distance to be travelled: *It's a long haul to Sydney.* **2** an act of dragging something with effort or difficulty. **3** an amount gained or seized at any one time, eg of items stolen. ○ **hauler** *n*.

haulage *n* **1** the act or labour of hauling. **2** a the business of transporting goods by road, esp in lorries; **b** the money charged for this.

haulier *n* a person or company that transports goods by road, esp in lorries.

haulm or **halm** /hɔːm/ *n, bot* **1** the stalks or stems of potatoes, peas, beans or grasses, collectively. **2** one such stalk or stem.

haunch *n* **1** the fleshy part of the buttock or thigh. **2** the leg and loin, esp of a deer, as a cut of meat: *a haunch of venison.*

haunt *vb* **1** of a ghost or spirit: to be present in (a place) or visit (a person or place) regularly. **2** of unpleasant thoughts, etc: to keep coming back to someone's mind: *haunted by the memory of his death.* **3** to visit (a place) frequently. **4** to associate with someone frequently. ➤ *n* **1** (*often* **haunts**) a place visited frequently. **2** the habitation or usual feeding-ground of deer, game, fowls, etc. ○ **haunted** *adj* **1** inhabited by ghosts or spirits. **2** constantly worried or obsessed.

haunting *adj* of a place, memory, piece of music, etc: making a very strong and moving impression.

haute couture /oʊt kuːˈtjʊə(r)/ *n* the leading fashion designers or their products, collectively.

haute cuisine /oʊt kwɪˈziːn/ *n* cookery, esp French cookery, of a very high standard.

hauteur /oʊˈtɜː(r)/ *n* haughtiness; arrogance.

have *vb* (**has, had, having**) **1** to possess or own: *They have a big house.* **2** to possess as a characteristic or quality: *He has brown eyes.* **3** to receive, obtain or take: *I'll have a drink* • *He had a look.* **4** to think of or hold in the mind: *I have an idea.* **5** to experience, enjoy or suffer: *You'll have a good time* • *I have a headache* • *I had my car stolen.* **6** to be in a specified state: *The book has a page missing.* **7** to arrange or hold: *I'm having a party.* **8** to take part in something: *We had a conversation.* **9** to cause, order or invite someone to do something or something to be done: *You should have your hair cut* • *They had him fired.* **10** to state or assert: *Rumour has it that they've only just met.* **11** to place: *I'll have the fridge in this corner.* **12** to eat or drink: *I had beans and chips.* **13** to gain an advantage over or control of someone: *You have me on that point.* **14** *colloq* to cheat or deceive: *You've been had.* **15** to show or feel: *I have no pity for them* • *She had the goodness to leave.* **16** *with negatives* to accept or tolerate: *I won't have any of that!* **17** to receive as a guest: *We're having people to dinner.* **18** to be pregnant with or give birth to (a baby, etc): *She had a boy.* **19** *coarse slang* to have sexual intercourse with someone. **20** to possess a knowledge of something: *I have some French.* ➤ *auxiliary vb* used with a past PARTICIPLE to show that the action or actions described have been completed, as in *I made the cake* and *She has been there many times.* ➤ *n* (**haves**) *colloq* people who have wealth and the security it brings: *the haves and the have-nots.* ◆ **have had it** *colloq* **1** to be dead, ruined or exhausted. **2** to have missed one's opportunity. **3** to become unfashionable. **have it off** or **away with sb** *Brit, coarse slang* to have sexual intercourse with them. **have it out** to settle a disagreement by arguing or discussing it frankly. **have to be** to surely be: *That has to be the reason.* **have to be** or **do sth** to be required to be or do it: *He had to run fast* • *We had to be gentle.* **I have it!** or **I've got it!** I have found the answer, solution, etc. **let sb have it** *colloq* to launch an attack on them, either physical or verbal. ◊ **have sb on** *colloq* to trick or tease them. **have sth on** to have an engagement or appointment. **have sth on sb** to have information about them, esp incriminating information. **have sb up for sth** *Brit, colloq* to bring them to court to answer (a charge): *He was had up for robbery.*

haven *n* **1** a place of safety or rest. **2** a harbour or other sheltered spot for ships.

have-nots *pl n* people with relatively little material wealth.

haven't *contraction* have not.

haver /ˈheɪvə(r)/ *esp Scot & N Eng, vb, intr* **1** to

babble; to talk nonsense. **2** to be slow or hesitant in making a decision. ➤ *n* (*usu* **havers**) foolish talk; nonsense.

haversack *n* a canvas bag carried over one shoulder or on the back.

havoc *n* **1** great destruction or damage. **2** *colloq* chaos; confusion. ♦ **play havoc with sth** to cause a great deal of damage or confusion to it.

haw¹ see HUM AND HAW at HUM

haw² *n* **1** a hawthorn berry. **2** the hawthorn.

haw-haw see HA-HA¹,²

hawk¹ *n* **1** a relatively small diurnal bird of prey with short rounded wings. **2** *pol* a person favouring force and aggression rather than peaceful means of settling disputes. Compare DOVE² (sense 2). **3** a ruthless or grasping person. ➤ *vb* **1** *intr* to hunt with a hawk. **2** to pursue or attack on the wing, as a hawk does. ○ **hawking** *n*. ○ **hawkish** *adj*. ○ **hawklike** *adj*.

hawk² *vb* **1** to carry (goods) round, usu from door to door, trying to sell them. ○ **hawker** *n*.

hawk³ *vb* **1** *intr* to clear the throat noisily. **2** to bring phlegm up from the throat. ➤ *n* an act or an instance of doing this.

hawser *n, naut* a thick rope or steel cable for tying ships to the quayside.

hawthorn *n* a thorny tree or shrub with pink or white flowers and red berries.

hay *n* grass, clover, etc that has been cut and dried in the field before being baled and stored for use as winter fodder for livestock. ♦ **make hay while the sun shines** to take advantage of an opportunity while one has the chance.

hay fever *n* an allergic response to pollen characterized by itching and watering of the eyes, dilation of nasal blood vessels and increased nasal mucus.

haystack or **hayrick** *n* a large firm stack of hay in an open field.

haywire *adj, colloq* (*often* **go haywire**) **1** of things: out of order; not working properly. **2** of people: crazy or erratic.

hazard *n* **1** a risk of harm or danger. **2** something which is likely to cause harm or danger. **3** *golf* an obstacle on a golf course, such as water, a bunker, etc. **4** chance; accident. ➤ *vb* **1** to put forward (a guess, suggestion, etc). **2** to risk. **3** to expose to danger. ○ **hazardous** *adj*.

haze *n* **1** a thin mist, vapour or shimmer in the atmosphere which obscures visibility. **2** a feeling of confusion or of not understanding. ➤ *vb, tr & intr* to make or become hazy.

hazel *n* **1** a small deciduous shrub or tree with edible nuts. **2** its wood. **3** a hazelnut. **4** a greenish-brown colour.

hazelnut *n* the edible nut of the hazel tree, with a smooth hard shiny shell.

hazy *adj* (**-ier, -iest**) **1** misty. **2** vague; not clear: *a bit hazy about what happened*. ○ **hazily** *adv*. ○ **haziness** *n*.

He *symbol, chem* helium.

he *pron* **1** a male person or animal already referred to. **2** a person or animal of unknown or unstated sex, esp after pronouns such as

'someone' or 'whoever'. ➤ *n, also in compounds* a male person or animal: *Is the kitten a he or a she?* ♦ *he-goat.*

head *n* **1** the uppermost or foremost part of an animal's body, containing the brain and the organs of sight, smell, hearing and taste. **2** the head thought of as the seat of intelligence, imagination, ability, etc: *Use your head* ♦ *a head for heights.* **3** something like a head in form or function, eg the top of a tool. **4** the person with the most authority in an organization, family, etc. **5** the position of being in charge. **6** *colloq* a head teacher or principal teacher. **7** the top or upper part of something, eg a table or bed. **8** the highest point of something: *the head of the pass.* **9** the front or forward part of something, eg a queue. **10** the foam on top of a glass of beer, lager, etc. **11** the top part of a plant which produces leaves or flowers. **12** a culmination or crisis: *Things came to a head.* **13** the pus-filled top of a boil or spot. **14** (*pl* **head**) a person, animal or individual considered as a unit: *600 head of cattle* ♦ *The meal cost £10 a head.* **15** *colloq* a headache. **16** the source of a river, lake, etc. **17** the height or length of a head, used as a measurement: *He won by a head* ♦ *She's a head taller than her brother.* **18** a headland: *Beachy Head.* **19 a** the height of the surface of a liquid above a specific point, esp as a measure of the pressure at that point: *a head of six metres*; **b** water pressure, due to height or velocity, measured in terms of a vertical column of water; **c** any pressure: *a full head of steam.* **20** an electromagnetic device in a tape recorder, video recorder, computer, etc for converting electrical signals into the recorded form on tapes or disks, or vice versa, or for erasing recorded material. **21** (**heads**) the side of a coin bearing the head of a monarch, etc. Compare TAILS at TAIL¹ (*noun* sense 7). **22** a headline or heading. **23** a main point of an argument, discourse, etc. **24** (*often* **heads**) *naut* a ship's toilet. **25** *colloq* a user of a specified drug: *acid head* ♦ *smack head.* **26** *also in compounds* the final point of a route: *railhead.* ➤ *adj* **1** for or belonging to the head: *headband* ♦ *head cold.* **2** chief; principal: *head gardener.* **3** at, or coming from, the front: *head wind.* ➤ *vb* **1** to be at the front of or top of something: *to head the queue.* **2** to be in charge of, or in the most important position. **3** *tr & intr* to move or cause to move in a certain direction: *heading for work* ♦ *heading home.* **4** *tr & intr* to turn or steer (a vessel) in a particular direction: *They headed into the wind.* **5** to provide with or be (a headline or heading) at the beginning of a chapter, top of a letter, etc. **6** *football* to hit (the ball) with the head. ○ **headless** *adj*. ♦ **above** or **over one's head** too difficult for one to understand. **bring** or **come to a head** to reach or cause to reach a climax or crisis. **give sb his** or **her head** to allow them to act freely and without restraint. **go to one's head 1** of alcoholic drink: to make one slightly intoxicated. **2** of praise, success, etc: to make one conceited. **head and shoulders**

by a considerable amount; **to a considerable degree**: *head and shoulders above the rest*. **head over heels 1** rolling over completely with the head first. **2** completely: *head over heels in love*. **hold up one's head** to be confident or unashamed. **keep one's head** to remain calm and sensible in a crisis. **lose one's head** to become angry or excited or act foolishly, particularly in a crisis. **not make head or tail of sth** to be unable to understand it. **off one's head** *colloq* mad; crazy. **off the top of one's head** *colloq* without much thought or calculation. **on your,** *etc* **own head be it** you, etc will bear the full responsibility for your, etc actions. **out of one's head 1** *colloq* mad, crazy. **2** of one's own invention. **over sb's head 1** without considering the obvious candidate: *He was promoted over the head of his supervisor*. **2** referring to a higher authority without consulting the person in the obvious position. **3** too difficult for them to understand: *Her jokes are always over my head*. **put your** or **your** or **their heads together** to consult. **take** or **get it into one's head 1** to decide to do something, usu foolishly. **2** to come to believe something, usu wrongly. **turn sb's head 1** to make them vain and conceited. **2** to attract their attention. ◊ **head off** to leave: *I headed off before it got too dark*. **head sb off** to intercept them and force them to turn back. **head sth off** to prevent or hinder it.

headache *n* **1** a continuous pain felt in the head. **2** *colloq* someone or something that causes worry or annoyance. ○ **headachy** *adj*.

headbanger *n, colloq* **1** a fan of heavy metal or rock music. **2** a stupid or fanatical person.

headboard *n* a panel at the top end of a bed.

headcase *n, colloq* **1** someone who behaves in a wild or irrational way. **2** a mentally ill person.

head count *n* a count of people present.

headdress *n* a covering for the head, esp a highly decorative one used in ceremonies.

headed *adj* **1** having a heading: *headed notepaper*. **2** *in compounds*: *clear-headed*.

header *n* **1** *colloq* a fall or dive forward. **2** *football* the hitting of the ball with the head. **3** *building* a brick or stone laid across a wall so that the shorter side shows on the wall surface. Compare STRETCHER (sense 2). **4** a heading for a chapter, article, etc.

headfirst *adv* **1** moving esp quickly with one's head in front or bent forward. **2** without thinking; rashly.

headgear *n* anything worn on the head: *protective headgear*.

headhunting *n* **1** *anthropol* the practice in certain societies of taking the heads of one's dead enemies as trophies. **2** the practice of trying to attract a person away from their present job to work for one's own or a client's company. ○ **headhunt** *vb*. ○ **headhunter** *n*.

heading *n* **1** a title at the top of a page, letter, section of a report, etc. **2** a main division, eg in a speech.

headland *n* a strip of land which sticks out into a sea or other expanse of water.

headlight or **headlamp** *n* a powerful light on the front of a vehicle.

headline *n* **1 a** a title or heading of a newspaper article, written above the article in large letters; **b** a line at the top of a page, indicating the page number, title, etc. **2** (**headlines**) the most important points in a television or radio news broadcast, read out before the full broadcast. ➤ *vb, tr & intr* to have top billing in (a show, etc).

headlong *adj, adv* **1** moving esp quickly with one's head in front or bent forward. **2** quickly, and usu without thinking.

headmaster or **headmistress** *n* a HEAD TEACHER.

head on *adv* **1** head to head; with the front of one vehicle hitting the front of another. **2** in direct confrontation.

headphones *pl n* a device consisting of two small sound receivers, either held over the ears by a metal strap passed over the head, or inserted into the ear, for listening to a radio, CD player, personal stereo, etc.

headquarters *sing* or *pl n* the centre of an organization or group, from which activities are controlled.

headrest *n* a cushion which supports the head, fitted to the top of a car seat, etc.

headroom *n* **1** the space between the top of a vehicle and the underside of a bridge. **2** any space overhead, below an obstacle, etc.

headset *n* a pair of headphones, often with a microphone attached.

head start *n* an initial advantage in a race or competition.

headstone *n* **1** a GRAVESTONE. **2** *archit* a keystone.

headstrong *adj* **1** of a person: difficult to persuade; determined; obstinate. **2** of an action: heedless; rash.

head teacher *n* the principal teacher in charge of a school.

head to head *adv, adj, colloq* in direct competition: *a head-to-head clash*. ➤ *n* a competition involving two people, teams, etc.

headwaters *pl n* the tributary streams of a river, which flow from the area in which it rises.

headway *n* **1** progress. **2** a ship's movement forward.

heady *adj* (*-ier, -iest*) **1** of alcoholic drinks: tending to make one drunk quickly. **2** very exciting. **3** rash; impetuous. ○ **headily** *adv*. ○ **headiness** *n*.

heal *vb* **1** to cause (a person, wound, etc) to become healthy again. **2** *intr* (*also* **heal up** or **over**) of a wound: to become healthy again by natural processes, eg by scar formation. **3** to make (sorrow, etc) less painful. **4** *tr & intr* to settle (disputes, etc) and restore friendly relations, harmony, etc. ○ **healer** *n*. ○ **healing** *n, adj*.

health *n* **1** a state of physical, mental and social wellbeing accompanied by freedom from illness or pain. **2** a person's general mental or physical condition: *in poor health*. **3** the soundness, esp financial soundness, of an organization, country, etc. ○ **healthful** *adj*.

health farm *n* a place where people go to improve their health through diet and exercise.

health food *n* any food that is considered to be natural, free of additives and beneficial to health.

health service *n* a public service providing medical care, usu without charge.

health visitor *n* a trained nurse who visits people, eg new mothers and their babies, the elderly, etc, in their homes to check on their health and give advice on matters of health.

healthy *adj* (*-ier, -iest*) **1** having or showing good health. **2** causing good health. **3** in a good state: *a healthy economy*. **4** wise: *a healthy respect for authority*. **5** *colloq* considerable; satisfactory: *a healthy sum*. ○ **healthily** *adv*. ○ **healthiness** *n*.

heap *n* **1** a collection of things in an untidy pile or mass. **2** (*usu* **heaps**) *colloq* a large amount or number: *heaps of time*. **3** *colloq* something, esp a motor vehicle, that is very old and not working properly. ➤ *vb* **1** *tr & intr* (*also* **heap sth up** *or* **heap up**) to collect or be collected together in a heap. **2** (*often* **heap sth on sb** *or* **heap sb with sth**) to give them it in large amounts. ➤ *adv* (**heaps**) *colloq* very much: *I'm heaps better*. ○ **heaped** *adj* denoting a spoonful that forms a rounded heap on the spoon.

hear *vb* (**heard**) **1** *tr & intr* to perceive (sounds) with the ear. **2** to listen to something: *Did you hear what he said?* **3** *intr* (*usu* **hear about, of** *or* **that**) to be told or informed (of it). **4** *intr* (*usu* **hear from**) to be contacted (by them), esp by letter or telephone. **5** *law* to listen to and judge (a case). ○ **hearer** *n*. ♦ **hear! hear!** an expression of agreement or approval. **not hear of sth** not to allow it to happen. ◊ **hear sb out** to listen to them until they have said all they wish to say.

hearing *n* **1** the sense that involves the perception of sound. **2** the distance within which something can be heard: *within hearing*. **3** an opportunity to state one's case: *We gave him a fair hearing*. **4** a judicial investigation and listening to evidence and arguments, esp without a jury.

hearing aid *n* a small electronic device consisting of a miniature sound receiver, an amplifier and a power source, worn in or behind the ear by a partially deaf person to help them hear more clearly.

hearken *or* (*sometimes US*) **harken** *vb, intr* (*often* **hearken to**) *old use* to listen or pay attention (to someone or something).

hearsay *n* rumour; gossip.

hearse *n* a vehicle used for carrying a coffin at a funeral.

heart *n* **1** in vertebrates: a muscular organ that contracts and pumps blood round the body. **2** the corresponding organ or organs that pump circulatory fluid in invertebrates. **3** this organ considered as the centre of a person's

thoughts, emotions, conscience, etc. **4** emotional mood: *a change of heart*. **5** ability to feel tenderness or pity: *You have no heart*. **6** courage and enthusiasm: *take heart*. **7** the most central part: *the heart of the old town*. **8** the most important part: *the heart of the problem*. **9** the compact inner part of some vegetables. **10** a symbol (♥), usu red in colour, representing the heart, with two rounded lobes at the top curving down to meet in a point at the bottom. **11 a** (**hearts**) one of the four suits of playing-cards, with a red heart-shaped symbol (♥); **b** a playing-card of this suit. ♦ **at heart** really; basically. **break sb's heart** to cause them great sorrow. **by heart** by or from memory. **lose heart** to become discouraged or disillusioned over something. **take sth to heart** to pay great attention to it or be very affected by it. **to one's heart's content** as much as one wants. **with all one's heart** very willingly or sincerely.

heartache *n* great sadness or mental suffering.

heart attack *n, non-technical* a sudden severe chest pain caused by failure of part of the heart muscle to function.

heartbeat *n* **1** the pulsation of the heart, produced by the alternate contraction and relaxation of the heart muscle. **2** a single pumping action of the heart.

heartbreak *n* very great sorrow or grief. ○ **heartbreaking** *adj*. ○ **heartbroken** *adj*.

heartburn *n* a feeling of burning in the chest caused by indigestion.

hearten *vb, tr & intr* to make or become happier, more cheerful or encouraged. ○ **heartening** *adj*.

heartfelt *adj* sincerely and deeply felt.

hearth *n* **1** the floor of a fireplace, or the area surrounding it. **2** the home. **3** the lowest part of a blast-furnace.

heartland *n* a central or vitally important area or region.

heartless *adj* cruel; very unkind. ○ **heartlessly** *adv*. ○ **heartlessness** *n*.

heart-rending *adj* causing great sorrow or pity.

heart-searching *n* the close examination of one's deepest feelings and conscience.

heartstrings *pl n* a person's deepest feelings.

heart-throb *n, colloq* someone, esp a male actor or singer, many people find very attractive.

heart-to-heart *n* an intimate and candid conversation.

heart-warming *adj* gratifying; pleasing; emotionally moving.

heartwood *n, bot* the dark, hard wood at the centre of a tree.

hearty *adj* (*-ier, -iest*) **1** very friendly and warm in manner. **2** strong, vigorous or enthusiastic: *hale and hearty*. **3** heartfelt: *a hearty dislike*. **4** of a meal or an appetite: large. ○ **heartily** *adv*. ○ **heartiness** *n*.

heat *n* **1** a form of energy that is stored as the

energy of vibration or motion of the atoms or molecules of a material. **2** a high temperature; warmth; the state of being hot. **3** hot weather. **4** intensity of feeling, esp anger or excitement: *the heat of the argument*. **5** the most intense part: *in the heat of the battle*. **6** *sport* **a** a preliminary race or contest which eliminates some competitors; **b** a single section in a contest. ➤ *vb, tr & intr* **1** to make or become hot or warm. **2** to make or become intense or excited. ◆ **in** or **on heat** of some female mammals: ready to mate. **in the heat of the moment** without pausing to think.

heated *adj* **1** having been made hot or warm. **2** angry or excited. ○ **heatedly** *adv.* ○ **heatedness** *n.*

heater *n* an apparatus for heating a room, building, water in a tank, etc.

heath *n* **1** an area of open land, usu with acidic soil, dominated by low-growing evergreen shrubs, esp heathers. **2** a low evergreen shrub found esp on open moors and heaths.

heathen *n* (**heathens** or **heathen**) **1** someone who does not adhere to a particular religion, esp when regarded by a person or community that does follow that religion. **2** *colloq* an ignorant or uncivilized person. ➤ *adj* having no religion; pagan.

heather *n* a low evergreen moor or heath shrub with small pink or purple bell-shaped flowers.

Heath-Robinson *adj* of a machine or device: ludicrously complicated and impractical in design, esp when its function is a simple one.

heating *n* **1** any of various systems for maintaining the temperature inside a room or building at a level higher than that of the surroundings. **2** the heat generated by such a system.

heatstroke *n* a condition caused by overexposure to unaccustomed heat, characterized by progressively severe symptoms of lassitude, fainting and high fever.

heatwave *n* a prolonged period of unusually hot dry weather.

heave *vb* (**heaved** or (*in naut senses*) **hove**) **1** to lift or pull with great effort. **2** *colloq* to throw something heavy. **3** *intr* to rise and fall heavily or rhythmically. **4** to make something rise and fall heavily or rhythmically. **5** *intr, colloq* to retch or vomit. ➤ *n* an act or instance of heaving. ◆ **heave a sigh** to sigh heavily or with effort. **heave into sight** *esp naut* to move in a particular direction. **the heave** or **the heave-ho** *colloq* dismissal or rejection. ◊ **heave to** *esp naut* to bring or be brought to a stop or standstill.

heaven *n* **1** the place believed to be the abode of God, angels and the righteous after death. **2** (*usu* **the heavens**) the sky. **3** a place or the state of great happiness or bliss. **4** often used in exclamations: God or Providence: *heaven forbid.*

heavenly *adj* **1** *colloq* very pleasant; beautiful.

2 situated in or coming from heaven or the sky: *heavenly body*. **3** holy. ○ **heavenliness** *n.*

heaven-sent *adj* very lucky or convenient; timely.

heavy *adj* (**-ier, -iest**) **1** having great weight. **2** of breathing: loud, because of excitement, exhaustion, etc. **3** great in amount, size, power, etc: *heavy traffic* • *a heavy crop*. **4** great in amount, frequency, etc: *a heavy drinker*. **5** considerable: *heavy emphasis*. **6** hard to bear, endure or fulfil: *a heavy fate*. **7** ungraceful and coarse: *heavy features*. **8** severe, intense or excessive: *heavy fighting*. **9** sad or dejected: *with a heavy heart*. **10** difficult to digest: *a heavy meal*. **11** having a great or relatively high density: *a heavy metal*. **12** forceful or powerful: *a heavy sea* • *heavy rain*. **13** intense or deep: *a heavy sleep*. **14** of the sky: dark and cloudy. **15** needing a lot of physical or mental effort. **16** of literature, music, etc: **a** serious in tone and content; **b** not immediately accessible or appealing. **17** physically and mentally slow. **18** fat; solid. **19** of soil: wet and soft due to its high clay content. **20** *colloq* strict; severe: *Don't be heavy on him.* **21** *mil* **a** equipped with powerful weapons, armour, etc; **b** of guns: large and powerful. **22** of cakes and bread: dense through not having risen enough. ➤ *n* (**-ies**) **1** *slang* a large, violent man: *They sent in the heavies*. **2** *Scot* a beer like bitter but darker in colour and gassier. ➤ *adv* heavily: *Time hangs heavy on my hands.* ○ **heavily** *adv* **1** in a heavy way; with or as if with weight. **2** intensely, severely or violently. ○ **heaviness** *n.* ◆ **make heavy weather of sth** see under WEATHER.

heavy-duty *adj* designed to resist or withstand very hard wear or use.

heavy going *n* difficult or slow progress.

heavy-handed *adj* **1** clumsy and awkward. **2** too severe or strict; oppressive. ○ **heavy-handedly** *adv.* ○ **heavy-handedness** *n.*

heavy industry *n* a factory or factories involving the use of large or heavy equipment, eg coal-mining, ship-building, etc.

heavy metal *n* loud repetitive rock music with a strong beat.

heavyweight *n* **1** a class for boxers, wrestlers, and weightlifters of more than a specified weight. **2** a boxer, etc of this weight. **3** *colloq* an important, powerful or influential person. **4** a person who is heavier than average.

hebdomadal /hɛbˈdɒmədəl/ *adj* weekly.

Hebrew *n* **1** a member of an ancient people, orig based in Palestine, and claiming descent from Abraham. **2** the ancient language of the Hebrews, or its modern form spoken esp by Jews in Israel. ➤ *adj* relating or referring to the Hebrew language or people.

heck *exclam, colloq* mildly expressing anger, annoyance, surprise, etc.

heckle *vb, tr & intr* to interrupt (a public speaker) with critical or abusive shouts and jeers. ○ **heckler** *n.*

hectare *n* a metric unit of land measurement,

equivalent to 100 ares (see ARE^2), or 10,000 square metres (2.471 acres).

hectic adj agitated; very excited, flustered or rushed. ○ **hectically** adv.

hector vb, tr & intr to bully, intimidate or threaten.

he'd contraction **1** he had. **2** he would.

hedge n **1** a boundary formed by bushes and shrubs planted close together, esp between fields. **2** a barrier or protection against loss, criticism, etc. ➤ vb **1** to enclose or surround (an area of land) with a hedge. **2** to avoid making a decision or giving a clear answer. **3** to protect oneself from possible loss or criticism by backing both sides: *to hedge one's bets*. **4** intr to make hedges. **5** intr to be evasive or shifty, eg in an argument. ○ **hedged** adj. ○ **hedger** n.

hedgehog n a small, prickly-backed, insectivorous, nocturnal mammal with a hoglike snout.

hedge-hop vb, intr to fly at a very low altitude as if hopping over hedges, eg when crop-spraying.

hedgerow n a row of bushes, hedges or trees forming a boundary.

hedonism n **1** the belief that pleasure is the most important achievement or the highest good in life. **2** the pursuit of and devotion to pleasure. ○ **hedonist** n. ○ **hedonistic** adj.

the heebie-jeebies pl n, slang feelings or fits of nervousness or anxiety.

heed vb **1** to pay attention to or take notice of (something, esp advice or a warning, etc). **2** intr to mind or care. ➤ n careful attention; notice: *Take heed of what she says*. ○ **heedful** adj. ○ **heedfully** adv. ○ **heedfulness** n.

heedless adj taking no care; careless. ○ **heedlessly** adv. ○ **heedlessness** n.

hee-haw n the bray of a donkey, or an imitation of this sound. ➤ vb, intr to bray.

heel^1 n **1** the rounded back part of the foot below the ankle. **2** the part of a sock, shoe, etc that covers or supports the heel. **3** anything shaped or functioning like the heel, eg that part of the palm near the wrist. **4** a heel-like bend, as on a golf club. **5** the end of a loaf of bread. **6** slang a despicable person; someone who is untrustworthy or who lets others down. ➤ vb **1** to execute or strike with the heel. **2** to repair or fit a new heel on (a shoe, etc). **3** intr to move one's heels in time to a dance rhythm. **4** rugby to kick (the ball) backwards out of the scrum with the heel. ♦ **at, on** or **upon sb's heels** following closely behind them. **cool** or **kick one's heels** to be kept waiting indefinitely. **dig one's heels in** to behave stubbornly. **down at heel** untidy; in poor condition or circumstances. **take to one's heels** to run away. **to heel 1** esp of a dog: walking obediently at the heels of the person in charge of it. **2** under control; submissive. **turn on one's heel** to turn round suddenly or sharply. **under the heel** crushed; ruled over tyrannically.

heel^2 vb **1** intr (often **heel over**) of a vessel: to lean over to one side; to list. **2** to cause (a vessel) to tilt.

heel^3 vb (usu **heel in**) to temporarily cover (the roots of a plant) with soil to keep them moist.

hefty adj (-ier, -iest) colloq **1** of a person: strong, robust or muscular. **2** of an object, blow, etc: large, heavy or powerful; vigorous. **3** large or considerable in amount: *a hefty sum of money*. ○ **heftily** adv. ○ **heftiness** n.

hegemony /hɪˈɡɛmənɪ/ n (-ies) authority or control, esp of one state over another within a confederation.

heifer /ˈhɛfə(r)/ n a cow over one year old that has either not calved, or has calved only once.

height n **1** the condition of being high. **2** the distance from the base of something to the top. **3** the distance above the ground from a recognized point. **4** relatively high altitude. **5** a high place or location. **6** the highest point of elevation; the summit. **7** the most intense part or climax: *the height of battle*. **8** an extremely good, bad or serious example: *the height of stupidity*. ○ **heighten** vb to make higher, greater, stronger, etc.

heinous /ˈheɪnəs, ˈhiː-/ adj extremely wicked or evil; odious. ○ **heinously** adv. ○ **heinousness** n.

heir /ɛə(r)/ n **1** someone who by law receives or is entitled to receive property, wealth, a title, etc when the previous owner or holder dies. **2** someone who is successor to a position, eg leadership, or who continues a tradition. ○ **heirless** adj. ♦ **fall heir to sth** to inherit it.

heir apparent n (**heirs apparent**) law an heir whose claim to an inheritance cannot be challenged by the birth of another heir.

heiress /ˈɛərɛs/ n a female heir, esp a woman who has inherited or will inherit considerable wealth.

heirloom n an object that has been handed down through a family over many generations.

heir presumptive n (**heirs presumptive**) law an heir whose claim to an inheritance may be challenged by the birth of another heir more closely related to the holder.

heist /haɪst/ n, N Am, slang a robbery. ➤ vb to steal or rob in a heist.

helical adj relating to or like a helix; coiled.

helicopter n an aircraft that is lifted and propelled by rotating blades above its body.

heliograph n an instrument which uses mirrors to reflect light from the Sun in flashes as a way of sending messages.

heliotrope n **1** a garden plant of the borage family, with small fragrant lilac-blue flowers which grow towards the sun. **2** the colour of these flowers.

helium n, chem a colourless odourless inert gas found in natural gas deposits, also formed in stars by nuclear fusion.

helix /ˈhiːlɪks/ n (**helices** /-siːz/ or **helixes**) **1** a spiral or coiled structure, eg the thread of a screw. **2** geom a spiral-shaped curve that lies on the lateral surface of a cylinder or cone.

hell *n* **1** the place or state of infinite punishment for the wicked after death. **2** the abode of the dead and evil spirits. **3** any place or state which causes extensive pain, misery and discomfort. ➤ *exclam, colloq* **1** expressing annoyance or exasperation. **2** (**the hell**) an expression of strong disagreement or refusal: *The hell I will!* ✦ **a hell of a** or **one hell of a** *colloq* a very great or significant: *one hell of a row.* **all hell breaks** or **is let loose** there is chaos and uproar. **as hell** absolutely; extremely: *He's as mad as hell.* **for the hell of it** *colloq* for the fun or sake of it. **from hell** considered to be the most awful example of its kind imaginable: *boyfriend from hell.* **give sb hell** *colloq* **1** to punish or rebuke them severely. **2** to make things extremely difficult for them. **hell for leather** *colloq* at an extremely fast pace: *We drove hell for leather to the airport.* **hell to pay** serious trouble or consequences. **like hell 1** very much, hard, fast, etc: *I ran like hell.* **2** not at all or in any circumstances: *Like hell I will.* **to hell with sb** or **sth 1** an expression of angry disagreement with them or it. **2** an intention to ignore or reject them or it. **what the hell 1** what does it matter?; who cares? **2** an expression of amazement: *What the hell are you doing?*

he'll *contraction* **1** he will. **2** he shall.

hellbent *adj* (*usu* **hellbent on sth**) *colloq* recklessly determined or intent about it.

Hellenistic or **Hellenistical** *adj* relating to Greek culture after Alexander the Great.

hellfire *n* the fire or punishment of hell.

hellhole *n* a disgusting, evil, frightening, etc place.

hellish *adj* **1** relating to or resembling hell. **2** *colloq* very unpleasant, horrifying or difficult.

hello, hallo or **hullo** *exclam* used as a greeting, to attract attention or to start a telephone conversation. **2** used to express surprise or discovery: *Hello! What's going on here?*

hellraiser *n, colloq* a boisterously debauched person.

helm *n, naut* the steering apparatus of a boat or ship, such as a wheel or tiller. ✦ **at the helm** in charge.

helmet *n* a protective head covering, worn eg by police officers, firefighters, soldiers, motorcyclists, cyclists, etc. ○ **helmeted** *adj.*

helmsman *n* someone who steers a boat or ship.

help *vb* **1** to contribute towards the success of something; to assist or aid. **2** to give the means to do something. **3** to relieve a difficult situation or burden; to improve or lighten (a predicament). **4** to provide or supply with a portion; to deal out. **5** (**help oneself to sth**) to take it without authority or permission. **6** to remedy; to mitigate or alleviate. **7** to refrain from something: *I couldn't help laughing.* **8** to prevent or control: *I can't help the bad weather.* **9** *intr* to contribute. ➤ *n* **1** an act of helping. **2** means or strength given to another for a particular purpose. **3** someone who is employed to help,

esp a domestic help. **4** a remedy or relief. ○ **helper** *n.* ◊ **help out** or **help sb out** to offer help, usu for a short time, and esp by sharing a burden or the cost of something.

helpful *adj* giving help or aid; useful.

helping *n* a single portion of food served at a meal.

helping hand *n* help or assistance.

helpless *adj* **1** unable or unfit to do anything for oneself. **2** weak and defenceless; needing assistance.

helpline *n* a telephone service that people with a particular problem can call, often free of charge, in order to contact advisers and counsellors who are qualified in that specific field: *victim support helpline.*

helpmate *n* a friend or partner, esp a husband or wife.

helter-skelter *adj* hurried and disorderly. ➤ *adv* in a hurried and disorientated manner. ➤ *n, Brit* a spiral slide on the outside of a tower in a fairground or playground.

hem[1] *n* a bottom edge or border of a garment, piece of cloth, etc, folded over and sewn down. ➤ *vb* (**hemmed, hemming**) *tr & intr* to form a border or edge on a garment, piece of cloth, etc. ◊ **hem sth** or **sb in** to surround it or them closely, preventing movement.

hem[2] *exclam* a slight clearing of the throat or cough to show hesitation or to draw attention. ➤ *n* such a sound. ➤ *vb* (**hemmed, hemming**) *intr* to utter this kind of cough or sound.

he-man *n* (**he-men**) *colloq* a man of exaggerated or extreme strength, stamina and virility.

hemiplegia *n, pathol* paralysis of one side of the body only. Compare PARAPLEGIA, QUADRIPLEGIA. ○ **hemiplegic** *adj, n.*

hemisphere *n* **1** one half of a sphere. **2** either half of the Earth's sphere, when divided by the equator into the northern and southern hemispheres, or by a meridian into the eastern and western hemispheres. ○ **hemispheric** or **hemispherical** *adj.*

hemline *n* the height, level or line of a hem on a dress or skirt, etc.

hemlock *n* **1** a poisonous umbelliferous plant with small white flowers and a spotted stem. **2** the poison extracted from this plant.

hemp *n* **1** any of a genus of Asian plants. **2** any drug obtained from some species of this plant, esp marijuana. **3** the fibre obtained from this plant, used to make rope, paper, fine cloth, etc. **4** its seeds and oil, used as a source of food, fabric, biofuel, etc.

hemstitch *n* a decorative finishing stitch used on the inner side of a hem. ➤ *vb, tr & intr* to use this stitch to secure a hem.

hen *n* a female bird of any kind, esp a domestic fowl.

hence *adv* **1** for this reason or cause. **2** from this time onwards. **3** *old use* from this place or origin.

henceforth or **henceforward** *adv* from now on.

henchman *n* a faithful supporter or right-hand man, esp one who obeys and assists without question.

henge *n* a prehistoric monument consisting of large upright stones or wooden posts, usu forming a circle.

hen harrier *n* the common harrier.

hen house *n* a house or coop for fowl.

henna *n* **1** an Asian and N African shrub. **2** reddish-brown dye obtained from the leaves of this shrub, used for colouring the hair and decorating the skin. ➤ *vb* (**hennaed**) to dye or stain using henna.

hen party or **hen night** *n* a party attended by women only, esp one to celebrate the imminent marriage of one of the group.

henpecked *adj, colloq* usu of a man: constantly harassed, criticized and dominated by a woman, esp a wife, girlfriend, etc.

henry *n* (**henry, henrys** or **henries**) the SI unit of electrical inductance.

hepatic *adj* **1** relating or referring to the liver. **2** liver-coloured.

hepatitis *n* inflammation of the liver, the symptoms of which include jaundice, fever and nausea.

heptagon *n* a plane figure with seven angles and sides. ○ **heptagonal** *adj*.

heptathlon *n* an athletic contest comprising seven events.

her *pron* **1** the objective form of SHE: *We all like her • Send it to her.* **2** the possessive form of SHE: *Her car is outside.* ➤ *adj* referring to a female person or animal, or something personified or thought of as female, eg a ship: *I went to her house • She gave the cat her milk • She tried to keep her head into the wind.*

herald *n* **1** a person who announces important news, or an officer whose task it is to make public proclamations and arrange ceremonies. **2** someone or something that is a sign of what is to come. **3** an officer responsible for keeping a record of the genealogies and coats of arms of noble families. ➤ *vb* to be a sign of the approach of something; to proclaim or usher in: *dark clouds heralding a storm.* ○ **heraldic** *adj*.

heraldry *n* the art of recording genealogies, and blazoning coats of arms.

herb *n* **1** a flowering plant which, unlike a shrub or tree, has no woody stem above the ground. **2** an aromatic plant such as rosemary, mint and parsley, used in cookery or in herbal medicine. ○ **herbal** *adj*.

herbaceous *adj* relating to or having the characteristics of a HERB (sense 1).

herbage *n* herbs collectively; herbaceous vegetation covering a large area, esp for use as pasture.

herbalist or **herbist** *n* **1** a person who researches, collects and sells herbs and plants. **2** a person who practises herbal medicine. **3** an early botanist. ○ **herbalism** *n*.

herbarium /hɜːˈbɛərɪəm/ *n* (**herbaria** /-rɪə/ or **herbariums**) **1** a classified collection of preserved plants (in a room or building, etc). **2** the room or building used to house such a collection.

herbicide *n* a substance used to kill weeds, etc.

herbivore *n* an animal that feeds on plants. ○ **herbivorous** *adj*.

herd *n* **1** a company of animals, esp large ones, that habitually remain together. **2** a collection of livestock or domestic animals, eg cows or pigs. **3** (*also in combination*) a person who looks after a herd: *The herd grazed his flock on the hillside • a lonely goatherd.* **4** a large crowd of people. **5** (**the herd**) people in general, esp when considered as behaving in an unimaginative and conventional way. ➤ *vb* **1** *intr* to gather in a crowd like an animal in a herd. **2** to look after or tend a herd of (animals). **3** to group (animals) together. ○ **herdsman** *n*.

here *adv* **1** at, in or to this place. **2** in the present life or state; at this point, stage or time. **3** used with *this, these,* etc for emphasis: **a** after a noun: *this chair here;* **b** *colloq, dialect* between a noun and *this, that,* etc: *this here chair.* ➤ *n* this place or location. ➤ *exclam* **1** calling for attention. **2** calling attention to one's own presence, or to something one is about to say. ♦ **here and now** the present moment; straight away. **here and there** in various places; irregularly or thinly. **neither here nor there** of no particular importance or relevance.

hereabouts or **hereabout** *adv* around or near this place; within this area.

hereafter *adv, formal* **1** after this time; in a future time, life or state. **2** in a legal document or case: from this point on. ♦ **the hereafter** the after-life.

hereby *adv, formal* **1** not far off. **2** as a result of this or by this.

hereditable *adj* relating to something that may be inherited.

hereditary *adj* **1** descending or acquiring by inheritance. **2** passed down or transmitted genetically to offspring: *a hereditary disease.* **3** succeeding to a title or position, etc by inheritance. **4** passed down according to inheritance.

heredity *n* (**-ies**) **1** the transmission of recognizable and genetically based characteristics from one generation to the next. **2** the total quantity of such characteristics inherited.

herein *adv* **1** *formal* in this case or respect. **2** *law & formal* contained within this letter or document, etc.

hereinafter *adv, law & formal* later in this document or form, etc.

hereof *adv, law & formal* relating to or concerning this.

hereon *adv, formal* on, upon or to this point.

heresy /ˈhɛrəsɪ/ *n* (**-ies**) **1** an opinion or belief contrary to the authorized teaching of a particular religion. **2** an opinion that contradicts a conventional or traditional belief.

heretic /ˈherətɪk/ n someone who believes in, endorses or practises heresy. ○ **heretical** adj.

hereto adv, law & formal **1** to this place or document. **2** for this purpose.

heretofore adv, law & formal before or up to this time; formerly.

hereupon adv, law & formal **1** on this. **2** immediately after or as a result of this.

herewith adv, law & formal with this; enclosed or together with this letter, etc.

heritable adj **1** of property: able to be inherited or passed down. **2** of people: able or in a position to inherit property.

heritage n **1** something that is inherited. **2** the characteristics, qualities, property, etc inherited at birth. **3** the buildings, countryside, cultural traditions, etc seen as a people's or country's defining qualities.

hermaphrodite n a person, plant or animal that has both male and female reproductive organs.

hermetic or **hermetical** adj perfectly closed or sealed so as to be airtight. ○ **hermetically** adv.

hermit n **1** an ascetic who leads an isolated life for religious reasons. **2** someone who lives a solitary life. ○ **hermitic** adj.

hermitage n **1** the dwelling-place of a hermit. **2** a secluded place or abode; a retreat.

hernia n the protrusion of an organ (esp part of the viscera) through an opening or weak spot in the wall of its surroundings. ○ **herniated** adj.

hero n (**heroes**) **1** a man distinguished by his bravery and strength. **2** in novels, plays, films, etc: a principal male character or one whose life is the theme of the story. Compare HEROINE.

heroic adj **1** supremely courageous and brave. **2** relating to or concerning heroes or heroines. ○ **heroically** adv.

heroics pl n **1** over-dramatic or extravagant speech. **2** excessively bold behaviour.

heroin n a powerful analgesic drug produced from MORPHINE, used illegally as a highly addictive narcotic.

heroine n **1** a woman distinguished by her bravery or her achievements; any illustrious woman. **2** in novels, plays, films, etc: a principal female character or one whose life is the theme of the story. Compare HERO.

heroism n the qualities of a hero.

heron n a large wading bird with a long neck and legs, and usu with grey and white plumage.

hero-worship n **1** an excessive fondness and admiration for someone. **2** the worship of heroes in antiquity. ➤ vb to idealize or to have a great admiration for someone.

herpes /ˈhɜːpiːz/ n any of various contagious skin diseases caused by a virus which gives rise to watery blisters.

herpetology n the study of reptiles and amphibians.

herring n (**herring** or **herrings**) a small edible silvery sea fish, found in large shoals in northern waters.

herringbone n a zigzag pattern, like the spine of a herring, woven into cloth.

hers pron the one or ones belonging to HER. ♦ **of hers** relating to or belonging to HER.

herself pron **1** the reflexive form of HER and SHE: She made herself a dress. **2** used for emphasis: She did it herself. **3** her normal self or true character: She isn't feeling herself. **4** (also **by herself**) alone; without help.

hertz n (pl **hertz**) the SI unit of frequency, equal to one cycle per second.

he's contraction **1** he is. **2** he has.

hesitant adj uncertain; holding back; doubtful. ○ **hesitance** and **hesitancy** n. ○ **hesitantly** adv.

hesitate vb, intr **1** to falter or delay in speaking, acting or making a decision; to be in doubt. **2** to be unwilling to do or say something, often because one is uncertain if it is right. ○ **hesitatingly** adv. ○ **hesitation** n.

hessian n a coarse cloth, similar to sacking, made from hemp or jute.

heterocyclic adj, chem of a compound: having a closed chain of atoms where at least one is not the same as the others. Compare HOMOCYCLIC.

heterodoxy n (-ies) a belief, esp a religious one, that is different from the one most commonly accepted.

heterodyne adj, electronics in radio communication: superimposing one wave on another continuous wave of slightly different wavelength, creating beats.

heterogamy n **1** genetics reproduction from unlike reproductive cells. **2** bot the presence of different kinds of flowers (eg male, female, hermaphrodite, neuter) in the same inflorescence. **3** bot CROSS-POLLINATION. ○ **heterogamous** adj.

heterogeneous adj composed of parts, people, things, etc that are not related to each other, or are of different kinds. ○ **heterogeneity** n.

heterologous adj not homologous; different in form and origin.

heterosexual adj **1** having a sexual attraction to people of the opposite sex. **2** of a relationship: between a man and a woman. ➤ n a heterosexual person. ○ **heterosexuality** n. ○ **heterosexually** adv.

het up adj, colloq angry; agitated.

heuristic /hjʊəˈrɪstɪk/ adj **1** serving or leading to discover or find out. **2** of a teaching method: encouraging a desire in learners to find their own solutions.

hew vb (past participle **hewn**) **1** to cut, fell or sever something using an axe, etc. **2** to carve or shape something from wood or stone.

hex n **1** a witch, wizard or wicked spell. **2** anything that brings bad luck. ➤ vb to bring misfortune; to bewitch.

hexad n any group or series of six.

hexadecimal *adj, comput* relating to or being a number system with a base of 16 (see BASE[1] *noun* sense 8). ➤ *n* 1 such a system. 2 the notation used in the system. 3 a number expressed using the system.

hexagon *n* a plane figure with six sides and angles. ○ **hexagonal** /hɛk'saɡənəl/ *adj.*

hexameter /hɛk'samɪtə(r)/ *n* a line or verse with six feet.

hey *exclam, colloq* 1 a shout expressing joy, surprise, interrogation or dismay. 2 a call to attract attention. ♦ **hey presto!** a conjuror's expression, usu used at the successful finale of a trick.

heyday *n* a period of great success, power, prosperity, popularity, etc.

Hf *symbol, chem* hafnium.

Hg *symbol, chem* mercury.

HGV *abbrev, Brit* heavy goods vehicle.

hi *exclam, colloq* 1 a casual form of greeting. 2 a word used to attract attention.

hiatus /haɪ'eɪtəs/ *n* (**hiatus** or **hiatuses**) an opening or gap; a break in something which should be continuous.

hibernal *adj* referring or belonging to the winter; wintry.

hibernate *vb, intr* of certain animals: to pass the winter in a dormant state; to be completely inactive. ○ **hibernation** *n.*

Hibernian *literary, adj* relating to Ireland. ➤ *n* a native of Ireland.

hibiscus *n* a tropical tree or shrub with large brightly coloured flowers.

hiccup or **hiccough** /'hɪkʌp/ *n* 1 a an involuntary spasm of the diaphragm; b a burping sound caused by this. 2 *colloq* a temporary and usu minor setback, difficulty or interruption. ➤ *vb* (**hiccuped, hiccuping**) 1 *intr* to produce a hiccup or hiccups. 2 *intr* to falter, hesitate or malfunction.

hick *n, colloq* 1 someone from the country. 2 an unsophisticated person.

hickory *n* (**-ies**) 1 a N American tree of the walnut family, with edible nutlike fruits. 2 its heavy strong wood.

hide[1] *vb* (**hid, hidden**) 1 to put, keep or conceal (something) from sight: *I hid the key under the doormat.* 2 to keep secret: *She hid her prison record from her employer.* 3 *intr* to conceal (oneself); to go into or stay in concealment: *I hid in the cellar.* 4 to make (something) difficult to see; to obscure: *Trees hid the cottage from the road.* ➤ *n* a concealed shelter used for observing wildlife. ○ **hidden** *adj.*

hide[2] *n* the skin of an animal, esp a large one, either raw or treated. ♦ **not** or **neither hide nor hair of sb** or **sth** not the slightest trace of them or it.

hide-and-seek or (*N Am*) **hide-and-go-seek** *n* a game in which one person seeks the others who have hidden themselves.

hideaway or **hideout** *n* a refuge or retreat; concealment.

hidebound *adj, derog* reluctant to accept new ideas or opinions, esp because of a petty, stubborn or conservative outlook.

hideous *adj* 1 dreadful; revolting; extremely ugly. 2 frightening; horrific; ghastly.

hiding[1] *n* 1 the state of being hidden or concealed. 2 concealment; a secret location. ➤ *vb, present participle of* HIDE[1].

hiding[2] *n, colloq* a severe beating. ♦ **be on a hiding to nothing** *colloq* to be in a situation in which a favourable outcome is impossible.

hie *vb* (**hied, hieing** or **hying**) *archaic* 1 *intr* to hasten or hurry. 2 to urge.

hierarchy *n* (**-ies**) 1 a system that classifies people or things according to rank, importance, etc. 2 the operation of such a system or the people who control it. ○ **hierarchical** or **hierarchic** *adj.*

hieroglyph or **hieroglyphic** *n* a character or symbol representing a word, syllable, sound or idea, esp in ancient Egyptian.

hi-fi *adj* of high fidelity. ➤ *n* a set of equipment, usu consisting of an amplifier, tape deck, CD player, record player, etc, for sound reproduction that has such a high quality that it is virtually indistinguishable from the original sound.

higgledy-piggledy *adv, adj, colloq* haphazard; in confusion; disorderly.

high *adj* 1 elevated; tall; towering: *high buildings.* 2 being a specific height: *a hundred feet high.* 3 far up from a base point, such as the ground or sea level: *a high branch • a high mountain.* 4 intense or advanced; more forceful than normal: *a high wind.* 5 at the peak or climax: *high summer.* 6 (*also* **High**) of a period or era; at the height of its development: *High Renaissance.* 7 significant; exalted or revered: *high art.* 8 of sound: acute in pitch. 9 fully developed in terms of emotions and content: *high drama.* 10 of meat: partially decomposed or tainted. 11 elated or euphoric; over-excited. 12 *colloq* under the influence of drugs or alcohol: *high on E.* 13 taller or bigger than average: *a high-necked sweater.* ➤ *adv* at or to a height; in or into an elevated position: *The plane flew high.* ➤ *n* 1 a high point or level. 2 the maximum or highest level. 3 *colloq* a state of ecstasy and euphoria, often produced by drugs or alcohol: *on a high.* 4 *meteorol* an ANTICYCLONE. ♦ **high and dry** 1 stranded or helpless; defenceless. 2 of boats: out of the water. **high and mighty** arrogant; pompous. **high as a kite** *colloq* 1 over-excited or ecstatic. 2 under the influence of drugs or alcohol. **on high** above or aloft; in heaven. **on one's high horse** *colloq* having an attitude of arrogance and imagined superiority.

highball *n, chiefly N Am* an alcoholic drink of spirits and soda served with ice in a long glass.

highbrow *often derog, n* an intellectual or learned person. ➤ *adj* of art, literature, etc: intellectual; cultured.

highchair *n* a tall chair with a small attached table for young children to eat from.

High Church *n* a section within the Church of

England which places great importance on holy ceremony and priestly authority.

high-class *adj* **1** of very high quality. **2** superior and distinguished.

high court *n* **1** a supreme court. **2** (**the High Court**) the supreme court for civil cases in England and Wales.

high-density *adj, comput* of a disk: having a large data-storage capacity.

higher education *n, Brit* education beyond secondary school level, ie at university or college, usu studying for a degree. Compare FURTHER EDUCATION.

high explosive *n* a detonating explosive of immense power and extremely rapid action, eg dynamite, TNT, etc.

highfalutin or **highfaluting** *adj, colloq* ridiculously pompous or affected.

high fidelity *n* an accurate and high quality reproduction of sound.

high-five *n, esp N Am* a sign of greeting or celebration, involving the slapping together of raised palms.

high-flier or **high-flyer** *n* **1** an ambitious person, likely to achieve their goals. **2** someone naturally skilled and competent in their career. ○ **high-flying** *adj*.

high-flown *adj* often of language: sounding grand but lacking real substance; rhetorical; extravagant.

high frequency *n* a radio frequency between 3 and 30 megahertz.

high-handed *adj* overbearing and arrogant; arbitrary. ○ **high-handedness** *n*.

high jump *n* **1** an athletic event where competitors jump over a high bar which is raised after each successful jump. **2** *colloq* a severe punishment or reproof: *He's for the high jump.* ○ **high-jumper** *n*.

highland *n* **1** (*often* **highlands**) a mountainous area of land. **2** (**the Highlands**) the mountainous area of northern Scotland. ○ **highlander** or **Highlander** *n*.

high-level language *n, comput* a programming language which allows users to employ instructions that more closely resemble their own language, rather than machine code.

high life *n* (*usu* **the high life**) luxurious living associated with the very wealthy.

highlight *n* **1** the most memorable or outstanding feature, event, experience, etc. **2** (**highlights**) lighter patches or streaks in the hair, often bleached or dyed. ➢ *vb* **1** to draw attention to or emphasize something. **2** to overlay sections of (a text) with a bright colour for special attention. **3** to put highlights in (someone's hair).

highly *adv* **1** very; extremely: *highly gratified.* **2** with approval: *He spoke highly of her.* **3** at or to a high degree; in a high position: *He is rated highly in his office.*

highly strung or **highly-strung** *adj* excitable; extremely nervous; easily upset or sensitive.

High Mass *n, RC Church* an esp elaborate form of the mass involving music, ceremonies and incense.

high-minded *adj* having or showing noble and moral ideas and principles, etc.

highness *n* **1** (**Highness**) an address used for royalty, usu as **Her Highness**, **His Highness** and **Your Highness**. **2** the state of being high.

high-pitched *adj* **1** of sounds, voices, etc: high or acute in tone. **2** of a roof: steeply angled.

high point *n* the most memorable, pleasurable, successful, etc moment or occasion.

high-powered *adj* **1** very powerful or energetic. **2** very important or responsible.

high-pressure *adj* **1** having, using or allowing the use of air, water, etc at a pressure higher than that of the atmosphere: *high-pressure water reactor.* **2** *colloq* forceful and persuasive: *high-pressure negotiations.* **3** involving considerable stress or intense activity: *a high-pressure job.*

high priest or **high priestess** *n* the chief priest or priestess of a religious group.

high-rise *adj* of a building: having many storeys: *high-rise flats.*

high-risk *adj* potentially very dangerous; particularly vulnerable to danger: *high-risk sports.*

high road *n* a public or main road; a road for general traffic.

high school *n* a secondary school, formerly often called **grammar school**.

high seas *pl n* the open ocean not under the control of any country.

high season *n* the busiest time of year at a holiday resort, tourist town, etc; the peak tourist period.

high society *n* fashionable wealthy society; the upper classes.

high-spirited *adj* daring or bold; naturally cheerful and vivacious.

high spirits *pl n* a positive, happy and exhilarated frame of mind.

high spot *n* an outstanding feature, moment, location, etc.

high street *n* **1** (*also* **High Street**) the main shopping street of a town. **2** (**the high street**) **a** shops generally; the retail trade; **b** the public, when regarded as consumers.

hightail *vb, N Am colloq* (*usu* **hightail it**) to hurry away: *Let's hightail it out of here.*

high tea *n, Brit* a meal served in the late afternoon, usu consisting of a cooked dish, with bread, cakes and tea.

high-tech, **hi-tech** or **hi-tec** *adj* employing, designed by, etc advanced and sophisticated technology.

high-tension *adj* carrying high-voltage electrical currents.

high tide or **high water** *n* **1** the highest level of a tide. **2** the time when this occurs.

high time *adv, colloq* the right or latest time by which something ought to have been done: *It's high time you went home.*

high treason *n* treason against one's sovereign or country.

high-up *n, colloq* someone in a high or advanced position.

high-voltage *adj* having or concerning a voltage large enough to cause damage or injury.

high-water mark *n* **1 a** the highest level reached by a tide, river, etc; **b** a mark indicating this. **2** the highest point reached by anything.

highway *n, chiefly N Am* a main public road.

highwayman *n, hist* a robber, usu on horseback, who robbed people travelling on public roads.

high wire *n* a tightrope stretched high above the ground for performing.

hijack *vb* **1** to take control of a vehicle, esp an aircraft, and force it to go to an unscheduled destination, often taking any passengers present as hostages. **2** to stop and rob (a vehicle). **3** to steal (goods) in transit. ○ **hijacker** *n.* ○ **hijacking** *n.*

hike *n* a long walk or tour, often for recreation, and usu in the country. ➢ *vb* **1** *intr* to go on or for a hike. **2** (*often* **hike sth up**) to pull up, raise or lift it with a jerk. **3** to increase (prices) suddenly. ○ **hiker** *n.*

hilarious *adj* extravagantly funny or humorous; merry. ○ **hilariously** *adv.* ○ **hilariousness** *n.* ○ **hilarity** *n.*

hill *n* **1** a raised area of land, smaller than a mountain. **2** an incline on a road. ○ **hilliness** *n.* ○ **hilly** *adj.* ♦ **over the hill** *colloq* past one's peak or best.

hillbilly *n* (*-ies*) *esp US derog* any unsophisticated person, particularly from a remote, mountainous or rustic area.

hillock *n* **1** a small hill. **2** a small heap or pile.

hillwalking *n* the activity of walking in hilly or mountainous country.

hilt *n* the handle, esp of a sword, dagger, knife, etc. ♦ **up to the hilt** completely; thoroughly.

him *pron* the object form of HE: *We saw him • We gave it to him.*

himself *pron* **1** the reflexive form of HIM and HE: *He made himself a drink.* **2** used for emphasis: *He did it himself.* **3** his normal self: *He's still not feeling himself after the operation.* **4** (*also* **by himself**) alone; without help.

hind¹ *adj* at the back; referring to the area behind: *hind legs.*

hind² *n* (**hind** or **hinds**) a female red deer, usu older than three years of age.

hinder¹ /ˈhɪndə(r)/ *vb* **1** to delay or hold back; to prevent the progress of something. **2** *intr* to be an obstacle; to obstruct.

hinder² /ˈhaɪndə(r)/ *adj* **1** placed at the back. **2** further back: *the hinder region.*

Hindi *n* **1** one of the official languages of India, a literary form of Hindustani, and including terms from SANSKRIT. **2** a group of Indo-European languages spoken in N India.

hindquarters *pl n* the rear parts of an animal, esp a four-legged one.

hindrance *n* **1** someone or something that hinders; an obstacle or prevention. **2** the act or an instance of hindering.

hindsight *n* wisdom or knowledge after an event.

Hindu *n* **1** someone who practises HINDUISM. **2** a native or citizen of Hindustan or India. ➢ *adj* relating or referring to Hindus or Hinduism.

Hinduism *n* the main religion of India, that includes the worship of several gods, a belief in reincarnation, and the arrangement of society into a caste system.

hinge *n* the movable hook or joint by which eg a door is fastened to a door-frame or a lid is fastened to a box, etc and also on which they turn when opened or closed. ➢ *vb* (**hinging**) **1** to provide a hinge or hinges for something. **2** *intr* (*usu* **hinge on sth**) to depend on it: *Everything hinges on their decision.*

hinny *n* (*-ies*) the offspring of a stallion and a female donkey or ass.

hint *n* **1** a distant or indirect indication or allusion; an insinuation or implication. **2** a helpful suggestion or tip. **3** a small amount; a slight impression or suggestion of something: *a hint of perfume.* ➢ *vb* **1** to indicate indirectly. **2** *intr* (*often* **hint at sth**) to suggest or imply it, esp indirectly. ♦ **take** or **get the hint** *colloq* to understand and act on what a person is hinting at.

hinterland *n* **1** the region lying inland from the coast or the banks of a river. **2** an area dependent on a nearby port, commercial site, or any centre of influence.

hip¹ *n* **1** the haunch or upper fleshy part of the thigh just below the waist. **2** the joint between the thigh bone and the pelvis. **3** *archit* the external angle created where the sloping end of a roof meets the sloping sides.

hip² *n* the red fruit of a rose, esp a wild variety.

hip³ *exclam* used to encourage a united cheer: *Hip, hip, hooray!*

hip⁴ *adj* (**hipper, hippest**) *colloq* informed about or following current fashions in music, fashion, political ideas, etc.

hip bath *n* a bath for sitting in.

hip flask *n* a flask, esp for alcoholic drink, small enough to be carried in the hip pocket.

hip-hop *n* a popular culture movement originating in the US in the early 1980s, incorporating rap music, breakdancing and graffiti art, etc.

hippie or **hippy** *n* (*-ies*) *colloq* a member of a 1960s youth subculture, typically with long hair and wearing brightly-coloured clothes, stressing the importance of self-expression and love, and rebelling against the more conservative standards and values of society.

hippo *n, colloq* short for HIPPOPOTAMUS.

hippodrome *n* **1** a variety theatre or circus. **2** in ancient Greece and Rome: a racecourse for horses and chariots.

hippopotamus *n* (**hippopotamuses** or **hippopotami** /hɪpəˈpɒtəmaɪ/) a hoofed mammal with a thick skin, large head and muzzle, and short stout legs, found in rivers and lakes in parts of Africa.

hipsters *pl n* trousers which hang from the hips rather than the waist.

hire *vb* **1** to procure the temporary use of (something belonging to someone else) in exchange for payment. **2** to employ or engage (someone) for wages. **3** (**hire sth out**) to grant the temporary use of it for payment. ➤ *n* **1** payment for the use or hire of something. **2** wages paid for services. **3** an act or instance of hiring. ○ **hirable** or **hireable** *adj*. ○ **hirer** *n*. ◆ **for hire** ready for hiring. **on hire** hired out.

hireling *n, derog* **1** a hired servant. **2** someone whose work is motivated solely by money.

hire-purchase *n, Brit* a system where a hired article becomes owned by the hirer after a specified number of payments.

hirsute /ˈhɜːsjuːt, hɜːˈsjuːt/ *adj* hairy; shaggy.

his *adj* referring or belonging to a male person or animal. ➤ *pron* the one or ones belonging to HIM. ◆ **of his** relating or belonging to HIM.

Hispanic *adj* relating to or deriving from Spain, the Spanish or Spanish-speaking communities. ➤ *n, N Am* an American of Latin-American or Spanish descent.

hiss *n* **1** a sharp sibilant sound like a sustained *s*. **2** an unwanted noise in audio reproduction: *tape hiss.* ➤ *vb* **1** *intr* of an animal, such as a snake or goose, or a person: to make such a sound, esp as a sign of disapproval or anger. **2** to show (one's disapproval of someone or something) by hissing.

histamine *n, biochem* a chemical compound released by body tissues during allergic reactions, injury, etc.

histogram *n* a statistical graph in which vertical rectangles of differing heights are used to represent a frequency distribution.

histology *n* the study of the microscopic structure of cells and tissues of living organisms. ○ **histologic** or **histological** *adj*. ○ **histologically** *adv*. ○ **histologist** *n*.

historian *n* a person who studies or writes about history.

historic *adj* famous, important or significant in history.

historical *adj* **1** relevant to or about history. **2** relevant to or about people or events in history. **3** of the study of a subject: based on its development over a period of time. **4** referring to something that actually existed or took place; authentic. ○ **historically** *adv*.

historicism *n* **1** the idea that historical events are determined by natural laws. **2** the theory that sociological circumstances are historically determined.

historicity *n* historical truth or actuality.

history *n* (*-ies*) **1** an account of past events and developments. **2** a methodical account of the origin and progress of a nation, institution, the world, etc. **3** the knowledge of past events associated with a particular nation, the world, a

person, etc. **4** the academic discipline of understanding and interpreting past events. **5** a past full of events of more than common interest: *a building with a fascinating history.* ◆ **be history** *colloq* to be finished, over, dead, etc: *He's history.* **make history** to do something significant or memorable, esp to be the first person to do so.

histrionic *adj* **1** of behaviour, etc: theatrical; melodramatic; expressing too much emotion. **2** *formerly* referring or relating to actors or acting. ➤ *n* (**histrionics**) theatrical or dramatic behaviour expressing excessive emotion and done to get attention. ○ **histrionically** *adv*.

hit *vb* (*past tense, past participle* **hit**, *present participle* **hitting**) **1** to strike (someone or something). **2** to come into forceful contact with (something). **3** of a blow, missile, etc: to reach (a target). **4** to knock (eg oneself or part of oneself) against something, esp hard or violently: *She hit her head on the door.* **5** to affect suddenly and severely: *The sad news hit her hard.* **6** *intr* to strike or direct a blow. **7** *colloq* to find or attain (an answer, etc) by chance: *You've hit it!* **8** to reach or arrive at: *They hit an all-time low.* **9** *sport* to drive (a ball) with a stroke of the bat. **10** *colloq* to reach (a place): *We'll hit the city tomorrow.* ➤ *n* **1** a stroke or blow. **2** *sport* a successful stroke or shot. **3** *colloq* something of extreme popularity or success: *The new cinema is a real hit.* **4** an effective remark, eg a sarcasm or witticism. **5** *slang* a murder, esp one by organized gangs. **6** *slang* a dose of a hard drug. ◆ **hit it off** (**with sb**) to get on well (with them). ◇ **hit back** to retaliate. **hit out** at or **against sb** or **sth** to attack them or it physically or verbally.

hit-and-miss or **hit-or-miss** *adj, colloq* without any order or planning; random.

hitch *vb* **1** to move (something) jerkily. **2** (*also* **hitch up**) to move or lift (something, esp an article of clothing) with a jerk. **3** (*also* **hitch up**) to hook, fasten or tether: *We hitched the caravan to the car.* **4** *colloq* **a** *intr* to hitchhike; **b** to obtain (a lift) as a hitchhiker. ➤ *n* **1** a small temporary setback or difficulty. **2** a jerk; a sudden movement. **3** a knot for attaching two pieces of rope together. ○ **hitcher** *n*. ◆ **get hitched** *colloq* to get married.

hitchhike *vb, intr* to travel, esp long distances, by obtaining free lifts from passing vehicles. ○ **hitchhiker** *n*.

hi-tec or **hi-tech** see HIGH-TECH

hither *adv, old use* to this place. ◆ **hither and thither** in different directions; this way and that.

hitherto *adv* up to this or that time.

hit list *n, colloq* a list of targeted victims.

hit man *n, colloq* someone hired to assassinate or attack others.

HIV *abbrev* human immunodeficiency virus, a virus which breaks down the human body's natural immune system, often leading to AIDS.

hive *n* **1** a box or basket for housing bees. **2** a colony of bees living in such a place. **3** a scene of extreme animation, eg where people are working busily: *a hive of activity.* ◊ **hive sth off 1** to separate (a company, etc) from a larger organization. **2** to divert (assets or sectors of an industrial organization) to other organizations, esp private ones. **3** to assign (work) to a subsidiary company.

hives *pl n* raised red or white itchy patches on the skin.

hiya *exclam, slang* a familiar greeting.

HM *abbrev* Her or His Majesty or Majesty's.

Ho *symbol, chem* holmium.

ho or **hoh** *exclam* **1** a call or shout to attract attention or indicate direction or destination. **2** (*esp* **ho-ho**) representation of laughter.

hoar *adj, esp poetic* white or greyish-white, esp with age or frost.

hoard *n* a store of money, food or treasure, usu one hidden away for use in the future. ➤ *vb, tr & intr* to store or gather (food, money or treasure), often secretly, and esp for use in the future. ◊ **hoarder** *n.*

> **hoard** There is sometimes a spelling confusion between **hoard** and **horde**.

hoarding *n* **1** a screen of light boards, eg round a building site. **2** a similar wooden surface for displaying advertisements, posters, etc.

hoarfrost *n* the white frost on grass, leaves, etc in the morning formed by freezing dew after a cold night.

hoarse *adj* **1** of the voice: rough and husky, esp because of a sore throat or excessive shouting. **2** of a person: having a hoarse voice. ◊ **hoarsely** *adv.* ◊ **hoarseness** *n.*

hoary *adj* (*-ier, -iest*) **1** white or grey with age. **2** ancient. **3** overused and trite.

hoax *n* a deceptive trick played either humorously or maliciously. ➤ *vb* to trick or deceive with a hoax. ◊ **hoaxer** *n.*

hob *n* the flat surface on which pots are heated, either on top of a cooker or as a separate piece of equipment.

hobbit *n* one of an imaginary race of people, half the size of humans and hairy-footed, living below the ground.

hobble *vb* **1** *intr* to walk awkwardly and unsteadily by taking short unsteady steps. **2** to loosely tie the legs of (a horse) together, to inhibit its movement. **3** to hamper or impede. ➤ *n* **1** an awkward and irregular gait. **2** something used to hamper an animal's feet.

hobbledehoy *n* an awkward youth.

hobby[1] *n* (*-ies*) an activity or occupation carried out in one's spare time for amusement or relaxation.

hobby[2] *n* (*-ies*) a small species of falcon.

hobby-horse *n* **1** a child's toy consisting of a long stick with a horse's head at one end that they prance about with, as if riding a horse. **2** a subject which a person talks about frequently.

hobgoblin *n* a mischievous or evil spirit.

hobnail *n* a short nail with a large strong head for protecting the soles of boots, shoes and horseshoes. ◊ **hobnailed** *adj.*

hobnob *vb* (**hobnobbed, hobnobbing**) *intr* (*also* **hobnob with**) to associate or spend time socially or talk informally (with someone).

hobo *n* (**hobos** or **hoboes**) *N Am* a tramp or homeless person.

Hobson's choice *n* the choice of taking the thing offered, or nothing at all.

hock[1] *n* **1** the joint on the hind leg of horses and other hoofed mammals, corresponding to the ankle joint on a human leg. **2** the joint of meat extending upwards from the hock joint.

hock[2] *n* a German white wine from the Rhine valley.

hock[3] *vb, colloq* to pawn. ➤ *n* (*always* **in hock**) *colloq* **1** in debt. **2** in prison. **3** in pawn; having been pawned.

hockey *n* **1** a ball game played by two teams of eleven players with long clubs curved at one end, each team attempting to score goals. **2** *N Am* ICE HOCKEY.

hocus-pocus *n, colloq* **1** the skill of trickery or deception. **2** a conjurer's chant while performing a magic trick.

hod *n* an open V-shaped box on a pole, used for carrying bricks, etc.

hodgepodge see HOTCHPOTCH

hoe *n* a long-handled tool with a narrow blade, used for loosening soil, weeding, etc. ➤ *vb* (**hoed, hoeing**) **1** to dig, loosen or weed (the ground, etc) using a hoe. **2** *intr* to use a hoe.

hoedown *n, esp US* **1** a country dance, esp a square dance. **2** a gathering for performing such dances.

hog *n* **1** *N Am* a general name for a PIG. **2** a castrated boar. **3** a pig reared specifically for slaughter. **4** *colloq* a greedy, inconsiderate and often coarse person. ➤ *vb* (**hogged, hogging**) *colloq* to take, use, occupy, etc selfishly. ♦ **go the whole hog** to carry out or do something completely.

hogback or **hog's-back** *n* a steep-sided hill-ridge.

Hogmanay *n, Scot* New Year's Eve or a celebration of this time.

hogshead *n* **1** a large cask for liquids. **2** a liquid or dry measure of capacity (usu about 63 gallons or 238 litres).

hogtie *vb* **1** to tie (someone) up by fastening all four limbs together. **2** to frustrate, obstruct or impede.

hogwash *n, colloq* worthless nonsense.

hoh see HO

hoi see HOY

hoick or **hoik** *vb, colloq* to lift up abruptly.

hoi polloi *pl n* (*usu* **the hoi polloi**) the masses; the common people.

hoist *vb* **1** to lift or heave up. **2** to raise or heave up using lifting equipment. ➤ *n* **1** *colloq* the act of hoisting. **2** equipment for hoisting heavy articles.

hoity-toity *adj* arrogant; superciliously haughty.

hokum *n, N Am slang* **1** nonsense. **2** pretentious or over-sentimental material in a play, film, etc.

hold¹ *vb (past tense & past participle **held**)* **1** to have or keep in one's hand or hands. **2** to have in one's possession. **3** to think or believe. **4** to retain or reserve. **5** *tr & intr* to keep or stay in a specified state or position: *hold firm*. **6** *intr* to remain in position, esp when under pressure. **7** to detain or restrain. **8** to contain or be able to contain: *This bottle holds three pints*. **9** to conduct or carry on: *to hold a conversation • to hold a meeting*. **10** to have (a position of responsibility, a job, etc): *She held office for two years*. **11** to have or possess: *He holds the world record*. **12** to keep or sustain (a person's attention). **13** to affirm or allege. **14** to maintain one's composure and awareness, and not suffer any bad effects, even after large amounts of (alcohol): *She can hold her drink*. **15** *intr* of weather: to continue. **16** to consider to be; to think or believe. **17** *intr* to continue to be valid or apply: *The law still holds*. **18** to defend from the enemy. **19** to cease or stop: *hold fire*. **20** *mus* to continue (a note or pause). **21** *intr* of a telephone caller: to wait without hanging up. **22** to have in store or readiness: *Who knows what the future holds?* ➤ *n* **1** an act of holding. **2** a power or influence: *They have a hold over him*. **3** a way of holding someone, esp in certain sports, eg judo. **4** a place of confinement; a prison cell. **5** an object to hold on to. ♦ **get hold of sb** *colloq* to manage to find and speak to them. **get hold of sth** to find, obtain or buy it. **hold good** or **hold true** to remain true or valid; to apply. **hold one's own** to maintain one's position, eg in an argument, etc. **hold one's peace** or **tongue** to remain silent. **on hold** in a state of suspension; temporarily postponed: *She put the trip on hold*. **with no holds barred** without any restrictions. ◊ **hold back** to hesitate; to restrain oneself. **hold sb back** to restrain them from doing something. **hold sth back** to keep it in reserve. **hold sth down** to manage to keep it: *to hold down a job*. **hold sth in** to restrain or check it. **hold off** or **hold off doing sth** to delay or not begin to do it. **hold on** *colloq* to wait. **hold on to sth** to keep or maintain it in one's possession. **hold out** **1** to stand firm, esp resisting difficulties: *They held out against the enemy*. **2** to endure or last. **hold out for sth** to wait persistently for something one wants or has demanded. **hold out on sb** *colloq* to keep back money, information, etc from them. **hold sth over** to postpone or delay it. **hold sb up** **1** to delay or hinder them. **2** to stop and rob them. **hold sth up** to delay or hinder it. **hold sb** or **sth up as sth** to exhibit them or it as an example: *She held them up as models of integrity*. **hold with sth** *(with negatives and in questions)* to endorse or approve of it: *I don't hold with violence*.

hold² *n* a storage cavity in ships and aeroplanes.

holdall *n* a large strong bag for carrying miscellaneous articles, esp clothes when travelling.

holder *n* **1** someone or something that holds or grips. **2** *law* someone who has ownership or control of something, eg a shareholder.

holdfast *n* **1** something that holds fast or firmly. **2** a device for fixing or holding something together, eg a long nail or a hook.

holding *n* **1** land held by lease. **2** an amount of land, shares, etc owned by a person or company.

hold-up *n* **1** a delay or setback. **2** a robbery, usu with violence or threats of violence.

hole *n* **1** a hollow area or cavity in something solid. **2** an aperture or gap in or through something: *a hole in the sock*. **3** an animal's nest or refuge. **4** *colloq* an unpleasant or contemptible place. **5** *colloq* an awkward or difficult situation. **6** *colloq* a fault or error: *a hole in the argument*. **7** *golf* **a** a hollow in the middle of each green, into which the ball is hit; **b** each section of a golf course extending from the tee to the green. ➤ *vb* **1** to make a hole in something. **2** to hit or play (a ball, etc) into a hole. ♦ **make a hole in sth** *colloq* to use up a large amount of it, eg money. **pick holes in sth** to find fault with it. ◊ **hole out** *golf* to play the ball into the hole. **hole up** *colloq* to go to earth; to hide.

hole-and-corner *adj* secret; underhand.

hole in one *n, golf* a hit of the ball from the tee which results in it going straight into the hole.

hole in the wall *n, colloq* an automated cash dispensing machine sited in a wall, eg outside a bank, etc.

holey *adj (-ier, -iest)* full of holes.

holiday *n* **1** *(often **holidays**)* a period of recreational time spent away from work, study or general routine. **2** a day when no work is done, orig a religious festival. ➤ *vb, intr* to spend or go away for a holiday in a specified place or at a specified time: *They holiday every year in Cornwall*.

holidaymaker *n* a person on holiday.

holier-than-thou *adj* of a person, attitude, etc: self-righteous, often sanctimoniously or patronizingly so.

holiness *n* **1** the state of being holy; sanctity. **2** *(**Holiness**)* a title of the Pope, used to address or refer to him, in the form of **Your Holiness** and **His Holiness**.

holism *n, philos* **1** the theory that a complex entity or system is more than merely the sum of its parts or elements. **2** the treatment of a disease, etc by taking social, economic, psychological, etc factors into consideration, rather than just the person's ailment or condition. ○ **holistic** *adj*. ○ **holistically** *adv*.

hollandaise sauce /ˈhɒləndeɪz/ *n* a sauce made from egg yolks, butter and lemon juice or vinegar.

holler *vb, tr & intr, colloq* to shout or yell. ➤ *n* a shout or yell.

hollow *adj* **1** containing an empty space within

or below; not solid. **2** sunken or depressed: *hollow cheeks*. **3** of a sound: echoing as if made in a hollow place. **4** without any great significance: *a hollow victory*. **5** insincere: *hollow promises*. ➤ *n* **1** a hole or cavity in something. **2** a valley or depression in the land. ➤ *adv, colloq* completely: *beaten hollow*. ➤ *vb* (*usu* **hollow out**) to make hollow. ○ **hollowly** *adv.* ○ **hollowness** *n*.

holly *n* (*-ies*) an evergreen tree or shrub with dark shiny prickly leaves and red berries.

hollyhock *n* a tall garden plant of the mallow family, with thick hairy stalks and colourful flowers.

holmium *n, chem* a soft silver-white metallic element.

holocaust *n* **1** a large-scale slaughter or destruction of life, often by fire. **2** (**the Holocaust**) the mass murder of Jews by the Nazis during World War II.

Holocene *n* the most recent geological period, during which modern human civilization began.

hologram *n, photog* a three-dimensional photographic image produced without a lens, by the interference between two split laser beams.

holograph *n* a document completely in the handwriting of the author.

holography *n* the process or study of producing or using holograms. ○ **holographic** *adj.*

hols *pl n, colloq* holidays.

holster *n* a leather case for a gun, often a belt round a person's hips or shoulders.

holt *n* an animal's den, esp that of an otter.

holy *adj* (*-ier, -iest*) **1** associated with God or gods; religious or sacred. **2** morally pure and perfect; saintly. **3** sanctified or sacred. ○ **holily** *adv.*

holy day *n* a religious festival.

the Holy Ghost, the Holy Spirit *or* **the Spirit** *n, Christianity* the third person in the Trinity.

the Holy Land *n, Christianity* Palestine, esp Judea, the scene of Christ's ministry in the New Testament.

holy of holies *n* any place or thing regarded as especially sacred.

holy orders *pl n* the office of an ordained member of the clergy.

the Holy See *n, RC Church* the see or office of the Pope in Rome.

holy war *n* a war waged in the name of or in support of a religion.

holy water *n* water blessed for use in religious ceremonies.

homage *n* a display of great respect towards someone or something; an acknowledgement of their superiority.

home *n* **1** the place where one lives, often with one's family. **2** the country or area one orig comes from, either a birthplace or where one grew up. **3** a place where something first occurred, or was first invented. **4** an institution for people who need care or rest, eg the elderly,

orphans, etc. **5** the den, base or finishing point in some games and races. ➤ *adj* **1** being at or belonging to one's horse, country, family, sports ground, etc. **2** made or done at home or in one's own country: *home baking*. **3** of a sporting event: played on one's own ground, etc: *a home match*. ➤ *adv* **1** to or at one's home. **2** to the target place, position, etc: *to hit the point home*. **3** to the furthest or final point; as far as possible: *to hammer the nail home*. ➤ *vb, intr* **1** of an animal, esp a bird: to return home safely. **2** (*often* **home in on sth**) to identify (a target or destination) and focus on attempting to reach it. ♦ **bring sth home to sb** to make it clear or obvious to them. **home and dry** having achieved one's goal. **home from home** a place where one feels completely comfortable, relaxed, and happy, as if at home. **nothing to write home about** *colloq* unremarkable.

homecoming *n* an arrival home, usu of someone who has been away for a long time.

home economics *sing n* the study of domestic science, household skills and management.

home farm *n, Brit* a farm, usu one of several on a large estate, set aside to produce food, etc for the owner of the estate.

home help *n, Brit* a person who is hired, often by the local authority, to help sick, aged, etc people with domestic chores.

homeland *n* **1** one's native country; the country of one's ancestors. **2** *hist* in South Africa: an area of land reserved by the government for the Black population.

homeless *adj* **1** of a person: without a home and living, sleeping, etc in public places or squats. **2** of an animal: without an owner. ○ **homelessness** *n*.

homely *adj* (*-ier, -iest*) **1** relating to home; familiar. **2** making someone feel at home. **3** of a person: honest and unpretentious; pleasant. **4** *N Am* of a person: plain and unattractive.

home-made *adj* **1** of food, clothes, etc: made at home. **2** made in one's native country.

home movie *n* a motion picture made by an amateur, usu using a portable cine camera or camcorder.

homeopathy *or* **homoeopathy** *n* a system of alternative medicine where a disease is treated by prescribing small doses of drugs which produce symptoms similar to those of the disease itself. ○ **homeopath** *n*. ○ **homeopathic** *adj.* ○ **homeopathically** *adv.* ○ **homeopathist** *n*.

homer *n* **1** a breed of pigeon that can be trained to return home from a distance. **2** *baseball* a home run. **3** *colloq* an out-of-hours job illicitly done by a tradesman for cash-in-hand payment.

home rule *n* the government of a country and its internal affairs by its own citizens.

homesick *adj* pining for one's home and family when away from them. ○ **homesickness** *n*.

homespun *adj* **1** of character, advice, thinking,

etc: artless, simple and straightforward. **2** *old use* of cloth: woven at home. ➤ *n* a cloth produced at home.

homestead *n* **1** a dwelling-house and its surrounding land and buildings. **2** *N Am, hist* an area of land granted to a settler for development as a farm.

home town *n* the town where one lives or lived; the place of one's birth.

home truth *n* (*usu* **home truths**) a true but unwelcome fact, usu about oneself.

homeward *adj* going home. ➤ *adv* (*also* **homewards**) towards home.

homework *n* **1** work or study done at home, esp for school. **2** paid work, esp work paid for according to quantity rather than time, done at home.

home worker *n* someone who works at home, but under similar terms and conditions to a worker in a conventional office, and linked to an office by a computer. ○ **homeworking** *n*.

homey or **homy** *adj* (**-ier, -iest**) homelike; homely.

homicide *n* **1** the murder or manslaughter of one person by another. **2** a person who commits this act. ○ **homicidal** *adj*.

homily *n* (**-ies**) **1** a sermon. **2** a long, tedious talk.

homing *vb, present participle of* HOME. ➤ *adj* **1** of animals, esp pigeons: trained to return home, usu from a distance. **2** of navigational devices on missiles, crafts, etc: guiding towards a target.

hominid *n* a primate belonging to the family which includes modern humans and their fossil ancestors.

hominoid *n* any animal resembling a human.

hominy *n, N Am* dried maize kernels or GRITS, cooked by boiling.

homo *n, adj, colloq, usu derog* short form of HOMOSEXUAL.

homocyclic *adj, chem* of a compound: having a closed chain of similar atoms. Compare HETEROCYCLIC.

homoeopathy see HOMEOPATHY

homogeneous *adj* **1** made up of parts or elements that are all of the same kind or nature. **2** made up of similar parts or elements. ○ **homogeneity** *n*.

homogenize or **-ise** *vb* **1** to make or become homogeneous. **2** to break up the fat droplets of (a liquid, esp milk) into smaller particles so that they are evenly distributed throughout the liquid.

homograph *n* a word with the same spelling as another, but with a different meaning, origin, and sometimes a different pronunciation, eg *tear* (rip) and *tear* (teardrop).

homologous *adj* **1** having a related or similar function or position. **2** of plant or animal structures: having a common origin, but having evolved in such a way that they no longer perform the same functions or resemble each other, eg a human arm and a bird's wing.

○ **homology** *n* (**-ies**).

homologue or (*US*) **homolog** *n* anything which is homologous to something else.

homonym *n* a word with the same sound and spelling as another, but with a different meaning, eg *kind* (helpful) and *kind* (sort).

homophobe *n* a person with a strong aversion to or hatred of homosexuals. ○ **homophobia** *n*. ○ **homophobic** *adj*.

homophone *n* **1** a word which sounds the same as another word but is different in spelling and/or meaning, eg *bear* and *bare*. **2** a character or characters that represent the same sound as another, eg *f* and *ph*.

homophony *n, mus* a style of composition in which one part or voice carries the melody, and other parts or voices add texture with simple accompaniment. Compare POLYPHONY.

homosexual *n* a person who is sexually attracted to people of the same sex. ➤ *adj* **1** having a sexual attraction to people of the same sex. **2** relating to or concerning a homosexual or homosexuals. ○ **homosexuality** *n*. ○ **homosexually** *adv*.

honcho *n, N Am colloq* an important person, esp someone in charge; a big shot.

hone *n* a smooth stone used for sharpening tools. ➤ *vb* to sharpen with or as if with a hone.

honest *adj* **1** not inclined to steal, cheat or lie; truthful and trustworthy. **2** fair or justified: *an honest wage*. **3** sincere and respectable: *an honest attempt*. **4** ordinary and undistinguished; unremarkable: *an honest wine*. ➤ *adv, colloq* honestly: *I do like it, honest*.

honest broker *n* an impartial and objective mediator in a dispute.

honestly *adv* **1** in an honest way. **2** in truth. ➤ *exclam* expressing annoyance or disbelief.

honesty *n* **1** the state of being honest and truthful. **2** integrity and candour. **3** a common garden plant with silvery leaf-like pods.

honey *n* **1** a sweet viscous fluid made by bees from the nectar of flowers, and stored in honeycombs. **2** *N Am colloq* a term of endearment used to address a loved one.

honeycomb *n* **1** the structure made up of rows of hexagonal wax cells in which bees store their eggs and honey. **2** anything like a honeycomb. **3** a bewildering maze of cavities, rooms, passages, etc. ➤ *vb* to form like a honeycomb.

honeyed or **honied** *adj* of a voice, words, etc: sweet, flattering or soothing.

honeymoon *n* **1** the first weeks after marriage, often spent on holiday, before settling down to the normal routine of life. **2** a period of unusual or temporary goodwill, enthusiasm and harmony at the start eg of a new business relationship. ➤ *vb, intr* to spend time on a honeymoon, usu on holiday. ○ **honeymooner** *n*.

honeysuckle *n* a climbing garden shrub with sweet-scented white, pale-yellow or pink flowers.

honk *n* **1** the cry of a wild goose. **2** the sound

made by a car horn. ➢ *vb, tr & intr* to make or cause something to make a honking noise.

honky or **honkie** *n* (*-ies*) *N Am, dated Black slang, offensive* a white person.

honky-tonk *n, colloq* **1** a style of jangly popular piano music based on RAGTIME. **2** *N Am slang* a cheap seedy nightclub.

honorarium *n* (**honorariums** or **honoraria** /ɒnəˈrɛərɪə/) a fee paid to a professional person in return for services carried out on a voluntary basis.

honorary *adj* **1** conferring or bestowing honour. **2** of a title, etc: given as a mark of respect, and without the usual functions, dues, etc. **3** of an official position: receiving no payment.

honorific *adj* showing or giving honour or respect. ➢ *n* a form of title, address or mention.

Honour *n* a title of respect given to judges, mayors, etc, in the form of **Your Honour, His Honour** and **Her Honour.**

honour or (*US*) **honor** *n* **1** the esteem or respect earned by or paid to a worthy person. **2** great respect or public regard. **3** a source of credit, such as fame, glory or distinction, or an award, etc in recognition of this. **4** a scrupulous sense of what is right; a high standard of moral behaviour or integrity. **5** a pleasure or privilege. **6** *old use* a woman's chastity or virginity, or her reputation for this. ➢ *vb* **1** to respect or venerate; to hold in high esteem. **2** to confer an award, title, etc on someone as a mark of respect for an ability, achievement, etc. **3** to pay (a bill, debt, etc) when it falls due. **4** to keep or meet (a promise or agreement). ◆ **do the honours** *colloq* to perform or carry out a task, esp that of a host. **in honour of sb** or **sth** out of respect for or in celebration of them or it. **on one's honour** under a moral obligation.

honourable or (*US*) **honorable** *adj* **1** deserving or worthy of honour. **2** having high moral principles. **3** (**Honourable**) a prefix to the names of certain people as a courtesy title. ○ **honourableness** *n*. ○ **honourably** *adv.*

honour-bound *adj* obliged to do something by duty or by moral considerations.

honours *pl n* **1** a higher grade of university degree with distinction for specialized or advanced work. **2** a mark of civility or respect, esp at a funeral. **3** in some card games: any of the top four or five cards.

hooch or **hootch** *n, N Am colloq* any strong alcoholic drink, such as whisky, esp when distilled or obtained illegally.

hood[1] *n* **1** a flexible covering for the whole head and back of the neck, often attached to a coat at the collar. **2** a folding and often removable roof or cover on a car, pushchair, etc. **3** *N Am* a car bonnet. **4** an ornamental loop of material worn as part of academic dress, specifically coloured according to the university and degree obtained. **5** a covering of a hawk's head. **6** any projecting or protective covering. **7** an expanding section of a cobra's neck. ➢ *vb* to cover with a hood.

hood[2] *n, slang* a hoodlum.

hood[3] or **'hood** /hʊd/ *n, US slang* a shortened form of NEIGHBOURHOOD.

hooded *adj* having, covered with, or shaped like a hood.

hoodie *n, colloq* a hooded jacket or sweatshirt.

hoodlum *n* **1** *N Am* a small-time criminal. **2** a violent, destructive or badly behaved youth.

hoodoo *n* **1** voodoo. **2** a jinx or bad luck. **3** a thing or person that brings such. ➢ *vb* (**hoodoos, hoodooed**) to bring bad luck to someone.

hoodwink *vb* to trick or deceive.

hooey *n, slang* nonsense.

hoof *n* (**hoofs** or **hooves**) the horny structure that grows beneath and covers the ends of the digits in the feet of certain mammals, eg horses. ◆ **hoof it** *slang* **1** to go on foot. **2** to dance. **on the hoof** of cattle, horses, etc: alive.

hoofer *n, slang* a professional dancer.

hoo-ha or **hoo-hah** *n, colloq* excited and noisy talk; a commotion.

hook *n* **1** a curved piece of metal or similar material, used for catching or holding things. **2** a snare, trap, attraction, etc. **3** a curved tool used for cutting grain, branches, etc. **4** a sharp bend or curve, eg in land or a river. **5** *boxing* a swinging punch with the elbow bent. **6** *sport* a method of striking the ball causing it to curve in the air. **7** *cricket, golf* a shot that causes the ball to curve in the direction of the swing. **8** *pop mus* a catchy or easily memorized phrase. ➢ *vb* **1** to catch, fasten or hold with or as if with a hook. **2** to form into or with a hook. **3** to ensnare, trap, attract, etc. **4 a** *golf, cricket* to hit (the ball) out round the other side of one's body, to the left if the player is right-handed, and vice versa; **b** of the ball: to curve in this direction. **5** in a rugby scrum: to catch (the ball) with the foot and kick it backwards. **6** *tr & intr* to bend or curve. **7** *tr & intr* to pull abruptly. ◆ **by hook or by crook** by some means or other. **hook and eye** a device used to fasten clothes by means of a hook that catches in a loop or eye. **hook, line and sinker** *colloq* completely. **off the hook 1** *colloq* out of trouble or difficulty; excused of the blame for something. **2** of a telephone receiver: not on its rest, and so not able to receive incoming calls.

hookah or **hooka** *n* an oriental tobacco pipe consisting of a tube which passes through water, used to cool the smoke before it is inhaled.

hooked *adj* **1** curved like a hook. **2** *colloq* physically, emotionally, etc dependent.

hooker *n* **1** *colloq* a prostitute. **2** *rugby* the forward whose job is to hook the ball out of a scrum.

hookey or **hooky** *n, N Am colloq* absence from school without permission: *playing hookey.*

hook-up *n* a temporary link-up of different broadcasting stations, esp the radio and a television channel, for a special transmission.

hookworm *n* a parasitic worm with hook-like

parts in its mouth, which lives in the intestines of animals and humans, causing mild anaemia.

hooligan *n* a violent, destructive or badly-behaved youth. ○ **hooliganism** *n*.

hoop *n* **1** a thin ring of metal, wood, etc, esp those used round casks. **2** anything similar to this in shape. **3** a large ring made of light wood or plastic, used for amusement. **4** an iron arch through which the ball is hit in croquet. **5** a horizontal band of colour running round a sportsperson's shirt. ➢ *vb* to bind or surround with a hoop or hoops. ♦ **go** or **be put through the hoops** *colloq* to undergo or suffer a thorough and difficult test or ordeal.

hoop-la *n* **1** *Brit* a fairground game in which small rings are thrown at objects, with the thrower winning any objects encircled by the rings. **2** *US colloq* loud and excited activity or reaction.

hoorah or **hooray** see HURRAH

hoot *n* **1** the call of an owl, or a similar sound. **2** the sound of a car horn, siren, steam whistle, etc, or a similar sound. **3** a loud shout of laughter, scorn or disapproval. **4** *colloq* a hilarious person, event or thing. ➢ *vb* **1** *intr* of an owl: to make a hoot. **2** to sound (a car horn, etc). **3** *intr* of a person: to shout or laugh loudly, often expressing disapproval, scorn, etc. ♦ **not care** or **give a hoot** or **two hoots** *colloq* not to care at all.

hooter *n* **1** a person or thing that makes a hooting sound. **2** *Brit colloq* a nose.

Hoover *n*, *trademark* (*also* **hoover**) a VACUUM CLEANER. ➢ *vb* (**hoover**) *tr & intr* to clean (a carpet, etc) with a vacuum cleaner.

hooves see HOOF

hop¹ *vb* (**hopped, hopping**) **1** *intr* of a person: to jump up and down on one leg, esp forward as a form of movement. **2** *intr* of certain small birds, animals and insects: to move by jumping on both or all legs simultaneously. **3** to jump over something. **4** *intr* (*usu* **hop in, out,** *etc*) *colloq* to move in a lively or agile way in the specified direction. ➢ *n* **1** an act of hopping; a jump on one leg. **2** *colloq* a distance travelled in an aeroplane without stopping; a short journey by air. **3** *old use, colloq* an informal dance. ♦ **catch sb on the hop** *colloq* to catch them unawares or by surprise. **hop it** *Brit slang* to take oneself off; to leave. **hopping mad** *colloq* very angry or furious. **on the hop** in a state of restless activity.

hop² *n* **1** a climbing plant of the mulberry family, grown for its green cone-shaped female flowers, which are used to give a bitter flavour to beer. **2** (*usu* **hops**) these flowers. ➢ *vb* (**hopped, hopping**) **1** *intr* to pick or gather hops. **2** to flavour (beer) with hops.

hope *n* **1** a desire for something, with some confidence or expectation of success. **2** a person, thing or event that gives one good reason for hope. **3** a reason for justifying the belief that the thing desired will still occur. **4** something desired or hoped for. ➢ *vb* **1** (*also* **hope for**

sth) to wish or desire that something may happen, esp with some reason to believe that it will. **2** *intr* to have confidence.

hopeful *adj* **1** feeling, or full of, hope. **2** having qualities that excite hope. **3** likely to succeed; promising. ➢ *n* a person, esp a young one, who is ambitious or expected to succeed. ○ **hopefulness** *n*.

hopefully *adv* **1** in a hopeful way. **2** *colloq* it is to be hoped, if all goes according to plan.

hopeless *adj* **1** without hope. **2** having no reason or cause to expect a good outcome or success. **3** *colloq* having no ability; incompetent: *He is hopeless at maths.* **4** of a disease, etc: incurable. **5** of a problem: unresolvable. ○ **hopelessly** *adv*. ○ **hopelessness** *n*.

hopper¹ *n* **1** a person, animal or insect that hops. **2** *esp agric* a funnel-like device used to feed material into a container below it, or on to the ground.

hopper² *n* a person or machine that picks hops.

hopscotch *n* a children's game in which players take turns at throwing a stone into one of a series of squares marked on the ground, and hopping in the others around it in order to fetch it.

horde *n* **1** *often derog* a huge crowd or multitude, esp a noisy one. **2** a group of nomads.

> **horde** There is sometimes a spelling confusion between **horde** and **hoard**.

horizon *n* **1** the line at which the Earth and sky seem to meet. **2** the limit of a person's knowledge, interests or experience.

horizontal *adj* **1** at right angles to vertical. **2** relating to or parallel to the horizon; level or flat. **3** measured in the plane of the horizon. ➢ *n* a horizontal line, position or object. ○ **horizontally** *adv*.

hormone *n* **1** a substance secreted by an endocrine gland, and carried in the bloodstream to organs and tissues in the body, where it performs a specific physiological action. **2** an artificially manufactured chemical compound which has the same function as such a substance. **3** a substance in plants which influences their growth and development. ○ **hormonal** *adj*.

horn *n* **1** one of a pair of hard hollow outgrowths, usu pointed, on the heads of many ruminant animals, such as cattle, sheep, etc. **2** any similar structure growing on the head of another animal, such as the growth on the snout of a rhinoceros, a male deer's antlers, or a snail's tentacle. **3** the bony substance (KERATIN) of which horns are made. **4** something resembling a horn in shape. **5** a horn-shaped area of land or sea. **6** an object made of horn, or an equivalent of horn, eg a drinking vessel. **7** *mus* a wind instrument orig made from horn, now usu made of brass, specifically: **a** *Brit* a FRENCH HORN; **b** *jazz* any wind instrument. **8** an apparatus for making a warning sound, esp on motor vehicles. **9** *US slang* a telephone. ➤ *vb* **1** to fit with a horn or horns. **2** to injure or gore with a horn or horns. ➤ *adj* made of horn. ○ **horned** *adj*. ♦ **on the horns of a dilemma** having to make a choice between two equally undesirable alternatives. **pull** or **draw in one's horns 1** to control one's strong emotions. **2** to restrict or confine one's activities, esp spending, etc.

hornbeam *n* a tree similar to a beech, with hard tough wood.

hornblende *n* a dark green or black mineral that is a major component of many metamorphic and igneous rocks.

hornet *n* a large social wasp, with a brown and yellow striped body. ♦ **stir up a hornets' nest** to do something that causes trouble or hostile reactions.

horn of plenty see CORNUCOPIA (sense 1)

hornpipe *n* a lively solo jig, conventionally regarded as popular amongst sailors, or the music for this dance.

horny *adj* (**-ier, -iest**) **1** relating to or resembling horn, esp in hardness. **2** *slang* sexually excited.

horology *n* the art of measuring time or of making clocks, watches, etc.

horoscope *n* **1** an astrologer's prediction of someone's future based on the position of the stars and planets at the time of their birth. **2** a map or diagram showing the positions of the stars and planets at a particular moment in time.

horrendous *adj* causing great shock, fear or terror; dreadful or horrifying.

horrible *adj* **1** causing horror, dread or fear. **2** *colloq* unpleasant, detestable or foul. ○ **horribleness** *n*. ○ **horribly** *adv*.

horrid *adj* **1** revolting; detestable or nasty. **2** *colloq* unpleasant; distasteful. **3** spiteful or inconsiderate.

horrific *adj* **1** causing horror; terrible or frightful. **2** *colloq* very bad; awful. ○ **horrifically** *adv*.

horrify *vb* (**-ies, -ied**) to shock greatly; to cause a reaction of horror. ○ **horrified** *adj*. ○ **horrifying** *adj*.

horror *n* **1** intense fear, loathing or disgust. **2** intense dislike or hostility. **3** someone or something causing horror. **4** *colloq* a bad, distasteful or ridiculous person or thing. ➤ *adj* of literature, films, etc: with horrifying, frightening or bloodcurdling themes: *a horror film*.

horror-stricken or **horror-struck** *adj* shocked, horrified or dismayed.

hors d'oeuvre /ɔː ˈdɜːvr/ *n* (*pl* **hors d'oeuvre** or **hors d'oeuvres**) a savoury appetizer, usu served at the beginning of a meal, to whet the appetite.

horse *n* **1** a large hoofed mammal, with a long neck, a mane and long legs, used for riding or for pulling or carrying loads. **2** an adult male of this species. **3** cavalry. **4** *gymnastics* a piece of apparatus used for vaulting over, etc. **5** *in compounds* any of various types of supporting apparatus: *clothes-horse • saw-horse*. ♦ **hold**

your horses wait a moment; not so fast or hasty. **straight from the horse's mouth** directly from a well-informed and reliable source. ◊ **horse about** or **around** *colloq* to fool about.

horseback *n* the back of a horse. ♦ **on horseback** mounted on or riding a horse.

horsebox *n* a closed trailer, designed to carry horses.

horse chestnut see under CHESTNUT

horseflesh *n* **1** the flesh of a horse used as food. **2** horses as a group.

horsefly *n* (**-ies**) a large biting fly, especially troublesome to horses.

horsehair *n* hair from the mane or tail of a horse, formerly used as padding or stuffing, eg for mattresses.

horseman or **horsewoman** *n* **1** a horse rider. **2** a person skilled in riding and managing horses. ○ **horsemanship** *n*.

horseplay *n* rough boisterous play.

horsepower *n* **1** an imperial unit of power equal to 745.7 watts. **2** the power of a vehicle's engine so expressed.

horseradish *n* a plant with a pungent root, which is crushed and used to make a savoury sauce.

horse sense *n*, *colloq* plain common sense.

horseshoe *n* **1** a piece of curved iron nailed to the bottom of a horse's hoof to protect the hoof. **2** anything shaped like a horseshoe, esp as a symbol of good luck.

horse-trading *n* hard bargaining.

horsewhip *n* a long whip, used for driving or managing horses. ➤ *vb* to beat, esp severely, with a horsewhip.

horsey or **horsy** *adj* (**-ier, -iest**) **1** referring or relating to horses. **2** *often derog* of people: like a horse, esp in appearance. **3** *Brit colloq* very interested in or devoted to horses, or to racing or breeding them. ○ **horsiness** *n*.

hortative or **hortatory** *adj* giving advice or encouragement.

horticulture *n* **1** the intensive cultivation of fruit, vegetables, flowers and ornamental shrubs. **2** the art of gardening or cultivation. ○ **horticultural** *adj*. ○ **horticulturist** *n*.

hosanna *n*, *exclam* a shout of adoration and praise to God.

hose[1] *n* (*also* **hosepipe**) a flexible tube for conveying water, eg for watering plants. ➤ *vb* (*often* **hose down**) to water, clean or soak with a hose.

hose[2] *n* (*hose* or (*archaic*) *hosen*) a covering for the legs and feet, such as stockings, socks and tights.

hosiery *n* **1** stockings, socks and tights collectively. **2** knitted underwear.

hospice *n* **1** a home that specializes in the care of the sick, esp the terminally ill. **2** *hist* a HOSPITAL (sense 3).

hospitable *adj* **1** generous and welcoming towards guests. **2** showing kindness to strangers. ○ **hospitableness** *n*. ○ **hospitably** *adv*.

hospital *n* **1** an institution, staffed by doctors

and nurses, for the treatment and care of people who are sick or injured. **2** *archaic* a charitable institution providing shelter for the old and destitute, and education for the young. **3** *hist* a hostel offering lodging and entertainment for travellers, esp one kept by monks or a religious order.

hospitality *n* (*-ies*) the friendly welcome and entertainment of guests or strangers, which usu includes offering them food and drink.

hospitalize or **-ise** *vb* **1** to take or admit (someone) to hospital for treatment. **2** to injure (someone) so badly that hospital treatment is necessary. ○ **hospitalization** *n*.

host¹ *n* **1** someone who entertains someone. **2** *old use* an innkeeper or publican. **3** someone who introduces performers and participants, chairs discussions and debates, etc on a TV or radio show. **4** *biol* a plant or animal on which a parasite lives. **5** *med* the recipient of a tissue graft or organ transplant. ➤ *vb* to be the host of (an event, programme, show, etc).

host² *n* **1** a very large number; a multitude. **2** *old use* an army.

host³ *n*, *RC Church* the consecrated bread of the Eucharist, used in a Holy Communion service.

hostage *n* **1** someone who is held prisoner as a guarantee or security that the captor's demands and conditions are carried out and fulfilled. **2** the condition of being a hostage.

hostel *n* **1** a residence providing shelter for the homeless. **2** a residence for students, nurses, etc. **3** a YOUTH HOSTEL.

hosteller or (*US*) **hosteler** *n* **1** someone who lives in or regularly uses a hostel, esp a youth hostel. **2** *archaic* the keeper of a hostel or inn.

hostelling *n* the use of youth hostels when on holiday.

hostelry *n* (*-ies*) *old use, now facetious* an inn or public house.

hostess *n* **1** a female host. **2** a woman employed as a man's companion for the evening at a nightclub, dance hall, etc.

hostile *adj* **1** expressing enmity, aggression or angry opposition. **2** relating or belonging to an enemy. **3** resistant or strongly opposed to something. **4** of a place, conditions, atmosphere, etc: harsh, forbidding or inhospitable.

hostility *n* (*-ies*) **1** enmity, aggression or angry opposition. **2** (**hostilities**) acts of warfare; battles.

hot *adj* (**hotter, hottest**) **1** having or producing a great deal of heat; having a high temperature. **2** having a higher temperature than is normal or desirable. **3** of food: spicy or fiery. **4** easily made angry; excitable or passionate: *a hot temper*. **5** *slang* sexually attractive or excited. **6** of a contest or fight: intense and animated. **7** of news: recent, fresh and of particular interest. **8** strongly favoured: *a hot favourite*. **9** of jazz music: having strong and exciting rhythms, with complex improvisations. **10** of a colour: bright and fiery. **11** *slang* of goods: recently sto-

len or illegally acquired. **12** of a scent in hunting: fresh and strong, suggesting the quarry is not far ahead. **13** *slang* of information: up-to-date and reliable: *a hot tip*. **14** *colloq* of a situation: difficult, unpleasant, or dangerous: *making life hot for him*. **15** *slang* highly radioactive. **16** in certain games, etc: very close to guessing the answer or finding the person or thing sought. ➤ *adv* in a hot way; hotly: *a dish served hot*. ➤ *vb* (**hotted, hotting**) *colloq* to heat. ○ **hotly** *adv*. ○ **hotness** *n*. ♦ **go** or **sell like hot cakes** to sell or disappear rapidly; to be extremely popular. **have** or **get the hots for sb** *slang* to have a strong sexual desire for them. **hot and bothered** *colloq* anxious and confused; agitated. **hot on sth** interested in, skilled at or well-informed about it. **hot on the heels of sb** *colloq* following or pursuing them closely. **hot under the collar** *colloq* indignant or annoyed; uncomfortable. **in hot pursuit** chasing as fast or as closely as one can. ◊ **hot up** or **hot sth up** to increase in excitement, energy, danger, etc.

hot air *n*, *colloq* empty, unsubstantial or boastful talk.

hotbed *n* **1** a glass-covered bed of earth heated by a layer of fermenting manure, to encourage rapid plant growth. **2** a place where something, esp something undesirable, flourishes: *a hotbed of discontent*.

hot-blooded *adj* having strong and passionate feelings; high-spirited.

hotchpotch or **hodgepodge** *n* **1** a confused mass or jumble. **2** a mutton stew, containing many different vegetables.

hot cross bun *n* a fruit bun marked with a pastry cross on top, customarily eaten on Good Friday.

hot dog *n* a sausage in a long soft bread roll.

hotel *n* a commercial building providing accommodation, meals and other services to visitors for payment.

hotelier /hoʊˈtɛliei/ *n* a person who owns or manages a hotel.

hotfoot *colloq*, *adv* in haste; as fast as possible. ➤ *vb* (*usu* **hotfoot it**) to rush or hasten.

hothead *n* **1** an easily angered or agitated person. **2** an impetuous or headstrong person. ○ **hotheaded** *adj*. ○ **hotheadedness** *n*.

hothouse *n* **1** a greenhouse which is kept warm for growing tender or tropical plants. **2** any establishment or environment promoting rapid growth or development, eg of skills, ideas, etc.

hotline *n* **1** a direct and exclusive telephone link between political leaders. **2** an emergency telephone number for inquiries about a particular incident or accident.

hotplate *n* **1** the flat top surface of a cooker on which food is cooked. **2** a portable heated surface for keeping food, dishes, etc hot.

hotpot *n* chopped meat and vegetables, seasoned and covered with sliced potatoes, and cooked slowly in a sealed pot.

hot potato *n, colloq* a difficult or controversial problem or situation.

hot rod *n* a motor car modified for extra speed by increasing the engine power.

the hot seat *n colloq* an uncomfortable or difficult situation.

hotshot *n, chiefly US* a person who is, often boastfully or pretentiously, successful or skilful.

hot spot *n* **1** an area with higher than normal temperature, eg, in an engine, etc. **2** *colloq* a popular or trendy nightclub. **3** an area of potential trouble or conflict.

hot spring *n* a spring of water heated naturally underground.

hot stuff *n, colloq* **1** a person, object or performance of outstanding ability, excellence or importance. **2** a person who is sexually attractive or exciting.

hot-tempered *adj* easily angered or provoked.

hot water *n, colloq* trouble; bother.

hot-water bottle *n* a container, usu made of rubber, filled with hot water and used to warm a bed.

hot-wire *vb, colloq* to start (a vehicle engine) by touching electrical wires together, rather than using the ignition switch.

hound *n* **1** *colloq* a dog. **2** a type of dog used in hunting. **3** an assiduous hunter, tracker or seeker of anything. **4** *colloq* a despicable or contemptible man. **5** *often in compounds* **a** a hunting dog: *foxhound;* **b** an addict or devotee: *newshound.* **6** (**the hounds**) a pack of foxhounds. ➤ *vb* **1** to chase or bother relentlessly. **2** to set or urge on in chase.

houndstooth *n* a textile pattern of small broken checks.

hour *n* **1** sixty minutes, or a twenty-fourth part of a day. **2** the time indicated by a clock or watch. **3** an occasion or a point in time: *an early hour.* **4** a special occasion or point in time: *his finest hour.* **5** (**hours**) the time allowed or fixed for a specified activity: *office hours.* **6** the distance travelled in an hour: *two hours away from the airport.* **7** a time for action: *The hour has come.* **8** (**hours**) CANONICAL HOURS. ♦ **at the eleventh hour** at the last or latest moment. **on the hour** at exactly one, two, etc, o'clock: *The train departs on the hour.*

hourglass *n* an instrument that measures time, consisting of two reversible glass containers connected by a narrow glass tube, and filled with sand that takes a specified time, not necessarily an hour, to pass from one container to the other.

houri /ˈhʊərɪ/ *n* **1** a nymph in the Muslim Paradise. **2** any voluptuous and beautiful young woman.

hourly *adj* **1** happening or done every hour. **2** measured by the hour: *an hourly wage.* **3** frequent or constant: *I live in hourly fear of discovery.* ➤ *adv* **1** every hour. **2** frequently.

house *n* /haʊs/ **1** a building in which people,

esp a single family, live. **2** the people living in such a building. **3** an inn or public house. **4** *in compounds* a building used for a specified purpose: *an opera-house.* **5** a business firm: *a publishing house.* **6** the audience in a theatre, a theatre itself or a performance given there. **7** (*often* **the House**) the legislative body that governs a country, esp either chamber in a bicameral system. **8** (**the House**) **a** in Oxford: Christ Church College; **b** in London: the Stock Exchange; **c** in London: the Houses of Parliament. **9** (**House**) a family, esp a noble or royal one: *the House of Hanover.* **10** *astrol* one of the twelve divisions of the heavens. **11** *Brit* one of several divisions of pupils at a large school. **12** a building at a college, university or boarding-school in which students live. **13** a building in which members of a religious community live; a convent. **14** HOUSE MUSIC. ➤ *vb* /haʊz/ **1** to provide with a house or similar shelter. **2** to store. **3** to protect by covering. ♦ **bring the house down** *colloq* to evoke loud applause in a theatre; to be a great success. **keep house** to manage a household. **keep open house** to be hospitable or provide entertainment for all visitors. **like a house on fire** *colloq* **1** very well: *They get on like a house on fire.* **2** very quickly. **on the house** of food, drink, etc: at the expense of the manager or owner; free of charge. **put** or **set one's house in order** to organize or settle one's affairs.

house arrest *n* confinement in one's own home instead of imprisonment.

houseboat *n* a barge or boat, usu stationary, with a deck-cabin designed and built for living in.

housebound *adj* confined to one's house because of illness, carer's duties, etc.

housebreaking *n* the act or process of unlawfully breaking into and entering a house or building with the intention to steal. ○ **housebreaker** *n*.

housecoat *n* a woman's long loose garment similar to a dressing-gown, worn in the home.

house guest *n* a guest staying in a private house, usu for several nights.

household *n* the people who live together in a house, making up a family. ➤ *adj* relating to the house or family living there; domestic.

householder *n* **1** the owner or tenant of a house. **2** the head of a family or household.

household name or **household word** *n* a familiar name, word or saying.

house husband *n* a man who looks after the house and family instead of having a paid job.

housekeeper *n* a person who is paid to manage a household's domestic arrangements.

housekeeping *n* **1** the management of a household's domestic arrangements. **2** money set aside to pay for this.

housemaid *n* a maid employed to keep a house clean and tidy.

houseman *n* a recently qualified doctor holding a junior resident post in a hospital to complete their training.

housemaster or **housemistress** n in Britain: a male or female teacher in charge of a house in a school, esp a boarding-school.

house music n a style of dance music that features a strong beat in 4/4 time and often incorporates edited fragments of other recordings.

houseplant n a plant grown indoors.

house-proud adj taking an often excessive amount of pride in the condition and appearance of one's house.

houseroom n. ♦ **not give sth houseroom** to refuse to have anything to do with it.

house-sit vb, intr to look after someone's house by living in it while they are away. ○ **housesitter** n.

housetrain vb to train (a puppy, kitten, etc) to urinate and defecate outside or in a special tray, etc. ○ **housetrained** adj.

house-warming n a party given to celebrate moving into a new house.

housewife n a wife who looks after the house and family and who often does not have a paid job outside the home.

housework n the work involved in keeping a house clean and tidy.

housing vb, present participle of HOUSE. ➤ n 1 houses and accommodation collectively. 2 the act, or process of providing living accommodation. 3 anything designed to cover, contain or protect machinery, etc.

housing estate n a planned residential estate, esp one built by a local authority.

hovel n a small, dirty, run-down dwelling.

hover vb, intr 1 of a bird, helicopter, etc: to remain in the air without moving in any direction. 2 (also **hover about, around** or **round**) to linger, esp anxiously or nervously (near someone or something). 3 to be or remain undecided (usu between two options). ➤ n 1 an act or state of hovering. 2 a condition of uncertainty or indecision.

hovercraft n a vehicle which is able to move over land or water, supported by a cushion of air.

hoverfly n (-ies) a wasp-like fly that hovers and feeds on pollen and nectar.

how adv 1 in what way; by what means: How did it happen? 2 to what extent: How old is he? • How far is it? 3 in what condition, esp of health: How is she feeling now? 4 to what extent or degree is something good, successful, etc: How was your holiday? 5 for what cause or reason; why: How can you behave like that? 6 using whatever means are necessary: Do it how best you can. ➤ conj 1 colloq that: He told me how he'd done it on his own. 2 in which manner or condition: How did you get there? ➤ n a manner or means of doing something: The hows and whys of it. ♦ **how about** would you like; what do you think of: How about another piece of cake? • How about going to see a film? **how are you?** a conventional greeting to someone,

sometimes referring specifically to their state of health. **how come?** colloq for what reason?; how does that come about?: How come you're not going tomorrow? **how do you do?** a formal greeting to a person one is meeting for the first time. **how's that? 1** what is your opinion of that? **2** cricket an appeal to the umpire to give the batsman out.

howdah or **houdah** n a seat, usu with a sunshade, used for riding on an elephant's back.

howdy exclam, N Am, colloq hello.

however adv, conj 1 in spite of that; nevertheless. 2 colloq esp implying surprise: in what way; by what means: However did you do that? 3 by whatever means: Do it however you like. 4 to no matter what extent: You must finish this however long it takes.

howitzer n a short heavy gun which fires shells high in the air and at a steep angle, esp used in trench warfare.

howl n 1 a long mournful cry of a wolf or dog. 2 a long loud cry made by the wind, etc. 3 a prolonged cry of pain or distress. 4 a loud peal of laughter. 5 electronics a vibrant sound made by loudspeakers caused by feedback. ➤ vb, intr 1 to make a howl. 2 to laugh or cry loudly. ◊ **howl sb down** to prevent a speaker from being heard by shouting loudly and angrily.

howler n 1 (also **howler monkey**) the largest of the S American monkeys, with black, brown or reddish fur. 2 colloq an outrageous and amusing blunder.

howling adj, colloq very great; tremendous: a howling success.

hoy or **hoi** exclam used to attract someone's attention.

hoyden n a wild lively girl; a tomboy. ○ **hoydenish** adj.

HP or **hp** abbrev 1 high pressure. 2 Brit hire purchase. 3 horsepower.

HQ or **hq** abbrev headquarters.

http abbrev in Internet addresses: hypertext transfer protocol.

hub n 1 the centre of a wheel. 2 the focal point of activity, interest, discussion, etc.

hubbub n 1 a confused noise of many sounds, esp voices. 2 uproar; commotion.

hubby n (-ies) colloq an affectionate contraction of HUSBAND.

hubris /'hju:brıs/ n arrogance or over-confidence, esp when likely to result in disaster or ruin. ○ **hubristic** adj.

huckleberry n (-ies) 1 a low-growing American woodland plant. 2 its dark blue or blackish fruit.

huckster n 1 an aggressive seller. 2 a mercenary person. ➤ vb to sell aggressively.

huddle vb 1 tr & intr (usu **huddle together** or **up**) to nestle or crowd closely, eg because of cold. 2 intr to sit curled up or curl oneself up. ➤ n 1 a confused mass or crowd. 2 colloq a secret or private conference. 3 a gathering together of esp football players during a game, in order to receive instructions, etc.

hue *n* 1 a colour, tint or shade. 2 the feature of a colour that distinguishes it from other colours. 3 a view or aspect.

hue and cry *n* a loud public protest or uproar.

huff *n* a fit of anger, annoyance or offended dignity: *in a huff.* ◆ *vb* 1 *intr* to blow or puff loudly. 2 *tr & intr* to give or take offence. 3 *draughts* to remove (an opponent's piece) for failing to capture one's own piece. ◆ **huffing and puffing** loud empty threats or objections.

huffy or **huffish** *adj* (*-ier, -iest*) 1 offended. 2 easily offended; touchy. ○ **huffily** or **huffishly** *adv.* ○ **huffiness** *n.*

hug *vb* (**hugged, hugging**) 1 *tr & intr* to hold tightly in one's arms, esp to show love. 2 to keep close to something: *The ship was hugging the shore.* 3 to hold or cherish (a belief, etc) very firmly. ➤ *n* 1 a tight grasp with the arms; a close embrace. 2 *wrestling* a squeezing type of grip.

huge *adj* very large or enormous. ○ **hugely** *adv.* ○ **hugeness** *n.*

hugger-mugger *n* 1 confusion or disorder. 2 secrecy. ➤ *adj, adv* 1 secret; in secret. 2 confused; in confusion or disorder.

huh *exclam, colloq* expressing disgust, disbelief or inquiry.

hula or **hula-hula** *n* a Hawaiian dance in which the dancer, usu a woman, sways their hips and moves their arms gracefully.

hula hoop *n* a light hoop, usu made of plastic, which is kept spinning round the waist by a swinging movement of the hips.

hulk *n* 1 the dismantled body of an old ship. 2 a ship which is or looks unwieldy or difficult to steer. 3 *derog, colloq* a large, awkward and ungainly person or thing. 4 *hist* the body of an old ship used as a prison.

hulking *adj, colloq* big and clumsy.

hull[1] *n* 1 the frame or body of a ship or airship. 2 the armoured body of a tank, missile, rocket, etc.

hull[2] *n* 1 the outer covering or husk of certain fruit and seeds, esp the pods of beans and peas. 2 the calyx of a strawberry, etc. ➤ *vb* to remove the hulls from (strawberries, etc).

hullabaloo *n, colloq* an uproar or clamour.

hum *vb* (**hummed, humming**) 1 *intr* to make a low, steady murmuring sound similar to that made by a bee. 2 *tr & intr* to sing (a tune) with closed lips. 3 *intr* to speak indistinctly or stammer, esp through embarrassment or hesitation. 4 *intr, colloq* to be full of activity: *The whole building was humming.* 5 *intr, slang* to have an unpleasant smell or odour. ➤ *n* 1 a humming sound. 2 an inarticulate sound or murmur. 3 *slang* a bad smell. ◆ **hum and haw** or **ha** or **hah** to make inarticulate sounds expressing doubt, uncertainty or hesitation; to hesitate.

human *adj* 1 relating or belonging to people. 2 having or showing the qualities and limitations typical of a person. 3 having or showing the better qualities of people, eg in being kind, thoughtful, etc. ➤ *n* a human being. ○ **humanness** *n.*

human being *n* a member of the human race.

humane *adj* 1 kind and sympathetic. 2 of a killing: done with as little pain and suffering as possible. ○ **humanely** *adv.*

humanism *n* a system of thought that rejects the divine, the supernatural, etc, in favour of the notion that human beings are paramount, esp in their capability to decide what is or is not moral. ○ **humanist** *n.*

humanitarian *adj* concerned with improving people's lives and welfare: *humanitarian aid.* ➤ *n* a person who tries to improve the quality of people's lives by means of reform, charity, etc; a philanthropist. ○ **humanitarianism** *n.*

humanity *n* (*-ies*) 1 humans as a species or a collective group. 2 typical human nature. 3 the typical qualities of human beings, eg kindness, mercy, etc. 4 (**humanities**) the subjects involving the study of human culture, esp language, literature, philosophy, and Latin and Greek.

humanize or **-ise** *vb* 1 to render, make or become human. 2 to make humane. ○ **humanization** *n.*

humankind *n* 1 the human species. 2 people generally or collectively.

humanly *adv* 1 in a human or humane way. 2 by human agency or means. 3 with regard to human limitations: *if it is humanly possible.*

humanoid *n* 1 any of the ancestors from which modern human beings are descended and to which they are more closely related than to ANTHROPOIDS. 2 an animal or machine with human characteristics.

human resources *pl n* 1 people collectively in terms of their skills, training, knowledge, etc in the work place. 2 the workforce of an organization.

human rights *pl n* the rights every person has to justice, freedom, etc.

humble *adj* 1 having a low opinion of oneself and one's abilities, etc. 2 having a low position in society. 3 lowly, modest or unpretentious. ➤ *vb* 1 to make humble or modest. 2 to abase or degrade. ○ **humbleness** *n.* ○ **humbling** *adj.* ○ **humbly** *adv.*

humble pie or **umble pie** *n* a pie made from deer offal. ◆ **eat humble pie** to be forced to humble or abase oneself, or to make a humble apology.

humbug *n* 1 a trick or deception. 2 nonsense or rubbish. 3 an impostor or fraud. 4 *Brit* a hard, peppermint-flavoured sweet.

humdinger /ˈhʌmˈdɪŋə(r)/ *n, slang* an exceptionally good person or thing.

humdrum *adj* dull or monotonous; ordinary.

humerus *n* (**humeri** /ˈhjuːməraɪ/) the bone in the upper arm.

humid *adj* damp; moist. ○ **humidly** *adv.* ○ **humidness** *n.*

humidifier *n* a device for increasing or maintaining the humidity of a room, etc.

humidity *n* **1** the amount of water vapour in the atmosphere, usu expressed as a percentage. **2** a large amount of moisture in the air.

humiliate *vb* to injure (someone's pride), or make (someone) feel ashamed or look foolish, esp in the presence of others. ○ **humiliating** *adj*. ○ **humiliatingly** *adv*. ○ **humiliation** *n*.

humility *n* (**-ies**) **1** the quality or state of being humble. **2** a lowly self-opinion; modesty or meekness.

hummingbird *n* a very small American bird with brilliant plumage that feeds on nectar and tiny insects.

hummock *n* a low hill; a hillock.

hummus, **hoummos** or **houmus** /'hʊməs, 'hʌ-/ *n* a Middle-Eastern hors d'oeuvre or dip made using puréed cooked chickpeas.

humongous or **humungous** *adj*, *colloq* huge or enormous.

humoresque *n* a humorous piece of music; a musical caprice.

humorist *n* someone with a talent for talking or writing humorously.

humorous *adj* **1** funny or amusing. **2** of a person, joke, etc: having the ability or quality to cause humour. ○ **humorously** *adv*. ○ **humorousness** *n*.

humour or (*US*) **humor** *n* **1** the quality of being amusing. **2** the ability to appreciate and enjoy something amusing. **3** a specified temperament or state of mind: *He is in good humour today.* **4** a specified type of fluid in the body: *aqueous humour.* **5** *old* any of the four bodily fluids formerly believed to determine a person's physical health and character. ➤ *vb* **1** to please or gratify someone by doing what they wish. **2** to adapt to eg the mood or ideas of someone else. ○ **humourless** *adj*.

hump *n* **1** a large rounded lump of fat on the back of a camel that serves as an energy store when food is scarce. **2** an abnormal curvature of the spine that gives the back a hunched appearance, due to spinal deformity. **3** a rounded raised area of a road, etc. ➤ *vb* **1** to hunch or bend in a hump. **2** (*usu* **hump about** or **around**) to shoulder or carry (esp something awkward or heavy) with difficulty. **3** *tr & intr, coarse slang* to have sexual intercourse with. ○ **humpy** *adj*. ◆ **have** or **give sb the hump** to be in, or put someone in, a bad mood or sulk. **over the hump** *colloq* past the crisis; over the worst.

humph *exclam* expressing doubt, displeasure or hesitation.

humus /'hjuːməs/ *n* dark-brown organic material produced in the topmost layer of soil due to the decomposition of plant and animal matter.

hunch *n* **1** an idea, guess or belief based on feelings, suspicions or intuition rather than on actual evidence. ➤ *vb* **1** to bend or arch; to hump. **2** *intr* (*also* **hunch up** or **over**) to sit with the body hunched or curled up.

hunchback *n* someone with a large rounded lump on their back, due to spinal deformity. ○ **hunchbacked** *adj*.

hundred *n* (**hundreds** or after a number **hundred**) **1** the number which is ten times ten. **2** a numeral, figure or symbol representing this, eg *100* or *C*. **3** a set of a hundred people or things. **4** (**hundreds**) *colloq* a large but indefinite number: *hundreds of people*. **5** (**hundreds**) *in compounds* the hundred years of a specified century: *the thirteenth-hundreds*. **6** *hist* a division of an English county orig containing a hundred families. ➤ *adj* **1** totalling or aged one hundred. **2** *colloq* very many: *I've told you a hundred times to stop.* ○ **hundredth** *adj, n.* ◆ **a** or **one hundred per cent** completely. **one, two,** *etc* **hundred hours** one, two, etc o'clock.

hundredweight *n* (**hundredweight** or **hundredweights**) **1** *Brit* a measure of weight equal to 112 pounds (50.8kg). **2** *N Am* a measure of weight equal to 100 pounds (45.4kg). **3** a metric measure of weight equal to 50kg.

hung *vb*, *past tense*, *past participle of* HANG. ➤ *adj* of a parliament or jury: with neither side having a majority. ◆ **be hung over** *colloq* to be suffering from a hangover. **be hung up on** or **about sb** or **sth** *colloq* **1** to be extremely anxious or upset about it. **2** to be obsessed with them or it: *She is completely hung up on him.*

hung See note at **hang**.

hunger *n* **1** the desire or need for food. **2** a strong desire for anything. ➤ *vb*, *intr* (*usu* **hunger for** or **after**) to crave.

hungry *adj* (**-ier**, **-iest**) **1** having a need or craving for food. **2** (*usu* **hungry for**) having a great desire (for something): *He is hungry for success.* **3** eager; greedy: *hungry eyes.* ○ **hungrily** *adv*. ○ **hungriness** *n*.

hunk *n* **1** a lump or piece, sometimes broken or cut off from a larger piece. **2** *colloq* a strong, muscular, sexually attractive man. ○ **hunky** *adj* (**-ier**, **-iest**).

hunky-dory *adj*, *colloq* of a situation, condition, etc: fine; excellent.

hunt *vb* **1** *tr & intr* to chase and kill (wild birds or animals) for food or sport. **2** *Brit* to hunt and kill (an animal, esp a fox) on horseback, using hounds. **3** to seek out and pursue game over (a certain area). **4** of an animal or bird: to search for and chase (its prey). **5** *mech* to oscillate around a middle point, or to vary in speed. ➤ *n* **1** an act of hunting. **2** a group of people meeting together, often on horses, to hunt animals for sport, eg foxes. **3** a search. ○ **hunting** *n.* ◇ **hunt sb** or **sth down** **1** to pursue and capture them or it. **2** to persecute them or it out of existence. **hunt sb** or **sth out** or **up** to search or seek for them or it.

hunter *n* **1 a** someone who hunts; **b** *esp in compounds* someone who seeks someone or something out: *bounty hunter*. **2** an animal that hunts (usu other animals) for food. **3** a horse used in hunting, esp fox-hunting. **4** a watch with a hinged metal cover to protect the glass over its face.

hunter-gatherer *n, anthropol* a member of a society which lives by hunting animals from the land and sea, and by gathering wild plants.

hurdle *n* **1** *athletics, horse-racing* one of a series of portable frames, hedges or barriers to be jumped in a race. **2** an obstacle, problem or difficulty to be overcome. **3** (**hurdles**) a race with hurdles. **4** a light frame with bars or wire across it, used as a temporary fence. ➤ *vb* **1** *tr & intr* to jump over (a hurdle in a race, an obstacle, etc) **2** to enclose with hurdles. ○ **hurdler** *n.* ○ **hurdling** *n.*

hurdy-gurdy *n* (*-ies*) a musical instrument whose strings make a droning sound when a wheel is turned by a handle.

hurl *vb* **1** to fling violently. **2** to utter with force and spite: *hurl abuse*. ➤ *n* an act of hurling.

hurling or **hurley** *n* a traditional Irish game resembling hockey.

hurly-burly *n* noisy activity; confusion or uproar.

hurrah, hoorah or **hooray** *exclam* a shout of joy, enthusiasm or victory. ➤ *n* such a shout.

hurricane *n* an intense, often devastating, cyclonic tropical storm with average wind speeds exceeding 118kph.

hurricane lamp *n* an oil lamp whose flame is enclosed in glass to protect it from the wind.

hurry *vb* (*-ies, -ied*) **1** to urge forward or hasten; to make (someone or something) move or act quickly. **2** *intr* to move or act with haste, esp with excessive speed. ➤ *n* **1** great haste or speed. **2** the necessity for haste or speed. ○ **hurried** *adj.*

hurt *vb* (*past tense & past participle* **hurt**) **1** to injure or cause physical pain to. **2** to cause emotional, etc pain to: *I hurt her feelings*. **3** *intr* to be injured or painful: *The wound hurts.* ➤ *n* **1** an injury or wound. **2** mental or emotional pain or suffering. ➤ *adj* **1** injured: *a hurt leg.* **2** aggrieved; upset: *a hurt expression.*

hurtful *adj* causing mental pain; emotionally harmful.

hurtle *vb, tr & intr* to move or throw very quickly or noisily.

husband *n* a man to whom a woman is married. ➤ *vb* to manage (money, resources, etc) wisely and economically.

husbandry *n* **1** the farming business. **2** the economical and wise management of money, resources, etc.

hush *exclam* silence!; be still! ➤ *n* silence or calm, esp after noise. ➤ *vb, tr & intr* to make or become silent, calm or still. ○ **hushed** *adj.*

hush-hush *adj, colloq* top-secret or extremely private.

hush money *n, colloq* money paid to someone to guarantee that something remains secret.

husk *n* **1** the thin dry covering of certain fruits and seeds. **2** a case, shell or covering, esp one that is worthless.

husky[1] *adj* (*-ier, -iest*) **1** of a voice: rough and dry in sound. **2** *colloq* usu of a man: big, tough and strong. **3** resembling or full of husks. ○ **huskily** *adv.* ○ **huskiness** *n.*

husky[2] *n* (*-ies*) a dog with a thick coat and curled tail, used as a sledge-dog in the Arctic.

hussar /hʊ'zɑː(r)/ *n* a soldier in a cavalry regiment who carries only light weapons.

hussy *n* (*-ies*) *derog* a forward, immoral or promiscuous girl or woman.

hustings *sing or pl n* speeches, campaigning, etc prior to a political election, or a platform, etc from which such speeches are given.

hustle *vb* **1 a** to push or shove quickly and roughly; to jostle; **b** to push or shove in a specified direction or into a specified position: *He hustled her out of the room.* **2** to act hurriedly or hastily. **3** *colloq* to coerce or pressure someone to act or deal with something quickly: *They hustled us into agreeing.* **4** to earn money or one's living illicitly. **5** *intr, slang* to work as a prostitute. ➤ *n* **1** lively or frenzied activity. **2** *slang* a swindle or fraud.

hustler *n, slang* **1** a lively or energetic person. **2** a swindler. **3** a prostitute.

hut *n* **1** a small and crudely built house, usu made of wood. **2** a small temporary dwelling.

hutch *n* a box, usu made of wood and with a wire-netting front, in which small animals, eg rabbits, are kept.

hyacinth *n* a bulbous plant with sweet-smelling clusters of blue, pink or white flowers.

hybrid *n* **1** an animal or plant produced by crossing two different species, varieties, etc. **2** something composed of disparate elements. ➤ *adj* bred or produced by combining elements from different sources. ○ **hybridism** or **hybridity** *n.* ○ **hybridization** *n.* ○ **hybridize** *vb.*

hydra *n* (*hydras* or **hydrae** /'haɪdriː/) **1** a freshwater polyp with a tube-like body and tentacles round the mouth, remarkable for its ability to multiply when cut or divided. **2** any manifold or persistent evil.

hydrant *n* a pipe connected to the main water supply, esp in a street, with a nozzle for attaching, eg, a firefighter's hose.

hydrate *chem, n* a compound containing water which is chemically combined, and which may be expelled without affecting the composition of the other substance. ➤ *vb* **1** to form (such a compound) by combining with water. **2** to cause something to absorb water. ○ **hydration** *n.*

hydraulic *adj* **1** relating to hydraulics. **2** worked by the pressure of water or other fluid carried in pipes: *hydraulic brakes.* **3** relating to something that sets in water: *hydraulic cement.* ○ **hydraulically** *adv.*

hydraulics *sing n, eng* the science of the mechanical properties of fluids, esp water, at rest or in motion, and their practical applications, eg to water pipes.

hydride *n* a chemical compound of hydrogen with another element or RADICAL (*noun sense* 3).

hydro[1] *n* hydroelectric power.

hydro[2] *n, Brit* a hotel or clinic, often situated near a spa, providing hydropathic treatment.

hydrocarbon *n, chem* an organic chemical compound containing carbon and hydrogen.

hydrocephalus *n, med* an accumulation of fluid in the brain, usu occurring in young children. ○ **hydrocephalic** or **hydrocephalous** *adj.*

hydrochloric acid *n, chem* a strong corrosive acid, formed by dissolving hydrogen and chlorine in water.

hydrodynamics *sing n* the science of the movement, equilibrium and power of liquids.

hydroelectricity or **hydroelectric power** *n* electricity generated by turbines that are driven by the force of falling water. ○ **hydroelectric** *adj.*

hydrofoil *n* 1 a device on a boat which raises it out of the water as it accelerates. 2 a boat fitted with such a device.

hydrogen *n* a flammable colourless odourless gas which is the lightest of all known substances and by far the most abundant element in the universe. ○ **hydrogenous** *adj.*

hydrogen bomb or **H-bomb** *n* a bomb which releases vast amounts of energy as a result of hydrogen nuclei being converted into helium nuclei by fusion.

hydrogen peroxide *n, chem* an unstable colourless viscous liquid, used in rocket fuel and as a bleach for hair and textiles.

hydrogen sulphide *n, chem* a colourless, toxic gas composed of hydrogen and sulphur with a characteristic smell of bad eggs, produced by decaying organic matter, and also found in natural gas.

hydrography *n* the science of charting and mapping seas, rivers and lakes, and of studying tides, currents, winds, etc.

hydrology *n* the scientific study of the occurrence, movement and properties of water on the Earth's surface, and in the atmosphere.

hydrolysis /haɪˈdrɒlɪsɪs/ *n* the chemical decomposition of organic compounds caused by the action of water. ○ **hydrolytic** *adj.*

hydrometer *n, physics* a device used for measuring the density of a liquid.

hydropathy *n* the treatment of disease or illness using large amounts of water both internally and externally. ○ **hydropathic** *adj.*

hydrophilic *adj, chem* relating to a substance that absorbs, attracts or has an affinity for water.

hydrophobia *n* 1 a fear or horror of water. 2 the inability to swallow water, esp as a symptom of rabies. 3 rabies.

hydroplane *n* 1 a motorboat with a flat bottom or hydrofoils which, at high speeds, skims along the surface of the water. 2 a fin-like device on a submarine allowing it to rise and fall in the water.

hydroponics *sing n, bot* the practice of growing plants without using soil, by immersing the roots in a chemical solution of essential nutrients. ○ **hydroponic** *adj.*

hydrosphere *n* the water, such as seas and rivers, on the surface of the Earth.

hydrotherapy *n, med* the treatment of diseases and disorders by the external use of water, esp through exercising in water.

hydrous *adj* of a substance: containing water.

hydroxide *n, chem* a chemical compound containing hydrogen and oxygen atoms in a group.

hyena or **hyaena** *n* a dog-like mammal that feeds on carrion.

hygiene *n* 1 the practice or study of preserving health and preventing the spread of disease. 2 sanitary principles and practices. ○ **hygienic** *adj.* ○ **hygienically** *adv.*

hygroscope *n* a device which indicates changes in air humidity without measuring it.

hygroscopic or **hygroscopical** *adj* 1 relating to the hygroscope. 2 of a substance: able to absorb moisture from the air. 3 of some movements of plants: indicating or caused by absorption or loss of moisture.

hymen *n, anat* a thin membrane partially covering the opening of the vagina, that is usu broken during the first instance of penetrative sexual intercourse.

hymn *n* a song of praise, esp to God, but also to a nation, etc. ➤ *vb* 1 to celebrate in song or worship. 2 *intr* to sing in adoration.

hymnal *n* a book containing hymns.

hype *colloq, n* 1 intensive, exaggerated or artificially induced excitement about, or enthusiasm for, something or someone. 2 exaggerated and usu misleading publicity or advertising; a sales gimmick. ➤ *vb* to promote or advertise intensively.

hyped up *adj, slang* stimulated or highly excited.

hyper *adj, colloq* of a person: over-excited; over-stimulated.

hyperactive *adj* of, esp, a child: abnormally or pathologically active. ○ **hyperactivity** *n.*

hyperbola /haɪˈpɜːbələ/ *n* (**hyperbolas, hyperbolae** /-liː/) *geom* the curve produced when a PLANE[2] cuts through a cone so that the angle between the base of the cone and the plane is greater than the angle between the base and the sloping side of the cone. ○ **hyperbolic** *adj.*

hyperbole /haɪˈpɜːbəlɪ/ *n, rhetoric* an overstatement or exaggeration used for effect and not meant to be taken literally. ○ **hyperbolic** *adj.* ○ **hyperbolically** *adv.*

hypercritical *adj* too critical, esp of small faults.

hyperglycaemia or (*N Am*) **hyperglycemia** /haɪpəglaɪˈsiːmɪə/ *n, pathol* a condition in which the sugar concentration in the blood is abnormally high.

hyperlink *n, comput* a link between documents or items within a document created using hypertext.

hypermarket *n, Brit* a very large supermarket

with a wide range of goods, usu on the edge of a town.

hypermedia *n, comput* a computer file and related software which identifies and links information in various media, such as text, graphics, sound, video clips, etc.

hypersensitive *adj* excessively sensitive; more sensitive than normal. ○ **hypersensitiveness** or **hypersensitivity** *n.*

hypersonic *adj* **1** of speeds: greater than Mach number 5. **2** *aeronautics* of an aircraft or rocket: capable of flying at such speeds. **3** of sound waves: having a frequency greater than 1000 million hertz. ○ **hypersonics** *pl n.*

hypertension *n pathol* a condition in which the blood pressure is abnormally high. ○ **hypertensive** *adj, n.*

hypertext *n, comput* computer-readable text in which cross-reference links (HYPERLINKs) have been inserted, enabling the user to call up relevant data from other files, or parts of the same file, by clicking on a coded word or symbol, etc.

hyperventilation *n* a condition in which the speed and depth of breathing becomes abnormally rapid, causing dizziness, a feeling of suffocation and sometimes unconsciousness. ○ **hyperventilate** *vb.*

hyphen *n* a punctuation mark (-) used to join two words to form a compound (eg, *booby-trap, double-barrelled*) or, in texts, to split a word between the end of one line and the beginning of the next. ➤ *vb* to hyphenate.

hyphenate *vb* to join or separate (two words or parts of words) with a hyphen. ○ **hyphenated** *adj.* ○ **hyphenation** *n.*

hypnosis *n* (*-ses* /-si:z/) an induced state of deep relaxation, in which the mind responds to external suggestion and can recover subconscious memories.

hypnotherapy *n* the treatment of illness or altering of habits, eg smoking, by hypnosis. ○ **hypnotherapist** *n.*

hypnotic *adj* **1** relating to, causing or caused by, hypnosis. **2** causing sleepiness; soporific. ➤ *n* **1** a drug that produces sleep. **2** someone who is subject to hypnosis. **3** someone in a state of hypnosis. ○ **hypnotically** *adv.*

hypnotism *n* **1** the science or practice of hypnosis. **2** the art or practice of inducing hypnosis. ○ **hypnotist** *n.*

hypnotize or **-ise** *vb* **1** to put someone in a state of hypnosis. **2** to fascinate, captivate or bewitch.

hypo *n, colloq* a hypodermic syringe or injection.

hypochondria or **hypochondriasis** *n* a condition characterized by excessive or morbid concern over one's health and sometimes belief that one is seriously ill. ○ **hypochondriac** *n, adj.*

hypocrisy *n* (*-ies*) **1** the practice of pretending to have feelings, beliefs or principles which one does not actually have. **2** an act or instance of this.

hypocrite *n* a person who practises hypocrisy. ○ **hypocritical** *adj.* ○ **hypocritically** *adv.*

hypodermic *adj* **a** of a drug: injected under the skin; **b** of a syringe; designed for use under the skin. ➤ *n* a hypodermic injection or syringe.

hypoglycaemia or **hypoglycemia** /haɪpoʊˌglaɪˈsiːmɪə/ *n, pathol* a condition in which the sugar content of the blood is abnormally low, usu occurring in diabetics after an insulin overdose. ○ **hypoglycaemic** *adj.*

hypotenuse /haɪˈpɒtənjuːz/ *n, maths* the longest side of a right-angled triangle, opposite the right angle.

hypothalamus *n* (*hypothalami* /haɪpoʊˈθaləmaɪ/) *anat* the region of the brain which is involved in the regulation of involuntary functions, such as body temperature.

hypothermia *n* a condition where the body temperature becomes abnormally and sometimes dangerously low.

hypothesis *n* (*-ses* /-siːz/) **1** a statement or proposition assumed to be true for the sake of argument. **2** a statement or theory to be proved or disproved by reference to evidence or facts. **3** a provisional explanation of anything.

hypothesize or **-ise** *vb* **1** *intr* to form a hypothesis. **2** to assume as a hypothesis.

hypothetical or **hypothetic** *adj* **1** based on or involving hypothesis. **2** assumed but not necessarily true. ○ **hypothetically** *adv.*

hyssop *n* a small shrubby aromatic plant with narrow leaves and clusters of long blue flowers, formerly cultivated as a medicinal herb.

hysterectomy *n* (*-ies*) the surgical removal of the womb.

hysteresis *n, physics* the delay or lag between the cause of an effect, and the effect itself, eg when a magnetic material becomes magnetized. ○ **hysteretic** *adj.*

hysteria *n* **1** *psychol* a psychoneurosis characterized by hallucinations, convulsions, amnesia or paralysis. **2** any state of emotional instability caused by acute stress or a traumatic experience. **3** any extreme emotional state, such as laughter or weeping.

hysteric *n* **1** (**hysterics**) *psychol* a bout of hysteria. **2** (**hysterics**) *colloq* a bout of uncontrollable laughter: *The film had us in hysterics.* **3** someone suffering from hysteria.

hysterical *adj* **1** relating to or suffering from hysteria. **2** characterized by hysteria: *a hysterical laugh.* **3** *colloq* extremely funny or amusing: *a hysterical joke.* ○ **hysterically** *adv.*

Hz *abbrev* hertz.

Ii

I¹ or **i** n (**Is, I's** or **i's**) the ninth letter of the English alphabet.

I² pron used to refer to oneself.

> **I, me** After prepositions, the object form **me** should always be used:
> ✓ with you and me
> ✗ with you and I
> ✓ for John and me
> ✗ for John and I
> If in doubt, try the phrase without the you, and you will see that with I and for I are not correct.

I³ abbrev **1** Institute or Institution. **2** International. **3** Island or Isle.

I⁴ symbol **1** chem iodine. **2** the Roman numeral for one.

iambus n (/aɪˈæmbəs/ or **iamb** /ˈaɪamb/ n (**iambuses, iambi** /-baɪ/ and **iambs**) a metrical foot containing a short or unstressed syllable followed by a long or stressed one. ○ **iambic** adj of or using iambuses. ➤ n **1** an iambus. **2** (usu **iambics**) iambic verse.

Iberian adj relating to Portugal and Spain, their inhabitants, languages or culture. ➤ n a Spanish or Portuguese person.

ibex n (**ibex, ibexes** or **ibices** /ˈaɪbɪsiːz/) a wild mountain goat with backward-curving horns.

ibis /ˈaɪbɪs/ n (**ibis** or **ibises**) a large wading bird with a long slender downward-curving beak.

ice n **1** solid frozen water. **2** ICE CREAM or a portion of this. **3** coldness of manner. ➤ vb **1** to cover (a cake) with icing. **2** intr (usu **ice over** or **up**) to become covered with ice. **3** to cool or mix something with ice. ♦ **on ice 1** to be used later. **2** awaiting preferred attention.

ice age n, geol **1** any period when ice sheets and glaciers covered large areas of the Earth. **2** (**the Ice Age**) the period during which this happened in the PLEISTOCENE epoch.

iceberg n **1** a huge mass of ice floating in the sea. **2** a type of lettuce with crisp leaves.

icebox n **1** a refrigerator compartment where food is kept frozen and ice is made. **2** a container packed with ice for keeping food, drink, etc cold. **3** N Am a refrigerator.

icebreaker n **1** a ship that cuts channels through ice. **2** something or someone that breaks down shyness or formality. ○ **icebreaking** adj, n.

icecap n a thick permanent covering of ice.

ice cream n a sweet creamy flavoured frozen dessert.

iced adj **1** covered or cooled with, or affected by, ice. **2** covered with icing.

ice floe n a sheet of ice floating on the sea.

ice hockey n a form of hockey played on ice, with a PUCK² instead of a ball.

ice lolly n, Brit colloq a portion of flavoured water or ice cream frozen on a small stick.

ice pack n **1** med a bag of crushed ice, used to reduce swelling, lower a person's temperature, etc. **2** geog an area of PACK ICE. **3** a gel-filled pack that stays frozen for long periods, used to keep food cool.

ice skate n a boot with a metal blade, used for skating on ice. ➤ vb (**ice-skate**) intr to skate on ice. ○ **ice-skater** n. ○ **ice-skating** n.

ichthyology /ɪkθɪˈɒlədʒɪ/ n the study of fishes. ○ **ichthyological** adj. ○ **ichthyologist** n.

icicle n a long hanging spike of ice.

icing n a sugar-based coating for cakes, etc. ♦ **the icing on the cake** colloq an agreeable addition to something which is already satisfactory.

icing sugar n very fine powdered sugar.

icky adj (**-ier, -iest**) colloq **1** sickly; cloying or sticky. **2** repulsive, nasty or unpleasant.

icon or (sometimes) **ikon** n **1** relig art esp in the Orthodox Church: an image of Christ, the Virgin Mary or a saint. **2** a a person or thing uncritically revered or admired; **b** someone or something regarded as a symbol of a particular culture, sphere, etc. **3** comput a symbol on a computer screen. **4** a picture, image or representation. ○ **iconic** adj.

iconoclast n **1** esp church hist someone who rejects the use of religious images, often destroying them. **2** someone who is opposed to, and attacks, traditional and cherished beliefs and superstitions. ○ **iconoclasm** n. ○ **iconoclastic** adj.

icosahedron n (**icosahedrons** or **icosahedra** /aɪkɒsəˈhiːdrə/) geom a solid figure with 20 faces.

icy adj (**-ier, -iest**) **1** very cold. **2** covered with ice. **3** unfriendly. ○ **icily** adv. ○ **iciness** n.

ID abbrev identification or identity.

I'd contraction **1** I had. **2** I would.

id n, psychoanal the unconscious source of primitive biological instincts and urges. Compare EGO (sense 2), SUPEREGO.

idea n **1** a thought, image or concept formed by the mind. **2** a plan or notion. **3** an aim or purpose: The idea of the game is to win cards. **4** an opinion, belief or vague fancy. **5** someone's conception of something: not my idea of fun.

ideal adj 1 perfect; best possible or conceivable. 2 existing only in the mind. 3 theoretical; conforming to theory. ➤ n 1 the highest standard of behaviour, perfection, beauty, etc. 2 someone or something considered perfect. 3 something existing only in the imagination. ○ **ideally** adv.

idealism n 1 a tendency to see things in an ideal or idealized form rather than as they really are. 2 the practice of forming, and living according to, ideals. 3 impracticality. 4 philos the theory that objects and the external world are products of the mind. Compare REALISM. ○ **idealist** n. ○ **idealistic** adj.

idealize or **-ise** vb to regard or treat someone or something as perfect or ideal. ○ **idealization** n.

identical adj 1 exactly similar in every respect. 2 being the very same one. 3 of twins: developed from a single fertilized egg, therefore of the same sex and closely resembling each other. Compare FRATERNAL (sense 2). ○ **identically** adv.

identify vb (-ies, -ied) 1 to recognize or establish someone or something as being a particular person or thing. 2 to associate (one person, thing or group) closely with another. 3 to see clearly (a problem, method, solution, etc). 4 intr (**identify with sb**) to feel sympathy and understanding for someone because of shared personal characteristics or experiences. ○ **identifiable** adj. ○ **identification** n.

identity n (-ies) 1 who or what a person or thing is: The winner's identity is not yet known. 2 the characteristics by which a person or thing can be identified. 3 the state of being exactly the same: identity of interests. 4 maths a (**in full identity element**) an element that, when combined with another element x, leaves x unchanged; b an equation that is valid for all possible values of the variables involved.

ideogram n a symbol for a concept or object, but not a direct representation of it. Also called **ideograph**.

ideology n (-ies) 1 the ideas and beliefs which form the basis for a social, economic or political system. 2 the opinions, beliefs and way of thinking characteristic of a particular person, group or nation. ○ **ideological** adj. ○ **ideologically** adv. ○ **ideologist** n.

idiocy n (-ies) a foolish action or foolish behaviour.

idiom n 1 an expression with a meaning which cannot be derived from the meanings of the words which form it. 2 the forms of expression peculiar to a language, dialect, group, etc. 3 the characteristic style or forms of expression of a particular artist, musician, artistic or musical school, etc. ○ **idiomatic** adj 1 characteristic of a particular language. 2 tending to use idioms; using idioms correctly. ○ **idiomatically** adv.

idiosyncrasy n (-ies) a personal peculiarity or

eccentricity. ○ **idiosyncratic** adj. ○ **idiosyncratically** adv.

idiot n 1 colloq a foolish or stupid person. 2 nontechnical a person with a severe learning disability. ○ **idiotic** adj. ○ **idiotically** adv.

idle adj 1 not in use; unoccupied. 2 not wanting to work. 3 worthless: idle chatter. 4 without cause, basis or good reason: an idle rumour. 5 having no effect or result; not taken seriously: an idle threat. ➤ vb 1 (usu **idle away time**, etc) to spend (time) idly. 2 intr to do nothing or be idle. 3 intr of an engine, machinery, etc: to run gently while out of gear or without doing any work. 4 to make (an engine, etc) idle. ○ **idleness** n. ○ **idler** n. ○ **idly** adv.

idol n 1 an image or symbol used as an object of worship. 2 an object of excessive love, honour or devotion.

idolatry /aɪˈdɒlətrɪ/ n (-ies) 1 the worship of idols. 2 excessive love, honour or admiration. ○ **idolater** and (now rare) **idolatress** n. ○ **idolatrous** adj. ○ **idolatrously** adv.

idolize or **-ise** vb 1 to love, honour, admire, etc someone or something too much. 2 to make an idol of someone or something. ○ **idolization** n.

idyll /ˈɪdɪl/ n 1 a short poem or prose work describing a simple, pleasant, usu rural scene. 2 a story, episode or scene of happy innocence or love. 3 a work of this character in another art form, esp music. ○ **idyllic** /ɪˈdɪlɪk/ adj 1 relating to or typical of an idyll. 2 charming; picturesque.

ie or **i.e.** abbrev: id est (Latin), that is; that is to say.

if conj 1 in the event that; on condition that; supposing that. 2 although; even though: very enjoyable, if overpriced. 3 whenever: She jumps if the phone rings. 4 whether. 5 (usu **if only**) used to express a wish. 6 used to make a polite request or suggestion: if you wouldn't mind waiting. 7 used in exclamations, to express surprise or annoyance: Well, if it isn't John! ➤ n 1 a condition or supposition: ifs and buts. 2 an uncertainty.

iffy adj (-ier, -iest) colloq uncertain; dubious.

igloo n a dome-shaped Inuit house built with blocks of hard snow.

igneous adj 1 relating to or like fire. 2 geol of a rock: formed by the solidification of molten MAGMA.

ignite vb 1 to set fire to something or heat it to the point of combustion. 2 intr to catch fire. 3 to excite (feelings, emotions, etc). ○ **ignitable** or **ignitible** adj.

ignition n 1 chem the point at which combustion begins. 2 (usu **the ignition**) a system that produces the spark which ignites the mixture of fuel and air in an INTERNAL-COMBUSTION ENGINE. 3 an act or the means or process of igniting something.

ignoble adj 1 dishonourable. 2 of humble or low birth. ○ **ignobly** adv.

ignominy /ˈɪɡnəmɪnɪ/ n (-ies) 1 public shame, disgrace or dishonour. 2 dishonourable conduct. ○ **ignominious** /ˌɪgnəˈmɪnɪəs/ *adj.*

ignoramus *n* an ignorant or unintelligent person.

ignorant *adj* 1 knowing very little; uneducated. 2 (*usu* ignorant of sth) knowing little or nothing about it. 3 rude. ○ **ignorance** *n*. ○ **ignorantly** *adv.*

ignore *vb* to take no notice of someone or something.

iguana *n* (**iguanas** *or* **iguana**) a large lizard with a crest of spines along its back.

ikon see ICON

ileum *n* (**ilea**) *anat* the lowest part of the small intestine.

ilex /ˈaɪlɛks/ *n*, *bot* a shrub or tree of the genus that includes HOLLY.

ilium *n* (**ilia**) *anat* one of the bones that form the upper part of the pelvis.

ilk *n* type; class. ◆ **of that ilk** *Scot* of the place of the same name: *Macdonald of that ilk (ie Macdonald of Macdonald)*.

I'll *contraction* I will or I shall.

ill *adj* (**worse, worst;** *colloq* **iller, illest**) 1 unwell. 2 of health: not good. 3 bad; harmful: *ill effects*. 4 hostile; unfriendly: *ill feeling*. 5 causing or heralding bad luck: *an ill omen*. 6 of manners: incorrect; improper. ➢ *adv* (**worse, worst**) 1 badly; wrongly: *ill-fitting*. 2 unfavourably: *speak ill of someone*. 3 not easily: *ill able to afford the money.* ➢ *n* 1 evil; trouble: *the ills of modern society.* 2 an injury, ailment or misfortune. ◆ **ill at ease** uneasy; uncomfortable; embarrassed.

ill-advised *adj* foolish; done, or doing things, with little thought or consideration. ○ **ill-advisedly** *adv.*

ill-bred *adj* badly brought up or educated; rude. ○ **ill-breeding** *n*.

ill-considered *adj* not well planned.

ill-disposed *adj* (*esp* ill-disposed towards sb or sth) unfriendly; unsympathetic.

illegal *adj* 1 not legal. 2 not authorized by law. ○ **illegality** /ˌɪlɪˈgalɪtɪ/ *n* (-**ies**). ○ **illegally** *adv.*

illegible *adj* difficult or impossible to read. ○ **illegibility** *n*. ○ **illegibly** *adv.*

illegitimate *adj* 1 born of unmarried parents. 2 of a birth: happening outside marriage. 3 unacceptable or not allowed; illegal. 4 *logic* not properly reasoned. 5 improper. ○ **illegitimacy** *n*.

ill-equipped *adj* poorly provided with the necessary tools, skills, etc.

ill-fated *adj* ending in or bringing bad luck or ruin.

ill-favoured *adj* unattractive.

ill-founded *adj* without sound basis or reason.

ill-gotten *adj* obtained dishonestly.

illiberal *adj* 1 narrow-minded; prejudiced. 2 not generous. 3 uncultured. ○ **illiberality** *n*.

illicit *adj* not permitted by law, rule or social custom.

ill-informed *adj* 1 lacking knowledge or information. 2 made without the relevant or necessary information.

illiterate *adj* 1 unable to read and write. 2 uneducated. ➢ *n* an illiterate person. ○ **illiteracy** *n*.

ill-judged *adj* done without proper consideration.

ill-mannered *adj* rude.

illness *n* 1 a disease. 2 the state of being ill.

illogical *adj* 1 not based on careful reasoning. 2 against the principles of logic. ○ **illogicality** *n*. ○ **illogically** *adv.*

ill-timed *adj* said or done at an unsuitable time.

ill-treat *vb* to abuse. ○ **ill-treatment** *n*.

illuminance *n*, *physics* the luminous FLUX on a given surface per unit area.

illuminate *vb* 1 to light something up or make it bright. 2 to decorate something with lights. 3 to decorate (a manuscript) with elaborate designs. 4 to make something clearer and more easily understood. 5 to enlighten someone spiritually or intellectually. ○ **illuminating** *adj.* ○ **illuminative** *adj.*

illumination *n* 1 illuminating or being illuminated. 2 any source of light; lighting. 3 (*usu* illuminations) decorative lights hung in streets and towns, eg at times of celebration. 4 the art of decorating manuscripts with elaborate designs and letters. 5 such a design or letter in a manuscript.

illusion *n* 1 a deceptive or misleading appearance: *an optical illusion.* 2 a false or misleading impression, idea or belief: *under the illusion he worked here.*

> **illusion** A word often confused with this one is **allusion**.

illusionist *n* a conjurer who plays tricks, performs optical illusions, etc.

illusive *or* **illusory** *adj* 1 seeming to be or like an illusion. 2 deceptive; unreal. ○ **illusively** *or* **illusorily** *adv.* ○ **illusiveness** *or* **illusoriness** *n*.

illustrate *vb* 1 to provide pictures and/or diagrams for (a book, lecture, etc). 2 to make (a statement, etc) clearer by providing examples. 3 to be an example of, or an analogy for, something. ○ **illustrated** *adj.* ○ **illustrative** *adj.* ○ **illustrator** *n*.

illustration *n* 1 a picture or diagram. 2 an example. 3 illustrating or being illustrated.

illustrious *adj*, *rather formal* distinguished; celebrated; noble.

ill will *n* hostile feeling.

I'm *contraction* I am.

image *n* 1 a likeness of a person or thing, esp a portrait or statue. 2 someone or something that closely resembles another: *He's the image of his father.* 3 an idea or picture in the mind. 4 the visual display produced by a television. 5 the impression that people in general have of someone's character, behaviour, etc. 6 a simile or metaphor. 7 *optics* an optical reproduction of a physical object. 8 *physics* a reproduction of an object formed by sound waves or electromagnetic radiation. **9** a typical example or embodiment of something. ➤ *vb* **1** to form a likeness or image of something or someone. **2** *med* to produce a pictorial representation of (a body part) using eg X-ray or ultrasound scanning. **3** to form a mental or optical image of something or someone. **4** to portray; to be a typical example of something. ○ **imaging** *n*.

imagery *n* (*-ies*) **1** figures of speech in writing, literature, etc that produce a particular effect: *Heaney's use of agricultural imagery.* **2** the making of images, esp in the mind. **3** mental images. **4** images in general. **5** statues, carvings, etc.

imaginary *adj* existing only in the mind or imagination; not real.

imagination *n* **1** the forming or ability to form mental images of things, people, events, etc that one has not seen or of which one has no direct knowledge. **2** the creative ability of the mind. **3** the ability to cope resourcefully with unexpected events.

imaginative *adj* **1** showing, done with or created by imagination. **2** having a lively imagination.

imagine *vb* **1** to form a mental picture of something: *I can't imagine her wearing a hat.* **2** to see, hear or think something which is not true or does not exist: *You're imagining things.* **3** to think, suppose or guess: *I can't imagine where she is.* **4** *intr* to use the imagination. **5** used as an exclamation of surprise: *Imagine that!* ○ **imaginable** *adj*.

imago /ɪˈmeɪgoʊ/ *n* (**imagos** or **imagines** /-dʒɪˈniːz/) *biol* a sexually mature adult insect.

imam /ɪˈmɑːm/ *n, Islam* **1** a leader of prayers in a mosque. **2** (**Imam**) a title given to various Muslim leaders.

imbalance *n* a lack of balance or proportion.

imbecile *n* **1** *old use* someone of very low intelligence. **2** *colloq* a fool. ○ **imbecility** *n* (*-ies*).

imbibe *vb* **1** *now facetious or formal* to drink, esp alcoholic drinks. **2** *formal or literary* to take in or absorb something (eg ideas).

imbroglio /ɪmˈbroʊlioʊ/ *n* **1** a confused and complicated situation. **2** a misunderstanding or disagreement.

imbue *vb* (**imbued**, **imbuing**) **1** (*esp* **imbue sb with sth**) to inspire someone, esp with ideals or principles. **2** to soak or saturate something, esp with dye.

imitate *vb* **1** to copy the behaviour, appearance, etc of someone. **2** to make a copy of something. ○ **imitable** *adj*. ○ **imitator** *n*.

imitation *n* **1** an act of imitating. **2** something which is produced by imitating. ➤ *adj* sham or artificial: *imitation leather.* ○ **imitative** *adj*.

immaculate *adj* **1** perfectly clean and neat. **2** free from blemish, flaw or error. **3** free from any moral stain or sin. ○ **immaculately** *adv*.

immanent *adj* **1** existing or remaining within something. **2** of a Supreme Being: permanently present throughout the universe. ○ **immanence** *n*.

immaterial *adj* **1** not important or relevant. **2** not formed of matter.

immature *adj* **1** not fully grown or developed. **2** not fully developed emotionally or intellectually. ○ **immaturity** *n*.

immeasurable *adj* too great to be measured; very great. ○ **immeasurably** *adv*.

immediacy *n* (*-ies*) the quality of being immediate or appealing directly to the emotions, understanding, etc.

immediate *adj* **1** happening or done without delay. **2** nearest or next in space, time, relationship, etc: *the immediate family.* **3** belonging to the current time: *deal with the immediate problems first.* **4** having a direct effect: *the immediate cause of death.*

immediately *adv* **1** at once. **2** without anything between: *immediately next to me.* ➤ *conj* as soon as: *Immediately he arrived, the meeting began.*

immemorial *adj* extending far back in time, beyond anyone's memory or written records.

immense *adj* **1** very or unusually large or great. **2** *dated colloq* very good. ○ **immensely** *adv*. ○ **immenseness** or **immensity** *n* (*-ies*).

immerse *vb* (*esp* **immerse sth** or **sb in sth**) to dip it or them into a liquid completely. ○ **immersible** *adj*. ○ **immersion** *n*. ✦ **be immersed in sth** to be occupied, involved or absorbed in it.

immigrant *n* someone who immigrates or has immigrated. ➤ *adj* **1** belonging or relating to immigrants. **2** immigrating or having recently immigrated.

immigrate *vb, intr* to come to a foreign country with the intention of settling in it. ○ **immigration** *n* **1** the process of immigrating. **2** *colloq* **a** the immigration checkpoint at an airport, etc; **b** the immigration authorities.

| **immigrate** | A related word often confused with this one is **emigrate**. |

imminent *adj* likely to happen in the near future. ○ **imminence** *n*. ○ **imminently** *adv*.

immiscible *adj, chem* of liquids, eg oil and water: forming separate layers and not mixing when shaken together.

immobile *adj* **1** not able to move or be moved. **2** motionless. ○ **immobility** *n*.

immobilize or **-ise** *vb* to make or keep something or someone immobile. ○ **immobilization** *n*.

immoderate *adj* excessive or extreme.

immodest *adj* **1** shameful; indecent. **2** boastful and conceited; forward.

immolate *vb* to kill or offer as a sacrifice. ○ **immolation** *n*.

immoral *adj* **1** morally wrong. **2** not conforming to the sexual standards of society. **3** unscrupulous; unethical. ○ **immorality** *n*.

| **immoral** | See note at **amoral**. |

immortal *adj* **1** living forever. **2** lasting forever. **3** to be remembered forever. ➤ *n* **1** someone who will live forever or who will always be remembered. **2** someone whose greatness or genius will be remembered forever. **3** (**the immortals**) the ancient Greek and Roman gods. ○ **immortality** n.

immortalize or **-ise** vb **1** to make (a person, etc) famous for ever, eg in a work of art or literature. **2** to make someone immortal. ○ **immortalization** n.

immovable or **immoveable** adj **1** impossible to move; not meant to be moved. **2** steadfast; unyielding. **3** incapable of feeling or showing emotion. **4** law of property: consisting of land or houses. ○ **immovability** n.

immune adj **1** (esp **immune to sth**) having a natural resistance to or protected by inoculation from (a particular disease). **2** (esp **immune from sth**) free, exempt or protected from it. **3** (esp **immune to sth**) unaffected by or not susceptible to it: *immune to criticism*. **4** physiol relating to or concerned with producing immunity: *the immune system*. ○ **immunity** n.

immunize or **-ise** vb, med to produce artificial immunity to a disease in someone by injecting them with eg a treated antigen. ○ **immunization** n.

immunodeficiency n, physiol, med a deficiency or breakdown in the body's ability to fight infection.

immunology n the scientific study of immunity and the defence mechanisms that the body uses to resist infection and disease. ○ **immunological** adj. ○ **immunologist** n.

immunotherapy n the treatment of disease, esp cancer, by antigens which stimulate the patient's own natural immunity.

immure vb **1** to enclose or imprison someone within, or as if within, walls. **2** to shut someone away.

immutable adj **1** unable to be changed. **2** not susceptible to change. ○ **immutability** n. ○ **immutably** adv.

imp n **1** a small mischievous or evil spirit. **2** a mischievous child. ○ **impish** adj.

impact n /ˈɪmpakt/ **1** the collision of an object with another object. **2** the force of such a collision. **3** a strong effect or impression. ➤ vb /ɪmˈpakt/ **1 a** to press (two objects) together with force; **b** to force (one object) into (another). **2** intr to come forcefully into contact with another body or surface, etc. **3** to have an impact or effect on. ○ **impacted** adj. ○ **impaction** n.

impair vb to damage or weaken something, esp in terms of its quality or strength. ○ **impairment** n.

impala /ɪmˈpɑːlə/ n (**impalas** or **impala**) an antelope of S and E Africa.

impale vb **a** to pierce with, or as if with, a long, pointed object; **b** to put someone to death by this method. ○ **impalement** n.

impalpable adj **1** not able to be felt by touch. **2** difficult to understand. ○ **impalpability** n. ○ **impalpably** adv.

impart vb **1** to make (information, knowledge, etc) known. **2** to give or transmit (a particular quality).

impartial adj fair and unbiased. ○ **impartiality** n. ○ **impartially** adv.

impassable adj of a road, path, etc: not able to be travelled along. ○ **impassability** n.

impasse /ˈɪmpas, amˈpas; French ɛ̃pas/ n a situation with no possible progress or escape.

impassioned adj **1** fervent, zealous or animated. **2** deeply moved by emotion.

impassive adj **1** incapable of feeling and expressing emotion. **2** showing no feeling or emotion. ○ **impassively** adv. ○ **impassiveness** or **impassivity** n.

impasto n, art in painting and pottery: **a** the technique of laying paint or pigment on thickly; **b** paint applied thickly.

impatient adj **1** unwilling to wait or delay. **2** (usu **impatient of** or **with sth** or **sb**) intolerant; showing a lack of patience. **3** (often **impatient to do** or **for sth**) restlessly eager and anxious. ○ **impatience** n. ○ **impatiently** adv.

impeach vb **1** Brit law to charge someone with a serious crime, esp against the state. **2** N Am to accuse (a public official) of misconduct while in office. **3** to cast doubt upon (eg a person's honesty). ○ **impeachable** adj. ○ **impeachment** n.

impeccable adj faultless; perfect.

impecunious adj having little or no money.

impedance /ɪmˈpiːdəns/ n **1** elec the effective RESISTANCE of an electric circuit or component. **2** anything that impedes.

impede vb to prevent or delay the start or progress of (an activity, etc); to obstruct or hinder something or someone.

impediment n **1** an obstacle or hindrance. **2** (also **speech impediment**) a defect in a person's speech.

impedimenta pl n objects which impede progress or movement, eg military baggage and equipment, legal obstructions, etc.

impel vb (**impelled, impelling**) **1** to push, drive or urge something forward. **2** to force or urge someone into action.

impend vb, intr **1** to be about to happen. **2** of a danger, etc: to be threateningly close. ○ **impending** adj.

impenetrable adj **1** incapable of being entered or passed through. **2** not capable of being understood or explained. **3** not capable of receiving or being touched by intellectual ideas and influences: *impenetrable ignorance*.

impenitent adj not sorry for having done something wrong. ➤ n an unrepentant person; a hardened sinner. ○ **impenitence** n.

imperative adj **1** absolutely essential; urgent. **2** having or showing authority: *an imperative manner*. **3** gram of the MOOD² of a verb: used for giving orders. ➤ n **1** gram a mood of verbs used for giving orders. **2** a verb form of this kind. **3** something imperative, esp a command or order. ○ **imperatively** adv.

imperceptible adj 1 too small, slight or gradual to be seen, heard, noticed, etc. 2 not able to be perceived by the senses. ○ **imperceptibly** adv.

imperfect adj 1 having faults; spoilt. 2 lacking the full number of parts; incomplete or unfinished. 3 gram of the tense of a verb: expressing a continuing state or incomplete action in the past. ➤ n, gram **a** the imperfect tense; **b** a verb in the imperfect tense. ○ **imperfection** n.

imperial adj 1 relating to an empire, emperor or empress. 2 having supreme authority. 3 commanding. 4 regal; magnificent. 5 Brit of a non-metric measure or weight, or of the non-metric system: conforming to standards fixed by parliament. ○ **imperially** adv.

imperialism n 1 the power of, or rule by, an emperor or empress. 2 the policy or principle of having or extending control or influence over other nations, eg by conquest, trade or diplomacy. 3 the spirit, character, motivation, etc of empire. ○ **imperialist** n, adj. ○ **imperialistic** adj.

imperil vb (**imperilled, imperilling;** US **imperiled, imperiling**) to endanger. ○ **imperilment** n.

imperious adj arrogant, haughty and domineering. ○ **imperiously** adv.

imperishable adj not subject to decay; lasting forever. ○ **imperishability** n. ○ **imperishably** adv.

impermanent adj not lasting or remaining. ○ **impermanence** n.

impermeable adj of a material, etc: not allowing substances, esp liquids, to pass through it. ○ **impermeability** n.

impersonal adj 1 having no reference to any particular person; objective. 2 without or unaffected by personal or human feelings, warmth, sympathy, etc. 3 without personality. 4 gram of a verb: used without a subject or with a purely formal one (as in It's snowing); **b** of a pronoun: not referring to a particular person. ○ **impersonality** n. ○ **impersonally** adv.

impersonate vb to pretend to be, or copy the behaviour and appearance of, someone, esp in order to entertain or deceive other people. ○ **impersonation** n. ○ **impersonator** n.

impertinent adj disrespectful. ○ **impertinence** n.

imperturbable adj always calm and unruffled. ○ **imperturbability** n. ○ **imperturbably** adv.

impervious adj (usu **impervious to sth**) 1 of a substance, material, etc: not allowing (eg water) to pass through or penetrate it. 2 not influenced or affected by it.

impetigo /ɪmpɪ'taɪgoʊ/ n, pathol a contagious skin disease characterized by pustules and yellow crusty sores.

impetuous adj 1 acting or done hurriedly and without due consideration. 2 moving or acting forcefully or with great energy. ○ **impetuosity** n.

impetus n 1 the force or energy with which something moves. 2 a driving force. 3 an incentive or encouragement.

impinge vb (**impinging**) intr (usu **impinge against** or **on sth** or **sb**) 1 to interfere with or encroach on it or them. 2 to make an impression on it or them. ○ **impingement** n.

impious adj lacking respect or proper reverence. ○ **impiety** n (**-ies**).

implacable adj not able to be calmed, satisfied or placated. ○ **implacability** n. ○ **implacably** adv.

implant vb /ɪm'plɑːnt/ 1 to fix or plant something securely; to embed it. 2 to fix or instil (ideas, beliefs, etc) in someone's mind. 3 surgery to insert or graft (an object, tissue, etc) into the body. ➤ n /'ɪmplɑːnt/ surgery an implanted object, tissue, etc. ○ **implantation** n.

implausible adj not easy to believe. ○ **implausibly** adv.

implement n a tool or utensil. ➤ vb to carry out, fulfil or perform. ○ **implementation** n.

implicate vb 1 to show or suggest that someone is or was involved in eg a crime. 2 to imply. ○ **implicative** adj.

implication n 1 implicating someone or being implicated. 2 implying something or being implied. 3 something that is implied.

implicit adj 1 implied but not stated directly. 2 present, although not explicit or immediately discernible: There was a threat implicit in her words. 3 unquestioning; complete: implicit faith. ○ **implicitly** adv.

implode vb, tr & intr to collapse or make something collapse inwards.

implore vb to beg someone.

imply vb (**-ies, -ied**) 1 to suggest or express something indirectly. 2 to suggest or involve something as a necessary result or consequence: These privileges imply a heavy responsibility.

imply See note at **infer**.

impolite adj rude, disrespectful. ○ **impolitely** adv. ○ **impoliteness** n.

impolitic adj unwise; not to be advised.

imponderable adj having influence or importance that cannot be assessed. ➤ n something imponderable.

import vb /ɪm'pɔːt/ 1 to bring (goods, etc) into a country from another country. 2 to bring something in from an external source. 3 comput to load (a file, text, data, etc) into a program. 4 formal or old use to signify, imply or portend. ➤ n /'ɪmpɔːt/ 1 an imported commodity, article, etc. 2 the act or business of importing goods. 3 formal importance: a matter of great import. 4 formal or old use meaning. ○ **importation** n. ○ **importer** n.

important adj 1 having great value, influence, significance or effect. 2 having high social rank or status. 3 rather formal or literary pompous or pretentious. ○ **importance** n. ○ **importantly** adv.

importunate adj, formal 1 persistent or excessively demanding. **2** extremely urgent or pressing.

importune *vb, tr & intr, formal* **1** to make persistent and usu annoying requests of someone. **2** to solicit for immoral purposes, eg prostitution. ○ **importunity** *n* (*-ies*).

impose *vb* **1** (*usu* **impose sth on** or **upon sb**) to make payment of (a tax, fine, etc) or performance of (a duty) compulsory. **2** (*esp* **impose oneself on** or **upon sb**) to force one's opinions, company, etc on them. **3** (*esp* **impose on** or **upon sb** or **sth**) *intr* to take advantage of them or it; to set unreasonable burdens or tasks on them: *We mustn't impose on your good nature.*

imposing *adj* impressive, esp in size, dignity, etc.

imposition *n* **1** the act or process of imposing. **2** an unfair or excessive demand, burden or requirement. **3** a tax or duty.

impossible *adj* **1** not capable of happening, being done, etc. **2** not capable of being true; difficult to believe. **3** *colloq* unacceptable, unsuitable or difficult to bear. ○ **impossibility** *n*. ○ **impossibly** *adv.*

impostor or **imposter** *n* someone who pretends to be someone else in order to deceive others. ○ **imposture** *n*.

impotent *adj* **1** powerless; lacking the necessary strength. **2** of an adult male: **a** unable to maintain a sexual erection; **b** unable to have an orgasm. ○ **impotence** *n*.

impound *vb* **1** to shut (eg an animal) up in, or as if in, a POUND². **2** to take legal possession of something; to confiscate it.

impoverish *vb* **1** to make poor or poorer. **2** to reduce the quality, richness or fertility of something (eg soil). ○ **impoverished** *adj*.

impracticable *adj* **1** not able to be done, put into practice, used, etc. **2** not in a suitable condition for use. ○ **impracticability** *n*.

impractical *adj* **1** not effective in actual use. **2** of a person, plan, etc: lacking common sense. ○ **impracticality** *n* (*-ies*).

imprecation *n, formal or old use* a curse. ○ **imprecatory** *adj*.

imprecise *adj* inaccurate. ○ **imprecision** *n*.

impregnable *adj* **1** of a city, fortress, etc: not able to be taken by force. **2** not affected by criticism, doubts, etc. ○ **impregnability** *n*.

impregnate *vb* **1** to make (a woman or female animal) pregnant; to fertilize (eg a female cell or plant). **2** to permeate something completely. **3** to fill or imbue something. ○ **impregnation** *n*.

impresario *n* **1** someone who organizes public concerts, etc. **2** the manager of an opera or theatre company.

impress *vb* /ɪmˈprɛs/ **1** to produce a strong and usu favourable impression on someone. **2** (*esp* **impress sth on** or **upon sb**) to make it very clear or emphasize it to them. **3** to make or stamp (a mark, pattern, etc) on something by pressure. **4** (*often* **impress sth on** or **upon sb**) to fix (a fact, belief, etc) firmly or deeply in their mind or memory. ➤ *n* /ˈɪmprɛs/ **1** the act or process of

impressing. **2** something (eg a mark or impression) made by impressing. ○ **impressible** *adj*.

impression *n* **1** an idea or effect, esp a favourable one, produced in the mind or made on the senses. **2** a vague or uncertain idea or belief: *I got the impression he was lying.* **3** an act or the process of impressing. **4** a mark or stamp produced by, or as if by, pressure. **5** an imitation of a person, thing or sound, done for entertainment: *He does impressions of pop stars.* **6** the number of copies of a book, newspaper, etc printed at one time.

impressionable *adj* easily impressed or influenced. ○ **impressionability** *n*.

Impressionism *n* (*sometimes* **impressionism**) in art, music or literature: a 19c style aiming to give a general impression of feelings and events rather than a formal treatment of them.

impressionist *n* **1** (*usu* **Impressionist**) a painter, writer or composer in the style of Impressionism. **2** someone who imitates, or performs impressions of, other people. ➤ *adj* (*usu* **Impressionist**) relating to Impressionism.

impressionistic *adj* based on impressions or feelings rather than facts or knowledge.

impressive *adj* **1** capable of making a deep impression on a person's mind, feelings, etc. **2** producing admiration, wonder or approval. ○ **impressively** *adv.*

imprimatur /ɪmprɪˈmeɪtə(r), -ˈmɑːtə(r)/ *n* **1** permission to print or publish a book, now esp one granted by the Roman Catholic Church. **2** approval; permission.

imprint *n* /ˈɪmprɪnt/ **1** a mark made by pressure. **2** a permanent effect, eg on the mind. **3** a publisher's name and address, and often the date and place of publication, as printed eg at the bottom of a book's title page. ➤ *vb* /ɪmˈprɪnt/ (*usu* **imprint sth on sth**) **1** to mark or print an impression of it on (eg a surface). **2** to fix it firmly in (the mind, etc).

imprison *vb* **1** to put in prison. **2** to confine as if in a prison. ○ **imprisonment** *n*.

improbable *adj* **1** unlikely to happen or exist. **2** hard to believe. ○ **improbability** *n* (*-ies*). ○ **improbably** *adv.*

improbity *n* dishonesty; wickedness.

impromptu *adj* made or done without preparation or rehearsal. ➤ *adv* without preparation; spontaneously.

improper *adj* **1** not conforming to accepted standards of modesty and moral behaviour. **2** not correct: *improper use of funds.* **3** not suitable: *We consider jeans improper dress for the occasion.* ○ **improperly** *adv.*

improper fraction *n, maths* a fraction in which the NUMERATOR has a value equal to or higher than that of the DENOMINATOR, eg $^5/_4$. Compare PROPER FRACTION.

impropriety *n* (*-ies*) **1** an improper act. **2** the state of being improper.

improve *vb* **1** *tr & intr* to make or become better or of higher quality or value; to make or cause something to make progress. **2** *tr & intr* (*esp* **im-**

prove on sth) to produce something better, or of higher quality or value, than a previous example. **3** to increase the value or beauty of (land or property) by cultivation, building, etc.

improvement *n* **1** improving or being improved. **2** someone or something considered better than a previous example. **3** something that improves, esp by adding value, beauty, quality, etc: *home improvements*.

improvident *adj* **1** not considering or providing for likely future needs. **2** careless; thoughtless. ○ **improvidence** *n*. ○ **improvidently** *adv*.

improving *adj* **1** tending to cause improvement. **2** uplifting or instructive, esp in regard to someone's morals.

improvise *vb* **1** *tr & intr* to compose, recite or perform (music, verse, etc) without advance preparation. **2** to make or provide something quickly, without preparation and using whatever materials are to hand. ○ **improvisation** *n*.

imprudent *adj* lacking good sense or caution. ○ **imprudence** *n*.

impudent *adj* insolent or impertinent. ○ **impudence** *n*.

impugn /ɪmˈpjuːn/ *vb* to call into question or raise doubts about (the honesty, integrity, etc of someone or something).

impulse *n* **1** a sudden push forwards; a force producing sudden movement forwards. **2** the movement produced by such a force or push. **3** a sudden desire or urge to do something without thinking of the consequences: *I bought the dress on impulse*. **4** an instinctive or natural tendency. **5** *physiol* an electrical signal that travels along a nerve fibre.

impulsive *adj* **1** tending or likely to act suddenly and without considering the consequences. **2** done without consideration of consequences. **3** having the power to urge or push forwards, into motion or into action. ○ **impulsively** *adv*. ○ **impulsiveness** *n*.

impunity *n* freedom or exemption from punishment, injury, loss, etc.

impure *adj* **1** mixed with something else; tainted. **2** dirty. **3** immoral; not chaste. **4** *relig* ritually unclean. ○ **impurity** *n* (*-ies*).

impute *vb* (*usu* **impute sth to sb** or **sth**) to regard (something unfavourable or unwelcome) as being brought about by them or it. ○ **imputable** *adj*. ○ **imputation** *n*.

In *symbol, chem* indium.

in *prep* **1** used to express position with regard to what encloses, surrounds or includes someone or something. **2** into. **3** after (a period of time): *Come back in an hour*. **4** during; while: *lost in transit*. **5** used to express arrangement or shape: *in a square*. **6** from; out of something: *one in every eight*. **7** by the medium or means of, or using, something: *in code*. **8** wearing: *in costume*. **9** used to describe a state or manner: *in a hurry*. **10** used to state an occupation: *She's in banking*. **11** used to state a purpose: *in memory of his wife*. **12** of some animals: pregnant with (young): *in calf*. ➤ *adv* **1** to or towards

the inside; indoors. **2** at home or work: *Is John in?* **3** so as to be added or included: *beat in the eggs*. **4** so as to enclose or conceal: *The fireplace was bricked in*. **5** in or into political power or office: *when the Tories were in*. **6** in or into fashion. **7** in favour: *He kept in with the boss*. **8** in certain games: batting. **9** into a proper, required or efficient state: *run a new car in*. **10** of the tide: at its highest point. **11** *in compounds* expressing prolonged activity, esp by many people gathered in one place, originally as a form of protest: *a sit-in*. ➤ *adj* **1** inside; internal; inward: *the in door*. **2** fashionable: *Orange is the in colour*. **3** *in compounds* used for receiving things coming in: *an in-tray*. **4** *in compounds* shared by a particular group of people: *an in-joke*. ♦ **be in for it** or **sth** *colloq* to be going to experience some trouble or difficulty. **have it in for sb** *colloq* to want to make trouble for someone one dislikes. **in as far as** or **in so far as ...** (*sometimes written* **insofar as ...**) to the degree that ... **in as much as ...** or **inasmuch as ...** because ... ; considering that ... **in itself** intrinsically; considered on its own. **in on sth** *colloq* knowing about it; sharing in it. **ins and outs** the complex and detailed facts of a matter. **insomuch that** or **insomuch as 1** in as much as. **2** to such an extent that. **in that ...** for the reason that ...

in. *abbrev* inch.

inability *n* the lack of sufficient power, means or ability.

inaccessible *adj* **1** difficult or impossible to approach, reach or obtain. **2** of a person: difficult to understand. ○ **inaccessibility** *n*.

inaccurate *adj* containing errors. ○ **inaccuracy** *n* (*-ies*). ○ **inaccurately** *adv*.

inaction *n* lack of action; sluggishness.

inactive *adj* **1** taking little or no exercise. **2** no longer operating or functioning. **3** not taking part in or available for duty or operations. **4** *chem* of a substance: showing little or no chemical reactivity. ○ **inactively** *adv*. ○ **inactivity** *n*.

inadequate *adj* **1** not sufficient or adequate. **2** not competent or capable. ○ **inadequacy** *n* (*-ies*).

inadmissible *adj* not allowable or able to be accepted.

inadvertent *adj* **1** not deliberate. **2** not paying attention. ○ **inadvertently** *adv*.

inadvisable *adj* not wise; not advisable.

inalienable *adj* not capable of being taken or given away: *an inalienable right*.

inane *adj* **1** without meaning or point. **2** silly or senseless. ○ **inanity** *n*.

inanimate *adj* **1** without life; not living. **2** dull; spiritless. ○ **inanimately** *adv*. ○ **inanimation** *n*.

inapplicable *adj* not applicable or suitable.

inapposite *adj, rather formal* not suitable; out of place.

inappreciable *adj* too small or slight to be noticed or to be important.

inappropriate *adj* not suitable or appropriate.

inapt *adj* **1** not apt or appropriate. **2** lacking skill; unqualified. ○ **inaptitude** *n*.

inarticulate *adj* **1** unable to express oneself clearly or to speak distinctly. **2** badly expressed; not pronounced clearly. **3** not jointed or hinged.

inasmuch see under IN

inattentive *adj* not paying attention; neglectful. ○ **inattention** or **inattentiveness** *n*.

inaudible *adj* not loud enough to be heard.

inaugural *adj* **1** officially marking the beginning of something. **2** of a speech, lecture, etc: given by someone on taking office or at their inauguration ceremony. ➤ *n* an inaugural speech or lecture.

inaugurate *vb* **1** to place (a person) in office with a formal ceremony. **2** to mark the beginning of (some activity) with a formal ceremony, dedication, etc. ○ **inauguration** *n*.

inauspicious *adj* not promising future success.

inboard *adj, adv* esp of a boat's motor or engine: situated inside the hull. Compare OUTBOARD.

inborn *adj* of an attribute or characteristic: possessed from birth.

in-box *n, comput* a file for storing incoming electronic mail.

inbred *adj* **1** INBORN. **2** *biol* of a plant or animal: produced by inbreeding.

inbreed *vb (past tense & past participle inbred)* *biol* to allow or be involved in reproduction between closely related individuals, esp over several generations. ○ **inbreeding** *n*.

in-built *adj* integral.

incalculable *adj* **1** not able to be estimated in advance. **2** too great to be measured. ○ **incalculability** *n*. ○ **incalculably** *adv*.

in camera *adv* in secret; in private.

incandescent *adj* **1** white-hot; glowing with intense heat. **2** shining brightly. **3** of a substance: emitting light as a result of being heated to a high temperature. ○ **incandescence** *n*.

incandescent lamp *n* an electric lamp with a filament of highly resistive wire that becomes white hot and emits light when a current passes through it.

incantation *n* **1** a spell. **2** the use of spells and magical formulae.

incapable *adj (often incapable of sth)* **1** lacking the ability, power, character, etc to do it. **2** unable or unfit to do it.

incapacitate *vb (often incapacitate sb for sth)* **1** to take away strength, power or ability; to make unfit (eg for work). **2** to disqualify someone legally.

incapacity *n (-ies)* **1** a lack of the necessary strength, power, ability, etc. **2** legal disqualification.

incapsulate see ENCAPSULATE

incarcerate *vb* to shut in or keep in prison. ○ **incarceration** *n*.

incarnate *adj (usu placed after a noun)* **1** in bodily, esp human, form: *God incarnate*. **2** personified; typified: *She is laziness incarnate*. ➤ *vb* **1** to give bodily, esp human, form to (a spirit or god). **2** to personify or typify something.

incarnation *n* **1** the bodily form, esp human form, taken by a spirit or god. **2** someone or something that typifies a quality or idea. **3** a period spent in a particular bodily form or state.

incautious *adj* acting or done without thinking.

incendiary *adj* **1** relating to the deliberate and illegal burning of property or goods. **2** capable of catching fire and burning readily. **3** causing, or likely to cause, trouble or violence. ➤ *n (-ies)* **1** someone who deliberately and illegally sets fire to buildings or property. **2** *(also incendiary bomb)* a device containing a highly inflammable substance, designed to burst into flames on striking its target.

incense[1] /ˈɪnsɛns/ *n* **1** a spice or other substance which gives off a pleasant smell when burned, used esp during religious services. **2** the smell or smoke given off by burning spices, etc. ➤ *vb* **1** to offer incense to (a god). **2** to perfume or fumigate something with incense.

incense[2] /ɪnˈsɛns/ *vb* to make someone very angry.

incentive *n* something, such as extra money, that motivates or encourages an action, work, etc. ➤ *adj* serving to motivate or encourage: *an incentive scheme*.

inception *n* beginning.

incessant *adj* going on without stopping. ○ **incessantly** *adv*.

incest *n* sexual intercourse between people who are too closely related to be allowed to marry. ○ **incestuous** *adj*.

inch *n* **1** a unit of length equal to 2.54cm or one-twelfth of a foot. **2** *meteorol* the amount of rain or snow that will cover a surface to the depth of one inch. **3** *meteorol* a unit of pressure equal to the amount of atmospheric pressure required to balance the weight of a column of mercury one inch high. **4** *(also inches)* a small amount or distance. **5** *(inches)* stature. ➤ *vb, tr & intr (esp inch along, forward, out, etc)* to move or be moved slowly, carefully and by small degrees. ◆ **every inch** completely; in every way. **inch by inch** or **by inches** by small degrees. **within an inch of sth** very close to or almost as far as it.

inchoate /ɪnˈkoʊeɪt/ *adj, formal or technical* **1** at the earliest stage of development; just beginning. **2** not fully developed; unfinished; rudimentary.

incidence *n* **1** the frequency with which something happens or the extent of its influence. **2** *physics* the way in which something moving in a line (eg a ray of light) comes into contact with a surface or plane. **3** the fact or manner of falling on, striking or affecting something.

incident *n* **1** an event or occurrence; a relatively minor event or occurrence which might have serious consequences. **2** a brief violent conflict or disturbance. ➤ *adj* **1** (*esp* **incident to sth**) belonging naturally to it or being a natural consequence of it. **2** *physics* of light rays, particles, etc: falling on a surface, etc.

incidental *adj* **1** happening, etc by chance in connection with something else, and of secondary importance: *incidental expenses*. **2** (*usu* **incidental to sth**) occurring or likely to occur as a minor consequence of it. **3** (*usu* **incidental on** or **upon sth**) following or depending upon it, or caused by it, as a minor consequence. ➤ *n* **1** anything that occurs incidentally. **2** (**incidentals**) minor expenses, details, items, etc. ○ **incidentally** *adv*.

incidental music *n* music which accompanies the action of a film, play, etc.

incinerate *vb, tr & intr* to burn to ashes. ○ **incineration** *n*.

incinerator *n* a furnace for burning rubbish, etc.

incipient *adj* beginning to exist.

incise *vb, esp technical* **1** to cut into, esp precisely with a sharp tool. **2** to engrave (an inscription, stone, etc).

incision *n* **1** a cut, esp one made by a surgeon. **2** an act of cutting, esp by a surgeon.

incisive *adj* clear and sharp; to the point. ○ **incisively** *adv*. ○ **incisiveness** *n*.

incisor *n* in mammals: a sharp chisel-edged tooth in the front of the mouth, used for biting and nibbling.

incite *vb* (*esp* **incite sb to sth**) to stir up or provoke to action, etc. ○ **incitement** *n*.

incivility *n* (*-ies*) **1** rudeness. **2** a rude act or remark.

incl. or (*sometimes*) **inc.** *abbrev* **1** included. **2** including. **3** inclusive.

inclement /ɪŋˈklɛmənt/ *adj, formal* of weather: stormy or severe.

inclination *n* **1** (*often* **an inclination for** or **towards sth** or **to do sth**) a tendency or feeling; a liking, interest or preference. **2** the degree to which an object slopes. **3** a slope. **4** a bow or nod (of the head, etc). **5** the act of inclining; being inclined.

incline /ɪŋˈklaɪn/ *vb* **1** *tr & intr* (*esp* **incline to** or **towards sth**) to lean or make someone lean towards or be disposed towards (a particular opinion or conduct): *He inclined towards radicalism.* **2** *tr & intr* to slope or make something slope. **3** to bend (the head, one's body, etc) forwards or downwards. ➤ *n* /ˈɪŋklaɪn/ a slope. ○ **inclined** *adj*.

inclose, inclosure see ENCLOSE, ENCLOSURE

include *vb* **1** to count, take in or consider something or someone as part of a group. **2** to contain or be made up of something, or to have it as a part of the whole. ○ **including** *prep* which includes.

inclusion *n* **1** including or being included. **2** something that is included.

inclusive *adj* **1** (*usu* **inclusive of sth**) incorporating; taking it in. **2** counting the items or

terms forming the limits. **3** comprehensive.

incognito *adj, adv* keeping one's identity secret, eg by using a disguise and a false name. ➤ *n* **1** the disguise and false name of a person who wishes to keep their identity secret. **2** someone who is incognito.

incognizant or **-isant** *adj, formal* not aware of something. ○ **incognizance** *n*.

incoherent *adj* **1** not expressed clearly or logically. **2** unable to speak clearly and logically.

income *n* money received over a period of time as salary or wages, interest or profit.

incomer *n* someone who comes to live in a place, not having been born there.

income tax *n* a tax levied on income.

incoming *adj* **1** coming in: *the incoming train*. **2** next or following. **3** of an official, politician, etc: coming into office.

incommensurable *adj* (*esp* **incommensurable with sth**) **1** having no common standard or basis and not able to be compared with it. **2** *maths* of a quantity or magnitude: having no common factor with another. ○ **incommensurability** *n*.

incommensurate *adj* **1** (*esp* **incommensurate with** or **to sth**) out of proportion to it; inadequate for it. **2** INCOMMENSURABLE.

incommodious *adj, formal* of eg accommodation: uncomfortable; too small.

incommunicado *adv, adj* not able or allowed to communicate with other people, esp when in solitary confinement.

incomparable *adj* **1** having no equal. **2** lacking a basis for comparison.

incompatible *adj* **1** unable to live, work or get on together in harmony. **2** (*often* **incompatible with sth**) not in agreement; inconsistent. **3** of eg drugs: not able to be used together. **4** of eg machines, computer software or hardware, etc: incapable of functioning together. ○ **incompatibility** *n*.

incompetent *adj* **1** lacking the necessary skill, ability or qualifications, esp for a job. **2** not legally qualified or COMPETENT. ➤ *n* an incompetent person. ○ **incompetence** *n*. ○ **incompetently** *adv*.

incomplete *adj* not complete or finished.

incomprehensible *adj* difficult or impossible to understand. ○ **incomprehensibility** *n*.

inconceivable *adj* **1** unable to be imagined or believed. **2** *colloq* extremely unlikely. ○ **inconceivability** *n*.

inconclusive *adj* not leading to a definite conclusion, result or decision. ○ **inconclusiveness** *n*.

incongruous *adj* **1** out of place; unsuitable. **2** (*often* **incongruous with** or **to sth**) incompatible or out of keeping with it. ○ **incongruity** *n* (*-ies*).

inconsequent *adj* **1** not following logically or reasonably. **2** irrelevant. **3** (also **inconsequential**) not connected or related. ○ **inconsequently** *adv*.

inconsequential *adj* **1** of no importance, value or CONSEQUENCE. **2** INCONSEQUENT (sense 3).

inconsiderable adj, often with negatives not worth considering; small in amount, value, etc: *Her father lent her a not inconsiderable sum.* ○ **inconsiderably** adv.

inconsiderate adj thoughtless, esp in not considering the feelings, etc of others. ○ **inconsiderateness** or **inconsideration** n.

inconsistent adj 1 not in agreement or accordance with something. 2 containing contradictions. 3 not consistent in thought, speech, behaviour, etc; changeable. ○ **inconsistency** n (-ies).

inconsolable adj not able to be comforted.

inconspicuous adj not easily noticed.

inconstant adj 1 having frequently changing feelings. 2 subject to frequent change. ○ **inconstancy** n.

incontestable adj indisputable; undeniable.

incontinent adj 1 unable to control one's bowels and/or bladder. 2 formal or old use unable to control oneself, esp one's sexual desires. ○ **incontinence** n.

incontrovertible adj not able to be disputed or doubted. ○ **incontrovertibly** adv.

inconvenience n 1 trouble or difficulty. 2 something that causes trouble or difficulty. ➤ vb to cause trouble or difficulty to someone. ○ **inconvenient** adj. ○ **inconveniently** adv.

incorporate vb /ɪŋ'kɔ:pəreɪt/ 1 tr & intr to include or contain something, or be included, as part of a whole. 2 tr & intr to combine something, or be united thoroughly, in a single mass. 3 to admit someone to membership of a legal corporation. 4 to form (a company or other body) into a legal corporation. 5 intr to form a legal corporation. ➤ adj /-rət/ (also **incorporated**) 1 united in one body or as a single whole. 2 forming a legal corporation. ○ **incorporation** n.

incorporeal adj 1 without bodily or material form or substance. 2 spiritual.

incorrect adj 1 not accurate; containing errors or faults. 2 not in accordance with normal or accepted standards.

incorrigible adj of a person, their bad behaviour or a bad habit: not able to be improved, corrected or reformed. ○ **incorrigibility** n.

incorruptible adj 1 incapable of being bribed or morally corrupted. 2 not liable to decay. ○ **incorruptibility** n. ○ **incorruptibly** adv.

increase vb /ɪŋ'kri:s/ tr & intr to make or become greater in size, intensity or number. ➤ n /'ɪŋkri:s/ 1 increasing or becoming increased; growth. 2 the amount by which something increases or is increased. ○ **increasing** adj. ○ **increasingly** adv.

incredible adj 1 difficult or impossible to believe. 2 colloq amazing; unusually good. ○ **incredibility** n. ○ **incredibly** adv.

| incredible, incredulous | These words are often confused with each other.

incredulous adj 1 showing or expressing dis-

belief. 2 (often **incredulous of sth**) unwilling to believe or accept that it is true. ○ **incredulity** n. ○ **incredulously** adv.

increment n 1 an increase, esp of one point or level on a scale, eg a regular increase in salary. 2 the amount by which something is increased. 3 maths a small positive or negative change in the value of a variable. ○ **incremental** adj.

incriminate vb 1 (sometimes **incriminate sb in sth**) a to show that they were involved in it (esp in a crime); b to involve or implicate them (esp in a crime). 2 to charge someone with a crime or fault. ○ **incriminating** or **incriminatory** adj. ○ **incrimination** n.

incrust see ENCRUST

incubate vb 1 tr & intr of birds: to hatch (eggs) by sitting on them to keep them warm. 2 to encourage (germs, bacteria, etc) to develop, eg in a culture medium in a laboratory. 3 intr of germs, etc: to remain inactive in an organism before the first signs of disease appear. 4 tr & intr to develop slowly or gradually. ○ **incubation** n.

incubator n 1 med a transparent boxlike container in which a premature baby can be nurtured under controlled conditions. 2 a cabinet or room that can be maintained at a constant temperature, used for culturing microorganisms, hatching eggs, etc.

incubus /'ɪŋkjʊbəs/ n (**incubuses, incubi** /-baɪ/) 1 folklore an evil male spirit which is supposed to have sexual intercourse with sleeping women. Compare SUCCUBUS. 2 something which oppresses or weighs heavily upon one, esp a nightmare.

inculcate vb (esp **inculcate sth in** or **into** or **upon sb**) rather formal to teach or fix (ideas, habits, etc) firmly in their mind by constant repetition. ○ **inculcation** n.

inculpate vb, formal to blame someone or show them to be guilty of a crime. ○ **inculpation** n. ○ **inculpatory** adj.

incumbent adj, rather formal 1 (esp **incumbent on** or **upon sb**) imposed as a duty or responsibility on them: *I feel it incumbent upon me to defend him.* 2 currently occupying a specified position or office: *the incumbent bishop.* ➤ n a holder of an office, esp a church office. ○ **incumbency** n (-ies).

incur vb (**incurred, incurring**) 1 to bring (something unpleasant) upon oneself. 2 to become liable for (debts, payment of a fine, etc). ○ **incurrable** adj.

incurable adj 1 of eg a disease: not curable. 2 of a person: incapable of changing a specified aspect of their character: *an incurable optimist.* ➤ n an incurable person or thing. ○ **incurably** adv.

incursion n 1 a brief or sudden attack made into enemy territory. 2 a damaging invasion into or using up of something. 3 the action of leaking or running into something. ○ **incursive** adj.

Ind. *abbrev* **1** Independent. **2** India or Indian.

indebted *adj* (*usu* **indebted to sb**) **1** having reason to be grateful or obliged to them. **2** owing them money. ○ **indebtedness** *n*.

indecent *adj* **1** offensive to accepted standards of morality or sexual behaviour. **2** in bad taste; improper: *He remarried with indecent haste*. ○ **indecency** *n* (*-ies*). ○ **indecently** *adv*.

indecent assault *n, law* a sexual attack which falls short of rape.

indecipherable *adj* unable to be read, deciphered or understood.

indecisive *adj* **1** not producing a clear or definite decision or result. **2** of a person: unable to make a firm decision. ○ **indecision** *n*. ○ **indecisively** *adv*. ○ **indecisiveness** *n*.

indecorous *adj, formal* in bad taste; unseemly.

indeed *adv* **1** without any question; in truth. **2** in fact; actually. **3** used for emphasis: *very wet indeed*. ➤ *exclam* expressing irony, surprise, disbelief, disapproval, etc, or simple acknowledgement of a previous remark: *I'm going whether you like it or not. — Indeed?*

indefatigable *adj* **1** without tiring. **2** never stopping. ○ **indefatigably** *adv*.

indefensible *adj* **1** unable to be excused or justified. **2** of an opinion, position, etc: unable to be defended. **3** *literally* not possible to defend against attack. ○ **indefensibility** *n*. ○ **indefensibly** *adv*.

indefinable *adj* unable to be clearly or exactly defined or described. ○ **indefinably** *adv*.

indefinite *adj* **1** without fixed or exact limits or clearly marked outlines: *off sick for an indefinite period*. **2** uncertain; vague: *indefinite about her plans*. **3** *gram* not referring to a particular person or thing. ○ **indefinitely** *adv*.

indefinite article *n, gram* in English *a* or *an*, or any equivalent word in another language. Compare DEFINITE ARTICLE.

indehiscent / ɪndɪˈhɪsnt / *adj, bot* of a fruit, not splitting open to scatter its seeds.

indelible *adj* **1** unable to be removed or rubbed out. **2** designed to make an indelible mark. ○ **indelibly** *adv*.

indelicate *adj* **1** tending to embarrass or offend. **2** slightly coarse. ○ **indelicacy** *n* (*-ies*). ○ **indelicately** *adv*.

indemnify *vb* (*-ies, -ied*) **1** (*esp* **indemnify sb against** or **from sth**) to provide them with security or protection against (loss or misfortune). **2** (*usu* **indemnify sb for sth**) to pay them compensation for (esp loss or damage). ○ **indemnification** *n*.

indemnity *n* (*-ies*) **1 a** compensation for loss or damage; **b** money paid in compensation. **2** security or protection from loss or damage; insurance. **3** legal exemption from liabilities or penalties.

indent[1] *vb* / ɪnˈdɛnt / **1** *printing, typing* to begin (a line or paragraph) further in from the margin than the main body of text. **2** to divide (a document drawn up in duplicate in two columns) along a zigzag line. **3** to draw up (a document, deed, etc) in duplicate. **4** *tr & intr, Brit, commerce* to make out a written order (for goods). **5** to indenture someone as an apprentice. **6** to notch (eg a border). ➤ *n* / ˈɪndɛnt / **1** *Brit, commerce* a written order or official requisition for goods. **2** *printing, typing* an indented line or paragraph. **3** a notch. **4** an indenture.

indent[2] *vb* / ɪnˈdɛnt / to form a dent in something or mark it with dents. ➤ *n* / ˈɪndɛnt / a hollow, depression or dent.

indentation *n* **1** a cut or notch, often one of a series. **2** a deep, inward curve or recess, eg in a coastline. **3** the act or process of indenting. **4** INDENTION.

indention *n, printing, typing* **1** the indenting of a line or paragraph. **2** the blank space at the beginning of a line caused by indenting a line or paragraph.

indenture *n* **1** (*usu* **indentures**) a contract binding an apprentice to a master. **2** an indented document, agreement or contract. ➤ *vb, chiefly old use* **1** to bind (eg an apprentice) by indentures. **2** to bind (eg another party) by an indented contract or agreement.

independent *adj* (*sometimes* **independent of sth** or **sb**) **1 a** not under the control or authority of others; **b** of a country, etc: self-governing. **2** not relying on others for financial support, care, help or guidance. **3** thinking and acting for oneself and not under an obligation to others. **4** *maths, etc* not dependent on something else for value, purpose or function. **5** of two or more people or things: not related to or affected by the others. **6** of private income or resources: large enough to make it unnecessary to work for a living: *a man of independent means*. **7** not belonging to a political party. **8** of a school or broadcasting company: not belonging to the state system. ➤ *n* an independent person or thing. ○ **independence** *n*. ○ **independently** *adv*.

in-depth *adj* thorough; exhaustive.

indescribable *adj* unable to be put into words. ○ **indescribably** *adv*.

indestructible *adj* not able to be destroyed.

indeterminable *adj* **1** not able to be fixed, decided or measured. **2** unable to be settled. ○ **indeterminably** *adv*.

indeterminate *adj* **1** not precisely fixed or settled. **2** doubtful; vague: *an indeterminate outlook*. **3** *maths* of an equation: having more than one variable and an infinite number of possible solutions. **4** *maths* denoting an expression that has no defined or fixed value or no quantitative meaning, eg 0/0.

index *n* (**indexes** or *technical* **indices** / ˈɪndɪsiːz /) **1** an alphabetical list of names, subjects, etc dealt with in a book, with the page numbers on which each item appears. **2** in a library, etc: a catalogue which lists each book, magazine, etc alphabetically and gives details of where it is shelved. **3** anything which points to, identifies or highlights a particular trend or condition. **4** a scale of numbers which shows

changes in price, wages, etc: *retail price index*.
5 *maths* an EXPONENT (sense 3). **6** *physics* a numerical quantity that indicates the magnitude of an effect: *refractive index*. ➤ *vb* **1** to provide (a book, etc) with an index. **2** to list something in an index. **3** to make something INDEX-LINKED. ○ **indexation** *n*. ○ **indexer** *n*.

index finger *n* the finger next to the thumb.

index-linked *adj, econ* of prices, wages, rates of interest, etc: rising or falling by the same amount as the cost of living.

Indian *adj* **1** relating to India or the Indian subcontinent, its inhabitants, languages or culture. **2** *chiefly old use* relating to the indigenous peoples of America, their languages or culture. Now NATIVE AMERICAN. ➤ *n* **1** a citizen or inhabitant of, or person born in, India or the Indian subcontinent, or someone belonging to the same races. **2** *chiefly old use* a NATIVE AMERICAN or someone belonging to one of the indigenous peoples of America. **3** *chiefly old use* any of the Native American languages. **4** *colloq* **a** a restaurant that specializes in Asian food, esp curries; **b** a meal in, or a takeaway from, this type of restaurant.

Indian club *n* one of a pair of heavy bottle-shaped clubs swung to develop the arm muscles.

Indian corn *n* another name for MAIZE.

Indian file see SINGLE FILE

Indian ink or (*N Am*) **India ink** *n* a black ink.

Indian summer *n* **1** a period of unusually warm weather in late autumn. **2** a period of happiness and success towards the end of someone's life, an era, etc.

India rubber *n* a RUBBER[1] (sense 2).

indicate *vb* **1** to point out or show. **2** to be a sign or symptom of something. **3** of a gauge, dial, etc: to show something as a reading. **4** to show or state something: *He indicated his consent.* **5** *med, etc (esp in the passive)* to point to something as a treatment: *A course of steroids was indicated.* **6** *intr* to use an INDICATOR (sense 2) on a motor vehicle. ○ **indication** *n*.

indicative *adj* **1** (*usu indicative of sth*) serving as a sign or indication of it. **2** *gram* **a** of the MOOD[2] of a verb: used to state facts, describe events or ask questions; **b** of a verb, tense, etc: in this mood. ➤ *n, gram* **1** the indicative MOOD[2]. **2** a verb form of this kind. ○ **indicatively** *adv*.

indicator *n* **1** an instrument or gauge that shows the level of temperature, fuel, pressure, etc; **b** a needle or pointer on such a device. **2** a flashing light on a motor vehicle which shows that the vehicle is about to change direction. **3** any sign, condition, situation, etc which shows or indicates something: *an economic indicator*. **4** a board or diagram giving information, eg in a railway station. **5** *chem* a substance (eg LITMUS) that changes colour depending on the pH of a solution.

indict /ɪnˈdaɪt/ *vb, law* to accuse someone of, or charge them formally with, a crime, esp in writing. ○ **indictable** *adj*.

indictment *n* **1** a formal written accusation or charge. **2** an act of indicting someone. **3** something which deserves severe criticism or censure, or which serves to criticize or condemn something or someone.

indie *n, colloq* **1** a small independent and usu non-commercial record or film company. **2** a type of music produced predominantly by such companies. ➤ *adj* produced by small independent companies; not mainstream or commercial: *indie music*.

indifferent *adj* **1** (*esp indifferent to or towards sth or sb*) showing no interest in or concern for it or them. **2** neither good nor bad; average. **3** fairly bad; inferior. **4** unimportant. **5** neutral. ○ **indifference** *n*. ○ **indifferently** *adv*.

indigenous *adj* **1** *biol* of plants or animals: belonging naturally to or occurring naturally in a country or area. **2** of a person: born in a region, area, country, etc.

indigent *adj, formal* very poor. ○ **indigence** *n* poverty.

indigestible *adj* **1** difficult or impossible to digest. **2** not easily understood. ○ **indigestibility** *n*.

indigestion *n* discomfort or pain in the abdomen or lower region of the chest caused by difficulty in digesting food.

indignant *adj* feeling or showing anger or a sense of having been treated unjustly. ○ **indignantly** *adv*. ○ **indignation** *n*.

indignity *n* (*-ies*) **1** any act or treatment which makes someone feel shame or humiliation. **2** a feeling of shame, disgrace or dishonour.

indigo *n* (*indigos* or *indigoes*) **1** a violet-blue dye. **2** a plant whose leaves yield this dye. **3** the deep violet-blue colour of this dye. ➤ *adj* violet-blue in colour.

indirect *adj* **1** of a route, line, etc: not direct or straight. **2** not going straight to the point; not straightforward or honest. **3** not directly aimed at or intended: *indirect consequences*.

indirect object *n, gram* a noun, phrase or pronoun which is affected indirectly by the action of a verb, usu standing for the person or thing to whom something is given or for whom something is done. Compare DIRECT OBJECT.

indirect question *n* a question reported in indirect speech, as in *They're asking who you are.*

indirect speech *n, gram* a speaker's words as reported by another person, eg *We will come* becomes *They said they would come* in indirect speech. Also called **reported speech**. Compare DIRECT SPEECH.

indirect tax *n* a tax levied on goods and services when they are purchased. Compare DIRECT TAX.

indiscernible *adj* unable to be noticed or recognized as being distinct, esp because too small.

indiscipline *n* lack of discipline.

indiscreet *adj* **1** giving away too many secrets or too much information. **2** not wise or cautious. ○ **indiscreetly** adv. ○ **indiscretion** n.

indiscriminate adj **1** making no distinctions; not making careful choice or showing discrimination. **2** confused; not differentiated. ○ **indiscriminately** adv. ○ **indiscriminateness** n.

indispensable adj necessary; essential. ○ **indispensability** n. ○ **indispensably** adv.

indisposed adj, rather formal **1** slightly ill. **2** (esp **indisposed to do sth**) reluctant to do it. ○ **indisposition** n.

indisputable adj certainly true; beyond doubt.

indissoluble adj incapable of being dissolved or broken; permanent.

indistinct adj not clear to a person's eye, ear or mind. ○ **indistinctly** adv. ○ **indistinctness** n.

indistinguishable adj not able to be distinguished or told apart from something.

indium n, chem a soft, silvery-white metallic element.

individual adj **1** intended for or relating to a single person or thing: jam served in individual portions. **2** particular to one person; showing or having a particular person's unique qualities or characteristics. **3** separate; single. ➤ n **1** a particular person, animal or thing, esp in contrast to the group to which it belongs: the rights of the individual. **2** colloq a person. ○ **individualize** or **-ise** vb. ○ **individually** adv.

individualism n **1 a** the belief that individual people should lead their lives as they want and should be independent; **b** behaviour governed by this belief. **2** self-centredness. ○ **individualist** n.

individuality n (**-ies**) **1** the qualities and character which distinguish one person or thing from others. **2** a separate and distinct existence or identity.

indivisible adj **1** not able to be divided or separated. **2** maths of a number: not divisible (by a given number) without leaving a remainder. ➤ n, maths an indefinitely small quantity.

indoctrinate vb to teach (an individual or group) to accept and believe a particular set of beliefs, etc uncritically. ○ **indoctrination** n.

indolent adj disliking and avoiding work and exercise. ○ **indolence** n. ○ **indolently** adv.

indomitable adj unable to be conquered or defeated. ○ **indomitably** adv.

indoor adj used, belonging, done, happening, etc inside a building.

indoors adv in or into a building.

indorse see ENDORSE

indrawn adj **1** esp of the breath: drawn in. **2** of a person: aloof or introspective.

indubitable adj unable to be doubted; certain. ○ **indubitably** adv.

induce vb **1** to persuade, influence or cause someone to do something. **2** obstetrics to initiate or hasten (labour) by artificial means. **3** to make something happen or appear. **4** to produce or transmit (an electromotive force) by INDUCTION. **5** logic to infer (a general conclu-

sion) from particular cases. ○ **inducible** adj.

inducement n something that persuades or influences; an incentive or motive.

induct vb **1** to place (eg a priest) formally and often ceremonially in an official position. **2** to initiate someone as a member of eg a society or profession.

inductance n, physics the property of an electric circuit or circuit component that causes an ELECTROMOTIVE force to be generated in it when a changing current is present.

induction n **1** inducting or being inducted, esp into office. **2** obstetrics the initiation of labour by artificial means. **3** elec the production of an electric current in a conductor as a result of its close proximity to a varying magnetic field. **4** elec magnetization caused by close proximity either to a magnetic field or to the electromagnetic field of a current-carrying conductor. **5** logic the forming of a general conclusion from particular cases. Compare DEDUCTION. ○ **inductional** adj.

induction coil n, physics a type of TRANSFORMER that can produce a high-voltage alternating current from a low-voltage direct current source.

induction course n a course of introductory formal instruction given to familiarize a new employee.

inductor n **1** elec a component of an electrical circuit that shows INDUCTANCE. **2** someone or something that inducts.

indulge vb **1** tr & intr (esp **indulge in sth** or **indulge sb in sth**) to allow oneself or someone else pleasure or the pleasure of (a specified thing). **2** to allow someone to have or do anything they want. **3** to give in to (a desire, taste, wish, etc) without restraint. **4** intr, colloq to eat or drink something one should not: No, I won't indulge. I'm driving.

indulgence n **1** the state of being indulgent; generosity; favourable or tolerant treatment. **2** an act or the process of indulging a person, desire, etc. **3** a pleasure that is indulged in. **4** RC Church a special grant of remission from the punishment which remains due for a sin after it has been absolved.

indulgent adj quick or too quick to overlook or forgive faults or gratify the wishes of others. ○ **indulgently** adv.

industrial adj **1** relating to or suitable for industry. **2** of a country, city, etc: having highly developed industry.

industrial action n, Brit action taken by workers as a protest, eg a STRIKE, GO-SLOW or WORK TO RULE.

industrial estate n an area in a town which is developed for industry and business.

industrialism n a social system in which industry forms the basis of commerce and the economy.

industrialist n someone who owns a large industrial organization or who is involved in its management at a senior level.

industrialize or **-ise** *vb, tr & intr* to develop industrially; to introduce industry to (a place). ○ **industrialization** *n.*

industrial relations *pl n* relations between management and workers.

industrious *adj* busy and hard-working. ○ **industriously** *adv.* ○ **industriousness** *n.*

industry *n* (*-ies*) **1** the business of producing goods. **2** a branch of manufacturing and trade which produces a particular product: *the coal industry.* **3** organized commercial exploitation or use of natural or national assets: *the tourist industry.* **4** hard work or effort.

inebriate *vb* /ɪn'iːbrɪeɪt/ **1** to make someone drunk. **2** to exhilarate someone greatly. ➤ *adj* /ɪn'iːbrɪət/ (*now usu* **inebriated**) drunk, esp habitually drunk. ➤ *n* /ɪn'iːbrɪət/ *formal* someone who is drunk, esp regularly so. ○ **inebriation** *n.*

inedible *adj* not fit or suitable to be eaten.

ineffable *adj, esp literary or formal* **1** unable to be described or expressed in words, esp because of size, magnificence, etc. **2** not supposed or not allowed to be said, esp because too sacred. ○ **ineffably** *adv.*

ineffective *adj* **1** having no effect; not able or likely to produce a result, or the result or effect intended. **2** not capable of achieving results. ○ **ineffectiveness** *n.*

ineffectual *adj* **1** not producing a result or the intended result. **2** lacking the ability and confidence needed to achieve results. ○ **ineffectuality** or **ineffectualness** *n.* ○ **ineffectually** *adv.*

inefficient *adj* lacking the power or skill to do or produce something in the best, most economical, etc way. ○ **inefficiency** *n.* ○ **inefficiently** *adv.*

inelegant *adj* lacking grace or refinement. ○ **inelegance** *n.* ○ **inelegantly** *adv.*

ineligible *adj* **1** not qualified to stand for election. **2** not suitable to be chosen. ○ **ineligibility** *n.*

ineluctable *adj, esp literary or formal* unavoidable, irresistible or inescapable. ○ **ineluctably** *adv.*

inept *adj* **1** awkward; done without, or not having, skill. **2** not suitable or fitting. **3** silly; foolish. ○ **ineptitude** *n.*

inequable *adj* **1** not fair or just. **2** changeable; not even or uniform.

inequality *n* (*-ies*) **1** a lack of equality, fairness or evenness, or an instance of this. **2** *maths* a statement that the values of two numerical quantities, algebraic expressions, functions, etc are not equal.

inequitable *adj, rather formal* not fair or just.

inequity *n* (*-ies*) *rather formal* **1** an unjust action. **2** lack of fairness or equity.

inert *adj* **1** *physics* tending to remain in a state of rest or uniform motion in a straight line unless acted upon by an external force. **2** not wanting to move, act or think; indolent. **3** *chem* unreactive or showing only a limited ability to

react with other chemical elements.

inert gas see NOBLE GAS

inertia *n* **1** *physics* the tendency of an object to be INERT. **2** the state of not wanting to move, act or think; indolence. ○ **inertial** *adj.*

inescapable *adj* unable to be avoided. ○ **inescapably** *adv.*

inessential *adj* not necessary. ➤ *n* an inessential thing.

inestimable *adj, rather formal* too great, or of too great a value, to be estimated, measured or fully appreciated. ○ **inestimably** *adv.*

inevitable *adj* **1** unable to be avoided; certain to happen. **2** *colloq* tiresomely regular or predictable. ➤ *n* (*esp* **the inevitable**) something that is certain to happen and is unavoidable. ○ **inevitability** *n.* ○ **inevitably** *adv.*

inexact *adj* not quite correct or true.

inexcusable *adj* too bad to be excused, justified or tolerated. ○ **inexcusably** *adv.*

inexhaustible *adj* **1** of eg a supply: incapable of being used up. **2** tireless; never failing or giving up.

inexorable *adj* **1** refusing to change opinion, course of action, etc. **2** unable to be altered or avoided. ○ **inexorably** *adv.*

inexpensive *adj* cheap or reasonable in price.

inexperience *n* lack of skill or knowledge gained from experience. ○ **inexperienced** *adj.*

inexpert *adj* (*often* **inexpert at** or **in sth**) unskilled at it. ○ **inexpertly** *adv.*

inexplicable *adj* impossible to explain or understand. ○ **inexplicably** *adv.*

inexpressible *adj* unable to be expressed or described. ○ **inexpressibly** *adv.*

in extremis *adv* **1** at, or as if at, the point of death. **2** in desperate circumstances.

inextricable *adj* **1** of a situation, etc: unable to be escaped from. **2** of a knot, dilemma, etc: unable to be disentangled. ○ **inextricably** *adv.*

infallible *adj* **1** of a person: incapable of error. **2** *RC Church* of the Pope: unable to err when pronouncing officially on dogma. **3** of a plan, method, etc: always, or bound to be, successful or effective. ○ **infallibility** *n.*

infamous *adj* **1** notoriously bad. **2** *formal* vile; disgraceful. ○ **infamously** *adv.* ○ **infamy** *n* (*-ies*).

infancy *n* (*-ies*) **1** the state or time of being an infant. **2** an early period of existence, growth and development: *when television was still in its infancy.* **3** *law* MINORITY (sense 4).

infant *n* **1** a very young child. **2** *Brit* a schoolchild under the age of seven or eight. **3** *law* a MINOR (noun sense 1). ➤ *adj* **1** relating to or involving infants: *infant mortality.* **2** at an early stage of development.

infanticide *n* **1** the murder of a child. **2** someone who commits this act. **3** the practice of killing newborn children. ○ **infanticidal** *adj.*

infantile *adj* **1** relating to infants or infancy. **2** very childish; immature.

infantry *n* (*-ies*) soldiers trained and equipped to fight on foot.

infantryman *n* a soldier in the infantry.

infarction *n, pathol* the death of a localized area of tissue as a result of the blocking of its blood supply.

infatuate *vb* to make someone feel passionate, foolish, intense, etc love or admiration. ○ **infatuated** *adj* (*esp* **infatuated with sb** or **sth**) filled with intense love. ○ **infatuation** *n*.

infect *vb* (*often* **infect sth** or **sb with sth**) **1** *biol, med, etc* to contaminate (a living organism) with a bacterium, virus, etc and thereby cause disease. **2** to taint or contaminate (eg water, food or air) with a bacterium, pollutant, etc. **3** to pass on a feeling or opinion, esp a negative one, to someone. **4** *comput* to affect with a VIRUS (sense 4).

infection *n* **1** infecting or being infected. **2** *biol, med, etc* the invasion of a human, animal or plant by disease-causing micro-organisms. **3** a disease caused by such micro-organisms.

infectious *adj* **1** of a disease: caused by bacteria, viruses or other micro-organisms, and therefore capable of being transmitted through air, water, etc. **2** eg of a person: capable of infecting others. **3** of an emotion, opinion, etc: likely to be passed on to others: *Laughter is infectious.*

> **infectious, contagious** There is often confusion between **infectious** and **contagious**: an **infectious** disease is spread through the air, while a **contagious** disease is spread by touch, although when used figuratively, of laughter for example, they mean the same thing.

infelicitous *adj* **1** not happy, fortunate or lucky. **2** not suitable, fitting or apt.

infer *vb* (**inferred, inferring**) **1** *tr & intr* to conclude or judge from facts, observation and deduction. **2** *colloq* to imply or suggest. ○ **inferable** or **inferrable** *adj*.

> **infer** The meaning given in sense 2 is common, but is still subject to disapproval. Use **imply** or **suggest** if you are talking or writing to someone who is likely to be precise about the use of language.

inference *n* **1** an act of inferring. **2** something which is inferred. ○ **inferential** *adj*.

inferior *adj* (*often* **inferior to sth** or **sb**) **1** poor or poorer in quality. **2** low or lower in value, rank or status. **3** low or lower in position. **4** of letters or figures: printed or written slightly below the line. ➤ *n* someone or something which is inferior. ○ **inferiority** *n*.

inferiority complex *n* **1** *psychol* a disorder arising from the conflict between the desire to be noticed and the fear of being shown to be inadequate, characterized by aggressive behaviour or withdrawal. **2** *loosely* a general feeling of inadequacy or worthlessness.

infernal *adj* **1** belonging or relating to the underworld. **2** belonging or relating to hell. **3** wicked; hellish. **4** *colloq* extremely annoying, unpleasant, etc.

inferno *n* **1** (*often* **the Inferno**) hell. **2** a place or situation of horror and confusion. **3** a raging fire.

infertile *adj* **1** of soil, etc: lacking the nutrients required to support the growth of crops, etc. **2** unable to produce offspring. ○ **infertility** *n*.

infest *vb* **1** of fleas, lice, etc: to invade and occupy an animal or plant. **2** of someone or something harmful or unpleasant: to exist in large numbers or quantities. ○ **infestation** *n*.

infidel *n* **1** someone who rejects a particular religion, esp Christianity or Islam. **2** someone who rejects all religions. ➤ *adj* relating to unbelievers; unbelieving.

infidelity *n* (*-ies*) **1** unfaithfulness, esp of a sexual nature, or an instance of this. **2** lack of belief or faith in a religion.

infield *n* **1** *cricket* **a** the area of the field close to the wicket; **b** the players positioned there. **2** *baseball* **a** the diamond-shaped area of the pitch enclosed by the four bases; **b** the players positioned there. Compare OUTFIELD. ○ **infielder** *n*.

in-fighting *n* **1** fighting or competition between members of the same group, organization, etc. **2** *boxing* fighting at close quarters. ○ **in-fighter** *n*.

infill *n* (*also* **infilling**) **1** the act of filling or closing gaps, holes, etc. **2** the material used to fill a gap, hole, etc. ➤ *vb* to fill in (a gap, hole, etc).

infiltrate *vb* **1** of troops, agents, etc: to get into (territory or an organization) secretly to gain influence or information. **2** to filter (eg liquid or gas) slowly through the pores of (a substance). **3** *intr* eg of liquid or gas: to filter in. ○ **infiltration** *n*. ○ **infiltrator** *n*.

infinite *adj* **1** having no limits in size, extent, time or space. **2** too great to be measured or counted. **3** very great. **4** *maths* of a number, series, etc: having an unlimited number of elements, digits or terms. **5** all-encompassing; complete: *God in his infinite wisdom.* ➤ *n* anything which has no limits, boundaries, etc. ○ **infinitely** *adv*.

infinitesimal *adj* **1** infinitely small; with a value too close to zero to be measured. **2** *colloq* extremely small. ➤ *n* an infinitesimal amount. ○ **infinitesimally** *adv*.

infinitive *gram, n* a verb form that expresses an action but which does not refer to a particular subject or time, in English often used with *to* (eg *go* in *Tell him to go* • *Let her go*). ➤ *adj* of a verb: having this form. Compare FINITE (sense 3).

infinity *n* (*-ies*) **1** space, time or distance that is without limit. **2** *loosely* a quantity, space, time or distance that is too great to be measured. **3** *maths* (symbol ∞) **a** a number that is larger than any FINITE value; **b** the RECIPROCAL of zero. **4** the quality or state of being infinite.

infirm *adj* weak or ill, esp from old age.

infirmary n (-ies) 1 a hospital. 2 a room or ward, eg in a boarding school, monastery, etc, where the sick and injured are treated.

infirmity n (-ies) 1 the state or quality of being sick, weak or infirm. 2 a disease or illness.

inflame vb 1 to arouse strong or violent emotion in someone or something. 2 to make something more heated or intense. 3 tr & intr to become or to make (part of the body) red, heated, swollen and painful.

inflammable adj 1 easily set on fire. 2 easily excited or angered. ➤ n an inflammable substance or thing. ○ **inflammability** n.

inflammable See note at **flammable**.

inflammation n 1 pathol a response of body tissues to injury, infection, etc in which the affected part becomes inflamed. 2 inflaming or being inflamed.

inflammatory adj 1 likely to cause strong or violent emotion, esp anger. 2 pathol relating to, causing or caused by inflammation of part of the body.

inflatable adj able to be inflated for use. ➤ n an inflatable object.

inflate vb 1 tr & intr to swell or cause something to swell or expand with air or gas. 2 econ a to increase (prices generally) by artificial means; b to increase (the volume of money in circulation). Compare DEFLATE (sense 3), REFLATE. 3 to exaggerate the importance or value of something. 4 to raise (the spirits, etc).

inflation n 1 econ a general increase in the level of prices caused by an increase in the amount of money and credit available. 2 loosely the rate at which the level of prices is rising. 3 inflating or being inflated. ○ **inflationary** adj.

inflect vb 1 gram a to change the form of (a word) to show eg tense, number, gender or grammatical case; b intr of a word, language, etc: to change, or be able to be changed, in this way. 2 to vary the tone or pitch of (the voice, a note, etc). 3 to bend inwards.

inflection or **inflexion** n 1 gram a the change in the form of a word which shows tense, number, gender, grammatical case, etc; b an inflected form of a word; c a suffix which is added to a word to form an inflected form, eg -s, -ing. 2 a change in the tone, pitch, etc of the voice. 3 the act of inflecting or state of being inflected. ○ **inflectional** adj.

inflexible adj 1 incapable of being bent. 2 derog unyielding; obstinate. 3 unable to be changed. ○ **inflexibility** n. ○ **inflexibly** adv.

inflict vb (esp inflict sth on sb) to impose (something unpleasant) on them, or make them suffer it.

inflorescence n, bot 1 the flower-head and stem of a flowering plant. 2 any of the various possible arrangements of the flowers on a flowering plant.

inflow n 1 the act or process of flowing in. 2 something that flows in. ○ **inflowing** n, adj.

influence n 1 (esp influence on or over sb or sth) the power that one person or thing has to affect another. 2 a person or thing that has such a power. 3 power resulting from political or social position, wealth, ability, etc. ➤ vb 1 to have an effect on (a person, their work, events, etc). 2 to exert influence on someone or something. ♦ **under the influence** colloq drunk.

influential adj 1 having influence or power. 2 (esp influential in sth) making an important contribution to it. ○ **influentially** adv.

influenza n, pathol a viral infection, with symptoms including fever, catarrh and muscular aches and pains. Commonly shortened to **flu**.

influx n 1 a continual stream or arrival of large numbers of people or things. 2 a flowing in or inflow.

info n, colloq information.

inform vb 1 tr & intr, (esp inform sb about or of sth) to tell them about it. 2 intr (often inform against or on sb) to give incriminating evidence about them to the authorities. 3 literary or formal to animate, inspire or give life to something. 4 formal to give an essential quality to something.

informal adj 1 without ceremony or formality; relaxed and friendly. 2 of language, clothes, etc: suitable for and used in relaxed, everyday situations. ○ **informality** n (-ies). ○ **informally** adv.

informant n someone who informs, eg against another person, or who gives information.

information n 1 knowledge gained or given; news. 2 the communicating or receiving of knowledge.

information technology n the use, study or production of technologies such as computer systems, digital electronics and telecommunications to store, process and transmit information.

informative adj giving useful or interesting information. ○ **informatively** adv. ○ **informativeness** n.

informed adj 1 esp of a person: having or showing knowledge. 2 also in compounds of eg a newspaper article, a guess or estimate, opinion, etc: based on sound information: well-informed.

informer n someone who informs against another, esp to the police.

infra adv in books, texts, etc: below; lower down on the page or further on in the book.

infraction n, formal the breaking of a law, rule, etc.

infrared or (sometimes) **infra-red** adj 1 of electromagnetic radiation: with a wavelength between the red end of the visible spectrum and microwaves and radio waves. 2 relating to, using, producing or sensitive to radiation of this sort: infrared camera. ➤ n 1 infrared radiation. 2 the infrared part of the spectrum.

infrasonic adj relating to or having a frequency below the range which can normally be heard by the human ear.

infrastructure n 1 the basic inner structure of a society, organization or system. 2 the roads, railways, bridges, factories, schools, etc needed for a country to function properly.

infrequent adj occurring rarely or occasionally. ○ **infrequency** n. ○ **infrequently** adv.

infringe vb 1 to break or violate (eg a law or oath). 2 intr (esp **infringe on** or **upon** sth) to encroach or trespass; to interfere with (a person's rights, freedom, etc) in such a way as to limit them. ○ **infringement** n.

infuriate vb to make someone very angry. ○ **infuriating** adj.

infuse vb 1 tr & intr to soak, or cause (eg herbs or tea) to be soaked, in hot water to release flavour or other qualities. 2 (esp **infuse sb with sth** or **infuse sth into sb**) to inspire them with (a positive feeling, quality, etc). ○ **infusible** adj.

infusion n 1 an act or the process of infusing something. 2 a solution produced by infusing eg herbs or tea.

ingenious adj showing or having skill, originality and inventive cleverness. ○ **ingeniously** adv. ○ **ingeniousness** or **ingenuity** n.

ingenuous adj innocent and childlike, esp in being incapable of deception. ○ **ingenuously** adv. ○ **ingenuousness** n.

ingest vb, technical to take (eg food or liquid) into the body. ○ **ingestible** adj. ○ **ingestion** n.

inglorious adj 1 bringing shame. 2 chiefly old use ordinary; not glorious or noble.

ingot / 'ɪŋɡət / n a brick-shaped block of metal, esp of gold or silver.

ingrained adj 1 difficult to remove or wipe off or out. 2 instilled or rooted deeply.

ingratiate vb (esp **ingratiate oneself with sb**) to gain or try to gain their favour or approval. ○ **ingratiating** adj.

ingratitude n lack of due gratitude.

ingredient n a component of a mixture or compound, esp in cooking.

ingress n, formal 1 the act of going in or entering. 2 the power or right to go in or enter. ○ **ingression** n.

ingrowing adj esp of a toenail: growing abnormally so that it becomes embedded in the flesh. ○ **ingrown** adj.

inhabit vb to live in or occupy (a place). ○ **inhabitable** adj HABITABLE. ○ **inhabitant** n.

inhalant n a medicinal preparation in the form of a vapour or aerosol, inhaled for its therapeutic effect.

inhale vb, tr & intr to draw (air, tobacco smoke, etc) into the lungs; to breathe in. ○ **inhalation** n.

inhaler n, med a small, portable device used for inhaling certain medicinal preparations.

inharmonious adj 1 not sounding well together. 2 not agreeing or going well together; not compatible.

inhere vb, formal or technical, intr of character, a quality, etc: to be an essential or permanent part.

inherent adj of a quality, etc: existing as an essential, natural or permanent part. ○ **inherently** adv.

inherit vb (inherited, inheriting) 1 to receive (money, property, a title, etc) after someone's death. 2 to receive (genetically transmitted characteristics) from the previous generation. 3 colloq to receive something second-hand from someone. ○ **inheritable** adj. ○ **inheritor** n.

inheritance n 1 something (eg money, property, a title, a physical or mental characteristic) that is or may be inherited. 2 the legal right to inherit something. 3 HEREDITY. 4 the act of inheriting.

inhibit vb (inhibited, inhibiting) 1 to make someone feel unable to act freely or spontaneously. 2 to hold back, restrain or prevent (an action, desire, progress, etc). 3 to prohibit or forbid someone from doing something. ○ **inhibited** adj. ○ **inhibitor** n.

inhibition n 1 a feeling of fear or embarrassment which prevents one from acting, thinking, etc freely or spontaneously. 2 inhibiting or being inhibited. 3 something which inhibits, prevents progress, holds back or forbids, etc.

inhospitable adj 1 not friendly or welcoming to others, esp in not offering them food, drink and other home comforts. 2 of a place: offering little shelter, eg from harsh weather.

in-house adv, adj within a particular company, organization, etc.

inhuman adj 1 cruel and unfeeling. 2 not human.

inhumane adj showing no kindness, sympathy or compassion. ○ **inhumanity** n.

inimical adj, formal 1 tending to discourage. 2 not friendly; hostile or in opposition.

inimitable adj too good, skilful, etc to be satisfactorily imitated by others.

iniquity n (-ies) 1 an unfair, unjust, wicked or sinful act. 2 wickedness; sinfulness. ○ **iniquitous** adj.

initial adj relating to or at the beginning. ➤ n the first letter of a word, esp of a name: Write your initials at the bottom. ➤ vb (initialled, initialling; (N Am) initialed, initialing) to mark or sign something with the initials of one's name.

initially adv 1 at first. 2 as a beginning.

initiate vb /ɪ'nɪʃɪeɪt/ 1 to begin (eg a relationship, project, conversation, etc). 2 (usu **initiate sb into sth**) to accept (a new member) into a society, organization, etc, esp with secret ceremonies. 3 (usu **initiate sb in sth**) to give them instruction in the basics of a skill, science, etc. ➤ n /ɪ'nɪʃɪət/ someone who has recently been or is soon to be initiated. ○ **initiation** n.

initiative n 1 the ability to initiate things, take decisions or act resourcefully. 2 (esp in **take the initiative**) a first step or move towards an end or aim. 3 (esp **the initiative**) the right or power to begin something. ➤ adj serving to begin.

inject vb 1 to introduce (a liquid, eg medicine) into the body using a hypodermic syringe. 2 to force (fuel) into an engine. **3** to introduce (a quality, element, etc): *inject a note of optimism*. ○ **injectable** *adj*. ○ **injection** *n*.

injudicious *adj* not wise.

injunction *n* **1** *law* an official court order that forbids or commands. **2** any authoritative order or warning.

injure *vb* **1** to do physical harm or damage to someone or something. **2** to harm, spoil or weaken something: *Only his pride was injured.* **3** to do an injustice or wrong to someone.

injurious *adj* causing injury or damage.

injury *n* (*-ies*) **1 a** physical harm or damage; **b** an instance of this: *Jenny did herself an injury playing squash.* **2** a wound: *He has a serious head injury.* **3** something that harms, spoils or hurts something: *a cruel injury to her feelings.* **4** *now chiefly law* a wrong or injustice.

injustice *n* **1** unfairness or lack of justice. **2** an unfair or unjust act.

ink *n* **1** a coloured liquid used for writing, drawing or printing. **2** *biol* a dark liquid ejected by octopus, squid, etc to confuse predators. ➤ *vb* **1** to mark something with ink. **2** to cover (a surface to be printed) with ink.

inkjet printer *n, comput* a printer which produces characters by spraying a fine jet of ink.

inkling *n* a slight idea or suspicion.

inkwell *n* a small container for ink, esp in a desk.

inky *adj* (*-ier, -iest*) **1** covered with ink. **2** like ink; black or very dark. ○ **inkiness** *n*.

inland *adj* **1** not beside the sea. **2** *esp Brit* not abroad. ➤ *n* that part of a country that is not beside the sea. ➤ *adv* in or towards the parts of a country away from the sea.

in-laws *pl n, colloq* relatives by marriage, esp one's mother- and father-in-law.

inlay *vb* (*past tense & past participle* **inlaid**) **1** to set or embed (eg pieces of wood, metal, etc) flush in another material. **2** to decorate (eg a piece of furniture) by inlaying pieces of coloured wood, ivory, metal, etc in its surface. ➤ *n* **1** a decoration or design made by inlaying. **2** the pieces used to create an inlaid design. **3** *dentistry* a filling shaped to fit a cavity in a tooth.

inlet *n* **1** *geog* a narrow arm of water running inland from a sea coast or lake shore or between two islands. **2** a narrow opening or valve through which a gas or liquid enters a device. **3** *dressmaking* an extra piece of material sewn into a garment to make it larger.

inmate *n* someone living in or confined to an institution, esp a prison.

in memoriam *prep* in memory of (a specified person).

inmost *adj* INNERMOST.

inn *n, esp Brit* a public house or small hotel providing food and accommodation.

innards *pl n, colloq* **1** the inner organs of a person or animal, esp the stomach and intestines. **2** the inner workings of a machine.

innate *adj* **1** existing from birth. **2** natural or

instinctive, rather than learnt or acquired. ○ **innately** *adv*.

inner *adj* **1** further in; situated inside, close or closer to the centre. **2** of thoughts, feelings, etc: secret, hidden and profound, or more secret, profound, etc.

inner city *n* the central area of a city, esp if densely populated and very poor, with bad housing, roads, etc.

innermost or **inmost** *adj* **1** furthest within; closest to the centre. **2** most secret or hidden.

inning *n* in a baseball game: any of the nine divisions per game in which each team may bat.

innings *n* **1** *cricket* **a** a team's or player's turn at batting; **b** the runs scored during such a turn. **2** *Brit* a period during which someone has an opportunity for action or achievement.

innocent *adj* **1** free from sin; pure. **2** not guilty, eg of a crime. **3** not causing, or intending to cause, harm or offence: *an innocent remark*. **4** simple and trusting. **5** lacking, free or deprived of something: *innocent of all knowledge of the event*. ➤ *n* an innocent person, esp a young child or trusting adult. ○ **innocence** *n*. ○ **innocently** *adv*.

innocuous *adj* harmless; inoffensive.

innovate *vb, intr* to introduce new ideas, methods, etc. ○ **innovation** *n*. ○ **innovative** *adj*. ○ **innovator** *n*. ○ **innovatory** *adj*.

innuendo *n* (*innuendos* or *innuendoes*) **1 a** an indirectly unpleasant, critical or spiteful remark, eg about someone's character; **b** a rude or smutty allusion or insinuation. **2** the act or practice of making such remarks.

innumerable *adj* too many to be counted.

innumerate *adj* having no understanding of mathematics. ○ **innumeracy** *n*.

inoculate *vb* **1** *med* to inject a harmless form of an ANTIGEN into (a person or animal). **2** *biol, etc* to introduce a micro-organism into (a medium) in order to start a CULTURE, or into another organism in order to produce antibodies. ○ **inoculation** *n*.

inoffensive *adj* harmless; not objectionable or provocative.

inoperable *adj, med* of a disease or condition: not able to be treated by surgery.

inoperative *adj* **1** of a machine, etc: not working or functioning. **2** of rule, etc: having no effect.

inopportune *adj* not suitable or convenient.

inordinate *adj* greater than or beyond what is normal or acceptable.

inorganic *adj* **1** not composed of living or formerly living material. **2** not caused by natural growth. **3** *chem* not containing chains or rings of carbon atoms.

inpatient *n* a patient temporarily living in hospital while receiving treatment there. Compare OUTPATIENT.

input *n* **1** *comput* the data that is entered into the main memory of a computer. **2** something which is put or taken in, eg a contribution to a discussion: *Your input would be valuable at the meeting*. **3** the money, power, materials, labour, etc required to produce something; the power or electrical current put into a machine. **4** an act or process of putting something in. ➤ *vb* to enter (data) into the main memory of a computer. Compare OUTPUT.

inquest *n* **1** a coroner's investigation into an incident, eg a sudden death. **2** *colloq, esp facetious* analysis of the result of a game, campaign, etc and discussion of mistakes made.

inquietude /ɪŋˈkwaɪətʃuːd/ *n, formal* restlessness or uneasiness.

inquire or **enquire** *vb* **1** *tr & intr* to seek or ask for information. **2** *intr* (*often* **inquire into sth**) to try to discover the facts of (a crime, etc), esp formally. **3** *intr* (**inquire after sb**) to ask about their health or happiness.

> **inquire, enquire** Inquire and **enquire** are to a great extent interchangeable variants. **Inquire** is used more than **enquire**, especially in formal writing such as reports, with reference to formal or systematic investigating. The distinction is more apparent in the nouns **enquiry** and **inquiry**.

inquiring or **enquiring** *adj* **1** eager to discover or learn things: *an inquiring mind*. **2** esp of a look: appearing to be asking a question. ○ **inquiringly** *adv*.

inquiry or **enquiry** *n* (*-ies*) **1** an act or the process of asking for information. **2** (*often* **an inquiry into sth**) an investigation, esp a formal one.

> **inquiry, enquiry** Inquiry and **enquiry** are interchangeable variants in the more general sense 1. **Inquiry** and not **enquiry** is used in the more formal and specific sense 2.

inquisition *n* **1** a searching or intensive inquiry or investigation. **2** an official or judicial inquiry. ○ **inquisitional** *adj*.

inquisitive *adj* **1** over-eager to find out things, esp about other people's affairs. **2** eager for knowledge or information. ○ **inquisitively** *adv*. ○ **inquisitiveness** *n*.

inquisitor *n, usu derog* someone who carries out an inquisition or inquiry, esp harshly or intensively. ○ **inquisitorial** *adj*.

inroad *n* **1** (*usu* **inroads into sth**) a large or significant using up or consumption of it, or encroachment on it. **2** a hostile attack or raid.

insane *adj* **1** mad; mentally ill. **2** *colloq* esp of actions: extremely foolish; stupid. **3** relating to or for the mentally ill. ○ **insanely** *adv*. ○ **insanity** *n*.

insanitary *adj* so dirty as to be dangerous to health. ○ **insanitariness** *n*.

insatiable /ɪnˈseɪʃəbəl/ *adj* not able to be satisfied.

inscribe *vb* **1** to write, print or engrave (words) on (paper, metal, stone, etc). **2** to enter (a name) on a list or in a book. **3** (*often* **inscribe sth to sb**) to dedicate or address (a book, etc) to them, usu by writing in the front of it. **4** *geom* to draw (a figure) within another figure so as to touch all or some of its sides or faces.

inscription *n* **1** words written, printed or engraved, eg as a dedication in a book or as an epitaph on a gravestone. **2** the act of inscribing, esp of writing a dedication in the front of a book or of entering a name on a list.

inscrutable *adj* hard to understand or explain. ○ **inscrutability** *n*.

insect *n* **1** *zool* an invertebrate animal, such as a fly, beetle, ant or bee, typically with a segmented body and two pairs of wings. **2** *loosely* any other small invertebrate, eg a spider.

insecticide *n* any substance used to kill insects. ○ **insecticidal** *adj*.

insectivore *n* **1** an animal or bird that feeds on insects. **2** a plant that traps and digests insects. ○ **insectivorous** /ɪnsɛkˈtɪvərəs/ *adj*.

insecure *adj* **1** not firmly fixed. **2** lacking confidence; anxious about possible loss or danger. **3** under threat or in danger or likely to be so: *insecure jobs*. ○ **insecurity** *n* (*-ies*).

inseminate *vb* to introduce SEMEN into (a female). ○ **insemination** *n*.

insensate *adj, formal or literary* **1** not able to perceive physical sensations; not conscious. **2** insensitive and unfeeling.

insensible *adj, formal or literary* **1** not able to feel pain; not conscious. **2** (*usu* **insensible of** or **to sth**) unaware of it; not caring about it. **3** incapable of feeling emotion; callous. **4** too small or slight to be noticed. ○ **insensibility** *n*.

insensitive *adj* **1** not aware of, or not capable of responding sympathetically or thoughtfully to, other people's feelings, etc. **2** not feeling or reacting to (stimulation, eg touch or light). ○ **insensitivity** *n*.

inseparable *adj* **1** incapable of being separated. **2** unwilling to be apart; constantly together. ○ **inseparability** *n*. ○ **inseparably** *adv*.

insert *vb* /ɪnˈsɜːt/ **1** to put or fit something inside something else. **2** to introduce (text, words, etc) into the body of other text, words, etc. ➤ *n* /ˈɪnsɜːt/ something inserted, esp a loose sheet in a book or magazine. ○ **insertion** *n*.

in-service *adj* carried on while a person is employed.

inset *n* /ˈɪnsɛt/ **1** something set in or inserted. **2** a small map or picture put in the corner of a larger one. ➤ *vb* /ɪnˈsɛt/ (**inset, insetting**) to put in, add or insert something.

inshore *adv, adj* in or on water, but near or towards the shore: *inshore shipping*. Compare OFFSHORE.

inside *n* **1** the inner side, surface or part of something. Opposite of OUTSIDE. **2** the side of a road nearest to the buildings, pavement, etc. **3** the part of a pavement or path away from the road. **4** *sport* the inside track, or the equivalent part of any racetrack. **5** (**insides**) *colloq* the inner organs, esp the stomach and bowels. **6** *colloq* a position which gains one the confidence of and otherwise secret information from people in authority: *Those on the inside knew his plans.* ➤ *adj* **1 a** being in, near, towards or from the inside; **b** indoor. **2** *colloq* coming from, concerned with or planned by a person or people within a specific organization or circle: *inside knowledge.* ➤ *adv* **1** to, in or on the inside or interior. **2** indoors. **3** *colloq* in or into prison. ➤ *prep* **1** to or on the interior or inner side of something. **2** in less than (a specified time).

inside out *adv* **1** (*also* **outside in**) with the inside surface turned out. **2** *colloq* thoroughly.

insider *n* a member of an organization or group who has access to confidential or exclusive information about it.

insidious *adj* **1** developing gradually without being noticed but causing great harm. **2** attractive but harmful. ○ **insidiously** *adv.* ○ **insidiousness** *n.*

insight *n* **1** the ability to gain a relatively rapid, clear and deep understanding of the real, often hidden and usu complex nature of a situation, problem, etc. **2** an instance or example of this.

insignia *sing or pl n* (**insignia** *or* **insignias**) badges or emblems of office, honour or membership.

insignificant *adj* **1** of little or no meaning, value or importance. **2** relatively small in size or amount. ○ **insignificance** *n.*

insincere *adj* not genuine; hypocritical. ○ **insincerely** *adv.* ○ **insincerity** *n* (*-ies*).

insinuate *vb* **1** to suggest or hint (something unpleasant) in an indirect way. **2** to introduce (eg an idea) in an indirect, subtle or devious way. **3** (*esp* **insinuate oneself into sth**) to succeed in gaining (eg acceptance or favour) by gradual, careful and often cunning means. ○ **insinuation** *n.*

insipid *adj* **1** having little or no interest or liveliness. **2** having little or no taste or flavour. ○ **insipidness** *or* **insipidity** *n.*

insist *vb* **1** *tr & intr* to maintain or assert something firmly. **2** (*usu* **insist on** *or* **upon sth**) to demand it firmly.

insistent *adj* **1** making continual forceful demands. **2** demanding attention. ○ **insistence** *or* **insistency** *n.* ○ **insistently** *adv.*

in situ /ɪn ˈsɪtjuː/ *adv* in the natural or original position.

insole *n* an inner sole in a shoe or boot.

insolent *adj* rude or insulting; showing a lack of respect. ○ **insolence** *n.* ○ **insolently** *adv.*

insoluble *adj* **1** of a substance: not able to be dissolved in a particular solvent (esp water). **2** of a problem or difficulty: not able to be solved or resolved. ○ **insolubility** *n.*

insolvent *adj* **1** not having enough money to pay debts, etc. **2** relating to insolvent people or insolvency. ○ **insolvency** *n.*

insomnia *n* the chronic inability to sleep or to

have enough sleep. ○ **insomniac** *n, adj.*

insomuch see under IN.

insouciant /ɪnˈsuːsɪənt; *French* ɛ̃susjɑ̃/ *adj, rather formal or literary* without cares or worries; light-hearted. ○ **insouciance** *n.*

inspect *vb* **1** to look at or examine closely, often to find faults or mistakes. **2** to look at or examine (a body of soldiers, etc) officially or ceremonially. ○ **inspection** *n.*

inspector *n* **1** someone whose job is to inspect something. **2** (*often* **Inspector**) *Brit* a police officer below a superintendent and above a sergeant in rank.

inspectorate *n* **1** a body of inspectors. **2** the office or post of inspector. Also called **inspectorship**.

inspiration *n* **1** someone or something that inspires; a supposed power which stimulates the mind, esp to artistic activity or creativity. **2** the state of being inspired. **3** a brilliant or inspired idea. **4** *physiol* **a** the act of drawing breath into the lungs; **b** a breath taken in this way. ○ **inspirational** *adj.*

inspire *vb* **1** (*often* **inspire sb to sth** *or* **to do sth**) to stimulate them into activity, esp into artistic or creative activity. **2** to fill someone with a feeling of confidence, encouragement and exaltation. **3** (*esp* **inspire sb with sth** *or* **inspire sth into sb**) to create (a particular feeling) in them. **4** to be the origin or source of (a poem, piece of music, etc). **5** *tr & intr* to breathe in (air, etc); to inhale. ○ **inspired** *adj* so good, skilful, etc as to seem to be the result of inspiration.

instability *n* lack of physical or mental steadiness or stability.

install *or* (*sometimes*) **instal** *vb* (**installed, installing**) **1** to put (equipment, machinery, etc) in place and make it ready for use. **2** to place (a person) in office with a formal ceremony. **3** to place (something, oneself, etc) in a particular position, condition or place. ○ **installation** *n.*

instalment *or* (*US*) **installment** *n* **1** one of a series of parts into which a debt is divided for payment. **2** one of several parts published, issued, broadcast, etc at regular intervals.

instance *n* **1** an example, esp one of a particular condition or circumstance. **2** a particular stage in a process or a particular situation: *in the first instance.* **3** *formal* request: *at the instance of your partner.* ◆ **for instance** for example.

instant *adj* **1** immediate. **2** of food and drink, etc: quickly and easily prepared, esp by reheating or the addition of boiling water. **3** of the current month. ➤ *n* **1** a particular moment in time. **2** a moment: *I'll be there in an instant.* ○ **instantly** *or* **this instant** *adv* immediately.

instantaneous *adj* done, happening or occurring at once, very quickly or in an instant.

instead *adv* as a substitute or alternative; in place of something or someone.

instep *n* **1** the prominent arched middle section of the human foot, between the ankle and the toes. **2** the part of a shoe, sock, etc that covers this.

instigate *vb* **1** to urge someone on or incite them, esp to do something wrong or evil. **2** to set in motion or initiate (eg an inquiry). ○ **instigation** *n*. ○ **instigator** *n*.

instil or (*US*) **instill** *vb* (*instilled, instilling*) (*esp* **instil sth in** or **into sb**) to impress, fix or plant (ideas, feelings, etc) slowly or gradually in their mind. ○ **instillation** or **instilment** *n*. ○ **instiller** *n*.

instinct *n* **1** in animal behaviour: an unlearned and inherited response to a stimulus. **2** in humans: a basic natural drive that urges a person towards a specific goal, such as survival or reproduction. **3** intuition: *Instinct told me not to believe him*.

instinctive *adj* **1** prompted by instinct or intuition. **2** involuntary; automatic. ○ **instinctively** *adv*.

institute *n* **1** a society or organization which promotes research, education or a particular cause. **2** a building or group of buildings used by an institute. **3** an established law, principle, rule or custom. ➤ *vb, rather formal* **1** to set up, establish or organize something: *They instituted a trust fund*. **2** to initiate something or cause it to begin: *to institute legal proceedings*. **3** to appoint someone to, or install them in, a position or office.

institution *n* **1** an organization or public body founded for a special purpose, esp for a charitable or educational purpose or as a hospital. **2** a hospital, old people's home, etc, regarded as impersonal or bureaucratic. **3** a custom or tradition; something which is well-established: *the institution of marriage*. **4** *colloq* a familiar and well-known object or person. **5** the act of instituting or process of being instituted. ○ **institutional** *adj* **1** like or typical of an institution, esp in being dull or regimented: *institutional food*. **2** depending on, or originating in, an institution. ○ **institutionalism** *n*.

institutionalize or **-ise** *vb* **1** to place someone in an institution. **2** to cause someone to lose their individuality and ability to cope with life by keeping them in a place (eg a long-stay hospital or prison) for too long. **3** to make something into an institution.

instruct *vb* **1 a** to teach or train someone in a subject or skill; **b** (*usu* **instruct sb in sth**) to give them information about or practical knowledge of it. **2** to direct or order, eg someone to do something. **3** *law* to give (a lawyer) the facts concerning a case. **4** *law* to engage (a lawyer) to act in a case.

instruction *n* **1** (*often* **instructions**) a direction, order or command: *She's always issuing instructions*. **2** teaching; the act or process of instructing. **3** *comput* a command that activates a specific operation. **4** (**instructions**) guidelines on eg how to operate a piece of equipment. **5** (**instructions**) *law* the information, details, etc of a case, given to a lawyer. ○ **instructional** *adj*.

instructive *adj* giving knowledge or information.

instructor *n* **1** someone who gives instruction: *driving instructor*. **2** *N Am* a college or university teacher ranking below an assistant professor.

instrument *n* **1** a tool, esp one used for delicate scientific work or measurement. **2** (*also* **musical instrument**) a device used to produce musical sounds. **3** a device which measures, shows and controls speed, temperature, direction, etc. **4** a means of achieving or doing something: *She was the instrument of his downfall*. **5** a formal or official legal document.

instrumental *adj* **1** (*often* **instrumental in** or **to sth**) being responsible for it or an important factor in it. **2** of music: performed by or for musical instruments only. **3** relating to or done with an instrument or tool. ➤ *n* a piece of music for or performed by musical instruments only.

instrumentalist *n* someone who plays a musical instrument.

instrumentation *n* **1** the way in which a piece of music is written or arranged to be played by instruments. **2** the instruments used to play a piece of music. **3** the use, design or provision of instruments or tools.

insubordinate *adj* refusing to take orders or submit to authority. ○ **insubordination** *n*.

insubstantial *adj* **1** not solid, strong or satisfying: *insubstantial evidence*. **2** not solid or real. ○ **insubstantially** *adv*.

insufferable *adj* too unpleasant, annoying, etc to tolerate. ○ **insufferably** *adv*.

insufficient *adj* not enough or not adequate. ○ **insufficiency** *n*. ○ **insufficiently** *adv*.

insular *adj* **1** relating to an island or its inhabitants. **2** narrow-minded; isolated. ○ **insularity** *n*.

insulate *vb* **1** to surround (a body, device or space) with a material that prevents or slows down the flow of heat, electricity or sound. **2** to remove or set someone or something apart. ○ **insulation** *n*. ○ **insulator** *n*.

insulin *n* a HORMONE which controls the concentration of sugar in the blood.

insult *vb* /ɪnˈsʌlt/ **1** to speak rudely or offensively to or about someone or something. **2** to behave in a way that offends or affronts. ➤ *n* /ˈɪnsʌlt/ **1** a rude or offensive remark or action. **2** an affront: *an insult to the intelligence*.

insuperable *adj* too difficult to be overcome, defeated or dealt with successfully.

insupportable *adj* **1** intolerable. **2** not justifiable.

insurance *n* **1** an agreement by which a company promises to pay a person, etc money in the event of loss, theft, damage to property, injury or death, etc. **2** the contract for such an agreement. **3** the protection offered by such a contract. **4** an insurance PREMIUM. **5** the sum which will be paid according to such an agreement. **6** the business of providing such contracts for clients. **7** anything done, any measure taken, etc to try to prevent possible loss, disappointment, problems, etc. **8** an act or instance of insuring.

insurance See note at **assurance**.

insure *vb* **1** *tr & intr* to arrange for the payment of an amount of money in the event of the loss or theft of or damage to (property), injury to or the death of (a person), etc by paying regular amounts of money to an insurance company. **2** to take measures to try to prevent (an event leading to loss, damage, difficulties, etc). ○ **insurable** *adj*.

insurer *n* (*esp* **the insurer**) *law, etc* a person or company that provides insurance.

insurgence or **insurgency** *n* (*insurgences* or *insurgencies*) an uprising or rebellion.

insurgent *adj* opposed to and fighting against the government of the country. ➤ *n* a rebel.

insurmountable *adj* too difficult to be dealt with; impossible to overcome.

insurrection *n* an act of rebellion against authority.

intact *adj* whole; not broken or damaged.

intaglio /ɪnˈtɑːlɪoʊ/ *n* **1** a stone or gem which has a design engraved into its surface. Compare CAMEO (sense I). **2 a** the art or process of engraving designs into the surface of objects, esp jewellery; **b** an engraved design.

intake *n* **1** a thing or quantity taken in or accepted. **2 a** a number or the amount taken in; **b** the people, etc taken in. **3** an opening through which liquid or gas (eg air) enters a pipe, engine, etc. **4** an act of taking in.

intangible *adj* **1** not perceptible by touch. **2** difficult for the mind to grasp. **3** of eg a business asset: having value but no physical existence.

integer *n* **1** *maths* a positive or negative whole number. **2** any whole or complete entity.

integral *adj* **1** being a necessary part of a whole. **2** forming a whole; supplied as part of a whole. **3** complete.

integrate *vb* **1** to fit (parts) together to form a whole. **2** *tr & intr* to mix (people) or cause (people) to mix freely with other groups in society, etc. ○ **integration** *n*.

integrated circuit *n, electronics* a circuit on a chip of semiconductor material, usu silicon.

integrity *n* **1** moral uprightness. **2** the quality or state of being whole and unimpaired.

integument *n, zool, bot* a protective outer layer of tissue.

intellect *n* **1** the part of the mind that thinks, reasons and understands. **2** the capacity to use this part of the mind. **3** someone who has great mental ability.

intellectual *adj* **1** involving or appealing to the intellect. **2** having a highly developed ability to think, reason and understand. ➤ *n* an intellectual person.

intelligence *n* **1** the ability to use one's mind to solve problems, etc. **2** news or information. **3 a** the gathering of secret information about an enemy; **b** the government department, army personnel, etc responsible for this.

intelligence quotient *n* a measure of a person's intellectual ability.

intelligent *adj* **1** having highly developed mental ability. **2** of a machine, computer, etc: able to vary its behaviour according to the situation. ○ **intelligently** *adv*.

intelligentsia *n* (*usu* **the intelligentsia**) the most highly educated and cultured people in a society.

intelligible *adj* able to be understood. ○ **intelligibility** *n*. ○ **intelligibly** *adv*.

intemperate *adj* **1** going beyond reasonable limits. **2** habitually drinking too much alcohol. **3** of a climate or region: having extreme and severe temperatures. ○ **intemperance** *n*.

intend *vb* **1** to plan or have in mind as one's purpose or aim. **2** (**intend sth for sb** or **sth**) to set it aside or destine it for some person or thing. **3** to mean.

intended *adj* meant; done on purpose or planned. ➤ *n, colloq* someone's future husband or wife.

intense *adj* **1** very great or extreme. **2** feeling or expressing emotion deeply. **3** very deeply felt: *intense happiness*. ○ **intensely** *adv*.

intensifier *n, gram* an adverb or adjective which adds emphasis to or intensifies the word or phrase which follows it, eg *very*. Also called **intensive**.

intensify *vb* (*-ies, -ied*) *tr & intr* to make or become intense or more intense. ○ **intensification** *n*.

intensity *n* (*-ies*) **1** the quality or state of being intense. **2** *physics* the rate per unit area at which power or energy is transmitted, eg loudness or brightness. **3** *chem* the concentration of a solution. **4** *physics* the power per unit area transmitted by a wave.

intensive *adj* **1** *often in compounds* using, done with or requiring considerable amounts of thought, effort, time, etc within a relatively short period: *labour-intensive*. **2** thorough; intense; concentrated. **3** using large amounts of capital and labour (rather than more land or raw materials) to increase production: *intensive farming*. **4** *gram* of an adverb or adjective: adding force or emphasis, eg *extremely, quite*. ➤ *n, gram* an INTENSIFIER. ○ **intensively** *adv*. ○ **intensiveness** *n*.

intensive care *n* **1** the care of critically ill patients who require continuous attention. **2** (*in full* **intensive-care unit**) a hospital unit that provides such care.

intent *n* **1** an aim, intention or purpose. **2** *law* the purpose of committing a crime: *loitering with intent*. ➤ *adj* **1** (*usu* **intent on** or **upon sth**) firmly determined to do it. **2** (*usu* **intent on sth**) having one's attention fixed on it. **3** showing concentration; absorbed: *an intent look*. ○ **intently** *adv*. ○ **intentness** *n*. ♦ **to all intents and purposes** in every important respect; virtually.

intention n 1 an aim or purpose. 2 (**intentions**) *colloq* a man's purpose with regard to marrying a particular woman.

intentional *adj* said, done, etc on purpose. ○ **intentionally** *adv.*

inter *vb* (**interred, interring**) to bury (a dead person, etc).

interact *vb, intr* to act with or on one another. ○ **interaction** n. ○ **interactive** *adj* 1 characterized by interaction. 2 involving or allowing a continuous exchange of information between a computer and its user. ○ **interactively** *adv.*

interbreed *vb, tr & intr* to breed within a single family or strain so as to control the appearance of certain characteristics in the offspring. 2 to cross-breed.

intercede *vb, intr* 1 to act as a peacemaker between (two people, groups, etc). 2 (*usu* **intercede for sb**) to make an appeal on their behalf. ○ **intercession** n.

intercept *vb* 1 **a** to stop or catch (eg a person, missile, aircraft, etc) on their or its way from one place to another; **b** to prevent (a missile, etc) from arriving at its destination, often by destroying it. 2 *maths* to mark or cut off (a line, plane, curve, etc) with another line, plane, etc that crosses it. ➤ n, *maths* 1 the part of a line or plane that is cut off by another line or plane crossing it; the distance from the origin to the point where a straight line or a curve crosses one of the axes of a coordinate system. 2 the point at which two figures intersect. ○ **interception** n. ○ **interceptive** *adj.*

interceptor n someone or something that intercepts, esp a small light aircraft used to intercept approaching enemy aircraft.

interchange *vb, tr & intr* to change or cause to change places with something or someone. ➤ n 1 an act of interchanging; an exchange. 2 a road junction consisting of roads and bridges designed to prevent streams of traffic from directly crossing one another. ○ **interchangeability** n. ○ **interchangeable** *adj.* ○ **interchangeably** *adv.*

intercom n an internal system which allows communication within a building, aircraft, ship, etc.

interconnect *vb, tr & intr* to connect (two things) or be connected with one another. ○ **interconnection** n.

intercontinental *adj* travelling between or connecting different continents.

intercourse n 1 SEXUAL INTERCOURSE. 2 communication, connection or dealings between people, groups, etc.

interdenominational *adj* involving (members of) different religious denominations.

interdepartmental *adj* involving (members of) different departments within a single organization, etc.

interdependent *adj* depending on one another. ○ **interdependence** n. ○ **interdependently** *adv.*

interdict n / ˈɪntədɪkt / 1 an official order forbidding someone to do something. 2 *RC Church* a sentence or punishment removing the right to most sacraments (including burial but not communion) from the people of a place or district. 3 *Scots law* an INJUNCTION (sense 1). ➤ *vb* / ɪntəˈdɪkt / to place under an interdict; to forbid or prohibit. ○ **interdiction** n. ○ **interdictory** *adj.*

interdisciplinary *adj* involving two or more subjects of study.

interest n 1 the desire to learn or know about someone or something; curiosity. 2 the power to attract attention and curiosity. 3 something which arouses attention and curiosity, a pastime. 4 a charge for borrowing money or using credit. 5 (*often* **interests**) advantage, benefit or profit, esp financial: *It is in your own interests to be truthful.* 6 a share or claim in a business and its profits, or a legal right to property. 7 (*also* **interest group**) a group of people or organizations with common, esp financial, aims and concerns: *the banking interest.* ➤ *vb* 1 to attract the attention and curiosity of someone. 2 (*often* **interest sb in sth**) to cause them to take a part in or be concerned about some activity.

interested *adj* 1 showing concern or having an interest. 2 personally involved; not impartial. ○ **interestedly** *adv.*

interesting *adj* attracting interest; holding the attention. ○ **interestingly** *adv.*

interface n 1 a surface forming a common boundary between two regions, things, etc. 2 a common boundary or meeting-point. 3 *comput* a link between a computer and a peripheral device, such as a printer, or a user. ➤ *vb, tr & intr* to connect (a piece of equipment, etc) with another so as to make them compatible. ○ **interfacial** *adj.*

interfacing n a piece of stiff fabric sewn between two layers of material to give shape and firmness.

interfere *vb, intr* 1 (*often* **interfere with** or **in sth**) **a** of a person: to meddle with something not considered their business; **b** of a thing: to hinder or adversely affect something else: *The weather is interfering with picture reception.* 2 (**interfere with sb**) *euphem* to assault or molest them sexually. 3 *physics* of sound waves, rays of light, etc: to combine together to cause disturbance or interference. 4 of a horse: to strike a foot against the opposite leg in walking. ○ **interfering** *adj.*

interference n 1 the act or process of interfering. 2 *physics* the interaction between two or more waves of the same frequency. 3 *telecomm* the distortion of transmitted radio or television signals by an external power source.

intergalactic *adj* happening or situated between galaxies.

interim *adj* provisional, temporary. ♦ **in the interim** in the meantime.

interior *adj* 1 on, of, suitable for, happening or acting in, or coming from the inside: *interior design.* 2 away from the shore or frontier; inland.

3 concerning the domestic or internal affairs of a country. **4** belonging to or existing in the mind or spirit; belonging to the mental or spiritual life. ➤ *n* **1** an internal or inner part; the inside. **2** the part of a country or continent that is furthest from the coast. **3** the internal or home affairs of a country. **4** a picture or representation of the inside of a room or building, esp with reference to its decoration or style: *a typical southern French interior.*

interj *abbrev* interjection.

interject *vb* to say or add abruptly; to interrupt with something.

interjection *n* **1** an exclamation of surprise, sudden disappointment, pain, etc. **2** an act of interjecting.

interlace *vb* **1** *tr & intr* to join by lacing or by crossing over. **2** to mix or blend with something: *a story interlaced with graphic descriptions.*

interlard *vb* to add foreign words, quotations, unusual phrases, etc to (a speech or piece of writing), esp to do so excessively.

interlay *vb* to lay (eg layers) between.

interleaf *n* (*interleaves*) a usu blank leaf of paper inserted between two leaves of a book.

interleave *vb* (*interleaved, interleaving*) to insert interleaves between the pages of a book.

interline[1] *vb* to insert (words) between the lines of (a document, book, etc). ○ **interlineation** *n.*

interline[2] *vb* to put an extra lining between the first lining and the fabric of (a garment), esp for stiffness. ○ **interlining** *n.*

interlink *vb, tr & intr* to join or connect together.

interlock *vb, tr & intr* to fit, fasten or connect together, esp by the means of teeth or parts which fit into each other. ➤ *n* a device or mechanism that connects and co-ordinates the functions of the parts or components of eg a machine. ➤ *adj*, of a fabric or garment: knitted with closely locking stitches. ○ **interlocking** *adj.*

interlocutor *n* **1** someone who takes part in a conversation or dialogue. **2** *Scots law* **a** *strictly* a judgement coming just short of the final decree; **b** *loosely* any order of the court. ○ **interlocution** *n.*

interloper *n* someone who interferes with other people's affairs, or goes to places where they have no right to be; an intruder.

interlude *n* **1** a short period of time between two events or a short period of a different activity; a brief distraction. **2** a short break between the acts of a play or opera or between items of music. **3** a short piece of music, or short item of entertainment, played during such a break. **4** a short dramatic or comic piece, formerly often performed during this interval.

intermarry *vb, intr* **1** of different races, social or religious groups, etc: to become connected by marriage. **2** to marry someone from one's own family. ○ **intermarriage** *n.*

intermediary *n* (*-ies*) **1** someone who mediates between two people or groups, eg to try to settle a dispute or get agreement. **2** any intermediate person or thing.

intermediate /ɪntəˈmiːdɪət/ *adj* in the middle; placed between two points, stages or extremes. ➤ *n* **1** an intermediate thing. **2** *chem* a short-lived chemical compound formed during one of the middle stages of a series of chemical reactions. **3** *chem* the precursor of a particular end-product, eg a dye. ➤ *vb* /ɪntəˈmiːdɪeɪt/ *intr* to act as an intermediary. ○ **intermediation** *n.*

interment *n* burial, esp with appropriate ceremony.

intermezzo /ɪntəˈmɛtsoʊ/ *n* (*intermezzi* /-tsiː/ or *intermezzos*) *mus* a short instrumental piece usu performed between the sections of a symphonic work, opera or other dramatic musical entertainment.

interminable *adj* seemingly without an end, esp because of being extremely dull and tedious.

intermingle *vb, tr & intr* to mingle or mix together.

intermission *n* a short period of time between two things, eg two parts of a film, play, etc.

intermittent *adj* happening occasionally; not continuous. ○ **intermittently** *adv.*

intern *vb* **1** /ɪnˈtɜːn/ to confine within a country, restricted area or prison, esp during a war. **2** /ˈɪntɜːn/ *intr, chiefly US* to train or work as an intern. ➤ *n* (*also* **interne**) /ˈɪntɜːn/ **1** *chiefly US* an advanced student or graduate who gains practical experience by working, eg in a hospital. **2** an inmate. ○ **internee** *n.* ○ **internment** *n.* ○ **internship** *n.*

internal *adj* **1** on, in, belonging to or suitable for the inside; inner. **2** on, in, belonging to or suitable for the inside of the body. **3** relating to a nation's domestic affairs. **4** for, belonging to or coming from within an organization. **5** relating to the inner nature or feelings or of the mind or soul. ○ **internally** *adv.*

internal-combustion engine *n* an engine that produces power by burning a mixture of fuel and air within an enclosed space.

internalize or **-ise** *vb* **1** to make (a type of behaviour, a characteristic, etc) part of one's personality. **2** to keep (an emotion, etc) inside oneself rather than express it. ○ **internalization** *n.*

international *adj* involving or affecting two or more nations. ➤ *n* **1** a sports match or competition between two national teams. **2** (*also* **internationalist**) someone who takes part in, or has taken part in, such a match or competition.

internationalism *n* the view that the nations of the world should co-operate and work towards greater mutual understanding. ○ **internationalist** *n.*

internationalize or **-ise** *vb* to make international, esp to bring under the control of two or more countries. ○ **internationalization** *n.*

internecine /ɪntəˈniːsaɪn/ *adj* **1** of a fight, war,

etc: destructive and damaging to both sides. **2** of a conflict or struggle: within a group or organization.

the Internet *n* a global computer communications network. Often shortened to **the net**.

interpersonal *adj* concerning or involving relationships between people.

interplanetary *adj* **1** relating to the solar system. **2** happening or existing in the space between the planets.

interplay *n* the action and influence of two or more things on each other.

interpolate *vb* **1** to add (words) to a book or manuscript, esp to make the text misleading or corrupt. **2** to alter (a text) in this way. **3** to interrupt a conversation, a person speaking, etc with (a comment). **4** *maths* to estimate (the value of a function) at a point between values that are already known. ○ **interpolation** *n*.

interpose *vb* **1** *tr & intr* to put something, or come, between two other things. **2** to interrupt a conversation or argument with (a remark, comment, etc). **3** *intr* to act as mediator; to intervene. ○ **interposition** *n*.

interpret *vb* **1** to explain the meaning of (a foreign word, dream, etc). **2** *intr* to act as an interpreter. **3** to consider or understand (behaviour, a remark, etc): *He interpreted her silence as disapproval.* **4** to convey one's idea of the meaning of (eg a dramatic role, piece of music) in one's performance. ○ **interpretable** *adj.* ○ **interpretation** *n.* ○ **interpretative** or **interpretive** *adj.*

interpreter *n* **1** someone who translates foreign speech as the words are spoken and relays the translation orally. **2** *comput* a program that translates a statement written in a high-level language into machine code and then executes it.

interracial *adj* between different races of people.

interregnum *n* (*interregnums* or *interregna*) **1** the time between two monarchs' reigns when the throne is unoccupied. **2** the time between rule by one government and rule by the next. **3** any interval or pause in events.

interrelate *vb, tr & intr* to be in or be brought into a mutually dependent or reciprocal relationship.

interrogate *vb* **1** to question closely and thoroughly. **2** of a radar set, etc: to send out signals to (a radio beacon) to work out a position. ○ **interrogation** *n.* ○ **interrogator** *n.*

interrogative *adj* **1** like a question; asking or seeming to ask a question. **2** *gram* of an adjective or pronoun: used to introduce a question, eg *what, whom*, etc. ➤ *n, gram* an interrogative word, sentence or construction. ○ **interrogatively** *adv.*

interrupt *vb* **1** *tr & intr* to break into (a conversation or monologue) by asking a question or making a comment. **2** *tr & intr* to make a break in the continuous activity of (an event), or to disturb someone from some action. **3** to de-

stroy (a view, eg of a clear sweep of land) by getting in the way. ○ **interrupter** or **interruptor** *n* **1** someone who interrupts. **2** *electronics* a device for opening and closing an electric circuit at set intervals and so produce pulses. ○ **interruption** *n.* ○ **interruptive** *adj.*

intersect *vb* **1** to divide (lines, an area, etc) by passing or cutting through or across. **2** *intr* esp of lines, roads, etc: to run through or cut across each other.

intersection *n* **1** a place where things meet or intersect, esp a road junction. **2** the act of intersecting. **3** *geom* the point or set of points where two or more lines or plane surfaces cross each other. **4** *geom* a set of points common to two or more geometrical figures. **5** *maths* the set of elements formed by the elements common to two or more other sets.

intersperse *vb* to scatter or insert something here and there. ○ **interspersion** *n.*

interstate *adj* between two or more states. ➤ *n, esp US* a major road that crosses a state boundary.

interstellar *adj* happening or existing in the space between individual stars within galaxies.

interstice /ɪnˈtɜːstɪs/ *n* a very small gap or space.

intertwine *vb, tr & intr* to twist or be twisted together.

interval *n* **1** a period of time between two events. **2** a space or distance between two things. **3** *Brit* a short break between the acts of a play or opera, or between parts of a concert or long film. **4** *mus* the difference in pitch between two notes or tones.

intervene *vb, intr* **1** (*often* **intervene in sth**) to involve oneself in something which is happening in order to affect the outcome. **2** (*often* **intervene in sth** or **between people**) to involve oneself or interfere in a dispute between other people in order to settle it or prevent more serious conflict. **3** to come or occur between two things in place or time. ○ **intervention** *n.*

interventionism *n* the belief that a government should, or should be allowed to, interfere in the economic affairs of the country or in the internal affairs of other countries. ○ **interventionist** *n, adj.*

interview *n* **1** a formal meeting and discussion with someone, esp one at which an employer meets and judges a prospective employee. **2** a conversation or discussion which aims at obtaining information, esp one for broadcasting or publication in which a famous or important person is questioned. ➤ *vb* to hold an interview with someone. ○ **interviewee** *n.* ○ **interviewer** *n.*

interweave *vb, tr & intr* to weave or be woven together.

intestate *law, adj* of a person: not having made a valid will before their death. ➤ *n* someone who dies without making a valid will. ○ **intestacy** *n.*

intestine *n* the muscular tube-like part of the alimentary canal between the stomach and the anus. ○ **intestinal** *adj*.

intimacy *n* (*-ies*) **1** warm close personal friendship. **2** an intimate or personal remark. **3** *euphem* sexual intercourse. **4** the state or quality of being intimate.

intimate[1] /'ɪntɪmət/ *adj* **1** marked by or sharing a close and affectionate friendship. **2** very private or personal. **3** of a place: small and quiet with a warm, friendly atmosphere. **4** (*often* **intimate with sb**) sharing a sexual relationship with them. **5** of knowledge: deep and thorough. ➤ *n* a close friend. ○ **intimately** *adv*.

intimate[2] /'ɪntɪmeɪt/ *vb* **1** to announce or make known. **2** to hint or suggest indirectly. ○ **intimation** *n*.

intimidate *vb* **1** to coerce, esp with threats. **2** to frighten, scare or overawe. ○ **intimidation** *n*.

into *prep* **1** to or towards the inside or middle of something. **2** against; making contact or colliding with something or someone. **3** used to express a change of state or condition: *get into difficulties*. **4** having reached a certain period of time: *into extra time*. **5** *maths* used to express division: *Four into twenty makes five*. **6** *colloq* involved with, interested in or enthusiastic about: *into golf in a big way*.

intolerable *adj* too bad, difficult, painful, etc to be put up with. ○ **intolerably** *adv*.

intolerant *adj* refusing or unwilling to accept ideas, beliefs, behaviour, etc different from one's own. ○ **intolerance** *n*.

intonation *n* **1** the rise and fall of the pitch of the voice in speech. **2** an act of intoning. **3** the correct pitching of musical notes.

intone *vb, tr & intr* **1** to recite (a prayer, etc) in a solemn monotonous voice or in singing tones. **2** to say something with a particular intonation or tone.

intoxicate *vb* **1** to make drunk. **2** to excite or elate. ○ **intoxicant** *n, adj*. ○ **intoxicating** *adj*. ○ **intoxication** *n*.

intractable *adj* **1** difficult to control or influence; obstinate. **2** difficult to solve, cure or deal with. ○ **intractability** *n*.

intramural *adj* within or amongst the people in an institution, esp a school, college or university.

intranet *n, comput* a restricted website, eg within a company.

intransigent *adj* refusing to change or compromise one's beliefs. ➤ *n* an intransigent person. ○ **intransigence** *n*.

intransitive *gram, adj* of a verb: not taking or having a direct object. ➤ *n* such a verb. Compare TRANSITIVE. ○ **intransitively** *adv*.

intrauterine /ɪntrəˈjuːtəraɪn/ *adj, med* located or occurring within the uterus.

intravenous /ɪntrəˈviːnəs/ *adj, med* located within or introduced into a vein or veins. ○ **intravenously** *adv*.

in-tray *n, Brit* a tray, eg on a desk, that incoming mail, etc is put in before it is dealt with.

intrench see ENTRENCH

intrepid *adj* bold and daring; brave. ○ **intrepidity** *n*. ○ **intrepidly** *adv*.

intricate *adj* full of complicated, interrelating or tangled details or parts and therefore difficult to understand, analyse or sort out. ○ **intricacy** *n* (*-ies*). ○ **intricately** *adv*.

intrigue *n* /'ɪntriːg/ **1** secret plotting or underhand scheming. **2** a secret plot or plan. **3** a secret illicit love affair. ➤ *vb* /ɪn'triːg/ (*intrigued, intriguing*) **1** to arouse the curiosity or interest of someone. **2** *intr* to plot secretly. ○ **intriguing** *adj*. ○ **intriguingly** *adv*.

intrinsic *adj* being an inherent and essential part of something or someone. ○ **intrinsically** *adv*.

intro *n, colloq* an introduction, esp to a piece of music.

introduce *vb* **1** (*usu* introduce sb to sb else) to present them to one another by name. **2** to announce or present (eg a radio or television programme) to an audience. **3** to bring (something) into a place, situation, etc for the first time. **4** to bring into operation, practice or use. **5** to put forward or propose (a possible law or bill) for consideration or approval. **6** (*usu* introduce sb to sth) to cause someone to experience or discover something for the first time. **7** to start or preface: *Introduce the play with a brief analysis of the plot*. **8** (*usu* introduce one thing into another) to insert or put something into something else. ○ **introductory** *adj*.

introduction *n* **1** the act or process of introducing or process of being introduced. **2** a presentation of one person to another or others. **3** a section at the beginning of a book which explains briefly what it is about, why it was written, etc. **4** a book which outlines the basic principles of a subject. **5** a short passage of music beginning a piece or song, or leading up to a movement. **6** something which has been introduced.

introspection *n* the examination of one's own thoughts, feelings, etc. ○ **introspective** *adj*.

introvert *n* **1** *psychol* someone who is more interested in the self and inner feelings than in the outside world and social relationships. **2** someone who tends not to socialize and who is uncommunicative and withdrawn. ➤ *adj* (*also* **introverted**) concerned more with one's own thoughts and feelings than with other people and outside events. Compare EXTROVERT. ○ **introversion** *n*. ○ **introverted** *adj*.

intrude *vb, tr & intr* (*often* intrude into or on sb or sth) to force or impose (oneself, one's presence or something) without welcome or invitation. ○ **intruder** *n*. ○ **intrusion** *n*.

intrusive *adj* tending to intrude. ○ **intrusively** *adv*. ○ **intrusiveness** *n*.

intrust see ENTRUST

intuit *vb* to know or become aware of something by intuition. ○ **intuitable** *adj*.

intuition *n* **1** the power of understanding or realizing something without conscious rational thought or analysis. **2** something understood or realized in this way. **3** immediate instinctive understanding or belief. ○ **intuitive** *adj.* ○ **intuitively** *adv.* ○ **intuitiveness** *n.*

intumesce /ɪntʃʊˈmɛs/ *vb, intr* to swell up. ○ **intumescence** *n.* ○ **intumescent** *adj.*

Inuit or **Innuit** *n* (*pl* **Inuit** or **Innuit**) **1** a member of a people of the Arctic and sub-Arctic regions of Canada, Greenland and Alaska. **2** their language. ▷ *adj* belonging or relating to this people or their language.

inundate *vb* **1** to cover with water. **2** to swamp: *The company was inundated with applications for the job.* ○ **inundation** *n.*

inure or **enure** *vb* (*often* **inure sb to sth**) to accustom them to something unpleasant or unwelcome. ○ **inurement** *n.*

invade *vb* **1** *tr & intr* to enter (a country) by force with an army. **2** *tr & intr* to attack or overrun: *Angry supporters invaded the pitch.* **3** to interfere with (a person's rights, privacy, etc). ○ **invader** *n.*

invalid[1] /ˈɪnvəlɪd/ *n* someone who is constantly ill or who is disabled. ▷ *adj* suitable for or being an invalid. ▷ *vb* (**invalided, invaliding**) **1 a** (*usu* **invalid sb out**) to discharge (a soldier, etc) from service because of illness; **b** (*usu* **invalid sb home**) to send (a soldier, etc) home because of illness. **2** to affect with disease. ○ **invalidity** *n.*

invalid[2] /ɪnˈvalɪd/ *adj* **1** of a document, agreement, etc: having no legal force. **2** of an argument, reasoning, etc: based on false reasoning or a mistake and therefore not valid, correct or reliable. ○ **invalidity** *n.* ○ **invalidly** *adv.*

invalidate *vb* to make (a document, agreement, argument, etc) invalid. ○ **invalidation** *n.*

invaluable *adj* having a value that is too great to be measured.

invariable *adj* not prone to change or alteration. ○ **invariably** *adv.*

invasion *n* **1** invading, or being invaded, eg by a hostile country or by something harmful. **2** an encroachment or violation. ○ **invasive** *adj.*

invective *n* **1** sarcastic or abusive language. **2** a denunciation or critical attack using such words. ▷ *adj* characterized by such an attack.

inveigh /ɪnˈveɪ/ *vb, intr* (*usu* **inveigh against sb** or **sth**) to speak strongly or passionately against them or it, esp in criticism or protest.

inveigle *vb* (*usu* **inveigle sb into sth**) to trick, deceive or persuade them into doing it. ○ **inveiglement** *n.*

invent *vb* **1** to be the first person to make or use (a machine, game, method, etc). **2** to think or make up (an excuse, false story, etc). ○ **invention** *n.* ○ **inventive** *adj.* ○ **inventively** *adv.* ○ **inventiveness** *n.* ○ **inventor** *n.*

inventory /ˈɪnvəntəri/ *n* (*-ies*) **1** a list of the articles, goods, etc in a particular place. **2** the items on such a list. ▷ *vb* (*-ies, -ied*) to make an inventory of (items); to list in an inventory.

inverse *adj* opposite or reverse in order, sequence, direction, effect, etc. ▷ *n* **1** a direct opposite. **2** the state of being directly opposite or reversed. **3** *maths* a mathematical function that is opposite in effect or nature to another function. ○ **inversely** *adv.*

invert *vb* **1** to turn upside down or inside out. **2** to reverse in order, sequence, direction, effect, etc. ○ **inversion** *n.*

invertebrate *n, zool* any animal that does not possess a backbone, such as an insect, worm, snail or jellyfish. ▷ *adj* (*also* **invertebral**) relating to an animal without a backbone.

inverted commas *n* another name for QUOTATION MARKS.

invest *vb* **1** *tr & intr* to put (money) into a company or business, eg by buying shares in it, in order to make a profit. **2** *tr & intr* to devote (time, effort, energy, etc) to something. **3** *intr* (**invest in sth**) *colloq* to buy it. **4** (*often* **invest sb with sth**) to give them the symbols of power, rights, rank, etc officially. **5** (*usu* **invest sth in sb**) to place power, rank, a quality or feeling, etc in somebody. **6** to clothe or adorn. **7** *mil* to besiege (a stronghold). ○ **investor** *n.*

investigate *vb, tr & intr* to carry out a thorough and detailed inquiry into or examination of something or someone. ○ **investigation** *n.* ○ **investigative** or **investigatory** *adj.* ○ **investigator** *n.*

investiture *n* a formal ceremony giving a rank or office to someone.

investment *n* **1** a sum of money invested. **2** something, such as a business, house, etc, in which one invests money, time, effort, etc. **3** the act of investing.

inveterate *adj* **1** of a habit, etc: firmly established. **2** of a person: firmly fixed in a habit by long practice. ○ **inveterately** *adv.*

invidious *adj* likely to cause envy, resentment or indignation, esp by being or seeming to be unfair. ○ **invidiously** *adv.* ○ **invidiousness** *n.*

invigilate *vb, tr & intr, Brit* to keep watch over people sitting an examination, esp to prevent cheating. ○ **invigilation** *n.* ○ **invigilator** *n.*

invigorate *vb* to give fresh life, energy and health to something or someone; to strengthen or animate. ○ **invigorating** *adj.* ○ **invigoration** *n.*

invincible *adj* indestructible; unable to be defeated. ○ **invincibility** *n.* ○ **invincibly** *adv.*

inviolable *adj* not to be broken or violated; sacred. ○ **inviolability** *n.* ○ **inviolably** *adv.*

inviolate *adj* not broken, violated or injured.

invisible *adj* **1** not able to be seen. **2** unseen. **3** *econ* relating to services (eg insurance, tourism) rather than goods: *invisible exports.* **4** *econ* not shown in regular statements: *invisible assets.* ▷ *n* an invisible item of trade. ○ **invisibility** *n.* ○ **invisibly** *adv.*

invitation *n* **1** a request to a person to come or go somewhere, eg to a party, meal, etc. **2** the form such a request takes, eg written on a card, etc. **3** an act of inviting. **4** encouragement; inducement.

invite *vb* /ɪnˈvaɪt/ **1** to request the presence of

someone at one's house, at a party, etc, esp formally or politely. **2** to ask politely or formally for (eg comments, advice, etc). **3** to bring on or encourage (something unwanted or undesirable). **4** to attract or tempt. ➤ *n* /'mvaɪt/ *colloq* an invitation.

inviting *adj* attractive or tempting. ○ **invitingly** *adv.*

in vitro /m 'vi:troʊ/ *adj, adv, biol* of biological techniques or processes: performed outside a living organism in an artificial environment created by means of scientific equipment, eg in a test tube: *in-vitro fertilization.*

invoice *n* a list of goods supplied, delivered with the goods and giving details of price and quantity, usu treated as a request for payment. ➤ *vb* **1** to send an invoice to (a customer). **2** to provide an invoice for (goods).

invoke *vb* **1** to make an appeal to (God, some deity, a Muse, authority, etc) for help, support or inspiration. **2** to appeal to (a law, principle, etc) as an authority or reason for eg one's behaviour. **3** to make an earnest appeal for (help, support, inspiration, etc). **4** to conjure up (a spirit) by reciting a spell. **5** to put (a law, decision, etc) into effect. ○ **invocation** *n.*

involuntary *adj* done without being controlled by the will; not able to be controlled by the will. ○ **involuntarily** *adv.*

involute *adj* **1** entangled; intricate. **2** *bot* of petals, etc: rolled in at the edges. **3** of shells: curled up in a spiral shape, so that the axis is concealed. ➤ *vb, intr* to become involute or undergo involution.

involution *n* **1** involving or being involved or entangled. **2** *zool* degeneration. **3** *physiol* the shrinking of an organ after its purpose has been served or as a result of ageing.

involve *vb* **1** to require as a necessary part. **2** (*usu* **involve sb in sth**) to cause them to take part or be implicated in it. **3** to have an effect on someone or something. **4** (*often* **involve oneself in sth**) to become emotionally concerned in it. ○ **involved** *adj* **1** concerned, implicated. **2** complicated. ○ **involvement** *n.*

invulnerable *adj* incapable of being hurt, damaged or attacked. ○ **invulnerability** *n.*

inward *adj* **1** placed or being within. **2** moving towards the inside. **3** relating or belonging to the mind or soul. ➤ *adv* (*also* **inwards**) **1** towards the inside or the centre. **2** into the mind, inner thoughts or soul.

inwardly *adv* **1** on the inside; internally. **2** in one's private thoughts; secretly.

iodine *n* **1** *chem* a non-metallic element consisting of dark-violet crystals that form a violet vapour when heated. **2** *med* a solution of iodine in ethanol, used as an antiseptic.

iodize or **-ise** *vb* to treat something with iodine, esp common salt so as to provide iodine as a nutritional supplement.

ion *n, chem* an atom or group of atoms that has acquired a net positive charge as a result of losing one or more electrons, or a net negative charge as a result of gaining one or more electrons. ○ **ionic** *adj.*

ionize or **-ise** *vb, tr & intr, chem* to produce or make something produce ions. ○ **ionization** *n.*

ionosphere *n, meteorol* the upper layer of the Earth's atmosphere, which contains many ions and free electrons produced by the ionizing effects of solar radiation.

iota /aɪˈoʊtə/ *n* **1** the ninth letter of the Greek alphabet. **2** a very small amount: *Nothing she said makes an iota of difference.*

IOU *n* (**IOUs, IOU's**) *colloq* a written and signed note that serves as an acknowledgement of a debt.

ipecacuanha /ɪpɪkakjʊˈanə/ or **ipecac** /'ɪpɪkak/ *n* **1** a small Latin American shrub. **2** the dried root of this plant prepared as a tincture or syrup, which is used in small doses as an expectorant or as a purgative or emetic.

IQ *abbrev* intelligence quotient.

Ir *symbol, chem* iridium.

irascible *adj* easily made angry. ○ **irascibility** *n.* ○ **irascibly** *adv.*

irate *adj* very angry. ○ **irately** *adv.* ○ **irateness** *n.*

ire *n, literary* anger.

iridescent *adj* having many bright rainbow-like colours which seem to shimmer and change constantly. ○ **iridescence** *n.* ○ **iridescently** *adv.*

iridium *n, chem* a silvery metallic element that is resistant to corrosion.

iris *n* **1** (**irises**, *technical* **irides** /'aɪərɪdi:z/) a plant that has flattened sword-shaped leaves and large brilliantly coloured flowers. **2** *anat* an adjustable pigmented ring of muscle lying in front of the lens of the eye, surrounding the pupil. **3** (*in full* **iris diaphragm**) a device consisting of a series of thin overlapping crescent-shaped plates surrounding a central aperture, used to control the amount of light entering an optical instrument.

Irish *adj* belonging or relating to Ireland, its inhabitants, their Celtic language or their dialect of English. ➤ *n* **1** (*in full* **Irish Gaelic**) the Celtic language of Ireland. **2** (**the Irish**) the people of Ireland. **3** whiskey made in Ireland.

Irishman or **Irishwoman** *n* someone who is Irish by birth or descent.

irk *vb* to annoy or irritate, esp persistently.

irksome *adj* annoying, irritating or boring.

iron *n* **1** a strong hard greyish metallic element that is naturally magnetic. **2** a tool, weapon or other implement made of iron. **3** a triangular, flat-bottomed, now usu electrical, household tool used for smoothing out creases and pressing clothes. **4** *golf* any of various clubs with an angled iron head. **5** a BRAND (*noun* sense 4). **6** great physical or mental strength. **7** (**irons**) chains; fetters. ➤ *adj* **1** made of iron. **2** very strong, inflexible, unyielding, etc: *iron determination.* ➤ *vb* **1** to smooth the creases out of or press (eg clothes) with an iron. **2** *intr* of clothing or fabric: to react or respond in the way specified to being ironed: *shiny material which irons badly.* ♦ **have several irons in the fire** to have several commitments. **strike while the iron is hot** to act while the situation is to one's advantage. ◊ **iron sth out** 1 to remove or put right (problems, etc) so that progress becomes easier. 2 to remove creases in it by ironing.

Iron Age *n* the period in history following the Bronze Age and beginning about 1200 BC, when weapons and tools were made of iron.

ironclad *adj* 1 covered with protective iron plates. 2 inflexible; set firm. ➤ *n, hist* a 19c warship covered with protective iron plates.

ironic or **ironical** *adj* 1 containing, characterized by or expressing irony. 2 of a person: given to frequent use of irony. ○ **ironically** *adv.*

ironing *n* 1 clothes, household linen, etc which need to be or have just been ironed. 2 the act or process of ironing.

ironmonger *n, Brit* a dealer in articles made of metal, eg tools, locks, etc, and other household hardware. ○ **ironmongery** *n.*

iron rations *pl n* food with a high energy value, carried for emergencies by climbers, walkers, military personnel, etc.

ironstone *n* hard, white earthenware.

ironware *n* things made of iron, esp household hardware.

ironwork *n* 1 articles made of iron, such as gates and railings. 2 (**ironworks**) a factory where iron is smelted.

irony *n* (*-ies*) 1 a linguistic device or form of humour that takes its effect from stating the opposite of what is meant. 2 a dramatic device by which information is given to the audience that is not known to all the characters in the drama, or in which words are meant to convey different meanings to the audience and to the characters. 3 awkward or perverse circumstances applying to a situation that is in itself satisfactory or desirable.

irradiate *vb* 1 *med* to subject (a part of the body) to IRRADIATION. 2 to preserve food by IRRADIATION. 3 to shed light on something; to light up. 4 to make bright or clear intellectually or spiritually.

irradiation *n* 1 *med* exposure of part of the body to electromagnetic radiation or a radioactive source, for diagnostic or therapeutic purposes. 2 a method of preserving food by exposing it to ultraviolet or ionizing radiation.

irrational *adj* 1 not the result of clear, logical thought. 2 unable to think logically and clearly. 3 *maths* not commensurable with natural numbers. 4 *maths* of a root, expression, etc: involving irrational numbers. ➤ *n, maths* an irrational number. ○ **irrationality** *n.* ○ **irrationally** *adv.*

irreconcilable *adj* 1 not agreeing or able to be brought into agreement; incompatible. 2 hostile and opposed; unwilling to be friendly. ➤ *n* 1 a hostile or obstinate opponent. 2 any of various opinions, ideas, etc that cannot be

brought into agreement. ○ **irreconcilability** *n.* ○ **irreconcilably** *adv.*

irrecoverable *adj* 1 not able to be recovered or regained. 2 not able to be corrected. ○ **irrecoverably** *adv.*

irredeemable *adj* 1 of a person: too evil to be saved; beyond help. 2 incapable of being recovered, repaired or cured. 3 of shares, etc: unable to be bought back from the shareholder by the issuing company for the sum originally paid. 4 of paper money: unable to be exchanged for coin. ○ **irredeemably** *adv.*

irreducible *adj* 1 unable to be reduced or made simpler. 2 unable to be brought from one state into another, usu desired, state. ○ **irreducibly** *adv.*

irrefutable *adj* not able to be denied or proved false. ○ **irrefutability** *n.* ○ **irrefutably** *adv.*

irregular *adj* 1 not happening or occurring at regular or equal intervals. 2 not smooth, even or balanced. 3 not conforming to rules, custom, accepted or normal behaviour, or routine. 4 *gram* of a word: not changing its form (eg to show tenses or plurals) according to the usual patterns in the language. 5 of troops: not belonging to the regular army. ➤ *n* an irregular soldier. ○ **irregularity** *n.* ○ **irregularly** *adv.*

irrelevant *adj* not connected with the subject in hand. ○ **irrelevance** *n.* ○ **irrelevantly** *adv.*

irreligious *adj* 1 lacking religion. 2 lacking respect for religion.

irremediable *adj* unable to be cured, corrected or made better. ○ **irremediably** *adv.*

irremovable *adj* not able to be removed. ○ **irremovability** *n.* ○ **irremovably** *adv.*

irreparable *adj* not able to be restored or put right. ○ **irreparability** *n.* ○ **irreparably** *adv.*

irreplaceable *adj* not able to be replaced, esp because too rare or valuable or of sentimental value. ○ **irreplaceably** *adv.*

irrepressible *adj* not able to be controlled, restrained or repressed, esp because of being too lively and full of energy or strength. ○ **irrepressibility** *n.* ○ **irrepressibly** *adv.*

irreproachable *adj* free from faults; blameless. ○ **irreproachability** *n.* ○ **irreproachably** *adv.*

irresistible *adj* 1 too strong to be resisted. 2 very attractive or enticing. ○ **irresistibility** or **irresistibleness** *n.* ○ **irresistibly** *adv.*

irresolute *adj* hesitating or doubtful; not able to take firm decisions. ○ **irresolutely** *adv.* ○ **irresoluteness** or **irresolution** *n.*

irrespective *adj* (*always* **irrespective of sth**) without considering or taking it into account. ➤ *adv, colloq* nevertheless; regardless. ○ **irrespectively** *adv.*

irresponsible *adj* 1 done without, or showing no, concern for the consequences; reckless; careless. 2 not reliable or trustworthy. ○ **irresponsibility** *n.* ○ **irresponsibly** *adv.*

irretrievable *adj* not able to be recovered or put right. ○ **irretrievability** *n.* ○ **irretrievably** *adv.*

irreverent *adj* lacking respect or reverence (eg for things considered sacred or for important people). ○ **irreverence** *n.* ○ **irreverently** *adv.*

irreversible *adj* 1 not able to be changed back to a former or original state. 2 not able to be recalled or annulled. ○ **irreversibility** or **irreversibleness** *n.* ○ **irreversibly** *adv.*

irrevocable *adj* unable to be changed, stopped or undone. ○ **irrevocability** *n.* ○ **irrevocably** *adv.*

irrigate *vb* 1 to provide (land) with a supply of water. 2 *med* to wash out (the eye, a wound, body cavity, etc) with a flow of water or antiseptic solution. ○ **irrigation** *n.*

irritable *adj* 1 easily annoyed, angered or excited. 2 extremely or excessively sensitive. ○ **irritability** or **irritableness** *n.* ○ **irritably** *adv.*

irritant *n* 1 any chemical, physical or biological agent that causes irritation of a tissue, esp inflammation of the skin or eyes. 2 something or someone that causes physical or mental irritation. ➤ *adj* irritating.

irritate *vb* 1 to make someone angry or annoyed. 2 to make (part of the body, an organ, etc) sore and swollen or itchy. ○ **irritating** *adj.* ○ **irritatingly** *adv.* ○ **irritation** *n.* ○ **irritative** *adj.*

irrupt *vb, intr* to burst into or enter a place, etc suddenly with speed and violence. ○ **irruption** *n.*

isinglass /ˈaɪzɪŋglɑːs/ *n* 1 gelatine from the dried swim bladders of certain fish, eg sturgeon. 2 thin transparent sheets of MICA used in furnace and stove doors.

Islam *n* 1 the monotheistic religion of the MUSLIMS, as revealed by the prophet Muhammad, and set forth in the KORAN. 2 a Muslims collectively; b the parts of the world in which Islam is the main or recognized religion. ○ **Islamic** *adj.*

island *n* 1 a piece of land, smaller than a continent, which is completely surrounded by water. 2 anything which is like an island, esp in being isolated or detached. 3 (*in full* **traffic island**) a small raised area in the middle of a street on which people may safely stand when crossing the road.

islander *n* someone who lives on an island.

isle *n* an island, esp a small one.

> **isle** There is sometimes a spelling confusion between **isle** and **aisle**.

islet *n* 1 a small island. 2 any small group of cells which has a different nature and structure to the cells surrounding it.

ism *n, colloq, often derog* a distinctive and formal set of ideas, principles or beliefs.

isn't *contraction* is not.

isobar *n* a line on a weather chart connecting points that have the same atmospheric pressure. ○ **isobaric** *adj.*

isolate *vb* 1 to separate from others; to cause to be alone. 2 to place in quarantine. 3 to separate or detach, esp to allow closer examination: *isolate the problem*. 4 to separate so as to obtain in a pure or uncombined form. ➤ *n* someone or something that is isolated. ○ **isolation** *n.*

isolated *adj* 1 placed or standing alone or apart. 2 separate. 3 solitary.

isolationism *n* the policy of not joining with other countries in international political and economic affairs. ○ **isolationist** *n, adj.*

isomer /ˈaɪsəmə(r)/ *n* 1 *chem* one of two or more chemical compounds that have the same molecular composition but different three-dimensional structures. 2 *physics* one of two or more atomic nuclei with the same atomic number and mass number, but with different energy states and radioactive properties. ○ **isomeric** /aɪsəˈmɛrɪk/ *adj.*

isometric *adj* 1 having equal size or measurements. 2 of a three-dimensional drawing: having all three axes equally inclined to the surface of the drawing and all lines drawn to scale. 3 *physiol* relating to muscular contraction that generates tension but does not produce shortening of the muscle fibres. 4 relating to ISOMETRICS.

isometrics *sing or pl n* a system of physical exercises for strengthening and toning the body in which the muscles are pushed either together or against an immovable object and are not contracted, flexed or made to bend limbs.

isomorph *n* 1 any object that is similar or identical in structure or shape to another object. 2 *chem* any of two or more substances having the same crystalline structure but differing in chemical composition. 3 *biol* any of two or more individuals that appear similar in form, although they belong to different races or species.

isosceles /aɪˈsɒsəliːz/ *adj* of a triangle: having two sides of equal length.

isotherm *n* 1 a line on a weather map connecting places where the temperature is the same at a particular time or for a particular period of time. 2 *physics* a line on a graph linking all places or points having a certain temperature.

isotonic *adj, physiol* of muscles: having the same tension.

isotope *n, chem* one of two or more atoms of the same chemical element that contain the same number of protons but different numbers of neutrons in their nuclei. ○ **isotopic** *adj.* ○ **isotopically** *adv.* ○ **isotopy** *n.*

isotropic *adj* 1 having physical properties that are identical in all directions. 2 tending to show equal growth in all directions. ○ **isotropy** *n.*

Israeli *adj* belonging or relating to Israel, a modern state in the Middle East, or its inhabitants. ➤ *n* a citizen or inhabitant of, or person born in, Israel.

Israelite *n, Bible, hist* someone born or living in the ancient kingdom of Israel, esp a person claiming descent from Jacob. ➤ *adj* belonging or relating to the ancient kingdom of Israel or its inhabitants.

issue *n* **1** the giving out, publishing or making available of something, eg stamps, a magazine, etc. **2** something given out, published or made available. **3** one item in a regular series. **4** a subject for discussion or argument. **5** a result or consequence. **6** *formal* children; offspring. **7** an act of going or flowing out. ➤ *vb* **(issued, issuing) 1** to give or send out, distribute, publish or make available, esp officially or formally. **2** (*usu* **issue sb with sth**) to supply them with the required item. **3** *intr* (*often* **issue forth** or **out**) to flow or come out, esp in large quantities. **4** *intr* (*usu* **issue in sth**) to end or result in it. **5** *intr* (*often* **issue from sb** or **sth**) to come or descend from them or it; to be produced or caused by them or it. ♦ **at issue 1** in dispute or disagreement. **2** under discussion. **force the issue** to act so as to force a decision to be taken. **join** or **take issue with sb** to disagree with them. **make an issue of sth** to make it the explicit subject of an argument or disagreement.

isthmus /ˈɪsməs, ˈɪsθməs/ *n* a narrow strip of land, bounded by water on both sides, that joins two larger areas of land.

IT *abbrev* information technology.

it *pron* **1** the thing, animal, baby or group already mentioned. **2** the person in question: *Who is it?* **3** used as the subject with impersonal verbs and when describing the weather or distance or telling the time: *It's a bit blustery today.* **4** used as the grammatical subject of a sentence when the real subject comes later, eg *It's very silly to run away.* **5** used to refer to a general situation or state of affairs: *How's it going?* **6** used to emphasize a certain word or phrase in a sentence: *When is it that her train's due?* **7** exactly what is needed, suitable or available: *That's it!* **8** used with many verbs and prepositions as an object with little meaning: *run for it.* ➤ *n* **1** the person in a children's game who has to oppose all the others, eg by trying to catch them. **2** *old use, colloq* sex appeal. **3** *colloq* sexual intercourse.

Italian *adj* belonging or relating to Italy, its inhabitants or their language. ➤ *n* **1** a citizen or inhabitant of, or person born in, Italy. **2** the official language of Italy, also spoken in parts of Switzerland. **3** *colloq* **a** a restaurant that serves Italian food; **b** a meal in one of these restaurants.

Italianate *adj* esp of decoration, architecture or art: done in an Italian style.

italic *adj* **1** of a typeface: containing characters which slope upwards to the right. **2** (**Italic**) belonging or relating to ancient Italy. **3** (**Italic**) denoting a group of Indo-European languages spoken in ancient Italy, including Latin. ➤ *n* **1** (*usu* **italics**) a typeface with characters which slope upwards to the right. **2** a character written or printed in this typeface. **3** the Italic languages.

italicize or **-ise** *vb* to print or write in italics; to change (characters, words, etc in normal typeface) to italics. ○ **italicization** *n*.

itch *n* **1** an unpleasant or ticklish irritation on the surface of the skin which makes one want to scratch. **2** *colloq* a strong or restless desire. **3** a skin disease or condition which causes a constant unpleasant irritation, esp scabies. ➤ *vb* **1** *intr* to have an itch and want to scratch. **2** *tr & intr* to cause someone to feel an itch. **3** *intr, colloq* to feel a strong or restless desire. ○ **itchiness** *n*. ○ **itchy** *adj* (**-ier, -iest**).

itchy feet *pl n, colloq* the strong desire to leave, move or travel.

it'd *contraction* **1** it had. **2** it would.

item *n* **1** a separate object or unit, esp one on a list. **2** a separate piece of information or news. **3** *colloq* a couple regarded as having a romantic or sexual relationship.

itemize or **-ise** *vb* to list (things) separately, eg on a bill. ○ **itemization** *n*. ○ **itemizer** *n*.

iterate *vb* to say or do again. ○ **iteration** *n*. ○ **iterative** *adj*.

itinerant *adj* travelling from place to place, eg on business. ➤ *n* a person whose work involves going from place to place or who has no fixed address.

itinerary *n* (**-ies**) **1** a planned route for a journey or trip. **2** a diary or record of a journey. **3** a guidebook. ➤ *adj* belonging or relating to journeys.

it'll *contraction* **1** it will. **2** it shall.

its *adj* belonging to it. ➤ *pron* the one or ones belonging to it.

---

its, it's Confusion between **its** and **it's** is still the most common error in the English language. **Its** = belonging to it, **it's** = 'it is' or in informal use, 'it has'.

---

it's *contraction* **1** it is. **2** *colloq* it has.

itself *pron* **1** the reflexive form of IT. **2** used for emphasis: *His behaviour itself was bad.* **3** its usual or normal state: *The puppy was soon itself again.* **4** (*also* **by itself**) alone; without help.

itsy-bitsy or **itty-bitty** *adj, colloq* very small.

IUD *abbrev* intrauterine device, a contraceptive device inserted into the womb, which prevents implantation of the fertilized egg.

IV *abbrev, med* intravenous.

I've *contraction* I have.

ivory *n* (**-ies**) **1** a hard white material that forms the tusks of the elephant, walrus, etc. **2** the creamy-white colour of this substance. **3** an article made from this substance. **4** (**ivories**) *colloq* the keys on a piano. ➤ *adj* **1** made of ivory: *ivory statuette.* **2** ivory-coloured, often with the implication of smoothness: *ivory skin.*

ivory tower *n* a hypothetical place where the unpleasant realities of life can be ignored.

ivy *n* (**-ies**) **1** a woody evergreen climbing or trailing plant. **2** any of several other climbing plants, such as poison ivy.

Jj

J¹ or **j** *n* (*Js, J's* or *j's*) the tenth letter of the English alphabet.

J² *abbrev* joule.

jab *vb* (*jabbed, jabbing*) (*also* **jab at**) **1** to poke or prod someone or something. **2** to strike someone or something with a short quick punch. ➤ *n* **1** a poke or prod. **2** *colloq* an injection or inoculation.

jabber *vb, tr & intr* to talk or utter rapidly and indistinctly. ➤ *n* rapid indistinct speech. ○ **jabbering** *n, adj*.

jack *n* **1** a device for raising a heavy weight, such as a car, off the ground. **2** a winch. **3** *elec, telecomm, etc* a socket with two or more terminals into which a **jack plug** can be inserted in order to make or break a circuit or circuits. **4** *cards* the court card of least value, bearing a picture of a young man. **5** *bowls* the small white ball that the players aim at. **6** a small national flag flown at the bows of a ship. ➤ *vb* to raise something with a jack. ◊ **jack sth in** or **up** *slang* to give it up, or abandon it. **jack up** to increase (prices, etc).

jackal *n* a scavenging mammal, closely related to the dog and wolf, that lives in Asia and Africa.

jackass *n* **1** a male ass or donkey. **2** *colloq* a foolish person.

jackboot *n* **1** a tall knee-high military boot. **2** such a boot as a symbol of oppressive military rule.

jackdaw *n* a bird of the crow family with black plumage shot with blue on the back and head, and a reputation for stealing bright objects.

jacket *n* **1** a short coat, esp a long-sleeved, hip-length one. **2** something worn over the top half of the body: *life jacket*. **3** a DUST JACKET. **4** the skin of an unpeeled cooked potato.

jack-in-the-box *n* (*jack-in-the-boxes*) a box containing a doll attached to a spring, which jumps out when the lid is opened.

jackknife *n* **1** a large pocket knife with a folding blade. **2** a dive in which the body is bent double and then straightened before entering the water. ➤ *vb, intr* of an articulated vehicle: to go out of control in such a way that the trailer swings round against the cab.

jack-of-all-trades *n* (*jacks-of-all-trades*) someone who turns their hand to a variety of different jobs.

jackpot *n* the maximum win to be made in a lottery, card game, etc.

Jack tar *n, old use* a sailor.

Jacobean *adj* belonging or relating to the reign of James I of England (also VI of Scotland) (1603–25).

Jacobite *Brit hist, n* an adherent of the **Jacobites**, supporters of James II, his son or grandson, the Stuart claimants to the British throne. ➤ *adj* relating to the Jacobites.

jacquard /ˈdʒɑkɑːd/ *n* **1** a piece of equipment consisting of a set of coded perforated cards that can be fitted to a loom to produce a fabric with an intricate woven pattern. **2** (*in full* **jacquard loom**) a loom fitted with this kind of device. **3** fabric produced on this kind of loom.

Jacuzzi /dʒəˈkuːzɪ/ *n, trademark* a large bath or pool with underwater jets that massage and invigorate the body.

jade *n* **1** a very hard, green, white, brown or yellow semi-precious stone used to make vases and carved ornaments. **2** the intense green colour of jade.

jaded *adj* fatigued; dull and bored.

jag *n* **1** a sharp projection. **2** *Scots* an injection. ➤ *vb* (*jagged, jagging*) **1** to cut something unevenly. **2** to make indentations in something.

jagged /ˈdʒagɪd/ *adj* having a rough or sharp uneven edge. ○ **jaggedness** *n*.

jaguar *n* the largest of the American big cats, with a deep yellow or tawny coat covered with black spots.

jail or **gaol** *n* prison. ➤ *vb* to imprison. ○ **jailer**, **jailor** or **gaoler** *n*.

jailbird or **gaolbird** *n, colloq* a person who is, or has been, frequently in prison.

jalopy or **jaloppy** /dʒəˈlɒpɪ/ *n* (*-ies*) *colloq* a worn-out old car.

jam¹ *n* a thick sticky food made from fruit boiled with sugar, used as a spread on bread, etc.

jam² *vb* (*jammed, jamming*) **1** *often in passive* to stick or wedge something so as to make it immovable. **2** *tr & intr* of machinery, etc: to stick or make it stick and stop working. **3** to push or shove; to cram, press or pack. **4** (*also* **jam up**) to fill (eg a street) so full that movement comes to a stop. **5** to cause interference to (a radio signal, etc), esp deliberately. **6** *intr, colloq* to play jazz in a JAM SESSION.

jamb /dʒam/ *n* the vertical post at the side of a door, window or fireplace.

jamboree *n* **1** a large rally of Scouts, Guides, etc. **2** *colloq* a large and lively gathering.

jammy *adj* (*-ier, -iest*) **1** covered or filled with jam. **2** *colloq* of a person: lucky.

jam-packed *adj, colloq* packed tight.

jam session *n, slang* a session of live, esp improvised, jazz or popular music.

jangle *vb* **1** *tr & intr* to make or cause to make an irritating, discordant ringing noise. **2** to upset or irritate (a person's nerves). ➤ *n* an unpleasant dissonant ringing sound.

janitor *n* **1** *N Am, Scot* a caretaker, esp of a school. **2** a doorkeeper.

January *n* the first month of the year.

japan *n* a hard glossy black lacquer, orig from Japan, used to coat wood and metal. ➤ *vb* (*japanned, japanning*) to lacquer something with japan.

Japanese *adj* belonging or relating to Japan, its inhabitants or their language. ➤ *n* **1** a citizen or inhabitant of, or person born in, Japan. **2** the official language of Japan.

jape *n, old use* a trick, prank or joke.

japonica *n* **1** an ornamental, red-flowered shrub which bears round green, white or yellow fruit. **2** the CAMELLIA.

jar¹ *n* a wide-mouthed cylindrical container, usu made of glass.

jar² *vb* (*jarred, jarring*) **1** *intr* to have a harsh effect; to grate. **2** *tr & intr* to jolt or vibrate. **3** *intr* (*esp jar with sth*) to clash or conflict with something. ➤ *n* a jarring sensation, shock or jolt.

jargon *n* **1** the specialized vocabulary of a particular trade, profession, group or activity. **2** *derog* language which uses this type of vocabulary in a pretentious or meaningless way.

jasmine *n* a shrub or vine whose fragrant flowers are used as a source of oil in perfumery and also to scent tea.

jasper *n, geol* a semi-precious gemstone, used to make jewellery and ornaments.

jaundice *n, pathol* a condition which turns the skin and the whites of the eyes a yellowish colour, caused by an excess of bile pigments in the blood.

jaundiced *adj* **1** suffering from jaundice. **2** of a person or attitude: bitter or resentful.

jaunt *n* a short journey for pleasure. ➤ *vb, intr* to go for a jaunt.

jaunty *adj* (*-ier, -iest*) **1** of someone's manner or personality: breezy and exuberant. **2** of dress, etc: smart; stylish. ○ **jauntily** *adv.* ○ **jauntiness** *n.*

javelin *n* **1** a light spear for throwing, either as a weapon or in sport. **2** (**the javelin**) the athletic event of throwing the javelin.

jaw *n* **1** *zool, biol* in most vertebrates: either of the two bony structures that form the framework of the mouth and in which the teeth are set. **2** the lower part of the face round the mouth and chin. **3** (**jaws**) the mouth, esp of an animal. **4** (**jaws**) a threshold, esp of something terrifying: *the jaws of death.* **5** (**jaws**) in a machine or tool: a pair of opposing parts used for gripping, crushing, etc. **6** *colloq* a long conversation; talk; chatter. ➤ *vb, intr, colloq* to chatter, gossip or talk.

jawbone *n, zool, non-technical* the upper or lower bone of the jaw.

jay *n* a bird of the crow family which has pinkish-brown plumage and blue, black and white bands on its wings.

jaywalk *vb, intr* to cross streets wherever one likes, regardless of traffic signals. ○ **jaywalker** *n.* ○ **jaywalking** *n.*

jazz *n* **1** a type of popular music of Black American origin, with strong catchy rhythms, performed with much improvisation. **2** *colloq* talk; nonsense; business, stuff, etc. ➤ *vb* (*usu jazz up*) *colloq* **1** to enliven or brighten something. **2** to give something a jazzy rhythm.

jazzy *adj* (*-ier, -iest*) **1** in the style of, or like, jazz. **2** *colloq* showy; flashy; stylish. ○ **jazzily** *adv.*

JCB *n* a type of mobile excavator used in the building industry, with a hydraulic shovel at the front and a digging arm at the back.

jealous *adj* (*often jealous of sb*) **1** envious (of someone else, their possessions, success, talents, etc). **2** suspicious and resentful (of possible rivals): *a jealous husband.* **3** anxiously protective (of something one has). **4** caused by jealousy: *a jealous fury.* Compare ENVIOUS. ○ **jealously** *adv.* ○ **jealousy** *n.*

jeans *pl n* casual trousers made esp of denim.

Jeep *n, trademark* a light military vehicle capable of travelling over rough country.

jeer *vb* **1** to mock or deride (a speaker, performer, etc). **2** *intr* (*jeer at sb* or *sth*) to laugh unkindly at them or it: *jeered at his accent.* ➤ *n* a taunt or hoot of derision.

jejune /dʒɪˈdʒuːn/ *adj, derog* **1** of writing, ideas, etc: dull, unoriginal and empty of imagination. **2** childish; naive.

jejunum /dʒɪˈdʒuːnəm/ *n, anat* in mammals: the part of the SMALL INTESTINE between the duodenum and the ileum.

Jekyll and Hyde /ˈdʒekɪl ənd haɪd; *US* ˈdʒiːkɪl/ *n* a person with two distinct personalities, one good, the other evil.

jell or **gel** *vb, intr* **1** to become firm; to set. **2** *colloq* to take definite shape.

jellied *adj* set in jelly: *jellied eels.*

jelly *n* (*-ies*) **1** a wobbly, transparent, fruit-flavoured dessert set with gelatine. **2** a clear jam made by boiling and straining fruit. **3** meat stock or other savoury medium set with gelatine. **4** any jelly-like substance.

jellyfish *n, zool* any of various marine COELENTERATES, usu having an umbrella-shaped body and tentacles containing stinging cells.

jemmy *n* (*-ies*) a small crowbar used esp by burglars for forcing open windows, etc. ➤ *vb* (*jemmies, jemmied*) to force (a door, window, etc) open with a jemmy or similar tool.

jenny *n* (*-ies*) a name given to the female of certain animals, esp the donkey and wren.

jeopardize or **-ise** *vb* to put something at risk of harm, loss or destruction.

jeopardy *n* danger of harm, loss or destruction.

jeremiad *n, colloq* a lengthy and mournful tale of woe.

jerk *n* **1** a quick tug or pull. **2** a sudden movement; a jolt. **3** *derog slang* a useless or idiotic person. ➤ *vb* **1** to pull or tug something sharply. **2** *intr* to move with sharp suddenness.

jerkin *n* a sleeveless jacket, short coat or close-fitting waistcoat.

jerky *adj* (**-ier, -iest**) making sudden movements or jerks. ○ **jerkily** *adv*. ○ **jerkiness** *n*.

Jerry *n* (**-ies**) *Brit war slang* **a** a German; **b** the Germans collectively.

jerry-built *adj* of a building: cheaply and quickly built.

jerry can *n* a flat-sided can used for carrying water, petrol, etc.

jersey *n* (**-eys**) a knitted garment worn on the upper part of the body, pulled on over the head.

Jerusalem artichoke *n* **1** a tall plant widely cultivated for its edible tubers. **2** the underground tuber of this plant, with white flesh and knobbly brownish or reddish skin, which can be eaten as a vegetable.

jest *n* a joke or prank. ➤ *vb, intr* to make a jest; to joke.

jester *n, hist* a professional clown, employed by a king or noble to amuse the court.

Jesuit *n* a member of the Society of Jesus (**the Jesuits**), a male religious order founded in 1540 by Ignatius of Loyola. ○ **Jesuitical** *adj*.

Jesus *n* Jesus Christ, the central figure of the Christian faith. ➤ *exclam* an exclamation of surprise, anger, etc.

jet¹ *n, geol* a hard black variety of LIGNITE that can be cut and polished, used to make jewellery and ornaments.

jet² *n* **1** a strong continuous stream of liquid or gas, forced under pressure from a narrow opening. **2** an orifice, nozzle or pipe through which such a stream is forced. **3** any device powered by such a stream of liquid or gas, esp a jet engine. **4** (*also* **jet aircraft**) an aircraft powered by a jet engine. ➤ *vb* (**jetted, jetting**) *tr & intr, colloq* to travel or transport something by jet aircraft.

jet-black *adj* deep glossy black.

jet engine *n* any engine, esp in an aircraft, which generates all or most of its forward thrust by ejecting a jet of gases formed as a result of fuel combustion.

jet lag *n* the tiredness and lethargy that result from the body's inability to adjust to the rapid changes of TIME ZONE that go with high-speed, long-distance air travel. ○ **jet-lagged** *adj*.

jet propulsion *n* the forward thrust of a body brought about by means of a force produced by ejection of a jet of gas or liquid to the rear of the body. ○ **jet-propelled** *adj*.

jetsam *n* goods jettisoned from a ship and washed up on the shore. Compare FLOTSAM.

the jet set *sing or pl n, colloq* wealthy people who lead a life of fast travel and expensive enjoyment. ○ **jet-setter** *n*. ○ **jet-setting** *n, adj*.

jet ski *n* a powered craft, similar to a motor-bike, adapted for skimming across water on a ski-like keel. ○ **jet-ski** *vb*.

jettison *vb* **1** to throw (cargo) overboard to lighten a ship, aircraft, etc in an emergency. **2** *colloq* to abandon, reject or get rid of someone or something.

jetty *n* (**-ies**) **1** a landing stage. **2** a barrier built out into the sea to protect a harbour from currents and high waves.

Jew *n* **1** a member of the Hebrew race. **2** someone who practises Judaism. ○ **Jewish** *adj*.

jewel *n* **1** a precious stone. **2** a personal ornament made with precious stones and metals. **3** someone or something greatly prized. ○ **jewelled** *adj*.

jeweller or (*US*) **jeweler** *n* a person who deals in, makes or repairs jewellery.

jewellery or (*US*) **jewelry** *n* articles worn for personal adornment, eg necklaces and rings.

Jew's harp *n* a tiny, lyre-shaped musical instrument held between the teeth, with a narrow metal tongue that is twanged with the finger.

Jezebel *n, derog* a shamelessly immoral woman.

jib¹ *n, naut* a small three-cornered sail in front of the mainsail of a yacht. ➤ *vb* (**jibbed, jibbing**) *intr* (**jib at sth**) of a person: to object to it.

jib² *n* the projecting arm of a crane from which the lifting gear hangs.

jibe see GIBE¹, GYBE

jiffy *n* (**-ies**) *colloq* a moment: *in a jiffy*.

jig *n* **1** a lively country dance or folk dance. **2** music for such a dance. **3** a jerky movement. **4** *mech* a device that holds a piece of work in position and guides the tools being used on it. ➤ *vb* (**jigged, jigging**) **1** *intr* to dance a jig. **2** *tr & intr* to jerk rapidly up and down.

jigger *n* **a** a small quantity of alcoholic spirits; **b** a glass for measuring this.

jiggered *adj, colloq* exhausted.

jiggery-pokery *n, colloq* trickery or deceit.

jiggle *vb, tr & intr* to jump or make something jump or jerk about. ➤ *n* a jiggling movement.

jigsaw *n* **1** (*also* **jigsaw puzzle**) a picture, mounted on wood or cardboard and cut into interlocking irregularly shaped pieces, to be fitted together again. **2** a fine-bladed saw for cutting intricate patterns.

jihad or **jehad** /dʒɪˈhɑːd/ *n* a holy war fought by Muslims on behalf of Islam.

jilt *vb* to leave and abruptly discard (a lover).

jingle *n* **1** a light ringing or clinking sound, eg of coins, keys, etc. **2** a simple rhyming verse, song or tune, esp one used to advertise a product, etc. ➤ *vb, tr & intr* to make, or cause something to make, a ringing or clinking sound.

jingoism *n* over-enthusiastic or aggressive patriotism. ○ **jingoistic** *adj*.

jink *vb* **1** *intr* to dodge. **2** to elude someone or something. ➤ *n* a dodge; a jinking movement.

jinni, jinnee or **djinni** /ˈdʒɪni/ or **djinn** /dʒɪn/ *n* (*pl* **jinn** or **djinn**) in Muslim folklore: a supernatural being able to adopt human or animal form.

jinx *n* **1** (*usu* **a jinx on sth** or **sb**) an evil spell or influence, held responsible for misfortune. **2** someone or something that appears to bring bad luck. ➤ *vb* to bring bad luck to someone or something. ○ **jinxed** *adj*.

jitter *colloq, vb, intr* to behave in an agitated or nervous way. ➤ *n* (*usu* **the jitters**) an attack of nervousness. ○ **jittery** *adj*.

jitterbug *n, US* an energetic dance like the JIVE, popular in the 1940s. ➤ *vb* (**jitterbugged, jitterbugging**) *intr* to dance the jitterbug.

jive *n* **1** a lively style of jazz music or swing, popular in the 1950s. **2** the style of dancing done to this music. ➤ *vb, intr* to dance in this style. ○ **jiver** *n*.

Jnr or **jnr** *abbrev* Junior or junior.

job *n* **1** a person's regular paid employment. **2** a piece of work. **3** a completed task: *You made a good job of the pruning*. **4** a function or responsibility. **5** *colloq* a problem; difficulty: *I had a job finding it*. **6** a crime, esp a burglary: *an inside job*. **7** an underhand scheme: *a put-up job*. **8** *colloq* a surgical operation, usu involving plastic surgery: *a nose job*. ♦ **just the job** exactly what is required.

jobless *adj* having no paid employment.

job lot *n* a mixed collection of objects sold as one item at an auction, etc.

job-sharing *n* the practice of sharing one full-time job between two or more part-time workers.

jock *n, colloq* **1** *US* a male athlete. **2** a jock-strap.

jockey *n* (**-eys**) a rider, esp a professional one, in horse races. ➤ *vb* **1** to ride (a horse) in a race. **2** *tr & intr* to manipulate someone or something skilfully or deviously.

jockstrap *n* a garment for supporting the genitals, worn by male athletes.

jocose /dʒəˈkoʊs/ *adj formal* playful; humorous. ○ **jocosely** *adv*.

jocular *adj* **1** of a person: given to joking; good-humoured. **2** of a remark, etc: intended as a joke. ○ **jocularity** *n*.

jocund /ˈdʒɒkənd/ *adj, formal* cheerful; merry; good-humoured.

jodhpurs /ˈdʒɒdpəz/ *pl n* riding-breeches that are loose-fitting over the buttocks and thighs, and tight-fitting from knee to calf.

joey *n, Aust* a young animal, esp a kangaroo.

jog *vb* (**jogged, jogging**) **1** to knock or nudge someone or something slightly. **2 a** to remind someone; **b** to prompt (a person's memory). **3** *intr* (*also* **jog along** or **on**) to progress slowly and steadily; to plod. **4** *intr* to run at a slowish steady pace, esp for exercise. ➤ *n* **1** a period or spell of jogging: *go for a jog*. **2** a nudge, knock or jolt. ○ **jogger** *n*. ○ **jogging** *n*.

joggle *vb, tr & intr* to jolt, shake or wobble.

john *n, N Am colloq* (*usu* **the john**) a lavatory.

johnny *n* (**-ies**) **1** *Brit colloq, old use* a chap; a fellow. **2** a condom.

joie de vivre /ˌʒwɑː də ˈviːvrə/ *n* enthusiasm for living.

join *vb* **1** to connect, attach, link or unite. **2** *tr &*

intr to become a member of (a society, firm, etc). **3** *tr & intr* of roads, rivers, etc: to meet. **4** to come together with someone or something; to enter the company of (a person or group of people): *joined them for supper*. **5** to take part in something. ➤ *n* a seam or joint. ◊ **join in** to take part. **join up** to enlist as a member of an armed service.

joiner *n* a craftsman who makes and fits wooden doors, window frames, shelves, etc. ○ **joinery** *n*.

joint *n* **1** the place where two or more pieces join. **2** *anat* in vertebrates: the point of contact or articulation between two or more bones, together with the ligaments that surround it. **3** a piece of meat, usu containing a bone, for cooking or roasting. **4** *slang* a cheap shabby café, bar, nightclub, etc. **5** *slang* a cannabis cigarette. ➤ *vb* **1** to connect to something by joints. **2** to divide (a bird or animal) into, or at, the joints for cooking. ➤ *adj* owned, done, etc in common; shared: *joint responsibility*. ○ **jointed** *adj*. ○ **jointly** *adv*. ♦ **out of joint 1** of a bone: dislocated. **2** in disorder.

joist *n* any of the beams supporting a floor or ceiling.

jojoba /həˈhoʊbə/ *n* a shrub whose edible seeds contain a waxy oil, used in the manufacture of cosmetics and lubricants.

joke *n* **1** a humorous story. **2** anything said or done in jest. **3** an amusing situation. **4** *colloq* something or someone ludicrous. ➤ *vb, intr* **1** to make jokes. **2** to speak in jest, not in earnest. ○ **jokey** *adj* (**-ier, -iest**). ○ **jokingly** *adv*.

joker *n* **1** *cards* an extra card in a pack, usu bearing a picture of a jester, used in certain games. **2** a cheerful person, always full of jokes. **3** *colloq* an irresponsible or incompetent person.

jollify *vb* (**jollifies, jollified**) to make something jolly. ○ **jollification** *n*.

jollity *n* **1** merriment. **2** (**jollities**) festivities.

jolly *adj* (**-ier, -iest**) **1** good-humoured; cheerful. **2** happy; enjoyable; convivial. ➤ *adv, Brit colloq* very: *jolly good*. ➤ *vb* (**jollies, jollied**) (**jolly sb** or **sth along**) to keep them or it going in a cheerful way.

jolt *vb* **1** *intr* to move along jerkily. **2** to shock someone emotionally. ➤ *n* **1** a jarring shake. **2** an emotional shock.

Jonah *n* a person who seems to bring bad luck.

jonquil *n* a small daffodil with fragrant white or yellow flowers.

josh *vb, tr & intr, colloq, orig N Am* to tease.

joss-stick *n* a stick of dried scented paste, burnt as incense.

jostle *vb* **1** *intr* to push and shove. **2** to push against someone roughly.

jot *n* (*usu with negatives*) the least bit: *not a jot of sympathy*. ➤ *vb* (**jotted, jotting**) (**jot sth down**) to write it down hastily.

jotter *n* a school notebook for rough work and notes.

jotting *n* (*usu* **jottings**) something jotted down.

joule /dʒuːl/ *n, physics* in the SI system: the unit of work and energy.

journal *n* **1** a magazine or periodical, eg one dealing with a specialized subject. **2** a diary in which one recounts one's daily activities.

journalese *n, derog* the language, typically full of clichés and jargon, used in newspapers and magazines.

journalism *n* the profession of writing for newspapers and magazines, or for radio and television. ○ **journalist** *n.* ○ **journalistic** *adj.*

journey *n* (*-eys*) **1** a process of travelling from one place to another. **2** the distance covered by, or time taken for, a journey. ➤ *vb, intr* to make a journey.

journeyman *n* a craftsman qualified in a particular trade and working for an employer.

joust *n, hist* a contest between two knights on horseback armed with lances. ➤ *vb, intr* to take part in a joust.

Jove *n* JUPITER (sense I). ◆ **by Jove!** *Brit colloq, old use* an exclamation expressing surprise or emphasis.

jovial *adj* good-humoured; merry; cheerful. ○ **joviality** *n.* ○ **jovially** *adv.*

jowl *n* **1** the lower jaw. **2** the cheek. **3** loose flesh under the chin.

joy *n* **1** a feeling of happiness; intense gladness. **2** someone or something that causes delight: *She's a joy to live with.* **3** *Brit colloq* satisfaction; success: *Any joy at the enquiry desk?*

joyful *adj* **1** happy; full of joy. **2** expressing or resulting in joy. ○ **joyfully** *adv.* ○ **joyfulness** *n.*

joyous *adj* filled with, causing or showing joy. ○ **joyously** *adv.* ○ **joyousness** *n.*

joyride *n* a jaunt, esp a reckless drive in a stolen vehicle. ➤ *vb, intr* to go for such a jaunt. ○ **joyrider** *n.* ○ **joyriding** *n.*

joystick *n, colloq* **1** the controlling lever of an aircraft, machine, etc. **2** *comput* a lever for controlling the movement of an image on a computer screen.

JP *abbrev* justice of the peace.

Jr or **jr** *abbrev* Junior or junior: *John Smith, Jr.*

jubilant *adj* showing and expressing triumphant joy; rejoicing. ○ **jubilantly** *adv.*

jubilation *n* triumphant rejoicing.

jubilee *n* a special anniversary of a significant event, esp the 25th (**silver jubilee**) or 50th (**golden jubilee**).

Judaic *adj* relating to the Jews or Judaism.

Judaism /ˈdʒuːdeɪɪzəm/ *n* the Jewish religion, based on a belief in one God, or way of life.

Judas *n* a traitor.

judder *vb, intr* to jolt, shake, shudder or vibrate. ➤ *n* an intense jerking motion.

judge *n* **1** a public official who hears and decides cases in a law court. **2** a person appointed to decide the winner of a contest. **3** someone qualified to assess something; someone who shows discrimination. ➤ *vb* **1** to try (a legal case) in a law court as a judge; to decide (questions of guiltiness, etc). **2** to decide the winner of (a contest). **3** *intr* to act as judge or

adjudicator. **4** to assess; to form an opinion about something or someone. **5** to consider or state (something to be the case), after consideration: *He judged her fit to travel.* **6** to criticize someone or something, esp severely; to condemn.

judgement or **judgment** *n* **1** the decision of a judge in a court of law. **2** the act or process of judging. **3** the ability to make wise or sensible decisions; good sense: *I value his judgement.* **4** an opinion: *in my judgement.* ◆ **pass judgement on sb** or **sth** to give an opinion about them.

judgemental or **judgmental** *adj* apt to pass judgement, esp to make moral judgements.

judicial *adj* relating or referring to a court of law, judges or the decisions of judges. ○ **judicially** *adv.*

judiciary *n* (*-ies*) **1** the branch of government concerned with the legal system and the administration of justice. **2** a country's body of judges.

judicious *adj* shrewd, sensible, wise or tactful. ○ **judiciously** *adv.*

judo *n* a Japanese sport and physical discipline based on unarmed self-defence techniques. ○ **judoist** *n.*

jug *n* **1** a deep container for liquids, with a handle and a shaped lip for pouring. **2** (*also* **jugful**) the amount a jug holds. **3** *slang* prison.

juggernaut *n* **1** *Brit colloq* a very large articulated lorry. **2** a mighty force sweeping away and destroying everything in its path.

juggle *vb* **1** to keep several objects simultaneously in the air by skilful throwing and catching. **2** (*also* **juggle with sth**) to adjust (facts or figures) to create a misleading impression. ○ **juggler** *n.* ○ **juggling** *n, adj.*

jugular *n, anat* any of several veins that carry deoxygenated blood from the head to the heart.

juice *n* **1** the liquid or sap from fruit or vegetables. **2** a natural fluid in the body: *digestive juices.* **3** *slang* power or fuel, esp electricity or petrol. **4** *US slang* alcoholic drink. ➤ *vb* to squeeze juice from (a fruit, etc).

juicy *adj* (*-ier, -iest*) **1** full of juice; rich and succulent. **2** *colloq* full of gossip: intriguing; spicy. ○ **juiciness** *n.*

ju-jitsu or **jiu-jitsu** /dʒuːˈdʒɪtsuː/ *n* a martial art founded on the ancient Japanese system of combat and self-defence without weapons.

jujube /ˈdʒuːdʒuːb/ *n* a soft fruit-flavoured sweet made with gelatine.

jukebox *n* a coin-operated machine that plays the song or video one selects.

julep /ˈdʒuːlɪp/ *n* **1** a sweet drink, often a medicated one. **2** (*also* **mint julep**) esp in N America: an iced drink of spirits and sugar, flavoured esp with mint.

julienne /dʒuːlɪˈɛn/ *n* a clear soup, with shredded vegetables. ➤ *adj* of vegetables: in thin strips; shredded.

July *n* the seventh month of the year.

jumble *vb* 1 to mix or confuse (things or people), physically or mentally. 2 to throw (things) together untidily. ➤ *n* 1 a confused mass. 2 unwanted possessions collected, or suitable, for a jumble sale.

jumble sale *n* a sale of unwanted possessions, usu to raise money for charity.

jumbo *colloq, adj* extra-large. ➤ *n* a jumbo jet.

jumbo jet *n, colloq* the popular name for a large wide-bodied jet airliner.

jump *vb* 1 *intr* to spring off the ground, pushing off with the feet. 2 *intr* to leap or bound. 3 to get over or across something by jumping. 4 to make (esp a horse) leap. 5 *intr* of prices, levels, etc: to rise abruptly. 6 *intr* to make a startled movement. 7 *intr* to twitch, jerk or bounce. 8 *tr & intr* to omit or skip something: *jump the next chapter.* 9 *colloq* to pounce on someone or something. 10 *colloq* of a car: to pass through (a red traffic light). ➤ *n* 1 an act of jumping. 2 an obstacle to be jumped, esp a fence to be jumped by a horse. 3 the height or distance jumped. 4 a jumping contest: *the long jump.* 5 a sudden rise in amount, cost or value. 6 an abrupt change or move. 7 a startled movement; a start: *gave a jump of surprise.* ◆ **jump down sb's throat** *colloq* to snap at them impatiently. **jump the gun** to get off one's mark too soon; to act prematurely; to take an unfair advantage. **jump the queue** to get ahead of one's turn. ◊ **jump at sth** to accept it eagerly.

jumped-up *adj, derog colloq* having an inflated view of one's own importance.

jumper *n* 1 a knitted garment for the top half of the body. 2 *N Am* a pinafore dress.

jump jet *n* a jet aircraft capable of taking off and landing vertically.

jumpsuit *n* a one-piece garment combining trousers and top.

jumpy *adj* (*-ier, -iest*) nervy; anxious.

junction *n* a place where roads or railway lines meet or cross.

juncture *n* 1 a joining; a union. 2 a point in time, esp a critical one.

June *n* the sixth month of the year.

jungle *n* 1 an area of dense vegetation, esp in a tropical region. 2 a mass of complexities difficult to penetrate: *the jungle of building regulations.* 3 a complex or hostile environment where toughness is needed for survival: *the concrete jungle.* 4 a type of fast rhythmic dance music.

junior *adj* 1 a low or lower in rank; b younger. 2 relating or belonging to, or for, schoolchildren aged between 7 and 11: *junior schools.* 3 used after the name of a person with the same forename as their father. ➤ *n* 1 a person of low or lower rank in a profession, organization, etc. 2 a pupil in a junior school. 3 *N Am* a third-year college or high-school student. 4 a person younger than the one in question: *She's three years his junior.* 5 (*often* Junior) *N Am* a name used to address or refer to the son of a family.

juniper *n* an evergreen coniferous tree or shrub with purple berry-like cones, oils from which are used to flavour gin.

junk[1] *n, colloq* 1 worthless or rejected material; rubbish. 2 nonsense. 3 *slang* narcotic drugs, esp heroin. ➤ *vb, colloq* 1 to treat something as junk. 2 to discard or abandon something as useless.

junk[2] *n* a flat-bottomed square-sailed boat from the Far East.

junket / 'dʒʌŋkɪt/ *n* 1 a dessert made from sweetened and curdled milk. 2 a feast or celebration. 3 a trip made by a government official, businessman, etc which they do not pay for themselves. ➤ *vb* (**junketed, junketing**) *intr* to feast, celebrate or make merry.

junk food *n* food with little nutritional value.

junkie or **junky** *n* (*-ies*) 1 *slang* a drug addict or drug-pusher. 2 *colloq* someone who is addicted to something: *a TV junkie.*

junk mail *n* unsolicited mail, such as advertising circulars.

junta / 'dʒʌntə, 'hʊntə/ *n, derog* a group or faction, usu of army officers, in control of a country after a coup d'état.

Jupiter *n* 1 the chief god of the ancient Romans. 2 *astron* the fifth planet from the Sun, and the largest in the solar system.

Jurassic *geol, n* in the Mesozoic era, the period of geological time between the Triassic and Cretaceous periods, lasting from about 210 to 140 million years ago. ➤ *adj* belonging or relating to this period.

juridical or **juridic** *adj* relating or referring to the law or the administration of justice. ○ **juridically** *adv.*

jurisdiction *n* 1 the right or authority to apply laws and administer justice. 2 the district or area over which this authority extends. 3 authority generally.

jurisprudence *n* 1 knowledge of or skill in law. 2 a speciality within law: *medical jurisprudence.*

jurist *n* 1 an expert in the science of law. 2 *US* a lawyer.

juror *n* 1 a member of a jury in a court of law. 2 someone who takes an oath.

jury *n* (*-ies*) 1 a body of people sworn to give an honest verdict on the evidence presented to a court of law on a particular case. 2 a group of people selected to judge a contest.

just[1] *adj* 1 fair; impartial. 2 reasonable; based on justice. 3 deserved. ○ **justly** *adv.* ○ **justness** *n.*

just[2] *adv* 1 exactly; precisely. 2 a short time before: *He had just gone.* 3 at this or that very moment: *I was just leaving.* 4 and no earlier, more, etc: *only just enough.* 5 barely; narrowly: *The bullet just missed him.* 6 only; merely: *just a brief note.* 7 *colloq* used for emphasis: *That's just not true.* 8 *colloq* absolutely: *just marvellous.* ◆ **just about** almost: *I'm just about ready.* **just about to do sth** on the point of doing it. **just a minute** or **second,** *etc* an instruction to wait a short while. **just now** at this particular moment. **just**

so 1 a formula of agreement. **2** neat and tidy: *They like everything just so*. **just the same** nevertheless.

justice *n* **1** the quality of being just; fairness. **2** the quality of being reasonable. **3** the law, or administration of or conformity to the law: *a miscarriage of justice*. **4** a justice of the peace. **5** *N Am* a judge.

justice of the peace *n* (*justices of the peace*) a person authorized to judge minor criminal cases.

justifiable *adj* able to be justified. ○ **justifiably** *adv.*

justify *vb* (*justifies, justified*) **1** to prove something to be right, just or reasonable. **2** *printing* to arrange (text) so that the margins are even-edged. ○ **justification** *n.*

jut *vb* (*jutted, jutting*) *intr* (*also* **jut out**) to stick out; to project.

jute *n* fibre from certain types of tropical bark, used for making sacking, etc.

juvenile *adj* **1** young; youthful. **2** suitable for young people. **3** *derog* childish; immature. ➤ *n* a young person.

juvenile delinquent *n, dated* a young person who is guilty of an offence, esp vandalism or antisocial behaviour.

juxtapose *vb* to place (things) side by side. ○ **juxtaposition** *n.*

Kk

K¹ or **k** *n* (*Ks, K's* or *k's*) the eleventh letter of the English alphabet.

K² *n* (*pl* **K**) *colloq* **1** one thousand, esp £1000. **2** *comput* a unit of memory equal to 1024 bits, bytes or words.

K³ *abbrev* **1** *physics* kelvin, or a degree on the Kelvin scale. **2** kilo. **3** *comput* kilobyte.

K⁴ *symbol* **1** *chem* potassium. **2** *chess* king.

k *abbrev* **1** karat or CARAT. **2** kilo.

kaftan see CAFTAN

kagoule see CAGOULE

Kaiser /ˈkaɪzə(r)/ *n, hist* any of the emperors of Germany, Austria or the Holy Roman Empire.

Kalashnikov *n* a type of submachine-gun manufactured in the Soviet Union.

kale or **kail** *n* a variety of cabbage with loose wrinkled or curled leaves.

kaleidoscope *n* **1** an optical toy consisting of long mirrors fixed at an angle to each other inside a tube containing small pieces of coloured plastic, glass or paper, so that multiple reflections produce random regular patterns when the tube is viewed through an eyepiece at one end and rotated or shaken. **2** any colourful and constantly changing scene or succession of events. ○ **kaleidoscopic** *adj.*

kalends see CALENDS

kamikaze /kamɪˈkɑːzɪ/ *n* **1** in World War II: a Japanese plane loaded with explosives that the pilot would deliberately crash into an enemy target. **2** the pilot of this kind of plane. ➤ *adj* **1** relating or referring to such an attack or the pilot concerned. **2** *colloq* of exploits, missions, etc: suicidally dangerous.

kangaroo *n* a marsupial mammal with a thick tail and large powerful hind legs adapted for leaping, native to Australia, Tasmania and New Guinea.

kangaroo court *n* a court that has no legal status and which is usu perceived as delivering unfair or biased judgements.

kaolin or **kaoline** *n* a soft white clay used for making fine porcelain, and medicinally to treat diarrhoea and vomiting.

kapok /ˈkeɪpɒk/ *n* the light waterproof silky fibres that surround the seeds of certain trees, used for padding and stuffing eg pillows.

kaput /kəˈpʊt/ *adj, colloq* ruined; destroyed.

karakul /ˈkɑːrəkuːl/ *n* **1** a breed of sheep, native to central Asia. **2** the soft curly fleece of a lamb of this breed.

karaoke /karɪˈoʊkɪ/ *n* a form of entertainment in which amateur performers sing to the accompaniment of pre-recorded music.

karat *n* another spelling of CARAT.

karate /kəˈrɑːtɪ/ *n* a system of unarmed self-defence, using blows and kicks.

karma *n, Buddhism, Hinduism* **1** the sum of someone's lifetime's actions, seen as governing their fate in the next life. **2** destiny; fate. **3** *popularly* an aura or quality that is perceived to be given off by someone or something.

kart *n, colloq* a GO-KART. ○ **karting** *n.*

kasbah /ˈkazbɑː/ *n* **1** a castle or fortress in a N African town. **2** the area around it.

katydid /ˈkeɪtɪdɪd/ *n, N Am* a grasshopper with long antennae.

kauri /ˈkaʊərɪ/ *n* **1** a tall coniferous tree, native to SE Asia and Australasia. **2** the brownish resin of this tree, used mainly in varnishes and in the manufacture of linoleum.

kayak /ˈkaɪak/ *n* **1** a sealskin-covered canoe for one person used by the Inuit. **2** a similar craft used in the sport of canoeing.

kazi /ˈkɑːzɪ/ *n, slang* a lavatory.

kazoo *n* a crude wind instrument which makes a buzzing sound when blown.

KB *abbrev, comput* kilobyte.

kebab *n* **1** (*in full* **shish kebab**) a dish of small pieces of meat and vegetables grilled on a skewer. **2** a DONER KEBAB.

kedge *vb, tr & intr* to manoeuvre by means of a hawser attached to a light anchor. ➤ *n* a light anchor used for kedging.

kedgeree *n, cookery* a dish consisting of rice, fish and eggs.

keel *n* the timber or metal strut extending from stem to stern along the base of a ship, from which the hull is built up. ♦ **on an even keel** calm and steady. ◊ **keel over 1** of a ship: to tip over sideways. **2** *colloq* to fall over, eg in a faint.

keelhaul *vb* to drag someone under the keel of a ship from one side to the other, as a naval punishment. ➤ *n* a lament for the dead.

keen¹ *adj* **1** eager; willing. **2** of competition, rivalry, etc: fierce. **3** of the wind: bitter. **4** of a blade, etc: sharp. **5** of the mind or senses: quick; acute. **6** of prices: competitive. ◦ **keenness** *n*. ♦ **keen on sb** or **sth** enthusiastic about them or it.

keen² *vb, tr & intr* to lament or mourn in a loud wailing voice. ➤ *n* a lament for the dead.

keep *vb* (**kept**) **1** to have; to possess. **2** to continue to have something. **3** to maintain or retain: *keep one's temper.* **4** to store. **5** *tr & intr* to remain or cause something to remain in a certain state, position, place, etc. **6** *intr* to continue or be frequently doing something: *keep smiling.* **7** of a shopkeeper, etc: to have something regularly in stock. **8** to own and look after (an animal, etc): *keep hens.* **9** to own or run (a shop, boarding-house, etc). **10** to look after something: *keep this for me.* **11** *intr* of food: to remain fit to be eaten: *This cake keeps well.* **12** to preserve (a secret). **13** to stick to (a promise or appointment). **14** to celebrate (a festival, etc) in the traditional way; to follow (a custom). **15** to support someone financially. ➤ *n* **1** the cost of one's food and other daily expenses: *earn one's keep.* **2** the central tower or stronghold in a Norman castle. ♦ **for keeps** *colloq* permanently; for good. **keep to oneself** to avoid the company of others. ◊ **keep at sth** to persevere at or persist in it. **keep sth back** to conceal information, etc. **keep sb down** to prevent their development, progress, etc. **keep sth down** to manage not to vomit (food, etc). **keep off sth 1** to avoid (a harmful food, awkward topic, etc). **2** to stay away from it: *Keep off my books!* **keep sb on** to continue to employ them. **keep on at sb** to nag or harass them. **keep to sth** not to leave it: *Keep to the path.* **keep sth up 1** to prevent (eg spirits, morale, etc) from falling. **2** to maintain (a habit, friendship, pace, etc). **3** to maintain (a house, garden, etc) in good condition. **keep up with sb 1** not to be left behind by them. **2** to maintain the pace or standard set by them.

keeper *n* **1** a person who looks after something, eg a collection in a museum. **2** a person who looks after animals or birds in captivity. **3** a gamekeeper. **4** *colloq* a goalkeeper. **5** a wicketkeeper.

keep fit *n* a series or system of exercises intended to improve the circulation and respiratory system, suppleness and stamina, etc.

keeping *n* care or charge. ♦ **in keeping with sth** in harmony with it.

keepsake *n* something kept in memory of the giver.

kefuffle see CARFUFFLE

keg *n* a small barrel, usu for transporting and storing beer.

kelp *n* any large brown seaweed that grows below the low-tide mark.

kelpie or **kelpy** *n* (*-ies*) *Scot folklore* a malignant water spirit in the form of a horse.

kelson *n* a timber fixed along a ship's keel for strength.

kelvin *n, physics* in the SI system: a unit of temperature.

Kelvin scale *n* a temperature scale starting at ABSOLUTE ZERO.

ken *vb* (**kent** or **kenned, kenning**) *Scot & N Eng dialect* **1** to know. **2** to understand. ➤ *n* range of knowledge: *beyond our ken.*

kendo *n* a Japanese art of fencing using bamboo staves or sometimes real swords.

kennel *n* **1** a small shelter for a dog. **2** (**kennels**) an establishment where dogs are boarded or bred. ➤ *vb* (**kennelled, kennelling**; *N Am* **kenneled, kenneling**) to put or keep (an animal) in a kennel.

kept man or **kept woman** *n, derog* a man or woman supported financially by someone in return for being available to them as a sexual partner.

keratin *n, biochem* a tough fibrous protein forming the main component of hair, nails, claws, horns, feathers and the dead outer layers of skin cells.

kerb or (*esp N Am*) **curb** *n* **1** the row of stones or concrete edging forming the edge of a pavement. **2** a kerbstone.

kerb-crawling *n* the practice of driving slowly alongside the kerb in order to lure potential sexual partners into the car. ◦ **kerb-crawler** *n*.

kerbstone *n* one of the stones used to form a kerb.

kerchief *n* a square of cloth or a scarf for wearing over the head or round the neck.

kerfuffle see CARFUFFLE

kermes /ˈkɜːmiːz/ *n* **1** the dried bodies of the female scale insect used as a red dye. **2** (*also* **kermes oak**) a small evergreen oak tree on which the insects breed.

kernel *n* **1** the inner part of a seed, eg the edible part of a nut. **2** in cereal plants such as corn: the entire grain or seed. **3** the important, essential part of anything.

kerosine *n* **1** a combustible oily mixture of hydrocarbons obtained mainly by distillation of petroleum, used as a fuel for jet aircraft, domestic heating systems and lamps, and as a solvent. **2** *N Am* PARAFFIN.

kestrel *n* a small falcon with a long tail and broad pointed wings.

ketch *n* a small two-masted sailing boat, the foremast being the taller.

ketchup *n, popularly* a thick sauce made from tomatoes, vinegar, spices, etc.

ketone *n, chem* any of a class of organic chemical compounds that are formed by the oxidation of secondary alcohols.

kettle *n* **1** a container with a spout, lid and handle, for boiling water. **2** a metal container for heating liquids or cooking something in liquid. ○ **kettleful** *n*. ♦ **a different kettle of fish** *colloq* an entirely different matter. **a pretty** or **fine kettle of fish** *colloq* an awkward situation.

kettledrum *n* a large cauldron-shaped drum with a skin or other membrane stretched over the top, tuned by adjusting screws that alter the tension of the skin.

key¹ *n* **1** a device for opening or closing a lock, or for winding up, turning, tuning, tightening or loosening. **2** one of a series of buttons or levers pressed to sound the notes on a musical instrument, or to print or display a character on a computer, calculator, etc. **3** a system of musical notes related to one another in a scale. **4** pitch, tone or style: *spoke in a low key*. **5** something that provides an answer or solution. **6** a means of achievement: *the key to success*. **7** a table explaining signs and symbols used on a map, etc. **8** a pin or wedge for fixing something. ➢ *adj* centrally important: *key questions*. ➢ *vb* **1** (*also* **key sth in**) to enter (data) into a computer, calculator, etc by means of a keyboard. **2** to lock or fasten something with a key. ♦ **keyed up** *colloq* excited; tense; anxious. **under lock and key 1** safely stored. **2** in prison.

key² or **cay** /keɪ, kiː/ *n* a small low island or reef formed of sand, coral, rock or mud.

keyboard *n* **1** the set of keys on a piano, etc. **2** the bank of keys for operating a typewriter or computer. **3** an electronic musical instrument with a keyboard. ➢ *vb* **1** *intern* to operate the keyboard of a computer. **2** to set (text) using a computer keyboard. ○ **keyboarder** *n*.

keyhole *n* **1** the hole through which a key is inserted into a lock. **2** any small hole similar to this.

keyhole surgery *n* internal surgery performed with minimal external excision through a small opening.

keynote *n* **1** the note on which a musical scale or key is based. **2** a central theme, principle or controlling thought. ➢ *adj* of fundamental importance.

keypad *n* a small device with push-button controls, eg a TV remote control unit.

key ring *n* a ring for keeping keys on.

key signature *n, mus* the sharps and flats shown on the stave at the start of a piece of music indicating the key it is to be played in.

keystone *n, archit* the central supporting stone at the high point of an arch.

keystroke *n* a single press of a key on a keyboard.

keyword *n* **1** a word that sums up or gives an indication of the nature of the passage in which it occurs. **2** *comput* a group of letters or numbers that is used to identify a database record.

kg *abbrev* kilogram.

khaki /ˈkɑːkɪ/ *n* **1** a dull brownish-yellow or brownish-green colour. **2 a** cloth of this colour; **b** military uniform made of such cloth.

khan /kɑːn/ *n* the title of a ruler or prince in central Asia.

kHz *abbrev* kilohertz.

kibble *vb* to grind (cereal, etc) fairly coarsely.

kibbutz /kɪˈbʊts/ *n* (**kibbutzim** /-ˈsiːm/) in Israel: a communal farm or other concern owned and run jointly as a co-operative by its workers.

kibosh or **kybosh** /ˈkaɪbɒʃ/ *colloq, n* rubbish; nonsense. ♦ **put the kibosh on sth** to put an end to it.

kick *vb* **1** to hit or propel with the foot. **2** *intr* to strike out or thrust with one or both feet, eg when swimming, struggling, etc. **3** *tr & intr* esp in dancing: to jerk (the leg) vigorously or swing it high. **4** *intr* of a gun, etc: to recoil when fired. **5** *intr* (*sometimes* **kick against sth**) to resist it: *kick against discipline*. **6** to get rid of (a habit, etc). ➢ *n* **1** a blow or fling with the foot. **2** *dancing, gymnastics, etc* a swing of the leg: *high kicks*. **3** *swimming* any of various leg movements. **4** the recoil of a gun, etc after firing. **5** *colloq* a thrill of excitement: *He gets a kick out of violence*. **6** *colloq* the powerful effect of certain drugs or strong drink: *That fruit punch has quite a kick*. ♦ **for kicks** for thrills. **kick in the teeth** *colloq* a humiliating snub. **kick the bucket** *colloq* to die. ◊ **kick about** or **around** *colloq* **1** to lie around unused or neglected. **2** to pass time idly: *kicking about with his mates*. **kick in** to take effect: *as the effects of the pay freeze kick in*. **kick off 1** to start, or restart, a football game by kicking the ball away from the centre. **2** *colloq* (*also* **kick sth off**) to begin a discussion or other activity involving several people.

kickback *n* part of a sum of money received that is paid to someone else for help or favours already received or to come, esp if this is illegally given.

kick-off *n* **1** the start or restart of a football match. **2** *colloq* the start of anything.

kick-start *n* **1** (*also* **kick-starter**) a pedal on a motorcycle that is kicked vigorously downwards to start the engine. **2** the starting of an engine with this pedal. ➢ *vb* **1** to start (a motorcycle) using this pedal. **2** to get something moving; to give an advantageous, and sometimes sudden, impulse to something.

kid¹ *n* **1** *colloq* a child; a young person. **2** a young goat, antelope or other related animal. **3** the smooth soft leather made from the skin of such an animal. ➢ *adj, colloq* younger: *my kid sister*.

kid² *vb* (**kidded, kidding**) *colloq* (*sometimes* **kid sb on** or **along**) **1** to fool or deceive them, esp light-heartedly or in fun. **2** *intr* to bluff; to pretend.

kiddie or **kiddy** *n* (*-ies*) *colloq* a small child.

kid glove *n* a glove made of kids' skin. ♦ **handle sb with kid gloves** to treat them with special care or caution.

kidnap *vb* (**kidnapped, kidnapping;** *N Am* **kidnaped, kidnaping**) to seize and hold someone prisoner illegally, usu demanding a ransom for their release. ○ **kidnapper** *n*.

kidney *n* **1** *anat* either of a pair of organs at the back of the abdomen whose function is to remove waste products from the blood, and excrete them from the body in the form of urine. **2** animal kidneys as food.

kidney bean *n* a dark-red kidney-shaped seed, eaten as a vegetable.

kidney machine *n, med* a machine that removes toxic waste products from the blood of someone whose kidneys do not function properly.

kidology *n, colloq* the art of deceiving or bluffing.

kilim /ˈkiːliːm/ *n* a woven rug without any pile.

kill *vb* **1** *tr & intr* to cause the death of (an animal or person); to murder; to destroy someone or something. **2** *colloq* to cause severe pain to someone: *My feet are killing me.* **3** *colloq* to cause something to fail; to put an end to it: *to kill the conversation.* **4** to defeat (a parliamentary bill). **5** *colloq* to deaden (pain, noise, etc.). **6** to pass (time), esp aimlessly or wastefully, while waiting for some later event: *killing an hour in the pub.* **7** *colloq, esp ironic* to exhaust or put a strain on someone: *Don't kill yourself doing unpaid overtime.* **8** *colloq* to overwhelm someone with admiration, amazement, laughter, etc. ➤ *n* **1** an act of killing. **2** the prey killed by any creature. **3** game killed. ○ **killer** *n* **1** a person or creature that kills. **2** a habitual murderer. ♦ **kill two birds with one stone** to accomplish two things by one action.

killer whale *n* a toothed whale, having a black body with white underparts and white patches on its head, and a narrow triangular dorsal fin similar to that of a shark.

killing *n* an act of slaying. ➤ *adj, colloq* **1** exhausting. **2** highly amusing. **3** deadly; fatal. ♦ **make a killing** *colloq* to make a large amount of money, esp quickly from a single transaction.

killjoy *n* someone who spoils the pleasure of others.

kiln *n* a heated oven or furnace used for drying timber, grain or hops, or for firing bricks, pottery, etc.

kilo *n* a KILOGRAM.

kilobyte *n, comput* a unit of memory equal to 1024 BYTES.

kilogram or **kilogramme** *n* in the SI system: the basic unit of mass, equal to 1000 grams (2.205 lb).

kilohertz *n* (*pl* **kilohertz**) an SI unit of frequency equal to 1000 HERTZ or 1000 cycles per second, used to measure the frequency of

sound and radio waves.

kilojoule *n* 1000 joules, an SI unit used to measure energy, work and heat.

kilolitre or (*N Am*) **kiloliter** *n* a metric unit of liquid measure equal to 1000 litres.

kilometre or (*N Am*) **kilometer** *n* a metric unit of length equal to 1000 metres (0.62 miles).

kiloton or **kilotonne** *n* a metric unit of explosive power equivalent to that of 1000 tonnes of TNT.

kilovolt *n* an SI unit used to measure electric potential: 1000 volts.

kilowatt *n* an SI unit of electrical power equal to 1000 watts or about 1.34 horsepower.

kilowatt hour *n* a commercial metric unit of electrical energy, based on the WATT, equal to the energy consumed when an electrical appliance with a power of one kilowatt operates for one hour.

kilt *n* **1** a pleated tartan knee-length skirt, traditionally worn by men as part of Scottish Highland dress. **2** any similar garment.

kilter *n* good condition. ♦ **out of kilter** out of order; not working properly.

kimono /kɪˈmoʊnoʊ/ *n* **1** a long, loose, wide-sleeved Japanese garment fastened by a sash at the waist. **2** a dressing-gown, etc, imitating this in style.

kin *n* **1** one's relatives. **2** people belonging to the same family.

kind[1] *n* **1** a group, class, sort, race or type. **2** a particular variety or a specimen belonging to a specific variety. **3** nature, character or distinguishing quality: *differ in kind.* ♦ **in kind 1** of payment: in goods instead of money. **2** of repayment or retaliation: in the same form as the treatment received. **kind of** *colloq* somewhat; slightly. ♦ **of a kind 1** of the same sort: *three of a kind.* **2** of doubtful worth: *an explanation of a kind.*

kind[2] *adj* **1** friendly, helpful, generous or considerate. **2** warm; cordial: *kind regards.* ○ **kindness** *n*.

kindergarten *n* a school for young children, usu those aged between 4 and 6.

kindle *vb, tr & intr* **1** to start or make something start burning. **2** of feelings: to stir or be stirred. ○ **kindling** *n* materials for starting a fire, eg dry twigs or leaves, sticks, etc.

kindly *adv* **1** in a kind manner: *She kindly offered me a lift.* **2** please: *Kindly remove your feet from the desk.* ➤ *adj* (*-ier, -iest*) kind, friendly, generous or good-natured. ○ **kindliness** *n*. ♦ **not take kindly to sth** to be unwilling to put up with it.

kindred *n* **1** one's relatives; family. **2** relationship by blood or, less properly, by marriage. ➤ *adj* **1** related. **2** having qualities in common.

kindred spirit *n* someone who shares one's tastes, opinions, etc.

kinematics *sing n, physics* the study of the motion of objects, without consideration of the forces acting on them. ○ **kinematic** or **kinematical** *adj*.

kinetic adj **1** physics relating to or producing motion. **2** chem relating to the speed of chemical reactions. ○ **kinetically** adv.

kinetic art or **kinetic sculpture** n art and sculpture which has movement as an essential feature.

kinetic energy n the energy that an object possesses because of its motion.

kinetics sing n, physics the branch of MECHANICS concerned with moving objects, their masses and the forces acting on them.

kinfolk or **kinfolks** see KINSFOLK

king n **1** a male ruler of a nation, esp a hereditary monarch. **2** a ruler or chief. **3** a creature considered supreme in strength, ferocity, etc: the lion, king of beasts. **4** a leading or dominant figure in a specified field, eg a wealthy manufacturer or dealer: the diamond king. **5** cards the court card bearing a picture of a king. **6** chess the piece which must be protected from checkmate. ➤ adj signifying a large, or the largest, variety of something: king penguin. ○ **kingly** adj. ○ **kingship** n.

kingdom n **1** a region, state or people ruled, or previously ruled, by a king or queen. **2** biol any of the divisions corresponding to the highest rank in the classification of plants and animals. **3** the domain of, or area associated with, something: the kingdom of the imagination. ◆ **to** or **till kingdom come** colloq **1** into the next world: blow them all to kingdom come. **2** until the coming of the next world; for ever: wait till kingdom come.

kingfisher n a brightly coloured fish-eating bird with a long pointed bill and short wings.

kingpin n **1** the most important person in an organization, team, etc. **2** mech a bolt serving as a pivot. **3** the tallest or most prominently placed pin, such as the front pin in TENPIN BOWLING.

king prawn n a large prawn.

king-size or **king-sized** adj of a large or larger-than-standard size.

kink n **1** a bend or twist in hair or in a string, wire, etc. **2** colloq an oddness of personality. ➤ vb, tr & intr to develop, or cause something to develop, a kink.

kinky adj (-ier, -iest) **1** colloq interested in or practising unusual or perverted sexual acts. **2** colloq eccentric; crazy. **3** of cable, hair, etc: twisted; in loops. ○ **kinkiness** n.

kinsfolk, (NAm) **kinfolk** or **kinfolks** pl n one's relations.

kinship n **1** family relationship. **2** a state of having common properties or characteristics.

kinsman or **kinswoman** n a relative.

kiosk n **1** a small booth or stall for the sale of sweets, newspapers, etc. **2** a public telephone box.

kip colloq, n **1** sleep or a sleep. **2** somewhere to sleep; a bed. ➤ vb (**kipped, kipping**) intr **1** to sleep. **2** (also **kip down**) to go to bed; to doss down.

kipper n a fish, esp a herring, that has been split open, salted and smoked.

kirk n, Scot **1** a church. **2** (**the Kirk**) the Church of Scotland.

kirsch /kɪəʃ/ n a clear liqueur distilled from black cherries.

kismet n **1** Islam the will of Allah. **2** fate or destiny.

kiss vb **1** to touch someone with the lips, or to press one's lips against them, as a greeting, sign of affection, etc. **2** intr to kiss one another on the lips. **3** to express something by kissing: kissed them goodbye. **4** intr of billiard or snooker balls: to touch each other gently while moving. ➤ n **1** an act of kissing. **2** a gentle touch. ○ **kisser** n, slang the mouth or face. ◆ **kiss sth goodbye** or **kiss goodbye to sth** to lose the chance of having it, esp through folly, mismanagement, etc: we can kiss goodbye to a holiday.

kiss curl n a flat curl of hair pressed against the cheek or forehead.

kiss of death n, colloq someone or something that brings failure or ruin on some enterprise.

kiss of life n **1** MOUTH-TO-MOUTH resuscitation. **2** a means of restoring vitality.

kit¹ n **1** a set of instruments, equipment, etc needed for a purpose. **2** a set of special clothing and personal equipment, eg for a soldier, footballer, etc. **3** a set of parts ready for assembling. ➤ vb (**kitted, kitting**) (also **kit sb out**) to provide someone with clothes and equipment.

kit² n **1** a kitten. **2** the young of various smaller fur-bearing animals, eg the ferret or fox.

kitbag n a soldier's or sailor's bag, usu cylinder-shaped and made of canvas, for holding kit.

kitchen n a room or an area in a building where food is prepared and cooked.

kitchenette n a small kitchen, or a section of a room serving as a kitchen.

kitchen garden n a garden where vegetables, and sometimes fruit, are grown.

kitchenware n pots and pans, cutlery and utensils, etc, that are used in kitchens.

kite n **1** a bird of prey of the hawk family, noted for its long pointed wings, deeply forked tail, and soaring graceful flight. **2** a light frame covered in paper or some other light material, with a long holding string attached to it, for flying in the air for fun, etc. **3** (also **box kite**) a more complicated structure built of boxes, sometimes used for carrying recording equipment or a person in the air. **4** slang an aircraft.

kith n friends. ◆ **kith and kin** friends and relations.

kitsch /kɪtʃ/ n sentimental, pretentious or vulgar tastelessness. ➤ adj tastelessly or vulgarly sentimental. ○ **kitschy** adj (-ier, -iest).

kitten n **1** a young cat. **2** the young of various other small mammals, eg the rabbit. ○ **kittenish** adj **1** like a kitten; playful. **2** of a woman: affectedly playful; flirtatious.

kittiwake n a type of gull which has white plumage with dark-grey back and wings.

kitty¹ n (-ies) **1** a fund contributed to jointly, for communal use by a group of people. **2** *cards* a pool of money used in certain games.

kitty² *n* an affectionate name for a cat or kitten.

kiwi *n* **1** a nocturnal flightless bird, found in New Zealand, with hair-like brown or grey feathers, a long slender bill and no tail. **2** *colloq* a New Zealander. **3** *colloq* a kiwi fruit.

kiwi fruit *n* an oval edible fruit with pale-green juicy flesh enclosed by a brown hairy skin.

kJ *abbrev* kilojoule.

kl *abbrev* kilolitre.

klaxon *n* a loud horn used as a warning signal on ambulances, fire engines, etc.

kleptomania *n* an irresistible urge to steal, esp objects that are not desired for themselves and are of little monetary value. ○ **kleptomaniac** *n*, *adj*.

klutz /klʌts/ *n*, *US*, *slang* an idiot; an awkward, stupid person. ○ **klutzy** *adj* (*-ier*, *-iest*).

km *abbrev* kilometre.

km/h *abbrev* kilometres per hour.

kn *abbrev*, *naut* knot (see KNOT *noun* sense 9).

knack *n* **1** the ability to do something effectively and skilfully. **2** a habit or tendency, esp an intuitive or unconscious one.

knacker *n* a buyer of old horses for slaughter. ➤ *vb*, *colloq* **1** to exhaust: *I was knackered after the climb.* **2** to break or wear out: *This clock is knackered.*

knapsack *n* a hiker's or traveller's bag for food, clothes, etc, carried on the back or over the shoulder.

knave *n*, *old use* **1** *cards* the JACK. **2** a scoundrel. ○ **knavish** *adj*.

knead *vb* **1** to work (dough) with one's fingers and knuckles into a uniform mass. **2** to massage (flesh) with firm finger-movements.

knee *n* **1** in humans: the joint in the middle of the leg where the lower end of the FEMUR meets the upper end of the TIBIA. **2 a** the corresponding joint in the hind limb of other vertebrates; **b** in a horse's foreleg: the joint corresponding to the wrist. **3** the area surrounding this joint. **4** the lap: *with the child on her knee.* **5** the part of a garment covering the knee. ➤ *vb* (**kneed, kneeing**) to hit, nudge or shove someone or something with the knee. ◆ **bring sb to their knees** to defeat, prostrate, humiliate or ruin them utterly. **go weak at the knees** *colloq* to be overcome by emotion. **on one's knees** **1** kneeling. **2** exhausted. **3** begging.

kneecap *n* a small plate of bone situated in front of and protecting the knee joint in humans and most other mammals. ➤ *vb* to shoot or otherwise damage someone's kneecaps as a form of revenge, torture or unofficial punishment.

knee-deep *adj*, *adv* **1** rising or reaching to someone's knees. **2** sunk to the knees: *standing knee-deep in mud.* **3** deeply involved.

knee-high *adj* rising or reaching to the knees.

knee-jerk *n* an involuntary kick of the lower leg, caused by a reflex response when the tendon just below the kneecap is tapped sharply.

➤ *adj* of a response or reaction: automatic.

kneel *vb* (**knelt** or **kneeled**) *intr* (*often* **kneel down**) to support one's weight on, or lower oneself onto, one's knees.

knee-length *adj* coming down or up as far as the knees.

knees-up *n*, *Brit*, *colloq* a riotous party or dance.

knell *n* **1** the tolling of a bell announcing a death or funeral. **2** something that signals the end of anything.

knickerbockers *pl n* baggy trousers tied just below the knee or at the ankle.

knickers *pl n* an undergarment with two separate legs or legholes, worn by women and girls, and covering part or all of the lower abdomen and buttocks.

knick-knack or **nick-nack** *n* a little trinket or ornament.

knife *n* (**knives**) a cutting instrument, typically in the form of a blade fitted into a handle or into machinery, and sometimes also used for spreading. ➤ *vb* **1** to cut. **2** to stab or kill with a knife.

knife edge *n* the cutting edge of a knife. ◆ **on a knife edge** in a state of extreme uncertainty; at a critical point.

knight *n* **1** a man who has been awarded the highest or second highest class of distinction in any of the four British orders of chivalry. **2** *hist* in medieval Europe: a man-at-arms of high social status, usu mounted, serving a feudal lord. **3** *hist* the armed champion of a lady, devoted to her service. **4** *chess* a piece shaped like a horse's head. ➤ *vb* to confer a knighthood on someone. ○ **knighthood** *n* **1** the rank of a knight, just below that of a baronet, conferring the title 'Sir'. **2** the order of knights. ○ **knightly** *adj* (*-ier*, *-iest*).

knight errant *n* (**knights errant**) *hist* a knight who travelled about in search of opportunities for daring and chivalrous deeds.

knit *vb* (**knitted** or *old use* **knit, knitting**) **1** *tr* & *intr* to produce a fabric composed of interlocking loops of yarn. **2** to make (garments, etc) by this means. **3** to unite something: *The tragedy served to knit them closer together.* **4** *tr* & *intr* of broken bones: to grow or make them grow together again. **5** to draw (one's brows) together in a frown. ➤ *n* a fabric or a garment made by knitting. ○ **knitting** *n* **1** a garment, etc that is in the process of being knitted. **2** the art or process of producing something knitted.

knitwear *n* knitted clothing.

knives *pl of* KNIFE

knob *n* **1** a hard rounded projection. **2** a handle, esp a rounded one, on a door or drawer. **3** a button on mechanical or electrical equipment that is pressed or rotated to operate it. **4** a small roundish lump: *a knob of butter.*

knobbly *adj* (*-ier*, *-iest*) covered with or full of knobs.

knock *vb* **1** *intr* to tap or rap with the knuckles or some object, esp on a door for admittance. **2** to strike and so push someone or something, esp accidentally. **3** to put someone or something into a specified condition by hitting them or it: *knocked him senseless.* **4** *tr & intr* (*usu* **knock against** or **on** or **into sth** or **sb**) to strike, bump or bang against it or them. **5** *colloq* to find fault with or criticize someone or something, esp unfairly. **6** *intr* of an internal-combustion engine: to make a metallic knocking sound caused by a fault. ➤ *n* **1** an act of knocking. **2** a tap or rap. **3** a push or shove. **4** *colloq* a personal misfortune, setback, etc. **5** in an internal-combustion engine: a metallic knocking sound. **6** *colloq* a criticism. ◆ **knock sth on the head** *colloq* to put an end to it. ◊ **knock about** or **around** *colloq* to lie about unused; to be idle: *knocking about the streets.* **knock sb about** or **around** *colloq* to hit or batter them. **knock sb back 1** *colloq* to cost them (a specified amount): *That knocked me back 500 quid.* **2** to rebuff or reject them; to turn them down. **knock sth back** *colloq* to eat or drink it quickly. **knock sth down** *colloq* to reduce its price: *They've knocked these down to a fiver each.* **knock off** *colloq* to finish work: *We knock off at 5pm.* **knock sb off** *slang* to kill them. **knock sth off 1** *colloq* to produce it or them at speed or in quick succession, apparently quite easily: *He knocks off several books a year.* **2** *colloq* to deduct (a certain amount): *I'll knock off £15 for a quick sale.* **knock on** *rugby* to commit the foul of pushing the ball forward with the hand. **knock sb out 1** to make them unconscious, esp by hitting them. **2** *boxing* to make them unconscious or render them incapable of rising in the required time. **3** to defeat them in a knockout competition. **4** *colloq* to amaze them; to impress them greatly. **knock up** *tennis* to exchange practice shots with one's opponent before a match. **knock sb up 1** to wake them by knocking. **2** *coarse slang* to make them pregnant. **knock sth up** *colloq* to make it hurriedly.

knockabout *adj* of comedy: boisterous; slapstick. ➤ *n* a boisterous performance with horseplay.

knock-back *n* a setback; a rejection or refusal.

knockdown *adj, colloq* very low; cheap: *knockdown prices.*

knocker *n* **1** (also **doorknocker**) a heavy piece of metal, usu of a decorative shape, fixed to a door by a hinge and used for knocking. **2** someone who knocks. **3** (**knockers**) *slang* a woman's breasts.

knock knee or (*popularly*) **knock knees** *n* a condition in which the lower legs curve inwards, causing the knees to touch when the person is standing with their feet slightly apart. ◊ **knock-kneed** *adj.*

knock-on effect *n* a secondary or indirect effect of some action, etc on one or more indirectly related matters or circumstances.

knockout *n* **1** *colloq* someone or something stunning. **2** a competition in which the defeated teams or competitors are dropped after

each round. **3** *boxing, etc* **a** the act of rendering someone unconscious; **b** a blow that renders the opponent or victim unconscious. ➤ *adj* **1** of a competition: in which the losers in each round are eliminated. **2** of a punch, etc: leaving the victim unconscious. **3** *colloq* attractive; excellent.

knoll *n* a small round hill.

knot *n* **1** a join or tie in string, etc made by looping the ends around each other and pulling tight. **2** a bond or uniting link. **3** a coil or bun in the hair. **4** a decoratively tied ribbon, etc. **5** a tangle in hair, string, etc. **6** a difficulty or complexity. **7** a hard mass of wood at the point where a branch has grown out from a tree trunk. **8** a scar on a piece of timber, representing a cross-section through such a mass. **9** used in meteorology and in navigation by aircraft and at sea: a unit of speed equal to one nautical mile (1.85km) per hour. **10** a tight feeling, eg in the stomach, caused by nervousness. ➤ *vb* (**knotted, knotting**) **1** to tie something in a knot. **2** *tr & intr* to tangle; to form knots. **3** *intr* of the stomach: to become tight with nervousness. ◊ **knotty** *adj* (**-ier, -iest**). ◆ **at a rate of knots** *colloq* very fast. **tie sb** or **oneself in knots** to bewilder, confuse or perplex them or oneself. **tie the knot** *colloq* to get married.

know *vb* (**knew, known**) **1** *tr & intr* (*usu* **know sth** or **know of** or **about sth**) to be aware of it; to be certain about it. **2** to have learnt and remembered something. **3** to have an understanding or grasp of something. **4** to be familiar with someone or something: *I know her well.* **5** to be able to recognize or identify someone or something. **6** to be able to distinguish someone or something, or to tell them apart: *I wouldn't know him from Adam.* **7** *intr* to have enough experience or training: *I knew not to question him further.* **8** to experience or be subject to something: *to know poverty.* ◊ **knowable** *adj.* ◆ **in the know** *colloq* **1** having information not known to most people. **2** initiated. **know better than to do sth** to be wiser, or better instructed, than to do it. **know the ropes** to understand the detail or procedure. **know what's what** to be shrewd, wise or hard to deceive. **know which side one's bread is buttered on** to be fully aware of one's own best interests.

know-all *n, derog* someone who seems, or claims, to know more than others.

know-how *n, colloq* ability; skill.

knowing *adj* **1** shrewd; canny; clever. **2** of a glance, etc: signifying secret awareness. **3** deliberate. ◊ **knowingly** *adv.* ◊ **knowingness** *n.*

knowledge *n* **1** the fact of knowing; awareness; understanding. **2** the information one has acquired through learning or experience. **3** learning; the sciences: *a branch of knowledge.* **4** specific information about a subject.

knowledgeable or **knowledgable** *adj* well-informed. ◊ **knowledgeably** *adv.*

known *adj* **1** widely recognized. **2** identified by the police: *a known thief*.

knuckle *n* **1** a joint of a finger, esp one that links a finger to the hand. **2** *cookery* the knee or ankle joint of an animal, esp with the surrounding flesh, as food. ◆ **near the knuckle** *colloq* bordering on the indecent. ◇ **knuckle down to sth** to begin to work hard at it. **knuckle under** *colloq* to submit, yield or give way.

knuckle-duster *n* a set of metal links or other metal device worn over the knuckles as a weapon.

knurl *n* a ridge.

KO or **k.o.** *abbrev* **1** kick-off. **2** knockout.

koala /kəʊˈɑːlə/ *n* an Australian tree-climbing marsupial with thick grey fur and bushy ears.

kohl /kəʊl/ *n* a cosmetic for darkening the eyelids.

kohlrabi /kəʊlˈrɑːbɪ/ *n* (**kohlrabis** or **kohlrabi**) a variety of cabbage with a short swollen green or purple edible stem.

kola see COLA

kook *n*, *N Am*, *colloq* a crazy or eccentric person. ○ **kooky** or **kookie** *adj* (**-ier**, **-iest**).

kookaburra *n* a large kingfisher, found in Australia and New Guinea and known for its chuckling cry.

kopeck or **kopek** *n* a coin or unit of currency of Russia, and the former USSR, worth one-hundredth of a rouble.

Koran or **Qur'an** /kɔːˈrɑːn, kəˈrɑːn/ *n*, *Islam* the holy book of Islam, believed by Muslims to be composed of the true word of Allah as dictated to Muhammad.

korfball *n* a game similar to basketball, played by two teams, consisting each of six men and six women.

korma *n* in Indian cookery: meat or vegetables braised in stock, yoghurt or cream.

kosher /ˈkəʊʃə(r)/ *adj* **1** in accordance with Jewish law. **2** of food: prepared as prescribed by Jewish dietary laws. **3** *colloq* legitimate.

kowtow *vb* **1** *intr* (*usu* **kowtow to sb**) *colloq* to defer to them, esp in an over-submissive way. **2** to touch the forehead to the ground in a gesture of submission, orig a Chinese ceremonial custom. ➤ *n* an act of kowtowing.

kph *abbrev* kilometres per hour.

Kr *symbol*, *chem* krypton.

kraal /krɑːl/ *n* **1** a S African village of huts surrounded by a fence. **2** *S Afr* an enclosure for cattle, sheep, etc.

kraft or **kraft paper** *n* a type of strong brown wrapping paper.

kraken *n* a legendary gigantic sea monster.

kremlin *n* the citadel of a Russian town, esp (**the Kremlin**) that of Moscow.

krill *n* (*pl* **krill**) a shrimp-like crustacean that feeds on plankton and lives in enormous swarms.

krona *n* (**kronor**) the standard unit of currency of Sweden.

krone /ˈkrəʊnə/ *n* (**kroner**) the standard unit of currency of Denmark and Norway.

krypton *n* a colourless odourless tasteless noble gas that is almost inert, used in lasers, fluorescent lamps and discharge tubes.

kT *abbrev* kiloton.

kt *abbrev* **1** kiloton. **2** karat or carat. **3** *naut* knot.

kudos /ˈkjuːdɒs/ *n* credit, honour or prestige.

kudu /ˈkuːduː/ *n*, *zool* a lightly striped African antelope.

kümmel /ˈkʊməl/ *n* a German liqueur flavoured with cumin and caraway seeds.

kumquat /ˈkʌmkwɒt/ *n* **1** a small spiny citrus shrub or tree, native to China. **2** the small orange citrus fruit produced by this plant.

kung fu *n* a Chinese martial art with similarities to karate and judo.

kV *abbrev* kilovolt.

kW *abbrev* kilowatt.

kWh *abbrev* kilowatt hour.

kybosh see KIBOSH

kyle *n*, *Scot* a sea channel or sound.

Ll

L¹ or **l** *n* (**Ls**, **L's** or **l's**) the twelfth letter of the English alphabet.

L² *abbrev* **1** lake. **2** learner driver. **3** as a clothes size, etc: large.

L³ *symbol* the Roman numeral for 50.

l *abbrev* **1** left. **2** length. **3** line. **4** litre.

La *symbol*, *chem* lanthanum.

la see LAH

lab *n*, *colloq* short form of LABORATORY.

label *n* **1** a tag, etc attached to something specifying its contents, etc or how to use it, wash it, etc. **2** a descriptive word or short phrase. **3** a small strip of material on a garment, etc with the name of the maker or designer. **4** a recording company's trademark. ➤ *vb* (**labelled, labelling** or *US* **labeled, labeling**) **1 a** to mark something in a specified way with a special tag, sticker, etc; **b** to attach a tag, sticker, etc to something. **2** to call (someone or some group) by a specified name.

labial *adj* **1** relating to or beside the lips. **2** *phonetics* of a sound: produced by the active use of one or both lips. ➤ *n*, *phonetics* a labial sound.

labiate *n*, *bot* a plant, eg mint and thyme,

where the COROLLA of petals is divided into two lips. ➤ *adj* **1** *bot* referring or relating to this type of plant. **2** *biol* having or resembling lips.

labium *n* (*labia* /'leɪbɪə/) **1** a lip or lip-like structure. **2** (*usu* **labia**) one section of the two pairs of fleshy folds which form part of the VULVA.

laboratory *n* (-*ies*) a room or building specially equipped for scientific experiments, the preparation of drugs, etc.

laborious *adj* of a task, etc: requiring hard work or much effort. ○ **laboriously** *adv.*

labour or (*esp N Am*) **labor** *n* **1** strenuous and prolonged work. **2** (*usu* **labours**) the amount of effort put into doing something. **3** working people or their productive output regarded collectively. **4** the process of giving birth. **5** (**Labour**) *Brit* the Labour Party. ➤ *vb, intr* **1** to work hard or with difficulty. **2** to progress or move slowly and with difficulty. **3** to spend time and effort achieving something. ◆ **labour a** or **the point** to spend excessive time on one particular subject, etc.

laboured or (*esp N Am*) **labored** *adj* **1** showing signs of effort or difficulty. **2** not natural or spontaneous: *laboured prose.*

labourer or (*esp N Am*) **laborer** *n* someone employed to do heavy, usu unskilled, physical work.

Labour Party *n* **1** *Brit* a political party on the left of the political spectrum, founded by members of trades unions and socialist organizations. **2** (*often* **Labor Party**) any similar party in several other countries.

labour-saving *adj* having the effect of reducing the amount of work or effort needed.

Labrador *n* a medium-sized retriever dog with a short black or golden coat.

laburnum *n* a small tree with hanging clusters of yellow flowers and poisonous seeds.

labyrinth /'labɪrɪnθ/ *n* **1** a network of interconnected, sometimes underground, passages. **2** anything that is complicated, intricate or difficult to negotiate. ○ **labyrinthine** *adj.*

lac *n* a resinous substance produced by certain tropical Asian insects.

lace *n* **1** a delicate material made by knotting, looping or twisting thread into open intricate symmetrical patterns. **2** a string or cord drawn through holes or round hooks and used for fastening shoes, etc. ➤ *vb* **1** *tr & intr* to fasten or be fastened with a lace or laces. **2** to put a lace or laces into (shoes, etc). **3** to flavour, strengthen, adulterate, etc (with alcohol, drugs, poison, etc): *She laced the trifle with sherry.* ◊ **lace sth up** to tighten or fasten shoes, etc with laces.

lacerate *vb* **1** to tear or cut (esp flesh) roughly. **2** to wound or hurt (someone's feelings). ○ **laceration** *n.*

lace-up *n* a shoe fastened with a lace. ➤ *adj* of a shoe: fastened with a lace.

lachrymal /'lakrɪməl/ *adj* (*also* **lacrimal**) *anat* referring or relating to tears.

lachrymose /'lakrɪmoʊs/ *adj, literary* **1** prone

to crying. **2** of a novel, play, film, etc: likely to make someone cry.

lack *n* a deficiency or want. ➤ *vb* to be without or to have too little of something.

lackadaisical /lakə'deɪzɪkəl/ *adj* **1** showing little energy, interest, enthusiasm, etc. **2** lazy or idle, esp in a nonchalant way.

lackey *n* **1** *derog* a servile follower. **2** *old use* a male servant, esp a footman or valet.

lacklustre or (*US*) **lackluster** *adj* having or showing little energy, enthusiasm, brightness, etc.

laconic *adj* using few words; neatly concise and to the point. ○ **laconically** *adv.*

lacquer *n* **1** a substance made by dissolving natural or man-made resins in alcohol and used to form a hard, shiny covering on wood and metal. **2** the sap from some trees, used as a varnish for wood. **3** HAIRSPRAY. ➤ *vb* to cover with lacquer.

lacrimal *see* LACHRYMAL

lacrosse *n* a team game similar to hockey but played with a stick with a netted pocket.

lactate¹ *vb, intr* of mammary glands: to secrete milk. ○ **lactation** *n.*

lactate² *n, biochem* a salt or ester of lactic acid.

lacteal *adj* referring or relating to, or consisting of, milk or a milky fluid.

lactic *adj* relating to, derived from or containing milk.

lactic acid *n, biochem* an organic acid produced during the souring of milk and in muscle tissue when there is insufficient oxygen available to break down carbohydrates.

lactose *n, biochem* a white crystalline sugar found in milk.

lacuna /lə'kjuːnə/ *n* (*lacunae* /-niː/ or *lacunas*) a gap or a space where something is missing, esp in printed text.

lacy *adj* (-*ier*, -*iest*) like, made of or trimmed with lace.

lad *n* **1** a boy or youth. **2** *Brit* someone who works in a stable, regardless of their age or sex. ◆ **a bit of a lad** *colloq* a man with a boisterous lifestyle. **the lads** *colloq* a group of male friends.

ladder *n* **1** a structure used for climbing up or down, consisting of a set of parallel horizontal rungs set between two vertical supports. **2** *chiefly Brit* a long narrow flaw, esp in a stocking, tights or other knitted garment, where a row of stitches has broken. **3** a graded route of advancement or progress: *the social ladder.* ➤ *vb, chiefly Brit* **a** to cause a ladder to appear in (a stocking, etc); **b** *intr* of a stocking, etc: to develop a ladder.

lade *vb* (*past tense* **laded**, *past participle* **laden**, *present participle* **lading**) **1 a** to load cargo on to (a ship); **b** *intr* of a ship: to take cargo on board. **2** to put a burden, esp one of guilt, on someone.

laden *adj* **1** of a ship: loaded with cargo. **2** of a person, an animal, the sky, a vehicle, etc: heavily loaded, weighed down, burdened. **3** of a person: oppressed, esp with guilt, worry, etc.

la-di-da or **lah-di-dah** adj, colloq pretentiously snobbish.

ladies sing and pl n, colloq a women's public lavatory.

lading n the cargo or load that a ship, etc carries.

ladle n a large spoon with a long handle and deep bowl, for serving soup, etc. ➢ vb to serve with a ladle. ◊ **ladle sth out** to serve or distribute praise, blame, etc generously or excessively.

lady n (-ies) **1** a woman who is regarded as having good manners and refined behaviour. **2** a polite word for a woman generally. **3** hist a woman of the upper classes. **4** (**Lady**) Brit a title of honour used for peeresses, wives and daughters of peers and knights, etc. ➢ adj, now rather dated of the female gender: **a** used for occupations, etc formerly considered to be the domain of men: a lady doctor; **b** used when the attendant noun fails to signal gender: his lady friend.

ladybird or (N Am) **ladybug** n a small beetle whose body is usu red or yellow with black spots.

Lady Day n, Christianity 25 March, the feast of THE ANNUNCIATION.

lady-in-waiting n (**ladies-in-waiting**) a woman who attends a queen, princess, etc.

lady-killer n, colloq a man who is irresistibly attractive to women.

ladylike adj showing attributes, eg refinement, politeness, etc, appropriate to a lady.

Ladyship n (usu **Your** or **Her Ladyship**) a title used to address or refer to peeresses and the wives and daughters of peers, knights, etc.

lady's man or **ladies' man** n a man who enjoys the company of women.

lady's-slipper n an orchid with a large yellow slipper-like lip.

lag¹ vb (**lagged, lagging**) intr (usu **lag behind**) to move or progress so slowly as to become separated or left behind. ➢ n a delay or the length of a delay.

lag² vb (**lagged, lagging**) to cover (a boiler, water pipes, etc) with thick insulating material in order to minimize heat loss.

lager n a light-coloured effervescent beer.

laggard n someone or something that lags behind.

lagging n insulating cover for pipes, boilers, etc.

lagoon n a relatively shallow body of water separated from the open sea by a barrier such as a reef or a narrow bank of sand.

lah or **la** n, mus in SOL-FA notation: the sixth note of the major scale.

laid-back adj, colloq relaxed; easy-going.

laid paper n a type of paper that has faint lines running across the surface.

laid-up adj confined to bed because of illness or injury.

lair n **1** a wild animal's den. **2** colloq a place of refuge or hiding.

laird n, Scot someone who owns a large country estate.

laissez-faire or **laisser-faire** /lɛseɪˈfɛə(r)/ n a policy of not interfering in what others are doing.

laity /ˈleɪtɪ/ n (usu **the laity**) the people who are not members of a particular profession, esp the clergy.

lake¹ n a large area of fresh or salt water, surrounded by land.

lake² n **1** a reddish dye, orig obtained from LAC, but now more usu obtained from COCHINEAL. **2** a dye made by combining animal, vegetable or coal-tar pigment with a metallic oxide or earth.

lam vb (**lammed, lamming**) slang to thrash.

lama n a Buddhist priest or monk in Tibet and Mongolia.

the Lamb or **the Lamb of God** n, Christianity a title given to Christ because of the sacrificial nature of his death.

lamb n **1** a young sheep. **2** the flesh of a lamb used as food. **3** colloq a kind, gentle, good, sweet, etc person. ➢ vb, intr of a ewe: to give birth to a lamb or lambs. ◆ **like a lamb to the slaughter** innocently and without resistance.

lambaste or **lambast** /lamˈbast/ vb **1** to beat severely. **2** to criticize severely.

lambent adj of a flame or light: flickering over a surface.

lame adj **1** not able to walk properly, esp due to an injury or defect. **2** of an excuse, etc: not convincing. ➢ vb to make lame. ○ **lamely** adv. ○ **lameness** n.

lamé /ˈlɑːmeɪ/ n a fabric which has metallic threads, usu gold or silver, woven into it.

lame duck n someone who depends on the help of others to an excessive extent.

lament vb, tr & intr to feel or express regret or sadness. ➢ n **1** an expression of sadness, grief, regret, etc. **2** a poem, song, etc which expresses great grief, esp following someone's death. ○ **lamentation** n.

lamentable adj regrettable, shameful or deplorable. ○ **lamentably** adv.

lamina n (**laminae** /ˈlamɪniː/) a thin plate or layer, esp of bone, rock or metal.

laminate vb /ˈlamɪneɪt/ **1** to beat (a material, esp metal) into thin sheets. **2** to form (a composite material) by bonding together two or more sheets of that material. **3** to cover or overlay (a surface) with a thin sheet of protective material, eg transparent plastic film. **4** tr & intr to separate or be separated into thin layers. ➢ n /-nət/ a laminated sheet, material, etc. ➢ adj /-nət/ of a material: composed of layers or beaten into thin sheets. ○ **lamination** n.

Lammas n, Christianity a former church feast day held on 1 August, one of the four QUARTER DAYS in Scotland.

lamp n **1** a piece of equipment designed to give out light. **2** any piece of equipment that produces ultraviolet or infrared radiation and which is used in the treatment of certain medical conditions.

lampblack *n* soot obtained from burning carbon and used as a pigment.

lampoon *n* an attack, usu in the form of satirical prose or verse, on someone or something. ➤ *vb* to satirize.

lamppost *n* a tall post that supports a streetlamp.

lamprey *n* (*-eys*) *zool* an eel-like fish with a sucker-like mouth.

lampshade *n* a shade placed over a lamp or light bulb to soften or direct the light coming from it.

Lancastrian *n* **1** someone who comes from or lives in Lancaster or Lancashire. **2** *hist* a supporter of the House of Lancaster in the Wars of the Roses. Compare YORKIST. ➤ *adj* relating to Lancaster, the House of Lancaster or Lancashire.

lance *n* a long spear used as a cavalry weapon. ➤ *vb* **1** to cut open (a boil, abscess, etc) with a lancet. **2** to pierce with, or as if with, a lance.

lance corporal *n* a British army rank between private and corporal, being the lowest rank of non-commissioned officer.

lanceolate *adj* shaped like a spear-head, tapering at both ends.

lancer *n*, *formerly* a cavalry soldier armed with a lance.

lancet *n* a small pointed surgical knife which has both edges sharpened.

lancet arch *n*, *archit* a high, narrow, pointed arch.

lancet window *n*, *archit* a high, narrow, pointed window.

land *n* **1** the solid part of the Earth's surface as opposed to the area covered by water. **2** ground or soil, esp with regard to its use or quality: *farm land*. **3** ground that is used for agriculture. **4** a country, state or region. **5** (**lands**) estates. **6** *in compounds* any area of ground that is characterized in a specified way: *gangland • hinterland*. ➤ *vb* **1** *tr & intr* to come or bring to rest on the ground or water, or in a particular place, after flight through the air. **2** *intr* to end up in a specified place or position, esp after a fall, jump, throw, etc. **3** *tr & intr* to end up or cause someone to end up in a certain position or situation, usu unwelcome or unfavourable: *They landed themselves in trouble.* **4** to bring on to the land from a ship. **5** to bring (a hooked fish) out of the water. **6** *colloq* to be successful in getting (a job, contract, prize, etc). **7** *colloq* to give someone (a punch or slap). ◊ **land up** *colloq* to come to be in a specified position or situation: *Don landed up homeless after losing his job.* **land sb with sth** *colloq* to give or pass (something unpleasant or unwanted) to them: *She landed us with all the bills to pay.*

land agent *n* **1** someone who manages a large estate for the owner. **2** someone who takes care of the sale of estates.

landau /ˈlandɔː/ *n* a four-wheeled horse-drawn carriage with two folding hoods.

landed *adj* **1** owning land or estates: *landed gentry.* **2** consisting of or derived from land: *landed estates.*

landfall *n* the first land visible towards the end of a journey by sea or air, or an approach to or sighting of this.

landfill *n* **1** a site where rubbish is disposed of by burying it under layers of earth. **2** the rubbish that is disposed of in this way.

landing *n* **1** the act of coming or being put ashore or of returning to the ground. **2** a place for disembarking, esp from a ship. **3** a level part of a staircase either between two flights of steps, or at the very top.

landlady *n* (*-ies*) **1** a woman who rents property out to a tenant or tenants. **2** a woman who owns or runs a public house or hotel.

landlocked *adj* of a country or a piece of land: completely enclosed by land.

landlord *n* **1** a man who rents property out to a tenant or tenants. **2** a man who owns or runs a public house or hotel.

landlubber *n* someone who has no sea-going experience.

landmark *n* **1** a distinctive feature, esp one used by sailors or travellers as an indication of where they are. **2** an event or development of importance, esp one that is significant in the history or progress of something.

landmass *n* a large area of land unbroken by seas.

land mine *n* an explosive device that is laid near the surface of the ground and which detonates if it is disturbed from above.

landowner *n* someone who owns land.

landscape *n* **1** the area and features of land that can be seen in a broad view, esp when they form a particular type of scenery. **2 a** a painting, drawing, photograph, etc of the countryside; **b** this genre of art. **3** an orientation of a page, illustration, etc that is wider than it is tall or deep. Compare PORTRAIT. ➤ *vb* to improve the look of (a garden, park, etc) by enhancing the existing natural features or by artificially creating new ones.

landscape gardening *n* the art or practice of laying out grounds, etc, esp to produce the effect of a natural landscape. ○ **landscape gardener** *n*.

landslide *n* **1** (*also* **landslip**) **a** a sudden downward movement of a mass of soil and rock material, esp in mountainous areas; **b** the accumulation of soil and rock material from a landslide. **2** a victory in an election by an overwhelming majority.

lane *n* **1** a narrow road. **2** a subdivision of a road for a single line of traffic. **3** a regular course taken by ships across the sea, or by aircraft through the air. **4** a marked subdivision of a running track or swimming pool for one competitor.

language *n* **1** a formalized system of communication, esp one that uses sounds or written symbols which the majority of a particular community will readily understand. **2** the speech and writing of a particular nation or social group. **3** the faculty of speech. **4** a specified style of speech or verbal expression: *elegant language*. **5** any other way of communicating or expressing meaning: *sign language*. **6** professional or specialized vocabulary: *legal language*. **7** a system of signs and symbols used to write computer programs.

language laboratory *n* a room with separate cubicles equipped with tape recorders and prerecorded tapes, used for language learning.

languid *adj* **1** lacking in energy or vitality. **2** slow-moving.

languish *vb, intr* **1** to spend time in hardship or discomfort. **2** to grow weak. **3** to pine.

languor /'laŋgə(r)/ *n* a feeling of dullness or lack of energy. ○ **languorous** *adj*.

lank *adj* **1** long and thin. **2** of hair, etc: long, straight and dull.

lanky *adj* (*-ier, -iest*) thin and tall, esp in an ungainly way. ○ **lankiness** *n*.

lanolin *n* a fat that occurs naturally in sheep's wool, used in cosmetics, ointments and soaps.

lantern *n* **1** a lamp or light contained in a transparent case. **2** the top part of a lighthouse, where the light is kept. **3** a structure, esp on the top of a dome, that admits light and air.

lantern jaws *pl n* long thin jaws that give the face a hollow drawn appearance. ○ **lantern-jawed** *adj*.

lanthanide *n, chem* any of a group of 15 highly reactive metallic elements with atomic numbers ranging from 57 (lanthanum) to 71 (lutetium).

lanthanum *n, chem* a silvery-white metallic element.

lanyard *n* **1** a cord for hanging a knife, whistle, etc round the neck, esp as worn by sailors. **2** *naut* a short rope for fastening rigging, etc.

lap[1] *vb* (*lapped, lapping*) **1** usu of an animal: to drink (milk, water, etc) using the tongue. **2** *tr & intr* of water, etc: to wash or flow against (a shore or other surface) with a light splashing sound. ➤ *n* the sound, act or process of lapping. ◊ **lap sth up** to drink or consume it eagerly or greedily.

lap[2] *n* **1** the front part of the body from the waist to the knees, when in a sitting position. **2** the part of someone's clothing, esp of a skirt or dress, which covers this part of the body.

lap[3] *n* **1** one circuit of a racecourse or other track. **2** one section of a journey. **3** a part which overlaps or the amount it overlaps by. ➤ *vb* **1** to get ahead of (another competitor in a race) by one or more laps. **2** to make something overlap something else. **3** *intr* to lie with an overlap.

lapdog *n* a small pet dog.

lapel /lə'pɛl/ *n* the part of a collar on a coat or jacket that is folded back towards the shoulders.

lapidary *n* (*-ies*) someone whose job is to cut

and polish gemstones. ➤ *adj* relating to stones.

lapis lazuli /'lapɪs 'lazjʊlɪ/ *n* **1** *geol* a deep-blue mineral used as a gemstone. **2** a bright-blue colour.

lap of honour *n* (*laps of honour*) a ceremonial circuit of a racecourse or sports ground by the winner or winners.

Lapp *n* **1** (*also* **Laplander**) a member of a mainly nomadic people who live chiefly in the far north of Scandinavia. **2** (*also* **Lappish**) the language spoken by this people. ➤ *adj* referring or relating to this people, their language or their culture.

lapse *n* **1** a slight mistake or failure. **2** a perceived decline in standards of behaviour, etc. **3** a passing of time. **4** *law* the loss of a right or privilege because of failure to renew a claim to it. ➤ *vb, intr* **1** to fail to behave in what is perceived as a proper or morally acceptable way. **2** to turn away from a faith or belief. **3** *law* of a right, privilege, etc: to become invalid because the claim to it has not been renewed. **4** of a membership of a club, society, etc: to become invalid, usu because the fees have not been paid. ○ **lapsed** *adj*.

laptop *n* a portable personal computer, small enough to be used on someone's lap.

lapwing *n* a crested bird of the plover family.

larceny *n* (*-ies*) *law, old use* theft of personal property. ○ **larcenist** *n*.

larch *n* **1** a deciduous coniferous tree with rosettes of short needles and egg-shaped cones. **2** the wood of this tree.

lard *n* a soft white preparation made from pig fat, used in cooking and baking. ➤ *vb* **1** to insert strips of bacon or pork fat into (lean meat) in order to make it more moist once it is cooked. **2** to sprinkle (a piece of writing, etc) with technical details or over-elaborate words.

larder *n* a cool room or cupboard for storing food.

large *adj* **1** occupying a comparatively big space. **2** comparatively big in size, extent, amount, etc. **3** broad in scope; wide-ranging. ➤ *adv* importantly; prominently: *looming large*. ○ **largeness** *n*. ♦ **as large as life** *colloq* in person. **at large 1** of prisoners, etc: free and threatening. **2** in general; as a whole: *people at large*. **3** in full detail.

large intestine *n* in mammals: the part of the alimentary canal comprising the CAECUM, COLON[2] and RECTUM.

largely *adv* **1** mainly or chiefly. **2** to a great extent.

large-scale *adj* **1** of maps, models, etc: made on a relatively large scale, though small in comparison with the original. **2** extensive; widespread.

largesse *or* **largess** *n* **1** generosity. **2** gifts, money, etc given generously.

largo *mus, adv* slowly and with dignity. ➤ *adj* slow and dignified. ➤ *n* a piece of music to be played in this way.

lariat *n* **1** a lasso. **2** a rope used for tethering animals.

lark¹ *n* any of various gregarious, brownish birds, esp the skylark.

lark² *n*, *colloq* **1** a joke or piece of fun. **2** *Brit colloq* a job or activity: *I'm really getting into this gardening lark now.* ➣ *vb*, *intr* (*usu* **lark about** or **around**) *colloq* to play or fool about frivolously.

larkspur *n* a plant with blue, white or pink flowers.

larva *n* (*larvae* /ˈlɑːviː/) *zool* the immature stage in the life cycle of many insects between the egg and pupa stages. ○ **larval** *adj*.

laryngeal /ləˈrɪndʒəl/ *adj* relating to the LARYNX.

laryngitis /larɪnˈdʒaɪtɪs/ *n* inflammation of the larynx.

larynx /ˈlarɪŋks/ *n* (*larynges* /ləˈrɪndʒiːz/ or *larynxes*) in mammals and other higher vertebrates: the upper part of the trachea containing the vocal cords.

lasagne or **lasagna** /ləˈzanjə/ *n* **1** pasta in the form of thin flat sheets. **2** a dish made of layers with these sheets alternating with minced beef or vegetables in a tomato sauce and cheese sauce.

lascivious /ləˈsɪvɪəs/ *adj* **1** of behaviour, thoughts, etc: lewd. **2** of poetry, prose, art, etc: causing or inciting lewd behaviour, thoughts, etc.

laser *n* a device that produces a very powerful narrow beam of light.

laser printer *n*, *comput* a type of printer that uses a laser beam to produce text, etc and transfers this to paper.

lash¹ *n* **1** a stroke or blow, usu made by a whip as a form of punishment. **2** the flexible part of a whip. **3** an eyelash. ➣ *vb* **1** to hit or beat with a lash. **2** *tr & intr* to move suddenly, restlessly, uncontrollably, etc. **3** to attack with harsh scolding words. **4** *intr* to make a sudden whip-like movement. **5** *tr & intr* of waves or rain: to beat with great force. **6** to urge on as if with a whip. ◊ **lash out 1 a** to hit out violently; **b** to speak in a very hostile or aggressive manner. **2** *colloq* to spend money extravagantly.

lash² *vb*, *chiefly naut* to fasten with a rope or cord.

lashing¹ *n* **1** a beating with a whip. **2** (**lashings**) a generous amount.

lashing² *n* a rope used for tying things fast.

lass *n*, *Scot & N Eng dialect* a girl or young woman.

Lassa fever *n* a viral disease, sometimes fatal, of tropical Africa.

lassie *n*, *Scot & N Eng dialect*, *colloq* a girl.

lassitude *n* physical or mental tiredness; a lack of energy and enthusiasm.

lasso /laˈsuː/ *n* (*lassos* or *lassoes*) a long rope with a sliding noose at one end used for catching cattle, horses, etc. ➣ *vb* (*lassoes*, *lassoed*) to catch with a lasso.

last¹ *adj* **1** being, coming or occurring at the end of a series or after all others. **2** most recent; happening immediately before the present (week, month, year, etc). **3** only remaining after all the rest have gone or been used up: *her last fiver.* **4** least likely, desirable, suitable, etc: *She's the last person you'd expect help from.* **5** final: *He administered the last rites.* ➣ *adv* **1** most recently: *When did you see her last?* **2** lastly; at the end (of a series of events, etc): *and last she served the coffee.* ➣ *n* **1** a person or thing that is at the end or behind the rest. **2** (**the last**) the end; a final moment, part, etc: *the last of the milk.* **3** (**the last**) the final appearance or mention: *We haven't heard the last of him.* ◆ **at last** or **at long last** in the end, esp after a long delay. **to the last** until the very end, esp until death.

last² *vb*, *tr & intr* **1** to take (a specified amount of time) to complete, happen, come to an end, etc. **2** to be adequate for someone: *enough water to last us a week.* **3** to be or keep fresh or in good condition: *The bread will only last one more day.*

last³ *n* a foot-shaped piece of wood or metal used in making and repairing shoes, etc.

last-ditch *adj* done as a last resort: *a last-ditch attempt.*

lasting *adj* existing or continuing for a long time or permanently: *It had a lasting effect.*

lastly *adv* used to introduce the last item or items in a series or list: finally.

last-minute *adj* made, done or given at the latest possible moment.

last name *n* a SURNAME.

the last post *n*, *mil* **1** a final bugle call of a series given to signal that it is time to retire at night. **2** a farewell bugle call at military funerals.

the last rites *pl n*, *Christianity* the formalized ceremonial acts performed for someone who is dying.

the last straw *n*, *colloq* a minor inconvenience which, if it occurs after a series of other misfortunes, difficulties, etc, serves to make the whole situation intolerable.

lat. *abbrev* latitude.

latch *n* **1** a door catch consisting of a bar which is lowered or raised from its notch by a lever or string. **2** a door lock by which a door may be opened from the inside using a handle, and from the outside using a key. ➣ *vb*, *tr & intr* to fasten or be fastened with a latch. ◊ **latch on** *colloq* to understand. **latch on to sth** *colloq* to cling to it, often obsessively.

latchkey child *n* a child who comes home from school while the parent or parents are still out at work.

late *adj* **1** coming, arriving, etc after the expected or usual time. **2 a** far on in the day or night; **b** well into the evening or night; **c** *in compounds* occurring towards the end of a specified historical period, etc: *late-Georgian architecture*; **d** written, painted, etc towards the end of someone's life or towards the end of their active career: *a late Picasso.* **3** happening, growing, etc at a relatively advanced time: *the late showing.* **4** dead: *his late father.* **5** former: *the late prime minister.* **6** recent: *a late model of car.* ➤ *adv* **1** after the expected or usual time: *He arrived late for the meeting.* **2** far on in the day or night: *late on Thursday.* **3** at an advanced time: *They flower late in the season.* **4** recently: *The letter was sent as late as this morning.* **5** formerly, but no longer: *late of Glasgow.* ○ **lateness** *n.* ◆ **late in the day** at a late stage, esp when it is too late to be of any use.

lateen *adj, naut* denoting a triangular sail on a long sloping yard.

lately *adv* in the recent past.

latent *adj* **1** of a characteristic, tendency, etc: present or existing in an undeveloped or hidden form. **2** *pathol* of a disease: failing to present or not yet presenting the usual or expected symptoms. ○ **latency** *n.*

later *adj* more late. ➤ *adv* at some time after, or in the near future.

lateral *adj* at, from or relating to a side or the side of something: *lateral fins.* ○ **laterally** *adv.*

lateral thinking *n* an indirect or seemingly illogical approach to problem-solving or understanding something.

latest *adj* most recent. ➤ *n* (**the latest**) the most recent news, occurrence, fashion, etc. ◆ **at the latest** not later than a specified time

latex *n* (**latexes** or **latices** /ˈleɪtɪsiːz/) **1** a thick milky juice that is produced by some plants and used commercially, esp in the manufacture of rubber. **2** a synthetic product that has similar properties to rubber.

lath /lɑːθ/ *n* a thin narrow strip of wood, esp one of a series used to support plaster, tiles, slates, etc.

lathe *n* a machine tool used to cut, drill or polish a piece of metal, wood or plastic that is rotated against its cutting edge.

lather /ˈlɑːðə(r)/ *n* **1** a foam made by mixing water and soap or detergent. **2** foamy sweat, eg, on a horse during exercise. ➤ *vb* **1** *intr* to form a lather. **2** to cover something with lather. ○ **lathery** *adj.* ◆ **in a lather** *colloq* extremely agitated or excited.

Latin *n* **1** the language of ancient Rome and its empire. **2** a person of Italian, Spanish, Portuguese or Latin American extraction. ➤ *adj* **1** relating to, or in, the Latin language. **2** applied to languages derived from Latin, esp Italian, Spanish and Portuguese. **3** of a person: Italian, Spanish, Portuguese or Latin American in origin. **4** belonging or relating to the Roman Catholic Church.

Latin American *n* an inhabitant of Latin America, the areas in America where languages such as Spanish and Portuguese are spoken. ○ **Latin-American** *adj.*

latish *adj, adv* slightly late.

latitude *n* **1** *geog* angular distance north or south of the equator, measured from 0 degrees at the equator to 90 degrees at the north and

south poles. Compare LONGITUDE. **2** (*usu* **latitudes**) *geog* a region or area thought of in terms of its distance from the equator or its climate: *warm latitudes.* **3** scope for freedom of action or choice. ○ **latitudinal** *adj.*

latitudinarian *n* someone who believes in freedom of thought, action, etc, esp in religious matters.

latrine *n* a lavatory, esp in a barracks or camp.

latte /ˈlɑːteɪ, ˈlateɪ/ *n* espresso coffee with frothy hot milk.

latter *adj* **1** nearer the end than the beginning: *the latter part of the holiday.* **2** used when referring to two people or things: mentioned, considered, etc second. ◆ **the latter** of two people or things: the second one mentioned, considered, etc. Compare FORMER.

latter-day *adj* recent or modern.

Latter-day Saints *pl n* the name that the Mormons prefer to call themselves.

latterly *adv* **1** recently. **2** towards the end.

lattice *n* **1** (*also* **lattice-work**) an open frame made by crossing narrow strips of wood or metal over each other to form an ornamental pattern and used esp in gates and fences. **2** (*also* **lattice window**) a window with small diamond-shaped panels of glass held in place with strips of lead. **3** *chem* the regular three-dimensional grouping of atoms, ions or molecules that forms the structure of a crystalline solid. ○ **latticed** *adj.*

laud *formal, vb* to praise highly. ➤ *n* glorification or praise.

laudable *adj* worthy of praise. ○ **laudably** *adv.*

laudanum /ˈlɔːdənəm/ *n* a solution of morphine in alcohol, formerly used to relieve pain, aid sleep, etc.

laudatory *adj* containing or expressing praise.

laugh *vb* **1** *intr* to make spontaneous sounds associated with happiness, amusement, scorn, etc. **2** to express (a feeling, etc) by laughing: *David laughed his contempt.* **3** *intr* (**laugh at sb** or **sth**) **a** to make fun of or ridicule them or it; **b** to find them or it funny. ➤ *n* **1** an act or sound of laughing. **2** *colloq* someone or something that is good fun, amusing, etc. ◆ **have the last laugh** *colloq* to win or succeed in the end, esp after setbacks; to be finally proved right. ◊ **laugh sth off** to treat an injury, embarrassment, etc lightly or trivially.

laughable *adj* **1** deserving to be laughed at. **2** absurd; ludicrous. ○ **laughably** *adv.*

laughing gas *n* NITROUS OXIDE, esp when used as an anaesthetic.

laughing stock *n* someone or something that is the object of ridicule.

laughter *n* the act or sound of laughing.

launch[1] *vb* **1 a** to send (a ship or boat) into the water at the beginning of a voyage; **b** to send a newly-built ship or boat) into the water for the first time. **2** to send (a spacecraft, missile, etc) into space or into the air. **3** to start someone or something off in a specified direction. **4** to bring (a new product) on to the market, esp with publicity. **5** to begin (an attack, etc). **6** *intr* (**launch into sth**) **a** to begin (an undertaking, etc) with vigour and enthusiasm; **b** to begin (a story or speech, esp a long one). ➤ *n* **1** the action or an instance of a ship, spacecraft, missile, etc being sent off into the water or into the air. **2** the start of something. ○ **launcher** *n*.

launch² *n* a large powerful motorboat.

launching pad or **launch pad** *n* the area or platform for launching a spacecraft or missile.

launder *vb* **1** to wash and iron (clothes, linen, etc). **2** *colloq* to transfer (illegally obtained money, etc) to cover up its origins.

launderette or **laundrette** *n* a place where clothes can be washed and dried using coin-operated machines.

laundry *n* (*-ies*) **1** a place where clothes, linen, etc are washed. **2** clothes, linen, etc for washing or newly washed.

laureate *adj* **1** *often following a noun* honoured for artistic or intellectual distinction: *poet laureate*. **2** crowned with laurel leaves as a sign of honour or distinction. ➤ *n* someone honoured for artistic or intellectual achievement, esp a **poet laureate**.

laurel *n* **1** a small evergreen tree with smooth dark shiny leaves. **2** a crown of laurel leaves worn as a symbol of victory or mark of honour. **3** (**laurels**) honour; praise. ♦ **look to one's laurels** to beware of losing one's reputation by being outclassed. **rest on one's laurels** to be satisfied with one's past successes and so not bother to achieve anything more.

lav *n*, *colloq* short form of LAVATORY.

lava *n* **1** *geol* MAGMA that has erupted from a volcano or fissure. **2** the solid rock that forms as a result of cooling of this material.

lavatorial *adj* of humour: rude, esp in making use of references to excrement.

lavatory *n* (*-ies*) **1** a piece of equipment, usu bowl-shaped with a seat, where urine and faeces are deposited and then flushed away by water. **2** a room or building containing one or more of these.

lavender *n* **1** a plant or shrub with sweet-smelling pale bluish-purple flowers. **2** the dried flowers from this plant, used to perfume clothes or linen. **3** a pale bluish-purple colour. **4** a perfume made from the distilled flowers of this plant.

lavish *adj* **1** spending or giving generously. **2** gorgeous or luxurious: *lavish decoration*. **3** extravagant or excessive. ➤ *vb* to spend (money) or give (praise, etc) freely or generously. ○ **lavishly** *adv*.

law *n* **1** a customary rule recognized as allowing or prohibiting certain actions. **2** a collection of such rules according to which people live or a country is governed. **3** the control which such rules exercise: *law and order*. **4** a controlling force: *Their word is law*. **5** a collection of laws as a social system or a subject for study. **6** one of a group of rules which set out

how certain games, sports, etc should be played. **7** the legal system as a recourse: *to go to law*. **8** a rule in science, philosophy, etc, based on practice or observation, which says that under certain conditions certain things will always happen. ♦ **the law 1** people who are knowledgeable about law, esp professionally. **2** *colloq* the police or a member of the police.

law-abiding *adj* obeying the law.

lawcourt *n* (*also* **court of law**) a place where people accused of crimes are tried and legal disagreements settled.

lawful *adj* **1** allowed by or according to law. **2** just or rightful. ○ **lawfully** *adv*.

lawless *adj* **1** breaking the law, esp violently. **2** having no laws. ○ **lawlessness** *n*.

Law Lord *n* **1** a peer in the House of Lords who sits in the highest Court of Appeal. **2** *Scot* a judge in the Court of Session.

lawn¹ *n* an area of smooth mown grass, esp as part of a garden or park.

lawn² *n* fine linen or cotton.

lawnmower *n* a machine for cutting grass.

lawn tennis *n* TENNIS (sense 1).

lawrencium *n*, *chem* a synthetic radioactive metallic element.

lawsuit *n* an argument or disagreement taken to a court of law to be settled.

lawyer *n* a person employed in the legal profession, esp a solicitor.

lax *adj* **1** showing little care or concern over behaviour, morals, etc. **2** loose, slack or flabby. **3** negligent. ○ **laxity** *n*.

laxative *adj* inducing movement of the bowels. ➤ *n* a medicine or food that induces movement of the bowels.

lay¹ *vb* (**laid**) **1** to place something on a surface, esp in a horizontal position. **2** to put or bring something to a stated position or condition: *She laid her hand on his arm*. **3** to design, arrange or prepare. **4** to put plates, cutlery, etc on (a table) ready for a meal. **5** to prepare (a fire) by putting coal, etc in the grate. **6** *tr & intr* of a female bird: to produce (eggs). **7** to present: *He laid his case before the court*. **8** to set down as a basis: *She laid the ground rules*. **9** *colloq* to place (a bet): *I'll lay 20 quid you can't do it*. **10** *slang* to have sexual intercourse with. ➤ *n* **1** the way or position in which something is lying: *the lay of the surrounding countryside*. **2** *slang* **a** a partner in sexual intercourse; **b** an act of sexual intercourse. ♦ **lay bare** to reveal or explain (a plan or intention that has been kept secret). **lay down one's arms** to surrender or call a truce. **lay down the law** to dictate in a forceful and domineering way. **lay it on thick** *colloq* to exaggerate, esp in connection with flattery, praise, etc. **lay oneself open to sth** to expose oneself to criticism or attack. **lay one's hands on sb** or **sth** *colloq* to succeed in getting hold of them or it. **lay sth on sb 1** to assign or attribute it to them: *She laid the blame on his friends*. **2** *colloq* to give it to them. **lay sb low** of

.an illness: to affect them severely. **lay to rest** to bury (a dead body). **lay waste** to destroy or devastate completely. ◊ **lay sth down 1** to put it on the ground or some other surface. **2** to give it as a deposit, pledge, etc. **3** to give it up or sacrifice it: *He laid down his life*. **4** to formulate or devise it: *to lay down a plan*. **5** to store (wine) in a cellar. **lay sth in** to get and store a supply of it. **lay into sb** *colloq* to attack or scold them severely. **lay sb off** to dismiss (an employee) when there is no work available. **lay off sth** *colloq* to stop it. **lay off sb** *colloq* to leave them alone. **lay sth on** to provide a supply of it. **lay sb out 1** *colloq* to knock them unconscious. **2** to prepare their dead body for burial. **lay sth out 1** to plan and arrange (esp land or natural features). **2** to spread it out or display it. **3** *colloq* to spend it. **lay sb up** *colloq* to force them to stay in bed or at home. **lay sth up 1** to keep or store it. **2** to put a ship out of use, esp for repairs.

> **lay, lie** These two verbs are commonly confused because their meanings are close and their forms overlap, since **lay** is also the past of **lie**:
>
> ✓ *Lucy lay on the bed to review the situation.*
>
> ✗ *I got so tired I used to lay down on the bunk.*
>
> ✓ *Many individual units began to lay down their arms.*
>
> Another cause of confusion is the closeness in form of **laid** and **lain**, and the fact that **laid** is the past and past participle of **lay**; but **lain** is only the past participle of **lie**:
>
> ✓ *He paused, then laid a hand on her shoulder.*
>
> ✗ *He had lain the saw aside and was hammering.*
>
> ✓ *He had lain on his bed all afternoon.*

---

lay² *past tense of* LIE²

lay³ *adj* **1** relating to or involving people who are not members of the clergy. **2** not having specialized or professional knowledge of a particular subject.

lay⁴ *n* a short narrative or lyric poem, esp one that is meant to be sung.

layabout *n, colloq* a habitually lazy person.

lay-by *n* (**lay-bys**) *Brit* an area off to the side of a road where cars can stop safely.

layer *n* **1** a thickness or covering, esp one of several on top of each other. **2** *in compounds* someone or something that lays something specified: *bricklayer*. **3** a hen that regularly lays eggs. **4** a shoot from a plant fastened into the soil so that it can take root while still attached to the parent plant. ➤ *vb* **1** to arrange or cut in layers. **2** to produce (a new plant) by preparing a layer from the parent plant.

layette *n* a complete set of clothes, blankets, etc for a new baby.

layman, laywoman or **layperson** *n* **1** someone who is not a member of the clergy. **2** someone who does not have specialized or professional knowledge of a particular subject.

lay-off *n* a dismissal of employees when there is no work available.

layout *n* **1** an arrangement or plan of how land, buildings, pages of a book, etc are to be set out. **2** the things displayed or arranged in this way. **3** the general appearance of a printed page.

laze *vb, intr* (*often* **laze about** or **around**) to be idle or lazy. ➤ *n* a period of time spent lazing.

lazy *adj* (**-ier, -iest**) **1** disinclined to work or do anything requiring effort. **2** idle. ○ **lazily** *adv.* ○ **laziness** *n*.

lazybones *n* (*pl* **lazybones**) *colloq* someone who is lazy.

lb *abbrev* **1** *libra* (Latin), a pound weight. **2** *cricket* leg bye.

lbw *abbrev, cricket* leg before wicket.

LCD *abbrev* **1** liquid crystal display. **2** (*also* **lcd**) lowest common denominator.

LCM or **lcm** *abbrev* lowest common multiple.

lea *n, poetic* a field, meadow or piece of arable or pasture land.

leach *vb* **1** *chem* to wash (a soluble substance) out of (a solid) by allowing a suitable liquid solvent to percolate through it. **2** to make (liquid) seep through (ash, soil, etc), in order to remove substances from that material.

lead¹ /liːd/ *vb* (**led**) **1** *tr & intr* to guide by going in front. **2** to precede. **3** to guide or make someone or something go in a certain direction by holding or pulling with the hand, etc. **4** to guide. **5** to conduct. **6** to induce. **7** to cause to live or experience. **8** *tr & intr* to direct or be in control of something. **9** to cause someone to act, feel or think in a certain way. **10** to live, pass or experience: *to lead a miserable existence*. **11** *tr & intr* to go or take someone in a certain direction: *The road leads to the village*. **12** *intr* (**lead to sth**) to result in it. **13** *tr & intr* to be foremost or first; to be the most important or influential in (a group, etc). **14** *intr* (*usu* **lead with** or **on**) of a newspaper: to have (a particular story) as its most important article: *The tabloids all lead with the latest scandal*. **15** *tr & intr, cards* to begin a round of cards by playing (the first card, esp of a particular suit). ➤ *n* **1** an instance of guidance given by leading. **2** the first, leading or most prominent place; leadership. **3** the amount by which someone or something is in front of others in a race, contest, etc. **4** a strap or chain for leading or holding a dog, etc. **5** an initial clue or piece of information which might help solve a problem, mystery, etc. **6** the principal part in a play, film, etc; the actor playing this role. **7** the most important story in a newspaper. **8** a precedent or example. **9** precedence. **10** an indication. **11** direction. **12** initiative. **13** a wire or conductor taking electricity from a source to an appliance. **14** *cards* the act or right of playing first, the first card played or the turn of someone who plays first. **15** the first player in some team sports and games. ◊ **lead off** to begin. **lead sb on 1** to persuade them to go further than intended. **2** to deceive or mislead them. **lead up to sth 1** to approach (a topic of conversation, etc) reluctantly or by gradual steps or stages. **2** to be an underlying cause of it.

lead² /lɛd/ *n* **1** a soft, heavy, bluish-grey, highly toxic metallic element used in building and in the production of numerous alloys. **2** graphite. **3** a thin stick of graphite, or some other coloured substance, used in pencils. **4** a lump of lead used for measuring the depth of the water, esp at sea. **5** (**leads**) a sheet of lead for covering roofs; a roof covered with lead sheets. **6** a lead frame for a small window-pane, eg in stained glass windows. ➤ *vb* **1** to fit or surround with lead. **2** to cover or weight with lead. **3** to set (eg window-panes) in lead.

leaden *adj* **1** made of lead. **2** dull grey in colour. **3** heavy or slow. **4** depressing; dull.

leader *n* **1** someone or something that leads or guides others. **2** someone who organizes or is in charge of a group. **3** *Brit* the principal violinist in an orchestra. **4** *Brit* an article in a newspaper, etc written to express the opinions of the editor. **5** a short blank strip at the beginning and end of a film or tape. **6** a long shoot growing from the stem or branch of a plant. ○ **leadership** *n*.

lead-in /ˈliːd-/ *n* an introduction, opening, etc.

leading¹ /ˈliːdɪŋ/ *adj* chief; most important.

leading² /ˈlɛdɪŋ/ *n, printing* a thin strip of metal used to produce a space between lines of metal type.

leading aircraftman or **leading aircraftwoman** *n* a man or woman with the rank above aircraftman or aircraftwoman.

leading light *n* someone who is very important and influential in a particular field or subject.

leading question *n* a question asked in such a way as to suggest the answer wanted.

leaf *n* (**leaves**) **1** an expanded outgrowth, usu green and flattened, from the stem of a green plant. **2** anything like a leaf, such as a scale or a petal. **3** leaves regarded collectively. **4** a single sheet of paper forming two pages in a book. **5** a very thin sheet of metal. **6** a hinged or sliding extra part or flap on a table, door, etc. ➤ *vb, intr* **1** of plants: to produce leaves. **2** (**leaf through sth**) to turn the pages of (a book, magazine, etc) quickly and cursorily. ✦ **turn over a new leaf** to begin a new and better way of behaving or working.

leaflet *n* **1** a single sheet of paper, or several sheets of paper folded together, giving information, advertising products, etc, usu given away free. **2** a small or immature leaf. **3** a division of a compound leaf. ➤ *vb* (**leafleted, leafleting**) *tr & intr* to distribute leaflets.

leaf mould *n* earth formed from rotted leaves, used as a compost for plants.

leafy *adj* (**-ier, -iest**) **1** having or covered with leaves. **2** shaded by leaves. **3** like a leaf.

league¹ *n* **1** a union of people, nations, etc formed for the benefit of the members. **2** a group of sports clubs which compete over a period for a championship. **3** a class or group, considered in terms of ability, importance, etc. ✦ **in league with sb** acting or planning with them, usu for some underhand purpose.

league² *n, old use* a unit of distance, usu taken to be about 4.8km (3 miles).

league table *n* **1** a list where people or clubs are placed according to performance or points gained. **2** any grouping where relative success or importance is compared or monitored.

leak *n* **1 a** an unwanted crack or hole in a container, pipe, etc where liquid or gas can pass in or out; **b** the act or fact of liquid or gas escaping in this way; **c** liquid or gas which has escaped in this way. **2 a** a revelation of secret information, esp when unauthorized; **b** information revealed in this way; **c** someone who reveals information in this way. ➤ *vb* **1 a** *intr* of liquid, gas, etc: to pass accidentally in or out of an unwanted crack or hole; **b** to allow (liquid, gas, etc) to pass accidentally in or out. **2 a** to reveal (secret information) without authorization; **b** *intr* of secret information: to become known. ○ **leaky** *adj*. ✦ **have** or **take a leak** *slang* to urinate.

leakage *n* **1** an act or instance of leaking. **2** something that enters or escapes through a leak.

lean¹ *vb* (**leant** or **leaned**) **1** *tr & intr* to slope or be placed in a sloping position. **2** *tr & intr* to rest or be rested against something for support. **3** *intr* (usu **lean towards**) to have an inclination to, a preference for or tendency towards. ➤ *n* an act or condition of leaning.

lean² *adj* **1** of a person or animal: thin. **2** of meat: containing little or no fat. **3** producing very little food, money, etc: *lean years.* ➤ *n* meat with little or no fat. ○ **leanness** *n*.

leaning *n* a liking or preference.

lean-to *n* (**lean-tos**) a shed built against another building or a wall.

leap *vb* (**leapt** or **leaped**) **1** *intr* to jump or spring suddenly or with force. **2** to jump over something. **3** *intr* of prices: to go up by a large amount suddenly and quickly. ➤ *n* an act of leaping or jumping. ✦ **by leaps and bounds** extremely rapidly. **a leap in the dark** an action, decision, etc whose results cannot be guessed in advance. ◊ **leap at sth** *colloq* to accept it eagerly.

leapfrog *n* a children's game in which each player in turn jumps over the back of the player in front. ➤ *vb* (**leapfrogged, leapfrogging**) **1** to jump over (someone's back) in this way. **2** to advance past someone or something.

leap year *n* a year, occurring once in every four years, of 366 days, with an extra day on 29 February.

learn *vb* (**learnt** or **learned**) **1** *tr & intr* (often **learn about** or **of sth**) to be or become informed of or to hear of something. **2** *tr & intr* to gain knowledge of or skill in something through study, teaching, instruction or experience. **3** to get to know by heart. ○ **learner** *n*.

learned /'lɜːnɪd/ *adj* **1** having great knowledge or learning, esp through years of study. **2** scholarly.

learning *n* knowledge gained through study.

lease *n* a contract by which the owner of a house, land, etc agrees to let someone else use it for a stated period of time in return for payment. ➤ *vb* **1** of an owner: to allow someone else to use (a house, land, etc) under the terms of a lease. **2** of an occupier: to borrow (a house, land, etc) from the owner under the terms of a lease. ○ **leaser** *n* a LESSEE. ♦ **a new lease of life** a longer or better life or period of usefulness than might have been expected.

leasehold *n* **1** the holding of land or buildings by lease. **2** the land or buildings held by lease. Compare FREEHOLD. ○ **leaseholder** *n*.

leash *n* a strip of leather or chain used for leading or holding a dog or other animal. ➤ *vb* **1** to put a leash on (a dog, etc). **2** to control or restrain. ♦ **straining at the leash** impatient or eager to begin.

least *adj* smallest; slightest. ➤ *adv* in the smallest or lowest degree. ➤ *pron* the smallest amount: *He has least to offer.* ♦ **at least 1** if nothing else; at any rate. **2** not less than: *at least half an hour late.* **not in the least** or **not in the least bit** not at all. **the least** the minimum: *The least you could do is visit from time to time.*

leather *n* **1** the skin of an animal made smooth by tanning. **2** a small piece of leather for polishing or cleaning. **3** (*usu* **leathers**) clothes made of leather, esp as worn by motorcyclists. ➤ *vb* **1** to cover or polish with leather. **2** *colloq or dialect* to thrash.

leathery *adj* **1** tough. **2** looking or feeling like leather.

leave¹ *vb* (**left**) **1** *intr* to go away from someone or somewhere. **2** to allow something to remain behind, esp by mistake: *I left the keys at home.* **3** to move out of (an area). **4** to abandon. **5** to resign or quit. **6** to allow someone or something to be or remain in a particular state, etc: *leave the window open.* **7** to deliver to or deposit: *I'll leave the keys with a neighbour.* **8** to cause: *It may leave a scar.* **9** to have as a remainder: *Three minus one leaves two.* **10** to make a gift of in a will: *She left all her money to charity.* **11** to be survived by: *He leaves a wife and daughter.* **12** to cause (esp food or drink) to remain unfinished: *She left half her dinner.* **13** to hand or turn something over to someone else: *I left the driving to her.* ♦ **leave sb** or **sth alone** to allow them or it to remain undisturbed. ◊ **leave sb** or **sth behind 1** to go without taking them or it, either intentionally or accidentally. **2** to advance faster than them. **leave off sth** to stop doing it. **leave sb** or **sth out** to exclude or omit them or it.

leave² *n* **1** permission to do something. **2 a** permission to be absent, esp from work or military duties; **b** permitted absence from work or mil-

itary duties; **c** the length of time this lasts: *a week's leave.* ♦ **on leave** officially absent from work. **take one's leave** *formal, old use* to depart.

leaven /'lɛvən/ *n* **1** a substance, esp yeast, added to dough to make it rise. **2** anything which is an influence and causes change. ➤ *vb* **1** to cause (dough) to rise with leaven. **2** to influence or cause change in something.

leaves *pl of* LEAF

leavings *pl n, colloq* things which are left over.

lecherous *adj* having or showing great or excessive sexual desire, esp in ways which are offensive. ○ **lecher** *n*. ○ **lechery** *n*.

lecithin /'lɛsɪθɪn/ *n, biochem* an organic chemical compound that is a major component of cell membranes in higher animals and plants, and is used in foods, pharmaceuticals, cosmetics and paints.

lectern *n* a stand with a sloping surface for holding a book, notes, etc for someone to read from, esp in a church or lecture-hall.

lecture *n* **1** a formal talk on a particular subject given to an audience. **2** a lesson or period of instruction, esp as delivered at a college or university. **3** a long and tedious scolding or warning. ➤ *vb* **1** *tr & intr* to give or read a lecture or lectures (to a group of people). **2** to scold someone at length. **3** to instruct by lectures, esp in a college or university. ○ **lecturer** *n*. ○ **lectureship** *n*.

LED *abbrev, electronics* light-emitting diode, a semiconductor diode used in the displays of calculators, digital watches, etc.

ledge *n* **1** a narrow horizontal shelf or shelf-like part. **2** a ridge or shelf of rock, esp one on a mountain side or under the sea.

ledger *n* the chief book of accounts of an office or shop, in which details of all transactions are recorded.

ledger line or **leger line** *n, mus* a short line added above or below a musical stave on which to mark a note higher or lower than the stave allows.

lee *n* **1** shelter given by a neighbouring object. **2** the sheltered side, away from the wind.

leech *n* **1** a worm with suckers at each end, esp a blood-sucking parasite formerly used medicinally. **2** a person who befriends another in the hope of personal gain.

leek *n* a long thin vegetable with broad flat leaves and a white base, closely related to the onion.

leer *n* a lecherous look or grin. ➤ *vb, intr* to look or grin lecherously.

lees *pl n* sediment at the bottom of wine bottles, etc.

leeward *naut, adj, adv* in or towards the direction in which the wind blows. ➤ *n* the sheltered side.

leeway *n* **1** scope for freedom of movement or action. **2** *naut* a ship's drift sideways.

left¹ *adj* **1** referring, relating to or indicating the side facing west from the point of view of someone or something facing north. **2** relatively liberal, democratic or progressive. **3** inclined towards socialism or communism. ➤ *adv* on or towards the left side. ➤ *n* **1** the left side, part, direction, etc. **2** the region to the left side. **3** (**the Left**) **a** political parties, political parties, etc in favour of socialism; **b** the members of any political party that holds the most progressive, democratic, socialist, radical or actively innovating views. **4** a blow with the left hand. **5** a glove, shoe, etc which fits the left hand or foot. **6** a turning to the left.

left² *past tense, past participle of* LEAVE¹

left-hand *adj* **1** relating to, on or towards the left. **2** done with the left hand.

left-handed *adj* **1** having the left hand stronger and more skilful than the right. **2** for use by left-handed people, or the left hand. **3** awkward; clumsy. **4** of compliments, etc: dubious or ambiguous. **5** anti-clockwise.

leftism *n* principles and policies of the political left. ○ **leftist** *n, adj.*

left-luggage *n* (*in full* **left-luggage office**) in an airport or a railway or coach station: an area with lockers where luggage can be stored for collection at a later time.

leftover *adj* not used up or not eaten. ➤ *n* (**leftovers**) food that remains uneaten.

left wing *n* **1** the members of a political party or group who are most inclined towards a socialist viewpoint. **2** *sport* **a** the extreme left side of a pitch or team in a field game; **b** (*also* **left-winger**) a player playing on this side. ○ **left-wing** *adj.*

lefty *n* (*-ies*) *colloq, often derog* **1** a person with socialist leanings. **2** a left-handed person.

leg *n* **1** one of the limbs on which animals, birds and people walk and stand. **2** an animal's or bird's leg used as food. **3** the part of a piece of clothing that covers one of these limbs. **4** a long narrow support of a table, chair, etc. **5** one stage in a journey. **6** a section of a competition or lap of a race. **7** *cricket* (*also* **leg side**) the side of the field that is to the left of a right-handed batsman or to the right of a left-handed batsman. **8** a branch or limb of a forked or jointed object. ◆ **leg it** *colloq* to walk briskly, to run or dash away. **not have a leg to stand on** *colloq* to have no way of excusing behaviour or supporting an argument, etc. **pull sb's leg** *colloq* to try to make them believe something which is not true.

legacy *n* (*-ies*) **1** an amount of property or money left in a will. **2** something handed on or left unfinished by a past owner or predecessor: *a legacy of mismanagement.*

legal *adj* **1** allowed by the law. **2** referring or relating to the law or lawyers. **3** created by law. ○ **legally** *adv.*

legal aid *n* financial assistance from public funds for those who cannot afford to pay for legal advice or proceedings.

legalese *n* technical legal jargon.

legalism *n* the tendency to observe the letter or form of the law rather than the spirit.

○ **legalist** *n, adj.* ○ **legalistic** *adj.*

legality *n* (*-ies*) **1** the state of being legal. **2** a legal obligation.

legalize or **-ise** *vb* to make something legal or lawful. ○ **legalization** *n.*

legal tender *n* currency which, by law, must be accepted in payment of a debt.

legate *n* an ambassador or representative, esp from the Pope.

legatee *n* the recipient of a legacy.

legation *n* **1** a diplomatic mission or group of delegates. **2** the official residence of such a mission or group.

legato /lɪˈɡɑːtoʊ/ *mus, adv* smoothly, with the notes running into each other. ➤ *adj* smooth and flowing. ➤ *n* **1** a piece of music to be played in this way. **2** a legato style of playing.

leg before wicket *n, cricket* a way of being given out for having prevented the ball from hitting the wicket with any part of the body other than the hand.

leg bye *n, cricket* a run made when the ball touches any part of the batsman's body apart from the hand.

legend *n* **1** a traditional story which is popularly regarded as true, but not confirmed as such. **2** such stories collectively. **3** someone famous about whom popularly believed stories are told. **4** words accompanying a map, picture, etc which explain the symbols used. **5** an inscription on a coin, medal or coat of arms.

legendary *adj* **1** relating to or in the nature of legend. **2** described or spoken about in legend. **3** *colloq* very famous.

leger line see LEDGER LINE

leggings *pl n* **1** close-fitting stretch coverings for the legs, worn by girls and women. **2** outer and extra protective coverings for the lower legs.

leggy *adj* (*-ier, -iest*) **1** of a woman: having attractively long slim legs. **2** of a plant: having a long stem.

legible *adj* esp of handwriting: clear enough to be read. ○ **legibly** *adv.*

legion *n* **1** *hist* a unit in the ancient Roman army, containing between three and six thousand soldiers. **2** a very great number. **3** a military force: *the French Foreign Legion.* ➤ *adj* great in number: *Books on this subject are legion.* ○ **legionary** *adj, n* (*-ies*).

legionnaire *n* a member of a legion.

Legionnaires' Disease or **Legionnaire's Disease** *n, pathol* a severe and sometimes fatal disease caused by a bacterial infection of the lungs.

legislate *vb, intr* to make laws. ○ **legislator** *n.* ◆ **legislate for sth** to make provision for it.

legislation *n* **1** the process of legislating. **2** a group of laws.

legislative *adj* **1** relating to or concerned with law-making. **2** having the power to make laws: *a legislative assembly.*

legislature *n* the part of the government which has the power to make laws.

legitimate adj /lɪˈdʒɪtɪmət/ **1** lawful. **2** born to parents who are married to each other. **3** of an argument, conclusion, etc: reasonable or logical. ➤ vb /-meɪt/ to make lawful or legitimate. ○ **legitimacy** n. ○ **legitimately** adv. ○ **legitimation** n.

legitimize or **-ise** vb **1** to make legitimate. **2** to make (an argument, etc) valid. ○ **legitimization** n.

legless adj **1** colloq very drunk. **2** having no legs.

Lego n, trademark a toy construction system consisting of small plastic bricks, etc which can be fastened together.

leg-pull n, colloq a joking attempt to make someone believe something which is not true.

legroom n the amount of space available for someone's legs, esp in a confined area such as a car, etc.

legume n **1** any of a family of flowering plants with fruit in the form of a pod, eg pea, bean, lentil. **2** the fruit of such a plant, containing edible seeds rich in protein. **3** an edible seed of this plant. ○ **leguminous** adj.

lei /leɪ/ n a Polynesian garland of flowers worn round the neck.

leisure n free time, esp when a person can relax, pursue a hobby, etc. ♦ **at leisure 1** not occupied. **2** without hurrying. **at one's leisure** at a time one finds convenient.

leisure centre n a centre providing sport and recreational facilities.

leisurely adj not hurried. ➤ adv without hurrying. ○ **leisureliness** n.

leitmotif or **leitmotiv** /ˈlaɪtməʊtiːf/ n a recurring theme, image, etc in a piece of music, novel, etc that is associated with a particular person, idea, feeling, etc.

lemming n **1** a small rodent which occasionally participates in huge migrations once popularly but erroneously believed to result in mass drownings at sea. **2** someone who blindly follows others on a course to predictable disaster.

lemon n **1** a small oval citrus fruit with a yellow rind enclosing sour-tasting juicy flesh. **2** the small evergreen tree that produces this fruit. **3** a pale yellow colour. **4** colloq someone or something thought of as worthless, disappointing, unattractive or defective. ➤ adj **1** pale yellow in colour. **2** tasting of or flavoured with lemon. ○ **lemony** adj.

lemonade n a fizzy or still drink flavoured with or made from lemons.

lemon curd or **lemon cheese** n a thick creamy paste made from lemons, sugar, butter and egg.

lemon sole n a European FLATFISH used as food.

lemur n a nocturnal tree-dwelling PRIMATE, now confined to Madagascar, with large eyes and a long bushy tail.

lend vb (**lent**) **1** to allow someone to use something on the understanding that it (or its equivalent) will be returned. **2** to give someone

the use of (usu money), esp in return for interest paid on it. **3** to give or add (interest, beauty, etc) to: The lighting lends a calming atmosphere. ○ **lender** n. ♦ **lend a hand** to help. **lend an ear** to listen. **lend itself to sth** to be suitable for (a purpose): The hall lends itself to staging live bands.

length n **1** the distance from one end of an object to the other, normally the longest dimension. Compare BREADTH. **2** often in compounds the distance something extends. **3** the quality of being long. **4** a long piece of something or a stated amount of something long: a length of rope. **5** the extent from end to end of a horse, boat, etc, as a way of measuring one participant's lead over another in a race: She won by two lengths. **6** (often in length) a stretch or extent. **7** swimming **a** the longer measurement of a swimming pool; **b** this distance swum. **8 a** an extent of time; **b** phonetics, music the amount of time a vowel, syllable, note, etc sounds. ♦ **at length 1** at last. **2** in great detail.

lengthen vb, tr & intr to make or become longer.

lengthways or **lengthwise** adv, adj in the direction of or according to something's length.

lengthy adj (**-ier, -iest**) **1** of great, often excessive, length. **2** of speech, etc: long and tedious. ○ **lengthily** adv. ○ **lengthiness** n.

lenient adj mild and tolerant, esp in punishing. ○ **lenience** or **leniency** n. ○ **leniently** adv.

lens n **1 a** an optical device consisting of a piece of glass, clear plastic, etc curved on one or both sides, used for converging or diverging a beam of light; **b** a contact lens. **2** in a camera: a mechanical equivalent of the lens of an eye which allows the image to fall on the photographer's eye or, when the shutter is open, on the film plane.

Lent n, Christianity the time, lasting from Ash Wednesday to Easter Sunday, of fasting or abstinence in remembrance of Christ's fast in the wilderness. ○ **Lenten** adj.

lentil n **1** a small orange, brown or green seed used as food. **2** a leguminous plant which produces these seeds.

lento mus, adv slowly. ➤ adj slow.

Leo n, astrol **a** the fifth sign of the zodiac; **b** a person born between 24 July and 23 August, under this sign.

leonine adj relating to or like a lion.

leopard n a large member of the cat family of Africa and Asia, with a black-spotted tawny coat or a completely black coat.

leopardess n a female leopard.

leotard n a stretchy one-piece tight-fitting garment worn for dancing, exercise, etc.

leper n **1** med someone who has leprosy. **2** derog someone who is avoided, esp on moral grounds.

lepidopterist n a person who studies butterflies and moths.

lepidopterous adj relating or belonging to the

order of insects that includes butterflies and moths. ○ **lepidopteran** adj, n.

leprechaun n, Irish folklore a small mischievous elf.

leprosy n an infectious disease of the skin, mucous membranes and nerves which, before drug treatment was available, often led to severe disfigurement. ○ **leprous** adj.

lesbian n a woman who is sexually attracted to other women. ➢ adj for, relating to or referring to lesbians. ○ **lesbianism** n.

lesion n 1 an injury or wound. 2 pathol an abnormal change in the structure of an organ or tissue as a result of disease or injury.

less adj 1 smaller in size, quantity, duration, etc. 2 colloq fewer in number: smoke less cigarettes. ➢ adv not so much; to a smaller extent: He exercises less nowadays. ➢ pron a smaller amount or number: She tried to eat less. ➢ prep without; minus: £100 less the discount.

lessee n someone granted the use of property by lease.

lessen vb, tr & intr to make or become less.

lesser adj used in names, esp plant, animal and place names, to denote: smaller in size, quantity or importance: lesser celandine.

lesson n 1 an amount taught or learned at one time. 2 a period of teaching. 3 (**lessons**) instruction in a particular subject given over a period of time. 4 an experience or example which one should take as a warning or encouragement: Let that be a lesson to you. 5 a passage from the Bible read during a church service.

lessor n someone who rents out property by lease.

lest conj, formal or literary in case: speak quietly lest they hear us.

let¹ vb (let, letting) 1 a to allow, permit or cause: She let her daughter borrow the car, b used in commands, orders, warnings, etc: let him go. 2 Brit to give the use of (rooms, a building or land) in return for payment. 3 maths, philos used to suggest that a symbol or a hypothesis be understood as something: Let 'D' be the distance travelled. ➢ n, Brit 1 the leasing of a property, etc: We got the let of the cottage for £100 a week. 2 the period of time for which a property, etc is leased: a two-week let. ◆ **let alone** used to link alternatives so that disapproval, surprise, etc is emphasized: He didn't even clear the table let alone do the washing up. **let fly at sb** to attack them physically or verbally. **let go of sth** to release or stop holding it. **let oneself go** 1 to act without restraint. 2 to allow one's appearance, lifestyle, etc to deteriorate. **let sb alone** or **let sb be** to avoid disturbing or worrying them. **let sb off the hook** to free them from a responsibility, commitment or promise. **let sth drop** to make secret information, etc known, esp unintentionally. ◊ **let sb** or **sth down** 1 to disappoint or fail to help someone at a crucial time. 2 to lower them or it. 3 to allow the air to escape from (something in-

flated): let down the tyres. 4 to make longer: let the skirt down. **let sb in on sth** colloq to share a secret, etc with them. **let sb off** 1 to allow them to go without punishment, etc. 2 to release them from work, duties, etc. **let sth off** 1 to fire (a gun) or explode (a bomb, etc). 2 to release liquid or gas. **let sth out** 1 to enlarge it: She let out the waist of the jeans. 2 to emit (a sound): Jane let out a horrible scream. **let up** to stop or to become less strong or violent: The rain let up at last.

let² n, sport esp in racket games: an obstruction during service that requires the ball, etc to be served again. ◆ **without let or hindrance** without anything hindering or preventing action or progress.

let-down n a disappointment.

lethal adj causing or enough to cause death. ○ **lethally** adv.

lethargy n 1 lack of energy and vitality. 2 pathol a state of abnormal drowsiness and inactivity caused by inadequate rest, etc. ○ **lethargic** adj. ○ **lethargically** adv.

let-out n a chance to escape or avoid keeping an agreement, contract, etc.

let's contraction let us, used esp in suggestions: let's go.

letter n 1 a conventional written or printed mark, usu part of an alphabet, used to represent a speech sound or sounds. 2 a written or printed message normally sent by post in an envelope. 3 (**the letter**) the strict literal meaning of words, esp in legal documents, or how such words can be interpreted: according to the letter of the law. 4 printing type. ➢ vb to write or mark letters on. ○ **lettering** n. ◆ **to the letter** exactly; in every detail: I followed the instructions to the letter.

letter bomb n an envelope containing a device that is designed to explode when someone opens it.

letter box n, Brit 1 a slot in a door through which letters are delivered. 2 (also **pillar box**) a large box, with a slot in the front, for people to post letters.

letterhead n a printed heading on notepaper giving a company's or an individual's name, address, etc.

letter of credit n (**letters of credit**) a letter authorizing a bank, etc to issue a person with credit or money up to a set amount.

letterpress n a technique of printing where ink is applied to raised surfaces and then pressed onto paper.

lettuce n a green plant with large edible leaves used in salads.

let-up n end; respite; relief.

leucocyte or **leukocyte** /'luːkəsaɪt/ n, anat a white blood cell or CORPUSCLE.

leukaemia or (esp US) **leukemia** /luːˈkiːmɪə/ n a malignant disease which affects the bone marrow and other blood-forming organs, resulting in the overproduction of abnormal white blood cells.

levee[1] n **1** US esp on the Lower Mississippi: the natural embankment of silt and sand that is deposited along the banks of a river during flooding. **2** an artificial embankment constructed along a watercourse. **3** a quay.

levee[2] n, hist the first official meeting of a sovereign or other high-ranking person after they have risen from bed.

level n **1** a horizontal plane or line. **2** a specified height, value or extent. **3** position, status or importance in a scale of values. **4** a stage or degree of progress. **5** any device for checking whether a surface is horizontal or not: *spirit level.* **6** (**the level**) a flat area of land. **7** a storey of a building. ➢ adj (**leveller, levellest**) **1** having a flat smooth even surface. **2** horizontal. **3** having or being at the same height (as something else). **4** having the same standard (as something else); equal. **5** steady; constant; regular. **6** *cookery* of measurements: filled so as to be even with the rim. ➢ vb (**levelled, levelling**) **1** to make flat, smooth or horizontal. **2** to make equal. **3** to pull down or demolish. **4** (*often* **level sth at sb**) to point (a gun, etc) at them. **5** (*usu* **level sth at** or **against sb**) to direct (an accusation, criticism, etc) at them. **6** *intr, colloq* to speak honestly with someone: *Let me level with you – I'm leaving.* ◆ **do one's level best** *colloq* to make the greatest possible effort. **on the level** *slang* honest; genuine. ◊ **level off** or **level sth off** to make become flat, even, steady, regular, etc. **level out** or **level sth out** to make or become level.

level crossing n, Brit, Aust & NZ a place where a road and a railway line, or two railway lines, cross at the same level.

level-headed adj sensible; well-balanced.

leveller n someone or something that flattens or makes equal.

lever n **1** a simple device for lifting and moving heavy loads, consisting of a rigid bar supported by and pivoting about a FULCRUM at some point along its length, so that an effort applied at one point can be used to move an object (the load) at another point. **2** a strong bar for moving heavy objects, prising things open, etc. **3** a handle for operating a machine. **4** anything that can be used to gain an advantage. ➢ vb to move or open using a lever.

leverage n **1** the mechanical power or advantage gained through using a lever. **2** power or advantage.

leveret n a young hare.

leviathan or **Leviathan** /lə'vaɪəθən/ n **1** Bible a sea monster. **2** anything which is large or powerful.

levitate vb, tr & intr to float or cause to float in the air, esp by invoking some supernatural power. ◊ **levitation** n.

levity n a lack of seriousness.

levy vb (**levies, levied**) **1** to calculate and then collect (a tax, etc). **2** to raise (an army or the money needed to fund a war). ➢ n (**-ies**) **1** the collection of a tax, etc. **2** the amount of money raised by collecting a tax, etc. **3** soldiers or money collected in preparation for a war.

lewd adj **1** feeling, expressing or designed to stimulate crude sexual desire. **2** obscene; indecent. ◊ **lewdly** adv. ◊ **lewdness** n.

lexical adj **1** referring or relating to the words in a language. **2** referring or relating to a lexicon. ◊ **lexically** adv.

lexicography n the writing, compiling and editing of dictionaries. ◊ **lexicographer** n.

lexicon n **1** a dictionary, esp one for Arabic, Greek, Hebrew or Syriac. **2** the vocabulary of terms as used in a particular branch of knowledge or by a particular person, group, etc.

Li symbol, chem lithium.

liability n (**-ies**) **1** the state of being legally liable or responsible for something. **2** a debt or obligation. **3** someone or something one is responsible for. **4** someone or something that is a problem or that causes a problem.

liable adj **1** legally bound or responsible. **2** given or inclined: *She is liable to outbursts of temper.* **3** likely. **4** susceptible.

liaise vb, tr & intr (*usu* **liaise with** or **between**) to communicate with or be in contact with someone.

liaison n **1** communication or co-operation between individuals or groups. **2** an adulterous or illicit sexual or romantic relationship.

liar n someone who tells lies.

lib n, colloq used esp in the names of movements: short form of **liberation** (see under LIBERATE): *gay lib.*

libation /laɪ'beɪʃən/ n **1** the pouring out of wine, etc in honour of a god. **2** a drink so poured. **3** facetious an alcoholic drink.

libel n **1** Brit, law the publication of a statement in some permanent form which has the potential to damage someone's reputation and which is claimed to be false. **2** any false or potentially damaging description of someone. ➢ vb (**libelled, libelling** or US **libeled, libeling**) **1** law to publish a libellous statement about someone. **2** to accuse wrongly and spitefully. Compare SLANDER. ◊ **libellous** or (US) **libelous** adj.

liberal adj **1** given or giving generously. **2** tolerant of different opinions. **3** lavish; extensive: *liberal glasses of wine.* **4** in favour of social and political reform, progressive. **5** (**Liberal**) belonging to the LIBERAL PARTY. **6** of education: aiming to develop general cultural interests and to broaden the mind, as opposed to being technically or professionally orientated. **7** free from restraint; not rigorous: *a liberal interpretation.* ➢ n **1** someone who has liberal views, either politically or in general. **2** (**Liberal**) a member or supporter of the LIBERAL PARTY. ◊ **liberalism** n. ◊ **liberally** adv.

Liberal Democrat or **Lib Dem** n, Brit pol a member or supporter of a political party (the **Liberal Democrats**), slightly to the left of centre.

liberality n **1** the quality of being generous. **2** the quality of being open-minded.

liberalize or **-ise** *vb, tr & intr* to make or become more liberal or less strict. ○ **liberalization** *n*.

Liberal Party *n* 1 *Brit* a political party advocating liberal policies and which in 1989 became the LIBERAL DEMOCRATS. **2** any similar political party in other countries.

liberate *vb, tr & intr* **1** to set free. **2** to free (a country from enemy occupation). **3** to free from accepted moral or social conventions or from traditional gender-based roles. ○ **liberation** *n*. ○ **liberator** *n*.

liberated *adj* **1** not bound by traditional ideas about sexuality, morality, etc. **2** freed from enemy occupation.

libertarian *n* someone who believes that people should be completely free to express themselves as they like.

libertine *n, old use* someone who is not bound by the generally accepted codes of morality.

liberty *n* (*-ies*) **1** freedom from captivity, slavery, restrictions, etc. **2** freedom to act and think as one pleases. **3** (*usu* **liberties**) a natural right or privilege. **4** an action or utterance thought of as over-familiar or presumptuous. ♦ **at liberty** **1** free from prison or control; **2** allowed or permitted: *at liberty to use the car*. **take liberties** **1** to treat someone with too much familiarity. **2** to act in an unauthorized way; to be deliberately inaccurate. **take the liberty to** or **of** to do or venture to do something, usu without permission.

libidinous /lɪˈbɪdɪnəs/ *adj* lustful. ○ **libidinously** *adv*.

libido /lɪˈbiːdəʊ/ *n* sexual desire. ○ **libidinal** *adj*.

Libra *n, astrol* **a** the seventh sign of the zodiac; **b** a person born between 24 September and 22 October, under this sign.

librarian *n* someone who works in or is in charge of a library. ○ **librarianship** *n*.

library *n* (*-ies*) **1** a room, rooms or building where books, films, records, videos, etc are kept for study, reference, reading or for lending. **2** a collection of books, films, records, videos, etc for public or private use. **3** a group of books published as a series. **4** *comput* a collection of computer programs, software, files, etc.

libretto *n* (**libretti** /lɪˈbrɛtiː/ or **librettos**) the words or text of an opera, oratorio or musical. ○ **librettist** *n*.

lice *pl of* LOUSE

licence or (*US*) **license** *n* **1** an official document that allows someone to own something or that gives permission to do something. **2** permission or leave in general. **3** excessive freedom of action or speech. **4** a departure from a rule or convention, esp by writers and artists, for effect: *poetic licence*.

license *vb* **1** to give a licence or permit for something. **2** to give a licence or permit to someone to do something such as drive, get married, etc.

licensee *n* someone who has been given a licence, esp to sell alcohol.

licentiate *n* someone who holds a certificate of competence to practise a profession.

licentious *adj* immoral or promiscuous. ○ **licentiousness** *n*.

lichee see LYCHEE

lichen /ˈlaɪkən, ˈlɪtʃən/ *n* a primitive plant form, usu found on rocks, walls or tree trunks.

licit *adj* lawful; permitted.

lick *vb* **1** to pass the tongue over in order to moisten, taste or clean. **2** of flames, etc: to flicker over or around. **3** *colloq* to defeat. **4** *colloq* to beat or hit repeatedly. ➤ *n* **1** an act of licking with the tongue. **2** *colloq* a small amount. **3** *colloq* a quick speed: *He drove away at some lick*. **4** *colloq* a sharp blow. ♦ **lick into shape** *colloq* to make more efficient or satisfactory. **lick one's wounds** to recover after having been thoroughly defeated or humiliated.

licorice see LIQUORICE

lid *n* **1** a removable or hinged cover for a pot, box, etc. **2** an eyelid. ○ **lidded** *adj*. ♦ **put the lid on it 1** to put an end to something. **2** to be the last in a series of injustices or misfortunes: *and the flat tyre just put the lid on it*.

lido /ˈliːdəʊ/ *n* a public open-air swimming pool.

lie¹ *n* **1** a false statement made with the intention of deceiving. **2** anything misleading; a fraud: *He lived a lie*. ➤ *vb* (**lied**, **lying**) *intr* **1** to say things that are not true with the intention of deceiving. **2** to give a wrong or false impression: *The camera never lies*. ♦ **give the lie to** to show (a statement, etc) to be false.

lie² *vb* (*past tense* **lay**, *past participle* **lain**, *present participle* **lying**) *intr* **1** to be in or take on a flat or more or less horizontal position on a supporting surface. **2** to be situated: *The village lies to the west of here*. **3** to stretch or be spread out to view: *The harbour lay before us*. **4** of subjects for discussion: to remain undiscussed: *let matters lie*. **5** **a** to be or remain in a particular state: *to lie dormant*; **b** to be buried: *Jim's remains lie in a cemetery in Paris*. **6** (*usu* **lie in sth**) to consist of it or have it as an essential part: *Success lies in hard work*. **7** (**lie with sb**) of a duty or responsibility: to rest with them. ➤ *n* **1** **a** the way or direction in which something is lying; **b** *golf* the relative position of a ball that has been struck: *a good lie*. **2** an animal's or bird's hiding place. ♦ **lie in wait** (**for sb** or **sth**) to hide before ambushing them or it. **lie low** to stay quiet or hidden. **take sth lying down** *often with negatives* to accept a rebuke or disappointment, etc meekly and without protest. ◊ **lie down** to take a flat or horizontal position, esp to sleep or have a short rest. **lie in** to stay in bed later than usual.

> **lie** See note at **lay**.

lied /liːd; *German* liːt/ *n* (**lieder** /ˈliːdə(r)/; *German* /ˈliːdə/) a German song for solo voice and piano accompaniment.

lie detector *n* a machine for measuring changes in someone's blood pressure, perspiration, pulse, etc, taken as indications that they are giving dishonest replies to questions.

lie-down *n* a short rest taken lying down.

liege /liːdʒ/ *adj* **1** of a feudal lord: entitled to receive service, etc from a vassal. **2** of a vassal: bound to give service, etc to a feudal lord. ➤ *n* **1** (*also* **liege lord**) a feudal superior, lord or sovereign. **2** (*also* **liege man**) a feudal subject or vassal.

lie-in *n* a longer than usual stay in bed.

lien /liːn/ *n, law* a right to keep someone's property until a debt has been paid.

lie of the land *n* the current state of affairs.

lieu /ljuː, luː/ *n* **1** (**in lieu**) instead. **2** (**in lieu of**) in place of.

Lieut or **Lieut.** *abbrev* Lieutenant.

lieutenant /lɛfˈtɛnənt; *US* luː-/ *n* **1** a deputy acting for a superior. **2** an army officer of the rank below captain. **3** a naval officer of the rank below lieutenant commander. **4** *US* a police officer or fireman of the rank below captain.

lieutenant colonel *n* an army officer of the rank below colonel.

lieutenant commander *n* a naval officer of the rank below commander.

lieutenant general *n* an army officer of the rank below general.

life *n* (*lives*) **1 a** the quality or state which distinguishes living animals and plants from dead ones; **b** collectively, the characteristics which distinguish living animals, plants, etc from inanimate objects, esp the ability to grow, develop and reproduce. **2 a** the period between birth and death; **b** the period between birth and the present time: *She has led a very sheltered life;* **c** the period between the present time and death: *He had his life carefully mapped out.* **3** the length of time a thing exists or is able to function: *a long shelf life.* **4** living things in general or as a group: *marine life.* **5** a living thing, esp a human: *many lives lost in war.* **6** a way or manner of living: *He leads a very busy life.* **7** *in compounds* a specified aspect of someone's life: *her love-life.* **8** liveliness: *full of life.* **9** a source of liveliness, energy or high spirits: *the life and soul of the party.* **10** a written account of someone's life. **11** *colloq* a LIFE SENTENCE. ◆ **for life** until death: *friends for life.* **to the life** exactly like the original.

life-and-death *adj* extremely serious or critical.

life assurance or **life insurance** *n* an insurance policy that guarantees that a sum of money will be paid to the policyholder when they reach a certain age, or to the policyholder's named dependant(s) if the policyholder dies before that age.

lifebelt *n* a ring or belt used to support someone who is in danger of drowning.

lifeblood *n* **1** the blood necessary for life. **2** anything that is an essential part or factor.

lifeboat *n* **1** a boat for rescuing people who are in trouble at sea. **2** a small boat carried on a larger ship for use in emergencies.

lifebuoy *n* a float for supporting someone in the water until they are rescued.

life cycle *n* the sequence of stages through which a living organism passes in each generation.

lifeguard *n* an expert swimmer employed at a swimming pool or beach to rescue people in danger of drowning.

life jacket *n* an inflatable sleeveless jacket for supporting someone in the water.

lifeless *adj* **1** dead. **2** unconscious. **3** having no energy or vivacity.

lifelike *adj* of a portrait, etc: very like the person or thing represented.

lifeline *n* **1** a rope for support in dangerous operations or for saving lives. **2** a vital means of communication or support.

lifelong *adj* lasting the whole length of someone's life.

life peer or **life peeress** *n* a peer whose title is not hereditary. ○ **life peerage** *n.*

life raft *n* a raft kept on a ship, for use in emergencies.

life sciences *pl n* the branches of science concerned with the study of living organisms, eg biochemistry, genetics, etc.

life sentence *n, Brit* a prison sentence that is for the rest of the offender's life, but which is often less than that.

life-size or **life-sized** *adj* of a copy, drawing, etc: having the same size as the original.

lifestyle *n* the particular way a group or individual lives.

life-support *adj* of machines, etc: allowing someone to remain alive, eg in an unfavourable environment such as space, or when seriously ill: *a life-support system.*

lifetime *n* the duration of someone's life.

lift *vb* **1** *tr & intr* to raise or rise to a higher position. **2** to move (esp one's eyes or face) upwards. **3** to take and carry away; to remove. **4** to raise to a better or more agreeable level: *It lifted my spirits.* **5** *intr* **a** of cloud, fog, etc: to clear; **b** of winds: to become less strong. **6** to remove or annul. **7** to dig up (potatoes, etc). **8** *colloq* to plagiarize from someone else's work or from published material. **9** *slang* to arrest. **10** *colloq* to steal. ➤ *n* **1** an act of lifting. **2** lifting power. **3** the upward force of the air on an aircraft, etc. **4** *Brit* a device for moving people and goods between floors of a building. **5** *Brit* a ride in a person's car or other vehicle, often given without payment as a favour. **6** a boost to the spirits.

lift-off *n* the vertical launching of a spacecraft or rocket.

ligament *n anat* a band of tough connective tissue that holds two bones together at a joint.

ligature *n* **1** anything that binds or ties. **2** *mus* a SLUR (*noun* sense 3b). **3** *printing* a character formed from two or more characters joined together, eg, æ.

light¹ n 1 a form of electromagnetic radiation that travels freely through space, and can be absorbed and reflected, esp that part of the spectrum which can be seen with the human eye. 2 any source of this, such as the sun, a lamp, a candle, etc. 3 an appearance of brightness; a gleam: *a light in the distance*. 4 (**the lights**) traffic lights. 5 the time during the day when it is daylight. 6 dawn. 7 a particular quality or amount of light: *a good light for taking photographs*. 8 a flame or spark for igniting. 9 a means of producing a flame for igniting, such as a match. 10 a way in which something is thought of or regarded: *I see the problem in a new light*. 11 a hint, clue or help towards understanding. 12 a glow in the eyes or on the face as a sign of liveliness, happiness or excitement. 13 someone who is well regarded in a particular field: *a leading light*. 14 an opening in a wall that lets in light, such as a window. ➢ *adj* 1 having light. 2 of a colour: pale. ➢ *vb* (*past tense & past participle* **lit** or **lighted**, *present participle* **lighting**) 1 to provide light for: *lit the stage*. 2 *tr & intr* to begin to burn or make something begin to burn: *light the fire*. 3 to guide or show someone (the way) using a light or torch. 4 *tr & intr* to make or become bright or sparkling with liveliness, happiness or excitement. ♦ **come to light** to be made known or discovered. **in a good** or **bad light** putting a favourable or unfavourable construction on something. **in the light of sth** taking it into consideration. **light at the end of the tunnel** an indication of success or completion. **lights out** 1 *mil* a bugle or trumpet call for lights to be put out. 2 the time at night when lights in a dormitory or barracks have to be put out. **see the light** 1 to understand something. 2 to have a religious conversion. **see the light of day** 1 to be born, discovered or produced. 2 to come to public notice. ◊ **light up** *colloq* to light (a cigarette, etc) and begin smoking.

light² *adj* 1 weighing little. 2 low in weight, amount or density: *light rain*. 3 not pressing heavily; gentle: *a light touch*. 4 easy to bear, suffer or do: *light work*. 5 weighing less than is correct or proper. 6 equipped with only hand-held weapons: *light infantry*. 7 without problems, sorrow, etc; cheerful: *a light heart*. 8 graceful and quick; nimble: *a light skip*. 9 not serious or profound, but for amusement only: *light reading*. 10 thoughtless or trivial: *a light remark*. 11 not thinking clearly or seriously; giddy: *a light head*. 12 easily digested: *a light meal*. 13 denoting a weight category in boxing, etc that is slightly below one of the standard categories: *light middleweight*. 14 of cakes, etc: spongy and well risen. 15 (*also* **lite**) of alcoholic drinks: low in alcohol. 16 (*also* **lite**) of food and non-alcoholic drinks: containing little fat and/or sugar. ➢ *adv* 1 in a light manner. 2 with little luggage: *travel light*. ○ **lightly** *adv*. ○ **lightness** *n*. ♦ **make light of sth** to treat it as unimportant or trivial.

light³ *vb* (*past tense & past participle* **lit** or **lighted**, *present participle* **lighting**) 1 of birds, etc: to come to rest after flight. 2 (**light on** or **upon sth**) to come upon or find it by chance: *I suddenly lit upon the idea*.

light bulb *n* a glass bulb with an electric filament which emits light when a current is passed through it.

lighten¹ *vb* 1 *tr & intr* to make or become brighter. 2 to cast light on. 3 *intr* to shine or glow.

lighten² *vb* 1 *tr & intr* to make or become less heavy. 2 *tr & intr* to make or become happier. 3 to make (a problem, unhappy mood, etc) less: *He tried to lighten her sadness*. ◊ **lighten up** *colloq* 1 to relax. 2 to become less serious, etc.

lighter¹ *n* a device for lighting cigarettes, etc.

lighter² *n* a large open boat used for transferring goods between ships, or between a ship and a wharf.

light-fingered *adj* having a habitual tendency to steal.

light-footed *adj* nimble; active.

light-headed *adj* having a dizzy feeling in the head.

light-hearted *adj* 1 of entertainment, etc: cheerful and amusing. 2 happy and carefree.

lighthouse *n* a building on the coast with a flashing light to guide ships or warn them of rocks, etc.

light industry *n* factories producing small or light goods.

lighting *n* 1 equipment for providing light. 2 light, usu of a specified kind: *subdued lighting*.

lighting-up time *n* the time of day when road vehicles must have their lights turned on.

lightning *n*, *meteorol* a bright flash of light produced by the discharge of static electricity between or within clouds, or between a cloud and the Earth's surface. ➢ *adj* very quick and sudden: *lightning speed*.

light pen *n* *comput* a light-sensitive pen-like device that can be used to generate or modify images and move them about on a computer screen by touching the screen with the device.

lights *pl n* the lungs of an animal, used as food.

lightship *n* a ship with a beacon, which acts as a lighthouse.

lightweight *adj* 1 light in weight. 2 *derog* having little importance or authority. 3 belonging to or relating to the lightweight class of boxing, etc. ➢ *n* 1 a person or thing of little physical weight. 2 *derog* a person or thing having little importance or authority. 3 a class for boxers, wrestlers and weightlifters of not more than a specified weight, for example 61.2kg (135 lb) in professional boxing. 4 a boxer, etc competing in one of these classes.

light year *n* the distance travelled by a beam of light in a vacuum in one year, equal to about 9.46 trillion km.

ligneous *adj* resembling or composed of wood.

lignite *n*, *geol* a soft brown low-grade form of coal, intermediate between peat and bituminous coal.

like¹ *adj* **1** similar: *as like as two peas*. **2** typical of: *It's just like them to forget*. **3** used in asking someone for a description of someone or something: *What's he like?* ➢ *prep* **1** in the same manner as: *to run like a deer*. **2** such as: *animals like cats and dogs*. ➢ *adv, colloq* approximately. ➢ *conj, colloq* **1** as if; as though: *It's like I've been here before*. **2** in the same way as: *She's not pretty like you are*. ➢ *n, usu preceded by a possessive pronoun*: the counterpart or equal of someone or something: *people of their like*. ◆ **the like a** things of the same kind: *TVs, radios and the like*; **b** with negatives and in questions anything similar: *We'll never see the like again*. **the likes of** *usu contemptuous* people or things such as: *She wouldn't have much to do with the likes of them*. **more like it a** nearer to what is wanted or required: *Tea? A brandy would be more like it*; **b** nearer to the truth: *He calls her his research assistant, but dogsbody is more like it*.

like² *vb* **1** to enjoy or be pleased with something. **2** to be fond of someone or something. **3** to prefer: *She likes her tea without sugar*. **4** to wish, or wish for: *if you like*. ➢ *n* (**likes**) things that someone has a preference for: *likes and dislikes*. ○ **likeable** or **likable** *adj*.

likelihood or **likeliness** *n* probability.

likely *adj* **1** probable. **2** suitable for a particular purpose: *a likely spot for a picnic*. **3** *ironic* credible: *a likely tale*. ➢ *adv* probably.

like-minded *adj* sharing a similar outlook, opinion, purpose, etc.

liken *vb* to compare or point to the similarities between (two things or people).

likeness *n* **1** a similarity: *a family likeness*. **2** *formerly* a portrait or formal photograph.

likewise *adv* **1** in the same or a similar manner. **2** also; in addition.

liking *n* **1** a fondness: *a liking for chocolates*. **2** taste: *Is it to your liking?*

lilac *n* **1** a small tree or shrub with white or pale pinkish-purple sweet-smelling flowers. **2** a pale pinkish-purple colour.

Lilliputian *n* someone or something very small. ➢ *adj* (*also* **lilliputian**) very small.

Lilo or **Li-lo** *n* (*Lilos*) *trademark* a type of inflatable mattress.

lilt *n* **1** a light graceful swinging rhythm. **2** a tune, song or voice with such a rhythm. **3** a springing quality in someone's walk. ➢ *vb, intr* to speak, sing or move with a lilt. ○ **lilting** *adj*.

lily *n* (*-ies*) **1** *strictly* a plant with an underground bulb, narrow leaves, and white or brightly coloured flowers. **2** *loosely* any of various other plants with flowers superficially resembling those of a lily, eg water lily.

lily-livered *adj* cowardly.

lily-of-the-valley *n* (**lilies-of-the-valley**) a spring plant with small white bell-shaped flowers that have a sweet smell.

limb¹ *n* **1** an arm, leg or wing. **2** a projecting part. **3** a main branch on a tree. **4** a branch or section of a larger organization. ○ **limbless** *adj*.

◆ **out on a limb** exposed or isolated, esp as regards an opinion or attitude.

limb² *n* an edge of the disk of the Sun, Moon or a planet.

limber¹ *adj* flexible and supple. ◊ **limber up** to stretch and warm up before taking exercise.

limber² *n* the detachable front part of a gun carriage, consisting of an axle, pole and two wheels.

limbo¹ or **Limbo** *n Christianity* an area between heaven and hell that is believed to be reserved for the unbaptized dead. ◆ **in limbo** in a state of uncertainty or waiting.

limbo² *n* a West Indian dance in which the object is to lean backwards and shuffle under a rope or bar.

lime¹ *n* **1** *loosely* calcium oxide. **2** *loosely* SLAKED LIME. **3** *loosely* LIMESTONE. **4** BIRD-LIME. ➢ *vb* to apply ground limestone as a fertilizer to (soil).

lime² *n* **1** a small, round or oval, green or yellowish-green citrus fruit with a sour taste. **2** a small evergreen tree that bears this fruit. **3** the yellowish-green colour of this fruit.

lime³ *n* (*also* **lime tree**) a deciduous tree or shrub with clusters of fragrant flowers.

limelight *n* **1** formerly used in theatres: a bright white light produced by heating a block of lime in a flame. **2** the glare of publicity: *in the limelight*.

limerick *n* a humorous poem with five lines rhyming *aabba*, the opening line usu beginning something like: *There was a young lady from …*

limestone *n, geol* a sedimentary rock composed mainly of CALCIUM CARBONATE.

limey *n* (*-eys*) *N Am, Aust & NZ slang* a British person.

limit *n* **1** a point, degree, amount or boundary, esp one which cannot or should not be passed. **2** a restriction or boundary. **3** (**the limit**) *colloq, sometimes facetious* someone or something that is intolerable or extremely annoying. ➢ *vb* (**limited, limiting**) **1** to be a limit or boundary to. **2** to restrict. ○ **limitable** *adj*.

limitation *n* **1** an act of limiting or the condition of being limited. **2** *law* a specified period within which an action must be brought. **3** (*often* **limitations**) someone's weakness, lack of ability, etc: *know your limitations*.

limited *adj* **1** having a limit or limits. **2** restricted: *a limited understanding*.

limited company or **limited liability company** *n* a company owned by its shareholders, who have liability for debts, etc only according to the extent of their stake in the company.

limited edition *n* an edition of a book, etc of which only a certain number of copies is printed or made.

limo /'lɪməʊ/ *n, colloq* short form of LIMOUSINE.

limousine *n* a large, luxurious motor car, esp one with a screen separating the driver from the passengers.

limp[1] *vb, intr* **1** to walk with an awkward or uneven step, often because one leg is weak or injured. **2** of a damaged ship or aircraft: to move with difficulty. ➤ *n* the walk of someone who limps.

limp[2] *adj* **1** not stiff or firm; hanging loosely. **2** without energy or vitality. **3** of a book: with a soft cover. ○ **limply** *adv.*

limpet *n* a marine mollusc with a conical shell, which clings to rock surfaces, etc by a muscular foot.

limpid *adj* **1** of water, eyes, etc: clear; transparent. **2** of speeches, writing, etc: easily understood.

linchpin *n* **1** a pin-shaped rod passed through an axle to keep a wheel in place. **2** someone or something essential to a business, plan, etc.

linctus *n, Brit* a syrupy medicine taken to relieve coughs, etc.

linden *n* another name for LIME[3].

line[1] *n* **1** a long narrow mark, streak or stripe. **2** *often in compounds* a length of thread, rope, wire, etc used for a specified purpose: *a washing line • telephone lines.* **3** a wrinkle or furrow, esp on the skin. **4** *maths* something that has length but no breadth or thickness. **5** the path which a moving object is considered to leave behind it, having length but no breadth. **6** a row. **7** a row of words or printed or written characters: *a line from Shakespeare.* **8** (**lines**) the words of an actor's part. **9** (*often* **lines**) an outline or shape: *a car of stylish lines.* **10** (**lines**) a punishment at school where a sentence has to be written out a set number of times. **11** *mus* any one of the five horizontal marks forming a musical stave. **12** *mus* a series of notes forming a melody. **13** *colloq* a short letter or note: *drop him a line.* **14** a series or group of people coming one after the other, esp in the same family or profession: *He's from a long line of doctors.* **15** a field of activity, interest, study or work: *his line of business.* **16** a course or way of acting, behaving, thinking or reasoning: *think along different lines.* **17** the rules or limits of acceptable behaviour: *Don't overstep the line.* **18** a group or class of goods for sale: *a new line in tonic water.* **19** a production line. **20** one of several white marks outlining a pitch, race-track, etc on a field. **21a** a single track for trains or trams; **b** a branch or route of a railway system. **22** a route, track or direction of movement: *line of fire.* **23a** a continuous system, eg of telephone cables, connecting one place with another; **b** a telephone connection; **c** *in compounds* a telephone number that connects the caller to some kind of special service: *the ticket line.* **24** a company running regular services of ships, buses or aircraft between two or more places. **25** an arrangement of troops or ships side by side and ready to fight. **26** (*always* **lines**) a connected series of military defences: *behind enemy lines.* **27** *N Am* a QUEUE (*noun* sense 1). **28** *slang* a remark, usu insincere, that someone uses in the hope of getting some kind of benefit: *He spun her a line.* ➤ *vb* **1** to mark or cover something with lines. **2** to form a line along something: *Crowds lined the streets.* ♦ **all along the line** at every point. **bring sb** or **sth into line** to make them or it conform. **get a line on sb** or **sth** *colloq* to get information about them or it. **hard lines!** *colloq* bad luck! **in line for sth** likely to get it: *in line for promotion.* **in line with sb** or **sth** in agreement or harmony with them or it. **lay it on the line** to speak frankly. **lay** or **put sth on the line** to risk one's reputation or career over it. **out of line 1** not aligned. **2** impudent. **3** exhibiting unacceptable behaviour. ◊ **line up** to form a line. **line people** or **things up 1** to form them into a line. **2** to align them. **line sth up** to organize it: *He lined up a new job.*

line[2] *vb* **1** to cover the inside of (clothes, boxes, curtains, etc) with some other material. **2** to cover as if with a lining: *We'll line the walls with books.* **3** *colloq* to fill, esp with large amounts. ♦ **line one's pocket** or **pockets** to make a profit, esp by dishonest means.

lineage /'lɪnɪɪdʒ/ *n* ancestry, esp when it can be traced from one particular ancestor.

lineal *adj* **1** of family descent: in a direct line. **2** referring to or transmitted by direct line of descent or legitimate descent. **3** of or in lines.

lineament *n* (*usu* lineaments) a distinguishing feature, esp on the face.

linear *adj* **1** referring to, consisting of or like a line or lines. **2** in or of one dimension only. **3** sequential.

line drawing *n* a drawing in pen or pencil using lines only.

linen *n* **1** cloth made from flax. **2** articles, eg sheets, tablecloths, etc, orig made from linen, now more likely to be made from cotton or artificial fibres. ➤ *adj* made of or like linen. ♦ **wash one's dirty linen in public** to let personal problems and quarrels, often of a sordid nature, become generally known.

liner[1] *n* a large passenger ship or aircraft.

liner[2] *n, often in compounds* something used for lining: *bin-liner.*

liner[3] *n, often in compounds* colouring used to outline the eyes or the lips: *eyeliner.*

linesman *n* an official at a boundary line in some sports whose job is to indicate when the ball has gone out of play.

line-up *n* **1** an arrangement of things or people in line. **2** a list of people selected for a sports team. **3** the artistes appearing in a show.

ling[1] *n* (**ling** or **lings**) a long slender edible marine fish, related to the cod.

ling[2] *n* same as HEATHER.

linger *vb, intr* **1** of sensations: to remain for a long time. **2** to be slow or reluctant to leave. **3** (**linger over sth**) to spend a long time with it or doing it. **4** of someone who is dying: to die very slowly. ○ **lingering** *n.*

lingerie /'lɛ̃ʒərɪ/ *n* women's underwear and nightclothes.

lingo *n, colloq* **1** a language, esp one that is not highly thought of or that is not understood: *She* *doesn't speak the lingo.* **2** the specialized vocabulary of a particular group, profession, etc: *medical lingo.*

lingua franca *n* (*lingua francas*) a language, often a simplified form, used as a means of communication amongst the speakers of different languages.

lingual *adj* **1** referring or relating to the tongue. **2** relating to speech or language. ○ **lingually** *adv.*

linguini or **linguine** *pl n* pasta in long flat strips.

linguist *n* someone skilled in languages or linguistics.

linguistic *adj* relating to language or linguistics. ○ **linguistically** *adv.*

linguistics *sing n* the study of language.

liniment *n* a thin oily cream applied to the skin to ease muscle pain, etc.

lining *n* **1** material used for lining something. **2** an inner covering, eg of a bodily organ.

link *n* **1** a ring of a chain or in chain-mail. **2** someone or something that connects. **3** a means of communication or travel. ➤ *vb* **1** to connect or join. **2** *intr* (*often* **link up**) to be or become connected.

linkage *n* **1** an act, method, etc of linking. **2** a chemical bond.

links *pl n* a golf course by the sea.

link-up *n* a connection or union, esp between military units, broadcasting systems, etc.

linnet *n* a small brown songbird of the finch family.

lino /ˈlaɪnoʊ/ *n, colloq* LINOLEUM.

linocut *n* a design cut in relief in linoleum.

linoleum *n, dated* a smooth hard-wearing covering for floors, made by impregnating a fabric with a mixture of substances such as linseed oil and cork.

linseed *n* a seed of the flax plant.

linseed oil *n* oil extracted from linseed and used in paints, varnishes, enamels, etc.

lint *n* **1** linen or cotton with a raised nap on one side, for dressing wounds. **2** fine, very small pieces of wool, cotton, etc; fluff.

lintel *n* a horizontal wooden or stone supporting beam over a doorway or window.

lion *n* **1** a large member of the cat family, found mainly in Africa, with a tawny coat, a tufted tail, and, in the male, a thick mane. **2** the male of this species, as opposed to the female. **3** someone who is brave.

lioness *n* a female lion.

lionize or **-ise** *vb* to treat someone as a celebrity or hero.

lip *n* **1** either of the two fleshy parts which form the edge of the mouth. **2** the edge or rim of something: *the lip of the milk jug.* **3** *colloq* cheek.

lipid *n, biochem* any of a group of organic compounds, mainly oils and fats, that occur naturally in living organisms and are generally insoluble in water.

liposuction *n* the removal for cosmetic reasons of excess fat from the body by sucking it out through an incision in the skin.

lip-read *vb* to make sense of (what someone is saying) by watching the movement of their lips. ○ **lip-reader** *n.* ○ **lip-reading** *n.*

lip-service *n* insincere or feigned approval, acceptance, etc.

lipstick *n* cosmetic colouring for the lips.

liquefy *vb* (*liquefies, liquefied*) *tr & intr* to make or become liquid. ○ **liquefaction** *n.*

liqueur /lɪˈkjʊə(r)/ *n* a sweet, strong alcoholic drink.

liquid *n* **a** a state of matter between SOLID and GAS, where the volume remains constant, but the shape depends on that of its container; **b** any substance in a water-like state. ➤ *adj* **1** of a substance: able to flow and change shape. **2** like water in appearance, esp in being clear. **3** flowing and smooth. **4** of assets: able to be easily changed into cash. ○ **liquidity** *n.*

liquidate *vb* **1** to bring to an end the trading of (an individual or a company), and have debts and assets calculated. **2** to turn (assets) into cash. **3** to pay off (a debt). **4** to eliminate or kill. ○ **liquidation** *n.* ○ **liquidator** *n.*

liquid crystal *n, chem* an organic compound that flows like a liquid but resembles solid crystalline substances in its optical properties.

liquid crystal display *n* in digital watches, calculators, etc: a display of numbers or letters produced by applying an electric field across a LIQUID CRYSTAL solution sandwiched between two transparent electrodes.

liquidize or **-ise** *vb* **1** to make liquid. **2** to make (food, etc) into a liquid or purée. ○ **liquidizer** *n.*

liquor *n* **1** strong alcoholic, esp distilled, drink. **2** any fluid substance, esp liquid produced in cooking.

liquorice or **licorice** *n* **1** a plant with sweet roots used in confectionery and medicine. **2** a black sticky sweet made from the juice of the roots of this plant.

lira *n* **1** (*lire*) the former standard unit of currency of Italy, replaced in 2002 by the euro. **2** (*liras*) the standard unit of currency of Turkey.

lisp *vb* **1** *intr* to pronounce the sounds of *s* and *z* in the same way as the *th* sounds in *thin* and *this* respectively. **2** to say or pronounce (words, an answer, etc) in this way. ➤ *n* a speech defect distinguished by lisping.

lissom or **lissome** *adj* graceful and supple in shape or movement.

list¹ *n* **1** a series of names, numbers, prices, etc printed out, written down or said one after the other. **2** *comput* an arrangement of data in a file. ➤ *vb* **1** to make a list of something. **2** to add (an item, etc) to a list. **3** to include in a list.

list² *vb, intr* of a ship, etc: to lean over to one side. ➤ *n* an act of listing or a listing position.

listed building *n* a building which, because of its architectural or historical interest, cannot, by law, be destroyed or changed.

listen *vb, intr* **1** to try to hear. **2** to pay attention.

3 to follow advice: *I warned him but he wouldn't listen.* ○ **listener** *n*.

listeria *n* a bacterium sometimes found in certain foods, eg chicken and soft cheese, which if not killed in cooking may cause the serious disease **listeriosis**.

listing *n* **1** a list. **2** a position in a list. **3** *comput* a printout of a file or a program. **4** (**listings**) a guide to what is currently available in entertainment, eg on television or radio.

listless *adj* tired and lacking energy or interest. ○ **listlessly** *adv*.

lists *pl n, hist* the barriers enclosing an area used for jousting and tournaments. ◆ **enter the lists** to start or become involved in a fight or controversy.

litany *n* (*-ies*) **1** *Christianity* a series of prayers or supplications with a response which is repeated several times by the congregation. **2** a long tedious recital or list.

litchi see LYCHEE.

liter *n* the *US* spelling of LITRE.

literacy *n* the ability to read and write.

literal *adj* **1** of words or a text: following the exact meaning, without allegorical or metaphorical interpretation. **2** of a translation: following the words of the original exactly. **3** true; exact: *the literal truth*. ➤ *n, printing* a misprint of one letter. ○ **literally** *adv*.

literalism *n* strict adherence to the literal meaning of words. ○ **literalist** *n*.

literary *adj* **1** referring or relating to, or concerned with, literature or writing. **2** of a person: knowing a great deal about literature. **3** of a word: formal; used in literature.

literate *adj* **1** able to read and write. **2** educated. **3** *in compounds* competent and experienced in something specified: *computer-literate*. ➤ *n* someone who is literate.

literati *pl n* literary or learned people.

literature *n* **1** written material, such as novels, poems and plays, that is valued for its language, content, etc. **2** the whole body of written works of a particular country, period in time, subject, etc. **3** the art or works produced by a writer. **4** *colloq* any printed matter, esp advertising leaflets.

lithe *adj* supple and flexible.

lithium *n, chem* a soft silvery metallic element.

litho /ˈlaɪθoʊ/ *n* **1** a LITHOGRAPH. **2** LITHOGRAPHY. ➤ *adj* lithographic.

lithograph *n* a picture or print made by lithography. ➤ *vb* to print (images, etc) using lithography. ○ **lithographic** *adj*.

lithography *n* a method of printing using a stone or metal plate which has been treated so that the ink adheres only to the design or image to be printed. ○ **lithographer** *n*.

litigant *n* someone involved in a lawsuit.

litigate *vb* **1** *intr* to be involved in a lawsuit. **2** to contest (a point, claim, etc) in a lawsuit. ○ **litigation** *n*. ○ **litigator** *n*.

litigious /lɪˈtɪdʒəs/ *adj* inclined to taking legal action over arguments, problems, etc.

litmus *n, chem* a dye obtained from certain lichens, widely used as an indicator to distinguish between acid solutions, in which it turns red, and alkaline ones, in which it turns blue.

litmus paper *n, chem* paper that has been treated with litmus, used to test for acidity and alkalinity.

litmus test *n* **1** *chem* a chemical test for relative acidity or alkalinity using litmus paper. **2** *colloq* a definitive test or trial of something.

litotes /ˈlaɪtoʊtiːz/ *n, rhetoric* understatement used for effect, esp by negating the opposite, as in *not a little angry* meaning *furious*.

litre or (*US*) **liter** *n* **1** the basic metric unit of volume, equal to one cubic decimetre (1000 cubic centimetres) or about 1.76 pints. **2** *in compounds*, denoting the capacity of the cylinders of a motor vehicle engine: *a three-litre engine*.

litter *n* **1** discarded paper, rubbish, etc lying in a public place. **2** a number of animals born to the same mother at the same time. **3** any scattered or confused collection of objects. **4 a** straw, hay, etc used as bedding for animals; **b** absorbent material put in a tray for a cat to urinate and defecate in. **5** *old use* a framework consisting of cloth stretched tight between two long poles, used to carry sick or wounded people. **6** *old use* a framework consisting of a couch covered by curtains, with poles on either side, for transporting a single passenger. ➤ *vb* **1** to make something untidy by spreading litter or objects about. **2** of objects: to lie untidily around (a room, etc). **3** of animals: to give birth to (young). **4** to give bedding litter to (animals).

little *adj* (often having connotations of affection or another emotion and used instead of the more formal *small*) **1** small in size, extent or amount. **2** young; younger: *a little girl* • *her little brother*. **3** small in importance: *a little mishap*. ➤ *adv* (**less, least**) not much or at all: *They little understood the implications*. ➤ *pron* not much: *little to be gained from that course of action*. ◆ **a little** (with a noun such as *bit, while, way* understood but not expressed) **1** a small amount: *do a little to help out*. **2** a short time: *He'll be here in a little*. **3** a short distance: *down the road a little*. **4** a small degree or extent: *run around a little to keep warm*. **little by little** gradually; by degrees. **make little of sth 1** to treat it as unimportant or trivial. **2** to understand only a little of it. **think little of sth or sb** to have a low opinion of it or them.

little people *pl n, folklore* fairies, leprechauns, etc.

littoral *adj* on or near the shore of a sea or lake. ➤ *n* an area of land on a shore or coast.

liturgy *n* (*-ies*) the standard form of service in a church. ○ **liturgical** *adj*.

live¹ /lɪv/ *vb* **1** *intr* to have life. **2** *intr* to be alive. **3** *intr* to continue to be alive. **4** *intr* to survive or to escape death. **5** *intr* to have a home or dwelling: *We live in a flat.* **6** (often **live on**) to continue or last: *Memories live on.* **7** *intr* to lead life in a certain way: *We live well.* **8** (**live off sth** or **sb**) to be supported by them or it: *They live off the land.* **9** to pass or spend: *I live a happy life in the country.* **10** *intr* to enjoy life passionately or to the full: *They really know how to live.* **11** to express something through a way of living: *She lived a lie.* ◆ **live and let live** *colloq* to be tolerant of others and expect toleration in return. ◇ **live sth down** to carry on living until something in the past has been forgotten or forgiven by other people: *He lived down the shame of his arrest.* **live in** to live in accommodation supplied at one's place fo work. **live up to sb** to become as respected as them: *He could never live up to his brother.* **live up to sth** to turn out in a manner worthy of them or it: *She tried to live up to her parents' expectations.* **live with sth 1** to continue to suffer from or be haunted by the memory of it: *He will live with the mistake for the rest of his life.* **2** to put up with it: *He has to live with psoriasis.*

live² /laɪv/ *adj* **1** having life; not dead. **2** of a radio or TV broadcast: heard or seen as the event takes place and not from a recording. **3** of a record, video, etc: recorded during a performance. **4** of a wire: connected to a source of electrical power. **5** of coal, etc: still glowing or burning. **6** of a bomb, etc: still capable of exploding. **7** up-to-date; relevant: *The programme tackles live issues.* **8** of a volcano: still liable to erupt. **9** of entertainments: playing to an audience: *a good live band.* ➤ *adv* at, during or as a live performance: *They had to perform live on stage.*

liveable *adj* **1** of a house, etc: fit to live in. **2** of life: worth living.

lived-in *adj* **1** of a room, etc: having a comfortable, homely feeling. **2** *colloq* of a face: marked by life's experiences.

live-in *adj* **1** living at a one's place of work: *a live-in nanny.* **2** of a sexual partner: sharing the same home.

livelihood *n* a means of earning a living.

livelong /ˈlɪvlɒŋ/ *adj, poetic* of the day or night: complete, in all its pleasant or tedious length.

lively *adj* (*-ier, -iest*) **1** active and full of life, energy and high spirits. **2** brisk. **3** vivid or bright. **4** interesting or stimulating: *a lively debate.* ◇ **liveliness** *n*.

liven *vb, tr & intr* (*usu* **liven up**) to make or become lively.

liver¹ *n* **1** in vertebrates: a large dark red glandular organ whose main function is to regulate the chemical composition of the blood. **2** this organ in certain animals, used as food.

liver² *n* someone who lives in a specified way: *a riotous liver.*

liverish *adj* **1** *old use* suffering from a disordered liver. **2** irritable.

liver sausage *n* finely minced liver combined with either pork or veal and made into a sausage shape.

liverwort *n* a small spore-bearing plant, closely related to mosses, typically growing in moist shady conditions.

livery *n* (*-ies*) **1** a distinctive uniform worn by male servants belonging to a particular household or by the members of a particular trade guild, etc. **2** any distinctive uniform or style, esp as used by companies so that their employees, vehicles, etc can be easily identified. **3** the distinctive colours and decoration used to identify the buses, aircraft, etc operated by a particular company. **4** the feeding, care, stabling and hiring out of horses for money.

lives *pl of* LIFE

livestock *sing or pl n* domesticated farm animals.

live wire *n, colloq* someone who is full of energy and enthusiasm.

livid *adj* **1** *colloq* extremely angry. **2** having the greyish colour of lead. **3** of a bruise: black and blue.

living *adj* **1** having life. **2** currently in existence, use or activity. **3** of a likeness: exact. ➤ *n* **1** livelihood or means of subsisting. **2** a manner of life: *riotous living.* **3** *C of E* a position as a vicar or rector which has an income or property attached to it.

living room *n* a room in a house, etc where people sit and relax.

living wage *n* a wage which can support a wage-earner and family.

lizard *n* a reptile closely related to the snake.

'll *vb,* contraction of SHALL and WILL: *I'll* ◆ *they'll.*

llama *n* a hoofed S American mammal kept for its meat, milk and wool, and used as a beast of burden.

lo *exclam, old use* look! see! ◆ **lo and behold** *usu facetious* an exclamation used to introduce some startling revelation.

loach *n* a small edible freshwater fish of the carp family.

load *n* **1** something that is carried or transported. **2 a** an amount that is or can be carried or transported at one time; **b** in compounds: *lorryload of bricks.* **3** a burden. **4** a cargo. **5** a specific quantity, varying according to the type of goods. **6** the weight carried by a structure, etc. **7** (**loads**) *colloq* a large amount. **8** something, eg a duty, oppressive or difficult to bear: *a load off my mind.* **9** an amount or number of things to be dealt with at one time. **10** the power carried by an electric circuit. **11** the power output of an engine. **12** the amount of work imposed on or expected of someone: *a heavy teaching load.* ➤ *vb* **1** to put (cargo, passengers, etc) on (a ship, vehicle, plane, etc). **2** *intr* (*also* **load up**) to take or pick up a load. **3** to fill: *load the dishwasher.* **4** *photog* to put (film) in (a camera). **5** to weigh down or overburden. **6** to be a weight on or burden to someone or something. **7** *comput* **a** to put (a disk, computer tape, etc) into a drive, so that it may be used; **b** to transfer (a program or data) into main memory, so that it may be used. **8** to put (ammunition) into (a gun). **9** to give weight or bias to (dice, a roulette wheel, a question, etc). **10** *insurance* to add charges to. ♦ **a load of sth** *colloq* a lot of it: *a load of rubbish.* **get a load of sth** *slang* to pay attention to, listen to, or look at it: *Get a load of those leggings!*

loaded *adj* **1** carrying a load. **2** of a gun: containing bullets. **3** of a camera: containing film. **4** *colloq* very wealthy.

loaded question *n* a question that is designed to bring out a specific kind of response.

loadstar see LODESTAR

loadstone see LODESTONE

loaf[1] *n* (**loaves**) **1** a shaped lump of dough, esp after it has risen and been baked. **2** *in compounds* a quantity of food formed into a regular shape: *meatloaf.* **3** *colloq* the head or brains: *Use your loaf.*

loaf[2] *vb, intr* (*often* **loaf about** or **around**) to loiter or stand about idly.

loafer *n* **1** someone who loafs about. **2** a light casual leather shoe.

loam *n* **1** a dark fertile easily worked soil. **2** a mixture basically of moist clay and sand used in making bricks, casting moulds, etc. ○ **loamy** *adj.*

loan *n* **1** something lent, esp money lent at interest. **2** an act or the state of lending or being lent. ➢ *vb* to lend (esp money). ♦ **on loan** given as a loan.

loan shark *n, colloq* someone who lends money at exorbitant rates of interest.

loath or **loth** /loʊθ/ *adj* unwilling; reluctant: *They were loath to admit it.*

> **loath, loathe** These words are often confused with each other.

loathe *vb* **1** to dislike intensely. **2** to find someone or something disgusting.

loathing *n* intense dislike or disgust.

loathsome *adj* causing intense dislike or disgust.

loaves *pl of* LOAF[1]

lob *n* **1** *tennis* a ball hit in a high overhead path. **2** *sport* any high looping ball. ➢ *vb* (**lobbed, lobbing**) **1** to hit, kick or throw (a ball) in this way. **2** to send a high ball over (an opponent): *He lobbed the goalkeeper.*

lobar *adj* relating to or affecting a lobe, esp in the lungs.

lobate *adj* having lobes.

lobby *n* (**-ies**) **1** a small entrance hall, passage or waiting room. **2** a common entrance giving access to several flats or apartments. **3** an antechamber of a legislative hall. **4** *Brit* (*also* **division lobby**) either of two corridors in the House of Commons that members pass into when they vote. **5** a group of people who try to influence the Government, politicians, legislators, etc to favour their particular cause. **6** the particular cause that such a group tries to promote. ➢ *vb* (**lobbies, lobbied**) **1** to try to influence (the Government, politicians, legislators, etc) to favour a particular cause. **2** *intr* to conduct a campaign in order to influence public officials. ○ **lobbyist** *n.*

lobe *n* **1** (*also* **earlobe**) the soft lower part of the outer ear. **2** a division of an organ or gland in the body, esp the lungs, brain or liver. **3** a division of a leaf. ○ **lobed** *adj.*

lobelia *n* a garden plant with red, white, purple, blue or yellow flowers.

lobotomy *n* (**-ies**) *surgery* an operation that involves cutting into a lobe of an organ or gland.

lobster *n* **1** a large edible marine crustacean with two large pincer-like claws. **2** its flesh used as food.

lobster pot *n* a basket for catching lobsters.

local *adj* **1** relating or belonging to a particular place. **2** relating or belonging to someone's home area. **3** of a train or bus: stopping at all the stations or stops in a neighbourhood. **4** *med* affecting or confined to a small area or part of the body: *a local infection.* ➢ *n* **1** someone who lives in a particular area. **2** *Brit* someone's nearest and most regularly visited pub. ○ **localization** *n.* ○ **localize** or **-ise** *vb.* ○ **locally** *adv.*

local anaesthetic *n, med* an injection that anaesthetizes only a limited part of the body. Compare GENERAL ANAESTHETIC.

local authority *n* the elected local government body in an area.

locale /loʊˈkɑːl/ *n* a scene of some event or occurrence.

local government *n* government of town or county affairs by a locally elected authority.

locality *n* (**-ies**) **1** a district or neighbourhood. **2** the scene of an event. **3** the position of a thing.

locate *vb* **1** to set in a particular place or position. **2** to find the exact position of. **3** to establish something in a place or position.

location *n* **1** a position or situation. **2** the act of locating or process of being located. ♦ **on location** *cinema* at an authentic site as opposed to in the studio.

loc. cit. *abbrev: loco citato* (Latin), in the passage just quoted.

loch /lɒk; *Scot* lɒx/ *n, Scot* **1** a lake. **2** (*also* **sea loch**) a long narrow arm of the sea surrounded by land on three sides.

loci *pl of* LOCUS

lock[1] *n* **1** a mechanical device, usu consisting of a sliding bolt moved by turning a key, dial, etc, that secures a door, lid, machine, etc. **2** an enclosed section of a canal or river in which the water level can be altered by means of gates. **3** a state of being jammed or fixed together, and completely immovable. **4** the part of a gun that explodes the charge. **5** *wrestling* a tight hold which prevents an opponent from moving. **6** the full amount by which the front wheels of a vehicle will turn. **7** (*also* **lock forward**) *rugby* either of the two inside players in the second row of a scrum. ➢ *vb* **1** to fasten (a door, box, etc) with a lock. **2** *intr* of a door, window, etc: to become or have the means of becoming locked. **3** (*also* **lock sth up**) to shut up or secure (a building, etc) by locking all doors and windows. **4** tr & intr to jam or make something jam. **5** tr & intr to fasten or make something be fastened so as to prevent movement. ○ **lockable** adj. ◆ **lock, stock and barrel** completely. **under lock and key** securely locked up. ◊ **lock sb up** to confine them or prevent them from leaving by locking them in.

lock² n **1** a section or curl of hair. **2** (**locks**) hair.

locker n a small lockable cupboard for storage, eg of luggage at a station.

locket n a small decorated case for holding a photograph or memento, worn on a chain round the neck.

lockjaw n difficulty in opening the mouth, caused by spasm of the jaw muscles, often a symptom of tetanus.

lockout n the exclusion of employees by the management from their place of work during an industrial dispute, as a means of imposing certain conditions.

locksmith n someone who makes and mends locks.

lockup n, Brit **1** a building, etc that can be locked up. **2** a small shop with no living quarters attached.

loco¹ n, colloq a locomotive.

loco² adj, slang crazy.

locomotion n the power, process or capacity of moving from one place to another.

locomotive n a railway engine used for pulling trains. ➢ adj relating to, capable of or causing locomotion.

locum /ˈloʊkəm/ (in full **locum tenens**) /ˈtɛnɛnz/ n (**locums** or **locum tenentes** /tɛnˈɛntiːz/) someone who temporarily stands in for someone else, esp in the medical and clerical professions.

locus n (**loci** /ˈloʊsaɪ/) **1** law an exact place or location, esp one where some incident has taken place. **2** maths the set of points or values that satisfy an equation or a particular set of conditions.

locust n a grasshopper noted for its tendency to form dense swarms that eat all the vegetation in their path.

locution n **1** a style of speech. **2** an expression, word or phrase.

lode n a thin band of rock containing metallic ore.

lodestar or **loadstar** n **1** a star used as a guide by sailors and astronomers, esp the Pole Star. **2** any guide or guiding principle.

lodestone or **loadstone** n **1** a form of magnetite which exhibits polarity, behaving, when freely suspended, as a magnet. **2** a magnet. **3** something that attracts.

lodge n **1** a cottage at the gateway to the grounds of a large house or mansion. **2** a small house in the country orig used by people taking part in field sports. **3** a porter's room in a university, college, etc. **4** a the meeting-place of a local branch of certain societies, eg the FREEMASONS and the Orange Order; **b** the members of a branch of one of these societies.

5 a beaver's nest. ➢ vb **1** intr to live, usu temporarily, in rented accommodation, esp in someone else's home. **2** tr & intr **a** to become or cause to become firmly fixed; **b** of feelings, ideas, thoughts, etc: to become implanted: The idea was firmly lodged in his mind. **3** a to bring (a charge or accusation) against someone; **b** to make (a complaint) officially. **4** to provide with rented accommodation, esp in one's home. **5** (usu **lodge sth with sb**) to deposit money or valuables with them, esp for safe-keeping. **6** intr (usu **lodge in** or **with sb**) of power, authority, etc: to be in or under their control: The power to hire and fire lodges with the board.

lodger n someone who rents accommodation in someone else's home.

lodging n **1** (usu **lodgings**) a room or rooms rented in someone else's home. **2** temporary accommodation.

loess /ˈloʊɪs/ n, geol a loose quartz-based loam found esp in river basins.

loft n **1** a room or space under a roof. **2** a gallery in a church or hall: an organ loft. **3** a room used for storage, esp one over a stable for storing hay. **4** (also **pigeon loft**) a room or shed where pigeons are kept. **5** golf the relative backward slant of the face of a golf club. **6** golf the amount of height that a player gives a ball. ➢ vb to strike, kick or throw (a ball, etc) high up in the air.

lofty adj (-ier, -iest) **1** very tall; of great or imposing height. **2** high or noble in character: lofty thoughts. **3** haughty or proud. ○ **loftily** adv. ○ **loftiness** n.

log n **1** a a part of a tree trunk or branch that has been cut, esp for firewood; **b** a tree trunk or large branch that has fallen to the ground. **2** a detailed record of events occurring during the voyage of a ship, aircraft, etc. **3** a logbook. **4** a float, orig made of wood, attached by a line to a ship and used for measuring its speed. ➢ vb (**logged, logging**) **1** a to record (distances covered on a journey, events, etc) in a book or logbook; **b** to record (speed) over a set distance. **2** to cut (trees or branches) into logs. **3** intr to cut logs. ◆ **sleep like a log** to sleep very soundly. ◊ **log in** or **on** comput to start a session on a computer system or make a connection with another computer. **log out** or **off** comput to end a session on a computer system or close a connection with another computer.

loganberry n (-ies) a large edible dark red berry.

logarithm /ˈlɒɡərɪðəm/ n (often **log**) maths the power to which a real number, called the BASE¹ (noun sense 9), must be raised in order to give another number or variable, eg the logarithm of 100 to the base 10 is 2 (written log₁₀ 100 = 2). ○ **logarithmic** adj.

logbook n **1** a book containing an official record of the voyage of a ship, aircraft, etc. **2** Brit, formerly the registration documents of a motor vehicle, now called **Vehicle Registration Document**.

loggerhead n (in full **loggerhead turtle**) a large sea turtle. ♦ **at loggerheads** disagreeing fiercely.

logging n the work of cutting trees and preparing timber. ○ **logger** n.

logic n 1 a philos the exploration of the validity or otherwise of arguments and reasoning; **b** maths the analysis of the principles of reasoning on which mathematical systems are based. 2 the reasoning governing a particular subject or activity. 3 a the extent to which someone's reasoning is sound: I didn't understand his logic; **b** the convincing and compelling force of an argument: The logic for having exams is dubious; **c** rationalized thinking: Logic dictated that she shouldn't go. 4 the way that related events or facts are interconnected. 5 the system underlying the design and operation of computers. ○ **logician** n.

logical adj 1 relating or according to logic: a logical truth. 2 correctly reasoned or thought out: a logical conclusion. 3 able to reason correctly: a logical mind. 4 following reasonably or necessarily from facts or events: the logical choice. ○ **logically** adv.

logistics sing or pl n 1 the organizing of everything needed for any large-scale operation. 2 the art of moving and supplying troops and military equipment. ○ **logistic** adj. ○ **logistical** adj. ○ **logistically** adv.

logo n a small design used as the symbol for a company, organization, etc.

loin n 1 (**loins**) the area of the body in humans and some animals stretching from the bottom rib to the pelvis. 2 a cut of meat from the lower back area of an animal.

loincloth n a piece of material worn round the hips.

loiter vb, intr 1 to wait around, esp furtively. 2 to stand around or pass time doing nothing.

loll vb, intr 1 (often **loll about**) to lie or sit about lazily. 2 of the tongue: to hang out.

lollipop n a boiled sweet on a stick.

lollipop lady or **lollipop man** n someone employed to see that children get across roads safely.

lollop vb (**lolloped, lolloping**) intr, colloq to bound around, esp with big ungainly strides.

lolly n (**-ies**) 1 colloq a LOLLIPOP or an ICE LOLLY. 2 slang money.

lone adj 1 without a partner, spouse or companion: a lone parent. 2 only: the lone car on the road. 3 poetic of a place: isolated and unfrequented.

lonely adj (**-ier, -iest**) 1 of a person: sad because they have no companions or friends. 2 solitary and without companionship. 3 of a place: isolated and unfrequented: a lonely street. ○ **loneliness** n.

loner n a person or animal that prefers to be alone.

lonesome adj 1 sad and lonely. 2 causing feelings of loneliness.

long¹ adj 1 a measuring a great distance in space from one end to the other; **b** of time: lasting for an extensive period. 2 often in compounds **a** measuring a specified amount: six centimetres long; **b** lasting a specified time: a three-hour-long movie. 3 having a large number of items: a long list. 4 a measuring more than is usual, expected or wanted: long hair; **b** lasting a greater time than is usual, expected or wanted: a really long journey. 5 of a cold drink: large and thirst-quenching. 6 of stocks: bought in large amounts in expectation of a rise in prices. 7 a phonetics of a vowel: having the greater of two recognized lengths; **b** of a syllable in verse: stressed. ➣ adv 1 for, during or by a long period of time: They had long expected such news. 2 throughout the whole time: all night long. ➣ n a comparatively long time: He won't be there for long. ♦ **as long as** or **so long as** 1 provided that. 2 while. **the long and the short of it** the most important facts in a few words.

long² vb, intr (often **long for** or **to**) to desire very much: I longed to hear from her.

longboat n, formerly the largest boat carried by a sailing ship.

longbow n a large bow, drawn by hand, for shooting arrows.

longevity /lɒnˈdʒɛvɪtɪ/ n great length of life.

long face n a miserable expression.

longhand n ordinary handwriting as opposed to SHORTHAND, typing or word-processing.

longing n an intense desire or yearning. ➣ adj having or exhibiting this feeling: a longing look. ○ **longingly** adv.

longitude n the angular distance east or west of the meridian that passes through Greenwich, measured from 0 degrees at this meridian to 180 degrees east or west of it. Compare LATITUDE.

longitudinal adj 1 relating to longitude; measured by longitude. 2 relating to length. 3 lengthways. ○ **longitudinally** adv.

long johns pl n, colloq underpants with long legs.

long jump n an athletics event in which competitors take a running start and try to jump as far as possible.

long-life adj of food and drink: treated so that, even without refrigeration, it may be stored for a long time in an unopened container.

long-lived adj having a long life.

long-playing adj denoting a RECORD (noun sense 4) where each side lasts approximately 25 minutes.

long-range adj 1 of predictions, etc: looking well into the future. 2 of a missile or weapon: able to reach far-off targets.

longship n, hist a long narrow Viking warship with oars and a large squarish sail.

long shot n 1 colloq **a** a guess, attempt, etc that is unlikely to be successful; **b** a bet made in the knowledge that there is only a slim chance of winning; **c** a participant in a competition, etc generally thought to have little chance of winning. 2 cinematog a camera shot that makes viewers feel they are at a considerable distance from the scene.

long-sighted *adj* **1** only able to see distant objects clearly. Compare SHORT-SIGHTED. **2** tending to consider what effect actions, etc might have on the future. ○ **long-sightedness** *n*.

long-standing *adj* having existed or continued for a long time.

long-suffering *adj* patiently tolerating difficulties, hardship, etc.

long-term *adj* of a plan, etc: occurring in or concerning the future.

long wave *n* an electromagnetic wave, esp a radio wave, with a wavelength greater than 1000m. Compare MEDIUM WAVE, SHORT WAVE.

longways *adv, adj* in the direction of a thing's length.

long-winded *adj* of a speaker or speech: tediously using or having far more words than are necessary. ○ **long-windedness** *n*.

loo *n, Brit colloq* a lavatory.

loofah *n* the roughly cylindrical dried inner part of a tropical gourd-like fruit, used as a bath sponge.

look *vb* **1** *intr* (*often* **look at sth**) to direct one's sight towards it: *I looked out of the window.* **2** *intr* (*often* **look at sth**) to direct one's attention towards it: *look at all the implications.* **3** *intr* (**look to sb or sth**) to rely on, turn to or refer to them or it: *He looked to her for support.* **4** to seem to be; to have the appearance of being: *She looked much younger than she was.* **5** *intr* to face or be turned in a specified direction: *The window looks south.* **6** to express by a look: *She was looking daggers at him.* **7** to consider or realize: *Just look what you've done!* **8** *intr* (**look for sb or sth**) **a** to search for them or it; **b** *colloq* to be hoping for it: *He was looking for £100 for the bike.* ➤ *n* **1 a** an act or the action of looking; a glance or view: *We had a look through his photos;* **b** a glance or stare that conveys a particular feeling or emotion: *an impatient look.* **2** (*sometimes* **looks**) the outward appearance of something or someone: *She always has that tired look* • *She didn't like the looks of the restaurant.* **3** (**looks**) beauty; attractiveness. **4** a particular way of dressing, etc, esp one that is different or particularly up-to-date: *They went for a punk look.* **5 a** a search: *I'll have another look for that missing CD;* **b** a browse. **6** (*sometimes* **Look here!**) used as an exclamation to call for attention or to express protest: *Look, you just can't behave like that!* • *Look here! What do you think you're doing?* ♦ **by the look** or **looks of sb** or **sth** *colloq* going by appearances: *By the look of him, he's in need of a rest.* **by the look of things** *colloq* going by how things stand at the moment: *By the look of things, we won't get this finished today.* **look like 1** to seem probable: *It looks like it will rain.* **2** to appear to be similar to: *She looks like her sister.* **3** to seem to be: *He looks like a nice guy.* **look**

oneself to seem to be as healthy as usual. **look the part** to appear to be very well suited (to do or be something). **look right** or **straight through sb** *colloq* to ignore them on purpose. **look sharp** *colloq* to hurry up: *We'd better look sharp if we're going to be there for seven.* **not know where to look** to feel acutely embarrassed. ◊ **look after sb** or **sth** to attend to or take care of them or it. **look down on** or **upon sb** or **sth** to consider them or it inferior or contemptible. **look forward to sth** to anticipate it with pleasure. **look in on sb** to visit them briefly. **look into sth** to investigate it. **look on** or **upon sb** or **sth in a certain way** to think of or consider them or it in that way: *look on it as a bonus.* **look out 1** to keep watch and be careful. **2** used as an exclamation warning of imminent danger. **look out sth** to find it by searching: *I'll look out that magazine for you.* **look out for sb** or **sth 1** to be alert about finding them or it. **2** *colloq* to protect: *He has always looked out for his brother.* **look over sth** to check it quickly or cursorily: *She looked over her daughter's homework.* **look through sth** to read or examine it. **look up** to show signs of improving: *The weather's looking up at last.* **look sb up** *colloq* to visit or get in touch with them. **look sth up** to search for an item of information, etc in a reference book, etc. **look up to sb** to respect their behaviour, opinions, etc.

lookalike *n* someone or something that looks very much like someone or something else.

look-in *n* **1** a chance of joining in, being included, or doing something: *He never gives her a look-in.* **2** a quick visit.

looking-glass *n, old use* a mirror.

lookout *n* **1** a careful watch. **2** a place from which such a watch can be kept. **3** someone who has to keep watch, eg on board ship. **4** *colloq* a personal concern or problem: *That's your lookout.* ♦ **be on the lookout for sb** or **sth** to be watching for them or it.

loom[1] *n* a machine that weaves thread into fabric.

loom[2] *vb, intr* **1** to appear indistinctly and usu in some enlarged or threatening form. **2** of an event: to be imminent, esp in some menacing way.

loon *n, N Am* a DIVER (sense 3).

loony *slang, n* (*-ies*) someone who is mad. ➤ *adj* (*-ier, -iest*) **1** crazy; mad. **2** overzealous; fanatical: *a loony fringe group.*

loop *n* **1** a rounded or oval-shaped single coil in a piece of thread, string, rope, etc, formed as it crosses over itself. **2** any similar oval-shaped or U-shaped bend, eg in a river. **3** a manoeuvre in which an aircraft describes a complete vertical circle in the sky. **4** a strip of magnetic tape or motion-picture film whose ends have been spliced together to form a loop so that the sound or images on it can be continually repeated. **5** *electronics* a closed circuit which a signal can pass round, as, for example, in a FEEDBACK (sense 3) control system. **6**

comput a series of instructions in a program that is repeated until a certain condition is met. **7** *maths* a line on a graph which begins and ends at the same point. **8** *physics* a closed curve on a graph, such as a HYSTERESIS loop. **9** in knitting and crochet: a STITCH. ➣ *vb* **1** to fasten with or enclose in a loop. **2** to form into a loop or loops. ◆ **loop the loop** of an aircraft, pilot, etc: to make a vertical loop in the sky.

loophole *n* a means of escaping a responsibility, duty, etc without infringing a law, regulation, etc.

loopy *adj* (*-ier, -iest*) *slang* mad; crazy.

loose *adj* **1** not or no longer tied up or attached to something else. **2** of clothes, etc: not tight or close-fitting. **3 a** not held together; not fastened or firmly fixed in place: *a loose tooth*; **b** not packaged: *loose oranges*. **4** not tightly packed or compact: *loose soil*. **5** vague or inexact: *a loose translation*. **6** promiscuous. **7** indiscreet: *loose talk*. **8** *sport* of a ball, etc: in play but not under a player's control. **9** hanging; droopy; baggy. ➣ *adv* in an unrestrained way: *The dog can run loose in the park.* ➣ *vb* **1** to release or set free. **2** to unfasten or untie. **3** to make less tight, compact or dense. **4** to relax: *She loosed her hold.* **5** to discharge (a gun, bullet, arrow, etc). ◇ **loosely** *adv* ◇ **looseness** *n*. ◆ **on the loose** free from confinement or control.

loose A word often confused with this one is **lose**.

loose box *n* a part of a stable or horse box where horses are kept untied.

loose-leaf *adj* of a folder, etc: having clips or rings which open to allow pages to be taken out or put in.

loosen *vb* **1** *tr & intr* (*sometimes* **loosen up** or **loosen sth up**) to make or become loose or looser. **2** to free; to cause to become free or freer: *Drink always loosened his tongue.* ◇ **loosen up** *colloq* to relax or become more relaxed.

loot *vb, tr & intr* to steal from (shops, warehouses, etc), often during or following rioting, a battle, etc. ➣ *n* **1 a** money, goods or supplies stolen from shops, warehouses, etc, esp when taken during or following rioting; **b** money or goods stolen from an enemy in wartime. **2** *slang* money. ◇ **looter** *n*.

lop *vb* (*lopped, lopping*) (*usu* **lop sth off**) **1** to cut off (esp the branches of a tree). **2** to cut away the unnecessary or superfluous parts of something: *He lopped five pages off the article.*

lope *vb, intr* to run with long bounding steps. ➣ *n* a bounding leap.

lop-eared *adj* of animals: having ears that droop.

lopsided *adj* **1** with one side smaller, lower or lighter than the other. **2** leaning over to one side.

loquacious *adj* very talkative. ◇ **loquacity** *n*.

lord *n* **1** a master or ruler. **2** *hist* someone in a superior position in a feudal system. **3** *chiefly*

Brit **a** a man who is a member of the aristocracy; **b** (**Lord**) a title used to address certain members of the aristocracy. **4** (**My Lord** or **my lord**) **a** a conventional way for lawyers, etc to address a judge in court; **b** a formal way of addressing certain members of the clergy and aristocracy. **5** (**Lord** or **Our Lord** or **the Lord**) *Christianity* a way of addressing or referring to God or Jesus Christ. **6** (**Lord**) *in compounds* forming part of the titles of some high-ranking officials: *Lord Privy Seal.* **7** (**Lord!**) expressing shock, surprise, dismay, etc: *Good Lord!* ◆ **lord it over sb** to behave in a condescending or overbearing manner towards them.

Lord Advocate *n* a Scottish law officer, equivalent to the ATTORNEY GENERAL.

Lord Chief Justice *n, Brit* the head of the Queen's Bench division.

Lord Lieutenant *n, Brit* the crown representative in a county in England and Wales.

lordly *adj* (*-ier, -iest*) **1** grand or haughty. **2** belonging, relating or suitable to a lord or lords. ◇ **lordliness** *n*.

Lord Mayor *n* the title of the mayor of London and the mayors of certain other English cities.

Lord Privy Seal *n* a senior British cabinet minister without official duties.

the Lords *sing n* the House of Lords.

Lordship *n* (**His** or **Your Lordship**) a title used to address bishops, judges and all peers except dukes.

the Lord's Prayer *n, Christianity* the prayer that begins, 'Our Father, who art in heaven'.

Lords Spiritual *pl n, Brit* the English and Welsh Anglican archbishops and bishops entitled to sit in the House of Lords. Compare LORDS TEMPORAL.

the Lord's Supper *n, Christianity* the EUCHARIST.

Lords Temporal *pl n, Brit* all the members of the House of Lords who are not archbishops or bishops. Compare LORDS SPIRITUAL.

lore *n* the whole body of knowledge on a particular subject, esp the kind of knowledge that has been enhanced by legends, traditional beliefs, etc: *classical lore.*

lorgnette /lɔːnˈjɛt/ *n* a pair of spectacles that are held up to the eyes using a long handle.

lorry *n* (*-ies*) *Brit* a large road vehicle for transporting heavy loads.

lose *vb* (*lost*) **1 a** to fail to keep or obtain something, esp because of a mistake, carelessness, etc: *He lost his money through a hole in his pocket*; **b** to stop or begin to stop having (some distinguishing quality, characteristic or property): *She was losing her nerve*; **c** to become less marked, noticeable, intense, etc in (a specified way): *These roses have lost their scent.* **2 a** to misplace, esp temporarily: *I've lost the car keys*; **b** to be unable to find; **c** to leave accidentally: *I lost the umbrella at the cinema.* **3 a** to suffer the loss of (usu a close friend or relative) through death; **b** to suffer the loss of (an unborn baby) through miscarriage or stillbirth; **c** to fail to save the life of (esp a patient); **d** to be deprived of (life, possessions, etc), esp in a war, fire, natural disaster, etc: *The village lost half its population in the earthquake*; **e** (**be lost**) to be killed or drowned, esp at sea. **4** to miss (an opportunity, etc). **5 a** *tr & intr* to fail to win (a game, vote, proposal, election, battle, bet, etc); **b** to give away: *I lost £50 on the horses*. **6 a** to be unable or no longer able to hear, see, understand, etc: *Sorry, I lost what you said when that bus went by*; **b** to confuse or bewilder someone: *Sorry, you've lost me there*. **7 a** to escape or get away from someone or something; **b** of a competitor in a race, etc: to leave (the rest of the field, etc) behind. **8** of a clock or watch: to become slow by (a specified amount). ♦ **lose one's cool** *colloq* to become upset. **lose face** to be humiliated or discredited. **lose one's grip (on sth)** to be unable to control or understand things. **lose ground** to slip back or fall behind. **lose one's head** to become angry or irrational. **lose heart** to become discouraged. **lose one's heart (to sb)** to fall in love (with them). **lose one's mind** or **reason** to behave irrationally, esp temporarily. **lose one's** or **the rag** *Brit colloq* to become very angry. **lose sight of sb** or **sth 1** to be unable or no longer able to see them or it. **2** to forget or ignore the importance of them or it: *They lost sight of their original aims*. **lose one's touch** to forget how to do something or to be less proficient at doing something than one used to be. **lose touch with sb** or **sth** to no longer be in contact with them or it. **lose track of sb** or **sth** to fail to notice or monitor the passing or progress of them or it. **lose one's** or **the way** to stray from one's route by mistake. ◊ **lose out** *colloq* **1** to suffer loss or be at a disadvantage. **2** to fail to get something one wants.

> **lose** A word often confused with this one is **loose**.

loser *n* **1** someone or something that is defeated. **2** *colloq* someone who is habitually unsuccessful. ♦ **a bad, poor** or **good loser** someone who loses in bad, poor or good spirit.

losing *adj* never likely to be successful: *We're fighting a losing battle*.

loss *n* **1** an act or instance of losing or being lost: *the loss of his driving licence*. **2** the thing, amount, etc lost: *His loss of hearing was severe*. **3** the disadvantage that results when someone or something loses: *She's a great loss to the company*. **4 a** the death of a close friend or relative: *the loss of his mother*; **b** the sadness felt after such a death: *He did his best to console her in her loss*. ♦ **at a loss 1** puzzled; uncertain: *Her tantrums left me at a complete loss*. **2** of a selling price, etc: lower than the buying price: *We sold the house at a loss*. **3** of a company, etc: losing more money than it is making: *They're trading at a loss*.

loss leader *n, commerce* an item on sale at a loss, as a means of attracting custom for a wider range of goods.

lost cause *n* an aim, ideal, person, etc that has no chance of success.

lot *n* **1** *colloq* (*usu* **a lot** or **lots**) a large number or amount of something: *an awful lot of work to do*: *lots of children*. **2 a** (**the lot**) everything; the total; the whole number or amount: *I ate the lot*; **b** (**one's lot**) *colloq* all one is getting: *That's your lot!* **3** a group of people or things that have something, often a specified attribute or quality, in common: *Get a move on, you lazy lot*. **4 a** a straw, slip of paper, etc that is drawn from a group of similar objects, in order to reach a fair and impartial decision: *They drew lots to see who'd go first*; **b** the use of lots to arrive at a decision, choice, etc: *They made their selection by lot*. **5** someone's fortune, destiny, plight, etc: *the lot of the homeless*. **6** an item or set of items for sale by auction, usu identified by a number. **7** *N Am* an area of land for a specified purpose: *parking lot*. ♦ **a bad lot** a group or person considered to be dishonest, immoral, etc. **cast** or **throw in one's lot with sb** to decide to share their fortunes.

loth see LOATH

lotion *n* any liquid, used either as a medicine or a cosmetic, for healing or cleaning the skin.

lottery *n* (**-ies**) **1** a system for raising money which involves randomly drawing numbers and giving prizes to those who hold the tickets with the same numbers as the ones that have been picked out. **2** anything which is thought of as being a matter of chance.

lotto *n* **1** an earlier name for the game now usu called BINGO. **2** a name used for various lotteries.

lotus *n* **1** *Greek myth* a fruit which was thought to produce a state of dreamy forgetfulness. **2** a water lily sacred to the ancient Egyptians. **3** a water lily traditionally associated with Buddhism and Hinduism.

lotus-eater *n* someone who lives a lazy and indulgent life.

lotus position *n, yoga* a seated position with the legs crossed and each foot resting on the opposite thigh.

loud *adj* **1** making a relatively great sound; noisy. **2** capable of making a relatively great sound: *a loud horn*. **3** emphatic and insistent: *loud complaints*. **4** of colours, clothes, designs, etc: tastelessly bright, garish or gaudy. **5** of someone or their behaviour: aggressively noisy and coarse. ➤ *adv* in a loud manner. ○ **loudly** *adv*. ○ **loudness** *n*.

loudhailer *n* a portable device for amplifying the voice.

loudmouth *n, colloq* someone who is very noisy and aggressively boastful. ○ **loud-mouthed** *adj*.

loudspeaker (*often just* **speaker**) *n* an electronic device that converts electrical signals into audible sound waves.

lough /lɒk; *Irish* lɒx/ *n, Irish* also LOCH.

lounge *vb, intr* **1** to lie, sit, recline, etc in a relaxed and comfortable way. **2** to pass the time without doing very much. ➤ *n* **1** a sitting room in a private house. **2** a large room in a public building, such as a hotel, where people can sit and relax. **3** (*also* **departure lounge**) an area in an airport, ferry terminal, etc, where passengers can relax prior to boarding. **4** *Brit* (*also* **lounge bar**) the more up-market bar of a pub or hotel.

lounge suit *n*, *Brit* a man's suit for everyday wear.

lour or **lower** *vb, intr* **1** of the sky: to darken or threaten rain. **2** to scowl or look angry or gloomy.

louse *n* **1** (*pl* **lice**) a wingless parasitic insect infesting human hair and skin. **2** (*pl* **louses**) *slang* a scornful term of abuse for a person. ◊ **louse sth up** *slang* to spoil or ruin it.

lousy *adj* (*-ier, -iest*) **1** having lice. **2** *slang* very bad, unpleasant or disgusting. **3** *colloq* poor or second-rate.

lout *n* someone, usu a teenage male, whose behaviour, esp in public, is generally considered unacceptable. ○ **loutish** *adj*.

louvre or (*N Am*) **louver** / 'luːvə(r)/ *n* **1** any one of a set of overlapping slats in a door, etc which let air in but keep rain and light out. **2** a dome-like structure on a roof for letting smoke out and air in. ○ **louvred** *adj*.

lovage *n* a European flowering plant used medicinally and for flavouring.

lovat *n* a pale dusky green colour.

love *vb* **1** to feel great affection for someone. **2 a** to enjoy very much: *I love to boogie*; **b** to like very much: *I love chocolate biscuits.* ➤ *n* **1** a feeling of great affection: *brotherly love.* **2** a strong liking: *a love of the outdoors.* **3** used as an affectionate term of address: *my love.* **4** *tennis, squash, whist, etc* no score. ○ **lovable** or **loveable** *adj*. ○ **loveless** *adj*. ◆ **fall in love with sb** to develop feelings of love and sexual attraction for them. **make love to** or **with sb** to have sexual intercourse with them.

love affair *n* a romantic or sexual relationship, esp one that is fleeting or illicit.

lovebird *n* a small parrot sometimes kept as a cage bird.

love bite *n* a patch of bruised skin caused by a sucking kiss.

lovelorn *adj* sad because the love felt for someone else is not returned.

lovely *adj* (*-ier, -iest*) **1** strikingly attractive. **2** *colloq* delightful or pleasing. ➤ *n* (*-ies*) *colloq* a pretty woman.

lover *n* **1** someone who is in love with someone else, esp in a romantic or sexual way. **2** (**lovers**) two people who are in love with one another or who are sharing a sexual relationship. **3** someone who enjoys or is fond of a specified thing: *a lover of fine wine.*

lovesick *adj* **1** infatuated with someone. **2** lovelorn.

lovey-dovey *adj, colloq* of a couple: openly displaying affection, esp in a sentimental way.

loving *adj* **1** affectionate and caring. **2** *in com-*

pounds enjoying or appreciating a specified thing: *fun-loving.* ○ **lovingly** *adv.*

low¹ *adj* **1** of a building, hill, etc: measuring comparatively little from top to bottom. **2** close to the ground, sea level, the horizon, etc: *low cloud.* **3** of a temperature, volume of water, score, etc: measuring comparatively less than is usual or average: *The river is low.* **4** having little value. **5** of numbers: small. **6** not near the top: *Shopping was low on her list of priorities.* **7** coarse, rude, vulgar, etc. **8** being of humble rank or position. **9** not very advanced: *a low form of animal life.* **10** of the neckline of a garment: leaving the neck and upper part of the chest bare. **11** of a sound, note, voice, etc: **a** quiet; soft: *a low hum*; **b** produced by slow vibrations and having a deep pitch. **12** a weak; lacking in energy or vitality: *Mum was feeling low after the operation*; **b** depressed: *He is feeling low after losing his job.* **13** unfavourable: *a low opinion.* **14** underhanded; unprincipled: *How low can you get?* **15** giving a relatively slow engine speed: *a low gear.* **16** subdued: *low lighting.* **17** not prominent or conspicuous: *I'm keeping a low profile.* **18** of latitudes: near the equator. ➤ *adv* **1** in or to a low position, state or manner: *He aimed low and fired • We were brought low by his gambling debts.* **2** in a small quantity or to a small degree. **3** of a sound, etc: **a** quietly; **b** with or in a deep pitch. **4** *in compounds* **a** not measuring much in a specified respect: *low-voltage*; **b** not far off the ground: *low-slung*; **c** deeply: *low-cut*; **d** lowly: *low-born.* ➤ *n* **1** a depth, position, level, etc which is low or lowest: *The pound has reached an all-time low.* **2** *meteorol* a CYCLONE (sense 1). ○ **lowness** *n*. ◆ **low in sth** containing less than the average amount, etc of it: *low in fat.* **low on sth 1** *sometimes euphem* not having much of it: *low on courage.* **2** not having much of it left: *We're running low on petrol.*

low² *vb, intr* of cattle: to make a gentle mooing sound. ➤ *n* the gentle mooing sound made by cattle. ○ **lowing** *n*.

lowbrow *adj* lacking cultural or intellectual values. ➤ *n* a lowbrow person.

Low Church *n* a group within the Church of England which puts little value on ceremony, but which stresses evangelical theology.

the lowdown *n, colloq* information about someone or something: *the lowdown on their affair.*

low-down *adj, colloq* mean and dishonourable: *a low-down dirty trick.*

lower¹ *adj* **1** not as high in position, status, height, value, etc: *lower middle class.* **2** of an animal or plant: less highly developed than other species. **3** of part of a river or the land around it: relatively far from the source: *lower Deeside.* **4** in place names: **a** relatively far south; **b** geographically not so high. ➤ *adv* in or to a lower position. ➤ *vb* **1** *tr & intr* to lessen or become less in amount, value, status, sound, etc. **2 a** to pull down: *We'd better lower* *the window;* **b** to cause or allow something to come down: *The crew lowered the lifeboat.* **3** to reduce or cause to be reduced: *The rejection lowered his confidence.*

lower² see LOUR.

lower case *printing, adj* referring or relating to small letters as opposed to capitals. ➤ *n* a letter or letters of this kind: *a novel written entirely in lower case.* Compare UPPER CASE.

lower class *n* a social group that traditionally includes manual workers. ➤ *adj* (**lower-class**) referring or relating to this social group.

lower house or **lower chamber** *n* in a BI-CAMERAL parliament: usu the larger section, more representative of the population as a whole, such as the House of Commons in the United Kingdom.

lowest common denominator *n, maths* in a group of fractions, the lowest common multiple of all the denominators.

lowest common multiple *n, maths* the smallest number into which every member of a group of numbers will divide exactly.

low frequency *n* a radio band where the number of cycles per second is between 30 and 300 kilohertz.

low-key *adj* restrained or subdued.

lowland *n* **1** (*also* **lowlands**) land which is comparatively low-lying and flat. **2** (**the Lowlands**) the less mountainous region of Scotland lying to the south and east of the Highlands. ➤ *adj* (**lowland** or **Lowland**) belonging or relating to lowlands or the Scottish Lowlands. ○ **lowlander** or **Lowlander** *n.*

low-level language *n, comput* a programming language in which each instruction represents a single MACHINE-CODE operation.

lowly *adj* (**-ier, -iest**) **1** humble in rank, status or behaviour. **2** simple, modest. ○ **lowliness** *n.*

low-pitched *adj* **1** of a sound: low in pitch. **2** of a roof: having a gentle slope.

low profile *n* a deliberate avoidance of publicity and attention. ➤ *adj* (**low-profile**) getting little publicity: *low-profile talks.*

low-spirited *adj* dejected or depressed.

low-tech *adj, colloq* not involving the use of the latest technology.

low tide *n* the tide at its lowest level or the time when this occurs.

loyal *adj* **1** faithful and true. **2** personally devoted to a sovereign, government, leader, friend, partner, etc. **3** expressing or showing loyalty: *the loyal toast to the Queen.* ○ **loyally** *adv.*

loyalist *n* **1** a loyal supporter, esp of a sovereign or an established government. **2** (**Loyalist**) in N Ireland: a person in favour of continuing the parliamentary union with Great Britain. Compare REPUBLICAN. ○ **loyalism** *n.*

loyalty *n* (**-ies**) **1** the state or quality of being loyal. **2** (*often* **loyalties**) a feeling of loyalty or duty: *divided loyalties.*

lozenge /'lɒzɪndʒ/ *n* **1** a small medicated tablet which dissolves in the mouth. **2** *maths* a less

common term for a RHOMBUS.

LP *abbrev* **1** long-playing. **2** long-playing record.

L-plate *n, Brit* a small square white sign with a red letter *L* on it which a learner driver must display on the back and front of a car.

Lr *symbol, chem* lawrencium.

LSD *abbrev* lysergic acid diethylamide, an illegal hallucinatory drug.

Lt or **Lt.** *abbrev* Lieutenant.

Ltd or **Ltd.** *abbrev* Limited, as used at the end of the names of limited liability companies.

Lu *symbol, chem* lutetium.

lubricant *n* oil, grease, etc used to reduce friction.

lubricate *vb* **1** to coat (engine parts, etc) with oil, grease, etc in order to reduce friction. **2** *intr* to act as a lubricant. ○ **lubrication** *n.*

lubricious *adj* lewd.

lucerne /luːˈsɜːn/ *n, Brit* ALFALFA.

lucid *adj* **1** clearly presented and easily understood. **2** not confused, esp in contrast to bouts of insanity or delirium. ○ **lucidity** *n.* ○ **lucidly** *adv.*

Lucifer *n* the Devil.

luck *n* **1** chance, esp as it is perceived as influencing someone's life at specific times: *luck was on his side.* **2** good fortune. **3** events in life which cannot be controlled and seem to happen by chance: *She's had nothing but bad luck.* ○ **luckless** *adj.* ♦ **down on one's luck** experiencing problems or suffering hardship. **no such luck** *colloq* unfortunately not. **try** or **test one's luck** to attempt something without being sure of the outcome. **worse luck** *colloq* unfortunately.

lucky *adj* (**-ier, -iest**) **1** having good fortune. **2** bringing good fortune. **3** happening by chance, esp when the outcome is advantageous: *It was lucky the weather was good.* ○ **luckily** *adv.*

lucky dip *n* a chance to rummage around in a container full of shredded paper, etc in which prizes have been hidden, and to draw out a prize at random.

lucrative *adj* affording financial gain. ○ **lucratively** *adv.*

lucre /'luːkə(r)/ *n, derog* wealth or money.

Luddite *n* **1** (**the Luddites**) *hist* a group of artisans who, in the early 19c, destroyed machinery, because they feared that it threatened their jobs. **2** anyone who opposes new technology.

ludicrous *adj* completely ridiculous or absurd.

ludo *n, Brit* a board game where counters are moved according to the number shown by each throw of the dice.

lug¹ *vb* (**lugged, lugging**) to carry, pull or drag with difficulty or effort.

lug² *n* **1** *dialect* or *colloq* an ear. **2** a protruding part on something, esp one that acts as a kind of handle.

luge /luːʒ/ *n* a kind of toboggan on which riders lie back in an almost flat position.

luggage *n, Brit* suitcases, bags, etc used when travelling.

lugger *n* a small vessel with square sails.

lughole *n, colloq* an ear.

lugubrious *adj* sad and gloomy.

lugworm *n* a large worm which burrows on seashores and river estuaries and which is often used as fishing bait.

lukewarm *adj* 1 of liquids: moderately warm. 2 of interest, support, response, etc: not enthusiastic.

lull *vb* 1 to soothe or induce a feeling of well-being in someone: *I lulled the baby to sleep.* 2 to allay (suspicions), esp falsely. 3 to deceive someone: *We lulled them into a false sense of security.* ➢ *n* a period of calm and quiet: *a lull before the storm.*

lullaby *n (-ies)* a soft soothing song to help send a child to sleep.

lumbago *n* chronic pain in the lower region of the back.

lumbar *adj, anat* relating to or situated in the region of the lower back.

lumbar puncture *n, med* the withdrawal of spinal fluid through a needle inserted into the lower region of the spine as an aid to diagnosing a disease.

lumber[1] *n* 1 disused articles of furniture or odds and ends that are no longer used and which have been stored away. 2 *N Am* timber, esp when partly cut up ready for use. ➢ *vb* 1 to fill something with lumber or other useless items. 2 *tr & intr, chiefly N Am* to fell trees and saw the wood into timber for transportation. 3 (**lumber sb with sth**) *colloq* to burden them with (something unwanted, difficult, etc).

lumber[2] *vb, intr* to move about heavily and clumsily. ○ **lumbering** *adj.*

lumberjack *n* someone who works at felling trees, sawing them up and moving them.

luminary *n (-ies)* 1 someone who is considered an expert or authority in a particular field. 2 a famous or prominent member of a group.

luminescence *n, physics* the emission of light by a substance in the absence of a rise in temperature. ○ **luminescent** *adj.*

luminous *adj* 1 full of or giving out light. 2 *non-technical* glowing in the dark: *a luminous clock face.* 3 *non-technical* of colours: very bright and garish. ○ **luminosity** *n (-ies).*

lump[1] *n* 1 a small solid mass that has no definite shape. 2 a swelling or tumour. 3 a number of things taken as a single whole. 4 a heavy, dull or awkward person. ➢ *vb (often **lump things together**)* to gather (esp dissimilar things) into a group or pile, often without any legitimate reason for doing so. ◆ **a lump in one's throat** a sensation of tightness in one's throat, usu caused by great emotion.

lump[2] *vb, colloq* to put up with (something unpleasant): *like it or lump it.*

lumpectomy *n (-ies)* surgery the removal of a lump from the breast.

lumpish *adj* heavy, dull or awkward.

lump sum *n* a comparatively large single payment, as opposed to several smaller ones.

lumpy *adj (-ier, -iest)* full of lumps. ○ **lumpiness** *n.*

lunacy *n (-ies)* 1 insanity. 2 great foolishness or stupidity.

lunar *adj* relating to, like or caused by the Moon.

lunatic *adj* 1 *formerly* insane. 2 foolish or wildly eccentric. ➢ *n* 1 someone who is foolish or highly eccentric. 2 *formerly* someone considered insane.

lunatic fringe *n* the most extreme, fanatical or eccentric members of any group.

lunch *n* a light meal eaten in the middle of the day. ➢ *vb, intr* to eat lunch.

luncheon *n* 1 a formal meal served in the middle of the day. 2 *formal* lunch.

luncheon meat *n* a type of pre-cooked meat, processed and mixed with cereal.

luncheon voucher *n, Brit* a voucher given by employers to workers for part-payment for food at participating restaurants, etc.

lung *n* in the chest cavity of air-breathing vertebrates: one of a pair of respiratory organs which remove carbon dioxide from the blood and replace it with oxygen.

lunge *n* 1 a sudden plunge forwards. 2 *fencing* a sudden thrust with a sword. ➢ *vb, intr* 1 to make a sudden strong or thrusting movement forwards. 2 *fencing* to make a sudden forward movement with a sword.

lupin *n* a garden plant with long spikes of brightly coloured flowers.

lupine *adj* relating to or like a wolf.

lupus *n (lupuses or lupi / 'luːpaɪ /)* any of a variety of skin diseases characterized by the formation of ulcers and lesions.

lurch[1] *vb, intr* 1 of a person: to stagger unsteadily. 2 of ships, etc: to make a sudden roll to one side. ➢ *n* 1 an act of staggering. 2 a sudden roll to one side.

lurch[2] *n, cards* a state of play in cribbage, whist, etc where one side or player is being roundly beaten by the other. ◆ **leave sb in the lurch** *colloq* to abandon them in a difficult situation.

lure *vb* to tempt or entice, often by the offer of some reward. ➢ *n* 1 someone or something which tempts, attracts or entices: *He left teaching for the lure of more money.* 2 *falconry* a piece of meat attached to a bunch of feathers used for encouraging a hawk, etc to return to its falconer.

lurid *adj* 1 glaringly bright, esp when the surroundings are dark: *a lurid light in the sky.* 2 horrifying or sensational: *lurid details.* 3 of someone's complexion: pale or wan. ○ **luridly** *adv.*

lurk *vb* 1 to lie in wait, esp in ambush, with some sinister purpose in mind. 2 to linger unseen or furtively: *The idea lurked at the back of his mind.*

luscious *adj* 1 of a smell, taste, etc: richly sweet. 2 voluptuously attractive: *luscious lips.*

lush[1] *adj* 1 of grass, foliage, etc: green and

growing abundantly. **2** of fruit, etc: ripe and succulent. **3** luxurious.

lush² *n, slang* an alcoholic.

lust *n* **1** strong sexual desire. **2** enthusiasm; relish: *a lust for life.* ➢ *vb, intr* (*usu* lust after) to have a strong desire for. ○ **lustful** *adj.* ○ **lustfully** *adv.*

lustre or (*US*) **luster** *n* **1** the shiny appearance of something in reflected light. **2** shine, brightness or gloss. **3** splendour and glory, on account of beauty, accomplishments, etc. **4** a glaze for pottery that imparts a shiny appearance. ○ **lustrous** *adj.*

lusty *adj* (*-ier, -iest*) **1** vigorous or loud: *a baby's lusty cries.* **2** strong and healthy. ○ **lustily** *adv.*

lute *n, mus* a stringed instrument with a long neck and a pear-shaped body. ○ **lutenist** *n.*

lutetium /luːˈtiːʃɪəm/ *n, chem* a very rare soft silvery metallic element, belonging to the LANTHANIDE series.

Lutheran *n* a follower of Martin Luther, German protestant reformer. ➢ *adj* relating to Luther or his teaching. ○ **Lutheranism** *n.*

luvvie or **luvvy** *n* (*-ies*) *Brit, facetious* an actor, esp one who speaks and behaves in an overly pretentious or camp manner.

luxe see DE LUXE

luxuriant *adj* **1** of plants, etc: growing abundantly. **2** of someone's writing, imagination, language, etc: full of metaphors and very elaborate. **3** of material things: ornate. ○ **luxuriance** *n.* ○ **luxuriantly** *adv.*

luxuriate *vb, intr* **1** to live in great comfort or luxury. **2** (**luxuriate in sth**) to enjoy it greatly or revel in it.

luxurious *adj* **1** expensive and opulent: *a luxurious hotel.* **2** enjoying luxury. ○ **luxuriously** *adv.*

luxury *n* (*-ies*) **1** expensive, rich and extremely comfortable surroundings and possessions. **2** habitual indulgence in or enjoyment of luxurious surroundings. **3** something that is pleasant and enjoyable but not essential.

lychee, lichee or **litchi** /laɪˈtʃiː/ *n* a small fruit with sweet white juicy flesh.

Lycra *n, trademark* a stretchy fibre or fabric made from lightweight polyurethane and used in the manufacture of sportswear, tights, etc.

lye *n* **1** an alkaline solution made by leaching water through wood ash, etc. **2** a strong solution of sodium or potassium hydroxide.

lymph *n, anat* in animals: a colourless fluid that bathes all the tissues and drains into the vessels of the LYMPHATIC SYSTEM, and which contains LYMPHOCYTES and antibodies which prevent the spread of infection. ○ **lymphatic** *adj.*

lymphatic system *n, anat* the network of vessels that transports LYMPH around the body.

lymph node or **lymph gland** *n, anat* a small rounded structure that produces antibodies in immune responses and filters bacteria and foreign bodies from lymph.

lymphocyte *n* a type of white blood cell present in large numbers in lymphatic tissues, and involved in immune responses.

lymphoma *n* (**lymphomas** or **lymphomata** /lɪmˈfoʊmətə/) *pathol* any tumour of the lymphatic tissues, esp a malignant tumour of the lymph nodes.

lynch *vb* of a group of people: to execute (someone thought guilty of a crime), usu by hanging, without recourse to the law. ○ **lynching** *n.*

lynx *n* (**lynxes** or **lynx**) a wild cat with yellowish-grey or reddish fur, a stubby tail, and tufted ears.

lynx-eyed *adj* sharp-sighted.

lyre *n* a small U-shaped stringed musical instrument.

lyrebird *n* an Australian bird, the male of which spreads its tail into a lyre-shaped fan during courtship.

lyric *adj* **1** *poetry* expressing personal, private or individual emotions. **2** having the form of a song; intended for singing, orig to the lyre. **3** referring or relating to the words of songs rather than the music. ➢ *n* **1** a short poem or song, usu written in the first person and expressing a particular emotion: *a love lyric.* **2** (**lyrics**) the words of a song.

lyrical *adj* **1** lyric; song-like. **2** full of enthusiastic praise: *waxing lyrical.* ○ **lyrically** *adv.*

lyricism *n* **1** the state or quality of being lyrical. **2** an affected pouring out of emotions.

lyricist *n* someone who writes the words to songs.

Mm

M¹ or **m** *n* (*Ms*, *M's* or *m's*) the thirteenth letter of the English alphabet.

M² *abbrev* **1** Master. **2** as a clothes size, etc: medium. **3** million. **4** Monsieur. **5** *Brit* Motorway, followed by a number, as in **M1**.

M³ *symbol* the Roman numeral for 1000.

m or **m.** *abbrev* **1** male. **2** married. **3** masculine. **4** metre. **5** mile. **6** million. **7** minute. **8** month.

MA *abbrev* Master of Arts.

ma *n, colloq* a mother.

ma'am /mam or (*mainly in addressing female royalty*) mɑːm/ *contraction* used as a polite or respectful form of address to a lady: madam.

mac *n, colloq* short form of MACKINTOSH.

macabre /mə'kɑːbrə/ *adj* causing fear or anxiety; gruesome.

macadam *n, esp US* **1** a road-making material consisting of layers of compacted broken stones, usu bound with tar. **2** a road surface made with this. ○ **macadamize** *vb*.

macadamia *n* **1** an evergreen tree belonging to a native Australian genus. **2** the round edible oily nut of the macadamia.

macaque /mə'kɑːk/ *n* a type of short-tailed or tailless monkey of Asia and Africa, with large cheek-pouches.

macaroni *n* (*macaronis* or *macaronies*) pasta in the form of short narrow tubes.

macaroon *n* a sweet cake or biscuit made with sugar, eggs and crushed almonds.

macaw *n* any of numerous large brilliantly-coloured parrots with long tails, found mainly in tropical Central and S America.

mace¹ *n* **1** a ceremonial staff carried by some public officials. **2** *hist* a heavy club, usu with a spiked metal head, used as a weapon in medieval times.

mace² *n* a spice made from the layer around the nutmeg seed, dried and ground up.

macerate /'masəreɪt/ *vb, tr & intr, technical* to break up or make something break up or become soft by soaking it. ○ **maceration** *n*.

machete /mə'ʃɛtɪ/ *n* a long heavy broad-bladed knife used as a weapon or cutting tool.

Machiavellian /makɪə'vɛlɪən/ *adj* of a person or their conduct: crafty, amoral and opportunist. ○ **Machiavellianism** *n*.

machinations *pl n* a crafty scheme or plot, esp a sinister one.

machine *n* **1** a device with moving parts, and usu powered, designed to perform a particular task: *a flying machine • a sewing machine*. **2** a group of people or institutions, or a network of equipment, under a central control: *the party's political machine*. **3** *colloq* a motor vehicle, esp a motorcycle. ➤ *vb* to make, shape or cut something with a machine.

machine code or **machine language** *n, comput* a numerical code used for writing instructions in a form that a computer can process. ○ **machine-code** *adj*.

machine-gun *n* any of various portable guns that fire a continuous rapid stream of bullets when the trigger is pressed.

machine-readable *adj, comput* of data, text, etc: in a form that can be directly processed by a computer.

machinery *n* (*-ies*) **1** machines in general. **2** the working or moving parts of a machine. **3** the combination of processes, systems or people that keeps anything working.

machine tool *n* any stationary power-driven machine used to shape or finish metal, wood or plastic parts by cutting, planing, etc.

machinist *n* **1** someone who operates a machine. **2** someone who makes or repairs machines.

machismo /ma'tʃɪzmoʊ, ma'kɪzmoʊ/ *n, usu derog* exaggerated manliness.

Mach number /mɑːk, mak/ *n* (often shortened to **Mach**) *aeronautics* a ratio of the speed of an object (such as an aircraft) to the speed of sound in the same medium.

macho /'matʃoʊ/ *adj, often derog* exaggeratedly or aggressively manly. ➤ *n* **1** *colloq* a macho man. **2** MACHISMO.

mackerel *n* (*mackerels* or *mackerel*) an important food fish with a streamlined body.

mackintosh or **macintosh** *n* **1** *chiefly Brit* a waterproof raincoat. **2** a kind of rubberized waterproof material.

macramé /mə'krɑːmeɪ/ *n* **1** the art of knotting string or coarse thread into patterns. **2** decorative articles made in this way.

macro *n, comput* a single instruction that brings a set of instructions into operation.

macrobiotics *sing n* the science of devising diets using whole grains and organically-grown fruit and vegetables. ○ **macrobiotic** *adj*.

macrocosm *n* **1** (**the macrocosm**) the universe as a whole. **2** any large or complex system or structure made up of similar smaller systems or structures. Compare MICROCOSM.

macron *n* a straight horizontal bar (¯) placed over a letter to show that it is a long or stressed vowel.

macroscopic *adj, technical* **1** large enough to be seen by the naked eye. Compare MICROSCOPIC. **2** considered in terms of large units or elements.

macula /ˈmakjʊlə/ n (*maculae* /-liː/) *technical* a coloured mark or spot, eg a freckle. ○ **macular** *adj*.

mad *adj* (*madder, maddest*) **1** mentally disturbed. **2** foolish or senseless; extravagantly carefree. **3** *colloq, orig & esp US* (*often* **mad at** or **with sb**) very angry. **4** *colloq* (*usu* **mad about** or **on sth**) extremely enthusiastic. **5** marked by extreme confusion, haste or excitement: *a mad dash for the door.* **6** of a dog, etc: infected with rabies. ○ **madly** *adv* **1** in a mad way. **2** *colloq* passionately. ○ **madness** *n*. ◆ **go mad 1** to become insane or demented. **2** *colloq* to become very angry. **like mad** *colloq* frantically; very energetically: *We ran like mad for the bus.*

madam *n* (*pl* in sense 1 *mesdames* /ˈmeɪdam/ or in other senses *madams*) **1** a polite form of address to any woman, esp any female customer in a shop, etc, used instead of a name. **2** a form of address to a woman in authority, often prefixed to an official title: *Madam Chairman.* **3** a woman who manages a brothel. **4** *colloq, esp Brit* an arrogant or spoiled girl: *Cheeky little madam!*

Madame /məˈdɑːm, ˈmadəm/ n (*Mesdames* /meɪdam/) a title equivalent to MRS, used esp of a French or French-speaking woman.

madcap *adj* foolishly impulsive, wild or reckless. ➤ *n* a foolishly impulsive person.

mad cow disease *n, colloq* BSE.

madden *vb* to make (a person, etc) mad, esp to enrage them. ○ **maddening** *adj*. ○ **maddeningly** *adv*.

madder *n* **1** a plant with yellow flowers and a red root. **2** a dark red dye, orig made from the root of this plant.

made *vb, past tense, past participle of* MAKE. ➤ *adj* **1** (*esp* **made from, in** or **of sth**) artificially produced or formed. **2** *in compounds*, denoting produced, constructed or formed in a specified way or place: *handmade.* **3** of a person, etc: whose success or prosperity is certain: *a made man.* ◆ **have it made** *colloq* to enjoy, or be assured of, complete success, happiness, etc.

Mademoiselle /madəmwəˈzɛl, madməˈzɛl/ n (*Mesdemoiselles* /meɪ-/) **1** a title equivalent to Miss, used of an unmarried French or French-speaking woman. **2** (**mademoiselle**) a French governess or teacher.

made up *adj* **1** of a person: wearing make-up. **2** of a story, etc: not true; invented. **3** *colloq* of a person: extremely pleased.

madhouse *n* **1** *colloq* a place of great confusion and noise. **2** *old use* a mental hospital.

madman or **madwoman** *n* **1** an insane person. **2** a very foolish person.

Madonna *n* **1** (**the Madonna**) *esp RC Church* the Virgin Mary, mother of Christ. **2** (*sometimes* **madonna**) a picture, statue, etc of the Virgin Mary.

madras *n* a kind of medium-hot curry.

madrigal *n, mus* an unaccompanied PART SONG, popular in the 16c and 17c.

maelstrom /ˈmeɪlstrəʊm/ n, *esp literary* **1** a

place or state of uncontrollable confusion or destruction. **2** a violent whirlpool.

maestro /ˈmaɪstrəʊ/ n (*maestros* or *maestri* /-rɪ/) someone who is regarded as being specially gifted in a specified art, esp a distinguished musical composer, conductor, etc.

Mae West *n* an inflatable life jacket.

Mafia *n* **1** (**the Mafia**) a secret international criminal organization, originating in Sicily, that controls numerous illegal activities worldwide, esp in Italy and the US. **2** (*often* **mafia**) any group that exerts a secret and powerful influence, esp one that uses unscrupulous or ruthless criminal methods.

Mafioso or (*sometimes*) **mafioso** *n* (*Mafiosi* or *Mafiosos*) a member of the Mafia or a mafia.

mag *n, colloq* a MAGAZINE.

magazine *n* **1** a paperback periodical publication, usu a heavily illustrated one, containing articles, stories, etc by various writers. **2** *TV, radio* a regular broadcast in which reports are presented on a variety of subjects. **3** in some automatic firearms: a metal container for several cartridges. **4 a** a storeroom for ammunition, explosives, etc; **b** any place, building, etc in which military supplies are stored. **5** *photog* a removable container from which slides are automatically fed through a projector.

magenta *adj* dark, purplish-red in colour. ➤ *n* this colour.

maggot *n* the worm-like larva of various flies, esp that of the housefly. ○ **maggoty** *adj*.

magi or **Magi** see under MAGUS.

magic *n* **1** the supposed art or practice of using the power of supernatural forces, spells, etc to affect people, objects and events. **2** the art or practice of performing entertaining illusions and conjuring tricks. **3** the quality of being wonderful, charming or delightful. **4** a secret or mysterious power over the imagination or will. ➤ *adj* **1** belonging or relating to, used in, or done by, sorcery or conjuring. **2** causing wonderful, startling or mysterious results. **3** *colloq* excellent; great. ➤ *vb* (*magicked, magicking*) to produce something by using, or as if by using, sorcery or conjuring: *He magicked a rabbit out of his hat.* ○ **magical** *adj*. ○ **magically** *adv*. ◆ **like magic 1** mysteriously. **2** suddenly and unexpectedly. **3** excellently.

magician *n* **1** an entertainer who performs conjuring tricks, illusions, etc. **2** someone who practises black or white magic, or who uses supernatural powers.

magisterial *adj* **1** belonging or relating to a magistrate. **2** authoritative. ○ **magisterially** *adv*.

magistracy *n* (*-ies*) **1** the rank or position of a magistrate. **2** (*usu* **the magistracy**) magistrates as a whole.

magistrate *n* **1** in England and Wales: a judge who presides in a lower court of law, dealing with minor criminal and civil cases. **2** any public official administering the law.

magma *n* (*magmas* or *magmata*) *geol* hot molten rock material generated deep within the Earth's crust or mantle. ○ **magmatic** *adj*.

magnanimous *adj* having or showing admirable generosity of spirit towards another person or people. ○ **magnanimity** *n*.

magnate *n* someone of high rank or great power, esp in industry.

> **magnate** There is sometimes a spelling confusion between **magnate** and **magnet**.

magnesia *n, chem* **1** a white light powder, magnesium oxide. **2** *pharmacol* magnesium carbonate, as an antacid and laxative.

magnesium *n, chem* a reactive silvery-grey metallic element that burns with a dazzling white flame.

magnet *n* **1** a piece of metal with the power to attract and repel iron. **2** someone or something that attracts: *That rubbish bin is a magnet to flies.*

> **magnet** There is sometimes a spelling confusion between **magnet** and **magnate**.

magnetic *adj* **1** having the powers of or operated by a magnet or magnetism. **2** of a metal, etc: able to be made into a magnet. **3** of a person, personality, etc: extremely charming or attractive.

magnetic disk *n, comput* a flat circular sheet of material used to store programs and data.

magnetic field *n, physics* the region of physical space surrounding a magnet, within which magnetic forces may be detected.

magnetic mine *n* a mine detonated by a pivoted MAGNETIC NEEDLE when it detects a magnetic field created by the presence of a large metal object.

magnetic needle *n* the slim rod in a nautical compass which, because it is magnetized, always points to the north, or in other instruments is used to indicate the direction of a magnetic field.

magnetic north *n* the direction in which a compass's MAGNETIC NEEDLE always points.

magnetic pole *n, geol* either of two points on the Earth's surface to or from which a MAGNETIC NEEDLE points.

magnetic tape *n, electronics* a narrow plastic ribbon, coated on one side with a magnetic material, used to record and store data in audio and video tape recorders and computers.

magnetism *n* **1** the properties of attraction possessed by magnets. **2** the scientific study of magnets and magnetic phenomena. **3** strong personal charm.

magnetite *n, geol* a black, strongly magnetic mineral form of iron oxide.

magnetize or **-ise** *vb* **1** to make something magnetic. **2** to attract something or someone strongly. ○ **magnetization** *n*.

magneto / mag'ni:toʊ / *n, elec* a simple electric generator consisting of a rotating magnet that induces an alternating current in a coil surrounding it, used to provide the spark in the ignition system of petrol engines without batteries, eg in lawnmowers, etc.

magnetron *n, physics* a device for generating MICROWAVES, developed for use in radar transmitters, and now widely used in microwave ovens.

magnification *n* **1** *optics* a measure of the extent to which an image of an object produced by a lens or optical instrument is enlarged or reduced. **2** the action or an instance of magnifying, or the state of being magnified.

magnificent *adj* **1** splendidly impressive in size, extent or appearance. **2** *colloq* excellent; admirable. ○ **magnificence** *n*. ○ **magnificently** *adv*.

magnify *vb* (*-ies, -ied*) **1** to make something appear larger, eg by using a microscope or telescope. **2** to exaggerate something.

magnifying glass *n* a convex lens, esp a hand-held one, through which objects appear larger.

magniloquent *adj, formal* speaking or spoken in a grand or pompous style. ○ **magniloquence** *n*.

magnitude *n* **1** importance or extent. **2** physical size; largeness. **3** *astron* the degree of brightness of a star.

magnolia *n* **1** a tree or shrub with large sweet-smelling usu white or pink flowers; **b** one of its flowers. **2** a very pale, pinkish-white or beige colour. ➤ *adj* having the colour magnolia.

magnox *n* **a** a material consisting of an aluminium-based alloy containing a small amount of magnesium, from which certain nuclear reactor fuel containers are made; **b** such a container or reactor.

magnum *n* a champagne or wine bottle that holds approximately 1.5 litres.

magpie *n* **1** a black-and-white bird of the crow family, known for its habit of collecting shiny objects. **2** a person who hoards, steals or collects small objects.

magus / 'meɪgəs / *n* (*magi* / 'meɪdʒaɪ /) (*usu* the **Magi**) *Christianity* the three wise men from the east who in tradition brought gifts to the infant Jesus, guided by a star. **2** *hist* a sorcerer. **3** *hist* a Persian priest.

maharajah or **maharaja** *n, hist* an Indian prince, esp any of the former rulers of the states of India.

maharani or **maharanee** *n* **1** the wife or widow of a maharajah. **2** a woman of the same rank as a maharajah in her own right.

maharishi *n* a Hindu religious teacher or spiritual leader.

mahatma *n* a wise and holy Hindu leader.

mah-jong or **mah-jongg** *n* an old game of Chinese origin, usu played by four players using a set of 144 small patterned tiles.

mahogany *n* (*-ies*) **1** a tall evergreen tree of tropical Africa and America, grown commercially for timber. **2** the hard, attractively marked wood of this tree. **3** the colour of the wood, a dark reddish-brown. ➤ *adj* **1** made from this wood. **2** dark reddish-brown in colour.

mahout /mə'haʊt/ *n* someone who drives, trains and looks after elephants.

maid *n* **1** a female servant. **2** *literary & old use* an unmarried woman.

maiden *n* **1** *literary* a young, unmarried woman. **2** *literary* a virgin. **3** *horse-racing* a horse that has never won a race. ➤ *adj* **1** first ever: *maiden voyage*. **2** unmarried: *maiden aunt*. ○ **maidenly** *adj*.

maidenhair *n* a fern with delicate, fan-shaped leaves.

maidenhead *n, literary* **1** virginity. **2** the HYMEN.

maiden name *n* the surname of a married woman at birth.

maid of honour *n* (*maids of honour*) **1** an unmarried female servant of a queen or princess. **2** the principal bridesmaid at a wedding.

maidservant *n, old use* a female servant.

mail¹ *n* **1** the postal system. **2** letters, parcels, etc sent by post. **3** a single collection or delivery of letters, etc: *Has the mail arrived yet?* **4** a vehicle carrying letters, etc. **5** short for ELECTRONIC MAIL. ➤ *vb, esp N Am* to send (a letter, parcel, etc) by post.

mail² *n* flexible armour made of small linked metal rings. ○ **mailed** *adj*.

mailbox *n* **1** *esp N Am* a public or private letter box or postbox. **2** *comput* in an electronic mail system: a facility that allows computer messages from one user to be stored in the file of another.

mailing list *n* a list of the names and addresses of people to whom an organization regularly sends information, advertising material, etc.

mailman *n, esp N Am* a POSTMAN.

mail order *n* a system of buying and selling goods by post. ➤ *adj* (**mail-order**) relating to, bought, sold, sent or operating by mail order: *mail-order catalogue*.

mailshot *n* **1** an unrequested item sent by post, esp a piece of advertising material. **2** the action or an instance of sending out a batch of such post.

maim *vb* to wound (a person or animal) seriously, esp to disable, mutilate or cripple them. ○ **maiming** *n*.

main *adj* **1** most important; chief. **2** (**mains**) belonging or relating to the mains (see *noun* senses 1 and 2): *mains supply*. ➤ *n* **1** (*often* **the mains**) the chief pipe, conduit or cable in a branching system: *not connected to the mains*. **2** (*usu* **the mains**) *chiefly Brit* the network by which power, water, etc is distributed. **3** *old use* great strength, now usu only in the phrase **with might and main**. See under MIGHT². ♦ **in the main** mostly.

mainbrace *n, naut* the rope controlling the movement of a ship's mainsail.

main clause *n, gram* a clause which can stand alone as a sentence. Compare SUBORDINATE CLAUSE.

main course *n* the most substantial course in a meal.

mainframe *n, comput* a large powerful computer that is capable of handling very large amounts of data at high speed.

mainland *n* (*esp* **the mainland**) a country's principal mass of land, as distinct from a nearby island or islands forming part of the same country. ○ **mainlander** *n*.

mainline *vb, tr & intr, slang* to inject (a drug) into a principal vein.

main line *n* **1** the principal railway line between two places. **2** *US* a principal route, road, etc. **3** *slang* a major vein.

mainly *adv* chiefly; largely.

mainmast /'meɪnməst, -mɑːst/ *n, naut* the principal mast of a sailing ship. Compare FOREMAST.

mainsail /'meɪnsəl, 'meɪnseɪl/ *n, naut* the largest and lowest sail on a sailing ship.

mainspring *n* **1** the chief spring in a watch or clock, or other piece of machinery, that gives it motion. **2** a chief motive, reason or cause.

mainstay *n* **1** *naut* a rope stretching forward and down from the top of the MAINMAST. **2** a chief support: *He has been my mainstay during this crisis.*

mainstream *n* **1** (*usu* **the mainstream**) the chief trend, or direction of development, in any activity, business, movement, etc. **2** the principal current of a river which has tributaries. **3** mainstream jazz (see *adj* sense 3 below). ➤ *adj* **1** belonging or relating to the mainstream. **2** in accordance with what is normal or standard: *Joel takes a mainstream view on this subject.* **3** *jazz* said of swing, etc: belonging or relating to a style that developed between early and modern jazz.

maintain *vb* **1** to continue; to keep something in existence: *Adam must maintain this level of commitment.* **2** to keep something in good condition. **3** to pay the expenses of someone or something: *a duty to maintain his children.* **4** to continue to argue something; to assert (eg an opinion, one's innocence, etc). ○ **maintained** *adj, esp in compounds* of a school, etc: financially supported, eg from public funds: *grant-maintained*.

maintenance *n* **1** the process of keeping something in good condition. **2** money paid by one person to support another, as ordered by a court of law, eg money paid to an ex-spouse and/or children, following a divorce. **3** the process of continuing something or keeping it in existence.

maisonette or **maisonnette** *n* a flat within a larger house or block, esp one on two floors. *US equivalent* **duplex**.

maître d'hôtel /meɪtrədoʊˈtel/ *n* the manager or head waiter of a hotel or restaurant.

maize *n* **1** a tall cereal plant, widely grown for its edible yellow grain which grows in large spikes called CORNCOBS. **2** the grain of this plant, eaten ripe and unripe as a vegetable.

majestic adj stately, dignified or grand.

majesty n (**-ies**) **1** great and impressive dignity, sovereign power or authority. **2** splendour; grandeur. **3** His, Her or Your Majesty (Their or Your Majesties) the title used when speaking of or to a king or queen.

majolica /məˈdʒɒlɪkə/ or **maiolica** /məˈjɒl-/ n colourfully glazed or enamelled earthenware, esp that of the early 16c decorated with scenes in the Renaissance style.

major adj **1** great, or greater, in number, size, extent, value, importance, etc. **2** mus **a** of a scale: having two full tones between the first and third notes; **b** of a key, chord, etc: based on such a scale. In all senses compare MINOR. ➢ n **1 a** an army officer of the rank below lieutenant colonel; **b** an officer who is in charge of a military band: pipe major. **2** mus a major key, chord or scale. **3** esp N Am **a** a student's main or special subject of study: English is his major; **b** a student studying such a subject: He's a psychology major. **4** someone who has reached the age of full legal responsibility. Compare MINOR (noun sense I). ➢ vb, intr (always major in sth) esp US to specialize in (a particular subject of study).

major-domo n a chief servant or steward in charge of the management of a household.

majorette n a member of a group of girls who march in parades, performing elaborate displays of baton-twirling, etc.

major-general n an army officer of the rank below lieutenant general.

majority n (**-ies**) **1** the greater number; the largest group: The majority of the population is in favour. **2** the difference between the greater and the lesser number. **3** the winning margin of votes in an election: a Labour majority of 2549. **4** the age at which someone legally becomes an adult. ◆ in the majority forming the larger group or greater part.

make vb (**made**) **1** to form, create, manufacture or produce something by combining or shaping materials: make the tea. **2** to cause, bring about or create something by one's actions, etc: He's always making trouble. **3** to force, induce or cause someone to do something: He makes me laugh. **4** (often make sth or sb into sth) to cause it or them to change into something else; to transform or convert it or them. **5** to cause something or someone to be, do or become a specified thing: It made me cross. **6** to be capable of turning or developing into or serving as (a specified thing); to have or to develop the appropriate qualities for something: This box makes a good table. **7** (always make sb sth) to appoint them as something: They made her deputy head. **8** (also make sth or sth into sth) to cause them or it to appear to be, or to represent them or it as being (a specified thing): Long hair makes her look younger. **9** to gain,

earn or acquire something: Ted makes £400 a week. **10** to add up to or amount to something; to constitute: 4 and 4 makes 8 • The book makes interesting reading. **11** to calculate, judge or estimate something to be (a specified thing): I make it three o'clock. **12** (always make of sth or sb) to understand by it or them: What do you make of their comments? **13** to arrive at or reach something, or to succeed in doing so: Julia can't make the party. **14** to score or win (points, runs, card tricks, etc). **15** to tidy (a bed) after use by smoothing out and tucking in the sheets, etc. **16** to bring about or ensure the success of something; to complete something: It made my day. **17** to propose something or propose something to someone: make me an offer. **18** to engage in something; to perform, carry out or produce something: make a speech • make a decision. ➢ n **1** a manufacturer's brand: What make of car is it? **2** applied to a physical object, a person's body, etc: structure, type or build; the way in which it is made. ○ **maker** n.

◆ make as if or as though, or (US) make like sth or make like to do sth to act or behave in a specified way: She made as if to leave. **make do** colloq to manage or get by: always having to make do. **make do without sth** colloq to manage without it. **make do with sth** colloq to manage with, or make the best use of, a second or inferior choice. **make it** colloq **1** to be successful: to make it in show business. **2** to survive. **make it up to sb** to repay them for difficulties, etc which they have experienced on one's account, or for kindness, etc which they have shown to one. **make or break sth** or **sb** to be the crucial test that brings it or them either success or failure: The takeover will either make or break the company. **on the make** colloq of a person: seeking a large or illegal personal profit. ◇ **make away with sb** to kill them. **make for sth** or **sb** to go towards it or them, esp rapidly, purposefully or suddenly. **make off** to leave, esp in a hurry or secretly. **make off** or **away with sth** or **sb** to run off with it or them; to steal or kidnap it or them. **make out 1** colloq to progress or get along: How did you make out in the exam? **2** colloq, chiefly N Am to manage, succeed or survive: It's been tough, but we'll make out. **make out sth** or **that sth** to pretend or claim that it is so: He made out that he was ill. **make out sth** or **make sth out 1** to begin to discern it, esp to see or hear it. **2** to write or fill in a document, etc: I made out a cheque for £20. **make sth** or **sb out to be sth** to portray them, or cause them to seem to be, what they are not: They made us out to be liars. **make over sth** or **make sth over 1** to transfer ownership of it: I made over my shares to her when I retired. **2** N Am to convert or alter it. **make up for sth** to compensate or serve as an apology for it. **make up to sb** colloq to seek their friendship or favour; to flirt with them. **make up with sb** to resolve a disagreement with someone. **make sth up 1** to fabricate or invent it: Tom made up the story. **2** to prepare or assemble it. **3** to constitute it; to be the parts of it: *The three villages together make up a district.* **4** to form the final element in something; to complete it: *another player to make up the team.*

make-believe *n* pretence, esp playful or innocent imaginings. ➤ *adj* imaginary.

makeover *n* **1** a complete change in a person's style of dress, appearance, make-up, hair, etc. **2** a remake or reconstruction.

Maker *n* God, the Creator: *go to meet his Maker.*

makeshift *adj* serving as a temporary and less adequate substitute for something: *a makeshift bed.*

make-up *n* **1 a** cosmetics such as mascara, lipstick, etc applied to the face; **b** cosmetics worn by actors to give the required appearance for a part. **2** the combination of characteristics or ingredients that form something, eg a temperament: *Greed is not in his make-up.*

making *n* the materials or qualities from which something can be made. ♦ **be the making of sb** to ensure their success. **in the making** in the process of being made, formed or developed: *She is a star in the making.*

makings *pl n.* ♦ **have the makings of sth** to have the ability to become a specified thing.

malachite /ˈmaləkaɪt/ *n, geol* a bright green copper mineral that is used as a gemstone and as a minor ore of copper.

maladjusted *adj* of a person: psychologically unable to deal with everyday situations and relationships. ○ **maladjustment** *n.*

maladminister *vb* to manage (eg public affairs) badly, dishonestly or incompetently. ○ **maladministration** *n.*

maladroit *adj, rather formal* clumsy; tactless. ○ **maladroitness** *n.*

malady /ˈmalədɪ/ *n (-ies) rather formal or old use* an illness or disease.

malaise *n* a feeling of uneasiness, discontent, or despondency.

malapropism *n* **1** the unintentional misuse of a word, usu with comic effect, through confusion with another word that sounds similar but has a different meaning. **2** a word misused in this way.

malaria *n* an infectious disease that produces recurring bouts of fever, caused by the bite of the mosquito. ○ **malarial** *adj.*

malarkey or **malarky** *n, colloq* nonsense; absurd behaviour or talk.

malcontent *adj (also* **malcontented***)* of a person: dissatisfied and inclined to rebel. ➤ *n* a dissatisfied or rebellious person.

male *adj* **1** belonging or relating to the sex that produces sperm and fertilizes the egg cell produced by the female. **2** denoting the reproductive structure of a plant that produces the male GAMETE. **3** belonging to or characteristic of men: *male hormones.* **4** for or made up of men or boys: *male college.* **5** *eng* of a piece of machinery, etc: having a projecting part that fits into another part (the FEMALE *adj* sense 4).

➤ *n* a male person, animal or plant. ○ **maleness** *n.*

male chauvinist or *(colloq)* **male chauvinist pig** *n, derog* a man who believes in the superiority of men over women. ○ **male chauvinism** *n.*

malediction /malɪˈdɪkʃən/ *n, literary or formal* **1** a curse or defamation. **2** the uttering of a curse. ○ **maledictory** *adj.*

malefactor /ˈmalɪfaktə(r)/ *n, literary or formal* a criminal; a wrongdoer.

malevolent /məˈlɛvələnt/ *adj* wishing to do evil to others. ○ **malevolence** *n.* ○ **malevolently** *adv.*

malfeasance *n, law* wrongdoing; the committing of an unlawful act, esp by a public official. ○ **malfeasant** *adj.*

malformation *n* **1** the state or condition of being badly or wrongly formed or shaped. **2** a badly or wrongly formed part. ○ **malformed** *adj.*

malfunction *vb, intr* to work imperfectly; to fail to work. ➤ *n* failure of, or a fault or failure in, the operation of a machine, etc.

malice /ˈmalɪs/ *n* the desire or intention to harm or hurt another or others. ○ **malicious** /məˈlɪʃəs/ *adj.*

malign /məˈlaɪn/ *vb* to say or write bad or unpleasant things about someone, esp falsely. ➤ *adj* **1** of a person: evil in nature or influence. **2** of a disease: harmful.

malignant /məˈlɪgnənt/ *adj* **1** of a person: feeling or showing hatred or the desire to do harm to another or others. **2** *med* esp of a cancerous tumour: of a type that, esp if left untreated, destroys the surrounding tissue and may spread elsewhere in the body. Compare BENIGN. ○ **malignancy** *n.*

malinger /məˈlɪŋgə(r)/ *vb, intr* to pretend to be ill, esp in order to avoid having to work. ○ **malingerer** *n.*

mall /mɔːl, mal/ *n* a shopping centre that is closed to vehicles.

mallard *n (mallard* or *mallards)* a common wild duck, the male of which has a green head.

malleable /ˈmalɪəbəl/ *adj* **1** of certain metals and alloys, etc: able to be beaten into a different shape, etc without breaking. **2** eg of a person or personality: easily influenced. ○ **malleability** *n.*

mallet *n* **1** a hammer with a large head, usu made of wood. **2** in croquet, polo, etc: a long-handled wooden hammer used to strike the ball.

mallow *n* a plant with pink, purple or white flowers.

malnourished *adj* suffering from MALNUTRITION.

malnutrition *n, med* a disorder resulting from inadequate food intake, an unbalanced diet or inability to absorb nutrients from food.

malodorous *adj, formal* foul-smelling.

malpractice *n, law* improper, careless, illegal or unethical professional conduct.

malt *n* **1** *brewing* a mixture, used in brewing, prepared from barley or wheat grains that have been soaked in water, allowed to sprout and then dried in a kiln. **2** MALT WHISKY, or another liquor made with malt. ➤ *vb* to make (a grain) into malt. ○ **malted** *adj.* ○ **malty** *adj.*

Maltese cross *n* a cross with four arms of equal length that taper towards the centre, each with a V cut into the end.

maltose *n, biochem* a hard white crystalline sugar that occurs in starch and glycogen.

maltreat *vb* to treat someone or something roughly or cruelly. ○ **maltreatment** *n.*

malt whisky *n* whisky made entirely from malted barley.

mam *n, dialect or colloq* mother.

mama or (*chiefly US*) **mamma** or **mammy** *n* (*mamas, mammas* or *mammies*) **1** *rather dated* now used chiefly by young children: mother. **2** *slang, chiefly US* a woman.

mamba *n* a large, poisonous, black or green African snake.

mambo *n* **1** a rhythmic Latin American dance resembling the RUMBA. **2** a piece of music for this dance.

mammal *n, zool* any warm-blooded, vertebrate animal characterized by the possession in the female of MAMMARY GLANDs which secrete milk to feed its young. ○ **mammalian** /mə'meɪlɪən/ *adj.*

mammary *adj, biol, med* belonging to, of the nature of, or relating to the breasts or other milk-producing glands.

mammary gland *n, biol, anat* the milk-producing gland of a mammal.

mammography *n, med* the process of X-raying the breast, usu in order to detect any abnormal or malignant growths at an early stage.

mammon *n, chiefly literary or Bible* **1** wealth when considered as the source of evil and immorality. **2** (**Mammon**) the personification of this in the New Testament as a false god, the god of riches.

mammoth *n* an extinct shaggy-haired, prehistoric elephant, with long curved tusks. ➤ *adj* huge; giant-sized.

man *n* (*men*) **1** an adult male human being. **2** human beings as a whole or as a genus; the human race: *when man first walked the earth.* **3** any subspecies of, or type of creature belonging to, the human genus *Homo.* **4** a human being; a person: *the right man for the job.* **5** an ordinary employee, worker or member of the armed forces. **6** an adult male human being displaying typical or expected masculine qualities, such as strength and courage: *Stand up and be a man.* **7** in various board games, eg draughts and chess: one of the movable pieces. **8** *colloq* a husband or boyfriend. **9** *colloq* used as a form of address to an adult male, in various contexts, eg indicating impatience: *Damn it, man!* **10** *colloq* the perfect thing or person, esp for a specified job or purpose: *If you want to know about films, Dave's your man.* ➤ *vb* (**manned, manning**) **1** to provide (eg a ship, industrial plant, fortress, etc) with workers, operators, defenders, etc. **2** to operate (a piece of equipment, etc) or to make it ready for action: *man the pumps.* ➤ *exclam, colloq, esp US* used to intensify a statement that follows it: *Man, is she gorgeous!* ○ **manned** *adj* of a ship, machine, spacecraft, etc: provided with men, operators, crew, etc. ♦ **as one man** simultaneously; all together. **be sb's man** to be exactly the person they are looking for to do a particular job: *You're my man.* **man and boy** from childhood to manhood. **sort out** or **separate the men from the boys** *colloq* to serve as a test that will prove someone's ability, calibre, quality, etc or otherwise. **to a man** *slightly formal or old use* without exception.

manacle *n* a shackle for the hand or wrist. Compare FETTER. ➤ *vb* to restrain someone with manacles.

manage *vb* **1** to be in overall control or charge of, or the manager of, something or someone. **2** to deal with something or handle it successfully or competently: *I can manage my own affairs.* **3** *tr & intr* to succeed in doing or producing something: *Can you manage the food if I organize the drink?* **4** to have, or to be able to find, enough room, time, etc for something: *Can you manage another sandwich?* **5** *intr* (*usu* **manage on sth**) to succeed in living on (a specified amount of money, etc). ○ **manageable** *adj.*

management *n* **1** the skill or practice of controlling, directing or planning something, esp a commercial enterprise or activity. **2** the managers of a company, etc, as a group. **3** manner of directing, controlling or using something.

manager *n* **1** someone who manages a commercial enterprise, organization, etc. **2** someone who manages eg actors, musicians, sportsmen and sportswomen, or a particular team, etc. ○ **managerial** *adj.*

manageress *n* a female manager of a business, etc.

managing director *n* a director in overall charge of an organization and its day-to-day running. *N Am equivalent* **chief executive officer**.

man-at-arms *n* (**men-at-arms**) *hist* a soldier, esp a heavily-armed, mounted soldier.

manatee *n* a large plant-eating marine mammal of the tropical waters of America, Africa and the W Indies.

mandarin *n* **1** (*also* **mandarin orange**) a small citrus fruit, similar to the tangerine. **2** a high-ranking official or bureaucrat, esp one who is thought to be outside political control: *at the mercy of the mandarins at Whitehall.* **3** a person of great influence, esp a reactionary or pedantic literary figure. **4** *hist* a senior official belonging to any of the nine ranks of officials under the Chinese Empire.

mandate *n* a right or authorization given to a

nation, person, etc to act on behalf of others.
➤ *vb* **1** to give authority or power to someone or something. **2** to assign (territory) to a nation under a mandate.

mandatory *adj* **1** not allowing any choice. **2** referring to the nature of, or containing, a MANDATE or command.

mandible *n, zool* **1** the lower jaw of a vertebrate. **2** the upper or lower part of a bird's beak. **3** one of a pair of jaw-like mouthparts in insects, crustaceans, etc.

mandolin or **mandoline** *n* a musical instrument like a small guitar, with eight metal strings tuned in pairs.

mandrake *n* a plant with purple flowers and a forked root, formerly thought to have magical powers.

mandrel or **mandril** *n, technical* **1** the rotating shaft on a lathe that the object being worked on is fixed to. **2** the axle of a circular saw or grinding wheel.

mandrill *n* a large W African baboon with distinctive red and blue striped markings on its muzzle and hindquarters.

mane *n* **1** on a horse, lion or other animal: the long hair growing around the neck. **2** on a human: a long, thick head of hair.

maneuver, maneuvered, *etc* the N Am spellings of MANOEUVRE, etc.

man Friday *n* (**man Fridays**) **1** a faithful or devoted manservant or male assistant. **2** a junior male worker given various duties, esp in an office.

manful *adj* brave and determined. ○ **manfully** *adv.*

manganese *n, chem* a hard brittle pinkish-grey metallic element, widely used to make alloys that are very hard and resistant to wear.

mange /meɪndʒ/ *n, vet med* a skin disease that affects hairy animals such as cats and dogs, causing itching and loss of hair. ○ **mangy** or **mangey** *adj* **1** suffering from mange. **2** *derog* shabby; scruffy.

mangel-wurzel or (*US*) **mangel** *n* a variety of beet with a large yellow root, used as cattle food.

manger *n* an open trough from which cattle or horses feed.

mangetout /mɒndʒ'tu:/ *n* a variety of garden pea with an edible pod.

mangle[1] *vb* **1** to damage or destroy something or someone by crushing, tearing, etc. **2** to spoil, ruin or bungle something. ○ **mangled** *adj.*

mangle[2] *n* **1** *dated* a device, usu hand-operated, that consists of two large heavy rotating rollers which have wet laundry fed between them so as to squeeze most of the water out. **2** *esp US* a machine that presses laundry by passing it between two large heated rollers. ➤ *vb* to pass (laundry, etc) through a mangle.

mango *n* (**mangos** or **mangoes**) a heavy oblong fruit with a central stone surrounded by sweet, soft juicy orange flesh and a thick green, yellow or red skin.

mangrove *n* a tropical evergreen tree that grows in salt marshes and on mudflats, producing aerial roots from its branches that form a dense tangled network.

manhandle *vb* **1** to treat someone or something roughly; to push them or it. **2** to move or transport something using manpower, not machinery.

manhole *n* an opening large enough to allow a person through, esp one that leads down into a sewer.

manhood *n* **1** the state of being an adult male. **2** manly qualities.

man-hour *n* a unit of work equal to the work done by one person in one hour.

manhunt *n* an intensive and usu large-scale organized search for someone, esp a criminal or fugitive.

mania *n* **1** *psychol* a mental disorder characterized by great excitement and violence. **2** *loosely* (*esp* **a mania for sth**) a great enthusiasm for it; a craze.

maniac *n* **1** *colloq* a person who behaves wildly. **2** an extremely keen enthusiast.

manic *adj* **1** *psychol* characteristic of, relating to or suffering from MANIA (sense I). **2** *colloq* very energetic or active. ○ **manically** *adv.*

manic-depressive *psychiatry, adj* affected by or suffering from an illness which produces alternating phases of extreme elation (MANIA sense I) and severe depression. ➤ *n* someone who is suffering from this illness.

manicure *n* **1** the care and cosmetic treatment of the hands, esp the fingernails. **2** an individual treatment of this kind. ➤ *vb* to carry out a manicure on (a person or their hands).

manifest *vb, formal* **1** to show or display something clearly. **2** (*usu* **manifest itself**) to reveal itself. **3** to be evidence of something: *an act which manifested his sincerity.* ➤ *adj* easily seen or perceived: *a manifest lie.* ➤ *n* **1** a customs document that gives details of a ship or aircraft, its cargo and destination. **2** a passenger list, for an aeroplane, etc. ○ **manifestation** *n.* ○ **manifestly** *adv* obviously.

manifesto *n* (**manifestos** or **manifestoes**) a written public declaration of policies, intentions, opinions or motives, esp one produced by a political party or candidate.

manifold *adj, formal or literary* many and various: *manifold pleasures.* ➤ *n, technical* a pipe with several inlets and outlets.

manikin or **mannikin** *n* **1** a model of the human body, used in teaching art and anatomy, etc. **2** *old use* an abnormally small person.

manila or **manilla** *n* (*also* manila paper or **manilla paper**) a type of thick strong brown paper.

the man in the street *n* the ordinary or average man.

manipulate *vb* **1** to handle something, or move or work it with the hands, esp in a skilful way. **2** to control someone or something cleverly and unscrupulously, esp to one's own advantage. **3** to give false appearance to something, etc: *manipulating the statistics to suit his argument*. ○ **manipulation** *n*. ○ **manipulative** or **manipulatory** *adj*. ○ **manipulator** *n*.

mankind *n* **1** the human race as a whole. **2** human males collectively.

manly *adj* (**-ier, -iest**) **1** displaying qualities considered admirable in a man, such as strength, determination, courage, etc. **2** considered suitable for or characteristic of a man. ○ **manliness** *n*.

man-made *adj* made by or originated by humans: *man-made fibre*.

manna *n* **1** in the Old Testament: the food miraculously provided by God for the Israelites in the wilderness (Exodus 16:14–36). **2** any unexpected gift or windfall: *manna from heaven*.

mannequin *n* **1** a fashion model, esp a woman, employed to model clothes, etc. **2** a lifesize dummy of the human body, used in the making or displaying of clothes.

manner *n* **1** way; fashion: *an unusual manner of walking*. **2** (*often* **manners**) behaviour towards others: *Judy has a very pleasant manner*. **3** (**manners**) good or polite social behaviour. **4** *formal or dated* kind or kinds: *all manner of things*. ◆ **in a manner of speaking** in a way; to some degree. **to the manner born** of a person: naturally suited to a particular occupation, lifestyle, etc.

mannered *adj*, *formal* **1** *usu derog* unnatural and artificial. **2** *in compounds* having or displaying a specified kind of social behaviour: *bad-mannered*.

mannerism *n* **1** an individual characteristic, such as a gesture or facial expression. **2** *derog* esp in art or literature: noticeable or excessive use of a mannered style.

mannerly *adj*, *old use* polite; showing good manners. ○ **mannerliness** *n*.

mannish *adj* of a woman: having an appearance or qualities regarded as more typical of a man.

manoeuvre or (*N Am*) **maneuver** /mə-ˈnuːvə(r)/ *n* **1** a movement requiring, or performed with, skill or intelligence. **2** a clever or skilful handling of affairs, often one involving deception or inventiveness. **3** *mil, navy* **a** (*usu* **manoeuvres**) a large-scale battle-training exercise by armed forces; **b** a skilful or clever tactical movement of troops or ships, etc. ➤ *vb* **1** *tr & intr* to move something accurately and with skill. **2** *tr & intr* to use ingenuity, and perhaps deceit, in handling something or someone. ○ **manoeuvrability** *n*. ○ **manoeuvrable** *adj*.

man-of-war or **man-o'-war** *n*, *hist* an armed sailing ship used as a warship.

manor *n* **1** (*also* **manor house**) the principal residence on a country estate, often the former home of a medieval lord. **2** *hist* in medieval Europe: an area of land under the control of a lord. **3** *Brit, colloq* the area in which a particular police unit or criminal operates.

manpower *n* the number of available employees or people fit and ready to work.

manqué /ˈmɒŋkeɪ; *French* māke/ *adj*, following its noun, *literary* applied to a specified kind of person: having once had the ambition or potential to be that kind of person, without achieving it: *an artist manqué*.

mansard *n*, *archit* (*in full* **mansard roof**) a four-sided roof, each side of which is in two parts, the lower part sloping more steeply.

manse *n* esp in Scotland: the house of a religious minister.

manservant *n* (**menservants**) *old use* a male servant, esp a valet.

mansion *n* **1** a large house, usu a grand or luxurious one. **2** (**mansions** or **Mansions**) *Brit* used eg as the name or address of a residential property: a large building divided into apartments.

manslaughter *n*, *law* the crime of HOMICIDE without malice aforethought, eg as a result of gross negligence or diminished responsibility.

mantel *n*, *chiefly old use* a mantelpiece.

mantelpiece *n* the ornamental frame around a fireplace, esp the top part which forms a shelf.

mantilla /manˈtɪlə; *Spanish* manˈtiːja/ *n* a lace or silk scarf worn by women as a covering for the hair and shoulders, esp in Spain and S America.

mantis *n* (**mantises** or **mantes**) a tropical insect-eating insect that sits in wait for prey with its two front legs raised.

mantissa *n*, *maths* the part of a logarithm comprising the decimal point and the figures following it.

mantle *n* **1** a cloak or loose outer garment. **2** *literary* a covering: *a mantle of snow*. **3** *geol* the part of the Earth between the crust and the core. **4** a fireproof mesh around a gas or oil lamp, that glows when the lamp is lit. **5** *literary* a position of responsibility: *The leader's mantle passed to him*. ➤ *vb*, *literary* to cover, conceal or obscure something or someone.

man-to-man *adj* esp of personal discussion: open and frank. ➤ *adv* in an open and frank manner.

mantra *n* **1** *Hinduism, Buddhism* a sacred phrase, word or sound chanted repeatedly as part of meditation and prayer as an aid to concentration. **2** *Hinduism* any of the hymns of praise in the VEDAS.

manual *adj* **1** belonging or relating to the hand or hands: *manual skill*. **2** using the body, rather than the mind. **3** worked, controlled or operated by hand. ➤ *n* **1** a book of instructions, eg for repairing a car or operating a machine. **2** an organ keyboard or a key played by hand not by foot. ○ **manually** *adv*.

manufacture *vb* **1** to make something from raw materials, esp in large quantities using machinery. **2** to invent or fabricate something. ➤ *n* **1** the practice, act or process of manufacturing something. **2** anything manufactured. ○ **manufacturer** *n*. ○ **manufacturing** *adj, n*.

manumit *vb* (**manumitted, manumitting**) *formal* to release (a person) from slavery. ○ **manumission** *n*.

manure *n* any substance, esp animal dung, used on soil as a fertilizer. ➤ *vb* to apply manure to (land, soil, etc).

manuscript *n* 1 an author's hand-written or typed version of a book, play, etc before it has been printed. 2 a book or document written by hand.

Manx *adj* 1 belonging or relating to the Isle of Man or its inhabitants. 2 relating to the Manx language.

many *adj* (**more, most**) consisting of a large number: *Many teenagers smoke.* ➤ *pron* a great number (of things or people): *The sweets were so rich that I couldn't eat many.* ♦ **the many** the majority of ordinary people.

map *n* 1 a diagram of any part of the Earth's surface, showing geographical and other features. 2 a similar diagram of the surface of the Moon or a planet. 3 a diagram showing the position of the stars in the sky. 4 a diagram of the layout of anything. ➤ *vb* (**mapped, mapping**) 1 to make a map of something. 2 *maths* to place (the elements of a SET² (*noun* sense 2)) in one-to-one correspondence with the elements of another set. ♦ **put sth** or **sb on the map** *colloq* to cause (eg a town, an actor, etc) to become well-known or important. ◊ **map sth out** to plan (a route, course of action, etc) in detail.

maple *n* 1 (*also* **maple tree**) a broad-leaved deciduous tree of northern regions. 2 the hard light-coloured wood of these trees.

maple leaf *n* the leaf of a maple tree, esp as the national emblem of Canada.

maple syrup *n, esp N Am* the distinctively flavoured syrup made from the sap of the sugar-maple tree.

maquis /ˈmɑːkiː/ *n* (*pl* **maquis**) 1 a type of thick, shrubby vegetation found in coastal areas of the Mediterranean. 2 (**the maquis** or **the Maquis**) *hist* a the French resistance movement that fought against German occupying forces during World War II; b a member of this movement.

mar *vb* (**marred, marring**) to spoil something.

marabou or **marabout** *n* 1 a large black-and-white African stork. 2 its feathers, used to decorate clothes.

maraca *n* a hand-held percussion instrument, usu one of a pair, consisting of a gourd filled with dried beans, pebbles, etc.

maraschino /marəˈʃiːnoʊ, -ˈskiːnoʊ/ *n* a liqueur made from cherries.

maraschino cherry *n* a cherry preserved in MARASCHINO, used for decorating cocktails, cakes, etc.

marathon *n* 1 (*sometimes* **marathon race**) a long-distance race on foot, usu 42.195km (26ml 385yd). 2 any lengthy and difficult task. ➤ *adj* 1 belonging or relating to a marathon race. 2 requiring or displaying great powers of endurance: *a marathon effort.*

maraud *vb* 1 *intr* to wander in search of people to attack and property to steal or destroy. 2 to plunder (a place). ○ **marauder** *n*. ○ **marauding** *adj, n*.

marble *n* 1 a *geol* a hard, metamorphic rock, usu mottled or streaked; b any such rock that can be highly polished, used in building and sculpture. 2 in children's games: a small hard ball, now usu made of glass. 3 a work of art, tombstone, tomb or other object made of marble. ➤ *vb* to stain or paint something (esp paper) to resemble marble. ○ **marbled** *adj*. ○ **marbling** *n* 1 a marbled appearance or colouring. 2 the practice or act of staining or painting (esp the edges of a book) in imitation of marble.

marbles *sing n* any of several children's games played with marbles. ♦ **have all**, or **lose, one's marbles** to be in full possession of, or to lack, one's mental faculties.

marc *n* 1 *technical* the leftover skins and stems of grapes used in winemaking. 2 a kind of brandy made from these.

marcasite *n* 1 *geol* a pale yellow mineral, a compound of iron, formerly used in jewellery. 2 a polished gemstone made from this or any similar mineral.

March *n* the third month of the year.

march¹ *vb* 1 *intr* to walk in a stiff, upright, formal manner, usu at a brisk pace. 2 to make or force someone, esp a soldier or troop of soldiers, to walk in this way. 3 *intr* to walk in a purposeful and determined way: *suddenly marched out of the room.* 4 *intr* to advance or continue, steadily or irresistibly: *Events marched on.* ➤ *n* 1 an act of marching. 2 a distance travelled by marching. 3 a brisk walking pace. 4 a procession of people moving steadily forward. 5 *mus* a piece of music written in a marching rhythm. 6 steady and unstoppable progress or movement: *the march of time.* ○ **marcher** *n*.

march² *n* 1 a boundary or border. 2 a border district.

March hare *n* a hare during its breeding season in March, noted for its excitable and erratic behaviour: *mad as a March hare.*

marching orders *pl n* 1 orders to march in a certain way, given to soldiers, etc. 2 *colloq* dismissal from a job, house, relationship, etc.

marchioness /ˈmɑːʃənəs/ *n* 1 the wife or widow of a MARQUIS. 2 a woman who holds the rank of marquis in her own right.

mare¹ *n* an adult female horse, ass, zebra, etc.

mare² /ˈmɑːreɪ/ *n* (**maria**) *astron* any of numerous large, flat areas on the surface of the Moon or Mars.

mare's nest *n* 1 a discovery that proves to be untrue or without value. 2 *chiefly US* a disordered or confused place or situation.

marg or **marge** *contraction, colloq* margarine.

margarine *n* a food, usu made from vegetable oils with water, flavourings, etc, used as a substitute for butter.

margin n 1 the blank space around a page of writing or print. 2 any edge, border or fringe. 3 an extra amount beyond what should be needed: *allow a margin for error.* 4 an amount by which one thing exceeds another: *win by a large margin.* 5 *business* the difference between the selling and buying price of an item. 6 *econ, etc* an upper or lower limit, esp one beyond which it is impossible for a business, etc to operate.

marginal adj 1 small and unimportant or insignificant. 2 near to the lower limit. 3 *chiefly Brit* of a political constituency: whose current MP was elected by only a small majority of votes at the last election. 4 of a note, design, etc: appearing in the margin of a page of text. 5 in, on, belonging or relating to a margin. ➤ n, *chiefly Brit* a marginal constituency or seat. ○ **marginality** n. ○ **marginally** adv.

marginalize or **-ise** vb to push something or someone to the edges of anything, in order to reduce its or their effect, significance, etc. ○ **marginalization** n.

marigold n a garden plant with bright orange or yellow flowers.

marijuana or **marihuana** /marɪ'wɑːnə/ n CANNABIS.

marimba n, *mus* a type of XYLOPHONE consisting of a set of hardwood strips which, when struck with hammers, vibrate metal plates underneath.

marina n a harbour for berthing private pleasure boats.

marinade n, *cookery* any liquid mixture, esp a mixture of oil, herbs, wine, etc, in which meat or fish is soaked before cooking. ➤ vb, tr & intr to soak (meat or fish, etc) in a marinade.

marinate vb to MARINADE something.

marine adj 1 belonging to or concerned with the sea: *marine landscape.* 2 inhabiting, found in or obtained from the sea: *marine mammal.* 3 belonging or relating to ships, shipping trade or the navy: *marine insurance.* ➤ n 1 (*often* **Marine**) a a soldier trained to serve on land or at sea; b a member of the Royal Marines or the US Marine Corps. 2 the merchant or naval ships of a nation collectively.

mariner /'marɪnə(r)/ n a seaman.

marionette n a puppet with jointed limbs moved by strings.

marital adj belonging or relating to marriage: *marital status.* ○ **maritally** adv.

maritime adj 1 belonging or relating to the sea or ships, etc. 2 of plants, etc: living or growing near the sea.

marjoram n (*in full* **wild marjoram**) a pungent plant used to season food, esp pasta dishes.

mark¹ n 1 a visible blemish. 2 a a grade or score awarded according to the proficiency of a student or competitor, etc; b a letter, number or percentage used to denote this: *What mark did you get? Only a C.* 3 a sign or symbol: *a question mark.* 4 an indication or representation: *a mark of respect.* 5 the position from

which a competitor starts in a race. 6 an object or thing to be aimed at or striven for: *It fell wide of the mark.* 7 a required or normal standard: *up to the mark.* 8 an impression, distinguishing characteristic or influence: *Your work bears his mark.* 9 (*often* **Mark**) applied esp to vehicles: a type of design; a model: *driving a Jaguar Mark II.* ➤ vb 1 tr & intr to spoil something with, or become spoiled by, a mark. 2 a to read, correct and award (a grade) to a piece of written work, etc; b to allot a score to someone or something. 3 to show; to be a sign of something: *events marking a new era.* 4 (*often* **mark sth down**) to make a note of something; to record it. 5 to pay close attention to something: *mark my words.* 6 *sport* to stay close to (an opposing player) in order to try and prevent them from getting or passing the ball. 7 to characterize or label someone or something: *This incident marks him as a criminal.* ✦ **make** or **leave one's mark** to make a strong or permanent impression. **mark time** to move the feet up and down as if marching, but without going forward. 2 merely to keep things going, without making progress. **off the mark** 1 not on target; off the subject. 2 of an athlete, etc: getting away from the mark in a race, etc: *slow off the mark.* **on your marks** or **mark** *athletics* said to the runners before a race begins: get into your position, ready for the starting signal. **up to the mark** 1 of work, etc: of a good standard. 2 of a person: fit and well. ◊ **mark sb down** to give them or their work a lower mark. **mark sth down** 1 to reduce its price: *a jacket marked down from £75 to £55.* 2 to note it. **mark sth up** to increase its price.

mark² n the former currency unit in Germany.

marked adj 1 obvious or noticeable: *a marked change in her attitude.* 2 of a person: watched with suspicion; selected as a target: *a marked man.* ○ **markedly** /'mɑːkɪdlɪ/ adv.

marker n 1 a pen with a thick point, for writing signs, etc. 2 anything used to mark the position of something.

market n 1 a gathering of people that takes place periodically, where stalls, etc are set up allowing them to buy and sell goods. 2 a public place in which this regularly takes place. 3 a particular region, country or section of the population, considered as a potential customer: *the teenage market.* 4 buying and selling; a level of trading: *The market is slow.* 5 opportunity for buying and selling; demand: *no market for these goods.* 6 *esp N Am* a shop or supermarket. ➤ vb (**marketed, marketing**) 1 to offer something for sale; to promote (goods, etc). 2 intr to trade or deal, esp at a market. 3 intr, esp US to shop. ○ **marketable** adj. ✦ **be in the market for sth** to wish to buy it. **on the market** on sale.

marketeer n 1 someone who trades at a market. 2 *econ* someone who is involved with, or who promotes, a particular kind of market: *black marketeer.*

market garden n an area of land, usu near a

large town or city, that is used commercially to grow produce. ○ **market gardener** n.

marketing n **1** business the techniques or processes by which a product or service is sold, including responsibility for its promotion, distribution and development. **2** esp N Am an act or process of shopping.

market price n the price for which a thing can be sold at a particular time.

market research n analysis of the habits, needs and preferences of customers, often in regard to a particular product. ○ **market researcher** n.

market town n a town, often at the centre of a farming area, where a market is held regularly.

marking n **1** (often **markings**) a distinctive pattern of colours on an animal or plant. **2** the act or process of giving marks (eg to school work) or making marks on something.

marksman or **markswoman** n someone who can shoot a gun or other weapon accurately. ○ **marksmanship** n.

mark-up n, commerce an increase in price, esp in determining level of profit.

marl n, geol a mixture of clay and limestone.

marlin n (**marlin** or **marlins**) a large fish found in tropical seas which has a long spear-like upper jaw.

marlinspike or **marlinespike** n, naut a pointed metal tool for separating the strands of rope to be spliced.

marmalade n jam made from the pulp and rind of any citrus fruit.

marmoreal /maː'mɔːrɪəl/ adj, formal or literary **1** like marble. **2** made of marble.

marmoset n a small S American monkey with a long bushy tail and tufts of hair around the head and ears.

marmot n a stout, coarse-haired, burrowing rodent of Europe, Asia and N America.

maroon¹ adj dark brownish-red or purplish-red in colour. ➤ n this colour.

maroon² vb **1** to leave someone in isolation in a deserted place, esp on a desert island. **2** to leave someone helpless or without support.

marque /maːk/ n applied esp to cars: a brand or make.

marquee /maː'kiː/ n a very large tent used for circuses, parties, etc.

marquess /'maːkwɪs/ n, Brit a member of the nobility ranking below a duke.

marquetry /'maːkətrɪ/ n (-**ies**) the art or practice of making decorative patterns out of pieces of different-coloured woods, ivory, etc, esp set into the surface of wooden furniture.

marquis /'maːkwɪs; French maʁki/ n (**marquis** or **marquises**) **1** in various European countries: a nobleman next in rank above a count. **2** sometimes a MARQUESS.

marquise /maː'kiːz/ n **1** in various European countries: a MARCHIONESS. **2** a gemstone cut to form a pointed oval.

marriage n **1** the state or relationship of being

husband and wife. **2** the act, or legal contract, of becoming husband and wife. **3** the civil or religious ceremony during which this act is performed. **4** a joining together.

marriageable adj of a woman, or sometimes a man: suitable for marriage, esp in terms of being at a legal age for marriage. ○ **marriageability** n.

marriage guidance n professional counselling given to couples with marital problems.

married adj **1** having a husband or wife. **2** belonging or relating to the state of marriage: married life. **3** (esp **married to sth**) closely fixed together; joined, esp inseparably or intimately, to it: He's married to his work.

marrow n **1** (also **bone marrow**) the soft tissue that fills the internal cavities of bones. **2** (also **vegetable marrow**) **a** a plant cultivated for its large, oblong, edible fruit; **b** the fruit of this plant which has a thick, green or striped skin, and soft white flesh, and is cooked as a vegetable.

marrowfat or **marrowfat pea** n **1** a variety of large, edible pea. **2** the plant that bears it.

marry¹ vb (-**ies**, -**ied**) **1** to take someone as one's husband or wife. **2** of a priest, minister, official, etc: to perform the ceremony of marriage between two people: My uncle married us. **3** intr to become joined in marriage: We married last June. **4** intr (also **marry sth up**) to fit together, join up, or match (usu two things) correctly. ◊ **marry sb off** (colloq) to find a husband or wife for them.

marry² exclam, archaic an expression of surprise or earnest declaration; indeed!.

Mars n, astron the fourth planet from the Sun, and the nearest planet to the Earth.

marsh n a poorly-drained, low-lying, often flooded area of land. ○ **marshy** adj.

marshal n **1** (often **Marshal**) in compounds **a** high-ranking officer in the armed forces: Air Vice-Marshal; **b** Brit a high-ranking officer of State: Earl Marshal. **2** an official who organizes, or controls crowds at, public events. **3** US in some states: a chief police or fire officer. **4** a law-court official with various duties: judge's marshal. ➤ vb (**marshalled, marshalling**; US **marshaled, marshaling**) **1** to arrange (troops, competitors, facts, etc) in order. **2** to direct, lead or show the way to (a crowd, procession, etc), esp in a formal or precise way.

marsh fever n MALARIA.

marsh gas n METHANE.

marshmallow n a spongy pink or white sweet.

marsh mallow n a pink-flowered plant that grows wild in coastal marshes.

marsh marigold n a marsh plant with yellow flowers like large buttercups.

marsupial n, zool a mammal, such as the kangaroo, in which the young is carried in an external pouch on the mother's body until it is mature enough to survive independently. ➤ adj belonging to or like a marsupial.

mart *n* a trading place; a market or auction.

martello *n* a small circular fortified tower used for coastal defence.

marten *n* **1** a small, tree-dwelling, predatory mammal with a long thin body and a bushy tail. **2** its highly-valued, soft, black or brown fur.

martial *adj* belonging or relating to, or suitable for, war or the military. ○ **martialism** *n.* ○ **martially** *adv.*

martial art *n* a fighting sport or self-defence technique of Far Eastern origin.

martial law *n* law and order strictly enforced by the military powers, eg when ordinary civil law has broken down.

Martian *adj* belonging or relating to the planet MARS.

martin *n* a small bird of the swallow family, with a square or slightly forked tail.

martinet *n, derog* someone who maintains strict discipline.

martingale *n* a strap that is passed between a horse's forelegs and fastened to the girth and to the bit, used to keep the horse's head down.

martini *n* a cocktail made of gin and vermouth.

Martinmas *n* St Martin's Day, 11 November.

martyr *n* **1** someone who chooses to be put to death as an act of witness to their faith. **2** someone who suffers or dies, esp for their beliefs, or for a particular cause. **3** (*usu* a martyr to sth) *colloq* someone who suffers greatly on account of something (eg an illness): *She is a martyr to arthritis.* ➤ *vb* to put someone to death as a martyr. ○ **martyrdom** *n.*

marvel *vb* (**marvelled, marvelling**; *US* **marveled, marveling**) *intr* (*esp* **marvel at sth**) to be filled with astonishment or wonder. ➤ *n* an astonishing or wonderful person or thing.

marvellous or (*US*) **marvelous** *adj* **1** so wonderful or astonishing as to be almost beyond belief. **2** *colloq* excellent. ○ **marvellously** *adv.*

marzipan *n* a sweet paste made of ground almonds, sugar and egg whites, used to decorate cakes, make sweets, etc.

masala *n, cookery* **1** a blend of spices ground into a powder or paste used in Indian cookery. **2** a dish using this: *chicken tikka masala.*

masc. *abbrev* masculine.

mascara *n* a cosmetic for darkening, lengthening and thickening the eyelashes, applied with a brush.

mascarpone /maskəˈpoʊnɪ/ *n* a soft Italian cream cheese.

mascot *n* a person, animal or thing thought to bring good luck and adopted for this purpose by a person, team, etc.

masculine *adj* **1** belonging to, typical of, peculiar to or suitable for a man or the male sex. **2** of a woman: mannish. **3** *gram* in some languages: belonging or relating to one of the GENDERS into which most words for animate males fall. Compare FEMININE, NEUTER. ➤ *n, gram* **1** the masculine gender. **2** a word belonging to this gender. ○ **masculinity** *n.*

maser *n* a device for increasing the strength of MICROWAVES.

mash *vb* (*also* **mash sth up**) to beat or crush it into a pulpy mass. ➤ *n* **1** a boiled mixture of grain and water used to feed farm animals. **2** a mixture of crushed malt and hot water, used in brewing. **3** any soft or pulpy mass. **4** *colloq* mashed potatoes. ○ **mashed** *adj.* ○ **masher** *n.*

mask *n* **1 a** any covering for the face or for part of the face, worn for amusement, protection or as a disguise: *Hallowe'en mask*; **b** a covering for the mouth and nose. **2** a pretence; anything that disguises the truth: *a mask of kindliness.* **3** a moulded or sculpted cast of someone's face: *death-mask.* **4** a cosmetic face pack. ➤ *vb* **1** to put a mask on someone or something. **2** to disguise, conceal or cover. **3** to protect something with a mask, or as if with a mask.

masking tape *n* sticky tape, used eg in painting to cover the edge of a surface to be left unpainted.

masochism /ˈmasəkɪzəm/ *n* **1** *psychol* the practice of deriving sexual pleasure from pain or humiliation inflicted by another person. Compare SADISM. **2** *colloq* a tendency to take pleasure in one's own suffering. ○ **masochist** *n.* ○ **masochistic** *adj.*

mason *n* **1** a STONEMASON. **2** (**Mason**) a FREEMASON. ○ **masonic** /məˈsɒnɪk/ *adj* (*often* **Masonic**) belonging or relating to Freemasons.

masonry *n* **1** structures made of stone and brick. **2** the craft of a stonemason.

masque /mɑːsk/ *n, hist* in English royal courts during the 16c and 17c: a kind of dramatic entertainment performed to music by masked actors.

masquerade /maskəˈreɪd/ *n* **1** a pretence or false show. **2 a** a formal dance at which the guests wear masks and costumes; **b** *chiefly US* any party or gathering to which costumes or disguises are worn. **3** *chiefly US* the costume or disguise worn at a masquerade, etc. ➤ *vb, intr* (*esp* **masquerade as sb** or **sth**) **1** to disguise oneself. **2** to pretend to be someone or something else: *He was masquerading as a vicar.*

mass¹ *n* **1** *physics* the amount of matter that an object contains, which is a measure of its INERTIA. **2** a large quantity, usu a shapeless quantity, gathered together. **3** (*often* **masses**) *colloq* a large quantity or number: *He has masses of books.* **4** (*usu* **the mass of sth**) the majority or bulk of it. **5** *technical* a measure of the quantity of matter in a body. **6** (**the masses**) ordinary people; the people as a whole. ➤ *adj* **a** involving a large number of people: *a mass meeting* • *mass murder*; **b** belonging or relating to a mass, or to large quantities or numbers: *mass production.* ➤ *vb, chiefly intr* (*sometimes* **mass together**) to gather or form in a large quantity or number.

mass² or **Mass** *n* **1** *Christianity* in the Roman Catholic and Orthodox Churches: **a** the EUCHARIST, a celebration of Christ's Last Supper; **b** the ceremony in which this occurs. **2** a part of the text of the Roman Catholic liturgy set to music and sung by a choir or congregation: *a requiem mass*.

massacre /'masəkə(r)/ *n* **1** a cruel and indiscriminate killing of large numbers of people or animals. **2** *colloq* in a game, sports match, etc: an overwhelming defeat. ➤ *vb* **1** to kill (people or animals) cruelly, indiscriminately and in large numbers. **2** *colloq* to defeat (the opposition or enemy, etc) overwhelmingly.

massage /'masɑːʒ/ *n* **1** a technique of easing pain or stiffness in the body, esp the muscles, by rubbing, kneading and tapping with the hands. **2** a body treatment using this technique. ➤ *vb* **1** to perform massage on someone. **2** to alter something (esp statistics or other data) to produce a more favourable result.

masseur /ma'sɜː(r)/ or **masseuse** /-'sɜːz/ *n* someone who is trained to carry out massage.

massif /'masiːf/ *n, geol* a mountainous plateau.

massive *adj* **1** of physical objects: very big, bulky, solid and heavy. **2** *colloq* very large: *a massive explosion*. ○ **massively** *adv.* ○ **massiveness** *n*.

mass market *n, econ* the market for goods that have been mass-produced. ○ **mass-marketing** *n*.

mass noun *n, gram* a noun which cannot be qualified in the singular by the indefinite article and cannot be used in the plural, eg *furniture*. Compare COUNT NOUN.

mass number *n, chem* the total number of protons and neutrons in the nucleus of an atom.

mass-produce *vb* to produce (goods, etc) in a standard form in great quantities. ○ **mass-produced** *adj.* ○ **mass production** *n*.

mass spectrometer *n, chem, physics* a device used to measure the relative atomic masses of isotopes of chemical elements.

mast[1] *n* any upright wooden or metal supporting pole, esp one carrying the sails of a ship, or an aerial. ◆ **before the mast** *naut* serving as an apprentice seaman or ordinary sailor.

mast[2] *n* the nuts of various forest trees, esp beech, oak and chestnut, used as food for pigs.

mastaba *n, archaeol* an ancient Egyptian tomb built of brick or stone with sloping sides and a flat roof.

mastectomy *n* (*-ies*) *surgery* the surgical removal of a woman's breast.

master *n* **1** someone, esp a man, who commands or controls. **2** the owner, esp a male owner, of a dog, slave, etc. **3** someone with outstanding skill in a particular activity, eg art. **4** a fully qualified craftsman or tradesman, allowed to train and direct others. **5** *rather dated* a male teacher. **6** the commanding officer on a merchant ship. **7** (**Master**) **a** a degree of the level above BACHELOR (sense 2). Usually called **Masters**: *He has a Masters in geophysics*; **b** someone who holds this degree: *Master of Science*. **8** (**Master**) a title for a boy too young to be called MR. ➤ *adj* **1** fully qualified; highly skilled. **2** main: *master bedroom*. **3** controlling: *master switch*. ➤ *vb* **1** to overcome or defeat (eg feelings or an opponent). **2** to become skilled in something.

masterful *adj* showing the authority, skill or power of a master. ○ **masterfully** *adv.* ○ **masterfulness** *n*.

masterly *adj* showing the skill of a master.

mastermind *n* **1** someone who has great intellectual ability. **2** the person responsible for devising a complex plan. ➤ *vb* to originate, think out and direct something.

master of ceremonies *n* (**masters of ceremonies**) an announcer, esp one who announces the speakers at a formal dinner or the performers in a stage entertainment.

masterpiece *n* an extremely skilful piece of work.

mastery *n* (*-ies*) **1** (*usu* **mastery of sth**) great skill or knowledge in it. **2** (*esp* **mastery over sb** or **sth**) control over them or it.

masthead *n* **1** *naut* the top of a ship's mast. **2** *journalism* the title of a newspaper or periodical, and other information such as logo, price and place of publication, printed at the top of its front page.

mastic *n* **1** a gum obtained from a Mediterranean evergreen tree, used in making varnish. **2** *building* a waterproof, putty-like paste used as a filler.

masticate *vb, tr & intr, formal or technical* to chew (food). ○ **mastication** *n*.

mastiff *n* a large powerful short-haired breed of dog.

mastitis *n* inflammation of a woman's breast or an animal's udder.

mastodon *n* any of several, now extinct, mammals from which elephants are thought to have evolved.

mastoid *anat, adj* like a nipple or breast. ➤ *n* the raised area of bone behind the ear.

masturbate *vb, tr & intr* to rub or stroke the genitals of (oneself or someone else) so as to produce sexual arousal. ○ **masturbation** *n*.

mat *n* **1** a flat piece of any carpet-like material, used as a decorative or protective floor-covering or for absorbing impact on landing in gymnastics, etc. **2** a smaller piece of fabric, or a harder material, used under a plate, vase, etc to protect a surface. ➤ *vb* (**matted, matting**) *tr & intr* to become, or make something become, tangled. ○ **matted** *adj* of hair: tangled.

matador *n* the principal TOREADOR who kills the bull in bullfighting.

match[1] *n* **1** a formal contest or game. **2** (*esp* a **match for sb** or **sth**) a person or thing that is similar or identical to, or combines well with, another. **3** a person or thing able to equal, or surpass, another: *He met his match*. **4** a partnership or pairing; a suitable partner, eg in marriage. **5** a condition of exact agreement, compatibility or close resemblance, esp between two colours. ➤ *vb* **1** *tr & intr* (*also* **match up** *or* **match sth up**) to combine well; to be well suited. **2** to set (people or things) in competition. **3** to be equal to something; to make, produce, etc an equivalent to something: *We cannot match, let alone beat, the offer.* ○ **matching** *adj.* ◆ **be a match for sb** to be as good at something as them; to be as successful, strong, forceful, etc as them.

match² *n* **1** a short thin piece of wood or strip of card coated on the tip with a substance that ignites when rubbed against a rough surface. **2** a slow-burning fuse used in cannons, etc.

matchbox *n* a small cardboard box for holding matches.

matchless *adj* having no equal; superior to all.

matchmaker *n* someone who tries to arrange romantic partnerships or marriages between people. ○ **matchmaking** *n, adj.*

matchstick *n* the stem of a wooden MATCH² (sense I). ➤ *adj* **1** very thin, like a matchstick: *matchstick legs.* **2** of figures in a drawing, etc: with limbs represented by single lines: *matchstick men.*

matchwood *n* **1** wood suitable for making matches. **2** splinters.

mate *n* **1** an animal's breeding partner. **2** *colloq* a person's sexual partner. **3 a** *colloq* a companion or friend; **b** used as a form of address, esp to a man: *alright, mate.* **4** *in compounds* a person someone shares something with: *workmate* ◆ *flatmate.* **5** a tradesman's assistant: *plumber's mate.* **6** one of a pair. **7** *naut* any officer below the rank of master on a merchant ship: *first mate.* ➤ *vb* **1** *intr* of animals: to copulate. **2** to bring (male and female animals) together for breeding. **3** *tr & intr* to marry. **4** to join (two things) as a pair.

material *n* **1** any substance out of which something is, or may be, made. **2** cloth; fabric. **3** (**materials**) instruments or tools needed for a particular activity or task. **4** information that provides the substance from which a book, TV programme, etc is prepared. **5** someone who is suitable for a specified occupation, training, etc: *He is management material.* ➤ *adj* **1** relating to or consisting of physical objects, etc; not abstract or spiritual: *the material world.* **2** (*usu* **material to sth**) *technical* important; relevant: *facts not material to the discussion.* ○ **materially** *adv.*

materialism *n* **1** *often derog* excessive interest in or devotion to material possessions and financial success. **2** *philos* the theory stating that only material things exist, esp denying the existence of a soul or spirit. ○ **materialist** *n, adj.* ○ **materialistic** *adj.*

materialize *or* **-ise** *vb* **1** *intr* to become real, visible or tangible; to appear or take shape. **2** *intr, loosely* to become fact. ○ **materialization** *n.*

matériel /mətɪərɪˈɛl/ *n* materials and equipment, esp for an army.

maternal *adj* **1** belonging to, typical of or like a mother. **2** of a relative: related on the mother's side of the family: *my maternal grandfather.* Compare PATERNAL. ○ **maternally** *adv.*

maternity *n* **1** the state of being or becoming a mother. **2** the qualities typical of a mother. ➤ *adj* relating to pregnancy or giving birth: *maternity hospital* ◆ *maternity wear.*

matey *or* **maty** *adj* (**matier, matiest**) *colloq* friendly or familiar. ➤ *n* (**mateys** *or* **maties**) *colloq* usu used in addressing a man: friend.

math *n, N Am colloq* mathematics. *Brit equivalent* **maths**.

math. *abbrev* mathematics.

mathematical *adj* **1** belonging or relating to, or using, mathematics. **2** of calculations, etc: very accurate. ○ **mathematically** *adv.*

mathematician *n* someone who specializes in or studies mathematics.

mathematics *sing n* the science dealing with measurements, numbers, quantities, and shapes, usu expressed as symbols.

maths *sing n, Brit colloq* mathematics. *N Am equivalent* **math**.

matinée *or* **matinee** /ˈmatɪneɪ/ *n* an afternoon performance of a play or showing of a film.

matinée jacket *or* **matinée coat** *n* a baby's short jacket or coat.

matins *sing or pl n, C of E* the daily morning service.

matriarch /ˈmeɪtrɪɑːk/ *n* the female head of a family, community or tribe. ○ **matriarchal** *adj.*

matriarchy /ˈmeɪtrɪɑːkɪ/ *n* (**-ies**) a social system in which women are the heads of families or tribes, and property and power passes from mother to daughter.

matricide *n* **1** the act of killing one's own mother. **2** someone who commits this act.

matriculate *vb, intr* to register as a student at a university, college, etc. ○ **matriculation** *n.*

matrimony *n* (**-ies**) *formal* the state of being married. ○ **matrimonial** *adj.*

matrix /ˈmeɪtrɪks/ *n* (**matrices** /-trɪsiːz/ *or* **matrixes**) **1** *maths* a square or rectangular arrangement of symbols or numbers, in rows or columns, used to summarize relationships between different quantities, etc. **2** *geol* the rock in which a mineral or fossil is embedded. **3** *printing* a mould, esp one from which printing type is produced.

matron *n* **1** the former title of the head of the nursing staff in a hospital. Now usu called **senior nursing officer**. **2** a woman in charge of nursing in an institution such as a boarding school or old people's home. **3** any dignified, worthy or respectable middle-aged or elderly woman, esp a married one. ○ **matronly** *adj.*

matron of honour *n* (**matrons of honour**) a married woman who is a bride's chief attendant at a wedding.

matt *or* (*sometimes*) **matte** *adj* eg of paint: having a dull surface.

matter *n* **1** the substance from which all physical things are made. **2** material of a particular kind: *reading matter*. **3** a subject or topic; a concern, affair or question: *It's a matter of money*. **4** content, as distinct from style or form. **5** (*usu a* **matter of sth**) **a** an approximate quantity or amount of (time, etc): *I'll be there in a matter of minutes*; **b** used in saying what is involved or necessary: *It's just a matter of asking her to do it*. **6** (**the matter** or **the matter with sb** or **sth**) something that is wrong; the trouble or difficulty: *What is the matter?* **7** *med* pus or discharge. ➤ *vb intr* to be important or significant. ◆ **a matter of opinion** something about which different people have different opinions. **as a matter of fact** in fact; actually. **for that matter** used when referring to some alternative or additional possibility, etc: as far as that is concerned. **no matter** it is not important. **no matter how, what** or **where,** *etc* regardless of how or what, etc.

matter-of-fact *adj* calm and straightforward. ○ **matter-of-factly** *adv*.

matting *vb*, present participle of MAT. ➤ *n* material of rough woven fibres used for making mats.

mattock *n* a kind of pickaxe with a blade flattened horizontally at one end, used for breaking up soil, etc.

mattress *n* a large flat fabric-covered pad, now often made of foam rubber or springs, used for sleeping on.

mature *adj* **1** fully grown or developed. **2** having or showing adult good sense, emotional and social development, etc. **3** of cheese, wine, etc: having a fully developed flavour. **4** of bonds, insurance policies, etc: paying out, or beginning to pay out, money to the holder. ➤ *vb* **1** *tr & intr* to make or become fully developed or adult in outlook. **2** *intr* of a life insurance policy, etc: to begin to produce a return. ○ **maturation** *n*. ○ **maturity** *n*.

matzo *n* **1** unleavened bread. **2** a wafer or cracker made of this, now usu a large, thin, square one, eaten esp during Passover, etc.

maudlin *adj* esp of a drunk person: foolishly sad or sentimental.

maul *vb* **1** to attack someone or something fiercely, usu tearing the flesh. **2** to handle someone or something roughly or clumsily. **3** to subject someone to fierce criticism. ➤ *n*, *rugby* a gathering of players from both teams around a player who is holding the ball.

maunder *vb*, *intr* **1** (*also* **maunder on**) to talk in a rambling way. **2** to wander about, or behave, in an aimless way. ○ **maundering** *adj*.

mausoleum /mɔːzə'lɪəm/ *n* (**mausoleums** or **mausolea** /-lɪə/) a grand or monumental tomb.

mauve /moʊv/ *adj* pale purple in colour. ➤ *n* this colour.

maverick *n* **1** *N Am* an unbranded stray animal, esp a calf. **2** a determinedly independent person; a nonconformist.

maw *n* the jaws, throat or stomach of a voracious animal.

mawkish *adj* **1** weakly sentimental, maudlin or insipid. **2** sickly or disgusting. ○ **mawkishly** *adv*. ○ **mawkishness** *n*.

max. *abbrev* maximum.

maxi *adj*, *often in compounds* of a skirt, coat, etc: **a** extra long; full length; **b** extra large. ➤ *n* a maxi garment.

maxilla /mak'sɪlə/ *n* (**maxillae** /-liː/) *biol* **1** the upper jaw or jawbone in animals. **2** the chewing organ or organs of an insect, just behind the mouth. ○ **maxillary** *adj*.

maxim *n* **1** a saying that expresses a general truth. **2** a general rule or principle.

maximal *adj* belonging or relating to a MAXIMUM; having the greatest possible size, value, etc.

maximize or **-ise** *vb* to make something as high or great, etc as possible. ○ **maximization** *n*.

maximum *adj* greatest possible. ➤ *n* (**maximums** or **maxima**) the greatest or most; the greatest possible number, quantity, degree, etc. Also (*chiefly US colloq*) called the **max**.

maxwell *n*, *physics* a unit of magnetic flux, equal to 10^{-8} weber.

May *n* the fifth month of the year.

may¹ *auxiliary vb* (*past tense* **might**) **1** used to express permission: *You may go now*. **2** (*sometimes* **may well**) used to express a possibility: *I may come with you if I get this finished*. **3** used to express an offer: *May I help you?* **4** *formal* used to express a wish: *May you prosper!* **5** *formal & old use* used to express purpose or result: *Listen, so that you may learn*. **6** *affected, old use* or *facetious* used to express a question: *And who may you be?* **7** used to express the idea of 'although': *You may be rich, but you're not happy*. ◆ **be that as it may** in spite of that. **come what may** whatever happens. **That's as may be** That may be so.

> **may** See note at **can**.

may² *n* **1** the blossom of the HAWTHORN tree. **2** any variety of hawthorn tree.

maybe *adv* it is possible; perhaps. ➤ *n* a possibility.

May Day *n* the first day of May, a national holiday in many countries, on which socialist and labour demonstrations are held, and traditionally a day of festivities.

mayday or **Mayday** *n* the international radio distress signal sent out by ships and aircraft.

mayfly *n* (*-ies*) a short-lived insect with transparent wings, which appears briefly in spring.

mayhem *n* **1** a state of great confusion and disorder. **2** *US & formerly law* the crime of maiming someone.

mayn't *contraction, colloq* may not.

mayonnaise *n*, *cookery* a cold, creamy sauce made of egg yolk, oil, vinegar or lemon juice and seasoning. Sometimes (*colloq*) shortened to **mayo**.

mayor *n* **1** in England, Wales and N Ireland: the

head of the local council in a city, town or borough. **2** in other countries: the head of any of various communities. ○ **mayoral** adj.

mayoress n **1** a mayor's wife. **2** old use a female mayor.

maypole n a tall, decorated pole traditionally set up for dancing round on MAY DAY.

maze n **1** a confusing network of paths bordered by high walls or hedges, laid out in a garden as a puzzling diversion in which a person might become lost. **2** any confusingly complicated system, procedure, etc.

mazurka n **1** a lively Polish dance in triple time. **2** a piece of music for this dance.

MB abbrev, comput megabyte.

mbar abbrev millibar.

MBE abbrev Member of the Order of the British Empire.

MC abbrev master of ceremonies.

MD abbrev managing director.

Md symbol, chem mendelevium.

ME abbrev, med myalgic encephalomyelitis.

me¹ pron **1** the object form of I², used by a speaker or writer to refer to himself or herself: She asked me a question. **2** used for I after the verb BE or when standing alone: It's only me.

me² or **mi** n, mus in sol-fa notation: the third note of the major scale.

mea culpa /meɪə ˈkʊlpə/ exclam, literary or facetious as an acknowledgement of one's own guilt or mistake: I am to blame.

mead¹ n an alcoholic drink made by fermenting honey and water, usu with spices added.

mead² n, poetic or old use a meadow.

meadow n **1** a low-lying field of grass, used for grazing animals or making hay. **2** any moist, grassy area near a river.

meagre or (US) **meager** adj **1** lacking in quality or quantity. **2** of a person: thin, esp unhealthily so. ○ **meagrely** adv. ○ **meagreness** n.

meal¹ n **1** an occasion on which food is eaten, eg lunch, supper, dinner, etc. **2** an amount of food eaten on one such occasion. ♦ **make a meal of sth** colloq to exaggerate the importance of it.

meal² n, often in compounds **1** the edible parts of any grain, usu excluding wheat, ground to a coarse powder: oatmeal. **2** any other food substance in ground form: bone meal. ○ **mealy** adj.

meal ticket n **1** colloq a person or situation that provides a source of income or other means of living. **2** N Am a LUNCHEON VOUCHER.

mealy-mouthed adj, derog of a person: afraid to speak plainly or openly; not frank or sincere.

mean¹ vb (**meant**) **1** to express or intend to express, show or indicate something. **2** to intend something; to have it as a purpose: I didn't mean any harm. **3** to be serious or sincere about something: He means what he says. **4** to be important to the degree specified; to represent something: Your approval means a lot to me. **5** to entail something necessarily; to in-

volve or result in it: War means hardship. **6** to foretell something: Cold cloudless evenings mean overnight frost. ♦ **be meant for sth** to be destined to it. **mean well** to have good intentions.

mean² adj **1** not generous. **2** low; despicable. **3** poor; shabby. **4** colloq, esp N Am vicious; malicious. **5** colloq good; skilful: Joe plays a mean guitar. ○ **meanly** adv. ○ **meanness** n. ♦ **no mean sth** colloq **1** an excellent one: He's no mean singer. **2** not an easy one: That was no mean feat.

mean³ adj **1** midway; intermediate. **2** average. ➢ n **1** a midway position or course, etc between two extremes. **2** maths, stats a mathematical AVERAGE, in particular: **a** the average value of a set of numbers; **b** the value which is midway between the highest and lowest numbers in a set. Compare MEDIAN (sense 3), MODE (sense 5).

meander /mɪˈandə(r)/ vb, intr **1** of a river: to bend and curve. **2** (also **meander about**) to wander randomly or aimlessly. ➢ n (often **meanders**) a bend; a winding course.

meanie or **meany** n (-ies) colloq **1** a selfish or ungenerous person. **2** esp N Am a malicious or bad-tempered person.

meaning n **1** the sense in which a statement, action, word, etc is intended to be understood. **2** significance, importance or purpose, esp when hidden or special.

meaningful adj **1** having meaning; significant. **2** full of significance. ○ **meaningfully** adv.

meaningless adj **1** without meaning or reason. **2** having no importance. **3** having no purpose. ○ **meaninglessly** adv.

means sing or pl n **1** the instrument or method used to achieve some object. **2** wealth; resources. ♦ **a means to an end** something treated merely as a way of achieving a desired result, considered unimportant in every other respect. **by all means** rather formal yes, of course. **by any means** using any available method. **by means of sth** with the help or use of it. **by no means** or **not by any means** not at all; definitely not.

means test n an official inquiry into someone's wealth or income to determine their eligibility for financial benefit from the state.

meantime n (esp **in the meantime**) the time or period in between. ➢ adv MEANWHILE.

meanwhile adv **1** during the time in between. **2** at the same time.

measles sing n a highly infectious viral disease characterized by fever, a sore throat and a blotchy red rash.

measly adj (-ier, -iest) **1** derog, colloq of an amount, value, etc: very small. **2** relating to, or suffering from, measles. ○ **measliness** n.

measure n **1** size, volume, etc determined by comparison with something of known size, etc, usu an instrument graded in standard units. **2** such an instrument for taking a measurement of something. **3** a standard unit of size, etc; a standard amount: *a measure of whisky.* **4** a system of such units: *metric measure.* **5** (*usu* **measures**) an action; a step: *We must take drastic measures.* **6** a limited, or appropriate, amount or extent: *a measure of politeness.* **7** an enactment or bill. **8** *mus* time or rhythm; a bar. **9** *poetry* rhythm or metre. ➤ *vb* **1** *tr & intr* (*often* **measure sth up**) to determine the size, volume, etc of, usu with a specially made instrument or by comparing it to something else. **2** *intr* to be a specified size. **3** (*also* **measure off sth** or **measure sth off** or **out**) to mark or divide something into units of a given size, etc. **4** to set something in competition with something else: *measure his strength against mine.* ○ **measurable** *adj.* ○ **measuring** *n.* ◆ **for good measure** as something extra, or above the minimum necessary. ◇ **measure up to sth** to reach the required standard.

measured *adj* **1** slow and steady. **2** carefully chosen or considered: *a measured response.* ○ **measuredly** *adv.*

measurement *n* **1** (*often* **measurements**) a size, amount, etc determined by measuring: *measurements for the new bedroom carpet.* **2** (*often* **measurements**) the size of a part of the body. **3** the act of measuring. **4** a standard system of measuring.

meat *n* **1** the flesh of any animal used as food. **2** the basic or most important part. ○ **meatless** *adj.*

meatball *n, cookery* a small ball of minced meat mixed with breadcrumbs and seasonings.

meat loaf *n* a loaf-shaped food made from chopped or minced meat, seasoning, etc, cooked and usu eaten cold in slices.

meaty *adj* (*-ier, -iest*) **1** full of, containing or resembling meat. **2** of a person: heavily built. **3** full of interesting information or ideas: *a meaty article.*

mecca or **Mecca** *n* any place of outstanding significance to a particular group of people, esp one which they feel they have to visit.

mechanic *n* a skilled worker who repairs, maintains or constructs machinery.

mechanical *adj* **1** belonging to or concerning machines or mechanics. **2** worked by, or performed with, machinery or a mechanism. **3** of an action or movement, etc: done without or not requiring much thought. ○ **mechanically** *adv.*

mechanics *sing n* **1** the branch of physics that deals with the motion of bodies and the forces that act on them. **2** the art or science of machine construction. ➤ *pl n* **1** the system on which something works. **2** *colloq* routine procedures.

mechanism *n* **1** a working part of a machine or its system of working parts. **2** the arrangements and action by which something is produced or achieved. **3** *psychol* an action that serves some purpose, often a subconscious

purpose: *Laughter is a common defence mechanism.* ○ **mechanistic** *adj.*

mechanize or **-ise** *vb* **1** to change (the production of something, a procedure, etc) from a manual to a mechanical process. **2** *mil* to provide (troops etc) with armoured armed vehicles. ○ **mechanization** *n.*

medal *n* a flat piece of metal decorated with a design or inscription and awarded, eg to a soldier, sportsperson, etc, or produced in celebration of a special occasion. ○ **medallist** *n, sport* someone who is awarded a medal.

medallion *n* **1** a large medal-like piece of jewellery, usu worn on a chain. **2** in architecture or on textiles: an oval or circular decorative feature. **3** *cookery* a thin circular cut of meat.

meddle *vb, intr* **1** (*usu* **meddle in sth**) to interfere in it. **2** (*usu* **meddle with sth**) to tamper with it. ○ **meddler** *n.* ○ **meddlesome** *adj, derog* fond of meddling. ○ **meddling** *n, adj.*

media *pl n: pl of* MEDIUM. ➤ *sing or pl n* (*usu* **the media** or **the mass media**) the means by which news and information, etc is communicated to the public, usu considered to be TV, radio and the press collectively.

---

media When referring to newspapers and broadcasting, **media** is still more commonly treated as a plural noun:
✓ *The media are highly selective in their focus on sexual violence.*
Occasionally, however, it is used as a singular noun, especially when a unified concept is intended:
These people have fears which the media has shamelessly played on over the years.

---

mediaeval a less common spelling of MEDIEVAL

medial /'miːdɪəl/ *adj, technical* belonging to or situated in the middle. ○ **medially** *adv.*

median /'miːdɪən/ *n* **1** a middle point or part. **2** *geom* a straight line between any VERTEX of a triangle and the centre of the opposite side. **3** *stats* **a** the middle value in a set of numbers or measurements arranged from smallest to largest, eg the median of 1, 5 and 11 is 5; **b** of an even number of measurements: the AVERAGE of the middle two measurements. Compare MEAN³ (*noun* sense 2), MODE (sense 5). ➤ *adj* (*also* **medial**) **1** situated in or passing through the middle. **2** *stats* belonging or relating to the median.

mediate /'miːdɪeɪt/ *vb* **1 a** *intr* to act as the agent seeking to reconcile the two sides in a disagreement; **b** to intervene in or settle (a dispute) in this way. **2** *intr* to hold an intermediary position. ○ **mediation** *n.* ○ **mediator** *n.*

medic *n, colloq* a doctor or medical student.

medical *adj* **1** belonging or relating to doctors or the science or practice of medicine. **2** concerned with medicine, or treatment by medicine, rather than surgery. ➤ *n* a medical examination to discover a person's physical health. ○ **medically** adv.

medical certificate n **1** a certificate outlining a person's state of health, provided by a doctor who has carried out a medical examination on them. **2** a certificate from a doctor stating that a person is, or has been, unfit for work.

medicament /mə'dɪkəmənt/ n, formal a medicine.

medicate vb **1** to treat someone with medicine. **2** to add a healing or health-giving substance to something. ○ **medication** n.

medicinal /mə'dɪsɪnəl/ adj having healing qualities; used as a medicine. ○ **medicinally** adv.

medicine n **1** any substance used to treat or prevent disease or illness. **2** the science or practice of treating or preventing illness, esp using prepared substances rather than surgery. **3** in primitive societies: something regarded as magical or curative. ◆ **have** or **get a taste** or **dose of one's own medicine** to suffer the same unpleasant treatment that one has given to other people.

medicine man n a person believed to have magic powers, used for healing or sorcery.

medieval or (less commonly) **mediaeval** adj **1** belonging or relating to, or characteristic of, THE MIDDLE AGES. **2** colloq extremely old and primitive. ○ **medievalist** n.

mediocre /miːdɪ'ovkə(r)/ adj only ordinary or average. ○ **mediocrity** /miːdɪ'ɒkrɪtɪ/ n (-**ies**).

meditate vb **1** intr to spend time in deep religious or spiritual thought, often with the mind in a practised state of emptiness. **2** (often **meditate about** or **on sth**) to think deeply and carefully about something. ○ **meditative** adj.

meditation n **1** the act or process of meditating. **2** contemplation, esp on a spiritual or religious theme.

Mediterranean adj **1** in, belonging or relating to the area of the Mediterranean Sea, a large inland sea lying between S Europe, N Africa and SW Asia. **2** characteristic of this area. **3** of a human physical type: of slight to medium stature and with a dark complexion.

medium n (pl in all senses except 2 and 5 **mediums** or, in all senses except 3, **media**) **1** something by or through which an effect is produced. **2** see MEDIA. **3** someone through whom the spirits of dead people are said to communicate with the living. **4** art a particular category of materials seen as a means of expression, eg watercolours, photography or clay. **5** comput (usu **media**) any material on which data is recorded, eg magnetic disk. **6** a middle position, condition or course: a happy medium. ➢ adj **1** intermediate; average. **2** moderate.

medium wave n a radio wave with a wavelength between 200 and 1000 metres. Compare LONG WAVE, SHORT WAVE.

medlar n a small brown apple-like fruit eaten only when already decaying.

medley n **1** a piece of music made up of pieces from other songs, tunes, etc. **2** a mixture or miscellany. **3** a race in stages with each stage a different length or, in swimming, with each stage swum using a different stroke.

medulla /mɛ'dʌlə/ n (**medullae** /-liː/ or **medullas**) biol the central part of an organ or tissue, when this differs in structure or function from the outer layer, eg the pith of a plant stem.

medusa /mə'djuːzə, -səə/ n (**medusas** or **medusae** /-siː/) zool a free-swimming, disc-shaped or bell-shaped organism with marginal tentacles, being the sexually-reproducing stage in the life cycle of a jellyfish.

meek adj **1** having a mild and gentle temperament. **2** submissive. ○ **meekly** adv.

meerkat n any of several species of mongoose-like carnivores native to S Africa.

meerschaum /'mɪəʃəm, -ʃaʊm/ n **1** a fine, whitish, clay-like mineral. **2** a tobacco pipe with a bowl made of this.

meet¹ vb (**met**) **1** tr & intr to be introduced to someone for the first time. **2** tr & intr **a** (also **meet up with sb** or US **meet with sb**) to come together with them by chance or by arrangement; **b** of two people, groups, etc: to come together, either by chance or arrangement. **3** to be present at the arrival of (a vehicle, etc): Alex met the train. **4** tr & intr (often **meet with sth**) to come into opposition against it: My plan met with fierce resistance. **5** tr & intr to join; to come into contact with something: where the path meets the road. **6** to satisfy: meet your requirements. **7** to pay: meet costs. **8** to come into the view, experience or presence of something: the sight that met my eyes. **9** (also **meet with sth**) to encounter or experience it: met with disaster. **10** (also **meet with sth**) to receive it: My suggestions met with approval. ➢ n a sporting event, esp a series of athletics competitions. ◆ **more than meets the eye** or **ear** more complicated, interesting, etc than it first appears or sounds.

meet² adj, old use proper, correct or suitable. ○ **meetly** adv.

meeting n **1** an act of coming together. **2** a gathering at a prearranged time, usu to discuss specific topics. **3** a sporting event, esp an athletics or horse-racing event: race meeting.

meg n, colloq a megabyte.

mega- pfx, denoting **1** in the metric system: ten to the power of six (10⁶), ie one million: megahertz. **2** comput two to the power of twenty (2²⁰).

megabuck n, N Am colloq **1** a million dollars. **2** (usu **megabucks**) a huge sum of money.

megabyte n, comput a unit of storage capacity equal to 2²⁰ or 1,048,576 bytes.

megahertz n (pl **megahertz**) a unit of frequency equal to one million hertz.

megalith n, archaeol a very large stone, esp one that forms part of a prehistoric monument. ○ **megalithic** adj.

megalomania n **1** med a mental condition

characterized by an exaggerated sense of power and self-importance. **2** *colloq* greed for power. ○ **megalomaniac** *n, adj*.

megaphone *n* a funnel-shaped device which, when someone speaks into it, amplifies the voice.

megastore *n* a very large shop.

megaton *n* **1** a unit of weight equal to one million tons. **2** a unit of explosive power equal to one million tons of TNT.

meiosis /maɪˈoʊsɪs/ *n* (*-ses* /-siːz/) *biol* a type of cell division in which four daughter nuclei are produced, each containing half the number of chromosomes of the parent nucleus and resulting in the formation of male and female GAMETES. Compare MITOSIS. ○ **meiotic** /maɪˈɒtɪk/ *adj*.

melamine *n*, *chem* a white crystalline organic compound used to form artificial resins that are resistant to heat, water and many chemicals.

melancholia /mɛlənˈkoʊlɪə/ *n, old use* mental depression.

melancholy /ˈmɛlənkɒlɪ, -kəlɪ/ *n* (*-ies*) **1** a tendency to be gloomy or depressed. **2** prolonged sadness. **3** a sad, pensive state of mind. ➤ *adj* sad; causing or expressing sadness. ○ **melancholic** /mɛlənˈkɒlɪk/ *adj*.

melange or **mélange** /meɪˈlɑːnʒ, *French* melɑ̃ʒ/ *n* a mixture.

melanin *n*, *physiol, chem* the black or dark brown pigment found to varying degrees in the skin, hair and eyes of humans and animals.

melanoma *n* (*melanomas* or *melanomata*) *med* a cancerous tumour, usu of the skin.

meld *vb, tr & intr* to merge or blend.

melee or **mêlée** /ˈmɛleɪ/ *n* **1** a riotous brawl involving large numbers of people. **2** any confused or muddled collection.

mellifluous /mɪˈlɪfluəs/ or **mellifluent** /-fluənt/ *adj* of sounds, speech, etc: having a smooth sweet flowing quality.

mellow *adj* **1** of a person or their character: calm and relaxed with age or experience. **2** of sound, colour, light, etc: soft, rich and pure. **3** of wine, cheese, etc: fully flavoured with age. **4** of fruit: sweet and ripe. **5** of a person: pleasantly relaxed or warm-hearted through being slightly drunk or affected by a recreational drug. ➤ *vb, tr & intr* to make or become mellow. ○ **mellowness** *n*.

melodeon or **melodion** *n* **1** a small reed-organ; a harmonium. **2** a kind of accordion.

melodic *adj* **1** relating or belonging to melody. **2** pleasant-sounding. ○ **melodically** *adv*.

melodious *adj* **1** pleasant to listen to. **2** having a recognizable melody. ○ **melodiousness** *n*.

melodrama *n* **1** a play or film containing sensational events, and also usu with an emphasis on appealing to the emotions. **2** *derog* excessively dramatic behaviour. ○ **melodramatic** *adj*.

melody *n* (*-ies*) **1** *mus* the sequence of single notes forming the core of a tune. **2** pleasantness of sound. **3** esp in poetry: pleasant arrangement or combination of sounds.

melon *n* **1** any of several plants of the gourd family, cultivated for their fruits. **2** the large rounded edible fruit of any of these plants, which generally have a thick skin, sweet juicy flesh and many seeds.

melt *vb, tr & intr* **1** (*sometimes* **melt down** or **melt sth down**) to make or become soft or liquid, esp through the action of heat; to dissolve (something solid). **2** (*often* **melt into sth**) to combine or fuse, or make something combine or fuse with something else, causing a loss of distinctness. **3** (*also* **melt away** or **melt sth away**) to disappear or make something disappear or disperse: *Support for the scheme melted away.* **4** *colloq* to make or become emotionally or romantically tender or submissive: *Her smile melted my heart.* ➤ *n* **1** the act of melting. **2** the quantity or material melted. ○ **melting** *n, adj*. ○ **meltingly** *adv*. ◆ **melt in the mouth** of food: to be especially delicious, eg in lightness of texture. ◊ **melt down** to turn (metal, or metal articles) to a liquid state so that the raw material can be reused.

meltdown *n, colloq* a major disaster or failure.

melting point *n* the temperature at which a particular substance changes from a solid to a liquid.

melting pot *n* a place or situation in which varying beliefs, cultures, etc come together.

member *n* **1** someone who belongs to a group or organization. **2** (*often* **Member**) an elected representative of a governing body, eg a Member of Parliament, or of a local council. **3** a part of a whole, esp a limb of an animal or a petal of a plant. **4** a plant or animal belonging to a specific class or group.

Member of Parliament *n* (abbrev **MP**) **1** in the UK: a person elected to represent the people of a CONSTITUENCY in the House of Commons. **2** (*also* **member of parliament**) a person elected to a legislative assembly in various countries.

membership *n* **1** the state of being a member. **2 a** the members of an organization collectively; **b** the number of members.

membrane *n* **1** a thin sheet of tissue that lines a body cavity or surrounds a body part, organ, etc. **2** *biol* a thin layer of lipid and protein molecules that forms the boundary between a cell and its surroundings. ○ **membranous** *adj*.

memento *n* (*mementos* or *mementoes*) a thing that serves as a reminder of the past.

memento mori /məˈmɛntoʊ ˈmɔːriː/ *n* an object intended as a reminder of the inevitability of death.

memo *contraction* a short note.

memoir /ˈmɛmwɑː(r)/ *n* **1** a written record of events in the past, esp one based on personal experience. **2** (*usu* **memoirs**) a person's written account of his or her own life.

memorabilia *pl n* souvenirs of people or events.

memorable *adj* worth remembering; easily remembered.

memorandum n (*memorandums* or *memoranda*) 1 a written statement or record, esp one circulated for the attention of colleagues at work. 2 a note of something to be remembered. 3 *law* a brief note of some transaction, recording the terms, etc.

memorial n a thing that honours or commemorates a person or an event, eg a statue or monument. ➢ *adj* 1 serving to preserve the memory of a person or event: *a memorial fund*. 2 relating to or involving memory.

memorize or **-ise** vb to learn something thoroughly, so as to be able to reproduce it exactly from memory.

memory n (*-ies*) 1 the ability of the mind to remember. 2 the mind's store of remembered events, impressions, knowledge and ideas. 3 the mental processes of memorizing information, retaining it, and recalling it on demand. 4 any such impression reproduced in the mind: *I have no memory of the event*. 5 *comput* the part of a computer that is used to store data and programs. 6 the limit in the past beyond which one's store of mental impressions does not extend: *not within my memory*. 7 the act of remembering: *in memory of old friends*. 8 reputation after death: *Her memory lives on*.

memsahib /'mɛmsɑːɪb/ n, *formerly* in India: a married European woman. Also used as a polite form of address.

men *pl of* MAN

menace n 1 a source of threatening danger. 2 a threat. 3 *colloq* something or someone that is very annoying. ➢ vb, *tr & intr* to threaten. ○ **menacing** *adj*.

menagerie /mə'nadʒərɪ/ n a a collection of wild animals caged for exhibition; b the place where they are kept.

mend vb 1 to repair something. 2 *intr* to heal or recover. 3 to improve or correct something: *mend one's ways*. ➢ n on a garment, etc: a repaired part or place. ◆ **on the mend** getting better, esp in health.

mendacious *adj* lying, or likely to lie. ○ **mendaciously** *adv*. ○ **mendacity** n.

mendelevium n, *chem* an artificially-produced radioactive metallic element.

mendicant n 1 a monk who is a member of an order that is not allowed to own property and is therefore entirely dependent on charity. 2 *formal* a beggar. ➢ *adj* 1 dependent on charity. 2 *formal* begging.

menfolk *pl* n men collectively, esp the male members of a particular group, family, etc.

menhir /'mɛnhɪə(r)/ n a prehistoric monument in the form of a single upright standing stone.

menial /'miːnɪəl/ *adj* of work: unskilled, uninteresting and of low status. ➢ n, *derog* a domestic servant.

meninges /mɛ'nɪndʒiːz/ *pl* n (*sing* **meninx** /'mɛnɪŋks/) *anat* the three membranes that cover the brain and spinal cord. ○ **meningeal** *adj*.

meningitis /mɛnɪn'dʒaɪtɪs/ n, *pathol* inflammation of the MENINGES, usu caused by infection, the main symptoms being severe headache, fever, stiffness of the neck and aversion to light.

meniscus /mə'nɪskəs/ n (*meniscuses* or *menisci* /-skaɪ, -saɪ/) 1 *physics* the curved upper surface of a liquid in a partly-filled narrow tube, caused by the effects of surface tension. 2 *optics* a lens that is convex on one side and concave on the other.

menopause n the period in a woman's life, typically between the ages of 45 and 55, when menstruation ceases and pregnancy is no longer possible. ○ **menopausal** *adj*.

menorah /mə'nɔːrə/ n a candelabrum with seven branches regarded as a symbol of Judaism.

menses /'mɛnsiːz/ *pl* n, *biol*, *med* 1 the fluids discharged from the womb during menstruation. 2 the time of menstruation.

menstrual *adj* relating to or involving menstruation.

menstruation n, *biol* 1 in women of childbearing age: the discharge through the vagina of blood that takes place at approximately monthly intervals if fertilization of an OVUM has not occurred. 2 the time or occurrence of menstruating. ○ **menstruate** vb.

mensuration n 1 *technical* the application of geometric principles to the calculation of measurements such as length, volume and area. 2 *formal* the process of measuring.

menswear n clothing for men.

mental *adj* 1 belonging or relating to, or done by using, the mind or intelligence: *mental arithmetic*. 2 *old use* belonging to, or suffering from, an illness or illnesses of the mind: *a mental patient*. 3 *colloq* foolish; stupid. 4 *colloq* ridiculous; unimaginable. ○ **mentally** *adv*.

mental age n, *psychol* the age at which an average child would have reached the same stage of mental development as the individual in question: *He is 33, with a mental age of 10*.

mentality n (*-ies*) 1 a certain way of thinking. 2 intellectual ability.

menthol n a sharp-smelling substance obtained from peppermint oil, used as a decongestant and a painkiller. ○ **mentholated** *adj*.

mention vb 1 to speak of or make reference to something or someone. 2 to remark on something or someone, usu briefly or indirectly. ➢ n 1 a remark, usu a brief reference: *He made no mention of it*. 2 a reference made to an individual's merit in an official report, esp a military one: *a mention in dispatches*. ○ **mentionable** *adj*. ◆ **don't mention it** *colloq* no apologies or words of thanks are needed. **not to mention sth** used to introduce (a subject or facts that the speaker is about to mention), usu for emphasis.

mentor n a trusted teacher or adviser.

menu n 1 a the range of dishes available in a restaurant, etc; b a list of these dishes. 2 *com-*

put a set of options displayed on a computer screen.

menu-driven *adj, comput* applied to an interactive program in which the command choices are displayed as MENUS (sense 2).

meow, meowed or **meowing** see under MIAOW

MEP *abbrev* Member of the European Parliament.

mercantile *adj, formal* belonging or relating to trade or traders.

mercenary *adj* 1 *derog* excessively concerned with the desire for personal gain, esp money. 2 hired for money. ➤ *n (-ies)* a soldier available for hire by a country or group.

mercerize or **-ise** *vb* to treat a material, esp cotton, with a substance which strengthens it and gives it a silky appearance. ○ **mercerized** *adj.*

merchandise *n* commercial goods. ➤ *vb, tr & intr* 1 to trade. 2 to plan the advertising or supplying of, or the selling campaign for (a product). ○ **merchandising** *n.*

merchant *n* 1 a trader, esp a wholesale trader. 2 *N Am & Scot* a shopkeeper. 3 *colloq* someone who indulges in a specified activity, esp one that is generally not acceptable or appropriate: *gossip merchant.* ➤ *adj* used for trade: *merchant ship.* ○ **merchantable** *adj.*

merchant bank *n* a bank whose main activities are financing international trade, lending money to industry and assisting in company takeovers, etc. ○ **merchant banker** *n.*

merchantman *n* a ship that carries merchandise.

merchant navy or **merchant service** *n* the ships and crews that are employed in a country's commerce.

merciful *adj* showing or exercising mercy. ○ **mercifully** *adv* 1 luckily; thankfully. 2 in a merciful way. ○ **mercifulness** *n.*

merciless *adj* without mercy. ○ **mercilessly** *adv.*

mercurial *adj* 1 relating to or containing mercury. 2 of someone or their personality, mood, etc: lively, active and unpredictable. ○ **mercurially** *adv.*

mercury *n* 1 a dense, silvery-white metallic element, and the only metal that is liquid at room temperature. 2 (**Mercury**) *astron* the closest planet to the Sun.

mercy *n (-ies)* 1 kindness or forgiveness shown when punishment is possible or justified. 2 an act or circumstance in which these qualities are displayed, esp by God. 3 a tendency to be forgiving. 4 a piece of good luck: *grateful for small mercies.* ◆ **at the mercy of sb** or **sth** wholly in their or its power; liable to be harmed by them or it.

mere¹ *adj* nothing more than: *a mere boy.* ○ **merely** *adv.*

mere² *n, old use, poetic* often in English place names: a lake or pool.

meretricious *adj, formal* bright or attractive on the surface, but of no real value. ○ **meretriciously** *adv.*

merge *vb* 1 *tr & intr* (*often* **merge with sth**) to blend, combine or join with something else. 2 *intr* (**merge into sth**) to become part of it and therefore impossible to distinguish from it.

merger *n* a joining together, esp of business firms.

meridian *n* 1 *geog* **a** an imaginary line on the Earth's surface passing through the poles at right angles to the equator; a line of longitude; **b** a representation of this, eg on a map. 2 in Chinese medicine: any of several pathways through the body along which life energy flows. ○ **meridional** *adj* 1 *technical* belonging or relating to, or along, a meridian. 2 *literary* belonging or relating to the south, esp to S Europe.

meringue /məˈraŋ/ *n* 1 a crisp, cooked mixture of sugar and egg-whites. 2 a cake or dessert made from this, often with a filling of cream.

merino *n* 1 a type of sheep bred for its long, fine wool. 2 fine yarn or fabric made from its wool.

merit *n* 1 worth, excellence or praiseworthiness. 2 (*often* **merits**) a good point or quality: *He got the job on his own merits.* ➤ *vb* (**merited, meriting**) to deserve; to be worthy of something.

meritocracy /merɪˈtɒkrəsɪ/ *n (-ies)* a social system based on leadership by people of great talent or intelligence. ○ **meritocrat** /ˈmerɪtəkrət/ *n.* ○ **meritocratic** *adj.*

meritorious *adj, formal* deserving reward or praise. ○ **meritoriously** *adv.*

merlin *n* a small, dark-coloured falcon with a black-striped tail.

mermaid *n, folklore* a mythical sea creature with a woman's head and upper body and a fish's tail. ○ **merman** *n.*

merry *adj* (*-ier, -iest*) 1 cheerful and lively. 2 *colloq* slightly drunk. 3 causing or full of laughter. ○ **merrily** *adv.* ○ **merriment** *n.* ○ **merriness** *n.*

merry-go-round *n* 1 a fairground ride consisting of a revolving platform fitted with rising and falling seats in the form of horses or other figures. 2 a whirl of activity.

merrymaking *n* cheerful celebration. ○ **merrymaker** *n.*

mescal *n* 1 a globe-shaped cactus of Mexico and the SW USA, with button-like tubercles on its stems. 2 a colourless Mexican spirit made from the sap of this and certain other plants.

mescaline or **mescalin** *n* a hallucinogenic drug obtained from the MESCAL cactus.

Mesdames *pl of* MADAME

mesdames *pl of* MADAM

Mesdemoiselles *pl of* MADEMOISELLE

mesh *n* 1 netting, or a piece of netting made of wire or thread. 2 each of the openings between the threads of a net. 3 (*usu* **meshes**) a network. ➤ *vb* 1 *intr, technical* of the teeth on gear wheels: to engage. 2 *intr* (*often* **mesh with sth**) to fit or work together. 3 *intr* to become entangled.

mesmerize or **-ise** vb **1** to grip the attention of someone. **2** old use to hypnotize someone. ○ **mesmerism** n. ○ **mesmerizing** adj.

Mesolithic or **mesolithic** adj belonging or relating to the middle period of the Stone Age.

meson /'mi:zɒn/ n, physics any of a group of unstable, strongly-interacting, elementary particles, with a mass between that of an ELECTRON and a NUCLEON.

Mesozoic /mɛsəʊ'zəʊɪk/ adj **1** geol belonging or relating to the era of geological time between the PALAEOZOIC and CENOZOIC eras. **2** relating to the rocks formed during this era.

mess n **1** an untidy or dirty state: The kitchen's in a mess. **2** a state of disorder or confusion: The accounts are in a mess. **3** a badly damaged state. **4** something or someone in a damaged, disordered or confused state: My hair is a mess. **5** a communal dining room, esp in the armed forces: the sergeants' mess. **6** old use a portion of any pulpy food: a mess of potage. ➤ vb **1** (often **mess sth up**) to put or get it into an untidy, dirty, confused or damaged state. **2** (usu **mess with sth**) to meddle, tinker or interfere in it. **3** (**mess with sb**) colloq to become involved in argument or conflict with them. **4** intr of soldiers, etc: to eat, or live, together. ○ **messy** adj (**-ier, -iest**). ◊ **mess about** or **around** colloq to behave in an annoyingly foolish way. **mess about** or **around with sb** colloq to flirt or have sexual intercourse with someone. **mess about** or **around with sth** to play or tinker with something.

message n **1** a spoken or written communication sent from one person to another. **2** the instructive principle contained within a story, poem, religious teaching, work of art, etc. **3** (usu **messages**) chiefly Scot household shopping. ♦ **get the message** colloq to understand.

messenger n someone who carries communications between people.

Messiah n (usu **the Messiah**) **1** Christianity Jesus Christ. **2** Judaism the king of the Jews still to be sent by God to free his people and restore Israel. **3** someone who sets a country or a people free. ○ **Messianic** /mɛsɪ'anɪk/ adj **1** belonging or relating to, or associated with, a Messiah. **2** relating to any popular or inspirational leader, esp a liberator.

Messieurs pl of MONSIEUR

Messrs pl of MR

metabolism /mə'tabəlɪzəm/ n, biochem the sum of all the chemical reactions that occur within the cells of a living organism. ○ **metabolic** adj.

metabolize or **-ise** vb, tr & intr, biochem to break down complex organic compounds into simpler molecules.

metacarpus n (**metacarpi**) anat the set of five bones in the human hand between the wrist and the knuckles. Compare METATARSUS. ○ **metacarpal** adj.

metal n **1** any of a class of chemical elements with certain shared characteristic properties,

most being shiny, malleable, ductile and good conductors of heat and electricity, and all (except MERCURY) being solid at room temperature. **2** road metal, broken rock for making and mending roads. ➤ adj made of, or mainly of, metal. ○ **metallic** adj **1** made of metal. **2** characteristic of metal, eg in sound or appearance.

metalanguage n a language or system of symbols used to discuss another language or symbolic system.

metalloid n, chem a chemical element that has both metallic and non-metallic properties.

metallurgy /mɛ'talədʒɪ, 'mɛtələːdʒɪ/ n the scientific study of the nature and properties of metals and their extraction from the ground. ○ **metallurgic** or **metallurgical** adj. ○ **metallurgist** n.

metalwork n **1** the craft, process or practice of shaping metal and making items of metal. **2** articles made of metal. ○ **metalworker** n.

metamorphic adj **1** relating to METAMORPHOSIS. **2** geol of any of a group of rocks: formed by METAMORPHISM.

metamorphism n, geol the transformation of the structure of rock by the action of the Earth's crust.

metamorphose vb, tr & intr to undergo or cause something to undergo metamorphosis.

metamorphosis /mɛtə'mɔːfəsɪs/ n (**-ses** /-siːz/) **1** a change of form, appearance, character, etc. **2** biol the change of physical form that occurs during the development into adulthood of some creatures, eg butterflies.

metaphor n **1** an expression in which the person, action or thing referred to is described as if it really were what it merely resembles, eg a rejection described as 'a slap in the face', or a ferocious person as 'a tiger'. **2** such expressions in general. ○ **metaphorical** adj. ○ **metaphorically** adv.

metaphysical adj **1** belonging or relating to METAPHYSICS. **2** abstract. ○ **metaphysically** adv.

metaphysics sing n **1** the branch of philosophy dealing with the nature of existence and the basic principles of truth and knowledge. **2** colloq any type of abstract discussion, writing or thinking.

metastasis /mɛ'tastəsɪs/ n (**-ses** /-siːz/) med the spread of a disease, esp of a malignant tumour, from one part of the body to another.

metatarsus n (**metatarsi**) anat the set of five long bones in the human foot between the ankle and the toes. Compare METACARPUS. ○ **metatarsal** adj.

metathesis /mɛ'taθəsɪs/ n, ling alteration of the normal order of sounds or letters in a word.

metazoan /mɛtə'zəʊən/ n, zool any many-celled animal that has specialized differentiated body tissues.

mete vb, rather formal (now always **mete sth out** or **mete out sth**) to give out or dispense something, esp punishment.

meteor *n, astron* the streak of light seen when a meteoroid enters into the Earth's atmosphere, where it burns up as a result of friction.

meteoric /miːˈtɒrɪk/ *adj* **1** belonging or relating to meteors. **2 a** of success, etc: very rapid; **b** like a meteor in terms of brilliance, speed, transience, etc. ○ **meteorically** *adv.*

meteorite *n, astron* the remains of a METEOROID which has survived burn-up in its passage through the Earth's atmosphere as a METEOR. ○ **meteoritic** *adj.*

meteoroid *n, astron* in interplanetary space: a small, moving, solid object or dust particle, which becomes visible as a METEORITE or a METEOR if it enters the Earth's atmosphere.

meteorology *n* the scientific study of weather and climate over a relatively short period. ○ **meteorological** *adj.* ○ **meteorologist** *n.*

meter¹ *n* **1** an instrument for measuring and recording, esp quantities of electricity, gas, water, etc used. **2** a parking-meter. ➤ *vb* to measure and record (eg electricity) using a meter.

meter² the *US* spelling of METRE¹, METRE²

meth *n, slang* short for METHAMPHETAMINE.

methadone *n* a drug similar to MORPHINE, but less addictive, used as a painkiller and as a heroin substitute for drug addicts.

methamphetamine *n* a derivative of AMPHETAMINE with rapid and long-lasting action, used as a stimulant.

methanal *n, chem* FORMALDEHYDE.

methane *n, chem* a colourless odourless flammable gas, used as a cooking and heating fuel (in the form of NATURAL GAS of which it is the main component).

methanol *n, chem* a colourless flammable toxic liquid used as a solvent and antifreeze.

methinks *vb* (**methought**) *old use or humorous* it seems to me (that).

method *n* **1** a way of doing something, esp an ordered set of procedures or an orderly system. **2** good planning; efficient organization. **3** (*often* **methods**) a technique used in a particular activity: *farming methods.* ○ **methodical** *adj* efficient and orderly; done in a systematic way. ○ **methodically** *adv.*

Methodist *Christianity, n* **1** a member of the Methodist Church, a denomination founded by John Wesley as an evangelical movement within the Church of England. **2** a supporter of Methodism. ➤ *adj* belonging or relating to Methodism. ○ **Methodism** *n.*

methodology *n* (**-ies**) **1** the system of methods and principles used in a particular activity, science, etc. **2** the study of method and procedure.

meths *sing n, colloq, esp Brit* methylated spirits.

methylate *vb* to mix or impregnate something with methanol.

methylated spirits or **methylated spirit** *sing n* ethanol treated with additives, used as a fuel and solvent.

meticulous *adj* paying, or showing, very careful attention to detail. ○ **meticulously** *adv.* ○ **meticulousness** *n.*

métier /ˈmeːtieː; *French* metje/ *n* **1** a person's business or line of work. **2** the field or subject, etc in which one is especially skilled.

metonymy /mɪˈtɒnɪmɪ/ *n* (**-ies**) *ling* the use of a word referring to an element or attribute of something to mean the thing itself, eg *the bottle* for 'the drinking of alcohol' or *the Crown* for 'the sovereign'.

metre¹ or (*US*) **meter** *n* in the SI system: the principal unit of length, equal to 39.37in or 1.094yd.

metre² or (*US*) **meter** *n* **1** *poetry* the arrangement of words and syllables, or feet (see FOOT sense 8), in a rhythmic pattern according to their length and stress; a particular pattern or scheme. **2** *mus* **a** the basic pattern or structure of beats; **b** tempo.

metric¹ *adj* relating to or based on the METRE¹ or the metric system. ○ **metrically** *adv.*

metric² see METRICAL

metrical or **metric** *adj, technical* **1** in or relating to verse as distinct from prose. **2** belonging or relating to measurement.

metricate *vb, tr & intr* to convert (a non-metric measurement, system, etc) to a metric one using units of the metric system. ○ **metrication** *n.*

metric system *n* a standard system of measurement, based on DECIMAL units, in which each successive multiple of a unit is 10 times larger than the one before it. *Technical equivalent* SI.

metro *n* an urban railway system, usu one that is mostly underground.

metronome *n* a device that indicates musical tempo by means of a ticking pendulum that can be set to move at different speeds.

metropolis /məˈtrɒpəlɪs/ *n* (**-ses** /-lɪsɪz/) a large city, esp the capital city of a nation or region.

metropolitan *adj* **1** belonging or relating to, typical of, or situated in, a large city. **2** belonging or referring to a country's mainland, as opposed to its overseas territories. ➤ *n* **1** *Christianity* in the Roman Catholic and Orthodox Churches: a bishop, usu an archbishop, with authority over all the bishops in a province. **2** an inhabitant of a metropolis.

mettle *n, literary* **1** courage, determination and endurance. **2** character; personal qualities: *show one's mettle.* ♦ **put sb on their mettle** *literary* to encourage or force them to make their best effort.

mew *vb, intr* to make the cry of a cat. ➤ *n* a cat's cry.

mews *sing n* (**mews** or **mewses**) a set of stables around a yard or square, esp one converted into residential accommodation or garages.

mezzanine /ˈmɛzəniːn/ *n, archit* in a building: a small storey between two main floors.

mezzo /ˈmɛtsoʊ/ *adv, mus* moderately, quite or

rather, as in **mezzo-forte** rather loud.

mezzo-soprano *n, mus* **1** a singing voice with a range between soprano and contralto. **2** a singer with this range or type of voice.

mezzotint /'mɛtsoutɪnt/ *n, chiefly hist* **1** a method of engraving a copper plate, by polishing and scraping to produce areas of light and shade. **2** a print made from a plate engraved in this way.

Mg *symbol, chem* magnesium.

mg *abbrev* milligram.

Mgr *abbrev* **1** manager. **2** Monseigneur. **3** (*also* **Monsig.**) Monsignor.

MHz *abbrev* megahertz.

mi see ME[2]

miaow or **meow** /mɪ'aʊ/ *vb, intr* to make the cry of a cat. ➤ *n* a cat's cry.

miasma /mɪ'azmə/ *n* (**miasmata** or **miasmas**) *literary* **1** a thick foul-smelling vapour. **2** an evil influence or atmosphere.

mica /'maɪkə/ *n, geol* any of a group of silicate minerals that split easily into thin flexible sheets and are used as electrical insulators.

mice *pl of* MOUSE

Michaelmas /'mɪkəlməs/ *n, Christianity* a festival in honour of St Michael the archangel, held on 29 September.

mick *n, offensive slang* **1** an Irishman. **2** *esp Aust* a Roman Catholic.

mickey *n.* ♦ **take the mickey** or **take the mickey out of sb** *colloq* to tease or make fun of them.

mickle or **muckle** *archaic or N Eng dialect & Scot, adj* much or great. ➤ *adv* much. ➤ *n* a great quantity.

micro *n, colloq* **1** a microcomputer or microprocessor. **2** a microwave oven.

microbe *n, loosely* any micro-organism, esp a bacterium that is capable of causing disease. ○ **microbial** or **microbic** *adj.*

microbiology *n* the branch of biology dealing with the study of micro-organisms.

microchip see under SILICON CHIP

microcircuit *n* an electronic circuit with components formed in one microchip.

microcomputer *n* a small, relatively inexpensive computer designed for use by one person at a time. Now usu called **personal computer**.

microcosm *n* **1** any structure or system which contains, in miniature, all the features of the larger structure or system that it is part of. **2** *philos* humankind regarded as a model or epitome of the universe. Compare MACROCOSM. ○ **microcosmic** *adj.*

microdot *n* a photograph, eg one taken of secret documents, reduced to the size of a pinhead.

microelectronics *sing n* the branch of electronics dealing with the design and use of small-scale electrical circuits or other very small electronic devices.

microfibre *n* a synthetic, very closely woven fabric.

microfiche /'maɪkrəfiːʃ, -rou-/ *n* (**microfiche** or **microfiches**) *photog* a flat sheet of film with printed text on it that has been photographically reduced, used for storing library catalogues, newspaper texts, etc.

microfilm *n* a length of thin photographic film on which printed material is stored in miniaturized form. ➤ *vb* to record something on microfilm.

microlight *n* a very lightweight, small-engined aircraft, like a powered hang-glider.

micrometer /maɪ'krɒmɪtə(r)/ *n* an instrument of various kinds used for accurately measuring very small distances, thicknesses or angles. ○ **micrometry** *n.*

microminiaturize or **-ise** *vb* to reduce (scientific or technical equipment, etc, or any part of such equipment) to an extremely small size.

micro-organism *n* any living organism that can only be observed with the aid of a microscope.

microphone *n* an electromagnetic transducer that converts sound waves into electrical signals.

microphotography *n* photography, esp of documents and plans, in the form of greatly reduced images of small area which have to be viewed by magnification.

microprocessor *n, comput* a single circuit performing most of the basic functions of a CPU.

microscope *n* an instrument consisting of a system of lenses which produce a magnified image of objects that are too small to be seen with the naked eye. ○ **microscopy** /maɪ'krɒskəpɪ/ *n.*

microscopic *adj* **1** too small to be seen without the aid of a microscope. Compare MACRO-SCOPIC. **2** *colloq* extremely small. ○ **microscopically** *adv.*

microsecond *n* in the SI or metric system: a unit of time equal to one millionth part of a second.

microsurgery *n, med* any intricate surgical procedure that is performed by means of a powerful microscope and small specialized instruments.

microwave *n* **1** a form of electromagnetic radiation with wavelengths in the range 1mm to 0.3m, used in radar, communications and cooking. **2** a microwave oven. ➤ *vb* to cook something in a microwave oven.

microwave oven *n* an electrically operated oven that uses microwaves to cook food more rapidly than is possible in a conventional oven.

micturate *vb, intr, formal* to urinate. ○ **micturition** *n.*

mid[1] *adj, often in compounds* (sometimes with hyphen) referring to the middle point or in the middle of something: *mid-March* • *in mid sentence.*

mid[2] or **'mid** *prep, poetic* a short form of AMID.

mid-air *n* any area or point above the ground: *caught it in mid-air.*

midday *n* the middle of the day; twelve o'clock.

midden *n* 1 *chiefly old use or dialect* a rubbish heap; a pile of dung. 2 *colloq* an untidy mess.

middle *adj* 1 at, or being, a point or position between two others, usu two ends or extremes, and esp the same distance from each. 2 intermediate; neither at the top or at the bottom end of the scale: *middle income.* ➢ *n* 1 the middle point, part or position of something: *the middle of the night.* 2 *colloq* the waist. ◆ **be in the middle of sth** to be busy with it and likely to remain so for some time.

middle age *n* the years between youth and old age, usu thought of as between the ages of 40 and 60. ○ **middle-aged** *adj.*

the Middle Ages *pl n* in European history: 1 the period (c. 500–1500AD) between the fall of the Roman Empire in the West and the Renaissance. 2 *sometimes strictly* the period between 1100 and 1500.

middle-age spread or **middle-aged spread** *n* fat around the waist, often regarded as a consequence of reaching middle age.

middlebrow *derog, adj* intended for, or appealing to, people with conventional tastes and average intelligence. ➢ *n* a middlebrow person.

middle class *n* (*esp* **the middle class**) a social class between the working class and the upper class, traditionally thought of as being made up of educated people with professional or business careers. ➢ *adj* (**middle-class**) belonging or relating to, or characteristic of, the middle class.

middle distance *n* in a painting, photograph, etc: the area between the foreground and the background. ➢ *adj* (**middle-distance**) 1 of an athlete: competing in races of distances of 400, 800 and 1500m. 2 of a race: run over any of these distances.

middle ear *n, anat* in vertebrates: an air-filled cavity that lies between the eardrum and the inner ear.

middleman *n* 1 a dealer who buys goods from a producer and sells them to shopkeepers or to the public. 2 any intermediary.

middle name *n* 1 a name which comes between a FIRST NAME and a SURNAME. 2 a quality or feature for which a person is well-known: *Punctuality is his middle name.*

middle-of-the-road *adj, often derog* 1 eg of politics or opinions: not extreme. 2 eg of music: **a** of widespread appeal; **b** boringly average or familiar.

middle school *n, England & Wales* a school for children between the ages of 8 or 9 and 12 or 13.

middle-sized *adj* characterized by being of average or medium size.

middleweight *n* 1 a class for boxers, wrestlers and weightlifters of not more than a specified weight, for example 73kg (160lb) in professional boxing. 2 a boxer, wrestler, etc of this weight.

middling *colloq, adj* average; moderate.

➢ *adv* esp of a person's health: moderately: *middling good.*

midfield *n, football* the middle area of the pitch, not close to the goal of either team. ○ **midfielder** *n.*

midge *n* a small insect that gathers with others near water, esp one of the kinds that bite people.

midget *n* 1 an unusually small person whose limbs and features are of normal proportions. 2 anything that is smaller than others of its kind.

midi *n, colloq, fashion* a skirt or coat of medium length or medium size.

midland *adj* belonging or relating to the central, inland part of a country.

midmost *literary, adv* in the very middle. ➢ *adj* nearest the middle.

midnight *n* twelve o'clock at night.

mid-on or **mid-off** *n, cricket* a fielder in a roughly-horizontal line with, but at a certain distance from, the non-striking batsman, on the on or off side respectively (see ON *adj* sense 6, OFF *adj* sense 4).

midpoint *n* a point at or near the middle in distance or time.

midriff *n* 1 the part of the body between the chest and waist. 2 the DIAPHRAGM.

midshipman *n, naut* a trainee naval officer, stationed on land.

midst *n* 1 (*always* **in the midst of sth**) a among it or in the centre of it; **b** at the same time as something; during it. 2 (*always* **in sb's midst**) among them or in the same place as them.

midstream *n* the area of water in the middle of a river or stream. ◆ **in midstream** before a sentence, action, etc is finished.

midsummer *n* the period of time in the middle of summer.

midterm *n* 1 the middle of an academic term or term of office, etc. 2 the middle of a particular period of time, esp of a pregnancy.

midway *adj, adv* halfway between two points in distance or time.

midweek *n* the period of time in the middle of the week, esp Wednesday.

mid-wicket *n, cricket* a fielder placed on the on side (see ON *adj* sense 6), roughly level with the middle of the pitch and halfway to the boundary.

midwife *n* a nurse trained to assist women in childbirth and to provide care and advice for women before and after childbirth. ○ **midwifery** /'mɪdwɪfərɪ/ *n.*

midwinter *n* the period of time in the middle of winter.

mien /miːn/ *n, formal or literary* an appearance, expression or manner, esp one that reflects a mood: *her thoughtful mien.*

miff *vb, intr, colloq* (usu **be miffed at, about** or **with sb** or **sth**) to be offended. ○ **miffed** *adj* offended, upset or annoyed.

might¹ *auxiliary vb* 1 past tense of MAY¹: *He asked if he might be of assistance.* 2 (*sometimes*

might well) used to express a possibility: *He might win if he tries hard.* **3** used to request permission: *Might I speak to you a moment?*

might² *n* power or strength. ♦ **with might and main** *literary* with great strength.

mightn't *contraction* might not.

mighty *adj* (*-ier, -iest*) **1** having great strength or power. **2** very large. **3** very great or important. ➤ *adv, N Am, colloq* very: *mighty pretty.* ○ **mightily** *adv.* ○ **mightiness** *n.*

migraine *n* a throbbing headache that usu affects one side of the head and is often accompanied by nausea or vomiting, and sometimes preceded by visual disturbances.

migrant *n* a person or animal that migrates. ➤ *adj* regularly moving from one place to another.

migrate *vb, intr* **1** of animals, esp birds: to travel from one region to another at certain times of the year. **2** of people: to leave one place and settle in another, esp another country. ○ **migration** *n.* ○ **migratory** *adj.*

mikado or (*often*) **Mikado** /mɪˈkɑːdoʊ/ *n* a title formerly given by foreigners to an emperor of Japan.

mike *contraction, colloq* short for MICROPHONE.

mil *n* a millimetre.

milady *n* (*-ies*) *dated* a term formerly used to address, or to refer to, a rich or aristocratic English woman.

milch /mɪltʃ/ *adj* of cattle: producing milk.

mild *adj* **1** gentle in temperament or behaviour. **2** not sharp or strong in flavour or effect. **3** not great or severe. **4** of climate, etc: not characterized by extremes. ➤ *n* (*also* **mild ale**) dark beer less flavoured with hops than BITTER. ○ **mildly** *adv.* ○ **mildness** *n.* ♦ **to put it mildly** to understate the case.

mildew *n* **a** a parasitic fungus that produces a fine white powdery coating on the surface of infected plants; **b** similar white or grey patches on the surface of paper which has been exposed to damp conditions. ➤ *vb, tr & intr* to affect or become affected by mildew. ○ **mildewy** *adj.*

mild steel *n* steel that contains little carbon and is easily worked.

mile *n* **1** in the imperial system: a unit of distance equal to 1760yd (1.61km). **2** a race over this distance, esp a race on foot. **3** *colloq* a great distance; a large margin: *You missed by a mile.* ➤ *adv* (**miles**) **a** at a great distance: *She lives miles away*; **b** *colloq* very much: *I feel miles better.*

mileage *n* **1** the number of miles travelled or to be travelled. **2** the number of miles a motor vehicle will travel on a fixed amount of fuel; **b** the total number of miles a car has done since new, as shown on the mileometer. **3** *colloq* use; benefit: *We can get a lot of mileage out of that story.*

mileometer or **milometer** /maɪˈlɒmɪtə(r)/ *n* in a motor vehicle: an instrument for recording the total number of miles travelled.

milestone *n* **1** a very important event; a significant point. **2** a stone pillar at a roadside showing distances in miles to various places.

milieu /ˈmiːljɜː/ *n* (*milieus* or *milieux*) *literary* a social environment or set of surroundings.

militant *adj* **1** taking, or ready to take, strong or violent action. **2** *formal* engaged in warfare. ➤ *n* a militant person. ○ **militancy** *n.* ○ **militantly** *adv.*

militarism *n, often derog* **1** an aggressive readiness to engage in warfare. **2** the vigorous pursuit of military aims and ideals. ○ **militarist** *n.* ○ **militaristic** *adj.*

militarize or **-ise** *vb* **1** to provide (a country, body, etc) with a military force. **2** to make something military in nature or character. ○ **militarization** *n.*

military *adj* **1** by, for, or belonging or relating to the armed forces or warfare: *military encounter.* **2** characteristic of members of the armed forces: *military bearing.* ➤ *n* (*-ies*) (*usu* **the military**) the armed forces. ○ **militarily** *adv.*

military police or **Military Police** *n* (abbrev **MP**) a police force within an army, enforcing army rules.

militate *vb, intr* (*usu* **militate for** or **against sth**) of facts, etc: to have a strong influence or effect: *The evidence militates against your sworn statement.*

militia /mɪˈlɪʃə/ *n* a civilian fighting force used to supplement a regular army in emergencies. ○ **militiaman** *n.*

milk *n* **1** a whitish liquid that is secreted by the MAMMARY GLANDs of female mammals to provide their young with nourishment. **2** the whiteish, milk-like juice or sap of certain plants: *coconut milk.* **3** any preparation that resembles milk: *milk of magnesia.* ➤ *vb* **1** to take milk from (an animal). **2** to extract or draw off a substance (eg venom or sap) from something. **3** *colloq* to obtain money, information or any other benefit from someone or something, cleverly or relentlessly: *They milked the scandal for all it was worth.* **4** *intr* of cattle: to yield milk. ○ **milker** *n.* ○ **milkiness** *n.* ○ **milking** *n.* ○ **milky** *adj* (*-ier, -iest*).

milk chocolate *n* chocolate containing milk.

milk float *n, Brit* a vehicle, usu an electrically-powered one, used for delivering milk.

milkmaid *n* a woman who milks cows, goats, etc.

milkman *n, Brit* a man who delivers milk to people's houses.

milk of magnesia *n* another name for MAGNESIA (sense 2).

milkshake *n* a drink consisting of a mixture of milk, flavouring and sometimes ice cream, whipped together until creamy.

milksop *n, derog, old use* a weak, effeminate or ineffectual man or youth.

milk tooth *n* any of a baby's or young mammal's first set of teeth.

mill *n* **1** **a** a large machine that grinds grain into flour; **b** a building containing such a machine: *windmill.* **2** a smaller machine or device for grinding a particular thing: *a pepper mill.* **3** a factory, esp one with one or more large machines that press, roll or otherwise shape something: *a woollen mill.* ➤ *vb* **1** to grind (grain, etc). **2** to shape (eg metal) in a mill. **3** to cut grooves into the edge of (a coin). **4** *intr, colloq* (*esp* **mill about** or **around**) to move in an aimless or confused manner. ○ **miller** *n* someone who owns or operates a mill, esp a grain mill. ◆ **go** or **put sb** or **sth through the mill** to undergo or make them or it undergo an unpleasant experience or difficult test.

millennium *n* (**millenniums** or **millennia**) **1** a period of a thousand years. **2** (**the millennium**) **a** a future period of a thousand years during which some Christians believe Christ will rule the world; **b** a future golden age of worldwide peace and happiness. ○ **millennial** *adj.*

millepede see MILLIPEDE

millesimal /mɪˈlɛsɪməl/ *adj* **1** thousandth. **2** consisting of or relating to thousandths. ➤ *n* a thousandth part.

millet *n* a cereal grass which is grown as an important food crop, and also widely used as animal fodder.

millibar *n, physics, meteorol, etc* a unit of atmospheric pressure equal to 10^{-3} (one thousandth) of a bar.

milligram or **milligramme** *n* a unit of weight equal to one thousandth of a gram.

millilitre or (*US*) **milliliter** *n* a unit of volume, equal to one thousandth of a litre.

millimetre or (*US*) **millimeter** *n* a unit of length equal to one thousandth of a metre.

milliner *n* someone who makes or sells women's hats. ○ **millinery** *n.*

million *n* (**millions** or after a number **million**) **1 a** the cardinal number 10^6; **b** the quantity that this represents, being a thousand thousands. **2** a numeral, figure or symbol representing this, eg *1 000 000.* **3** (*often* **millions**) *colloq* a great number: *He's got millions of friends.* ➤ *adj* **1** totalling one million. **2** *colloq* very many: *I've told you a million times.* ○ **millionth** *adj, n.* ◆ **one in a million** something or someone very rare of their kind, and therefore very valuable or special.

millionaire or **millionairess** *n* someone whose wealth amounts to a million pounds, dollars, etc or more.

millipede or **millepede** *n* (**millipedes** or **millepedes**) a small wormlike creature with a many-jointed body and numerous pairs of legs.

millisecond *n* a unit of time equal to one thousandth of a second.

millpond *n* a pond containing water which is, or used to be, used for driving a mill. ◆ **like** or **as calm as a millpond** of a stretch of water: completely smooth and calm.

millstone *n* **1** either of the large, heavy stones between which grain is ground in a mill. **2** (*esp*

a millstone around sb's neck) any heavy burden which someone has to bear and which slows their progress.

millstream *n* a stream of water that turns a millwheel.

millwheel *n* a wheel, esp a waterwheel, used to drive a mill.

milometer see MILEOMETER

milord *n, dated* a term formerly used on the continent to address or refer to a rich or aristocratic English gentleman.

milt *n* the testis or sperm of a fish.

mime *n* **1** the theatrical art of conveying meaning without words through gesture, movement and facial expression. **2** a play or dramatic sequence performed in this way. **3** an actor who practises this art. ➤ *vb, tr & intr* **1** to act or express (feelings, etc) without words through gesture, movement and facial expression. **2** to mouth the words to a song in time with a recording, giving the illusion of singing.

mimeograph /ˈmɪmɪəɡrɑːf/ *n* **1** a machine that produces copies of printed or hand-written material from a stencil. **2** a copy produced in this way. ➤ *vb* to make a copy of something in this way.

mimesis /mɪˈmiːsɪs/ *n* in art or literature: imitative representation. ○ **mimetic** *adj* consisting of, showing, or relating to imitation.

mimic *vb* (**mimicked, mimicking**) **1** to imitate someone or something, esp for comic effect. **2** to copy. **3** to simulate. ➤ *n* someone who is skilled at imitating other people, esp in a comic manner. ➤ *adj* **1** imitative. **2** mock or sham. ○ **mimicry** *n* (*-ies*).

mimosa *n* (**mimosas** or **mimosae**) a tropical shrub or tree which has leaves that droop when touched, and clusters of flowers, typically yellow ones.

Min. *abbrev* **1** Minister. **2** Ministry.

min. *abbrev* **1** minimum. **2** minute.

minaret *n* a tower or attached to a mosque, with a balcony from which the MUEZZIN calls Muslims to prayer.

minatory *adj, formal* threatening.

mince *vb* **1** to cut or shred something (esp meat) into very small pieces. **2** (*esp* **mince words with sb** or **mince one's words**), *chiefly with negatives* to restrain or soften the impact of (one's words, opinion, remarks, etc) when addressing someone: *not one to mince his words.* **3** *intr, usu derog* to walk or speak with affected delicateness. ➤ *n* minced meat. ○ **mincer** *n.*

mincemeat *n* a spiced mixture of dried fruits, apples, candied peel, etc and often suet, used as a filling for pies. ◆ **make mincemeat of sb** or **sth** *colloq* to destroy or defeat them or it thoroughly.

mince pie *n* a pie filled with mincemeat or with minced meat.

mincing *adj, usu derog* of a manner of walking or behaving: over-delicate and affected.

mind *n* **1** the power of thinking and understanding. **2** the place where thoughts, feelings and creative reasoning exist. **3** memory; recollection: *to call something to mind.* **4** opinion: *It's unjust, to my mind.* **5** attention: *Keep your mind on the job.* **6** wish; inclination: *I have a mind to go.* **7** right senses; sanity: *He has lost his mind.* ➢ *vb* **1** to look after or care for something or someone: *Stay here and mind the luggage.* **2** *tr & intr* to be upset, concerned or offended by something or someone: *I don't mind the noise.* **3** (*also* **mind out** *or* **mind out for sth**) to be careful or wary of it: *Mind where you step.* **4** to take notice of or pay attention to something or someone: *Mind your own business.* **5** to take care to control something: *Mind your language.* **6** *tr & intr* to take care to protect something or someone: *Mind your jacket near this wet paint!* ➢ *exclam* (*often* **mind out!**) be careful; watch out!: *Mind! There's a car reversing.* ♦ **bear sth in mind** to remember or consider it. **do you mind!** an exclamation expressing disagreement or objection. **in one's mind's eye** in one's imagination. **make up one's mind** to come to a decision. **on one's mind** referring to something that is being thought about, considered, worried about, etc. **to my mind** in my opinion.

mind-blowing *adj, colloq* **1** very surprising, shocking, or exciting. **2** of a drug: producing a state of hallucination or altered consciousness.

mind-boggling *adj, colloq* too difficult, large, strange, etc to imagine or understand.

minded *adj, in compounds* having the specified kind of mind or attitude: *open-minded • like-minded.*

minder *n* **1** *in compounds* someone who takes care of or supervises someone or something: *childminder.* **2** *colloq* a bodyguard.

mindful *adj* (*usu* **mindful of sth**) keeping it in mind.

mindless *adj* **1** *derog* senseless; done without a reason: *mindless violence.* **2** *derog* needing no effort of mind: *watching mindless rubbish on TV.* **3** (*usu* **mindless of sth**) taking no account of it: *mindless of his responsibilities.* ○ **mindlessly** *adv.*

mind-numbing *adj, colloq* so boring that it seems to deaden the brain. ○ **mind-numbingly** *adv.*

mind-reader *n* someone who claims to be able to know other people's thoughts. ○ **mind-reading** *n.*

mindset *n* an attitude or habit of mind, esp a firmly fixed one.

mine¹ *pron* **1** something or someone belonging to, or connected with, me: *That coat is mine.* **2** my family or people: *as long as it doesn't affect me or mine.* ➢ *adj, old use, poetic* used in place of MY before a vowel sound or *h*: *mine host.*

mine² *n* **1** an opening or excavation in the ground, used to remove minerals, metal ores, coal, etc, from the Earth's crust. **2** an explosive device that is placed just beneath the ground surface or in water, designed to destroy tanks, ships, etc, when detonated. **3** a rich source: *He's a mine of information.* ➢ *vb* **1** *tr & intr* to dig for (minerals, etc). **2** (*also* **mine somewhere for sth**) to dig (a particular area) in order to extract minerals, etc. **3** to lay exploding mines in (land or water): *The beach has been mined.* ○ **miner** *n* someone who mines or works in a mine, esp a coal mine. ○ **mining** *n.*

minefield *n* **1** an area of land or water in which mines (see MINE² *noun* sense 2) have been laid. **2** a subject or situation that presents many problems or dangers, esp hidden ones.

mineral *n* **1** *technical* a naturally occurring substance that is inorganic, and has characteristic physical and chemical properties by which it may be identified. **2** *loosely* any substance obtained by mining. **3** any inorganic substance, ie one that is neither animal nor vegetable. ➢ *adj* belonging or relating to the nature of a mineral; containing minerals.

mineralogy /mɪnəˈralədʒɪ/ *n* the scientific study of minerals. ○ **mineralogical** *adj.* ○ **mineralogist** *n.*

mineral water *n* water containing small quantities of dissolved minerals, esp water that occurs naturally in this state at a spring.

minestrone /mɪnəˈstrəʊnɪ/ *n, cookery* a soup containing a variety of chunky vegetables and pasta.

minesweeper *n* a ship equipped to clear mines from an area. ○ **minesweeping** *n.*

mingle *vb* (*often* **mingle with sth** *or* **sb**) **1** *tr & intr* to become or make something become blended or mixed. **2** *intr* to move from person to person at a social engagement, briefly talking to each.

mingy /ˈmɪndʒɪ/ *adj* (*-ier, -iest*) *Brit derog, colloq* ungenerous; mean.

mini *colloq, n* something small or short of its kind, esp a MINISKIRT, or a type of small car. ➢ *adj* small or short of its kind.

mini- *pfx, forming nouns, denoting* smaller or shorter than the standard size.

miniature *n* **1** a small copy, model or breed of anything. **2** a very small painting, esp a portrait on a very small scale. ➢ *adj* minute or small-scale; referring to the nature of a miniature. ○ **miniaturist** *n* an artist who paints miniatures. ♦ **in miniature** on a small scale.

miniaturize *or* **-ise** *vb* **1** to make (eg technical equipment) on a small scale. **2** to make something very small. ○ **miniaturization** *n.*

minibus *n* a small bus.

minicab *n* a taxi that is ordered by telephone from a private company, not one that can be stopped in the street.

minidisk *n, comput* a very compact magnetic disk storage medium for microcomputers.

minim *n* **1** *mus* a note half the length of a SEMI-BREVE. **2** in the imperial system: a unit of liquid volume, equal to ⅟₆₀ of a fluid drachm (0.06ml).

minimal *adj* very little indeed: *minimal damage.* ○ **minimally** *adv.*

minimalism n esp in art, music and design: the policy of using the minimum means, eg the fewest and simplest elements, to achieve the desired result. ○ **minimalist** n, adj.

minimize or **-ise** vb **1** to reduce something to a minimum. **2** to treat something as being of little importance.

minimum n (**minimums** or **minima**) **1** the lowest possible number, value, quantity or degree. **2** (sometimes **a minimum of sth**) the lowest number, value, quantity or degree reached or allowed: There must be a minimum of three people present. ➤ adj **1** relating or referring to the nature of a minimum; lowest possible: minimum waste. **2** lowest reached or allowed: minimum age.

minimum wage n the lowest wage an employer is allowed to pay, by law or union agreement.

minion n, derog an employee or follower, esp one who is subservient.

miniseries n a short series of TV programmes, usu broadcast over consecutive days.

miniskirt n a very short skirt, with a hemline well above the knee.

minister n **1** the political head of, or a senior politician with responsibilities in, a government department. **2** a member of the clergy in certain branches of the Christian Church. **3** a high-ranking diplomat, esp the next in rank below an ambassador. ➤ vb, intr, formal (esp **minister to sb**) to provide someone with help or some kind of service. ○ **ministerial** /mɪnɪ-ˈstɪərɪəl/ adj.

ministration n, formal **1** the act or process of ministering. **2** (usu **ministrations**) help or service given.

ministry n (**-ies**) **1 a** a government department; **b** the premises it occupies. **2** (**the ministry**) **a** the profession, duties or period of service of a religious minister; **b** religious ministers collectively. **3** the act of ministering.

mink n (pl **mink**) **1** a European or N American mammal with a slender body and thick fur. **2** the highly valued fur of this animal. **3** a garment made of this fur.

minneola n an orange-like citrus fruit which is a cross between a grapefruit and a tangerine.

minnow n a small freshwater fish of the carp family.

minor adj **1** not as great in importance or size; fairly small or insignificant: only a minor problem. **2** mus **a** of a scale: having a semitone between the second and third, fifth and sixth, and seventh and eighth notes; **b** of a key, chord, etc: based on such a scale. **3** Brit, esp formerly used after the surname of the younger of two brothers attending the same school: junior: Simcox minor. **4** of a person: below the age of legal majority or adulthood. ➤ n **1** someone who is below the age of legal majority. **2** mus a minor key, chord or scale. **3** esp US **a** a student's minor or subsidiary subject of study; **b** a student studying such a subject: a history minor. ➤ vb, esp

US (always **minor in sth**) to study a specified minor or subsidiary subject at college or university. Compare MAJOR.

minority n (**-ies**) **1** a small number, or the smaller of two numbers, sections or groups. **2** a group of people who are different, esp in terms of race or religion, from most of the people in a country, region, etc. **3** the state of being the smaller or lesser of two groups: in a minority. **4** the state of being below the age of legal majority.

minster n a large church or cathedral, esp one that was orig attached to a monastery: York Minster.

minstrel n, hist **1** in the Middle Ages: a travelling singer, musician and reciter of poetry, etc. **2** formerly in the USA and Britain: any of a group of white-skinned entertainers made up to look black, who performed song and dance routines superficially of Negro origin.

mint¹ n **1** an aromatic plant with small, white or purple flowers, widely grown as a garden herb. **2** cookery the pungent-smelling leaves of this plant, used fresh or dried as a flavouring. **3** a sweet flavoured with mint, or with a synthetic substitute for mint. ○ **minty** adj (**-ier, -iest**).

mint² n **1** a place where coins are produced under government authority. **2** colloq a very large sum of money. ➤ vb **1** to manufacture (coins). **2** to invent or coin (a new word, phrase, etc). ○ **mintage** n. ♦ **in mint condition** or **state** in perfect condition, as if brand new.

minuet /mɪnjʊˈɛt/ n **1** a slow formal dance with short steps in triple time, popular in the 17c and 18c. **2** a piece of music for this dance.

minus prep **1** with the subtraction of (a specified number): Eight minus six equals two. **2** colloq without: He arrived minus his wife. ➤ adj **1** negative or less than zero. **2** of a student's grade, and placed after the grade: indicating a level slightly below that indicated by the letter: I got a B minus for my essay. **3** colloq characterized by being a disadvantage: a minus point. ➤ n **1** a sign (–) indicating a negative quantity or that the quantity which follows it is to be subtracted. **2** colloq a negative point; a disadvantage. **3** a negative quantity or term.

minuscule adj extremely small.

minute¹ /ˈmɪnɪt/ n **1** a unit of time equal to $\frac{1}{60}$ of an hour; 60 seconds. **2** colloq a short while: Wait a minute. **3** a particular point in time: At that minute the phone rang. **4** the distance that can be travelled in a minute: a house five minutes away. **5** (usu **the minutes**) the official written record of what is said at a formal meeting. **6** geom (symbol ′) a unit of angular measurement equal to $\frac{1}{60}$ of a degree; 60 seconds. ➤ vb to make an official written record of what is said in (eg a meeting); to take or record something in the minutes of (eg a meeting). ♦ **up to the minute** or **up-to-the-minute** very modern or up-to-date.

minute² /maɪˈnjuːt/ adj **1** very small. **2** precise; detailed.

minutiae /mɪˈnjuːʃɪaɪ/ pl n small and often unimportant details.

minx n, humorous or rather dated a cheeky, playful, sly or flirtatious young woman.

Miocene /ˈmaɪəsiːn/ geol, n the fourth epoch of the Tertiary period. ➤ adj 1 belonging or relating to this epoch. 2 relating to rocks formed during this epoch.

MIPS or **mips** /mɪps/ abbrev, comput millions of instructions per second.

miracle n 1 an act or event that breaks the laws of nature, and is therefore thought to be caused by the intervention of God or another supernatural force. 2 colloq an act or event that breaks the laws of nature, and is therefore thought to be caused by the intervention of God or another supernatural force. 2 colloq a fortunate happening; an amazing event. 3 colloq an amazing example or achievement of something: a miracle of modern technology.

miracle play n a MYSTERY PLAY.

miraculous adj 1 brought about by, relating to, or like a miracle. 2 colloq amazing; amazingly fortunate: a miraculous escape. ○ **miraculously** adv.

mirage /ˈmɪrɑːʒ, mɪˈrɑːʒ/ n 1 an optical illusion that usu resembles a pool of water on the horizon reflecting light from the sky, commonly experienced in deserts, and caused by the refraction of light by very hot air near to the ground. 2 anything illusory or imaginary.

mire n 1 deep mud; a boggy area. 2 trouble; difficulty. ➤ vb, tr & intr to sink, or to make something or someone sink, in a mire.

mirror n 1 a smooth highly-polished surface, such as glass, coated with a thin layer of metal, that reflects an image of what is in front of it. 2 any surface that reflects light. 3 a faithful representation or reflection: when art is a mirror of life. ➤ vb 1 to represent or depict something faithfully. 2 to reflect something or someone as in a mirror.

mirror image n a reflected image as produced by a mirror, ie one in which the right and left sides are reversed.

mirth n laughter; merriment. ○ **mirthful** adj. ○ **mirthless** adj.

misadventure n, formal 1 an unfortunate happening. 2 law an accident, with total absence of negligence or intent to commit crime: death by misadventure.

misalign vb to align something wrongly. ○ **misalignment** n.

misalliance n, formal a relationship, esp a marriage, in which the parties are not suited to each other.

misanthrope /ˈmɪzənθroʊp/ or **misanthropist** /mɪzˈanθrəpɪst/ n someone who has an irrational hatred or distrust of people in general. ○ **misanthropic** adj. ○ **misanthropy** n.

misapply vb 1 to apply something wrongly. 2 to use something unwisely or for the wrong purpose.

misapprehend vb, formal to misunderstand something. ○ **misapprehension** n.

misappropriate vb, formal, esp law to put something (eg funds) to a wrong use. ○ **mis-**

appropriation n embezzlement or theft.

misbegotten adj 1 literary foolishly planned or thought out. 2 old use illegitimate.

misbehave vb, intr to behave badly. ○ **misbehaviour** or (US) **misbehavior** n.

miscalculate vb, tr & intr to calculate or estimate something wrongly. ○ **miscalculation** n.

miscall vb to call by the wrong name.

miscarriage n 1 med the expulsion of a fetus from the uterus before it is capable of independent survival. 2 an act or instance of failure or error.

miscarry vb, intr 1 of a woman: to have a MISCARRIAGE (sense 1). 2 formal of a plan, etc: to go wrong or fail.

miscellaneous /mɪsəˈleɪnɪəs/ adj made up of various kinds.

miscellany /mɪˈsɛlənɪ/ n (-ies) a mixture of various kinds.

mischance n 1 bad luck. 2 an instance of bad luck.

mischief n 1 behaviour that annoys or irritates people but does not mean or cause any serious harm. 2 the desire to behave in this way: full of mischief. 3 damage or harm; an injury: You'll do yourself a mischief.

mischievous /ˈmɪstʃɪvəs/ adj 1 of a child, etc: tending to make mischief. 2 of behaviour: playfully troublesome. 3 rather dated of a thing: damaging or harmful. ○ **mischievously** adv.

miscible /ˈmɪsɪbəl/ adj, formal, chem of a liquid or liquids: capable of dissolving in each other or mixing with each other.

misconceive vb 1 tr & intr (also **misconceive of sth**) to have the wrong idea or impression about it. 2 to plan or think something out badly. ○ **misconceived** adj.

misconception n a wrong or misguided attitude, opinion or view.

misconduct n improper or unethical behaviour.

misconstrue vb to interpret something wrongly or mistakenly.

miscount vb, tr & intr to count something wrongly; to miscalculate. ➤ n an act or instance of counting wrongly.

miscreant /ˈmɪskrɪənt/ n, literary or old use a malicious person. ➤ adj villainous or wicked.

miscue n an error or failure.

misdeed n, literary or formal an example of bad or criminal behaviour.

misdemeanour or (US) **misdemeanor** n 1 formal a wrongdoing. 2 old use, law a crime less serious than a FELONY.

misdiagnose vb 1 to diagnose something (eg a disease) wrongly. 2 to wrongly diagnose the condition of (eg a patient). ○ **misdiagnosis** n.

misdirect vb, formal to give wrong directions to someone; to direct, address or instruct something or someone wrongly. ○ **misdirection** n.

miser n someone who stores up their wealth and hates to spend any of it. ○ **miserly** adj.

miserable adj 1 of a person: a very unhappy; b

habitually bad-tempered or depressed. **2** marked by great unhappiness: *a miserable life.* **3** causing unhappiness or discomfort: *miserable weather.* **4** marked by poverty or squalor: *miserable living conditions.* **5** *dialect* ungenerous; mean. ○ **miserably** *adv.*

misericord /mɪˈzɛrɪkɔːd/ *n* in a church: a ledge on the underside of a seat in the choir stalls which a standing person can use as a support when the seat is folded up.

misery *n* (-*ies*) **1** great unhappiness or suffering. **2** a cause of unhappiness: *His biggest misery is the cold.* **3** poverty or squalor: *living in misery.* **4** *colloq* a habitually sad or bad-tempered person.

misfire *vb, intr* **1** of a gun, etc: to fail to fire, or to fail to fire properly. **2** of an engine or vehicle: to fail to ignite the fuel at the right time. **3** of a plan, practical joke, etc: to produce the wrong effect. ➤ *n* an instance of misfiring.

misfit *n* someone who is not suited to the situation, job, social environment, etc that they are in.

misfortune *n* **1** bad luck. **2** an unfortunate incident.

misgiving *n* (*often* **misgivings**) a feeling of uneasiness, doubt or suspicion.

misguided *adj* acting from or showing mistaken or bad judgement. ○ **misguidedly** *adv.*

mishandle *vb* to deal with something or someone carelessly or without skill.

mishap *n* an unfortunate accident, esp a minor one; a piece of bad luck.

mishear *vb* to hear something or someone incorrectly.

mishit *vb* /mɪsˈhɪt/ *sport, etc* to fail to hit (eg a ball) cleanly or accurately. ➤ *n* /ˈmɪshɪt/ **1** an act of mishitting. **2** a wrongly-hit ball, shot, etc.

mishmash *n, colloq* a jumbled assortment or mixture.

misinform *vb* to give someone incorrect or misleading information. ○ **misinformation** *n.*

misinterpret *vb* to understand or explain something incorrectly or misleadingly. ○ **misinterpretation** *n.*

misjudge *vb* to judge something or someone wrongly, or to have an unfairly low opinion of them. ○ **misjudgement** or **misjudgment** *n.*

mislay *vb* to lose something, usu temporarily, esp by forgetting where it was put.

mislead *vb* to cause someone to have a false impression or belief. ○ **misleading** *adj* likely to mislead.

mismanage *vb* to manage or handle something or someone badly or carelessly. ○ **mismanagement** *n.*

mismatch *vb* /mɪsˈmætʃ/ to match (things or people) unsuitably or incorrectly. ➤ *n* /ˈmɪsmætʃ/ an unsuitable or incorrect match.

misnomer /mɪsˈnoʊmə(r)/ *n* **1** a wrong or unsuitable name. **2** the use of an incorrect name or term.

misogyny /mɪˈsɒdʒɪnɪ/ *n* hatred of women. ○ **misogynist** *n.*

misplace *vb* **1** to lose something, usu temporarily, esp by forgetting where it was put. **2** to give (trust, affection, etc) unwisely or inappropriately. **3** to put something in the wrong place or an unsuitable place.

misprint *n* /ˈmɪsprɪnt/ a mistake in printing, eg an incorrect or damaged character. ➤ *vb* /mɪsˈprɪnt/ to print something wrongly.

mispronounce *vb* to pronounce (a word, etc) incorrectly. ○ **mispronunciation** *n.*

misquote *vb* to quote something or someone inaccurately, sometimes with the intention of deceiving.

misread *vb* **1** to read something incorrectly. **2** to misunderstand or misinterpret something.

misrepresent *vb* to represent something or someone falsely, esp to give a misleading account or impression of it or them. ○ **misrepresentation** *n.*

misrule *n, formal* **1** bad or unjust government. **2** civil disorder. ➤ *vb* to govern (eg a country) in a disorderly or unjust way.

miss¹ *vb* **1** *tr & intr* to fail to hit or catch something: *Tom missed the ball.* **2** to fail to get on something: *I missed my train.* **3** to fail to take advantage of something: *You missed your chance.* **4** to feel or regret the absence or loss of someone or something: *I miss you when you're away.* **5** to notice the absence of someone or something. **6** to fail to hear or see something: *I missed his last remark.* **7** to refrain from going to (a place or an event): *I'll have to miss the next class.* **8** to avoid or escape (esp a specified danger): *She just missed being run over.* ➤ *n* a failure to hit or catch something, etc. ♦ **give sth a miss** *colloq* to avoid it or refrain from it. **miss the boat** or **bus** *colloq* to miss an opportunity, esp by being too slow to act. ◊ **miss out** to fail to benefit from something enjoyable or worthwhile, etc: *Buy some now; don't miss out!* **miss out on sth** to fail to benefit from it or participate in it.

miss² *n* **1** a girl or unmarried woman. **2** (**Miss**) a term used when addressing an unmarried woman (esp in front of her surname).

missal *n, RC Church* a book containing all the texts used in the service of mass throughout the year.

misshapen *adj* badly shaped; deformed.

missile *n* **1** a self-propelled flying bomb. **2** any weapon or object that is thrown or fired.

missing *adj* **1** absent; lost. **2** of a soldier, military vehicle, etc: not able to be located, but not known to be dead or destroyed. ♦ **go missing** to disappear, esp unexpectedly and inexplicably.

mission *n* **1** a purpose for which a person or group of people is sent. **2 a** a journey made for a scientific, military or religious purpose; **b** a group of people sent on such a journey. **3** a flight with a specific purpose, such as a bombing raid or a task assigned to the crew of a spacecraft. **4** a group of people sent somewhere to have discussions, esp political ones.

5 (*usu* **mission in life**) someone's chosen, designated or assumed purpose in life. **6** a centre run by a charitable or religious organization, etc to provide a particular service in the community.

missionary *n* (*-ies*) a member of a religious organization seeking to carry out charitable works and religious teaching.

missive *n, literary or law, etc* a letter, esp a long or official one.

misspell *vb* to spell something incorrectly. ○ **misspelling** *n*.

misspend *vb* to spend (money, time, etc) foolishly or wastefully.

missus or (*sometimes*) **missis** *n, colloq* **1** humorous a wife: *Bring the missus.* **2** *old use* a term used to address an adult female stranger.

missy *n* (*-ies*) *colloq, old use, usu facetious or derog* a term used to address a girl or young woman.

mist *n* **1** condensed water vapour in the air near the ground; thin fog. **2** a mass of tiny droplets of liquid, eg one forced from a pressurized container. **3** condensed water vapour on a surface. **4** *literary* a watery film: *a mist of tears.* ➤ *vb, tr & intr* (*also* **mist up** or **over**) to cover or become covered with mist, or as if with mist. ○ **misty** *adj* (*-ier, -iest*).

mistake *n* **1** an error. **2** a regrettable action. **3** an act of understanding or interpreting something wrongly. ➤ *vb* (**mistook, mistaken**) **1** to misinterpret or misunderstand something: *I mistook your meaning.* **2** to make the wrong choice of something: *He mistook the turning in the fog.* ○ **mistakable** *adj.* ◆ **by mistake** accidentally.

mistaken *adj* **1** understood, thought, named, etc wrongly: *mistaken identity.* **2** guilty of, or displaying, a failure to understand or interpret correctly: *You are mistaken in saying that he's English.* ○ **mistakenly** *adv.*

mister *n* **1** (**Mister**) the full form of the abbreviation MR. **2** *colloq* a term used when addressing an adult male stranger: *Can I have my ball back please, mister?*

mistime *vb* **1** to do or say something at a wrong or unsuitable time. **2** *sport* to misjudge the timing of (a stroke, etc) in relation to the speed of an approaching ball.

mistletoe *n* an evergreen shrub that grows as a parasite on trees and produces clusters of white berries in winter.

mistreat *vb* to treat someone or something cruelly or without care. ○ **mistreatment** *n*.

mistress *n* **1** the female lover of a man married to another woman. **2** *rather dated* a female teacher: *She is the French mistress.* **3** a woman in a commanding or controlling position; a female head or owner. **4** (*esp* **Mistress**) *formerly* a term used when addressing any woman, esp one in authority.

mistrial *n, law* a trial not conducted properly according to the law and declared invalid.

mistrust *vb* to have no trust in, or to be suspi-

cious of, someone or something. ➤ *n* a lack of trust. ○ **mistrustful** *adj.* ○ **mistrustfully** *adv.*

misunderstand *vb, tr & intr* to fail to understand something or someone properly. ○ **misunderstanding** *n* **1** a failure to understand properly. **2** a slight disagreement.

misunderstood *vb, past tense, past participle of* MISUNDERSTAND. ➤ *adj* usu of a person: not properly understood or appreciated as regards character, feelings, intentions, purpose, etc.

misuse *n* /mɪsˈjuːs/ improper or inappropriate use: *the misuse of funds.* ➤ *vb* /mɪsˈjuːz/ **1** to put something to improper or inappropriate use. **2** to treat something or someone badly.

mite[1] *n* a small, often microscopic, animal with a simple rounded body and eight legs.

mite[2] *n* **1** any small person or animal. **2** a small amount of anything, esp of money.

miter the US spelling of MITRE[1], MITRE[2].

mitigate *vb* to make (pain, anger, etc) less severe. ○ **mitigation** *n*.

mitochondrion *n* (**mitochondria**) *biol* in the cytoplasm of most cells: a specialized oval structure, consisting of a central matrix surrounded by two membranes. ○ **mitochondrial** *adj.*

mitosis *n* (*-ses*) *biol* a type of cell division in which two new nuclei are produced, each containing the same number of chromosomes as the parent nucleus. Compare MEIOSIS.

mitre[1] or (*US*) **miter** *n* the ceremonial headdress of a bishop or abbot, a tall pointed hat with separate front and back sections.

mitre[2] or (*US*) **miter** *n* in joinery, etc: a corner joint between two lengths of wood, made by fitting together two 45° sloping surfaces cut into their ends. ➤ *vb* to join (two lengths of wood, etc) with a mitre.

mitt *n* **1** *colloq* a hand: *Keep your mitts off!* **2** *baseball* a large padded leather glove worn by the catcher. **3** a thick loosely-shaped glove designed for a specific purpose: *oven mitt.* **4** a mitten or fingerless glove.

mitten *n* a glove with one covering for the thumb and a large covering for all the other fingers together.

mix *vb* **1** (*esp* **mix sth with sth else**, or **mix sth and sth else together** or **up together**) to put (things, substances, etc) together or to combine them to form one mass: *mix a cake.* **3** *intr* to blend together to form one mass: *Water and oil do not mix.* **4** *intr* of a person: **a** to meet with people socially; **b** to feel at ease in social situations. **5** to do something at the same time as something else; to combine: *I'm mixing business with pleasure.* **6** to drink (different types of alcoholic drink) on one occasion: *Don't mix your drinks!* **7** *technical* to adjust (separate sound elements, eg the sounds produced by individual musicians) electronically to create an overall balance or particular effect. ➤ *n* **1** a collection of people or things mixed together. **2**

a collection of ingredients, esp dried ingredients, from which something is prepared: *cake mix*. **3** *technical* in music, broadcasting, cinema, etc: the combined sound or soundtrack, etc produced by mixing various recorded elements. ◆ **be mixed up** *colloq* to be upset or emotionally confused. **be mixed up in sth** or **with sth** or **sb** *colloq* to be involved in it or with them, esp when it is something illicit or suspect. ◊ **mix sth** or **sb up 1** to confuse it or them for something else. **2** *colloq* to upset or put into a state of confusion: *The divorce really mixed me up*.

mixed *adj* **1** consisting of different and often opposite kinds of things, elements, characters, etc: *a mixed reaction*. **2** done, used, etc by people of both sexes: *mixed bathing*. **3** mingled or combined by mixing.

mixed bag *n, colloq* a collection of people or things of different kinds, standards, backgrounds, etc.

mixed blessing *n* something which has both advantages and disadvantages.

mixed metaphor *n* a combination of two or more metaphors which produces an inconsistent or incongruous mental image, and is often regarded as a stylistic flaw, eg *There are concrete steps in the pipeline*.

mixed-up *adj* **1** mentally or emotionally confused. **2** badly adjusted socially.

mixer *n* **1** a machine used for mixing: *a cement mixer*. **2** a soft drink for mixing with alcoholic drinks. **3** *colloq* someone considered in terms of their ability to mix socially: *a good mixer*. **4** *electronics* a device which combines two or more input signals into a single output signal.

mixture *n* **1** a blend of ingredients prepared for a particular purpose: *cake mixture* • *cough mixture*. **2** a combination: *a mixture of sadness and relief*. **3** the act of mixing. **4** the product of mixing.

mix-up *n* a confusion or misunderstanding.

mizzenmast *n, naut* on a ship with three or more masts: the third mast from the front of the ship.

ml *abbrev* **1** mile. **2** millilitre.

Mlle *abbrev*: (**Mlles**) Mademoiselle (French), Miss.

mm *abbrev* millimetre.

Mme *abbrev*: (**Mmes**) Madame (French), Mrs.

Mn *symbol, chem* manganese.

mnemonic /nɪ'mɒnɪk/ *n* a device or form of words, often a short verse, used as a memory-aid. ➤ *adj* serving to help the memory.

Mo *symbol, chem* molybdenum.

mo *n, chiefly Brit colloq* a short while; a moment.

moa *n* an extinct flightless ostrich-like bird of New Zealand.

moan *n* **1** a low prolonged sound expressing sadness, grief or pain. **2** any similar sound, eg made by the wind or an engine. **3** *colloq* a complaint or grumble. **4** *colloq* someone who complains a lot. ➤ *vb* **1** *intr* to utter or produce a

moan. **2** *intr, colloq* to complain, esp without good reason. **3** to utter something with a moan or moans. ○ **moaner** *n*. ○ **moaning** *adj, n*.

moat *n* a deep trench, often filled with water, dug round a castle or other fortified position to provide extra defence.

mob *n* **1** a large, disorderly crowd. **2** *colloq* any group or gang. **3** (**the mob**) *colloq* ordinary people; the masses. **4** (**the mob**) an organized gang of criminals, esp the MAFIA. **5** *Aust, NZ* a large herd or flock. ➤ *vb* (**mobbed, mobbing**) **1** to attack something or someone as a mob. **2** to crowd round someone or something, esp curiously or admiringly. **3** *esp N Am* to crowd into (a building, shop, etc). ○ **mobbed** *adj, colloq* densely crowded.

mobile *adj* **1** able to be moved easily; not fixed. **2** set up inside a vehicle travelling from place to place: *mobile shop*. **3** of a face: that frequently changes expression. **4** moving, or able to move, from one social class to another: *upwardly mobile*. **5** *colloq* provided with transport and able to travel. ➤ *n* **1** a hanging decoration or sculpture, etc made up of parts that are moved around by air currents. **2** *colloq* a mobile phone, shop, etc. ○ **mobility** *n*.

mobile home *n* a type of house, similar to a large caravan, which can be towed but is usu kept in one place and connected to the local utilities.

mobile phone *n* a portable telephone that operates by means of a cellular radio system.

mobilize or **-ise** *vb* **1** to organize or prepare something or someone for use, action, etc. **2 a** to assemble and make (forces, etc) ready for war; **b** *intr* of forces, etc: to assemble and become ready for war. ○ **mobilization** *n*.

mobster *n, slang* a member of a gang or an organized group of criminals, esp the MAFIA.

moccasin *n* **1** a soft leather shoe with a continuous sole and heel, as worn by Native Americans. **2** any slipper or shoe in this style.

mocha /'mɒkə/ *n* **1** a flavouring made from coffee and chocolate. **2** a deep brown colour. **3** dark brown coffee of fine quality.

mock *vb* **1** *tr & intr* (*also* **mock at sb** or **sth**) to speak or behave disparagingly, derisively or contemptuously towards someone or something. **2** to mimic someone, usu in a way that makes fun of them. ➤ *adj* **1** false: *mock sincerity*. **2** serving as practice for the similar but real thing, event, etc which is to come later: *a mock examination*. ➤ *n, colloq* in England and Wales: a mock examination. *Scot equivalent* **prelim**. ○ **mocking** *adj, n*.

mockers *pl n* ◆ **put the mockers on sth** or **sb** *colloq* to spoil or end its or their chances of success.

mockery *n* (**-ies**) **1** an imitation, esp a contemptible or insulting one. **2 a** any ridiculously inadequate person, action or thing; **b** the subject of ridicule or contempt: *make a mockery of someone*. **3** ridicule; contempt.

mock turtle soup *n, cookery* soup made in

the style of turtle soup, but using a calf's head.

mock-up *n* **1** a full-size model of something, built for experimental purposes. **2** a rough layout of a printed text or item, showing the size, colours, etc.

mod¹ *adj, colloq, dated* short form of MODERN.
➤ *n* (**Mod**) orig in the 1960s: a follower of a British teenage culture characterized by a liking for smart clothes and motor scooters.

mod² or **Mod** *n* a Scottish Gaelic literary and musical festival, held annually.

modal /ˈmoʊdəl/ *adj* **1** *gram* belonging or relating to, or concerning, MOOD² or a mood. **2** of music: using or relating to a particular mode. ➤ *n, gram* a verb used as the auxiliary of another verb to express grammatical mood such as condition, possibility and obligation, eg *can, could, may, shall, will, must, ought to.* ○ **modally** *adv.*

modality *n* (*-ies*) **1** *mus* the quality or characteristic of music as determined by its MODE (sense 4). **2** *gram* the modal property of a verb or construction.

mod cons *pl n, colloq* modern household conveniences, eg central heating, washing machine, etc.

mode *n* **1** *rather formal* a way of doing something, or of living, acting, etc: *a new mode of transport.* **2** a fashion or style, eg in clothes or art: *the latest mode.* **3** *comput* a method of operation as provided by the software: *print mode.* **4** *mus* any of several systems according to which notes in an octave are or were arranged. **5** *stats* the value of greatest frequency in a set of numbers. Compare MEAN³ (*noun* sense 2), MEDIAN (sense 3).

model *n* **1** a small-scale representation of something that serves as a guide in constructing the full-scale version. **2** a small-scale replica. **3** one of several types or designs of manufactured article: *the latest model of car.* **4** a person whose job is to display clothes to potential buyers by wearing them. **5** a person who is the subject of an artist's or photographer's work, etc. **6** a thing from which something else is to be derived. **7** an excellent example; an example to be copied: *She's a model of loyalty.* ➤ *vb* (**modelled, modelling;** US **modeled, modeling**) **1** *tr & intr* to display (clothes) by wearing them. **2** *intr* to work as a model for an artist, photographer, etc. **3** *tr & intr* to make models of something. **4** (*esp* **model sth on sth else**) to plan, build or create it according to a model. ○ **modelling** *n.*

modem *n, comput* an electronic device that transmits information from one computer to another along a telephone line, converting digital data into audio signals and back again.

moderate *adj* /ˈmɒdərət/ **1** not extreme; not strong or violent. **2** average: *moderate intelligence.* ➤ *n* /ˈmɒdərət/ someone who holds moderate views, esp on politics. ➤ *vb* /ˈmɒdəreɪt/ **1** *tr & intr* to make or become less extreme, violent or intense. **2** *intr* (*also* **moderate**

over sth) to act as a moderator in any sense, eg over an assembly. ○ **moderately** *adv.*

moderation *n* **1** the quality or state of being moderate. **2** an act of becoming or making something moderate or less extreme. **3** lack of excess.

moderato /mɒdəˈrɑːtoʊ/ *mus, adv, adj* at a restrained and moderate tempo.

moderator *n* **1** *Christianity* in a Presbyterian Church: a minister who presides over a court or assembly. **2** someone who settles disputes. **3** a person or thing that moderates in any other sense.

modern *adj* **1** belonging to the present or to recent times. **2** of techniques, equipment, etc: involving, using or being the very latest available. ➤ *n* a person living in modern times, esp someone who follows the latest trends. ○ **modernity** *n.*

modernism *n* **1** modern spirit or character. **2** a modern usage, expression or trait. **3** (**Modernism**) in early 20c art, literature, architecture, etc: a movement characterized by the use of unconventional subject matter and style, experimental techniques, etc. ○ **modernist** *n, adj.*

modernize or **-ise** *vb* **1** to bring something up to modern standards, or adapt it to modern style, conditions, etc. **2** *intr* to switch to more modern methods or techniques. ○ **modernization** *n.*

modest *adj* **1** not having or showing pride; not pretentious or showy. **2** not large; moderate: *a modest income.* **3** unassuming; shy or diffident. **4** *old use* esp of clothing: plain and restrained: *a modest dress.* ○ **modestly** *adv.* ○ **modesty** *n.*

modicum *n, formal or facetious* a small amount.

modifier *n* **1** *gram* a word or phrase that modifies or identifies the meaning of another word, eg *in the green hat* in the phrase *the man in the green hat,* and *vaguely* in the phrase *He was vaguely embarrassed.* **2** a person or thing that modifies in any sense.

modify *vb* (*-ies, -ied*) **1** to change the form or quality of something, usu only slightly. **2** *gram* to act as a modifier of (a word). **3** to moderate. ○ **modifiable** *adj.* ○ **modification** *n.*

modish /ˈmoʊdɪʃ/ *adj, rather formal* stylish; fashionable. ○ **modishly** *adv.* ○ **modishness** *n.*

modulate *vb* **1** *technical* to alter the tone or volume of (a sound, or one's voice). **2** *formal* to change or alter. **3** *radio* to cause modulation of a CARRIER WAVE. ○ **modulator** *n.*

modulation *n* **1** the act or process of, or an instance of, modulating something. **2** *technical* in radio transmission: the process whereby the frequency or amplitude, etc of a CARRIER WAVE is increased or decreased in response to variations in the signal being transmitted.

module *n* **1** a separate self-contained unit that combines with others to form a larger unit, structure or system. **2** in a space vehicle: a separate self-contained part used for a particular purpose: *lunar module*. **3** *educ* a set course forming a unit in a training scheme, degree programme, etc. ○ **modular** *adj*.

modulus *n* (*moduli*) *maths* the absolute value of a real number, whether positive or negative.

moggy or **moggie** *n* (*-ies*) *Brit colloq* a cat, esp an ordinary domestic cat of mixed breeding.

mogul *n* **1** an important, powerful, or influential person: *a movie mogul*. **2** (**Mogul**) *hist* a Muslim ruler of India between the 16c and 19c.

mohair *n* **1** the long soft hair of the Angora goat. **2** a yarn or fabric made of this, either pure or mixed with wool.

mohican *n* a hairstyle popular amongst PUNKs, in which the head is partially shaved, leaving a central, front-to-back band of hair, usu coloured and formed into a spiky crest.

moiety /ˈmɔɪətɪ/ *n* (*-ies*) *literary* or *law* a half; one of two parts or divisions.

moist *adj* **1** damp or humid. **2** of a climate: rainy. ○ **moistness** *n*.

moisten *vb, tr & intr* to make something moist, or become moist.

moisture *n* liquid in vapour or spray form, or condensed as droplets.

moisturize or **-ise** *vb* **1** to make something less dry; to add moisture to it. **2** *tr & intr* to apply a cosmetic moisturizer to the skin. ○ **moisturizer** *n*.

mol *symbol, chem* MOLE[3].

molar *n* any of the large back teeth in humans and other mammals, used for chewing and grinding. ➤ *adj* belonging or relating to a molar.

molasses *sing n* **1** the thickest kind of treacle, left over at the very end of the process of refining raw sugar. **2** *N Am* treacle.

mold, moldy, etc the *N Am* spelling of MOULD, MOULDY, etc.

mole[1] *n* **1** a small insectivorous burrowing mammal with velvety greyish-black fur and strong front legs with very broad feet adapted for digging. **2** *colloq* a spy who works inside an organization and passes secret information to people outside it.

mole[2] *n* a raised or flat, dark, permanent spot on the skin, caused by a concentration of melanin.

mole[3] *n, chem* the SI unit of amount of substance, equal to the amount of a substance (in grams) that contains as many atoms, molecules, etc, as there are atoms of carbon in 12 grams of the isotope carbon-12.

mole[4] *n* **1** a pier, causeway or breakwater made of stone. **2** a harbour protected by any of these.

molecule /ˈmɒlɪkjuːl/ *n* **1** *chem, physics* the smallest particle of an element or compound that can exist independently and participate in a reaction, consisting of two or more atoms bonded together. **2** *loosely* a tiny particle. ○ **molecular** /məˈlɛkjʊlə(r)/ *adj*.

molehill *n* a little pile of earth thrown up by a burrowing mole (see MOLE[1]).

moleskin *n* **1** mole's fur. **2 a** a heavy twilled cotton fabric with a short nap; **b** (**moleskins**) trousers made of this fabric.

molest *vb* **1** to attack or interfere with someone sexually. **2** *formal* to attack someone, causing them physical harm. ○ **molestation** *n*. ○ **molester** *n*.

moll *n, slang, old use* a gangster's girlfriend.

mollify *vb* (*-ies, -ied*) **1** to make someone calmer or less angry. **2** to soothe, ease, or soften something (eg someone's anger, etc). ○ **mollification** *n*. ○ **mollifier** *n*.

mollusc *n, zool* an invertebrate animal with a soft unsegmented body, with its upper surface often protected by a hard, chalky shell, eg the snail, mussel, etc.

mollycoddle *vb, colloq* to treat someone with fussy care and protection.

molt the *N Am* spelling of MOULT

molten *adj* in a melted state; liquefied: *molten metal*.

molto *adv, adj, mus* very; much: *molto allegro*.

molybdenum /məˈlɪbdənəm/ *n, chem* a hard silvery metallic element that is used as a hardening agent in various alloys, etc.

mom, momma or **mommy** *n* (*moms, mommas,* or *mommies*) *N Am colloq* mother. *Brit equivalents* mum, mummy.

moment *n* **1** a short while: *It will only take a moment*. **2** a particular point in time: *at that moment*. **3** (**the moment**) the present point, or the right point, in time: *She cannot be disturbed at the moment*. **4** *formal* importance or significance: *a literary work of great moment*. ♦ **of the moment** currently very popular, important, fashionable, etc.

momentarily *adv* **1** for a moment: *He paused momentarily*. **2** every moment: *He kept pausing momentarily*. **3** *N Am* at any moment.

momentary *adj* lasting for only a moment.

moment of truth *n* a very important or significant point in time, esp one when a person or thing is faced with stark reality or is put to the test.

momentous *adj* describing something of great importance or significance.

momentum *n* (*momentums* or *momenta*) **1 a** continuous speed of progress: *The campaign gained momentum*; **b** the force that an object gains in movement. **2** *physics* the product of the mass and the velocity of a moving object.

monad *n* **1** *philos* any self-contained non-physical unit of being, eg God, or a soul. **2** *biol* a single-celled organism. **3** *chem* a univalent element, atom or RADICAL (*noun* sense 3).

monandrous *adj* **1** *bot* having only one stamen in each flower. **2** *sociol* having or allowing only one husband or male sexual partner at a time.

monarch *n* a king, queen or other non-elected sovereign with a hereditary right to rule. ○ **monarchic** or **monarchical** *adj*.

monarchism *n* **1** the principles of monarchic government. **2** support for monarchy.

○ **monarchist** *n* a supporter of the monarchy.

monarchy *n* (*-ies*) **1** a form of government in which the head of state is a MONARCH. **2** a country which has this form of government.

monastery *n* (*-ies*) the home of a community of monks.

monastic *adj* **1** belonging or relating to monasteries, monks or nuns. **2** marked by simplicity and self-discipline, like life in a monastery. ○ **monasticism** *n*.

Monday *n* the second day of the week.

monetarism *n*, *econ* the theory or practice of basing an economy on, and curbing inflation by, control of the MONEY SUPPLY rather than by fiscal policy. ○ **monetarist** *n*, *adj*.

monetary *adj* belonging or relating to, or consisting of, money.

money *n* (*pl* in sense 1b and 4 *monies* or *moneys*) **1 a** coins or banknotes used as a means of buying things; **b** any currency used as LEGAL TENDER. **2** wealth in general. **3** *colloq* a rich person; rich people: *marry money.* **4** *commerce, law* (*always* **monies** or **moneys**) sums of money. ○ **moneyed** or **monied** *adj*. ♦ **be in the money** *colloq* to be wealthy. **for my, our,** *etc* **money** *colloq* in my, our, etc opinion. **made of money** *colloq* of a person: extremely rich. **money for old rope** *colloq* money obtained without any effort. **money talks** an expression used to convey the idea that people with money have power and influence over others. **on the money** *US slang* spot-on; exactly right. **put money on sth** *colloq* to bet on it. **put one's money where one's mouth is** to support what one has said by risking or investing money, or giving other material or practical help.

moneybags *sing n*, *colloq* a very rich person.

money-grubber *n*, *derog*, *colloq* someone who greedily acquires as much money as possible. ○ **money-grubbing** *adj*, *n*.

moneylender *n* a person or small business that lends money to people at interest, esp at rates higher than general commercial interest rates. ○ **moneylending** *n*.

moneymaker *n*, *colloq* a project or company, etc that makes, or is expected to make, a large profit. ○ **moneymaking** *adj*, *n*.

money order *n* a written order for the transfer of money from one person to another, through a post office or bank.

money-spinner *n*, *colloq* an idea or project, etc that brings in large sums of money. ○ **money-spinning** *adj*, *n*.

money supply *n*, *econ* the amount of money in circulation in an economy at a given time.

Mongol *n* **1** *hist* any member of the tribes of central Asia and S Siberia that were united under Genghis Khan in 1206. **2** (**mongol** or **Mongoloid**) *old use, now offensive* a person affected by DOWN'S SYNDROME. ○ **mongolism** *n*, *old use, now offensive* DOWN'S SYNDROME.

mongoose *n* (*mongooses*) a small mammal that preys on snakes, etc, and has a long, slen-

der body, pointed muzzle and a bushy tail.

mongrel *n* **1** an animal, esp a dog, of mixed breeding. **2** *derog* a person or thing of mixed origin or nature. ➤ *adj* **1** characterized by being of mixed breeding, origin or nature. **2** neither one thing nor another.

monied or **monies** see under MONEY

moniker *n*, *slang* a nickname.

monism *n*, *philos* the theory that reality exists in one form only, esp that there is no difference in substance between body and soul. ○ **monist** *n*. ○ **monistic** *adj*.

monitor *n* **1** any instrument designed to check, record or control something on a regular basis. **2** a high-quality screen used in closed-circuit television systems, in TV studios, etc to view the picture being transmitted, etc. **3** the visual display unit of a computer, used to present information to the user. **4** someone whose job is to monitor eg a situation, process, etc. ➤ *vb* to check, record, track or control something on a regular basis; to observe or act as a monitor of something. ○ **monitorial** *adj*. ○ **monitorship** *n*.

monk *n* a member of a religious community of men living under vows of poverty, chastity and obedience.

monkey *n* **1** any mammal belonging to the PRIMATES other than a human, ape, chimpanzee, gibbon, orang-utan or lemur. **2** *colloq* a mischievous child. **3** *Brit slang* £500. **4** *US slang* an oppressive burden or habit, esp a drug addiction. ➤ *vb, intr, colloq* (*esp* **monkey about** or **around with sth**) to play, fool, interfere, etc with it.

monkey business *n*, *colloq* mischief; illegal or dubious activities.

monkey nut *n* a peanut in its shell.

monkey wrench *n* a spanner-like tool with movable jaws.

mono *colloq*, *adj* short form of MONOPHONIC and MONOUNSATURATED. ➤ *n* monophonic sound reproduction, ie on one channel only.

monochromatic *adj*, *physics* **a** of light: having only one wavelength; **b** of radiation or oscillation: having a unique or very narrow band of frequency.

monochrome *adj* **1** of visual reproduction: using or having one colour, or in black and white only. **2** esp of painting: using shades of one colour only. **3** lacking any variety or interest. ➤ *n* **1** a monochrome picture, photograph, drawing, etc. **2** representation in monochrome. **3** the art or technique of working in monochrome.

monocle *n* a lens for correcting the sight in one eye only, held in place between the bones of the cheek and brow. ○ **monocled** *adj*.

monocline *n*, *geol* in rock strata: a fold with one side that dips steeply, after which the strata resume their original direction. ○ **monoclinal** *adj*.

monocotyledon *n*, *bot* a flowering plant with an embryo that has one COTYLEDON, eg daffodil, grasses and palms. Compare DICOTY-LEDON.

monocracy /mɒˈnɒkrəsɪ/ n (-ies) **1** government by one person only. **2** a country, state, society, etc that is governed by one person. ○ **monocrat** n. ○ **monocratic** adj.

monocular adj for the use of, or relating to, one eye only.

monoculture n, agric the practice of growing the same crop each year on a given area of land, rather than growing different crops in rotation.

monody n (-ies) **1** literary esp in Greek tragedy: a mournful song or speech performed by a single actor. **2** mus a song in which the melody is sung by one voice only, with other voices accompanying. ○ **monodist** n.

monogamy n the state or practice of having only one husband or wife at any one time. Compare POLYGAMY. ○ **monogamist** n. ○ **monogamous** adj.

monoglot n a person who only knows and speaks one language.

monogram n a design composed from letters, usu a person's initials, often used on personal belongings, etc.

monograph n a book or essay dealing with one particular subject or a specific aspect of it.

monolingual adj **1** of a person: able to speak one language only. **2** expressed in, or dealing with, a single language: a monolingual dictionary.

monolith n **1** a single, tall block of stone, esp one shaped like a column or pillar. **2** anything resembling one of these in its uniformity, immovability or massiveness. ○ **monolithic** adj.

monologue or (US) **monolog** n **1** theat, etc **a** a long speech by one actor in a film or play; **b** a drama for one actor. **2** usu derog any long, uninterrupted piece of speech by one person, usu a tedious or opinionated speech that prevents any conversation.

monomania n, psychol domination of the mind by a single subject, to an excessive degree. ○ **monomaniac** n, adj.

monomer n, chem a simple molecule that can be joined to many others to form a much larger molecule known as a POLYMER.

mononucleosis n, pathol a condition in which an abnormally large number of lymphocytes are present in the blood.

monophonic adj of a recording or broadcasting system, record, etc: reproducing sound or records on one channel only.

monoplane n an aeroplane with a single set of wings.

monopolize or **-ise** vb **1** to have a monopoly or exclusive control of trade in (a commodity or service). **2** to dominate (eg a conversation or a person's attention), while excluding all others. ○ **monopolization** n.

monopoly n (-ies) **1** the right to be, or the fact of being, the only supplier of a specified commodity or service. **2** a business that has such

a monopoly. **3** a commodity or service controlled in this way. **4** exclusive possession or control of anything: You don't have a monopoly on the truth!

monorail n a railway system in which the trains run on, or are suspended from, a single rail.

monosaccharide n, biochem a simple sugar, eg GLUCOSE or FRUCTOSE, that cannot be broken down into smaller units.

monosodium glutamate n (abbrev **MSG**) a white crystalline chemical substance used to enhance the flavour of many processed savoury foods.

monosyllable n a word consisting of only one syllable. ○ **monosyllabic** adj.

monotheism n the belief that there is only one God. ○ **monotheist** n. ○ **monotheistic** adj.

monotone n **1** in speech or sound: a single unvarying tone. **2** a sequence of sounds of the same tone. **3** esp in colour: sameness; lack of variety. ➤ adj **1** lacking in variety; unchanging. **2** in monotone.

monotonous adj **1** lacking in variety; tediously unchanging. **2** of speech or sound, etc: in one unvaried tone. ○ **monotonously** adv.

monotony n (-ies) **1** the quality of being monotonous. **2** routine or dullness or sameness.

monounsaturated adj esp of an oil or fat: containing only one double or triple bond per molecule. Compare POLYUNSATURATED.

monovalent adj, chem of an atom of an element: with a valency of one; capable of combining with one atom of hydrogen or its equivalent. ○ **monovalence** or **monovalency** n.

monoxide n, chem a compound that contains one oxygen atom in each molecule.

Monseigneur /mɒnˈsɛnjə(r)/ n (**Messeigneurs** /meɪˈsɛn-/) a title equivalent to My Lord, used to address a French man of high rank or birth, eg a prince.

Monsieur /məˈsjɜː(r)/ n (**Messieurs** /meɪˈsjɜːs/) **1** a French title equivalent to MR. **2** (**monsieur**) a Frenchman, when not used with a surname.

Monsignor /mɒnˈsiːnjə(r)/ n (**Monsignors** or **Monsignori** /-ˈnjɔːrɪ/) a title given to various high-ranking male members of the Roman Catholic Church.

monsoon n **1** esp in India, etc and S Asia: a wind that blows from the NE in winter (the **dry monsoon**) and from the SW in summer (the **wet monsoon**). **2** in India: the heavy rains that accompany the summer monsoon.

monster n **1** esp in fables and folklore: any large and frightening imaginary creature. **2** a cruel or evil person. **3** any unusually large thing. **4** old use a deformed person, animal or plant. ➤ adj huge; gigantic.

monstrance n, RC Church a gold or silver cup in which the HOST³ is displayed to the congregation during Mass.

monstrosity n (-ies) any very ugly or outrageous thing.

monstrous adj **1** like a monster; huge and hor-

rible. **2** outrageous; absurd. **3** extremely cruel.
4 *old use* deformed; abnormal. ○ **monstrously**
adv.

montage /mɒnˈtɑːʒ/ *n* **1 a** the process of creating a picture by assembling and piecing together elements from other pictures, photographs, etc, and mounting them on to canvas, etc; **b** a picture made in this way. **2** the process of editing film material. **3** *cinema, TV* a film sequence made up of short clips, or images superimposed, dissolved together, etc, esp one used to condense events that take place over a long period. **4** *cinema, TV* extensive use of changes in camera position to create an impression of movement or action in a filmed scene.

month *n* **1** any of the 12 named divisions of the year, which vary in length between 28 and 31 days. **2** a period of roughly four weeks or 30 days. **3** (also **calendar month**) the period between identical dates in consecutive months.

monthly *adj* **1** happening, published, performed, etc once a month. **2** lasting one month. ➤ *adv* once a month. ➤ *n* (*-ies*) **1** a monthly periodical. **2** *colloq* a menstrual period.

monument *n* **1** something, eg a statue, built to preserve the memory of a person or event. **2** any ancient building or structure preserved for its historical value. **3** *formal* a tombstone.

monumental *adj* **1** like a monument, esp huge and impressive. **2** belonging or relating to, or taking the form of, a monument. **3** *colloq* very great: *monumental arrogance.* ○ **monumentally** *adv.*

moo *n* the long low sound made by a cow, etc. ➤ *vb, intr* to make this sound. ○ **mooing** *n.*

mooch *vb, colloq* **1** *intr* (*usu* **mooch about** or **around**) to wander around aimlessly. **2** *tr & intr* to cadge or scrounge.

mood[1] *n* **1** a state of mind at a particular time. **2** (*esp* **the mood**) a suitable or necessary state of mind: *not in the mood for dancing.* **3** a temporary grumpy state of mind: *Now he's gone off in a mood.* **4** an atmosphere: *The mood in the factory is tense.*

mood[2] *n, gram* each of several forms of a verb, indicating whether the verb is expressing a fact (see INDICATIVE), a wish, possibility or doubt (see SUBJUNCTIVE) or a command (see IMPERATIVE).

moody *adj* (*-ier, -iest*) **1** tending to change mood often. **2** frequently bad-tempered or sulky. ○ **moodily** *adv.* ○ **moodiness** *n.*

moon[1] *n* **1** (*often* **Moon**) the Earth's natural satellite, illuminated to varying degrees by the Sun depending on its position and often visible in the sky, esp at night. **2** the appearance of the Moon to an observer on Earth, esp in terms of its degree of illumination, eg HALF-MOON, FULL MOON. **3** a natural satellite of any planet: *the moons of Jupiter.* **4** *literary or old use* a month. ◆ **over the moon** *colloq* thrilled; delighted.

moon[2] *vb, intr* (*usu* **moon about** or **around**) to wander around aimlessly; to spend time idly.

moonbeam *n* a ray of sunlight reflected from the moon.

moonlight *n* sunlight reflected by the moon. ➤ *vb, intr, colloq* to work at a second job outside the working hours of one's main job, often evading income tax on the extra earnings. ○ **moonlighter** *n.* ○ **moonlighting** *n.*

moonlit *adj* illuminated by moonlight.

moonshine *n, colloq* **1** foolish talk; nonsense. **2** *chiefly N Am* smuggled or illegally-distilled alcoholic spirit.

moonshot *n* a launching of an object, craft, etc to orbit or land on the moon.

moonstone *n, geol* a transparent or opalescent, silvery or bluish FELDSPAR, used as a semi-precious gemstone.

moonstruck *adj, colloq* behaving in an unusually distracted, dazed, or wild way, as if affected by the moon.

moony *adj* (*-ier, -iest*) *colloq* in a dreamy, distracted mood.

moor[1] *n* a large area of open, uncultivated upland with an acid peaty soil.

moor[2] *vb* **1** to fasten (a ship or boat) by a rope, cable or anchor. **2** *intr* of a ship, etc: to be fastened in this way. ○ **moorage** *n.*

moorhen *n* a small black water bird with a red beak.

mooring *n* **1** a place where a boat is moored. **2** (**moorings**) the ropes, anchors, etc used to moor a boat.

moose *n* (*pl* **moose**) a large deer with flat, rounded antlers, found in N America.

moot *vb* to suggest; to bring something up for discussion. ➤ *adj* open to argument; debatable: *a moot point.*

mop *n* **1** a tool for washing or wiping floors, consisting of a large sponge or a set of thick threads fixed on to the end of a long handle. **2** a similar smaller tool for washing dishes. **3** *colloq* a thick or tangled mass of hair. ➤ *vb* (**mopped, mopping**) **1** to wash or wipe (eg a floor) with a mop. **2** to wipe, dab or clean (eg a sweaty brow). ◊ **mop up** or **mop sth up 1** to clean something up (eg a spillage) with a mop. **2** *colloq* to capture or kill (remaining enemy troops) after a victory. **3** *colloq* to deal with or get rid of (anything that remains).

mope *vb, intr* **1** (*esp* **mope about** or **around**) to behave in a depressed, sulky or aimless way. **2** to move in a listless, aimless or depressed way. ○ **mopy** *adj.*

moped /ˈmoʊpɛd/ *n* a small-engined motorcycle, esp one that is started by using pedals.

moppet *n* a term of affection used to a small child.

moquette /mɒˈkɛt/ *n* thick velvety material used to make carpets and upholstery.

moraine *n, geol* a ridge of rock and earth formed by the gradual movement of a glacier down a valley.

moral *adj* **1** belonging or relating to the principles of good and evil, or right and wrong. **2** conforming to what is considered by society to be good, right or proper. **3** having a psychological rather than a practical effect: *moral support*. **4** considered in terms of psychological effect, rather than outward appearance: *a moral victory*. **5** of a person: capable of distinguishing between right and wrong. ➤ *n* **1** a principle or practical lesson that can be learned from a story or event. **2** (**morals**) a sense of right and wrong, or a standard of behaviour based on this, esp in relation to sexual conduct: *loose morals*. ○ **morally** *adv.*

morale /mə'rɑːl/ *n* the level of confidence or optimism in a person or group: *The news boosted morale in the camp.*

moralist *n* **1** someone who lives according to strict moral principles. **2** someone who tends to lecture others on their low moral standards. ○ **moralistic** *adj.*

morality *n* (*-ies*) **1** the quality of being moral. **2** behaviour in relation to accepted moral standards. **3** a particular system of moral standards.

moralize or **-ise** *vb* **1** *intr* to write or speak, esp critically, about moral standards. **2** to explain something in terms of morals. **3** to make someone or something moral or more moral. ○ **moralization** *n.*

morass *n* **1** an area of marshy or swampy ground. **2** *literary* a dangerous or confused situation.

moratorium *n* (**moratoriums** or **moratoria**) **1** an agreed temporary break in an activity. **2 a** a legally-authorized postponement of payment of a debt for a given time; **b** the period of time authorized for this.

moray *n* a sharp-toothed eel of warm coastal waters.

morbid *adj* **1** displaying an unhealthy interest in unpleasant things, esp death. **2** *med* relating to, or indicating the presence of, disease. ○ **morbidity** *n.* ○ **morbidly** *adv.*

mordant *adj* sharply sarcastic or critical. ➤ *n* **1** *chem* a chemical compound, usu a metallic oxide or salt, that is used to fix colour on textiles, etc that cannot be dyed directly. **2** a corrosive substance. ○ **mordancy** *n.*

more (used as the comparative of MANY and MUCH) *adj* greater; additional: *Don't use more than two bags.* ➤ *adv* **1** used to form the comparative form of many adjectives and most adverbs, esp those of two or more syllables: *a more difficult problem.* **2** to a greater degree; with greater frequency: *I miss him more than ever.* **3** again: *Do it once more.* ➤ *pron* a greater, or additional, number or quantity of people or things: *If we run out, I'll have to order more.* Compare MOST. ◆ **more and more** increasingly. **more or less 1** almost: *more or less finished.* **2** roughly: *It'll take two hours, more or less.*

moreish or **morish** *adj, Brit colloq* esp of a

food: so tasty, delicious, etc that one wants to keep eating more of it.

morel *n, bot* an edible fungus whose fruiting body has a pale stalk and a ridged egg-shaped head.

morello *n* a bitter-tasting, dark-red cherry.

moreover *adv, slightly formal or old use* also; besides; and what is more important.

mores /'mɔːreɪz/ *pl n, formal* social customs that reflect the basic moral and social values of a particular society.

morganatic *adj, technical* of marriage: between a person of high social rank and one of low rank, and allowing neither the lower-ranking person nor any child from the marriage to inherit the title or property of the higher-ranking person.

morgue /mɔːg/ *n* **1** a MORTUARY. **2** in a newspaper office, etc: a place where miscellaneous information is stored for reference.

moribund *adj* **1** dying; near the end of existence. **2** lacking strength or vitality.

Mormon *n* a member of the Church of Jesus Christ of Latter-Day Saints, a religious sect.

morn *n, poetic* morning.

mornay or (*sometimes*) **Mornay** *adj* (following its noun) *cookery* served in a cheese sauce: *cod mornay.*

morning *n* **1** the part of the day from sunrise to midday, or from midnight to midday. **2** sunrise; dawn. ◆ **the morning after** *colloq* the morning after a celebration, esp when one is affected by a hangover or other unpleasant after-effects.

morning-after pill *n, med* a contraceptive drug, which can be taken within 72 hours of unprotected sexual intercourse by a woman wanting to prevent conception.

morning coat *n* a man's black or grey TAILCOAT worn as part of morning dress.

morning dress *n* men's formal dress for the daytime, consisting of morning coat, grey trousers and usu a top hat.

mornings *adv, colloq, dialect or US* in the morning, esp on a regular basis: *I don't work mornings.*

morning sickness *n, colloq* nausea and vomiting or both, often experienced during the early stages of pregnancy, frequently in the morning.

morning star *n* a planet, usu Venus, seen in the eastern sky just before sunrise.

morocco *n* a type of soft fine leather, made from the skin of goats.

moron *n* **1** *derog, colloq* a very stupid person. **2** *old use, now very offensive* a person with a mild degree of mental handicap. ○ **moronic** *adj.*

morose /mə'rəʊs/ *adj* silently gloomy or bad-tempered. ○ **morosely** *adv.*

morpheme *n, ling* any of the grammatically or lexically meaningful units forming or underlying a word, not divisible themselves into smaller meaningful units. ○ **morphemic** *adj.*

morphine *n* a highly-addictive, narcotic drug obtained from opium, used medicinally as a powerful analgesic and as a sedative.

morphing *n, cinematog* the use of computer graphics to blend one screen image into another, eg to transform or manipulate an actor's body.

morphology *n* **1** *ling* the study of MORPHEMES and the rules by which they combine to form words. **2** *biol* the scientific study of the structure of plants and animals. ○ **morphological** *adj*. ○ **morphologist** *n*.

the morrow *n, old use or poetic* **1** the following day. **2** the morning.

Morse or **Morse code** *n* a code used for sending messages, each letter of a word being represented as a series of short or long radio signals or flashes of light.

morsel *n* a small piece of something, esp of food.

mortal *adj* **1** esp of human beings: certain to die at some future time. **2** causing or resulting in death: *mortal combat*. **3** extreme: *mortal fear*. **4** characterized by intense hostility: *mortal enemies*. **5** used for emphasis: conceivable; single: *every mortal thing*. ➤ *n* a mortal being, esp a human being. ○ **mortally** *adv*.

mortality *n* (*-ies*) **1** the state of being mortal. **2** the number of deaths, eg in a war or epidemic. **3** death, esp on a broad scale.

mortal sin *n, RC Church* a serious sin, for which there can be no forgiveness from God. Compare VENIAL SIN.

mortar *n* **1** *building* a mixture of sand, water and cement or lime, used to bond bricks or stones. **2** the small heavy dish in which substances are ground with a PESTLE. **3** a type of short-barrelled artillery gun for firing shells over short distances. ➤ *vb* **1** to fix something (esp bricks) in place with mortar. **2** to plaster (eg a wall) with mortar. **3** to bombard (a place or target, etc) using a mortar.

mortarboard *n* **1** *building* a flat board used by bricklayers to carry mortar, held horizontally by a handle underneath. **2** a black cap with a hard, square, flat top, worn by academics at formal occasions.

mortgage /'mɔːɡɪdʒ/ *n* **1 a** a legal agreement by which a building society or bank, the (**mortgagee**) grants a client the **mortgagor** or **mortgager**) a loan for the purpose of buying property, ownership of the property being held by the mortgagee until the loan is repaid; **b** the deed that brings such a contract into effect. **2 a** the money borrowed for this; **b** the regular amounts of money repaid. ➤ *vb* to give ownership of (property) as security for a loan. ○ **mortgageable** *adj*.

mortician *n, N Am* an undertaker.

mortify *vb* (*-ies, -ied*) **1** to make someone feel humiliated or ashamed. **2** *relig* to control (physical desire) through self-discipline and self-inflicted hardship: *mortify the flesh*. **3** *intr, pathol, old use* of a limb, etc: to be affected by gangrene. ○ **mortification** *n*.

mortise lock *n* a lock fitted into a hole cut in

the side edge of a door, rather than on to the door's surface.

mortuary *n* (*-ies*) a building or room in which dead bodies are laid out for identification or kept until they are buried or cremated.

Mosaic /moʊˈzeɪɪk/ *adj* relating to Moses, the biblical prophet and lawgiver, or to the laws attributed to him.

mosaic /moʊˈzeɪɪk/ *n* **1** a design or piece of work formed by fitting together lots of small pieces of coloured stone, glass, etc. **2** anything that resembles a mosaic or is pieced together in a similar way.

mosey *vb, intr* (*usu* **mosey along**) *colloq, orig & esp US* to walk in a leisurely way.

Moslem see MUSLIM

mosque *n* a Muslim place of worship.

mosquito *n* (**mosquitos** or **mosquitoes**) a type of small two-winged insect with thin, feathery antennae, long legs and a slender body, the female of which has piercing mouthparts for sucking blood.

moss *n* **1** the common name for a type of small spore-bearing plant, typically found growing in dense, spreading clusters in moist shady habitats. **2** *dialect, esp Scot & N Eng* an area of boggy ground. ○ **mosslike** *adj*. ○ **mossy** *adj* (*-ier, -iest*).

most (*used as the superlative of* MANY *and* MUCH) *adj denoting* the greatest number, amount, etc: *Most people enjoy parties*. ➤ *adv* **1** (*also* **the most**) used to form the superlative of many adjectives and most adverbs, esp those of more than two syllables: *the most difficult problem of all*. **2** (*also* **the most**) to the greatest degree; with the greatest frequency: *I miss him most at Christmas*. **3** extremely: *a most annoying thing*. ➤ *pron* the greatest number or quantity, or the majority of people or things: *Most of them are here*. Compare MORE. ♦ **at the most** or **at most** certainly not more than (a specified number). **for the most part** mostly. **make the most of sth** to take the greatest possible advantage of it.

mostly *adv* **1** mainly; almost completely. **2** usually.

mote *n* a speck, esp a speck of dust.

motel *n* a hotel situated near a main road and intended for overnight stops by motorists.

motet *n* a short piece of sacred music for several voices.

moth *n* the common name for one of many winged insects belonging to the same order as butterflies but generally duller in colour and night-flying.

mothball *n* a small ball of camphor or naphthalene that is hung in wardrobes, etc to keep away clothes moths. ➤ *vb* **1** to postpone work on something (eg a project), or to lay it aside, esp for an indefinitely long time. **2** to put (clothes, linen, etc), with mothballs, into a place for long-term storage.

moth-eaten *adj* **1** of cloth, etc: damaged by clothes moths. **2** *colloq* old and worn.

mother n 1 a female parent. 2 (also Mother) as a term of address or a title for: one's female parent or stepmother, foster-mother, etc. 3 the cause or origin; the source from which other things have sprung or developed: *Necessity is the mother of invention*. ➤ vb 1 to give birth to or give rise to someone or something. 2 to treat someone with care and protection, esp excessively so. ○ **motherhood** n. ○ **motherless** adj. ○ **motherly** adj. ♦ **the mother of all sths** colloq one that is bigger than any other.

motherboard n, comput a printed circuit board that can be plugged into the back of a computer, and into which other boards can be slotted to allow the computer to operate various peripheral devices.

mother-in-law n (mothers-in-law) the mother of one's husband or wife.

mother-of-pearl n a hard shiny iridescent substance that forms the inner layer of the shell of some molluscs (eg oysters).

mother-to-be n (mothers-to-be) a pregnant woman, esp one who is expecting her first child.

mother tongue n one's native language.

mothproof adj of cloth: treated with chemicals which resist attack by clothes moths. ➤ vb to treat (fabric) in this way.

motif /mou'ti:f/ n 1 on clothing, etc: a single design or symbol. 2 a shape repeated many times within a pattern. 3 in the arts: something that is often repeated throughout a work or works, eg a theme in a novel.

motile adj, biol of a living organism: capable of independent spontaneous movement. ○ **motility** n.

motion n 1 the act, state, process or manner of moving. 2 a single movement, esp one made by the body; a gesture or action. 3 the ability to move a part of the body. 4 a proposal for formal discussion at a meeting. 5 law an application made to a judge during a court case for an order or ruling to be made. 6 Brit a an act of discharging faeces from the bowels; b (motions) faeces. ➤ vb, tr & intr (often motion to sb) to give a signal or direction. ○ **motionless** adj. ♦ **go through the motions 1** to pretend to do something; to act something out. 2 to perform a task mechanically or half-heartedly. **in motion** moving; operating.

motion picture n, N Am a cinema film.

motion sickness n travel sickness.

motivate vb 1 to be the motive of something or someone. 2 to cause or stimulate (a person) to act; to be the underlying cause of (an action). ○ **motivation** n.

motive n 1 a reason for, or underlying cause of, action of a certain kind. 2 a MOTIF (sense 2). ➤ adj causing motion: *motive force*.

motley adj 1 made up of many different kinds: *a motley crew*. 2 many-coloured.

motocross n a form of motorcycle racing in which specially-adapted motorcycles compete across rough terrain.

motor n 1 an engine, esp the INTERNAL-COMBUSTION ENGINE of a vehicle or machine. 2 colloq a car. 3 a device that converts electrical energy into mechanical energy. ➤ adj 1 anat a of a nerve: transmitting impulses from the CENTRAL NERVOUS SYSTEM to a muscle or gland; b of a nerve cell: forming part of such a nerve. 2 giving or transmitting motion. ➤ vb, intr 1 to travel by motor vehicle, esp by private car. 2 colloq to move or work, etc fast and effectively. ○ **motoring** n. ○ **motorist** n.

motorbike n, colloq a MOTORCYCLE.

motorboat n a boat that is driven by a motor.

motorcade n a procession of cars carrying VIPs, esp political figures.

motor car n, old use a CAR.

motorcycle n any two-wheeled vehicle powered by an internal-combustion engine that runs on petrol. ○ **motorcyclist** n.

motorize or **-ise** vb to fit a motor or motors to something. ○ **motorization** n.

motormouth n, derog, slang a person who talks non-stop or too much.

motorway n, Brit, Aust & NZ a major road for fast-moving traffic, esp one with three lanes per carriageway and limited access and exit points.

motte and bailey n, hist a type of fortification, orig of earth and timber, consisting of an artificial mound (the **motte**) surrounded by a ditch, with a walled outer court (the BAILEY) adjoining it to one side.

mottled adj having a pattern of different coloured blotches or streaks.

motto n (mottos or mottoes) 1 a a phrase adopted by a person, family, etc as a principle of behaviour; b such a phrase appearing on a coat of arms, crest, etc. 2 a printed phrase or verse contained in a paper cracker. 3 a quotation at the beginning of a book or chapter, hinting at what is to follow.

mould¹ or (N Am) **mold** n 1 a fungus that produces an abundant woolly network of threadlike strands which may be white, grey-green or black in colour. 2 a woolly growth of this sort on foods, plants, etc.

mould² or (N Am) **mold** n 1 a hollow, shaped container into which a liquid substance, eg jelly, is poured so that it takes on the container's shape when it cools and sets. 2 nature, character or personality: *We need a leader in the traditional mould*. 3 a framework on which certain manufactured objects are built up. ➤ vb 1 to shape something in or using a mould. 2 a to shape (a substance) with the hands: *Sue moulded the clay in her hands*; b to form something by shaping a substance with the hands: *She moulded a pot out of the clay*. 3 tr & intr to fit, or make something fit, tightly: *The dress was moulded to her body*. 4 (esp mould sth or sb into sth) to exercise a controlling influence over the development of something or someone.

mould³ or (N Am) **mold** n loose soft soil that is

rich in decayed organic matter: *leaf mould.*

moulder or (*N Am*) **molder** *vb, intr* (*also* **moulder away**) to become gradually rotten with age.

moulding or (*N Am*) **molding** *n* a shaped, decorative strip, esp one made of wood or plaster.

mouldy or (*N Am*) **moldy** *adj* (*-ier, -iest*) **1** covered with mould. **2** old and stale. **3** *derog, colloq* rotten or bad; a general term of dislike.

moult or (*N Am*) **molt** *vb, intr, zool* of an animal: to shed feathers, hair or skin to make way for a new growth. ➣ *n* **1** the act or process of moulting. **2** the time taken for this.

mound *n* **1** any small hill, or bank of earth or rock. **2** a heap or pile.

mount¹ *vb* **1** *tr & intr* to go up: *mounting the stairs.* **2** *tr & intr* to get up on to (a horse, bicycle, etc). **3** *intr* (*also* **mount up**) to increase in level or intensity: *when pressure mounts up.* **4** to put (a picture, slide, etc) in a frame or on a background for display; to hang or put something up on a stand or support. **5** to organize or hold (a campaign, etc). **6** to carry out (an attack, etc); to put something into operation. ➣ *n* **1** a support or backing on which something is placed for display or use, etc. **2** a horse that is ridden. ○ **mounted** *adj* **1** of a person, etc: on horseback. **2** of a picture, etc: hung on a wall, or placed in a frame or on a background.

mount² *n, chiefly poetic or old use* a mountain.

mountain *n* **1** a very high, steep hill, often one of bare rock. **2** (*also* **mountains of sth**) *colloq* a large heap or mass: *a mountain of washing.* **3** a huge surplus of some commodity: *a butter mountain.* ○ **mountainous** *adj.* ♦ **make a mountain out of a molehill** to exaggerate the seriousness or importance of some trivial matter.

mountain ash see under ROWAN

mountain bike *n* a sturdy bicycle with thick, deep-tread tyres and straight handlebars, designed for riding in hilly terrain.

mountaineer *n* someone who climbs mountains. ➣ *vb, intr* to climb mountains. ○ **mountaineering** *n.*

mountain lion see under PUMA

mountebank *n, literary, derog* **1** *formerly* a medically unqualified person who sold supposed medicines from a public platform. **2** any person who swindles or deceives.

mourn *vb* **1** *tr & intr* (*esp* **mourn for** or **over sb** or **sth**) to feel or show deep sorrow at the death or loss of them or it. **2** *intr* to be in mourning or wear mourning. ○ **mourner** *n.*

mournful *adj* **1** feeling or expressing grief. **2** suggesting sadness or gloom: *mournful music.* ○ **mournfully** *adv.*

mourning *n* **1** grief felt or shown over a death. **2** a symbol of grief, esp black clothing or a black armband. **3** a period of time during which someone is officially mourning a death.

mouse *n* (*mice* or in sense 3 *mouses*) **1** a small rodent with a grey or brown coat, pointed muz-

zle, bright eyes and a long hairless tail. **2** *colloq* a very shy, quiet person. **3** *comput* an input device which can be used to move the CURSOR (sense I) or choose different functions on-screen. ➣ *vb, intr* of an animal, esp a cat: to hunt mice. ○ **mouser** *n* a cat that catches mice, or is kept esp for catching mice.

mousemat or **mousepad** *n, comput* a small flat piece of fabric, used as a surface on which to move a MOUSE (sense 3).

mousetrap *n* a mechanical trap for catching or killing mice.

moussaka *n, cookery* a dish made with minced meat, aubergines, onions, tomatoes, etc, covered with a cheese sauce and baked.

mousse *n* **1** *cookery* **a** a dessert made from a whipped mixture of cream, eggs and flavouring, eaten cold: *strawberry mousse;* **b** a similar but savoury dish, made with meat, fish, etc: *salmon mousse.* **2** (*also* **styling mousse**) a foamy or frothy chemical preparation applied to hair to add body or to make styling easier.

moustache or (*N Am*) **mustache** /məˈstɑːʃ, mʌˈstɑːʃ/ *n* unshaved hair growing across the top of the upper lip. ○ **moustached** *adj.*

mousy or **mousey** *adj* (*-ier, -iest*) **1** like a mouse, or belonging or relating to a mouse. **2** of hair: light dullish brown in colour. **3** of a person: shy, quiet or timid. ○ **mousiness** *n.*

mouth *n* /maʊθ/ **1** in humans, animals, etc: an opening in the head through which food is taken in and speech or sounds emitted. **2** the lips; the outer visible parts of the mouth. **3** an opening, eg of a bottle. **4** the part of a river that widens to meet the sea. **5** a person considered as a consumer of food: *five mouths to feed.* **6** *derog, colloq* boastful talk: *He's all mouth.* **7** *colloq* use of language; way of speaking: *a foul mouth.* ➣ *vb* /maʊð/ **1** to form (words) without actually speaking. **2** *tr & intr, derog* to speak (words) pompously or insincerely: *He is always mouthing platitudes.* ◊ **mouth off** *slang, esp US* **1** to express opinions forcefully or loudly. **2** to boast or brag.

mouthful *n* **1** as much food or drink as fills the mouth or is in one's mouth. **2** a small quantity, esp of food. **3** *colloq* a word or phrase that is difficult to pronounce. **4** *colloq* an outburst of forceful and often abusive language: *She gave me such a mouthful.*

mouth organ see under HARMONICA

mouthpiece *n* **1** the part of a musical instrument, telephone receiver, tobacco pipe, etc that is held in or against the mouth. **2** a person or publication that is used to express the views of a group.

mouth-to-mouth *adj* of a method of resuscitation: involving someone breathing air directly into the mouth of the person to be revived in order to inflate their lungs. ➣ *n* mouth-to-mouth resuscitation.

mouthwash *n* an antiseptic liquid used for gargling or for rinsing or freshening the mouth.

mouth-watering *adj* **1** of food: having a delicious appearance or smell. **2** *colloq* highly desirable.

movable or **moveable** *adj* **1** not fixed in one place. **2** *esp Scots law* of property: able to be removed; personal. **3** of a religious festival: taking place on a different date each year: *Easter is a movable feast.*

move *vb* **1** *tr & intr* to change position or make something change position or go from one place to another. **2** *intr* to make progress of any kind: *move towards a political solution.* **3** *chiefly intr* (*often* **move on, out** or **away,** *etc*) to change one's place of living, working, operating, etc. **4** to affect someone's feelings or emotions. **5** (*usu* **move sb to do sth**) to prompt them or affect them in such a way that they do it: *What moved him to say that?* **6** *tr & intr* to change the position of (a piece in a board game). **7** *tr & intr, formal* (*usu* **move for** or **that sth**) to propose or request it formally, at a meeting, etc. **8** *intr* to spend time; to associate with people: *move in fashionable circles.* **9** *intr, colloq* to take action; to become active or busy: *We must move on this matter straight away.* **10** *intr, colloq* to travel or progress fast: *That bike can really move.* **11 a** *intr* of the bowels: to be evacuated; **b** to cause (the bowels) to evacuate. ➤ *n* **1** an act of moving the body. **2** an act of changing homes or premises: *How did your move go?* **3** *games* **a** an act of moving a piece on the board; **b** a particular player's turn to move a piece. ◆ **mover** *n*. ◆ **make a move 1** *colloq* to start on one's way; to leave. **2** to begin to proceed. **on the move 1** moving from place to place. **2** advancing or making progress. ◇ **move in** or **into sth** or **somewhere** to begin to occupy new premises. **move out** to vacate premises; to leave. **move over** to move so as to make room for someone else.

movement *n* **1** a process of changing position or going from one point to another. **2** an act or manner of moving. **3** an organization, association or group, esp one that promotes a particular cause: *the women's movement.* **4** a general tendency or current of opinion, taste, etc: *a movement towards healthy eating.* **5** *mus* a section of a large-scale piece, eg a symphony. **6** (**movements**) a person's actions during a particular time. **7 a** an act of evacuating the bowels; **b** the waste matter evacuated. **8** the moving parts of a watch or clock.

movie *n*, *esp US* **1** a cinema film. *Brit equivalent* **film**. **2** (*esp* **the movies**) cinema films in general.

moving *adj* **1** having an effect on the emotions: *a moving story.* **2** in motion: *a moving staircase.* ◇ **movingly** *adv.*

mow *vb* (**mown**) to cut (grass, a lawn, etc) by hand or with a machine. ◇ **mower** *n.* ◇ **mow sb** or **sth down** *colloq* to kill them or it in large numbers.

mozzarella /mɒtsəˈrɛlə/ *n* a soft, white, Italian curd cheese, esp used as a topping for pizza and in salads.

MP *abbrev* **1** Member of Parliament. **2** *Eng* Metropolitan Police. **3** Military Police. **4** mounted police.

mpg *abbrev* miles per gallon.

mph *abbrev* miles per hour.

Mr /ˈmɪstə(r)/ *n* (**Messrs** /ˈmɛsəz/) **1** the standard title given to a man, used as a prefix before his surname: *Mr Brown.* **2** a title given to a man who holds one of various official positions, used as a prefix before his designation: *Mr Speaker.*

Mrs /ˈmɪsɪz/ *n* the standard title given to a married woman, used as a prefix before her surname, or before her full name with either her own or her husband's first name.

MS or **ms.** *abbrev* **1** (*pl* **MSS** or **mss.**) manuscript. **2** Master of Surgery. **3** multiple sclerosis.

Ms /məz, mɪz/ *n* the standard title given to a woman, married or not, used as a prefix before her surname in place of *Mrs* or *Miss*: *Ms Brown.*

ms. *abbrev* **1** see under MS. **2** millisecond.

MSc *abbrev* Master of Science.

MSG *abbrev* monosodium glutamate.

Mt *abbrev* Mount: *Mt Etna.*

much *adj, pron* (**more, most**) esp with negatives and in questions: **1** a great amount or quantity of something: *You don't have much luck.* **2** (*only as pronoun*) a great deal; anything of significance or value: *Can you see much?* ➤ *adv* **1** by a great deal: *That looks much prettier.* **2** to a great degree: *I don't like her much.* **3** (*often* **much the same**) nearly the same: *Things look much as I left them.* ◆ **a bit much** *colloq* rather more that can be tolerated or accepted: *His constant teasing is a bit much.* **(as) much as** although: *I cannot come, much as I would like to.* **make much of sth** or **sb 1** to cherish or take special interest in them or it, or to treat them or it as very important. **2** *with negatives* to find much sense in, or to succeed in understanding, them or it: *I couldn't make much of what he was saying.* **not much of a sth** *colloq* not a very good example of it; a rather poor one: *I'm not much of a singer.* **not up to much** *colloq* of a poor standard. **too much** *colloq* more than can be tolerated or accepted. **too much for sb** more than a match for them.

muchness *n* ◆ **much of a muchness** *colloq* very similar.

mucilage /ˈmjuːsɪlɪdʒ/ *n*, *bot* a type of gum-like substance that becomes viscous and slimy when added to water, present in or secreted by various plants. ◇ **mucilaginous** *adj.*

muck *n* **1** *colloq* dirt, esp wet or clinging dirt. **2** animal dung; manure. **3** *derog, colloq* anything disgusting or of very poor quality: *How can you read that muck?* ➤ *vb* to treat (soil) with manure. ◇ **muck about** or **around** *colloq* to behave foolishly. **muck about** or **around with sth** *colloq* to interfere, tinker or fiddle about with it. **muck sb about** or **around** to treat them inconsiderately. **muck in** or **muck in with sb** *colloq* to take a share of the work or responsibilities with others. **muck out** or **muck sth out**

to clear dung from (a farm building, etc) or clear dung from the stall, etc of (animals). **muck sth up** *colloq* **1** to do it badly or wrongly; to ruin or spoil it. **2** to make it dirty.

muckle see MICKLE

muckraking *n*, *colloq* the practice of searching for and exposing scandal. ○ **muckraker** *n*.

mucky *adj* (**-ier, -iest**) *colloq* **1** very dirty: *mucky hands*. **2** eg of films or magazines: featuring explicit sex.

mucous /'mjuːkəs/ *adj* consisting of, like or producing MUCUS. ○ **mucosity** *n*.

> **mucous, mucus** These words are sometimes confused with each other.

mucous membrane *n*, *zool*, *anat* in vertebrates: the moist, mucus-secreting lining of various internal cavities of the body.

mucus /'mjuːkəs/ *n* the thick slimy substance that protects and lubricates the surface of MUCOUS MEMBRANES and traps bacteria and dust particles.

mud *n* **1** soft, wet earth. **2** *colloq* insults; slanderous attacks: *throw mud at someone*.

mudbath *n* a medical treatment in which the body is covered in mud, esp hot mud, rich in minerals.

muddle *vb* (*also* **muddle sth** or **sb up**) **1** to put it or them into a disordered or confused state. **2 a** to confuse the mind of someone: *You'll muddle him with all those figures*; **b** to confuse (different things) in the mind: *I always muddle their names*. ➤ *n* a state of disorder or mental confusion. ◇ **muddle along** *colloq* to manage or make progress slowly and haphazardly. **muddle through** *colloq* to succeed by persevering in spite of difficulties.

muddle-headed *adj* of a person: not capable of clear thinking.

muddy *adj* (**-ier, -iest**) **1** covered with or containing mud. **2** of a colour, a liquid, etc: dull, cloudy or dirty. **3** of thoughts, etc: not clear. ➤ *vb* (**-ies, -ied**) to make something muddy, esp to make it unclear or difficult to understand. ○ **muddiness** *n*.

mudflap *n* a flap of rubber, etc fixed behind the wheel of a vehicle to prevent mud, etc being thrown up behind. *N Am equivalent* **splash guard**.

mudflat *n* (*often* **mudflats**) a relatively flat area of land which is covered by a shallow layer of water at high tide, but not covered at low tide.

mudguard *n* a curved, metal guard over the upper half of the wheel of a bicycle or motorcycle to keep rain or mud from splashing up.

mud-slinging *n*, *colloq* the act or process of making slanderous personal attacks or allegations to discredit someone else. ○ **mud-slinger** *n*.

muesli *n* a mixture of crushed grain, nuts and dried fruit, eaten with milk.

muezzin /muˈɛzɪn/ *n*, *Islam* the Muslim official

who calls worshippers to prayer, usu from a MINARET.

muff[1] *n* a wide fur tube which the wearer places their hands inside for warmth.

muff[2] *colloq*, *vb* **1** to bungle something. **2** to miss (an opportunity, etc).

muffin *n* **1** *Brit* a small round flat bread-like cake, usu eaten toasted or hot with butter. **2** *N Am* a cup-shaped sweet cake, usu of a specified flavour: *blueberry muffins*.

muffle *vb* **1** to make something quieter; to suppress (sound). **2** to prevent someone from saying something. ○ **muffled** *adj*. **muffler** *n* **1** a thick scarf. **2** *US* a SILENCER.

mufti *n*, *old use* civilian clothes when worn by people who usu wear a uniform.

mug[1] *n* **1** a drinking-vessel with a handle, used without a saucer. **2** *colloq* a face or mouth. **3** *colloq* someone who is easily fooled. ➤ *vb* (**mugged, mugging**) to attack and rob someone violently or under threat of violence. ○ **mugger** *n*. **mugging** *n*.

mug[2] *vb* (**mugged, mugging**) *tr & intr* (*esp* **mug sth up** *or* **mug up on sth**) *colloq* to study or revise (a subject, etc) thoroughly, esp for an examination.

muggins *n*, *Brit colloq* a foolish person, used esp to describe oneself when one has been taken advantage of by others.

muggy *adj* (**-ier, -iest**) of the weather: unpleasantly warm and damp. ○ **mugginess** *n*.

mugshot *n*, *colloq*, *orig US* a photograph of a criminal's face, taken for police records.

mujaheddin, mujahedin *or* **mujahadeen** /muːdʒəhəˈdiːn/ *pl n* (*usu* **the Mujaheddin**) in Afghanistan, Iran and Pakistan: Muslim fundamentalist guerillas.

mulatto /muːˈlatəʊ, mjuː-/ *n* (**mulattos** *or* **mulattoes**) *old use*, *now usu offensive* a person of mixed race, esp someone with one black and one white parent. ➤ *adj* relating to a mulatto.

mulberry *n* (**-ies**) **1** a tree that produces small edible purple berries. **2** such a berry. **3** a dark purple colour. ➤ *adj* **1** belonging or relating to the tree or its berries. **2** having a dark purple colour.

mulch *n* straw, compost, shredded bark, etc laid on the soil around plants to retain moisture and prevent the growth of weeds. ➤ *vb* to cover (soil, etc) with mulch.

mule[1] *n* **1** the offspring of a male donkey and a female horse. **2** a stubborn person. **3** a cotton-spinning machine that produces yarn on spindles.

mule[2] *n* a shoe or slipper with no back part covering the heel.

muleteer *n* someone whose job is to drive mules.

mulish *adj* stubborn; obstinate.

mull[1] *vb* (*now always* **mull sth over**) to consider it carefully; to ponder on it.

mull[2] *vb* to spice, sweeten and warm (wine or beer).

mull³ n, Scot a headland or promontory: the Mull of Kintyre.

mullah n a Muslim scholar and adviser in Islamic religion and sacred law.

mullet n any of a family of thick-bodied edible marine fish.

mulligatawny n, cookery a thick curry-flavoured meat soup, orig made in E India from chicken stock.

mullion n, archit a vertical bar or post separating the panes or casements of a window. ○ **mullioned** adj.

multicoloured adj having many colours.

multicultural adj esp of a society, community, etc: made up of, involving or relating to several distinct racial or religious cultures, etc.

multifarious /mʌltɪ'fɛərɪəs/ adj, formal consisting of many different kinds.

multigym n an apparatus consisting of an arrangement of weights and levers, designed for exercising and toning up all the muscles of the body.

multilateral adj 1 involving or affecting several people, groups, parties or nations: a multilateral treaty. 2 many-sided.

multilingual adj 1 written or expressed in several different languages. 2 of a person: able to speak several different languages.

multimedia adj 1 in entertainment, education, etc: involving the use of a combination of different media, eg TV, radio, slides, hi-fi, visual arts. 2 comput of a computer system: able to present and manipulate data in a variety of forms, eg text, graphics and sound, often simultaneously. ➤ sing n a number of different media taken collectively.

multimillionaire n someone whose wealth is valued at several million pounds, dollars, etc.

multinational adj esp of a large business company: operating in several different countries. ➤ n a multinational corporation, business or organization.

multiparous /mʌl'tɪpərəs/ adj, zool of a mammal: producing several young at one birth.

multipartite adj divided into many parts or segments.

multiple adj 1 having, involving or affecting many parts. 2 many, esp more than several. 3 multiplied or repeated. ➤ n, maths a number or expression for which a given number or expression is a FACTOR (sense 2), eg 24 is a multiple of 12.

multiple-choice adj of a test, exam or question: giving a list of possible answers from which the candidate has to try to select the correct one.

multiple sclerosis n (abbrev MS) a progressive disease of the central nervous system, producing symptoms such as inability to co-ordinate movements and weakness of the muscles.

multiplex n a large cinema building divided into several smaller cinemas. ➤ adj, formal having very many parts.

multiplicand n, maths a number to be multiplied by a second number (the MULTIPLIER).

multiplication n 1 maths a an operation in which one number is added to itself as many times as is indicated by a second number, written using the MULTIPLICATION SIGN; b the process of performing this operation. 2 the act or process of multiplying.

multiplication sign n, maths the symbol × used between two numbers to indicate that they are to be multiplied.

multiplicity n (-ies) formal 1 a great number and variety. 2 the state of being many and various.

multiplier n 1 maths a number indicating by how many times another number (the MULTIPLICAND), to which it is attached by a multiplication sign, is to be multiplied. 2 a person or thing that multiplies.

multiply vb (-ies, -ied) 1 (esp multiply sth by sth) a to add (one number or amount) to itself a specified number of times: Two multiplied by two equals four; b (sometimes multiply sth and sth together) to combine (two numbers) by the process of MULTIPLICATION. 2 intr to increase in number, esp by breeding.

multipurpose adj having many uses.

multiracial adj for, including, or consisting of, people of many different races. ○ **multiracialism** n.

multistorey adj of a building: having many floors or levels. ➤ n, colloq a car park that has several levels.

multitasking n, comput the action of running several processes or jobs simultaneously on one system.

multitude n 1 a great number of people or things. 2 (**the multitude**) ordinary people. ○ **multitudinous** adj.

multi-user adj, comput of a system: consisting of several terminals linked to a central computer, allowing access by several users at the same time.

multivitamin n a pill containing several vitamins, taken as a dietary supplement.

mum¹ n 1 colloq a mother. 2 a term used to address or refer to one's own mother.

mum² adj, colloq silent: Keep mum about it. ♦ **mum's the word!** colloq an entreaty or warning to someone to keep quiet about something.

mumble vb, tr & intr to speak or say something unclearly, esp with the mouth partly closed. ➤ n the sound of unclear, muffled or hushed speech. ○ **mumbling** n, adj.

mumbo-jumbo n, colloq 1 foolish talk, esp of a religious or spiritual kind. 2 baffling jargon.

mummer n, hist in medieval England: one of a group of masked actors who visited houses during winter festivals, performing dances, etc. ○ **mumming** n.

mummify vb (-ies, -ied) to preserve (a corpse) as a MUMMY². ○ **mummification** n.

mummy¹ n (-ies) chiefly Brit a child's word for

mother. *N Am equivalent* **mommy**.

mummy² *n* (*-ies*) esp in ancient Egypt: a corpse preserved with embalming spices and bandaged, in preparation for burial.

mumps *sing n* (*also* **the mumps**) *med* an infectious viral disease causing fever, headache and painful swelling of the salivary glands on one or both sides of the face.

mumsy *adj* (*-ier, -iest*) *colloq* **1** homely. **2** maternal, in an old-fashioned cosy way.

munch *vb, tr & intr* to chew with a steady movement of the jaws, esp noisily.

mundane *adj* **1** ordinary; dull; everyday. **2** belonging or relating to this world.

mung bean *n* **1** an E Asian plant that produces beans and beansprouts. **2** the edible green or yellow bean of this plant.

municipal *adj* belonging or relating to, or controlled by, the local government of a town or region.

municipality *n* (*-ies*) **1** a town or region that has its own local government. **2** the local government itself.

munificent *adj, formal* extremely generous. ○ **munificence** *n.*

muniments *pl n, law* official papers that prove ownership.

munitions *pl n* military equipment, esp ammunition and weapons.

muon /ˈmjuːɒn/ *n, physics* an elementary particle that behaves like a heavy ELECTRON, but decays to form an electron and NEUTRINO. ○ **muonic** *adj.*

mural /ˈmjʊərəl/ *n* (*also* **mural painting**) a painting that is painted directly on to a wall. ➤ *adj, formal* belonging or relating to, on or attached to, a wall or walls.

murder *n* **1** the act of unlawfully and intentionally killing a person. **2** *colloq* something, or a situation, which causes hardship or difficulty: *The traffic in town was murder today.* ➤ *vb* **1** *tr & intr* to kill someone unlawfully and intentionally. **2** *colloq* to vent one's fury on someone: *I'll murder him when he gets home.* **3** *colloq* to spoil or ruin something (eg a piece of music), by performing it very badly. **4** *colloq* to defeat someone easily and by a huge margin. ○ **murderer** *n.* ○ **murderess** *n.* ◆ **get away with murder** *colloq* to behave very badly or dishonestly and not be caught or punished. **scream, shout** or **cry blue murder** *colloq* to protest loudly or angrily.

murderous *adj* **1** of a person, weapon, etc: intending, intended for, or capable of, causing or committing murder: *a murderous look.* **2** *colloq* very unpleasant; causing hardship or difficulty. ○ **murderously** *adv.*

murk or (*rarely*) **mirk** *n* darkness; gloom.

murky *adj* (*-ier, -iest*) **1** dark; gloomy. **2** of water: dark and dirty. **3** suspiciously vague or unknown: *her murky past.* ○ **murkily** *adv.* ○ **murkiness** *n.*

murmur *n* **1** a quiet, continuous sound, eg of running water or low voices. **2** anything said in a low, indistinct voice. **3** a complaint, esp a

subdued, muttering one. **4** *med* an abnormal rustling sound made by the heart. ➤ *vb* *tr & intr* to speak (words) softly and indistinctly. ○ **murmuring** *n, adj.* ○ **murmurous** *adj.*

murrain /ˈmʌrɪn/ *n, vet med* any infectious cattle disease, esp foot-and-mouth disease.

mus. *abbrev* **1** music. **2** musical.

muscle *n* **1** an animal tissue composed of bundles of fibres that are capable of contracting to produce movement of part of the body. **2** a body structure or organ composed of this tissue. **3** bodily strength. **4** power or influence of any kind: *financial muscle.* ➤ *vb, colloq* (*always* **muscle in on sth**) to force one's way into it.

muscle-bound *adj* having over-enlarged muscles that are stiff and difficult to move.

muscleman *n* a man with very big muscles, esp one employed to intimidate people.

muscular *adj* **1** belonging or relating to, or consisting of, muscle. **2** having well-developed muscles. ○ **muscularity** *n.*

muscular dystrophy *n, med* a hereditary disease in which there is progressive wasting of certain muscles, which are eventually replaced by fatty tissue.

musculature *n* the arrangement, or degree of development, of muscles in a body or organ.

Muse *n, Greek myth, also literary, art, etc* any of the nine goddesses of the arts, said to be a source of creative inspiration to all artists.

muse *vb* **1** *intr* (*often* **muse on sth**) to ponder silently. **2** to say something in a reflective way. **3** *intr* to gaze contemplatively.

museum *n* a place where objects of artistic, scientific or historical interest are displayed to the public, preserved and studied.

museum piece *n* an article or specimen displayed in a museum, or something fit for this because of its special quality, age or interest.

mush¹ *n* **1** a soft half-liquid mass of anything. **2** *derog, colloq* sloppy sentimentality.

mush² *exclam, N Am* used esp to a team of dogs: go on! go faster! ➤ *vb, intr* to travel on a sledge pulled by dogs.

mushroom *n* **1 a** a type of FUNGUS which consists of a short white stem supporting an umbrella-shaped cap; **b** the edible species of such fungi. **2** anything resembling this in shape. **3** anything resembling this in the speed of its growth or development. ➤ *vb, intr* to develop or increase with alarming speed.

mushy *adj* (*-ier, -iest*) **1** in a soft half-liquid state. **2** sentimental in a sickly way.

music *n* **1** the art of making sound in a rhythmically organized, harmonious form, either sung or produced with instruments. **2** such sound, esp that produced by instruments. **3 a** any written form or composition in which such sound is expressed; **b** musical forms or compositions collectively. **4** the performance of musical compositions. **5** pleasing, harmonious or melodic sound.

musical *adj* **1** consisting of, involving, relating to or producing music. **2** pleasant to hear; melodious. **3** of a person: having a talent or aptitude for music. ➤ *n* a play or film that features singing and dancing. ○ **musicality** *n*. ○ **musically** *adv*.

musical box *n* a small box containing a mechanical device that plays music when the box is opened.

musical chairs *sing n* **1** a party game in which the participants walk or run round a decreasing number of chairs while the music plays, and when the music stops, try to grab a chair, with the player left without a seat being eliminated. **2** a series of position-changes involving a number of people, seen as a comical thing.

music hall *n* **1** VARIETY (sense 4) entertainment. **2** a theatre in which variety entertainment can be seen.

musician *n* **1** someone who is skilled in music, esp in performing or composing it. **2** someone who performs or composes music as their profession.

musicology *n* the academic study of music in all its aspects. ○ **musicologist** *n*.

musk *n* **1** a strong-smelling substance much used in perfumes, secreted by the glands of various animals, esp the male musk deer. **2** any similar synthetic substance.

musket *n*, *hist* an early rifle-like gun that was loaded through the barrel and fired from the shoulder. ○ **musketeer** *n*.

muskrat or **musquash** *n* **1** a large, N American water rodent, which produces a musky smell. **2** its highly-prized thick brown fur.

musky *adj* (*-ier, -iest*) containing, or like the smell of, musk. ○ **muskily** *adv*. ○ **muskiness** *n*.

Muslim or **Moslem** *n* a follower of the religion of Islam. ➤ *adj* belonging or relating to Muslims or to Islam.

muslin *n* a fine cotton cloth with a gauze-like appearance.

muss *vb*, N Am, *colloq*, (*usu* **muss sth up**) to make something (esp clothes or hair) untidy; to mess up.

mussel *n* an edible marine BIVALVE mollusc that has a bluish-black shell and anchors itself to rocks, etc.

must[1] *auxiliary vb* **1** used to express necessity: *I must earn some extra money.* **2** used to express duty or obligation: *You must help him.* **3** used to express certainty: *You must be Charles.* **4** used to express determination: *I must remember to go to the bank.* **5** used to express probability: *She must be there by now.* **6** used to express inevitability: *We must all die some time.* **7** used to express an invitation or suggestion: *You must come and see us soon.* ➤ *n* (*always* **a must**) a necessity: *Fitness is a must in professional sport.*

must[2] *n* the juice of grapes or other fruit before it is completely fermented to become wine.

mustache the *N Am* spelling of MOUSTACHE.

mustachio /məˈstɑːʃɪəʊ/ *n* (*often* **mustachios**) an elaborately curled moustache. ○ **mustachioed** *adj*.

mustang *n* a small wild or half-wild horse native to the plains of the western US.

mustard *n* **1** a plant with bright yellow flowers. **2** a hot-tasting paste used as a condiment or seasoning, made from powdered seeds of black or white mustard or both. **3** a light yellow or brown colour. ➤ *adj* having a light yellow or brown colour. ♦ **as keen as mustard** *colloq* extremely keen or enthusiastic.

mustard gas *n* a highly poisonous gas, or the colourless oily liquid of which it is the vapour, that causes severe blistering of the skin, widely used as a CHEMICAL WARFARE agent in World War I.

muster *vb* **1** *tr & intr* esp of soldiers: to gather together for duty or inspection, etc. **2** (*also* **muster sth up** or **muster up sth**) to summon or gather (eg courage or energy). ➤ *n* any assembly or gathering, esp of troops for duty or inspection. ♦ **pass muster** to be accepted as satisfactory, eg at an inspection.

mustn't *contraction* must not.

musty *adj* (*-ier, -iest*) **1** mouldy or damp. **2** smelling or tasting stale or old. ○ **mustiness** *n*.

mutable *adj* subject to or able to change. ○ **mutability** *n*.

mutagen *n*, *biol* a chemical or physical agent that induces or increases the frequency of mutations in living organisms. ○ **mutagenic** *adj*.

mutant *n* a living organism or cell that carries a specific mutation of a gene which usu causes it to differ from previous generations in one particular characteristic. ➤ *adj* of an organism or cell: carrying or resulting from a mutation.

mutate *vb*, *tr & intr* **1** *biol* to undergo or cause to undergo MUTATION (sense 1). **2** *formal* to change.

mutation *n* **1** *genetics* in a living organism: a change in the structure of a single gene, the arrangement of genes on a chromosome or the number of chromosomes, which may result in a change in the appearance or behaviour of the organism. **2** *formal* a change of any kind.

mute *adj* **1** of a person: unable to speak. **2** silent. **3** felt, but not expressed in words: *mute anger*. **4** of a letter in a word: not sounded, like the final *e* in many English words, eg *bite*. ➤ *n* **1** *med* someone who is physically unable to speak. **2** *psychol* someone who refuses to speak, eg as a result of psychological trauma. **3** a device that softens or deadens the sound of a musical instrument). ➤ *vb* to soften or deaden the sound of (a musical instrument). ○ **mutely** *adv*. ○ **muteness** *n*.

muted *adj* **1** of sound or colour: not loud or harsh. **2** of feelings, etc: mildly expressed: *muted criticism*.

mutilate *vb* **1** to cause severe injury to (a person or animal), esp by removing a limb or organ. **2** to damage something severely, esp to alter (eg a text, song, etc) beyond recognition. ○ **mutilation** *n*. ○ **mutilator** *n*.

mutinous *adj* **1** of a person, soldier, crew, etc: having mutinied or likely to mutiny. **2** belonging or relating to mutiny.

mutiny n (-ies) rebellion, or an act of rebellion, against established authority, esp in the armed services. ➢ vb (-ies, -ied) intr to engage in mutiny. ○ **mutineer** n.

mutt n, slang 1 a dog, esp a mongrel. 2 a foolish, clumsy person.

mutter vb 1 tr & intr to utter (words) in a quiet, barely audible voice. 2 intr to grumble or complain, esp in a low voice. ➢ n 1 a soft, barely audible or indistinct tone of voice. 2 a muttered complaint. ○ **muttering** n, adj.

mutton n the flesh of an adult sheep, used as food.

muttonhead n, derog, colloq a stupid person.

mutual adj 1 felt by each of two or more people about the other or others. 2 to, towards or of each other: mutual supporters. 3 colloq shared by each of two or more; common: a mutual friend. ○ **mutuality** n. ○ **mutually** adv.

muzak see under PIPED MUSIC

muzzle n 1 the projecting jaws and nose of an animal, eg a dog. 2 an arrangement of straps fitted round an animal's jaws to prevent it biting. 3 the open end of a gun barrel. ➢ vb 1 to put a muzzle on (eg a dog). 2 to prevent someone from speaking or being heard.

muzzy adj (-ier, -iest) 1 not thinking clearly. 2 blurred; hazy. ○ **muzzily** adv. ○ **muzziness** n.

MW abbrev 1 medium wave. 2 megawatt.

mx abbrev, physics maxwell.

my adj 1 belonging to or relating to ME[1]: my book. 2 used with nouns in various exclams: My goodness!: My foot! 3 used in respectful terms of address such as my lord. ➢ exclam (also **my word, my goodness** or, more strongly, **my God**) expressing surprise or amazement: My, how grown-up you look!

myalgia n, med pain in the muscles or a muscle. ○ **myalgic** adj.

myalgic encephalomyelitis n (abbrev **ME**) a virus-associated debilitating disorder, characterized by extreme fatigue, muscular pain, lack of concentration, memory loss and depression.

mycelium n (mycelia) biol in fungi: a mass or network of thread-like filaments formed when the non-reproductive tissues are growing.

mycology n, biol the study of fungi. ○ **mycologist** n.

myelin n, zool, anat a soft white substance that forms a thin insulating sheath around the nerve fibres of vertebrates.

myeloma n (myelomas or myelomata) med, pathol a tumour of the bone marrow.

myna or **mynah** n a large bird of the starling family which can be taught to imitate human speech.

myopia n, ophthalmology short-sightedness, in which rays of light entering the eye are brought to a focus in front of the retina rather than on it, so that distant objects appear blurred. ○ **myopic** adj.

myriad n (esp **myriads** or **a myriad of sth**) an exceedingly great number. ➢ adj innumerable: her myriad admirers.

myriapod n, zool a crawling, many-legged ARTHROPOD, eg the centipede or millipede.

myrrh /mɜː(r)/ n 1 a type of African and Asian tree and shrub that produces a bitter, brown, aromatic resin. 2 the resin produced by these, used in medicines, perfumes, etc.

myrtle n an evergreen shrub with pink or white flowers and dark blue, aromatic berries.

myself pron 1 the reflexive form of I (used instead of me when the speaker or writer is the object of an action he or she performs): I burnt myself. 2 used with I or me, to add emphasis or to clarify something: I prefer tea myself. 3 my normal self: I am not myself today. 4 (also **by myself**) alone; without any help.

mysterious adj 1 difficult or impossible to understand or explain. 2 creating, containing or suggesting mystery. ○ **mysteriously** adv.

mystery n (-ies) 1 an event or phenomenon that cannot be, or has not been, explained. 2 someone about whom very little is known or understood. 3 a story about a crime that is difficult to solve. 4 a religious rite, esp the Eucharist.

mystery play n a medieval play telling a story from the Bible.

mystic n, relig someone whose life is devoted to meditation or prayer in an attempt to achieve direct communication with and knowledge of God, regarded as the ultimate reality. ➢ adj mystical.

mystical adj (also **mystic**) 1 relig **a** relating to or involving truths about the nature of God and reality revealed only to those people with a spiritually-enlightened mind; **b** relating to the mysteries or to mysticism. 2 mysterious. 3 wonderful or awe-inspiring.

mysticism n 1 relig the practice of gaining direct communication with God through prayer and meditation. 2 the belief in the existence of a state of reality hidden from ordinary human understanding.

mystify vb (-ies, -ied) 1 to puzzle or bewilder. 2 to make something mysterious or obscure. ○ **mystification** n.

mystique /mɪˈstiːk/ n a mysterious, distinctive or compelling quality possessed by a person or thing.

myth n 1 an ancient story that deals with gods and heroes, esp one used to explain some natural phenomenon. 2 such stories in general; mythology. 3 a commonly held false notion. 4 a non-existent, fictitious person or thing. ○ **mythical** adj.

mythology n (-ies) 1 myths in general. 2 a collection of myths, eg about a specific subject. 3 the study of myths. ○ **mythological** adj.

myxomatosis /ˌmɪksəməˈtəʊsɪs/ n, vet med, biol an infectious, usu fatal, viral disease of rabbits, causing the growth of numerous tumours through the body.

Nn

N¹ or **n** *n* (*Ns, N's* or *n's*) the fourteenth letter of the English alphabet.

N² *abbrev* **1** National. **2** Nationalist. **3** New. **4** *physics* newton. **5** North. **6** Northern.

N³ *symbol* **1** *chess* knight. **2** *chem* nitrogen.

n¹ *n* **1** *maths* an indefinite number. **2** *colloq* a large number.

n² *abbrev* **1** *gram* neuter. **2** *physics* neutron. **3** *gram* nominative. **4** note. **5** *gram* noun.

Na *symbol, chem* sodium.

n/a *abbrev* not applicable.

naan see NAN

nab *vb* (**nabbed, nabbing**) *colloq* **1** to catch someone doing wrong. **2** to arrest someone. **3** to grab or take something.

nabob /'neɪbɒb/ *n, colloq* a wealthy influential person.

nachos *pl n, cookery* tortilla chips topped with chillis, melted cheese, etc.

nacre /'neɪkə(r)/ *n* MOTHER-OF-PEARL.

nadir /'neɪdɪə(r)/ *n* **1** *astron* the point on the celestial sphere directly opposite the zenith. **2** the lowest point; the depths, eg of despair or degradation.

naevus or (*US*) **nevus** /'niːvəs/ *n* (*naevi* /-vaɪ/) a birthmark or mole.

naff *adj, slang* **1** of poor quality; worthless. **2** tasteless; vulgar. ◆ **naff off!** *offensive* go away!

nag¹ *n* **1** *derog* a broken-down old horse. **2** a small riding-horse.

nag² *vb* (**nagged, nagging**) **1** (*also* **nag at sb**) *tr & intr* to keep finding fault with them. **2** (*also* **nag at sb**) *intr* to worry them or cause them anxiety. **3** *intr* of pain: to persist. ➤ *n* someone who nags. ○ **nagging** *adj*.

naiad /'naɪad/ *n* (*naiades* /-ədiːz/ or *naiads*) *Greek myth* a water nymph.

nail *n* **1** the hard structure at the tip of a finger or toe. **2** a metal spike for hammering into something, eg to join two objects together. ➤ *vb* **1** to fasten something with, or as if with, a nail or nails. **2** *colloq* to catch, trap or corner someone. **3** to detect, identify or expose (a lie, deception, etc). ◆ **a nail in one's** or **the coffin** a contributory factor in someone's or something's death or downfall. **hit the nail on the head 1** to pinpoint a problem or issue exactly. **2** to sum something up precisely. **on the nail** *colloq* immediately. ◊ **nail sb down** *colloq* to extract a definite decision or promise from them. **nail sth down** to define or identify it clearly.

nail-biting *adj* excitingly full of suspense.

nailfile *n* a FILE² (*noun* sense 2).

naive or **naïve** /naɪ'iːv/ *adj* **1** simple, innocent or unsophisticated. **2** *derog* too trusting.

○ **naively** *adv*. ○ **naivety** /-vətɪ/ or **naïveté** /-vətɛr, naɪ'iːvtɪ/ *n*.

naked *adj* **1** wearing no clothes. **2** without fur, feathers or foliage. **3** barren; blank; empty. **4** simple; without decoration; artless. **5** undisguised or flagrant: *naked greed*. **6** of a light or flame: uncovered; exposed. **7** of the eye: unaided by an optical instrument. **8** *literary* vulnerable; defenceless. **9** without confirmation or supporting evidence. ○ **nakedly** *adv*. ○ **nakedness** *n*.

namby-pamby *adj, derog* **1** feebly sentimental; soppy. **2** prim; over-demure. ➤ *n* (*-ies*) a namby-pamby person.

name *n* **1** a word or words by which a person, place or thing is identified and referred to. **2** reputation: *You'll get a bad name*. **3** a famous or important person, firm, etc: *the big names in fashion*. ➤ *vb, tr & intr* **1** to give a name to someone or something. **2** to mention or identify someone or something by name. **3** to specify or decide on someone or something. **4** to choose or appoint. ◆ **call sb names** to insult or abuse them verbally. **in all but name** in practice, though not officially. **in name only** officially, but not in practice. **in the name of sb** or **sth 1** by their or its authority. **2** on their or its behalf. **3** using them or it as justification. **make a name for oneself** to become famous. **name names** to identify eg culprits by name. **the name of the game** *colloq* the essential aspect or aim of some activity. **to one's name** belonging to one. ◊ **name sb** or **sth after** or (*N Am*) **for sb else** to give (eg a child or a place) the same name as someone, as an honour or commemoration.

name-dropping *n, derog* the practice of casually referring to well-known people as if they were friends, to impress one's hearers. ○ **name-dropper** *n*.

nameless *adj* **1** having no name. **2** unidentified. **3** anonymous; undistinguished. **4** too awful to specify.

namely *adv* used to introduce an expansion or explanation of what has just been mentioned.

nameplate *n* a plate on or beside the door of a room etc, bearing the name, and sometimes occupation, etc, of the occupant.

namesake *n* someone with the same name as, or named after, another person.

nan or **naan** /nɑːn/ or **nan bread** *n* a slightly leavened Indian and Pakistani bread, baked in a flat round or teardrop shape.

nancy or **nancy boy** *n* (*nancies* or *nancy boys*) *colloq, offensive* **1** an effeminate young man or boy. **2** a homosexual youth.

nanny n (-ies) a children's nurse. ➤ adj, derog protective to an intrusive extent. ➤ vb (-ies, -ied) to overprotect or oversupervise.

nanny goat n an adult female goat.

nanometre or (US) **nanometer** n a unit of length equal to one thousand millionth of a metre.

nanotechnology n the manufacture and measuring of extremely tiny objects.

nap[1] n a short sleep. ➤ vb (**napped, napping**) intr to have a nap. ◆ **catch sb napping** colloq to find them unprepared.

nap[2] n a woolly surface on cloth.

nap[3] n 1 a card game like whist. 2 horse-racing a tip that is claimed to be a certainty. ➤ vb (**napped, napping**) horse-racing to name (a particular horse) as certain to win.

napalm /'neɪpɑːm/ n an incendiary agent used in bombs and flamethrowers.

nape n the back of the neck.

naphtha /'nafθə, 'napθə/ n, chem a flammable liquid distilled from coal or petroleum and used as a solvent.

naphthalene n, chem a white crystalline hydrocarbon distilled from coal tar, used eg in mothballs and dyes.

napkin n a piece of cloth or paper for wiping one's mouth and fingers or to protect one's clothing at mealtimes.

nappy n (-ies) a pad of disposable material or soft cloth secured round a baby's bottom to absorb urine and faeces.

narcissism n excessive admiration for oneself or one's appearance. ○ **narcissistic** adj.

narcissus /nɑː'sɪsəs/ n (**narcissuses** or **narcissi** /-saɪ/) a plant similar to the daffodil, with white or yellow flowers.

narcosis n (-ses) pathol drowsiness, unconsciousness, or other effects produced by a narcotic.

narcotic n 1 a drug which causes numbness, drowsiness and unconsciousness, deadens pain or produces a sense of well-being. 2 loosely any addictive or illegal drug. 3 any substance that has a narcotic effect, eg alcohol. ➤ adj 1 relating to narcotics or the users of narcotics. 2 relating to NARCOSIS.

nark n, slang 1 a spy or informer working for the police. 2 a habitual grumbler. ➤ vb, colloq 1 tr & intr to annoy. 2 intr to grumble. 3 intr to inform or spy, esp for the police. ○ **narky** adj (-ier, -iest) colloq irritable.

narrate vb, tr & intr 1 to tell (a story). 2 to give a running commentary on (a film, etc). ○ **narration** n. ○ **narrator** n.

narrative n 1 an account of events. 2 those parts of a book, etc that recount events. ➤ adj 1 telling a story; recounting events. 2 relating to the telling of stories.

narrow adj 1 not wide. 2 of interests or experience: restricted; limited. 3 of attitudes or ideas: illiberal, unenlightened or intolerant. 4 of the use of a word: restricted to its precise or original meaning. 5 close; only just achieved,

etc: a narrow escape. ➤ n 1 a narrow part or place. 2 (**narrows**) a narrow part of a channel, river, etc. ➤ vb, tr & intr 1 to make or become narrow. 2 (also **narrow sth down**) to reduce or limit (eg a range of possibilities), or be reduced or limited. ○ **narrowness** n.

narrowboat n a canal barge.

narrowcast vb, tr & intr to transmit (TV programmes, etc) to a particular audience, eg on a cable network. ○ **narrowcasting** n.

narrowly adv 1 only just; barely. 2 with close attention: She eyed him narrowly. 3 in a narrow or restricted way.

narrow-minded adj, derog 1 intolerant. 2 bigoted; prejudiced. ○ **narrow-mindedness** n.

narwhal n an arctic whale, the male of which has a long spiral tusk.

NASA /'nasə/ abbrev National Aeronautics and Space Administration.

nasal adj 1 relating to the nose. 2 pronounced through, or partly through, the nose. 3 of a voice, etc: abnormally or exceptionally full of nasal sounds. ➤ n 1 a nasal sound. 2 a letter representing such a sound. ○ **nasally** adv.

nascent adj coming into being; in the early stages of development. ○ **nascency** n.

nasturtium /nə'stɜːʃəm/ n a climbing garden plant with red, orange or yellow trumpet-like flowers.

nasty adj (-ier, -iest) 1 unpleasant; disgusting. 2 malicious; ill-natured. 3 worrying; serious: a nasty wound. 4 of weather: wet or stormy. ➤ n (-ies) someone or something unpleasant, disgusting or offensive: a video nasty. ○ **nastily** adv. ○ **nastiness** n.

natal /'neɪtl/ adj connected with birth.

nation n 1 the people of a single state. 2 a race of people of common descent, history, language, culture, etc. ○ **nationhood** n.

national adj 1 belonging to a particular nation. 2 concerning or covering the whole nation. 3 public; general. ➤ n 1 a citizen of a particular nation. 2 a national newspaper. ○ **nationally** adv.

national anthem n a nation's official song.

national insurance n, Brit a system of state insurance to which employers and employees contribute, to provide for the sick, unemployed, etc.

nationalism n 1 great pride in or loyalty to one's nation; patriotism. 2 extreme or fanatical patriotism. 3 a policy of, or movement aiming at, national independence. ○ **nationalist** n, adj. ○ **nationalistic** adj.

nationality n (-ies) 1 citizenship of a particular nation. 2 a group that has the character of a nation. 3 the racial or national group to which one belongs. 4 national character.

nationalize or **-ise** vb 1 to bring (eg an industry) under state ownership and control. 2 to make something national. ○ **nationalization** n.

national park n an area of countryside, usu important for its natural beauty, wildlife, etc, under the ownership and care of the nation.

national service n compulsory service in the armed forces.

nationwide adj, adv extending over the whole of a nation.

native adj **1** being in or belonging to the place of one's upbringing. **2** born a citizen of a particular place: *a native Italian.* **3** inborn or innate: *native wit.* **4** being a person's first language. **5** originating in a particular place: *native to Bali.* **6** belonging to the original inhabitants of a country: *native Balinese music.* **7** natural; in a natural state. ➤ n **1** someone born in a certain place. **2** a plant or animal originating in a particular place. **3** an original inhabitant of a place as distinct from later, esp European, settlers.

Native American n a member of any of the indigenous peoples of America, esp in the United States, or the languages they speak.

nativity n (-ies) **1** birth, advent or origin. **2** (**Nativity**) **a** the birth of Christ; **b** a picture representing it; **c** Christmas.

NATO or **Nato** /ˈneɪtoʊ/ abbrev North Atlantic Treaty Organization.

natter colloq, vb, intr to chat busily. ➤ n an intensive chat.

natterjack n, zool a European toad with a yellow stripe down its spine.

natty adj (-ier, -iest) colloq **1** of clothes: flashily smart. **2** clever; ingenious. ○ **nattily** adv.

natural adj **1** normal; unsurprising. **2** instinctive; not learnt. **3** born in one; innate. **4** being such because of inborn qualities. **5** of manner, etc: simple, easy and direct; not artificial. **6** of looks: not improved on artificially. **7** relating to nature, or to parts of the physical world not made or altered by man: *natural sciences • areas of natural beauty.* **8** following the normal course of nature. **9** of materials, products, etc: derived from plants and animals; not manufactured. **10** wild; uncultivated or uncivilized. **11** related by blood: *one's natural parents.* **12** euphem ILLEGITIMATE. **13** mus not sharp or flat. ➤ n **1** colloq someone with an inborn feel for something. **2** an obvious choice for something. **3** someone or something that is assured of success; a certainty. **4** mus **a** a sign (♮) indicating a note that is not to be played sharp or flat; **b** such a note. ○ **naturalness** n.

natural-born adj native.

natural gas n a fuel gas found under the ground or sea-bed.

natural history n the study of plants, animals and minerals.

naturalism n realistic treatment of subjects in art, sculpture, etc. ○ **naturalistic** adj.

naturalist n **1** someone who studies animal and plant life. **2** a follower of naturalism.

naturalize or **-ise** vb **1** to confer citizenship on (a foreigner). **2** tr & intr of a word of foreign origin: to come to be considered as part of a language. **3** to gradually admit (a custom) among established traditions. **4** of an introduced species of plant or animal: to adapt to the local en-

vironment. **5** to make something natural or lifelike. ○ **naturalization** n.

naturally adv **1** of course; not surprisingly. **2** in accordance with the normal course of things. **3** by nature; as a natural characteristic. **4** by means of a natural process, as opposed to being produced by a man-made process. **5** in a relaxed or normal manner.

natural philosophy n physics.

natural resources pl n sources of energy and wealth that occur naturally in the earth.

natural science n the science of nature (including biology, chemistry, geology and physics).

natural selection n the process by which plant and animal species that adapt most successfully to their environment survive, while others die out; the basis for EVOLUTION.

natural wastage n, business failure to replace employees that leave or retire, as a means of reducing staffing levels.

nature n **1** (also **Nature**) the physical world and the forces that have formed and control it. **2** animal and plant life as distinct from human life. **3** what something is or consists of. **4** a fundamental tendency; essential character; attitude or outlook. **5** a kind, sort or type. ♦ **in the nature of sth** with the characteristics of it; like it.

nature reserve n an area of land specially managed to preserve the flora and fauna in it.

naturism n nudism. ○ **naturist** n.

naturopathy n the promotion of health and healing by methods such as nutrition, herbal medicine, and a range of natural therapies. ○ **naturopath** n. ○ **naturopathic** adj.

naught n, old use nothing.

naughty adj (-ier, -iest) **1** mischievous; disobedient. **2** mildly shocking or indecent; titillating. ○ **naughtily** adv. ○ **naughtiness** n.

nausea /ˈnɔːzɪə/ n **1** a feeling that one is about to vomit. **2** disgust.

nauseate vb **1** to make someone feel nausea. **2** to disgust someone. ○ **nauseating** adj.

nauseous adj **1** affected by nausea. **2** sickening; disgusting.

nautical adj relating to ships, sailors or navigation.

nautical mile n a measure of distance traditionally used at sea, equal to about 1.85km.

nautilus n (**nautiluses** or **nautili**) a sea creature related to the squid and octopus.

naval adj relating to a navy or to ships generally.

nave[1] n, archit the main central part of a church.

nave[2] n the central part of a wheel.

navel n **1** the small hollow or scar at the point where the umbilical cord was attached to the fetus. **2** the central point of something.

navigable adj **1** able to be sailed along or through. **2** seaworthy. **3** steerable.

navigate vb **1** intr to direct the course of a ship, aircraft or other vehicle. **2** intr to find one's way and hold one's course. **3** to steer (a ship or aircraft). **4 a** to manage to sail along or through (a river, channel, etc); **b** to find one's way through, along, over or across something, etc. **5** *intr* of a vehicle passenger: to give the driver directions on the correct route. ○ **navigator** *n*.

navigation *n* **1** the act, skill or science of navigating. **2** the movement of ships and aircraft. ○ **navigational** *adj*.

navvy /'navɪ/ *n* (*-ies*) a labourer, esp one building roads or canals. ➤ *vb* (*-ies, -ied*) *intr* to work as or like a navvy.

navy /'neɪvɪ/ *n* (*-ies*) **1** (*often* **the Navy**) a the warships of a state, and their personnel; **b** the organization to which they belong. **2** a body or fleet of ships with their crews. **3** (*also* **navy blue**) a dark blue colour.

nawab /nə'wɑːb/ *n, hist* a Muslim ruler or landowner in India.

nay *exclam, old use or dialect* **1** no. **2** rather; to put it more strongly. ➤ *n* **1** a vote against something, esp in the House of Commons. **2** someone who votes against something. Opposite of AYE.

Nazi /'nɑːtsɪ/ *n* **1** *hist* a member of the German National Socialist Party, which came to power in Germany in 1933 under Adolf Hitler. **2** *derog colloq* someone with extreme racist and dogmatic opinions. ○ **Nazism** *n*.

NB *abbrev*: nota bene (Latin), note well; take note.

Nb *symbol, chem* niobium.

NCO *n* (*NCOs* or *NCO's*) non-commissioned officer.

Nd *symbol, chem* neodymium.

NE *abbrev* **1** north-east. **2** north-eastern.

Ne *symbol, chem* neon.

Neanderthal /nɪ'andətɑːl/ *adj* **1** denoting a primitive type of human living in Europe during the PALAEOLITHIC period of the Stone Age. **2** (*sometimes* **neanderthal**) *colloq, derog* extremely primitive, old-fashioned or chauvinistic.

neap tide or **neap** *n* a tide occurring at the first and last quarters of the moon, when there is the least variation between high and low water. Compare SPRING TIDE.

near *prep* close to (someone or something). ➤ *adv* **1** close: *He came near to hitting her.* **2** *old use or colloq* almost; nearly: *She damn near died.* ➤ *adj* **1** being a short distance away; close. **2** closer of two. **3** similar; comparable: *the nearest thing to a screwdriver.* **4** closely related to one. **5** almost amounting to, or almost turning into, the specified thing. ➤ *vb, tr & intr* to approach. ○ **nearness** *n*. ♦ **near at hand** conveniently close.

nearby *adj, adv* a short distance away.

nearly *adv* almost. ♦ **not nearly** very far from; nothing like.

near miss *n* **1** something not quite achieved, eg a shot that almost hits the target. **2** something (eg an air collision) only just avoided.

nearside *n* the side of a vehicle, horse or team of horses nearer the kerb.

near-sighted *adj* short-sighted.

near thing *n* a narrow escape or a success only just achieved.

neat *adj* **1** tidy; clean; orderly. **2** pleasingly small or regular. **3** elegantly or cleverly simple. **4** skilful or efficient: *Neat work!* **5** *N Am* excellent: *That's neat!* **6** esp of an alcoholic drink: undiluted. ○ **neatly** *adv*. ○ **neatness** *n*.

neaten *vb* to make something neat and tidy.

neath or **'neath** *prep, dialect or poetry* beneath.

neb *n, Scot & N Eng* **1** a beak or bill. **2** the nose.

nebula /'nɛbjʊlə/ *n* (**nebulae** /-liː/ or **nebulas**) *astron* a luminous or dark patch in space representing a mass of dust or particles. ○ **nebular** *adj*.

nebulizer *n, med* a device with a mouthpiece or face mask, through which a drug is administered as a fine mist.

nebulous *adj* vague; lacking distinct shape, form or nature.

necessarily *adv* as a necessary or inevitable result.

necessary *adj* **1** needed; essential; indispensable. **2** inevitable; inescapable. **3** logically required or unavoidable. **4** of eg an agent: not free. ➤ *n* (*-ies*) **1** (*usu* **necessaries**) something that is necessary. **2** (**the necessary**) *humorous, colloq* **a** money needed for a purpose; **b** action that must be taken.

necessitate *vb* to make something necessary or unavoidable.

necessity *n* (*-ies*) **1** something necessary or essential. **2** circumstances that make something necessary, obligatory or unavoidable. **3** a pressing need. **4** poverty; want; need. ♦ **of necessity** necessarily; unavoidably.

neck *n* **1** the part of the body between the head and the shoulders. **2** the part of a garment at or covering the neck. **3** a narrow part; a narrow connecting part. **4** *horse-racing* a head-and-neck's length: *won by a neck.* **5** meat from the neck of an animal. **6** *colloq* impudence; boldness. ➤ *vb, tr & intr, slang* to hug and kiss amorously. ○ **necking** *n*. ♦ **get it in the neck** *colloq* to be severely rebuked or punished. **neck and neck** of competitors: exactly level. **up to one's neck in sth** *colloq* deeply involved in (*esp* a troublesome situation); busy.

neckerchief *n* (**neckerchiefs** or **neckerchieves**) a cloth worn round the neck.

necklace *n* a string of beads, chain, etc, worn round the neck as jewellery.

neckline *n* the edge of a garment at the neck, or its shape.

neck of the woods *n, humorous* a neighbourhood or locality.

necktie *n, esp US* a man's TIE.

necromancy *n* **1** divination or prophecy through communication with the dead. **2** black magic; sorcery. ○ **necromancer** *n*.

necrophilia *n* sexual interest in or intercourse with dead bodies.

necropolis /nɛ'krɒpəlɪs/ *n* a cemetery or burial site.

necrosis n (-ses) pathol the death of living tissue or bone. ○ **necrotic** adj.

nectar n 1 a sugary substance produced in flowers, collected by bees to make honey. 2 Greek myth the special drink of the gods. 3 any delicious drink. 4 anything delightful to the senses, esp taste or smell.

nectarine n a variety of peach with a shiny downless skin.

née or **nee** /neɪ/ adj used in giving a married woman's maiden name: born.

need vb 1 to lack; to require. 2 intr (also as auxiliary verb) to be required or obliged to be or do something: We need to find a replacement. ➢ n 1 something one requires. 2 (**need of** or **for sth**) a condition of lacking or requiring it; an urge or desire. 3 (**need for sth**) necessity or justification for it. ◆ **if need** or **needs be** if necessary. **in need** needing help or financial support. **needs must** one must do what is necessary, even if it is disagreeable.

needful adj necessary. ➢ n (**the needful**) humorous, colloq 1 whatever action is necessary. 2 money needed for a purpose.

needle n 1 a slender pointed sewing instrument with a hole for the thread. 2 a longer, thicker implement without a hole, for knitting, crocheting, etc. 3 a hypodermic syringe. 4 a gramophone STYLUS. 5 the moving pointer on a compass or other instrument. 6 anything slender, sharp and pointed. 7 the needle-shaped leaf of a tree such as the pine or fir. 8 (**the needle**) colloq a provocation; b irritation; anger; c dislike. ➢ vb, tr & intr, colloq to provoke or irritate someone, esp deliberately. ◆ **look for a needle in a haystack** to undertake a hopeless search.

needlepoint n 1 embroidery on canvas. 2 lace made with needles over a paper pattern.

needless adj unnecessary. ○ **needlessly** adv.

needlework n sewing and embroidery.

needn't contraction, colloq need not.

needy adj (-ier, -iest) 1 in severe need; poverty-stricken. 2 craving excessive attention or affection.

ne'er adv, poetic never.

ne'er-do-well n an idle irresponsible useless person.

nefarious /nɪ'feərɪəs/ adj wicked; evil. ○ **nefariously** adv.

neg. abbrev 1 negative. 2 negotiable.

negate vb 1 to cancel the effect of something. 2 to deny the existence of something. ○ **negation** n.

negative adj 1 meaning or saying 'no'. 2 unenthusiastic, defeatist or pessimistic. 3 maths less than zero. 4 contrary to, or cancelling the effect of, whatever is regarded as positive. 5 elec having the kind of electric charge produced by an excess of electrons. 6 photog of film: having the light and shade of the actual image reversed, or complementary colours in place of actual ones. ➢ n 1 a word, statement or grammatical form expressing 'no' or 'not'. 2 a photographic film with a negative image, from which prints are made. ○ **negativeness** or **negativity** n.

negative equity n, econ the situation when the market value of property is less than the value of the mortgage on it. Compare EQUITY (sense 3).

negative sign n the symbol of subtraction (−).

negativism n a tendency to deny and criticize without offering anything positive. ○ **negativistic** adj.

neglect vb 1 not to give proper care and attention to someone or something. 2 to leave (duties, etc) undone. 3 to fail (to do something). ➢ n 1 lack of proper care. 2 a state of disuse or decay. ○ **neglectful** adj inattentive or negligent.

négligée or **negligee** /'nɛglɪʒeɪ/ n a woman's thin light nightgown.

negligent adj 1 not giving proper care and attention. 2 careless or offhand. ○ **negligence** n. ○ **negligently** adv.

negligible adj small or unimportant enough to ignore.

negotiable adj 1 open to discussion. 2 able to be got past or through. 3 of a cheque, etc: that can be transferred to another person and exchanged for its value in money.

negotiate vb 1 intr to confer; to bargain. 2 to bring about (an agreement), or arrange (a treaty, price, etc), by conferring. 3 to pass safely (a hazard on one's way, etc). 4 colloq to cope with something successfully. ○ **negotiation** n. ○ **negotiator** n.

Negro n (**Negroes**) often offensive a person belonging to or descended from one of the black-skinned races orig from Africa.

neigh n the cry of a horse. ➢ vb, intr to make this cry or a sound like it.

neighbour or (N Am) **neighbor** n 1 someone who lives near or next door. 2 an adjacent territory, person, etc. 3 old use a fellow human: Love your neighbour. ○ **neighbouring** adj nearby. 2 adjoining.

neighbourhood or (N Am) **neighborhood** n 1 a district or locality. 2 the local community. 3 the area near something or someone. ◆ **in the neighbourhood of** approximately.

neighbourly or (N Am) **neighborly** adj friendly, esp to people living nearby.

neither adj, pron not the one nor the other thing or person: Neither proposal is acceptable ● Neither of the proposals is acceptable. ➢ conj (used to introduce the first of two or more alternatives) not: I neither know nor care. ➢ adv nor; also not: If you won't, then neither will I. ◆ **neither here nor there** irrelevant; unimportant.

| **neither** | Neither is followed by a singular or plural verb, although a singular verb is usually regarded as more correct: Neither of us likes the idea very much. Note that **neither** should be paired with **nor**, not with **or**: ✓ He possessed neither arms nor armour. |

nelly n, old slang life. ♦ **not on your nelly** certainly not.

nematode n, zool a long thin worm, a parasite in plants and animals as well as occurring in soil or sediment.

nemesis /'nɛməsɪs/ n (-ses /-siːz/) **1** retribution or just punishment. **2** something that brings this.

neoclassical adj of artistic or architectural style, esp in the late 18c and early 19c: imitating or adapting the styles of the ancient classical world. ○ **neoclassicism** n.

neocolonialism n the domination by powerful states of weaker but politically independent states by means of economic pressure. ○ **neocolonialist** adj, n.

neodymium n, chem a silvery metallic element, one of the rare earth elements.

neofascism n a movement attempting to reinstate the policies of FASCISM. ○ **neofascist** n, adj.

neolithic or **Neolithic** adj belonging or relating to the later Stone Age, in Europe lasting from about 4000 to 2400BC, and characterized by the manufacture of polished stone tools.

neologism /nɪ'ɒlədʒɪzəm/ n **1** a new word or expression. **2** a new meaning acquired by an existing word or expression.

neon n, chem an element, a colourless gas that glows red when electricity is passed through it, used eg in illuminated signs.

neonatal adj relating to newly born children. ○ **neonate** n, biol, med a newly born child.

Neo-Nazi n a supporter of any modern movement advocating the principles of the Nazis. ○ **Neo-Nazism** n.

neophyte n **1** a beginner. **2** a new convert to a religious faith. **3** a novice in a religious order.

Neozoic /niːoʊ'zoʊɪk/ n, geol the period between the MESOZOIC and the present age.

nephew n the son of one's brother or sister, or of the brother or sister of one's wife or husband.

nephrite n, geol a hard glistening mineral that occurs in a wide range of colours; JADE.

nephritis /nɪ'fraɪtɪs/ n, pathol inflammation of a kidney.

nepotism n the favouring of one's relatives or friends, esp in making official appointments. ○ **nepotistic** adj.

neptunium n, chem a metallic element obtained artificially in nuclear reactors during the production of PLUTONIUM.

nerd or **nurd** n, derog slang someone foolish or annoying, esp one who is wrapped up in something that isn't thought by others to be worthy of such interest. ○ **nerdy** adj.

nerve n **1** a cord that carries instructions and information between the brain or spinal cord and other parts of the body. **2** courage; assurance. **3** colloq cheek; impudence. **4** (**nerves**) colloq nervousness; tension or stress. **5** (**nerves**) colloq one's capacity to cope with stress or excitement. **6** bot a leaf-vein or rib. ➤ vb (often **nerve oneself for sth**) to prepare

(oneself) for (a challenge or ordeal). ♦ **get on sb's nerves** colloq to annoy them.

nerve agent n a NERVE GAS or similar substance.

nerve cell see under NEURONE

nerve centre n **1** a cluster of nerve cells responsible for a particular bodily function. **2** the centre of control within an organization, etc.

nerve gas n a poisonous gas that acts on the nerves, esp those controlling respiration, used as a weapon.

nerveless adj **1** lacking feeling or strength; inert. **2** fearless.

nerve-racking or **nerve-wracking** adj making one feel tense and anxious.

nervous adj **1** timid; easily agitated. **2** apprehensive; uneasy. **3** relating to the nerves. **4** consisting of nerves. ○ **nervously** adv ○ **nervousness** n.

nervous breakdown n a mental illness attributed loosely to stress, with intense anxiety, low self-esteem and loss of concentration.

nervous system n the network of communication, represented by the brain, nerves and spinal cord, that controls all one's mental and physical functions.

nervy adj (-ier, -iest) **1** excitable. **2** nervous.

ness n a headland.

nest n **1** a structure built by birds, rats, wasps, etc in which to lay eggs or give birth to and look after young. **2** a cosy habitation or retreat. **3** a den or haunt, eg of thieves, or secret centre, eg of vice, crime, etc. **4** a brood, swarm, gang, etc. **5** a set of things that fit together: a nest of tables. ➤ vb **1** intr to build and occupy a nest. **2** tr & intr to fit things together compactly, esp one inside another. **3** intr to go in search of birds' nests.

nest egg n **1** a real or artificial egg left in a nest to encourage laying. **2** colloq a sum of money saved up for the future.

nestle vb, intr to lie or settle snugly.

nestling n a young bird still unable to fly.

net¹ n **1** an open material made of thread, cord, etc knotted, twisted or woven to form mesh. **2** a piece of this, eg for catching fish, confining hair, etc. **3** a strip of net dividing a tennis or badminton court, etc. **4** sport the net-backed goal in hockey, football, etc. **5** (**nets**) cricket **a** a practice pitch enclosed in nets; **b** a practice session in nets. **6** a snare or trap. **7** (**the net**) short for THE INTERNET. ➤ vb (**netted, netting**) **1** to catch something in a net. **2** to acquire, as with a net. **3** to cover something with a net. **4** sport to hit, kick, etc (a ball) into the net or goal.

net² adj **1** of profit: remaining after all expenses, etc have been paid. **2** of weight: excluding the packaging or container. ➤ vb (**netted, netting**) to produce, or earn, (an amount) as clear profit. Opposite of GROSS.

netball n a game played by teams of women or girls, points being scored for the ball being thrown through a net hanging from a ring at the top of a pole.

nether adj, literary or old use lower or under. ○ **nethermost** adj lowest; farthest down.

netting n any material with meshes, made by knotting or twisting thread, cord or wire, etc.

nettle n a plant covered with hairs that sting if touched. ♦ **grasp the nettle** to deal boldly with a difficult situation.

network n **1** any system that resembles a mass of criss-crossing lines. **2** any co-ordinated system involving large numbers of people or branches, etc: a telecommunications network. **3** a group of radio or TV stations that broadcast the same programmes at the same time. **4** comput a linked set of computers capable of sharing power or storage facilities. ➤ vb **1** to broadcast something on a network. **2** intr to build or maintain relationships with a network of people for mutual benefit. **3** to link (computer terminals, etc) to operate interactively.

neural adj relating to the nerves or nervous system.

neuralgia n, pathol pain originating along the course of a nerve. ○ **neuralgic** adj.

neuritis /njʊəˈraɪtɪs/ n, pathol inflammation of a nerve or nerves, in some cases with defective functioning of the affected part.

neurology n, med the study of the CENTRAL NERVOUS SYSTEM, and the peripheral nerves. ○ **neurological** adj. ○ **neurologist** n.

neurone or **neuron** n, anat a specialized cell that transmits nerve impulses from one part of the body to another.

neurosis n (-ses) **1** a mental disorder that causes obsessive fears, depression and unreasonable behaviour. **2** colloq an anxiety or obsession.

neurotic adj **1** relating to, or suffering from, a neurosis. **2** colloq overanxious, oversensitive or obsessive. ➤ n someone suffering from a neurosis.

neuter adj **1** gram belonging to the GENDER which is neither MASCULINE nor FEMININE. **2** sexless or apparently sexless. ➤ n **1** gram a the neuter gender; **b** a word belonging to this gender. **2** a neuter plant, animal or insect, eg a worker bee or ant. ➤ vb to castrate (an animal).

neutral adj **1** not taking sides in a quarrel or war. **2** not belonging or relating to either side: neutral ground. **3** of colours: indefinite enough to blend easily with brighter ones. **4** with no strong or noticeable qualities; not distinctive. **5** elec with no positive or negative electrical charge. **6** chem neither acidic nor alkaline. ➤ n **1** a neutral person or nation, not allied to any side. **2** the disengaged position of an engine's gears, with no power being transmitted to the moving parts. ○ **neutrality** n.

neutralize or **-ise** vb to cancel out the effect of something.

neutrino n, physics a stable SUBATOMIC particle that has no electric charge, virtually no mass, and travels at or near the speed of light.

neutron n, physics one of the electrically uncharged particles in the nucleus of an atom.

neutron bomb n a type of bomb that destroys life by intense radiation, without the blast and heat that destroy buildings.

never adv **1** not ever; at no time. **2** emphatically not: This will never do. **3** surely not: Those two are never twins! ♦ **well I never!** an expression of astonishment.

nevermore adv, formal or literary never again.

never-never n, colloq the hire-purchase system.

never-never land n an imaginary place or conditions too fortunate to exist in reality.

nevertheless adv in spite of that.

nevus see NAEVUS

new adj **1** recently made, bought, built, opened, etc. **2** recently discovered. **3** never having existed before; just invented, etc. **4** fresh; additional; supplementary: a new consignment. **5** recently arrived, installed, etc: a new prime minister. **6** (chiefly **new to sb** or **sth**) unfamiliar; experienced, or experiencing something, for the first time. **7** of a person: changed physically, mentally or morally for the better. **8** renewed: gave us new hope. **9** modern: the new generation. **10** used in naming a place after an older one: New York. ➤ adv, usu in compounds **1** only just; freshly: new-baked bread. **2** anew. ○ **newly** adv **1** only just; recently. **2** again; anew: newly awakened desire. ○ **newness** n.

new blood see BLOOD (noun sense 5b)

newborn adj **1** just or very recently born. **2** of faith, etc: reborn.

new broom n a new person in charge, bent on making sweeping improvements.

newcomer n **1** someone recently arrived. **2** a beginner.

newel n **1** the central spindle round which a spiral stair winds. **2** a post at the top or bottom of a flight of stairs, supporting the handrail.

newfangled adj modern, esp objectionably so.

new moon n **1** the moon when it is visible as a narrow waxing crescent. Compare FULL MOON. **2** the time when the moon becomes visible in this form.

news sing n **1** information about recent events, esp as reported by newspapers, radio, TV or the Internet. **2** (**the news**) a radio or TV broadcast report of news. **3** any fresh interesting information. **4** a currently celebrated person, thing or event: He's big news in America. ♦ **that's news to me** colloq I have not heard that before.

news agency n an agency that collects news stories and supplies them to newspapers, etc.

newsagent n a shop, or the proprietor of a shop, that sells newspapers and usu also confectionery, etc.

newscast n a radio or TV broadcast of news items. ○ **newscaster** n.

news conference see PRESS CONFERENCE

newsflash n a brief announcement of important news that interrupts a radio or TV broadcast.

newsgroup *n*, *comput* a group of people who exchange views and information by means of the Internet.

newsletter *n* a sheet containing news, issued to members of an organization, etc.

newspaper *n* a daily or weekly publication composed of folded sheets, containing news, advertisements, topical articles, correspondence, etc.

newspeak *n*, *ironic* the ambiguous language used by politicians and other persuaders.

newsprint *n* **1** the paper on which newspapers are printed. **2** the ink used to print newspapers.

newsreader *n* a radio or television news announcer.

newsreel *n* a film of news events, once a regular cinema feature.

newsroom *n* an office in a newspaper office or broadcasting station where news stories are received and edited.

news stand *n* a stall or kiosk that sells newspapers and magazines, etc.

newsworthy *adj* interesting or important enough to be reported as news.

newsy *adj* (*-ier, -iest*) full of news, esp gossip.

newt *n* a small amphibious animal with a long body and tail and short legs.

New Testament *n* the part of the Bible concerned with the teachings of Christ and his earliest followers.

newton *n*, *physics* a unit of force which gives a one kilogram mass an acceleration of one second every second.

new town *n* a town built to relieve congestion in nearby cities.

new wave *n* an artistic, musical or cultural movement or grouping that abandons traditional ideas.

New Year *n* the first day of the year or the days, usu festive ones, immediately following or preceding it.

next *adj* **1** following in time or order: *next on the list*. **2** following this one: *next week*. **3** adjoining; neighbouring: *in the next compartment*. **4** first, counting from now: *the next person I meet*. ➤ *n* someone or something that is next. ➤ *adv* **1** immediately after or this. **2** on the next occasion: *when I next saw her*. **3** following, in order of degree: *Walking is the next best thing to cycling.* ◆ **next to sth** or **sb 1** beside it or them. **2** after it or them, in order of degree: *Next to swimming, I like dancing.* **3** almost: *wearing next to no clothes.*

next-door *adj* occupying or belonging to the next room, house, shop, etc. ➤ *adv* (**next door**) to or in the next room, house, shop, etc. ◆ **next door to sth** bordering on or very near it.

next of kin *n* one's closest relative or relatives.

nexus *n* (**nexus** or **nexuses**) **1** a connected series or group. **2** a bond or link.

NHS *abbrev* National Health Service.

NI *abbrev* **1** National Insurance. **2** Northern Ireland.

Ni *symbol*, *chem* nickel.

nib *n* **1** the writing-point of a pen, esp a metal one with a divided tip. **2** a point or spike. **3** (**nibs**) crushed coffee or cocoa beans.

nibble *vb, tr & intr* **1** to take very small bites of something; to eat a little at a time. **2** to bite gently.

nibs *sing n* (*usu* **his** or **her nibs**) *facetious* a derogatory title for an important or would-be important person.

nice *adj* **1** pleasant; agreeable; respectable. **2** *often ironic* good; satisfactory. **3** *ironic* nasty: *a nice mess*. **4** fine; subtle: *nice distinctions*. **5** exacting; particular: *nice in matters of etiquette*. ○ **niceness** *n*. ◆ **nice and …** *colloq* satisfactorily …; commendably …: *nice and firm.*

nicely *adv* **1** in a nice or satisfactory way. **2** precisely; carefully: *We judged it nicely*. **3** suitably; effectively: *That will do nicely.*

nicety /'naɪsətɪ/ *n* (*-ies*) **1** precision. **2** a subtle point of detail. ◆ **to a nicety** exactly.

niche /niːʃ, nɪtʃ/ *n* **1** a shallow recess in a wall. **2** a position in life in which one feels fulfilled or at ease. **3** a group identified as a market for a particular range of products or services. ➤ *vb* **1** to place something in a niche. **2** to ensconce (oneself).

Nick or **Old Nick** *n* the Devil.

nick *n* **1** a small cut; a notch. **2** *colloq* a prison or police station. **3** *slang* state of health or condition: *She's kept the car in good nick.* ➤ *vb* **1** to make a small cut in something. **2** *slang* to arrest (a criminal). **3** *slang* to steal. ◆ **in the nick of time** just in time.

nickel *n* **1** *chem* a greyish-white metallic element used esp in alloys and for plating. **2** an American or Canadian coin worth five cents. ➤ *vb* (**nickelled, nickelling;** *US* **nickeled, nickeling**) to plate something with nickel.

nickelodeon *n*, *US old use* **1** an early form of jukebox. **2** a type of mechanical piano.

nicker *n* (*pl* **nicker**) *old slang* a pound sterling.

nick-nack see KNICK-KNACK

nickname *n* a name given to a person or place in fun, affection or contempt. ➤ *vb* to give a nickname to someone.

nicotine *n* a poisonous alkaline substance contained in tobacco.

niece *n* the daughter of one's sister or brother, or the sister or brother of one's husband or wife.

niff *n*, *slang* a bad smell. ➤ *vb, intr* to smell bad. ○ **niffy** *adj*.

nifty *adj* (*-ier, -iest*) **1** clever; adroit; agile. **2** stylish. ○ **niftily** *adv*.

niggardly *adj* **1** stingy; miserly. **2** meagre. ○ **niggard** *n* a stingy person. ○ **niggardliness** *n*.

nigger *n*, *extremely offensive* a person of Black African origin or race.

niggle *vb, intr* **1** to complain about small or unimportant details. **2** to bother or irritate, esp slightly but continually. ➤ *n* **1** a slight nagging worry. **2** a small complaint or criticism. ○ **niggling** *adj.*

nigh *adv, old use, dialect or poetic* near. ♦ **nigh on** or **well nigh** nearly; almost.

night *n* **1** the time of darkness between sunset and sunrise. **2** the time between going to bed and getting up in the morning. **3** evening: *last night.* **4** nightfall. **5** *poetic* darkness, evil, etc. ○ **nightly** *adj, adv* done or happening at night or every night. ○ **nights** *adv, colloq* at night; most nights or every night. ♦ **make a night of it** *colloq* to celebrate late into the night.

nightcap *n* **1** a drink, esp an alcoholic one, taken before going to bed. **2** *old use* a cap worn in bed at night.

nightclass *n* a class at NIGHT SCHOOL.

nightclothes *pl n* clothes for sleeping in.

nightclub *n* a club open in the evening and running late into the night for drinking, dancing, entertainment, etc. ○ **nightclubber** *n.* ○ **nightclubbing** *n.*

nightdress *n* a loose garment for sleeping in, worn by women and girls.

nightfall *n* the beginning of night; dusk.

nightgown *n* a loose garment for sleeping in.

nightie or **nighty** *n* (**nighties**) *colloq* a nightdress.

nightingale *n* a small brown thrush known for its melodious song, heard esp at night.

nightjar *n* a nocturnal bird of the swift family that has a harsh discordant cry.

nightlife *n* entertainment available in a city or resort, etc, late into the night.

night light *n* a dim-shining lamp or slow-burning candle that can be left lit all night.

nightmare *n* **1** a frightening dream. **2** an intensely distressing or frightful experience or situation. ○ **nightmarish** *adj.*

night owl *n* someone who likes to stay up late at night or who is more alert and active, etc, at night.

night school *n* **1** educational classes held in the evening, esp for those who are at work during the day. **2** an institution providing such classes.

nightshade *n* any of various wild plants, some with poisonous berries, including BELLA-DONNA.

night shift *n* **1** a session of work during the night. **2** the staff working during this period.

nightshirt *n* a loose garment like a long shirt for sleeping in.

night-time *n* the time of darkness between sunset and sunrise.

nihilism /ˈnaɪɪlɪzəm/ *n* **1** the rejection of moral and religious principles. **2** a 19c Russian movement aimed at overturning all social institutions. ○ **nihilist** *n.* ○ **nihilistic** *adj.*

nil *n, games, sport, etc* a score of nothing; zero.

nimble *adj* **1** quick and light in movement; agile. **2** of wits: sharp; alert. ○ **nimbly** *adv.*

nimbostratus *n* (**nimbostrati** /-taɪ:/) *meteorol* a low dark-coloured layer of cloud bringing rain.

nimbus *n* (**nimbuses** or **nimbi** /-baɪ:/) **1** *meteor-*ol a heavy dark type of cloud bringing rain or snow. **2** a luminous mist or halo surrounding a god or goddess.

nincompoop *n* a fool; an idiot.

nine *n* **1 a** the cardinal number 9; **b** the quantity that this represents, being one more than eight. **2** any symbol for this, eg *9* or *IX.* **3** the ninth hour after midnight or midday. **4** a set or group of nine people or things. ⊳ *adj* **1** totalling nine. **2** aged nine. ○ **ninth** *adj, n, adv.* ♦ **dressed up to the nines** *colloq* wearing one's best clothes; elaborately dressed.

nine days' wonder *n* something that grips everyone's attention for a brief time.

ninefold *adj* **1** equal to nine times as much or many. **2** divided into, or consisting of, nine parts. ⊳ *adv* by nine times as much.

ninepins *sing n* a game similar to skittles, using a wooden ball to knock down nine skittles arranged in a triangle.

nineteen *n* **1 a** the cardinal number 19; **b** the quantity that this represents, being one more than eighteen, or the sum of ten and nine. **2** any symbol for this, eg *19* or *XIX.* ⊳ *adj* **1** totalling nineteen. **2** aged nineteen. ○ **nineteenth** *adj, n, adv.* ♦ **talk nineteen to the dozen** *colloq* to chatter away animatedly.

nineties (often written **90s** or **90's**) *pl n* **1** (**one's nineties**) the period of time between one's ninetieth and hundredth birthdays. **2** (**the nineties**) the range of temperatures between ninety and a hundred degrees. **3** (**the nineties**) the period of time between the ninetieth and hundredth years of a century.

ninety *n* **1 a** the cardinal number 90; **b** the quantity that this represents, being one more than eighty-nine, or the product of ten and nine. **2** any symbol for this, eg *90* or *XC.* ⊳ *adj* **1** totalling ninety. **2** aged ninety. ○ **ninetieth** *adj, n, adv.*

ninja *n* (**ninja** or **ninjas**) esp in medieval Japan: one of a body of professional assassins trained in martial arts and stealth.

ninny *n* (**-ies**) a foolish person.

niobium *n, chem* a relatively unreactive soft greyish-blue metallic element.

nip¹ *vb* (**nipped, nipping**) **1** to pinch or squeeze something or someone sharply. **2** to give a sharp little bite to something. **3** (*often* **nip off sth**) to remove or sever it by pinching or biting. **4** *tr & intr* to sting; to cause smarting. **5** *colloq* to go quickly: *nip round to the shop.* ⊳ *n* **1** a pinch or squeeze. **2** a sharp little bite. **3** a sharp biting coldness, or stinging quality. ♦ **nip sth in the bud** to halt its growth or development at an early stage.

nip² *n* a small quantity of alcoholic spirits.

nip and tuck *colloq, n* a surgical operation carried out for cosmetic reasons. ⊳ *adj, adv, N Am* neck and neck.

nipper *n* **1** the large claw of a crab, lobster, etc. **2** (**nippers**) pincers, tweezers, forceps, or other gripping or severing tool. **3** *old colloq use* a small child.

nipple n 1 the deep-coloured pointed projection on a breast. 2 N Am the teat on a baby's feeding-bottle. 3 mech any small projection with a hole through which a flow is regulated or machine parts lubricated.

nippy adj (-ier, -iest) colloq 1 cold; chilly. 2 quick-moving; nimble. 3 of flavour: pungent or biting.

nirvana or **Nirvana** n 1 Buddhism, Hinduism the ultimate state of spiritual tranquillity attained through release from everyday concerns and extinction of individual passions. 2 colloq a place or state of perfect bliss.

nit¹ n the egg or young of a louse, found eg in hair.

nit² n, slang an idiot.

nit-picking n petty criticism or fault-finding. ➤ adj fussy.

nitrate n, chem 1 a salt or ester of NITRIC ACID. 2 sodium nitrate or potassium nitrate, used as a soil fertilizer or meat preservative.

nitre n, chem potassium nitrate; saltpetre.

nitric adj, chem belonging to or containing nitrogen.

nitric acid n, chem a colourless acid used as an oxidizing agent and for making explosives, fertilizers and dyes.

nitrify vb (-ies, -ied) tr & intr, chem usu of ammonia: to convert or be converted into nitrates or nitrites through the action of bacteria. ○ **nitrification** n.

nitrogen /'naɪtrədʒən/ n, chem an element, the colourless, odourless and tasteless gas making up four-fifths of the air we breathe. ○ **nitrogenous** adj.

nitroglycerine or **nitroglycerin** n, chem an explosive liquid compound used in dynamite.

nitrous adj, chem relating to or containing nitrogen in a low valency.

nitrous oxide n, chem dinitrogen oxide, used as an anaesthetic and popularly known as **laughing gas**.

the nitty-gritty n, colloq the fundamental issue or essential part of any matter, situation, etc.

nitwit n a stupid person.

nm abbrev 1 nanometre. 2 nautical mile.

No¹, No. or **no.** abbrev number.

No² symbol, chem nobelium.

no¹ exclam 1 used as a negative reply, expressing denial, refusal or disagreement. 2 colloq used as a question tag expecting agreement: It's a deal, no? 3 used as an astonished rejoinder: No! You don't say! ➤ adv 1 not any: no bigger than one's thumb. 2 used to indicate a negative alternative: not: willing or no. ➤ n (noes) a negative reply or vote: The noes have it. ♦ **no more** 1 destroyed; dead. 2 never again; not any longer. **not take no for an answer** to continue with an activity in spite of refusals; to insist.

no² adj 1 not any. 2 certainly not or far from something specified: He's no fool. 3 hardly any: do it in no time. 4 not allowed: no smoking.

♦ **no go** colloq impossible; no good. **no one** no single: No one candidate is the obvious choice. **no way** colloq no; definitely not.

n.o. abbrev, cricket not out.

nob¹ n, slang someone of wealth or high social rank.

nob² n, slang the head.

no-ball n, cricket a ball bowled in a manner that is not allowed by the rules.

nobble vb, colloq 1 horse-racing to drug or otherwise interfere with (a horse) to stop it winning. 2 to persuade someone by bribes or threats. 3 to obtain something dishonestly. 4 to catch (a criminal). 5 to swindle someone.

nobelium n, chem a radioactive element produced artificially.

nobility n (-ies) 1 the quality of being noble. 2 (**the nobility**) people of noble birth.

noble adj 1 honourable. 2 generous. 3 of high birth or rank. 4 grand, splendid or imposing in appearance. ➤ n a person of noble rank. ○ **nobly** adv.

noble gas n, chem any of the gases helium, neon, argon, krypton, xenon and radon. Also called **inert gas**.

nobleman or **noblewoman** n a member of the nobility.

noble metal n a metal such as gold, silver or platinum that is highly unreactive and so does not easily tarnish. Compare BASE METAL.

noblesse oblige /nou'blɛs ou'bliːʒ/ n, usu ironic it is the duty of the privileged to help the less fortunate.

nobody pron no person; no one. ➤ n (-ies) someone of no significance.

nock n a notch, or a part carrying a notch, esp on an arrow or a bow.

nocturnal adj 1 of animals, etc: active at night. 2 happening at night. 3 belonging or relating to the night.

nocturne n 1 mus a dreamy piece of music, usu for the piano. 2 art a night or moonlight scene.

nod vb (**nodded, nodding**) 1 tr & intr to make a brief bowing gesture with (the head) in agreement, greeting, etc. 2 intr to let the head droop with sleepiness; to become drowsy. 3 intr to make a mistake through momentary loss of concentration. 4 to indicate or direct by nodding. 5 intr of flowers, plumes, etc: to sway or bob about. ➤ n a quick bending forward of the head as a gesture of assent, greeting or command. ♦ **on the nod** colloq of the passing of a proposal, etc: by general agreement, without the formality of a vote. **the Land of Nod** sleep. ◊ **nod off** intr to fall asleep. **nod sb** or **sth through** to pass something without a discussion, vote, etc.

noddle n, colloq the head or brain.

noddy n (-ies) 1 a tropical bird of the tern family, so unafraid of humans as to seem stupid. 2 a simpleton.

node n 1 a knob, lump, swelling or knotty mass. 2 bot a swelling where a leaf is attached to a stem. 3 geom the point where a curve crosses itself. **4** *astron* a point where the orbit of a body intersects the apparent path of the sun or another body. **5** *physics* in a vibrating body: the point of least movement. ○ **nodal** *adj*.

nodule *n* **1** a small round lump. **2** *bot* a swelling in a root of a leguminous plant, inhabited by bacteria that convert nitrogen to the plant's use. ○ **nodular** *adj*.

Noel or **Noël** *n* in Christmas cards and carols, etc: Christmas.

no-fault *adj* of insurance compensation payments, etc: made without attachment or admission of blame.

no-frills *adj* basic, not elaborate or fancy.

nog *n* an alcoholic drink made with whipped eggs.

noggin *n* **1** a small measure or quantity of alcoholic spirits. **2** a small mug or wooden cup. **3** *colloq* one's head.

no-go area *n* an area to which normal access is prevented.

nohow *adv, colloq or dialect* in no way, not at all.

noise *n* **1** a sound. **2** a harsh disagreeable sound; a din. **3** *radio* interference in a signal. **4** *comput* irrelevant or meaningless material appearing in output. **5** something one says as a conventional response, vague indication of inclinations, etc: *make polite noises*. ➤ *vb* (*usu* **noise abroad** or **about**) to make something generally known; to spread (a rumour, etc). ○ **noiseless** *adj*. ○ **noiselessly** *adv*.

noisette /nwa'zɛt/ *n* **1** a small piece of meat (usu lamb) cut off the bone and rolled. **2** a nutlike or nut-flavoured sweet. ➤ *adj* flavoured with or containing hazelnuts.

noisome *adj* **1** disgusting; offensive; stinking. **2** harmful; poisonous.

noisy *adj* (*-ier, -iest*) **1** making a lot of noise. **2** full of noise; accompanied by noise. ○ **noisily** *adv*.

nomad *n* **1** a member of a people without a permanent home, who travel from place to place seeking food and pasture. **2** a wanderer. ○ **nomadic** *adj*.

no-man's-land *n* **1** neutral territory between opposing armies or between two countries with a common border. **2** a state or situation that is neither one thing nor another.

nom-de-plume or **nom de plume** /nɒm də 'pluːm/ *n* (**noms-de-plume** or **noms de plume** /nɒm-/) a pseudonym used by a writer; a pen-name.

nomenclature /noʊ'mɛŋklətʃə(r)/ *n* **1** a classified system of names, esp in science; terminology. **2** a list or set of names.

nominal *adj* **1** in name only; so called, but not actually. **2** very small in comparison to actual cost or value: *a nominal rent*. **3** *gram* being or relating to a noun. **4** being or relating to a name. **5** *space flight* according to plan. ➤ *n*, *gram* a noun, or a phrase, etc standing for a noun. ○ **nominally** *adv*.

nominal value *n* the stated or face value on a bond, share certificate, etc.

nominate *vb* **1** (*usu* **nominate sb for sth**) to propose them formally as a candidate for election, a job, etc. **2** (*usu* **nominate sb to sth**) to appoint them to (a post or position). **3** to specify formally (eg a date). ○ **nomination** *n*.

nominative *n, gram* **1** in certain languages: the form or CASE² used to mark the subject of a verb. **2** a noun, etc in this case. ➤ *adj* **1** *gram* belonging to or in this case. **2** appointed by nomination rather than election.

nominee *n* **1** someone nominated to, or nominated as a candidate for, a job, position, etc. **2** a person or organization appointed to act on behalf of another. **3** someone on whose life an annuity or lease depends.

nonage *n, law* the condition of being under age; one's minority or period of immaturity.

nonagenarian *n* someone between the ages of 90 and 99 years old.

nonagon *n, geom* a nine-sided figure.

non-aligned *adj* not allied to any of the major power blocs in world politics; neutral.

nonce *n* (**the nonce**) the present time. ♦ **for the nonce** for the time being; for the present.

nonce-word *n* a word coined for one particular occasion.

nonchalant /'nɒnʃələnt/ *adj* calmly or indifferently unconcerned. ○ **nonchalance** *n*. ○ **nonchalantly** *adv*.

non-combatant *n* **1** a member of the armed forces whose duties do not include fighting. **2** in time of war: a civilian.

non-commissioned officer *n* an officer such as a corporal or sergeant, appointed from the lower ranks of the armed forces, not by being given a COMMISSION.

non-committal *adj* avoiding expressing a definite opinion or decision.

non compos mentis *adj, often humorous* not of sound mind.

nonconformist *n* **1** someone who refuses to conform to generally accepted practice. **2** (**Nonconformist**) in England and Wales: a member of a Protestant Church that has separated from the Church of England. ○ **nonconformity** *n*.

non-contributory *adj* **1** of a pension scheme: paid for by the employer, without contributions from the employee. **2** of a state benefit: not dependent on the payment of National Insurance contributions.

non-denominational *adj* not linked with any particular religious denomination.

nondescript *adj* with no strongly noticeable characteristics or distinctive features. ➤ *n* a nondescript person or thing.

none¹ /nʌn/ *pron* (*with sing* or *pl verb*) **1** not any. **2** no one; not any people: *None were as kind as she*. ♦ **none but** only. **none of** I won't put up with: *None of your cheek!* **none other than** sb or sth the very person or thing mentioned or thought of. **none the** (*followed by a comparative*) not any: *none the worse for his adventure*. **none the less** or **nonetheless** nevertheless; in spite of that. **none too** by no means: *none too clean.*

---

none When **none** refers to a number of individual people or things, it can be followed by a singular or a plural verb, rather like a collective noun, depending on whether the individuals or the group as a whole are intended:
The hotel is half a mile from the beach and none of the rooms overlook the sea.
None of us has time for much else but the work in hand.

---

none² /noʊn/ *or* **nones** /noʊnz/ *n, esp RC Church* the fifth of the CANONICAL HOURS.

nonentity *n (-ies)* **1** *derog* someone of no significance, character, ability, etc. **2** *derog* a thing of no importance. **3** a thing which does not exist. **4** the state of not being.

nonesuch or **nonsuch** *n, literary* a unique, unparalleled or extraordinary thing.

nonet /noʊˈnɛt/ *n, mus* **1** a composition for nine instruments or voices. **2** a group of nine instrumentalists or singers.

nonetheless see under NONE¹

non-event *n* an event that fails to live up to its promise.

non-feasance *n, law* omission of something which ought to be, or ought to have been, done.

non-fiction *n* literature concerning factual characters or events.

non-flammable *adj* not liable to catch fire or burn easily.

non-invasive *adj* of medical treatment: not involving surgery or the insertion of instruments, etc into the patient.

non-negotiable *adj* **1** not open to negotiation. **2** of a cheque, etc: not NEGOTIABLE.

no-no *n (no-nos or no-noes) colloq* something which must not be done, said, etc.

nonpareil /nɒnpəˈreɪl/ *adj* having no equal; matchless. ➤ *n* a person or thing without equal.

nonplus *vb (nonplussed, nonplussing; US nonplused, nonplusing)* to puzzle; to disconcert.

non-proliferation *n* lack or limitation of the production or spread of something, esp the policy of limiting the production and ownership of nuclear or chemical weapons.

non-renewable resource *n* any naturally occurring substance that is economically valuable, but which forms over such a long period of time that for all practical purposes it cannot be replaced.

non-returnable *adj* **1** of a bottle or other container: on which a returnable deposit is not paid and which will not be accepted after use by the vendor for recycling. **2** of a deposit, etc: that will not be returned in case of cancellation, etc.

nonsense *n* **1** words or ideas that do not make sense. **2** foolishness; silly behaviour. ➤ *exclam*

you're quite wrong. ♦ **make a nonsense of sth** to destroy the effect of it; to make it pointless.

nonsensical *adj* making no sense; absurd.

non sequitur *n* **1** an illogical step in an argument. **2** a conclusion that does not follow from the premises.

non-specific *adj* **1** not specific. **2** of a disease: not caused by any specific agent that can be identified.

non-standard *adj* **1** not standard. **2** of language: different to the usage of educated speakers and considered by some to be incorrect.

non-starter *n* **1** a person, thing or idea, etc that has no chance of success. **2** a horse which, though entered for a race, does not run.

non-stick *adj* of a pan, etc: that has a coating to which food does not stick during cooking.

non-stop *adj* without a stop; continuous. ➤ *adv* without stopping; continuously.

nonsuch see NONESUCH

noodle¹ *n (usu noodles) cookery* a thin strip of pasta, often made with egg.

noodle² *n, colloq* **1** a simpleton. **2** *N Am* the head.

nook *n* **1** a secluded retreat. **2** a corner or recess. ♦ **every nook and cranny** absolutely everywhere.

nooky or **nookie** *n, slang* sexual activity.

noon *n* midday; twelve o'clock.

noonday *n* midday.

no one or **no-one** *n* no person.

noose *n* a loop made in the end of a rope, etc, with a sliding knot. ➤ *vb* to tie someone or something in a noose.

nope *exclam, slang* emphatic form of NO¹.

nor *conj* **1** *(used to introduce alternatives after* NEITHER): *He neither knows nor cares.* **2** and not: *It didn't look appetizing, nor was it.* ➤ *adv* not either: *If you won't, nor shall I.*

---

nor See note at **neither.**

Nordic *adj* **1** relating or belonging to Scandinavia or its inhabitants. **2** Germanic or Scandinavian in appearance, typically tall, blond and blue-eyed. **3** (**nordic**) denoting a type of competitive skiing with cross-country racing and ski-jumping.

norm *n* **1** (**the norm**) a typical pattern or situation. **2** an accepted way of behaving, etc. **3** a standard, eg for achievement in industry: *production norms.*

normal *adj* **1** usual; typical; not extraordinary. **2** mentally or physically sound: *a normal baby.* **3** (**normal to sth**) *geom* perpendicular. ➤ *n* **1** what is average or usual. **2** *geom* a perpendicular line or plane. ○ **normality** and (*N Am*) **normalcy** *n*. ○ **normalize** or **-ise** *vb*. ○ **normally** *adv* **1** in an ordinary or natural way. **2** usually.

Norman *n* **1** a person from Normandy, esp one of the descendants of the Scandinavian settlers of N France, who then conquered England in 1066. **2** Norman French. ➤ *adj* **1** relating to the Normans, their language, etc, or to Normandy. **2** *archit* signifying or relating to a building style typical in 10c and 11c Normandy and 11c and 12c England, with round arches and heavy massive pillars.

normative *adj* establishing a guiding standard or rules.

Norse *adj* **1** relating or belonging to ancient or medieval Scandinavia. **2** Norwegian. ➤ *n* **1** the Germanic language group of Scandinavia. **2** the language of this group used in medieval Norway and its colonies.

Norseman *n* a Scandinavian; a VIKING.

north *n* (*also* **North** or **the North**) **1** the direction to one's left when one faces the rising sun. **2** MAGNETIC NORTH. **3** any part of the earth, a country or a town, etc lying in the direction of north. ➤ *adj* **1** situated in the north; on the side that is on or nearest the north. **2** facing or toward the north. **3** esp of wind: coming from the north. ➤ *adv* in, to or towards the north.

northbound *adj* going or leading towards the north.

north-east *n* (*sometimes* **North-East**) **1** the compass point or direction that is midway between north and east. **2** an area lying in this direction. ➤ *adj* **1** in the north-east. **2** from the direction of the north-east: *a north-east wind.* ➤ *adv* in, to or towards the north-east. ○ **north-eastern** *adj*.

northeaster or **nor'easter** *n* a strong wind or storm from the north-east.

northerly *adj* **1** of a wind, etc: coming from the north. **2** looking or lying, etc towards the north; situated in the north. ➤ *adv* to or towards the north. ➤ *n* (*-ies*) a northerly wind.

northern or **Northern** *adj* situated in, directed towards or belonging to the north or the North. ○ **northerner** or **Northerner** *n*. ○ **northernmost** *adj*.

the northern lights *pl n* an AURORA (sense I) sometimes observed in northern regions.

northing *n*, *chiefly naut* **1** motion, distance or tendency northward. **2** distance of a heavenly body from the equator northward. **3** difference of LATITUDE made by a ship in sailing. **4** deviation towards the north.

the North Pole *n* the northernmost point of the Earth's axis of rotation.

northward *adv* (*also* **northwards**) towards the north. *adj* towards the north.

north-west *n* (*sometimes* **North-West**) **1** the compass point or direction that is midway between north and west. **2** an area lying in this direction. ➤ *adj* **1** in the north-west. **2** from the direction of the north-west: *a north-west wind.* ➤ *adv* in, to or towards the north-west. ○ **north-western** *adj*.

northwester *n* a strong wind from the north-west.

Nos, Nos. or **nos** *abbrev* numbers.

nose *n* **1** the projecting organ above the mouth, with which one smells and breathes. **2** an animal's snout or muzzle. **3** the sense of smell. **4** a scent or aroma, esp a wine's bouquet. **5** the front or projecting part of anything, eg a motor vehicle. **6** the nose as a symbol of inquisitiveness or interference: *poke one's nose into something.* ➤ *vb* **1** *tr & intr* to move carefully forward: *I nosed the car out of the yard.* **2** to detect something by smelling. **3** of an animal: to sniff at something or nuzzle it. **4** *intr* (*often* **nose about** or **around**) to pry. ♦ **a nose for sth** a faculty for detecting or recognizing something. **by a nose** by a narrow margin. **cut off one's nose to spite one's face** to act from resentment in a way that can only cause injury to oneself. **get up sb's nose** *colloq* to annoy them. **keep one's nose clean** *colloq* to avoid doing anything that might get one into trouble. **look down** or **turn up one's nose at sth** or **sb** *colloq* to show disdain for it or them. **not see beyond** or **further than the end of one's nose** not to see the long-term consequences of one's actions. **on the nose** of bets made in horse-racing: to win only, ie not to come second, etc. **pay through the nose** *colloq* to pay an exorbitant price. **put sb's nose out of joint** *colloq* to affront them. **under one's (very) nose** in full view and very obviously in front of one; close at hand. ◊ **nose sth out** to discover it by prying; to track it down.

nosebag *n* a food bag for a horse, hung over its head.

noseband *n* the part of a bridle that goes over the horse's nose.

nosebleed *n* a flow of blood from the nose.

nosedive *n* **1** a steep nose-downward plunge by an aircraft. **2** a sharp plunge or fall. **3** a sudden drop, eg in prices. ➤ *vb*, *intr* to plunge or fall suddenly.

nosegay *n*, *old use* a posy of flowers.

nosey see NOSY

nosh *colloq*, *n* food. ➤ *vb*, *intr* to eat.

nostalgia *n* **1** a yearning for the past. **2** homesickness. ○ **nostalgic** *adj*. ○ **nostalgically** *adv*.

nostril *n* either of the two external openings in the nose, through which one breathes and smells, etc.

nostrum *n* a patent medicine; a panacea or cure-all.

nosy or **nosey** *adj* (*nosier, nosiest*) *derog* inquisitive; prying. ➤ *n* (*nosies* or *noseys*) a prying person. ○ **nosiness** *n*.

nosy parker *n*, *derog*, *colloq* a nosy person; a busybody.

not *adv* (*often shortened to* **-n't**) **1** used to make a negative statement, etc. **2** used in place of a negative clause or predicate: *We might be late, but I hope not.* **3** (indicating surprise, an expectation of agreement, etc) surely it is the case that …: *Haven't you heard?* **4** used to contrast the untrue with the true: *It's a cloud, not a mountain.* **5** barely: *with his face not two inches from mine.* **6** *colloq* used to emphatically deny what has just been said: *looks a lot like Brad Pitt … not.* ♦ **not a** absolutely no: *not a sound.* **not**

at all don't mention it; it's a pleasure. **not just** or **not only**, *etc* used to introduce what is usu the lesser of two points, etc: *not just his family, but his wider public*. **not on** *colloq* 1 not possible. 2 not morally or socially acceptable. **not that** though it is not the case that: *not that I care*.

notable /'nəʊtəbəl/ *adj* 1 worth noting; significant. 2 distinguished. ➤ *n* a notable person. ○ **notability** *n*. ○ **notably** *adv* as something or someone notable, esp in a list or group: *several people, notably my father*.

notary /'nəʊtərɪ/ *n* (*-ies*) (*in full* **notary public**) (*pl* **notaries public**) a public official with the legal power to draw up and witness official documents, and to administer oaths, etc.

notation *n* 1 the representation of quantities, numbers, musical sounds or movements, etc by symbols. 2 any set of such symbols.

notch *n* 1 a small V-shaped cut or indentation. 2 a nick. 3 *colloq* a step or level. ➤ *vb* 1 to cut a notch in something. 2 (*also* **notch something up**) to record something with, or as if with, a notch. 3 (*usu* **notch something up**) to achieve it. 4 to fit (an arrow) to a bowstring. ○ **notched** *adj*.

note *n* 1 (*often* **notes**) a brief written record made for later reference. 2 a short informal letter. 3 *often in compounds* a brief comment explaining a textual point, etc: *a footnote*. 4 a short account or essay. 5 a a banknote; b a promissory note. 6 esp in diplomacy: a formal communication. 7 attention; notice: *buildings worthy of note*. 8 distinction; eminence. 9 *mus* a a written symbol indicating the pitch and length of a musical sound; b the sound itself; c a key on a keyboard instrument. 10 *esp poetic* the call or cry of a bird or animal. 11 an impression conveyed; a hint or touch: *with a note of panic in her voice*. ➤ *vb* 1 (*also* **note sth down**) to write it down. 2 to notice something. 3 to pay close attention to something. 4 to mention or to remark upon something. ○ **noted** *adj* 1 famous; eminent: *noted for his use of colour*. 2 notorious. ○ **notedly** *adv*. ◆ **compare notes** to exchange ideas and opinions about a particular person, event or thing. **of note** 1 well-known; distinguished. 2 significant; worthy of attention. **strike a false note** to act or speak inappropriately. **strike the right note** to act or speak appropriately. **take note** (*often* **take note of sth**) to observe it carefully, to pay attention to it.

notebook *n* 1 a small book in which to write notes, etc. 2 a small portable computer; a LAPTOP.

notecase *n* a wallet.

notelet *n* a folded piece of notepaper.

notepad *n* a block of writing-paper for making notes on.

notepaper *n* paper for writing letters on.

noteworthy *adj* worthy of notice; remarkable.

nothing *n* 1 no thing; not anything. 2 a zero; the figure 0. 3 a very little; b something of no

importance or not very impressive; c no difficulty or trouble. ➤ *adv* not at all: *nothing daunted*. ○ **nothingness** *n*. ◆ **come to nothing** to fail or peter out. **for nothing** 1 free; without payment. 2 for no good reason; in vain. **nothing doing** *colloq* 1 an expression of refusal. 2 no hope of success. **think nothing of sth** 1 to regard it as normal or straightforward. 2 to feel no hesitation, guilt or regret about it.

notice *n* 1 an announcement displayed or delivered publicly. 2 one's attention: *It escaped my notice*. 3 a a warning or notification given: *will continue until further notice*; b warning or notification given before leaving, or dismissing someone from, a job. 4 a review of a performance or book, etc. ➤ *vb* 1 to observe; to become aware of something. 2 to remark on something. 3 to show signs of recognition of someone, etc. 4 to treat someone with polite attention. ◆ **at short notice** with little warning or time for preparation, etc. **take notice** to take interest in one's surroundings, etc.

noticeable *adj* easily seen. ○ **noticeably** *adv*.

noticeboard *n* a board on which notices are displayed.

notify *vb* (*-ies, -ied*) to tell or to inform. ○ **notifiable** *adj* of infectious diseases: that must be reported to the public health authorities. ○ **notification** *n*.

notion *n* 1 an impression, conception or understanding. 2 a belief or principle. 3 an inclination, whim or fancy. 4 (**notions**) small items such as pins, needles, threads, etc. ○ **notional** *adj* 1 existing in imagination only. 2 theoretical. 3 hypothetical. ○ **notionally** *adv*.

notorious *adj* famous for something disreputable: *a notorious criminal*. ○ **notoriety** *n*. ○ **notoriously** *adv*.

not-out *adj, adv, cricket* still in; at the end of the innings without having been put out.

not proven /'prəʊvən/ *n, Scots law* a verdict delivered when there is insufficient evidence to convict, resulting in the freedom of the accused.

no-trump *bridge, n* (*also* **no-trumps**) a call for the playing of a hand without any trump suit. ➤ *adj* of a hand: possible to play without trumps.

notwithstanding *prep* in spite of. ➤ *adv* in spite of that; however. ➤ *conj* although.

nougat /'nuːgɑː, 'nʌɡət/ *n* a chewy sweet containing chopped nuts, cherries, etc.

nought *n* 1 the figure 0; zero. 2 *old use* nothing; NAUGHT.

noughts and crosses *sing n* a game for two players, the aim being to complete a row of three noughts (for one player) or three crosses (for the other) within a framework of nine squares.

noun *n, gram* a word used as the name of a person, animal, thing, place or quality.

nourish *vb* 1 to supply someone or something with food. 2 a to encourage the growth of something; b to foster (an idea, etc).

○ **nourishing** adj. ○ **nourishment** n.

nous /naʊs/ n, colloq common sense; gumption.

nouveau riche /ˈnuːvoʊ riːʃ/ n, derog (usu in pl **nouveaux riches** /ˈnuːvoʊ riːʃ/) people who have recently acquired wealth but lack the upper-class breeding to go with it.

nova /ˈnoʊvə/ n (**novae** /-viː/ or **novas**) astron a normally faint star that flares into brightness and then fades again.

novel¹ n 1 a book-length fictional story. 2 (**the novel**) such writing as a literary genre. ○ **novelist** n.

novel² adj new; original.

novelette n, derog a short novel, esp one that is trite or sentimental.

novella n a short story or short novel.

novelty n (**-ies**) 1 the quality of being new and intriguing. 2 something new and strange. 3 a small, cheap toy or souvenir.

November n the eleventh month of the year.

novena /noʊˈviːnə/ n, RC Church a series of special prayers and services held over a period of nine days.

novice /ˈnɒvɪs/ n 1 someone new in anything; a beginner. 2 a probationary member of a religious community. 3 horse-racing a horse that has not won a race in a season prior to the current season.

noviciate or **novitiate** n 1 the period of being a novice, esp in a religious community. 2 the state of being a novice.

now adv 1 at the present time or moment. 2 immediately. 3 in narrative: then: He now turned from journalism to fiction. 4 in these circumstances; as things are: I planned to go, but now I can't. 5 up to the present: He has now been teaching 13 years. 6 used in conversation to accompany explanations, warnings, commands, rebukes, words of comfort, etc: Now, this is what happened • Careful now! ➢ n the present time. ➢ conj (also **now that**) because at last; because at this time: Now we're all here, we'll begin. ♦ **any day** or **moment** or **time now** at any time soon. **for now** until later; for the time being. **just now** 1 a moment ago. 2 at this very moment. **now and again** or **now and then** sometimes; occasionally. **now, now!** 1 used to comfort someone: Now, now, don't cry! 2 (also **now then!**) a warning or rebuke: Now, now! Less noise please!

nowadays adv in these present times.

Nowell or **Nowel** n NOEL.

nowhere adv in or to no place; not anywhere. ➢ n a non-existent place. ♦ **from** or **out of nowhere** suddenly and inexplicably: They appeared from nowhere. **get nowhere** colloq to make no progress. **in the middle of nowhere** colloq isolated; remote from towns or cities, etc. **nowhere near** colloq not nearly; by no means: nowhere near enough. **nowhere to be found** or **seen** lost.

no-win adj of a situation: in which one is bound to fail or lose, whatever one does.

nowt n, colloq or dialect nothing.

noxious adj harmful; poisonous.

nozzle n an outlet tube or spout, esp as a fitting attached to the end of a hose, etc.

Np symbol, chem neptunium.

NT abbrev New Testament.

-n't contraction not.

nth /ɛnθ/ adj 1 denoting an indefinite position in a sequence: to the nth degree. 2 many times more than the first: I'm telling you for the nth time.

nuance /ˈnjuːɑːns/ n a subtle variation in colour, meaning, expression, etc.

the nub n the central and most important issue.

nubile /ˈnjuːbaɪl/ adj of a young woman: 1 sexually mature. 2 marriageable. 3 sexually attractive.

nuclear /ˈnjuːklɪə(r)/ adj 1 having the nature of, or like, a NUCLEUS. 2 relating to atoms or their nuclei: nuclear physics. 3 relating to or produced by the fission or fusion of atomic nuclei: nuclear energy.

nuclear disarmament n a country's act of giving up its nuclear weapons.

nuclear energy n energy produced through a nuclear reaction. Also called **atomic energy**.

nuclear family n the basic family unit, mother, father and children. Compare EXTENDED FAMILY.

nuclear fission n a reaction in which an atomic nucleus of a radioactive element splits with simultaneous release of large amounts of energy.

nuclear fuel n material such as URANIUM or PLUTONIUM used to produce nuclear energy.

nuclear fusion n a THERMONUCLEAR reaction in which two atomic nuclei combine with a release of large amounts of energy.

nuclear physics n the study of atomic nuclei, esp relating to the generation of NUCLEAR ENERGY.

nuclear power n power, esp electricity, obtained from reactions by NUCLEAR FISSION or NUCLEAR FUSION. ○ **nuclear-powered** adj.

nuclear reaction n a process of NUCLEAR FUSION or NUCLEAR FISSION.

nuclear reactor n an apparatus for producing nuclear energy, eg to generate electricity, by means of sustained and controlled NUCLEAR FISSION.

nuclear waste n radioactive waste material.

nuclear weapon n a weapon that derives its destructive force from the energy released during NUCLEAR FISSION or NUCLEAR FUSION.

nuclear winter n a period without light, heat or growth, predicted as a likely after-effect of nuclear war.

nucleate vb, tr & intr to form, or form something into, a nucleus. ➢ adj having a nucleus.

nuclei pl of NUCLEUS

nucleic acid n a complex compound, either DNA or RNA, found in all living cells.

nucleolus n (**nucleoli**) biol a spherical body in the nucleus of most plant and animal cells, concerned with the production of protein.

nucleon n, physics a PROTON or NEUTRON.

nucleonics sing n the study of the uses of radioactivity and nuclear energy.

nucleus n (**nuclei** /'njuːklıaı/) **1** physics the central part of an atom, consisting of neutrons and protons. **2** biol the central part of a plant or animal cell, containing genetic material. **3** chem a stable group of atoms in a molecule acting as a base for the formation of compounds. **4** a core round which things grow or accumulate.

nuclide n, physics one of two or more atoms that contain the same number of PROTONS and NEUTRONs in their nuclei.

nude adj **1** wearing no clothes; naked. **2** uncovered; bare. ➤ n **1** a representation of one or more naked figures in painting or sculpture, etc. **2** someone naked. **3** the state of nakedness: in the nude. ○ **nudity** n.

nudge vb **1** to poke or push someone gently, esp with the elbow, to get attention, etc. **2** to give someone a gentle reminder or persuasion. ➤ n a gentle prod.

nudism n the practice of not wearing clothes, as a matter of principle. ○ **nudist** n, adj.

nugatory /'njuːgətərı/ adj, formal **1** worthless; trifling. **2** ineffective; futile. **3** invalid.

nugget n **1** a lump, esp of gold. **2** a small piece of something precious: nuggets of wisdom.

nuisance n **1** an annoying or troublesome person, thing or circumstance. **2** law something obnoxious to the community or an individual, that is disallowed by law.

nuke slang, vb to attack with nuclear weapons. ➤ n a nuclear weapon.

null adj **1** legally invalid: declared null and void. **2** with no significance or value. **3** maths of a set: with no members; empty. ○ **nullity** n **1** the state of being null or void. **2** (-ies) something without legal force or validity. **3** lack of existence, force or efficacy. ○ **nullness** n.

nullify vb (-ies, -ied) **1** to cause or declare something to be legally invalid. **2** to make something ineffective; to cancel it out. ○ **nullification** n.

numb adj **1** deprived completely, or to some degree, of sensation. **2** too stunned to feel emotion; stupefied: numb with shock. ➤ vb **1** to make something numb. **2** to deaden something. ○ **numbly** adv. ○ **numbness** n.

number n **1** a specific quantity that can be counted. **2** a symbol representing this, eg 5 or V; a numeral. **3** a numeral or set of numerals identifying something or someone within a series: telephone numbers. **4** (before a numeral) the person, animal, vehicle, etc bearing the specified numeral: Number 2 is pulling ahead. **5** a single one of a series, eg an issue of a magazine. **6** a quantity of individuals. **7** an act or a piece of music. **8** colloq an article or person considered appreciatively: driving a white sports number. **9** a group or set: She isn't one of our number. **10** (**numbers**) numerical superiority: overwhelmed by sheer weight of numbers. **11** gram the property of expressing, or classification of word forms into, SINGULAR and PLURAL. ➤ vb **1** to give a number to something; to mark it with a number. **2** to amount to (a specified number). **3** tr & intr to list, include or be included: I number her among my enemies. ○ **numberless** adj **1** too many to count; innumerable. **2** without a number. ♦ **any number of sth** many of it. **get** or **have sb's number** colloq to understand them; to have them sized up. **one's days are numbered** one is soon to die, or come to the end of (eg a job) unpleasantly. **one's number is up** colloq one is due for some unpleasant fate, eg death or ruin. **without number** more than can be counted; countless.

number one n, colloq, ironic oneself. ➤ adj (**number-one**) first; of primary importance: Give it number-one priority.

number plate n a plate on a motor vehicle bearing its registration number.

numbskull see NUMSKULL

numerable adj that may be numbered or counted. ○ **numerably** adv.

numeral n an arithmetical symbol or group of symbols used to express a number, eg 5 or V, 29 or XXIX. ➤ adj relating to, consisting of, or expressing a number.

numerate adj **1** able to perform arithmetical operations. **2** having some understanding of mathematics and science. ○ **numeracy** /'njuː-mərəsı/ n.

numeration n **1** the process of counting or numbering. **2** a system of numbering.

numerator n the number above the line in a fraction. Compare DENOMINATOR.

numeric or **numerical** adj relating to, using, or consisting of, numbers. ○ **numerically** adv.

numerology n the study of numbers as supposed to predict future events or influence human affairs. ○ **numerologist** n.

numerous adj **1** many. **2** containing a large number of people.

numismatics or **numismatology** n the study or collecting of coins and medals.

numskull or **numbskull** n, colloq a stupid person.

nun n a member of a female religious order living within a community, in obedience to certain vows.

nuncio /'nʌnsɪoʊ/ n an ambassador from the pope.

nunnery n (-ies) a house in which a group of nuns live; a CONVENT.

nuptial adj **1** relating to marriage. **2** zool relating to mating. ➤ n (usu **nuptials**) a marriage ceremony.

nurd see NERD

nurse n **1** someone trained to look after sick, injured or helpless people. **2** someone, esp a woman, who looks after small children in a household, etc. **3** a worker ant, bee, etc, that tends the young in the colony. ➢ *vb* **1** to look after (sick or injured people) esp in a hospital. **2** *intr* to follow a career as a nurse. **3** *tr & intr* **a** to breastfeed a baby; **b** of a baby: to feed at the breast. **4** to hold something with care: *gave him the bag of meringues to nurse*. **5** to tend something with concern: *I was at home nursing a cold*. **6** to encourage or indulge (a feeling) in oneself: *nursing her jealousy*. ○ **nursing** *adj, n.*

nursemaid or **nurserymaid** *n* a children's nurse in a household.

nursery *n* (*-ies*) **1 a** a place where children are looked after while their parents are at work, etc; **b** a NURSERY SCHOOL. **2** a room in a house, etc, set apart for young children and, where appropriate, their nurse or other carer. **3** a place where plants are grown for sale. **4** a place where young animals are reared or tended.

nurseryman *n* someone who grows plants for sale.

nursery rhyme *n* a short simple traditional rhyme or song for young children.

nursery school *n* a school for young children, usu those aged between three and five.

nursery slopes *pl n, skiing* the lower, more gentle slopes, used for practice by beginners.

nursing home *n* a small private hospital or home, esp one for old people.

nurture *n* care, nourishment and encouragement given to a growing child, animal or plant. ➢ *vb* **1** to nourish and tend (a growing child, animal or plant). **2** to encourage the development of (a project, idea or feeling, etc).

nut *n* **1** *popularly* **a** a fruit consisting of a kernel contained in a hard shell, eg a hazelnut or walnut; **b** the kernel itself. **2** *bot* a hard dry one-seeded fruit. **3** *popularly* a roasted peanut. **4** a small, usu hexagonal, piece of metal with a hole through it, for screwing on the end of a bolt. **5** *colloq* a person's head. **6** *colloq* (*also* **nutter**) a crazy person. **7** *colloq, usu in compounds* an enthusiast: *a football nut*. **8** a small lump: *a nut of butter*. **9** (**nuts**) *colloq* testicles. ➢ *vb, colloq* (**nutted, nutting**) to butt someone with the head. ♦ **a hard** or **tough nut to crack** *colloq* a difficult problem or person. **do one's nut** *colloq*

to be furious. **for nuts** *colloq* at all: *can't sing for nuts*. **off one's nut** *colloq* mad. See also NUTS, NUTTY.

nutcase *n, colloq* a crazy person.

nutcracker *n* (*usu* **nutcrackers**) a utensil for cracking nuts.

nuthatch *n* a bird that feeds on insects, nuts and seeds.

nuthouse *n, colloq, offensive* a mental hospital.

nutmeg *n* the hard aromatic seed of the fruit of an E Indian tree, used ground or grated as a spice.

nutria *n* **1** the coypu. **2** its fur.

nutrient *n* any nourishing substance. ➢ *adj* nourishing.

nutriment *n* nourishment; food.

nutrition *n* **1** the act or process of nourishing. **2** the study of the body's dietary needs. **3** food. ○ **nutritional** *adj.* ○ **nutritionist** *n.*

nutritious *adj* nourishing; providing nutrition.

nutritive *adj* **1** nourishing. **2** relating to nutrition.

nuts *colloq, adj* insane; crazy.

the nuts and bolts *pl n, colloq* the essential or practical details.

nutshell *n* the case containing the kernel of a nut. ♦ **in a nutshell** concisely or very briefly expressed.

nutty *adj* (*-ier, -iest*) **1** full of, or tasting of, nuts. **2** *colloq* crazy. ○ **nuttiness** *n.*

nuzzle *vb, tr & intr* **1** to push or rub someone or something with the nose. **2** (*usu* **nuzzle up to** or **against sb**) to snuggle up against them.

nylon *n* **1** a polymer that can be formed into fibres, bristles or sheets. **2** a yarn or cloth made of nylon. **3** (**nylons**) nylon stockings.

nymph *n* **1** *myth* a goddess that inhabits mountains, water, trees, etc. **2** *poetic* a beautiful young woman. **3** *zool* the immature larval form of certain insects.

nymphet *n* a sexually attractive and precocious girl in early adolescence.

nympho *n, colloq* a nymphomaniac.

nymphomania *n* in women: overpowering sexual desire. ○ **nymphomaniac** *n, adj.*

Oo

O¹ or **o** *n* (*Oes, O's* or *o's*) **1** the fifteenth letter of the English alphabet. **2** in telephone, etc jargon: zero.

O² *symbol, chem* oxygen.

oaf *n* a stupid, awkward or loutish person. ○ **oafish** *adj.*

oak *n* **1** any tree which produces acorns. **2** the hard durable wood of this tree.

oaken *adj, old use* made of oak wood.

oakum *n* pieces of old untwisted rope, used to

fill small cracks in wooden ships.

OAP *abbrev, Brit* old age pensioner.

oar *n* a long pole with a broad flat blade at one end, used for rowing a boat. ♦ **put** or **stick one's oar in** *colloq* to interfere or meddle.

oasis *n* (*oases*) **1** a fertile area in a desert, where water is found and plants grow. **2** any place or period of rest or calm, etc.

oast *n* a kiln for drying hops.

oat *n* **1** a cereal and type of grass cultivated as a food crop. **2** (**oats**) the grains of this plant, used to make porridge, etc, and for feeding livestock. ♦ **feel one's oats** *chiefly N Am colloq* **1** to feel lively. **2** to feel self-important. **sow one's oats** or **wild oats** *colloq* to indulge in excessive drinking or promiscuity, etc during youth and before settling down.

oatcake *n* a thin dry savoury biscuit made from oatmeal.

oath *n* **1** a solemn promise to tell the truth or to be loyal, etc, usu naming God as a witness. **2** swear-word, obscenity or blasphemy. ♦ **on** or **under oath 1** having sworn to tell the truth, eg in a court of law. **2** attested by oath. **take an oath** to pledge formally.

oatmeal *n* **1** meal ground from oats, used to make oatcakes, etc. **2** the pale brownish-yellow flecked colour of oatmeal.

obbligato or **obligato** /ɒblɪˈgɑːtoʊ/ *mus, n* (**obbligatos** or **obbligati** /-tiː/) an accompaniment that forms an essential part of a piece of music. ➢ *adj* played with an obbligato.

obdurate *adj* **1** hard-hearted. **2** stubborn; difficult to influence or change. ○ **obduracy** *n*. ○ **obdurately** *adv*.

OBE *abbrev, Brit* Officer of the Order of the British Empire.

obedient *adj* obeying; willing to obey. ○ **obedience** *n*. ○ **obediently** *adv*.

obeisance /oʊˈbeɪsəns/ *n* a bow or other expression of obedience or respect. ○ **obeisant** *adj*.

obelisk *n* **1** a tall tapering, usu four-sided, stone pillar with a pyramidal top. **2** an OBELUS.

obelus /ˈɒbələs/ *n* (*pl* **obeli** /-laɪ/) *printing* a dagger-shaped mark (†) used esp for referring to footnotes.

obese /oʊˈbiːs/ *adj* very or abnormally fat. ○ **obesity** *n*.

obey *vb* **1** to do what one is told to do by someone. **2** to carry out (a command). **3** *intr* to do what one is told.

obfuscate *vb* **1** to darken or obscure (something). **2** to make (something) difficult to understand. ○ **obfuscation** *n*. ○ **obfuscatory** *adj*.

obituary *n* (*-ies*) a notice or announcement, esp in a newspaper, of a person's death, often with a short account of their life. ○ **obituarist** *n*.

object /ˈɒbdʒɪkt, ˈɒbdʒɛkt/ *n* **1** a material thing that can be seen or touched. **2** an aim or purpose. **3** a person or thing to which action, feelings or thought are directed: *the object of his affections*. **4** *gram* a noun, noun phrase or pronoun affected by the action of the verb; **b** a noun, noun phrase or pronoun affected by a preposition. Compare SUBJECT (*noun* sense 6). ➢ *vb* /əbˈdʒɛkt/ **1** *intr* (*usu* **object to** or **against sth**) to feel or express dislike or disapproval of it. **2** to state something as a ground for disapproval or objection. ○ **objector** *n*. ♦ **no object** not a difficulty or obstacle: *Money's no object*.

objection *n* **1** the act of objecting. **2** an expression or feeling of disapproval, opposition or dislike, etc.

objectionable *adj* unpleasant; offensive.

objective *adj* **1 a** not depending on, or influenced by, personal opinions or prejudices; **b** relating to external facts, etc as opposed to internal thoughts or feelings. **2** *philos* having existence outside the mind; **b** based on fact or reality. Compare SUBJECTIVE. **3** *gram* of a case or word: **a** indicating the object; **b** in the relation of object to a verb or preposition. ➢ *n* **1** a thing aimed at or wished for; a goal. **2** something independent of or external to the mind. **3** *gram* **a** the objective case; **b** a word or form in that case. ○ **objectively** *adv*. ○ **objectivity** or **objectiveness** *n*.

object lesson *n* an instructive experience or event.

oblate *adj, geom* of something approximately spherical: flattened at the poles, like the Earth. Compare PROLATE.

oblation *n* **1** *Christianity* the offering of the bread and wine to God at a Eucharist. **2** a religious or charitable offering. ○ **oblational** or **oblatory** /ˈɒblətərɪ/ *adj*.

obligate *vb* **1** to bind or oblige (someone) by contract, duty or moral obligation. **2** to bind (someone) by gratitude.

obligation *n* **1** a moral or legal duty or tie. **2** the binding power of such a duty or tie. **3** a debt of gratitude for a service: *be under obligation to her*.

obligatory *adj* **1** legally or morally binding. **2** compulsory.

oblige *vb* **1** to bind (someone) morally or legally; to compel. **2** to bind (someone) by a service or favour. **3** to please or do a favour for (someone): *Please oblige me by leaving at once*. **4** to do something as a favour or contribution for (someone): *She obliged us with a song*.

obliging *adj* ready to help others. ○ **obligingly** *adv*.

oblique /əˈbliːk/ *adj* **1** sloping; not vertical or horizontal. **2** *geom* of lines and planes, etc: not at a right angle. **3** not straight or direct. ➢ *n* **1** an oblique line (/). **2** anything that is oblique. ○ **obliquely** *adv*. ○ **obliqueness** *n*.

obliterate *vb* to destroy (something) completely. ○ **obliteration** *n*.

oblivion *n* **1** the state or fact of having forgotten or of being unconscious. **2** the state of being forgotten.

oblivious *adj* (*usu* **oblivious of** or **to sth**) unaware or forgetful of it. ○ **obliviousness** *n*.

oblong *adj* rectangular with adjacent sides of unequal length. ➢ *n, non-technical* something that has this shape.

obloquy /ˈɒbləkwɪ/ *n* (*-quies*) **1** abuse, blame or censure. **2** disgrace; loss of honour or reputation.

obnoxious *adj* offensive; objectionable. ○ **obnoxiousness** *n*.

oboe *n* (**oboes**) a double-reed treble woodwind instrument with a penetrating tone. ○ **oboist** *n*.

obscene *adj* **1** offensive to accepted standards

of behaviour or morality, esp sexual morality. **2** *colloq* indecent; disgusting. **3** *Brit law* of a publication: tending to cause moral corruption. ○ **obscenely** *adv.* ○ **obscenity** *n* (*-ies*).

obscure *adj* **1** dark; dim. **2** not clear; hidden. **3** not well known. **4** difficult to understand. ➤ *vb* **1** to make (something) dark or dim. **2** to overshadow (something). **3** to make (something) difficult to understand. ○ **obscurity** *n*.

obsequies /'ɒbsəkwɪz/ *pl n* funeral rites.

obsequious /əb'si:kwɪəs/ *adj* submissively obedient. ○ **obsequiously** *adv.* ○ **obsequiousness** *n*.

observance *n* **1** the fact or act of obeying rules or keeping customs, etc. **2** a custom or religious rite observed.

observant *adj* quick to notice.

observation *n* **1 a** the act of noticing or watching; **b** the state of being observed. **2** the ability to observe. **3** a remark or comment. **4** the noting of behaviour, symptoms or phenomena, etc as they occur. ○ **observational** *adj*.

observatory *n* (*-ies*) a room or building specially equipped for making observations of natural phenomena, esp the stars and other celestial objects.

observe *vb* **1** to notice or become conscious of (something). **2** to watch (something) carefully. **3** *tr & intr* to examine and note (behaviour, symptoms or phenomena, etc). **4** to obey, follow or keep (a law, custom or religious rite, etc). **5** *tr & intr* to make (a remark): *She observed that he was late again.* ○ **observable** *adj.* ○ **observer** *n*.

obsess *vb* **1** to occupy (someone's thoughts or mind) completely, persistently or constantly: *She is obsessed by football.* **2** *tr & intr* to think or worry constantly (about something).

obsession *n* **1** a persistent or dominating thought, idea, feeling, etc. **2** *psychol* a recurring thought, feeling or impulse that preoccupies a person against their will and is a source of constant anxiety. **3** the act of obsessing or state of being obsessed. ○ **obsessional** *adj*.

obsessive *adj* **1** relating to or resulting from obsession. **2** of a person: affected by an obsession. ➤ *n* someone affected or characterized by obsessive behaviour.

obsidian *n, geol* a volcanic glass, usu black.

obsolescent *adj* going out of use; becoming out of date. ○ **obsolescence** *n*.

obsolete *adj* no longer in use or in practice.

obstacle *n* someone or something that obstructs or hinders.

obstetrics *sing n* the branch of medicine and surgery that deals with pregnancy, childbirth and the care of the mother. ○ **obstetric** *adj.* ○ **obstetrician** *n*.

obstinate *adj* **1** refusing to change one's opinion or course of action. **2 a** difficult to defeat or remove; **b** esp of a disease or medical condition, etc: difficult to treat. ○ **obstinacy** *n*. ○ **obstinately** *adv.*

obstreperous *adj* noisy and hard to control.

obstruct *vb* **1** to block or close (a passage or opening, etc). **2** to prevent or hinder the movement or progress of (someone or something). **3** to block or impede (a view or line of vision, etc). ○ **obstruction** *n*.

obstructive *adj* causing or designed to cause an obstruction. ○ **obstructively** *adv.* ○ **obstructiveness** *n*.

obtain *vb* **1** to get (something); to become the owner, or come into possession, of (something). **2** *intr* to be established, exist or hold good. ○ **obtainable** *adj*.

obtrude *vb* **1** *intr* to be or become unpleasantly noticeable or prominent. **2** to push (oneself or one's opinions, etc) forward, esp when they are unwelcome. ○ **obtrusion** *n*.

obtrusive *adj* unpleasantly noticeable or prominent. ○ **obtrusiveness** *n*.

obtuse *adj* **1** stupid and slow to understand. **2** *chiefly bot & zool* of eg a leaf or other flat part: rounded at the tip. **3** *geom* of an angle: greater than 90° and less than 180°. Compare ACUTE (*adj* sense 6). ○ **obtuseness** *n*.

obverse *n* **1** the side of a coin with the head or main design on it. **2** an opposite or counterpart, eg of a fact or truth.

obviate *vb* to prevent or remove (a potential difficulty or problem, etc) in advance.

obvious *adj* easily seen or understood. ➤ *n* (**the obvious**) something which is obvious: *to state the obvious.* ○ **obviously** *adv.* ○ **obviousness** *n*.

ocarina *n* a small simple fluty-toned wind instrument that has an egg-shaped body with fingerholes.

occasion *n* **1** a particular event or happening, or the time at which it occurs: *They met on three occasions.* **2** a special event or celebration. **3** a suitable opportunity or chance. **4** a reason; grounds: *You have no occasion to be angry.* ➤ *vb* to cause something. ♦ **on occasion 1** as the need or opportunity arises. **2** from time to time.

occasional *adj* **1** happening irregularly and infrequently. **2** produced on or for a special occasion. ○ **occasionally** *adv.*

Occident *n* (**the Occident**) the countries in the west, esp those in Europe and America regarded as culturally distinct from eastern countries. ○ **Occidental** *adj*.

occipital /ɒk'sɪpɪtəl/ *anat, adj* relating to or in the region of the back of the head. ➤ *n* (*also* **occipital bone**) the bone that forms the back of the skull and part of its base, and encircles the spinal column.

occiput /'ɒksɪpʌt/ *n, anat* the back of the head or skull.

occlude *vb, technical* **1** to block up or cover (an opening or passage). **2** to shut (something) in or out. ○ **occlusion** *n*.

occult *adj* **1** involving, using or dealing with that which is magical, mystical or supernatural. **2** beyond understanding or esoteric. **3** secret, hidden or esoteric. ➤ *n* (**the occult**) the knowledge and study of magical, mystical or supernatural things. ○ **occultism** n.

occupancy n (-ies) **1** the act or condition of occupying (a house or flat, etc), or the fact of its being occupied. **2** the period of time during which a house, etc is occupied.

occupant n someone who occupies or resides in property, or holds a particular position, etc.

occupation n **1** a person's job or profession. **2** an activity that occupies a person's attention or free time, etc. **3** the act of occupying or state of being occupied: *the terrorists' occupation of the embassy.* **4** the act of taking and keeping control of a foreign country by military power. ○ **occupational** adj related to or caused by a person's job.

occupational hazard n a risk or danger accepted as a consequence of the nature or working conditions of a particular job.

occupational therapy n a form of rehabilitation in which patients participate in selected activities that will equip them to function independently in everyday life. ○ **occupational therapist** n.

occupy vb (-ies, -ied) **1** to have possession of or live in (a house, etc). **2** to be in or fill (time or space, etc). **3** to take possession of (a town, foreign country, etc) by force. **4** to enter and take possession of (a building, etc) often by force and without authority. **5** to hold (a post or office). ○ **occupier** n someone who lives in a building.

occur vb (**occurred, occurring**) intr **1** to happen or take place. **2** to be found or exist. **3** (**occur to sb**) to come into their mind, esp unexpectedly or by chance.

occurrence n **1** anything that occurs; an event. **2** the act or fact of occurring.

ocean n **1** the continuous expanse of salt water that covers about 70% of the Earth's surface. **2** any one of its five main divisions: the Atlantic, Indian, Pacific, Arctic and Antarctic. **3** the sea. **4** (*often* **oceans**) a very large number, amount or expanse. ○ **oceanic** adj.

oceanarium n (**oceanariums** or **oceanaria**) orig US a large saltwater aquarium, or an enclosed part of the sea, in which sea creatures are kept for research purposes or for display to the public.

ocean-going adj of a ship, etc: suitable for sailing across oceans.

oceanography n the scientific study of the oceans. ○ **oceanographer** n. ○ **oceanographic** or **oceanographical** adj.

ocelot /ˈɒsəlɒt, ˈoʊ-/ n **1** a medium-sized wild cat, found in Central and S America, that has dark-yellow fur marked with spots and stripes. **2** its fur.

och /ɒx/ exclam, Scot & Irish expressing surprise, impatience, disagreement, annoyance or regret, etc.

oche /ˈɒki/ n, darts the line, groove or ridge on the floor behind which a player must stand to throw.

ochre /ˈoʊkə(r)/ or (*N Am*) **ocher** n **1** a fine earth or clay used as a red, yellow or brown pigment. **2** a pale brownish-yellow colour. ➢ adj pale brownish-yellow in colour.

o'clock adv after a number from one to twelve: used in specifying the time, indicating the number of hours after midday or midnight: *three o'clock.*

OCR abbrev, comput optical character recognition.

oct. abbrev octavo.

octad n a group, series or set of eight things.

octagon n a plane figure with eight straight sides and equal angles. ○ **octagonal** adj.

octahedron or **octohedron** /ɒktəˈhiːdrən/ n (**octahedra** /-drə/ or **octahedrons**) a solid figure with eight plane faces. ○ **octahedral** adj.

octane n, chem a colourless liquid which is present in petroleum.

octave /ˈɒktɪv, ˈɒkteɪv/ n **1** mus **a** the range of sound, or the series of notes, between the first and the eighth notes of a major or minor scale, eg from C to the C above; **b** a musical note that is an eighth above or below another. **2** poetry **a** a verse with eight lines; **b** the first eight lines of a sonnet.

octavo n, printing, publishing **1** a size of book or page produced by folding a standard-sized sheet of paper three times to give eight leaves. **2** a book or page of this size.

octet n **1** any group of eight people or things. **2** mus **a** a group of eight musicians or singers who perform together; **b** a piece of music written for eight instruments or voices.

October n the tenth month of the year.

octogenarian n someone who is 80 years old, or between 80 and 89 years old. ➢ adj **1** between 80 and 89 years old. **2** relating to an octogenarian or octogenarians.

octopus n (**octopuses**) a marine mollusc with a soft rounded body, no external shell, and eight arms with suckers.

octuplet n **1** mus a group of eight notes to be played in the time of six. **2** one of eight children or animals born at one birth.

ocular adj relating to or in the region of the eye.

oculist n a specialist in diseases and defects of the eye.

OD[1] /oʊˈdiː/ slang, n (**ODs** or **OD's**) an overdose of drugs. ➢ vb (**OD's, OD'd, OD'ing**) intr to take a drug overdose.

OD[2] or **O/D** abbrev **1** on demand. **2** overdrawn.

odalisque or **odalisk** /ˈoʊdəlɪsk/ n, hist a female slave or concubine in a harem.

odd adj **1** left over when others are put into groups or pairs. **2** not matching: *odd socks.* **3** not one of a complete set. **4** maths of a whole number: not exactly divisible by two. **5** unusual; strange: *an odd face.* ○ **oddly** adv **1** in an odd way or manner. **2** strangely; surprisingly: *Oddly, he refused to stay.* ○ **oddness** n.
♦ **odd man** or **odd one out** someone that is

set apart or in some way different from others forming a particular group.

oddball *colloq, n* a strange or eccentric person. ➢ *adj* of a thing, a plan or circumstances, etc: eccentric.

oddity *n (-ies)* **1** a strange person or thing. **2** an odd quality or characteristic. **3** the state of being odd or unusual.

odd job *n (usu* **odd jobs)** casual or occasional pieces of work, often routine or domestic.

oddment *n* something left over or remaining from a greater quantity: *oddments of fabric.*

odds *pl n* **1** the chance or probability, expressed as a ratio, that something will or will not happen: *The odds are 10–1 against.* **2** the difference, expressed as a ratio, between the amount placed as a bet and the money which might be won: *offer odds of 2 to 1.* **3** an advantage that is thought to exist, esp in favour of one competitor over another: *The odds are in her favour.* **4** likelihood: *The odds are he'll be late again.* ♦ **against all (the) odds** in spite of great difficulty or disadvantage. **at odds** in disagreement or dispute. **over the odds** more than is normal, required or expected.

odds and ends *pl n, colloq* miscellaneous objects or pieces of things, etc, usu of little value or importance.

odds-on *adj* very likely to succeed, win or happen, etc.

ode *n* a lyric poem with lines of different lengths and complex rhythms, addressed to a particular person or thing.

odious *adj* extremely unpleasant or offensive. ○ **odiously** *adv.* ○ **odiousness** *n.*

odium *n* hatred, strong dislike, or disapproval of a person or thing.

odometer /ɒˈdɒmɪtə, oʊˈdɒmɪtə/ *n, N Am* a device for measuring and displaying the distance travelled by a wheeled vehicle or a person. ○ **odometry** *n.*

odontology *n, anat* the study of the structure, development and diseases of the teeth. ○ **odontologist** *n.*

odoriferous *adj* with or giving off a smell, usu a pleasant smell.

odour or *(N Am)* **odor** *n* a distinctive smell. ○ **odorous** *adj.* ○ **odourless** *adj.*

odyssey /ˈɒdɪsɪ/ *n* a long and adventurous journey or series of wanderings.

oedema or **edema** /ɪˈdiːmə/ *n (oedemata /-mətə/* or *oedemas) pathol* an abnormal accumulation of fluid within body tissues or body cavities, causing swelling.

Oedipus complex /ˈiːdɪpəs/ *n, psychoanal* the repressed sexual desire of a son for his mother. ○ **Oedipal** or **oedipal** *adj.*

oenology /iːˈnɒlədʒɪ/ *n* the study or knowledge of wine. ○ **oenological** *adj.* ○ **oenologist** *n.*

o'er *prep, adv, poetic* or *old use* short form of OVER.

oesophagus /ɪˈsɒfəgəs/ or *(esp N Am)* **esophagus** *n (oesophagi /-gaɪ, -dʒaɪ/) anat* a nar-

row muscular tube through which food passes from the mouth to the stomach. ○ **oesophageal** /-fəˈdʒɪəl/ *adj.*

oestrogen /ˈiːstrədʒən/ or *(N Am)* **estrogen** *n, biochem* a hormone, produced mainly by the ovaries, that controls the growth and functioning of the female sex organs, and that regulates the menstrual cycle.

oestrus /ˈiːstrəs/ or *(N Am)* **estrus** *n, zool, physiol* a regularly occurring period of sexual receptivity that occurs in most female mammals apart from humans. ○ **oestrous** *adj.*

of *prep* **1** used to show origin, cause or authorship: *people of Glasgow • die of hunger.* **2** belonging to or connected with something or someone. **3** used to specify a component, ingredient or characteristic, etc: *built of bricks • a heart of gold.* **4** at a given distance or amount of time from something: *within a minute of arriving.* **5** about; concerning: *tales of Rome.* **6** belonging to or forming a part of something: *most of the story.* **7** existing or happening at, on, in or during something: *Battle of Hastings.* **8** used with words denoting loss, removal or separation, etc: *cured of cancer.* **9** used to show the connection between a verbal noun and the person or thing that is performing, or that is the object of, the action stated: *the eating of healthy food.* **10** aged: *a boy of twelve.* **11** *N Am* in giving the time: to; before a stated hour: *a quarter of one.*

off *adv* **1** away; at or to a distance. **2** in or into a position which is not attached; separate: *The handle came off.* **3** in or into a state of no longer working or operating: *Turn the radio off.* **4** in or into a state of being stopped or cancelled: *The match was rained off.* **5** in or into a state of sleep: *nod off.* **6** to the end, so as to be completely finished: *Finish the work off.* **7** away from work or one's duties: *Take an hour off.* **8** situated as regards money: *well off • badly off.* ➢ *adj* **1** of an electrical device: not functioning or operating; disconnected: *The radio was off.* **2** cancelled: *The meeting's off.* **3** not good; not up to standard: *an off day.* **4** *cricket* on the side of the field towards which the batsman's feet are pointing, usu the bowler's left. **5** in a restaurant, on a menu, etc: no longer available as a choice: *Peas are off.* **6** esp of food or drink: in a state of decay; gone bad or sour: *The milk was off.* ➢ *prep* **1** from or away from something: *Lift it off the shelf.* **2** removed from or no longer attached to something. **3** opening out of, leading from, or not far from something: *a side street off the main road.* **4** not wanting or no longer attracted by something: *off one's food.* **5** no longer using something, etc: *be off the tablets.* ➢ *n* **1** *(usu* **the off)** the start, eg of a race or journey: *ready for the off.* **2** *cricket* the side of a field towards which the batsman's feet are pointing, usu the bowler's left. ♦ **a bit off** *colloq* of behaviour, etc: unacceptable or unfair. **off and on** now and then.

offal *n* the heart, brains, liver and kidneys, etc of an animal, used as food.

offbeat adj, colloq unusual; unconventional.

off-centre adj not quite central.

off-colour adj 1 Brit slightly unwell. 2 chiefly N Am (**off-color**) of humour: rude.

offcut n a small piece of eg wood or cloth, etc cut off or left over from a larger quantity.

offence or (chiefly US) **offense** n 1 a the breaking of a rule or law, etc; b a crime. 2 any cause of anger, annoyance or displeasure. 3 displeasure, annoyance or resentment: I mean no offence. ◆ **give offence** to cause displeasure or annoyance. **take offence at sth** to be offended by it.

offend vb 1 to make (someone) feel hurt or angry. 2 to be unpleasant or annoying to (someone). 3 intr (usu **offend against sb** or **sth**) to commit a sin or crime against them. ○ **offender** n. ○ **offending** adj.

offensive adj 1 giving or likely to give offence. 2 unpleasant, disgusting and repulsive, esp to the senses: an offensive smell. 3 sport, military, etc used for attacking: offensive weapons. ➢ n 1 an aggressive action or attitude: go on the offensive. 2 an attack. ○ **offensively** adv. ○ **offensiveness** n.

offer vb 1 to put forward (a gift, payment or suggestion, etc) for acceptance, refusal or consideration. 2 formal to provide: a site offering the best view. 3 intr to state one's willingness (to do something). 4 to present (something) for sale. 5 to provide (an opportunity) (for something): a job offering rapid promotion. 6 intr to present itself; to occur: if opportunity offers. 7 tr & intr to propose (a sum of money) as payment (to someone): offer him £250 for the car. 8 to present (a prayer or sacrifice) (to God). ➢ n 1 an act of offering. 2 something that is offered, esp an amount of money offered to buy something. **on offer** for sale, esp at a reduced price. **under offer** of a property, etc for sale: for which a possible buyer has made an offer, but with the contracts still to be signed.

offering n 1 the act of making an offer. 2 anything offered, esp a gift. 3 a gift of money given to a church during a religious service, used for charity, etc. 4 a sacrifice made to God, a saint or a deity, etc in the course of worship.

offertory n (**-ies**) Christianity 1 the offering of bread and wine to God during a Eucharist. 2 money collected during a church service.

offhand or **offhanded** adj casual or careless, often with the result of being rude: an offhand manner. ➢ adv impromptu: I can't remember his name offhand. ○ **offhandedness** n.

office n 1 the room, set of rooms or building in which the business of a firm is done, or in which a particular kind of business, clerical work, etc is done. 2 a local centre or department of a large business. 3 a position of authority, esp in the government or in public service: run for office. 4 a the length of time for which an official position is held; b of a political party: the length of time for which it forms the govern-

ment: hold office. 5 (**Office**) a government department: the Home Office. 6 the group of people working in an office. 7 a function or duty. 8 (usu **offices**) an act of kindness or service: through her good offices. 9 (often **Office**) an authorized form of Christian worship or service, esp one for the dead.

officer n 1 someone in a position of authority in the armed forces. 2 someone with an official position in an organization, society or government department. 3 a policeman or policewoman.

official adj 1 relating or belonging to an office or position of authority. 2 given or authorized by a person in authority: an official report. 3 formal; suitable for or characteristic of a person holding office: official dinners. ○ **officially** adv.

officialdom n 1 officials and bureaucrats as a group. 2 excessive devotion to official routine and detail.

officialese n unclear, wordy and pompous language or jargon, thought to be typical of officials or official letters and documents, etc.

officiate vb, intr 1 a to act in an official capacity; b to perform official duties, esp at a particular function. 2 to conduct a religious service.

officious adj too ready to offer help or advice, etc, esp when it is not wanted. ○ **officiousness** n.

offing n, naut the more distant part of the sea that is visible from the shore. ◆ **in the offing** likely to happen soon.

off-key adj, adv 1 mus a in the wrong key; b out of tune. 2 colloq not quite suitable.

off-licence n, Brit a shop, or a counter in a pub or hotel, that is licensed to sell alcohol to be drunk elsewhere.

off-limits adj, esp mil not to be entered. ➢ adv (**off limits**) in or into an area that is out of bounds.

off-line computi, adj 1 not connected to a computer network, esp the Internet. 2 of a peripheral device, eg a printer: not connected to the central processing unit. ➢ adv (**off line**) without a connection to the Internet.

offload vb 1 tr & intr to unload. 2 to get rid of (something, esp something unpleasant or unwanted) by passing it on to someone else.

off-peak adj of services, eg electricity, etc: used at a time when there is little demand, and therefore usu cheaper: off-peak travel.

off-putting adj, colloq 1 disconcerting; distracting. 2 unpleasant; repulsive.

off-road adj 1 of vehicle use: not on public roads; esp on rough ground or terrain. 2 of a car, bike or other vehicle: suitable for such use. ○ **off-roader** n.

off-season n the less popular and less busy period in a particular business or for a particular activity. ➢ adj relating to such a period: off-season reductions.

offset n /ˈɒfset/ 1 a start. 2 a side-shoot on a plant, used for developing new plants. 3 print-

ing a process in which an image is inked on to a rubber roller which then transfers it to paper, etc. ➤ *vb* /ɒfˈsɛt/ **1** to counterbalance or compensate for (something): *price rises offset by tax cuts*. **2** to print (something) using an offset process.

offshoot *n* **1** a shoot growing from a plant's main stem. **2** anything which has developed from something else.

offshore *adv, adj* **1** situated in, at, or on the sea, not far from the coast: *offshore industries*. **2** of the wind: blowing away from the coast. Compare INSHORE.

offside *adj, adv, football, rugby, etc* in an illegal position between the ball and the opponents' goal. Compare ONSIDE. ➤ *n* the side of a vehicle or horse nearest the centre of the road, in the UK the right side.

offspring *n* (*pl* **offspring**) **1** a person's child or children. **2** the young of an animal. **3** a result or outcome.

off-stage *adj, adv, theat* not on the stage and so unable to be seen by the audience.

off-the-peg *adj* of clothing: ready to wear.

off-the-wall *adj, slang* of humour, etc: unorthodox.

often *adv* **1** many times; frequently. **2** in many cases. ♦ **as often as not** in about half the cases. **every so often** sometimes. **more often than not** in most of the cases.

ogle *vb* **1** to look at or eye (someone) in an amorous or lecherous way. **2** to stare at (something).

ogre or **ogress** *n* **1** in fairy stories: a frightening, cruel, ugly giant. **2** a cruel, frightening or ugly person. ○ **ogreish** or **ogrish** *adj*.

oh *exclam* expressing surprise, admiration, pleasure, anger or fear, etc.

ohm *n* the SI unit of electrical resistance.

oil *n* **1** any greasy, viscous and usu flammable substance, insoluble in water, that is derived from animals, plants or mineral deposits, or manufactured artificially. **2** PETROLEUM. **3 a** (*often* **oils**) OIL PAINT; **b** an oil painting. ➤ *vb* to apply oil to (something); to lubricate (something) with oil. ♦ **burn the midnight oil** to work or study late into the night. **oil the wheels** to do something in order to make things go more smoothly or successfully, etc. **pour oil on troubled waters** to calm a person or situation.

oilcloth *n* cloth, often cotton, treated with oil to make it waterproof.

oilfield *n* an area of land or seabed that contains reserves of petroleum.

oil-fired *adj* of central heating, etc: using oil as a fuel.

oil paint *n* paint made by mixing ground pigment with oil.

oilseed rape *n* a plant with vivid yellow flowers, the seed of which contains large amounts of oil and is used in margarine and cooking oils.

oilskin *n* **1** cloth treated with oil to make it waterproof. **2** (*often* **oilskins**) an outer garment made of oilskin.

oily *adj* (**-ier, -iest**) **1 a** like oil; greasy; **b** containing or consisting of oil. **2** soaked in or covered with oil. **3** *derog* of a person or behaviour, etc: servile and flattering. ○ **oiliness** *n*.

oink *n* a representation of the characteristic grunting noise made by a pig.

ointment *n* any greasy or oily semi-solid preparation, usu medicated, that can be applied to the skin in order to heal, soothe or protect it.

OK or **okay** *colloq, adj* all right; satisfactory: *an okay song*. ➤ *adv* well; satisfactorily. ➤ *exclam* expressing agreement or approval; yes: *OK! I'll do it!* ➤ *n* (**OKs, OK's** or **okays**) approval, sanction or agreement. ➤ *vb* (**OK'd** or **OK'ed, OK'ing; okayed, okaying**) to approve or pass (something) as satisfactory.

okapi /oʊˈkɑːpɪ/ *n* (**okapis** or **okapi**) an animal related to the giraffe, but with a shorter neck, and which has a reddish coat, with irregular horizontal black and white stripes on the hindquarters.

okey-doke or **okey-dokey** *adv, adj, exclam, colloq* OK.

okra *n* **1** a tall plant that has red and yellow flowers. **2** the edible fruit of this plant, consisting of long green seed pods.

old *adj* (**older** or **elder, oldest** or **eldest**) **1** advanced in age; that has existed for a long time. **2** having a stated age: *five years old*. **3** belonging or relating to the end period of a long life or existence: *old age*. **4** worn out or shabby through long use: *old shoes*. **5** no longer in use; out of date; old-fashioned. **6** belonging to the past. **7** former or previous; earliest of two or more things: *They went back to see their old house*. **8** of long standing or long existence: *an old member of the society*. **9** with the characteristics, eg experience, maturity or appearance, of age: *be old beyond one's years*. **10** (**Old**) of a language: relating to or denoting its earliest form: *Old English*. **11** *colloq, jocular* used in expressions of familiar affection or contempt, etc: *silly old fool*. ➤ *n* an earlier time: *men of old*.

| **older** | See note at **elder**[1]. |

old age *n* the later part of life.

old age pension *n* a retirement pension. ○ **old age pensioner** *n*.

old boy *n* **1** *Brit* a former male pupil of a school. **2** *colloq* an elderly man. **3** *colloq* an affectionate or familiar form of address to a man.

olden *adj, archaic* former; past: *in olden days*.

Old English see under ANGLO-SAXON.

old-fashioned *adj* **1** belonging to, or in a style common to, some time ago. **2** of a person: in favour of, or living and acting according to, the habits and moral views of the past.

old flame *n, colloq* a former boyfriend or girlfriend.

old girl *n* **1** *Brit* a former female pupil of a school. **2** *colloq* an elderly woman.

old guard *n* the original or most conservative members of a society, group or organization.

old hand *n, colloq* an experienced person.

old hat *adj, colloq* tediously familiar or well known.

oldie *n, colloq* an old person, song or film.

old maid *n, derog, colloq* 1 a woman who is not married and is probably unlikely ever to marry. 2 a woman or man who is prim and fussy.

old man *n, slang* someone's husband or father.

old master *n, art* 1 any of the great European painters from the period stretching from the Renaissance to about 1800. 2 a painting by one of these painters.

old moon *n* the moon in its last quarter, before the NEW MOON.

Old Nick *n, colloq* the devil.

old school *n* a group of people or section of society with traditional or old-fashioned ways of thinking, ideas or beliefs, etc.

Old Testament *n* the first part of the Christian Bible, containing the Hebrew scriptures.

old-time *adj* belonging to or typical of the past.

old-timer *n, colloq* 1 someone who has been in a job, position or profession, etc, for a long time. 2 *US* esp as a form of address: an old man.

old wives' tale *n* an old belief, superstition or theory considered foolish and unscientific.

old woman *n, slang* 1 someone's wife or mother. 2 *derog* a person, esp a man, who is timid or fussy.

old-world *adj* belonging to earlier times, esp in being considered quaint or charming: *old-world charm.*

oleaginous /oʊliˈadʒɪnəs/ *adj* 1 like or containing oil. 2 producing oil. 3 obsequious.

olfactory *adj* relating to the sense of smell.

oligarchy /ˈɒlɪɡɑːkɪ/ *n* (*-ies*) 1 government by a small group of people. 2 a state or organization governed by a small group of people. 3 a small group of people which forms a government. ○ **oligarch** *n*. ○ **oligarchic** or **oligarchical** *adj*.

Oligocene /ˈɒlɪɡoʊsiːn/ *geol, n* the third epoch of the Tertiary period. ➤ *adj* relating to this epoch or rocks formed during it.

oligopoly *n* (*-ies*) *econ* a situation in which there are few sellers of a particular product or service, and a small number of competitive firms control the market.

olive *n* 1 a small evergreen tree cultivated mainly in the Mediterranean region for its fruit and the oil obtained from the fruit. 2 the small green or black oval edible fruit of this tree. 3 the wood of this tree. 4 (*also* **olive green**) a dull yellowish-green colour like that of unripe olives. ➤ *adj* 1 (*also* **olive-green**) dull yellowish-green in colour. 2 of a complexion: sallow.

olive branch *n* a sign or gesture that indicates a wish for peace.

olive oil *n* the pale-yellow oil obtained by pressing ripe olives.

olivine *n, geol* any of a group of hard glassy rock-forming silicate minerals, typically olive-green.

oloroso /ɒlɔˈroʊsoʊ/ *n* a golden-coloured medium-sweet sherry.

Olympiad *n* 1 a celebration of the modern Olympic Games. 2 a regular international contest, esp in chess or bridge.

Olympian *n* 1 someone who competes in the Olympic Games. 2 *Greek myth* any of the twelve ancient Greek gods thought to live on Mount Olympus in N Greece. ➤ *adj* 1 *Greek myth* relating or belonging to Mount Olympus or to the ancient Greek gods thought to live there. 2 godlike, esp in being superior or condescending.

Olympic *adj* 1 relating to the Olympic Games. 2 relating to ancient Olympia.

Olympic Games *sing* or *pl n* 1 *hist* games celebrated every four years at Olympia in Greece, that included athletic, musical and literary competitions. 2 (*also* **the Olympics**) a modern international sports competition held every four years.

ombudsman *n* an official appointed to investigate complaints against public authorities, government departments or the people who work for them.

omega /ˈoʊmɪɡə; *US* oʊˈmiːɡə/ *n* 1 the 24th and last letter of the Greek alphabet. 2 the last of a series.

omelette or (*N Am*) **omelet** *n, cookery* a dish made of beaten eggs fried in a pan.

omen *n* 1 a circumstance, phenomenon, etc that is regarded as a sign of a future event, either good or evil. 2 threatening or prophetic character: *bird of ill omen.*

ominous *adj* threatening; containing a warning of something evil or bad. ○ **ominously** *adv*.

omission *n* 1 something that has been left out or neglected. 2 the act of leaving something out or neglecting it. ○ **omissive** *adj*.

omit *vb* (*omitted, omitting*) 1 to leave (something) out, either by mistake or on purpose. 2 to fail to do (something).

omnibus *n* 1 *old use or formal* a BUS. 2 (*also* **omnibus book** or **omnibus volume**) a book that contains reprints of a number of works by a single author, or several works on the same subject or of a similar type. 3 a TV or radio programme made up of the preceding week's editions of a particular serial.

omnipotent /ɒmˈnɪpətənt/ *adj* 1 of God or a deity: all-powerful. 2 with very great power or influence. ○ **omnipotence** *n*.

omnipresent *adj* esp of a god: present everywhere at the same time. ○ **omnipresence** *n*.

omniscient /ɒmˈnɪsɪənt/ *adj* 1 esp of God: with infinite knowledge or understanding. 2 with very great knowledge. ○ **omniscience** /-sɪəns/ *n*.

omnivore *n* a person or animal that eats any type of food. ○ **omnivorous** *adj*.

on *prep* 1 touching, supported by, attached to, covering, or enclosing: *a chair on the floor* • *a dog on a lead.* 2 in or into (a vehicle, etc): *She got on the bus.* 3 *colloq* carried with (a person):

I've got no money on me. **4** very near to or along the side of something: *a house on the shore.* **5** at or during (a certain day or time, etc): *on Monday.* **6** immediately after, at or before: *He found the letter on his return.* **7** within the (given) limits of something: *a picture on page nine.* **8** about: *a book on Jane Austen.* **9** through contact with or as a result of something: *He cut himself on the broken bottle.* **10** in the state or process of something: *on fire • on a journey.* **11** using as a means of transport: *Claire goes to work on the bus.* **12** using as a means or medium: *talk on the telephone.* **13** having as a basis or source: *on good authority.* **14** working for or being a member of something: *on the committee • work on the case.* **15** at the expense of or to the disadvantage of something or someone: *treatment on the National Health • The drinks are on me.* **16** supported by something: *live on bread and cheese.* **17** regularly taking or using something: *on tranquillizers.* **18** staked as a bet: *put money on a horse.* ➤ *adv* **1** esp of clothes: in or into contact or a state of enclosing, covering or being worn, etc: *with no clothes on.* **2** ahead, forwards or towards in space or time: *later on.* **3** continuously; without interruption: *keep on about something.* **4** in or into operation or activity: *put the radio on.* ➤ *adj* **1** working, broadcasting or performing: *You're on in two minutes.* **2** taking place: *Which films are on this week?* **3** colloq possible, practicable or acceptable: *That just isn't on.* **4** colloq talking continuously, esp to complain or nag: *always on at him to try harder.* **5** in favour of a win: *odds of 3 to 4 on.* **6** cricket on the side of the field towards which the bat is facing, usu the batsman's left and the bowler's right. ♦ **be on to sb** or **sth** colloq **1** to realize their or its importance or intentions. **2** to be in touch with them: *We'll be on to you about the party.* **get on to sb** colloq to get in touch with them. **on and off** now and then. **on and on** continually; at length. **on time** at the right time.

onanism *n* **1** sexual intercourse in which the penis is withdrawn from the vagina before ejaculation. **2** masturbation. ○ **onanist** *n.* ○ **onanistic** *adj.*

once *adv* **1 a** a single time: *I'll say this only once;* **b** on one occasion: *They came once.* **2** multiplied by one. **3** at some time in the past; formerly: *I lived in London once.* **4** by one degree of relationship: *a cousin once removed.* ➤ *conj* as soon as: *Once you have finished you can go out.* ➤ *n* one time or occasion: *just this once.* ♦ **all at once 1** suddenly. **2** all at the same time. **at once 1** immediately. **2** all at the same time. **for once** on this one occasion if on no other; as an exception. **once again** or **once more** one more time, as before. **once (and) for all** for the last time; now and never again. **once in a while** occasionally. **once** or **twice** a few times. **once upon a time** the usual way to begin fairy tales: at an unspecified time in the past.

once-over *n, colloq* a quick, often casual, examination or appraisal: *give the car the once-over.*

oncology *n* the branch of medicine that deals with the study of tumours. ○ **oncologist** *n.*

oncoming *adj* approaching; advancing.

one *n* **1 a** the cardinal number l; **b** the quantity that this represents, being a single unit. **2** a unity or unit. **3** any symbol for this, eg *I* or *l*. **4** the first hour after midnight or midday: *Come at one o'clock • 1pm.* ➤ *adj* **1** being a single unit, number or thing. **2** being a particular person or thing, esp as distinct from another or others of the same kind: *lift one leg and then the other.* **3** being a particular but unspecified instance or example: *visit him one day soon.* **4** being the only such: *the one woman who can beat her.* **5** the same: *of one mind.* **6** forming a single whole: *They sang with one voice.* **7** first: *page one.* **8** colloq an exceptional example of something: *That was one big fellow.* **9** totalling one. ➤ *pron* **1** (often referring to a noun already mentioned or implied) an individual person, thing or instance: *buy the blue one.* **2** anybody: *One can't do better than that.* **3** formal or facetious I; me: *One doesn't like to pry.* ♦ **at one with sb** or **sth 1** in complete agreement with them or it. **2** in harmony with them. **for one as** one person: *I for one don't agree.* **one and all** everyone without exception. **one and only** used for emphasis: only. **one another** used as the object of a verb or preposition when an action takes place between two (or more than two) people, etc: *Chris and Pat love one another.* **one by one** one after the other. **one or two** colloq a few.

one-armed bandit *n* a fruit machine with a long handle at the side which is pulled down hard to make the machine work.

one-horse race *n* a race or competition, etc in which one particular competitor or participant is certain to win.

one-liner *n, colloq* a short amusing remark or joke made in a single sentence.

one-man, **one-woman** or **one-person** *adj* consisting of, for or done by one person: *a one-person tent.*

oneness *n* **1** the state or quality of being one. **2** agreement. **3** the state of being the same. **4** the state of being unique.

one-night stand *n* **1** colloq a sexual encounter that lasts only one night. **2** a performance given only once in any place, the next performance taking place elsewhere.

one-off colloq, chiefly Brit, *adj* made or happening, etc on one occasion only. ➤ *n* something that is one-off.

one-on-one see ONE-TO-ONE

onerous /ˈəʊnərəs, ˈɒnərəs/ *adj* heavy; difficult to do or bear.

oneself or **one's self** *pron* **1** the reflexive form of ONE (pronoun): *not able to help oneself.* **2** the emphatic form of ONE (pronoun): *One hasn't been there oneself.* **3** one's normal self: *not feeling oneself after an operation.*

one-sided *adj* **1** of a competition, etc: with one person or side having a great advantage over the other. **2** seeing, accepting, representing or favouring only one side of a subject or argument, etc. **3** occurring on or limited to one side only.

one-stop *adj* of a shop, etc: able to provide the complete range of goods or services that a customer might require.

one-time *adj* former: *one-time lover.*

one-to-one *adj* **1** with one person or thing exactly corresponding to or matching another. **2** in which a person is involved with only one other person: *one-to-one teaching.* *N Am equivalent* **one-on-one**.

one-track *adj, colloq* of a person's mind: **a** incapable of dealing with more than one subject or activity, etc at a time; **b** obsessed with one idea.

one-upmanship *n, colloq* the art of gaining psychological, social or professional advantages over other people.

one-way *adj* **1 a** of a road or street, etc: on which traffic is allowed to move in one direction only; **b** relating to or indicating such a traffic system: *one-way sign.* **2** of a feeling or relationship: not reciprocated. **3** *N Am* of a ticket: valid for travel in one direction only.

ongoing *adj* in progress.

onion *n* **1** a plant belonging to the lily family. **2** the edible bulb of this plant, which consists of white fleshy scales surrounded by a brown papery outer layer. ○ **oniony** *adj.* ♦ **know one's onions** *colloq* to know one's subject or job well.

online *comput, adj* **1** connected to a computer network, esp the Internet. **2** of a peripheral device, eg a printer: connected to the central processing unit. ➤ *adv* by means of a connection to the Internet.

onlooker *n* someone who watches and does not take part. ○ **onlooking** *adj.*

only *adj* **1** without any others of the same type. **2** of a person: having no brothers or sisters. **3** *colloq* best: *Flying is the only way to travel.* ➤ *adv* **1** not more than; just. **2** alone; solely. **3** not longer ago than; not until: *only a minute ago.* **4** merely; with no other result than: *I arrived only to find he had already left.* ➤ *conj* **1** but; however: *Come if you want to, only don't complain if you're bored.* **2** if it were not for the fact that: *I'd come too, only I know I'd slow you down.* ♦ **if only** I wish. **only too** very; extremely: *only too ready to help.*

o.n.o. *abbrev* or near offer; or nearest offer.

onomatopoeia /ɒnəmatə'pɪə/ *n* the formation of words whose sounds imitate the sound or action they represent, eg *hiss, squelch.* ○ **onomatopoeic** *adj.*

onrush *n* a sudden and strong movement forward.

onscreen *adj, adv* relating to information that is displayed on a TV screen or VDU.

onset *n* **1** an attack. **2** a beginning, esp of something unpleasant.

onshore *adv* /ɒn'ʃɔː(r)/ towards, on, or on to

the shore. ➤ *adj* /'ɒnʃɔː(r)/ found or occurring on the shore or land.

onside *adj, adv, football, rugby, etc* of a player: in a position where the ball may legally be played. Compare OFFSIDE.

onslaught *n* a fierce attack.

on-stage *adj, adv, theat* on the stage and visible to the audience.

onto *prep* on to. ♦ **be onto sb** to be suspicious or aware of their (usu underhand) actions.

ontology *n, philos* the branch of metaphysics that deals with the nature and essence of things or of existence. ○ **ontological** *adj.* ○ **ontologically** *adv.*

onus /'əʊnəs/ *n* a responsibility or burden: *The onus is on you to prove it.*

onward *adj* moving forward in place or time. ➤ *adv* (*also* **onwards**) **1** towards or at a place or time which is advanced or in front. **2** continuing to move forwards or progress.

onyx *n, geol* a very hard variety of agate with alternating bands of colours, used as a gemstone.

oodles *pl n, colloq* lots: *oodles of money.*

ooh *exclam* expressing pleasure, surprise, excitement or pain. ➤ *vb* (*often* **ooh and aah**) to make an ooh sound to show surprise or excitement, etc.

oomph *n, colloq* energy; enthusiasm.

oops *exclam, colloq* expressing surprise or apology, eg when one makes a mistake or drops something, etc.

ooze¹ *vb* **1** *intr* to flow or leak out gently or slowly. **2** *intr* of a substance: to give out moisture. **3** to give out (a liquid, etc) slowly. **4** to overflow with (a quality or feeling): *He oozed charm.* ➤ *n* a slow gentle leaking or oozing. ○ **oozy** *adj.*

ooze² *n* mud, esp the kind found on the beds of rivers or lakes.

op *n, colloq* **1** a surgical operation. **2** a military operation.

opacity /oʊ'pasɪtɪ/ *n* **1** opaqueness. **2** the state of being difficult to understand. **3** dullness.

opal *n, geol* a usu milky-white stone, used as a gemstone.

opalescent *adj* reflecting different colours as the surrounding light changes. ○ **opalescence** *n.*

opaque *adj* **1** not allowing light to pass through. **2** difficult to understand.

open *adj* **1 a** of a door or barrier, etc: not closed or locked; **b** of a building or an enclosed space, etc: allowing people or things to go in or out. **2** of a container, etc: **a** not sealed or covered; **b** with the insides visible: *an open cupboard.* **3** of a space or area of land, etc: not enclosed, confined or restricted: *the open sea.* **4** not covered, guarded or protected: *an open wound.* **5** expanded, spread out or unfolded: *an open newspaper.* **6** of a shop, etc: ready for business. **7** *mus* **a** of a string: not stopped by a finger; **b** of a note: played on an open string, or without holes on the instrument being covered. **8** generally known; public. **9** (*usu* **open to sth**) liable or susceptible to it; defenceless against it: *leave oneself open to abuse*. **10** of a competition: not restricted; allowing anyone to compete or take part. **11** free from restraint or restrictions of any kind: *the open fishing season* • *an open marriage* • *the open market*. **12** unprejudiced: *have an open mind*. **13** (*usu* **open to**) amenable to or ready to receive (eg new ideas or impressions): *open to suggestion*. **14** of a person: ready and willing to talk honestly. ➤ *vb* **1 a** to unfasten or move (eg a door or barrier) to allow access; **b** *intr* of a door or barrier, etc: to become unfastened to allow access. **2** *tr & intr* to become or make (something) become open or more open, eg by removing obstructions, etc. **3** (*also* **open out**) *tr & intr* to spread (something) out or become spread out or unfolded, esp so as to make or become visible. **4** *tr & intr* to start or begin working: *The office opens at nine*. **5** to declare (something) open with an official ceremony: *open the new hospital*. **6** *tr & intr* to begin (something) or start speaking or writing, etc: *He opened his talk with a joke*. **7** to arrange (a bank account, etc), usu by making an initial deposit. **8** *tr & intr, cricket* to begin (the batting) for one's team. ➤ *n* **1** (**the open**) an area of open country; an area not obstructed by buildings, etc. **2** (**the open**) public notice or attention (*esp* **bring something into the open** or **out into the open**). **3** (**Open**) *often in compounds* a sports contest which both amateurs and professionals may enter: *the British Open*. ○ **openly** *adv.* ○ **openness** *n.* ♦ **open fire** to start shooting. **with open arms** warmly: *We welcomed him with open arms*. ◊ **open up 1** to open a shop for the day. **2** to start firing. **3** to begin to reveal one's feelings and thoughts or to behave with less restraint.

open air *n* unenclosed space outdoors. ➤ *adj* (**open-air**) in the open air: *open-air theatre*.

open-and-shut *adj* easily proved, decided or solved: *an open-and-shut case*.

open book *n* someone who keeps no secrets and is easily understood.

opencast *adj, mining* using or relating to a method in which the substance to be mined is exposed by removing the overlying layers of material, without the need for shafts or tunnels.

open day *n* a day when members of the public can visit an institution (eg a school) usu closed to them.

open-ended *adj* **1** with an open end or ends. **2** of a question or debate, etc: not limited to strictly 'yes' or 'no' answers.

opener *n* **1** *often in compounds* a device for opening something: *a bottle-opener* • *a tin-opener*. **2** *cricket* either of the two batsmen who begins the batting for their team. **3** an opening remark, etc.

open-eyed *adj* **1** with the eyes wide open, eg in surprise or amazement. **2** fully aware.

open-handed *adj* generous.

open-hearted *adj* **1** honest, frank and hiding nothing. **2** kind; generous.

open-heart surgery *n* surgery performed on a heart that has been stopped while the blood circulation is maintained by a heart-lung machine.

open house *n* the state of being willing to welcome and entertain visitors at any time.

opening *n* **1** the act of making or becoming open. **2** a hole or gap, esp one that can serve as a passageway. **3** a beginning or first stage of something. **4** *theat* the first performance of a play or opera, etc. **5** an opportunity or chance. **6** a vacancy. **7** *chiefly US* an area of ground in a forest, etc in which there are very few or no trees. ➤ *adj* relating to or forming an opening; first: *opening night at the opera* • *opening batsman*.

open letter *n* a letter, esp one of protest, addressed to a particular person or organization but intended to be published in a newspaper or magazine.

open-minded *adj* willing to consider or receive new ideas. ○ **open-mindedness** *n.*

open-plan *adj* of a building or office, etc: with few internal walls and with large undivided rooms.

open prison *n* a prison which allows prisoners who are considered to be neither dangerous nor violent greater freedom of movement than in normal prisons.

open question *n* a matter that is undecided.

open secret *n* something that is supposedly a secret but that is in fact widely known.

opera[1] *n* **1** a dramatic work set to music, in which the singers are usu accompanied by an orchestra. **2** operas as an art-form. **3** a company that performs opera. ○ **operatic** *adj* **1** relating to or like opera. **2** dramatic or overly theatrical. ○ **operatically** *adv.*

opera[2] *pl of* OPUS

opera glasses *pl n* small binoculars used at the theatre or opera, etc.

operand *n, maths, logic* a quantity on which an OPERATION (sense 7) is performed.

operate *vb* **1** *intr* to function or work. **2** to make (a machine, etc) function or work; to control the functioning of (something). **3** to manage, control or direct (a business, etc). **4** (*usu* **operate on sb**) *intr* to perform a surgical operation on them. **5** *intr* to perform military, naval or police, etc operations. ○ **operable** *adj* **1** *med* of a disease or injury, etc: that can be treated by surgery. **2** that can be operated.

operating system *n, comput* a software system that controls all the main activities of a computer.

operating theatre or **operating room** *n* the specially equipped room in a hospital, etc where surgical operations are performed.

operation *n* **1** an act, method or process of working or operating. **2** the state of working or being active: *The factory is not yet in operation*. **3** an activity; something done. **4** an action or series of actions which have a particular effect. **5** *med* any surgical procedure that is performed in order to treat a damaged or diseased part of the body. **6** (*often* **operations**) one of a series of military, naval or police, etc actions performed as part of a much larger plan. **7** *maths* a specific procedure, such as addition or multiplication, whereby one numerical value is derived from another value or values. **8** *comput* a series of actions that are specified by a single computer instruction.

operational *adj* **1** relating to an operation or operations. **2** able or ready to work or perform an intended function.

operative *adj* **1** working; in action; having an effect. **2** of a word: esp important or significant: *'Must' is the operative word.* **3** relating to a surgical operation. ➤ *n* **1** a worker, esp one with special skills. **2** *N Am* a private detective.

operator *n* **1** someone who operates a machine or apparatus. **2** someone who operates a telephone switchboard. **3** someone who runs a business. **4** *maths* any symbol used to indicate that a particular mathematical operation is to be carried out, eg ×, which shows that two numbers are to be multiplied. **5** *colloq* a calculating, shrewd and manipulative person.

operetta *n* a short light opera, with spoken dialogue and often dancing.

ophthalmic *adj* pertaining or relating to the eye.

ophthalmic optician *n* an optician qualified both to examine the eyes and test vision, and to prescribe, make and sell glasses or contact lenses.

ophthalmology *n, med* the study, diagnosis and treatment of diseases and defects of the eye. ○ **ophthalmologist** *n*.

opiate /ˈəʊpɪət/ *n* **1** a drug containing or derived from opium that depresses the central nervous system. **2** anything that dulls physical or mental sensation.

opine *vb, formal* to suppose or express (something) as an opinion.

opinion *n* **1** a belief or judgement which seems likely to be true, but which is not based on proof. **2** (*usu* **opinion on** or **about sth**) what one thinks about it. **3** a professional judgement given by an expert: *medical opinion.* **4** estimation or appreciation: *Joe has a high opinion of himself.* ♦ **a matter of opinion** a matter about which people have different opinions.

opinionated *adj* with very strong opinions that one is very unwilling to change.

opinion poll see under POLL

opium *n* a highly addictive narcotic drug extracted from the seed capsules of the **opium poppy**, used in medicine to bring sleep and relieve pain.

opossum *n* (**opossums** or **opossum**) **1** a small tree-dwelling American marsupial with thick fur and a hairless prehensile tail. **2** any similar marsupial, native to Australasia.

opponent *n* someone who belongs to the op-

posing side in an argument, contest or battle, etc.

opportune *adj* **1** of an action: happening at a time which is suitable, proper or correct. **2** of a time: suitable; proper.

opportunist *n* someone whose actions and opinions are governed by the particular events and circumstances, etc of the moment rather than being based on settled principles. ➤ *adj* referring to such actions or opinions. ○ **opportunism** *n*. ○ **opportunistic** *adj*.

opportunity *n* (*-ies*) **1** an occasion offering a possibility. **2** favourable or advantageous conditions.

opposable *adj* of a digit, esp the thumb: able to be placed in a position so that it faces and can touch the ends of the other digits of the same hand or foot. ○ **opposability** *n*.

oppose *vb* **1** to resist or fight against (someone or something) by force or argument. **2** *intr* to compete in a game or contest, etc against another person or team. ○ **opposer** *n*. ○ **opposing** *adj*. ♦ **as opposed to** in contrast to.

opposite *adj* **1** placed or being on the other side of, or at the other end of, a real or imaginary line or space. **2** facing in a directly different direction: *opposite sides of the coin.* **3** completely or diametrically different. **4** referring to something that is the other of a matching or contrasting pair: *the opposite sex.* **5** *maths* of a side of a triangle: facing a specified angle. ➤ *n* an opposite person or thing. ➤ *adv* in or into an opposite position: *live opposite.* ➤ *prep* **1** (*also* **opposite to sb** or **sth**) in a position across from and facing them or it: *a house opposite the station.* **2** of an actor: in a role which complements that taken by another actor: *He played opposite Olivier.*

opposite number *n* someone with an equivalent position or job in another company or country, etc.

opposition *n* **1** the act of fighting against someone or something by force or argument. **2** the state of being hostile or in conflict. **3** a person or group of people who are opposed to something. **4** (*usu* **the Opposition**) a political party which opposes the party in power. **5** *astron, astrol* the position of a planet or star when it is directly opposite another, esp the Sun, as seen from the Earth.

oppress *vb* **1** to govern with cruelty and injustice. **2** to worry, trouble or make (someone) anxious. **3** to distress or afflict (someone). ○ **oppression** *n*. ○ **oppressor** *n*.

oppressive *adj* **1** cruel, tyrannical and unjust: *an oppressive regime.* **2** causing worry or mental distress. **3** of the weather: heavy, hot and sultry. ○ **oppressiveness** *n*.

opprobrium *n* (*pl* in sense 2 **opprobria**) **1** public shame, disgrace or loss of favour. **2** anything that brings such shame or disgrace, etc. ○ **opprobrious** *adj*.

oppugn /əˈpjuːn/ *vb* to call into question.

opt *vb, intr* (*usu* **opt for sth** or **to do sth**) to decide between several possibilities. ◊ **opt in** to choose to take part or participate in something. **opt out** 1 to choose not to take part in something. 2 of a school or hospital: to leave local authority control and become, respectively, a grant-maintained school or a hospital trust.

optic *adj* relating to the eye or vision.

optical *adj* 1 relating to sight or to what one sees. 2 relating to light or optics. 3 of a lens: designed to improve vision. ○ **optically** *adv.*

optical character recognition *n, comput* the scanning, identification and recording of printed characters by a photoelectric device attached to a computer.

optical fibre *n, telecomm* a thin flexible strand of glass used to convey information, eg in the cables for telephones, cable TV, etc.

optical illusion *n* 1 something that has an appearance which deceives the eye. 2 a misunderstanding caused by such a deceptive appearance.

optician *n* 1 (*also* **dispensing optician**) someone who fits and sells glasses and contact lenses but is not qualified to prescribe them. 2 *loosely* an OPHTHALMIC OPTICIAN.

optic nerve *n, anat* in vertebrates: a cranial nerve, responsible for the sense of vision, which transmits information from the retina of the eye to the visual cortex of the brain.

optics *sing n, physics* the study of light and its practical applications.

optimal *adj* most favourable.

optimism *n* 1 the tendency to take a bright, hopeful view of things and expect the best possible outcome. 2 the theory that good will ultimately triumph over evil. Compare PESSIMISM. ○ **optimist** *n.* ○ **optimistic** *adj.* ○ **optimistically** *adv.*

optimize or **-ise** *vb* 1 to make the most or best of (a particular situation or opportunity, etc). 2 *comput* to prepare or modify (a computer system or program) so as to achieve the greatest possible efficiency. ○ **optimization** *n.*

optimum *n* (**optimums** or **optima**) the condition, situation, amount or level, etc that is the most favourable or gives the best results. ➤ *adj* best or most favourable.

option *n* 1 an act of choosing. 2 that which is or which may be chosen. 3 the power or right to choose: *You have no option.* 4 *commerce* the exclusive right to buy or sell something, eg stocks, at a fixed price and within a specified time-limit. ➤ *vb, chiefly US* 1 to buy or sell (something) under option. 2 to have or grant an option on (something). ◆ **keep** or **leave one's options open** to avoid making a choice or committing oneself to a particular course of action. **soft option** the easiest choice or course of action.

optional *adj* left to choice; not compulsory.

optional extra *n* an available accessory, that is useful or desirable, but not essential.

opt-out *n* 1 a the action or an act of opting out of something; b of a school or hospital: the act of leaving local authority control. 2 *TV, radio* a programme broadcast by a regional station in place of the main network transmission.

opulent *adj* 1 rich. 2 abundant. ○ **opulence** *n.* ○ **opulently** *adv.*

opus *n* (**opuses** or **opera**) an artistic work, esp a musical composition, often used with a number to show the order in which a composer's works were written or catalogued.

or *conj* used to introduce: 1 alternatives: *red or pink.* 2 a synonym or explanation: *a puppy or young dog.* 3 the second part of an indirect question: *Ask her whether she thinks he'll come or not.* 4 because if not: *Run or you'll be late.* ◆ **or else** 1 otherwise. 2 *colloq* expressing a threat or warning: *Give it to me or else!* **or so** about: *I'd been there two hours or so.*

oracle *n* 1 in ancient Greece or Rome: a holy place where a god was believed to give advice and prophecy. 2 a priest or priestess at an oracle, through whom the god was believed to speak. 3 someone who is believed to have great wisdom or be capable of prophesying the future.

oral *adj* 1 spoken. 2 relating to or used in the mouth. 3 of a medicine or drug, etc: taken in through the mouth: *oral contraceptive.* ➤ *n* a spoken test or examination. ○ **orally** *adv.*

oral A word often confused with this one is **aural**.

orange *n* 1 a round citrus fruit with a tough reddish-yellow outer peel filled with juicy flesh. 2 the evergreen tree that bears this fruit. 3 a reddish-yellow colour like that of the skin of an orange. 4 an orange-flavoured drink. ➤ *adj* 1 orange-coloured. 2 orange-flavoured. ○ **orangey** *adj.*

orangery *n* (**-ies**) a greenhouse or other building in which orange trees can be grown in cool climates.

orang-utan or **orang-outang** *n* a large tree-dwelling ape with long reddish hair and long strong arms.

oration *n* a formal or ceremonial public speech delivered in dignified language.

orator /ˈɒrətə(r)/ *n* someone who is skilled in persuading, moving or exciting people through public speech.

oratorio /ɒrəˈtɔːrɪəʊ/ *n* a musical composition, usu based on a religious theme, sung by soloists and a chorus accompanied by an orchestra.

oratory[1] /ˈɒrətərɪ/ *n* (**-ies**) a small place set aside for private prayer.

oratory[2] /ˈɒrətərɪ/ *n* 1 the art of public speaking. 2 rhetorical style or language.

orb *n* 1 a globe with a cross on top that is decorated with jewels and is carried as part of a monarch's regalia. 2 anything in the shape of a globe or sphere.

orbit *n* 1 *astron* in space: the elliptical path of

one celestial body around another or of an artificial satellite, spacecraft, etc around a celestial body. **2** a sphere of influence or action. **3** *anat* in the skull of vertebrates: one of the two bony hollows in which the eyeball is situated. ➤ *vb* **1** of a celestial body, or a spacecraft, etc: to circle (the Earth or another planet, etc) in space. **2** to put (a spacecraft, etc) into orbit. ○ **orbiter** *n* a spacecraft or satellite that orbits the Earth or another planet but does not land on it.

orbital *adj* **1** relating to or going round in an orbit. **2** of a road: forming a circle or loop round a city.

orchard *n* a garden or piece of land where fruit trees are grown.

orchestra *n* **1** a large group of instrumentalists who play together. **2** (*also* **orchestra pit**) the part of a theatre where the musicians sit, usu in front of, or under the front part of, the stage. ○ **orchestral** *adj*.

orchestrate *vb* **1** to arrange, compose or score (a piece of music) for an orchestra. **2** to organize or arrange (elements of a plan, etc) so as to get the desired or best result. ○ **orchestration** *n*. ○ **orchestrator** *n*.

orchid *n* a plant which is best known for its complex and exotic flowers.

ordain *vb* **1** *Christianity* to appoint or admit (someone) as priest or vicar, etc. **2** to order, command or decree (something) formally. ○ **ordainment** *n*.

ordeal *n* **1** a difficult, painful or testing experience. **2** *hist* a method of trial in which the accused person was subjected to physical danger, survival of which was taken as a sign from God of the person's innocence.

order *n* **1** a state in which everything is in its proper place. **2** an arrangement of objects according to importance, value or position, etc. **3** a command, instruction or direction. **4** a state of peace and harmony in society, characterized by the absence of crime and the general obeying of laws. **5** the condition of being able to function properly: *in working order*. **6** a social class or rank making up a distinct social group: *the lower orders*. **7** a kind or sort: *of the highest order*. **8** an instruction to a manufacturer, supplier or waiter, etc to provide something. **9** the goods or food, etc supplied. **10** an established system of society: *a new world order*. **11** *biol* in taxonomy: any of the groups into which a CLASS (*noun* sense 9) is divided, and which is in turn subdivided into one or more families (see FAMILY *noun* sense 7). **12** *commerce* a written instruction to pay money. **13** the usual procedure followed at esp official meetings and during debates: *a point of order*. **14** (**Order**) a religious community living according to a particular rule and bound by vows. **15** any of the different grades of the Christian ministry. **16** (**orders**) HOLY ORDERS. **17** the specified form of a religious service: *order of marriage*. **18** (**Order**) a group of people to which new members are admitted as a mark of honour or reward for services to the sovereign or country: *Order of the British Empire*. **19** any of the five classical styles of architecture (Doric, Ionic, Corinthian, Tuscan and Composite). **20** any of the nine ranks of angel (seraph, cherub, dominion, virtue, power, principality, throne, archangel, angel). ➤ *vb* **1** to give a command to (someone). **2** to command (someone) to go to a specified place: *order the regiment to Germany*. **3** to instruct a manufacturer, supplier or waiter, etc to supply or provide (something): *I ordered the fish*. **4** to arrange or regulate: *order one's affairs*. **5** *intr* to give a command, request or order, esp to a waiter for food: *ready to order*. ◆ **a tall order** *colloq* a difficult or demanding job or task. **in order 1** in accordance with the rules; properly arranged. **2** suitable or appropriate: *Her conduct just isn't in order*. **3** in the correct sequence. **in order that** so that. **in order to do sth** so as to be able to do it. **in the order of** approximately (the number specified). **on order** of goods: having been ordered but not yet supplied. **out of order 1** of a machine, etc: not working. **2** not correct, proper or suitable. **to order** according to a customer's particular requirements. **under orders** having been commanded or instructed (to do something). ◇ **order sb about** *or* **around** to give them orders continually and officiously.

orderly *adj* **1** in good order; well arranged. **2** well behaved. ➤ *n* (*-ies*) **1** an attendant, usu without medical training, who does various jobs in a hospital, such as moving patients. **2** *mil* a soldier who carries an officer's orders and messages. ○ **orderliness** *n*.

ordinal *n*, *RC Church* a service book.

ordinal number *n* a number which shows a position in a sequence, eg *first*, *second*, *third*, etc. Compare CARDINAL NUMBER.

ordinance *n* a law, order or ruling.

ordinary *adj* **1** of the usual everyday kind. **2** plain; uninteresting. ➤ *n* (*-ies*) **1** *law* a judge of ecclesiastical or other causes who acts in his own right, such as a bishop or his deputy. **2** (**Ordinary**) *RC Church* those parts of the Mass which do not vary from day to day. **3** *heraldry* a simple type of armorial charge. ○ **ordinarily** *adv* usually; normally. ◆ **out of the ordinary** unusual.

ordinary seaman *n* a sailor of the lowest rank in the Royal Navy.

ordinate *n*, *maths* on a graph: the second of a pair of numbers x and y, known as the y-coordinate, which specifies the distance of a point from the horizontal or x-axis. Compare ABSCISSA.

ordination *n* the act or ceremony of ordaining a priest or minister of the church.

ordnance *n* **1** heavy guns and military supplies. **2** the government department responsible for military supplies.

Ordovician /ɔːdəʊˈvɪʃən/ *adj, geol* relating to the second period of the Palaeozoic era.

ordure *n* waste matter from the bowels.

ore *n*, *geol* a solid naturally occurring mineral deposit from which one or more economically valuable substances can be extracted.

oregano /ɒrɪˈɡɑːnoʊ; *US* əˈrɛɡənoʊ/ *n* a sweet-smelling herb, used as a flavouring in cooking.

organ *n* **1** a part of a body or plant which has a special function, eg a kidney. **2** a musical instrument with a keyboard and pedals, in which sound is produced by air being forced through pipes of different lengths. **3** any similar instrument without pipes, such as one producing sound electronically. **4** a means of spreading information, esp a newspaper or journal of a particular group or organization, etc.

organdie or **organdy** *n* a very fine stiffened cotton fabric.

organic *adj* **1** *biol* relating to, derived from, or with the characteristics of a living organism. **2** *agric* **a** relating to farming practices that avoid the use of synthetic fertilizers and pesticides, etc; **b** relating to food produced in this way. **3** being or formed as an inherent or natural part. **4** systematically organized. ○ **organically** *adv*.

organism *n* **1** any living structure, such as a plant, animal, fungus or bacterium. **2** any establishment, system or whole made up of parts that depend on each other.

organist *n* a person who plays an organ.

organize or **-ise** *vb* **1** to give an orderly structure to (something): *Adam organized the books into a neat pile.* **2** to arrange, provide or prepare (something): *Val organized the tickets.* **3** to form or enrol (people or a person) into a society or organization. **4** *intr* to form a society or organization, esp a trade union. ○ **organization** *n*. ○ **organizer** *n*.

organza *n* a very fine stiff dress material made of silk or synthetic fibres.

orgasm *n* the climax of sexual excitement. ○ **orgasmic** *adj*.

orgy *n* (*-ies*) **1** a wild party involving indiscriminate sexual activity and excessive drinking. **2** any act of excessive or frenzied indulgence: *an orgy of shopping.*

oriel *n* **1** a small room or recess with a polygonal bay window. **2** (*also* **oriel window**) the window of an oriel.

orient *n* (**the Orient**) the countries in the east, esp those of E Asia regarded as culturally distinct from western countries. ➤ *vb* **1** to place (something) in a definite position in relation to the points of the compass or some other fixed or known point. **2** to acquaint (oneself or someone) with one's position or their position relative to points known, or relative to the details of a situation.

oriental *adj* (*also* **Oriental**) from or relating to the Orient; eastern. ➤ *n* (*usu* **Oriental**) *often offensive* a person born in the Orient; an Asiatic.

orientate *vb* to orient. ○ **orientation** *n*.

orienteering *n* a sport in which contestants race on foot over an unfamiliar cross-country course, finding their way to official check points using a map and compass. ○ **orienteer** *vb*.

orifice /ˈɒrɪfɪs/ *n* a usu small opening or hole, esp one in the body.

origami *n* the Japanese art of folding paper into decorative shapes.

origin *n* **1** a beginning or starting-point. **2** (*usu* **origins**) a person's family background or ancestry. **3** *maths* in coordinate geometry: the point on a graph where the horizontal x-axis and the vertical y-axis cross each other, having a value of zero on both axes.

original *adj* **1** relating to an origin or beginning. **2** existing from the beginning; first. **3** of an idea or concept, etc: not thought of before; fresh. **4** of a person: creative or inventive. **5** being the first form from which copies, reproductions or translations are made; not copied or derived, etc from something else. ➤ *n* **1** the first example of something, such as a document, photograph or text, etc, which is copied, reproduced or translated to produce others. **2** a work of art or literature that is not a copy or imitation. ○ **originality** *n*. ○ **originally** *adv*.

original sin *n*, *Christianity* the supposed innate sinfulness of the human race, inherited from Adam, who disobeyed God.

originate *vb*, *tr & intr* to bring or come into being; to start. ○ **origination** *n*. ○ **originator** *n*.

oriole *n* a songbird with bright yellow and black plumage.

ormolu /ˈɔːməluː/ *n* a gold-coloured alloy that is used to decorate furniture, make ornaments, etc.

ornament *n* /ˈɔːnəmənt/ **1** something that decorates or adds grace or beauty to a person or thing. **2** embellishment or decoration. **3** a small, usu decorative object. **4** someone whose talents add honour to the group or company, etc to which they belong. **5** *mus* a note or notes that embellish the melody but do not belong to it, eg a trill. ➤ *vb* /-ment/ to decorate (something) with ornaments or serve as an ornament to (something). ○ **ornamental** *adj*. ○ **ornamentation** *n*.

ornate *adj* **1** highly or excessively decorated. **2** of language: using many elaborate words or expressions. ○ **ornately** *adv*.

ornithology *n* the scientific study of birds and their behaviour. ○ **ornithological** *adj*. ○ **ornithologist** *n*.

orotund *adj* **1** of the voice: full, loud and grand. **2** of speech or writing: boastful or self-important. ○ **orotundity** *n*.

orphan *n* a child who has lost both parents. ➤ *vb*, *usu in passive* to make (a child) an orphan.

orphanage *n* a home for orphans.

orrery *n* (*-ies*) a clockwork model of the Sun and the planets which revolve around it.

orris *n* **1** an iris which has white flowers and fragrant rhizomes. **2** (*also* **orrisroot**) the dried sweet-smelling rhizome of this plant, used in perfumes.

orthodontics *sing n, dentistry* the branch of dentistry concerned with the prevention and correction of irregularities in the alignment of the teeth or jaws. ○ **orthodontist** *n.*

orthodox *adj* **1** believing in, living according to, or conforming with established or generally accepted opinions. **2** (*usu* **Orthodox**) belonging or relating to a group of Christian churches that recognize the primacy of the Patriarch of Constantinople. **3** (*usu* **Orthodox**) belonging or relating to the branch of Judaism which keeps to strict traditional interpretations of doctrine and scripture.

orthography *n* (*-ies*) **1** correct or standard spelling. **2** a particular system of spelling. **3** the study of spelling. ○ **orthographer** or **orthographist** *n.*

orthopaedics or (*US*) **orthopedics** /ɔːθə-ˈpiːdɪks/ *sing n, med* the correction of deformities arising from injury or disease of the bones and joints. ○ **orthopaedic** *adj.* ○ **orthopaedist** *n.*

oryx *n* (**oryxes** or **oryx**) any large grazing antelope typically with very long slender horns.

OS *abbrev* **1** *comput* operating system. **2** outsize.

Os *symbol, chem* osmium.

oscillate /ˈɒsɪleɪt/ *vb* **1** *tr & intr* to swing or make (something) swing backwards and forwards like a pendulum. **2** *tr & intr* to vibrate. **3** *intr* to waver between opinions, choices, courses of action, etc. **4** *intr, electronics* of an electrical current: to vary regularly in strength or direction between certain limits. ○ **oscillation** *n.* ○ **oscillator** *n.*

oscilloscope /əˈsɪləskoʊp/ *n* a device that measures the changing values of an oscillating electrical current and displays the varying electrical signals graphically on the fluorescent screen of a cathode-ray tube.

osier /ˈoʊzɪə(r)/ *n* **1** a species of willow tree. **2** a flexible branch or twig from this tree.

osmium *n, chem* a very hard dense bluish-white metal, the densest known element.

osmosis *n* **1** *chem* the movement of a solvent, eg water, across a semipermeable membrane from a more dilute solution to a more concentrated one. **2** a gradual, usu unconscious, process of assimilation of ideas or knowledge, etc. ○ **osmotic** *adj.*

osprey *n* a large fish-eating bird of prey, with a dark-brown body, white head and legs.

osseous *adj* relating to, like, containing, or formed from bone.

ossify *vb* (*-ies, -ied*) **1** *tr & intr* to turn into or make (something) turn into bone. **2** *intr* of one's opinions or habits, etc: to become rigid, fixed or inflexible. ○ **ossification** *n.*

ostensible *adj* of reasons, etc: stated or claimed, but not necessarily true. ○ **ostensibly** *adv.*

ostensive *adj* **1** *logic* directly or manifestly demonstrative. **2** of a definition: giving examples of things to which the defined word properly applies. ○ **ostensively** *adv.*

ostentation *n* pretentious display of wealth, knowledge, etc. ○ **ostentatious** *adj.* ○ **ostentatiously** *adv.*

osteoarthritis *n, pathol* a chronic disease of bones, in which degeneration of the cartilage at a joint leads to deformity of the bone surface, causing pain and stiffness. ○ **osteoarthritic** *adj.*

osteology /ɒstɪˈɒlədʒɪ/ *n* **1** the branch of human anatomy that deals with the study of bones and the skeleton. **2** (*-ies*) the structure and arrangement of an animal's bones. ○ **osteological** *adj.* ○ **osteologist** *n.*

osteopathy /ɒstɪˈɒpəθɪ/ *n, med* a system of healing or treatment, mainly involving manipulation of the bones and joints and massage of the muscles, that provides relief for many bone and joint disorders. ○ **osteopath** *n.*

osteoporosis /ɒstɪoʊpəˈroʊsɪs/ *n, pathol* a disease in which the bones become porous, brittle and liable to fracture, owing to loss of calcium.

ostinato *adj, mus* frequently repeated.

ostler /ˈɒslə(r)/ *n, hist* someone who attends to horses at an inn.

ostracize or **-ise** *vb* to exclude (someone) from a group or society, etc. ○ **ostracism** *n.*

ostrich *n* (**ostriches** or **ostrich**) **1** the largest living bird, native to Africa, having an extremely long neck and legs, and only two toes on each foot. **2** *colloq* someone who refuses to face or accept unpleasant facts.

OT *abbrev* Old Testament.

other *adj* **1** remaining from a group of two or more when one or some have been specified already: *Now close the other eye.* **2** different from the one or ones already mentioned, understood or implied: *other people.* **3** additional: *I need to buy one other thing.* **4** far or opposite: *the other side of the world.* ➣ *pron* **1 a** another person or thing; **b** (**others**) other people or things. **2** (**others**) further or additional ones: *I'd like to see some others.* **3** (*usu* **the others**) the remaining people or things of a group: *Go with the others.* ➣ *adv* (*usu* **other than**) otherwise; differently: *He couldn't do other than hurry home.* ○ **otherness** *n.* ♦ **every other** each alternate: *We see him every other week.* **in other words** this means: *In other words, you won't do it?* **other than ... 1** except ...; apart from ...: *Other than that, there's no news.* **2** different from ...: *do something other than watch TV.* **the other day** or **week**, *etc* a few days or weeks, etc ago.

otherwise *conj* or else; if not. ➣ *adv* **1** in other respects: *He is good at languages but is otherwise not very bright.* **2** in a different way: *She couldn't act otherwise than as she did.* **3** under different circumstances: *I might otherwise have been late.* ➣ *adj* different: *The truth is otherwise.*

otherworldly *adj* **1** belonging or relating to, or resembling, a world supposedly inhabited after death. **2** concerned with spiritual or intellectual rather than practical matters. ○ **other-worldliness** n.

otiose /'ouţıous/ adj, formal serving no useful function.

OTT abbrev, slang over the top (see under OVER).

otter n (**otters** or **otter**) a carnivorous semi-aquatic mammal with a long body covered with smooth fur, a broad flat head and large webbed hind feet.

oubliette /u:blɪ'ɛt/ n, hist a secret dungeon with a single, often concealed, opening at the top.

ouch exclam expressing sudden sharp pain.

ought auxiliary vb used to express: **1** duty or obligation: You ought to help if you can. **2** advisability: You ought to see a doctor. **3** probability or expectation: She ought to be here soon. **4** shortcoming or failure: He ought to have been here hours ago. **5** enthusiastic desire on the part of the speaker: You really ought to read this book. **6** logical consequence: The answer ought to be 'four'. ♦ **ought not to …** used to express moral disapproval: You ought not to speak to him like that.

Ouija /'wi:dʒə/ or **Ouija board** n, trademark a board with the letters of the alphabet printed round the edge, on which messages from the dead are supposed to be spelt out.

ounce n **1** in the imperial system: a unit of weight equal to one sixteenth of a pound (28.35g). **2** short form of FLUID OUNCE. **3** a small amount.

our adj **1** relating or belonging to, associated with, or done by us: our children. **2** relating or belonging to people in general, or to humanity: our planet. **3** formal used by a sovereign: my: our royal will.

ours pron the one or ones belonging to us: They're ours • Ours are better.

ourselves pron **1** reflexive form of we: We helped ourselves to cakes. **2** used for emphasis: we personally; our particular group of people: We ourselves know nothing about that. **3** our normal selves: We can relax and be ourselves. **4** (also **by ourselves**) **a** alone: We went by ourselves; **b** without anyone else's help: We did it all by ourselves.

oust vb to force (someone) out of a position and take their place.

out adv **1** away from the inside; not in or at a place: Go out into the garden. **2** not in one's home or place of work: I called but you were out. **3** to or at an end; to or into a state of being completely finished, etc: The milk has run out • before the day is out. **4** aloud: She cried out in surprise. **5** with care or taking care: watch out. **6** in all directions from a central point: Share out the sweets. **7** to the fullest extent or amount: Spread the blanket out. **8** to public attention or notice; revealed: The secret is out. **9** sport of a person batting: no longer able to bat, eg because of having the ball caught by an opponent. **10** in or into a state of being removed,

omitted or forgotten: Rub out the mistake. **11** not to be considered; rejected: That idea's out. **12** removed; dislocated: have a tooth out. **13** not in authority; not having political power: We voted them out of office. **14** into unconsciousness: pass out in the heat. **15** in error: Your total is out by three. **16** colloq existing: the best car out. **17** of a flower: in bloom. **18** of a book: published: It will be out in the autumn. **19** visible: the moon's out. **20** no longer in fashion: Drainpipes are out, flares are in. **21** of workers: on strike. **22** of a jury: considering its verdict. **23** old use of a young woman: introduced into fashionable society. **24** of a tide: at or towards the lowest level of water: going out. ➣ adj **1** external. **2** directing or showing direction outwards. ➣ prep, colloq, esp US out of something: Get out the car. ➣ exclam expressing: **1** sport that the batsman is dismissed. **2** that a radio transmission has finished: over and out. ➣ n a way out, a way of escape; an excuse. ➣ vb **1** intr to become publicly known: Murder will out. **2** to make public the homosexuality of (a famous person who has been attempting to keep their homosexuality secret). ♦ **out and about** active outside the house, esp after an illness. **out for sth** colloq determined to achieve it: He's out for revenge. **out of sth 1** from inside it: drive out of the garage. **2** not in or within it: be out of the house. **3** having exhausted a supply of it: We're out of butter. **4** from among several: two out of three cats. **5** from a material: made out of wood. **6** because of it: out of anger. **7** beyond the range, scope or bounds of it: out of reach. **8** excluded from it: leave him out of the team. **9** no longer in a stated condition: out of practice. **10** at a stated distance from a place: a mile out of town. **11** without or so as to be without something: cheat him out of his money. **out of date** old-fashioned and no longer of use. **out of it 1** colloq not part of, or wanted in, a group or activity, etc. **2** slang unable to behave normally or control oneself, usu because of drink or drugs. **out of pocket** having spent more money than one can afford. **out of the way 1** difficult to reach or arrive at. **2** unusual; uncommon. **out with it!** an exhortation to speak openly.

outage /'auţɪdʒ/ n a period of time during which a power supply fails to operate.

out-and-out adj complete; thorough: an out-and-out liar.

outback n isolated remote areas of a country, esp in Australia.

outbid vb to offer a higher price than (someone else), esp at an auction.

outboard adj **1** of a motor or engine: portable and designed to be attached to the outside of a boat's stern. **2** of a boat: equipped with such a motor or engine. ➣ adv, adj nearer or towards the outside of a ship or aircraft. ➣ n **1** an outboard motor or engine. **2** a boat equipped with an outboard motor or engine. Compare INBOARD.

outbound adj of a vehicle, flight, carriageway,

etc: going away from home or a station, etc; departing.

outbreak *n* a sudden beginning or occurrence of something unpleasant, eg a disease.

outbuilding *n* a building such as a barn, stable, etc that is separate from the main building of a house but within the grounds surrounding it.

outburst *n* **1** a sudden violent expression of strong emotion, esp anger. **2** an eruption or explosion.

outcast *n* someone who has been rejected by their friends or by society.

outclass *vb* **1** to be or become of a much better quality or class than (something else). **2** to defeat (someone) easily.

outcome *n* the result of some action or situation, etc.

outcrop *n* a rock or group of rocks which sticks out above the surface of the ground.

outcry *n* (*-ies*) a widespread and public show of anger or disapproval.

outdated *adj* no longer useful or in fashion.

outdo *vb* to do much better than (someone or something else).

outdoor *adj* **1** done, taking place, situated or for use, etc in the open air: *outdoor pursuits*. **2** preferring to be in the open air or fond of outdoor activities and sport, etc: *an outdoor person.*

outdoors *adv* (*also* **out-of-doors**) in or into the open air. ➤ *sing n* the open air: *the great outdoors.*

outer *adj* **1** external; belonging to or for the outside. **2** further from the centre or middle.

outermost *adj* nearest the edge; furthest from the centre.

outer space *n* any region of space beyond the Earth's atmosphere.

outface *vb* to stare at (someone) until they look away.

outfield *n* **1** *cricket* the area of the pitch far from the part where the stumps, etc are laid out. **2** *baseball* the area of the field beyond the diamond-shaped pitch where the bases are laid out. Compare INFIELD. ○ **outfielder** *n*.

outfit *n* **1** a set of clothes worn together, esp for a particular occasion. **2** a set of articles, tools or equipment, etc for a particular task. **3** *colloq* a group of people working as a single unit or team. ○ **outfitter** *n*.

outflank *vb* **1** *mil* to go round the side or sides of (an enemy's position). **2** to get the better of (someone or something), esp by a surprise action.

outfox *vb* to get the better of (someone) by being more cunning.

outgoing *adj* **1** of a person: friendly and sociable. **2** leaving. **3** of an official, politician, etc: about to leave office: *the outgoing president.* ➤ *n* the act of going out.

outgoings *pl n* money spent.

outgrow *vb* **1** to grow too large for (one's clothes). **2** to become too old for (childish ailments or children's games, etc). **3** to grow larger or faster than (someone or something else).

outhouse *n* a building, usu a small one such as a shed, built close to a house.

outing *n* **1** a short pleasure trip or excursion. **2** *colloq* the act of making public the homosexuality of a prominent person, often against their will.

outlandish *adj* of appearance, etc: very strange.

outlaw *n* **1** *orig* someone excluded from, and deprived of the protection of, the law. **2** a criminal who is a fugitive from the law. ➤ *vb* **1** to deprive (someone) of the benefit and protection of the law. **2** to forbid (something) officially.

outlay *n* money, or occasionally time, spent on something.

outlet *n* **1** a vent or way out, esp for water or steam. **2** a way of releasing or using energy, talents or strong feeling, etc. **3** a market for, or a shop that sells, the goods produced by a particular manufacturer. **4** an electrical power point.

outline *n* **1** a line that forms or marks the outer edge of an object. **2** a drawing with only the outer lines and no shading. **3** the main points, etc without the details: *an outline of the plot.* **4** (*usu* **outlines**) the most important features of something. ➤ *vb* **1** to draw the outline of (something). **2** to give a brief description of the main features of (something).

outlive *vb* **1** to live longer than (someone or something else). **2** to survive the effects of (a disease, etc).

outlook *n* **1** a view from a particular place. **2** someone's mental attitude or point of view. **3** a prospect for the future.

outmoded *adj* no longer in fashion.

outpatient *n* a patient who receives treatment at a hospital but does not stay there overnight. Compare INPATIENT.

outpost *n* **1** *mil* a group of soldiers stationed at a distance from the main body. **2** a distant or remote settlement or branch.

outpouring *n* **1** (*usu* **outpourings**) a powerful or violent show of emotion. **2** the amount that pours out.

output *n* **1** the quantity or amount of something produced. **2** *comput* data transferred from the main memory of a computer to a disk, tape or output device such as a VDU or printer. **3** the power or energy produced by an electrical component or apparatus. ➤ *vb, comput* to transfer (data from the main memory of a computer) to a disk or tape, or to an output device. Compare INPUT.

outrage *n* **1** an act of great cruelty or violence. **2** an act which breaks accepted standards of morality, honour and decency. **3** great anger or resentment. ➤ *vb* to insult, shock or anger (someone) greatly.

outrageous *adj* **1** not moderate in behaviour. **2** greatly offensive to accepted standards of morality, honour and decency. **3** colloq terrible; shocking. ○ **outrageously** adv.

outrank vb to have a higher rank than (someone).

outré /ˈuːtreɪ/ adj not conventional; shocking.

outrider n an attendant or guard who rides a horse or motorcycle at the side or ahead of a carriage or car conveying an important person.

outrigger n, naut a beam or framework sticking out from the side of a boat to help balance the vessel and prevent it capsizing.

outright adv /aʊtˈraɪt/ **1** completely: be proved outright. **2** immediately; at once: killed outright. **3** openly; honestly: ask outright. ➤ adj /ˈaʊtraɪt/ **1** complete: an outright fool. **2** clear: the outright winner. **3** open; honest: outright disapproval.

outset n a beginning or start.

outside n /ˈaʊtsaɪd/ **1** the outer surface; the external parts. **2** everything that is not inside or within the bounds or scope of something. **3** the farthest limit. **4** the side of a pavement next to the road. ➤ adj /ˈaʊtsaɪd/ **1** relating to, on or near the outside. **2** not forming part of a group, organization or one's regular job, etc: outside interests. **3** unlikely; remote. ➤ adv /aʊtˈsaɪd/ **1** on or to the outside. **2** slang not in prison. ➤ prep /aʊtˈsaɪd/ **1** on or to the outside of something. **2** beyond the limits of something. **3** except; apart from. ♦ **at the outside** at the most.

outside broadcast n a radio or TV programme that is recorded somewhere other than in a studio.

outsider n **1** someone who is not part of a group, etc or who refuses to accept the general values of society. **2** in a race or contest, etc: a competitor who is not expected to win.

outsize adj over normal or standard size. ➤ n anything, esp a garment, that is larger than standard size.

outskirts pl n the outer parts of a town or city.

outsmart vb, colloq to outwit.

outsource vb of a business, company, etc: **1** to subcontract (work) to another company. **2** to buy in (parts for a product) from another company rather than manufacture them. ○ **outsourcing** n.

outspoken adj **1** of a person: saying exactly what they think. **2** of a remark or opinion, etc: frank. ○ **outspokenness** n.

outspread adj stretched or spread out widely or fully.

outstanding adj **1** excellent; remarkable. **2** not yet paid or done, etc: outstanding debts. ○ **outstandingly** adv.

outstay vb **1** to stay longer than the length of (one's invitation, etc): outstay one's welcome. **2** to stay longer than (other people).

outstretch vb **1** to stretch or spread out. **2** to reach or stretch out (esp one's hand). ○ **outstretched** adj.

outstrip vb **1** to go faster than (someone or something else). **2** to leave behind.

outtake n, cinema, TV a section of film or tape removed from the final edited version of a motion picture or video.

outvote vb to defeat (someone or something) by obtaining more votes.

outward **1** on or towards the outside. **2** of a journey: away from a place. **3** apparent or seeming: outward appearances. ➤ adv (also **outwards**) towards the outside; in an outward direction. ○ **outwardly** adv.

outweigh vb **1** to be greater than (something) in weight. **2** to be greater than (something) in value, importance or influence.

outwit vb to get the better of or defeat (someone) by being cleverer or more cunning than they are.

outworn adj esp of an idea, belief or institution: no longer useful or in fashion.

ouzo /ˈuːzoʊ/ n a Greek alcoholic drink flavoured with aniseed and usu drunk diluted with water.

ova pl of OVUM

oval adj **1** shaped like an egg. **2** loosely elliptical. ➤ n any egg-shaped figure or object.

ovary n (-ies) **1** in a female animal: the reproductive organ in which the ova are produced. **2** bot the hollow base of the carpel of a flower, which contains the ovules. ○ **ovarian** adj.

ovate adj egg-shaped.

ovation n sustained applause or cheering to express approval, etc.

oven n **1** a closed compartment or arched cavity in which substances may be heated, used esp for baking or roasting food, drying clay, etc. **2** a small furnace.

ovenproof adj of dishes and plates, etc: suitable for use in a hot oven.

oven-ready adj of food: prepared beforehand so as to be ready for cooking in the oven immediately.

over adv **1** above and across. **2** outwards and downwards: knock him over. **3** across a space; to or on the other side: fly over from Australia. **4** from one person, side or condition to another: turn the card over. **5** through, from beginning to end, usu with concentration: think it over thoroughly. **6** again; in repetition: do it twice over. **7** at an end: The game is over. **8** so as to cover completely: paper the cracks over. **9** beyond a limit; in excess (of): go over budget. **10** remaining: left over. ➤ prep **1** in or to a position which is higher in place, importance, authority, value or number, etc. **2** above and from one side to another: fly over the sea. **3** so as to cover: Hair flopped over his eyes. **4** out and down from: fall over the edge. **5** throughout the extent of: read over that page again. **6** during a specified time or period: sometime over the weekend. **7** until after a specified time: stay over Monday night. **8** more than: over a year ago. **9** concerning; about: argue over who would pay. **10** while occupied with something: chat about it over cof-

fee. **11** occupying time with something: *spend a day over the preparations.* **12** recovered from the effects of something: *She's over the accident.* **13** by means of something: *hear about it over the radio.* **14** divided by: *Six over three is two.* ➤ *adj* **1** upper; higher. **2** outer. **3** excessive. ➤ *exclam* used during two-way radio conversations: showing that one has finished speaking and expects a reply. ➤ *n, cricket* **1** a series of six balls bowled by the same bowler from the same end of the pitch. **2** play during such a series of balls. ♦ **over again** once more. **over and above sth** in addition to it. **over and above again** repeatedly. **over the top** *colloq* excessive.

overact *vb, tr & intr* to act (a part) with too much expression or emotion.

overall *n* /'ouvərɔːl/ **1** *Brit* a loose-fitting coat-like garment worn over ordinary clothes to protect them. **2** (**overalls**) a one-piece garment with trousers to cover the legs and either a dungaree-type top, or a top with sleeves, worn to protect clothes. ➤ *adj* /'ouvərɔːl/ **1** including everything: *the overall total.* **2** from end to end: *the overall length.* ➤ *adv* /ouvər'ɔːl/ as a whole; in general: *quite good, overall.*

overawe *vb* to subdue or restrain (someone) by filling them with awe, fear or astonishment.

overbalance *vb, tr & intr* to lose or cause (someone or something) to lose balance and fall.

overbearing *adj* **1** domineering; too powerful and proud. **2** having particularly great importance.

overblown *adj* overdone; excessive.

overboard *adv* over the side of a ship or boat into the water: *fall overboard.* ♦ **go overboard** *colloq* to be very or too enthusiastic. **throw sth or sb overboard** to abandon or get rid of it or them.

overburden *vb* to give (someone) too much to do, carry or think about.

overcast *adj* of the sky or weather: cloudy.

overcharge *vb* **1** *tr & intr* to charge (someone) too much. **2** to overload (something).

overcoat *n* a warm heavy coat worn esp in winter.

overcome *vb* **1** to defeat (someone or something; to succeed in a struggle against (them or it). **2** to deal successfully with (something): *He overcame his problems.* **3** *intr* to be victorious. **4** to affect (someone) strongly; to overwhelm (them).

overdo *vb* **1** to do (something) too much; to exaggerate. **2** to cook (food) for too long. **3** to use too much of (something). ♦ **overdo it** or **things** to work too hard.

overdose *n* an excessive dose of a drug, etc. ➤ *vb, tr & intr* to take an overdose or give an excessive dose to (someone).

overdraft *n* **1** a state in which one has taken more money out of one's bank account than was in it. **2** the excess of money taken from one's account over the sum that was in it.

overdraw *vb, tr & intr* to draw more money from (one's bank account) than is in it. ○ **overdrawn** *adj.*

overdrive *n* an additional very high gear in a motor vehicle's gearbox, which saves fuel when travelling at high speeds.

overdue *adj* of bills or work, etc: not yet paid, done or delivered, etc, although the date for doing this has passed.

overestimate *vb* to estimate or judge, etc (something) too highly. ➤ *n* too high an estimate.

overexpose *vb* **1** to expose (someone) to too much publicity. **2** to expose (photographic film) to too much light. ○ **overexposure** *n.*

overflow *vb* **1** to flow over (a brim) or go beyond (the limits or edge of something). **2** *intr* of a container, etc: to be filled so full that the contents spill over or out. **3** (**overflow with sth**) *intr* to be full of it: *He was overflowing with gratitude.* ➤ *n* **1** something that overflows. **2** a pipe or outlet for surplus water. **3** an excess of something.

overgrown *adj* **1** of a garden, etc: dense with plants that have grown too large and thick. **2** grown too large or beyond the normal size. ○ **overgrowth** *n.*

overhang *vb, tr & intr* to project or hang out over (something). ➤ *n* **1** a piece of rock or part of a roof, etc that overhangs. **2** the amount by which something overhangs.

overhaul *vb* **1** to examine carefully and repair (something). **2** to overtake. ➤ *n* a thorough examination and repair.

overhead *adv, adj* above; over one's head. ➤ *n* (**overheads**) the regular costs of a business, such as rent, wages and electricity.

overhear *vb, tr & intr* to hear (a person or remark, etc) without the speaker knowing.

overheat *vb* **1** to heat (something) excessively. **2** *intr* to become too hot. **3** *econ* to overstimulate (the economy) with the risk of increasing inflation. ○ **overheated** *adj* of an argument, discussion, etc: angry and excited.

overjoyed *adj* very glad.

overkill *n* action, behaviour or treatment, etc that is far in excess of what is required.

overladen *adj* overloaded.

overlap *vb* **1** of part of an object: to partly cover (another object). **2** *intr* of two parts: to have one part partly covering the other. **3** *intr* of two things: to have something in common; to partly coincide.

overlay *vb* /ouvə'leɪ/ to lay (one thing) on or over (another). ➤ *n* /'ouvə-/ **1** a covering; something that is laid over something else. **2** a layer, eg of gold leaf, applied to something for decoration. **3** *comput* **a** the process by which segments of a large program are brought from backing store for processing, with only those segments currently requiring processing being held in the main store; **b** a segment of a program transferred in this way.

overleaf *adv* on the other side of the page.

overload vb **1** to load (something) too heavily. **2** to put too great an electric current through (a circuit). ➤ n too great an electric current flowing through a circuit.

overlook vb **1** to give a view of (something) from a higher position: *overlooks the garden.* **2** to fail to see or notice (something). **3** to allow (a mistake or crime, etc) to go unpunished.

overlord n a lord or ruler with supreme power.

overly adv too; excessively.

overnight adv **1** during the night. **2** for the duration of the night. **3** suddenly: *Success came overnight.* ➤ adj **1** done or occurring in the night. **2** sudden: *an overnight success.* **3** for use overnight: *an overnight bag.*

overpass see under FLYOVER.

overplay vb **1** to exaggerate or overemphasize (the importance of something). **2** tr & intr to exaggerate (an emotion, etc); to act in an exaggerated way. ♦ **overplay one's hand** to overestimate one's talents or assets, etc.

overpower vb **1** to defeat or subdue (someone or something) by greater strength. **2** to weaken or reduce (someone or something) to helplessness. ○ **overpowering** adj.

overrate vb to value too highly. ○ **overrated** adj.

overreach vb to defeat (oneself) by trying to do too much.

overreact vb, intr to react too strongly. ○ **overreaction** n.

override vb **1** to dominate or assume superiority over (someone). **2** to annul something or set it aside. **3** to take manual control of (a normally automatically controlled operation). ○ **overriding** adj dominant; most important.

overrule vb **1** to rule against or cancel (esp a previous decision or judgement) by higher authority. **2** to impose a decision on (a person) by higher authority.

overrun vb **1** to spread over or through (something): *overrun with weeds.* **2** to occupy an area, country, etc quickly and by force. **3** tr & intr to go beyond (a fixed limit).

overseas adv in or to a land beyond the sea; abroad: *working overseas.* ➤ adj (also **oversea**) across or from beyond the sea; foreign: *an overseas posting.* ➤ n a foreign country or foreign countries in general.

oversee vb to supervise (someone or something). ○ **overseer** n.

oversew vb to sew (two edges) together with close stitches that pass over both edges.

overshadow vb **1** to seem much more important than (someone or something else). **2** to cast a shadow over (something); to make (it) seem more gloomy.

overshoe n a shoe, usu made of rubber or plastic, worn over a normal shoe to protect it in wet weather.

overshoot vb to shoot or go farther than (a target aimed at).

oversight n a mistake or omission, esp one made through a failure to notice something.

oversize adj (also **oversized**) larger than normal.

overspill n, Brit the people leaving an overcrowded town area to live elsewhere.

overstate vb to state (something) too strongly. ○ **overstatement** n.

overstep vb (esp **overstep the mark**) to go beyond (a certain limit, or what is prudent or reasonable).

oversubscribe vb to apply for or try to purchase (eg shares, etc) in larger quantities than are available.

overt adj not hidden or secret; open. ○ **overtly** adv.

overtake vb **1** tr & intr, chiefly Brit to catch up with and go past (a car or a person, etc) moving in the same direction. **2** to draw level with and begin to do better than (someone). **3** to come upon (someone) suddenly or without warning: *overtaken by bad weather.*

overtax vb **1** to demand too much tax from (someone). **2** to put too great a strain on (someone or oneself).

over-the-counter adj of goods, eg drugs and medicines: legally sold directly to the customer.

overthrow vb **1** to defeat completely (an established order or a government, etc). **2** to upset or overturn (something). ➤ n the act of overthrowing or state of being overthrown.

overtime n **1** time spent working beyond the regular hours. **2** money paid for this. **3** sport, N Am extra time. ➤ adv in addition to regular hours: *work overtime.*

overtone n **1** (often **overtones**) a subtle hint, quality or meaning: *political overtones.* **2** mus a tone that contributes towards a musical sound and adds to its quality.

overture n **1** mus **a** an orchestral introduction to an opera, oratorio or ballet; **b** a single-movement orchestral composition in a similar style. **2** (usu **overtures**) a proposal or offer intended to open a discussion, negotiations or a relationship, etc.

overturn vb **1** tr & intr to turn or cause (something) to be turned over or upside down. **2** to bring down or destroy (a government). **3** to overrule or cancel (a previous legal decision).

overview n a brief general account or description.

overweening adj **1** of a person: arrogant. **2** of pride: excessive.

overweight adj above the desired or usual weight.

overwhelm vb **1** to crush mentally; to overpower (a person's emotions or thoughts, etc). **2** to defeat completely by superior force or numbers. **3** to supply or offer (something) in great amounts. ○ **overwhelming** adj. ○ **overwhelmingly** adv.

overwind vb to wind (a watch, etc) too far.

overwork vb **1** intr to work too hard. **2** to make (someone) work too hard. **3** to make too much use of (something). ➤ n excessive work.

overwrite vb **1** to write on top of (something else). **2** comput to record new information over (existing data), thereby destroying (it).

overwrought adj very nervous or excited.

oviduct n, anat, zool the tube through which ova are conveyed from the ovary.

oviform adj egg-shaped.

ovine adj relating to or characteristic of a sheep or sheep.

oviparous /ouˈvɪpərəs/ adj, zool of many birds, reptiles, amphibians, bony fishes, etc: laying eggs that develop and hatch outside the mother's body. Compare OVOVIVIPAROUS, VIVIPAROUS.

ovoid /ˈouvɔɪd/ adj, chiefly zool & bot egg-shaped.

ovoviviparous /ouvouvɪˈvɪpərəs/ adj, zool of many insects and of certain fish and reptiles: producing eggs that hatch within the body of the mother. Compare OVIPAROUS, VIVIPAROUS.

ovulate vb, intr, physiol **1** to release an ovum or egg cell from the ovary. **2** to form or produce ova. ○ **ovulation** n.

ovule n, bot in flowering plants: the structure that develops into a seed after fertilization. ○ **ovular** adj.

ovum n (**ova**) an unfertilized egg or egg cell.

ow exclam expressing sudden pain.

owe vb **1** tr & intr to be under an obligation to pay (money) (to someone): She owes him £5. **2** to feel required by duty or gratitude to do or give (someone) (something): I owe you an explanation. **3** (**owe sth to sb** or **sth**) to have or enjoy it as a result of them or it.

owing adj still to be paid; due. ◆ **owing to sth** because of it; on account of it.

owl n a nocturnal bird of prey with a flat face, large forward-facing eyes and a short hooked beak. ○ **owlish** adj.

own adj often used for emphasis: belonging to or for oneself or itself: my own sister. ➤ pron one belonging (or something belonging) to oneself or itself: Jack lost his own, so I lent him mine. ➤ vb **1** to have (something) as a possession or property. **2** (usu **own to sth**) intr to admit or confess to it: He owned to many weaknesses. ○ **owner** n. ○ **ownership** n. ◆ **come into one's own 1** to take possession of one's rights or what is due to one. **2** to have one's abilities or talents, etc duly recognized, or to realize one's potential. **hold one's own** to maintain one's position, esp in spite of difficulty or opposition, etc; not to be defeated. **on one's own 1** alone. **2** without help. ◇ **own up** or **own up to sth** to confess; to admit a wrongdoing, etc.

owner-occupier n someone who owns the property they are living in.

own goal n **1** sport a goal scored by mistake for the opposing side. **2** colloq an action that turns out to be to the disadvantage of the person who took it.

ox n (**oxen**) an adult castrated bull, used for pulling loads or as a source of meat.

oxbow n (also **oxbow lake**) a shallow curved lake on a river's flood plain formed when one of the meanders of the river has been cut off.

Oxbridge n, Brit the universities of Oxford and Cambridge considered together.

oxen pl of OX

oxidation n, chem the process of oxidizing.

oxide n, chem any compound of oxygen and another element.

oxidize or **-ise** vb, tr & intr, chem **1** to undergo, or cause (a substance) to undergo, a chemical reaction with oxygen. **2** to lose or cause (an atom or ion) to lose electrons. **3** to become, or make (something) become, rusty as a result of the formation of a layer of metal oxide. ○ **oxidization** n.

oxtail n the tail of an ox used as food.

oxyacetylene n a mixture of oxygen and acetylene which burns with an extremely hot flame and is used in torches for cutting, welding or brazing metals.

oxygen n a colourless odourless tasteless gas, which is an essential requirement of most forms of plant and animal life.

oxygenate vb to combine, treat, supply or enrich (eg the blood) with oxygen.

oxymoron n a rhetorical figure of speech in which contradictory terms are used together, often for emphasis or effect, eg horribly good.

oyez or **oyes** /ouˈjez, ouˈjes/ exclam, hist a cry for silence and attention, usu shouted three times by an official before a public announcement.

oyster n a marine mollusc with a soft fleshy body enclosed by a hinged shell, eaten as food, certain types of which produce pearls.

Oz or **Ozzie** adj, n, slang Australian.

oz abbrev OUNCE (sense 1).

ozone n, chem a pungent ALLOTROPE of oxygen formed when an electric spark acts on oxygen.

ozone-friendly adj of products such as aerosols, etc: not harmful to the ozone layer; free from chemicals, eg chlorofluorocarbons, that deplete the ozone layer.

ozone layer or **ozonosphere** n a layer of the upper atmosphere where ozone is formed, which filters harmful ultraviolet radiation from the Sun and prevents it from reaching the Earth.

Pp

P[1] or **p** *n* (**Ps, P's** or **p's**) the sixteenth letter of the English alphabet. ◆ **mind one's p's and q's** *colloq* to behave politely.

P[2] *abbrev* as a street sign: parking.

P[3] *symbol* **1** *chess* pawn. **2** *chem* phosphorus.

p *abbrev* **1** page. **2** penny or pence.

PA *abbrev* **1** personal assistant. **2** public-address system.

Pa[1] *abbrev* pascal.

Pa[2] *symbol, chem* protactinium.

pa *n* a familiar word for FATHER.

p.a. *abbrev* per annum.

pace[1] /'peɪs/ *n* **1** a single step. **2** the distance covered by one step when walking. **3** rate of walking or running, etc: *at a slow pace.* **4** rate of movement or progress: *at your own pace.* **5** any of the gaits used by a horse. ➤ *vb* **1** *tr & intr* (*often* **pace about** or **around**) to keep walking about, in a preoccupied or frustrated way. **2** *intr* to walk steadily. **3** to set the pace for (others) in a race, etc. **4** (*often* **pace sth out**) to measure out (a distance) in paces. ◆ **go through** or **show one's paces** to demonstrate one's skills at something. **keep pace with sb** to go as fast as them. **put sb through their paces** to test them in some activity. **set the pace** to be ahead of, and so set the rate for, others.

pace[2] /'peɪsiː, 'paːkeɪ/ *prep* with due respect to (someone with whom one is disagreeing).

pacemaker *n* **1** *med* an electronic device that stimulates the heart muscle to contract at a specific and regular rate, used to correct weak or irregular heart rhythms. **2** the leader in a race.

pachyderm /'pakɪdɜːm/ *n* any large thick-skinned non-ruminant mammal, esp the elephant, rhinoceros or hippopotamus.

pacific *adj* tending to make peace or keep the peace; peaceful; peaceable.

pacifist *n* someone who believes that violence is unjustified and refuses to take part in making war. ○ **pacifism** *n*.

pacify *vb* (**-ies, -ied**) **1** to calm, soothe or appease someone. **2** to restore something to a peaceful condition. ○ **pacification** *n*.

pack[1] *n* **1** a collection of things tied into a bundle for carrying. **2** a rucksack; a backpack. **3** a set of playing cards, usu 52. **4** a group of animals living and hunting together, eg wolves. **5** a compact package, eg of equipment for a purpose: *a first-aid pack.* **6** *in compounds* a collection of things of a specified number or for a specified purpose: *a four-pack* • *a party-pack.* **7** *derog* a collection or bunch: *a pack of lies.* **8** a group of Brownie Guides or Cub Scouts. **9** *rugby* the forwards in a team. **10** a medicinal or cosmetic skin preparation: *a face pack.* ➤ *vb* **1** to stow (goods, clothes, etc) compactly in cases, etc for transport or travel. **2** *intr* to put one's belongings into a suitcase, rucksack, etc, ready for a journey: *Have you packed yet?* **3** to put (goods, food, etc) into a container, or to wrap them, ready for sale. **4** (*usu* **pack sth in**) **a** to push and cram it into something that is already quite full; **b** to cram (a great deal of activity) into a limited period. **5** *intr* to be capable of being formed into a compact shape. **6** to fill something tightly or compactly: *The hall was packed.* **7** *tr & intr, N Am colloq* to make a habit of carrying (a gun). ◆ **packed out** of a place: very busy. **send sb packing** *colloq* to send them away unceremoniously. ◊ **pack sb off** to send them off hastily. **pack up 1** to stop work, etc at the end of the day or shift, etc. **2** *colloq* of machinery, etc: to break down.

pack[2] *vb* to fill (a jury, meeting, etc) illicitly with people one can rely on to support one's cause.

package *n* **1** something wrapped and secured with string, adhesive tape, etc; a parcel. **2** a case, box or other container for packing goods in. **3** *comput* a group of related computer programs designed to perform a particular complex task.

package holiday or **package tour** *n* a holiday or tour for which one pays a fixed price that includes travel, accommodation, meals, etc.

packaging *n* the wrappers or containers in which goods are packed and presented for sale.

pack animal *n* an animal, eg a donkey, mule or horse, used to carry luggage or goods.

packet *n* **1** a wrapper or container made of paper, cardboard or plastic, with its contents. **2** a small pack or package. **3** a boat that transports mail and also carries cargo and passengers, travelling a regular fixed route. **4** *colloq* a large sum of money: *It cost a packet.*

pack ice *n* a large area of free-floating sea ice consisting of pieces that have been driven together to form a solid mass.

packing *n* materials used for padding or wrapping goods for transport, etc.

pact *n* an agreement reached between two or more parties, states, etc for mutual advantage.

pad[1] *n* **1** a wad of material used to cushion, protect, shape or clean. **2** a leg-guard for a cricketer, etc. **3** *also in compounds* a quantity of sheets of paper fixed together in a block: *notepad.* **4** a rocket-launching platform. **5** the soft fleshy underside of an animal's paw. **6** *N Am* a large water lily leaf. **7** *slang* the place where someone lives. ➤ *vb* (**padded, padding**) **1** to cover, fill, stuff, cushion or shape something with layers of soft material. **2** (*also* **pad sth out**) *derog* to include unnecessary or irrelevant material in (a piece of writing, speech, etc) for the sake of length.

pad² *vb* (**padded, padding**) **1** *intr* to walk softly or with a quiet or muffled tread. **2** *tr & intr* to tramp along (a road); to travel on foot.

padding *n* **1** material for cushioning, shaping or filling. **2** *derog* irrelevant or unnecessary matter in a speech or piece of writing, added to extend it to the desired length.

paddle¹ *vb* **1** *intr* to walk about barefoot in shallow water. **2** to trail or dabble (fingers, etc) in water. ➢ *n* a spell of paddling.

paddle² *n* **1** a short light oar with a blade at one or both ends, used to propel and steer a canoe, kayak, etc. **2** one of the slats fitted round the edge of a paddle wheel or mill wheel. **3** a paddle-shaped instrument for stirring, beating, etc. ➢ *vb, tr & intr* **1** to propel (a canoe, kayak, etc) with paddles. **2** *intr* (*also* **paddle along**) to move through water using, or as if using, a paddle or paddles.

paddock *n* **1** a small enclosed field for keeping a horse in. **2** *horse-racing* an enclosure beside a race track where horses are saddled and walked round before a race.

paddy¹ *n* (**-ies**) *colloq* a fit of rage.

paddy² *n* (**-ies**) **1** (*also* **paddy field**) a field filled with water in which rice is grown. **2** rice as a growing crop; harvested rice grains that have not been processed in any way.

padlock *n* a detachable lock with a U-shaped bar that pivots at one side so that it can be passed through a ring or chain and locked in position. ➢ *vb* to fasten (a door, cupboard, etc) with a padlock.

padre /'pɑːdreɪ/ *n* a chaplain in any of the armed services.

paean or (*US*) **pean** /pɪən/ *n* a song of triumph, praise or thanksgiving.

paederasty see PEDERASTY

paediatrics or (*N Am*) **pediatrics** /piːdɪ-'ætrɪks/ *sing n, med* the branch of medicine concerned with the health and care of children. ○ **paediatric** or (*N Am*) **pediatric** *adj.*

paedophilia /piːdou'fɪlɪə/ *n* sexual attraction to children. ○ **paedophile** *n.*

paella /paɪ'ɛlə/ *n, cookery* a Spanish dish of rice with fish or chicken and vegetables and saffron.

pagan *adj* **1 a** not Christian, Jewish, or Muslim; **b** belonging or relating to, or following, a religion in which a number of gods are worshipped. **2** without religious belief. ➢ *n* a pagan person. ○ **paganism** *n.*

page¹ *n* **1** one side of a leaf in a book, etc. **2** a leaf of a book, etc.

page² *n* **1** *hist* a boy attendant serving a knight and training for knighthood. **2** a boy attending the bride at a wedding. **3** a boy who carries messages or luggage, etc in hotels, clubs, etc. ➢ *vb* to summon someone by calling their name out loud, or through a PUBLIC-ADDRESS SYSTEM or PAGER.

pageant /'pædʒənt/ *n* **1** a series of tableaux or dramatic scenes, usu depicting local historical events or other topical matters. **2** any colourful and varied spectacle, esp involving a procession.

pageantry /'pædʒəntrɪ/ *n* splendid display.

pageboy *n* **1** a PAGE² (*noun sense* 2). **2** a smooth jaw-length hairstyle with the ends curled under.

pager *n, telecomm* a small individually-worn radio receiver and transmitter that enables its user to receive a signal (typically a 'beep' or a short message) to which they can respond with a phone call, etc to the sender.

paginate *vb* to give consecutive numbers to the pages of (a text), carried out by a command within a word-processing package, or as part of the printing process, etc. ○ **pagination** *n.*

pagoda *n* a Buddhist shrine or memorial-building in India, China and parts of SE Asia, esp in the form of a tall tower with many storeys.

paid *vb, past tense, past participle of* PAY. ♦ **put paid to sth** to destroy any chances of success in it.

paid-up *adj* of a society member, etc: having paid a membership fee.

pail *n* **1** a bucket. **2** the amount contained in a pail: *a pail of milk.* ○ **pailful** *n.*

pain *n* **1** an uncomfortable, distressing or agonizing sensation caused by the stimulation of specialized nerve endings by heat, cold, pressure or other strong stimuli. **2** emotional suffering. **3** *derog colloq* an irritating or troublesome person or thing. **4** (**pains**) trouble taken or efforts made in doing something. ➢ *vb, rather formal* to cause distress to someone: *It pained me to see the injured donkey.* ♦ **on pain of sth** at the risk of incurring it as a punishment. **take pains** to be careful to do something properly.

pained *adj* of an expression, tone of voice, etc: expressing distress or disapproval.

painful *adj* **1** causing pain: *a painful injury.* **2** of part of the body: affected by some injury, etc which causes pain. **3** causing distress: *a painful duty.* **4** laborious and slow: *painful progress.* ○ **painfully** *adv.*

pain in the neck *n, slang* **1** an exasperating circumstance. **2** an annoying, irritating or tiresome person.

painkiller *n* any drug or other agent that relieves pain; an ANALGESIC.

painless *adj* without pain. ○ **painlessly** *adv.*

painstaking *adj* conscientious and thorough, ie taking pains or care: *painstaking work.* ○ **painstakingly** *adv.*

paint *n* **1** colouring matter, esp in the form of a liquid, which is applied to a surface and dries forming a hard surface. **2** a dried coating of this. **3** *old use* face make-up. ➢ *vb* **1** to apply a coat of paint to (walls, woodwork, etc). **2** to turn something a certain colour by this means:

I'll paint the door yellow. **3** *tr & intr* to make (pictures) using paint. **4** to depict (a person, place or thing) in paint. **5** to describe (a scene, place or person) as if in paint. **6** *tr & intr, old use* to put make-up on (one's face). ♦ **paint the town red** to go out and celebrate something lavishly.

paintball *n* a game in which players shoot each other with pellets of paint fired from compressed-air guns.

painter *n* **1** someone who decorates houses with paint. **2** an artist who paints pictures.

painting *n* **1** a painted picture. **2** the art or process of applying paint to walls, etc. **3** the art of creating pictures in paint.

pair *n* **1** a set of two identical or corresponding things, eg shoes or gloves, intended for use together. **2** something consisting of two joined and corresponding parts: *a pair of trousers • a pair of scissors.* **3** one of a matching pair: *Where's this earring's pair?* a couple. **5** two mating animals, birds, fishes, etc. **6** two horses harnessed together: *a coach and pair.* **7** two playing cards of the same denomination. **8** in a parliament: two voters on opposite sides who have an agreement to abstain from voting on a specific motion. ➤ *vb* **1** *tr & intr (often* **pair off** *or* **pair sth** *or* **sb off**) to divide into groups of two; to sort out in pairs. **2** *intr* of two opposing voters in a parliament: to agree a PAIR (*noun* sense 8) or to have such an agreement. ○ **paired** *adj.* ♦ **in pairs** in twos.

paisley or **paisley pattern** *n* a design featuring an ornate device which looks like a tree cone with a curving point, used mainly on fabrics.

pajamas see PYJAMAS

pakora /pə'kɔːrə/ *n* an Indian dish of vegetables, chicken, etc formed into balls, coated in batter and deep-fried.

pal *colloq, n* a friend. ➤ *vb* (**palled, palling**) *intr* (*usu* **pal up with sb**) to make friends with them. ○ **pally** *adj.*

palace *n* **1** the official residence of a sovereign, bishop, archbishop or president. **2** a spacious and magnificent residence or other building.

paladin *n, hist* **1** any of the 12 peers of Charlemagne's court. **2** a KNIGHT ERRANT; a champion of a sovereign.

Palaeocene *adj, geol* the earliest epoch of the TERTIARY period, during which time many reptiles became extinct and mammals became the dominant vertebrates.

palaeography /palɪ'ɒgrəfɪ/ *n* the study of ancient writing and manuscripts. ○ **palaeographer** *n.*

palaeolithic or **Palaeolithic** *adj* relating or belonging to an early period of the Stone Age, extending from about 2.5 million years ago to about 10,000 years ago, characterized by the use by primitive people of tools made of unpolished chipped stone.

palaeontology *n, geol* the scientific study of the structure, distribution, environment and

evolution of extinct life forms by interpretation of their fossil remains. ○ **palaeontologist** *n.*

Palaeozoic /palɪoʊ'zoʊɪk/ *adj, geol* relating to the era of geological time extending from about 580 million to 250 million years ago, during which time the first vertebrates appeared.

palamino see PALOMINO

palanquin or **palankeen** /palən'kiːn/ *n, hist* a light covered litter used in the Orient.

palatable *adj* **1** having a pleasant taste. **2** acceptable; agreeable.

palate /'palat/ *n* **1** the roof of the mouth. **2** the sense of taste.

palatial *adj* like a palace in magnificence, spaciousness, etc.

palatine *adj* **1** referring to a palace. **2** having royal privileges or jurisdiction.

palaver /pə'lɑːvə(r)/ *n* a long, boring, complicated and seemingly pointless exercise.

pale¹ *adj* **1** of a person, face, etc: having less colour than normal, eg from illness, fear, shock, etc. **2** of a colour: whitish; closer to white than black; light: *pale-green.* **3** lacking brightness or vividness; subdued: *pale sunlight.* ➤ *vb, intr* **1** to become pale. **2** to fade or become weaker or less significant: *My worries pale by comparison.* ○ **paleness** *n.*

pale² *n* **1** a wooden or metal post or stake used for making fences. **2** a fence made of these; a boundary fence. ♦ **beyond the pale** outside the limits of acceptable behaviour.

palette /'palat/ *n* **1** a hand-held board with a thumb-hole, on which an artist mixes colours. **2** the range of colours used by a particular artist, in a particular picture, etc.

palimpsest *n* a parchment or other ancient writing surface re-used after the original content has been erased.

palindrome *n* a word or phrase that reads the same backwards and forwards, eg *Hannah.*

paling *n* **1** the act of constructing a fence with pales (see PALE² sense 1). **2** a fence of this kind. **3** an upright stake or board in a fence.

palisade *n* a tall fence of pointed wooden stakes fixed edge to edge, for defence or protection.

pall¹ /pɔːl/ *n* **1 a** the cloth that covers a coffin at a funeral; **b** the coffin itself. **2** anything spreading or hanging over: *a pall of smoke.*

pall² /pɔːl/ *vb* **1** *intr* to begin to bore or seem tedious. **2** to cloy; to bore.

palladium *n, chem* a soft silvery-white metallic element used as a catalyst, and in gold dental alloys, jewellery, electrical components, and catalytic converters for car exhausts.

pall-bearer *n* one of the people carrying the coffin or walking beside it at a funeral.

pallet¹ *n* **1** a small wooden platform on which goods can be stacked for lifting and transporting, esp by fork-lift truck. **2** a flat-bladed wooden tool used for shaping pottery.

pallet² *n* **1** a straw bed. **2** a small makeshift bed.

palliasse or **paillasse** *n* a straw-filled mattress.

palliate *vb* **1** to ease the symptoms of (a disease) without curing it. **2** to serve to lessen the gravity of (an offence, etc). **3** to reduce the effect of (anything disagreeable).

palliative *n* anything used to reduce pain or anxiety. ➤ *adj* having the effect of alleviating or reducing pain.

pallid *adj* **1** pale, esp unhealthily so. **2** lacking vigour or conviction.

pallor *n* paleness, esp of complexion.

palm[1] *n* **1** the inner surface of the hand between the wrist and the fingers. **2** the part of a glove covering this. ➤ *vb* to conceal something in the palm of one's hand. ♦ **in the palm of one's hand** in one's power. ◊ **palm sth off on sb** or **palm sb off with sth** *colloq* to give them something unwanted or unwelcome, esp by trickery.

palm[2] *n* a tropical tree with a woody unbranched trunk bearing a crown of large fan-shaped or feather-shaped leaves.

palmate /'palmeɪt/ or **palmated** *adj*, *bot* of a leaf: divided into lobes that radiate from a central point, resembling an open hand.

palmetto *n* (*palmettos* or *palmettoes*) a small palm tree with fan-shaped leaves.

palmistry *n* the art of telling someone's fortune by reading the lines on the palm of their hand. ◊ **palmist** *n*.

palm oil *n* the oil obtained from the outer pulp of the fruit of some palm trees, used in cooking fats.

Palm Sunday *n*, *Christianity* the Sunday before Easter.

palmtop *n* a portable computer small enough to be held in the hand.

palmy *adj* (*-ier, -iest*) effortlessly successful and prosperous: *one's palmy days*.

palomino or **palamino** *n* (*palominos* or *palaminos*) a golden or cream horse, largely of Arab blood, with a white or silver tail and mane.

palpable *adj* **1** easily detected; obvious. **2** *med* eg of an internal organ: able to be felt. ◊ **palpably** *adv*.

palpate *vb*, *med* to examine (the body or a part of it) by touching or pressing.

palpitate *vb*, *intr* **1** *med* of the heart: to beat abnormally rapidly, eg as a result of physical exertion, fear, emotion or heart disease. **2** to tremble or throb. ◊ **palpitation** *n*.

palsy /'pɔːlzɪ/ *n* (*-ies*) paralysis, or loss of control or feeling in a part of the body. ➤ *vb* (*-ies, -ied*) to affect someone or something with palsy.

paltry *adj* (*-ier, -iest*) insignificant or insultingly inadequate.

pampas grass *n* a large S American grass bearing silvery-white or pink plume-like panicles.

pamper *vb* to treat (a person or animal) overindulgently.

pamphlet *n* a booklet or leaflet providing information or dealing with a current topic.

pan[1] *n* **1** a pot, usu made of metal, used for cooking. **2** a panful, the amount a pan will hold. **3** *often in compounds* a vessel, usu shallow, used for domestic, industrial and other purposes: *dustpan • bedpan*. **4** the bowl of a lavatory. **5** either of the two dishes on a pair of scales. **6** a shallow hollow in the ground: *a salt pan*. ➤ *vb* (*panned, panning*) **1** (*often* **pan for sth**) *tr & intr* to wash (river gravel) in a shallow metal vessel in search for (eg gold). **2** *colloq* to criticize something or review (a performance, book, etc) harshly. ◊ **panful** *n*. ◊ **pan out 1** to result or turn out. **2** to come to an end; to be exhausted.

pan[2] *vb* (*panned, panning*) *tr & intr* of a film camera, camcorder, etc: to swing round so as to follow a moving object or show a panoramic view. ➤ *n* a panning movement or shot.

panacea /panə'sɪə/ *n* a cure for any ill, problem, etc.

panache /pə'naʃ/ *n* a flamboyant and self-assured manner.

panama or **panama hat** *n* a lightweight brimmed hat made from the plaited leaves of a palm-like Central American tree.

panatella *n* a long slim cigar.

pancake *n* a thin cake made from a batter of eggs, flour and milk, cooked on both sides in a frying pan or on a griddle.

Pancake Day *n* SHROVE TUESDAY, when pancakes are traditionally eaten.

panchromatic *adj*, *photog* of a film: sensitive to all colours.

pancreas /'paŋkrɪəs/ *n*, *anat* in vertebrates: a large carrot-shaped gland lying between the duodenum and the spleen, that secretes pancreatic juice serving hormonal and digestive functions. ◊ **pancreatic** *adj*.

panda *n* **1** (*also* **giant panda**) a black-and-white bearlike animal, native to China. **2** (*also* **red panda**) a related species, smaller and with reddish brown coat, native to forests of S Asia.

pandemic *adj*, *med* describing a widespread epidemic of a disease, one that affects a whole country, continent, etc.

pandemonium *n* **1** any very disorderly or noisy place or assembly. **2** noise, chaos and confusion.

pander *n* someone who obtains a sexual partner for someone else. ➤ *vb* (**pander to sb** or **sth**) to indulge or gratify them or their wishes or tastes.

pandit see under PUNDIT

Pandora's box *n* any source of great and unexpected troubles.

p & p *abbrev* postage and packing.

pane *n* a sheet of glass, esp one fitted into a window or door.

panegyric /panɪ'dʒɪrɪk/ *n* a speech or piece of writing in praise of someone or something. ◊ **panegyric** or **panegyrical** *adj*.

panel *n* **1** a rectangular wooden board forming a section, esp an ornamentally sunken or raised one, of a wall or door. **2** one of several strips of fabric making up a garment. **3** any of the metal sections forming the bodywork of a vehicle. **4** a board bearing the instruments and dials for controlling an aircraft, etc: *control panel.* **5** rectangular divisions on the page of a book, esp for illustrations. **6** a team of people selected to judge a contest, or to participate in a discussion, quiz or other game before an audience. **7 a** a list of jurors; **b** the people serving on a jury. ➤ *vb* (**panelled, panelling;** *esp N Am* **paneled, paneling**) to fit (a wall or door) with wooden panels.

panel-beating *n* the removal of dents from metal, esp from the bodywork of a vehicle, using a soft-headed hammer. ○ **panel-beater** *n.*

panelling or (*N Am*) **paneling** *n* **1** panels covering a wall or part of a wall, usu as decoration. **2** material for making these.

panellist or (*N Am*) **panelist** *n* a member of a panel of people, esp in a panel game on TV or radio.

pang *n* a brief but painfully acute feeling of hunger, guilt, remorse, etc: *a pang of guilt.*

pangolin *n* a toothless mammal that is covered with large overlapping horny plates and can curl into an armoured ball when threatened by a predator.

panhandle *n, esp US* a narrow strip of territory stretching out from the main body into another territory, eg part of a state which stretches into another.

panic *n* a sudden overpowering fear that affects an individual, or esp one that grips a crowd or population. ➤ *vb* (**panicked, panicking**) *tr & intr* to feel panic, or make someone feel panic. ○ **panicky** *adj.*

panicle *n, bot* a branched flower-head, common in grasses, in which the youngest flowers are at the tip of the flower-stalk.

panic-stricken *adj* struck with sudden fear.

panini *pl n* an Italian dish of grilled sandwiches.

pannier *n* **1** one of a pair of baskets carried over the back of a donkey or other pack animal. **2** one of a pair of bags carried on either side of the wheel of a bicycle, etc.

panoply /'panəplɪ/ *n* (*-ies*) the full assemblage, got together for a ceremony, etc.

panorama *n* **1** an open and extensive or all-round view, eg of a landscape. **2** a view of something in all its range and variety: *the panorama of history.* ○ **panoramic** *adj.*

panpipes, Pan pipes or **Pan's pipes** *pl n* a musical instrument, made of reeds of different lengths bound together and played by blowing across their open ends.

pansy *n* (*-ies*) **1** a garden plant which has flat flowers with five rounded white, yellow or purple petals. **2** *offensive slang* an effeminate man or boy; a male homosexual.

pant *vb* **1** *intr* to breathe in and out with quick, shallow, short gasps as a result of physical exertion. **2** to say something breathlessly. ➤ *n* a gasping breath. ○ **panting** *n, adj.*

pantaloons *pl n* **1** baggy trousers gathered at

the ankle. **2** tight-fitting trousers for men with buttons or ribbons below the calf, worn at the turn of the 19c.

pantechnicon *n* a large furniture-removal van.

pantheism *n* **1** the belief that equates all the matter and forces in the Universe with God. **2** readiness to believe in all or many gods. ○ **pantheist** *n.* ○ **pantheistic** or **pantheistical** *adj.*

pantheon *n* **1** all the gods of a particular people: *the ancient Greek pantheon.* **2** a temple sacred to all the gods. **3** a building in which the glorious dead of a nation have memorials or are buried.

panther *n* **1** a LEOPARD, esp a black one, formerly believed to be a different species. **2** *N Am* a PUMA.

panties *pl n* thin light knickers, mainly for women and children.

pantihose see PANTY HOSE

pantile *n, building* a roofing tile with an S-shaped cross section.

panto *n, colloq* short form of PANTOMIME.

pantograph *n* **1** a device consisting of jointed rods forming an adjustable parallelogram, for copying maps, plans, etc to any scale. **2** a similarly shaped metal framework on the roof of an electric train, transmitting current from an overhead wire.

pantomime *n* **1** a Christmas entertainment usu based on a popular fairy tale, with songs, dancing, comedy acts, etc. **2** a farcical or confused situation: *What a pantomime!*

pantry *n* (*-ies*) a small room or cupboard for storing food, cooking utensils, etc.

pants *pl n* **1** *Brit* an undergarment worn over the buttocks and genital area; underpants. **2** *N Am* trousers. ♦ **scare, bore,** *etc* **the pants off sb** *slang* to scare, bore, etc them to a great extent.

panty hose or **pantihose** *pl n, N Am* women's tights.

pap¹ *n* **1** soft semi-liquid food for babies and sick people. **2** *derog* trivial or worthless reading matter or entertainment.

pap² *n* **1** *old use* a nipple or teat. **2** *Scot* in place-names: a round conical hill.

papa /pə'pɑ:/ *n, old use or jocular* a child's word for father.

papacy /'peɪpəsɪ/ *n* (*-ies*) **1** the position, power or period of office of a POPE. **2** government by popes.

papal *adj* referring or relating to the POPE (*noun* sense I) or the PAPACY.

paparazzo /papə'ratsoʊ/ *n* (**paparazzi** /-tsiː/) a newspaper photographer who follows famous people about in the hope of photographing them in unguarded moments.

papaw /pə'pɔː/ or **pawpaw** /'pɔːpɔː/ *n* a large oblong yellow or orange fruit, which has sweet orange flesh and a central cavity filled with black seeds.

paper *n* **1** a material manufactured in thin

sheets from pulped wood, rags, or other forms of cellulose, used for writing and printing on, wrapping things, etc. **2** a loose piece of paper, eg a wrapper or printed sheet. **3** other material used for a similar purpose or with a similar appearance, eg PAPYRUS, RICE PAPER. **4** wallpaper. **5 a** a newspaper; **b** (**the papers**) newspapers collectively; the press. **6** a set of questions on a certain subject for a written examination. **7 a** a written article dealing with a certain subject, esp for reading to an audience at a meeting, conference, etc; **b** an essay written eg by a student. **8** (**papers**) personal documents establishing one's identity, nationality, etc. **9** (**papers**) a person's accumulated correspondence, diaries, etc. ➢ *adj* **1** consisting of or made of paper. **2** paper-like, esp like paper. **3** on paper. ➢ *vb* **1** to decorate (a wall, a room, etc) with wallpaper: *to paper the hall.* **2** to cover something with paper. ○ **papery** *adj.* ◆ **on paper 1** in theory or in abstract as distinct from practice: *The plans looked good on paper.* **2** in written form: *I'll get my ideas down on paper.* ◊ **paper over sth** or **paper over the cracks in sth** to conceal or avoid (an awkward fact, mistake, etc).

paperback *n* a book with a thin flexible paper binding, as opposed to a HARDBACK.

paper clip *n* a metal clip formed from bent wire, for holding papers together.

paper hanger *n* someone who puts up wallpaper.

paperless *adj* using electronic means, rather than paper, for recording, etc: *a paperless office.*

paper money *n* bank notes, as opposed to coins.

paperweight *n* a small heavy object kept on a desk for holding papers down.

paperwork *n* routine written work, eg filling in forms, keeping files, writing reports, etc.

papier-mâché /ˈpapɪəˈmaʃeɪ, papjeɪ-/ *n* a light hard material consisting of pulped paper mixed with glue, moulded into shape while wet and left to dry, and used to make boxes, masks, etc.

papilla /pəˈpɪlə/ *n* (**papillae** /-liː/) *anat, biol* **1** a small nipple-like projection from the surface of a structure. **2** a protuberance at the base of a hair, feather, tooth, etc. ○ **papillary** *adj.*

papist *n, offensive* a Roman Catholic. ○ **papism** or **papistry** *n, often offensive* Roman Catholicism.

papoose *n, often offens* a Native American baby or young child.

pappadom see POPPADUM

paprika *n* a powdered hot spice made from red peppers.

papyrus /pəˈpaɪərəs/ *n* (**papyri** /pəˈpaɪəraɪ/ or **papyruses**) **1** a tall plant, common in ancient Egypt. **2** the writing material prepared from the pith of the flowering stems of this plant, used by the ancient Egyptians, Greeks and Romans. **3** an ancient manuscript written on this material.

par *n* **1** a normal level or standard. **2** *golf* the standard number of strokes that a good golfer would take for a certain course or hole. **3** *commerce* (*also* **par of exchange**) the established value of the unit of one national currency against that of another. ◆ **below** or **not up to par** *colloq* **1** not up to the usual or required standard. **2** slightly unwell. **par for the course** *colloq* only to be expected.

para *n, colloq* a paratrooper.

parable *n* a story intended to convey a moral or religious lesson.

parabola /pəˈrabələ/ *n, geom* a CONIC SECTION produced when a plane intersects a cone and the plane is parallel to the cone's sloping side.

paracetamol *n* **1** a mild analgesic drug, used to relieve pain or to reduce fever. **2** a tablet of this drug.

parachute *n* **1** an umbrella-shaped apparatus consisting of light fabric, with a harness for attaching to, and slowing the fall of, a person or package dropped from an aircraft. **2** any structure that serves a similar purpose. ➢ *vb, tr & intr* to drop from the air by parachute. ○ **parachutist** *n.*

parade *n* **1** a ceremonial procession of people, vehicles, etc. **2** of soldiers, etc: **a** the state of being drawn up in rank for formal marching or inspection; **b** a group or body of soldiers, etc drawn up in this way. **3** a self-advertising display. **4** a row of shops, a shopping street, etc. ➢ *vb* **1** *tr & intr* to walk or make (a body of soldiers, etc) walk or march in procession, eg across a square, etc. **2** to flaunt.

paradigm /ˈparədaɪm/ *n* **1** an example, model or pattern. **2** *gram* **a** a table of the inflected forms of a word serving as a pattern for words of the same declension or conjugation; **b** the words showing a particular pattern.

paradise *n* **1** heaven. **2** a place of utter bliss or delight. **3** the Garden of Eden.

paradox *n* **1** a statement that seems to contradict itself, eg *More haste, less speed.* **2** a situation involving apparently contradictory elements. **3** *logic* a proposition that is essentially absurd or leads to an absurd conclusion. ○ **paradoxical** *adj.* ○ **paradoxically** *adv.*

paraffin *n* a fuel oil obtained from petroleum or coal and used in aircraft, domestic heaters, etc.

paragliding *n* a sport in which the participant is towed through the air by a light aircraft while wearing a modified parachute, then released to glide in the air and eventually drift to the ground. ○ **paraglider** *n.*

paragon *n* someone who is a model of excellence.

paragraph *n* **1** a section of a piece of writing of variable length, starting on a fresh, often indented, line, and dealing with a distinct point or idea. **2** a short report in a newspaper. **3** *mus* a musical passage forming a unit. **4** (*also* **paragraph mark**) *printing* a sign (¶), indicating the start of a new paragraph. ➤ *vb* to divide (text) into paragraphs.

parakeet *n* a small brightly-coloured parrot with a long pointed tail.

parallax *n* 1 *physics* the apparent change in the position of an object, relative to a distant background, when it is viewed from two different positions. **2** *astron* the angle between two straight lines joining two different observation points to a celestial body, used to measure the distance of stars from the Earth. ○ **parallactic** *adj*.

parallel *adj* (*often* **parallel to sth**) 1 of lines, planes, etc: the same distance apart at every point; alongside and never meeting or intersecting. **2** similar; exactly equivalent; corresponding: *parallel careers*. ➤ *adv* (*often* **parallel to sth**) alongside and at an unvarying distance from it. ➤ *n* 1 *geom* a line or plane parallel to another. **2** a corresponding or equivalent instance of something. **3** any of the lines of LATITUDE circling the Earth parallel to the equator and representing a particular angular degree of distance from it. ➤ *vb* (**paralleled, paralleling**) 1 to equal. **2** to correspond to or be equivalent to something. **3** to run parallel to something. ♦ **in parallel** 1 of electrical appliances: so co-ordinated that terminals of the same polarity are connected. **2** simultaneously.

parallelism *n* 1 the state or fact of being parallel. **2** resemblance in corresponding details.

parallelogram *n*, *geom* a two-dimensional four-sided figure in which opposite sides are parallel and equal in length, and opposite angles are equal.

the Paralympics *n* a multi-sport competition for people with physical and learning disabilities. ○ **Paralympic** *adj*.

paralyse or (*N Am*) **paralyze** *vb* 1 to affect (a person or bodily part) with paralysis. **2** of fear, etc: to have an immobilizing effect on someone. **3** to disrupt something or bring it to a standstill.

paralysis *n* (**-ses**) 1 a temporary or permanent loss of muscular function or sensation in any part of the body, usu caused by nerve damage, eg as a result of disease or injury. **2** a state of immobility; a standstill.

paralytic *adj* 1 relating to, caused by or suffering from paralysis. **2** *colloq* helplessly drunk. ➤ *n* a person affected by paralysis.

paramedic *n* a person, esp one trained in emergency medical procedures, whose work supplements and supports that of the medical profession. ○ **paramedical** *adj*.

parameter /pə'ræmɪtə(r)/ *n* 1 *maths* a constant or variable that, when altered, affects the form of a mathematical expression in which it appears. **2** a limiting factor that serves to define the scope of a task, project, discussion, etc.

paramilitary *adj* organized like a professional military force without actually being one. ➤ *n*

(**-ies**) 1 a group organized in this way. **2** a member of such a group.

paramount *adj* foremost; supreme; of supreme importance.

paramour *n* a lover.

paranoia *n* 1 *psychol* a rare mental disorder, characterized by delusions of persecution by others. **2** a strong, usu irrational, feeling that one is being persecuted by others, resulting in a tendency to be suspicious and distrustful.

paranoid, paranoiac /parə'nɔɪak/ or **paranoic** /parə'nɔɪk/ *adj* relating to or affected by paranoia. ➤ *n* a person affected by paranoia.

paranormal *adj* of phenomena, observations, occurrences, etc: beyond the normal scope of scientific explanation, and therefore not possible to explain in terms of current understanding of scientific laws. ➤ *n* (**the paranormal**) paranormal occurrences.

parapet *n* 1 a low wall along the edge of a bridge, balcony, roof, etc. **2** an embankment of earth or sandbags protecting the soldiers in a military trench.

paraphernalia *pl n*, *sometimes used as a sing n* 1 the equipment and accessories associated with a particular activity, etc. **2** personal belongings.

paraphrase *n* a restatement of something using different words, esp in order to clarify. ➤ *vb* to express something in other words.

paraplegia /parə'pliːdʒɪə/ *n*, *med* paralysis of the lower half of the body, usu caused by injury or disease of the spinal cord. Compare HEMIPLEGIA, QUADRIPLEGIA. ○ **paraplegic** *adj*, *n*.

parapsychology *n* the study of mental phenomena, such as telepathy and clairvoyance, that suggest the mind can gain knowledge by means other than the normal processes of perception. ○ **parapsychologist** *n*.

parasite *n* 1 a plant or animal that for all or part of its life obtains food and physical protection from a living organism of another species (the HOST[1] *noun* sense 4) which never benefits from its presence. **2** *derog* a person who lives at the expense of others, contributing nothing in return. ○ **parasitic** or **parasitical** *adj*. ○ **parasitically** *adv*. ○ **parasitism** *n*.

parasitology /parəsaɪ'tɒlədʒɪ/ *n*, *zool* the scientific study of parasites. ○ **parasitologist** *n*.

parasol *n* a light umbrella used as a protection against the sun.

paratroops *pl n* a division of soldiers trained to parachute from aircraft into enemy territory or a battle zone. ○ **paratrooper** *n* a member of such a division.

paratyphoid *n*, *med* an infectious disease, similar to but milder than TYPHOID fever, caused by a bacterium.

parboil *vb* to boil something until it is partially cooked.

parcel *n* 1 something wrapped in paper, etc and secured with string or sticky tape; a package. **2** a portion of something, eg of land. **3** a group of people, etc. **4** a lot or portion of goods for sale; a deal or transaction. ➤ *vb* (**parcelled, parcelling**) **1** (*also* **parcel sth up**) to wrap it up in a parcel. **2** (*also* **parcel sth out**) to divide it into portions and share it out.

parch *vb* **1** to dry something up; to deprive (soil, plants, etc) of water. **2** to make something or someone hot and very dry.

parched *adj* **1** *colloq* very thirsty. **2** very dry.

parchment *n* **1 a** a material formerly used for bookbinding and for writing on, made from the skin of goats, calves or sheep; **b** a piece of this, or a manuscript written on it. **2** stiff off-white writing-paper resembling this. ➤ *adj* made of, or resembling, parchment: *parchment paper*.

pardon *vb* **1** to forgive or excuse someone for a fault or offence: *Pardon me for interrupting.* **2** to allow someone who has been sentenced to go without the punishment. **3** *intr* to grant pardon. ➤ *n* **1** forgiveness. **2** the cancellation of a punishment. ○ **pardonable** *adj.* ♦ **pardon me 1** a formula of apology. **2** (*also* **pardon**) a request to someone to repeat something said.

pare *vb* **1** to trim off (skin, etc) in layers. **2** to cut (fingernails or toenails). **3** to peel (fruit). **4** (*also* **pare sth down**) to reduce (expenses, funding, etc) gradually, in order to economize.

parent *n* **1** a father or mother. **2** the adopter or guardian of a child. **3** an animal or plant that has produced offspring. **4** a source or origin. ➤ *vb, tr & intr* to be or act as a parent; to care for someone or something as a parent. ○ **parental** *adj.* ○ **parenthood** *n.* ○ **parenting** *n.*

parentage *n* **1** descent from parents. **2** rank or character derived from one's parents or ancestors. **3** the state or fact of being a parent.

parenthesis /pəˈrɛnθəsɪs/ *n* (*-ses* /-siːz/) **1** a word or phrase inserted into a sentence as a comment, usu marked off by brackets or dashes. **2** (**parentheses**) a pair of round brackets ( ), used to enclose such a comment.

parenthetic or **parenthetical** *adj* **1** referring to the nature of a parenthesis. **2** using parenthesis. ○ **parenthetically** *adv.*

par excellence /paːˈrɛksəlɑːs, -ləns/ *adv* beyond compare.

pariah /pəˈraɪə/ *n* **1** someone scorned and avoided by others; a social outcast. **2** in S India and Burma: a member of a caste lower than the four Brahminical castes.

parietal /pəˈraɪətəl/ *adj, med, anat* relating to, or forming, the wall of a bodily cavity, eg the skull: *the parietal bones.*

parish *n* **1** a district or area served by its own church and priest or minister, usu the established church of that particular area. **2** esp in England: the smallest unit of local government. **3** the inhabitants of a parish. ➤ *adj* **1** belonging or relating to a parish. **2** employed or supported by the parish. ○ **parishioner** *n.*

parity *n* (*-ies*) **1** equality in status, eg in pay. **2** precise equivalence; exact correspondence. **3** *commerce* an established equivalence be-

tween a unit of national currency and an amount in another national currency.

park *n* **1** an area in a town with grass and trees, for public recreation. **2** an area of land kept in its natural condition as a nature reserve, etc. **3** the woodland and pasture forming the estate of a large country house. **4** a place where vehicles can be left temporarily: *a bus park.* **5** an area containing a group of buildings housing related enterprises: *a science park.* **6** *chiefly N Am* a sports field or stadium. **7** (**the park**) *colloq* the pitch in use in a football game. ➤ *vb* **1** *tr & intr* **a** to leave (a vehicle) temporarily at the side of the road or in a car park; **b** to manoeuvre (a vehicle) into such a position. **2** *colloq* to lay or leave something somewhere temporarily. **3** (**park oneself**) *colloq* to sit or install oneself.

parka *n* **1** a hooded jacket made of skins, worn by the Inuit and Aleut people of the Arctic. **2** a windproof jacket, esp a quilted one with a fur-trimmed hood.

parkin or **perkin** *n, Scot & N Eng* a moist ginger-flavoured oatmeal cake made with treacle.

parkinsonism *n, med* an incurable disorder, usu occurring later in life, and characterized by trembling of limbs, rigidity of muscles, a mask-like facial expression, a slow shuffling gait and stooping posture.

Parkinson's disease *n, med* the commonest form of PARKINSONISM, caused by degeneration of brain cells.

parkland *n* pasture and woodland forming part of a country estate.

parky *adj* (*-ier, -iest*) *Brit colloq* of the weather: chilly.

parlance *n* a particular style or way of using words: *in legal parlance.*

parley *vb, intr* to discuss peace terms, etc with an enemy, esp under truce. ➤ *n* a meeting with an enemy to discuss peace terms, etc.

parliament *n* **1** the highest law-making assembly of a nation. **2** (**Parliament**) in the UK: the Houses of Commons and Lords. ○ **parliamentary** *adj.*

parliamentarian *n* **1** an expert in parliamentary procedure. **2** an experienced parliamentary debater.

parlour or (*US*) **parlor** *n* **1** *usu in compounds* a shop or commercial premises providing specified goods or services: *an ice-cream parlour* • *a funeral parlour.* **2** *dated* a sitting-room for receiving visitors.

parlous *adj, archaic or facetious* precarious; perilous; dire.

Parmesan /ˈpɑːməzan/ *n* a hard dry Italian cheese, grated on pasta, etc.

parochial *adj* **1** *derog* of tastes, attitudes, etc: concerned only with local affairs; narrow, limited or provincial in outlook. **2** referring or relating to a parish. ○ **parochialism** *n.*

parody *n* (*-ies*) **1** a comic or satirical imitation of a work, or the style, of a particular writer, composer, etc. **2** a poor attempt at something.

➤ *vb* (*-ies, -ied*) to ridicule something through parody. ○ **parodist** *n*.

parole *n* **1 a** the release of a prisoner before the end of their sentence, on promise of good behaviour: *released on parole*; **b** the duration of this conditional release. **2** the promise of a prisoner so released to behave well. ➤ *vb* to release or place (a prisoner) on parole. ○ **parolee** *n*.

parotid *adj, anat* situated beside or near the ear. ➤ *n* the **parotid gland**, a salivary gland in front of the ear.

paroxysm *n* **1** a sudden emotional outburst, eg of rage or laughter. **2** a spasm, convulsion or seizure, eg of coughing or acute pain. **3** a sudden reappearance of or increase in the severity of the symptoms of a disease or disorder. ○ **paroxysmal** *adj*.

parquet /ˈpɑːkeɪ/ *n* flooring composed of small inlaid blocks of wood arranged in a geometric pattern. ➤ *adj* made of parquet: *parquet floor*.

parquetry /ˈpɑːkətrɪ/ *n* inlaid work in wood arranged in a geometric pattern, used esp to cover floors or to decorate furniture, etc.

parr *n* (*parr* or *parrs*) a young salmon aged up to two years, before it becomes a SMOLT.

parricide *n* **1** the act of killing one's own parent or near relative. **2** someone who commits this act.

parrot *n* **1** a brightly-coloured bird, native to forests of warmer regions, with a large head and a strong hooked bill. **2** a person who merely imitates or mimics others. ➤ *vb* (*parroted, parroting*) to repeat or mimic (another's words, etc) unthinkingly.

parrot-fashion *adv* by mindless, unthinking repetition: *We learnt our tables parrot-fashion*.

parry *vb* (*-ies, -ied*) **1** to fend off (a blow). **2** to sidestep (a question) adeptly. ➤ *n* (*-ies*) an act of parrying, esp in fencing.

parse *vb, tr & intr, gram* to analyse (a sentence) grammatically; to give the part of speech of and explain the grammatical role of (a word).

parsec *n, astron* a unit of astronomical measurement equal to 3.26 light years or 3.09×10^{13} km.

parsimony *n* reluctance or extreme care in spending money. ○ **parsimonious** *adj*.

parsley *n* a plant with finely-divided bright green curly aromatic leaves, used as a culinary herb and as a garnish.

parsnip *n* a plant widely grown for its thick fleshy tap root, eaten as a vegetable.

parson *n* **1** a parish priest in the Church of England. **2** any clergyman.

parsonage *n* the residence of a parson.

part *n* **1** a portion, piece or bit; some but not all. **2** one of a set of equal divisions or amounts that compose a whole: *five parts sand to two of sand*. **3** an essential piece; a component: *vehicle spare parts*. **4** a section of a book; any of the episodes of a story, etc issued or broadcast as a serial. **5 a** a performer's role in a play, etc; **b** the words, actions, etc belonging to the role. **6** the melody, etc given to a particular instrument or voice in a musical work. **7** one's share, responsibility or duty in something. **8** (*usu* **parts**) a region: *foreign parts*. **9** (**parts**) talents; abilities: *a man of many parts*. ➤ *vb* **1** to divide; to separate. **2** *intr* to become divided or separated. **3** to separate (eg curtains, combatants, etc). **4** *intr* of more than one person: to leave one another; to go in different directions. **5** *intr* (**part from** or **with sb**) to leave them or separate from them. **6** *intr* (**part with sth**) to give it up or hand it over. **7** to put a parting in (hair). **8** *intr* to come or burst apart. ➤ *adj* in part; partial: *part payment*. ♦ **for my part** as far as I am concerned. **for the most part 1** usually. **2** mostly or mainly. **in part** partly; not wholly but to some extent. **on the part of sb 1** as done by them. **2** so far as they are concerned. **part and parcel of sth** an essential part of it. **take part in sth** to participate in it; to share in it.

partake *vb* (**partook, partaken**) *intr* (*usu* **partake in** or **of sth**) **1** to participate in it. **2** to eat or drink.

parterre /pɑːˈteə(r)/ *n* a formal flower-garden with lawns and paths.

part exchange *n* a purchase or sale of new goods made by exchanging used goods for part of the value of the new goods.

Parthian shot SEE PARTING SHOT

partial *adj* **1** incomplete; in part only. **2** (*always* **partial to sth**) having a liking for it. **3** favouring one side or person unfairly. ○ **partially** *adv* not completely.

partiality *n* **1** being partial. **2** favourable bias or prejudice. **3** fondness.

participate *vb, intr* (*often* **participate in sth**) to take part or be involved in it. ○ **participant** or **participator** *n*. ○ **participation** *n*.

participle *n, gram* a word formed from a verb, which has adjectival qualities as well as verbal ones. There are two participles in English, the **present participle**, formed with the ending -*ing*, as in *going, swimming* or *shouting*, and the **past participle**, generally ending in -*d*, -*ed*, -*t* or -*n*, as in *chased, shouted, kept* and *shown*, but also with irregular forms such as *gone, swum*, etc. ○ **participial** /pɑːtɪˈsɪpɪəl/ *adj* having the role of a participle: *a participial clause*.

particle *n* **1** a tiny piece; a minute piece of matter. **2** *physics* a tiny unit of matter such as a MOLECULE, ATOM or ELECTRON. **3** *gram* a word which does not have any inflected forms, eg a PREPOSITION, CONJUNCTION or INTERJECTION. **4** *gram* an AFFIX, such as *un-, de-, -fy* and -*ly*.

particoloured *adj* partly one colour, partly another.

particular *adj* **1** specific; single; individually known or referred to: *that particular day*. **2** especial: *I took particular care*. **3** difficult to satisfy; fastidious; exacting: *He's very particular*. **4** exact; detailed. ➤ *n* **1** a detail. **2** (**particulars**) personal details, eg name, date of birth, etc.

♦ **in particular** particularly; especially; specifically; in detail.

particularity n **1** the quality of being particular. **2** minuteness of detail. **3** (often **particularities**) a single instance or case; a detail: *the particularities of the case*.

particularize or **-ise** vb **1** to specify individually. **2** to give specific examples of something. **3** intr to go into detail.

particularly adv **1** more than usually: *particularly good*. **2** specifically; especially: *She particularly wanted red*.

parting n **1** the act of taking leave. **2** a divergence or separation: *a parting of the ways*. **3** a line of exposed scalp that divides sections of hair brushed in opposite directions: *a middle parting*. ➤ adj referring to, or at the time of, leaving; departing: *a parting comment*.

parting shot n (also **Parthian shot**) a final hostile remark made on departing.

partisan n **1** an enthusiastic supporter of a party, person, cause, etc. **2** a member of an armed resistance group in a country occupied by an enemy. ➤ adj strongly loyal to one side, esp blindly so. ○ **partisanship** n.

partition n **1** something which divides an object into parts. **2** a screen or thin wall dividing a room. **3** the dividing of a country into two or more independent states. ➤ vb **1** to divide (a country) into independent states. **2** (also **partition sth off**) to separate it off with a partition.

partly adv in part, or in some parts; to a certain extent, not wholly.

partner n **1** one of two or more people who jointly own or run a business or other enterprise on an equal footing. **2** a person with whom one has a sexual relationship, esp a long-term one. **3** a person one dances with: *dance partner*. **4** a person who is on the same side as oneself in a game of bridge, tennis, etc. ➤ vb to join as a partner with someone; to be the partner of someone.

partnership n **1** a relationship in which two or more people or groups operate together as partners. **2** the status of a partner: *They offered her a partnership*. **3** a business or other enterprise jointly owned or run by two or more people, etc.

part of speech n (**parts of speech**) gram any of the grammatical classes of words, eg noun, adjective, verb or preposition.

partridge n (**partridge** or **partridges**) a ground-dwelling bird, with brown or grey plumage, unfeathered legs and feet, and a very short tail.

part song n a song for singing in harmonized parts.

part-time adj done, attended, etc during only part of the full working week. ➤ adv (**part time**) for only part of the working week. Compare FULL-TIME. ○ **part-timer** n.

parturient adj, med **1** referring or relating to childbirth. **2** giving birth or about to give birth.

parturition n, med the process of giving birth; childbirth.

party n (**-ies**) **1** a social gathering, esp of invited guests, for enjoyment or celebration. **2** a group of people involved in a certain activity together: *search party*. **3** (often **Party**) an organization, esp a national organization, of people united by a common, esp political, aim. **4** law each of the individuals or groups concerned in a contract, agreement, lawsuit, etc: *There's no third party involved*. **5** old facetious use a person: *an elderly party*. ➤ vb (**-ies, -ied**) intr, colloq to gather as a group to drink, chat, dance, etc for enjoyment.

parvenu or **parvenue** /'pɑːvənjuː, -nuː/ n (**parvenus** or **parvenues**) derog respectively a man or woman who has recently acquired wealth but lacks the social refinement sometimes thought necessary to go with it.

pascal /'paskəl/ n in the SI system: a unit of pressure, equal to a force of one newton per square metre.

paschal /'paskəl/ adj **1** relating to the Jewish festival of PASSOVER. **2** relating to Easter.

pasha n, hist placed after the name in titles: a high-ranking Turkish official in the Ottoman Empire.

pass vb **1** tr & intr to come alongside and progress beyond something or someone: *I passed her on the stairs*. **2** intr to run, flow, progress, etc: *blood passing through our veins*. **3** tr & intr (also **pass through, into**, etc sth or **pass sth through, into**, etc sth) to go or make it go, penetrate, etc: *to pass through a filter*. **4** (sometimes **pass sth round, on**, etc) to circulate it; to hand or transfer it from one person to the next in succession. **5** tr & intr to move lightly across, over, etc something: *to pass a duster over the furniture*. **6** intr to move from one state or stage to another. **7** to exceed or surpass: *We passed the target*. **8** tr & intr of a vehicle: to overtake. **9** a tr & intr to achieve the required standard in (a test, etc); **b** to award (a student, etc) the marks required for success in a test, etc. **10** intr to take place: *what passed between them*. **11** tr & intr of time: to go by; to use up (time) in some activity, etc. **12** tr & intr (usu **pass down** or **pass sth down**) to be inherited; to hand it down. **13** tr & intr, sport to throw or kick (the ball, etc) to another player in one's team. **14** tr & intr to agree to (a proposal or resolution) or be agreed to; to vote (a law) into effect. **15** of a judge or law court: to pronounce (judgement). **16** intr (sometimes **pass off**) to go away after a while: *Her nausea passed*. **17** intr to be accepted, tolerated or ignored: *Let it pass*. **18** intr to choose not to answer in a quiz, etc or bid in a card game. **19** to make a (comment, etc). **20** to discharge (urine or faeces). ➤ n **1** a route through a gap in a mountain range. **2** an official card or document permitting one to enter somewhere, be absent from duty, etc. **3** a successful result in an examination, but usu without distinction or honours. **4** sport a throw, kick, hit, etc to another player in one's team. **5** a state of affairs: *Things came to a sorry pass.* **6** a decision not to answer in a quiz, etc, or not to bid in a card game. ♦ **come or be brought to pass** to happen. **make a pass at sb** to make a casual sexual advance towards them. **pass the time of day** to exchange an ordinary greeting with someone. ◊ **pass away** or **on** *euphem* to die. **pass sth** or **sb by** to overlook or ignore them. **pass off** of an arranged event: to take place with the result specified: *The party passed off very well.* **pass oneself off as sb** or **sth** to represent oneself as that person or thing: *They passed themselves off as students.* **pass sth off** to successfully present (something which is fraudulent). **pass out 1** to faint. **2** to leave a military or police college having successfully completed one's training. **pass over sth** to overlook it; to ignore it. **pass sth up** *colloq* to neglect or sacrifice (an opportunity).

passable *adj* **1** barely adequate. **2** *colloq* fairly good. **3** of a road, etc: able to be travelled along, crossed, etc.

passage *n* **1** a route through; a corridor, narrow street, or channel. **2** a tubular vessel in the body. **3** a piece of a text or musical composition of moderate length. **4** the process of passing: *the passage of time.* **5 a** a journey, esp by ship or aeroplane; **b** the cost of such a journey. **6** permission or freedom to pass through a territory, etc. **7** the voting of a law, etc into effect: *passage of the bill.*

passageway *n* a narrow passage or way, etc, usu with walls on each side; a corridor; an alley.

passé /ˈpɑseɪ, ˈpɑːseɪ/ *adj* outmoded; old-fashioned.

passenger *n* **1** a traveller in a vehicle, boat, aeroplane, etc, driven, sailed or piloted by someone else. **2** *derog* someone not doing their share of the work in a joint project, etc. ➢ *adj* relating to, or for, passengers: *passenger trains.*

passer-by *n* (**passers-by**) someone who is walking past a house, shop, incident, etc.

passerine *ornithol, adj* belonging or relating to the largest order of birds, characterized by a perching habit, and which includes the songbirds. ➢ *n* any bird belonging to this order.

passim *adv* of a word, reference, etc: occurring frequently throughout the literary or academic work in question.

passing *adj* **1** lasting only briefly. **2** casual; transitory: *a passing glance.* ➢ *n* **1** a coming to the end. **2** *euphem* death. ♦ **in passing** while dealing with something else; casually; by allusion rather than directly.

passion *n* **1** a violent emotion, eg anger or envy. **2** a fit of anger. **3** sexual love or desire. **4 a** an enthusiasm: *He has a passion for bikes;* **b** the subject of great enthusiasm: *Bikes are his passion.* **5** (*usu* **the Passion**) the suffering and death of Christ.

passionate *adj* **1** easily moved to passion; strongly emotional. **2** keen, enthusiastic; intense. ◊ **passionately** *adv.*

passion fruit *n* the round yellow or purple edible fruit of a tropical plant.

passive *adj* **1** lacking positive or assertive qualities. **2** lethargic; inert. **3** *gram* **a** denoting or relating to a verbal construction which in English consists of *be* and the past participle, which carries a meaning in which the subject undergoes, rather than performs, the action of the verb, such as '*the letter*' in *The letter was written by John.* Compare ACTIVE (sense 6a); **b** denoting or relating to the verb in such a construction. ➢ *n, gram* **1** (*also* **passive voice**) the form or forms that a passive verb takes. **2** a passive verb or construction. ◊ **passively** *adv.* ◊ **passivity** *n.*

passive smoking *n* the involuntary breathing in of tobacco smoke by non-smokers.

Passover *n* an annual Jewish festival held 15–22 Nisan (in March or April), commemorating the deliverance of the Israelites from bondage in Egypt.

passport *n* **1** an official document issued by the government, giving proof of the holder's identity and nationality, and permission to travel abroad with its protection. **2** an asset that guarantees one something, esp a privilege: *A degree is your passport to a good job.*

password *n* **1** *esp mil* a secret word allowing entry to a high-security area or past a checkpoint, etc. **2** *comput* a set of characters personal to a user which they input to gain access to a computer or network.

past *adj* **1** referring to an earlier time; of long ago. **2** recently ended; just gone by: *the past year.* **3** over; finished. **4** former; previous: *past presidents.* **5** *gram* of the tense of a verb: indicating an action or condition which took place or began in the past. ➢ *prep* **1** up to and beyond: *They went past me.* **2** after in time or age: *It's past your bedtime.* **3** beyond; farther away than: *the one past the library.* **4** having advanced too far for something: *She's past playing with dolls.* **5** beyond the reach of something: *past help* ♦ *What he did was past belief.* ➢ *adv* **1** so as to pass by: *She watched me go past.* **2** ago: *two months past.* ➢ *n* **1** (*usu* **the past**) **a** the time before the present; **b** events, etc belonging to this time. **2** one's earlier life or career. **3** a disreputable period earlier in one's life: *a woman with a past.* **4** *gram* **a** the past tense; **b** a verb in the past tense. ♦ **not put it past sb** *colloq* to believe them quite liable or disposed to do a certain thing. **past it** *colloq* having lost the vigour of one's youth or prime.

pasta *n* a dough made with flour, water and eggs, shaped into a variety of forms such as spaghetti, macaroni, lasagne, etc.

paste *n* **1** a stiff moist mixture made from a powder, traditionally flour, and water, and used as an adhesive: *wallpaper paste.* **2** a spread for sandwiches, etc made from ground meat or fish, etc. **3** any fine, often sweet, dough like mixture: *almond paste.* **4** a hard brilliant glass used in making imitation gems.

➤ *vb* **1** to stick something with paste. **2** (*also* **paste sth up**) *printing* to mount (text, illustrations, etc) on a backing as a proof for printing from or photographing, etc. **3** *word-processing* to insert text, etc which has been copied or cut from another part of the document, etc. **4** *colloq* to thrash or beat soundly.

pastel *n* **1** a chalk-like crayon made from ground pigment. **2** a picture drawn with pastels. ➤ *adj* **1** of colours: delicately pale; soft, quiet. **2** drawn with pastels.

pastern *n* the part of a horse's foot between the hoof and the fetlock.

pasteurize or **-ise** / 'pɑːstjʊəraɪz/ *vb* to partially sterilize (food, esp milk) by heating it to a specific temperature for a short period before rapidly cooling it. ○ **pasteurization** *n*.

pastiche / pa'stiːʃ/ *n* a musical, artistic or literary work in someone else's style, or in a mixture of styles.

pastille *n* a small fruit-flavoured sweet, sometimes medicated: *fruit pastilles*.

pastime *n* a hobby.

pasting *n, colloq* a thrashing.

past master *n* an expert.

pastor *n* a member of the clergy, esp in churches other than Anglican and Catholic, with responsibility for a congregation.

pastoral *adj* **1 a** relating to the countryside or country life; **b** of a poem, painting, musical work, etc: depicting the countryside or country life, esp expressing nostalgia for an idealized simple rural existence. **2** relating to a member of the clergy or their work. **3** relating to shepherds or their work. **4** of land: used for pasture. ➤ *n* **1** a pastoral poem or painting. **2** *mus* a PASTORALE. **3** a letter from a bishop to the clergy and people of the diocese.

pastorale / pastə'rɑːl/ *n, mus* a musical work that evokes the countryside.

pastrami *n* a smoked highly-seasoned cut of beef.

pastry *n* (*-ies*) **1** dough made with flour, fat and water, used for piecrusts. **2** a sweet baked article made with this.

pasturage *n* **1** an area of land where livestock is allowed to graze. **2** grass for feeding.

pasture *n* an area of grassland suitable or used for the grazing of livestock. ➤ *vb* **1** to put (animals) in pasture to graze. **2** *intr* of animals: to graze.

pasty[1] / 'pastɪ, 'pɑːstɪ/ *n* (*-ies*) a pie consisting of pastry folded round a savoury or sweet filling: *a Cornish pasty*.

pasty[2] / 'peɪstɪ/ *adj* (*-ier, -iest*) **1** like a paste in texture. **2** of the complexion: unhealthily pale. ○ **pastiness** *n*.

pat *vb* (**patted, patting**) **1** to strike (a person or animal) lightly or affectionately with the palm of one's hand. **2** to shape something by striking it lightly with the palm or a flat instrument: *to pat it into shape*. ➤ *n* **1** a light blow, esp an affectionate one, with the palm of the hand. **2** a round flat mass: *a pat of butter*. ➤ *adv* esp of

things said: immediately and fluently, as if memorized: *Their answers came too pat*. ➤ *adj* of answers, etc: quickly and easily supplied.
♦ **a pat on the back** an approving word or gesture. **have** or **know sth off pat** to have memorized it and know it perfectly.

patch *n* **1** a piece of material sewn on or applied, eg to a garment or piece of fabric, etc, so as to cover a hole or reinforce a worn area. **2** a plot of earth: *a vegetable patch*. **3** a pad or cover worn as protection over an injured eye. **4** a small expanse contrasting with its surroundings: *patches of ice*. **5** a scrap or shred. **6** *colloq* a phase or period of time: *We went through a bad patch*. **7** *slang* the area patrolled by a police officer or covered by a particular police station. **8** *comput* a set of instructions added to a program to correct an error. ➤ *vb* **1** to mend (a hole or garment) by sewing a patch or patches on or over it. **2** (*also* **patch sth up**) to repair it hastily and temporarily. **3** *comput* to make a temporary correction in (a program). ○ **patchy** *adj*. ♦ **not a patch on sb** or **sth** *colloq* not nearly as good as them. ◊ **patch sth up** *colloq* to settle (a quarrel, etc).

patchwork *n* **1** needlework done by sewing together small pieces of contrasting patterned fabric. **2** a piece of work produced in this way. **3** a variegated expanse: *a patchwork of fields*.

pate *n, old use or facetious* the head or skull.

pâté / 'pateɪ/ *n* a spread made from minced meat, fish or vegetables blended with herbs, spices, etc.

pâté de foie gras see under FOIE GRAS

patella / pə'telə/ *n* (*patellae* /-'teliː/ or *patellas*) *anat* the KNEECAP.

paten / 'patən/ *n, relig* a circular metal plate on which the bread is placed in the celebration of the Eucharist.

patent / 'peɪtənt, 'patənt/ *n* **1** an official licence from the government granting a person or business the sole right, for a certain period, to make and sell a particular article. **2** the right so granted. **3** the invention so protected. ➤ *vb* to obtain a patent for (an invention, design, etc). ➤ *adj* **1** very evident: *a patent lie*. **2** concerned with the granting of, or protection by, patents. **3** of a product: made or protected under patent. **4** open for inspection: *letters patent*. ○ **patentable** *adj*. ○ **patently** *adv* openly; clearly: *patently obvious*.

patent leather *n* leather made glossy by varnishing.

patent medicine *n, technical* a patented medicine which is available without prescription.

pater *n, old use or facetious* father.

paternal *adj* **1** referring, relating, or appropriate to a father: *paternal instincts*. **2** of a relation or ancestor: related on one's father's side: *my paternal grandmother*. Compare MATERNAL.

paternalism *n* governmental or managerial benevolence towards its citizens, employees, etc taken to the extreme of overprotectiveness and authoritarianism. ○ **paternalistic** *adj*.

paternity n **1** the quality or condition of being a father. **2** the relation of a father to his children. **3** the authorship, source or origin of something.

paternoster n **1** THE LORD'S PRAYER. **2** every eleventh bead in a rosary at which the Lord's Prayer is repeated.

path n **1** (*also* **pathway**) a track trodden by, or specially surfaced for, walking. **2** the line along which something is travelling: *the path of Jupiter*. **3** a course of action: *the path to ruin*.

pathetic adj **1** touching, heart-rending, poignant or pitiful: *her pathetic sobs*. **2** derog, colloq hopelessly inadequate. ○ **pathetically** adv.

pathname n, comput the description of the location of a file in terms of a computer's disk drives and directory structure.

pathogen n, pathol any micro-organism, esp a bacterium or virus, that causes disease in a living organism. ○ **pathogenic** adj.

pathological adj **1** relating to pathology. **2** caused by, or relating to, illness. **3** colloq compulsive; habitual: *a pathological liar*. ○ **pathologically** adv.

pathology n (*-ies*) **1** the branch of medicine concerned with the study of the nature of diseases. **2** the manifestations, characteristic behaviour, etc of a disease. ○ **pathologist** n.

pathos n a quality in a situation, etc, esp in literature, that moves one to pity.

> **pathos** A word sometimes confused with this one is **bathos**.

patience n **1** the ability to endure delay, trouble, pain or hardship in a calm and contained way. **2** tolerance and forbearance. **3** perseverance. **4** cards a solo game in which the player, in turning each card over, has to fit it into a certain scheme.

patient adj having or showing patience. ➤ n a person who is being treated by, or is registered with, a doctor, dentist, etc. ○ **patiently** adv.

patina n **1** a coating formed on a metal surface by oxidation. **2** a mature shine on wood resulting from continual polishing and handling. **3** any fine finish acquired with age.

patio n **1** an open paved area beside a house. **2** an inner courtyard in a Spanish or Spanish-American house.

patisserie /pəˈtiːsəri/ n **1** a shop or café selling fancy cakes, sweet pastries, etc in the continental style. **2** such cakes.

patois /ˈpatwɑː/ n (*pl* **patois**) **1** the local dialect of a region, used usu in informal everyday situations. **2** jargon.

patriarch n **1** the male head of a family or tribe. **2** in the Eastern Orthodox Church: a high-ranking bishop. **3** in the Roman Catholic Church: the pope. **4** in the Old Testament: any of the ancestors of the human race or of the tribes of Israel, eg Adam, Abraham or Jacob. **5** a venerable old man. ○ **patriarchal** adj.

patriarchate n the office, authority, or residence of a church patriarch.

patriarchy n (*-ies*) **1** a social system in which a male is head of the family and descent is traced through the male line. **2** a society based on this system.

patrician n **1** hist a member of the aristocracy of ancient Rome. **2** an aristocrat. **3** someone who is thought of as refined and sophisticated. ➤ adj **1** belonging or relating to the aristocracy, esp that of ancient Rome. **2** refined and sophisticated.

patricide n **1** the act of killing one's own father. **2** someone who kills their own father.

patrimony n (*-ies*) **1** property inherited from one's father or ancestors. **2** something inherited; a heritage.

patriot n someone who loves and serves their fatherland or country devotedly. ○ **patriotic** adj. ○ **patriotically** adv. ○ **patriotism** n.

patrol vb (**patrolled, patrolling**) **1** tr & intr to make a regular systematic tour of (an area) to maintain security or surveillance. **2** intr of a police officer: to be on duty on a beat. ➤ n **1** the act of patrolling: *on patrol*. **2** a person or group of people performing this duty. **3** a body of aircraft, ships, etc carrying out this duty. **4** any of the units of six or so into which a troop of Scouts or Guides is divided.

patron n **1** someone who gives financial support and encouragement eg to an artist, the arts, a movement or charity: *a patron of the arts*. **2** a regular customer of a shop, attender at a theatre, etc.

patronage n **1** the support given by a patron. **2** regular custom given to a shop, theatre, etc. **3** the power of bestowing, or recommending people for, offices.

patronize or **-ise** /ˈpatrənaɪz; N Am ˈpeɪtrənaɪz/ vb **1** to treat someone condescendingly. **2** to act as a patron towards (an organization, individual, etc). **3** to give custom, esp regularly, to (a shop, theatre, restaurant, etc). ○ **patronizing** adj. ○ **patronizingly** adv.

patron saint n the guardian saint of a country, profession, etc.

patronymic n a name derived from one's father's or other male ancestor's name, usu with a suffix or prefix, as in *Donaldson* or *Macdonald*.

patsy n (*-ies*) slang, chiefly N Am an easy victim; a scapegoat or fall guy.

patter[1] vb, intr **1** of rain, footsteps, etc: to make a light rapid tapping noise. **2** to move with light rapid footsteps. ➤ n the light rapid tapping of footsteps or rain.

patter[2] n **1** the fast persuasive talk of a salesman, or the quick speech of a comedian. **2** the jargon or speech of a particular group or area: *Glasgow patter*. ➤ vb, tr & intr to say or speak rapidly or glibly.

pattern n **1** a model, guide or set of instructions for making something: *a dress pattern*. **2** a decorative design, often consisting of repeated motifs, eg on wallpaper or fabric. **3** a piece, eg of fabric, as a sample. **4** any excellent example suitable for imitation. **5** a coherent series of occurrences or set of features: *a pattern of events.* ➤ *vb* (*usu* **pattern sth on another thing**) to model it on another type, design, etc.

patty *n* (*-ies*) **1** *N Am* a flat round cake of minced meat, vegetables, etc. **2** a small meat pie.

paucity *n* (*-ies*) smallness of quantity; a scarcity or lack.

paunch *n* a protruding belly, esp in a man. ○ **paunchy** *adj* (*-ier, -iest*).

pauper *n* **1** a poverty-stricken person. **2** *hist* someone living on charity or publicly provided money.

pause *n* **1** a relatively short break in some activity, etc. **2** *mus* a the prolonging of a note or rest beyond its normal duration; **b** a sign (⌒) indicating this, usu placed above the note, etc. ➤ *vb, intr* **1** to have a break; to stop briefly. **2** to hesitate. ◆ **give sb pause** to make them hesitate before acting.

pave *vb* to surface (esp a footpath, but also a street, etc) with stone slabs, cobbles, etc. ○ **paved** *adj.* ◆ **pave the way for sth** or **sb** to prepare for and make way for its introduction or their arrival.

pavement *n* **1** a raised footpath edging a road, etc, often but not always paved. **2** a paved road, area, expanse, etc: *a mosaic pavement.* **3** a road surface; road-surfacing material.

pavilion *n* **1** a building in a sports ground in which players change their clothes, store equipment, etc. **2** a light temporary building such as a marquee, in which to display exhibits at a trade fair, etc. **3** a summerhouse or ornamental shelter. **4** a large ornamental building for public pleasure and entertainment. **5** a large and elaborate tent.

paving *n* **1** stones or slabs used to pave a surface. **2** a paved surface.

paw *n* **1** the foot, usu clawed, of a four-legged mammal. **2** *colloq* a hand, esp when used clumsily. ➤ *vb* **1** to finger or handle something clumsily; to touch or caress someone with unwelcome familiarity. **2** (*also* **paw at sth**) of an animal: to scrape or strike it with a paw.

pawn[1] *vb* **1** to deposit (an article of value) with a pawnbroker as a pledge for a sum of money borrowed. **2** to pledge or stake something. ➤ *n* **1** the condition of being deposited as a pledge: *in pawn.* **2** an article pledged in this way.

pawn[2] *n* **1** *chess* a chess piece of lowest value. **2** a person used and manipulated by others.

pawnbroker *n* someone who lends money in exchange for pawned articles.

pawnshop *n* a pawnbroker's place of business.

pawpaw see under PAPAW

pay *vb* (**paid**) **1** *tr & intr* to give (money) to someone in exchange for goods, services, etc. **2** *tr & intr* to settle (a bill, debt, etc). **3** *tr & intr* to give (wages or salary) to an employee. **4** *tr & intr* to make a profit, or make something as profit: *businesses that don't pay.* **5** *tr & intr* to benefit; to be worthwhile: *It pays one to be polite* ● *Dis-*

honesty doesn't pay. **6** *tr & intr* (*also* **pay for sth**) to suffer a penalty on account of it; to be punished for it. **7 a** to do someone the honour of (a visit or call): *I paid her a visit in hospital;* **b** to offer someone (a compliment, one's respects, etc). **8** to give (heed or attention). ➤ *n* money given or received for work, etc; wages; salary. ○ **payable** *adj* that can or must be paid: *Make cheques payable to me* ● *payable by 31st July.* ◆ **in the pay of sb** employed by them. **pay one's way** to pay all of one's own debts and living expenses. **pay through the nose** to pay a very high price. **put paid to sth** or **sb** *colloq* to put an end to them; to deal effectively or finally with them. ◇ **pay sb back** to revenge oneself on them. **pay sth back** to return (money owed). **pay off** to have profitable results. **pay sth off** to finish paying (a debt, etc). **pay sth out 1** to spend or give (money), eg to pay bills, debts, etc. **2** to release or slacken (a rope, etc) esp by passing it little by little through one's hands. **pay up** *colloq* to pay the full amount that is due, esp reluctantly.

payee *n* someone to whom money is paid or a cheque is made out.

paying guest *n, euphem* a lodger.

payload *n* **1** the part of a vehicle's load which earns revenue. **2** the operating equipment carried by a spaceship or satellite. **3** the quantity and strength of the explosive carried by a missile. **4** the quantity of goods, passengers, etc carried by an aircraft.

paymaster *n* an official in charge of the payment of wages and salaries.

payment *n* **1** a sum of money paid. **2** the act of paying or process of being paid. **3** a reward or punishment.

payoff *n, colloq* **1** a fruitful result. **2** a bribe. **3** a climax, outcome or final resolution.

payola *n* **1** a bribe for promoting a product. **2** the practice of giving or receiving such bribes.

payout *n* **1** the act of paying out money. **2** an amount of money paid out.

pay-per-view *adj* referring or relating to PAY TV.

payphone *n* a telephone that is operated by coins or a plastic card.

payroll *n* a register of employees that lists the wage or salary due to each.

payslip *n* a note of an employee's pay, showing deductions for tax or national insurance.

pay TV or **pay television** *n* TV programmes, video entertainment, etc distributed to an audience which pays for the programmes viewed by subscribing to a cable or satellite network.

pazzazz or **pazazz** see PIZZAZZ

Pb *symbol, chem* lead.

PC *abbrev* **1** personal computer. **2** Police Constable. **3 a** political correctness; **b** politically correct.

pc *abbrev* **1** per cent. **2** *colloq* postcard.

Pd *symbol, chem* palladium.

pd *abbrev* paid.

PE *abbrev* physical education.

pea *n* 1 a climbing plant of the pulse family, cultivated for its edible seeds, which are produced in long pods. 2 the round protein-rich seed of this plant, eaten as a vegetable.

peace *n* 1 freedom from or absence of war. 2 a treaty or agreement ending a war. 3 freedom from or absence of noise, disturbance or disorder; quietness or calm. 4 freedom from mental agitation; serenity: *peace of mind*. ♦ **at peace 1** not at war; not fighting. 2 in harmony or friendship. 3 in a calm or serene state. 4 freed from earthly worries; dead. **hold one's peace** to remain silent. **keep the peace 1** *law* to preserve law and order. 2 to prevent, or refrain from, fighting or quarrelling. **make peace** to end a war or quarrel, etc.

peaceable *adj* peace-loving; mild; placid. ○ **peaceably** *adv*.

peaceful *adj* 1 calm and quiet. 2 unworried; serene. 3 free from war, violence, disturbance, disorder, etc.

peacemaker *n* 1 someone who makes or brings about peace with the enemy. 2 someone who reconciles enemies. ○ **peacemaking** *n, adj*.

peace pipe *n* a CALUMET.

peacetime *n* periods that are free of war.

peach *n* 1 a small deciduous tree, widely cultivated for its edible fruit or for ornament. 2 the large round fruit of this tree, consisting of a hard stone surrounded by sweet juicy yellow flesh and a yellowish-pink velvety skin. 3 the yellowish-pink colour of this fruit. 4 *colloq* something delightful: *a peach of a day*. ➤ *adj* yellowish-pink in colour: *a peach blouse*.

peachy *adj* (*-ier, -iest*) 1 coloured like or tasting like a peach. 2 *colloq* very good.

peacock *n* (*peacock* or *peacocks*) 1 a large bird, the male of which has a train of green and gold feathers with large spots which it fans showily during courtship. 2 the male of this species (the female being the **peahen**). 3 *derog* a vain person.

peak[1] *n* 1 a a sharp pointed summit; b a pointed mountain or hill. 2 a maximum, eg in consumer use: *Consumption reaches its peak at around 7pm*. 3 a time of maximum achievement, etc: *His peak was in his early twenties*. 4 the front projecting part of a cap. ➤ *adj* referring or relating to the period of highest use or demand: *peak viewing time*. ➤ *vb, intr* 1 to reach a maximum. 2 to reach the height of one's powers or popularity.

peak[2] *vb, intr* to droop; to look thin or sickly.

peaky *adj* (*-ier, -iest*) ill-looking; pallid.

peal *n* 1 the ringing of a bell or set of bells. 2 *non-technical* a set of bells, each with a different note. 3 a burst of noise: *a peal of thunder*. ➤ *vb* 1 to ring or resound. 2 to sound or signal (eg a welcome) by ringing.

pean see PAEAN

peanut *n* 1 a low-growing plant of the pulse family, widely cultivated for its edible seeds

which are produced under the ground in pods. 2 the protein-rich seed of this plant. 3 (**peanuts**) *colloq* a something small, trivial or unimportant; b a paltry amount of money.

peanut butter *n* a savoury spread made from ground roasted peanuts.

pear *n* 1 a deciduous tree, widely cultivated for its edible fruit and ornamental flowers. 2 the edible cone-shaped fruit of this tree, consisting of a core of small seeds surrounded by sweet juicy white pulp.

pearl[1] *n* 1 a bead of smooth hard lustrous material found inside the shell of certain molluscs, eg oysters, and used as a gem. 2 an artificial imitation of this. 3 (**pearls**) a necklace of pearls. 4 mother-of-pearl. 5 something resembling a pearl. 6 something valued or precious: *pearls of wisdom*. ➤ *adj* 1 like a pearl in colour or shape. 2 made of or set with pearls or mother-of-pearl. ➤ *vb* 1 to set something with, or as if with, pearls. 2 *intr* to fish for pearls.

pearl[2] see PURL[1] (*noun* sense 3).

pearl barley *n* seeds of barley ground into round polished grains, used in soups and stews.

pearly *adj* (*-ier, -iest*) 1 like a pearl or pearl. 2 covered in pearl.

pearly gates *pl n, colloq* the gates of Heaven.

peasant *n* 1 in poor agricultural societies: a farm worker or small farmer. 2 *derog* a rough unmannerly or culturally ignorant person. ○ **peasantry** *n* 1 the peasant class. 2 the condition of being a peasant.

pease *n* (*pl pease*) *archaic* a pea or pea-plant.

pease pudding *n* a purée made from split peas.

pea-shooter *n* a short tube through which to fire dried peas by blowing, used as a toy weapon.

pea-souper *n, colloq* a very thick yellowish fog.

peat *n* a mass of dark-brown or black fibrous plant material, produced by the compression of partially decomposed vegetation, used in compost and in dried form as a fuel. ○ **peaty** *adj* (*-ier, -iest*).

pebble *n* a small fragment of rock, esp one worn round and smooth by the action of water. ➤ *vb* to cover with pebbles. ○ **pebbled** *adj*. ○ **pebbly** *adj* (*-ier, -iest*).

pebbledash *n, Brit* a coating for exterior walls of cement or plaster with small stones embedded in it.

pec *n* (*usu* **pecs**) *colloq* a PECTORAL MUSCLE.

pecan *n* 1 a deciduous N American tree, widely cultivated for its edible nut. 2 the oblong reddish-brown edible nut, with a sweet oily kernel, produced by this tree.

peccadillo *n* (*peccadillos* or *peccadilloes*) a minor misdeed.

peck[1] *vb* 1 (*also* **peck at sth**) of a bird: to strike, nip or pick at it with the beak. 2 to poke (a hole) with the beak. 3 to kiss someone or something in a quick or perfunctory way. 4 *intr* (*often* **peck at sth**) a to eat (food) in a cursory, inattentive or dainty way, without enjoyment or application; **b** to quibble at it. ➤ *n* **1** a tap or nip with the beak. **2** a perfunctory kiss.

peck² *n* in the imperial system: a measure of capacity of dry goods, esp grain, equal to two gallons (9.1 litres) or a quarter of a BUSHEL.

pecker *n* **1** something that pecks; a beak. **2** a woodpecker. **3** *colloq* spirits; resolve: *Keep your pecker up!*

pecking order *n* any social hierarchy in animals or humans, or system of ranks and associated privileges.

peckish *adj, colloq* quite hungry.

pectin *n, biochem* a complex carbohydrate that functions as a cement-like material within and between plant cell-walls. It forms a gel at low temperatures and is widely used in jam-making.

pectoral *adj* **1** referring or relating to the breast or chest. **2** worn on the breast. ➤ *n* **1** a pectoral muscle. **2** a pectoral fin. **3** a neck ornament worn covering the chest. **4** armour for the breast of a person or a horse.

pectoral fin *n* in fishes: one of a pair of fins situated just behind the gills, used to control the angle of ascent or descent in the water, and for slowing down.

pectoral muscle *n, anat* either of two muscles situated on either side of the top half of the chest.

peculate *vb, tr & intr, formal* to appropriate something dishonestly for one's own use. ○ **peculation** *n.*

peculiar *adj* **1** strange; odd. **2** (**peculiar to sb or sth**) exclusively or typically belonging to or associated with them: *habits peculiar to cats.* **3** special; individual: *their own peculiar methods.* **4** especial; particular: *of peculiar interest.* ○ **peculiarly** *adv.*

peculiarity *n* (*-ies*) **1** the quality of being strange or odd. **2** a distinctive feature, characteristic or trait. **3** an eccentricity or idiosyncrasy.

pecuniary *adj* relating to, concerning or consisting of money.

pedagogue *n, old derog use* a teacher, esp a strict or pedantic one. ○ **pedagogic** *adj.*

pedagogy /'pɛdəgɒdʒɪ/ *n* the science, principles or work of teaching.

pedal /'pɛdl/ *n* **1** a lever operated by the foot, eg on a machine, vehicle or musical instrument. ➤ *vb* (**pedalled, pedalling;** or *esp N Am*) **pedaled, pedaling**) *tr & intr* to move or operate by means of a pedal or pedals. ➤ *adj* /'piːdəl/ *zool* referring or relating to the foot or feet.

pedant *n, derog* someone who is overconcerned with correctness of detail, esp in academic matters. ○ **pedantic** *adj.*

pedantry *n* **1** excessive concern with correctness. **2** a pedantic expression.

peddle *vb* **1** *tr & intr* to go from place to place selling (a selection of small goods). **2** *colloq* to deal illegally in (narcotic drugs). **3** *colloq* to

publicize and try to win acceptance for (ideas, theories, etc).

peddler *n* **1** the usual *N Am* spelling of PEDLAR. **2** someone who deals illegally in narcotics.

pederasty or **paederasty** *n* sexual relations between adults and children. ○ **pederast** or **paederast** *n* an adult who practises pederasty.

pedestal *n* the base on which a vase, statue, column, etc is placed or mounted. ♦ **put** or **place sb on a pedestal** to admire them extremely.

pedestrian *n* someone travelling on foot, esp in a street; someone who is walking. ➤ *adj* **1** referring to, or for, pedestrians. **2** dull; unimaginative; uninspired.

pedestrian crossing *n* a specially marked crossing-place for pedestrians, where they have priority over traffic.

pedestrianize or **-ise** *vb* to convert (a shopping street, etc) into an area for pedestrians only by excluding through-traffic and usu paving over the street. ○ **pedestrianization** *n.*

pedestrian precinct *n* a shopping street or similar area from which traffic is excluded.

pedicure *n* a medical or cosmetic treatment of the feet and toenails.

pedigree *n* **1** a person's or animal's line of descent, esp if long and distinguished, or proof of pure breeding. **2** a genealogical table showing this.

pediment *n, archit* a wide triangular gable set over a classical portico or the face of a building. ○ **pedimented** *adj.*

pedlar or (*chiefly N Am*) **peddler** *n* someone who peddles.

pedometer /pɪ'dɒmɪtə(r)/ *n* a device that measures distance walked by recording the number of steps taken.

peduncle *n* **1** *bot* a short stalk, eg carrying an inflorescence or a single flower-head. **2** *anat, pathol* any stalk-like structure. ○ **peduncular** or **pedunculated** *adj.*

pee *colloq, vb* (**peed, peeing**) *intr* to urinate. ➤ *n* **1** an act of urinating. **2** urine.

peek *vb, intr* (*also* **peek at sth**) to glance briefly and surreptitiously at it. ➤ *n* a brief furtive glance.

peel *vb* **1** to strip the skin or rind off (a fruit or vegetable). **2** *intr* to be able to be peeled: *Grapes don't peel easily.* **3** (*also* **peel sth away** or **off**) to strip off (an outer layer). **4** *intr* of a wall or other surface: to shed its outer coating in flaky strips. **5** *intr* of skin, paint or other coverings: to flake off in patches. **6** *intr* of a person or part of the body: to shed skin in flaky layers after sunburn. ➤ *n* the skin or rind of vegetables or fruit, esp citrus fruit: *candied peel.* ○ **peeler** *n* a small knife or device for peeling fruit and vegetables. ◊ **peel off 1** of an aircraft or vehicle: to veer away from the main group. **2** *colloq* to undress.

peelings *pl n* strips of peel removed from a fruit or vegetable.

peen or **pein** n the end of a hammer-head opposite the hammering face.

peep[1] vb, intr **1** (often **peep at sth** or **sb** or **peep out**) to look quickly or covertly, eg through a narrow opening or from a place of concealment; to peek. **2** (also **peep out**) to emerge briefly or partially. ⮞ n **1** a quick covert look. **2** a first faint glimmering: at peep of day.

peep[2] n **1** the faint high-pitched cry of a baby bird, etc. **2** the smallest utterance: Not another peep out of you! ⮞ vb, intr **1** of a young bird, etc: to utter a high-pitched cry; to cheep. **2** colloq to sound or make something sound: The driver peeped the horn.

peephole n a hole, crack, aperture, etc through which to peep.

peeping Tom n a man who furtively spies on other people.

peepshow n a box with a peephole through which a series of moving pictures, esp erotic or pornographic ones, can be watched.

peer[1] n **1** a member of the nobility, such as, in Britain, a DUKE, MARQUESS, EARL, VISCOUNT or BARON. **2** a member of the House of Lords. **3** someone who is one's equal in age, rank, etc; a contemporary, companion or fellow.

peer[2] vb, intr **1** (also **peer at sth** or **sb**) to look hard at it or them, esp through narrowed eyes, as if having difficulty in seeing. **2** (sometimes **peer out**) literary to peep out or emerge briefly or partially.

peerage n **1** the title or rank of a peer. **2** sing or pl the members of the nobility as a group.

peerless adj without equal; excelling all.

peer pressure n compulsion to do or obtain the same things as others in one's peer group.

peeve colloq, vb to irritate, annoy or offend. ⮞ n a cause of vexation or irritation. ○ **peeved** adj.

peevish adj irritable; inclined to whine or complain. ○ **peevishly** adv.

peg n **1** a little shaft of wood, metal or plastic shaped for fixing, fastening or marking uses. **2** a coat hook fixed to a wall, etc. **3** a wooden or plastic clip for fastening washing to a line to dry. **4** a small stake for securing tent ropes, marking a position, boundary, etc. **5** any of several wooden pins on a stringed instrument, which are turned to tune it. **6** a pin for scoring, used eg in cribbage. **7** colloq a leg. **8** colloq a PEG LEG (sense l). **9** old colloq a drink of spirits. ⮞ vb (**pegged, pegging**) **1** to insert a peg into something. **2** to fasten something with a peg or pegs. **3** (sometimes **peg sth out**) to mark out (ground) with pegs. **4** to set or freeze (prices, incomes, etc) at a certain level. ◆ **a square peg in a round hole** a person who does not fit in well in their environment, job, etc. **off the peg** of clothes: ready to wear; ready-made. **take sb down a peg or two** colloq to humiliate or humble them. ◇ **peg away at sth** colloq to work steadily at it. **peg out 1** colloq to die. **2** to become exhausted.

peg leg n, colloq **1** an artificial leg. **2** a person with an artificial leg.

pein see PEEN

pejorative /pə'dʒɒrətɪv/ adj of a word or expression: disapproving, derogatory, disparaging or uncomplimentary. ⮞ n a word or affix with derogatory force.

pelargonium n a plant with hairy stems, rounded or lobed aromatic leaves, and conspicuous scarlet, pink or white fragrant flowers, often cultivated under the name GERANIUM.

pelican n (**pelican** or **pelicans**) a large aquatic bird that has an enormous beak with a pouch below it, and mainly white plumage.

pelican crossing n a PEDESTRIAN CROSSING with a set of pedestrian-controlled traffic lights.

pelisse /pɛ'liːs/ n, hist **1** a long mantle of silk, velvet, etc, worn esp by women. **2** a fur or fur-lined garment, esp a military cloak.

pellagra n, med a disease characterized by scaly discoloration of the skin, diarrhoea, vomiting, and psychological disturbances.

pellet n **1** a small rounded mass of compressed material, eg paper. **2** a piece of small shot for an airgun, etc. **3** a ball of undigested material regurgitated by an owl or hawk. ⮞ vb (**pelleted, pelleting**) to form (esp seeds) into pellets by coating it with a substance, eg to aid planting.

pell-mell adv headlong; in confused haste. ⮞ adj confusedly mingled; headlong.

pellucid adj **1** transparent. **2** absolutely clear in expression and meaning.

pelmet n a strip of fabric or a narrow board fitted along the top of a window to conceal the curtain rail.

pelota n a game in which players use their hand or a basket-like device strapped to their wrist to catch and throw a ball against a specially marked wall.

pelt[1] vb **1** to bombard with missiles: He was pelted with stones. **2** intr to rush along at top speed: We were pelting along the motorway. **3** intr (often **pelt down**) to rain heavily. ⮞ n an act or spell of pelting. ◆ **at full pelt** as fast as possible.

pelt[2] n **1** the skin of a dead animal, esp with the fur still on it. **2** the coat of a living animal. **3** a hide stripped of hair for tanning.

pelvic adj relating to or in the region of the pelvis.

pelvis n (**pelvises** or **pelves**) anat the basin-shaped cavity formed by the SACRUM and the COCCYX.

pen[1] n **1** a writing instrument that uses ink. **2** this instrument as a symbol of the writing profession. ⮞ vb (**penned, penning**) formal to compose and write (a letter, poem, etc) with a pen. ○ **penned** adj written.

pen[2] n **1** a small enclosure, esp for animals. **2** often in compounds any small enclosure or area of confinement for the specified purpose:

a playpen. ➤ *vb* (**penned** or **pent, penning**) (*often* **pen sb** or **sth in** or **up**) to enclose or confine them in a pen, or as if in a pen.

pen³ *n, N Am colloq* a PENITENTIARY.

pen⁴ *n* a female swan.

penal /'pi:nəl/ *adj* relating to punishment, esp by law. ○ **penally** *adv.*

penalize or **-ise** *vb* **1** to impose a penalty on someone, for wrongdoing, cheating, breaking a rule, committing a foul in sport, etc. **2** to disadvantage someone.

penalty *n* (**-ies**) **1** a punishment, such as imprisonment, a fine, etc, imposed for wrongdoing, breaking a contract or rule, etc. **2** a punishment that one brings on oneself through ill-advised action: *I paid the penalty for my error.* **3** *sport* a handicap imposed on a competitor or team for an infringement of the rules, in team games taking the form of an advantage awarded to the opposing side. ◆ **under** or **on penalty of sth** with liability to the penalty of a particular punishment in case of violation of the law, etc: *He swore on penalty of death.*

penance *n* **1** repentance or atonement for an offence or wrongdoing, or an act of repentance. **2** *RC Church* a sacrament involving confession, repentance, forgiveness, and the performance of a penance suggested by one's confessor.

pence *a pl of* PENNY

penchant /'pɑ̃ʃɑ̃/ *n* a taste, liking, or tendency: *a penchant for childish pranks.*

pencil *n* **1** a writing and drawing instrument consisting of a wooden shaft containing a stick of graphite or other material. **2** something with a similar function or shape, eg for medical or cosmetic purposes: *an eyebrow pencil.* **3** something long, fine and narrow in shape. ➤ *vb* (**pencilled, pencilling;** N Am **penciled, penciling**) to write, draw or mark something with a pencil. ◊ **pencil sth** or **sb in** to note down a provisional commitment in one's diary for later confirmation.

pendant or (*sometimes*) **pendent** *n* **1 a** an ornament suspended from a neck chain, bracelet, etc; **b** a necklace with such an ornament hanging from it. **2** any of several hanging articles, eg an earring, ceiling light, etc.

pendent or (*sometimes*) **pendant** *adj* **1** hanging; suspended; dangling. **2** projecting; jutting; overhanging. **3** undetermined or undecided; pending.

pending *adj* **1** remaining undecided; waiting to be decided or dealt with. **2** of a patent: about to come into effect. ➤ *prep* until; awaiting; during: *He was held in prison pending trial.*

pendulous *adj* hanging down loosely; drooping; swinging freely.

pendulum *n* **1** *physics* a weight, suspended from a fixed point, that swings freely back and forth. **2** a swinging lever used to regulate the movement of a clock. **3** anything that undergoes obvious and regular shifts or reversals in direction, attitude, opinion, etc.

penes *a pl of* PENIS

penetrate *vb* **1** (*also* **penetrate into sth**) to find a way into it; to enter it, esp with difficulty. **2** to gain access into and influence within (a country, organization, market, etc) for political, financial, etc purposes. **3** to find a way through something; to pierce or permeate: *Troops penetrated enemy lines.* **4** *intr* to be understood: *The news didn't penetrate at first.* **5** to see through (a disguise). **6** to fathom, solve, or understand (a mystery). **7** of a man: to insert his penis into the vagina of (a woman) or anus of (a man or a woman). ○ **penetrative** *adj.*

penetrating *adj* **1** of a voice, etc: all too loud and clear; strident; carrying. **2** of a person's mind: acute; discerning. **3** of the eyes or of a look: piercing; probing.

penetration *n* **1** the process of penetrating or being penetrated. **2** mental acuteness; insight.

pen friend or **pen pal** *n* someone, usu living abroad, with whom one corresponds by letter, and whom one may not have met in person.

penguin *n* a flightless sea bird with a stout body, small almost featherless wings, short legs, bluish-grey or black plumage, and a white belly.

penicillin *n* any of various ANTIBIOTICs, derived from a mould or produced synthetically, that are widely used to treat bacterial infections.

peninsula *n* a piece of land projecting into water from a larger landmass and almost completely surrounded by water. ○ **peninsular** *adj.*

penis *n* (**penises** or **penes** /'pi:ni:z/) in higher vertebrates: the male organ of copulation which is used to transfer sperm to the female reproductive tract and also contains the URETHRA through which urine is passed. ○ **penile** *adj.*

penitent *adj* regretful for wrong one has done, and feeling a desire to reform. ➤ *n* **1** a repentant person, esp one doing penance on the instruction of a confessor. **2** *RC Church* a member of one of various orders devoted to penitential exercises, etc. ○ **penitence** *n.*

penitential *adj* referring to, showing or constituting penance: *penitential psalms.*

penitentiary *n* (**-ies**) *N Am* a federal or state prison. ➤ *adj* **1** referring or relating to punishment or penance. **2** penal or reformatory.

penknife *n* a pocket knife with blades that fold into the handle.

penmanship *n* the ability to write beautifully or to write well.

pen name *n* a pseudonym used by a writer.

pennant *n* **1** *naut* a dangling line from the masthead, etc, with a block for tackle, etc. **2** *naut* a small narrow triangular flag, used on vessels for identification or signalling.

pennate *adj, biol* **1** winged; feathered; shaped like a wing. **2** PINNATE.

penne *n* pasta in the form of short thick tubes.

penniless *adj* without money; poverty-stricken.

pennon n **1** hist a long narrow flag with a tapering divided tip, eg borne on his lance by a knight. **2** a PENNANT (sense 2).

penny / 'pɛnɪ/ n (**pence** in senses 1 and 2, or **pennies**) **1** (sing and pl abbrev **p**) in the UK: a hundredth part of £1, or a bronze coin having this value. **2** (sing and pl symbol **d**) in the UK before decimalization in 1971: $^{1}/_{12}$ of a shilling or $^{1}/_{240}$ of £1, or a bronze coin having this value. **3** with negatives the least quantity of money: It won't cost a penny. **4** N Am one cent, or a coin having this value. **5** / 'pɛnɪ, pənɪ/ in compounds denoting a specified number of pennies (as a value): a five-penny piece. ◆ **a pretty penny** ironic a huge sum. **spend a penny** euphem, colloq to urinate. **the penny dropped** colloq understanding about something finally came. **two a penny** or **ten a penny** in abundant supply and of little value.

penny-pinching adj, derog too careful with one's money. ○ **penny-pincher** n.

penny whistle n a tiny whistle or flageolet.

pen pal see PEN FRIEND

pen pusher n a clerk or minor official whose job includes much tedious paperwork. ○ **pen-pushing** n, adj.

pension / 'pɛnʃən/ n **1** a government allowance to a retired, disabled or widowed person. **2** a regular payment by an employer to a retired employee. **3** a regular payment from a private pension company to a person who contributed to a pension fund for much of their working life. **4** /French pãsjõ/ a boarding house in continental Europe. ➤ vb to grant a pension to (a person). ○ **pensioner** n someone who is in receipt of a pension. ◊ **pension sb off** to put them into retirement, or make them redundant, on a pension.

pensive adj preoccupied with one's thoughts; thoughtful. ○ **pensively** adv.

pentacle n a PENTANGLE.

pentad n **1** a set of five things. **2** a period of five years or five days.

pentagon n, geom a plane figure (see PLANE² adj sense 3) with five sides and five angles. ○ **pentagonal** / pɛn'tagənəl/ adj.

pentagram n **1** a figure in the shape of a star with five points and consisting of five lines. **2** such a figure used as a magic symbol; a PENTACLE.

pentahedron n (**pentahedrons** or **pentahedra**) geom a five-faced solid figure. ○ **pentahedral** adj.

pentameter / pɛn'tamɪtə(r)/ n, poetry a line of verse with five metrical feet.

pentangle n a PENTAGRAM or similar figure or amulet used as a defence against demons.

Pentateuch / 'pɛntətjuːk/ n the first five books of the Old Testament. ○ **Pentateuchal** adj.

pentathlon n an athletic competition comprising five events all of which the contestants must compete in.

pentatonic adj, mus of a musical scale: having five notes to the octave.

pentavalent adj, chem of an atom of a chemical element: having a valency of five.

Pentecost n, Christianity a festival on Whit Sunday, the seventh Sunday after Easter, commemorating the descent of the Holy Spirit on the Apostles.

Pentecostal adj **1** denoting any of several fundamentalist Christian groups that put emphasis on God's gifts through the Holy Spirit, characterized by their literal interpretation of the Bible and informal worship. **2** relating to Pentecost. ○ **Pentecostalist** n, adj.

penthouse n an apartment, esp a luxuriously appointed one, built on to the roof of a tall building.

pent-up (also **pent up**) adj of feelings, energy, etc: repressed or stifled; bursting to be released.

penultimate adj last but one. ➤ n the last but one.

penumbra n (**penumbrae** / pɛ'nʌmbriː/ or **penumbras**) **1** the lighter outer shadow that surrounds the dark central shadow produced by a large unfocused light-source shining on an opaque object. **2** astron the lighter area around the edge of a sunspot. ○ **penumbral** or **penumbrous** adj.

penury n extreme poverty. ○ **penurious** adj.

peon n **1** in India and Ceylon: an office messenger; an attendant. **2** in Latin America: a farm labourer.

peony n (-ies) a plant with large round red, pink, yellow or white flowers.

people n, usu pl **1** a set or group of persons. **2** men and women in general. **3** a body of persons held together by belief in common origin, speech, culture, political union, or by common leadership, etc. **4 a** (**the people**) ordinary citizens without special rank; the general populace; **b** in compounds denoting that the specified thing belongs or relates to the people, general populace, etc: people-power • people-oriented. **5** (**the people**) voters as a body. **6** subjects or supporters of a monarch, etc. **7** sing a nation or race: a warlike people. **8** colloq one's parents, or the wider circle of one's relations. ➤ vb **1** to fill or supply (a region, etc) with people; to populate. **2** to inhabit. ◆ **of all people 1** especially; more than anyone else: You, of all people, should know that. **2** very strangely or unexpectedly: He chose me, of all people, as spokesperson.

pep n, colloq energy; vitality; go. ➤ vb (**pepped**, **pepping**) (always **pep sb** or **sth up**) to enliven or invigorate them or it. ○ **peppy** adj (-ier, -iest).

peplum n (**peplums** or **pepla**) a short skirt-like section attached to the waistline of a dress, blouse or jacket.

pepper n **1 a** a climbing shrub, widely cultivated for its small red berries which are dried to form PEPPERCORNS; **b** a pungent seasoning prepared by grinding the dried berries of this plant. **2 a** a tropical shrub cultivated for its large red, green, yellow or orange edible fruits; **b** the fruit of this plant, eaten raw in salads or cooked as a vegetable. ➤ *vb* **1** to bombard something or someone (with missiles). **2** to sprinkle liberally: *The text was peppered with errors*. **3** to season (a dish, etc) with pepper.

peppercorn *n* **1** the dried berry of the pepper plant. **2** something nominal or of little value.

peppermill *n* a device for grinding peppercorns.

peppermint *n* **1** a species of mint with dark-green leaves and spikes of small purple flowers, widely cultivated for its aromatic oil. **2** a food flavouring prepared from the aromatic oil produced by this plant. **3** a sweet flavoured with peppermint.

pepperoni or **peperoni** *n* a hard, spicy beef and pork sausage.

peppery *adj* **1** well seasoned with pepper; tasting of pepper; hot-tasting or pungent. **2** short-tempered. ○ **pepperiness** *n*.

pep pill *n* a pill containing a stimulant drug.

pepsin *n, biochem* in the stomach of vertebrates: a digestive enzyme produced by the gastric glands that catalyses the partial breakdown of dietary protein.

pep talk *n* a brief talk intended to raise morale for a cause or course of action.

peptic *adj* **1** referring or relating to digestion. **2** referring or relating to the stomach. **3** referring or relating to pepsin.

peptide *n, biochem* a molecule that consists of a relatively short chain of amino acids.

per *prep* **1** out of every: *two per thousand*. **2** for every: *£5 per head*. **3** in every: *60 miles per hour • 100 accidents per week*. **4** through; by means of: *per post*. ♦ **as per …** according to …: *proceed as per instructions*. **as per usual** *colloq* as always.

perambulate *vb, formal* **1** to walk about (a place). **2** *intr* to stroll around. ○ **perambulation** *n*.

perambulator *n, formal* a **PRAM**.

per annum *adv* for each year; yearly.

per capita *adv, adj* for each person: *income per capita*.

perceive *vb* **1** to observe, notice, or discern. **2** to understand, interpret or view: *It's how I perceive my role*. ○ **perceivable** *adj*.

per cent *adv, adj* (symbol **%**) **1** in or for every 100: *Sales are 20 per cent down*. **2** on a scale of 1 to 100: *90 per cent certain*. ➤ *n* (*usu* **percent**) **1** a percentage or proportion. **2** one part in or on every 100: *half a percent*.

percentage *n* **1** an amount, number or rate stated as a proportion of one hundred. **2** a proportion: *a large percentage of students fail*. **3** *colloq* commission: *What percentage do you take?* **4** profit; advantage.

percentile *n, stats* one of the points or values that divide a collection of statistical data, arranged in order, into 100 equal parts.

perceptible *adj* able to be perceived; noticeable; detectable. ○ **perceptibly** *adv*.

perception *n* **1** *psychol* the process whereby information about one's environment, is received by the senses, is organized and interpreted so that it becomes meaningful. **2** one's powers of observation; insight. **3** one's view or interpretation of something.

perceptive *adj* quick to notice or discern. ○ **perceptively** *adv*. ○ **perceptiveness** *n*.

perch[1] *n* **1** a branch or other narrow support above ground for a bird to rest or roost on. **2** any place selected, esp temporarily, as a seat. **3** a high position or vantage point. ➤ *vb* **1** *intr* of a bird: to alight and rest on a perch. **2** *intr* to sit, esp insecurely or temporarily. **3** *tr & intr* to sit or place high up.

perch[2] *n* a freshwater fish which has a stream-lined body and a silvery-white belly.

percipient *adj* perceptive; acutely observant; discerning. ○ **percipience** *n*.

percolate *vb* **1** *tr & intr* to undergo or subject (a liquid) to the process of filtering, oozing or trickling. **2** *intr* (*also* **percolate through**) *colloq* of news or information: to trickle or spread slowly. **3** *tr & intr* of coffee: to make or be made in a percolator.

percolator *n* a pot for making coffee, in which boiling water circulates up through a tube and down through ground coffee beans.

percussion *n* **1** the striking of one hard object against another. **2 a** musical instruments played by striking, eg drums, cymbals, xylophone, etc; **b** these instruments collectively as a section of an orchestra. ○ **percussionist** *n*. ○ **percussive** *adj*.

percussion cap *n* a metal case containing a material that explodes when struck, formerly used for firing rifles.

perdition *n* everlasting punishment after death; hell.

peregrinate *vb, literary* **1** *intr* to travel, voyage or roam; to wander abroad. **2** to travel through (a place, region, etc). ○ **peregrination** *n*. ○ **peregrinator** *n*.

peregrine *n* a large falcon with greyish-blue plumage on its back and wings and paler underparts.

peremptory *adj* **1** of an order: made in expectation of immediate compliance: *a peremptory summons*. **2** of a tone or manner: arrogantly impatient. **3** of a statement, conclusion, etc: allowing no denial or discussion; dogmatic.

perennial *adj* **1** *bot* referring or relating to a plant that lives for several to many years. **2** lasting throughout the year. **3** constant; continual. ➤ *n* a perennial plant.

perfect *adj* /ˈpɜːfɪkt/ **1** complete in all essential elements. **2** faultless; flawless. **3** excellent; absolutely satisfactory. **4** exact: *a perfect circle*. **5** *colloq* absolute; utter: *perfect nonsense*. **6** *gram* of the tense or aspect of a verb: denoting an action completed at some time in the past or prior to the time spoken of. ➤ *n* /ˈpɜːfɪkt/ *gram* **1** the perfect tense, in English formed with the auxiliary verb *have* and the past PARTICIPLE, denoting an action completed in the past (**present perfect**, eg *I have written the letter*) or one that was or will be completed at the time being spoken of (**past perfect** or **pluperfect**, eg *I had written the letter*; **future perfect**, eg *I will have written the letter*). **2** a verb in a perfect tense. ➤ *vb* /pəˈfɛkt/ **1** to improve something to one's satisfaction: *I'm perfecting my Italian.* **2** to finalize or complete. **3** to develop (a technique, etc) to a reliable standard. ○ **perfectible** *adj*.

perfection *n* **1** the state of being perfect. **2** the process of making or being made perfect, complete, etc. **3** flawlessness. **4** *colloq* an instance of absolute excellence: *The meal was perfection.* ♦ **to perfection** perfectly.

perfectionism *n* **1** the doctrine that perfection is attainable. **2** an expectation of the very highest standard. ○ **perfectionist** *adj, n*.

perfectly *adv* **1** in a perfect way. **2** completely; quite: *It was a perfectly reasonable reaction.*

perfidious *adj* treacherous, double-dealing or disloyal. ○ **perfidy** *n*.

perforate *vb* **1** to make a hole or holes in something. **2** to make a row of holes in something, for ease of tearing. ○ **perforation** *n*.

perforce *adv, chiefly old use* necessarily; inevitably or unavoidably.

perform *vb* **1** to carry out (a task, job, action, etc); to do or accomplish. **2** to fulfil (a function) or provide (a service, etc). **3** *tr & intr* to act, sing, play, dance, etc (a play, song, piece of music, dance, etc) to entertain an audience. **4** *intr* eg of an engine: to function. **5** *intr* to conduct oneself, esp when presenting oneself for assessment. **6** *intr* of commercial products, shares, etc: to fare in competition. ○ **performer** *n*. ○ **performing** *adj*.

performance *n* **1 a** the performing of a play, part, dance, piece of music, etc before an audience; **b** a dramatic or artistic presentation or entertainment. **2** the act or process of performing a task, etc. **3** a level of achievement, success or, in commerce, profitability. **4** manner or efficiency of functioning. **5** *derog* an instance of outrageous behaviour, esp in public.

perfume *n* /ˈpɜːfjuːm/ **1** a sweet smell; a scent or fragrance. **2** a fragrant liquid prepared from the extracts of flowers, etc, for applying to the skin or clothes; scent. ➤ *vb* /pəˈfjuːm/ to give a sweet smell to something; to apply perfume to something. ○ **perfumed** *adj*. ○ **perfumer** *n* a maker or seller of perfumes. ○ **perfumery** *n*.

perfunctory *adj* done merely as a duty or routine, without genuine care or feeling. ○ **perfunctorily** *adv*. ○ **perfunctoriness** *n*.

pergola *n* an arched framework constructed from slender branches.

perhaps *adv* possibly; maybe.

perianth *n, bot* the outer part of a flower, usu consisting of a circle of petals within a circle of SEPALS.

pericardium *n* (**pericardia**) *anat* the sac, composed of fibrous tissue, that surrounds the heart. ○ **pericardiac** or **pericardial** *adj*.

pericarp *n, bot* in plants: the wall of a fruit, which develops from the ovary wall after fertilization.

perigee *n, astron* the point in the orbit of the Moon or a satellite around the Earth when it is closest to the Earth. Compare APOGEE.

perihelion *n* (**perihelia**) *astron* the point in the orbit of a planet round the Sun when it is closest to the Sun. Compare APHELION.

peril *n* **1** grave danger. **2** a hazard. ○ **perilous** *adj*. ○ **perilously** *adv*. ♦ **at one's peril** at the risk of one's life or safety.

perimeter /pəˈrɪmɪtə(r)/ *n* **1** the boundary of an enclosed area. **2** *geom* **a** the boundary or circumference of any plane figure; **b** the length of this boundary.

perinatal *adj, med* denoting or relating to the period extending from the 28th week of pregnancy to about one month after childbirth.

perineum /pɛrɪˈnɪəm/ *n* (**perinea** /-ˈnɪə/) *anat* the region of the body between the genital organs and the anus. ○ **perineal** *adj*.

period *n* **1** a portion of time. **2** a phase or stage, eg in history, or in a person's life and development, etc. **3** an interval of time at the end of which events recur in the same order. **4** *geol* a unit of geological time that is a subdivision of an ERA. **5** any of the sessions of equal length into which the school day is divided, and to which particular subjects or activities are assigned. **6** *esp N Am* a FULL STOP. **7** *colloq* added to a statement to emphasize its finality: *You may not go, period.* **8** the periodic discharge of blood during a woman's menstrual cycle. **9** *chem* in the periodic table: any of the seven horizontal rows of chemical elements. **10** *physics* the time interval after which a cyclical phenomenon, eg a wave motion, repeats itself; the reciprocal of the frequency. ➤ *adj* dating from, or designed in the style of, the historical period in question: *period furniture.*

periodic *adj* happening at intervals, esp regular intervals. ○ **periodicity** *n*.

periodical *n* a magazine published weekly, monthly, quarterly, etc. ➤ *adj* **1** referring or relating to such publications. **2** published at more or less regular intervals. **3** periodic. ○ **periodically** *adv*.

periodic table *n, chem* a table of all the chemical elements in order of increasing atomic number.

peripatetic /pɛrɪpəˈtɛtɪk/ *adj* **1** travelling about from place to place. **2** of a teacher: employed by several schools and so obliged to travel between them. ➤ *n* a peripatetic teacher. ○ **peripatetically** *adv*.

peripheral /pəˈrɪfərəl/ *adj* **1** relating or belonging to the outer edge or outer surface: *peripheral nerves.* **2** (**peripheral to sth**) not central to the issue in hand. **3** *comput* supplementary; auxiliary. **4** relating to the outer edge of the field of vision. ➤ *n, comput* a device concerned with the input, output or backup storage of data, eg a printer, mouse or disk drive.

periphery /pə'rɪfərɪ/ n (-ies) **1** the edge or boundary of something. **2** the external surface of something. **3** a surrounding region.

periphrasis /pə'rɪfrəsɪs/ n (-ses /-siːz/) a roundabout way of saying something. ○ **periphrastic** adj.

periscope n, optics a system of prisms or mirrors that enables the user to view objects that are above eye-level or obscured by a closer object, used in submarines, military tanks, etc.

perish vb **1** intr to die; to be destroyed or ruined. **2 a** intr of materials: to decay; **b** tr to cause (materials) to decay or rot.

perishable adj of commodities, esp food: liable to rot or go bad quickly.

perishing adj **1** colloq of weather, etc: very cold. **2** old use, colloq damned, infernal or confounded.

peristalsis /perɪ'stalsɪs/ n (-ses /-siːz/) physiol in hollow tubular organs, eg the intestines: the waves of involuntary muscle contractions that force the contents of the tube, eg food, further forward. ○ **peristaltic** adj.

peritoneum /perɪtə'niːəm/ n (peritonea /-'niːə/ or peritoneums) anat a SEROUS membrane that lines the abdominal cavity. ○ **peritoneal** adj.

peritonitis /perɪtə'naɪtɪs/ n, pathol inflammation of the peritoneum.

periwig n a man's wig of the 17c and 18c.

periwinkle[1] n a climbing plant with slender trailing stems, oval shiny green leaves, and single bluish-purple flowers.

periwinkle[2] n a small marine mollusc with a spirally coiled shell, esp the common edible variety, the **winkle**.

perjure vb (now always **perjure oneself**) to forswear oneself in a court of law, ie lie while under oath.

perjury /'pɜːdʒərɪ/ n (-ies) the crime of lying while under oath in a court of law. ○ **perjurer** n.

perk[1] vb, tr & intr (always **perk up**) to become or make (someone) more lively and cheerful. ○ **perky** adj (-ier, -iest).

perk[2] n, colloq a benefit, additional to income, derived from employment, such as the use of a company car.

perk[3] vb, tr & intr, colloq to PERCOLATE (coffee).

perkin see PARKIN

perm[1] n a hair treatment using chemicals that give a long-lasting wave or curl. ➤ vb to curl or wave (hair) with a perm.

perm[2] colloq, n short form of PERMUTATION (sense 2). ➤ vb short form of PERMUTE.

permafrost n, geol an area of subsoil or rock that has remained frozen for at least a year, and usu much longer.

permanent adj **1** lasting, or intended to last, indefinitely; not temporary. **2** of a condition, etc: unlikely to alter. ○ **permanence** n. ○ **permanently** adv.

permanent wave n, old use a PERM[1].

permanganate n, chem any of the salts of **permanganic acid** used as an oxidizing and bleaching agent and disinfectant.

permeable adj of a porous material or membrane: allowing certain liquids or gases to pass through it. ○ **permeability** n.

permeate vb (also **permeate through sth**) **1** of a liquid or gas: to pass, penetrate or diffuse through (a fine or porous material or a membrane). **2** tr & intr of a smell, gas, etc: to spread through a room or other space; to fill or impregnate. ○ **permeation** n.

Permian adj **1** geol relating to the last period of the PALAEOZOIC era, during which reptiles became more abundant. **2** relating to the rocks formed during this period.

permissible adj allowable; permitted.

permission n consent, agreement or authorization.

permissive adj **1** tolerant; liberal. **2** allowing usu excessive freedom, esp in sexual matters: the permissive society. ○ **permissively** adv. ○ **permissiveness** n.

permit vb /pə'mɪt/ (permitted, permitting) **1** to consent to or give permission for something. **2** to give (someone) leave or authorization. **3** to allow someone something: She permitted him access to his children. **4** (also **permit of sth**) formal to enable it to happen or take effect; to give scope or opportunity for it: an outrage that permits of no excuses. ➤ n /'pɜːmɪt/ a document that authorizes something: a fishing permit.

permutation n **1** maths **a** any of several different ways in which a set of objects or numbers can be arranged; **b** any of the resulting combinations. **2** a fixed combination in football pools for selecting the results of matches.

permute or **permutate** vb to rearrange (a set of things) in different orders, esp in every possible order in succession.

pernicious adj harmful; destructive; deadly.

pernickety adj **1** of a person: overparticular about small details. **2** of a task: tricky; intricate.

peroration n the concluding section of a speech, in which the points made are summed up.

peroxide n **1** chem a strong oxidizing agent that releases hydrogen peroxide when treated with acid, used in rocket fuels, antiseptics, disinfectants and bleaches. **2** a solution of hydrogen peroxide used as a bleach for hair and textiles. ➤ vb to bleach (hair) with hydrogen peroxide.

perpendicular adj **1** vertical; upright; in the direction of gravity. **2** (also **perpendicular to sth**) at right angles; forming a right angle with (a particular line or surface). **3** of a cliff, etc: precipitous; steep. **4** (usu **Perpendicular**) archit referring or relating to the form of English Gothic architecture from late 14c to 16c, characterized by the use of slender vertical lines and vaulting. ➤ n **1** a perpendicular line, position or direction. **2** an instrument for determining the vertical line. ○ **perpendicularity** n. ○ **perpendicularly** adv.

perpetrate vb to commit, or be guilty of (a crime, misdeed, error, etc). ○ **perpetration** n. ○ **perpetrator** n.

perpetual adj **1** everlasting; eternal; continuous; permanent. **2** continual; continually recurring: perpetual quarrels. ○ **perpetually** adv.

perpetuate vb **1** to make something last or continue. **2** to preserve the memory of (a name, etc). **3** to repeat and pass on (an error, etc). ○ **perpetuation** n.

perpetuity n (-ies) **1** the state of being perpetual. **2** eternity. **3** duration for an indefinite period. **4** something perpetual, eg an allowance to be paid indefinitely. ♦ **in perpetuity** for ever.

perplex vb **1** to puzzle, confuse or baffle someone with intricacies or difficulties. **2** to complicate. ○ **perplexed** adj. ○ **perplexing** adj. ○ **perplexity** n.

perquisite n **1** a PERK². **2** a customary tip expected on some occasions.

perry n (-ies) an alcoholic drink made from fermented pear juice.

per se /pɜː seɪ/ adv in itself; intrinsically: not valuable per se.

persecute vb **1** to ill-treat, oppress, torment or put to death (a person or people), esp for their religious or political beliefs. **2** to harass, pester or bother someone continually. ○ **persecution** n. ○ **persecutor** n.

perseverance n the act or state of persevering; continued effort to achieve something one has begun, despite setbacks.

persevere vb, intr (also **persevere in** or **with sth**) to keep on striving for it; to persist steadily with (an endeavour).

persiflage /ˈpɜːsɪflɑːʒ/ n flippancy or frivolous talk.

persimmon n **1** a tall tree, widely cultivated for its hard wood and edible fruits. **2** the plum-like fruit of this tree.

persist vb, intr **1** (also **persist in** or **with sth**) to continue with it in spite of resistance, difficulty, discouragement, etc. **2** of rain, etc: to continue steadily. **3** eg of a mistaken idea: to remain current. **4** to continue to exist. ○ **persistence** n.

persistent adj **1** continuing with determination in spite of discouragement; dogged; tenacious. **2** constant; unrelenting: persistent questions. **3** zool, bot of parts of animals and plants, such as horns, hair, leaves, etc: remaining after the time they usu fall off, wither or disappear. ○ **persistently** adv.

person n (**persons** or in sense 1 also **people**) **1** an individual human being. **2** the body, often including clothes: A knife was found hidden on his person. **3** gram each of the three classes into which pronouns and verb forms fall, **first person** denoting the speaker (or the speaker and others, eg I and we), **second person** the person addressed (with or without others, eg you) and

third person the person(s) or thing(s) spoken of (eg she, he, it or they). ♦ **in person 1** actually present oneself. **2** doing something oneself.

persona /pəˈsəʊnə/ n (**personae** /-niː/ or **personas**) in psychology: one's character as one presents it to the world, masking one's inner thoughts, feelings, etc.

personable adj good-looking or likeable.

personage n a well-known, important or distinguished person.

personal adj **1** of a comment, opinion, etc: coming from someone as an individual, not from a group or organization: my personal opinion. **2** done, attended to, etc by the individual person in question, not by a substitute: I'll give it my personal attention. **3** relating to oneself in particular: a personal triumph. **4** relating to one's private concerns: details of her personal life. **5** of remarks: referring, often disparagingly, to an individual's physical or other characteristics. **6** relating to the body: personal hygiene. **7** gram indicating PERSON (sense 3): personal pronouns.

personal assistant n (abbrev **PA**) a secretary or administrator, esp one who helps a senior executive.

personal column n a newspaper column or section in which members of the public may place advertisements, enquiries, etc.

personal computer n (abbrev **PC**) a microcomputer designed for use by one person.

personal identification number see PIN

personality n (-ies) **1** a person's nature or disposition; the qualities that give one's character individuality. **2** strength or distinctiveness of character: lots of personality. **3** a well-known person.

personalize or **-ise** vb **1** to mark something distinctively, eg with name, initials, etc, as the property of a particular person. **2** to focus a discussion, etc) on personalities instead of the matter in hand. **3** to personify. ○ **personalization** n.

personally adv **1** as far as one is concerned: Personally, I disapprove. **2** in person. **3** as a person. **4** as directed against one: He took my remark personally.

personal pronoun n, gram any of the pronouns that represent a person or thing, eg I, you, she, her, he, it, they, us.

personal stereo n a small cassette or CD player with earphones, that can be worn attached to a belt or carried in a pocket.

persona non grata /nɒn ˈɡrɑːtə/ n (**personae non gratae** /-tiː/) someone who is not wanted or welcome within a particular group.

personify vb (-ies, -ied) **1** in literature, etc: to represent (an abstract quality, etc) as a human being or as having human qualities. **2** of a figure in art, etc: to represent or symbolize (a quality, etc). **3** to embody something in human form; to be the perfect example of it: She's patience personified. ○ **personification** n.

personnel pl n the people employed in a business company, an armed service or other organization. ➤ *sing n* a department within such an organization that deals with matters concerning employees.

perspective *n* 1 the observer's view of objects in relation to one another, esp with regard to the way they seem smaller the more distant they are. 2 the representation of this phenomenon in drawing and painting. 3 the balanced or objective view of a situation, in which all its elements assume their due importance. 4 an individual way of regarding a situation, eg one influenced by personal experience or considerations.

Perspex *n, trademark* polymethylmethacrylate, a tough transparent plastic used to make windscreens, visors, etc.

perspicacious /pɜːspɪˈkeɪʃəs/ *adj* shrewd; astute; perceptive or discerning. ○ **perspicacity** /-ˈkasɪtɪ/ *n*.

perspicuous /pəˈspɪkjʊəs/ *adj* of speech or writing: clearly expressed and easily understood. ○ **perspicuity** /pɜːspɪˈkjuːətɪ/ *n*.

perspiration *n* 1 the secretion of fluid by the sweat glands of the skin, usu in response to heat or physical exertion. 2 the fluid secreted in this way.

perspire *vb, intr* to sweat.

persuade *vb* 1 (*also* **persuade sb to do sth**) to urge successfully; to prevail on or induce someone. 2 (*often* **persuade sb of sth**) to convince them that it is true, valid, advisable, etc. ○ **persuadable** *adj*.

persuasion *n* 1 the act of urging, coaxing or persuading. 2 a creed, conviction, or set of beliefs, esp that of a political group or religious sect.

persuasive *adj* having the power to persuade; convincing or plausible. ○ **persuasiveness** *n*.

pert *adj* 1 impudent; cheeky. 2 of clothing or style: jaunty; saucy. ○ **pertness** *n*.

pertain *vb, intr* (*often* **pertain to sb or sth**) 1 to concern or relate to them or it; to have to do with them or it. 2 to belong to them or it: *skills pertaining to the job.* 3 to be appropriate; to apply.

pertinacious /pɜːtɪˈneɪʃəs/ *adj* determined in one's purpose. ○ **pertinacity** /-ˈnasɪtɪ/ *n*.

pertinent *adj* (*also* **pertinent to sb or sth**) relating to or concerned with them or it. ○ **pertinence** *n*.

perturb *vb* to make someone anxious, agitated, worried, etc. ○ **perturbation** *n*.

peruse *vb* 1 to read through (a book, magazine, etc) carefully. 2 to browse through something casually. 3 to examine or study (eg someone's face) attentively. ○ **perusal** *n*.

pervade *vb* to spread or extend throughout something; to affect throughout something; to permeate. ○ **pervasion** *n*. ○ **pervasive** *adj*.

perverse *adj* 1 deliberately departing from what is normal and reasonable. 2 unreasonable; awkward; stubborn or wilful. ○ **perversely** *adv*. ○ **perversity** *n*.

perversion *n* 1 the process of perverting or condition of being perverted. 2 a distortion. 3 an abnormal sexual activity.

pervert *vb* /pəˈvɜːt/ 1 to divert something or someone illicitly from what is normal or right: *to pervert the course of justice.* 2 to lead someone into evil or unnatural behaviour; to corrupt them. 3 to distort or misinterpret (words, etc). ➤ *n* /ˈpɜːvɜːt/ someone who is morally or sexually perverted.

peseta /pəˈseɪtə/ *n* (**peseta** or **pesetas**) the former standard unit of currency of Spain, replaced in 2002 by the euro.

pesky *adj* (**-ier, -iest**) *N Am colloq* troublesome or infuriating.

peso /ˈpeɪsoʊ/ *n* the standard unit of currency of many Central and S American countries and the Philippines.

pessary *n* (**-ies**) a vaginal SUPPOSITORY.

pessimism *n* 1 the tendency to emphasize the gloomiest aspects of anything, and to expect the worst to happen. 2 the belief that this is the worst of all possible worlds, and that evil is triumphing over good. Compare OPTIMISM. ○ **pessimist** *n*. ○ **pessimistic** *adj*.

pest *n* 1 a living organism, such as an insect, fungus or weed, that has a damaging effect on animal livestock, crop plants or stored produce. 2 *colloq* a person or thing that is a constant nuisance.

pester *vb* 1 to annoy constantly. 2 to harass or hound someone with requests.

pesticide *n* any of various chemical compounds that are used to kill pests.

pestilence *n* a virulent epidemic or contagious disease, such as bubonic plague.

pestilent *adj* 1 deadly, harmful or destructive. 2 (*also* **pestilential**) *colloq, often facetious* infuriating; troublesome.

pestle *n* a club-shaped utensil for pounding, crushing and mixing substances in a MORTAR.

pesto *n* an Italian sauce made with basil leaves, pine kernels, olive oil, garlic and Parmesan cheese.

pet¹ *n* 1 a tame animal or bird kept as a companion. 2 someone's favourite: *the teacher's pet.* 3 a darling or love. 4 a term of endearment. ➤ *adj* 1 kept as a pet: *a pet lamb.* 2 relating to pets or for pets: *pet food.* 3 favourite; own special: *her pet subject.* ➤ *vb* (**petted, petting**) 1 to pat or stroke (an animal, etc). 2 to treat someone indulgently; to make a fuss of them. 3 *intr* of two people: to fondle and caress each other. ○ **petting** *n*.

pet² *n* a fit of bad temper or sulks.

petal *n, bot* in a flower: one of the modified leaves, often scented and brightly coloured, which in insect-pollinated plants attract passing insects.

petard *n, hist* a small bomb for blasting a hole in a wall, door, etc. ♦ **hoist with one's own petard** blown up by one's own bomb, ie the victim of one's own trick or cunning; caught in one's own trap.

peter *vb, intr (always* **peter out**) to dwindle away to nothing.

Peter Pan *n* a youthful, boyish or immature man.

pethidine /ˈpɛθɪdiːn/ *n* a mildly sedative pain-relieving drug, widely used in childbirth.

petiole *n* **1** *bot* the stalk that attaches a leaf to the stem of a plant. **2** *zool* a stalk-like structure, esp that of the abdomen in wasps, etc.

petite /pəˈtiːt/ *adj* of a woman or girl: small and dainty.

petit four /ˈpɛtɪ fʊə(r), fɔː(r), ˈpɒtɪ/ *n (petits fours* /fʊəz, fɔːz/ *)* a small sweet biscuit, usu decorated with icing.

petition *n* **1** a formal written request to an authority to take some action, signed by a large number of people. **2** any appeal to a higher authority. **3** *law* an application to a court for some procedure to be set in motion. ➤ *vb, tr & intr (also* **petition sb for** *or* **against sth)** to address a petition to them for or against some cause; to make an appeal or request. ○ **petitioner** *n.*

petit mal /ˈpɛtɪ mal/ *n, med* a mild form of EPI-LEPSY, without convulsions. Compare GRAND MAL.

petits pois /ˈpɛtɪ pwɑː/ *pl n* small young green peas.

pet name *n* a special name used as an endearment.

petrel *n* a small seabird with a hooked bill and external tube-shaped nostrils, esp the storm petrel.

Petri dish /ˈpiːtrɪ, ˈpɛtrɪ/ *n, biol* a shallow glass or plastic plate used in laboratories for culturing bacteria, etc.

petrifaction or **petrification** *n, geol* a type of fossilization whereby organic remains are turned into stone as the original tissue is gradually replaced by minerals.

petrify *vb (-ies, -ied)* **1** to terrify; to paralyse someone with fright. **2** *tr & intr* of organic remains: to turn into stone by the process of petrifaction. **3** *tr & intr* to fix or become fixed in an inflexible mould.

petrochemical *n* any organic chemical derived from petroleum or natural gas. ➤ *adj* **1** referring or relating to such chemicals. **2** referring or relating to the petrochemical industry.

petrol *n* a volatile flammable liquid mixture of hydrocarbons, used as a fuel in most internal-combustion engines.

petrolatum /pɛtrəˈleɪtəm/ *n* a PARAFFIN-base PETROLEUM used as a lubricant or medicinally as an ointment.

petroleum *n* a naturally occurring oil consisting of a thick dark liquid mixture of hydrocarbons, distillation of which yields a wide range of petrochemicals, eg liquid and gas fuels, asphalt, and raw materials for the manufacture of plastics, solvents, drugs, etc.

petrology *n, geol* the scientific study of the structure, origin, distribution and history of rocks. ○ **petrologist** *n.*

petrol station *n* a FILLING STATION.

petticoat *n* a woman's underskirt.

pettifogger *n* **1** a lawyer who deals with unimportant cases, esp somewhat deceitfully or quibblingly. **2** *derog* someone who argues over trivial details. ○ **pettifog** *vb (pettifogged, pettifogging) intr* to act as a pettifogger. ○ **pettifogging** *n, adj.*

pettish *adj* peevish; sulky.

petty *adj (-ier, -iest)* **1** being of minor importance. **2** small-minded or childishly spiteful. **3** referring to a low or subordinate rank. ○ **pettily** *adv.* ○ **pettiness** *n.*

petty cash *n* money kept for small everyday expenses in an office, etc.

petty officer *n* a non-commissioned officer in the navy.

petulant *adj* ill-tempered; peevish. ○ **petulance** *n.* ○ **petulantly** *adv.*

petunia *n* a plant with large funnel-shaped, often striped, flowers in a range of bright colours.

pew *n* **1** one of the long benches with backs used as seating in a church. **2** *colloq* a seat: *Take a pew.*

pewter *n* **1** a silvery alloy with a bluish tinge, composed of tin and lead, used to make tableware (eg tankards), jewellery and other decorative objects. **2** articles made of pewter. ➤ *adj* made of pewter: *pewter goblets.*

PG *abbrev* as a film classification: parental guidance, ie containing scenes possibly unsuitable for children.

pg. *abbrev* page.

pH or **pH value** *n, chem* a measure of the relative acidity or alkalinity of a solution expressed as the logarithm of the reciprocal of the hydrogen-ion concentration of the solution.

phagocyte /ˈfagəsaɪt/ *n, biol* a cell, esp a white blood cell, that engulfs and destroys micro-organisms and other foreign particles. ○ **phagocytic** *adj.*

phalanger *n* a nocturnal tree-dwelling marsupial, with thick fur, small fox-like ears and large forward-facing eyes.

phalanx /ˈfalaŋks, ˈfeɪlaŋks/ *n (phalanxes* or **phalanges** /-dʒiːz/ *)* **1** *hist* in ancient Greece: a body of infantry in close-packed formation. **2** a solid body of people, esp one representing united support or opposition.

phallic *adj* relating to or resembling a phallus.

phallus *n (phalluses* or **phalli)** **1** a penis. **2** a representation or image of an erect penis, esp as a symbol of male reproductive power.

Phanerozoic /fanərəˈzoʊɪk/ *adj, geol* relating to the eon consisting of the Palaeozoic, Mesozoic and Cenozoic eras, extending from about 570 million years ago until the present time.

phantasm *n* **1** an illusion or fantasy. **2** a ghost or phantom. ○ **phantasmal** *adj.*

phantasmagoria *n* a fantastic succession of real or illusory images seen as if in a dream. ○ **phantasmagoric** or **phantasmagorical** *adj.*

phantom *n* **1** a ghost or spectre. **2** an illusory image or vision. ➤ *adj* **1** referring to the nature of a phantom. **2** imaginary; fancied; not real: *a phantom pregnancy*.

Pharaoh /ˈfɛərəʊ/ *n* the title of the kings of ancient Eygpt, specifically the god-kings from the time of the New Kingdom (c.1500BC) onwards. ○ **Pharaonic** /fɛəreɪˈɒnɪk/ *adj*.

Pharisee *n* **1** a member of an ancient Jewish sect whose strict interpretation of the Mosaic law led to an obsessive concern with the rules covering the details of everyday life. **2** *derog* anyone more careful of the outward forms than of the spirit of religion. **3** *derog* a self-righteous or hypocritical person. ○ **Pharisaic** /farɪˈseɪk/ *adj*.

pharmaceutical or **pharmaceutic** *adj* referring or relating to the preparation of drugs and medicines.

pharmaceutics *sing n* the preparation and dispensing of drugs and medicine.

pharmacist *n* someone who is trained and licensed to prepare and dispense drugs and medicines.

pharmacology *n* the scientific study of medicines and drugs and their effects and uses. ○ **pharmacological** *adj*. ○ **pharmacologist** *n*.

pharmacopoeia /fɑːməkəˈpiːə/ *n*, *med* an authoritative book that contains a list of drugs, together with details of their properties, uses, preparation and recommended dosages.

pharmacy *n* (*-ies*) **1** the mixing and dispensing of drugs and medicines. **2** a dispensary in a hospital, etc. **3** a pharmacist's or chemist's shop.

pharynx /ˈfarɪŋks/ *n* (*pharynxes* or *pharynges* /-ɪndʒiːz/) **1** *anat* in mammals: the part of the alimentary canal that links the mouth and nasal passages with the oesophagus and trachea. **2** the throat. ○ **pharyngeal** *adj*.

phase *n* **1** a stage or period in growth or development. **2** the appearance or aspect of anything at any stage. **3** *astron* any of the different shapes assumed by the illuminated surface of a celestial body, eg the Moon. **4** *physics* the stage that a periodically varying wave has reached at a specific moment, usu in relation to another wave of the same frequency. ➤ *vb* to organize or carry out (changes, etc) in stages. ◊ **phase sth in** or **out** to introduce it, or get rid of it, gradually and in stages.

PhD *abbrev*: *philosophiae doctor* (Latin), Doctor of Philosophy.

pheasant *n* (*pheasant* or *pheasants*) a ground-dwelling bird, the male of which is usu brightly coloured and has a long pointed tail.

phenobarbitone or (*chiefly N Am*) **phenobarbital** *n* a hypnotic and sedative drug used to treat insomnia, anxiety and epilepsy.

phenol *n*, *chem* **1** a colourless crystalline toxic solid used in the manufacture of resins, solvents, explosives, drugs, dyes and perfumes. **2** any member of a group of weakly acidic organic chemical compounds, many of which are used as antiseptics, eg trichlorophenol (TCP).

phenomenal *adj* **1** remarkable; extraordinary; abnormal. **2** referring to the nature of a phenomenon. **3** relating to phenomena. ○ **phenomenally** *adv*.

phenomenon *n* (*phenomena*) **1** a happening perceived through the senses, esp something unusual. **2** an extraordinary or abnormal person or thing. **3** a feature of life, social existence, etc: *stress as a work-related phenomenon*.

> **phenomenon** Note that **phenomena** is plural. 'A phenomena' is often heard, but is not correct.

phenotype *n*, *genetics* the observable characteristics of an organism, determined by the interaction between its GENOTYPE and environmental factors.

phenyl /ˈfiːnɪl/ *n*, *chem* an organic RADICAL (*noun* sense 3) found in benzene, phenol, etc.

pheromone *n*, *zool* any chemical substance secreted by an animal which has a specific effect on the behaviour of other members of the same species.

phew *exclam* used to express relief, astonishment or exhaustion.

phial *n* a little medicine bottle.

philander *vb*, *intr* of men: to flirt or have casual love affairs with women. ○ **philanderer** *n*.

philanthropy /fɪˈlanθrəpɪ/ *n* a charitable regard for one's fellow human beings, esp in the form of benevolence to those in need. ○ **philanthropic** /-lənˈθrɒpɪk/ *adj* benevolent. ○ **philanthropist** *n*.

philately /fɪˈlatəlɪ/ *n* the study and collecting of postage stamps. ○ **philatelic** /fɪləˈtɛlɪk/ *adj*. ○ **philatelist** *n*.

philharmonic *adj* used as part of the name of choirs and orchestras: dedicated to music.

philippic *n* a speech making a bitter attack on someone or something.

philistine *adj* having no interest in or appreciation of art, literature, music, etc. ➤ *n* a philistine person. ○ **philistinism** *n*.

philology *n* **1** the study of language, its history and development; the comparative study of related languages; linguistics. **2** the study of texts, esp older ones. ○ **philological** *adj*. ○ **philologist** *n*.

philosopher *n* someone who studies philosophy, esp one who develops a particular set of doctrines or theories.

philosophical or **philosophic** *adj* **1** referring or relating to philosophy or philosophers. **2** calm and dispassionate in the face of adversity; resigned, stoical or patient. ○ **philosophically** *adv*.

philosophize or **-ise** *vb*, *intr* **1** to form philosophical theories. **2** to reason or speculate in the manner of a philosopher. ○ **philosophizer** *n*.

philosophy *n* (*-ies*) **1** the search for truth and knowledge concerning the universe, human existence, perception and behaviour, pursued by means of reflection, reasoning and argument. **2** any particular system or set of beliefs established as a result of this. **3** a set of principles that serves as a basis for making judgements and decisions: *one's philosophy of life.*

philtre /ˈfɪltə(r)/ *n* a magic potion for arousing sexual desire.

phlebitis /flɪˈbaɪtɪs/ *n, pathol* inflammation of the wall of a vein, often resulting in the formation of a blood clot at the affected site.

phlegm /flɛm/ *n* **1** a thick yellowish substance produced by the mucous membrane that lines the air passages, brought up by coughing. **2** calmness or impassiveness; stolidity or sluggishness of temperament.

phlegmatic /flɛgˈmatɪk/ or **phlegmatical** *adj* of a person: calm; not easily excited.

phloem /ˈfloʊəm/ *n, bot* the plant tissue that is responsible for the transport of sugars and other nutrients from the leaves to all other parts of the plant.

phobia *n* an obsessive and persistent fear of a specific object or situation, eg spiders, open spaces, etc. ○ **phobic** *adj.*

phoenix /ˈfiːnɪks/ *n* in Arabian legend: a bird which every 500 years sets itself on fire and is reborn from its ashes to live a further 500 years.

phone *n* a telephone. ➤ *vb* (*also* **phone sb up**) *tr & intr* to telephone someone.

phone-in *n* a radio or TV programme in which telephoned contributions from listeners or viewers are invited and discussed live by an expert or panel in the studio.

phoneme *n, ling* the smallest unit of sound in a language that has significance in distinguishing one word from another. ○ **phonemic** *adj.*

phonetic *adj* **1** referring or relating to the sounds of a spoken language. **2** eg of a spelling: intended to represent the pronunciation. **3** denoting a pronunciation scheme using symbols each of which represents one sound only. ○ **phonetically** *adv.*

phonetics *sing n* the branch of linguistics that deals with speech sounds, esp how they are produced and perceived. ○ **phonetician** /foʊnɪˈtɪʃən/ *n.*

phoney or (*US*) **phony** *adj* (*-ier*, *-iest*) not genuine; fake, sham, bogus or insincere. ➤ *n* (**phoneys** or **phonies**) someone or something bogus; a fake or humbug.

phonograph *n, N Am, old use* a record player.

phonology *n* (*-ies*) **1** the study of speech sounds in general, or of those in any particular language. **2** any particular system of speech sounds. ○ **phonological** *adj.*

phooey *exclam, colloq* an exclamation of scorn, contempt, disbelief, etc.

phosgene /ˈfɒsdʒiːn/ *n, chem* a poisonous gas, carbonyl chloride, used in the manufacture of pesticides and dyes.

phosphate *n, chem* any salt or ester of phosphoric acid, found in living organisms and in many minerals, and used in fertilizers, detergents, etc.

phosphor *n, chem* any substance that is cap-

able of phosphorescence, used to coat the inner surface of television screens and fluorescent light tubes, and as a brightener in detergents.

phosphorescence *n* **1** the emission of light from a substance after it has absorbed energy from a source such as ultraviolet radiation, and which continues for some time after the energy source has been removed. **2** a general term for the emission of light by a substance in the absence of a significant rise in temperature. ○ **phosphoresce** *vb.* ○ **phosphorescent** *adj.*

phosphoric *adj, chem* referring to or containing phosphorus in higher VALENCY.

phosphorous *adj, chem* referring to or containing phosphorus in lower VALENCY.

phosphorus *n, chem* a non-metallic element that exists as several different allotropes, including a whitish-yellow soft waxy solid that ignites spontaneously in air.

photo *n, colloq* a PHOTOGRAPH.

photocell *n,* a PHOTOELECTRIC CELL.

photocopier *n* a machine that makes copies of printed documents or illustrations by any of various photographic techniques, esp XEROGRAPHY.

photocopy *n* (*-ies*) a photographic copy of a document, drawing, etc. ➤ *vb* (*-ies*, *-ied*) to make a photographic copy of (a document, etc).

photoelectric *adj* referring or relating to the electrical effects of light, eg the emission of electrons or a change in resistance. ○ **photoelectricity** *n.*

photoelectric cell *n* a light-sensitive device that converts light energy into electrical energy, used in light meters, burglar alarms, etc.

photoengraving *n* a technique for producing metal printing plates or cylinders carrying the image of continuous-tone and half-tone text and illustrations.

photo finish *n* a race finish in which the runners are so close that the result must be decided by looking at a photograph taken at the finishing line.

photogenic *adj* **1** esp of a person: characterized by the quality of photographing well or looking attractive in photographs. **2** *biol* producing, or produced by, light.

photograph *n* a permanent record of an image that has been produced on photosensitive film or paper by the process of photography. ➤ *vb, tr & intr* to take a photograph of (a person, thing, etc).

photographic *adj* **1** relating to or similar to photographs or photography. **2** of memory: retaining images in exact detail. ○ **photographically** *adv.*

photography *n* the process of creating an image on light-sensitive film or some other sensitized material using visible light, X-rays, or some other form of radiant energy. ○ **photographer** *n.*

photogravure *n* a method of engraving in

which the design is photographed on to a metal plate, and then etched in.

photojournalism *n* journalism consisting mainly of photographs to convey the meaning of the article, with written material playing a small role. ○ **photojournalist** *n*.

photolithography *n* a process of lithographic printing from a photographically produced plate.

photometry /foʊˈtɒmɪtrɪ/ *n, physics* the measurement of visible light and its rate of flow, which has important applications in photography and lighting design. ○ **photometric** *adj*.

photon *n, physics* a particle of electromagnetic radiation that travels at the speed of light, used to explain phenomena that require light to behave as particles rather than as waves.

photophobia *n, med* a fear of or aversion to light.

photosensitive *adj* readily stimulated by light or some other form of radiant energy.

photosphere *n, astron* the outermost visible layer of the Sun, representing the zone from which light is emitted.

Photostat *n, trademark* 1 a photographic apparatus for copying documents, drawings, etc. 2 a copy made by this. ➤ *vb* (**photostat**) (**photostatted, photostatting**) to make a Photostat of (a document, etc).

photosynthesis *n, bot* the process whereby green plants manufacture carbohydrates from carbon dioxide and water, using the light energy from sunlight trapped by the pigment CHLOROPHYLL in specialized structures known as CHLOROPLASTs. ○ **photosynthesize** or **-ise** *vb*.

phototropism *n, bot* the growth of the roots or shoots of plants in response to light.

photovoltaic cell *n* a SOLAR CELL.

phrasal verb *n, gram* a phrase consisting of a verb plus an adverb or preposition, or both, frequently with a meaning or meanings that cannot be determined from the meanings of the individual words, eg *let on* or *come up with something*.

phrase *n* 1 a set of words expressing a single idea, forming part of a sentence though not constituting a CLAUSE (sense 1). 2 an idiomatic expression: *What is the phrase she used?* 3 manner or style of speech or expression: *ease of phrase.* 4 *mus* a run of notes making up an individually distinct part of a melody. ➤ *vb* 1 to express; to word something: *He phrased his reply carefully.* 2 *mus* to bring out the phrases in (music) as one plays. ○ **phrasal** *adj*.

phraseology /freɪzɪˈɒlədʒɪ/ *n* (**-ies**) 1 one's choice of words and way of combining them, in expressing oneself. 2 the language belonging to a particular subject, group, etc: *legal phraseology.*

phrasing *n* 1 the wording of a speech or passage. 2 *mus* the grouping of the parts, sounds, etc into musical phrases.

phrenetic see FRENETIC

phrenology *n* the practice, now discredited, of assessing someone's character and aptitudes by examining the shape of their skull. ○ **phrenological** *adj*. ○ **phrenologist** *n*.

phut *n, colloq* the noise of a small explosion. ♦ **go phut** 1 to break down or cease to function. 2 to go wrong.

phylactery *n* (**-ies**) *Judaism* either of two small boxes containing religious texts worn on the left arm and forehead by Jewish men during prayers.

phylum *n* (**phyla**) *biol, zool* in taxonomy: any of the major groups, eg *Chordata* (the vertebrates), into which the animal KINGDOM (sense 2) is divided and which in turn is subdivided into one or more CLASSes (*noun* sense 9).

physical *adj* 1 relating to the body rather than the mind: *physical strength.* 2 relating to objects that can be seen or felt: *the physical world.* 3 relating to nature or to the laws of nature: *physical features • a physical impossibility.* 4 involving bodily contact. 5 relating to PHYSICS. ○ **physically** *adv*.

physical education *n* (abbrev **PE**) instruction in sport and gymnastics.

physical training *n* (abbrev **PT**) instruction in sport and gymnastics.

physician *n* 1 in the UK: a registered medical practitioner who specializes in medical as opposed to surgical treatment of diseases and disorders. 2 in other parts of the world: anyone who is legally qualified to practise medicine.

physics *sing n* the scientific study of the properties and interrelationships of matter, energy, force and motion. ○ **physicist** *n*.

physio *n, colloq* 1 physiotherapy. 2 a physiotherapist.

physiognomy /fɪzɪˈɒnəmɪ/ *n* (**-ies**) the face or features, esp when used or seen as a key to someone's personality.

physiology *n, biol* the branch of biology that is concerned with the internal processes and functions of living organisms, as opposed to their structure. ○ **physiological** *adj*. ○ **physiologist** *n*.

physiotherapy *n, med* the treatment of injury and disease by external physical methods, such as remedial exercises, manipulation or massage, rather than by drugs or surgery. ○ **physiotherapist** *n*.

physique *n* the structure of the body with regard to size, shape, proportions and muscular development.

pi¹ /paɪ/ *n* 1 the sixteenth letter of the Greek alphabet. 2 *maths* this symbol (π), representing the ratio of the circumference of a circle to its diameter, in numerical terms 3.14159.

pi² see PIE²

pianissimo *mus, adv* performed very softly. ➤ *adj* very soft. ➤ *n* a piece of music to be performed in this way.

pianist *n* someone who plays the piano.

piano¹ *n* a large musical instrument with a keyboard, the keys being pressed down to operate a set of hammers that strike tautened wires to produce the sound.

piano² *mus, adv* softly. ➤ *adj* soft. ➤ *n* a passage of music to be played or performed softly.

piano accordion *n* an ACCORDION whose melody is produced by means of a keyboard.

pianoforte /pɪanoʊˈfɔːtɪ/ *n* the full formal term for a PIANO¹.

piazza /pɪˈatsə/ *n* **1** a public square in an Italian town. **2** *mainly Brit* a covered walkway.

pibroch /ˈpiːbrɒx/ *n* a series of variations on a martial theme or lament, played on the Scottish bagpipes.

pic *n* (**pics** or **pix**) *colloq* a photograph or picture.

pica /ˈpaɪkə/ *n, printing* an old type-size, giving about six lines to the inch, approximately 12-point and still used synonymously for that point size.

picador *n, bullfighting* a TOREADOR who weakens the bull by wounding it with a lance.

picaresque *adj* of a novel, etc: telling of the adventures of a usu likeable rogue in separate, only loosely connected, episodes.

piccalilli *n* a pickle consisting of mixed vegetables in a mustard sauce.

piccolo *n* a small transverse FLUTE pitched one octave higher than the standard flute and with a range of about three octaves.

pick¹ *vb* **1** *tr & intr* to choose or select. **2** to detach and gather (flowers from a plant, fruit from a tree, etc). **3** to open (a lock) with a device other than a key, often to gain unauthorized entry. **4** to get, take or extract whatever is of use or value from something: *The dog picked the bone clean* • *I need to pick your brains*. **5** to steal money or valuables from (someone's pocket). **6** to undo; to unpick. **7** to make (a hole) by unpicking. **8** to remove pieces of matter from (one's nose, teeth, a scab, etc) with one's fingernails, etc. **9** *intr* (*often* **pick at sth**) **a** to eat only small quantities of (one's food); **b** to keep pulling at (a scab, etc) with one's fingernails. **10** to provoke (a fight, quarrel, etc) with someone. ➤ *n* **1** the best of a group: *the pick of the bunch*. **2** one's own preferred selection. ○ **picker** *n*. ◆ **pick and choose** to be over-fussy in one's choice. **pick holes in sth** to find fault with it. **pick up the pieces** to have to restore things to normality or make things better after some trouble or disaster. ◊ **pick on sb 1** to blame them unfairly. **2** to bully them. **pick sb out 1** to select them from a group. **2** to recognize or distinguish them among a group or crowd. **pick up** of a person, a person's health, or a situation: to recover or improve. **pick up** or **pick sth up** to resume: *Let's pick up where we left off*. **pick sb up 1** to arrest or seize them. **2** to go and fetch them from where they are waiting. **3** to stop one's vehicle for them and give them a lift. **4** *colloq* to successfully invite them, eg to go home with one, esp with a view to sexual relations. **pick sth up 1** to lift or raise it from a surface, from the ground, etc. **2** to learn

or acquire (a habit, skill, language, etc) over a time. **3** to notice or become aware of it: *I picked up a faint odour*. **4** to obtain or acquire it casually, by chance, etc: *She picked up a bargain* • *I picked up an infection*. **5** to go and fetch (something waiting to be collected). **6** *telecomm* to receive (a signal, programme, etc). **7** *colloq* to agree to pay (a bill, etc): *I'll pick up the tab*.

pick² *n* **1** a tool with a long metal head pointed at one or both ends, for breaking ground, rock, ice, etc. **2** a poking or cleaning tool: *a toothpick*. **3** a plectrum.

pickaback see PIGGYBACK

pickaxe *n* a large pick.

picket *n* **1** a person or group of people stationed outside a place of work to persuade other employees not to go in during a strike. **2** a body of soldiers on patrol or sentry duty. **3** a stake fixed in the ground, eg as part of a fence. ➤ *vb* (**picketed, picketing**) **1** to station pickets or act as a PICKET (*noun* sense 1) at (a factory, etc). **2** to guard or patrol with, or as, a military picket. **3** to fence (an area, etc) with PICKETS (*noun* sense 3).

picket line *n* a line of people acting as pickets in an industrial dispute.

pickings *pl n, colloq* profits made easily or casually from something: *rich pickings*.

pickle *n* **1** (*also* **pickles**) a preserve of vegetables in vinegar, salt water or a tart sauce. **2** a vegetable preserved in this way. **3** the liquid used for this preserve. **4** *colloq* a mess; a predicament: *She got herself in a terrible pickle*. ➤ *vb* to preserve something in vinegar, salt water, etc.

pickled *adj* **1** preserved in pickle. **2** *colloq* drunk.

pick-me-up *n* **1** a stimulating drink, such as tea, a whisky, etc. **2** anything that revives.

pickpocket *n* a thief who steals from people's pockets, usu in crowded areas.

pick-up *n* **1** the STYLUS on a record player. **2** a TRANSDUCER on electric musical instruments. **3** a small lorry, truck or van. **4** *colloq* an acquaintance made casually, esp with a view to sexual relations; **b** the making of such an acquaintance. **5 a** a halt or place to load goods or passengers; **b** the goods or passengers loaded.

picky *adj* (**-ier, -iest**) *colloq* choosy or fussy, esp excessively so; difficult to please.

picnic *n* **1** an outing on which one takes food for eating in the open air. **2** food taken or eaten in this way. ➤ *vb* (**picnicked, picnicking**) *intr* to have a picnic. ○ **picnicker** *n*. ◆ **no picnic** or **not a picnic** *colloq* a disagreeable or difficult job or situation.

picot /ˈpiːkoʊ/ *n* **1** a loop in an ornamental edging. **2** *embroidery* a raised knot.

pictograph or **pictogram** *n* **1** a picture or symbol that represents a word, as in Chinese writing. **2** a pictorial or diagrammatic representation of values, statistics, etc. ○ **pictographic** *adj*. ○ **pictography** *n*.

pictorial *adj* relating to, or consisting of, pictures. ➢ *n* a periodical with a high proportion of pictures as opposed to text.

picture *n* **1** a representation of someone or something on a flat surface; a drawing, painting or photograph. **2** someone's portrait. **3** a view; mental image: *a clear picture of the battle*. **4** a situation or outlook: *a gloomy financial picture*. **5** a person or thing strikingly like another: *She is the picture of her mother*. **6** a visible embodiment: *She was the picture of happiness*. **7** an image of beauty: *It looks a picture*. **8** the image received on a television screen: *We get a good picture*. **9** a cinema film. **10** (**the pictures**) *colloq* the cinema. ➢ *vb* **1** to imagine or visualize: *Just picture that settee in our lounge*. **2** to describe something or someone vividly; to depict. **3** to represent or show someone or something in a picture or photograph. ♦ **get the picture** *colloq* to understand something. **in the picture** informed of all the facts, etc.

picture card *n* a COURT CARD.

picturesque *adj* **1** of places or buildings: charming to look at, esp if rather quaint. **2** of language: **a** colourful, expressive or graphic; **b** *facetious* vivid or strong to the point of being offensive.

picture window *n* an unusually large window with a plate-glass pane, usu affording an extensive view.

piddle *colloq, vb, intr* to urinate. ➢ *n* **1** urine. **2** the act of urinating.

piddling *adj* trivial; trifling: *piddling excuses*.

pidgin *n* **1** a type of simplified language used esp for trading purposes between speakers of different languages, commonly used in the East and West Indies, Africa and the Americas. **2** (*also* **pigeon**) *colloq* one's own affair, business or concern.

pidgin English *n* a PIDGIN (sense 1) in which one element is English.

pie¹ *n* a savoury or sweet dish, usu cooked in a container, consisting of a quantity of food with a covering of pastry, a base of pastry, or both. ♦ **easy as pie** very easy. **pie in the sky** hoped-for but unguaranteed future prospect.

pie² or **pi** *n* **1** *printing* confusedly mixed type. **2** a mixed state; confusion.

piebald *adj* having contrasting patches of colour, esp black and white. ➢ *n* a horse with black and white markings.

piece *n* **1** a portion of some material; a bit. **2** any of the sections into which something (eg a cake) is divided; a portion taken from a whole. **3** a component part: *a jigsaw piece*. **4** an item in a set. **5** an individual member of a class of things represented by a collective noun: *a piece of fruit* • *a piece of clothing*. **6** a specimen or example of something: *a fine piece of Chippendale*. **7** an instance: *a piece of nonsense*. **8** a musical, artistic, literary or dramatic work. **9** an article in a newspaper, etc. **10** a coin: *a 50 pence piece* • *pieces of eight*. **11** one of the tokens or men used in a board game. **12** a cannon

or firearm. **13** *offensive, colloq* a woman. ➢ *vb* (**pieced, piecing**) (**piece sth** or **things together**) to join it or them together to form a whole. ♦ **a piece of one's mind** a frank and outspoken reprimand. **go to pieces** *colloq* to lose emotional control; to panic. **of a piece with sth** consistent or uniform with it. **say one's piece** to make one's contribution to a discussion.

piecemeal *adv* a bit at a time.

piece of cake *n* something that is easy, simple, etc.

piecework *n* work paid for according to the amount done, not the time taken to do it.

pie chart, **pie diagram** or **pie graph** *n* a diagram used to display statistical data, consisting of a circle divided into sectors, each of which contains one category of information. Compare BAR CHART.

pied *adj* of a bird: having variegated plumage, esp of black and white.

pie-eyed *adj, colloq* drunk.

pier *n* **1 a** a structure projecting into water for use as a landing stage or breakwater; **b** such a structure used as a promenade with funfair-like sideshows, amusement arcades, etc. **2** a pillar supporting a bridge or arch. **3** the masonry between two openings in the wall of a building.

pierce *vb* (*also* **pierce through sth**) **1** of a sharp object or a person using one: to make a hole in or through; to puncture; to make (a hole) with something sharp. **2** to penetrate or force a way through or into something: *The wind pierced through her thin clothing*. **3** of light or sound: to burst through (darkness or silence). **4** to affect or touch (someone's heart, soul, etc) keenly or painfully.

piercing *adj* **1** referring to something that pierces. **2** penetrating, acute, keen or sharp: *a piercing cry*. ➢ *n* the practice of piercing parts of the body to insert studs or rings. ○ **piercingly** *adv*.

pietism *n* pious feeling or an exaggerated show of piety. ○ **pietist** *n*.

piety *n* **1** dutifulness; devoutness. **2** the quality of being pious, dutiful or religiously devout. **3** sense of duty towards parents, benefactors, etc.

piezoelectricity /paɪɪˌzəʊɪlɛkˈtrɪsɪtɪ, piːˌzəʊ-/ *n* electricity produced by stretching or compressing quartz crystals and other non-conducting crystals. ○ **piezoelectric** *adj*.

piffle *n, colloq* nonsense.

piffling *adj, colloq* trivial, trifling or petty.

pig *n* **1** a hoofed mammal with a stout bristle-covered body and a protruding flattened snout, kept for its meat. **2** an abusive term for a person, esp someone greedy, dirty, selfish or brutal. **3** *slang* an unpleasant job or situation. **4** *offensive slang* a policeman. **5 a** a quantity of metal cast into an oblong mass; **b** the mould into which it is run. ➢ *vb* (**pigged, pigging**) **1** of a pig: to produce young. **2** *tr & intr* of a person: to eat greedily. ♦ **a pig in a poke** *colloq* a purchase made without first inspecting it to see whether it is suitable. **make a pig of oneself** *colloq* to eat greedily. **make a pig's ear of sth** *colloq* to make a mess of it. ◊ **pig out** to eat a large amount with relish and overindulgence.

pigeon[1] *n* 1 a medium-sized bird with a plump body, a rounded tail and dense soft grey, brown or pinkish plumage. 2 *slang* a dupe or simpleton.

pigeon[2] see PIDGIN (sense 2)

pigeon-breasted or **pigeon-chested** *adj* of humans: having a narrow chest with the breastbone projecting, as a pigeon has.

pigeonhole *n* 1 any of a set of compartments, eg in a desk or on a wall, for filing letters or papers in. 2 a compartment of the mind or memory. ➢ *vb* 1 to put something into a pigeonhole. 2 to put someone or something mentally into a category, esp too readily or rigidly.

pigeon-toed *adj* of a person: standing and walking with their toes turned in.

piggery *n* (**-ies**) 1 a place where pigs are bred. 2 *colloq* greediness or otherwise disgusting behaviour.

piggish *adj*, *derog* greedy, dirty, selfish, mean or ill-mannered. ○ **piggishness** *n*.

piggy or **piggie** *n* (**-ies**) a child's diminutive: **a** a pig; a little pig; **b** a toe. ➢ *adj* (**-ier**, **-iest**) 1 piglike. 2 of the eyes: small and mean-looking.

piggyback or **pickaback** *n* a ride on someone's back, with the legs supported by the bearer's arms. ➢ *adj* carried on the back of someone else. ➢ *adv* on the back of someone else.

piggy bank *n* a child's pig-shaped container for saving money in.

pigheaded *adj* stupidly obstinate. ○ **pigheadedly** *adv*. ○ **pigheadedness** *n*.

pig-in-the-middle or **piggy-in-the-middle** *n* 1 a game in which one person stands between two others and tries to intercept the ball they are throwing to each other. 2 (**pigs**-or **piggies-in-the-middle**) any person helplessly caught between two contending parties.

pig iron *n*, *metallurgy* an impure form of iron produced by smelting iron in a BLAST FURNACE.

piglet *n* a young pig.

pigment *n* 1 any insoluble colouring matter that is used in suspension in water, oil or other liquids to give colour to paint, paper, etc. 2 a coloured substance that occurs naturally in living tissues, eg the red blood pigment HAEMOGLOBIN, or CHLOROPHYLL in the leaves of green plants. ➢ *vb* to colour something with pigment; to dye or stain. ○ **pigmentary** or **pigmented** *adj*. ○ **pigmentation** *n*.

pigmy see PYGMY

pigskin *n* leather made from the skin of a pig.

pigsty *n* (**-ies**) 1 a pen where pigs are kept. 2 *colloq* a filthy and disordered place.

pigtail *n* a plaited length of hair, esp one of a pair, worn hanging at the sides or back of the head.

pike[1] *n* (**pike** or **pikes**) a large predatory freshwater fish with a narrow pointed head and a small number of large teeth in the lower jaw.

pike[2] *n* 1 *hist* a weapon like a spear, consisting of a metal point mounted on a long shaft. 2 a point or spike. 3 *N Eng dialect* a sharp-pointed hill or summit.

pike[3] *n* 1 a TURNPIKE. 2 *US* a main road.

pike[4] *adj*, *diving*, *gymnastics* (also **piked**) of a body position: bent sharply at the hips with the legs kept straight at the knees and toes pointed. ➢ *vb*, *intr* to move into this position.

pikestaff *n* the shaft of a PIKE[2]. ◆ **plain as a pikestaff** all too obvious.

Pilates /pɪˈlɑːtiːz/ *n* an exercise system for improving posture, stretching muscles, etc.

pilau /pɪˈlaʊ/, **pilaf** or **pilaff** /pɪˈlaf/ *n* an oriental dish of spiced rice with, or to accompany, chicken, fish, etc.

pilchard *n* a small edible marine fish of the herring family, bluish-green above and silvery below, covered with large scales.

pile[1] *n* 1 a number of things lying on top of each other; a quantity of something in a heap or mound. 2 (**a pile** or **piles**) *colloq* a large quantity. 3 *colloq* a fortune: *I made a pile on the horses*. 4 a massive or imposing building. 5 a PYRE. 6 a NUCLEAR REACTOR, orig the graphite blocks forming the moderator for the reactor. ➢ *vb* 1 *tr & intr* (*usu* **pile up** or **pile sth up**) to accumulate into a pile. 2 *intr* (**pile in** or **into sth** or **pile off, out**, *etc*) to move in a crowd or confused bunch into or off it, etc. ◆ **pile it on** *colloq* to exaggerate.

pile[2] *n* a heavy wooden shaft, stone or concrete pillar, etc driven into the ground as a support for a building, bridge, etc.

pile[3] *n* 1 the raised cropped threads that give a soft thick surface to carpeting, velvet, etc. 2 soft fine hair, fur, wool, etc.

pile-driver *n* a machine for driving piles (see PILE[2]) into the ground.

piles *pl n* haemorrhoids.

pile-up *n* a vehicle collision in which following vehicles also crash, causing a number of collisions.

pilfer *vb*, *tr & intr* to steal in small quantities. ○ **pilfering** *n*.

pilgrim *n* 1 someone who makes a journey to a holy place as an act of reverence. 2 a traveller. ○ **pilgrimage** *n*.

pill *n* 1 a small ball or tablet of medicine, for swallowing. 2 something unpleasant that one must accept. 3 (**the pill**) an oral contraceptive, usu taken by women.

pillage *vb*, *tr & intr* to plunder or loot. ➢ *n* 1 the act of pillaging. 2 loot, plunder or booty. ○ **pillager** *n*.

pillar *n* 1 a vertical post of wood, stone, metal or concrete serving as a support to a main structure. 2 any slender vertical mass of something, eg of smoke, rock, etc. 3 a strong and reliable supporter of a particular cause or organization: *He is a pillar of the village commu-*

nity. ◆ **from pillar to post** from one place to another, esp moving between these in desperation, frustration, etc.

pillar box see LETTER BOX

pillbox *n* **1** a small round container for pills. **2** *mil* a small, usu circular, concrete shelter for use as a lookout post and gun emplacement. **3** a small round flat-topped hat.

pillion *n* a seat for a passenger on a motorcycle or horse, behind the driver or rider. ➤ *adv* on a pillion: *to ride pillion.*

pillock *n, Brit slang* a foolish person.

pillory *n* (*-ies*) *hist* a wooden frame with holes for the hands and head, into which wrong-doers were locked as a punishment and publicly ridiculed. ➤ *vb* (*-ies, -ied*) **1** to hold someone up to public ridicule. **2** to put someone in a pillory.

pillow *n* a cushion for the head, esp a large rectangular one on a bed.

pillowcase or **pillowslip** *n* a removable washable cover for a pillow.

pillow talk *n* confidential conversation with a sexual partner in bed.

pilot *n* **1** someone who flies an aircraft, hovercraft, spacecraft, etc. **2** someone employed to conduct or steer ships into and out of harbour. **3** someone who is qualified to act as pilot. **4** a guide. ➤ *adj* of a scheme, programme, test, etc: serving as a preliminary test which may be modified before the final version is put into effect: *a pilot project.* ➤ *vb* (*piloted, piloting*) **1** to act as pilot to someone. **2** to direct, guide or steer (a project, etc).

pilot light *n* **1** a small permanent gas flame, eg on a gas cooker, that ignites the main burners when they are turned on. **2** an indicator light on an electrical apparatus showing when it is switched on.

pilot officer *n, Brit* an air-force officer of the lowest commissioned rank.

pimento *n* **1** a small tropical evergreen tree, cultivated mainly in Jamaica. **2** any of the dried unripe berries of this tree which are a source of allspice. ➤ the PIMIENTO.

pimiento /pɪmɪˈɛntoʊ/ *n* **1** a variety of sweet pepper, widely cultivated for its mild-flavoured red fruit. **2** the fruit of this plant, eaten raw or cooked.

pimp *n* a man who finds customers for a prostitute or a brothel and lives off the earnings. ➤ *vb, intr* to act as a pimp.

pimpernel *n* a small sprawling plant, esp the scarlet pimpernel.

pimple *n* a small raised often pus-containing swelling on the skin. ○ **pimply** *adj* (*-ier, -iest*).

PIN /pɪn/ *abbrev* personal identification number, a number used to authorize electronic transactions, such as a withdrawal from a cash dispenser.

pin *n* **1** a short slender implement with a sharp point and small round head, usu made of stainless steel, for fastening, attaching, etc, and used esp in dressmaking. **2** *in compounds* a

fastening device consisting of or incorporating a slender metal or wire shaft: *hatpin* • *safety pin.* **3** a narrow brooch. **4** *in compounds* any of several cylindrical wooden or metal objects with various functions: *a rolling pin.* **5** a peg. **6** any or either of the cylindrical or square-sectioned legs on an electric plug. **7** a club-shaped object set upright for toppling with a ball: *ten-pin bowling.* **8** the clip on a grenade, that is removed before it is thrown. **9** *golf* the metal shaft of the flag marking a hole. **10** (**pins**) *colloq* one's legs: *I'm shaky on my pins.* ➤ *vb* (**pinned, pinning**) **1** to secure it with a pin. **2** to make a small hole in something. **3** (**pin sth on sb**) *colloq* to put the blame (for a crime or offence) on them. ◆ **pin one's hopes** or **faith on sth** or **sb** to rely on or trust in them entirely. ◇ **pin sb down** to force a commitment or definite expression of opinion from them. **pin sth down** to identify or define it precisely. **pin sth** or **sb down** to hold them fast or trap them.

pinafore *n* **1** an apron, esp one with a bib. **2** (*also* **pinafore dress**) a sleeveless dress for wearing over a blouse, sweater, etc.

pinball *n* a game played on a slot machine, in which a small metal ball is propelled by flippers round a course, the score depending on what hazards it avoids and targets it hits; a form of BAGATELLE (sense 1).

pince-nez /ˈpænsneɪ/ *pl n* spectacles that are held in position by a clip gripping the nose.

pincers *pl n* **1** a hinged tool with two claw-like jaws joined by a pivot, used for gripping objects, pulling nails, etc. **2** the modified claw-like appendage of a decapod crustacean, eg a crab or lobster, adapted for grasping.

pinch *vb* **1** to squeeze or nip the flesh of someone or something, between thumb and finger. **2** to compress or squeeze something painfully. **3** of cold or hunger: to affect someone or something painfully or injuriously. **4** *tr & intr* of tight shoes: to hurt or chafe. **5** *tr & intr, colloq* to steal. **6** *intr* of controls, restrictions, shortages, etc: to cause hardship. **7** *intr* to economize: *I had to pinch and scrape to get by.* **8** *colloq* to arrest someone. ➤ *n* **1** a nip or squeeze. **2** the quantity of something (eg salt) that can be held between thumb and finger. **3** a very small amount. **4** a critical time of difficulty or hardship. ◆ **at a pinch** *colloq* if absolutely necessary. **feel the pinch** *colloq* to find life, work, etc difficult because of lack of money.

pinchbeck *n* a copper-zinc alloy with the appearance of gold, used in cheap jewellery. ➤ *adj* cheap, sham, counterfeit or imitation.

pinched *adj* of a person's appearance: pale and haggard from tiredness, cold or other discomfort.

pincushion *n* a pad into which to stick dressmaking pins for convenient storage.

pine¹ *n* **1** (*also* **pine tree**) an evergreen coniferous tree with narrow needle-like leaves. **2** (*also* **pinewood**) the pale durable wood of this tree, used to make furniture, telegraph poles, paper pulp, etc, and widely used in construction work.

pine² vb, intr **1** (also **pine for sb** or **sth**) to long or yearn for them or it. **2** (also **pine away**) to waste away from grief or longing.

pineal gland or **pineal body** /ˈpɪnɪəl/ n, anat in vertebrates: a small outgrowth from the brain which produces hormones.

pineapple n **1** a tropical S American plant with spiky sword-shaped leaves, widely cultivated for its large edible fruit. **2** the fruit of this plant, which has sweet juicy yellow flesh covered by a yellowish-brown spiny skin.

pine nut or **pine kernel** n the edible oily seed of various species of pine trees.

ping n a sharp ringing sound like that made by plucking a taut wire, lightly striking glass or metal, etc. ➤ vb, tr & intr to make or cause something to make this sound.

ping-pong n TABLE TENNIS.

pinhead n **1** the little rounded or flattened head of a pin. **2** slang a stupid person. ○ **pinheaded** adj.

pinhole n a tiny hole made by, or as if by, a pin.

pinion¹ vb **1** to immobilize someone by holding or binding their arms; to hold or bind (someone's arms). **2** to hold fast or bind. ➤ n **1** the extreme tip of a bird's wing. **2** a bird's flight feather.

pinion² n a small cogwheel that engages with a larger wheel or rack.

pink¹ n **1** a light or pale-red colour, between red and white. **2** a plant, eg a CARNATION, which has grass-like bluish-green leaves and flowers with five spreading toothed or slightly frilled pink, red, white, purple, yellow, orange or variegated petals. **3 a** a scarlet hunting coat or its colour; **b** the person wearing it. **4** the highest point: *in the pink of condition.* ➤ adj **1** having, being or referring to the colour pink. **2** slightly left-wing. **3** of or relating to homosexuals: *the pink vote.* ♦ **in the pink** colloq in the best of health.

pink² vb to cut (cloth) with a notched or serrated edge that frays less readily than a straight edge.

pink³ vb, intr of a vehicle engine: to KNOCK (verb sense 6).

pink eye see CONJUNCTIVITIS

pinkie or **pinky** n (-ies) Scot & N Am the little finger.

pinking shears pl n scissors with a serrated blade for cutting a zigzag edge in cloth.

pin money n extra cash earned for spending on oneself, on luxury items, etc.

pinnace /ˈpɪnəs/ n a small boat carried on a larger ship.

pinnacle n **1** a slender spire crowning a buttress, gable, roof or tower. **2** a rocky peak. **3** a high point of achievement: *the pinnacle of her success.*

pinnate adj, bot denoting a compound leaf that consists of pairs of leaflets arranged in two rows on either side of a central axis.

pinny n, colloq an apron.

pinpoint vb to place, define or identify something precisely.

pinprick n **1** a tiny hole made by, or as if by, a pin. **2** a slight irritation.

pins and needles pl n an abnormal tingling or prickling sensation in a limb, etc, felt as the flow of blood returns to it after being temporarily obstructed.

pinstripe n **1** a very narrow stripe in cloth. **2** cloth with such stripes. ○ **pinstriped** adj.

pint n **1** in the UK, in the imperial system: a unit of liquid measure equivalent to ⅛ of a gallon or 20 fl oz, equivalent to 0.568 litre (liquid or dry). **2** in the US: a unit of liquid measure equivalent to ⅛ of a gallon or 16 US fl oz, equivalent to 0.473 litre (liquid) or 0.551 litre (dry). **3** colloq a drink of beer of this quantity.

pinta n, colloq a pint of milk.

pintle n a bolt or pin, esp one which is turned by something.

pint-size or **pint-sized** adj, humorous of a person: very small.

pin tuck n a narrow decorative tuck in a garment.

pin-up n **1** a picture of a pop star or a famous, glamorous or otherwise admirable person that one pins on one's wall. **2** someone whose picture is pinned up in this way.

pioneer n **1** an explorer of, or settler in, hitherto unknown or wild country. **2** someone who breaks new ground in anything. **3** bot a plant or species that is characteristically among the first to establish itself on bared ground. ➤ vb **1** intr to be a pioneer. **2** to explore and open up (a route, etc). **3** to try out, originate or develop (a new technique, etc).

pious adj **1** religiously devout. **2** dutiful. **3** derog ostentatiously virtuous. ○ **piously** adv ○ **piousness** n.

pip¹ n the small seed of a fruit such as an apple, pear, orange or grape. ○ **pipless** adj.

pip² n **1** one of a series of short high-pitched signals on the radio, telephone, etc. **2** (**the pips**) colloq the six pips broadcast as a time-signal by BBC radio.

pip³ vb (**pipped**, **pipping**) to defeat someone narrowly. ♦ **pipped at the post** colloq overtaken narrowly in the closing stages of a contest, etc.

pip⁴ n **1** one of the emblems or spots on playing-cards, dice or dominoes. **2** mil in the British army: a star on a uniform indicating rank. **3** on a radar screen: a mark, eg a spot of light, that indicates the presence of an object.

pip⁵ n, old use a disease of fowl. ♦ **give sb the pip** colloq to irritate them.

pipe n **1** a tubular conveyance for water, gas, oil, etc. **2 a** a little bowl with a hollow stem for smoking tobacco, etc; **b** a quantity of tobacco smoked in one of these. **3** a wind instrument consisting of a simple wooden or metal tube. **4** (**the pipes**) the BAGPIPES. **5** any of the vertical metal tubes through which sound is produced on an organ. **6** a boatswain's whistle. **7** a pipe-like vent forming part of a volcano. **8** *old use or in compounds* any of the air passages in an animal's body: *the windpipe.* ➢ *vb* **1** to convey (gas, water, oil, etc) through pipes. **2** *tr & intr* to play on a pipe or the pipes. **3** (*also* **pipe sb** *or* **sth in**) to welcome or convey with music from a pipe or the bagpipes: *He piped in the haggis.* **4** *tr & intr* of a child: to speak or say in a small shrill voice. **5** *intr* to sing shrilly as a bird does. **6 a** to use a bag with a nozzle in order to force (icing or cream, etc from the bag) into long strings for decorating a cake, dessert, etc; **b** to make (designs, etc) on a cake, etc by this means. ◊ **pipe down** *colloq* to stop talking: *Will you please pipe down!* **pipe up** to speak unexpectedly, breaking a silence, etc.

pipeclay *n* fine white clay for making tobacco pipes and delicate crockery.

piped music *n* light recorded music played continuously through loudspeakers, esp in public places.

pipe dream *n* a delightful fantasy of the kind indulged in while smoking a pipe, orig one filled with opium.

pipeful *n* the amount a pipe can hold.

pipeline *n* a series of connected pipes laid underground to carry oil, natural gas, water, etc, across large distances. ♦ **in the pipeline** *colloq* under consideration; forthcoming or in preparation.

piper *n* a player of a pipe or the bagpipes.

pipette *n* a small laboratory device usu consisting of a narrow tube into which liquid can be sucked and from which it can subsequently be dispensed in known amounts.

piping *n* **1** a length of pipe, or a system or series of pipes conveying water, oil, etc. **2** covered cord forming a decorative edging on upholstery or clothing. **3** strings and knots of icing or cream decorating a cake or dessert. **4** the art of playing a pipe or the bagpipes. ➢ *adj* of a voice: small and shrill. ♦ **piping hot** of food: satisfyingly hot.

pipistrelle *n* the smallest and most widespread European bat, which has a reddish-brown body and short triangular ears.

pipit *n* a small ground-dwelling songbird with a slender body, streaked brown plumage and a long tail.

pippin *n* any of several varieties of eating apple with a green or rosy skin.

pipsqueak *n, derog colloq* someone or something insignificant or contemptible.

piquant /'pi:kənt/ *adj* **1** having a pleasantly spicy taste or tang. **2** amusing, intriguing, provocative or stimulating. ◊ **piquancy** *n* the state of being piquant.

pique /pi:k/ *n* resentment; hurt pride. ➢ *vb* **1** to hurt someone's pride; to offend or nettle them. **2** to arouse (curiosity or interest). **3** to pride (oneself) on something: *He piqued himself on his good taste.*

piqué /'pi:keɪ/ *n* a stiff corded fabric, esp of cotton.

piquet /pɪ'ket, pɪ'keɪ/ *n* a card game for two, played with 32 cards.

piracy *n* (*-ies*) **1** the activity of pirates, such as robbery on the high seas. **2** unauthorized publication or reproduction of copyright material.

piranha /pɪ'rɑːnə/ *or* **piraña** /pə'rɑːnjə/ *n* an extremely aggressive S American freshwater fish, with sharp saw-edged teeth.

pirate *n* **1** someone who attacks and robs ships at sea. **2** the ship used by pirates. **3** someone who publishes material without permission from the copyright-holder, or otherwise uses someone else's work illegally. **4** someone who runs a radio station without a licence. ➢ *vb* to publish, reproduce or use (someone else's literary or artistic work, or ideas) without legal permission. ◊ **piratic** *or* **piratical** *adj*.

pirouette /pɪru'et/ *n* a spin or twirl executed on tiptoe in dancing. ➢ *vb, intr* to execute a pirouette.

piscatorial *or* **piscatory** *adj, formal* relating to fish or fishing.

Pisces /'paɪsiːz/ *n, astrol* **a** the twelfth sign of the zodiac; **b** someone born between 20 February and 20 March, under this sign.

pisciculture /'pɪsɪkʌltʃʊə(r)/ *n* the rearing of fish by artificial methods or under controlled conditions.

piscina /pɪ'siːnə/ *n* (*piscinae* /-niː/ *or* **piscinas**) a stone basin with a drain, found in older churches, in which to empty water used for rinsing the sacred vessels.

piscine /pɪ'saɪn/ *adj* referring or relating to, or resembling, a fish or fishes.

piss *vb* **1** *intr, coarse slang, sometimes considered taboo* to urinate. **2** to discharge something (eg blood) in the urine. **3** to wet something with one's urine. **4** *intr* (*also* **piss down**) to rain hard. ➢ *n* **1** urine. **2** an act of urinating. ♦ **take the piss out of sb** *or* **sth** to ridicule them or it. ◊ **piss about** *or* **around** to mess about; to waste time. **piss off** to go away. **piss sb off** *Brit* to irritate or bore them.

pissed *adj* **1** *Brit coarse slang* drunk. **2** *N Am* (*often* **pissed at sb** *or* **sth**) annoyed with them or it.

pistachio /pɪ'stɑːʃɪəʊ/ *n* **1** a small deciduous tree with greenish flowers and reddish-brown nut-like fruits containing edible seeds. **2** the edible greenish seed of this tree.

piste /piːst/ *n* a ski slope or track of smooth compacted snow.

pistil *n, bot* in a flowering plant: the female reproductive structure.

pistol *n* a small gun held in one hand when fired.

pistol-whip *vb* to hit someone with a pistol.

piston *n* **1** *eng* a cylindrical device that moves up and down in the cylinder of a petrol, diesel or steam engine. **2** a sliding valve on a brass wind instrument.

pit¹ *n* **1** a big deep hole in the ground. **2** a mine, esp a coalmine. **3** a cavity sunk into the ground from which to inspect vehicle engines, etc. **4** (**the pits**) *motor sport* any of a set of areas beside a racetrack where vehicles can refuel, have wheel changes, etc. **5** an enclosure in which fighting animals or birds are put. **6 a** the floor of the auditorium in a theatre; **b** the people sitting there. **7** *anat* a hollow, indentation or depression, eg the **armpit**. **8** a scar left by a smallpox or acne pustule. **9** (**the pit**) *old use* hell. **10** (**the pits**) *slang* an awful or intolerable situation, person, etc. ➤ *vb* (**pitted, pitting**) **1** (*often* **pit oneself against sb**) to set or match oneself against them in competition. **2** to mark something with scars and holes.

pit² *n, N Am* the stone in a peach, apricot, plum, etc. ➤ *vb* (**pitted, pitting**) to remove the stone from (a piece of fruit).

pit-a-pat *n* **1** a noise of pattering. **2** a succession of light taps. ➤ *adv* with a pattering or tapping noise: *The rain was falling pit-a-pat.* ➤ *vb* (**pit-a-patted, pit-a-patting**) to make a succession of quick light taps.

pitch¹ *vb* **1** to set up (a tent or camp). **2** to throw or fling. **3** *tr & intr* to fall or make someone or something fall heavily forward. **4** *intr* of a ship: to plunge and lift alternately at bow and stern. **5** *tr & intr* of a roof: to slope. **6** to give a particular musical pitch to (one's voice or a note) in singing or playing, or to set (a song, etc) at a higher or lower level within a possible range: *The tune is pitched too high for me.* **7** to choose a level, eg of difficulty, sophistication, etc at which to present (a talk, etc). **8 a** *cricket* to bowl (the ball) so that it lands in front of the batsman; **b** *golf* to hit (the ball) high and gently, so that it stays where it is on landing; **c** *tr & intr, baseball* of the PITCHER²: to throw the ball to the person batting. ➤ *n* **1** the field or area of play in any of several sports. **2** an act or style of pitching or throwing. **3** a degree of intensity; a level: *The crowd reached such a pitch of excitement.* **4 a** the angle of steepness of a slope; **b** such a slope. **5** *mus* the degree of highness or lowness of a note that results from the frequency of the vibrations producing it. **6** a street trader's station. **7** a line in sales talk, esp one often made use of. **8** the plunging and rising motion of a ship. ◊ **pitchy** *adj* (**-ier, -iest**). ◊ **pitch in** *colloq* **1** to begin enthusiastically. **2** to join in; to make a contribution. **pitch into sb** *colloq* to rebuke or blame them angrily.

pitch² *n* **1** a thick black sticky substance obtained from coal tar, used for filling ships' seams, etc. **2** any of various bituminous substances.

pitch-black or **pitch-dark** *adj* utterly, intensely or unrelievedly black or dark.

pitchblende *n, geol* a radioactive glossy brown or black form of uraninite, the main ore of uranium and radium.

pitched battle *n* a prearranged battle between two sides on chosen ground.

pitcher¹ *n* a large earthenware jug with either one or two handles.

pitcher² *n, baseball* the player who throws the ball to the person batting to hit.

pitchfork *n* a long-handled fork with two or three sharp prongs, for tossing hay.

piteous *adj* arousing one's pity; moving, poignant, heartrending or pathetic. ◊ **piteously** *adv.* ◊ **piteousness** *n*.

pitfall *n* a hidden danger, unsuspected hazard or unforeseen difficulty.

pith *n* **1** the soft white tissue that lies beneath the rind of many citrus fruits, eg orange. **2** *bot* in the stem of many plants: a central cylinder of generally soft tissue. **3** the most important part of an argument, etc. **4** substance, forcefulness or vigour as a quality in writing, etc.

pithead *n* the entrance to a mine-shaft and the machinery round it.

pithy *adj* (**-ier, -iest**) **1** of a saying, comment, etc: brief, forceful and to the point. **2** referring to, resembling or full of pith. ◊ **pithily** *adv.* ◊ **pithiness** *n*.

pitiable *adj* **1** arousing pity. **2** miserably inadequate; contemptible.

pitiful *adj* **1** arousing pity; wretched or pathetic: *His clothes were in a pitiful state.* **2** sadly inadequate or ineffective: *a pitiful attempt.* ◊ **pitifully** *adv.* ◊ **pitifulness** *n*.

pitiless *adj* showing no pity. ◊ **pitilessly** *adv.*

piton /ˈpiːtɒn/ *n, mountaineering* a metal peg or spike with an eye for passing a rope through, hammered into a rock face as an aid to climbers.

pitstop *n, motor sport* a pause made at a refuelling PIT¹ (*noun* sense 4) by a racing driver.

pitta *n* a Middle-Eastern slightly leavened bread, usu in a hollow oval shape that can be filled with other foods.

pittance *n* a meagre allowance or wage.

pitter-patter *n* the sound of pattering. ➤ *adv* with this sound. ➤ *vb, intr* to make such a sound.

pituitary *n* (**-ies**) short form of PITUITARY GLAND. ➤ *adj* relating to this gland.

pituitary gland or **pituitary body** *n, physiol* in vertebrates: an endocrine gland at the base of the brain that is responsible for the production of a number of important hormones.

pity *n* (**-ies**) **1** a feeling of sorrow for the troubles and sufferings of others. **2** a cause of sorrow or regret. ➤ *vb* (**-ies, -ied**) to feel or show pity for someone or something. ◊ **pitying** *adj.* ◊ **pityingly** *adv.* ◆ **have** or **take pity on sb** to feel or show pity for them, esp in some practical way.

pivot *n* **1** a central pin, spindle or pointed shaft round which something revolves, turns, balances or oscillates. **2** someone or something crucial, on which everyone or everything else depends. ➤ *vb* (**pivoted, pivoting**) **1** *intr* (*often* **pivot on sth**) **a** to turn, swivel or revolve; **b** to depend. **2** to mount something on a pivot.

pivotal *adj* **1** constructed as or acting like a pivot. **2** crucially important: *a pivotal moment in our history.*

pix[1] *n* a PYX.

pix[2] *a pl of* PIC

pixel *n, electronics* the smallest element of the image displayed on a computer or TV screen, consisting of a single dot which may be illuminated (ie on) or dark (off).

pixie or **pixy** *n* (*-ies*) *myth* a kind of fairy, traditionally with mischievous tendencies.

pizza *n* a circle of dough spread with cheese, tomatoes, etc and baked, made orig in Italy.

pizzazz, pazzazz, pizazz or **pazazz** *n, colloq* a quality that is a combination of boldness, vigour, dash and flamboyance.

pizzeria *n* a restaurant specializing in pizzas.

pizzicato /pɪtsɪˈkɑːtoʊ/ *mus, adj, adv* of music for stringed instruments: played using the fingers to pluck the strings. ➢ *n* **1** a passage of music to be played in this way. **2** the playing or technique of playing a piece by plucking.

pl. *abbrev* plural.

placable *adj* easily appeased.

placard *n* a board or stiff card bearing a notice, advertisement, slogan, message of protest, etc, carried or displayed in public. ➢ *vb* **1** to put placards on (a wall, etc). **2** to announce (a forthcoming event, etc) by placard.

placate *vb* to pacify or appease (someone who is angry, etc). ○ **placatory** *adj*.

place *n* **1** a portion of the earth's surface, particularly one considered as a unit, such as an area, region, district, locality, etc. **2** a geographical area or position, such as a country, city, town, village, etc. **3** a building, room, piece of ground, etc, particularly one assigned to some purpose: *a place of business* • *a place of worship.* **4** *colloq* one's home or lodging: *Let's go to my place.* **5** *in compounds* somewhere with a specified association or function: *one's birthplace* • *a hiding place.* **6** a seat or space, eg at table: *I laid three places.* **7** a seat in a theatre, on a train, bus, etc. **8** an area on the surface of something, eg on the body. **9** the customary position of something or someone: *Put it back in its place.* **10** a point reached, eg in a conversation, narrative, series of developments, etc: *a good place to stop.* **11** a point in a book, etc, esp where one stopped reading: *She made me lose my place.* **12** a position within an order eg of competitors in a contest, a set of priorities, etc: *They finished in third place* • *He lost his place in the queue.* **13** social or political rank: *I know my place.* **14** a vacancy at an institution, on a committee, in a firm, etc: *a university place.* **15** one's role, function, duty, etc: *It's not my place to tell him.* **16** an open square or a row of houses: *the market place.* **17** *maths* the position of a number in a series, esp of decimals after the point. ➢ *vb* **1** to put, position etc in a particular place. **2** to submit: *Let's place an order.* **3** to find a place, home, job, publisher, etc for someone. **4** to assign final positions to (contestants, etc): *I was placed fourth.* **5** to identify or categorize: *It was a familiar voice that I couldn't quite place.* **6** *commerce* to find a

buyer for (stocks or shares, usu a large quantity of them). **7** to arrange (a bet, loan, etc). **8** *intr, esp N Am* to finish a race or competition (in a specified position or, if unspecified, in second position). ◆ **all over the place** in disorder or confusion. **go places** *colloq* **1** to travel. **2** to be successful. **in place** in the correct position. **in place of sth** or **sb** instead of it or them. **in places** here and there. **know one's place** to show proper subservience (to someone, an organization, etc). **lose one's place** to falter in following a text, etc; not to know what point has been reached. **out of place 1** not in the correct position. **2** inappropriate. **put** or **keep sb in their place** to humble them as they deserve because of their arrogance, conceit, etc. **take one's place** to assume one's usual or rightful position. **take place** to happen, occur, be held, etc. **take the place of sb** or **sth** to replace or supersede them.

placebo /pləˈsiːboʊ/ *n, med* a substance that is administered as a drug but has no medicinal content, either given to a patient for its reassuring and therefore beneficial effect (the **placebo effect**), or used in a clinical trial of a real drug, in which participants who have been given a placebo serve as untreated CONTROL subjects for comparison with those actually given the drug.

placement *n* **1** the act or process of placing or positioning. **2** the finding of a job or home for someone. **3** a temporary job providing work experience, esp for someone on a training course.

placename *n* the name of a town, village, hill, lake, etc.

placenta /pləˈsɛntə/ *n* (**placentas** or **placentae** /-tiː/) in mammals: a disc-shaped organ attached to the lining of the uterus during pregnancy and through which the embryo obtains nutrients and oxygen. ○ **placental** *adj*.

place setting *n*, a SETTING (*noun* sense 2).

placid *adj* calm; tranquil. ○ **placidity** or **placidness** *n*. ○ **placidly** *adv*.

placket *n, dressmaking* **1** an opening in a skirt for a pocket or at the fastening. **2** a piece of material sewn behind this.

plagiarize or **-ise** /ˈpleɪdʒəraɪz/ *vb, tr & intr* to copy (ideas, passages of text, etc) from someone else's work and use them as if they were one's own. ○ **plagiarism** *n*. ○ **plagiarist** *n*.

plague *n* **1** *med* **a** any of several epidemic diseases with a high mortality rate; **b** specifically, an infectious epidemic disease of rats and other rodents, caused by a bacterium and transmitted to humans by flea bites, eg BUBONIC PLAGUE. **2** an overwhelming intrusion by something unwelcome: *a plague of tourists.* **3** *colloq* a nuisance. **4** an affliction regarded as a sign of divine displeasure: *a plague on both your houses.* ➢ *vb* **1** to afflict severely: *She's plagued by headaches.* **2** to pester someone; to annoy them continually. ◆ **avoid sth like the plague** to keep well away from it.

plaice *n* (*pl* **plaice**) **1** a flatfish that has a brown upper surface covered with bright orange spots, and is an important food fish. **2** *N Am* any of several related fishes.

plaid /plad/ *n* **1** tartan cloth. **2** a long piece of woollen cloth worn over the shoulder, usu tartan and worn with a kilt as part of Scottish Highland dress. ➤ *adj* with a tartan pattern or in tartan colours: *plaid trousers*.

plain *adj* **1** all of one colour; unpatterned; undecorated. **2** simple; unsophisticated; without improvement, embellishment or pretensions: *plain food*. **3** obvious; clear. **4** straightforward; direct: *plain language* • *plain dealing*. **5** frank; open. **6** of a person: lacking beauty. **7** sheer; downright: *plain selfishness*. ➤ *n* **1** a large area of relatively smooth flat land without significant hills or valleys. **2** *knitting* the simpler of two basic stitches, with the wool passed round the front of the needle. ➤ *adv* utterly; quite: *just plain stupid*. ○ **plainly** *adv.* ○ **plainness** *n*.

plain chocolate *n* dark-coloured chocolate made without milk.

plain clothes *pl n* ordinary clothes worn by police officers on duty, as distinct from a uniform. ➤ *adj* (**plain-clothes** or **plain-clothed**) of police officers on duty: wearing ordinary clothes, not uniformed.

plain flour *n* flour that contains no raising agent.

plain sailing *n* **1** easy unimpeded progress. **2** *naut* sailing in unobstructed waters.

plainsong *n* in the medieval Church, and still in the Roman Catholic and some Anglican Churches: music for unaccompanied voices, sung in unison.

plain-spoken *adj* frank to the point of bluntness.

plaint *n* **1** *poetic* an expression of woe. **2** *law* a written statement of grievance against someone, submitted to a court of law.

plaintiff *n, law* someone who brings a case against another person in a court of law.

plaintive *adj* mournful-sounding; sad; wistful. ○ **plaintively** *adv.*

plait /plat/ *vb* to arrange something (esp hair) by interweaving three or more lengths of it. ➤ *n* a length of hair or other material interwoven in this way. ○ **plaited** *adj.*

plan *n* **1** a thought-out arrangement or method for doing something. **2** (*usu* **plans**) intentions: *What are your plans for today?* **3** a sketch, outline, scheme or set of guidelines. **4** *often in compounds* a large-scale detailed drawing or diagram of a floor of a house, the streets of a town, etc done as though viewed from above: *a floor plan* • *a street plan*. ➤ *vb* (**planned, planning**) **1** (*also* **plan for sth**) to devise a scheme for it. **2** (*also* **plan for sth**) to make preparations or arrangements for it. **3** *intr* to prepare; to make plans: *to plan ahead*. **4** (*also* **plan on sth**) to intend or expect it. **5** to draw up plans for (eg a building); to design.

plane¹ *n* an AEROPLANE.

plane² *n* **1** *geom* a flat surface, either real or imaginary, such that a straight line joining any two points lies entirely on it. **2** a level surface. **3** a level or standard: *She's on a higher intellectual plane*. ➤ *adj* **1** flat; level. **2** having the character of a plane. **3** *maths* lying in one plane: *a plane figure* • *plane geometry.* ➤ *vb, intr* **1** of a boat: to skim over the surface of the water. **2** of a bird: to wheel or soar with the wings motionless.

plane³ *n* a carpenter's tool for smoothing wood by shaving away unevennesses. ➤ *vb* (*also* **plane sth down**) to smooth (a surface, esp wood) with a plane. ○ **planer** *n* a tool or machine for planing.

plane⁴ *n* a large deciduous tree with thin bark which is shed in large flakes, revealing creamy or pink patches on the trunk.

planet *n, astron* **a** a celestial body, in orbit around the Sun or another star; **b** one of nine such bodies, Mercury, Venus, Earth, Mars, Jupiter, Saturn, Uranus, Neptune and Pluto, that revolve around the Sun in the solar system.

planetarium *n* (**planetaria** or **planetariums**) **1** a special projector by means of which the positions and movements of stars and planets can be projected on to a hemispherical domed ceiling in order to simulate the appearance of the night sky to an audience seated below. **2** the building that houses such a projector.

planetary *adj* **1** *astron* **a** relating to or resembling a planet; **b** consisting of or produced by planets; **c** revolving in an orbit. **2** *astrol* under the influence of a planet.

plangent *adj* of a sound: deep, ringing and mournful. ○ **plangency** *n*. ○ **plangently** *adv.*

plank *n* **1** a long flat piece of timber thicker than a board. **2** any of the policies forming the programme of a political party. ➤ *vb* to fit or cover something with planks.

planking *n* planks, or a surface, etc constructed of them.

plankton *n, biol* microscopic animals and plants that passively float or drift with the current in the surface waters of seas and lakes. ○ **planktonic** *adj.*

planner *n* **1** someone who draws up plans or designs: *a town planner*. **2** a wall calendar showing the whole year, on which holidays, etc can be marked.

plant *n* **1** any living organism that is capable of manufacturing carbohydrates by the process of photosynthesis and that typically possesses cell walls containing cellulose. **2** a relatively small organism of this type, eg a herb or shrub as opposed to a tree. **3** the buildings, equipment and machinery used in the manufacturing or production industries, eg a factory, a power station, etc. **4** *colloq* something deliberately placed for others to find and be misled by. **5** *colloq* a spy placed in an organization in order to gain information, etc. ➤ *vb* **1** to put (seeds or plants) into the ground to grow. **2** (*often* **plant sth out**) to put plants or seeds into (ground, a garden, bed, etc). **3** to introduce (an idea, doubt, etc) into someone's mind. **4** to place something firmly. **5** (*usu* **plant sth on sb**) to give them (a kiss or blow). **6** to post someone as a spy in an office, factory, etc. **7** *colloq* to place something deliberately so as to mislead the finder, esp as a means of incriminating an innocent person.

plantain *n* **1** a plant belonging to the banana family, widely cultivated for its edible fruit. **2** the green-skinned banana-like edible fruit of this plant, which can be cooked and eaten as a vegetable.

plantation *n* **1** an estate, esp in the tropics, that specializes in the large-scale production of a single cash crop, eg coffee or rubber. **2** an area of land planted with a certain kind of tree for commercial purposes: *a conifer plantation.* **3** *hist* a colony.

planter *n* **1** the owner or manager of a plantation. **2** a device for planting bulbs, etc. **3** a container for house plants.

plaque *n* **1** a commemorative inscribed tablet fixed to or set into a wall. **2** *dentistry* a thin layer of food debris, bacteria and calcium salts that forms on the surface of teeth and may cause tooth decay.

plasma *n* **1** *physiol* the colourless liquid component of blood or lymph, in which the blood cells are suspended. **2** *physics* a gas that has been heated to a very high temperature so that most of its atoms or molecules are broken down into free electrons and positive ions. **3** *geol* a bright green CHALCEDONY.

plaster *n* **1** a material consisting of lime, sand and water that is applied to walls when soft and dries to form a hard smooth surface. **2** a strip of material, usu with a lint pad and an adhesive backing, that is used for covering and protecting small wounds. **3** PLASTER OF PARIS. ➣ *vb* **1** to apply plaster to (walls, etc). **2** (*usu* **plaster sth with** or **on sth**) *colloq* to coat or spread thickly. **3** to fix something with some wet or sticky substance: *His hair was plastered to his skull.* **4** (*often* **plaster sth with sth**) to cover it liberally. ○ **plasterer** *n.*

plasterboard *n* a material consisting of hardened plaster faced on both sides with paper or thin board, used to form or line interior walls.

plaster cast *n* **1** a copy of an object, eg a sculpture, obtained by pouring a mixture of PLASTER OF PARIS and water into a mould formed from that object. **2** a covering of plaster of Paris for a broken limb, etc.

plastered *adj* **1** covered with plaster. **2** *colloq* drunk.

plaster of Paris *n* a white powder consisting of a hydrated form of calcium sulphate (GYPSUM), mixed with water to make a paste that sets hard, used for sculpting and for making casts for broken limbs.

plastic *n* **1** any of a large number of synthetic materials that can be moulded by heat and/or pressure into a rigid or semi-rigid shape. **2** *colloq* a credit card, or credit cards collectively: *Can I pay with plastic?* ➣ *adj* **1** made of plastic.

2 easily moulded or shaped. **3** easily influenced. **4** *derog* artificial; lacking genuine substance. **5** of money: in the form of, or funded by, a credit card. **6** relating to sculpture and modelling. ○ **plasticity** *n.*

plastic arts *pl n* arts involving modelling or shaping in three dimensions, such as ceramics or sculpture.

plastic bullet *n* a solid plastic cylinder fired by the police to disperse riots, etc.

plastic explosive *n* an explosive substance resembling putty that can be moulded by hand.

plasticizer or **-iser** *n, chem* an organic compound that is added to a rigid polymer in order to make it flexible and so more easily workable. ○ **plasticize** *vb.*

plastic surgery *n, med* the branch of surgery concerned with the repair or reconstruction of deformed or damaged tissue or body parts, the replacement of missing parts, and cosmetic surgery. ○ **plastic surgeon** *n.*

plate *n* **1** *also in compounds* a shallow dish, esp one made of earthenware or porcelain, for serving food on: *a side plate* • *dinner plates.* **2 a** the amount held by this; a plateful; **b** a portion served on a plate. **3** (*also* **collection plate**) a shallow vessel in which to take the collection in church. **4** a sheet of metal, glass or other rigid material. **5** *often in compounds* a flat piece of metal, plastic, etc inscribed with a name, etc: *nameplate* • *bookplate.* **6** gold and silver vessels or cutlery. **7 a** a gold or silver cup as the prize in a horse race, etc; **b** a race or contest for such a prize. **8** a thin coating of gold, silver or tin applied to a base metal. **9** an illustration on glossy paper in a book. **10** *photog* a sheet of glass prepared with a light-sensitive coating for receiving an image. **11 a** a sheet of metal with an image engraved on it; **b** a print taken from one of these. **12** a surface set up with type ready for printing. **13 a** a rigid plastic fitting to which false teeth are attached; **b** a denture. **14** *geol* any of the rigid sections that make up the Earth's crust. **15** *anat* a thin flat piece of bone or horn. **16** *baseball* a five-sided white slab at the home base. ➣ *vb* **1** to coat (a base metal) with a thin layer of a precious one. **2** to cover something with metal plates. ○ **plateful** *n.* ♦ **hand** or **give sb sth on a plate** *colloq* to present them with it without their having to make the least effort. **have a lot** or **much on one's plate** *colloq* to have a great deal of work, commitments, etc.

plateau /ˈplatoʊ/ *n* (*plateaux* /-toʊ/ or *plateaus* /-toʊz/) **1** *geog* an extensive area of relatively flat high land, usu bounded by steep sides. **2** *econ* a stable unvarying condition of prices, etc after a rise: *The production rate reached a plateau in August.* ➣ *vb, intr* (*sometimes* **plateau out**) to reach a level; to even out.

plated *adj* **1** covered with plates of metal. **2** *usu in compounds* covered with a coating of another metal, esp gold or silver.

plate glass *n* a high-quality form of glass that

has been ground and polished to remove defects, used in shop windows, mirrors, etc.

platelayer *n* someone who lays and repairs railway lines.

platelet *n, physiol* in mammalian blood: any of the small disc-shaped cell fragments that are responsible for starting the formation of a blood clot when bleeding occurs.

platen *n* **1** in some printing-presses: a plate that pushes the paper against the type. **2** the roller of a typewriter.

plate tectonics *sing n, geol* a geological theory according to which the Earth's crust is composed of a small number of large plates of solid rock, whose movements in relation to each other are responsible for continental drift.

platform *n* **1** a raised platform for speakers, performers, etc. **2** the raised walkway alongside the track at a railway station, giving access to trains. **3** *often in compounds* a floating installation moored to the sea bed, for oil-drilling, marine research, etc: *an oil platform* • *a production platform*. **4** an open step at the back of some buses, esp older ones, for passengers getting on or off. **5** a very thick rigid sole for a shoe, fashionable particularly in the 1970s. **6** the publicly declared principles and intentions of a political party, forming the basis of its policies.

platinum *n, chem* a silvery-white precious metallic element that does not tarnish or corrode, used to make jewellery, coins, electrical contacts, etc.

platinum-blonde or **platinum-blond** *adj* of hair: having a silvery fairness.

platitude *n* an empty, unoriginal or redundant comment, esp one made as though it were important. ◦ **platitudinous** *adj*.

Platonic *adj* **1** belonging or relating to the Greek philosopher Plato. **2** (*usu* **platonic**) of human love: not involving sexual relations. ◦ **platonically** *adv*.

platoon *n* **1** *mil* a subdivision of a COMPANY. **2** a squad of people acting in co-operation.

platter *n* **1** a large flat dish. **2** *N Am colloq* a RECORD (*noun* sense 4).

platypus *n* an Australian egg-laying amphibious mammal with dense brown fur, a long flattened toothless snout, webbed feet and a broad flat tail. Also called **duck-billed platypus**.

plaudit *n* (*usu* **plaudits**) a commendation; an expression of praise.

plausible *adj* **1** of an explanation, etc: credible, reasonable or likely. **2** of a person: characterized by having a pleasant and persuasive manner; smooth-tongued or glib. ◦ **plausibility** *n*. ◦ **plausibly** *adv*.

play *vb* **1** *intr* esp of children: to spend time in recreation, eg dancing about, kicking a ball around, doing things in make-believe, generally having fun, etc. **2** *intr* to pretend for fun; to behave without seriousness. **3** (*also* **play at sth**) to take part in (a recreative pursuit, game, sport, match, round, etc): *We played rounders* • *They played at rounders*. **4** (*also* **play against**

sb) to compete against them in a game or sport. **5** (**play with sth**) to contemplate (an idea, plan, etc). **6** *intr, colloq* to co-operate: *He refuses to play*. **7** *tr, sport* to include someone as a team member: *Newcastle played Given in goal.* **8** *sport* to hit or kick (the ball), deliver (a shot), etc in a sport. **9** *cards* to use (a card) in the course of a game: *He played the three of clubs.* **10** to speculate or gamble on (the stock exchange, etc): *I'm playing the market.* **11** *tr & intr* **a** to act or behave in a certain way: *He's playing it cool* • *You're not playing fair*; **b** to pretend to be someone or something: *She likes to play the dumb blonde.* **12** to act (a particular role): *The hotel will play host to the delegates.* **13** (*usu* **play sb in sth**) *tr & intr* to perform (a role) in a play: *I played Oliver in the school play.* **14** *tr & intr* esp of a pop group: to perform in (a particular place or venue): *She plays the sax.* **15** *intr* of a film, play, etc: to be shown or performed publicly: *It's playing all next week.* **16** *mus* **a** to perform (a specified type of music) on an instrument: *Lisa plays jazz on the saxophone*; **b** to perform on (an instrument): *He plays the sax.* **17** to turn on (a radio, a tape-recording, etc). **18** *intr* **a** of recorded music, etc: to be heard from a radio, etc; **b** of a radio, etc: to produce sound. **19** *intr* of a fountain: to be in operation. **20** *angling* to allow (a fish) to tire itself by its struggles to get away. ➤ *n* **1** playing games for fun and amusement: *children at play.* **2** the playing of a game, performance in a sport, etc: *Rain stopped play.* **3** *colloq* behaviour; conduct: *fair play* • *foul play.* **4** a dramatic piece for the stage or a performance of it. **5** fun; jest: *It was said in play.* **6** range; scope: *to give full play to the imagination.* **7** freedom of movement; looseness: *There's too much play in the steering.* **8** action or interaction: *the play of sunlight on water.* **9** use: *He brought all his cunning into play.* ◦ **playable** *adj*. ✦ **play ball** *colloq* to co-operate. **play for time** to delay action or decision in the hope or belief that conditions will become more favourable later. **play hard to get** to make a show of unwillingness to co-operate or lack of interest, with a view to strengthening one's position. **play into the hands of sb** to act so as to give, usu unintentionally, an advantage to them. **play it by ear** to improvise a plan of action to meet the situation as it develops. **play safe** to take no risks. **play with fire** to take foolish risks. ◇ **play about** or **around with sb** to behave irresponsibly towards them, their affections, etc. **play about** or **around with sth** to fiddle or meddle with it. **play sb along** to manipulate them, usu for one's own advantage. **play along with sb** to co-operate with them for the time being. **play sth back** to play (a film or sound recording) through immediately after making it. **play sth down** to represent it as unimportant; to minimize, make light of or discount it. **play on sth 1** to exploit (someone's fears, feelings, sympathies, etc) for one's own benefit. **2** to make a pun on it: *He played on the two mean-*

ings of 'batter'. **play up 1** *colloq* to behave uncooperatively. **2** *colloq* to cause one pain or discomfort: *His stomach is playing up again.* **3** *colloq* of a machine, etc: to function faultily. **4** to try one's hardest in a game, match, etc. **play sth up** to highlight it or give prominence to it. **play up to sb** to flatter them; to ingratiate oneself with them.

play-act *vb, intr* to behave in an insincere fashion, disguising one's true feelings or intentions.

playback *n* a playing back of a sound recording or film.

playboy *n* a man of wealth, leisure and frivolous lifestyle.

player *n* **1** someone who plays. **2** someone who participates in a game or sport, particularly as their profession. **3** *colloq* a participant in a particular activity, esp a powerful one: *a major player in the Mafia.* **4** a performer on a musical instrument: *a guitar player.* **5** *old use* an actor.

playful *adj* **1** full of fun; frisky. **2** of a remark, etc: humorous. ○ **playfully** *adv.* ○ **playfulness** *n.*

playground *n* an area for children's recreation, esp one that is part of a school's grounds.

playgroup *n* an organized group of preschool children that meets for regular supervised play.

playhouse *n, old use* a theatre.

playing-card *n* a rectangular card belonging to a PACK[1] (*noun* sense 3) used in card games.

playing field *n* a grassy outdoor area prepared and marked out for playing games on.

playmate *n* a companion to play with.

play-off *n* a match or game played to resolve a draw or other undecided contest.

play on words *n* **1** a pun. **2** punning.

playpen *n* a collapsible frame that when erected forms an enclosure inside which a baby may safely play.

playschool *n* a PLAYGROUP, or a school for children between the ages of two and five.

plaything *n* a toy, or a person or thing treated as if they were a toy.

playtime *n* a period for recreation, esp a set period for playing out of doors as part of a school timetable.

playwright *n* an author of plays.

plaza *n* a large public square or market place, esp one in a Spanish town.

PLC or **plc** *abbrev* public limited company.

plea *n* **1** an earnest appeal. **2** *law* a statement made in a court of law by or on behalf of the defendant.

plead *vb* (**pleaded** or *esp N Am & Scot* **pled**) **1** (*usu* **plead with sb for sth**) to appeal earnestly to them for it: *pleading for mercy.* **2** *intr* of an accused person: to state in a court of law that one is guilty or not guilty. **3** (*also* **plead for sth**) to argue in defence of it: *I'll plead my case.* **4** to give something as an excuse: *She pleaded ignorance.*

pleadings *pl n, law* the formal statements submitted by defendant and plaintiff in a lawsuit.

pleasant *adj* **1** giving pleasure; enjoyable;

agreeable. **2** of a person: friendly; affable. ○ **pleasantly** *adv.*

pleasantry *n* (*-ies*) **1** a remark made for the sake of politeness or friendliness. **2** humour; teasing.

please *vb* **1** *tr & intr* to give satisfaction, pleasure or enjoyment; to be agreeable to someone. **2** (with *it* as subject) *formal* to be the inclination of someone or something: *if it should please you to join us.* **3** *tr & intr* to choose; to like: *Do as you please.* ➤ *adv, exclam* used politely to accompany a request, order, acceptance of an offer, protest, a call for attention, etc. ○ **pleased** *adj.* ○ **pleasing** *adj.* ◆ **please oneself** to do as one likes.

pleasurable *adj* enjoyable; pleasant.

pleasure *n* **1** a feeling of enjoyment or satisfaction. **2** a source of such a feeling: *I'd like the pleasure of your company.* **3** one's will, desire, wish, preference or inclination. **4** recreation; enjoyment. **5** gratification of a sensual kind: *pleasure and pain.* ➤ *vb, old use* **1** to give pleasure to someone, esp sexual pleasure. **2** (*usu* **pleasure in sth**) to take pleasure in it. ◆ **with pleasure** gladly; willingly; of course.

pleat *n* a fold sewn or pressed into cloth, etc. ➤ *vb* to make pleats in (cloth, etc).

pleb *n, derog* someone who has coarse or vulgar tastes, manners or habits.

plebeian /plə'bɪən/ *n* **1** a member of the common people, esp ancient Rome. **2** *derog* someone who lacks refinement or culture. ➤ *adj* **1** referring or belonging to the common people. **2** *derog* coarse; vulgar; unrefined.

plebiscite /'plɛbɪsaɪt/ *n* a vote of all the electors, taken to decide a matter of public importance.

plectrum *n* (**plectrums** or **plectra**) a small flat implement of metal, plastic, horn, etc used for plucking the strings of a guitar.

pledge *n* **1** a solemn promise. **2** something left as security with someone to whom one owes money, etc. **3** something put into pawn. **4** a token or symbol. ➤ *vb* **1** to promise (money, loyalty, etc) to someone. **2** to bind or commit (oneself, etc). **3** to offer or give something as a pledge or guarantee.

Pleiocene see PLIOCENE

Pleistocene /'plaɪstəʊsiːn/ *adj, geol* denoting the first epoch of the Quaternary period, which contains the greatest proportion of fossil molluscs of living species and during which modern man evolved.

plenary *adj* **1** full; complete: *plenary powers.* **2** of a meeting, assembly, council, etc: to be attended by all members, delegates, etc.

plenipotentiary *adj* entrusted with, or conveying, full authority to act on behalf of one's government or other organization. ➤ *n* (*-ies*) someone, eg an ambassador, invested with such authority.

plenitude *n* **1** abundance; profusion. **2** completeness; fullness.

plenteous *adj, literary* plentiful; abundant.

plentiful adj in good supply; copious; abundant. ○ **plentifully** adv.

plenty n **1** (often **plenty of** sth) a lot: Plenty of folk would agree. **2** wealth or sufficiency; a sufficient amount: in times of plenty. ➤ pron **1** enough, or more than enough: That's plenty, thank you. **2** a lot; many: I'm sure plenty would agree with me (ie plenty of folk; many people). ➤ adv, colloq fully: That should be plenty wide enough.

plenum n (**plenums** or **plena**) **1** a meeting attended by all members. **2** physics a space completely filled with matter.

pleonasm /'pliːənazəm/ n, gram, rhetoric **1** the use of more words than are needed to express something. **2** a superfluous word or words. ○ **pleonastic** adj.

plethora /'plɛθərə/ n a large or excessive amount.

pleura /'plʊərə/ n (**pleurae** /-riː/) anat in mammals: the double membrane that covers the lungs and lines the chest cavity. ○ **pleural** adj.

pleurisy n, pathol, med inflammation of the pleura. ○ **pleuritic** adj.

Plexiglas n, US trademark PERSPEX.

plexus n (**plexus** or **plexuses**) anat a network of nerves or blood vessels, eg the SOLAR PLEXUS behind the stomach.

pliable adj **1** easily bent; flexible. **2** adaptable or alterable. **3** easily persuaded or influenced. ○ **pliability** n.

pliant adj **1** bending easily; pliable, flexible or supple. **2** easily influenced. ○ **pliancy** n.

pliers pl n a hinged tool with jaws for gripping small objects, bending or cutting wire, etc.

plight¹ n a danger, difficulty or situation of hardship that one finds oneself in.

plight² vb, old use to promise something solemnly. ◆ **plight one's troth** to pledge oneself in marriage.

plimsoll or **plimsole** n, old use a light rubber-soled canvas shoe worn for gymnastics, etc.

plinth n **1** archit a square block serving as the base of a column, pillar, etc. **2** a base or pedestal for a statue or other sculpture, or for a vase.

Pliocene or **Pleiocene** /'plaɪəusiːn/ adj, geol the last epoch of the Tertiary period, during which the climate became cooler, many mammals became extinct and primates that walked upright appeared.

plod vb (**plodded, plodding**) intr **1** to walk slowly with a heavy tread. **2** to work slowly, methodically and thoroughly, if without inspiration. ○ **plodder** n.

plonk¹ colloq, n the resounding thud made by a heavy object falling. ➤ vb **1** to put or place something with a thud or with finality. **2** intr to place oneself or to fall with a plonk. ➤ adv with a thud: He banged the plonk beside her.

plonk² n, colloq cheap, undistinguished wine.

plonker n, slang a foolish person.

plop n the sound of a small object dropping into water without a splash. ➤ vb (**plopped,**

plopping) tr & intr to fall or drop with this sound. ➤ adv with a plop.

plot¹ n **1** a secret plan, esp one laid jointly with others, for contriving something illegal or evil. **2** the story or scheme of a play, film, novel, etc. ➤ vb (**plotted, plotting**) **1** tr & intr to plan something (esp something illegal or evil), usu with others. **2** to make a plan of something; to mark the course or progress of something. **3** maths to mark (a series of individual points) on a graph, or to draw a curve through them. ○ **plotter** n.

plot² n, often in compounds a piece of ground for any of various uses: a vegetable plot.

plough or (N Am) **plow** /plaʊ/ n **1** a bladed farm implement used to turn over the surface of the soil and bury stubble, weeds, etc, in preparation for the cultivation of a crop. **2** any similar implement, esp a SNOWPLOUGH. **3** (the Plough) astron the seven brightest stars in the constellation Ursa Major. ➤ vb **1** (also **plough sth up**) to till or turn over (soil, land, etc) with a plough. **2** intr to make a furrow or to turn over the surface of the soil with a plough. **3** intr (usu **plough through sth**) **a** to move through it with a ploughing action; **b** colloq to make steady but laborious progress with it. **4** intr (usu **plough into sth**) colloq of a vehicle or its driver: to crash into it at speed. ◇ **plough on** colloq to continue with something although progress is laborious.

ploughman or (N Am) **plowman** n someone who steers a plough.

ploughman's lunch n a cold meal of bread, cheese, and pickle.

ploughshare or (N Am) **plowshare** n a blade of a plough.

plover n a wading bird with boldly patterned plumage and a short straight bill.

plow the N Am spelling of PLOUGH.

ploy n a stratagem, dodge or manoeuvre to gain an advantage.

pluck vb **1** to pull the feathers off (a bird) before cooking it. **2** to pick (flowers or fruit) from a plant or tree. **3** (often **pluck sth out**) to remove it by pulling. **4** to shape (the eyebrows) by removing hairs from them. **5** (usu **pluck** or **pluck at** sth) to pull or tug at it. **6** to sound (the strings of a violin, etc) using the fingers or a plectrum. ➤ n **1** courage. **2** a little tug. **3** the heart, liver and lungs of an animal. ◆ **pluck up courage** to strengthen one's resolve for a difficult undertaking, etc.

plucky adj (**-ier, -iest**) colloq courageous; spirited. ○ **pluckily** adv. ○ **pluckiness** n.

plug n **1** a piece of rubber, plastic, etc shaped to fit a hole as a stopper, eg in a bath or sink. **2** often in compounds any device or piece of material for a similar purpose: earplugs. **3 a** the plastic or rubber device with metal pins, fitted to the end of the flex of an electrical apparatus, that is pushed into a socket to connect with the power supply; **b** loosely the socket or power point: Switch it off at the plug. **4** colloq a piece of favourable publicity given to a product, programme, etc, eg on television. **5** a SPARK PLUG. **6** an accumulation of solidified magma which fills the vent of a volcano. ➤ *n* a lump of tobacco for chewing. ➤ *vb* (**plugged, plugging**) **1** (*often* **plug sth up**) to stop or block up (a hole, etc) with something. **2** *colloq* to give favourable publicity to (a product, programme, etc), esp repeatedly: *She plugged her new book.* **3** *intr* (*usu* **plug away** or **along**) *colloq* to work or progress steadily. **4** *slang* to shoot someone with a gun. ○ **plugger** *n.* ◊ **plug sth in** to connect (an electrical appliance) to the power supply by an electrical plug.

plug-and-play *adj, comput* of a component, software, etc: able to be used immediately without any complex installation process.

plughole *n* the hole in a bath or sink through which water flows into the waste-pipe.

plum *n* **1** a shrub or small tree, cultivated in temperate regions for its edible fruit, or for its ornamental flowers or foliage. **2** the smooth-skinned red, purple, green or yellow fruit of this tree, which has a hard central stone surrounded by sweet juicy flesh, eg damson, greengage. **3** *in compounds* a raisin used in cakes, etc: *plum pudding.* **4** *colloq* something especially valued or sought. **5** a deep dark red colour. ➤ *adj* **1** dark red in colour. **2** highly sought-after: *a plum job.*

plumage *n* a bird's feathers, esp with regard to colour.

plumb *n* a lead weight, usu suspended from a line, used for measuring water depth or for testing a wall, etc for perpendicularity. ➤ *adj* straight, vertical or perpendicular. ➤ *adv* **1** in a straight, vertical or perpendicular way: *It dropped plumb to the sea bed.* **2** *colloq* exactly: *plumb in the middle.* **3** *N Am colloq* utterly: *The guy is plumb crazy.* ➤ *vb* **1** to measure, test or adjust something using a plumb. **2** to penetrate, probe or understand (a mystery, etc). **3** (*usu* **plumb sth in**) to connect (a water-using appliance) to the water supply or waste pipe.
♦ **out of plumb** not vertical. **plumb the depths of sth** to experience the worst extreme of (a bad feeling, etc): *They plumbed the depths of misery.*

plumbago *n, chem* another name for GRAPHITE.

plumber *n* someone who fits and repairs water pipes, and water- or gas-using appliances.

plumbing *n* **1** the system of water and gas pipes in a building, etc. **2** the work of a plumber.

plumbline *n* a line with a PLUMB attached, used for measuring depth or testing whether something is vertical.

plume *n* **1** a conspicuous feather of a bird. **2** such a feather, or bunch of feathers, worn as an ornament or crest, represented in a coat of arms, etc. **3** a curling column (of smoke etc). ➤ *vb* **1** of a bird: to clean or preen (itself or its

feathers). **2** to decorate with plumes. **3** (*usu* **plume oneself on sth**) to pride or congratulate oneself on it, usu on something trivial. ○ **plumy** *adj.*

plummet *vb* (**plummeted, plummeting**) *intr* to fall or drop rapidly; to plunge or hurtle downwards. ➤ *n* the weight on a plumbline or fishing line.

plummy *adj* (**-ier, -iest**) **1** *colloq* of a job, etc: desirable; worth having. **2** *derog* of a voice: affectedly or excessively rich and deep. **3** full of plums.

plump¹ *adj* full, rounded or chubby; not unattractively fat. ➤ *vb* (*often* **plump sth up**) to shake (cushions or pillows) to give them their full soft bulk. ○ **plumply** *adv.* ○ **plumpness** *n.*

plump² *colloq, vb* **1** *tr & intr* (*sometimes* **plump down** or **plump sth down**) to put down, drop, fall, or sit heavily. **2** *intr* (**plump for sth** or **sb**) to decide on or choose them; to make a decision in their favour. ➤ *n* a sudden heavy fall or the sound this makes. ➤ *adv* **1** suddenly; with a plump. **2** in a blunt or direct way. ➤ *adj* blunt or direct.

plunder *vb, tr & intr* to steal (valuable goods) or loot (a place), esp with open force during a war; to rob or ransack. ➤ *n* the goods plundered; loot; booty. ○ **plunderer** *n.*

plunge *vb* **1** *intr* (*usu* **plunge in** or **into sth**) to dive, throw oneself, fall or rush headlong in or into it. **2** *intr* (*usu* **plunge in** or **into sth**) to involve oneself rapidly and enthusiastically. **3** to thrust or push something. **4** *tr & intr* to put something or someone into a particular state or condition: *They plunged the town into darkness.* **5** to dip something briefly into water or other liquid. **6** *intr* to dip steeply: *The ship plunged and rose.* ➤ *n* **1** an act of plunging; a dive. **2** *colloq* a dip or swim. ♦ **take the plunge** *colloq* to commit oneself finally after hesitation; to take an irreversible decision.

plunger *n* a rubber suction cup at the end of a long handle, used to clear blocked drains, etc.

plunk *vb* **1** to pluck (the strings of a banjo, etc). **2** (*often* **plunk sth down**) to drop it, esp suddenly. ➤ *n* the act of plunking or the sound this makes.

pluperfect *gram, adj* of the tense of a verb: formed in English by the auxiliary verb *had* and a past PARTICIPLE, and referring to action already accomplished at the time of a past action being referred to, as in *They had often gone there before, but this time they lost their way.* ➤ *n* **a** the pluperfect tense; **b** a verb in the pluperfect tense.

plural *adj* **1** *gram* denoting or referring to two or more people, things, etc as opposed to only one. **2** consisting of more than one, or of different kinds. ➤ *n, gram* a word or form of a word expressing the idea or involvement of two or more people, things, etc. Compare SINGULAR. ○ **pluralize** or **-ise** *vb.*

pluralism *n* **1** the existence within a society of

a variety of ethnic, cultural and religious groups. **2** the holding of more than one post, esp in the Church. ○ **pluralist** *n, adj.* ○ **pluralistic** *adj.*

plurality *n* (*-ies*) **1** the state or condition of being plural. **2** PLURALISM (sense 2). **3** a large number or variety.

plus *prep* **1** *maths* with the addition of (a specified number): *2 plus 5 equals 7.* **2** in combination with something; with the added factor of (a specified thing): *Bad luck, plus his own obstinacy, cost him his job.* ➤ *adv* after a specified amount: with something more besides: *Helen earns £20 000 plus.* ➤ *adj* **1** denoting the symbol '+': *the plus sign.* **2** mathematically positive; above zero: *plus 3.* **3** advantageous: *a plus factor.* **4** in grades: denoting a slightly higher mark than the letter alone: *B plus.* **5** *physics, elec* electrically positive. ➤ *n* **1** (*also* **plus sign**) the symbol '+', denoting addition or positive value. **2** *colloq* something positive or good; a bonus, advantage, surplus, or extra: *The free crèche was a definite plus.* ➤ *conj, colloq* in addition to the fact that.

plus fours *pl n* loose breeches gathered below the knee, still occasionally used as golfing wear.

plush *n* a fabric with a long velvety pile. ➤ *adj* **1** made of plush. **2** *colloq* plushy.

plushy *adj* (*-ier, -iest*) *colloq* luxurious, opulent, stylish or costly.

plutocracy *n* (*-ies*) **1** government or domination by the wealthy. **2** a state governed by the wealthy. **3** an influential group whose power is backed by their wealth.

plutocrat *n* **1** a member of a plutocracy. **2** *colloq* a wealthy person. ○ **plutocratic** *adj.*

plutonium *n, chem* a dense highly poisonous silvery-grey radioactive metallic element, whose isotope **plutonium-239** is used as an energy source for nuclear weapons and some nuclear reactors.

pluvial *adj* relating to or characterized by rain; rainy. ➤ *n, geol* a period of prolonged rainfall.

ply[1] *n* (*plies*) **1** thickness of yarn, rope or wood, measured by the number of strands or layers that compose it. **2** a strand or layer. ➤ *adj, in compounds* specifying the number of strands or layers involved: *four-ply wool.*

ply[2] *vb* (*plies, plied*) **1** (*usu* ply sb with sth) to keep supplying them with something or making a repeated, often annoying, onslaught on them: *He plied them with drinks • They were plying me with questions.* **2** *tr & intr* (*often* ply between one place and another) to travel a route regularly; to go regularly to and fro between destinations. **3** *dated or literary* to work at (a trade). **4** *dated or literary* to use (a tool, etc). ○ **plier** *n.*

plywood *n* wood which consists of thin layers glued together, widely used in the construction industry.

PM *abbrev* **1** Paymaster. **2** Postmaster. **3** Prime Minister.

Pm *symbol, chem* promethium.

p.m. or **pm** *abbrev* **1** (*also* **P.M.** or **PM**) post meridiem. **2** post mortem.

PMS *abbrev* premenstrual syndrome.

PMT *abbrev* premenstrual tension.

pneumatic /njʊˈmatɪk/ *adj* **1** relating to air or gases. **2** containing or inflated with compressed air: *pneumatic tyres.* **3** of a tool or piece of machinery: operated or driven by compressed air: *a pneumatic drill.* ○ **pneumatically** *adv.*

pneumonia /njʊˈmoʊnɪə/ *n, pathol* inflammation of one or more lobes of the lungs, usu as a result of bacterial or viral infection.

PO *abbrev* **1** Petty Officer. **2** Pilot Officer. **3** Post Office.

Po *symbol, chem* polonium.

po[1] *n, colloq* a chamberpot.

po[2] or **p.o.** *abbrev* postal order.

poach[1] *vb, cookery* **1** to cook (an egg without its shell) in or over boiling water. **2** to simmer (fish) in milk or other liquid.

poach[2] *vb* **1** *tr & intr* to catch (game or fish) illegally on someone else's property. **2** to steal (ideas, etc). **3** to lure away (personnel at a rival business, etc) to work for one. ○ **poacher** *n.*

pock *n* **1** a small inflamed area on the skin, containing pus, esp one caused by smallpox. **2** POCKMARK.

pocket *n* **1** an extra piece sewn into or on to a garment to form a pouch for carrying things in. **2** any container similarly fitted or attached. **3** one's financial resources: *It's well beyond my pocket.* **4** a rock cavity filled with ore. **5** in conditions of air turbulence: a place in the atmosphere where the air pressure drops or rises abruptly. **6** an isolated patch or area of something: *pockets of unemployment.* **7** *billiards, etc* any of the holes, with nets or pouches beneath them, situated around the edges of the table and into which balls are potted. ➤ *adj* small enough to be carried in a pocket; smaller than standard: *a pocket calculator.* ➤ *vb* **1** to put in one's pocket. **2** *colloq* to take something dishonestly. **3** *billiards, etc* to drive (a ball) into a pocket. ○ **pocketful** *n.* ◆ **in one another's pockets** of two people: in close intimacy with, or dependence on, one another. **in** or **out of pocket** having gained, or lost, money on a transaction. **in sb's pocket** influenced or controlled by them. **put one's hand in one's pocket** to be willing to contribute money.

pocketbook *n* **1** *N Am, esp US* a wallet for money and papers. **2** *N Am, esp US* a woman's strapless handbag or purse. **3** a notebook.

pocket knife *n* a knife with folding blades.

pocket money *n* **1** *Brit* a weekly allowance given to children by their parents. **2** money carried for occasional expenses.

pockmark *n* a small pit or hollow in the skin left by a pock, esp one caused by chickenpox or smallpox. ○ **pockmarked** *adj.*

pod *n* **1** *bot* **a** the long dry fruit produced by leguminous plants, eg peas and beans, consisting of a seed-case which splits down both sides to release its seeds; **b** the seedcase itself. **2** *aeronautics* in an aeroplane or space vehicle: a detachable container or housing, eg for an engine.

podcast *n* a sound broadcast published on the Internet so that it can be downloaded and played at the listener's convenience. ○ **podcasting** *n*.

podgy or **pudgy** *adj* (**-ier, -iest**) *derog* short and fat.

podium *n* (**podiums** or **podia**) a small platform for a public speaker, orchestra conductor, etc.

poem *n* **1** a literary composition, typically, but not necessarily, in verse, often with elevated and/or imaginatively expressed content. **2** an object, scene or creation of inspiring beauty.

poesy *n* (**-ies**) *old use* poetry.

poet or **poetess** *n* a male or female writer of poems.

poetic or **poetical** *adj* **1** relating or suitable to poets or poetry. **2** possessing grace, beauty or inspiration suggestive of poetry. **3** written in verse. ○ **poetically** *adv*.

poet laureate *n* (**poets laureate** or **poet laureates**) in the UK: an officially appointed court poet, commissioned to produce poems for state occasions.

poetry *n* (**-ies**) **1** the art of composing poems. **2** poems collectively. **3** poetic quality, feeling, beauty or grace.

po-faced *adj, derog colloq* wearing a disapproving or solemn expression.

pogo stick *n* a spring-mounted pole with a handlebar and foot rests, on which to bounce.

pogrom *n* an organized persecution or massacre of a particular group of people, orig that of Jews in 19c Russia.

poignant /ˈpɔɪnjənt/ *adj* **1** painful to the feelings: *a poignant reminder*. **2** deeply moving; full of pathos. **3** of words or expressions: sharp; penetrating. **4** sharp or pungent in smell or taste. ○ **poignancy** *n*. ○ **poignantly** *adv*.

point *n* **1** a sharp or tapering end or tip. **2** a dot, eg inserted (either on the line or above it) before a decimal fraction, as in *2.1* or *2·1* (two point one). **3** a punctuation mark, esp a full stop. **4** *geom* a position found by means of co-ordinates. **5** *often in compounds* a position, place or location: *a look-out point*. **6** a moment: *Sandy lost his temper at that point*. **7** a stage in a process, etc. **8** *in compounds* a stage, temperature, etc: *boiling point*. **9** the right moment for doing something: *She lost courage when it came to the point*. **10** a feature or characteristic. **11** in a statement, argument, etc: a detail, fact or particular used or mentioned. **12** aim or intention: *What is the point of this?* **13** use or value: *There's no point in trying to change her mind*. **14** the significance (of a remark, story, joke, etc). **15** a unit or mark in scoring. **16** any of the 32 directions marked on, or indicated by, a compass. **17** (*often* **points**) an adjustable tapering rail by means of which a train changes lines. **18** *elec* a socket where an appliance may be connected to the mains. **19** (*usu* **points**) in an internal-combustion engine: either of the two electrical contacts which complete the circuit in the distributor. **20** *printing* a unit of type measurement, equal to ¹/₁₂ of a PICA. **21** *cricket* an off-side fielding position at right angles to the batsman. **22** (*usu* **points**) *ballet* **a** the tip of the toe; **b** a block inserted into the toe of a ballet shoe. **23** a headland or promontory. Often in place names: *Lizard Point*. ➤ *vb* **1** to aim something: *The hitman pointed a gun at her*. **2** *tr & intr* **a** to extend (one's finger or a pointed object) towards someone or something, so as to direct attention there; **b** of a sign, etc: to indicate (a certain direction): *a weather vane pointing south*. **3** *intr* to extend or face in a certain direction: *his toes were pointing upward*. **4** *intr* of a gun dog: to stand with the nose turned to where the dead game lies. **5** *often facetious* to direct someone: *Just point me to the grub*. **6** (*usu* **point to sth** or **sb**) to indicate or suggest it or them: *It points to one solution*. **7** in dancing, etc: to extend (the toes) to form a point. **8** to fill gaps or cracks in (stonework or brickwork) with cement or mortar. ◆ **beside the point** irrelevant. **come** or **get to the point** to cut out the irrelevancies and say what one wants to say. **in point of fact** actually; in truth. **make a point of doing sth** to be sure of doing it or take care to do it. **make one's point** to state one's opinion forcefully. **on the point of doing sth** about to do it. **score points off sb** to argue cleverly and successfully against them. **to the point** relevant. **up to a point** to a limited degree. ◊ **point sth out** to indicate or draw attention to it.

point-blank *adj* **1** of a shot: fired at very close range. **2** of a question, refusal, etc: bluntly worded and direct. ➤ *adv* **1** at close range. **2** in a blunt, direct manner: *She refused point-blank*.

point duty *n* the task or station of a police officer or traffic warden who is directing traffic.

pointed *adj* **1** having or ending in a point. **2** of a remark, etc: intended for, though not directly addressed to, a particular person. **3** keen or incisive. ○ **pointedly** *adv*.

pointer *n* **1** a rod used by a speaker for indicating positions on a wall map, chart, etc. **2** the indicating finger or needle on a measuring instrument. **3** *colloq* a suggestion or hint. **4** a gun dog trained to point its muzzle in the direction where the dead game lies.

pointing *n* the cement or mortar filling the gaps between the bricks or stones of a wall.

pointless *adj* **1** without a point. **2** lacking purpose or meaning. ○ **pointlessly** *adv*.

point of view *n* (**points of view**) **1** one's own particular way of looking at or attitude towards something, influenced by personal considerations and experience. **2** the physical position from which one looks at something.

point-to-point *n* a horse race across open

country, from landmark to landmark.

poise n 1 self-confidence, calm or composure. 2 grace of posture or carriage. 3 a state of equilibrium, balance or stability, eg between extremes. ➤ vb 1 tr & intr, often in passive to balance or suspend. 2 in passive to be in a state of readiness: *She was poised to take over as leader.*

poised adj 1 of behaviour, etc: calm and dignified. 2 ready for action.

poison n 1 any substance that damages tissues or causes death when injected, absorbed or swallowed by living organisms. 2 any destructive or corrupting influence: *a poison spreading through society.* ➤ vb 1 to harm or kill with poison. 2 to put poison into (food, etc). 3 to contaminate or pollute: *rivers poisoned by effluents.* 4 to corrupt or pervert (someone's mind). 5 (*esp* **poison one person against another**) to influence them to be hostile. 6 to harm or spoil in an unpleasant or malicious way: *Jealousy poisoned their relationship.* ○ **poisoner** n.

poison ivy n a N American woody vine or shrub, all parts of which produce a toxic chemical that causes an itching rash on contact with human skin.

poisonous adj 1 liable to cause injury or death if swallowed, inhaled or absorbed by the skin. 2 containing or capable of injecting a poison: *poisonous snakes.* 3 colloq of a person, remark, etc: malicious.

poke¹ vb 1 (often **poke at sth**) to thrust: *Kevin poked at the hole with a stick.* 2 to prod or jab. 3 to make (a hole) by prodding. 4 tr & intr to project or make something project: *Her big toe poked through a hole in her sock.* 5 to make (a fire) burn more brightly by stirring it with a poker. 6 intr (esp **poke about** or **around**) to search; to pry or snoop. ➤ n a jab or prod. ♦ **poke fun at sb** to tease or laugh at them unkindly. **poke one's nose into sth** colloq to pry into or interfere in it.

poke² n, Scot a paper bag.

poker¹ n a metal rod for stirring a fire to make it burn better.

poker² n a card game in which players bet on the hands they hold, relying on bluff to outwit their opponents.

poker face n a blank expressionless face that shows no emotion. ○ **poker-faced** adj.

poky adj (**-ier, -iest**) colloq of a room, house, etc: small and confined or cramped. ○ **pokiness** n.

polar adj 1 belonging or relating to the North or South Pole, or the regions round them. 2 relating to or having electric or magnetic poles. 3 having polarity. 4 as different as possible: *polar opposites.*

polarity n (**-ies**) 1 the state of having two opposite poles: *magnetic polarity.* 2 the condition of having two properties that are opposite. 3 the tendency to develop differently in different directions along an axis. 4 *physics* the status,

whether positive or negative, of the poles of a magnet, the terminals of an electrode, etc: *negative polarity.* 5 the tendency to develop, or be drawn, in opposite directions; oppositeness or an opposite.

polarize or **-ise** vb 1 to give magnetic or electrical polarity to something. 2 *physics* to restrict the vibrations of (electromagnetic waves, eg light) to one direction only. 3 tr & intr of people or opinions: to split according to opposing views. ○ **polarization** n.

Polaroid n, *trademark* a plastic material that polarizes light, used in sunglasses, etc to reduce glare.

Polaroid camera n, *trademark* a camera with a special film containing a pod of developing agents which bursts when the film is ejected, producing a finished print within seconds of exposure to daylight.

polder n an area of low-lying land which has been reclaimed from the sea, a river or lake.

pole¹ n 1 either of two points representing the north and south ends of the axis about which the Earth rotates, known as the **North Pole** and **South Pole** respectively. 2 a MAGNETIC POLE. 3 either of the two terminals of a battery. 4 either of two opposite positions in an argument, etc. ♦ **poles apart** colloq widely different; as far apart as it is possible to be.

pole² n a rod, esp one that is cylindrical in section and fixed in the ground as a support.

poleaxe n 1 a short-handled axe with a spike or hammer opposite the blade, used, esp formerly, for slaughtering cattle. 2 hist a long-handled battle-axe. ➤ vb to strike, fell or floor (an animal or person) with, or as if with, a poleaxe.

polecat n 1 a mammal resembling a large weasel that produces a foul-smelling discharge when alarmed or when marking territory. 2 N Am, esp US a skunk.

polemic /pə'lɛmɪk/ n 1 a controversial speech or piece of writing that fiercely attacks or defends an idea, opinion, etc. 2 writing or oratory of this sort. ➤ adj (also **polemical**) relating to or involving polemics or controversy. ○ **polemicist** n.

polemics sing n the art of verbal dispute or debate.

pole vault n, *athletics* a field event in which athletes attempt to jump over a high horizontal bar with the help of a long flexible pole to haul themselves into the air. ➤ vb (**pole-vault**) intr to perform a pole vault or take part in a pole vault competition. ○ **pole vaulter** n.

police pl n 1 the body of men and women employed by the government of a country to keep order, enforce the law, prevent crime, etc. 2 members of this body. ➤ vb 1 to keep law and order in (an area) using the police, army, etc. 2 to supervise (an operation, etc) to ensure that it is fairly or properly run.

policeman or **policewoman** n a male or female member of a police force.

police officer n a member of a police force.

police state n a state with a repressive government that operates through SECRET POLICE to eliminate opposition to it.

policy[1] n (-ies) a plan of action, usu based on certain principles, decided on by a body or individual.

policy[2] n (-ies) 1 an insurance agreement. 2 the document confirming such an agreement. ○ **policy-holder** n.

polio n short form of POLIOMYELITIS.

poliomyelitis /ˌpəʊlɪəʊmaɪəˈlaɪtɪs/ n, pathol a viral disease of the brain and spinal cord, which in some cases can result in permanent paralysis.

polish /ˈpɒlɪʃ/ vb 1 tr (also polish sth up) to make it smooth and glossy by rubbing: I'm polishing my shoes. 2 intr to become smooth and glossy by rubbing. 3 tr (also polish up sth) to improve or perfect. it. 4 tr to make cultivated, refined or elegant: Henrietta polished her vowels before the speech day. ➤ n 1 also in compounds a substance used for polishing surfaces: boot polish. 2 a smooth shiny finish; a gloss. 3 an act of polishing. 4 refinement or elegance. ◊ **polish off sth** or **polish sth off** to finish it quickly and completely, esp speedily.

polite adj 1 of a person or their actions, etc: well-mannered; considerate towards others; courteous. 2 well-bred, cultivated or refined: polite society. ○ **politely** adv. ○ **politeness** n.

politic adj 1 of a course of action: prudent; wise; shrewd. 2 of a person: cunning; crafty. 3 old use political. ➤ vb (also **politik**) (**politicked, politicking**) intr, derog to indulge in politics, esp to strike political bargains or to gain votes for oneself.

political adj 1 relating or belonging to government or public affairs. 2 relating to POLITICS. 3 interested or involved in POLITICS. 4 of a course of action: made in the interests of gaining or keeping power. 5 of a map: showing political and social structure rather than physical features. ○ **politically** adv.

political correctness n (abbrev **PC**) the avoidance of expressions or actions that may be understood to exclude or denigrate certain people or groups of people on the grounds of race, gender, disability, sexual orientation, etc. ○ **politically correct** adj.

political prisoner n someone imprisoned for their political beliefs, activities, etc.

political science n the study of politics and government, in terms of its principles, aims, methods, etc.

politician n 1 someone engaged in POLITICS, esp as a member of parliament. 2 derog, chiefly US someone who enters politics for personal power and gain.

politicize or **-ise** vb 1 intr to take part in political activities or discussion. 2 to give a political nature to something. 3 to make someone aware of or informed about politics. ○ **politicization** n.

politico n (**politicos** or **politicoes**) colloq, usu derog a politician or someone who is keen on politics.

politics sing n 1 the science or business of government. 2 POLITICAL SCIENCE. 3 a political life as a career: He entered politics in 1961. ➤ sing or pl n political activities, wrangling, etc. ➤ pl n also in compounds moves and manoeuvres concerned with the acquisition of power or getting one's way, eg in business: office politics. 2 one's political sympathies or principles: What are your politics?

polity n (-ies) 1 a politically organized body such as a state, church or association. 2 any form of political institution or government.

polka n 1 a lively dance performed with a partner, which has a pattern of three steps followed by a hop. 2 a piece of music for this dance. ➤ vb (**polkaed, polkaing**) intr to dance a polka.

polka dot n any one of numerous regularly spaced dots forming a pattern on fabric, etc.

poll n 1 (**polls**) a political election: another Tory disaster at the polls. 2 the voting or votes cast at an election: a heavy poll. 3 (also **opinion poll**) a survey of public opinion carried out by directly questioning a representative sample of the populace. ➤ vb 1 to win (a number of votes) in an election. 2 to register the votes of (a population). 3 tr & intr to cast (one's vote). 4 to conduct an opinion poll among (people, a specified group, etc). 5 to cut off the horns of (cattle). 6 to cut the top off (a tree).

pollard n 1 a tree whose branches have been cut back, in order to produce a crown of shoots at the top of the trunk. 2 an animal whose horns have been removed. ➤ vb to make a pollard of (a tree or animal).

pollen n the fine, usu yellow, dust-like powder produced by the ANTHERs of flowering plants, and by the male cones of cone-bearing plants.

pollinate vb, bot in flowering and cone-bearing plants: to transfer pollen from ANTHER to STIGMA, or from the male to the female cone in order to achieve fertilization and subsequent development of seed. ○ **pollination** n.

pollster n someone who organizes and carries out opinion polls.

poll tax n a fixed tax levied on each adult member of a population.

pollutant n any substance or agent that pollutes. ➤ adj polluting: pollutant emissions.

pollute vb 1 to contaminate something with harmful substances or impurities; to cause pollution in something. 2 to corrupt (someone's mind, etc). 3 to defile. ○ **pollution** n.

polo n a game, similar to hockey, played on horseback by two teams of four players, using long-handled mallets to propel the ball along the ground.

polonaise n 1 a stately Polish marching dance. 2 a piece of music for this dance.

polo neck n 1 a high close-fitting band of material at the neck of a sweater or shirt, which is doubled over. **2** a sweater or shirt with such a neck.

polonium *n, chem* a rare radioactive metallic element that emits ALPHA PARTICLES.

polo shirt *n* a short-sleeved open-necked casual shirt with a collar, esp one made of a knitted cotton fabric.

poltergeist /'pɔʊltəgaɪst/ *n* a type of mischievous ghost supposedly responsible for otherwise unaccountable noises and the movement of objects.

poltroon *n, literary or old use* a despicable coward.

poly *n, colloq* a polytechnic.

polyandrous *adj* **1** *sociol* having more than one husband at the same time. **2** *bot* of a flower: having many STAMENS.

polyandry *n, anthropol, etc* the custom or practice of having more than one husband at the same time. Compare POLYGYNY.

polychromatic *adj* **1** POLYCHROME. **2** of electromagnetic radiation: composed of a number of different wavelengths.

polychrome *adj* (*also* **polychromatic**) multicoloured. ➤ *n* **1** varied colouring. **2** a work of art, esp a statue, in several colours.

polyester *n* a synthetic resin used to form strong durable crease-resistant artificial fibres, such as Terylene, widely used in textiles for clothing, etc.

polyethylene see under POLYTHENE

polygamy /pə'lɪgəmɪ/ *n* the custom or practice of having more than one husband or wife at the same time. Compare MONOGAMY. ○ **polygamist** *n*. ○ **polygamous** *adj*.

polyglot *adj* speaking, using or written in many languages. ➤ *n* someone who speaks many languages.

polygon *n, geom* a plane figure (see PLANE² *adj* sense 3) with a number of straight sides, usu more than three, eg a PENTAGON or a HEXAGON. ○ **polygonal** *adj*.

polygraph *n, med* a device, sometimes used as a lie-detector, that monitors several body functions simultaneously, eg pulse, blood pressure and conductivity of the skin.

polygyny *n, anthropol, etc* the condition or custom of having more than one wife at the same time. Compare POLYANDRY.

polyhedron *n* (**polyhedrons** *or* **polyhedra**) *geom* a solid figure with four or more faces, all of which are polygons, eg a TETRAHEDRON. ○ **polyhedral** *adj*.

polymath *n* someone who is well educated in a wide variety of subjects.

polymer *n, chem* a very large molecule consisting of a long chain of MONOMERS linked end to end to form a series of repeating units. ○ **polymeric** *adj*. ○ **polymerization** *or* **-isation** *n*.

polynomial *maths, adj* of an expression: consisting of a sum of terms each containing a CONSTANT and one or more VARIABLES raised to a power. ➤ *n* an expression of this sort.

polyp *n* **1** *zool* a sessile COELENTERATE with a more or less cylindrical body and a mouth surrounded by tentacles. **2** *pathol* a small abnormal but usu benign growth projecting from a mucous membrane.

polyphone *n* a letter which can be pronounced or sounded in more than one way, eg the letter *g* in English.

polyphonic *adj* **1** having many voices. **2** relating to polyphony. **3** denoting a polyphone.

polyphony /pə'lɪfənɪ/ *n* a style of musical composition in which each part or voice has an independent melodic value. Compare HOMOPHONY.

polysaccharide *n, biochem* a large carbohydrate molecule consisting of many MONOSACCHARIDES linked together to form long chains, eg starch and cellulose.

polysemy /pə'lɪsɪmɪ/ *n, ling* the existence of more than one meaning for a single word, such as *table*. ○ **polysemous** *adj*.

polystyrene *n, chem* a tough transparent THERMOPLASTIC that is a good thermal and electrical insulator, used in packaging, insulation, ceiling tiles, etc.

polysyllable *n* a word of three or more syllables. ○ **polysyllabic** *adj*.

polytechnic *n, Brit education, formerly* a college of higher education providing courses in a large range of subjects, esp of a technical or vocational kind. In 1992 the polytechnics became universities. ➤ *adj* relating to technical training.

polytheism *n* belief in or worship of more than one god. ○ **polytheist** *n*. ○ **polytheistic** *adj*.

polythene *n* a waxy translucent easily-moulded THERMOPLASTIC, used in the form of film or sheeting to package food products, clothing, etc, and to make pipes, moulded articles and electrical insulators.

polyunsaturated *adj, chem* of a compound, esp a fat or oil: containing two or more double bonds per molecule: *polyunsaturated margarine*. Compare MONOUNSATURATED.

polyurethane *n, chem* a polymer that contains the URETHANE group, and is used in protective coatings, adhesives, paints, etc.

polyvinyl chloride *n, chem* (abbrev **PVC**) a tough white THERMOPLASTIC, resistant to fire and chemicals and easily dyed and softened, used in pipes and other moulded products, RECORDS (*noun* sense 4), food packaging etc.

pomace *n* **a** crushed apples for cider-making; **b** the residue of these or of any similar fruit after pressing.

pomade *hist, n* a perfumed ointment for the hair and scalp. ➤ *vb* to put pomade on (a person's hair, etc).

pomander *n* **1** a perfumed ball composed of various aromatic substances, orig carried as scent or to ward off infection. **2** a perforated container for this.

pomegranate *n* **1** a small deciduous tree or shrub widely cultivated for its edible fruit. **2**

the round fruit of this plant, which has tough red or brown skin surrounding a mass of seeds, each of which is enclosed by red juicy edible flesh.

pomelo /'pɒməloʊ/ *n* a round yellow citrus fruit, resembling a grapefruit.

pommel *n* **1** the raised front part of a saddle. **2** a rounded knob forming the end of a sword hilt. ➤ *vb* (**pommelled, pommelling**) to pummel.

pommy *n* (*-ies*) *Aust & NZ derog colloq* a British, or esp English, person.

pomp *n* **1** ceremonial grandeur. **2** vain ostentation.

pompom or **pompon** *n* **1** a ball made of cut wool or other yarn, used as a trimming on clothes, etc. **2** a variety of chrysanthemum with globe-like flowers.

pompous *adj* **1** solemnly self-important. **2** said of language: inappropriately grand and flowery. ○ **pomposity** *n*.

ponce *offensive slang, n* **1** a pimp. **2** an effeminate man. ➤ *vb, intr* (*usu* **ponce about** or **around**) **1** to mince about in an effeminate manner. **2** to mess around.

poncho *n* an outer garment, orig S American, made of a large piece of cloth with a hole in the middle for the head to go through.

pond *n* a small area of still fresh water surrounded by land.

ponder *vb, tr & intr* (*often* **ponder on** or **over** sth) to consider or contemplate it deeply.

ponderous *adj* **1** of speech, humour, etc: heavy-handed, laborious, over-solemn or pompous. **2** heavy or cumbersome; lumbering in movement. **3** weighty; important. ○ **ponderously** *adv*.

pong *colloq, n* a bad smell. ➤ *vb, intr* to smell badly. ○ **pongy** *adj* (*-ier, -iest*) stinking.

pontiff *n* a title for the Pope.

pontifical *adj* **1** belonging or relating to a pontiff. **2** *derog* pompously opinionated; dogmatic.

pontificate *vb* /pɒn'tɪfɪkeɪt/ *intr* **1** to pronounce one's opinion pompously and arrogantly. **2** to perform the duties of a pontiff. ➤ *n* /pɒn'tɪfɪkət/ the office of a pope.

pontoon¹ *n* any of a number of flat-bottomed craft, punts, barges, etc, anchored side by side across a river, to support a temporary bridge or platform.

pontoon² *n, cards* a game in which the object is to collect sets of cards that add up to or close to 21, without going over that total.

pony *n* (*-ies*) **1** any of several small hardy breeds of horse. **2** *Brit slang* a sum of £25. **3** *US slang* a crib or a translation prepared for use in an exam, etc.

ponytail *n* a hairstyle in which a person's hair is drawn back and gathered by a band at the back of the head, so that it hangs free like a pony's tail.

poo see POOP³

pooch *n, colloq* a dog.

poodle *n* **1** a breed of lively pet dog of various sizes which has a narrow head with pendulous

ears and a long curly coat, often clipped into an elaborate style. **2** *derog* a lackey.

poof or **poofter** *n, offensive slang* a male homosexual. ○ **poofy** *adj* (*-ier, -iest*) effeminate.

pooh *exclam, colloq* indicating scorn or disgust, esp at an offensive smell.

pooh-pooh *vb, colloq* to express scorn for (a suggestion, etc).

pool¹ *n* **1** a small area of still water. **2** a patch of spilt liquid: *pools of blood*. **3** a swimming pool. **4** a deep part of a stream or river.

pool² *n* **1** *also in compounds* a reserve of money, personnel, vehicles, etc used as a communal resource: *a typing pool*. **2** the combined stakes of those betting on something; a jackpot. **3** *commerce* a group of businesses with a common arrangement to maintain high prices, so eliminating competition and preserving profits. **4** a game like BILLIARDS played with a white cue ball and usu 15 numbered coloured balls, the aim being to shoot specified balls into specified pockets using the cue ball. ➤ *vb* to put (money or other resources) into a common supply for general use.

poop¹ *n, naut* **1** the raised enclosed part at the stern of old sailing ships. **2** the high deck at the stern of a ship.

poop² *vb, colloq* **1** *in passive* to become winded or exhausted: *Sheena was pooped after walking up the hill.* **2** (*also* **poop sb out**) to make them exhausted or winded.

poop³ or **poo** *slang, n* faeces. ➤ *vb, intr* to defecate.

poor *adj* **1** not having sufficient money or means to live comfortably. **2** (**poor in sth**) not well supplied with it. **3** not good; weak; unsatisfactory: *poor eyesight.* **4** unsatisfactorily small or sparse: *a poor attendance.* **5** used in expressing pity or sympathy: *poor fellow!* ○ **poorness** *n*. ♦ **poor man's ...** *derog* a substitute of lower quality or price than the specified thing: *poor man's caviare.*

poorhouse *n, hist* an institution maintained at public expense, for housing the poor; a WORKHOUSE.

poor law *n, hist* a law or set of laws concerned with the public support of the poor.

poorly *adv* not well; badly: *I speak French poorly.* ➤ *adj, colloq or dialect* unwell: *Do you feel poorly?*

pop¹ *n* **1** a sharp explosive noise, like that of a cork coming out of a bottle. **2** *colloq, esp N Am* any sweet non-alcoholic fizzy drink such as ginger beer. ➤ *vb* (**popped, popping**) **1** *tr & intr* to make or cause something to make a pop. **2** *tr & intr* to burst with a pop. **3** (*esp* **pop out** or **up**) to spring out or up; to protrude. **4** *intr, colloq* to go quickly in a direction specified: *I'll just pop next door for a second.* **5** *colloq* to put something somewhere quickly or briefly: *to pop it in the oven.* ➤ *adv* with a pop. ♦ **pop the question** *humorous, colloq* to propose marriage. ◊ **pop off** *colloq* **1** to leave quickly or suddenly.

2 to die. **pop up** to appear or occur, esp unexpectedly.

pop² n (*in full* **pop music**) a type of music, primarily commercial, usu with a strong beat and characterized by its use of electronic equipment such as guitars and keyboards. ➤ *adj* popular: *pop culture*.

pop³ n, *colloq, esp N Am* **1** father; dad. **2** often as a form of address: *an elderly man*.

popcorn n **1** (*also* **popping corn**) maize grains that puff up and burst open when heated. **2** the edible puffed-up kernels of this grain.

pope n **1** (*often* **Pope**) the Bishop of Rome, the head of the Roman Catholic Church. **2** a priest in the Eastern Orthodox Church.

popery n, *offensive* Roman Catholicism.

popgun n a toy gun that fires a cork or pellet with a pop.

popinjay n, *old use, derog* a vain or conceited person; a dandy or fop.

popish *adj, offensive* belonging or relating to Roman Catholicism.

poplar n **1** a tall slender deciduous tree found in northern temperate regions, with broad simple leaves which tremble in a slight breeze. **2** the soft fine-grained yellowish wood of this tree.

poplin n a strong cotton cloth with a finely ribbed finish.

pop music see POP²

poppadum, poppadom or **pappadom** n a paper-thin pancake, grilled or fried till crisp, served with Indian dishes.

popper n **1** someone or something that pops. **2** *colloq* a PRESS STUD. **3** *esp N Am* a container used to make popcorn.

poppet n a term of endearment for someone lovable.

poppy n (*-ies*) a plant with large brightly-coloured bowl-shaped flowers and a fruit in the form of a capsule.

poppycock n, *colloq* nonsense.

populace n the body of ordinary citizens.

popular *adj* **1** liked or enjoyed by most people. **2** of beliefs, etc: accepted by many people: *a popular misconception*. **3** catering for the tastes and abilities of ordinary people as distinct from specialists, etc: *a popular history of science*. **4** of a person: generally liked and admired. **5** involving the will or preferences of the public in general: *by popular demand*. ○ **popularity** n. ○ **popularly** *adv*.

popularize or **-ise** *vb* **1** to make something popular. **2** to present something in a simple easily understood way, so as to have general appeal. ○ **popularization** n.

populate *vb* **1** of people, animals or plants: to inhabit or live in (a certain area). **2** to supply (uninhabited places) with inhabitants.

population n **1** all the people living in a particular country, area, etc. **2** the number of people living in a particular area, country, etc. **3** a group of animals or plants of the same species living in a certain area; the total number of these: *the declining elephant population*.

populist n **1** a person who believes in the right and ability of the common people to play a major part in government. **2** a person who studies, supports or attracts the support of the common people. ➤ *adj* of a political cause, programme, etc: appealing to the majority of the people. ○ **populism** n.

populous *adj* densely inhabited.

pop-up *adj* **1** of a picture book, greetings card, etc: having cut-out parts designed to stand upright as the page is opened. **2** of appliances, etc: having a mechanism which causes a component, or the item being prepared, to pop up.

porcelain n **1** a fine white translucent earthenware, orig made in China. **2** objects made of this.

porch n **1** a structure that forms a covered entrance to the doorway of a building. **2** *N Am* a verandah.

porcine /ˈpɔːsaɪn/ *adj* relating to or or resembling a pig.

porcupine n a large nocturnal rodent with long black-and-white spikes or quills on the back and sides of its body.

pore¹ n **1** a small, usu round opening in the surface of a living organism, eg in the skin, through which fluids, gases and other substances can pass. **2** any tiny cavity or gap, eg in rock.

pore² *vb, intr* (*always* **pore over sth**) to study (books, papers, etc) with intense concentration.

pork n the flesh of a pig used as food.

porker n a pig reared for fresh meat as opposed to processed meats such as bacon.

porky *adj* (*-ier, -iest*) **1** resembling pork. **2** *colloq* plump.

porn or **porno** *colloq, n* pornography. ➤ *adj* pornographic.

pornography n books, pictures, films, etc designed to be sexually arousing, often offensive owing to their explicit nature. ○ **pornographer** n. ○ **pornographic** *adj*.

porous *adj* **1** referring or relating to a material that contains pores or cavities. **2** capable of being permeated by liquids or gases. ○ **porosity** n.

porphyry /ˈpɔːfɪrɪ/ n, *geol* **1** loosely any igneous rock that contains large crystals surrounded by much smaller ones. **2** a very hard purple and white rock used in sculpture. ○ **porphyritic** /pɔːfɪˈrɪtɪk/ *adj*.

porpoise n **1** a beakless whale, smaller than a dolphin, with a blunt snout. **2** *loosely* a DOLPHIN.

porridge n **1** a dish of oatmeal or some other cereal which is boiled in water or milk until it reaches a thick consistency. **2** *Brit slang* a jail sentence.

porringer n a bowl, with a handle, for soup or porridge.

port¹ n **1** a harbour. **2** a town with a harbour.

port² n the left side of a ship or aircraft. Compare STARBOARD.

port³ n **1** an opening in a ship's side for loading, etc. **2** a PORTHOLE. **3** *comput* a socket that connects the CPU of a computer to a peripheral device.

port⁴ n a sweet dark-red or tawny fortified wine.

portable *adj* **1** easily carried or moved, and usu designed to be so. **2** *comput* of a program: adaptable for use in a variety of systems. ➤ n a portable radio, television, typewriter, etc. ◦ **portability** n.

portal n, *formal* an entrance, gateway or doorway, esp an imposing or awesome one.

portcullis n, *hist* a vertical iron or wooden grating fitted into a town gateway or castle entrance, which lowered to keep intruders out.

portend vb to warn of (usu something bad); to signify or foreshadow it.

portent n **1** a prophetic sign; an omen. **2** fateful significance: *an event of grim portent*. **3** a marvel or prodigy.

portentous *adj* **1** ominous or fateful; relating to portents. **2** weighty, solemn or pompous. **3** amazing or marvellous. ◦ **portentously** *adv*.

porter¹ n a doorman, caretaker or janitor at a college, office or factory.

porter² n **1** someone employed to carry luggage or parcels, eg at a railway station. **2** in a hospital: someone employed to move patients when required and to carry out other general duties. **3** a heavy dark-brown beer brewed from black malt. **4** *N Am* on a train: a sleeping-car attendant.

porterhouse n **1** (*in full* **porterhouse steak**) a choice cut of beef from the back of the sirloin. **2** *formerly* a public house where porter, beer, etc and steaks were served.

portfolio n **1** a flat case for carrying papers, drawings, photographs, etc. **2** the contents of such a case, as a demonstration of a person's work. **3** *pol* the post of a government minister with responsibility for a specific department. **4** a list of the investments or securities held by an individual, company, etc.

porthole n **1** an opening, usu a round one, in a ship's side to admit light and air. **2** an opening in a wall through which a gun can be fired.

portico n (*porticos* or *porticoes*) *archit* a colonnade forming a porch or covered way alongside a building.

portion n **1** a piece or part of a whole: *12 equal portions*. **2** a share; a part allotted to one. **3** an individual helping of food. **4** *literary* one's destiny or fate. **5** *law* a woman's dowry. ➤ vb (*now usu* **portion sth out**) to divide it up; to share it out.

portly *adj* (*-ier*, *-iest*) esp of a man: somewhat stout.

portmanteau /pɔːt'mantoʊ/ n (*portmanteaus* or *portmanteaux* /-toʊz/) a large travelling bag that opens flat in two halves. ➤ *adj* combining or covering two or more things of the same kind: *portmanteau statistics*.

portmanteau word n a word formed by combining the sense and sound of two separate words, eg BRUNCH (for *breakfast* and *lunch*).

portrait n **1** a drawing, painting or photograph of a person, esp of the face only. **2** a written description, film depiction, etc of someone or something: *a portrait of country life*. ➤ *adj*, *printing* of a page, illustration, etc: taller than it is wide. Compare LANDSCAPE.

portraiture n **1** the art or act of making portraits. **2** a portrait, or portraits collectively.

portray vb **1** to make a portrait of someone or something. **2** to describe or depict something. **3** to act the part of (a character) in a play, film, etc. ◦ **portrayal** n.

Portuguese /pɔːtʃʊ'giːz/ *adj* belonging or relating to Portugal, its inhabitants or their language. ➤ n **1** (**the Portuguese**) the people of Portugal. **2** the official language of Portugal.

pose n **1** a position or attitude of the body: *a relaxed pose*. **2** an artificial way of behaving, adopted for effect: *His cynicism is just a pose*. ➤ vb **1** *tr & intr* to take up a position oneself, or position (someone else), for a photograph, portrait, etc. **2** *intr, derog* to behave in an exaggerated or artificial way so as to draw attention to oneself. **3** *intr* (*usu* **pose as sb** or **sth**) to pretend to be someone or something that one is not. **4** to ask or put forward (a question). **5** to cause (a problem, etc) or present (a threat, etc). ♦ **strike a pose** to adopt a position or attitude, esp a commanding or impressive one.

poser¹ n **1** someone who poses. **2** *derog* someone who tries to impress others by putting on an act and by dressing, behaving, etc so as to be noticed.

poser² n a puzzling or perplexing question.

poseur /poʊ'zɜː(r)/ n, *derog* someone who behaves in an affected or insincere way, esp to impress others.

posh *colloq, adj* **1** high-quality, expensive, smart or stylish. **2** upper-class. ➤ *adv* in a way associated with the upper class: *Bert talks posh when he's on the telephone*.

posit /'pɒzɪt/ vb (*posited, positing*) to lay down or assume something as a basis for discussion. ➤ n, *philos* a statement made on the assumption that it will be proved valid.

position n **1** a place where someone or something is: *The mansion was in a fine position overlooking the bay*. **2** the right or proper place: *Volume 2 was out of position*. **3** the relationship of things to one another in space; arrangement. **4** a way of sitting, standing, lying, facing, being held or placed, etc: *an upright position*. **5** *mil* a place occupied for strategic purposes. **6** one's opinion or viewpoint. **7** a job or post. **8** rank; status; importance in society: *wealth and position*. **9** the place of a competitor in the finishing order, or at an earlier stage in a contest: *fourth position*. **10** *sport* an allotted place in a team, esp on the pitch or playing-area: *the centre-forward position*. **11** the set of circumstances in which one is placed: *I'm not in a posi-*

tion to help. ➢ *vb* to put something or someone in position. ○ **positional** *adj.* ◆ **be in no position to do sth** to have no right to (complain, criticize, etc).

positive *adj* **1** sure; certain; convinced. ○ **2** definite; allowing no doubt: *positive proof of her guilt.* **3** expressing agreement or approval. **4** optimistic: *I'm feeling more positive.* **5** forceful or determined; not tentative. **6** constructive; contributing to progress or improvement; helpful. **7** clear and explicit: *positive directions.* **8** *colloq* downright: *a positive scandal.* **9** of the result of a chemical test: confirming the existence of the suspected condition. **10** *maths* of a number or quantity: greater than zero. **11** *physics, elec* having a deficiency of electrons, and so being able to attract them, ie attracted by a negative charge. **12** *photog* of a photographic image: in which light and dark tones and colours correspond to those in the original subject. **13** *gram* expressing a quality in the simple form, as distinct from the COMPARATIVE or SUPERLATIVE forms.

positivism *n* a school of philosophy maintaining that knowledge can come only from observable phenomena and positive facts. ○ **positivist** *n, adj.*

positron *n, physics* an ANTIPARTICLE that has the same mass as an electron, and an equal but opposite charge.

posse /'pɒsɪ/ *n* **1** *N Am, hist* a mounted troop of men at the service of a local sheriff. **2** *colloq* any group or band of people, esp friends.

possess *vb* **1** to own. **2** to have something as a feature or quality: *Frances possesses a quick mind.* **3** of an emotion, evil spirit, etc: to occupy and dominate the mind of someone: *What possessed you to behave like that?* ○ **possessor** *n.*

possessed *adj* **1** (**possessed of sth**) *formal* owning it; having it: *She's possessed of great wealth.* **2** *following its noun* controlled or driven by demons, etc: *He was screaming like a man possessed.*

possession *n* **1** the condition of possessing something; ownership: *It came into my possession.* **2** the crime of possessing something illegally. **3** occupancy of property: *They'll take possession of the house.* **4** *sport* control of the ball, puck, etc by one or other team in a match. **5** something owned. **6** (**possessions**) one's property or belongings. **7** (**possessions**) *formal* a country's dominions abroad: *foreign possessions.* ◆ **be in possession of sth** to hold or possess it.

possessive *adj* **1** relating to possession. **2** of a person or of character: unwilling to share, or allow others to use, things they own: *I'm very possessive about my car.* **3** of a person or of character: inclined to dominate, monopolize and allow no independence to one's wife, husband, child, etc: *a possessive husband.* **4** *gram* denoting the form or CASE[2] of a noun, pronoun or adjective which shows possession, eg *Kurt's, its, her.* ➢ *n, gram* **1** the possessive form or case

of a word. **2** a word in the possessive case or in a possessive form. ○ **possessiveness** *n.*

possibility *n* (*-ies*) **1** something that is possible. **2** the state of being possible. **3** a candidate for selection, etc. **4** (**possibilities**) promise or potential: *This idea has definite possibilities.*

possible *adj* **1** achievable; able to be done: *a possible target of 50%.* **2** capable of happening: *the possible outcome.* **3** imaginable; conceivable: *It's possible that he's dead.* ➢ *n* someone or something potentially selectable or attainable; a possibility.

possibly *adv* **1** perhaps; maybe. **2** within the limits of possibility: *We'll do all we possibly can.* **3** used for emphasis: at all: *How could you possibly think that?*

possum *n, colloq* **1** an OPOSSUM. **2** a PHALANGER. ◆ **play possum** to pretend to be unconscious, asleep or unaware of what is happening.

post[1] *n* **1** a shaft or rod fixed upright in the ground, as a support or marker, etc. **2** *often in compounds* a vertical timber supporting a horizontal one: *a doorpost.* **3** an upright pole marking the beginning or end of a race track. **4** a GOALPOST. ➢ *vb* **1** (*sometimes* **post sth up**) to put up (a notice, etc) on a post or board, etc for public viewing. **2** to announce the name of someone among others in a published list: *He was posted missing.*

post[2] *n* **1** a job: *a teaching post.* **2** a position to which one is assigned for military duty: *He never left his post.* **3** *often in compounds* a settlement or establishment, esp one in a remote area: *a trading post • a military post.* **4** *mil* a bugle call summoning soldiers to their quarters at night. ➢ *vb* (*usu* **post sb to**, **at** or in some-where) to station them there on duty; to transfer (personnel) to a new location.

post[3] *n* (*esp* the post) **1** the official system for the delivery of mail. **2** letters and parcels delivered by this system. **3** a collection of mail, eg from a postbox: *It'll catch the next post.* **4** a delivery of mail: *The letter came by the second post.* **5** a place for mail collection; a postbox or post office: *I took it to the post.* ➢ *vb* **1** to put (mail) into a postbox; to send something by post. **2** *bookkeeping* **a** to enter (an item) in a ledger; **b** (*now usu* **post up sth**) to update (a ledger). **3** to supply someone with the latest news: *He kept us posted.*

postage *n* the charge for sending a letter, etc through the POST[3].

postage stamp *n* a small printed gummed label stuck on a letter, etc indicating that the appropriate postage charge has been paid.

postal *adj* **1** relating or belonging to the POST OFFICE or to delivery of mail. **2** sent by post: *a postal vote.*

postal code same as POSTCODE

postal order *n* a money order available from, and payable by, a post office.

postbag *n* **1** a bag for carrying mail. **2** the letters received by eg a radio or TV programme, magazine or celebrated person, etc.

postbox n a large box, with a slot in the front, for people to post letters.

postcard n a card for writing messages on, often with a picture on one side, designed for sending through the post without an envelope.

postcode n a code used to identify a postal address, made up of a combination of letters and numerals.

postdate vb 1 to put a future date on (a cheque, etc). 2 to assign a later date than that previously accepted to (an event, etc). 3 to occur at a later date than (a specified date).

poster n 1 a large notice or advertisement for public display. 2 a large printed picture.

posterior adj 1 placed behind, after or at the back of something. 2 formal or old use coming after in time. Compare ANTERIOR. ➤ n, facetious the buttocks.

posterity n 1 future generations. 2 one's descendants.

postern n, hist a back door, back gate or private entrance.

postgraduate n a person studying for an advanced degree or qualification after obtaining a first degree. ➤ adj relating to such a person or degree: a postgraduate diploma.

posthaste adv with the utmost speed.

posthumous /ˈpɒstjʊməs/ adj 1 of a work: published after the death of the author, composer, etc. 2 of a child: born after its father's death. 3 coming or occurring after death: posthumous fame. ○ **posthumously** adv.

postilion or **postillion** n, hist a rider on the nearside horse of one of the pairs of horses drawing a carriage, who, in the absence of a coachman, guides the team.

postimpressionism or **Post-Impressionism** n, art an imprecise term used to describe the more progressive forms of painting since c.1880, which developed as a reaction against IMPRESSIONISM, with the aim of conveying the essence of their subjects through a simplification of form.

postman or **postwoman** n a man or woman whose job is to deliver mail.

postmark n a mark stamped on mail by the post office, cancelling the stamp and showing the date and place of posting. ➤ vb to mark (mail) in this way.

postmaster or **postmistress** n the man or woman in charge of a local post office.

post meridiem n indicating the time from midday to midnight. Compare ANTE MERIDIEM.

post mortem n 1 (in full post mortem examination) the dissection and examination of the internal organs of the body after death, in order to determine the cause of death. 2 colloq an after-the-event discussion. ➤ adj coming or happening after death.

postnatal adj relating to or occurring during the period immediately after childbirth. ○ **postnatally** adv.

post office n 1 a local office that handles postal business, the issuing of various types of licence, etc. 2 (**Post Office**) the government department in charge of postal services.

post-operative adj relating to or occurring during the period immediately following a surgical operation.

postpone vb to delay or put off something until later. ○ **postponement** n.

postprandial adj, facetious following a meal: a postprandial doze.

postscript n (abbrev PS or ps) a message added to a letter as an afterthought, after one's signature.

postulant n someone who asks or petitions for something, esp a candidate for holy orders or for admission to a religious community. ○ **postulancy** n (-ies).

postulate vb /ˈpɒstjʊleɪt/ 1 to assume or suggest something as the basis for discussion; to take it for granted. 2 to demand; to claim. ➤ n /ˈpɒstjʊlət/ 1 a stipulation or prerequisite. 2 a position assumed as self-evident. ○ **postulation** n.

posture n 1 the way one holds one's body while standing, sitting or walking. 2 a particular position or attitude of the body. 3 an attitude adopted towards a particular issue, etc. 4 a pose adopted for effect. ➤ vb 1 to take up a particular bodily attitude. 2 intr, derog to pose, strike attitudes, etc so as to draw attention to oneself. ○ **postural** adj.

postwar adj relating or belonging to the period following a war.

posy n (-ies) a small bunch of flowers.

pot¹ n 1 a domestic container, usu a deep round one, used as a cooking or serving utensil, or for storage. 2 (also **potful**) the amount a pot can hold: a pot of tea. 3 pottery any handmade container. 4 the pool of accumulated bets in any gambling game. 5 in snooker, billiards, pool, etc: a shot that pockets a ball. 6 a casual shot: to take a pot at something. 7 a CHAMBERPOT. 8 a FLOWERPOT. 9 (**pots**) colloq a great deal, esp of money. 10 colloq a trophy, esp a cup. 11 a POTBELLY. ➤ vb (**potted, potting**) 1 to plant something in a plant pot. 2 to preserve (a type of food) in a pot. 3 in snooker, billiards, pool, etc: to shoot (a ball) into a pocket. 4 a colloq to shoot at (an animal, bird, etc), esp indiscriminately or wildly; b to win or secure, esp by shooting: The Duke potted six grouse. ♦ **go to pot** colloq to degenerate badly.

pot² n, colloq CANNABIS.

potable /ˈpəʊtəbl/ adj fit or suitable for drinking.

potash n a compound of potassium.

potassium n, chem a soft silvery-white metallic element, compounds of which are used in fertilizers, explosives, laboratory reagents, soaps and some types of glass.

potation n, formal or humorous 1 the act or an instance of drinking. 2 a drink, esp an alcoholic one. 3 a drinking binge.

potato n (**potatoes**) **1** a plant that produces edible TUBERS and is a staple crop of temperate regions worldwide. **2** the starch-rich round or oval tuber of this plant, which is cooked for food.

potato crisp see CRISP (*noun*)

potbelly n (**-ies**) *colloq* **1** a large overhanging belly. **2** someone who has such a belly. ○ **pot-bellied** *adj*.

potboiler n, *derog* an inferior work of literature or art produced by a writer or artist capable of better work, simply to make money.

poteen /pɒ'tiːn, pɒ'tʃiːn/ n, *Irish* illicitly distilled Irish whiskey.

potent *adj* **1** strong; effective; powerful. **2** of an argument, etc: persuasive; convincing. **3** of a drug or poison: powerful and swift in effect. **4** of a male: capable of sexual intercourse. ○ **potency** n (**-ies**) **1** the state of being potent; power. **2** strength or effectiveness, eg of a drug. **3** the capacity for development.

potentate n, *esp hist or literary* a powerful ruler; a monarch.

potential *adj* possible or likely, though as yet not tested or actual: *a potential customer.* ➢ n **1** the range of capabilities that someone or something has; powers or resources not yet developed or made use of: *Try to fulfil your potential.* **2** *physics* the energy required to move a unit of mass, electric charge, etc from an infinite distance to the point in a gravitational or electric field where it is to be measured. ○ **potentiality** n. ○ **potentially** *adv*.

potential energy n, *physics* the energy stored by an object by virtue of its position.

pother n a fuss or commotion.

pot-herb n any plant whose leaves or stems are used in cooking to season or garnish food.

pothole n **1** a circular hole worn in the bedrock of a river. **2** a vertical cave system or deep hole eroded in limestone. **3** a hole worn in a road surface. ○ **potholing** n the activity of exploring deep caves and potholes.

potion n a draught of medicine, poison or some magic elixir.

pot luck n whatever happens to be available.

pot plant n a plant grown in a pot and usu kept indoors for decoration.

potpourri /pou'puɒrɪ/ n **1** a fragrant mixture of dried flowers, leaves, etc placed in containers and used to scent rooms. **2** a medley or mixture.

potsherd n, *archaeol* a fragment of pottery.

pot shot n **1** an easy shot at close range. **2** a shot made without taking careful aim.

pottage n a thick soup.

potted *adj* **1** abridged: *a potted history.* **2** of food: preserved in a pot or jar: *potted meat.* **3** of a plant: growing or grown in a pot: *a potted begonia.*

potter[1] n someone who makes pottery.

potter[2] vb, intr **1** (*usu* **potter about**) to busy oneself in a mild way with trifling tasks. **2** (*usu*

potter about or **along**) to progress in an unhurried manner. ○ **potterer** n.

pottery n (**-ies**) **1** containers, pots or other objects of baked clay. **2** the art or craft of making such objects. **3** a factory where such objects are produced commercially.

potty[1] *adj* (**-ier, -iest**) *colloq* **1** mad; crazy. **2** (*usu* **potty about sb** or **sth**) intensely interested in or keen on them or it. **3** trifling; insignificant. ○ **pottiness** n.

potty[2] n (**-ies**) *colloq* a child's chamberpot.

potty-train vb to teach (usu a toddler) to use a potty or the toilet. ○ **potty-trained** *adj*.

pouch n **1** *chiefly old use* a purse or small bag: *a tobacco pouch.* **2** in marsupials such as the kangaroo: a pocket of skin on the belly, in which the young are carried until they are weaned. **3** a fleshy fold in the cheek of hamsters and other rodents, for storing undigested food. ➢ vb **1** to form, or form into, a pouch. **2** *colloq* to take possession of something.

pouf or **poufter** n a POOF.

pouffe or **pouf** /puːf/ n a firmly stuffed drum-shaped or cube-shaped cushion for use as a low seat.

poulterer n a dealer in poultry and game.

poultice /'pəultɪs/ n, *med* a hot, semi-liquid mixture spread on a bandage and applied to the skin to reduce inflammation.

poultry n **1** *collective* domesticated birds kept for their eggs or meat, or both, eg chickens, ducks, etc. **2** the meat of such birds.

pounce vb, intr (*often* **pounce on sth** or **sb**) **1** to leap or swoop on (a victim or prey), esp when trying to capture them or it. **2** to seize on it or them; to grab eagerly. ➢ n an act of pouncing.

pound[1] n **1** (symbol £) the standard unit of currency of the UK. **2** the English name for the principal currency unit in several other countries, including Egypt. **3** (abbrev **lb**) a measure of weight equal to 16 ounces (0.45kg) avoirdupois, or 12 ounces (0.37kg) troy.

pound[2] n **1** an enclosure where stray animals or illegally parked cars that have been taken into police charge are kept for collection. **2** a place where people are confined.

pound[3] vb **1** tr & intr (*often* **pound on** or **at sth**) to beat and bang vigorously: *pounding on the door.* **2** *intr* to walk or run with heavy thudding steps. **3** to crush or grind something to a powder. **4** to thump or beat esp with the fists: *Jake pounded him senseless.* **5** of the heart: to beat with heavy thumping pulses, esp through fear, excitement, etc.

poundage n a fee or commission charged per POUND[1] in weight or money.

pour vb **1** tr & intr to flow or cause something to flow in a downward stream. **2** tr & intr of a jug, teapot, etc: to discharge (liquid) in a certain way: *It doesn't pour very well.* **3** (*also* **pour sth out**) to serve (a drink, etc) by pouring. **4** *intr* to rain heavily. **5** *intr* (*usu* **pour in** or **out**) to come or go in large numbers. **6** *intr* (*also* **pour in** or

out, *etc*) to flow or issue plentifully. **7** *tr* (**pour sth into sth**) to invest eg money, energy, etc liberally into it. ○ **pourer** *n*. ◊ **pour sth out** to reveal without inhibition: *She poured out her feelings*.

poussin /*French* pusĕ/ *n* a young chicken killed and eaten at the age of four to six weeks.

pout *vb* **1** *tr* & *intr* to push the lower lip or both lips forward as an indication of sulkiness or seductiveness. **2** *intr* of the lips: to stick out in this way. ➣ *n* **1** an act of pouting. **2** a pouting expression.

poverty *n* **1** the condition of being poor. **2** poor quality. **3** inadequacy; deficiency: *poverty of imagination*.

poverty-stricken *adj* suffering from poverty.

POW *abbrev* prisoner of war.

powder *n* **1** any substance in the form of fine dust-like particles: *talcum powder*. **2** (*also* **face powder**) a cosmetic that is patted on to the skin to give it a soft smooth appearance. **3** GUN-POWDER. **4** a dose of medicine in powder form. ➣ *vb* **1** to apply powder to (eg one's face); to sprinkle or cover something with powder. **2** to reduce something to a powder by crushing. ○ **powdery** *adj*.

powder keg *n* **1** a barrel of gunpowder. **2** a potentially dangerous or explosive situation.

powder room *n* a women's cloakroom or toilet in a restaurant, hotel, etc.

power *n* **1** control and influence exercised over others. **2** strength, vigour, force or effectiveness. **3** *usu in compounds* military strength: *sea power • air power*. **4** the physical ability, skill, opportunity or authority to do something. **5** an individual faculty or skill: *the power of speech*. **6** a right, privilege or responsibility: *the power of arrest*. **7** political control. **8** *also in compounds* a state that has an influential role in international affairs. **9** a person or group exercising control or influence. **10** *colloq* a great deal: *The rest did her a power of good*. **11** *often in compounds* any form of energy, esp when used as the driving force for a machine: *nuclear power*. **12** *maths* a number that indicates how many times a given quantity is to be multiplied by itself. **13** *physics* the rate of doing work or converting energy from one form into another. **14** mechanical or electrical energy, as distinct from manual effort. **15** *optics* a measure of the extent to which a lens, optical instrument or curved mirror can deviate light rays and so magnify an image of an object. ➣ *vb* **1** *also in compounds* to supply something with power: *wind-powered*. **2** *tr* & *intr*, *colloq* to move or cause something to move with great force, energy or speed. ◆ **in power** elected; holding office. **the powers that be** the people who are in control or in authority. ◊ **power sth up** to recharge its power supply (esp that of a laptop computer) by attaching it to the mains electricity supply.

powerboat *n* a small boat fitted with a high-powered engine.

power cut *n* a temporary break or reduction in an electricity supply.

powerful *adj* **1** having great power, strength or vigour. **2** very effective or efficient: *a powerful argument*. ➣ *adv*, *dialect* extremely: *June was powerful hot*.

powerhouse *n* **1** a power station. **2** *colloq* a forceful or vigorous person.

powerless *adj* **1** deprived of power or authority. **2** completely unable (usu to do something).

power of attorney *n* the right to act for another person in legal and business matters.

power station *n* a building where electricity is generated on a large scale from another form of energy, such as coal, nuclear fuel, moving water, etc.

powwow *n* **1** *colloq* a meeting for discussion. **2** a meeting of Native Americans. ➣ *vb*, *intr* to hold a powwow.

pox *n* **1** *med*, *often in compounds* an infectious viral disease that causes a skin rash consisting of pimples containing pus: *chickenpox • smallpox*. **2** (*often* **the pox**) a former name for SYPHILIS.

poxy *adj* (**-ier**, **-iest**) *Brit colloq* worthless, second-rate, trashy.

pp *abbrev* **1** pages: *pp9–12*. **2** usu written when signing a letter in the absence of the sender: *per procurationem* (Latin), for and on behalf of (the specified person). **3** *mus* pianissimo.

ppm *abbrev* parts per million.

PPS *abbrev* **1** Parliamentary Private Secretary. **2** (*also* **pps**) *post postscriptum* (Latin), after the postscript, ie an additional postscript.

PR *abbrev* **1** proportional representation. **2** public relations.

Pr *symbol*, *chem* praseodymium.

practicable *adj* capable of being done, used or successfully carried out; feasible. ○ **practicability** *n*. ○ **practicably** *adv*.

practical *adj* **1** concerned with or involving action rather than theory: *She put her knowledge to practical use*. **2** effective, or capable of being effective, in actual use. **3** eg of clothes: designed for tough or everyday use; sensibly plain. **4** of a person: **a** sensible and efficient in deciding and acting; **b** good at doing manual jobs. **5** in effect: *a practical walkover*. ➣ *n* a practical lesson or examination, eg in a scientific subject. ○ **practicality** *n* (**-ies**).

practical joke *n* a trick which is played on someone to make them look silly. ○ **practical joker** *n*.

practically *adv* **1** almost; very nearly. **2** in a practical manner.

practice *n* **1** the process of carrying something out: *putting ideas into practice*. **2** a habit, activity, procedure or custom: *Don't make a practice of it!* **3** repeated exercise to improve technique in an art or sport, etc. **4** the business or clientele of a doctor, dentist, lawyer, etc. ◆ **be in** or **out of practice** to have maintained, or failed to maintain, one's skill in an art or sport, etc.

practice, practise In British English, **practice** is the spelling of the noun, and **practise** the verb. American English uses **practice** for both.

practise or (*US*) **practice** *vb* **1** *tr & intr* to do exercises repeatedly in (an art or sport, etc) so as to improve one's performance. **2** to make a habit of something: *I need to practise self-control.* **3** to go in for something as a custom: *tribes that practise bigamy.* **4** to work at or follow (an art or profession, esp medicine or law). **5** to perform (a wrongful act) against someone: *He practised a cruel deception on them.*

practised or (*US*) **practiced** *adj* (*often practised at sth*) skilled; experienced; expert.

practising or (*US*) **practicing** *adj* actively engaged in or currently pursuing or observing: *a practising lawyer.* ➤ *n* an act or the process of doing something for PRACTICE (sense 3): *Download the program into your computer for practising.*

practitioner *n* someone who practises an art or profession, esp medicine.

praetor /ˈpriːtə(r)/ *n, Roman hist* one of the chief law officers of the state, elected annually, and second to the CONSULS in importance. ○ **praetorian** *adj, n.*

pragmatism *n* **1** a practical matter-of-fact approach to dealing with problems, etc. **2** *philos* a school of thought that assesses the truth of concepts in terms of their practical implications. ○ **pragmatic** *adj.* ○ **pragmatist** *n.*

prairie *n* in N America: a large expanse of flat or rolling natural grassland, usu without trees.

praise *vb* **1** to express admiration or approval of someone or something. **2** to worship or glorify (God) with hymns or thanksgiving, etc. ➤ *n* **1** the expression of admiration or approval; commendation. **2** worship of God. ♦ **sing sb's** or **sth's praises** to commend them or it enthusiastically.

praiseworthy *adj* deserving praise.

praline /ˈprɑːliːn/ *n* a sweet consisting of nuts in caramelized sugar.

pram *n* a wheeled baby carriage pushed by someone on foot.

prance *vb, intr* **1** esp of a horse: to walk with lively springing steps. **2** to frisk or skip about. **3** to parade about in a swaggering manner.

prandial *adj, often facetious* belonging or relating to dinner.

prang *colloq, vb* **1** to crash (a vehicle). **2** to bomb something from the air. ➤ *n* **1** a vehicle crash. **2** a bombing raid.

prank *n* a playful trick; a practical joke. ○ **prankster** *n.*

praseodymium *n, chem* a soft silvery metallic element.

prat *n, slang* **1** *offensive* a fool; an ineffectual person. **2** the buttocks.

prate *vb, tr & intr* to talk or utter foolishly. ➤ *n* idle chatter.

prattle *vb, tr & intr* to chatter or utter childishly or foolishly. ➤ *n* childish or foolish chatter. ○ **prattler** *n.*

prawn *n* a small edible shrimp-like marine crustacean.

pray *vb* (*often pray for sth* or **sb**) **1** *now usu intr* to address one's god, making earnest requests or giving thanks. **2** *old use, tr & intr* to entreat or implore: *Stop, I pray you!* **3** *tr & intr* to hope desperately. ➤ *exclam, old use* (now often uttered with quaint politeness or cold irony) please, or may I ask: *Pray come in • Who asked you, pray?*

pray A word often confused with this one is **prey**.

prayer¹ /ˈpreə(r)/ *n* **1** an address to one's god, making a request or giving thanks. **2** the activity of praying. **3** an earnest hope, desire or entreaty.

prayer² /ˈpreɪə(r)/ *n* someone who prays.

prayerful *adj* **1** of someone: devout; tending to pray a lot or often. **2** said of a speech, etc: imploring.

praying mantis see under MANTIS.

preach *vb* **1** *tr & intr* to deliver (a sermon) as part of a religious service. **2** (*often preach at sb*) to give them advice in a tedious or obtrusive manner. **3** to advise or advocate something. ○ **preacher** *n* someone who preaches, esp a minister of religion.

preamble *n* an introduction or preface, eg to a speech or document.

prearrange *vb* to arrange something in advance. ○ **prearrangement** *n.*

prebend /ˈprebənd/ *n* **1** an allowance paid out of the revenues of a cathedral or collegiate church to its canons or chapter members. **2** the piece of land, etc which is the source of such revenue. **3** a prebendary. ○ **prebendal** /prɪˈbendəl/ *adj.*

prebendary /ˈprebəndərɪ/ *n* (*-ies*) **1** a clergyman of a cathedral or collegiate church who is in receipt of a PREBEND. **2** *C of E* the honorary holder of a prebend.

Precambrian *geol, adj* **1** relating to the earliest geological era, during which primitive forms of life appeared on earth. **2** relating to the rocks formed during this period. ➤ *n* (**the Precambrian**) the Precambrian era.

precancerous *adj* esp of cells: showing early indications of possible malignancy.

precarious *adj* **1** unsafe; insecure; dangerous. **2** uncertain; chancy. ○ **precariously** *adv.*

precaution *n* **1** a measure taken to ensure a satisfactory outcome, or to avoid a risk or danger. **2** caution exercised beforehand. ○ **precautionary** *adj.*

precede *vb, tr & intr* to go or be before someone or something, in time, order, position, rank or importance.

precedence /ˈpresɪdəns/ *n* **1** priority. **2** the right to precede others.

precedent n /ˈprɛsɪdənt/ **1** a previous incident or legal case, etc that has something in common with one under consideration, serving as a basis for a decision in the present one. **2** the judgement or decision given in such a case.

precentor n, relig someone who leads the singing of a church congregation, or the prayers in a synagogue.

precept n **1** a rule or principle, esp one of a moral kind, that is seen or used as a guide to behaviour. **2** law the written warrant of a magistrate.

preceptor or **preceptress** n a teacher or instructor. ○ **preceptorial** adj.

precession n **1** physics the gradual change in direction of the axis of rotation of a spinning body. **2** astron the progressively earlier occurrence of the equinoxes, resulting from the gradual change in direction of the Earth's axis of rotation. **3** the act of preceding. ○ **precessional** adj.

precinct n **1** (also **precincts**) the enclosed grounds of a large building, etc: the cathedral precinct. **2** (also **precincts**) the neighbourhood or environs of a place. **3** a PEDESTRIAN PRECINCT. **4** N Am, esp US **a** any of the districts into which a city is divided for administrative or policing purposes; **b** the police station of one of these districts.

precious adj **1** valuable. **2** dear; beloved; treasured. **3** derog of speech or manner: affected or over-precise. **4** colloq, ironic **a** confounded: Him and his precious goldfish! **b** substantial: And a precious lot you'd care! ➣ n a rather sickly form of address: And how's my little precious today? ◆ **precious few** or **little** colloq almost none.

precious metal n gold, silver or platinum.

precious stone n a gemstone, such as a diamond, ruby, etc, valued for its beauty and rarity, esp with regard to its use in jewellery or ornamentation.

precipice n a steep, vertical or overhanging cliff or rock face.

precipitate vb /prɪˈsɪpɪteɪt/ **1** to cause something or hasten its advent: They precipitated a war. **2** to throw or plunge: Jim precipitated himself into the controversy. **3** tr & intr, chem to form or cause something to form a suspension of small solid particles in a solution, as a result of certain chemical reactions. **4** meteorol of moisture, etc: to condense and fall as rain, snow, etc. ➣ adj /prɪˈsɪpɪtət/ of actions or decisions: recklessly hasty or ill-considered. ➣ n /prɪˈsɪpɪtət/ **1** chem a suspension of small solid particles formed in a solution as a result of certain chemical reactions. **2** meteorol moisture deposited as rain or snow, etc.

precipitation n **1** rash haste. **2** meteorol water that falls from clouds in the atmosphere to the Earth's surface in the form of rain, snow, etc. **3** the act of precipitating or process of being precipitated. **4** chem the formation of a precipitate.

precipitous adj **1** dangerously steep. **2** of actions or decisions: rash; precipitate. ○ **precipitously** adv.

précis /ˈpreɪsiː/ n (pl **précis**) a summary of a piece of writing. ➣ vb to make a précis of something.

precise adj **1** exact; very: at this precise moment. **2** clear; detailed: precise instructions. **3** accurate: precise timing. **4** of someone: careful over details. ○ **preciseness** n.

precisely adv **1** exactly: It began at eight o'clock precisely. **2** in a precise manner. **3** said in response to a remark: you are quite right.

precision n accuracy. ➣ adj designed to operate with minute accuracy: precision tools.

preclude vb **1** to rule out or eliminate something or make it impossible. **2** (often **preclude sb from sth**) to prevent their involvement in it. ○ **preclusion** n. ○ **preclusive** adj.

precocious adj eg of a child: unusually advanced in mental development, speech, behaviour, etc. ○ **precociously** adv. ○ **precociousness** or **precocity** n.

precognition n the supposed ability to foresee events before they happen. ○ **precognitive** adj.

preconceive vb to form (an idea, etc) of something before having direct experience of it. ○ **preconceived** adj.

preconception n **1** an assumption about something not yet experienced. **2** (often **preconceptions**) a prejudice.

precondition n a condition to be satisfied in advance.

precursor n something that precedes, and is a sign of, an approaching event. ○ **precursive** or **precursory** adj.

predacious adj of animals: predatory.

predate vb **1** to write an earlier date on (a document, cheque, etc). **2** to occur at an earlier date than (a specified date or event).

predation n the killing and consuming of other animals for survival; the activity of preying.

predator /ˈprɛdətə(r)/ n **1** any animal that obtains food by catching, usu killing, and eating other animals. **2** derog a predatory person.

predatory /ˈprɛdətərɪ/ adj **1** of an animal: obtaining food by catching and eating other animals. **2** of a person: cruelly exploiting the weakness or goodwill of others for personal gain.

predecessor n **1** the person who formerly held a job or position now held by someone else. **2** the previous version, model, etc of a particular thing or product. **3** an ancestor.

predestination n **1** the act of predestining or fact of being predestined. **2** relig the doctrine that whatever is to happen has been unalterably fixed by God from the beginning of time.

predestine vb **1** to determine something beforehand. **2** to ordain or decree by fate.

predetermine vb **1** to decide, settle or fix in advance. **2** to influence, shape or bias something in a certain way. ○ **predeterminate** adj.

○ **predetermination** n. ○ **predetermined** adj.

predicable adj able to be predicated or affirmed.

predicament n a difficulty, plight or dilemma.

predicate n /'prɛdɪkət/ **1** gram the word or words in a sentence that make a statement about the subject, usu consisting of a verb and its complement, eg ran in John ran and knew exactly what to do in The people in charge knew exactly what to do. **2** logic what is stated as a property of the subject of a proposition. ➤ vb /'prɛdɪkeɪt/ **1** to assert. **2** to imply; to entail the existence of something. **3** logic to state something as a property of the subject of a proposition. **4** (usu **predicate on** or **upon sth**) to make the viability of (an idea, etc) depend on something else being true: Their success was predicated on the number of supporters they had. ○ **predication** n.

predicative /prɪ'dɪkətɪv/ adj **1** gram of an adjective: forming part of a PREDICATE, eg 'asleep' in They were asleep. **2** relating to predicates. ○ **predicatively** adv, gram with a predicative function.

predict vb to prophesy, foretell or forecast.

predictable adj **1** able to be predicted; easily foreseen. **2** derog boringly consistent in behaviour or reactions, etc. ○ **predictability** n. ○ **predictably** adv.

prediction n **1** the act or art of predicting. **2** something foretold.

predilection n a special liking or preference for something.

predispose vb **1** to incline someone to react in a particular way: Clear handwriting will predispose the examiners in your favour. **2** to make someone susceptible to something (esp illness). ○ **predisposition** n.

predominant adj **1** more numerous, prominent or powerful. **2** more frequent; prevailing. ○ **predominance** n. ○ **predominantly** adv.

predominate vb, intr **1** to be more numerous. **2** to be more noticeable or prominent. **3** to have more influence.

pre-eminent adj outstanding; better than all others. ○ **pre-eminence** n. ○ **pre-eminently** adv.

pre-empt vb **1** to do something ahead of someone else and so make pointless (an action they had planned). **2** to obtain something in advance.

pre-emptive adj **1** having the effect of pre-empting. **2** mil of an attack: effectively destroying the enemy's weapons before they can be used: a pre-emptive strike.

preen vb **1** tr & intr of a bird: to clean and smooth (feathers, etc) with its beak. **2** of a person: to groom (oneself, hair, clothes, etc), esp in a vain manner.

prefab n a prefabricated building.

prefabricate vb to manufacture standard sections of (a building) for later quick assembly.

preface /'prɛfəs/ n **1** an explanatory statement at the beginning of a book. **2** anything of an in-

troductory or preliminary character. ➤ vb **1** to provide (a book, etc) with a preface. **2** to introduce or precede something with some preliminary matter.

prefatory adj **1** relating to a preface. **2** serving as a preface or introduction. **3** introductory.

prefect n **1** in a school: a senior pupil with minor disciplinary powers. **2** in some countries: the senior official of an administrative district. ○ **prefectoral** and **prefectorial** adj.

prefecture n **1** the office or term of office of a prefect. **2** the district presided over by a prefect. **3** the official residence of a prefect.

prefer vb (**preferred, preferring**) **1** to like someone or something better than another: I prefer tea to coffee. **2** law to submit (a charge, accusation, etc) to a court of law for consideration. **3** formal to promote someone, esp over their colleagues.

> **prefer** **Prefer** should be followed by to, not than, as in He prefers tea to coffee.

preferable adj more desirable, suitable or advisable; better. ○ **preferably** adv.

preference n **1** the preferring of one person, thing, etc to another. **2** one's choice of, or liking for, someone or something particular. **3** favourable consideration. ♦ **in preference to** rather than.

preferential adj bestowing special favours or advantages: preferential treatment.

preferment n promotion to a more responsible position.

prefix n **1** gram an element such as un-, pre-, non-, de-, etc which is added to the beginning of a word to create a new word. Compare SUFFIX (noun sense 1). **2** a title such as Mr, Dr, Ms, etc used before someone's name. ➤ vb **1** to add something as an introduction. **2** gram to attach something as a prefix to a word. **3** to add (a prefix) to something.

pregnancy n (-ies) biol in female mammals, including humans: the period between fertilization or conception and birth, during which a developing embryo is carried in the womb.

pregnant adj **1** of a female mammal, including humans: carrying a child or young in the womb. **2** of a remark or pause, etc: loaded with significance. **3** fruitful in results. ○ **pregnantly** adv.

preheat vb to heat (an oven, etc) before use.

prehensile adj denoting a part of an animal that is adapted for grasping, eg the tail of certain vertebrates.

prehistoric or **prehistorical** adj belonging or relating to the period before written records. ○ **prehistory** n.

prejudge vb **1** to form an opinion on (an issue, etc) without having all the relevant facts. **2** to condemn someone unheard. ○ **prejudgement** n.

prejudice n **1** a biased opinion, based on insufficient knowledge. **2** hostility, eg towards a particular racial or religious group. **3** law harm;

detriment; disadvantage. ➤ *vb* **1** to make someone feel prejudice; to bias. **2** to harm or endanger.

prejudicial *adj* **1** causing prejudice. **2** harmful. ○ **prejudicially** *adv.*

prelate /'prɛlət/ *n, Christianity* a bishop, abbot or other high-ranking ecclesiastic. ○ **prelatic** /prɪ'latɪk/ and **prelatical** *adj.*

prelim *n, colloq* **1** in Scotland: any one of a set of school examinations taken before the public ones. **2** the first public examination in certain universities. **3** (**prelims**) *printing* the title page, contents page and other matter preceding the main text of a book.

preliminary *adj* occurring at the beginning; introductory or preparatory. ➤ *n* (*-ies*) **1** (*usu* **preliminaries**) something done or said by way of introduction or preparation: *He had no time for the usual preliminaries.* **2** a preliminary round in a competition.

prelude *n* **1** *mus* an introductory passage or first movement, eg of a fugue or suite. **2** a name sometimes given to a short musical piece or a poetic composition, etc. **3** (*esp* **a prelude to sth**) some event that precedes, and prepares the ground for, something of greater significance. ➤ *vb* **1** *tr & intr* to act as a prelude to something. **2** to introduce something with a prelude.

premarital *adj* belonging to or occurring in the period before marriage.

premature *adj* **1** *med* of human birth: occurring less than 37 weeks after conception. **2** occurring before the usual or expected time: *premature senility.* **3** of a decision, etc: overhasty; impulsive. ○ **prematurely** *adv.*

premedication *n, med* drugs, usu including a sedative, given to a patient in preparation for a GENERAL ANAESTHETIC prior to surgery.

premeditate *vb* to think something out beforehand. ○ **premeditated** *adj* esp of a crime: planned beforehand. ○ **premeditation** *n.*

premenstrual *adj* **1** relating to or occurring during the days immediately before a MENSTRUAL period. **2** of a woman: in the days immediately before a menstrual period.

premenstrual tension or **premenstrual syndrome** *n* (abbrev PMT or PMS) *med* a group of symptoms associated with hormonal changes and experienced by some women before the onset of menstruation, characterized by fluid retention, headache, food cravings, depression and irritability.

premier *adj* **1** first in rank; most important; leading. **2** *Brit* denoting the top division in some football, etc leagues. **3** first in time; earliest. ➤ *n* **1** a prime minister. **2** in Australia and Canada: the head of government of a state or province. ○ **premiership** *n.*

première or **premiere** /'prɛmɪɛə(r)/ *n* the first public performance of a play or showing of a film. ➤ *vb* **1** to present a première of (a film, etc). **2** *intr* of a play, film, etc: to open.

premise *n* /'prɛmɪs/ **1** (*also* **premiss**) some-

thing assumed to be true as a basis for stating something further. **2** *logic* either of the propositions introducing a syllogism. ➤ *vb* /prɪ'maɪz/ to assume or state as a premise.

premises *pl n* **1** a building and its grounds, esp as a place of business. **2** *law* **a** the preliminary matter in a document, etc; **b** matters explained or property referred to earlier in the document.

premium *n* **1** an amount paid, usu annually, on an insurance agreement. **2** an extra sum added to wages or to interest. **3** a prize. ➤ *adj* finest; exceptional: *premium quality.* ♦ **be at a premium** to be scarce and greatly in demand.

premolar *n* any of the teeth between the canine teeth and the molars. ➤ *adj* situated in front of a MOLAR tooth.

premonition *n* a feeling that something is about to happen, before it actually does.

prenatal *adj* relating to or occurring during the period before childbirth. ○ **prenatally** *adv.*

prenuptial *adj* relating to or occurring during the period before marriage.

preoccupation *n* **1** the state or condition of being preoccupied. **2** something that preoccupies.

preoccupied *adj* **1** lost in thought. **2** (*often* **preoccupied by** or **with sth**) having one's attention completely taken up. **3** already occupied.

preoccupy *vb* **1** to occupy the attention of someone wholly. **2** to occupy or fill something before others.

preordain *vb* to decide or determine beforehand.

prep¹ *n, colloq* **1** short for PREPARATION (sense 3). **2** short for PREPARATORY: *prep school.*

prep² *vb* (**prepped, prepping**) to prep (a patient) ready for an operation, etc, esp by giving a sedative.

prepack *vb* to pack (food, etc) before offering it for sale.

preparation *n* **1** the process of preparing or being prepared. **2** (*usu* **preparations**) something done by way of preparing or getting ready. **3** *Brit* chiefly in public schools: school work done out of school hours, done either in school or as HOMEWORK. **4** a medicine, cosmetic or other such prepared substance.

preparatory /prə'parətərɪ/ *adj* **1** serving to prepare for something. **2** introductory; preliminary.

prepare *vb* **1** *tr & intr* to make or get ready. **2** to make (a meal). **3** to clean or chop (vegetables or fruit). **4** to get someone or oneself into a fit state to receive a shock, surprise, etc: *We prepared ourselves for bad news.* **5** *intr* to brace oneself (to do something).

prepared *adj* **1** (*usu* **be prepared to do sth**) of a person: to be willing and able: *I'm not prepared to lend any more.* **2** (*usu* **prepared for sth**) expecting it or ready for it: *We were prepared for the worst.*

prepay *vb* to pay for something, esp postage, in advance. ○ **prepaid** *adj.* ○ **prepayment** *n.*

preponderance *n* **1** the circumstance of predominating. **2** a superior number; a majority. ○ **preponderant** adj.

preponderate vb, intr **1** (often **preponderate over sth**) to be more numerous than it. **2** to weigh more.

preposition n, gram a word, or words, such as to, from, into, out of, etc, typically preceding nouns and pronouns, and describing their position, movement, etc in relation to other words in the sentence. ○ **prepositional** adj.

prepossess vb, rather formal **1** to charm. **2** to win over; to incline or bias. **3** to preoccupy someone in a specified way.

prepossessing adj attractive; winning.

preposterous adj ridiculous, absurd or outrageous. ○ **preposterously** adv.

preppy adj (-ier, -iest) colloq, esp N Am of dress sense, etc: neat and conservative.

preprandial adj, facetious preceding a meal.

prep school n in the UK: a private school that prepares pupils for public school.

prepuce /'priːpjuːs/ n, anat **1** the fold of skin that covers the top of the penis. **2** the fold of skin that surrounds the clitoris.

prequel n a book or film produced after one that has been a popular success, but with the story beginning prior to the start of the original story.

prerecord vb to record (a programme for radio or TV) in advance of its scheduled broadcasting time.

prerequisite n a preliminary requirement that must be satisfied. ➤ adj of a condition, etc: required to be satisfied beforehand.

prerogative /prɪ'rɒɡətɪv/ n **1** an exclusive right or privilege arising from one's rank or position. **2** any right or privilege.

presage /'presɪdʒ/ vb **1** to warn of or be a warning sign of something; to foreshadow. **2** to have a premonition about something. ➤ n, formal or literary **1** a portent, warning or omen. **2** a premonition.

presbyter n, Christianity **1** in the early Christian Church: an administrative official with some teaching and priestly duties. **2** in Episcopal Churches: a priest. **3** in Presbyterian Churches: an elder.

presbyterian adj **1** referring or relating to church administration by presbyters or elders. **2** (often **Presbyterian**) designating a Church governed by elders. ➤ n (**Presbyterian**) a member of a Presbyterian Church.

presbytery n, Christianity (-ies) **1** in a Presbyterian Church: an area of local administration. **2** a body of ministers and elders, esp one sitting as a local church court. **3** archit the eastern section of a church, beyond the choir. **4** the residence of a Roman Catholic priest.

preschool adj denoting or relating to children before they are old enough to attend school: preschool playgroups.

prescience /'presɪəns/ n the ability to predict events; foresight. ○ **prescient** adj.

prescribe vb **1** esp of a doctor: to advise (a

medicine) as a remedy, esp by completing a prescription. **2** to recommend officially (eg a text for academic study). **3** to lay down or establish (a duty, penalty, etc) officially. ○ **prescriber** n.

> **prescribe** A word sometimes confused with this one is **proscribe**.

prescript n, formal a law, rule, principle, etc that has been laid down.

prescription n **1 a** a set of written instructions from a doctor to a pharmacist regarding the preparation and dispensing of a drug, etc for a particular patient; **b** the drug, etc prescribed in this way by a doctor. **2** a set of written instructions for an optician stating the type of lenses required to correct a patient's vision. **3** the act of prescribing.

prescriptive adj **1** authoritative; laying down rules. **2** of a right, etc: established by custom.

presence n **1** the state or circumstance of being present. **2** someone's company or nearness: He said so in my presence • Your presence is requested. **3** physical bearing, esp if it is commanding or authoritative: people with presence. **4** a being felt to be close by, esp in a supernatural way. **5** a situation or activity demonstrating influence or power in a place: Britain will maintain a military presence in the area.

presence of mind n the ability to act calmly and sensibly, esp in an emergency.

present¹ /'prezənt/ adj **1** being at the place or occasion in question. **2** existing, detectable or able to be found. **3** existing now: the present situation. **4** now being considered: the present subject. **5** gram of the tense of a verb: indicating action that is taking place now, or action that is continuing or habitual, as in I walk the dog every morning and He's going to school. ➤ n **1** the present time. **2** gram **a** the present tense; **b** a verb in the present tense. ◆ **at present** now. **for the present** for the time being.

present² /prɪ'zent/ vb **1** to give or award something, esp formally or ceremonially: He presented them with gold medals. **2** to introduce (a person), esp formally. **3** to introduce or compère (a TV or radio show). **4** to stage (a play), show (a film), etc. **5** to offer something for consideration; to submit. **6** to pose; to set: It shouldn't present any problem. **7** of an idea: to suggest (itself). **8** to hand over (a cheque) for acceptance or (a bill) for payment. **9** to set out something: She presents her work neatly. **10** to depict or represent something or someone. **11** to put on (a specified appearance) in public. **12** to offer (one's compliments) formally. **13** to hold (a weapon) in aiming position. ◆ **present arms** to hold a weapon vertically in front of one as a salute.

present³ /'prezənt/ n a gift.

presentable adj **1** fit to be seen or to appear in company, etc. **2** passable; satisfactory. ○ **presentability** n.

presentation n **1** the act of presenting. **2** the

manner in which something is presented, laid out, explained or advertised. **3** something performed for an audience, eg a play, show or other entertainment. **4** a formal report, usu delivered verbally.

present-day *adj* modern; contemporary.

presenter *n, broadcasting* someone who introduces a programme and provides a linking commentary between items.

presentiment /prɪ'zɛntɪmənt/ *n* a feeling that something, esp something bad, is about to happen, just before it does.

presently *adv* **1** soon; shortly. **2** *N Am, esp US* at the present time; now.

preservative *n* a chemical substance that, when added to food or other perishable material, slows down or prevents its decay. ➤ *adj* having the effect of preserving.

preserve *vb* **1** to save something from loss, damage, decay or deterioration. **2** to treat (food), eg by freezing, smoking, drying, etc, so that it will last. **3** to maintain (eg peace, the status quo, standards, etc). **4** to keep safe from danger or death. ➤ *n* **1** an area of work or activity that is restricted to certain people: *Politics was once a male preserve.* **2** an area of land or water where creatures are protected for private hunting, shooting or fishing: *a game preserve.* **3** a jam, pickle or other form in which fruit or vegetables are preserved by cooking in sugar, salt, vinegar, etc. ○ **preservation** *n*. ○ **preserver** *n*.

preset *vb* /priː'sɛt/ to adjust (a piece of electronic equipment, etc) so that it will operate at the required time. ➤ *n* /'priːsɛt/ a device or facility for presetting.

preside *vb, intr (often* **preside at** *or* **over sth)** **1** to take the lead at (an event), the chair at (a meeting, etc); to be in charge. **2** to dominate; to be a dominating presence in (a place, etc).

president *n* **1** *(often* **President)** the elected head of state in a republic. **2** the chief officebearer in a society or club. **3** *esp US* the head of a business organization, eg the chairman of a company, governor of a bank, etc. **4** the head of some colleges or other higher-education institutions. ○ **presidency** *n*. ○ **presidential** *adj*.

presidium or **praesidium** *n (presidiums* or *presidia) (often with capital)* in a Communist state: a standing executive committee.

press¹ *vb* **1** a *tr & intr* to push steadily, esp with the finger; **b** *(often* **press against** *or* **on** *or* **down on sth)** to push it; to apply pressure to it: *Press down on the accelerator.* **2** to hold something firmly against something; to flatten: *She pressed her nose against the glass.* **3** to compress or squash. **4** to squeeze (eg someone's hand) affectionately. **5** to preserve (plants) by flattening and drying, eg between the pages of a book. **6** a to squeeze (fruit) to extract juice; **b** to extract (juice) from fruit by squeezing. **7** to iron (clothes, etc). **8** to urge or compel someone; to ask them insistently. **9** to insist on

something; to urge recognition or discussion of it: *I'll press the point.* **10** *intr (press for sth)* to demand it. **11** *(press sth on sb)* to insist on giving it to them. **12** *intr (usu press on, ahead* or *forward)* to hurry on; to continue, esp in spite of difficulties. **13** *law* to bring (charges) officially against someone. **14** to produce (eg a RECORD *noun* sense 4) from a mould by a compressing process. ➤ *n* **1** an act of pressing. **2** any apparatus for pressing, flattening, squeezing, etc. **3** a machine for printing books, newspapers, etc. **4** the process or art of printing. **5** **(the press)** newspapers or journalists in general. **6** newspaper publicity or reviews received by a show, book, etc: *It got a poor press.* **7** a crowd: *a press of onlookers.* **8** *Scot* a cupboard. ➤ *adj* belonging or relating to the newspaper industry: *press photographers.*

press² *vb* **1** to force (men) into the army or navy. **2** *(esp* **press sth** *or* **sb into service)** to put it or them to use in a way that was not originally intended.

press agent *n* someone who arranges newspaper advertising or publicity for a performer or other celebrity, etc.

press conference or **news conference** *n* an interview granted to reporters by a politician or other person in the news.

press cutting *n* a paragraph or article cut from a newspaper, etc.

pressed *adj* of a person: under pressure; in a hurry. ♦ **be hard pressed** to be in difficulties. **be pressed for sth** *colloq* to be short of it, esp time or money.

pressgang *n, hist* a gang employed to seize men and force them into the army or navy. ➤ *vb* **1** to force (men) into the army or navy. **2** *facetious* to coerce someone into something.

pressie or **prezzie** *n, colloq* a present or gift.

pressing *adj* urgent: *pressing engagements.* ➤ *n* in the music industry: a number of records produced from a single mould.

press release *n* an official statement given to the press by an organization, etc.

press stud *n* a type of button-like fastener, one part of which is pressed into the other.

press-up *n* an exercise performed face down, raising and lowering the body on the arms while keeping the trunk and legs rigid.

pressure *n* **1** *physics* the force exerted on a surface divided by the area of the surface to which it is applied. **2** the act of pressing or process of being pressed. **3** force or coercion; forceful persuasion. **4** urgency; strong demand: *I work well under pressure.* **5** tension or stress: *the pressures of family life.* ➤ *vb* to try to persuade; to coerce, force or pressurize.

pressure cooker *n* a thick-walled pan with an airtight lid, in which food is cooked at speed by steam under high pressure.

pressure group *n* a number of people who join together to influence public opinion and government policy on some issue.

pressurize or **-ise** *vb* **1** to adjust the pressure within (an enclosed compartment such as an aircraft cabin) so that nearly normal atmospheric pressure is constantly maintained. **2** to put pressure on someone or something; to force or coerce.

prestidigitation *n* SLEIGHT OF HAND. ○ **prestidigitator** *n*.

prestige / prɛˈstiːʒ/ *n* **1** fame, distinction or reputation due to rank or success. **2** influence; glamour: *a job with prestige.* ○ **prestigious** / prɛˈstɪdʒəs/ *adj*.

presto *mus, adv* in a very fast manner. ➤ *adj* very fast. ➤ *n* a piece of music to be played in this way.

presumably *adv* I suppose; probably.

presume *vb* **1** to suppose (something to be the case) without proof; to take something for granted: *She presumed he was dead.* **2** to be bold enough; esp without the proper right or knowledge: *He wouldn't presume to advise the experts.* **3** *intr* (**presume on** or **upon sb** or **sth**) **a** to rely or count on them or it, esp unduly; **b** to take unfair advantage of (someone's good nature, etc). ○ **presumption** *n*.

presumptive *adj* **1** presumed rather than absolutely certain. **2** giving grounds for presuming.

presumptuous *adj* overbold in behaviour, esp towards others; insolent or arrogant.

presuppose *vb* **1** to take for granted; to assume as true. **2** to require as a necessary condition; to imply the existence of something. ○ **presupposition** *n*.

pretence or (*US*) **pretense** *n* **1** the act of pretending. **2** make-believe. **3** an act someone puts on deliberately to mislead. **4** a claim, esp an unjustified one: *I make no pretence to expert knowledge.* **5** show, affectation or ostentation; pretentiousness. **6** (*usu* **pretences**) a misleading declaration of intention: *She won their support under false pretences.* **7** appearance or show: *They abandoned all pretence of fair play.*

pretend *vb* **1** *tr & intr* to make believe; to act as if, or give the impression that, something is the case when it is not: *I pretended to be asleep.* **2** *tr & intr* to imply or claim falsely: *He pretended not to know.* **3** to claim to feel something; to profess something falsely: *She pretends friendship towards her.* **4** *intr* (**pretend to sth**) **a** to claim to have (a skill, etc), esp falsely; **b** *hist* to lay claim, esp doubtful claim, to (eg the throne). ➤ *adj, colloq* esp used by or to children: imaginary: *a pretend cave.*

pretender *n* someone who pretends or pretended to something, esp the throne.

pretension *n* **1** foolish vanity, self-importance or affectation; pretentiousness. **2** a claim or aspiration: *She had no pretensions to elegance.*

pretentious *adj* **1** pompous, self-important or foolishly grandiose. **2** phoney or affected. **3** showy; ostentatious. ○ **pretentiously** *adv.* ○ **pretentiousness** *n*.

preterite / ˈprɛtərɪt/ *gram, n* **1** a verb tense that

expresses past action, eg *hit, moved, ran.* **2** a verb in this tense. ➤ *adj* denoting this tense.

preternatural *adj* **1** exceeding the normal; uncanny; extraordinary. **2** supernatural. ○ **preternaturally** *adv.*

pretext *n* a false reason given for doing something in order to disguise the real one.

prettify *vb* (**-ies, -ied**) to attempt to make something or someone prettier by superficial ornamentation.

pretty *adj* (**-ier, -iest**) **1** usu of a woman or girl: facially attractive, esp in a feminine way. **2** charming to look at; decorative. **3** of music, sound, etc: delicately melodious. **4** neat, elegant or skilful: *a pretty solution.* **5** *ironic* grand; fine: *a pretty mess.* ➤ *adv* fairly; satisfactorily; decidedly. ○ **prettily** *adv.* ○ **prettiness** *n*.

pretzel *n* a crisp salted biscuit in the shape of a knot.

prevail *vb, intr* **1** (*often* **prevail over** or **against sb** or **sth**) to be victorious; to win through: *Common sense prevailed.* **2** to be the common, usual or generally accepted thing. **3** to be predominant. **4** (**prevail on** or **upon sb** or **sth**) to persuade them or appeal to it.

prevailing *adj* most common or frequent.

prevalent / ˈprɛvələnt/ *adj* common; widespread. ○ **prevalence** *n*.

prevaricate *vb, intr* to avoid stating the truth or coming directly to the point. ○ **prevarication** *n*. ○ **prevaricator** *n*.

prevent *vb* **1** to stop someone from doing something, or something from happening. **2** to stop the occurrence of something beforehand or to make it impossible. ○ **preventable** or **preventible** *adj.* ○ **prevention** *n*. ○ **preventive** *adj.*

preview *n* **1** an advance view. **2** an advance showing of a film, play, exhibition, etc before it is presented to the general public. ➤ *vb* to show or view (a film, etc) in advance to a select audience.

previous *adj* **1** earlier: *a previous occasion.* **2** former: *the previous chairman.* **3** prior: *a previous engagement.* **4** *facetious* premature; overprompt or overhasty. **5** (*usu* **previous to sth**) before (an event, etc). ○ **previously** *adv.*

prey *sing or pl n* **1** an animal or animals hunted as food by another animal: *It's in search of prey.* **2** a victim or victims: *easy prey for muggers.* **3** (*usu* **a prey to sth**) someone liable to suffer from (an illness, a bad feeling, etc). ➤ *vb, intr* (*now esp* **prey on** or **upon sth** or **sb**) **1** of an animal: to hunt or catch (another animal) as food. **2 a** to bully, exploit or terrorize as victims; **b** to afflict in an obsessive way: *I'm preyed on by anxieties.*

> **prey** A word often confused with this one is **pray**.

price *n* **1** the amount, usu in money, for which a thing is sold or offered. **2** what must be given up or suffered in gaining something. **3** the sum by which someone may be bribed. **4** *betting odds.*

➤ *vb* **1** to fix a price for or mark a price on something. **2** to find out the price of something.

priceless *adj* **1** too valuable to have a price. **2** *colloq* hilariously funny.

pricey or **pricy** *adj* (*-ier, -iest*) *colloq* expensive.

prick *vb* **1** to pierce slightly with a fine point. **2** to make (a hole) by this means. **3** *tr & intr* to hurt something or someone by this means. **4** *tr & intr* to smart or make something smart. **5** *tr & intr* (*also* **prick up**) **a** of a dog, horse, etc: to stick (its ears) upright in response to sound; **b** of a dog's, etc ears: to stand erect in this way. **6** to mark out (a pattern) in punctured holes. **7** to trouble: *His conscience must be pricking him.* **8** to plant (seedlings, etc) in an area of soil that has had small holes marked out in it. ➤ *n* **1** an act of pricking or feeling of being pricked. **2** the pain of this. **3** a puncture made by pricking. **4** *slang* the penis. **5** *derog slang* an abusive term for a man, esp a self-important fool. ◆ **prick up one's ears** *colloq* to start listening attentively.

prickle *n* **1** a hard pointed structure growing from the surface of a plant or animal. **2** a pricking sensation. ➤ *vb, tr & intr* to cause, affect something with or be affected with a prickling sensation.

prickly *adj* (*-ier, -iest*) **1** covered with or full of prickles. **2** causing prickling. **3** *colloq* of a person: irritable; over-sensitive. **4** of a topic: liable to cause controversy. ○ **prickliness** *n*.

prickly heat *n* an itchy skin rash, most common in hot humid weather, caused by blockage of the sweat ducts.

pride *n* **1** a feeling of pleasure and satisfaction at one's own or another's accomplishments, possessions, etc. **2** the source of this feeling: *That car is my pride and joy.* **3** self-respect. **4** an unjustified assumption of superiority. **5** *poetic* the finest state; the prime. **6** the finest item: *the pride of the collection.* **7** a number of lions keeping together as a group. ➤ *vb* (*always* **pride oneself on sth**) to congratulate oneself on account of it. ◆ **take pride** or **take a pride in sth** or **sb 1** to be proud of it or them. **2** to be conscientious about maintaining high standards in (one's work, etc).

pride of place *n* special prominence; the position of chief importance.

priest *n* **1 a** in the Roman Catholic and Orthodox Churches: an ordained minister authorized to administer the sacraments; **b** in the Anglican Church: a minister ranking between deacon and bishop. **2** in non-Christian religions: an official who performs sacrifices and other religious rites. ○ **priestly** *adj*.

priestess *n* in non-Christian religions: a female priest.

priesthood *n* **1** the office of a priest. **2** the role or character of a priest. **3** priests collectively.

prig *n* someone who is self-righteously moralistic. ○ **priggish** *adj*.

prim *adj* (**primmer, primmest**) **1** stiffly formal, over-modest or over-proper. **2** prudishly disapproving. ○ **primly** *adv*. ○ **primness** *n*.

prima ballerina /ˈpriːmə/ *n* the leading female dancer in a ballet company.

primacy *n* (*-ies*) **1** the condition of being first in rank, importance or order. **2** the rank, office or area of jurisdiction of a PRIMATE of the Church.

prima donna /ˈpriːmə ˈdɒnə/ *n* (**prima donnas**) **1** a leading female opera singer. **2** someone difficult to please, esp someone given to melodramatic tantrums when displeased.

primaeval see PRIMEVAL

prima facie /ˈpraɪmə ˈfeɪʃɪ/ *esp law, adv* at first sight; on the evidence available. ➤ *adj* apparent; based on first impressions: *prima-facie evidence.*

primal *adj* **1** relating to the beginnings of life; original. **2** basic; fundamental.

primarily *adv* **1** chiefly; mainly. **2** in the first place; initially.

primary *adj* **1** first or most important; principal. **2** earliest in order or development. **3** (**Primary**) *geol* PALAEOZOIC. **4** basic; fundamental. **5** at the elementary stage or level. **6** of education, schools, classes etc: for children aged between 5 and 11. **7** of a bird's wing feather: outermost and longest. **8** first-hand; direct: *primary sources of information.* **9** of a product or industry: being or concerned with produce in its raw natural state. **10** *elec* **a** of a battery or cell: producing electricity by an irreversible chemical reaction; **b** of a circuit or current: inducing a current in a neighbouring circuit. ➤ *n* (*-ies*) **1** something that is first or most important. **2** *US* a preliminary election, esp to select delegates for a presidential election. **3** *Brit colloq* a primary school. **4** a bird's primary feather. **5** (**the Primary**) the PALAEOZOIC era.

primary colour *n* any of the pigments red, yellow and blue, which can be combined in various proportions to give all the other colours of the spectrum.

primary school *n* a school, esp a state one, for pupils aged between 5 and 11.

primate *n* **1** *zool* any member of an order of mammalian vertebrates which have a large brain, forward-facing eyes, nails instead of claws, and hands with grasping thumbs facing the other digits, eg a human, ape, etc. **2** *Christianity* an archbishop.

prime *adj* **1** chief; fundamental. **2** the best quality. **3** excellent: *He's in prime condition.* **4** supremely typical: *a prime example.* **5** having the greatest potential for attracting interest or custom: *prime sites on the high street.* ➤ *n* the best, most productive or active stage in the life of a person or thing: *She was cut down in her prime.* ➤ *vb* **1** to prepare something for use or treatment (eg a gun for firing or wood for painting). **2** to supply with the necessary facts in advance; to brief.

prime minister *n* the chief minister of a government.

prime mover *n* the force that is most effective in setting something in motion.

prime number *n, maths* a whole number that can only be divided by itself and 1, eg 3, 5, 7, 11, etc.

primer[1] *n* a first or introductory book of instruction.

primer[2] *n* 1 any material that is used to provide an initial coating for a surface before it is painted. 2 any device that ignites or detonates an explosive charge.

primeval or **primaeval** /praɪˈmiːvəl/ *adj* 1 relating or belonging to the Earth's beginnings. 2 primitive. 3 instinctive.

primitive *adj* 1 relating or belonging to earliest times or the earliest stages of development. 2 simple, rough, crude or rudimentary. 3 *art* simple, naive or unsophisticated in style. 4 *biol* original; belonging to an early stage of development. ➤ *n* 1 an unsophisticated person or thing. 2 a a work by an artist in naive style; b an artist who produces such a work. ○ **primitively** *adv*. ○ **primitiveness** *n*.

primitivism *n, art* the deliberate rejection of Western techniques and skills in pursuit of stronger effects found, for example, in African tribal or Oceanic art.

primogeniture *n* 1 the fact or condition of being the first-born child. 2 the right or principle of succession or inheritance of an eldest son.

primordial *adj* 1 existing from the beginning; formed earliest: *primordial matter*. 2 *biol* relating to an early stage in growth.

primp *vb, tr & intr* to groom, preen or titivate.

primrose *n* 1 a small plant with a rosette of oval leaves, and long-stalked pale-yellow flowers. 2 (*in full* **primrose yellow**) the pale-yellow colour of these flowers.

primula *n* (**primulae** or **primulas**) a plant with white, pink, purple or yellow flowers with five spreading petals, eg the primrose.

prince *n* 1 in the UK: the son of a sovereign. 2 a non-reigning male member of a royal or imperial family. 3 a sovereign of a small territory. 4 a nobleman in certain countries. 5 someone or something celebrated or outstanding within a type or class: *the prince of pop*.

princedom *n* a PRINCIPALITY; the estate, jurisdiction, sovereignty or rank of a prince.

princely *adj* 1 characteristic of or suitable for a prince. 2 *often ironic* lavish; generous: *the princely sum of five pence*.

princess *n* 1 the wife or daughter of a prince. 2 the daughter of a sovereign. 3 a non-reigning female member of a royal or imperial family.

principal *adj* first in rank or importance; chief; main. ➤ *n* 1 the head of an educational institution. 2 a leading actor, singer or dancer in a theatrical production. 3 *law* the person on behalf of whom an agent is acting. 4 *law* someone ultimately responsible for fulfilling an obligation. 5 someone who commits or participates

in a crime. 6 *commerce* the original sum of money on which interest is paid. 7 *mus* the leading player of each section of an orchestra. ○ **principally** *adv*.

principal, principle These words are often confused with each other.

principal clause see under MAIN CLAUSE

principality *n* (*-ies*) 1 a territory ruled by a prince, or one that he derives his title from. 2 (**the Principality**) in the UK: Wales.

principle *n* 1 a general truth or assumption from which to argue. 2 a scientific law, esp one that explains a natural phenomenon or the way a machine works. 3 a a general rule of morality that guides conduct; b the having of or holding to such rules: *a woman of principle*. 4 (**principles**) a set of such rules. 5 a fundamental element or source: *the vital principle*. 6 *chem* a constituent of a substance that gives it its distinctive characteristics. ♦ **in principle** esp of agreement or disagreement to a plan, decision or action: in theory; in general, although not necessarily in a particular case. **on principle** on the grounds of a particular principle of morality or wisdom.

principled *adj* holding, or proceeding from principles, esp high moral principles.

print *vb* 1 to reproduce (text or pictures) on paper with ink, using a printing press or other mechanical means. 2 (*also* **print sth out**) to produce a printed version, eg of computer data. 3 to publish (a book, article, etc). 4 *tr & intr* to write in separate, as opposed to joined-up, letters. 5 to make (a positive photograph) from a negative. 6 to mark (a shape, pattern, etc) in or on a surface by pressure. 7 to mark designs on (fabric). 8 to fix (a scene) indelibly (on the memory, etc). ➤ *n* 1 *often in compounds* a mark made on a surface by the pressure of something in contact with it: *a pawprint*. 2 a FINGERPRINT. 3 hand-done lettering with each letter written separately. 4 mechanically printed text, esp one produced on a printing press: *small print*. 5 a printed publication. 6 a design or picture printed from an engraved wood block or metal plate. 7 a positive photograph made from a negative. 8 a fabric with a printed or stamped design. ♦ **be in** or **out of print** of a publication: to be currently available, or no longer available, from a publisher.

printed circuit *n, electronics* an electronic circuit in which circuit components are connected by thin strips of a conducting material that are printed or etched on to the surface of a thin board of insulating material.

printer *n* 1 a person or business engaged in printing books, newspapers, etc. 2 a machine that prints, eg photographs. 3 *comput* a type of output device that produces printed copies of text or graphics on to paper.

printing *n* 1 the art or business of producing books, etc in print. 2 the run of books, etc printed all at one time; an impression. 3 the form of handwriting in which the letters are separately written.

printout *n, comput* output from a computer system in the form of a printed paper copy.

prior¹ *adj* **1** of an engagement: already arranged for the time in question; previous. **2** more urgent or pressing: *a prior claim.* ◆ **prior to sth** before an event.

prior² *n, Christianity* **1** the head of a community of certain orders of monks and friars. **2** in an abbey: the deputy of the abbot. ○ **prioress** *n.*

priority *n (-ies)* **1** the right to be or go first; precedence or preference. **2** something that must be attended to before anything else. **3** the fact or condition of being earlier. ○ **prioritize** or **-ise** *vb.*

priory *n (-ies) Christianity* a religious house under the supervision of a prior or prioress.

prise or *(US)* **prize** *vb* **1** to lever something open, off, out, etc, usu with some difficulty: *She prised open the lid.* **2** to get with difficulty: *I prised the truth out of her.*

prism *n* **1** *geom* a solid figure in which the two ends are matching parallel polygons (eg triangles or squares) and all other surfaces are parallelograms. **2** *optics* a transparent block, usu of glass and with triangular ends and rectangular sides, that separates a beam of white light into the colours of the visible spectrum.

prison *n* **1** a building for the confinement of convicted criminals and certain accused persons awaiting trial. **2** any place of confinement or situation of intolerable restriction. **3** custody; imprisonment.

prisoner *n* **1** someone who is under arrest or confined in prison. **2** a captive, esp in war. ◆ **take sb prisoner** to capture and hold them as a prisoner.

prisoner of conscience *n* someone imprisoned for their political beliefs.

prisoner of war *n* someone taken prisoner during a war, esp a member of the armed forces.

prissy *adj (-ier, -iest)* insipidly prim and prudish. ○ **prissily** *adv.*

pristine *adj* **1** fresh, clean, unused or untouched. **2** original; unchanged or unspoilt: *It's still in its pristine state.*

privacy *n* **1 a** freedom from intrusion by the public, esp as a right; **b** someone's right to this: *He should respect her privacy.* **2** seclusion; secrecy.

private *adj* **1** not open to, or available for the use of, the general public. **2** of a person: not holding public office. **3** kept secret from others; confidential. **4** relating to someone's personal, as distinct from their professional, life: *a private engagement.* **5** of thoughts or opinions: personal and usu kept to oneself. **6** quiet and reserved by nature. **7** of a place: secluded. **8 a** not coming under the state system of education, healthcare, social welfare, etc; **b** paid for or paying individually by fee, etc. ➤ *n*

1 a private soldier. **2 (privates)** *colloq* the PRIVATE PARTS. ○ **privately** *adv.* ◆ **in private** not in public; confidentially.

private detective or **private investigator** *n* someone who is not a member of the police force, engaged to do detective work.

private enterprise *n* the management and financing of industry, etc by private individuals or companies, not by the state.

privateer *n, hist* **1** a privately owned ship engaged by a government to seize and plunder an enemy's ships in wartime. **2** the commander or a crew member of such a ship.

private member *n* a member of a legislative body who does not hold a government office.

private parts *pl n, euphem* the external genitals and excretory organs.

private school *n* a school run independently by an individual or group, esp for profit.

private sector *n* that part of a country's economy consisting of privately owned businesses, etc.

privation *n* the condition of not having, or being deprived of, life's comforts or necessities; a lack of something particular.

privative /ˈprɪvətɪv/ *adj* lacking some quality that is usu, or expected to be, present.

privatize or **-ise** *vb* to transfer (a state-owned business) to private ownership. ○ **privatization** *n.*

privet *n* a shrub with glossy lance-shaped dark-green leaves, used esp in garden hedges.

privilege *n* **1** a right granted to an individual or a select few, bestowing an advantage not enjoyed by others. **2** advantages and power enjoyed by people of wealth and high social class. **3** an opportunity to do something that brings one delight; a pleasure or honour. ➤ *vb, tr & intr* to grant a right, privilege or special favour to someone or something. ○ **privileged** *adj.*

privy *adj* **1** *(usu* **privy to sth***)* allowed to share in (secret discussions, etc) or know about secret plans, happenings, etc. **2** *old use* secret; hidden. ➤ *n (-ies) old use* a lavatory.

prize¹ *n* **1** something won in a competition, lottery, etc. **2** a reward given in recognition of excellence. **3** something striven for, or worth striving for. **4** something captured or taken by force, esp a ship in war; a trophy. ➤ *adj* **1** deserving, or having won, a prize: *a prize bull.* **2** highly valued: *her prize possession.* **3** *ironic* perfect; great: *a prize fool.* **4** belonging or relating to, or given as, a prize: *prize money.* ➤ *vb* to value or regard highly.

prize² see PRISE

prizefight *n* a boxing-match fought for a money prize. ○ **prizefighter** *n.*

pro¹ *prep* in favour of something. ➤ *n* a reason, argument or choice in favour of something. ➤ *adv, colloq* in favour: *I thought he would argue pro.* Compare ANTI.

pro² *n, colloq* **1** a professional. **2** a prostitute.

pro- *pfx, signifying* **1** in favour of: *pro-hunting.*

Compare ANTI- (sense I). **2** in place of: *pro-vice-chancellor*.

proactive *adj* actively initiating change in anticipation of future developments, rather than merely reacting to events as they occur.

probability *n* (*-ies*) **1** the state of being probable; likelihood. **2** something that is probable. **3** *stats* a mathematical expression of the likelihood or chance of a particular event occurring, usu expressed as a fraction or numeral: *a probability of one in four*. ◆ **in all probability** most probably.

probable *adj* **1** likely to happen: *a probable outcome*. **2** likely to be the case; likely to have happened. **3** of an explanation, etc: likely to be correct; feasible. ➢ *n* someone or something likely to be selected. ○ **probably** *adv.*

probate *n* **1** *law* the process of establishing that a will is valid. **2** an official copy of a will, with the document certifying its validity.

probation *n* **1** the system whereby offenders, esp young or first offenders, are allowed their freedom under supervision, on condition of good behaviour. **2** in certain types of employment: a trial period during which a new employee is observed on the job, to confirm whether or not they can do it satisfactorily. ○ **probationary** *adj.*

probationer *n* someone on probation.

probe *n* **1** a long, slender and usu metal instrument used by doctors to examine a wound, locate a bullet, etc. **2** a comprehensive investigation. **3** (*also* **space probe**) an unmanned spacecraft designed to study conditions in space, esp around one or more planets or their natural satellites. **4** an act of probing; a poke or prod. ➢ *vb* (*often* **probe into sth**) **1** to investigate it closely. **2** *tr & intr* to examine it with a probe. **3** *tr & intr* to poke or prod it.

probity *n* integrity; honesty.

problem *n* **1** a situation or matter that is difficult to understand or deal with: *a problem with the software* • *a drink problem*. **2** someone or something that is difficult to deal with. **3** a puzzle or mathematical question set for solving. ➢ *adj* **1** of a child, etc: difficult to deal with, esp in being disruptive or antisocial. **2** of a play, etc: dealing with a moral or social problem. ◆ **no problem** *colloq* **1** said in response to a request, or to thanks: it's a pleasure, no trouble, etc. **2** easily: *We found our way, no problem*.

problematic or **problematical** *adj* **1** causing problems. **2** uncertain.

proboscis /prəʊˈbɒsɪs/ *n* (**proboscises** or **proboscides** /-sɪdiːz/) **1** *zool* the flexible elongated snout of certain animals, eg the elephant. **2** *biol* the elongated tubular mouthparts of certain insects, eg the butterfly.

procedure *n* **1** the method and order followed in doing something. **2** an established routine for conducting business at a meeting or in a law case. **3** a course of action; a step or measure taken. ○ **procedural** *adj.*

proceed *vb, intr* **1** *formal* to make one's way: *I proceeded along the road*. **2** (*often* **proceed with sth**) to go on with it; to continue after stopping. **3** to set about a task, etc. **4** *colloq* to begin: *He proceeded to question her*. **5** (**proceed from sth**) to arise from it. **6** (*often* **proceed against sb**) *law* to take legal action against them.

proceeding *n* **1** an action; a piece of behaviour. **2** (**proceedings**) a published record of the business done or papers read at a meeting of a society, etc. **3** (**proceedings**) legal action: *divorce proceedings*.

proceeds *pl n* money made by an event, sale, transaction, etc.

process *n* **1** a series of operations performed during manufacture, etc. **2** a series of stages which a product, etc passes through, resulting in the development or transformation of it. **3** an operation or procedure: *a slow process*. **4** *anat* a projection or outgrowth, esp one on a bone: *the mastoid process*. **5** *law* a writ by which a person or matter is brought into court. **6** any series of changes, esp natural ones: *the aging process*. ➢ *vb* **1** to put something through the required process; to deal with (eg an application) appropriately. **2** to prepare (agricultural produce) for marketing, eg by canning, bottling or treating it chemically. **3** *comput* to perform operations on (data, etc). ◆ **in the process of sth** in the course of it.

procession *n* **1** a file of people or vehicles proceeding ceremonially in orderly formation. **2** this kind of succession or sequence.

processor *n* **1** *often in compounds* a machine or person that processes something: *word processor* • *food processor*. **2** *comput* a CENTRAL PROCESSING UNIT.

pro-choice *adj* supporting the right of a woman to have an abortion. Compare PRO-LIFE.

proclaim *vb* **1** to announce something publicly. **2** to declare someone to be something: *He was proclaimed a traitor*. **3** to attest or prove something all too clearly: *Cigar smoke proclaimed his presence*. ○ **proclamation** *n.*

proclivity *n* (*-ies*) *rather formal* a tendency, liking or preference.

procrastinate *vb, intr* to put off doing something that should be done straight away. ○ **procrastination** *n.* ○ **procrastinator** *n.*

procreate *vb, tr & intr* to produce (offspring); to reproduce. ○ **procreation** *n.* ○ **procreative** *adj.*

proctor *n* in some English universities: an official whose functions include enforcement of discipline. ○ **proctorial** *adj.*

procurator *n* an agent with power of attorney in a law court.

procurator fiscal *n, Scot* a district official who combines the roles of coroner and public prosecutor.

procure *vb* **1** to manage to obtain something or bring it about. **2** *tr & intr* to get (women or girls) to act as prostitutes. ○ **procurable** *adj.* ○ **procurement** *n.*

prod vb (**prodded, prodding**) 1 (often **prod at sth**) to poke or jab it. 2 to nudge, prompt or spur (a person or animal) into action. ➤ n 1 a poke, jab or nudge. 2 a reminder. 3 a pointed instrument.

prodigal adj 1 heedlessly extravagant or wasteful. 2 (often **prodigal of sth**) formal or old use lavish in bestowing it; generous. ➤ n 1 a squanderer, wastrel or spendthrift. 2 (also **prodigal son**) a repentant ne'er-do-well or a returned wanderer. ○ **prodigality** n. ○ **prodigally** adv.

prodigious adj 1 extraordinary or marvellous. 2 enormous; vast. ○ **prodigiously** adv.

prodigy n (**-ies**) 1 something that causes astonishment. 2 someone, esp a child, of extraordinary talent.

produce vb / prə'dʒuːs/ 1 to bring out or present something to view. 2 to bear (children, young, leaves, etc). 3 tr & intr to yield (crops, fruit, etc). 4 to secrete (a substance), give off (a smell), etc. 5 tr & intr to make or manufacture something. 6 to give rise to or prompt (a reaction) from people. 7 to direct (a play), arrange (a radio or television programme) for presentation, or finance and schedule the making of (a film). ➤ n / 'prɒdʒuːs/ foodstuffs derived from crops or animal livestock, eg fruit, vegetables, eggs and dairy products. ○ **producible** adj.

producer n a person, organization or thing that produces.

product n 1 something produced, eg through manufacture or agriculture. 2 a result: the product of much thought. 3 maths the value obtained by multiplying two or more numbers.

production n 1 a the act of producing; b the process of producing or being produced: The new model goes into production next year. 2 the quantity produced or rate of producing it. 3 something created; a literary or artistic work. 4 a particular presentation of a play, opera, ballet, etc.

productive adj 1 yielding a lot; fertile; fruitful. 2 useful; profitable: a productive meeting. 3 (usu **productive of sth**) giving rise to it; resulting in it: productive of ideas.

productivity n the rate and efficiency of work, esp in industrial production, etc.

proem / 'prəʊem/ n an introduction, prelude or preface, esp at the beginning of a book.

Prof. abbrev Professor.

prof n, colloq a professor.

profane adj 1 showing disrespect for sacred things. 2 not sacred or spiritual; temporal or worldly. 3 esp of language: vulgar; blasphemous. ➤ vb 1 to treat (something sacred) irreverently. 2 to violate or defile (what should be respected). ○ **profanation** n. ○ **profanity** n (**-ies**).

profess vb 1 to make an open declaration of (beliefs, etc). 2 to declare adherence to something. 3 to claim or pretend: I don't profess to be an expert.

professed adj 1 self-acknowledged; self-confessed. 2 claimed by oneself; pretended. 3 having taken the vows of a religious order.

profession n 1 an occupation, esp one that requires specialist academic and practical training, eg medicine, teaching, etc. 2 the body of people engaged in a particular one of these. 3 an act of professing; a declaration: a profession of loyalty. 4 a declaration of religious belief made upon entering a religious order.

professional adj 1 earning a living in the performance, practice or teaching of something that is usu a pastime: a professional golfer. 2 belonging to a trained profession. 3 like, appropriate to or having the competence, expertise or conscientiousness of someone with professional training: She did a very professional job. ➤ n 1 someone who belongs to one of the skilled professions. 2 someone who makes their living in an activity, etc that is also carried on at an amateur level. ○ **professionalism** n. ○ **professionally** adv.

professor n 1 a teacher of the highest rank in a university; the head of a university department. 2 N Am, esp US a university teacher. ○ **professorial** / profɛ'sɔːrɪəl/ adj. ○ **professorship** n.

proffer vb to offer something for someone to accept.

proficient adj fully trained and competent. ○ **proficiency** n.

profile n 1 a a side view of something, esp of a face or head; b a representation of this. 2 a brief outline, sketch or assessment. ➤ vb 1 to represent in profile. 2 to give a brief outline (of a person, their career, a company, prospects, etc). ♦ **in profile** from the side view. **keep a low profile** to maintain a unobtrusive presence.

profit n 1 the money gained from selling something for more than it originally cost. 2 an excess of income over expenses. 3 advantage or benefit. ➤ vb (**profited, profiting**) intr (often **profit from** or **by sth**) to benefit from it.

profitable adj 1 of a business, etc: making a profit. 2 useful; fruitful. ○ **profitability** n.

profiteer n someone who takes advantage of a shortage or other emergency to make exorbitant profits. ➤ vb, intr to make profits in such a way.

profligate / 'prɒflɪgət/ adj 1 immoral and irresponsible; licentious or dissolute. 2 scandalously extravagant. ➤ n a profligate person. ○ **profligacy** n.

profound adj 1 radical, extensive, farreaching: profound changes. 2 deep; far below the surface. 3 of a feeling: deeply felt or rooted. 4 of comments, etc: showing understanding or penetration. 5 penetrating deeply into knowledge. 6 intense; impenetrable: profound deafness. 7 of sleep: deep; sound. ○ **profoundly** adv. ○ **profundity** n.

profuse adj 1 overflowing; exaggerated; excessive: profuse apologies. 2 copious: profuse bleeding. ○ **profusely** adv. ○ **profusion** or **profuseness** n.

progenitor n 1 an ancestor, forebear or forefather. 2 the founder or originator of a movement, etc.

progeny n (-ies) 1 children; offspring; descendants. 2 a result or conclusion.

progesterone n, biochem a steroid sex hormone that prepares the lining of the uterus for implantation of a fertilized egg.

prognosis n (-ses) 1 an informed forecast of developments in any situation. 2 a doctor's prediction regarding the probable course of a disease, disorder or injury.

prognostic adj serving as an informed forecast.

prognosticate vb 1 to foretell. 2 to indicate in advance; to be a sign of something. ○ **prognostication** n. ○ **prognosticator** n.

programmable adj capable of being programmed to perform a task automatically.

programme or (US) **program** n 1 a the schedule of proceedings for, and list of participants in, a theatre performance, entertainment, ceremony, etc; **b** a leaflet or booklet describing these. 2 an agenda, plan or schedule. 3 a series of planned projects to be undertaken. 4 a scheduled radio or TV presentation. 5 (usu **program**) comput a set of coded instructions to a computer for the performance of a task or a series of operations, written in a PROGRAMMING LANGUAGE. ➢ vb 1 to include something in a programme; to schedule. 2 to draw up a programme for something. 3 to set (a computer) by program to perform a set of operations. 4 to prepare a program for a computer. 5 to set (a machine) so as to operate at the required time. 6 to train to respond in a specified way.

programmer n someone who writes computer programs (see PROGRAMME noun sense 5).

programming language n, comput any system of codes, symbols, rules, etc designed for writing computer programs (see PROGRAMME noun sense 5).

progress n /ˈprəʊɡrɛs; N Am ˈprɒ-/ 1 movement while travelling in any direction. 2 course: I followed the progress of the trial. 3 movement towards a destination, goal or state of completion: She made slow progress. 4 advances or development. ➢ vb /prəˈɡrɛs/ 1 intr to move forwards or onwards; to proceed towards a goal. 2 intr to advance or develop. 3 intr to improve. 4 to put (something planned) into operation. ◆ **in progress** taking place.

progression n 1 an act or the process of moving forwards or advancing in stages. 2 improvement. 3 maths a sequence of numbers, each of which bears a specific relationship to the preceding term.

progressive adj 1 advanced in outlook; using or favouring new methods. 2 moving forward or advancing continuously or by stages. 3 of a disease: continuously increasing in severity or complication. 4 of a dance or game: involving changes of partner at intervals. 5 of taxation:

increasing as the sum taxed increases. 6 gram of a verbal aspect or tense: expressing continuing action or a continuing state, formed in English with be and the present PARTICIPLE, as in I am doing it and they will be going. ➢ n 1 someone with progressive ideas. 2 gram a the progressive aspect or tense; **b** a verb in a progressive aspect or tense. ○ **progressively** adv. ○ **progressivist** n, adj.

prohibit vb (**prohibited, prohibiting**) 1 to forbid something, esp by law. 2 to prevent or hinder.

prohibition n 1 the act of prohibiting or state of being prohibited. 2 a law or decree that prohibits something. 3 a ban by law, esp in the US from 1920–1933, on the manufacture and sale of alcoholic drinks. ○ **prohibitionist** n.

prohibitive or **prohibitory** adj 1 banning; prohibiting. 2 tending to prevent or discourage. 3 of prices, etc: unaffordably high. ○ **prohibitively** adv.

project n /ˈprɒdʒɛkt/ 1 a plan, scheme or proposal. 2 a research or study assignment. ➢ vb /prəˈdʒɛkt/ 1 intr to jut out. 2 to throw something forwards; to propel. 3 to throw (a shadow, image, etc) on to a surface, screen, etc. 4 to propose or plan. 5 to forecast something from present trends and other known data. 6 to imagine (oneself) in another situation, esp a future one. 7 to cause (a sound, esp the voice) to be heard clearly at some distance.

projectile n an object designed to be projected by an external force, eg a guided missile, bullet, etc. ➢ adj 1 capable of being, or designed to be, hurled. 2 projecting.

projection n 1 the act of projecting or process of being projected. 2 something that protrudes from a surface. 3 the process of showing of a film or transparencies on a screen. 4 a forecast based on present trends and other known data. 5 maths esp on maps: the representation of a solid object, esp part of the Earth's sphere, on a flat surface. 6 psychol the reading of one's own emotions and experiences into a particular situation. ○ **projectionist** n someone who operates a projector.

projector n an instrument containing a system of lenses that projects an enlarged version of an illuminated still or moving image on to a screen.

prolapse n, pathol the slipping out of place or falling down of an organ, esp the slipping of the uterus into the vagina. ➢ vb, intr of an organ: to slip out of place.

prolate adj, geom of something approximately spherical: more pointed at the poles. Compare OBLATE.

prole n, adj, derog colloq proletarian.

proletarian /prəʊləˈtɛərɪən/ adj relating to the proletariat. ➢ n a member of the proletariat.

proletariat /prəʊləˈtɛərɪət/ n 1 the working class, esp unskilled labourers and industrial workers. 2 hist in ancient Rome: the lowest class of people.

pro-life adj of a person or an organization: opposing abortion, euthanasia and experimentation on human embryos. Compare PRO-CHOICE.

proliferate *vb* **1** *intr* of a plant or animal species: to reproduce rapidly. **2** *intr* to increase in numbers; to multiply. **3** to reproduce (cells, etc) rapidly. ○ **proliferation** *n*.

prolific *adj* **1** abundant in growth; producing plentiful fruit or offspring. **2** of a writer, artist, etc: constantly producing new work. **3** (*often* **prolific of** or **in sth**) productive of it; abounding in it. ○ **prolifically** *adv.*

prolix *adj* of speech or writing: tediously long-winded. ○ **prolixity** *n*.

prologue *n* **1** *theat* **a** a speech addressed to the audience at the beginning of a play; **b** the actor delivering it. **2** a preface to a literary work. **3** an event serving as an introduction or prelude.

prolong *vb* to make something longer; to extend or protract. ○ **prolongation** *n*.

prom *n*, *colloq* **1** a walkway or promenade. **2** a concert at which the audience stands and can move about. **3** *orig N Am* a formal school or college dance at the end of the academic year.

promenade *n* **1** a broad paved walk, esp along a seafront. **2** *facetious* a stately stroll. ➤ *vb* **1** *intr* to stroll in a stately fashion. **2** to walk (the streets, etc). **3** to take someone out for some fresh air. ○ **promenader** *n*.

Promethean *adj* daring and skilfully inventive.

promethium *n*, *chem* a radioactive metallic element that occurs naturally in minute amounts and is manufactured artificially by bombarding neodymium with neutrons.

prominence *n* **1** the state or quality of being prominent. **2** a prominent point or thing. **3** a projection.

prominent *adj* **1** jutting out; projecting; protruding; bulging. **2** noticeable; conspicuous. **3** leading; notable.

promiscuous *adj* **1** indulging in casual or indiscriminate sexual relations. **2** haphazardly mixed. ○ **promiscuity** /prɒmɪˈskjuːɪtɪ/ *n*. ○ **promiscuously** *adv.*

promise *vb* **1** *tr & intr* to give an undertaking (to do or not do something). **2** to undertake to give something to someone: *I promised him a treat.* **3** to show signs of bringing something: *Those clouds promise rain.* **4** to look likely (to do something): *It promises to have a great future.* **5** to assure or warn: *I promise nothing bad will happen.* ➤ *n* **1** an assurance to give, do or not do something. **2** a sign: *the promise of spring in the air.* **3** signs of future excellence.

promised land *n* **1** *Bible* in the Old Testament: the fertile land promised by God to the Israelites. **2** *Christianity* heaven. **3** any longed-for place of contentment and prosperity.

promising *adj* **1** showing promise; talented; apt. **2** seeming to bode well for the future: *a promising start.*

promissory *adj* containing, relating to or expressing a promise.

promo *n*, *colloq* something which is used to publicize a product, esp a video for a pop single.

promontory *n* (*-ies*) a usu hilly part of a coastline that projects into the sea.

promote *vb* **1 a** to raise someone to a more senior position; **b** *sport, esp football* to transfer (a team) to a higher division or league. **2** to contribute to something: *Exercise promotes health.* **3** to work for the cause of something: *He tirelessly promotes peace.* **4** to try to boost the sales of (a product) by advertising. ○ **promotion** *n*. ○ **promotional** *adj.*

promoter *n* the organizer or financer of a sporting event or other undertaking.

prompt *adj* **1** immediate; quick; punctual. **2** instantly willing; ready; unhesitating. ➤ *adv* punctually. ➤ *n* **1** something serving as a reminder. **2** *theat* words supplied by a prompter to an actor. **3** *theat* a prompter. **4** *comput* a sign on the screen indicating that the computer is ready for input. ➤ *vb* **1** to cause, lead or remind someone to do something. **2** to produce or elicit (a reaction or response). **3** *tr & intr* to help (an actor) to remember their next words by supplying the first few. ○ **promptly** *adv.* ○ **promptness** *n*.

prompter *n* **1** *theat* someone positioned offstage to prompt actors if they forget their lines. **2** someone or something that prompts.

promulgate *vb* **1** to make (a decree, etc) effective by means of an official public announcement. **2** to publicize or promote (an idea, theory, etc) widely. ○ **promulgation** *n*. ○ **promulgator** *n*.

prone *adj* **1** lying flat, esp face downwards. **2** (*often* **prone to sth**) predisposed to it, or liable to suffer from it. **3** inclined or liable to do something.

prong *n* **1** a point or spike, esp one of those making up the head of a fork. **2** any pointed projection.

pronominal *adj*, *gram* referring to or of the nature of a pronoun.

pronoun *n*, *gram* a word such as *she*, *him*, *they*, *it*, etc used in place of, and to refer to, a noun, phrase, clause, etc.

pronounce *vb* **1** to say or utter (words, sounds, letters, etc); to articulate or enunciate. **2** to declare something officially, formally or authoritatively: *He pronounced her innocent.* **3** to pass or deliver (judgement). **4** *intr* (*usu* **pronounce on sth**) to give an opinion or verdict on it. ○ **pronounceable** *adj.*

pronounced *adj* **1** noticeable; distinct: *a pronounced limp.* **2** spoken; articulated.

pronouncement *n* **1** a formal announcement. **2** a declaration of opinion; a verdict.

pronto *adv*, *colloq* immediately.

pronunciation *n* **1** the act or a manner of pronouncing words, sounds, letters, etc. **2** the correct way of pronouncing a word, sound, etc in a given language.

proof *n* **1** evidence, esp conclusive evidence,

that something is true or a fact. **2** *law* the accumulated evidence on which a verdict is based. **3** the activity or process of testing or proving. **4** a test, trial or demonstration. **5** *maths* a step-by-step verification of a proposed mathematical statement. **6** *printing* a trial copy of printed text used for examination or correction. **7** a trial print from a photographic negative. **8** a trial impression from an engraved plate. **9** a measure of the alcohol content of a distilled liquid, esp an alcoholic beverage, equal to 49.28% of alcohol by weight. ➢ *adj, esp in compounds* able or designed to withstand, deter or be free from or secure against a specified thing: *proof against storms • leakproof*. ➢ *vb* **1** *often in compounds* to make something resistant to or proof against a specified thing: *They damp-proofed the walls*. **2** to take a proof of (printed material). **3** to proof-read.

proof-read *vb, tr & intr* to read and mark for correction the proofs of (a text, etc). ○ **proof-reader** *n.* ○ **proof-reading** *n.*

proof spirit *n* a standard mixture of alcohol and water containing 49.28% alcohol by weight or 57.1% by volume.

prop¹ *n* **1** a rigid support, esp a vertical one: *a clothes prop*. **2** a person or thing that one depends on for help or emotional support. **3** (*also* **prop forward**) *rugby* **a** the position at either end of the front row of the scrum; **b** a player in this position. ➢ *vb* (**propped, propping**) **1** (*often* **prop sth up**) to support or hold it upright with, or as if with, a prop. **2** (*usu* **prop against sth**) to lean against it; to put something against something else. **3** to serve as a prop to something.

prop² *n, colloq* (*in full* **property**) *theat* a portable object or piece of furniture used on stage.

prop³ *n, colloq* a propeller.

propaganda *n* **1 a** the organized circulation by a political group, etc of doctrine, information, misinformation, rumour or opinion, intended to influence public feeling, raise public awareness, bring about reform, etc; **b** the material circulated in this way. **2** (**Propaganda**) a Roman Catholic committee responsible for foreign missions and the training of missionaries. ○ **propagandist** *n.*

propagate *vb* **1** *tr & intr, bot* of a plant: to multiply. **2** *bot* to grow (new plants), either by natural means or artificially. **3** to spread or popularize (ideas, etc). **4** *physics* to transmit energy, eg sound or electromagnetism, over a distance in wave form. ○ **propagation** *n.* ○ **propagator** *n.*

propane *n, chem* a colourless odourless flammable gas, obtained from petroleum and used as a fuel.

propanone *n* ACETONE.

propel *vb* (**propelled, propelling**) **1** to drive or push something forward. **2** to steer or send someone or something in a certain direction.

propellant *n* **1** *chem* a compressed inert gas in an aerosol that is used to release the liquid contents as a fine spray when the pressure is released. **2** *eng* the fuel and oxidizer that are burned in a rocket in order to provide thrust. **3** something that propels.

propeller *n* a device consisting of a revolving hub with radiating blades that produce thrust or power, used to propel aircraft, ships, etc.

propensity *n* (**-ies**) a tendency or inclination.

proper *adj* **1** real; genuine; able to be correctly described as (a specified thing). **2** right; correct. **3** appropriate: *at the proper time*. **4** own; particular; correct: *in its proper place*. **5** socially accepted; respectable. **6** *derog* morally strict; prim. **7** (*usu* **proper to sth**) belonging or appropriate to it; suitable: *the form of address proper to her rank*. **8** used immediately after a noun: strictly so called; itself, excluding others not immediately connected with it: *We are now entering the city proper*. **9** *colloq* utter; complete; out-and-out: *a proper idiot*.

proper fraction *n, maths* a fraction in which the NUMERATOR is less than the DENOMINATOR, eg ½ or ³/₇. Compare IMPROPER FRACTION.

properly *adv* **1** suitably; appropriately; correctly. **2** with strict accuracy. **3** fully; thoroughly; completely.

proper noun or **proper name** *n, gram* the name of a particular person, place or thing, eg *Kurt, Clapham*.

property *n* (**-ies**) **1** something someone owns. **2** possessions collectively. **3** the concept of ownership. **4 a** land or real estate; **b** an item of this. **5** a quality or attribute: *It has the property of dissolving easily*. **6** a PROP².

prophecy *n* (**-ies**) **1 a** the interpretation of divine will; **b** the act of revealing such interpretations. **2 a** the foretelling of the future; **b** something foretold; a prediction. **3** a gift or aptitude for predicting the future.

prophesy *vb* (**-ies, -ied**) **1** *tr & intr* to foretell (future happenings); to predict. **2** *intr* to utter prophecies; to interpret divine will.

prophet *n* **1** someone who is able to express the will of God or a god. **2** *Bible* **a** any of the writers of prophecy in the Old Testament; **b** any of the books attributed to them. **3** *Islam* (**the Prophet**) Muhammad. **4** someone who claims to be able to tell what will happen in the future: *a prophet of doom*. **5** a leading advocate of or spokesperson for a movement or cause. ○ **prophetess** *n.*

prophetic *adj* **1** foretelling the future. **2** relating or belonging to prophets or prophecy. ○ **prophetically** *adv.*

prophylactic *adj* guarding against or tending to prevent disease or other mishap. ➢ *n* **1** a prophylactic drug or device; a precautionary measure. **2** a condom.

propinquity *n* **1** nearness in place or time. **2** closeness of kinship.

propitiate /prə'pɪʃɪeɪt/ *vb* to appease or placate (an angry or insulted person or god).

○ **propitiable** adj. ○ **propitiation** n. ○ **pro-pitiator** n. ○ **propitiatory** adj.

propitious /prə'pɪʃəs/ adj 1 favourable; auspicious; advantageous. 2 (often **propitious for** or **to sth**) likely to favour or encourage it. ○ **propitiously** adv.

proponent n a supporter or advocate of something.

proportion n 1 a comparative part of a total: a large proportion of the population. 2 the size of one element or group in relation to the whole or total. 3 the size of one group or component in relation to another: in a proportion of two parts to one. 4 the correct balance between parts or elements: out of proportion. 5 (**proportions**) size; dimensions: a garden of large proportions. 6 maths correspondence between the ratios of two pairs of quantities, as expressed in 2 is to 8 as 3 is to 12. ➤ vb to adjust the proportions, or balance the parts, of something. ◆ **in proportion to sth** 1 in relation to it; in comparison with it. 2 in parallel with it; in correspondence with it; at the same time.

proportional adj 1 corresponding or matching in size, rate, etc. 2 in correct proportion; proportionate.

proportional representation n (abbrev **PR**) any electoral system in which the number of representatives each political party has in parliament is in direct proportion to the number of votes it receives.

proportionate adj (**proportionate to sth**) due or in correct proportion. ○ **proportionately** adv.

proposal n 1 the act of proposing something. 2 something proposed or suggested. 3 an offer of marriage.

propose vb 1 to offer (a plan, etc) for consideration; to suggest. 2 to suggest or nominate someone for a position, task, etc. 3 to be the proposer of (the motion in a debate). 4 to intend (to do something): I don't propose to sell. 5 to suggest (a specified person, topic, etc) as the subject of a toast. 6 intr (often **propose to sb**) to make them an offer of marriage. ○ **proposer** n.

proposition n 1 a proposal or suggestion: an awkward proposition. 2 something to be dealt with or undertaken: an awkward proposition. 3 euphem, colloq an invitation to have sexual intercourse. 4 logic a form of statement affirming or denying something, that can be true or false; a premise. 5 maths a statement of a problem or theorem, esp one that incorporates its solution or proof. ➤ vb, euphem, colloq to propose sexual intercourse to someone.

propound vb to put forward (an idea or theory, etc) for consideration.

proprietary adj 1 of rights: belonging to an owner or proprietor. 2 suggestive or indicative of ownership. 3 of medicines, etc: marketed under a tradename. 4 esp Aust, NZ & S Afr (abbrev **Pty**) of a company etc: privately owned and managed.

proprietary name n a TRADENAME.

proprietor or **proprietress** n an owner, esp of a shop, hotel, business, etc. ○ **proprietorial** adj.

propriety n (**-ies**) 1 conformity to socially acceptable behaviour, esp between the sexes; modesty or decorum. 2 correctness; moral acceptability. 3 (**proprieties**) accepted standards of conduct.

propulsion n 1 the act of causing something to move forward. 2 also in compounds a force exerted against a body which makes it move forward: jet propulsion. ○ **propulsive** adj.

pro rata adv in proportion; in accordance with a certain rate.

prorogue /prou'roug/ vb, formal 1 to discontinue the meetings of (a legislative assembly) for a time, without dissolving it. 2 intr of a legislative assembly: to suspend a session. ○ **prorogation** n.

prosaic /prou'zeɪk/ adj 1 unpoetic; unimaginative. 2 dull, ordinary and uninteresting. ○ **prosaically** adv.

pros and cons pl n the various advantages and disadvantages of a course of action, idea, etc.

proscenium /prou'si:nɪəm/ n (**prosceniums** or **proscenia** /-ə/) theat 1 the part of a stage in front of the curtain. 2 (also **proscenium arch**) the arch framing the stage and separating it from the auditorium.

proscribe vb 1 to prohibit or condemn something (eg a practice). 2 hist to outlaw or exile someone. ○ **proscription** n. ○ **proscriptive** adj.

proscribe A word sometimes confused with this one is **prescribe**.

prose n 1 the ordinary form of written or spoken language as distinct from verse or poetry. 2 a passage of prose set for translation into a foreign language. 3 uninteresting discussion or speech, etc.

prosecute vb 1 tr & intr to bring a criminal action against someone. 2 formal to carry on or carry out something (eg enquiries). ○ **prosecutable** adj. ○ **prosecutor** n.

prosecution n 1 the act of prosecuting or process of being prosecuted. 2 the bringing of a criminal action against someone. 3 a the prosecuting party in a criminal case; b the lawyers involved in this. 4 formal the process of carrying something out.

proselyte /'prɒsəlaɪt/ n a convert, esp a Gentile turning to Judaism. ○ **proselytism** /'prɒsəlɪtɪzəm/ n.

proselytize or **-ise** /'prɒsəlɪtaɪz/ vb, tr & intr to try to convert someone from one faith to another; to make converts. ○ **proselytizer** n.

prosody /'prɒsədɪ/ n 1 the study of verse composition, esp poetic metre. 2 (also **prosodics** /prə'sɒdɪks/) the study of rhythm, stress and intonation in speech. ○ **prosodic** /-'sɒdɪk/ adj. ○ **prosodist** n.

prospect n /'prɒspekt/ 1 an expectation of

something due or likely to happen. **2** an outlook for the future. **3** (**prospects**) chances of success, improvement, recovery, etc. **4** (**prospects**) opportunities for advancement, promotion, etc: *a job with prospects.* **5** a potentially selectable candidate, team member, etc: *He's a doubtful prospect for Saturday's match.* **6** a potential client or customer. **7** a broad view. ➢ *vb* /prə'spɛkt/ **1** *tr & intr* to search or explore (an area, region, etc) for gold or other minerals. **2** *intr* to hunt for or look out for (eg a job). ◆ **in prospect** expected soon.

prospective *adj* likely or expected; future.

prospector *n* someone prospecting for oil, gold, etc.

prospectus *n* **1** a brochure giving information about a school or other institution, esp about the courses on offer. **2** a document outlining a proposal for something, eg an issue of shares.

prosper *vb, intr* **1** of someone: to do well, esp financially. **2** of a business, etc: to thrive or flourish. ○ **prosperity** *n*.

prosperous *adj* wealthy and successful. ○ **prosperously** *adv.*

prostate *n* (*in full* **prostate gland**) *anat* in male mammals: a muscular gland around the base of the bladder which produces an alkaline fluid that activates sperm during ejaculation.

prostate, prostrate These words are often confused with each other.

prosthesis /prɒs'θiːsɪs/ *n* (*-ses* /-siːz/) *med* an artificial substitute for a part of the body that is missing or non-functional, eg dentures, an artificial limb or breast or a pacemaker. ○ **prosthetic** /-'θɛtɪk/ *adj.*

prosthetics *sing n* the branch of surgery concerned with supplying and fitting prostheses.

prostitute *n* **1** also in compounds someone who performs sexual acts or intercourse in return for money. **2** someone who offers their skills or talents, etc for unworthy ends. ➢ *vb* **1** to offer (oneself or someone else) as a prostitute. **2** to put (eg one's talents) to an unworthy use. ○ **prostitution** *n.*

prostrate *adj* /'prɒstreɪt/ **1** lying face downwards in an attitude of abject submission, humility or adoration. **2** distraught with illness, grief, exhaustion, etc. ➢ *vb* /prə'streɪt/ **1** to throw (oneself) face down in submission or adoration. **2** of exhaustion, illness, grief, etc: to overwhelm someone physically or emotionally. ○ **prostration** *n.*

prosy *adj* (*-ier, -iest*) of speech or writing: **1** prose-like. **2** dull and tedious.

protactinium *n, chem* a white highly toxic radioactive metallic element.

protagonist *n* **1** the main character in a play, story, film, etc. **2** any person at the centre of a story or event. **3** *non-standard* a leader or champion of a movement or cause, etc.

protean /'prəʊtɪən/ *adj* **1** readily able to change shape or appearance; variable; changeable. **2** esp of a writer, artist, actor, etc: versatile.

protect *vb* **1** to shield someone or something from danger; to guard them or it against injury, destruction, etc; to keep safe. **2** to shield (home industries) from foreign competition by taxing imports.

protection *n* **1** the action of protecting or condition of being protected; shelter, refuge, cover, safety or care. **2** something that protects. **3** (*also* **protectionism**) the system of protecting home industries against foreign competition by taxing imports. **4** *colloq* **a** the criminal practice of extorting money from shop-owners, etc in return for leaving their premises unharmed; **b** (*also* **protection money**) the money extorted in this way. ○ **protectionist** *n.*

protective *adj* **1** giving or designed to give protection: *protective clothing.* **2** inclined or tending to protect. ➢ *n* **1** something which protects. **2** a condom. ○ **protectively** *adv.* ○ **protectiveness** *n.*

protector or **protectress** *n* **1** someone or something that protects. **2** a patron or benefactor. **3** someone who rules a country during the childhood, absence or incapacity of a sovereign. ○ **protectorship** *n.*

protectorate *n* **1** the office or period of rule of a protector. **2 a** a protectorship of a weak country assumed by a more powerful one without actual annexation; **b** the territory that is so protected.

protégé or **protégée** /'prəʊtəʒeɪ/ *n* a person (male and female respectively) under the guidance, protection, patronage, etc of someone wiser or more important.

protein *n, biochem* any of thousands of different organic compounds, characteristic of all living organisms, that have large molecules consisting of long chains of amino acids.

Proterozoic /prəʊtərəʊ'zəʊɪk/ *geol, adj* **1** relating to the geological era from which the oldest forms of life date. **2** *sometimes* denoting the entire PRECAMBRIAN period. ➢ *n* (**the Proterozoic**) the Proterozoic era.

protest *vb* /prə'tɛst/ **1** *intr* to express an objection, disapproval, opposition or disagreement. **2** *N Am, esp US* to challenge or object to (eg a decision or measure). **3** to declare something solemnly, eg in response to an accusation: *She protested her innocence.* ➢ *n* /'prəʊtɛst/ **1** a declaration of disapproval or dissent; an objection. **2** an organized public demonstration of disapproval. **3** the act of protesting. ○ **protestation** *n.* ○ **protester** or **protestor** *n.* ◆ **under protest** reluctantly; unwillingly.

Protestant or **protestant** *n* **1** a member of any of the Christian Churches which embraced the principles of the Reformation and, rejecting the authority of the Pope, separated from the Roman Catholic Church. **2** a member of any body descended from these. ➢ *adj* relating or belonging to Protestants. ○ **Protestantism** *n.*

protocol *n* **1** correct formal or diplomatic etiquette or procedure. **2** a first draft of a diplomatic document, eg one setting out the terms of a treaty. **3** *N Am, esp US* a plan of a scientific experiment or other procedure.

proton *n, physics* any of the positively charged subatomic particles that are found inside the nucleus at the centre of an atom.

protoplasm *n, biol* the mass of protein material of which cells are composed, consisting of the cytoplasm and usu a nucleus. ◇ **protoplasmic** *adj*.

prototype *n* **1** an original model from which later forms are copied, developed or derived. **2** a first working version, eg of a vehicle or aircraft. ◇ **prototypical** *adj*.

protozoan /prəʊtəˈzəʊən/ *n* (**protozoa** /-ˈzəʊə/) a single-celled organism, eg an amoeba.

protract *vb* **1** to prolong; to cause something to last a long time. **2** to lengthen something out. ◇ **protracted** *adj*. ◇ **protraction** *n*.

protractor *n, geom* an instrument, usu a transparent plastic semicircle marked in degrees, used to draw and measure angles.

protrude *vb* **1** *intr* to project; to stick out. **2** to push something out or forward. ◇ **protrusion** *n*. ◇ **protrusive** *adj*.

protuberant *adj* projecting; bulging; swelling out. ◇ **protuberance** *n*.

proud *adj* **1** (*often* **proud of sb** or **sth**) feeling satisfaction, delight, etc with one's own or another's accomplishments, possessions, etc. **2** of an event, occasion, etc: arousing justifiable pride: *a proud day.* **3** arrogant; conceited. **4** concerned for one's dignity and self-respect. **5** honoured; gratified; delighted. **6** splendid; imposing; distinguished: *a proud sight.* **7** *technical* projecting slightly from the surrounding surface. ◇ **proudly** *adv*. ◆ **do sb proud** to entertain or treat them grandly.

prove *vb* (*past participle* **proved** or **proven**) **1** to show something to be true, correct or a fact. **2** to show something to be (a specified thing): *He was proved innocent.* **3** *intr* to be found to be (a specified thing) when tried; to turn out to be the case: *Her advice proved sound.* **4** to show (oneself) to be (of a specified type or quality, etc): *He proved himself reliable.* **5** to show (oneself) capable or daring. **6** *law* to establish the validity of (a will). **7** of dough: to rise when baked. ◇ **provable** or **proveable** *adj*.

proven *adj* shown to be true, worthy, etc: *of proven ability.*

provenance /ˈprɒvənəns/ *n* the place of origin (of a work of art, archaeological find, etc).

provender *n* **1** dry food for livestock. **2** *now usu facetious* food.

proverb *n* any of a body of well-known neatly-expressed sayings that give advice or express a supposed truth.

proverbial *adj* **1** belonging or relating to a proverb. **2** referred to in a proverb; traditionally quoted; well known: *He turned up like the proverbial bad penny.*

provide *vb* **1** to supply. **2** of a circumstance or situation, etc: to offer (a specified thing): *It pro-*

vided an opportunity. **3** *intr* (*often* **provide against** or **for sth**) to be prepared for (an unexpected contingency, an emergency, etc). **4** *intr* (**provide for sb** or **sth**) to support or keep (a dependant, etc), or arrange for the means to do so. ◇ **provider** *n*.

provided or **providing** *conj* **1** on the condition or understanding (that a specified thing happens, etc). **2** if and only if: *Providing Joe gives me the money, I'll go.*

providence *n* **1** (**Providence**) God or Nature regarded as an all-seeing protector of the world. **2** the quality of being provident.

provident *adj* **1** having foresight and making provisions for the future. **2** careful and thrifty.

providential *adj* due to providence; fortunate; lucky; opportune. ◇ **providentially** *adv*.

province *n* **1** an administrative division of a country. **2** someone's allotted range of duties or field of knowledge or experience, etc. **3** (**the provinces**) the parts of a country away from the capital, typically thought of as culturally backward.

provincial *adj* **1** belonging or relating to a province. **2** relating to the parts of a country away from the capital: *a provincial accent.* **3** *derog* supposedly typical of provinces in being culturally backward, unsophisticated or narrow in outlook: *provincial attitudes.* ◇ **provincialism** *n*. ◇ **provincially** *adv*.

provision *n* **1** the act or process of providing. **2** something provided or made available; facilities. **3** measures taken in advance: *Let's make provision for the future.* **4** (**provisions**) food and other necessities. **5** *law* a condition or requirement; a clause stipulating or enabling something. ➤ *vb* to supply (eg an army, country, boat) with food.

provisional *adj* temporary; for the time being or immediate purposes only; liable to be altered. ◇ **provisionally** *adv*.

proviso /prəˈvaɪzəʊ/ *n* **1** a condition or stipulation. **2** *law* a clause stating a condition. ◇ **provisory** *adj*.

provocation *n* **1** the act of provoking or state of being provoked; incitement. **2** a cause of anger, irritation or indignation.

provocative *adj* **1** tending or intended to cause anger; deliberately infuriating. **2** sexually arousing or stimulating, esp by design. ◇ **provocatively** *adv*.

provoke *vb* **1** to annoy or infuriate someone, esp deliberately. **2** to incite or goad. **3** to rouse (someone's anger, etc). **4** to cause, stir up or bring about something: *The invasion provoked a storm of protest.* ◇ **provoking** *adj*.

provost *n* **1** the head of some university colleges. **2** in Scotland: **a** the chief councillor of a district council; **b** *formerly* the chief magistrate of a burgh.

provost marshal *n* an officer in charge of military police.

prow *n* the projecting front part of a ship; the BOW³.

prowess n 1 skill; ability; expertise. 2 valour; dauntlessness.

prowl vb, intr 1 to go about stealthily, eg in search of prey. 2 intr to pace restlessly. ➤ n an act of prowling. ◦ **prowler** n. ♦ **on the prowl** lurking about, esp menacingly.

prox. abbrev proximo.

proximate adj 1 nearest. 2 immediately before or after in time, place or chronology. ◦ **proximately** adv.

proximity n (-ies) nearness; closeness in space or time.

proximo adv (abbrev **prox.**) used mainly in formal correspondence: in or during the next month. Compare ULTIMO.

proxy n (-ies) 1 a a person authorized to act or vote on another's behalf; b the agency of such a person. 2 a the authority to act or vote for someone else; b a document granting this.

prude n someone who is, or affects to be, shocked by improper behaviour, mention of sexual matters, etc. ◦ **prudery** n. ◦ **prudish** adj. ◦ **prudishness** n.

prudent adj 1 wise or careful in conduct. 2 shrewd or thrifty in planning ahead. 3 wary; discreet. ◦ **prudence** n.

prudential adj, old use characterized by or exercising careful forethought. ◦ **prudentially** adv.

prune¹ vb 1 to cut off (branches, etc) from (a tree or shrub) in order to stimulate its growth, improve the production of fruit or flowers, etc. 2 to cut out (superfluous matter) from (a piece of writing, etc). 3 to cut back on (expenses, etc). ➤ n an act of pruning. ◦ **pruner** n.

prune² n 1 a PLUM that has been preserved by drying, which gives it a black wrinkled appearance. 2 colloq a silly foolish person.

prurient adj 1 unhealthily or excessively interested in sexual matters. 2 tending to arouse such unhealthy interest. ◦ **prurience** n. ◦ **pruriently** adv.

pry¹ vb (**pries, pried**) intr 1 (also **pry into sth**) to investigate, esp the personal affairs of others; to nose or snoop. 2 to peer inquisitively.

pry² vb (**pries, pried**) N Am to prise.

PS abbrev postscript.

psalm /sɑːm/ n a sacred song, esp one from the Book of Psalms in the Old Testament.

psalmist /'sɑːmɪst/ n a composer of psalms.

psalmody /'sɑːmədɪ/ n (-ies) 1 the art of singing psalms. 2 a collected body of psalms.

psalter /'sɔːltə(r)/ n a book containing psalms.

psaltery /'sɔːltərɪ/ n (-ies) an old stringed instrument similar to the ZITHER, played by plucking.

psephology /sɪ'fɒlədʒɪ/ n the statistical study of elections and voting patterns. ◦ **psephologist** n.

pseud /sjuːd, suːd/ Brit, colloq, n a pretentious person; a bogus intellectual. ➤ adj bogus, sham or phoney.

pseudo /'sjuːdəʊ, 'suːdəʊ/ adj, colloq false; sham; phoney.

pseudo- or (before a vowel) **pseud-** comb form, forming nouns and adjs, denoting 1 false; pretending to be something: pseudo-intellectuals. 2 deceptively resembling: pseudo-scientific jargon.

pseudonym /'sjuːdənɪm/ n a false or assumed name, esp one used by an author. ◦ **pseudonymous** /-'dɒnɪməs/ adj.

psittacosis /sɪtə'kəʊsɪs/ n, pathol a contagious disease of birds, esp parrots, that can be transmitted to human beings as a form of pneumonia.

psoriasis /sə'raɪəsɪs/ n, pathol a skin disease characterized by red patches covered with white scales.

psst or **pst** exclam used to draw someone's attention quietly or surreptitiously.

psych or **psyche** /saɪk/ vb, colloq to psychoanalyse someone. ◊ **psych sb out** to undermine the confidence of (an opponent, etc). **psych oneself** or **sb up** to prepare or steel oneself, or them, for a challenge, etc.

psyche /'saɪkɪ/ n the mind or spirit.

psychedelia /saɪkɪ'diːlɪə/ pl n psychedelic items such as posters, paintings, etc collectively or generally.

psychedelic /saɪkɪ'dɛlɪk/ adj 1 a of a drug, esp LSD: inducing a state of altered consciousness characterized by an increase in perception, eg of colour, sound, etc, and hallucinations; b of an event or experience, etc: resembling such effects: a psychedelic vision; c belonging or relating to this kind of drug, experience, etc: the psychedelic 60s. 2 of perceived phenomena, eg colour, music; etc: startlingly clear and vivid, often with a complex dazzling pattern.

psychiatry /saɪ'kaɪətrɪ/ n the branch of medicine concerned with the study, diagnosis, treatment and prevention of mental and emotional disorders. ◦ **psychiatric** /saɪkɪ'atrɪk/ adj. ◦ **psychiatrist** n.

psychic /'saɪkɪk/ adj 1 (also **psychical**) relating to mental processes or experiences that are not scientifically explainable, eg telepathy. 2 of a person: sensitive to influences that produce such experiences; having mental powers that are not scientifically explainable. ➤ n someone who possesses such powers.

psycho /'saɪkəʊ/ colloq, n a psychopath. ➤ adj psychopathic.

psychoanalyse or (US) **psychoanalyze** vb to examine or treat someone by psychoanalysis.

psychoanalysis n, psychol a theory and method of treatment for mental and emotional disorders, which explores the effects of unconscious motivation and conflict on a person's behaviour. ◦ **psychoanalyst** n. ◦ **psychoanalytic** or **psychoanalytical** adj.

psychogenic adj of symptoms, etc: originating in the mind.

psychokinesis n the apparent power to move objects, etc by non-physical means.

psychological adj 1 relating or referring to PSYCHOLOGY. 2 relating or referring to the mind or mental processes. ○ **psychologically** *adv.*

psychology *n* **1** the scientific study of the mind and behaviour of humans and animals. **2** the mental attitudes and associated behaviour characteristic of a certain individual or group. ○ **psychologist** *n.*

psychopath *n* **1** *technical* someone with a personality disorder characterized by extreme callousness, who is liable to behave antisocially or violently in getting their own way, without any feelings of remorse. **2** *colloq* someone who is dangerously unstable mentally or emotionally. ○ **psychopathic** *adj.*

psychosis /saɪˈkoʊsɪs/ *n* (*-ses* /-siːz/) *psychol* one of the two divisions of psychiatric disorders, characterized by a loss of contact with reality, in the form of delusions or hallucinations and belief that only one's own actions are rational.

psychosomatic *adj, med* of physical symptoms or disorders: strongly associated with psychological factors, esp mental stress.

psychotherapy *n* the treatment of mental disorders and emotional and behavioural problems by psychological means, rather than by drugs or surgery. ○ **psychotherapist** *n.*

psychotic *adj* relating to or involving a PSYCHOSIS. ➢ *n* someone suffering from a psychosis.

PT *abbrev* physical training.

Pt *symbol, chem* platinum.

PTA *abbrev* Parent-Teacher Association.

ptarmigan /ˈtɑːmɪɡən/ *n* a mountain-dwelling game bird with white winter plumage.

pterodactyl /tɛrəˈdaktɪl/ *n* a former name for PTEROSAUR.

pterosaur /ˈtɛrəsɔː(r)/ *n* an extinct flying reptile with narrow leathery wings, known from the late Triassic to the end of the Cretaceous period.

PTO or **pto** *abbrev* please turn over.

ptomaine /ˈtoʊmeɪn/ *n, biochem* any of a group of organic compounds, some of which are poisonous, produced during the bacterial decomposition of dead animal and plant matter.

Pu *symbol, chem* plutonium.

pub *n, colloq* a PUBLIC HOUSE.

puberty *n, biol* in humans and other primates: the onset of sexual maturity.

pubes /ˈpjuːbiːz/ *n* (*pl* **pubes**) **1** *anat* the pubic region of the lower abdomen; the groin. **2** (*also colloq* treated as *pl n* /ˈpjuːbz/) the hair that grows on this part from puberty onward.

pubescence *n* **1** the onset of puberty. **2** *biol* a soft downy covering on plants and animals. ○ **pubescent** *adj.*

pubic *adj* belonging or relating to the pubis or pubes.

pubis *n* (*pl* **pubes** /ˈpjuːbiːz/) *anat* in most vertebrates: one of the two bones forming the lower front part of each side of the pelvis.

public *adj* **1** relating to or concerning all the

people of a country or community: *public health.* **2** relating to the organization and administration of a community. **3** provided for the use of the community: *public library.* **4** well known through exposure in the media: *a famous public figure.* **5** made, done or held, etc openly, for all to see, hear or participate in: *a public inquiry.* **6** known to all: *public knowledge* • *He made his views public.* **7** open to view; not private or secluded: *It's too public here.* **8** provided by or run by central or local government: *under public ownership.* ➢ *sing or pl n* **1** the people or community. **2** a particular class of people: *the concert-going public.* **3** an author's or performer's, etc audience or group of devotees: *I mustn't disappoint my public.* ♦ **go public 1** *business* to become a public company. **2** to make something previously private known to everyone. **in public** in the presence of other people. **in the public eye** of a person, etc: well known through media exposure.

public-address system *n* a system of microphones, amplifiers and loudspeakers, used to communicate public announcements, etc over a large area.

publican *n, Brit* the keeper of a PUBLIC HOUSE.

publication *n* **1** the act of publishing a printed work; the process of publishing or of being published. **2** a book, magazine, newspaper or other printed and published work. **3** the act of making something known to the public.

public bar *n* in a public house: a bar which is less well furnished and serves drinks more cheaply than a lounge bar (see LOUNGE *noun* sense 4).

public company or **public limited company** (*abbrev* **PLC** or **plc**) *n, business* a company whose shares are available for purchase on the open market by the public.

public convenience *n* a public toilet.

public enemy *n* someone whose behaviour threatens the community, esp a criminal.

public house *n, Brit* an establishment licensed to sell alcoholic drinks for consumption on the premises.

publicity *n* **1** advertising or other activity designed to rouse public interest in something. **2** public interest attracted in this way.

publicize or **-ise** *vb* **1** to make something generally or widely known. **2** to advertise.

public limited company see PUBLIC COMPANY

public relations (*abbrev* **PR**) *sing or pl n* the process of creating a good relationship between an organization, etc and the public. ➢ *sing n* the department within an organization that is responsible for this.

public school *n* **1** in the UK: a secondary school, run independently of the state, financed by endowments and by pupils' fees. **2** in the US: a school run by a public authority.

public sector *n* the part of a country's economy which consists of nationalized industries and of institutions and services run by the state or local authorities.

public servant n an elected or appointed holder of public office; a government employee.

public-spirited adj acting from or showing concern for the general good of the whole community.

public works pl n buildings, roads, etc built by the state for public use.

publish vb, tr & intr 1 to prepare, produce and distribute (printed material, computer software, etc) for sale to the public. 2 tr & intr of an author: to have (their work) published. 3 to publish the work of (an author). 4 to announce something publicly. ○ **publishing** n.

publisher n 1 a person or company engaged in the business of publishing books, newspapers, music, software, etc. 2 N Am a newspaper proprietor.

puce n a colour anywhere between deep purplish-pink and purplish-brown. ➤ adj puce-coloured.

puck[1] n a goblin or mischievous sprite. ○ **puckish** adj.

puck[2] n, sport a thick disc of hard rubber used in ice hockey instead of a ball.

pucker vb, tr & intr to gather into creases, folds or wrinkles. ➤ n a wrinkle, fold or crease.

pud n, Brit colloq pudding.

pudding n 1 often in compounds any of several sweet or savoury foods usu made with flour and eggs and cooked by steaming, boiling or baking: rice pudding • steak and kidney pudding. 2 a any sweet food served as dessert; b the dessert course. 3 in compounds a type of sausage made with minced meat, spices, blood, etc: black pudding.

puddle n 1 a small pool, esp one of rainwater on the road. 2 (also **puddle clay**) a non-porous watertight material consisting of thoroughly mixed clay, sand and water. ➤ vb 1 to make something watertight by means of puddle clay. 2 to knead (clay, sand and water) to make puddle clay. 3 metallurgy to produce (wrought iron) from molten clay by stirring to remove carbon.

pudenda pl n (rare sing **pudendum**) the external sexual organs, esp those of a woman.

pudgy see PODGY

puerile / 'pjʊəraɪl / adj childish; silly; immature.

puerperal / pjuː'ɜːpərəl / adj 1 referring or relating to childbirth. 2 referring or relating to a woman who has just given birth.

puff n 1 a a small rush, gust or blast of air or wind, etc; b the sound made by it. 2 a small cloud of smoke, dust or steam emitted from something. 3 colloq breath: I'm out of puff. 4 an act of inhaling and exhaling smoke from a pipe or cigarette. 5 in compounds a light pastry, often containing a sweet or savoury filling: jam puffs. ➤ vb 1 tr & intr to blow or breathe in small blasts. 2 intr of smoke or steam, etc: to emerge in small gusts or blasts. 3 tr & intr to inhale and exhale smoke from, or draw at (a cigarette,

etc). 4 intr of a train or boat, etc: to go along emitting puffs of steam. 5 intr to pant, or go along panting. 6 (often **puff sb out**) colloq to leave them breathless after exertion. 7 tr & intr (also **puff out** or **up**) to swell or cause something to swell. ○ **puffy** adj (-**ier**, -**iest**).

puffball n, bot the spore-bearing structure of certain fungi, consisting of a hollow ball of fleshy tissue from which spores are released as puffs of fine dust through a hole in the top.

puffin n a small black-and-white seabird with a large brightly coloured bill.

puff pastry n, cookery light flaky pastry made with a high proportion of fat.

pug n a small breed of dog with a flattened face with a wrinkled snout and a short curled tail.

pugilism / 'pjuːdʒɪlɪzəm / n, old use or facetious the art or practice of boxing or prizefighting. ○ **pugilist** n.

pugnacious adj given to fighting; quarrelsome, belligerent or combative. ○ **pugnacity** n.

pug nose n a short upturned nose. ○ **pug-nosed** adj.

puissance / 'pwiːsɑːns / n, showjumping a competition that tests the horse's ability to jump high fences.

puke colloq, vb, tr & intr to vomit. ➤ n 1 vomit. 2 an act of vomiting.

pukka adj, colloq 1 high-quality. 2 upper-class. 3 genuine.

pulchritude n, literary or formal beauty of face and form.

pull vb 1 tr & intr to grip something or someone strongly and draw or force it or them towards oneself. 2 (also **pull sth out** or **up**) to remove or extract (a cork, tooth, weeds, etc) with this action. 3 to operate (a trigger, lever or switch) with this action. 4 to draw (a trailer, etc). 5 to open or close (curtains or a blind). 6 (often **pull sth on sb**) to produce (a weapon) as a threat to them. 7 a tr & intr to row; b intr (often **pull away**, **off**, etc) of a boat: to be rowed or made to move in a particular direction. 8 to draw (beer, etc) from a cask by operating a lever. 9 intr a of a driver or vehicle: to steer or move (in a specified direction): I pulled right, b of a vehicle or its steering: to go or direct (towards a specified direction), usu because of some defect. 10 sport in golf, snooker, etc: to hit (a ball) so that it veers off its intended course. 11 intr of an engine or vehicle: to produce the required propelling power. 12 (usu **pull at** or **on sth**) to inhale and exhale smoke from (a cigarette, etc); to draw or suck at it. 13 to attract (a crowd, votes, etc). 14 to strain (a muscle or tendon). 15 printing to print (a proof). 16 tr & intr, slang to pick up (a sexual partner). ➤ n 1 an act of pulling. 2 attraction; attracting force. 3 useful influence: She has some pull with the education department. 4 a drag at a pipe; a swallow of liquor, etc. 5 a tab, etc for pulling. 6 a stroke made with an oar. 7 printing a proof. 8 slang a sexual partner, esp a casual one. ♦ **pull a fast**

one to trick or cheat someone. **pull one's punches** to be deliberately less hard-hitting than one might be. **pull the other one** a dismissive expression used by the speaker to indicate that they are not being fooled by what has just been said. **pull sb up short 1** to check someone, often oneself. **2** to take them aback. ◊ **pull sth back** to withdraw it or make it withdraw or retreat. **pull sth down** to demolish (a building, etc). **pull in 1** of a train: to arrive and halt at a station. **2** of a driver or vehicle: to move to the side of the road. **pull sth off** colloq to arrange or accomplish it successfully: *We pulled off the deal.* **pull over** of a driver or vehicle: to move to the side of or off the road and stop. **pull round** or **through** to recover from an illness. **pull together** to work together towards a common aim. **pull up** of a driver, vehicle or horse: to stop. **pull sb up** to criticize them or tell them off. **pull sth up** to make (a vehicle or horse) stop.

pullet *n* a young female hen in its first laying year.

pulley *n* a simple mechanism for lifting and lowering weights, consisting of a wheel with a grooved rim over which a rope or belt runs.

Pullman *n* a type of luxurious railway carriage.

pull-out *n* **1** a self-contained detachable section of a magazine designed to be kept for reference. **2** a withdrawal from combat or competition, etc.

pullover *n* a knitted garment pulled on over the head.

pulmonary *adj* **1** belonging or relating to, or affecting, the lungs. **2** having the function of a lung.

pulp *n* **1** the flesh of a fruit or vegetable. **2** a soft wet mass of mashed food or other material. **3** *derog* worthless literature, novels, magazines, etc printed on poor paper. **4** *anat* the tissue in the cavity of a tooth, containing nerves. ➤ *vb* **1** *tr & intr* to reduce or be reduced to a pulp. **2** to remove the pulp from (fruit, etc). ○ **pulpy** *adj* (*-ier, -iest*).

pulpit *n* **1** a small enclosed platform in a church, from which the preacher delivers the sermon. **2** (*usu* **the pulpit**) the clergy in general.

pulsar *n*, *astron* a star that emits electromagnetic radiation in brief regular pulses, mainly at radio frequency.

pulsate *vb*, *intr* **1** to beat or throb. **2** to contract and expand rhythmically. **3** to vibrate. ○ **pulsation** *n*.

pulse[1] *n* **1** *physiol* the rhythmic beat that can be detected in an artery, as the heart pumps blood around the body. **2** *med*, *etc* the rate of this beat, often measured as an indicator of a person's state of health. **3** a regular throbbing beat in music. **4** *physics* a signal, eg one of light or electric current, of very short duration. **5** the hum or bustle of a busy place. **6** a thrill of excitement, etc. **7** the attitude or feelings of a group or community at any one time. ➤ *vb* **1** *intr* to throb or pulsate. **2** to drive something by pulses.

pulse[2] *n* **1** the edible dried seed of a plant belonging to the pea family, eg pea, bean, lentil, etc. **2** any plant that bears this seed.

pulverize or **-ise** *vb* **1** *tr & intr* to crush or crumble to dust or powder. **2** *colloq* to defeat utterly. ○ **pulverization** *n*.

puma *n* one of the large cats of America, with short yellowish-brown or reddish fur, found in mountain regions, forests, plains and deserts.

pumice /ˈpʌmɪs/ *n* (*also* **pumice stone**) *geol* a very light porous white or grey form of solidified lava, used as an abrasive and polishing agent. ➤ *vb* to polish or rub something with pumice.

pummel *vb* (*pummelled, pummelling*) to beat something repeatedly with the fists.

pump[1] *n* a piston-operated or other device for forcing or driving liquids or gases into or out of something, etc. ➤ *vb* **1** *tr & intr* to raise, force or drive (a liquid or gas) out of or into something with a pump. **2** (*usu* **pump sth up**) to inflate (a tyre, etc) with a pump. **3** to force something in large gushes or flowing amounts. **4** to pour (money or other resources) into a project, etc. **5** to force out the contents of (someone's stomach) to rid it of a poison, etc. **6** to try to extract information from someone by persistent questioning. **7** to work something vigorously up and down, as though operating a pump handle. **8** to fire (bullets, etc), often into someone or something: *He pumped six bullets into her.* ♦ **pump iron** *colloq* to exercise with weights; to go in for weight-training.

pump[2] *n* **1** a light dancing shoe. **2** a plain, low-cut flat shoe for women. **3** a PLIMSOLL.

pumpernickel *n* a dark heavy coarse rye-bread.

pumpkin *n* **1** a trailing or climbing plant which produces yellow flowers and large round fruits at ground level. **2** the fruit of this plant, which contains pulpy flesh and many seeds, enclosed by a hard leathery orange rind.

pun *n* a form of joke consisting of the use of a word or phrase that can be understood in two different ways, esp one where an association is created between words of similar sound but different meaning. ➤ *vb* (*punned, punning*) *intr* to make a pun.

punch[1] *vb* **1** *tr & intr* to hit someone or something with the fist. **2** *esp US & Aust* to poke or prod with a stick; to drive (cattle, etc). **3** to prod, poke or strike smartly, esp with a blunt object, the foot, etc. ➤ *n* **1** a blow with the fist. **2** vigour and effectiveness in speech or writing.

punch[2] *n* **1** a tool for cutting or piercing holes or notches, or stamping designs, in leather, paper, metal, etc. **2** a tool for driving nail-heads well down into a surface. ➤ *vb* to pierce, notch or stamp something with a punch.

punch[3] *n* a drink, usu an alcoholic one, made up of a mixture of other drinks, which can be served either hot or cold.

punchbag *n* **1** a heavy stuffed leather bag, used for boxing practice. **2** someone who is physically or emotionally abused.

punch-drunk adj **1** of a boxer: disorientated from repeated blows to the head, with resultant unsteadiness and confusion. **2** dazed from over-intensive work or some other shattering experience.

punchline n the words that conclude a joke or funny story and contain its point.

punch-up n, colloq a fight.

punchy adj (**-ier, -iest**) of speech or writing: vigorous and effective; forcefully expressed. ○ **punchily** adv. ○ **punchiness** n.

punctilious adj carefully attentive to details of correct, polite or considerate behaviour; making a point of observing a rule or custom. ○ **punctiliously** adv.

punctual adj **1** arriving or happening at the arranged time; not late. **2** of a person: making a habit of arriving on time. ○ **punctuality** n. ○ **punctually** adv.

punctuate vb **1** tr & intr to put punctuation marks into (a piece of writing). **2** to interrupt something repeatedly: Bursts of applause punctuated his speech.

punctuation n **1** a system of conventional marks used in a text to clarify its meaning for the reader, indicating pauses, intonation, missing letters, etc. **2 a** the use of such marks; **b** the process of inserting them.

punctuation mark n any of the set of marks such as the FULL STOP, COMMA, QUESTION MARK, etc that in written text conventionally indicate the pauses and intonations that would be used in speech.

puncture n **1** a small hole pierced in something with a sharp point. **2 a** a perforation in an inflated object, esp one in a pneumatic tyre; **b** the resulting flat tyre. ➤ vb **1** tr & intr to make a puncture in something, or to be punctured. **2** to deflate (someone's pride, self-importance, etc).

pundit n **1** an authority or supposed authority on a particular subject, esp one who is regularly consulted. **2** (also **pandit**) a Hindu learned in Hindu culture, philosophy and law.

pungent adj **1** of a taste or smell: sharp and strong. **2** of remarks or wit, etc: cleverly caustic or biting. **3** of grief or pain: keen or sharp. ○ **pungency** n.

punish vb **1** to cause (an offender) to suffer for an offence. **2** to impose a penalty for (an offence). **3** colloq to treat something or someone roughly. **4** to beat or defeat (an opponent, etc) soundly. ○ **punishable** adj. ○ **punishing** adj harsh; severe.

punishment n **1** the act of punishing or process of being punished. **2** a method of punishing; a type of penalty. **3** colloq rough treatment; suffering or hardship.

punitive /ˈpjuːnɪtɪv/ adj **1** relating to, inflicting or intended to inflict punishment. **2** severe; inflicting hardship. ○ **punitively** adv.

punk n **1** a youth-orientated, anti-establishment movement, at its height in the mid- to late-1970s, which was characterized by aggressive music and dress style. **2** a follower of punk styles or punk rock. **3** (in full **punk rock**) a type of loud aggressive rock music, popular in the mid- to late-1970s. **4** N Am a worthless or stupid person. ➤ adj **1** relating to or characteristic of punk as a movement. **2** N Am worthless; inferior.

punka or **punkah** n **1** a fan made from leaf-palm. **2** a large mechanical fan for cooling a room.

punnet n a small container for soft fruit.

punster n someone who makes PUNS, esp habitually.

punt¹ n a long, flat-bottomed open boat with square ends, propelled by a pole pushed against the bed of the river, etc. ➤ vb **1** intr to travel by or operate a punt. **2** to propel (a punt, etc) with a pole.

punt² n, rugby a kick given with the toe of the boot to a ball dropped directly from the hands. ➤ vb, tr & intr to kick in this way.

punt³ vb, intr **1** colloq to bet on horses. **2** cards to bet against the bank. ➤ n a gamble or bet.

punt⁴ n the former standard unit of currency of the Republic of Ireland, replaced in 2002 by the euro.

punter n, colloq **1** someone who places bets. **2 a** the average consumer, customer or member of the public; **b** a prostitute's client.

puny adj (**-ier, -iest**) **1** small, weak or undersized. **2** feeble or ineffective.

pup n **1** a young dog. **2** the young of other animals, eg the seal, wolf and rat. ➤ vb (**pupped, pupping**) intr to give birth to pups.

pupa /ˈpjuːpə/ n (**pupae** /ˈpjuːpiː/ or **pupas**) zool in the life cycle of certain insects, eg butterflies and moths: the inactive stage during which a larva is transformed into a sexually mature adult while enclosed in a protective case. ○ **pupal** adj.

pupil¹ n **1** someone who is being taught; a schoolchild or student. **2** someone studying under a particular expert, etc. **3** Scots law a girl under the age of 12 or boy under the age of 14, who is in the care of a guardian.

pupil² n, anat in the eye of vertebrates: the dark circular opening in the centre of the IRIS (sense 2), which varies in size allowing more or less light to pass to the retina.

puppet n **1** a type of doll that can be moved in a number of ways, eg one operated by strings or sticks attached to its limbs, or one designed to fit over the hand. **2** a person, company, country, etc, being controlled or manipulated by someone or something else. ○ **puppeteer** n.

puppy n (**-ies**) **1** a young dog. **2** colloq, dated a conceited young man.

puppy fat n a temporary plumpness in children, usu at the pre-adolescent stage, which disappears with maturity.

puppy love n romantic love between adolescents, or of an adolescent for an older person. Also called **calf love**.

purblind *adj* **1** nearly blind; dim-sighted. **2** dull-witted.

purchase *vb* **1** to obtain something in return for payment; to buy. **2** to get or achieve something through labour, effort, sacrifice or risk. ➢ *n* **1** something that has been bought. **2** the act of buying. **3** firmness in holding or gripping; a sure grasp or foothold. **4** *mech* the advantage given by a device such as a pulley or lever. ○ **purchaser** *n.*

purdah *n* in some Muslim and Hindu societies: **1** the seclusion or veiling of women from public view. **2** a curtain or screen used to seclude women.

pure *adj* **1** consisting of itself only; unmixed with anything else. **2** unpolluted; uncontaminated; wholesome. **3** virtuous; chaste; free from sin or guilt. **4** utter; sheer: *pure lunacy*. **5** of mathematics or science: dealing with theory and abstractions rather than practical applications. Compare APPLIED. **6** of unmixed blood or descent: *pure Manx stock*. **7** of sound, eg a sung note: clear, unwavering and exactly in tune. **8** absolutely true to type or style. ○ **pureness** *n.*

pure-bred *adj* of an animal or plant: that is the offspring of parents of the same breed or variety.

purée /'pjʊəreɪ/ *cookery, n* a quantity of fruit, vegetables, meat, fish, etc reduced to a smooth pulp by liquidizing or rubbing through a sieve. ➢ *vb* (**purées, puréed, puréeing**) to reduce something to a purée.

purely *adv* **1** in a pure way. **2** wholly; entirely. **3** merely.

purgative *n* **1** a medicine that causes the bowels to empty. **2** something that cleanses or purifies. ➢ *adj* **1** of a medicine, etc: having this effect. **2** of an action, etc: having a purifying, cleansing or cathartic effect.

purgatory *n* (*-ies*) **1** (**Purgatory**) *chiefly RC Church* a place or state into which the soul passes after death, where it is cleansed of pardonable sins before going to heaven. **2** *humorous, colloq* any state of discomfort or suffering; an excruciating experience. ○ **purgatorial** *adj.*

purge *vb* **1 a** to rid (eg the soul or body) of unwholesome thoughts or substances; **b** to rid (anything) of impurities. **2** to rid (a political party, community, etc) of (undesirable members). **3** *old use* **a** to empty (the bowels), esp by taking a laxative; **b** to make someone empty their bowels, esp by giving them a laxative. **4** *relig* to rid (oneself) of guilt by atoning for an offence. **5** *law* to clear (oneself or someone else) of an accusation. ➢ *n* **1** an act of purging. **2** the process of purging a party or community of undesirable members. **3** *old use* the process of purging the bowels. **4** *old use* a LAXATIVE.

purify *vb* (*-ies, -ied*) **1** *tr & intr* to make or become pure. **2** to cleanse something of contaminating or harmful substances. **3** to rid

something of intrusive elements. **4** *relig* to free someone from sin or guilt. ○ **purification** *n.* ○ **purifier** *n.*

purism *n* insistence on the traditional elements of the content and style of a particular subject, esp of language. ○ **purist** *n.*

puritan *n* **1** (**Puritan**) *hist* in the 16c and 17c: a supporter of the Protestant movement in England and America that sought to rid church worship of ritual. **2** someone of strict, esp over-strict, moral principles. ➢ *adj* **1** (**Puritan**) belonging or relating to the Puritans. **2** characteristic of a puritan. ○ **puritanical** *adj.*

purity *n* **1** the state of being pure or unmixed. **2** freedom from contamination, pollution or unwholesome or intrusive elements. **3** chasteness or innocence.

purl¹ *n* **1** *knitting* a reverse PLAIN (*noun* sense 2) stitch. **2** cord made from gold or silver wire. **3** (*also* **pearl**) a decorative looped edging on lace or braid, etc. ➢ *vb* to knit in purl.

purl² *vb, intr* **1** to flow with a murmuring sound. **2** to eddy or swirl.

purlieu /'pɜːljuː/ *n* **1** (*usu* **purlieus**) the surroundings or immediate neighbourhood of a place. **2** (*usu* **purlieus**) someone's usual haunts. **3** *Eng hist* an area of land on the edge of a forest.

purlin or **purline** *n, building* a roof timber stretching across the principal rafters or between the tops of walls.

purloin *vb* to steal or pilfer.

purple *n* **1** a colour that is a mixture of blue and red. **2** *hist* a crimson dye obtained from various shellfish. **3** crimson cloth, or a robe made from it, worn eg by emperors and cardinals, symbolic of their authority. ➢ *adj* **1** purple-coloured. **2** of writing: especially fine in style; over-elaborate.

purple patch *n* **1** a passage in a piece of writing which is over-elaborate and ornate. **2** any period of time characterized by good luck.

purport *vb* /pɜː'pɔːt/ **1** of a picture, piece of writing, document, etc: to profess by its appearance, etc (to be something): *a manuscript that purports to be written by Camus*. **2** of a piece of writing, or a speech, etc: to convey; to imply (that). ➢ *n* /'pɜːpɔːt/ meaning, significance, point or gist.

purpose *n* **1** the object or aim in doing something. **2** the function for which something is intended. **3** the intentions, aspirations, aim or goal: *He has no purpose in life.* **4** determination; resolve: *a woman of purpose.* ➢ *vb* to intend (to do something). ○ **purposeless** *adj* without purpose; aimless. ○ **purposely** *adv* intentionally. ◆ **on purpose** intentionally.

purpose-built *adj* designed or made to meet specific requirements.

purposeful *adj* determined; intent; resolute; showing a sense of purpose. ○ **purposefully** *adv.*

purposefully, purposely | **Purposefully**
(= with purpose) refers to a person's manner or determination:
He stood up and began to pace purposefully round the room.
Purposely (= on purpose) refers to intention:
Earlier estimates had been purposely conservative.

purposive *adj* **1** having a clear purpose. **2** purposeful.

purr *vb* **1** *intr* of a cat: to make a soft low vibrating sound associated with contentment. **2** *intr* of a vehicle or machine: to make a sound similar to this, suggestive of good running order. **3** *tr & intr* to express pleasure, or say something, in a tone vibrating with satisfaction. ➤ *n* a purring sound.

purse *n* **1** a small container carried in the pocket or handbag, for keeping cash, etc in. **2** *N Am* a woman's handbag. **3** funds available for spending; resources. **4** a sum of money offered as a present or prize. ➤ *vb* to draw (the lips) together in disapproval or deep thought.

purser *n* the ship's officer responsible for keeping the accounts and, on a passenger ship, seeing to the welfare of passengers.

purse strings *pl n*. ♦ **hold** or **control the purse strings** to be in charge of the financial side of things, eg in a family.

pursuance *n* the process of pursuing: *in pursuance of his duties*.

pursue *vb* **1** *tr & intr* to follow someone or something in order to overtake, capture or attack them or it, etc; to chase. **2** to proceed along (a course or route). **3** to put effort into achieving (a goal, aim, etc). **4** to occupy oneself with (one's career, etc). **5** to continue with or follow up (investigations or enquiries, etc). ○ **pursuer** *n*.

pursuit *n* **1** the act of pursuing or chasing. **2** an occupation or hobby.

purulent /'pjʊərʊlənt/ *adj, med, etc* belonging or relating to, or full of, pus. ○ **purulence** *n*.

purvey *vb, tr & intr* to supply (food or provisions, etc) as a business. ○ **purveyor** *n*.

purview *n, formal or technical* **1** scope of responsibility or concern, eg of a court of law. **2** the range of someone's knowledge, experience or activities.

pus *n* the thick, usu yellowish liquid that forms in abscesses or infected wounds.

push *vb* **1** (*often* **push against, at** or **on sth**) to exert pressure to force it away from one; to press, thrust or shove it. **2** (**push sb** or **sth over**) to knock them down. **3** to hold (a wheelchair, trolley, etc) and move it forward in front of one. **4** *tr & intr* (*often* **push through, in** or **past, etc**) to force one's way, thrusting aside people or obstacles. **5** *intr* to progress, esp laboriously. **6** to force in a specified direction: *This will push*

up prices. **7** (*often* **push sb into sth**) to coax, urge, persuade or goad them to do it: *She pushed me into agreeing.* **8** to pressurize someone (or oneself) into working harder, achieving more, etc. **9** (*usu* **push for sth**) to recommend strongly; to campaign or press for it. **10** to promote (products) or urge (acceptance of ideas). **11** to sell (drugs) illegally. ➤ *n* **1** an act of pushing; a thrust or shove. **2** a burst of effort towards achieving something. **3** determination, aggression or drive. ♦ **at a push** *colloq* if forced; at a pinch. **be pushed for sth** *colloq* to be short of (eg time or money). **be pushing** *colloq* to be nearly (a specified age): *She is pushing 30.* **get the push** *colloq* to be dismissed from a job, etc; to be rejected by someone. **give sb the push** to dismiss or reject them. ◊ **push sb around** or **about** *colloq* **1** to bully them; to treat them roughly. **2** to dictate to them; to order them about. **push off** or **along** *colloq* to go away. **push on** to continue on one's way or with a task, etc. **push sth through** to force acceptance of (a proposal or bill, etc) by a legislative body, etc.

pushbike *n, colloq* a bicycle propelled by pedals alone.

push button *n* a button pressed to operate a machine, etc.

pushchair *n* a small folding wheeled chair for a toddler.

pusher *n, colloq* someone who sells illegal drugs.

pushover *n, colloq* **1** someone who is easily defeated or outwitted. **2** a task that is easily accomplished.

pushy *adj* (*-ier, -iest*) *colloq* aggressively self-assertive or ambitious.

pusillanimous /pjuːsɪ'lanɪməs/ *adj* timid, cowardly or faint-hearted. ○ **pusillanimity** /-lə-'nɪmətɪ/ *n*.

puss *n, colloq* a cat.

pussy *n* (*-ies*) **1** (*also* **pussycat**) *colloq* a cat. **2** *coarse slang* **a** the female genitals; the vulva; **b** women considered sexually.

pussyfoot *vb, intr* **1** to behave indecisively. **2** to pad about stealthily.

pustule *n* a small inflammation on the skin, containing pus. ○ **pustular** *adj*.

put *vb* (*past tense & past participle* **put,** *present participle* **putting**) **1** to place something or someone in or convey them to a specified position or situation. **2** to fit: *Put a new lock on the door.* **3** to cause someone or something to be in a specified state: *Let's put him at ease.* **4** to apply. **5** to set or impose: *to put a tax on luxuries* • *They put an end to free lunches.* **6** to lay (blame, reliance, emphasis, etc) on something. **7** to set someone to work, etc or apply something to a good purpose, etc. **8** to translate: *Put this into French.* **9** to invest or pour (energy, money or other resources) into something. **10** to classify or categorize something or put it in order: *I put accuracy before speed.* **11** to submit (questions for answering or ideas for considering) to someone; to suggest: *I put it to her that she was lying*. **12** to express something. **13** *colloq* to write or say: *I don't know what to put*. **14** *athletics* to throw (the shot). ♦ **put it across sb** or **put one over on sb** *colloq* to trick, deceive or fool them. **put it on** to feign or exaggerate: *She said she'd been ill but she was putting it on*. **put sth right** to mend it or make it better. **put sb up to sth** to urge them to do something they ought not to do. ◊ **put about** *naut* to turn round; to change course. **put sth about** to spread (a report or rumour). **put sth across** to communicate (ideas, etc) to other people. **put sth aside 1** to save (money), esp regularly, for future use. **2** to discount or deliberately disregard (problems, differences of opinion, etc) for the sake of convenience or peace, etc. **put sb away** *colloq* **1** to imprison them. **2** to confine them in a mental institution. **put sth away 1** to replace it tidily where it belongs. **2** to save it for future use. **3** *colloq* to consume (food or drink), esp in large amounts. **4** *old use* to reject, discard or renounce it. **put sth back 1** to replace it. **2** to postpone (a match or meeting, etc). **3** to adjust (a clock, etc) to an earlier time. **put sb down 1** to humiliate or snub them. **put sb down 1** to lay it on a surface after holding it, etc. **2** to crush (a revolt, etc). **3** to kill (an animal) painlessly, esp when it is suffering. **4** to write it down. **put sb forward** to propose their name for a post, etc; to nominate them. **put sth forward** to offer (a proposal or suggestion). **put sth in 1** to fit or install it. **2** to spend (time) working at something: *I put in four hours' practice*. **3** to submit (a claim, etc). **put in for sth** to apply for it. **put sb off 1** to cancel or postpone an engagement with them. **2** to make them lose concentration; to distract them. **3** to cause them to lose enthusiasm or to feel disgust for something: *I was put off by its smell*. **put sth off** to postpone (an event or arrangement). **put sth on 1** to switch on (an electrical device, etc). **2** to dress in it. **3** to gain (weight or speed). **4** to present (a play, show, etc). **5** to assume (an accent, manner, etc) for effect or to deceive. **6** to bet (money) on a horse, etc. **put sb out 1** to inconvenience them. **2** to offend or annoy them. **put sth out 1** to extinguish (a light or fire). **2** to publish (a leaflet, etc). **3** to strain or dislocate (a part of the body). **put sth over** to communicate (an idea, etc) to someone else. **put sb through** to connect them by telephone. **put sb up** to stay for the night. **put sb up** to give them a bed for the night. **put sth up 1** to build it. **2** to raise (prices). **3** to present (a plan, etc). **4** to provide (funds) for a project, etc. **5** to show (resistance); to offer (a fight). **put sb** or **oneself up for sth** to offer or nominate them, or oneself, as a candidate. **put upon sb** to take unfair advantage of them. **put up with sb** or **sth** to tolerate them or it, esp reluctantly.

putative *adj* supposed; assumed.

put-down *n, colloq* a snub or humiliation.

put-on *adj* of an accent or manner, etc: assumed; pretended.

putrefy *vb* (**-ies, -ied**) *intr* of flesh or other organic matter: to go bad, rot or decay, esp with a foul smell. ○ **putrefaction** *n*.

putrescent *adj* decaying; rotting.

putrid *adj* **1** of organic matter: decayed; rotten. **2** stinking; foul; disgusting. **3** *colloq* repellent; worthless.

putsch /pʊtʃ/ *n* a secretly planned sudden attempt to remove a government from power.

putt *golf, vb, tr & intr* to send (the ball) gently forward on the green and into or nearer the hole. ➤ *n* a putting stroke.

puttee *n* a long strip of cloth worn by wrapping it around the leg from the ankle to the knee and used as protection or support.

putter *n, golf* **1** a club used for putting. **2** someone who putts.

putting *n* **1** the act of putting a ball towards a hole. **2** a game played on a PUTTING GREEN using only putting strokes.

putting green *n* **1** on a golf course: a smoothly mown patch of grass surrounding a hole. **2** an area of mown turf where PUTTING is played.

putty *n* (**-ies**) a paste of ground chalk and linseed oil, used for fixing glass in window frames, filling holes in wood, etc. ➤ *vb* (**-ies, -ied**) to fix, coat or fill something with putty.

put-up job *n* something dishonestly prearranged to give a false impression.

puzzle *vb* **1** to perplex, mystify, bewilder or baffle. **2** *intr* (*usu* **puzzle about** or **over sth**) to brood, ponder, wonder or worry about it. **3** (**puzzle sth out**) to solve it after prolonged thought. ➤ *n* **1** a baffling problem. **2** a game or toy that takes the form of something for solving. ○ **puzzlement** *n*. **puzzling** *adj*.

PVC *abbrev* polyvinyl chloride.

pygmy or **pigmy** *n* (**-ies**) **1** (**Pygmy**) a member of one of the unusually short peoples of equatorial Africa. **2** an undersized person. **3** *derog* someone insignificant, esp in a specified field: *an intellectual pygmy*. ➤ *adj* belonging or relating to a small-sized breed: *a pygmy hippopotamus*. ○ **pygmaean** or **pygmean** *adj*.

pyjamas or (*N Am*) **pajamas** *pl n* a sleeping suit consisting of a loose jacket or top, and trousers.

pylon *n* a tall steel structure for supporting electric power cables.

pyorrhoea or (*esp US*) **pyorrhea** /paɪə'rɪə/ *n, dentistry* a discharge of pus, esp from the gums or tooth sockets.

pyramid *n* **1** any of the huge ancient Egyptian royal tombs built on a square base, with four sloping triangular sides meeting in a common apex. **2** *geom* a solid of this shape, with a square or triangular base. **3** any structure, pile, etc of similar shape. ○ **pyramidal** /pɪ'ramɪdəl/ *adj*.

pyre *n* a pile of wood on which a dead body is ceremonially cremated.

pyretic /paɪə'rɛtɪk/ *adj, med* relating to, accompanied by or producing fever.

Pyrex *n, trademark* a type of heat-resistant

glass widely used to make laboratory apparatus and cooking utensils.

pyrite /ˈpaɪəraɪt/ *n, geol* the commonest sulphide mineral, used in the production of sulphuric acid.

pyrites /paɪəˈraɪtiːz/ *n* **1** *geol* PYRITE. **2** *chem* any of a large class of mineral sulphides: *copper pyrites*.

pyromania *n, psychol* an obsessive urge to set fire to things. ○ **pyromaniac** *n*.

pyrotechnics *sing n* the art of making fire-works. ➤ *sing or pl n* **1** a fireworks display. **2** a display of fiery brilliance in speech, music, etc.

Pyrrhic victory /ˈpɪrɪk/ *n* a victory won at so great a cost in lives, etc that it can hardly be regarded as a triumph at all.

python *n* a snake that coils its body around its prey and squeezes it until the victim suffocates.

pyx *n, Christianity* a container in which the consecrated Communion bread is kept.

Qq

Q¹ or **q** *n* (*Qs, Q's* or *q's*) the seventeenth letter of the English alphabet.

Q² *abbrev* Queen or Queen's.

q or **q.** *abbrev* **1** quart. **2** quarter.

QC *abbrev, law* Queen's Counsel, a senior barrister.

QED *abbrev: quod erat demonstrandum* (Latin), which was the thing that had to be proved.

qi, chi or **ch'i** /tʃiː/ *n, Chinese med* the life force that is believed to flow along a network of meridians in a person's body and is vital to their physical and spiritual health.

qr *abbrev* quarter.

qt *abbrev* quart.

quack¹ *n* the noise that a duck makes. ➤ *vb, intr* to make this noise.

quack² *n* **1** someone who practises medicine or who claims to have medical knowledge, but who has no formal training in the subject. **2** *colloq, often derog* a term for any doctor or medical practitioner. **3** anyone who pretends to have a knowledge or skill that they do not possess. ○ **quackery** *n*.

quad¹ *n, colloq* a quadruplet.

quad² *n, colloq* a quadrangle.

quad³ *colloq, adj* quadraphonic. ➤ *n* quadraphonics.

quadrangle *n* **1** *geom* a square, rectangle or other four-sided two-dimensional figure. **2** an open rectangular courtyard, esp one that is in the grounds of a college or school. ○ **quadrangular** *adj*.

quadrant *n* **1** *geom* **a** a quarter of the circumference of a circle; **b** a plane figure (see PLANE² *adj* sense 3) that is a quarter of a circle, ie an area bounded by two perpendicular radii and the arc between them; **c** a quarter of a sphere, ie a section cut by two planes that intersect at right angles at the centre. **2** any device or mechanical part in the shape of a 90° arc. **3** an instrument that was formerly used in astronomy and navigation and which consists of a graduated 90° arc allowing angular measurements, eg of the stars, to be taken and altitude calculated.

quadraphonic or **quadrophonic** *adj* of a stereophonic sound recording or reproduction: using four loudspeakers that are fed by four separate channels. ○ **quadraphonically** *adv*. ○ **quadraphonics** *n*.

quadrate *n, anat, zool* a muscle or bone that has a square or rectangular shape. ➤ *adj, bot* square or almost square in cross-section or face view.

quadratic *maths, n* **1** (*in full* **quadratic equation**) an algebraic equation that involves the square, but no higher power, of an unknown quantity or variable. **2** (**quadratics**) the branch of algebra that deals with this type of equation. ➤ *adj* **1** involving the square of an unknown quantity or variable but no higher power. **2** square.

quadrennial *adj* **1** lasting four years. **2** occurring every four years.

quadriceps *n* (**quadricepses** or **quadriceps**) *anat* a large four-part muscle that extends the leg and which runs down the front of the thigh.

quadrilateral *geom, n* a two-dimensional figure that has four sides. ➤ *adj* four-sided.

quadrille *n* **1** a square dance for four couples, in five or six movements. **2** music for this kind of dance.

quadripartite *adj* divided into or composed of four parts.

quadriplegia *n, pathol* paralysis that affects both arms and both legs. Compare HEMIPLEGIA, PARAPLEGIA. ○ **quadriplegic** *adj, n*.

quadruped /ˈkwɒdrʊpɛd/ *n* an animal, esp a mammal, that has its four limbs specially adapted for walking. ➤ *adj* four-footed.

quadruple *adj* **1** four times as great, much or many. **2** made up of four parts or things. **3** *mus* of time: having four beats to the bar. ➤ *vb, tr & intr* to make or become four times as great, much or many.

quadruplet *n* one of four children or animals born to the same mother at the same time.

quaff *vb, tr & intr, literary* to drink eagerly or deeply. ○ **quaffer** *n*.

quagga *n* an extinct member of the zebra family which had stripes around the head and shoulders.

quagmire /ˈkwɒɡmaɪə(r)/ *n* **1** an area of soft marshy ground; a bog. **2** a dangerous, difficult or awkward situation.

quail¹ *n* (*quail* or *quails*) a small migratory game bird of the partridge family.

quail² *vb, intr* to lose courage; to be apprehensive with fear.

quaint *adj* old-fashioned, strange or unusual, esp in a charming way. ○ **quaintness** *n*.

quake *vb, intr* **1** of people: to shake or tremble with fear, etc. **2** of a building, etc: to rock or shudder. ➢ *n, colloq* an earthquake. ○ **quaking** *adj, n*.

Quaker *n* a member of the Religious Society of Friends, a pacifist Christian organization. ○ **Quakerism** *n*.

qualification *n* **1** an official record that one has completed a training course or performed satisfactorily in an examination, etc. **2** a skill or ability that fits one for some job, etc. **3** the act, process or fact of qualifying. **4** an addition to a statement, etc that modifies, narrows or restricts its implications; a condition.

qualify *vb* (*-ies, -ied*) **1** *intr* to complete a training course or pass an examination, etc, esp in order to practise a specified profession. **2 a** (*often* **qualify sb for sth**) to give or provide them with the necessary competence, ability, attributes, etc to do it; **b** to entitle: *that qualifies you to get £10 discount*. **3** *intr* **a** to meet or fulfil the required conditions, guidelines, etc (in order to receive an award, privilege, etc); **b** (*usu* **qualify as sth**) to have the right characteristics to be a specified thing. **4 a** to modify (a statement, document, agreement, etc) in such a way as to restrict, limit or moderate it; **b** to add reservations to something; to tone it down. **5** *gram* of a word or phrase: to modify, define or describe (another word or phrase). **6** *tr & intr, sport* to proceed or allow someone to proceed to the later stages or rounds (of a competition, etc). ○ **qualified** *adj*. ○ **qualifier** *n*. ○ **qualifying** *adj, n*.

qualitative *adj* relating to, affecting or concerned with distinctions of the quality or standard of something. Compare QUANTITATIVE.

quality *n* (*-ies*) **1** the degree or extent of excellence of something. **2** general excellence; high standard: *articles of consistent quality*. **3 a** a distinctive or distinguishing talent, attribute, etc; **b** the basic nature of something. ➢ *adj* being of or exhibiting a high quality or standard: *the quality newspapers*.

quality control *n* a system or process that involves regular sampling of the output of an industrial process in order to detect any variations in quality.

qualm /kwɑːm/ *n* **1 a** a sudden feeling of nervousness or apprehension; **b** a feeling of uneasiness about whether a decision, course of action, etc is really for the best; **c** a scruple, misgiving or pang of conscience. **2** a feeling of faintness or nausea.

quandary *n* (*-ies*) **1** (*usu* **in a quandary about, over, as to,** *etc* **sth**) a state of indecision, uncertainty, doubt or perplexity. **2** a situation that involves some kind of dilemma or predicament.

quango *n* a semi-public administrative body that functions outside the civil service but which is government-funded.

quantify *vb* (*-ies, -ied*) **1** to determine the quantity of something or to measure or express it as a quantity. **2** *logic* to stipulate the extent of (a term or proposition) by using a word such as *all, some,* etc. ○ **quantifiable** *adj*.

quantitative *adj* **1** relating to or involving quantity. **2** estimated, or measurable, in terms of quantity. Compare QUALITATIVE.

quantity *n* (*-ies*) **1** the property that things have that allows them to be measured or counted; size or amount. **2** a specified amount or number: *a tiny quantity*. **3** largeness of amount; bulk: *buy in quantity*. **4** *maths* a value that may be expressed as a number, or the symbol or figure representing it.

quantity surveyor *n* a person whose job is to estimate the amount and cost of the various materials, labour, etc that a specified building project will require.

quantum *n* (*quanta*) **1** an amount or quantity, esp a specified one. **2** *physics* **a** the minimal indivisible amount of a specified physical property (eg momentum or electromagnetic radiation energy) that can exist; **b** a unit of this, eg the PHOTON.

quantum leap or **quantum jump** *n* **1** a sudden transition; a spectacular advance. **2** *physics* a sudden transition from one quantum state in an atom or molecule to another.

quantum theory *n, physics* a theory that is based on the principle that in physical systems, the energy associated with any QUANTUM is proportional to the frequency of the radiation.

quarantine *n* **1** the isolation of people or animals to prevent the spread of any infectious disease that they could be developing. **2** the duration or place of such isolation. ➢ *vb* to put (a person or animal) into quarantine.

quark¹ /kwɑːk, kwaːk/ *n, physics* the smallest known bit of matter, being any of a group of subatomic particles which, in different combinations, are thought to make up all protons, neutrons and other hadrons.

quark² /kwɑːk/ *n* a type of low-fat soft cheese that is made from skimmed milk.

quarrel *n* **1** an angry disagreement or argument. **2** a cause of such disagreement. **3** a break in a friendship. ➢ *vb* (**quarrelled, quarrelling**; *US* **quarreled, quarreling**) *intr* **1** to argue or dispute angrily. **2** to fall out; to disagree and remain on bad terms. **3** (*usu* **quarrel with sb** or **sth**) to find fault with them or it. ○ **quarrelsome** *adj*.

quarry¹ *n* (*-ies*) **1** an open excavation for the

purpose of extracting stone or slate for building. **2** a place from which stone, etc can be excavated. ➤ *vb* (*-ies, -ied*) **1** to extract (stone, etc) from a quarry. **2** to excavate a quarry in (land). ○ **quarrying** *n*.

quarry² *n* (*-ies*) **1** an animal or bird that is hunted, esp one that is the usual prey of some other animal or bird. **2** someone or something that is the object of pursuit.

quarry tile *n* an unglazed floor tile.

quart *n* **1** in the UK: **a** in the imperial system: a liquid measure equivalent to one quarter of a gallon, two pints (1.136 litres) or 40fl oz; **b** a container that holds this amount. **2** in the US: **a** a unit of liquid measure that is equivalent to two pints (0.946 litres) or 32fl oz; **b** a unit of dry measure that is equivalent to two pints (1.101 litres), an eighth of a peck.

quarter *n* **1 a** one of four equal parts that an object or quantity is or can be divided into; **b** (often written ¼) the number one when it is divided by four. **2** any of the three-month divisions of the year, esp one that begins or ends on a QUARTER DAY. **3** *N Am* **a** 25 cents, ie a quarter of a dollar; **b** a coin of this value. **4 a** a period of 15 minutes; **b** a point of time 15 minutes after or before any hour. **5** *astron* **a** a fourth part of the Moon's cycle; **b** either of the two phases of the Moon when half its surface is lit and visible at the point between the first and second and the third and fourth quarters of its cycle. **6** any of the four main compass directions. **7** a district of a city: *the Spanish quarter.* **8** (*also* **quarters**) a section of the public or society: *no sympathy from that quarter.* **9** (**quarters**) lodgings or accommodation, eg for soldiers and their families: *married quarters.* **10** in the imperial system: **a** a unit of weight equal to a quarter of a hundredweight, ie (*Brit*) 28lb or (*US*) 25lb; **b** *Brit colloq* four ounces or a quarter of a pound; **c** *Brit* a unit of measure for grain equal to eight bushels. **11 a** any of the four sections that an animal's or bird's carcass is divided into, each section having a leg or a wing; **b** (**quarters**) *hist* the four similar sections that a human body was divided into, esp after execution for treason. **12** mercy that is shown or offered, eg to a defeated enemy, etc: *give no quarter.* **13** *heraldry* any of the four sections of a shield which are formed by two perpendicular horizontal and vertical lines. **14** *sport* any of the four equal sections that some games are divided into. ➤ *vb* **1** to divide something into quarters. **2 a** to accommodate or billet (troops, etc) in lodgings; **b** *intr* esp of military personnel: to be accommodated in lodgings. **3** *hist* to divide (the body of a hanged traitor, etc) into four parts. **4** *heraldry* **a** to divide (a shield) into quarters using one horizontal and one vertical line; **b** to fill (each quarter of a shield) with bearings. **5** of a hunting dog or a bird of prey: to cross and recross (an area) searching for game.

quarterback *n, Amer football* a player who directs the attacking play.

quarter day *n, Brit* any of the four days when one of the QUARTERS (*noun* sense 2) of the year begins or ends, traditionally days on which rent or interest fell due.

quarterdeck *n, naut* the stern part of a ship's upper deck which is usu reserved for officers.

quarter final *n* a match or the round that involves the eight remaining participants or teams in a competition, cup, etc and which precedes the semifinal.

quarterly *adj* produced, occurring, published, paid or due once every quarter of a year. ➤ *adv* once every quarter. ➤ *n* (*-ies*) a quarterly publication.

quartermaster *n* **1** an army officer who is responsible for soldiers' accommodation, food and clothing. **2** *naut* a petty officer who is responsible for navigation and signals.

quarter note *n, N Am, mus* a crotchet.

quartet *n* **1** *mus* **a** an ensemble of four singers or instrumentalists; **b** a piece of music for four performers. **2** any group or set of four.

quarto *n, printing* **1** a size of paper produced by folding a sheet in half twice to give four leaves or eight pages. **2** a book that has pages of this size of paper.

quartz *n, geol* a common colourless mineral that is often tinged with impurities that give a wide variety of shades making it suitable as a gemstone.

quartz clock or **quartz watch** *n* a clock or watch that has a mechanism which is controlled by the vibrations of a QUARTZ CRYSTAL.

quartz crystal *n* a disc or rod cut from quartz that is ground so that it vibrates at a specified frequency when a suitable electrical signal is applied to it.

quartzite *n, geol* **1** a highly durable rock that is composed largely or entirely of quartz. **2** a sandstone consisting of grains of quartz cemented together by silica.

quasar /'kweızɑː(r)/ *n, astron* a highly intense luminous star-like source of light and radio waves that exists thousands of millions of light years outside the Earth's galaxy.

quash *vb* **1** to subdue, crush or suppress (eg a rebellion or protest). **2** to reject (a verdict, etc) as invalid. **3** to annul (a law, etc).

quaternary *adj* **1** having or consisting of four parts. **2** fourth in a series. **3** (**Quaternary**) *geol* belonging or relating to the most recent period of geological time when humans evolved. ➤ *n, geol* the Quaternary period or rock system.

quatrain *n, poetry* a verse or poem of four lines.

quatrefoil /'katrəfɔıl/ *n* **1** *bot* a flower or leaf with four petals or leaflets. **2** *archit* a four-lobed design, esp one that is used in open stonework.

quattrocento /kwatrou'tʃɛntou/ *n* the 15c, esp with reference to Italian Renaissance art.

quaver *vb, intr* of a voice, a musical sound, etc: to shake or tremble. ➤ *n* **1** *mus* a note that lasts half as long as a CROTCHET. **2** a tremble in the voice.

quay /kiː/ n an artificial structure that projects into the water for the loading and unloading of ships.

quayside n the area around a quay.

queasy adj (-ier, -iest) **1** of a person: feeling slightly sick. **2** of the stomach or digestion: easily upset. ○ **queasily** adv. ○ **queasiness** n.

queen n **1 a** a woman who rules a country, having inherited her position by birth; **b** (in full **queen consort**) the wife of a king; **c** (usu **Queen**) the title applied to someone who holds either of these positions. **2** a woman, place or thing considered supreme in some way: the new queen of tennis. **3** a large fertile female ant, bee or wasp that lays eggs. **4** chess a piece that is able to move in any direction. **5** cards any of the four cards that have a picture of a queen on them. **6** derog an effeminate homosexual man. ➤ vb, chess to advance (a pawn) to the opponent's side of the board and convert it into a queen.

Queen Anne adj, denoting a style of English architecture and furniture, etc that was popular in the early 18c.

queen bee n **1** the fertile female in a beehive. **2** the dominant, superior or controlling woman in an organization.

queenly adj (-ier, -iest) **1** suitable for or appropriate to a queen. **2** majestic; like a queen.

queen mother n the widow of a king who is also the mother of the reigning king or queen.

queen-size or **queen-sized** adj esp of a bed or other piece of furniture: larger than the usual or normal size but not as large as king-size.

queer adj **1** slang of a man: homosexual. **2** odd, strange or unusual. **3** colloq slightly mad. **4** faint or ill. ➤ n, slang a homosexual. ◆ **in queer street** Brit, colloq **1** in financial difficulties. **2** in trouble. **queer sb's pitch** colloq to spoil their plans.

quell vb **1** to crush or subdue (riots, opposition, etc). **2** to suppress or put an end to (unwanted feelings, etc).

quench vb **1** to satisfy (thirst, a desire, etc). **2** to extinguish (a fire or light). **3** metallurgy to cool (hot metal) rapidly by plunging in cold liquid in order to alter its properties.

quenelle /kəˈnɛl/ n, cookery a sausage-shaped dumpling made from spiced meat-paste.

quern n **1** a mill, usu consisting of two circular stones (**quernstones**) one on top of the other, used for grinding grain by hand. **2** a small hand mill for grinding pepper, mustard, etc.

querulous /ˈkwɛrjʊləs, -rʊləs/ adj **1** of someone or their disposition: inclined or ready to complain. **2** of a voice, tone, comment, etc: complaining or whining. ○ **querulously** adv.

query n (-ies) **1** a question, esp one that raises a doubt or objection. **2** a request for information. **3** a less common name for a QUESTION MARK. ➤ vb (-ies, -ied) **1** to raise a doubt about something. **2** to ask.

quest n **1** a search or hunt. **2** a journey, esp one undertaken by a medieval knight, that involves searching for something. **3** the object of a search; an aim or goal. ➤ vb, intr **1** (usu **quest after** or **for sth**) to roam around in search of it. **2** of a dog: to search for game.

question n **1 a** a written or spoken sentence that is worded in such a way as to request information or an answer; **b** the form of words in which this is expressed. **2** a doubt or query. **3** a problem or difficulty: the Iraq question. **4** a problem set for discussion or solution in an examination paper, etc. **5** an investigation or search for information. **6** a matter, concern or issue: a question of safety. ➤ vb **1** to ask someone questions; to interrogate them. **2** to raise doubts about something; to query it. ○ **questioner** n. ◆ **call sth in** or **into question** to suggest reasons for doubting its validity, truth, etc. **in question 1** presently under discussion or being referred to: I was away at the time in question. **2** in doubt: Her ability is not in question. **out of the question** impossible and so not worth considering.

questionable adj **1** doubtful; debatable. **2** suspect; disreputable. ○ **questionably** adv.

questioning n an act or the process of asking a question or questions. ➤ adj **1** characterized by doubt or uncertainty; mildly confused: We exchanged questioning looks. **2** esp of a person's mind: inquisitive; keen to learn.

question mark n **1** the punctuation mark (?) which is used to indicate that the sentence that comes before it is a question. **2** a doubt: There is still a question mark over funds.

questionnaire n a set of questions that has been specially formulated as a means of collecting information, surveying opinions, etc.

queue /kjuː/ n **1** Brit a line or file of people, vehicles, etc, esp ones that are waiting for something. **2** comput a list of items, eg programs or data, held in a computer system in the order in which they are to be processed. ➤ vb, intr **1** (also **queue up**) **a** to form a queue; **b** to stand or wait in a queue. **2** comput to line up tasks for a computer to process.

quibble vb, intr to argue over trifles; to make petty objections. ➤ n a trifling objection.

quiche /kiːʃ/ n a type of open tart that is usu made with a filling of beaten eggs and cream with various savoury flavourings.

quick adj **1** taking little time. **2** brief. **3** fast; speedy. **4** not delayed; immediate. **5** intelligent; alert. **6** of the temper: easily roused to anger. **7** nimble, deft or brisk. **8** not reluctant or slow (to do something): quick to take offence. ➤ adv, colloq rapidly. ➤ n **1** an area of sensitive flesh, esp at the base of the fingernail or toenail. **2** the site where someone's emotions or feelings are supposed to be located: Her words wounded him to the quick. **3** (usu **the quick**) old use those who are alive: the quick and the dead. ○ **quickly** adv. ○ **quickness** n.

quicken vb **1** tr & intr to make or become quicker; to accelerate. **2** to stimulate, rouse or stir (interest, imagination, etc).

quick-fire *adj* **1** esp of repartee, etc: very rapid. **2** of a gun, etc: able to fire shots in rapid succession.

quickie *n, colloq* **1** something that is dealt with or done rapidly or in a short time. **2** (*also* **a quick one**) a measure of alcohol that is drunk quickly.

quicksand *n* loose, wet sand that can suck down anything that lands or falls on it, often swallowing it up completely.

quickset *n* **1** a living slip or cutting from a plant that is put into the ground with others where they will grow to form a hedge. **2** a hedge that is formed from such slips or cuttings. ➢ *adj* of a hedge: formed from such slips or cuttings.

quicksilver *n* MERCURY (sense I). ➢ *adj* of someone's mind, temper, etc: fast, esp unpredictably so; volatile.

quickstep *n* **1** a fast modern ballroom dance in quadruple time. **2** a piece of music suitable for this kind of dance. ➢ *vb, intr* to dance the quickstep.

quick-tempered *adj* easily angered.

quick-witted *adj* **1** having fast reactions. **2** able to grasp or understand situations, etc quickly. ○ **quick-wittedness** *n*.

quid¹ *n* (*pl* **quid**) *colloq* a pound sterling. ◆ **quids in** well-off; in a profitable or advantageous position.

quid² *n* a bit of tobacco that is kept in the mouth and chewed.

quiddity *n* (*-ies*) **1** the essence of something; the distinctive qualities, etc that make a thing what it is. **2** a trifling detail or point.

quid pro quo /kwɪd prou kwoʊ/ *n* something that is given or taken in exchange for something else of comparable value or status.

quiescent /kwɪˈɛsənt/ *adj* quiet, silent, at rest or in an inactive state, usu temporarily. ○ **quiescence** *n*.

quiet *adj* **1 a** making little or no noise; **b** of a sound, voice, etc: not loud. **2** of a place, etc: tranquil; without noise or bustle. **3** of someone or their nature or disposition: reserved; shy. **4** of the weather, sea, etc: calm. **5** not disturbed by trouble or excitement. **6** without fuss or publicity. **7** of business or trade: not flourishing or busy. **8** secret; private. **9** undisclosed or hidden: *a quiet satisfaction.* **10** enjoyed in peace: *a quiet read.* **11** not showy or gaudy: *quiet tones of beige.* ➢ *n* **1** absence of, or freedom from, noise, commotion, etc. **2** calm, tranquillity or repose. ➢ *vb, tr & intr* (*usu* **quiet down**) to make or become quiet or calm: *He told the class to quiet down.* ○ **quietly** *adv.* ○ **quietness** *n*. ◆ **keep quiet about sth** or **keep sth quiet** to remain silent or say nothing about it. **on the quiet** secretly; discreetly.

quieten *vb* **1** (*often* **quieten down**) *tr & intr* to make or become quiet. **2** to calm (doubts, fears, etc).

quietism *n* a state of calmness and passivity.

quietude *n* quietness; tranquillity.

quietus *n* **1 a** release from life; death; **b** something that brings about death. **2** release or discharge from debts or duties.

quiff *n* a tuft of hair at the front of the head that is brushed up into a crest and which is sometimes made to hang over the forehead.

quill *n* **1 a** a large stiff feather from a bird's wing or tail; **b** the hollow base part of this. **2** (*in full* **quill pen**) a pen that is made by sharpening and splitting the end of a feather, esp a goose feather. **3** a porcupine's long spine.

quilt *n* **1** a type of bedcover that is made by sewing together two layers of fabric, usu with some kind of soft padding in between them. **2** a bedspread that is made in this way but which tends to be thinner. **3** *loosely* a duvet. ➢ *vb, tr & intr* **1** to sew (two layers of material, etc) together with a filling in between. **2** to cover or line something with padding. ○ **quilted** *adj*. ○ **quilter** *n*.

quin *n, colloq* a quintuplet.

quince *n* **1** a small Asian tree of the rose family. **2** the acidic hard yellow fruit of this tree, which is used in making jams, jellies, etc.

quincentenary *n* (*-ies*) **1** a 500th anniversary. **2** a celebration that is held to mark this. ○ **quincentennial** *adj*.

quincunx *n* **a** an arrangement in which each of the four corners of a square or rectangle and the point at its centre are all indicated by some object; **b** five objects that are arranged in this way.

quinine /ˈkwɪniːn/ or (*esp US*) /ˈkwaɪnaɪn/ *n* **1** an alkaloid that is found in the bark of the CINCHONA. **2** *med* a bitter-tasting toxic drug obtained from this alkaloid, formerly taken as a tonic and widely used in treating malaria.

quinquennial *adj* **1** lasting for five years. **2** recurring once every five years.

quinquennium *n* (*quinquennia*) a period of five years.

quinquereme *n, hist* a type of ancient Roman or Greek galley ship that had five banks of oars.

quinquevalent *adj, chem* alternative for PENTAVALENT.

quinsy *n, pathol* inflammation of the tonsils and the area of the throat round about them, accompanied by the formation of an abscess or abscesses on the tonsils.

quintal *n* **1** a unit of weight that is equal to a hundredweight, 112lb in Britain or 100lb in the US. **2** in the metric system: a unit of weight that is equal to 100kg.

quintessence *n* **1** (*usu* **quintessence of sth**) a perfect example or embodiment of it. **2** the fundamental essential nature of something. **3** *old use* the purest, most concentrated extract of a substance. ○ **quintessential** *adj*. ○ **quintessentially** *adv*.

quintet *n* **1** a group of five singers or musicians. **2** a piece of music for five such performers. **3** any group or set of five.

quintuple *adj* **1** five times as great, much or many. **2** made up of five parts or things. **3** *mus* of time: having five beats to the bar. ➤ *vb, tr & intr* to make or become five times as great, much or many. ➤ *n* an amount that is five times greater than the original, usual, etc amount.

quintuplet *n* one of five children or animals born to the same mother at the same time.

quip *n* **1** a witty saying. **2** a sarcastic or wounding remark. ➤ *vb* (**quipped, quipping**) **1** *intr* to make a quip or quips. **2** to answer someone with a quip.

quire *n* **1** a measure for paper that is equivalent to 25 (formerly 24) sheets and one-twentieth of a REAM. **2 a** a set of four sheets of parchment or paper folded in half together to form eight leaves; **b** *loosely* any set of folded sheets that is grouped together with other similar ones and bound into book form.

quirk *n* **1** an odd habit, mannerism or aspect of personality, etc. **2** an odd twist in affairs or turn of events. ○ **quirkiness** *n*. ○ **quirky** *adj* (*-ier, -iest*).

quisling *n* **1** a traitor. **2** someone who collaborates with an enemy.

quit *vb* (**quitted** or **quit, quitting**) **1** to leave or depart from (a place, etc). **2** *tr & intr* to leave, give up or resign (a job). **3** to exit (a computer program, application, game, etc). **4** *N Am, colloq* to cease something or doing something. **5** *tr & intr* of a tenant: to move out of rented premises. ○ **quitter** *n*.

quitch *n* (*in full* **quitch grass**) another name for COUCH[2].

quite *adv* **1** completely; entirely: *I quite understand*. **2** to a high degree: *quite exceptional*. **3** to some or a limited degree: *quite a nice day*. **4** (*also* **quite so**) used in a reply: I agree, see your point, etc. ♦ **not quite** hardly; just short of or less than a specified thing. **quite a** or **an** a striking, impressive, daunting, challenging, etc: *That was quite a night*. **quite a few** *colloq* a reasonably large number of (people or things). **quite some** a considerably large amount of: *quite some time*. **quite something** very impressive.

quits *adj, colloq* **1** on an equal footing. **2** even, esp where money is concerned. ♦ **call it quits** to agree to stop arguing and accept that the outcome is even.

quittance *n* **1** release from debt or other obligation. **2** a document that acknowledges this.

quiver[1] *vb* **1** (*often* **quiver with sth**) *intr* to shake or tremble slightly because of it; to shiver: *Her voice quivered with fear*. **2** *intr* to shake or flutter. ➤ *n* a tremble or shiver.

quiver[2] *n* a long narrow case for carrying arrows.

quixotic /kwɪk'sɒtɪk/ *adj* **1** absurdly generous or chivalrous. **2** naively romantic, idealistic, impractical, etc. ○ **quixotically** *adv*.

quiz *n* (**quizzes**) **1** an entertainment in which the knowledge of a panel of contestants is tested through a series of questions. **2** any series of questions as a test of general or specialized knowledge. **3** an interrogation. ➤ *vb*

(**quizzes, quizzed, quizzing**) to question or interrogate someone.

quizzical *adj* of a look, expression, etc: mildly amused or perplexed. ○ **quizzically** *adv*.

quod *n, Brit, slang* prison.

quod erat demonstrandum see under QED

quoin /kɔɪn/ *n* **1** the external angle of a wall or building. **2** a cornerstone. **3** a wedge.

quoit /kɔɪt/ *n* **1** a ring made of metal, rubber or rope used in the game of quoits. **2** (**quoits**) a game that involves throwing these rings at pegs with the aim of encircling them or landing close to them.

quorate *adj, Brit* of a meeting, etc: attended by or consisting of enough people to form a quorum.

quorum *n* the fixed minimum number of members of an organization, society, etc who must be present at a meeting for its business to be valid.

quota *n* **1** the proportional or allocated share or part that is, or that should be, done, paid, contributed, etc out of a total amount. **2** the maximum or prescribed number or quantity that is permitted or required, eg of imported goods.

quotation *n* **1** a remark or a piece of writing, etc that is quoted. **2** the act or an instance of quoting. **3** *business* an estimated price for a job submitted by a contractor to a client. **4** *stock exchange* an amount that is stated as the current price of a commodity, stock, security, etc.

quotation marks *pl n* a pair of punctuation marks which can be either single (' ') or double (" "), used to mark the beginning and end of a quoted passage.

quote *vb, tr & intr* **1** to cite or offer (someone else or the words, ideas, etc of someone else) to substantiate an argument. **2** to repeat in writing or speech (the exact words, etc of someone else). **3** to cite or repeat (figures, data, etc). **4** *tr & intr* of a contractor: to submit or suggest (a price) for doing a specified job or for buying something: *They quoted her £600 as a trade-in*. **5** *stock exchange* to state the price of (a security, commodity, stock, etc). ♦ **quote sth at sth** to give (a racehorse) betting odds as specified: *quoted at 2/1*. **7 a** to put quotation marks around (a written passage, word, title, etc); **b** (*also* **quote … unquote**) to indicate (in speech) that a specified part has been said by someone else. ➤ *n* **1** a quotation. **2** a price quoted. **3** (**quotes**) quotation marks.

quoth *vb, old use* said: *'Alas!' quoth he*.

quotidian *adj* **1** everyday; common-place. **2** daily. **3** recurring daily.

quotient /'kwoʊʃənt/ *n, maths* the result of a division sum, eg when 72 (the DIVIDEND) is divided by 12 (the DIVISOR), the quotient is 6.

qv or **q.v.** *abbrev: quod vide* (Latin), which see.

qwerty or **QWERTY** *adj* of an English-language typewriter, word processor or other keyboard: having the standard arrangement of keys, ie with the letters *q w e r t y* appearing in that order at the top left of the letters section.

Rr

R¹ or **r** (*Rs*, *R's* or *r's*) the eighteenth letter of the English alphabet.

R² or **R.** *abbrev* **1** rand. **2** *physics, electronics* resistance. **3 a** *Regina* (Latin), Queen; **b** *Rex* (Latin), King. **4** River.

r or **r.** *abbrev* **1** radius. **2** right.

Ra *symbol, chem* radium.

rabbi /'rabaɪ/ *n* **1** a Jewish religious leader. **2** a Jewish scholar or teacher of the law. ○ **rabbinical** /rə'bɪnɪkəl/ *adj*.

rabbit *n* **1** a small burrowing herbivorous mammal with long ears and a small stubby tail. **2** its flesh as food. **3** its fur. ➤ *vb* (**rabbited, rabbiting**) *intr* **1** to hunt rabbits. **2** (*usu* **rabbit on** or **away**) *colloq* to talk at great length.

rabble *n* **1** a noisy disorderly crowd. **2** (**the rabble**) the lowest class of people.

rabble-rouser *n* someone who agitates for social or political change. ○ **rabble-rousing** *adj, n*.

rabid *adj* **1** of dogs, etc: suffering from rabies. **2** fanatical.

rabies *n* a potentially fatal viral disease affecting mammals, esp dogs, and communicable to humans.

raccoon or **racoon** *n* (**raccoons** or **raccoon**) **1** a nocturnal American mammal with characteristic black eye patches. **2** its dense fur.

race¹ *n* **1** a contest of speed between runners, cars, etc. **2** (*usu* **the races**) a series of such contests over a fixed course, esp for horses. **3** any contest, esp to be the first to do or get something: *the space race*. **4** a strong current of water. **5** a channel conveying water to and from a mill wheel. ➤ *vb* **1** *intr* to take part in a race. **2** to have a race with. **3** to cause (a horse, car, etc) to race. **4** *intr* (*usu* **race about** or **along** or **around**) to move quickly and energetically. **5** *intr* of an engine, etc: to run too fast. ○ **racer** *n*. ○ **racing** *n, adj*.

race² *n* **1** any of the major divisions of humankind distinguished by a particular set of physical characteristics. **2** a nation or similar group of people thought of as distinct from others. **3** (**the human race**) human beings as a group. **4** a group of animals or plants within a species, which have characteristics distinguishing them from other members of that species.

racecourse or **racetrack** *n* a course or track used for racing horses, cars, etc.

racehorse *n* a horse bred and used for racing.

raceme /ra'siːm/ *n, bot* a flower head consisting of individual flowers attached to a main unbranched stem.

race meeting *n* a series of races, esp horse races, taking place over the same course.

race relations *pl n* social relations between people of different races living in the same community.

racetrack see RACECOURSE

racial *adj* **1** relating to a particular race. **2** based on race. ○ **racialism** *n*. ○ **racialist** *n, adj*.

racism *n* **1** hatred, rivalry or bad feeling between races. **2** belief in the inherent superiority of a particular race or races. **3** discriminatory treatment based on such a belief. ○ **racist** *n, adj*.

rack¹ *n* **1** a framework with rails, shelves, hooks, etc for holding things. **2** a cogged or toothed bar connecting with a cogwheel or pinion for changing the position of something. **3** (**the rack**) *hist* a device for torturing people by stretching their bodies. ➤ *vb* **1** to put in a rack. **2** to move or adjust by rack and pinion. **3** *hist* to torture on a rack. **4** to cause pain or suffering to. ♦ **on the rack** extremely anxious or distressed. **rack one's brains** to think as hard as one can.

rack² *n* destruction. ♦ **go to rack and ruin** to get into a state of neglect and decay.

rack and pinion *n* a means of turning rotary motion into linear motion or vice versa by means of a toothed wheel engaging in a rack.

racket¹ or **racquet** *n* a bat with a handle ending in a rounded head with a network of strings used in tennis, badminton, squash, etc.

racket² *n* **1** *colloq* a loud confused noise or disturbance. **2** an illegal means of making money. **3** *slang* a job or occupation.

racketeer *n* someone who makes money in an illegal way. ○ **racketeering** *n*.

rackets *sing n* a game derived from REAL TENNIS played by two or four players in a walled court.

raconteur /rakɒn'tɜː(r)/ or **raconteuse** /-'tɜːz/ *n* someone who tells anecdotes.

racoon see RACCOON

racquet see RACKET¹

racy *adj* (**-ier, -iest**) **1** lively or spirited. **2** slightly indecent. ○ **racily** *adv*. ○ **raciness** *n*.

rad *abbrev* radian.

radar *n* **1** a system for detecting the presence of ships, aircraft, etc by transmitting short pulses of high-frequency radio waves. **2** the equipment for sending and receiving such radio waves.

radar trap *n* the use of radar to detect vehicles travelling faster than the speed limit.

raddle *vb* **1** to colour or mark with red ochre. **2** to wear out or cause to become untidy.

radial *adj* **1** spreading out like rays. **2** relating to rays, a radius or radii. **3** along or in the direction of a radius or radii. **4** *anat* relating to the RA-DIUS (sense 5). ➤ *n* **1** a radiating part. **2** (*in full* **radial-ply tyre**) a tyre with fabric cords laid at right angles to the tread, giving the walls flexibility. ○ **radially** *adv*.

radian *n, geom* the SI unit of plane angular measurement defined as the angle that is made at the centre of a circle by an arc whose length is equal to the radius of the circle.

radiant *adj* **1** emitting electromagnetic radiation, eg rays of light or heat. **2** shining. **3** of a person: beaming with joy, love or health. **4** transmitted by or as radiation. ➤ *n* a point or object which emits electromagnetic radiation, eg light or heat. ○ **radiance** *n*. ○ **radiantly** *adv*.

radiant heat *n* heat transmitted by electromagnetic radiation.

radiate *vb* **1** to send out rays of light, heat, electromagnetic radiation, etc. **2** *intr* of light, heat, radiation, etc: to be emitted in rays. **3** of a person: to manifestly exhibit (happiness, good health, etc): *radiate vitality*. **4** *tr & intr* to spread or cause to spread out from a central point. ➤ *adj* having rays, radii or a radial structure.

radiation *n* **1** energy, usu electromagnetic radiation, eg radio waves, visible light or X-rays, that is emitted from a source and travels in the form of waves or particles. **2** a stream of particles emitted by a radioactive substance.

radiation sickness *n* illness caused by exposure to high levels of radiation.

radiator *n* **1** an apparatus for heating, consisting of a series of pipes through which hot water or hot oil is circulated. **2** an apparatus for cooling an engine, eg in a car, consisting of a series of water-filled tubes and a fan.

radical *adj* **1** concerning or relating to the basic nature of something. **2** thoroughgoing: *radical changes*. **3** in favour of or tending to produce reforms. **4** relating to a political, etc group in favour of extreme reforms. **5** *med* of treatment: with the purpose of removing the source of a disease: *radical surgery*. **6** *maths* relating to the root of a number. ➤ *n* **1** a root or basis in any sense. **2** someone who is a member of a radical political group. **3** *chem* within a molecule: a group of atoms which remains unchanged during a series of chemical reactions, but is normally incapable of independent existence: *free radical*. **4** *maths* the root of a number. ○ **radicalism** *n*. ○ **radicalize** or **-ise** *vb*. ○ **radically** *adv*.

radicchio /ra'di:kɪoʊ/ *n* a variety of chicory with purplish leaves used in salads.

radicle *n, bot* the part of a plant embryo which develops into the main root.

radii *pl of* RADIUS

radio *n* **1** the use of radio waves to transmit and receive information such as television or radio programmes, telecommunications, and computer data, without connecting wires. **2** a wireless device that receives, and may also transmit, information in this manner. **3** a message or broadcast that is transmitted in this manner. **4** the business or profession of sound broadcasting: *to work in radio*. ➤ *adj* **1** relating to radio. **2** for transmitting by, or transmitted by, radio. **3** controlled by radio. ➤ *vb* **1** to send (a message) to someone by radio. **2** *intr* to broadcast or communicate by radio.

radio- *comb form, denoting* **1** radio or broadcasting. **2** radioactivity. **3** rays or radiation.

radioactive *adj* relating to or affected by radioactivity.

radioactivity *n* **1** the spontaneous disintegration of the nuclei of certain atoms, accompanied by the emission of alpha particles, beta particles or gamma rays. **2** the subatomic particles or radiation emitted during this process.

radiocarbon *n* a radioactive isotope of carbon, esp carbon-14.

radiocarbon dating *n* CARBON DATING.

radio frequency *n* a frequency of electromagnetic waves used for radio and television broadcasting.

radiogram *n, old use* an apparatus consisting of a radio and record player.

radiography /reɪdɪˈɒɡrəfɪ/ *n, med* the examination of the interior of the body by means of recorded images produced by X-rays on photographic film. ○ **radiographer** *n*.

radioisotope *n, physics* a naturally occurring or synthetic radioactive isotope of a chemical element.

radiology /reɪdɪˈɒlədʒɪ/ *n* the branch of medicine concerned with the use of RADIATION (eg X-rays) and radioactive isotopes to diagnose and treat diseases. ○ **radiological** *adj*. ○ **radiologist** *n*.

radiophonic /reɪdɪəˈfɒnɪk/ *adj* **1** of sound, esp of music: produced electronically. **2** producing electronic music. ○ **radiophonics** *pl n*.

radioscopy /reɪdɪˈɒskəpɪ/ *n* the examination of the inside of the body, or of opaque objects, using X-rays.

radio telephone *n* a telephone which works by radio waves.

radio telescope *n* a large aerial, together with amplifiers and recording equipment, that is used to study distant stars, etc by detecting the radio waves they emit.

radiotherapy or **radiotherapeutics** *n* the treatment of disease, esp cancer, by X-rays and other forms of radiation. Compare CHEMOTHERAPY.

radio wave *n, physics* an electromagnetic wave that has a low frequency and a long wavelength, widely used for communication.

radish *n* a plant with pungent-tasting red-skinned white roots which are eaten raw in salads.

radium *n, chem* a silvery-white highly toxic radioactive metallic element, obtained from uranium ores.

radius /'reɪdɪəs/ *n* (*radii* /-dɪaɪ/ or *radiuses*) **1** *geom* **a** a straight line running from the centre of a circle or sphere to any point on its circumference; **b** the length of such a line. **2** a radiating line. **3** anything placed like a radius, such as the spoke of a wheel. **4** a distance from a central point, thought of as defining, limiting, etc an area: *houses within a radius of 10km.* **5** *anat* the shorter of the two bones in the forearm.

radon /'reɪdɒn/ *n, chem* a highly toxic radioactive gas that is formed by the decay of radium.

RAF *abbrev* Royal Air Force.

raffia *n* ribbon-like fibre obtained from the leaves of a palm, used for weaving mats, baskets, etc.

raffish *adj* **1** of appearance, dress, behaviour, etc: slightly shady or disreputable. **2** flashy.

raffle *n* a LOTTERY in which numbered tickets, which are drawn from a container holding all the numbers sold, win prizes for the holders of the tickets that match the numbers drawn. ➤ *vb* (*also* **raffle off**) to offer in a raffle.

raft[1] *n* **1** a flat structure of logs, timber, etc, fastened together so as to float on water. **2** a flat, floating mass of ice, vegetation, etc.

raft[2] *n* (*often* **a raft of**) a large amount or collection.

rafter *n* a sloping beam supporting a roof.

rag[1] *n* **1** a worn, torn or waste scrap of cloth. **2** a shred, scrap or tiny portion of something. **3** (*usu* **rags**) an old or tattered garment. **4** *colloq* a newspaper.

rag[2] *vb* (**ragged, ragging**) **1** to tease. **2** to scold. ➤ *n* **1** *Brit* a series of stunts and events put on by university students to raise money for charity. **2** a prank.

ragamuffin *n* a person, usu a child, dressed in rags.

rag-and-bone man *n* someone who collects and deals in old clothes, furniture, etc.

ragbag *n, colloq* a random collection.

rag doll *n* a doll made from scraps of cloth.

rage *n* **1** anger. **2** a passionate outburst, esp of anger. **3** *in compounds* uncontrolled anger or aggression in a particular environment: *air rage.* **4** a violent, stormy action, esp of weather, the sea, etc. **5** an intense desire or passion for something. **6** *colloq* a widespread, usu temporary, fashion. ➤ *vb, intr* **1** to be violently angry. **2** to speak wildly with anger or passion. **3** of the wind, the sea, a battle, etc: to be stormy. ○ **raging** *adj, n.* ♦ **all the rage** *colloq* very much in fashion.

ragged /'ragɪd/ *adj* **1** of clothes: old, worn and tattered. **2** of a person: dressed in old, worn, tattered clothing. **3** with a rough and irregular edge. **4** untidy. **5** of a performance or ability: not of consistent quality.

raglan *adj* **1** of a sleeve: attached to a garment by two seams running diagonally from the neck to the armpit. **2** of a garment: having such sleeves.

ragout /ra'gu:/ *n* a highly seasoned stew of meat and vegetables.

ragtag *n* (*usu* **ragtag and bobtail**) the rabble.

ragtime *n* a type of jazz piano music with a highly syncopated rhythm.

rag trade *n, colloq* the business of designing, making and selling clothes.

raid *n* **1** a sudden unexpected attack. **2** an incursion by police, etc for the purpose of making arrests, or searching for suspected criminals or illicit goods. ➤ *vb* **1** to make a raid on (a person, place, etc). **2** *intr* to go on a raid. ○ **raider** *n.*

rail[1] *n* **1** a bar, usu horizontal and supported by vertical posts. **2** a horizontal bar used to hang things on: *a picture rail.* **3** either of a pair of lengths of metal forming a track for the wheels of a train or other vehicle. **4** the railway as a means of travel or transport: *go by rail.* **5** a horizontal section in panelling or framing. **6** (**the rails**) the fence which forms the inside barrier of a racecourse. ➤ *vb* **1** to provide with rails. **2** (*usu* **rail in** or **off**) to enclose or separate (eg a space) within a rail or rails. ♦ **off the rails** mad; eccentric.

rail[2] *vb, intr* (*usu* **rail at** or **against**) to complain bitterly.

rail[3] *n* a bird with a short neck and long legs, usu found near water.

railcar *n* **1** *US* a railway carriage. **2** a self-propelled railway carriage.

railing *n* **1** fencing or material for building fences. **2** (*often* **railings**) a barrier or ornamental fence.

raillery *n* (*-ies*) good-humoured teasing.

railroad *n, N Am* a railway. ➤ *vb* to rush or force someone or something unfairly (into doing something).

railway *n* **1** a track or set of tracks for trains to run on. **2** a system of such tracks, plus all the trains, buildings and people required for it to function. **3** a company responsible for operating such a system. **4** a similar set of tracks for a different type of vehicle: *funicular railway.*

raiment *n, archaic, poetic* clothing.

rain *n* **1** a condensed moisture falling as water droplets from the atmosphere; **b** a fall of this. **2** a fall, esp a heavy one, of something: *a rain of bullets.* **3** (**rains**) the season of heavy rainfall in tropical countries. ➤ *vb* **1** *intr* of rain: to fall. **2** *tr & intr* to fall or cause to fall like rain: *He rained compliments on her head.* ♦ **right as rain** *colloq* perfectly all right.

rainbow *n* an arch of red, orange, yellow, green, blue, indigo and violet seen in the sky when falling raindrops reflect and refract sunlight. ➤ *adj* multicoloured like a rainbow.

rainbow trout *n* a large freshwater trout.

rain check *n, chiefly N Am* a ticket for future use, given to spectators when a game or sports meeting is cancelled or stopped due to bad weather. ♦ **take a rain check (on sth)** *colloq, orig N Am* to ask for (an invitation) to be postponed.

raincoat *n* a waterproof or water-resistant coat.

raindrop *n* a single drop of rain.

rainfall *n* **1** the amount of rain that falls in a certain place over a certain period, measured by depth of water. **2** a shower of rain.

rainforest *n* forest in tropical regions, which has heavy rainfall.

rainy *adj* (**-ier, -iest**) characterized by periods of rain or by the presence of much rain: *a rainy afternoon.* ◆ **save** or **keep sth for a rainy day** to keep it for a future time of potential need.

raise *vb* **1** to move or lift to a higher position or level. **2** to put in an upright position. **3** to build. **4** to increase the value, amount or strength of something: *raise prices* • *raise one's voice.* **5** to put forward for consideration or discussion: *raise an objection.* **6** to gather together: *raise an army.* **7** to collect together (funds, money, etc): *raise money for charity.* **8** to stir up: *raise a protest.* **9** to bring into being; to provoke: *raise a laugh* • *raise the alarm.* **10** to promote to a higher rank. **11** to awaken or arouse from sleep or death. **12** to grow (vegetables, a crop, etc). **13** to bring up (a child, children, etc): *raise a family.* **14** to bring to an end or remove: *raise the siege.* **15** to cause (bread or dough) to rise with yeast. **16** to establish radio contact with. **17** *maths* to increase (a quantity to a given power): *3 raised to the power of 4 is 81.* **18** *cards* to increase a bet. ➤ *n* **1** an act of raising a bet, etc. **2** *colloq, esp N Am* an increase in salary. ◆ **raise Cain** or **the roof** *colloq* **1** to make a lot of noise. **2** to be extremely angry.

raise There is often a spelling confusion between **raise** and **raze**.

raisin *n* a dried grape.

raison d'être /ˈreɪzɑ̃ˈdɛːtrə/ *n* (**raisons d'être** /ˈreɪzɑ̃ˈdɛːtrə/) a purpose or reason that justifies someone's or something's existence.

Raj *n* (*usu* **the Raj**) the British rule of India, 1858–1947.

raja or **rajah** *n, hist* an Indian king or prince.

rake¹ *n* **1** a long-handled garden tool with a comb-like part at one end, used for smoothing or breaking up earth, gathering leaves together, etc. **2** any tool with a similar shape or use, eg one used by a croupier. ➤ *vb* **1** (*usu* **rake up** or **together**) to collect, gather or remove with, or as if with, a rake. **2** (*usu* **rake over**) to make smooth with a rake. **3** *intr* to work with, or as if with, a rake. **4** *tr & intr* (*often* **rake through**) to search carefully. **5** to sweep gradually along (the length of something), esp with gunfire or one's eyes. **6** to scrape. ◊ **rake sth in** *colloq* to earn or acquire (esp money) in large amounts: *She must be raking it in!* **rake sth up** *colloq* to revive or uncover (something forgotten or lost).

rake² *n, old use* a fashionable man who lives a dissolute life. ○ **rakish** *adj.* ○ **rakishly** *adv.*

rake³ *n* **1** a sloping position. **2** *theat* the slope of a stage. **3** the amount by which something slopes. ➤ *vb* **1** to set or construct at a sloping angle. **2** *intr* **a** of a ship's mast or funnel: to slope backwards towards the stern; **b** of a ship's bow or stern: to project out beyond the keel.

rake-off *n, colloq* a share of the profits, esp when dishonest or illegal.

rallentando *mus, adj, adv* as a musical direction: becoming gradually slower. ➤ *n* (**rallentandos, rallentandi**) in a piece of music: a passage to be played in this way.

rally *vb* (**-ies, -ied**) **1** *tr & intr* to come or bring together again after being dispersed. **2** *tr & intr* to come or bring together for some common cause or action. **3** *tr & intr* to revive (spirits, strength, abilities, etc) by making an effort. **4** *intr* to recover lost health, strength, etc, esp after an illness. **5** *intr* of share prices: to increase again after a fall. ➤ *n* (**-ies**) **1** a reassembling of forces to make a new effort. **2** a mass meeting of people with a common cause or interest. **3** a recovering of lost health, strength, etc, esp after an illness. **4** *tennis* a series of strokes between players before one of them finally wins the point. **5** a competition to test skill in driving. ◊ **rally round sb** to come together to offer support or help them at a time of crisis, etc.

RAM *abbrev, comput* random access memory, a temporary memory which allows programs to be loaded and run, and data to be changed. Compare ROM.

ram *n* **1** an uncastrated male sheep. **2** a BATTERING-RAM. **3** the falling weight of a pile-driver. **4** the striking head of a steam hammer. **5 a** a piston or plunger operated by hydraulic or other power; **b** a machine with such a piston. ➤ *vb* (**rammed, ramming**) **1** to force something down or into position by pushing hard. **2** to strike or crash something violently (against, into, etc something or someone): *ram the car into the wall.* ◆ **ram sth down sb's throat** *colloq* to force them to believe, accept or listen to a statement, idea, etc by talking about it constantly. **ram sth home** to emphasize it forcefully.

Ramadan or **Ramadhan** *n* **1** the ninth month of the Muslim year, during which Muslims fast between sunrise and sunset. **2** the fast itself.

ramble *vb, intr* **1** to go for a long walk or walks, esp in the countryside, for pleasure. **2** (*often* **ramble on**) to speak or write, often at length, in an aimless way. ➤ *n* a walk, usu in the countryside, for pleasure. ○ **rambler** *n* **1** someone who rambles. **2** a climbing plant, esp a rose.

rambling *n* walking for pleasure, esp in the countryside. ➤ *adj* **1** wandering. **2** of a building, etc: extending without any obvious plan: *a large rambling castle.* **3** of speech, etc: confused and disorganized. **4** of a plant: climbing, trailing or spreading freely: *a rambling rose.*

ramekin /ˈræmɪkɪn/ *n* **1** a small round straight-sided baking dish for a single serving of food. **2** food served in such a dish.

ramification *n* **1** an arrangement of branches. **2** a single part or section of a complex subject, plot, situation, etc. **3** (*usu* **ramifications**) a consequence, esp a serious, complicated and unwelcome one.

ramp¹ n 1 a sloping surface between two different levels. 2 a set of movable stairs for entering and leaving an aircraft. 3 a low hump across a road, designed to slow traffic down. ➤ vb 1 to provide with a ramp. 2 intr to slope from one level to another.

ramp² vb, commerce (usu **ramp up**) to increase greatly (the price of shares, etc), usu dishonestly and for financial advantage.

rampage vb /ram'peɪdʒ/ intr to rush about wildly, angrily, violently or excitedly. ➤ n /'rampeɪdʒ/ (chiefly **on the rampage**) storming about or behaving wildly and violently in anger, excitement, etc.

rampant adj 1 uncontrolled; unchecked: rampant discrimination. 2 heraldry, following its noun of an animal: in profile and standing erect on the left hind leg with the other legs raised: lion rampant.

rampart n 1 a broad mound or wall for defence. 2 anything which performs such a defensive role.

ramrod n a rod for ramming charge down into, or for cleaning, the barrel of a gun.

ramshackle adj of a building, car, etc: badly made or poorly maintained.

ranch n 1 esp N Am & Aust an extensive grassland farm where sheep, cattle or horses are raised. 2 any large farm that specializes in the production of a particular crop or animal: a mink ranch. ➤ vb to farm on a ranch. ○ **rancher** n.

rancid adj of stale butter, oil, etc: tasting or smelling sour. ○ **rancidity** or **rancidness** n.

rancour or (US) **rancor** n a long-lasting feeling of bitterness or dislike. ○ **rancorous** adj.

rand n (**rand** or **rands**) the standard monetary unit used in South Africa and some neighbouring countries.

R & B abbrev rhythm and blues.

random adj lacking a definite plan, system or order. ○ **randomly** adv. ○ **randomness** n. ♦ **at random** without any particular plan, system or purpose: chosen at random.

random access n, comput a method of accessing data stored on a disk or in the memory of a computer without having to read all the data in sequence.

random access memory n see RAM

R & R abbrev, orig US colloq rest and recreation.

randy adj (-ier, -iest) colloq sexually excited. ○ **randily** adv. ○ **randiness** n.

ranee see RANI

range n 1 a an area between limits within which things may move, function, etc; b the limits forming this area. 2 a number of items, products, etc forming a distinct series. 3 mus the distance between the lowest and highest notes which may be produced by a musical instrument or a singing voice. 4 the distance to which a gun may be fired or an object thrown. 5 the distance between a weapon and its target. 6 the distance that can be covered by a vehicle without it needing to refuel. 7 an area

where shooting may be practised and rockets tested: firing range. 8 a group of mountains forming a distinct series or row. 9 N Am a large area of open land for grazing livestock. 10 the region over which a plant or animal is distributed. 11 maths the set of values that a function or dependent variable may take. 12 an enclosed kitchen fireplace fitted with a large cooking stove with one or more ovens and a flat top for pans. ➤ vb 1 to put in a row or rows. 2 to put someone, oneself, etc into a specified category or group. 3 intr to vary between specified limits. 4 (usu **range over** or **through**) to roam freely. 5 intr to stretch in a specified direction or over a specified area.

ranger n 1 someone who looks after a royal or national forest or park. 2 N Am a member of a group of armed men who patrol and police a region. 3 (**Ranger** or **Ranger Guide**) Brit a member of the senior branch of the Guides.

rangy adj (-ier, -iest) of a person: with long thin limbs and a slender body.

rani or **ranee** n, hist 1 an Indian queen or princess. 2 the wife or widow of a RAJA.

rank¹ n 1 a line of people or things. 2 a line of soldiers standing side by side. 3 a position of seniority within an organization, society, the armed forces, etc. 4 a distinct class or group, eg according to ability. 5 high social position or status. 6 (**the ranks**) ordinary soldiers. 7 Brit a place where taxis wait for passengers. 8 chess a row of squares along the player's side of a chessboard. Compare FILE¹ (noun sense 5). ➤ vb 1 to arrange (people or things) in a row. 2 tr & intr to give or have a particular grade, position or status in relation to others. 3 to have a higher position, status, etc than someone else. ♦ **close ranks** of a group of people: to keep their solidarity. **pull rank** to use rank or status to achieve something. **the rank and file** the ordinary members of an organization or society.

rank² adj 1 of plants, etc: coarsely overgrown. 2 offensively strong in smell or taste. 3 bold, open and shocking: rank disobedience. 4 complete: a rank beginner.

rankle vb, intr to continue to cause feelings of annoyance or bitterness.

ransack vb 1 to search (a house, etc) thoroughly and often destructively. 2 to rob or plunder. ○ **ransacker** n.

ransom n money demanded in return for the release of a kidnapped person, or for the return of property, etc. ➤ vb to pay, demand or accept a ransom for someone. ♦ **hold sb to ransom** 1 to keep them prisoner until a ransom is paid. 2 to blackmail them into agreeing to demands.

rant vb 1 intr to talk in a loud, angry way. 2 tr & intr to declaim in a loud, self-important way. ➤ n 1 loud, empty speech. 2 an angry tirade. ○ **ranting** n, adj.

rap¹ n 1 a a quick short tap or blow; b the sound made by this. 2 slang blame or punishment: take the rap. 3 a fast rhythmic monologue recited over a musical backing with a pronounced beat. **4** a style of music that has a strong background beat and rhythmic monologues. ➤ *vb* (**rapped, rapping**) **1** to strike sharply. **2** *intr* to make a sharp tapping sound. **3** to criticize sharply. **4** *intr, colloq* to talk or have a discussion. ○ **rapper** *n* a performer of rap music.

rap² *n* the least bit: *not care a rap*.

rapacious *adj* **1** greedy, esp for money. **2** of an animal or bird: living by catching prey. ○ **rapaciously** *adv*. ○ **rapaciousness** or **rapacity** *n*.

rape¹ *n* **1** the crime of forcing a person, esp a woman, to have sexual intercourse against their will. **2** violation or abuse. ➤ *vb* **1** to commit rape on someone. **2** to violate or despoil (esp a country or place in wartime). ○ **rapist** *n*.

rape² *n* OILSEED RAPE.

rapid *adj* **1** moving, acting or happening quickly. **2** requiring or taking only a short time. ➤ *n* (*usu* **rapids**) a part of a river where the water flows quickly. ○ **rapidity** or **rapidness** *n*.

rapid-fire *adj* fired, asked, etc in quick succession.

rapier /'reɪpɪə(r)/ *n* a long thin sword for thrusting. ➤ *adj* sharp: *rapier wit*.

rapport /ra'pɔː(r)/ *n* a feeling of sympathy and understanding.

rapprochement /ra'prɒʃmɑ̃/ *n* the establishment or renewal of a close, friendly relationship, esp between states.

rapscallion *n, old use* a rascal.

rapt *adj* **1** enraptured; entranced. **2** completely absorbed. ○ **raptly** *adv*.

raptor *n* a bird of prey.

rapture *n* **1** great delight. **2** (**raptures**) great enthusiasm or pleasure. ○ **rapturous** *adj*.

rare¹ *adj* **1** not done, found or occurring very often. **2** unusually good: *a rare old treat*. **3** of a gas, etc: lacking the usual density. ○ **rarely** *adv*. ○ **rareness** *n*.

rare² *adj* of meat, esp a steak: lightly cooked, and often still bloody.

rarebit see WELSH RABBIT.

rare earth *n, chem* **1** a metallic element in the lanthanide series. **2** an oxide of such an element.

rarefied /'reərɪfaɪd/ *adj* **1** of the air, atmosphere, etc: with a very low oxygen content. **2** refined; exclusive: *She moves in rarefied circles*.

rare gas *n* a NOBLE GAS.

raring *adj, colloq* (**raring to go**) keen; very willing and ready.

rarity *n* (*-ies*) **1** uncommonness. **2** something valued because it is rare.

rascal *n* **1** a rogue. **2** a mischievous child. ○ **rascally** *adj*.

rase *vb* see RAZE.

rash¹ *adj* **1** of an action, etc: **a** overhasty; reckless; **b** done without considering the consequences. **2** of a person: lacking in caution. ○ **rashly** *adv*. ○ **rashness** *n*.

rash² *n* **1** an outbreak of red spots or patches on the skin. **2** a large number of instances (of something happening) at the same time or in the same place: *a rash of burglaries*.

rasher *n* a thin slice of bacon or ham.

rasp *n* **1 a** a coarse file; **b** any tool with a similar surface. **2** a harsh, rough, grating sound. ➤ *vb* **1** to scrape roughly, esp with a rasp. **2** to grate upon or irritate (eg someone's nerves). **3** to speak or utter in a harsh, grating voice. ○ **rasping** *adj*.

raspberry *n* (*-ies*) **1** a cone-shaped berry, usu reddish in colour. **2** a deciduous shrub with thorny canes that is cultivated for these berries. **3** a sound expressing disapproval or contempt, made by blowing through the lips.

rat *n* **1** a rodent, similar to a mouse but larger. **2** any of various unrelated but similar rodents, eg the kangaroo rat. **3** *colloq* someone who is disloyal to a friend, political party, etc. **4** *colloq* a despicable person. ➤ *vb* (**ratted, ratting**) *intr* **1** to hunt or chase rats. **2** (*usu* **rat on sb**) *colloq* to betray or inform on them.

ratafia /ratə'fiə/ *n* **1** a liqueur flavoured with fruit kernels and almonds. **2** an almond-flavoured biscuit or small cake.

ratan see RATTAN.

rat-a-tat-tat *n* a sound of knocking on a door.

ratatouille /ratə'tuːɪ/ *n* a vegetable dish made with tomatoes, peppers, courgettes, aubergines, onions and garlic simmered in olive oil.

ratbag *n, slang* a despicable person.

ratchet *n* **1** a bar which fits into the notches of a toothed wheel causing the wheel to turn in one direction only. **2** (*also* **ratchet-wheel**) a wheel with a toothed rim. **3** the mechanism of such a bar and toothed wheel together.

rate¹ *n* **1** the number of times something happens, etc within a given period of time; the amount of something considered in relation to, or measured according to, another amount: *a high suicide rate* • *at the rate of 40kph*. **2** a price or charge, often measured per unit: *the rate of pay for the job*. **3** a price or charge fixed according to a standard scale: *rate of exchange*. **4** class or rank: *second-rate*. **5** the speed of movement or change: *rate of progress*. ➤ *vb* **1** to give a value to: *They rate him number two in the world*. **2** to be worthy of: *an answer that doesn't rate full marks*. **3** *intr* (*usu* **rate as**) to be placed in a certain class or rank: *This rates as the best book on the subject*. ◆ **at any rate** in any case.

rate² *vb* to scold or rebuke severely.

rateable or **ratable** *adj* **1 a** of property: able to have its value assessed for the purpose of payment of RATES; **b** liable to payment of rates. **2** able to be rated or evaluated.

rates *pl n* in the UK: a tax paid by a business, based on the assessed value of property and land owned or leased and collected by a local authority to pay for public services.

rather *adv* **1 a** more readily; more willingly; **b** in preference: *I'd rather go to the cinema than watch TV*. **2** more truly or correctly: *my parents, or rather my mother and stepfather*. **3** to a limited degree: *It's rather good.* **4** on the contrary: *She said she'd help me; rather, she just sat around watching TV.* ➤ *exclam* yes indeed: *Would you like a chocolate? Rather!*

ratify *vb* (*-ies, -ied*) to give formal consent to (a treaty, agreement, etc). ○ **ratification** *n*.

rating *n* **1** a classification according to order, rank or value. **2** *Brit* an ordinary seaman. **3** an estimated value of a person's position, esp as regards credit. **4** a measure of a TV or radio programme's popularity based on its estimated audience.

ratio *n* the number or degree of one class of things in relation to another, or between one thing and another, expressed as a proportion.

ration *n* **1** a fixed allowance of food, clothing, petrol, etc during a time of war or shortage. **2** (**rations**) a daily allowance of food, esp in the army. ➤ *vb* **1** (*often* **ration out**) to distribute or share out (esp something that is in short supply). **2** to restrict (the supply of provisions, etc).

rational *adj* **1** related to or based on reason or logic. **2** able to think, form opinions, make judgements, etc. **3** sensible; reasonable. **4** sane. **5** *maths* of a quantity, ratio or root: able to be expressed as a ratio of whole numbers. ○ **rationality** *n*. ○ **rationally** *adv*.

rationale /ˌraʃəˈnɑːl/ *n* the underlying reason on which something is based.

rationalism *n* the theory that an individual's actions and beliefs should be based on reason. ○ **rationalist** *n*.

rationalize or **-ise** *vb* **1** to attribute something to sensible, well-thought-out reasons, esp after the event. **2** *intr* to explain one's behaviour, etc in this way. **3** to make something logical or rational. **4** to make (an industry or organization) more efficient and profitable by reorganization to lower costs, etc. ○ **rationalization** *n*.

rat race *n*, *colloq* the fierce, unending competition for success, wealth, etc in business, society, etc.

rattan or **ratan** *n* **1** a climbing palm with very long thin tough stems. **2** a cane made from the stem of this palm.

rattle *vb* **1** *intr* to make a series of short sharp hard sounds in quick succession. **2** to cause (eg crockery) to make such a noise. **3** *intr* to move along rapidly, often with a rattling noise. **4** *intr* (*usu* **rattle on**) to chatter thoughtlessly. **5** *colloq* to make anxious, nervous or upset. ➤ *n* **1** a series of short sharp sounds. **2** a baby's toy made of a container filled with small pellets which rattle when it is shaken. **3** a device for making a whirring sound, used esp at football matches. ◇ **rattle sth off** to say, recite or write it rapidly. ◇ **rattle through sth** to complete it quickly.

rattlesnake *n* a poisonous American snake with a series of dry horny structures at the end of its tail, producing a characteristic rattling sound.

rattling *adj, adv, colloq, old use* as a general

intensifying word: good; very: *He told us a rattling good yarn.*

ratty *adj* (*-ier, -iest*) **1** like a rat. **2** *colloq* irritable.

raucous *adj* of a sound, esp a voice: hoarse. ○ **raucously** *adv*.

raunchy *adj* (*-ier, -iest*) *colloq* coarsely or openly sexual. ○ **raunchiness** *n*.

ravage *vb, tr & intr* to destroy or cause extensive damage to something. ➤ *n* (*usu* **ravages**) damage or destruction: *the ravages of time.*

rave *vb* **1** *intr* to talk wildly as if mad or delirious. **2** *intr* (*usu* **rave about** or **over sth**) to talk enthusiastically or passionately about something. ➤ *n, colloq* **1** extravagant praise. **2** a gathering in a large warehouse or open-air venue for dancing to amplified music. ➤ *adj, colloq* extremely enthusiastic: *rave reviews.*

ravel *vb* (**ravelled, ravelling;** *US* **raveled, raveling**) **1** *tr & intr* to tangle or become tangled up. **2** (*usu* **ravel sth out**) **a** to untangle, unravel or untwist; **b** to resolve, explain or make clear. **3** *intr* to fray.

raven *n* a large blue-black bird of the crow family. ➤ *adj* glossy blue-black in colour: *raven hair.*

ravenous *adj* **1** extremely hungry or greedy. **2** of hunger, a desire, etc: intensely strong. **3** of an animal, etc: living on prey. ○ **ravenously** *adv*.

raver *n, colloq* **1** someone who leads a full, very lively and often wild social life. **2** someone who attends a **RAVE** (*noun* sense 2).

rave-up *n, colloq* a lively party or celebration.

ravine /rəˈviːn/ *n* a deep narrow steep-sided gorge.

raving *vb, present participle of* RAVE. ➤ *adj & adv* **1** frenzied; delirious. **2** *colloq* great; extreme: *a raving beauty.* ➤ *n* (*usu* **ravings**) wild, frenzied or delirious talk.

ravioli *sing or pl n* small square pasta cases with a savoury filling.

ravish *vb* **1** to overwhelm with joy, delight, etc. **2** to rape. ○ **ravishing** *adj* delightful; lovely.

raw *adj* **1** of meat, vegetables, etc: not cooked. **2** not processed, purified or refined: *raw silk.* **3** of alcoholic spirit: undiluted. **4** of statistics, data, etc: not analysed. **5** of a person: not trained or experienced. **6** of a wound, etc: with a sore, inflamed surface. **7** of the weather: cold and damp. **8** of an edge of material: not finished off and so liable to fray. **9** particularly sensitive: *She touched a raw nerve.* ◆ **get a raw deal** *colloq* to get harsh, unfair treatment. **in the raw** in a natural or crude state.

rawboned *adj* lean and gaunt.

rawhide *n* **1** untanned leather. **2** a whip made from this.

raw material *n* a substance in its natural state, used as the basis for a manufacturing process.

ray[1] *n* **1** a narrow beam of light or radioactive particles. **2** a set of lines fanning out from a central point. **3** a small amount (of hope, understanding, etc).

ray[2] *n* a cartilaginous fish with a flattened body.

ray³ or **re** *n, mus* in sol-fa notation: the second note of the major scale.

rayon *n* an artificial fibre or fabric used to make clothing, conveyor belts, hoses, etc.

raze or **rase** *vb* to destroy (buildings, a town, etc) completely.

> **raze** There is often a spelling confusion between **raze** and **raise**.

razor *n* a sharp-edged instrument used for shaving. ➤ *vb* **1** to use a razor on. **2** to shave or cut, esp closely.

razorbill *n* a seabird with a sharp-edged bill.

razor edge *n* **1** a very fine sharp edge. **2** *colloq* a delicately balanced situation.

razzle *n, slang* a lively spree, outing or party, esp involving a lot of drinking: *out on the razzle*.

razzle-dazzle *n, slang* **1** excitement, dazzling show, etc. **2** a lively spree.

razzmatazz *n* razzle-dazzle.

Rb *symbol, chem* rubidium.

RC *abbrev* **1** Red Cross. **2** Roman Catholic.

Rd *abbrev* used in street names: Road.

RE *abbrev* religious education.

Re *symbol, chem* rhenium.

re¹ *prep* with regard to; concerning: *re your letter of 18 March*.

re² see RAY³

're *vb* contraction of ARE¹: *We're going to Paris.*

reach *vb* **1** to arrive at or get as far as (a place, position, etc). **2** *tr & intr* to be able to touch or get hold of something. **3** *tr & intr* to project or extend to a point. **4** *intr* (*usu* **reach across**, **out**, **up**, *etc*) to stretch out one's arm to try to touch or get hold of something. **5** *colloq* to hand or pass: *Can you reach me that CD, please?* **6** to make contact or communicate with, esp by telephone: *I couldn't reach her.* ➤ *n* **1** the distance one can stretch one's arm, etc: *out of reach.* **2** a distance that can be travelled easily: *within reach of London.* **3** an act of reaching out. **4** range of influence, power, understanding or abilities. **5** (*usu* **reaches**) a section with clear limits, eg part of a river. **6** (*usu* **reaches**) level or rank: *the upper reaches of government.*

react *vb* **1** *intr* (*chiefly* **react to sth**) to act in response to it. **2** *intr* (*usu* **react against sth**) **a** to respond to it adversely; **b** to act in a contrary or opposing way. **3** *intr, physics* to exert an equal force in the opposite direction. **4** *tr & intr, chem* to undergo or cause to undergo chemical change produced by a REAGENT.

reaction *n* **1** a response to a stimulus. **2** an action or change in the opposite direction. **3** a change of opinions, feelings, etc. **4** a response showing how someone feels or thinks. **5** opposition to change and a tendency to revert to a former system or state of affairs. **6** a physical or psychological effect caused by a drug, allergy, etc. **7** *chem* **a** a chemical process in which the electrons surrounding the nuclei in the atoms of one or more elements or compounds react to form one or more new compounds; **b** chem-

ical change. **8** *physics* a nuclear reaction involving a change in an atomic nucleus. **9** *physics* the force offered by a body that is equal in magnitude but opposite in direction to the force applied to it.

reactionary *adj* of a person or policies: opposed to change. ➤ *n* (**-ies**) a reactionary person.

reactive *adj* showing a reaction; liable to react.

read /riːd/ *vb* (**read** /rɛd/) **1** to look at and understand (printed or written words). **2** to speak (words which are printed or written). **3** to learn or gain knowledge of by reading: *We read the election results in the newspaper.* **4** *intr* to pass one's leisure time reading: *She doesn't read much.* **5** to look at or be able to see something and get information: *I can't read the clock without my glasses.* **6** to interpret or understand the meaning of: *to read a map.* **7** to interpret or understand (signs, marks, etc) without using one's eyes: *to read Braille.* **8** *intr* to have a certain wording: *The letter reads as follows.* **9** *tr & intr* to think that (a statement, etc) has a particular meaning: *He read it as criticism.* **10** *intr* of writing: to convey meaning in a specified way: *an essay that reads well.* **11** of a dial, instrument, etc: to show a particular measurement: *The barometer reads 'fair'.* **12** to replace (a word, phrase, etc) by another: *For 'three' read 'four'.* **13** to study (a subject) at university. **14** to hear and understand: *Do you read me?* **15** *comput* to retrieve (data) from a storage device. ➤ *n* **1** a period or act of reading. **2** a book, magazine, etc considered in terms of how enjoyable it is: *a good read.* ◆ **read between the lines** to perceive a meaning that is not stated. **take sth as read** /rɛd/ to accept or assume it. ◊ **read sth in** or **out** *comput* to transfer data from a disk or other storage device into the main memory of a computer or vice versa. **read sth out** to read it aloud. **read up on sth** to learn a subject by reading books about it.

reader *n* **1** someone who reads. **2** (*also* **Reader**) *Brit* a university lecturer of a rank between professor and senior lecturer. **3** someone who reads lessons in a church. **4** a book containing short texts, used for learning to read or for learning a foreign language: *a German reader.*

readership *n* **1** the total number of people who read a newspaper, etc. **2** (*also* **Readership**) *Brit* the post of reader in a university.

reading *n* **1** the action of someone who reads. **2** the ability to read: *His reading is poor.* **3** any book, printed material, etc that can be read. **4** an event at which a play, poetry, etc is read to an audience. **5** *Brit pol* any one of the three stages in the passage of a bill through Parliament, when it is respectively introduced, discussed and reported on by a committee. **6** an understanding or interpretation of something.

readjust *vb* to alter. ◊ **readjustment** *n*.

read-only memory see ROM

read-out *n, comput* the copying of data from

the main memory of a computer into an external storage device, eg a disk or tape.

read-write head see under DISK DRIVE

ready *adj* (**-ier, -iest**) **1** prepared and available for use or action. **2** willing; eager: *always ready to help.* **3** prompt; quick, usu too quick: *He's always ready to find fault.* **4** likely or about to: *a plant just ready to flower.* ➤ *n* (**readies**) *colloq* short form of READY MONEY. ➤ *adv* prepared or made beforehand: *ready cooked meals.* ➤ *vb* (**-ies, -ied**) to make ready. ○ **readily** *adv.* ○ **readiness** *n.* ♦ **at the ready 1** of a gun: aimed and ready to be fired. **2** ready for immediate action.

ready-made *adj* **1** (*also* **ready-to-wear**) of clothes: made to a standard size. **2** convenient: *a ready-made excuse.*

ready money *n, colloq* cash for immediate use.

reafforest *vb* to replant trees in a cleared area of land that was formerly forested. ○ **reafforestation** *n.*

reagent /riːˈeɪdʒənt/ *n, chem* **1** a chemical compound that participates in a chemical reaction. **2** a common laboratory chemical with predictable characteristic reactions.

real¹ /rɪəl/ *adj* **1** actually or physically existing. **2** actual; true: *the real reason.* **3** not imitation; genuine: *real leather.* **4 a** great, important or serious; **b** deserving to be so called: *a real problem.* **5** *law* consisting of or relating to immoveable property, such as land and houses. **6** of income, etc: measured in terms of its buying power: *in real terms.* ➤ *adv, N Am, Scot* really: *real nice.* ♦ **for real** *slang* in reality; seriously.

real² /reɪˈɑːl/ *n* (**reals** or **reales**) **1** the standard monetary unit of Brazil. **2** *hist* a small silver Spanish or Spanish-American coin.

real ale *n* ale or beer which is allowed to continue to ferment and mature in the cask after brewing.

realign *vb* **1** to put back into alignment. **2** to regroup politically. ○ **realignment** *n.*

realism *n* **1** the tendency to consider, accept or deal with things as they really are. **2** a style in art, literature, etc that represents things in a lifelike way. Compare IDEALISM. ○ **realist** *n.*

realistic *adj* **1** showing awareness or acceptance of things as they really are. **2** representing things as they actually are. **3** based on facts.

reality *n* (**-ies**) **1** the state or fact of being real. **2** the real nature of something. **3** something that is not imaginary. ♦ **in reality** as a fact.

realize or **-ise** *vb* **1** to become aware of; to know or understand: *to realize the danger.* **2** to accomplish or bring into being: *to realize my ambitions.* **3** to make real or appear real. **4** to cause to seem real. **5** to convert (property or goods) into money. **6** to make (a sum of money): *He realized £145,000 on the sale of the house.* ○ **realizable** *adj.* ○ **realization** *n.*

really *adv* **1** actually; in fact. **2** very: *a really*

lovely day. ➤ *exclam* expressing surprise, doubt or mild protest.

realm *n* **1** a kingdom. **2** a domain, province or region. **3** a field of interest, study or activity.

real tennis *n* an early form of tennis played on a walled indoor court.

real time *n* the actual time during which an event takes place, esp a period which is analysed by a computer as it happens, the data produced during it being processed as it is generated.

realtor *n, N Am* an estate agent.

ream *n* **1** 500 sheets of paper. **2** (**reams**) *colloq* a large quantity: *I wrote reams.*

reap *vb* **1** to cut or gather (grain, etc). **2** to clear (a field) by cutting a crop. **3** to receive as a consequence of one's actions.

reaper *n* **1** someone who reaps. **2** a reaping machine. **3** (**the Reaper** or **the Grim Reaper**) the personification of death.

rear¹ *n* **1** the back part; the area at the back. **2** a position behind or to the back. **3** *colloq* the buttocks. ➤ *adj* situated or positioned at the back: *rear window.*

rear² *vb* **1** to bring up (offspring). **2 a** to breed (animals); **b** to grow (crops). **3** to build or erect something. **4** *intr* (*also* **rear up**) of an animal, esp a horse: to rise up on the hind legs. **5** *intr* to reach a great height. **6** to move or hold upwards.

rear admiral *n* a naval officer of the rank below vice-admiral.

rearguard *n* a group of soldiers who protect the rear of an army.

rearguard action *n* **1** military action undertaken by the rearguard. **2** an effort to prevent or delay defeat, eg in an argument.

rearm *vb* to arm again, esp with new or improved weapons. ○ **rearmament** *n.*

rearmost *adj* nearest the back.

rearward *adj* positioned in or at the rear. ➤ *adv* (*also* **rearwards**) towards the rear.

reason *n* **1** a justification or motive for an action, belief, etc. **2** an underlying explanation or cause. **3** the power to think, form opinions and judgements, etc. **4** sanity: *to lose one's reason.* ➤ *vb* **1** *intr* to form opinions, judgements, etc. **2** *intr* (*usu* **reason with sb**) to try to persuade them by means of reasonable argument. **3** (*usu* **reason sth out**) to think it through logically. ♦ **within reason** within the limits of what is sensible or possible.

reasonable *adj* **1** sensible; showing reason or good judgement. **2** willing to listen to reason or argument. **3** in accordance with reason. **4** fair or just; moderate: *a reasonable price.* **5** satisfactory or equal to what one might expect. ○ **reasonably** *adv.*

reasoned *adj* well thought out or argued.

reasoning *n* **1** the forming of judgements or opinions using reason or careful argument. **2** the act or process of deducing logically from evidence. **3** the opinions or judgements formed, or deductions made, in this way.

reassure vb **1** to dispel or alleviate the anxiety or worry of. **2** to confirm someone in opinion, etc: *Sonia reassured him that he was correct.* ○ **reassurance** n. ○ **reassuring** adj. ○ **reassuringly** adv.

rebate n /ˈriːbeɪt/ **1** a refund of part of a sum of money paid. **2** a discount. ➤ vb /rɪˈbeɪt/ to pay as a rebate.

rebel vb /rɪˈbel/ intr (**rebelled, rebelling**) (*often* **rebel against sth**) **1** to resist or fight against authority or oppressive conditions. **2** to refuse to conform to conventional rules of behaviour, dress, etc. ➤ n /ˈrebəl/ someone who rebels. ○ **rebellion** n.

rebellious adj rebelling or having a tendency to rebel.

rebirth n **1 a** a second or new birth; **b** reincarnation. **2** any revival or renewal.

reboot vb, *comput* to restart (a computer), esp when the computer has crashed.

reborn adj **1 a** born again; **b** reincarnated. **2** revived or spiritually renewed.

rebound vb /rɪˈbaʊnd/ intr **1** to bounce or spring back after an impact. **2** to recover after a setback. **3** (*also* **rebound on** or **upon sb**) of an action: to have a bad effect (on the person performing the action). ➤ n /ˈriːbaʊnd/ an instance of rebounding. ♦ **on the rebound** while still recovering from an emotional shock, esp the ending of a love affair.

rebuff n **1** a snub. **2** a refusal or rejection, esp of someone's help, advice, etc. ➤ vb to give a rebuff to.

rebuke vb to let (someone thought to have done wrong) know that the action, behaviour, etc is unacceptable. ➤ n a stern reprimand or reproach.

rebus /ˈriːbəs/ n a puzzle where pictures, etc represent words or syllables.

rebut vb (**rebutted, rebutting**) **1** to disprove or refute (a charge or claim), esp by offering opposing evidence. **2** to drive back. ○ **rebuttal** n.

recalcitrant adj not willing to accept authority or discipline. ○ **recalcitrance** n.

recall vb **1** to call back. **2** to order to return. **3** US to remove someone from office by vote. **4** to remember. **5** to cancel or revoke. ➤ n /ˈriːkɔːl/ **1** an act of recalling. **2** the ability to remember accurately and in detail: *total recall.*

recant vb **1** intr to revoke a former declaration, belief, etc. **2** tr & intr to withdraw or retract (a statement, belief, etc). ○ **recantation** n.

recap colloq, vb (**recapped, recapping**) to recapitulate. ➤ n recapitulation.

recapitulate vb **1** to go over the chief points of (an argument, statement, etc) again. **2** to summarize. ○ **recapitulation** n.

recapture vb **1** to capture again. **2** to convey, recreate or re-experience (an image, sensation, etc from the past). ➤ n the act of recapturing or fact of being recaptured.

recce /ˈreki/ colloq, n reconnaissance. ➤ vb (**recced** or **recceed, recceing**) to reconnoitre.

recede vb, intr **1** to go or move back or backwards. **2** to become more distant. **3** to bend or slope backwards. **4 a** of hair: to stop growing above the forehead and at the temples; **b** of a person: to go bald gradually in this way. ○ **receding** adj.

receipt /rɪˈsiːt/ n **1** a note acknowledging that money, goods, etc have been received. **2** the act of receiving or being received: *We acknowledge receipt of the goods.* **3** (*usu* **receipts**) money received during a given period of time. ➤ vb to mark (a bill) as paid.

receive vb **1** to get, be given or accept (something offered, sent, etc). **2** to experience, undergo or suffer: *to receive injuries.* **3** to give attention to or consider: *to receive a petition.* **4** to learn of or be informed of: *We finally received word of their arrival.* **5** to react to in a specified way: *The film was badly received.* **6** to admit or accept (an idea, principle, etc) as true. **7** to be awarded (an honour, etc): *to receive the OBE.* **8** to support or bear the weight of something. **9** tr & intr to be at home to (guests or visitors). **10** tr to welcome or greet (guests), esp formally. **11** to permit someone to become part of a particular body or group: *to be received into the priesthood.* **12** tr & intr, tennis, badminton to be the player who returns (the opposing player's service). **13** tr & intr, Christianity to participate in communion. **14** tr & intr, chiefly Brit to buy or deal in (goods one knows are stolen). **15** to change (radio or television signals) into sounds or pictures.

received adj generally accepted: *received wisdom.*

Received Pronunciation n (abbrev **RP**) the form of British English spoken by educated people in Southern England.

receiver n **1** someone or something that receives. **2** (*in full* **official receiver**) a person appointed by a court to take control of the business of someone who has gone bankrupt. **3** the part of a telephone held to the ear. **4** the equipment in a telephone, radio or television that changes signals into sounds and pictures, or both. **5** chiefly Brit a person who receives stolen goods.

receivership n **1** (*usu* **in receivership**) the status of a business that is under the control of an official receiver. **2** the office of official receiver.

recent adj **1** happening, done, having appeared, etc not long ago. **2** fresh; new. **3** modern. **4** (**Recent**) geol HOLOCENE. ○ **recency** n. ○ **recently** adv.

receptacle n **1** anything that holds something. **2** bot the top of a flower stalk, from which the different flower parts arise.

reception n **1** the act of receiving or fact of being received. **2** a response, reaction or welcome; the manner in which a person, information, an idea, etc is received: *a hostile reception.* **3** a formal party or social function to welcome guests, esp after a wedding. **4** the quality of radio or television signals received. **5** an area, office or desk where visitors or clients are welcomed on arrival: *Ask at reception.*

receptionist *n* someone employed in a hotel, office, surgery, etc to deal with clients, visitors and guests, arrange appointments, etc.

receptive *adj* willing to accept new ideas, suggestions, etc. ○ **receptively** *adv.* ○ **receptiveness** or **receptivity** *n.*

receptor *n, biol* a cell or body part adapted to respond to external stimuli.

recess *n* /rɪ'sɛs, 'riːsɛs/ **1** a space set in a wall. **2** part of a room formed by a receding of the wall: *dining recess.* **3** (*often* **recesses**) a hidden, inner or secret place: *the dark recesses of her mind.* **4** a temporary break from work, esp of a law-court, Parliament, etc during a vacation: *summer recess.* **5** *N Am* a short break between school classes. ➤ *vb* /rɪ'sɛs/ **1** to make a recess in (a wall, etc). **2** *intr* of a law-court, Parliament, etc: to take a break.

recession *n* **1** the act of receding or state of being set back. **2** a temporary decline in economic activity, trade and prosperity.

recessive *adj* **1** tending to recede. **2** *biol* denoting a characteristic that is only present when it comes from a gene that is paired with a gene that gives the same characteristic. Compare DOMINANT (*adj* sense 4).

recherché /rə'ʃeəʃeɪ/ *adj* **1** rare, exotic or particularly exquisite. **2** obscure and affected.

recidivism /rɪ'sɪdɪvɪzəm/ *n* the habit of relapsing into crime. ○ **recidivist** *n, adj.*

recipe *n* directions for making something, esp for preparing and cooking food.

recipient *n* a person or thing that receives something.

reciprocal /rɪ'sɪprəkəl/ *adj* **1 a** giving and receiving, or given and received; **b** complementary. **2** *gram* of a pronoun: expressing a relationship between two people or things, or mutual action, eg *one another* in *John and Mary love one another.* ➤ *n* **1** something that is reciprocal. **2** *maths* the value obtained when 1 is divided by the number concerned, eg the reciprocal of 4 is ¼.

reciprocate *vb* **1 a** to give and receive mutually; **b** to return (affection, love, etc). **2** *intr* of part of a machine: to move backwards and forwards. ○ **reciprocation** *n.*

reciprocity *n* **1** reciprocal action. **2** a mutual exchange of privileges or advantages between countries, trade organizations, etc.

recital /rɪ'saɪtl/ *n* **1** a public performance of music, usu by a soloist or a small group. **2** a detailed statement or list of something. **3** an act of reciting something learned or prepared. ○ **recitalist** *n.*

recitation *n* **1** an act or instance of reciting something. **2** something recited or a particular style of reciting something.

recitative /rɛsɪtə'tiːv/ *n, mus* **1** a style of singing resembling speech, used for narrative passages in opera. **2** a passage sung in this way.

recite *vb* **1** to repeat aloud (a poem, etc) from memory. **2** to make a detailed statement of something: *He recited his grievances.*

reckless *adj* without consideration of the consequences, danger, etc.

reckon *vb* **1** (*also* **reckon up**) to calculate, compute or estimate. **2** to consider as: *I reckon him among my friends.* **3** (*usu* **reckon that**) *colloq* to think or suppose: *I reckon it's going to rain.* **4** *intr* (*usu* **reckon on sb** or **sth**) to rely on or expect them or it: *We reckoned on their support.* ♦ **to be reckoned with** of considerable importance or power that is not to be ignored.

reckoning *n* **1 a** a calculation; **b** estimation: *By my reckoning, we must be about eight miles from the town.* **2** an account. **3** a settling of an account, debt, grievance, etc.

reclaim *vb* **1** to seek to regain possession of. **2** to make (land) available for agricultural or commercial use. **3** to recover useful materials from waste. ➤ *n* the action of reclaiming something or someone, or the state of being reclaimed. ○ **reclamation** *n.*

recline *vb* **1** *intr* to lean or lie back. **2** to lean or lay something in a sloping position.

recluse *n* someone who lives alone and has little contact with society. ○ **reclusive** *adj.*

recognition *n* the act or state of recognizing or being recognized.

recognizance or **recognisance** /rɪ'kɒgnɪzəns/ *n* **1** a legally binding promise made to a magistrate or court to do or not do something specified. **2** money pledged as a guarantee of such a promise being kept.

recognize or **-ise** *vb* **1** to identify (a person or thing known or experienced before). **2** to admit or be aware of: *He recognized his mistakes.* **3** to show approval of and gratitude for: *They recognized her courage with the award of a medal.* **4** to acknowledge the status or legality of (esp a government or state). **5** to accept: *to recognize the authority of the court.* ○ **recognizable** *adj.*

recoil *vb* /rɪ'kɔɪl/ *intr* **1** to spring back or rebound. **2** of a gun: to spring powerfully backwards under the force of being fired. **3** to shrink back, esp in fear, disgust, etc. ➤ *n* /rɪ'kɔɪl, 'riːkɔɪl/ an act of recoiling.

recollect *vb* to remember, esp with an effort.

recommend *vb* **1** to suggest as being suitable, acceptable, etc: *Can you recommend a good restaurant?* **2** to make desirable or pleasing: *It has very little to recommend it.* **3** to advise as a particular course of action: *She recommended he went home.* ○ **recommendation** *n.*

recompense *vb* **1** to repay or reward for service, work done, etc. **2** to compensate for loss, injury or hardship suffered. ➤ *n* **1** repayment or reward. **2** compensation for loss, injury, etc.

reconcile *vb* **1** to put on friendly terms again, esp after a quarrel. **2** to bring (two or more different aims, points of view, etc) into agreement. ○ **reconciliation** *n.*

recondite *adj* **1** of a subject or knowledge: difficult to understand. **2** dealing with profound, abstruse or obscure knowledge.

recondition vb to restore (an engine, piece of equipment, etc) to good working condition.

reconnaissance /rɪˈkɒnɪsəns/ n **1** mil a survey, eg of land or the position of troops, to obtain information about the enemy before advancing. **2** a preliminary survey.

reconnoitre or (US) **reconnoiter** /ˌrekəˈnɔɪtə(r)/ vb to examine or survey (land, enemy troops, etc), esp with a view to military operations, etc. ➤ n the act of reconnoitring.

reconsider vb to consider (a decision, opinion, etc) again, esp for a possible change. ○ **reconsideration** n.

reconstitute vb **1** to restore (esp dried foods or concentrates, by adding water) to the original form. **2** to form or make up again. ○ **reconstitution** n.

reconstruct vb **1** to construct or form again. **2** to create a description or idea of (a crime, past event, etc) from the evidence available. **3** to re-enact (an incident, esp a crime). ○ **reconstruction** n. ○ **reconstructive** adj.

record n /ˈrekɔːd/ **1** a formal written report of facts, events or information. **2** (often **records**) information, facts, etc collected usu over a fairly long period of time: *dental records*. **3** the state or fact of being recorded: *for the record*. **4** a thin plastic disc used as a recording medium for reproducing music or other sound. **5** esp in sports: a performance which is officially recognized as the best of a particular kind. **6** a description of the history and achievements of a person, company, etc. **7** a list of the crimes a person has been convicted of. **8** comput in database systems: a subdivision of a file that can be treated as a single unit of stored information. **9** anything that recalls or commemorates past events. ➤ vb /rɪˈkɔːd/ **1** to set down in writing or some other permanent form. **2** tr & intr to register (sound, music, speech, etc) on a record or tape so that it can be listened to in the future. **3** of a dial, instrument, person's face, etc: to show or register (a particular figure, feeling, etc). ◆ **off the record** of information, statements, etc: not intended to be repeated or made public. **on record** officially recorded; publicly known.

recorder n **1** a wooden or plastic wind instrument. **2** (usu **Recorder**) a solicitor or barrister who sits as a part-time judge in a court. **3** someone who records. **4** a device for recording, esp a tape recorder or video recorder.

recording n **1** the process of registering sounds or images on a record, tape, video, etc. **2** sound or images which have been recorded.

recount vb to tell (a story, etc) in detail.

re-count vb /riːˈkaʊnt/ to count again. ➤ n /ˈriːkaʊnt/ a second or new counting, esp of votes in an election to check a very close result.

recoup vb **1** to get back (something lost, eg

money). **2** to compensate or reimburse someone (eg for something lost).

recourse n **a** an act of turning to someone, or resorting to a particular course of action, for help or protection; **b** a source of help or protection.

recover vb **1** to get or find again. **2** intr to regain one's good health, spirits or composure. **3** intr to regain a former and usu better condition: *The economy recovered slightly last year*. **4** to regain control of: *He recovered his senses*. **5** law to gain (compensation or damages) by legal action. **6** to obtain (a usable substance) from a waste product. ○ **recoverable** adj.

recovery n (**-ies**) an act, instance or process of recovering, or the state of having recovered.

recreate or **re-create** vb to create something again. ○ **re-creation** n.

recreation n **1** a pleasant activity. **2** the process of having an enjoyable time. ○ **recreational** adj.

recrimination n the act of returning an accusation. ○ **recriminatory** adj.

recruit n **1** mil a newly enlisted member of the army, air force, navy, etc. **2** a new member of a society, company, etc. ➤ vb, tr & intr **1** mil **a** to enlist (people) as recruits; **b** to raise or reinforce (eg an army) by enlisting recruits. **2** to enrol new members, employees, etc. ○ **recruitment** n.

rectangle n a four-sided plane figure with opposite sides of equal length and all its angles right angles. ○ **rectangular** adj.

rectify vb (**-ies, -ied**) **1 a** to put (a mistake, etc) right; **b** to adjust. **2** chem to purify (alcohol, etc) by repeated distillation. **3** elec to change (alternating current) into direct current. ○ **rectification** n.

rectilineal or **rectilinear** adj **1** in or forming a straight line or straight lines. **2** bounded by straight lines.

rectitude n **1** correctness of behaviour or judgement. **2** moral integrity.

recto n, printing **1** the right-hand page of an open book. **2** the front of a sheet of printed paper. Compare VERSO.

rector n **1** in the Church of England: a clergyman in charge of a parish. **2** in the Roman Catholic Church: a priest in charge of a congregation or a religious house. **3** the headmaster of some schools and colleges, esp in Scotland. **4** Scot a senior university official elected by and representing the students.

rectory n (**-ies**) the residence of a rector.

rectum n (**recta** or **rectums**) the lower part of the alimentary canal, ending at the anus. ○ **rectal** adj.

recumbent adj lying down.

recuperate vb **1** intr to recover, esp from illness. **2** to recover (health, something lost, etc). ○ **recuperation** n.

recur vb (**recurred, recurring**) intr **1** to happen or come round again. **2** of a thought, etc: to come back into one's mind.

recurrent *adj* happening often or regularly. ○ **recurrence** *n*.

recycle *vb* to process or treat (waste material) for re-use. ○ **recyclable** *adj*. ○ **recycling** *n*.

red *adj* (**redder, reddest**) **1** having the colour of blood, or a colour similar to it. **2** of hair, fur, etc: between a golden brown and a deep reddish-brown colour. **3** of the eyes: bloodshot or with red rims. **4** having a flushed face, esp from shame or anger, or from physical exertion. **5** of wine: made with black grapes. **6** *colloq* communist. ➢ *n* **1** the colour of blood, or a similar shade. **2** red dye or paint. **3** red material or clothes. **4** the red traffic light. **5** (*usu* **the red**) the debit side of an account; the state of being in debt. Compare BLACK (*noun sense 6*). **6** *colloq* (*often* **Red**) a communist or socialist. ○ **reddish** *adj*. ○ **redness** *n*. ♦ **see red** *colloq* to become angry.

red alert *n* a state of readiness to deal with imminent crisis or emergency.

red blood cell or **red corpuscle** *n* a blood cell containing the pigment haemoglobin which gives the cell its red colour.

red-blooded *adj, colloq* full of vitality; manly.

redbreast *n* a robin.

redbrick *adj* of a British university: established in the late 19c or early 20c.

red card *n, football* a piece of red plastic shown by the referee to a player to indicate that they are being sent off. ➢ *vb* (**red-card**) of a referee: to show (a player) a red card.

red carpet *n* special treatment given to an important person.

redcoat *n, hist* a British soldier.

redcurrant *n* a widely cultivated European shrub, or its small edible red berry.

redden *vb* **1** to make red or redder. **2** *intr* to become red.

redeem *vb* **1** to buy back. **2** to recover (eg something that has been pawned or mortgaged) by payment or service. **3** to fulfil (a promise). **4** to set free or save someone by paying a ransom. **5** to free someone or oneself from blame or debt. **6** to free from sin. **7** to make up or compensate for (something bad or wrong). **8** to exchange (tokens, vouchers, etc) for goods. **9** to exchange (bonds, shares, etc) for cash. ○ **redeemable** *adj*. ○ **redeeming** *adj* making up for faults or shortcomings: *one of her redeeming features*.

redeemer *n* **1** someone who redeems. **2** (**the Redeemer**) a name for Jesus Christ.

redemption *n* **1** the act of redeeming or state of being redeemed. **2** *Christianity* the freeing of humanity from sin by Christ's death on the Cross. ○ **redemptive** *adj*.

redeploy *vb* to transfer (soldiers, supplies, etc) to another place or job. ○ **redeployment** *n*.

redevelop *vb* to develop again (esp a run-down urban area). ○ **redeveloper** *n*. ○ **redevelopment** *n*.

red flag *n* **1** a symbol of socialism or of revolution. **2** a flag used to warn of danger or as a signal to stop.

red-handed *adj* in the very act of committing a crime or doing something wrong.

redhead *n* a person with red hair. ○ **redheaded** *adj*.

red herring *n* a misleading idea, clue, etc.

red-hot *adj* **1** of metal, etc: heated until it glows red. **2** feeling or showing intense emotion or excitement. **3** *colloq* feeling or showing great enthusiasm. **4** strongly tipped to win: *a red-hot favourite*. **5** of news, etc: completely up to date.

Red Indian *n, offensive* a Native American.

red-letter day *n* a memorable or special day.

red light *n* a red warning light, esp the red traffic light at which vehicles have to stop. ➢ *adj* (**red-light**) *colloq* relating to brothels or containing many brothels: *red-light district*.

red meat *n* dark-coloured meat, eg beef or lamb. Compare WHITE MEAT.

redneck *n, derog* a poor white farm worker from the southern USA.

redo *vb* (**redoes, redid, redone**) **1** to do again or differently. **2** to redecorate (a room, etc).

redolent *adj* **1** fragrant. **2** (*usu* **redolent of** or **with**) **a** smelling strongly; **b** strongly suggestive or reminiscent. ○ **redolence** *n*.

redouble *vb* to make or become greater or more intense.

redoubt *n* a fortification, esp a temporary one defending a pass or hilltop.

redoubtable *adj* inspiring fear or respect. ○ **redoubtably** *adv*.

red pepper *n* **1** CAYENNE pepper. **2** a red CAPSICUM or SWEET PEPPER, eaten as a vegetable.

red rag *n* (*usu* **red rag to a bull**) something which is likely to provoke someone or make them angry.

redress *vb* **1** to set right or compensate for (something wrong). **2** to make even or equal again: *to redress the balance*. ➢ *n* **1** the act of redressing or being redressed. **2** money, etc paid as compensation for loss or wrong done.

red shift *n, astron* an increase in the wavelength of light or other electromagnetic radiation emitted by certain galaxies or quasars.

redskin *n, offensive colloq* a Native American.

red tape *n, colloq* unnecessary rules and regulations which result in delay.

reduce *vb* **1** *tr & intr* to make or become less, smaller, etc. **2** to change into a worse or less desirable state: *He reduced her to tears*. **3** *mil* to lower the rank, status or grade of: *reduced to the ranks*. **4** to bring into a state of obedience. **5** to make weaker or poorer. **6** to lower (the price of something). **7** *intr* to lose weight by dieting. **8** to convert (a substance) into a simpler form. **9** to simplify. **10** *tr & intr, cookery* to thicken (a sauce) by slowly boiling off the excess liquid. **11** *chem* to cause (a substance) to undergo a chemical reaction whereby it gains hydrogen or loses oxygen. ○ **reducible** *adj*.

reduction *n* **1** an act, instance or process of reducing; the state of being reduced. **2** the amount by which something is reduced. **3** a copy of a picture, document, etc made on a smaller scale. ○ **reductive** *adj*.

redundant *adj* **1** not needed. **2** of an employee: no longer needed and therefore dismissed. ○ **redundancy** *n*.

reduplicate *vb* to repeat, copy or double something. ○ **reduplication** *n*.

redwood *n* **1** an extremely tall and long-lived SEQUOIA, native to California. **2** its reddish-brown wood.

reed *n* **1 a** a grass that grows in the margins of streams, lakes and ponds; **b** a stalk of one of these plants used to make thatched roofs and furniture. **2** a thin piece of cane or metal in certain musical instruments which vibrates and makes a sound when air passes over it. **3** a wind instrument or organ pipe with reeds.

reedy *adj* (*-ier, -iest*) **1** full of reeds. **2** having a tone like a reed instrument, esp in being thin and piping. ○ **reediness** *n*.

reef[1] *n* a mass of rock, coral, sand, etc that either projects above the surface at low tide, or is permanently covered by shallow water.

reef[2] *naut, n* a part of a sail which may be folded in or let out so as to alter the area of sail exposed to the wind. ➢ *vb* to take in a reef or reefs of (a sail).

reefer *n* **1** (*in full* **reefer jacket**) a thick woollen double-breasted jacket. **2** *colloq* a cigarette containing marijuana.

reef knot *n* a knot made by passing one end of a rope over and under the other end, then back over and under it again.

reek *n* **1** a strong, unpleasant smell. **2** *Scot & N Eng dialect* smoke. ➢ *vb, intr* **1** to give off a strong, usu unpleasant smell. **2** *Scot & N Eng dialect* to give off smoke. **3** (*often* **reek of**) to suggest or hint at (something unpleasant): *a scheme that reeks of corruption.*

reel *n* **1** a round wheel-shaped or cylindrical object on which thread, film, fishing lines, etc can be wound. **2** the quantity of film, thread, etc wound on one of these. **3** a device for winding and unwinding a fishing line. **4** a lively Scottish or Irish dance, or the music for it. ➢ *vb* **1** to wind something on a reel. **2** (*usu* **reel sth in** or **up**) to pull in or up using a reel: *to reel in a fish.* **3** *intr* to stagger or sway. **4** *intr* to whirl or appear to move. **5** *intr* to be shaken physically or mentally. **6** *intr* to dance a reel. ◊ **reel sth off** to say, repeat or write it rapidly and often with little effort.

re-entry *n* (*-ies*) the return of a spacecraft to the Earth's atmosphere.

reeve *n, hist* **1** the chief magistrate of a town or district. **2** an official who supervises a lord's manor or estate.

ref *n, colloq* a sports referee.

refectory *n* (*-ies*) a dining hall, esp one in a monastery or university.

refer *vb* (*referred, referring*) **1** *intr* (**refer to sth**) **a** to mention or make allusion to it; **b** to look to it for information, facts, etc: *He referred to his notes.* **c** to be relevant or relate to it. **2** (**refer sb to sb** or **sth**) to direct them to them or it. **3** (**refer sth to sb**) **a** to hand it over to them for consideration: *She referred the query to the manager;* **b** to hand it back to the person from whom it came because it is unacceptable. **4** to fail (an examination candidate).

referee *n* **1** a person to whom reference is made to settle a dispute, etc. **2** an umpire or judge. **3** someone who is willing to testify to a person's character, talents and abilities. ➢ *vb* (*refereed, refereeing*) *tr & intr* to act as a referee in (a game, dispute, etc).

reference *n* **1** a mention of or an allusion to something. **2** a direction in a book to another passage or another book where information can be found. **3** a book or passage referred to. **4** the act of referring to a book or passage for information. **5** a written report on a person's character, talents, abilities, etc. **6 a** the providing of facts and information; **b** a source of facts or information. **7** the directing of a person, question, etc to some authority for information, a decision, etc. **8** relation, correspondence or connection: *with reference to your last letter.* **9** a standard for measuring or judging: *a point of reference.* ➢ *vb* **1** to make a reference to something. **2** to provide (a book, etc) with references to other sources. ○ **referential** *adj*.

reference book *n* a book, such as an encyclopedia or dictionary, consulted occasionally for information.

referendum *n* (*referendums* or *referenda*) the practice of giving people a chance to state their opinions on a particular matter by voting for or against it.

referral *n* the act of referring someone to someone else, esp the sending of a patient by a GP to a specialist for treatment.

refill *n* /ˈriːfɪl/ a new filling for something which has become empty through use. ➢ *vb* /riːˈfɪl/ to fill again. ○ **refillable** *adj*.

refine *vb* **1** to make pure by removing dirt, waste, etc. **2** *tr & intr* to become or make more elegant, polished or subtle.

refined *adj* **1** very polite; well-mannered. **2** with all the dirt, waste, etc removed. **3** improved.

refinement *n* **1** an act or the process of refining. **2** good manners or good taste; polite speech. **3** an improvement. **4** a subtle distinction.

refinery *n* (*-ies*) a plant where raw materials, esp sugar and oil, are purified.

refit *vb* /riːˈfɪt/ (*refitted, refitting*) **1** to repair or fit new parts to (esp a ship). **2** *intr* of a ship: to undergo repair or the fitting of new parts. ➢ *n* /ˈriːfɪt/ the process of refitting or being refitted. ○ **refitment** or **refitting** *n*.

reflate *vb* to bring about reflation of (an economy). Compare INFLATE (sense 2), DEFLATE (sense 3).

reflation *n* an increase in economic activity and in the amount of money and credit available, designed to increase industrial production after a period of deflation. ○ **reflationary** *adj.*

reflect *vb* **1** *tr & intr* of a surface: to send back (light, heat, sound, etc). **2** *tr & intr* of a mirror, etc: to give an image of someone or something. **3** *intr* of a sound, image, etc: to be sent back. **4** to have as a cause or be a consequence of. **5** to show or give an idea of. **6** *intr* (*also* **reflect on** or **upon sth**) to consider carefully. **7** *intr* (**reflect on** or **upon sb**) of an action, etc: to bring about a specified result, attitude, etc: *His behaviour during all the trouble reflects well on him.*

reflection or **reflexion** *n* **1** the change in direction of a particle or wave, eg the turning back of a ray of light when it strikes a mirror. **2** the act of reflecting. **3** a reflected image. **4** careful and thoughtful consideration.

reflective *adj* **1** of a person: thoughtful. **2** of a surface: able to reflect images, light, sound, etc. **3** reflected. ○ **reflectively** *adv.*

reflector *n* **1** a polished surface that reflects light, heat, etc. **2** a piece of plastic or glass attached to a bicycle that glows when light shines on it. **3** a telescope that uses a mirror to produce images, or the mirror itself.

reflex *n* **1** (*also* **reflex action**) *physiol* a response to a sensory, physical or chemical stimulus. **2** the ability to respond rapidly to a stimulus. **3 a** reflected light, sound, heat, etc; **b** a reflected image. ➤ *adj* **1** occurring as an automatic response without being thought about. **2** bent or turned backwards. **3** directed back on the source. **4** *geom* denoting an angle that is greater than 180° but less than 360°.

reflexive *adj* **1** *gram* of a pronoun: showing that the object of a verb is the same as the subject, eg in *He cut himself, himself* is a reflexive pronoun. **2** *gram* of a verb: used with a reflexive pronoun as object, eg *shave* in *shave oneself.* **3** *physiol* relating to a reflex. ➤ *n, gram* a reflexive pronoun or verb.

reflexology *n* the massaging of the reflex points on the soles of the feet, the hands and the head as a form of therapy. ○ **reflexologist** *n.*

reform *vb* **1** to improve or remove faults from (a person, behaviour, etc). **2** to improve (a law, institution, etc) by making changes to it. **3** *intr* to give up bad habits; to improve one's behaviour, etc. **4** to stop (misconduct, an abuse, etc). ➤ *n* **1** a correction or improvement, esp in some social or political system. **2** improvement in behaviour, morals, etc. ○ **reformable** *adj.* ○ **reformative** *adj.* ○ **reformer** *n.*

re-form *vb, tr & intr* to form again or in a different way. ○ **re-formation** *n.*

reformation /rɛfə'meɪʃən/ *n* **1** the act or process of reforming or being reformed; improvement. **2** (**the Reformation**) the great religious

and political revolution that took place in Europe in the 16c and resulted in the establishment of the Protestant Churches.

reformatory *n* (*-ies*) *old use* (*also* **reform school**) a school where young people who had broken the law were sent to be reformed. ➤ *adj* with the function or purpose of reforming.

reformism *n, pol* any doctrine or movement that advocates gradual social and political change. ○ **reformist** *n.*

refract *vb* of a medium, eg water or glass: to deflect (a wave of light, sound, etc) when it crosses the boundary between this medium and another. ○ **refraction** *n.* ○ **refractive** *adj.*

refractor *n* **1** anything that refracts. **2** a telescope that uses a lens to produce an image, or the lens itself.

refractory *adj* **1** difficult to control; stubborn. **2** *med* of a disease: resistant to treatment. **3** of a material: resistant to heat.

refrain¹ *n* **1** a phrase or group of lines repeated at the end of each verse in a poem or song. **2** the music for this.

refrain² *vb, intr* (*usu* **refrain from**) to stop or avoid doing something.

refrangible *adj* able to be refracted.

refresh *vb* **1** to make fresh again. **2** of drink, food, rest, etc: to give renewed strength, energy, etc to. **3** to revive (someone, oneself, etc) with drink, food, rest, etc. **4** to make (one's memory) clearer and stronger by reading or listening to the source of information again. **5** *comput* to update (esp a screen display) with data.

refresher course *n* a course of training intended to update previous knowledge.

refreshing *adj* **1** giving new strength, energy and enthusiasm. **2** cooling. **3** particularly pleasing because of being different, unexpected, new, etc: *His attitude was refreshing.* ○ **refreshingly** *adv.*

refreshment *n* **1** the act of refreshing or state of being refreshed. **2** anything that refreshes. **3** (**refreshments**) food and drink, esp a light meal.

refrigerant *n* **1** a fluid that vaporizes at low temperatures and is used in the cooling mechanism of refrigerators. **2** *med* a substance used for reducing fever. ➤ *adj* cooling.

refrigerate *vb* **1** *a tr* to freeze or make cold; **b** *intr* to become cold. **2** to make or keep (esp food) cold or frozen to slow down decay. ○ **refrigeration** *n.*

refrigerator *n* an insulated cabinet or room maintained at a low temperature in order to slow down the decay of its contents, esp food. Often shortened to **fridge.**

refuel *vb* **1** to supply (an aircraft, car, etc) with more fuel. **2** *intr* of an aircraft, car, etc: to take on more fuel.

refuge *n* **1** shelter or protection from danger or trouble. **2** any place, person or thing offering help or shelter. **3** an establishment offering emergency accommodation, protection, support, etc, eg for the homeless, victims of domestic violence, etc. **4** a traffic island for pedestrians.

refugee *n* someone who seeks refuge, esp from religious or political persecution, in another country.

refulgent *adj, literary* shining brightly. ○ **refulgence** *n*.

refund *vb* /rɪ'fʌnd/ to pay (money, etc) back, esp because something bought was faulty, etc. ➤ *n* /'riːfʌnd/ **1** the paying back of money, etc. **2** money, etc that is paid back. ○ **refundable** /rɪ'fʌndəbəl/ *adj*.

refurbish *vb* **1** to renovate. **2** to redecorate or brighten something up. ○ **refurbishment** *n*.

refusal *n* **1** an act or instance of refusing. **2** (*usu* **first refusal**) the opportunity to buy, accept or refuse something before it is offered, given, sold, etc to anyone else: *I'll give you first refusal if I decide to sell it.*

refuse[1] /rɪ'fjuːz/ *vb* **1** *tr & intr* to indicate unwillingness to do something. **2** to decline to accept: *She refused their offer of help.* **3** not to allow someone or something (access, permission, etc). **4** *tr & intr* of a horse: to stop at a fence and not jump over it.

refuse[2] /'rɛfjuːs/ *n* **1** rubbish; waste. **2** anything that is thrown away.

refute *vb* **1** to prove that (a person, theory, etc) is wrong. **2** *colloq* to deny. ○ **refutation** *n*.

regain *vb* **1** to get back again or recover: *He regained consciousness.* **2** to get back to (a place, position, etc): *She regained her place as the world's number one.*

regal *adj* **1** relating to, like or suitable for a king or queen. **2** royal. ○ **regality** *n*. ○ **regally** *adv*.

regale *vb* **1** (*usu* **regale sb with sth**) to amuse (eg with stories, etc). **2** to entertain lavishly.

regalia *pl n* **1** the insignia of royalty, eg the crown, sceptre and orb. **2** any ornaments, ceremonial clothes, etc worn as a sign of importance or authority, eg by a mayor.

regard *vb* **1** to consider in a specified way: *She regarded him as a friend.* **2** to esteem or respect: *I regarded him highly.* **3 a** to pay attention to or take note of; **b** to heed. **4** to look attentively or steadily at. **5** to have a connection with or to relate to. ➤ *n* **1 a** esteem; **b** respect and affection. **2** thought or attention. **3** care or consideration. **4** a gaze or look. **5** connection or relation. **6** (**regards**) **a** greetings; **b** respectful good wishes. ◆ **as regards** concerning. **with regard to 1** about or concerning. **2** as concerns.

regarding *prep* about; concerning.

regardless *adv* **1** not thinking or caring about problems, dangers, etc. **2** nevertheless; in spite of everything. ➤ *adj* (*usu* **regardless of**) taking no notice of.

regatta *n* a meeting for yacht or boat races.

regency *n* (*-ies*) **1** (**Regency**) a period when a regent is head of state, eg, in Britain, from 1811–20. **2** government by a regent; any period when a regent rules or ruled. **3** the office of a regent. ➤ *adj* (*also* **Regency**) of art, furniture, etc: belonging to, or in the style prevailing during, the period of the Regency.

regenerate *vb* /rɪ'dʒɛnəreɪt/ **1** to produce again or anew. **2** *tr & intr* to make or become morally or spiritually improved. **3** *tr & intr* **a** to develop or give new life or energy to; **b** to be brought back or bring back to life or original strength. **4** *tr & intr, physiol* to regrow or cause (new tissue) to regrow. ➤ *adj* /-rət/ **1** regenerated, esp morally, spiritually or physically. **2** reformed. ○ **regeneration** *n*. ○ **regenerative** *adj*.

regent *n* someone who governs a country during a monarch's childhood, absence or illness. ➤ *adj* acting as regent: *Prince regent.*

reggae *n* popular music of W Indian origin with a strongly accented upbeat.

regicide *n* **1** the act of killing a king. **2** someone who kills a king.

regime or **régime** /reɪ'ʒiːm/ *n* **1** a system of government. **2** a particular government or administration. **3** a regimen.

regimen *n, med* a course of treatment, esp of diet and exercise, which is recommended for good health.

regiment *n* **1** *mil* a body of soldiers consisting of several companies, etc. **2 a** large number of people or things formed into an organized group. ➤ *vb* **1** to organize or control (people, etc) strictly. **2** *mil* to form or group (soldiers, an army, etc) into a regiment or regiments. ○ **regimentation** *n*.

regimental *adj* belonging or relating to a regiment. ➤ *n* (**regimentals**) a military uniform, esp that of a particular regiment. ○ **regimentally** *adv*.

region *n* **1** an area of the world or of a country: *a mountainous region • a deprived region of the country.* **2** (**Region**) esp (1973–96) in Scotland: an administrative area. **3** *anat* an area of the body, esp when described as being in or near a specified part, organ, etc: *the abdominal region.* **4** an area of activity, interest, study, etc. ○ **regional** *adj*. ○ **regionalization** or **-isation** *n*. ○ **regionally** *adv*. ◆ **in the region of** approximately: *in the region of a hundred pounds.*

register *n* **1 a** a written list or record of names, events, etc; **b** a book containing such a list. **2 a** machine or device which records and lists information, eg a CASH REGISTER. **3** *mus* the range of tones produced by the human voice or a musical instrument. **4** *mus* **a** an organ stop; **b** the set of pipes controlled by an organ stop. **5** a style of speech or language. **6** *comput* a device for storing small amounts of data. ➤ *vb* **1** to enter (an event, name, etc) in an official register. **2** *intr* to enter one's name and address in a hotel register on arrival. **3** *tr & intr* to enrol formally: *Please register for the conference by Friday.* **4** of a device: to record and usu show (speed, information, etc) automatically. **5** of a person's face, expression, etc: to show (a particular feeling). **6** *intr, colloq* to make an impression on someone, eg by being understood, remembered, etc: *The name didn't register.*

register office *n, Brit* an office where records of births, deaths and marriages are kept and where marriages may be performed. Also called **registry office**.

registrar *n* **1** someone who keeps an official register, esp of births, deaths and marriages. **2** a senior administrator in a university, responsible for student records, enrolment, etc. **3** *Brit* a middle-ranking hospital doctor who is training to become a specialist. ○ **registrarship** *n*.

registration *n* **1** an act or instance or the process of registering. **2** something registered.

registry *n* (*-ies*) **1** an office or place where registers are kept. **2** registration.

regress *vb* /rɪˈgrɛs/ **1** *intr* **a** to go back; **b** to return. **2** *intr* to revert to a former state or condition, usu a less desirable one. **3** *tr & intr, psychol* to return to an earlier, less advanced stage of development or behaviour. ➤ *n* /ˈriːgrɛs/ an act or instance or the process of regressing.

regret *vb* (**regretted, regretting**) **1 a** to feel sorry, repentant, etc about (something one has done or that has happened); **b** to wish that things had been otherwise. **2** to remember someone or something with a sense of loss. ➤ *n* **1 a** a feeling of sorrow, repentance, etc; **b** a wish that things had been otherwise. **2** a sense of loss. **3** (**regrets**) a polite expression of sorrow, disappointment, etc, used esp when declining an invitation.

regretful *adj* feeling or displaying regret. ○ **regretfully** *adv.*

regrettable *adj* unwelcome; unfortunate: *a regrettable mistake.*

regular *adj* **1** usual; normal; customary. **2** arranged, occurring, acting, etc in a fixed pattern of predictable or equal intervals of space or time: *at regular intervals.* **3** agreeing with some rule, established practice, etc, and commonly accepted as correct. **4** symmetrical or even. **5** of a geometric figure: having all the sides, angles, etc the same. **6** of bowel movements or menstrual periods: occurring with normal frequency. **7** *orig US* medium-sized: *a regular portion of fries.* **8** *colloq* complete: *a regular little monster.* **9** *gram* of a noun, verb, etc: following one of the usual patterns of formation, inflection, etc. **10** *mil* of troops, the army, etc: belonging to or forming a permanent professional body. **11 a** officially qualified or recognized; **b** professional. **12** *N Am, colloq* behaving in a generally acceptable or likeable way: *a regular guy.* ➤ *n* **1** *mil* a soldier in a professional permanent army. **2** *colloq* a frequent customer, esp of a pub, bar, shop, etc. ○ **regularity** *n*. ○ **regularize** or **-ise** *vb.* ○ **regularly** *adv.*

regulate *vb* **1** to control or adjust (the amount of available heat, sound, etc). **2** to control or adjust (a machine) so that it functions correctly. **3** to control or direct (a person, thing, etc) according to a rule or rules. **4** *intr* to make or lay down a rule. ○ **regulative** /ˈrɛgjʊlətɪv/ or **regulatory** *adj.* ○ **regulator** *n*.

regulation *n* **1** an act or instance or the process or state of regulating or being regulated. **2** a rule or instruction.

regurgitate *vb* **1 a** to pour back; **b** to cast out again. **2** to bring back (food) into the mouth after it has been swallowed. **3** to repeat exactly (something already said). ○ **regurgitation** *n*.

rehabilitate *vb* **1** to help (someone who has been ill, etc or a former prisoner) adapt to normal life again. **2** to rebuild or restore (buildings, etc) to good condition. **3** to lift (the reputation of someone or something) to a better status or rank. ○ **rehabilitation** *n*.

rehash *colloq, vb* /riːˈhaʃ/ to re-use (material which has been used before), but with no significant changes or improvements. ➤ *n* /ˈriːhaʃ/ a re-use of such material.

rehearse *vb* **1** *tr & intr* to practise (a play, piece of music, etc) before performing it in front of an audience. **2** to train (a person) for performing in front of an audience. **3** to give a list of: *Mark rehearsed his grievances.* **4** to repeat or say over again. ○ **rehearsal** *n*.

rehouse *vb* to provide with new and usu better accommodation. ○ **rehousing** *n*.

reign *n* **1** the period of time when a king or queen rules. **2** the period during which someone or something rules, is in control or dominates: *reign of terror.* ➤ *vb, intr* **1** to be a ruling king or queen. **2** to prevail, exist or dominate: *silence reigns.* ○ **reigning** *adj* **1 a** a ruling; **b** prevailing. **2** of a winner, champion, etc: currently holding the title of champion, etc.

reimburse *vb* **1** to repay (money spent). **2** to pay (a person) money to compensate for or cover (expenses, losses, etc): *We will reimburse you your costs.* ○ **reimbursable** *adj.* ○ **reimbursement** *n*.

rein *n* **1** (*often* **reins**) the strap attached to a bridle and used to guide and control a horse. **2** (*usu* **reins**) a harness with straps for guiding a small child. **3** any means of controlling, governing or restraining. ➤ *vb* **1** to provide with reins. **2** to guide or control (esp a horse) with reins. **3** (*usu* **rein sth in**) to stop or restrain it with, or as if with, reins. **4** *intr* (*usu* **rein in**) to stop or slow up. ♦ **give (a free) rein to sb** or **sth** to allow them or it to do as they like. **keep a tight rein on sb** or **sth** to keep strict control of them or it.

reincarnation *n* in some beliefs: the transference of someone's soul after death to another body. ○ **reincarnate** *vb, adj.*

reindeer *n* (**reindeer** or **reindeers**) a large deer, antlered in both sexes, found in arctic and subarctic regions.

reinforce *vb* **1** to strengthen or give additional support to something. **2** to stress or emphasize: *It reinforced his argument.* **3** to make (an army, workforce, etc) stronger by providing additional soldiers, weapons, workers, etc.

reinforced concrete *n, eng* concrete in which steel bars or wires have been embedded to increase its tensile strength.

reinstate vb **1** to place in a previous position. **2** to restore someone to a position, status or rank formerly held. ○ **reinstatement** n.

reiterate vb to do or say again or repeatedly. ○ **reiteration** n.

reject vb /rɪˈdʒɛkt/ **1** to refuse to accept, agree to, admit, believe, etc. **2** to throw away or discard. **3** med of the body: to fail to accept (new tissue or an organ from another body). ➤ n /ˈriːdʒɛkt/ **1** someone or something that is rejected. **2** an imperfect article offered for sale at a discount. ○ **rejection** n.

rejig vb (**rejigged, rejigging**) **1** to re-equip or refit (a factory, etc). **2** to rearrange something.

rejoice vb **1** intr to feel, show or express great happiness or joy. **2** (usu **rejoice that**) to be glad. **3** (**rejoice in sth**) often ironic to revel or take delight in it: He rejoices in the name Ben Pink Dandelion.

rejoin¹ /rɪˈdʒɔɪn/ vb **1 a** to say in reply, esp abruptly or wittily; **b** to retort. **2** intr, law to reply to a charge or pleading. ○ **rejoinder** n.

rejoin² /riːˈdʒɔɪn/ vb, tr & intr to join again.

rejuvenate vb to make young again. ○ **rejuvenation** n.

relapse vb, intr **1** to fall back into a former state, esp one involving bad habits, etc. **2** to become ill again after apparent or partial recovery. ➤ n an act or instance or the process of relapsing into bad habits, etc or poor health. ○ **relapser** n.

relate vb **1** to tell (a story, etc). **2** to show or form a connection between facts, events, etc: He related his unhappiness to a deprived childhood. **3** intr, colloq (**relate to sb**) **a** to get on well with them; **b** to react favourably or sympathetically to them. **4** intr (**relate to sth**) **a** to be about it or concerned with it: I have information that relates to their activities; **b** to be able to understand it or show some empathy towards it: I can relate to her angry response.

related adj **1** belonging to the same family, by birth or marriage. **2** connected.

relation n **1** an act of relating. **2** a telling. **3** the state or way of being related. **4** a connection between one person or thing and another. **5** someone who belongs to the same family through birth or marriage. **6** kinship. **7** (**relations**) social, political or personal contact between people, countries, etc. **8** (**relations**) euphemistic sexual intercourse. ♦ **in** or **with relation to sth** in reference to it; with respect to it.

relationship n **1** the state of being related. **2** the state of being related by birth or marriage. **3** the friendship, communications, etc which exist between people, countries, etc. **4** an emotional or sexual affair.

relative n a person who is related to someone else by birth or marriage. ➤ adj **1** compared with something else: the relative speeds of a car and train. **2** existing only in relation to something else: 'Hot' and 'cold' are relative terms. **3** (chiefly **relative to**) in proportion to: sal-

ary relative to experience. **4** relevant: information relative to the problem. **5** gram **a** of a pronoun or adjective: referring to someone or something that has already been named and attaching a subordinate clause to it, eg who in the children who are playing; **b** of a clause or phrase: attached to a preceding word, phrase, etc by a relative word such as which and who, or whose in the man whose cat was lost. ○ **relatively** adv.

relativity n **1** the condition of being relative to and therefore affected by something else. **2** two theories of motion, **special theory of relativity** and **general theory of relativity**, which recognize the dependence of space, time and other physical measurements on the position and motion of the observer who is making the measurements.

relax vb **1 a** to make (part of the body, one's grip, etc) less tense or stiff; **b** intr of muscles, a grip, etc: to become less tense. **2** tr & intr to make or become less tense, nervous or worried. **3** intr of a person: to become less formal. **4** to make (discipline, rules, etc) less strict. **5** to lessen the force, strength or intensity of something: He relaxed his vigilance. ○ **relaxed** adj. ○ **relaxing** adj.

relaxation n **1** an act or the process of relaxing or the state of being relaxed. **2** recreation. **3** a relaxing activity.

relay¹ n /ˈriːleɪ/ **1** a set of workers, animals, etc that replace others doing some task, etc. **2** a RELAY RACE. **3** electronics an electrical switching device that, in response to a change in an electric circuit, opens or closes one or more contacts in the same or another circuit. **4** telecomm a device fitted at regular intervals along TV broadcasting networks, etc to amplify weak signals and pass them on from one communication link to the next. **5 a** something which is relayed, esp a signal or broadcast; **b** the act of relaying it. ➤ vb /rɪˈleɪ, ˈriːleɪ/ **1** to receive and pass on (news, a TV programme, etc). **2** radio to rebroadcast (a programme received from another station or source).

relay² or **re-lay** /riːˈleɪ/ vb (**relaid**) to lay again.

relay race n a race between teams of runners, swimmers, etc in which each member of the team covers part of the total distance to be covered.

release vb **1** to free (a prisoner, etc) from captivity. **2** to relieve someone of a duty, burden, etc. **3** to loosen one's grip and stop holding something. **4** to make (news, information, etc) known publicly. **5** to offer (a film, recording, book, etc) for sale, performance, etc. **6** to move (a catch, brake, etc) so that it no longer prevents something from moving, operating, etc. **7** to give off or emit (heat, gas, etc). ➤ n **1** an act or the process of releasing or the state of being released. **2** an item of news made public, or a document containing this: press release. ○ **releaser** n.

relegate vb **1** to move down to a lower grade,

position, status, etc. **2** *sport, esp football* to move (a team) down to a lower league or division. ○ **relegation** *n*.

relent *vb, intr* **1** to become less severe or unkind. **2** to give way and agree to something one initially would not accept. ○ **relenting** *n, adj*.

relentless *adj* **1 a** without pity; **b** harsh. **2** never stopping: *a relentless fight against crime*. ○ **relentlessly** *adv*. ○ **relentlessness** *n*.

relevant *adj* directly connected with or related to the matter in hand. ○ **relevance** or **relevancy** *n*. ○ **relevantly** *adv*.

reliable *adj* **1** dependable; trustworthy. **2** consistent in character, quality, etc. ○ **reliability** *n*. ○ **reliably** *adv*.

reliance *n* **1** dependability, trust or confidence. **2** the state of relying on someone or something: *She overcame her reliance on drugs*.

relic *n* **1** a fragment or part of an object left after the rest has decayed: *relics from the stone-age village*. **2** an object valued as a souvenir of the past. **3** something left from a past time, esp a custom, belief, etc. **4** part of the body of a saint or martyr, or of some object connected with them, preserved as an object of veneration.

relief *n* **1** the lessening or removal of pain, worry, etc or the feeling that comes from this. **2** anything lessening pain, worry, boredom, etc. **3** help, often in the form of money, food, clothing and medicine, given to people in need. **4** someone who takes over a job or task from another person. **5** the freeing of a besieged or endangered town, fortress, etc. **6** *art* a method of sculpture in which figures project from a flat surface. **7** a clear, sharp outline caused by contrast.

relief map *n* a map which shows the variations in the height of the land by shading rather than contour lines.

relieve *vb* **1** to lessen or stop (pain, worry, boredom, etc). **2** to remove a physical or mental burden from someone: *He relieved her of many responsibilities*. **3** to give assistance to. **4** to make less monotonous, esp by providing a contrast. **5** to free or dismiss from a duty or restriction. **6** to take over a job or task from. **7** to come to the help of (a besieged town, fortress, etc). ○ **relieved** *adj*. ◆ **relieve oneself** to urinate or defecate.

relievo /rɪˈliːvoʊ/ or **rilievo** /rɪˈljeɪvoʊ/ *n, art* **1** relief. **2** a work in relief. **3** appearance of relief.

religion *n* **1** a belief in, or the worship of, a god or gods. **2** a particular system of belief or worship, such as Christianity or Judaism. **3** the monastic way of life.

religious *adj* **1** relating to religion. **2 a** following the rules or forms of worship of a particular religion very closely; **b** pious; devout. **3** conscientious. **4** belonging or relating to the monastic way of life. ➤ *n* (*pl* **religious**) a person bound by monastic vows, eg a monk or nun. ○ **religiously** *adv*.

relinquish *vb* **1** to give up or abandon (a belief,

task, etc). **2** to release one's hold of something. **3** to renounce possession or control of (a claim, right, etc). ○ **relinquishment** *n*.

reliquary /ˈrɛlɪkwəri/ *n* (**-ies**) a container for holy relics.

relish *vb* **1** to enjoy greatly or with discrimination. **2** to look forward to with great pleasure. ➤ *n* **1** pleasure; enjoyment. **2 a** a spicy appetizing flavour; **b** a sauce or pickle which adds such a flavour to food. **3** zest, charm or gusto.

relive *vb* **1** *intr* to live again. **2** to experience again, esp in the imagination.

relocate *vb* **1** to locate again. **2** *tr & intr* to move (oneself, a business, home, etc) from one place, town, etc to another. ○ **relocation** *n*.

reluctant *adj* unwilling or disinclined: *reluctant to leave*. ○ **reluctance** *n*. ○ **reluctantly** *adv*.

rely *vb* (**-ies, -ied**) *intr* (*always* **rely on** or **upon**) **1** to depend on or need. **2** to trust. **3** to be certain of.

remain *vb, intr* **1** to be left after others, or other parts, have been used up, taken away, etc. **2 a** to stay behind; **b** to stay in the same place. **3** to stay the same or unchanged. **4** to continue to need to be done, dealt with, etc: *That remains to be decided*.

remainder *n* **1** what is left after others, or other parts, have gone, been used up, etc. **2** *maths* the amount left over when one number cannot be divided exactly by another number. **3** *maths* the amount left when one number is subtracted from another. **4** the copies of a book left unsold or sold at a reduced price because sales have fallen off. ➤ *vb* to sell (copies of a book) at a reduced price because sales have fallen off.

remains *pl n* **1** what is left after part has been eaten, destroyed, etc. **2** a dead body. **3** relics.

remake *vb* /riːˈmeɪk/ to make again or in a new way. ➤ *n* /ˈriːmeɪk/ something that is made again, eg a new version of an existing film.

remand *vb* to send (an accused person) back into custody to await trial. ➤ *n* an act or the process of remanding someone. ◆ **on remand** in custody or on bail awaiting trial.

remark *vb* **1** *tr & intr* to notice and comment on something. **2** to make a casual comment. ➤ *n* **1** a comment, often a casual one. **2** an observation. **3** noteworthiness.

remarkable *adj* **1** worth mentioning or commenting on. **2** very unusual or extraordinary. ○ **remarkably** *adv*.

remedial *adj* **1** affording a remedy. **2** *formerly* relating to or concerning the teaching of children with learning difficulties. ○ **remedially** *adv*.

remedy *n* (**-ies**) **1** a drug or treatment which cures or controls a disease. **2** something which solves a problem or gets rid of something undesirable. **3** legal redress. ➤ *vb* (**-ies, -ied**) **1** to cure or control (a disease, etc). **2** to put right or correct (a problem, error, etc). ○ **remediable** /rɪˈmiːdɪəbəl/ *adj*.

remember vb 1 to bring something from the past to mind. 2 to keep (a fact, idea, etc) in one's mind: *Remember to phone.* 3 to reward or make a present to someone, eg in a will or as a tip. 4 to commemorate. 5 (**remember sb to sb else**) to pass on their good wishes and greetings to the other person.

remembrance n 1 the act of remembering or being remembered. 2 a something which reminds a person of something or someone; b a souvenir.

remind vb 1 to cause someone to remember something or to do something: *Remind me to speak to him.* 2 to make someone think about someone or something similar: *She reminds me of her sister.*

reminder n 1 something that reminds or is meant to remind: *We got a reminder for the gas bill.* 2 a memento.

reminisce vb, intr to think, talk or write about things remembered from the past.

reminiscence n 1 the act of thinking, talking or writing about the past. 2 something from the past that is remembered. 3 (often **reminiscences**) a written account of things remembered from the past.

reminiscent adj (usu **reminiscent of**) similar: *a painting reminiscent of Turner.*

remiss adj careless; failing to pay enough attention.

remission n 1 a lessening in force or effect, esp in the symptoms of a disease such as cancer. 2 a reduction of a prison sentence. 3 a pardon; b forgiveness from sin. 4 the act of remitting or state of being remitted.

remit vb /rɪˈmɪt/ (**remitted, remitting**) 1 to cancel or refrain from demanding (a debt, punishment, etc). 2 tr & intr to make or become loose or relaxed. 3 to send (money) in payment. 4 to refer (a matter for decision, etc) to some other authority. 5 law to refer (a case) to a lower court. 6 intr of a disease, pain, rain, etc: to become less severe for a time. 7 to send or put back into a previous state. 8 of God: to forgive (sins). ➤ n /ˈriːmɪt, rɪˈmɪt/ the authority or terms of reference given to an official, committee, etc in dealing with a matter.

remittance n 1 the sending of money in payment. 2 the money sent.

remix vb /riːˈmɪks/ to mix again in a different way, esp to mix (a recording) again, changing the balance of the different parts, etc. ➤ n /ˈriːmɪks/ a remixed recording.

remnant n (often **remnants**) 1 a remaining small piece or amount of something larger. 2 a remaining piece of fabric from the end of a roll. 3 a surviving trace or vestige.

remonstrate vb, tr & intr (often **remonstrate with sb**) to protest forcefully (to someone): *They remonstrated that they knew nothing about it.* ○ **remonstration** n.

remorse n 1 a deep feeling of guilt, regret and bitterness for something wrong or bad. 2 compassion or pity. ○ **remorseful** adj.

remorseless adj 1 without remorse. 2 cruel. 3 without respite. ○ **remorselessness** n.

remote adj 1 far away; distant in time or place. 2 far from civilization. 3 operated or controlled from a distance. 4 comput of a computer terminal: located separately from the main processor but having a communication link with it. 5 distantly related or connected. 6 very small, slight or faint: *a remote chance.* 7 aloof or distant. ➤ n a remote control device, eg for a TV. ○ **remotely** adv. ○ **remoteness** n.

remote access n, comput access to a computer from a computer terminal at another site.

remote control n 1 the control of machinery or electrical devices from a distance, by the making or breaking of an electric circuit or by means of radio waves. 2 a battery-operated device for transmitting such waves. ○ **remote-controlled** adj.

remould vb /riːˈmoʊld/ 1 to mould again. 2 to bond new tread onto (a worn tyre). ➤ n /ˈriːmoʊld/ a tyre that has had new tread bonded onto it.

removal n 1 the act or process of removing or state of being removed. 2 the moving of possessions, furniture, etc to a new house.

remove vb 1 to move to a different place. 2 to take off (a piece of clothing). 3 to get rid of. 4 to dismiss from a job, position, etc. ➤ n 1 a removal. 2 the degree, usu specified, of difference separating two things: *a government only one remove from tyranny.* 3 Brit in some schools: an intermediate form or class. ○ **removable** adj. ○ **remover** n.

removed adj 1 separated, distant or remote. 2 usu of cousins: separated by a specified number of generations or degrees of descent: *first cousin once removed.*

remunerate vb 1 to recompense. 2 to pay someone for services rendered. ○ **remuneration** n. ○ **remunerative** adj.

renaissance /rɪˈneɪsəns/ n 1 a rebirth or revival, esp of learning, culture and the arts. 2 (**the Renaissance**) the revival of arts and literature during the 14th-16th centuries.

renal /ˈriːnəl/ adj relating to the kidneys.

renascence n the fact or process of being born again or entering on new life. ○ **renascent** adj.

rend vb (**rent**) old use 1 tr & intr to tear something, esp using force or violence. 2 tr & intr to divide or split: *War had rent the country in two.* 3 of a noise: to disturb (the silence, etc) with a loud, piercing sound.

render vb 1 to cause something to be or become: *to render things more agreeable.* 2 to give or provide (a service, help, etc). 3 to show (obedience, honour, etc). 4 to pay (money) or perform (a duty), esp in return for something: *to render thanks to God.* 5 to give back or return something. 6 to give in return or exchange. 7 (*also* **render up**) to give up, release or yield: *The grave will never render up its dead.* 8 to translate: *How do you render that in German?* 9 to perform (a role in a play, a piece of music, etc). **10** to portray or reproduce, esp in painting or music. **11** to present or submit for payment, approval, etc. **12** to cover (brick or stone) with a coat of plaster. **13 a** to melt (fat), esp to clarify it; **b** to remove (fat) by melting.

rendezvous /'rādeɪvuː, 'ron-/ n (pl **rendezvous** /-vuːz/) **1 a** an appointment to meet at a specified time and place; **b** the meeting itself; **c** the place where such a meeting is to be. **2** a place where people generally meet. ➤ vb, intr to meet at an appointed place or time.

rendition n a performance or interpretation of a piece of music, a dramatic role, etc.

renegade n someone who deserts the religious, political, etc group which they belong to, and joins a rival group.

renege or **renegue** /rɪ'neɪg/ vb **1** intr (often **renege on**) to go back on one's word, an agreement, etc. **2** to renounce (a promise, etc) or desert (a person, faith, etc).

renew vb **1 a** to make fresh or like new again; **b** to restore to the original condition. **2 a** to begin to do again; **b** to repeat. **3** tr & intr to begin (some activity) again after a break. **4** tr & intr to make (a licence, lease, loan, etc) valid for a further period of time. **5** to replenish or replace. ○ **renewable** adj. ○ **renewal** n.

rennet n a substance that curdles milk, obtained either from the stomachs of calves or from some fungi.

renounce vb **1** to give up (a claim, title, right, etc), esp formally and publicly. **2** to refuse to recognize or associate with someone. **3** to give up (a bad habit). ○ **renouncement** n.

renovate vb **1** to renew or make new again. **2** to restore (esp a building) to a former and better condition. ○ **renovation** n. ○ **renovator** n.

renown n fame. ○ **renowned** adj.

rent¹ n money paid periodically to the owner of a property by a tenant in return for the use or occupation of that property. ➤ vb **1** to pay rent for (a building, house, flat, etc). **2** (also **rent out**) to allow someone the use of (property) in return for payment of rent. **3** intr to be hired out for rent.

rent² n, old use **1** an opening or split made by tearing. **2** a fissure. ➤ vb, past tense, past participle of REND.

rental n **1** the act of renting. **2** money paid as rent.

rent boy n a young male prostitute.

renunciation n **1** an act of renouncing. **2** a formal declaration of renouncing something.

rep¹ n, colloq a representative, esp a travelling salesperson.

rep² n a REPERTORY COMPANY.

repair¹ vb **1** to restore (something damaged or broken) to good working condition. **2** to put right, heal or make up for (some wrong that has been done). ➤ n **1** an act or the process of repairing. **2** a condition or state: in good repair. **3** a part or place that has been mended or repaired. ○ **repairable** adj. ○ **repairer** n.

repair² vb, intr (usu **repair to**) old use to go.

reparation n **1** an act or instance of making up for some wrong that has been done. **2** money paid or something done for this purpose. **3** (usu **reparations**) compensation paid after a war by a defeated nation for the damage caused. ○ **reparable** /'rɛpərəbəl/ adj.

repartee n **1** the practice or skill of making spontaneous witty retorts. **2** a quick witty retort. **3** conversation with many such replies.

repast n, formal or old use a meal.

repatriate vb to send (a refugee, prisoner of war, etc) back to their country of origin. ○ **repatriation** n.

repay vb **1** to pay back or refund (money). **2** to do or give something to someone in return for something they have done or given: We must repay his kindness. ○ **repayable** adj. ○ **repayment** n.

repeal vb to make (a law, etc) no longer valid. ➤ n the act of repealing a law, etc.

repeat vb **1** to say, do, etc, again or several times. **2** to say again exactly (the words already said by someone else). **3** to tell (something, esp a secret) to someone else. **4 a** to quote from memory; **b** to recite (a poem, etc). **5** intr of food: to be tasted again some time after being swallowed. **6** intr to occur again or several times. **7** (usu **repeat itself**) of an event, etc: to happen in exactly the same way more than once: History repeats itself. **8** intr of a gun: to fire several times without being reloaded. **9** intr of a clock: to strike the hour or quarter hour. **10** (**repeat oneself**) to say the same thing more than once, esp with the result of being tedious. **11** of a TV or radio company: to broadcast (a programme, etc) again. ➤ n **1 a** the act of repeating; **b** a repetition. **2** something that is repeated, esp a television or radio programme. **3** mus **a** a passage in a piece of music that is to be repeated; **b** a sign that marks such a passage. **4** an order for goods, etc that is exactly the same as a previous one. ➤ adj second or subsequent: a repeat showing. ○ **repeatable** adj. ○ **repeated** adj. ○ **repeatedly** adv.

repeater n **1** someone or something that repeats. **2** a clock that strikes the hour or quarter hour.

repel vb (**repelled, repelling**) **1 a** to force or drive back or away; **b** to repulse. **2** tr & intr to provoke a feeling of disgust in someone. **3** to fail to mix with, absorb or be attracted by something else: Oil repels water. **4** to reject or rebuff.

repellent n **1** something that drives away insects, etc. **2** a substance used to treat fabric so as to make it resistant to water. ➤ adj **1** forcing or driving back or away. **2** provoking a feeling of disgust.

repent vb **1** tr & intr **a** (usu **repent of**) to feel great sorrow or regret for something one has done; **b** to wish (an action, etc) undone. **2** intr to feel regret (for the bad things one has done) and change one's behaviour. ○ **repentance** n. ○ **repentant** adj.

repercussion n 1 (usu **repercussions**) a bad, unforeseen, indirect, etc result or consequence of some action, event, etc. 2 an echo or reverberation. 3 a recoil or repulse after an impact.

repertoire /'rɛpətwɑː(r)/ n 1 the list of songs, plays, etc that a singer, group of actors, etc is able or ready to perform. 2 the range or stock of skills, techniques, talents, etc that someone or something has. 3 comput the total list of codes and commands that a computer can accept and execute.

repertory n (-ies) 1 a repertoire, esp of a theatre company. 2 the performance of a repertoire of plays at regular, short intervals. 3 a storehouse. 4 short form of REPERTORY COMPANY.

repertory company n a group of actors who perform a series of plays from their repertoire in the course of a season at one theatre.

repetition n 1 the act of repeating or being repeated. 2 something that is repeated. 3 a recital from memory, eg of a poem, piece of music, etc. 4 a copy or replica.

repetitious adj inclined to repetition, esp when boring, etc. ○ **repetitiously** adv.

repetitive adj happening, done, said, etc over and over again. ○ **repetitively** adv.

rephrase vb to express in different words, esp as a way of improving sense, etc.

replace vb 1 to put back in a previous or proper position. 2 to take the place of or be a substitute for. 3 to supplant. 4 to substitute (a person or thing) in place of (an existing one). ○ **replaceable** adj.

replacement n 1 the act of replacing something. 2 someone or something that replaces another.

replay n /'riːpleɪ/ 1 an act or instance of playing a game, etc again, usu because there was no clear winner the first time. 2 an act or instance of playing a recording. ➤ vb /riː'pleɪ/ to play (a tape, football match, etc) again.

replenish vb to fill up or make complete again, esp a supply of something which has been used up. ○ **replenishment** n.

replete adj 1 (often **replete with**) completely or well supplied. 2 formal having eaten enough or more than enough. ○ **repleteness** or **repletion** n.

replica n 1 an exact copy, esp of a work of art. 2 a copy or model, esp a scaled-down one.

replicate vb 1 to make a replica of. 2 to repeat (a scientific experiment). 3 intr of a molecule, virus, etc: to make a replica of itself. ○ **replication** n.

reply vb (-ies, -ied) 1 intr to answer or respond in words, writing or action. 2 to say or do in response. ➤ n (-ies) 1 an answer or response. 2 an act or instance of replying.

report n 1 a detailed statement, description or account, esp one made after some form of investigation. 2 a detailed account of the discussions of a committee or other group of people.

3 an account of news, etc: a newspaper report. 4 a statement of a pupil's work and behaviour at school. 5 rumour; general talk. 6 character or reputation. 7 a loud explosive noise, eg of a gun firing. ➤ vb 1 to bring back (information, etc) as an answer, news or account: He reported that fighting had broken out. 2 to state. 3 tr & intr (often **report on**) to give a formal account of (findings, information, etc), esp after an investigation. 4 a to give an account of (news, etc), esp for a newspaper or TV or radio broadcast; b intr to act as a newspaper, TV or radio reporter. 5 to make a complaint about someone. 6 intr to present oneself at an appointed place or time or to a specified person: Report to reception on arrival. 7 intr (usu **report to sb**) to be under (a specified superior): Liz reports directly to the manager. 8 intr to account for oneself in a particular way: to report sick. ○ **reportedly** adv.

reported speech n, gram INDIRECT SPEECH.

reporter n 1 someone who reports, esp for a newspaper, TV or radio. 2 law someone whose job is to prepare reports on legal proceedings.

repose[1] n 1 a state of rest, calm or peacefulness. 2 composure. ➤ vb 1 intr to rest. 2 to lay (oneself, one's head, etc) down to rest. ○ **reposeful** adj.

repose[2] vb to place (confidence, trust, etc) in someone or something.

reposition vb 1 to move to or put in a new or different place. 2 to alter the position of one's body.

repository n (-ies) 1 a storage place or container. 2 a a place where things are stored for exhibition; b a museum. 3 a warehouse. 4 someone or something thought of as a store of information, knowledge, etc.

repossess vb of a creditor: to regain possession of (property or goods), esp because the debtor has defaulted on payment. ○ **repossession** n.

reprehensible adj deserving blame or criticism. ○ **reprehensibly** adv.

represent vb 1 a to serve as a symbol or sign for: Letters represent sounds; b to stand for or correspond to: A thesis represents years of hard work. 2 to speak or act on behalf of someone else. 3 a to be a good example of; b to typify: What he said represents the feelings of many people. 4 to present an image of or portray, esp through painting or sculpture. 5 to bring clearly to mind: a film that represents all the horrors of war. 6 to describe in a specified way; to attribute a specified character or quality to: They represented themselves as experts. 7 to show, state or explain: to represent the difficulties forcibly to the committee. 8 to be an elected Member of Parliament for (a constituency). 9 to act out or play the part of on stage. ○ **representable** adj.

re-present vb to present something again.

representation n 1 an act or process of representing, or the state or fact of being represented. **2** a person or thing that represents someone or something else. **3 a** an image; **b** a picture or painting. **4** a dramatic performance. **5** (*often* **representations**) a strong statement made to present facts, opinions, complaints or demands. ○ **representational** *adj*.

representative *adj* **1** representing. **2** a standing as a good example of something; **b** typical. **3** standing or acting as a deputy for someone. **4** of government: comprised of elected people. ➢ *n* **1 a** someone who represents someone or something else, esp someone who sells the goods of a business; **b** someone who acts as a person's agent. **2** someone who represents a constituency in Parliament. **3** a typical example.

repress *vb* **1 a** to keep (an impulse, desire, etc) under control; **b** to restrain (an impulse, desire, etc). **2** to put down, esp using force: *to repress an insurrection*. **3** *psychol* to exclude (unacceptable thoughts, feelings, etc) from the conscious mind. ○ **repression** *n*. ○ **repressive** *adj*.

reprieve *vb* **1** to delay or cancel (punishment). **2** to give temporary relief from (trouble, pain, etc). ➢ *n* an act or instance or the process of delaying or cancelling a criminal sentence, esp a death sentence; **b** a warrant granting this.

reprimand *vb* to criticize or rebuke angrily or severely. ➢ *n* an angry or severe rebuke.

reprint *vb* /riː'prɪnt/ **1** to print something again. **2** to print more copies of (a book, etc). **3** *intr* of a book, etc: to have more copies printed. ➢ *n* /'riːprɪnt/ **1** the act of reprinting. **2** a copy of a book made by reprinting the original without any changes. **3** the total number of copies made of a reprinted book: *a reprint of 3000*.

reprisal *n* revenge or retaliation or an act involving this.

reprise *mus*, *n* the repeating of a passage or theme. ➢ *vb* to repeat (an earlier passage or theme).

reproach *vb* **a** to express disapproval of or disappointment with; **b** to blame. ➢ *n* **1** an act of reproaching. **2** (*often* **reproaches**) a rebuke or expression of disapproval. **3** a cause of disgrace or shame. ○ **reproachful** *adj*. ○ **reproachfully** *adv*. ♦ **beyond reproach** too good to be criticized.

reprobate /'reprəbeɪt/ *n* an immoral unprincipled person. ○ **reprobation** *n*.

reproduce *vb* **1** to make or produce again. **2 a** to make or produce a copy of; **b** to duplicate. **3** *tr & intr* to produce (offspring).

reproduction *n* **1** an act or the process of reproducing. **2** a copy or imitation, esp of a work of art. **3** the quality of reproduced sound: *a stereo that gives excellent reproduction*. ➢ *adj* of furniture, etc: made in imitation of an earlier style. ○ **reproductive** *adj*.

reproof *n* **1** blame or censure. **2** a rebuke.

reprove *vb* **1** to rebuke. **2** to blame or condemn for a fault, wrongdoing, etc. ○ **reprovingly** *adv*.

reptile *n* **1** *zool* a cold-blooded scaly vertebrate

animal, eg a lizard, snake, etc. **2** a despicable person. ○ **reptilian** /rep'tɪlɪən/ *adj, n*.

republic *n* a form of government in which supreme power is held by the people or their elected representatives, esp one in which the head of state is an elected or nominated president.

republican *adj* **1** relating to or characteristic of a republic. **2** in favour of or supporting the republic as a form of government. **3** (**Republican**) *US* relating to the Republican Party. ➢ *n* **1** someone who favours the republic as a form of government. **2** (**Republican**) *US* a member or supporter of the Republican Party. Compare DEMOCRAT. **3** (**Republican**) someone who advocates the union of N Ireland and Eire. Compare LOYALIST. ○ **republicanism** *n*.

repudiate /rɪ'pjuːdɪeɪt/ *vb* **1** to deny or reject as unfounded: *They repudiate the suggestion*. **2** to refuse to recognize or have anything to do with (a person). **3** to refuse or cease to acknowledge (a debt, etc). ○ **repudiation** *n*.

repugnant *adj* disgusting. ○ **repugnance** *n*. ○ **repugnantly** *adv*.

repulse *vb* **1** to drive or force back (an enemy, etc). **2** to reject (someone's offer of help, etc) with coldness and discourtesy. **3** to bring on a feeling of disgust in someone. ➢ *n* **1** an act or instance of repulsing or the state of being repulsed. **2** a cold discourteous rejection.

repulsion *n* **1** an act or the process of forcing back or of being forced back. **2** a feeling of disgust. **3** *physics* a force that tends to push two objects further apart, such as that between like electric charges or like magnetic poles. Opposite of ATTRACTION.

repulsive *adj* provoking a feeling of disgust. ○ **repulsively** *adv*. ○ **repulsiveness** *n*.

reputable /'repjʊtəbəl/ *adj* well thought of.

reputation *n* **1** a generally held opinion about someone's abilities, moral character, etc. **2** (*often* **reputation for** or **of**) fame or notoriety, esp because of a particular characteristic. **3** a high opinion generally held about someone or something.

repute *vb* to consider (as having some specified quality, etc): *She is reputed to be a fine tennis player*. ➢ *n* **1** general opinion or impression. **2** reputation.

reputed *adj* **1** supposed. **2** generally considered to be.

request *n* **1** an act or an instance of asking for something. **2** something asked for. **3 a** a letter, etc sent to a radio station, etc asking for a specified song to be played; **b** the song played in response to this. ➢ *vb* to ask for, esp politely or as a favour. ♦ **on** or **by request** if or when requested.

requiem /'rekwɪəm/ *n* **1** (*also* **Requiem**) *RC Church* **a** a mass for the souls of the dead; **b** a piece of music written for this. **2** any piece of music composed or performed to commemorate the dead.

require *vb* **1** to need or wish to have. **2** to demand, exact or command by authority. **3** to have as a necessary or essential condition for success, fulfilment, etc.

requirement *n* **1 a** a need; **b** something that is needed. **2** something that is asked for, essential, etc. **3** a necessary condition.

requisite /'rɛkwɪzɪt/ *adj* required or necessary. ➤ *n* something that is required or necessary.

requisition *n* **1** a formal demand for supplies or the use of something, eg by the army. **2** an official form on which such a demand is made. ➤ *vb* to demand, take or order (the use of something, etc) by official requisition.

requite *vb, formal* **1** to make a suitable return in response to (someone's kindness or injury). **2** to repay someone for something. **3** to repay (good with good, evil with evil, hate with love, etc). ○ **requital** *n*.

reredos /'rɪədɒs/ *n* an ornamental screen behind an altar.

rerun *vb* /riː'rʌn/ **1** to cause (a race, etc) to be run again or to run (a race, etc) again. **2** to broadcast (a TV or radio programme or series) again. ➤ *n* /'riːrʌn/ **1** a race that is run again. **2** a TV or radio programme or series broadcast again.

rescind *vb* to cancel, annul or revoke (an order, law, etc).

rescue *vb* to save or set free from danger, captivity, etc. ➤ *n* an act or an instance or the process of rescuing or being rescued. ○ **rescuer** *n*.

research *n* detailed and careful investigation into some subject with the aim of discovering and applying new facts. ➤ *vb, tr & intr* to do research (on a specified subject, etc). ○ **researcher** *n*.

resemblance *n* likeness or similarity or the degree of likeness or similarity.

resemble *vb* to be like or similar to (someone or something else).

resent *vb* **1** to take or consider as an insult or an affront. **2** to feel anger or bitterness towards or about someone or something. ○ **resentful** *adj*. ○ **resentfully** *adv*. ○ **resentment** *n*.

reservation *n* **1** an act of reserving something for future use. **2 a** an act of booking or ordering a hotel room, a table in a restaurant, a ticket, etc in advance; **b** something reserved or booked in advance. **3** (*often* **reservations**) a doubt or objection. **4** a limiting condition or exception to an agreement, etc. **5** an area of land set aside for a particular purpose, eg for Native Americans.

reserve *vb* **1** to keep back or set aside, eg for a future, special use. **2** to book or order (a hotel room, a table in a restaurant, a ticket, etc) in advance. **3** to delay or postpone (a legal judgement, etc). **4** to maintain or secure: *I reserve the right to silence*. ➤ *n* **1** something kept back or set aside, esp for future use or possible need. **2** the state or condition of being reserved or an act of reserving. **3** an area of land set aside for a particular purpose, esp for the protection of wildlife: *a nature reserve*. **4** coolness, dis-

tance or restraint. **5** *sport* **a** an extra player or participant who can take another's place if needed; **b** (*usu* **the reserves**) the second team: *playing for the reserves*. **6** (*also* **reserves**) *mil* a part of an army or force kept out of immediate action to provide reinforcements when needed; **b** forces in addition to a nation's regular armed services that may be called upon if necessary; **c** a member of such a force. **7** (*often* **reserves**) *finance* a company's assets, or a country's gold and foreign currency, held at a bank to meet future liabilities. **8** (*usu* **reserves**) a supply of oil, gas, coal, etc known to be present in a particular region and as yet unexploited. **9** (*usu* **reserves**) extra physical or mental power, stamina, etc that can be drawn upon in a difficult situation: *reserves of strength*. ♦ **in reserve** unused, but available if necessary.

reserved *adj* **1** kept back, set aside or destined for a particular use or for a particular person. **2** of a person or their manner: cool, distant or restrained; diffident.

reserve price *n* the lowest price that the owner of something which is being sold by auction is prepared to accept.

reservist *n, mil* a member of a reserve force.

reservoir /'rɛzəvwɑː(r)/ *n* **1** a large lake or tank in which water is collected and stored for public use, etc. **2** a chamber in a machine, device, etc where liquid is stored. **3** a supply, eg of information. **4** a place where fluid or vapour collects.

reshuffle *vb* /riː'ʃʌfəl/ **1** to shuffle (cards) again. **2** to reorganize or redistribute (esp government posts). ➤ *n* /'riːʃʌfəl/ an act of reshuffling: *a cabinet reshuffle*.

reside *vb, intr* **1** *formal* to live or have one's home (in a place), esp permanently. **2** of power, authority, etc: to rest with someone or be attributable to someone.

residence *n* **1** *formal* a house or dwelling, esp a large, imposing one. **2 a** an act or an instance of living in a particular place; **b** the period of time someone lives there. ♦ **in residence 1** living in a particular place, esp officially. **2** of a creative writer, artist, etc: working in a particular place for a certain period of time: *The prison has an artist in residence*.

resident *n* **1** someone who lives permanently in a particular place. **2** a registered guest in a hotel, esp one staying a relatively long time. **3** a non-migratory bird or animal. **4** *med* **a** a doctor who works at and usu lives in a hospital; **b** *N Am* a doctor undergoing advanced training in a hospital. ➤ *adj* **1** living or dwelling in a particular place. **2** living or required to live in the place where one works. **3** of birds and animals: not migrating.

residential *adj* **1** of a street, an area of a town, etc: containing private houses rather than factories, etc. **2** requiring residence in the same place as one works or studies: *a residential course*. **3** used as a residence: *a residential* *home for the elderly.* **4** relating to or connected with residence or residences. ○ **residentially** *adv.*

residual *adj* remaining. ○ **residually** *adv.*

residue *n* **1** what remains or is left over when a part has been taken away, etc. **2** *law* what is left of a dead person's estate after debts and legacies have been paid. **3** *chem* a RESIDUUM. ○ **residuary** /rɪˈzɪdjʊərɪ/ *adj.*

residuum *n* (*residua*) *chem* a substance remaining after evaporation, combustion or distillation.

resign *vb* **1** *intr* to give up a job, etc. **2** to give up or relinquish (a right, claim, etc). **3** (*usu* **resign oneself to sth**) to come to accept a situation, etc with patience, tolerance, etc.

resignation *n* **1** an act of resigning from a job, etc. **2** a signed notification of intention to resign from a job, etc. **3** uncomplaining acceptance of something unpleasant, inevitable, etc.

resigned *adj* (*often* **resigned to sth**) prepared to accept something unpleasant, inevitable, etc without complaining. ○ **resignedly** /rɪˈzaɪnɪdlɪ/ *adv.*

resilient *adj* **1** of a person: able to recover quickly from, or to deal readily with, illness, unexpected difficulties, etc. **2** of an object, a material, etc: able to return quickly to its original shape, position, etc. ○ **resilience** or **resiliency** *n.* ○ **resiliently** *adv.*

resin /ˈrɛzɪn/ *n* **1** a sticky aromatic substance secreted by various plants and trees. **2** (*in full* **synthetic resin**) *chem* an organic compound used in the production of plastics, paints, textiles, etc. ➤ *vb* to treat with resin. ○ **resinous** *adj.*

resist *vb* **1** *tr & intr* to oppose or refuse to comply with something. **2** to withstand (something damaging): *a metal which resists corrosion.* **3** to impede: *to resist arrest.* **4** to refrain from or turn down: *I can't resist chocolate.*

resistance *n* **1** an act or the process of resisting. **2** the ability to resist, esp the extent to which damage, etc can be withstood: *Resistance is low during the winter months.* **3** *physics* in damped harmonic motion: the ratio of the frictional forces to the speed. **4** *elec* a measure of the extent to which a material or an electrical device opposes the flow of an electric current through it. **5** a measure of the extent to which a material opposes the flow of heat through it. **6** an underground organization fighting for the freedom of a country occupied by an enemy force. ○ **resistant** *adj.*

resistor *n*, *elec* a device which introduces a known value of resistance to electrical flow into a circuit.

resit *vb* /riːˈsɪt/ *tr & intr* to take (an examination) again. ➤ *n* /ˈriːsɪt/ an act or instance of taking an examination again or the examination itself.

resoluble *adj* able to be resolved.

resolute *adj* determined; with a fixed purpose or belief. ○ **resolutely** *adv.* ○ **resoluteness** *n.*

resolution *n* **1** an act or instance or the process of making a firm decision. **2** a firm decision. **3** determination. **4** an act or instance or the process of solving a mathematical problem, etc. **5** an answer to a mathematical problem, etc. **6** the ability of a television screen, photographic film, etc to reproduce an image in very fine detail. **7** a formal decision, expression of opinion, etc by a group of people, eg at a public meeting. **8** *mus* the passing of a chord from discord to concord. **9** an act or the process of separating something, eg a chemical compound, into its constituent parts. **10** *physics* the ability of a microscope, telescope, etc to distinguish between objects which are very close together.

resolve *vb* **1** to decide firmly or make up one's mind. **2** to find an answer to (a problem, etc). **3** to take away (a doubt, difficulty, etc). **4** to bring (an argument, etc) to an end. **5** *tr & intr* to decide, or pass (a resolution), esp formally by vote. **6** of a television screen, photographic film, etc: to produce an image in fine detail. **7** of a microscope, telescope, etc: to distinguish clearly (eg objects which are very close together). **8** *tr & intr, mus* of a chord: to pass from discord into concord. **9** to break up or cause to break up into separate or constituent parts. ➤ *n* **1** determination. **2** a firm decision.

resolved *adj* determined. ○ **resolvedly** /rɪˈzɒlvɪdlɪ/ *adv.*

resonant *adj* **1** of sounds: continuing to sound; resounding. **2** producing echoing sounds: *resonant walls.* **3** full of or intensified by a ringing quality: *a resonant voice.* ○ **resonance** *n.* ○ **resonantly** *adv.*

resonate *vb*, *tr & intr* to resound or cause to resound or echo. ○ **resonator** *n.*

resort *vb*, *intr* (*usu* **resort to**) **1** to use something as a means of solving a problem, etc. **2** *formal* to frequent (a place), esp habitually or in great numbers. ➤ *n* **1** a place visited by many people. **2** someone or something used or looked to for help. ♦ **the last resort** the only remaining course of action or means of overcoming a difficulty, etc.

resound /rɪˈzaʊnd/ *vb* **1** *intr* of sounds: to ring or echo. **2** *intr* (**resound with** or **to**) to reverberate: *The hall resounded to their cheers.* **3** *intr* to be widely known or celebrated: *Her fame resounded throughout the country.* **4** of a place: to make (a sound) echo or ring.

resounding *adj* **1** echoing and ringing. **2** clear and decisive: *a resounding victory.*

resource *n* **1** someone or something that provides a source of help, support, etc when needed. **2** a means of solving problems, etc. **3** skill at finding ways of solving problems, etc. **4** something useful. **5** (*usu* **resources**) a means of support, esp money or property. **6** (*usu* **resources**) a country's, business's, etc source of wealth or income: *natural resources.* ➤ *vb* to provide with support, usu financial.

resourceful *adj* skilled in finding ways of overcoming difficulties, solving problems, etc. ○ **resourcefully** *adv.* ○ **resourcefulness** *n.*

respect *n* **1** admiration; good opinion: *held in great respect.* **2** the state of being honoured, admired or well thought of. **3** (**respect for**) consideration, thoughtfulness or attention: *She showed no respect for his feelings.* **4** (*often* **respects**) *formal* a polite greeting or expression of admiration and esteem. **5** a particular detail, feature or characteristic: *In what respect are they different?* **6** reference, relation or connection. ➤ *vb* **1** to show or feel high regard for. **2** to show consideration for, or attention to: *We must respect her wishes.* **3** to pay proper attention to (a rule, law, etc). ○ **respecter** *n.* ♦ **in respect of** or **with respect to sth** with reference to, or in connection with (a particular matter, etc). **pay one's last respects to sb** to show respect for someone who has died by attending their funeral. **with respect** or **with all due respect** a polite expression indicating disagreement and used before presenting one's own opinion.

respectable *adj* **1** worthy of or deserving respect. **2** having a reasonably good social standing. **3** having a good reputation or character. **4** of behaviour: correct; acceptable. **5** of a person's appearance: presentable. **6** fairly or relatively good or large: *a respectable turnout.* ○ **respectability** *n.* ○ **respectably** *adv.*

respectful *adj* having or showing respect. ○ **respectfully** *adv.* ○ **respectfulness** *n.*

respecting *prep* about; with regard to.

respective *adj* belonging to or relating to each person or thing mentioned: *our respective homes.* ○ **respectively** *adv.*

respiration *n* **1** an act or instance or the process of breathing. **2** a breath, in and out. **3** (*also* **external respiration**) *physiol* a metabolic process in plants and animals whereby compounds are broken down to release energy.

respirator *n* **1** a mask worn over the mouth and nose to prevent poisonous gas, dust, etc being breathed in. **2** *med* an apparatus that does a sick or injured person's breathing for them.

respire *vb* **1** *tr & intr* to inhale and exhale (air, etc); to breathe. **2** *intr, biochem* to release energy as a result of the breakdown of organic compounds. ○ **respiratory** /ˈrɛspɪrətəri/ *adj.*

respite *n* **1** a period of rest or relief from, or a temporary stopping of, something unpleasant, difficult, etc. **2** a temporary delay.

resplendent *adj* brilliant or splendid in appearance. ○ **resplendence** or **resplendency** *n.*

respond *vb* **1** *tr & intr* to answer or reply; to say or do in reply. **2** *intr* (*usu* **respond to**) to react favourably or well: *to respond to treatment.* **3** *intr, relig* to utter liturgical responses. ○ **responder** *n.*

respondent *n, law* a defendant, esp in a divorce suit.

response *n* **1** an act of responding, replying or reacting. **2** a reply or answer. **3** a reaction: *This met with little response.* **4** (*usu* **responses**) *Christianity* an answer or reply made by the congregation to something said by the minister during a service.

responsibility *n* (-**ies**) **1** the state of being responsible or of having important duties for which one is responsible. **2** something or someone for which one is responsible.

responsible *adj* **1** (*usu* **responsible for** or **to**) accountable: *responsible to her immediate superior.* **2** of a job, position, etc: with many important duties. **3** (*often* **responsible for**) being the main or identifiable cause: *Who was responsible for the accident?* **4** of a person: **a** able to be trusted; **b** capable of rational and socially acceptable behaviour: *She's very responsible for her age.* ○ **responsibly** *adv.*

responsive *adj* **1** of a person: ready and quick to react or respond. **2** reacting readily to a stimulus. **3** reacting well or favourably: *a disease responsive to drugs.* **4** made as or constituting a response: *a responsive smile.* ○ **responsively** *adv.* ○ **responsiveness** *n.*

respray *vb* to spray or paint (esp the bodywork of a vehicle) again. ➤ *n* **1** the action of respraying. **2** the result of respraying.

rest[1] *n* **1** a period of relaxation or freedom from work, activity, etc. **2** sleep; repose. **3** calm. **4** a pause from some activity: *We stopped halfway up the hill for a rest.* **5** death, when seen as repose. **6** a support, eg for a snooker cue. **7** a place or thing which holds or supports. **8** a pause in reading, speaking, etc. **9** *mus* **a** an interval of silence in a piece of music: *two bars' rest;* **b** a mark indicating the duration of this. ➤ *vb* **1** *tr & intr* to stop or cause to stop working or moving. **2** *intr* to relax, esp by sleeping or stopping some activity. **3** *tr & intr* to set, place or lie on or against something for support, etc: *She rested her arm on the chair.* **4** *intr* to be calm and free from worry. **5** *tr & intr* to give or have as a basis or support: *I will rest my argument on practicalities.* **6** *intr* to depend or be based on: *The decision rests with the board.* **7** *intr* to be left without further attention, discussion or action: *Let the matter rest there.* **8** *intr* to lie dead or buried. **9** *intr, euphemistic* of an actor: to be unemployed. ♦ **at rest 1** not moving or working. **2** free from trouble, worry, etc: *I set his mind at rest.* **3** asleep. **4** dead. **lay sb to rest** to bury or inter them.

rest[2] *n* (*usu* **the rest**) **1** what is left when part of something is taken away, used, etc. **2** the others. ➤ *vb, intr* to continue to be: *rest assured.*

restaurant *n* an establishment where meals may be bought and eaten.

restaurant car *n* a carriage on a train in which meals are served to travellers.

restaurateur /rɛstərəˈtɜː(r)/ *n* an owner or manager of a restaurant.

restful *adj* **1** bringing or giving rest, or producing a sensation of calm, peace and rest. **2** relaxed. ○ **restfulness** *n.*

resting adj 1 not moving, working, etc. 2 euphemistic of an actor: unemployed.

restitution n 1 the act of giving something stolen, lost, etc back to its rightful owner. 2 compensation for loss or injury: to make restitution for the damage. ○ **restitutive** adj.

restive adj 1 restless; nervous. 2 unwilling to accept control or authority.

restless adj 1 constantly moving about or fidgeting; unable to stay still or quiet. 2 constantly active or in motion. 3 giving no rest; disturbed: a restless night. 4 worried, nervous and uneasy. ○ **restlessly** adv. ○ **restlessness** n.

restoration n 1 an act or instance or the process of restoring or being restored. 2 a model or reconstruction (eg of a ruin, extinct animal, etc). 3 (usu **the Restoration**) Brit hist the re-establishment of Charles II on the English throne in 1660, or the period of his reign.

restorative adj tending or helping to restore or improve health, strength, spirits, etc. ➤ n a restorative food or medicine.

restore vb 1 to return (a building, painting, etc) to a former condition by repairing, cleaning, etc. 2 to bring someone or something back to a normal or proper state: to be restored to health. 3 to bring back (a normal, desirable, etc state): restore discipline. 4 to return (something lost or stolen) to the rightful owner. 5 to bring or put back to a former and higher status, etc. ○ **restorer** n.

restrain vb 1 to prevent (someone, oneself, etc) from doing something. 2 to keep (one's temper, ambition, etc) under control. 3 to confine. ○ **restrainer** n.

restrained adj controlled; able to control one's emotions.

restraint n 1 an act or instance of restraining or the state of being restrained. 2 a limit or restriction. 3 the avoidance of exaggeration or excess.

restrict vb 1 to keep within certain limits. 2 to limit or regulate; to withhold from general use. ○ **restricted** adj. ○ **restriction** n.

restrictive adj restricting or intended to restrict, esp excessively.

rest room n, N Am a room with lavatories and wash basins, eg in a shop or theatre, for the use of the staff or public.

restructuring n the reorganization of a business, company, etc in order to improve efficiency, cut costs, etc.

result n 1 an outcome or consequence of something. 2 (often **results**) colloq a positive or favourable outcome or consequence: His action got results. 3 a number or quantity obtained by calculation, etc. 4 (**results**) a list of scores, examination outcomes, etc. ➤ vb, intr 1 (usu **result from**) to be a consequence or outcome. 2 (usu **result in**) to lead (to a specified thing, condition, etc).

resultant adj resulting. ➤ n, maths, physics a single force which is the equivalent of two or more forces acting on an object.

resume vb 1 tr & intr to return to or begin again after an interruption. 2 to take back or return to (a former position, etc): to resume one's seat. ○ **resumption** n.

résumé /ˈrezjumeɪ/ n 1 a summary. 2 N Am a curriculum vitae.

resurgence n an act or instance of returning to a state of importance, influence, etc after a period of decline. ○ **resurgent** adj.

resurrect vb 1 to bring someone back to life from the dead. 2 to bring (a custom, memory, etc) back.

resurrection n 1 an act or instance or the process of resurrecting. 2 (**the Resurrection**) Christianity Christ's rising from the dead.

resuscitate vb 1 to bring back to life or consciousness. 2 intr to revive or regain consciousness. ○ **resuscitation** n.

retail n /ˈriːteɪl/ the sale of goods to customers buying them for personal use. Compare WHOLESALE. ➤ adj relating to, concerned with or engaged in selling such goods. ➤ adv 1 by retail. 2 at a retail price. ➤ vb 1 /ˈriːteɪl/ a to sell (goods) in small quantities; b intr to be sold in small quantities to customers. 2 /riːˈteɪl/ to recount (a story, gossip, etc) in great detail. ○ **retailer** n.

retain vb 1 to keep or continue to have: to retain a sense of humour. 2 to be able to hold or contain: a substance that retains moisture. 3 to keep (facts, etc) in one's memory. 4 to hold back or keep in place. 5 to secure the services of (a person, esp a barrister) by paying a preliminary fee.

retainer n 1 someone or something that retains. 2 hist a dependant of a person of rank. 3 a domestic servant who has been with a family for a long time. 4 a fee paid to secure professional services, esp of a lawyer or barrister. 5 a reduced rent paid for property while it is not occupied in order to reserve it for future use.

retake vb /riːˈteɪk/ 1 a to take again; b to take back. 2 to capture (eg a fortress) again. 3 to sit (an examination) again. 4 to film (eg a scene) again. ➤ n /ˈriːteɪk/ 1 the action of retaking something. 2 an examination that someone sits again. 3 a an act or the process of filming a scene, etc again; b the scene, etc resulting from this.

retaliate vb, intr to repay an injury, wrong, etc in kind. ○ **retaliation** n. ○ **retaliatory** adj.

retard vb to slow down or delay something. ○ **retardant** adj, n. ○ **retardation** or **retardment** n.

retarded adj backward in physical or esp mental development.

retch vb, intr to strain as if to vomit, but without actually doing so. ➤ n an act of retching.

retention n 1 the act of retaining something or the state of being retained. 2 the power of retaining or capacity to retain something. 3 the ability to remember experiences and things learnt.

retentive adj 1 able to retain or keep, esp

memories or information. **2** tending to retain (fluid, etc).

rethink *vb* /riːˈθɪŋk/ to think about or consider (a plan, etc) again. ➤ *n* /ˈriːθɪŋk/ an act of rethinking.

reticent *adj* **1** not saying very much. **2** not willing to communicate. **3** not communicating everything that is known. ○ **reticence** *n*.

reticulate *adj* like a net or network, esp in having lines, veins, etc: *a reticulate leaf.* ○ **reticulation** *n*.

retina /ˈrɛtɪnə/ *n* (**retinas** or **retinae** /ˈrɛtɪniː/) the light-sensitive tissue that lines the back of the eyeball. ○ **retinal** *adj*.

retinue *n* the servants, officials, etc who travel with and attend an important person.

retire *vb* **1** *tr & intr* to stop or make someone stop working permanently: *She retired at 60.* **2** *intr, formal* to go to bed. **3** *intr, formal* to go away (from or to a place): *to retire to the drawing room.* **4** *tr & intr* to withdraw or make someone withdraw from a sporting contest, esp because of injury. **5** *tr & intr* of a military force, etc: to withdraw from a dangerous position.

retired *adj* no longer working.

retirement *n* **1** an act of retiring or the state of being retired from work. **2** seclusion and privacy.

retiring *adj* shy and reserved.

retort¹ *vb* **1** *intr* to make a quick and clever or angry reply. **2** to turn (an argument, criticism, etc) back on the person who first used it. ➤ *n* **1** a quick and clever or angry reply. **2** an argument, criticism, blame, etc which is turned back on the originator.

retort² *n* **1** a glass vessel with a long neck which curves downwards, used in distilling. **2** *metallurgy* a vessel for heating metals to obtain steel, or for heating coal to produce gas.

retouch *vb* /riːˈtʌtʃ/ to improve or repair (a photograph, painting, etc) by making small alterations. ➤ *n* /ˈriːtʌtʃ/ **1** an act of retouching. **2** a photograph, painting, etc that has been retouched.

retrace *vb* **1** to go back over (a route, etc). **2** to trace back to a source or origin: *She wants to retrace her roots.* **3** to go over (events, etc) again in one's memory.

retract *vb* **1** to draw (an animal's body part, an aircraft's landing gear, etc) in or back. **2** *tr & intr* to withdraw (a statement, claim, etc). ○ **retraction** *n*.

retractile *adj* of a cat's, etc claws: able to be drawn in, back or up.

retrain *vb* **1** to teach (a person or animal) new skills. **2** *intr* to learn new skills, esp with a view to finding alternative employment.

retread *vb, n* same as REMOULD

retreat *vb* **1** *intr* of a military force, army, etc: to move back or away from the enemy or retire after defeat. **2** *intr* to retire or withdraw to a place of safety or seclusion. **3** *intr* to recede; to slope back. ➤ *n* **1** an act or instance or the process of retreating. **2** *mil* a signal to retreat,

esp one given on a bugle. **3** a place of privacy or seclusion. **4 a** a period of retirement or withdrawal from the world, esp for prayer, meditation, etc; **b** a place for this.

retrench *vb, tr & intr* to economize; to reduce (expenses). ○ **retrenchment** *n*.

retrial *n* a second or subsequent trial for the same offence.

retribution *n* **1** the act of punishing or taking vengeance for sin or wrongdoing. **2** deserved punishment. ○ **retributive** /rɪˈtrɪbjʊtɪv/ *adj*.

retrieve *vb* **1** to get or bring back again. **2** to rescue or save: *to retrieve the situation.* **3** *comput* to recover (information) from storage in a computer memory. **4** to remember. **5** *tr & intr* of a dog: to search for and bring back (shot game, a thrown stick, etc). ○ **retrievable** *adj*. ○ **retrieval** *n*.

retriever *n* a large dog that can be trained to retrieve game: *a golden retriever.*

retro *adj* reminiscent of, recreating or imitating a style, etc from the past.

retro- *pfx, denoting* **1** back or backwards in time or space. **2** behind.

retroactive *adj* applying to or affecting things from a date in the past: *retroactive legislation.* ○ **retroactively** *adv*.

retrograde *adj* **1** being, tending towards or causing a worse, less advanced or less desirable state. **2** moving or bending backwards. **3** in a reversed or opposite order. ➤ *vb, intr* **1** to move backwards. **2** to deteriorate or decline.

retrogress *vb, intr* **1** to go back to an earlier, worse or less advanced state. **2** to recede or move backwards. ○ **retrogression** *n*. ○ **retrogressive** *adj*.

retrospect *n* a survey of what has happened in the past. ♦ **in retrospect** with the benefit of hindsight.

retrospective *adj* **1** of a law, etc: applying to the past as well as to the present and to the future. **2** of an art exhibition, music recital, etc: showing how the work of the artist, composer, etc has developed over their career. **3** inclined to look back on and evaluate past events. ➤ *n* a retrospective exhibition, etc. ○ **retrospectively** *adv*.

retroussé /rəˈtruːseɪ/ *adj* of a nose, etc: turned up at the end.

retsina *n* a Greek white or rosé wine flavoured with pine resin.

return *vb* **1** *intr* to come or go back again to a former place, state, owner, etc. **2** to give, send, put back, etc in a former position. **3** *intr* to come back in thought or speech. **4** to repay: *to return the compliment.* **5** *tr & intr* to answer or reply. **6** to report officially. **7** to earn or produce (profit, interest, etc). **8** to elect as a Member of Parliament. **9** *law* of a jury: to deliver (a verdict). ➤ *n* **1** an act of coming back from a place, state, etc. **2** an act of returning something, esp to its former place, state, ownership, etc. **3** something returned. **4** profit from work, a business or investment. **5** a statement of income and allowances, used for calculating tax. **6** (*usu* **returns**) a statement of the votes polled in an election. **7** *Brit* (*in full* **return ticket**) a ticket entitling a passenger to travel to a place and back to the starting point. **8** an answer or reply. **9** (*in full* **return key**) **a** a key on a keyboard that takes the operator from the end of one line to the beginning of the line below; **b** a key on a computer keyboard used for various functions including the loading of software: *Type 'install' and press 'Return'.* ○ **returnable** *adj.* ◆ **in return** in exchange; as compensation. **many happy returns (of the day)** an expression of good wishes on someone's birthday.

returning officer *n* an official in charge of running an election in a constituency, counting the votes and declaring the result.

reunion *n* **1** a meeting of people (eg relatives or former colleagues) who have not met for some time. **2** an act of reuniting or the state of being reunited.

reunite *vb, tr & intr* to bring or come together again after being separated.

Rev or **Revd** *abbrev* Reverend.

rev *n, colloq* (*often* **revs**) a revolution of an engine. ➤ *vb* (**revved, revving**) *colloq* (*also* **rev up**) **1** to increase the speed of revolution of (a car engine, etc). **2** *intr* of an engine or vehicle: to run faster.

revalue *vb* to adjust the exchange rate of (a currency), esp making it more valuable with respect to other currencies.

revamp *vb* to revise, renovate or improve. ➤ *n* an act of revamping.

reveal[1] *vb* **1** to make (a secret, etc) known. **2** to show or allow to be seen. **3** of a deity: to make known through divine inspiration or by supernatural means. ○ **revealingly** *adv.*

reveal[2] *n, archit* a vertical side surface of a recess in a wall, esp in the opening for a doorway or window.

reveille /rɪ'vali/ *n* a military wake-up call, usu by a drum or bugle.

revel *vb* (**revelled, revelling**) *intr* **1** (**revel in sth**) to take great delight in it. **2** to have fun in a noisy lively way. ➤ *n* (*usu* **revels**) an occasion of revelling. ○ **reveller** *n.* ○ **revelry** *n* (*-ies*).

Revelation or (*popularly*) **Revelations** *sing n* the last book of the New Testament.

revelation *n* **1** an act of revealing, showing or disclosing something previously unknown or unexpected. **2** something revealed or disclosed in this way.

revenge *n* **1** malicious injury, harm or wrong done in return for injury, harm or wrong received. **2** something that is done as a means of returning like injury, harm, etc. **3** the desire to do such injury, harm, etc. ➤ *vb* **1** to do similar injury, harm, etc in return for injury, harm, etc received. **2** to take revenge on behalf of oneself or someone else.

revengeful *adj* keen for revenge.

revenue *n* **1** money from a property, shares, etc. **2 a** money raised by the government of a country or state from taxes, etc; **b** (*often* **Revenue**) a government department responsible for collecting this money.

reverberate *vb* **1** *intr* of a sound, light, heat, etc: to be echoed, repeated or reflected repeatedly. **2** to echo, repeat or reflect (a sound, light, etc) repeatedly. **3** *intr* of a story, scandal, etc: to circulate or be repeated many times. ○ **reverberation** *n.*

revere *vb* to feel or show great respect or reverence for.

reverence *n* **1** great respect or veneration, esp that shown to something sacred or holy. **2** a feeling of, or the capacity to feel, such respect. ➤ *vb* to regard with great reverence.

reverend *adj* deserving reverence, esp used before proper names as a title for members of the clergy. ➤ *n, colloq* a member of the clergy.

reverent *adj* showing or feeling reverence.

reverential *adj* reverent or very respectful. ○ **reverentially** *adv.*

reverie /'rɛvərɪ/ *n* **1** a state of dreamy and absent-minded thought. **2** a daydream or absent-minded idea or thought.

revers /rɪ'vɪə(r)/ *n* (*pl* **revers**) any part of a garment that is turned back, esp a lapel.

reverse *vb* **1** *tr & intr* to move or make something move backwards or in an opposite direction: *He reversed the car.* **2** to run (a mechanism, piece of machinery, etc) backwards or in the opposite direction from normal. **3** to put or arrange in an opposite position, state, order, etc. **4** to turn (an item of clothing, etc) inside out. **5** to change (a policy, decision, etc) to the exact opposite. **6** *law* to set aside or overthrow (a legal decision, etc). ➤ *n* **1** the opposite or contrary of something. **2** a change to an opposite or contrary position, direction, state, etc. **3** the back or rear side of something, eg the back cover of a book. **4** the side of a coin, medal, note, etc that has a secondary design on it. **5** a mechanism, esp a car gear, which makes a vehicle, piece of machinery, etc move or operate in a backwards direction. ○ **reversal** *n.* ○ **reversible** *adj.*

reversion *n* **1** a return to an earlier state, belief, etc. **2** *law* **a** the legal right (eg of an original owner or their heirs) to possess a property again at the end of a certain period; **b** property to which someone has such a right. **3** *biol* of individuals, organs, etc: a return to an earlier ancestral, and usu less advanced, type.

revert *vb* (*usu* **revert to**) **1** to return (to something in thought or conversation). **2** to return (to a former and usu worse state, practice, etc). **3** *law* of property, etc: to return (to an original owner or their heirs) after belonging temporarily to someone else.

review *n* **1** an act of examining, reviewing or revising, or the state of being examined, reviewed or revised. **2** a general survey of a particular subject, situation, etc. **3** a survey of the past and past events. **4** a critical report of a recent book, play, film, etc. **5** a magazine or newspaper, or a section of one, with reviews of books, etc. **6** an additional study or consideration of certain facts, events, etc. **7** *mil* a formal or official inspection of troops, ships, etc. **8** *law* a re-examination of a case, esp by a superior court. ➤ *vb* **1** to see or view again. **2** to examine or go over, esp critically or formally. **3** to look back on and examine (events in the past). **4** to write reviews of (books, plays, etc), esp professionally. **5** *mil* to inspect (troops, ships, etc), esp officially. **6** *law* to re-examine (a case). ○ **reviewable** *adj*. ○ **reviewer** *n*. ◆ **in** or **under review** undergoing consideration, negotiation, etc.

revile *vb* **1** to abuse or criticize bitterly or scornfully. **2** *intr* to speak scornfully.

revise *vb* **1** to examine or re-examine (a text, etc) in order to identify and correct faults, make improvements, etc. **2** *tr & intr* to study or look at (a subject, notes, etc) again, esp in preparation for an examination. **3** to reconsider or amend (an opinion, etc).

revision *n* **1** an act or the result of revising, or the process of revising. **2** an act or the process of studying a subject or notes on it again, esp in preparation for an examination. **3** a revised book, article, etc. ○ **revisionary** *adj*.

revisionism *n*, *pol* a policy or practice of revising established political ideas, doctrines, etc. ○ **revisionist** *n*, *adj*.

revitalize or **-ise** *vb* to give new life or energy to.

revival *n* **1** an act or the process of reviving or the state of being revived. **2** a renewed interest, esp in old customs, fashions, etc. **3** a new production or performance, esp of an old play. **4** a period of renewed religious faith and spirituality.

revivalism *n* the promotion of renewed religious faith and spirituality through evangelistic meetings. ○ **revivalist** *n*.

revive *vb* **1** *tr & intr* to come or bring back to consciousness, strength, health, etc. **2** *tr & intr* to come or bring back into use or fashion, etc. **3** to perform (an old play) again.

revivify *vb* (**-ies, -ied**) to put new life, vigour, etc into. ○ **revivification** *n*.

revoke *vb* **1** to cancel (a will, agreement, etc). **2** *intr, cards* to fail to follow suit in cards when able to do so. ➤ *n*, *cards* an act of revoking. ○ **revocable** *adj*. ○ **revocation** /rɛvə'keɪʃən/ *n*.

revolt *vb* **1** *intr* to rebel or rise up (against a government, authority, etc). **2** *tr & intr* to feel, or provoke a feeling of, disgust, loathing or revulsion. ➤ *n* a rebellion or uprising against a government, authority, etc.

revolting *adj* causing a feeling of disgust, loathing, etc. ○ **revoltingly** *adv*.

revolution *n* **1** the overthrow of a government or political system. **2** any complete economic, social, etc change: *the Industrial Revolution*. **3 a** an act or the process of turning about an axis; **b** a single turn about an axis; **c** the time taken to make one such movement. **4** a cycle of events.

revolutionary *adj* **1** relating to or causing a revolution. **2** completely new or different. ➤ *n* (**-ies**) someone who takes part in or is in favour of a political, social, etc revolution.

revolutionize or **-ise** *vb* to bring about a great change in: *Computers have revolutionized many businesses.*

revolve *vb* **1** *tr & intr* to move or turn, or cause to move or turn, in a circle around a central point. **2** *intr* (*usu* **revolve around** or **about sth**) to have it as a centre, focus or main point. **3** *intr* to occur in cycles or at regular intervals. **4** to consider. ➤ *n*, *theat* a section of a stage that can be rotated, providing a means of scene-changing. ○ **revolving** *adj* able, designed, etc to revolve.

revolver *n* a pistol with a revolving cylinder holding several bullets.

revue *n* a humorous theatrical show that includes songs, sketches, etc.

revulsion *n* **1** a feeling of complete disgust, distaste or repugnance. **2** a sudden and often violent change of feeling, esp from love to hate.

reward *n* **1** something given or received in return for work done, good behaviour, etc. **2** a sum of money offered for finding or helping to find a criminal, stolen or lost property, etc. **3** something given or received in return for a good or evil deed, etc. ➤ *vb* to give something to someone as a show of gratitude or in recompense.

rewarding *adj* giving personal pleasure or satisfaction: *a rewarding job.*

rewind *vb* /riː'waɪnd/ (**rewound**) to wind (thread, tape, film, etc) back. ➤ *n* /'riːwaɪnd/ **1** the action or process of rewinding. **2** a mechanism for rewinding tape, film, etc.

rewire *vb* to fit (a house, etc) with new electrical wiring.

reword *vb* to express in different words.

rework *vb* **1** to work something again. **2** to alter or refashion something in order to use it again. **3** to revise or rewrite something. ○ **reworking** *n* **1** the action of working something again, or of altering, revising it, etc. **2** something that is reworked, esp something that is revised or rewritten.

rewrite *vb* /riː'raɪt/ **1** to write something again or in different words. **2** *comput* to retain (data) in an area of store by recording it in the location from which it has been read. ➤ *n* /'riːraɪt/ **1** the action of rewriting. **2** something that is rewritten.

Rh¹ *abbrev* rhesus.

Rh² *symbol, chem* rhodium.

rhapsodize or **-ise** *vb*, *tr & intr* to speak or write with great enthusiasm or emotion.

rhapsody *n* (**-ies**) **1** *mus* a piece of music, emotional in character and usu written to suggest a free form or improvisation. **2** an exaggeratedly enthusiastic and emotional speech, piece of writing, etc. ○ **rhapsodic** /rap'spdɪk/ or **rhapsodical** *adj*.

rhea /rɪə/ *n* a S American flightless bird, like an ostrich but smaller.

rhenium *n, chem* a rare silvery-white metallic element with a very high melting point.

rheostat *n, elec* a device for varying resistance in an electric circuit, used, eg, in dimming light bulbs, etc. ○ **rheostatic** *adj.*

rhesus factor or **Rh factor** *n, med* an ANTIGEN that is present on the surface of red blood cells of about 84% of the human population, who are said to be **rhesus positive**, and absent in the remaining 16%, who are said to be **rhesus negative**.

rhetoric /ˈrɛtərɪk/ *n* **1** the art of using language elegantly, effectively or persuasively. **2** language of this kind, sometimes with overtones of insincerity or exaggeration: *mere rhetoric*. ○ **rhetorician** /rɛtəˈrɪʃən/ *n.*

rhetorical /rɪˈtɒrɪkəl/ *adj* **1** relating to or using rhetoric. **2** persuasive or insincere in style.

rhetorical question *n* a question that is asked for effect rather than to gain information.

rheum /ruːm/ *n* a watery mucous discharge from the nose or eyes. ○ **rheumy** *adj.*

rheumatic *adj* **1** relating to, like or caused by rheumatism. **2** affected with rheumatism. ➤ *n* **1** someone who suffers from rheumatism. **2** (**rheumatics**) *colloq* rheumatism or pain caused by it. ○ **rheumatically** *adv.*

rheumatism *n* a disease causing painful swelling of the joints, muscles and fibrous tissues. ○ **rheumatoid** *adj.*

rhinestone *n* an imitation diamond, usu made from glass or plastic.

rhino *n* (**rhinos** or **rhino**) short form of RHINOCEROS.

rhinoceros *n* (**rhinoceroses** or **rhinoceros**) a large herbivorous mammal with very thick skin and either one or two horns on its snout.

rhizome *n, bot* a thick horizontal underground stem which produces both roots and leafy shoots.

rhodium *n, chem* a hard, silvery-white metallic element, used for making alloys, plating jewellery, etc.

rhododendron *n* (**rhododendrons** or **rhododendra**) a widely cultivated shrub with evergreen leaves and large colourful flowers.

rhomboid *n* a quadrilateral where only the opposite sides and angles are equal. ➤ *adj* (*also* **rhomboidal**) shaped like a rhomboid or rhombus.

rhombus /ˈrɒmbəs/ *n* (**rhombuses** or **rhombi** /-baɪ/) **1** *geom* a quadrilateral with four equal sides and two angles greater than and two angles smaller than a right angle. **2** a lozenge or diamond shape, or an object with this shape.

rhubarb *n* a plant with large poisonous leaves or its long fleshy edible leafstalks.

rhumba see RUMBA

rhyme *n* **1** a pattern of words which have the same final sounds at the ends of lines in a poem. Compare ASSONANCE. **2** the use of such patterns in poetry, etc. **3** a word which has the same final sound as another: *'Beef' is a rhyme for 'leaf'.* **4** a short poem, verse or jingle written in rhyme. ➤ *vb* **1** *intr* of words: to have the same final sound. **2** to use (a word) as a rhyme for another. **3** *intr* to write using rhymes. **4** to put (a story, etc) into rhyme. ◆ **without rhyme or reason** lacking sense, reason or logic.

rhymester *n* a poet, esp one who writes simple verses or who is not very talented.

rhyming slang *n* slang, esp Cockney slang, where one word is replaced by a phrase that rhymes with it.

rhythm *n* **1** a regularly repeated pattern, movement, beat, sequence of events, etc. **2 a** the regular arrangement of stress, notes of different lengths, and pauses in a piece of music; **b** a particular pattern of stress, notes, etc in music: *tango rhythm.* **3** a regular arrangement of sounds, and of stressed and unstressed syllables, giving a sense or feeling of movement. **4** ability to sing, speak, move, etc rhythmically. ○ **rhythmic** or **rhythmical** *adj.* ○ **rhythmically** *adv.*

rhythm and blues *sing n, mus* (abbrev **R & B**) a style of popular music combining blues elements with more lively rhythms.

rib[1] *n* **1** in vertebrates: any of the curved paired bones that articulate with the spine and form the chest wall. **2** a cut of meat containing one or more ribs. **3** a section of an object or structure that resembles a rib in form or function, eg in the hull of a ship or an umbrella. **4** *knitting* a series of ridges produced by alternating plain and purl stitches. ➤ *vb* (**ribbed, ribbing**) **1** to provide, support or enclose (an object, structure, etc) with ribs. **2** *knitting* to knit ribs or in ribs. ○ **ribbed** *adj* with ribs or ridges. ○ **ribbing** *n.*

rib[2] *vb* (**ribbed, ribbing**) *colloq* to tease. ○ **ribbing** *n.*

ribald /ˈrɪbəld/ *adj* of language, a speaker, humour, etc: humorous in an obscene, vulgar or indecently disrespectful way. ○ **ribaldry** *n.*

riband or **ribband** *n* a ribbon, esp as a prize in sport, etc.

ribbon *n* **1 a** a material such as silk, etc, formed into a long narrow strip; **b** a strip of such material used for tying hair, parcels, etc. **2** a long narrow strip of anything: *hanging in ribbons* ◆ *a typewriter ribbon.* **3** a small strip of coloured cloth, worn to show membership of a team, as a sign of having won an award, etc.

ribcage *n* the chest wall, formed by the ribs.

ribonucleic acid *n, biochem* (abbrev **RNA**) a nucleic acid, present in all living cells, that plays an important part in the synthesis of proteins.

rice *n* **1** an important cereal plant of the grass family, native to SE Asia. **2** its edible starchy seeds used as food. ➤ *vb, cookery* to press (eg cooked potatoes) through a coarse sieve to form strands. ○ **ricer** *n.*

rice paper *n* a thin, edible paper made from the pith of an Asiatic tree, used in baking biscuits and cakes.

rich adj **1** having a lot of money, property or possessions. **2** of decoration, furnishings, etc: luxurious, costly and elaborate: rich clothes. **3** high in value or quality: a rich harvest. **4** (**rich in** or **with sth**) abundant in (esp a natural resource): rich in minerals. **5** of soil, a region, etc: very productive. **6** of colour, sound, smell, etc: vivid and intense: rich red. **7 a** of food: heavily seasoned or strongly flavoured; **b** of food or a diet: containing a lot of fat, oil or dried fruit. **8** of a remark, suggestion, event, etc: ridiculous: That's rich, coming from you! **9** of the mixture in an internal-combustion engine: with a high proportion of fuel to air. ○ **richness** n.

riches pl n wealth in general, or a particular form of abundance or wealth: family riches • architectural riches.

richly adv **1** in a rich way. **2** fully and suitably: richly deserved.

rick¹ n a stack or heap, eg of hay or corn. ➤ vb to stack or heap (esp hay, corn, etc).

rick² vb to sprain or wrench (one's neck, back, etc). ➤ n a sprain or wrench.

rickets sing or pl n a disease caused by vitamin D deficiency, characterized by imperfect formation of the bones.

rickety adj **1** of a construction, piece of furniture, etc: unsteady and likely to collapse. **2** of the mind, etc: feeble. **3** suffering from rickets. ○ **ricketiness** n.

rickshaw or **ricksha** n a small two-wheeled hooded carriage, either drawn by a person on foot, or attached to a bicycle or motorcycle.

ricochet /ˈrɪkəʃeɪ, -ʃet/ n **1** the action, esp of a bullet or other missile, of hitting a surface and then rebounding. **2** a sound or hit made by such an action. ➤ vb, intr (**ricocheted** /-ʃeɪd/ or **ricochetted, ricocheting** /-ʃeɪŋ/ or **ricochetting**) of an object, esp a bullet, etc: to glance off a surface and rebound.

ricotta n a soft white unsalted Italian curd cheese.

rid vb (**rid** or (archaic) **ridded, ridding**) (**rid of**) to free (someone, oneself, something or somewhere) from something undesirable or unwanted.

riddance n the act of getting rid of something. ♦ **good riddance** a welcome relief from someone or something undesirable or unwanted.

riddle¹ n **1** a short and usu humorous puzzle, often in the form of a question, which can only be solved or understood using ingenuity. **2** a person, thing or fact that is puzzling or difficult to understand. ➤ vb, intr to speak enigmatically or in riddles. ○ **riddler** n.

riddle² n a large coarse sieve for sifting soil, grain, etc. ➤ vb **1** to pass through a riddle. **2** (usu **riddle with**) to pierce with many holes: Snipers had riddled the wall with bullets. **3** (usu **riddle with**) to spread through: a government department riddled with corruption.

ride vb (**rode, ridden**) **1** to sit, usu astride, on and control the movements of (esp a horse, bicycle, etc). **2** intr to travel or be carried (on a horse, bicycle, etc or in a car, train or other vehicle). **3** chiefly N Am to travel on (a vehicle). **4** intr to go on horseback, esp regularly. **5** to ride (a horse) in a race. **6** to move across or be carried over (the sea, sky, etc): a ship riding the waves. **7** of a ship: **a** intr to float at anchor; **b** to be attached to (an anchor). **8** intr of the moon: to appear to float: The moon was riding high. **9** intr to travel by horse, car, etc: They rode across the desert on camels. **10** intr (**ride on sth**) to depend completely upon it: It all rides on his answer. **11** to bend before (a blow, punch, etc) to reduce its impact. **12** to infest or dominate: a cellar ridden with rats • ridden with remorse. ➤ n **1 a** a journey or certain distance covered on horseback, on a bicycle or in a vehicle; **b** the duration of this: a long ride home. **2** a horse, vehicle, etc as a means of transport. **3** an experience or series of events of a specified nature: a rough ride. **4** esp N Am a LIFT (noun sense 5). **5** the type of movement a vehicle, etc gives: a very smooth ride. **6** a path or track reserved for horseback riding. **7** a fairground machine, such as a rollercoaster or big wheel. ♦ **take sb for a ride** colloq to trick, cheat or deceive them. ◊ **ride sth out** to come through (a difficult period, situation, etc) successfully: to ride out the storm. **ride up** intr of clothing, etc: to move gradually out of the correct position.

rider n **1** someone who rides. **2** an extra or subsequent clause, etc added to a document as a qualification, amendment, etc. ○ **riderless** adj.

ridge n **1** a strip of ground raised either side of a ploughed furrow. **2** any long narrow raised area on an otherwise flat surface. **3** the top edge of something where two upward sloping surfaces meet, eg on a roof. **4** a long narrow strip of relatively high ground with steep slopes on either side. **5** meteorol a long narrow area of high atmospheric pressure. Compare TROUGH (sense 4). ➤ vb, tr & intr to form or make into ridges. ○ **ridged** adj. ○ **ridging** n.

ridgepole n a horizontal pole at the top of a tent.

ridicule n contemptuous mockery or derision. ➤ vb to subject or expose someone or something to ridicule.

ridiculous adj **1** deserving or provoking ridicule. **2** absurd or unreasonable: ridiculous prices. ○ **ridiculously** adv. ○ **ridiculousness** n.

riding¹ n **1** the art and practice of riding a horse. **2** a track or path for horseback riding.

riding² n **1** any of the three former administrative divisions of Yorkshire, **East Riding, North Riding** and **West Riding. 2** Can a political constituency.

rife adj **1** very common or numerous. **2** (**rife with sth**) teeming in (usu something bad or undesirable): The garden was rife with weeds.

riff n, pop music a short passage of music played repeatedly. ➤ vb, intr to play riffs.

riffle vb **1** tr & intr (often **riffle through sth**) to turn (pages) rapidly. **2** to shuffle (playing-cards) by dividing the pack into two equal piles and allowing them to fall together more or less alternately. ➢ *n* an act or instance of riffling.

riff-raff *n* worthless, disreputable or undesirable people.

rifle[1] *n* a large gun with a long barrel, usu fired from the shoulder.

rifle[2] *vb* **1** *tr & intr* (*often* **rifle through sth**) to search (through a house, drawer, etc). **2** to steal and take away.

rifleman *n* a soldier armed with a rifle.

rift *n* **1** a split or crack, esp one in the earth. **2** a gap in mist or clouds. **3** a break in previously friendly relations. ➢ *vb* to tear or split apart.

rift valley *n*, *geol* a long steep-sided valley with a flat floor, formed when part of the Earth's crust subsides between two faults.

rig *vb* (**rigged, rigging**) **1** *naut* to fit (a ship, masts, etc) with ropes, sails and rigging. **2** *aeronautics* to position correctly the various parts and components of (an aircraft, etc). **3** *intr, naut, aeronautics* of a ship, aircraft, etc: to be made ready for use. **4** to control or manipulate for dishonest purposes, or for personal advantage. ➢ *n* **1** *naut* the particular arrangement of sails, ropes and masts on a ship. **2** an installation for drilling oil wells. **3** gear or equipment, esp for a specific task. **4** *N Am* a lorry or truck. ◊ **rig sb out 1** to dress them in clothes of a stated or special kind. **2** to provide them with special equipment. **rig sth up** to build or prepare it, esp hastily.

rigging *n* the system of ropes, wires, etc which support and control a ship's masts and sails.

right *adj* **1** indicating, relating to or on the side facing east from the point of view of someone or something facing north. **2** of a part of the body: on or towards the right side. **3** of an article of clothing, etc: worn on the right hand, foot, etc. **4 a** on, towards or close to an observer's right; **b** on a stage: on or towards the performers' right. **5** of a river bank: on the right side of a person facing downstream. **6** correct; true. **7** of a clock or watch: showing the correct time. **8** suitable; proper. **9** most appropriate or favourable. **10** in a correct, proper or satisfactory state or condition. **11** sound or stable: *not in his right mind*. **12** morally correct or good. **13** legally correct or good. **14** on the side of a fabric, garment, etc which is intended to be seen: *Turn the dress right side out.* **15** (*also* **Right**) conservative. **16** socially acceptable: *to know all the right people.* **17** *Brit, colloq* complete; real: *a right mess.* ➢ *adv* **1** on or towards the right side. **2** correctly; properly; satisfactorily. **3** exactly or precisely: *It happened right there.* **4** immediately: *He'll be right over.* **5** completely: *It went right out of my mind.* **6** all the way: *It went right through him.* **7** of movement, a direction, etc: straight; without deviating from a straight line: *right to the top.* **8** favourably or satisfactorily: *It turned out right in the end.* **9** esp in religious titles: most; very: *right reverend.* ➢ *n* **1** (*often* **rights**) a power, privilege, title, etc. **2** (*often* **rights**) a just or legal claim. **3** fairness; truth.

4 something that is correct, good or just: *the rights and wrongs of the case.* **5** (*often* **the Right**) the political party, or a group of people within a party, etc which has the most conservative views. **6** the right side, part or direction of something. **7** *boxing* **a** the right hand: *He was lethal with his right;* **b** a punch with the right hand: *He knocked him out with a right.* **8** a glove, shoe, etc worn on the right hand or foot: *Can I try on the right?* **9** (*often* **rights**) *commerce* the privilege given to a company's existing shareholders to buy new shares, usu for less than the market value. **10** (**rights**) the legal permission to print, publish, film, etc a book. ➢ *vb* **1** *tr & intr* to put or come back to the correct or normal, esp upright, position: *They soon righted the boat.* **2** to avenge or compensate for (some wrong done). **3** to correct or rectify. **4** to put in order or return to order. ➢ *exclam* expressing agreement or readiness. ○ **rightness** *n*. ◆ **by right** or **rights** rightfully; properly. **in the right** with justice, reason, etc on one's side. **put** or **set right** or **to rights** to make correct or proper. **right away** or **now** immediately.

right angle *n* an angle of 90°, formed by two lines which are perpendicular to each other. ○ **right-angled** *adj*.

right arm *n* a most trusted and reliable helper, etc.

righteous /'raɪtʃəs/ *adj* **1** of a person: virtuous; free from sin or guilt. **2** of an action: morally good. **3** justifiable morally: *righteous indignation.* ○ **righteously** *adv.* ○ **righteousness** *n*.

rightful *adj* **1** having a legally just claim. **2** of property, a privilege, etc: held legally. **3** fair; just.

right-hand *adj* **1** relating to, on or towards the right. **2** done with the right hand.

right-handed *adj* **1** of a person: using the right hand more easily than the left. **2** of a tool, etc: designed to be used in the right hand. **3** of a blow, etc: done with the right hand. **4** of a screw: fixed by turning clockwise.

right-hand man or **right-hand woman** *n* an indispensable and trusted assistant.

rightism *n* the political opinions of conservatives. ○ **rightist** *n, adj*.

rightly *adv* **1** correctly. **2** justly. **3** fairly; properly. **4** with good reason.

right-minded *adj* thinking, judging and acting according to principles which are just, honest and sensible.

right of way *n* (**rights of way**) **1 a** the right of the public to use a path that crosses private property; **b** a path used by this right. **2** the right of one vehicle to proceed before other vehicles coming from different directions.

right-on *slang, adj* **1** excellent. **2** up to date or politically correct. ➢ *exclam* (**right on**) expressing enthusiastic agreement or approval.

rightward or **rightwards** *adj, adv* on or towards the right.

right wing *n* **1** the more conservative members of a group or political party. **2** *sport* **a** the extreme right side of a pitch or team in a field game; **b** (*also* **right-winger**) the member of a team who plays in this position. **3** the right side of an army. ➤ *adj* (**right-wing**) belonging or relating to the right wing.

rigid *adj* **1** completely stiff and inflexible. **2** of a person: strictly and inflexibly adhering to ideas, rules, etc. ○ **rigidity** *n*. ○ **rigidly** *adv*. ○ **rigidness** *n*.

rigmarole *n* **1** an unnecessarily or absurdly long, complicated series of actions or procedures. **2** a long rambling statement.

rigor mortis *n* a stiffening of the body soon after death.

rigorous *adj* **1** showing or having rigour. **2** strictly accurate. ○ **rigorously** *adv*. ○ **rigorousness** *n*.

rigour or (*US*) **rigor** *n* **1** stiffness; hardness. **2** strictness or severity of temper, behaviour or judgement. **3** strict enforcement of rules or the law. **4** (*usu* **rigours**) of a particular situation or circumstances, eg of weather: harshness or severity.

rig-out *n* a set of clothes.

rile *vb* to anger or annoy.

rilievo see RELIEVO

rill *n* a small stream.

rim *n* **1** a raised edge, esp of something curved, eg a cup. **2** the outer circular edge of a wheel to which the tyre is attached. ➤ *vb* (**rimmed, rimming**) to form or provide an edge to something. ○ **rimless** *adj*. ○ **rimmed** *adj*.

rime¹ *n* thick white frost. ➤ *vb* to cover with rime. ○ **rimy** *adj* (**-ier, -iest**).

rime² *archaic* variant of RHYME

rind *n* a thick hard outer layer on fruit, cheese or bacon. ○ **rindless** *adj*.

ring¹ *n* **1** a small circle of gold, silver, etc worn on the finger. **2** a circle of metal, wood, plastic, etc for holding, connecting, hanging, etc. **3** any object, mark or figure which is circular in shape. **4** a circular course or route. **5** a group of people or things arranged in a circle. **6** an enclosed and usu circular area in which circus acts are performed. **7** a square area on a platform, marked off by ropes, where boxers or wrestlers fight. **8** (**the ring**) boxing as a profession. **9** an enclosure for bookmakers at a racecourse. **10** at agricultural shows, etc: an enclosure where cattle, horses, etc are paraded. **11** a group of people who act together: *a drugs ring • a spy ring*. **12** a circular electric element or gas burner on top of a cooker. **13** a circular mark, seen when a tree trunk is examined in section, that represents one year's growth. ➤ *vb* **1** to make, form, draw, etc a ring round something or to form into a ring. **2** to cut into rings. **3** to put a ring on (a bird's leg) as a means of identifying it. **4** to fit a ring in (a bull's nose) so that it can be led easily. ○ **ringed** *adj*. ◆ **make** or **run rings round sb** *colloq* to beat them or be much better than them.

ring² *vb* (**rang, rung**) **1 a** to sound (a bell, etc); **b** *intr* of a bell: to sound. **2 a** to make (a metal object, etc) give a resonant bell-like sound by striking it; **b** *intr* of a metal object, etc: to sound in this way when struck. **3** *intr* of a large building, etc: to be filled with a particular sound: *The theatre rang with laughter*. **4** *intr* of a sound or noise: to resound: *Applause rang round the theatre*. **5** *intr* (*usu* **ring out**) to make a sudden clear loud sound: *Shots rang out*. **6** *intr* to sound repeatedly: *Her criticisms rang in his ears*. **7** *intr* of the ears: to be filled with a buzzing, humming or ringing sound. **8** (*also* **ring up**) *chiefly Brit* to call by telephone. ➤ *n* **1** an act of ringing a bell. **2** an act or sound of ringing. **3** a clear resonant sound of a bell, etc. **4** *Brit* a telephone call. **5** a suggestion or impression: *a story with a ring of truth about it*. ○ **ringing** *n, adj*. ○ **ringingly** *adv*. ◆ **ring a bell** to bring to mind a vague memory of having been seen, heard, etc before: *His name rings a bell*. **ring the changes** to vary the way something is done, used, said, etc. **ring the curtain down** or **up 1** *theat* to give the signal for lowering, or raising, the curtain. **2** (*usu* **ring the curtain down** or **up on sth**) *colloq* to put an end to, or to begin (a project, relationship, etc). ◊ **ring sb back** to telephone them again. **ring off** to end a telephone call. **ring sth up** to record the price of an item sold, etc on a cash register.

ring binder *n* a loose-leaf binder with metal rings which can be opened to add or take out pages.

ringer *n* **1** someone or something that rings a bell, etc. **2** (*also* **dead ringer**) someone or something that is almost identical to another: *He's a dead ringer for Robbie Williams*. **3** *chiefly US* a horse or athlete entered into a race or competition under a false name or other false pretences. **4** *chiefly US colloq* an impostor or fake.

ringleader *n* a person who leads or incites a group, esp in wrongdoing.

ringlet *n* a long spiral curl of hair.

ringmaster *n* a person who presents performances in a circus ring.

ring pull *n* a metal ring on a can, etc which, when pulled, breaks a seal. ➤ *adj* (**ring-pull**) of a can, etc: with a ring pull attached.

ring road *n, Brit* a road that bypasses a town centre and so keeps it relatively free of traffic.

ringside *n* the seating area immediately next to a boxing ring, circus ring, etc.

ringtone *n* a sound or tune made by a mobile phone when ringing.

ringworm *n* a fungal infection that causes dry, red, itchy patches on the skin.

rink *n* **1 a** an area of ice prepared for skating, curling or ice hockey; **b** a building containing this. **2 a** an area of smooth floor for roller-skating; **b** a building containing this. **3** *bowls, curling* **a** a strip of grass or ice allotted to a team of players; **b** a team of players using such a strip of grass or ice.

rinse *vb* **1** to wash (soap, etc) out of (clothes,

hair, etc) with clean water. **2** to remove (traces of dirt, etc) from by dipping in clean water, usu without soap. **3** (*also* **rinse out**) to clean or freshen (a cup, one's mouth, etc) with a swirl of water. ➢ *n* **1** an act or instance or the process of rinsing. **2** liquid used for rinsing. **3** a temporary tint for the hair.

riot *n* **1** a noisy public disturbance or disorder. **2** uncontrolled or wild revelry. **3** a striking display: *a riot of colour*. **4** *colloq* someone or something that is very amusing, esp in a boisterous way. ➢ *vb, intr* **1** to take part in a riot. **2** to take part in boisterous revelry. ○ **rioter** *n*. ♦ **read the riot act** *jocular* to give an angry warning. **run riot 1** to act, speak, etc in a wild or unrestrained way: *He let the children run riot.* **2** of plants, vegetation, etc: to grow in an uncontrolled way: *The weeds were running riot.*

riotous *adj* **1** participating in, likely to start, or like a riot. **2** very active, noisy and wild: *a riotous party.* **3** filled with wild revelry, etc: *riotous living*. ○ **riotously** *adv*.

RIP *abbrev*: *requiescat* (or *requiescant*) *in pace* (Latin), may he, she (or they) rest in peace.

rip *vb* (**ripped, ripping**) **1** *tr & intr* to tear or come apart violently or roughly. **2** *intr, colloq* to rush along or move quickly without restraint. **3 a** to make (a hole, etc) by tearing roughly; **b** to make a long ragged tear in. **4** (**rip sth off, out, up,** *etc*) to remove it quickly and violently. ➢ *n* **1** a violent or rough tear or split. **2** an unrestrained rush. ♦ **let rip** to speak, behave, etc violently or unrestrainedly. ◊ **rip sb off** to cheat someone. **rip sth off** to steal it. **rip sth up** to shred or tear it into pieces.

riparian /raɪ'pɛərɪən/ *adj* relating to, occurring or living on a river bank.

ripcord *n* a cord which, when pulled, releases a parachute.

ripe *adj* **1** of fruit, grain, etc: fully matured and ready to be eaten. **2** of cheese, wine, etc: having been allowed to age to develop a full flavour. **3** of a flavour, eg that of wine: rich or strong. **4** of a person's age: very advanced. ○ **ripely** *adv*. ○ **ripeness** *n*. ♦ **ripe for sth** suitable or appropriate for a particular action or purpose: *ripe for reform*.

ripen *vb, tr & intr* to make or become ripe or riper.

rip-off *n* **1** an act or instance of stealing, cheating or defrauding. **2** an item which is outrageously overpriced.

riposte /rɪ'pɒst/ *n* **1** a quick sharp reply. **2** *fencing* a quick return thrust after a parry. ➢ *vb, intr* to deliver a riposte.

ripple *n* **1** a slight wave on the surface of water. **2** a similar wavy appearance or motion in material, hair, etc. **3** of laughter or applause: a sound that rises and falls gently. **4** a type of ice cream marbled with a coloured flavoured syrup: *raspberry ripple*. ➢ *vb* **1 a** to ruffle or agitate the surface of (water, etc); **b** to mark with ripples, or form ripples in (a surface, material, etc). **2** *intr* to form ripples or move with an un-

dulating motion. **3** *intr* of a sound: to rise and fall gently.

rip-roaring *adj, colloq* wild, noisy and exciting.

ripsaw *n* a saw for cutting along the grain of timber.

rise *vb* (**rose, risen**) *intr* **1** to get or stand up, from a sitting, etc position. **2** to get up from bed. **3** to move upwards. **4** to increase in size, amount, strength, degree, etc. **5** of the sun, moon, planets, etc: to appear above the horizon. **6** to stretch or slope upwards. **7** to rebel. **8** to move from a lower position, rank, level, etc to a higher one. **9** to begin or originate: *a river that rises in the mountains.* **10** of a person's spirits: to become more cheerful. **11** of an animal's fur, a person's hair, etc: to become straight and stiff, esp from fear or anger. **12** of a committee, court, parliament, etc: to finish a session. **13** to come back to life. **14** of fish: to come to the surface of the water. **15** of birds: to fly up from the ground, etc. **16** of dough, a cake, etc: to swell up. **17** to be built. **18** (*usu* **rise to sth**) to respond (to provocation, criticism, etc). ➢ *n* **1** an act of rising. **2** an increase in size, amount, volume, strength, status, rank, etc. **3** *Brit* an increase in salary. **4** a piece of rising ground. **5** a beginning or origin. **6** the vertical height of a step or flight of stairs. ♦ **get** or **take a rise out of sb** *colloq* to make them angry or upset, esp by teasing them. **give rise to sth** to cause it or bring it about. ◊ **rise above sth** to remain unaffected by teasing, provocation, criticism, etc.

riser *n* **1** someone who gets out of bed, usu at a specified time: *a late riser.* **2** a vertical part between the horizontal steps of a staircase. **3** a vertical pipe on a building, oil rig, etc.

risible *adj* laughable.

rising *n* a rebellion. ➢ *adj* **1** moving or sloping upwards. **2** approaching greater status, reputation or importance. **3** approaching a specified age: *rising seven.*

rising damp *n, Brit* wetness which rises up through the bricks or stones of a wall.

risk *n* **1** the chance or possibility of suffering loss, injury, damage, etc. **2** someone or something likely to cause loss, injury, damage, etc. ➢ *vb* **1** to expose someone or something to risk. **2** to act in spite of (something unfortunate): *He risked being caught.* ♦ **run the risk of sth** to be in danger of it: *You run the risk of being late.*

risky *adj* (**-ier, -iest**) likely to cause loss, damage, mishap, etc. ○ **riskily** *adv*. ○ **riskiness** *n*.

risotto *n* an Italian dish of rice cooked in stock with meat, vegetables or seafood.

risqué /'rɪskeɪ/ *adj* of a story, joke, etc: rather rude, but usu not offensive.

rissole *n* a small fried cake of chopped meat coated in breadcrumbs.

rite *n* **1** a formal ceremony or observance, esp a religious one. **2** the required words or actions for such a ceremony. **3** a body of such acts or ceremonies which are characteristic of a particular church.

rite of passage n (*rites of passage*) a ritual event marking an important transition in a person's life.

ritual n 1 a set order or words used in a religious ceremony. 2 a series of actions performed compulsively, habitually, etc. ➤ *adj* relating to, like or used for religious, social or other rites or ritual. ○ **ritualize** or **-ise** *vb.* ○ **ritually** *adv.*

ritualism n excessive belief in the importance of, or excessive practice of, ritual. ○ **ritualist** n. ○ **ritualistic** *adj.*

ritzy *adj* (*-ier, -iest*) *colloq* 1 very smart and elegant. 2 ostentatiously rich. ○ **ritzily** *adv.* ○ **ritziness** n.

rival n 1 a person or group of people competing with another. 2 someone or something that is comparable with or equals another in quality, ability, etc. ➤ *vb* (*rivalled, rivalling; US rivaled, rivaling*) 1 to try to equal or be better than. 2 to equal or be comparable with, in terms of quality, ability, etc. ○ **rivalry** n (*-ies*).

rive *vb* (*past participle rived* or *riven*) *poetic, archaic* to tear or tear apart: *a family riven by feuds.*

river n 1 a large permanent body of flowing water, originating at a source, travelling along a fixed course, and emptying into a lake or the sea. 2 an abundant flow: *a river of tears.*

riverside n a bank of a river or an area of ground along a river.

rivet n a metal pin or bolt for joining pieces of metal, etc. ➤ *vb* (*riveted, riveting*) 1 to fasten (pieces of metal, etc) with a rivet. 2 to fix securely. 3 to attract and hold (attention, etc). 4 to render motionless, esp with fascination, horror, fear, etc: *I was riveted to the spot.*

riveting *adj* fascinating; enthralling.

riviera /ɪrɪvɪ'eərə/ n a coastal area with a warm climate, esp the Mediterranean coasts of France and Italy.

rivulet n a small river.

Rn *symbol, chem* radon.

RNA *abbrev, biochem* ribonucleic acid.

roach¹ n (*roaches* or *roach*) a silvery freshwater fish of the carp family.

roach² n, *colloq* 1 *N Am* a cockroach. 2 a butt of a cannabis cigarette.

road n 1 a an open way, usu specially surfaced, for people, vehicles or animals to travel on; b the part of this designated for the use of vehicles. 2 a route or course: *the road to ruin.* 3 (*usu roads*) a relatively sheltered area of water near the shore where ships may be anchored. ◆ **one for the road** a final, usu alcoholic, drink before leaving. **on the road** travelling from place to place.

roadblock n a police, army, etc barrier across a road for stopping and checking vehicles and drivers.

road hog n, *colloq* an aggressive, selfish or reckless driver.

roadholding n the extent to which a vehicle remains stable when turning corners at high speed, in wet conditions, etc.

roadhouse n a public house at the side of a major road.

roadie n, *colloq* a person who helps move and organize the instruments and equipment for a rock or pop group, esp on tour.

road rage n uncontrolled anger or aggression between road users.

roadshow n 1 a live radio or TV broadcast, usu in front of an audience, presented from one of a series of venues on a tour. 2 a promotional tour to publicize an organization's policies, products, etc.

roadside n the ground beside a road.

road sign n a sign beside or over a road, motorway, etc that gives information.

roadstead n same as ROAD (sense 3).

roadster n, *orig US, old use* an open sports car for two people.

road test n 1 a test of a vehicle's performance and roadworthiness. 2 a practical test of a product, etc. ➤ *vb* (*road-test*) 1 to test the performance and roadworthiness of (a vehicle). 2 to test out the practicalities, suitability, etc of (a new product, etc).

roadway n the part of a road or street used by traffic.

roadworks *pl* n the building or repairing of a road.

roadworthy *adj* of a vehicle: safe to be used on the road. ○ **roadworthiness** n.

roam *vb* 1 *intr* to ramble, esp over a large area, with no fixed purpose. 2 to wander about, over, through, etc (a particular area) in no fixed direction. ➤ n 1 the act of roaming. 2 a ramble.

roan *adj* of an animal, esp a horse: having a coat whose colour is flecked with many grey or white hairs. ➤ n a roan animal, esp a horse.

roar *vb* 1 *intr* of a lion or other animal: to give a loud growling cry. 2 of a person: a *intr* to give a deep loud cry, esp in anger or pain; b to say something with a deep loud cry, esp in anger. 3 *intr* to laugh loudly and wildly. 4 *intr* of traffic, wind, a fiercely burning fire, etc: to make a deep loud sound. 5 *intr* to move or be moving very fast and noisily: *Traffic roared past.* ➤ n an act or the sound of roaring.

roaring n an act or the sound of making a loud deep cry. ➤ *adj* 1 uttering or emitting roars. 2 *colloq* riotous. 3 *colloq* proceeding with great activity or success. ◆ **do a roaring trade** to do very brisk and profitable business. **roaring drunk** *colloq* rowdily or boisterously drunk.

roast *vb* 1 to cook (meat, etc) by exposure to dry heat, esp in an oven. 2 to dry and brown (coffee beans, nuts, etc) by exposure to dry heat. 3 *intr* of meat, coffee beans, nuts, etc: to be cooked or dried and made brown by exposure to dry heat. 4 *colloq* to heat (oneself or something else) to an extreme degree: *to roast oneself in the sun.* 5 *colloq* to criticize severely. ➤ n 1 a piece of meat which has been roasted or is suitable for roasting. 2 *N Am* a party in the open air at which food is roasted and eaten.

roasting adj extremely or uncomfortably hot. ➤ n a dose of severe criticism.

rob vb (**robbed, robbing**) **1** to steal from (a person or place). **2** intr to commit robbery. **3** to deprive of something expected as a right or due: It robbed her of her dignity. ○ **robber** n.

robbery n (**-ies**) an act or instance or the process of robbing. Compare BURGLARY.

robe n **1** (often **robes**) a long loose flowing garment, esp the official vestment worn by peers, judges, the clergy, etc. **2** a dressing-gown or bathrobe. ➤ vb to clothe (oneself or someone else) in a robe or robes.

robin n **1** (also **robin redbreast**) a small brown European thrush with a red breast. **2** a larger N American thrush with a brick-red breast and white rings around its eyes.

robot n **1** esp in science fiction: a machine that vaguely resembles a human being and which can be programmed to carry out tasks. **2** an automatic machine that can be programmed to perform specific tasks. **3** colloq someone who works efficiently but who lacks human warmth. ○ **robotic** adj.

robotics sing n the branch of engineering concerned with the design, construction, operation and use of industrial robots.

robust adj **1** of a person: strong and healthy. **2** strongly built or constructed. **3** of exercise, etc: requiring strength and energy. **4** of language, humour, etc: rough; earthy. **5** of wine, food, etc: with a full, rich quality. ○ **robustly** adv. ○ **robustness** n.

roc n in Arabian legends: an enormous bird that was strong enough to carry off an elephant.

rock¹ n **1** geol a mass of one or more minerals that forms part of the Earth's crust, eg granite, limestone, etc. **2** a large natural mass of this material. **3** a large stone. **4** someone or something that provides support and can be depended upon. **5** Brit a hard sweet usu made in the form of long, cylindrical sticks. **6** slang a precious stone, esp a diamond. ♦ **on the rocks** colloq **1** of a marriage: broken down. **2** of an alcoholic drink: served with ice cubes. **3** of a business, etc: in a state of great financial difficulty.

rock² vb **1** tr & intr to sway or make something sway gently backwards and forwards or from side to side: to rock the baby to sleep. **2** tr & intr to move or make something move or shake violently. **3** colloq to disturb or shock: The news rocked the sporting world. **4** intr to dance to or play rock music. ➤ n **1** a rocking movement. **2** (also **rock music**) a form of popular music with a very strong beat. **3** rock and roll.

rockabilly n a style of music that combines elements from both rock and roll and hillbilly.

rock and roll or **rock'n'roll** n **1** a form of popular music originating in the 1950s, with a lively jive beat and simple melodies. **2** the type of dancing done to this music.

rock bottom or **rock-bottom** n **1** bedrock. **2**

colloq the lowest possible level. ➤ adj, colloq of prices: the lowest possible.

rock cake n a small round bun with a rough surface, containing fruit and spices.

rock crystal n, mineralogy a transparent colourless quartz.

rocker n **1** a curved support on which a chair, cradle, etc rocks. **2** something that rocks on such supports, esp a rocking chair. **3** someone or something that rocks. **4** a device which is operated with a rocking movement. **5** (**Rocker**) Brit in the 1960s: a member of a teenage movement, typically wearing a leather jacket and riding a motorcycle. **6** a devotee of rock music or a rock musician. ♦ **off one's rocker** colloq crazy.

rockery n (**-ies**) a garden or an area in a garden with large stones placed in the earth, and small plants growing between them.

rocket¹ n **1** a cylinder containing inflammable material, which is projected through the air, used for signalling, in a firework display, etc. **2** a projectile or vehicle that obtains its thrust from a backward jet of hot gases. **3** a missile propelled by a rocket system. **4** Brit colloq a severe reprimand. ➤ vb (**rocketed, rocketing**) **1** to propel (a spacecraft, etc) by means of a rocket. **2** intr to move, esp upwards, extremely quickly. **3** intr of prices, etc: to rise very quickly. **4** to attack with rockets. **5** Brit colloq to reprimand severely.

rocket² n a Mediterranean salad plant.

rocketry n the scientific study and use of rockets.

rocking chair n a chair which rocks backwards and forwards on two curved supports.

rocking horse n a toy horse mounted on two curved supports on which a child can sit and rock backwards and forwards.

rock salmon n a dogfish, esp when sold as food.

rock salt n common salt occurring as a mass of solid mineral.

rock-solid adj **1** very firmly fixed. **2** of a relationship, etc: firmly established.

rocky¹ adj (**-ier, -iest**) **1 a** full of rocks; **b** made of rock; **c** like rock. **2** colloq full of problems and obstacles. ○ **rockiness** n.

rocky² adj (**-ier, -iest**) shaky; unsteady. ○ **rockily** adv. ○ **rockiness** n.

rococo /rə'kəʊkəʊ/ n (also **Rococo**) a style of architecture, decoration and furniture-making originating in France in the early 18c, characterized by elaborate ornamentation and asymmetry. ➤ adj relating to, or in, this style.

rod n **1** a long slender bar of wood, metal, etc. **2** a stick or bundle of twigs used to beat people as a punishment. **3** a stick, wand or sceptre carried as a symbol of office or authority. **4** a fishing rod. **5** in surveying: a unit of length equivalent to 5.5yd (5.03m). **6** anat in the retina of the vertebrate eye: a rod-shaped cell involved in seeing in dim light. ○ **rodlike** adj.

rodent n, zool an animal, eg a rat or squirrel,

with strong, continually growing incisors adapted for gnawing.

rodeo n 1 a round-up of cattle in order to count or brand them. 2 a place where cattle are assembled for this. 3 a show or contest of skills such as riding, lassoing and animal-handling.

roe[1] n 1 (also **hard roe**) the mass of mature eggs contained in the ovaries of a female fish. 2 (also **soft roe**) the testis of a male fish containing mature sperm. 3 either of these used as food.

roe[2] or **roe deer** n (**roes** or **roe**) a small European and Asian deer.

roentgen or **röntgen** /'rɜːntjən/ n a former unit for measurement of X-rays or gamma rays.

roentgen rays pl n X-rays.

rogation n, Christianity (usu **rogations**) solemn supplication, esp in ceremonial form.

roger[1] exclam 1 in radio communications, etc: message received and understood. 2 colloq OK: Roger, will do – see you later.

roger[2] vb, coarse slang of a man: to have sexual intercourse with someone.

rogue n 1 a dishonest or unscrupulous person. 2 someone who is playfully mischievous. 3 someone or something, esp a plant, which is not true to its type and is of inferior quality. 4 a horse, person or object that is troublesome and unruly. 5 a vicious wild animal that lives apart from, or has been driven from, its herd. 6 someone or something that has strayed or that is found in an unusual place. ○ **roguery** n (**-ies**).

rogues' gallery n a collection of photographs of known criminals, kept by the police and used to identify suspects.

roguish adj 1 characteristic of a rogue. 2 dishonest; unprincipled. 3 playfully mischievous: a roguish grin. ○ **roguishly** adv.

roister vb, to enjoy oneself noisily and boisterously. ○ **roisterer** n. ○ **roistering** n.

role or **rôle** n 1 an actor's part or character in a play, film, etc. 2 a function, or a part played or taken on by someone or something in life, business, etc: in her role as head of the household • the role of television in education.

role model n someone whose character, life, behaviour, etc is taken as a good example to follow.

role-play or **role-playing** n the assuming and performing of imaginary roles, usu as a method of instruction, therapy, etc.

roll n 1 a cylinder or tube formed by rolling up anything flat. 2 a rolled document. 3 a small individually baked portion of bread: a crusty roll. 4 a folded piece of pastry or cake with a filling: Swiss roll • sausage roll. 5 a rolled mass of something: rolls of fat. 6 an undulation in a surface or of a landscape. 7 a an official list of names, eg of school pupils or people eligible to vote; b the total number registered on such a list. 8 a swaying or rolling movement. 9 a long low prolonged sound: a roll of thunder. 10 (also **drum roll**) a series of quick beats on a drum. 11 a complete rotation around its longitudinal

axis by an aircraft. 12 a an act of rolling: Sparky had a roll in the sand; b a gymnastic exercise similar to, but less strenuous than, a somersault: a backward roll. ➢ vb 1 tr & intr to move or make something move by turning over and over, as if on an axis, and often in a specified direction: Jack rolled the dice. 2 tr & intr to move or make something move on wheels, rollers, etc, or in a vehicle with wheels. 3 intr (also **roll over**) of a person, animal, etc that is lying down: to turn with a rolling movement to face in another direction. 4 tr & intr to move or make something move or flow gently and steadily. 5 intr (usu **roll by, on, past**, etc) of time: to pass or follow steadily and often quickly: The weeks rolled by. 6 intr to seem to move like or in waves: a garden rolling down to the river. 7 intr of a ship: to rock gently from side to side. 8 intr to walk with a swaying movement: Tom rolled in drunk at six o'clock. 9 tr & intr to begin to operate or work: The cameras rolled. 10 tr & intr to move or make (one's eyes) move in a circle, eg in disbelief or amazement. 11 tr & intr to form, or form something, into a tube or cylinder by winding or being wound round and round. 12 (also **roll up**) a to wrap something by rolling: Spike rolled a spliff; b to curl around: The hamster rolled itself up into a ball. 13 (also **roll out**) to spread out or make flat, esp by pressing with something heavy: Mum rolled out the pastry. 14 intr to make a series of long low rumbling sounds. 15 to pronounce (esp an 'r' sound) with a trill. 16 slang to rob someone who is helpless, usu because they are drunk or asleep. 17 a to make (the credits) appear on a screen; b intr to appear on a screen. 18 a to make (a car) do a somersault; b intr of a car: to overturn. ○ **rolled** adj. ♦ **be rolling in sth** colloq to have large amounts of it, esp money. **on a roll** chiefly US, colloq going through a period of continuous good luck or success. **roll on ...** may a specified event, time, etc come soon: Roll on the holidays. ◊ **roll in** to arrive in large quantities. **roll sth out** to introduce (a product, programme, etc) over a period of time. **roll over 1** to overturn. 2 see verb (sense 3) above. 3 of a jackpot prize, eg in the UK National Lottery: to be carried across to the next week because it has not been won. **roll sth over** econ to defer demand for repayment of (a debt, loan, etc) for a further term. **roll up 1** colloq to arrive. 2 to come in large numbers.

roll-call n an act or the process of calling out names from a list to check who is present.

rolled gold n base metal covered with a very thin coating of gold.

roller n 1 a cylindrical object or machine used for flattening, applying paint, etc. 2 a small cylinder on which hair is rolled to make it curl. 3 a long heavy sea wave.

Rollerblades pl n, trademark a brand of in-line skates, roller skates with wheels set in a single line from front to back along the sole. ➢ vb (**rollerblade**) intr to move on Rollerblades. ○ **rollerblading** n.

roller blind *n* a window blind that wraps around a roller when not in use.

rollercoaster *n* a raised railway with sharp curves and steep inclines and descents, ridden on for excitement at funfairs, etc.

roller skate *n* a series of wheels attached to a framework which can be fitted onto a shoe, or a shoe with wheels attached to the sole. ➤ *vb* (**roller-skate**) *intr* to move on roller skates. ○ **roller-skater** *n.* ○ **roller-skating** *n.*

rollicking *n, colloq* a severe scolding.

rolling *adj* **1** of land, countryside, etc: with low, gentle hills. **2** *colloq* extremely wealthy. **3** *colloq* staggering with drunkenness. **4** of a contract: subject to review at regular intervals.

rolling mill *n* **1** a machine for rolling metal into sheets. **2** a factory with such machines.

rolling pin *n* a cylinder, usu made of wood, for flattening out pastry or dough.

rolling stock *n* the engines, wagons, coaches, etc used on a railway.

rolling stone *n* someone who leads an unsettled life.

rollmop *n* a rolled fillet of raw pickled herring.

rollneck *adj* of a garment: with a high neck which is folded over on itself.

roll-on *n* a deodorant, etc contained in a bottle with a rotating ball at the top, by means of which the liquid is applied.

roll-on roll-off *adj* of a passenger ferry: with entrances at both the front and back of the ship, so that vehicles can be driven on through one entrance and off through the other.

roll-over *n* **1** an instance of deferring demand for repayment of a debt, loan, etc for a further term. **2** in the UK National Lottery: a jackpot prize which, having not been won in one week, is carried forward to the draw in the following week and added to that week's jackpot.

roll-top desk *n* a desk with a flexible cover of slats that may be rolled down when the desk is not in use.

roll-up *n, Brit colloq* a hand-rolled cigarette.

roly-poly *adj* round and podgy. ➤ *n* (*-ies*) (*also* **roly-poly pudding**) suet pastry spread with jam and rolled up, then baked or steamed.

ROM / rom / *abbrev, comput* read-only memory, a storage device which holds data permanently and allows it to be read and used but not changed. Compare RAM.

Roman *adj* **1** belonging or relating to modern or ancient Rome, or to the Roman Empire. **2** relating to the Roman Catholic Church. **3** (**roman**) *printing* of type: relating to or indicating the ordinary, upright kind most commonly used for printed material. ➤ *n* **1** an inhabitant of modern or ancient Rome. **2** a Roman Catholic.

roman alphabet *n* the alphabet developed by the ancient Romans for writing Latin, and now used for most writing in W European languages, including English.

Roman candle *n* a firework that discharges a succession of flaming sparks.

Roman Catholic *adj* belonging or relating to the Roman Catholic Church, the Christian Church which recognizes the pope as its head. ➤ *n* a member of this Church. ○ **Roman Catholicism** *n.*

romance *n* **1** a love affair. **2** sentimentalized or idealized love, valued esp for its beauty, purity and the mutual devotion of the lovers. **3** the atmosphere, feelings or behaviour associated with romantic love. **4** a sentimental account, esp in writing or on film, of a love affair. **5** such writing, films, etc as a group or genre. **6** a fictitious story which deals with imaginary, adventurous and mysterious events, characters, etc. **7** a medieval verse narrative dealing with chivalry, highly idealized love and fantastic adventures. **8** (**Romance**) a group of languages, including French, Spanish and Italian, which have developed from Latin. ➤ *adj* (**Romance**) belonging or relating to the languages which have developed from Latin. ➤ *vb* **1** to try to win someone's love. **2** *intr* to speak or write extravagantly or fantastically. **3** *intr* to lie.

Romanesque *n* a style of European architecture from the 9c to the 12c, characterized by the use of round arches and massive walls and vaultings. ➤ *adj* in or relating to this style.

Roman nose *n* a high-bridged nose.

Roman numeral *n* an upper-case letter of the roman alphabet used to represent a cardinal number, eg I=1, V=5, X=10, etc. Compare ARABIC NUMERAL.

romantic *adj* **1** characterized by or inclined towards sentimental and idealized love. **2** dealing with or suggesting adventure, mystery and sentimentalized love: *romantic fiction.* **3** highly impractical or imaginative. **4** (**Romantic**) of literature, art, music, etc: relating to or in the style of romanticism. ➤ *n* **1** someone who has a romantic view of love, etc. **2** (**Romantic**) a Romantic poet, writer, artist, composer, etc. ○ **romantically** *adv.*

romanticism or **Romanticism** *n* a late 18c and early 19c movement in the arts with an emphasis on feelings, often using imagery from nature. ○ **romanticist** *n.*

romanticize or **-ise** *vb* **1** to make romantic. **2** *tr & intr* to describe, think of or interpret in an idealized way. **3** *intr* to hold or indulge in romantic ideas or act in a romantic way. ○ **romanticization** *n.*

Romany *n* (*-ies*) **1** a Gypsy. **2** the language spoken by Gypsies. ➤ *adj* of or relating to the Romanies, their language or culture.

Romeo *n* **1** an ardent young male lover. **2** a womanizer.

romp *vb, intr* **1** to play or run about in a lively boisterous way. **2** (*usu* **romp through sth**) *colloq* to complete (a task, etc) quickly and easily. ➤ *n* **1** an act of romping; boisterous playing or running about. **2** a light-hearted outing. **3** a swift pace. ♦ **romp in** or **home** *colloq* to win a race, competition, etc quickly and easily.

rompers *pl n* (*also* **romper suit**) *formerly* a baby's suit, usu one-piece, with short-legged trousers and either a short-sleeved top or a bib.

rondeau /ˈrɒndoʊ/ or **rondel** *n* (*rondeaux* /-doʊ, -doʊz/) a poem of 13 or sometimes 10 lines with only two rhymes, and with the first line used as a refrain.

rondo *n, mus* a piece of music with a recurring principal theme.

röntgen see ROENTGEN

roo *n, Aust colloq* a kangaroo.

rood *n* **1** a cross or crucifix, esp a large one set on a beam or screen at the entrance to a church chancel. **2** a former unit of area, equal to a quarter of an acre.

rood screen *n* in a church: an ornamental wooden or stone screen separating the choir from the nave.

roof *n* (**roofs** or *non-standard* **rooves**) **1 a** the top outside covering of a building; **b** the structure at the top of a building that supports this. **2** a similar top or covering for a vehicle, etc. **3** the interior overhead surface of a room, vault, cave, etc. **4** a dwelling. **5** the top inner surface of something, eg an oven or the mouth. ➤ *vb* **1** to cover or provide with a roof. **2** to serve as a roof or shelter for something. ○ **roofed** *adj*. ○ **roofless** *adj*. ◆ **go through the roof** *colloq* **1** to become very angry. **2** of a price, etc: to become very expensive. **raise** or **hit the roof** *colloq* **1** to make a great deal of noise or fuss. **2** to become very angry.

roofing *n* materials for building a roof.

roof rack *n* a frame attached to the roof of a car or other vehicle for carrying luggage, etc.

rooftop *n* the outside of a roof of a building.

roof tree *n* a beam running along a roof's ridge.

rook[1] *n* a large, noisy crow-like bird. ➤ *vb, colloq* **1** to cheat or defraud, esp at cards. **2** to charge (a customer) an excessively high price.

rook[2] *n, chess* a CASTLE.

rookery *n* (*-ies*) **1** a colony of rooks. **2** a colony of seals or seabirds.

rookie or **rooky** *n* (*-ies*) *colloq* **1** a new or raw recruit. **2** *sport, chiefly N Am* a new member of a team.

room *n* **1** an area within a building enclosed by a ceiling, floor and walls. **2** sufficient or necessary space: *no room for all her books.* **3** all the people present in a room: *The room suddenly became silent.* **4** opportunity, scope or possibility: *room for improvement.* **5** (**rooms**) rented lodgings: *He returned to his rooms at Oxford.* ➤ *vb, tr & intr, chiefly N Am* (*also* **room with sb**) to lodge (with someone); to share a room or rooms. ○ **-roomed** *adj*.

roommate *n* a person sharing a room or rooms with another or others.

room service *n* in a hotel: a facility for guests to order and be served food, drinks, etc in their rooms.

roomy *adj* (*-ier, -iest*) with plenty of room. ○ **roominess** *n*.

roost *n* a branch, perch, etc on which a bird perches, esp to rest at night. ➤ *vb, intr* of a bird: to settle on a roost. ◆ **come home to roost** of a scheme, etc: to have an unpleasant result for the originator.

rooster *n, chiefly N Am* a farmyard cock.

root[1] *n* **1** a structure in a plant which anchors the plant in the soil and absorbs water and nutrients. **2** a part by which something, eg a tooth or hair, is attached to or embedded in something larger. **3** a basic cause, source or origin of something: *the root of the problem.* **4** (**roots**) ancestry or family origins, etc: *to go back to one's roots.* **5** the basic element in a word to which affixes can be added, eg *love* is the root of *lovable, lovely, lover* and *unloved.* **6** *maths* a factor of a quantity that, when multiplied by itself a specified number of times, produces that quantity, eg 2 is the square root of 4 and the cube root of 8. ➤ *vb* **1** *intr* to grow a root. **2** *intr* to become firmly established. **3** (*usu* **root sth up** or **out**) to dig it up by the roots. **4** to fix with or as if with a root. **5** to provide with a root. ◆ **root and branch** thoroughly; completely. **take** or **strike root** **1** to grow roots. **2** to become firmly established. ◇ **root sth out** to find, remove or destroy it completely.

root[2] *vb, intr* **1** of pigs: to dig in the earth with the snout in search of food, truffles, etc. **2** *intr* (*usu* **root around** or **about**) *colloq* to look for something by rummaging. **3** (*usu* **root sb** or **sth out** or **up**) to find and remove them or it.

root[3] *vb, intr* (*always* **root for**) *colloq* to cheer on, encourage or back someone or something.

root canal *n* a passage through which the nerves and blood vessels of a tooth enter the pulp cavity.

root crop *n* any plant that is grown mainly for its edible root, tuber or corm, eg carrot, potato, etc.

rooted *adj* **1** fixed by or as if by roots. **2** firmly established.

rootstock *n, bot* **1** an underground plant stem that bears buds. **2** a stock onto which another plant has been grafted.

rope *n* **1 a** a strong thick cord made by twisting fibres together; **b** a length of this. **2** a number of objects, esp pearls or onions, strung together. **3** (**the rope**) **a** a hangman's noose; **b** execution by this means. **4** (**ropes**) the cords that mark off a boxing or wrestling ring, or the boundary of a cricket ground. ➤ *vb* **1** to tie, fasten or bind with rope or as if with rope. **2** (*usu* **rope in** or **off**) to enclose, separate or divide with a rope. **3** *mountaineering* to tie (climbers) together with a rope for safety. **4** *chiefly N Am* to catch (an animal) with a rope. ◆ **know the ropes** to be thoroughly conversant with a particular thing. ◇ **rope sb in** or **into sth** to persuade them to take part in some activity.

ropy or **ropey** *adj* (*-ier, -iest*) **1** rope-like. **2** *colloq* poor in quality. **3** *colloq* slightly unwell.

rorqual *n* a baleen whale with a small dorsal fin near the tail.

Rorschach test /'rɔːʃak/ *n, psychol* a test where a subject is asked to interpret a standard set of inkblots in order to determine personality type, mental state, etc.

rosaceous *adj* belonging to the rose family of plants or resembling a rose.

rosary *n* (*-ies*) *RC Church* **1** a series of prayers with a set form and order in which five or fifteen decades of Aves are recited. **2** a string of 55 or 165 beads used for counting such prayers.

rose¹ *n* **1** a thorny shrub that produces large, often fragrant, flowers. **2** a flower of this plant. **3** a rose as the national emblem of England. **4** a flowering plant that superficially resembles a rose, eg the Christmas rose. **5** a darkish pink colour. **6** (**roses**) a light-pink, glowing complexion: *to put the roses back in one's cheeks.* **7** a perforated nozzle, attached to the end of a hose, shower-head, etc so that water comes out in a spray. **8** a circular fitting in a ceiling through which an electric light flex hangs. **9** a circular moulding from which a door handle projects. ➤ *adj* relating to or like a rose or roses, esp in colour, scent or form.

rose² *past tense of* RISE

rosé /'rɔʊzeɪ/ *n* a pale pink wine.

roseate /'rɔʊzɪət/ *adj* **1** like a rose, esp in colour. **2** unrealistically hopeful or cheerful.

rosebud *n* **1** the bud of a rose. **2** *literary* a pretty young woman.

rose-coloured or **rose-tinted** *adj* **1** pink. **2** cheerful; overoptimistic.

rosehip *n* a red berry-like fruit of a rose.

rosemary *n* a fragrant evergreen shrub with stiff needle-like leaves, used in cookery and perfumery.

rosette *n* **1** a decoration made with coloured ribbon, awarded as a prize, etc. **2** *archit* a rose-shaped ornament on a wall or other surface. **3** a cluster of leaves radiating from a central point. **4** any rose-shaped structure, arrangement or figure.

rosewater *n* perfume distilled from roses.

rose window *n* a circular window with ornamental tracery radiating from the centre.

rosewood *n* **1** the valuable dark red wood of any of various tropical trees, used in making high quality furniture. **2** a tree from which this wood is obtained.

rosin *n* a clear hard resin produced by distilling turpentine. ➤ *vb* to rub rosin on (the bow of a violin, etc).

roster *n* a list of people's names that shows the order in which they are to do various duties, go on leave, etc. ➤ *vb* to put on a roster.

rostrum *n* (**rostrums** or **rostra**) a platform for a public speaker, orchestra conductor, etc.

rosy *adj* (*-ier, -iest*) **1** pink. **2** of the complexion: with a healthy pink colour: *rosy cheeks.* **3 a** hopeful or optimistic, often overly so: *a rosy view of things;* **b** promising: *The situation looks quite rosy.*

rot *vb* (**rotted, rotting**) **1** *tr & intr* to decay or cause to decay. **2** *intr* to become corrupt. **3** *intr*

to become physically weak, esp through being confined, etc: *left to rot in jail.* ➤ *n* **1 a** decay; **b** something which has decayed or decomposed. **2** *colloq* nonsense. ➤ *exclam* expressing contemptuous disagreement.

rota *n, Brit* a list of duties to be done with the names and order of the people who are to take turns doing them.

rotary *adj* turning on an axis like a wheel. ➤ *n* (*-ies*) **1** a rotary machine. **2** *N Am* a traffic roundabout.

rotate *vb* **1** *tr & intr* to turn or cause to turn about an axis like a wheel. **2** to arrange in an ordered sequence. **3** *intr* to change position, take turns in doing something, etc according to an ordered sequence. **4** to grow (different crops) in an ordered sequence on the same ground. ○ **rotation** *n.*

Rotavator or **Rotovator** *n, trademark* a machine with a rotating blade for breaking up the soil.

rote *n* (*often* **by rote**) habitual repetition: *to learn by rote.*

rotgut *n, slang* cheap alcoholic drink.

rotisserie *n* **1** a cooking apparatus with a spit on which meat, poultry, etc is cooked by direct heat. **2** a shop or restaurant that sells or serves meat cooked in this way.

rotor *n* **1** a rotating part of a machine, esp in an internal-combustion engine. **2** a system of blades providing the force to lift and propel a helicopter.

rotten *adj* **1** gone bad, decayed. **2** falling or fallen to pieces from age, decay, etc. **3** morally corrupt. **4** *colloq* miserably unwell: *I felt rotten.* **5** *colloq* unsatisfactory: *a rotten plan.* **6** *colloq* unpleasant: *rotten weather.* ➤ *adv, colloq* very much: *Kat fancied him rotten.*

rotter *n, dated, Brit slang* a thoroughly worthless or despicable person.

Rottweiler /'rɒtwaɪlə(r)/ *n* a large, powerfully built black-and-tan dog.

rotund *adj* **1** *chiefly bot, zool* round or rounded in form. **2** of a person, part of the body, etc: plump. **3** of speech, language, etc: impressive or grandiloquent. ○ **rotundity** *n.* ○ **rotundly** *adv.*

rotunda *n* a round, usu domed, building or hall.

rouble or **ruble** *n* the standard unit of currency in Russia and Belarus.

roué /'ruːeɪ/ *n, old use* a debauched, disreputable man.

rouge /ruːʒ/ *n* a pink or red cosmetic for colouring the cheeks. ➤ *vb* to apply rouge to.

rough *adj* **1** of a surface or texture: not smooth, even or regular. **2** of ground: covered with stones, tall grass, bushes and/or scrub. **3** of an animal: with shaggy or coarse hair. **4** of a sound: harsh or grating. **5** of a person's character, behaviour, etc: noisy, coarse or violent. **6** of the sea, etc: stormy. **7** requiring hard work or considerable physical effort, or involving great difficulty, tension, etc: *a rough day at work.* **8**

hard to bear: *a rough deal*. **9** of a guess, calculation, etc: approximate. **10** not polished or refined: *a rough draft*. **11** *colloq* slightly unwell. **12** not well-kept: *a rough area*. ➤ *n* **1** (**the rough**) rough ground, esp at the side of a golf fairway. **2** the unpleasant side of something: *We must take the rough with the smooth*. **3** a rough state. **4** a thug or hooligan. ➤ *vb* to make rough. ○ **roughness** *n*. ♦ **rough it** *colloq* to live in a very basic or primitive way, without the comforts one is accustomed to. **sleep rough** to sleep in the open without proper shelter. ◊ **rough sb up** *colloq* to beat them up.

roughage *n* FIBRE (sense 3).

rough-and-ready *adj* **1** quickly prepared, but usu good enough for the purpose. **2** of a person: friendly and pleasant but not refined.

rough-and-tumble *n* disorderly but usu friendly fighting. ➤ *adj* haphazard; disorderly.

roughcast *n* a mixture of plaster and small stones used to cover the outside walls of buildings. ➤ *vb* (**roughcast**) to cover (a wall) with roughcast.

rough diamond *n* **1** an uncut and unpolished diamond. **2** *colloq* a good-natured person with unrefined manners.

roughen *vb, tr & intr* to make or become rough.

rough-hewn *adj* crude, unrefined.

roughhouse *n, colloq* a disturbance or brawl.

roughly *adv* **1** in a rough way. **2** approximately.

roughneck *n, colloq* **1** a worker on an oil rig, esp an unskilled labourer. **2** a rough and rowdy person.

roughshod *adj* of a horse: with shoes that have projecting nails to prevent it slipping. ♦ **ride roughshod over** to behave arrogantly and without regard to other people's feelings, etc.

roulade /ruˈlɑːd/ *n* something cooked in the shape of a roll.

roulette *n* a gambling game in which a ball is dropped into a revolving wheel, the players betting on which of its small, numbered compartments the ball will come to rest in.

round *adj* **1** shaped like, or approximately like, a circle or a ball. **2** not angular; with a curved outline. **3** of a body or part of a body: curved and plump: *a round face*. **4** moving in or forming a circle. **5** of numbers: complete and exact: *a round dozen*. **6** of a number: without a fraction. **7** of a number: approximate; without taking minor amounts into account. **8** of a character in a story: fully and realistically developed. ➤ *adv* **1** in a circular direction or with a circular or revolving movement. **2** in or to the opposite direction, position or opinion: *to win someone round*. **3** in, by or along an indirect route. **4** on all sides so as to surround: *Gather round*. **5** from one person to another successively: *Pass it round*. **6** in rotation, so as to return to the starting point: *Wait until spring comes round*. **7** from place to place: *We drove round for hours*. **8** in circumference: *It meas-*

ures *six feet round*. **9** to a particular place, esp someone's home: *Come round for supper*. ➤ *prep* **1** on all sides of so as to surround or enclose. **2** so as to move or revolve around a centre or axis and return to the starting point: *Run round the field*. **3** *colloq* having as a central point or basis: *a story built round her experiences*. **4** from place to place in: *We went round the town shopping*. **5** in all or various directions from somewhere; close to it. **6** so as to pass, or having passed, in a curved course: *Drive round the corner*. ➤ *n* **1** something round, and often flat, in shape. **2 a** movement in a circle; **b** a complete revolution round a circuit or path. **3** a single slice of bread. **4** a sandwich, or two or more sandwiches, made from two slices of bread. **5** a cut of beef across the thigh bone of an animal. **6** *golf* the playing of all 18 holes on a course in a single session. **7** one of a recurring series of events, actions, etc: *a round of talks*. **8** a series of regular activities: *the daily round*. **9** a regular route followed, esp for the delivery of goods: *a milk round*. **10** (*usu* **rounds**) a sequence of visits made by a doctor to patients, either in a hospital or in their homes. **11** a stage in a competition: *They're through to the second round*. **12** a single turn by every member of a group of people playing a game, eg a card game. **13** a single period of play, competition, etc in a group of such periods, eg in boxing, wrestling, etc. **14** a burst of applause or cheering. **15** a single bullet or charge of ammunition. **16** a number of drinks bought at the same time for all the members of a group. **17** *mus* an unaccompanied song in which different people all sing the same part continuously but start, and therefore end, at different times. ➤ *vb* **1** *tr & intr* to make or become round. **2** to go round something: *The car rounded the corner*. ○ **roundness** *n*. ♦ **go** or **make the rounds 1** of news, information, a cold, etc: to be passed round from person to person. **2** to patrol. **in the round 1** with all details shown or considered. **2** *theat* with the audience seated on at least three, and often four, sides of the stage. **round about 1** on all sides. **2** the other way about. **3** approximately: *round about four o'clock*. ◊ **round sth down** to lower (a number) to the nearest convenient figure: *to round 15.47 down to 15*. **round sth off 1** to make (corners, angles, etc) smooth. **2** to complete it: *to round off the meal with a brandy*. **round on sb 1** to turn on or attack them. **2** to reply or attack them verbally. **round sth up 1** to raise (a number) to the nearest convenient figure: *to round 15.89 up to 16*. **2** to collect (people, livestock, facts, etc) together.

roundabout *n, Brit* **1** a junction of several roads where traffic must travel in the same direction, usu round a central traffic island. **2** a MERRY-GO-ROUND. ➤ *adj* not direct: *a roundabout way of explaining something*.

roundel *n* **1** a small circular window or design. **2** a coloured, round identification disc on a military aircraft.

roundelay *n* a simple song with a refrain.

rounders *n* a team game in which runs are scored by a batter running a complete circuit of bases.

roundly *adv* **1** thoroughly: *He was roundly defeated.* **2** bluntly: *She told him roundly that it wouldn't do.*

round robin *n* **1** a petition in which the names are written in a circle to conceal the ringleader. **2** *sport* a tournament in which every competitor plays each of the others in turn.

round-shouldered *adj* having shoulders that bend forward, giving a hunched appearance to the back.

round table *n* **1** (**Round Table**) an international group formed by business and professional people to do charitable work. **2** a meeting at which the participants meet on equal terms. ➤ *adj* (**round-table**) characterized by equality: *round-table talks.*

round-the-clock *adj* lasting through the day and night: *round-the-clock surveillance.*

round trip *n* a trip to a place and back again.

round-up *n* **1** a systematic gathering together of people or animals. **2** a summary of facts: *a round-up of the news.*

rouse *vb* **1** to arouse or awaken (oneself or someone else) from sleep or lethargy. **2** *intr* to awaken or become more fully conscious or alert. **3** to excite or provoke: *The injustice of it roused her anger.* **4** *intr* to become excited, provoked, etc.

rousing *adj* stirring; exciting.

roustabout *n* an unskilled labourer, eg on an oil rig or a farm.

rout¹ *vb* to defeat (an army, a sporting team, etc) completely. ➤ *n* a complete and overwhelming defeat.

rout² *vb* **1** *tr & intr* to dig something up, esp with the snout. **2** (**rout sb** or **sth out** or **up**) to find and drive them out or fetch them by searching.

route /ruːt; *Brit mil & US general* raʊt/ *n* **1** a way travelled on a regular journey. **2** a particular group of roads followed to get to a place. **3** *N Am* a regular series of calls, eg for the collection or sale of goods. ➤ *vb* (**routeing** or **routing**) **1** to arrange a route for (a journey, etc). **2** to send by a particular route.

route march *n* a long and tiring march, esp one for soldiers in training.

routine *n* **1** a regular or unvarying series of actions or way of doing things: *a daily routine.* **2** regular or unvarying procedure. **3** a set series of movements or steps in a dance, etc. **4** a comedian's, singer's, etc act. **5** *comput* a program or part of one which performs a specific function. ➤ *adj* **1** unvarying. **2** standard; ordinary: *a routine examination.* **3** done as part of a routine. ○ **routinely** *adv.*

roux *n* (*pl* **roux**) *cookery* a cooked mixture of flour and fat, usu butter, used to thicken sauces.

rove *vb* **1** *intr* to roam about aimlessly. **2** to wander over or through (a particular area, etc). **3** *intr* of the eyes: to keep looking in different directions.

rover *n* someone who roves; a wanderer.

row¹ /rəʊ/ *n* **1** a number of people or things arranged in a line. **2** in a cinema, theatre, etc: a line of seats. **3** a street with a continuous line of houses on one or both sides. **4** *maths* a horizontal arrangement of numbers, terms, etc. **5** in knitting: a complete line of stitches. ◆ **in a row 1** forming a row. **2** *colloq* in succession: *three telephone calls in a row.*

row² /rəʊ/ *vb* **1** to move (a boat) through the water using oars. **2** to carry (people, goods, etc) in a rowing boat. **3** *intr* to race in rowing boats for sport. **4** *intr* to compete in a rowing race. ➤ *n* **1** the action or an act of rowing a boat. **2 a** a period of rowing; **b** a distance of rowing. **3** a trip in a rowing boat. ○ **rower** *n.* ○ **rowing** *n.*

row³ /raʊ/ *n* **1** a noisy quarrel. **2** a loud unpleasant noise. **3** a severe reprimand. ➤ *vb, intr* to quarrel noisily.

rowan *n* **1** (*also* **rowan-tree**) a tree of the rose family, with white flowers. **2** (*also* **rowan-berry**) the small red berry-like fruit of this tree.

rowboat *n, N Am* a ROWING BOAT.

rowdy *adj* (**-ier, -iest**) loud and disorderly: *a rowdy party.* ➤ *n* (**-ies**) *colloq* a loud, disorderly person. ○ **rowdily** *adv.* ○ **rowdiness** *n.*

rowel *n* a small spiked wheel attached to a spur.

rowing boat *n, Brit* a small boat moved by oars.

rowlock /ˈrɒlək/ *n* a device that holds an oar in place.

royal *adj* **1** relating to or suitable for a king or queen. **2** (*often* **Royal**) under the patronage or in the service of a monarch: *Royal Geographical Society.* **3** regal; magnificent. **4** larger or of better quality, etc than usual. ➤ *n* (*often* **Royal**) *colloq* a member of a royal family. ○ **royally** *adv.*

royal blue *n* a bright deep blue.

royalist or **Royalist** *n* **1** a supporter of monarchy or of a specified monarchy. **2** *hist* during the English Civil War: a supporter of Charles I. ➤ *adj* relating to royalists. ○ **royalism** *n.*

royal jelly *n* a rich protein substance secreted by worker bees and fed to all very young larvae and, throughout their development, to certain female larvae destined to become queen bees.

royalty *n* (**-ies**) **1** the character, state, office or power of a king or queen. **2** members of a royal family or families, either individually or collectively. **3** royal authority. **4** a percentage of the profits from each copy of a book, piece of music, invention, etc that is sold, publicly performed or used, which is paid to the author, composer, inventor, etc. **5** a payment made by companies who mine minerals, oil or gas to the person who owns the land the company is mining or the mineral rights to it.

royal warrant *n* an official authorization to supply goods to a royal household.

RP *abbrev* Received Pronunciation.

rpm *abbrev* revolutions per minute.

RSVP *abbrev* often written on invitations: *répondez s'il vous plaît* (French), please reply.

Rt Hon *abbrev* Right Honourable.

Rt Rev *abbrev* Right Reverend.

Ru *symbol, chem* ruthenium.

rub *vb* (**rubbed, rubbing**) **1** to apply pressure and friction to something by moving one's hand or an object backwards and forwards. **2** *intr* (*usu* **rub against, on** or **along sth**) to move backwards and forwards against, on or along something with pressure and friction. **3** (*usu* **rub sth in**) **a** to apply (cream, polish, etc) to something; **b** *cookery* to mix (fat) into flour using the fingertips. **4** to clean, dry, smooth, etc by applying pressure and friction. **5** *tr & intr* to remove or be removed by pressure and friction. **6** *tr & intr* to be sore or cause to be sore through pressure and friction. **7** *tr & intr* to fray by pressure and friction. ➤ *n* **1** the process or an act of rubbing. **2** an obstacle or difficulty: *It will cost a lot and there's the rub.* ◆ **rub sb's nose in it** to persist in reminding someone of a mistake they have made. **rub shoulders** to come into social contact. **rub sb up the wrong way** to annoy or irritate them, esp by dealing with them tactlessly. ◊ **rub sth down 1** to rub (one's body, a horse, etc) briskly from head to foot, eg to dry it. **2** to prepare (a surface) to receive new paint or varnish by rubbing the old paint or varnish off. **rub sth in** *colloq* to insist on talking about or emphasizing (an embarrassing fact or circumstance). **rub off on sb** to have an effect on or be passed to someone by close association: *Some of his bad habits have rubbed off on you.* **rub sth out** to remove it by rubbing, esp with an eraser.

rubato /rʊ'bɑːtoʊ/ *n* (**rubatos** or **rubati** /-tiː/) *mus* a modified or distorted tempo.

rubber¹ *n* **1** a strong, elastic substance obtained from the latex of certain plants, esp the rubber tree, or manufactured synthetically. **2** *Brit* a small piece of rubber or plastic for rubbing out pencil or ink marks. **3** *slang* a condom. **4** (**rubbers**) *US* galoshes. ○ **rubbery** *adj*.

rubber² *n* **1** *bridge, whist, etc* a match to play for the best of three or sometimes five games. **2** a series of games in any of various sports, such as cricket, tennis, etc.

rubber band *n* an ELASTIC BAND.

rubberneck *n, orig US, slang* someone who stares or gapes inquisitively or stupidly. ➤ *vb* **1** *intr* to gape inquisitively or stupidly. **2** to stare at (the aftermath of an accident, etc).

rubber stamp *n* **1** a device used to stamp a name, date, etc on books, papers, etc. **2** an act or instance or the process of making an automatic, unthinking, etc agreement or authorization; **b** a person or group doing this. ➤ *vb* (**rubber-stamp**) *colloq* to approve or authorize automatically.

rubber tree *n* a tree that produces a milky white liquid that is used to make rubber.

rubbing *n* **1** the application of friction. **2** an impression or copy made by placing paper over a raised surface and rubbing the paper with crayon, wax, etc: *a brass rubbing*.

rubbish *n* **1** waste material; refuse. **2** worthless or useless material or objects. **3** *colloq* worthless or absurd talk, writing, etc. ➤ *vb, colloq* to criticize or dismiss as worthless. ○ **rubbishy** *adj*.

rubble *n* pieces of broken stones, bricks, plaster, etc.

rub-down *n* an act or the process of rubbing down.

rubella *n, med* a viral disease characterized by a pink rash and sore throat. Also called **German measles**.

Rubicon or **rubicon** *n* a boundary which, once crossed, signifies an irrevocable course of action.

rubicund /'ruːbɪkənd/ *adj* of the face or complexion: red or rosy.

rubidium *n, chem* a silvery-white, highly reactive metallic element, used in photoelectric cells.

ruble see ROUBLE

rubric /'ruːbrɪk/ *n* **1** a heading, esp one in a book or manuscript. **2** an authoritative rule or set of rules.

ruby *n* (*-ies*) **1** a valuable red gemstone. **2** a rich deep-red colour.

ruby wedding *n* a fortieth wedding anniversary.

ruche /ruːʃ/ *n* a pleated or gathered frill used as a trimming. ➤ *vb* to trim (clothing, etc) with a ruche or ruches. ○ **ruched** *adj*. ○ **ruching** *n*.

ruck¹ *n* **1** a heap or mass of indistinguishable people or things. **2** *rugby* a loose scrum that forms around a ball on the ground. ➤ *vb, intr* to form a ruck or play as a member of the ruck.

ruck² *n* a wrinkle or crease. ➤ *vb, tr & intr* to wrinkle or crease or become wrinkled or creased.

rucksack *n* a bag carried on the back with straps over the shoulders, used esp by climbers and walkers.

ruckus *n, orig chiefly N Am* a commotion.

ruction *n, colloq* **1** a noisy disturbance. **2** (**ructions**) a noisy and usu unpleasant argument or reaction.

rudder *n* **1** a movable flat device fixed vertically to a ship's stern for steering. **2** a movable aerofoil attached to the fin of an aircraft which helps control its movement along a horizontal plane. **3** anything that steers or guides. ○ **rudderless** *adj*.

ruddy *adj* (*-ier, -iest*) **1** of the face, complexion, etc: with a healthy rosy or pink colour. **2** red; reddish. **3** *chiefly Brit, colloq* bloody: *ruddy fool*. ○ **ruddiness** *n*.

rude *adj* **1** impolite or discourteous. **2** roughly made: *a rude shelter*. **3** ignorant, uneducated or primitive. **4** sudden and unpleasant: *a rude awakening*. **5** vigorous; robust: *rude health*. **6** vulgar: *a rude joke*. ○ **rudely** *adv*. ○ **rudeness** *n*.

rudiment n 1 (usu **rudiments**) a fundamental fact, rule or skill of a subject: the rudiments of cooking. 2 (usu **rudiments**) the early and incomplete stage of something. 3 biol an organ or part which does not develop fully. ○ **rudimentary** adj.

rue¹ vb (**ruing** or **rueing**) to wish something had not been said, had not happened, etc: She rued the day she ever met him.

rue² n a strongly scented evergreen plant with bitter leaves.

rueful adj feeling or showing regret. ○ **ruefully** adv.

ruff¹ n 1 a circular pleated or frilled collar, worn in the late 16c and early 17c, or more recently by the members of some choirs. 2 a a fringe of feathers growing on a bird's neck; b a similar fringe of hair on an animal's neck. 3 a type of domestic pigeon with a ruff.

ruff² cards, vb, tr & intr to trump. ➢ n an act of ruffing.

ruffian n a coarse, violent, brutal or lawless person.

ruffle vb 1 to wrinkle or make uneven. 2 tr & intr to make or become irritated, annoyed or discomposed. 3 of a bird: to make (its feathers) erect, usu in anger or display. 4 to gather (lace, linen, etc) into a ruff or ruffle. 5 to flick or turn (pages of a book, etc) hastily. ➢ n a frill of lace, etc worn either round the neck or wrists.

rufous adj of a bird or animal: reddish or brownish-red in colour.

rug n 1 a small carpet. 2 a thick blanket, esp one used for travelling, or as a protective covering for horses. 3 orig N Am, slang a toupee. ◆ **pull the rug (out) from under sb** to leave them without defence, support, etc, esp as a result of some sudden discovery, action or argument.

rugby or **rugby football** n a team game played with an oval ball which players may pick up and run with and may pass from hand to hand.

rugged adj 1 of landscape, hills, ground, etc: rough, steep and rocky. 2 of facial features: irregular and furrowed. 3 of character: stern, austere and unbending. 4 of manners, etc: unsophisticated. 5 involving physical hardships: a rugged life. 6 sturdy; robust. ○ **ruggedly** adv. ○ **ruggedness** n.

rugger n, colloq RUGBY.

ruin n 1 a broken, destroyed, decayed or collapsed state. 2 (often **ruins**) the remains of something which has been broken or destroyed or has decayed or collapsed, esp a building. 3 a complete loss of wealth, social position, power, etc; b a person, company, etc that has suffered this; c something or someone that causes this. ➢ vb 1 to reduce or bring someone or something to ruin. 2 to spoil.

ruination n 1 an act or the process of ruining. 2 the state of having been ruined.

ruinous adj 1 likely to bring about ruin: ruinous prices. 2 ruined; destroyed. ○ **ruinously** adv.

rule n 1 a governing or controlling principle, regulation, etc. 2 a government or control; b the period during which government or control is exercised. 3 a general principle, standard, guideline or custom: I make a rule always to be punctual. 4 Christianity the laws and customs which form the basis of a monastic or religious order: the Benedictine rule. 5 a RULER (sense 2). 6 printing a thin straight line or dash. 7 law an order made by a court and judge which applies to a particular case only. ➢ vb 1 tr & intr to govern; to exercise authority over. 2 to keep control of or restrain. 3 to make an authoritative and usu official or judicial decision. 4 intr to be common or prevalent: Chaos ruled. 5 to draw a straight line or a series of parallel lines, eg on paper. ◆ **as a rule** usually. ◇ **rule sth out** to leave it out; to preclude it.

rule of thumb n a method of doing something, based on practical experience rather than theory or careful calculation.

ruler n 1 someone, eg a sovereign, who rules or governs. 2 a strip of wood, metal or plastic with straight edges that is marked off in units (usu inches or centimetres) and used for drawing straight lines and measuring.

ruling n an official or authoritative decision. ➢ adj 1 governing; controlling. 2 most important or strongest.

rum¹ n a spirit distilled from fermented sugar-cane juice or from molasses.

rum² adj (**rummer, rummest**) chiefly Brit, colloq strange; odd.

rumba or **rhumba** n 1 a lively Afro-Cuban dance. 2 a a popular ballroom dance derived from this; b music for this dance, with a stressed second beat. ➢ vb, intr to dance the rumba.

rum baba n a small sponge cake soaked in a rum-flavoured syrup.

rumble vb 1 intr to make a deep low grumbling sound: Her stomach rumbled. 2 intr to move with a rumbling noise. 3 Brit slang to find out the truth about or see through someone or something. ➢ n 1 a deep low grumbling sound: a rumble of thunder. 2 N Am slang a street fight.

rumbustious adj, Brit colloq noisy and cheerful.

ruminant n a mammal, eg a cow, sheep or goat, that chews the cud. ➢ adj 1 relating or belonging to this group of mammals. 2 meditative or contemplative.

ruminate vb 1 intr to chew the cud. 2 tr & intr to think deeply about something. ○ **rumination** n. ○ **ruminative** /ˈruːmɪnətɪv/ adj. ○ **ruminatively** adv.

rummage vb 1 tr & intr (usu **rummage through sth**) to search messily through (a collection of things, a cupboard, etc). 2 intr (usu **rummage about** or **around**) to search: I rummaged around for a pen. ➢ n a search.

rummage sale n, N Am a jumble sale.

rummy n a card game in which each player

tries to collect sets or sequences of three or more cards.

rumour or (*US*) **rumor** *n* **1** a piece of information passed from person to person and which may or may not be true. **2** general talk or gossip. ➤ *vb* to report or spread (information, etc) by rumour: *She is rumoured to be having an affair.* • *It is rumoured she is having an affair.*

rump *n* **1** the rear part of an animal's or bird's body. **2** a person's buttocks. **3** (*also* **rump steak**) a cut of beef from the rump. **4** a small or inferior remnant.

rumple *vb, tr & intr* to become or make (hair, clothes, etc) untidy, creased or wrinkled. ➤ *n* a wrinkle or crease.

rumpus *n, colloq* a noisy disturbance, fuss, brawl or uproar.

run *vb* (**ran, run, running**) **1** *intr* to move so quickly that both or all feet are off the ground together for an instant during part of each step. **2** to cover (a specified distance, etc) by running: *to run the marathon.* **3** to perform (an action) as if by running: *to run an errand.* **4** *intr* of a vehicle: to move over a surface on, or as if on, wheels. **5** *intr* (*often* **run off**) to flee. **6** *tr & intr* to move or make something move in a specified way or direction or with a specified result: *Run the car up the ramp* • *Let the dog run free* • *They ran him out of town.* **7** *tr & intr* (*usu* **run** or **run sth along, over, through,** *etc* **sth**) to move or cause it to move or pass quickly, lightly or freely in the specified direction: *Run your eyes over the report* • *Excitement ran through the audience.* **8** *intr, chiefly N Am* to stand as a candidate in an election: *He is running for governor.* **9** *intr* of water, etc: to flow: *rivers running to the sea.* **10** to make or allow (liquid) to flow: *to run cold water into the bath.* **11** *intr* of the nose or eyes: to discharge liquid or mucus. **12** *intr* of wax, etc: to melt and flow. **13** *tr & intr* to give out or cause (a liquid, container, etc) to give out liquid: *Run the tap* • *Leave the tap running.* **14** to fill with water: *to run a hot bath.* **15** *metallurgy* **a** *tr & intr* to melt or fuse; **b** to form (molten metal) into bars, etc. **16** *tr & intr* to come to a specified state or condition by, or as if by, flowing or running: *to run dry* • *to run short of time* • *Her blood ran cold.* **17** to be full of or flow with. **18** *tr & intr* to operate or function: *The presses ran all night.* **19** *comput* to execute (a program). **20** *intr* (**run on sth**) of a vehicle: to use a (specified fuel). **21** to organize, manage or be in control of: *Diane runs her own business.* **22** *tr & intr* to continue or cause to continue or extend in a specified direction, for a specified time or distance, or over a specified range: *a road running south* • *colours running from pink to deep red* • *The play ran for ten years.* **23** *intr, law* to continue to have legal force: *a lease with a year still to run.* **24** *colloq* to drive someone or something in a vehicle: *I'll run you to the station.* **25** *intr* to spread or diffuse: *The colour in his shirt ran.* **26** *intr* to have as wording: *The report runs as follows.* **27** to be affected by or subjected to: *to run a high temperature* • *to run risks.* **28** *intr* to

be inherent or recur frequently: *Blue eyes run in the family.* **29** to own, drive and maintain (a vehicle): *Pete runs a sports car.* **30** to publish: *They threatened to run the story in the magazine.* **31** to show or broadcast (a programme, film, etc): *to run a repeat of the series.* **32** *intr* **a** of stitches: to come undone; **b** of a garment, eg tights: to have some of its stitches come undone and form a ladder. **33** to hunt or track down (an animal): *They ran the fox to ground.* **34** to get past or through an obstacle, etc: *to run a blockade.* **35** to smuggle or deal illegally in something: *to run guns.* **36** *cricket* to score a run by, or as if by, running. ➤ *n* **1** an act or instance or the process of running. **2** the distance covered or time taken up by an act of running. **3** a rapid pace quicker than a walk: *to break into a run.* **4** a manner of running. **5** a mark, streak, etc made by the flowing of some liquid, eg paint. **6** a trip in a vehicle, esp for pleasure: *a run to the seaside.* **7** a continuous and unbroken period or series of something: *a run of bad luck* • *The play had a run of six weeks.* **8** freedom to move about or come and go as one pleases: *We have the run of the house.* **9** a high or urgent demand (for a currency, commodity, etc): *a run on the pound.* **10** a route which is regularly travelled, eg by public transport, or as a delivery round, etc: *a coach on the London to Glasgow run.* **11** a LADDER (*noun* sense 2). **12** (**the runs**) *colloq* diarrhoea. **13** the length of time for which a machine, etc functions or is operated. **14** the quantity produced in a single period of production: *a print run.* **15** *cards* three or more playing-cards in a sequence. **16** *cricket* a point scored, usu by a batsman running from one wicket to the other. **17** a unit of scoring in baseball made by the batter successfully completing a circuit of four bases. **18** an enclosure or pen for domestic fowls or animals: *a chicken-run.* ◆ **a (good) run for one's money** *colloq* **1** fierce competition. **2** enjoyment or success from an activity. **on the run** fleeing. **run for it** *colloq* to try to escape. **run off one's feet** *Brit, colloq* extremely busy. ◇ **run across** or **into sb** to meet them unexpectedly. **run away** to escape or flee. **run away with sb** to elope with them. **run away with sth 1** to steal it. **2** of someone: to be carried away by (an idea, etc). **3** to win (a competition, etc) comfortably. **run down** of a clock, battery, etc: to cease to work because of a gradual loss of power. **run sb** or **sth down 1** of a vehicle or its driver: to knock them or it to the ground. **2** to speak badly of them or it. **3** to search for them or it until they are found. **run sth down** to allow (eg an operation or business) to be gradually reduced or closed. **run sb in** *colloq* to arrest them. **run into sb** *colloq* to meet them unexpectedly. **run into sb** or **sth** to collide with them or it. **run into sth** to be beset by (problems, etc): *Our plans quickly ran into problems.* **2** to reach as far as (an amount or quantity): *His debts run into hundreds.* **run sth off** to produce (esp printed material) quickly or promptly. **run**

off with sth to steal it. **run out** of a supply: to come to an end; to be used up. **run out of sth** to use up a supply of it: *I've run out of money.* **run sb out 1** *cricket* to put out (a batsman running towards a wicket) by hitting that wicket with the ball. **2** *chiefly N Am, colloq* to force them to leave: *We'll run them out of town.* **run out on sb** *colloq* to abandon or desert them. **run over 1** to overflow. **2** to go beyond (a limit, etc). **run over** or **through sth** to read or perform (a piece of music, a script, etc) quickly, esp for practice. **run sb** or **sth over** of a vehicle or driver: to knock them or it down and injure or kill them. **run sb through** to pierce them with a sword or similar weapon. **run to sth 1** to have enough money for it: *We can't run to a holiday this year.* **2** of money, resources, etc: to be sufficient for particular needs. **3** of a text: to extend to (a specified extent). **4** to tend towards it: *to run to fat.* **run sth up 1** to make (clothing, etc) quickly. **2** to amass or accumulate (bills, debts, etc). **3** to hoist (a flag). **run up against sb** or **sth** to be faced with (an opponent or difficulty).

runabout *n* a small light car, boat or aircraft.

runaround *n* a RUNABOUT. ◆ **give sb the runaround** *colloq* to behave repeatedly in a deceptive or evasive way towards them.

runaway *n* a person or animal that has run away. ➤ *adj* **1** in the process of running away; out of control: *a runaway train.* **2** of a race, victory, etc: easily and convincingly won.

run down *adj* **1** of a person: tired; in weakened health. **2** of a building: dilapidated. ➤ *n* (**rundown**) **1** a gradual reduction in numbers, size, etc. **2** a brief statement of the main points or items.

rune *n* **1** a letter of an early alphabet used by the Germanic peoples. **2** a mystical symbol or inscription. ○ **runic** *adj.*

rung *n* **1** a step on a ladder. **2** a crosspiece on a chair.

run-in *n* **1** an approach. **2** *colloq* a quarrel.

runnel *n* **1** a small stream. **2** a gutter.

runner *n* **1** someone or something that runs. **2** a messenger. **3** a groove or strip along which a drawer, sliding door, etc slides. **4** either of the strips of metal or wood running the length of a sledge, etc. **5** a blade on an ice skate. **6** in strawberry plants, etc: a stem that grows horizontally along the surface of the ground. **7** a long narrow strip of cloth or carpet used to decorate or cover a table, floor, etc. **8** a RUNNER BEAN. **9** a smuggler: *a drugs runner.* ◆ **do a runner** *slang* to leave a place hastily, esp without paying.

runner bean *n* **1** a climbing plant which produces bright red flowers and long green edible beans. **2** the bean this plant produces.

runner-up *n* (**runners-up**) a team or competitor that finishes in second place.

running *n* **1** the action of moving quickly. **2** the act of managing, organizing or operating. ➤ *adj* **1** relating to or for running: *running shoes.* **2** done or performed while running,

working, etc: *running repairs* • *a running jump.* **3** continuous: *a running dispute.* **4** consecutive: *two days running.* **5** flowing: *running water.* **6** of a wound or sore, etc: giving out pus. ◆ **in** or **out of the running** having, or not having, a chance of success. **make** or **take up the running** to take the lead or set the pace, eg in a competition, race, etc.

runny *adj* (**-ier, -iest**) **1** tending to run or flow with liquid. **2** liquid; too watery. **3** of the nose: discharging mucus.

run-of-the-mill *adj* ordinary; not special.

runt *n* **1** the smallest animal in a litter. **2** an undersized and weak person.

run-through *n* a practice or rehearsal.

run time *n*, *comput* the time during which a computer program is executed.

run-up *n* **1** *sport* a run made in preparation for a jump, throw, etc. **2** an approach to something or period of preparation: *the run-up to Christmas.*

runway *n* **1** a wide hard surface that aircraft take off from and land on. **2** in a theatre, etc: a narrow ramp projecting from a stage into the audience.

rupee *n* the standard unit of currency in several countries including India and Pakistan.

rupture *n* **1 a** a breaking or bursting; **b** the state of being broken or burst. **2** a breach of harmony or friendly relations. **3** a hernia, esp in the abdominal region. ➤ *vb* **1** to break, tear or burst. **2** to breach or break off (friendly relations). **3** to cause a rupture in (an organ, tissue, etc). **4** *intr* to be affected by a rupture.

rural *adj* relating to or suggestive of the countryside.

rural dean *n* in the Church of England: a clergyman with responsibility over a group of parishes.

ruse /ruːz/ *n* a clever stratagem intended to deceive.

rush¹ *vb* **1** *intr* to hurry; to move forward or go quickly. **2** to hurry someone or something on. **3** to send, transport, etc quickly or urgently: *They rushed her to hospital.* **4** to perform or deal with someone or something too quickly or hurriedly. **5** *intr* to come, flow, spread, etc quickly and suddenly: *Colour rushed to her cheeks.* **6** to attack someone or something suddenly. ➤ *n* **1** a sudden quick movement, esp forwards. **2** a sudden general movement or migration of people: *a gold rush.* **3** a sound or sensation of rushing. **4** hurry: *in a rush.* **5** a period of great activity. **6** a sudden demand for a commodity. **7** *slang* a feeling of euphoria after taking a drug. ➤ *adj* done, or needing to be done, quickly: *a rush job.*

rush² *n* **1** a densely tufted plant, typically found in cold wet regions. **2** a stalk or stalklike leaf of this plant, often used as a material for making baskets, etc. **3** rushes as a material.

rushes *pl n*, *cinematog* the first unedited prints of a scene or scenes.

rush hour *n* the period at the beginning or end

of a working day when traffic is at its busiest. ➤ *adj* (**rush-hour**) relating to or happening at either of these times.

rusk *n* a hard dry biscuit, esp as a baby food.

russet *n* **1** a reddish-brown colour. **2** a variety of apple with a reddish-brown skin.

Russian *adj* **1** belonging or relating to Russia or its inhabitants. **2** relating to the Russian language. ➤ *n* **1** a native of Russia. **2** the official language of Russia.

Russian roulette *n* an act of daring, esp that of spinning the cylinder of a revolver which is loaded with just one bullet, pointing the revolver at one's own head, and pulling the trigger.

rust *n* **1** a reddish-brown coating that forms on the surface of iron or steel that has been exposed to air and moisture. **2** a similar coating that forms on other metals. **3** the colour of rust, usu a reddish brown. **4** a fungus disease of cereals, etc, characterized by the appearance of reddish-brown patches on the leaves, etc. ➤ *vb* **1** *tr & intr* to become or cause to become coated with rust. **2** *intr* of a plant: to be affected by rust. **3** *intr* to become inefficient etc, usu through lack of use.

rustic *adj* **1** relating to, characteristic of or living in the country. **2** simple and unsophisticated. **3** awkward or uncouth. **4** made of rough untrimmed branches: *rustic furniture*. ➤ *n* a person from, or who lives in, the country, esp one who is thought to be simple and unsophisticated. ○ **rusticity** /rʌˈstɪsɪtɪ/ *n*.

rusticate *vb* **1** *Brit* to suspend (a student) temporarily from college or university. **2** *intr* to live or go to live in the country. **3** to make rustic. ○ **rustication** *n*.

rustle *vb* **1** *intr* to make a soft whispering sound like that of dry leaves. **2** *intr* to move with such a sound. **3** to make something move with, or make, such a sound: *He rustled the newspaper*. **4** *tr & intr*, *chiefly US* to round up and steal (cattle or horses). ➤ *n* a rustling sound. ○ **rustler** *n*. ◊ **rustle sth up 1** to gather (people or things) together, esp at short notice: *I rustled up a few people to go to the meeting*. **2** to arrange or prepare, esp at short notice.

rustproof *adj* **1** tending not to rust. **2** preventing rusting. ➤ *vb* to make rustproof.

rusty *adj* (**-ier, -iest**) **1** of iron, steel or other metals: covered with rust. **2** of a plant: affected by rust. **3** of a skill, knowledge of a subject, etc: impaired by lack of use or practice: *His French was rusty*. **4** rust-coloured. ○ **rustily** *adv*. ○ **rustiness** *n*.

rut[1] *n* a deep track or furrow in soft ground, esp one made by wheels. ➤ *vb* (**rutted, rutting**) to furrow (the ground) with ruts. ○ **rutty** *adj*. ♦ **in a rut** stuck in a boring routine.

rut[2] *n* in male ruminants, eg deer: a period of sexual excitement. ➤ *vb* (**rutted, rutting**) *intr* of male animals: to be in a period of sexual excitement.

ruthenium *n*, *chem* a brittle, silvery-white metallic element.

ruthless *adj* without pity. ○ **ruthlessly** *adv*. ○ **ruthlessness** *n*.

rye *n* **1 a** a cereal plant similar to barley but with longer, narrower ears; **b** its grain, used for making flour and in the distillation of whiskey, etc. **2** *esp US* whiskey distilled from fermented rye.

rye grass *n* a grass grown for fodder or used for lawns.

Ss

S[1] or **s** *n* (**Ss, S's** or **s's**) the nineteenth letter of the English alphabet.

S[2] *abbrev* **1** Saint. **2** siemens. **3** South.

S[3] *symbol*, *chem* sulphur.

s *abbrev* **1** a second of time. **2** *formerly* in the UK: shilling.

's[1] *sfx* **1** a word-forming element used to form the possessive: *the children's*. **2** a word-forming element used to form the plural of numbers and symbols: *3's, X's*.

's[2] *abbrev* **1** the shortened form of *is*, as in *he's not here*. **2** the shortened form of *has*, as in *she's taken it*. **3** the shortened form of *us*, as in *let's go*.

Sabbath *n* a day of the week set aside for religious worship and rest from work, Saturday among Jews and Sunday among most Christians.

sabbatical *n* a period of leave to undertake a special project.

sable[1] *n* (**sables** or **sable**) **1** a small carnivorous mammal, native to Europe and Asia, that is a species of the marten. **2** the dark brown or black coat of this animal, highly prized as fur.

sable[2] *adj* **1** *poetic* dark. **2** *heraldry* black.

sabotage /ˈsabətɑːʒ/ *n* **1** deliberate or underhand damage or destruction, esp for military or political reasons. **2** action designed to disrupt or destroy any plan or scheme. ➤ *vb* to deliberately destroy, damage or disrupt something. ○ **saboteur** /sabəˈtɜː(r)/ *n*.

sabre or (*US*) **saber** *n* **1** a curved single-edged cavalry sword. **2** a lightweight sword with a tapering blade used for fencing.

sac *n*, *biol* any bag-like part in a plant or animal.

saccharin /ˈsakərɪn/ *n* a white crystalline substance used as an artificial sweetener.

saccharine /ˈsakəriːn/ *adj* over-sentimental or sickly sweet.

sacerdotal /sasəˈdoutəl/ *adj* referring or relating to priests.

sachet /'saʃeɪ/ n a small sealed packet or bag containing a liquid, cream, etc.

sack[1] n 1 a large bag, esp one made of coarse cloth or paper. 2 a sackful. 3 (**the sack**) colloq dismissal from employment. 4 (**the sack**) slang bed. ➤ vb 1 to put into a sack or sacks. 2 colloq to dismiss from employment. ○ **sackful** n.

sack[2] vb to plunder, pillage and destroy a town. ➤ n the act of sacking a town.

sackbut n an early wind instrument with a slide like a trombone.

sackcloth n 1 coarse cloth used to make sacks. 2 a garment made from this, formerly worn in mourning or as a penance. ♦ **sackcloth and ashes** a display of mourning, sorrow or remorse.

sacking n coarse cloth used to make sacks.

sacrament n 1 Christianity a religious rite or ceremony, eg marriage or baptism. 2 (**Sacrament**) Christianity a the service of the Eucharist or Holy Communion; b the bread and wine consumed at Holy Communion. ○ **sacramental** adj.

sacred adj 1 devoted to a deity, saint, etc; consecrated. 2 connected with religion or worship: sacred music. 3 of rules, etc: not to be challenged, violated or breached in any circumstances.

sacred cow n, colloq a custom, institution, etc so revered as to be above criticism.

sacrifice n 1 the offering of a slaughtered person or animal on an altar to a god. 2 the person or animal slaughtered for such an offering. 3 any offering, symbolic or tangible, made to a god. 4 the destruction, surrender or giving up of something valued, esp for a higher consideration. ➤ vb 1 to offer someone or something as a sacrifice to a god. 2 to surrender or give up something for the sake of some other person or thing. ○ **sacrificial** adj.

sacrilege n 1 a profanation or extreme disrespect for something holy or greatly respected. 2 the breaking into a holy or sacred place and stealing from it. ○ **sacrilegious** adj.

sacristan or **sacrist** n a person responsible for the church buildings and churchyard; a sexton.

sacristy n (**-ies**) a room in a church where sacred utensils and vestments are kept; a vestry.

sacrosanct adj supremely holy or sacred; inviolable.

sacrum /'seɪkrəm/ n (**sacra**) anat a large triangular bone composed of fused vertebrae, forming the keystone of the pelvic arch in humans. ○ **sacral** adj.

SAD abbrev, psychol seasonal affective disorder, a depressive illness occurring during the winter months.

sad adj (**sadder, saddest**) 1 feeling unhappy or sorrowful. 2 causing unhappiness: sad news. 3 expressing or suggesting unhappiness: sad music. 4 very bad; deplorable: a sad state. 5 colloq lacking in taste; inspiring ridicule: He has such sad taste in music. ○ **sadly** adv 1 in a sad

manner. 2 unfortunately. ○ **sadness** n.

sadden vb 1 to make someone sad. 2 intr to become sad.

saddle n 1 a leather seat for horseriding, which fits on the horse's back and is secured under its belly. 2 a fixed seat on a bicycle or motorcycle. 3 a pad on the back of a draught animal, used for supporting the load. 4 a butcher's cut of meat including part of the backbone with the ribs. ➤ vb 1 to put a saddle on (an animal). 2 intr to climb into a saddle. 3 to burden someone with a problem, duty, etc. ♦ **in the saddle** in a position of power or control.

saddleback n 1 an animal or bird with a saddle-shaped marking on its back. 2 a hill or mountain with a dip in the middle.

saddlebag n a small bag carried at or attached to the saddle of a horse or bicycle.

saddler n a person who makes or sells saddles, harnesses and related equipment for horses.

saddlery n (**-ies**) 1 the occupation or profession of a saddler. 2 a saddler's shop or stock-in-trade.

saddle soap n a type of oily soap used for cleaning and preserving leather.

sadhu /'sɑːduː/ n a nomadic Hindu holy man, living an austere life and existing on charity.

sadism /'seɪdɪzəm/ n 1 the pleasure, esp sexual, gained by inflicting pain on others. 2 any infliction of suffering on others for one's own satisfaction. Compare MASOCHISM. ○ **sadist** n. ○ **sadistic** adj.

sado-masochism n the practice of deriving sexual pleasure from inflicting pain on another person, and having pain inflicted on oneself by another person. ○ **sado-masochist** n. ○ **sado-masochistic** adj.

safari n an expedition to hunt or observe wild animals, esp in Africa.

safari park n a large enclosed area in which wild animals roam freely and can be observed by the public from their vehicles.

safe adj 1 free from danger or harm. 2 unharmed. 3 giving protection from danger or harm; secure: a safe place. ➤ n a sturdily constructed cabinet, usu made of metal, in which valuables can be locked away. ○ **safely** adv. ○ **safeness** n. ○ **safety** n. ♦ **be or err on the safe side** to choose the safer alternative. **safe and sound** secure and unharmed. **safe as houses** colloq extremely safe and secure.

safe-deposit or **safety-deposit** n a vault, eg in a bank, in which valuables can be locked away.

safeguard n a person, device or arrangement giving protection against danger or harm. ➤ vb to protect from harm.

safekeeping n care and protection; safe custody: She put her jewellery in the bank for safekeeping.

safe sex n sexual intercourse or activity in which pregnancy and sexually transmitted diseases are guarded against, eg by the use of condoms.

safety catch *n* any catch to provide protection against something, eg the accidental firing of a gun.

safety curtain *n* a fireproof curtain between the stage and a theatre audience, lowered to control the spread of fire.

safety glass *n* toughened glass that leaves no sharp edges if it shatters.

safety lamp *n* a miner's oil lamp designed to prevent ignition of any flammable gases encountered in the mine by covering the flame with a wire gauze.

safety match *n* a match that only ignites when struck on a specially prepared surface.

safety net *n* **1** a large net stretched beneath acrobats, tightrope walkers, etc in case they fall. **2** any means of protecting against loss or failure.

safety pin *n* a U-shaped pin with an attached guard to cover the point.

safety razor *n* a shaving razor with the blade protected by a guard to prevent deep cutting of the skin.

safety valve *n* **1** a valve in a boiler or pipe system that opens when the pressure exceeds a certain level, and closes again when the pressure drops. **2** an outlet for harmlessly releasing strong emotion.

saffron *n* **1** a crocus which has lilac flowers with large bright orange stigmas. **2** the dried stigmas of this species, used to dye and flavour food. **3** a bright orange-yellow colour.

sag *vb* (**sagged, sagging**) *intr* to bend, sink or hang down, esp in the middle, under or as if under weight. ➤ *n* a sagging state or condition. ○ **saggy** *adj*.

saga *n* **1** a medieval prose tale of the deeds of legendary Icelandic or Norwegian heroes and events. **2** *colloq* any long detailed story or series of events.

sagacious *adj, formal* having or showing intelligence and good judgement; wise or discerning. ○ **sagacity** *n*.

sage¹ *n* **1** a shrub with greyish-green aromatic leaves. **2** these leaves used as a seasoning.

sage² *n* someone of great wisdom and knowledge, esp an ancient philosopher. ➤ *adj* extremely wise and shrewd. ○ **sagely** *adv*.

Sagittarius *n, astrol* **a** the ninth sign of the zodiac; **b** a person born between 23 November and 22 December, under this sign.

sago *n* **1** a starchy grain or powder obtained from the soft pith of the sago palm, a staple food in the tropics, and also widely used in desserts. **2** any of various species of palm that yield this.

sahib /ˈsɑːɪb/ *n* in India: a term of respect used after a man's name, equivalent to 'Mr' or 'Sir', and formerly used on its own to address or refer to a European man.

said *vb, past tense, past participle of* SAY. ➤ *adj, often formal* previously or already mentioned: *the said occasion*.

sail *n* **1** a sheet of canvas, or similar structure, spread to catch the wind as a means of propelling a boat or ship. **2** a trip or voyage in a boat or ship with or without sails. ➤ *vb* **1** *tr & intr* to travel by boat or ship. **2** to control (a boat or ship): *He sailed his ship around the world.* **3** *intr* to depart by boat or ship: *We sail at two-thirty.* **4** *intr* (**sail through sth**) *colloq* to succeed in it effortlessly. ♦ **sail close to** or **near the wind 1** *naut* to keep the boat's bow as close as possible to the direction from which the wind is blowing so that the sails catch as much wind as is safely possible. **2** to come dangerously close to overstepping a limit. **set sail 1** to begin a journey by boat or ship. **2** to spread the sails.

sailboard *n* a windsurfing board, like a surfboard with a sail attached, controlled by a hand-held boom. ○ **sailboarding** *n*.

sailcloth *n* **1** strong cloth, such as canvas, used to make sails. **2** heavy cotton cloth used for garments.

sailor *n* **1** any member of a ship's crew, esp one who is not an officer. **2** someone regarded in terms of ability to tolerate travel on a ship without becoming seasick: *a good sailor.*

sainfoin /ˈseɪnfɔɪn/ *n* a leguminous plant, widely cultivated as a fodder crop, having bright pink to red flowers veined with purple.

saint *n* **1** (*often* **Saint**) a person whose profound holiness is formally recognized after death by a Christian Church. **2** *colloq* a very good and kind person. ○ **sainthood** *n*. ○ **saintlike** *adj*.

sainted *adj* **1** formally declared a saint. **2** greatly respected or revered; hallowed.

saintly *adj* (**-ier, -iest**) **1** similar to, characteristic of or befitting a saint. **2** very good or holy. ○ **saintliness** *n*.

Saint Valentine's Day *n* 14 February, a day on which special greetings cards are sent to sweethearts.

Saint Vitus's dance *n, pathol* chorea.

saithe *n, Brit* the COLEY.

sake¹ *n* **1** benefit or advantage; behalf; account: *for my sake.* **2** purpose; object or aim. ♦ **for God's** or **heaven's,** *etc* **sake** exclamations used in annoyance or when pleading. **for the sake of sth** for the purpose of or in order to achieve or assure it: *You should take these exams for the sake of your future.*

sake² or **saki** /ˈsɑːkɪ/ *n* a Japanese fermented alcoholic drink made from rice.

salaam /səˈlɑːm/ *n* **1** a word used as a greeting in Eastern countries, esp by Muslims. **2** a Muslim greeting or show of respect in the form of a low bow with the palm of the right hand on the forehead. ➤ *vb, tr & intr* to perform the salaam to someone.

salacious *adj* **1** unnaturally preoccupied with sex. **2** seeking to arouse sexual desire, esp crudely or obscenely.

salad *n* a cold dish of vegetables or herbs, either raw or pre-cooked, eaten either on its own or as an accompaniment to a main meal.

salad days *pl n, literary* years of youthful inexperience and carefree innocence.

salad dressing n any sauce served with a salad, eg a mixture of oil and vinegar.

salamander n 1 a small amphibian resembling a lizard. 2 a mythical reptile or spirit believed to live in fire and be able to quench it with the chill of its body.

salami n a highly seasoned type of sausage, usu served very thinly sliced.

salaried adj receiving or providing a salary.

salary n (**-ies**) a fixed regular payment, usu made monthly, for esp non-manual work. ➢ vb (**-ies, -ied**) to pay a salary to someone.

sale n 1 the exchange of anything for a specified amount of money. 2 a period during which goods in shops, etc are offered at reduced prices. 3 the sale of goods by auction. 4 any event at which certain goods can be bought: a book sale. 5 (**sales**) the operations associated with, or the staff responsible for, selling. ➢ adj intended for selling, esp at reduced prices or by auction: sale items. ♦ **for** or **on sale** available for buying.

saleable or (US) **salable** adj 1 suitable for selling. 2 in demand. ○ **saleability** n.

salesman, salesgirl, saleswoman or **salesperson** n 1 a person who sells goods to customers, esp in a shop. 2 a person representing a company, who often visits people's homes, offices, etc.

salesmanship n the techniques used by a salesperson to present goods in an appealing way so as to persuade people to buy them.

salient /ˈseɪlɪənt/ adj striking; outstanding or prominent. ➢ n a projecting angle, part or section, eg of a fortification or a defensive line of troops.

saline /ˈseɪlaɪn/ adj 1 of a substance: containing common salt; salty. 2 of medicines: containing or having the nature of the salts of alkali metals and magnesium. ➢ n (also **saline solution**) a solution of sodium chloride in water, having the same pH and concentration as body fluids, used in intravenous drips, etc. ○ **salinity** n.

saliva n a clear liquid produced by the salivary glands of the mouth, which moistens and softens food and begins the process of digestion. ○ **salivary** adj.

salivary gland n a gland that secretes saliva.

salivate vb, intr 1 of the salivary glands: to produce a flow of saliva into the mouth in response to the thought or sight of food. 2 to drool. ○ **salivation** n.

sallow adj of a person's complexion: being a pale yellowish colour, often through poor health.

sally n (**-ies**) 1 a sudden rushing forward or advance of troops to attack besiegers. 2 an excursion or outing. 3 a witty comment or remark. ➢ vb (**-ies, -ied**) intr 1 of troops: to carry out a sally. 2 humorous (also **sally forth**) to rush out or surge forward. 3 to set off on an excursion.

salmon /ˈsamən/ n (**salmon** or **salmons**) 1 a large silvery fish that migrates to freshwater rivers and streams in order to spawn, highly prized as a food and game fish. 2 the reddish-orange flesh of this fish. 3 (also **salmon pink**) an orange-pink colour.

salmonella /salməˈnɛlə/ n (**salmonellae** /-liː/ or **salmonellas**) 1 (**Salmonella**) a form of bacteria that can cause food poisoning. 2 food poisoning caused by such bacteria.

salon n 1 a reception room, esp in a large house. 2 a social gathering of distinguished people in a fashionable household. 3 a shop or other establishment where clients are beautified in some way: a hairdressing salon.

saloon n 1 colloq (in full **saloon car**) any motor car with two or four doors and an enclosed compartment. 2 a large public cabin or dining room on a passenger ship. 3 (also **saloon bar**) a lounge bar; a quieter and more comfortable part of a public house, sometimes separated from it. 4 N Am a bar, esp formerly in the Wild West.

salsa n 1 rhythmic music of Latin-American origin, containing elements of jazz and rock. 2 a dance performed to this. 3 cookery a spicy Mexican sauce, made with raw tomatoes, onions, and chillies.

salsify n (**-ies**) a plant with a long white cylindrical tap root eaten as a vegetable.

salt n 1 SODIUM CHLORIDE, esp as used to season and preserve food. 2 chem a chemical compound that is formed when an acid reacts with a base. 3 liveliness; interest, wit or good sense: Her opinion added salt to the debate. 4 (also **old salt**) an experienced and usu old sailor. 5 (**salts**) SMELLING SALTS. ➢ adj containing, tasting of or preserved in salt: salt water • salt pork. ➢ vb 1 to season or preserve (food) with salt. 2 to cover (an icy road) with a scattering of salt to melt the ice. 3 to add piquancy, interest or wit to something. ○ **salted** adj. ♦ **rub salt in sb's wounds** to add to their discomfort, sorrow, shame, etc. **take sth with a pinch of salt** to treat a statement or proposition sceptically. **the salt of the earth** a consistently reliable or dependable person. **worth one's salt** competent or useful. ◊ **salt sth away** to store it up for future use; to hoard it, esp in a miserly way.

saltcellar n a container holding salt when used as a condiment.

saltpetre or (US) **saltpeter** n potassium nitrate.

salty adj (**-ier, -iest**) 1 tasting strongly or excessively of, or containing, salt. 2 of humour: sharp or witty; spirited.

salubrious adj 1 formal promoting health or wellbeing: a salubrious climate. 2 decent or respectable; pleasant: not a very salubrious neighbourhood.

salutary adj beneficial; bringing or containing a timely warning.

salutation n a word, act or gesture of greeting. ○ **salutatory** adj.

salute vb 1 to greet with friendly words or a gesture. **2** to pay tribute to something or someone: *We salute your bravery.* **3** *intr, mil* to pay formal respect to someone or something with a set gesture, esp with the right arm. ➤ *n* **1** a greeting. **2** a military gesture of respect, for a person or an occasion.

salvage *n* **1** the rescue of a ship or its cargo from the danger of destruction or loss. **2** the reward paid by a ship's owner for saving the ship. **3** the rescue of any property from fire or other danger. **4** the saving and utilization of waste material. **5** the property salvaged. ➤ *vb* **1** to rescue (property or a ship) from potential destruction or loss, eg in a fire or shipwreck, or from disposal as waste. **2** to manage to retain (eg one's pride) in adverse circumstances. ○ **salvageable** *adj.*

salvation *n* **1** the act of saving someone or something from harm. **2** a person or thing that saves another from harm. **3** *relig* the liberation or saving of man from the influence of sin.

salve *n* **1** an ointment or remedy to heal or soothe: *lip salve.* **2** anything that comforts, consoles or soothes. ➤ *vb* to ease or comfort: *salve one's conscience.*

salver *n* a small ornamented tray.

salvo *n* (*salvos* or *salvoes*) a burst of gunfire from several guns firing simultaneously.

sal volatile /sal vɒˈlatɪlɪ/ *n* a former name for ammonium carbonate, esp in a solution used as smelling salts.

Samaritan *n* (*in full* **Good Samaritan**) a kind, considerate or helpful person.

samarium *n, chem* a soft silvery metallic element, used in alloys with cobalt to make strong permanent magnets.

samba *n* **1** a lively Brazilian dance in duple time. **2** a piece of music written for this.

same *adj* **1** identical or very similar: *This is the same film we saw last week.* **2** used as emphasis: *He went home the very same day.* **3** unchanged: *This town is still the same as ever.* **4** previously mentioned; the actual one in question: *this same man.* ➤ *pron* the same person or thing, or the one previously referred to: *She drank whisky, and I drank the same.* ➤ *adv* (**the same**) **1** similarly; likewise: *I feel the same.* **2** *colloq* equally: *We love each of you the same.* ○ **sameness** *n.* ♦ **all** or **just the same** nevertheless; anyhow. **at the same time** still; however; on the other hand. **be all the same to sb** to make no difference to them; to be of little or no importance.

samey *adj, colloq* boringly similar or unchanging; monotonous.

samizdat *n* **1** in the former Soviet Union: the secret printing and distribution of banned writings. **2** the writings themselves.

samosa *n* (*samosas* or *samosa*) a deep-fried triangular pastry turnover, of Indian origin, filled with spicy meat or vegetables.

samovar *n* a Russian water boiler, used for making tea, etc, often elaborately decorated, and heated by a central pipe filled with charcoal.

sampan or **sanpan** *n* a small Oriental boat propelled by oars.

sample *n* a small portion or part used to represent the quality and nature of others or of a whole. ➤ *vb* **1** to take or try as a sample. **2** to get experience of something: *He has sampled life abroad.* **3** *pop music* **a** to mix a short extract from one recording into a different backing track; **b** to record a sound and program it into a synthesizer which can then reproduce it at the desired pitch.

sampler *n* **1** a collection of samples. **2** *pop music* the equipment used for sampling sound. **3** a piece of embroidery produced as a show or test of skill. ○ **sampling** *n.*

samurai /ˈsamʊraɪ/ *n* (*pl* **samurai**) *hist* an aristocratic caste of Japanese warriors.

sanatorium *n* (*sanatoriums* or *sanatoria*) **1** a hospital for the chronically ill or convalescents. **2** *Brit* a room for sick people in a boarding school, etc.

sanctify *vb* (*-ies, -ied*) to make, consider or show to be sacred or holy. ○ **sanctification** *n.*

sanctimonious *adj* affecting or simulating holiness or virtuousness, esp hypocritically. ○ **sanctimoniously** *adv.* ○ **sanctimoniousness** or **sanctimony** *n.*

sanction *n* **1** official permission or authority. **2** the act of giving permission or authority. **3** aid; support. **4** (*esp* **sanctions**) *pol* an economic or military measure taken by one nation against another as a means of coercion: *trade sanctions.* ➤ *vb* **1** to authorize or confirm formally. **2** to countenance or permit.

---

sanction This does not mean 'impose sanctions on'; this meaning is expressed by **embargo** or **boycott**.

---

sanctity *n* (*-ies*) **1** the quality of being holy or sacred. **2** purity or godliness; inviolability.

sanctuary *n* (*-ies*) **1** a holy or sacred place, eg a church or temple. **2** a place providing protection from arrest, persecution, etc. **3** a place of retreat: *the sanctuary of the garden.* **4** a nature reserve in which animals or plants are protected by law.

sanctum *n* (*sanctums* or *sancta*) (*esp* **inner sanctum**) **1** a sacred place. **2** a place providing total privacy.

sand *n* **1** *geol* tiny rounded particles or grains of rock, esp quartz. **2** (**sands**) an area of land covered with these particles or grains, such as a seashore or desert. ➤ *adj* **1** made of sand. **2** having the colour of sand, a light brownish-yellow colour. ➤ *vb* **1** to smooth or polish a surface with sandpaper or a sander. **2** to sprinkle, cover or mix with sand.

sandal *n* a type of lightweight shoe consisting of a sole attached to the foot by straps.

sandalwood *n, bot* the hard pale fragrant timber obtained from an evergreen tree, used for ornamental carving and incense, and yielding an aromatic oil used in perfumes.

sandbag *n* a sack filled with sand or earth,

used with others to form a protective barrier against gunfire or floods, or used as ballast. ➤ *vb* to barricade or weigh down with sandbags.

sandbank or **sandbar** *n* a bank of sand in a river, river mouth or sea, formed by currents and often above the water level at low tide.

sandblast *vb* to clean or engrave (glass, metal, stone surfaces, etc) with a jet of sand forced from a tube by air or steam pressure. ○ **sandblasting** *n*.

sander *n* a power-driven tool fitted with sandpaper or an abrasive disc, used for sanding wood, etc.

S and M *abbrev* sado-masochism.

sandman *n, folklore* a man who supposedly sprinkles magical sand into children's eyes at bedtime to make them sleepy.

sandpaper *n* abrasive paper with a coating of sand or crushed glass, used for smoothing and polishing surfaces. ➤ *vb* to smooth or polish with sandpaper.

sandstone *n, geol* a sedimentary rock consisting of compacted sand cemented together with clay, silica, etc, widely used in the construction of buildings.

sandwich *n* a snack consisting of two slices of bread or a roll with a filling of cheese, meat, etc. ➤ *vb* to place, esp with little or no gap, between two layers.

sandy *adj* (*-ier, -iest*) **1** covered with or containing sand. **2** having the colour of sand, a light brownish-yellow colour: *sandy hair*. ○ **sandiness** *n*.

sane *adj* **1** sound in mind; not mentally impaired. **2** sensible or rational; sound in judgement. ○ **sanely** *adv*.

sangfroid /sɒŋ'frwɑː/ *n* calmness or composure; cool-headedness.

sanguinary *adj* **1** bloody; involving much bloodshed. **2** bloodthirsty; taking pleasure in bloodshed.

sanguine /'saŋgwɪn/ *adj* **1** cheerful, confident and full of hope. **2** of a complexion: ruddy or flushed.

sanitary *adj* **1** concerned with and promoting hygiene, good health and the prevention of disease. **2** relating to health, esp drainage and sewage disposal. ○ **sanitarily** *adv*.

sanitary towel or (*US*) **sanitary napkin** *n* an absorbent pad worn during menstruation.

sanitation *n* **1** standards of public hygiene. **2** measures taken to promote and preserve public health, esp through drainage and sewage disposal.

sanitize or **-ise** *vb* **1** to make hygienic or sanitary. **2** to make less controversial or more acceptable by removing potentially offensive elements, etc.

sanity *n* **1** soundness of mind; rationality. **2** good sense and reason.

sanserif or **sans serif** /san'serɪf/ *n, printing* a type in which the letters have no serifs.

Sanskrit *n* the ancient Indo-European reli-

gious and literary language of India.

sap¹ *n* **1** *bot* a vital liquid containing sugars and other nutrients that circulates in plants. **2** energy or vitality. **3** *slang* a weak or easily fooled person. ➤ *vb* (*sapped, sapping*) **1** to drain or extract sap from something. **2** to weaken or exhaust; to drain energy from something. ○ **sappy** *adj*.

sap² *n* a hidden trench by means of which an attack is made on an enemy position. ➤ *vb* (*sapped, sapping*) **1** *intr* to attack by means of a sap. **2** to undermine or weaken.

sapient /'seɪpɪənt/ *adj, formal, often ironic* having or showing good judgement; wise.

sapling *n* a young tree.

saponify *vb* (*-ies, -ied*) *chem* to convert fats into soap using an alkali. ○ **saponification** *n*.

sapper *n* **1** *Brit* a soldier in the Royal Engineers. **2** a soldier responsible for making saps (see SAP²).

sapphire /'safaɪə(r)/ *n* **1** a hard transparent blue gem, prized as a gemstone. **2** the deep blue colour of this stone.

saprophyte *n, biol* a plant, esp a fungus, that feeds on dead and decaying organic matter.

saraband or **sarabande** *n* **1** a slow formal Spanish dance. **2** a piece of music written for this dance.

sarcasm *n* **1** an often ironical expression of scorn or contempt. **2** the use of such an expression.

sarcastic *adj* **1** containing sarcasm. **2** tending to use sarcasm. ○ **sarcastically** *adv*.

sarcoma *n* (*sarcomas* or *sarcomata*) *pathol* a cancerous tumour arising in connective tissue.

sarcophagus /sɑː'kɒfəgəs/ *n* (*sarcophagi* /-gaɪ/ or *sarcophaguses*) a stone coffin or tomb.

sardine *n* (*sardines* or *sardine*) a young pilchard, an important food fish, commonly tinned in oil.

sardonic *adj* mocking or scornful; sneering. ○ **sardonically** *adv*.

sargasso *n* (*sargassos* or *sargassoes*) a brown seaweed with branching ribbon-like fronds that floats freely in huge masses.

sarge *n, colloq* sergeant.

sari or **saree** *n* (*saris* or *sarees*) a traditional garment of Hindu women, consisting of a single long piece of fabric wound round the waist and draped over one shoulder and sometimes the head.

sarky *adj* (*-ier, -iest*) *colloq* sarcastic.

sarnie *n, colloq* a sandwich.

sarong *n* **1** a Malay garment worn by both sexes, consisting of a long piece of fabric wrapped around the waist or chest. **2** a Western adaptation of this garment, often worn by women as beachwear.

SARS *abbrev* severe acute respiratory syndrome, a contagious lung infection.

sarsaparilla *n* **1** a climbing tropical American plant with an aromatic root used as a flavouring or tonic. **2** *US* a soft drink flavoured with this root.

sartorial *adj* referring or relating to a tailor, tailoring or clothes in general: *sartorial elegance*.

sash[1] *n* a broad band of cloth, worn round the waist or over the shoulder.

sash[2] *n* a glazed frame, esp a sliding one, forming part of a SASH WINDOW.

sashay *vb, intr* to walk or move in a gliding or ostentatious way.

sashimi *n* a Japanese dish of thinly sliced raw fish.

sash window *n* a window consisting of two sashes (see SASH[2]), one of which can slide vertically past the other.

sass *US colloq, n* impertinent talk or behaviour. ➤ *vb, intr* to speak or behave impertinently. ○ **sassy** *adj* (*-ier, -iest*).

sassafras *n* a deciduous North American tree, various parts of which are used in teas, remedies, and as a flavouring.

Sassenach /ˈsasənax, -ak/ *Scot, usu derog, n* an English person. ➤ *adj* English.

Satan *n* the Devil.

satanic or **satanical** *adj* **1** referring or relating to Satan. **2** evil; abominable. ○ **satanically** *adv*.

Satanism *n* (*also* **satanism**) the worship of Satan. ○ **Satanist** *n, adj*.

satchel *n* a small briefcase-like bag for schoolbooks, often leather, and usu with shoulder straps.

sate *vb* to satisfy (a longing or appetite) to the full or to excess.

satellite *n* **1** a celestial body that orbits a much larger celestial body, eg the Moon is a satellite of the Earth. **2** a man-made device launched into space by a rocket, etc, and placed in orbit around a planet, esp the Earth, used for communication, photography, etc. **3** a nation or state dependent on a larger neighbour.

satellite dish *n* a saucer-shaped aerial for receiving television signals broadcast by satellite.

satellite TV, satellite television or **satellite broadcasting** *n, telecomm* the broadcasting of television by means of an artificial satellite.

satiable /ˈseɪʃəbl/ *adj* able to be satisfied or satiated.

satiate /ˈseɪʃɪeɪt/ *vb* to gratify fully; to satisfy to excess.

satin *n* silk or rayon closely woven to produce a shiny finish, showing much of the warp. ○ **satiny** *adj*.

satinwood *n* **1** a shiny light-coloured hardwood used for fine furniture. **2** the tree that yields it.

satire *n* **1** a literary composition, orig in verse, which holds up follies and vices for criticism, ridicule and scorn. **2** the use of sarcasm, irony, wit, humour, etc in such compositions. **3** satirical writing as a genre. ○ **satirical** *adj*. ○ **satirist** *n*.

satirize or **-ise** *vb* **1** *intr* to write satire. **2** to

mock, ridicule or criticize using satire. ○ **satirization** *n*.

satisfaction *n* **1** the act of satisfying, or the state or feeling of being satisfied. **2** something that satisfies. **3** gratification or comfort. **4** compensation for mistreatment or an insult.

satisfactory *adj* **1** adequate or acceptable. **2** giving satisfaction. ○ **satisfactorily** *adv*.

satisfy *vb* (*-ies, -ied*) **1** *intr* to fulfil the needs, desires or expectations of someone. **2** to give enough to or be enough for someone or something. **3** to meet the requirements or fulfil the conditions of someone or something. **4** to remove the doubts of someone. ○ **satisfying** *adj*.

satsuma *n* **1** a thin-skinned seedless type of mandarin orange. **2** the tree that bears this fruit.

saturate *vb* **1** to soak. **2** to fill or cover with a large amount of something. **3** to charge (air or vapour) with moisture to the fullest extent possible. **4** *chem* to add a solid, liquid or gas to (a solution) until no more of that substance can be dissolved at a given temperature.

saturation *n* **1** the state of being saturated; saturating. **2** *chem* the point at which a solution contains the maximum possible amount of dissolved solid, liquid or gas at a given temperature.

Saturday *n* the seventh day of the week.

Saturn *n, astron* the sixth planet from the Sun.

saturnalia *n* a scene of rowdy celebration; an orgy.

saturnine *adj* having a grave and gloomy temperament; melancholy in character.

satyr /ˈsatə(r)/ *n* **1** *Greek myth* a lecherous woodland god, part man, part goat. **2** a lustful or lecherous man.

sauce *n* **1** any liquid, often thickened, cooked or served with food. **2** anything that adds relish, interest or excitement. **3** *colloq* impertinent language or behaviour; cheek.

saucepan *n* a deep cooking pot with a long handle and usu a lid.

saucer *n* **1** a shallow round dish, esp one for placing under a cup. **2** anything of a similar shape. ○ **saucerful** *n*.

saucy *adj* (*-ier, -iest*) *colloq* **1** impertinent or cheeky; bold or forward. **2** referring to sex, esp in an amusing way: *saucy postcards*. ○ **saucily** *adv*. ○ **sauciness** *n*.

sauerkraut /ˈsaʊəkraʊt/ *n* a popular German dish, consisting of shredded cabbage pickled in salt water.

sauna *n* a Finnish-style bath where the person is exposed to dry heat, with occasional short blasts of steam created by pouring water on hot coals.

saunter *vb, intr* to walk, often aimlessly, at a leisurely pace. ➤ *n* a leisurely walk or stroll.

saurian *adj, zool* referring or relating to lizards.

sausage *n* **1** a mass of chopped or minced seasoned meat, sometimes with fat, cereal, vegetables, etc, stuffed into a tube of gut. **2** any object of a similar shape. ♦ **not a sausage** *colloq* nothing at all.

sausage roll *n, Brit* sausage meat baked in a roll of pastry.

sauté /'sooteɪ/ *vb* (**sautéed, sautéing** or **sautéeing**) to fry lightly for a short time.

savage *adj* **1** of animals: untamed or undomesticated. **2** ferocious or furious: *He has a savage temper.* **3** of eg behaviour: uncivilized; coarse. **4** cruel; barbaric. **5** of land: uncultivated; wild and rugged. ➤ *n* **1** *now offensive* a member of a primitive people. **2** an uncultured, fierce or cruel person. ➤ *vb* to attack ferociously, esp with the teeth, causing severe injury. ○ **savagely** *adv.* ○ **savageness** *n.*

savanna or **savannah** *n* an expanse of level grassland, often dotted with trees and bushes, characteristic of Africa.

savant /'savənt or *French* savã/ or **savante** /'savənt or *French* savãt/ *n* a wise and learned man or woman respectively.

save *vb* **1** to rescue, protect or preserve someone or something from danger, evil, loss or failure. **2** to use economically so as to prevent or avoid waste or loss. **3** *intr* (*also* **save up**) to be economical: *We're saving up for a holiday abroad next year.* **4** to reserve or store for later use. **5** to spare from potential unpleasantness or inconvenience: *That will save you having to make another trip.* **6** to obviate or prevent. **7** *sport* to prevent (a ball or shot) from reaching the goal; to prevent (a goal) from being scored by the opposing team. **8** *tr & intr, relig* to deliver from the influence or consequences of sin. **9** *comput* to transfer (data, etc) onto a disk or tape for storage. ➤ *n* **1** an act of saving a ball or shot, or of preventing a goal: *He made a great save in that match.* **2** *comput* the saving of data onto a disk or tape. ➤ *prep* (*sometimes* **save for**) except: *We found all the tickets save one.* ○ **savable** or **saveable** *adj.* ○ **saver** *n.* ♦ **save one's** or **sb's face** to prevent oneself or them from appearing foolish or wrong; to avoid humiliation. **save one's** or **sb's skin** or **neck** to save one's or their life. **save the day** to prevent something from disaster, failure, etc.

saveloy /'savələɪ/ *n* a spicy smoked pork sausage, orig made from brains.

saving *vb, present participle of* SAVE. ➤ *adj* **1** protecting or preserving. **2** economical or frugal. ➤ *n* **1** something saved. **2** (**savings**) money set aside for future use.

saving grace *n* a desirable virtue or feature that compensates for undesirable ones.

saviour or (*N Am*) **savior** *n* **1** a person who saves someone or something else from danger or destruction. **2** (**the Saviour**) *Christianity* Christ.

savoir-faire /savwaː'fɛə(r)/ *n* instinctively knowing exactly what to do and how to do it; expertise.

savory *n* (*-ies*) a plant whose leaves are used as a herb.

savour or (*US*) **savor** *n* **1** the characteristic

taste or smell of something. **2** a faint but unmistakable quality. ➤ *vb* **1** to taste or smell with relish. **2** to take pleasure in something. **3** to flavour or season. **4** to relish. **5** *intr* (*chiefly* **savour of** *sth*) to show signs of it; to smack of it. ○ **savourless** *adj.*

savoury or (*US*) **savory** *adj* **1** having a salty, sharp or piquant taste or smell: *a savoury snack.* **2** having a good savour or relish; appetizing. **3** pleasant or attractive, esp morally pleasing or respectable. ➤ *n* (*-ies*) a savoury course or snack. ○ **savouriness** *n.*

savoy *n* a winter variety of cabbage with a large compact head and wrinkled leaves.

savvy *slang, vb* (*-ies, -ied*) *tr & intr* to know or understand. ➤ *n* **1** general ability or common sense; shrewdness. **2** skill; know-how.

saw[1] *past tense of* SEE[1]

saw[2] *n* any of various toothed cutting tools, either hand-operated or power-driven, used esp for cutting wood. ➤ *vb* (*past participle* **sawn** or **sawed**) **1** to cut with, or as if with, a saw. **2** to shape by sawing. **3** *intr* to use a saw. **4** *intr* to make to-and-fro movements, as if using a saw.

sawdust *n* small particles of wood, made by sawing.

sawmill *n* a factory in which timber is cut into planks.

sawn-off or (*esp US*) **sawed-off** *adj* shortened by cutting with a saw: *sawn-off shotgun.*

sawyer /'sɔːjə(r)/ *n* a person who saws timber, esp in a sawmill.

sax *n, colloq* short for SAXOPHONE.

Saxon *n* **1** a member of a Germanic people which conquered Britain in the 5c and 6c. **2** any of their Germanic dialects. ➤ *adj* of the Saxons or the ANGLO-SAXONS, or their languages or culture.

saxophone *n* a single-reeded wind instrument with a long S-shaped metal body, usu played in jazz and dance bands. ○ **saxophonist** /sak'spfənɪst/ *n.*

say *vb* (**said**) **1** to speak, utter or articulate: *He said he would come.* **2** to express in words: *Say what you mean.* **3** to assert or declare; to state as an opinion: *I say we should give it a try.* **4** to suppose: *Say he doesn't come, what do we do then?* **5** to recite or repeat: *Don't forget to say your prayers.* **6** to judge or decide: *It's difficult to say which is best.* **7** to convey information: *She talked for ages but didn't actually say much.* **8** to indicate: *The clock says 10 o'clock* **9** to report or claim: *Elvis Presley is said by some to be still alive.* **10** *tr & intr* to make a statement; to tell: *I'd rather not say.* ➤ *n* **1** a chance to express an opinion: *You've had your say.* **2** the right to an opinion; the power to influence a decision: *to have no say in the matter.* ♦ **to say nothing of** *sth* not to mention it: *He wastes all his money on alcohol, to say nothing of all those cigarettes.* **to say the least** at least; without exaggeration: *She is, to say the least, a rather irresponsible per-*

son. **you can say that again!** *colloq* you are absolutely right!

saying *n* a proverb or maxim.

say-so *n* **1** an authorized decision. **2** an unsupported claim or assertion.

Sb *symbol, chem* antimony.

Sc *symbol, chem* scandium.

scab *n* **1** a crust of dried blood formed over a healing wound. **2** a contagious skin disease of sheep caused esp by mites, characterized by pustules or scales. **3** a plant disease caused by a fungus, producing crusty spots. **4** *derog, slang* a worker who defies a union's instruction to strike. ➤ *vb* (**scabbed, scabbing**) *intr* **1** (*also* **scab over**) to become covered by a scab. **2** *slang* to work or behave as a scab.

scabbard *n* a sheath, esp for a sword or dagger.

scabby *adj* (**-ier, -iest**) **1** covered with scabs. **2** *derog, colloq* contemptible; worthless.

scabies /'skeɪbiːz/ *n, pathol* a contagious skin disease characterized by severe itching, caused by a secretion of the itch mite, which bores under the skin to lay its eggs.

scabrous /'skeɪbrəs/ *adj* **1** of skin, etc: rough and flaky or scaly. **2** bawdy; smutty or indecent.

scaffold *n* **1** a temporary framework of metal poles and planks used as a platform from which building repairs or construction can be carried out. **2** any temporary platform. **3** a raised platform for eg performers or spectators. **4** (**the scaffold**) a platform on which a person is executed. ○ **scaffolding** *n* **1** an arrangement of scaffolds. **2** materials used for building scaffolds.

scalar *n, maths* a quantity that has magnitude but not direction, such as distance, speed and mass. Compare VECTOR (sense I).

scald *vb* **1** to injure with hot liquid or steam. **2** to treat with hot water so as to sterilize. **3** to cook or heat to just short of boiling point. ➤ *n* an injury caused by scalding. ○ **scalding** *n, adj.*

scale[1] *n* **1** a system or series of markings or divisions at regular intervals, for use in measuring. **2** a measuring device with such markings. **3** the relationship between actual size and the size as represented on a model or drawing. **4** *mus* **a** a defined series of notes; **b** (*usu* **scales**) a succession of these notes performed in ascending or descending order of pitch through one or more octaves. **5** any graded system, eg of employees' salaries. **6** *maths* a numeral system: *logarithmic scale.* **7** extent or level relative to others: *on a grand scale.* ➤ *vb* **1** to climb. ○ (*also* **scale up** and **scale down**) to change something's size according to scale, making it either bigger or smaller than the original. ◆ **on a large, small,** *etc* **scale** in a great, small, etc way. **to scale** in proportion to the actual dimensions.

scale[2] *n* **1** any of the small thin plates that provide a protective covering on the skin of fish and reptiles and on the legs of birds. **2** any readily or easily detached flake. **3** tartar on the teeth. **4** a crusty white deposit formed when hard water is heated, esp in kettles. ➤ *vb* **1** to clear something of scales. **2** to remove in thin layers. **3** *intr* to come off in thin layers or flakes. **4** *intr* to become encrusted with scale. ○ **scaly** *adj.*

scale[3] *n* **1** (**scales**) a device for weighing. **2** the pan, or either of the two pans, of a balance. ➤ *vb* to weigh or weigh up.

scalene *adj, geom* of a triangle: having each side a different length.

scallion *n* a spring onion.

scallop, scollop or **escallop** *n* **1** a marine bivalve mollusc with a strongly ribbed shell consisting of two valves with wavy edges. **2** any of a series of curves forming a wavy edge, eg on fabric. **3** *cookery* an ESCALOPE. ➤ *vb* to shape (an edge) into scallops or curves.

scallywag *n, colloq* a rascal or scamp; a good-for-nothing.

scalp *n* **1** the area of the head covered, or usu covered, by hair. **2** the skin itself on which the hair grows. **3** a piece of this skin with its hair, formerly taken from slain enemies as a trophy, esp by Native Americans. ➤ *vb* **1** to remove the scalp of someone or something. **2** *chiefly US colloq* to buy cheaply in order to resell quickly at a profit.

scalpel *n* a small surgical knife with a thin blade.

scam *n, slang* a trick or swindle.

scamp *n* a cheeky or mischievous person, esp a child.

scamper *vb, intr* to run or skip about briskly, esp in play. ➤ *n* an act of scampering.

scampi *pl n* large prawns. ➤ *sing n* a dish of these prawns, usu deep-fried in breadcrumbs.

scan *vb* (**scanned, scanning**) **1** to read through or examine something carefully or critically. **2** to look or glance over something quickly. **3** to examine (all parts or components of something) in a systematic order. **4** to analyse (verse) metrically. **5** to recite (verse) so as to bring out or emphasize the metrical structure. **6** *intr* of verse: to conform to the rules of metre or rhythm. **7** *med* to examine (parts, esp internal organs, of the body) using techniques such as ultrasound. **8** *comput* to examine (data) eg on a magnetic disk. ➤ *n* **1** an act of scanning. **2** *med* an image obtained by scanning.

scandal *n* **1** widespread public outrage and loss of reputation. **2** any event or fact causing this. **3** any extremely objectionable fact, situation, person or thing. **4** malicious gossip or slander; a false imputation. ○ **scandalous** *adj.*

scandalize or **-ise** *vb* **1** to give or cause scandal or offence to. **2** to shock or outrage.

scandalmonger *n* someone who spreads or relishes malicious gossip.

scandium *n, chem* a soft silvery-white metallic element with a pinkish tinge.

scanner *n* **1** *radar* the rotating aerial by which the beam is made to scan an area. **2** *comput* any device capable of recognizing characters, etc, in documents and generating signals corresponding to them, used esp to input text and graphics directly. **3** *med* any device that produces an image of an internal organ.

scansion *n* **1** the act or practice of scanning poetry. **2** the division of a verse into metrical feet.

scant *adj* in short supply; deficient. ➢ *adv* barely; scantily.

scanty *adj* (*-ier, -iest*) small or lacking in size or amount; barely enough: *a scanty meal.* ○ **scantily** *adv.*

scapegoat *n* someone made to take the blame or punishment for the errors and mistakes of others.

scapula /'skapjʊlə/ *n* (*scapulae* /-liː/ or *scapulas*) *anat* the broad flat triangular bone at the back of the shoulder.

scar¹ *n* **1** a mark left on the skin after a sore or wound has healed. **2** any permanent damaging emotional effect. **3** any mark or blemish. **4** a mark on a plant where a leaf was formerly attached. ➢ *vb* (*scarred, scarring*) *tr & intr* to mark or become marked with a scar.

scar² *n* a steep rocky outcrop or crag on the side of a hill or mountain.

scarab /'skarəb/ *n* **1** a dung beetle, which was regarded as sacred by the ancient Egyptians. **2** an image or carving of the sacred beetle, or a gemstone carved in its shape.

scarce *adj* **1** not often found; rare. **2** in short supply. ➢ *adv* scarcely; hardly ever: *We could scarce see it through the mist.* ○ **scarcity** *n.* ♦ **make oneself scarce** *colloq* to leave quickly or stay away, often for reasons of prudence, tact, etc.

scarcely *adv* **1** only just. **2** hardly ever. **3** not really; not at all: *That is scarcely a reason to hit him.*

scare *vb* **1** *tr & intr* to make or become afraid. **2** to startle. **3** (*usu* **scare sb** or **sth away** or **off**) to drive them away by frightening them. ➢ *n* **1** a fright or panic. **2** a sudden, widespread and often unwarranted public alarm: *a bomb scare.*

scarecrow *n* **1** a device, usu in the shape of a human figure, set up in fields to scare birds. **2** *colloq* a shabbily dressed person.

scaremonger *n* an alarmist, or someone who causes panic or alarm by initiating or spreading rumours of disaster. ○ **scaremongering** *n.*

scarf¹ *n* (*scarves* or *scarfs*) a strip or square of fabric, worn around the neck, shoulders or head.

scarf² *n* a joint made between two ends, esp of timber, cut so as to overlap, producing the effect of a continuous surface. ➢ *vb* to join by means of such a joint.

scarify *vb* (*-ies, -ied*) **1** *chiefly surgery* to make a number of scratches, shallow cuts, or lacerations in (the skin, etc). **2** to break up the surface of soil with a wire rake, etc, without turning the soil over. **3** to hurt someone with severe criticism. ○ **scarification** *n.*

scarlatina *n, pathol* SCARLET FEVER.

scarlet *n* a brilliant red colour.

scarlet fever *n* an acute infectious disease, caused by bacterial infection, and characterized by fever, sore throat, vomiting and a bright red skin rash.

scarp *n* **1** the steep side of a hill or rock; an escarpment. **2** *fortification* the inner side of a defensive ditch, nearest to the rampart.

scarper *vb, intr, colloq* to run away or escape.

scary *adv* (*-ier, -iest*) *colloq* causing fear or anxiety; frightening. ○ **scarily** *adv.* ○ **scariness** *n.*

scat¹ *vb* (*scatted, scatting*) *intr, colloq* esp as a command: to go away; to run off.

scat² *n* a form of jazz singing consisting of improvised sounds rather than words. ➢ *vb* (*scatted, scatting*) *intr* to sing jazz in this way.

scathing *adj* scornfully critical; detrimental: *a scathing attack.*

scatology *n* a morbid interest in or preoccupation with the obscene, esp with excrement, or with literature referring to it. ○ **scatological** *adj.*

scatter *vb* **1** to disperse. **2** to strew, sprinkle or throw around loosely. **3** *tr & intr* to depart or send off in different directions. ➢ *n* **1** an act of scattering. **2** a quantity of scattered items.

scatterbrain *n, colloq* a person incapable of organized thought. ○ **scatterbrained** *adj.*

scatty *adj* (*-ier, -iest*) *Brit colloq* mentally disorganized.

scavenge *vb, tr & intr* to search among waste for (usable items).

scavenger *n* **1** a person who searches among waste for usable items. **2** an animal that feeds on refuse or decaying flesh.

scenario *n* **1** a rough outline of a dramatic work, film, etc; a synopsis. **2** any hypothetical situation or sequence of events.

scene *n* **1** the setting in which a real or imaginary event takes place. **2** the representation of action on the stage. **3** a division of a play, indicated by the fall of the curtain, a change of place or the entry or exit of an important character. **4** a unit of action in a book or film. **5** any of the pieces making up a stage or film set, or the set as a whole. **6** a landscape, situation or picture of a place or action as seen by someone: *A delightful scene met their eyes.* **7** an embarrassing and unseemly display of emotion in public: *make a scene.* **8** *colloq* the publicity, action, etc surrounding a particular activity or profession: *the current music scene.* **9** *colloq* a liked or preferred area of interest or activity: *Rock concerts are just not my scene.* ♦ **behind the scenes 1** out of sight of the audience; backstage. **2** unknown to the public. **come on the scene** to arrive; to become part of the current situation: *Everything was fine until he came on the scene.* **set the scene** to describe the background to an event.

scenery *n* (*-ies*) **1** a picturesque landscape, esp one that is rural. **2** the items making up a stage or film set.

scenic *adj* referring to, being or including attractive natural landscapes: *the scenic route.*

scent n 1 the distinctive smell of a person, animal or plant. 2 a trail of this left behind. 3 a series of clues or findings leading to a major discovery: *The police are on the scent of the drug baron.* 4 perfume. ➢ vb 1 to smell; to discover or discern by smell. 2 to sense; to be aware of something by instinct or intuition. 3 *intr* to give out a smell, esp a pleasant one. 4 to perfume. ○ **scented** adj having a smell; fragrant or perfumed. ♦ **put** or **throw sb off the scent** to deliberately mislead them.

sceptic or (*N Am*) **skeptic** /'skɛptɪk/ n 1 someone with a tendency to disbelieve or doubt the veracity or validity of other people's motives, ideas, opinions, etc. 2 someone who questions widely accepted, esp religious, doctrines and beliefs. ○ **sceptical** adj. ○ **scepticism** n.

sceptre or (*US*) **scepter** n a ceremonial staff or baton carried by a monarch as a symbol of sovereignty. ○ **sceptred** adj.

schedule n 1 a list of events or activities planned to take place at certain times. 2 the state of an event or activity occurring on time, according to plan: *We are well behind schedule.* ➢ vb 1 to plan or arrange something to take place at a certain time. 2 to put something on a schedule.

schema /'ski:mə/ n (*schemata*) 1 a scheme or plan. 2 a diagrammatic outline or synopsis.

schematic adj 1 following or involving a particular plan or arrangement. 2 represented by a diagram or plan. ○ **schematically** adv.

scheme n 1 a plan of action. 2 a system or programme: *a pension scheme.* 3 a careful arrangement of different components: *a colour scheme.* 4 a secret plan intended to cause harm or damage. 5 a diagram or table. ➢ vb, intr to plan or act secretly and often maliciously. ○ **schemer** n. ○ **scheming** adj, n.

scherzo /'skɛətsoʊ/ n (*scherzos* or *scherzi* /-siː/) a lively piece of music, generally the second or third part of a symphony, sonata, etc, replacing the minuet.

schilling n the former standard unit of currency of Austria, replaced in 2002 by the euro.

schism /'skɪzəm/ n, relig a breach or separation from the main group, or into opposing groups. ○ **schismatic** adj.

schist /ʃɪst/ n, geol a coarse-grained metamorphic rock that splits readily into layers.

schistosomiasis /ʃɪstəsoʊ'maɪəsɪs/ n, pathol a tropical disease, transmitted by contaminated water and caused by infestation with parasitic flukes.

schizo /'skɪtsoʊ/ colloq, n a schizophrenic person. ➢ adj schizophrenic.

schizoid /'skɪtsɔɪd/ adj displaying some symptoms of schizophrenia, such as introversion or tendency to fantasy, but without a diagnosed mental disorder.

schizophrenia /skɪtsə'friːnɪə/ n a severe mental disorder characterized by loss of contact with reality, impairment of thought processes, a marked personality change, loss of emotional responsiveness and social withdrawal. ○ **schizophrenic** n, adj.

schmaltz n, colloq extreme or excessive sentimentality, esp in music or other art. ○ **schmaltzy** adj.

schnapps n a strong dry alcoholic spirit, esp Dutch gin distilled from potatoes.

schnitzel n a veal cutlet.

scholar n 1 a learned person, esp an academic. 2 a person who studies; a pupil or student. 3 a person receiving a scholarship. ○ **scholarliness** n. ○ **scholarly** adj.

scholarship n 1 the achievements or learning of a scholar. 2 a sum of money awarded, usu to an outstanding student, for the purposes of further study.

scholastic adj referring or relating to learning institutions, such as schools or universities, and to their teaching and education methods.

school¹ n 1 a place or institution where education is received, esp primary or secondary education. 2 the building or room used for this purpose. 3 the work of such an institution. 4 the body of students and teachers that occupy such a place. 5 the period of the day or year during which such a place is open to students: *Stay behind after school.* 6 the disciples or adherents of a particular teacher. 7 a group of painters, writers or other artists sharing the same style. 8 any activity or set of surroundings as a provider of experience: *Factories are the schools of life.* ➢ vb 1 to educate in a school. 2 to give training or instruction of a particular kind to. 3 to discipline. ○ **schooling** n.

school² n a group of fish, whales or other marine animals swimming together. ➢ vb, intr to gather into or move about in a school.

schoolmaster or **schoolmistress** n respectively, a male or female schoolteacher.

schoolteacher n a person who teaches in a school.

schooner n 1 a fast sailing ship with two or more masts, and rigged fore-and-aft. 2 Brit a large sherry glass. 3 N Am a large beer glass.

schottische /ʃɒ'tiːʃ/ n a German folk dance, similar to a slow polka.

sciatic /saɪ'atɪk/ adj 1 referring or relating to the hip region. 2 affected by sciatica.

sciatica /saɪ'atɪkə/ n, pathol pain in the lower back, buttocks and backs of the thighs caused by pressure on the sciatic nerve.

science n 1 the systematic observation and classification of natural phenomena in order to learn about them and bring them under general principles and laws. 2 a department or branch of such knowledge or study developed in this way, eg astronomy, genetics or chemistry. 3 any area of knowledge obtained using, or arranged according to, formal principles: *political science.* 4 acquired skill or technique, as opposed to natural ability. ○ **scientist** n.

science fiction n imaginative fiction presenting a view of life in the future, based on great scientific and technological advances.

scientific adj 1 referring or relating to, or used in, science. 2 displaying the kind of principled approach characteristic of science. ○ **scientifically** adv.

sci-fi n, colloq science fiction.

scimitar n a sword with a short curved single-edged blade, broadest at the point end.

scintilla /sɪnˈtɪlə/ n, literary a hint or trace; an iota.

scintillate vb, intr 1 to sparkle or emit sparks. 2 to capture attention or impress with one's vitality or wit. ○ **scintillating** adj brilliant or sparkling; full of interest or wit.

scion /ˈsaɪən/ n 1 bot the detached shoot of a plant inserted into a cut in the outer stem of another plant when making a graft. 2 a descendant or offspring; a younger member of a family.

scissors pl n a one-handed cutting device with two long blades pivoted in the middle so the cutting edges close and overlap.

sclera /ˈsklɪərə/ n the outermost membrane of the eyeball.

sclerosis /sklɪˈrəʊsɪs/ n, pathol abnormal hardening or thickening of an artery or other body part, esp as a result of inflammation or disease.

scoff¹ vb, intr (often scoff at sb or sth) to express scorn or contempt for them; to jeer. ➤ n an expression of scorn; a jeer. ○ **scoffer** n.

scoff² vb, tr & intr, colloq to eat (food) rapidly and greedily.

scold vb 1 to reprimand or rebuke. 2 intr to use strong or offensive language. ➤ n, old use a nagging or quarrelsome person, esp a woman. ○ **scolding** n.

scollop see SCALLOP

sconce n a candlestick or lantern fixed by a bracket to a wall, or one with a handle.

scone /skɒn, skəʊn/ n a small flattish plain cake, sometimes containing dried fruit.

scoop vb 1 (also scoop sth up) to lift, dig or remove it with a sweeping circular movement. 2 (also scoop sth out) to empty or hollow it with such movements. 3 to do better than (rival newspapers) in being the first to publish a story. ➤ n 1 a spoonlike implement for handling or serving food. 2 a hollow shovel or lipped container for lifting loose material. 3 anything of a similar shape. 4 a scooping movement. 5 a quantity scooped. 6 a news story printed by one newspaper in advance of all others.

scoot vb, intr, colloq to make off speedily. ➤ n the act of scooting.

scooter n 1 a child's toy vehicle consisting of a board on a two-wheeled frame, with tall handlebars connected to the front wheel, propelled by pushing against the ground with one foot. 2 (in full motor scooter) a small-wheeled motorcycle with a protective front shield curving back to form a support for the feet.

scope n 1 the size or range of a subject or topic covered. 2 the aim, intention or purpose of

something. 3 the limits within which there is the opportunity to act. 4 range of understanding: beyond his scope.

scorch vb 1 tr & intr to burn or be burned slightly or superficially. 2 to dry up, parch or wither. 3 to injure with severe criticism or scorn. ➤ n 1 an act of scorching. 2 a scorched area or burn. 3 a mark made by scorching. ○ **scorcher** n, colloq an extremely hot day. ○ **scorching** adj, colloq 1 of the weather: very hot. 2 of a criticism, etc: harsh.

score n 1 a total number of points gained or achieved eg in a game. 2 an act of gaining or achieving a point, etc. 3 a scratch or shallow cut. 4 a set of twenty: three score. 5 (scores) very many; lots: I have scores of letters to write. 6 (the score) colloq the current situation; the essential facts: What's the score with your job? 7 a written or printed copy of music for several parts, set out vertically down the page. 8 the music from a film or play. 9 (the score) a reason; grounds: rejected on the score of expense. 10 a grievance or grudge: He has an old score to settle. 11 a record of amounts owed. ➤ vb 1 tr & intr to gain or achieve (a point) in a game. 2 intr to keep a record of points gained during a game. 3 to make cuts or scratches in the surface of something; to mark (a line) by a shallow cut. 4 to be equivalent to (a number of points): A black king scores three. 5 mus to adapt music for instruments or voices other than those originally intended. 6 to compose music for a film or play. 7 intr to achieve a rating; to be judged or regarded: This film scores high for entertainment value. 8 (often score with sb) slang to succeed in having sexual intercourse with them. ○ **scorer** n. ♦ **know the score** to know or be aware of the facts of a situation. **on that score** as regards that matter or concern: She has no worries on that score. **over the score** colloq beyond reasonable limits; unfair. **settle a score** to repay an old grudge or debt. ◊ **score off sb** to humiliate them for personal advantage; to get the better of them.

scoreboard n a board on which the score in a game is displayed.

scorn n extreme or mocking contempt. ➤ vb 1 to treat someone or something with scorn; to express scorn for. 2 to refuse or reject with scorn. ○ **scornful** adj contemptuous. ○ **scornfully** adv.

Scorpio n, astrol a the eighth sign of the zodiac; b a person born between 23 October and 22 November, under this sign.

scorpion n an invertebrate animal, found in hot regions, with eight legs, powerful claw-like pincers and a long thin segmented abdomen or 'tail', bearing a poisonous sting, that is carried arched over its back.

Scot n a native or inhabitant of Scotland.

Scotch adj of things, esp products, but not usu of people: Scottish: Scotch broth • Scotch eggs. ➤ n Scotch whisky.

scotch vb 1 to ruin or hinder eg plans. 2 to reveal (something, esp rumours) to be untrue.

scot-free *adj* unpunished or unharmed.

Scots *adj* **1** Scottish by birth. **2** esp of law and language: Scottish. ➤ *n* Lowland Scots. ○ **Scotsman** and **Scotswoman** *n*.

Scottish *adj* belonging or relating to Scotland or its inhabitants.

scoundrel *n* an unprincipled or villainous rogue.

scour[1] *vb* **1** to clean, polish or remove by hard rubbing. **2** to flush clean with a jet or current of water.

scour[2] *vb* **1** to make an exhaustive search of (an area). **2** to range over or move quickly over (an area).

scourge /skɜːdʒ/ *n* **1** a cause of great suffering and affliction, esp to many people. **2** a whip used for punishing. ➤ *vb* **1** to cause suffering to; to afflict. **2** to whip.

scout *n* **1** *mil* a person or group sent out to observe the enemy and bring back information. **2** (*often* **Scout**, *formerly* **Boy Scout**) a member of the Scout Association. **3** in the US: a member of the **Girl Scouts**, an organization similar to the Guides. **4** a TALENT SCOUT. **5** *colloq* a search. ➤ *vb, intr* **1** to act as a scout. **2** (*often* **scout about** or **around**) *colloq* to make a search.

scowl *vb, intr* to look disapprovingly, angrily or menacingly. ➤ *n* a scowling expression. ○ **scowling** *adj*.

scrabble *vb, intr* **1** to scratch, grope or struggle frantically. **2** to scrawl. ➤ *n* an act of scrabbling.

scrag *n* **1** the thin part of a neck of mutton or veal, providing poor quality meat. **2** an unhealthily thin person or animal. **3** *slang* the human neck. ○ **scraggy** *adj* (*-ier, -iest*) unhealthily thin; scrawny.

scram *vb* (**scrammed, scramming**) *intr, colloq* often as a command: to go away at once; to be off.

scramble *vb* **1** *intr* to crawl or climb using hands and feet, esp hurriedly or frantically. **2** *intr* to struggle violently against others: *starving people scrambling to find food*. **3** to cook (eggs) whisked up with milk, butter, etc. **4** to throw or jumble together haphazardly. **5** to re-write (a message) in code form, for secret transmission. **6** to transmit (a message) in a distorted form intelligible only by means of an electronic scrambler. **7** *intr* of military aircraft or air crew: to take off immediately in response to an emergency. ➤ *n* **1** an act of scrambling. **2** a dash or struggle to beat others in getting something. **3** a walk or hike over rough ground. **4** an immediate take-off in an emergency. **5** a cross-country car or motorcycle race. ○ **scrambling** *adj, n*.

scrambler *n, electronics* a device that modifies radio or telephone signals so that they can only be made intelligible using a special decoding device.

scrap[1] *n* **1** a small piece; a fragment. **2** waste material, esp metal, for recycling or re-using. **3** (**scraps**) leftover pieces of food. ➤ *vb* (**scrapped, scrapping**) to discard or cease to use; to abandon as unworkable. ♦ **not a scrap** not even the smallest amount.

scrap[2] *colloq, n* a fight or quarrel, usu physical. ➤ *vb* (**scrapped, scrapping**) *intr* to fight or quarrel.

scrapbook *n* a book with blank pages for pasting in cuttings, pictures, etc.

scrape *vb* **1** (*also* **scrape sth along, over**, *etc* sth) to push or drag (esp a sharp object) along or over (a hard or rough surface). **2** *intr* to move along a surface with a grazing action. **3** to graze (the skin) by a scraping action. **4** to move along (a surface) with a grating sound. **5** *intr* to make a grating sound. **6** (*also* **scrape sth off**) to remove it from or smooth (a surface) with such an action. **7** to make savings through hardship: *We managed to scrape enough for a holiday*. ➤ *n* **1** an instance, process or act of dragging or grazing. **2** a part damaged or cleaned by scraping. **3** a scraped area in the ground. **4** a graze (of the skin). **5** *colloq* a difficult or embarrassing situation or predicament. **6** *colloq* a fight or quarrel. ○ **scraper** *n*. ♦ **bow and scrape** to be over-obsequious. **scrape the bottom of the barrel** to utilize the very last and worst of one's resources, opinions, etc. ◊ **scrape through** or **by** to manage or succeed in doing something narrowly or with difficulty. **scrape sth together** or **up** to collect it little by little, usu with difficulty.

scrap heap *n* **1** a place where unwanted and useless objects, eg old furniture, are collected. **2** the state of being discarded or abandoned: *They consigned the idea to the scrap heap*. ♦ **throw sth** or **sb on the scrap heap** to reject or discard it or them as useless.

scrappy *adj* (*-ier, -iest*) fragmentary or disjointed; not uniform or flowing. ○ **scrappiness** *n*.

scratch *vb* **1** to draw a sharp or pointed object across (a surface), causing damage or making marks. **2** to make (a mark) by such action. **3** *tr & intr* to rub the skin with the fingernails, esp to relieve itching. **4** to dig or scrape with the claws. **5** (*usu* **scratch sth out** or **off**) to erase or cancel it. **6** *intr* to make a grating noise. **7** *intr* to withdraw from a contest, competition, etc. ➤ *n* **1** an act of scratching. **2** a mark made by scratching. **3** a scratching sound. **4** a superficial wound or minor injury. ➤ *adj* **1** casually or hastily got together; improvised: *a scratch meal*. **2** of a competitor: not given a handicap. ○ **scratchy** *adj*. ♦ **come up to scratch** *colloq* to meet the required or expected standard. **from scratch** from the beginning; without the benefit of any preparation or previous experience. **scratch the surface** to deal only superficially with an issue or problem.

scratchcard *n* a lottery card covered with a thin opaque film, which is scratched off to reveal symbols or numbers which may correspond to prizes.

scrawl vb, tr & intr to write or draw illegibly, untidily or hurriedly. ➤ n untidy or illegible handwriting.

scrawny adj (-ier, -iest) unhealthily thin and bony.

scream vb 1 tr & intr to cry out in a loud high-pitched voice, as in fear, pain or anger. 2 intr to laugh shrilly or uproariously. 3 (often **scream at sb**) usu of something unpleasant or garish: to be all too obvious or apparent: *Those colours really scream at you.* ➤ n 1 a sudden loud piercing cry or noise. 2 colloq an extremely amusing person, thing or event.

scree n, geol a sloping mass of rock debris that piles up at the base of cliffs or on the side of a mountain.

screech n a harsh, shrill and sudden cry, voice or noise. ➤ vb 1 tr & intr to utter a screech or make a sound like a screech. 2 to speak in such a way.

screed n a long and often tedious spoken or written passage.

screen n 1 a set of hinged panels that can be folded and unfolded to partition off part of a room for privacy. 2 a single panel used for protection against strong heat or light, or any other outside influence. 3 a WINDSCREEN. 4 a wire netting placed over windows for keeping out insects. 5 the surface on which the images are formed on a television or computer. 6 a white surface onto which films or slides are projected. 7 (**the screen**) the medium of cinema or television: *She is a star of the stage and the screen.* ➤ vb 1 to shelter or conceal. 2 to subject someone to tests in order to discern their ability, reliability, worthiness, etc. 3 to test someone in order to check for the presence of disease. 4 to show or project (a film, programme, etc) at the cinema or on TV. ○ **screening** n.

screenplay n the script of a film, comprising dialogue, stage directions and details for characters and sets.

screen printing, **screen process** or **silk-screen printing** n a stencil technique in which coloured ink is forced through a fine silk or nylon mesh.

screen saver n, comput a program which temporarily blanks out a screen display, or displays a preset pattern, when a computer is switched on but is not in active use.

screen test n a filmed audition to test whether or not an actor or actress is suitable for cinema work.

screw n 1 a small fastening device consisting of a metal cylinder with a spiral ridge down the shaft and a slot in its head, driven into position in wood, etc by rotation using a screwdriver. 2 any object similar in shape or function. 3 the turn or twist of a screw. 4 snooker, billiards a shot in which the cue ball is subjected to sidespin or backspin. 5 slang a prison officer. 6 coarse slang an act of sexual intercourse. ➤ vb 1 to twist (a screw) into place. 2 to push

or pull with a twisting action. 3 colloq to swindle or cheat. 4 snooker, billiards to put sidespin or backspin on (the cue ball). 5 tr & intr, coarse slang to have sexual intercourse with someone. ◆ **have a screw loose** colloq to be slightly mad or crazy. **have one's head screwed on (the right way)** colloq to be a sensible person. **put the screws on sb** colloq to use force or pressure on them. ◊ **screw sth up** slang to bungle it.

screwball n, slang, N Am a crazy person; an eccentric. ➤ adj crazy; eccentric.

screwdriver n a hand-held tool with a metal shaft with a shaped end that fits into the slot, etc on a screw's head, turned repeatedly to twist a screw into position.

screwed-up adj, slang of a person: extremely anxious, nervous or psychologically disturbed.

screwy adj (-ier, -iest) colloq crazy; eccentric.

scribble vb 1 tr & intr to write quickly or untidily; to scrawl. 2 intr to draw meaningless lines or shapes absent-mindedly. ➤ n 1 untidy or illegible handwriting; scrawl. 2 meaningless written lines or shapes.

scribe n 1 a person employed to make handwritten copies of documents before printing was invented. 2 in biblical times: a Jewish lawyer or teacher of law.

scrimmage or **scrummage** n 1 a noisy brawl or struggle. 2 a spell of play in American football. 3 rugby a SCRUM (sense 1). ➤ vb, intr to take part in a scrimmage.

scrimp vb, intr to live economically; to be frugal or sparing. ◆ **scrimp and save** to be sparing and niggardly, often out of necessity.

scrip n 1 colloq a doctor's prescription. 2 commerce a provisional certificate issued before a formal share certificate is drawn up.

script n 1 a piece of handwriting. 2 type which imitates handwriting, or vice versa. 3 the printed text of a play, film or broadcast. 4 a set of characters used for writing; an alphabet: Cyrillic script. 5 a candidate's examination answer paper. ➤ vb to write the script of (a play, film or broadcast).

scripture or **Scripture** n 1 the sacred writings of a religion. 2 (also **the Scriptures**) the Christian Bible. ○ **scriptural** adj.

scriptwriter n a person who writes scripts. ○ **scriptwriting** n.

scrofula n, pathol the former name for tuberculosis of the lymph nodes, esp of the neck.

scroll n 1 a roll of paper or parchment usu containing an inscription, now only a ceremonial format, eg for academic degrees. 2 an ancient text in this format: *the Dead Sea Scrolls.* 3 a decorative spiral shape, eg carved in stonework or in handwriting. ➤ vb 1 to roll or cut into a scroll or scrolls. 2 tr & intr, comput (often **scroll up** or **down**) to move the text displayed on a VDU up or down to bring into view data that cannot all be seen at the same time.

Scrooge n a miserly person.

scrotum n (scrota or scrotums) biol the sac of

skin that encloses the testicles.

scrounge vb **1** tr & intr, colloq to get something by asking or begging; to cadge or sponge. **2** intr (often **scrounge for sth**) to hunt or search around for it. ○ **scrounger** n.

scrub¹ vb (**scrubbed, scrubbing**) **1** tr & intr to rub something hard in order to remove dirt. **2** to wash or clean by hard rubbing. **3** colloq to cancel or abandon (plans, etc). ➢ n an act of scrubbing. ◊ **scrub up** of a surgeon, etc, before an operation: to wash the hands thoroughly.

scrub² n **1** vegetation consisting of stunted trees and evergreen shrubs collectively. **2** (also **scrubland**) an area, usu with poor soil or low rainfall, containing such vegetation. ➢ adj small or insignificant.

scrubber n, offensive slang a woman who regularly indulges in casual sex.

scrubby adj (**-ier, -iest**) **1** covered with scrub. **2** of trees, shrubs, etc: stunted.

scruff¹ n the back or nape of the neck.

scruff² n, colloq a dirty untidy person.

scruffy adj (**-ier, -iest**) shabby and untidy. ○ **scruffily** adv. ○ **scruffiness** n.

scrum n **1** rugby the restarting of play when the forwards from both teams hunch together and tightly interlock their arms and heads in readiness for the ball being thrown in. **2** colloq a riotous struggle.

scrummage see SCRIMMAGE

scrummy adj (**-ier, -iest**) chiefly Brit colloq delicious; scrumptious.

scrumptious adj, colloq **1** delicious. **2** delightful. ○ **scrumptiously** adv.

scrumpy n (**-ies**) strong dry cider with a harsh taste made from small sweet apples.

scrunch vb **1** tr & intr to crunch or crush, esp with relation to the noise produced. **2** intr to make a crunching sound. ➢ n an act or the sound of scrunching.

scruple n (usu **scruples**) a sense of moral responsibility making one reluctant or unwilling to do wrong: He has no scruples. ➢ vb, intr to be reluctant or unwilling because of scruples: I would scruple to steal even if we were starving.

scrupulous adj **1** having scruples; being careful to do nothing morally wrong. **2** extremely conscientious and meticulous. ○ **scrupulously** adv.

scrutinize or **-ise** vb to subject to scrutiny.

scrutiny n (**-ies**) **1** a close, careful and thorough examination or inspection. **2** a penetrating or searching look.

scuba n a device consisting of one or two cylinders of compressed air connected by a tube to a mouthpiece allowing divers to breathe under water.

scud vb (**scudded, scudding**) intr **1** esp of clouds: to sweep quickly and easily across the sky. **2** esp of sailing vessels: to sail swiftly driven by the force of a strong wind.

scuff vb, tr & intr to drag (the feet) when walking. **2** to brush, graze or scrape (esp shoes or heels) while walking. ➢ n **1** the act of scuffing.

2 an area worn away by scuffing.

scuffle n a confused fight or struggle. ➢ vb, intr to take part in a scuffle.

scull n **1** either of a pair of short light oars used by one rower. **2** a small light racing boat propelled by one rower using a pair of such oars. **3** a large single oar over the stern of a boat, moved from side to side to propel it forward. **4** an act or spell of sculling. ➢ vb to propel with a scull or sculls. ○ **sculler** n.

scullery n (**-ies**) a room attached to the kitchen where basic chores are carried out.

sculpt vb **1** tr & intr to carve or model. **2** to sculpture.

sculptor or **sculptress** n a person who practises the art of sculpture.

sculpture n **1** the art or act of carving or modelling with clay, wood, stone, plaster, etc. **2** a work, or works, of art produced in this way. ➢ vb **1** to carve, mould or sculpt. **2** to represent in sculpture. ○ **sculptural** adj.

scum n **1** dirt or waste matter floating on the surface of a liquid, esp in the form of foam or froth. **2** colloq, derog a worthless or contemptible person or such people. ➢ vb (**scummed, scumming**) **1** to remove the scum from (a liquid). **2** intr to form or throw up a scum. ○ **scummy** adj (**-ier, -iest**).

scupper¹ vb **1** colloq to ruin or put an end to (a plan, an idea, etc). **2** to deliberately sink (a ship).

scupper² n (usu **scuppers**) naut a hole or pipe in a ship's side through which water is drained off the deck.

scurf n **1** small flakes of dead skin, esp DANDRUFF. **2** any flaking or peeling substance.

scurrilous adj indecently insulting or abusive, and unjustly damaging to the reputation.

scurry n (**-ies**) **1** an act of or the sound of scurrying. **2** a sudden brief gust or fall, eg of wind or snow; a flurry.

scurvy n, pathol a disease caused by deficiency of vitamin C and characterized by swollen bleeding gums, amnesia, bruising and pain in the joints. ➢ adj (**-ier, -iest**) vile; contemptible.

scut n a short tail, esp of a rabbit, hare or deer.

scuttle¹ n (in full **coal scuttle**) a container for holding coal, usu kept near a fire.

scuttle² vb, intr to move quickly with haste; to scurry. ➢ n a scuttling pace or movement.

scuttle³ n a lidded opening in a ship's side or deck. ➢ vb **1** naut to deliberately sink (a ship) by making holes in it or by opening the lids of the scuttles. **2** to ruin or destroy (eg plans).

scythe /saɪð/ n a tool with a wooden handle and a long curved blade set at right angles, for cutting tall crops or grass. ➢ vb to cut with a scythe.

SE abbrev south-east or south-eastern.

Se symbol, chem selenium.

sea n **1** (usu **the sea**) the large expanse of salt water covering the greater part of the Earth's surface. **2** any geographical division of this, eg the Mediterranean Sea. **3** an area of this with reference to its calmness or turbulence: *choppy seas*. **4** a large inland saltwater lake, eg the Dead Sea. **5** anything resembling the sea in its seemingly limitless mass or expanse: *a sea of paperwork*. ♦ **at sea 1** away from land; in a ship on the sea or ocean. **2** completely disorganized or bewildered. **go to sea** to become a sailor.

sea anemone *n* a marine invertebrate with a round brightly-coloured body and stinging tentacles.

seaboard *n* a coast; the boundary between land and sea.

sea dog *n* an old or experienced sailor.

seafaring *adj* travelling by or working at sea. ○ **seafarer** *n*.

seafood *n* shellfish and other edible marine fish.

seafront *n* the side of the land, a town or a building facing the sea.

seagoing *adj* of a ship: suitable for sea travel.

seagull see GULL

seahorse *n* a small fish with a horse-like head and neck.

seal¹ *n* **1** a piece of wax, lead or other material, attached to a document and stamped with an official mark to show authenticity. **2** such a mark: *the royal seal*. **3** an engraved metal stamp for making such a mark eg on wax. **4** a similar piece of material, with or without an official stamp, for keeping something closed. **5** a piece of rubber or other material serving to keep a joint airtight or watertight. **6** a token or object given, or a gesture made, as a pledge or guarantee. ➢ *vb* **1** to fix a seal to something. **2** to fasten or stamp something with a seal. **3** to decide, settle or confirm: *seal someone's fate*. **4** (*sometimes* **seal sth up**) to make it securely closed, airtight or watertight with a seal. **5** to close, esp permanently. **6** (**seal sth off**) to isolate an area, preventing entry by unauthorized persons.

seal² *n* **1** a marine mammal with a smooth-skinned or furry streamlined body and limbs modified to form webbed flippers. **2** sealskin. ➢ *vb, intr* to hunt seals.

sealant *n* any material used for sealing a gap to prevent the leaking of water, etc.

sea legs *pl n* **1** the ability to resist seasickness. **2** the ability to walk steadily on the deck of a pitching ship.

sea level *n* the mean level of the surface of the sea between high and low tides, therefore the point from which land height is measured.

seal of approval *n, often facetious* official approval.

sealskin *n* the prepared skin of a furry seal, or an imitation of it.

seam *n* **1** a join between edges, esp one that has been welded. **2** a similar join where pieces of fabric have been stitched together. **3** *geol* a layer of coal or ore in the earth. ➢ *vb* **1** to join edge to edge. **2** to scar or wrinkle. ○ **seamless** *adj*.

seaman *n* a sailor below the rank of officer. ○ **seamanship** *n* sailing skills.

seamstress *n* a woman who sews, esp as a profession.

seamy *adj* (**-ier, -iest**) sordid; disreputable.

séance or **seance** /ˈseɪɒns/ *n* a meeting at which a person, esp a spiritualist, attempts to contact the spirits of dead people on behalf of other people present.

seaplane *n* an aeroplane designed to take off from and land on water.

sear *vb* **1** to scorch. **2** to dry out or wither. ➢ *n* a mark made by scorching. ○ **searing** *adj* burning or intense: *searing heat*.

search *vb* **1** *tr & intr* to explore something thoroughly in order to try to find someone or something. **2** to check the clothing or body of someone for concealed objects. **3** to examine closely or scrutinize: *search one's conscience*. **4** to ransack. ➢ *n* an act of searching.

searching *adj* seeking to discover the truth by intensive examination or observation: *a searching inquiry*.

searchlight *n* a lamp and reflector throwing a powerful beam of light for illuminating an area in darkness.

search party *n* a group of people participating in an organized search for a missing person or thing.

seashell *n* the empty shell of a marine invertebrate, esp a mollusc.

seashore *n* the land immediately adjacent to the sea.

seasick *adj* suffering from nausea caused by the rolling or dipping motion of a ship. ○ **seasickness** *n*.

seaside *n* (*usu* **the seaside**) a coastal area or town, esp a holiday resort.

season *n* **1** any of the four major periods (SPRING, SUMMER, AUTUMN and WINTER) into which the year is divided according to changes in weather patterns and other natural phenomena. **2** any period having particular characteristics: *our busy season*. **3** a period of the year during which a particular sport, activity, etc is played or carried out: *holiday season*. **4** a period during which a particular fruit or vegetable is in plentiful supply. **5** any particular period of time. ➢ *vb* **1** to flavour (food) by adding salt, pepper and/or other herbs and spices. **2** to prepare something, esp timber, for use by drying it out. **3** to add interest or liveliness to something. ♦ **in season 1** of food, esp fruit and vegetables: readily available, as determined by its growing season. **2** of game animals: legally allowed to be hunted and killed, according to the time of year. **3** of a female animal: ready to mate; on heat. **out of season 1** of food, esp fruit and vegetables: not yet available. **2** of game animals: legally not yet to be hunted.

seasonable *adj* **1** of weather: appropriate to the particular season. **2** coming or occurring at the right time.

seasonable, seasonal | **Seasonable**
means appropriate to the season, ie opportune; **seasonal** is a more neutral word relating to the seasons of the year.

seasonal *adj* available, taking place or occurring only at certain times of the year. ○ **seasonally** *adv.*

seasoned *adj* **1** of food: flavoured. **2** matured or conditioned: *seasoned wood.* **3** experienced: *seasoned travellers.*

seasoning *n* any substance such as salt, pepper, herbs, spices, etc used to season food.

season ticket *n* a ticket, usu bought at a reduced price, allowing a specified or unlimited number of visits or journeys during a fixed period.

seat *n* **1** anything designed or intended for sitting on, eg a chair, bench, saddle, etc. **2** the part of it on which a person sits. **3** a place for sitting, eg in a cinema or theatre, esp a reservation for such a place: *We booked early to get the good seats.* **4** the buttocks. **5** the part of a garment covering the buttocks. **6** the base of an object, or any part on which it rests or fits. **7** a parliamentary or local government constituency. **8** a position on a committee or other administrative body. **9** a large country house or mansion. ➤ *vb* **1** to place on a seat. **2** to cause to sit down. **3** to assign a seat to someone, eg at a dinner table. **4** to provide seats for (a specified number of people): *My car seats five.* ◆ **by the seat of one's pants** instinctively; by intuition. **take a seat** to sit down.

seat belt *n* a safety belt that prevents a passenger in a car, aeroplane, etc from being thrown violently forward in the event of an emergency stop, a crash, etc.

seating *n* **1** the provision of seats. **2** the number, allocation or arrangement of seats, eg in a dining room.

sea urchin *n* a small ECHINODERM with a spherical or heart-shaped shell covered by protective spines.

seaward *adj* facing or moving towards the sea. ➤ *adv* (*also* **seawards**) towards the sea.

seaweed *n* the common name for any of numerous species of marine algae.

seaworthy *adj* of a ship: fit for a voyage at sea. ○ **seaworthiness** *n.*

sebaceous *adj* similar to, characteristic of or secreting sebum.

sebaceous gland *n, anat* in mammals: any of the tiny glands in the skin that protect the skin by secretion of SEBUM.

sebum /ˈsiːbəm/ *n, biol* the oily substance secreted by the sebaceous glands that lubricates and waterproofs the hair and skin.

sec¹ *n, colloq* short for SECOND² (sense 3): *wait a sec.* ➤ *abbrev* SECOND² (sense 1).

sec² *abbrev* secant.

secant /ˈsiːkənt/ *n* **1** *geom* a straight line that cuts a curve at one or more places. **2** *maths* for a given angle in a right-angled triangle: the ratio of the length of the hypotenuse to the length of the side adjacent to the angle under consideration; the reciprocal of the cosine of an angle.

secateurs /sɛkəˈtɜːz/ *pl n* small sharp shears for pruning bushes, etc.

secede *vb, intr* to withdraw formally, eg from a political or religious body or alliance. ○ **secession** *n.*

seclude *vb* **1** to keep away or isolate from other contacts, associations or influences. **2** to keep out of view.

secluded *adj* **1** protected or away from people and noise; private and quiet. **2** hidden from view.

seclusion *n* **1** the state of being secluded or the act of secluding. **2** a private place.

second¹ /ˈsɛkənd/ (*often written* **2nd**) *adj* **1** in counting: next after or below the first, in order of sequence or importance. **2** alternate; other: *every second week.* **3** additional; supplementary: *Have a second go.* **4** subordinate; inferior: *second to none.* ➤ *n* **1** someone or something next in sequence after the first; someone or something of second class. **2** a person coming second, eg in a race or exam: *He finished a poor second.* **3** (**the second**) the second day of the month. **4** an assistant to a boxer or duellist. **5** *mus* the interval between successive notes of the diatonic scale. **6** a flawed or imperfect article sold at reduced price. **7** (**seconds**) *colloq* a second helping of food. ➤ *vb* **1** to declare formal support for (a proposal, or the person making it). **2** to give support or encouragement to someone or something. **3** to act as second to (a boxer or duellist). ➤ *adv* secondly. ○ **secondly** *adv* **1** used to introduce the second point in a list. **2** in the second place; as a second consideration. ◆ **second to none** best or supreme; unsurpassed or exceptional.

second² /ˈsɛkənd/ *n* **1** a unit of time equal to ¹⁄₆₀ of a minute. **2** *geom* (*symbol* ″) a unit of angular measurement equal to ¹⁄₃₆₀₀ of a degree or ¹⁄₆₀ of a minute. **3** a moment: *wait a second.*

second³ /səˈkɒnd/ *vb* to transfer someone temporarily to a different post, place or duty. ○ **secondment** *n.*

secondary *adj* **1** being of lesser importance than the principal or primary concern; subordinate. **2** developed from something earlier or original: *a secondary infection.* **3** of education: between primary and higher or further, for pupils aged between 11 and 18. **4** *geol* (**Secondary**) relating to the MESOZOIC era. ➤ *n* (*-ies*) **1** a subordinate person or thing. **2** a delegate or deputy. **3** (**the Secondary**) the MESOZOIC era.

secondary colour *n* a colour obtained by mixing or superimposing two primary colours.

second class *n* the next class or category after the first in quality or worth. ➤ *adj* (**second-class**) **1** referring or relating to the class below the first. **2** being of a poor standard; inferior. **3** of mail: sent at a cheaper rate than first class, therefore taking longer for delivery. ➤ *adv* by second-class mail or transport: *sent it second class.*

second cousin see COUSIN

second-degree *adj* **1** *med* denoting the second most serious of the three degrees of burning with blistering but not permanent damage to the skin. **2** *N Am law* denoting unlawful killing with intent, but no premeditation.

seconder *n* a person who seconds (see SECOND[1] *verb* sense 1) a proposal or the person making it.

second hand *n* the pointer on a watch or clock that measures and indicates the time in seconds.

second-hand *adj* **1** previously owned or used by someone else. **2** dealing or trading in second-hand goods. **3** not directly received or obtained, but known through an intermediary: *second-hand information.* ➤ *adv* **1** in a second-hand state: *It's cheaper to buy second-hand.* **2** not directly, but from someone else: *They heard it second-hand.*

second lieutenant *n* an army or navy officer of the lowest commissioned rank.

second nature *n* a habit or tendency so deeply ingrained as to seem an innate part of a person's nature.

second person see under PERSON

second-rate *adj* inferior or mediocre; having a substandard quality.

second sight *n* the power believed to enable someone to see into the future or to see things happening elsewhere.

second thoughts *pl n* **1** doubts. **2** a process of reconsideration leading to a different decision being made: *On second thoughts I think I'll stay.*

second wind *n* a burst of renewed energy or enthusiasm.

secrecy *n* **1** the state or fact of being secret. **2** confidentiality: *I'm sworn to secrecy.* **3** the tendency to keep information secret.

secret *adj* **1** kept hidden or away from the knowledge of others. **2** unknown or unobserved by others: *a secret army.* **3** tending to conceal things from others; private or secretive. **4** guarded against discovery or observation: *a secret location.* ➤ *n* **1** something not disclosed, or not to be disclosed, to others. **2** an unknown or unrevealed method of achievement: *the secret of eternal youth.* **3** a central but sometimes elusive principle, etc: *the secret of a good marriage.* ○ **secretly** *adv.* ♦ **in secret** secretly; unknown to others. **keep a secret** not to disclose or reveal it.

secret agent *n* a member of the secret service; a spy.

secretaire *n* a cabinet which folds out to form a writing desk.

secretariat *n* **1** the administrative department of any council, organization or legislative body. **2** its staff or premises. **3** a secretary's office.

secretary *n* (*-ies*) **1** a person employed to perform administrative or clerical tasks for a company or individual. **2** the member of a club or

society committee responsible for its correspondence and business records. **3** a senior civil servant assisting a government minister or ambassador. ○ **secretarial** *adj.*

secrete[1] *vb, biol, zool* of a gland or similar organ: to form and release (a substance).

secrete[2] *vb* to hide away or conceal.

secretion *n* **1** the process whereby glands of the body discharge or release particular substances. **2** any of the substances produced by such glands, eg sweat, saliva, mucus or bile.

secretive *adj* inclined to or fond of secrecy; reticent. ○ **secretively** *adv.* ○ **secretiveness** *n.*

secret police *n* a police force operating in secret to suppress opposition to the government.

secret service *n* a government department responsible for espionage and national security matters.

sect *n* **1** a religious or other group whose views and practices differ from those of an established body or from those of a body from which it has separated. **2** a subdivision of one of the main religious divisions of mankind.

sectarian *adj* **1** referring, relating or belonging to a sect. **2** having, showing or caused by hostility towards those outside one's own group or belonging to a particular group or sect. ○ **sectarianism** *n.*

section *n* **1** the act or process of cutting, or the cut or division made. **2** any of the parts into which something is or can be divided or of which it may be composed. **3** *geom* the surface formed when a plane cuts through a solid figure. **4** the act of cutting through a solid figure. **5** a plan or diagram showing a view of an object as if it had been cut through. ➤ *vb* **1** to divide something into sections. **2** *med* to issue an order for the compulsory admission of (a mentally ill person) to a psychiatric hospital.

sectional *adj* **1** made in sections. **2** referring or relating to a particular section. **3** restricted to a particular group or area.

sector *n* **1** *geom* a portion of a circle bounded by two radii and an arc. **2** a division or section of a nation's economic operations. **3** a part of an area divided up for military purposes. **4** a mathematical measuring instrument consisting of two graduated rules hinged together at one end.

secular *adj* **1** relating to the present world rather than to heavenly or spiritual things. **2** not religious or ecclesiastical; civil or lay. **3** of clergy: not bound by vows to a particular monastic or religious order. ○ **secularize** or **-ise** *vb.*

secularism *n* the view or belief that society's values and standards should not be influenced or controlled by religion or the Church. ○ **secularist** *n.*

secure *adj* **1** free from danger; providing safety. **2** free from trouble, worry or uncertainty. **3** firmly fixed or attached. **4** not likely to be lost or taken away; safe or assured: *a secure job.* **5** in custody, usu of the police. ➤ *vb* **1** to fasten or attach firmly. **2** to get or assure possession of something: *She's secured a place on the course for next year.* **3** to make free from danger or risk; to make safe. **4** to contrive to get something. **5** to guarantee. ○ **securely** *adv.*

security *n* (*-ies*) **1** the state of being secure. **2** protection from the possibility of future financial difficulty, physical harm or theft. **3** the staff providing protection against attack or theft. **4** something given as a guarantee, esp to a creditor giving them the right to recover a debt. **5** (*usu* **securities**) a certificate stating ownership of stocks or shares, or the value represented by such certificates. ➤ *adj* providing security: *security guard.*

sedan *n, N Am* a saloon car.

sedate *adj* **1** calm and dignified in manner. **2** slow and unexciting. ➤ *vb* to calm or quieten someone by means of a sedative. ○ **sedately** *adv.*

sedation *n, med* the act of calming or the state of having been calmed, esp by means of sedatives.

sedative *n, med* any agent, esp a drug, that has a calming effect.

sedentary /'sɛdəntərɪ/ *adj* **1** of work: involving much sitting. **2** of a person: spending much time sitting; taking little exercise.

sedge *n* a plant, resembling grass, which grows in bogs, fens, marshes and other poorly drained areas.

sediment *n* **1** insoluble solid particles that have settled at the bottom of a liquid in which they were previously suspended. **2** *geol* solid material that has been deposited by the action of gravity, wind, water or ice. ○ **sedimentary** *adj.* ○ **sedimentation** *n.*

sedition *n* public speech, writing or action encouraging public disorder, esp rebellion against the government. ○ **seditious** *adj.*

seduce *vb* **1** to lure or entice someone into having sexual intercourse. **2** to lead astray; to tempt, esp into wrongdoing. ○ **seducer** or **seductress** *n.* ○ **seduction** *n.*

seductive *adj* **1** sexually attractive and charming. **2** tempting; enticing.

sedulous *adj, formal* assiduous and diligent; steadily hardworking.

see[1] *vb* (*past tense* **saw**, *past participle* **seen**) **1** to perceive by the eyes. **2** *intr* to have the power of vision. **3** *tr & intr* to understand or realize. **4** to watch: *We're going to see a play.* **5** to be aware of or know, esp by looking or reading: *I see from your letter that you're married.* **6** *tr & intr* to find out; to learn: *We'll have to see what happens.* **7** to predict; to expect: *We could see what was going to happen.* **8** to meet with someone. **9** to spend time with someone regularly, esp romantically: *He's seeing Carole.* **10** to speak to someone; to consult: *He's asking to see the manager.* **11** to receive as a visitor or client: *The doctor will see you now.* **12** to make sure of something: *See that you lock the door.* **13** to imagine, and often also to regard as likely: *I can't see him agreeing.* **14** to consider: *I see her more as an acquaintance than*

a friend. **15** to encounter or experience: *She's seen too much pain in her life.* **16** to be witness to something as a sight or event: *We're now seeing huge wage rises.* **17** to escort: *I'll see you home.* **18** to refer to (the specified page, etc) for information: *See page five.* **19** *intr* (**see to sth**) to attend to it; to take care of it. **20** *cards* to match the bet of someone by staking the same sum: *I'll see you and raise you five.* ◆ **see fit to do sth** to think it appropriate or proper to do it. **see things** to have hallucinations. ◇ **see about sth** to attend to a matter or concern. **see sb off 1** to accompany them to their place of departure. **2** *colloq* to get rid of them by force. **see sb out** to outlive them. **see sth out** to stay until the end of it. **see through sth 1** to discern what is implied by an idea or scheme, etc. **2** to detect or determine the truth underlying a lie. **see sth through** to participate in it to the end.

see[2] *n* **1** the area under the religious authority of a bishop or archbishop. **2** THE HOLY SEE.

seed *n* (**seeds** or **seed**) **1** *bot* in flowering and cone-bearing plants: the structure that develops from the ovule after fertilization, and is capable of developing into a new plant. **2** a small hard fruit or part in a fruit; a pip. **3** a source or origin: *the seeds of the plan.* **4** *sport* a seeded player: *the number one seed.* ➤ *vb* **1** *intr* of a plant: to produce seeds (**seeds**). **2** to sow or plant (seeds). **3** to remove seeds from (eg a fruit). **4** to scatter particles of some substance into (a cloud) in order to induce rainfall, disperse a storm or freezing fog, etc. **5** *sport* to arrange (a tournament) so that high-ranking players only meet each other in the later stages of the contest. ○ **seeded** *adj.* ○ **seedless** *adj.* ◆ **go** or **run to seed 1** *bot* of a plant: to stop flowering prior to the development of seed. **2** *colloq* to allow oneself to become unkempt or unhealthy through lack of care.

seedling *n* a young plant grown from seed.

seedy *adj, colloq* (*-ier, -iest*) **1** mildly ill or unwell. **2** shabby; dirty or disreputable: *a seedy club.* ○ **seediness** *n.*

seeing *n* the ability to see; the power of vision. ➤ *conj* (*usu* **seeing that**) given (that); since: *Seeing you are opposed to the plan, I shall not pursue it.*

seek *vb* (**sought**) **1** to look for someone or something. **2** to try to find, get or achieve something. **3** to ask for something: *We sought his advice.* ○ **seeker** *n.* ◇ **seek sb** or **sth out** to search intensively for and find them.

seem *vb, intr* **1** to appear to the eye; to give the impression of (being): *She seems happy today.* **2** to be apparent; to appear to the mind: *There seems to be no good reason for refusing.* **3** to think or believe oneself (to be, do, etc): *I seem to know you from somewhere.*

seeming *adj* apparent; ostensible. ○ **seemingly** *adv.*

seemly *adj* (*-ier, -iest*) fitting or suitable; becoming.

seep *vb, intr* of a liquid: to escape slowly or

ooze through, or as if through, a narrow opening. ○ **seepage** n.

seer n 1 a person who predicts future events; a clairvoyant. 2 a person of great wisdom and spiritual insight; a prophet.

seersucker n lightweight Indian cotton or linen fabric with a crinkly appearance, often with stripes.

seesaw n 1 a plaything consisting of a plank balanced in the middle allowing people seated on the ends to propel each other up and down by pushing off the ground with the feet. 2 an alternate up-and-down or back-and-forth movement. ➤ vb, intr to move alternately up-and-down or back-and-forth.

seethe vb, intr 1 to be extremely agitated or upset, esp with anger. 2 of a liquid: to churn and foam as if boiling. ○ **seething** adj.

see-through adj esp of a fabric or clothing: able to be seen through; transparent or translucent.

segment n /'sɛgmənt/ 1 a part, section or portion. 2 geom in a circle or ellipse: the region enclosed by an arc and its chord. 3 zool in certain animals, eg some worms: each of a number of repeating units of which the body is composed. ➤ vb /sɛg'mɛnt/ to divide into segments. ○ **segmental** adj. ○ **segmentation** n.

segregate vb 1 to set apart or isolate. 2 intr to separate out into a group or groups. ○ **segregation** n. ○ **segregationist** n.

seigneur /sɛn'jɜː(r)/ or **seignior** /'seɪnjə(r)/ n a feudal lord, esp in France or French Canada.

seine /seɪn/ n a large vertical fishing net held underwater by floats and weights, and whose ends are brought together and hauled. ➤ vb, tr & intr to catch or fish with a seine.

seismic /'saɪzmɪk/ adj relating to or characteristic of earthquakes.

seismology /saɪz'mɒlədʒɪ/ n, geol the scientific study of earthquakes. ○ **seismological** or **seismologic** adj. ○ **seismologist** n.

seize vb 1 to take or grab suddenly, eagerly or forcibly. 2 to take by force; to capture. 3 to affect suddenly and deeply; to overcome: *He was seized by panic.* 4 to take legal possession of someone or something. 5 (often **seize on** or **upon sth**) to use or exploit it eagerly: *She seized on the idea as soon as it was suggested.* 6 intr (often **seize up**) a of a machine or engine: to become stiff or jammed; b of part of the body: to become stiff through over-exertion; c of a person: to become overwhelmed with nerves, fear, etc: *As soon as I stepped on the stage I just seized up.*

seizure n 1 the act of seizing. 2 a capture. 3 pathol a sudden attack of illness, esp producing spasms as in an epileptic fit.

seldom adv rarely.

select vb to choose from several by preference. ➤ adj 1 picked out or chosen in preference to others. 2 having a restricted entrance or membership; exclusive: *She mixes with a very select group.* ○ **selectness** n. ○ **selector** n.

selection n 1 the act or process of selecting or being selected. 2 a thing or set of things selected. 3 a range from which to select. 4 biol the process by which some individuals contribute more offspring than others to the next generation.

selective adj 1 tending to select or choose; discriminating: *a selective school.* 2 involving only certain people or things; exclusive. ○ **selectively** adv. ○ **selectivity** n.

selenium n, chem a metalloid element that is a semiconductor, used in electronic devices, photoelectric cells and photographic exposure meters.

self n (**selves**) 1 personality, or a particular aspect of it. 2 a person's awareness of their own identity; ego. 3 a person as a whole, comprising a combination of characteristics of appearance and behaviour: *He was his usual happy self.* 4 personal interest or advantage. ➤ pron, colloq myself, yourself, himself or herself. ➤ adj being of the same material or colour.

self-absorbed adj wrapped up in one's own thoughts, affairs or circumstances.

self-abuse n, derog or humorous masturbation.

self-addressed adj addressed by the sender for return to themselves.

self-appointed adj acting on one's own authority, without the choice or approval of others.

self-assurance n self-confidence. ○ **self-assured** adj.

self-catering adj of a holiday, accommodation, etc: providing facilities allowing guests and residents to prepare their own meals.

self-centred adj interested only in oneself and one's own affairs; selfish.

self-coloured adj having the same colour all over.

self-confessed adj as openly acknowledged and admitted by oneself: *a self-confessed cheat.*

self-confidence n confidence in or reliance on one's own abilities. ○ **self-confident** adj.

self-conscious adj ill at ease in company as a result of irrationally believing oneself to be the subject of observation to others.

self-contained adj 1 of accommodation: having no part that is shared with others. 2 needing nothing added; complete in itself.

self-control n the ability to control one's emotions and impulses. ○ **self-controlled** adj.

self-defence n the act or techniques of protecting or defending oneself from attack.

self-denial n the act or practice of denying one's own needs or desires.

self-determination n 1 the freedom to make one's own decisions without intervention from others. 2 a nation's freedom to decide its own government and political relations.

self-drive adj of a hired motor vehicle: to be driven by the hirer.

self-effacing adj tending to avoid making others aware of one's presence or achievements out of shyness or modesty. ○ **self-effacement** n.

self-employed adj working for oneself and under one's own control, rather than as an employee. ○ **self-employment** n.

self-esteem n one's good opinion of oneself.

self-evident adj clear or evident enough without need for proof or explanation. ○ **self-evidently** adv.

self-explanatory or **self-explaining** adj easily understood or obvious; needing no further explanation.

self-expression n the giving of expression of one's personality, esp in art, poetry, etc.

self-government n a government run by the people of a nation without any outside control or interference. ○ **self-governing** adj.

self-help n the practice of solving one's own problems using abilities developed in oneself rather than relying on assistance from others.

self-image n one's idea or perception of oneself.

self-important adj having an exaggerated sense of one's own importance or worth; arrogant or pompous. ○ **self-importance** n.

self-imposed adj taken voluntarily on oneself; not imposed by others.

self-indulgent adj giving in to or indulging one's own whims or desires. ○ **self-indulgence** n.

self-inflicted adj inflicted by oneself on oneself.

self-interest n 1 regard for oneself and one's own interests. 2 one's own personal welfare or advantage.

selfish adj 1 concerned only with one's personal welfare, with total disregard for that of others. 2 of an act: revealing such a tendency. ○ **selfishly** adv. ○ **selfishness** n.

selfless adj tending to consider the welfare of others before one's own; altruistic. ○ **selflessness** n.

self-made adj having achieved wealth or success by working one's way up from poverty and obscurity, rather than by advantages acquired by birth.

self-pity n pity for oneself.

self-possessed adj calm, controlled and collected, esp in an emergency. ○ **self-possession** n.

self-preservation n 1 the protection and care of one's own life. 2 the instinct underlying this.

self-propelled adj of a vehicle or craft: having its own means of propulsion. ○ **self-propelling** adj.

self-raising adj of flour: containing an ingredient to make dough or pastry rise.

self-reliant adj never needing or seeking help from others; independent. ○ **self-reliance** n.

self-respect n respect for oneself and one's character, and concern for one's dignity and reputation. ○ **self-respecting** adj.

self-righteous adj having too high an opinion of one's own merits, and being intolerant of other people's faults. ○ **self-righteousness** n.

self-sacrifice n the forgoing of one's own needs, interests or happiness for the sake of others. ○ **self-sacrificing** adj.

selfsame adj the very same; identical: He left that selfsame day.

self-satisfied adj feeling or showing complacent or arrogant satisfaction with oneself or one's achievements. ○ **self-satisfaction** n.

self-seeking adj preoccupied with one's own interests and opportunities for personal advantage. ➢ n the act of self-seeking.

self-service n a system in which customers serve themselves and pay at a checkout.

self-serving adj benefiting or seeking to benefit oneself, often to the disadvantage of others.

self-starter n 1 in a vehicle's engine: an automatic electric starting device. 2 colloq a person with initiative and motivation, requiring little supervision in a job.

self-styled adj called or considered so only by oneself: a self-styled superstar.

self-sufficient adj of a person or thing: able to provide for oneself or itself without outside help. ○ **self-sufficiency** n.

self-supporting adj 1 earning enough money to meet all one's own expenses; self-sufficient. 2 of a structure, plant, etc: needing no additional supports or attachments to stay fixed or upright. ○ **self-support** n.

self-willed adj stubbornly or obstinately determined to do or have what one wants, esp to the disadvantage of others. ○ **self-will** n.

self-winding adj of a watch: containing a device that automatically rewinds it.

sell vb (**sold**) 1 to give something to someone in exchange for money. 2 to have available for buying: Do you sell batteries? 3 intr to be in demand among customers; to be sold: This particular style sells well. 4 to promote the sale of something; to cause to be bought: The author's name sells the book. 5 to convince or persuade someone to acquire or agree to something, esp by emphasizing its merits or advantages: It was difficult to sell them the idea. 6 to lose or betray (eg one's principles) in the process of getting something, esp something dishonourable. ➢ n 1 the act or process of selling. 2 the style of persuasion used in selling: the hard sell. ○ **seller** n. ✦ **sell sb down the river** colloq to betray them. **sell sb, sth** or **oneself short** colloq to understate their good qualities; to belittle them. **sold on sth** colloq convinced or enthusiastic about it. ◊ **sell sth off** to dispose of remaining goods by selling them quickly and cheaply. **sell out of sth** to sell one's entire stock of it. **sell out to sb** to betray one's principles or associates to another party. **sell up** to sell one's house or business, usu because of debts.

sell-by date n a date stamped on a manufacturer's or distributor's label indicating when goods, esp foods, are considered no longer fit to be sold.

Sellotape or **sellotape** n, trademark a form of usu transparent adhesive tape, esp for use on paper. ➤ vb to stick using Sellotape.

sell-out n an event for which all the tickets have been sold.

selvage or **selvedge** n an edge of a length of fabric sewn or woven so as to prevent fraying.

semantic adj 1 referring or relating to meaning, esp of words. 2 referring or relating to semantics. ○ **semantically** adv.

semantics sing n the branch of linguistics that deals with the meaning of words.

semaphore n a system of signalling in which flags or the arms are held in positions that represent individual letters and numbers. ➤ vb, tr & intr to signal using semaphore.

semblance n 1 outer appearance, esp when superficial or deceptive. 2 a hint or trace.

semen n a thick whitish liquid carrying spermatozoa, ejaculated from the penis.

semester n an academic term lasting for half an academic year.

semi /ˈsɛmɪ, US ˈsɛmaɪ/ n, colloq 1 a semi-detached house. 2 a semifinal.

semi-automatic adj 1 partially automatic. 2 of a firearm: continuously reloading itself, but only firing one bullet at a time. ○ **semi-automatically** adv.

semibreve n, mus the longest note in common use, equal to half a breve, two minims or four crotchets.

semicircle n 1 one half of a circle. 2 an arrangement of anything in this form. ○ **semicircular** adj.

semicolon n a punctuation mark (;) indicating a pause stronger than that marked by a comma but weaker than that marked by a full stop.

semiconductor n, electronics a crystalline material that behaves either as an electrical conductor or as an insulator. ○ **semiconducting** adj.

semi-detached adj of a house: forming part of the same building, with another house on the other side of the shared wall.

semifinal n in competitions, sports tournaments, etc: either of two matches, the winners of which play each other in the final. ○ **semifinalist** n.

seminal adj 1 referring or relating to seed, semen or reproduction in general. 2 referring or relating to the beginnings or early developments of an idea, study, etc. 3 highly original and at the root of a trend or movement: seminal writings.

seminar n 1 a group of advanced students working in a specific subject of study under the supervision of a teacher. 2 any meeting set up for the discussion of any topic.

seminary n (-ies) 1 a college for the training of priests, ministers and rabbis. 2 old use a secondary school, esp for girls. ○ **seminarian** n.

semiotics or **semiology** sing n, ling the study of human communication, esp the relationship between words and the objects or concepts they represent. ○ **semiotic** adj.

semi-permeable adj, biol of a membrane: allowing only certain molecules to pass.

semi-precious adj of a gem: considered less valuable than a precious stone.

semi-professional adj 1 of a person: engaging only part-time in a professional activity. 2 of an activity: engaged in only by semi-professionals. ➤ n a semi-professional person.

semiquaver n a musical note equal to half a quaver or one-sixteenth of a semibreve.

semi-skilled adj having or requiring a degree of training less advanced than that needed for specialized work.

semitone n, mus 1 half a tone. 2 the interval between adjacent notes on a keyboard instrument, and the smallest interval in a normal musical scale.

semi-tropical adj subtropical.

semivowel n a speech sound having the qualities of both a vowel and a consonant, eg y and w in English.

semolina n the hard particles of wheat not ground into flour during milling, used for thickening soups, making puddings, etc.

Sen. abbrev 1 senate. 2 senator. 3 senior.

senate n (often Senate) in the USA, Australia and other countries: a legislative body, esp the upper chamber of the national assembly.

senator n (often Senator) a member of a senate. ○ **senatorial** adj.

send vb (sent) 1 to cause, direct or order to go or be conveyed. 2 (also send sth off) to dispatch it, eg by post. 3 intr a (send for sb) to ask or order them to come; b (send for sth) to order it to be brought or delivered. 4 to force or propel: He sent me flying. 5 to cause to pass into a specified state: She sent him into fits of laughter. ○ **sender** n. ◊ **send away** or **off for sth** to order (goods) by post. **send sb off** in football, rugby, etc: to order a player to leave the field with no further participation in the game, usu after infringement of the rules. **send sb** or **sth up** Brit colloq to make fun of or parody them.

send-off n a display of good wishes from a gathering of people to a departing person or group.

send-up n, Brit colloq a parody or satire.

senescent adj, formal 1 growing old; ageing. 2 characteristic of old age. ○ **senescence** n.

senile adj displaying the feebleness and decay of mind or body brought on by old age. ○ **senility** n.

senile dementia n a psychological disorder caused by irreversible degeneration of the brain, usu commencing after late middle age, and characterized by loss of memory and impaired intellectual ability.

senior adj 1 older than someone. 2 higher in rank or authority than someone. 3 for or pertaining to schoolchildren over the age of 11. 4 N Am referring to final-year high school, college or university students. 5 (Senior) older than another person of the same name, esp distinguishing parent from child: *James Smith, Senior.* ➤ *n* **1** a person who is older or of a higher rank. **2** a pupil in a senior school, or in the senior part of a school. **3** *N Am* a final-year student in a high school, college or university.

senior citizen *n* an elderly person; an old age pensioner.

seniority *n* **1** the state or fact of being senior. **2** a privileged position earned through long service in a profession or with a company.

senior nursing officer *n* a MATRON (sense 1).

senior service *n* (*usu* **the senior service**) the Royal Navy.

senna *n* the dried leaves or pods of a plant native to Africa and Arabia, used as a laxative.

sensation *n* **1** an awareness of an external or internal stimulus as a result of its perception by the senses. **2** a physical feeling: *I've a burning sensation in my mouth.* **3** an emotion or general feeling; a thrill: *a sensation of doubt.* **4** a sudden widespread feeling of excitement or shock: *His presence caused quite a sensation.* **5** the cause of such excitement or shock. ○ **sensational** *adj.*

sensationalism *n* the practice of or methods used in deliberately setting out to cause widespread excitement, intense interest or shock. ○ **sensationalist** *n, adj.* ○ **sensationalize** or **-ise** *vb.*

sense *n* **1** any of the five main faculties used by a person or animal to obtain information about their external or internal environment, namely sight, hearing, smell, taste and touch. **2** an awareness or appreciation of, or an ability to make judgements regarding, some specified thing: *She has a good sense of direction.* **3** (**senses**) soundness of mind; one's wits or reason: *He's lost his senses.* **4** wisdom; practical worth: *There's no sense in doing it now.* **5** a general feeling or emotion, not perceived by any of the five natural powers: *a sense of guilt.* **6** general, overall meaning: *They understood the sense of the poem.* **7** specific meaning: *In what sense do you mean?* ➤ *vb* **1** to detect a stimulus by means of any of the five main senses. **2** to be aware of something by means other than the five main senses: *I sensed that someone was following me.* ◆ **bring sb to their senses** to make them recognize the facts; to make them understand that they must rectify their behaviour. **come to one's senses 1** to act sensibly and rationally after a period of foolishness. **2** to regain consciousness. **in a sense** in one respect; in a way. **make sense** to be understandable, rational or wise. **make sense of sth** to understand it; to see the purpose or explanation in it. **take leave of one's senses** to begin behaving irrationally; to go mad.

senseless *adj* **1** unconscious. **2** unwise; without good sense or foolish. ○ **senselessly** *adv.* ○ **senselessness** *n.*

sensibility *n* (**-ies**) **1** the ability or capacity to feel or have sensations or emotions. **2** a delicacy of emotional response; sensitivity: *There was a general sensibility to his grief.* **3** (**sensibilities**) feelings that can easily be offended or hurt.

sensible *adj* **1** having or showing reasonableness or good judgement; wise. **2** perceptible by the senses. **3** having the power of sensation; sensitive: *sensible to pain.* ○ **sensibly** *adv.*

sensitive *adj* **1** feeling or responding readily, strongly or painfully: *sensitive to our feelings.* **2** *biol* responding to a stimulus. **3** easily upset or offended. **4** stimulating much strong feeling or difference of opinion: *sensitive issues.* **5** of documents, etc: secret or confidential. **6** of scientific instruments: reacting to or recording extremely small changes. **7** *photog* responding to the action of light. ○ **sensitivity** *n.*

sensitize or **-ise** *vb* to make sensitive or more sensitive.

sensor *n, elec* any of various devices that detect or measure a change in a physical quantity, usu by converting it into an electrical signal.

sensory *adj* referring or relating to the senses or sensation.

sensual *adj* **1** relating to the senses. **2** of pleasures: connected with often undue gratification of the bodily senses. **3** pursuing physical pleasures, esp those derived from sex or food and drink.

sensuality *n* **1** the quality of being sensual. **2** indulgence in physical, esp sexual, pleasures.

sensuous *adj* **1** appealing to the senses aesthetically, with no suggestion of sexual pleasure. **2** affected by or pleasing to the senses. **3** aware of what is perceived by the senses. ○ **sensuously** *adv.*

sentence *n* **1** a sequence of words forming a meaningful grammatical structure that can stand alone as a complete utterance, and which in written English usu begins with a capital letter and ends with a full stop, question mark or exclamation mark. **2** a punishment pronounced by a court or judge; its announcement in court. **3** a judgement, opinion or decision. ➤ *vb* **1** to announce the judgement or sentence to be given to someone. **2** to condemn someone to a punishment. ◆ **pass sentence on sb** to announce the punishment to be given to someone.

sententious *adj* **1** fond of using or full of sayings or proverbs. **2** tending to lecture others on morals.

sentient /ˈsɛnʃənt, ˈsɛntɪənt/ *adj* capable of sensation or feeling; conscious or aware of something: *sentient beings.* ○ **sentience** *n.*

sentiment *n* **1** a thought or emotion. **2** emotion or emotional behaviour in general, esp when considered excessive, self-indulgent or insincere. **3** (*often* **sentiments**) an opinion or view.

sentimental *adj* **1** readily feeling, indulging in or expressing tender emotions or sentiments, esp love, friendship and pity. **2** provoking or designed to provoke such emotions, esp in large measure and without subtlety. **3** closely associated with or moved by fond memories of the past; nostalgic: *objects of sentimental value.* ○ **sentimentally** *n.* ○ **sentimentally** *adv.*

sentimentalize or **-ise** *vb* **1** *intr* to behave sentimentally or indulge in sentimentality. **2** to make sentimental.

sentinel *n* someone posted on guard; a sentry.

sentry *n* (*-ies*) a person, usu a soldier, posted on guard to control entry or passage.

sepal *n, bot* in a flower: one of the modified leaves, usu green but sometimes brightly coloured, that together form the CALYX which surrounds the petals.

separable *adj* able to be separated or disjoined.

separate *vb* / 'sɛpəreɪt/ **1** to take, force or keep apart (from others or each other): *A hedge separates the two fields.* **2** *intr* of a couple: to cease to be together or live together. **3** to disconnect or disunite; to sever. **4** to isolate or seclude: *He should be separated from the others.* **5** *tr & intr* (*also* **separate up**) to divide or become divided into parts: *The building is separated up into smaller apartments.* ➤ *adj* /-rət/ **1** separated; divided. **2** distinctly different or individual; unrelated: *That is a separate issue.* **3** physically unattached; isolated. ➤ *n* /-rət/ (*usu* **separates**) individual items which form a unit and are often purchased separately to mix and match, eg separate parts of an outfit or of a hi-fi system. ○ **separately** *adv.* ○ **separateness** *n.* ○ **separation** *n.*

separatist *n* a person who encourages, or takes action to achieve, independence from an established church, federation, organization, etc. ○ **separatism** *n.*

sepia *n* **1** a rich reddish-brown pigment, obtained from a fluid secreted by the cuttlefish. **2** this colour.

sepoy *n, hist* an Indian soldier serving with a European (esp British) army.

sepsis *n* (*-ses*) *med* the presence of disease-causing micro-organisms, esp viruses or bacteria, and their toxins in the body tissues.

sept *n* esp in Scotland or Ireland: a clan; a division of a tribe.

September *n* the ninth month of the year.

septennial *adj* **1** occurring once every seven years. **2** lasting seven years.

septet *n* **1** a group of seven musicians. **2** a piece of music for seven performers. **3** any group or set of seven.

septic *adj* **1** *med* of a wound: contaminated with pathogenic bacteria. **2** putrefying.

septicaemia /sɛptɪ'siːmɪə/ *n, pathol* the presence of pathogenic bacteria; blood poisoning.

septic tank *n* a tank, usu underground, in which sewage is decomposed by the action of bacteria.

septuagenarian /sɛptʃʊədʒə'nɛərɪən/ *n* a person between 70 and 79 years old.

septum *n* (*septa*) *biol, anat* any partition between cavities, eg nostrils, areas of soft tissue, etc.

septuple *adj* being seven times as much or as many; sevenfold. ➤ *vb, tr & intr* to multiply or increase sevenfold.

septuplet *n* **1** any of seven children or animals born at the same time to the same mother. **2** *mus* a group of seven notes played in the time of four or six.

sepulchral /sɪ'pʌlkrəl/ *adj* **1** referring or relating to a tomb or burial. **2** suggestive of death or burial; gloomy or funereal.

sepulchre or (*US*) **sepulcher** /'sɛpəlkə(r)/ *n* a tomb or burial vault. ➤ *vb* to bury in a sepulchre; to entomb.

sequel *n* **1** a book, film or play that continues an earlier story. **2** anything that follows on from a previous event, etc.

sequence *n* a series or succession of things in a specific order.

sequential *adj* in, having or following a particular order or sequence.

sequester *vb* **1** to set aside or isolate. **2** *law* to sequestrate. ○ **sequestered** *adj* secluded.

sequestrate *vb, law* to remove or confiscate (something, esp property) from someone's possession until a dispute or debt has been settled. ○ **sequestration** *n.*

sequin *n* a small round shiny disc of foil or plastic, sewn on a garment for decoration. ○ **sequined** *adj.*

sequoia /sɪ'kwɔɪə/ *n* either of two species of massive evergreen trees, native to N America, the Californian REDWOOD and the **giant sequoia**.

seraglio /sə'rɑːlɪəʊ/ *n* **1** women's quarters in a Muslim house or palace; a harem. **2** *hist* a Turkish palace, esp that of the sultans at Constantinople.

seraph *n* (*seraphs* or *seraphim*) an angel of the highest rank. ○ **seraphic** *adj.*

serenade *n* **1** a song or piece of music performed at night under a woman's window by her suitor. **2** any musical piece with a gentle tempo suggestive of romance and suitable for such a performance. ➤ *vb* **1** to entertain someone with a serenade. **2** *intr* to perform a serenade.

serendipity *n* the state of frequently making lucky or beneficial finds. ○ **serendipitous** *adj.*

serene *adj* **1** of a person: calm and composed; at peace. **2** of a sky: cloudless. ○ **serenely** *adv.* ○ **serenity** /sɪ'rɛnətɪ/ *n.*

serf *n* in medieval Europe: a worker in modified slavery, bought and sold with the land on which they worked. ○ **serfdom** *n.*

serge *n* a strong twilled fabric, esp of wool or worsted.

sergeant or **serjeant** *n* **1** in the armed forces: a non-commissioned officer of the rank next above corporal. **2** in Britain: a police officer of the rank between constable and inspector.

sergeant-at-arms or **serjeant-at-arms** *n* an

officer of a court or parliament who is responsible for keeping order.

sergeant-major *n* a non-commissioned officer of the highest rank in the armed forces.

serial *n* **1** a story, television programme, etc published or broadcast in regular instalments. **2** a periodical. ➢ *adj* **1** appearing in instalments. **2** forming a series or part of a series. **3** in series; in a row.

> **serial, series** There is often confusion between **serial** and **series**: a **serial** is a single story presented in separate instalments, whereas a **series** is a set of separate stories featuring the same characters.

serialize or **-ise** *vb* to publish or broadcast (a story, television programme, etc) in instalments. ○ **serialization** *n*.

serial killer *n* someone who commits a succession of murders.

serial number *n* the individual identification number on each of a series of identical products.

series *n* (*pl* **series**) **1** a number of similar, related or identical things arranged or produced in line or in succession. **2** a television or radio programme in which the same characters appear, or a similar subject is addressed, in regularly broadcast shows. **3** a set of things that differ progressively. **4** *maths* in a sequence of numbers: the sum obtained when each term is added to the previous ones.

> **series** See note at **serial**.

serif *n*, *printing* a short decorative line or stroke on the end of a printed letter, as opposed to SANSERIF.

seriocomic /ˌsɪərɪəʊˈkɒmɪk/ *adj* containing both serious and comic elements or qualities.

serious *adj* **1** grave or solemn; not inclined to flippancy or lightness of mood. **2** dealing with important issues: *a serious newspaper*. **3** severe: *a serious accident*. **4** important; significant: *There were serious differences of opinion*. **5** sincere or earnest: *I am serious about doing it*. **6** *colloq* notable, renowned or in significant quantities: *serious money*. ○ **seriously** *adv*. ○ **seriousness** *n*.

serjeant see SERGEANT

sermon *n* **1** a public speech or discourse, esp one forming part of a church service. **2** a lengthy moral or advisory speech, esp a reproving one.

serology /sɪəˈrɒlədʒɪ/ *n*, *biol* the study of blood serum and its constituents, esp antibodies and antigens. ○ **serologist** *n*.

serotonin *n*, *physiol* a hormone that transmits impulses in the central nervous system.

serous /ˈsɪərəs/ *adj* characteristic of, relating to or containing serum.

serpent *n* **1** a snake. **2** a sneaky, treacherous or malicious person.

serpentine /ˈsɜːpəntaɪn/ *adj* **1** snakelike. **2** winding; full of twists and bends. ➢ *n*, *geol* a soft green or white rock-forming mineral derived from magnesium silicates, often mottled like a snake's skin.

serrate *adj* /ˈsɛreɪt/ notched like the blade of a saw. ➢ *vb* /səˈreɪt/ to notch. ○ **serration** *n*.

serried *adj* closely packed or grouped together.

serum /ˈsɪərəm/ *n* (**serums** or **sera**) **1** (*in full* **blood serum**) *anat* the yellowish fluid component of blood, which contains specific antibodies and can therefore be used in a vaccine. **2** *bot* the watery part of a plant fluid.

servant *n* **1** a person employed by another to do household or menial work for them. **2** a person who acts for the good of others in any capacity. **3** a PUBLIC SERVANT.

serve *vb* **1** to work for someone as a domestic servant; to be in the service of someone. **2** *intr* to be a servant. **3** *tr & intr* to work for the benefit of someone; to aid or benefit: *He serves the community well.* • *These shoes have served me well.* • *to serve the country.* **4** *tr & intr* to attend to customers in a shop, etc. **5** *intr* (**serve as sth**) to act as or take the place of it: *This box will serve as a chair.* **6** *tr & intr* (*also* **serve up**) to bring, distribute or present (food or drink) to someone: *I'm ready to serve up now.* **7** to provide with or supply materials. **8** *intr* to carry out duties as a member of some body or organization: *They serve on a committee.* **9** *intr* to act as a member of the armed forces: *We served in the marines.* **10** to provide with specified facilities: *There are trams serving the entire city.* **11** *intr* to have a specific effect or result: *His speech just served to make matters worse.* **12** to undergo as a requirement: *You have to serve an apprenticeship.* **13** *tr & intr* in racket sports: to put (the ball) into play. **14** *law* to deliver or present (a legal document) to someone: *to serve a writ.* **15** of a male animal: to copulate with (a female). ➢ *n* in racket sports: an act of serving. ♦ **serve one's time** to undergo an apprenticeship or term in office. **serve sb right** *colloq* to be the misfortune or punishment that they deserve. **serve time** to undergo a term of imprisonment.

server *n* **1** a person who serves. **2** in racket sports: the person who serves the ball. **3** in computer networks: a dedicated computer that stores communal files, processes electronic mail, etc.

service *n* **1** the condition or occupation of being a servant or someone who serves. **2** work carried out for or on behalf of others: *Your services are no longer required.* **3** the act or manner of serving. **4** use or usefulness: *Can I be of service?* **5** a favour or any beneficial act: *to do someone a service.* **6** employment as a member of an organization working to serve or benefit others in some way; such an organization: *the civil service.* **7** the personnel employed in such an organization. **8** assistance given to customers in a shop, restaurant, etc. **9** a facility provided: *British Rail ran an excellent service*. **10** an occasion of worship or other religious ceremony; the words, etc used on such an occasion: *the marriage service*. **11** a complete set of cutlery and crockery: *a dinner service*. **12** (*usu* **service**) the supply eg of water, public transport, etc. **13** a periodic check and sometimes repair of the workings of a vehicle or other machine. **14** in racket sports: the act of putting the ball into play, or the game in which it is a particular player's turn to do so. **15** a SERVICE CHARGE, eg in a restaurant: *service not included*. **16** (*often* **services**) any of the armed forces. **17** (**services**) an area providing facilities for motorway users. ➤ *vb* **1** to subject (a vehicle, etc) to a periodic check. **2** of a male animal: to mate with (a female). ◆ **at sb's service** ready to serve or give assistance to them. **be of service to sb** to help or be useful to them. **in service 1** in use or operation. **2** working as a domestic servant. **out of service** broken; not in operation.

serviceable *adj* **1** capable of being used. **2** able to give long-term use; durable.

service charge *n* a percentage of a restaurant or hotel bill added on to cover the cost of service.

service industry *n* an industry whose business is providing services rather than manufacturing products, eg entertainment, transport, etc.

serviceman or **servicewoman** *n* a member of any of the armed forces.

service station *n* a petrol station providing facilities for motorists, esp refuelling, car-washing, etc.

serviette *n* a table napkin.

servile *adj* slavishly respectful or obedient; fawning or submissive. ○ **servility** *n*.

serving *n* a portion of food or drink served at one time; a helping.

servitude *n* **1** slavery. **2** subjection to irksome or taxing conditions.

servo *adj* denoting a system in which the main mechanism is set in operation by a subsidiary mechanism and is able to develop a force greater than the force communicated to it: *servo brakes*.

sesame /'sɛsəmɪ/ *n* **1** a plant with solitary white flowers, usu marked with purple or yellow. **2** the small edible seeds of this plant, used as a garnish and flavouring and as a source of sesame oil.

sessile *adj* **1** of a flower or leaf: attached directly to the plant, rather than by a stalk. **2** of an animal: stationary or immobile.

session *n* **1** a meeting of a court, council or parliament, or the period during which such meetings are regularly held. **2** *colloq* a period of time spent engaged in any particular activity: *a drinking session*. **3** an academic term or year. **4** the period during which classes are taught. ○ **sessional** *adj*. ◆ **in session** of a court, committee, etc: conducting or engaged in a meeting.

sestet *n* **1** the last six lines of a sonnet. **2** *mus* a SEXTET.

set[1] *vb* (**set, setting**) **1** to put, place or fix into a specified position or condition: *set them straight*. **2** to array or arrange: *Everything was set out beautifully*. ◆ *Please set the table*. **3** *tr & intr* to make or become solid or motionless: *The jelly has set*. **4** to fix, establish or settle: *Let's set a date*. **5** to embed: *set firmly in the cement*. **6** to stud or sprinkle. **7** to ordain, regulate or fix (a procedure, etc). **8** to adjust (a measuring device, eg a clock) to the correct reading. **9** in Scotland and Ireland: to lease or let to a tenant. **10** to put something upon a course or start it off: *I set it going*. **11** to incite or direct. **12** to fix (a broken bone) in its normal position for healing. **13** to impose or assign as an exercise or duty: *to set a test*. **14** to present as a lead to be followed: *We must set an example*. **15** to place on or against a certain background or surroundings: *diamonds set in a gold bracelet*. **16** to decorate: *She wore a bracelet set with diamonds*. **17** to stir, provoke or force into activity: *That set me thinking*. **18** to treat (hair) when wet so that it stays in the required style when dry. **19** *intr* of the sun or moon: to disappear below the horizon. **20** to put down or advance (a pledge or deposit). **21** to compose or fit music to (words). **22** to place (a novel, film, etc) in a specified period, location, etc: *The Great Gatsby is set in the 1920s*. **23** of a gun dog: **a** to point out (game); **b** *intr* to indicate the location of game by crouching. **24** *tr & intr* of a colour in dyeing: to become, or to make it become, permanent or to prevent it running. ➤ *n* **1** the act or process of setting or the condition of being set. **2** a setting. **3** form, shape or posture: *the set of his jaw*. **4** *theat, cinematog* the scenery and props used to create a particular location. ➤ *adj* **1** fixed or rigid; allowing no alterations: *a set menu* ◆ *set in his ways*. **2** predetermined or conventional: *set phrases*. **3** ready or prepared: *We're all set to go*. **4** about to receive or experience something; due: *We're set for a pay rise*. ◆ **be set on sth** to be determined to do it. ◊ **set about sb** to attack them. **set about sth** to start or begin it: *They set about digging the garden*. **set sb against sb else** to make them mutually hostile. **set sth against sth else** to compare or contrast them. **set sth or sb apart** to separate or put them aside as different, esp superior. **set sth aside 1** to disregard or reject it. **2** to reserve it or put it away for later use. **set sb back** *slang* to cost (in money): *How much did that set you back?* **set sth back 1** to delay or hinder its progress. **2** to cause it to return to a previous and less advanced stage. **set sb down** to allow them to leave or alight from a vehicle at their destination. **set sth down** to record it in writing. **set in** to become firmly established: *We must leave before darkness sets in*. **set off** to start out on a journey. **set sb off** to provoke them into action or behaviour of a specified kind: *He can always set us off laughing.* **set sth off 1** to detonate (an explosive). **2** to show it off to good advantage or enhance its appearance: *The colour of the dress sets off your eyes.* **set on sb** to attack them. **set sb** or **sth on sb** to order them to attack: *I'll set the dogs on you!* **set out 1** to begin a journey. **2** to resolve (to do something): *She set out to cause trouble.* **set sth out 1** to present or explain it: *She set out her proposals plainly.* **2** to lay it out for display. **set to 1** to start working; to apply oneself to a task. **2** to start fighting or arguing. **set sb up 1** to put them into a position of guaranteed security: *The inheritance has set him up for life.* **2** to enable them to begin a new career. **3** *slang* to trick them into becoming a target for blame, or into feeling foolish. **set sth up 1** to bring it into being or operation; to establish it: *He set the company up by himself.* **2** to arrange it. **3** to put up or erect something: *Let's set the tents up over here.*

set² *n* **1** a group of related people or things, esp of a kind that usu associate, occur or are used together: *The class has two sets of twins.* **2** *maths* a group of objects, or elements, that have at least one characteristic in common, eg the set of even numbers. **3** a complete collection or series of pieces needed for a particular activity: *a chess set.* **4** the songs or tunes performed by a singer or a band at a concert: *They played quite a varied set.* **5** *tennis, darts, etc* a group of games in which the winning player or players have to win a specified number, with a match lasting a certain number of sets. **6** a device for receiving or transmitting television or radio broadcasts.

set³ or **sett** *n* **1** a badger's burrow. **2** a block of stone or wood used in paving.

setback *n* a delay, check or reversal to progress.

set piece *n* **1** a carefully prepared musical or literary performance. **2** *sport* a practised sequence of passes, movements, etc performed after a stoppage in play.

set square *n* a right-angled triangular plate used as an aid for drawing or marking lines and angles.

settee *n* a long indoor seat with a back and arms, usu able to hold two or more people; a sofa.

setter *n* a large sporting dog with a long smooth coat.

setting *n* **1 a** a situation or background within or against which action takes place; **b** *theat, cinematog* the scenery and props used in a single scene. **2** a set of cutlery, crockery and glassware laid out for use by one person. **3** a position in which a machine's controls are set. **4** a mounting for a jewel. **5** the music composed specifically for a song, etc.

settle¹ *vb* **1** *tr & intr* to make or become securely, comfortably or satisfactorily positioned or established. **2** *tr & intr* (*also* **settle on sth**) to come to an agreement about it: *to settle an argument* • *to settle on a date.* **3** *intr* to come to

rest. **4** *intr* to subside: *Wait till the dust has settled.* **5** *intr* to establish a practice or routine: *You'll soon settle into the job.* **6** *tr & intr* (*also* **settle down** or **settle sb down**) to make or become calm, quiet or disciplined after a period of noisy excitement or chaos. **7** to conclude or decide: *Let's settle this matter once and for all.* **8** *tr & intr* to establish or take up a permanent home or residence. **9** *tr & intr* (*also* **settle up**) to pay off or clear (a bill or debt). **10** *intr* of particles in a liquid: to sink to the bottom or form a scum. **11** to secure by gift or legal act. ◊ **settle for sth** to accept it as a compromise or instead of something more suitable. **settle in** to adapt to a new living environment. **settle with sb** to come to an agreement or deal with them.

settle² *n* a wooden bench with arms and a solid high back.

settlement *n* **1** the act of settling or the state of being settled. **2** a recently settled community or colony. **3** an agreement, esp one ending an official dispute.

settler *n* someone who settles in a country that is being newly populated.

set-to *n* **1** *colloq* a fight or argument. **2** a fierce contest.

set-up *n* **1** *colloq* an arrangement or set of arrangements. **2** *slang* a trick to make a person unjustly blamed, accused or embarrassed.

seven *n* **1 a** the cardinal number 7; **b** the quantity that this represents, being one more than six. **2** any symbol for this, eg *7* or *VII*. **3** the seventh hour after midnight or midday. **4** a set or group of seven people or things. ➢ *adj* **1** totalling seven. **2** aged seven. ○ **seventh** *adj, n, adv.*

sevenfold *adj* **1** equal to seven times as much or as many. **2** divided into, or consisting of, seven parts. ➢ *adv* by seven times as much.

seventeen *n* **1 a** the cardinal number 17; **b** the quantity that this represents, being one more than sixteen, or the sum of ten and seven. **2** any symbol for this, eg *17* or *XVII*. ➢ *adj* **1** totalling seventeen. **2** aged seventeen. ○ **seventeenth** *adj, n, adv.*

seventh heaven *n* a state of extreme or intense happiness or joy.

seventies (often written **70s** or **70's**) *pl n* **1** (one's **seventies**) the period of time between one's seventieth and eightieth birthdays. **2** (**the seventies**) the range of temperatures between seventy and eighty degrees. **3** (**the seventies**) the period of time between the seventieth and eightieth years of a century: *born in the seventies.*

seventy *n* (*-ies*) **1 a** the cardinal number 70; **b** the quantity that this represents, being one more than sixty-nine, or the product of ten and seven. **2** any symbol for this, eg *70* or *LXX*. ➢ *adj* **1** totalling seventy. **2** aged seventy. ○ **seventieth** *adj, n, adv.*

sever *vb* **1** to cut off physically. **2** to separate or isolate. **3** to break off or end: *He's completely severed relations with them.*

several *adj* **1** more than a few, but not a great

number: *I had several drinks.* **2** various or assorted: *They were all there with their several backgrounds.* **3** different and distinct; respective: *They went their several ways.* **4** *law* separate; not jointly. ➤ *pron* quite a few people or things.

severe *adj* **1** extreme and difficult to endure; marked by extreme conditions. **2** very strict towards others. **3** suggesting seriousness: *a severe appearance.* **4** having serious consequences: *a severe injury.* **5** conforming to a rigorous standard. ○ **severely** *adv.* ○ **severity** *n.*

sew /soʊ/ *vb* (*past participle* **sewed** or **sewn**) **1** to stitch, attach or repair (esp fabric) with thread, either by hand with a needle or by machine. **2** to make (garments) by stitching pieces of fabric together. **3** *intr* to work using a needle and thread, or a sewing machine. ○ **sewer** *n.* ◊ **sew sth up** *slang* to arrange or complete it successfully and satisfactorily.

sewage /'suːɪdʒ/ *n* any liquid-borne waste matter, esp human excrement, carried away in drains.

sewer /soʊə(r)/ *n* a large underground pipe that carries away sewage from drains and water from road surfaces.

sewerage /'soʊərɪdʒ/ *n* **1** a system or network of sewers. **2** drainage of sewage and surface water using sewers.

sewing *n* **1** the act of sewing. **2** something that is being sewn: *I keep my sewing in the basket.*

sex *n* **1** either of the two classes, male and female, into which animals and plants are divided according to their role in reproduction. **2** membership of one of these classes, or the characteristics that determine this. **3** sexual intercourse, or the activities, feelings, desires, etc associated with it. ➤ *adj* **1** referring or relating to sexual matters in general: *sex education.* **2** due to or based on the fact of being male or female: *sex discrimination.* ➤ *vb* to identify or determine the sex of (an animal).

sexagenarian *n* a person aged between 60 and 69.

sex appeal *n* the power of exciting sexual desire in other people; sexual attractiveness.

sexism *n* contempt shown for or discrimination against a particular sex, usu by men of women, based on prejudice or stereotype. ○ **sexist** *n, adj.*

sexless *adj* **1** neither male nor female. **2** having no desire to engage in sexual activity. **3** *derog* lacking in sexual attractiveness.

sexology *n* the study of human sexual behaviour, sexuality and relationships. ○ **sexologist** *n.*

sextant *n* a device used in navigation and surveying for measuring angular distances.

sextet *n* **1 a** a group of six singers or musicians; **b** a piece of music for this group. **2** any set of six.

sexton *n* someone responsible for the church buildings and churchyard, often also having bell-ringing, grave-digging and other duties.

sextuple *n* a value or quantity six times as much. ➤ *adj* **1** sixfold. **2** made up of six parts. ➤ *vb, tr & intr* to multiply sixfold.

sextuplet *n* **1** any of six children or animals born at the same time to the same mother. **2** *mus* a group of six notes performed in the time of four.

sexual *adj* **1** concerned with or suggestive of sex. **2** referring or relating to reproduction involving the fusion of two gametes. **3** concerned with, relating to or according to membership of the male or female sex. ○ **sexuality** *n.*

sexual intercourse *n* a joining of sexual organs, esp the insertion of a man's penis into a woman's vagina.

sexually transmitted disease *n* any disease that is transmitted by sexual intercourse.

sexy *adj* (**-ier, -iest**) *colloq* **1** of a person: sexually attractive; stimulating or arousing sexual desire. **2** of an object, idea, etc: currently popular or interesting; attractive or tempting: *sexy products.* ○ **sexily** *adv.* ○ **sexiness** *n.*

Sgt *abbrev* Sergeant.

sh *exclam* hush; be quiet.

shabby *adj* (**-ier, -iest**) **1** esp of clothes or furnishings: old and worn; threadbare or dingy. **2** of a person: wearing such clothes; scruffy. **3** of behaviour, conduct, etc: unworthy, discreditable or contemptible. ○ **shabbily** *adv.* ○ **shabbiness** *n.*

shack *n* a crudely built hut or shanty. ➤ *vb, intr* (*always* **shack up with**) *slang* to live with a sexual partner, usu without being married.

shackle *n* **1** (*usu* **shackles**) a metal ring locked round the ankle or wrist of a prisoner or slave to limit movement, usu one of a pair joined by a chain. **2** (*usu* **shackles**) anything that restricts freedom; a hindrance or constraint. **3** a U-shaped metal loop or staple closed over by a **shackle-bolt**, used for fastening ropes or chains together. **4** the curved movable part of a padlock. ➤ *vb* **1** to restrain with or as if with shackles. **2** to connect or couple.

shad *n* (**shad** or **shads**) any of various marine fish resembling a large herring but with a deeper body.

shade *n* **1** the blocking or partial blocking out of sunlight, or the relative darkness caused by this. **2** an area from which sunlight has been completely or partially blocked. **3** any device used to modify direct light, eg a lampshade. **4** a device, eg a screen, used as a shield from direct heat, light, etc. **5** *US* a window-blind. **6** a dark or shaded area in a drawing or painting. **7** the state of appearing less impressive than something or someone else: *Her singing puts mine in the shade.* **8** a colour, esp one similar to but slightly different from a principal colour: *a lighter shade of blue.* **9** a small amount; a touch: *My house is a shade smaller than that.* **10** (**shades**) *colloq* sunglasses. **11** *literary* a ghost. ➤ *vb* **1** to block or partially block out sunlight from someone or something. **2** to draw or paint so as to give the impression of shade or shadows, eg by close parallel lines.

shading *n* in drawing and painting: the representation of areas of shade or shadows, eg by close parallel lines.

shadow *n* **1** a dark shape cast on a surface when an object stands between the surface and the source of light. **2** an area darkened by the blocking out of light. **3** the darker areas of a picture. **4** a slight amount; a hint or trace: *without a shadow of a doubt.* **5** a sense of gloom, trouble or foreboding: *The incident cast a shadow over the proceedings.* **6** a weakened person or thing that has wasted away to almost nothing: *She's a shadow of her former self.* **7** a constant companion. **8** a person following another closely and secretively, esp a spy or detective. ➤ *vb* **1** to put into darkness by blocking out light. **2** to cloud or darken. **3** to follow closely and secretively. ➤ *adj, pol* in the main opposition party: denoting a political counterpart to a member or section of the government: *shadow Chancellor* • *shadow cabinet.* ♦ **afraid of one's own shadow** extremely or excessively timid.

shadow-boxing *n* boxing against an imaginary opponent as training. ○ **shadow-box** *vb.*

shadowy *adj* **1** dark and shady; not clearly visible: *a shadowy figure.* **2** secluded; darkened by shadows.

shady *adj* (**-ier, -iest**) **1** sheltered or giving shelter from heat or sunlight. **2** *colloq* underhand or disreputable, often dishonest or illegal: *a shady character.* **3** shadowy or mysterious; sinister. ○ **shadiness** *n.*

shaft *n* **1** the long straight part or handle of anything. **2** a ray or beam of light. **3** in vehicle engines: a rotating rod that transmits motion. **4** a vertical passageway in a building, esp one through which a lift moves. **5** a well-like excavation or passage, eg into a mine. **6** either of the projecting parts of a cart, etc to which a horse is attached. ➤ *vb, US slang* to dupe, cheat or swindle.

shag¹ *n* **1** a ragged mass of hair. **2** a long coarse pile or nap on fabric. **3** a type of tobacco cut into coarse shreds.

shag² *n* a cormorant with glossy dark-green plumage, a long neck, webbed feet and an upright stance.

shag³ *coarse slang, vb* (**shagged, shagging**) to have sexual intercourse with someone. ➤ *n* an act of sexual intercourse.

shaggy *adj* (**-ier, -iest**) **1** of hair, fur, wool, etc: long and coarse; rough and untidy in appearance. **2** having shaggy hair or fur. ○ **shagginess** *n.*

shagreen *n* **1** a coarse granular leather, often dyed green, made from the skin of animals, esp a horse or donkey. **2** the skin of a shark, ray, etc, used as an abrasive.

shah *n, hist* a title of the former rulers of Iran and other Eastern countries.

shake *vb* (**shook, shaken**) **1** to move with quick, often forceful to-and-fro or up-and-down movements. **2** (*also* **shake sth up**) to mix it in this way. **3** to wave violently and threateningly; to brandish: *He shook his fist at them.* **4** *tr & intr* to tremble or make something or someone tremble, totter or shiver. **5** to cause intense shock to; to agitate profoundly: *the accident that shook the nation.* **6** (*also* **shake sb up**) to disturb, unnerve or upset them greatly. **7** to make something or someone waver; to weaken: *The experience shook my confidence.* **8** *intr* to shake hands. **9** *intr, mus* to trill. ➤ *n* **1** an act or the action of shaking. **2** *colloq* a very short while; a moment. **3** (**the shakes**) *colloq* a fit of uncontrollable trembling. **4** a milk shake. **5** *mus* a trill. ○ **shakeable** *or* **shakable** *adj.* ♦ **no great shakes** *colloq* not of great importance, ability or worth. **shake a leg** *colloq* to hurry up or get moving. **shake one's head** to turn one's head from side to side as a sign of rejection, disagreement, disapproval, denial, etc. **two shakes (of a lamb's tail)** *colloq* a very short time. ◊ **shake sth** *or* **sb off 1** to get rid of them; to free oneself from them. **2** to escape from them. **shake sb up** *colloq* to stimulate them into action, esp from a state of lethargy or apathy. **shake sth up 1** to mix it. **2** *colloq* to reorganize it thoroughly.

shakedown *n, colloq* **1** a makeshift or temporary bed, orig made by shaking down straw. **2** an act of extortion.

shaker *n* **1** a container from which something, eg salt, is dispensed by shaking. **2** a container in which something, eg a cocktail, is mixed by shaking.

Shakespearean *or* **Shakespearian** *adj* relating to or characteristic of the works of William Shakespeare.

shake-up *or* **shake-out** *n, colloq* a fundamental change, disturbance or reorganization.

shaky *adj* (**-ier, -iest**) **1** trembling or inclined to tremble with, or as if with, weakness, fear or illness. **2** *colloq* wavering; not solid, sound or secure. **3** disputable or uncertain: *shaky knowledge.* ○ **shakily** *adv.*

shale *n, geol* a fine-grained sedimentary rock, easily split into thin layers, formed as a result of the compression of clay, silt or sand by overlying rocks.

shall *auxiliary vb* expressing: **1** the future tense of other verbs, esp when the subject is *I* or *we.* **2** determination, intention, certainty and obligation, esp when the subject is *you, he, she, it* or *they. They shall succeed* • *You shall not kill.* **3** a question implying future action, often with the sense of an offer or suggestion, esp when the subject is *I* or *we: What shall we do?* • *Shall I give you a hand?*

> **shall** The rule about **shall** and **will** used to be as follows: to express the simple future, use **shall** with **I** and **we**, and **will** with **you, he, she, it** and **they**; to express per-

mission, obligation or determination, use **will** with **I** and **we**, and **shall** with **you**, **he**, **she**, **it** and **they**.

Nowadays, **I will** and **we will** are commonly used to express the simple future.

Note that **shall** is often used in questions in the second person to show that the question is really a neutral request for information rather than a request for something be done:

Shall you tell him about it?

shallot or **shalot** /ʃə'lɒt/ *n* a small onion, widely used in cooking and for making pickles.

shallow *adj* 1 having no great depth. 2 not profound or sincere; superficial. ➢ *n* (*often* **shallows**) a shallow place or part, esp in water. ○ **shallowness** *n*.

sham *adj* false, counterfeit or pretended; insincere. ➢ *vb* (**shammed, shamming**) *tr & intr* to pretend or feign. ➢ *n* 1 anything not genuine. 2 a person who shams, esp an impostor.

shaman /'ʃeɪmən/ *n* a traditional healer among some indigenous peoples, esp one who attempts to journey to the spirit world.

shamble *vb, intr* (*usu* **shamble along, past**, *etc*) to walk with slow awkward scuffing steps. ➢ *n* a shambling walk or pace. ○ **shambling** *n, adj*.

shambles *sing n* 1 *colloq* a confused mess or muddle; a state of total disorder: *The whole event was a shambles*. 2 a slaughterhouse. 3 a scene or place of slaughter or carnage. ○ **shambolic** *adj, colloq* totally disorganized.

shame *n* 1 the humiliating feeling of having appeared unfavourably in one's own eyes, or those of others, as a result of one's own offensive or disrespectful actions, or those of an associate. 2 susceptibility to such a feeling or emotion. 3 fear or scorn of incurring or bringing disgrace or dishonour. 4 disgrace or loss of reputation: *He's brought shame on the whole family*. 5 modesty or bashfulness. 6 a regrettable or disappointing event or situation: *It's such a shame that he failed his exam*. ➢ *vb* 1 to make someone feel shame. 2 to bring disgrace on someone or something. ♦ **put sb to shame** 1 to disgrace them. 2 to make them seem inadequate by comparison. **shame on you, them**, *etc* you, they, etc should be ashamed.

shamefaced *adj* showing shame or embarrassment; abashed.

shameful *adj* bringing or deserving shame; disgraceful: *shameful behaviour*. ○ **shamefully** *adv*.

shameless *adj* 1 incapable of feeling shame; showing no shame. 2 carried out or done without shame; brazen or immodest. ○ **shamelessly** *adv*.

shammy *n* (-*ies*) *colloq* (*in full* **shammy leather**) a chamois leather.

shampoo *n* 1 a soapy liquid for washing the hair and scalp. 2 a similar liquid for cleaning carpets or upholstery. 3 the act or an instance of treating with either liquid. ➢ *vb* to wash or clean with shampoo.

shamrock *n* a plant with leaves divided into three rounded leaflets, esp various species of clover, adopted as the national emblem of Ireland.

shandy *n* (-*ies*) a mixture of beer or lager with lemonade or ginger beer.

shanghai *vb* (**shanghais, shanghaied, shanghaiing**) *colloq* 1 to kidnap and drug or make drunk and send to sea as a sailor. 2 to trick into any unpleasant situation.

shank *n* 1 the lower leg between the knee and the foot. 2 the same part of the leg in an animal, esp a horse. 3 the main section of the handle of a tool.

Shanks's pony or (*US*) **Shank's mare** *n, colloq* the use of one's own legs as a means of travelling.

shan't *contraction, colloq* shall not.

shantung *n* a plain and usu undyed fabric of wild silk with a rough finish.

shanty[1] *n* (-*ies*) a roughly built hut or cabin; a shack.

shanty[2] *n* (-*ies*) a rhythmical song with chorus and solo verses, formerly sung by sailors while working together.

shape *n* 1 the outline or form of anything. 2 a person's body or figure. 3 a form, person, etc: *I had an assistant in the shape of my brother*. 4 a desired form or condition: *We like to keep in shape*. 5 a general condition: *in bad shape*. 6 an unidentifiable figure; an apparition: *shapes lurking in the dark*. 7 a mould or pattern. 8 a geometric figure. ➢ *vb* 1 to form or fashion; to give a particular form to something. 2 to influence: *the event that shaped history*. 3 to devise, determine or develop to suit a particular purpose. ♦ **out of shape** 1 unfit; in poor physical condition. 2 deformed or disfigured. **take shape** 1 to take on a definite form. 2 to finally become recognizable as the desired result of plans or theories. ◊ **shape up** *colloq* 1 to appear to be developing in a particular way: *This project is shaping up well*. 2 to be promising; to progress or develop well. 3 to lose weight; to tone up: *I'm trying to shape up for summer*.

shapeless *adj* 1 having an ill-defined or irregular shape. 2 unattractively shaped. ○ **shapelessness** *n*.

shapely *adj* (-*ier*, -*iest*) having an attractive, well-proportioned shape or figure. ○ **shapeliness** *n*.

shard *n* a fragment of something brittle, usu glass or pottery.

share[1] *n* 1 a part allotted, contributed or owned by each of several people or groups. 2 a portion, section or division. 3 (*usu* **shares**) the fixed units into which the total wealth of a business company is divided, ownership of which gives the right to receive a portion of the company's profits. ➢ *vb* 1 to have in common. 2 to use something with someone else: *We had to share a book in class*. 3 (*also* **share in sth**) to have joint possession or responsibility for it, with another or others. **4** (*often* **share sth out**) to divide it into portions and distribute it among several people or groups. ○ **sharer** *n*. ◆ **share and share alike 1** to give everyone their due share. **2** with or in equal shares.

share² *n* a PLOUGHSHARE.

shareholder *n* someone who owns shares in a company. ○ **shareholding** *n*.

shareware *n, comput* software readily available for free, esp for a limited trial period.

shark *n* **1** a large, usu fierce, fish with a long body covered with tooth-like scales, and a prominent dorsal fin. **2** *colloq* a ruthless or dishonest person.

sharkskin *n* **1** leather made from a shark's skin; shagreen. **2** smooth rayon fabric with a dull sheen.

sharp *adj* **1** having a thin edge or point that cuts or pierces. **2** having a bitter pungent taste. **3** severely or harshly felt; penetrating: *sharp pain*. **4** sudden and acute: *a sharp bend*. **5** abrupt or harsh in speech; sarcastic. **6** easily perceived; clear-cut or well-defined: *a sharp contrast*. **7** keen or perceptive. **8** eager; alert to one's own interests. **9** barely honest; cunning. **10** *colloq* stylish: *a sharp dresser*. **11** *mus* higher in pitch by a semitone: *C sharp*. Compare FLAT¹ (*adj* sense 11b). **12** *mus* slightly too high in pitch. ➤ *n* **1** *mus* a note raised by a semitone, or the sign indicating this (♯). **2** *mus* the key producing this note. **3** *colloq* a practised cheat; a SHARPER: *a card sharp*. ➤ *adv* **1** punctually; on the dot: *at 9 o'clock sharp*. **2** suddenly: *pull up sharp*. **3** *mus* high or too high in pitch. ○ **sharply** *adv*. ○ **sharpness** *n*.

sharpen *vb, tr & intr* to make or become sharp. ○ **sharpener** *n*.

sharper *n, colloq* a practised cheat; a sharp.

sharpish *adj* quite sharp. ➤ *adv* quickly; promptly: *I'd get there sharpish if I were you!*

sharpshooter *n* an expert marksman, esp a soldier, policeman, etc with this skill. ○ **sharpshooting** *n, adj*.

sharp-witted *adj* quick to perceive, act or react; keenly intelligent or alert. ○ **sharp-wittedly** *adv*.

shatter *vb* **1** *tr & intr* to break into tiny fragments, usu suddenly or with force. **2** to destroy completely; to wreck. **3** to upset greatly. **4** *colloq* to tire out or exhaust. ○ **shattered** *adj, colloq* **1** exhausted. **2** extremely upset. ○ **shattering** *adj*.

shave *vb* **1** to cut off (hair) from (esp the face) with a razor or shaver. **2** *intr* to remove one's facial hair in this way. **3** to graze the surface of something in passing. ➤ *n* **1** an act or the process of shaving one's facial hair. **2** a tool for shaving wood.

shaver *n* **1** an electrical device with a moving blade or set of blades for shaving hair. **2** *old use, colloq* a young boy.

shawl *n* a large single piece of fabric used to cover the head or shoulders or to wrap a baby.

she *pron* a female person or animal, or a thing thought of as female (eg a ship), named before or understood from the context. ➤ *n* a female person or animal.

sheaf *n* (*sheaves*) **1** a bundle of things tied together, esp reaped corn. **2** a bundle of papers. ➤ *vb* (*sheafed, sheafing; sheaved, sheaving*) **1** to tie up in a bundle. **2** *intr* to make sheaves.

shear *vb* (*past participle* **sheared** or **shorn**) **1** to clip or cut off something, esp with a large pair of clippers. **2** to cut the fleece off (a sheep). **3** (*usu* **shear sb of sth**) to strip or deprive them of it. **4** *tr & intr, eng, physics* (*also* **shear off**) to subject to a shear. ➤ *n* **1** the act of shearing. **2** (**shears**) a large pair of clippers, or a scissor-like cutting tool with a pivot or spring. **3** *eng, physics* a force acting parallel to a plane rather than at right angles to it. ○ **shearer** *n* someone who shears sheep.

sheath *n* **1** a case or covering for the blade of a sword or knife. **2** a condom. **3** (*also* **sheath-dress**) a straight tight-fitting dress. **4** *biol* in plants and animals: any protective or encasing structure.

sheathe *vb* to put into a sheath or case.

shebang /ʃɪˈbaŋ/ *n, orig US slang* an affair or matter; a situation: *the whole shebang*.

shebeen /ʃəˈbiːn/ *n* **1** an illicit liquor-shop. **2** in Ireland: illicit and usu home-made alcohol.

shed¹ *n* a wooden or metal outbuilding, usu small, sometimes open-fronted, for working in, for storage or for shelter.

shed² *vb* (*shed, shedding*) **1** to release or make something flow: *to shed tears*. **2** to get rid of or cast off something: *to shed a skin*. **3** to allow to flow off: *This fabric sheds water*. ◆ **shed light on sth** to cause (a problem, situation, etc) to become easier to comprehend.

she'd *contraction* **1** she had. **2** she would.

sheen *n* shine, lustre or radiance; glossiness.

sheep *n* (*pl* **sheep**) **1** a herbivorous mammal with a stocky body covered with a thick woolly fleece, kept as a farm animal for its meat and wool. **2** a meek person, esp one who follows or obeys unquestioningly, like a sheep in a flock.

sheep-dip *n* a disinfectant insecticidal preparation in a dipping bath, used for washing sheep in order to control parasitic diseases such as sheep scab.

sheepdog *n* **1** a working dog that is used to guard sheep from wild animals or to assist in herding. **2** any of several breeds of dog orig developed to herd sheep.

sheepish *adj* embarrassed through having done something wrong or foolish. ○ **sheepishly** *adv*. ○ **sheepishness** *n*.

sheepshank *n* a nautical knot used for shortening a rope.

sheepskin *n* the skin of a sheep, either with or without the fleece attached to it.

sheer¹ *adj* **1** complete; absolute or downright: *sheer madness*. **2** of a cliff, etc: vertical or nearly vertical: *a sheer drop*. **3** eg of a fabric: so thin or

fine as to be almost transparent: *sheer tights*.
➤ *adv* **1** completely. **2** vertically or nearly vertically.

sheer² *vb* **1** to make something change course or deviate. **2** *intr* (*usu* **sheer off** or **away**) to change course suddenly.

sheet¹ *n* **1** a large rectangular piece of fabric, esp for covering the mattress of a bed. **2** any large wide piece or expanse. **3** a piece of paper, esp if large and rectangular. **4** a pamphlet, broadsheet or newspaper. ➤ *vb* **1** to wrap or cover with or as if with a sheet. **2** *intr* of rain, ice, etc: to form in or fall in a sheet.

sheet² *n*, *naut* a controlling rope attached to the lower corner of a sail.

sheeting *n* fabric used for making sheets.

sheikh or **sheik** / ʃeɪk / *n* **1** the chief of an Arab tribe, village or family. **2** a Muslim leader.
○ **sheikhdom** *n*.

sheila *n*, *Aust*, *NZ colloq* a woman or girl.

shelf *n* (**shelves**) **1** a usu narrow, flat board fixed to a wall or part of a cupboard, bookcase, etc, for storing or laying things on. **2** a ledge of land, rock, etc; a sandbank. ♦ **on the shelf 1** of a person or thing: too old or worn out to be of any use. **2** no longer likely to marry, esp because of being too old.

shelf life *n* the length of time that a product remains usable, edible, etc.

shell *n* **1** the hard protective structure covering an egg. **2** *zool* the hard protective structure covering the body of certain animals, esp shellfish, snails,and tortoises. **3** *bot* the hard protective structure covering the seed or fruit of some plants. **4** any hard protective cover. **5** a round of ammunition for a large-bore gun, eg a mortar. **6** a shotgun cartridge. **7** *comput* a program that acts as a user-friendly interface between an operating system and the user. ➤ *vb* **1** to remove the shell from something. **2** to bombard with (eg mortar) shells. ♦ **come out of one's shell** to cease to be shy and become more friendly or sociable. ◇ **shell out** or **shell out for sth** *colloq* to pay out (money) or spend (money) on it.

she'll *contraction* **1** she will. **2** she shall.

shellac / ʃə'lak / *n* **1** a yellow or orange resin produced by the lac insect. **2** a solution of this in alcohol, used as a varnish. ➤ *vb* (**shellacked**, **shellacking**) to coat with shellac.

shellfish *n* (*pl* **shellfish**) a shelled edible aquatic invertebrate, eg a prawn, crab, shrimp or lobster.

shellshock *n* a psychological disorder caused by prolonged exposure to military combat conditions. ○ **shellshocked** *adj*.

shelter *n* **1** protection against weather or danger. **2** a place or structure providing this. **3** a place of refuge, retreat or temporary lodging in distress. ➤ *vb* **1** to protect someone or something from the effects of weather or danger. **2** to give asylum or lodging. **3** *intr* to take cover.

sheltered *adj* **1** protected from the effects of

weather. **2** protected from the harsh realities and unpleasantnesses of the world: *a sheltered life*.

shelve *vb* **1** to place or store on a shelf. **2** to fit with shelves. **3** to postpone or put aside; to abandon. **4** to remove from active service.

shelving *n* **1** material used for making shelves. **2** shelves collectively.

shenanigans *pl n*, *colloq* **1** foolish behaviour; nonsense. **2** underhand dealings; trickery.

shepherd *n* **1** someone who looks after, or herds, sheep. **2** *literary* a religious minister or pastor. ➤ *vb* **1** to watch over or herd (sheep). **2** to guide or herd (a group or crowd).

shepherdess *n*, *old use* a female shepherd.

shepherd's pie *n* a dish consisting of minced meat baked with mashed potatoes on the top.

sherbet *n* **1** a fruit-flavoured powder eaten as confectionery, or made into an effervescent drink. **2** *N Am* a kind of water-ice.

sheriff *n* **1** in a US county: the chief elected police officer. **2** in England: the chief officer of the monarch in the shire or county, whose duties are now mainly ceremonial. **3** in Scotland: the chief judge of a sheriff court of a town or region.

sheriff court *n* in a Scottish town or region: a court trying all but the most serious crimes.

sherry *n* (**-ies**) a fortified wine ranging in colour from pale gold to dark brown.

she's *contraction* **1** she is. **2** she has.

shiatsu or **shiatzu** *n*, *med* a Japanese healing massage technique similar to ACUPUNCTURE but using pressure instead of needles.

shibboleth *n* **1** a common saying. **2** a slogan, custom or belief, esp if considered outdated. **3** a peculiarity of speech. **4** a use of a word, phrase or pronunciation that characterizes members of a particular group.

shield *n* **1** a piece of armour consisting of a broad plate, carried to deflect weapons. **2** a protective plate, screen, pad or other guard. **3** any shield-shaped design or object, esp one used as an emblem or coat of arms. **4** a shield-shaped plate or medal presented as a prize. **5** someone or something that protects from danger or harm. ➤ *vb* **1** to protect from danger or harm. **2** to ward off something.

shift *vb* **1** *tr* & *intr* to change the position or direction of something; to change position or direction. **2** to transfer, switch or redirect: *He tried to shift the blame on to someone else*. **3** in a vehicle: to change (gear). **4** to remove or dislodge someone or something: *Nothing will shift that mark*. **5** *intr*, *colloq* to move quickly. **6** to take appropriate or urgent action. **7** *intr* to manage or get along; to do as best one can. ➤ *n* **1** a change, or change of position. **2** one of a set of consecutive periods into which a 24-hour working day is divided. **3** the group of workers on duty during any one of these periods. **4** *comput* displacement of an ordered set of data to the left or right. **5** a loose, usu straight, dress.

shiftless adj 1 having no motivation or initiative. 2 inefficient.

shifty adj (-ier, -iest) of a person or behaviour: evasive, sly or shady.

shilling n 1 in the UK: a monetary unit and coin, before the introduction of decimal currency in 1971, worth one-twentieth of a pound or 12 old pence. 2 the standard unit of currency in Kenya, Tanzania, Uganda and Somalia, equal to 100 cents.

shilly-shally vb (-ies, -ied) intr to be indecisive; to vacillate.

shim n a thin washer or slip of metal, wood, plastic, etc used to adjust or fill a gap between machine parts, esp gears.

shimmer vb, intr to shine tremulously and quiveringly with reflected light; to glisten. ➤ n a tremulous or quivering gleam of reflected light. ○ **shimmery** adj.

shin n 1 the bony front part of the leg below the knee. 2 the lower part of a leg of beef. ➤ vb (**shinned, shinning**) tr & intr (usu **shin up**) to climb by gripping with the hands and legs.

shinbone n the TIBIA.

shindig n, colloq 1 a lively party or celebration. 2 a noisy disturbance or row.

shine vb (**shone** or in sense 4 **shined**) 1 intr to give out or reflect light; to beam with a steady radiance. 2 to direct the light from something: *They shone the torch around the room.* 3 to be bright; to glow: *Her face shone with joy.* 4 to make bright and gleaming by polishing. 5 intr to be outstandingly impressive in ability; to excel: *She shines at maths.* 6 intr to be clear or conspicuous: *Intelligence shines from their faces.* ➤ n 1 shining quality; brightness or lustre. 2 an act or process of polishing. ○ **shiny** adj. ◆ **take a shine to sb** colloq to like or fancy them on first acquaintance.

shiner n, colloq a black eye.

shingle[1] n 1 a thin rectangular tile, esp made of wood, laid with others in overlapping rows on a roof or wall. 2 these tiles collectively. 3 US a small sign hung outside a shop or business premises. 4 a woman's short hairstyle, cropped at the back into overlapping layers. ➤ vb 1 to tile with shingles. 2 to cut in a shingle.

shingle[2] n, geol 1 small pebbles that have been worn smooth by water. 2 a beach, bank or bed covered in gravel or stones.

shingles sing n, med a disease which produces a series of blisters along the path of the nerve, esp in the area of the waist and ribs.

shinty n (-ies) 1 a game, orig Scottish, similar to hockey, played by two teams of 12. 2 (also **shinty-stick**) the stick used for this game.

ship n 1 a large engine-propelled vessel, intended for sea travel. 2 a large sailing vessel, esp a three-masted, square-rigged sailing vessel. 3 colloq a spaceship or airship. ➤ vb (**shipped, shipping**) 1 to send or transport by ship. 2 to send or transport by land or air. 3 naut of a boat: to take in (water, eg waves) over the side. 4 naut to bring on board a boat or ship:

ship oars. 5 to engage for service on board ship. ◆ **when one's ship comes in** or **comes home** when one becomes rich.

shipboard n the side of a ship. ➤ adj occurring or situated on board a ship.

shipbuilder n a person or company that constructs ships. ○ **shipbuilding** n.

shipmate n a fellow sailor.

shipment n 1 the act or practice of shipping cargo. 2 a cargo or consignment transported, not necessarily by ship.

shipping n 1 the commercial transportation of freight, esp by ship. 2 ships as traffic.

shipshape adj in good order; neat and tidy.

shipwreck n 1 the accidental sinking or destruction of a ship. 2 the remains of a sunken or destroyed ship. 3 wreck or ruin; disaster. ➤ vb 1 tr & intr to be or make someone the victim of a ship's accidental sinking or destruction. 2 to wreck, ruin or destroy (eg plans).

shipwright n a skilled worker who builds or repairs (esp wooden) ships.

shipyard n a place where ships are built and repaired.

shire n a county.

shirk vb, tr & intr to evade (work, a duty, etc). ○ **shirker** n.

shirt n a garment for the upper body, typically with buttons down the front, and usu a fitted collar and cuffs. ◆ **keep one's shirt on** colloq to remain calm. **put one's shirt on sth** colloq to bet all one has on it.

shirtwaister n a woman's tailored dress with a shirt-like bodice.

shirty adj (-ier, -iest) colloq ill-tempered or irritable.

shish kebab see KEBAB

shit or **shite** coarse slang, n 1 excrement or faeces. 2 an act of defecating. 3 derog rubbish; nonsense. 4 derog a despicable person. ➤ vb (**shit, shitted** or **shat, shitting; shited, shiting**) intr to defecate.

shiver[1] vb, intr 1 to quiver or tremble, eg with fear. 2 to make an involuntary muscular movement in response to the cold. ➤ n 1 an act of shivering; a shivering movement or sensation. 2 (**the shivers**) colloq a fit of shivering. ○ **shivery** adj.

shiver[2] n a splinter or other small fragment. ➤ vb, tr & intr to shatter.

shoal[1] n 1 a multitude of fish swimming together. 2 a huge crowd; a multitude, flock or swarm. ➤ vb, intr to gather or move in a shoal; to swarm.

shoal[2] n 1 an area of shallow water in a river, lake or sea where sediment has accumulated. 2 such an accumulation of sediment, esp one exposed at high tide. ➤ vb 1 tr & intr to make or become shallow. 2 intr, naut to sail into shallow water. ➤ adj shallow.

shock[1] n 1 a strong emotional disturbance, esp a feeling of extreme surprise, outrage or disgust. 2 a cause of such a disturbance. 3 a heavy and violent impact, orig of charging warriors. 4

(*in full* **electric shock**) the passage of an electric current through the body. **5** *med* a state of extreme physical collapse, characterized by lowered blood pressure and body temperature and a sweaty pallid skin, occurring as a result of severe burns, drug overdose, extreme emotional disturbance, etc. ➤ *vb* **1** to give a shock to someone. **2** *tr & intr* to feel or make someone feel extreme surprise, outrage or disgust.

shock² *n* a bushy mass of hair.

shock³ *n* a number of sheaves of corn propped up against each other to dry.

shock absorber *n* in a vehicle: a device, such as a coiled spring, that damps vibrations caused by the wheels passing over bumps in the road.

shocker *n, colloq* **1** a very sensational tale. **2** any unpleasant or offensive person or thing.

shocking *adj* **1** giving a shock. **2** extremely surprising, outrageous or disgusting. **3** *colloq* deplorably bad: *His handwriting is shocking.* ○ **shockingly** *adv.*

shockproof *adj* protected against or resistant to the effects of shock or impact. ○ **shockproofing** *n.*

shock tactics *pl n* any course of action that seeks to achieve its object by means of suddenness and force.

shock therapy or **shock treatment** *n* another name for ELECTROCONVULSIVE THERAPY.

shock wave *n* **1** *physics* an exceptionally intense sound wave, caused by a violent explosion or the movement of an object at a speed greater than that of sound. **2** a feeling of shock which spreads through a community, etc, after some disturbing event.

shoddy *adj* (**-ier, -iest**) of poor quality; carelessly done or made. ○ **shoddiness** *n.*

shoe *n* **1** either of a pair of shaped outer coverings for the feet, esp ones made of leather or other stiff material, usu finishing below the ankle. **2** anything like this in shape or function. **3** a horseshoe. ➤ *vb* (**shod, shoeing**) **1** to provide with shoes. **2** to fit (a horse) with shoes. ◆ **in sb's shoes** in the same situation as them: *I wouldn't like to be in his shoes now.*

shoehorn *n* a curved piece of metal, plastic or (orig) horn, used for levering the heel into a shoe. ➤ *vb* to fit, squeeze or compress into a tight space.

shoelace *n* a string or cord passed through eyelet holes to fasten a shoe.

shoemaker *n* someone who makes or repairs shoes and boots.

shoeshine *n* the act of polishing shoes.

shoestring *n, N Am* a shoelace. ◆ **on a shoestring** *colloq* with or using a very small amount of money.

shoe tree *n* a support put inside a shoe to preserve its shape when it is not being worn.

shoo *exclam* an expression used to scare or chase away a person or animal. ➤ *vb* (**shooed, shooing**) (*usu* **shoo** *sb* or *sth* **away** or **off**) to

chase them away by, or as if by, shouting 'Shoo!'

shoot *vb* (**shot**) **1** *tr & intr* to fire a gun or other weapon. **2** to fire bullets, arrows or other missiles. **3** to hit, wound or kill with a weapon or missile. **4** to let fly with force: *The geyser shot water high into the air.* **5** to launch or direct forcefully and rapidly: *He shot questions at them.* **6** *tr & intr* (*also* **shoot up**) to move, grow or progress quickly, or make someone or something do this: *Prices shot up.* **7** *tr & intr, sport* to strike (the ball, etc) at goal. **8** *tr & intr* to film (motion pictures), or take photographs of someone or something. **9** *intr* of pain: to dart with a stabbing sensation. **10** *intr* to dart forth or forwards. ➤ *n* **1** an act of shooting. **2** a shooting match or party. **3** an outing or expedition to hunt animals with firearms. **4** an area of land for this. **5** the shooting of a film or a photographic modelling session. **6** a new or young plant growth. **7** the sprouting of a plant. ◆ **be** or **get shot of** *sb* or *sth* *colloq* to be rid of them. **shoot ahead** to advance quickly in front of others, eg in a race. **shoot from the hip** *colloq* to speak hastily, bluntly or directly, without preparation or concern for the consequences. **shoot it out** to settle (a dispute, competition, etc) by military action. **shoot oneself in the foot** *colloq* to injure or harm one's own interests by ineptitude. **shoot one's mouth off** *colloq* to speak freely, indiscreetly or boastfully. **the whole shoot** or **shooting-match** *colloq* the whole lot.

shooter *n* **1** someone or something that shoots. **2** *colloq* a gun. **3** *colloq* a small drink of alcoholic spirit.

shooting gallery *n* a long room fitted out with targets used for practice or amusement with firearms.

shooting star *n* a METEOR.

shop *n* **1** a room or building where goods are sold or services are provided. **2** a spell of shopping. ➤ *vb* (**shopped, shopping**) **1** *intr* to visit a shop or shops, esp in order to buy goods. **2** *slang* to betray or inform on someone to the police, etc. ◆ **all over the shop** *colloq* scattered everywhere. **set up shop** to establish or open a trading establishment. **shut up shop** *colloq* to stop trading, either at the end of the working day or permanently. **talk shop** *colloq* to talk about one's work or business, esp in a tedious way. ◊ **shop around 1** to compare the price and quality of goods in various shops. **2** *colloq* to explore the full range of options available.

shop assistant *n* someone serving customers in a shop.

shop floor *n* **1** the part of a factory or workshop where the manual work is carried out. **2** the workers in a factory, as opposed to the management.

shopkeeper *n* someone who owns and manages a shop.

shoplift *vb, tr & intr* to steal (goods) from shops. ○ **shoplifter** *n.* ○ **shoplifting** *n.*

shopper n 1 someone who shops. 2 a shopping bag or basket.

shopping n 1 the act of visiting shops to look at or buy goods. 2 goods bought in shops.

shop-soiled adj slightly dirty, faded or spoiled from being used as a display in a shop.

shop steward n a worker elected by others to be an official trade union representative in negotiations with the management.

shop window n 1 a window of a shop in which goods are arranged in a display. 2 any arrangement which displays something to advantage.

shore¹ n 1 a narrow strip of land bordering on the sea, a lake or any other large body of water. 2 land as opposed to the sea. 3 (**shores**) lands; countries: foreign shores. ➤ vb to set on shore: shore a boat.

shore² n a prop. ➤ vb (usu **shore sth up**) 1 to support it with props. 2 to give support to it; to sustain or strengthen it.

shoreline n the line formed where land meets water.

short adj 1 having little physical length; not long. 2 having little height. 3 having little extent or duration; brief. 4 of a temper: quickly and easily lost. 5 rudely abrupt; curt: She was very short with him. 6 of the memory: tending not to retain things for long. 7 of pastry: crisp and crumbling easily. 8 in short supply; in demand: We are two tickets short. 9 phonetics of a vowel sound: being the briefer of two possible lengths of vowel. 10 lacking in money: I'm a bit short at the moment. ➤ adv 1 abruptly; briefly: I stopped short. 2 on this or the near side: The dart fell short of the board. ➤ n 1 something that is short. 2 shortness; abbreviation or summary. 3 colloq a drink of an alcoholic spirit. 4 a short cinema film shown before the main film. 5 a SHORT CIRCUIT. ➤ vb, tr & intr to SHORT-CIRCUIT. ○ **shortness** n. ♦ **fall short** to be insufficient; to be less than a required, expected or stated amount. **for short** as an abbreviated form: She gets called Jenny for short. **in short** concisely stated; in a few words. **make short work of sb** or **sth** to settle or dispose of them quickly and thoroughly. **short and sweet** colloq agreeably brief. **short of** or **on sth** lacking in it. **short of sth** without going as far as it; except it: We tried every kind of persuasion short of threats. **stop short** to come to an abrupt halt or standstill.

shortage n a lack or deficiency.

shortbread n a rich crumbly biscuit made with flour, butter and sugar.

shortcake n 1 shortbread or other crumbly cake. 2 US a cake like a scone, prepared in layers with fruit between, served with cream.

short-change vb 1 to give (a customer) less than the correct amount of change, either by accident or intentionally. 2 colloq to cheat someone.

short circuit n, electronics a connection across an electric circuit with a very low resistance, which may damage electrical equip-

ment or be a fire hazard. ➤ vb (**short-circuit**) 1 to cause a short circuit in something. 2 to provide with a short cut or bypass.

shortcoming n a fault or defect.

short cut n 1 a quicker route than normal between two places. 2 a method that saves time or effort. ➤ vb (**short-cut**) to use a shorter route or method.

shorten vb, tr & intr to make or become shorter.

shortening n butter, lard or other fat used for making pastry more crumbly.

shortfall n 1 a failure to reach a desired or expected level or specification. 2 the amount or margin by which something is deficient: There is a shortfall of £100.

shorthand n any of various systems of combined strokes and dots representing speech sounds, used as a fast way of recording speech.

short-handed adj understaffed; short of workers.

shorthorn n a breed of beef and dairy cattle with very short horns.

shortlist n a selection of the best candidates from the total number submitted or nominated, from which the successful candidate will be chosen. ➤ vb (**short-list**) to place on a shortlist.

short-lived adj living or lasting only for a short time.

shortly adv 1 soon: He'll arrive shortly. 2 in a curt or abrupt manner.

short-range adj referring or relating to a short distance or length of time: a short-range telescope.

shorts pl n trousers extending from the waist to anywhere between the upper thigh and the knee.

short shrift n discourteously brief or disdainful consideration: Their suggestions were given short shrift. ♦ **make short shrift of sth** to discard it without due consideration.

short-sighted adj 1 capable of seeing only near objects clearly. Compare LONG-SIGHTED. 2 of a person, plan, etc: lacking or showing a lack of foresight. ○ **short-sightedness** n.

short-staffed adj lacking enough workers.

short-tempered adj easily made angry.

short-term adj 1 concerned only with the near or immediate future. 2 lasting only a short time.

short wave n 1 a radio wave with a wavelength between 10 and 100 metres. Compare LONG WAVE, MEDIUM WAVE. 2 physics an electromagnetic wave with a wavelength no longer than that of visible light.

short-winded adj easily and quickly running out of breath.

shot¹ n 1 an act of shooting or firing a gun. 2 the sound of a gun being fired. 3 small metal pellets collectively, fired in clusters from a SHOTGUN. 4 a person considered in terms of their ability to fire a gun accurately: a good shot. 5 a photographic exposure. 6 a single piece of filmed action recorded without a break by one camera. **7** *sport* an act or instance of shooting or playing a stroke eg in tennis, snooker, etc. **8** *athletics* a heavy metal ball thrown in the SHOT PUT. **9** *colloq* an attempt: *I'll have a shot at it.* **10** *colloq* an injection. **11** *colloq* a small drink of alcoholic spirit. ◆ **a long shot** a bet, attempt, etc with little chance of success: *It's a long shot, but I'll have a try.* **a shot in the arm** *colloq* an uplifting or reviving influence; a boost. **a shot in the dark** a wild guess. **like a shot** extremely quickly or eagerly.

shot² *adj* **1** of a fabric: woven with different-coloured threads in the warp and weft so that movement produces the effect of changing colours: *shot silk.* **2** streaked with a different colour.

shotgun *n* a gun with a long, wide, smooth barrel for firing small shot.

shot put *n, athletics* a field event in which a heavy metal ball is thrown from the shoulder as far as possible. ○ **shot-putter** *n*.

should *auxiliary vb* expressing: **1** obligation, duty or recommendation; ought to: *You should brush your teeth regularly.* **2** likelihood or probability: *He should have left by now.* **3** condition: *If she should die before you, what would happen?* **4** *with first person pronouns* a past tense of *shall* in reported speech: *I told them I should be back soon.* See note at SHALL. **5** statements in clauses with *that*, following expressions of feeling or mood: *It seems odd that we should both have had the same idea.*

shoulder *n* **1** in humans and animals: the part on either side of the body, just below the neck, where the arm or front limb joins the trunk. **2** the part of a garment that covers this. **3** a cut of meat consisting of the animal's upper foreleg. **4** either edge of a road. ➤ *vb* **1** to bear (eg a responsibility). **2** to carry on one's shoulders. **3** to thrust with the shoulder. ◆ **a shoulder to cry on** a person to tell one's troubles to. **put one's shoulder to the wheel** *colloq* to get down to some hard work; to make a great effort. **rub shoulders with sb** *colloq* to meet or associate with them. **shoulder to shoulder** together in friendship or agreement.

shoulder blade *n* the SCAPULA.

shouldn't contraction, *colloq* should not.

shout *n* **1** a loud cry or call. **2** *colloq* a turn to buy a round of drinks. ➤ *vb* **1** *tr & intr* (*also* **shout out**) to utter a loud cry or call. **2** *intr* to speak in raised or angry tones. ○ **shouter** *n*. ◇ **shout sb down** to force them to give up speaking, or prevent them from being heard, by means of persistent shouting.

shove *vb* **1** *tr & intr* to push or thrust with force. **2** *colloq* to place or put, esp roughly: *Just shove it in the bag.* ➤ *n* a forceful push. ◇ **shove off** *colloq* to go away.

shovel *n* **1** a tool with a deep-sided spade-like blade and a handle, for lifting and carrying loose material. **2** a machine, machine part or device with a scooping action. **3** a shovelful. ➤ *vb* (**shovelled, shovelling**) **1** to lift or carry

with, or as if with, a shovel. **2** to rapidly and crudely gather in large quantities: *She shovelled food into her mouth.* ○ **shovelful** *n*.

show *vb* (*past participle* **shown** *or* **showed**) **1** *tr & intr* to make or become visible, known or noticeable: *Does my embarrassment show?* **2** to present to view. **3** to display or exhibit. **4** to prove, indicate or reveal: *This shows us that man evolved from the ape.* **5** to prove oneself or itself to be: *He always shows himself to be such a gentleman.* **6** to teach by demonstrating. **7** to lead, guide or escort: *I'll show you to the door.* **8** to give: *Show him some respect.* **9** *intr* of a cinema film, theatre production, etc: to be part of a current programme: *Her latest film is now showing at smaller cinemas.* **10** *intr, slang* to appear or arrive: *What time did he show?* ➤ *n* **1** an act of showing. **2** any form of entertainment or spectacle. **3** an exhibition. **4** a pretence: *a show of friendship.* **5** a sign or indication: *a show of emotion.* **6** *colloq* proceedings; affair. **7** *old use, colloq* effort; attempt: *a jolly good show.* ◆ **for show** for the sake of outward appearances. **on show** on display. **run the show** *colloq* to be in charge; to dominate. ◇ **show off** to display oneself or one's talents precociously, with the aim of inviting attention or admiration. **show sth off 1** to display it proudly, inviting admiration. **2** to display it to good effect: *The cream rug shows off the red carpet nicely.* **show up 1** *colloq* to arrive; to turn up. **2** to be clearly visible. **show sb up** to embarrass them in public.

showbiz *n, adj, colloq* show business.

show business *n* the entertainment industry, esp light entertainment in film, theatre and television.

showcase *n* **1** a glass case for displaying objects. **2** any setting in which someone or something is displayed to good advantage.

showdown *n, colloq* a confrontation or fight by which a long-term dispute may be finally settled.

shower *n* **1** a device that produces a spray of water for bathing under, usu while standing. **2** a room or cubicle fitted with such a device or devices. **3** an act or an instance of bathing under such a device. **4** a sudden but short and usu light fall of rain, snow or hail. **5** a fall of drops of any liquid. **6** a sudden (esp heavy) burst or fall: *a shower of abuse.* **7** *N Am* a party at which wedding or baby gifts are presented. **8** *slang* a detestable or worthless person or group of people. ➤ *vb* **1** *tr & intr* to bestow, fall or come abundantly. **2** *intr* to bathe under a shower. **3** *intr* to rain in showers. ○ **showery** *adj*.

showgirl *n* a girl who performs in variety entertainments, usu as a dancer or singer.

showing *n* **1** an act of exhibiting or displaying. **2** a screening of a cinema film. **3** a display of behaviour as evidence of a fact: *On this showing, he certainly won't get the job.*

showjumping *n* a competitive sport in which riders on horseback take turns to jump a variety of obstacles, usu against the clock. ○ **showjumper** n.

showman n **1** someone who owns, exhibits or manages a circus or other entertainment. **2** someone skilled in displaying things, esp personal abilities. ○ **showmanship** n.

show-off n, colloq someone who shows off to attract attention; an exhibitionist.

showpiece n **1** an item on display; an exhibit. **2** an item presented as an excellent example of its type, to be copied or admired.

showroom n a room where examples of goods for sale, esp large and expensive items, are displayed.

show-stopper n an act or performance that is very well received by the audience. ○ **show-stopping** adj.

showy adj (-ier, -iest) **1** making an impressive or exciting display. **2** attractively and impressively bright; flashy. ○ **showily** adv. ○ **showiness** n.

shrapnel n **1** a shell, filled with pellets or metal fragments, which explodes shortly before impact. **2** flying fragments of the casing of this or any exploding shell.

shred n **1** a thin scrap or strip cut or ripped off. **2** the smallest piece or amount: There's not a shred of evidence. ➤ vb (**shredded, shredding**) to cut, tear or scrape into shreds. ○ **shredder** n.

shrew n **1** a small nocturnal mammal with velvety fur, small eyes and a pointed snout. **2** a quarrelsome or scolding woman. ○ **shrewish** adj.

shrewd adj possessing or showing keen judgement gained from practical experience; astute. ○ **shrewdly** adv. ○ **shrewdness** n.

shriek vb, tr & intr to cry out with a piercing scream. ➤ n such a piercing cry.

shrift n absolution; confession.

shrike n any of various small perching birds with a powerful slightly hooked beak.

shrill adj of a voice, sound, etc: high-pitched and piercing. ➤ vb to utter in such a high-pitched manner. ○ **shrillness** n.

shrimp n **1** a small edible crustacean with a cylindrical semi-transparent body and five pairs of jointed legs. **2** colloq a very small slight person. ➤ vb, intr to fish for shrimps.

shrine n **1** a sacred place of worship. **2** the tomb or monument of a saint or other holy person. **3** any place or thing greatly respected because of its associations.

shrink vb (**shrank, shrunk**) **1** tr & intr to make or become smaller in size or extent, esp through exposure to heat, cold or moisture. **2** tr & intr to contract or make something contract. **3** intr to shrivel or wither. **4** intr (often **shrink from sth**) to move away in horror or disgust; to recoil. **5** intr (often **shrink from sth**) to be reluctant to do it. ➤ n **1** an act of shrinking. **2** colloq a psychiatrist. ○ **shrinkable** adj.

shrinkage n **1** the act of shrinking. **2** the amount by which something shrinks.

shrinking violet n, colloq a shy hesitant person.

shrink-wrap vb to wrap (goods) in clear plastic film that is then shrunk, eg by heating, so that it fits tightly.

shrivel vb (**shrivelled, shrivelling**) tr & intr (also **shrivel up**) to make or become shrunken and wrinkled, esp as a result of drying out.

shroud n **1** a garment or cloth in which a corpse is wrapped. **2** anything that obscures, masks or hides: shrouds of fog. ➤ vb **1** to wrap in a shroud. **2** to obscure, mask or hide: proceedings shrouded in secrecy.

Shrove Tuesday n in the Christian calendar: the day before Ash Wednesday, on which it was customary to confess one's sins.

shrub n, bot a woody plant or bush, without any main trunk, which branches into several main stems at or just below ground level. ○ **shrubby** adj.

shrubbery n (-ies) **1** a place, esp a part of a garden, where shrubs are grown. **2** a collective name for shrubs.

shrug vb (**shrugged, shrugging**) tr & intr to raise up and drop the shoulders briefly as an indication of doubt, indifference, etc. ➤ n an act of shrugging. ◊ **shrug sth off 1** to get rid of it easily. **2** to dismiss (esp criticism) lightly.

shrunken adj having shrunk or having been shrunk.

shudder vb, intr to shiver or tremble, esp with fear, cold or disgust. ➤ n **1** such a trembling movement or feeling. **2** a heavy vibration or shaking. ○ **shuddering** adj.

shuffle vb **1** tr & intr to move or drag (one's feet) with short sliding steps; to walk in this fashion. **2** intr to shamble or walk awkwardly. **3** to rearrange or mix up roughly or carelessly: shuffle papers. **4** tr & intr to jumble up (playing-cards) randomly. ➤ n **1** an act or sound of shuffling. **2** a short quick sliding of the feet in dancing.

shufti or **shufty** n, colloq a look or glance.

shun vb (**shunned, shunning**) to intentionally avoid someone or something.

shunt vb **1** to move (a train or carriage) from one track to another. **2** to bypass or sidetrack. **3** to get rid of or transfer (eg a task) on to someone else, as an evasion. ➤ n **1** an act of shunting. **2** electronics a conductor diverting part of an electric current. **3** colloq a minor collision between vehicles. ○ **shunter** n.

shush exclam be quiet! ➤ vb to make someone or something quiet by, or as if by, saying 'Shush!'

shut vb (**shut, shutting**) **1** tr & intr to place or move so as to close an opening: Shut the door. **2** tr & intr to close or make something close over, denying access to the contents or inside: I shut the book. **3** tr & intr (often **shut up**) not to allow access to something; to forbid entrance into it: They shut up the building. **4** to fasten or bar; to lock. **5** to confine: He shuts himself in his room for hours. **6** to catch or pinch in a fastening: I shut my finger in the window. **7** intr of a business, etc: to cease to operate at the end of the day. ➤ adj **1** not open; closed. **2** made fast;

secure. ◊ **shut down** or **shut sth down** to stop or make it stop operating, either for a time or permanently. **shut sth off** to switch it off; to stop the flow of it. **shut sb** or **shut sth 1** to prevent them or it entering a room, building, etc. **2** to exclude them or it. **shut up** *colloq* to stop speaking. **shut sb up 1** *colloq* to make them stop speaking; to reduce them to silence. **2** to confine them, usu against their will.

shutdown *n* a temporary closing of a factory or business.

shuteye *n*, *colloq* sleep.

shutter *n* **1** someone or something that shuts. **2** a movable internal or external cover for a window, esp one of a pair of hinged wooden or metal panels. **3** a device in a camera that regulates the opening and closing of the aperture, exposing the film to light. ➣ *vb* to fit or cover (a window) with a shutter or shutters.

shuttle *n* **1** *weaving* the device that carries the horizontal thread (the WEFT) backwards and forwards between the vertical threads (the WARP). **2** the device that carries the lower thread through the loop formed by the upper in a sewing machine. **3** an aircraft, train or bus that runs a frequent service between two places, usu at a relatively short distance from one another. ➣ *vb, tr & intr* to convey or travel in a shuttle.

shuttlecock *n* a cone of feathers or of feathered plastic attached to a rounded cork, hit backwards and forwards with battledores or badminton rackets.

shy¹ *adj* **1** of a person: embarrassed or unnerved by the company or attention of others. **2** easily scared; bashful or timid. **3** (**shy of sth**) wary or distrustful of it. **4** warily reluctant. ➣ *vb* (**shies, shied**) *intr* **1** eg of a horse: to jump suddenly aside or back in fear. **2** (*usu* **shy away** or **off**) to shrink from something or recoil, showing reluctance. ➣ *n* (**shies**) an act of shying. ◊ **shyly** *adv*. ◊ **shyness** *n*.

shy² *vb* (**shies, shied**) to fling or throw. ➣ *n* (**shies**) a fling or throw.

shyster *n*, *N Am, slang* an unscrupulous or disreputable person, esp a lawyer.

SI *abbrev* Système International d'Unités, the modern scientific system of units, used in the measurement of all physical quantities.

Si *symbol, chem* silicon.

Siamese twins see CONJOINED TWINS

sibilant *adj* similar to, having or pronounced with a hissing sound. ➣ *n, phonetics* a consonant with such a sound, eg *s* and *z*. ◊ **sibilance** *n*.

sibling *n* a brother or sister.

sic *adv* a term used in brackets after a word or phrase in a quotation to indicate that it is quoted accurately, even if it appears to be a mistake.

sick *adj* **1** vomiting; feeling the need to vomit. **2** ill; unwell. **3** referring or relating to ill health: *sick pay*. **4** (*often* **sick for sb** or **sth**) pining or longing for them or it. **5** (*often* **sick of sb** or **sth**)

extremely annoyed, disgusted or fed up with them or it: *I'm sick of your attitude*. **6** mentally deranged. **7** of humour, comedy, jokes, etc: exploiting gruesome subjects in an unpleasant way. ➣ *n, colloq* vomit. ➣ *vb, tr & intr* (*usu* **sick up**) to vomit. ♦ **make sb sick** *colloq* to disgust or upset them. **sick to one's stomach 1** nauseated; about to vomit. **2** upset; disgusted.

sick bay *n* a compartment, eg on board a ship, for sick and wounded people.

sicken *vb* **1** to make someone or something feel like vomiting. **2** to annoy greatly or disgust. **3** *intr* (*usu* **sicken for sth**) to show symptoms of an illness: *I'm sickening for the flu*.

sickening *adj* **1** causing nausea. **2** causing extreme annoyance or disgust. ◊ **sickeningly** *adv*.

sickle *n* a tool with a short handle and a curved blade for cutting grain crops.

sick leave *n* time taken off work as a result of sickness.

sickly *adj* (**-ier, -iest**) **1** susceptible or prone to illness; ailing or feeble. **2** unhealthy-looking; pallid. **3** weakly sentimental; mawkish. ➣ *adv* to an extent that suggests illness: *sickly pale*.

sickness *n* **1** the condition of being ill; an illness. **2** vomiting. **3** nausea.

sick pay *n* payment made to a worker who is absent through illness.

side *n* **1** any of the usu flat or flattish surfaces that form the outer extent of something; any of these surfaces other than the front, back, top or bottom. **2** an edge or border, or the area adjoining this: *My car's at the side of the road*. **3** either of the parts or areas produced when the whole is divided up the middle: *I'll take the left side of the room*. **4** the part of the body between the armpit and hip. **5** the area of space next to someone or something: *He's round the side of the house*. **6** half of a carcass divided along the medial plane: *a side of beef*. **7** either of the broad surfaces of a flat or flattish object: *two sides of a coin*. **8** any of the lines forming a geometric figure. **9** any of the groups or teams, or opposing positions, in a conflict or competition. **10** an aspect: *We've seen a different side to him*. **11** a page: *My essay covered 5 sides*. **12** *Brit colloq* a television channel. **13** either of the two playing surfaces of a record or cassette. ➣ *adj* **1** located at the side: *side entrance*. **2** subsidiary or subordinate: *side road*. ➣ *vb, intr* (*usu* **side with sb**) to take on their position or point of view; to join forces with them. ♦ **on** or **to one side** removed to a position away from the main concern. **on the side** in addition to ordinary occupation or income, often illegal. **side by side 1** close together. **2** with sides touching. **take sides** to support one particular side in a conflict, argument or dispute.

sideboard *n* **1** a large piece of furniture, often consisting of shelves or cabinets mounted above drawers or cupboards, for holding

plates, ornaments, etc. **2** (**sideboards**) SIDE-
BURNS.

sideburn n (usu **sideburns**) the hair that grows
on each side of a man's face in front of the ears.

sidecar n a small carriage for one or two passengers, attached to the side of a motorcycle.

side effect n **1** an additional and usu undesirable effect, esp of a drug, eg nausea or drowsiness. **2** any undesired additional effect.

sidekick n, colloq a close or special friend; a
partner or deputy.

sideline n **1** a line marking either side boundary of a sports pitch. **2** a business, occupation
or trade in addition to regular work.

sidelong adj, adv from or to one side; not direct or directly: a sidelong glance.

sidereal /saɪˈdɪərɪəl/ adj referring or relating
to, or determined by the stars.

side-saddle n a horse's saddle designed to enable a woman in a skirt to sit with both legs on
the same side. ➤ adv sitting in this way.

sideshow n **1** an exhibition or show subordinate to a larger one. **2** any subordinate or incidental activity or event.

sidespin n the spinning of a ball in a sideways
direction.

side-splitting adj provoking uproarious and
hysterical laughter.

sidestep vb **1** to avoid by, or as if by, stepping
aside: You're sidestepping the issue. **2** intr to step
aside. ➤ n a step taken to one side.

sidetrack vb to divert the attention of someone
away from the matter in hand.

sidewalk n, N Am a pavement.

sideways adv, adj **1** from, to or towards one
side. **2** with one side foremost: We skidded sideways into the hedge.

siding n a short dead-end railway line on to
which trains, wagons, etc can be shunted temporarily from the main line.

sidle vb, intr to go or edge along sideways, esp
in a cautious, furtive or ingratiating manner.

siege n **1** the act or process of surrounding a
fort or town with troops, cutting off its supplies
and subjecting it to persistent attack with the
intention of forcing its surrender. **2** a police operation using similar tactics, eg to force a criminal out of a building. ♦ **lay siege to a place** to
subject it to a siege.

siemens n the SI unit of conductance.

sienna n a pigment obtained from a type of
earth with a high clay and iron content, **raw
sienna** being yellowish-brown, and **burnt sienna** being the reddish-brown colour of the
roasted pigment.

sierra n esp in Spanish-speaking countries and
the US: a mountain range, esp when jagged.

siesta n in hot countries: a sleep or rest after
the midday meal.

sieve /sɪv/ n a utensil with a meshed or perforated bottom, used for straining solids from liquids or for sifting large particles from smaller
ones. ➤ vb to strain or sift with a sieve.

sift vb **1** to pass through a sieve in order to sep-

arate out lumps or larger particles. **2** tr & intr to
examine closely and discriminatingly: to sift
through applications. ○ **sifter** n.

sigh vb **1** intr to release a long deep audible
breath, expressive of sadness, longing, tiredness or relief. **2** intr to make a similar sound:
We heard the engine sigh. **3** to express with such
a sound. ➤ n an act or the sound of sighing.

sight n **1** the power or faculty of seeing; vision.
2 a thing or object seen; view or spectacle: It's a
lovely sight. **3** someone's field of view or vision,
or the opportunity to see things that this provides: out of sight. **4** (usu **sights**) places, buildings, etc that are particularly interesting or
worth seeing: to see the sights of the city. **5** a device on a firearm through or along which one
looks to take aim. **6** a similar device used as a
guide to the eye on an optical or other instrument. **7** colloq a person or thing unpleasant to
look at: He looked a sight without his teeth in.
➤ vb **1** to get a look at or glimpse of someone
or something. **2** to aim (a firearm) using the
sight. ♦ **a sight for sore eyes** a very welcome
sight. **catch sight of sb** or **sth** to get a glimpse
of them or it. **know sb** or **sth by sight** to recognize them only by their appearance. **set one's
sights on sth** to decide on it as an ambition.

sighted adj having the power of sight; not
blind.

sightless adj blind.

sightly adj pleasing to the eye.

sight-reading n playing or singing from
printed music that one has not previously
seen. ○ **sight-read** vb.

sightsee vb, intr to visit places of interest, esp
as a tourist. ○ **sightseeing** n. ○ **sightseer** n.

sign n **1** a printed mark with a meaning; a symbol: a multiplication sign. **2** a gesture expressing a meaning; a signal. **3** an indication:
signs of improvement. **4** an omen; a miraculous
token. **5** a board or panel displaying information for public view. **6** med any external evidence or indication of disease. **7** astrol any of
the twelve parts of the zodiac. ➤ vb **1** tr & intr
to give a signal or indication. **2** to write a signature on something; to confirm one's assent to
something with a signature. **3** to write (one's
name) as a signature. **4** tr & intr to employ or
become employed with the signing of a contract: Stoke City have signed a new player. **5** tr
& intr to communicate using sign language. **6**
to make the sign of the cross over (oneself or
someone else). ◊ **sign sth away** to give it away
or transfer it by signing a legal document. **sign
in** or **out** to record one's arrival or departure by
signing one's name. **sign sb in** to allow someone official entry to a club, etc by signing one's
name. **sign off 1** to bring a broadcast to an end.
2 to stop work, etc. **sign on** colloq to register as
unemployed. **sign up 1** to join the army. **2** to join
an organization by signing a contract.

signal n **1** a message in the form of a gesture,
light, sound, etc. **2** (**signals**) the apparatus
used to send such a message, eg coloured

lights or movable arms or poles on a railway network. **3** an event marking the moment for action to be taken: *Their arrival was a signal for the party to begin.* **4** any set of transmitted electrical impulses received as a sound or image, eg in television; the message conveyed by them. ➤ *vb* (**signalled, signalling**) **1** *tr & intr* to transmit or convey (a message) using signals. **2** to indicate. ➤ *adj* notable: *a signal triumph.*

signal box *n* the cabin from which signals on a railway line are controlled.

signalman *n* a controller who works railway signals.

signatory /'sɪɡnətrɪ/ *n* (*-ies*) a person, organization or state that is a party to a contract, treaty or other document.

signature *n* **1** one's name written by oneself as a formal authorization, etc. **2** an indication of key or time at the beginning of a line of music. **3** a large sheet of paper with printed pages on it, each with a numeral or letter at the bottom, which when folded forms a section of a book.

signature tune *n* a tune used to identify or introduce a specified radio or television programme or performer.

signet *n* a small seal used for stamping documents, etc.

signet ring *n* a finger ring carrying a signet.

significance *n* meaning or importance.

significant *adj* **1** important; worth noting or considering. **2** having some meaning; indicating or implying something. ○ **significantly** *adv.*

signify *vb* (*-ies, -ied*) **1** to be a sign or symbol for something or someone; to suggest or mean. **2** *intr* to be important or significant.

sign language *n* any form of communication using gestures to represent words and ideas, esp an official system of hand gestures used by deaf people.

sign of the zodiac see under ZODIAC

signpost *n* **1** a post supporting a sign that gives information or directions to motorists or pedestrians. **2** an indication or clue. ➤ *vb* **1** to mark (a route) with signposts. **2** to give directions to someone.

Sikh /siːk/ *n* an adherent of the monotheistic religion established in the 16c by Guru Nanak. ➤ *adj* belonging or relating to the Sikhs, their beliefs or customs. ○ **Sikhism** *n.*

silage /'saɪlɪdʒ/ *n* animal fodder made from forage crops such as grass, maize, etc compressed and preserved by controlled fermentation, eg in a silo.

sild *n* a young herring.

silence *n* **1** absence of sound or speech. **2** a time of such absence of sound or speech. **3** failure or abstention from communication, disclosing information or secrets, etc. ➤ *vb* to make someone or something stop speaking, making a noise or giving away information. ➤ *exclam* be quiet!

silencer *n* a device fitted to a gun barrel or engine exhaust to reduce or eliminate the noise made.

silent *adj* **1** free from noise; unaccompanied by sound. **2** refraining from speech; not mentioning or divulging something. **3** unspoken but expressed: *silent joy.* **4** not pronounced: *the silent p in pneumonia.* ○ **silently** *adv.*

silhouette /ˌsɪluːˈɛt/ *n* **1** a dark shape or shadow seen against a light background. **2** an outline drawing of an object or esp a person, in profile, usu filled in with black. ➤ *vb* to represent, or make appear, as a silhouette.

silica *n, geol* a hard white or colourless glassy solid that occurs naturally as quartz, sand and flint, and also as silicate compounds, and is used in the manufacture of glasses, glazes and enamels.

silicate *n, chem* a chemical compound containing silicon, oxygen and one or more metals.

silicon *n* a non-metallic element that occurs naturally as silicate minerals in clays and rocks, and as silica in sand and quartz, used as a semiconductor to make transistors and silicon chips for the integrated circuits of computers, etc.

silicon, silicone These words are often confused with each other.

silicon chip *n, electronics, comput* a very thin piece of silicon or other semiconductor material on which all the components of an integrated circuit are arranged.

silicone *n, chem* a synthetic polymer, used in lubricants, electrical insulators, paints, adhesives and surgical breast implants.

silicosis *n, pathol* a lung disease caused by prolonged inhalation of dust containing silica.

silk *n* **1** a fine soft fibre produced by the larva of the silkworm. **2** a synthetic imitation of this. **3** thread or fabric made from such fibres. **4** a garment made from such fabric. **5 a** the silk gown worn by a Queen's or King's Counsel; **b** the rank conferred by this. ♦ **take silk** of a barrister: to be appointed a Queen's or King's Counsel.

silken *adj, literary* **1** made of silk. **2** as soft or smooth as silk.

silkworm *n* the caterpillar of the silk moth, which spins a cocoon of unbroken silk thread.

silky *adj* (*-ier, -iest*) **1** soft and shiny like silk. **2** of a person's manner or voice: suave.

sill *n* **1** the bottom part of the framework around the inside of a window or door. **2** the ledge of wood, stone or metal forming this.

silly *adj* (*-ier, -iest*) **1** not sensible; foolish; trivial or frivolous. **2** *cricket* in a fielding position very near the batsman: *silly mid-on.* ➤ *n* (*-ies*) *colloq* (*also* **silly-billy**) a foolish person. ○ **silliness** *n.*

silo *n* **1** a tall round airtight tower for storing green crops and converting them into silage. **2** an underground chamber housing a missile ready for firing.

silt *n* sedimentary material, finer than sand and coarser than clay, consisting of very small rock fragments or mineral particles, deposited by or suspended in running or still water. ➤ *vb,* *intr (often **silt up**)* to become blocked up with silt.

Silurian /sɪ'lʊərɪən/ *adj, geol* denoting the period of geological time between the ORDOVICIAN and DEVONIAN periods, during which marine life predominated and the first jawed fish and primitive land plants appeared.

silvan see SYLVAN

silver *n* **1** an element, a soft white lustrous precious metal that is an excellent conductor of heat and electricity, and is used in jewellery, ornaments, mirrors and coins. **2** coins made of this metal. **3** articles made of or coated with this metal, esp cutlery and other tableware. **4** a silver medal. ➤ *adj* **1** having a whitish-grey colour. **2** denoting a 25th wedding or other anniversary. ➤ *vb* **1** to apply a thin coating of silver to something; to plate with silver. **2** to give a silvery sheen to something. **3** *intr* to become silvery. ♦ **born with a silver spoon in one's mouth** born to affluence or wealthy surroundings.

silverfish *n* a primitive wingless insect with a tapering body covered with silvery scales, commonly found in houses.

silver jubilee *n* a 25th anniversary.

silver lining *n* a positive aspect of an otherwise unpleasant or unfortunate situation.

silver medal *n* a medal of silver awarded to a person or team in second place.

silver plate *n* **1** a thin coating of silver or a silver alloy on a metallic object, eg cutlery. **2** such objects coated with silver. ○ **silver-plated** *adj*.

the silver screen *n, colloq* the film industry or films in general.

silverside *n* a fine cut of beef from the rump, just below the aitchbone.

silversmith *n* someone who makes or repairs articles made of silver.

silverware *n* objects, esp cutlery or tableware, made from or coated with silver.

silvery *adj* **1** having the colour or shiny quality of silver. **2** having a pleasantly light ringing sound: *silvery bells*.

silviculture *n, bot* the cultivation of forest trees, or the management of woodland to produce timber, etc.

simian *n* a monkey or ape. ➤ *adj* belonging or relating to, or resembling, a monkey or ape.

similar *adj* **1** having a close resemblance to something; being of the same kind, but not identical. **2** *geom* exactly corresponding in shape, regardless of size. ○ **similarity** *n*. ○ **similarly** *adv*.

simile /'sɪmɪlɪ/ *n* a figure of speech in which a thing is described by being likened to something, usu using *as* or *like*, as in *eyes sparkling like diamonds*.

similitude *n, formal* resemblance.

simmer *vb* **1** *tr & intr* to cook or make something cook gently at just below boiling point. **2** *intr* to be close to an outburst of emotion, usu anger. ➤ *n* a simmering state. ◊ **simmer down**

to calm down, esp after a commotion, eg an angry outburst.

simnel *n* a sweet fruit cake covered with marzipan, traditionally baked at Easter or Mid-Lent.

simony /'saɪmənɪ/ *n* the practice of buying or selling a religious post, benefice or privilege.

simper *vb* **1** *intr* to smile in a weak affected manner. **2** to express by or while smiling in this way. ➤ *n* a simpering smile.

simple *adj* **1** easy; not difficult. **2** straightforward; not complex or complicated. **3** plain or basic: *a simple outfit*. **4** down-to-earth; unpretentious; honest. **5** *often ironic* foolish; gullible; lacking intelligence: *He's a bit of a simple lad*. **6** plain; straightforward; not altered or adulterated: *the simple facts*. **7** consisting of one thing or element.

simple fraction *n, maths* a fraction with whole numbers as numerator and denominator.

simple fracture *n* a fracture of the bone that does not involve an open skin wound. Compare COMPOUND FRACTURE.

simple interest *n* interest calculated only on the basic sum initially borrowed. Compare COMPOUND INTEREST.

simple-minded *adj* **1** lacking intelligence; foolish. **2** guileless; unsophisticated. ○ **simple-mindedness** *n*.

simple sentence *n* a sentence consisting of one MAIN CLAUSE.

simpleton *n* a foolish or unintelligent person.

simplicity *n* a simple state or quality.

simplify *vb* (*-ies, -ied*) to make something less difficult or complicated; to make it easier to understand. ○ **simplification** *n*.

simplistic *adj* unrealistically straightforward or uncomplicated. ○ **simplistically** *adv*.

simply *adv* **1** in a straightforward, uncomplicated manner. **2** just: *It's simply not true*. **3** absolutely: *simply marvellous*. **4** merely: *We simply wanted to help*.

simulate *vb* **1** to convincingly re-create (a set of conditions or a real-life event), esp for the purposes of training. **2** to pretend to have, do or feel: *She simulated anger*. ○ **simulated** *adj*. ○ **simulation** *n*.

simulator *n* a device that simulates a system, process or set of conditions, esp in order to test it, or for training purposes: *a flight simulator*.

simultaneous *adj* happening, or carried out, at exactly the same time. ○ **simultaneously** *adv*.

sin[1] *n* **1** an act that breaches a moral and esp a religious law or teaching. **2** the condition of offending a deity by committing a moral offence. **3** an act that offends common standards of morality or decency; an outrage. **4** a great shame. ➤ *vb* (**sinned, sinning**) *intr* to commit a sin. ○ **sinner** *n*.

sin[2] *abbrev* sine (see SINE[1]).

since *conj* **1** from the time that; seeing that. **2** as; because: *I'm not surprised you failed, since you* *did no work.* ➢ *prep* during or throughout the period between now and some earlier stated time: *I've been there several times since her death.* ➢ *adv* **1** from that time onwards: *I haven't been back since.* **2** ago: *five years since.*

sincere *adj* genuine; not pretended or affected. ○ **sincerely** *adv.* ○ **sincerity** *n.*

sine¹ /saɪn/ *n, trig* in a right-angled triangle: a FUNCTION (*noun sense 4*) of an angle, defined as the length of the side opposite the angle divided by the length of the hypotenuse.

sine² /ˈsaɪnɪ, ˈsɪnɛ/ *prep* without.

sinecure /ˈsɪnɪkjʊə(r)/ *n* a paid job involving little or no work.

sinew *n* **1** a strong piece of fibrous tissue joining a muscle to a bone; a tendon. **2** (**sinews**) physical strength; muscle. ○ **sinewy** *adj.*

sinful *adj* wicked; involving sin; morally wrong. ○ **sinfully** *adv.* ○ **sinfulness** *n.*

sing *vb* (*past tense* **sang**, *past participle* **sung**) **1** *tr & intr* to make music with the voice. **2** *intr* to do this as a profession: *Her mother was a dancer, but she sings.* **3** to make someone or something pass into a particular state with such sound: *The mother sang her baby to sleep.* **4** *intr* to make a sound like a musical voice; to hum, ring or whistle: *The kettle was singing on the stove.* **5** *intr* to suffer a ringing sound: *a loud bang that made their ears sing.* **6** *intr, esp US slang* to inform or confess; to squeal. **7** *intr* of birds, specific insects, etc: to produce calls or sounds. ○ **singer** *n.* ◊ **sing out** to shout or call out.

sing. *abbrev* singular.

singe *vb* (**singeing**) *tr & intr* to burn lightly on the surface; to scorch or become scorched. ➢ *n* a light surface burn.

single *adj* **1** comprising only one part; solitary. **2** having no partner; unmarried, esp never having been married. **3** for use by one person only: *a single room.* **4** of a travel ticket: valid for an outward journey only; not return. **5** unique; individual. **6** even one: *Not a single person turned up.* ➢ *n* **1** (*often* **singles**) a person without a partner, either marital or otherwise. **2** a single room, eg in a guest house. **3** a ticket for an outward journey only. **4** a recording of an individual pop song released for sale, usu with one or more supplementary tracks. **5** *Brit* a pound coin or note. **6** *US* a one-dollar note. **7** *cricket* a hit for one run. ➢ *vb* (*always* **single out**) to pick someone or something from among others.

single-breasted *adj* of a coat or jacket: having only one row of buttons and a slight overlap at the front.

single cream *n* cream which does not thicken when beaten.

single-decker *n* a vehicle, esp a bus, with only one deck.

single figures *pl n* the numbers from 1 to 9.

single file or **Indian file** *n* a line of people, animals, etc standing or moving one behind the other.

single-handed *adj, adv* done, carried out, etc by oneself, without any help from others. ○ **single-handedly** *adv.*

single-minded *adj* determinedly pursuing one specific aim or object. ○ **single-mindedly** *adv.*

single parent *n* a mother or father bringing up a child alone.

singles *n* in tennis, etc: a match where one player competes against another.

singles bar or **singles club** *n* an establishment intended as a meeting place for unmarried or unattached people.

singlet *n* a sleeveless vest or undershirt.

singleton *n* **1** the only playing-card of a particular suit in a hand. **2** a solitary person or thing.

singly *adv* **1** one at a time; individually. **2** alone; by oneself.

singsong *n* an informal gathering at which friends, etc sing together for pleasure. ➢ *adj* of a speaking voice, etc: having a fluctuating intonation and rhythm.

singular *adj* **1** single; unique. **2** extraordinary; exceptional. **3** strange; odd. **4** *gram* denoting or referring to one person, thing, etc as opposed to two or more. ➢ *n, gram* a word or form of a word expressing the idea or involvement of one person, thing, etc as opposed to two or more. Compare PLURAL. ○ **singularity** *n.* ○ **singularly** *adv.*

sinister *adj* **1** suggesting or threatening evil or danger; malign. **2** *heraldry* on the left side of the shield from the bearer's point of view, as opposed to that of the observer. Compare DEXTER.

sink *vb* (*past tense* **sank** or **sunk**, *past participle* **sunk**) **1** *tr & intr* to fall or cause to fall and remain below the surface of water, either partially or completely. **2** *intr* to collapse downwardly or inwardly; to fall because of a collapsing base or foundation. **3** *intr* to be or become inwardly withdrawn or dejected: *My heart sank at the news.* **4** to embed: *They sank the pole into the ground.* **5** *intr* to pass steadily into a worse level or state: *He sank into depression after her death.* **6** *intr* to diminish or decline: *My opinion of him sank after that incident.* **7** to invest (money) heavily: *We sank a lot of money into this project.* **8** *colloq* to ruin: *We are sunk.* **9** *colloq* to drink (esp alcohol) usu quickly: *We sank four beers within the hour.* **10** *colloq* to send (a ball) into a pocket in snooker, billiards, etc and into the hole in golf. **11** to excavate (a well, shaft, etc). **12** to let in or insert: *screws sunk into the wall.* ➢ *n* a basin with built-in water supply and drainage, for washing dishes, etc. ◊ **sink in** *colloq* to be fully understood or realized: *The bad news took a few days to sink in.* **2** to penetrate or be absorbed: *Wait for the ink to sink in first.*

sinker *n* a weight used to sink something, eg a fishing line.

Sino- *comb form, denoting* Chinese: *Sino-Soviet.*

Sinology /saɪˈnɒlədʒɪ/ *n* the study of China in

all its aspects, esp cultural and political.

sinuous *adj* wavy; winding.

sinus /'saɪnəs/ *n, anat* a cavity or depression filled with air, esp in the bones of mammals.

sinusitis *n* inflammation of the lining of the sinuses, esp the nasal ones.

sip *vb* (**sipped, sipping**) *tr & intr* to drink in very small mouthfuls. ➤ *n* **1** an act of sipping. **2** an amount sipped at one time.

siphon or **syphon** *n* **1** a tube held in an inverted U-shape that can be used to transfer liquid from one container at a higher level into another at a lower level, used to empty car petrol tanks, etc. **2** (*in full* **soda siphon**) a bottle with a device for releasing a liquid, esp soda water, by pressure of gas. ➤ *vb* (*usu* **siphon sth off**) **1** to transfer (liquid) from one container to another using such a device. **2** to take (money, funds, etc) slowly and continuously from a store or fund.

sir *n* **1** a polite and respectful address for a man. **2** (**Sir**) a title used before the Christian name of a knight or baronet.

sire *n* **1** the father of a horse or other animal. **2** *hist* a term of respect used in addressing a king. ➤ *vb* of an animal: to father (young).

siren *n* **1** a device that gives out a loud wailing noise, usu as a warning signal. **2** an irresistible woman thought capable of ruining men's lives.

sirloin *n* a fine cut of beef from the loin or the upper part of the loin.

sirocco *n* in S Europe: a dry hot dusty wind blowing from N Africa, and becoming more moist as it moves further north.

sis *n, colloq* short for SISTER.

sisal /'saɪzəl/ *n* a strong coarse durable yellowish fibre obtained from the leaves of **sisal hemp** or **sisal grass**, used to make ropes, twine, brush bristles, sacking, etc.

sissy or **cissy** *n* (*-ies*) *derog* a feeble, cowardly or effeminate male.

sister *n* **1** a female child of the same parents as another. **2** a nun. **3** a senior female nurse, esp one in charge of a ward. **4** a fellow female member of a profession, class or racial group. ➤ *adj* being of the same origin, model or design: *a sister ship.*

sisterhood *n* **1** the state of being a sister or sisters. **2** a religious community of women; a body of nuns. **3** a group of women with common interests or beliefs.

sister-in-law *n* (**sisters-in-law**) **1** the sister of one's husband or wife. **2** the wife of one's brother.

sisterly *adj* like a sister, esp in being kind and affectionate.

sit *vb* (**sat, sitting**) **1** *intr* to rest the body on the buttocks, with the upper body more or less vertical. **2** *intr* of an animal: to position itself on its hindquarters in a similar manner. **3** *intr* of a bird: to perch or lie. **4** *intr* of a bird: to brood. **5** *intr* of an object: to lie or rest: *There are a few cups sitting on the shelf.* **6** *intr* to lie unused: *I've got all my tools sitting in the shed.* **7** *intr* to hold a meeting or other session: *The court sits tomorrow.* **8** *intr* to be a member, taking regular part in meetings: *to sit on a committee.* **9** *intr* to have a seat, as in parliament. **10** *intr* to have a specific position: *The TV sits on this stand.* **11** to take (an examination); to be a candidate for (a degree or other award): *I'm sitting my first exam tomorrow.* **12** to conduct to a seat; to assign a seat to someone: *They sat me next to him.* **13** *intr* to be or exist in a specified comparison or relation: *His smoking sits awkwardly with his being a doctor.* **14** *intr* to pose as an artist's or photographer's model. ♦ **be sitting pretty** *colloq* to be in a very advantageous position. **sit tight 1** to maintain one's position and opinion determinedly. **2** to wait patiently. ◊ **sit back 1** to sit comfortably, esp with the head and back rested. **2** to observe rather than take an active part, esp when action is needed. **sit down** or **sit sb down** to take, or make them take, a sitting position. **sit down under sth** to submit meekly to (an insult, etc). **sit in on sth** to be present at it as a visitor or observer, esp without participating. **sit in for sb** to act as a substitute for them. **sit on sth** *colloq* to delay taking action over it. **sit sth out** to take no part, esp in a dance or game. **sit up 1** to move oneself from a slouching or lying position into an upright sitting position. **2** to take notice suddenly or show a sudden interest.

sitar *n* a guitar-like instrument of Indian origin, with a long neck, rounded body and two sets of strings.

sitcom *n, colloq* short for SITUATION COMEDY.

sit-down *n, colloq* a short rest in a seated position. ➤ *adj* **1** of a meal: for which the diners are seated. **2** of a strike: in which the workers occupy their place of work until an agreement is reached.

site *n* **1** the place where something was, is, or is to be situated: *the site of the museum* • *a Roman site.* **2** an area set aside for a specific activity: *a camping site.* ➤ *vb* to position or situate.

sit-in *n* the occupation of a public building, factory, etc as a form of protest.

sitter *n* **1** a person who poses for an artist or photographer. **2** a babysitter. **3** *in compounds* a person who looks after a house, pet, etc in the absence of its owner: *a flat sitter.*

sitting *vb, present participle of* SIT. ➤ *n* **1** the act or state of being seated. **2** a period of continuous activity, usu while sitting or in a similar position: *He wrote it at one sitting.* **3** a turn to eat for any of two or more sections of a group too large to eat all at the same time in the same place, or the period set aside for each turn. **4** a period of posing for an artist or photographer. **5** a session or meeting of an official body. ➤ *adj* **1** currently holding office: *He's the sitting MP for this constituency.* **2** seated: *in a sitting position.*

sitting duck or **sitting target** *n* someone or something in a defenceless or exposed position.

sitting room *n* a room, esp in a private house, for relaxing in, entertaining visitors, etc.

sitting tenant *n*, *Brit* a tenant occupying a property when it changes ownership.

situate *vb* to place in a certain position, context or set of circumstances.

situation *n* **1** a set of circumstances or state of affairs. **2** a place, position or location. **3** a job; employment: *situations vacant.*

situation comedy *n* a radio or TV comedy in which the same characters appear in more or less the same surroundings, and which depends for its humour on the behaviour of the characters in particular, sometimes contrived, situations.

sit-up *n* a physical exercise in which the body is raised up and over the thighs from a lying position, often with the hands behind the head.

six *n* **1 a** the cardinal number 6; **b** the quantity that this represents, being one more than five. **2** any symbol for this, eg *6* or *VI.* **3** the sixth hour after midnight or midday. **4** a set or group of six people or things. **5** *cricket* a hit scoring six runs. ➤ *adj* **1** totalling six. **2** aged six. ◦ **sixth** *adj, n.* ♦ **at sixes and sevens** in a state of total disorder or confusion. **hit** or **knock sb for six** *colloq* **1** to defeat or ruin them completely. **2** to shock or surprise them completely. **six of one and half a dozen of the other** equal; equally acceptable or unacceptable; the same on both sides.

sixfold *adj* **1** equal to six times as much or many. **2** divided into, or consisting of, six parts. ➤ *adv* by six times as much.

six-pack *n* **1** a pack containing six items sold as one unit, esp a pack of six cans of beer. **2** *colloq* a set of well-defined abdominal muscles.

sixpence *n* in Britain: a former small silver coin worth six old pennies (6d), equivalent in value to 2½p.

sixteen *n* **1 a** the cardinal number 16; **b** the quantity that this represents, being one more than fifteen, or the sum of ten and six. **2** any symbol for this, eg *16* or *XVI.* ➤ *adj* **1** totalling sixteen. **2** aged sixteen. ◦ **sixteenth** *adj, n, adv.*

sixth form *n* in secondary education: the stage in which school subjects are taught to a level that prepares for higher education. ◦ **sixth-former** *n.*

sixth sense *n* an unexplained power of intuition by which one is aware of things that are not seen, heard, touched, smelled or tasted.

sixties (often written **60s** or **60's**) *pl n* **1** (**one's sixties**) the period of time between one's sixtieth and seventieth birthdays. **2** (**the sixties**) the range of temperatures between sixty and seventy degrees. **3** (**the sixties**) the period of time between the sixtieth and seventieth years of a century.

sixty *n* **1 a** the cardinal number 60; **b** the quantity that this represents, being one more than fifty-nine, or the product of ten and six. **2** any symbol for this, eg *60* or *LX.* ➤ *adj* **1** totalling

sixty. **2** aged sixty. ◦ **sixtieth** *adj, n, adv.*

size¹ *n* **1** length, breadth, height or volume, or a combination of these; the dimensions of something. **2** largeness; magnitude: *We were amazed at its size.* **3** any of a range of graded measurements into which esp garments and shoes are divided. ➤ *vb* **1** to measure something in order to determine size. **2** to sort or arrange something according to size. ◦ **sized** *adj.* ◊ **size sb** or **sth up 1** to take a mental measurement of them or it. **2** *colloq* to mentally judge their or its nature, quality or worth.

size² *n* a weak kind of glue used to stiffen paper and fabric, and to prepare walls for plastering and wallpapering. ➤ *vb* to cover or treat with size.

sizeable or **sizable** *adj* fairly large; being of a considerable size.

sizzle *vb, intr* **1** to make a hissing sound when, or as if when, frying in hot fat. **2** to be extremely hot: *sizzling weather.* **3** *colloq* to be in a state of intense emotion, esp anger or excitement. ➤ *n* a sizzling sound. ◦ **sizzler** *n.*

skate¹ *n* an ICE SKATE or ROLLER SKATE. ➤ *vb, intr* to move around on skates. ◦ **skater** *n.* ◦ **skating** *n.* ♦ **get one's skates on** *colloq* to hurry up. **skate on thin ice** to risk danger, harm or embarrassment, esp through lack of care or good judgement. ◊ **skate over sth** to hurry or rush over it: *We'll skate over this next chapter.* **skate round sth** to avoid dealing with something or considering (a difficulty, etc).

skate² *n* (**skate** or **skates**) a large edible flatfish with a greyish-brown upper surface with black flecks, a long pointed snout, large wing-like pectoral fins and a long slim tail.

skateboard *n* a narrow shaped board mounted on sets of small wheels, usu ridden in a standing position.

skating rink *n* a large surface covered in ice for the use of ice skaters.

skedaddle *vb, intr, colloq* to run away or leave quickly. ➤ *n* a hurried departure.

skein *n* **1** a loosely tied coil of wool or thread. **2** a flock of geese in flight.

skeletal *adj* **1** similar to or like a skeleton. **2** painfully or extremely thin. **3** existing in outline only.

skeleton *n* **1** the framework of bones that supports the body of an animal, and to which the muscles are usu attached. **2** the supporting veins of a leaf. **3** an initial basic structure, outline or idea upon or around which anything is built. **4** *colloq* an unhealthily thin person or animal.

skeleton in the cupboard or (*US*) **skeleton in the closet** *n* a shameful or slanderous fact concerning oneself or one's family that one tries to keep secret.

skeleton key *n* a key whose edge is filed in such a way that it can open many different locks.

skeptic an alternative *N Am* spelling of SCEPTIC.

skerry n (**-ies**) a reef of rock or a small rocky island.

sketch n 1 a rough drawing quickly done, esp one without much detail used as a study towards a more finished work. 2 a rough plan. 3 a short account or outline: *She gave us a quick sketch of the story*. 4 any of several short pieces of comedy presented as a programme. ⊳ vb 1 tr & intr to do a rough drawing or drawings of something. 2 to give a rough outline of something. ○ **sketcher** n.

sketchy adj (**-ier, -iest**) lacking detail; not complete or substantial. ○ **sketchily** adv.

skew adj slanted; oblique; askew. ⊳ vb, tr & intr to slant or cause to slant. ⊳ n a slanting position: *on the skew*. ○ **skewed** adj.

skewbald adj of an animal, esp a horse: marked with patches of white and another colour (other than black). ⊳ n an animal, esp a horse, with such markings.

skewer n a long wooden or metal pin pushed through chunks of meat or vegetables which are to be grilled or roasted. ⊳ vb to fasten or pierce with, or as if with, a skewer.

skew-whiff adj, adv, colloq lying in a slanted position; crooked; awry.

ski n 1 one of a pair of long narrow runners of wood, metal or plastic, upturned at the front and attached to each of a pair of boots or to a vehicle for gliding over snow. 2 a WATER-SKI. ⊳ vb (**skis, skied** or **ski'd, skiing**) intr to move on skis. ○ **skier** n. ○ **skiing** n.

skid vb (**skidded, skidding**) 1 intr of a vehicle or person: to slip or slide at an angle, esp out of control. 2 to cause a vehicle to slide out of control. ⊳ n an instance of skidding. ◆ **put the skids under sb** colloq to bring about their downfall.

skidoo n a motorized sledge, fitted with tracks at the rear and steerable skis at the front. ⊳ vb (**skidooed, skidooing**) to use a skidoo.

skid row n, esp US colloq the poorest or most squalid part of a town where vagrants, drunks, etc live.

skiff n a small light boat.

skilful or (US) **skillful** adj having or showing skill. ○ **skilfully** adv. ○ **skilfulness** n.

ski lift n a device for carrying skiers, either by towing or on chairs, to the top of a slope so that they can ski down.

skill n 1 expertness; dexterity. 2 a talent, craft or accomplishment, naturally acquired or developed through training. 3 (**skills**) aptitudes and abilities appropriate for a specific job.

skilled adj 1 of people: possessing skills; trained or experienced. 2 of a job: requiring skill or showing the use of skill.

skillet n 1 a small long-handled saucepan. 2 esp N Am a frying pan.

skim vb (**skimmed, skimming**) 1 to remove floating matter from the surface of (a liquid). 2 (often **skim off**) to take something off by skimming. 3 tr & intr to brush or cause something to brush against or glide lightly over (a surface):

He skimmed the table as he went past. 4 to throw an object over a surface so as to make it bounce: *We skimmed stones on the river*. 5 (usu **skim through sth**) **a** to glance through (eg a book); **b** to deal with or discuss it superficially. ○ **skimming** n.

skimmed milk or **skim milk** n milk from which the fat has been removed.

skimp vb 1 intr (often **skimp on sth**) to spend, use or give too little or only just enough of it. 2 intr to stint or restrict. 3 to carry out hurriedly or recklessly. ⊳ adj scanty.

skimpy adj (**-ier, -iest**) 1 inadequate; barely enough. 2 of clothes: leaving much of the body uncovered; scanty. ○ **skimpily** adv. ○ **skimpiness** n.

skin n 1 the tough flexible waterproof covering of the human or animal body. 2 an animal hide, with or without the fur or hair attached. 3 the outer covering of certain fruits and vegetables. 4 any outer covering or integument: *sausage skin*. 5 complexion: *greasy skin*. 6 a semi-solid coating or film on the surface of a liquid. 7 a container for liquids made from an animal hide. ⊳ vb (**skinned, skinning**) 1 to remove or strip the skin from something. 2 to injure by scraping the skin: *He skinned his elbow when he fell*. 3 slang to cheat or swindle. ◆ **by the skin of one's teeth** very narrowly; only just. **get under sb's skin** colloq 1 to greatly annoy them. 2 to become their consuming passion or obsession. **no skin off one's nose** colloq not a cause of even slight concern or nuisance to one: *It's no skin off my nose if he decides to resign*.

skin-deep adj superficial; shallow or not deeply fixed. ⊳ adv superficially.

skinflint n, colloq a very ungenerous or stingy person.

skinhead n a person, esp a white youth and generally one of a gang, with closely cropped hair, tight jeans, heavy boots and antisocial attitudes.

skinny adj (**-ier, -iest**) of a person or animal: very thin.

skinny-dip vb, intr, colloq to go swimming naked. ○ **skinny-dipping** n.

skint adj, slang without money; hard up; broke.

skin-tight adj of a piece of clothing: very tight-fitting.

skip¹ vb (**skipped, skipping**) 1 intr to move along with light springing or hopping steps on alternate feet. 2 intr to make jumps over a skipping-rope. 3 to omit, leave out or pass over. 4 colloq not to attend (eg a class in school). 5 to make (a stone) skim over a surface. 6 intr of a stone: to skim over a surface. ⊳ n 1 a skipping movement. 2 the act of omitting or leaving something out. ◆ **skip it!** colloq forget it; ignore it.

skip² n 1 Brit a large metal container for rubbish from eg building work. 2 a lift in a coal mine for raising minerals.

ski pants n trousers made from a stretch fabric

and kept taut by a band under the foot, orig designed for skiing but often worn as casual wear.

skipper n 1 a ship's captain. 2 the captain of an aeroplane. 3 the captain of a team. ➤ vb to act as skipper of something.

skipping n the art or activity of skipping using a skipping-rope.

skipping-rope n a rope swung backwards and forwards or twirled in a circular motion, either by the person skipping or by two others each holding an end, for jumping over as exercise or as a children's game.

skirl Scot, n the high-pitched sound of bagpipes. ➤ vb 1 intr to make this sound. 2 tr & intr to shriek or sing in a high-pitched manner.

skirmish n a minor fight or dispute. ➤ vb, intr to engage in a skirmish.

skirt n 1 a woman's or girl's garment that hangs from the waist. 2 the part of a woman's dress, coat, gown, etc from the waist down. 3 any part or attachment resembling a skirt. 4 the flap around the base of a hovercraft containing the air-cushion. 5 a cut of beef from the rear part of the belly; the midriff. 6 slang a a woman or women collectively; b (also a bit of skirt) a woman regarded as an object of sexual desire. ➤ vb 1 to pass along or around the edge of something. 2 to avoid confronting (eg a problem): skirting the issue. 3 tr & intr (usu skirt along, around, etc sth) to be on or pass along the border of something.

skirting-board n the narrow wooden board next to the floor round the walls of a room.

skit n a short satirical piece of writing or drama.

skittish adj 1 lively and playful; spirited. 2 frequently changing mood or opinion; fickle or capricious. 3 of a horse: easily frightened. ○ **skittishly** adv. ○ **skittishness** n.

skittle n 1 each of the upright bottle-shaped wooden or plastic targets used in a game of skittles. 2 (skittles) a game in which balls are rolled down an alley towards a set of these targets, the object being to knock over as many as possible.

skive vb, tr & intr, Brit colloq (also **skive off**) to evade work or a duty, esp through laziness: I'm going to skive French today. ➤ n the act or an instance of skiving: I chose drama because it's such a skive. ○ **skiver** n. ○ **skiving** n.

skivvy colloq, n 1 derog a servant, esp a woman, who does unpleasant household jobs. 2 (skivvies) esp US slang men's underwear. 3 Aust, NZ a knitted cotton polo-necked sweater. ➤ vb (-ies, -ied) intr to work as, or as if as, a skivvy.

skua /'skjuːə/ n a large predatory gull-like seabird.

skulduggery or (N Am) **skullduggery** n (-ies) unscrupulous, underhand or dishonest behaviour; trickery.

skulk vb, intr 1 to sneak off out of the way. 2 to hide or lurk, planning mischief. ○ **skulking** n.

skull n the hard cartilaginous or bony framework of the head. ♦ **out of one's skull 1** mad or crazy. **2** extremely drunk.

skull and crossbones n a representation of a human skull with two femurs arranged like an X underneath, used formerly as a pirate's symbol, now as a symbol of death or danger.

skullcap n a small brimless cap fitting closely on the head.

skunk n (skunk or skunks) 1 a small American mammal related to the weasel, best known for the foul-smelling liquid which it squirts from musk glands at the base of its tail in order to deter predators. 2 derog a despised person.

sky n (skies) 1 the apparent dome of space over our heads. 2 (skies) the heavens. 3 the maximum limit or aim: Aim for the sky. ➤ vb (skies, skied) cricket to mishit (a ball) high into the air. ♦ **the sky's the limit** there is no upper limit, eg to the amount of money that may be spent, or achievements to be made. **to the skies** in a lavish or extremely enthusiastic manner: He praised him to the skies.

sky-high adj, adv esp of prices: very high.

skylark n a small lark which inhabits open country and is known for its loud clear warbling song, performed in flight. ➤ vb, intr, old use to lark about; to frolic.

skylight n a (usu small) window in a roof or ceiling.

skyline n the outline of buildings, hills and trees seen against the sky; the horizon.

skyrocket n a firework that explodes very high in the sky. ➤ vb, intr to rise high and fast.

skyscraper n an extremely tall building.

skyward adj directed towards the sky. ➤ adv (also **skywards**) towards the sky.

slab n 1 a thick flat rectangular piece of stone, etc. 2 a thick slice, esp of cake. ➤ vb (slabbed, slabbing) to pave with concrete slabs.

slack¹ adj 1 limp or loose; not pulled or stretched tight. 2 not careful or diligent; remiss. 3 not busy: Business is a bit slack these days. 4 of the tide, etc: still; neither ebbing nor flowing. ➤ adv in a slack manner; partially. ➤ n 1 a loosely hanging part, esp of a rope. 2 a period of little trade or other activity. ➤ vb (also **slacken**) (often **slack off**) 1 intr (also **slack up**) to become slower; to slow one's working pace through tiredness or laziness: Stop slacking! 2 tr & intr to make or become looser. 3 intr to become less busy: work is slackening off for the winter.

slack² n coal dust or tiny fragments of coal.

slacken see under SLACK¹ (verb)

slacker n an idle person; a shirker.

slacks pl n, dated a type of loose casual trousers, worn by both males and females.

slag¹ n 1 the layer of waste material that forms on the surface of molten metal ore during smelting and refining. 2 waste left over from coal mining.

slag² vb (slagged, slagging) slang (usu **slag sb off**) to criticize or deride them harshly or speak disparagingly about them.

slag³ *n, derog slang* someone, esp a woman, who regularly has casual sex with many different people.

slag heap *n* a hill or mound formed from coal-mining waste.

slake *vb* **1** *literary* to satisfy or quench (thirst, desire or anger). **2** to cause (lime) to crumble by adding water.

slaked lime *n* calcium hydroxide, **Ca(OH)₂**, used in the production of cements.

slalom *n* a race, on skis or in canoes, in and out of obstacles on a winding course designed to test tactical skill.

slam¹ *vb* (**slammed, slamming**) **1** *tr & intr* to shut loudly and with violence: *She slammed the window shut.* **2** *tr & intr* (*usu* **slam against, down, into,** *etc*) *colloq* to make or cause something to make loud heavy contact: *He slammed his books down.* **3** *slang* to criticize severely. ➤ *n* **1** the act or sound of slamming. **2** a severe criticism.

slam² *n* short for **grand slam**.

slammer *n, slang* (**the slammer**) prison.

slander *n* **1** *law* damaging defamation by spoken words, or by looks or gestures. **2** a false, malicious and damaging spoken statement about a person. **3** the making of such statements. ➤ *vb* to speak about someone in such a way. Compare LIBEL. ○ **slanderer** *n*. ○ **slanderous** *adj*.

slang *n* very informal words and phrases used by any class, profession or set of people. ➤ *vb* to speak abusively to someone using coarse language. ○ **slangy** *adj*.

slanging match *n, colloq* an angry exchange of insults or abuse.

slant *vb* **1** *intr* to be at an angle as opposed to horizontal or vertical; to slope. **2** *intr* to turn, strike or fall obliquely or at an angle. **3** to present (information, etc) in a biased way, or for a particular audience or readership. ➤ *n* **1** a sloping position, surface or line. **2** a point of view, opinion or way of looking at a particular thing. ➤ *adj* sloping; lying at an angle.

slap *n* **1** a blow with the palm of the hand or anything flat. **2** the sound made by such a blow, or by the impact of one flat surface on another. **3** a snub or rebuke. ➤ *vb* (**slapped, slapping**) **1** to strike with the open hand or anything flat. **2** to bring or send with a slapping sound: *He slapped the newspaper down on the table.* **3** (*often* **slap sth on**) *colloq* to apply thickly and carelessly: *She slapped cream on her face.* ➤ *adv, colloq* **1** exactly or precisely: *slap in the middle.* **2** heavily or suddenly; with a slap: *He fell slap on his face.* ♦ **a slap in the face** *colloq* an insult or rebuff. **a slap on the back** *colloq* congratulations. **a slap on the wrist** *colloq, often facetious* a mild reprimand.

slap and tickle *n, humorous colloq* kissing and cuddling; sexual activity of any kind.

slap-bang *adv, colloq* **1** exactly or precisely: *slap-bang in the middle.* **2** violently; directly and with force: *He drove slap-bang into the wall.*

slapdash *adv* in a careless and hurried manner. ➤ *adj* careless and hurried: *a slapdash piece of work.*

slap-happy *adj, colloq* cheerfully carefree or careless; happy-go-lucky.

slapstick *n* comedy in which the humour is derived from boisterous antics of all kinds.

slap-up *adj, colloq* of a meal: lavish; extravagant.

slash¹ *vb* **1** *tr & intr* to make sweeping cuts or cutting strokes, esp repeatedly. **2** to cut by striking violently and often randomly. **3** *colloq* to reduce (prices, etc) suddenly and drastically. ➤ *n* **1** a sweeping cutting stroke. **2** a long and sometimes deep cut. **3** (*also* **slash mark**) an oblique line (/) in writing or printing; a solidus.

slash² *coarse slang, vb, intr* to urinate. ➤ *n* an act of urinating.

slat *n* a thin strip, esp of wood or metal. ○ **slatted** *adj*.

slate¹ *n* **1** *geol* a shiny dark grey metamorphic rock that is easily split into thin flat layers, formed by the compression of clays and shales, and used for roofing and flooring. **2** a roofing tile made of this. **3** *formerly* a piece of this for writing on. **4** a record of credit given to a customer: *Put it on my slate.* **5** a dull grey colour. ➤ *vb* to cover (a roof) with slates. ➤ *adj* **1** made of slate. **2** slate-coloured. ○ **slating** *n*. ○ **slaty** *adj*. ♦ **on the slate** on credit. **wipe the slate clean** to enable a person to make a fresh start by ignoring past mistakes, acts of crime, etc.

slate² *vb, colloq* to criticize extremely harshly; to abuse or reprimand.

slattern *n, old use* a woman of dirty or untidy appearance or habits; a slut. ○ **slatternly** *adj*.

slaughter *n* **1** the killing of animals, esp for food. **2** cruel and violent murder. **3** the large-scale indiscriminate killing of people or animals. ➤ *vb* **1** to subject to slaughter. **2** *colloq* to defeat resoundingly; to trounce: *I was slaughtered at tennis yesterday.* ○ **slaughterer** *n*.

slaughterhouse *n* a place where animals are killed for food; an abattoir.

slave *n* **1** *hist* someone owned by and acting as servant to another, with no personal freedom. **2** a person who is submissive under domination. **3** a person who works extremely hard for another; a drudge. **4** (*also* **a slave to sth**) a person whose life is dominated by a specific activity or thing: *She's a slave to her work.* ➤ *vb, intr* to work like or as a slave; to work hard and ceaselessly.

slave-driver *n* **1** *hist* someone employed to supervise slaves to ensure they work hard. **2** *colloq* someone who demands very hard work from others.

slaver /ˈslavə(r)/ *n* spittle running from the mouth. ➤ *vb, intr* **1** to let spittle run from the mouth; to dribble. **2** (*also* **slaver over sb**) to fawn over them, esp lustfully. **3** *colloq* to talk nonsense.

slavery n 1 the state of being a slave. 2 the practice of owning slaves. 3 toil or drudgery.

slavish adj 1 characteristic of, belonging to or befitting a slave. 2 very closely copied or imitated; unoriginal. ○ **slavishly** adv.

slay vb (past tense **slew**, past participle **slain**) tr & intr, archaic or literary to kill. ○ **slayer** n.

sleaze n, colloq 1 sleaziness. 2 a disreputable person.

sleazy adj (-**ier**, -**iest**) colloq 1 looking dirty and neglected. 2 cheaply suggestive of sex or crime; disreputable and considered to be of low standards, esp with regard to morals: a sleazy bar. ○ **sleaziness** n.

sledge or **sled** n 1 a vehicle with ski-like runners for travelling over snow, drawn by horses or dogs. 2 a smaller vehicle of a similar design for children, for sliding on the snow; a toboggan. ➤ vb, intr to travel or play on a sledge.

sledgehammer n a large heavy hammer swung with both arms.

sleek adj 1 of hair, fur, etc: smooth, soft and glossy. 2 having a well-fed and prosperous appearance. 3 insincerely polite or flattering; slick in manner. ➤ vb to smooth (esp hair). ○ **sleekly** adv. ○ **sleekness** n.

sleep n 1 a readily reversible state of natural unconsciousness during which the body's functional powers are restored, and physical movements are minimal. 2 a period of such rest. 3 colloq mucus that collects in the corners of the eyes during such rest. 4 poetic death. ➤ vb (**slept**) intr 1 to rest in a state of sleep. 2 to be motionless, inactive or dormant. 3 (**sleep with sb**) to have sexual relations with them. 4 to provide or contain sleeping accommodation for (the specified number): The caravan sleeps four. 5 colloq to be in a dreamy state, not paying attention, etc. 6 poetic to be dead. ◆ **lose sleep over sth** colloq, usu with negatives to be worried or preoccupied by it. **put sb** or **sth to sleep** 1 to anaesthetize them. 2 euphem to kill (an animal) painlessly with an injected drug. **sleep on it** to delay taking a decision about it until the following morning in the hope that one might have a better intuitive feel for the best course of action. ◇ **sleep around** to engage in casual sexual relations. **sleep in** to sleep later than usual in the morning. **sleep sth off** to recover from it by sleeping.

sleeper n 1 someone who sleeps, esp in a specified way: a heavy sleeper. 2 any of the horizontal wooden or concrete beams supporting the rails on a railway track. 3 a a railway carriage providing sleeping accommodation for passengers; b a train with such carriages: We took the sleeper to London. 4 a small gold hoop worn in a pierced ear to prevent the hole from closing up.

sleeping bag n a large quilted sack for sleeping in when camping, etc.

sleeping partner n a business partner who invests money in a business without taking part in its management.

sleeping pill n a pill which contains a sedative drug that induces sleep.

sleeping policeman n, colloq each of a series of low humps built into the surface of a road, intended to slow down motor traffic in residential areas, parks, etc.

sleeping sickness n an infectious disease transmitted by the tsetse fly, so called because the later stages of the disease are characterized by extreme drowsiness, and eventually death.

sleepless adj 1 characterized by an inability to sleep: a sleepless night. 2 unable to sleep. ○ **sleeplessly** adv. ○ **sleeplessness** n.

sleepwalking n the act of walking about in one's sleep. ○ **sleepwalker** n.

sleepy adj (-**ier**, -**iest**) 1 feeling the desire or need to sleep; drowsy. 2 suggesting sleep or drowsiness: sleepy music. 3 characterized by quietness and a lack of activity: a sleepy village. ○ **sleepily** adv. ○ **sleepiness** n.

sleepyhead n, colloq a person who seems in need of sleep.

sleet n rain mixed with snow and/or hail. ➤ vb, intr to rain and snow simultaneously.

sleeve n 1 the part of a garment that covers the arm. 2 eng a tube fitted inside a metal cylinder or tube, either as protection or to decrease the diameter. 3 the cardboard or paper envelope in which a RECORD (noun sense 4) is stored. ○ **sleeveless** adj. ◆ **have sth up one's sleeve** to have something in secret reserve. **laugh up one's sleeve** to laugh privately or secretly.

sleigh esp N Am, n a large horse-drawn sledge. ➤ vb, intr to travel by sleigh.

sleight /slaɪt/ n dexterity; cunning or trickery.

sleight of hand n the quick and deceptive movement of the hands in the performing of magic tricks.

slender adj 1 attractively slim. 2 thin or narrow; slight: by a slender margin. 3 meagre: slender means. ○ **slenderness** n.

sleuth /sluːθ/ colloq, n a detective. ➤ vb, intr to work as a detective.

slew¹ past tense of SLAY

slew² or **slue** vb, tr & intr to twist or cause to twist or swing round, esp suddenly and uncontrollably. ➤ n an instance of slewing.

slice n 1 a thin broad piece, wedge or segment that is cut off. 2 colloq a share or portion: a slice of the business. 3 a kitchen utensil with a broad flat blade for sliding under and lifting solid food, esp fish. 4 a slash or swipe. 5 in golf and tennis: a stroke causing a ball to spin sideways and curve away in a particular direction; the spin itself. ➤ vb 1 to cut up into slices. 2 (also **slice sth off**) to cut it off as or like a slice: slice a piece off the end. 3 intr to cut deeply and easily; to move easily and forcefully: a boat slicing through the water. 4 intr to slash. 5 to strike (a ball) with a slice. ○ **slicer** n.

slick adj 1 dishonestly or slyly clever. 2 glib; smooth-tongued or suave: a slick operator. 3 impressively and superficially smart or efficient: *a slick organization*. **4** esp of hair: smooth and glossy; sleek. ➤ *vb* (*usu* **slick sth back** or **down**) to smooth (esp hair). ➤ *n* a wide layer of spilled oil floating on water. ○ **slickness** *n*.

slicker *n* **1** a sophisticated city-dweller. **2** a shifty or swindling person.

slide *vb* (*slid*) **1** *tr & intr* to move or cause to move or run smoothly along a surface. **2** *intr* to lose one's footing, esp on a slippery surface; to slip. **3** *tr & intr* to move or place softly and unobtrusively: *I slid the letter into his pocket*. **4** *intr* to pass gradually, esp through neglect or laziness; to lapse: *He slid back into his old habits*. ➤ *n* **1** an act or instance of sliding. **2** a polished slippery track, eg on ice. **3** any part of something that glides smoothly, eg the moving part of a trombone. **4** an apparatus for children to play on, usu with a ladder to climb up and a narrow sloping part to slide down; a chute. **5** a small glass plate on which specimens are mounted to be viewed through a microscope. **6** a small transparent photograph viewed in magnified size by means of a projector. **7** a sliding clasp for a girl's or woman's hair. ○ **slidable** *adj*. ○ **slider** *n*.

slide rule *n* a hand-held mechanical device used to perform quick numerical calculations.

sliding scale *n* a scale, eg of fees charged, varying according to changes in conditions, eg unforeseen difficulties in performing the service requested, etc.

slight *adj* **1** small in extent, significance or seriousness: *a slight problem*. **2** slim or slender. **3** lacking solidity, weight or significance; flimsy. ➤ *vb* to insult someone by ignoring or dismissing them abruptly; to snub them. ➤ *n* an insult by snubbing or showing neglect. ○ **slightly** *adv* to a small extent; in a small way. ○ **slightness** *n*. ◆ **not in the slightest** not at all.

slim *adj* (*slimmer, slimmest*) **1** of people: attractively thin; slender. **2** characterized by little thickness or width. **3** not great; slight or remote: *a slim chance*. ➤ *vb* (*slimmed, slimming*) *intr* **1** (*sometimes* **slim down**) to make oneself slimmer, esp by diet and/or exercise. **2** to try to lose weight. ○ **slimmer** *n*. ○ **slimming** *n*. ○ **slimness** *n*.

slime *n* **1** any thin, unpleasantly slippery or gluey, mud-like substance. **2** any mucus-like substance secreted, eg by snails, slugs and certain fishes. ➤ *vb* to smear or cover with slime.

slimy *adj* (*-ier, -iest*) **1** similar to, covered with or consisting of slime. **2** *colloq* exaggeratedly obedient or attentive; obsequious. ○ **slimily** *adv*. ○ **sliminess** *n*.

sling[1] *n* **1** a cloth hoop that hangs from the neck to support an injured arm. **2 a** a weapon for hurling stones, consisting of a strap or pouch in which the stone is placed and swung round fast; **b** a catapult. **3** a strap or loop for hoisting, lowering or carrying a weight. ➤ *vb* (*slung*) **1** to hang something loosely: *a jacket slung over his*

shoulder. **2** to throw, hurl, fling or toss. ◆ **sling one's hook** *slang* to go away or remove oneself.

sling[2] *n* a drink of alcoholic spirit and water, usu sweetened and flavoured.

slink *vb* (*slunk*) *intr* **1** to go or move sneakingly or ashamedly. **2** to move in a lithe and seductive manner. ➤ *n* a slinking gait.

slinky *adj* (*-ier, -iest*) *colloq* **1** of clothing: attractively close-fitting: *a slinky dress*. **2** slender. **3** of a person: walking in a slow and seductive manner. ○ **slinkily** *adv*. ○ **slinkiness** *n*.

slip[1] *vb* (*slipped, slipping*) **1** *intr* to lose one's footing and slide accidentally. **2** *intr* (*also* **slip up**) to make a slight mistake inadvertently rather than due to ignorance. **3** *intr* to slide, move or drop accidentally. **4** to place smoothly, quietly or secretively: *She slipped the envelope into her pocket*. **5** *tr & intr* to move or cause to move quietly, smoothly or unobtrusively with a sliding motion: *He slipped into the church in the middle of the service*. **6** to pull free from someone or something smoothly and swiftly; to suddenly escape from them or it: *The name has slipped my mind*. **7** *colloq* to give or pass secretly: *She slipped him a fiver*. **8** *intr, colloq* to lose one's former skill or expertise, or control of a situation. **9** to dislocate (a spinal disc). ➤ *n* **1** an instance of losing one's footing and sliding accidentally. **2** a minor and usu inadvertent mistake. **3** a slight error or transgression. **4** an escape. **5** a slight dislocation. **6** a woman's undergarment, worn under a dress or skirt. **7** a loose covering for a pillow. **8** a SLIPWAY. ◆ **give sb the slip** *colloq* to escape from them skilfully or adroitly. **let sth slip 1** to reveal it accidentally. **2** to fail to take advantage of something, esp an opportunity. **slip of the tongue** or **pen** a word, phrase, etc said or written in error when something else was intended.

slip[2] *n* **1** a small strip or piece of paper. **2** a small pre-printed form. **3** a young or exceptionally slender person: *She's just a slip of a girl*.

slip[3] *n* a creamy mixture of clay and water used for decorating pottery.

slipknot *n* a knot finishing off a noose, and slipping along the cord to adjust the noose's tightness.

slip-on *n* a shoe or other item of clothing that is easily put on due to having no laces, buttons or other fastenings.

slipped disc *n* a dislocation of one of the flat circular plates of cartilage situated between any of the vertebrae, resulting in painful pressure on a spinal nerve.

slipper *n* a soft loose laceless indoor shoe.

slippery *adj* **1** so smooth, wet, etc as to cause or allow slipping. **2** difficult to catch or keep hold of; elusive or evasive. **3** unpredictable or untrustworthy: *a slippery character*. ○ **slipperiness** *n*.

slippy *adj* (*-ier, -iest*) *colloq* of a thing: liable to slip; slippery.

slip road *n* a road by which vehicles join or leave a motorway.

slipshod *adj* untidy and careless; carelessly done.

slipstream *n* a stream of air driven back by an aircraft propeller.

slip-up *n, colloq* a minor and usu inadvertent mistake.

slipway *n* a ramp in a dock or shipyard that slopes into water, for launching boats.

slit *n* a long narrow cut or opening. ➤ *vb* (**slit, slitting**) to cut a slit in something, esp lengthwise.

slither *vb, intr* **1** to slide or slip unsteadily while walking, esp on ice. **2** to move slidingly, like a snake. ➤ *n* a slithering movement. ○ **slithery** *adj*.

sliver *n* a long thin piece cut or broken off. ➤ *vb, tr & intr* to break or cut into slivers.

slob *colloq, n* a lazy, untidy and slovenly person. ➤ *vb* (**slobbed, slobbing**) *intr* (*usu* **slob about** or **around**) to move or behave in a lazy, untidy or slovenly way.

slobber *vb, intr* **1** to let saliva run from the mouth; to dribble. **2** (*usu* **slobber over sth**) *colloq* to express extreme or excessive enthusiasm or admiration for it. ➤ *n* dribbled saliva; slaver. ○ **slobbery** *adj*.

sloe *n* the blackthorn bush or its fruit.

slog *colloq, vb* (**slogged, slogging**) **1** to hit hard and wildly. **2** *intr* to labour or toil. ➤ *n* **1** a hard wild blow or stroke. **2** extremely tiring work. ○ **slogger** *n*.

slogan *n* a phrase used to identify a group or organization, or to advertise a product.

sloop *n* a single-masted sailing boat with fore-and-aft sails.

slop *vb* (**slopped, slopping**) **1** (*often* **slop about** or **around**) *tr & intr* to splash or cause to splash or spill violently. **2** *intr* to walk carelessly in slush or water. ➤ *n* **1** spilled liquid; a puddle. **2** (**slops**) waste food. **3** (**slops**) semi-liquid food fed to pigs. ◊ **slop about** or **around** *colloq* to move or behave in an untidy or slovenly manner.

slope *n* **1** a slanting surface; an incline. **2** a position or direction that is neither level nor upright. **3** the side of a hill or mountain. ➤ *vb, intr* **1** to rise or fall at an angle. **2** to be slanted or inclined. ○ **sloping** *adj*. ◊ **slope off** *colloq* to leave stealthily or furtively.

sloppy *adj* (**-ier, -iest**) **1** wet or muddy. **2** watery. **3** over-sentimental. **4** of language, work, etc: inaccurate or careless; shoddy. **5** of clothes: baggy; loose-fitting. ○ **sloppily** *adv*. ○ **sloppiness** *n*.

slosh *vb* **1** *tr & intr* (*often* **slosh about** or **around**) to splash or cause to splash or spill noisily. **2** *slang* to hit or strike with a heavy blow. ➤ *n* **1** the sound of splashing or spilling. **2** slush; a watery mess. **3** *slang* a heavy blow.

sloshed *adj, colloq* drunk; intoxicated.

slot *n* **1** a long narrow rectangular opening into which something is fitted or inserted. **2** a (usu regular) time, place or position within a schedule, eg of radio or TV broadcasts. ➤ *vb*

(**slotted, slotting**) **1** to make a slot in. **2** (*usu* **slot sth in**) to fit or insert it, or place it in a slot.

sloth /sloʊθ/ *n* **1** a tree-dwelling mammal with long slender limbs and hook-like claws, noted for its very slow movements. **2** the desire to avoid all activity or exertion; laziness; indolence. ○ **slothful** *adj* lazy; inactive.

slot machine *n* a machine operated by inserting a coin in a slot, eg a fruit machine.

slouch *vb, intr* to sit, stand or walk with a tired, lazy or drooping posture. ➤ *n* such a posture. ○ **slouching** *adj*. ♦ **no slouch at sth** *colloq* of a person: able or competent in some respect: *He's no slouch at cooking*.

slough[1] *n* **1** /slaʊ/ a mud-filled hollow. **2** /sluː/ *N Am* an area of boggy land; a marsh or mire. **3** /slaʊ/ *literary* a state of deep and gloomy emotion: *a slough of depression*.

slough[2] /slʌf/ *n* any outer part of an animal cast off or moulted, esp a snake's dead skin. ➤ *vb* **1** to shed (eg a dead skin). **2** to cast off or dismiss (eg worries).

sloven /ˈslʌvən/ *n* someone who is carelessly or untidily dressed; a person of shoddy appearance.

slovenly *adj* **1** careless, untidy or dirty in appearance. **2** careless or shoddy in habits or methods of working. ➤ *adv* in a slovenly manner. ○ **slovenliness** *n*.

slow *adj* **1** having little speed or pace; not fast. **2** taking a long time, or longer than usual or expected. **3** of a watch or clock: showing a time earlier than the correct time. **4** of a mind: unable to quickly and easily understand or appreciate. **5** of wit or intellect: dull; unexciting or uninteresting. **6** progressing at a tediously gentle pace: *a slow afternoon*. **7** boring or dull; tedious: *a slow film*. **8** needing much provocation in order to do something: *He's slow to get angry*. **9** of business: slack. **10** of photographic film: needing a relatively long exposure time. ➤ *adv* in a slow manner. ➤ *vb, tr & intr* (*also* **slow down** or **up**) to reduce or make something reduce speed, pace or rate of progress. ○ **slowly** *adv*. ○ **slowness** *n*.

slowcoach *n, colloq* someone who moves or works at a slow pace.

slow motion *n* in film or television: a speed of movement that is much slower than real-life movement.

slowworm *n* a harmless species of legless lizard with a small mouth and a smooth shiny brownish-grey to coppery body.

sludge *n* **1** soft slimy mud or mire. **2** muddy sediment. **3** sewage. **4** half-melted snow; slush. ○ **sludgy** *adj*.

slug[1] *n* a mollusc, similar to a snail, but which has a long fleshy body and little or no shell.

slug[2] *n* **1** *colloq* **a** an irregularly formed bullet; **b** a bullet. **2** *printing* a solid line or section of metal type produced by a composing machine.

slug[3] *colloq, n* a heavy blow. ➤ *vb* (**slugged, slugging**) to strike with a heavy blow. ○ **slugger** *n*.

slug⁴ *n, esp US colloq* a large gulp or mouthful of alcohol, esp spirit.

sluggard *n* a habitually lazy or inactive person.

sluggish *adj* **1** unenergetic; habitually lazy or inactive. **2** less lively, active or responsive than usual: *This engine is a bit sluggish.* ○ **sluggishness** *n*.

sluice /sluːs/ *n* **1** a channel or drain for water. **2** (*in full* **sluicegate**) a valve or sliding gate for regulating the flow of water in such a channel. **3** a trough for washing gold or other minerals out of sand, etc. **4** an act of washing down or rinsing. ➤ *vb* **1** to let out or drain by means of a sluice. **2** to wash down or rinse by throwing water on.

slum *n* **1** a run-down, dirty and usu overcrowded house. **2** (*often* **slums**) an area or neighbourhood containing such housing. ➤ *vb* (**slummed, slumming**) *intr* to visit an area of slums, esp out of curiosity or for amusement. ○ **slummy** *adj.* ◆ **slum it** *colloq* to experience conditions that are less affluent or more squalid than one is used to.

slumber *chiefly poetic, n* sleep. ➤ *vb, intr* to sleep.

slump *vb, intr* **1** to drop or sink suddenly and heavily, eg with tiredness: *He slumped into an armchair.* **2** of prices, trade, etc: to decline suddenly and sharply. ➤ *n* **1** an act or instance of slumping. **2** a serious and usu long-term decline, esp in a nation's economy. ○ **slumped** *adj.*

slur *vb* (**slurred, slurring**) **1** to pronounce (words) indistinctly. **2** to speak or write about something very disparagingly; to cast aspersions on it. **3** (*often* **slur over sth**) to mention it only briefly or deal with it only superficially. **4** *mus* to sing or play (notes) as a flowing sequence without pauses. ➤ *n* **1** a disparaging remark intended to damage a reputation. **2** a slurred word or slurring way of speaking. **3** *mus* **a** a flowing pauseless style of singing or playing; **b** the curved line under the notes indicating this style.

slurp *vb* to eat or drink noisily with a sucking action. ➤ *n* a slurping sound.

slurry *n* (**-ies**) **1** a thin paste or semi-fluid mixture, esp watery concrete. **2** liquid manure that is treated so that it can be distributed on to fields.

slush *n* **1** half-melted snow. **2** any watery half-liquid substance, eg liquid mud. **3** sickly sentimentality. ○ **slushy** *adj.*

slush fund *n* a fund of money used for dishonest purposes, eg bribery, esp by a political party.

slut *n, derog* a woman who regularly engages in casual sex. ○ **sluttish** *adj.*

sly *adj* **1** of people: clever; cunning or wily. **2** surreptitious; secretively deceitful or dishonest. **3** playfully mischievous: *a sly smile.* ○ **slyly** *adv.* ○ **slyness** *n.* ◆ **on the sly** *colloq* secretly or furtively.

Sm *symbol, chem* samarium.

smack¹ *vb* **1** to slap loudly and smartly. **2** *tr & intr, colloq* to hit loudly and heavily: *Her head smacked against the wall.* **3** to kiss loudly. **4** to part (the lips) loudly in pleasant anticipation. ➤ *n* **1** an act or the sound of smacking. **2** a loud enthusiastic kiss. ➤ *adv, colloq* **1** directly and with force: *He drove smack into the tree.* **2** precisely: *smack in the middle.* ○ **smacking** *n, adj.*

smack² *vb, intr* (*always* **smack of sth**) **1** to have the flavour of it. **2** to have a trace of it. ➤ *n* a hint or trace.

smack³ *n* a small single-masted fishing boat.

smacker *n* **1** *colloq* a loud enthusiastic kiss. **2** *slang* a pound note or a dollar bill.

small *adj* **1** little in size or quantity. **2** little in extent, importance or worth. **3** slender: *of small build.* **4** humble: *small beginnings.* **5** young: *a small child.* **6** minor; insignificant: *a small problem.* **7** of a printed or written letter: lower-case; not capital. **8** humiliated: *feel small.* ➤ *n* **1** the narrow part, esp of the back. **2** (**smalls**) *colloq* underclothes. ➤ *adv* into small pieces. ○ **smallness** *n.*

small beer *n, colloq* something unimportant.

small change *n* coins of little value.

small fry *sing or pl n, colloq* **1** people or things of little importance or influence. **2** young children.

smallholding *n* an area of cultivated land smaller than an ordinary farm. ○ **smallholder** *n.*

small hours *pl n* (**the small hours**) the hours immediately after midnight, very early in the morning.

small intestine *n, anat* in mammals: the part of the intestine whose main function is to digest and absorb food.

small-minded *adj* narrow-minded; petty.

smallpox *n, pathol* a highly contagious viral disease, characterized by fever and a rash that usu leaves pitted scars.

small print *n* the details of a contract or other undertaking, often printed very small, esp when considered likely to contain unattractive conditions that the writer of the contract does not want to be noticed.

the small screen *n* television, as opposed to cinema.

small talk *n* polite conversation about trivial matters.

small-time *adj* operating on a small scale; insignificant.

smarm *vb* **1** *intr, colloq* to be exaggeratedly and insincerely flattering. **2** (*often* **smarm sth down**) to flatten (the hair) with an oily substance. ➤ *n, colloq* exaggerated or insincere flattery.

smarmy *adj* (**-ier, -iest**) *colloq* nauseatingly charming.

smart *adj* **1** neat and well-dressed. **2** clever; witty; shrewd. **3** expensive, sophisticated and fashionable: *a smart hotel.* **4** quick, adept and efficient in business. **5** of pain, etc: sharp and stinging. **6** brisk: *He walked at a smart pace.* **7** *comput* technologically advanced. **8** guided by computers or controlled by electronics: *a smart bomb.* ➤ *vb, intr* **1** to feel or be the cause of a sharp stinging pain. **2** to feel or be the cause of acute irritation or distress: *He's still smarting from the insult.* ➤ *n* a sharp stinging pain. ➤ *adv* in a smart manner. ○ **smartly** *adv.* ○ **smartness** *n.* ♦ **look smart** to hurry up.

smart alec or **smart aleck** *n, colloq* a person who thinks that they are cleverer than others.

smart card *n* a plastic card like a bank card, fitted with a microprocessor (including a memory) used in commercial transactions, telecommunications, etc.

smarten *vb, tr & intr* (*usu* **smarten up**) to make or become smarter.

smartypants *sing n, colloq* a know-all.

smash *vb* **1** *tr & intr* to break violently into pieces; to destroy or be destroyed in this way. **2** *tr & intr* to strike with violence, often causing damage; to burst with great force: *They smashed through the door.* **3** *colloq* to break up or ruin completely: *Police have smashed an international drugs ring.* **4** in racket sports: to hit (a ball) with a powerful overhead stroke. **5** to crash (a car). ➤ *n* **1** an act, or the sound, of smashing. **2** in racket sports: a powerful overhead stroke. **3** *colloq* a road traffic accident. **4** *colloq* a SMASH HIT. ➤ *adv* with a smashing sound.

smash-and-grab *colloq, adj* of a robbery: carried out by smashing a shop window and snatching the items on display. ➤ *n* a robbery carried out in this way.

smasher *n, colloq* someone or something very much liked or admired.

smash hit *n, colloq* a song, film, play, etc that is an overwhelming success.

smashing *adj, colloq* excellent; splendid.

smash-up *n, colloq* a serious road traffic accident.

smattering *n* a few scraps.

smear *vb* **1** to spread (something sticky or oily) thickly over (a surface). **2** *tr & intr* to make or become blurred; to smudge. **3** to say or write damaging things about someone. ➤ *n* **1** a greasy mark or patch. **2** a damaging criticism or accusation. **3** an amount of a substance, esp of cervical tissue, placed on a slide for examination under a microscope. ○ **smeary** *adj.*

smear test *n* the use of a cervical smear to detect cancer.

smell *n* **1** the sense that allows different odours to be recognized by specialized receptors in the mucous membranes of the nose. **2** the characteristic odour of a particular substance: *It has a strong smell.* **3** an unpleasant odour: *What a smell!* **4** an act of using this sense: *Have a smell of this.* **5** a sense, savour or suggestion of something: *The smell of money always brings him back.* ➤ *vb* (**smelled** or **smelt**) **1** to apply the sense of smell to something. **2** to recognize (a substance) by its odour. **3** *intr* to give off an un-

pleasant odour. **4** to give off a specified odour: *The perfume smells flowery.* **5** to be aware of something by intuition: *I smell a government cover-up.* ◊ **smell sb** or **sth out** to track them down by smell, or as if by smell.

smelling salts *pl n* a preparation of ammonium carbonate with a strong sharp odour, used to stimulate a return to consciousness after fainting.

smelly *adj* (**-ier, -iest**) *colloq* having an unpleasant smell. ○ **smelliness** *n.*

smelt[1] *vb* to process (an ore), esp by melting it, in order to separate out the crude metal.

smelt[2] *n* (**smelts** or **smelt**) a small edible fish with a slender silvery body.

smelt[3] *past tense, past participle of* SMELL

smelter *n* an industrial plant where smelting is done.

smidgen, smidgeon or **smidgin** *n, colloq* a very small amount.

smile *vb* **1** *intr* to turn up the corners of the mouth, usu as an expression of pleasure, favour or amusement. **2** to show or communicate with such an expression: *He smiled his agreement.* **3** *intr* (*usu* **smile on sb** or **sth**) to show favour towards them. ➤ *n* an act or way of smiling.

smiley *n, comput slang* a symbol created from characters on a keyboard, eg :-) intended to look like a smiling face (sideways on), used in e-mails and text messages.

smirch *vb* **1** to make dirty. **2** to damage (a reputation, etc). ➤ *n* **1** a stain. **2** a smear on a reputation.

smirk *vb* to smile in a self-satisfied, affected or foolish manner. ➤ *n* such a smile.

smite *vb* (*past tense* **smote**, *past participle* **smitten**) *literary* **1** to strike with a heavy blow. **2** to kill. **3** to afflict. **4** to cause someone to fall immediately and overpoweringly in love: *He could not fail to be smitten by such beauty.* ○ **smitten** *adj* in love; obsessed.

smith *n* **1** *in compounds* a person who makes articles in the specified metal: *silversmith.* **2** a BLACKSMITH. **3** *in compounds* a person who makes skilful use of anything: *wordsmith.*

smithereens *pl n, colloq* tiny fragments.

smithy *n* (**-ies**) a blacksmith's workshop.

smock *n* **1** any loose shirt-like garment worn over other clothes for protection esp by artists, etc. **2** a woman's long loose-fitting blouse. **3** *hist* a loose-fitting overall of coarse linen worn by farm-workers.

smocking *n* honeycomb-patterned stitching used on gathered material for decoration.

smog *n* a mixture of smoke and fog, esp in urban or industrial areas. ○ **smoggy** *adj* (**-ier, -iest**).

smoke *n* **1** a visible cloud given off by a burning substance. **2** a cloud of fumes. **3** the act or process of smoking tobacco. **4** *colloq* something that can be smoked, such as a cigarette. ➤ *vb* **1** *intr* to give off smoke or fumes. **2** *tr & intr* to inhale and then exhale the smoke from burning tobacco or other substances in a cigarette, pipe, etc. **3** *tr & intr* to do this frequently, as a habit. **4** to preserve or flavour food by exposing it to smoke. ○ **smoky** *adj (-ier, -iest)*.

smokeless *adj* of a fuel: giving off little or no smoke when burned.

smoker *n* someone who smokes tobacco products.

smokescreen *n* **1** a cloud of smoke used to conceal the movements of troops, etc. **2** anything said or done to hide or deceive.

smolt *n* a young salmon migrating from fresh water to the sea.

smooch *vb, intr, colloq* **1** to kiss and cuddle. **2** to dance slowly while in an embrace.

smoochy *adj (-ier, -iest)* of music: sentimental and romantic.

smooth *adj* **1** having an even regular surface; not rough, coarse, bumpy or wavy. **2** having few or no lumps; having an even texture: *smooth sauce.* **3** free from problems: *a smooth journey.* **4** characterized by steady movement and a lack of jolts: *a smooth ferry crossing.* **5** of skin: having no hair, spots, blemishes, etc. **6** extremely charming, esp excessively or insincerely so: *a smooth talker.* **7** *slang* very classy or elegant: *a smooth dresser.* ➣ *vb* **1** *(also **smooth sth down** or **out**)* to make it smooth. **2** *(often **smooth over sth**)* to cause a difficulty, etc to seem less serious or important. **3** to free from lumps or roughness. **4** *(often **smooth sth away**)* to remove (esp problems) by smoothing; to calm or soothe. **5** to make easier. **6** *intr* to become smooth. ➣ *adv* smoothly. ➣ *n* **1** the act or process of smoothing. **2** the easy, pleasurable or trouble-free part (eg of a situation): *to take the rough with the smooth.* ○ **smoothly** *adv.* ○ **smoothness** *n*.

smoothie or **smoothy** *n (-ies) colloq* **1** a person who is very elegant and charming, esp one excessively or insincerely so. **2** a thick drink made from fruit and yoghurt, ice cream or milk.

smooth-talking, **smooth-spoken** or **smooth-tongued** *adj* **1** exaggeratedly and insincerely flattering. **2** charmingly persuasive. ○ **smooth-talker** *n*.

smorgasbord *n* a Swedish-style buffet of hot and cold savoury dishes.

smother *vb* **1** *tr & intr* to kill with or die from lack of air, esp with an obstruction over the mouth and nose. **2** to extinguish (a fire) by cutting off the air supply. **3** to cover something with a thick layer: *She loved her bread smothered with jam.* **4** to give an oppressive or stifling amount to someone: *She smothered the children with love.* **5** to suppress or contain.

smoulder *vb, intr* **1** to burn slowly or without flame. **2** of emotions: to linger on in a suppressed state. **3** of a person: to harbour suppressed emotions: *He sat smouldering in the corner.*

smudge *n* **1** a mark or blot caused or spread by

rubbing. **2** a faint or blurred shape, eg an object seen from afar. ➣ *vb* **1** to make a smudge on or of something. **2** *intr* to become or cause a smudge: *These pens smudge easily.* ○ **smudgy** *adj*.

smug *adj (smugger, smuggest)* arrogantly self-complacent or self-satisfied. ○ **smugly** *adv.* ○ **smugness** *n*.

smuggle *vb* **1** to take (goods) into or out of a country secretly and illegally, eg to avoid paying duty. **2** to bring, take or convey secretly: *He smuggled his notes into the exam.* ○ **smuggler** *n*. ○ **smuggling** *n*.

smut *n* **1** a speck of dirt, soot, etc. **2** mildly obscene language, jokes or pictures. **3** a serious disease of cereal crops, characterized by the appearance of masses of black spores, resembling soot.

smutty *adj (-ier, -iest)* **1** dirtied by smut. **2** mildly obscene: *a smutty sense of humour.* ○ **smuttiness** *n*.

Sn *symbol, chem* tin.

snack *n* a light meal often taken quickly, or a bite to eat between meals. ➣ *vb, intr* to eat a snack.

snack bar or **snack counter** *n* a café, kiosk or counter serving snacks.

snaffle *n (in full snaffle-bit)* a simple bridle bit for a horse. ➣ *vb* **1** to fit (a horse) with a snaffle. **2** *slang* to take sneakily or without permission.

snafu *n, US slang, orig mil* chaos.

snag *n* **1** a problem or drawback. **2** a protruding sharp edge on which clothes, etc could get caught. **3** a tear in clothes (esp tights, etc) caused by such catching. **4** a part of a tree submerged in water, hazardous to boats. ➣ *vb (snagged, snagging)* to catch or tear on a snag.

snaggletooth *n* a broken, irregular or projecting tooth. ○ **snaggletoothed** *adj*.

snail *n* **1** a mollusc with a coiled or conical shell on its back. **2** a sluggish person or animal. ♦ **at a snail's pace** extremely slowly.

snail mail *n, comput slang* the ordinary postal service, as opposed to electronic mail.

snake *n* **1** a limbless carnivorous reptile which has a long narrow body covered with scaly skin, and a forked tongue. **2** any long and flexible or winding thing or shape. **3** a SNAKE IN THE GRASS. ➣ *vb, intr* to move windingly or follow a winding course. ○ **snaky** *adj*.

snake-charmer *n* a street entertainer who appears to induce snakes to perform rhythmical movements, esp by playing music.

snake in the grass *n, colloq* an apparent friend revealed to be an enemy.

snap *vb (snapped, snapping)* **1** *tr & intr* to break suddenly and cleanly with a sharp cracking noise: *He snapped the stick over his knee.* **2** *tr & intr* to make or cause to make a sharp noise. **3** *tr & intr* to move quickly and forcefully into place with a sharp sound: *The lid snapped shut.* **4** *intr* to speak sharply in sudden irritation. **5** *colloq* to take a photograph of someone or something. **6** *intr, colloq* to lose one's senses or self-control suddenly. ➣ *n* **1** the act or sound of snapping.

2 *colloq* a photograph. **3** a catch or other fastening that closes with a snapping sound. **4** a sudden bite. **5** a crisp biscuit. **6** a card game in which all the cards played are collected by the first player to shout the word 'snap' on spotting a pair of matching cards laid down by consecutive players. ➤ *exclam* **1** the word shouted in the card game (see *noun* sense 6 above). **2** the word used to highlight any matching pairs, etc. ➤ *adj* taken or made spontaneously, without long consideration: *a snap decision.* ➤ *adv* with a snapping sound. ◆ **snap one's fingers** to show contempt or defiance. **snap out of it** *colloq* to bring oneself out of a state, eg of sulking or depression. ◊ **snap sth up** to acquire, purchase or seize it eagerly: *He snapped up the opportunity.*

snapper *n* **1** someone or something that snaps. **2** a deep-bodied food fish, found in tropical seas. **3** *US* a party cracker.

snappy *adj* (*-ier, -iest*) **1** irritable; inclined to snap. **2** smart and fashionable: *a snappy dresser.* **3** lively: *a snappy tempo.* ◆ **look snappy!** or **make it snappy!** *colloq* hurry up!, be quick about it!

snapshot *n*, *colloq* a photograph.

snare *n* **1** an animal trap, esp one with a noose to catch the animal's foot. **2** anything that traps or entangles. **3** anything that lures or tempts. **4** (*in full* **snare drum**) a medium-sized drum sitting horizontally, with a set of wires fitted to its underside that rattle sharply when the drum is struck. ➤ *vb* to catch, trap or entangle in, or as if in, a snare.

snarl¹ *vb* **1** *intr* of an animal: to growl angrily, showing the teeth. **2** *tr & intr* to speak aggressively. ➤ *n* **1** an act of snarling. **2** a snarling sound or facial expression.

snarl² *n* a knotted or tangled mass. ➤ *vb*, *tr & intr* (*also* **snarl sb** or **sth up** or **snarl up**) to make or become knotted, tangled, confused or congested.

snarl-up *n*, *colloq* any muddled or congested situation, esp a traffic jam.

snatch *vb* **1** to seize or grab suddenly. **2** *intr* to make a sudden grabbing movement. **3** to pull suddenly and forcefully: *She snatched her hand away.* **4** *colloq* to take or have as soon as the opportunity arises: *snatch a bite to eat.* ➤ *n* **1** an act of snatching. **2** a fragment overheard or remembered: *snatches of conversation.* **3** a brief period: *snatches of rest between long shifts.* **4** *colloq* a robbery.

snazzy *adj* (*-ier, -iest*) *colloq* fashionably and often flashily smart or elegant.

sneak *vb* (**sneaked** or (*colloq*) **snuck**) **1** (*often* **sneak away, off, out,** *etc*) *intr* to move, go or depart quietly, furtively and unnoticed. **2** to bring or take secretly, esp breaking a rule or prohibition: *He tried to sneak a look at the letter.* **3** *intr*, *colloq* to tell tales. ➤ *n*, *colloq* someone who sneaks.

sneakers *pl n*, *esp US* sports shoes; soft-soled, usu canvas, shoes.

sneaking *adj* **1** of a feeling, etc: slight but not easily suppressed: *a sneaking suspicion.* **2** secret: *a sneaking admiration.* **3** underhand.

sneak thief *n* a thief who enters premises through unlocked doors or windows, without actually breaking in.

sneaky *adj*, *-iest* done or operating with secretive unfairness.

sneer *vb* **1** *intr* (*often* **sneer at sb** or **sth**) to show scorn or contempt, esp by drawing the top lip up at one side. **2** *intr* to express scorn or contempt. **3** to say scornfully or contemptuously. ➤ *n* **1** an act of sneering. **2** an expression of scorn or contempt made with a raised lip, or in other ways.

sneeze *vb*, *intr* to blow air out through the nose suddenly, violently and involuntarily, esp because of irritation in the nostrils. ➤ *n* an act or the sound of sneezing. ◆ **not to be sneezed at** *colloq* not to be disregarded or overlooked lightly.

snib *n*, *chiefly Scot* a small catch for a door or window.

snick *n* **1** a small cut. **2** *cricket* **a** a glancing contact with the edge of the bat; **b** the shot hit in this way. ➤ *vb* **1** to make a small cut in something. **2** *cricket* to hit with a snick.

snicker *vb*, *intr* to SNIGGER. ➤ *n* a giggle.

snide *adj* expressing criticism or disapproval in an offensive, sly or malicious manner.

sniff *vb* **1** to draw in air with the breath through the nose. **2** *tr & intr* (*often* **sniff sth** or **sniff at sth**) to smell it in this way. **3** *intr* to draw up mucus or tears escaping into the nose. ➤ *n* **1** an act or the sound of sniffing. **2** a smell. **3** a small quantity inhaled by the nose. **4** a slight intimation or suspicion. ○ **sniffer** *n*. ◆ **not to be sniffed at** *colloq* not to be disregarded or overlooked lightly. ◊ **sniff sb** or **sth out** to discover them or it by, or as if by, the sense of smell.

sniffle *vb*, *intr* to sniff repeatedly, eg because of having a cold. ➤ *n* **1** an act or the sound of sniffling. **2** (*also* **the sniffles**) a slight cold. ○ **sniffly** *adj*.

sniffy *adj* (*-ier, -iest*) *colloq* contemptuous or disdainful, or inclined to be so.

snifter *n* **1** *slang* a drink of alcohol, esp alcoholic spirit. **2** *US* a brandy glass.

snigger *vb*, *intr* to laugh in a stifled or suppressed way, often mockingly. ➤ *n* such a laugh.

snip *vb* (**snipped, snipping**) to cut, esp with a quick action or actions, with scissors. ➤ *n* **1** an act or the action of snipping. **2** the sound of a stroke of scissors while snipping. **3** a small piece snipped off. **4** a small cut, slit or notch. **5** *colloq* a bargain: *It's a snip at £10.*

snipe *n* (**snipe** or **snipes**) **1** a wading bird with a long straight bill and relatively short legs. **2** a sniping shot, ie a shot from a hidden position. **3** a quick verbal attack. ➤ *vb*, *intr* **1** to shoot snipe for sport. **2** (*often* **snipe at sb**) **a** to shoot at them from a hidden position; **b** to criticize them bad-temperedly. ○ **sniper** *n* someone who shoots from a concealed position.

snippet *n* a scrap, eg of information, news, etc.

snitch *slang, n* an informer. ➤ *vb* **1** *intr* to inform on or betray others. **2** to steal.

snivel *vb* (**snivelled, snivelling**) *intr* **1** to whine or complain tearfully. **2** to have a runny nose. **3** to sniff or snuffle. ➤ *n* an act of snivelling.

snob *n* **1** someone who places too high a value on social status, treating those higher up the social ladder obsequiously and those lower down the social ladder with contempt. **2** someone having similar pretensions as regards specific tastes: *an intellectual snob.* ○ **snobbery** *n*. ○ **snobbish** *adj*.

snog *slang, vb* (**snogged, snogging**) *intr* to embrace, kiss and cuddle. ➤ *n* a kiss and cuddle.

snood *n* a decorative pouch of netting worn by women on the back of the head, keeping the hair in a bundle.

snook¹ or **snoek** *n* (**snook** or **snooks; snoek**) a marine fish.

snook² *n* the gesture of putting the thumb to the nose and waving the fingers as an expression of derision, contempt or defiance. ♦ **cock a snook at sb** *colloq* **1** to make this gesture at them. **2** to express open contempt for them.

snooker *n* **1** a game played with cues and coloured balls, the object being to use the white ball to knock the non-white balls in a certain order into any of the six pockets of the table. **2** in this game: a position in which the path between the white ball and the target ball is obstructed by another ball. ➤ *vb* **1** in snooker: to force (an opponent) to attempt to hit an obstructed target ball. **2** *colloq* to thwart (a person or a plan).

snoop *vb, intr* to go about sneakingly and inquisitively. ➤ *n* **1** an act of snooping. **2** someone who snoops. ○ **snooper** *n*.

snooty *adj* (**-ier, -iest**) *colloq* haughty; snobbish.

snooze *vb, intr* to sleep lightly. ➤ *n* a brief period of light sleeping.

snore *vb, intr* to breathe heavily and with a snorting sound while sleeping. ➤ *n* an act or the sound of snoring.

snorkel *n* a rigid tube through which air from above the surface of water can be drawn into the mouth while one is swimming just below the surface. ➤ *vb* (**snorkelled, snorkelling**) *intr* to swim with a snorkel.

snort *vb* **1** *intr* esp of animals: to force air violently and noisily out through the nostrils; to make a similar noise while taking air in. **2** *tr & intr* to express contempt or anger in this way. **3** *slang* to inhale (a powdered drug, esp cocaine) through the nose. ➤ *n* an act or the sound of snorting.

snot *n* **1** mucus of the nose. **2** a contemptible person.

snotty *adj* (**-ier, -iest**) *colloq* **1** covered or messy with nasal mucus. **2** haughty; having or showing contempt: *a snotty attitude.* ○ **snottily** *adv*. ○ **snottiness** *n*.

snout *n* **1** the projecting nose and mouth parts of certain animals, eg the pig. **2** *colloq* the human nose. **3** any projecting part.

snow *n* **1** precipitation in the form of ice crystals falling to the ground in soft white flakes, or lying on the ground as a soft white mass. **2** a fall of this: *There's been a lot of snow this year.* **3** *colloq* a flickering speckled background on a TV or radar screen, caused by interference or a poor signal. ➤ *vb, intr* of snow: to fall. ♦ **snowed under** overwhelmed with work, etc.

snowball *n* a small mass of snow pressed hard together, often used for fun as a missile. ➤ *vb, intr* to increase rapidly.

snowboard *n* a board resembling a skateboard without wheels, used on snow and guided with movements of the feet and body. ➤ *vb, intr* to ski on a snowboard. ○ **snowboarding** *n*.

snowbound *adj* shut in or prevented from travelling because of heavy falls of snow.

snowdrift *n* a bank of snow blown together by the wind.

snowdrop *n* a plant with small solitary drooping white bell-shaped flowers.

snowfall *n* **1** a fall of snow. **2** *meteorol* an amount of fallen snow in a given time: *annual snowfall.*

snowflake *n* any of the single small feathery clumps of crystals of snow.

snowman *n* a figure, resembling a person, made from packed snow.

snowmobile *n* a motorized vehicle, on skis or tracks, designed for travelling on snow.

snowplough *n* a vehicle or train fitted with a large shovel-like device for clearing snow from roads or railway tracks.

snowshoe *n* either of a pair of racket-like frameworks strapped to the feet for walking over deep snow.

snowy *adj* (**-ier, -iest**) **1** abounding or covered with snow. **2** white like snow. **3** pure.

Snr or **snr** *abbrev* senior.

snub *vb* (**snubbed, snubbing**) to insult by openly ignoring, rejecting or otherwise showing contempt. ➤ *n* an act of snubbing. ➤ *adj* short and flat.

snub nose *n* a broad flat nose. ○ **snub-nosed** *adj*.

snuff¹ *vb* **1** *intr* to draw in air violently and noisily through the nose. **2** to examine or detect by sniffing. ➤ *n* **1** a sniff. **2** powdered tobacco for inhaling through the nose.

snuff² *vb* **1** (*often* **snuff sth out**) to extinguish (a candle). **2** to snip off the burnt part of the wick of (a candle or lamp). **3** (*usu* **snuff sth out**) to put an end to it: *He tried to snuff out all opposition.* ➤ *n* the burnt part of the wick of a lamp or candle. ♦ **snuff it** *slang* to die.

snuffle *vb* **1** *intr* to breathe, esp breathe in, through a partially blocked nose. **2** *tr & intr* to say or speak nasally. **3** *intr* to snivel. ➤ *n* an act or the sound of snuffling.

snug *adj* (**snugger, snuggest**) **1** warm, cosy and

comfortable. **2** well protected and sheltered: *a snug boat.* **3** compact and comfortably organized: *a snug kitchen.* **4** close-fitting: *a snug dress.* ➤ *n* a small comfortable room in a pub. ○ **snugly** *adv.*

snuggle *vb, intr* **1** (*usu* **snuggle down** or **in**) to settle oneself into a position of warmth and comfort. **2** (*sometimes* **snuggle up**) to hug close.

so¹ *adv* **1** to such an extent: *It's so expensive that nobody buys it.* **2** to this, that or the same extent: *This one is lovely, but that one is not so nice.* **3** extremely: *She is so talented!* **4** in that state or condition: *He promised to be faithful, and has remained so.* **5** also; likewise: *She's my friend and so are you.* **6** used to avoid repeating a previous statement: *You've to go upstairs because I said so.* **7** *colloq* used to add vehemence to a statement: *I am so not going to his stupid party!* ➤ *conj* **1** therefore: *He insulted me, so I hit him.* **2** (*also* **so that** ...) in order that ...: *Give me more time so I can finish it.* ➤ *adj* true: *You think I'm mad, but it's not so.* ➤ *exclam* used to express discovery: *So, that's what you've been doing!* ♦ **and so on** or **and so forth** or **and so on and so forth** and more of the same; continuing in the same way. **just so** neatly, precisely or perfectly: *with her hair arranged just so.* **so as to** ... in order to ...; in such a way as to ... **so be it** used to express acceptance or defiant resignation. **so much** or **many 1** such a lot: *There's so much work to do!* **2** just; mere: *politicians squabbling like so many children.* **so much for** ... nothing has come of ...; that has disposed of or ruined ...: *So much for all our plans!* **so what?** *colloq* that is of no importance or consequence at all.

so² see SOH

soak *vb* **1** *tr & intr* to stand or leave to stand in a liquid for some time. **2** to make someone or something thoroughly wet. **3** to penetrate or pass through: *The rain soaked through my coat.* **4** (**soak sth up**) to absorb it. ➤ *n* **1** an act of soaking. **2** a drenching. **3** *colloq* a long period of lying in a bath. ○ **soaking** *n, adj, adv.*

so-and-so *n* (*so-and-sos*) *colloq* **1** someone whose name one does not know or cannot remember: *He's gone with so-and-so.* **2** used in place of a vulgar word: *You crafty little so-and-so!*

soap *n* **1** a cleaning agent consisting of a fatty acid that is soluble in water, in the form of a solid block, liquid or powder. **2** *colloq* a SOAP OPERA. ➤ *vb* to apply soap to something.

soapbox *n* **1** a crate for packing soap. **2** an improvised platform for public speech-making.

soap opera *n* a radio or TV series concerning the domestic and emotional lives and troubles of a regular group of characters.

soapstone *n* a soft usu grey or brown variety of the mineral talc, widely used for ornamental carvings.

soapy *adj* (*-ier, -iest*) **1** like soap. **2** containing soap. **3** smeared or covered with soap. **4** *colloq* like a soap opera.

soar *vb, intr* **1** to rise or fly high into the air. **2** to glide through the air at a high altitude. **3** to rise sharply to a great height or level: *Temperatures are soaring.*

sob *vb* (**sobbed, sobbing**) **1** *intr* to cry uncontrollably with gulps for breath. **2** (*often* **sob sth out**) to say something while crying in this way. ➤ *n* a gulp for breath between bouts of crying.

sober *adj* **1** not at all drunk. **2** serious, solemn or restrained; not frivolous or extravagant. **3** suggesting sedateness or seriousness rather than exuberance or frivolity: *sober colours.* **4** plain; unembellished: *the sober truth.* ➤ *vb, tr & intr* (*always* **sober down** or **sober sb down**) to become, or make someone, quieter, less excited, etc. **2** (*always* **sober up** or **sober sb up**) to become, or make someone, free from the effects of alcohol. ○ **sobering** *adj* causing someone to become serious or thoughtful: *a sobering thought.*

sobriety *n* the state of being sober, esp not drunk.

sobriquet /'soʊbrɪkeɪ/ or **soubriquet** /'suː-brɪkeɪ/ *n, literary* a nickname.

so-called *adj* known or presented as such with the implication that the term is wrongly used: *a panel of so-called experts.*

soccer *n* ASSOCIATION FOOTBALL.

sociable *adj* **1** fond of the company of others. **2** characterized by friendliness.

social *adj* **1** relating to or for people or society as a whole: *social policies.* **2** relating to the organization and behaviour of people in societies: *social studies.* **3** tending or needing to live with others: *social creatures.* **4** intended for or promoting friendly gatherings of people: *a social club.* **5** convivial. ➤ *n* **1** a social gathering. **2** (**the social**) *colloq* social security. ○ **socially** *adv.*

social climber *n, often derog* someone who seeks to gain higher social status.

socialism *n* a political doctrine or system which aims to create a classless society by moving ownership of the nation's wealth into public hands. ○ **socialist** *n, adj.*

socialite *n* someone who mixes with people of high social status.

socialize or **-ise** *vb* **1** *intr* to meet with people on an informal, friendly basis. **2** *intr* to mingle or circulate among guests at a party. **3** to organize into societies. ○ **socialization** *n.*

social sciences *pl n* the subjects that deal with the organization and behaviour of people in societies, including sociology, anthropology, economics and history.

social security *n* **1** a system by which each member of society makes regular contributions from their earned income into a common fund, from which payments are made to those who are unemployed, ill, disabled or elderly. **2** a payment or scheme of payments from such a fund.

social services *pl n* **1** services provided by local or national government for the general welfare of people in society. **2** the public bodies providing these services.

social work *n* work in any of the services provided by local government for the care of underprivileged people. ○ **social worker** *n*.

society *n* (*-ies*) **1** humankind as a whole, or a part of it such as one nation, considered as a single community. **2** a division of humankind with common characteristics, eg of nationality, race or religion. **3** an organized group, meeting to share a common interest or activity. **4 a** the rich and fashionable section of the upper class; **b** the social scene of this class section. **5** *formal* company: *He prefers the society of women.*

socioeconomic *adj* referring or relating to social and economic aspects.

sociology *n* the scientific study of the nature, structure and workings of human society. ○ **sociological** *adj*. ○ **sociologist** *n*.

sock[1] *n* a fabric covering for the foot and ankle, sometimes reaching to the knee, worn inside a shoe. ◆ **pull one's socks up** *colloq* to make an effort to do better. **put a sock in it** *slang* to be quiet.

sock[2] *slang*, *vb* to hit with a powerful blow. ➤ *n* a powerful blow. ◆ **sock it to sb** *slang* to make a powerful impression on them.

socket *n* **1** a specially shaped hole or set of holes into which something is inserted: *an electrical socket.* **2** *anat* a hollow structure into which another part fits.

sod[1] *n* **1** a slab of earth with grass growing on it. **2** *poetic* the ground.

sod[2] *slang*, *n* **1** a term of abuse for a person. **2** a person in general: *lucky sod.* ◆ **sod all** nothing at all. **sod it** an expression of annoyance or contempt. ◇ **sod off** to go away.

soda *n* **1** any of various compounds of sodium in everyday use, eg SODIUM CARBONATE or BICARBONATE OF SODA. **2** *colloq* SODA WATER. **3** *N Am* any fizzy soft drink.

soda ash *n*, *chem* the common name for the commercial grade of anhydrous SODIUM CARBONATE.

soda siphon see SIPHON (*noun* sense 2)

soda water *n* water made fizzy by the addition of carbon dioxide.

sodden *adj* **1** thoroughly soaked. **2** made sluggish, esp through excessive consumption of alcohol.

sodium *n*, *chem* a soft silvery-white metallic element used in alloys.

sodium bicarbonate *n*, *chem* BICARBONATE OF SODA.

sodium carbonate *n*, *chem* a water-soluble white powder or crystalline solid, used as a water softener and food additive, in glass making and in photography.

sodium chloride *n*, *chem* a water-soluble white crystalline salt, used for seasoning and preserving food.

sodium hydroxide *n*, *chem* a white crystalline solid that dissolves in water to form a highly corrosive alkaline solution, and is used

in the manufacture of soap, detergents, etc. Also called **caustic soda**.

sodomy *n* anal intercourse with a man or woman. ○ **sodomite** *n*. ○ **sodomize** or **-ise** *vb*.

Sod's law *n*, *slang* a facetious maxim stating that if something can go wrong it will, or that the most inconvenient thing that could happen will happen.

sofa *n* an upholstered seat with a back and arms, for two or more people.

soft *adj* **1** easily yielding or changing shape when pressed. **2** easily yielding to pressure. **3** easily cut. **4** of fabric, etc: having a smooth surface producing little or no friction. **5** pleasing or soothing to the senses; quiet: *a soft voice.* **6** having little brightness: *soft colours.* **7** kind or sympathetic, esp excessively so. **8** not able to endure rough treatment or hardship. **9** lacking strength of character; easily influenced. **10** *colloq* weak in the mind: *soft in the head.* **11** of a person: out of training; unfit. **12** weakly sentimental. **13** of water: low in mineral salts. **14** tender; affectionate: *soft words.* ➤ *adv* softly; gently: *She speaks soft.* ○ **softly** *adv.* ○ **softness** *n*. ◆ **be** or **go soft on sb** *colloq* **1** to be lenient towards them. **2** to be infatuated with them.

softball *n* a game similar to baseball, played with a larger, softer ball which is pitched underarm.

soft drink *n* a non-alcoholic drink.

soften *vb*, *tr* & *intr* **1** to make or become soft or softer. **2** to make or become less severe. ○ **softener** *n* a substance added to another to increase its softness, etc, such as fabric softener. ◇ **soften sb up** *colloq* to prepare them for an unwelcome or difficult request.

soft focus *n*, *photog*, *cinematog* the deliberate slight blurring of a picture or scene.

soft fruit *pl n*, *Brit* small stoneless edible fruit, such as berries, currants, etc.

soft furnishings *pl n* rugs, curtains, cushion covers and other articles made of fabric.

soft-hearted *adj* kind-hearted; compassionate.

soft landing *n* a landing by a spacecraft without damaging impact.

softly-softly *adj* cautious or careful: *a softly-softly approach.*

soft option *n* the easier or easiest of two or several alternative courses of action.

soft palate *n*, *anat* the fleshy muscular back part of the palate.

soft pedal *n* a pedal on a piano pressed to make the tone less lingering or ringing. ➤ *vb* (**soft-pedal**) **1** *mus* to play (the piano) using the soft pedal. **2** *colloq* to tone down, or avoid emphasizing something: *The government were soft-pedalling the scheme's disadvantages.*

soft sell *n* the use of gentle persuasion as a selling technique.

soft soap *n* **1** a semi-liquid soap. **2** *colloq* flattery. ➤ *vb* (**soft-soap**) *colloq* to speak flatteringly to someone.

soft-spoken *adj* **1** having a soft voice, and usu

a mild manner. **2** suave or smooth-tongued.

soft spot *n, colloq* a special liking: *She has a soft spot for him.*

soft touch *n, colloq* someone easily taken advantage of or persuaded.

software *n, comput* the programs that are used in a computer system, and the magnetic disks, tapes, etc, on which they are recorded. Compare HARDWARE (sense 2).

softwood *n, bot* the wood of a coniferous tree.

softy or **softie** *n* (*-ies*) *colloq* **1** a weakly sentimental, soft-hearted or silly person. **2** someone not able to endure rough treatment.

soggy *adj* (*-ier, -iest*) **1** thoroughly soaked or wet. **2** of ground: waterlogged. ○ **sogginess** *n*.

soh, so or **sol** *n, mus* in sol-fa notation: the fifth note of a scale.

soil[1] *n* **1** the mixture of fragmented rock, plant and animal debris that lies on the surface of the earth. **2** *literary* country; land: *on foreign soil.*

soil[2] *vb* **1** to stain or make dirty. **2** to bring discredit on. ➤ *n* **1** a spot or stain. **2** dung; sewage.

soirée or **soiree** /ˈswɑːreɪ/ *n* a formal party held in the evening.

sojourn /ˈsɒdʒən, -ɜːn/ *formal, n* a short stay. ➤ *vb, intr* to stay for a short while.

sol[1] see SOH

sol[2] *n, chem* a type of colloid that consists of small solid particles dispersed in a liquid.

solace /ˈsɒləs/ *n* **1** comfort in time of disappointment or sorrow. **2** a source of comfort. ➤ *vb* to provide with such comfort.

solar *adj* **1** referring or relating to the Sun. **2** relating to, by or using energy from the Sun's rays: *solar-powered.*

solar cell *n, elec* an electric cell that converts solar energy directly into electricity.

solar energy *n* energy radiated from the Sun.

solarium *n* (**solariums** or **solaria**) a room equipped with sunbeds.

solar plexus *n, anat* an area in the abdomen in which there is a concentration of nerves radiating from a central point.

solar system *n, astron* the Sun and the system of nine major planets, and the asteroids, comets and meteors that revolve around it.

solder *eng, n* an alloy with a low melting point, applied when molten to the joint between two metals to form an airtight seal. ➤ *vb* to join (two pieces of metal) without melting them, by applying solder to the joint between them.

soldier *n* **1** a member of a fighting force, esp a national army. **2** a member of an army below officer rank. **3** (**soldiers**) narrow strips of bread-and-butter or toast, esp for dipping into a soft-boiled egg. ○ **soldierly** *adj.* ◇ **soldier on** to continue determinedly in spite of difficulty and discouragement.

soldier of fortune *n* a mercenary.

sole[1] *n* **1** the underside of the foot. **2** the underside of a shoe or boot. ➤ *vb* to fit (a shoe or boot) with a sole.

sole[2] *n* (**sole** or **soles**) an edible flatfish with a slender brown body and both eyes on the left side of the head.

sole[3] *adj* **1** alone; only. **2** exclusive: *sole rights to the story.*

solecism /ˈsɒlɪsɪzəm/ *n* **1** a mistake in the use of language. **2** an instance of incorrect behaviour. ○ **solecistic** *adj.*

solely *adv* **1** alone; without others: *solely to blame.* **2** only: *done solely for profit.*

solemn *adj* **1** done, made or carried out in earnest and seriousness: *a solemn vow.* **2** being of a very serious and formal nature; suggesting seriousness: *a solemn occasion.* **3** marked by special (esp religious) ceremonies. ○ **solemnly** *adv.*

solemnity *n* (*-ies*) **1** the state of being solemn. **2** a solemn ceremony.

solemnize or **-ise** *vb* **1** to perform (esp a marriage) with a formal or religious ceremony. **2** to make something solemn.

solenoid *n, physics* a cylindrical coil of wire that produces a magnetic field when an electric current is passed through it.

sol-fa *n* a system of musical notation, either written down or sung, in which the notes of a scale are represented by the syllables *doh, re, mi, fah, soh, la, ti.*

solicit *vb* **1** *formal* to ask for something, or for something from someone: *She solicited me for advice.* **2** *intr* of a prostitute: to approach people with open offers of sex for money. ○ **solicitation** *n.* ○ **soliciting** *n.*

solicitor *n* **1** in Britain: a lawyer who prepares legal documents, gives legal advice and, in the lower courts only, speaks on behalf of clients. **2** someone who solicits. **3** in N America: someone who canvasses. **4** in N America: someone responsible for legal matters in a town or city.

solicitous *adj* **1** (solicitous about or for sb or sth) anxious or concerned about them. **2** eager to do something. ○ **solicitously** *adv.*

solicitude *n* **1** anxiety or uneasiness of mind. **2** the state of being solicitous.

solid *adj* **1** in a form other than liquid or gas, and resisting changes in shape. **2** having the same nature or material throughout; uniform or pure: *solid oak.* **3** not hollow: *a solid chocolate egg.* **4** firmly constructed or attached; not easily breaking or loosening. **5** *geom* having or pertaining to three dimensions. **6** difficult to undermine or destroy: *solid support.* **7** without any breaks: *We waited for four solid hours.* **8** of a character: reliable; sensible. **9** of a character: worthy of credit: *He has a solid presence.* **10** financially secure. ➤ *n* **1** a solid substance or body. **2** *geom* a three-dimensional geometric figure. **3** (**solids**) non-liquid food. ○ **solidity** *n.*

solidarity *n* (*-ies*) mutual support and unity of interests, aims and actions among members of a group.

solidify *vb* (*-ies, -ied*) *tr & intr* to make or become solid. ○ **solidification** *n.*

solid-state *adj, electronics* denoting an electronic device or component that functions by the movement of electrons through solids and contains no heated filaments or vacuums.

solidus n (**solidi** /'sɒlɪdaɪ/) a printed line sloping from right to left, eg separating alternatives, as in *and/or*.

soliloquy n (**-quies**) 1 a speech, esp in a play, etc, in which someone reveals their thoughts by talking aloud. 2 the use of such speeches as a device in drama. ○ **soliloquize** or **-ise** vb.

solipsism /'sɒlɪpsɪzəm/ n, philos the theory that one's own existence is the only certainty. ○ **solipsist** n, adj. ○ **solipsistic** adj.

solitaire n 1 any of several games for one player only, esp one whose object is to eliminate pegs or marbles from a board and leave only one. 2 a single gem in a setting on its own. 3 N Am the card game PATIENCE.

solitary adj 1 single; lone. 2 preferring to be alone; not social. 3 without companions; lonely. ➤ n, colloq solitary confinement. ○ **solitariness** n.

solitary confinement n imprisonment in a cell by oneself.

solitude n the state of being alone.

solo n (**solos** or **soli** /'souliː/) 1 a piece of music, or a passage within it, for a single voice or instrument. 2 any performance in which no other person or instrument participates. 3 (in full **solo whist**) a card game based on WHIST, in which various declarations are made and the declarer does not have a partner. ➤ adj performed alone, without assistance or accompaniment. ➤ adv alone: *flying solo*. ➤ vb, intr 1 to fly solo. 2 to play a solo. ○ **soloist** n.

so long or **so-long** exclam, colloq goodbye; farewell.

solstice n either of the times when the Sun is furthest from the equator: the longest day (**summer solstice**) and the shortest day (**winter solstice**). ○ **solstitial** adj.

soluble adj 1 denoting a substance that is capable of being dissolved in a liquid. 2 capable of being solved or resolved.

solute n, chem any substance that is dissolved in a SOLVENT.

solution n 1 the process of finding an answer to a problem or puzzle. 2 the answer sought or found. 3 chem a homogeneous mixture consisting of a solid or gas (the SOLUTE) and the liquid (the SOLVENT) in which it is completely dissolved. 4 maths in an equation: the value that one or more of the variables must have for that equation to be valid.

solve vb 1 to discover the answer to (a puzzle) or a way out of (a problem). 2 to clear up or explain something. ○ **solvable** adj.

solvent adj able to pay all one's debts. ➤ n, chem 1 in a solution: the liquid in which a solid or gas is dissolved. 2 a substance which may act in this way, eg for removing glue. ○ **solvency** n the ability to pay one's debts.

somatic adj, med, biol referring or relating to the body.

sombre adj 1 sad and serious. 2 dark and gloomy. 3 eg of colours: dark. ○ **sombrely** adv. ○ **sombreness** n.

sombrero n a wide-brimmed straw or felt hat, esp popular in Mexico.

some adj 1 signifying an unknown or unspecified amount or number of something: *She owns some shares.* 2 signifying a certain undetermined category: *Some films are better than others.* 3 having an unknown or unspecified nature or identity: *some problem with the engine.* 4 quite a lot of something: *We have been waiting for some time.* 5 at least a little: *Try to feel some enthusiasm.* ➤ pron 1 certain unspecified things or people: *Some say he should resign.* 2 an unspecified amount or number: *Give him some, too.* ➤ adv 1 to an unspecified extent: *Play some more.* 2 approximately: *some twenty feet deep.*

somebody pron 1 an unknown or unspecified person. 2 someone of importance: *He always strove to be somebody.*

someday adv at an unknown or unspecified time in the future.

somehow adv 1 in some way not yet known. 2 for a reason not easy to explain. 3 (also **somehow or other**) in any way necessary or possible: *I'll get there somehow or other.*

someone pron somebody.

somersault n a leap or roll in which the whole body turns a complete circle forwards or backwards, leading with the head. ➤ vb, intr to perform such a leap or roll.

something pron 1 a thing not known or not stated: *Take something to eat.* 2 an amount or number not known or not stated: *something short of 500 people.* 3 a person or thing of importance: *make something of oneself.* 4 a certain truth or value: *There is something in what you say.* ➤ adv to some degree: *The garden looks something like a scrapyard.*

sometime adv at an unknown or unspecified time in the future or the past: *I'll finish it sometime.* ➤ adj former: *the sometime king.*

sometimes adv occasionally.

somewhat adv rather: *He seemed somewhat unsettled.*

somewhere adv in or to some place or degree, or at some point, not known or not specified.

somnambulism n sleepwalking. ○ **somnambulist** n.

somniferous or **somnific** adj causing sleep.

somnolent adj, formal sleepy or drowsy. ○ **somnolence** n.

son n 1 a male child or offspring. 2 a male person closely associated with, or seen as developing from, a particular activity or set of circumstances: *a son of the Russian Revolution.* 3 a familiar and sometimes patronizing term of address used to a boy or man. 4 (the **Son**) Christianity the second person of the Trinity, Jesus Christ.

sonar n a system that is used to locate underwater objects by transmitting ultrasound signals and measuring the time taken for their echoes to return from an obstacle.

sonata n a piece of music written in three or more movements for a solo instrument, esp the piano.

song n 1 a set of words, short poem, etc to be sung, usu with accompanying music. 2 the music to which these words are set. 3 singing: *poetry and song*. 4 the musical call of certain birds. ♦ **going for a song** *colloq* at a bargain price. **make a song and dance about sth** *colloq* to make an unnecessary fuss about it.

songbird n a bird that has a musical call.

songster or **songstress** n, *old use* a talented singer.

sonic adj relating to or using sound or sound waves.

sonic boom or **sonic bang** n a loud boom that is heard when an aircraft flying through the Earth's atmosphere reaches supersonic speed.

son-in-law n (*sons-in-law*) the husband of one's daughter.

sonnet n a short poem with 14 lines of 10 or 11 syllables each and a regular rhyming pattern.

sonny n a familiar and often condescending term of address used to a boy or man.

sonorous adj 1 sounding impressively loud and deep. 2 giving out a deep clear sound when struck: *a sonorous bell*. 3 of language: impressively eloquent. ○ **sonority** /sə'nɒrɪtɪ/ n.

soon adv 1 in a short time from now or from a stated time. 2 quickly. 3 readily or willingly. ♦ **as soon as …** at or not before the moment when …: *I will pay you as soon as I receive the goods.*

sooner adv 1 earlier than previously thought. 2 preferably: *I'd sooner die than go back there.* ♦ **sooner or later** eventually.

soot n a black powdery substance produced when coal or wood is imperfectly burned. ○ **sooty** adj (*-ier, -iest*).

soothe vb 1 to bring relief from (a pain, etc). 2 to comfort, calm or compose someone. 3 *intr* to have a calming, tranquillizing or relieving effect. ○ **soothing** n, adj. ○ **soothingly** adv.

soothsayer n someone who predicts the future.

sop n 1 (*often sops*) a piece of food, esp bread, soaked in a liquid. 2 something given or done as a bribe or in order to pacify someone. 3 a feeble person. ➤ vb (*sopped, sopping*) tr & intr to soak or become soaked.

sophism n a convincing but false argument or explanation, esp one intended to deceive. ○ **sophist** n. ○ **sophistic** adj.

sophisticate vb 1 to make someone sophisticated. 2 to adulterate or falsify an argument. ➤ n /-kət/ a sophisticated person.

sophisticated adj 1 having or displaying a broad knowledge and experience of the world and its culture. 2 appealing to or frequented by people with such knowledge and experience. 3 of a person: accustomed to an elegant life-style. 4 esp of machines: complex; equipped with the most up-to-date devices: *sophisticated weaponry*. ○ **sophistication** n.

sophistry n (*-ies*) 1 plausibly deceptive or fallacious reasoning, or an instance of this. 2 the art of reasoning speciously.

sophomore n, *N Am* a second-year student at a school or university.

soporific adj 1 causing sleep. 2 extremely boring: *a soporific speech*. ➤ n a sleep-inducing drug.

sopping adj, adv (*also* **sopping wet**) thoroughly wet.

soppy adj (*-ier, -iest*) *colloq* weakly sentimental. ○ **soppily** adv. ○ **soppiness** n.

soprano n (*sopranos* or *soprani*) 1 a singing voice of the highest pitch for a woman or a boy. 2 a person having this voice pitch. 3 a musical part for such a voice. 4 a musical instrument high or highest in pitch in relation to others in its family. ➤ adj referring or relating to a soprano pitch.

sorbet /'sɔːbeɪ/ n a water ice.

sorcery n the art or use of magic. ○ **sorcerer** or **sorceress** n.

sordid adj 1 repulsively filthy. 2 morally revolting or degraded: *a sordid affair*.

sore adj 1 of a wound, injury, part of the body, etc: painful or tender. 2 of a blow, bite, sting, etc: painful or causing physical pain. 3 causing mental anguish, grief or annoyance: *a sore point*. 4 *N Am* angry or resentful: *He got sore at the kids*. 5 urgent: *in sore need of attention*. ➤ n a diseased or injured spot or area.

sorely adv very much: *I'm sorely tempted to tell her*.

sore point n a subject that causes great anger, resentment, etc whenever it is raised.

sorghum n a grass which is grown as a cereal crop and a source of syrup.

sorority n (*-ies*) a women's society, esp one affiliated to a US university, college or church. Compare FRATERNITY.

sorrel n a plant with spear-shaped leaves which are used in medicine and cooking.

sorrow n 1 a feeling of grief or deep sadness, esp one that arises from loss or disappointment. 2 someone or something that is the cause of this. ➤ vb, intr to have or express such feeling. ○ **sorrowful** adj. ○ **sorrowfully** adv.

sorry adj (*-ier, -iest*) 1 distressed or full of regret or shame, esp over something that one has done or said, something that has happened, etc: *I'm sorry if I hurt you*. 2 (*usu* **sorry for sb**) full of pity or sympathy. 3 pitifully bad: *in a sorry state*. ➤ exclam 1 given as an apology. 2 used when asking for something that has just been said to be repeated.

sort n 1 a kind, type or class. 2 *colloq* a type of person: *He's not a bad sort*. ➤ vb 1 to arrange into different groups according to some specified criterion. 2 *colloq* to fix something or put it back into working order: *Dad tried to sort the* *car himself.* **3** (*also* **sort out**) *colloq* to resolve (a problem, etc): *You caused the problem, so you'd better sort it.* ♦ **a sort of …** a thing like a …: *A cafetière is a sort of pot for making coffee.* **nothing of the sort** no such thing: *I did nothing of the sort.* **of a sort** or **of sorts** of an inferior or untypical kind: *an author of a sort.* **out of sorts** *colloq* slightly unwell. **sort of** *colloq* rather; in a way: *sort of embarrassed.* ◊ **sort sb out 1** *colloq* to deal with them firmly and sometimes violently. **2** to put them right: *A good night's sleep will soon sort you out.* **sort sth out 1** to separate things out from a mixed collection into a group or groups according to their kind. **2** to put things into order; to arrange them systematically or methodically: *You must sort out your priorities.*

sortie /ˈsɔːtɪ/ *n* **1** a sudden attack by besieged troops. **2** *colloq* a short return trip: *We're just going on a quick sortie to the shops.* ➢ *vb* (**sortied, sortieing**) *intr* to make a sortie.

SOS *n* **1** an internationally recognized distress call that consists of these three letters repeatedly transmitted in Morse code. **2** *colloq* any call for help.

so-so *colloq, adj* neither very good nor very bad. ➢ *adv* in an indifferent or unremarkable way.

sot *n, old use* someone who habitually drinks a lot of alcohol. ○ **sottish** *adj.*

soubriquet see SOBRIQUET

soufflé /ˈsuːfleɪ/ *n* a light fluffy sweet or savoury dish that is made by gently combining egg yolks and other ingredients with stiffly beaten egg-whites.

sough /saʊ, sʌf; *Scot* suːx/ *vb, intr* usu of the wind: to make a sighing, rustling or murmuring sound.

sought-after *adj* desired; in demand.

souk /suːk/ *n* an open-air market or market-place in Muslim countries.

soul *n* **1 a** the spiritual part of someone, which is often regarded as the source of personality, will, emotions and intellect, and which is believed by some people to survive after death; **b** this entity when thought of as having separated from the body after death. **2** emotional sensitivity: *a singer with no soul.* **3** the essential nature or a motivating force (of or behind something): *Brevity is the soul of wit.* **4** *colloq* a person: *a kind soul.* **5** (*also* **soul music**) a type of music that has its roots in African-American urban rhythm and blues and has elements of jazz, gospel, pop, etc.

soul-destroying *adj* **1** of a job, task, etc: extremely boring or repetitive. **2** of an on-going situation: difficult to tolerate or accept emotionally: *Being unemployed was completely soul-destroying.*

soulful *adj* having, expressing, etc deep feelings.

soulless *adj* **1** having, showing, etc no emotional sensitivity, etc. **2** of a place: bleak.

soul mate *n* someone who shares the same ideas, outlook, tastes, etc as someone else.

soul-searching *n* the process of critically examining one's own motives, actions, etc.

sound¹ *n* **1** *physics* periodic vibrations that are propagated through a medium, eg air, as pressure waves. **2** the noise that is heard as a result of such periodic vibrations. **3** audible quality: *The guitar has a nice sound.* **4** the mental impression created by something heard: *I don't like the sound of that.* **5** (*also* **sounds**) *colloq* music, esp pop music: *the sounds of the 60s.* ➢ *vb* **1** *tr & intr* to produce or cause to produce a sound: *The bugle sounded.* **2** *intr* to create an impression in the mind: *That sounds like fun.* **3** to pronounce: *He doesn't sound his h's.* **4** to announce or signal with a sound: *to sound the alarm.* **5** *med* to examine by tapping or listening. ◊ **sound off** *colloq* to state one's opinions, complaints, etc forcefully or angrily.

sound² *adj* **1** not damaged or injured; in good condition: *The kitten was found safe and sound.* **2 a** sensible; well-founded; reliable: *a sound investment*; **b** of an argument, opinion, etc: well researched or thought through; logical and convincing. **3** acceptable or approved of. **4** severe, hard or thorough: *a sound telling-off.* **5** of sleep: deep and undisturbed. ➢ *adv* deeply: *sound asleep.* ○ **soundly** *adv.* ○ **soundness** *n.*

sound³ *vb, tr & intr* **1** to measure the depth of (esp the sea). **2** *med* to examine (a hollow organ, etc) with a probe. ➢ *n* a probe for examining hollow organs. ◊ **sound sb** or **sth out** to try to discover (opinions, intentions, etc).

sound⁴ *n* a narrow passage of water that connects two large bodies of water or that separates an island from the mainland.

sound barrier *n, non-technical* the increase in drag that an aircraft experiences when it travels close to the speed of sound.

soundbite *n* a short succinct statement extracted from a longer speech and quoted on TV or radio or in the press.

soundcard *n, comput* a printed circuit board added to a computer to provide or enhance sound effects.

sound effects *pl n* artificially produced sounds used in film, broadcasting, theatre, etc.

sounding *n* **1 a** the act or process of measuring depth, esp of the sea, eg by using echo; **b** an instance of doing this; **c** (**soundings**) measurements that are taken or recorded when doing this. **2** (*usu* **soundings**) a sampling of opinions or (eg voting) intentions.

sounding board *n* someone or a group used for testing the acceptability or popularity of ideas or opinions.

soundproof *adj* of a room or building: not allowing sound to escape.

soundtrack *n* **1** the recorded sound that accompanies a motion picture. **2** a recording of the music from a film, broadcast, etc.

soup *n* a liquid food that is made by boiling meat, vegetables, grains, etc together in stock or in water. ➢ *vb* (*usu* **soup up**) *colloq* to make changes to a vehicle or its engine in order to increase its speed or power. ♦ **in the soup** *slang* in trouble.

soupçon /'suːpsɒn/ *n, often humorous* the slightest amount.

soup kitchen *n* a place where volunteers supply free or very cheap food to people in need.

sour *adj* **1** having an acid taste or smell, similar to that of lemon juice or vinegar. **2** rancid because of fermentation: *sour milk.* **3** sullen; embittered: *a sour expression.* **4** unpleasant, unsuccessful or inharmonious: *The marriage turned sour.* ➤ *vb, tr & intr* to make or become sour. ○ **sourly** *adv.* ○ **sourness** *n.*

source *n* **1** the place, thing, person, circumstance, etc that something begins or develops from. **2** a spring or place where a river or stream begins. **3** a person, book or document that can be used to provide information, evidence, etc. ➤ *vb* to originate in someone or something. ♦ **at source** at the point of origin.

sour cream *n* cream that has been deliberately made sour by the addition of lactic acid bacteria.

sour grapes *pl n* a hostile attitude towards something or someone, esp when motivated by envy, resentment, etc: *He says he wouldn't have taken the job anyway, but that's just sour grapes.*

sourpuss *n, colloq* a habitually sullen or miserable person.

souse *vb* **1** to steep or cook something in vinegar or white wine. **2** to pickle. **3** to plunge in a liquid. **4** to make thoroughly wet; to drench. ➤ *n* **1** an act of sousing. **2** the liquid in which food is soused. **3** *N Am* any pickled food. ○ **soused** *adj, slang* drunk.

soutane /suːˈtɑːn/ *n, RC Church* a long plain robe that a priest wears.

south *n* (*also* **South** or **the South**) **1** the direction to one's right when one faces the rising sun, directly opposite north. **2** any part of the earth, a country, a town, etc that lies in this direction. ➤ *adj* **1** situated in the south; on the side which is on or nearest the south. **2** facing or toward the south. **3** esp of wind: coming from the south. ➤ *adv* in, to or towards the south.

southbound *adj* going or leading towards the south.

south-east *n* (*sometimes* **South-East**) **1** the compass point or direction that is midway between south and east. **2** an area lying in this direction. ➤ *adj* **1** in the south-east. **2** from the direction of the south-east: *a south-east wind.* ➤ *adv* in, to or towards the south-east. ○ **south-eastern** *adj.*

southeaster *n* a strong wind that blows from the south-east.

southerly *adj* **1** of a wind, etc: coming from the south. **2** looking, lying, etc towards the south; situated in the south. ➤ *adv* to or towards the south. ➤ *n* (*-ies*) a southerly wind.

southern or **Southern** *adj* situated in, directed towards or belonging to the south or the South. ○ **southerner** or **Southerner** *n.* ○ **southernmost** *adj.*

southpaw *n, colloq* someone whose left hand is stronger than their right, esp a boxer.

the South Pole *n* the southernmost point of the Earth's axis of rotation, which is in central Antarctica.

southward *adv* (*also* **southwards**) towards the south. ➤ *adj* towards the south.

south-west *n* (*sometimes* **South-West**) **1** the compass point or direction that is midway between south and west. **2** an area lying in this direction. ➤ *adj* **1** in the south-west. **2** from the direction of the south-west: *a south-west wind.* ➤ *adv* in, to or towards the south-west. ○ **south-western** *adj.*

southwester *n* a wind that blows from the south-west.

souvenir *n* something that is bought, kept or given as a reminder of a place, person, occasion, etc.

sou'wester *n* **1** a type of waterproof hat that has a large flap at the back and which is usu worn by seamen. **2** a SOUTHWESTER.

sovereign *n* **1** a supreme ruler or head, esp a monarch. **2** a former British gold coin worth £1. ➤ *adj* **1** having supreme power or authority: *a sovereign ruler.* **2** politically independent: *a sovereign state.* **3** outstanding; unrivalled: *sovereign intelligence.* **4** effective: *a sovereign remedy.*

sovereignty *n* (*-ies*) **1** supreme and independent political power. **2** a politically independent state. **3** self-government.

soviet *n* **1** any of the councils that made up the local and national governments of the former Soviet Union. **2** (**Soviet**) a citizen or inhabitant of the former Soviet Union. ➤ *adj* (**Soviet**) belonging, relating or referring to the former Soviet Union.

sow¹ /soʊ/ *vb* (**sown** or **sowed**) **1** *tr & intr* to scatter or place (plant seeds, a crop, etc) on or in the earth, in a plant pot, etc. **2** *tr & intr* to plant (a piece of land) with seeds, a crop, etc. **3** to introduce: *It sowed the seeds of doubt in his mind.* ○ **sower** *n.*

sow² /saʊ/ *n* an adult female pig.

soy *n* **1** (*also* **soy sauce**) a salty dark brown sauce that is made from fermented soya beans. **2** SOYA.

soya or **soy** *n* **1** a plant of the pulse family, widely cultivated for its edible seeds. **2** (*also* called **soya bean**) the edible protein-rich seed of this plant, which is used in making soya flour, soya milk, bean curd, etc, and which yields an oil that is used in the manufacture of margarine, soap, paints, etc.

sozzled *adj, colloq* drunk.

spa *n* **1** a mineral water spring. **2** a town where such a spring is or was once located.

space *n* **1** the limitless three-dimensional expanse where all matter exists. **2** a restricted portion of this: *There's no space in the garden for a pool.* **3** an interval of distance: *Sign in the space below.* **4** any of a restricted number of seats, places, etc. **5** a period of time: *within the space of ten minutes.* **6** (*also* **outer space**) all the regions of the Universe that lie beyond the Earth's atmosphere. ➢ *vb* **1** to set or place at intervals: *They spaced the interviews over three days.* **2** to separate or divide with a space or spaces, eg in printing, etc. ○ **spacing** *n*.

space age *n* (*usu* **the space age**) the present era thought of in terms of being the time when space travel became possible. ➢ *adj* (**space-age**) **1** technologically very advanced. **2** having a futuristic appearance.

space bar *n* the long key that is usu situated below the character keys on a keyboard, which inserts a space in the text when it is pressed.

spacecraft *n* a vehicle that is designed to travel in space.

spaced *adj* **1** (*also* **spaced out**) *colloq* being, acting, appearing to be, etc in a stupefied or dreamlike state, esp one that is or seems to be induced by drugs. **2** set, placed, arranged, occurring, etc at intervals.

spaceman or **spacewoman** *n* someone who travels in space.

spaceship *n*, *esp sci fi* a spacecraft.

space suit *n* a sealed and pressurized suit of clothing that is specially designed for space travel.

space walk *n* an instance of manoeuvring or other physical activity by an astronaut outside the spacecraft while in space.

spacial SEE SPATIAL

spacious *adj* having ample room or space. ○ **spaciousness** *n*.

spade¹ *n* a long-handled digging tool with a broad blade which is pushed into the ground with the foot. ➢ *vb* to dig or turn over (ground) with a spade. ◆ **call a spade a spade** to speak plainly and frankly.

spade² *n, cards* a (**spades**) one of the four suits of playing-card, with a black spade-shaped symbol (♠); **b** a playing-card of this suit.

spadework *n* hard or boring preparatory work.

spadix /ˈspeɪdɪks/ *n* (**spadices** /ˈspeɪdɪsiːz/) *bot* a spike of tiny flowers on a fleshy stem.

spaghetti *n* **1** a type of pasta that is in the form of long thin string-like strands. **2** a dish made from this kind of pasta.

spaghetti western *n* a film set in the American wild west, with an international cast and an Italian director.

Spam *n, trademark* a type of tinned processed cold meat, mainly pork, with added spices.

spam *comput, n* electronic junk mail. ➢ *vb* (**spammed, spamming**) *tr & intr* to send electronic junk mail to people.

span *n* **1** the distance, interval, length, etc between two points in space or time. **2** the length between the supports of a bridge, arch, etc. **3** the extent to which, or the duration of time for which, someone can concentrate, process information, listen attentively, etc. **4** the maximum distance between the tip of one wing and the tip of the other, eg in birds and planes. **5** a measure of length equal to the distance between the tips of thumb and little finger on an extended hand, which is conventionally taken as 9in (23cm). ➢ *vb* (**spanned, spanning**) **1** a of a bridge, ceiling, rainbow, etc: to extend across or over, esp in an arched shape; **b** to bridge (a river, etc). **2** to last: *The feud spanned more than 30 years.* **3** to measure or cover, eg by using an extended hand.

spangle *n* a small piece of glittering material, esp a sequin. ➢ *vb* to decorate (eg a piece of clothing) with spangles. ○ **spangly** *adj*.

spaniel *n* a dog with a wavy coat and long silky ears.

Spanish *adj* **1** belonging or relating to Spain or its inhabitants. **2** relating to the Spanish language. ➢ *n* the official language of Spain and various other countries.

spank *vb* to smack, usu on the buttocks with the flat of the hand, a slipper, etc. ➢ *n* such a smack.

spanking¹ *n* an act or instance or the process of delivering a series of smacks, eg as a punishment to a child.

spanking² *colloq, adv* absolutely; strikingly: *a spanking new watch.* ➢ *adj* **1** brisk: *a spanking pace.* **2** impressively fine: *a spanking performance.*

spanner *n* a metal hand tool that is used for gripping, tightening or loosening nuts, bolts, etc. ◆ **throw, put, chuck,** *etc* **a spanner in the works** to frustrate, annoy, irritate, etc, esp by causing a plan, system, etc that is already in place to change.

spar¹ *n* a strong thick pole of wood or metal, esp one used as a mast or beam on a ship.

spar² *vb* (**sparred, sparring**) *intr* (*often* **spar with sb** or **sth**) **1** a to box, esp in a way that deliberately avoids heavy blows, for practice; **b** to box against an imaginary opponent, for practice. **2** to engage in lively and light-hearted argument, banter, etc. ➢ *n* **1** an act or instance of sparring. **2** a light-hearted argument, banter, etc.

spar³ *n* any of various translucent nonmetallic minerals that split easily into layers.

spare *adj* **1** kept for occasional use: *the spare room.* **2** kept for use as a replacement: *a spare wheel.* **3** available for use; extra: *There's a spare seat next to me.* **4** lean; thin. **5** frugal; scanty. **6** furious or distraught to the point of distraction: *He went spare when he found out I'd borrowed his car.* ➢ *vb* **1** to afford to give, give away or do without: *I can't spare the time.* **2** a to refrain from harming, punishing, killing or destroying: *spare their feelings;* **b** to avoid causing or bringing on something: *It will spare you the embarrassment.* **3** to avoid incurring something: *no expense spared.* ➢ *n* a duplicate kept in reserve for use as a replacement. ◆ **to spare** left over; surplus to what is required: *I have one cake to spare.*

spare part *n* a component for a car, machine, etc that is designed to replace an existing identical part that is lost or that has become worn or faulty.

spare rib *n* a cut of meat, esp pork, that consists of ribs with very little meat on them.

spare time *n* the hours that are spent away from work or other commitments, which can be spent doing what one wants to do.

spare tyre *n* **1** an extra tyre for a motor vehicle, bicycle, etc that can be used to replace a punctured tyre. **2** *colloq* a roll of fat just above someone's waist.

sparing *adj* inclined to be economical or frugal, often to the point of inadequacy or meanness. ○ **sparingly** *adv.*

spark[1] *n* **1** a tiny fiery particle that jumps out from some burning material. **2 a** a flash of light that is produced by a discontinuous electrical discharge flashing across a short gap between two conductors; **b** this kind of electrical discharge, eg in the engine of a motor vehicle, etc where its function is to ignite the explosive mixture. **3** a trace or glimmer: *a spark of recognition.* ➢ *vb* **1** *intr* to emit sparks of fire or electricity. **2** (*usu* **spark sth off**) to stimulate or start: *The film sparked off great controversy.*

spark[2] *n*, often *ironic* (*usu* **bright spark**) someone who is lively, witty, intelligent, etc: *What bright spark left the oven on?*

sparkle *vb*, *intr* **1** to give off sparks. **2** to shine with tiny points of bright light: *Her eyes sparkled in the moonlight.* **3** of wine, mineral water, etc: to give off bubbles of carbon dioxide. **4** to be impressively lively or witty. ➢ *n* **1** a point of bright shiny light; an act of sparkling; sparkling appearance. **2** liveliness; vivacity; wit. ○ **sparkling** *adj.* ○ **sparkly** *adj* (*-ier, -iest*).

sparkler *n* **1** a type of small hand-held firework that produces gentle showers of silvery sparks. **2** *colloq* a diamond or other impressive jewel.

spark plug or **sparking plug** *n* a device that discharges a spark between the two electrodes at its end which ignites the mixture of fuel and air in the cylinder of an internal-combustion engine.

sparrow *n* a small grey or brown bird with a short conical beak.

sparse *adj* thinly scattered or dotted about. ○ **sparsely** *adv.*

spartan *adj* **1** (**Spartan**) belonging, relating to or characteristic of ancient Sparta or its inhabitants, customs, etc. **2** of living conditions, a regime, etc: harsh and basic. ➢ *n* **1** someone who shows these qualities. **2** (**Spartan**) a citizen or inhabitant of ancient Sparta.

spasm *n* **1** a sudden uncontrollable contraction of a muscle or muscles. **2** a short period of activity. **3** a sudden burst (of emotion, etc): *spasm of anger.* ➢ *vb*, *intr* to twitch or go into a spasm.

spasmodic or **spasmodical** *adj* being or occurring in, or consisting of, short periods; not

constant or regular: *spasmodic gunfire.* ○ **spasmodically** *adv.*

spastic *n* someone who suffers from CEREBRAL PALSY. ➢ *adj* **a** affected by or suffering from cerebral palsy; **b** relating to, affected by, etc a spasm or spasms.

spat[1] *past tense, past participle of* SPIT[1]

spat[2] *colloq, n* a trivial quarrel. ➢ *vb* (**spatted, spatting**) *intr* to engage in a trivial quarrel.

spate *n* a sudden rush or increased quantity: *a spate of complaints.* ♦ **in spate** of a river: in a fast-flowing state that is brought on by flooding or melting snow.

spathe *n, bot* a large bract that surrounds the inflorescence.

spatial or **spacial** *adj* belonging, referring or relating to space. ○ **spatially** *adv.*

spats *pl n, hist* cloth coverings that go around the ankles and over the tops of shoes.

spatter *vb, tr & intr* **1** of mud, etc: to spray or splash in scattered drops. **2** to cause (mud, etc) to fly in scattered drops: *The wheels of the bike spattered mud everywhere.* ➢ *n* **1** a quantity spattered. **2** the act or process of spattering.

spatula *n* **1** *cookery* an implement that has a broad, blunt and often flexible blade. **2** *med* a flat, usu wooden, implement that is used for holding down the tongue during a throat examination, etc.

spawn *n* **1** the jelly-like mass of eggs that amphibians, fish, molluscs, crustaceans, etc lay in water. **2** *derisive* something that is the product of something else and is regarded with a degree of contempt: *the spawn of the devil.* ➢ *vb* **1** *intr* of amphibians, fish, etc: to lay eggs. **2** to give rise to something: *The film's success spawned several sequels.* **3** to give birth to someone or something: *They'd spawned three equally useless sons.*

spay *vb* to remove the ovaries from (esp a domestic animal) in order to prevent it from breeding. ○ **spayed** *adj.*

speak *vb* (**spoke, spoken**) **1** *tr & intr* **a** to utter words in an ordinary voice, as opposed to shouting, singing, screaming, etc; **b** to talk: *He speaks a load of rubbish.* **2** *intr* to have a conversation: *We spoke on the phone.* **3** *intr* to deliver a speech: *She spoke about rising urban crime.* **4** to communicate, or be able to communicate, in (a particular language): *He speaks French.* **5** *intr* to convey meaning: *Actions speak louder than words.* ♦ **so to speak** in a way; as it were: *We had a bit of a tiff, so to speak.* ◊ **speak for 1** to give an opinion on behalf of (another or others). **2** to articulate in either spoken or written words the commonly held feelings, beliefs, views, etc of (others). **speak out 1** to speak openly; to state one's views forcefully. **2** to speak more loudly. **speak up 1** to speak more loudly. **2** to make something known: *If you've any objections, speak up now.* **speak up for sb** or **sth 1** to vouch for or defend them or it. **2** to represent them or it.

speakeasy n (-ies) colloq a place where alcohol was sold illicitly, esp during Prohibition in the US.

speaker n 1 someone who speaks, esp someone who gives a formal speech. 2 a shortened form of LOUDSPEAKER. 3 (usu the Speaker) the person who presides over debate in a lawmaking assembly such as the House of Commons.

spear[1] n a weapon that consists of a long pole with a hard sharp point, which is thrown from the shoulder. ➤ vb to pierce with a spear or something similar.

spear[2] n a spiky plant shoot.

spearhead n 1 the leading part of an attacking force. 2 the tip of a spear. ➤ vb to lead (a campaign, attack, etc).

spearmint n 1 a plant of the mint family with spikes of purple flowers. 2 the aromatic oil obtained from its leaves used as a flavouring in confectionery, toothpaste, etc.

spec n, colloq a commercial venture. ♦ on spec as a speculation or gamble, in the hope of success.

special adj 1 distinct from, and usu better than, others of the same kind: a special occasion. 2 designed for a particular purpose: You can get a special program to do that. 3 not ordinary or common: special circumstances. 4 particular; great: make a special effort. ➤ n 1 something that is special, eg an extra edition of a newspaper, etc, an extra train, a dish on a menu, etc. 2 a special person, such as a member of the special police constabulary: The specials were drafted in to control the fans. ○ **specially** adv.

special delivery n a delivery of post, etc outside normal delivery times.

special effects pl n, cinematog 1 techniques, such as those that involve computer-generated imagery, manipulation of film or sound, etc, used to contribute to the illusion in films, TV programmes, etc. 2 the resulting illusion that these techniques produce.

specialist n 1 someone whose work, interest or expertise is concentrated on a particular subject. 2 a doctor who is trained in specific diseases, diseases of a particular part of the body, etc: a heart specialist.

speciality or (chiefly US) **specialty** n (-ies) 1 something such as a particular area of interest, quality, product, etc that a company, individual, etc has special knowledge of or that they excel in studying, teaching, producing, etc: The restaurant's speciality is seafood. 2 a special feature, skill, characteristic, service, etc.

specialize or **-ise** vb, intr 1 (also **specialize in sth**) to be or become an expert in a particular activity, field of study, etc. 2 of an organism, body part, etc: to adapt or become adapted for a specified purpose or to particular surroundings. ○ **specialization** n.

special licence n a licence that allows a marriage to take place without the normal legal formalities.

specie /'spiː.ʃiː/ n money in the form of coins as opposed to notes. ♦ in specie 1 in kind. 2 in coin.

species n (pl species) 1 biol a any of the groups into which a GENUS (sense I) is divided, in which all the members are capable of interbreeding and producing fertile offspring; b the members of one of these units of classification thought of collectively. 2 (usu species of) a kind or type.

specific adj 1 particular; exact; precisely identified. 2 precise in meaning. ➤ n 1 (usu specifics) a specific detail, factor or feature. 2 a drug that is used to treat one particular disease, condition, etc. ○ **specifically** adv. ○ **specificity** /ˌspɛsɪ'fɪsɪtɪ/ n.

specification n 1 (often specifications) a a detailed description of the methods, materials, dimensions, quantities, etc that are used in the construction, manufacture, planning, etc of something; b the standard, etc of the construction, manufacture, etc of something: high safety specifications. 2 an act or instance of the process of specifying.

specify vb (-ies, -ied) 1 to refer to, name or identify precisely. 2 (usu specify that) to state as a condition or requirement.

specimen n 1 a sample or example of something. 2 med a sample of blood, urine, tissue, etc that is taken so that tests can be carried out on it. 3 colloq a person of a specified kind: an ugly specimen.

specious adj superficially or apparently convincing, sound or just, but really false, flawed or lacking in sincerity: specious arguments.

speck n 1 a small spot, stain or mark. 2 a particle of something: a speck of dirt. ➤ vb to mark with specks: a blue carpet specked with grey.

speckle n a little spot, esp one of several on a different-coloured background. ➤ vb to mark with speckles. ○ **speckled** adj.

specs pl n, colloq a shortened form of SPECTACLES.

spectacle n 1 something that can be seen; a sight, esp one that is impressive, ridiculous, etc. 2 a public display or exhibition. 3 someone or something that attracts attention. ♦ make a spectacle of oneself to behave in a way that attracts attention, esp ridicule.

spectacles pl n a frame that holds two lenses designed to correct defective vision, and which has two legs that hook over the ears.

spectacular adj 1 impressively striking to see. 2 remarkable; huge. ➤ n a spectacular show or display, esp one with lavish costumes, sets, music, etc: an old-fashioned musical spectacular. ○ **spectacularly** adv.

spectate vb, intr to be a spectator.

spectator n someone who watches an event or incident.

spectre or (US) **specter** n 1 a ghost. 2 a haunting fear: The spectre of famine was never far away. ○ **spectral** adj.

spectrometer n a device that is designed to

produce spectra, esp one that can measure wavelength, energy and intensity.

spectroscope n, chem an optical device that is used to produce a spectrum for a particular chemical compound, allowing the spectrum to be analysed.

spectrum n (**spectra** or **spectrums**) 1 physics (in full **visible spectrum**) the band of colours (red, orange, yellow, green, blue, indigo and violet) that is produced when white light is split into its constituent wavelengths by passing it through a prism. 2 a continuous band representing the wavelengths or frequencies of electromagnetic radiation (eg visible light, X-rays, radio waves) emitted or absorbed by a particular substance. 3 any full range: the whole spectrum of human emotions.

speculate vb, intr 1 (often **speculate on** or **about sth**) to consider the circumstances or possibilities regarding it, usu without coming to a definite conclusion. 2 to engage in risky financial transactions in the hope of making a quick profit. ○ **speculation** n. ○ **speculative** adj. ○ **speculator** n.

speculum n (**specula** or **speculums**) 1 optics a mirror with a reflective surface usu of polished metal. 2 med a device that is used to enlarge the opening of a body cavity so that the interior may be inspected.

speech n 1 the act or an instance of speaking; the ability to speak. 2 a way of speaking: slurred speech. 3 something that is spoken. 4 spoken language, esp that of a particular group, region, etc: Doric speech. 5 a talk that is addressed to an audience.

speechify vb (-ies, -ied) intr, colloq to make a long or tedious speech.

speechless adj 1 often euphem temporarily unable to speak, because of surprise, shock, etc. 2 not able to speak at all.

speech therapy n the treatment of people with speech disorders. ○ **speech therapist** n.

speed n 1 rate of movement or action. 2 rapidity: with speed. 3 a gear setting on a vehicle: a five-speed gearbox. 4 a photographic film's sensitivity to light. 5 drug-taking slang an AMPHETAMINE. ➤ vb, intr 1 (**sped**) to move quickly. 2 (**speeded**) to drive at a speed higher than the legal limit. ♦ **at speed** quickly. ◇ **speed up** or **speed sth up** to increase in speed or make it increase in speed.

speedboat n a motor boat that has an engine designed to make it capable of high speeds.

speeding n an act, instance or the process of going fast or too fast. ➤ adj moving, acting, etc fast: a speeding car.

speed limit n the designated maximum speed at which a vehicle may legally travel on a given stretch of road.

speedo n, colloq a SPEEDOMETER.

speedometer n a device which indicates the speed that a motor vehicle is travelling at.

speed trap n a stretch of road where police monitor the speed of vehicles.

speedway n 1 the sport of racing round a cinder track on lightweight motorcycles. 2 the track that is used for this. 3 N Am a racetrack for cars. 4 N Am a highway.

speedwell n a plant with small bluish flowers.

speedy adj (-ier, -iest) fast; prompt. ○ **speedily** adv.

speleology or **spelaeology** n 1 the scientific study of caves. 2 the activity or pastime of exploring caves.

spell¹ vb 1 to write or name (the constituent letters of a word) in their correct order. 2 of letters: to form (a word) when written in sequence: I T spells 'it'. 3 to indicate something clearly: His angry expression spelt trouble. ○ **speller** n. ◇ **spell sth out** 1 to read, write or speak the constituent letters of a word) one by one. 2 to explain something clearly and in detail.

spell² n 1 a set of words which is believed to have magical power: a magic spell. 2 any strong attracting influence: the spell of her personality. ♦ **cast a spell (on** or **upon sb)** to direct the words of a spell (towards them). **under a spell** held by the influence of a spell that has been cast. **under sb's spell** captivated by their influence.

spell³ n 1 (often **for a spell** or **a spell of**) a period of illness, work, weather, etc: I hope this spell of sunshine continues. 2 now chiefly Aust, NZ & N Eng dialect an interval or short break from work.

spellbinding adj captivating, enchanting or fascinating. ○ **spellbound** adj.

spellchecker n, comput a program that checks the operator's spelling against a store of words in a word-processor's database. ○ **spellcheck** vb.

spelling n 1 the ability to spell: His spelling is awful. 2 a way a word is spelt: an American spelling.

spelunker n someone who takes part in the activity of exploring caves. ○ **spelunking** n.

spend vb (**spent**) 1 tr & intr (often **spend on**) to pay out (money, etc). 2 to use or devote (eg time, energy, effort, etc): He spent hours trying to fix the car. 3 to use up completely: Her anger soon spends itself. ➤ n an act or the process of spending (esp money): She went on a massive spend after winning the lottery. ○ **spender** n. ○ **spending** n. ○ **spent** adj used up; exhausted: a spent match.

spendthrift n someone who spends money wastefully.

sperm n 1 a SPERMATOZOON. 2 SEMEN.

spermaceti /spɜːməˈsiːtɪ/ n a white translucent waxy substance obtained from the snout of the sperm whale, formerly used for making candles, soap, cosmetics, etc.

spermatozoon /spɜːmətəˈzəʊɒn/ n (**spermatozoa** /-ˈzəʊə/) zool in male animals: the small male gamete that locates, penetrates and fertilizes the female gamete.

spermicide n a substance that can kill sperm

and which is used in conjunction with various methods of barrier contraception. ○ **spermicidal** adj.

spew vb, tr & intr **1** to vomit. **2** to pour or cause to pour or stream out. ➤ n vomit.

sphagnum n (**sphagna**) a moss that grows on boggy ground, and which forms peat when it decays.

sphere n **1** maths a round three-dimensional figure where all points on the surface are an equal distance from the centre. **2** a globe or ball. **3** a field of activity: Rugby's not really my sphere. **4** a class or circle within society: We don't move in the same sphere any more.

spherical adj having or being in the shape of a sphere.

spheroid n, geom a figure or body characterized by having, or being in, almost the shape of a sphere.

sphincter n, anat a ring of muscle that, when it contracts, closes the entrance to a cavity in the body.

sphinx n **1** (also **Sphinx**) any representation in the form of a human head and lion's body, esp the huge recumbent statue near the Egyptian pyramids at Giza. **2** a mysterious person.

spice n **1** an aromatic or pungent substance that is derived from plants and used for flavouring food. **2** such substances collectively. **3** something that adds interest or enjoyment: Variety is the spice of life. ➤ vb **1** to flavour with spice. **2** (also **spice up**) to add interest or enjoyment to something.

spick and span adj neat, clean and tidy.

spicy or **spicey** adj (**-ier, -iest**) **1** flavoured with or tasting or smelling of spices; piquant. **2** colloq characterized by, or suggestive of, scandal, sensation, etc: Got any spicy gossip?

spider n any of numerous species of invertebrate animals that have eight legs and two main body parts, many of which produce silk and spin webs to trap their prey.

spidery adj **1** thin and straggly: spidery handwriting. **2** full of spiders.

spiel / ʃpiːl, spiːl/ n, colloq a long rambling, often implausible, story, esp from a salesman.

spigot n **1** a plug used for stopping the vent hole in a barrel. **2** a US a tap; **b** a tap for controlling the flow of liquid, eg in a cask, pipe, etc.

spike¹ n **1** a any thin sharp point; **b** a pointed piece of metal. **2** (**spikes**) a pair of running-shoes with spiked soles. **3** a large metal nail. ➤ vb **1** to strike, pierce or impale with a pointed object. **2** colloq **a** to make (a drink) stronger by adding alcohol or extra alcohol; **b** to lace (a drink) with a drug. ○ **spiky** adj.

spike² n, bot a pointed flower head which consists of a cluster of small individual flowers.

spill¹ vb (**spilt** or **spilled**) **1** tr & intr to run or flow or cause (a liquid, etc) to run or flow out from a container, esp accidentally. **2** intr to come or go in large crowds: The spectators spilled onto the pitch. **3** to shed (blood). ➤ n **1** an act of spilling. **2** colloq a fall, esp from a horse. ◆ **spill the**

beans colloq to reveal confidential information.

spill² n a thin strip of wood or twisted paper for lighting a fire, pipe, etc.

spillage n **1** the act or process of spilling. **2** something that is spilt or an amount spilt.

spin vb (past tense, past participle **spun,** present participle **spinning**) **1** tr & intr to rotate or cause to rotate repeatedly, esp quickly: We spun a coin to see who would go first. **2** intr (usu **spin round**) to turn around, esp quickly. **3** to draw out and twist (fibres, etc) into thread. **4** of spiders, silkworms, etc: to construct (a web, cocoon, etc) from the silky thread they produce. **5** a to bowl, throw, kick, strike, etc (a ball) so that it rotates while moving forward, causing a change in the expected direction or speed; **b** intr of a ball, etc: to be delivered in this way. **6** intr of someone's head, etc: to become dizzy. **7** to dry (washing) in a spin dryer. ➤ n **1** an act or process of spinning or a spinning motion. **2** rotation in a ball thrown, struck, etc. **3** a nose-first spiral descent in an aircraft. **4** colloq a short trip in a vehicle, for pleasure. **5** of information, a news report, etc: a favourable bias: The PR department will put a spin on it. ○ **spinning** n. ◆ **spin a yarn, tale,** etc to tell a story, esp a long improbable one.

spina bifida / ˈspaɪnə ˈbɪfɪdə/ n, pathol a condition existing from birth in which there is a protrusion of the spinal column through the backbone, often causing permanent paralysis.

spinach n a dark green leafy vegetable.

spinal column n the spine.

spinal cord n a cord-like structure of nerve tissue that is enclosed by the spinal column and which connects the brain to nerves in all other parts of the body.

spindle n **1** a notched or tapered rod for twisting the fibres in hand-spinning. **2** a pin or axis which turns.

spindly adj (**-ier, -iest**) colloq long, thin and frail-looking.

spin doctor n, colloq someone, esp in politics, who tries to influence public opinion by putting a favourable bias on information when it is presented to the public or to the media.

spindrift n spray that is blown from the crests of waves.

spin dryer or **spin drier** n an electrically powered machine that takes water out of wet laundry by spinning it at high speed in a drum.

spine n **1** in vertebrates: the flexible bony structure that surrounds and protects the spinal cord. **2** the narrow middle section in the cover of a book that hides the part where the pages are glued or stitched. **3** in certain plants and animals: one of many sharply pointed structures that protect it against predators. ○ **spinal** adj.

spine-chiller n a frightening story, thought, etc. ○ **spine-chilling** adj.

spineless adj **1** invertebrate. **2** colloq of a person, their attitude, behaviour, etc: lacking courage or strength of character. ○ **spinelessly** *adv.*

spinet *n* a musical instrument like a small harpsichord.

spinnaker *n* a large triangular sail set at the front of a yacht.

spinner *n* **1** someone or something that spins. **2** an angler's lure that spins in the water when the line is pulled. **3** *cricket* **a** a bowler who spins the ball; **b** a ball that is bowled with spin.

spinneret *n, zool* in spiders, silkworms, etc: a small tubular organ that produces the silky thread which they use in making webs, cocoons, etc.

spinney *n* a small wood.

spinning wheel *n* a machine with a spindle driven by a wheel operated either by hand or by the foot, used for spinning thread or yarn.

spin-off *n* **1** a side effect or by-product. **2** something that comes about because of the success of an earlier product or idea, eg a television series derived from a successful film.

spinster *n* a woman who has never been married.

spiny *adj* (*-ier, -iest*) **1** of plants or animals: covered with spines. **2** difficult to deal with: *a spiny problem.*

spiracle /ˈspaɪrəkəl/ *n, zool* an aperture used for respiration in certain insects and fishes, whales, etc.

spiral *n* **1** the pattern that is made by a line winding outwards from a central point in circles or near-circles of regularly increasing size. **2** a curve or course that makes this kind of a pattern. **3** a gradual but continuous rise or fall, eg of prices, etc. ➣ *adj* being in or having the shape or nature of a spiral: *a spiral staircase.* ➣ *vb* (**spiralled, spiralling;** or (*US*) **spiraled, spiraling**) *intr* **1** to follow a spiral course or pattern. **2** esp of prices, etc: to go up or down, usu quickly.

spire *n* a tall thin structure tapering upwards to a point, esp the top of a tower on a church roof.

spirit *n* **1** the animating force that motivates, invigorates or energizes someone or something. **2** this force as an independent part of a person, widely believed to survive the body after death. **3** a supernatural being without a body: *Evil spirits haunted the house.* **4** a temperament, frame of mind, etc, usu of a specified kind: *She always had a very independent spirit*; **b** the dominant mood, attitude, etc: *public spirit*; **c** the characteristic essence, nature, etc of something: *the spirit of Christmas.* **5** a distilled alcoholic drink, eg whisky, gin, etc. ➣ *vb* (*usu* **spirit sth** or **sb away** or **off**) to carry or convey them mysteriously or magically. ◆ **in good** or **high,** *etc* **spirits** in a happy, etc mood. **in spirit** as a presence that is perceived to be there: *I'll be with you in spirit, if not in person.*

spirited *adj* **1** full of courage or liveliness. **2** *in compounds* having or showing a specified kind of mood, attitude, etc: *high-spirited.*

spirit gum *n* a quick-drying sticky substance that is esp used for securing false facial hair.

spirit lamp *n* a lamp that burns methylated or other spirit.

spirit level *n* a device used for testing that surfaces are level, made up of a flat bar into which is set a liquid-filled glass tube with a large air bubble which lies between two markings on the tube when laid against a level surface.

spiritual *adj* **1** belonging, referring or relating to the spirit or soul rather than to the body or to physical things. **2** belonging, referring or relating to religion; holy or divine. **3 a** belonging, referring or relating to, or arising from, the mind or intellect; **b** highly refined in thought, feelings, etc. **4** belonging, referring or relating to spirits, ghosts, etc: *the spiritual world.* ➣ *n* (*also* **Negro spiritual**) a type of religious song that is characterized by voice harmonies and which developed from the communal singing traditions of African American people in the southern states of the USA. ○ **spirituality** *n.* ○ **spiritually** *adv.*

spiritualism *n* the belief that it is possible to have communication with the spirits of dead people. ○ **spiritualist** *n.*

spirituous *adj* having a high alcohol content.

spirograph *n, med* a device for measuring and recording breathing movements.

spirogyra /spaɪroʊˈdʒaɪərə/ *n* a green alga found in ponds and streams.

spit¹ *vb* (*past tense, past participle* **spat** or (*US*) **spit,** *present participle* **spitting**) **1 a** *tr & intr* to expel (saliva) from the mouth; **b** *intr* to do this as a gesture of contempt: *She spat in his face.* **2** (*also* **spit out**) to eject (eg food) forcefully out of the mouth. **3** of a fire, fat or oil in a pan, etc: to throw off (a spark, oil, etc) in a spurt or spurts. **4** to utter with contempt, hate, etc. **5** *intr* of rain or snow: to fall in light intermittent drops or flakes. ➣ *n* **1** saliva that has been spat from the mouth. **2** an act of spitting. ◆ **spit it out** *colloq* to say what one has been hesitating to say.

spit² *n* **1** a long thin metal rod on which meat is skewered for roasting. **2** a long narrow strip of land that juts out into the water.

spit and polish *n, colloq, often derog* exceptional cleanliness, tidiness, etc.

spite *n* **1** the desire to hurt or offend. **2** an instance of this. ➣ *vb, chiefly used in the infinitive form:* to annoy, offend, etc: *She did it to spite him.* ◆ **in spite of** notwithstanding: *We decided to go in spite of the rain.*

spiteful *adj* motivated by spite. ○ **spitefully** *adv.* ○ **spitefulness** *n.*

spitfire *n* someone who has a quick or fiery temper.

spitting image *n, colloq* an exact likeness.

spittle *n* saliva, esp when it has been spat from the mouth.

spittoon *n* a container for spitting into.

spiv *n, colloq* a man who sells, deals in or is otherwise involved in the trading of illicit, black-market or stolen goods, and who is usu dressed in a very flashy way.

splash *vb* **1 a** to make (a liquid or semi-liquid substance) fly around or land in drops; **b** *intr* of a liquid or semi-liquid substance: to fly around or land in drops. **2** to make someone or something wet or dirty (with drops of liquid or semi-liquid): *The bus splashed them with mud.* **3** to print or display something boldly: *The photograph was splashed across the front page.* ➤ *n* **1** a sound of splashing. **2** an amount splashed. **3** an irregular patch: *splashes of colour.* **4** *colloq* a small amount of liquid: *tea with just a splash of milk.* ♦ **make a splash** to attract a great deal of attention. ◊ **splash out** or **splash out on sth** *colloq* to spend a lot of money.

splat *n* the sound made by a soft wet object striking a surface. ➤ *adv* with this sound. ➤ *vb* (**splatted, splatting**) to hit, fall, land, etc with a splat.

splatter *vb* **1** *tr & intr* to make something dirty with lots of small scattered drops. **2** of water, mud, etc: to wet or dirty: *The mud splattered him from head to toe.* ➤ *n* a splash or spattering.

splay *vb* to spread (eg the fingers).

splay foot *n* a foot that turns outwards. ○ **splay-footed** *adj*.

spleen *n* **1** a delicate organ located beneath the diaphragm on the left side, which destroys red blood cells that are no longer functional. **2** bad temper: *He vented his spleen by punching the wall.*

splendid *adj* **1** very good; excellent. **2** magnificent; impressively grand.

splendiferous *adj*, *now colloq, humorous* splendid.

splendour or (*US*) **splendor** *n* magnificence, opulence or grandeur.

splenetic *adj* bad-tempered; spiteful.

splice *vb* **1** to join (two pieces of rope) by weaving the strands of one into the other. **2** to join (two pieces of timber, etc) by overlapping and securing the ends. **3** to join the neatened ends of (two pieces of film, magnetic tape, wire, etc) using solder, adhesive, etc. ➤ *n* a join made in one of these ways. ♦ **get spliced** *colloq* to get married.

splint *n* a piece of rigid material that is strapped to a broken limb, etc to hold it in position while the bone heals. ➤ *vb* to bind or hold (a broken limb, etc) in position using a splint.

splinter *n* **1** a small thin sharp piece that has broken off a hard substance, eg wood or glass. **2** a fragment of an exploded shell, etc. ➤ *vb, tr & intr* **1** to break into splinters. **2** of a group: to divide or become divided: *The party splintered over green issues.*

splinter group *n* a small group, esp a political one, that is formed by individuals who have broken away from the main group.

split *vb* (**split, splitting**) **1** *tr & intr* to divide or break or cause to divide or break apart or into usu two pieces, esp lengthways. **2** to divide or share (money, etc). **3** (*also* **split up**) *tr & intr* **a** to divide or separate into smaller amounts,

groups, parts, etc; **b** to divide or separate or cause to divide or separate, eg because of disagreement, etc: *European policy split the party.* **4** *intr* (*usu* **split away** or **split off**) to separate from or break away from the main part: *The road splits off to the right.* **5** *intr, colloq* to go away or leave: *Let's split and go back for a drink.* ➤ *n* **1 a** an act or the process of separating or dividing; **b** a division, esp of money, etc: *a two-way split on the lottery winnings.* **2** a lengthways break or crack. **3** a separation or division through disagreement. **4** a dessert that consists of fruit, esp a banana, sliced open and topped with cream and/or ice cream, nuts, etc. **5** (**the splits**) an acrobatic drop to the floor so that the legs form a straight line. ➤ *adj* divided, esp in two. ♦ **split hairs** to make or argue about fine distinctions. **split one's sides** *colloq* to laugh uncontrollably.

split infinitive *n, gram* an INFINITIVE that has an adverb or other word coming in between the particle *to* and the verb, as in *to really believe, to boldly go,* etc.

split-level *adj* of a house, room, etc: being on or having more than one floor.

split personality *n, psychol* a condition in which two or more distinct personalities or types of behaviour are displayed by a single person.

split second *n* a fraction of a second: *In a split second she was gone.*

splitting *adj* **1** of a headache: very painful. **2** of a head: gripped by severe pain: *My head is absolutely splitting.*

splodge or **splotch** *n* a large splash, stain or patch. ➤ *vb, tr & intr* to mark with splodges.

splurge *n* **1** an ostentatious display. **2** a bout of extravagance, eg a spending spree. ➤ *vb, tr & intr* to spend extravagantly or ostentatiously.

splutter *vb* **1** *intr* to put or throw out drops of liquid, bits of food, sparks, etc with spitting sounds. **2** *intr* to make intermittent noises or movements, esp as a sign of something being wrong: *The car spluttered to a halt.* **3** *tr & intr* to speak or say haltingly or incoherently. ➤ *n* the act or noise of spluttering.

spoil *vb* (**spoilt** or **spoiled**) **1** to impair, ruin or make useless or valueless. **2** to mar or make less enjoyable: *The contrived ending spoiled the film.* **3** to harm (eg the character of a child) by overindulgence. **4** *intr* of food: to become unfit to eat. ➤ *n* (*always* **spoils**) **1** possessions taken by force: *the spoils of war.* **2** any benefits or rewards: *A company car is just one of the spoils of the new job.* ♦ **spoiled** or **spoilt for choice** having so many options that it is hard to decide which to choose. **spoiling for sth** seeking out (a fight, argument, etc) eagerly.

spoilage *n* **1** decay or deterioration of food. **2** waste, esp waste paper caused by bad printing.

spoiler *n* **1** a flap on an aircraft wing that is used for increasing drag and so assists in its descent by reducing the air speed. **2** a fixed horizontal structure on a car that is designed to put pressure on the wheels and so increase its roadholding capacity. **3** someone or something that spoils.

spoilsport n, colloq someone who mars or detracts from the fun or enjoyment of others.

spoke¹ past tense of SPEAK

spoke² n **1** any of the radiating rods that fan out from the hub of a wheel and attach it to the rim. **2** a rung of a ladder. ♦ **put a spoke in sb's wheel** to upset their plans, esp intentionally or maliciously.

spoken adj **1** uttered or expressed in speech. **2** in compounds speaking in a specified way: well-spoken. ➤ vb, past participle of SPEAK. ♦ **be spoken for** to be married, engaged or in a steady relationship.

spokesperson n someone, a **spokesman** or **spokeswoman**, who is appointed to speak on behalf of other people.

spoliation n an act, instance or the process of robbing, plundering, etc.

spondee n, prosody a metrical foot of two long syllables or two stressed syllables and which in English verse tends to suggest weariness, depression, slowness, etc.

spondulicks /spɒn'dju:lɪks/ pl n, colloq, chiefly US money; cash.

sponge n **1** a marine invertebrate animal that consists of a large cluster of cells supported by an often porous skeleton. **2 a** a piece of the soft porous skeleton of this animal which is capable of holding comparatively large amounts of water and which remains soft when wet, making it particularly suitable for washing, etc; **b** a piece of similarly absorbent synthetic material that is used in the same way. **3** a light, fluffy cake or pudding. **4** a wipe with a cloth or sponge in order to clean something. ➤ vb **1** (also **sponge sth down**) to wash it with a cloth or sponge and water. **2** to mop up. **3** tr & intr (usu **sponge off** or **on sb**) colloq to borrow money, etc from them, often without any intention of paying it back. ○ **spongy** adj.

sponger n, colloq someone who survives by habitually imposing on other people, expecting them to pay for things, etc.

sponsor n **1** a person or organization that finances an event or broadcast in return for advertising. **2 a** someone who promises a sum of money to a participant in a forthcoming fundraising event; **b** a company that provides backing for a sports team or individual, in return for the team or individual displaying the company's name or logo on their shirts. **3** someone who offers to be responsible for another, esp in acting as a godparent. ➤ vb to act as a sponsor for someone or something. ○ **sponsorship** n.

spontaneity /spɒntə'neɪtɪ/ n natural or unrestrained behaviour.

spontaneous adj **1** unplanned and voluntary or instinctive, not provoked or invited by others. **2** occurring naturally, not caused or influenced from outside.

spontaneous combustion n an act or instance or the process of a substance or body catching fire as a result of heat that is generated within it.

spoof colloq, n **1** a satirical imitation. **2** a light-hearted hoax. ➤ vb to parody; to play a hoax on.

spook colloq, n **1** a ghost. **2** N Am a spy. ➤ vb **1** to frighten or startle. **2** to haunt. **3** to make someone feel nervous or uneasy. ○ **spooky** adj (-ier, -iest).

spool n a small cylinder, usu with a hole down the centre and with extended rims at either end, on which thread, film, tape, etc is wound.

spoon n **1** a metal, wooden or plastic utensil that has a handle with a shallow bowl-like part at one end and which is used for eating, serving or stirring food. **2** the amount a spoon will hold. ➤ vb **1** to lift or transfer (food) with a spoon. **2** intr, old use to kiss and cuddle. ♦ **be born with a silver spoon in one's mouth** to be born into a family with wealth and/or high social standing.

spoonerism n an accidental slip of the tongue where the positions of the first sounds in a pair of words are reversed, such as par cark for car park, and which often results in an unintentionally comic or ambiguous expression.

spoon-feed vb **1** to feed (eg a baby) with a spoon. **2** to supply someone with everything they need or require, so that any effort on their part is unnecessary.

spoonful n the amount a spoon will hold.

spoor n the track or scent left by an animal.

sporadic adj occurring from time to time, at irregular intervals. ○ **sporadically** adv.

spore n one of the tiny reproductive bodies produced by certain micro-organisms and non-flowering plants, which are capable of developing into new individuals.

sporran n a pouch that is traditionally worn hanging from a belt in front of the kilt in Scottish Highland dress.

sport n **1 a** an activity, competition, etc that usu involves a degree of physical exertion, and which people take part in for exercise and/or pleasure; **b** such activities collectively: Dad enjoys watching sport on TV. **2** good-humoured fun: It was just meant to be a bit of sport. **3** colloq **a** someone who is thought of as being generous, easy-going, etc: Be a sport and lend me your car; **b** someone who behaves in a specified way: Even when he loses, he's a good sport; **c** Aust, NZ a form of address that is esp used between men: How's it going, sport? ➤ vb **1** to wear or display, esp proudly: She sported a small tattoo. **2** biol to vary from, or produce a variation from, the parent stock.

sporting adj **1** belonging, referring or relating to sport: sporting dogs. **2** of someone or their behaviour, attitude, nature, etc: characterized by fairness, generosity, etc: It was sporting of him to lend me the car. **3** keen or willing to gamble: I'm not a sporting man, but I like a bet on the Grand National.

sporting chance n (usu **a sporting chance**) a reasonable possibility of success.

sportive adj playful.

sports Brit, sing n in schools and colleges: a day or afternoon that each year is dedicated to competitive sport, esp athletics: Parents may attend the school sports. ➤ adj 1 belonging, referring or relating to sport: sports pavilion. 2 used in or suitable for sport: sports holdall. 3 casual: sports jacket.

sports car n a small fast car, usu a two-seater, often with a low-slung body.

sports ground n an area of land that is used for outdoor sport.

sports jacket n a man's casual jacket, often made from tweed.

sportsman n 1 a man who plays sport, esp professionally. 2 someone who plays fair, sticks to the rules and accepts defeat without any rancour or bitterness. ○ **sportsmanlike** adj. ○ **sportsmanship** n.

sportswear n clothes that are designed for or suitable for sport or for wearing casually.

sportswoman n a woman who plays sport, esp professionally.

sporty adj (-ier, -iest) 1 of someone: habitually taking part in sport, or being particularly fond of, good at, etc sport. 2 of clothes: casual; suitable for wearing when playing a sport. 3 of a car: looking, performing or handling like a sports car.

spot n 1 a small mark or stain. 2 a drop of liquid. 3 a small amount, esp of liquid. 4 an eruption on the skin. 5 a place: We found a secluded spot. 6 colloq a small amount of work: I did a spot of ironing. 7 a place or period in a schedule or programme: a five-minute comedy spot. 8 colloq a spotlight. ➤ vb (**spotted, spotting**) 1 to mark with spots. 2 to see. 3 usu in compounds to watch for and record the sighting of (eg trains, planes, etc). 4 to search for (new talent). 5 intr of rain: to fall lightly. ♦ **in a spot** colloq in trouble or difficulty. **knock spots off sb** or **sth** colloq to be overwhelmingly better than them. **on the spot 1** immediately and often without warning: Motorists caught speeding are fined on the spot. **2** at the scene of some notable event. **3** in an awkward situation, esp one requiring immediate action or response: to put someone on the spot.

spot check n an inspection made at random and without warning. ➤ vb (**spot-check**) to carry out a random check: The police were spot-checking for worn tyres.

spotless adj 1 absolutely clean. 2 unblemished: a spotless working record. ○ **spotlessly** adv.

spotlight n 1 a concentrated circle of light that can be directed onto a small area, esp of a theatre stage. 2 a lamp that casts this kind of light. ➤ vb (**spotlit** or **spotlighted**) 1 to illuminate with a spotlight. 2 to direct attention to something. ♦ **be in the spotlight** to have the attention of others, the media, etc focused on one.

spot-on adj, Brit colloq precisely what is required; very accurate.

spotted adj 1 patterned or covered with spots. 2 stained: a tie spotted with tomato sauce.

spotter n, usu in compounds someone who watches for and records the sighting of trains, planes, etc.

spotty adj (-ier, -iest) 1 marked with a pattern of spots. 2 of someone's skin: covered in pimples, etc.

spot-weld vb to join metal with single circular welds. ➤ n a weld that is made in this way.

spouse n a husband or wife.

spout n 1 a projecting tube or lip that allows liquid to pass through. 2 a jet or stream of liquid. ➤ vb 1 tr & intr to flow or make something flow out in a jet or stream. 2 tr & intr to speak or say, esp at length and boringly. 3 intr of a whale: to squirt air through a blowhole. ♦ **up the spout** slang 1 ruined; no longer a possibility. 2 pregnant.

sprain vb to injure (a joint) by the sudden overstretching or tearing of a ligament. ➤ n such an injury, usu causing painful swelling.

sprat n a small edible fish of the herring family.

sprawl vb, intr 1 to sit or lie lazily with the arms and legs spread out wide. 2 to fall in an ungainly way. 3 to spread or extend in an irregular, straggling or untidy way. ➤ n 1 a sprawling position. 2 a straggling expansion, esp one that is unregulated, uncontrolled, etc: an urban sprawl.

spray¹ n 1 a fine mist of small flying drops of liquid. 2 a liquid designed to be applied as a mist: body spray. 3 a device for dispensing a liquid as a mist. 4 a shower of small flying objects: a spray of pellets. ➤ vb 1 to squirt (a liquid) in the form of a mist. 2 to apply a liquid in the form of a spray to something. 3 to subject someone or something to a heavy burst: They sprayed the car with bullets.

spray² n 1 a a small branch of a tree or plant which has delicate leaves and flowers growing on it; b any decoration that is an imitation of this. 2 a small bouquet of flowers.

spread vb (past tense, past participle **spread**) 1 tr & intr to apply, or be capable of being applied, in a smooth coating over a surface: Spread the butter on the toast. 2 tr & intr (also **spread out** or **spread sth out**) to extend or make it extend or scatter, often more widely or more thinly. 3 (also **spread sth out**) to open it out or unfold it, esp to its full extent: I spread the sheet on the bed. 4 tr & intr to transmit or be transmitted or distributed: Rumours began to spread. ➤ n 1 the act, process or extent of spreading. 2 a food in paste form, for spreading on bread, etc. 3 a a pair of facing pages in a book, newspaper or magazine; b loosely an article in a newspaper or magazine: a huge spread on Madonna. 4 colloq a lavish meal. 5 N Am a farm and its lands, usu one given over to cattle-rearing. 6 colloq increased fatness around the waist and hips: middle-age spread. 7 a cover, esp for a bed.

spread-eagled *adj* in a position where the arms and legs are stretched out away from the body.

spreadsheet *n, comput* a program that displays data in a grid, allowing various kinds of calculation, projection, etc.

spree *n* a period of extravagance or excess, esp one that involves spending a lot of money or drinking a lot of alcohol: *a spending spree.*

sprig *n* a small shoot or twig.

sprightly *adj* (*-ier, -iest*) lively; vivacious.

spring *vb* (*past tense* **sprang** or (*US*) **sprung,** *past participle* **sprung**) 1 *intr* to leap with a sudden quick launching action. 2 *intr* to move suddenly and swiftly, esp from a stationary position: *She sprang into action.* 3 to set off (a trap, etc) suddenly. 4 to fit (eg a mattress) with springs. 5 (*also* **spring sth on sb**) to present or reveal something suddenly and unexpectedly: *Jo sprang the idea on me without warning.* 6 *slang* to engineer the escape of (a prisoner) from jail. 7 *intr* (**spring from somewhere**) to develop or originate from (a place, etc): *an idea that had sprung from one of his students.* ➤ *n* 1 a metal coil that can be stretched or compressed, and which will return to its original shape when the pull or pressure is released. 2 any place where water emerges from under ground. 3 (*also* **Spring**) the season between winter and summer. 4 a sudden vigorous leap. 5 a the ability of a material to return rapidly to its original shape after a distorting force, such as stretching, bending or compression, has been removed: *The elastic has lost its spring;* b a lively bouncing or jaunty quality: *a spring in his step.*

springboard *n* 1 a a long narrow pliable board that projects over a swimming pool and which is used in diving; b a similar but shorter board that is used in gymnastics and which is placed in front of a piece of apparatus to give extra height and impetus. 2 anything that serves to get things moving.

springbok *n* (*springbok* or *springboks*) 1 (*also* **springbuck**) a type of South African antelope that is renowned for its high springing leap when it runs. 2 (**Springbok**) a nickname for a member of a S African sporting team, esp their national rugby union side.

spring chicken *n* a very young chicken valued for its tender flesh. ✦ **no spring chicken** no longer young.

spring-clean *vb, tr & intr* to clean and tidy (a house) thoroughly. ➤ *n* an act of doing this. ○ **spring-cleaning** *n.*

spring onion *n* an immature onion that is picked when it is just a tiny white bulb with long thin green shoots, and which is usu eaten raw in salads.

spring roll *n* a type of deep-fried folded Chinese pancake that can have a variety of savoury fillings.

spring tide *n* a tidal pattern that occurs twice a month when the Moon is full and again when it is new. Compare NEAP TIDE.

springtime or **springtide** *n* the season of spring.

springy *adj* (*-ier, -iest*) having the ability to readily spring back to the original shape when any pressure that has been exerted is released. ○ **springiness** *n.*

sprinkle *vb* 1 to scatter in, or cover with a scattering of, tiny drops or particles. 2 to arrange or distribute in a thin scattering: *The hillside was sprinkled with houses.* ➤ *n* 1 an act of sprinkling. 2 a very small amount.

sprinkler *n* a person or device that sprinkles, esp one that sprinkles water over a lawn, etc or one for extinguishing fires.

sprinkling *n* a small amount of something.

sprint *n* 1 *athletics* a race at high speed over a short distance. 2 a burst of speed at a particular point, usu the end, of a long race. 3 a fast run. ➤ *vb, tr & intr* to run at full speed.

sprinter *n* an athlete, cyclist, etc who sprints.

sprit *n* a small diagonal spar used to spread a sail.

sprite *n* 1 *folklore* a playful fairy. 2 a number of PIXELs that can be moved around a screen in a group, eg those representing a figure in a computer game.

spritzer *n* a drink of white wine and soda water.

sprocket *n* 1 any of a set of teeth on the rim of a driving wheel, eg fitting into the links of a chain. 2 (*also* **sprocket wheel**) a wheel with sprockets.

sprog *n, slang* a child.

sprout *vb* 1 *tr & intr* to develop (a new growth, eg of leaves or hair). 2 *intr* (*also* **sprout up**) to grow or develop: *Cybercafés are sprouting up everywhere.* ➤ *n* 1 a new growth. 2 a shortened form of BRUSSELS SPROUT.

spruce[1] *n* 1 an evergreen pyramid-shaped tree which has needle-like leaves. 2 the valuable white-grained timber of this tree.

spruce[2] *adj* neat and smart. ➤ *vb* (*usu* **spruce up**) to make oneself, someone or something neat and tidy.

sprung *adj* fitted with a spring or springs. ➤ *vb, past tense, past participle of* SPRING.

spry *adj* 1 lively; active. 2 light on one's feet; nimble.

spud *n, colloq* a potato.

spume *n* foam or froth, esp on the sea. ➤ *vb, tr & intr* to foam or froth.

spun *adj* formed or made by a spinning process: *spun gold.*

spunk *n, colloq* courage. ○ **spunky** *adj.*

spur *n* 1 a device with a spiky metal wheel, fitted to the heel of a horse-rider's boot, which is used for pressing into the horse's side to make it go faster. 2 anything that urges or encourages greater effort or progress. 3 a spike or pointed part. 4 a ridge of high land that projects out into a valley. ➤ *vb* (**spurred, spurring**) 1 (*often* **spur sb** or **sth on**) to urge or encourage them or it. **2** to hurry up. ♦ **on the spur of the moment** suddenly; on an impulse.

spurge *n* a plant which produces a bitter milky juice formerly used as a laxative.

spurious *adj* false, counterfeit or untrue.

spurn *vb* to reject (eg a person's love) scornfully. ➤ *n* an act or instance of spurning.

spurt or **spirt** *vb, tr & intr* to flow out or make something flow out in a sudden sharp jet. ➤ *n* **1** a jet of liquid that suddenly gushes out. **2** a short spell of intensified activity or increased speed: *Business tends to come in spurts.*

spurtle or **spirtle** *n, Scot* a wooden stick used for stirring porridge, soup, etc.

sputter same as SPLUTTER.

sputum *n* (*sputa*) a mixture of saliva and mucus.

spy *n* (*spies*) **1** someone who is employed to gather information about political enemies, competitors, etc. **2** someone who observes others in secret. ➤ *vb* (*spies, spied*) **1** *intr* to act or be employed as a spy. **2** *intr* (**spy on sb** or **sth**) to keep a secret watch on them or it. **3** to catch sight of someone or something.

spyglass *n* a small hand-held telescope.

spyhole *n* a peephole.

sq *abbrev* **1** square. **2** (**Sq.**) in addresses: Square.

squab *n* a young unfledged bird.

squabble *vb, intr* to quarrel noisily, esp about something trivial. ➤ *n* a noisy quarrel, esp a petty one.

squad *n* **1** a small group of soldiers who work together. **2** any group of people who work together in some specified field: *the drug squad.* **3** a set of players from which a sporting team is selected.

squaddy or **squaddie** *n* (*-ies*) *slang* an ordinary soldier.

squadron *n* the principal unit of an air force.

squadron leader *n* an air-force officer who ranks below wing commander.

squalid *adj* esp of places to live: disgustingly filthy and neglected. **2** morally repulsive: *gossip about their squalid affair.*

squall[1] *n, meteorol* a sudden or short-lived violent gust of wind, usu accompanied by rain or sleet. ○ **squally** *adj*.

squall[2] *vb, tr & intr* to yell.

squalor *n* the condition or quality of being disgustingly filthy.

squander *vb* to use up (money, time, etc) wastefully.

square *n* **1** a two-dimensional figure with four sides of equal length and four right angles. **2** anything shaped like this. **3** an open space in a town and the buildings that surround it. **4** an L-shaped or T-shaped instrument which is used for measuring angles, drawing straight lines, etc. **5** the number that is formed when a number is multiplied by itself. **6** *colloq, old use* someone who has old-fashioned tastes, ideas, etc. ➤ *adj* **1** shaped like a square or, sometimes, like a cube. **2** used with a defining measurement to denote the area of something: *The area of a rectangle whose sides are 2 feet by 3 feet would be 6 square feet.* **3** angular: *a square jaw.* **4** measuring almost the same in breadth as in length or height. **5** fair; honest: *a square deal.* **6** of debts: completely paid off: *now we're square.* **7** set at right angles. **8** *colloq, old use* having old-fashioned tastes, ideas, etc. ➤ *vb* **1** to make square in shape. **2** to multiply (a number) by itself. **3** to pay off or settle (a debt). **4** to make the scores level in (a match). **5** to mark with a pattern of squares. ➤ *adv* **1** solidly and directly: *He hit me square on the jaw.* **2** fairly; honestly. ○ **squarely** *adv*. ♦ **all square** *colloq* **1** equal. **2** not in debt; with each side owing nothing. **a square peg in a round hole** something or someone that cannot or does not perform its or their function very well. ◊ **square up** to settle a bill, etc. **square up to sb** to prepare to fight them. **square up to sth** to prepare to tackle it. **square with sth** to agree or correspond with it. **square sth with sb** to get their approval or permission for it.

square-bashing *n, slang* military drill on a barracks square.

square bracket *n* either of a pair of characters ([ ]), chiefly used in mathematical notation or to contain special information.

square dance *chiefly N Am, n* any of various folk dances that are performed by couples in a square formation. ➤ *vb* (**square-dance**) *intr* to take part in this type of dance. ○ **square-dancing** *n*.

square deal *n, colloq* an arrangement that is considered to be fair by all the parties involved.

square meal *n* a good nourishing meal.

square number *n, maths* an integer, such as 1, 4, 9, 16, 25, etc, that is the square of another integer.

square-rigged *adj* of a sailing ship: fitted with large square sails set at right angles to the length of the ship.

square root *n, maths* (symbol √) a number or quantity that when multiplied by itself gives one particular number, eg 2 is the square root of 4, and 3 is the square root of 9.

squash[1] *vb* **1** to crush or flatten by pressing or squeezing. **2** *tr & intr* to force someone or something into a confined space: *I managed to squash everything into one bag.* **3** to suppress or put down (eg a rebellion). **4** to force someone into silence with a cutting reply. ➤ *n* **1** a concentrated fruit syrup, or a drink made by diluting this. **2** a crushed or crowded state. **3** SQUASH RACKETS. **4 a** an act or the process of squashing something; **b** the sound of something being squashed.

squash[2] *n, N Am* **1** any of various trailing plants widely cultivated for their marrow-like gourds. **2** the fruit of any of these plants, which can be cooked and used as a vegetable.

squash rackets or **squash racquets** *sing n* a game for two players who use small-headed rackets to hit a little rubber ball around an indoor court.

squashy *adj* (**-ier, -iest**) soft and easily squashed.

squat *vb* (**squatted, squatting**) *intr* **1** to take up, or be sitting in, a low position with the knees fully bent and the weight on the soles of the feet. **2** usu of homeless people: to occupy an empty building without legal right. ➣ *n* **1** a squatting position. **2 a** a building or part of a building that is unlawfully occupied; **b** the unlawful occupation of such a building. ➣ *adj* short and broad or fat.

squatter *n* someone who unlawfully occupies a building, usu an empty one.

squaw *n, offensive* a Native American woman or wife.

squawk *n* **1** a loud screeching noise, esp one made by a bird. **2** a loud protest or complaint. ➣ *vb, intr* **1** to make a loud screeching noise. **2** to complain loudly.

squeak *n* **1** a short high-pitched cry or sound, like that made by a mouse or a rusty gate. **2** (*also* **narrow squeak**) a narrow escape or success. ➣ *vb* **1** *tr & intr* to utter a squeak or with a squeak. **2** *intr* (**squeak through sth**) to succeed in it by a very narrow margin.

squeaky clean *adj, colloq* **1** spotlessly clean. **2** virtuous, above reproach or criticism, but often with an implication that this impression is for show.

squeal *n* **1** a long high-pitched noise, cry or yelp, like that of a pig, a child, etc. **2** a screeching sound: *the squeal of brakes.* ➣ *vb* **1** *tr & intr* to utter a squeal or with a squeal. **2** *intr, colloq* to inform on someone or to report an incident to the police or other authority. **3** *intr* to complain or protest loudly.

squeamish *adj* **1** slightly nauseous. **2** easily offended.

squeegee *n* a device with a rubber blade for scraping water off a surface, eg a window.

squeeze *vb* **1** to grasp or embrace tightly. **2** to press forcefully, esp from at least two sides. **3** to press or crush so as to extract (liquid, juice, toothpaste, etc). **4** to press gently, esp as an indication of affection, etc: *She squeezed his hand.* **5** *tr & intr* to force or be forced into or through a confined space: *Ten of us squeezed into a phone box.* **6** to put under financial pressure: *Tom squeezed his elderly mother for money.* **7** (*usu* **squeeze sth out of sb**) to extract it, esp by exerting pressure: *They eventually squeezed a confession out of him.* ➣ *n* **1** an act of squeezing. **2** a crowded or crushed state. **3** an amount (of fruit juice, etc) that is obtained by squeezing: *a squeeze of lemon.* **4** a restriction, esp on spending or borrowing money. ✦ **put the squeeze on sb** *colloq* to pressurize them into paying something.

squeeze-box *n, colloq* an accordion or concertina.

squeezy *adj* of a bottle, container, etc: soft and flexible so that its contents can be squeezed out.

squelch *n* a loud gurgling or sucking sound made by contact with a thick sticky substance. ➣ *vb, intr* **1** to walk through wet ground or with water in one's shoes and so make this sound. **2** to make this sound. ○ **squelchy** *adj.*

squib *n* **1** a small firework that jumps around on the ground before exploding. **2** a satirical criticism or attack.

squid *n* (**squid** or **squids**) **1** a marine mollusc with a torpedo-shaped body, eight sucker-bearing arms and two longer tentacles. **2** the flesh of this animal used as food.

squidge *vb* to squash; to squeeze together.

squidgy *adj* (**-ier, -iest**) soft, pliant and sometimes soggy.

squiffy *adj* (**-ier, -iest**) *old use* slightly drunk.

squiggle *n* a wavy scribbled line. ○ **squiggly** *adj.*

squillion *n* (**squillions** or after a number *squillion*) *colloq* a very large number.

squint *n* **1** *non-technical* the condition of having one or both eyes set slightly off-centre, preventing parallel vision. **2** *colloq* a quick look. ➣ *vb, intr* **1** to be affected by a squint. **2** to look with eyes half-closed. ➣ *adj* **1** having a squint. **2** *colloq* not being properly straight or centred. ➣ *adv, colloq* in a way or manner that is not properly straight or centred.

squire *n* **1** *hist* in England and Ireland: an owner of a large area of rural land. **2** (in the feudal system) a young man of good family who ranked next to a knight and who would attend upon him. **3** *colloq* a term of address esp used between men.

squirm *vb, intr* **1** to wriggle along. **2** to feel or show embarrassment, shame, etc, often with slight wriggling movements. ➣ *n* a wriggling movement.

squirrel *n* a rodent that has a bushy tail, beady eyes and tufty ears, and usu lives in trees. ➣ *vb* (**squirrelled, squirrelling** or (*chiefly US*) **squirreled, squirreling**) (*often* **squirrel away** or **squirrel up**) to store or put away something for future use.

squirt *vb* **1 a** to shoot (a liquid, etc) out in a narrow jet; **b** *intr* of a liquid, etc: to shoot out in a narrow jet: *Paint squirted everywhere.* **2** *intr* to press the nozzle, trigger, etc of a container, etc so that liquid comes shooting out of it. **3** to cover something with a liquid: *Mum squirted the table with polish.* ➣ *n* **1 a** an act or instance of squirting; **b** an amount of liquid squirted. **2** *colloq* a small, insignificant or despicable person.

squish *n* a gentle splashing or squelching sound. ➣ *vb* **1** *intr* to make this sound; to move with this sound. **2** to crush (eg an insect, etc). ○ **squishy** *adj.*

Sr¹ *abbrev* used after a name: Senior.

Sr² *symbol, chem* strontium.

St *abbrev* **1** Saint. **2** in addresses: Street.

st *abbrev* stone (the imperial unit of weight).

stab *vb* (**stabbed, stabbing**) **1 a** to wound with a sharp or pointed instrument; **b** of a sharp instrument, etc: to wound; **c** to push (a sharp implement) into (someone or something). **2** (*often* **stab at sth**) to make a quick thrusting movement with something sharp at something. ➤ *n* **1** an act of stabbing. **2** a stabbing sensation: *She felt a sudden stab of pain.* ♦ **have** or **make a stab at sth** to try to do it. **stab sb in the back** to betray them, esp after posing as their friend.

stability *n* the state or quality of being stable.

stabilize or **-ise** *vb, tr & intr* to make or become stable or more stable. ○ **stabilization** *n*.

stabilizer or **-iser** *n* **1** a device used to give stability to an aircraft, ship or child's bicycle. **2** a substance that encourages food ingredients that would not otherwise mix well to remain together.

stable[1] *adj* **1** firmly balanced or fixed. **2** firmly established; not likely to be abolished, overthrown or destroyed: *a stable government* • *a stable relationship*. **3 a** regular or constant; not erratic or changing: *The patient's condition is stable*; **b** of someone or their disposition, judgement, etc: not moody, impulsive, etc.

stable[2] *n* **1** a building where horses are kept. **2** a place where horses are bred and trained. **3** *colloq* a number of people or things with a common background or origin. ➤ *vb* to put (a horse) into or back into its stable. ○ **stabling** *n*.

staccato /stə'kɑːtəʊ/ *mus, adv* in a short, abrupt manner. ➤ *adj* short and abrupt.

stack *n* **1** a large pile. **2** a large pile of hay or straw. **3** (*sometimes* **stacks**) *colloq* a large amount: *stacks of money*. **4** a large industrial chimney. **5** a hi-fi system where the individual components are placed on top of each other. **6** *chiefly N Am* an exhaust pipe on a truck that sticks up behind the driver's cab. ➤ *vb* **1** (*also* **stack things up**) to arrange them in a stack or stacks. **2** to arrange (circumstances, etc) to favour or disadvantage a particular person. **3** to arrange (aircraft that are waiting to land) into a queue in which each circles the airport at a different altitude. **4** to fill something: *She stacked the fridge with goodies*. ○ **stacker** *n*.

stadium *n* (*stadiums* or *stadia*) a large sports arena in which the spectators' seats are arranged in rising tiers.

staff *n* (*pl* in senses 1–3 **staffs**, in senses 4–6 **staffs** or **staves**) **1 a** the total number of employees working in an organization; **b** the employees working for a manager. **2** the teachers, lecturers, etc of a school, university, etc as distinct from the students. **3** *mil* the officers assisting a senior commander. **4** any stick or rod, esp one that is carried in the hand as a sign of authority, etc. **5** (*also* **flagstaff**) a pole that a flag is hung from. **6** *mus* a set of lines and spaces on which music is written. ➤ *vb* to provide (an establishment) with staff.

staff nurse *n* a qualified nurse of the rank below SISTER.

staff sergeant *n, mil* the senior sergeant in an army company.

stag *n* an adult male deer.

stage *n* **1** a platform on which a performance takes place, esp one in a theatre. **2** any raised area or platform. **3** the scene of a specified event: *a battle stage*. **4** any of several distinct and successive periods: *the planning stage*. **5** (**the stage**) the theatre as a profession or art form. **6 a** part of a journey: *The last stage of the trip entails a short bus ride*; **b** *Brit* a major stop on a bus route that involves a change in ticket prices. **7** *colloq* a stagecoach. ➤ *vb* **1** to present a performance of (a play). **2** to organize and put on something or set it in motion: *It was a huge undertaking to stage the festival*. **3** to prearrange something to happen in a particular way: *She tried to stage her colleague's downfall*.

stagecoach *n, formerly* a large horse-drawn coach carrying passengers and mail on a regular fixed route.

stage door *n* the back or side entrance to a theatre.

stage fright *n* nervousness felt by an actor or other performer when about to appear in front of an audience.

stagehand *n* someone who is responsible for moving scenery and props in a theatre.

stage-manage *vb* **1** to supervise the arrangement of scenery and props for a play. **2** to prearrange for something to happen in a certain way, in order to create a particular effect. ○ **stage-management** *n*. ○ **stage manager** *n*.

stage name *n* a name assumed by an actor, performer, etc.

stage-struck *adj* filled with awe of the theatre, esp in having an overwhelming desire to become an actor.

stage whisper *n* **1** an actor's loud whisper that is intended to be heard by the audience. **2** any loud whisper that is intended to be heard by people other than the person addressed.

stagey see STAGY

stagflation *n* inflation in an economy without the expected growth in employment or demand for goods.

stagger *vb* **1** *intr* to walk or move unsteadily. **2** *colloq* to cause extreme shock or surprise to someone. **3** to arrange (a series of things) so that they take place or begin at different times. ➤ *n* the action or an act of staggering. ○ **staggering** *adj*. ○ **staggeringly** *adv*.

staggers *sing n* a disease of the brain in horses and cattle that causes them to stagger.

staging *n* scaffolding, esp the horizontal planks used for walking on.

stagnant *adj* **1** of water: not flowing; dirty and foul-smelling because of a lack of movement. **2** not moving or developing: *a stagnant market*.

stagnate *vb, intr* to be or become stagnant. ○ **stagnation** *n*.

stag night or **stag party** *n* a night out for men only, esp one held to celebrate the end of bachelorhood of a man about to get married.

stagy or **stagey** *adj, N Am* (*-ier, -iest*) theatrical; artificial or affectedly pretentious.

staid *adj* serious or sober in character or manner.

stain *vb* **1** *tr & intr* to make or become discoloured. **2** to change the colour of (eg wood) by applying a liquid chemical. **3** to tarnish: *The affair stained his previously good name.* ➤ *n* **1** a mark or discoloration. **2** a liquid chemical applied (eg to wood) to bring about a change of colour. **3** a cause of shame: *a stain on his reputation.*

stained glass *n* decorative glass that has been coloured by a chemical process.

stainless steel *n* a type of steel that contains a high percentage of chromium, making it resistant to rusting.

stair *n* **1** any of a set of indoor steps connecting the floors of a building. **2** (*also* **stairs**) a set of these.

staircase *n* a set of stairs.

stairway *n* a way into a building or part of a building that involves going up a staircase.

stairwell *n* **1** the vertical shaft containing a staircase. **2** the floor area at the foot of a flight of stairs.

stake¹ *n* **1** a stick or post, usu with one pointed end, that is knocked into the ground as a support, eg for a young tree or a fence. **2** (**the stake**) *formerly* a post that is set into materials for a bonfire and to which a person is tied before being burned alive as a punishment. ➤ *vb* to support or fasten to the ground with a stake. ♦ **stake a claim** to assert or establish a right or ownership. ◊ **stake sth out 1** to mark the boundary of (a piece of land) with stakes. **2** to keep (a building, etc) under surveillance.

stake² *n* **1** a sum of money risked in betting. **2** an interest, esp a financial one: *a stake in the project's success.* **3** (**stakes**) **a** a prize, esp in horse-racing, where the horses' owners put up the money that is to be won; **b** a race of this kind; **c** a specified area, esp one where there is pressure to succeed: *It all depends on how he fares in the promotion stakes.* ➤ *vb* **1** to risk, esp as a bet. **2** to support, esp financially. ♦ **at stake** at risk.

stakeout *n, colloq* an act or period of surveillance of a person, building, etc, usu carried out by the police or a private detective.

stalactite *n* an icicle-like mass of calcium carbonate that hangs from the roof of a cave, etc, and which is formed by water continuously dripping through and partially dissolving limestone rock.

stalagmite *n* a spiky mass of calcium carbonate that sticks up from the floor of a cave, etc, and which is formed by water containing limestone that drips from a stalactite.

stale *adj* **1** of food: past its best because it has been kept too long. **2** of air: not fresh. **3** of words, phrases, ideas, etc: overused and no longer interesting or original. **4** of someone: lacking in energy because of overfamiliarity, etc with the job in hand. **5** of news, gossip, etc: out-of-date.

stalemate *n* **1** *chess* a position where either player cannot make a move without putting their king in check and which results in a draw. **2** a position in any contest or dispute where no progress can be made: *The staff and management had reached a stalemate over pay.*

stalk¹ *n* **1** *bot* **a** the main stem of a plant; **b** a stem that attaches a leaf, flower or fruit to the plant. **2** any slender connecting part.

stalk² *vb* **1** to hunt, follow or approach stealthily. **2** *intr* to walk or stride stiffly, proudly, disdainfully, etc: *She stalked out of the meeting.* **3** to pervade, penetrate or spread over (a place): *Fear stalked the neighbourhood.* ➤ *n* **1** an act or the process of stalking. **2** a striding way of walking. ◦ **stalker** *n*. ◦ **stalking** *n, adj*.

stalking-horse *n* a person or thing that is used to conceal real intentions, esp a planned attack.

stall¹ *n* **1** a compartment in a cowshed, stable, etc for housing a single animal. **2** a stand, often with a canopy, set up temporarily in a marketplace, etc for the selling of goods. **3** (**stalls**) the seats on the ground floor of a theatre or cinema. ➤ *vb, tr & intr* **1 a** of a motor vehicle or its engine: to cut out or make it cut out unintentionally; **b** to come, bring or be brought to a standstill: *Plans for the expansion had stalled.* **2** *chiefly US* to stick or to make something stick in snow, mud, etc.

stall² *vb* **1** to delay. **2** *intr* to do something in order to delay something else: *Quit stalling and answer the question.* ➤ *n* an act of stalling; a delaying tactic.

stallion *n* an uncastrated adult male horse, esp one kept for breeding.

stalwart /ˈstɔːlwət/ *adj* **1** strong and sturdy. **2** unwavering in commitment and support. ➤ *n* a long-standing and committed supporter: *the stalwarts of the right.*

stamen *n* (**stamens** or **stamina** /ˈstæmɪnə/) *bot* in flowering plants: the male reproductive structure where the pollen grains are produced.

stamina *n* energy and staying power.

stammer *vb, tr & intr* to speak or say something in a faltering way, often by repeating words or parts of words, usu because of heightened emotion or a pathological disorder that affects the speech organs or the nervous system. ➤ *n* a speech disorder that is characterized by this kind of faltering. ◦ **stammerer** *n*. ◦ **stammering** *adj, n*.

stamp *vb* **1** *tr & intr* to bring (the foot) down with force: *Katie stamped her feet in rage.* **2** *intr* to walk with a heavy tread. **3 a** to imprint or impress (a mark or design); **b** to imprint or impress something with a mark or design. **4** to fix or mark deeply: *The event was stamped on his memory.* **5** to fix a postage or other stamp on something. ➤ *n* **1 a** a small piece of gummed paper bearing an official mark and indicating that a tax or fee has been paid, esp a POSTAGE STAMP; **b** a similar piece of gummed paper that is given away free, eg by petrol stations, and which can be collected and exchanged for a gift. **2 a** a device for stamping a mark or design; **b** the mark or design that is stamped on something. **3** a characteristic mark or sign: *The crime bears the stamp of a professional.* **4** an act or the process of stamping with the foot. ◊ **stamp sth out 1** to put out (a fire) by stamping on it. **2** to put an end to (an activity or practice): *They tried to stamp out the use of drugs.* **3** to eradicate (a disease): *Smallpox has now been stamped out.*

stamp duty or **stamp tax** *n* a tax that is incurred when certain legal documents are drawn up.

stampede *n* **1** a sudden dash made by a group of startled animals. **2** an excited or hysterical rush by a crowd of people. ➢ *vb, tr & intr* to rush or make (animals or people) rush in a herd or crowd.

stamping-ground *n* someone's usual or favourite meeting place.

stance *n* **1** point of view; a specified attitude towards something. **2 a** the position that the body of a person or an animal takes up; **b** a position or manner of standing.

stanchion /'stanʃən/ *n* an upright beam or pole that functions as a support.

stand *vb* (**stood**) **1** *intr* to be in, remain in or move into an upright position supported by the legs or a base. **2** *tr & intr* to place or situate, or be placed or situated, in a specified position: *I stood the vase on the table.* **3** *intr* to be a specified height: *The tower stands 300 feet tall.* **4** to tolerate or put up with someone or something: *How can you stand that awful noise?* **5** *intr* to be in a specified state or condition: *I stand corrected.* **6** *intr* to be in a position (to do something): *We stand to make a lot of money.* **7** *intr* to continue to apply or be valid: *The decision stands.* **8** to withstand or survive something: *It stood the test of time.* ➢ *n* **1** a base on which something sits or is supported. **2** a stall on which goods or services for sale are displayed. **3 a** a structure at a sports ground, etc which has sitting or standing accommodation for spectators; **b** (**the stand**) a witness box. **4** a rack, etc where coats, hats, umbrellas, etc may be hung. **5** an opinion, attitude or course of action that is adopted resolutely: *He took a stand against animal testing.* **6** *cricket* a partnership between batsmen, expressed in terms of the time it lasts or the number of runs scored. **7** an act of resisting attack. ♦ **make a stand** to adopt a determined attitude (against or towards something): *They made a stand for higher pay.* **stand guard** to keep a lookout for danger, an enemy, etc. **stand one's ground** to maintain a position resolutely. **stand on one's own feet** or **own two feet** to be or become independent. **stand to reason** to be the logical or obvious assumption to make. **stand trial** to go through the usual legal processes in order to establish guilt or innocence. **take the stand** to enter a witness box and give evidence. ◊ **stand by 1** to be in a state of readiness to act. **2** to look on without taking the required or expected action: *She just stood by and never offered to help.* **stand by sb** to give them loyalty or support, esp when they are in difficulty. **stand down** to resign. **stand for sth 1** to be in favour of promoting it. **2** of a symbol, letter, device, etc: to represent, mean or signify something: *The red ribbon stands for AIDS awareness.* **3** to tolerate or allow it. **stand in for sb** to act as a substitute for them. **stand off** to keep at a distance. **stand out** to be noticeable or prominent. **stand to** to be ready (to start work, etc). **stand up 1** to assume a standing position. **2** to prove to be valid on examination: *an argument that will stand up in court.* **stand sb up** *colloq* to fail to keep a date with them. **stand up for sb 1** to back them in a dispute, argument, etc. **2** *chiefly US* to act as best man or be a witness at their wedding. **stand up for sth** to support it. **stand up to sb** to face or resist them. **stand up to sth** to withstand it (eg hard wear or criticism).

stand-alone *adj* esp of a computer: able to work independently of a network or other system.

standard *n* **1** an established or accepted model: *Size 14 is the standard for British women.* **2** something that functions as a model of excellence for other similar things to be compared to, measured by or judged against: *the standard by which all other dictionaries will be measured.* **3** (*often* **standards**) **a** a degree or level of excellence, value, quality, etc: *Standards of living have fallen*; **b** a principle, eg of morality: *moral standards.* **4** a flag or other emblem, esp one carried on a pole: *the royal standard.* **5** an upright pole or support. **6** an authorized model of a unit of measurement or weight. ➢ *adj* **1** having features that are generally accepted as normal or expected; typical: *A month's notice is standard practice.* **2** accepted as supremely authoritative: *the standard text of Shakespeare.* **3** of language: accepted as correct by educated native speakers.

standard-bearer *n* **1** someone who carries a flag. **2** the leader of a movement or cause.

standardize or **-ise** *vb* to make (all the examples of something) conform in size, shape, etc. ○ **standardization** *n*.

standard lamp *n* a lamp at the top of a pole which has a base that sits on the floor.

standard of living *n* a measurement of the comparative wealth of a class or community, usu taken from their ability to afford certain commodities.

stand-by *n* (**stand-bys**) **1 a** a state of readiness to act; **b** a person or thing that takes on this kind of role. **2 a** of air travel: a system of allocating spare seats to passengers who do not have reservations; **b** a ticket that has been allocated in this way. ♦ **on stand-by** ready and prepared to do something if necessary: *The emergency team were on stand-by.*

stand-in n a substitute.

standing n 1 position, status or reputation. 2 the length of time something has been in existence, someone has been doing something, etc: *a professor of long standing.* ➤ *adj* 1 done, taken, etc in or from a standing position: *a standing ovation.* 2 permanent; regularly used: *a standing order.*

standing joke n a subject that causes hilarity or jeering whenever it is mentioned.

standing order n 1 *finance* an instruction from an account-holder to a bank to make fixed payments from the account to a third party at regular intervals. Compare DIRECT DEBIT. 2 (**standing orders**) regulations that govern the procedures that a legislative assembly adopts.

stand-off n a stalemate or the condition of being in stalemate.

stand-offish adj unfriendly or aloof.

standpipe n a vertical pipe leading from a water supply, esp one that provides an emergency supply in the street when household water is cut off.

standpoint n a point of view.

standstill n a complete stop, with no progress being made at all.

stand-up adj 1 in a standing position. 2 of a verbal or physical fight: earnest; passionate. 3 of a comedian: performing solo in front of a live audience.

stanza n a verse in poetry.

staple[1] n a squared-off U-shaped wire fastener for holding sheets of paper together and which is forced through the paper from a special device that has several of these loaded into it. ➤ *vb* to fasten or attach with a staple or staples.

staple[2] adj 1 principal: *staple foods.* 2 of a traded article, industry, etc of a specified individual, company, region, etc: rated and established as being of prime economic importance: *Shipbuilding was once one of our staple industries.* ➤ *n* 1 an economically important food, product, export, etc. 2 a major constituent of a particular community's diet.

stapler n a device for driving staples through paper.

star n 1 a any celestial body that can be seen in a clear night sky as a twinkling white light, which consists of a sphere of gaseous material that generates heat and light energy; b used more loosely to refer to: any planet, comet or meteor, as well as any of these bodies. 2 a representation of such a body in the form of a figure with five or more radiating points, often used as a symbol of rank or excellence, etc. 3 a a celebrity, esp in the world of entertainment or sport: *a film star;* b someone or something that is distinguished or thought well of in a specified field: *Her brilliant paper made her the star of the conference.* 4 (**the stars**) a the planets regarded as an influence on people's fortunes: *He believed his fate was in the stars;* b a horoscope:

According to my stars, I'm going to win the lottery. 5 an asterisk. ➤ *vb* (**starred, starring**) 1 *tr & intr* to feature someone as a principal performer or to appear in a film, TV programme, theatre production, etc as a principal performer. 2 to decorate something with stars. 3 to asterisk. ○ **starring** adj. ♦ **see stars** to see spots of light before one's eyes.

starboard n the right side of a ship or aircraft as you look towards the front of it. ➤ *adj, adv* relating to, on or towards the right side. Compare PORT[2].

starch n 1 a *biochem* a carbohydrate that occurs in all green plants, where it serves as an energy store; b the fine white powder form of this substance that is extracted from potatoes and cereals and which is widely used in the food industry; c a preparation of this substance used to stiffen fabrics and to make paper. 2 stiffness of manner. ➤ *vb* to stiffen with starch.

starchy adj (**-ier, -iest**) 1 like or containing starch. 2 of someone's manner, etc: overformal.

star-crossed adj, *literary* ill-fated.

stardom n the state of being a celebrity.

stardust n an imaginary dust that blinds someone's eyes to reality and fills their mind with romantic illusions.

stare *vb, intr* to look with a fixed gaze. ➤ *n* 1 an act of staring. 2 a fixed gaze. ♦ **be staring sb in the face** of a solution, etc: to be readily apparent, but unnoticed. ◊ **stare sb out** or **down** to stare more fixedly at (someone staring back), causing them to look away.

starfish n the popular name for a star-shaped marine invertebrate animal.

stargaze *vb, intr* 1 to study the stars. 2 *colloq* to daydream.

stark adj 1 barren or severely bare: *a stark landscape.* 2 plain: *the stark truth.* 3 utter; downright: *an act of stark stupidity.* ➤ *adv* utterly: *stark staring bonkers.*

starkers adj, *colloq* stark-naked.

stark-naked adj without any clothes on at all.

starlet n a young film actress.

starlight n the light from the stars.

starling n a common songbird which has dark glossy speckled feathers.

starlit adj lit by the stars.

starry adj (**-ier, -iest**) 1 relating to or like a star or the stars; filled with or decorated with stars. 2 shining brightly.

starry-eyed adj naively idealistic or optimistic.

starship n in science fiction: a vehicle for interstellar travel.

star-studded adj 1 *colloq* of the cast of a film, theatre production, etc: featuring many well-known performers. 2 covered with stars.

start *vb* 1 *tr & intr* to begin; to bring or come into being. 2 *intr* (**start with sth**) to have it at the beginning: *The book starts with a gruesome murder.* 3 *tr & intr* to set or be set in motion, or put or be put into a working state: *She started the car.* **4** to establish or set up: *He started his own business.* **5** to initiate or get going; to cause or set off: *Harry started the quarrel.* **6** *intr* to begin a journey: *We started for home at midday.* **7** *intr* to flinch or shrink back suddenly and sharply. **8** *intr, colloq* to begin to behave in an annoying way, eg by picking a quarrel, raising a disagreeable subject, etc: *Come on, don't start.* ➤ *n* **1** the first or early part. **2** a beginning, origin or cause. **3** the time or place at which something starts: *We made an early start.* **4** an advantage given at the beginning of a race or contest: *a two metre start.* **5** sudden flinching or shrinking back. ♦ **for a start** as an initial consideration; in the first place. ◇ **start off** or **out 1** to be initially: *The film starts off in black and white.* **2** to begin a journey, etc. **start sth off 1** to be the cause of it: *Anger over the tax started the riots off.* **2** to begin it. **start on sb** to become suddenly and violently hostile towards them. **start up** or **start sth up 1** of a car, engine, etc: to run or get it running. **2** to establish it; to put it into action: *The mums started up their own playgroup.*

starter *n* **1** an official who gives the signal for a race to begin. **2** any of the competitors, horses, etc that assemble for the start of a race. **3** (*also* **starter motor**) an electric motor that is used to start the engine of a motor vehicle. **4** the first course of a meal. ♦ **for starters** *colloq* in the first place.

startle *vb, tr & intr* to be or cause to be slightly shocked or surprised, often with an attendant jump or twitch. ◇ **startled** *adj.* ◇ **startling** *adj.*

starve *vb* **1** *tr & intr* **a** to die or cause to die because of a lack of food; **b** to suffer or cause to suffer because of a lack of food. **2** *intr, colloq* to be very hungry. **3** to deprive someone or something of something that is vital: *They starved the project of funds.* ◇ **starvation** *n.* ◇ **starving** *adj, n.*

stash *slang, vb* to put into a hiding place. ➤ *n* a hidden supply or store of something, or its hiding place.

stat *n* (*usu* **stats**) *colloq* a statistic.

state *n* **1** the condition, eg of health, appearance, etc, that someone or something is in at a particular time. **2** a territory governed by a single political body. **3** any of a number of locally governed areas making up a nation or federation under the ultimate control of a central government, as in the US. **4** (**the States**) the United States of America. **5** (*also* **State** or **the State**) the political entity of a nation, including the government, the civil service and the armed forces. **6** *colloq* **a** an emotionally agitated condition: *He was in a right state*; **b** a confused or untidy condition: *What a state your room's in!* ➤ *vb* **1** to express clearly, either in written or spoken form. **2** to specify. ♦ **lie in state** of a dead person: to be ceremonially displayed to the public before burial.

stateless *adj* having no nationality or citizenship.

stately *adj* (**-ier, -iest**) noble, dignified and impressive in appearance or manner.

stately home *n* a large grand old house, esp one that is open to the public.

statement *n* **1** a thing stated, esp a formal written or spoken declaration: *He made a statement to the press.* **2 a** a record of finances, esp one sent by a bank to an account-holder detailing the transactions within a particular period; **b** an account that gives details of the costs of materials, services, etc and the amount that is due to be paid. **3** the act of stating.

state-of-the-art *adj* in the most advanced form: *state-of-the-art technology.*

stateroom *n* **1** a large room in a palace, etc that is used for ceremonial occasions. **2** a large private cabin on a ship.

state school *n* a school that is state-funded and where the education is free.

statesman or **stateswoman** *n* an experienced and distinguished politician. ◇ **statesmanlike** *adj.* ◇ **statesmanship** *n.*

static *adj* **1** not moving. **2** fixed; not portable. **3** relating to statics. **4** characteristic of or relating to television or radio interference. ➤ *n* **1** (*in full* **static electricity**) an accumulation of electric charges that remain at rest instead of moving to form a flow of current. **2** a sharp crackling or hissing sound that interferes with radio and television signals, and which is caused by static electricity or atmospheric disturbance.

statics *sing n* the branch of mechanics that deals with the action of balanced forces on bodies such that they remain at rest or in unaccelerated motion.

station *n* **1** a place where trains or buses regularly stop so that people can get off and on, etc. **2** a local headquarters or depot, eg of a police force, etc. **3** a building equipped for some particular purpose: *a power station* • *a petrol station.* **4 a** a radio or TV channel; **b** the building or organization that broadcasts particular radio or TV programmes. **5** a position in a specified structure, organization, etc: *He had ideas above his station.* **6** someone's profession, etc. **7** a post or place of duty. **8** *Aust & NZ* a large farm that specializes in rearing sheep or cattle. ➤ *vb* to assign or appoint to a post or place of duty.

stationary *adj* not moving; still.

stationer *n* a person or shop that sells stationery.

stationery *n* paper, envelopes, pens and other writing materials.

stationmaster *n* the official who is in charge of a railway station.

station wagon *n, N Am* an ESTATE CAR.

statistic *n* a specified piece of information or data. ◇ **statistical** *adj.* ◇ **statistically** *adv.*

statistics *pl n* (*sometimes* **stats**) items of related information that have been collected, collated, interpreted, analysed and presented to show particular trends. ➤ *sing n* the branch of mathematics concerned with drawing inferences from numerical data, based on probability theory. ○ **statistician** *n*.

statuary *n* statues collectively. ➤ *adj* belonging or referring to statues or to the sculpting of them.

statue *n* a sculpted, moulded or cast figure, esp of a person or animal, usu life-size or larger.

statuesque /statʃʊˈɛsk/ *adj* of someone's appearance: tall and well-proportioned.

statuette *n* a small statue.

stature *n* 1 the height of a person, animal, tree, etc. 2 greatness; importance. 3 the level of achievement someone has attained.

status *n* 1 rank or position in relation to others within society, an organization, etc: *social status*. 2 legal standing. 3 a high degree or level of importance: *Her huge salary reflects the status of the job*.

status quo *n* (*usu* the status quo) the existing situation at a given moment.

status symbol *n* a possession or privilege that represents prestige, wealth, high social standing, etc.

statute *n* 1 a a law made by the legislative assembly of a country and recorded in a formal document; b the formal document where such a law is recorded. 2 a permanent rule drawn up by an organization, esp one that governs its internal workings or the conduct of its members.

statute law *n* law in the form of statutes, as distinct from CASE LAW.

statutory *adj* 1 required or prescribed by law or a rule. 2 usual or regular, as if prescribed by law.

staunch[1] *adj* 1 loyal; steadfast. 2 watertight. ○ **staunchly** *adv*. ○ **staunchness** *n*.

staunch[2] *vb* to stop the flow of (something, such as blood from a wound).

stave *n* 1 any of the vertical wooden strips that are joined together to form a barrel, boat hull, etc. 2 *mus* a STAFF (*noun* sense 6). 3 a verse of a poem or song. ➤ *vb* (*staved* or *stove*) 1 (*often* **stave in**) a to smash (a hole, etc in something); b to break (a stave or the staves of a barrel or boat). 2 (in this sense *past tense* only *staved*) (*often* **stave off**) a to delay the onset of something: *He tried to stave off his downfall by calling an election*; b to ward off something: *She staved her hunger with an apple*.

stay[1] *vb*, *intr* 1 to remain in the same place or condition, without moving or changing. 2 a to reside temporarily, eg as a guest; b *Scot* to live permanently: *She's stayed in Edinburgh all her life*. ➤ *n* 1 a period of temporary residence. 2 a suspension of legal proceedings or a postponement of a legally enforceable punishment: *to grant a stay of execution*. ♦ **stay put** *colloq* to remain in the same place. **stay the course** to have the stamina for something demanding. ◊ **stay over** *colloq* to spend the night. **stay up** to remain out of bed.

stay[2] *n* 1 a prop or support. 2 (**stays**) a corset stiffened with strips of bone or metal.

stay[3] *n* a rope or cable that is used for anchoring something, eg a mast, and to keep it upright.

stay-at-home *colloq, adj* tending to prefer the peaceful routine of domestic life to a busy and varied social life. ➤ *n* a stay-at-home person.

staying power *n* stamina; endurance.

stead *n* (*usu* in sb's stead) in place of them. ♦ **stand sb in good stead** to prove useful to them.

steadfast *adj* firm; resolute. ○ **steadfastly** *adv*. ○ **steadfastness** *n*.

steady *adj* (*-ier, -iest*) 1 firmly fixed or balanced; not wobbling. 2 regular; constant: *a steady job*. 3 stable; not easily disrupted or undermined. 4 having a serious or sober character. 5 continuous: *a steady stream*. ➤ *vb* (*-ies, -ied*) *tr & intr* to make or become steady or steadier. ➤ *adv* in a steady manner: *steady as she goes*. ➤ *exclam* (*also* **steady on!** or **steady up!**) used to urge someone to be careful or restrained. ○ **steadily** *adv*. ○ **steadiness** *n*. ♦ **go steady with sb** *colloq* to have a steady romantic relationship with them. **go steady with sth** *colloq* to use it sparingly.

steak *n* 1 a fine quality beef for frying or grilling; b a thick slice of this: *fillet steak*. 2 beef that is cut into chunks and used for stewing or braising. 3 a thick slice of any meat or fish: *salmon steaks*.

steakhouse *n* a restaurant that specializes in serving steaks.

steal *vb* (*past tense* **stole**, *past participle* **stolen**) 1 *tr & intr* to take away (another person's property) without permission or legal right. 2 to obtain something by cleverness or trickery: *to steal a kiss*. 3 to present (another person's work, ideas, etc) as one's own. 4 *intr* (*often* **steal away**) to go stealthily: *He stole down to the basement*. ➤ *n*, *colloq* 1 a bargain; something that can be easily obtained: *The silk shirt was a steal at £25*. 2 *N Am* an act of stealing. ♦ **steal sb's thunder** to divert attention and praise away from someone by presenting or using the same idea, plan, etc before they have an opportunity to do so. **steal the show** to attract the most applause, attention, etc.

stealth *n* 1 softness and quietness of movement in order to avoid being noticed. 2 secretive or deceitful behaviour. ○ **stealthily** *adv*. ○ **stealthy** *adj* (*-ier, -iest*).

steam *n* 1 a the colourless gas formed by vaporizing water at 100°C; b any similar vapour. 2 *colloq* power, energy or speed: *I haven't got the steam to climb any further*. ➤ *adj* a powered by steam: *a steam generator*; b using steam: *a steam iron*. ➤ *vb* 1 *intr* to give off steam. 2 to cook, etc using steam. 3 *intr* to move under the power of steam. 4 *intr*, *colloq* to go at speed: *She steamed up the road to catch the bus*. ♦ **be** or **get steamed up** or **all steamed up** *colloq* to be very angry or excited. **full steam ahead** forward as fast as possible or with as much energy, enthusiasm, etc as possible. **get up steam** of the boiler of a steam ship, locomotive, etc: to be in the process of heating up. **let off steam** to release bottled-up energy or emotions. **run out of steam** to become depleted of energy, enthusiasm, etc. **under one's own steam** unassisted by anyone else. ◊ **steam up** of a transparent or reflective surface: to become clouded by tiny water droplets formed from condensed steam: *His glasses steamed up.*

steamboat or **steamship** *n* a vessel that is driven by steam.

steam engine *n* **1** an engine that is powered by steam from a boiler that is heated by a furnace. **2** a steam locomotive engine.

steamer *n* **1** a ship whose engines are powered by steam. **2** a two-tier pot in which food in the upper tier is cooked by the action of steam from water heated in the lower tier.

steamroller *n* a large vehicle, often steam-driven, that has huge heavy solid metal cylinders for wheels so that when it is driven over newly made roads it smooths, flattens and compacts the surface. ➤ *vb, colloq* **1** to use overpowering force or persuasion to secure the speedy movement or progress of something. **2** (*often* **steamroller sb into sth**) to make them do it, using forceful persuasion to overcome their reluctance.

steamy *adj* (**-ier, -iest**) **1** full of, clouded by, emitting, etc steam. **2** *colloq* sexy; erotic.

steatite /ˈstiːətaɪt/ *n* another name for SOAPSTONE.

steed *n* a horse, esp one that is lively and bold.

steel *n* **1** an iron alloy that contains small amounts of carbon and, in some cases, additional elements. **2** a rough-surfaced rod, made of this alloy, that knives are sharpened on by hand. **3** esp of someone, their character, determination, etc: hardness, strength, etc: *a man of steel*. ➤ *vb* (*usu* **steel oneself**) to harden oneself or prepare oneself emotionally, esp for something unpleasant or unwelcome. ○ **steely** *adj* (**-ier, -iest**).

steel band *n* a group, orig in the W Indies, who play music on oil or petrol drums which have had the tops specially beaten so that striking different areas produces different notes.

steel wool *n* thin strands of steel in a woolly mass that is used for polishing, scrubbing and scouring.

steelworks *sing or pl n* a factory where steel is manufactured. ○ **steelworker** *n*.

steelyard *n* a type of weighing machine that has one short arm, which the object to be weighed is put onto, and another longer graduated arm, which has a single weight on it that is pushed along the arm until the balance is established.

steep¹ *adj* **1** sloping sharply. **2** *colloq* of a price, rate, etc: unreasonably high. **3** *colloq* of a story or someone's version of events: hard to believe. ○ **steeply** *adv.* ○ **steepness** *n.*

steep² *vb, tr & intr* to soak something thor-

oughly in liquid. ◆ **be steeped in sth** to be deeply involved in it: *a castle steeped in history.*

steepen *vb, tr & intr* to make or become steep or steeper.

steeple *n* **1** a tower, esp one that forms part of a church. **2** the spire of such a tower.

steeplechase *n* **1** a horse race round a course with hurdles, usu in the form of man-made hedges. **2** a track running race where athletes have to jump hurdles and, usu, a water jump. ➤ *vb, intr* to take part in a steeplechase. ○ **steeplechaser** *n.* ○ **steeplechasing** *n.*

steeplejack *n* a person whose job is to construct and repair steeples and tall chimneys.

steer¹ *vb* **1** *tr & intr* to guide or control the direction of (a vehicle or vessel) using a steering wheel, rudder, etc. **2** *intr* **a** to tend towards a specified direction: *This car steers to the right*; **b** to move in a specified way: *This car steers badly.* **3** to guide or encourage (someone, a conversation, etc) to move in a specified direction: *She steered the conversation round to the subject of money.* ○ **steerable** *adj.* ○ **steering** *n.* ◆ **steer clear of sb** or **sth** *colloq* to avoid them or it.

steer² *n* a young castrated bull or male ox.

steerage *n* **1** *old use* the cheapest accommodation on board a passenger ship. **2** an act or the practice of steering.

steering committee *n* a committee that decides on the nature and order of topics to be discussed by a parliament, etc.

steering wheel *n* a wheel that is turned to direct the wheels of a vehicle or the rudder of a vessel.

stein /staɪn; *German* ʃtaɪn/ *n* a large metal or earthenware beer mug, often with a hinged lid.

stele /ˈstiːlɪ, stiːl/ *n* (**stelae** /ˈstiːliː/) an ancient stone pillar or upright slab, usu carved or engraved.

stellar *adj* **1** referring or relating to or resembling a star or stars. **2** referring or relating to the famous.

stem¹ *n* **1 a** the central part of a plant that grows upward from its root; **b** the part that connects a leaf, flower or fruit to a branch. **2** any long slender part, eg of a wine glass, etc. **3** *ling* the base form of a word that inflections are added to; for example *love* is the stem of *loved, lover, lovely, unloved*, etc and of *luvvie*, despite the distortion of the spelling. ➤ *vb* (**stemmed, stemming**) *intr* (**stem from sth** or **sb**) to originate or derive from it or them.

stem² *vb* (**stemmed, stemming**) to stop (the flow of something).

stench *n* a strong and extremely unpleasant smell.

stencil *n* **1** a card or plate that has shapes cut out of it to form a pattern, letter, etc and which is put onto a surface and ink or paint applied so that the cut-out design is transferred to the surface. **2** the design that is produced using this technique. ➤ *vb* (**stencilled, stencilling** or (*US*) **stenciled, stenciling**) **1** to mark or decorate (a surface) using a stencil. **2** to produce (a design, lettering, etc) using a stencil.

stenographer *n, US* someone who is skilled in shorthand and typing.

stentorian *adj, literary* of a voice: loud and strong.

step *n* **1** a single complete action of lifting then placing down the foot in walking or running. **2** the distance covered in the course of such an action. **3** a movement of the foot (usu one of a pattern of movements) in dancing. **4** a single action or measure that is taken in proceeding towards an end or goal: *a step in the right direction*. **5** (*often* **steps**) **a** a single (often outdoor) stair, or any stair-like support used to climb up or down; **b** a STEPLADDER; **c** a rung on a ladder. **6** the sound or mark of a foot being laid on the ground, etc in walking. **7** a degree or stage in a scale or series: *Nick moved up a step on the payscale.* **8** a way of walking: *Zoe always has a bouncy step.* ➤ *vb* (**stepped, stepping**) **1** *intr* to move by lifting up each foot alternately and setting it down in a different place. **2** *intr* to go or come on foot: *Step right this way.* **3** to perform (a dance). **4** to arrange in such a way as to avoid overlap. ◆ **in step 1** walking, marching, etc in time with others or with the music. **2** in harmony, unison, agreement, etc with another or others. **out of step 1** not walking, marching, etc in time with others or with the music. **2** not in harmony, unison, agreement, etc with another or others. **step by step** gradually. **step on it** *colloq* to hurry up. **step out of line** to behave in an inappropriate way; to disobey or offend. **watch one's step 1** to walk with careful steps in order to avoid danger, etc. **2** to proceed with caution, taking care not to anger, offend, etc others. ◊ **step down** to resign from a position of authority. **step in 1** to take up a position or role as a substitute. **2** to intervene in an argument. **step into sth** to enter into it or become involved in it, esp easily: *Jill stepped into a high-flying job.* **step out 1** to walk quickly and confidently with long strides. **2** *colloq* to go out socially. **step up** to increase the rate, intensity, etc of something.

stepbrother or **stepsister** *n* a son or daughter of someone's step-parent.

stepchild, **stepdaughter** or **stepson** *n* a child of someone's spouse or partner who is the offspring of a previous relationship.

stepfather *n* a husband or partner of a person's mother who is not that person's biological father.

stepladder *n* a short ladder with flat steps made free-standing by means of a supporting frame attached by a hinge at the ladder's top where there is usu a platform to stand on.

stepmother *n* a wife or partner of a person's father who is not that person's biological mother.

step-parent *n* a stepfather or stepmother.

steppe *n* an extensive dry grassy and usu treeless plain, esp one found in SE Europe and Asia.

stepping-stone *n* **1** a large stone that has a surface which is above the water level of a stream, etc and which can be used for crossing it. **2** something that functions as a means of progress: *She thought of the job as a stepping-stone to better things.*

stepson *see* STEPCHILD

steradian *n, geom* the SI unit that is used for measuring solid (three-dimensional) angles.

stereo *n* **1** stereophonic reproduction of sound. **2** a DVD player, cassette player, hi-fi system, etc that gives a stereophonic reproduction of sound. ➤ *adj* a shortened form of STEREOPHONIC.

stereophonic *adj* of a system for reproducing or broadcasting sound: using two or more independent sound channels leading to separate loudspeakers.

stereoscope *n* a binocular instrument that presents a slightly different view of the same object to each eye thus producing an apparently 3-D image. ○ **stereoscopic** *adj.*

stereotype *n* **a** an overgeneralized and preconceived idea of what characterizes someone or something; **b** someone or something that conforms to such an idea, etc. ➤ *vb* to attribute overgeneralized and preconceived characteristics to someone or something. ○ **stereotypical** *adj.* ○ **stereotypically** *adv.*

sterile *adj* **1** biologically incapable of producing offspring, fruit or seeds. **2** free of germs. **3** producing no results; having no new ideas. ○ **sterility** *n.*

sterilize or **-ise** *vb* **1** to make something germ-free. **2** to make someone or something infertile. ○ **sterilization** *n.* ○ **sterilizer** *n.*

sterling *n* British money. ➤ *adj* **1** good quality; worthy: *a sterling performance.* **2** of silver: conforming to the official level of purity, which is set at a minimum of 92.5 per cent. **3** authentic; genuine.

stern[1] *adj* **1** extremely strict. **2** harsh, severe or rigorous. **3** unpleasantly serious or unfriendly in appearance or nature. ○ **sternly** *adv* ○ **sternness** *n.*

stern[2] *n* the rear of a ship or boat.

sternum *n* (**sternums** or **sterna**) *anat* in humans: the broad vertical bone in the chest that the ribs and collarbone are attached to.

steroid *n* **1** *biochem* any of a large group of organic compounds that have a complex molecular structure (17-carbon-atom, four-linked ring system). **2** *med* a class of drug containing such a compound.

sterol *n, biochem* any of a group of colourless waxy solid STEROID alcohols that are found in plants, animals and fungi, eg cholesterol.

stertorous *adj, formal* of breathing: noisy.

stet *n* a conventionalized direction given in the margin of a text to indicate that something which has been changed or marked for deletion is to be retained in its original form after all. ➤ *vb* (**stetted, stetting**) to mark (text which has been changed or marked for deletion) with this direction.

stethoscope *n, med* an instrument that consists of a small concave disc that has hollow tubes attached to it and which, when it is placed on the body, carries sounds.

stevedore /'sti:vədɔ:(r)/ *n* a person whose job is to load and unload ships; a docker.

stew *vb* 1 *tr & intr* to cook (esp meat) by long simmering. 2 **a** to cause (tea) to become bitter and over-strong by letting it brew for too long; **b** *intr* of tea: to become bitter and over-strong because it has been left brewing for too long. 3 *intr, colloq* to be in a state of worry or agitation. ➤ *n* 1 a dish of food, esp a mixture of meat and vegetables, that has been cooked by stewing. 2 *colloq* a state of worry or agitation.

steward *n* 1 someone whose job is to look after the needs of passengers on a ship or aircraft. 2 someone whose duties include supervising crowd movements during sporting events, gigs, etc. 3 someone whose job is to oversee the catering arrangements, etc in a hotel or club. 4 *esp hist* someone whose job is to manage another person's property and affairs, eg on a country estate. ➤ *vb* to serve as a steward of something. ○ **stewardship** *n*.

stewardess *n* a female steward on a ship, aircraft, etc.

stewed *adj* 1 of meat, vegetables, fruit, etc: cooked by stewing. 2 of tea: bitter and over-strong because it has been brewed for too long.

stick¹ *n* 1 a twig or thin branch of a tree. 2 **a** any long thin piece of wood; **b** *in compounds* a shaped piece of wood or other material which has a designated purpose: *a hockey stick • the gear stick*. 3 a long thin piece of anything: *a stick of rock*. 4 a piece of furniture, esp when it is one of few. 5 *colloq* verbal abuse, criticism or mockery. 6 (**the sticks**) *colloq* a rural area that is considered remote or unsophisticated. 7 *colloq* a person: *a funny old stick*. ➤ *vb* to support (a plant) using a stick or sticks. ♦ **get hold of the wrong end of the stick** to misunderstand. **give sb stick** *colloq* to criticize or punish them. **up sticks** *colloq* to move away, esp without warning: *He just upped sticks and left.*

stick² *vb* (**stuck**) 1 to push or thrust (esp something long and thin or pointed). 2 to fasten by piercing with a pin or other sharp object: *Stick it up with drawing pins*. 3 *tr & intr* to fix, or be or stay fixed, with an adhesive. 4 *intr* to remain persistently: *an episode that sticks in my mind*. 5 *tr & intr* to make or be unable to move: *The car got stuck in the snow*. 6 to confine: *stuck in the house all day*. 7 *colloq* to place or put: *Just stick it on the table*. 8 *colloq* to bear or tolerate: *She couldn't stick it any longer*. 9 to cause to be at a loss: *He's never stuck for something to say*. ♦ **stick in one's throat** *colloq* to be extremely difficult to say or accept, usu for reasons of principle. **stick one's neck out (for sb or sth)** to put oneself in a dangerous or tricky position (for them or it). **stick one's nose in** or **into sth**

to interfere or pry, or to interfere with it or pry into it. **stick out a mile** or **stick out like a sore thumb** to be glaringly obvious. ◊ **stick to one's guns** to be adamant. ◊ **stick around** *colloq* to remain or linger. **stick by sb** or **sth** to remain loyal or supportive towards them or it: *She sticks by him no matter what he does*. **stick out** 1 to project or protrude. 2 to be obvious or noticeable. 3 to endure. **stick out for sth** to continue to insist on it. **stick to sth** 1 to remain faithful to it, eg a promise: *She stuck to the same story throughout the questioning*. 2 to keep to it. **stick up for sb** or **oneself** to speak or act in their or one's own defence.

sticker *n* an adhesive label or small poster, card etc.

stick insect *n* a tropical insect with a long slender body and legs that are camouflaged to look like twigs.

stick-in-the-mud *n, colloq* someone who is opposed to anything new or adventurous and is therefore seen as boring.

stickleback *n* a small spiny-backed fish found in many northern rivers.

stickler *n* (*usu* **a stickler for sth**) someone who fastidiously insists on something.

sticky *adj* (**-ier, -iest**) 1 covered with something that is tacky. 2 able or likely to stick to other surfaces. 3 of the weather: warm and humid. 4 *colloq* of a situation, etc: difficult; unpleasant. ○ **stickiness** *n*. ♦ **come to** or **meet a sticky end** *colloq* to suffer an unpleasant end or death.

sticky wicket *n, colloq* a difficult situation.

stiff *adj* 1 not easily bent or folded. 2 of limbs, joints, etc: not moving or bending easily. 3 of a punishment, etc: harsh; severe. 4 of a task, etc: difficult. 5 of a wind: blowing strongly. 6 of someone or their manner: not natural and relaxed. 7 thick in consistency. 8 *colloq* of an alcoholic drink: not diluted or only lightly diluted. 9 of a price: excessively high. ➤ *adv, colloq* to an extreme degree: *scared stiff*. ➤ *n, slang* a corpse. ○ **stiffly** *adv*. ○ **stiffness** *n*.

stiffen *vb* 1 *tr & intr* to make or become stiff or stiffer. 2 *intr* to become nervous or tense.

stiff-necked *adj* arrogantly obstinate.

stifle *vb* 1 **a** to suppress (a feeling or action): *Kerry stifled a laugh*; **b** to conceal: *He stifled the truth*. 2 *tr & intr* to experience or cause to experience difficulty in breathing, esp because of heat and lack of air. 3 to kill or nearly kill by stopping the breathing. 4 to stamp out: *Police stifled the riot*.

stifling *adj* 1 unpleasantly hot or airless. 2 overly oppressive. ○ **stiflingly** *adv*.

stigma *n* 1 shame or social disgrace. 2 *bot* in a flowering plant: the sticky surface that receives pollen and which is situated at the tip of the STYLE (*noun* sense 6).

stigmata *pl n, Christianity* marks that are said to have appeared on the bodies of certain holy people and are thought to resemble Christ's crucifixion wounds.

stigmatize or **-ise** *vb* to describe, regard, etc

someone as bad, shameful, etc.

stile n a step, or set of steps, that is incorporated into a fence or wall so that people can cross but animals cannot.

stiletto n 1 (in full **stiletto heel**) a high thin heel on a woman's shoe. 2 colloq a shoe with such a heel. 3 a dagger with a narrow tapering blade.

still[1] adj 1 motionless; inactive; silent. 2 quiet and calm. 3 of a drink: not having escaping bubbles of carbon dioxide. ➤ adv 1 continuing as before, now or at some future time: Do you still live in Edinburgh? 2 up to the present time, or the time in question: I still don't understand. 3 even then; nevertheless: Seb knows the dangers but still continues to smoke. 4 quietly and without movement: to sit still. 5 to a greater degree; even: older still. ➤ vb 1 tr & intr to make or become still, silent, etc. 2 to calm, appease or put an end to something. ➤ n 1 stillness; tranquility: the still of the countryside. 2 a photograph, esp of an actor in, or a scene from, a cinema film, used for publicity purposes. ○ **stillness** n.

still[2] n an apparatus for the distillation of alcoholic spirit.

stillbirth n 1 the birth of a dead baby or fetus. 2 a baby or fetus that is dead at birth.

stillborn adj 1 of a baby or fetus: dead when born. 2 of a project, etc: doomed from the start.

still life n 1 a painting, drawing or photograph of an object or objects. 2 this kind of art or photography.

still room n 1 a room where distilling is carried out. 2 a housekeeper's pantry in a large house.

stilt n 1 either of a pair of long poles that have supports for the feet part of the way up so that someone can walk around supported high above the ground. 2 any of a set of props on which a building, jetty, etc is supported above ground or water level.

stilted adj 1 of language: unnatural-sounding and over-formal. 2 laboured; not flowing: a stilted conversation.

stimulant n 1 any substance, such as a drug, that produces an increase in the activity of a particular body organ or function. 2 anything that causes an increase in excitement, activity, interest, etc.

stimulate vb 1 to cause physical activity, or increased activity, in (eg an organ of the body). 2 to initiate or get going. 3 to excite or arouse the senses of someone; to animate or invigorate them. 4 to create interest and enthusiasm in someone or something. ○ **stimulation** n.

stimulating adj exciting; invigorating.

stimulus /'stɪmjʊləs/ n (**stimuli** /-laɪ/) 1 something that acts as an incentive, inspiration, provocation, etc. 2 something, such as a drug, heat, light, etc, that causes a specific response in a cell, tissue, organ, etc.

sting n 1 a defensive puncturing organ that is found in certain animals and plants, which can inject poison or venom. 2 the injection of poison from an animal or plant. 3 a painful wound resulting from the sting of an animal or plant. 4 any sharp tingling pain. 5 anything that is hurtful: Bob felt the sting of her wicked words. 6 slang a trick, swindle or robbery. ➤ vb (**stung**) 1 to pierce, poison or wound with a sting. 2 intr to produce a sharp tingling pain. 3 slang to cheat, swindle or rob; to cheat by overcharging: They stung him for 50 quid.

stinging nettle n a NETTLE.

stingray n a RAY[2] with a long whip-like tail tipped with spikes that are capable of inflicting severe wounds.

stingy /'stɪndʒɪ/ adj (**-ier, -iest**) ungenerous; mean. ○ **stingily** adv. ○ **stinginess** n.

stink n 1 a strong and very unpleasant smell. 2 colloq an angry complaint or outraged reaction. ➤ vb (past tense **stank** or **stunk**, past participle **stunk**) intr 1 to give off an offensive smell. 2 colloq to be contemptibly bad or unpleasant: The idea of going with Harry stinks. ○ **stinky** adj. ◆ **kick up, raise** or **make a stink** to cause trouble, esp in public. ◊ **stink out** or **up** to fill (a room, etc) with an offensive smell.

stinker n, colloq 1 a very difficult task, question, etc. 2 someone who behaves in a dishonest, cheating or otherwise unscrupulous unpleasant way.

stinking adj 1 offensively smelly. 2 colloq very unpleasant, disgusting, etc. ➤ adv, colloq extremely; disgustingly: stinking rich.

stint vb, intr (**stint on**) to be mean or grudging in giving or supplying something: Don't stint on the chocolate sauce. ➤ n 1 an allotted amount of work or a fixed time for it: a twelve hour stint. 2 a turn: Adam did his stint yesterday.

stipend /'staɪpɛnd/ n a salary or allowance, now esp one that is paid to a member of the clergy. ○ **stipendiary** adj.

stipple vb to paint, engrave or draw something in dots or dabs. ➤ n a painting, engraving, drawing, etc that has been produced using this technique. ○ **stippled** adj.

stipulate vb in a contract, agreement, etc: to specify as a necessary condition. ○ **stipulation** n.

stir[1] vb (**stirred, stirring**) 1 to mix or agitate (a liquid or semi-liquid substance) by repeated circular strokes with a spoon or other utensil. 2 to arouse the emotions of someone. 3 tr & intr to make or cause to make a slight or single movement: She stirred in her sleep. 4 intr to get up after sleeping. 5 to rouse (oneself) to action. 6 to evoke something: The photos stirred happy memories. 7 intr, colloq to make trouble. ➤ n 1 an act of stirring a liquid, etc. 2 an excited reaction. ◊ **stir up sth** to cause or provoke (eg trouble).

stir[2] n, slang prison.

stir-crazy adj, orig N Am slang emotionally disturbed through long confinement.

stir-fry vb to cook (small pieces of meat, vegetables etc) lightly by brisk frying in a wok or large frying pan on a high heat. ➤ n a dish of food that has been cooked in this way.

stirrer *n*, *colloq* someone who enjoys making trouble or who deliberately goes about making trouble.

stirring *adj* **1** arousing strong emotions. **2** lively.

stirrup *n* **1** either of a pair of metal loops suspended from straps attached to a horse's saddle, used as footrests for the rider. **2** any strap that supports or passes under the foot: *ski-pants with stirrups.*

stirrup pump *n* a portable hand-operated pump that draws water from a bucket, etc, and which is used in fighting small fires.

stitch *n* **1** a single loop of thread or yarn in sewing or knitting. **2** a complete movement of the needle or needles to create such a loop. **3** a sharp ache in the side resulting from physical exertion. **4** *non-technical* a. SUTURE. ➢ *vb* (*sometimes* **stitch sth up**) **1** to join, close, decorate, etc with stitches. **2** to sew. **3** *non-technical* to close a cut, wound, etc with stitches. ♦ **in stitches** *colloq* helpless with laughter. **without a stitch** or **not a stitch** *colloq* without any clothing or no clothing at all. ◊ **stitch sb up** *slang* **1** to incriminate, trick, betray or double-cross them. **2** to swindle or overcharge them.

stoat *n* a small flesh-eating mammal that has a long slender body and reddish-brown fur with white underparts.

stock *n* **1** (*sometimes* **stocks**) goods or raw material that a shop, factory, warehouse, etc has on the premises at a given time. **2** a supply kept in reserve: *an impressive stock of fine wine.* **3** equipment or raw material in use. **4** liquid in which meat or vegetables have been cooked and which can then be used as a base for soup, a sauce, etc. **5** the shaped wooden or plastic part of a rifle or similar gun that the user rests against the shoulder. **6** farm animals. **7** the money raised by a company through the selling of shares. **8** the total shares issued by a particular company or held by an individual shareholder. **9** a group of shares bought or sold as a unit. **10** ancestry; descent: *of peasant stock.* **11** any of various Mediterranean plants of the wallflower family that are cultivated for their bright flowers. **12** (**the stocks**) *formerly* a wooden device that was used for securing offenders who were held by the head and wrists or by the wrists and ankles, so that they could be displayed for public ridicule as a punishment. **13** reputation. ➢ *adj* **1** being of a standard type, size, etc, constantly in demand and always kept in stock. **2** of a phrase, etc: much used. ➢ *vb* **1** to keep a supply for sale. **2** to provide with a supply: *Pete stocked the drinks cabinet with expensive brandies.* ♦ **out of** or **in stock** not currently, or currently, held for sale on the premises. **take stock of sth** to make an overall assessment of one's circumstances, etc. ◊ **stock up on sth** to acquire or accumulate a large supply of it.

stockade *n* a defensive fence or enclosure

built of upright tall heavy posts.

stockbroker *n* someone whose profession is to buy and sell stocks and shares on behalf of customers in return for a fee.

stock car *n* a car that has been specially strengthened and modified for competing in a kind of track racing where deliberate colliding is allowed.

stock exchange *n* **1 a** a market where the trading of stocks and shares by professional dealers on behalf of customers goes on; **b** a building where this type of trading is done. **2** (*usu* **the stock exchange**) the level of prices in this type of market or the amount of activity that this type of market generates.

stocking *n* either of a pair of close-fitting coverings for women's legs which are made of fine semi-transparent nylon or silk. ♦ **in stockinged feet** without shoes.

stocking stitch *n*, *knitting* a way of joining loops together that involves the alternation of plain and purl rows.

stock-in-trade *n* **1** something that is seen as fundamental to a particular trade or activity. **2** all the goods that a shopkeeper, etc has for sale.

stockist *n* a person or shop that stocks a particular item or brand.

stock market *n* the STOCK EXCHANGE.

stockpile *n* a reserve supply that has been accumulated. ➢ *vb* to accumulate a large reserve supply of something.

stockroom *n* a storeroom.

stock-still *adj*, *adv* completely motionless.

stocktaking *n* **1** the process of making a detailed inventory and valuation of all the goods, raw materials, etc that are held on the premises of a shop, factory, etc at a particular time. **2** the process of making an overall assessment eg of the present situation with regard to one's future prospects, etc.

stocky *adj* (**-ier, -iest**) of a person or animal: broad, strong-looking and usu not very tall.

stockyard *n* a large yard or enclosure that is usu sectioned off into pens, where livestock are kept temporarily.

stodge *n* food that is heavy, filling and usu fairly tasteless.

stodgy *adj* (**-ier, -iest**) **1** of food: heavy and filling but usu fairly tasteless. **2** of someone or their attitude, conversation, etc: boringly conventional or serious.

stoic /'stəʊɪk/ *n* **1** someone who can repress emotions and show patient resignation under difficult circumstances. **2** (**Stoic**) *philos* a member of the Greek school of philosophy that was founded by Zeno around 300BC.

stoical *adj* **1** accepting suffering or misfortune uncomplainingly. **2** indifferent to both pain and pleasure.

stoicism /'stəʊɪsɪzm/ *n* **1 a** brave or patient acceptance of suffering and misfortune; **b** repression of emotion. **2** (**Stoicism**) the philosophy of the Stoics, which was characterized by an emphasis on the development of self-sufficiency in the individual.

stoke *vb* **1** to put coal or other fuel on (a fire, the furnace of a boiler, etc). **2** to arouse or intensify (eg passion or enthusiasm). ○ **stoker** *n*.

stole¹ *n* a woman's scarf-like garment, worn around the shoulders.

stole² *past tense of* STEAL

stolid *adj* showing little or no interest or emotion.

stoma /'stəʊmə/ *n* (**stomata** /'stəʊmətə/) **1** *bot* one of many tiny pores that are found on the stems and leaves of vascular plants, where water loss from the plant and gaseous exchange between plant tissue and the atmosphere take place. **2** *biol* any small opening or pore in the surface of a living organism.

stomach *n* **1** in the alimentary canal of vertebrates: a large sac-like organ where food is temporarily stored until it is partially digested. **2** *loosely* the area around the abdomen. ➣ *vb* **1** *colloq* to bear or put up with: *I can't stomach his arrogance*. **2** to be able to eat, drink or digest easily: *I find red meat very hard to stomach*. ◆ **have the stomach for sth** *colloq* to have the inclination, desire, courage, etc for it: *Ben has the stomach for dangerous sports*.

stomach pump *n* an apparatus that includes a long tube which is inserted down the throat and into the stomach, used medically for sucking out the contents of the stomach, esp in cases of suspected poisoning.

stomp *vb, intr* to stamp or tread heavily.

stone *n* (**stones** or in sense 7 **stone**) **1** the hard solid material that rocks are made of. **2** a a small fragment of rock, eg a pebble; **b** anything that resembles this: *hailstone*. **3** *usu in compounds* a shaped piece of stone that has a designated purpose, eg a *paving stone* or *milestone*. **4** a gemstone. **5** the hard woody middle part of some fruits, eg peach, which contains the seed. **6** a hard mass that sometimes forms in the gall bladder, kidney, etc, which often causes pain and requires surgical removal. **7** a UK measure of weight equal to 14 pounds or 6.35 kilograms. **8** a dull light grey colour. ➣ *vb* **1** to pelt with stones as a punishment. **2** to remove the stone from (fruit). ➣ *adv, in compounds* completely: *stone-cold*. ◆ **a stone's throw** *colloq* a short distance. **leave no stone unturned** to try all the possibilities imaginable or make every possible effort.

stone-cold *adj* completely cold.

stoned *adj* **1** *slang* in a state of drug-induced euphoria. **2** of a fruit: with the stone removed.

stone-deaf *adj* unable to hear at all.

stoneground *adj* of flour: produced by grinding between millstones.

stonemason *n* someone who is skilled in shaping stone for building work. ○ **stonemasonry** *n*.

stonewall *vb* **1** *tr & intr* to hold up progress, esp in parliament, intentionally, eg by giving long irrelevant speeches, etc. **2** *intr, cricket* of a batsman: to bat extremely defensively.

stoneware *n* a type of hard coarse pottery made from clay that has a high proportion of silica, sand or flint in it.

stonewashed *adj* of new clothes or a fabric, esp denim: having a faded and worn appearance because of the abrasive action of the small pieces of pumice stone that they have been washed with.

stonework *n* **1** a structure or building part that has been made out of stone. **2** the process of working in stone.

stonking *colloq, adj* excellent. ➣ *adv* extremely: *a stonking big cup of coffee*.

stony or **stoney** *adj* (**-ier, -iest**) **1** covered with stones. **2** relating to or resembling stone or stones. **3** unfriendly; unfeeling: *a stony expression*. **4** a fixed: *a stony stare*; **b** unrelenting: *a stony silence*.

stony-broke *adj, Brit colloq* absolutely without money.

stooge *n* **1** a performer who provides a comedian with opportunities for making jokes and is often also the butt of the jokes. **2** an assistant, esp one who is exploited in some way.

stool *n* **1** a simple seat without a back. **2** faeces. **3** *US* a hunter's decoy.

stool pigeon *n* a police informer.

stoop¹ *vb, intr* **1** (*sometimes* **stoop down**) to bend the upper body forward and down. **2** to walk with head and shoulders bent forward. **3** (*often* **stoop to sth**) **a** to degrade oneself to do it: *How could you stoop to shoplifting?*; **b** to deign or condescend to do it. ➣ *n* **1** a bent posture. **2** a downward swoop. ○ **stooped** *adj* bent.

stoop² *n, N Am* an open platform, usu a wooden one, with steps leading up to it that runs along the front of a house.

stoop³ see STOUP

stop *vb* (**stopped, stopping**) **1** *tr & intr* to bring or come to rest, a standstill or an end; to cease or cause to cease moving, operating or progressing. **2** to prevent. **3** to withhold or keep something back. **4** to block, plug or close something. **5** to instruct a bank not to honour (a cheque). **6** *intr, colloq* to stay or reside temporarily: *I stopped the night with friends*. **7** *mus* to adjust the vibrating length of (a string) by pressing down with a finger. ➣ *n* **1** an act of stopping. **2** a regular stopping place, eg on a bus route. **3** the state of being stopped. **4** a device that prevents further movement: *a door stop*. **5** a temporary stay, esp when it is en route for somewhere else. **6** FULL STOP. **7 a** a set of organ pipes that have a uniform tone; **b** a knob that allows the pipes to be brought into and out of use. **8** *phonetics* any consonant sound that is made by the sudden release of air that has built up behind the lips, teeth, tongue, etc. ◆ **pull out all the stops** to try one's best. **put a stop to sth** to cause it to end, esp abruptly. **stop at nothing** to be prepared to do anything, no matter how unscrupulous, in order to achieve an aim, outcome, etc. ◊ **stop off, in** or **by** to visit, esp on the way to somewhere else. **stop over** to make a break in a journey.

stopcock *n* a valve that controls the flow of liquid, gas, steam, etc in a pipe.

stopgap *n* a temporary substitute.

stop-off or **stop-over** *n* a brief or temporary stop during a longer journey.

stoppage *n* **1** an act of stopping or the state of being stopped. **2** an amount deducted from wages. **3** an organized withdrawal of labour.

stopper *n* a cork, plug or bung.

stop press *n* late news that can be placed in a specially reserved space of a newspaper even after printing has begun.

stopwatch *n* a watch that is used for accurately recording the elapsed time in races, etc.

storage *n* **1** the act of storing or the state of being stored. **2** space reserved for storing things. **3** *comput* the act or process of storing information in a computer's memory.

storage device *n, comput* any piece of equipment, such as a magnetic disk, that data can be stored on.

storage heater *n* a device that encloses a stack of bricks which accumulate and store heat (usu generated from overnight off-peak electricity) which is then slowly released by convection during the daytime.

store *n* **1** a supply, usu one that is kept in reserve for use in the future. **2 a** *Brit* a shop, esp a large one that is part of a chain: *department store*; **b** *N Am* a small grocery, often also selling a wide variety of other goods. **3** (*also* **stores**) a place where stocks or supplies are kept. **4** a computer's MEMORY. ➢ *vb* **1** (*also* **store away** or **store up**) to put aside for future use. **2** to put something, eg furniture, into a warehouse for temporary safekeeping. **3** to put something into a computer's memory. ♦ **in store 1** kept in reserve; ready to be supplied. **2** destined to happen: *a surprise in store*. **set** or **lay store** or **great store by sth** to value it highly.

store card *n* a credit card that is issued by a department store for exclusive use in that store or any of its branches.

storehouse *n* a place where things are stored.

storeroom *n* a room that is used for keeping things in.

storey or (*N Am*) **story** *n* (**storeys** or **stories**) a level, floor or tier of a building.

stork *n* a large wading bird that has long legs, a long bill and neck, and usu black and white plumage.

storm *n* **1** an outbreak of violent weather, with severe winds and heavy falls of rain, hail or snow, often accompanied by thunder and lightning. **2** a violent reaction, outburst or show of feeling: *a storm of protest*. **3** a furious burst, eg of gunfire or applause. ➢ *vb* **1** *intr* **a** to go or come loudly and angrily: *Sarah stormed out of the meeting*; **b** to come or go forcefully: *Rooney stormed through the defence to score*. **2** to say or shout something angrily. **3** *mil* to make a sudden violent attack on something: *Police*

stormed the embassy. ○ **storming** *n, adj.* ♦ **a storm in a teacup** *colloq* a big fuss about something unimportant. **take sb** or **sth by storm 1** to enthral or captivate them or it totally and instantly. **2** *mil* to capture them or it by storming.

stormtrooper *n, hist* a member of a paramilitary wing of the Nazi Party.

stormy *adj* (**-ier, -iest**) **1** affected by storms or high winds. **2** of a person or their temperament, etc or of circumstances, etc: characterized by violence, passion, etc: *a stormy relationship.*

story[1] *n* (**-ies**) **1** a written or spoken description of an event or series of events which can be real or imaginary. **2** the plot of a novel, play, film, etc. **3** an incident, event, etc that has the potential to be interesting, amusing, etc. **4** a news article. **5** *colloq* a lie. ♦ **cut a long story short** to omit the finer details when telling something.

story[2] see STOREY

storybook *n* a book that contains a tale or a collection of tales for children.

storyline *n* the plot of a novel, play or film.

story-teller *n* **1** someone who tells stories. **2** *colloq* a liar.

stoup or **stoop** /stuːp/ *n* a basin for holy water.

stout *adj* **1** of someone: fattish. **2** hard-wearing; robust. **3** courageous; steadfastly reliable. ➢ *n* dark beer that has a strong malt flavour. ○ **stoutly** *adv.* ○ **stoutness** *n.*

stout-hearted *adj* courageous; steadfastly reliable.

stove[1] *n* **1** a domestic cooker. **2** any cooking or heating apparatus.

stove[2] see STAVE

stovepipe *n* **1** a metal funnel that takes smoke away from a stove. **2** (*in full* **stovepipe hat**) a tall cylindrical silk dress hat worn by men.

stow *vb* (*often* **stow sth away**) to pack or store it, esp out of sight. ◊ **stow away** to hide on a ship, aircraft or vehicle in the hope of travelling free.

stowage *n* **1** a place, charge, space, etc for stowing things. **2** the act or an instance of stowing.

stowaway *n* someone who hides on a ship, aeroplane, etc in the hope of being able to get to the destination undetected and so avoid paying the fare.

strabismus *n, med* the technical term for a SQUINT of the eye, which is caused by a muscular defect that prevents parallel vision.

straddle *vb* **1** to have one leg or part on either side of something or someone: *He straddled the horse.* **2** *colloq* **a** to adopt a neutral or non-committal attitude towards something; **b** to seem to be in favour of or see the advantage of both sides of something at once.

strafe *vb* to attack someone or something with heavy machine-gun fire from a low-flying aircraft.

straggle *vb, intr* **1** to grow or spread untidily. **2** to lag behind or stray from the main group or path, etc. ○ **straggler** n. ○ **straggly** adj.

straight adj **1** not curved, bent, curly or wavy, etc: *straight hair.* **2** without deviations or detours: *a straight road.* **3** level; not sloping, leaning or twisted: *Is the picture straight?* **4** frank; direct: *a straight answer.* **5** respectable; not dishonest or criminal: *a straight deal.* **6** neat; tidy; in good order. **7** successive; in a row: *I won three straight games.* **8** of a drink, esp alcoholic: undiluted. **9** having all debts and favours paid back. **10** not comic. **11** *colloq* conventional in tastes and opinions. **12** *colloq* heterosexual. ➤ *adv* **1** in or into a level, upright, etc position or posture: *Is the picture hung straight?* **2** following an undeviating course; directly: *He went straight home.* **3** immediately: *I'll come round straight after work.* **4** honestly; frankly: *I told him straight that it was over.* **5** seriously: *He played the part straight.* ➤ *n* **1** a straight line or part, eg of a race track. **2** *colloq* a heterosexual person. ○ **straightness** n. ◆ **go straight** *colloq* to stop taking part in criminal activities and live an honest life. **straight away** immediately. **straight off** without thinking, researching, etc: *I couldn't say straight off.* **straight out** without any equivocation: *I asked her straight out if she was seeing someone else.* **straight up** *colloq* honestly; really. **the straight and narrow** the honest, respectable, etc way of life or behaving.

> **straight** A word sometimes confused with this one is **strait**.

straighten vb **1** tr & intr to make or become straight. **2** (*sometimes* **straighten out sth**) to resolve, disentangle, make something less complicated or put it into order. **3** intr (*often* **straighten up**) to stand upright, esp after bending down.

straight face n an unsmiling expression which is usu hiding the desire to laugh.

straightforward adj **1** without difficulties or complications. **2** honest and frank.

straight¹ man n a comedian's stooge.

strain¹ vb **1** tr to injure or weaken (oneself or a part of one's body) through overexertion. **2** intr to make violent efforts. **3** to make extreme use of or demands on something. **4** to pass something through or pour something into a sieve or colander. **5** (*often* **strain sth off**) to remove it by the use of a sieve or colander. **6** to stretch or draw something tight. **7** (*usu* **strain at sth**) to tug it forcefully. **8** intr to feel or show reluctance or disgust. ➤ n **1** an injury caused by overexertion. **2** an act of forceful mental or physical perseverance or effort: *Talking to her is such a strain.* **3** the fatigue resulting from such an effort. **4** mental tension. **5** *physics* a measure of how much an object is deformed when it is subjected to stress, which is equal to the change in dimension divided by the original dimension. **6** (*also* **strains**) a melody or tune, or a snatch of one: *the strains of distant pipes.* **7** one's tone in speech or writing. ○ **strained** adj.

strain² n **1** a group of animals (esp farm livestock) or plants (esp crops) that is maintained by inbreeding, etc so that particular characteristics can be retained. **2** an inherited trait or tendency: *a strain of madness in the family.*

strainer n a small sieve or colander.

strait n **1** (*often* **straits**) a narrow strip of water that links two larger areas of ocean or sea. **2** (**straits**) difficulty: *dire straits.*

> **strait** A word sometimes confused with this one is **straight**.

straiten vb **1** to distress, esp financially. **2** to restrict.

straitjacket n **1** a jacket which has very long sleeves that can be crossed over the chest and tied behind the back and which is used for restraining someone who has violent tendencies. **2** anything that prevents freedom of development or expression.

strait-laced adj of someone or their attitude, opinions, etc: strictly correct in moral behaviour and attitudes.

strand¹ vb **1** to run (a ship) aground. **2** to leave someone in a helpless position, eg without transport. ➤ n, *literary* a shore or beach.

strand² n **1** a single thread, fibre, length of hair, etc, either alone or twisted or plaited with others to form a rope, cord or braid. **2** a single element or part.

stranded adj **1** left without any money, means of transport, etc. **2** driven ashore, etc.

strange adj **1** not known or experienced before. **2** unfamiliar or alien. **3** not usual, ordinary or predictable. **4** difficult to explain or understand. ○ **strangely** adv. ○ **strangeness** n.

stranger n **1** someone that one does not know. **2** someone who comes from a different place, family, etc. ◆ **a stranger to sth** someone who is unfamiliar with or inexperienced in something: *He's no stranger to trouble.*

strangle vb **1** to kill or attempt to kill by squeezing the throat with the hands, a cord, etc. **2** to hold back or suppress (eg a scream or laughter). **3** to hinder or stop the development or expression of something: *The job strangled her creativity.* ○ **strangler** n.

stranglehold n **1** a choking hold in wrestling. **2** a position of total control; a severely repressive influence.

strangulate vb **1** *med* to press or squeeze so as to stop the flow of blood or air. **2** to STRANGLE. ○ **strangulation** n.

strap n **1** a narrow strip of leather or fabric which can be used for hanging something from, carrying or fastening something, etc. **2** (*also* **shoulder strap**) either of a pair of strips of fabric by which a garment hangs from the shoulders. **3 a** a leather belt that is used for giving a beating as punishment; **b** (**the strap**) a beating of this kind. **4** a loop that hangs down on a bus or train to provide a hand-hold for a standing passenger. ➤ vb (**strapped, strapping**) **1** (*also* **strap up**) to fasten or bind something with a strap or straps. **2** to beat someone with a strap. ○ **strapless** adj.

straphanger n, colloq **1** a standing passenger on a bus, train, etc who holds onto a strap. **2** a commuter who uses public transport.

strapped adj, colloq short of money. ♦ **strapped for sth** in dire need of it, esp money, staff, etc.

strapping adj tall and strong-looking.

stratagem n a trick or plan, esp one for deceiving an enemy.

strategic /strə'ti:dʒɪk/ adj **1** characteristic of or relating to strategy or a strategy. **2** of weapons: designed for a direct long-range attack on an enemy's homeland, rather than for close-range battlefield use. ○ **strategically** adv.

strategy n (-ies) **1** the process of, or skill in, planning and conducting a military campaign. **2** a long-term plan for future success or development. ○ **strategist** n.

strath n, Scot a broad flat valley with a river running through it.

strathspey n **1** a Scottish folk dance that has a similar format to the reel but with slower, more gliding steps. **2** a piece of music for this kind of dance.

stratify vb (-ies, -ied) **1** geol to deposit (rock) in layers or strata. **2** to classify or arrange things into different grades, levels or social classes. ○ **stratification** n. ○ **stratified** adj.

stratocumulus /stratoʊ'kju:mjʊləs/ n (**stratocumuli** /-laɪ/) meteorol a cloud that occurs as a large globular or rolled mass.

stratosphere n, meteorol the layer of the Earth's atmosphere that extends from about 12km to about 50km above the Earth's surface and contains the ozone layer. ○ **stratospheric** adj.

stratum /'strɑːtəm/ n (**strata** /-tə/) **1** a layer of sedimentary rock. **2** a layer of cells in living tissue. **3** a layer of the atmosphere or the ocean. **4** a level, grade or social class.

stratus /'streɪtəs/ n (**strati** /-taɪ/) meteorol a wide horizontal sheet of low grey layered cloud.

straw n **1** the parts of cereal crops that remain after threshing. **2** a single stalk of dried grass or cereal crop. **3** a thin hollow tube for sucking up a drink. **4** a pale yellow colour. ♦ **clutch** or **grasp at straws** to resort to an alternative option, remedy, etc in desperation, even though it is unlikely to succeed. **draw, get, pick,** etc **the short straw** to be the person chosen from a group to carry out an unpleasant task, duty, etc.

strawberry n (-ies) **1** a juicy red fruit which has tiny pips embedded in the surface. **2** the flavour or colour of this fruit.

strawberry blonde adj mainly of human hair: reddish-blonde. ➣ n a woman who has hair of this colour.

strawberry mark n a reddish birthmark.

straw poll or **straw vote** n an unofficial vote taken among a small number of people to get

some idea of general opinion on a specified issue.

stray vb, intr **1** to wander away from the right path or place, usu unintentionally. **2** to move away unintentionally from the main or current topic: He usually strays a bit from the subject during a lecture. **3** to depart from the accepted or required pattern of behaviour, living, etc. ➣ n an ownerless or lost pet, farm animal, etc. ➣ adj **1** of a pet, etc: ownerless; lost. **2** not the result of a regular or intended process: stray gunfire.

streak n **1** a long irregular stripe or band. **2** a flash of lightning. **3** an element or characteristic: a cowardly streak. **4** a short period: a streak of bad luck. **5** colloq a naked dash through a public place. ➣ vb **1** to mark with a streak or streaks. **2** intr to move at great speed. **3** intr, colloq to make a naked dash through a public place. ○ **streaked** adj.

streaker n, colloq someone who makes a naked dash in public.

streaky adj (-ier, -iest) **1** marked with streaks. **2** of bacon: with alternate layers of fat and meat.

stream n **1** a very narrow river. **2** any constant flow of liquid: streams of tears. **3** anything that moves continuously in a line or mass: a stream of traffic. **4** an uninterrupted and unrelenting burst or succession: a stream of questions. **5** general direction, trend or tendency. **6** Brit, educ any of several groups that pupils in some schools are allocated to, so that those of a broadly similar ability can be taught together. ➣ vb **1** intr to flow or move continuously and in large quantities or numbers. **2** intr to float or trail in the wind. **3** Brit to divide (pupils) into streams.

streamer n **1** a long paper ribbon used to decorate a room. **2** a roll of coloured paper that uncoils when thrown. **3** a long thin flag.

streamlined adj **1** of a vehicle, aircraft or vessel: shaped so as to move smoothly and efficiently with minimum resistance to air or water. **2** of an organization, process, etc: extremely efficient, with little or no waste of resources, etc.

street n **1** (also in addresses **Street**) a public road with pavements and buildings at the side or sides, esp one in a town. **2** the road and the buildings together. **3** the area between the opposite pavements that is used by traffic. **4** the people in the buildings or on the pavements: Don't tell the whole street. ➣ adj relating to, happening on, etc a street or streets: a street map. ♦ **streets ahead of sb** or **sth** colloq much more advanced than or superior to them. **up** or **right up sb's street** colloq ideally suited to them.

streetcar n, N Am a tram.

street cred n, colloq (in full **street credibility**) approval of those in tune with modern urban culture.

streetlamp or **streetlight** n a light at the top of a lamppost that lights up the road for motorists and pedestrians at night.

street value *n* the price something, such as illegal drugs, etc, is likely to be sold for to the person who will use it.

streetwalker *n, colloq* a prostitute who solicits on the streets.

streetwise *adj, colloq* experienced in and well able to survive the ruthlessness of modern urban life, esp in areas such as drugs, crime, etc.

strength *n* 1 the quality or degree of being physically or mentally strong. 2 the ability to withstand pressure or force. 3 degree or intensity, eg of emotion or light. 4 potency, eg of a drug or alcoholic drink. 5 forcefulness of an argument. 6 a highly valued quality or asset. 7 the number of people, etc needed or normally expected in a group, esp in comparison to those actually present or available: *It cannot be done with the workforce only at half strength.* ♦ **go from strength to strength** to achieve a series of successes, each surpassing the last. **on the strength of sth** on the basis of it; judging by it.

strengthen *vb, tr & intr* to make or become strong or stronger.

strenuous *adj* 1 characterized by the need for or the use of great effort or energy. 2 performed with great effort or energy and therefore very tiring. ○ **strenuously** *adv.*

streptococcus /streptoʊˈkɒkəs/ *n* (*streptococci* /-ˈkɒksaɪ/) any of several species of bacterium that cause conditions such as scarlet fever and throat infections. ○ **streptococcal** or **streptococcic** *adj.*

streptomycin *n* an antibiotic used to treat various bacterial infections.

stress *n* 1 physical or mental overexertion. 2 importance, emphasis or weight laid on or attached to something: *The stress was on speed not quality.* 3 the comparatively greater amount of force that is used in the pronunciation of a particular syllable: *The stress is on the first syllable.* 4 *physics* the force that is exerted per unit area on a body causing it to change its dimensions. ➤ *vb* 1 to emphasize or attach importance to something. 2 to pronounce (a sound, word, etc) with emphasis. ○ **stressed** *adj.* ○ **stressful** *adj.* ○ **stressless** *adj.* ◊ **stress sb out** to put them under severe mental, emotional, etc pressure.

stressed-out *adj* debilitated or afflicted by emotional, nervous or mental tension.

stretch *vb* 1 *tr & intr* to make or become temporarily or permanently longer or wider by pulling or drawing out. 2 *intr* to extend in space or time. 3 *tr & intr* to straighten and extend the body or part of the body. 4 *tr & intr* to make or become tight or taut. 5 *intr* to lie at full length. 6 *intr* to be extendable without breaking. 7 *tr & intr* to last or make something last longer through economical use. 8 (*also* **stretch out**) to prolong or last. 9 to make extreme demands on or severely test (eg resources or physical abilities): *The course stretched even the brightest students.* 10 to exaggerate (the truth, a story,

etc). ➤ *n* 1 an act of stretching, esp (a part of) the body. 2 a period of time. 3 an expanse, eg of land or water. 4 capacity to extend or expand. 5 *horse-racing* a straight part on a racetrack or course. 6 *colloq* a difficult task or test: *It'll be a bit of a stretch to get there by six.* 7 *slang* a term of imprisonment. ♦ **at a stretch** 1 continuously; without interruption. 2 with difficulty. **stretch a point** 1 to agree to something not strictly in keeping with the rules. 2 to exaggerate. **stretch one's legs** to take a short walk to invigorate oneself after inactivity.

stretcher *n* 1 a device that is used for carrying a sick or wounded person in a lying position. 2 *building* a brick, block or stone that is laid so that the longer side shows on the wall face. Compare HEADER (sense 3). ➤ *vb* to carry someone on a stretcher.

stretcher-bearer *n* someone who carries a stretcher.

stretch limo *n* an elongated and very luxurious car.

stretchy *adj* (*-ier, -iest*) of materials, clothes, etc: characterized by having the ability or tendency to stretch.

strew *vb* (*past participle* **strewed** or **strewn**) 1 to scatter untidily: *Papers were strewn across the floor.* 2 to cover with an untidy scattering: *The floor was strewn with papers.*

stria /ˈstraɪə/ *n* (*striae* /ˈstraɪiː/) *geol, biol* any of a series of parallel grooves in rock, or furrows or streaks of colour in plants and animals. ○ **striated** *adj.* ○ **striation** *n.*

stricken *adj, often in compounds* 1 deeply affected, esp by grief, panic, etc: *horror-stricken.* 2 afflicted by or suffering from disease, sickness, injury, etc: *a typhoid-stricken community.*

strict *adj* 1 demanding obedience or close observance of rules. 2 observing rules or practices very closely: *strict Catholics.* 3 exact: *in the strict sense of the word.* 4 meant or designated to be closely obeyed: *strict instructions.* 5 complete: *in the strictest confidence.* ○ **strictly** *adv.* ○ **strictness** *n.*

stricture *n* a severe criticism.

stride *n* 1 a single long step in walking. 2 the length of such a step. 3 a way of walking in long steps. 4 (*usu* **strides**) a measure of progress or development: *to make great strides.* 5 a rhythm, eg in working, that someone or something aims for or settles into: *Jack soon got into his stride.* 6 (**strides**) *chiefly Aust slang* trousers. ➤ *vb* (*past tense* **strode**, *past participle* **stridden**) *intr* 1 to walk with long steps. 2 to take a long step. ♦ **take sth in one's stride** to achieve it or cope with it effortlessly.

strident *adj* 1 of a sound, esp a voice: loud and harsh. 2 loudly assertive: *a strident clamour for reforms.* ○ **stridency** *n.*

strife *n* 1 bitter conflict or fighting. 2 *colloq* trouble of any sort.

strike *vb* (**struck**) 1 to hit someone or something. 2 to come or bring into heavy contact with someone or something: *The car struck the* *lamppost.* **3** to make a particular impression on someone: *They struck me as a strange couple.* **4** to come into one's mind; to occur to someone: *It struck me as strange.* **5** to cause (a match) to ignite through friction. **6** *tr & intr* of a clock: to indicate the time with chimes, etc. **7** *intr* to happen suddenly: *Disaster struck.* **8** *intr* to make a sudden attack. **9** to afflict someone suddenly; to cause to become by affliction: *The news struck him dumb.* **10** to introduce or inject suddenly: *The thought struck terror into them.* **11** to arrive at or settle (eg a bargain or a balance): *We struck a fair deal for the car.* **12** to find a source of (eg oil, gold, etc). **13** *intr* to stop working as part of a collective protest against an employer, working conditions, etc: *The factory has been striking for two weeks.* **14** to dismantle (a camp). **15** to make (a coin) by stamping metal. **16** to adopt (a posture or attitude). **17** *tr & intr* to draw (a line) in order to cross something out. ➤ *n* **1** an act of hitting or dealing a blow. **2** a situation where a labour force refuses to work in order to protest against an employer, working conditions, etc in the hope that, by doing this, their demands will be met. **3** a prolonged refusal to engage in a regular activity in order to make some kind of a protest: *a hunger strike.* **4** a military attack, esp one that is carried out by aircraft: *a pre-emptive strike on the ground troops.* **5** a discovery of a source, eg of gold, oil, etc. **6** *cricket* the position of being the batsman bowled at: *to take strike.* **7** *baseball* a ball that the batter has taken a swing at but missed. ◆ **on strike** taking part in an industrial or other strike. **strike it lucky** or **rich** to enjoy luck or become rich suddenly and unexpectedly. ◊ **strike back** to retaliate. **strike sb off 1** to remove (the name of a member of a professional body, eg a lawyer or doctor) from the appropriate register, esp because of misconduct. **2** to remove (someone's name from an official list, register, etc). **strike out** *baseball* of a batter: to be dismissed by means of three strikes (see STRIKE *noun* sense 7). **strike sb out** *baseball* to dismiss (a batter) by means of three strikes. **strike sth out** to draw a line through (eg a name) in order to show a cancellation, deletion, etc. **strike out for sth** to head towards it, esp in a determined way. **strike up** of a band, etc: to begin to play. **strike sth up** to start (a conversation, friendship, etc).

strike-breaker *n* someone who continues to work while others STRIKE (*verb* sense 13), or who is brought in to do the job of a striking worker.

striker *n* **1** someone who takes part in a strike. **2** *football* a player who has an attacking role.

striking *adj* **1** impressive; attractive, esp in an unconventional way. **2** noticeable; marked: *a striking omission.* **3** on strike. ◆ **be** or **come within striking distance** to be close, possible, achievable, etc.

string *n* **1** thin cord, or a piece of this. **2** any of a set of pieces of stretched wire, catgut or other material that can vibrate to produce sound in various musical instruments such as the guitar, violin, piano, etc. **3** (**strings**) **a** the orchestral instruments in which sound is produced in this way, usu the violins, violas, cellos and double basses collectively; **b** the players of these instruments. **4** a group of similar things: *a string of racehorses.* **5** a series or succession: *a string of disasters.* **6** *comput* a group of characters that a computer can handle as a single unit. **7** one of several pieces of taut gut, etc that are used in sports rackets. **8** a set of things that are threaded together, eg beads. **9** any cord-like thing. ➤ *vb* (**strung**) **1** to fit or provide with a string or strings. **2** (*often* **string sth up**) to hang, stretch or tie it with string. **3** to thread (eg beads) onto a string. **4** to extend something in a string: *She strung the onions.* ◆ **no strings attached** of eg an offer: having no undesirable conditions or limitations. **pull strings** *colloq* to use one's influence, or relationships with influential people, to get something done. ◊ **string sb along** to keep them in a state of deception or false hope. **string sb up** *colloq* to kill them by hanging.

stringed *adj* of a musical instrument: having strings.

stringent / ˈstrɪndʒənt / *adj* **1** of rules, terms, etc: severe; strictly enforced. **2** marked by a lack of money. ○ **stringency** *n.* ○ **stringently** *adv.*

stringer *n* **1** a horizontal beam in a framework. **2** a journalist employed part-time to cover a particular town or area.

string quartet *n* a musical ensemble that is made up of two violins, a cello and a viola.

stringy *adj* (*-ier, -iest*) **1** like string, esp thin and thread-like. **2** of meat or other food: full of chewy fibres.

strip[1] *vb* (**stripped, stripping**) **1** to remove (a covering, etc) from something: *Strip the beds.* **2** (*sometimes* **strip sth off**) to remove (the surface or contents of something): *He stripped the varnish* ◆ *We stripped off the wallpaper.* **3 a** to remove (the clothing) from someone: *They stripped him, then flogged him;* **b** *intr* (*also* **strip off**) *colloq* to take one's clothes off. **4** (*also* **strip sth down**) to take it to pieces: *Joe stripped the engine.* **5** (*usu* **strip sb of sth**) to take it away from them: *They stripped her of her dignity.* ➤ *n* **1** an act of undressing. **2** a striptease performance. ○ **stripped** *adj.* ○ **stripping** *n.*

strip[2] *n* **1** a long narrow, usu flat, piece of material, paper, land, etc. **2** *sport* lightweight distinctive clothing that is worn by a team. ◆ **tear strips off sb** to reprimand them severely and often angrily.

strip cartoon *n* a sequence of drawings, eg in a newspaper or magazine, that tell a story.

stripe *n* **1** a band of colour. **2** a chevron or coloured band on a uniform that indicates rank. ➤ *vb* to mark with stripes.

strip lighting *n* lighting given off by tube-shaped FLUORESCENT LIGHTS.

stripling *n, literary* a boy or youth.

stripper n 1 colloq a striptease performer. 2 a substance or appliance for removing paint, varnish, etc.

striptease n a type of titillating show where a performer gradually takes their clothes off while moving in an erotic way to music.

stripy adj (-ier, -iest) marked with stripes.

strive vb, intr (past tense **strove**, past participle **striven**) 1 to try extremely hard: We will strive to be the best in Wales. 2 (**strive against sth**) to fight against it: He strove against his addiction.

stroboscope n an instrument with a flashing light which, when the speed of the light is equal to that of a rotating object, makes the object appear to be stationary. Often shortened to **strobe**.

stroganoff n, cookery a dish that is traditionally made with strips of fillet steak, onions and mushrooms, cooked in a creamy white wine sauce.

stroke n 1 a any act or way of striking; b a blow. 2 sport a an act of striking a ball: He took six strokes at the par four; b the way a ball is struck: a well-timed ground stroke. 3 a single movement with a pen, paintbrush, etc, or the mark produced. 4 a a single complete movement in a repeated series, as in swimming or rowing; b usu in compounds a particular named style of swimming: backstroke. 5 the total linear distance travelled by a piston in the cylinder of an engine. 6 a the action of a clock, etc striking, or the sound of this; b the time indicated or which would be indicated by a clock striking: out the door on the stroke of five. 7 a gentle caress or other touching movement. 8 a sloping line used to separate alternatives in writing or print. 9 pathol a sudden interruption to the supply of blood to the brain that results in loss of consciousness, often with accompanying paralysis and loss of speech, caused by bleeding from or rupture of an artery. 10 colloq the least amount of work: Dave hasn't done a stroke all day. ➤ vb 1 to caress in kindness or affection, often repeatedly. 2 to strike (a ball) smoothly and with seeming effortlessness. ♦ **a stroke of sth** a significant or impressive instance of it, esp of genius or luck. **at a stroke** with a single action.

stroll vb, intr to walk in a slow leisurely way. ➤ n a leisurely walk.

stroller n a pushchair.

strong adj 1 exerting or capable of great force or power. 2 able to withstand rough treatment. 3 of views, etc: firmly held or boldly expressed. 4 of taste, light, etc: sharply felt or experienced. 5 of coffee, alcoholic drink, etc: relatively undiluted with water or other liquid. 6 of an argument, etc: having much force. 7 of language: bold or straightforward; rude or offensive. 8 of prices, values, etc: steady or rising: a strong dollar. 9 of a group: made up of about the specified number: a gang fifty strong. 10 of a colour: deep and intense. 11 of a wind: blowing hard. 12 impressive: a strong candidate for the

job. 13 characterized by ability, stamina, good technique, etc: a strong swimmer. 14 of an urge, desire, feeling, etc: intense; powerful: a strong feeling of distrust. ○ **strongly** adv. ♦ **come on strong** colloq to be highly persuasive or assertive, often in a way that others might find disconcerting. **going strong** colloq flourishing; thriving: He's still going strong at 95.

strongarm adj, colloq 1 aggressively forceful. 2 making use of physical violence or threats.

strongbox n a safe, or some other sturdy lockable box for storing money or valuables in.

stronghold n 1 a fortified place of defence, eg a castle. 2 a place where there is strong support (eg for a political party): a Labour stronghold.

strong-minded adj resolutely determined.

strong point n something that someone is especially good at: Maths was never my strong point.

strongroom n a room where valuables, prisoners, etc can be held for safekeeping.

strontium n, chem a soft silvery-white highly reactive metallic element that is a good conductor of electricity.

strop¹ n a strip of coarse leather used for sharpening razors. ➤ vb (**stropped, stropping**) to sharpen (a razor) on a strop.

strop² n a bad temper, when the person concerned is awkward to deal with: She went off in a strop.

stroppy adj (-ier, -iest) colloq quarrelsome, bad-tempered and awkward to deal with. ○ **stroppily** adv.

structural adj belonging or relating to structure or a basic structure or framework. ○ **structurally** adv.

structuralism n an approach to various areas of study, eg literary criticism and linguistics, which seeks to identify underlying patterns or structures. ○ **structuralist** n, adj.

structure n 1 the way in which the parts of a thing are arranged or organized. 2 a thing built or constructed from many smaller parts. 3 a building. ➤ vb to put into an organized form or arrangement.

strudel /ˈstruːdəl, German ˈʃtruːdəl/ n a baked roll of thin pastry with a filling of fruit, esp apple.

struggle vb, intr 1 to strive vigorously under difficult conditions. 2 to make one's way with great difficulty. 3 to fight or contend. 4 to move the body around violently, eg in an attempt to get free. ➤ n 1 an act of struggling. 2 a task requiring strenuous effort. 3 a fight or contest.

strum vb (**strummed, strumming**) tr & intr to play (a stringed musical instrument, such as a guitar, or a tune on it) with sweeps of the fingers or thumb rather than with precise plucking. ➤ n an act or bout of strumming.

strumpet n, old use a prostitute or a woman who engages in casual sex.

strung vb, past tense, past participle of STRING. ➤ adj 1 of a musical instrument: fitted with strings. 2 in compounds of a person or animal: characterized by a specified type of temperament: *highly-strung*.

strung-up *adj, colloq* tense; nervous.

strut *vb* (**strutted, strutting**) *intr* to walk in a proud way. ➢ *n* **1** a strutting way of walking. **2** a bar or rod whose function is to support weight or take pressure. ♦ **strut one's stuff** *colloq* **1** to dance in a sexually provocative way. **2** to flaunt a talent, attribute, etc.

strychnine /ˈstrɪkniːn/ *n* a deadly poison that can be used medicinally in small quantities as a stimulant.

stub *n* **1** a short piece of something that remains when the rest of it has been used up, eg a cigarette, a pencil, etc. **2** the part of a cheque, ticket, etc that the holder retains as a record, etc. ➢ *vb* (**stubbed, stubbing**) **1** to accidentally bump the end of (one's toe) against a hard surface. **2** (*usu* **stub out**) to extinguish (eg a cigarette) by pressing the end against a surface.

stubble *n* **1** the mass of short stalks left in the ground after a crop has been harvested. **2** a short early growth of beard.

stubborn *adj* **1** resolutely or unreasonably unwilling to change one's opinions, ways, plans, etc. **2** determined; unyielding. **3** difficult to treat, remove, deal with, etc: *stubborn stains*. ○ **stubbornly** *adv*. ○ **stubbornness** *n*.

stubby *adj* (**-ier, -iest**) **1** short and broad. **2** small and worn down: *a stubby pencil*. ➢ *n* (**-ies**) *Aust colloq* a small squat bottle of beer or the beer contained in such a bottle. ○ **stubbiness** *n*.

stucco *n* (**stuccos** or **stuccoes**) **1** a fine plaster that is used for coating indoor walls and ceilings and for forming decorative cornices, mouldings, etc. **2** a rougher kind of plaster or cement used for coating outside walls. ➢ *vb* (**stuccos** or **stuccoes, stuccoed**) to coat with or mould out of stucco. ○ **stuccoed** *adj*.

stuck *adj* **1** unable to give an answer, reason, etc. **2** unable to move. ➢ *vb, past tense, past participle* of STICK². ♦ **be stuck for sth** *colloq* to be in need of it or at a loss for it. **stuck on sb** *colloq* fond of or infatuated with them.

stuck-up *adj, colloq* snobbish; conceited.

stud¹ *n* **1** a rivet-like metal peg that is fitted on to a surface, eg of a garment, for decoration. **2** any of several peg-like projections on the sole of a sports boot that give added grip when playing football, etc. **3** a type of small round plain earring or nose-ring. **4** a fastener consisting of two small discs on either end of a short bar or shank, eg for fixing a collar to a shirt. **5** a short form of PRESS STUD. ➢ *vb* (**studded, studding**) to fasten or decorate with a stud or studs.

stud² *n* **1** a male animal, esp a horse, kept for breeding. **2** (*also* **stud farm**) a place where animals, esp horses, are bred. **3** a collection of animals kept for breeding. **4** *colloq* a man who has, or who sees himself as having, great sexual prowess.

student *n* someone who is following a formal course of study, esp in higher or further education.

studied *adj* **1** of an attitude, expression, etc: carefully practised or thought through and adopted for effect. **2** carefully considered: *Jones gave a studied report to the board*.

studio *n* **1** the room where an artist or photographer works. **2** a room in which music recordings, or TV or radio programmes, are made. **3 a** a company that produces films; **b** the premises where films are produced.

studio couch *n* a couch, often backless, that converts into a bed.

studio flat *n* a small flat with one main room with open-plan living, eating and sleeping areas.

studious *adj* **1** characterized by a serious hardworking approach, esp to study. **2** carefully attentive. ○ **studiously** *adv*.

study *vb* (**-ies, -ied**) **1** *tr & intr* to set one's mind to acquiring knowledge and understanding, esp by reading, research, etc. **2** to take an educational course in (a subject): *She studied French to A level*. **3** to look at or examine closely, or think about carefully: *I studied her face*. ➢ *n* (**-ies**) **1** the act or process of studying. **2** (**studies**) work done in the process of acquiring knowledge: *Having to work interfered with her studies*. **3** a careful and detailed examination or consideration: *He undertook a careful study of the problem*. **4** a work of art produced for the sake of practice, or in preparation for a more complex work. **5** a piece of music intended to exercise and develop the player's technique. **6** a private room where quiet work or study is carried out.

stuff *n* **1 a** any material or substance: *the stuff that dreams are made of*; **b** something that is suitable for, relates to or is characterized by whatever is specified: *kids' stuff*. **2** movable belongings: *I'll just get my stuff*. **3** the characteristics that define someone, esp positive ones: *made of stronger stuff*. ➢ *vb* **1** to cram or thrust: *He stuffed the clothes in the wardrobe*. **2** to fill to capacity; to overfill. **3** to put something away: *Helen stuffed the letter in the drawer*. **4** to fill the hollow or hollowed-out part of (a chicken, pepper, etc) with a mixture of other foods. **5** to fill out the disembodied skin of (an animal, bird, fish, etc) to recreate its living shape. **6** to feed (oneself) greedily: *Mike stuffed himself until he felt sick*. **7** (*also* **stuff up**) to block something, eg a hole, the nose with mucus, etc. **8** *slang* to defeat someone convincingly. ♦ **do one's stuff** *colloq* **1** to display one's talent or skill. **2** to perform the task that one is required to do. **know one's stuff** *colloq* to have a thorough understanding of the specific subject that one is concerned or involved with.

stuffed *adj* **1** of a food: having a filling: *stuffed aubergines*. **2** of a dead animal, bird, fish, etc: having had its internal body parts replaced by stuffing. **3** of a toy, cushion, etc: filled with soft stuffing. **4** (*also* **stuffed-up**) of the nose:

blocked with mucus. ♦ **get stuffed** *colloq* an exclamation expressing contempt, dismissal, anger, etc.

stuffed shirt *n* a conservative or pompous person.

stuffing *n* **1** any material that children's toys, cushions, animal skins, etc are filled with. **2** *cookery* any mixture that is used as a filling for poultry, vegetables, etc. ♦ **knock the stuffing out of sb** to deprive them rapidly of strength, mental well-being, etc.

stuffy *adj* (*-ier, -iest*) **1** of a room, atmosphere, etc: lacking fresh, cool air. **2** of someone or their attitude, etc: boringly formal, conventional or unadventurous.

stultify *vb* (*-ies, -ied*) **1** to cause something to be useless, worthless, etc. **2** to dull the mind of someone, eg with tedious tasks.

stumble *vb, intr* **1** to lose one's balance and trip forwards after accidentally catching or misplacing one's foot. **2** to walk unsteadily. **3** to speak with frequent hesitations and mistakes. **4** to make a mistake in speech or action. **5** (**stumble across, into** or **upon sth**) to arrive at, find, etc it by chance. ➤ *n* an act of stumbling.

stumbling-block *n* **1** an obstacle or difficulty. **2** a cause of failure or faltering.

stump *n* **1** the part of a felled or fallen tree that is left in the ground. **2** the short part of anything, eg a limb, that is left after the larger part has been removed, used up, etc. **3** *cricket* **a** any of the three thin vertical wooden posts that form the wicket; **b** (**stumps**) the whole wicket, including the bails. ➤ *vb* **1** to baffle or perplex. **2** *intr* to walk stiffly and unsteadily, or heavily and noisily. **3** *cricket* of a fielder, esp a wicket-keeper: to dismiss (a batter) by disturbing the wicket with the ball while they are away from the crease. **4** *intr, N Am* to go round making political speeches. ♦ **on the stump** busy with political campaigning, esp by going round delivering speeches. ◊ **stump up** *colloq* to pay.

stumpy *adj* (*-ier, -iest*) short and thick.

stun *vb* (**stunned, stunning**) **1** to make someone unconscious, eg by a blow to the head. **2** to make someone unable to speak or think clearly, eg through shock. **3** *colloq* to astound someone. ➤ *n* the act of stunning or state of being stunned.

stunner *n, colloq* someone or something that is extraordinarily beautiful, etc.

stunning *adj, colloq* **1** extraordinarily beautiful, etc. **2** extremely impressive. ○ **stunningly** *adv.*

stunt[1] *vb* to curtail the growth or development of (a plant, animal, someone's mind, etc) to its full potential. ○ **stunted** *adj.*

stunt[2] *n* **1** a daring act or spectacular event that is intended to show off talent or attract publicity. **2** a dangerous or acrobatic feat that is performed as part of the action of a film or television programme.

stupefaction *n* **1** stunned surprise, etc. **2** the act of stupefying or state of being stupefied.

stupefy *vb* (*-ies, -ied*) **1** to stun with amazement, fear or confusion. **2** to make someone senseless, eg with drugs or alcohol.

stupendous *adj* **1** astounding. **2** *colloq* astoundingly huge or excellent. ○ **stupendously** *adv.*

stupid *adj* **1** having or showing a lack of common sense, comprehension, perception, etc: *a stupid mistake.* **2** slow to understand. **3** *colloq* silly; unimportant; boring: *a stupid quarrel.* ○ **stupidity** *n.* ○ **stupidly** *adv.*

stupor *n* **1** a state of unconsciousness or near-unconsciousness, esp one caused by drugs, alcohol, etc. **2** *colloq* a daze, esp one brought on by shock, lack of sleep, etc.

sturdy *adj* (*-ier, -iest*) **1** of limbs, etc: thick and strong-looking. **2** strongly built. **3** healthy; hardy. ○ **sturdiness** *n.*

sturgeon *n* a large long-snouted fish which is used as food and valued as the source of true caviar.

stutter *vb, tr & intr* to speak or say something in a faltering way, often by repeating parts of words, esp the first consonant, usu because of indecision, heightened emotion or some pathological disorder that affects the speech organs or the nervous system. ➤ *n* a way of speaking that is characterized by this kind of faltering. ○ **stuttering** *adj, n.*

sty[1] *n* (*sties*) a pen where pigs are kept.

sty[2] or **stye** *n* (*sties* or *styes*) an inflamed swelling on the eyelid at the base of the lash.

Stygian /'stɪdʒɪən/ *adj, literary* dark and gloomy.

style *n* **1** a manner or way of doing something. **2** a distinctive manner that characterizes a particular author, painter, film-maker, etc. **3** kind; type; make. **4** a striking quality, often elegance or lavishness, that is considered desirable or admirable: *She dresses with style.* **5** the state of being fashionable: *It has gone out of style.* **6** *bot* in flowers: the part of the CARPEL that connects the STIGMA (sense 2) to the OVARY (sense 2). ➤ *vb* **1** to design, shape, groom, etc something in a particular way. **2** to name or designate someone: *He styled himself an expert.*

stylish *adj* elegant; fashionable. ○ **stylishly** *adv.* ○ **stylishness** *n.*

stylist *n* **1** a trained hairdresser. **2** a writer, artist, etc who pays a lot of attention to style.

stylistic *adj* relating to artistic or literary style.

stylized *adj* conventionalized and unnaturalistic: *Cubism is a highly stylized art form.*

stylus *n* (*styluses* or *styli*) **a** a hard pointed device at the tip of the arm of a record player, which picks up the sound from a record's grooves; **b** the cutting tool that is used to produce the grooves in a record.

stymie *vb* (**stymieing** or **stymying**) to prevent, thwart, hinder or frustrate: *Plans for expansion were stymied by cash-flow problems.* ➤ *n, golf, formerly* a situation on the green where an opponent's ball blocks the path between one's own ball and the hole. ○ **stymied** *adj*.

styptic *med, adj* of a drug or other substance: having the effect of stopping, slowing down or preventing bleeding: *a styptic pencil.* ➤ *n* a drug or other substance that has this type of effect.

suave /swɑːv/ *adj* of someone, esp a man, or their manner, attitude, etc: polite, charming and sophisticated. ○ **suavely** *adv*.

sub *colloq, n* **1** a submarine. **2** a substitute player. **3** a small loan; an advance payment, eg from someone's wages to help them subsist. **4** a subeditor. **5** (*usu* **subs**) a subscription fee. ➤ *vb* (**subbed, subbing**) **1** *intr* to act as a substitute. **2** *tr & intr* to subedit or work as a subeditor. **3** to lend (esp a small amount of money): *Can you sub me a quid till tomorrow?*

subaltern /ˈsʌbəltən/ *n* any army officer below the rank of captain.

subaqua *adj* belonging, relating or referring to underwater activities: *subaqua diving*.

subatomic *adj* **1** smaller than an atom: *subatomic particle.* **2** relating to an atom; existing or occurring in an atom.

subconscious *n, psychoanal* the part of the mind where memories, experiences, feelings, etc are stored and from which such things can be retrieved to the level of conscious awareness. ➤ *adj* denoting mental processes which a person is not fully aware of. ○ **subconsciously** *adv*.

subcontinent *n* a large part of a continent that is distinctive in some way, eg by its shape, culture, etc: *the Indian subcontinent*.

subcontract *n* /ˈsʌbˈkɒntrakt/ a secondary contract where the person or company that is initially hired to do a job then hires another to carry out the work. ➤ *vb* /sʌbkənˈtrakt/ (*also* **subcontract out**) to employ (a worker) or pass on (work) under the terms of a subcontract. ○ **subcontractor** *n*.

subculture *n* a group within a society, esp one seen as an underclass, whose members share the same, often unconventional, beliefs, lifestyle, tastes, etc. ○ **subcultural** *adj*.

subcutaneous /sʌbkjuːˈteɪnɪəs/ *adj, med* situated, used, introduced, etc under the skin.

subdivide *vb* to divide (esp something that is already divided) into even smaller parts. ○ **subdivision** *n*.

subdue *vb* **1** to overpower and bring under control. **2** to suppress or conquer (feelings, an enemy, etc).

subdued *adj* **1** of lighting, colour, noise, etc: not intense, bright, loud, etc. **2** of a person: quiet, shy, restrained or in low spirits.

subedit *vb, tr & intr* to prepare (copy) for the ultimate sanction of the editor-in-chief, esp on a newspaper. ○ **subeditor** *n*.

subheading or **subhead** *n* a subordinate title in a book, chapter, article, etc.

subhuman *adj* **1** relating or referring to animals that are just below humans on the evolutionary scale. **2** of a person or their behaviour,

attitude, etc: barbaric; lacking in intelligence.

subject *n* /ˈsʌbdʒɪkt/ **1 a** a matter, topic, person, etc that is under discussion or consideration or that features as the major theme in a book, film, play, etc; **b** the person that a biography is written about. **2** an area of learning that forms a course of study. **3** someone or something that an artist, sculptor, photographer, etc chooses to represent. **4** someone who undergoes an experiment, operation, form of treatment, etc. **5** someone who is ruled by a monarch, government, etc: *a British subject.* **6** *gram* a word, phrase or clause which indicates the person or thing that performs the action of an active verb or that receives the action of a passive verb, eg *The doctor* is the subject in *The doctor saw us*, and *We* is the subject in *We were seen by the doctor*. Compare OBJECT (*noun sense* 4). ➤ *adj* /ˈsʌbdʒɪkt/ **1** (*often* **subject to sth**) **a** liable; showing a tendency: *subject to huge mood swings*; **b** exposed; open: *He left himself subject to ridicule*; **c** conditional upon something. **2** dependent; ruled by a monarch or government: *a subject nation.* ➤ *adv* /ˈsʌbdʒɪkt/ (*always* **subject to**) conditionally upon something: *You may go, subject to your parents' permission.* ➤ *vb* /səbˈdʒɛkt/ **1** (*usu* **subject sb** or **sth to sth**) to cause them or it to undergo or experience something unwelcome, unpleasant, etc: *He subjected them to years of abuse.* **2** to make (a person, a people, nation, etc) subordinate to or under the control of another.

subject heading *n* in an index, catalogue, etc: a caption under which all the related topics are collected and referenced.

subjection *n* an act of domination; the state of being dominated: *the subjection of women.*

subjective *adj* **1** based on personal opinion, thoughts, feelings, etc; not impartial. Compare OBJECTIVE. **2** *gram* indicating or referring to the subject of a verb. ○ **subjectively** *adv*.

sub judice /sʌb ˈdʒuːdɪsɪ/ *adj* of a court case: under judicial consideration and therefore not to be publicly discussed.

subjugate *vb* **1** esp of one country, people, etc in regard to another: to dominate them; to bring them under control: *As a nation, the Poles have often been subjugated.* **2** to make someone obedient or submissive. ○ **subjugation** *n*.

subjunctive *gram, adj* of the mood of a verb: used in English for denoting the conditional or hypothetical (eg 'If he *were* in hospital, I would certainly visit him' or 'If I *were* you') or the mandatory (eg 'I insist he *leave* now'), although in other languages it has a wider application. ➤ *n* **1** the subjunctive mood. **2** a verb in this mood.

sublet *vb, tr & intr* to rent out (property one is renting from someone else) to another person.

sublieutenant *n* a naval officer of the rank below lieutenant.

sublimate *vb, psychol* to channel a morally or socially unacceptable impulse towards something else that is considered more appropriate. ○ **sublimation** n.

sublime adj **1** of someone: displaying the highest or noblest nature. **2** of something in nature or art: overwhelmingly great; awe-inspiring. **3** loosely unsurpassed. ➤ vb, tr & intr, chem of a substance: to change from a solid to a vapour without passing through the liquid state. ○ **sublimely** adv.

subliminal adj existing in, resulting from or targeting the area of the mind that is below the threshold of ordinary awareness: subliminal advertising.

submachine-gun n a lightweight portable machine-gun that can be fired from the shoulder or hip.

submarine n a vessel, esp a military one, that is designed for underwater travel. ➤ adj **1** of plants, animals, etc: living under the sea. **2** used, fixed in place, etc underwater: North Sea submarine piping. ○ **submariner** n.

submerge or **submerse** vb **1** tr & intr to plunge or sink or cause to plunge or sink under the surface of water or other liquid. **2** to overwhelm or inundate someone, eg with too much work. ○ **submersion** n.

submersible adj of a vessel: designed to operate under water. ➤ n a submersible vessel.

submission n **1** an act of submitting. **2** something, eg a plan, idea, etc, put forward for consideration or approval. **3** readiness or willingness to surrender.

submissive adj willing or tending to submit. ○ **submissively** adv. ○ **submissiveness** n.

submit vb (**submitted, submitting**) **1** intr (also **submit to sb**) to surrender; to give in, esp to the wishes or control of another person. **2** tr & intr to offer (oneself) as a subject for an experiment, treatment, etc. **3** a to offer, suggest or present (eg a proposal) for formal consideration by others; **b** to hand in (eg a piece of written work) for marking, etc.

subnormal adj esp of someone's level of intelligence with regard to possible academic achievement: lower than normal. ➤ n, derog someone of this type.

subordinate adj /sə'bɔːdɪnət/ (often **subordinate to sb**) lower in rank, importance, etc. ➤ n /sə'bɔːdɪnət/ someone or something that is characterized by being lower or secondary in rank, status, importance, etc. ➤ vb /-neɪt/ **1** to regard or treat someone as being lower or secondary in rank, status, importance, etc; to put someone into this kind of position. **2** to cause or force someone or something to become dependent, subservient, etc. ○ **subordination** n.

subordinate clause n, gram a CLAUSE which cannot stand on its own as an independent sentence and which functions in a sentence in the same way as a noun, adjective or adverb, eg 'The book that you gave me for Christmas was fascinating' or 'What you see is what you get'. Compare MAIN CLAUSE.

suborn vb to persuade someone to commit perjury, a crime or some other wrongful act, eg by bribing them.

subplot n a minor storyline that runs parallel to the main plot in a novel, film, play, etc.

subpoena /sə'piːnə, səb'piːnə/ n a legal document that orders someone to appear in a court of law at a specified time. ➤ vb (**subpoenaed** or **subpoena'd**) to serve with a subpoena.

sub rosa adv in secret.

subroutine n, comput a self-contained part of a computer program which performs a specific task and which can be called up at any time during the running of the main program.

subscribe vb **1** tr & intr to contribute (a sum of money) on a regular basis. **2** (usu **subscribe to sth**) to undertake to receive (regular issues of a magazine, etc) in return for payment. **3** (usu **subscribe to sth**) to agree with or believe in (a theory, idea, etc). ○ **subscriber** n.

subscript printing, adj of a character, esp one in chemistry and maths: set below the level of the line, eg the number 2 in H_2O. ➤ n a character that is in this position.

subscription n **1** an act or instance of subscribing; **b** a payment made in subscribing. **2** Brit a set fee for membership of a society, club, etc. **3** a an agreement to take a magazine, etc, usu for a specified number of issues; **b** the money paid for this. **4** an advance order, esp of a book before its official publication.

subsequent adj (also **subsequent to sth**) happening after or following. ○ **subsequently** adv.

subservient adj **1** ready or eager to submit to the wishes of others, often excessively so. **2** (usu **subservient to sth**) functioning as a means to an end. **3** (usu **subservient to sb** or **sth**) a less common term for SUBORDINATE (adj). ○ **subservience** or **subserviency** n.

subset n, maths a set (see SET² sense 2) that forms one part of a larger set, eg set X is said to be a subset of a set Y if all the members of set X can be included in set Y.

subside vb, intr **1** of land, buildings, etc: to sink to a lower level. **2** of noise, feelings, wind, a storm, etc: to become less loud or intense. ○ **subsidence** /'sʌbsɪdəns, səb'saɪdəns/ n the sinking of land, buildings, etc to a lower level.

subsidiarity /sʌbsɪdɪ'arɪtɪ/ n the principle that a central governing body will permit its member states, local government, etc to have control over those issues deemed more appropriate to the local level.

subsidiary adj **1** of secondary importance. **2** serving as an addition or supplement. ➤ n (**-ies**) **1** a subsidiary person or thing. **2** (sometimes **subsidiary of sth**) a company controlled by another, usu larger, company or organization.

subsidize or **-ise** vb **1** to provide or support with a subsidy. **2** to pay a proportion of the cost of (a thing supplied) in order to reduce the price paid by the customer: The company subsidized the meals in the canteen.

subsidy n (-ies) 1 a sum of money given, eg by a government to an industry, to help with running costs or to keep product prices low. 2 financial aid of this kind.

subsist vb, intr (usu **subsist on sth**) to live or manage to stay alive by means of it. ○ **subsistence** n.

subsoil n, geol the layer of soil that lies beneath the TOPSOIL.

subsonic adj relating to, being or travelling at speeds below the speed of sound.

substance n 1 the matter or material that a thing is made of. 2 a particular kind of matter with a definable quality: a sticky substance. 3 the essence or basic meaning of something spoken or written. 4 touchable reality: Ghosts have no substance. 5 solid quality or worth: food with no substance. 6 foundation; truth: There is no substance in the rumours. 7 wealth and influence: woman of substance. ◆ in substance in actual fact.

substandard adj not reaching the expected standard.

substantial adj 1 considerable in amount, extent, importance, etc. 2 of real value or worth. 3 of food: nourishing. 4 solidly built. 5 existing as a touchable thing. 6 belonging or relating to something's basic nature. ○ **substantially** adv.

substantiate vb to prove or support something; to confirm the truth of something. ○ **substantiation** n.

substantive adj 1 having or displaying significant importance, value, etc. 2 belonging or relating to the essential nature of something. 3 gram expressing existence. ➤ n, gram a noun or any linguistic unit that functions as a noun.

substitute n someone or something that takes the place of, or is used instead of, another. ➤ vb (usu **substitute sth for sth else**) to use or bring something into use as an alternative, replacement, etc for something else. ○ **substitution** n.

substrate n 1 biol the material that a living organism, such as a plant, bacterium, etc, grows on or is attached to. 2 biochem the substance that an enzyme acts on during a biochemical reaction. 3 SUBSTRATUM.

substratum n (substrata) 1 an underlying layer. 2 a foundation or foundation material. 3 a layer of soil or rock that lies just below the surface.

substructure n, archit the part of a building or other construction that supports the framework.

subsume vb to include (an example, idea, etc) in or regard it as part of a larger, more general group, rule, etc.

subtenant n someone who rents or leases a property from someone who already holds a lease for that property. ○ **subtenancy** n.

subtend vb, geom of the line opposite a specified angle in a triangle or the chord of an arc: to be opposite and bounding.

subterfuge n a trick or deception that evades, conceals or obscures: a clever subterfuge.

subterranean adj 1 situated, existing, operating, etc underground. 2 hidden; operating, etc in secret.

subtext n 1 the implied message that the author, director, painter, etc of a play, film, book, picture, etc creates at a level below that of plot, character, language, image, etc. 2 more loosely anything implied but not explicitly stated in ordinary speech or writing.

subtitle n 1 (usu **subtitles**) a printed version or translation of the dialogue of a film, TV programme, etc that appears bit by bit at the bottom of the screen. 2 a subordinate title that usu expands on or explains the main title. ➤ vb to give a subtitle to (a literary work, film, etc).

subtle /'sʌtəl/ adj 1 not straightforwardly or obviously stated or displayed. 2 of distinctions, etc: difficult to appreciate or perceive. 3 of a smell, flavour, colour, etc: delicate; understated. 4 capable of making fine distinctions: a subtle mind. ○ **subtlety** n (-ies). ○ **subtly** adv.

subtotal n the amount that a column of figures adds up to and which forms part of a larger total.

subtract vb to take (one number, quantity, etc) away from another. ○ **subtraction** n.

subtropics pl n the areas of the world that lie between the tropics and the temperate zone. ○ **subtropical** adj.

suburb n a residential district that lies on the edge of a town or city. ○ **suburban** adj.

suburbia n the suburbs and their inhabitants and way of life thought of collectively, esp in terms of lacking sophistication, etc.

subvention n a grant or subsidy, esp a government-funded one.

subversion n 1 an act or instance of overthrowing a law, government, etc. 2 the act or practice of subverting (usu a government).

subversive adj of a person, action, thinking, etc: characterized by a likelihood or tendency to undermine authority. ➤ n someone who is subversive.

subvert vb to undermine or overthrow (esp a government or other legally established body).

subway n 1 an underground passage or tunnel that pedestrians or vehicles can use for crossing under a road, railway, etc. 2 chiefly N Am an underground railway.

subzero adj esp of a temperature: below zero degrees.

succeed vb 1 intr to achieve an aim or purpose. 2 intr to develop or turn out as planned. 3 intr (also **succeed in sth**) to do well in a particular area or field: She succeeded at university. 4 to come next after (something). 5 tr & intr (also **succeed to sb or sth**) to take up a position, etc, following on from someone else: The Queen succeeded her father • She succeeded to the throne.

success n 1 the quality of succeeding or the state of having succeeded. 2 any favourable development or outcome. 3 someone who attains fame, power, wealth, etc or is judged favourably by others: *He became an overnight success.* **4** something that turns out well or that is judged favourably by others.

successful *adj* **1** achieving or resulting in the required outcome. **2** prosperous, flourishing: *a successful business.* ○ **successfully** *adv.*

succession *n* **1 a** a series of people or things that come, happen, etc one after the other; **b** the process or an instance of this. **2 a** the right or order by which one person or thing succeeds another; **b** the process or act of doing this. ◆ **in succession** one after the other.

successive *adj* immediately following another or each other. ○ **successively** *adv.*

successor *n* someone who follows another, esp someone who takes over another's job, title, etc.

succinct /sək'sɪŋkt/ *adj* of someone or of the way they write or speak: brief, precise and to the point. ○ **succinctly** *adv.*

succour or (*US*) **succor** /'sʌkə(r)/ *formal, n* **1** help or relief in time of distress or need. **2** someone or something that gives this kind of help. ➤ *vb* to give help or relief to someone or something.

succubus /'sʌkjʊbəs/ or **succuba** /-bə/ *n* (*succubi* /-baɪ/ or **succubuses; succubae** /-biː/ or **succubas**) a female evil spirit which was believed to have sexual intercourse with sleeping men and so conceive demonic children. Compare INCUBUS.

succulent *adj* **1** juicy; tender and tasty. **2** *bot* of a plant: characterized by having thick fleshy leaves or stems. **3** *colloq* attractive; inviting. ➤ *n, bot* a plant that is specially adapted to living in arid conditions by having thick fleshy leaves or stems, which allow it to store water. ○ **succulence** *n.*

succumb *vb, intr* (*often* **succumb to sth**) **1** to give in to (pressure, temptation, etc): *He succumbed to her charms.* **2** to fall victim to or to die of (a disease, old age, etc).

such *adj* **1** of that kind or a similar kind: *You cannot reason with such a person.* **2** so great; of a more extreme type, degree, extent, etc than is usual, etc: *You're such a good friend.* **3** of a type, degree, extent, etc that has already been indicated, spoken about, etc: *I did no such thing.* ➤ *pron* a person or thing, or people or things, like that or those which have just been mentioned: *chimps, gorillas and such.* ◆ **as such** as it is usu thought of, described, etc: *There's no spare bed as such, but you can use the sofa.* **such as** for example.

such-and-such *adj* of a particular but unspecified kind. ➤ *pron* a person or thing of this kind.

suchlike *pron* things of the same kind: *I went to the chemist for soap, toothpaste and suchlike.* ➤ *adj* of the same kind: *soap, toothpaste and suchlike things.*

suck *vb* **1** *tr & intr* to draw (liquid) into the mouth. **2** to draw liquid from (eg a juicy fruit)

with the mouth. **3** (*also* **suck sth in** or **up**) to draw in by suction or an action similar to suction: *The roots sucked up the water.* **4** to rub (eg one's thumb) with the tongue and inside of the mouth, using an action similar to sucking in liquids. **5** to draw the flavour from (eg a sweet) with squeezing and rolling movements inside the mouth. **6** to take milk from (a breast or udder) with the mouth. **7** *intr, slang* to be contemptible or contemptibly bad: *That movie sucks!* ➤ *n* an act or bout of sucking. ◊ **suck sb into sth** to drag them into it: *It sucked him into the world of politics.* **suck up to sb** *colloq* to flatter them in order to gain favour.

sucker *n* **1** *colloq* someone who can be easily deceived or taken advantage of. **2** (*usu* **sucker for sth**) *colloq* someone who finds a specified type of thing or person irresistible: *a sucker for chocolate ice cream.* **3** *zool* a specially adapted organ that helps an insect, sea creature, etc adhere to surfaces by suction. **4** a rubber cup-shaped device that is designed to adhere to a surface by creating a vacuum. **5** *bot* a shoot that sprouts from the parent stem or root. ➤ *vb* **1** to remove the suckers (from a plant). **2** *colloq* to deceive, trick or fool: *She suckered him out of £50.*

suckle *vb* **1** to feed (a baby or young mammal) with milk from the nipple or udder. **2** *tr & intr* to suck milk from (a nipple or udder).

suckling *n* **1** a baby or young animal that is still being fed with its mother's milk. **2** the process of feeding a baby or young animal with its mother's milk.

sucrose /'suːkrəʊs/ *n, biochem* a white soluble crystalline sugar.

suction *n* **1** an act, an instance or the process of sucking. **2 a** the production of an adhering or sucking force that is created by a difference or reduction in air pressure; **b** the amount of force that this creates.

suction pump *n* a pumping device for raising water, etc.

sudden *adj* happening or done quickly, without warning or unexpectedly. ○ **suddenly** *adv.* ○ **suddenness** *n.* ◆ **all of a sudden** without any warning; unexpectedly.

sudden infant death syndrome *n* (abbrev **SIDS**) *med* the sudden unexpected death of an apparently healthy baby without any identifiable cause.

Sudoku /sədəʊ'kuː/ *n* a type of puzzle in which numbers must be entered into a square grid.

sudorific /suːdə'rɪfɪk/ *med, adj* of a drug: causing sweating. ➤ *n* a drug, remedy or substance that causes sweating.

suds *pl n* **1** (*also* **soap-suds**) a mass of bubbles produced on water when soap or other detergent is dissolved. **2** water that has detergent in it.

sue *vb* **1** *tr & intr* to take legal proceedings against (a person or company). **2** *intr* (*usu* **sue for sth**) to make a claim for it.

suede /sweɪd/ *n* a soft leather, where the flesh

side is brushed so that it has a velvety finish.

suet n hard fat from around the kidneys of sheep or cattle, used for making pastry, puddings, etc.

suffer vb 1 tr & intr to undergo or endure (pain or other unpleasantness). 2 intr to deteriorate (as a result of something). 3 to tolerate: She doesn't suffer fools gladly. 4 old use to allow: Suffer the little children to come unto me. ○ **sufferer** n. ○ **suffering** n.

sufferance n consent that is given tacitly or that is understood to be given through the lack of objection. ♦ **on sufferance** with reluctant toleration.

suffice vb 1 intr to be adequate, sufficient, good enough, etc for a particular purpose. 2 to satisfy.

sufficient adj enough; adequate. ○ **sufficiency** n. ○ **sufficiently** adv.

suffix n 1 gram a word-forming element that can be added to the end of a word or to the base form of a word, eg as a grammatical inflection such as -ed or -s in walked and monkeys. Compare PREFIX (noun sense 1). 2 maths an INDEX that is placed below the other figures in an equation, etc, eg the n in x_n. ➤ vb 1 gram to attach something as a suffix to a word. 2 to add (a suffix) to something.

suffocate vb 1 tr & intr to kill or be killed by a lack of air, eg because the air passages are blocked. 2 intr to experience difficulty in breathing because of heat and lack of air. 3 to subject to an oppressive amount of something. ○ **suffocation** n.

suffragan n (in full **suffragan bishop** or **bishop suffragan**) a bishop considered as subordinate to an archbishop or metropolitan.

suffrage n the right to vote in political elections: They fought for universal suffrage. ○ **suffragist** n.

suffragette n a woman who is in favour of or who campaigns for women having the same voting rights as men, esp one who acted militantly for this in Britain in the early years of the 20th century.

suffuse vb (often **be suffused with sth**) to be covered or spread over or throughout with (colour, light, liquid, etc). ○ **suffusion** n.

sugar n 1 a white crystalline carbohydrate that is soluble in water, typically having a sweet taste and widely used as a sweetener. 2 the common name for SUCROSE. 3 a measure of sugar: Gary takes three sugars in his tea. 4 colloq a term of endearment. ➤ vb 1 to sweeten something with sugar. 2 to sprinkle or coat something with sugar. ○ **sugared** adj. ○ **sugaring** n. ♦ **sugar the pill** to make something unpleasant easier to deal with or accept.

sugar beet n a variety of beet that is widely cultivated for its large white root, which is an important source of sugar.

sugar cane n a tall tropical grass which resembles bamboo and is a main source of sugar.

sugar daddy n, colloq a wealthy elderly man

who lavishes money and gifts on a friend who is much younger than him, esp in return for companionship or sex.

sugar-free adj containing no sugar, but instead often containing some form of artificial sweetener: sugar-free chewing gum.

sugary adj 1 like sugar in taste or appearance. 2 containing much or too much sugar. 3 colloq exaggeratedly or insincerely pleasant or affectionate.

suggest vb 1 (often **suggest that**) to put forward as a possibility or recommendation. 2 to create an impression of something: a painting that suggests the artist's anguish. 3 to give a hint of something: an expression that suggests guilt.

suggestible adj easily influenced by suggestions made by others.

suggestion n 1 a something that is suggested; a proposal, recommendation, etc; b the act of suggesting. 2 a hint or trace: delicately flavoured with just a suggestion of coriander. 3 a the creation of a belief or impulse in the mind; b the process by which an idea, belief, etc can be instilled in the mind of a hypnotized person.

suggestive adj 1 (often **suggestive of sth**) causing one to think of it. 2 capable of a tacitly erotic or provocative interpretation. ○ **suggestively** adv.

suicidal adj 1 involving or indicating suicide. 2 characterized by behaviour that might result in suicide or ruin; irresponsibly rash or self-destructive. 3 of a person: inclined or likely to commit suicide.

suicide n 1 the act or an instance of killing oneself deliberately. 2 someone who deliberately kills or tries to kill himself or herself. 3 ruin or downfall: The minister's speech was political suicide.

suit n 1 a set of clothes designed to be worn together, usu consisting of a jacket and either trousers or a skirt. 2 often in compounds an outfit worn on specified occasions or for a specified activity: wet suit • suit of armour. 3 any of the four groups (clubs, diamonds, hearts or spades) that a pack of playing-cards is divided into. 4 a legal action taken against someone. 5 disparaging a businessman. ➤ vb 1 tr & intr to be acceptable to or what is required by someone. 2 to be appropriate to, in harmony with or attractive to someone or something. ○ **suited** adj. ♦ **follow suit** to do the same as someone else has done. **suit oneself** to do what one wants to do, esp without considering others.

suitable adj appropriate, proper, etc. ○ **suitability** n. ○ **suitably** adv.

suitcase n a stiffened portable travelling case that is used for carrying clothes.

suite /swiːt/ n 1 a set of rooms forming a self-contained unit within a larger building, esp a hotel: bridal suite. 2 a set of matching furniture, etc: three-piece suite. 3 mus a set of instrumental movements in related keys.

suitor n 1 old use a man who woos a woman,

esp with the intention of asking her to marry him. **2** someone who sues.

Sukkoth /ˈsukoʊt/ n a Jewish harvest festival commemorating the period when the Israelites lived in tents in the desert during the Exodus from Egypt.

sulk vb, intr to be silent, grumpy, unsociable, etc, esp because of some petty resentment, etc. ➤ n (also **the sulks**) a bout of sulking.

sulky adj (**-ier, -iest**) inclined to moodiness, esp when taking the form of grumpy silence, etc. ○ **sulkily** adv. ○ **sulkiness** n.

sullen adj **1** silently and stubbornly angry, serious, moody or unsociable. **2** of skies, etc: heavy and dismal. ○ **sullenly** adv. ○ **sullenness** n.

sully vb (**-ies, -ied**) **1** to tarnish or mar (a reputation, etc). **2** now chiefly literary to dirty something.

sulphate or (US) **sulfate** n a salt or ester of sulphuric acid.

sulphide or (US) **sulfide** n a compound that contains sulphur and another element.

sulphite or (US) **sulfite** n a salt or ester of sulphurous acid.

sulphonamide or (US) **sulfonamide** n, med any of a group of drugs that prevent the growth of bacteria.

sulphur or (US) **sulfur** n, chem a yellow solid non-metallic element that is used in the vulcanization of rubber and the manufacture of sulphuric acid, insecticides and sulphonamide drugs. ➤ vb to treat or fumigate using sulphur. ○ **sulphuric** /sʌlˈfjʊərɪk/ adj.

sulphur dioxide n, chem a colourless, pungent, toxic gas, used as a food preservative and also in the manufacture of sulphuric acid.

sulphuric acid or (US) **sulfuric acid** n, chem a colourless odourless oily liquid that is widely used in the manufacture of organic chemicals, fertilizers, explosives, paints and dyes.

sulphurous or (US) **sulfurous** /ˈsʌlfərəs/ adj relating to, like or containing sulphur.

sultan n the ruler of any of various Muslim countries.

sultana n **1 a** a pale seedless raisin that is used in making cakes, puddings, etc; **b** the grape that this type of dried fruit comes from. **2** the wife, concubine, mother, sister or daughter of a sultan.

sultry adj (**-ier, -iest**) **1** of the weather: hot and humid. **2** characterized by a sensual, passionate or sexually suggestive appearance, manner, etc.

sum n **1** the total that is arrived at when two or more numbers, quantities, etc are added together. **2** an amount of money, often a specified one: the grand sum of 50p. **3 a** an arithmetical calculation, esp of a basic kind; **b** (**sums**) colloq arithmetic. ➤ vb (**summed, summing**) to calculate the sum of something. ◆ **in sum** briefly; to sum up. ◊ **sum up 1** to summarize before finishing a speech, argument, etc. **2** of a judge: to review the main points of a case for the jury before they retire to consider their

verdict. **sum up sb** or **sth 1** to express or embody the complete character or nature of them or it: That kind of pettiness just sums her up. **2** to make a quick assessment of (a person, situation, etc).

summarize or **-ise** vb to make, present or be a summary of something.

summary n (**-ies**) a short account that outlines or picks out the main points. ➤ adj done or performed quickly and without the usual attention to details or formalities. ○ **summarily** adv.

summation n **1** the process of finding the sum. **2** a summary or summing-up.

summer n **1** (also **Summer**) the warmest season of the year, between spring and autumn. **2** the warm sunny weather that is associated with summer: a beautiful summer's day. ○ **summery** adj.

summerhouse n any small building in a park or garden where people can sit during warm weather and which provides some shade.

summer school n, Brit a course of study held during the summer vacation.

summer solstice n the longest day of the year in either hemisphere, either 21 June for the N hemisphere, or 22 December for the S hemisphere.

summing-up n a review of the main points, esp of a legal case by the judge before the members of the jury retire to consider their verdict.

summit n **1** the highest point of a mountain or hill. **2** the highest possible level of achievement or development. **3** a meeting, conference, etc between heads of government or other senior officials.

summon vb **1** to order someone to come or appear, eg in a court of law as a witness, defendant, etc. **2** to order or request someone to do something; to call someone to something; to ask for something: He had to summon help. **3** (often **summon up sth**) to gather or muster (eg one's strength or energy): She summoned up the nerve to tell him.

summons n (**summonses**) **1** a written order that legally obliges someone to attend a court of law at a specified time. **2** any authoritative order that requests someone to attend a meeting, etc or to do something specified. ➤ vb, law to serve someone with a summons.

sumo n a style of traditional Japanese wrestling where contestants of great bulk try to force an opponent out of the ring or to make them touch the floor with any part of their body other than the soles of the feet.

sump n **1** a small depression inside a vehicle's engine that acts as a reservoir so that lubricating oil can drain into it. **2** any pit into which liquid drains or is poured.

sumptuary adj **1** relating to or regulating expense. **2** of a law, etc: controlling extravagance.

sumptuous adj wildly expensive; extravagantly luxurious. ○ **sumptuously** adv.

sum total n the complete or final total.

sun n **1** (**the Sun**) the star that the planets revolve around and which gives out the heat and light energy necessary to enable living organisms to survive on Earth. **2** the heat and light of this star. **3** any star with a system of planets revolving around it. **4** someone or something that is regarded as a source of radiance, warmth, etc. ➢ vb (**sunned, sunning**) to expose (something or oneself) to the sun's rays. ○ **sunless** adj. ♦ **catch the sun** to become burnt or tanned by the sun. **under the sun** anywhere on earth.

sunbathe vb, intr to expose one's body to the sun in order to get a suntan. ○ **sunbather** n. ○ **sunbathing** n.

sunbeam n a ray of sunlight.

sunbed n **1** a device that has sun-lamps fitted above and often beneath a transparent screen and which someone can lie on in order to artificially tan the whole body. **2** a SUN-LOUNGER.

sunblock n a lotion, cream, etc that completely or almost completely protects the skin from the harmful effects of the sun's rays.

sunburn n soreness and reddening of the skin caused by overexposure to the sun's rays. ○ **sunburnt** or **sunburned** adj.

sundae /ˈsʌndeɪ/ n a portion of ice cream topped with fruit, nuts, syrup, etc.

Sunday n the first day of the week. ♦ **a month of Sundays** a very long time.

Sunday best n, jocular one's best clothes, formerly considered the most suitable for wearing to church.

Sunday school n a class for the religious instruction of children that is held on Sundays.

sundial n an instrument that uses sunlight to tell the time, by the changing position of the shadow that it casts on a plate with markings that indicate the hours.

sundown n sunset.

sun-dried adj dried or preserved by exposure to the sun: *sun-dried tomatoes*.

sundry adj various; miscellaneous. ➢ n (**sundries**) various small unspecified items. ♦ **all and sundry** everybody.

sunflower n a tall plant which produces large yellow flowerheads with closely-packed seeds (which yield **sunflower oil**) in the middle.

sunglasses pl n spectacles that have tinted lenses, which are worn to protect the eyes from sunlight.

sun-god or **sun-goddess** n the sun when it is thought of as a deity.

sunken adj **1** situated or fitted at a lower level than the surrounding area: *a sunken bath*. **2** submerged in water: *sunken treasure*. **3** of eyes, cheeks, etc: abnormally fallen in, eg because of ill health, old age, etc.

sun-lamp n an electric lamp that emits ultraviolet rays and which is used therapeutically and for artificially tanning the skin.

sunlight n light from the sun. ○ **sunlit** adj.

sun-lounger n, Brit a lightweight usu plastic sunbathing seat that can often be adjusted to a variety of positions and which usu supports the whole body.

sunny adj (**-ier, -iest**) **1** of a day, the weather, etc: characterized by long spells of sunshine. **2** of a place, etc: exposed to, lit or warmed by plenty of sunshine: *a lovely sunny room*. **3** cheerful; good-humoured.

sunrise n **1** the sun's appearance above the horizon in the morning. **2** the time of day when this happens.

sunrise industry n any new and rapidly expanding industry, esp one that involves computing, electronics, etc.

sunroof n a panel in the roof of a car that lets sunlight in and can usu open for ventilation.

sunscreen n a preparation that protects the skin and minimizes the possibility of sunburn because it blocks out some of the sun's harmful rays.

sunset n **1** the sun's disappearance below the horizon in the evening. **2** the time of day when this happens.

sunshade n **1** a type of umbrella that is used as protection in strong sunshine. **2** an awning.

sunshine n **1** the light or heat of the sun. **2** fair weather, with the sun shining brightly. **3** an informal term of address, often used in a mockingly scolding tone.

sunspot n **1** astron a relatively dark cool patch on the Sun's surface. **2** colloq a holiday resort that is renowned for its sunny weather.

sunstroke n a condition of collapse brought on by overexposure to the sun and sometimes accompanied by fever.

suntan n a browning of the skin through exposure to the sun or a sun-lamp.

suntrap n, Brit a sheltered sunny place.

sun-up n, US sunrise.

sup[1] vb (**supped, supping**) to drink in small mouthfuls. ➢ n a small quantity of something liquid.

sup[2] vb (**supped, supping**) intr, old use (often **sup off** or **on sth**) to eat supper; to eat for supper.

super adj, colloq extremely good; wonderful. ➢ exclam excellent! ➢ n **1** something of superior quality or grade, eg petrol. **2** colloq a short form of SUPERINTENDENT. **3** colloq a SUPERNUMERARY, esp an extra in the theatre or on a film set.

superabundant adj excessively or very plentiful. ○ **superabundance** n.

superannuated adj **1** of a post, vacancy, job, etc: with a pension as an integral part of the employment package. **2** made to retire and given a pension. **3** old and no longer fit for use.

superannuation n **1** an amount that is regularly deducted from someone's wages as a contribution to a company pension. **2** the pension someone receives when they retire. **3** retirement: *He took early superannuation*.

superb adj 1 colloq outstandingly excellent. 2 magnificent; majestic. ○ **superbly** adv.

supercharge vb 1 to increase the power and performance of (a vehicle engine). 2 (usu **supercharge sth with sth**) to charge or fill (eg an atmosphere, a remark, etc) with an intense amount of an emotion, etc.

supercharger n, eng a device that is used to increase the amount of air taken into the cylinder of an internal-combustion engine, in order to burn the fuel more rapidly and so increase the power output.

supercilious adj arrogantly disdainful or contemptuous. ○ **superciliousness** n.

superconductivity n, physics the property of having no electrical resistance that is displayed by many metals and alloys at temperatures close to absolute zero, and that other substances, such as ceramics, display at higher temperatures. ○ **superconductor** n.

superego n, psychoanal that aspect of the psyche where someone's moral standards are internalized and which acts as an often subconscious check on the ego. Compare EGO (sense 2), ID.

supererogation /suːpərɛrəˈgeɪʃən/ n doing more than duty, circumstances, etc require.

superficial adj 1 belonging or relating to, or on or near, the surface: a superficial wound. 2 not thorough or in-depth: a superficial understanding. 3 only apparent; not real or genuine: a superficial attempt to apologize. 4 lacking the capacity for sincere emotion or serious thought: a superficial person. ○ **superficiality** n (-ies). ○ **superficially** adv.

superfluous /suːˈpɜːfluəs/ adj more than is needed or wanted. ○ **superfluity** n. ○ **superfluously** adv.

superglue n a type of quick-acting extra strong adhesive. ➤ vb to bond something with superglue.

supergrass n, slang someone who gives the police so much information that a large number of arrests follow, often in return for the informer's own immunity or so that they will face lesser charges.

superhero n a character in a film, novel, comic, etc that has extraordinary powers, esp for saving the world from disaster.

superhighway n 1 US a wide road, with at least two carriageways going in either direction, that is meant for fast-moving traffic. 2 (in full **information superhighway**) electronic telecommunication systems collectively such as telephone links, cable and satellite TV, and computer networks, esp the Internet, over which information in digital form can be transferred rapidly.

superhuman adj beyond ordinary human power, ability, knowledge, etc.

superimpose vb to lay or set (one thing) on top of another.

superintend vb, tr & intr to look after and manage someone or something.

superintendent n 1 a Brit a police officer above the rank of chief inspector; b US a high ranking police officer, esp a chief of police. 2 someone whose job is to look after and manage, eg a department, a group of workers, etc. 3 N Am someone whose job is to act as caretaker of a building.

superior adj (often **superior to sb** or **sth**) 1 better in some way. 2 higher in rank or position: I reported him to his superior officer. 3 of high quality. 4 arrogant. 5 printing of a character: set above the level of the line. ➤ n 1 someone who is of higher rank or position. 2 the head of a religious community. ○ **superiority** n.

superlative /suːˈplatɪv/ adj 1 gram of adjectives or adverbs: expressing the highest degree of a particular quality, eg nicest, best, most beautiful. 2 superior to all others. ➤ n, gram 1 a superlative adjective or adverb. 2 the superlative form of a word. Compare POSITIVE (sense 13), COMPARATIVE (adj sense 4).

superman n 1 philos an ideal man as he will have evolved in the future. 2 a man who appears to have superhuman powers.

supermarket n a large self-service store that sells food, household goods, etc.

supermodel n an extremely highly paid, usu female, fashion model.

supernatural adj belonging or relating to or being phenomena that cannot be explained by the laws of nature or physics.

supernova /suːpəˈnoʊvə/ n (**supernovae** /-viː/ or **supernovas**) astron a vast stellar explosion which takes a few days to complete and which results in the star becoming temporarily millions of times brighter than it was.

supernumerary adj additional to the normal or required number. ➤ n (-ies) 1 someone or something that is extra or surplus to requirements. 2 an actor who does not have a speaking part. 3 someone who is not part of the regular staff, but who can be called on to work or serve when necessary.

superordinate adj of higher grade, status, importance, etc. ➤ n someone or something that is of higher grade, status, importance, etc.

superpower n a nation or state that has outstanding political, economic or military influence, esp the USA.

superscript printing, adj of a character: set above the level of the line that the other characters sit on, eg the number 2 in 10^2. ➤ n a superscript character.

supersede vb to take the place of (something, esp something outdated or no longer valid): DVDs will supersede videos.

supersonic adj 1 faster than the speed of sound. 2 of aircraft: able to travel at supersonic speeds. ○ **supersonically** adv.

superstar n an internationally famous celebrity, esp from the world of film, popular music or sport. ○ **superstardom** n.

superstition n 1 belief in an influence that certain (esp commonplace) objects, actions or occurrences have on events, people's lives, etc. **2** a particular opinion or practice based on such belief. ○ **superstitious** adj. ○ **superstitiously** adv.

superstore n **1** a very large supermarket that often sells clothes, etc as well as food and household goods. **2** a very large store that sells a specified type of goods such as DIY products, electrical products, furniture, etc.

superstructure n **1** a building thought of in terms of it being above its foundations. **2** anything that is based on or built above another part, eg those parts of a ship above the main deck.

supertanker n a large ship for transporting oil or other liquid.

supertax n, colloq a surtax.

supervene vb, intr to occur as an interruption to some process, esp unexpectedly. ○ **supervention** n.

supervise vb **1** to be in overall charge of (employees, etc). **2** to oversee (a task, project, etc). ○ **supervision** n. ○ **supervisor** n. ○ **supervisory** adj.

supine /'su:pam/ adj **1** lying on one's back. **2** lazy.

supper n an evening meal, esp a light one.

supplant vb to take the place of someone.

supple adj of a person, their joints, a material, etc: bending easily. ○ **suppleness** n.

supplement n **1** something that is added to make something else complete or that makes up a deficiency: vitamin supplement. **2** an extra section added to a book to give additional information or to correct previous errors. **3 a** a separate part that comes with a newspaper, esp a Sunday one; **b** a separate part that comes with a magazine, esp one that covers a specific topic. **4** an additional charge for a specified service, etc. ➤ vb to add to something; to make up a lack of something. ○ **supplementary** adj.

supplicate vb, tr & intr **1** (usu **supplicate for** sth) to humbly and earnestly request it. **2** (usu **supplicate sb for sth**) to humbly and earnestly request them for it. ○ **supplicant** n. ○ **supplication** n.

supply vb (**-ies, -ied**) **a** to provide or furnish (something believed to be necessary): I'll supply the wine if you bring some beers; **b** (also **supply sb with sth**) to provide or furnish them with it: The garden supplied them with all their vegetables. ➤ n (**-ies**) **1** an act or instance of providing. **2** an amount provided, esp regularly. **3** an amount that can be drawn from and used. **4** (**supplies**) necessary food, equipment, etc that is stored, taken on a journey, etc. **5** a source, eg of water, electricity, gas, etc: They cut off our gas supply. **6** econ the total amount of a commodity that is produced and available for sale. Compare DEMAND (noun sense 4). ○ **supplier** n.

support vb **1** to keep something upright or in place. **2** to keep from falling. **3** to bear the weight of someone or something. **4** to give ac-

tive approval, encouragement, money, etc to (an institution, belief, theory, etc). **5** to provide someone or something with the means necessary for living or existing: She supports a large family. **6** to maintain a loyal and active interest in the fortunes of (a particular sport or team). **7** to reinforce the accuracy or validity of (a theory, claim, etc): The evidence supports the prosecution's case. **8** to speak in favour of (a proposal, etc). **9** to play a part subordinate to (a leading actor). **10** to perform before (the main item in a concert, show, etc). **11** comput of a computer, an operating system, etc: to allow for the use of (a specified language, program, etc). **12** to bear or tolerate something. ➤ n **1** the act of supporting; the state of being supported. **2** someone or something that supports. **3** someone or something that helps, comforts, etc. **4** (often **the support**) a group, singer, film, etc that accompanies or comes on before the main attraction. ○ **supporting** adj, n. ○ **supportive** adj.

supporter n someone who gives a specified institution such as a sport, a team, a political party, etc their active backing, etc: football supporters.

suppose vb **1** to consider something likely, even when there is a lack of tangible evidence for it to be so. **2** to think, believe, agree, etc reluctantly or unwillingly (that something could be true). **3** to assume, often wrongly: He supposed she wouldn't find out. **4** of a theory, proposition, policy, etc: to require (some vital factor or assumption) to be the case before it can work, be valid, etc: Your idea for expansion supposes more money to be available. ♦ **I suppose so** an expression of reluctant agreement.

supposed adj generally believed to be so or true, but considered doubtful by the speaker: They couldn't find him at his supposed address. ○ **supposedly** adv. ♦ **be supposed to be** or **do** sth to be expected or allowed to be or do it: You were supposed to be here an hour ago.

supposition n **1** the act of supposing. **2** something that is supposed. **3** conjecture.

suppositious adj based on supposition.

suppository n (**-ies**) med a soluble preparation of medicine that remains solid at room temperature, but which dissolves when it is inserted into the rectum or vagina, where its active ingredients are then released.

suppress vb **1** to hold back or restrain (feelings, laughter, a yawn, etc). **2** to put a stop to something. **3** to crush (eg a rebellion). **4** to prevent (news, etc) from being broadcast, from circulating or from otherwise being made known. **5** to moderate or eliminate (interference) in an electrical device. ○ **suppression** n.

suppressant n a substance that suppresses or restrains.

suppurate vb, intr of a wound, boil, ulcer, etc: to gather and release pus. ○ **suppuration** n.

supremacy n **1** supreme power or authority. **2** the state or quality of being supreme.

supreme *adj* **1** highest in rank, power, importance, etc: *the Supreme Court*. **2** most excellent: *a supreme effort*. **3** greatest in degree: *supreme stupidity*. ○ **supremely** *adv*.

supremo *n, colloq* **1** a supreme head or leader. **2** a boss.

surcharge *n* **1** an extra charge, often as a penalty for late payment of a bill. **2** an amount over a permitted load. ➤ *vb* **1** to impose a surcharge on someone. **2** to overload something.

surd *maths, adj* of a number: unable to be expressed in finite terms; irrational. ➤ *n* an IRRATIONAL (sense 3) number.

sure *adj* **1** confident beyond doubt in one's belief or knowledge: *He felt sure he'd picked up the keys*. **2** undoubtedly true or accurate: *a sure sign*. **3** reliably stable or secure: *on a sure footing*. ➤ *adv, colloq* certainly; of course. ○ **sureness** *n*. ◆ **be sure to** to be guaranteed or certain to (happen, etc): *Whenever we plan a picnic it's sure to rain*. **for sure** *colloq* undoubtedly. **make sure** to take the necessary action to remove all doubt or risk. **sure of oneself** acting in a very self-confident way. **to be sure** admittedly.

sure-fire *adj, colloq* destined to succeed.

sure-footed *adj* **1** not stumbling or likely to stumble. **2** not making, or not likely to make, mistakes.

surely *adv* **1** without doubt. **2** used in questions and exclamations: to express incredulous disbelief: *Surely you knew he was just joking?* ◆ **slowly but surely** slowly and steadily.

surety /ˈʃʊərəti/ *n* (*-ies*) **1** someone who agrees to become legally responsible for another person's behaviour, debts, etc. **2** security, usu in the form of a sum of money, against loss, damage, etc or as a guarantee that a promise will be kept.

surf *n* **1** the sea as it breaks against the shore, etc. **2** the foam produced by breaking waves. **3** an act or instance of surfing. ➤ *vb* **1** *intr* to take part in a sport or recreation where the object is to stand or lie on a long narrow board, try to catch the crest of a wave and ride it to the shore. **2** to browse through (the Internet) randomly. ○ **surfer** *n* **1** someone who goes surfing. **2** someone who browses on the Internet. ○ **surfing** *n* **1** the sport or recreation of riding a surfboard on the crests of large breaking waves. **2** browsing on the Internet.

surface *n* **1 a** the upper or outer side of anything, often with regard to texture or appearance; **b** the size or area of such a side. **2** the upper level of a body or container of liquid or of the land. **3** the external appearance of something, as opposed to its underlying reality: *On the surface everything seems fine.* **4** *maths* a geometric figure that is two-dimensional, having length and breadth but no depth. ➤ *vb* **1** *intr* to rise to the surface of a liquid. **2** *intr* to become apparent; to come to light: *The scandal first surfaced in the press.* **3** *intr, colloq* to get out of bed: *He never surfaces*

till the afternoon. **4** to give the desired finish or texture to the surface of something.

surface mail *n* mail that is sent overland or by ship.

surface tension *n, physics* the film-like tension on the surface of a liquid that is caused by the cohesion of its particles, which has the effect of minimizing its surface area.

surfboard *n* a long narrow fibreglass board that a surfer stands or lies on. ➤ *vb, intr* to ride on a surfboard.

surfeit /ˈsɜːfɪt/ *n* **1** (*usu* **a surfeit of sth**) an excess. **2** the stuffed or sickened feeling that results from any excess, esp overeating. ➤ *vb* to indulge, esp in an excess of food or drink, until stuffed or disgusted.

surge *n* **1** a sudden powerful mass movement of a crowd, esp forward. **2** a sudden sharp increase, eg in prices, electrical current, etc. **3** a sudden rush of emotion: *I felt a surge of indignation.* **4** a rising and falling of a large area of sea. ➤ *vb, intr* **1** of the sea, waves, etc: to move up and down or swell with force. **2** of a crowd, etc: to move forward in a mass. **3** (*also* **surge up**) of an emotion, etc: to rise up suddenly and often uncontrollably: *Sorrow surged up inside him.* **4** of prices, electricity, etc: to increase, esp suddenly.

surgeon *n* a person who is professionally qualified to practise surgery.

surgery *n* (*-ies*) **1** the branch of medicine that is concerned with treating disease, disorder or injury by cutting into the patient's body to operate directly on or remove the affected part. **2** the performance or an instance of this type of treatment: *The surgery took 10 hours.* **3** *Brit* **a** the place where a doctor, dentist, etc sees their patients and carries out treatment; **b** the time when they are available for consultation. **4** *Brit* a time when a professional person such as an MP, lawyer, etc can be consulted.

surgical *adj* belonging or relating to, involving, caused by, used in, or by means of surgery: *surgical instruments*. ○ **surgically** *adv*.

surgical spirit *n* methylated spirit which is used for cleaning wounds and sterilizing medical equipment.

surly *adj* (*-ier, -iest*) grumpily bad-tempered and impolite. ○ **surliness** *n*.

surmise *vb* to conclude something from the information available, esp when the information is incomplete or insubstantial. ➤ *n* a conclusion drawn from such information.

surmount *vb* **1** to overcome (problems, obstacles, etc). **2** to be set on top of something. ○ **surmountable** *adj*.

surname *n* a family name or last name, as opposed to a forename or Christian name.

surpass *vb* **1** to go or be beyond in degree or extent. **2** to be better than: *a holiday that surpassed all expectations.*

surplice *n* a loose wide-sleeved white linen garment worn by members of the clergy and choir singers.

surplus *n* **1** an amount that exceeds the amount required or used; an amount that is left over after requirements have been met. **2** *commerce* the amount by which a company's income is greater than expenditure. ▷ *adj* left over after needs have been met. ♦ **surplus to requirements 1** in excess of what is needed. **2** *euphem* no longer needed or wanted.

surprise *n* **1** a sudden, unexpected, amazing, etc event, gift, etc. **2** a feeling of mental disorientation caused by something of this nature. **3 a** the act of catching someone unawares; **b** the process of being caught unawares. ▷ *vb* **1** to cause someone to experience surprise by presenting them with or subjecting them to something unexpected, amazing, etc: *He surprised her with a kiss.* **2** to come upon something or someone unexpectedly or catch unawares. **3** to capture or attack with a sudden unexpected manoeuvre. ○ **surprised** *adj.* ○ **surprising** *adj.* ○ **surprisingly** *adv.* ♦ **take sb by surprise** to catch them unawares.

surreal *adj* **1** dream-like; very odd or bizarre. **2** being in the style of surrealism.

surrealism *n* (*sometimes* **Surrealism**) a movement in art and literature that sprang up between the first and second World Wars, and whose most prominent aim was to allow the artist's or writer's unconscious to be expressed with complete creative freedom. ○ **surrealist** *adj, n.* ○ **surrealistic** *adj.*

surrender *vb* **1** *intr* to admit defeat by giving oneself up to an enemy. **2** to give or hand over someone or something, either voluntarily or under duress: *weapons surrendered under the arms amnesty.* **3** to lose or give up something: *We surrendered all hope of being rescued.* **4** *intr* (**surrender to sth**) to allow oneself to be influenced or overcome by a desire or emotion: *He surrendered to her beauty.* ▷ *n* an act, instance or the process of surrendering.

surreptitious *adj* secret, sneaky or clandestine.

surrogate *n* someone or something that takes the place of another. ○ **surrogacy** *n.*

surround *vb* to extend all around. ▷ *n* a border or edge, or an ornamental structure fitted round this. ○ **surrounding** *adj.*

surroundings *pl n* the places and/or things that are usu round about someone or something.

surtax *n* **1** an additional tax, esp one that is levied on incomes above a certain level. **2** an additional tax on something that already has a tax or duty levied on it. ▷ *vb* to levy such a tax on someone or something.

surveillance *n* (*often* **under surveillance** or **under the surveillance of sb** or **sth**) a close watch over something (eg for security purposes) or someone (eg a suspected criminal).

survey *vb* /sɜːˈveɪ/ **1** to look at or examine at length or in detail, in order to get a general view. **2** to examine (a building) in order to assess its condition or value. **3** to measure land heights and distances in (an area) for the purposes of drawing a detailed map, etc. **4** to canvass (public opinion) and make a statistical assessment of the replies. ▷ *n* /ˈsɜːveɪ/ **1** a detailed examination or investigation, eg to find out public opinion or customer preference. **2** an inspection of a building to assess condition or value. **3 a** the collecting of land measurements for map-making purposes, etc; **b** the map, etc that is drawn up after this has been done. ○ **surveying** *n.* ○ **surveyor** *n.*

survival *n* **1** of an individual: the fact of continuing to live, esp after some risk that might have prevented this. **2** something, such as an old custom, etc, that continues to be practised: *It's a survival from Victorian times.* ♦ **survival of the fittest** *non-technical* the process or result of NATURAL SELECTION.

survive *vb* **1** *tr & intr* **a** to remain alive, esp despite (some risk that might prevent this): *the only one to survive the tragedy;* **b** *colloq* to come or get through (something arduous or unpleasant): *It was a tough course, but I survived it.* **2** to live on after the death of someone: *She survived her husband by 10 years.* **3** *intr* to remain alive or in existence: *How do they survive on such a small income?* ○ **survivor** *n.*

susceptibility *n* (-*ies*) **1** the state or quality of being susceptible. **2 a** the capacity or ability to feel emotions; **b** (**susceptibilities**) feelings.

susceptible *adj* **1** (**susceptible to sth**) prone to being, or likely to be, affected by it: *I've always been susceptible to colds.* **2** capable of being affected by strong feelings, esp of love. **3** (**susceptible to sth**) capable of being influenced by something, eg persuasion.

sushi /ˈsuːʃɪ/ *n* a Japanese dish of small rolls or balls of cold boiled rice topped with egg, raw fish or vegetables.

suspect *vb* /səˈspɛkt/ **1** to consider or believe likely. **2** to think (a particular person) possibly or probably guilty of a crime or other wrongdoing. **3** to doubt the truth or genuineness of someone or something. ▷ *n* /ˈsʌspɛkt/ someone who is suspected of committing a crime, etc. ▷ *adj* /ˈsʌspɛkt/ thought to be possibly false, untrue or dangerous: *His excuse sounds pretty suspect to me.*

suspend *vb* **1** to hang or hang up something. **2** to bring a halt to something, esp temporarily: *Services are suspended due to flooding.* **3** to remove someone from a job, school, team, etc temporarily, as punishment.

suspended animation *n* a state in which a body's main functions are temporarily slowed down to an absolute minimum, eg in hibernation.

suspended sentence *n* a judicial sentence that is deferred for a set time during which the offender is required to be of good behaviour.

suspenders *pl n* **1** elasticated straps that can be attached to the top of a stocking or sock to hold it in place. **2** *N Am* braces for holding up trousers.

suspense n **1** a state of nervous or excited tension or uncertainty. **2** tension or excitedness, esp as brought on by an eager desire to know the outcome of something. ◆ **keep sb in suspense** to deliberately delay telling them something or the outcome of something.

suspension n **1** the act of suspending or the state of being suspended. **2** a temporary exclusion from an official position, work, school, etc, esp while allegations of misconduct are being investigated. **3** a temporary cessation: *suspension of hostilities*. **4** a system of springs and shock absorbers that connects the axles of a vehicle to the chassis and absorbs some of the unwanted vibrations transmitted from the road surface. **5** a liquid or gas that contains small insoluble solid particles which are more or less evenly dispersed throughout it.

suspension bridge n a bridge that has a road or rail surface hanging from vertical cables which are themselves attached to thicker cables stretched between towers.

suspicion n **1** an act, instance or feeling of suspecting. **2** a belief or opinion that is based on very little evidence. **3** a slight quantity. ◆ **above suspicion** too highly respected to be suspected of a crime or wrongdoing. **on suspicion** as a suspect: *He was held on suspicion of murder*. **under suspicion** suspected of a crime or wrongdoing.

suspicious adj **1** inclined to suspect guilt, wrongdoing, etc: *a suspicious nature*. **2** inviting or arousing suspicion: *They found the body in suspicious circumstances*. ○ **suspiciously** adv.

suss or **sus** vb, slang (**susses, sussed, sussing**) **1** to discover, assess or establish something, esp by investigation or intuition: *We soon sussed how the TV worked*. **2** to suspect something. ◇ **suss sb** or **sth out 1** to investigate, inspect or examine: *He sussed out the nightlife*. **2** to work out or understand: *I couldn't suss out his motives*.

sustain vb **1** to keep going. **2** to withstand, tolerate or endure: *It can sustain impacts even at high speed*. **3** to bolster, strengthen or encourage: *Jim had a whisky to sustain his nerves*. **4** to suffer or undergo (an injury, loss, defeat, etc). **5** to declare that an objection in court is valid. **6** to support, ratify, back up (an argument, claim, etc). **7** to maintain or provide for something: *She couldn't sustain her family on such a low salary*. ○ **sustained** adj. ○ **sustaining** adj, n.

sustainable adj **1** capable of being sustained. **2** of economic development, renewable resources, etc: capable of being maintained at a set level. ○ **sustainability** n.

sustenance n **1** a something, eg food or drink, that nourishes the body or that keeps up energy or spirits; b the action or an instance of nourishment. **2** something that maintains, supports or provides a livelihood.

suture /'suːtʃə(r)/ n a a stitch that joins the edges of a wound, surgical incision etc together; b the joining of such edges together. ➤ vb to sew up (a wound, surgical incision, etc).

suzerain n **1** a nation, state or ruler that exercises some control over another state but which allows it to retain its own ruler or government. **2** a feudal lord. ○ **suzerainty** n.

svelte adj slim or slender, esp in a graceful or attractive way.

SW abbrev **1** short wave. **2** south-west, or southwestern.

swab n a a piece of cotton wool, gauze, etc that is used for cleaning wounds, applying antiseptics, etc; b a medical specimen, eg of some bodily fluid, that is taken for examination or testing. ➤ vb (**swabbed, swabbing**) **1** to clean (a wound) with, or as if with, a swab. **2** to mop something (eg a ship's deck).

swaddle vb to wrap (a baby) in or as if in swaddling-clothes.

swaddling-clothes pl n, hist strips of cloth wrapped round a newborn baby to restrict movement.

swag n **1** slang stolen goods. **2** Aust a traveller's pack or rolled bundle of possessions. ➤ vb (**swagged, swagging**) Aust (often **swag it**) to travel around on foot with one's possessions in a bundle.

swagger vb, intr to walk with an air of self-importance. ➤ n **1** a swaggering way of walking or behaving. **2** colloq the quality of being showily fashionable or smart.

swagman or **swaggie** n, Aust someone, esp an itinerant workman, who travels about on foot and who carries their belongings in a swag.

swain n, old use, poetic **1** a country youth. **2** a young male lover or suitor.

swallow[1] vb **1** to perform a muscular movement to make (food or drink) go from the mouth, down the oesophagus and into the stomach. **2** intr to move the muscles of the throat involuntarily, esp as a sign of emotional distress. **3** (also **swallow sth up**) to engulf or absorb it. **4** to repress (pride, tears, etc). **5** to accept or endure (eg an insult) without retaliation. **6** colloq to believe gullibly or unquestioningly. ➤ n **1** an act of swallowing. **2** an amount swallowed at one time.

swallow[2] n a small migratory bird that has long pointed wings and a long forked tail.

swallow dive n a dive during which the arms are held out to the side, at shoulder level, until just above the level of the water when they are pulled in to the sides and the diver enters the water head first.

swallowtail n **1** a large colourful butterfly that has the back wings extended into slender tails. **2** a tail that is forked like a swallow's.

swami /'swɑːmɪ/ n (**swamis** or **swamies**) an honorific title for a Hindu male religious teacher.

swamp n an area of land that is permanently waterlogged. ➤ vb **1** to overwhelm or inundate. **2** to cause (a boat) to fill with water. **3** to flood. ○ **swampy** adj (**-ier, -iest**).

swan n a large, generally white, graceful aquatic bird with a long slender elegant neck, powerful wings and webbed feet. ➤ vb (**swanned, swanning**) intr, colloq (usu **swan off, around, about,** etc) to spend time idly; to wander aimlessly.

swank colloq, vb, intr to boast or show off. ➤ n flashiness; boastfulness. ○ **swanky** adj (**-ier, -iest**) flashy, fashionable, etc.

swan song n the last performance or piece of work that a musician, artist, etc gives before their death or retirement.

swap or **swop** vb (**swapped, swapping; swopped, swopping**) tr & intr to exchange or trade something or someone for another. ➤ n **1** an exchange or trading. **2** something that is exchanged or traded.

sward n a large grassy area of land.

swarm[1] n **1** a large group of flying bees, led by a queen, that have left their hive in order to set up a new home. **2** any large group of insects or other small creatures, esp ones that are on the move. **3** a crowd of people, esp one that is on the move. ➤ vb, intr to gather, move, go, etc in a swarm. ◆ **be swarming (with people or things)** of a place: to be crowded or overrun.

swarm[2] vb, tr & intr (often **swarm up sth**) to climb (esp a rope or tree) by clasping with the hands and knees or feet.

swarthy adj (**-ier, -iest**) having a dark complexion.

swashbuckler n **1** a daring and flamboyant adventurer. **2** a film, novel, etc that portrays exciting scenes of adventure, usu in a romanticized historical setting. ○ **swashbuckling** adj.

swastika n **1** an ancient religious symbol, representing the sun and good luck. **2** a plain cross with arms of equal length which are bent at right angles, usu clockwise, at or close to their midpoint, used as the adopted badge of the former German Nazi Party.

swat[1] vb (**swatted, swatting**) to hit (esp a fly) with a heavy slapping blow. ➤ n a heavy slap or blow. ○ **swatter** n a device for swatting flies, usu consisting of a long thin handle and a wide flat flexible head.

swat[2] see SWOT

swatch n **1** a small sample, esp of fabric. **2** (also **swatchbook**) a collection of samples (esp of fabric) bound together to form a sort of book.

swath /swɔːθ/ or **swathe** /sweɪð/ n (**swaths** or **swathes**) **1 a** a strip of grass, corn, etc cut by a scythe, mower or harvester; **b** the width of this strip; **c** the cut grass, corn, etc left in such a strip. **2** a broad strip, esp of land.

swathe vb to bind or wrap someone or something in strips of cloth, eg bandages. ➤ n a wrapping, esp a strip of cloth.

sway vb **1** tr & intr to swing, or make something swing, backwards and forwards or from side to side, esp slowly and smoothly. **2** tr & intr to lean or bend, or make something lean or bend, to

one side or in one direction. **3** to persuade someone to take a particular view or decision, or dissuade them from a course of action. **4** intr (usu **sway towards sth**) to incline towards a particular opinion. **5** intr to waver between two opinions or decisions. ➤ n **1** a swaying motion. **2** control or influence. ◆ **hold sway** to have authority or influence.

swear vb (**swore, sworn**) **1** intr to use indecent or blasphemous language. **2** to assert something solemnly, sometimes with an oath. **3** to promise solemnly, usu by taking an oath. **4** to take (an oath). **5** intr (**swear by sth** or **sth**) colloq to have or put complete trust in (eg a certain product) or them (eg a doctor or therapist). ➤ n an act of swearing. ○ **swearing** n. ◇ **swear sb in** to introduce them formally into a post, or into the witness box, by requesting them to take an oath. **swear off sth** colloq to promise to give it up.

swear-word n a word regarded as obscene or blasphemous.

sweat n **1** the salty liquid produced by glands and given out through the pores of the skin, esp in response to heat, physical exertion, nervousness or fear. **2** the state, or a period, of giving off such moisture. **3** colloq any activity that causes the body to give off such moisture. **4** colloq any laborious activity. ➤ vb (**sweated** or **sweat**) intr **1** to give out sweat through the pores of the skin. **2** colloq to be nervous, anxious or afraid. ○ **sweaty** adj. ◆ **in a sweat** or **in a cold sweat** colloq in a worried or anxious state. **no sweat!** slang that presents no problems. **sweat blood** colloq **1** to work extremely hard. **2** to be in a state of great anxiety. **sweat it out** colloq to endure a difficult situation to the end. ◇ **sweat sth off** to remove (weight, fat, etc) by exercise that makes one sweat.

sweatband n a strip of elasticated fabric worn around the wrist or head to absorb sweat when playing sports.

sweater n a knitted jersey or pullover.

sweatshirt n a long-sleeved jersey of a thick soft cotton fabric, usu fleecy on the inside.

sweatshop n a workshop or factory where employees work for long hours with poor pay and conditions.

sweatsuit n a loose-fitting suit of sweatshirt and trousers.

swede n **1** a plant widely cultivated for its edible root. **2** the swollen edible root of this plant, which has orange-yellow flesh and can be cooked and eaten as a vegetable.

sweep vb (**swept**) **1** to clean (a room, a floor, etc) with a brush or broom. **2** to remove (dirt, dust, etc) with a brush or broom. **3** (usu **sweep sth aside** or **away**) to dismiss (ideas, suggestions, etc) or remove (problems, errors, etc): *She swept aside their objections.* **4** (often **sweep sb** or **sth away, off, past,** etc) to take, carry or push them suddenly and with irresistible force: *The current swept the boat through the narrows.* **5** (often **sweep sb** or **sth off, up,** etc) to lift, gather or clear with a forceful scooping movement: *He swept the child into his arms.* **6** *tr & intr* (*often* **sweep in, out,** *etc*) to move, pass or spread smoothly and swiftly, or strongly or uncontrollably: *Strong winds were sweeping in from the sea.* **7** *intr* to walk, esp with garments flowing, arrogantly, angrily, etc: *She swept across the room in her robes.* **8** *tr & intr* to pass quickly over something, making light contact: *Her dress swept the floor.* **9** *intr* of emotions, etc: to affect someone suddenly and overpoweringly: *She felt a chill sweep over her.* **10** to have a decisive electoral win: *They are expecting to sweep the country in next week's elections.* **11** to direct (eg one's gaze) with a scanning movement. **12** to make extensive searches over (an area) for mines, ships, etc. ➤ *n* **1** an act of sweeping. **2** a sweeping movement or action. **3** a sweeping line or broad sweeping stretch. **4** the range or area over which something moves, esp in a curving path. **5** *colloq* a sweepstake. **6** *colloq* a chimney-sweep. ♦ **a clean sweep** the winning of all prizes, political seats, etc. **sweep sb off their feet** to have a strong or sudden effect on their emotions, usu causing them to fall in love. **sweep sth under the carpet** to hide or ignore something (esp unwelcome facts, difficulties, etc).

sweeper *n* **1** someone who sweeps. **2** a device or machine used for sweeping. **3** *football* a player covering the whole area behind a line of defenders.

sweeping *adj* **1** of a search, change, etc: wide-ranging and thorough. **2** of a statement: too generalized. **3** of a victory, etc: impressive; decisive.

sweepstake *n* **1** a system of gambling in which the prize money is the sum of the stakes of all those betting. **2** a horse race in which the owner of the winning horse receives sums of money put up by the owners of all the other horses.

sweet *adj* **1** tasting like sugar; not sour, salty or bitter. **2** pleasing to any of the senses, esp smell and hearing. **3** likeable; charming. **4** of wine: having some taste of sugar or fruit; not dry. **5** *colloq* (*usu* **sweet on sb**) fond of them. **6** of air or water: fresh and untainted. ➤ *n* **1** any small sugar-based confection that is sucked or chewed. **2** a pudding or dessert. ➤ *adv* sweetly. ○ **sweetly** *adv.* ○ **sweetness** *n.*

sweet-and-sour *adj* cooked in a sauce that includes both sugar and vinegar or lemon juice. ➤ *n* a sweet-and-sour dish.

sweetbread *n* the pancreas or thymus of a young animal, esp a calf, used as food.

sweet chestnut see CHESTNUT

sweetcorn *n* kernels of a variety of maize eaten young while still sweet.

sweeten *vb* **1** to make (food) sweet or sweeter. **2** (*also* **sweeten sb up**) *colloq* to make them more agreeable or amenable, eg by flattery. **3** *colloq* to make (eg an offer) more acceptable or inviting, by making changes or additions.

sweetener *n* **1** a substance used for sweetening food, esp one other than sugar. **2** *colloq* an inducement, usu illicit, added to an offer to make it more attractive, esp a bribe.

sweetheart *n* **a** a person one is in love with; **b** used as a term of endearment.

sweetie *n, colloq* **1** a sweet. **2** (*also* **sweetie-pie**) a term of endearment. **3** a lovable person.

sweetmeat *n, old use* any small sugar-based confection or cake.

sweet nothings *pl n* the endearments that people in love say to each other.

sweet pea *n* a climbing plant that has brightly coloured butterfly-shaped flowers with a sweet scent.

sweet pepper *n* **1** a tropical American plant, widely cultivated for its edible fruit. **2** the hollow edible fruit of this plant, which can be eaten when red (or another colour such as orange or yellow) and ripe or when green and unripe.

sweet potato *n* **1** a plant with trailing or climbing stems and large purple funnel-shaped flowers. **2** the swollen edible root of this plant, which has sweet-tasting flesh and can be cooked and eaten as a vegetable.

sweet talk *n, colloq* words, often flattery, intended to coax or persuade. ➤ *vb* (**sweet-talk**) *colloq* to coax or persuade, or to try to do so, eg with flattering words.

sweet tooth *n* a fondness for sweet foods.

swell *vb* (*past participle* **swollen** or **swelled**) **1** *tr & intr* to make or become bigger or fatter through injury or infection, or by filling with liquid or air. **2** *tr & intr* to increase in number, size or intensity. **3** *intr* to become visibly filled with emotion, esp pride. **4** *intr* of the sea: to rise and fall in smooth masses without forming individual waves. **5** *intr* of a sound: to become louder and then die away. ➤ *n* **1** a heaving of the sea without waves. **2** an increase in number, size or intensity. **3** an increase in volume of sound or music, followed by a dying away. **4** *old colloq* someone who dresses smartly and fashionably. **5** *mus* a device in organs and some harpsichords for increasing and decreasing the volume of sound. ➤ *adj, exclam, chiefly N Am colloq* excellent. ○ **swelling** *n* an area of the body that is temporarily swollen as a result of injury or infection.

swelter *vb, intr* to sweat heavily or feel extremely or oppressively hot. ➤ *n* a sweltering feeling or state. ○ **sweltering** *adj* of the weather: extremely or oppressively hot.

swerve *vb, intr* to turn or move aside suddenly and sharply, eg to avoid a collision. ➤ *n* an act of swerving; a swerving movement.

swift *adj* **1** fast-moving; able to move fast. **2** done, given, etc quickly. **3** acting promptly: *His friends were swift to defend him.* ➤ *adv* swiftly. ➤ *n* a small fast-flying bird that has dark brown or grey plumage, long narrow pointed wings and a forked tail. ○ **swiftly** *adv.* ○ **swiftness** *n.*

swig *colloq, vb* (**swigged, swigging**) *tr & intr* to drink in gulps, esp from a bottle. ➤ *n* a large gulp.

swill *vb* **1** (*also* **swill sth out**) to rinse something by splashing water round or over it. **2** *colloq* to drink (esp alcohol) greedily. ➤ *n* **1** any mushy mixture of scraps fed to pigs. **2** disgusting food or drink.

swim *vb* (**swam, swum, swimming**) **1** *intr* to propel oneself through water by moving the arms and legs or (in fish) the tail and fins. **2** to cover (a distance) or cross (a stretch of water) in this way: *to swim the Channel*. **3** *intr* to float. **4** *intr* to be affected by dizziness: *His head was swimming*. **5** *intr* to move or appear to move about in waves or whirls. ➤ *n* a spell of swimming. ○ **swimmer** *n*. ○ **swimming** *n*. ♦ **in the swim** *colloq* up to date with, and often involved in, what is going on around one.

swimming baths *pl n* a swimming pool, usu indoors.

swimming costume *n* a swimsuit.

swimmingly *adv, colloq* smoothly and successfully.

swimming pool *n* an artificial pool for swimming in.

swimsuit *n* a garment worn for swimming.

swindle *vb* to cheat or trick someone in order to obtain money from them; to obtain (money, etc) by cheating or trickery. ➤ *n* an act of swindling. ○ **swindler** *n*.

swine *n* (**swine** in sense 1 or **swines** in sense 2) **1** a pig. **2** a despicable person.

swineherd *n, old use* someone who looks after pigs.

swing *vb* (**swung**) **1** *tr & intr* to move in a curving motion, pivoting from a fixed point: *The door swung shut behind her*. **2** *tr & intr* to move or make something move or turn with a curving movement or movements: *Jeb swung himself into the saddle*. **3** *tr & intr* to turn or make something turn around a central axis: *She swung round, surprised*. **4** *intr* to undergo, often suddenly or sharply, a change of opinion, mood, fortune or direction: *He swung between extremes of mood*. **5** (*also* **swing sb round**) to persuade them to have a certain opinion: *That should swing them round to our way of thinking*. **6** *colloq* to arrange or fix; to achieve the successful outcome of something: *It just needs a couple of free gifts to swing the sale*. **7 a** *colloq* to determine or settle the outcome of (eg an election in which voters were initially undecided); **b** *intr* of an electorate's voting pattern: to change in favour of a particular party: *The vote has swung decisively to the Green Party*. **8** *tr & intr* (*often* **swing at sb** or **sth**) **a** to attempt to hit or make a hit with a curving movement of a bat, etc: *Lucy swung wildly at the ball*; **b** *colloq* to attempt to punch someone or make (a punch) with a curving arm movement: *He swung a frustrated punch at the goalkeeper*. **9** *intr, colloq* of a social function, etc: to be lively and exciting. **10** *intr, colloq* to change sexual

partners in a group, esp habitually. **11** *intr, colloq* to be hanged. ➤ *n* **1** a seat suspended from a frame or branch for a child (or sometimes an adult) to swing on. **2** a change, usu a sudden and sharp change, eg in mood, support, etc. **3** a swinging stroke with a golf club, cricket bat, etc; the technique of a golfer. **4** a punch made with a curving movement. **5** an act, manner or spell of swinging. **6** a swinging movement. **7** *mus* jazz or jazz-like dance music with a simple regular rhythm, popularized by bands in the 1930s. **8** *cricket* a curving movement of a bowled ball. **9** a change in the voting pattern of the electorate in a particular constituency, at a particular election, etc: *a swing of 40% to Labour*. ➤ *adj* able to swing: *a swing mirror*. ♦ **in full swing** or **into full swing** at, or to, the height of liveliness. **swings and roundabouts** *colloq* a situation in which advantages and disadvantages, or successes and failures, are equal. **the swing of things** the usual routine or pace of activity.

swingeing /'swɪndʒɪŋ/ *adj* hard to bear; severe; extensive.

swipe *vb* **1** to hit with a heavy sweeping blow. **2** (*usu* **swipe at sb** or **sth**) to try to hit them or it. **3** *colloq* to steal. **4** to pass (a plastic card) through a device that electronically interprets the information encoded on the card. ➤ *n* a heavy sweeping blow.

swirl *vb, tr & intr* to flow or cause to flow with a circling motion. ➤ *n* **1** a circling motion. **2** a curling shape or pattern. ○ **swirling** *adj*.

swish¹ *vb, tr & intr* to move with a rustling, hissing or whooshing sound. ➤ *n* a rustling, hissing or whooshing sound, or movement causing such a sound.

swish² *adj, colloq* smart and stylish.

Swiss roll *n* a cylindrical cake made by rolling up a thin slab of sponge spread with jam or cream.

switch *n* **1** a manually operated or automatic device that is used to open or close an electric circuit. **2** a change. **3** an exchange or changeover, esp one involving a deception. **4** a long flexible twig or cane, esp one used for corporal punishment; a stroke with such a twig or cane. **5** *N Am* a set of railway points. ➤ *vb* **1** *tr & intr* to exchange (one thing or person for another), esp quickly and without notice in order to deceive. **2** *tr & intr* to transfer or change over (eg to a different system). ♦ **switched on** *colloq* well informed or aware. ◊ **switch off** *colloq* to stop paying attention. **switch sth off** to turn (an appliance) off by means of a switch. **switch sth on 1** to turn (an appliance) on by means of a switch. **2** *colloq* to bring on (eg charm or tears) at will in order to create the required effect.

switchback *n* **1** a road with many twists and turns and upward and downward slopes. **2** a rollercoaster.

switchboard *n* a board on which incoming telephone calls are connected manually or electronically.

swither *vb, intr, Scot* to hesitate; to be undecided.

swivel *n* a joint between two parts enabling one part to turn or pivot freely and independently of the other. ➤ *vb* (**swivelled, swivelling**) *tr & intr* to turn or pivot on a swivel or as if on a swivel.

swizz *n, colloq* a thing that, in reality, is disappointingly inferior to what was cheatingly promised.

swizzle-stick *n* a thin stick used to stir cocktailss.

swoon *vb, intr* **1** to faint, esp from overexcitement. **2** (*often* swoon over sb or sth) to go into raptures about them or it. ➤ *n* an act of swooning.

swoop *vb, intr* **1** to fly down with a fast sweeping movement. **2** to make a sudden forceful attack. **3** (*usu* swoop at sb or sth) to make a sudden and quick attempt to seize them or it. ➤ *n* **1** an act of swooping. **2** a swooping movement or feeling. ◆ **in one fell swoop** in one complete decisive action.

swoosh *n* the noise of a rush of air or water, or any noise resembling this. ➤ *vb, intr* to make or move with such a noise.

swop see SWAP

sword *n* **1** a weapon like a large long knife, with a sharp blade usu ending in a point. **2** (**the sword**) violence or destruction. ◆ **cross swords with sb** to argue or fight with them.

swordfish *n* a large marine fish with an upper jaw prolonged into a long flat sword-shaped snout.

sword of Damocles /ˈdaməkliːz/ *n, literary* any imminent danger or disaster.

swordplay *n* the activity or art of fencing.

swordsman *n* a man skilled in fighting with a sword. ○ **swordsmanship** *n*.

sworn *vb, past participle of* SWEAR. ➤ *adj* confirmed by, or as if by, having taken an oath: *sworn enemies*.

swot or **swat** *colloq, vb* (**swotted, swotting; swatted, swatting**) *tr & intr* **1** to study hard and seriously. **2** (*also* swot sth up) to study it intensively, esp just before an exam. ➤ *n* someone who studies hard, esp single-mindedly or in order to impress a teacher.

sybarite /ˈsɪbərʌt/ *n* someone devoted to a life of luxury and pleasure. ○ **sybaritic** *adj* luxurious.

sycamore *n* **1** a large tree with dark green leaves. **2** *N Am* any of various plane trees native to America. **3** the wood of any of these trees, used for furniture-making, etc.

sycophant *n* someone who flatters in a servile way. ○ **sycophancy** *n* the behaviour of a sycophant. ○ **sycophantic** *adj*.

syllabic *adj* relating to syllables or the division of words into syllables.

syllabify *vb* (**-ies, -ied**) to divide (a word) into syllables. ○ **syllabification** *n*.

syllable *n* **1** a segment of a spoken word consisting of one sound or of two or more sounds said as a single unit of speech (*segment* has two syllables; *consisting* has three syllables). **2** the slightest word or sound: *He hardly uttered a syllable all evening.* ◆ **in words of one syllable** in simple language; plainly.

syllabub or **sillabub** *n* a frothy dessert made with a sweetened mixture of cream or milk and wine.

syllabus *n* (**syllabuses** or **syllabi**) a series of topics prescribed for a course of study.

syllogism *n* an argument in which a conclusion, whether valid or invalid, is drawn from two independent statements using logic, as in *All dogs are animals, foxhounds are dogs, therefore foxhounds are animals.* ○ **syllogistic** *adj.*

sylph *n* **1** in folklore: a spirit of the air. **2** a slender graceful woman or girl.

sylvan or **silvan** *adj, literary* relating to woods or woodland.

symbiosis *n* (**-ses** /-siːz/) *biol* a close association between two organisms of different species, usu to the benefit of both partners, and often essential for mutual survival. ○ **symbiotic** *adj.*

symbol *n* **1** a thing that represents another, usu something concrete representing an idea or emotion. **2** a letter or sign used to represent a quantity, object, operation, etc, such as the £ used to represent pound sterling. ○ **symbolic** or **symbolical** *adj* **1** being a symbol of something; representing something. **2** relating to symbols or their use. ○ **symbolically** *adv.*

symbolism *n* **1** the use of symbols, esp to express ideas or emotions in literature, cinema, etc. **2** a system of symbols. **3** (*usu* Symbolism) a 19th-century movement in art and literature which made extensive use of symbols to indicate or evoke emotions or ideas. ○ **symbolist** *n* an artist or writer who uses symbolism.

symbolize or **-ise** *vb* **1** to be a symbol of something; to stand for something. **2** to represent something by means of a symbol or symbols.

symmetry *n* (**-ies**) **1** exact similarity between two parts or halves, as if one were a mirror image of the other. **2** the arrangement of parts in pleasing proportion to each other; also, the aesthetic satisfaction derived from this. ○ **symmetrical** *adj.*

sympathetic *adj* **1** (*often* sympathetic to sb or sth) feeling or expressing sympathy for them. **2** amiable, esp because of being kind-hearted. **3** acting or done out of sympathy. **4** in keeping with one's mood or feelings.

sympathize or **-ise** *vb, intr* **1** (*often* sympathize with sb) to feel or express sympathy for them. **2** (*often* sympathize with sb or sth) to support or be in agreement with them. ○ **sympathizer** *n.*

sympathy *n* (**-ies**) **1** (*often* sympathy for or with sb) an understanding of and feeling for the sadness or suffering of others, often shown in expressions of sorrow or pity. **2** (*often* sympathies) loyal or approving support for, or agreement with, an organization or belief. **3** affection between people resulting from their understanding of each other's personalities.

symphony *n* (*-ies*) **1** a long musical work divided into several movements, played by a full orchestra. **2** an instrumental passage in a musical work which consists mostly of singing. **3** *literary* a pleasing combination of parts, eg shapes or colours. **4** a symphony orchestra. ○ **symphonic** *adj*.

symphony orchestra *n* a large orchestra capable of playing large-scale orchestral music.

symposium *n* (*symposia* or *symposiums*) **1** a conference held to discuss a particular subject. **2** a collection of essays by different writers on a single topic.

symptom *n* **1** *med* an indication of the presence of a disease or disorder. **2** an indication of the existence of a state or condition: *The increase in crime is a symptom of moral decline*. ○ **symptomatic** *adj*.

synagogue *n* a Jewish place of worship and religious instruction.

synch or **sync** /sɪŋk/ *colloq, n* synchronization, esp of sound and picture in film and television. ➢ *vb* to synchronize.

synchromesh *n* a gear system which matches the speeds of the gear wheels before they are engaged, avoiding shock and noise in gear-changing.

synchronize or **-ise** *vb* **1** *tr & intr* to happen or cause to happen, move or operate in exact time with (something else or each other). **2** to project (a film), or broadcast (a TV programme), so that the action, actors' lip movements, etc precisely match the sounds or words heard. **3** to set (clocks or watches) so that they all show exactly the same time. ○ **synchronization** *n*.

synchronous *adj* occurring at the same time or rate. ○ **synchrony** *n*.

syncopate *vb, mus* to alter (rhythm) by putting the stress on beats not usu stressed. ○ **syncopation** *n*.

syndic *n* someone who represents a university, company or other body in business or legal matters.

syndicate *n* /'sɪndɪkət/ **1** any association of people or groups working together on a single project. **2** a group of business organizations jointly managing or financing a single venture. **3** an association of criminals organizing widespread illegal activities. **4** an agency selling journalists' material to a number of newspapers for publication at the same time. ➢ *vb* /-keɪt/ **1** to form into a syndicate. **2 a** to sell (an article, photograph, etc) for publication by a number of newspapers; **b** in the US: to sell (a programme) for broadcasting by a number of TV stations. ○ **syndication** *n*.

syndrome *n* **1** a group of symptoms whose appearance together usu indicates the presence of a particular disease or disorder. **2** a pattern or series of events, observed qualities, etc

characteristic of a particular problem or condition.

synecdoche /sɪ'nɛkdəkɪ/ *n* a figure of speech in which a part of something is used to refer to or denote the whole thing, or the whole to refer to or denote a part, eg the use of *wiser heads* to mean *wiser people*.

synergy *n* a phenomenon in which the combined action of two or more things is greater than the sum of the individual effects of each.

synod *n* **a** a local or national council of members of the clergy; **b** a meeting of this.

synonym *n* a word having the same meaning as another. ○ **synonymous** *adj* (*often synonymous with sth*) **1** having the same meaning. **2** very closely associated in the mind.

synopsis /sɪ'nɒpsɪs/ *n* (*-ses* /-siːz/) a brief outline, eg of the plot of a book. ○ **synoptic** *adj* being or like a synopsis; giving or taking an overall view.

syntax *n* **1 a** the positioning of words in a sentence and their relationship to each other; **b** the grammatical rules governing this. **2** the branch of linguistics that is concerned with the study of such rules. ○ **syntactic** or **syntactical** *adj*. ○ **syntactically** *adv*.

synthesis /'sɪnθəsɪs/ *n* (*-ses* /-siːz/) **1** the process of putting together separate parts to form a complex whole. **2** the result of such a process. **3** *chem* any process whereby a complex chemical compound is formed from simpler compounds or elements.

synthesize or **-ise** *vb* **1** to combine (simple parts) to form (a complex whole). **2** *chem* to form (a compound, product, etc) by a process of chemical synthesis.

synthesizer or **-iser** *n, mus* an instrument that produces sound electronically, esp one able to produce the sounds of other instruments.

synthetic *adj* **1** referring or relating to, or produced by, chemical synthesis; man-made. **2** not sincere. ➢ *n* a synthetic substance. ○ **synthetically** *adv*.

syphilis *n, med* a sexually transmitted disease caused by bacterial infection and characterized by painless ulcers on the genitals, fever and a faint red rash. ○ **syphilitic** *adj, n*.

syphon see SIPHON

syringe *n* **1** a medical instrument for injecting or drawing off liquid, consisting of a hollow cylinder with a plunger inside and a thin hollow needle attached. **2** a similar device used in gardening, cooking, etc. ➢ *vb* to clean, spray or inject using a syringe.

syrup *n* **1** a sweet, sticky, almost saturated solution of sugar. **2** a solution of sugar in water used to preserve canned fruit. **3** any sugar-flavoured liquid medicine. **4** *colloq* exaggerated sentimentality or pleasantness of manner. ○ **syrupy** *adj* **1** having the consistency of or like syrup. **2** over-sentimental.

system *n* **1** a set of interconnected or interrelated parts forming a complex whole: *the transport system*. **2** an arrangement of mechanical, electrical or electronic parts functioning as a unit: *a stereo system*. **3** a way of working; a method or arrangement of organization or classification: *a more efficient filing system*. **4** one's mind or body regarded as a set of interconnected parts: *Get the anger out of your system*. **5** (**the system**) society, or the network of institutions that control it, usu regarded as an oppressive force.

systematic *adj* **1** making use of, or carried out according to, a clearly worked-out plan or method. **2** methodical. ○ **systematically** *adv*.

systematize or **-ise** *vb* to organize or arrange in a methodical way. ○ **systematization** *n*.

systemic *adj, med* relating to or affecting the whole body: *a systemic illness*. ○ **systemically** *adv*.

systems analysis *n, comput* the detailed investigation and analysis of some human task in order to determine whether and how it can be computerized.

systole /ˈsɪstəlɪ/ *n, med* contraction of the heart muscle, during which blood is pumped from the ventricle into the arteries. ○ **systolic** /sɪˈstɒlɪk/ *adj*.

Tt

T¹ or **t** *n* (**Ts, T's** or **t's**) the twentieth letter of the English alphabet. ♦ **to a T** exactly; perfectly well.

T² *symbol, chem* tritium.

t *abbrev* **1** ton. **2** tonne.

Ta *symbol, chem* tantalum.

ta *exclam, Brit colloq* thank you.

tab¹ *n* **1** a small flap, tag, strip of material, etc attached to something, for hanging it up, opening, holding or identifying it, etc. **2** *chiefly US* a bill, eg, in a bar, restaurant, etc. **3** *chiefly US* a price; cost. **4** a stage curtain or a loop from which it hangs. ➤ *vb* (**tabbed, tabbing**) to fix a tab to. ♦ **keep tabs on** *colloq* to keep a close watch or check on. **pick up the tab** to pay the bill.

tab² *n* a key on a typewriter or word processor keyboard which sets and then automatically finds the position of margins and columns.

tabard *n* **1** a short loose sleeveless jacket or tunic, worn esp by a medieval knight or by a herald. **2** a woman's or girl's sleeveless or short-sleeved tunic or overgarment.

tabbouleh /taˈbuːleɪ/ *n* a Mediterranean salad made with cracked wheat and vegetables.

tabby *n* (**-ies**) (*also* **tabby cat**) a grey or brown cat with darker stripes.

tabernacle *n* **1** the tent carried by the Israelites across the desert during the Exodus. **2** *RC Church* a receptacle where the consecrated bread and wine are kept. **3** a place of worship of certain nonconformist Christian denominations.

tabla *n* a pair of small drums played with the hands in Indian music.

table *n* **1** a piece of furniture consisting of a flat horizontal surface supported by one or more legs. **2** the people sitting at a table. **3** the food served at a particular table or in a particular house: *She keeps a good table*. **4** a group of words or figures, etc arranged in columns and rows. **5** (*also* **multiplication table**) *maths* a list of the products created by multiplying a number by every number in turn. ➤ *vb* **1** *Brit* to put forward for discussion. **2** *N Am* to postpone discussion of (a bill, etc) indefinitely. ♦ **on the table** under discussion. **turn the tables on sb** to reverse a situation so that they are at a disadvantage where previously they had an advantage.

tableau /ˈtæbloʊ; *French* tablo/ *n* (**tableaux** /-bloʊz; *French* tablo/) *theat* a moment or scene in which the action is frozen for dramatic effect.

tablecloth *n* a cloth for covering a table, esp during meals.

tableland *n* a broad high plain or a plateau.

table licence *n* a licence to sell and serve alcohol only with meals.

tablespoon *n* **1** a large spoon used for measuring and serving food. **2** the amount a tablespoon can hold. ○ **tablespoonful** *n*.

tablet *n* **1** a small solid measured amount of a medicine or drug. **2** a solid flat piece of something, eg, soap. **3** a slab of stone or wood on which an inscription may be carved.

table tennis *n* a game based on tennis played indoors on a table with small bats and a light hollow ball.

tabloid *n* a newspaper with relatively small pages, usu having a sensationalist style and many photographs. ➤ *adj* relating to this type of newspaper or this style of journalism: *the tabloid press* • *tabloid television*. Compare BROADSHEET.

taboo or **tabu** *n* **1** something forbidden or disapproved of for religious reasons or by social custom. **2** a system in which certain actions, etc are forbidden. ➤ *adj* forbidden or prohibited as being a taboo.

tabor /ˈteɪbə(r)/ *n* a small drum, often accompanying a pipe or fife.

tabular *adj* arranged in systematic columns or lists.

tabulate *vb* to arrange (information) in tabular form. ○ **tabulation** *n*.

tabulator *n* a TAB².

tachograph *n* a device which keeps a record

of a vehicle's speed, esp a lorry, and the time it takes to cover a particular distance.

tachometer /ta'kɒmətə(r)/ n a device which measures speed, esp that of an engine in revolutions per minute.

tacit /'tasɪt/ adj 1 silent; unspoken. 2 understood but not actually stated.

taciturn /'tasɪtɜːn/ adj saying little; quiet and uncommunicative.

tack¹ n 1 a short nail with a sharp point and a broad flat head. 2 N Am a drawing pin. 3 a long loose temporary stitch. 4 a sailing ship's course, esp when taking advantage of winds from different directions. 5 a direction, course of action or policy: *to try a different tack*. ➤ vb 1 to fasten with a tack or tacks. 2 to sew with long loose temporary stitches. 3 (also **tack sth on**) to attach or add it as a supplement. 4 intr to use the wind direction to one's advantage when sailing. 5 naut to change the tack of (a ship) to the opposite one.

tack² n a horse's riding harness, saddle and bridle, etc.

tackle n 1 sport an act of trying to get the ball away from an opposing player. 2 the equipment needed for a particular sport or occupation. 3 a system of ropes and pulleys for lifting heavy objects. 4 the ropes and rigging on a ship. ➤ vb 1 to grasp or seize and struggle with. 2 to question (someone) (about a disputed, etc issue): *We tackled him about the missing money.* 3 to try to deal with or solve (a problem). 4 tr & intr, sport to try to get the ball from (an opposing player).

tacky¹ adj (-ier, -iest) slightly sticky. ○ **tackiness** n.

tacky² adj (-ier, -iest) colloq 1 shabby; shoddy. 2 vulgar; in bad taste. ○ **tackiness** n.

taco n a folded, usu crisp, maize tortilla with a filling.

tact n 1 an awareness of the best or most considerate way to deal with others so as to avoid offence, upset, antagonism or resentment. 2 skill or judgement in handling difficult situations; diplomacy. ○ **tactful** adj. ○ **tactless** adj.

tactic n a tactical manoeuvre.

tactical adj 1 relating to or forming tactics. 2 skilful; well planned and well executed.

tactics sing or pl n 1 the art of employing and manoeuvring troops to win or gain an advantage over the enemy. 2 plans, procedures, etc used in achieving something. ○ **tactician** n.

tactile adj 1 belonging or relating to, or having, a sense of touch. 2 perceptible to the sense of touch.

tad n, colloq a small amount: *just a tad of milk in my tea.*

tadpole n the larval stage of an amphibian, often initially having the appearance of just a head and a tail.

taekwondo n a Korean martial art.

taffeta n a stiff woven silk or silk-like material.

taffrail n, naut a rail round a ship's stern.

tag¹ n 1 a label attached to something and carrying information, eg, washing instructions, price, destination, etc. 2 an electronic device such as a bracelet or anklet which transmits radio signals and is used to supervise the movements of a prisoner or offender outside prison. ➤ vb (**tagged, tagging**) 1 to put a tag or tags on. 2 (usu **tag along** or **on**) intr to follow or accompany, esp when uninvited.

tag² n a children's chasing game. ➤ vb (**tagged, tagging**) to catch or touch in, or as if in, the game of tag.

tagliatelle /taljə'tɛlɪ/ n pasta in the form of long narrow ribbons.

t'ai chi /taɪ tʃiː/ n a Chinese system of exercise and self-defence involving extremely slow and controlled movements.

tail¹ n 1 the part of an animal's body that projects from the lower or rear end. 2 the feathers that project from the rear of a bird's body. 3 anything which has a similar form, function or position as a creature's tail: *shirt tail*. 4 a lower, last or rear part. 5 the rear part of an aircraft. 6 astron the trail of luminous particles following a comet. 7 (**tails**) the reverse side of a coin, that side which does not bear a portrait or head. Compare HEADS at HEAD (noun sense 21). 8 (**tails**) a TAILCOAT. 9 (**tails**) evening dress for men, usu including a tailcoat and white bow tie. 10 colloq someone who follows and keeps a constant watch on someone else. ➤ vb 1 to remove the stalks (from fruit or vegetables). 2 to follow and watch very closely. ○ **tailless** adj. ♦ **turn tail** to turn round and run away. **with one's tail between one's legs** completely defeated or humiliated. ◊ **tail away** or **off** to become gradually less, smaller or weaker.

tail² n, law the limitation of who may inherit property to one person and that person's heirs, or to some other particular class of heirs.

tailback n a long queue of traffic stretching back from an accident or roadworks, etc.

tailboard n a hinged or removable flap at the rear of a lorry, etc.

tailcoat n a man's formal black jacket with a long divided tapering tail.

tail end n the very end or last part.

tailgate n 1 a door which opens upwards at the back of an estate car or hatchback. 2 N Am a TAILBOARD.

tailor n someone whose job is making suits, jackets, trousers, etc to measure. ➤ vb 1 tr & intr to make (garments) so that they fit well. 2 to make suitable for particular or special circumstances. 3 intr to work as a tailor.

tailored adj of clothes: well-made or fitting the wearer exactly.

tailor-made adj 1 of clothes: made by a tailor to fit a particular person. 2 perfectly suited or adapted for a particular purpose.

tailplane n a small horizontal wing at the rear of an aircraft.

tailspin n 1 a spinning movement made by an

aircraft, either because it is out of control or as part of a display of aeronautical skills. **2** *colloq* a state of great agitation.

taint *vb* **1** *tr & intr* to affect or be affected by pollution, putrefaction or contamination. **2** to contaminate morally. **3** to affect or spoil slightly. ➤ *n* **1** a spot, mark or trace of decay, contamination, infection or something bad or evil. **2** a corrupt or decayed condition. ○ **tainted** *adj*.

take *vb* (**took, taken**) **1** to reach out for and grasp, lift or pull, etc: *take a book from the shelf*. **2** to carry, conduct or lead to another place. **3** to do or perform: *take a walk* • *take revenge*. **4** to get, receive, occupy, obtain, rent or buy. **5** to agree to have or accept: *take advice* • *take office*. **6** to accept as true or valid: *take her word for it*. **7** to adopt or commit oneself to: *take a wife* • *take a decision*. **8** to endure or put up with: *I cannot take his arrogance*. **9** to need or require: *It will take all day to finish*. **10** to use (eg a bus or train) as a means of transport. **11** to make a written note, etc of: *take the minutes of the meeting*. **12** to photograph: *take a few colour slides* • *Shall I take you standing by the bridge?* **13** to study or teach (a subject, etc). **14** to remove, use or borrow without permission. **15** to proceed to occupy: *take a seat*. **16** to come or derive from: *a quotation taken from Shakespeare*. **17** to have room to hold or strength to support, etc: *The shelf won't take any more books*. **18** to consider as an example. **19** to consider or think of in a particular way, sometimes mistakenly: *I took her to be a teacher* • *Do you take me for a fool?* **20** to capture or win. **21** to charm and delight: *She was very taken with the little cottage*. **22** to eat or drink: *take medicine* • *I don't take sugar in coffee*. **23** to conduct or lead: *This road will take you to the station*. **24** to be in charge or control of: *take the meeting*. **25** to react to or receive (news, etc) in a specified way. **26** to feel: *Lucy takes pride in her work*. **27** *intr* (**take to** or **sth**) to develop a liking for them or it. **28** to derive (help or refuge, etc): *Oliver takes refuge in his religion*. **29** *intr* (**take to sth**) to turn to it as a remedy or for refuge: *After the break-up, he took to drink*. **30** *intr* (**take to sth**) to begin to do it regularly. **31** to subtract or remove. **32** to make use of; to select (a route, etc): *We took the first road on the left*. **33** to deal with or consider: *take the first two questions together*. **34** *intr* to have or produce the expected or desired effect: *The vaccination didn't take*. **35** *intr* of seeds, etc: to begin to send out roots and grow. **36** to measure: *take a temperature*. **37** *intr* to become suddenly (ill, etc). **38** to understand: *I take him to mean he isn't coming*. **39** to have sexual intercourse with. ➤ *n* **1** a scene filmed or a piece of music recorded, etc in a single, uninterrupted period. **2** an amount or number (eg, of caught fish) taken at one time. **3** the amount of money taken in a shop or business, etc over a particular period of time: *the day's take*. ◆ **take it out of sb** *colloq* to exhaust their strength or energy. **take it out on sb** *colloq*

to vent one's anger or frustration on them, esp when they do not deserve it. **take it upon oneself** to assume responsibility. ◊ **take after** to resemble in appearance or character. **take against** to dislike immediately. **take sb apart** to criticize or defeat them severely. **take sth apart** to separate it into pieces or components. **take sb back 1** to make them remember the past. **2** to resume relations with (a former partner, lover, etc) after an estrangement. **take sth back 1** to withdraw or retract (a statement or promise). **2** to regain possession of it. **3** to return (something bought from a shop) for an exchange or refund. **take sth down 1** to make a written note or record of it. **2** to demolish or dismantle it. **3** to lower it. **take sb in 1** to include them. **2** to give them accommodation or shelter. **3** to deceive or cheat them. **take sth in 1** to include it. **2** to understand and remember it. **3** to make (a piece of clothing) smaller. **4** to do (paid work of a specified kind) in one's home: *take in washing*. **5** to include a visit to (a place). **take off 1** of an aircraft or its passengers: to leave the ground. **2** *colloq* to depart or set out. **3** *colloq* of a scheme or product, etc: to become popular and successful and expand quickly. **take sb off** to imitate or mimic them, esp for comic effect. **take sth off 1** to remove: *Dan took off his jacket*. **2** to deduct: *She took two pounds off the price*. **3** to spend a period of time away from work on holiday, resting, etc: *I took two days off*. **take sb on 1** to give them employment. **2** to challenge or compete with them: *We took them on at snooker*. **take sth on 1** to agree to do or undertake it. **2** to acquire (a new meaning, quality or appearance, etc). **3** of an aircraft, ship, etc: to admit (new passengers) or put (a new supply of fuel or cargo, etc) on board. **take sb out 1** to go out with them or escort them in public. **2** *slang* to kill, defeat or destroy them. **take sth out 1** to remove or extract it. **2** to obtain it on application: *take out a warrant*. **take over** to assume control, management or ownership of (a business, etc). **take sth up 1** to lift or raise it. **2** to use or occupy (space or time). **3** to become interested in (a sport, hobby, etc): *take up the violin*. **4** to shorten (a piece of clothing). **5** to resume (a story or account, etc) after a pause. **6** to assume or adopt: *take up residence*. **7** to accept (an offer). **take sb up on sth 1** to accept their offer, proposal or challenge, etc. **2** to discuss (a point or issue) first raised by them. **take up with sb** to become friendly with them; to begin to associate with them. **take sth up with sb** to discuss it with them.

takeaway *n* **1** a cooked meal prepared and bought in a restaurant but taken away and eaten somewhere else. **2** a restaurant which provides such meals.

take-off *n* **1** an instance or the process of an aircraft leaving the ground. **2** an act of mimicking.

takeover *n* an act of assuming control (esp of a business or company).

taker *n* someone who takes or accepts an offer, etc.

takings *pl n* the amount of money taken at a concert or in a shop, etc; receipts.

talc *n* 1 *geol* a mineral form of magnesium silicate. 2 TALCUM.

talcum *n* (*in full* **talcum powder**) a fine, often perfumed, powder made from purified talc, used on the body.

tale *n* 1 a story or narrative. 2 a false or malicious story or piece of gossip; a lie.

talent *n* 1 a special or innate skill, aptitude or ability. 2 high general or mental ability. 3 a person or people with such skill or ability. 4 *colloq* attractive people thought of as potential sexual or romantic partners. 5 an ancient measure of weight and unit of currency. ○ **talented** *adj*.

talent scout or **talent spotter** *n* someone whose job is to find and recruit talented people.

talisman *n* a small object, such as a stone, supposed to have magic powers to protect its owner from evil, bring good luck or work magic. ○ **talismanic** *adj*.

talk *vb* 1 *intr* to express ideas, etc by spoken words, or by sign language, etc. 2 to discuss: *Let's talk business.* 3 *intr* to use or be able to use speech: *Alex could talk at an early age.* 4 to utter: *Don't talk nonsense!* 5 *intr* to gossip. 6 *intr* to give away secret information. 7 to use (a language): *I can't talk Dutch.* 8 to get into a certain state by talking: *They talked themselves hoarse.* 9 *intr* to have influence: *Money talks.* 10 *intr* to give a talk or lecture: *Our speaker will talk on potholing.* ➤ *n* 1 a conversation or discussion. 2 (*often* **talks**) a formal discussion or series of negotiations. 3 an informal lecture. 4 gossip or rumour, or the subject of it: *the talk of the town.* 5 fruitless or impractical discussion or boasting: *His threats are just talk.* ○ **talker** *n*. ♦ **now you're talking** *colloq* now you are saying something I want to hear. **you can** or **can't talk** *colloq* you are in no position to criticize or disagree. ◊ **talk back** to answer rudely or boldly. **talk sb down** 1 to silence them by speaking more loudly or aggressively. 2 to help (a pilot or aircraft) to land by sending instructions over the radio. **talk down to sb** to talk condescendingly to them. **talk sb into** or **out of sth** to persuade them to do or not to do it. **talk sth out** 1 to resolve (a problem or difference of opinion) by discussion. 2 *Brit* to defeat (a bill or motion in parliament) by prolonging discussion of it until there is not enough time left to vote on it. **talk sth over** to discuss it thoroughly. **talk sb round** to bring them to another way of thinking by talking persuasively.

talkative *adj* fond of talking a lot; chatty.

talkie *n*, *dated colloq* a cinema film with sound.

talking-to *n*, *colloq* a ticking-off or reproof.

talk show *n*, *esp N Am* a CHAT SHOW.

tall *adj* 1 having a specified height: *six feet tall.* 2 above average height or higher than expected:

a tall tree. 3 difficult to believe; extravagant: *a tall story.* 4 difficult or demanding: *a tall order.*

tallboy *n* a tall chest of drawers, consisting of an upper section standing on a larger lower one.

tallow *n* hard animal fat melted down and used to make candles, soap, etc.

tally *n* (*-ies*) 1 a reckoning up (of work done, debts, or the score in a game). 2 *hist* a stick in which notches were cut to show debts and accounts, and which could then be split in half lengthways so that each party had a record of the deal. 3 a distinguishing or identifying mark or label. 4 a corresponding part. 5 a mark representing a score or number. ➤ *vb* (*-ies, -ied*) 1 *intr* to agree, correspond or match: *Our results don't tally.* 2 to count or mark (a number or score, etc) on, or as if on, a tally.

tally-ho *exclam* a cry to the hounds at a hunt when a fox has been sighted.

Talmud *n*, *Judaism* the body of Jewish civil and canon law. ○ **Talmudic** *adj*.

talon *n* a hooked claw, esp of a bird of prey.

tamarind *n* the fruit of a tropical evergreen tree, the acidic pulp of which is used medicinally and as a flavouring.

tamarisk *n* an evergreen shrub or small tree with tiny scale-like leaves and small pink or white flowers.

tambour *n* 1 a drum. 2 a an embroidery frame for holding fabric taut while stitches are sewn; b embroidery done on this.

tambourine *n* a musical instrument consisting of a circular frame with a skin stretched over it and small jingling metal discs along the rim, struck with the hand or shaken.

tame *adj* 1 of animals: living or working with people. 2 of land, etc: cultivated. 3 docile, meek and submissive. 4 dull and unexciting. ➤ *vb* 1 to make (an animal) used to living or working with people. 2 to make meek and humble. ○ **tamer** *n*.

tammy *n* (*-ies*) a tam-o'-shanter.

tam-o'-shanter *n*, *Scot* a flat round cloth or woollen cap which fits tightly round the brows.

tamp *vb* to pack or ram down hard.

tamper *vb*, *intr* (*usu* **tamper with**) 1 to interfere or meddle, esp in a harmful way. 2 to attempt to corrupt or influence, esp by bribery.

tampon *n* a plug of absorbent material inserted into a cavity or wound to absorb blood and other secretions, esp one for use in the vagina during menstruation.

tan¹ *n* 1 a SUNTAN. 2 a tawny-brown colour. 3 oak bark or other material, used esp for tanning hides. ➤ *adj* tawny-brown in colour. ➤ *vb* (**tanned, tanning**) 1 *tr & intr* to make or become brown by exposure to ultraviolet light. 2 to convert (hide) into leather. 3 *colloq* to beat or thrash. ○ **tanned** *adj*. ○ **tanning** *n*.

tan² *abbrev*, *maths* tangent.

tandem *n* 1 a bicycle or tricycle for two people. 2 a carriage-drawn tandem. 3 any two people or things which follow one behind the other.

➤ *adv* one behind the other, esp on a bicycle, or with two horses harnessed one behind the other.

tandoori *adj* cooked over charcoal in a clay oven: *tandoori chicken.*

tang *n* **1** a strong or sharp taste, flavour or smell. **2** a trace or hint. **3** a projecting part of a knife, chisel, etc that fits into the handle. ○ **tangy** *adj* (*-ier, -iest*).

tangent *n* **1** *geom* a straight or curved line or a curved surface that touches a curve, but does not pass through it. **2** *trig* a FUNCTION (*noun sense 4*) of an angle in a right-angled triangle, defined as the length of the side opposite the angle divided by the length of the side adjacent to it.

tangerine *n* **1** a small edible citrus fruit, similar to an orange. **2** a reddish-orange colour.

tangible *adj* **1** able to be felt by touch. **2** able to be grasped by the mind. **3** real or definite; material. ○ **tangibility** *n.* ○ **tangibly** *adv.*

tangle *n* **1** an untidy and confused or knotted state or mass, eg, of hair or fibres. **2** a confused or complicated state or situation. ➤ *vb* **1 a** *intr* of hair, fibres, etc: to become untidy, knotted and confused; **b** to cause (hair, fibres, etc) to get into this state. **2** (*usu* **tangle with**) *colloq* to become involved (esp in conflict, or an argument). ○ **tangled** *adj.*

tango *n* **1** a Latin-American dance with stylized body positions and long pauses. **2** a piece of music composed for this. ➤ *vb* (**tangos** or **tangoes**) *intr* to perform this dance.

tank *n* **1** a large container for storing or transporting liquids or gas. **2** the amount a tank can hold. **3** a heavy steel-covered vehicle armed with guns and which moves on Caterpillar tracks. ○ **tankful** *n.* ♦ **tanked up** *colloq* very drunk.

tankard *n* a large beer mug, sometimes with a hinged lid.

tanker *n* **1** a ship or large lorry which transports liquid in bulk. **2** an aircraft which transports fuel.

tannery *n* (*-ies*) a place where hides are tanned.

tannic *adj* relating to or containing tannin.

tannin *n* any of several substances obtained from certain tree barks, etc used in tanning leather, and which also occur in red wine and tea.

Tannoy *n, trademark* a communication system with loudspeakers, used for making announcements in public buildings.

tansy *n* (*-ies*) a plant with yellow flowers and aromatic leaves.

tantalize or **-ise** *vb* to tease or torment, esp by offering but then withholding an object, etc that is much desired. ○ **tantalizing** *adj.*

tantalum *n, chem* a hard bluish-grey metallic element with a high melting point, used esp in making dental and surgical instruments.

tantalus *n* a case for holding decanters of alcoholic drink so that they are visible but locked up.

tantamount *adj* (*always* **tantamount to**) producing the same effect or result as; equivalent to.

tantrum *n* an outburst of childish or petulant bad temper.

tap¹ *n* **1** a quick or light touch, knock or blow, or the sound made by this. **2** tap-dancing. **3** a piece of metal attached to the sole and heel of a tap-dancing shoe. ➤ *vb* (**tapped, tapping**) **1** *tr & intr* to strike or knock lightly, and often audibly. **2** (*also* **tap out**) to produce by tapping: *tap out a message.*

tap² *n* **1** a device attached to a pipe, barrel, etc for controlling the flow of liquid or gas. **2 a** a concealed receiver for listening to and recording private telephone conversations; an act of attaching such a receiver. **3** the withdrawal of fluid, eg, from a body cavity: *spinal tap.* **4** a screw for cutting an internal thread. ➤ *vb* (**tapped, tapping**) **1** to get liquid from (a barrel or a cavity in the body, etc) using a tap or tap-like device. **2** to let out (liquid) by opening a tap or tap-like device. **3** to get sap from (a tree) by cutting into it. **4** to attach a concealed receiver to (a telephone, etc). **5** to start using (a source, supply, etc). **6** *colloq* to obtain (money, etc) from: *Joe tapped his mum for £10.* ♦ **on tap** **1** of beer: stored in casks from which it is served. **2** available for immediate use.

tapas /ˈtapas/ *pl n* savoury snacks, orig a Spanish style.

tap dance *n* a dance performed wearing shoes with metal attached to the soles and toes so that the dancer's rhythmical steps can be heard clearly. ➤ *vb* (**tap-dance**) *intr* to perform a tap dance. ○ **tap-dancer** *n.* ○ **tap-dancing** *n.*

tape *n* **1** a narrow strip of cloth used for tying, fastening, etc. **2** (*also* **magnetic tape**) a strip of thin plastic or metal used for recording sounds or images: *video tape.* **3** an audio or video recording. **4** (*also* **adhesive tape**) a strip of thin paper or plastic with a sticky surface, used for fastening or sticking, etc. **5** a string, strip of paper or ribbon stretched above the finishing line on a race track. **6** a tape measure. ➤ *vb* **1** to fasten, tie or seal with tape. **2** *tr & intr* to record (sounds or images) on magnetic tape. ♦ **have sth** or **sb taped** *colloq* to understand it or them, or be able to deal with it or them.

tape measure *n* a strip of cloth or flexible metal marked off in inches and feet, centimetres and metres, etc, used for measuring length.

taper *n* **1** a long thin candle. **2** a waxed wick for lighting candles, fires, etc. **3** a lessening of diameter or width towards one end. ➤ *vb, tr & intr* (*also* **taper off**) **1** to make or become narrower towards one end. **2** to make or become gradually less.

tape recorder *n* a machine for recording and playing back sounds on magnetic tape. ○ **tape-recording** *n.*

tapestry *n* (*-ies*) **1** a thick woven textile with an ornamental design, often a picture, used for wall-hangings, etc. **2** embroidery, or an embroidery, imitating this.

tapeworm *n* a parasitic segmented flatworm living in the intestines of vertebrates.

tapioca *n* hard white grains of starch from the root of the cassava plant, used for puddings.

tappet *n, mech* a lever or projection that transmits motion from one part of a machine to another.

taproom *n* a bar that serves alcoholic drinks, esp beer direct from casks.

taproot *n* a long tapering main root of some plants.

tar¹ *n* **1** a dark sticky pungent distillation of coal, wood, etc, used in road construction, etc. **2** a similar substance, esp the residue formed from burning tobacco. ➤ *vb* (**tarred,** **tarring**) to cover with tar. ♦ **tar and feather** to cover with tar and then feathers as a punishment. **tarred with the same brush** possessing the same faults.

tar² *n, old colloq* a sailor.

taramasalata /tarəməsəˈlɑːtə/ *n* a creamy pink pâté made from smoked fish roe, olive oil and garlic.

tarantella *n* a lively country dance from S Italy.

tarantula *n* **1** a large European spider. **2** a very large tropical spider with long hairy legs.

tarboosh *n* a hat similar to a fez.

tardy *adj* (**-ier, -iest**) **1** slow to move, progress or grow; sluggish. **2** slower to arrive or happen than expected. ○ **tardiness** *n*.

tare¹ *n* **1** VETCH. **2** (*usu* **tares**) in the Bible: a weed which grows in cornfields.

tare² *n* **1** the weight of the container in which goods are packed. **2** the weight of a vehicle without its fuel, cargo or passengers.

target *n* **1** an object aimed at in shooting practice, etc, esp a flat round board marked with concentric circles. **2** someone or something that is the object of ridicule, criticism, abuse, etc. **3** a goal. ➤ *vb* (**targeted, targeting**) **1** to direct or aim. **2** to make (a person, place or thing) a target or the object of an attack.

tariff *n* **1** a list of fixed prices. **2** a a duty to be paid on a particular class of imports or exports; **b** a list of such duties.

tarmac *n* **1** *trademark* tarmacadam. **2** a surface covered with tarmac, esp an airport runway. ➤ *vb* (**tarmacked, tarmacking**) to apply tarmacadam to.

tarmacadam or **Tarmacadam** *n, trademark* a mixture of small stones bound together with tar, used to make road surfaces, etc.

tarn *n* a small mountain lake.

tarnish *vb* **1** a to make (metal) dull and discoloured; **b** *intr* of metal: to become dull, esp through the action of air or dirt. **2** to spoil or damage (a reputation, etc.) ➤ *n* **1** a loss of shine, reputation, etc. **2** a discoloured or dull film.

taro /ˈtɑːroʊ/ *n* a tropical plant with an edible rootstock.

tarot /ˈtaroʊ/ *n* a pack of 78 playing-cards, now used mainly in fortune-telling.

tarpaulin *n* **1** heavy canvas waterproofed with tar, etc. **2** a sheet of this.

tarragon *n* a bushy plant whose leaves are used to season vinegar and as a flavouring in salads, etc.

tarry /ˈtarɪ/ *vb* (**-ies, -ied**) *intr* **1** to linger or stay in a place. **2** to be slow or late in doing something, etc.

tarsal *n, anat* any of the bones of the tarsus.

tarsus *n* (**tarsi**) **1** the bones forming the upper part of the human foot and ankle. **2** the corresponding part in other mammals, in birds, and in some insects and amphibians.

tart¹ *adj* **1** sharp or sour in taste. **2** of a remark, etc: brief and sarcastic; cutting.

tart² *n* a pastry case, esp one without a top, with a sweet or savoury filling.

tart³ *slang, n* a prostitute or a promiscuous person. ➤ *vb* (*always* **tart up**) *colloq* to decorate or embellish, esp in an ostentatious or tasteless way. ○ **tarty** *adj* (**-ier, -iest**).

tartan *n* **1** a distinctive checked pattern, esp one peculiar to a specified Scottish clan. **2** woollen cloth or a garment woven with such a design.

tartar¹ *n* a hard deposit that forms on the teeth.

tartar² *n* a fierce, ill-tempered, etc person.

tartar sauce or **tartare sauce** *n* mayonnaise with chopped pickles, capers, etc, often served with fish.

tartrazine *n* a yellow powder used as an artificial colouring in foods, drugs and cosmetics.

task *n* **1** a piece of work to be done. **2** an unpleasant or difficult job; a chore. ➤ *vb* to overburden; to stretch (someone's capabilities, etc). ♦ **take sb to task** to scold or criticize them.

task force *n, mil* a temporary grouping of different units that undertake a specific mission.

taskmaster or **taskmistress** *n* a man or woman who sets and supervises the work of others, esp strictly or severely.

tassel *n* a decorative bunch of dangling threads, etc attached to a curtain, hat, etc.

taste *vb* **1** *tr & intr* to perceive the flavour of (food, drink, etc) in the mouth. **2** to try or test (a food or drink) by having a small amount. **3** to be aware of or recognize the flavour of (something). **4** (**taste of sth**) to have a specified flavour: *It tastes of vanilla.* **5** to eat or drink, esp in small quantities or with enjoyment: *I hadn't tasted food for days.* **6** to experience: *taste defeat.* ➤ *n* **1** a the particular sensation produced when food, drink, etc is in the mouth; **b** the sense by which this is detected. **2** the quality or flavour of a food, drink, etc as perceived by this sense: *I dislike the taste of onions.* **3** an act of tasting or a small quantity of food or drink tasted. **4** a first, usu brief, experience of something: *a taste of what was to come.* **5** the quality or flavour of something: *the sweet taste of victory.* **6** a liking or preference: *a taste for exotic* *holidays.* **7** ability to judge and appreciate what is suitable, elegant or beautiful: *a joke in poor taste.*

taste bud *n* a sensory organ on the surface of the tongue by which tastes are perceived.

tasteful *adj* showing, or done with, good judgement or taste. ○ **tastefully** *adv.*

tasteless *adj* **1** lacking flavour. **2** showing, or done with, a lack of good judgement or taste. ○ **tastelessly** *adv.*

taster *n* **1** someone whose job is to taste and judge the quality of food or drink. **2** a sample of something.

tasty *adj* (*-ier, -iest*) **1** having a good, esp savoury, flavour. **2** *colloq* interesting or attractive.

tat *n, Brit colloq* rubbish or junk.

ta-ta *exclam, Brit colloq* goodbye.

tatter *n* (*usu* **tatters**) a torn ragged shred of cloth, paper, etc. ♦ **in tatters 1** of clothes: in a torn and ragged condition. **2** of an argument, relationship, etc: completely destroyed.

tattered *adj* ragged or torn.

tattie *n, Scot* a potato.

tatting *n* delicate knotted lace made from sewing-thread and worked by hand with a small shuttle.

tattle *n* idle chatter or gossip. ➣ *vb* **1** *intr* to chat or gossip idly. **2** to utter (words) in idle chatter. ○ **tattler** *n.*

tattoo¹ *vb* (**tattoos, tattooed**) to mark (a coloured design, etc) on (the body) by pricking the skin and putting in indelible dyes. ➣ *n* a design tattooed on the skin. ○ **tattooist** *n.*

tattoo² *n* **1** a signal by drum or bugle calling soldiers to quarters, esp in the evening. **2** an outdoor military display. **3** a rhythmic beating or drumming.

tatty *adj* (*-ier, -iest*) *colloq* shabby and untidy.

taunt *vb* to tease or say unpleasant things to in a cruel and hurtful way. ➣ *n* a cruel, hurtful or provoking remark.

taupe /toʊp/ *n* a brownish-grey colour.

Taurus *n, astrol* **a** the second sign of the zodiac; **b** a person born between 21 April and 20 May, under this sign.

taut *adj* **1** pulled or stretched tight. **2** showing nervous strain or anxiety.

tauten *vb, tr & intr* to make or become taut.

tautology *n* (*-ies*) the use of words which repeat the meaning of words already used, as in *I myself personally am a vegetarian.* ○ **tautological** or **tautologous** *adj.*

tavern *n* an inn or public house.

tawdry *adj* (*-ier, -iest*) cheap, gaudy and of poor quality. ○ **tawdriness** *n.*

tawny *n* a yellowish-brown colour.

tax *n* **1** a compulsory contribution to state revenue levied on people's salaries, property, the sale of goods and services, etc. **2** a strain, burden or heavy demand. ➣ *vb* **1** to impose a tax on (a person, goods, etc) or take tax from (a salary, etc). **2** to put a strain on, or make a heavy demand on. **3** (**tax with**) *formal* to accuse

(someone) of (a wrongdoing, etc). ○ **taxable** *adj.* ○ **taxing** *adj.*

taxation *n* the levying or payment of taxes.

tax-free *adj, adv* without payment of tax.

taxi *n* (**taxis** or **taxies**) a car which may be hired along with its driver to carry passengers on usu short town journeys. ➣ *vb* (**taxis** or **taxies, taxiing** or **taxying**) **a** *intr* of an aircraft: to move slowly along the ground before take-off or after landing; **b** to make (an aircraft) move in this way.

taxidermy *n* the art of preparing, stuffing and mounting the skins of dead animals, birds, etc so that they present a lifelike appearance. ○ **taxidermist** *n.*

taxi rank *n* a place where taxis wait until hired.

taxonomy *n* (*-ies*) **1** the science of classification, eg, of animals, plants, fossils, languages, etc. **2** a particular scheme of classification. ○ **taxonomic** *adj.*

taxpayer *n* someone who pays or is liable for tax.

TB *abbrev* tuberculosis.

Tb *symbol, chem* terbium.

T-bone steak *n* a large beef steak with a T-shaped bone.

tbsp *abbrev* tablespoon, or tablespoonful.

Tc *symbol, chem* technetium.

Te *symbol, chem* tellurium.

te or **ti** /tiː/ *n, mus* in sol-fa notation: the seventh note of the major scale.

tea *n* **1 a** a small evergreen tree or shrub cultivated for its leaves; **b** its dried leaves; **c** a drink made by infusing these with boiling water. **2** a similar drink made from the leaves or flowers of other plants: *peppermint tea.* **3** (*also* **afternoon tea**) a light afternoon meal with tea, sandwiches, cakes, etc. **4** *Brit* **a** a cooked meal served early in the evening; **b** a main evening meal. See also **HIGH TEA.**

tea bag *n* a small bag or sachet of tea, which is infused in boiling water.

teacake *n, Brit* a currant bun, usu toasted.

teach *vb* (**taught**) **1** to give knowledge to (an individual, class, etc). **2** *tr & intr* to give lessons in (a subject), esp as a professional. **3** to make (someone) learn or understand, esp by example, experience or punishment. ○ **teachable** *adj.*

teacher *n* someone whose job is to teach, esp in a school.

tea chest *n* a light wooden box in which tea is packed for export.

teaching *n* **1** the work or profession of a teacher. **2** (*often* **teachings**) something that is taught, esp guidance or doctrine.

tea cosy *n* (*-ies*) a cover to keep a teapot warm.

teacup *n* **1** a medium-sized cup used for drinking tea. **2** the amount a teacup can hold. ○ **teacupful** *n.*

teak *n* the heavy yellowish-brown durable wood of a large tropical deciduous tree, used in furniture-making, etc.

teal *n* (**teals** or **teal**) **1** a small freshwater duck. **2**

a dark greenish-blue colour.

tea leaf n a leaf or part of a leaf of the tea plant.

team n **1** a group of people who form one side in a game. **2** a group of people working together. **3** two or more animals working together, esp in harness. ➤ vb **1** tr & intr (usu **team up with**) to form a team for some common action. **2** to harness (horses or oxen, etc) together. **3** (also **team up**) to match (clothes, etc).

teamwork n co-operation between those who are working together on a task.

teapot n a pot with a spout and handle used for making and pouring tea.

tear¹ /tɪə(r)/ n **1** a drop of clear saline liquid from the eye, esp when crying. **2** any pear-shaped drop or blob. ◆ **in tears** crying; weeping.

tear² /teə(r)/ vb (**tore, torn**) **1** to pull or rip apart by force; to pull violently or with tearing movements. **2** to make (a hole, etc) by pulling or ripping. **3** intr to come apart; to be ripped apart: material that tears easily. **4** to disrupt or divide: a family torn by feuding. **5** intr to rush; to move with speed or force. ➤ n **1** a hole or other damage caused by tearing. **2** an act of tearing. **3** damage: wear and tear. ◆ **tear one's hair out** to be in despair with impatience and frustration. ◊ **tear sb apart** to cause them severe suffering or distress. **tear sb away** to remove or take them by force. **tear sth down** to pull it down or demolish it using force. **tear into sb** to attack them physically or verbally. **tear sth up** to tear it into pieces.

tearaway /ˈteərəweɪ/ n, Brit colloq an undisciplined and reckless young person.

teardrop n **1** a single tear. **2** anything with a similar shape.

tearful adj **1** inclined to cry or weep. **2** with much crying or weeping; covered with tears. **3** causing tears to be shed; sad. ○ **tearfully** adv.

tear gas n a gas which causes stinging blinding tears, and temporary loss of sight, used in the control of riots and in warfare, etc.

tearing adj furious; overwhelming: a tearing hurry.

tear-jerker n, colloq a sentimental play, film or book, etc intended to make people cry.

tearoom and **teashop** n a restaurant where tea, coffee and cakes, etc are served.

tease vb **1** to annoy or irritate deliberately or unkindly. **2** to laugh at or make fun of playfully. **3** to arouse sexually and fail to satisfy, usu deliberately. **4** to comb (wool, flax or hair, etc) to remove tangles and open out the fibres. **5** to raise a nap on (cloth), esp with teasels. ➤ n someone or something that teases. ◊ **tease sth out** to clarify (an obscure point) by discussion, etc.

teasel, **teazel** or **teazle** n **1** a plant with flower heads surrounded by curved prickly bracts. **2** one of its dried flower heads, or a similar artificial substitute, used for raising the nap on cloth. ➤ vb to produce a nap on (cloth).

teaser n **1** a puzzle or tricky problem. **2** a person who enjoys teasing.

teaspoon n **1** a small spoon for use with a teacup. **2** the amount a teaspoon can hold. ○ **teaspoonful** n.

teat n **1** a nipple, esp of an animal. **2** a piece of rubber, etc shaped like a nipple, attached to a baby's feeding bottle.

tea towel n a towel for drying dishes.

tech n, colloq **1** a technical college. **2** technology.

tech. abbrev **1** technical. **2** technology.

technetium /tek'niːʃɪəm/ n, chem an artificially produced radioactive metallic element.

technical adj **1** relating to a practical skill or applied science. **2** requiring knowledge of a particular subject to be understood. **3** according to a strict interpretation of the law or rules. **4** belonging or relating to, or showing a quality of, technique. ○ **technically** adv.

technical college n a college of further education that teaches practical skills and applied sciences.

technical drawing n drawing of plans, machinery, electrical circuits, etc done with compasses and rulers.

technicality n (**-ies**) **1** a technical detail or term. **2** a usu petty detail arising from a strict interpretation of a law or rules. **3** the state of being technical.

technician n **1** someone skilled in a practical art or science. **2** someone employed to do practical work in a laboratory.

technique n **1** proficiency or skill in the practical or formal aspects of something, eg painting, music, etc. **2** mechanical or practical skill or method: the techniques of film-making. **3** a way of achieving a purpose skilfully; a knack.

techno n a style of dance music that makes use of electronic effects over a frenzied rhythm, and produces fast, but often unmelodic, sounds.

technocracy n (**-ies**) the government of a country or management of an industry by technical experts. ○ **technocrat** n. ○ **technocratic** adj.

technology n (**-ies**) **1** the practical use of scientific knowledge in industry and everyday life. **2** practical sciences as a group. **3** the technical skills and achievements of a particular time in history, of a civilization or a group of people. ○ **technological** adj. ○ **technologist** n.

technophobe n someone who dislikes, fears, or avoids technology. ○ **technophobia** n. ○ **technophobic** adj.

tectonics sing n, geol the study of the Earth's crust and the forces which shape it.

teddy¹ n (**-ies**) (in full **teddy bear**) a stuffed toy bear.

teddy² n (**-ies**) a woman's one-piece undergarment consisting of a chemise and panties.

tedious adj tiresomely long; monotonous.

tedium n tediousness.

tee¹ n a phonetic spelling for the letter T.

tee² *n, golf* **1** a small area of level ground at the start of each hole where the initial shot towards a green is taken. **2** a small peg, etc used to support a ball when this shot is taken. ➤ *vb* (**teed, teeing**) **1** (*often* **tee up**) to place a golf ball on a tee ready to be played. **2** (**tee off**) to play a first shot at the start of a golf hole.

tee-hee or **te-hee** *exclam* expressing amusement or mirth. ➤ *n* a laugh or giggle. ➤ *vb* (**tee-heed, tee-heeing**) *intr* to laugh.

teem¹ *vb, intr* **1** (*usu* **teem with**) to be full of or abound in: *a resort teeming with tourists.* **2** to be present in large numbers; to be plentiful: *Fish teem in this river.*

teem² *vb, intr* (*usu* **teem down**) of water, esp rain: to pour in torrents.

teen *n* **1** (**teens**) the years of a person's life between the ages of 13 and 19. **2** (**teens**) the numbers from 13 to 19. **3** *colloq* a teenager. ➤ *adj* for or relating to teenagers.

teenage *adj* **1** (*also* **teenaged**) between the ages of 13 and 19. **2** relating to or suitable for someone of this age. ○ **teenager** *n*.

teeny *adj* (**-ier, -iest**) *colloq* tiny.

teenybopper *n, colloq* a young teenage girl who enthusiastically follows the latest trends.

teeny-weeny *adj, colloq* very tiny.

teepee see TEPEE

tee shirt see T-SHIRT

teeter *vb, intr* **1** to stand or move unsteadily; to wobble. **2** to hesitate or waver.

teethe *vb, intr* to develop or cut teeth, esp milk teeth. ○ **teething** *n*.

teething troubles *pl n* initial problems with something, usu regarded as temporary.

teetotal *adj* abstaining completely from alcoholic drink. ○ **teetotaller** *n*.

Teflon *n, trademark* for polytetrafluoroethylene, a tough thermoplastic used to coat cooking utensils.

tel *abbrev* telephone number.

telebanking *n* a system which enables banking transactions to be carried out by means of a telecommunications network.

telecast *vb, tr & intr* to broadcast by TV. ➤ *n* a TV broadcast. ○ **telecaster** *n*.

telecommunication *n* **1** communication over a distance using cable, telephone, telegraph, fax, e-mail, etc. **2** (**telecommunications**) the branch of technology dealing with these.

telecommuter *n* someone who works at home and communicates with an office by telephone or computer link, etc. ○ **telecommuting** *n*.

teleconference *n* a conference between people in two or more locations using video, audio and/or computer links. ○ **teleconferencing** *n*.

telegram *n, formerly* a message sent by telegraph and delivered in printed form.

telegraph *n* a system of, or instrument for, sending messages or information over a distance, by sending electrical impulses along a wire. ➤ *vb* **1** *tr & intr* to send (a message) (to

someone) by telegraph. **2** to give a warning of. **3** *intr* to signal. ○ **telegraphic** *adj*.

telegraphy *n* the science or practice of sending messages by telegraph.

telekinesis *n* the moving of objects at a distance without using physical contact, eg, by willpower.

telemarketing *n* the marketing of goods and services by telephoning prospective clients.

telemeter /tə'lɛmɪtə(r)/ *n* an instrument for taking recorded measurements and sending them to a remote location, usu by electrical or radio signals. ➤ *vb* to record and transmit (data) in this way. ○ **telemetric** /-'mɛtrɪk/ *adj*. ○ **telemetry** *n*.

teleology *n* the doctrine that the universe is designed for and directed towards a goal. ○ **teleological** *adj*.

telepathy /tə'lɛpəθɪ/ *n* the apparent communication of thoughts directly from one person's mind to another's without using any of the five known senses. ○ **telepathic** /tɛlɪ'paθɪk/ *adj*. ○ **telepathically** *adv*.

telephone *n* an instrument for transmitting speech in the form of electrical signals or radio waves. ➤ *vb* **1** to seek or establish contact and speak to (someone) by telephone. **2** to send (a message, etc) by telephone. **3** *intr* to make a telephone call. ○ **telephonic** *adj*. ◆ **on the telephone 1** connected to the telephone system. **2** talking to someone by telephone.

telephonist /tə'lɛfənɪst/ *n* a telephone switchboard operator.

telephony /tə'lɛfənɪ/ *n* the use of telephones.

telephoto lens *n* a camera lens which produces magnified images.

teleprinter *n* an apparatus with a keyboard which types messages as they are received by telegraph and transmits them as they are typed.

Teleprompter *n, trademark* a device which allows a speaker to read a script while apparently looking into a TV camera.

telesales *sing and pl n* the selling of goods or services by telephone.

telescope *n* **1** an optical instrument with a powerful magnifying lens or mirror that makes distant objects appear larger. **2** a RADIO TELESCOPE. ➤ *vb, tr & intr* **1** to collapse part within part. **2** to crush or compress, or become crushed or compressed, under impact. ○ **telescopic** *adj*.

teleshopping *n* the purchase of goods, using a telephone or computer link.

teletext *n* a non-interactive news service, able to be viewed on a TV set with a receiver and decoder.

telethon *n* a TV programme, usu a day-long one, broadcast to raise money for charity.

televise *vb* to broadcast by television.

television *n* **1** an electronic system that converts moving images and sound into electrical signals, which are then transmitted to a distant receiver that converts these signals back to images and sound. **2** (*also* **television set**) a device used to receive picture and sound signals transmitted in this way. **3** television broadcasting in general: *He works in television.* ○ **televisual** *adj.*

teleworking *n* working at a distance using an electronic communication link with an office. ○ **teleworker** *n.*

telex or **Telex** *n* **1** an international telecommunications network that enables subscribers to send and receive typed messages. **2** a teleprinter used in such a network. **3** a message received or sent by such a network. ➤ *vb, tr & intr* to send (messages) or communicate by telex.

tell *vb* (**told**) **1** *tr & intr* to relate (something) in speech or writing (to someone): *I told him what happened.* **2** to command or instruct: *She told me how to fix it.* **3** to express in words: *to tell lies.* **4** *tr & intr* to discover or distinguish: *You can tell it by its smell.* **5** (*usu* **tell on**) *colloq* to inform against: *I'll tell the teacher on you.* **6** to make known or give away: *Promise not to tell.* **7** (*also* **tell on**) *intr* of an ordeal, etc: to have a noticeable effect: *The strain had begun to tell.* **8** *tr & intr* to know or recognize definitely: *I can never tell when he's lying.* **9** to assure: *I'm telling you, that's exactly what he said.* **10** (*usu* **tell against**) *intr* of evidence, circumstances, etc: to have an influence, effect, etc. ♦ **you're telling me!** *colloq* an exclamation of agreement. ◊ **tell sb** or **sth apart** to distinguish between them: *I can't tell the twins apart.* **tell sb off** to scold or reprimand them.

teller *n* **1** someone who tells, esp stories. **2** a bank employee who receives money from and pays it out to members of the public. **3** someone who counts votes.

telling *adj* producing a great or marked effect.

telling-off *n* a mild scolding.

telltale *n* someone who spreads gossip. ➤ *adj* revealing or indicating: *the telltale signs of work-related stress.*

tellurium *n, chem* a brittle silvery-white element obtained from gold, silver and copper ores.

telly *n* (*-ies*) *colloq* **1** television. **2** a television set.

temerity *n* **1** rashness or impetuosity. **2** boldness or impudence.

temp *n* a temporary employee. ➤ *vb, intr* to work as a temp.

temper *n* **1** a characteristic state of mind; mood or humour: *have an even temper.* **2** a state of calm; composure; self-control: *lose one's temper.* **3** a state of uncontrolled anger: *in a temper.* **4** a tendency to have fits of uncontrolled anger: *She has quite a temper.* **5** the degree of hardness and toughness of metal or glass. ➤ *vb* **1** to soften or make less severe. **2** to bring (metal, clay, etc) to the desired consistency.

tempera *n* **1** a method of painting using an emulsion. **2** this emulsion or a painting produced using it.

temperament *n* **1** someone's natural character or disposition. **2** a sensitive, creative or emotional personality.

temperamental *adj* **1** of a machine, etc: not working reliably or consistently. **2** relating to, or caused by, temperament. ○ **temperamentally** *adv.*

temperance *n* **1** moderation or self-restraint in controlling one's appetite or desires. **2** moderation or abstinence from alcohol.

temperate *adj* **1** moderate and self-restrained, esp in appetite, consumption of alcoholic drink, and behaviour. **2** of a climate or region: characterized by mild temperatures.

temperature *n* **1** the degree of hotness or coldness as measured by a thermometer. **2** *colloq* a body temperature above normal: *He's running a temperature.*

tempest *n* a violent storm with very strong winds.

tempestuous *adj* **1** very stormy. **2** violently emotional; passionate: *a tempestuous love affair.*

template *n* a piece of metal, plastic or wood cut in a particular shape and used as a pattern.

temple[1] *n* a building in which people worship.

temple[2] *n* the flat part at either side of the head in front of the ears.

tempo /ˈtɛmpoʊ/ *n* (**tempos** or **tempi** /-piː/) **1** the speed at which a piece of music is played. **2** rate or speed.

temporal *adj* **1** relating to time. **2** relating to worldly or secular life rather than to religious or spiritual life. **3** *gram* relating to tense. ○ **temporally** *adv.*

temporary *adj* lasting, acting or used etc for a limited period of time only. ○ **temporarily** *adv.* ○ **temporariness** *n.*

temporize or **-ise** *vb, intr* **1** to avoid taking a decision, etc to gain time and perhaps win a compromise. **2** to adapt to circumstances.

tempt *vb* **1** to seek to persuade (someone) to do something wrong, foolish, etc. **2** to attract or allure. **3** to risk provoking, esp by doing something foolhardy: *tempt fate.* ○ **tempter** *n.* ○ **temptress** *n.*

temptation *n* **1** an act of tempting or the state of being tempted. **2** something that tempts.

tempting *adj* attractive; inviting; enticing. ○ **temptingly** *adv.*

ten *n* **1 a** the cardinal number 10; **b** the quantity that this represents, being one more than nine. **2** any symbol for this, eg *10* or *X.* **3** the tenth hour after midnight or midday. **4** a set or group of ten people or things. ➤ *adj* **1** totalling ten. **2** aged ten.

tenable *adj* **1** able to be believed, upheld or maintained. **2** of a post or office: only to be held or occupied for a specified period or by a specified person.

tenacious *adj* **1** holding or sticking firmly. **2** determined. **3** of memory: retaining information extremely well. ○ **tenacity** *n.*

tenancy *n* (*-ies*) **1** the status of being a tenant or the property rented. **2** the period during which property is held by a tenant.

tenant *n* **1** someone who rents property or land. **2** an occupant.

tench *n* (*tench* or *tenches*) a European freshwater fish of the carp family.

tend[1] *vb* **1** to take care of or look after. **2** to wait on, serve at, manage, etc: *tend bar*. **3** (**tend to**) to attend to.

tend[2] *vb, intr* **1** (*usu* **tend to**) to be inclined to: *He tends to be late*. **2** to move slightly, lean or slope (in a specified direction).

tendency *n* (*-ies*) **1** an inclination to behave or think in a particular way. **2** a general course, trend or drift. **3** a faction or group within a political party, etc.

tendentious *adj* characterized by a particular bias, tendency or underlying purpose.

tender[1] *adj* **1** soft and delicate; fragile or sensitive. **2** of meat: easily chewed or cut. **3** easily hurt when touched, esp because of having been hurt before. **4** loving and gentle: *tender words*. **5** youthful and vulnerable: *of tender years*. ○ **tenderly** *adv*.

tender[2] *vb* **1** to offer or present (an apology, resignation, etc). **2** (*usu* **tender for**) to make a formal offer (to do work or supply goods) at a stated amount of money, etc. ➤ *n* a formal offer to do work or supply goods for a stated amount of money and time.

tender[3] *n* **1** a person who looks after something or someone: *bartender*. **2** a small boat which carries stores or passengers to and from a larger boat. **3** a wagon carrying fuel and water and attached to a steam locomotive.

tenderfoot *n* (*tenderfeet* or *tenderfoots*) an inexperienced newcomer or beginner.

tenderize or **-ise** *vb* to make tender.

tendon *n* a cord of strong fibrous tissue that joins a muscle to a bone or some other structure.

tendril *n* a long shoot-like extension that some climbing plants use for attaching themselves to objects for support.

tenement *n* **1** a large building divided into several self-contained flats or apartments. **2** a self-contained flat or room within such a building.

tenet *n* a belief, opinion or doctrine.

tenfold *adj* **1** equal to ten times as much or many. **2** divided into, or consisting of, ten parts. ➤ *adv* by ten times as much.

tenner *n, colloq* a £10 note.

tennis *n* **1** (*also* **lawn tennis**) a game in which two players or two pairs of players use rackets to hit a ball across a net on a rectangular grass, clay or cement court. **2** REAL TENNIS.

tenon *n* a projection at the end of a piece of wood, etc, formed to fit into a socket in another piece of wood, etc.

tenor *n* **1** a singer or singing voice of the highest normal range for an adult man. **2** an instrument, eg, a viola, recorder or saxophone, with a similar range. **3** the general course or meaning of something written or spoken.

tenpin bowling *n* a game in which ten skittles are set up at the end of an alley and a ball is rolled at them with the aim of knocking as many down as possible.

tense[1] *n, gram* a form or set of forms of a verb showing the time of its action in relation to the time of speaking and whether that action is completed or not.

tense[2] *adj* **1** suffering, etc emotional, nervous or mental strain. **2** tightly stretched; taut. ➤ *vb, tr & intr* (*also* **tense up**) to make or become tense. ○ **tensely** *adv*. ○ **tenseness** *n*.

tensile *adj* **1** able to be stretched. **2** relating to or involving stretching or tension.

tension *n* **1** an act of stretching, the state of being stretched or the degree to which something is stretched. **2** mental or emotional strain. **3** strained relations between people, countries, etc. ➤ *vb* to subject to tension.

tent *n* **1** a movable canvas, etc shelter supported by poles or a frame and fastened to the ground with ropes and pegs. **2** something resembling a tent in form or function: *an oxygen tent*.

tentacle *n* a long thin flexible appendage of many invertebrates, eg, the sea anemone, octopus, etc, used for feeling, grasping, moving, etc. ○ **tentacled** *adj*.

tentative *adj* **1** not finalized; provisional. **2** uncertain; hesitant; cautious. ○ **tentatively** *adv*. ○ **tentativeness** *n*.

tenterhook *n* one of a series of hooks on a frame used for drying cloth. ♦ **on tenterhooks** in a state of impatient suspense or anxiety.

tenth (often written **10th**) *adj* **1** in counting: **a** next after ninth; **b** last of ten. **2** in tenth position. **3** being one of ten equal parts: *a tenth share*. ➤ *n* **1** one of ten equal parts. **2** a FRACTION equal to one divided by ten (usu written $^1/_{10}$). **3** a person coming tenth, eg, in a race, exam, etc. **4** (**the tenth**) the tenth day of the month. ➤ *adv* tenthly. ○ **tenthly** *adv* used to introduce the tenth point in a list.

tenuous *adj* **1** slight; with little strength or substance. **2** thin.

tenure *n* **1** the holding of an office, position or property. **2** the length of time an office, position or property is held. **3** the holding of a position, esp a permanent university teaching job. **4** the conditions by which an office, position or property is held.

tepee or **teepee** /ˈtiːpiː/ *n* a conical tent formed by skins stretched over a frame of poles, used by some Native Americans.

tepid *adj* **1** slightly or only just warm. **2** unenthusiastic.

tequila /təˈkiːlə/ *n* a Mexican alcoholic spirit obtained from the agave plant.

terabyte *n, comput* a unit of storage capacity equal to 1000 gigabytes.

terbium *n, chem* a silvery metallic element of the LANTHANIDE series.

tercentenary *n* (*-ies*) a three-hundred year period or anniversary.

term *n* **1** a word or expression, esp one with a precise meaning in a specialized field. **2** (**terms**) language used; a particular way of speaking: *in no uncertain terms*. **3** a limited or clearly defined period of time: *a term of office*. **4** the end of a particular time, esp of pregnancy. **5** (**terms**) a relationship between people or countries: *be on good terms*. **6** (**terms**) the rules or conditions of an agreement: *terms of sale*. **7** (**terms**) fixed charges for work or a service. **8** one of the divisions into which an academic year is divided. **9** the time during which a court is in session. **10** *maths* a quantity joined to another by either addition or subtraction. **11** *maths* one quantity in a series or sequence. **12** *logic* a word or expression which may be a subject or a predicate of a proposition. ➢ *vb* to name or call. ♦ **come to terms with 1** to come to an agreement with. **2** to find a way of tolerating (some difficulty). **in terms of** in relation to.

termagant *n* a scolding, brawling and overbearing woman.

terminable *adj* able to be ended.

terminal *adj* **1** of an illness or injury: causing death; fatal. **2** of a patient: expected to die soon. **3** *colloq* extreme; acute: *terminal laziness*. **4** forming or occurring at an end, boundary or terminus. ➢ *n* **1** an arrival and departure building at an airport. **2** a large station at the end of a railway line or for long-distance buses and coaches. **3** a point in an electric circuit or electrical device at which the current leaves or enters it, or by which it may be connected to another device. **4** a device consisting usu of a keyboard and VDU, which connects with a remote computer. **5** an installation at the end of a pipeline or at a port, where oil is stored and from where it is distributed. ○ **terminally** *adv.*

terminate *vb* **1** *tr & intr* to end. **2** to end (a pregnancy) artificially and before the fetus is viable. ○ **termination** *n.*

terminology *n* (*-ies*) the words and phrases used in a particular field.

terminus /ˈtɜːmɪnəs/ *n* (*termini* /-naɪ/ or **terminuses**) **a** the end of a railway line or bus route; **b** the station at this point.

termite *n* an ant-like insect of mainly tropical areas, some of which cause damage to trees and buildings, etc.

tern *n* a sea-bird, related to the gull, with a long forked tail.

ternary *adj* **1** containing three parts. **2** *maths* of a number system: using three as a base.

terpsichorean *adj* relating to dancing.

terrace *n* **1** each of a series of raised level earth banks on a hillside used for cultivation. **2** *Brit* a row of usu identical and connected houses. **3** a raised level paved area by the side of a house. **4** (*usu* **terraces**) open areas rising in tiers round a sports ground, where spectators stand. ➢ *vb* to form into a terrace or terraces.

terracotta *n* **1** an unglazed brownish-orange earthenware used for pottery, roof tiles, etc. **2** a brownish-orange colour.

terra firma *n* dry land; solid ground.

terrain *n* a stretch of land, esp with regard to its physical features.

terrapin *n* a small freshwater turtle.

terrarium *n* (*terraria* or **terrariums**) **1** a container in which small land animals are kept. **2** a sealed jar in which plants are grown.

terrazzo /tɛˈratsoʊ/ *n* a mosaic covering for concrete floors consisting of marble chips set in cement and then polished.

terrestrial *adj* **1** relating to or living on dry land or the Earth. **2** belonging or relating to this world; mundane. **3** of broadcast signals: sent by a land transmitter as opposed to satellite. ➢ *n* an inhabitant of the Earth.

terrible *adj* **1** *colloq* very bad: *a terrible singer*. **2** *colloq* very great; extreme: *a terrible gossip*. **3** causing great fear or terror. **4** causing suffering: *a terrible struggle*. ○ **terribly** *adv.*

terrier *n* a breed of small dog orig bred to hunt animals in burrows.

terrific *adj*, *colloq* **1** marvellous; excellent. **2** very great or powerful: *a terrific storm*.

terrify *vb* (*-ies, -ied*) to make very frightened. ○ **terrified** *adj.* ○ **terrifying** *adj.*

terrine /tɛˈriːn/ *n* an earthenware dish in which food may be cooked and served.

territorial *adj* **1** relating to a territory. **2** limited or restricted to a particular area or district. **3** likely to establish and defend one's own territory. ➢ *n* (**Territorial**) *Brit* a member of the Territorial Army.

territorial waters *pl n* the area of sea surrounding and belonging to a country.

territory *n* (*-ies*) **1** a stretch of land; a region. **2** the land under the control of a ruler, government or state. **3** an area of knowledge, interest or activity. **4** an area or district in which a travelling salesman or distributor operates. **5** an area which a bird or animal treats as its own and defends against others of the same species. **6** (*often* **Territory**) part of a country without the full rights of a state.

terror *n* **1** very great fear or dread. **2** something or someone which causes such fear. **3** *colloq* a troublesome or mischievous person, esp a child.

terrorism *n* the systematic use of violence and intimidation to force a government or community, etc to act in a certain way or accept certain demands. ○ **terrorist** *n*, *adj.*

terrorize or **-ise** *vb* **1** to frighten greatly. **2** to use terrorism against.

terry *n* (*-ies*) an absorbent fabric with uncut loops on one side, used esp for towels.

terse *adj* **1** brief and concise; succinct. **2** abrupt and rude; curt. ○ **tersely** *adv.* ○ **terseness** *n.*

tertiary /ˈtɜːʃərɪ/ *adj* **1** third in order, degree, importance, etc. **2** (**Tertiary**) *geol* relating to the first period of the Cenozoic era. ➢ *n* (**Tertiary**) this geological period.

Terylene *n, trademark* a light tough synthetic fabric of polyester fibres.

tessellate *vb* to form into or mark like a mosaic, esp with tesserae or checks. ○ **tessellated** *adj*.

tessera /ˈtɛsərə/ *n* (**tesserae** /-riː/) a square piece of stone or glass, etc used in mosaics.

test¹ *n* **1 a** a critical examination or trial of qualities, abilities, etc; **b** something used as the basis for this: *a test of strength*. **2** a short minor examination, esp in school. **3** *sport* a TEST MATCH. **4** *chem* anything used to distinguish, detect or identify a substance; a reagent. ➣ *vb* **1** to examine, esp by trial. **2** *tr & intr* to examine (a substance) to discover whether another substance is present or not. **3** *intr* to achieve a stated result in a test: *He tested negative for the virus.* ○ **testable** *adj*. ○ **tester** *n*.

test² *n, biol* a hard outer covering or shell of certain invertebrates.

testa /ˈtɛstə/ (**testae** /-tiː/) *biol* the hard outer covering of a seed.

testament *n* **1 a** a written statement of someone's wishes, esp of what they want to be done with their property after death; **b** a will: *her last will and testament*. **2** proof, evidence or a tribute: *a testament to her hard work*. **3** a covenant between God and humankind. **4** (**Testament**) either of the two main divisions of the Bible, the Old Testament and the New Testament. ○ **testamentary** *adj*.

testate *law, adj* having made and left a valid will. ➣ *n* a testate person, esp at the time of death.

testator *n, law* someone who leaves a will at death.

test case *n, law* a case whose outcome will serve as a precedent for all similar cases in the future.

test drive *n* a trial drive of a car by a prospective owner to assess its performance. ➣ *vb* (**test-drive**) to take (a car) for a test drive.

testicle *n* a testis. ○ **testicular** *adj*.

testify *vb* (**-ies, -ied**) **1** *intr* to give evidence in court. **2** (*often* **testify to**) to serve as evidence or proof (of something). **3** *intr* to make a solemn declaration (eg of one's faith).

testimonial *n* **1** a letter or certificate giving details of a person's character, conduct and qualifications. **2** a gift presented as a sign of respect or as a tribute to personal qualities or services. **3** *sport* a match or series of matches held in honour of a player, who receives all the proceeds.

testimony *n* (**-ies**) **1** a statement made under oath, esp in a law court. **2** evidence: *testimony to her intelligence*. **3** a declaration of truth or fact.

testing *n* the assessment of an individual level of knowledge or skill, etc. ➣ *adj* **1** troublesome; difficult: *a testing time*. **2** mentally taxing: *a testing question*.

testis *n* (**testes**) *anat* in male animals: either of the two reproductive glands that produce sperm.

test match *n* in various sports, esp cricket: a match forming one of a series played between two international teams.

testosterone *n, physiol* the main male sex hormone, a steroid secreted primarily by the testes.

test pilot *n* a pilot who tests new aircraft by flying them.

test tube *n* a thin glass tube closed at one end, used in chemical tests or experiments.

testy *adj* (**-ier, -iest**) irritable; bad-tempered; touchy. ○ **testily** *adv*. ○ **testiness** *n*.

tetanus *n* an infectious and potentially fatal disease whose main symptoms are fever and painful muscle spasms.

tetchy *adj* (**-ier, -iest**) irritable; peevish. ○ **tetchily** *adv*. ○ **tetchiness** *n*.

tête-à-tête /ˌteɪtəˈteɪt, ˌtɛtəˈtɛt/ *n* a private conversation between two people. ➣ *adj* private; intimate. ➣ *adv* intimately.

tether *n* a rope, etc for tying an animal to a post. ➣ *vb* to tie or restrain with a tether. ♦ **at the end of one's tether** having reached the limit of one's patience, mental resources, etc.

tetragon *n, geom* a plane figure with four angles and four sides. ○ **tetragonal** /tɛˈtragənəl/ *adj*.

tetrahedron /ˌtɛtrəˈhiːdrən/ *n* (**tetrahedra** or **tetrahedrons**) *geom* a solid figure with four triangular plane faces. ○ **tetrahedral** *adj*.

tetrameter /tɛˈtramɪtə(r)/ *n, poetry* a line of verse with four metrical feet.

tetraplegia *n* another name for QUADRI-PLEGIA.

tetrapod *n, zool* an animal with four feet.

Teutonic /tʃuːˈtɒnɪk/ *adj* **1** belonging or relating to the Germanic languages or peoples speaking these languages. **2** German.

Tex-Mex *adj* of food, music, etc: typically Mexican, but with Texan elements.

text *n* **1** the main body of printed words in a book or document as opposed to the illustrations, etc. **2** the actual words of an author as opposed to commentary on them. **3** a short passage from the Bible taken as the starting-point for a sermon or quoted in authority. **4** a theme or subject. **5** a book, novel or play, etc that forms part of a course of study: *a set text*. **6** a text message. **7** a textbook. ➣ *vb* (**texted, texting**) *tr & intr* to send a text message (to). ○ **texter** *n*. ○ **texting** *n*. ○ **textual** *adj*.

textbook *n* a book that contains the standard principles and information of a subject. ➣ *adj* conforming to or as if conforming to the guidance of a textbook; exemplary: *textbook accountancy*.

textile *n* **1** a cloth or fabric made by weaving or knitting. **2** fibre or yarn, etc suitable for weaving into cloth. ➣ *adj* **1** relating to manufacturing cloth. **2** woven or suitable for being woven into cloth.

texture *n* **1** the way something feels. **2** the feel and appearance of a surface, esp when rough or complex: *Layers give the painting texture.* **3**

the structure of a substance as formed by the size and arrangement of the smaller particles which form it. ➤ *vb* to give a particular texture to (food, fabric, etc). ○ **textural** *adj*.

Th *symbol, chem* thorium.

thalamus *n* (*thalami*) *anat* either of two masses of grey matter in the brain that relay sensory nerve impulses to the cerebral cortex.

thalidomide *n* a drug formerly used as a sedative but withdrawn because it was found to cause birth defects.

thallium *n, chem* a soft bluish-white metallic element.

than *conj* 1 used to introduce the second part of a comparison, or that part which is taken as the basis of a comparison: *He's better than me.* 2 used to introduce the second, and usu less desirable or rejected, option in a statement of alternatives: *I would rather walk than drive.* 3 except; other than: *left with no alternative than to resign.* ➤ *prep* in comparison with: *someone older than him.*

thane *n, hist* 1 in Anglo-Saxon England: a man holding land from the king or some other superior in exchange for military service. 2 in medieval Scotland: a man holding land from a Scottish king, but not in return for military service; a Scottish feudal lord.

thank *vb* 1 to express gratitude to: *We thanked him for his help.* 2 to hold responsible for something: *He has only himself to thank for the mess.* ➤ *n* (*usu* **thanks**) 1 gratitude or an expression of gratitude: *to express my thanks.* 2 thank you. ◆ **thank God** or **goodness** or **heavens**, *etc* an expression of relief. **thanks to** as a result of; because of: *Thanks to Amy, we missed the train.* **thank you** a polite expression acknowledging a gift, help or offer.

thankful *adj* grateful; relieved and happy. ○ **thankfully** *adv.* ○ **thankfulness** *n*.

thankless *adj* bringing no thanks, pleasure or profit. ○ **thanklessly** *adv.* ○ **thanklessness** *n*.

thanksgiving *n* 1 a formal act of giving thanks, esp to God. 2 (**Thanksgiving**) *N Am* a public holiday for giving thanks, occurring on the fourth Thursday in November in the USA and the second Monday in October in Canada.

thankyou *n* an instance of thanking, or something that expresses thanks: *some flowers as a thankyou.* ➤ *adj* (**thank-you**) expressing thanks: *a thank-you card.*

that *adj* (*pl* **those**) 1 indicating the thing, person or idea already mentioned or understood: *There's that girl I was telling you about.* 2 indicating someone or something farther away or in contrast: *not this book, but that one.* ➤ *pron* (*pl* **those**) 1 the person, thing or idea already spoken of or understood: *When did that happen?* 2 a relatively distant or more distant person, thing or idea. ➤ *pron* used instead of *which*, *who* or *whom*, to introduce a relative clause which defines, distinguishes or restricts the person or thing mentioned in the preceding clause: *All the children that were late re-*

ceived detention. ➤ *conj* used to introduce a noun clause, or a clause showing reason, purpose, consequence or a result or expressing a wish or desire: *He spoke so quickly that I couldn't understand* • *Oh, that the day would never end!* ➤ *adv* 1 to the degree or extent shown or understood: *It won't reach that far.* 2 *colloq* or *dialect* to such a degree that; so: *He's that mean he never buys a round.* ◆ **all that** *colloq* very: *not all that good.* **that's that** that is the end of the matter.

thatch *n* 1 a roof covering of straw or reeds, etc. 2 something resembling this, esp a thick head of hair. ➤ *vb, tr & intr* to cover (a roof or building) with thatch. ○ **thatcher** *n*.

thaw *vb* 1 a *intr* of snow, ice, frozen food, etc: to melt; **b** to make (snow, ice, frozen food, etc) melt. 2 *intr* of the weather: to be warm enough to begin to melt snow and ice: *It's beginning to thaw.* 3 *tr & intr, colloq* to make or become less stiff and numb with cold: *Come and thaw out by the fire.* 4 *tr & intr, colloq* to make or become more friendly or relaxed. ➤ *n* 1 an act or the process of thawing. 2 a period of weather warm enough to begin to thaw ice and snow.

the *definite article* 1 used to refer to a particular person, thing or group already mentioned, implied or known: *Pass me the CD.* 2 used to refer to a unique person or thing: *the Pope.* 3 used before a singular noun to denote all the members of a group or class: *a history of the novel.* 4 used before an adjective to denote collectively people or things who have the specified attribute, etc: *the poor* • *the paranormal.* 5 used before certain titles and proper names. 6 used to identify a person: *Robert the Bruce.* 7 used after a preposition to refer to a unit of quantity or time, etc: *forty miles to the gallon* • *paid by the hour.* 8 *colloq* my; our: *I'd better check with the wife.* ➤ *adv* 1 used before comparative adjectives or adverbs to indicate (by) so much or (by) how much: *the sooner the better.* 2 used before superlative adjectives and adverbs to indicate an amount beyond all others: *I like this book the best.*

theatre or (*US*) **theater** *n* 1 a building or outside area specially designed for the performance of plays, operas, etc. 2 a large room with seats rising in tiers, for lectures, etc. 3 (*also* **the theatre**) the writing and production of plays in general or the world and profession of actors and theatre companies. 4 *Brit* a specially equipped room in a hospital where surgery is performed. 5 a scene of action or place where events take place: *theatre of war.* 6 *N Am* a cinema.

theatrical *adj* 1 relating to theatres or acting. 2 of behaviour or a gesture, etc: done only for effect; artificial and exaggerated. ➤ *n* (**theatricals**) 1 dramatic performances. 2 insincere or exaggerated behaviour. ○ **theatricality** *n*.

thee *pron* the objective form of THOU[1].

theft *n* an act or instance or the process of stealing.

their adj **1** belonging or relating to them: their opinion. **2** his or her: Has everyone got their books?

theirs pron a person or thing that belongs to them: That's theirs.

theism /'θiːɪzəm/ n the belief in the existence of God or a god. ○ **theist** n. ○ **theistic** adj.

them pron **1** the objective form of THEY: We met them. **2** colloq or dialect those: Them's the best, I reckon. **3** colloq him or her. **4** old use themselves.

theme n **1** a subject of a discussion, speech or piece of writing, etc. **2** mus a short melody developed and repeated with variations. **3** a repeated or recurring image or idea in literature or art. ○ **thematic** adj. ○ **thematically** adv.

theme park n a large amusement park in which all of the rides and attractions are based on a particular theme, eg, outer space.

theme song or **theme tune** n a song or melody associated with, and usu played at the beginning and end of, a film or a TV or radio programme, or which is associated with a particular character, etc.

themselves pron **1** the reflexive form of THEM: They helped themselves. **2** used for emphasis: They, themselves, are to blame. **3** their normal selves: not feeling themselves today. **4** colloq himself or herself: Nobody needs to blame themselves.

then adv **1** at that time. **2** soon or immediately after that: I looked at him, then turned away. **3** in that case; as a consequence: What would we do then? • If you're tired, then you should rest. **4** also; in addition: Then there's the cost to take into account. **5** used to continue a narrative after a break or digression. **6** used esp at the end of questions which ask for an explanation, opinion, etc, or which ask for or assume agreement: Your mind is made up, then? ➤ n that time: But, until then, stay away. ➤ adj being or acting at that time: the then Prime Minister.

thence adv, old use or formal **1** from that place or time. **2** from that cause; therefore.

thenceforth or **thenceforward** adv, old use or formal from that time or place forwards.

theocracy n (**-ies**) **1** government by a deity or by priests representing a deity. **2** a state ruled in this way. ○ **theocrat** n. ○ **theocratic** adj.

theodolite n, surveying an instrument for measuring horizontal and vertical angles.

theology n **1** the study of God and religious affairs. **2** a particular system of theology and religion. ○ **theologian** n. ○ **theological** adj.

theorem n a scientific or mathematical statement which makes certain assumptions in order to explain observed phenomena, and which has been proved to be correct.

theoretical or **theoretic** adj **1** concerned with or based on theory rather than practical knowledge or experience. **2** existing in theory only; hypothetical. **3** dealing with theory only; speculative. ○ **theoretically** adv.

theoretician n someone concerned with the theoretical aspects of a subject rather than its practical use.

theorize or **-ise** vb, intr to devise theories; to speculate. ○ **theorist** n.

theory n (**-ies**) **1** a series of ideas and general principles that seek to explain some aspect of the world: theory of relativity. **2** an idea or explanation which has not yet been proved; a conjecture: My theory is he's jealous! **3** the general and usu abstract principles or ideas of a subject: theory of music. **4 a** an ideal, hypothetical or abstract situation; **b** ideal, hypothetical or abstract reasoning: a good idea in theory.

theosophy n (**-ies**) a religious philosophy based on the belief that a knowledge of God can be achieved through intuition, mysticism and divine inspiration, esp a modern movement which combines this with elements from Hinduism and Buddhism. ○ **theosophist** n.

therapeutic /θɛrə'pjuːtɪk/ adj **1** relating to, concerning or contributing to healing or curing disease, etc. **2** bringing a feeling of general wellbeing. ○ **therapeutically** adv.

therapeutics sing n the treatment and curing of diseases.

therapy n (**-ies**) the treatment of physical, social, psychiatric and psychological diseases and disorders. ○ **therapist** n.

there /ðɛə(r)/ adv **1** at, in or to a place or position: You can sit there. **2** at that point in speech, writing or a performance, etc: Don't stop there. **3** in that respect: I agree with him there. **4** used to begin a sentence when the subject of the verb follows the verb instead of coming before it: There are no mistakes in this. **5** used at the beginning of a sentence to emphasize or call attention to that sentence: There goes the last bus. **6** used after a noun for emphasis: That book there is the one you need. **7** colloq or dialect used between a noun and this or that, etc for emphasis: that there tractor. ➤ n that place or point. ➤ exclam **1** used to express satisfaction, approval, triumph or encouragement, etc: There! I knew he would come. **2** used to express sympathy or comfort, etc: There, there! He's just not worth it. ◆ **there and then** at that very time and on that very spot.

thereabouts or **thereabout** adv near that place, number, amount, degree or time.

thereafter adv, formal from that time onwards.

thereby adv, formal **1** by that means. **2** in consequence.

therefore adv for that reason.

therein adv, formal in or into that place, circumstance, etc.

thereof adv, formal belonging or relating to, or from, that or it.

thereon adv, formal on or on to that or it.

thereto adv, formal to that or it; in addition.

thereunder adv, formal under that or it.

thereupon adv, formal **1** on that matter or

point. **2** immediately after it or that.

therm *n* a unit of heat equal to 1.055×10^8 joules, used to measure the amount of gas supplied.

thermal *adj* **1** relating to, caused by or producing heat. **2** of clothing: designed to prevent the loss of heat from the body. ➤ *n* **1** a rising current of warm air, used by birds, gliders, etc to move upwards. **2** (**thermals**) thermal clothing, esp underwear.

thermal imaging *n* the visualization of people, objects, etc by detecting the infrared energy they emit.

thermocouple *n* a device for measuring temperature, consisting of two different metallic conductors welded together at their ends to form a loop.

thermodynamics *sing n, physics* the branch of physics concerned with the relationship between heat and other forms of energy, esp mechanical energy, and the behaviour of physical systems in which temperature is an important factor. ○ **thermodynamic** *adj*.

thermoelectricity *n* an electric current generated by a difference in temperature in an electric circuit. ○ **thermoelectric** *adj*.

thermometer *n* an instrument for measuring temperature, often a glass tube filled with mercury which expands as the temperature increases.

thermonuclear *adj* using or showing nuclear reactions which can only be produced at extremely high temperatures.

thermoplastic *n, chem* a polymer that can be repeatedly softened and hardened by heating and cooling.

Thermos or **Thermos flask** *n, trademark* a kind of VACUUM FLASK.

thermostat *n* a device which keeps the temperature of a system constant, or which activates some other device when the temperature reaches a certain level. ○ **thermostatic** *adj*.

thesaurus /θɪˈsɔːrəs/ *n* (**thesauruses** or **thesauri** /-raɪ/) a book which lists words and their synonyms according to sense.

these *pl of* THIS

thesis /ˈθiːsɪs/ *n* (**-ses** /-siːz/) **1** a long written dissertation or report, esp one based on original research and presented for an advanced university degree. **2** an idea or proposition to be upheld in argument.

thespian *adj* belonging or relating to tragedy, or to drama and the theatre in general. ➤ *n, facetious* an actor and actress.

they *pron* **1** the people, animals or things already spoken about, being indicated, or known from the context. **2** people in general. **3** people in authority. **4** *colloq* he or she: *Anyone can help if they want.*

they'd *contraction* **1** they had. **2** they would.

they'll *contraction* **1** they will. **2** they shall.

they're *contraction* they are.

they've *contraction* they have.

thick *adj* **1** having a relatively large distance between opposite sides. **2** having a specified distance between opposite sides: *one inch thick*. **3** having a large diameter: *a thick rope*. **4** of a line or handwriting, etc: broad. **5** of a liquid: containing a lot of solid matter: *thick soup*. **6** having many single units placed very close together; dense: *thick hair*. **7** difficult to see through: *thick fog*. **8** of speech: not clear. **9** of an accent: pronounced. **10** *colloq* of a person: stupid. **11** *colloq* friendly or intimate: *He is very thick with the new manager.* **12** *colloq* unfair: *That's a bit thick!* ➤ *adv* thickly. ➤ *n* (**the thick**) the most active or intense part: *in the thick of the fighting.* ○ **thickly** *adv.* ◆ **as thick as thieves** very friendly. **thick and fast** frequently and in large numbers. **through thick and thin** in spite of any difficulties.

thicken *vb* **1** *tr & intr* to make or become thick or thicker. **2** *intr* to become more complicated: *The plot thickens.*

thickening *n* **1** something used to thicken liquid. **2** the process of making or becoming thicker. **3** a thickened part.

thicket *n* a dense mass of bushes and trees.

thickhead *n, colloq* a stupid person. ○ **thickheaded** *adj*.

thickness *n* **1** the state, quality or degree of being thick. **2** a layer. **3** the thick part of something.

thickset *adj* heavily built; having a thick, short body.

thick-skinned *adj* not easily hurt by criticism or insults.

thief *n* (**thieves**) a person who steals, esp secretly and usu without violence.

thieve *vb, tr & intr* to steal or be a thief. ○ **thievery** *n.* ○ **thieving** *adj*.

thigh *n* the part of the leg between the knee and hip in humans, or the corresponding part in animals.

thigh bone *n* the FEMUR.

thimble *n* a cap worn on the finger to protect it and push the needle when sewing. ○ **thimbleful** *n* a very small quantity of liquid.

thin *adj* (**thinner, thinnest**) **1** having a relatively short distance between opposite sides. **2** having a relatively small diameter: *thin string*. **3** of a line or handwriting, etc: narrow or fine. **4** of a person or animal: not fat; lean. **5** of a liquid: containing very little solid matter. **6** set far apart; sparse: *thin hair*. **7** having a very low oxygen content: *thin air*. **8** weak; lacking in body: *thin blood.* **9** not convincing or believable: *a thin disguise.* **10** *colloq* difficult; uncomfortable; unpleasant: *have a thin time of it.* ➤ *adv* thinly. ➤ *vb* (**thinned, thinning**) *tr & intr* (often **thin out**) to make or become thin, thinner, sparser or less dense.

thing *n* **1** an object. **2** a object that cannot, need not or should not be named. **3** a fact, quality or idea, etc that can be thought about or referred to. **4** an event, affair or circumstance: *Things are getting out of hand.* **5** a quality: *Generosity is a great thing*. **6** *colloq* a person or animal, esp when thought of as an object of pity: *Poor thing!* **7** a preoccupation, obsession or interest: *She's got a real thing about Brad Pitt!* **8** what is needed or required: *It's just the thing.* **9** an aim: *The thing is to do better next time.* **10** (**things**) personal belongings: *I'll just get my things.* **11** (**things**) affairs in general: *So, how are things?*

thingummy, thingamy, thingummyjig or **thingummybob** *n* (**thingummies,** *etc*) *colloq* someone or something whose name is unknown, forgotten or deliberately not used.

think *vb* (**thought**) **1** *tr & intr* a to have or form ideas in the mind; **b** to have as a thought in one's mind. **2** *tr & intr* to consider, judge or believe: *I thought you were kidding!* • *They think of themselves as great singers.* **3** *tr & intr* to intend or plan; to form an idea of: *I'm thinking about going to London* • *Think no harm.* **4** *tr & intr* to imagine, expect or suspect: *I didn't think there would be any trouble.* **5** to keep in mind; to consider: *Think of the children first.* **6** *tr & intr* a to remember: *I couldn't think of his name;* **b** to consider: *I didn't think to tell her.* **7** to form or have an idea: *to think of a plan.* **8** to bring into a specified condition by thinking: *tried to think himself thin.* ➣ *n, colloq* an act of thinking. ○ **thinker** *n.* ♦ **think better of sth** or **sb 1** to change one's mind about it or them on further thought. **2** to think that it or they would not be so bad as to do something wrong: *I thought better of him than that.* **think highly, well** or **badly,** *etc* **of sb** to have a high, good or bad, etc opinion of them. **think little of sth** or **not think much of sth** to have a very low opinion of it. **think twice** to hesitate before doing something; to decide in the end not to do it. ◊ **think sth over** or **through** to think carefully about all the possible consequences of (a plan or idea, etc). **think sth up** to invent or devise it.

thinking *n* **1** the act of using one's mind to produce thoughts. **2** opinion or judgement: *What is your thinking on this?* ➣ *adj* of people: using or able to use the mind intelligently and constructively.

thinner *n* a liquid that is added to paint or varnish to dilute it.

thin-skinned *adj* easily hurt or upset.

third (often written **3rd**) *adj* **1** in counting: a next after second; **b** last of three. **2** in third position. **3** being one of three equal parts: *a third share.* ➣ *n* **1** one of three equal parts. **2** a FRACTION equal to one divided by three (usu written ⅓). **3** a person coming third, eg in a race or exam. **4** (**the third**) the third day of the month. **5** *mus* a an interval of three notes along the diatonic scale; **b** a note at that interval from another. ➣ *adv* thirdly. ○ **thirdly** *adv* used to introduce the third point in a list.

third degree *n* (**the third degree**) prolonged and intensive interrogation, usu involving physical and mental intimidation. ➣ *adj* (**third-degree**) *med* denoting the most serious of the

three degrees of burning, with damage to the lower layers of skin tissue.

third party *n, law* someone indirectly involved, or involved by chance, in a legal action or contract, etc. ➣ *adj* (**third-party**) of insurance: covering damage done by or injury done to someone other than the insured.

third person see under PERSON

third-rate *adj* inferior; substandard.

Third World *n, now sometimes offensive* the developing or underdeveloped countries in Africa, Asia and Latin America; the **Developing World**.

thirst *n* **1** a need to drink, or the feeling of dryness in the mouth that this causes. **2** a strong and eager desire or longing: *a thirst for knowledge.* ➣ *vb, intr* to have a great desire or long for.

thirsty *adj* (**-ier, -iest**) **1** needing or wanting to drink. **2** eager or longing. **3** causing thirst.

thirteen *n* **1** a the cardinal number 13; **b** the quantity that this represents, being one more than twelve, or the sum of ten and three. **2** any symbol for this, eg *13* or *XIII.* ➣ *adj* **1** totalling thirteen. **2** aged thirteen. ○ **thirteenth** *adj, n, adv.*

thirties (often written **30s** or **30's**) *pl n* **1** (**one's thirties**) the period of time between one's thirtieth and fortieth birthdays. **2** (**the thirties**) the range of temperatures between thirty and forty degrees. **3** (**the thirties**) the period of time between the thirtieth and fortieth years of a century.

thirty *n* (**-ies**) **1** a the cardinal number 30; **b** the quantity that this represents, being one more than twenty-nine, or the product of ten and three. **2** any symbol for this, eg *30* or *XXX.* ➣ *adj* **1** totalling thirty. **2** aged thirty. ○ **thirtieth** *adj, n, adv.*

this *pron* (**these**) **1** a person, animal, thing or idea already mentioned, about to be mentioned, indicated or otherwise understood from the context. **2** a person, animal, thing or idea which is nearby, esp which is closer to the speaker than someone or something else. **3** the present time or place. **4** an action, event or circumstance: *What do you think of this?* ➣ *adj* **1** being the person, animal, thing or idea which is nearby, esp closer than someone or something else: *this book or that one.* **2** being the person, animal, thing or idea just mentioned, about to be mentioned, indicated or otherwise understood. **3** relating to today, or time in the recent past ending today: *this morning* • *I've been ill these last few days.* **4** *colloq* denoting a person, animal, thing, etc not yet mentioned: *then I had this bright idea.* ➣ *adv* to this degree or extent: *I didn't think it would be this easy.* ♦ **this and that** *colloq* various minor unspecified actions or objects, etc.

thistle *n* **1** a plant with prickly leaves and usu globular purple, red or white flower heads. **2** this plant as the national emblem of Scotland.

thistledown *n* the light fluffy hairs attached to thistle seeds.

thither *adv, old use, literary or formal* to or towards that place.

tho' or **tho** *conj, adv* short for THOUGH.

thole or **tholepin** *n* either one of a pair of pins in the side of a boat to keep an oar in place.

thong *n* **1** a narrow strip of leather used for fastening, etc. **2** a type of skimpy undergarment or bathing costume, similar to a G-string. **3** (**thongs**) *N Am, NZ, Austral* flip-flops.

thorax *n* (**thoraxes** or **thoraces** /ˈθɔːrəsiːz/) *anat, zool* in humans and other vertebrates: the part of the body between the neck and abdomen; the chest. ○ **thoracic** *adj*.

thorium *n, chem* a silvery-grey radioactive metallic element used in X-ray tubes, sun-lamps, etc.

thorn *n* **1** a hard sharp point sticking out from the stem or branch of certain plants. **2** a shrub bearing thorns. **3** a constant irritation or annoyance: *a thorn in one's side*.

thorny *adj* (*-ier, -iest*) **1** full of or covered with thorns. **2** difficult; causing trouble or problems.

thorough *adj* **1** of a person: extremely careful and attending to every detail. **2** of a task, etc: carried out with great care and great attention to detail. **3** complete; absolute: *a thorough waste of time*. ○ **thoroughly** *adv*.

thoroughbred *n* **1** an animal bred from the best specimens over many years. **2** (**Thoroughbred**) a breed of racehorse descended from English mares and Arab stallions.

thoroughfare *n* **1** a public road or street. **2 a** a road or path open at both ends; **b** the right of passage through this.

thoroughgoing *adj* **1** extremely thorough. **2** utter; out-and-out: *a thoroughgoing villain*.

those *pl of* THAT.

thou[1] /ðaʊ/ *pron, old use or dialect, also relig* you (singular).

thou[2] /θaʊ/ *n* (**thous** or **thou**) **1** *colloq* a thousand. **2** one thousandth of an inch.

though *conj* **1** (*often* **even though**) despite the fact that: *I ate it up though I didn't like it*. **2** if or even if: *I wouldn't marry him though he was the richest man in the world*. **3** and yet; but: *We like the new car, though not as much as the old one*. ➤ *adv* however; nevertheless. ◆ **as though** as if: *It's as though I've known him all my life*.

thought *n* **1** an idea, concept or opinion. **2** an act or the process of thinking. **3** serious and careful consideration: *I'll give some thought to the problem*. **4** the faculty or power of reasoning. **5** intellectual ideas which are typical of a particular place, time or group, etc: *recent scientific thought*. **6** intention, expectation or hope: *no thoughts of retiring yet*. ➤ *vb, past tense & past participle of* THINK.

thoughtful *adj* **1** thinking deeply; reflective. **2** showing careful thought: *a thoughtful reply*. **3** considerate. ○ **thoughtfully** *adv*. ○ **thoughtfulness** *n*.

thoughtless *adj* **1** inconsiderate. **2** showing a

lack of careful thought; rash. ○ **thoughtlessly** *adv*. ○ **thoughtlessness** *n*.

thousand *n* (**thousands** or *after a number* **thousand**) **1 a** the number 1000; **b** the quantity that this represents, being the product of ten and one hundred. **2** any symbol for this, eg *1000* or *M*. **3** a set of a thousand people or things. **4** (**thousands**) *colloq* a large but indefinite number: *thousands of people*. ○ **thousandth** *adj, n*.

thrall *n* **1** (*often* **in thrall to**) a slave or captive. **2** (*often* **in thrall**) a state of being in slavery or captivation: *held in thrall by her beauty*.

thrash *vb* **1** to beat soundly, esp with blows or a whip. **2** to defeat thoroughly or decisively. **3** *intr* to move around violently or wildly. **4** *tr & intr* to thresh (corn, etc). ➤ *n* **1** an act of thrashing. **2** *colloq* a party. ○ **thrashing** *n*. ◇ **thrash sth out** to discuss (a problem, etc) thoroughly to try to come to a solution.

thread *n* **1** a strand of silk, cotton, wool, etc for sewing. **2** a naturally formed strand of fibre, such as that spun by a spider. **3** anything like a thread in length, narrowness, continuity, etc. **4** the projecting spiral ridge round a screw or bolt, or in a nut. **5** a connecting element or theme in a story or argument, etc: *I lost the thread of what he was saying*. **6** (**threads**) *colloq* clothes, esp when flashy. ➤ *vb* **1** to pass a thread through the eye of (a needle). **2** (*usu* **thread through**) to pass (tape, film, etc) (into or through something). **3** to put (beads, etc) on a string, etc. **4** *tr & intr* to make (one's way): *I threaded my way through the crowd*. **5** to provide (a bolt, etc) with a screw thread.

threadbare *adj* **1** of material or clothes: worn thin; shabby. **2** of a person: wearing such clothes. **3** of a word, excuse, etc: commonly used and meaningless; feeble.

threadworm *n* a parasitic worm living in the human large intestine.

threat *n* **1** a warning of impending hurt or punishment. **2** a sign that something dangerous or unpleasant is or may be about to happen. **3** a person or thing seen as dangerous.

threaten *vb* **1** to make or be a threat to. **2** to warn. **3** *intr* of something unpleasant or dangerous: to seem likely to happen: *The storm threatened all morning*. ○ **threatening** *adj*. ○ **threateningly** *adv*.

three *n* **1 a** the cardinal number 3; **b** the quantity that this represents, being one more than two. **2** any symbol for this, eg *3* or *III*. **3** the third hour after midnight or midday. **4** a set or group of three people or things. ➤ *adj* **1** totalling three. **2** aged three.

three-dimensional *adj* having or appearing to have three dimensions, ie, height, width and depth.

threefold *adj* **1** equal to three times as much or many. **2** divided into, or consisting of, three parts. ➤ *adv* by three times as much.

three-legged race *n* a race run between pairs of runners who have their adjacent legs tied together.

three-ply n something with three layers or strands bound together, esp wood or wool. ➤ adj having three layers or strands.

three-point turn n a manoeuvre, usu done in three movements, in which a driver turns a motor vehicle using forward and reverse gears, to face in the opposite direction.

three-quarter adj consisting of three-quarters of the full amount, length, etc.

threescore n, adj, archaic sixty.

threesome n 1 a group of three. 2 a game, esp a round of golf, played by three people.

threnody n (**threnodies**) a song or ode of lamentation, esp for a person's death.

thresh vb 1 tr & intr to separate grain or seeds from (corn, etc) by beating. 2 to beat or strike. ○ **thresher** n.

threshold n 1 a piece of wood or stone forming the bottom of a doorway. 2 any doorway or entrance. 3 a starting-point: on the threshold of a new career. 4 the point, stage, level, etc at which something will happen or come into effect, etc: a tax threshold. 5 biol the point below which there is no response to a stimulus: a low pain threshold.

thrice adv, old use or literary 1 three times. 2 three times as much. 3 greatly; highly: thrice blessed.

thrift n 1 careful spending, use or management of resources, esp money. 2 a wild seaside plant with narrow bluish-green leaves and pink flowers. ○ **thriftless** adj.

thrifty adj (**-ier, -iest**) showing thrift; economical; frugal. ○ **thriftily** adv. ○ **thriftiness** n.

thrill vb 1 tr & intr to feel or cause to feel exhilaration. 2 tr & intr to vibrate or quiver. 3 intr of a feeling: to pass quickly with a glowing or tingling sensation: Excitement thrilled through her. ➤ n 1 a sudden tingling feeling of excitement, happiness or pleasure. 2 something causing this. 3 a shivering or trembling feeling. ○ **thrilling** adj.

thriller n an exciting novel, play, film, etc, usu involving crime, espionage or adventure.

thrips n (pl **thrips**) a minute black insect, which feeds by sucking sap from plants, and causes damage to crops.

thrive vb (**throve** or **thrived, thriven** or **thrived**) intr 1 to grow strong and healthy. 2 to prosper or be successful, esp financially.

thro' or **thro** prep, adv, adj short for THROUGH.

throat n 1 the top part of the windpipe or gullet. 2 the front part of the neck. 3 something similar to a throat, esp a narrow passageway or opening. ♦ **ram sth down sb's throat** to force them to listen to or pay attention to it.

throaty adj (**-ier, -iest**) of a voice: deep and hoarse; husky. 2 colloq indicating a sore throat: feeling a bit throaty. 3 from the throat.

throb vb (**throbbed, throbbing**) intr 1 to beat, esp with unusual force. 2 to beat or vibrate with a strong regular rhythm. ➤ n a regular beat; pulse.

throe n (usu **throes**) a violent pang or spasm, esp during childbirth or before death. ♦ **in the throes of** busy with, involved in or suffering under: in the throes of doing the ironing • in the throes of the storm.

thrombosis /θrɒm'bəʊsɪs/ n (**-ses** /-siːz/) an abnormal congealing of the blood within a blood vessel, causing a blood clot.

throne n 1 a ceremonial chair of a monarch, bishop, etc. 2 the office or power of the sovereign: come to the throne.

throng n a crowd of people or things. ➤ vb, tr & intr to crowd or fill: people thronging the streets • The audience thronged into the theatre.

throttle n a valve regulating the amount of fuel, steam, etc supplied to an engine. ➤ vb 1 to injure or kill by choking or strangling. 2 to prevent (something from being said, etc). 3 to control the flow of (fuel, steam, etc to an engine) using a valve.

through or (US) **thru** prep 1 going from one side or end of something to the other: a road through the village. 2 all over: We searched through the house. 3 from the beginning to the end of: read through the magazine. 4 N Am up to and including: Tuesday through Thursday. 5 because of: Tom lost his job through his own stupidity. 6 by way, means, or agency of: related through marriage. ➤ adv 1 into and out of; from one side or end to the other: go straight through. 2 from the beginning to the end. 3 into a position of having completed, esp successfully: She sat the exam again and got through. 4 to the core; completely: soaked through. ➤ adj 1 of a journey, route, train or ticket, etc: going or allowing one to go all the way to one's destination without requiring a change of line or train, etc or a new ticket. 2 of traffic: passing straight through an area or town, etc without stopping. 3 going from one surface, side or end to another: a through road. ♦ **be through with sb** to have no more to do with them. **be through with sth** to have finished or completed it. **put through** to connect by telephone: I'll put you through to that extension. **through and through** completely.

throughout prep 1 in all parts of: She decorated throughout the house. 2 during the whole of: They chattered throughout the film. ➤ adv 1 in every part; everywhere: a house with carpets throughout. 2 during the whole time: remain friends throughout.

throughput n the amount of material put through a computer or manufacturing process.

throw vb (**threw, thrown**) 1 tr & intr to propel or hurl through the air with force. 2 to move or hurl into a specified position. 3 to put into a specified condition: It threw them into confusion. 4 to direct, cast or emit: a candle throwing shadows on the wall • throw a glance. 5 colloq to puzzle or confuse. 6 of a horse: to make (its rider) fall off. 7 wrestling, judo to bring (an opponent) to the ground. 8 to move (a switch or lever) so as to operate a mechanism. 9 to make (pottery) on a potter's wheel. 10 colloq to lose (a contest) deliberately, esp in return for a bribe. **11 a** *tr & intr* to roll (dice) on to a flat surface; **b** to obtain (a specified number) by throwing dice. **12** to have or suffer: *throw a tantrum*. **13** to give (a party). **14** to deliver (a punch). **15** to cause (one's voice) to appear to come from elsewhere. ➢ *n* **1** an act of throwing or instance of being thrown. **2** a distance thrown. **3** *colloq* an article, item, turn, etc: *sell them at £2 a throw*. **4** a decorative fabric covering a piece of furniture, etc. ◆ **throw oneself into sth** to begin doing it with great energy or enthusiasm. ◇ **throw sth away 1** to discard it or get rid of it. **2** to fail to take advantage of it. **throw sth in 1** to add it as part of a deal at no extra cost. **2** to contribute (a remark) to a discussion. **throw off 1** to get rid of it: *throw off a cold*. **2** to say it in an offhand way. **throw out 1** to confuse or disconcert: *was thrown out by his attitude*. **2** to get rid of. **throw sb over** to leave or abandon (esp a lover). **throw people together** of circumstances, etc: to bring them into contact by chance. **throw sth together** to construct it hurriedly or temporarily. **throw up** *colloq* to vomit. **throw sth up 1** to give it up or abandon it. **2** to build or erect it hurriedly. **3** to bring up (eg a meal) by vomiting.

| throw | There is sometimes a spelling confusion between **throw** and **throe**. |

throwaway *adj* **1** meant to be thrown away after use. **2** said or done casually or carelessly.

throwback *n* someone or something that shows or reverts to earlier or ancestral characteristics.

throw-in *n, sport* in football, basketball, etc: an act of throwing the ball back into play from a sideline.

thru see THROUGH

thrum *vb* (**thrummed, thrumming**) **1** *tr & intr* to strum idly on (a stringed instrument). **2** *intr* to drum or tap with the fingers. **3** *intr* to hum monotonously. ➢ *n* repetitive strumming, or the sound of this.

thrush[1] *n* a songbird, typically with brown feathers and a spotted chest.

thrush[2] *n* **1** a fungal infection causing white blisters in the mouth, throat and lips. **2** a similar infection in the vagina.

thrust *vb* (**thrust**) **1** to push suddenly and violently. **2** (*usu* **thrust on** or **upon**) to force (someone) to accept (something). **3** to make (one's) way forcibly. ➢ *n* **1** a sudden or violent movement forward; a push or lunge. **2** *aeronautics* the force produced by a jet or rocket engine that propels an aircraft or rocket forward. **3** an attack or lunge with a pointed weapon; a stab. **4** a military or verbal attack. **5** the main theme or gist, eg, of an argument.

thud *n* a dull sound like something heavy falling to the ground. ➢ *vb* (**thudded, thudding**) *intr* to move or fall with a thud.

thug *n* a violent or brutal person. ○ **thuggery** *n*. ○ **thuggish** *adj*.

thulium /ˈθuːlɪəm, ˈθjuː-/ *n, chem* a soft silvery-white metallic element of the lanthanide series.

thumb *n* **1** in humans: the opposable digit on the inner side of the hand, set lower than the other four digits. **2** a part of a glove or mitten covering this. **3** in other animals: the digit corresponding to the human thumb. ➢ *vb* **1** (*often* **thumb through**) *tr & intr* to turn the pages of (a book or magazine, etc) and glance at the contents. **2** to smudge or wear away with the thumb. **3** (*also* **thumb a lift** or **ride**) *tr & intr* to hitchhike: *He thumbed to London*. ◆ **all (fingers and) thumbs** awkward and clumsy. **thumb one's nose** to cock a snook (see under SNOOK[2]). **thumbs down** a sign indicating failure, rejection or disapproval. **thumbs up** a sign indicating success, best wishes for success, satisfaction or approval. **under sb's thumb** completely controlled or dominated by them.

thumb nail *n* **1** the nail on the thumb. **2** *comput* (*also* **thumbnail**) a small version of a picture or layout. ➢ *adj* brief and concise: *a thumb-nail sketch*.

thumbscrew *n, hist* an instrument of torture which crushes the thumbs.

thump *n* a heavy blow, or the dull sound of a blow. ➢ *vb* **1** *tr & intr* to beat or strike with dull-sounding heavy blows. **2** *intr* to throb or beat violently. **3** (*often* **thump out**) to play (a tune), esp on a piano, by pounding heavily on the keys. **4** to move with heavy pounding steps.

thumping *colloq, adj* very big: *a thumping lie*. ➢ *adv* very: *a pair of thumping great boots*.

thunder *n* **1** a deep rumbling or loud cracking sound heard soon after a flash of lightning. **2** a loud deep rumbling noise. ➢ *vb* **1** *intr* of thunder: to sound or rumble. **2** *intr* to make a noise like thunder: *tanks thundering over a bridge*. **3** to say or utter in a loud, often aggressive, voice. ○ **thundery** *adj*.

thunderbolt *n* **1** a flash of lightning coming simultaneously with a crash of thunder. **2** a sudden and unexpected event. **3** a supposed destructive stone or missile, etc falling to earth in a flash of lightning.

thunderclap *n* **1** a sudden crash of thunder. **2** something startling or unexpected.

thundercloud *n* a large cloud charged with electricity which produces thunder and lightning.

thundering *colloq, adj* very great: *a thundering idiot*. ➢ *adv* very: *a thundering great error*.

thunderous *adj* **1** like thunder, esp in being very loud: *thunderous applause*. **2** threatening or violent.

thunderstorm *n* a storm with thunder and lightning, usu accompanied by heavy rain.

thunderstruck *adj* overcome by surprise; astonished.

Thursday *n* the fifth day of the week.

thus *adv* **1** in the way or manner shown or mentioned. **2** to this degree, amount or distance: *thus far*. **3** therefore; accordingly.

thwack n a blow with something flat, or the noise of this. ➤ vb to strike with such a noise.

thwart vb to prevent or hinder (someone or something). ➤ n a seat for a rower that lies across a boat.

thy adj, old use or dialect, also relig belonging or relating to THEE.

thyme /taɪm/ n a herb or shrub with aromatic leaves used to season food.

thymus /'θaɪməs/ n (**thymuses** or **thymi** /-maɪ/) in vertebrates: a gland in the chest controlling the development of lymphatic tissue.

thyroid n in vertebrates: a gland in the neck that secretes hormones which control growth, development and metabolic rate.

Ti symbol, chem titanium.

ti see TE

tiara n 1 a woman's jewelled head-ornament. 2 a three-tiered crown worn by a pope.

tibia n (**tibias** or **tibiae** /'tɪbiːiː/) 1 the inner and usu larger of the two human leg bones between the knee and ankle. 2 the corresponding bone in other vertebrates. Compare FIBULA. ○ **tibial** adj.

tic n a habitual nervous involuntary movement or twitch of a muscle, esp of the face.

tick¹ n 1 a regular tapping or clicking sound, such as that made by a watch or clock. 2 Brit colloq a moment: Wait a tick. 3 a small mark, usu a downward-sloping line with the bottom part bent upwards, used to show that something is correct, to mark off items on a list once they are dealt with, etc. ➤ vb 1 intr of a clock, etc: to make a tick or ticks. 2 intr of time: to pass steadily. 3 (often **tick off**) to mark (an item on a list, etc) with a tick, eg, when checking. ♦ **what makes sb tick** colloq their underlying character and motivation. ◊ **tick sb off** colloq to scold them. **tick over 1** to function quietly and smoothly at a moderate rate. 2 of an engine: to idle.

tick² n 1 a bloodsucking arachnid living esp on the skin of dogs and cattle. 2 a bloodsucking fly living on the skin of sheep, birds, etc.

tick³ n 1 a strong cover of a mattress, bolster, etc. 2 short for TICKING.

tick⁴ n, Brit colloq credit: buy it on tick.

ticker n, colloq the heart.

ticker tape n continuous paper tape with messages, esp up-to-date share prices, printed by a telegraph instrument.

ticket n 1 a card, etc entitling the holder to travel on a bus, train, etc, or to be admitted to a theatre, cinema, sports match, etc, or to use a library, etc. 2 an official notice stating that a traffic offence, eg, speeding or illegal parking, has been committed. 3 a tag or label showing the price, size, etc of the item to which it is attached. 4 N Am a list of candidates put up for election by a political party, or their policies. 5 colloq exactly what is required or best: just the ticket. ➤ vb to give or attach a ticket or label to.

ticking n a strong coarse, usu striped, cotton fabric used to cover mattresses, bolsters, etc.

ticking-off n, Brit colloq a mild scolding.

tickle vb 1 to touch (a person or body part) lightly and provoke a tingling or light prickling sensation, laughter, jerky movements, etc. 2 intr of a part of the body: to feel a tingling or light prickling sensation. 3 colloq to amuse or entertain. ➤ n 1 an act of tickling. 2 a tingling or light prickling sensation. ♦ **tickled pink** or **tickled to death** colloq very pleased or amused. **tickle sb's fancy** to attract or amuse them in some way.

ticklish adj 1 sensitive to tickling. 2 of a problem, etc: needing careful handling.

tidal adj relating to or affected by tides. ○ **tidally** adv.

tidal wave n 1 an unusually large ocean wave. 2 a widespread show of feeling, etc.

tiddler n, Brit colloq 1 a small fish, esp a stickleback or a minnow. 2 a small person or thing.

tiddly¹ adj (**-ier, -iest**) Brit colloq slightly drunk.

tiddly² adj (**-ier, -iest**) Brit colloq little.

tiddlywinks sing n a game in which players try to flick small flat discs into a cup using larger discs.

tide n 1 the twice-daily rise and fall of the water level in the oceans and seas. 2 the level of water, esp the sea, as affected by this: high tide. 3 a sudden or marked trend: tide of public opinion. 4 in compounds a time or season, esp of some festival: Whitsuntide. ➤ vb, intr to drift with or be carried on the tide. ◊ **tide sb over** to help them to deal with a difficult situation, etc: Here's some money to tide you over.

tidemark n 1 a mark showing the highest level that the tide has reached or usu reaches. 2 Brit colloq a a scummy ring round a bath indicating where the water had come up to; b a mark on the skin indicating the difference between a washed area and an unwashed one.

tidings pl n, old use news.

tidy adj (**-ier, -iest**) 1 neat and in good order. 2 methodical. 3 colloq large; considerable: a tidy sum of money. ➤ n (**-ies**) an act or the process of tidying: I gave the room a quick tidy. ➤ vb (**-ies, -ied**) (also **tidy away** or **up**) to make neat: He tidied up the toys • She tidied her hair. ○ **tidily** adv. ○ **tidiness** n.

tie vb (**tying**) 1 (also **tie up**) to fasten with a string, ribbon, rope, etc. 2 a to make (string, ribbon, etc) into a bow or knot; b to make (a bow or knot) in. 3 intr to be fastened in a specified way: a dress that ties at the back. 4 (usu **tie with**) intr to have the same score or final position as (another competitor or entrant) in a game or contest, etc. 5 to limit or restrict. 6 mus a to mark (notes of the same pitch) with a curved line showing that they are to be played as a continuous sound rather than individually; b to play (notes of the same pitch) in this way. ➤ n 1 a narrow strip of material worn, esp by men, round the neck under a shirt collar and tied in a knot or bow at the front. 2 a strip of ribbon, rope, cord or chain, etc for binding and fastening. **3** something that limits or restricts. **4** a link or bond: *ties of friendship.* **5 a** a match or competition, etc in which the result is an equal score for both sides; **b** the score or result achieved. **6** *Brit* a game or match to be played, esp in a knockout competition: *The third round ties were all postponed.* **7** a rod or beam holding parts of a structure together. **8** *mus* a curved line above two or more notes of the same pitch showing that they are to be played as a continuous sound rather than individually. ◊ **tie in** or **up with sth** to be in or be brought into connection with it; to correspond or be made to correspond with it. **tie up** to moor or dock. **tie sb** or **sth up 1** to keep them busy. **2** to block or restrict their movement or progress.

tie-break or **tie-breaker** *n* an extra game, series of games, question, etc to decide a drawn match, etc.

tied cottage *n, Brit* a cottage occupied by a tenant during the period that they are employed by its owner.

tie-dye *n* a technique of dyeing fabrics in which parts of the fabric are tied tightly to stop them absorbing the dye, so that a swirly pattern is produced. ➢ *vb* to dye like this.

tie-in *n* (*tie-ins*) **1** a connection or link. **2** something presented at the same time as something else, eg a book published to coincide with a TV programme.

tie-pin *n* an ornamental pin fixed to a tie to hold it in place.

tier /'tɪə(r)/ *n* a level, rank, row, etc, esp one of several positioned one above another to form a structure: *a wedding cake with three tiers • tiers of seats.*

tiff *n* a slight petty quarrel.

tiffin *n, Anglo-Indian* a light midday meal.

tig see under TAG[2]

tiger *n* **1** a large carnivorous Asian member of the cat family with a fawn or reddish coat, with black or brownish-black transverse stripes. **2** a fierce or passionate person.

tight *adj* **1** fitting very or too closely. **2** stretched so as not to be loose; tense; taut. **3** fixed or held firmly in place: *a tight knot.* **4** *usu in compounds* preventing the passage of air, water, etc: *watertight.* **5** difficult or awkward: *in a tight spot.* **6** strictly and carefully controlled. **7** of a contest or match: closely or evenly fought. **8** of a schedule or timetable, etc: not allowing much time. **9** *colloq* mean; miserly: *He's so tight with his money.* **10** *colloq* drunk. **11** of money or some commodity: in short supply; difficult to obtain. ➢ *adv* tightly; soundly; completely: *sleep tight.* ○ **tightly** *adv.* ○ **tightness** *n.*

tighten *vb, tr & intr* to make or become tight or tighter. ◆ **tighten one's belt** *colloq* to live more economically.

tight-fisted *adj* mean with money, etc.

tight-knit or **tightly-knit** *adj* closely organized or united: *a tight-knit family.*

tight-lipped *adj* saying or revealing nothing.

tightrope *n* a tightly stretched rope or wire on which acrobats perform.

tights *pl n* a close-fitting garment covering the feet, legs and body up to the waist, worn esp by women, dancers, acrobats, etc.

tigress *n* **1** a female tiger. **2** a fierce or passionate woman.

tikka *adj* of meat in Indian cookery: having been marinated in yoghurt and spices.

tilde /'tɪldə/ *n* a mark (∼) placed over *n* in Spanish to show that it is pronounced *ny* and over *a* and *o* in Portuguese to show they are nasalized.

tile *n* **1** a flat thin slab of fired clay, or a similar one of cork or linoleum, used to cover roofs, floors and walls, etc. **2** a small flat rectangular piece used in some games. ➢ *vb* to cover with tiles. ○ **tiler** *n.* ○ **tiling** *n.* ◆ **on the tiles** having a wild social time.

till[1] *prep* up to the time of: *wait till tomorrow.* ➢ *conj* up to the time when: *go on till you reach the station.*

till[2] *n* a container or drawer where money is taken from customers is put, now usu part of a CASH REGISTER.

till[3] *vb* to prepare and cultivate (soil or land) for the growing of crops.

tillage *n* **1** the preparing and cultivating of land for crops. **2** land which has been tilled.

tiller *n* a lever used to turn the rudder of a boat.

tilt *vb* **1** *tr & intr* to slope or cause to slope. **2** (*often* **tilt at**) *intr* to charge or attack. **3** *intr* to fight on horseback with a lance. ➢ *n* **1** a sloping position or angle. **2** an act of tilting. **3** a joust. ◆ **at full tilt** at full speed or with full force.

tilth *n, agric* **1** cultivation. **2** the condition of tilled soil.

timber *n* **1** wood, esp for building or carpentry. **2** trees suitable for this. **3** a wooden beam in the framework, esp of a ship or house. ➢ *exclam* a warning cry that a tree has been cut and is about to fall.

timbre /'tæmbə(r)/ *n* the distinctive quality of the tone produced by a musical instrument or voice, as opposed to pitch and loudness.

time *n* **1** the continuous passing and succession of minutes, days and years, etc. **2** a particular point in time expressed in hours and minutes, or days, months and years, as shown on a clock, watch, calendar, etc. **3** a specified system for reckoning or expressing time: *Eastern European Time.* **4** (*also* **times**) a point or period of time: *at the time of her marriage • olden times.* **5** *in compounds* a period of time allocated to an activity, etc: *playtime • lunchtime.* **6** an unspecified interval or period: *She stayed there for a time.* **7** one of a number or series of occasions or repeated actions: *been to Spain three times.* **8** a period or occasion of a specified kind: *a good time • hard times.* **9** a particular period being considered, esp the present. **10** *colloq* a prison sentence: *do time.* **11** an apprenticeship: *Kate served her time and became a* *motor mechanic.* **12** the point at which something, eg, a match, game, etc, ends or must end. **13** *Brit* the time when a public house must close. **14** *mus* a specified rhythm or speed: *waltz time.* ➤ *vb* **1** to measure the time taken by (an event or journey, etc). **2** to arrange, set or choose the time for (a journey, meeting, etc). **3** *tr & intr* to keep or beat or cause to keep or beat time. ♦ **all in good time** in due course; soon enough. **behind the times** out of date; old-fashioned. **for the time being** meanwhile; for the moment. **from time to time** occasionally; sometimes. **have no time for sb or sth** to have no interest in or patience with them or it; to despise them or it. **have the time of one's life** to enjoy oneself very much. **in good time** early. **in no time** very quickly. **in one's own time 1** in one's spare time. **2** at the speed one prefers. **in time** early enough. **in time with sb or sth** at the same speed or rhythm as them or it. **keep time 1** to correctly follow the required rhythm of a piece of music. **2** of a clock: to function accurately. **kill time** to pass time aimlessly. **make good time** to travel as quickly as, or more quickly than, expected or hoped. **no time at all** *colloq* a very short time. **on time** at the right time; not late. **pass the time of day** to have a brief casual conversation. **take one's time** to work, etc as slowly as one wishes. **time and time again** repeatedly.

time bomb *n* a bomb that has been set to explode at a particular time.

time capsule *n* a box containing objects chosen as typical of the current age, buried or otherwise preserved for discovery in the future.

time-consuming *adj* taking up a lot of time.

time-honoured *adj* respected and upheld because of custom or tradition.

timekeeper *n* **1** someone who records time, eg, as worked by employees or taken by a competitor in a game, etc. **2** a clock, watch or person thought of in terms of accuracy or punctuality: *a good timekeeper.* ○ **timekeeping** *n*.

timeless *adj* **1** not belonging to or typical of any particular time or date. **2** unaffected by time; ageless; eternal. ○ **timelessly** *adv.* ○ **timelessness** *n*.

timely *adj* (**-ier, -iest**) coming at the right or a suitable moment; opportune. ○ **timeliness** *n*.

time out *n, N Am* a brief pause or period of rest.

timepiece *n* an instrument for keeping time, such as a watch or clock.

timer *n* a device like a clock which switches an appliance on or off at preset times, or which makes a sound when a set amount of time has passed.

times *prep* expressing multiplication: *three times two makes six.*

timescale *n* the time envisaged for the completion of a particular project.

time-served *adj* having completed an ap-

prenticeship; fully trained: *a time-served electrician.*

timeserver *n* someone who changes their behaviour or opinions to fit those held by people in general or by someone in authority.

time-sharing *n* **1** a scheme whereby someone buys the right to use a holiday home for the same specified period each year for an agreed number of years. **2** *comput* a system which allows many users with individual terminals to use a single computer at the same time.

time signature *n, mus* a sign, usu placed after a clef, indicating rhythm.

timetable *n* **1** a list of the departure and arrival times of trains, buses, etc. **2** a plan showing the order of events. ➤ *vb* to arrange or include in a timetable.

timeworn *adj* worn out through long use; old.

time zone *n* any one of the 24 more or less parallel sections into which the world is divided longitudinally, with all places within a given zone having the same standard time.

timid *adj* easily frightened or alarmed; nervous; shy. ○ **timidity** *n*.

timing *n* the regulating or co-ordinating of actions, events, etc to achieve the best possible effect.

timorous *adj* very timid; frightened.

timpani or **tympani** /'tɪmpənɪ/ *pl n* a set of two or three kettledrums.

tin *n* **1** *chem* a soft silvery-white metallic element used in alloys, eg, bronze, pewter and solder. **2** an airtight metal container for storing food: *a biscuit tin.* **3** a sealed container for preserving food: *a tin of baked beans.* ➤ *vb* (**tinned, tinning**) to pack (food) in a tin. ○ **tinned** *adj.*

tincture *n* **1** a slight flavour, trace or addition. **2** a slight trace of colour; hue; tinge. **3** a solution of a drug in alcohol for medicinal use.

tinder *n* dry material, esp wood, easily set alight and used as kindling.

tinderbox *n, hist* a box containing tinder, a flint and steel for striking a spark to light a fire.

tine *n* a slender prong, eg, of a comb, fork or antler.

tinfoil *n* aluminium or other metal in the form of thin, paper-like sheets, used esp for wrapping food.

ting *n* a tinkling sound, eg, made by a small bell. ➤ *vb, tr & intr* to produce or cause to produce this sound.

tinge *n* **1** a trace or slight amount of colour. **2** a trace or hint of (a quality, feeling, etc). ➤ *vb* **1** to give a slight colour to. **2** to give a trace or hint of a feeling or quality, etc to.

tingle *vb, tr & intr* to feel or cause to feel a prickling or slightly stinging sensation, eg, due to cold, embarrassment, etc. ➤ *n* a prickling or slightly stinging sensation. ○ **tingling** *adj.*

tinker *n* **1** a travelling mender of pots, pans and other household utensils. **2** *colloq* a mischievous or impish person, esp a child. ➤ *vb, intr* to work in an unskilled way, esp in trying to make

tinkering minor adjustments or improvements: *tinkering with that old car.*

tinkle *vb, tr & intr* to make or cause to make a succession of jingling sounds. ➤ *n* **1** a jingling sound. **2** *Brit colloq* a telephone call: *I'll give you a tinkle tomorrow.*

tinnitus *n, med* an abnormal ringing, buzzing, etc noise in the ears, not caused by external sound.

tinny *adj (-ier, -iest)* **1** relating to or resembling tin. **2** flimsy: *a tinny old car.* **3** of sound: thin and high-pitched. ➤ *n (-ies) Aust slang* a can of beer.

tin-opener *n* a device for opening tins of food.

tin plate *n* thin sheet iron or steel coated with tin. ➤ *vb* (**tin-plate**) to cover with a layer of tin.

tinpot *adj, Brit colloq* cheap or poor quality; paltry or contemptible: *tinpot dictator.*

tinsel *n* **1** long decorative strips of glittering metal threads, used esp at Christmas. **2** something cheap and gaudy.

tinsmith *n* a worker in tin and tin plate.

tint *n* **1** a variety or slightly different shade of a colour, esp one made lighter by adding white. **2** a pale or faint colour. **3** a hair dye. ➤ *vb* to give a tint to (hair, etc); to colour slightly.

tintinnabulation *n* a ringing of bells.

tiny *adj (-ier, -iest)* very small.

tip¹ *n* **1** an end or furthermost point of something: *the tips of her fingers.* **2** a small piece forming an end or point: *a rubber tip on a walking-stick.* **3** a top or summit. **4** a leaf bud of tea. ➤ *vb* (**tipped, tipping**) to put or form a tip on. ◆ **on the tip of one's tongue** about to be said, but not able to be because not quite remembered.

tip² *vb* (**tipped, tipping**) **1** *tr & intr* to lean or cause to lean. **2** (*also* **tip out**) to empty (from a container, etc): *He tipped the dirty water out of the bucket.* **3** *Brit* to dump (rubbish). ➤ *n* **1** a place for tipping rubbish, etc. **2** *colloq* a very untidy place.

tip³ *n* **1** money given to a servant or waiter, etc in return for service done well. **2** a piece of useful information. **3** a piece of inside information, eg, the name of a horse likely to win a race. ➤ *vb* (**tipped, tipping**) to give a tip to. ◊ **tip sb off** to give them a piece of useful or secret information.

tip⁴ *n* a light blow or tap. ➤ *vb* (**tipped, tipping**) to hit or strike lightly. ◆ **tip the balance** to make the critical difference.

tip-off *n* a piece of useful or secret information, or the disclosing of this.

tippet *n* **1** a woman's shoulder-cape made from fur or cloth. **2** a long band of cloth or fur worn by some clergy.

tipple *colloq, vb, tr & intr* to drink (alcohol) regularly, esp in relatively small amounts. ➤ *n* alcoholic drink. ○ **tippler** *n.*

tipster *n* someone who gives tips, esp as to which horses to bet on.

tipsy *adj, colloq (-ier, -iest)* slightly drunk. ○ **tipsily** *adv.* ○ **tipsiness** *n.*

tiptoe *vb* (**tiptoed, tiptoeing**) *intr* to walk quietly or stealthily on the tips of the toes. ➤ *n* (*often* **tiptoes**) the tips of the toes. ➤ *adv* (*usu* **on tiptoe**) on the tips of the toes.

tip-top *colloq, adj, adv* excellent; first-class. ➤ *n* the very best; the height of excellence.

tirade *n* a long angry speech, harangue or denunciation.

tire¹ *vb* **1** *tr & intr* to make or become physically or mentally weary. **2** (**tire of**) to lose patience with or become bored with.

tire² *n* the *US* spelling of TYRE.

tired *adj* **1** wearied; exhausted. **2** lacking freshness: *tired, lazy prose.* ○ **tiredly** *adv.* ○ **tiredness** *n.* ◆ **be tired of** to have had enough of.

tireless *adj* never becoming weary or exhausted. ○ **tirelessly** *adv.*

tiresome *adj* troublesome and irritating; annoying; tedious.

'tis *contraction, old use or poetic* it is.

tissue *n* **1** a group of plant or animal cells with a similar structure and particular function: *muscle tissue.* **2** thin soft disposable paper used as a handkerchief or as toilet paper, or a piece of this. **3** (*also* **tissue paper**) fine thin soft paper, used for wrapping, etc. **4** an interwoven mass or collection: *a tissue of lies.*

tit¹ *n* a small songbird.

tit² *n* a blow or injury. ◆ **tit for tat** repayment of an injury by an injury.

tit³ *n* **1** *slang* a teat. **2** *coarse slang* a woman's breast.

titan *n* someone or something of very great strength, size, intellect or importance.

titanic *adj* having great strength or size; gigantic.

titanium /tɪˈteɪnɪəm/ *n, chem* a silvery-white metallic element used in making alloys for components of aircraft, missiles, etc.

titbit *n* a choice or small tasty morsel of something, eg, food or gossip.

titchy *adj (-ier, -iest) Brit colloq* very small.

tithe *n* **1** (*often* **tithes**) a tenth of someone's annual income or produce, paid to support the church. **2** a tenth part. ➤ *vb* **1** to demand a tithe or tithes from. **2** *tr & intr* to pay a tithe or tithes.

Titian /ˈtɪʃən/ *adj* of a bright reddish-gold colour: *Titian hair.*

titillate *vb* **1** to excite, esp in a mildly erotic way. **2** to tickle. ○ **titillating** *adj.* ○ **titillation** *n.*

titivate *vb, tr & intr, colloq* to smarten up or put the finishing touches to.

title *n* **1** the distinguishing name of a book, play, work of art, piece of music, etc. **2** an often descriptive heading, eg, of a chapter in a book or a legal document. **3** a word used before someone's name to show acquired or inherited rank, an honour, occupation, marital status, etc. **4** (**titles**) written material on film giving credits or dialogue, etc. **5** *law* a right to the possession or ownership of property. **6** *sport* a championship: *St Johnstone won the title.* **7** a book or publication. ➤ *vb* to give a title to.

titled *adj* having a title of nobility or rank.

title deed *n* a document that proves legal ownership, esp of real property.

title role *n* the name of the character in a play, film, etc that gives its title, eg, King Lear.

titrate /'tartreɪt/ *vb, chem* to determine the concentration of (a chemical substance in a solution) by adding measured amounts of another solution of known concentration. ○ **titration** *n*.

titter *colloq, vb, intr* to giggle or snigger in a stifled way. ➤ *n* an instance or noise of this.

tittle *n* a very small insignificant amount.

tittle-tattle *n* idle or petty gossip or chatter. ➤ *vb, intr* to gossip or chatter idly.

titular *adj* **1** having the title of an office or position, but none of the authority or duties. **2** relating to a title.

tizzy or **tizz** *n* (**tizzies** or **tizzes**) *colloq* a nervous, highly excited or confused state: *She got into a tizzy*.

Tl *symbol, chem* thallium.

TLC *abbrev, colloq* tender loving care.

Tm *symbol, chem* thulium.

TNT *abbrev* trinitrotoluene.

to *prep* **1** towards; in the direction of, or with the destination of somewhere or something: *go to the shop*. **2** used to express as a resulting condition, aim or purpose: *boil the fruit to a pulp • to my surprise*. **3** as far as; until: *from beginning to end • bears the scars to this day*. **4** used to introduce the indirect object of a verb: *He sent it to us*. **5** used to express addition: *add one to ten*. **6** used to express attachment, connection, contact or possession: *He put his ear to the door*. **7** before the hour of: *ten minutes to three*. **8** used to express response or reaction to a situation or event, etc: *rise to the occasion • dance to the music*. **9** used to express comparison or proportion: *We won by two goals to one. • second to none*. **10** used before an infinitive or instead of a complete infinitive: *He asked her to stay, but she didn't want to*. ➤ *adv* **1** in or into a nearly closed position: *Mum pulled the window to*. **2** back into consciousness: *He came to a few minutes later*. **3** near at hand. **4** in the direction required: *have to*. ◆ **to and fro** backwards and forwards.

toad *n* **1** a tailless amphibian, with a short squat head and body, and moist skin which may contain poison glands. **2** an obnoxious or repellent person.

toad-in-the-hole *n, Brit* a dish of sausages cooked in batter.

toadstool *n* a fungus with a stalk and a spore-bearing cap, most varieties of which are poisonous or inedible.

toady *n* (**-ies**) someone who flatters someone else, does everything they want and hangs on their every word. ➤ *vb* (**-ies, -ied**) *tr & intr* (**toady to sb**) to flatter them and behave obsequiously towards them.

toast *vb* **1 a** to make (bread, cheese, a marshmallow, etc) brown by exposing to direct heat; **b** *intr* to become brown in this way. **2** *tr & intr* to make or become warm by being exposed to heat. **3** to drink ceremonially in honour of (someone or something). ➤ *n* **1** bread which has been browned by exposure to direct heat. **2 a** an act of toasting someone, etc; **b** someone who is the subject of a toast. **3** a highly regarded person or thing: *Her singing is the toast of the festival*.

toaster *n* an electric machine for toasting bread.

toastie *n, colloq* a toasted sandwich.

toastmaster or **toastmistress** *n* a man or woman who proposes the toasts at a ceremonial dinner.

tobacco *n* (**tobaccos** or **tobaccoes**) **1** a genus of plant with very large leaves. **2** the dried nicotine-containing leaves of some varieties of this plant, used in cigarettes, cigars, pipe tobacco and snuff.

tobacconist *n* a person or shop selling tobacco, cigarettes, cigars and pipes, etc.

-to-be *adj, in compounds* future; soon to become: *a bride-to-be*.

toboggan *n* a long light sledge for riding over snow and ice. ➤ *vb, intr* to ride on a toboggan.

toby jug *n* a jug in the shape of a stout man wearing a three-cornered hat.

toccata /tɒˈkɑːtə/ *n* a piece of music for a keyboard instrument intended to show off the performer's skill.

tocsin *n* an alarm bell or warning signal.

tod *n, Brit colloq*. ◆ **on one's tod** alone.

today *n* **1** this day. **2** nowadays. ➤ *adv* **1** on or during this day. **2** nowadays: *It doesn't happen much today*.

toddle *vb, intr* **1** to walk with unsteady steps, as or like a young child. **2** *colloq* to take a casual walk. **3** (*usu* **toddle off**) *colloq* to leave; to depart. ➤ *n* **1** a toddling walk. **2** *colloq* a casual walk or stroll.

toddler *n* a child who is just beginning, or has just learned, to walk.

toddy *n* (**-ies**) an alcoholic drink with added sugar, hot water, etc.

to-do *n, colloq* a fuss or commotion.

toe *n* **1 a** one of the five digits at the end of the human foot; **b** a corresponding digit in an animal. **2** a part of a shoe, sock, etc covering the toes. **3** the lower end of a tool, area of land, etc. ➤ *vb* (**toed, toeing**) to kick, strike or touch with the toes. ◆ **on one's toes** alert and ready for action. **toe the line** *colloq* to act according to the rules.

toecap *n* a reinforced covering on the toe of a boot or shoe.

toehold *n* **1** a place where toes can grip, eg, when climbing. **2** a start or small beginning: *She got a toehold in the designing business*.

toenail *n* a nail covering the tip of a toe.

toerag *n, Brit colloq* **1** a rascal. **2** a despicable or contemptible person.

toff *n, Brit slang* an upper-class and usu smartly dressed person.

toffee *n* a sticky sweet, made by boiling sugar

and butter. ◆ **for toffee** *with negatives* at all: *He can't act for toffee.*

toffee-nosed *adj, Brit colloq* snobbish; stuck-up.

tofu *n* a curd made from soya beans.

tog¹ *n* (**togs**) clothes.

tog² *n* a unit for measuring the warmth of fabrics, clothes, duvets, etc.

toga /'toʊgə/ *n, hist* an ancient Roman's loose outer garment.

together *adv* **1** with someone or something else; in company: *travel together.* **2** at the same time: *They all arrived together.* **3** so as to be in contact, joined or united. **4** by action with one or more other people: *Together we managed to persuade him.* **5** in or into one place: *gather together.* **6** continuously; at a time: *for hours together.* **7** *colloq* into a proper or suitable order or state of being organized: *get things together.* ➢ *adj, colloq* well organized; competent. ◆ **together with sb** or **sth** in addition to them or it.

togetherness *n* a feeling of closeness, mutual sympathy and understanding, etc.

toggle *n* **1** a fastening, eg, for garments, consisting of a small bar passed through a loop. **2** a pin, bar or crosspiece through a link in a chain, etc to prevent it from slipping. **3** *comput* a keyboard command which allows the user to switch between one mode and another. ➢ *vb* **1** to provide or fasten (something) with a toggle. **2** *comput* to use a toggle to switch between one mode and another.

toil *vb, intr* **1** to work long and hard. **2** to make progress or move forwards with great difficulty or effort. ➢ *n* long hard work.

toilet *n* **1** a LAVATORY. **2** (*also* **toilette**) the process of washing, dressing and arranging one's hair.

toilet paper or **toilet tissue** *n* paper used for cleaning oneself after urination and defecation.

toiletry *n* (**-ies**) an article or cosmetic used when washing, arranging the hair, making up, etc.

toilet water *n* a light perfume similar to EAU DE COLOGNE.

toilsome *adj* involving long hard work.

token *n* **1** a mark, sign or distinctive feature. **2** a symbol: *a token of my esteem.* **3** a voucher worth a specified amount, exchanged for goods: *book token.* **4** a small coin-like piece of metal or plastic, used instead of money. ➢ *adj* **1** nominal; of no real value: *token gesture.* **2** included only for the sake of appearances: *a token woman.* ◆ **by the same token** for the same reason.

tokenism *n* the principle or practice of doing no more than the minimum in a particular area, in pretence that one is committed to it, eg, employing one black person in a company to avoid charges of racism.

tolerable *adj* **1** able to be endured. **2** fairly good. ○ **tolerably** *adv.*

tolerance *n* **1** the ability to be fair towards and accepting of other people's beliefs or opinions. **2** the ability to resist or endure pain or hardship. **3** *med* someone's ability to adapt to the effects of a drug, so that increasingly larger doses are required to produce the same effect.

tolerant *adj* **1** tolerating the beliefs and opinions of others. **2** capable of enduring unfavourable conditions, etc. **3** indulgent; permissive. ○ **tolerantly** *adv.*

tolerate *vb* **1** to endure. **2** to be able to resist the effects of (a drug). **3** to treat fairly and accept. ○ **toleration** *n.*

toll¹ *vb* **1** *tr & intr* to ring (a bell) with slow measured strokes. **2** of a bell: to announce, signal or summon by ringing with slow measured strokes. ➢ *n* an act or the sound of tolling.

toll² *n* **1** a fee or tax paid for the use of something, eg, a bridge, road, etc. **2** a cost, eg, in damage, injury, lives lost, esp in a war, disaster, etc.

tollbridge *n* a bridge at which a toll is charged.

tollgate *n* a gate or barrier across a road or bridge which is not lifted until travellers have paid the toll.

tolu /'toʊljuː/ *n* a sweet-smelling balsam obtained from a S American tree, used in medicine and perfume.

toluene /'tɒljuːiːn/ *n, chem* a colourless flammable liquid derived from benzene and used in explosives, etc.

tom *n* a male of various animals, esp a male cat.

tomahawk *n* a small axe once used as a weapon by some Native Americans.

tomato *n* (**tomatoes**) **1** a round fleshy red, orange or yellow fruit, eaten raw or cooked. **2** a plant of the nightshade family producing this fruit.

tomb /tuːm/ *n* **1** a chamber or vault for a dead body. **2** a hole cut in the earth for a dead body.

tombola *n* a lottery in which winning tickets are drawn from a revolving drum.

tomboy *n* a girl who dresses or behaves in a boyish way. ○ **tomboyish** *adj.*

tombstone *n* a stone placed over a grave, often having the dead person's name, dates, etc engraved on it.

tomcat *n* a male cat.

tome *n* a large, heavy and usu learned book.

tomfool *n* an absolute fool.

tomfoolery *n* (**-ies**) **1** stupid or foolish behaviour; nonsense. **2** an instance of this.

tommygun *n* a type of submachine-gun.

tommy-rot *n, colloq* absolute nonsense.

tomography *n, med* a technique for scanning internal structures in a single plane of body tissue as an aid to diagnosis.

tomorrow *n* **1** the day after today. **2** the future. ➢ *adv* **1** on the day after today. **2** in the future.

tomtit *n* a tit, esp a blue tit.

tom-tom *n* a tall drum, usu with a small head, beaten with the hands.

ton *n* **1** (**long ton**) *Brit* a unit of weight equal to 2240lb (approximately 1016.06kg). **2** (**short ton**) *N Am* a unit of weight equal to 2000lb (approx 907.2kg). **3** (**metric ton**) a unit of weight equal to 1000kg (approx 2204.6lb). **4** (**displacement ton**) a unit used to measure the amount of water a ship displaces, equal to 2240lb or 35 cubic feet. **5** (**register ton**) a unit used to measure a ship's internal capacity, equal to 100 cubic feet. **6** (**freight ton**) a unit for measuring the space taken up by cargo, equal to 40 cubic feet. **7** (*usu* **tons**) *colloq* a lot. **8** *colloq* a speed, score or sum, etc of 100.

tonal *adj* relating to tone or tonality.

tonality *n* (**-ies**) **1** *mus* the organization of all of the notes and chords of a piece of music in relation to a single tonic. **2** the colour scheme and tones used in a painting, etc.

tone *n* **1** a musical or vocal sound with reference to its quality and pitch. **2** *mus* a sound that has a definite pitch. **3** a quality or character of the voice expressing a particular feeling or mood, etc. **4** the general character or style of spoken or written expression. **5** *mus* the interval between, or equivalent to that between, the first two notes of the major scale. **6** high quality, style or character: *His coarse jokes lowered the tone of the meeting.* **7** the quality, tint or shade of a colour. **8** the harmony or general effect of colours. **9** firmness of the body, a bodily organ or muscle. ➤ *vb* **1** (*also* **tone in**) *intr* to fit in well; to harmonize. **2** to give tone or the correct tone to. **3** *intr* to take on a tone or quality. ○ **toneless** *adj.* ◊ **tone down** to become or make softer or less harsh in tone, colour or force, etc. **tone up** to become or make (muscles or the body) stronger, firmer, etc.

tone-deaf *adj* unable to distinguish accurately between notes of different pitch.

tone poem *n* a continuous orchestral piece based on a story or a literary or descriptive theme.

tong *n* a Chinese guild or secret society, esp in organized crime.

tongs *pl n* a tool, consisting of two joined arms, used for holding and lifting.

tongue *n* **1** a fleshy muscular organ in the mouth, used for tasting, licking and swallowing and, in humans, speech. **2** the tongue of esp ox and sheep, used as food. **3** the ability to speak. **4** a particular language. **5** a particular manner of speaking: *a sharp tongue.* **6** anything like a tongue in shape: *the tongue of a shoe • a tongue of flame.* **7** a narrow strip of land that reaches out into water. **8** the clapper in a bell. **9** a projecting strip along the side of a board that fits into a groove in another. ◆ **hold one's tongue** to say nothing. **lose one's tongue** to be left speechless with shock or horror, etc. **speak in tongues** *relig* to speak in an unknown language. **tongue in cheek** with ironic, insincere or humorous intention.

tongue-tied *adj* unable to speak, esp because of shyness or embarrassment.

tongue-twister *n* a phrase or sentence that is difficult to say quickly.

tonic *n* **1** a medicine that increases or revives strength, energy and general wellbeing. **2** anything refreshing or invigorating. **3** TONIC WATER. **4** *mus* the first note of a scale, the note on which a key is based.

tonic water *n* a carbonated soft drink flavoured with quinine.

tonight *n* the night of this present day. ➤ *adv* on or during the night of the present day.

tonnage *n* **1** the space available in a ship for carrying cargo, measured in tons. **2** a duty on cargo by the ton.

tonne *n* another spelling of TON (sense 3).

tonsil *n* either of two lumps of lymphoid tissue at the back of the mouth.

tonsillitis *n* inflammation of the tonsils.

tonsorial *adj, often facetious* relating to barbers or hairdressing.

tonsure *n* **1** the act of shaving the crown or the entire head, esp of a person about to enter the priesthood or a monastic order. **2** a patch or head so shaved. ➤ *vb* to shave the head of.

too *adv* **1** to a greater extent or more than is required, desirable or suitable: *too many things to do.* **2** in addition; as well; also: *She loves Keats and Shelley too.* **3** what is more; indeed: *They need a good holiday, and they'll get one, too!* **4** extremely: *You're too generous!*

tool *n* **1** an implement, esp one used by hand, for cutting, digging, etc, such as a spade or hammer. **2** the cutting part of a MACHINE TOOL. **3** a thing used in or necessary to a particular trade or profession: *Words are the tools of a journalist's trade.* ➤ *vb* **1** to work or engrave (stone, leather, etc) using tools. **2** *tr & intr* (*also* **tool up** or **tool sth up**) to equip it.

toolbar *n, comput* a bar at the top of a WINDOW (sense 6) displaying a range of features, functions, etc that can be selected.

toot *n* a quick sharp blast of a trumpet, whistle or horn, etc. ➤ *vb, tr & intr* to sound or cause (a trumpet or horn, etc) to sound with a quick sharp blast.

tooth *n* (**teeth**) **1** in vertebrates: any of the hard structures, usu embedded in the upper and lower jaw bones, used for biting and chewing food. **2** anything like a tooth in shape, arrangement, function, etc: *the teeth of a comb.* **3** an appetite or liking: *a sweet tooth.* **4** (**teeth**) enough power or force to be effective. ➤ *vb* **1** to provide with teeth. **2** *intr* of cogs: to interlock. ◆ **get one's teeth into sth** to deal with it vigorously or eagerly, etc. **in the teeth of sth** against it; in opposition to it. **long in the tooth** *colloq* old. **set sb's teeth on edge** to irritate them severely. **tooth and nail** fiercely and with all one's strength.

toothache *n* pain in a tooth, usu as a result of decay.

toothbrush *n* a brush for cleaning the teeth.

toothpaste *n* a paste for cleaning the teeth.

toothpick *n* a small sharp piece of wood or

plastic, esp for removing food stuck between the teeth.

toothsome *adj* appetizing; delicious; attractive.

toothy *adj (-ier, -iest)* showing or having a lot of teeth, esp large prominent ones: *a toothy grin*.

tootle *vb, intr* 1 to toot gently or continuously. 2 *colloq* to go about casually, esp by car. ➤ *n* an act or sound of tootling.

top¹ *n* 1 the highest part, point or level of anything. 2 a the highest or most important rank or position; b the person holding this. 3 the upper edge or surface of something. 4 a lid or piece for covering the top of something. 5 a garment for covering the upper half of the body, esp a woman's body. 6 the highest or loudest degree or pitch: *the top of one's voice*. 7 (**the tops**) *colloq* the very best person or thing. 8 the highest gear in a motor vehicle. ➤ *adj* at or being the highest or most important. ➤ *vb (**topped, top-ping**)* 1 to cover or form the top of. 2 to remove the top of (a plant, fruit, etc). 3 to rise above or be better than. 4 to reach the top of (a hill, etc). 5 *slang* to kill, esp by hanging. 6 *golf* to hit the upper half of (the ball). ♦ **on top of sth** 1 in control of it. 2 in addition to it. 3 very close to it. **top the bill** to head the list of performers in a show, as the main attraction. ◊ **top sth off** to put a finishing or decorative touch to it. **top sb** or **sth up** 1 to refill (someone's glass, etc). 2 to provide money to bring (a wage, etc) to the desirable total.

top² *n* a toy which spins on a pointed base. ♦ **sleep like a top** to sleep soundly.

topaz /'təʊpaz/ *n* an aluminium silicate mineral, the pale yellow variety of which is used as a gemstone.

top brass *n, colloq* the highest-ranking officers or personnel, esp in the military.

top dog *n, colloq* the most important or powerful person in a group.

the top drawer *n, colloq* high social position, family or origin. ➤ *adj* (**top-drawer**) of the highest quality.

top-dressing *n* 1 manure or fertilizer spread on soil as opposed to being ploughed or dug in. 2 an application of this. ◊ **top-dress** *vb*.

top-flight *adj* of the best or highest quality.

top hat *n* a tall cylindrical men's hat worn as part of formal dress.

top-heavy *adj* disproportionately heavy in the upper part in comparison with the lower.

topi or **topee** /'təʊpɪ/ *n* a lightweight hat, shaped like a helmet, worn in hot countries as protection against the sun.

topiary /'təʊpɪərɪ/ *n* the art of cutting trees, bushes and hedges into ornamental shapes.

topic *n* a subject or theme.

topical *adj* relating to matters of current interest. ◊ **topicality** *n*.

topknot *n* 1 *esp hist* a knot of ribbons, etc worn on the top of the head as decoration. 2 a tuft of hair, growing on top of the head.

topless *adj* 1 of a woman: with her breasts exposed. 2 of a place: where women go topless: *topless beaches*.

topmost *adj* the very highest of all.

top-notch *adj, colloq* the very best quality; superb.

topography *n (-ies)* 1 a description, map representation, etc of the natural and constructed features of a landscape. 2 such features collectively. ◊ **topographer** *n*. ◊ **topographic** or **topographical** *adj*.

topology *n* the branch of geometry concerned with those properties of a geometrical figure that remain unchanged even when the figure is deformed by bending, stretching or twisting, etc. ◊ **topological** *adj*.

topping *n* something that forms a covering or garnish for food: *cheese topping*.

topple *vb, tr & intr* 1 (*also* **topple over**) to fall, or cause to fall, by overbalancing. 2 to overthrow or be overthrown.

top-secret *adj* very secret, esp officially classified as such.

topside *n* 1 a lean cut of beef from the rump. 2 the side of a ship above the waterline. ➤ *adj, adv* on deck.

topsoil *n* the uppermost layer of soil, rich in organic matter, where most plant roots develop. Compare SUBSOIL.

topspin *n* a spin given to a ball to make it travel higher, further or faster.

topsy-turvy *adj, adv* 1 upside down. 2 in confusion.

toque /təʊk/ *n* a small close-fitting brimless hat worn by women.

tor *n* a tower-like rocky peak.

torch *n* 1 *Brit* a portable battery-powered light. 2 a piece of wood or bundle of cloth, etc set alight and used as a source of light. 3 any source of heat, light or enlightenment, etc. ➤ *vb, colloq, esp N Am* to set fire to deliberately. ♦ **carry a torch for sb** to feel love, esp unrequited love, for them.

toreador /'tɒrɪədɔː(r)/ *n* a bullfighter, esp one on horseback.

torment *n* /'tɔːment/ 1 great pain, suffering or anxiety. 2 something causing this. ➤ *vb* /tɔː'ment/ 1 to cause great pain, suffering or anxiety to. 2 to pester or harass. ◊ **tormentor** *n*.

tornado *n* (**tornadoes**) a violently destructive storm characterized by a funnel-shaped rotating column of air.

torpedo *n* (**torpedoes** or **torpedos**) 1 a long self-propelling underwater missile which explodes on impact with its target. 2 a similar device dropped from the air. ➤ *vb* (**torpedoes, torpedoed**) 1 to attack with torpedoes. 2 to wreck or make (a plan, etc) ineffectual.

torpid *adj* 1 sluggish and dull; lacking energy. 2 unable to move or feel; numb. 3 of a hibernating animal: dormant.

torpor *n* the state of being torpid.

torque /tɔːk/ *n* 1 *hist* a necklace made of metal twisted into a band, worn by the ancient Britons and Gauls. **2** *physics* force multiplied by the perpendicular distance from a point about which it causes rotation, measured in newton-metres.

torrent *n* **1** a great rushing stream or downpour of water or lava, etc. **2** a violent or strong flow (of questions, abuse, etc). ○ **torrential** *adj*.

torrid *adj* **1** of the weather: so hot and dry as to scorch the land. **2** of land: scorched and parched by extremely hot dry weather. **3** of language, a relationship, etc: passionate; intensely emotional.

torsion *n* twisting by applying force to one end while the other is held firm or twisted in the opposite direction. ○ **torsional** *adj*.

torso *n* the main part of the human body, without the limbs and head; the trunk.

tort *n*, *law* any wrongful act, other than breach of contract, for which an action for damages or compensation may be brought.

torte /tɔːt, ˈtɔːtə/ *n* (**torten** or **tortes**) a rich sweet cake or pastry, often garnished or filled with fruit, nuts, cream or chocolate, etc.

tortilla /tɔːˈtiːjə/ *n* a thin round Mexican maize cake.

tortoise *n* a slow-moving reptile with a domed shell into which the head, legs and tail can be withdrawn for safety.

tortoiseshell *n* **1** the brown and yellow mottled shell of a sea turtle, used in making combs, jewellery, etc. **2** a butterfly with mottled orange or red and brown or black wings. **3** a domestic cat with a mottled orange and creamy-brown coat. ➣ *adj* made of or mottled like tortoiseshell.

tortuous *adj* **1** full of twists and turns. **2** devious or involved.

torture *n* **1** the infliction of severe pain or mental suffering, esp as a punishment or as a means of persuasion. **2 a** great physical or mental suffering; **b** a cause of this. ➣ *vb* **1** to subject to torture. **2** to cause to experience great physical or mental suffering. ○ **torturous** *adj*. ○ **torturously** *adv*.

Tory *n* (*-ies*) **1** a member or supporter of the British Conservative Party. **2** *hist* a member or supporter of a major English political party from the 17c to mid-19c, superseded by the Conservative Party. ○ **Toryism** *n*.

tosh *n*, *colloq* twaddle; nonsense.

toss *vb* **1** to throw up into the air. **2** to throw away casually or carelessly. **3** *intr* to move restlessly or from side to side repeatedly. **4** *tr & intr* to be thrown or cause to be thrown from side to side repeatedly and violently: *a ship tossed by the storm*. **5** to jerk (the head). **6** *tr & intr* **a** (*also* **toss up**) to throw (a spinning coin) into the air and guess which side will land facing up, as a way of making a decision or settling a dispute; **b** to settle (with someone) by tossing a coin: *toss you for the last cake*. **7** to coat (food, esp salad) with oil or a dressing, etc by gently mixing or turning it. ➣ *n* **1** an act or an instance of tossing. **2** *slang* the slightest amount: *not give a*

toss. ◆ **argue the toss** to dispute a decision. ◊ **toss sth off 1** to drink it quickly, esp in a single swallow. **2** to produce it quickly and easily.

tosser *n*, *Brit coarse slang* a stupid or loathsome person.

toss-up *n* **1** *colloq* an even chance or risk; something doubtful. **2** an act of tossing a coin.

tot¹ *n* **1** a small child; a toddler. **2** a small amount of spirits: *a tot of whisky*.

tot² *vb* (**totted**, **totting**) (*esp* **tot up**) **1** to add together. **2** *intr* of money, etc: to increase.

total *adj* whole; complete. ➣ *n* the whole or complete amount. ➣ *vb* (**totalled**, **totalling**; *US* **totaled**, **totaling**) **1** *tr & intr* to amount to (a specified sum): *The figures totalled 385.* **2** (*also* **total up**) to add (figures, etc) up to produce a total. ○ **totally** *adv*.

totalitarian *adj* relating to a system of government by a single party which allows no opposition and which demands complete obedience to the State. ➣ *n* someone in favour of such a system. ○ **totalitarianism** *n*.

totality *n* (*-ies*) completeness.

tote *vb*, *colloq* to carry, drag or wear (esp something heavy).

totem *n* **1** in Native American culture: a natural object, esp an animal, that is the sign and usu spirit guardian of a tribe or an individual. **2** an image or representation of this.

totem pole *n* **1** in Native American culture: a large wooden pole that has totems carved and painted on it. **2** *colloq* a hierarchical system: *the social totem pole*.

totter *vb*, *intr* **1** to walk or move unsteadily, shakily or weakly. **2** to sway or tremble as if about to fall. **3** of a system of government, etc: to be on the verge of collapse. ○ **tottery** *adj*.

toucan *n* a tropical bird with a huge beak and brightly coloured feathers on its chest.

touch *vb* **1** to bring (a hand, etc) into contact with something. **2 a** *tr & intr* to be in physical contact or come into physical contact with, esp lightly; **b** to bring together in close physical contact: *They touched hands.* **3** *often with negatives* **a** to injure, harm or hurt: *I never touched him!* **b** to interfere with, move, disturb, etc: *Who's been touching my things?* **c** to have dealings with, be associated with or be a party to: *I wouldn't touch that kind of job*; **d** to make use of: *He never touches alcohol*; **e** to use (eg money, etc): *I don't touch the money in that account*; **f** to approach in excellence: *Nobody can touch her at chess.* **4** to concern or affect: *It's a matter that touches us all.* **5** (*usu* **touch on** or **upon**) to deal with (a matter, subject, etc), esp in passing or not very thoroughly. **6** to affect with pity, sympathy, gratitude, quiet pleasure, etc: *The story of his sad life touched her heart.* **7** to reach or go as far as, esp temporarily: *The temperature touched 100.* **8** to tinge, taint, mark, modify, etc slightly or delicately: *The sky was touched with pink* ● *a love touched with sorrow* ● *Frost had touched the early crop.* **9** (*often* **touch sb for sth**) *slang* to ask them for and receive (money, esp a specified amount, as a loan or gift): *She touched him for 50 quid.* ➤ *n* **1** an act of touching or the sensation of being touched. **2** the sense by which the existence, nature, texture and quality of objects can be perceived through physical contact with the hands, etc. **3** the particular texture and qualities of an object, etc: *the silky touch of the fabric against her skin.* **4** a small amount, quantity, distance, etc; a trace or hint: *move it left a touch.* **5** a slight attack (of an illness, etc): *a touch of the flu.* **6** a slight stroke or mark. **7** a detail which adds to or complements the general pleasing effect or appearance: *The flowers were an elegant touch.* **8** a distinctive or characteristic style or manner: *need the expert's touch.* **9** a musician's individual manner or technique of touching or striking the keys of a keyboard instrument or strings of a string instrument to produce a good tone. **10** the ability to respond or behave with sensitivity and sympathy: *a wonderful touch with animals.* **11** *sport* in rugby, etc: the ground outside the touchlines. **12** *slang* someone who can be persuaded to give or lend money: *a soft touch.* ○ **touchable** *adj.* ♦ **in touch (with) 1** in contact, communication, (with): *We still keep in touch although we haven't seen each other for 20 years.* **2** up to date: *She keeps in touch with the latest news.* **3** aware or conscious (of): *in touch with her inner self.* **lose touch (with) 1** to be no longer in contact, communication, etc (with). **2** to be no longer familiar (with) or well-informed (about). **out of touch (with) 1** not in contact, communication, etc (with). **2** not up to date (with). ◊ **touch down 1** of an aircraft, spacecraft, etc: to land. **2** *rugby* to carry the ball over the goal-line and touch the ground with it. **touch sth off** to cause it to explode or begin: *Police brutality touched off the riots.* **touch on** to verge towards: *That touches on the surreal.* **touch up 1** (*usu* **touch sb up**) *Brit slang* **a** to fondle them so as to excite sexually; **b** to sexually molest them. **2** (*usu* **touch up sth**) to improve it by adding small details, correcting or hiding minor faults, etc: *He touched up the painting.*

touch and go *adj* very uncertain in outcome; risky: *It was touch and go whether she'd survive.*

touchdown *n* **1** an act or instance of the process of an aircraft or spacecraft making contact with the ground when landing. **2** *Amer football* an act or instance of the process of carrying the ball over the touchline and hitting the ground with it to score.

touché /tuːˈʃeɪ/ *exclam* **1** *fencing* an acknowledgement of a hit. **2** a good-humoured acknowledgement of the validity of a point, made either in an argument or in retaliation.

touched *adj* **1** having a feeling of pity, sympathy, quiet pleasure, etc. **2** *colloq* slightly mad.

touching *adj* causing feelings of pity or sympathy; moving. ➤ *prep, old use* concerning; pertaining to.

touchline *n, sport, esp football & rugby* either of the two lines that mark the side boundaries of the pitch.

touchpaper *n* paper steeped in saltpetre and used for lighting fireworks or firing gunpowder.

touchstone *n* **1** a hard black flint-like stone used for testing the purity and quality of gold and silver alloys. **2** a test or standard for judging the quality of something.

touch-type *vb, intr* to use a typewriter without looking at the keyboard.

touchy *adj* (*-ier, -iest*) *colloq* **1** easily annoyed or offended. **2** needing to be handled or dealt with with care and tact: *a touchy subject.*

tough *adj* **1** strong and durable; not easily cut, broken, torn or worn out. **2** of food, esp meat: difficult to chew. **3** of a person, animal, etc: strong and fit and able to endure hardship. **4** difficult to deal with or overcome; testing: *a tough decision.* **5** severe and determined; unyielding; resolute: *a tough customer.* **6** rough and violent; criminal: *a tough area.* **7** *colloq* unlucky; unjust; unpleasant: *The divorce was tough on the kids.* ➤ *n* a rough violent person, esp a bully or criminal. ➤ *adv, colloq* aggressively; in a macho way: *Joe acts tough when he's with his mates.* ○ **toughly** *adv.* ○ **toughness** *n.* ◊ **tough sth out** to withstand (a difficult situation).

toughen *vb, tr & intr* (*also* **toughen up**) to become or cause to become tough or tougher.

tough luck *exclam* **1** expressing sympathy when something has gone wrong or not to plan. **2** expressing aggressive scorn: *Well, tough luck! I'm going.*

toupee /ˈtuːpeɪ/ *n* a small wig or hairpiece, usu worn by men to cover a bald patch.

tour *n* **1** an extended journey with stops at various places of interest. **2** a visit round a particular place: *a tour of the cathedral.* **3** a journey with frequent stops for business or professional engagements, eg, by a theatre company, sports team, rock band, etc. **4** an official period of duty or military service, esp abroad: *a tour of duty in Germany.* ➤ *vb, tr & intr* **1** to travel round (a place). **2** to travel from place to place giving performances. ○ **touring** *adj, n.* ♦ **on tour** performing at a series of venues.

tourism *n* **1** the practice of travelling to and visiting places for pleasure and relaxation. **2** the industry involved in offering services for tourists.

tourist *n* **1** someone who travels for pleasure and relaxation; a holidaymaker. **2** a member of a sports team visiting from abroad. ➤ *adj* relating or referring to or suitable for people on holiday: *tourist resort.*

touristy *adj, usu derog* designed for, appealing to, frequented by or full of tourists.

tourmaline *n* a mineral found in granites and gneisses and used as a gemstone.

tournament *n* **1** a competition, eg, in tennis or chess, that involves many players taking part in heats for a championship. **2** *hist* in the Middle Ages: a competition with jousting.

tournedos /'tʊənədoʊ/ n (**tournedos** /-doʊz/) a small round thick cut of beef fillet.

tourniquet /'tʊənɪkeɪ, 'tɔ:-/ n an emergency compression device for stopping the flow of blood through an artery.

tousle /'taʊzəl/ vb 1 to make (esp hair) untidy. 2 to tangle. ➤ n a tousled mass. ○ **tousled** adj.

tout /taʊt/ vb 1 intr (usu **tout for**) to solicit custom, support, etc persistently: tout for trade. 2 to solicit the custom of (someone) or for (something). 3 intr to spy on racehorses in training to gain information about their condition and likely future performance. ➤ n 1 (in full **ticket tout**) someone who buys up large numbers of tickets for a popular sporting event, concert, etc and sells them on at inflated prices. 2 someone who touts. ○ **touter** n.

tow¹ /toʊ/ vb 1 to pull (a ship, car, caravan, etc) along by rope, chain, cable, etc. 2 to pull (someone or something) behind one. ➤ n an act or the process of towing; the state of being towed. ○ **towage** n. ♦ **in tow 1** of a vehicle: being towed. **2** following or accompanying: She arrived late with several men in tow. **on tow** of a vehicle: being towed. **under tow** of a vessel: being towed.

tow² /toʊ, taʊ/ n coarse, short or broken fibres of flax, hemp or jute prepared for spinning.

towards or **toward** prep **1** in the direction of: Turn towards him. **2** in relation or regard to: She showed no respect toward her boss. **3** as a contribution to: He donated £1000 towards the costs. **4** near; just before: towards midnight.

tow bar /toʊ/ n a device fitted to the back of a car, etc enabling it to tow a trailer, caravan, etc.

towel n **1** a piece of absorbent cloth used for drying the body, dishes, etc: a bath towel • a tea towel • a paper towel. **2** Brit, dated a SAN-ITARY TOWEL. ➤ vb (**towelled, towelling**; US **toweled, toweling**) to rub, wipe or dry with a towel.

towelling n a highly absorbent material formed from many uncut loops of cotton, etc.

tower n **1 a** a tall narrow structure forming part of a larger, lower building, eg a church; **b** a similar free-standing structure: a control tower. **2** a fortress, used by one or more towers: the Tower of London. ➤ vb, intr (usu **tower above** or **over**) to reach a great height, or be vastly superior or considerably taller.

tower block n, Brit a very tall building comprised of many residential flats or offices.

towering adj **1** reaching a great height: towering mountains. **2** of rage, fury, a storm, the sea, etc: intense; violent. **3** very impressive, important or lofty: a towering intellect.

tower of strength n someone who is a great help or support.

tow-headed /taʊ-/ adj with very fair hair or tousled hair.

town n **1** an urban area smaller than a city but larger than a village. **2** the central shopping or business area in a neighbourhood: She went into town to buy new shoes. **3** the principal town in an area, or the capital city of a country, regarded as a destination. **4** the people living in a town or a city: The whole town turned out. ♦ **go to town** colloq to act, work, etc very thoroughly or with great enthusiasm, etc. **on the town** colloq enjoying the entertainments offered by a town, esp its restaurants, clubs and bars.

town council n the elected governing body of a town.

town crier n, hist someone whose job was to make public announcements in the streets.

townee or **townie** n, colloq, often derog someone who lives in a town, esp as opposed to someone who lives in the countryside.

town hall n the building where the official business of a town's administration is carried out.

town house n a terraced house, esp a fashionable one.

town planning n the planning and designing of the future development of a town. ○ **town planner** n.

township n **1** S Afr an urban area that was formerly set aside for non-white citizens. **2** N Am a subdivision of a county. **3** Aust a small town or settlement.

towpath n a path that runs alongside a canal or river where a horse can walk while towing a barge.

toxaemia or (US) **toxemia** /tɒk'si:mɪə/ n, med **1** blood poisoning. **2** a complication in some pregnancies characterized by a sudden increase in the mother's blood pressure.

toxic adj **1** poisonous. **2** relating to poisons or toxins. ○ **toxically** adv. ○ **toxicity** n.

toxicology n the scientific study of poisons. ○ **toxicological** adj. ○ **toxicologist** n.

toxin n a poison produced by a living organism.

toy n **1** an object for a child to play with. **2** often derog something intended or thought of as being for amusement or pleasure rather than practical use. **3** something which is very small, esp a dwarf breed of dog. ➤ vb, intr (usu **toy with**) **1** to flirt with or trifle: We toyed with the idea of getting a new car. **2** to move (something) in an idle, distracted, etc way: toying with his food.

toyboy n, colloq a woman's much younger male lover.

trace¹ n **1** a mark or sign that some person, animal or thing has been in a particular place. **2** a track or footprint. **3** a very small amount that can only just be detected. **4** a tracing. **5** a line marked by the moving pen of a recording instrument. **6** a visible line on a cathode-ray tube showing the path of a moving spot. ➤ vb **1** to track and discover by, or as if by, following clues, a trail, etc. **2** to follow step by step: trace the development of medicine. **3** to make a copy of (a drawing, design, etc) by covering it with a sheet of semi-transparent paper and drawing over the visible lines. **4** to outline or sketch (an idea, plan, etc). **5** to investigate and discover the cause, origin, etc of: *Susan traced her family back to Tudor times.* ○ **traceable** *adj*.

trace² *n* either of the two ropes, chains or straps by which an animal, esp a horse, pulls a carriage, cart, etc.

trace element *n* a chemical element only found or required in very small amounts.

tracery (*-ies*) **1** ornamental open stonework, esp in the top part of a Gothic window. **2** a finely patterned decoration or design.

trachea /trə'kɪə/ *n* (*tracheae* /-'kiː/) an air tube extending from the larynx to the lungs; the windpipe.

tracheotomy /trakɪ'ɒtəmɪ/ *n* a surgical incision into the trachea to make an alternative airway when normal breathing is not possible.

tracing *n* **1** a copy of a drawing, etc that is made on semi-transparent paper. **2** an act, instance or the process of making such a copy.

tracing-paper *n* thin semi-transparent paper designed to be used for tracing drawings, etc.

track *n* **1 a** a mark or series of marks or footprints, etc left behind: *a tyre track*; **b** a course of action, thought, etc taken: *Sita followed in her mother's tracks and studied medicine.* **2** a rough path: *a track through the woods.* **3** a specially prepared course: *a race track.* **4** the branch of athletics that comprises all the running events. **5** a railway line: *leaves on the track.* **6** a length of railing that a curtain, spotlight, etc moves along. **7 a** the groove cut in a RECORD (*noun* sense 4) by the recording instrument; **b** an individual song, etc on an album, CD, cassette, etc; **c** one of several paths on magnetic recording tape that receives information from a single input channel; **d** one of a series of parallel paths on magnetic recording tape that contains a single sequence of signals; **e** a SOUNDTRACK; **f** *comput* an area on the surface of a magnetic disk where data is stored and which is created during the process of formatting. **8** a line, path or course of travel, passage or movement: *the track of the storm.* **9** a line or course of thought, reasoning, etc: *I couldn't follow the track of his argument.* **10** a continuous band that tanks, mechanical diggers, etc have instead of individual tyres. ➤ *vb* **1** to follow (marks, footprints, etc left behind). **2** to follow and usu plot the course of (a spacecraft, satellite, etc) by radar. **3** *intr* (*often* **track in, out** or **back**) of a television or film camera or its operator: to move, esp in such a way as to follow a moving subject, always keeping them or it in focus. ◆ **keep** or **lose track of sth** or **sb** to keep, or fail to keep, oneself informed about the progress, whereabouts, etc of them or it: *I lost all track of time.* **make tracks** *colloq* to leave; to set out. **off the beaten track** away from busy roads and therefore difficult to access or find. **on the right** or **wrong track** pursuing the right or wrong line of inquiry. ◇ **track sb** or **sth down** to search for and find them or it after following clues, etc: *to track down an address.*

track and field *n* the branch of athletics that comprises all the running and jumping events plus the hammer, discus, javelin, shot put, etc.

tracking *n* **1** an act or process of adding pre-recorded music to a motion picture as opposed to having a soundtrack of specially commissioned music. **2** *elec eng* leakage of current between two insulated points caused by moisture, dirt, etc.

track record *n*, *colloq* someone's performance, achievements, etc in the past: *Her CV shows an impressive track record.*

track shoe *n* a running shoe with a spiked sole.

tracksuit *n* a loose suit worn by athletes, footballers, etc when exercising or warming up, etc.

tract¹ *n* **1** an area of land, usu of indefinite extent: *large tracts of wilderness.* **2** a system in the body with a specified function: *the digestive tract.*

tract² *n* a short essay or pamphlet, esp on religion, politics, etc and intended as propaganda.

tractable *adj* **1** of a person, etc: easily managed, controlled, etc; docile. **2** of a material, etc: pliant.

traction *n* **1** the action or process of pulling. **2** the state of being pulled or the force used in pulling. **3** *med* a treatment involving steady pulling on a muscle, limb, etc using a series of pulleys and weights: *Marie had her leg in traction.* **4** the grip of a wheel, tyre, etc on a road surface, etc.

traction engine *n* a heavy steam-powered vehicle formerly used for pulling heavy loads.

tractor *n* a motor vehicle for pulling farm machinery, heavy loads, etc.

trade *n* **1 a** an act or instance or the process of buying and selling; **b** buying and selling generally: *foreign trade.* **2 a** a job, etc that involves skilled work, esp as opposed to professional or unskilled work: *Gary left school at 16 to learn a trade*; **b** the people and businesses that are involved in such work: *the building trade.* **3 a** business and commerce, esp as opposed to a profession or the owning of landed property; **b** the people involved in this. **4** customers: *the lunch-time trade.* **5** business at a specified time, for a specified market or of a specified nature: *the tourist trade.* **6** (**trades**) the trade winds. ➤ *vb* **1** *intr* to buy and sell; to engage in trading: *He trades in securities.* **2 a** to exchange (one commodity) for another; **b** to exchange (blows, insults, etc); **c** *colloq* to swap. **3** *intr* (**trade on sth**) to take unfair advantage of it: *He traded on his sister's popularity.* ○ **trader** *n*. ◇ **trade sth off** to give it in exchange for something else, usu as a compromise.

trade deficit or **trade gap** *n* the amount by which a country's imports outstrip its exports.

trade-in *n* something, esp a used car, etc, given in part exchange for another.

trademark *n* **1** a name, word or symbol, esp one officially registered and protected by law, with which a company or individual identifies goods made or sold by them. **2** a distinguishing characteristic or feature.

tradename *n* **1** a name given to an article or product, or a group of these, by the trade which produces them. **2** a name that a company or individual does business under.

trade-off *n* a balance or compromise, esp between two desirable but incompatible things, situations, etc.

trade price *n* a wholesale cost that a retailer pays for goods.

trade secret *n* an ingredient, technique, etc that a company or individual will not divulge.

tradesman or **tradeswoman** *n* **1** someone engaged in trading, eg, a shopkeeper. **2** someone who follows a skilled trade, eg, a plumber, electrician, etc.

trade union or **trades union** *n* an organization for the employees of a specified profession, trade, etc that exists to protect members' interests and improve pay, working conditions, etc. ○ **trade unionism** *n*. ○ **trade unionist** *n*.

trade wind *n* a wind that blows continually towards the equator and which, in the N hemisphere, is deflected westwards by the eastward rotation of the earth.

trading estate *n*, *Brit* an INDUSTRIAL ESTATE.

tradition *n* **1 a** a belief, custom, story, etc passed on from generation to generation; **b** the action or process of handing down something in this way. **2** a particular body of beliefs, customs, etc. **3** *colloq* an established or usual practice or custom. **4** a body of artistic, etc principles or conventions: *a film in the tradition of the American road movie.*

traditional *adj* relating to or derived from tradition: *traditional costumes.* ○ **traditionally** *adv.*

traditionalist *n* someone who subscribes to tradition. ○ **traditionalism** *n*.

traduce *vb* to say or write unpleasant things about (someone or something).

traffic *n* **1** the vehicles that are moving along a route. **2** this movement. **3** illegal or dishonest trade: *the traffic of cocaine.* **4** trade; commerce. **5** the transporting of goods or people on a railway, air or sea route, etc. **6** the goods or people transported along a route. **7** communication between groups or individuals. ➤ *vb* (**trafficked, trafficking**) **1** (*usu* **traffic in**) to deal or trade in, esp illegally. **2** to deal in. ○ **trafficker** *n*.

traffic calming *n* the intentional curbing of the speed of road vehicles by having humps, bends, narrowed passing places, etc on roads.

traffic cone *n* a large plastic cone used for guiding diverted traffic, etc.

traffic jam *n* a queue of vehicles that are at a standstill, eg, because of overcrowded roads, an accident, roadworks, etc.

traffic lights *pl n* a system of red, amber and green lights controlling traffic at road junctions, pedestrian crossings, etc.

traffic warden *n*, *Brit* someone whose job is controlling traffic flow and putting parking tickets on vehicles that infringe parking restrictions, etc.

tragedian /trə'dʒiːdɪən/ or **tragedienne** /trədʒiːdɪ'ɛn/ *n* **1** a male or female actor specializing in tragic roles. **2** a writer of tragedies.

tragedy *n* (*-ies*) **1** a serious catastrophe, accident, natural disaster, etc. **2** *colloq* a sad, disappointing, etc event. **3 a** a serious play, film, opera, etc portraying tragic events and with an unhappy ending; **b** such plays, etc as a group or genre. **4** *loosely* any sad play, film, book, etc.

tragic or **tragical** *adj* **1** very sad; intensely distressing. **2** *theat* relating to or in the style of tragedy. ○ **tragically** *adv.*

tragicomedy *n* (*-ies*) **1** a play, film, event, etc that includes a mixture of both tragedy and comedy. **2** such plays, etc as a group or genre. ○ **tragicomic** *adj.*

trail *vb* **1** *tr & intr* to drag or be dragged loosely along the ground or other surface. **2** *tr & intr* to walk or move along slowly and wearily. **3** to drag (a limb, etc) esp slowly and wearily. **4** *tr & intr* to fall or lag behind in a race, contest, etc: *They trailed their opponents by 20 points.* **5** to follow the track or footsteps of. **6** *tr & intr* **a** of a plant or plant part: to grow so long that it droops over or along a surface towards the ground; **b** to encourage (a plant or plant part) to grow in this way. **7** to advertise (a forthcoming programme, film, etc) by showing chosen extracts, etc. ➤ *n* **1** a track, series of marks, footprints, etc left by a passing person, animal or thing, esp one followed in hunting. **2** a rough path or track through a wild or mountainous area. ◊ **trail away** or **off** of a voice, etc: to become fainter.

trailblazer *n* **1** someone who makes inroads into new territory; a pioneer. **2** an innovator in a particular field or activity. ○ **trailblazing** *n*, *adj.*

trailer *n* **1** a cart that can be hooked up behind a car, etc and used for carrying loads, transporting boats, etc. **2** the rear section of an articulated lorry. **3** *N Am* a mobile home or caravan. **4** *cinema, TV, radio* a promotional preview of a forthcoming film, programme, etc. **5** someone or something that trails behind.

train *n* **1 a** a string of railway carriages or wagons with a locomotive; **b** *loosely* a locomotive. **2** a back part of a long dress or robe that trails behind the wearer. **3** the attendants following or accompanying an important person. **4** a connected series of animals, events, actions, ideas, thoughts, etc: *a camel train* • *You interrupted my train of thought.* ➤ *vb* **1** to teach or prepare (a person or animal) through instruction, practice, exercises, etc. **2** *intr* to be taught through instruction, practice, exercises, etc: *I trained as a nurse.* **3** (*usu* **train for**) to prepare (for a performance, eg, in a sport) through practice, exercise, diet, etc. **4** to point or aim (eg a gun) at or focus (eg a telescope) on (a particular object, etc). **5** to make (a plant, tree, etc) grow in a particular direction: *train the ivy along the wall.* ○ **trainable** *adj*.

trainee *n* someone in the process of being trained.

trainer *n* **1** someone who trains racehorses, athletes, etc. **2** (**trainers**) *Brit* running shoes without spikes, often worn as casual shoes.

training *n* **1** an act or the process of preparing or being prepared for something, or of being taught or learning a particular skill: *go into training for the marathon.* **2** the state of being physically fit: *out of training.*

train-spotter *n* someone whose hobby is noting the numbers of railway locomotives, etc. ○ **train-spotting** *n*.

traipse *vb* **1** *intr* to walk or trudge along idly or wearily: *I traipsed round the shops.* **2** to wander aimlessly: *traipsing the streets.* ➤ *n* a long tiring walk.

trait *n* an identifying feature or quality, esp of someone's character.

traitor *n* **1** someone who betrays their country, sovereign, government, etc. **2** someone who betrays a trust. ○ **traitorous** *adj*.

trajectory *n* (*-ies*) *physics* the curved path that a moving object describes, eg, when it is projected into the air or when it is subjected to a given force, etc.

tram *n* an electrically-powered passenger vehicle that runs on rails laid in the streets.

tramline *n* **1** (*usu* **tramlines**) either of a pair of rails that form the track for trams to run on. **2** the route that a tram takes. **3** (**tramlines**) *colloq* the parallel lines at the sides of tennis and badminton courts.

trammel *n* **1** (*usu* **trammels**) something that hinders or prevents freedom: *trapped by the trammels of convention.* **2** a triple dragnet for catching fish. ➤ *vb* (**trammelled, trammelling;** *US* **trammeled, trammeling**) to hinder or catch with or as if with trammels.

tramp *vb* **1** *intr* to walk with firm heavy footsteps. **2** *tr & intr* to make a journey on foot, esp heavily or wearily: *tramping over the hills • tramping six miles across the open moor.* **3** to walk heavily and wearily on or through: *tramp the streets.* **4** to tread or trample. ➤ *n* **1** someone who has no fixed home or job. **2** a long, tiring walk. **3** the sound of heavy rhythmic footsteps. **4** *slang* a promiscuous woman.

trample *vb, tr & intr* **1** to tread heavily. **2** (*also* **trample on** or **over**) to crush underfoot: *trampled grapes • trampled on the flowers.* **3** (*also* **trample on** or **over**) to treat (someone or their feelings, etc) roughly, dismissively or with contempt.

trampoline *n* a piece of gymnastic equipment that consists of a sheet of tightly stretched canvas, etc attached to a framework by strong springs and used for jumping on, performing somersaults, etc. ➤ *vb, intr* to jump, turn

somersaults, etc on a trampoline.

trance *n* **1** a sleep-like or half-conscious state in which the ability to react to stimuli is temporarily lost. **2** a dazed or absorbed state. **3** a state, usu self-induced, in which religious or mystical ecstasy is experienced. **4** the state that a medium enters to attempt contact with the dead.

tranche /trɑːnʃ/ *n* **1** a part, piece or division. **2** *econ* **a** an instalment of a loan; **b** part of a block of shares.

trannie or **tranny** *n* (*-ies*) *Brit colloq* a transistor radio.

tranquil *adj* serenely quiet or peaceful; undisturbed. ○ **tranquillity** or (*US*) **tranquility** *n*. ○ **tranquilly** *adv*.

tranquillize, -ise or (*US*) **tranquilize** *vb* (**tranquillized, tranquillizing; tranquilized, tranquilizing**) to make or become calm, esp by administering a drug.

tranquillizer, -iser or (*US*) **tranquilizer** *n* a drug that has a tranquillizing effect.

transact *vb* to conduct or carry out (business).

transaction *n* **1** a business deal. **2** (**transactions**) the published reports of a meeting of a learned society.

transalpine *adj* beyond or stretching across the Alps.

transatlantic *adj* **1** crossing, or designed for or capable of crossing, the Atlantic. **2 a** beyond the Atlantic; **b** *N Am* linking North America with Europe; **c** *Brit* American.

transceiver *n* a piece of radio equipment designed to transmit and receive signals.

transcend *vb* **1** to be beyond the limits, scope, range, etc of: *It transcends the bounds of human decency.* **2** to surpass or excel. **3** to overcome or surmount: *transcend all difficulties.*

transcendent *adj* **1** excellent; surpassing others of the same or a similar kind. **2** beyond ordinary human knowledge or experience. **3** of a deity, etc: existing outside the material or created world. ○ **transcendence** *n*.

transcendental *adj* **1** going beyond usual human knowledge or experience. **2** supernatural or mystical. **3** vague, abstract or abstruse.

transcendentalism *n* a philosophical system concerned with what is constant, innate, and independent of and a necessary prerequisite to experience.

transcendental meditation *n* a method of meditating that involves silent repetition of a mantra to promote spiritual and mental wellbeing.

transcribe *vb* **1** to write or type out (a spoken or written text). **2** to transliterate. **3** *mus* to arrange (a piece of music) for an instrument or voice that it was not orig composed for. **4** *comput* to transfer (data) from one computer storage device to another. ○ **transcriber** *n*.

transcript *n* a written, typed or printed copy, eg of court proceedings.

transcription *n* **1** an act or the process of transcribing. **2** something transcribed.

transducer *n* any device that converts energy from one form to another, eg, a loudspeaker, where electrical energy is converted into sound waves.

transept *n* in a church with a cross-shaped floor plan: either of two arms at right angles to the nave.

transfer *vb* /trans'fɜː(r), trɑːns-/ (**transferred, transferring**) **1** *tr & intr* to move from one place, person, group, team, etc to another. **2** *intr* to change from one vehicle, line, passenger system, etc to another while travelling. **3** *law* to hand over (a title, rights, property, etc) to someone else by means of a legal document. **4** to transpose (a design, etc) from one surface to another. ➢ *n* /'transfɜː(r), 'trɑːns-/ **1** an act, instance or the process of transferring or the state of being transferred: *a transfer to another department*. **2** a design or picture that can be transferred from one surface to another. **3** someone or something transferred. **4** *law* **a** an act of handing over (eg, the legal right to property, etc) from one person to another; **b** any document which records this. **5** *N Am* a ticket that allows a passenger to continue a journey on another bus, etc. ○ **transferable** or **transferrable** *adj.* ○ **transference** *n.*

transfiguration *n* **1** a change in appearance, esp one that involves something becoming more beautiful, glorious, exalted, etc. **2** (**Transfiguration**) *Christianity* **a** the radiant change in Christ's appearance described in Matthew 17.2 and Mark 9.2–3; **b** a church festival held on 6 August to commemorate this.

transfigure *vb* to change or cause to change in appearance, esp in becoming more beautiful, glorious, exalted, etc.

transfix *vb* **1** to immobilize through surprise, fear, horror, etc. **2** to pierce with a pointed weapon, etc.

transform *vb* to change in appearance, nature, function, etc, often completely and dramatically. ○ **transformation** *n.*

transformer *n, elec* an electromagnetic device designed to transfer electrical energy from one alternating current circuit to another, with an increase or decrease in voltage.

transfuse *vb* **1** *med* **a** to transfer (blood or plasma) from one person or animal to another; **b** to treat (a person or animal) with this. **2** to permeate: *Pink and orange patterns transfused the dawn sky.*

transfusion *n, med* the process or an instance of introducing blood, plasma, etc into the bloodstream.

transgress *vb* **1** to break or violate (divine law, a rule, etc). **2** to go beyond or overstep (a limit or boundary). ○ **transgression** *n.* ○ **transgressor** *n.*

transient *adj* lasting, staying, etc for only a short time. ➢ *n* a temporary resident, worker, etc. ○ **transience** or **transiency** *n.*

transistor *n* **1** *electronics* a semiconductor device that has three or more electrodes, acting as a switch, amplifier or detector of electric current. **2** (*in full* **transistor radio**) a small portable radio that has transistors instead of valves and tubes.

transistorize or **-ise** *vb* to design or fit with a transistor or transistors. ○ **transistorized** *adj.*

transit *n* **1** an act or the process of carrying or moving goods, passengers, etc from one place to another. **2** a route or passage. **3** *astron* **a** the passage of a heavenly body across a meridian; **b** the passage of a smaller heavenly body across a larger one. ♦ **in transit** in the process of going or being taken from one place to another.

transition *n* a change or passage from one condition, state, subject, place, etc to another. ○ **transitional** or **transitionary** *adj.*

transitive *adj, gram* of a verb: taking a direct object, eg *make* in *They make lots of money.* Compare INTRANSITIVE. ○ **transitively** *adv.* ○ **transitivity** *n.*

transitory *adj* short-lived; lasting only for a short time.

translate *vb* **1** **a** to express (a word, speech, written text, etc) in another language; **b** *intr* to do this, esp as a profession. **2** *intr* of a written text, etc: to be able to be expressed in another language, format, etc: *Poetry doesn't always translate well.* **3** to put or express (an idea, etc) in other, usu simpler, terms. **4** to interpret: *He translated her expression as contempt.* **5** *tr & intr* to convert or be converted into: *to translate their ideas into reality* • *The price translates as roughly £50.* **6** *tr & intr* to change or move from one state, condition, person, place, etc to another. ○ **translatable** *adj.* ○ **translator** *n.*

translation *n* **1** a word, speech, written text, etc that has been put into one language from another. **2** an act or instance or the process of translating. ○ **translational** *adj.*

transliterate *vb* to replace (the characters of a word, etc) with the nearest equivalent characters of another alphabet. ○ **transliteration** *n.*

translucent *adj* **1** allowing light to pass diffusely. **2** clear. ○ **translucence** or **translucency** *n.*

transmigrate *vb, intr* **1** of a soul: to pass into another body or just after death. **2** to move from one home to another. ○ **transmigration** *n.*

transmission *n* **1** an act or the process of transmitting or the state of being transmitted. **2** something transmitted, esp a radio or TV broadcast. **3** the system of parts in a motor vehicle that transfers power from the engine to the wheels.

transmit *vb* (**transmitted, transmitting**) **1** to pass or hand on (esp a message or an infection). **2** to convey (emotion, etc). **3** *tr & intr* **a** to send out (signals) by radio waves; **b** to broadcast (a radio or television programme). ○ **transmissible** *adj.* ○ **transmissive** *adj.* ○ **transmittable** *adj.* ○ **transmittal** *n.*

transmitter *n* **1** someone or something that transmits. **2** the equipment that transmits the signals in radio and TV broadcasting.

transmogrify *vb* (*-ies, -ied*) *humorous* to transform, esp in a surprising or bizarre way. ○ **transmogrification** *n*.

transmute *vb* 1 to change the form, substance or nature of. 2 *alchemy* to change (base metal) into gold or silver. ○ **transmutation** *n*.

transom *n* 1 a horizontal bar of wood or stone across a window or the top of a door. 2 a lintel.

transparency *n* (*-ies*) 1 the quality or state of being transparent. 2 a small photograph on clear plastic in a frame, viewed using a slide projector. 3 a picture on a translucent background that can be seen when a light is shone behind it.

transparent *adj* 1 able to be seen through. 2 of a motive, excuse, disguise, etc: easily understood or recognized; obvious. 3 of a person: frank and open. ○ **transparently** *adv*.

transpire *vb* 1 *intr* of a secret, etc: to become known; to come to light. 2 *intr, loosely* to happen. 3 *tr & intr, bot* of a plant: to release water vapour. ○ **transpiration** *n*.

> **transpire** Some people reject the use of **transpire** to mean 'to happen', but it is now well established.

transplant *vb* /trans'plɑːnt/ 1 to take (living skin, tissue, an organ, etc) from someone and use it as an implant, either at another site in the donor's own body or in the body of another person. 2 to move (esp a growing plant) from one place to another. ➢ *n* /'trans-/ 1 *surgery* an operation which involves transplanting an organ, etc. 2 an organ, plant, etc which has been or is ready to be transplanted. ○ **transplantation** *n*.

transponder *n* a radio and radar device that receives a signal and then sends out its own signal in response.

transport *vb* /trans'pɔːt/ 1 to carry (goods, passengers, etc) from one place to another. 2 *hist* to send (a criminal) to a penal colony overseas. 3 to affect strongly or deeply: *She was transported with grief.* ➢ *n* /'transpɔːt/ 1 a system or business for taking people, goods, etc from place to place: *public transport.* 2 a means of getting or being transported from place to place. 3 (*often* **transports**) strong emotion, esp of pleasure. 4 a ship, aircraft, lorry, etc used to carry soldiers or military equipment and stores. ○ **transportable** *adj*.

transportation *n* 1 an act of transporting or the process of being transported. 2 a means of being transported; transport. 3 *hist* a form of punishment where convicted criminals were sent to overseas penal colonies.

transport café *n, Brit* an inexpensive roadside restaurant catering esp for long-distance lorry drivers.

transporter *n* a vehicle that carries other vehicles, large pieces of machinery, etc by road.

transpose *vb* 1 to cause (two or more things, letters, words, etc) to change places. 2 to

change the position of (an item) in a sequence or series. 3 *mus* to perform or rewrite (notes, a piece of music, etc) in a different key. ○ **transposition** *n*.

transputer *n, comput* a chip capable of all the functions of a microprocessor, including memory, designed for parallel processing rather than sequential processing.

transsexual *n* someone anatomically of one sex but who adopts the characteristics, behaviour, etc typical of the opposite sex, often having medical treatment to alter their physical attributes. ○ **transsexualism** *n*. ○ **transsexuality** *n*.

transubstantiation *n* 1 an act or the process of changing, or changing something, into something else. 2 *Christianity* esp in the Roman Catholic Church: **a** the conversion of bread and wine into the body and blood of Christ; **b** the doctrine which states that this happens.

transuranic /tranzju'ranɪk/ *adj, chem* of an element: having an atomic number greater than that of uranium.

transverse *adj* placed, lying, built, etc in a crosswise direction. ○ **transversely** *adv*.

transvestite *n* someone, esp a man, who dresses in clothes that are typical of the opposite sex. ○ **transvestism** *n*.

trap *n* 1 a device or hole, usu baited, for catching animals, sometimes killing them in the process. 2 a plan or trick for surprising someone into speech or action, or catching them unawares: *a speed trap.* 3 a trapdoor. 4 a bend in a pipe which fills with liquid to stop foul gases passing up the pipe. 5 a light, two-wheeled carriage, usu pulled by a single horse. 6 a device for throwing a ball or clay pigeon into the air. 7 one of the compartments where greyhounds wait at the beginning of a race. 8 *golf* a bunker or other hazard. 9 *slang* the mouth. 10 (**traps**) *jazz slang* drums or other percussion instruments. ➢ *vb* (**trapped, trapping**) 1 to catch (an animal) in a trap. 2 to catch (someone) out or unawares, esp with a trick. 3 to set traps in (a place). 4 to stop and hold in or as if in a trap.

trapdoor *n* a small door or opening in a floor, ceiling, etc, usu set flush with its surface.

trapeze *n* a swing-like apparatus consisting of a short horizontal bar hanging on two ropes, used by gymnasts and acrobats.

trapezium *n* (**trapeziums** or **trapezia**) 1 *Brit* a four-sided geometric figure that has one pair of its opposite sides parallel. 2 *N Am* a four-sided geometric figure that has no parallel sides. 3 any four-sided geometric figure that is not a parallelogram.

trapezius /trə'piːzɪəs/ *n* (**trapeziuses** or **-zii** /-zɪaɪ/) either of a pair of large flat triangular muscles that extend over the back of the neck and the shoulders.

trapezoid *n* 1 *Brit* a four-sided geometric figure that has no sides parallel. 2 *N Am* a four-sided geometric figure that has one pair of its opposite sides parallel. ○ **trapezoidal** adj.

trapper n someone who traps wild animals, usu with the intention of selling their fur.

trappings pl n 1 ornamental accessories denoting office, status, etc: the trappings of office. 2 a horse's ornamental harness.

Trappist n a member of a branch of monks who observe a severe rule which includes a vow of silence.

trash n 1 a rubbish; waste material or objects; b chiefly US domestic waste. 2 nonsense. 3 a worthless, contemptible, etc person or people: white trash. 4 a a worthless object or worthless objects; b art, drama, etc perceived as having no merit. ➤ vb 1 colloq to wreck. 2 colloq to criticize severely or expose as worthless. ○ **trashy** adj (**-ier, -iest**).

trashcan n, US a dustbin.

trattoria /tratəˈriːə/ n (**trattorias** or **trattorie** /-eɪ/) an informal Italian restaurant.

trauma n (**traumas** or **traumata**) 1 med a a severe physical injury or wound; b a state of shock brought on by this. 2 a a severe emotional shock that may have long-term effects on behaviour or personality; b the condition that can result from this. 3 loosely any event, situation, etc that is stressful, emotionally upsetting, etc. ○ **traumatize** or **-ise** vb.

traumatic adj 1 relating to, resulting from or causing trauma. 2 colloq distressing; emotionally upsetting. ○ **traumatically** adv.

travail n 1 painful or extremely hard work or labour. 2 the pain of childbirth; labour. ➤ vb, intr 1 to do hard work. 2 to undergo pain, esp in childbirth.

travel vb (**travelled, travelling; US traveled, traveling**) 1 tr & intr to go from place to place; to make a journey: to travel the world • to travel through France. 2 to journey across (a stated distance). 3 intr to be capable of withstanding a journey, esp a long one: not a wine that travels well. 4 intr to move: Light travels in a straight line • Her eyes travelled over the horizon. 5 intr, colloq to move quickly. ➤ n 1 an act or the process of travelling. 2 (usu **travels**) a journey or tour, esp abroad. 3 the range, distance, speed, etc of the motion of a machine or a machine part.

travel agency n a business that makes arrangements for travellers, holidaymakers, etc. ○ **travel agent** n.

traveller n 1 someone who travels. 2 old use a travelling salesman. 3 Brit colloq a Gypsy.

traveller's cheque n a cheque for a fixed sum that the bearer signs and can use in another country.

travelogue n a film, article, talk, etc about travel.

traverse vb 1 to go or lie across or through. 2 to examine or consider (a subject, problem, etc) carefully and thoroughly. ➤ n 1 an act or the process of crossing or traversing. 2 a path or passage across eg a rock face or slope. 3 some-

thing that lies across. 4 a sideways movement. ○ **traversal** n.

travesty n (**-ies**) a ridiculous or crude distortion; a mockery: a travesty of justice. ➤ vb (**-ies, -ied**) to make or be a travesty of.

trawl n 1 (in full **trawl-net**) a large bag-shaped net, used for catching fish at sea. 2 a wide-ranging or extensive search: a trawl through the library catalogue. ➤ vb, tr & intr 1 to fish (an area of sea, etc) using a trawl-net. 2 to search through (a large number of things, people, etc) thoroughly: We had to trawl through hundreds of applications.

trawler n 1 a fishing-boat used in trawling. 2 someone who trawls.

tray n a flat piece of wood, metal, plastic, etc, usu with a small raised edge, used for carrying dishes, etc.

treacherous adj 1 of someone, their conduct, etc: not to be trusted; ready or likely to betray. 2 hazardous: Black ice made the roads treacherous. ○ **treacherously** adv.

treachery n (**-ies**) 1 deceit, betrayal, cheating or treason. 2 an act or instance of this.

treacle n 1 the thick dark sticky liquid that remains after the crystallization of sugar from sugar cane or sugar beet. 2 molasses. 3 cloying sentimentality. ○ **treacly** adj.

tread vb (**trod, trodden** or **trod**) 1 intr (usu **tread on**) to walk or step: Ben trod on the cat's tail. 2 to step or walk on, over or along: They trod the primrose path. 3 to crush or press (into the ground, etc) with a foot or feet: treading ash into the carpet. 4 to wear or form (a path, hole, etc) by walking. 5 to perform by walking. 6 intr to suppress or treat cruelly. 7 of a male bird: to copulate with (a female bird). ➤ n 1 a manner, style or sound of walking. 2 an act of treading. 3 the horizontal part of a stair. 4 a mark made by treading; a footprint or track. 5 a the thick, grooved and patterned surface of a tyre that grips the road and disperses rain water; b the depth of this surface. ◆ **tread on sb's toes** 1 to encroach on their sphere of influence, etc. 2 to offend them. **tread water** to keep oneself afloat and upright in water by moving the hands and arms.

treadle n a mechanical foot pedal that can drive a machine, eg, a sewing machine.

treadmill n 1 an apparatus for producing motion that consists of a large wheel turned by people or animals treading on steps inside or around it. 2 a similar piece of equipment used for exercising. 3 a monotonous and dreary routine.

treason n 1 (in full **high treason**) disloyalty to or betrayal of one's country, sovereign or government. 2 any betrayal of trust or act of disloyalty. ○ **treasonable** adj. ○ **treasonous** adj.

treasure n 1 wealth and riches, esp in the form of gold, silver, jewels, etc, esp accumulated over a period of time and hoarded. 2 anything of great value. 3 colloq someone loved and valued, esp as a helper, friend, etc. ➤ *vb* to value greatly or think of as very precious: *She treasured him as a friend.* ○ **treasured** *adj.*

treasure hunt *n* **1** a game where the object is to find a prize by solving a series of clues about its hiding place. **2** a hunt for treasure.

treasurer *n* **1** a person in a club, society, etc in charge of the money and accounts. **2** an official responsible for public money, eg, in a local council.

treasure-trove *n* **1** *law* something valuable found hidden and of unknown ownership and therefore deemed to be the property of the Crown. **2** anything of value.

treasury *n* (*-ies*) **1** (**Treasury**) **a** the government department in charge of a country's finances, esp expenditure, taxes, etc; **b** the officials who comprise this; **c** the place where this money is kept. **2** the funds of a state, organization, etc.

treat *vb* **1** to deal with or behave towards (someone or something) in a specified manner: *treat it as a joke.* **2** to care for or deal with (a person, illness, injury, etc) medically. **3** to put (something) through a process, etc: *treat the wood with creosote.* **4** to provide with (food, entertainment, etc) at one's own expense: *I'll treat you to lunch.* **5** *tr & intr* (*often* **treat of**) to discuss. **6** *intr* (*usu* **treat with**) to negotiate. ➤ *n* **1** an outing, meal, present, etc that one person treats another to. **2** a source of pleasure or enjoyment, esp when unexpected. ○ **treatable** *adj.* ◆ **a treat** *colloq, sometimes ironic* very good or well: *He looked a treat in his kilt.*

treatise /'tri:tɪz, -tɪs/ *n* a formal piece of writing that deals systematically and in depth with a subject.

treatment *n* **1** the medical or surgical care given to cure an illness or injury. **2** an act or the manner or process of dealing with someone or something: *rough treatment.* **3** a way of presenting something, esp in literature, music, art, etc: *his sympathetic treatment of female characters.*

treaty *n* (*-ies*) a formal agreement between states or governments.

treble *n* **1** something that is three times as much or as many. **2** *mus* **a** a soprano; **b** someone, esp a boy, who has a soprano singing voice; **c** a part written for this type of voice; **d** an instrument that has a similar range; **e** in a family of instruments: the member that has the highest range. **3** a high-pitched voice or sound. **4** the higher part of the audio frequency range of a radio, record, etc. **5** *betting* a progressive bet on three horses from three different races where the stake money plus any winnings from one race is staked on the next race. ➤ *adj, adv* **1** three times as much or as many; threefold; triple. **2** relating to a treble voice. **3** of a voice: high-pitched. ➤ *vb, tr & intr* to make or become three times as much or as many. ○ **trebly** *adv.*

treble chance *n, Brit* a type of football pool

where competitors try to select eight score draws from the fixture list.

treble clef *n, mus* in musical notation: a sign (𝄢) at the beginning of a piece of written music placing the note G (a fifth above middle C) on the second line of the staff.

tree *n* **1** *bot* **a** a tall woody perennial plant that typically has one main stem or trunk and which, unlike a shrub, usu only begins to branch at some distance from the ground; **b** any plant, eg, the banana, plantain, palm, etc, that has a single non-woody stem which grows to a considerable height. **2 a** a frame or support: *a shoe tree*; **b** a branched structure or diagram: *a family tree • a mug tree.* ○ **treeless** *adj.*

tree diagram *n, maths* a diagram with a branching tree-like structure representing the relationship between the elements.

tree fern *n* a tropical fern with a tall thick woody stem.

tree surgery *n* the treatment and preservation of diseased or damaged trees. ○ **tree surgeon** *n.*

trefoil /'trɛfɔɪl/ *n* **1** a leaf divided into three sections. **2** a plant with such leaves, eg, clover: *bird's-foot trefoil.* **3** something with three lobes or sections.

trek *vb* (**trekked, trekking**) *intr* to make a long hard journey. ➤ *n* **1** a long hard journey: *It's a bit of a trek to the shops.* **2** *S Afr* a journey by ox-wagon.

trellis *n* (*in full* **trellis-work**) an open lattice framework, usu fixed to a wall, for supporting or training climbing plants, fruit trees, etc.

trematode *n* a parasitic flatworm living in the gut of animals and humans.

tremble *vb, intr* **1** to shake or shudder involuntarily, eg, with cold, fear, weakness, etc. **2** to quiver or vibrate: *The harebells trembled in the wind.* **3** to feel great fear or anxiety: *I trembled at the thought of going for another interview.* ➤ *n* a trembling movement or state. ○ **trembling** *adj.*

tremendous *adj* **1** *colloq* extraordinary, very good, remarkable, enormous, etc: *a tremendous relief.* **2** awe-inspiring; terrible: *an accident involving a tremendous loss of lives.* ○ **tremendously** *adv.*

tremolo *n, mus* **1** a trembling effect achieved by rapidly repeating a note or notes, or by quickly alternating notes. **2** a device in an organ or on an electric guitar used for producing this. Compare VIBRATO.

tremor *n* **1** a shaking or quivering: *He couldn't disguise the tremor in his voice.* **2** (*in full* **earth tremor**) a minor earthquake. **3** a thrill of fear or pleasure. ➤ *vb, intr* to shake.

tremulous *adj* **1** quivering, esp with fear, worry, nervousness, excitement, etc. **2** of someone's disposition, etc: shy, retiring, fearful, anxious, etc. **3** of a drawn line, writing, etc: produced by a shaky or hesitant hand. ○ **tremulously** *adv.*

trench *n* **1** a long narrow ditch in the ground. **2**

mil a large-scale version of this where the earth thrown up by the excavations is used to form a parapet to protect soldiers from enemy fire. **3** a long narrow steep-sided depression in the floor of an ocean, esp one parallel to a continent.

trenchant *adj* **1** incisive; penetrating: *a trenchant mind.* **2** forthright; vigorous: *a trenchant policy to improve efficiency.* **3** *poetic* cutting; keen.

trench coat *n* **1** a long loose raincoat, usu double-breasted and with a belt. **2** a military overcoat.

trencher *n, hist* a wooden platter or board for serving food.

trencherman *n* someone who eats well, heartily or in a specified manner.

trend *n* **1** a general direction or tendency. **2** the current general movement in fashion, style, taste, etc. ➤ *vb, intr* to turn or have a tendency to turn in a specified direction.

trendsetter *n* someone who starts off a fashion.

trendy *adj* (**-ier, -iest**) *colloq* **1** of someone: following the latest fashions. **2** of clothes, music, clubs, bars, etc: fashionable at a particular time. ➤ *n* (**-ies**) someone who is, or who tries to be, trendy.

trepidation *n* nervousness or apprehension.

trespass *vb, intr* **1** (*usu* **trespass on** or **upon**) to make an unlawful entry or intrude (on someone else's property, time, rights, etc). **2** *old use* to sin. ➤ *n* **1** an act or the process of entering someone else's property without the right or permission to do so. **2** an intrusion into someone's time, privacy, etc. **3** *old use* a sin. ○ **trespasser** *n*.

tress *n* a long lock or plait of hair.

trestle *n* **1** a supporting framework with a horizontal beam the end of which rests on a pair of legs which slope outwards. **2** (*in full* **trestle-table**) a table that consists of a board or boards supported by trestles.

trews *pl n, Brit* trousers, esp close-fitting, tartan ones.

triad *n* **1** a group of three people or things, esp a chord consisting of three notes. **2** (*also* **Triad**) **a** a Chinese secret society, esp for organized crime; **b** a member of such a society. ○ **triadic** *adj*.

trial *n* **1** a legal process in which someone who stands accused of a crime is judged in a court of law. **2** an act or the process of trying or testing. **3** trouble, worry or vexation, or a cause of this: *Her son is a great trial to her.* **4** a preliminary test of someone's skill, esp to decide whether they should be offered a job, team place, etc. **5** a test of a vehicle's performance held esp over a demanding course. **6** a competition, usu over rough ground, to test skills in handling high-performance cars or motorcycles. **7** (*usu* **trials**) a competition in which the skills of animals are tested: *sheepdog trials.* **8** an attempt. ➤ *vb* (**trialled, trialling;** *US*

trialed, trialing) *tr & intr* to put (a new product, etc) to the test. ◆ **on trial 1** in the process of undergoing legal action in court: *on trial for murder.* **2** in the process of undergoing tests or examination before being permanently accepted or approved. **trial and error** the process of trying various methods, alternatives, etc until a correct or suitable one is found.

trial run *n* a test of a new product, etc, esp to assess effectiveness, potential, etc prior to an official launch.

triangle *n* **1** *geom* a plane figure with three sides and three internal angles. **2** anything of a similar shape. **3** a simple musical percussion instrument made from a metal bar which has been bent into a triangular shape and played by a small metal hammer. **4** an emotional relationship or love affair that involves three people. ○ **triangular** *adj*.

triangulate *vb* **1** to mark off (an area of land) into a network of triangular sections with a view to making a survey. **2** to survey and map (a triangularly divided area of land). ○ **triangulation** *n*.

Triassic *n, geol* the earliest period of the Mesozoic era, when the first dinosaurs, large sea reptiles and small mammals appeared.

triathlon *n* an athletic contest of three events, usu swimming, running and cycling. ○ **triathlete** *n*.

tribalism *n* **1** the system of tribes as a way of organizing society. **2** the feeling of belonging to a tribe, racial group, etc, esp when leading to violence.

tribe *n* **1** an organized, usu hierarchical, group of people, families, clans, etc who share ancestral, social, cultural, linguistic, religious, economic, etc ties. **2** a large group with a shared interest, profession, etc: *a tribe of protesters.* ○ **tribal** *adj*.

tribesman or **tribeswoman** *n* a man or woman who belongs to a tribe.

tribulation *n* **1** great sorrow, trouble, affliction, misery, etc. **2** a cause or source of this.

tribunal *n* **1** a court of justice. **2** *Brit* a board of people appointed to look into a specified matter and to adjudicate on it. **3** a seat or bench in a court for a judge or judges.

tribune *n* **1** *hist* **a** a high official elected by the ordinary people of ancient Rome to defend their rights; **b** a leader of a Roman legion. **2** a champion or defender of the rights of the common people.

tributary *n* (**-ies**) **1** a stream or river that flows into a larger river or a lake. **2** *hist* a person or nation that pays tribute to another.

tribute *n* **1** a speech, gift, etc given as an expression of praise, thanks, etc. **2** a sign of something valuable; a testimony: *Her success was a tribute to all her hard work.* **3** *hist* a sum of money regularly paid by one nation or ruler to another in return for protection, etc.

trice *n* a moment. ◆ **in a trice** almost immediately.

triceps *n* (*tricepses* or *triceps*) a muscle that is attached in three places, esp the large muscle at the back of the upper arm.

trichology /trɪˈkɒlədʒɪ/ *n* the scientific study of the hair and its diseases. ○ **trichologist** *n*.

trick *n* **1** something done or said to cheat, deceive, fool or humiliate someone. **2** a deceptive appearance; an illusion. **3** a mischievous act or plan; a prank or joke. **4** a clever or skilful act or feat which astonishes, puzzles or amuses. **5** a peculiar habit or mannerism: *He has a trick of always saying inappropriate things.* **6** a special technique or knack: *a trick of the trade.* **7** a feat of skill which can be learned. **8** the cards played in one round of a card game and which are won by one of the players. **9** *slang* a prostitute's client. ➤ *vb* **1** to cheat or deceive. **2** (**trick into** or **out of**) to persuade or cheat by: *tricked into believing him • He tricked the old woman out of her savings.* ○ **trickery** *n*. ♦ **do the trick** *colloq* to do or be what is necessary. **how's tricks?** *colloq* a casual greeting. ◊ **trick out** or **up** to dress or decorate in a fancy way.

trickle *vb, tr & intr* **1** to flow or cause to flow in a thin slow stream or drops. **2** to move, come or go slowly and gradually. ➤ *n* a slow stream, flow or movement.

trick or treat *n, chiefly N Am* the children's practice of dressing up on Halloween to call at people's houses for sweets, formerly threatening to play a trick on them if they were not given one.

trickster *n* someone who deceives, cheats or plays tricks.

tricky *adj* (**-ier, -iest**) **1** difficult to handle or do; needing skill and care. **2** inclined to trickery; sly; deceitful. **3** resourceful; adroit. ○ **trickily** *adv.* ○ **trickiness** *n*.

tricolour or (*US*) **tricolor** /ˈtrɪkələ(r)/ *n* a three-coloured flag, esp one with three bands of equal size in three different colours, eg, the French flag.

tricycle *n* a pedal-driven vehicle with two wheels at the back and one at the front.

trident *n* a spear with three prongs.

triennial *adj* **1** happening once every three years. **2** lasting for three years. ➤ *n* **1** a period of three years. **2** an event that recurs every three years. ○ **triennially** *adv.*

trier *n* **1** someone who perseveres at something, esp something they have little talent or aptitude for. **2** someone who tries out food.

trifle *n* **1** something of little or no value. **2** a very small amount. **3** *Brit* a dessert of sponge-cake soaked in sherry, topped with jelly and fruit, and then custard and whipped cream. ➤ *vb* (*usu* **trifle with**) **a** to treat (someone, their feelings, etc) frivolously, insensitively or with a lack of seriousness or respect; **b** to talk or think about (a proposition, idea, project, etc) idly or not very seriously. ♦ **a trifle** slightly, rather: *He's a trifle upset.*

trifling *adj* **1** unimportant; trivial. **2** frivolous. ○ **triflingly** *adv.*

trigger *n* **1** a small lever which, when squeezed and released, sets a mechanism going, esp one that fires a gun. **2** something that starts off a train of events, reactions, etc. ➤ *vb* **1** (*also* **trigger off**) to start (a train of events, reactions, etc) in motion. **2** to fire or set off (a gun, detonator, etc).

trigger-happy *adj, colloq* liable to shoot a gun, etc, or to go into a rage, etc, with little provocation.

trigonometry *n, maths* the branch of mathematics concerned with the relationships between the sides and angles of triangles.

trike see under TRICYCLE

trilateral *adj* **1** three-sided. **2** of talks, an agreement, etc: involving three parties, countries, etc.

trilby *n* (**-ies**) *Brit* a soft felt hat with an indented crown and narrow brim.

trill *n* **1** *mus* a sound produced by repeatedly playing or singing a note and a note above in rapid succession. **2** a warbling sound made by a songbird. **3** a consonant sound, esp an 'r', made by rapidly vibrating the tongue. ➤ *vb, tr & intr* to play, sing, pronounce, etc with a trill.

trillion *n* (*pl* **trillion**) **a** chiefly *N Am* a million million (10^{12}). *Brit equivalent* **billion**; **b** chiefly *Brit* a million million million (10^{18}). *N Am equivalent* **quintillion**. ○ **trillionth** *adj, n*.

trilobite /ˈtraɪləbaɪt/ *n* an extinct marine arthropod with a flat oval body divided lengthwise into three lobes, or its fossilized remains.

trilogy *n* (**-ies**) a group of three related plays, novels, poems, operas, etc.

trim *vb* (**trimmed, trimming**) **1** to make (hair, etc) neat and tidy, esp by clipping. **2** (*also* **trim away, from** or **off**) to remove by, or as if by, cutting: *trim hundreds of pounds off the cost.* **3** to make less by, or as if by, cutting: *trim costs.* **4** to decorate with ribbons, lace, ornaments, etc: *I trimmed the dress with pink velvet.* **5** to adjust the balance of (a ship, submarine or aircraft) by moving its cargo, ballast, etc. **6** to arrange (a ship's sails) to suit the weather conditions. **7** *intr* to hold a neutral or middle course between two opposing individuals or groups. **8** *intr* to adjust one's behaviour to suit current trends or opinions, esp for self-advancement. ➤ *n* **1 a** a neatening haircut; **b** an act or the process of giving or having this type of haircut. **2** proper order or condition: *in good trim.* **3** material, ornaments, etc used as decoration. **4** the upholstery, internal and external colour schemes, and chrome and leather accessories, etc of a car. ➤ *adj* (**trimmer, trimmest**) **1** in good order; neat and tidy. **2** slim.

trimaran /ˈtraɪməran/ *n* a boat that has three hulls side by side.

trimester /trɪˈmɛstə(r)/ *n* a period of three months, esp one of the three of human gestation, or a period of roughly three months forming an academic term.

trimming *n* **1** decorative ribbon, lace, etc: *a tablecloth with lace trimming.* **2** (**trimmings**) a the traditional or usual accompaniments of a meal or specified dish: *turkey with all the trimmings*; **b** the expected accessories, perks, etc that come with something: *an executive post with all the trimmings*.

trinitrotoluene /traɪnɪtrəʊˈtɒljuːiːn/ or **trinitrotoluol** /-ˈtɒljʊɒl/ *n, chem* a highly explosive yellow crystalline solid, used as an explosive and in certain photographic chemicals and dyes. Often shortened to **TNT**.

trinity *n* (*-ies*) **1** the state of being three. **2** a group of three. **3** (**Trinity**) *Christianity* the unity of the Father, Son and Holy Spirit.

trinket *n* a small ornament, piece of jewellery, etc of little value.

trio *n* **1** a group or set of three. **2** *mus* **a** a group of three instruments, players or singers; **b** a piece of music composed for such a group.

trip *vb* (**tripped, tripping**) **1** *tr & intr* (*also* **trip over** or **up**) to stumble or cause to stumble. **2** *tr & intr* (*also* **trip up**) to make or cause to make a mistake. **3** to catch (someone) out, eg, in a fault or mistake. **4** *intr* (*often* **trip along**) to walk, skip or dance with short light steps. **5** *intr* to move or flow smoothly and easily: *words tripping off the tongue*. **6** *intr* to take a trip or excursion. **7** *intr, colloq* to experience the hallucinatory effects of a drug, esp LSD. **8** *tr & intr* to activate or cause (a switch or device) to be activated, esp suddenly. ➢ *n* **1 a** a short journey or excursion, esp for pleasure; **b** a journey of any length. **2** a stumble; an act or the process of accidentally catching the foot. **3** a short light step or skip. **4** a part or catch that can be struck in order to activate a mechanism. **5** an error or blunder. **6** *colloq* a hallucinatory experience, esp one brought on by a drug, eg, LSD: *a bad trip*. ♦ **trip the light fantastic** *jocular* to dance.

tripartite *adj* **1** composed of three parts. **2** of talks, an agreement, etc: involving, ratified by, etc three parts, groups, nations, etc.

tripe *n* **1** parts of the stomach of a cow or sheep, used as food. **2** *colloq* nonsense; rubbish.

triple *adj* **1** three times as great, as much or as many. **2** made up of three parts or things. **3** *mus* having three beats to the bar. ➢ *vb, tr & intr* to make or become three times as great, as much or as many. ➢ *n* **1 a** an amount that is three times greater than the original, usual, etc amount; **b** a measure (of spirits) three times greater than a single measure. **2** a group or series of three. ○ **triply** *adv*.

triple jump *n* an athletic event that involves doing a hop, followed by a skip and then a jump.

triplet *n* **1** one of three children or animals born to the same mother at one birth. **2** a group or set of three, esp three notes played in the time usu taken by two.

triplicate *adj* /ˈtrɪplɪkət/ **1** having three parts which are exactly alike. **2** being one of three identical copies. **3** tripled. ➢ *n* /ˈtrɪplɪkət/ any of three identical copies or parts. ➢ *vb* /ˈtrɪplɪkeɪt/ **1** to make three copies of. **2** to

multiply by three. ○ **triplication** *n*.

tripod *n* **1** a three-legged stand or support, eg for a camera, etc. **2** a stool, table, etc with three legs or feet.

tripos *n* the honours examination for the BA degree at Cambridge University.

tripper *n, Brit* someone who goes on a journey for pleasure; a tourist: *day trippers*.

triptych /ˈtrɪptɪk/ *n* a picture or carving that covers three joined panels to form a single work of art, often used as an altarpiece.

trip-wire *n* a hidden wire that sets off a mechanism, eg, of an alarm, bomb, etc, when someone trips over it.

trireme /ˈtraɪriːm/ *n* an ancient galley with three banks of rowers on each side, principally a warship.

trite *adj* of a remark, phrase, etc: having no meaning or effectiveness because of overuse.

tritium *n, chem* a radioactive isotope of hydrogen that has two neutrons as well as one proton in its nucleus, used in fusion reactors and as an isotopic label or tracer.

triumph *n* **1** a great or notable victory, success, achievement, etc. **2** the joy or feeling of elation that is felt after victory, etc. ➢ *vb, intr* **1** (*also* **triumph over**) to win a victory or be successful; to prevail. **2** to rejoice in a feeling of triumph; to exult. ○ **triumphal** *adj*.

triumphant *adj* **1** having won a victory or achieved success. **2** exultant; feeling or showing great joy or elation because of a victory, success, achievement, etc.

triumvirate /traɪˈʌmvərət/ *n* a group of three people who share an official position, power, authority, etc equally.

trivalent *adj, chem* having a valency of three.

trivet *n* a three-legged stand or bracket for standing a hot dish, pot, teapot, etc on.

trivia *pl n* unimportant or petty matters or details.

trivial *adj* **1** of very little importance or value. **2** of a person: only interested in unimportant things; frivolous. ○ **triviality** *n*. ○ **trivially** *adv*.

trivialize or **-ise** *vb* to make or treat as unimportant, worthless, etc. ○ **trivialization** *n*.

trochee /ˈtrəʊkiː/ *n, prosody* a metrical foot of one long or stressed syllable followed by one short or unstressed one. ○ **trochaic** *adj*.

troglodyte *n* **1** a cave-dweller, esp in prehistoric times. **2** *colloq* someone who has little to do with the outside world and has become eccentric and out of touch.

troika *n* **1 a** a Russian vehicle drawn by three horses abreast; **b** this team of three horses. **2** any group of three people.

Trojan Horse *n* **1** *hist* a hollow wooden horse that the Greeks used to infiltrate Troy. **2** someone or something that undermines an organization, etc, from within, esp to bring about the downfall of an enemy, rival, etc. **3** *comput* a program that contains hidden instructions that can lead to the destruction or corruption of data.

troll¹ *n, folklore* an ugly, evil-tempered, human-like creature that can take the form of either a dwarf or a giant.

troll² *vb, tr & intr* to fish by trailing bait on a line through water. ➤ *n* the bait used in trolling, or a line holding this.

trolley *n* **1** *Brit* a small cart or basket on wheels for conveying luggage, shopping, etc. **2** *Brit* a small wheeled table for conveying food, crockery, etc. **3** a wheeled stretcher for transporting patients in hospital. **4** *Brit* a small wagon or truck running on rails. **5** A TROLLEY WHEEL. **6** *Brit* A TROLLEY BUS. **7** *N Am* A TROLLEY CAR. ♦ **off one's trolley** *colloq* daft; crazy.

trolley bus *n* a public transport vehicle powered from overhead electric wires.

trolley car *n, N Am* a public transport vehicle that runs on rails like a tram and is powered by overhead electric wires.

trolley wheel *n* a small grooved wheel which collects current from an overhead electric wire and transmits it down a pole to power the vehicle underneath.

trollop *n* **1 a** a promiscuous or disreputable girl or woman; **b** a prostitute. **2** a slovenly or untidy girl or woman.

trombone *n* a large brass instrument with a sliding tube. ◦ **trombonist** *n*.

trompe l'oeil /tromp 'lɜːj/ *n* (**trompe l'oeils**) a painting or decoration which gives a convincing illusion of reality.

troop *n* **1** (**troops**) armed forces or individual soldiers. **2** a group or collection, esp of people or animals. **3** a division of a cavalry or armoured squadron. **4** a large group of Scouts divided into patrols. ➤ *vb, intr* (*usu* **troop along, off, in**, etc) to move as a group. ♦ **troop the colour** *Brit* to parade a regiment's flag ceremonially.

trooper *n* **1** a private soldier, esp one in a cavalry or armoured unit. **2** a cavalry soldier's horse. **3** *US* (**state trooper**) a state police officer. **4** *N Am* a policeman mounted on a horse or motorcycle.

troop-ship *n* a ship designed for transporting military personnel.

trope *n* a word or expression used figuratively, eg, a metaphor.

trophy *n* (*-ies*) **1** a cup, medal, plate, etc awarded as a prize, esp in sport. **2** something kept in memory of a victory or success, eg, in hunting. ➤ *adj* of a person's partner, spouse, etc: elevating the person's status: *a trophy wife.*

tropic *n* **1** either of two lines of latitude that encircle the earth at 23° 27' north (**tropic of Cancer**) and 23° 27' south (**tropic of Capricorn**) of the equator. **2** (**the Tropics**) the parts of the earth that lie between these two circles.

tropical *adj* **1** relating to, found in or originating from the tropics: *Paul keeps tropical fish.* **2** very hot: *a tropical climate.* **3** luxuriant: *tropical rainforest.* ◦ **tropically** *adv.*

tropism *n, biol* the change of direction of an organism, esp a plant or plant part, in response to an external stimulus such as gravity, light or heat.

troposphere *n, meteorol* the lowest layer of the Earth's atmosphere, situated below the STRATOSPHERE. ◦ **tropospheric** *adj.*

trot *vb* (**trotted, trotting**) **1** *intr* of a horse: to move at a steady, fairly fast pace, in a bouncy kind of walk. **2** to make (a horse) move in this way. **3** *intr* to move or proceed at a steady, fairly brisk pace. ➤ *n* **1** an act or the process of trotting. **2** (**the trots**) *colloq* a euphemistic name for an ongoing bout of diarrhoea. ♦ **on the trot** *colloq* **1** one after the other. **2** continually moving about; busy. ♦ **trot sth out** *colloq* to produce (a story, article, etc), esp without much thought or effort: *He trots out the same boring lectures every year.*

troth /trouθ/ *n, old use* faith or fidelity. ♦ **plight one's troth** to make a solemn promise, esp in betrothal or marriage.

trotter *n* **1 a** a pig's foot; **b** (*usu* pigs' **trotters**) pigs' feet used as food. **2** a horse trained to trot in harness.

troubadour /'truːbədʊə(r), -dɔː(r)/ *n* **1** *hist* one of a group of lyric poets in S France and N Italy during the 11–13c who wrote about love. **2** a poet or singer, esp one whose topic is love.

trouble *n* **1 a** distress, worry or concern; **b** a cause of this. **2** bother or effort, or a cause of this: *go to a lot of trouble • The dog was no trouble.* **3** a problem or difficulty: *Your trouble is that you're too generous.* **4** (*usu* **troubles**) public disturbances and unrest. **5 a** illness or weakness: *heart trouble;* **b** malfunction; failure: *engine trouble.* ➤ *vb* **1** to cause distress, worry, anger, sadness, etc to: *What's troubling you?* **2** to cause physical distress or discomfort to: *His knee always troubled him.* **3** used esp in polite requests: to put (someone) to the inconvenience of (doing, saying, etc something): *Could I trouble you to open the window?* **4** *intr* to make any effort or take pains: *He didn't even trouble to tell me what had happened.* **5** to disturb or agitate (eg the surface of water). ◦ **troubled** *adj.* ♦ **in trouble** in difficulties, esp because of doing something wrong or illegal. **take (the) trouble** to make an effort (to do something, esp to do it well).

troublemaker *n* someone who continually, and usu deliberately, causes trouble, worry, problems, etc to others.

troubleshoot *vb* **1 a** to trace and mend a fault (in machinery, etc); **b** to identify and solve problems. **2** to mediate (in disputes, etc). ◦ **troubleshooter** *n.* ◦ **troubleshooting** *n, adj.*

troublesome *adj* slightly worrying, annoying, difficult, etc. ◦ **troublesomely** *adv.*

trough /trof/ *n* **1** a long narrow open container that animal feed or water is put into. **2** a channel, drain or gutter. **3** a long narrow hollow between the crests of two waves. **4** *meteorol* a long narrow area of low atmospheric pressure. Compare RIDGE (sense 5). **5** a low point, eg, in an economic recession, etc.

trounce *vb* to beat or defeat completely; to thrash. ○ **trouncing** *n*.

troupe *n* a group or company of performers.

trouper *n* 1 a member of a troupe. 2 an experienced, hard-working and loyal colleague.

trousers *pl n* an outer garment for the lower part of the body, reaching from the waist and covering each leg separately, usu down to the ankle.

trouser suit *n* a woman's suit, consisting of a jacket and trousers.

trousseau /'tru:səʊ/ *n* (**trousseaux** /'tru:səʊ/ or **trousseaus** /-səʊz/) clothes, linen, etc that a woman engaged to be married collects and keeps for her wedding and married life.

trout *n* (**trout** or **trouts**) 1 a freshwater fish of the salmon family, highly valued as food and by anglers. 2 *derog* an unpleasant, interfering old person, usu a woman.

trowel *n* 1 a small hand-held tool with a flat blade for applying and spreading mortar, plaster, etc. 2 a similar tool with a blade that is slightly curved in on itself for potting plants, etc.

troy *n* (*in full* **troy weight**) a system of weights used for precious metals and gemstones in which there are 12 ounces or 5760 grains to the pound.

truant *n* someone who stays away from school or work without good reason or without permission. ➢ *vb, intr* to be a truant. ○ **truancy** *n*. ◆ **play truant** to be a truant.

truce *n* an agreement to stop fighting, usu temporarily.

truck[1] *n* 1 *Brit* an open railway wagon for carrying goods. 2 *chiefly N Am* a lorry. 3 a frame with wheels that supports a railway carriage. 4 any wheeled vehicle, trolley or cart for moving heavy goods. ➢ *vb* **a** to put on or into a truck; **b** to transport by truck. ○ **trucker** *n, N Am*.

truck[2] *n* 1 commercial dealings. 2 *colloq* odds and ends. ◆ **have no truck with sb** or **sth** to avoid or refuse to have anything to do with them.

truckle *n* (*in full* **truckle-bed**) a low bed, usu on wheels, that can be stored away under a larger bed. ➢ *vb, intr* to submit or give in passively or weakly.

truculent /'trʌkjʊlənt/ *adj* aggressively defiant, quarrelsome or discourteous. ○ **truculence** *n*. ○ **truculently** *adv*.

trudge *vb* 1 *intr* (*usu* **trudge through, along, over,** *etc*) to walk with slow and weary steps: *I trudged through the snow.* 2 to cover (a stated distance, etc) slowly and wearily: *I trudged three miles to the nearest shops.* ➢ *n* a long and tiring walk.

true *adj* 1 agreeing with fact or reality; not false or wrong. 2 real; genuine; properly so called: *The spider is not a true insect.* 3 accurate or exact: *The photograph doesn't give a true idea of the size of the building.* 4 faithful; loyal: *a true friend* • *be true to one's word.* 5 conforming to a standard, pattern, type or expectation: *She behaved true to type.* 6 in the correct position; well-fitting; accurately adjusted. 7 honest; sincere: *twelve good men and true.* ➢ *adv* 1 certainly: *True, she isn't very happy here.* 2 truthfully. 3 faithfully. 4 honestly. 5 accurately or precisely. 6 accurately in tune: *sing true.* 7 conforming to ancestral type: *breed true.*

true-blue *adj* extremely loyal; staunchly orthodox. ➢ *n* (**true blue**) someone of this type.

true north *n* the direction of the north pole, as opposed to MAGNETIC NORTH.

truffle *n* 1 a fungus that grows underground, considered a delicacy. 2 a type of chocolate sweet with a centre made with cream, butter, chocolate and often flavoured with rum, etc.

trug *n, Brit* a shallow rectangular basket with a handle, for carrying flowers, fruit, vegetables, small garden tools, etc.

truism *n* a statement so obviously true that it requires no discussion.

truly *adv* 1 really: *Truly, I have no idea …* 2 genuinely; honestly: *truly sorry.* 3 faithfully. 4 accurately; exactly. 5 properly.

trump[1] *n* 1 **a** (**trumps**) the suit of cards declared to be of a higher value than any other suit; **b** (*also* **trump card**) a card of this suit. 2 (*usu* **trump card**) a secret advantage. ➢ *vb* 1 to defeat by playing a trump. 2 to win a surprising victory or advantage over (a person, plan, idea, etc). ◆ **come up** or **turn up trumps** *colloq* to be unexpectedly good or useful.

trump[2] *n, old use, poetic* a trumpet blast.

trumped-up *adj* of evidence, etc: invented; false.

trumpery *n* (*-ies*) 1 flashy but worthless articles. 2 rubbish. ➢ *adj* flashy but worthless.

trumpet *n* 1 **a** a brass instrument with a narrow tube, flared bell and a set of valves; **b** a similar but simpler instrument used, esp by the military, for signalling, fanfares, etc. 2 the corona of a daffodil. 3 any conical device designed to amplify sound, eg, an ear trumpet. 4 the loud cry of an elephant. ➢ *vb* (**trumpeted, trumpeting**) 1 *intr* of an elephant: to make a loud cry. 2 *intr* to blow a trumpet. 3 to make known or proclaim loudly. ○ **trumpeter** *n*. ◆ **blow one's own trumpet** to boast about one's own skills, achievements, etc.

truncate *vb* to cut a part from (a tree, word, piece of writing, etc), esp in order to shorten: *He truncated his lecture.*

truncheon *n* a short thick heavy stick carried by police officers.

trundle *vb, tr & intr* to move or roll, or cause to move or roll, heavily and clumsily. ➢ *n* an act or the process of trundling.

trunk *n* 1 the main stem of a tree without the branches and roots. 2 the body of a person or animal, discounting the head and limbs. 3 the main part of anything. 4 a large chest, usu with a hinged lid, for storing or transporting clothes, etc. 5 *N Am* the boot of a car. 6 the long nose of an elephant. 7 (**trunks**) men's close-fitting shorts or pants worn esp for swimming.

trunk road *n* a main road between large towns.

truss *n* **1** a framework supporting a roof, bridge, etc. **2** a belt, bandage, etc worn to support a hernia. **3** a bundle of hay or straw. **4** a cluster of flowers or fruit. ➤ *vb* **1** (*often* **truss up**) to tie up or bind tightly. **2** to support with a truss.

trust *n* **1** belief or confidence in the truth, goodness, power, ability, etc of someone or something. **2** charge or care: *The child was placed in my trust.* **3** responsibility for the conscientious performance of some task: *be in a position of trust.* **4** a task of this kind. **5** an arrangement by which money or property is managed by one person for the benefit of someone else. **6** the amount of this money or property. **7** a group of business firms working together to control the market and maximize profits. ➤ *vb* **1** *tr & intr* to have confidence in; to rely on: *We can trust her to do a good job.* **2** (*usu* **trust with**) to allow (someone) to use or do (something) in the belief that they will behave responsibly, honestly, etc: *I wouldn't trust him with your new car.* **3** to give (someone or something) into the care of (someone): *trusted the children to their grandfather.* **4** *tr & intr* to be confident; to hope or suppose: *I trust you had a good journey.* **5** to give credit to (someone), esp in business. ◦ **trustable** *adj*.

trustee *n* **1** someone who manages money or property for someone else. **2** a member of a group of people managing the affairs and business of a company or institution. ◦ **trusteeship** *n*.

trust fund *n* money or property held in trust.

trustworthy *adj* able to be trusted or depended on; reliable. ◦ **trustworthiness** *n*.

trusty *adj* (**-ier, -iest**) *old use* **1** able to be trusted or depended on: *my trusty sword.* **2** loyal: *a trusty servant.* ➤ *n* (**-ies**) a trusted person, esp a convict granted special privileges for good behaviour.

truth *n* **1** the quality or state of being true, genuine or factual. **2** the state of being truthful; sincerity; honesty. **3** that which is true. **4** that which is established or generally accepted as true: *scientific truths.* **5** strict adherence to an original or standard.

truthful *adj* **1** telling the truth. **2** true; realistic. ◦ **truthfully** *adv*. ◦ **truthfulness** *n*.

try *vb* (**tries, tried**) **1** *tr & intr* to attempt; to seek to attain or achieve. **2** (*also* **try out**) to test or experiment with in order to assess. **3 a** to conduct the legal trial of: *They tried him for murder*; **b** to examine all the evidence of and decide (a case) in a law court. **4** to strain or stress: *She tried the limits of his patience.* ➤ *n* (**tries**) **1** an attempt. **2** *rugby* an act of carrying the ball over the opponent's goal line and touching it down on the ground. ◆ **try it on** *Brit colloq* to attempt to deceive someone, or to test their patience or tolerance. ◊ **try sth on** to put on (clothes, etc) in order to check the fit, appearance, etc. **try**

out to show one's talents to a team, etc. in the hope of being asked to join.

trying *adj* causing strain or anxiety.

try-on *n*, *Brit colloq* an attempt to deceive or to test someone's patience.

try-out *n*, *colloq* a test or trial.

tryst *old use or literary*, *n* **1** an arrangement to meet someone, esp a lover. **2** the meeting itself. **3** (*also* **trysting-place**) the place for such a meeting. ➤ *vb*, *intr* (*usu* **tryst with**) to arrange a tryst.

tsar, tzar *or* **czar** /zɑː(r), tsɑː(r)/ *n*, *hist* the title of the former emperors of Russia. ◦ **tsarism** *n*. ◦ **tsarist** *n*, *adj*.

tsarina, tzarina *or* **czarina** /zɑːˈriːnə, tsɑː-/ *n*, *hist* the title of a former Russian empress.

tsetse /ˈtsetsɪ/ *n* (*in full* **tsetse fly**) an African fly that feeds on blood and can transmit diseases.

T-shirt *or* **tee shirt** *n* a short-sleeved collarless top, usu cotton.

tsp *abbrev* teaspoon or teaspoonful.

T-square *n* a T-shaped ruler for drawing and testing right angles.

tsunami /tsuˈnɑːmiː/ *n* a large, fast-moving and often very destructive wave caused by movement in the Earth's surface, eg earthquake, volcanic eruption, landslide, etc.

TT *abbrev* **1 a** teetotal; **b** teetotaller. **2** Tourist Trophy (annual motorcycle races on the Isle of Man). **3** tuberculin-tested.

tub *n* **1** a large, low container for holding water, growing plants, etc. **2** a small container for cream, ice cream, yoghurt, margarine, etc. **3** the amount held by a tub: *He ate a whole tub of ice cream.* **4** (*also* **bathtub**) a bath. **5** *colloq* a slow-moving boat. ◦ **tubful** *n*.

tuba /ˈtʃuːbə/ *n* a bass brass instrument with valves and a wide bell that points upwards.

tubby *adj* (**-ier, -iest**) *colloq* of a person: plump. ◦ **tubbiness** *n*.

tube *n* **1** a long hollow flexible or rigid cylinder for holding or conveying air, liquids, etc. **2** a similar structure in the body of an animal or plant: *bronchial tubes.* **3** an approximately cylindrical container from which a paste, a semi-liquid substance, etc may be squeezed: *a tube of toothpaste.* **4** *Brit* **a** an underground railway system, esp the London one; **b** (*in full* **tube train**) an underground train. **5 a** a cathode ray tube; **b** *colloq* a television set. **6** *surfing* a rounded hollow formed by a breaking wave: *He tried to shoot the tube.* **7** *colloq* an extremely stupid person. ➤ *vb* to fit with or enclose in a tube or tubes. ◆ **go down the tubes** *colloq* to fail dismally.

tuber *n* **1** a swollen underground stem or rhizome, such as the potato, with buds that can develop into a new plant. **2** a similar structure formed from a root, eg, of a dahlia, but without buds.

tubercle *n* a small round swelling on a bone or in an organ, esp one in the lung in tuberculosis.

tubercular *adj* of tuberculosis.

tuberculin *n* a sterile liquid containing proteins from the bacillus that causes tuberculosis, used to test for the disease.

tuberculin-tested *adj* of milk: produced by cows that have been certified free from tuberculosis.

tuberculosis *n* an infectious disease of humans and animals caused by the tubercle bacillus, affecting the lungs and other body systems.

tubing *n* 1 a length of tube or a system of tubes. 2 material that tubes can be made from.

tub-thumper *n*, *colloq* a passionate or ranting public speaker or preacher. ○ **tub-thumping** *adj, n*.

tubular *adj* made of or shaped like a tube.

tubule *n* a small tube in the body of an animal or plant.

tuck *vb* 1 (*usu* tuck in, into, under, up, *etc*) to push or fold into a specified position: *She tucked the note into the envelope.* 2 to make a tuck or tucks in (a piece of material, etc). 3 to carry out a cosmetic operation to tighten a flabby part, smooth out wrinkles or remove fat. ➢ *n* 1 a flat pleat or fold sewn into a garment or piece of material. 2 *Brit colloq* food, esp sweets, cakes, etc, eaten as snacks. 3 a cosmetic operation to tighten a flabby part, smooth out wrinkles or remove fat: *She had a tummy tuck.* ◊ **tuck away** *colloq* 1 to eat (large quantities of food). 2 to store or conceal: *Their cottage was tucked away from prying eyes.* **tuck in** or **into** *colloq* to eat heartily or greedily: *Dave tucked into a huge plate of chips.* **tuck sb in** or **up** *colloq* to put them to bed by pulling up the covers snugly. **tuck sth up** to draw or put it into a folded position: *Zoe tucked her legs up.*

tucker¹ *n* 1 *hist* a piece of material, lace, etc drawn or fastened over the bodice of a low-cut dress. 2 *colloq* food. ♦ **best bib and tucker** *colloq* best clothes.

tucker² *vb* (*usu* tuck out) to tire.

tuck shop *n*, *Brit* a small shop that sells sweets, cakes, pastries etc in or near a school.

Tuesday *n* the third day of the week.

tufa *n*, *geol* a white spongy porous rock that forms in a calcium carbonate encrustation in areas around springs, streams, etc.

tuff *n* rock largely composed of fine volcanic fragments and dust.

tuffet *n* 1 a small grassy mound. 2 a low seat.

tuft *n* a small bunch or clump of grass, hair, feathers, wool, etc attached at the base or growing together. ○ **tufted** *adj*. ○ **tufty** *adj* (*-ier, -iest*).

tug *vb* (**tugged, tugging**) *tr & intr* 1 (*also* tug at or on) to pull sharply or strongly: *a dog tugging at the lead.* 2 to tow with a tugboat. ➢ *n* 1 a a strong sharp pull; b a sharp or sudden pang of emotion. 2 a hard struggle. 3 (*in full* tugboat) a small boat with a very powerful engine, for towing larger ships, barges, oil platforms, etc.

tug-of-war *n* (**tugs-of-war**) 1 a contest in which two people or teams pull at opposite ends of a rope and try to haul their opponents

over a centre line. 2 any hard struggle between two opposing sides.

tuition *n* instruction, esp when paid for: *driving tuition.*

tulip *n* 1 a spring-flowering bulbous plant that produces a single cup-shaped flower of various colours on a long stem. 2 this flower.

tulle /tjuːl, tuːl/ *n* a delicate thin netted silk for making veils, dresses, hats, etc.

tum *n*, *colloq* the stomach.

tumble *vb* 1 *tr & intr* (*often* tumble down, over, etc) to fall or cause to fall headlong. 2 *intr* to fall or collapse suddenly, esp in value or amount. 3 *tr & intr* (*often* tumble about, around, etc) to roll helplessly or haphazardly: *The kids tumbled around in the garden.* 4 *intr* to perform as an acrobat, esp somersaults. 5 *intr* to move or rush in a confused hasty way: *We tumbled out of the car.* 6 (*also* tumble to) *colloq* to become aware of suddenly: *He tumbled to their intentions.* ➢ *n* 1 a fall. 2 a somersault. 3 a confused or untidy state or heap.

tumbledown *adj* of a building, etc: falling to pieces; ramshackle.

tumble-dryer or **tumble-drier** *n* an electrically powered machine that dries wet laundry by tumbling it around in a current of warm air. ○ **tumble-dry** *vb*.

tumbler *n* 1 a a flat-bottomed drinking cup without a stem or handle, usu of glass; b the amount this holds: *a tumbler of milk.* 2 an acrobat, esp one who somersaults. 3 the part of a lock which holds the bolt until it is moved by a key.

tumbleweed *n* bushy plants that grow in arid areas and snap off above the root when dead and dry so that they roll about in the wind.

tumbrel or **tumbril** *n*, *hist* a two-wheeled cart used during the French Revolution to take people who had been sentenced to death to the guillotine.

tumescent /tjuˈmɛsənt/ *adj* swollen or becoming swollen, esp with blood as a response to sexual stimulation. ○ **tumescence** *n*.

tumid *adj* 1 of a body part: swollen. 2 of writing, speech, etc: bombastic; inflated.

tummy *n* (*-ies*) *colloq* the stomach.

tumour or (*US*) **tumor** *n* an abnormal growth of benign or malignant cells. ○ **tumorous** *adj*.

tumult *n* 1 a great or confused noise; an uproar. 2 a violent or angry commotion. 3 a state of extreme confusion, agitation, etc: *a mind in tumult.*

tumultuous *adj* 1 noisy and enthusiastic: *He arrived to a tumultuous welcome.* 2 disorderly; unruly. 3 agitated.

tumulus *n* (**tumuli**) *archaeol* an ancient burial mound or barrow.

tun *n* a large cask for holding beer or wine.

tuna *n* (**tuna** or **tunas**) 1 a large marine fish that lives in warm and tropical seas, related to the mackerel. 2 (*in full* tuna fish) its flesh used as food.

tundra *n* a vast relatively flat treeless zone lying to the south of the polar ice cap in America and Eurasia with permanently frozen subsoil.

tune n **1** a pleasing succession of musical notes; a melody. **2** the correct, or a standard, musical pitch. ➤ vb **1** tr & intr (also **tune up**) to adjust (a musical instrument or its keys or strings, etc) to the correct or a standard pitch. **2 a** to adjust (a radio, TV, video recorder, etc) so that it can pick up signals from a specified frequency or station; **b** intr (usu **tune in to**) to have a radio adjusted to receive (a specified signal, station, DJ, etc) and listen to (it or them): *She tunes in to Radio 4 in the mornings*. **3** to adjust (an engine, machine, etc) so that it runs properly and efficiently. ◊ **tuner** n. ◆ **call the tune** colloq to be in charge. **change one's tune** to change one's attitude, opinions, approach or way of talking. **in tune 1** of a voice or musical instrument: having or producing the correct or a required pitch: *sing in tune*. **2** having the same pitch as other instruments or voices: *The two guitars are not in tune*. **in tune with sb** or **sth** being aware of and able to relate to them or it. **out of tune 1** not having the correct pitch. **2** not having the same pitch as other instruments or voices. **out of tune with sb** or **sth** not being aware of and able to relate to them or it: *completely out of tune with the latest technology*. **to the tune of** to the (considerable) sum or total of: *We had to shell out to the tune of 500 quid for the repairs*.

tuneful adj **1** having a clear, pleasant, etc tune; melodious. **2** full of music.

tuneless adj lacking a good, pleasant, etc tune; not melodious.

tungsten n, chem a very hard silvery-white metallic element used in light bulbs, X-ray tubes, TV sets, alloying steel, etc.

tunic n **1** a close-fitting, usu belted jacket, often part of the uniform of the military, police, etc. **2** a loose garment, often sleeveless, that covers the upper body, usu coming down as far as the hip or knee, esp in ancient Greece and Rome, the Middle Ages, etc.

tuning fork n a small device used for tuning musical instruments, consisting of a stem with two prongs at the top, which, when made to vibrate, produce a specified note.

tunnel n **1** a constructed passage through or under a hill, river, road, etc, allowing access for pedestrians, vehicles, etc. **2** an underground passage that a mole, etc digs. ➤ vb (**tunnelled, tunnelling**; (US) **tunneled, tunneling**) **1** intr (**tunnel through, under**, etc) to make a tunnel through, under, etc (a hill, river, road, etc). **2** to make (one's way) by digging a tunnel.

tunnel vision n **1** a medical condition in which objects on the periphery of the field of vision are unable to be seen. **2 a** the inability or unwillingness to consider other opinions, viewpoints, etc; **b** single-minded determination.

tunny n (-ies) (in full **tunny-fish**) esp Brit tuna.

tup Brit, n a ram.

tuppence, tuppenny see TWOPENCE, TWO-PENNY

turban n **1** a headdress worn esp by Muslim and Sikh men and formed by wrapping a length of cloth around the head. **2** a woman's hat that looks similar to this. ◊ **turbaned** adj.

turbid adj **1** of liquid, etc: cloudy; not clear. **2** of writing, the construction of an argument, etc: confused; disordered; unclear. ◊ **turbidity** n.

turbine n a power-generating machine with a rotating wheel driven by water, steam, gas, etc.

turbo n **1** a short form of TURBOCHARGER. **2** colloq a car fitted with a turbocharger.

turbocharger n a supercharger driven by a turbine which is itself powered by the exhaust gases of the engine. ◊ **turbocharged** adj.

turbofan n **1** a jet engine driven by a gas turbine that increases thrust. **2** an aircraft powered by this.

turbojet n **1** (in full **turbojet engine**) a type of gas turbine that uses exhaust gases to provide the propulsive thrust. **2** an aircraft powered by this.

turboprop n **1** a jet engine in which the turbine drives a propeller. **2** an aircraft powered by this.

turbot n (**turbot** or **turbots**) a large scaleless flatfish with eyes on the left side of its head, highly valued as food.

turbulence n **1** a disturbed, wild or unruly state. **2** stormy weather caused by disturbances in atmospheric pressure. **3** the jolting or bumpy effect caused by irregularity in the flow of air across an aircraft wing.

turbulent adj **1** violently disturbed or unruly: *She's had a turbulent life*. **2** stormy.

turd n **1** colloq a lump of excrement. **2** slang someone considered worthless, despicable, etc.

tureen n a large deep dish with a cover that food, esp soup or vegetables, is served from.

turf n (**turfs** or **turves**) **1 a** the surface of an area of grassland that consists of a layer of grass, weeds, matted roots, etc plus the surrounding earth; **b** a square piece that has been cut from this. **2** a slab of peat used as fuel. **3** (**the turf**) horseracing, a race-course or the racing world generally. **4** slang territory. ➤ vb to cover (an area of land, garden, etc) with turf. ◊ **turf out** Brit colloq to throw out.

turf accountant n, Brit a BOOKMAKER.

turgid adj **1** swollen; inflated or distended. **2** of language: pompous. ◊ **turgidity** n.

turkey n **1** a large bird with dark plumage, a bald blue or red head with red wattles and, in the male, a fan-like tail. **2** its flesh used as food. **3** N Am colloq a stupid or inept person or thing. ◆ **talk turkey** N Am colloq to talk bluntly or frankly.

turmeric n **1** an E Indian plant of the ginger family. **2** its aromatic underground stem, dried and powdered, used as a spice and as a yellow dye.

turmoil n wild confusion, agitation or disorder; upheaval.

turn *vb* **1** *tr & intr* to move or go round in a circle or with a circular movement: *I turned the key and opened the door* • *a gate turning on its hinge.* **2** *tr & intr* to change or cause to change position so that a different side or part comes to the top, front, etc: *turn the pages slowly* • *turn to face the sun.* **3** to put into a specified position by, or as if by, inverting; to tip out: *She turned the dough on to the table.* **4** *intr* to change direction or take a new direction: *turn left at the corner.* **5** *tr & intr* to direct, aim or point, or be directed, aimed or pointed: *He turned his thoughts to the problems at work.* **6** *tr & intr* to become or cause to become: *Fame turned him into a real show-off* • *love which turned to hate.* **7** *tr & intr* of milk, etc: to make or become sour. **8** to shape using a lathe or potter's wheel. **9** to perform with a rotating movement: *turn somersaults.* **10** to become or pass (in age or time): *I turned forty this year.* **11** to appeal to or have recourse to (someone or something) for help, support, relief, etc: *Jack turned to drink after the divorce.* **12** *tr & intr* **a** of the stomach: to feel nausea or queasiness; **b** to cause (the stomach) to become nauseous or queasy: *That scene is enough to turn your stomach.* **13** to make (a profit, etc). ➤ *n* **1** an act, instance or the process of turning; a complete or partial rotation: *a turn of the wheel.* **2** a change of direction, course or position: *The road takes a turn to the right.* **3** a point or place where a change of direction occurs: *The house is just past the turn in the road.* **4** a direction, tendency or trend: *the twists and turns of the saga.* **5** a change in nature, character, condition, course, etc: *an unfortunate turn of events.* **6** an opportunity or duty that comes to each of several people in rotation or succession: *her turn to bat.* **7** inclination or tendency: *a pessimistic turn of mind.* **8** a distinctive style or manner: *a blunt turn of phrase.* **9** an act or service of a specified kind: *always doing good turns for others.* **10** *colloq* a sudden feeling of illness, nervousness, shock, etc: *It gave her quite a turn.* **11** a short walk or ride: *We went for a turn round the garden.* **12 a** each of a series of short acts or performances, eg, in a circus or variety theatre; **b** a performer who does one of these acts. **13** a single coil or twist of rope, wire, etc. **14** *mus* an ornament in which the principal note is preceded by that next above it and followed by that next below it. **15** *golf* the place on the course after the ninth hole when the players start heading back to the clubhouse. ○ **turner** *n.* ♦ **at every turn** everywhere, at every stage; continually. **in turn** or **by turns** one after the other in an orderly or prearranged manner: *The children will be examined in turn.* **on the turn 1** of the tide: starting to change direction. **2** of milk: on the point of going sour. **out of turn 1** out of the correct order or at the wrong time: *played his shot out of turn.* **2** inappropriately, discourteously, etc: *He apologized for speaking out of turn.* **serve its turn** to be adequate for the job in hand. **to a turn** to exactly the right degree; to perfection:

The steak was done to a turn. **turn (and turn) about** one after the other. **turn in one's grave** of a dead person: to be thought certain to have been distressed or offended, had they been alive, by circumstances such as those now in question. **turn one's back on sb** or **sth** to leave them or it for good. **turn one's hand to sth** to undertake a task, etc or have the ability for it: *She's very talented and can turn her hand to most things.* **turn tail** to flee. **turn the other cheek** to refuse to engage in retaliation. **turn the tide** to cause a change or reversal, in events, thinking, etc. ◇ **turn about** to move so as to face a different direction. **turn against sb** to become hostile or unfriendly towards them. **turn sb away** to send them away. **turn sth away** to reject or refuse to accept or consider it: *They turned away his pleas for leniency.* **turn back** to begin to go in the opposite direction: *We turned back because of snow.* **turn sb** or **sth back** to make them or it begin to go in the opposite direction: *The occupying forces turned back the aid convoy.* **turn sth back** to fold over or back: *She turned back the beds.* **turn sb** or **sth down** to refuse or reject them: *They turned him down at the interview.* **turn sth down 1** to reduce the level of light, noise, etc a machine produces: *Turn that telly down* • *Turn down the heat.* **2** to fold down or back: *I turned down the bedclothes.* **turn in** in *colloq* to go to bed. **turn sb** or **sth in** to hand (someone or something) over, esp to someone in authority: *He turned in the wallet to the police.* **turn sth in** to give, achieve, etc (a specified kind of performance, score, etc). **turn off** to leave a straight course or a main road: *The car turned off at the lights.* **turn sb off** *colloq* to make (someone) feel dislike, disgust or disinterest: *The violent scenes really turned me off.* **turn sth off 1** to stop (a flow of water, electricity, etc): *I turned off the tap.* **2** to make (a machine, appliance, etc) stop: *I turned off the microwave.* **turn on sb** or **sth 1** to attack them or it physically or verbally, usu suddenly: *The dogs turned on each other.* **2** to depend on them or it: *The whole argument turns on a single point.* **turn sb on** *colloq* to make them feel excitement, pleasure, interest, etc. **turn sth on 1** to start (the flow of water, electricity, etc). **2** to make (a machine, appliance, etc) start. **turn out 1** to happen or prove: *She turned out to be right.* **2** to finally be: *It turned out all right in the end.* **3** to gather or assemble, for a public meeting, event, etc: *Hundreds of people turned out to vote.* **4** *colloq* to get out of bed. **turn sb out 1** to send away. **2** to dress, equip, groom, etc: *He always turns the kids out nicely.* **3** to bend, fold, incline, etc outwards. **turn sth out 1** to switch off (a light, etc). **2** to make, manufacture, etc (usu specified quantities of goods): *They turn out around 50 cars a week.* **3** to empty, clear, etc: *The police made him turn out his pockets.* **turn over 1** to roll over when in a lying position. **2** of an engine: to start running at low speed. **turn sb over** *colloq* to surrender or transfer them (to another person, an authority, etc): *He* *turned the thief over to the police.* **turn sth over 1** to start (an engine) running at low speed. **2** to turn it so that a hidden or reverse side becomes visible or faces upwards: *turn over the page.* **3** to consider it, esp thoughtfully, carefully, etc: *She turned over his proposal in her mind.* **4** *slang* to rob it: *They turned over the off-licence.* **5** to handle or do business at (a specified amount): *The business turns over five million pounds per year.* **turn round 1** to turn to face in the opposite direction: *Peter, turn round and pay attention.* **2** of a loaded vehicle, ship, etc: to arrive, be unloaded, loaded with new cargo, passengers, etc and depart again: *The ship turned round in two hours.* **3** to adopt a different policy, opinion, etc. **turn sth round** to receive and deal with or process it in a specified manner, time, etc: *We're able to turn an order round in an hour • The ship was turned round in two hours.* **turn up 1** to appear or arrive: *Hardly anyone turned up for the match.* **2** to be found, esp by accident or unexpectedly: *The kitten turned up safe and well.* **turn sth up 1** to increase (the flow, intensity, strength, volume, etc, eg, of sound, light, etc produced by a machine): *Sally turned up the music.* **2** to shorten (clothing or a hem). **3** to discover or reveal it.

turnabout *n* **1** an act of turning to face the opposite way. **2** a complete change or reversal of direction, opinion, policy, etc.

turnaround *n* **1 a** an act or the operation of processing something, eg, unloading and reloading a ship, or completing a manufacturing procedure; **b** the time that this takes. **2** a TURNABOUT (sense 2).

turncoat *n* someone who turns against or leaves his or her political party, principles, etc and joins the opposing side.

turning *n* **1** a place where one road branches off from another. **2** a road which branches off from another. **3** an act or the process of using a lathe to form curves in wood, metal, etc.

turning circle *n* the smallest possible circle in which a vehicle can turn round.

turning-point *n* a time, place, event at which there is a significant change or something crucial happens: *This film was the turning-point in her career.*

turnip *n* **1** a plant of the cabbage family. **2** its root used as a vegetable or for animal fodder.

turnkey *n, hist* someone who keeps the keys in a prison; a gaoler.

turn-off *n* **1** a road that branches off from a main road. **2** *colloq* someone or something that causes dislike or disgust: *Her attitude is such a turn-off.*

turn of phrase *n* (*turns of phrase*) a way of talking, esp when distinctive.

turn-on *n, colloq* someone or something that causes excitement or interest, esp of a sexual nature.

turn-out *n* **1** the number of people who collectively attend a meeting, celebration, event, etc: *a poor turn-out at the match.* **2** the number of people voting in an election.

turnover *n* **1** the total value of sales in a business during a certain time. **2** the rate at which stock is sold and replenished. **3** the rate at which money, workers, etc pass through a business: *They pay low wages so there is a high staff turnover.* **4** a small pastry with a fruit or jam filling: *a yummy apple turnover.*

turnpike *n* **a** *hist* a tollgate or barrier; **b** *N Am* a road that has a toll system.

turnstile *n* a gate that allows only one person to pass through at a time.

turntable *n* **1** a revolving platform on a record player where records are placed. **2** a revolving platform used for turning railway engines and other vehicles.

turn-up *n, Brit* the bottom of a trouser-leg folded back on itself. ♦ **a turn-up for the books** a surprising event.

turpentine *n* **1** a thick oily resin obtained from certain trees, eg, pines. **2** a clear oil distilled from this resin and used in solvents, paint thinners and medicine.

turpitude *n, formal* vileness; depravity: *moral turpitude.*

turquoise *n* **1** an opaque semi-precious stone that comes in varying shades of light blue or green. **2** its greenish-blue colour.

turret *n* **1** a small tower projecting from a wall of a castle, etc. **2** (*in full* **gun-turret**) a small revolving structure on a warship, tank, etc with a gun mounted on it. **3** a part in a lathe that holds the cutting tools and which can be rotated so that the required tool can be selected. ○ **turreted** *adj.*

turtle *n* **1** a marine or freshwater reptile with a bony shell enclosing its body and which has flippers or webbed toes. **2** its flesh used as food. **3** *comput* a type of cursor that is moved around in on-screen drawing and plotting. ♦ **turn turtle** of a boat, etc: to turn upside down; to capsize.

turtledove *n* a wild dove noted for its soft cooing and for the affection shown to its mate.

turtle-neck *n* a round close-fitting neckline coming about a third of the way up the neck.

tusk *n* one of a pair of long, curved, pointed teeth which project from the mouth area of certain animals, eg, the elephant, walrus, etc.

tussle *n* a verbal or physical struggle or fight. ➤ *vb, intr* to engage in a tussle.

tussock *n* a clump of grass or other vegetation.

tut or **tut-tut** *exclam* expressing mild disapproval, annoyance or rebuke. ➤ *vb* (**tutted**, **tutting**) *intr* to express this by saying 'tut' or 'tut-tut'. ➤ *n* an act of saying 'tut' or 'tut-tut'.

tutelage / 'tjuːtɪlɪdʒ/ *n* **1** the state or office of being a guardian. **2** the state of being under the care of a guardian. **3** tuition or instruction, esp as given by a tutor.

tutelary / 'tjuːtɪlərɪ/ *adj* **1** having the power or role of a guardian. **2** belonging or relating to a guardian. **3** giving protection.

tutor *n* **1** a university or college teacher who

teaches undergraduate students individually or in small groups, or who is responsible for the general welfare and progress of a certain number of students. **2** a private teacher: *my piano tutor.* **3** *Brit* an instruction book. ➤ *vb, tr & intr* **1** to act or work as a tutor to. **2** to discipline. ○ **tutorship** *n.*

tutorial *n* **1** a period of instruction when a university or college tutor and an individual student or small group of students meet, usu to discuss an assignment, lectures, etc. **2** a printed or on-screen lesson that a learner works through at their own pace, eg, one that teaches the user how to use a computing program: *I found the Windows tutorials really useful.* ➤ *adj* belonging or relating to a tutor or tuition by a tutor: *He forgot his tutorial exercise.*

tutti /'tuti/ *mus, adv* with all the instruments and singers together. ➤ *n* a passage to be played or sung by all the instruments and singers together.

tutti-frutti *n* an ice cream or other sweet that contains or is flavoured with mixed fruits.

tut-tut see TUT

tutu *n* a very short protruding skirt consisting of layers of stiffened net frills and worn by female ballet dancers.

tuxedo /tʌk'siːdoʊ/ *n* (**tuxedos** or **tuxedoes**) *chiefly N Am* **1** a DINNER JACKET. **2** an evening suit with a dinner jacket.

TV *abbrev* television.

twaddle *n, colloq* nonsense.

twain *n, adj, old use* two.

twang *n* **1** a sharp ringing sound like that produced by plucking a tightly-stretched string or wire. **2** a nasal quality or tone of voice. ➤ *vb, tr & intr* **1** to make or cause to make a twang. **2** to play (a musical instrument or a tune) casually, informally, etc. ○ **twangy** *adj* (*-ier, -iest*).

twat *n, coarse slang* **1** the female genitals. **2** a term of contempt for someone considered worthless, unpleasant, despicable, etc.

tweak *vb* **1** to get hold of and pull or twist with a sudden jerk. **2** to make fine adjustments to. ➤ *n* an act or instance, or the process, of tweaking.

twee *adj, Brit colloq, disparaging* affectedly or pretentiously pretty, sweet, cute, quaint, sentimental, etc.

tweed *n* **1** a thick roughish woollen cloth, usu with coloured flecks. **2** (**tweeds**) clothes made of this.

tweedy *adj* (*-ier, -iest*) **1** relating to or like tweed. **2** relating to or typical of people who enjoy outdoor country activities and who are conventionally thought of as wearing tweed clothes. ○ **tweediness** *n.*

tweet *n* a melodious chirping sound made by a small bird. ➤ *vb, intr* to chirp melodiously.

tweeter *n, electronics* a loudspeaker designed to reproduce high-frequency sounds. Compare WOOFER.

tweezers *pl n* a small pair of pincers for pulling out individual hairs, holding small objects, etc.

twelfth (often written **12th**) *adj* **1** in counting: **a** next after eleventh; **b** last of twelve. **2** in twelfth position. **3** being one of twelve equal parts: *a twelfth share.* ➤ *n* **1** one of twelve equal parts. **2** a FRACTION equal to one divided by twelve (usu written $^1/_{12}$). **3** a person coming twelfth, eg in a race or exam. **4** (**the twelfth**) the twelfth day of the month.

Twelfth Night *n* the evening before the twelfth day after Christmas (5 January) or the evening of the day itself (6 January).

twelve *n* **1 a** the cardinal number 12; **b** the quantity that this represents, being one more than eleven. **2** any symbol for this, eg *12* or *XII*. **3** midnight or midday. **4** a set or group of twelve people or things. **5** (written **12**) *Brit* a film classified as suitable for people aged twelve or over. ➤ *adj* **1** totalling twelve. **2** aged twelve.

twelvemonth *n, old use* a year.

twelve-tone *adj, mus* belonging or relating to music based on a pattern formed from the 12 notes of the CHROMATIC SCALE.

twenties (often written **20s** or**20's**) *pl n* **1** (**one's twenties**) the period of time between one's twentieth and thirtieth birthdays. **2** (**the twenties**) the range of temperatures between twenty and thirty degrees. **3** (**the twenties**) the period of time between the twentieth and thirtieth years of a century.

twenty *n* (*-ies*) **1 a** the cardinal number 20; **b** the quantity that this represents, being one more than 19, or the product of ten and two. **2** any symbol for this, eg *20* or *XX*. ➤ *adj* **1** totalling twenty. **2** aged twenty. ○ **twentieth** *adj, n, adv.*

twerp or **twirp** *n, colloq* a contemptible person.

twice *adv* **1** two times: *Twice two is four.* **2** on two occasions. **3** double in amount or quantity: *twice as much.*

twiddle *vb* **1** to twist round and round: *twiddle the knob on the radio.* **2** to play with or twist round and round idly: *twiddling her hair.* ➤ *n* **1** an act of twiddling. **2** a curly mark or ornamentation. ♦ **twiddle one's thumbs** to have nothing to do.

twig[1] *n* a small shoot or branch of a tree, bush, etc. ○ **twiggy** *adj* (*-ier, -iest*).

twig[2] *vb* (**twigged, twigging**) *tr & intr, Brit colloq* to understand (a joke, situation, etc), esp suddenly.

twilight *n* **1** a faint diffused light in the sky when the sun is just below the horizon, esp just after sunset, but also just before sunrise. **2** the time of day when this occurs. **3** partial darkness. **4** a period or state of decline: *the twilight of his life.*

twill *n* a strong fabric woven to give a surface pattern of parallel diagonal ridges.

twin *n* **1** either of two people or animals that are born at the same time to the same mother. **2** either of two people or things that are very like each other or closely associated with each other. **3** (**the Twins**) the constellation GEMINI.

➤ vb (**twinned, twinning**) **1** tr & intr to bring or come together closely or intimately. **2** to link (a town) with a counterpart in another country to encourage cultural, social, etc exchanges.

twin bed n one of a pair of matching single beds.

twine n **1** strong string or cord of twisted cotton, hemp, etc. **2** a coil or twist. **3** an act of twisting or clasping. ➤ vb **1** to twist together; to interweave. **2** to form by twisting or interweaving. **3** tr & intr to twist or coil round.

twinge n **1** a sudden sharp stabbing or shooting pain. **2** a sudden sharp pang of emotional pain, bad conscience, etc.

twinkle vb **1** intr of a star, etc: to shine with a bright, flickering light. **2** intr of the eyes: to shine or sparkle with amusement, mischief, etc. **3** to give off (light) with a flicker. ➤ n **1** a gleam or sparkle in the eyes. **2** a flicker or glimmer of light. **3** an act of twinkling. ○ **twinkly** adj (-ier, -iest). ◆ **in the twinkling of an eye** in a very short time.

twinset n, Brit a woman's matching sweater and cardigan.

twirl vb, tr & intr to turn, spin or twist round: They twirled across the dance floor. ➤ n **1** an act of twirling: She did a twirl to show off her new dress. **2** a curly mark or ornament, eg, a flourish made with a pen. ○ **twirler** n. ○ **twirly** adj (-ier, -iest).

twist vb **1** tr & intr to wind or turn round, esp by moving only a single part or by moving different parts in opposite directions: twist the knob • He twisted round in his seat. **2** intr to follow a winding course: The road twists through the mountains. **3** to force or wrench out of the correct shape or position with a sharp turning movement: Adam twisted his ankle as he fell. **4** to distort: Smith twisted his face into an ugly sneer • He twisted her words. ➤ n **1** an act or the process of twisting. **2** something formed by twisting or being twisted. **3** a turn or coil; a bend. **4** a sharp turning movement which pulls something out of shape; a wrench. **5** an unexpected event, development or change, eg, of direction: a twist in the plot. **6** a distortion of form, nature or meaning. **7** an eccentricity or perversion. **8 a** a twisted roll of bread; **b** a twisted roll of tobacco; **c** a curl of citrus peel used to flavour a drink. **9** (**the twist**) a 1960s dance which involves making twisting movements of the legs and hips. ○ **twisty** adj. ◆ **round the twist** colloq mad; crazy. **twist sb's arm** colloq to persuade them by applying pressure.

twisted adj **1** full of twists; coiled or distorted: a tree with knarled and twisted branches. **2** colloq emotionally disturbed or perverted.

twister n **1** Brit colloq a dishonest or deceiving person; a swindler. **2** N Am colloq a tornado.

twit n, colloq a fool or idiot.

twitch vb **1** to move or cause to move with a spasm or jerk: My eye has been twitching all day. **2** to pull or pluck sharply or jerkily.

➤ n a sudden spasm, jerk or pang.

twitcher n, colloq a bird-watcher whose aim is to spot as many rare birds as possible.

twitchy adj (-ier, -iest) **1** colloq nervous, anxious or restless: a twitchy smile • feeling twitchy about the interview. **2** characterized by twitching: a twitchy eye. ○ **twitchily** adv.

twitter n **1** a light repeated chirping sound made esp by small birds. **2** colloq a nervous or excited state: go all of a twitter. ➤ vb **1** intr to make a light repeated chirping sound. **2** to say or utter with this sound. **3** (also **twitter on** or **away**) to talk rapidly and often trivially. ○ **twitterer** n. ○ **twittery** adj.

'twixt prep, old use a shortened form of BETWIXT: There's many a slip 'twixt cup and lip.

two n **1 a** the cardinal number 2; **b** the quantity that this represents, being one more than one. **2** any symbol for this, eg 2 or II. **3** the second hour after midnight or midday. **4** a set or group of two people or things. ➤ adj **1** totalling two. **2** aged two. ◆ **in two** in or into two pieces. **or two** an indefinite small number: I'll just be a minute or two. **put two and two together** to come to a conclusion, usu an obvious one, from the available evidence. **that makes two of us** colloq the same is true of me.

two-bit adj, orig N Am colloq cheap; petty; small-time.

two-dimensional adj **1** having, or appearing to have, breadth and length but no depth. **2** disparaging having little depth or substance.

two-faced adj deceitful; hypocritical; insincere.

twofold adj **1** equal to twice as much or as many. **2** divided into, or consisting of, two parts. ➤ adv by twice as much.

twopence n, Brit 1 /'tʌpəns/ (also **tuppence**) the sum of two pence, esp before the introduction of decimal coinage. **2** /tuːˈpɛns/ a decimal coin of the value of two pence. ◆ **not care** or **give tuppence** (/'tʌpəns/) colloq not to care at all: I don't give tuppence for what you think.

twopenny or **tuppenny** /'tʌpənɪ/ adj, Brit **1** worth or costing twopence. **2** colloq cheap; worthless.

two-piece adj of a suit, bathing costume, etc: consisting of two matching or complementary pieces or parts. ➤ n a two-piece suit, etc.

two-ply adj consisting of two strands or layers: two-ply wool • two-ply wood. ➤ n (-ies) knitting wool consisting of two strands twisted together, or wood consisting of two layers glued together.

twosome n **1** a game, dance, etc for two people. **2** a pair of people together.

two-step n a ballroom dance in duple time, or a piece of music for it.

two-stroke n an internal-combustion engine that takes one upward movement and one downward movement of the piston to complete the power cycle.

two-time vb, tr & intr, colloq **1** to deceive or be unfaithful to (a husband, wife, lover, etc). **2** to double-cross. ○ **two-timing** adj, n.

two-tone adj having two colours or two sounds: a car with a two-tone trim • a two-tone alarm.

two-way adj **1** of a street, etc: having traffic moving in both directions. **2** of a radio, etc: able to send and receive messages. **3** of a switch, wiring, etc: designed so that the electricity can be switched on or off from either of two points. **4** of a mirror: designed so that one side is like a normal mirror but with the other side allowing someone to see through without being observed.

tycoon n a business magnate.

tyke n **1** a dog, esp a mongrel. **2** Brit colloq a rough or coarse person. **3** Brit colloq a small child, esp a naughty or cheeky one.

tympani see TIMPANI

tympanum /ˈtɪmpənəm/ n (**tympana** /-nə/ or **tympanums**) **1** anat the middle ear. **2** archit a recessed usu triangular face of a pediment. **3** archit **a** the area between the lintel of a doorway or window and an arch over it; **b** a carving on this area. **4** a drum or the skin of a drum.

type n **1** a class or group of people, animals or things that share similar characteristics. **2** the general character, nature or form of a particular class or group; a kind or sort. **3** colloq a person of a specified kind: the silent type • He's not really my type. **4** a person, animal or thing that is typical of its group or class. **5** printing **a** a small metal block with a raised letter or character on one surface, used for printing; **b** a set of such blocks; **c** a set of such blocks that give printing of a specified kind: italic type. **6** printed letters, characters, words, etc: a leaflet with bold red type. ➤ vb **1** tr & intr to use a typewriter or word processor (to produce words, text, etc): Can you type? • She typed a letter. **2** to be a characteristic example or type of something; to typify. **3 a** biol to allocate (an animal, plant, etc) to a type; **b** med to classify: He typed the blood sample for cross-matching.

typecast vb to put (an actor or actress) regularly in the same kind of part.

typeface n, printing **1** a set of letters, characters, etc of a specified design or style. **2** the part of the type that is inked or the impression this leaves.

typescript n a typewritten document, manuscript or copy.

typeset vb (**typeset, typesetting**) printing to arrange (type) or set (a page, etc) in type ready for printing. ○ **typesetter** n.

typewriter n a machine with keys that the user strikes to produce characters on paper. ○ **typewritten** adj.

typhoid n, med (in full **typhoid fever**) a bacterial infection characterized by fever, a rash of red spots on the front of the body, abdominal pain and sometimes delirium. ○ **typhoidal** adj.

typhoon n a cyclonic tropical storm of the W Pacific.

typhus n, med an infectious disease caused by parasitic micro-organisms transmitted to humans by lice carried by rodents, and characterized by fever, severe headache, a reddish-purple rash and delirium.

typical adj **1** having or showing the usual features, traits, etc, or being a characteristic or representative example: We take in about £1000 on a typical day. **2** (often **typical of**) displaying the usual or expected behaviour, attitude, etc: It's typical of him to be late; **b** an exclamation expressing disdain, frustration, etc: Typical! It always rains when we plan a picnic. ○ **typicality** n. ○ **typically** adv.

typify vb (**-ies, -ied**) **1** to be an excellent or characteristic example of. **2** to represent by a type or symbol; to symbolize.

typist n **1** someone whose job is to type. **2** someone who types: I'm not a very fast typist.

typo n, colloq **1** a typographical error. **2** a typographer.

typography n **1** the art or occupation of setting type and arranging texts for printing. **2** the style and general appearance of printed matter. ○ **typographer** n. ○ **typographic** or **typographical** adj. ○ **typographically** adv.

tyrannical adj **1** relating to or like a tyrant. **2** oppressive; despotic. ○ **tyrannically** adv.

tyrannize or **-ise** vb, tr & intr to rule or treat in a cruel, unjust and oppressive way.

tyrannosaurus or **tyrannosaur** n a huge flesh-eating dinosaur that walked on its powerful hind legs and which had relatively small clawlike front legs.

tyranny n (**-ies**) **1** the use of cruelty, injustice, oppression, etc to enforce authority or power. **2 a** absolute, cruel and oppressive government by a single tyrant or group of tyrannical people; **b** a state under such government; **c** a period when this kind of government rules. **3** a cruel, unjust or oppressive act.

tyrant n **1** a cruel, unjust and oppressive ruler with absolute power. **2** someone who uses authority or power cruelly and unjustly.

tyre or (US) **tire** n **1** a rubber ring around the outside edge of a wheel, eg, on a bicycle, pram, wheelbarrow, etc. **2** a similar hollow structure with an inner tube filled with compressed air on the wheel of a car, lorry, etc.

tyro n a novice or beginner.

tzar, tzarina see TSAR, TSARINA

Uu

U¹ or **u** *n* (*Us*, *U's* or *u's*) the twenty-first letter of the English alphabet.

U² *adj, Brit colloq* esp of language: typical of or acceptable to the upper classes.

U³ *abbrev, Brit* universal, denoting a film designated as suitable for people of all ages.

U⁴ *symbol, chem* uranium.

ubiquitous /juːˈbɪkwɪtəs/ *adj* existing, found or seeming to be found everywhere at the same time. ○ **ubiquitously** *adv.* ○ **ubiquity** *n.*

U-boat *n* a German submarine, used esp in World Wars I and II.

udder *n* in certain mammals, eg cows, goats, etc: the bag-like structure, with two or more teats, containing the mammary glands that secrete milk.

UFO or **ufo** /ˈjuːfoʊ/ *n* an unidentified flying object.

ugh /ʌx, ʌg, ɜːx, ɜːg/ *exclam* expressing dislike or disgust.

ugly *adj* (*-ier, -iest*) **1** unpleasant to look at; extremely unattractive. **2** morally repulsive or offensive. **3** threatening, or involving danger or violence: *an ugly situation.* **4** angry; bad-tempered: *an ugly mood.* ○ **ugliness** *n.*

ugly duckling *n* someone or something, initially thought ugly or worthless, that later turns out to be outstandingly beautiful or highly valued.

UHF *abbrev, radio* ultrahigh frequency.

UHT *abbrev* ultra-heat-treated.

UK *abbrev* United Kingdom.

ukase /juːˈkeɪz/ *n* a command issued by a supreme ruler, esp the Tsar in Imperial Russia.

ukulele or **ukelele** /juːkəˈleɪlɪ/ *n* a small guitar, usu with four strings.

ulcer *n* **1** *pathol* a persistent open sore on the surface of the skin or of the mucous membranes lining a body cavity. **2** a continuing source of evil or corruption. ○ **ulcerous** *adj.*

ulna *n* (*ulnae* /ˈʌlniː/ or *ulnas*) *anat* **1** the thinner and longer of the two bones of the human forearm. **2** the corresponding bone in the front limb or wing of other vertebrates. ○ **ulnar** *adj.*

ulster *n* a man's loose heavy double-breasted overcoat, often worn with a belt.

ult. *abbrev* ultimo.

ulterior /ʌlˈtɪərɪə(r)/ *adj* of motives, etc: beyond or other than what is apparent or admitted.

ultimate *adj* **1** last or final in a series or process. **2** most important; greatest possible. **3** fundamental; basic. **4** *colloq* best; most advanced. ➤ *n* **1** the final point; the end or conclusion. **2** (**the ultimate**) *colloq* the best; the most advanced of its kind: *the ultimate in com-*

puter technology. ○ **ultimately** *adv* in the end; finally.

ultimatum *n* (*ultimatums* or *ultimata*) **1** in a dispute, negotiations, etc: a final statement from one of the parties involved to another, declaring an intention to take hostile action unless specified conditions are fulfilled. **2** any final terms, demand, etc.

ultimo *adj* (abbrev **ult.**) used mainly in formal correspondence: of or during last month: *your letter of the tenth ultimo.* Compare PROXIMO.

ultra-heat-treated *adj* (abbrev **UHT**) of milk, etc: sterilized by exposure to very high temperatures, and thus with its shelf life increased.

ultrahigh frequency *n* (abbrev **UHF**) a radio frequency between 300 and 3000MHz.

ultramarine *n* **1** a deep-blue pigment used in paints, orig made by grinding lapis lazuli. **2** the colour of this pigment. ➤ *adj* of the colour ultramarine.

ultramontane *adj* **1** situated or relating to an area beyond a mountain range, esp the Alps. **2** *RC Church* relating or belonging to a faction which is in favour of supreme papal authority on doctrinal matters. ➤ *n* **1** someone who lives beyond a mountain range, esp the Alps. **2** *RC Church* a member of the ultramontane faction.

ultrasonic *adj* relating to or producing ultrasound. ○ **ultrasonically** *adv.*

ultrasonics *sing n* the branch of physics that deals with the study of ultrasound.

ultrasound *n* sound consisting of waves with frequencies higher than 20,000Hz, widely used in medical diagnosis, in sonar systems, for cleaning industrial tools, and for detecting flaws and impurities in metals.

ultrasound scan *n* a medical examination of an internal part, esp a fetus, by directing ultrasound waves through it to produce an image on a screen.

ultraviolet *adj* **1** denoting electromagnetic radiation with wavelengths in the range 4 to 400nm, ie in the region between violet light and X-rays. **2** relating to or involving ultraviolet radiation or its use. ➤ *n* the ultraviolet part of the spectrum.

ululate /ˈjuːljʊleɪt, ˈʌl-/ *vb, intr* to howl, wail or screech. ○ **ululation** *n.*

umbel *n, bot* a flower head in which a cluster of flowers with stalks of equal length arise from the same point on the main stem.

umbelliferous *adj, bot* denoting or belonging to plants which typically have flowers arranged in umbels.

umber *n* **1** a dark yellowish-brown earthy mineral containing oxides of iron and manganese, used to make pigments. **2** any of these pigments or the brownish colours produced by them. ➤ *adj* referring to the colour of umber; dark brown.

umbilical cord *n* **1** a long flexible tube-like organ by which a fetus is attached to the placenta and through which it receives nourishment. **2** any cable, tube, servicing line, etc through which essential supplies are conveyed, eg the lifeline that connects astronauts to their spacecraft during a spacewalk.

umbilicus *n* (*umbilici* /ʌmˈbɪlɪsaɪ/ or *umbilicuses*) *anat* the navel.

umble pie *n* HUMBLE PIE.

umbles *pl n, archaic* the entrails (the liver, heart, lungs, etc) of an animal, esp a deer.

umbra *n* (*umbrae* /ˈʌmbriː/ or *umbras*) **1** *astron* the shadow cast by the moon on the earth during an eclipse of the sun. **2** the darker inner part of a sunspot.

umbrage *n* (*esp* **give** or **take umbrage**) annoyance; offence.

umbrella *n* **1** a device carried to give shelter from rain, etc, consisting of a rounded fabric canopy supported on a lightweight collapsible framework of ribs fitted around a central stick. **2** something, such as an organization, that provides protection or overall cover for a number of others. ➤ *adj* **1** referring to something that covers or protects a number of things: *an umbrella organization*. **2** of a word, term, etc: general; covering several meanings or ideas.

umlaut /ˈʊmlaʊt/ *n* in Germanic languages: **1** a change in the pronunciation of a vowel under the influence of a front vowel in a following syllable (esp in a suffix). **2** a mark consisting of two dots placed above a vowel (eg ö or ä) that undergoes or has undergone this change.

umpire *n* **1** an impartial person who supervises play in various sports, eg cricket and tennis, enforcing the rules and deciding disputes. **2** someone who judges or decides a dispute or deadlock. ➤ *vb, tr & intr* to act as umpire in a match, dispute, etc.

umpteen *adj, colloq* very many: *I've told you umpteen times!* ○ **umpteenth** *n, adj*.

UN *abbrev* United Nations.

unable *adj* (*chiefly* **unable to do sth**) not able; not having sufficient strength, skill or authority (to do something).

unaccompanied *adj* **1** not accompanied; not escorted or attended. **2** *mus* without instrumental accompaniment.

unaccountable *adj* **1** impossible to explain. **2** of a person: difficult to make out; puzzling in character. **3** not answerable or accountable. ○ **unaccountably** *adv*.

unaccounted *adj* (*usu* **unaccounted for**) **1** unexplained. **2** not included in an account.

unaccustomed *adj* **1** not usual or customary; unfamiliar. **2** (*usu* **unaccustomed to sth**) not used or accustomed to it.

unadulterated *adj* **1** pure; not mixed with anything else. **2** sheer; complete.

unadvised *adj* **1** not advised; without advice. **2**

unwise; ill-advised. ○ **unadvisedly** *adv*.

unaffected *adj* **1** sincere or genuine, not affected; free from pretentiousness. **2** not affected or influenced. ○ **unaffectedly** *adv*.

unalienable *adj* INALIENABLE.

unalloyed *adj* **1** not alloyed; pure. **2** of joy, pleasure, etc: pure; sheer; not mixed with feelings of sadness or anxiety.

unanimous /jʊˈnanɪməs/ *adj* **1** all in complete agreement; of one mind. **2** of an opinion, decision, etc: shared or arrived at by all, with none disagreeing. ○ **unanimity** *n*. ○ **unanimously** *adv*.

unannounced *adj* not announced; unexpectedly or without warning.

unapproachable *adj* **1** out of reach; inaccessible. **2** with a manner that discourages familiarity; aloof; unfriendly.

unarmed *adj* not armed; without weapons.

unasked-for *adj* not sought or invited.

unassailable *adj* **1** not able to be assailed or attacked. **2** not able to be challenged or denied. ○ **unassailably** *adv*.

unassuming *adj* modest or unpretentious.

unattached *adj* **1** not attached, associated or connected, esp to a particular group, organization, etc. **2** not in a steady romantic or sexual relationship.

unattended *adj* **1** not accompanied or watched over. **2** (*often* **unattended to**) not listened to or paid attention.

unavailing *adj* of efforts, etc: futile; of no avail.

unavoidable *adj* not able to be avoided; inevitable. ○ **unavoidably** *adv*.

unaware *adj* with no knowledge (of something); not aware or conscious (of it). ➤ *adv* unawares.

unaware, unawares These words are often confused with each other.

unawares *adv* **1** unexpectedly; by surprise. **2** without knowing or realizing; inadvertently.

unbalance *vb* **1** to throw someone or something off balance. **2** to upset someone's mental balance.

unbalanced *adj* **1** not in a state of physical balance. **2** lacking mental balance. **3** eg of a view or judgement: lacking impartiality. **4** *bookkeeping* not adjusted so as to show balance of debtor and creditor.

unbearable *adj* not bearable; unendurable. ○ **unbearably** *adv*.

unbeatable *adj* not able to be beaten or defeated.

unbeaten *adj* not beaten, esp not defeated or surpassed.

unbecoming *adj* (*also* **unbecoming for** or **to sb**) **1** not becoming; not suited to the wearer or showing them to advantage. **2** of behaviour, etc: not appropriate or fitting; unseemly.

unbeknown or **unbeknownst** *adv* (*usu* **unbeknown** or **unbeknownst to sb**) unknown to them; without their knowledge.

unbelievable *adj* **1** too unusual or unexpected to be believed. **2** *colloq* remarkable; astonishing. ○ **unbelievably** *adv.*

unbeliever *n* someone who does not believe, esp in a particular religion.

unbend *vb, tr & intr* **1** to relax (one's mind, behaviour, etc) from stiffness or formality; to make or become affable. **2** to straighten or release something from a bent or curved position.

unbending *adj* **1** not bending; unyielding or inflexible. **2** strict or severe.

unbiased or **unbiassed** *adj* not biased; unprejudiced or impartial.

unbidden *adj* **1** not commanded or ordered; spontaneous or voluntary. **2** not invited or solicited.

unbind *vb* **1** to release or free someone from a bond or restraint. **2** to unfasten or undo (a bond, manacle, etc).

unblinking *adj* without blinking; not showing emotion, esp fear.

unblushing *adj* **1** not blushing. **2** unashamed; shameless or brazen. ○ **unblushingly** *adv.*

unbolt *vb* to unfasten or open (a door, etc) by undoing or drawing back a bolt.

unborn *adj* of a baby: not yet born; still in the womb.

unbosom *vb* **1** to reveal or confess something. **2** *intr* (*often* **unbosom oneself**) to speak openly about what is on one's mind; to free oneself of worries or troubles by talking about them.

unbound *adj* **1** not bound or restrained. **2** loose; not tied or fastened with a band, etc. **3** of a book: without binding.

unbounded *adj* **1** without bounds or limits. **2** unchecked; unrestrained.

unbowed *adj* **1** not bowed or bent. **2** not conquered or forced to yield.

unbridled *adj* **1** of a horse: not wearing a bridle. **2** said of speech, emotion, etc: fully and freely felt or expressed.

unbroken *adj* **1** not broken; intact. **2** continuous or undisturbed. **3** not subdued in spirit or health. **4** of a horse or other animal: not broken in; untamed. **5** of a (sporting) record: not surpassed.

unburden *vb* **1** to remove a load or burden from someone or something. **2** (*often* **unburden oneself**) to relieve (oneself or one's mind) of worries, secrets, etc by confessing them to another person.

uncalled-for *adj* of a remark, etc: not warranted or deserved, esp unjustifiably rude or aggressive.

uncanny *adj* **1** weird, strange or mysterious, esp in an unsettling or uneasy way. **2** eg of skill or ability: beyond what is considered normal for an ordinary human being. ○ **uncannily** *adv.* ○ **uncanniness** *n.*

uncared-for *adj* not well looked-after.

unceasing *adj* never-ending.

unceremonious *adj* **1** without ceremony; informal. **2** with no regard for politeness or dignity; direct and abrupt. ○ **unceremoniously** *adv.*

uncertain *adj* **1** not sure, certain or confident. **2** not definitely known or decided. **3** not to be depended upon. **4** likely to change. ○ **uncertainly** *adv.* ○ **uncertainty** *n* (*-ies*) **1** the state or condition of being uncertain. **2** something that is uncertain. ♦ **in no uncertain terms 1** unambiguously. **2** strongly; emphatically.

uncharted *adj* **1** of territory, etc: **a** not fully explored or mapped in detail; **b** not shown on a map or chart. **2** of a non-physical area, a subject area, etc: not yet examined or fully investigated.

unchecked *adj* **1** not restrained. **2** not checked or verified.

unchristian *adj* **1** of a person, community, etc: not Christian. **2** not in accordance with the principles or spirit of Christianity; uncharitable or uncaring.

uncial /ˈʌnsɪəl/ *adj* of a form of writing: in large rounded letters with flowing strokes, of a kind used in ancient manuscripts. ➤ *n* **1** an uncial letter or form of writing. **2** a manuscript written in uncials.

uncivil *adj* rude or impolite.

uncivilized or **-ised** *adj* **1** of a people, tribe, etc: not civilized. **2** uncultured; rough.

unclassified *adj* **1** not classified. **2** of information: not classified as secret.

uncle *n* **1** the brother or brother-in-law of a father or mother. **2** the husband of an aunt. **3** *colloq* a form of address used by a child to a male friend of their parents. **4** *slang* a pawnbroker.

unclean *adj* **1** morally or spiritually impure. **2** of an animal: regarded for religious reasons as impure and unfit to be used as food. **3** dirty or foul.

Uncle Sam *n, colloq* the United States, its government or its people.

Uncle Tom *n, offensive* a Black person who behaves subserviently to Whites.

unclog *vb* to free something from an obstruction; to unblock it.

unclothe *vb* **1** to remove the clothes from someone. **2** to uncover or reveal something.

uncoil *vb, tr & intr* to untwist or unwind something, or to become untwisted.

uncomfortable *adj* **1** not comfortable. **2** feeling, involving or causing discomfort or unease. ○ **uncomfortably** *adv.*

uncommitted *adj* not bound or pledged to support any particular party, policy, action, etc.

uncommon *adj* **1** rare or unusual. **2** remarkably great; extreme. ○ **uncommonly** *adv* in an uncommon way or to an uncommon degree.

uncommunicative *adj* not communicative; not inclined to talk, express opinions, etc.

uncomplicated *adj* not complicated; straightforward.

uncompromising *adj* **1** unwilling to compromise or submit. **2** sheer; out-and-out. ○ **uncompromisingly** *adv.*

unconcern *n* lack of concern or interest.

unconcerned *adj* **1** lacking concern or interest; indifferent. **2** not anxious; untroubled. ○ **unconcernedly** /ˌʌnkənˈsɜːnɪdlɪ/ *adv.*

unconditional *adj* **1** not conditional; with no conditions or limits imposed. **2** complete or absolute. ○ **unconditionally** *adv.*

unconscionable /ʌnˈkɒnʃənəbəl/ *adj* **1** of a person, behaviour, etc: without conscience; unscrupulous. **2** outrageous; unthinkable. **3** unreasonably excessive. ○ **unconscionably** *adv.*

unconscious *adj* **1** of a person or animal: in a state of insensibility, characterized by loss of awareness of the external environment, and inability to respond to sensory stimuli. **2** of an action, behaviour, etc: characterized by lack of awareness; unintentional; not deliberate. **3** *psychol* relating to or produced by the unconscious. ➤ *n* (**the unconscious**) *psychol* in psychoanalysis: the part of the mind that contains memories, thoughts and feelings of which one is not consciously aware, but which may be manifested as dreams, psychosomatic symptoms or certain patterns of behaviour. ○ **unconsciously** *adv.* ○ **unconsciousness** *n.*

unconstitutional *adj* not allowed by or consistent with a nation's constitution. ○ **unconstitutionally** *adv.*

unconventional *adj* not conventional; not conforming to the normal or accepted standards, rules, etc; unusual. ○ **unconventionally** *adv.*

unco-ordinated *adj* **1** not co-ordinated. **2** of a person's movements: lacking co-ordination; clumsy or awkward.

uncork *vb* **1** to remove the cork from (a bottle, etc). **2** *colloq* to release (eg emotion) from a pent-up state.

uncountable *adj* **1** not able to be counted; innumerable. **2** *ling* of a noun: that cannot be used with the indefinite article or form a plural.

uncounted *adj* **1** not counted. **2** not able to be counted.

uncouple *vb* **1** to undo the coupling of, or between (two or more things); to disconnect or release. **2** *intr* to become unfastened or disconnected.

uncouth *adj* coarse or awkward in behaviour, manners or language; uncultured or lacking refinement.

uncover *vb* **1** to remove the cover or top from something. **2** to reveal or expose something.

uncovered *adj* **1** not covered; bare; revealed or exposed. **2** not protected by insurance.

uncross *vb* to change or move something from a crossed position: *He uncrossed his legs.*

uncrowned *adj* **1** of a monarch: not yet crowned. **2** with a specified status but not a formal title; denoting an acknowledged master or expert in something: *He's the uncrowned king of swindlers.*

unction *n* **1** *Christianity* **a** the act of ceremonially anointing a person with oil; **b** the oil used. **2** ointment of any kind. **3** anything that soothes, such as words or thoughts.

unctuous *adj* **1** insincerely and excessively charming. **2** oily; greasy. ○ **unctuously** *adv.*

uncut *adj* **1** not cut. **2** of a book: **a** with the pages not (yet) cut open; **b** with the margins untrimmed. **3** of a book, film, etc: with no parts cut out; unabridged. **4** of a gemstone, esp a diamond: not cut into a regular shape.

undaunted *adj* not daunted; not discouraged or put off. ○ **undauntedly** *adv.*

undead *adj* eg of a vampire, zombie, etc: supposedly dead but still able to move around, etc.

undeceive *vb* to free someone from a mistaken belief; to reveal the truth to them.

undecided *adj* **1** of a problem, question, etc: not (yet) decided; not settled. **2** of a person: not (yet) having decided or not able to decide; hesitating or irresolute. ○ **undecidedly** *adv.*

undeniable *adj* **1** not able to be denied; unquestionably or obviously true. **2** clearly and indisputably excellent. ○ **undeniably** *adv.*

under *prep* **1 a** below or beneath something but not in contact with it: *under the table*; **b** below or beneath something and in contact with it: *under the book*. **2** at the foot of: *under the column*. **3** less than; short of: *under 10 per cent*. **4** lower in rank than. **5** during the reign or administration of: *under Queen Elizabeth II*. **6** subjected to, receiving or sustaining: *under consideration • under pressure*. **7** in the category or classification of. **8** known by: *under the name of Colonel Villiers*. **9** according to: *under the terms of the agreement*. **10** in view of; because of: *under the circumstances*. **11** propelled by: *under sail*. **12** of a field: planted with (a particular crop). **13** *astrol* within the influence of (a sign of the zodiac). ➤ *adv* **1** in or to a lower place, position or rank. **2** into a state of unconsciousness. ➤ *adj* lower. ♦ **under way 1** of a process, activity, project, etc: in progress. **2** *naut* of a vessel: in motion.

underachieve *vb, intr* to be less successful than expected, esp academically; to fail to fulfil one's potential. ○ **underachiever** *n.*

under-age *adj* **1** of a person: below an age required by law; too young: *At seventeen he was under-age*. **2** of an activity, etc: carried on by an under-age person: *under-age drinking*.

underarm *adj* **1** of a style of bowling in sports, esp cricket, or of a service in tennis, etc: performed with the arm kept below the level of the shoulder. **2** eg of a bag, case, etc: placed or held under the arm. **3** relating to or for the armpit. ➤ *adv* with an underarm style or action. ➤ *n* the armpit.

underbelly *n* (**-ies**) **1** the part of an animal's belly that faces or is nearest the ground. **2** (*also* **soft underbelly**) any unprotected part vulnerable to attack.

undercarriage *n* **1** the landing gear of an aircraft, including wheels, shock absorbers, etc, used to take the impact on landing and support the aircraft on the ground. **2** the supporting framework or chassis of a carriage or vehicle.

undercharge vb **1** to charge someone too little money. **2** to put an insufficient charge in (eg an electrical circuit or explosive device).

underclass n a subordinate social class, esp a class of people disadvantaged in society through poverty, unemployment, etc.

underclothes pl n (also **underclothing**) UNDERWEAR.

undercoat n a layer of paint applied as preparation for the top or finishing coat. ➤ vb to apply an undercoat to (a surface).

undercook vb to cook (food) insufficiently or for too short a time.

undercover adj working, carried out, etc in secret: an undercover agent. ➤ adv in secret: working undercover for the secret police.

undercurrent n **1** an unseen current under the (often still) surface of a body of water. **2** an underlying trend or body of opinion, esp if different from the one generally perceived.

undercut vb /ˌʌndəˈkʌt/ **1** to offer goods or services at a lower price than (a competitor). **2** to cut away the underside of something. **3** sport to apply backspin to (a ball). ➤ n /ˈʌndəkʌt/ a part that is cut away underneath.

underdeveloped adj **1** insufficiently developed; immature or undersized. **2** of a country: with resources inadequately used, a low standard of living and, usu, also lacking capital and social organization to advance. **3** photog not sufficiently developed to produce a normal image.

underdog n **1** the competitor in a contest, etc who is considered unlikely to win. **2** anyone in adversity.

underdress vb to dress too plainly or with insufficient formality for a particular occasion. ○ **underdressed** adj.

underemployed adj **1** given less work than could realistically be done. **2** given work that fails to make good use of the skills possessed.

underestimate vb /ʌndərˈestɪmeɪt/ to make too low an estimate of (someone's or something's value, capacity, extent, etc). ➤ n /ʌndərˈestɪmət/ an estimate that is too low. ○ **underestimation** n.

underexpose vb, photog to expose (a film, plate or paper) for too little time or to too little light, resulting in a darkened photograph. ○ **underexposure** n.

underfelt n an old type of underlay, made of felt.

underfloor adj situated, operating, etc beneath the floor: underfloor heating.

underfoot adv **1** beneath the foot or feet; on the ground. **2** colloq in the way; always present and causing inconvenience.

underfund vb to provide (an organization, public service, etc) with insufficient funding to carry out all the planned activities. ○ **underfunding** n.

undergarment n any garment worn under other clothes, esp an item of underwear.

undergo vb to endure, experience or be subjected to something.

undergraduate n someone studying for a first degree in a higher education establishment.

underground n /ˈʌndəɡraʊnd/ **1** (often **the underground**; also **Underground**) a system of electric trains running in tunnels below ground. **2** a secret paramilitary organization fighting a government or occupying force. **3** any artistic movement seeking to challenge or overturn established views and practices. ➤ adj /ˈʌndəɡraʊnd/ **1** existing or operating below the surface of the ground: an underground station. **2** referring or relating to any political or artistic underground: underground music. ➤ adv /ʌndəˈɡraʊnd/ **1** to a position below ground level. **2** into hiding: They went underground.

undergrowth n a thick growth of shrubs and bushes among trees.

underhand adj **1** secretively deceitful or dishonest; sly. **2** sport UNDERARM. ➤ adv in an underhand way.

underhanded adv /ʌndəˈhandɪd/ UNDERHAND. ➤ adj /ˈʌndəhandɪd/ **1** UNDERHAND. **2** short of workers; undermanned.

underlay vb /ʌndəˈleɪ/ to lay underneath something, or support or provide with something laid underneath. ➤ n /ˈʌndəleɪ/ a thing laid underneath another, esp felt or rubber matting laid under a carpet for protection.

underlie vb **1** to lie underneath something. **2** to be the hidden cause or meaning of (an attitude, event, etc), beneath what is apparent, visible or superficial.

underline vb **1** to draw a line under (eg a word or piece of text). **2** to emphasize.

underling n, derog a subordinate.

underlying adj **1** lying under or beneath. **2** present though not immediately obvious: his underlying intentions. **3** fundamental; basic: the underlying causes.

undermanned adj provided with too few workers.

undermentioned adj mentioned or named below or later in the text.

undermine vb **1** to weaken or destroy something, esp gradually and imperceptibly: She undermined his confidence. **2** to dig or wear away the base or foundation of (land, cliffs, etc). **3** to tunnel or dig beneath (a wall, etc). ○ **undermining** adj, n.

underneath prep, adv beneath or below; under. ➤ adj lower. ➤ n a lower or downward-facing part or surface.

undernourished adj insufficiently nourished; living on less food than is necessary for normal health and growth. ○ **undernourishment** n.

underpaid adj not paid sufficiently; paid less than is due.

underpants pl n a man's undergarment covering the body from the waist or hips to (esp the tops of) the thighs.

underpart *n* (*usu* **underparts**) the lower side, esp the underside, or part of the underside, of an animal, bird, etc.

underpass *n, orig US* **1** a tunnel for pedestrians under a road or railway; a subway. **2** a road or railway passing under another.

underpay *vb* to pay less than is required or deserved. ○ **underpayment** *n*.

underperform *vb* **1** *intr* **a** to perform less well than expected; **b** of an investment: to be less profitable than expected. **2 a** to perform less well than (another); **b** of an investment: to be less profitable than (another investment). ○ **underperformance** *n*.

underpin *vb* **1** to support (a structure) from beneath, usu temporarily, with brickwork or a prop. **2** to support or corroborate. ○ **underpinning** *n*.

underplay *vb* **1** *tr & intr* to underact; to perform (a role) in a deliberately restrained or understated way. **2** to understate or play down the importance of something.

underprivileged *adj* deprived of the basic living standards and rights enjoyed by most people in society.

underrate *vb* to rate or assess something at a lower worth or value than it deserves; to have too low an opinion of something.

underrepresented *adj* esp of a minority social group or a specified type or specimen: not present in sufficient numbers, eg to accurately reflect opinions, statistics, etc.

underscore *vb* **1** to score or draw a line under something. **2** to stress or emphasize something. ➤ *n* a line inserted or drawn under a piece of text.

undersea *adj* situated or lying below the surface of the sea. ➤ *adv* below the sea or the surface of the sea.

underseal *n* /ˈʌndəsiːl/ an anti-rusting substance painted onto the underside of a motor vehicle. ➤ *vb* /ʌndəˈsiːl/ to apply such a substance to (a vehicle) in order to seal the metal for protection.

under-secretary *n* a junior minister or senior civil servant in a government department.

undersell *vb* **1** to sell goods or services at a lower price than (a competitor). **2** to sell (goods, etc) at less than their real value or for less than the usual price.

undershirt *n, chiefly N Am* a vest.

undershoot *vb* **1** of an aircraft: to land short of (a runway). **2** to fall short of (a target, etc).

underside *n* the downward-facing side or surface.

undersigned *adj* whose names are signed below: *we, the undersigned …*

undersized *adj* referring to something of less than the usual size.

underskirt *n* a thin skirt-like undergarment worn under a dress or skirt; a petticoat.

understaffed *adj* of a business, organization,

etc: provided with too few members of staff. ○ **understaffing** *n*.

understand *vb* **1** to grasp the meaning of (a subject, words, a person, a language, etc): *I've never understood trigonometry • Do you understand Polish?* **2** to make out the significance, cause, etc of something: *I don't understand what all the fuss is about.* **3** to have sympathetic awareness of someone or something: *I fully understand your point of view.* **4** to infer from the available information: *Did he really get the sack? I understood that he'd resigned.* ○ **understandable** *adj.* ○ **understandably** *adv.* ♦ **understand each other** or **one another 1** to know and accept each other's opinions, feelings, etc. **2** to agree.

understanding *n* **1** the act of understanding or the ability to understand. **2** someone's perception or interpretation of information received. **3** an informal agreement. **4** a sympathetic harmony of viewpoints. **5** a condition agreed upon: *It's on the understanding that you stay for six months.* ➤ *adj* sympathetic to, or keenly aware of, the feelings and opinions of others.

understate *vb* **1** to describe something as being less or more moderate than is really the case. **2** to express something in very restrained or moderate terms, often for ironic or dramatic effect. ○ **understatement** *n.*

understated *adj* **1** referring to something that understates. **2** of clothes, someone's appearance, etc: effective through simplicity; not showy.

understeer *vb, intr* of a motor vehicle: to have a tendency to turn less sharply than it should. ➤ *n* a tendency in a motor vehicle to understeer.

understood *adj* **1** implied but not expressed or stated. **2** realized without being, or needing to be, openly stated. ➤ *vb, past tense, past participle of* UNDERSTAND.

understudy *vb* **1** to study or prepare (a role or part) so as to be able to replace the actor or actress who usu plays that part, in case of absence, etc. **2** *tr & intr* to act as understudy to (an actor or actress). ➤ *n* (*-ies*) **1** an actor or actress who understudies a role. **2** any person who is trained to replace another in case of absence, etc.

undertake *vb* **1** to accept (a duty, responsibility or task). **2** to promise or agree.

undertaker *n* a person whose job is to organize funerals and prepare the bodies of the dead for burial or cremation.

undertaking *n* **1** a duty, responsibility or task undertaken. **2** a promise or guarantee. **3** the work of an undertaker. **4 a** using the nearside lane to pass a slow-moving vehicle; **b** an instance of this.

under-the-counter *adj* of goods: obtained or sold illicitly, surreptitiously, etc.

underthings *pl n* underclothes, esp a woman's or girl's.

undertone *n* **1** a quiet tone of voice. **2** an underlying quality, emotion or shade of a colour. **3** a subdued sound or shade of a colour.

undertow *n* an undercurrent in the sea that flows in the opposite direction to the surface current.

undervalue *vb* **1** to place too low a value on something. **2** to appreciate something insufficiently: *Everybody tends to undervalue Barry's contribution to the team.*

underwater *adj* situated, carried out, happening, etc under the surface of the water. ➤ *adv* below the surface of the water.

underwear *n* clothes, eg bras, pants, etc, worn under shirts, trousers, dresses and skirts, etc, and usu next to the skin.

underweight *n* /ˈʌndəweɪt/ lack or insufficiency of weight. ➤ *adj* /ʌndəˈweɪt/ **1** lacking in weight; not heavy enough. **2** of a person: weighing less than is normal or healthy for their height, build, etc.

underwhelm *vb, jocular* to fail to impress or make any impact on someone.

underwired *adj* of a bra: with a thin band of wire under each cup.

underworld *n* **1** *myth* a world imagined to lie beneath the earth's surface, the home of the souls of the dead. **2** a hidden sphere of life or stratum of society, etc, esp the world of criminals.

underwrite *vb* **1** to write (words, figures, etc) beneath other written matter. **2** to agree to finance (a commercial venture) and accept the loss in the event of failure. **3** to agree to buy, or find a buyer for, leftover shares from (a sale of shares to the public). **4** to issue (an insurance policy), accepting the risk involved. ○ **underwriter** *n*.

undesirable *adj* not desirable; unpleasant or objectionable in some way. ➤ *n* someone or something that is considered undesirable.

undies /ˈʌndɪz/ *pl n, colloq* items of underwear, esp women's bras, pants, etc.

undiluted *adj* **1** not diluted. **2** complete; utter: *He told a pack of undiluted lies.*

undine /ˈʌndiːn/ *n* a nymph; a female water spirit.

undo *vb* (*undoes, undid, undone*) **1** *tr & intr* to open, unfasten or untie (something). **2** to cancel or reverse the doing of something, or its effect or result; to annul. **3** *facetious or literary* to bring about the downfall or ruin of someone or something.

undoing *n* **1** the act or action of unfastening, untying, opening etc. **2** a downfall or ruin; **b** the cause of it. ◆ **be the undoing of sb** to bring about their downfall: *Alcohol will be the undoing of her.*

undone[1] *adj* not done; not achieved; unfinished or incomplete.

undone[2] *adj* **1** unfastened, untied, etc. **2** reversed; annulled. **3** destroyed; ruined: *I am undone!*

undoubted *adj* beyond doubt or question; clear; evident. ○ **undoubtedly** *adv*.

undreamed or **undreamt** *adj* (*usu undreamed-of* or *undreamt-of*) not even imagined or dreamed of, esp thought never to be likely or possible.

undress *vb* **1** to take the clothes off oneself (or another person). **2** *intr* to take one's clothes off. ➤ *n* **1** nakedness, or near-nakedness: *She walked out of the bathroom in a state of undress.* **2** casual or informal dress. **3** *mil* ordinary uniform as opposed to full military dress (as worn on ceremonial occasions).

undressed *adj* **1** of stone, animal hide, etc: not treated, prepared or processed for use. **2** of food, esp salad: without a dressing. **3** not wearing clothes; partially or completely naked. **4** *mil* not wearing formal dress or full dress uniform.

undue *adj* **1** unjustifiable; improper. **2** inappropriately or unjustifiably great; excessive: *undue criticism.* ○ **unduly** *adv* **1** unjustifiably. **2** excessively.

undulant or **undulating** *adj* rising and falling like waves.

undulate *vb* **1** *tr & intr* to move or to make something move in or like waves. **2** *tr & intr* to have or to give something a wavy surface, form, etc. ○ **undulatory** *adj*.

undulation *n* **1** the action of undulating. **2** a wave-like motion or form. **3** waviness. **4** a wave.

undying *adj* referring to something that does not die; eternal.

unearned *adj* not deserved or merited.

unearned income *n* income, such as dividends and interest earned on savings or from property, that is not remuneration for work done.

unearth *vb* **1** to dig something up out of the ground. **2** to discover something by investigation, or by searching or rummaging; to bring it to light.

unearthly *adj* **1** not of this earth; heavenly or sublime. **2** supernatural; weird; ghostly; mysterious. **3** *colloq* ridiculous or outrageous, esp outrageously early: *He woke me at an unearthly hour.* ○ **unearthliness** *n*.

unease *n* lack of ease; discomfort or apprehension.

uneasy *adj* (*-ier, -iest*) **1** nervous, anxious or unsettled; ill at ease. **2** unlikely to prove lasting; unstable. **3** causing anxiety; unsettling. ○ **uneasily** *adv*. ○ **uneasiness** *n*.

uneconomic *adj* not economic; not in accordance with sound economic principles, esp unprofitable.

uneconomical *adj* not economical; wasteful.

unemployable *adj* unable or unfit for paid employment.

unemployed *adj* **1** without paid employment. **2** not in use or not made use of.

unemployment *n* **1** the state or condition of being unemployed. **2** the number or percentage of unemployed people in a particular region, country, etc.

unenforceable adj of a law, contract, etc: not able to be enforced, esp legally.

unenviable adj not to be envied; not provoking envy, esp because unpleasant or disagreeable: an unenviable task.

unequal adj 1 not equal in quantity, value, rank, size, etc. 2 of a contest, etc: not evenly matched or balanced. 3 (usu **unequal to sth**) unable to carry it out, deal with it, etc; inadequate. ○ **unequally** adv.

unequalled adj without equal; not matched by any other; supreme.

unequivocal adj clearly stated or expressed. ○ **unequivocally** adv.

unerring adj 1 not missing the mark or target; sure or certain. 2 consistently true or accurate; never making an error. ○ **unerringly** adv.

uneven adj 1 of a surface, etc: not smooth or flat; bumpy. 2 of a contest: with contestants or sides poorly matched; unequal. 3 not equal; not matched or corresponding. ○ **unevenly** adv. ○ **unevenness** n.

uneventful adj during which nothing interesting or out of the ordinary happens; uninteresting or routine. ○ **uneventfully** adv.

unexampled adj 1 unprecedented. 2 unequalled; unparalleled.

unexceptionable adj impossible to criticize or object to; completely satisfactory, suitable, etc.

unexceptional adj 1 not admitting or forming an exception. 2 run-of-the-mill. ○ **unexceptionally** adv.

unexpected adj not expected; surprising; unforeseen. ○ **unexpectedly** adv. ○ **unexpectedness** n.

unfailing adj 1 remaining constant; never weakening or failing. 2 continuous. 3 certain; sure. ○ **unfailingly** adv.

unfair adj 1 not fair or just; inequitable. 2 involving deceit or dishonesty. ○ **unfairly** adv. ○ **unfairness** n.

unfaithful adj 1 not faithful to a sexual partner, usu by having a sexual relationship with someone else. 2 not loyal. 3 not true to a promise. ○ **unfaithfully** adv. ○ **unfaithfulness** n.

unfamiliar adj 1 not (already or previously) known, experienced, etc. 2 strange; unusual. 3 (usu **unfamiliar with sth**) of a person: not familiar or well acquainted with it. ○ **unfamiliarity** n.

unfasten vb 1 to undo or release something from a fastening. 2 intr to open or become loose. ○ **unfastened** adj 1 released from fastening. 2 not fastened; loose.

unfathomable adj 1 unable to be understood or fathomed; incomprehensible. 2 too deep or vast to measure or fathom. ○ **unfathomably** adv. ○ **unfathomed** adj 1 unsounded; of unknown depth or meaning. 2 not fully explored or understood.

unfavourable or (US) **unfavorable** adj 1 not favourable; adverse or inauspicious. 2 of features, appearance, etc: ill-favoured; disagreeable or unattractive. ○ **unfavourably** adv.

unfazed adj, colloq not disconcerted or perturbed.

unfeeling adj 1 without physical feeling or sensation. 2 hard-hearted. ○ **unfeelingly** adv.

unfettered adj not controlled or restrained.

unfiltered adj 1 not filtered. 2 of a cigarette: without a filter.

unfit adj 1 (often **unfit for** or **to** or **to do sth**) of a person: not suitably qualified for it; not good enough; incompetent. 2 (often **unfit for sth**) of a thing: not suitable or appropriate for it. 3 not fit; not in good physical condition.

unflappable adj, colloq never becoming agitated, flustered or alarmed; always remaining calm under pressure. ○ **unflappability** n.

unflinching adj not flinching; showing a fearless determination in the face of danger or difficulty. ○ **unflinchingly** adv.

unfold vb 1 to open out the folds of something; to spread it out. 2 intr to open out or be spread out. 3 to reveal (a mystery, idea, etc); to make something clear. 4 intr to develop or be revealed gradually.

unforced adj 1 not compelled. 2 natural.

unfortunate adj 1 unlucky; suffering misfortune or ill-luck. 2 resulting from or constituting bad luck: an unfortunate injury. 3 regrettable. ➤ n an unfortunate person. ○ **unfortunately** adv 1 in an unfortunate way; unluckily. 2 it's unfortunate that …; I'm sorry to say …: Unfortunately he can't come.

unfounded adj of allegations, ideas, rumours, etc: not based on fact; without foundation.

unfreeze vb 1 tr & intr to thaw or cause something to thaw. 2 to free (eg prices, wages or funds) from a restriction or control imposed, eg by a government.

unfriendly adj 1 not friendly; somewhat hostile. 2 not favourable. ○ **unfriendliness** n.

unfrock vb to defrock; to deprive (someone in holy orders) of ecclesiastical office or function.

unfurl vb, tr & intr to open, spread out or unroll something from a rolled-up or tied-up state.

unfurnished adj esp of a rented property: lacking furniture.

ungainly adj (-ier, -iest) awkward and ungraceful in movement; clumsy. ○ **ungainliness** n.

ungodly adj 1 wicked or sinful; irreligious. 2 colloq outrageous, esp outrageously early: an ungodly hour. ○ **ungodliness** n.

ungovernable adj esp of a person's temper, etc: uncontrollable; not able to be restrained.

unguarded adj 1 without guard; unprotected. 2 of speech, behaviour, etc: **a** showing a lack of caution or alertness; **b** revealing. ○ **unguardedly** adv. ○ **unguardedness** n.

unguent /'ʌŋgwənt/ n ointment or salve.

ungulate /'ʌŋgjʊlət/ adj, chiefly zool 1 with the form of a hoof; hoof-shaped. 2 of a mammal: hoofed. ➤ n a hoofed mammal.

unhallowed adj 1 of ground, etc: not formally hallowed or consecrated. 2 not of a hallowed character; unholy.

unhand *vb, archaic or jocular* to let go of someone; to release them from one's grasp or take one's hands off them.

unhappy *adj* **1** sad; in low spirits; miserable. **2** bringing sadness; unfortunate: *an unhappy ending to the film.* **3** inappropriate; infelicitous: *an unhappy choice of words.* ○ **unhappily** *adv.* ○ **unhappiness** *n.*

unhealthy *adj* **1** not conducive to health; harmful. **2** suffering from, or showing evidence of, ill health. **3** flouting or corrupting moral standards. **4** causing or likely to cause anxiety or worry; psychologically damaging: *an unhealthy attitude.* **5** *colloq* dangerous to life. ○ **unhealthily** *adv.* ○ **unhealthiness** *n.*

unheard *adj* **1** not heard; not perceived with the ear. **2** not listened to; not heeded; ignored.

unheard-of *adj* **1** not known to have ever happened or been done before; unprecedented. **2** not at all famous; unknown: *an unheard-of comedian.*

unhinge *vb* **1 a** to remove (a door, etc) from its hinges; **b** to remove the hinges from (a door, etc). **2** to unbalance or derange (a person or a person's mind). ○ **unhinged** *adj.*

unholy *adj* **1** not holy or sacred. **2** wicked; sinful; irreligious. **3** *colloq* outrageous; dreadful. ○ **unholiness** *n.*

unhook *vb* **1** to remove or free something from a hook or hooks. **2** to unfasten the hook or hooks of (eg a dress or other garment). **3** *intr* to unfasten or become unfastened.

uni *n, colloq* short form of UNIVERSITY.

unicameral *adj* of a parliamentary system: with only one law-making body or chamber.

unicellular *adj, biol* of organisms or structures, eg bacteria, protozoa and many spores: consisting of a single cell.

unicorn *n* a mythical animal in the form of a horse (usu a white one) with a long straight spiralled horn growing from its forehead.

unicycle *n* a cycle consisting of a single wheel with a seat and pedals attached, used esp in circus performances, etc. ○ **unicyclist** *n.*

unidentified *adj* **1** not identified. **2** too strange to identify. ○ **unidentifiable** *adj.*

unification *n* **1** an act or the process of unifying or uniting. **2** the state of being unified.

uniform *n* **1** distinctive clothing, always of the same colour, cut, etc, worn by all members of a particular organization or profession, eg by schoolchildren or soldiers. **2** a single set of such clothing. **3** the recognizable appearance, or a distinctive feature or way of dressing, that is typical of a particular group of people. ➤ *adj* **1** unchanging or unvarying in form, nature or appearance; always the same, regardless of changes in circumstances, etc. **2** alike all over or throughout. **3** with the same form, character, etc as another or others; alike or like. **4** forming part of a military or other uniform. ➤ *vb* **1** to make (several people or things) uniform or alike. **2** to fit out or provide (a number of soldiers, etc) with uniforms. ○ **uniformed**

adj wearing a uniform. ○ **uniformly** *adv.* ○ **uniformness** *n.*

uniformity *n* **1** the state or fact of being uniform; conformity or similarity between several things, constituent parts, etc; sameness. **2** monotony; lack of variation.

unify *vb* (*-ies, -ied*) to bring (two or more things) together to form a single unit or whole; to unite. ○ **unifiable** *adj.*

unilateral *adj* **1** occurring on, affecting or involving one side only. **2** affecting, involving or done by only one person or group among several: *unilateral disarmament.* ○ **unilaterally** *adv.*

unilateralism *n* a policy or the practice of unilateral action, esp of unilateral nuclear disarmament. ○ **unilateralist** *n* a supporter or advocate of unilateralism. *adj* relating to or involving unilateralism.

unimpeachable *adj* indisputably reliable or honest; impossible to blame, find fault with, etc. ○ **unimpeachably** *adv.*

uninterested *adj* not interested; indifferent. ○ **uninterestedly** *adv.*

uninterested See note at **disinterested**.

uninteresting *adj* boring; not able to raise, or capable of raising, any interest. ○ **uninterestingly** *adv.*

union *n* **1 a** the action or an act of uniting two or more things; **b** the state of being united. **2** a united whole. **3** *formal* **a** a marriage; the state of wedlock; **b** sexual intercourse. **4** an association, confederation, etc of people or groups for a common (esp political) purpose. **5** agreement or harmony. **6** a league or association, esp a TRADE UNION. **7** a device that connects one thing with another, esp a connecting part for pipes, etc. **8** (*also* Union) **a** an organization concerned with the interests and welfare of the students in a college, university, etc; **b** the building that houses such an organization. **9** a textile fabric made from more than one kind of fibre. **10** *maths* (symbol ∪) **a** a SET² (sense 2) comprising all the members (but no others) of two or more smaller sets; **b** the operation of forming such a set.

unionism or **Unionism** *n* **1** advocacy of combination into one body for the purposes of social or political organization. **2** *US* advocacy of or adherence to union between the States. **3** advocacy of or adherence to the principles of the former Unionist Party of Great Britain and Ireland or of any party advocating the continued political union of Great Britain and Northern Ireland. **4** advocacy of or support for continued political union between Scotland, England and Wales. **5** adherence to the principles and practices of trade unions. ○ **unionist** or **Unionist** *n, adj.*

unionize or **-ise** *vb* **1** to organize (a workforce) into a trade union or trade unions. **2** *intr* to join or constitute a trade union. ○ **unionization** *n.*

Union Jack *n* (*also* Union flag) the national flag

of the United Kingdom, combining the crosses of St Andrew, St George and St Patrick.

unique adj 1 sole or solitary; of which there is only one. 2 referring to something that is the only one of its kind; without equal; unparalleled, esp in excellence. 3 (usu **unique to sb** or **sth**) referring to something that belongs solely to, or is associated solely with, them or it. 4 colloq, loosely extremely unusual; excellent. ○ **uniquely** adv. ○ **uniqueness** n.

unisex adj suited to, for use by, or to be worn by, both men and women: a unisex sauna.

unisexual adj 1 relating to or restricted to one sex only. 2 bot, zool of certain organisms: with either male or female reproductive organs but not both. 3 unisex.

unison n 1 mus the interval between two notes of the same pitch, or which are one or more octaves apart. 2 the state of acting all in the same way at the same time. 3 (usu **in unison**) complete agreement.

unit n 1 a single item or element regarded as the smallest subdivision of a whole; a single person or thing. 2 a set of mechanical or electrical parts, or a group of workers, performing a specific function within a larger construction or organization. 3 a standard measure of a physical quantity, such as time or distance, specified multiples of which are used to express its size, eg an SI unit. 4 any whole number less than 10. 5 any subdivision of a military force. 6 a an item of furniture that combines with others to form a set; b a set of such items. 7 a standard measure used to calculate alcohol intake. 8 finance the smallest measure of investment in a UNIT TRUST.

Unitarian n a member of a religious group orig comprising Christians who believed God to be a single entity rather than a Trinity, now including members holding a broad spectrum of beliefs. ➤ adj relating to or characteristic of Unitarians. ○ **Unitarianism** n.

unitary adj 1 relating to, characterized by or based on unity. 2 referring or relating to the nature of a unit; individual. 3 relating to a unit or units.

unit cost n the actual cost of producing one item.

unite vb 1 tr & intr to make or become a single unit or whole. 2 tr & intr to bring or come together in a common purpose or belief. 3 to have or exhibit (features, qualities, etc) in combination. 4 tr & intr to join in marriage.

united adj 1 referring to something that is or has been united; joined together or combined. 2 relating or pertaining to, or resulting from, two or more people or things in union or combination. 3 (usu **United**) often in the names of churches, societies, etc and in the names of football clubs: made up of or resulting from the union of two or more parts: Dundee United.

United Kingdom n (in full **United Kingdom of Great Britain and Northern Ireland**) since 1922: the official title for the kingdom comprising England, Wales, Scotland and Northern Ireland.

United Nations sing or pl n an association of independent states formed in 1945 to promote peace and international co-operation.

United States sing or pl n (in full **United States of America**) a federal republic mostly in N America, comprising 50 states and the District of Columbia.

unit price n the price per unit of goods supplied.

unit trust n an investment scheme in which clients' money is invested in various companies, with the combined shares purchased divided into units which are allocated in multiples to each client according to the individual amount invested.

unity n (-ies) 1 the state or quality of being one; oneness. 2 a single unified whole. 3 the act, state or quality of forming a single unified whole from two or more parts. 4 agreement; harmony; concord. 5 maths the number or numeral 1.

Univ. abbrev University.

univalent adj, chem MONOVALENT.

universal adj 1 relating to the universe. 2 relating to, typical of, affecting, etc the whole world or all people. 3 relating to, typical of, affecting, etc all the people or things in a particular group. 4 colloq widespread; general: He won universal approval. 5 (abbrev **U**) in film classification: suitable for everyone. ➤ n 1 something that is universal. 2 philos a general term or concept, or the nature or type signified by such a term. ○ **universality** n. ○ **universally** adv.

universal joint or **universal coupling** n a joint or coupling, esp between two rotating shafts, that allows movement in all directions.

universe n 1 astron a (**the Universe**) all existing space, energy and matter; b a star system; a galaxy. 2 the world; all people.

university n (-ies) 1 a higher education institution with the authority to award degrees and usu having research facilities. 2 the buildings, staff or students of such an institution.

UNIX or **Unix** /ˈjuːnɪks/ n, trademark, comput a type of operating system designed to handle large file transfers and allow multi-user access of data.

unkempt adj 1 of hair: uncombed. 2 of general appearance: untidy; dishevelled.

unkind adj unsympathetic, cruel or harsh. ○ **unkindly** adv. ○ **unkindness** n.

unknowing adj 1 not knowing; ignorant. 2 (often **unknowing of sth**) ignorant or unaware of it. ○ **unknowingly** adv.

unknown adj 1 not known; unfamiliar. 2 not at all famous. ➤ n 1 an unknown person or thing. 2 (usu **the unknown**) something that is unknown, undiscovered, unexplored, etc.

unknown quantity n a person or thing whose precise identity, nature or influence is not known or cannot be predicted.

unlace vb 1 to undo or loosen the lace or laces

of (shoes, etc). **2** to unfasten or remove garments, etc from (oneself or someone else) by undoing the laces or lacing.

unlawful assembly *n, law* a meeting of three or more people that is considered likely to cause a breach of the peace or endanger the public.

unleaded *adj* (*also* **lead-free**) of petrol: free from lead additives, eg antiknocking agents.

unlearn *vb* **1** to try actively to forget something learned; to rid the memory of it. **2** to free oneself from (eg an acquired habit).

unlearned¹ /ʌnˈlɜːnɪd/ *adj* not well educated; uneducated.

unlearned² /ʌnˈlɜːnd/ *or* **unlearnt** /ʌnˈlɜːnt/ *adj* **1** of a lesson, etc: not learnt. **2** of a skill, etc: not acquired by learning; instinctive; innate.

unleash *vb* **1** to release (eg a dog) from a leash. **2** to release or give free expression to (eg anger).

unleavened /ʌnˈlɛvənd/ *adj* of bread: not leavened; made without yeast.

unless *conj* if not; except when; except if: *Unless you come in now you won't get any tea.*

unlettered *adj* **1** uneducated. **2** illiterate.

unlike *prep* **1** different from: *Unlike her, he's going shopping today.* **2** not typical or characteristic of: *It's unlike her to be late.* ➤ *adj* not like or alike; different; dissimilar. ○ **unlikeness** *n.*

unlikely *adj* **1** not expected or likely to happen. **2** not obviously suitable; improbable. **3** probably untrue; implausible. ○ **unlikeliness** *or* **unlikelihood** *n.*

unlimited *adj* **1** not limited or restricted. **2** *loosely* very great or numerous.

unlined¹ *adj* free from or not marked with lines: *a youthful unlined face • unlined paper.*

unlined² *adj* of a garment, etc: without any lining.

unlisted *adj* **1** not entered on a list. **2** *stock exchange* of securities: not dealt in on the Stock Exchange. **3** *chiefly N Am* of a telephone number: ex-directory.

unlit *adj* not lit; without lights or lighting.

unlived-in *adj* not lived in; not homely or comfortable: *That cottage looks unlived-in.*

unload *vb* **1** *tr & intr* to remove (a load or cargo) from (a vehicle, ship, etc). **2** to relieve (oneself or one's mind) of troubles or anxieties by telling them to another. **3** to remove the charge of ammunition from (a gun) without firing it. **4** to dispose or get rid of (something undesirable).

unlock *vb* **1** to undo the lock of (a door, etc). **2** to free someone or something from being locked up. **3** to release or reveal (eg emotions, etc): *The accident unlocked the memory of her father's death.*

unlooked-for *adj* **1** unexpected. **2** not deliberately encouraged or invited.

unloose *or* **unloosen** *vb* to set free; to release.

unlovely *adj* unattractive; unpleasant or ugly.

unlucky *adj* **1** bringing, resulting from or constituting bad luck. **2** having, or tending

to have, bad luck. **3** regrettable. ○ **unluckily** *adv.*

unmade *adj* **1** not yet made. **2** of a bed: with bedclothes not arranged neatly. **3** of a road: with no proper surface (eg of tarmac).

unmake *vb* to cancel or destroy the (esp beneficial) effect of something.

unman *vb, old use, literary* **1** to cause someone to lose self-control, esp to overcome with emotion. **2** to deprive of someone of their virility.

unmanly *adj* **1** not manly; not virile or masculine. **2** weak or cowardly. ○ **unmanliness** *n.*

unmanned *adj* esp of a vehicle or spacecraft: without personnel or a crew, esp controlled remotely or automatically; not manned.

unmannerly *adj* ill-mannered; impolite. ○ **unmannerliness** *n.*

unmapped *adj* **1** not appearing on a geographical or chromosome map. **2** unexplored; untried: *We're now entering unmapped territory.*

unmask *vb, tr & intr* **1** to remove a mask or disguise from (oneself or someone else). **2** to reveal the true identity or nature of (oneself or someone else).

unmentionable *adj* not fit to be mentioned or talked about, esp because considered indecent. ➤ *n* **1** (**unmentionables**) *humorous* underwear. **2** (*often* **unmentionables**) someone or something that cannot or should not be mentioned.

unmerciful *adj* **1** merciless; not merciful. **2** unpleasantly great or extreme. ○ **unmercifully** *adv.*

unmissable *adj* of a TV programme, film, etc: too good to be missed.

unmistakable *or* **unmistakeable** *adj* too easily recognizable to be mistaken for anything or anyone else; certain; unambiguous. ○ **unmistakably** *or* **unmistakeably** *adv.*

unmitigated *adj* **1** not lessened or made less severe. **2** unqualified; absolute; out-and-out: *an unmitigated disaster.*

unmoral *adj* not moral; with no relation to morality.

unmoved *adj* **1** still in the same place. **2** not persuaded. **3** not affected by emotion; calm.

unmoving *adj* **1** still; stationary. **2** lacking the power to affect the emotions.

unnatural *adj* **1** contrary to the way things usually happen in nature. **2** abnormal. **3** intensely evil or cruel. **4** insincere; affected. ○ **unnaturally** *adv.*

unnecessary *adj* **1** not necessary. **2** more than is expected or required: *She spoke with unnecessary caution.* ○ **unnecessarily** *adv.*

unnerve *vb* **1** to deprive of strength; to weaken. **2** to deprive someone of courage or confidence. ○ **unnervingly** *adv.*

unnumbered *adj* **1** too numerous to be counted; innumerable. **2** not marked with or given a number.

unoccupied *adj* **1** not doing any work or engaged in any activity. **2** of a building, etc: without occupants or inhabitants; empty. **3** of a country, region, etc: not occupied by foreign troops.

unofficial *adj* **1** not officially authorized or confirmed. **2** not official or formal in character. **3** of a strike: not called or sanctioned by the strikers' trade union. ○ **unofficially** *adv.*

unorganized or **-ised** *adj* **1** not organized; not brought into an organized state or form. **2** of a workforce: not formed into or represented by a trade union.

unpack *vb* **1** to take something out of a packed state. **2** to empty (eg a suitcase, bag, etc) of packed contents. **3** *comput* to UNZIP (sense 3).

unpalatable *adj* **1** of food, drink, etc: not having a pleasant taste. **2** of a suggestion, idea, film scene, etc: unacceptable; distasteful.

unparalleled *adj* so remarkable as to have no equal or parallel.

unparliamentary *adj* not in accordance with the established procedures by which, or with the spirit in which, a parliament is conducted.

unperson *n* someone whose existence is officially denied or ignored and who is deemed not to have existed.

unpick *vb* **1** to undo (stitches). **2** to take (a sewn or knitted article, seam, etc) to pieces by undoing the stitching.

unplanned *adj* **1** not planned or scheduled: *I made an unplanned stopover in Paris.* **2** of a pregnancy: accidental.

unpleasant *adj* not pleasant; disagreeable. ○ **unpleasantly** *adv.* ○ **unpleasantness** *n.*

unplug *vb* **1** to unblock or unstop (something that is plugged or blocked). **2** to disconnect (an electrical appliance) by removing its plug from a socket.

unplumbed *adj* **1** of a building, etc: without plumbing. **2** unfathomed; unsounded. **3** not fully understood.

unpolished *adj* **1** not polished. **2** unrefined; not cultured or sophisticated.

unpopular *adj* not popular; not popular or liked by an individual or by people in general. ○ **unpopularity** *n.*

unpractical *adj* with no practical skills; not good at practical tasks. ○ **unpractically** *adv.*

unpractised or (*US*) **unpracticed** *adj* **1** with little or no practice, experience or skill. **2** not, or not yet, put into practice.

unprecedented *adj* **1** without precedent; not known to have ever happened before. **2** unparalleled.

unprejudiced *adj* free from prejudice; impartial.

unprepossessing *adj* **1** unappealing; unattractive. **2** not creating or likely to create a good impression.

unprincipled *adj* without or showing a lack of moral principles.

unprintable *adj* not fit to be printed, esp because of being obscene or libellous.

unprofessional *adj* not in accordance with the rules governing, or the standards of conduct expected of, members of a particular pro-

fession. ○ **unprofessionally** *adv.*

unprotected *adj* **1** not protected. **2** of an act of sexual intercourse: performed without the use of a condom.

unputdownable *adj, colloq* of a book: so absorbing that it proves difficult to stop reading it.

unqualified *adj* **1** not having any formal qualifications; lacking the formal qualifications required for a particular job, etc. **2** not limited or moderated in any way. **3** absolute; out-and-out: *an unqualified success.* **4** not competent.

unquestionable *adj* beyond doubt or question. ○ **unquestionably** *adv.*

unquestioned *adj* **1** not questioned or interrogated. **2** not examined or inquired into. **3** not called into question; undisputed.

unquestioning *adj* not arguing or protesting; done, accepted, etc without argument, protest or thought. ○ **unquestioningly** *adv.*

unquote *vb* to indicate (in speech) the end of something that was said by someone else.

unravel *vb* **1** to separate out the strands of (a knitted or woven fabric). **2** to take something out of a tangled state. **3** to explain or make clear (something confusing or obscure, a mystery, etc). **4** *intr* to become unravelled.

unread *adj* **1** of a book, etc: not having been read. **2** of a person: not well-read; not educated or instructed through reading.

unreadable *adj* **1** too difficult or tedious to read. **2** illegible. **3** of facial expression, a remark, etc: uninterpretable.

unready *adj* **1** not ready. **2** not acting quickly; hesitant. ○ **unreadily** *adv.* ○ **unreadiness** *n.*

unreal *adj* **1** not real; illusory or imaginary. **2** *colloq* **a** exceptionally strange; incredible; **b** amazing; excellent. ○ **unreality** *n.*

unreasonable *adj* **1** not based on reason or good sense. **2** beyond what is reasonable or fair. ○ **unreasonably** *adv.*

unreasoning *adj* not reasoning; showing lack of reasoning; irrational.

unrelenting *adj* **1** refusing to change viewpoint or a chosen course of action. **2** not softened by feelings of mercy or pity. **3** constant; relentless; never stopping. ○ **unrelentingly** *adv.*

unremitting *adj* **1** not easing off or abating. **2** constant; never stopping. ○ **unremittingly** *adv.*

unrequited *adj* esp of love: not returned.

unreserved *adj* **1** not booked or reserved. **2** open and sociable in manner; showing no shyness or reserve. **3** not moderated or limited; unqualified. ○ **unreservedly** *adv.*

unrest *n* **1** a state of (esp public) discontent bordering on riotousness. **2** anxiety; unease.

unripe *adj* **1** not (yet) fully developed; not matured. **2** of fruit, etc: not (yet) ready to be harvested or eaten; not ripe.

unrivalled or (*US*) **unrivaled** *adj* far better than any other; unequalled.

unroll *vb* **1** to open something out from a rolled state. **2** *intr* to become unrolled. **3** *tr & intr* to become or make something visible or known; to unfold gradually.

unruffled *adj* **1** of a surface: smooth or still. **2** of a person: not agitated or flustered.

unruly *adj* (*-ier, -iest*) disobedient or disorderly, esp habitually. ○ **unruliness** *n.*

unsafe *adj* **1** not safe or secure; dangerous. **2** of a verdict, conclusion or decision: based on insufficient or suspect evidence.

unsaid *adj* not said, expressed, spoken, etc, esp when it might have been or should have been.

unsaturated *adj, chem* **1** of an organic chemical compound: containing at least one double or triple bond between its carbon atoms, eg unsaturated fats. **2** of a solution: not containing the maximum amount of a solid or gas (SOLUTE) that can be dissolved in it.

unsavoury or (*US*) **unsavory** *adj* unpleasant or distasteful; offensive. ○ **unsavouriness** *n.*

unsay *vb* (*unsaid*) to take back or withdraw (something said, eg a statement, etc).

unscathed *adj* **1** not harmed or injured. **2** without harm, injury or damage.

unschooled *adj* **1** not educated. **2** not skilled or trained in a specified field or area.

unscramble *vb* **1** to interpret (a coded or scrambled message). **2** to take something out of a jumbled state and put it in order. ○ **unscrambler** *n.*

unscrew *vb* **1** to remove or loosen something by taking out a screw or screws, or with a twisting or screwing action. **2** to loosen (a screw or lid). **3** *intr* to be removed or loosened by turning a screw or screws. **4** *intr* of a screw or lid: to be loosened or removed by a turning action.

unscripted *adj* of a speech, etc: made or delivered without a prepared script.

unscrupulous *adj* without scruples or moral principles. ○ **unscrupulously** *adv.*

unseal *vb* **1** to remove or break open the seal of (a letter, container, etc). **2** to free or open (something that is closed as if sealed).

unsealed *adj* not sealed; not closed, marked, etc with a seal.

unseasonable *adj* **1** (*also* **unseasonal**) esp of the weather: not appropriate to the time of year. **2** coming at a bad time. ○ **unseasonably** *adv.*

unseasoned *adj* **1** of food: without seasonings. **2** not matured: *unseasoned timber.* **3** not habituated through time or experience.

unseat *vb* **1** of a horse: to throw or knock (its rider) off. **2** to remove someone from an official post or position, esp from a parliamentary seat.

unseeded *adj, sport, esp tennis* not placed among the top players in the preliminary rounds of a tournament.

unseemly *adj* (*-ier, -iest*) not seemly; not becoming or fitting, esp because of being indecent. ○ **unseemliness** *n.*

unseen *adj* **1** not seen or noticed. **2** of a text for translation: not seen or prepared in advance.

➤ *n* **1** an unseen text for translation in an examination. **2** the translation of such a text.

unselfish *adj* **1** having or showing concern for others. **2** generous. ○ **unselfishly** *adv.* ○ **unselfishness** *n.*

unsettle *vb* **1** to make someone ill at ease; to disturb or disconcert them. **2** *intr* to become unsettled.

unsettled *adj* **1** lacking stability. **2** frequently changing or moving from place to place. **3** undecided or unresolved. **4** of the weather: changeable; unpredictable. **5** not relaxed or at ease. **6** of a debt: unpaid.

unshackle *vb* **1** to release someone from a shackle or shackles; to remove a shackle from them. **2** to set them free.

unsheathe *vb* to draw (esp a sword, knife, etc) from a sheath.

unsightly *adj* (*-ier, -iest*) not pleasant to look at. ○ **unsightliness** *n.*

unskilled *adj* not having or requiring any special skill or training: *unskilled jobs.*

unsmoked *adj* **1** of bacon, etc: not cured by smoking. **2** not used up by smoking: *an unsmoked cigar.*

unsociable *adj* **1** of a person: disliking or avoiding the company of other people. **2** not conducive to social intercourse. ○ **unsociably** *adv.*

unsocial *adj* **1** annoying, or likely to annoy, other people. **2** of working hours: falling outside the normal working day.

unsophisticated *adj* **1** not experienced or worldly; naive. **2** free from insincerity or artificiality. **3** lacking refinement or complexity; basic.

unsound *adj* **1** not reliable; not based on sound reasoning: *an unsound argument.* **2** not firm or solid. ○ **unsoundness** *n.* ♦ **of unsound mind** mentally ill; insane.

unsparing *adj* **1** giving generously or liberally. **2** showing no mercy; unrelenting. ○ **unsparingly** *adv.*

unspeakable *adj* **1** not able to be expressed in words; indescribable. **2** too bad, wicked or obscene to be spoken about. ○ **unspeakably** *adv.*

unsteady *adj* **1** not secure or firm. **2** of behaviour, character, etc: not steady or constant; erratic. **3** of movement, a manner of walking, etc: unsure or precarious. ○ **unsteadily** *adv.* ○ **unsteadiness** *n.*

unstick *vb* to free or separate something that is stuck to something else.

unstoppable *adj* unable to be stopped or prevented. ○ **unstoppably** *adv.*

unstructured *adj* without any formal structure or organization.

unstuck *adj* loosened or released from a stuck state. ♦ **come unstuck** *colloq* of a person, plan, etc: to suffer a setback; to go wrong.

unstudied *adj* not affected; natural and spontaneous.

unsubstantial *adj* **1** with no basis or foundation in fact. **2** without material substance. **3**

lacking strength or firmness.

unsung adj **1** of someone, an achievement, etc: not praised or recognized: *an unsung hero*. **2** not (yet) sung.

unsuspected adj **1** not suspected; not under suspicion. **2** not known or supposed to exist.

unswerving adj not deviating from a belief or aim; steadfast. ○ **unswervingly** adv.

untangle vb **1** to disentangle something; to free something from a tangled state. **2** to clear something of confusion.

untenable adj of an opinion, theory, argument, etc: not able to be maintained, defended or justified.

unthinkable adj **1** too unusual to be likely; inconceivable. **2** too unpleasant to think about.

unthinking adj **1** inconsiderate; thoughtless. **2** careless. ○ **unthinkingly** adv.

untidy adj not tidy; messy or disordered. ○ **untidily** adv. ○ **untidiness** n.

untie vb **1** to undo (a knot, parcel, etc) from a tied state. **2** intr of a knot, etc: to come unfastened. **3** to remove the constraints on something; to set something free.

until prep **1** up to the time of: *I worked until 8.* **2** up to the time of reaching (a place); as far as: *We slept until Paris.* **3** *with negatives* before: *not until Wednesday.* ➤ conj **1** up to the time that: *He waited until she emerged with the money.* **2** *with negatives* before: *not until I say so.*

untimely adj **1** happening before the proper or expected time: *an untimely death.* **2** coming at an inappropriate or inconvenient time. ○ **untimeliness** n.

unto prep, *archaic or literary* to.

untold adj **1** not told. **2** too severe to be described. **3** too many to be counted.

untouchable adj **1** not to be touched or handled. **2** discouraging physical contact. **3** above the law. **4** unable to be matched; unrivalled. ➤ n **1** an untouchable person or thing. **2** *formerly* in India: a member of the lowest social class or caste whose touch was regarded by members of higher castes as a contamination.

untoward adj **1** inconvenient; unfortunate. **2** adverse; unfavourable. **3** difficult to manage; unruly or intractable. **4** unseemly; improper.

untrue adj **1** not true. **2** not accurate. **3** unfaithful. ○ **untruly** adv.

untruth n **1** the fact or quality of being untrue. **2** something that is untrue; a lie.

untruthful adj not truthful; lying or untrue. ○ **untruthfully** adv.

untutored adj **1** uneducated; untaught. **2** unsophisticated.

unused adj **1** /ʌnˈjuːzd/ brand new; never used. **2** /ʌnˈjuːst/ (*always* **unused to sth**) not used or accustomed to it.

unusual adj not usual; uncommon; rare. ○ **unusually** adv.

unutterable adj so extreme or intense as to be impossible to express in words. ○ **unutterably** adv.

unvarnished adj **1** of an account, report, etc: not exaggerated or embellished. **2** not covered with varnish.

unveil vb **1** to remove a veil from (one's own or someone else's face). **2** to remove a curtain or other covering from (a plaque, monument, etc) as part of a formal opening ceremony. **3** to reveal something or make it known for the first time. ○ **unveiling** n **1** the action or an act of removing a veil. **2** the ceremony of opening or presenting something new for the first time.

unversed adj (*usu* **unversed in sth**) not experienced in it.

unvoiced adj **1** not spoken. **2** *phonetics* of a sound: pronounced without vibrating the vocal cords, like 'p'; voiceless.

unwaged adj **1** of work: unpaid. **2** of a person: **a** not in paid employment; out of work; **b** doing unpaid work.

unwarranted adj **1** not warranted; not justified. **2** not authorized.

unwary adj not wary; careless or incautious; not aware of possible danger. ○ **unwarily** adv. ○ **unwariness** n.

unwashed adj not washed; not clean. ◆ **the great unwashed** *colloq, jocular* the lower classes; the masses.

unwell adj not well; ill.

unwholesome adj **1** not conducive to physical or moral health; harmful. **2** of a person: of dubious character or morals. **3** diseased; not healthy-looking. **4** of food: of poor quality.

unwieldy adj **1** of an object: large and awkward to carry or manage. **2** of a person: clumsy; not graceful in movement; awkward or ungainly.

unwilling adj **1** reluctant; loath. **2** done, said, etc reluctantly. ○ **unwillingly** adv. ○ **unwillingness** n.

unwind vb **1** to undo, slacken, untwist, etc something that has been wound or coiled up. **2** intr of something that has been wound or coiled up: to come undone, to slacken, untwist, etc. **3** *tr & intr, colloq* to make or become relaxed.

unwise adj not prudent; ill-advised; foolish. ○ **unwisely** adv.

unwished adj (*usu* **unwished for**) **1** unwelcome; uninvited. **2** not wanted or desired.

unwitting adj **1** not realizing or being aware. **2** done without being realized or intended. ○ **unwittingly** adv.

unwonted /ʌnˈwountɪd/ adj not usual or habitual.

unworldly adj **1** not relating or belonging to this world; otherworldly. **2** not concerned with material things. **3** unsophisticated; naive. ○ **unworldliness** n.

unworthy adj **1** (*often* **unworthy of sth**) not deserving or worthy of it. **2** (*often* **unworthy of sb or sth**) not worthy or befitting to (a person's character, etc). **3** without worth; of little or no merit or value. **4** of treatment, etc: not warranted; undeserved or worse than is deserved.

○ **unworthily** *adv.* ○ **unworthiness** *n.*

unwrap *vb* **1** to remove the wrapping or covering from something; to open something by removing its wrapping. **2** *intr* of something that is wrapped: to become unwrapped; to have the covering come off.

unwritten *adj* **1** not recorded in writing or print. **2** of a rule or law: not formally enforceable, but traditionally accepted and followed.

unzip *vb* **1** to unfasten or open (a garment, etc) by undoing a zip. **2** *intr* to open or come apart by means of a zip. **3** (*also* **unpack**) *comput* to convert (data that has been compressed in order to save storage space) into a less compressed form.

up *prep* at or to a higher position on, or a position further along: *He climbed up the stairs • I'm walking up the road.* ➤ *adv* **1** at or to a higher position or level: *Lift it up • Turn up the volume • Prices went up.* **2** at or to a place higher up, or a more northerly place. **3** in or to a more erect position: *I stood up.* **4** fully or completely: *He used it up • eat up.* **5** into the state of being gathered together: *We saved up for it • I'll parcel up the presents.* **6** in or to a place of storage or lodging: *We can put them up for the night.* **7** out of bed: *He got up.* **8** to or towards: *He's travelling up to London • I walked up to him.* **9** formal to or at university: *She's up at Oxford.* ➤ *adj* (**upper, uppermost** or **upmost**) **1** placed in, or moving or directed to, a higher position. **2** out of bed: *He's not up yet.* **3** having an advantage; ahead: *two goals up.* **4** appearing in court: *up before the judge.* **5** of the sun: visible above the horizon. **6** relating to or involving (esp rail) transport to, rather than away from, a major place, esp London: *the up train • the up line.* ➤ *vb* (**upped, upping**) **1** to raise or increase something: *They upped the price.* **2** *intr, colloq* to start boldly or unexpectedly saying or doing something; to get up (and do something): *He upped and left her.* ➤ *n* **1** a success or advantage. **2** a spell of good luck or prosperity. ♦ **it's all up with sb** *colloq* there is no hope for them. **not up to much** *colloq* not good at all; no good. **on the up-and-up** *colloq* **1** steadily becoming more successful. **2** honest; on the level. **something's up** something is wrong or amiss. **up against sb** or **sth 1** situated or pressed close against them. **2** facing the difficulties, etc associated with them; having to cope with them. **up for sth 1** presented or offered for (eg discussion or sale). **2** under consideration for (a job or post). **3** prepared and eager to do it. **up to sb** their responsibility; dependent on them: *It's up to you.* **up to sth 1** immersed in or embedded as far as: *up to his eyes in work.* **2** capable of; equal to: *Are you up to meeting them?* **3** thinking about doing or engaged in doing: *What are you up to?* **4** as good as: *not up to his usual standard.* **5** as many or as much as: *up to two weeks.* **up to the minute** completely up to date. **up yours!** *coarse slang* an expression of strong refusal, defiance, contempt, etc. **what's up?** what's the matter?, what's wrong?

up-and-coming *adj* beginning to become successful or well known.

up-and-down *adj* **1** undulating. **2** moving or working both, or alternately, up and down.

upbeat *adj, colloq* cheerful; optimistic. ➤ *n, mus* **1** an unstressed beat, esp the last in a bar and so coming before the downbeat. **2** the upward gesture by a conductor which marks this.

upbraid *vb* to scold or reproach someone.

upbringing *n* the all-round instruction and education of a child, which influences their character and values.

upcoming *adj, colloq, esp N Am* forthcoming; approaching.

up-country *n* the inland part or regions of a country. ➤ *adj, adv* to or in the regions away from the coast; inland.

update *vb* /ʌpˈdeɪt/ to make or bring something or someone up to date. ➤ *n* /ˈʌpdeɪt/ **1** an act of updating. **2** something that is updated.

up-end *vb* **1** *tr & intr* to turn or place something, or become turned or placed, upside down. **2** to put something into disorder or disarray.

upfront *adj, colloq* (*also* **up-front**) **1** candid; open. **2** of money: paid in advance. ➤ *adv* (*also* **up front**) **1** candidly; openly. **2** of money or a payment: in advance.

upgrade *vb* /ʌpˈgreɪd/ **1** to promote someone. **2** to improve the quality of (machinery, equipment, a computer or its memory, etc), esp by adding or replacing features, components, etc. ➤ *n* /ˈʌpgreɪd/ **1** an act or the process of upgrading something. **2** an upgraded version of something, eg a piece of machinery or equipment.

upheaval *n* **1** a change or disturbance that brings about great disruption. **2** *geol* see UP-LIFT (*noun* sense 4).

uphill *adj* **1** sloping upwards; ascending. **2** of a task, etc: requiring great and sustained effort. ➤ *adv* **1** up a slope. **2** against problems or difficulties. ➤ *n* an upward slope; an ascent or incline.

uphold *vb* **1** to support (an action), defend (a right) or maintain (the law), esp against opposition. **2** to declare (eg a court judgement or verdict) to be correct or just; to confirm. **3** to hold something up; to support it. ○ **upholder** *n.*

upholster *vb* to fit (chairs, sofas, etc) with upholstery. ○ **upholstered** *adj.* ○ **upholsterer** *n.*

upholstery *n* **1** the springs, stuffing and covers of a chair or sofa. **2** the work of an upholsterer.

upkeep *n* **1** the task or process of keeping something in good order or condition; maintenance. **2** the cost of doing this.

upland *n* (*often* **uplands**) a high or hilly region. ➤ *adj* relating to or situated in such a region.

uplift *vb* /ʌpˈlɪft/ **1** to lift something up; to raise it. **2** to fill (a person or people) with an invigorating happiness, optimism or awareness of the spiritual nature of things. **3** *Scot, chiefly formal* to pick up; to collect. ➤ *n* /ˈʌplɪft/ **1** the action or result of lifting up. **2** a morally or spiritually uplifting influence, result or effect. **3** support given by a garment, esp a bra, that raises part of the body, esp the breasts. **4** (*also* **upheaval**) *geol* the process or result of land being raised, eg as in a period of mountain-building. ○ **uplifting** *adj* cheering; inspiring with hope.

uplighter or **uplight** *n* a type of lamp or wall light placed or designed so as to throw light upwards.

upload *vb, tr & intr, comput* to send (data, files, etc) from one computer to another, eg by means of a telephone line and modem.

up-market *adj* relating to or suitable for the more expensive end of the market; high in price, quality or prestige: *She lives in an up-market area of town.*

upon *prep* on or on to.

upper *adj* **1** higher; situated above. **2** high or higher in rank or status. **3** (*with capital* when part of a name) upstream, farther inland or situated to the north. **4** (*with capital* when part of a name) *geol, archaeol* designating a younger or late part or division, deposit, system, etc, or the period during which it was formed or deposited. ➤ *n* **1** the part of a shoe above the sole. **2** the higher of two people, objects, etc. **3** *slang* a drug that induces euphoria. ♦ **on one's uppers** *colloq* extremely short of money.

upper case *printing, adj* referring or relating to capital letters, as opposed to small letters. Compare LOWER CASE. ➤ *n* a letter or letters of this kind: *He wrote the sign all in upper case.*

upper class *n* the highest social class; the aristocracy.

upper crust *n, colloq* the upper class.

uppercut *n* a forceful upward blow with the fist, usu under the chin. ➤ *vb tr & intr* to hit someone with an uppercut.

upper hand *n* (*usu* **the upper hand**) a position of advantage or dominance.

upper house or **upper chamber** *n* (*often* **Upper House** and **Upper Chamber**) the higher but normally smaller part of a two-chamber (bicameral) parliament.

uppermost or **upmost** *adj, adv* at, in or into the highest or most prominent position.

uppish *adj* **1** arrogant or snobbish. **2** pretentious.

uppity *adj, colloq* self-important; arrogant; uppish.

upright *adj* **1** standing straight up; erect or vertical. **2** possessing integrity or moral correctness. ➤ *adv* into an upright position. ➤ *n* **1** a vertical (usu supporting) post or pole. **2** an UP-RIGHT PIANO. ○ **uprightness** *n*.

upright piano *n* a piano with strings arranged vertically in a case above the keyboard.

uprising *n* a rebellion or revolt.

uproar *n* an outbreak of noisy and boisterous behaviour, esp angry protest.

uproarious *adj* **1** making, or characterized by, an uproar. **2** of laughter: loud and unrestrained. **3** provoking such laughter; very

funny. ○ **uproariously** *adv.*

uproot *vb* **1** to displace (a person or people) from their usual surroundings or home: *Many Bosnians were uprooted by the war.* **2** to pull (a plant) out of the ground completely, with the root attached. **3** to eradicate or destroy something completely. **4** to move away from a usual location or home: *They uprooted and moved to the country.*

ups-a-daisy or **upsy-daisy** *exclam* expressing encouragement to a child who is being helped up or who is getting up, eg after a fall.

ups and downs *pl n* **1** rises and falls. **2** spells of alternating success and failure; changes of fortune.

upset *vb* /ʌpˈsɛt/ **1** to disturb or distress someone emotionally. **2** to ruin or spoil (eg plans, etc). **3** to disturb the proper balance or function of (a person's stomach or digestion). **4** to disturb something's normal balance or stability. **5** *tr & intr* to knock something over or overturn. ➤ *n* /ˈʌpsɛt/ **1** a disturbance or disorder, eg of plans, the digestion, etc. **2** an unexpected result or outcome, eg of a contest. ➤ *adj* **1** /ʌpˈsɛt/ emotionally distressed, angry or offended, etc. **2** /ˈʌpsɛt, ˈʌpsɛt/ disturbed: *an upset stomach.* ○ **upsetting** *adj.*

upshot *n* (*often* **the upshot**) the final outcome or ultimate effect.

upside *n* **1** the upper part or side of anything. **2** *colloq* a positive or favourable aspect.

upside down *adj* (*also* **upside-down**) **1** with the top part at the bottom; upturned or inverted. **2** *colloq* in complete confusion or disorder. ➤ *adv* **1** in an inverted way or manner: *Why does buttered toast always fall upside down on the floor?* **2** in a completely confused or disordered way.

upsides *adv* (*usu* **upsides with sb**) *Brit colloq* even with them, esp through revenge or retaliation.

upstage *adv* /ʌpˈsteɪdʒ/ **1** on, at or towards the back of a theatre stage. **2** *colloq* in an arrogant or haughty manner. ➤ *adj* /ˈʌpsteɪdʒ/ situated, occurring at or towards, relating to, the back of a theatre stage. ➤ *vb* /ʌpˈsteɪdʒ/ **1** of an actor: to move upstage and force (another actor) to turn their back to the audience. **2** *colloq* to direct attention away from someone on to oneself; to outshine them.

upstairs *adv* /ʌpˈstɛəz/ **1** up the stairs; to or on an upper floor or floors of a house, etc. **2** *colloq* to or in a senior or more senior position. ➤ *adj* /ˈʌpstɛəz/ (*also* **upstair**) on or relating to an upper floor or floors. ➤ *n* /ʌpˈstɛəz/ an upper floor or the upper floors of a building, esp the part of a house above the ground floor.

upstanding *adj* **1** standing up. **2** of a person: honest; respectable; trustworthy: *an upstanding member of society.* **3** with a healthily erect posture; vigorous; upright.

upstart *n, derog* someone who has suddenly acquired wealth or risen to a position of power or importance, esp one who is considered arrogant. ➤ *adj* belonging or relating to someone who is an upstart; typical or characteristic of an upstart.

upstate *US, adv* /ʌp'steɪt/ in, to or towards the part of a state remotest from, and usu to the north of, the principal city of the state. ➤ *adj* /'ʌpsteɪt/ in, relating to, or characteristic of this part of a state. ➤ *n* /'ʌpsteɪt/ the remoter, and usu northern, part of a state.

upstream *adv* /ʌp'striːm/ towards the source of a river or stream and against the current. ➤ *adj* /'ʌpstriːm/ situated towards the source of a river or stream.

upsurge *n* a sudden sharp rise or increase; a surging up. ○ **upsurgence** *n*.

upswing *n* **1** *econ* a recovery in the trade cycle or a period during which this occurs. **2** a swing or movement upwards, or a period of improvement.

upsy-daisy see UPS-A-DAISY

uptake *n* **1** an act of lifting up. **2** the act of taking up something on offer, or the extent of this. ♦ **quick** or **slow on the uptake** *colloq* quick or slow to understand or realize something.

up-tempo or **uptempo** *adj, adv, mus* with or at a fast tempo.

upthrust *n* **1** an upward thrust or push. **2** *geol* the action or an instance of thrusting up, esp by volcanic action.

uptight *adj, colloq* **1** nervous; anxious; tense. **2** angry; irritated. **3** strait-laced; conventional.

up to date or **up-to-date** *adj* **1** containing all the latest information. **2** following the latest trends.

uptown *chiefly N Am, adv* in, into or towards the part of a town or city that is away from the centre, usu the more prosperous or residential area. ➤ *adj* situated in, relating, or belonging to or characteristic of this part of a town or city. ➤ *n* the uptown part of a town or city.

upturn *n* /'ʌptɜːn/ **1** an upheaval. **2** an increase in (esp economic) activity; an upward trend. ➤ *vb* /ʌp'tɜːn/ **1** to turn something over, up or upside down. **2** *intr* to turn or curve upwards. ○ **upturned** *adj*.

upward *adv* (*usu* **upwards**) to or towards a higher place, a more important or senior position, or an earlier era. ➤ *adj* moving or directed upwards, to a higher position, etc. ○ **upwardly** *adv*. ♦ **upwards of** more than: *upwards of a thousand people*.

upwardly mobile *adj* moving, or in a position to move, into a higher social class or income bracket. ○ **upward mobility** *n*.

upwind *adv* /ʌp'wɪnd/ **1** against the direction of the wind; into the wind. **2** in front in terms of wind direction; with the wind carrying one's scent towards eg an animal one is stalking. ➤ *adj* /'ʌpwɪnd/ going against or exposed to the wind.

uranium *n, chem* a dense silvery-white radioactive metallic element chiefly used to produce nuclear energy. ○ **uranic** *adj*.

Uranus /'jʊərənəs/ *n, astron* the seventh planet from the Sun.

urban *adj* **1** relating or belonging to, constituting, or characteristic of a city or town: *the urban landscape*. **2** living in a city or town: *an urban fox*.

urbane *adj* **1** with refined manners; suave; courteous. **2** sophisticated; civilized; elegant. ○ **urbanely** *adv*. ○ **urbanity** *n*.

urbanism *n* the urban way of life.

urbanize or **-ise** *vb* to make (an area) less rural and more town-like. ○ **urbanization** *n*.

urchin *n* **1** a mischievous child. **2** a dirty raggedly dressed child. **3** a SEA URCHIN. ➤ *adj* relating to or like an urchin.

Urdu *n* an Indo-Aryan language, the official literary language of Pakistan, also spoken in Bangladesh and among Muslims in India.

urea /jʊə'rɪə/ *n, biochem* a compound, white and crystalline when purified, formed during amino-acid breakdown in the liver of mammals, and excreted in the urine. ○ **ureal** or **ureic** *adj*.

ureter /jʊə'riːtə(r)/ *n, anat* one of the two tubes through which urine is carried from the kidneys to the bladder. ○ **ureteral** or **ureteric** /jʊərɪ'terɪk/ *adj*.

urethane /'jʊərəθeɪn/ *n* **1** *chem* a crystalline substance used eg in pesticides and formerly as an anaesthetic. **2** short form of POLY-URETHANE.

urethra /jʊə'riːθrə/ *n* (**urethras** or **urethrae** /-riː/) *anat* the tube through which urine passes from the bladder out of the body and which, in males, also conveys semen. ○ **urethral** *adj*.

urethritis /jʊərɪ'θraɪtɪs/ *n, med* inflammation of the urethra. ○ **urethritic** /-'θrɪtɪk/ *adj*.

urge *vb* **1** (*also* **urge sb on**) to persuade someone forcefully or incite them (to do something). **2** to beg or entreat someone (to do something). **3 a** (*usu* **urge that**) to earnestly advise or recommend that; **b** (*usu* **urge sth**) to earnestly recommend it: *The Chancellor urged prudence.* **4** to drive or hurry (onwards, forwards, etc). ➤ *n* a strong impulse, desire or motivation (to do something).

urgent *adj* **1** requiring or demanding immediate attention, action, etc; pressing. **2** of a request, etc: forcefully and earnestly made. ○ **urgency** *n*. ○ **urgently** *adv*.

uric /'jʊərɪk/ *adj* relating to, present in, or derived from, urine.

uric acid *n, biochem* an organic acid, a product of protein metabolism, present in urine and blood.

urinal *n* **1** any receptacle or sanitary fitting, esp one attached to a wall, designed for men to urinate into. **2** a vessel for urine, esp one for use by an incontinent or bedridden person.

urinary *adj* **1** relating to urine or the passing of urine. **2** containing or contained in urine. **3** relating to or affecting the organs and structures that excrete and discharge urine.

urinate *vb, intr* to discharge urine. ○ **urination** *n*.

urine *n* the yellowish slightly acidic liquid consisting mainly of water and containing urea, uric acid, and other nitrogenous waste products filtered from the blood by the kidneys.

urinogenital /jʊərɪnoʊˈdʒɛnɪtəl/ or **urogenital** /jʊəroʊ-/ *adj* relating or pertaining to, or affecting, both the urinary and genital functions or organs.

urn *n* **1** a vase or vessel with a rounded body, usu a small narrow neck and a base or foot. **2** such a vase used to contain the ashes of a dead person. **3** a large cylindrical metal container with a tap and an internal heating element, used for heating water or making large quantities of tea or coffee.

urology /jʊəˈrɒlədʒɪ/ *n, med* the branch of medicine that deals with the study and treatment of diseases and disorders of the male and female urinary tracts, and of the male genital tract. ○ **urologic** or **urological** *adj*. ○ **urologist** *n*.

ursine *adj* belonging, relating or referring to a bear or bears.

US *abbrev* **1** Under-Secretary. **2** United States (of America).

us *pron* **1** the speaker or writer together with another person or other people; the object form of *we: He asked us the way* • *give it to us*. **2** all or any people; one: *Computers can help us to work more efficiently.* **3** *colloq* **a** me: *Give us a hand*; **b** ourselves: *We'll make us a pile of dough*. **4** *formal* used by monarchs, etc: me.

> **us** See note at **we**.

USA *abbrev* United States of America.

usable or **useable** *adj* able to be used. ○ **usability** *n*.

usage *n* **1** the act or way of using, or fact of being used; use; employment. **2** custom or practice. **3 a** the way that the vocabulary, constructions, etc of a language are actually used in practice; **b** an example of this. **4** the amount or quantity of use, or the rate at which something is used.

use *vb* /juːz/ **1** to put to a particular purpose. **2** to consume; to take something as fuel. **3** to treat someone as a means to benefit oneself; to exploit them. **4** *slang* to take (eg drugs or alcohol) regularly. **5** *old use* to behave (well or badly) towards someone. ➤ *n* /juːs/ **1** the act of using. **2** the state of being (able to be) used: *not in use*. **3** a practical purpose a thing can be put to. **4** the quality of serving a practical purpose: *It's no use complaining* • *Is this spanner any use?* **5** the ability or power to use something (eg a limb): *She lost the use of her leg after the accident.* **6** the length of time a thing is, will be or has remained serviceable: *It should give you plenty of use.* **7** the habit of using; custom. ♦ **have no use for sth** or **sb 1** to have no need of it or them. **2** *colloq* to dislike or despise it or them. **make use of sth** to put it to a practical

purpose. **used to sth** or **sb** or **to doing** or **being sth** accustomed to it or them, or to doing or being it: *The puppies haven't got used to us yet.* **used up** *colloq* tired or exhausted. ◊ **use sth up 1** to exhaust supplies, etc. **2** to finish off an amount left over.

used /juːzd/ *adj* not new; second-hand: *a used car*.

used to /ˈjuːstə/ *auxiliary vb* used with other verbs to express habitual actions or states that took place in the past: *They used to be friends, but they aren't any more* • *He didn't use to be as grumpy as he is now.*

> **used to** There is often uncertainty about the correct negative form of **used to**. The following are all acceptable (note that when an auxiliary verb is used, it is **did**, not **had**):
> ✓ *He used not to do it.*
> ✓ *He usedn't to do it.*
> ✓ *He didn't use to do it.*
> The following are usually considered incorrect:
> ✗ *He usen't to do it.*
> ✗ *He didn't used to do it.*

useful *adj* **1** able to be used advantageously; serving a helpful purpose; able to be put to various purposes. **2** *colloq* skilled or proficient: *a useful performance.* ○ **usefully** *adv.* ○ **usefulness** *n*. ♦ **come in useful** to prove to be useful.

useless *adj* **1** serving no practical purpose. **2** (*often* **useless at sth**) *colloq* not at all proficient: *I'm useless at maths.* ○ **uselessly** *adv.* ○ **uselessness** *n*.

user *n* **1** someone who uses a specified facility such as a leisure centre, a computer network, etc. **2** someone who regularly takes a specified drug: *a heroin user.*

user-friendly *adj* esp of a computer system: designed to be easy or pleasant to use, or easy to follow or understand: *user-friendly software.*

usher *n* **1 a** someone whose job is to show people to their seats, eg in a theatre, cinema, etc; **b** someone whose function is to direct wedding guests to their seats in church, and to look after them generally. **2** an official in a court of law who guards the door and maintains order. **3** an official who escorts, or introduces people to, dignitaries on ceremonial occasions. ➤ *vb* **1** (*usu* **usher sb in** or **out**) to conduct or escort them, eg into or out of a building, room, etc. **2** (*usu* **usher sth in**) *formal or literary* to be a portent of it; to herald it.

usherette *n* a woman who shows people to their seats in a theatre or cinema.

USSR *abbrev, hist* Union of Soviet Socialist Republics.

usual *adj* done, happening, etc most often; customary: *my usual route to work.* ➤ *n* **1** something which is usual, customary, etc. **2** (*usu* **the** or **my usual**) *colloq* the thing regularly requested, done, etc, esp the drink that someone regularly or most often orders. ○ **usually** *adv* ordinarily; normally. ♦ **as usual** as regularly happens; as is or was usual.

usurer /ˈjuːʒərə(r)/ *n* someone who lends money, esp one who charges exorbitant rates of interest. ○ **usury** *n*.

usurp /juˈzɜːp/ *vb* **1** to take possession of (eg land) or assume (eg power, authority, etc) by force, without right or unjustly. **2** to encroach on something (eg someone else's rights, sphere of interest, etc). ○ **usurpation** *n*. ○ **usurper** *n*.

utensil *n* an implement or tool, esp one for everyday or domestic use: *cooking utensils*.

uterine *adj* **1** *med* relating to, in the region of or affecting the uterus. **2** of siblings: born of the same mother but different fathers.

uterus /ˈjuːtərəs/ *n* (*uteri* /-raɪ/) *technical* the WOMB.

utilitarian *adj* **1** intended to be useful rather than beautiful. **2** concerned too much with usefulness and not enough with beauty; strictly or severely functional. **3** relating to or characterized by utilitarianism. ➤ *n* a believer in utilitarianism.

utilitarianism *n*, *ethics* a set of values based on the belief that an action is morally right if it benefits the majority of people.

utility *n* (*-ies*) **1** usefulness; practicality. **2** something that is useful. **3** *econ* the ability of a commodity to satisfy human needs or wants. **4** a company which provides a supply eg of gas, water or electricity, or other service, for a community. **5** *comput* a program designed to carry out a routine function. ➤ *adj* **1** designed for usefulness or practicality, rather than beauty. **2** of a breed of dog: orig bred to serve a practical purpose.

utility room *n* a room where things such as a washing machine, freezer, etc are kept.

utility truck or **utility vehicle** *n*, *Aust*, *NZ* a small truck, pick-up or van designed to carry both passengers and goods.

utilize or **-ise** *vb* to make practical use of something; to use it. ○ **utilization** *n*.

utmost *adj* **1** greatest possible in degree, number or amount: *the utmost urgency*. **2** furthest or most remote in position; outermost. ➤ *n* **1** (*often* **the utmost**) the greatest possible amount, degree or extent. **2** the best or greatest, eg in terms of power, ability, etc: *He tried his utmost to win*.

Utopia or **utopia** *n* any imaginary place, state or society of idealized perfection.

Utopian or **utopian** *adj* relating to Utopia, to a utopia or to some unrealistically ideal place, society, etc. ➤ *n* someone who advocates idealistic or impracticable social reforms. ○ **Utopianism** *n*.

utter¹ *vb* **1** to give audible vocal expression to (an emotion, etc); to emit (a sound) with the voice: *She uttered a piercing cry*. **2** to speak or say; to express something in words. **3** *law* to put (counterfeit money) into circulation.

utter² *adj* complete; total; absolute: *utter disbelief*. ○ **utterly** *adv*.

utterance *n* **1** the act of uttering or expressing something with the voice. **2** the ability to utter; the power of speech. **3** a person's manner of speaking. **4** something that is uttered or expressed.

uttermost *adj*, *n* UTMOST.

U-turn *n* **1** a manoeuvre in which a vehicle is turned to face the other way in a single continuous movement, the turn making the shape of a U. **2** a complete reversal of direction, eg of government policy.

UV *abbrev* ultraviolet.

uvula /ˈjuːvjʊlə/ *n* (*uvulas* or *uvulae* /-liː/) *anat* the small fleshy part of the soft palate that hangs over the back of the tongue at the entrance to the throat. ○ **uvular** *adj*.

uxorial /ʌkˈsɔːrɪəl/ *adj* **1** relating or pertaining to a wife or wives. **2** UXORIOUS.

uxorious /ʌkˈsɔːrɪəs/ *adj* excessively or submissively fond of one's wife.

Vv

V¹ or **v** *n* (*Vs*, *V's* or *v's*) the twenty-second letter of the English alphabet.

V² *abbrev* volt.

V³ *symbol* **1** *chem* vanadium. **2** the Roman numeral for 5.

v or **v.** *abbrev* **1** velocity. **2** versus. **3** very. **4** *vide* (Latin), see, refer to. **5** volume.

vac *n*, *colloq* short for VACATION.

vacancy *n* (*-ies*) **1** the state of being vacant; emptiness. **2** an unoccupied job or post. **3** an unoccupied room in a hotel or guesthouse.

vacant *adj* **1** empty or unoccupied. **2** having, showing or suggesting an absence of thought,

concentration or intelligence. **3** of a period of time: not assigned to any particular activity.

vacate *vb* **1** to make something empty; to empty something out. **2** *tr & intr* to leave or cease to occupy (a house or an official position).

vacation *n* **1** *N Am* a holiday. **2** a holiday between terms at a university, college or court of law. ➤ *vb*, *intr*, *N Am* to take a holiday.

vaccinate *vb* to administer to a person or an animal a vaccine that gives immunity from a disease. ○ **vaccination** *n*.

vaccine *n* **1** *med* a preparation containing killed

or weakened bacteria or viruses, or serum containing specific antibodies, used in vaccination to confer temporary or permanent immunity to a bacterial or viral disease by stimulating the body to produce antibodies to a specific bacterium or virus. **2** *comput* a piece of software designed to detect and remove computer viruses from a floppy disk, program, etc.

vacillate /'vasɪleɪt/ *vb, intr* to change opinions or decisions frequently; to waver. ○ **vacillation** *n*.

vacuity *n* (*-ies*) **1** the state or quality of being vacuous. **2** a foolish thought or idea.

vacuous *adj* **1** unintelligent; stupid. **2** of a look or expression: blank; conveying no feeling or meaning. **3** empty.

vacuum *n* (**vacuums** or *technical* **vacua**) **1** a space from which all matter has been removed. **2** a space from which all or almost all air or other gas has been removed. **3** a feeling or state of emptiness. **4** a condition of isolation from outside influences. **5** *colloq* a VACUUM CLEANER. ➤ *adj* relating to, containing or operating by means of a vacuum: *a vacuum pump.* ➤ *vb, tr & intr, colloq* to clean with a vacuum cleaner.

vacuum cleaner *n* an electrically powered cleaning device that lifts dust and dirt by suction.

vacuum flask *n* a container for preserving the temperature of liquids, esp drinks, consisting of a double-skinned bottle with a vacuum sealed between the layers, fitted inside a protective metal or plastic container.

vacuum-packed *adj* of food: sealed in a container from which most of the air has been removed.

vacuum tube *n, elec* an electron tube containing an electrically heated electrode (the CATHODE) that emits electrons which flow through a vacuum to a second electrode (the ANODE). Also called **valve**.

vagabond *n* someone with no fixed home who lives an unsettled wandering life, esp someone regarded as lazy or worthless.

vagary /'veɪɡərɪ/ *n* (*-ies*) an unpredictable and erratic act or turn of events.

vagina /və'dʒaɪnə/ *n* (**vaginas** or **vaginae** /-niː/) in the reproductive system of most female mammals: the muscular canal that leads from the cervix of the uterus to the exterior of the body. ○ **vaginal** *adj*.

vagrant /'veɪɡrənt/ *n* someone who has no permanent home or place of work. ➤ *adj* wandering. ○ **vagrancy** *n*.

vague *adj* **1** indistinct or imprecise. **2** thinking, expressing or remembering without clarity or precision. ○ **vaguely** *adv*. ○ **vagueness** *n*.

vain *adj* **1** having too much pride in one's appearance, achievements or possessions. **2** having no useful effect or result. ○ **vainly** *adv*.
♦ **in vain** without success; fruitlessly.

vainglory *n, literary* extreme boastfulness; excessive pride in oneself. ○ **vainglorious** *adj*.

valance /'valəns/ *n* a decorative strip of fabric hung over a curtain rail or round the frame of a bed.

vale *n, literary* a valley.

valediction /valɪ'dɪkʃən/ *n* **1** the act of saying farewell; a farewell. **2** a valedictory speech, etc. ○ **valedictory** *adj*.

valency /'veɪlənsɪ/ or (*esp N Am*) **valence** *n* (**valencies; valences**) *chem* a positive or negative whole number that denotes the combining power of an atom of a particular element, equal to the number of hydrogen atoms or their equivalent with which it could combine to form a compound.

valentine *n* **1** a card or other message given, often anonymously, as a token of love or affection on 14 February. **2** the person it is given to.

valerian /və'lɪərɪən, və'lɛərɪən/ *n* **a** a small flowering plant with pink tubular flowers and rhizome roots; **b** a sedative drug derived from the root.

valet /'valeɪ, 'valɪt/ *n* **1** a man's personal servant, who attends to his clothes, dressing, etc. **2** a man who carries out similar duties in a hotel. ➤ *vb* (**valeted, valeting**) **1** *intr* to work as a valet. **2** to clean the body-work and interior of (a car) as a service.

valetudinarian /valɪtʃuːdɪ'nɛərɪən/ *adj, formal* **1** relating to or suffering from a long-term or chronic illness. **2** anxious about one's health. ➤ *n* a valetudinarian person.

valiant *adj* outstandingly brave and heroic. ○ **valiantly** *adv*.

valid *adj* **1** of an argument, objection, etc: **a** based on truth or sound reasoning; **b** well-grounded; having some force. **2** of a ticket or official document: **a** legally acceptable for use: *a valid passport*; **b** not having reached its expiry date: *The ticket is still valid.* **3** of a contract: drawn up according to proper legal procedure. ○ **validity** *n*.

validate *vb* **1** to make (a document, a ticket, etc) valid, eg by marking it with an official stamp. **2** to confirm the validity of something. ○ **validation** *n*.

valise /və'liːz; *N Am* və'liːs/ *n, now chiefly N Am* a small overnight case or bag.

Valium *n, trademark* a type of tranquillizing drug.

valley *n* a long flat area of land, usu containing a river or stream, flanked on both sides by higher land.

valour or (*US*) **valor** *n* courage or bravery, esp in battle.

valuable *adj* having considerable value or usefulness. ➤ *n* (*usu* **valuables**) personal possessions of high financial or other value.

valuation *n* **1** an assessment of the monetary value of something, esp from an expert or authority. **2** the value arrived at.

value *n* **1** worth in monetary terms. **2** the quality of being useful or desirable; the degree of usefulness or desirability. **3** the exact amount of a variable quantity in a particular case. **4** for the quality of being a fair exchange: *value for money.* **5** (**values**) moral principles or standards. **6** *maths* a quantity represented by a symbol or set of symbols. **7** *mus* the duration of a note or rest. ➤ *vb* **1** to consider something to be of a certain value, esp a high value. **2** to assess the value of something. ○ **valued** *adj.* ○ **valueless** *adj.* ○ **valuer** *n.*

value judgement *n* an assessment of worth based on personal opinion rather than objective fact.

valve *n* **1 a** any device that regulates the flow of a liquid or gas through a pipe by opening or closing an aperture; **b** any such device that allows flow in one direction only. **2** *anat* in certain tubular organs: a flap of membranous tissue that allows flow of a body fluid, such as blood, in one direction only. **3** any of a set of finger-operated devices that control the flow of air through some brass musical instruments. **4** *zool* either half of the hinged shell of a bivalve mollusc such as a cockle or clam.

vamoose *vb, intr, N Am slang* to depart hurriedly; to clear off.

vamp[1] *n, colloq* a woman who flaunts her sexual charm, esp in order to exploit men.

vamp[2] *n* the part of a shoe or boot that covers the toes. ➤ *vb* to improvise (a musical accompaniment). ◊ **vamp sth up** to refurbish it or do it up.

vampire *n* a dead person who supposedly rises from the grave at night to suck the blood of the living.

van[1] *n* **1** a commercial road vehicle with luggage space at the rear, lighter than a lorry. **2** (*also* **luggage van**) *Brit* a railway carriage in which luggage and parcels are carried.

van[2] *n* **1** a vanguard. **2** the forefront: *in the van of progress.*

vanadium *n, chem* a soft silvery-grey metallic element that is used to increase the toughness and shock resistance of steel alloys.

vandal *n* someone who wantonly damages or destroys personal and public property. ○ **vandalism** *n.*

vandalize or **-ise** *vb* to inflict wilful and senseless damage on (property, etc).

vane *n* **1** a WEATHERVANE. **2** each of the blades of a windmill, propeller or revolving fan.

vanguard *n* **1** the part of a military force that advances first. **2 a** a person or group that leads the way, esp by setting standards or forming opinion; **b** a leading position: *in the vanguard of discovery.*

vanilla *n* **1 a** a Mexican climbing orchid having large fragrant white or yellow flowers followed by pod-like fruits; **b** (*in full* **vanilla pod**) its fruit. **2** a flavouring substance obtained from the pod, used in ice cream, chocolate and other foods. ➤ *adj* **1** flavoured with or like vanilla: *vanilla ice cream.* **2** *colloq* ordinary; plain.

vanish *vb, intr* **1** to disappear suddenly. **2** to cease to exist; to die out.

vanity *n* (*-ies*) **1** the quality of being vain or conceited. **2** a thing one is conceited about. **3** futility or worthlessness.

vanity unit *n* a piece of furniture combining a dressing table and washbasin.

vanquish *vb, literary* to defeat or overcome someone.

vantage point *n* a position affording a clear overall view or prospect.

vapid /ˈvapɪd/ *adj* dull; uninteresting; insipid.

vapour or (*US*) **vapor** *n* **1** a substance in the form of a mist, fume or smoke, esp one coming off from a solid or liquid. **2** *chem* a gas that can be condensed to a liquid by pressure alone, without being cooled: *water vapour.* **3** (**the vapours**) *old use* a feeling of depression, or of faintness, formerly thought to be caused by gases in the stomach. ○ **vaporize** or **-ise** *vb.*

variable *adj* **1** referring to something that varies or tends to vary; changeable. **2** referring to something that can be varied or altered. ➤ *n* **1** a thing that can vary unpredictably in nature or degree. **2** a factor which may change or be changed by another. **3** *maths* in an algebraic expression or equation: a symbol, usu a letter, for which one or more quantities or values may be substituted. ○ **variability** *n.*

variance *n* the state of being different or inconsistent. ♦ **at variance with sth** in disagreement or conflict with it.

variant *n* **1** a form of a thing that varies from another form. **2** an example that differs from a standard. ➤ *adj* **1** different. **2** differing from a standard.

variation *n* **1** the act or process of varying or changing. **2** something that varies from a standard. **3** the extent to which something varies from a standard. **4** a passage of music in which the main melody is repeated with some, usu only slight, changes.

varicella *n, med* chickenpox.

varicoloured *adj* having different colours in different parts.

varicose *adj, pathol* of a superficial vein: abnormally swollen and twisted so that it produces a raised and often painful knot on the skin surface, usu of the legs.

varied *adj* having variety; diverse.

variegated *adj, bot* of leaves or flowers: marked with patches of two or more colours.

variety *n* (*-ies*) **1** any of various types of the same thing; a kind or sort. **2** the quality of departing from a fixed pattern or routine; diversity. **3** a plant or animal differing from another in certain characteristics, but not enough to be classed as a separate species. **4** a form of theatrical entertainment consisting of a succession of acts of different kinds.

varifocals *pl n* a pair of glasses with **varifocal** lenses, whose variable focal lengths allow a wide range of focusing distances.

various *adj* **1** several different: *I worked for various companies.* **2** different; disparate; di-

verse: *Their interests are many and various.*
○ **variously** *adv.*

varlet *n, old use* a rascal or rogue.

varnish *n* **1** an oil-based liquid containing resin, painted on a surface such as wood to give a hard transparent and often glossy finish. **2** any liquid providing a similar finish: *nail varnish.* **3** a superficial attractiveness or impressiveness, esp masking underlying shoddiness or inadequacy. ➤ *vb* to apply varnish to something.

varsity *n (-ies) colloq* **1** *Brit* a university, esp with reference to sport. **2** *N Am* the principal team representing a college in a sport.

vary *vb (-ies, -ied)* **1** *intr* to change, or be of different kinds, esp according to different circumstances. **2** *tr & intr* to make or become less regular or uniform and more diverse.
○ **varying** *n, adj.*

vascular *adj, biol* **1** relating to the blood vessels of animals or the sap-conducting tissues of plants. **2** composed of or provided with such vessels.

vas deferens /vas ˈdɛfərɛnz/ *n* (**vasa deferentia** /ˈveɪzə dɛfəˈrɛnʃɪə/) *biol* the duct from each testicle that carries spermatozoa to the penis.

vase /vɑːz; *US* veɪz/ *n* an ornamental glass or pottery container, esp one for holding cut flowers.

vasectomy *n (-ies) med* a surgical operation involving the tying and cutting of the VAS DEFERENS as a means of sterilization.

Vaseline *n, trademark* an ointment consisting mainly of petroleum jelly.

vassal *n* **1** *hist* someone acting as a servant to, and fighting on behalf of, a medieval lord in return for land or protection or both. **2** a person or nation dependent on or subservient to another. ○ **vassalage** *n.*

vast *adj* **1** extremely great in size, extent or amount. **2** *colloq* considerable; appreciable: *a vast difference.* ○ **vastly** *adv.* **vastness** *n.*

vat *n* a large barrel or tank for storing or holding liquids.

Vatican *n (usu* **the Vatican**) **1** a collection of buildings on the Vatican Hill in Rome, including the palace and official residence of the Pope. **2** the authority of the Pope.

vaudeville *n, N Am* **1** variety entertainment (see VARIETY sense 4). **2** a music hall.

vault¹ *n* **1** an arched roof or ceiling, esp in a church. **2** an underground chamber used for storage or as a burial tomb. **3** a wine cellar. **4** a fortified room for storing valuables, eg in a bank.

vault² *vb, tr & intr* to spring or leap over something, esp assisted by the hands or a pole. ➤ *n* an act of vaulting.

vaulting¹ *n* a series of vaults (see VAULT¹ sense 1) considered collectively.

vaulting² *adj* esp referring to ambition or pride: excessive or immoderate.

vaunt *vb, tr & intr* to boast or behave boastfully about something. ➤ *n* a boast.

VCR *abbrev* video cassette recorder.

VD *abbrev* venereal disease.

VDU *abbrev* visual display unit.

've *contraction (usu* after pronouns) have: *they've.*

veal *n* the flesh of a calf, used as food.

vector *n* **1** *maths* a quantity which has both magnitude and direction, eg force, velocity, or acceleration. Compare SCALAR. **2** *aeronautics* the course of an aircraft or missile. **3** *med* any agent, such as an insect, that is capable of transferring a PATHOGEN from one organism to another.

Veda /ˈveɪdə/ *n* any one, or all of, four ancient holy books of the Hindus. ○ **Vedic** *adj.*

vee *n* **1** a representation of the twenty-second letter of the English alphabet, V. **2** an object or mark shaped like the letter V.

veer *vb, intr* **1** to move abruptly in a different direction: *The car veered off the road into the ditch.* **2** of the wind: to change direction clockwise. Compare BACK (*verb* sense 7). **3** *naut* to change course, esp away from the wind. ➤ *n* a change of direction.

veg /vɛdʒ/ *sing or pl n, colloq* a vegetable or vegetables: *meat and two veg.*

vegan /ˈviːgən/ *n* someone who does not eat meat, fish, dairy products or any foods containing animal fats or extracts, often also avoiding using leather and other animal-based substances. ➤ *adj* **1** referring to or for vegans. **2** of a meal or diet: excluding such foods.
○ **veganism** *n.*

vegetable *n* **1 a** a plant or any of its parts, other than fruits and seeds, that is used for food, eg roots, tubers, stems or leaves; **b** the edible part of such a plant. **2** *offensive, colloq* a person almost totally incapable of any physical or mental activity because of severe brain damage.

vegetable marrow see MARROW

vegetable oil *n* an oil obtained from a plant, used esp in cooking and cosmetics.

vegetarian *n* someone who does not eat meat or fish. ➤ *adj* **1** referring to or for vegetarians. **2** denoting food or a diet that contains no meat or fish. ○ **vegetarianism** *n.*

vegetate *vb, intr* of a person: to live a dull inactive life.

vegetation *n, bot* **1** a collective term for plants. **2** the plants of a particular area.

vegetative *adj* **1** referring to plants or vegetation. **2** *biol* denoting asexual reproduction in plants or animals, as in bulbs, corms, yeasts, etc. **3** *bot* denoting a phase of plant growth as opposed to reproduction. **4** *biol* denoting unconscious or involuntary bodily functions as resembling the process of vegetable growth.

veggie or **vegie** *n, colloq* **1** a vegetarian. **2** a vegetable. Also written **veggy.**

vehement *adj* expressed with strong feeling or firm conviction; forceful. ○ **vehemence** *n.*
○ **vehemently** *adv.*

vehicle *n* **1** a conveyance for transporting people or things, esp a self-powered one. **2** someone or something used as a means of communicating ideas or opinions: *newspapers as vehicles for political propaganda.* **3** *med* a neutral substance in which a drug is mixed in order to be administered, eg a syrup. **4** a substance in which a pigment is transferred to a surface as paint, eg oil. ○ **vehicular** *adj.*

veil *n* **1** a fabric covering for a woman's head or face, forming part of traditional dress in some societies. **2** the hoodlike part of a nun's habit. **3** anything that covers or obscures something: *a veil of secrecy.* ➤ *vb* **1** to cover something, or cover the face of someone, with a veil. **2** to conceal or partly conceal; to disguise or obscure something: *He veiled his threats in pleasantries.* ○ **veiled** *adj.* ♦ **take the veil** to become a nun.

vein *n* **1** *anat* a blood vessel that carries deoxygenated blood back towards the heart. **2** *loosely* any blood vessel. **3** a thin sheetlike deposit of one or more minerals, deposited in a fracture or joint in the surrounding rock. **4** a streak of different colour, eg in cheese. **5** in a leaf: any of a large number of thin branching tubes containing the vascular tissues. **6** in an insect: any of the tubes of chitin that stiffen and support the membranous structure of the wings. **7** a mood or tone: *written in a sarcastic vein.* **8** a distinct characteristic present throughout; a streak. ○ **veined** *adj.*

Velcro *n, trademark* a fastening material consisting of two nylon surfaces, one of tiny hooks, the other of thin fibres, which bond tightly when pressed together but are easily pulled apart.

veld or **veldt** /felt, velt/ *n* a wide grassy plain with few or no trees, esp in S Africa.

vellum *n* **1** a fine kind of parchment, orig made from the skin of calves. **2** thick cream-coloured writing-paper resembling such parchment.

velocity *n* (*-ies*) **1** *technical* rate of motion, ie distance per unit of time, in a particular direction. **2** *loosely* speed.

velour or **velours** /və'luə(r)/ *n* any fabric with a velvet-like pile, used esp for upholstery.

velvet *n* **1** a fabric with a very short soft closely woven pile on one side. **2** the soft skin that covers the growing antlers of deer. ➤ *adj* **1** made of velvet. **2** soft or smooth like velvet. ○ **velvety** *adj.*

velveteen *n* cotton fabric with a velvet-like pile.

venal /'vi:nəl/ *adj* **1** of a person: willing to be persuaded by corrupt means, esp bribery. **2** of behaviour: dishonest; corrupt. ○ **venality** *n.*

vend *vb* to sell or offer (esp small wares) for sale.

vendetta *n* **1** a bitter feud in which the family of a murdered person takes revenge by killing the murderer or one of the murderer's relatives. **2** any long-standing bitter feud or quarrel.

vending machine *n* a coin-operated machine that dispenses small items such as snacks and cigarettes.

vendor *n, law* a seller, esp of property.

veneer *n* **1** a thin layer of a fine material, esp wood, fixed to the surface of an inferior material to give an attractive finish. **2** a false or misleading external appearance, esp of a favourable quality: *a veneer of respectability.*

venerable *adj* deserving respect, esp on account of age or religious association.

venerate *vb* to regard someone or something with deep respect or awe. ○ **veneration** *n.*

venereal *adj* of a disease or infection: transmitted by sexual intercourse.

venereal disease *n, med* (abbrev **VD**) former name for a SEXUALLY TRANSMITTED DISEASE.

Venetian blind *n* a window blind consisting of horizontal slats strung together, one beneath the other, and tilted to let in or shut out light.

vengeance *n* punishment inflicted as a revenge. ♦ **with a vengeance 1** forcefully or violently. **2** to a great degree.

vengeful *adj* **1** eager for revenge. **2** carried out in revenge.

venial sin /'vi:niəl/ *n* a sin that is pardonable or excusable. Compare MORTAL SIN.

venison *n* the flesh of a deer, used as food.

venom *n* **1** a poisonous liquid that some creatures, including scorpions and certain snakes, inject in a bite or sting. **2** spitefulness, esp in language or tone of voice. ○ **venomous** *adj.*

venous /'vi:nəs/ *adj* relating to or contained in veins.

vent¹ *n* a slit in a garment, esp upwards from the hem at the back, for style or ease of movement.

vent² *n* **1** an opening that allows air, gas or liquid into or out of a confined space. **2** the passage inside a volcano through which lava and gases escape. **3** a chimney flue. ➤ *vb* **1** to make a vent in something. **2** to let something in or out through a vent. **3** to release and express (esp emotion) freely: *Tom vented his frustration by shaking his fists.*

ventilate *vb* **1** to allow fresh air to circulate throughout (a room, building, etc). **2** to cause (blood) to take up oxygen. **3** to supply air to (the lungs). **4** to expose (an idea, etc) to public examination or discussion. ○ **ventilation** *n.*

ventilator *n* **1** a device that circulates or draws in fresh air. **2** a machine that ventilates the lungs of a person whose respiratory system is damaged.

ventral *adj* **1** denoting the lower surface of an animal that walks on four legs, of any invertebrate, or of a structure such as a leaf or wing. **2** denoting the front surface of the body of an animal that walks upright, eg a human being. **3** denoting a structure that is situated on or just beneath such a surface.

ventral fin *n* either of the paired fins on the belly of a fish.

ventricle *n, anat* in mammals: either of the two lower chambers of the heart which have thick muscular walls. ○ **ventricular** *adj.*

ventriloquism *n* the art of speaking in a way

that makes the sound appear to come from elsewhere, esp a dummy's mouth. ○ **ventriloquist** *n*.

venture *n* **1** an exercise or operation involving danger or uncertainty. **2** a business project, esp one involving risk or speculation. **3** an enterprise attempted. ➤ *vb* **1** *tr & intr* to be so bold as to; to dare: *Nobody ventured to criticize the chairman.* **2** to put forward or present (a suggestion, etc) in the face of possible opposition: *I ventured a different opinion.* **3** to expose someone or something to danger or chance; to risk.

venture capital *n* money supplied by individual investors or business organizations for a new business enterprise.

venturesome *adj* **1** prepared to take risks; enterprising. **2** involving danger; risky.

venue *n* **1** the chosen location for a sports event, a concert or other entertainment. **2** a meeting-place.

Venus *n, astron* the second planet from the Sun.

veracious *adj, formal* truthful.

veracity *n, formal* truthfulness.

veranda or **verandah** *n* a sheltered terrace attached to a building.

verb *n* a word or group of words that belongs to a grammatical class denoting an action, experience, occurrence or state, eg *do, feel, happen, love.*

verbal *adj* **1** relating to or consisting of words: *verbal abuse.* **2** spoken, not written: *verbal communication.* **3** *gram* relating to or derived from a verb or verbs. **4** literal; word-for-word. **5** talkative; articulate. ○ **verbally** *adv.*

verbalize or **-ise** *vb* **1** to express (ideas, thoughts, etc) in words. **2** *intr* to use too many words; to be verbose. **3** to turn (any word) into a verb. ○ **verbalization** *n*.

verbatim /vɜːˈbeɪtɪm/ *adj, adv* using exactly the same words; word-for-word.

verbena *n* a plant with fragrant white, pink, red or purplish tubular flowers, used in herbal medicine and cosmetics.

verbiage *n* **1** the use of language that is wordy or needlessly complicated. **2** such language.

verbose *adj* using or containing too many words; boringly or irritatingly long-winded. ○ **verbosity** /vɜːˈbɒsɪtɪ/ *n*.

verdant *adj* **1** covered with lush green grass or vegetation. **2** of a rich green colour.

verdict *n* **1** a decision arrived at by a jury in a court of law. **2** any decision, opinion or judgement.

verdigris /ˈvɜːdɪɡriː, -ɡriːs/ *n, chem* a bluish-green coating of basic copper salts that forms as a result of corrosion when copper, brass or bronze surfaces are exposed to air and moisture for long periods.

verdure *n, literary* **1** lush green vegetation. **2** the rich greenness of such vegetation.

verge¹ *n* **1** a limit, boundary or border. **2** a strip of grass bordering a road. **3** a point or stage immediately beyond or after which something

exists or occurs: *on the verge of tears.* ➤ *vb, intr* (**verge on sth**) to be close to being or becoming something specified: *enthusiasm verging on obsession.*

verge² *vb, intr* to slope or incline in a specified direction.

verger *n, chiefly C of E* a church official who assists the minister and acts as caretaker.

verify *vb* (**-ies, -ied**) to check or confirm the truth or accuracy of something. ○ **verifiable** *adj.* ○ **verification** *n*.

verily *adv, old use* truly; really.

verisimilitude *n, formal* the appearance of being real or true.

veritable *adj, formal* accurately described as such; real: *a veritable genius!* ○ **veritably** *adv.*

verity *n* (**-ies**) truthfulness.

vermicelli /vɜːmɪˈtʃelɪ/ *n* **1** pasta in very thin strands, thinner than spaghetti. **2** (*also* **chocolate vermicelli**) tiny splinters of chocolate used for decorating cakes, etc.

vermiform *adj* like a worm; worm-shaped.

vermiform appendix *n, anat* a small blind tube leading off the CAECUM, part of the large intestine. Usually shortened to **appendix**.

vermilion *n* **1** a bright scarlet colour. **2** a pigment of this colour consisting of sulphide of mercury; cinnabar. ➤ *adj* referring to or having this colour.

vermin *sing* or *pl n* **1** a collective name for wild animals that spread disease or generally cause a nuisance, esp rats and other rodents. **2** detestable people. ○ **verminous** *adj.*

vermouth /ˈvɜːməθ, vəˈmuːθ/ *n* an alcoholic drink consisting of wine flavoured with aromatic herbs, orig wormwood.

vernacular *n* (*usu* **the vernacular**) **1** the native language of a country or people, as opposed to a foreign language that is also in use. **2** the form of a language as commonly spoken, as opposed to the formal language. ➤ *adj* **1** referring to or in the vernacular. **2** local; native: *vernacular architecture.*

vernal *adj* relating to or appropriate to spring; happening or appearing in spring.

vernier /ˈvɜːnɪə(r)/ *n* a small sliding device on some measuring instruments, eg barometers and theodolites, used to measure fractions of units.

veronica *n* a plant of the foxglove family, with small blue, pink or white flowers, including the SPEEDWELL.

verruca /vəˈruːkə/ *n* (**verrucas** or **verrucae** /-ˈruːseɪ or -ˈruːkiː/) *pathol* a wart, esp one on the sole of the foot.

versatile *adj* **1** adapting easily to different tasks. **2** having numerous uses or abilities. ○ **versatility** *n*.

verse *n* **1** a division of a poem; a stanza. **2** poetry, as opposed to prose. **3** a poem. **4** a division of a song. **5** any of the numbered subdivisions of the chapters of the Bible.

versed *adj* (*always* **versed in sth**) familiar with it or skilled in it: *well versed in chemistry.*

versify *vb* (*-ies, -ied*) **1** *intr* to write poetry. **2** to express something as, or turn it into, a poem. ○ **versification** *n*. ○ **versifier** *n*.

version *n* any of several types or forms in which a thing exists or is available, eg a particular edition or translation of a book, or one person's account of an incident.

verso *n, printing* **1** the back of a loose sheet of printed paper. **2** the left-hand page of two open pages. Compare RECTO.

versus *prep* **1** in a contest or lawsuit: against. **2** *colloq* in comparison to.

vertebra /'vɜːtəbrə/ *n* (*vertebrae* /-breɪ, -briː/) *anat* any of the small bones or cartilaginous segments that form the backbone. ○ **vertebral** *adj*.

vertebrate *n, zool* any animal, including fish, amphibians, reptiles, birds and mammals, that has a backbone. ➢ *adj* having a backbone.

vertex /'vɜːtɛks/ *n* (*vertexes* or *vertices* /-tɪsiːz/) **1** the highest point; the peak or summit. **2** *geom* **a** the point opposite the base of a geometric figure, eg the pointed tip of a cone; **b** the point where the two sides forming an angle meet in a POLYGON, or where three or more surfaces meet in a POLYHEDRON; **c** the intersection of a curve with its axis.

vertical *adj* **1** perpendicular to the horizon; upright. **2** running from top to bottom, not side to side. **3** referring to a vertex or at a vertex. **4** relating to, involving or running through all levels within a hierarchy, all stages of a process, etc, rather than just one. ➢ *n* a vertical line or direction. ○ **vertically** *adv*.

vertigo *n* a whirling sensation felt when the sense of balance is disturbed; dizziness; giddiness. ○ **vertiginous** *adj*.

vervain *n* a wild VERBENA with small white, lilac or purple flowers borne in long slender spikes.

verve *n* great liveliness or enthusiasm.

very *adv* **1** to a high degree or extent: *very kind*. **2** (used with *own, same* and with superlative adjectives) absolutely; truly: *my very own room* • *the very same day* • *my very best effort*. ➢ *adj* (*used for emphasis*) **1** absolute: *the very top*. **2** precise; actual: *this very minute*. **3** most suitable: *That's the very tool for the job*. **4** mere: *shocked by the very thought*. ◆ **not very** not at all; the opposite of. **very good** or **very well** expressions of consent and approval.

very high frequency *n* (abbrev VHF) **1** a band of radio frequencies between 30 and 300MHz. **2** a radio frequency lying between these frequencies.

Very light *n* a coloured flare fired from a pistol, as a signal or to illuminate an area.

very low frequency *n* (abbrev VLF) **1** a band of radio frequencies between 3 and 30kHz. **2** a radio frequency lying between these frequencies.

vesicle *n* **1** *biol* any small sac or cavity, esp one filled with fluid, within a living cell. **2** *med* a small blister.

vespers *sing n* **1** *now esp RC Church* the sixth of the CANONICAL HOURS, taking place towards evening. **2** an evening service in some Christian Churches.

vessel *n* **1** a container, esp for liquid. **2** a ship or large boat. **3** a tube or duct carrying liquid, eg blood or sap, in animals and plants.

vest *n* **1** an undergarment for the top half of the body. **2** *US, Aust* a waistcoat. ➢ *vb* (*usu* **vest sth in sb** or **sb with sth**) to give or bestow legally or officially: *by the power vested in me*.

vestal virgin *n, hist* in ancient Rome: one of the virgins consecrated to the goddess Vesta, who kept the sacred fire burning on her altar.

vested *adj, law* usu of property or money held in trust: recognized as belonging to a person, although not perhaps available to them until some future date.

vested interest *n* an interest a person has in the fortunes of a particular system or institution because that person is directly affected or closely associated.

vestibule *n* an entrance hall.

vestige /'vɛstɪdʒ/ *n* **1** a slight amount; a hint or shred. **2** *biol* a small functionless part in an animal or plant, which was a fully developed organ in ancestors. ○ **vestigial** /vəˈstɪdʒɪəl/ *adj*.

vestment *n* any ceremonial robe.

vestry *n* (*-ies*) a room in a church where the vestments are kept, often also used for meetings, Sunday school classes, etc.

vet[1] *n* short for VETERINARY SURGEON. ➢ *vb* (*vetted, vetting*) to check someone for suitability or reliability.

vet[2] *n, colloq N Am* short for VETERAN: *a Gulf War vet*.

vetch *n* a climbing plant of the pea family with blue or purple flowers, the pods of which are often used as fodder.

veteran *n* **1** someone with many years of experience in a particular activity. **2** an old and experienced member of the armed forces. **3** *N Am* an ex-serviceman or -woman.

veteran car *n* a very old motor car, specifically one made before 1905.

veterinary *adj* concerned with diseases of animals.

veterinary surgeon or (*N Am*) **veterinarian** *n* a person qualified to treat diseases of animals.

veto /'viːtəʊ/ *n* (*vetoes*) **1 a** the right to formally reject a proposal or forbid an action, eg in a law-making assembly; **b** the act of using such a right. **2** *colloq* any refusal of permission. ➢ *vb* (*vetoes, vetoed*) **1** to formally and authoritatively reject. **2** *loosely* to forbid.

vex *vb* **1** to annoy or irritate someone. **2** to worry someone. ○ **vexation** *n*. ○ **vexing** *adj*.

vexatious *adj* vexing; annoying; troublesome.

vexed *adj* **1** annoyed; angry; troubled. **2** of an issue, etc: much discussed or debated: *vexed question*.

VHF *abbrev, radio* very high frequency.

VHS *abbrev* video home system, a video cassette recording system.

via *prep* by way of or by means of; through: *from Edinburgh to London via York*.

viable *adj* 1 of a plan, etc: having a chance of success; feasible. 2 of a plant, etc: able to exist or grow in particular conditions. 3 of a fetus or baby: able to survive independently outside the womb. ○ **viability** *n*.

viaduct *n* a bridge-like structure of stone arches supporting a road or railway across a valley, etc.

vial *n* a PHIAL.

vibes *pl n* 1 (*also* **vibe** *sing n*) *colloq* feelings, sensations or an atmosphere experienced or communicated: *bad vibes in the room*. 2 the VIBRAPHONE.

vibrant *adj* 1 extremely lively or exciting; strikingly animated or energetic. 2 of a colour: strong and bright. 3 vibrating. ○ **vibrancy** *n*.

vibraphone *n, mus, esp jazz* a percussion instrument with pitched keys set over tuned resonating tubes and electrically driven rotating metal discs which produce a vibrato effect.

vibrate *vb* 1 *tr & intr* to move a short distance back and forth very rapidly. 2 *intr* to ring or resound when struck. 3 *intr* to shake or tremble. 4 *intr* to swing back and forth; to oscillate. ○ **vibratory** *adj*.

vibration *n* 1 a vibrating motion. 2 a a single movement back and forth in vibrating; b sometimes a half of this period, ie either of the back or forward movements. 3 (**vibrations**) *colloq* VIBES (sense I).

vibrato /vɪˈbrɑːtəʊ/ *n, mus* a faint trembling effect in singing or the playing of string and wind instruments, achieved by vibrating the throat muscles or the fingers. Compare TREMOLO.

vibrator *n* any device that produces a vibrating motion.

vicar *n* 1 *C* of *E* the minister of a parish. 2 *RC Church* a bishop's deputy.

vicarage *n* a vicar's residence or benefice.

vicarious /vɪˈkɛərɪəs/ *adj* 1 achieved through witnessing the experience of another person: *vicarious pleasure in seeing his children learn.* 2 undergone on behalf of someone else. 3 standing in for another. 4 of authority, etc: delegated to someone else.

vice[1] or (*N Am*) **vise** *n* a tool with heavy movable metal jaws, usu fixed to a bench, for gripping an object being worked on.

vice[2] /vaɪs/ *n* 1 a habit or activity considered immoral, evil or depraved, esp involving prostitution or drugs. 2 such activities collectively. 3 a bad habit; a fault in one's character.

vice-admiral *n* a naval officer of the rank below an admiral and above a rear admiral.

vice-chancellor *n* the deputy chancellor of a British university, responsible for administrative duties.

vice-president *n* 1 a president's deputy or assistant. 2 an officer next below the president.

viceregal *adj* relating to a viceroy.

viceroy *n* a governor of a province or colony ruling in the name of, and with the authority of, a monarch or national government.

vice squad *n* a branch of the police force that investigates crimes relating to VICE[2].

vice versa *adj* the other way round: *from me to you and vice versa.*

vicinity *n* (*-ies*) 1 a neighbourhood. 2 the area immediately surrounding a place. 3 the condition of being close; nearness.

vicious *adj* 1 violent or ferocious. 2 spiteful or malicious. 3 extremely severe or harsh. ○ **viciously** *adv*. ○ **viciousness** *n*.

vicious circle *n* a situation in which any attempt to resolve a problem creates others which in turn recreate the first one.

vicissitude *n* an unpredictable change of fortune or circumstance. ○ **vicissitudinous** *adj*.

victim *n* 1 a person or animal subjected to death, suffering, ill-treatment or trickery. 2 a person or animal killed in a sacrifice or ritual.

victimize or **-ise** *vb* to single someone or something out for hostile, unfair or vindictive treatment. ○ **victimization** *n*.

victor *n* the winner or winning side in a war or contest.

victoria *n* a large oval red and yellow variety of plum with a sweet flavour.

Victorian *adj* 1 relating to or characteristic of Queen Victoria or her reign (1837–1901). 2 of attitudes or values: a typical of the strictness or conventionality associated with this period; b typical of the hypocrisy and bigotry often thought to underlie these values. ➤ *n* someone who lived during this period.

Victoriana or **victoriana** *pl n* objects from the Victorian period in Britain.

victorious *adj* 1 having won a war or contest: *the victorious army.* 2 referring to, marking or representing a victory: *a victorious outcome.* ○ **victoriously** *adv*.

victory *n* (*-ies*) 1 success against an opponent in a war or contest. 2 an occurrence of this.

victual /ˈvɪtl/ *vb* (**victualled, victualling;** *US* **victualed, victualing**) 1 to supply with victuals. 2 *intr* to obtain supplies. 3 *intr* of animals: to eat victuals. ○ **victualler** or (*US*) **victualer** *n*.

victuals /ˈvɪtlz/ *pl n* (*occasionally* **victual**) food; provisions.

vicuña or **vicuna** /vɪˈkuːnjə/ *n* a ruminant mammal, resembling a LLAMA but smaller, with a light-brown coat and a yellowish-red bib.

videlicet see VIZ.

video *n* 1 short for VIDEO CASSETTE. 2 short for VIDEO CASSETTE RECORDER. 3 a film or programme prerecorded on video cassette. 4 the process of recording, reproducing or broadcasting of visual, esp televised, images on magnetic tape. ➤ *adj* relating to the process of or equipment for recording by video. ➤ *vb* (**videos, videoed**) to make a video cassette recording of (a TV programme, a film, etc).

video camera *n, photog* a portable camera

that records moving visual images directly on to videotape, which can then be played back on a video cassette recorder and viewed on the screen of a television receiver.

video cassette *n* a cassette containing videotape, for use in a video cassette recorder.

video cassette recorder *n* a machine for recording and playing back TV broadcasts, and playing prerecorded tapes of motion pictures.

videoconference *n* a live discussion between people in different locations using electronically linked telephones and video screens.

video game *n* any electronically operated game involving the manipulation of images produced by a computer program on a visual display unit, such as a computer screen, a TV screen, etc.

video recorder *n* a VIDEO CASSETTE RECORDER.

videotape *n* magnetic tape on which visual images and sound can be recorded.

vie *vb* (*vying*) *intr* (*often* vie with sb for sth) to compete or struggle with them for some gain or advantage.

view *n* 1 an act or opportunity of seeing without obstruction: *a good view of the stage.* 2 something, esp a landscape, seen from a particular point: *a magnificent view from the summit.* 3 a range or field of vision: *out of view.* 4 a scene recorded in photograph or picture form. 5 a description or impression: *The book gives a view of life in Roman times.* 6 an opinion; a point of view. 7 a way of considering or understanding something: *a short-term view of the situation.* ➤ *vb* 1 to see or look at something. 2 to inspect or examine something: *We viewed the house that was for sale.* 3 to consider or regard something. 4 *tr & intr* to watch (a programme) on TV; to watch TV. ○ **viewer** *n*. ♦ **in view of sth** taking account of it. **on view** displayed for all to see or inspect. **take a dim view of sth** to regard it disapprovingly or unfavourably. **with a view to sth** with the intention of achieving it.

viewfinder *n* a device forming part of a camera that shows the area covered by the lens.

viewing *n* an act or opportunity of seeing or inspecting something, eg a house for sale.

viewpoint *n* an opinion or point of view; a standpoint.

vigil *n* 1 a period of staying awake, usu to guard or watch over a person or thing. 2 a stationary, peaceful demonstration for a specific cause.

vigilance *n* the state of being watchful or observant.

vigilant *adj* ready for possible trouble or danger; alert; watchful.

vigilante /ˌvɪdʒɪˈlæntɪ/ *n* an unappointed private citizen who assumes responsibility for keeping order in a community.

vignette /viːˈnjɛt/ *n* 1 a decorative design on a book's title page, traditionally of vine leaves. 2 a photographic portrait with the background deliberately faded. 3 a short literary essay, esp one describing a person's character.

vigorous *adj* 1 strong and active. 2 forceful; energetic: *She had a vigorous approach to life.* ○ **vigorously** *adv.*

vigour or (*US*) **vigor** *n* 1 great strength and energy of body or mind. 2 liveliness or forcefulness of action. 3 in plants, etc: healthy growth.

Viking or **viking** *n* any of the Scandinavian seafaring peoples who raided and settled in much of NW Europe between the 8c and 11c.

vile *adj* 1 morally evil or wicked. 2 physically repulsive; disgusting. 3 *colloq* extremely bad or unpleasant.

vilify *vb* (*-ies, -ied*) to say insulting or abusive things about someone or something. ○ **vilification** *n.*

villa *n* 1 a country residence. 2 a holiday home, esp one abroad.

village *n* 1 a group of houses, shops and other buildings, smaller than a town and larger than a hamlet, esp in or near the countryside. 2 the people living in it, regarded as a community: *The village has started to gossip.* ○ **villager** *n.*

villain *n* 1 the principal wicked character in a story. 2 any violent, wicked or unscrupulous person. 3 *colloq* a criminal.

villainous *adj* like or worthy of a villain.

villainy *n* (*-ies*) 1 wicked or vile behaviour. 2 an act of this kind.

villein /ˈvɪlən/ *n, hist* a peasant worker bound to a lord and showing allegiance to him. ○ **villeinage** *n.*

villus *n* (*villi*) *anat* any of many tiny finger-like projections that line the inside of the small intestine and absorb the products of digestion.

vim *n, colloq* energy; liveliness.

vinaigrette /ˌvɪneɪˈɡrɛt/ *n* (*also* **vinaigrette sauce**) a salad dressing made by mixing oil, vinegar and seasonings.

vindaloo *n* a hot Indian curry.

vindicate *vb* 1 to clear someone of blame or criticism. 2 to show something to have been worthwhile or justified. 3 to maintain or uphold (a point of view, cause, etc). ○ **vindication** *n.*

vindictive *adj* 1 feeling or showing spite or hatred. 2 seeking revenge.

vine *n* 1 a woody climbing plant that produces grapes. 2 any climbing or trailing plant, including ivy.

vinegar *n* 1 a sour liquid produced by the fermentation of alcoholic beverages such as cider or wine, used as a condiment and preservative. 2 bad temper.

vineyard /ˈvɪnjəd/ *n* a plantation of grape-bearing vines, esp for wine-making.

viniculture *n* the cultivation of grapes for wine-making.

vino /ˈviːnoʊ/ *n, slang* wine, esp of poor quality.

vintage *n* 1 the grape-harvest of a particular year. 2 the wine produced from a year's harvest. 3 a particular period of origin, esp when regarded as productive: *literature of a postwar vintage.* ➤ *adj* 1 of wine: good quality and of a specified year. 2 typical of someone's best work or most characteristic behaviour: *That re-*

mark was vintage Churchill.

vintage car *n, Brit* an old motor car, specifically one built between 1919 and 1930.

vintner *n, formal* a wine-merchant.

vinyl /ˈvaɪnɪl/ *n* **1** any of a group of tough plastics manufactured in various forms, eg paint additives and carpet fibres. **2** *colloq* plastic records (see RECORD *noun* sense 4) regarded collectively, as distinct from cassettes and CDs.

viol /ˈvaɪəl/ *n* a stringed musical instrument of the Renaissance period, played with a bow.

viola¹ /vɪˈoʊlə/ *n* a musical instrument of the violin family, larger than the violin and lower in pitch.

viola² /ˈvaɪələ/ *n* any of various plants native to temperate regions, including the violet and pansy.

violate *vb* **1** to disregard or break (a law, agreement or oath). **2** to treat (something sacred or private) with disrespect. **3** to disturb or disrupt (eg a person's privacy). **4** to rape or sexually abuse someone. ○ **violation** *n*.

violence *n* **1** the state or quality of being violent. **2** violent behaviour.

violent *adj* **1** marked by or using extreme physical force. **2** using or involving the use of such force to cause physical harm. **3** impulsively aggressive and unrestrained in nature or behaviour. **4** intense; extreme: *They took a violent dislike to me.* ○ **violently** *adv*.

violet *n* **1** a plant with large purple, blue or white petals. **2** a bluish-purple colour. ➤ *adj* violet-coloured.

violin *n* a four-stringed musical instrument, which is usu held with one end under the chin and played with a bow. ○ **violinist** *n*.

violist *n* someone who plays the viol or viola.

violoncello /vaɪələnˈtʃɛloʊ/ *n, formal* a CELLO. ○ **violoncellist** *n*.

VIP *abbrev* very important person.

viper *n* **1** a poisonous snake with long fangs through which venom is injected into the prey. **2** an ADDER.

virago /vɪˈrɑːgoʊ/ *n* (**viragoes** or **viragos**) *literary* a loudly fierce or abusive woman.

viral /ˈvaɪərəl/ *adj* belonging or relating to or caused by a virus.

virgin *n* a person, esp a woman, who has never had sexual intercourse. ➤ *adj* in its original state; never having been used.

virginal¹ *adj* **1** belonging or relating or appropriate to a virgin. **2** in a state of virginity.

virginal² *n* a keyboard instrument used in the 16c and 17c.

virginity *n* (*-ies*) the state of being a virgin.

Virgo *n, astrol* **a** the sixth sign of the zodiac; **b** a person born between 24 August and 23 September, under this sign.

virile *adj* displaying or requiring qualities regarded as typically masculine, esp physical strength. ○ **virility** *n*.

virology *n, med* the branch of microbiology concerned with the study of viruses and viral diseases. ○ **virological** *adj*. ○ **virologist** *n*.

virtual *adj* **1** being so in effect or in practice, but not in name: *a virtual state of war.* **2** nearly so; almost but not quite: *the virtual collapse of the steel industry.* **3** *comput* referring or relating to interaction, connection, use, etc via the Internet: *pay by virtual money.* **4** *comput* of memory or storage: appearing to be internal but actually transferred a segment at a time as required from (and to) back-up storage into (and out of) the smaller internal memory. ○ **virtually** *adv*.

virtual reality *n* a computer simulation of a real or artificial environment that gives the user the impression of actually being within the environment and interacting with it, eg by way of a special visor and special gloves which are worn by the user.

virtue *n* **1** a quality regarded as morally good. **2** moral goodness; righteousness. **3** an admirable quality or desirable feature: *The virtue of this one is its long life.* ✦ **by virtue of sth** because of it; on account of it.

virtuoso *n* someone with remarkable artistic skill, esp a brilliant musical performer. ○ **virtuosity** *n*.

virtuous *adj* possessing or showing virtue; morally sound. ○ **virtuously** *adv*.

virulent /ˈvɪrʊlənt, ˈvɪrjʊ-/ *adj* **1** of a disease: having a rapidly harmful effect. **2** of a disease or the organism causing it: extremely infectious. **3** of a substance: highly poisonous. **4** bitterly hostile. ○ **virulence** *n*.

virus *n* **1** an infectious particle, only visible under an electron microscope, that invades the cells of animals, plants and bacteria, and can only survive and reproduce within such cells. **2** the organism that causes and transmits an infectious disease. **3** *loosely* a disease caused by such an organism. **4** (*in full* **computer virus**) a self-replicating program that attaches to a computer system and when activated can corrupt or destroy data stored on the hard disk.

visa /ˈviːzə/ *n* a permit stamped into a passport, or a similar document, allowing the holder to enter or leave the country which issues it.

visage /ˈvɪzɪdʒ/ *n, literary* **1** the face. **2** the usual expression of a face.

vis-à-vis /viːzɑːˈviː/ *prep* in relation to something or someone.

viscera /ˈvɪsərə/ *pl n, anat* the internal organs of the body, esp those found in the abdominal cavity.

visceral /ˈvɪsərəl/ *adj* **1** belonging or relating to the viscera. **2** belonging or relating to the feelings, esp the basic human instincts as distinct from the intellect.

viscid /ˈvɪsɪd/ *adj* glutinous; sticky.

viscose *n* cellulose in a viscous state, able to be made into thread.

viscosity *n* (*-ies*) a measure of the resistance of a fluid to flow, caused by internal friction.

viscount /ˈvaɪkaʊnt/ *n* a member of the British nobility ranked below an earl and above a baron. ○ **viscountcy** *n* (*-ies*).

viscountess /ˈvaɪkaʊntɪs/ *n* **1** the wife or widow of a viscount. **2** a woman of the rank of viscount in her own right.

viscous *adj* **1** with a thick semi-liquid consistency; not flowing easily. **2** of liquid: sticky.

vise the *N Am* spelling of VICE[1].

visibility *n* **1** the state or fact of being visible. **2** the range in which one can see clearly in given conditions of light and weather: *visibility down to 20 yards*.

visible *adj* **1** able to be seen. **2** able to be realized or perceived; apparent: *his visible discomfort*. **3** *econ* relating to goods rather than services. ○ **visibly** *adv.*

vision *n* **1** the ability or faculty of perceiving with the eye; sight. **2** an image conjured up vividly in the imagination. **3** the ability to perceive what is likely, and plan wisely for it. **4** an image communicated supernaturally, esp by God. **5 a** the picture on a TV screen; **b** the quality of such a picture. **6** someone or something of overwhelming beauty: *a vision in pink taffeta*.

visionary *adj* **1** showing great foresight or imagination. **2** possible only in the imagination; impracticable; fanciful. **3** capable of seeing supernatural images or apparitions. ➤ *n* (*-ies*) a visionary person.

visit *vb* **1** *tr & intr* to go or come to see (a person or place) socially or professionally. **2** *tr & intr* to go or come to stay with someone temporarily. **3** (*usu* visit sth on sb) to inflict (harm or punishment) on them. **4** (*usu* visit sb with sth) *old use* to afflict or trouble them. **5** *N Am colloq* (*usu* visit with sb) to have a chat with them. ➤ *n* **1** an act of visiting; a social or professional call. **2** a temporary stay. **3** a sightseeing excursion.

visitation *n* **1** an official visit or inspection. **2** an event regarded as a divine punishment or reward. **3** an instance of seeing a supernatural vision.

visiting card *n* a card with one's name, address, etc printed on it, which is left instead of a formal visit. *N Am equivalent* calling card.

visitor *n* **1** someone who visits a person or place. **2** (*also* **visitant**) a migratory bird present in a place for a time.

visor or **vizor** /ˈvaɪzə(r)/ *n* **1** the movable part of a helmet, covering the face. **2** a flap at the top of a vehicle's windscreen that can be lowered to shield the driver's eyes from the sun's rays. **3** a peaked shield that is worn on the head to protect the eyes from the sun's rays.

vista *n* a view into the distance.

visual *adj* **1** relating to or received through sight or vision: *a visual image*. **2** creating vivid mental images: *visual poetry*. ○ **visually** *adv.*

visual aid *n* a picture, film or other visual material used as an aid to teaching or presenting information.

visual display unit *n* (abbrev **VDU**) a screen on which information from a computer is displayed.

visualize or **-ise** *vb* to form a clear mental image of someone or something. ○ **visualization** *n.*

vital *adj* **1** relating to or essential for life: *the vital organs*. **2** determining life or death, or success or failure: *a vital error*. **3** essential; of the greatest importance. **4** full of life; energetic. ➤ *n* (**vitals**) the vital organs, including the brain, heart and lungs. ○ **vitally** *adv.*

vitality *n* **1** liveliness and energy. **2** the state of being alive; the ability to stay alive.

vitalize or **-ise** *vb* to fill someone with life or energy. ○ **vitalization** *n.*

vital statistics *pl n* **1** statistics concerning births, marriages, deaths and other matters relating to population. **2** *colloq* a woman's bust, waist and hip measurements.

vitamin *n* any of various organic compounds that occur in small amounts in many foods, are also manufactured synthetically and are essential in small amounts for the normal growth and functioning of the body.

vitiate /ˈvɪʃɪeɪt/ *vb* **1** to impair the quality or effectiveness of (eg an argument); to make something faulty or defective. **2** to make (eg a legal contract) invalid. ○ **vitiation** *n.*

viticulture *n* the cultivation of grapes for making wine; viniculture.

vitreous *adj* **1** relating to or consisting of glass. **2** like glass in hardness, sheen or transparency: *vitreous china*.

vitreous humour *n, anat* a gelatinous substance inside the eye, between the lens and the retina.

vitriol *n* **1** concentrated sulphuric acid. **2** extremely bitter or hateful speech or criticism.

vitriolic *adj* extremely bitter or hateful.

vituperate /vɪˈtʃuːpəreɪt/ *vb* **1** to attack someone with abusive criticism or disapproval. **2** *intr* to use abusive language. ○ **vituperation** *n.* ○ **vituperative** *adj.*

viva[1] /ˈviːvə/ *exclam* long live (someone or something named): *viva Rodriguez!*

viva[2] /ˈvaɪvə/ *n* a VIVA VOCE. ➤ *vb* (**vivas, vivaed, vivaing**) to give someone an oral examination.

vivacious *adj* attractively lively and animated. ○ **vivacity** *n.*

viva voce /ˈvaɪvə ˈvəʊtʃɪ/ *adv* in speech; orally. ➤ *n* an oral examination, usu for an academic qualification. Often shortened to **viva**.

vivid *adj* **1** of a colour: strong and bright. **2** creating or providing a clear and immediate mental picture: *He gave a vivid account of the incident.* ○ **vividly** *adv.* ○ **vividness** *n.*

vivify *vb* (*-ies, -ied*) **1** to give something life. **2** to make something more vivid or startling. ○ **vivification** *n.*

viviparous /vɪˈvɪpərəs, vaɪ-/ *adj, zool* of an animal: giving birth to live young, as in humans and most other mammals. Compare OVIPAROUS, OVOVIVIPAROUS.

vivisection *n* the practice of dissecting living animals for experimental purposes. ○ **vivisectionist** *n.*

vixen *n* **1** a female fox. **2** a fierce or spiteful woman.

viz. *adv* (*in full* **videlicet** /vɪˈdeɪlɪsɛt/) used esp in writing: namely; that is.

vizier /vɪˈzɪə(r)/ *n* a high-ranking government official in some Muslim countries.

vizor see VISOR

VLF *abbrev, radio* very low frequency.

V-neck *n* **1** the open neck of a garment cut or formed to a point at the front. **2** a garment, esp a pullover, with such a neck. ➤ *adj* (*also* **V-necked**) having such a neck: *a V-neck jumper.*

vocabulary *n* (*-ies*) **1** the words used in speaking or writing a particular language. **2** the words, or range of words, known to or used by a particular person or group. **3** a list of words with translations in another language alongside.

vocal *adj* **1** relating to or produced by the voice. **2** expressing opinions or criticism freely and forcefully: *She was very vocal in her support for the homeless.* **3** *phonetics* voiced. ➤ *n* (**vocals**) the parts of a musical composition that are sung, as distinct from the instrumental accompaniment.

vocal cords *pl n, anat* in mammals: the two folds of tissue within the larynx that vibrate and produce sound when air is expelled from the lungs.

vocalist *n* a singer, esp in a pop group or jazz band.

vocalize or **-ise** *vb* **1** to utter or produce something with the voice. **2** to express in words; to articulate. ○ **vocalization** *n.*

vocation *n* **1** a particular occupation or profession, esp one regarded as needing dedication and skill. **2** a feeling of being especially suited for a particular type of work. **3** *relig* a divine calling to adopt a religious life or perform good works. ○ **vocational** *adj.*

vocative *gram, n* **1** in some languages, eg Latin and Greek: the form or CASE² of a noun, pronoun or adjective used when a person or thing is addressed directly. **2** a noun, etc in this case. ➤ *adj* belonging to or in this case.

vociferous *adj* **1** loud and forceful, esp in expressing opinions. **2** noisy. ○ **vociferously** *adv.*

vodka *n* a clear alcoholic spirit of Russian origin, traditionally made from rye, but sometimes from potatoes.

vogue *n* (*usu* **the vogue**) the current fashion or trend in any sphere. ○ **voguish** *adj.* ♦ **in vogue** in fashion.

voice *n* **1** a sound produced by the vocal organs and uttered through the mouth, esp by humans in speech or song. **2** the ability to speak; the power of speech: *Alan lost his voice.* **3** a way of speaking or singing peculiar to each individual: *I couldn't recognize the voice.* **4** a tone of voice reflecting a particular emotion: *in a nervous voice.* **5** the sound of someone speaking: *We heard a voice.* **6** the ability to sing, esp to sing well: *Liz has a lovely voice.* **7** expression in the form of spoken words: *They gave voice to their feelings.* **8** a means or medium of expression or communication. **9** *gram* the status or function of a verb in being either ACTIVE or PASSIVE. ➤ *vb* **1** to express something in speech: *He voiced his disapproval.* **2** *phonetics* to pronounce (a sound) with a vibration of the vocal cords.

voice box *n, colloq* the larynx.

voiced *adj* **1** expressed in speech. **2** *phonetics* pronounced with a vibration of the vocal cords, as in *z, d, b.*

voiceless *adj* **1** without a voice. **2** *phonetics* produced without vibration of the vocal cords, as in *s, t, p.*

voice-over *n* the voice of an unseen narrator in a film, TV advertisement or programme, etc.

void *adj* **1** not valid or legally binding: *She declared the contract null and void.* **2** containing nothing; empty. **3** (*usu* **void of sth**) lacking in: *void of humour.* ➤ *n* **1** an empty space. **2** a feeling of absence or emptiness strongly felt. ➤ *vb* **1** to make empty or clear. **2** to invalidate or nullify. **3** to empty (the bladder or bowels).

voile /vɔɪl, vwɑːl/ *n* any very thin semi-transparent fabric.

vol. or **vol** *abbrev* **1** volume. **2** volunteer. **3** voluntary.

volatile *adj* **1** changing quickly from a solid or liquid into a vapour. **2** easily becoming angry or violent. **3** of a situation, etc: liable to change quickly, esp verging on violence. **4** *comput* of a memory: not able to retain data after the power supply has been cut off. ○ **volatility** *n.*

vol-au-vent /ˈvɒləʊvɑ̃/ *n* a small round puff-pastry case with a savoury filling.

volcanic *adj* **1** relating to or produced by a volcano or volcanoes. **2** easily erupting into anger or violence: *a volcanic temper.*

volcano *n* (**volcanoes**) a vent in the Earth's crust through which MAGMA is or has previously been forced out onto the surface, usu taking the form of a conical hill due to the build up of solidified lava.

vole *n* a small rodent with a blunt snout.

volition *n* the act of willing or choosing; the exercising of one's will: *She did it of her own volition.* ○ **volitional** *adj.*

volley *n* **1 a** a firing of several guns or other weapons simultaneously; **b** the bullets, missiles, etc discharged. **2** an aggressive outburst, esp of criticism or insults. **3** *sport* a striking of the ball before it bounces. ➤ *vb* **1** *tr & intr* to fire (weapons) in a volley. **2** *tr & intr, sport* to strike (a ball) before it bounces.

volleyball *n, sport* a game for two teams of six players each, in which a large ball is volleyed back and forth over a high net with the hands.

volt *n* in the SI system: a unit of electric potential, the difference in potential that will carry a current of one ampere across a resistance of one ohm.

voltage *n, elec* potential difference expressed as a number of volts.

volte-face /vɒlt'fɑːs/ n a sudden and complete reversal of opinion or policy.

voltmeter n, elec an instrument that measures electromotive force in volts.

voluble adj 1 speaking or spoken insistently or with ease. 2 tending to talk at great length. ○ **volubility** n. ○ **volubly** adv.

volume n 1 the amount of three-dimensional space occupied by an object, gas or liquid. 2 a loudness of sound; b the control that adjusts it on a radio, hi-fi system, etc. 3 a book, whether complete in itself or one of several forming a larger work. 4 an amount or quantity, esp when large: *the volume of traffic.*

voluminous adj 1 of clothing: flowing or billowing out; ample. 2 of writing: enough to fill many volumes. ○ **voluminously** adv.

voluntary adj 1 done or acting by free choice, not by compulsion. 2 working with no expectation of being paid or otherwise rewarded. 3 of work: unpaid. 4 of an organization: staffed by unpaid workers; supported by donations of money freely given. 5 of a movement, muscle or limb: produced or controlled by the will. 6 spontaneous; carried out without any persuasion. ➢ n (-ies) a piece of music, usu for an organ, played before, during or after a church service. ○ **voluntarily** adv.

volunteer vb 1 tr & intr (often **volunteer for sth**) to offer one's help or services freely, without being persuaded or forced. 2 intr to go into military service by choice, without being conscripted. 3 to give (information, etc) unasked. 4 colloq to assign someone to perform a task or give help without first asking them: *I'm volunteering you for playground duty.* ➢ n 1 someone who volunteers. 2 someone carrying out voluntary work. 3 a member of a non-professional army of voluntary soldiers.

voluptuary n (-ies) someone addicted to luxury and sensual pleasures. ➢ adj promoting or characterized by luxury and sensual pleasures.

voluptuous adj 1 relating to or suggestive of sensual pleasure. 2 of a woman: full-figured and sexually attractive; curvaceous. ○ **voluptuousness** n.

volute n a spiral.

vomit vb (**vomited, vomiting**) 1 tr & intr to eject the contents of the stomach forcefully through the mouth through a reflex action; to be sick. 2 to emit or throw something out with force or violence. ➢ n the contents of the stomach ejected during the process of vomiting.

voodoo n witchcraft of a type orig practised by Black peoples of the West Indies and southern US.

voracious adj 1 eating or craving food in large quantities. 2 extremely eager in some respect: *a voracious reader.* ○ **voraciously** adv. ○ **voracity** n.

vortex /'vɔːtɛks/ n (**vortexes** or **vortices** /-tɪsiːz/) 1 a whirlpool or whirlwind; any whirling mass or motion. 2 a situation or activity into

which all surrounding people or things are helplessly drawn.

vote n 1 a formal indication of choice or opinion, eg in an election or debate. 2 the right to express a choice or opinion, esp in a national election. 3 a choice or opinion expressed formally, eg by a show of hands, a mark on a ballot paper, etc: *a vote in favour of the motion.* 4 the support given by a certain sector of the population, or to a particular candidate or group, in this way: *the middle-class vote.* ➢ vb 1 intr to cast or register a vote. 2 to decide, state, grant or bring about something by a majority of votes: *They voted that the tax be abolished.* 3 colloq to declare or pronounce by general consent: *The show was voted a success.* 4 colloq to propose or suggest something: *I vote that we go for a swim.* ○ **voter** n. ◇ **vote sb** or **sth down** to defeat them or it by voting. **vote sb** or **sth in** to appoint them or it by voting.

votive adj, relig done or given in thanks to a deity, or to fulfil a vow or promise.

vouch vb 1 intr (usu **vouch for sb** or **sth**) to give a firm assurance or guarantee of their authenticity, trustworthiness, etc. 2 to give (evidence) in support of a statement, assertion, etc.

voucher n 1 a ticket or paper serving as proof, eg of the purchase or receipt of goods. 2 esp in compounds a ticket worth a specific amount of money, exchangeable for goods or services up to the same value: *gift voucher.*

vouchsafe vb, tr & intr, literary 1 to agree or condescend to do, give, grant or allow. 2 (usu **vouchsafe to do sth**) to condescend to do it.

vow n 1 a solemn and binding promise. 2 (often **vows**) a solemn or formal promise of fidelity or affection: *marriage vows.* ➢ vb, tr & intr to promise or declare solemnly, or threaten emphatically; to swear.

vowel n 1 any speech-sound made with an open mouth and no contact between mouth, lips, teeth or tongue. 2 a letter of the alphabet, used alone or in combination, representing such a sound, eg *a, e, i, o, u, ai, oa* and in some words *y.* Compare CONSONANT.

vox pop n, broadcasting 1 popular opinion derived from comments given informally by members of the public. 2 an interview in which such opinions are expressed.

voyage n a long journey to a distant place, esp by air or sea. ➢ vb, intr to go on a voyage. ○ **voyager** n.

voyeur /vwa:'jɜː(r)/ n someone who derives gratification from furtively watching the sexual attributes or activities of others. ○ **voyeurism** n. ○ **voyeuristic** adj.

VR abbrev virtual reality.

vs or **vs.** abbrev versus.

VTOL /'viːtɒl/ n 1 a system that allows an aircraft to take off and land vertically. 2 an aircraft that is fitted with this system.

vulcanite n hard black vulcanized rubber.

vulcanize or **-ise** vb to treat natural or artificial rubber with various concentrations of sulphur or sulphur compounds at high temperatures for specific times, so as to harden it and increase its elasticity. ◇ **vulcanization** *n*.

vulgar *adj* **1** marked by a lack of politeness or social or cultural refinement; coarse. **2** belonging or relating to the form of a language commonly spoken, rather than formal or literary language; vernacular.

vulgar fraction *n* a fraction expressed in the form of a numerator above a denominator, rather than in decimal form. Compare DECIMAL FRACTION.

vulgarian *n* a vulgar person, esp one who is rich.

vulgarism *n* **1** a vulgar expression in speech. **2** an example of vulgar behaviour.

vulgarity *n* (-*ies*) **1** coarseness in speech or behaviour. **2** an instance of it.

vulgarize or **-ise** *vb* **1** to make something vulgar. **2** to make something common or popular, or spoil it in this way. ◇ **vulgarization** *n*.

Vulgate *n* a Latin version of the Bible prepared mainly by St Jerome in the 4c.

vulnerable *adj* **1** easily hurt or harmed physically or emotionally. **2** easily tempted or persuaded. **3** (*often* **vulnerable to sth** or **sb**) unprotected against physical or verbal attack from them. ◇ **vulnerability** *n*. ◇ **vulnerably** *adv*.

vulpine *adj* belonging or relating to, or resembling, a fox.

vulture *n* **1** a large bird with a bare head and a strongly curved beak, which feeds on carrion. **2** someone who exploits the downfall or death of another.

vulva *n*, *anat* the two pairs of labia surrounding the opening to the vagina; the external female genitals.

Ww

W¹ or **w** *n* (**Ws, W's** or **w's**) the twenty-third letter of the English alphabet.

W² *symbol*, *chem* tungsten.

W³ *abbrev* **1** watt. **2** West. **3** Western.

w *abbrev* **1** week. **2** weight. **3** *cricket* wicket. **4** wide. **5** width. **6** with.

wacky or **whacky** *adj* (-*ier*, -*iest*) *colloq*, *orig N Am* mad or crazy; eccentric. ◇ **wackiness** *n*.

wad /wɒd/ *n* **1** a compressed mass of soft material used for packing or stuffing, etc. **2** a compact roll or bundle of banknotes, etc.

wadding *n* material used as padding or stuffing.

waddle /'wɒdəl/ *vb*, *intr* to sway from side to side in walking. ➤ *n* the act of waddling.

wade *vb* **1** *tr & intr* to walk through (something, esp water, which does not allow easy movement of the feet). **2** *intr* (*usu* **wade through sth**) to make one's way laboriously through it: *wading through legal documents*. ◊ **wade in** to involve oneself unhesitatingly and enthusiastically in a task, etc.

wader *n* **1** any long-legged bird that wades in marshes, or along shores. **2** (**waders**) thigh-high waterproof boots used by anglers.

wadi or **wady** /'wɒdɪ/ *n* (**wadies**) a rocky river bed in N Africa and Arabia, dry except during the rains.

wafer *n* **1** a thin light finely layered kind of biscuit. **2** *Christianity* a thin disc of unleavened bread or rice paper served at Holy Communion. **3** *comput* a thin disc of silicon from which chips are cut.

waffle¹ *n*, *cookery* a light-textured cake with a grid-like surface pattern from cooking between metal plates.

waffle² *colloq*, *vb*, *intr* (*also* **waffle on**) to talk or write at length but to little purpose. ➤ *n* talk or writing of this kind.

waft *vb*, *tr & intr* to float or make (something) float or drift gently, esp through the air. ➤ *n* a whiff, eg of perfume.

wag *vb* (**wagged, wagging**) **1** *tr & intr* to wave (something) to and fro vigorously. **2** *intr* of the tongue, chin or beard: to move in light or gossiping chatter. **3** *slang* to play truant: *We wagged school*. ➤ *n* **1** a wagging movement. **2** a habitual joker or a wit. ◇ **waggish** *adj*.

wage *vb* to engage in or fight (a war or battle). ➤ *n* (*often* **wages**) a regular, esp weekly, payment from an employer to an employee.

wager *n* a bet on the result of something. ➤ *vb*, *tr & intr* to bet; to stake (something) in a bet.

waggle *vb*, *tr & intr* to move or make (something) move to and fro.

wagon or **waggon** *n* **1** a four-wheeled vehicle, often horse-drawn, used esp for carrying loads; a cart. **2** an open truck or closed van for carrying railway freight. **3** *colloq* a car, esp an estate car. ◇ **wagoner** *n*. ♦ **on the wagon** *colloq* temporarily abstaining from alcohol.

wagtail *n* any of various birds which constantly wag their tails.

waif *n* **1** an orphaned, abandoned or homeless child. **2** any pathetically undernourished-looking person. ◇ **waif-like** *adj*.

wail *n* **1** a prolonged and high-pitched mournful or complaining cry. **2** any sound resembling this. ➤ *vb tr & intr* to make or utter such a cry or sound.

wain *n*, *usu poetic* an open wagon, esp for hay or other agricultural produce.

wainscot *n* wooden panelling covering the lower part of the walls of a room.

○ **wainscoting** or **wainscotting** n.

waist n **1** the narrow part of the human body between the ribs and hips. **2** the part of a garment that covers this.

waistband n the reinforced strip of cloth on a skirt, trousers, etc that fits round the waist.

waistcoat n a close-fitting sleeveless garment, usu waist-length, worn esp by men under a jacket. N Am equivalent **vest**.

waistline n **1** the line marking the waist. **2** the measurement of a waist.

wait vb **1** to be or remain in a particular place in readiness. **2** intr (often **wait for sth**) to delay action or remain in a certain place in expectation of, or readiness for, it. **3** intr of a task, etc: to remain temporarily undealt with: That can wait. **4** to postpone action for (a period of time). **5** intr (often **wait on sb**) to serve (them), esp as a waiter, waitress, or servant. ♦ **lie in wait** or **lay wait** to be in hiding ready to surprise or ambush someone. ◊ **wait up** US to slow down or wait: Wait up, I can't run that fast. **wait up for sb** to delay going to bed at night waiting for their arrival or return.

waiter or **waitress** n a man or woman who serves people with food at a hotel, restaurant, etc.

waiting list n a list of people waiting for something currently unavailable.

waiting room n a room for people to wait in.

waive vb, law to refrain from insisting upon (something); to voluntarily give up (a claim or right, etc).

waiver n **1** the act or an instance of waiving. **2** a written statement formally confirming this.

wake[1] vb (**woke**, **woken**) tr & intr **1** (also **wake** (**sb**) **up**) **a** to rouse (them) or be roused from sleep; **b** to stir or be stirred out of a state of inactivity or lethargy, etc. **2** (often **wake up** or **wake sb up to sth**) to become or make (them) aware of a fact or situation, etc. ➤ n a watch or vigil kept beside a corpse.

wake, waken, awake, awaken These four verbs are virtually synonymous, with **wake** being the most commonly used. All can be used with or without an object; all can be used both in the literal sense 'to rouse from sleep' and in the figurative sense 'to arouse or provoke (feelings)'. The only difference between them is that **awake** and **awaken** are never followed by **up**.

wake[2] n a trail of disturbed water left by a ship, or of disturbed air left by an aircraft. ♦ **in the wake of sb** or **sth** coming after them or it; resulting from them or it.

wakeful adj **1** not asleep or unable to sleep. **2** of a night: sleepless. **3** vigilant or alert. ○ **wakefulness** n.

waken vb, tr & intr to rouse (someone) or be roused from sleep, or from inactivity or lethargy.

walk vb **1** intr to go on foot, moving one's feet alternately and always having one foot on the ground. **2** to go about (the streets or countryside, etc) on foot; to ramble. **3** to lead, accompany or support (someone who is on foot). **4** to take (a dog) out for exercise. **5** intr, colloq to disappear or go away; to be stolen: My pen has walked. ➤ n **1** the motion or pace of walking. **2** an outing or journey on foot, esp for exercise. **3** a distance walked or for walking. **4** a person's distinctive manner of walking. **5** a route for walking. **6** a path, esp a broad one; a promenade. ○ **walker** n. ♦ **walk all over sb** colloq **1** to take advantage of them. **2** to defeat them easily. **walk on air** to feel euphoric and light-hearted. **walk the streets 1** to wander about aimlessly, or in search of work. **2** to be a prostitute. ◊ **walk into sth 1** to collide or meet with (eg a joke, trap) unexpectedly. **2** to involve oneself in trouble or difficulty through unwariness. **walk out** to depart abruptly, esp in protest. **walk out on sb** to abandon them.

walkabout n **1** a casual stroll through a crowd of ordinary people by a celebrity, a member of the royal family, a politician, etc. **2** a period of wandering.

walkie-talkie n, colloq a portable two-way radio.

walking-stick n **1** a stick or cane used for support or balance in walking. **2** US a STICK INSECT.

Walkman n, trademark a small portable music player with headphones.

walk-on adj of a part in a play or opera, etc: not involving any speaking or singing.

walkout n a sudden departure, esp of a workforce in declaration of a strike.

walkover n, colloq an easy victory.

walkway n a paved path or passage for pedestrians.

wall /wɔːl/ n **1** a solid vertical brick or stone construction serving as a barrier, division, protection, etc. **2** the vertical side of a building or room. **3** something similar to or suggestive of a wall: a wall of fire. **4** biol **a** an outer covering, eg of a cell; **b** the side of a hollow organ or cavity. **5** a psychological barrier. ➤ vb **1** to surround or fortify (something) with, or as if with, a wall. **2** (usu **wall sth off** or **in**) to separate or enclose it with a wall. **3** (**wall sth** or **sb up**) **a** to block (an opening) with a wall or bricks; **b** to confine them behind a wall. ○ **walled** adj. ♦ **have one's back to the wall** to be in a difficult or desperate situation. **up the wall** colloq angry; crazy or mad.

wallaby n (**wallabies** or **wallaby**) a marsupial of the kangaroo family, native to Australia and Tasmania.

wallah or **walla** n, Anglo-Indian, in compounds a person who performs a specified task: the tea wallah.

wallet n **1** a flat folding case, often of leather, for holding banknotes, credit cards, etc. **2** any of various kinds of folders for papers, etc.

walleye *n* an eye that squints away from the nose, so that an abnormal amount of the white shows. ○ **walleyed** *adj*.

wallflower *n* **1** a sweet-smelling flowering plant. **2** *colloq* someone who sits all evening at the edge of the dance floor, waiting in vain to be asked to dance.

Walloon /wɒˈluːn/ *n* **1** a member of the French-speaking population of S Belgium. **2** their language, a dialect of French.

wallop *colloq*, *vb* (**walloped, walloping**) **1** to hit or strike vigorously. **2** to defeat soundly. ➤ *n* **1** a hit or a thrashing. **2** a powerful impression.

walloping *n* a thrashing. ➤ *adj* great; whopping.

wallow *vb*, *intr* (*often* **wallow in sth**) **1** to lie or roll about (in water or mud, etc). **2** to revel or luxuriate (in admiration, etc). **3** to indulge excessively (in self-pity, etc). ➤ *n* **1** the act of wallowing. **2** the place, or the dirt, in which an animal wallows.

wallpaper *n* paper, often coloured or patterned, used to decorate interior walls and ceilings. ➤ *vb* to cover (walls) or the walls of (a room) with wallpaper.

wall-to-wall *adj* usu of carpeting: covering the entire floor of a room.

wally *n* (**-ies**) *Brit*, *colloq* an ineffectual, stupid or foolish person.

walnut *n* **1** a deciduous tree. **2** its edible round nut. **3** its hard durable golden-brown wood.

walrus *n* (**walruses** or **walrus**) a large marine mammal related to the seal, with thick wrinkled skin, webbed flippers and two long tusks.

waltz *n* **1** a slow or fast ballroom dance in triple time, in which the dancers spin round the room. **2** a piece of music for this. ➤ *vb*, *intr* **1** to dance a waltz. **2** (*often* **waltz in** or **off**) *colloq* to go or move with vivacity and easy confidence: *She just waltzed in and took over.*

wampum /ˈwɒmpəm, ˈwɔː-/ *n*, *hist* shells strung together for use as money among the Native Americans.

wan /wɒn/ *adj* (**wanner, wannest**) pale and pinched-looking, esp from illness, exhaustion or grief. ○ **wanly** *adv*.

wand *n* **1** a slender rod used by magicians, conjurors, fairies, etc for performing magic. **2** a conductor's baton.

wander *vb* **1** to walk or travel about, with no particular destination. **2** to stray or deviate, eg from the right path, or from the point of an argument, etc. **3** of thoughts, etc: to flit randomly. ➤ *n* a ramble or stroll. ○ **wanderer** *n*. ○ **wandering** *n*, *adj*.

wanderlust *n* an urge to rove or travel.

wane *vb*, *intr* **1** of the moon: to appear to grow narrower as the sun illuminates less of its surface. **2** to decline in glory, power or influence, etc. ➤ *n* the process of waning or declining. ○ **waning** *adj*. ♦ **on the wane** decreasing or declining.

wangle *vb*, *colloq* to contrive or obtain some-

thing by persuasiveness.

wank *coarse slang*, *vb*, *intr* to masturbate. ➤ *n* masturbation.

wanker *n*, *coarse slang* **1** someone who masturbates. **2** *derog* a worthless contemptible person.

wannabe or **wannabee** /ˈwɒnəbiː/ *n*, *colloq* someone who aspires to be something or who admires and imitates the appearance, mannerisms and habits, etc of another person.

want *vb* **1** to feel a need or desire for (something). **2** to need to be dealt with in a specified way: *The bin wants emptying.* **3** *colloq* ought; need: *You want to take more care.* **4** (*often* **want for sth**) to feel the lack of it: *That kid wants for nothing.* **5** to require the presence of (someone or something): *You are wanted next door.* ➤ *n* **1** a need or requirement. **2** a lack: *a want of discretion.* **3** a state of need; destitution. ♦ **for want of sth** in the absence of it. **in want of sth** needing it.

---

want There is often a spelling confusion between **want** and **wont**.

---

wanted *adj* **1** needed or desired. **2** of a person: sought by the police.

wanting *adj* **1** missing; lacking. **2** not up to requirements: *found wanting.*

wanton *adj* **1** thoughtlessly and needlessly cruel. **2** motiveless: *wanton destruction.* **3** sexually immoral; lewd or licentious. ➤ *n*, *old use* an immoral person, esp a woman.

wapiti /ˈwɒpɪtɪ/ *n* (**wapitis**) a type of large N American deer, locally referred to as an **elk**.

war *n* **1** an open state of armed conflict, esp between nations. **2** any long struggle or campaign. **3** fierce rivalry or competition. ➤ *vb* (**warred, warring**) *intr* **1** to fight wars. **2** to be in conflict. ♦ **have been in the wars** *colloq* to have been damaged.

warble *vb*, *tr* & *intr* **1** of a bird: to sing melodiously. **2** of a person: to sing in a high tremulous voice; to trill.

warbler *n* a small songbird with dull green, brown or grey upper plumage, and a slender pointed bill.

war crime *n* a crime committed during a war, esp ill-treatment of prisoners or massacre of civilians. ○ **war criminal** *n*.

war cry *n* **1** a cry used to rally or encourage troops, or as a signal for charging. **2** a slogan or watchword.

ward *n* **1** a room or department of a hospital. **2** any of the areas into which a town, etc is divided for administration or elections. **3** *law* someone, esp a minor, under the protection of a guardian or court. ➤ *vb* (*usu* **ward off**) to keep (trouble, hunger or disease, etc) away.

warden *n* **1** someone in charge of a hostel, student residence or old people's home, etc. **2** *in compounds* a public official responsible for maintaining order: *traffic warden* • *game warden.* **3** *N Am* the officer in charge of a prison.

warder or **wardress** *n* 1 *Brit* a prison officer. 2 a man or woman who guards someone or something.

wardrobe *n* 1 a tall cupboard for clothes. 2 a personal stock of garments or costumes.

wardroom *n* the officers' quarters on board a warship.

ware *n* 1 *in compounds* manufactured goods of a specified material or for a specified use: *kitchenware*. 2 a particular type of pottery. 3 (**wares**) goods for sale.

warehouse *n* 1 a large building or room for storing goods. 2 a large, usu wholesale, shop.

warfare *n* the activity or process of waging or engaging in war.

warhead *n* the front part of a missile or torpedo etc that contains the explosives.

warhorse *n* 1 *hist* a powerful horse on which a knight rode into battle. 2 an old soldier or politician.

warlike *adj* 1 fond of fighting; aggressive or belligerent. 2 relating to war; military.

warlock *n* a wizard, male magician or sorcerer.

warlord *n* a powerful military leader.

warm *adj* 1 moderately, comfortably or pleasantly hot. 2 providing and preserving heat. 3 kind-hearted and affectionate. 4 welcoming and congenial. 5 enthusiastic; whole-hearted. 6 of a colour: suggestive of comfortable heat, typically containing red or yellow. 7 in a game, etc: close to being correct. ➤ *vb* 1 *tr & intr* (*usu* warm up or warm sth up) a to make or become warm or warmer; b of a party, etc: to become or make it livelier; c of an engine: to reach an efficient working temperature; d to exercise gently in preparation for a strenuous workout, race, etc. 2 (*usu* warm to sth or sb) to gain in enthusiasm or affection for them. ○ **warmly** *adv*.

warm-blooded *adj* 1 *zool* maintaining internal body temperature at a relatively constant level, independent of environmental temperature. 2 passionate.

war memorial *n* a monument to those who died in a war.

warm front *n, meteorol* the edge of a mass of advancing warm air.

warm-hearted *adj* kind, affectionate and generous; sympathetic.

warmonger *n* someone who tries to precipitate war, or who generates enthusiasm for it.

warmth *n* 1 the condition of being warm. 2 affection or kind-heartedness.

warm-up *n* the act of gently exercising the body in preparation for a strenuous work-out or race, etc.

warn *vb* 1 (*usu* warn sb of or about) to make them aware of (possible or approaching danger or difficulty). 2 to rebuke or admonish (someone), with the threat of punishment for a repetition of the offence. 3 (*often* warn sb against sb or sth) to caution them about them or it. 4 (warn sb off) to order them to go or keep away, often with threats.

warning *n* a statement, action or event that serves to caution.

warp *vb, tr & intr* 1 to become or cause to become twisted out of shape through the shrinking and expanding effects of damp or heat, etc. 2 to become or make distorted, corrupted or perverted. ➤ *n* 1 the state or fact of being warped. 2 an unevenness or twist in wood, etc. 3 a distorted or abnormal twist in personality, etc. 4 a shift or displacement in a continuous dimension, esp time. 5 *weaving* the set of threads stretched lengthways in a loom, under and over which the widthways set of threads (the WEFT or WOOF²) are passed. ○ **warped** *adj*.

warpaint *n* 1 paint put on the face and body when going to war, esp by Native Americans. 2 *colloq* a woman's make-up.

warpath *n* a route taken by people, esp Native Americans, going to war. ◆ **on the warpath** *colloq* **a** in angry pursuit; **b** in an angry mood.

warrant *n* 1 a written legal authorization for doing something, eg searching property. 2 a certificate such as a licence, voucher or receipt, that authorizes, guarantees or confirms something. ➤ *vb* 1 to justify (something). 2 to guarantee (goods, etc) as being of the specified quality or quantity.

warrant officer *n* in the armed services: an officer ranked between a commissioned and non-commissioned officer.

warranty *n* (*-ies*) an assurance of the quality of goods being sold, usu with an acceptance of responsibility for repairs during an initial period of use.

warren *n* 1 an underground labyrinth of interconnecting rabbit burrows. 2 an overcrowded dwelling or district. 3 any maze of passages.

warrior *n* a skilled fighter.

warship *n* a ship armed with guns, etc for battle.

wart *n* a small and usu hard benign growth, transmitted by a virus, found on the skin, esp of the fingers, hands and face. ○ **warty** *adj*. ◆ **warts and all** *colloq* with any blemishes or defects showing and accepted.

warthog *n* a large wild pig with wart-like lumps on its face, a bristly mane and two pairs of backward-curving tusks.

wartime *n* a period during which a war is going on.

wary / 'wɛərɪ/ *adj* (*-ier, -iest*) 1 alert, vigilant or cautious; on one's guard. 2 distrustful or apprehensive. 3 (*often* wary of sth or sb) suspicious of it or them. ○ **warily** *adv*. ○ **wariness** *n*.

wash *vb* 1 to cleanse (someone or something) with water and usu soap or detergent. 2 *intr* to cleanse (oneself, or one's hands and face) this way. 3 *intr* of a fabric or dye: to withstand washing without change or damage. 4 (*also* wash off or out) a *tr* to remove (a stain, dirt, etc) esp by using soap and water; b *intr* of a stain, dirt, etc: to be removed in this way. 5 *tr & intr* of an animal: to lick (itself or its young, etc) clean. 6

of a river, the sea, waves, etc: to flow against or over (a place or land feature, etc). **7** of flowing water: to erode or gouge out (a channel, etc) in the landscape. **8** to apply a thin layer of metal, paint etc to. **9** intr, colloq to stand the test; to bear investigation: *That excuse just won't wash.* ➤ *n* **1** the process of washing or being washed. **2** a quantity of clothes, etc for washing, or just washed. **3** the breaking of waves against something; the sound of this. **4** the rough water or disturbed air left by a ship or aircraft. **5** often in compounds a lotion or other preparation for cleansing or washing: *facewash.* **6** art a thin application of watercolour. ◇ **washable** adj. ♦ **come out in the wash** colloq to turn out satisfactorily, or become known, in the end. ◊ **wash sth down 1** to wash it from top to bottom. **2** to ease (a pill) down one's throat, or accompany or follow (food), with a drink. **wash up** to wash (the dishes and cutlery) after a meal.

washbasin or **washhand basin** *n* a shallow sink in which to wash one's face and hands.

washed-out adj **1** colloq of a person: worn out and pale; lacking in energy. **2** of fabric: faded by, or as if by, washing.

washed-up adj (esp **all washed-up**) slang finished; unsuccessful.

washer *n* **1** someone who washes. **2** a washing machine. **3** a flat ring of rubber or metal for keeping a joint or nut secure.

washing *n* **1** the act of cleansing, wetting or coating with liquid. **2** clothes to be, or which have just been, washed.

washing line *n* a CLOTHESLINE.

washing machine *n* a machine for washing clothes, bed linen, etc.

washing powder or **washing liquid** *n* a powdered or liquid detergent for washing fabrics.

washing soda *n* crystals of SODIUM CARBONATE dissolved in water for washing and cleaning.

washing-up *n* **1** the washing of dishes and cutlery, etc after a meal. **2** dishes and cutlery, etc for washing.

washout *n* **1** colloq a flop or failure. **2** colloq a useless person. **3** a rained-off event.

washroom *n*, N Am a lavatory.

washstand *n*, hist a small table in a bedroom designed to hold a jug and basin for washing one's hands and face.

washy adj (-ier, -iest) colloq **1** watery or weak. **2** feeble. **3** faded-looking.

wasn't contraction was not.

wasp *n* a common stinging insect with a slender black-and-yellow striped body.

waspish adj sharp-tongued; caustic or venomous.

wassail /'wɒseɪl/ *n, old use* **1** a festive bout of drinking. **2** a toast made at such an occasion. **3** a liquor for such toasts, esp a warm spiced ale. ➤ *vb* to go from house to house at Christmas singing carols and festive songs.

wastage *n* **1** the process of wasting; loss

through wasting. **2** the amount lost through wasting. **3** (esp **natural wastage**) reduction of staff through retirement or resignation, as distinct from dismissal or redundancy.

waste *vb* **1** to use or spend purposelessly or extravagantly; to squander. **2** intr to be used to no, or little, purpose or effect. **3** to fail to use, make the best of or take advantage of (an opportunity, etc). **4** to throw away (something unused or uneaten, etc). **5** (also **waste away**) tr & intr to lose or cause (someone) to lose flesh or strength. **6** chiefly US, slang to murder (someone). ➤ *adj* **1** rejected as useless, unneeded or excess to requirements. **2** of ground: lying unused, uninhabited or uncultivated. **3** physiol denoting material excreted from the body, usu in the urine or faeces. ➤ *n* **1** the act or an instance of wasting, or the condition of being wasted. **2** failure to take advantage of something: *a waste of talent.* **3** material no longer needed in its present form that must be processed, eg nuclear waste. **4** refuse; rubbish. **5** physiol matter excreted from the body. **6** a devastated or barren region. **7** (often **wastes**) a vast tract of uncultivated land or expanse of ocean, etc. ♦ **go** or **run to waste** to be wasted. **lay sth waste** to devastate it.

wasted adj **1** not exploited; squandered. **2** shrunken or emaciated. **3** slang extremely drunk or high on drugs.

wasteful adj causing waste; extravagant.

wasteland *n* **1** a desolate and barren region. **2** a place or point in time that is culturally, intellectually and spiritually empty.

waste paper *n* used paper discarded as rubbish.

waster *n* **1** an idler; a good-for-nothing. **2** a person or thing that wastes.

wastrel /'weɪstrəl/ *n* an idle spendthrift; a good-for-nothing.

watch *vb* **1** tr & intr to look at or focus one's attention on (someone or something) that is moving or doing something, etc. **2** tr & intr to pass time looking at or observing (TV, a programme, etc). **3** to keep track of, follow or monitor (developments, progress, etc). **4** intr to keep vigil; to remain awake or on the alert. **5** (also **watch for**) **a** to await one's chance; to be on the alert to take advantage of (an opportunity); **b** to look out for or guard against (something). **6** to pay proper attention to (something): *Watch where you're going!* ➤ *n* **1** a small timepiece, usu strapped to the wrist or on a chain in the waistcoat pocket or attached to clothing. **2** the activity, duty, or shift of watching or guarding. **3** a wake; a vigil kept beside a corpse. ♦ **keep a watch on sth** or **sb** to keep it or them under observation. **on the watch for sth** seeking or looking out for it. **watch it!** be careful! **watch one's step 1** to step or advance with care. **2** colloq to act cautiously or warily. ◊ **watch out** to be careful. **watch out for sth** or **sb** to be on one's guard against it or them, or to look out for it or them. **watch over**

sb or **sth** to guard, look after or tend to them or it.

watchable *adj, colloq* of entertainment: enjoyable and interesting to watch.

watchdog *n* **1** a dog kept to guard premises, etc. **2** a person or organization that guards against unacceptable standards, inefficiency or illegality, etc.

watchful *adj* alert, vigilant and wary. ○ **watchfully** *adv.* ○ **watchfulness** *n*.

watchman *n* (*also* **nightwatchman**) a man employed to guard premises at night.

watchtower *n* a tower from which a sentry keeps watch.

watchword *n* a catchphrase or slogan of a party or profession, etc.

water *n* **1** a colourless odourless tasteless liquid that freezes to form ice at 0°C and boils to form steam at 100°C. **2** (*also* **waters**) an expanse of this; a sea, lake or river, etc. **3** the surface of a body of water. **4** (**waters**) the sea round a country's coasts, considered part of its territory: *in British waters.* **5** the level or state of the tide: *high water.* **6** (**waters**) the amniotic fluid that surrounds the fetus in the womb. **7** *finance* an increase in a company's stock issue without an increase in assets to back it up. ➢ *vb* **1** to wet, soak or sprinkle (something) with water. **2** (*also* **water sth down**) to dilute (wine, etc). **3** *intr* of the mouth: to produce saliva esp at the expectation of food. **4** *intr* of the eyes: to fill with tears in response to irritation. **5** a *tr* to let (animals) drink; **b** *intr* of animals: to drink: *fed and watered.* **6** *finance* to increase (the debt of a company) by issuing new stock without a corresponding increase in assets. ○ **waterless** *adj.* ◆ **hold water** of an explanation, etc: to be valid. **in deep water** in trouble, danger or difficulty. **like a fish out of water** uncomfortable in a particular environment. **like water off a duck's back** of a rebuke or scolding, etc: having no effect at all. **water under the bridge** experiences that are past and done with. ◊ **water sth down** to reduce the impact of it; to make it less offensive.

waterbed *n* a waterproof mattress filled with water.

water biscuit *n* a thin crisp plain biscuit made from water and flour, usu eaten with cheese, etc.

water buffalo *n* the common domestic buffalo, native to India, Sri Lanka and SE Asia, which has large ridged horns that curve backwards.

water cannon *n* a hosepipe that sends out a powerful jet of water, used for dispersing crowds.

water chestnut *n* the tuber of a Chinese sedge plant, eaten as a vegetable.

water closet *n* **1** a flush toilet. **2** a small room containing this.

watercolour *n* **1** paint thinned with water rather than oil. **2** a painting done with this.

water-cooled *adj* of an engine, etc: cooled by circulating water.

watercourse *n* **1** a stream, river or canal. **2** the bed or channel along which any of these flow.

watercress *n* **1** a plant with creeping stems and dark-green oval leaflets, that grows in watery regions. **2** its sharp-tasting leaves used in salads and soups, etc.

water-diviner *n* someone who detects underground sources of water, usu with a DIVINING ROD.

watered-down *adj* **1** very diluted. **2** reduced in force or vigour.

waterfall *n* a sudden interruption in the course of a river or stream where water falls more or less vertically, eg over the edge of a cliff.

waterfowl *sing n* a bird that lives on or near water, esp a duck or swan. ➢ *pl n* swimming birds collectively.

waterfront *n* the buildings or part of a town lying along the edge of a river, lake or sea.

waterhole *n* (*also* **watering hole**) a pool or spring in a dried-up or desert area, where animals can drink.

water ice *n* sweetened fruit juice or purée frozen and served as a dessert; a sorbet.

watering can *n* a container with a handle and spout used for watering plants.

watering hole *n* **1** a waterhole. **2** *slang* a public house.

watering place *n* **1** a place where animals obtain water. **2** *hist* a spa or other resort where people go to drink mineral water or bathe.

water jump *n* in a steeplechase, etc: a jump over a water-filled ditch or pool, etc.

water lily *n* an aquatic plant with large flat circular leaves and flowers that float on the surface.

waterline *n* the level reached by the water on the hull of a floating vessel.

waterlogged *adj* saturated with water.

water main *n* a large underground pipe that carries a public water supply.

watermark *n* **1** the limit reached by the sea at high or low tide. **2** a manufacturer's distinctive mark in paper, visible only when the paper is held up to the light.

water meadow *n* a meadow kept fertile by periodic flooding from a stream.

watermelon *n* a large round fruit with a hard green skin and sweet juicy pink or red flesh containing many black seeds.

watermill *n* a mill whose machinery is driven by a waterwheel.

water polo *n* a seven-a-side game for swimmers, in which the object is to propel the ball into the opposing team's goal.

water power *n* the power generated by moving water, used to drive machinery directly or indirectly.

waterproof *adj* impenetrable by water; treated or coated so as to resist water. ➢ *vb* to treat (fabric, etc) to make it waterproof. ➢ *n* a waterproof outer garment.

water rat *n* **1** any of various unrelated small

rodents that live near water, esp the WATER VOLE. **2** US the MUSKRAT.

watershed n **1** a ridge or mountain that separates two river basins. **2** the region that drains into a particular river. **3** a crucial point after which events take a different turn.

water-ski n a ski on which to glide over water, towed by a powered boat. ➤ vb, intr to travel on water skis. ○ **water-skier** n. ○ **water-skiing** n.

water softener n a substance or device used in water to remove minerals, esp calcium, that cause hardness and prevent lathering.

water-soluble adj able to be dissolved in water.

water sports pl n sports practised on or in the water, eg swimming and water-skiing, etc.

water table n, geol the level below which porous rocks are saturated with water.

watertight adj **1** so well sealed as to be impenetrable by water. **2** of an argument, etc: without any flaw, weakness or ambiguity, etc.

water tower n a tower that supports a water tank, from which water can be distributed at uniform pressure.

water vapour n water in the form of an air dispersion, esp where evaporation has occurred at a temperature below boiling point.

water vole n a species of vole which burrows into the banks of streams and ponds.

waterway n a navigable channel, eg a canal or river, used by ships or boats.

waterwheel n a wheel turned by the force of flowing or falling water on blades or buckets around its rim.

waterwings pl n a pair of inflatable armbands, used by people learning to swim.

waterworks sing n an installation where water is purified and stored for distribution. ➤ pl n euphem one's bladder and urinary system. ♦ **turn on the waterworks** to start crying or weeping.

watery adj (-ier, -iest) **1** relating to, consisting of or containing water. **2** containing too much water; weak or thin. **3** of eyes: moist; inclined to water.

watt n, physics in the SI system: a unit of power equal to one joule per second.

wattage n electrical power expressed in watts.

wattle n **1** rods or branches, etc forming eg a framework for a wall, fences or roofs, esp when interwoven. **2** a loose fold of skin hanging from the throat of certain birds and lizards. **3** an Australian acacia tree with leaves divided into numerous tiny leaflets, and many tiny yellow flowers.

wattle and daub n wattle plastered with mud or clay, used as a building material.

wave vb **1** tr & intr to move (one's hand) to and fro in greeting, farewell or as a signal. **2** to hold up and move (some other object) in this way for this purpose. **3** tr & intr to move or make (something) move or sway to and fro. **4** (esp **wave sb on** or **through**) to direct them with a

gesture of the hand. **5** intr of hair: to have a gentle curl or curls. **6** to put a gentle curl into (hair) by artificial means. ➤ n **1** any of a series of moving ridges on the surface of the sea or some other body of water. **2** an act of waving the hand, etc. **3** physics a regularly repeated disturbance or displacement in a medium, eg water or air. **4** any of the circles of disturbance moving outwards from the site of a shock, such as an earthquake. **5** a loose soft curl, or series of such curls, in the hair. **6** a surge or sudden feeling of an emotion or a physical symptom. **7** a sudden increase in something: a heat wave. **8** an advancing body of people. **9** any of a series of curves in an upward-and-downward curving line or outline. ♦ **make waves** to create a disturbance or cause trouble, etc; to aggravate a situation.

waveband n, radio a range of frequencies in the electromagnetic spectrum occupied by radio or TV broadcasting transmission of a particular type.

wavelength n, physics **1** the distance between two successive peaks or troughs of a wave. **2** the length of the radio wave used by a particular broadcasting station. ♦ **on the same wavelength** of two or more people: thinking in a similar way.

waver vb, intr **1** to move to and fro. **2** to falter, lessen or weaken, etc. **3** to hesitate through indecision. **4** of the voice: to become unsteady through emotion, etc. ○ **wavering** adj.

wavy adj (-ier, -iest) **1** of hair: full of waves. **2** of a line or outline: curving alternately upwards and downwards.

wax[1] n **1** chem any of various fatty substances of plant, animal or mineral origin that are typically shiny, have a low melting point, are easily moulded when warm, and are insoluble in water. **2** the sticky yellowish matter that forms in the ears. ➤ vb **1** to use or apply a natural or mineral wax on (something), eg prior to polishing. **2** to remove hair from (a part of the body) by coating with wax, which is then peeled off. ○ **waxy** adj.

wax[2] vb, intr **1** of the moon: to appear larger as more of its surface is illuminated by the sun. **2** to increase in size, strength or power. **3** facetious to become (eloquent or lyrical) in one's description of something. ♦ **wax and wane** to increase and decrease in alternating sequence.

waxcloth n, old use **1** OILCLOTH. **2** LINOLEUM.

waxen adj made of, resembling, or covered with wax.

wax paper n paper covered with a thin layer of white wax to make it waterproof.

waxwork n **1** a lifelike wax model, esp of a famous person. **2** (**waxworks**) an exhibition of these.

way n **1 a** a route, entrance or exit, etc that provides passage or access somewhere; **b** the passage or access provided. **2** the route, road or direction taken for a particular journey. **3**

(**Way**) used in street names. **4** *often in compounds* a direction or means of motion: *a waterway.* **5** an established position: *the wrong way up.* **6** a distance in space or time: *a little way ahead.* **7** one's district: *if you're round our way.* **8** the route or path ahead; room to move or progress. **9** a means. **10** a distinctive manner or style. **11** a method. **12** (**ways**) customs or rituals. **13** a characteristic piece of behaviour. **14** a mental approach: *different ways of looking at it.* **15** a respect: *correct in some ways.* **16** a state or condition. **17** progress; forward motion: *They made their way through the crowds.* ➤ *adv, colloq* far; a long way: *They met way back in the 60s.* ◆ **by the way** incidentally; let me mention while I remember. **by way of** as a form or means of: *He grinned by way of apology.* **get** or **have one's own way** to do, get or have what one wants, often as opposed to what others want. **give way 1** to collapse or subside. **2** to fail or break down under pressure, etc. **3** to yield to persuasion or pressure. **go out of one's way** to make special efforts; to do more than is needed. **have it both ways** to benefit from two actions, situations or arguments, etc, each of which excludes the possibility or validity, etc of the others. **in a bad way** *colloq* in a poor or serious condition; unhealthy. **in a big way** *colloq* with enthusiasm; on a large or grandiose scale. **in a way** from a certain viewpoint; to some extent. **make one's way 1** to go purposefully. **2** to progress or prosper: *making her way in life.* **no way** *slang* absolutely not. **out of the way** situated so as not to hinder or obstruct anyone. **2** remote; in the middle of nowhere. **under way** in motion; progressing.

waybill *n* a list that gives details of goods or passengers being carried by a public vehicle.

wayfarer *n, old use or poetic* a traveller, esp on foot. ○ **wayfaring** *n, adj.*

waylay *vb* **1** to lie in wait for and ambush (someone). **2** to delay (someone) with conversation.

way-out *adj, slang* excitingly unusual, exotic or new.

ways and means *pl n* **1** methods for obtaining funds to carry on a government. **2** methods and resources for carrying out and fulfilling any purpose.

wayside *n* the edge of a road, or the area to the side of it. ◆ **fall by the wayside** to fail or drop out.

wayward *adj* undisciplined or self-willed; headstrong or rebellious. ○ **waywardness** *n.*

Wb *symbol* weber.

WC *abbrev* water closet.

we *pron* **1** oneself in company with another or others: *We went to a party last night.* **2** people in general: *the times we live in.* **3** used by a royal person, and by writers and editors in formal use, to refer to themselves or the authority they represent.

we After prepositions, the object form **us** should always be used:
✓ *They're laying on a party for us workers.*
Remember that you would say *for us*, not *for we.*

weak *adj* **1** lacking physical strength. **2** lacking in moral, emotional or mental force. **3** not able to support a great weight. **4** not functioning effectively. **5** liable to give way. **6** lacking power. **7** *commerce* dropping in value. **8** too easily influenced or led by others. **9** lacking full flavour. **10** of an argument: unsound or unconvincing. ○ **weakly** *adv.*

weaken *vb, tr & intr* to make or become weaker.

weak-kneed *adj, colloq* cowardly; feeble.

weakling *n* **1** a sickly or physically weak person or animal. **2** someone weak in a certain respect: *a moral weakling.*

weak-minded *adj* **1** having feeble intelligence. **2** lacking will or determination.

weakness *n* **1** the condition of being weak. **2** a fault or failing; a shortcoming. **3** (*often a* **weakness for sth**) a particular, usu indulgent, liking for it.

weal¹ *n* a long raised reddened mark on the skin caused eg by a whip or sword.

weal² *n, old use* welfare or wellbeing.

wealth *n* **1** riches, valuables and property, or the possession of them. **2** abundance of resources: *the country's mineral wealth.* **3** a large quantity: *a wealth of examples.*

wealthy *adj* (*-ier, -iest*) **1** possessing riches and property; rich or prosperous. **2** (**wealthy in sth**) well supplied with it; rich in it.

wean *vb* **1** to accustom (a baby or young mammal) to taking food other than its mother's milk. **2** to gradually break someone of a bad habit, etc: *how to wean him off drugs.*

weapon *n* **1** an instrument or device used to kill or injure people, usu in a war or fight. **2** something one can use to get the better of others: *Patience is our best weapon.*

weaponry *n* (*-ies*) weapons collectively; armament.

wear *vb* (**wore, worn**) **1** to be dressed in (something), or have (it) on one's body. **2** to have (one's hair or beard, etc) cut a certain length or in a certain style. **3** to have (a certain expression). **4** *intr* of a carpet or garment: to become thin or threadbare through use. **5** to make (a hole or bare patch, etc) in something through heavy use. **6** *intr* to bear intensive use; to last in use. **7** *colloq* to accept (an excuse or story, etc) or tolerate (a situation, etc). **8** to tire: *worn to a frazzle.* ➤ *n* **1** the act of wearing or state of being worn. **2** clothes suitable for a specified purpose, person or occasion, etc: *evening wear.* **3** the amount or type of use that clothing or carpeting, etc gets: *subjected to heavy wear.* **4** damage caused through use. ○ **wearer** *n.*
◆ **wearing thin 1** becoming thin or threadbare. **2** of an excuse, etc: becoming unconvincing or

ineffective through overuse. ◊ **wear down** or **wear sth down** to make or become reduced or consumed by constant use, rubbing, friction, etc. **wear sb down** to tire or overcome them, esp with persistent objections or demands. **wear off** of a feeling or pain, etc: to become less intense; to disappear gradually. **wear out** or **wear sth out** to make or become unusable through use. **wear sb out** to exhaust them.

wear and tear *n* damage sustained in the course of continual or normal use.

wearing *adj* exhausting or tiring.

weary *adj* (**-ier, -iest**) **1** tired out; exhausted. **2** (*usu* **weary of sth**) tired by it; fed up with it. **3** tiring, dreary or irksome; wearing. ➤ *vb* (**-ies, -ied**) **1** *tr & intr* to make or become weary. **2** (*usu* **weary of sth**) *intr* to get tired of it. ○ **wearily** *adv.* ○ **weariness** *n.* ○ **wearisome** *adj.*

weasel *n* **1** a small carnivorous mammal with a slender body, short legs and reddish-brown fur with white underparts. **2** *colloq* a treacherous or sly person. ➤ *vb* (**weaselled, weaselling;** *US* **weaseled, weaseling**) to equivocate. ◊ **weasel out** *colloq* to extricate (oneself) from a responsibility, esp indefensibly.

weather *n* the atmospheric conditions in any area at any time, with regard to sun, cloud, temperature, wind and rain, etc. ➤ *vb* **1** *tr & intr* to expose or be exposed to the effects of wind, sun and rain, etc; to alter or be altered by such exposure. **2** to come safely through (a storm or difficult situation). ♦ **make heavy weather of sth** to make its progress unnecessarily slow and difficult. **under the weather** *colloq* not in good health; slightly unwell.

weatherbeaten or **weather-worn** *adj* **1** of the skin: tanned or lined by exposure to sun and wind. **2** worn or damaged by exposure to the weather.

weatherboard *n* any of a series of overlapping horizontal boards covering an exterior wall. ➤ *vb* to fit (something) with such boards or planks. ○ **weatherboarding** *n.*

weathercock *n* a weathervane in the form of a farmyard cock.

weather forecast *n* a forecast of the weather based on meteorological observations.

weathering *n, geol* the disintegration of rocks caused by exposure to wind, rain, etc.

weatherman or **weathergirl** *n, colloq* a man or woman who presents a weather forecast on radio or television.

weatherproof *adj* designed or treated so as to keep out wind and rain. ➤ *vb* to make (something) weatherproof.

weathervane *n* a revolving arrow that turns to point in the direction of the wind.

weave[1] *vb* (**wove, woven**) **1** *tr & intr* to make (cloth or tapestry) in a loom, passing threads under and over the threads of a fixed warp; to interlace (threads) in this way. **2** to depict (something) by weaving. **3** to construct (a basket, fence, etc) by interlacing or intertwining. **4** to devise (a story or plot, etc). **5** of a spider: to weave or spin (a web). ➤ *n* the pattern, compactness or texture of the weaving in a fabric. ○ **weaver** *n.*

weave[2] *vb, intr* to move to and fro, or wind in and out.

web *n* **1** a network of slender threads constructed by a spider to trap insects. **2** a membrane that connects the toes of a swimming bird or animal. **3** any intricate network: *a web of lies.* **4** (**the Web**) short for WORLD WIDE WEB. ○ **webbed** *adj.*

webbing *n* strong jute or nylon fabric woven into strips for use as belts, straps and supporting bands in upholstery.

weber /'veɪbə(r)/ *n, physics* in the SI system: a unit of magnetic flux (the total size of a magnetic field).

web-footed or **web-toed** *adj* of swimming birds, etc: having webbed feet.

weblog see BLOG

website *n* a person or organization's location on the WORLD WIDE WEB.

wed *vb* (**wedded** or **wed, wedding**) **1** *tr & intr, old use* to marry. **2** *old use* to join (someone) in marriage. **3** (*usu* **wed one thing to** or **with another**) to unite or combine them: *wed firmness with compassion.*

we'd *contraction of* we had, we would or we should.

wedded *adj* **1** married. **2** referring or relating to marriage. ♦ **wedded to** devoted or committed to (a principle or activity, etc).

wedding *n* **1** a marriage ceremony, esp with the associated celebrations. **2** *in compounds* any of the notable anniversaries of a marriage, eg *silver wedding*.

wedge *n* **1** a piece of solid wood or other material, tapering to a thin edge, driven into eg wood to split it, pushed into a narrow gap between moving parts to immobilize them, or used to hold a door open, etc. **2** anything shaped like a wedge, usu cut from something circular. **3** a shoe heel in the form of a wedge, tapering towards the sole. **4** *golf* a club with a steeply angled wedge-shaped head for lofting the ball. ➤ *vb* **1** to fix or immobilize (something) in position with, or as if with, a wedge. **2** to thrust, insert or squeeze, or be pushed or squeezed like a wedge: *She wedged herself into the corner.* ♦ **the thin end of the wedge** something that looks like the small beginning of a significant, usu unwanted, development.

wedlock *n* the condition of being married; marriage. ♦ **born out of wedlock** *dated* born to parents not married to each other; illegitimate.

Wednesday *n* the fourth day of the week.

wee[1] *adj* (**weer, weest**) *esp Scot* small; tiny.

wee[2] or **wee-wee** *colloq, vb* (**wees, weed**) *intr* to urinate. ➤ *n* **1** an act of urinating. **2** urine.

weed *n* **1** any plant growing where it is not wanted, esp one hindering the growth of cultivated plants. **2** *derog* a skinny, feeble or ineffectual man. **3** *slang* marijuana. **4** (**the weed**) *slang* tobacco. ➤ *vb* **1** *tr & intr* to uproot weeds from (a garden or flowerbed, etc). **2** (*also* **weed out**) to identify and eliminate (eg those who are unwanted or ineffective). ○ **weeding** *n*.

weedkiller *n* a substance, usu a chemical poison, used to kill weeds.

weedy *adj* (*-ier, -iest*) **1** overrun with weeds. **2** *derog* of a person: having a weak or lanky build.

week *n* **1** a sequence of seven consecutive days, usu beginning on Sunday. **2** any period of seven days. **3** (*also* **working week**) the working days of the week, as distinct from the WEEKEND. **4** the period worked per week: *She works a 45-hour week*. **5** (**weeks**) an indefinitely long period of time: *I haven't seen you for weeks!* ➤ *adv* by a period of seven days before or after a specified day: *We leave Tuesday week*.

weekday *n* any day except Sunday, or except Saturday and Sunday.

weekend *n* the period from Friday evening to Sunday night.

weekly *adj, adv* occurring, produced or issued every week, or once a week. ➤ *n* (*-ies*) a magazine or newspaper published once a week.

weeny *adj* (*-ier, -iest*) *colloq* very small; tiny.

weep *vb* (**wept**) **1** *intr* to shed tears as an expression of grief or other emotion. **2** to express (something) while, or by, weeping: *She wept her goodbyes*. **3** *tr & intr* of a wound, etc: to exude matter; to ooze. ➤ *n* a bout of weeping.

weeping willow *n* an ornamental Chinese willow with long drooping branches.

weepy or **weepie** *adj* (*-ier, -iest*) **1** tearful. **2** of a film or novel, etc: poignant or sentimental. ➤ *n* (*-ies*) *colloq* a film or novel, etc of this kind.

weevil *n* **1** a beetle with an elongated proboscis, which can damage fruit, grain, nuts and trees. **2** any insect that damages stored grain.

weft *n, weaving* the threads that are passed over and under the fixed threads of the warp in a loom; the **woof**.

weigh *vb* **1** to measure the weight of (something). **2** *tr & intr* to have (a certain weight). **3** (*often* **weigh sth out**) to measure out a specific weight of it. **4** (*often* **weigh up**) to consider or assess (facts or possibilities, etc). **5** *intr* (**weigh with sb**) to impress them favourably. **6** *intr* (*usu* **weigh on** or **upon sb**) to oppress them. **7** to raise (the anchor) of a ship before sailing. ◊ **weigh sb down** to burden, overload or oppress them. **weigh in** esp of a wrestler, boxer or jockey: to be weighed officially. **weigh in with sth** *colloq* to contribute (a comment, etc) to a discussion.

weighbridge *n* an apparatus for weighing vehicles with their loads.

weigh-in *n* the official weighing of a wrestler, boxer or jockey.

weight *n* **1** the heaviness of something; the amount that it weighs. **2** *physics* the gravitational force, measured in NEWTONS, acting on a body. **3** any system of units for measuring and expressing weight. **4** a piece of metal of a standard weight, against which to measure the weight of other objects. **5** a heavy load. **6** *athletics* a heavy object for lifting, throwing or tossing. **7** (**weights**) weightlifting or weight-training. **8** a standard amount that a boxer, etc should weigh. **9** a mental burden. **10** strength or significance in terms of amount. **11** influence, authority or credibility. ➤ *vb* **1** to add weight to (something), eg to restrict movement. **2** (*often* **weight sth down**) to hold it down in this way. **3** to burden or oppress (someone). **4** to organize (something) so as to have an unevenness or bias: *a tax system weighted in favour of the wealthy*. ♦ **pull one's weight** to do one's full share of work, etc. **throw one's weight about** *colloq* to behave in an arrogant or domineering manner.

weighting *n* a supplement to a salary, usu to compensate for high living costs: *London weighting*.

weightless *adj* **1** weighing nothing or almost nothing. **2** of an astronaut, etc in space: not subject to the Earth's gravity, so able to float freely. ○ **weightlessness** *n*.

weightlifting *n* a sport in which competitors lift, or attempt to lift, a barbell which is made increasingly heavier. ○ **weightlifter** *n*.

weight-training *n* muscle-strengthening exercises performed with the aid of adjustable weights and pulleys.

weighty *adj* (*-ier, -iest*) **1** heavy. **2** important or significant; having much influence. **3** grave; worrying.

weir *n* **1** a shallow dam constructed across a river to control its flow. **2** a fence of stakes built across a river or stream to catch fish.

weird *adj* **1** eerie or supernatural; uncanny. **2** strange or bizarre. ○ **weirdly** *adv*. ○ **weirdness** *n*.

weirdo *n* (**weirdos** or **weirdoes**) *derog, colloq* someone who behaves or dresses bizarrely or oddly.

welcome *vb* **1** to receive (a guest or visitor, etc) with a warm greeting or kind hospitality. **2** to invite (suggestions or contributions, etc). ➤ *exclam* expressing pleasure on receiving someone. ➤ *n* **1** the act of welcoming. **2** a reception: *a cool welcome*. ➤ *adj* **1** warmly received. **2** gladly permitted or encouraged (to do or keep something). **3** much appreciated. ○ **welcoming** *adj*. ♦ **outstay one's welcome** to stay too long. **you're welcome!** used in response to thanks: not at all; it's a pleasure.

weld *vb* **1** *eng* to join (two pieces of metal) by heating them to melting point and fusing them together, or by applying pressure alone, producing a stronger joint than soldering. **2** to unite or blend (two or more things) together firmly. ➤ *n* a joint between two metals formed by welding. ○ **welder** or **weldor** *n*.

welfare *n* **1** the health, comfort, happiness and general wellbeing of a person or group, etc. **2**

financial support given to those in need.

welfare state *n* a system in which the government uses tax revenue to look after citizens' welfare, with the provision of free healthcare, old-age pensions and financial support for the disabled or unemployed.

well¹ *adv* (**better, best**) **1** competently; skilfully. **2** satisfactorily. **3** kindly or favourably. **4** thoroughly, properly or carefully. **5** fully or adequately. **6** intimately: *I don't know her well.* **7** successfully; prosperously. **8** attractively. **9** by a long way: *well past midnight.* **10** justifiably: *You can't very well ignore him.* **11** conceivably; quite possibly: *She may well be right.* **12** understandably: *if she objects, as well she may.* **13** very much: *well worth doing.* ➤ *adj* (**better, best**) **1** healthy. **2** in a satisfactory state. ➤ *exclam* **1** used enquiringly in expectation of a response or explanation, etc. **2** used variously in conversation, eg to resume a narrative, preface a reply, express surprise, indignation or doubt, etc. ◆ **all very well** *colloq* used as an objecting response to a consoling remark: satisfactory or acceptable but only up to a point: *It's all very well to criticize.* **as well 1** too; in addition. **2** (*also* **just as well**) all the difference it makes: *I may as well tell you.* **3** (*also* **just as well**) a good thing; lucky: *It was just as well you came when you did.* **as well as …** in addition to … **well off 1** wealthy; financially comfortable. **2** fortunate; successful.

> **well** In compounds such as **well intentioned** and **well prepared**, a hyphen is used when the compound comes before the noun it qualifies, as in:
> *a well-intentioned person*
> *a well-prepared meal.*
> When the compound comes after a verb such as **be**, it is usually not hyphenated, as in:
> *They were well intentioned.*
> *The meal was well prepared.*
> Idiomatic expressions such as **well-heeled** are usually hyphenated in all positions.

well² *n* a lined shaft sunk to a considerable depth below ground in order to obtain water, oil or gas, etc. ➤ *vb, intr* (*often* **well up**) of a liquid: to spring, flow or flood to the surface.

we'll *contraction* we will; we shall.

well-adjusted *adj* **1** emotionally and psychologically sound. **2** having a good adjustment.

well-advised *adj* sensible; prudent.

well-appointed *adj* of a house, etc: well furnished or equipped.

wellbeing *n* the state of being healthy and contented, etc; welfare.

well-born *adj* descended from an aristocratic family.

well-bred *adj* having good manners; showing good breeding.

well-built *adj* **1** strongly built. **2** with a muscular or well-proportioned body.

well-connected *adj* having influential or aristocratic friends and relations.

well-disposed *adj* inclined to be friendly, agreeable or sympathetic.

well-done *adj* of food, esp beef: thoroughly cooked.

well-earned *adj* thoroughly deserved: *a well-earned break.*

well-founded *adj* of suspicions, etc: justified: *a well-founded belief.*

well-groomed *adj* of a person: with a smart and neat appearance.

well-grounded *adj* **1** of an argument, etc: soundly based. **2** (*usu* **well grounded in sth**) having had a good basic education in it.

wellhead *n* **1** the source of a stream; a spring. **2** an origin or source.

well-heeled *adj, colloq* prosperous; wealthy.

well-informed *adj* **1** having reliable information on something particular. **2** full of varied knowledge.

wellington or **wellington boot** *n* a waterproof rubber or plastic boot loosely covering the foot and calf.

well-intentioned *adj* having or showing good intentions, but often having an unfortunate effect.

well-known *adj* **1** familiar or famous. **2** fully known or understood.

well-loved *adj* thought of with great affection.

well-meaning or **well-meant** *adj* well-intentioned.

well-nigh *adv* almost; nearly.

well-preserved *adj* youthful in appearance; showing few signs of age.

well-read *adj* having read and learnt much.

well-rounded *adj* **1** pleasantly plump. **2** having had a broadly based and balanced upbringing and education.

well-spoken *adj* having a courteous, fluent and usu refined way of speaking.

wellspring *n* **1** a spring or fountain. **2** any rich or bountiful source.

well-thought-of *adj* approved of or esteemed; respected.

well-thumbed *adj* of a book: showing marks of repeated use and handling.

well-to-do *adj* wealthy; financially comfortable.

well-trodden *adj* often followed or walked along.

well-versed *adj* thoroughly trained; knowledgeable.

well-wisher *n* someone concerned for another's welfare.

well-worn *adj* **1** much worn or used; showing signs of wear. **2** of an expression, etc: overfamiliar from frequent use.

welly or **wellie** *n* (*-ies*) *colloq* a WELLINGTON. ◆ **give it (some) welly** *slang* to put a great deal of effort or energy into something.

Welsh *n* **1** (**the Welsh**) the people of Wales. **2** the

Celtic language of Wales. ➤ *adj* belonging or relating to Wales, its inhabitants or their language.

welsh or **welch** *vb* 1 *intr* (*usu* **welsh on**) to fail to pay (one's debts) or fulfil (one's obligations). 2 *intr* (*usu* **welsh on sb**) to fail to keep one's promise to them. 3 to cheat in such a way. ○ **welsher** *n*.

Welshman or **Welshwoman** *n* an inhabitant of, or a person born in, Wales.

Welsh rabbit or **Welsh rarebit** *n* a dish consisting of melted cheese, usu with butter, ale and seasoning mixed in, served on toast.

welt *n* 1 a reinforcing band or border fastened to an edge, eg the ribbing at the waist of a knitted garment. 2 a WEAL[1] raised by a lash or blow.

welter *n* a confused mass.

welterweight *n* 1 a class for boxers and wrestlers of not more than a specified weight, for example 66.7kg (114lb) in professional boxing. 2 a boxer, wrestler, etc of this weight.

wen *n*, *pathol* a sebaceous cyst on the skin, usu of the scalp.

wench *n* 1 *facetious* a girl; a woman. 2 *old use* a servant girl.

wend *vb*, *archaic* or *literary* to go or direct (one's course). ♦ **wend one's way** to go steadily and purposefully on a route or journey.

we're *contraction* we are.

weren't *contraction* were not.

werewolf /ˈweǝwʊlf/ *n*, *folklore* someone who changes into a wolf, usu at full moon.

west *n* (*also* **West** or **the West**) 1 the direction in which the sun sets. 2 any part of the earth, a country or town, etc lying in that direction. 3 (**the West**) the countries of Europe and N America, in contrast to those of Asia, Russia, and the Middle East. ➤ *adj* 1 situated in the west; on the side which is on or nearest the west. 2 facing or toward the west. 3 esp of wind: coming from the west. ➤ *adv* in, to or towards the west.

westbound *adj* going or leading towards the west.

westerly *adj* 1 of a wind, etc: coming from the west. 2 looking or lying, etc towards the west; situated in the west. ➤ *adv* to or towards the west. ➤ *n* (*-ies*) a westerly wind.

western or **Western** *adj* situated in, directed towards or belonging to the west of the West. ➤ *n* a film or novel featuring cowboys in the west of the USA, esp during the 19c. ○ **westerner** or **Westerner** *n*. ○ **westernmost** *adj*.

westernize or **-ise** *vb* to make or become like the people of Europe and America in customs, or like their institutions, practices or ideas. ○ **westernization** *n*.

Westminster *n* the British parliament.

westward *adv* (*also* **westwards**) towards the west. *adj* towards the west.

wet *adj* (**wetter, wettest**) 1 covered or soaked in water or other liquid. 2 of the weather: rainy. 3 of paint, cement or varnish, etc: not yet dried.

4 *derog slang* of a person: feeble; ineffectual. ➤ *n* 1 moisture. 2 rainy weather: *Don't stay outside in the wet!* 3 *derog, slang* a feeble ineffectual person. 4 *colloq* a moderate Conservative. ➤ *vb* (**wet** or **wetted, wetting**) 1 to make (someone or something) wet. 2 to urinate involuntarily on (something). ○ **wetly** *adv*. ○ **wetness** *n*. ♦ **wet behind the ears** *colloq* immature or inexperienced. **wet oneself** to make oneself wet by urinating inadvertently.

> **wet** There is often a spelling confusion between **wet** and **whet**.

wet blanket *n* a dreary and pessimistic person who dampens the enthusiasm and enjoyment of others.

wet dream *n* an erotic dream that causes the involuntary ejaculation of semen.

wether *n* a castrated ram.

wetland *n* (*often* **wetlands**) a region of marshy land.

wet nurse *n* a woman employed to breastfeed another's baby.

wet suit *n* a tight-fitting rubber suit that is permeable by water but conserves body heat, worn by divers and canoeists, etc.

we've *contraction* we have.

whack *colloq, vb* to hit (something or someone) sharply and resoundingly. ➤ *n* 1 a sharp resounding blow. 2 the sound of this. 3 one's share of the profits, etc: *They haven't had their whack yet.* ♦ **have a whack at sth** to try it; to have a go at it. **out of whack** *esp Aust & US* out of order. **top, full** or **the full whack** the highest price, wage or rate, etc.

whacked *adj, colloq* exhausted; worn out.

whacking *colloq, n* a beating. ➤ *adj* enormous. ➤ *adv* extremely.

whacky see WACKY.

whale *n* (**whale** or **whales**) a large marine mammal which has a torpedo-shaped body, and a blowhole on the top of the head for breathing. ➤ *vb, intr* to hunt whales. ○ **whaling** *n*. ♦ **a whale of a ...** *colloq* a hugely enjoyable (time or evening, etc).

whalebone *n* the light flexible horny substance consisting of the baleen plates in toothless whales, used esp formerly for stiffening corsets, etc.

whaler *n* a person or ship engaged in hunting and killing whales.

wham *n* a resounding noise made by a hard blow.

whammy *n* (*-ies*) *orig US colloq* (**double** or **triple whammy**) two or three powerful blows or serious problems that hit at the same time.

wharf *n* (**wharfs** or **wharves**) a landing stage built along a waterfront for loading and unloading vessels.

what *adj, pron* 1 used in questions, indirect questions and statements, identifying, or seeking to identify or classify, a thing or person:

What street are we in? **2** used in exclamations expressing surprise, sympathy or other emotions: *What! You didn't pass?* **3** used as a relative pronoun or adjective: that or those which; whatever; anything that: *It is just what I thought.* **4** used to introduce a suggestion or new information: *I know what – let's go to the zoo!* **5** used to ask for a repetition or confirmation of something said: *What? I didn't catch what you said.* ➤ *adv* used in questions, indirect questions and statements: to how great an extent or degree?: *What does that matter?* ◆ **so what?** or **what of it?** *colloq* why is that important? **what's up?** **1** what's the matter? **2** how are you? **what's with …?** *colloq* what's the matter with …?

whatever *pron, adj* **1** (*also* **what ever**) used as an emphatic form of WHAT: *Whatever shall I do?* **2** anything: *Take whatever you want.* **3** no matter what: *I must finish, whatever happens.* **4** with negatives at all: *has nothing whatever to do with you.* **5** *colloq* some or other: *She has disappeared, for whatever reason.* **6** used to express uncertainty: *a didgeridoo, whatever that is.* ◆ **… or whatever** *colloq* … or some such thing: *Use tape, glue or whatever.*

whatnot *n, colloq* and other similar things: *cakes, bread and whatnot.*

whatsoever *adj, pron* **1** *old use or literary* whatever; what. **2** *with negatives* at all: *none whatsoever.*

wheat *n* **1** a cereal grass. **2** the grain of this plant, which provides flour, etc.

wheaten *adj* made of wheat flour or grain.

wheat germ *n* the vitamin-rich germ or embryo of wheat, present in the grain.

wheatmeal *n* wheat flour containing most of the powdered whole grain (bran and germ).

wheedle *vb, tr & intr* to coax or cajole (someone), often by flattery. ○ **wheedler** *n*.

wheel *n* **1** a circular object or frame rotating on an axle, used eg for moving a vehicle along the ground. **2** such an object serving as part of a machine or mechanism. **3** (**wheels**) *colloq* a motor vehicle for personal use. **4** a disc or drum on the results of whose random spin bets are made: *a roulette wheel.* **5** any progression that appears to go round in a circle. ➤ *vb* **1** to fit (something) with a wheel or wheels. **2** to push (a wheeled vehicle or conveyance) or to push (someone or something) in or on it: *He wheeled the bike outside.* **3** to make (something) move in a circular course. **4** *intr* (*usu* **wheel about** or **round**) to turn around suddenly; to pivot on one's heel. ◆ **at** or **behind the wheel 1** in the driver's seat of a car, boat, etc. **2** in charge. **wheel and deal** to engage in tough business dealing or bargaining.

wheelbarrow *n* a hand-pushed cart with a wheel in front and two handles and legs at the rear.

wheelbase *n* the distance between the front and rear axles of a vehicle.

wheelchair *n* a chair with wheels in which disabled people can be conveyed or convey themselves.

wheelhouse *n* the shelter on a ship's bridge in which the steering-gear is housed.

wheelie *n* a trick performed on a motorbike or bicycle in which the front wheel is lifted off the ground, either while stationary or in motion.

wheelie bin or **wheely bin** *n, Brit* a large dustbin in a wheeled frame.

wheelwright *n* a craftsman who makes and repairs wheels and wheeled carriages.

wheeze *vb, intr* to breathe in a laboured way with a gasping noise. ➤ *n* **1** a wheezing breath or sound. **2** *colloq* a bright idea; a clever scheme. ○ **wheezy** *adj*.

whelk *n* a large marine snail with a pointed shell.

whelp *n* **1** the young of a dog or wolf. **2** an impudent boy or youth. ➤ *vb, intr* of a dog or wolf: to give birth.

when *adv* used in questions, indirect questions and statements: at what time?; during what period? ➤ *conj* **1** at the time, or during the period, that. **2** as soon as. **3** at any time that; whenever. **4** at which time. **5** in spite of the fact that; considering that: *Why just watch when you could be dancing?* ➤ *pron* **1** what or which time: *They stayed talking, until when I can't say.* **2** used as a relative pronoun: at; during, etc which time: *an era when life was harder.*

whence *old use, formal or literary, adv, conj* **1** used in questions, indirect questions and statements: from what place?: *I enquired whence they had come.* **2** used esp in statements: from what cause or circumstance: *He can't explain whence the mistake arose.* **3** to the place from which: *They returned whence they had come.*

whenever *conj* **1** at any or every time that: *Mark gets furious whenever he doesn't get his way.* **2** if ever; no matter when: *I'll be here whenever you need me.* ➤ *adv* **1** an emphatic form of WHEN: *Whenever could I have said that?* **2** used to indicate that one does not know when: *at Pentecost, whenever that is.*

where *adv* used in questions, indirect questions and statements: **1** in, at or to which place; in what direction: *Where is she going?* **2** in what respect: *She showed me where I'd gone wrong.* **3** from what source: *Where did you get that?* ➤ *pron* what place?: *Where have you come from?* ➤ *conj* **1** in, at or to the, or any, place that: *Ben went where he pleased.* **2** in any case in which: *keep families together where possible.* **3** the aspect or respect in which: *That's where you are wrong.*

whereabouts *adv* where or roughly where? ➤ *sing or pl n* the (rough) position of a person or thing.

whereas *conj* but, by contrast: *I'm a pessimist, whereas my husband is an optimist.*

whereby *pron* by means of which.

wherefore *conj, adv, formal, old use or law* for what reason?

wherein *formal, old use or law, adv, conj* in what place?; in what respect?: *Wherein is the justification?* ➤ *pron* in which place or thing.

whereof *pron, formal or old use* of which; of what: *the circumstances whereof I told you.*

whereupon *conj* at which point; in consequence of which.

wherever *pron* any or every place that: *I'll take it to wherever you like.* ➤ *conj* 1 in, at or to whatever place: *They were welcomed wherever they went.* 2 no matter where: *I won't lose touch, wherever I go.* ➤ *adv* 1 an emphatic form of WHERE: *Wherever can they be?* 2 used to indicate that one does not know where: *the Round House, wherever that is.*

wherewithal *pron, old use* with which. ➤ *n* (**the wherewithal**) the means or necessary resources.

whet *vb* (**whetted, whetting**) 1 to sharpen (a bladed tool) by rubbing it against stone, etc. 2 to arouse or intensify (someone's appetite, interest or desire).

> **whet** There is often a spelling confusion between **whet** and **wet**.

whether *conj* 1 used to introduce an indirect question: *I asked whether it was raining.* 2 used in constructions involving alternative possibilities: *She was uncertain whether he liked her or not* • *I'm going whether you like it or not.*

whetstone *n* a stone for sharpening bladed tools.

whew *exclam, colloq* expressing relief or amazement.

whey /weɪ/ *n* the watery content of milk, separated from the CURD in making cheese and junket, etc.

which *adj, pron* 1 used in questions, indirect questions and statements to identify or specify a thing or person, usu from a known set or group: *I can't decide which book is better: which did you choose?* 2 used to introduce a defining or identifying relative clause: *animals which hibernate.* 3 used to introduce a commenting clause, chiefly in reference to things or ideas rather than people: *The house, which lies back from the road, is red.* 4 used in a relative clause, meaning 'any that': *Take which books you want.*

whichever *pron, adj* 1 the one or ones that; any that: *Take whichever is suitable.* 2 according to which: *at 10.00 or 10.30, whichever is more convenient.* 3 no matter which: *I'll be satisfied, whichever you choose.* 4 used to express uncertainty: *It's in the 'To Do' folder, whichever that is.*

whiff *n* 1 a puff or slight rush of air or smoke, etc. 2 a hint or trace: *at the first whiff of scandal.*

Whig *n, hist* a member of one of the main British political parties that emerged 1679–80, superseded in 1830 by the LIBERAL PARTY.

while *conj* 1 at the same time as: *She held the bowl while I stirred.* 2 for as long as; for the whole time that: *He guards us while we sleep.* 3 during the time that: *It happened while we were abroad.* 4 whereas: *He likes camping, while she*

prefers sailing. ➤ *adv* at or during which: *all the months while I was ill.* ➤ *n* a space or lapse of time: *after a while.* ➤ *vb* (*often* **while away**) to pass (time or hours, etc) in a leisurely or undemanding way. ♦ **worth (one's) while** worth one's time and trouble.

whilst *conj* WHILE.

whim *n* a sudden fanciful idea.

whimper *vb* 1 *intr* to cry feebly or plaintively. 2 to say (something) plaintively. 3 to say (something) in a whining or querulous manner. ➤ *n* a feebly plaintive cry.

whimsical *adj* 1 delicately fanciful or playful. 2 odd, weird or fantastic. ○ **whimsically** *adv.*

whimsy or **whimsey** *n* (**whimsies** or **whimseys**) 1 quaint or fanciful humour. 2 a whim. ➤ *adj* (**-ier, -iest**) quaint or odd.

whin *n* GORSE.

whine *vb, intr* 1 to whimper. 2 to complain peevishly or querulously. ➤ *n* 1 a whimper. 2 a continuous shrill or high-pitched noise. 3 an affected, thin and ingratiating nasal tone of voice. ○ **whining** *n, adj.*

whinge *colloq, vb* (**whingeing**) *intr* to complain irritably; to whine. ➤ *n* a peevish complaint. ○ **whinger** *n.*

whinny *vb* (**-ies, -ied**) *intr* of a horse: to neigh softly. ➤ *n* (**-ies**) a gentle neigh.

whip *n* 1 a lash with a handle for driving animals or punishing people. 2 a stroke administered by, or as if by, such a lash. 3 a whipping action or motion. 4 *pol* a member of a parliamentary party responsible for members' discipline, and for their attendance to vote on important issues. 5 *pol* a notice sent to members by a party whip requiring their attendance for a vote, urgency being indicated (*in compounds*) by the number of underlinings: *a three-line whip.* 6 a dessert of any of various flavours made with beaten egg-whites or cream. ➤ *vb* (**whipped, whipping**) 1 to strike or thrash with a whip. 2 to punish (someone) with lashes or smacking. 3 to lash (someone or something) with the action or force of a whip: *a sharp wind whipped their faces.* 4 *tr & intr* to move or make (something) move with a sudden or whip-like motion: *The branch whipped back.* 5 (*usu* **whip sth off** or **out,** *etc*) to take or snatch it: *Dan whipped out a revolver.* 6 to rouse, goad, drive or force into a certain state: *He whipped the crowd into a fury.* 7 *colloq* to steal. 8 to beat (egg-whites or cream, etc) until stiff or frothy. 9 *colloq* to outdo, outwit or defeat. ○ **whipping** *n, adj.* ◇ **whip sth up** 1 to arouse (support, enthusiasm or other feelings) for something. 2 to prepare (a meal, etc) at short notice.

whip hand *n* (*often* **the whip hand**) the advantage in a situation.

whiplash *n* 1 the lash of a whip. 2 a popular term for a neck injury caused by the sudden jerking back of the head and neck.

whippersnapper *n, colloq* an insignificant and cheeky young lad or any lowly person who behaves impudently.

whippet *n* a small slender breed of dog, resembling a greyhound.

whipping boy *n* someone who is blamed for the faults and shortcomings of others.

whip-round *n* a collection of money made, often hastily, among a group of people.

whirl *vb* **1** *intr* to spin or revolve rapidly. **2** *tr & intr* to move with a rapid circling or spiralling motion. **3** *intr* of the head: to feel dizzy from excitement, etc. ➤ *n* **1** a circling or spiralling movement or pattern. **2** a round of intense activity. **3** a dizzy or confused state: *a whirl of emotion*. ◆ **give sth a whirl** *colloq* to try it out.

whirligig *n* **1** a spinning toy, esp a top. **2** anything that spins or revolves rapidly.

whirlpool *n* a violent circular eddy of water that occurs in a river or sea at a point where several strong opposing currents converge.

whirlwind *n* **1** a violently spiralling column of air over land or sea. **2** anything that moves in a similarly rapid or destructive way. ➤ *adj* referring or relating to anything that develops rapidly or violently: *a whirlwind courtship*.

whirr or **whir** *n* a rapid drawn-out whirling, humming or vibratory sound. ➤ *vb* **1** *intr* to turn or spin with a whirring noise. **2** to make (something) move with this sound.

whisk *vb* **1** to transport (someone or something) rapidly: *Mum was whisked into hospital*. **2** to move (something) with a brisk waving motion. **3** to beat (egg-whites or cream, etc) until stiff. ➤ *n* **1** a whisking movement or action. **2** a hand-held implement for whisking egg-whites or cream, etc.

whisker *n* **1** any of the long coarse hairs that grow round the mouth of a cat or mouse, etc. **2** (**whiskers**) a man's beard. **3** the tiniest possible margin: *He won by a whisker*. ○ **whiskered** or **whiskery** *adj*.

whisky or (*Irish & N Am, esp US*) **whiskey** *n* (**whiskies** or **whiskeys**) an alcoholic spirit distilled from a fermented mash of cereal grains, eg barley, wheat or rye.

whisper *vb* **1** *tr & intr* to speak or say (something) quietly, breathing rather than voicing the words. **2** *intr* of a breeze, etc: to make a rustling sound in leaves, etc. ➤ *n* **1** a whispered level of speech. **2** (*often* **whispers**) a rumour or hint; whispered gossip. **3** a soft rustling sound. ○ **whispering** *n*.

whist *n* a card game, usu for two pairs of players, in which the object is to take a majority of 13 tricks, each trick over six scoring one point.

whistle *n* **1 a** a shrill sound produced through pursed lips or through the teeth, used to signal or to express surprise, etc; **b** the act of making this sound. **2** any of several similar sounds, eg the call of a bird or the shrill sigh of the wind. **3** a small hand-held device used for making a similar sound, used esp as a signal. **4** any of several devices which produce a similar sound by the use of steam, eg a kettle. ➤ *vb* **1** *tr & intr* **a** to produce (a tune, etc) by passing air through a narrow constriction in the mouth, esp through pursed lips; **b** to signal (something) by doing this or by blowing a whistle. **2** *tr & intr* to blow or play on a whistle. **3** *intr* of a kettle, a locomotive or the wind: to emit a whistling sound. **4** *tr & intr* of a bird: to sing. **5** *intr* (*usu* **whistle for sth**) *colloq* to expect it in vain. ◆ **blow the whistle on** *colloq* to expose (someone or their illegal or dishonest practices) to the authorities. **wet one's whistle** *colloq* to have a drink. **whistle in the dark** to do something (eg whistle or talk brightly) to quell or deny one's fear.

whistle-stop *adj* **1** of a politician's tour: with a number of short stops, orig at railway stations, to deliver electioneering addresses. **2** of any tour: very rapid, with a number of brief stops.

Whit *n* Whitsuntide.

whit *n*, *with negatives* the least bit; the smallest particle imaginable: *not a whit worse*.

white *adj* **1** having the colour of snow, the colour that reflects all light. **2** (*often* **White**) **a** of people: belonging to one of the pale-skinned races; **b** referring or relating to such people. **3** abnormally pale, eg from shock or illness. **4** eg of a rabbit or mouse: albino. **5** of hair: lacking pigment, as in old age. **6** of a variety of anything, eg grapes: pale-coloured, as distinct from darker types. **7** of wine: made from white grapes or from skinned black grapes. **8 a** of flour: having had the bran and wheat germ removed; **b** of bread: made with white flour. **9** of coffee or tea: with milk or cream added. ➤ *n* **1** the colour of snow. **2** white colour or colouring matter, eg paint. **3** (*often* **White**) a white person. **4** (*in full* **egg-white**) the clear fluid surrounding the yolk of an egg; albumen. **5** the white part of the eyeball. **6** (**whites**) **a** household linen; **b** white clothes, eg those worn for cricket. ○ **whiteness** *n*.

whitebait *n* (*pl* **whitebait**) the young of any of various silvery fishes, esp herrings and sprats, often fried and eaten whole.

white blood cell or **white corpuscle** *n* a colourless blood cell whose main functions are to engulf invading micro-organisms and foreign particles, to produce antibodies, or to remove cell debris from sites of injury and infection.

whiteboard *n* a board with a white plastic surface for writing on, using felt-tipped pens.

white-collar *adj* of workers: not engaged in manual labour.

white dwarf *n*, *astron* a small dense hot star that has reached the last stage of its life.

white elephant *n* a possession that is useless or unwanted, esp one inconvenient or expensive to keep.

white feather *n* a symbol of cowardice.

white fish *n* a general name for edible sea fish, including whiting, cod, sole, haddock and halibut.

white flag *n* the signal used for offering surrender or requesting a truce.

whitefly *n* a small sap-sucking bug, whose

body and wings are covered with a white waxy powder.

white gold *n* a pale lustrous alloy of gold containing platinum, palladium, nickel or silver.

white goods *pl n* large kitchen appliances such as washing machines, refrigerators and cookers, traditionally white in colour.

white hope *n* someone of whom great achievements and successes are expected.

white horse *n* a wave with a white crest.

white-hot *adj* 1 of a metal, etc: so hot that white light is emitted. 2 intense; passionate.

white-knuckle *adj, colloq* causing or designed to cause extreme fear or anxiety.

white lie *n* a forgivable lie, esp one told to avoid hurting someone's feelings.

white light *n* light, such as that of the sun, that contains all the wavelengths in the visible range of the spectrum.

white matter *n, anat* pale fibrous nerve tissue in the brain and spinal cord. Compare GREY MATTER (sense 1).

white meat *n* pale-coloured meat, eg chicken. Compare RED MEAT.

whiten *vb, tr & intr* to make or become white or whiter; to bleach. ○ **whitener** *n*.

white noise *n* sound waves that contain a large number of frequencies of roughly equal intensity.

white-out *n* a phenomenon in snowy weather when the overcast sky blends imperceptibly with the white landscape to give poor visibility.

white paper *n* (*also* **White Paper**) in the UK: a government policy statement printed on white paper, issued for the information of parliament.

white pepper *n* light-coloured pepper made from peppercorns with the dark outer husk removed.

white sauce *n* a thick sauce made from flour, fat and a liquid such as milk or stock.

white spirit *n* a colourless liquid distilled from petroleum, and used as a solvent and thinner for paints and varnishes.

white tie *n* 1 a white bow tie worn as part of men's formal evening dress. 2 formal evening dress for men.

whitewash *n* 1 a mixture of lime and water, used to give a white coating to walls. 2 measures taken to cover up a disreputable affair or to clear a stained reputation, etc. ➤ *vb* 1 to coat (something) with whitewash. 2 to clean up or conceal (a disreputable affair). 3 *colloq* in a game: to beat (the opponent) so decisively that they fail to score at all.

white water *n* the foaming water as in rapids.

whither *old use or poetic, adv* to what place?: *Whither did they go?* ➤ *conj, pron* towards which place: *Some miles away lay London, whither they journeyed.*

whiting /ˈwaɪtɪŋ/ *n* (*pl* **whiting**) a small edible fish related to the cod, native to the waters of northern Europe.

whitlow *n* an inflammation of the finger or toe, esp near the nail.

Whitsun or **Whitsuntide** *n* in the Christian Church: the week beginning with Whit Sunday, particularly the first three days.

Whit Sunday or **Whitsunday** *n* PENTECOST.

whittle *vb* 1 to cut, carve or pare (a stick or piece of wood, etc) with a knife. 2 to shape or fashion (something) by this means. 3 (*usu* **whittle sth away** or **down**) to wear it away or reduce it gradually.

whizz or **whiz** *vb, intr* 1 to fly through the air, esp with a whistling or hissing noise. 2 to move rapidly. ➤ *n* 1 a whistling or hissing sound. 2 *colloq* an expert.

whizz kid, **whiz kid** or **wiz kid** *n, colloq* someone who achieves success quickly and early, through ability, inventiveness, dynamism or ambition.

who *pron* 1 used in questions, indirect questions and statements: which or what person; which or what people: *Who is at the door?* • *She asked who he had seen.* 2 used as a relative pronoun to introduce a defining clause: *the boy who was on the train.* 3 used as a relative pronoun to add a commenting clause: *Julius Caesar, who was murdered in 44BC.*

whoa *exclam* a command to stop, esp to a horse.

who'd *contraction* 1 who would. 2 who had.

whodunit or **whodunnit** *n, colloq* a detective novel or play, etc.

whoever *pron* 1 used in questions, indirect questions and statements as an emphatic form of WHO or WHOM: *Whoever is that at the door?* • *Ask whoever you like.* 2 no matter who: *I don't want to see them, whoever they are.* 3 used to indicate that one does not know who: *St Fiacre, whoever he was.*

whole *n* 1 all the constituents or components of something: *the whole of the time.* 2 something complete in itself, esp something consisting of integrated parts. ➤ *adj* comprising all of something; entire: *The whole street heard you.* ➤ *adv* 1 *colloq* completely; altogether; wholly: *found a whole new approach.* 2 in one piece: *swallow it whole.* 3 unbroken: *only two cups left whole.* ○ **wholeness** *n*. ♦ **on the whole** considering everything.

wholefood *n* (*sometimes* **wholefoods**) food processed as little as possible.

wholehearted *adj* sincere and enthusiastic. ○ **wholeheartedly** *adv*.

wholemeal or **wholewheat** *adj* of flour or bread: made from the entire wheat grain.

whole number *n, maths* an integral number, being one without fractions.

wholesale *n* the sale of goods in large quantities to a retailer. ➤ *adj, adv* 1 buying and selling in this way. Compare RETAIL. 2 on a huge scale and without discrimination: *wholesale destruction.* ○ **wholesaler** *n*.

wholesome *adj* 1 attractively healthy. 2 promoting health: *wholesome food.* 3 *old use* morally beneficial.

wholly /'hoʊllɪ/ *adv* completely; altogether: *not wholly satisfied.*

whom *pron* used as the object of a verb or preposition (but often replaced by WHO, esp in less formal usage): **1** in seeking to identify a person: *To whom are you referring?* **2** as a relative pronoun in a defining or commenting clause: *I am looking for the man whom I met earlier* • *The man, whom I met earlier, has already left.*

whomever or **whomsoever** *pron, formal or old use* used as the object of a verb or preposition to mean 'any person or people that': *I will write to whomever they appoint.*

whoop *n* a loud cry of delight, joy or triumph, etc. ➤ *vb, tr & intr* to utter or say (something) with a whoop. ♦ **whoop it up** *colloq* to celebrate noisily.

whoopee *exclam* /wʊ'piː/ expressing exuberant delight. ➤ *n* /'wʊpiː/ **1** exuberant delight or excitement. **2** a cry indicating this. ♦ **make whoopee** *colloq* **1** to celebrate exuberantly. **2** to make love.

whooping cough *n, pathol* a highly contagious disease that mainly affects children, characterized by bouts of violent coughing followed by a sharp drawing in of the breath which produces a characteristic 'whooping' sound. *Technical equivalent* pertussis.

whoops or **whoops-a-daisy** *exclam* expressing surprise, concern or apology, eg when one has a slight accident, makes an error, etc.

whopper *n, colloq* **1** anything very large of its kind. **2** a blatant lie.

whopping *adj, colloq* huge; enormous; unusually large. ➤ *n* a thrashing.

whore /hɔː(r)/ *n, offensive* **1** a prostitute. **2** a sexually immoral or promiscuous woman. ○ **whorish** *adj*.

whorehouse *n* a brothel.

whorl /wɔːl/ *n* **1** *bot* a COROLLA. **2** *zool* one complete coil in the spiral shell of a mollusc. **3** any type of twist or coil.

who's *contraction* **1** who is. **2** who has.

whose *pron, adj* **1** used in questions, indirect questions and statements: belonging to which person or people: *Whose is this jacket?* **2** used as a relative adjective to introduce a defining clause or add a commenting clause: of whom or which: *buildings whose foundations are sinking* • *my parents, without whose help I could not have succeeded.* **3** used as a relative adjective, meaning 'whoever's' or 'whichever's': *Take whose advice you will.*

> **whose** Whose is correctly used to mean both 'of whom' and 'of which':
> *the boy whose father is a policeman*
> *the book whose pages are torn*
> Note that **who else's** is more common than **whose else**, because **who else** is regarded as a unit and **whose else** is more awkward to say.

Note also that **who's**, which is pronounced the same way as **whose** and is sometimes confused with it, is a contraction of **who is** or **who has**:
Who's there?
I'm looking for the person who's taken my pen.

whosoever *pron, formal or old use* used in statements: WHOEVER.

why *adv* used in questions, indirect questions and statements: for what reason. ➤ *conj* for, or because of, which: *no reason why I should get involved.* ➤ *exclam* expressing surprise, indignation, impatience or recognition, etc: *Why, you little monster!*

wick *n* the twisted string running up through a candle or lamp, that burns and draws the fuel to the flame. ♦ **get on sb's wick** *slang* to be a source of irritation to them.

wicked *adj* **1** evil or sinful; immoral. **2** mischievous, playful or roguish. **3** *slang* excellent or cool. **4** *colloq* bad: *wicked weather.* ○ **wickedly** *adv*. ○ **wickedness** *n*.

wicker *adj* made of interwoven twigs, canes or rushes, etc.

wickerwork *n* articles made from wicker; basketwork of any kind.

wicket *n, cricket* **a** a row of three small wooden posts stuck upright in the ground behind either crease; **b** the playing area between these; **c** a batsman's dismissal by the bowler: *45 runs for two wickets.*

wicketkeeper *n, cricket* the fielder who stands immediately behind the wicket.

wide *adj* **1** large in extent from side to side. **2** measuring a specified amount from side to side: *three feet wide.* **3** of the eyes: open to the fullest extent. **4** of a range or selection, etc: covering a great variety: *There's a wide choice of films on.* **5** extensive; widespread: *wide support.* ➤ *adv* **1** to the fullest extent: *with the door wide open.* **2** off the mark: *His aim went wide.* ➤ *n, cricket* a ball bowled out of the batsman's reach. ○ **widely** *adv*. ○ **wideness** *n*.

wide-angle lens *n, photog, cinematog* a camera lens which takes pictures that cover a wider area than a normal lens.

wide-eyed *adj* **1** showing great surprise. **2** naive.

widen *vb, tr & intr* to make, or become, wide or wider.

wide-ranging *adj* covering a large variety of subjects or topics.

widespread *adj* **1** extending over a wide area. **2** involving large numbers of people.

widget *n* **1** a device in a can of beer that produces a foamy head like that of draught beer. **2** a gadget; any small manufactured item or component.

widow *n* a woman whose husband is dead and who has not remarried. ➤ *vb* to leave or make (someone) a widow or widower. ○ **widowhood** *n*.

widower n a man whose wife is dead and who has not remarried.

width n 1 extent from side to side; breadth. 2 the distance from side to side across a swimming pool: *She swam ten widths*.

wield vb 1 to brandish or use (a tool or weapon, etc). 2 to have or exert (power, authority or influence, etc).

wife n (*wives*) the woman to whom a man is married; a married woman. ○ **wifely** adj.

wig¹ n an artificial covering of natural or synthetic hair for the head.

wig² vb (**wigged, wigging**) colloq to scold (someone) severely.

wigeon or **widgeon** n (*wigeon* or *wigeons*; *widgeon* or *widgeons*) a freshwater duck with long pointed wings and a wedge-shaped tail.

wiggle vb, tr & intr, colloq to move or cause (something) to move, esp jerkily, from side to side or up and down. ➤ n a wiggling motion. ○ **wiggly** adj (-*ier*, -*iest*).

wigwam n a usu domed Native American dwelling made of a framework of arched poles covered with skins, bark or mats.

wilco exclam in signalling and telecommunications, etc: expressing compliance or acknowledgement of instructions.

wild adj 1 of animals: untamed or undomesticated; not dependent on humans. 2 of plants: growing in a natural uncultivated state. 3 of country: desolate, rugged or uninhabitable. 4 of peoples: savage; uncivilized. 5 unrestrained; uncontrolled: *wild fury*. 6 frantically excited. 7 distraught: *wild with grief*. 8 dishevelled; disordered: *wild attire*. 9 of the eyes: staring; distracted or scared-looking. 10 of a guess: very approximate, or quite random. 11 colloq furious; extremely angry. 12 slang enjoyable; terrific. ➤ n 1 (**the wild**) a wild animal's or plant's natural environment or life in it: *They returned the cub to the wild*. 2 (**wilds**) lonely, sparsely inhabited regions away from the city. ○ **wildly** adv. ○ **wildness** n. ◆ **run wild** 1 of a garden or plants: to revert to a wild, overgrown and uncultivated state. 2 of children, animals, etc: to live a life of freedom, with little discipline or control.

wild boar n a wild pig of Europe, NW Africa and S Asia, with prominent tusks.

wild card n 1 someone allowed to compete in a sports event, despite lacking the usual or stipulated qualifications. 2 comput a symbol representing any character or set of characters, used in searching or selecting data.

wildcat n (*wildcats* or *wildcat*) 1 a medium-sized undomesticated cat. 2 a short-tempered, fierce and aggressive person. ➤ adj of a business scheme: financially unsound or risky.

wild dog n any of several wild species of dog, esp the DINGO.

wildebeest /'wɪldəbiːst, 'vɪl-/ n (*wildebeest* or *wildebeests*) the GNU.

wilderness n 1 an uncultivated or uninhabited region. 2 pol the state of being without office or

influence after playing a leading role.

wildfire n a sweeping destructive fire. ◆ **spread like wildfire** to spread rapidly and extensively.

wildfowl sing or pl n a game bird or game birds.

wild-goose chase n a search that is bound to be unsuccessful and fruitless.

wild hyacinth n the BLUEBELL.

wildlife n wild animals, birds and plants in general.

wild rice n a tall aquatic grass that yields rice-like seeds.

Wild West or **the Wild West** n, hist the part of the US west of the Mississippi, settled during the 19c.

wile n (*wiles*) charming personal ways. 2 a cunning trick. ➤ vb to lure or entice.

wilful or (*US*) **willful** adj 1 deliberate; intentional. 2 headstrong, obstinate or self-willed. ○ **wilfully** adv. ○ **wilfulness** n.

will¹ auxiliary vb expressing or indicating: 1 the future tense of other verbs, esp when the subject is *you, he, she, it* or *they*: *They will no doubt succeed*. 2 intention or determination, when the subject is *I* or *we*: *We will not give in*. 3 a request: *Will you please shut the door?* 4 a command: *You will apologize to your mother immediately!* 5 ability or possibility: *The table will seat ten*. 6 readiness or willingness: *Any of our branches will exchange the goods*. 7 invitations: *Will you have a coffee?* 8 what is bound to be the case: *The experienced teacher will know when a child is unhappy*. 9 what applies in certain circumstances: *An unemployed youth living at home will not receive housing benefit*. 10 an assumption or probability: *That will be Vernon at the door*. 11 choice or desire: *Make what you will of that*.

will² n 1 the power of conscious decision and deliberate choice of action: *free will*. 2 one's own preferences, or one's determination in effecting them: *against my will*. 3 desire or determination: *the will to live*. 4 a wish or desire. 5 a instructions for the disposal of a person's property, etc after death; b the document containing these. ➤ vb 1 to try to compel (someone) by, or as if by, exerting one's will: *She willed herself to keep going*. 2 formal to desire or require that (something) be done, etc: *Her Majesty wills it*. 3 to bequeath (something) in one's will. ◆ **at will** as and when one wishes.

the willies pl n, colloq the creeps; a feeling of anxiety or unease.

willing adj 1 ready, glad or not disinclined to do something. 2 eager and co-operative. ○ **willingly** adv. ○ **willingness** n.

will-o'-the-wisp n (*wills-o'-the-wisp* or *will-o'-the-wisps*) 1 a light sometimes seen over marshes, caused by the combustion of marsh gas. 2 any elusive or deceptive person or thing.

willow n 1 a deciduous tree or shrub that generally grows near water, and has slender flexible branches. 2 the durable wood of this tree, used to make cricket bats and furniture.

willowy *adj* of a person: slender and graceful.

willpower *n* the determination, persistence and self-discipline needed to accomplish something.

willy or **willie** *n* (*-ies*) *colloq* a penis.

willy-nilly *adv* whether one wishes or not; regardless.

wilt *vb, intr* **1** *bot* of a plant: to droop or become limp because of insufficient water. **2** to droop from fatigue or heat. **3** to lose courage or confidence.

wily /ˈwaɪlɪ/ *adj* (*-ier, -iest*) cunning; crafty or devious. ○ **wiliness** *n*.

wimp *colloq, n* a feeble person. ➤ *vb, intr* (*always* **wimp out**) to back out (of doing something) through feebleness. ○ **wimpish** or **wimpy** *adj*.

wimple *n* a veil folded around the head, neck and cheeks, orig a women's fashion and still worn as part of a nun's dress.

win *vb* (**won, winning**) **1** *tr & intr* to be victorious or come first in (a war, contest, race, election, bet, etc). **2** to compete or fight for, and obtain (a victory or prize, etc). **3** to obtain or earn (something) by struggle or effort. ➤ *n, colloq* a victory or success. ○ **winnable** *adj*. ◇ **win sb over** or **round** to persuade them over to one's side or opinion.

wince *vb, intr* to shrink back, start or grimace, eg in pain or anticipation of it; to flinch. ➤ *n* a start or grimace in reaction to pain, etc.

winch *n* **1** a reel or roller round which a rope or chain is wound for hoisting or hauling heavy loads. **2** a crank or handle for setting a wheel, axle or machinery in motion. ➤ *vb* to hoist or haul (something or someone) with a winch.

wind¹ /wɪnd/ *n* **1** the movement of air across the Earth's surface as a result of differences in atmospheric pressure between one location and another. **2** a current of air produced artificially, by a fan, etc. **3** an influence that seems to pervade events: *a wind of change*. **4** one's breath or breath supply: *short of wind*. **5** gas built up in the intestines; flatulence. **6** empty, pompous or trivial talk. ➤ *vb* **1** to deprive (someone) of breath temporarily, eg by a punch or fall. **2** to burp (a baby). ◆ **break wind** to discharge intestinal gas through the anus. **get wind of sth** to have one's suspicions aroused or hear a rumour about it. **like the wind** swiftly. **put the wind up sb** *colloq* to make them nervous, anxious or alarmed.

wind² /waɪnd/ *vb* (**wound** /waʊnd/) **1** (*often* **wind round**) *tr & intr* to wrap or coil, or be wrapped or coiled. **2** *tr & intr* to move or cause (something) to move with many twists and turns. **3** (*also* **wind sth up**) to tighten the spring of (a clock, watch or other clockwork device) by turning a knob or key. ➤ *n* **1** an act of winding or the state of being wound. **2** a turn, coil or twist. ◇ **wind down 1** of a clock: to slow down and stop working. **2** of a person: to begin to relax. **wind sth down** to reduce the resources

and activities of (a business or enterprise). **wind up** *colloq* to end up: *He wound up in jail.* **wind sb up 1** to make them tense, nervous or excited. **2** *colloq* to taunt or tease them. **wind sth up** to conclude or close down a business or enterprise.

windbag *n, colloq* an excessively talkative person who communicates little of any value.

windbreak *n* a barrier, eg in the form of a screen, fence or line of trees, that provides protection from the wind.

windcheater *n* a windproof jacket with tightly fitting cuffs, neck and waistband.

windchill *n, meteorol* the extra chill given to air temperature by the wind.

windfall *n* **1** a fruit blown down from its tree. **2** an unexpected or sudden financial gain or other piece of good fortune.

wind farm *n* a concentration of wind-driven turbines generating electricity.

wind gauge *n* an ANEMOMETER.

winding-sheet /ˈwaɪndɪŋ-/ *n* a sheet for wrapping a corpse in; a shroud.

wind instrument *n* a musical instrument such as a clarinet, flute or trumpet, played by blowing air, esp the breath, through it.

windjammer /ˈwɪndʒæmə(r)/ *n, hist* a large fast merchant sailing-ship.

windlass /ˈwɪndləs/ *n* a drum-shaped axle round which a rope or chain is wound for hauling or hoisting weights.

windmill *n* **1** a mechanical device operated by wind-driven sails that revolve about a fixed shaft, used for grinding grain, pumping water and generating electricity. **2** a toy with a set of plastic or paper sails, mounted on a stick, that revolve in the wind.

window *n* **1** an opening in a wall to look through, or let in light and air, consisting of a wooden or metal frame fitted with panes of glass. **2** the frame itself. **3** the area immediately behind a shop's window, in which goods on sale are displayed. **4** a gap in a schedule, etc available for some purpose. **5** an opening in the front of an envelope, allowing the address written on the letter inside to be visible. **6** *comput* an enclosed rectangular area displayed on the VDU of a computer, which can be used as an independent screen.

window box *n* a box fitted along an exterior window ledge, for growing plants in.

window-dressing *n* **1** the art of arranging goods in a shop window. **2** the art or practice of giving something superficial appeal by skilful presentation.

windowpane *n* a sheet of glass set in a window.

window seat *n* **1** a seat placed in the recess of a window. **2** on a train or aeroplane, etc: a seat next to a window.

window-shopping *n* the activity of looking at goods in shop windows without buying them.

windowsill or **window ledge** *n* the interior

or exterior ledge that runs along the bottom of a window.

windpipe *n, anat* the TRACHEA.

windpower *n* a renewable energy source derived from winds in the Earth's atmosphere, used to generate electricity.

windscreen *n* the large sheet of curved glass at the front of the motor vehicle. *N Am equivalent* **windshield**.

windscreen-wiper *n* a device fitted to the windscreen of a motor vehicle, consisting of a rubber blade on an arm which moves in an arc, to keep the windscreen clear of rain, snow, etc.

windsock or **wind cone** *n* an open-ended cone of fabric flying from a mast, which shows the direction and speed of the wind.

windsurfing *n* the sport of riding the waves on a sailboard. ○ **windsurfer** *n*.

windswept *adj* **1** exposed to strong winds. **2** dishevelled from exposure to the wind.

wind-up /'waɪndʌp/ *n* the taunting or teasing of someone, eg the playing of a practical joke on them, or a joke, etc used in this.

windward *n* the side of a boat, etc facing the wind.

windy *adj* (*-ier*, *-iest*) **1** exposed to, or characterized by, strong wind. **2** suffering from, producing or produced by flatulence. **3** *colloq* of speech or writing: long-winded or pompous. **4** *colloq* nervous; uneasy.

wine *n* **1** an alcoholic drink made from fermented grape juice. **2** a similar drink made from other fruits or plants, etc. **3** the dark-red colour of red wine. ♦ **wine and dine** to partake of, or treat (someone) to, a meal, usu accompanied by wine.

wine bar *n* a bar which specializes in the selling of wine and often food.

wine cellar *n* **1** a cellar in which to store wines. **2** the stock of wine stored there.

wing *n* **1** one of the two modified front limbs of a bird or bat that are adapted for flight. **2** one of two or more membranous outgrowths that project from either side of the body of an insect enabling it to fly. **3** one of the flattened structures that project from either side of an aircraft body. **4** any of the corner sections of a vehicle body, forming covers for the wheels. **5** a part of a building projecting from the central or main section: *the west wing*. **6** *sport* in football and hockey, etc: **a** either edge of the pitch; **b** the player at either extreme of the forward line. **7** (**wings**) *theat* the area at each side of a stage, where performers wait to enter, out of sight of the audience. **8** a group with its own distinct views and character, within a political party or other body. ➤ *vb* **1** to make (one's way) by flying, or with speed. **2** to wound (a bird) in the wing or (a person) in the arm or shoulder; to wound (someone or something) superficially. **3** *poetic* to fly or skim lightly (over something). ○ **winged** *adj*. ○ **wingless** *adj*. ♦ **on the wing** flying. **spread one's wings 1** to use one's potential fully. **2** to escape from a confining environment in order to do this. **under sb's wing** under their protection or guidance.

wing chair *n* an armchair that has a high back with projections on both sides.

wing collar *n* a stiff collar worn upright with the points turned down.

wing commander *n* an air-force officer of the rank below group captain.

winger /'wɪŋə(r)/ *n, sport* a player in wing position.

wing mirror *n* a rear-view mirror attached to the wing, or more commonly the side, of a motor vehicle.

wing nut *n* a metal nut easily turned on a bolt by the finger and thumb by means of its flattened projections.

wingspan *n* the distance from tip to tip of the wings of an aircraft, or of a bird's wings when outstretched.

wink *vb, tr & intr* **1** to shut an eye briefly as an informal or cheeky gesture or greeting. **2** of lights and stars, etc: to flicker or twinkle. ➤ *n* **1** an act of winking. **2** a quick flicker of light. **3** a short spell of something, esp sleep. ♦ **tip sb the wink** *colloq* to give them a useful hint, esp in confidence.

winkle *n* a small edible snail-shaped shellfish; a periwinkle. ➤ *vb* (*always* **winkle sth out**) to force or prise it out.

winner *n* **1** a person, animal or vehicle, etc that wins a contest or race. **2** someone or something that is or seems destined to be a success.

winning *adj* **1** attractive or charming; persuasive. **2** securing victory. ➤ *n* (**winnings**) money or prizes won, esp in gambling. ○ **winningly** *adv*.

winnow *vb* **1** to separate (chaff) from (grain) by blowing a current of air through it. **2** to sift (evidence, etc).

wino /'waɪnəʊ/ *n, slang* someone addicted to cheap wine; an alcoholic.

winsome *adj* charming; captivating.

winter *n* (*also* **Winter**) the coldest season of the year, coming between autumn and spring. ➤ *adj* **1** referring, relating or belonging to winter: *a winter dish*. **2** of crops: sown in autumn so as to be reaped in the winter. ➤ *vb, intr* to spend the winter in a specified place. ○ **wintertime** *n*.

wintergreen *n* an evergreen plant yielding an aromatic oil which can be used medicinally or as a flavouring.

winter solstice *n* the shortest day of the year, when the sun reaches its lowest point in the N hemisphere (usu 21 December).

winter sports *pl n* sports held on snow or ice, such as skiing and ice-skating.

wintry or **wintery** *adj* (*-ier*, *-iest*) **1** of weather, etc: characteristic of winter. **2** unfriendly, cold or hostile.

wipe *vb* **1** to clean or dry (something) with a cloth, etc. **2** (**wipe sth away**, **off**, **out** or **up**) to remove it by wiping. **3** *comput, etc* to erase (data or a magnetic tape or disk). **4** to remove or get rid of (something): *He wiped the incident from his memory.* ➤ *n* **1** the act of cleaning something by rubbing. **2** a piece of fabric or tissue, usu specially treated, for wiping and cleaning. ◊ **wipe sb out** *slang* to kill or murder them. **wipe sth out** to get rid of or destroy it.

wipeout *n, colloq* a complete failure or disaster; total destruction.

wiper *n* a WINDSCREEN-WIPER.

wire *n* **1** metal drawn out into a narrow flexible strand. **2** a length of this, usu wrapped in insulating material, for carrying electric current. **3** *telecomm* a cable that connects one point with another. **4** *old use* a telegram or telegraph. ➤ *vb* **1a** to send a telegram to (someone); **b** to send (a message) by telegram. **2** (*also* **wire up**) to fit or connect up (an electrical apparatus or system, etc) with wires. **3** to fasten or secure (something) with wire. ◆ **get one's wires crossed** to misunderstand or be confused about something.

wired *adj, slang* highly-strung; stressed-out.

wire-haired *adj* of a breed of dog: with a coarse, wiry coat.

wireless *n, old use* a radio.

wire wool *n* a mass of fine wire used for scouring.

wireworm *n* a hard-bodied worm-like beetle larva, which lives in soil where it is extremely destructive to plant roots.

wiring *n* the arrangement of wires that connects the individual components of electric circuits into an operating system, eg the mains wiring of a house.

wiry *adj* (**-ier, -iest**) **1** of a person: of slight build, but strong and agile. **2** resembling wire. ○ **wiriness** *n*.

wisdom *n* **1** the quality of being wise. **2** the ability to make sensible judgements and decisions, esp on the basis of one's knowledge and experience. **3** learning; knowledge.

wisdom tooth *n* in humans: any of the last four molar teeth to come through, appearing at the back of each side of the upper and lower jaw.

wise¹ *adj* **1** having or showing wisdom; prudent; sensible. **2** learned or knowledgeable. **3** astute, shrewd or sagacious. **4** *in compounds* knowing the ways of something: *streetwise • worldly-wise.* ○ **wisely** *adv.* ◆ **be wise to sth** *colloq* to be aware of or informed about it. **none the wiser** knowing no more than before. ◊ **wise up to sb** or **sth** *colloq* to find out the facts about them or it.

wise² *n, old use* way: *in no wise to blame.*

wiseacre *n, derog* someone who assumes an air of superior wisdom.

wisecrack *n* a smart, clever or knowing remark. ➤ *vb, intr* to make a wisecrack.

wise guy *n, colloq* someone who is full of smart and cocky comments; a know-all.

wish *vb* **1** to want; to have a desire. **2** to desire, esp vainly or helplessly (that something were the case). **3** to express a desire for (luck, suc-

cess, happiness, etc) to come to (someone). **4** to say (good afternoon, etc) to (someone). ➤ *n* **1** a desire. **2** (*usu* **wishes**) what one wants to be done, etc. **3** (**wishes**) a hope expressed for someone's welfare: *best wishes.*

wishbone *n* a V-shaped bone in the breast of poultry.

wishful *adj* **1** having a desire or wish. **2** eager or desirous.

wishful thinking *n* an over-optimistic expectation, arising from one's desire.

wishy-washy *adj* **1** pale and insipid; bland. **2** watery; weak.

wisp *n* **1** a strand; a thin fine tuft or shred. **2** something slight or insubstantial. ○ **wispy** *adj* (**-ier, -iest**).

wisteria or **wistaria** *n* a climbing shrub with long pendulous clusters of lilac, violet or white flowers.

wistful *adj* sadly or vainly yearning. ○ **wistfully** *adv.* ○ **wistfulness** *n*.

wit¹ *n* **1** the ability to express oneself amusingly; humour. **2** someone who has this ability. **3** humorous speech or writing. **4** (*also* **wits**) common sense or intelligence or resourcefulness: *Will he have the wit to phone?* ◆ **at one's wits' end** *colloq* reduced to despair; completely at a loss. **have** or **keep one's wits about one** to be, or stay, alert. **live by one's wits** to live by cunning. **scared, frightened,** *etc* **out of one's wits** extremely scared, frightened, etc.

wit² *vb* (*1st and 3rd person present tense* **wot,** *past tense & past participle* **wist,** *present participle* **witting**) *archaic* to know how; to discern. ◆ **to wit** *law* that is to say; namely.

witch *n* **1** someone, esp a woman, supposed to have magical powers. **2** a frighteningly ugly or wicked old woman.

witchcraft *n* **1** magic or sorcery. **2** the use of this.

witch doctor *n* a member of a tribal society who is believed to have magical powers to cure people.

witch elm see WYCH-ELM.

witch hazel or **wych hazel** *n* an astringent lotion produced from the bark of a N American shrub.

witch hunt *n* a concerted campaign against an individual or group believed to hold views or to be acting in ways harmful to society.

with *prep* **1** in the company of (someone): *I went with her.* **2** used after verbs of partnering, co-operating, associating, etc: *dancing with him.* **3** used after verbs of mixing: *mingling with the crowd.* **4** by means of; using: *raise it with a crowbar.* **5** used after verbs of covering, filling, etc: *plastered with mud.* **6** used after verbs of providing: *equipped with firearms.* **7** as a result of (something): *shaking with fear.* **8** in the same direction as (something): *drift with the current.* **9** used after verbs of conflict: *She quarrelled with her brother.* **10** used after verbs of agreeing, disagreeing, and comparing: *compared with last year.* **11** used in describing (someone or something): *a man with a limp.* **12** in or under the specified circumstances: *I can't go abroad with my mother so ill.* **13** regarding: *What shall we do with this?* • *I can't do a thing with my hair.* **14** loyal to or supporting (someone or something): *We're with you all the way.*

withdraw *vb* (**withdrew, withdrawn**) **1** *intr* to move somewhere else, esp more private: *Ann withdrew into her bedroom.* **2** *intr* to leave; to go away: *We tactfully withdrew.* **3 a** *intr* of troops: to move back or retreat; **b** to order (troops, etc) to retreat. **4** to take (money) from a bank account for use. **5** *tr & intr* to back out or pull (something) out of an activity or contest, etc. **6** to take back (a comment) that one regrets making. **7** *intr* to become uncommunicative or unresponsive.

withdrawal *n* **1** the act or process of withdrawing. **2** a removal of funds from a bank account. **3** *med* the breaking of an addiction to drugs, etc, with associated physical and psychological symptoms. **4** a retreat into silence and self-absorption.

withdrawn *adj* unresponsive, shy or reserved.

wither *vb* **1 a** *intr* of plants: to fade, dry up and die; **b** to cause (a plant) to do this. **2** (*sometimes* **wither away**) *tr & intr* to fade or make (something) fade and disappear. **3** *tr & intr* to shrivel or make (something) shrivel and decay. **4** to humble or disconcert (someone) with a glaring or scornful, etc expression. ○ **withered** *adj*.

withers *pl n* the ridge between the shoulder blades of a horse.

withhold *vb* **1** to refuse to give or grant (something): *He withheld evidence.* **2** to hold back (something): *withholding payment.*

within *prep* **1** inside; enclosed by something: *within these four walls.* **2** not outside the limits of (something); not beyond: *within sight.* **3** in less than (a certain time or distance): *finished within a week.* ➤ *adv* **1** inside: *apply within.* **2** *old use* indoors: *There is someone within.*

without *prep* **1** not having the company of (someone): *She went home without him.* **2** deprived of (someone or something): *He can't live without her.* **3** not having (something): *a blue sky without a cloud* • *entering without permission.* **4** not (behaving as expected or in a particular way): *I answered without smiling* • *He did it without being told.* **5** not giving or showing, etc (something): *She complied without a murmur.* **6** free from (something): *He admitted it without shame.* **7** if it had not been for (someone or something): *I would have died without their help.* ➤ *adv, old use* outside: *He is without.*

withstand *vb* **1** to maintain one's position or stance against (someone or something). **2** to resist or brave (something): *She withstood his insults.*

witless *adj* **1** stupid; lacking wit, sense or wisdom. **2** crazy.

witness *n* **1** someone who sees, and can therefore give a direct account of, an event or occurrence, etc. **2** someone who gives evidence in a court of law. **3** someone who adds their own signature to confirm the authenticity of another. **4** proof or evidence of anything. ➤ *vb* **1** to be present as an observer at (an event or occurrence, etc). **2** to add one's own signature to confirm the authenticity of (a signature). **3** *intr* to give evidence. **4** of a period or place, or of a person: to be the setting for, or to live through, (certain events). ♦ **bear witness to sth 1** to be evidence of it. **2** to give confirmation of it.

witter *vb, intr* (*usu* **witter on**) to talk or mutter ceaselessly and ineffectually.

witticism *n* a witty remark or comment.

wittingly *adv* consciously; deliberately.

witty *adj* (**-ier, -iest**) able to express oneself cleverly and amusingly. ○ **wittily** *adv*.

wizard *n* **1** someone, esp a man, supposed to have magic powers. **2** *dated, colloq* (*often* **a wizard at** or **with sth**) someone extraordinarily skilled in a particular way. ○ **wizardry** *n*.

wizened *adj* shrivelled or wrinkled, esp with age.

woad *n* **1** a plant whose leaves yield a blue dye. **2** this dye, used by the ancient Britons to paint their bodies.

wobble *vb* **1** *tr & intr* to rock, sway or shake unsteadily. **2** *intr* to move or advance in this manner. ➤ *n* a wobbling, rocking or swaying motion.

wobbly *adj* (**-ier, -iest**) unsteady; shaky; inclined to wobble. ➤ *n* (**-ies**) *colloq* a fit of anger; a tantrum. ♦ **throw a wobbly** *colloq* to have a tantrum.

wodge *n, colloq* a large lump, wad or chunk.

woe *n* **1** grief; misery. **2** (*often* **woes**) affliction; calamity. ♦ **woe betide …** *old use, facetious* may evil befall, or evil will befall (whoever offends or acts in some specified way): *Woe betide anyone who disturbs him.*

woebegone *adj* dismal-looking; showing sorrow.

woeful *adj* **1** mournful; sorrowful. **2** causing woe: *a woeful story.* **3** disgraceful; pitiful: *a woeful lack of interest.* ○ **woefully** *adv*. ○ **woefulness** *n*.

woggle *n, chiefly Brit* a ring, usu of leather or plastic, through which Cubs, Scouts and Guides, etc thread their neckerchiefs.

wok *n* a large metal bowl-shaped pan used in Chinese cookery.

wold *n* a tract of open rolling upland.

wolf *n* (**wolves**) **1** a wild carnivorous mammal of the dog family which hunts in packs. **2** *colloq* a man with an insatiable appetite for sexual conquests. ➤ *vb* (*usu* **wolf sth down**) *colloq* to gobble it quickly and greedily. ♦ **cry wolf** to give a false alarm, usu repeatedly.

wolfhound *n* a very large domestic dog.

wolfram *n, chem* TUNGSTEN.

wolf whistle *n* a loud whistle used as an expression of admiration for a person's appearance. ➤ *vb* (**wolf-whistle**) to whistle in this way.

wolverine or **wolverene** *n* a large carnivorous animal of the weasel family, which inhabits forests in N America and Eurasia.

woman *n* (*women*) **1** an adult human female. **2** women generally; the female sex. **3** *colloq* someone's wife or girlfriend. **4** *old use* a female servant or domestic daily help. **5** *old use* a female attendant to a queen, etc. ➤ *adj* female: *a woman doctor.* ○ **womanhood** *n.*

womanish *adj* of a man, his behaviour or appearance: effeminate; unmanly.

womanize or **-ise** *vb, intr* of a man: to pursue and have casual affairs with women. ○ **womanizer** *n.*

womankind *n* women generally; the female sex.

womanly *adj* (*-ier, -iest*) **1** having characteristics specific to a woman; feminine. **2** considered natural or suitable to a woman. ○ **womanliness** *n.*

womb *n, anat* the organ in female mammals in which the young develop until birth. *Technical equivalent* **uterus.**

wombat *n* a nocturnal Australian marsupial, with a compact body, short legs, a large flat head and no tail.

womenfolk *pl n* **1** women generally. **2** the female members of a family or society.

women's liberation *n* (*also with caps*) part of the women's movement, aimed at freeing women from the disadvantages of a male-dominated society.

wonder *n* **1** the state of mind produced by something extraordinary, new or unexpected; amazement or awe. **2** something that is a cause of awe, amazement or bafflement; a marvel or prodigy. ➤ *adj* notable for accomplishing marvels: *a wonder drug.* ➤ *vb* **1** *tr & intr* to be curious: *wondering where you'd gone.* **2** (*wonder at someone* or *sth*) to be amazed or surprised by them or it: *I wonder at you sometimes!* **3** used politely to introduce requests: *I wonder if you could help me?* ○ **wonderment** *n.* ♦ **do** or **work wonders** to achieve marvellous results. **no** or **small wonder** it is hardly surprising.

wonderful *adj* **1** arousing wonder; extraordinary. **2** excellent; splendid. ○ **wonderfully** *adv.*

wonderland *n* **1** an imaginary place full of marvels. **2** a scene of strange unearthly beauty.

wondrous *adj* wonderful, strange or awesome.

wonky *adj* (*-ier, -iest*) *Brit colloq* **1** unsound, unsteady or wobbly. **2** crooked or awry; uneven.

wont /wount/ *chiefly formal, literary or old use, adj* habitually inclined; accustomed: *He is wont to retire to bed early.* ➤ *n* a habit: *It was her wont to rise early.* ➤ *vb, tr & intr* (*wont* or *wonts, wont* or *wonted*) to become or make (someone) become accustomed.

> **wont** There is often a spelling confusion between **wont** and **want.**

won't *contraction* will not.

woo *vb* (*wooed*) **1** *old use* of a man: to try to win the love and affection of (a woman) esp in the hope of marrying her. **2** to try to win the support of (someone): *woo the voters.* ○ **wooing** *n, adj.*

wood *n* **1** *bot* the hard tissue beneath the bark, that forms the bulk of woody trees and shrubs. **2** this material used for building timber, furniture-making, etc. **3** (*also* **woods**) an expanse of growing trees. **4** firewood. **5** *golf* a club with a head traditionally made of wood, now usu of metal, used for driving the ball long distances. ➤ *adj* made of, or using, wood. ➤ *vb* to cover (land, etc) with trees. ○ **wooded** *adj.*

woodbine *n* honeysuckle.

woodcarving *n* **1** the process of carving in wood. **2** an object or decoration carved in wood.

woodchuck *n* a N American marmot. Also called **groundhog.**

woodcock *n* a long-billed game bird.

woodcut *n* **1** a design cut into a wooden block. **2** a print taken from this.

woodcutter *n* **1** someone who fells trees and chops wood. **2** someone who makes woodcuts.

wooden *adj* **1** made of wood. **2** of an actor, performance, etc: stiff, unnatural and inhibited; lacking expression and liveliness. **3** clumsy or awkward. **4** esp of a facial expression: blank; expressionless. ○ **woodenly** *adv.*

wooden spoon *n* a booby prize.

woodland *n* (*also* **woodlands**) an area of land planted with relatively short trees that are more widely spaced than those in a forest.

woodlouse *n* a crustacean with a grey oval plated body, found in damp places.

woodpecker *n* a tree-dwelling bird which has a straight pointed chisel-like bill used to bore into tree bark in search of insects and to drill nesting holes.

woodpigeon *n* a common pigeon that lives in woods, with a white marking round its neck.

wood pulp *n* wood fibres that have been chemically and mechanically pulped for papermaking.

woodruff *n* a sweet-smelling plant with small white flowers and whorled leaves.

wood stain *n* a substance for staining wood.

woodwind *n* **1** the wind instruments in an orchestra, including the flute, oboe, clarinet and bassoon. **2 a** the section of the orchestra composed of these; **b** (*also* **woodwinds**) the players of these.

woodwork *n* **1** the art of making things out of wood; carpentry. **2** the wooden parts of any structure. ♦ **crawl out from the woodwork** of someone or something undesirable: to make themselves or their presence known.

woodworm *n* (*woodworm* or *woodworms*) **1** the larva of any of several beetles, that bores into wood. **2** the condition of wood caused by this.

woody *adj* (**-ier, -iest**) **1** of countryside: wooded; covered in trees. **2** resembling, developing into, or composed of wood: *plants with woody stems*. **3** similar to wood in texture, smell or taste, etc. ○ **woodiness** *n*.

woof¹ /wʊf/ *n* the sound of a dog's bark. ➢ *vb, intr* to bark.

woof² /wuːf/ *n, weaving* the weft.

woofer /'wʊfə(r)/ *n, electronics* a large loudspeaker for reproducing low-frequency sounds. Compare TWEETER.

wool *n* **1** the soft wavy hair of sheep and certain other animals. **2** this hair spun into yarn for knitting or weaving. **3** fabric or clothing woven or knitted from this yarn. ♦ **pull the wool over sb's eyes** *colloq* to deceive them.

wool-gathering *n* absent-minded daydreaming.

woollen or (*US*) **woolen** *adj* **1** made of or relating to wool. **2** producing, or dealing in, goods made of wool. ➢ *n* (*often* **woollens**) a woollen, esp knitted, garment.

woolly or (*US*) **wooly** *adj* (**-ier, -iest**) **1** made of, similar to, or covered with wool or wool-like fibres, etc; fluffy and soft. **2** vague and muddled; lacking in clarity: *woolly-minded* • *woolly argument*. ➢ *n* (**-ies**) *colloq* a woollen, usu knitted, garment. ○ **woolliness** *n*.

woozy *adj* (**-ier, -iest**) *colloq* **1** having blurred senses, due to drink or drugs, etc. **2** confused; dizzy.

word *n* **1** the smallest unit of spoken or written language that can be used independently, usu separated off by spaces in writing and printing. **2** a brief conversation on a particular matter. **3** any brief statement, message or communication: *a word of caution*. **4** news or notice: *any word of Jane?* **5** a rumour: *The word is he's bankrupt*. **6** one's solemn promise. **7** an order: *She expects her word to be obeyed*. **8** a word given as a signal for action: *Wait till I give the word*. **9** what someone says or said: *She remembered her mother's words*. **10** (**words**) language as a means of communication: *impossible to convey in words*. **11** (**words**) an argument or heated discussion; verbal contention: *We had words when he returned*. **12** (**words**) **a** the lyrics of a song, etc; **b** the speeches an actor must learn for a particular part. **13** (**the Word**) *Christianity* the teachings contained in the Bible. **14** *comput* **a** a group of bits or bytes processed as a unit by a computer, the size of a word varying according to the size of the computer; **b** in word-processing: any group of characters separated by spaces or punctuation, whether or not it is a real word. ➢ *vb* to express (something) in carefully chosen words. ♦ **have words with sb** *colloq* to quarrel with them. **in a word** briefly; in short. **my word** or **upon my word** an exclamation of surprise. **say the word** to give one's consent or approval for some action to proceed. **take sb at their word** to take their offer or suggestion, etc literally. **take sb's word for it** to accept what they say as true, without verification.

the last word 1 the final, esp conclusive, remark or comment in an argument. **2** the most up-to-date design or model, or most recent advance in something. **3** the finest example of eg a particular quality, etc: *the last word in good taste*. **word for word** repeated in exactly the same words, or translated into exactly corresponding words.

word-blindness *n* DYSLEXIA.

wordgame *n* any game or puzzle in which words are constructed or deciphered, etc.

wording *n* **1** the choice and arrangement of words used to express something. **2** the words used in this arrangement.

word of honour *n* a promise or assurance which cannot be broken without disgrace.

word of mouth *n* spoken, as opposed to written, communication.

word-perfect *adj* **1** able to repeat something accurately from memory. **2** of a recitation, etc: faultless.

word processor *n, comput* a computer application dedicated completely to the input, processing, storage and retrieval of text. ○ **word-processing** *n*.

wordy *adj* (**-ier, -iest**) using or containing too many words; long-winded.

work *n* **1** physical or mental effort to achieve or make something, eg labour, study, research, etc. **2** employment: *out of work*. **3** one's place of employment: *He leaves work at 4.30*. **4** tasks to be done: *She often brings work home with her*. **5** the product of mental or physical labour: *a lifetime's work*. **6** a manner of working, or WORKMANSHIP. **7 a** any literary, artistic, musical, or dramatic composition or creation; **b** (**works**) the entire collection of such material by an artist, composer or author, etc. **8** anything done, managed, made or achieved, etc; an activity carried out for some purpose: *works of charity*. **9** (**the works**) *colloq* everything possible, available or going; the whole lot: *She has a headache, fever, cold – the works!* **10** *physics* the transfer of energy that occurs when force is exerted on a body to move it, measured in JOULES. ➢ *adj* relating to, or suitable for, etc work: *work clothes*. ➢ *vb* **1** *intr* to do work; to exert oneself mentally or physically. **2** *tr & intr* to have a job. **3** to impose tasks on (someone): *She works her staff hard*. **4** *tr & intr* to operate, esp satisfactorily: *Does this radio work?* **5** *intr* of a plan or idea, etc: to be successful or effective. **6** *intr* to function in a particular way: *That's not how life works*. **7** to cultivate (land). **8** to extract materials from (a mine). **9** *colloq* to manipulate (a system or rules, etc) to one's advantage. **10** *intr* (**work on sb**) *colloq* to use one's powers of persuasion on them. **11** *intr* (**work on sth**) **a** to try to perfect, finish, or improve it; **b** to use it as a basis for one's decisions and actions: *Working on that assumption …* **12** *tr & intr* to make (one's way), or shift or make (something) shift gradually: *We worked through the crowd*. ○ **workless** *adj*. ◇ **work sth off** to get rid of (energy or the effects of a heavy meal) by energetic activity. **work out 1** to be successfully achieved or resolved: *It'll all work out in the end.* **2** to perform a set of energetic physical exercises: *She's working out at the gym.* **work sth out** to solve it; to sort or reason it out. **work sb over** *slang* to beat them up. **work sb up** to excite or agitate them. **work sth up** to summon up (an appetite, enthusiasm or energy, etc). **work up to sth** to approach (a difficult task or objective) by gradual stages.

workable *adj* **1** of a scheme, etc: able to be carried out. **2** of a material or mineral source, etc: able to be worked.

workaday *adj* ordinary or mundane.

workaholic *n, colloq* someone addicted to work.

workbench *n* a table, usu a purpose-built one, at which a mechanic, craftsman, etc works.

workday see WORKING DAY

worker *n* **1** someone who works. **2** someone employed in manual work. **3** an employee as opposed to an employer. **4** a female social insect, eg a bee or ant, that is sterile and whose sole function is to maintain the colony and forage for food.

work experience *n* a scheme under which school pupils or leavers work unpaid with a company or organization, etc for a short time in order to gain experience.

workforce *n* **1** the number of workers engaged in a particular industry, factory, etc. **2** the total number of workers potentially available.

workhorse *n* **1** a horse used for labour. **2** a person, machine, etc that carries out arduous work.

workhouse *n, hist* an institution where the poor were housed and given work to do.

working *n* **1** (*also* **workings**) the operation or mode of operation of something. **2** (**workings**) excavations at a mine or quarry. ➤ *adj* **1** engaged in or devoted to work. **2** adequate for one's purposes: *a working knowledge of French.*

working capital *n* money used to keep a business, etc going.

working class *n* the wage-earning section of the population, employed esp in manual labour.

working day or (*N Am*) **workday** *n* **1** a day on which people go to work as usual. **2** the part of the day during which work is done.

working party *n* a group of people appointed to investigate and report on something.

workload *n* the amount of work to be done by a person or machine, esp in a specified time.

workman *n* a man employed to do manual work.

workmanlike *adj* characteristic of a skilful workman.

workmanship *n* expertise shown in the making of something, or the refinement of the finished product.

workmate *n, colloq* someone who works with another or others; a fellow-worker.

work of art *n* **1** a painting or sculpture of high quality. **2** anything constructed or composed with obvious skill and elegance.

workout *n* a session of physical exercise.

workshop *n* **1** a room or building where construction and repairs are carried out. **2** a course of study or work, esp of an experimental or creative kind, for a group of people: *a theatre workshop.*

workshy *adj, colloq* lazy; inclined to avoid work.

workstation *n* an area in an office, etc where one person works, esp at a computer terminal.

work surface or **worktop** *n* a flat surface along the top of kitchen installations for the preparation of food, etc.

work to rule *vb, intr* of workers: to scrupulously observe all the regulations for the express purpose of slowing down work, as a form of industrial action. ○ **work-to-rule** *n.*

world *n* **1** the Earth. **2** the people inhabiting the Earth; humankind: *tell the world.* **3** any other planet or potentially habitable heavenly body. **4** human affairs: *the present state of the world.* **5** (*also* **World**) a group of countries characterized in a certain way: *the Third World.* **6** (*also* **World**) the people of a particular period, and their culture: *the Ancient World.* **7** a state of existence: *in this world or the next.* **8** someone's individual way of life or range of experience: *He's in a world of his own.* **9** an atmosphere or environment: *a world of make-believe.* **10** a particular area of activity: *the world of politics.* **11** a class of living things: *the insect world.* **12** *colloq* a great deal: *It did her a world of good.* ➤ *adj* relating to, affecting, or important throughout, the whole world. ♦ **for all the world as if ...** exactly as if ... **on top of the world** *colloq* supremely happy. **out of this world** *colloq* extraordinarily fine. **the best of both worlds** the benefits of both alternatives with the drawbacks of neither. **think the world of sb** to love or admire them immensely.

world-class *adj* being among or competing against those of the highest standard in the world.

world-famous *adj* well known throughout the world.

worldly *adj* (**-ier, -iest**) **1** relating to this world; material, as opposed to spiritual or eternal: *worldly possessions.* **2** shrewd about the ways of the world. ○ **worldliness** *n.*

worldly-wise *adj* knowledgeable about life; having the wisdom of those experienced in, and affected by, the ways of the world.

world power *n* a state, group of states or institution, etc strong enough to have influence in world affairs and politics.

worldweary *adj* tired of the world; bored with life.

worldwide *adj, adv* extending or known throughout the world.

World Wide Web *n* a network of HYPER-MEDIA files containing HYPERLINKS from one file to another over the Internet, which allows the user to browse files containing related information from all over the world.

worm n 1 zool a small soft-bodied limbless invertebrate that is characteristically long and slender. 2 any superficially similar but unrelated animal, eg the larva of certain insects. 3 a mean, contemptible, weak or worthless person. 4 mech the spiral thread of a screw. 5 (**worms**) pathol any disease characterized by the presence of parasitic worms in the intestines. 6 comput an unauthorized computer program, differing from a virus in that it is an independent program rather than a piece of coding, designed to sabotage a computer system, esp by reproducing itself throughout a computer network. ➤ vb 1 (also **worm out**) to extract (information, etc) little by little: I wormed the secret out of them. 2 to treat (an animal) to rid it of worms. ♦ **worm one's way** to wriggle or manoeuvre oneself gradually: They wormed their way to the front. **worm one's way into sth** to insinuate oneself into someone's favour or affections, etc.

wormcast n a coiled heap of sand or earth excreted by a burrowing earthworm or lugworm.

wormwood n a bitter-tasting herb, used to flavour absinthe.

wormy adj (-ier, -iest) infested by worms.

worn adj 1 haggard with weariness. 2 showing signs of deterioration through long use or wear. 3 exhausted.

worn out adj 1 damaged or rendered useless by wear. 2 extremely weary.

worrisome adj 1 causing worry. 2 inclined to worry.

worry vb (-ies, -ied) 1 intr to be anxious; to fret. 2 to make (someone) anxious. 3 to bother, pester or harass (someone). 4 of a dog: to chase and bite (sheep, etc). 5 (often **worry at**) to try to solve (a problem, etc). ➤ n (-ies) 1 a state of anxiety. 2 a cause of anxiety. ○ **worrier** n.

worry beads pl n a string of beads for fiddling with, as a means of relieving mental tension.

worse adj 1 more bad. 2 more ill. 3 more grave, serious or acute. 4 inferior in standard. ➤ n something worse: Worse was to follow. ➤ adv less well; more badly: He's doing worse at school. ♦ **none the worse for …** unharmed by (an accident or bad experience, etc). **the worse for wear** 1 worn or shabby from use. 2 in poor condition. 3 drunk. **worse off** in a worse situation, esp financially.

worsen vb, tr & intr to make or become worse.

worship vb (**worshipped, worshipping**) 1 tr & intr to honour (God or a god) with praise, prayer, hymns, etc. 2 to love, admire, or glorify (a person, money, etc), esp blindly. ➤ n 1 a the activity of worshipping; b the worship itself. 2 a religious service. 3 a title for a mayor or magistrate, in the form of **His, Her** or **Your Worship**. ○ **worshipper** n.

worshipful adj full of or showing reverence or adoration.

worst adj 1 most bad, awful or unpleasant, etc. 2 most grave, severe, acute or dire. 3 most inferior; lowest in standard. ➤ n 1 the worst thing, part or possibility. 2 the most advanced degree of badness. ➤ adv most severely; most badly. ➤ vb to defeat (someone); to get the better of (them). ♦ **at its, etc worst** in the worst state or severest degree. **at (the) worst 1** in the worst possible circumstances. 2 taking the most pessimistic view.

worsted /ˈwɜːstɪd/ n 1 a fine strong twisted yarn spun out from long combed wool. 2 fabric woven from this.

wort n 1 in compounds a plant: liverwort. 2 brewing a dilute solution or infusion of malt, fermented to make beer and whisky.

worth n 1 importance or usefulness. 2 financial value. 3 the quantity of anything that can be bought for a certain sum, accomplished in a certain time, etc. ➤ adj 1 having a value of a specified amount. 2 colloq having money and property to a specified value. 3 justifying, deserving or warranting something: worth consideration.

worthless adj 1 having no financial value. 2 having no merit or virtue; useless. ○ **worthlessness** n.

worthwhile adj 1 worth the time, money or energy expended. 2 useful, beneficial or rewarding.

worthy adj (-ier, -iest) admirable, excellent or deserving. ➤ n (-ies) an eminent or distinguished person. ○ **worthily** adv. ○ **worthiness** n. ♦ **worthy of sb** suitable to their status or position. **worthy of sth** deserving it.

would auxiliary vb 1 in reported speech, used as the past tense of WILL[1]: Kathy said she would leave at 10. 2 used to indicate willingness, readiness, or ability: Roy was asked to help, but wouldn't. 3 used to indicate habitual action: Mum would always telephone at six. 4 used to express frustration at some happening: It would rain, just as we're setting out. 5 used to make polite invitations, offers or requests: Would you ring her back? 6 used when politely expressing or seeking an opinion: Would you not agree?

would-be adj hoping, aspiring or professing to be a specified thing: a would-be actor.

wouldn't contraction would not.

wound[1] /waʊnd/ past tense, past participle of WIND[2].

wound[2] /wuːnd/ n 1 any local injury to a human, animal or plant, caused by an external means such as cutting, crushing or tearing. 2 an injury caused to pride, feelings or reputation, etc. ➤ vb, tr & intr to inflict a wound on (a person, creature or limb, etc). 2 to injure (feelings, etc). ○ **wounding** n, adj.

wow colloq, exclam an exclamation of astonishment, admiration or wonder. ➤ n a huge success. ➤ vb to impress or amaze hugely.

WPC abbrev Woman Police Constable.

wrack n 1 a type of seaweed, esp one of the

large brown varieties. **2** destruction or devastation.

wraith n **1** a ghost. **2** any apparition, esp of a living person, believed to appear shortly before their death. ○ **wraithlike** adj.

wrangle vb, intr to quarrel, argue or debate noisily or bitterly. ➢ n **1** the act of disputing noisily. **2** a bitter dispute.

wrap vb (**wrapped, wrapping**) **1** to fold or wind (something) round (someone or something). **2** (also **wrap sth up**) to cover or enfold it with cloth, paper etc. **3** intr (**wrap round**) comput of text on a screen: to start a new line automatically as soon as the last character space on the previous line is filled. ➢ n **1** a warm garment, esp a shawl or stole for the shoulders. **2** a protective covering. **3** a wrapper. **4** cinematog, TV the completion of filming or recording. ♦ **keep sth under wraps** colloq to keep it secret. ◊ **wrap up 1** to dress warmly: Wrap up warm before you leave! **2** slang to be quiet. **wrap sth up** colloq to finish it off or settle it finally.

wrapper n a paper or Cellophane cover round a packet or sweet, etc.

wrapping n (usu **wrappings**) any of various types of cover, wrapper or packing material.

wrasse n (**wrasses** or **wrasse**) a brightly coloured sea fish with powerful teeth.

wrath /rɒθ/ n violent anger; resentment or indignation. ○ **wrathful** adj.

wreak vb **1** (esp **wreak havoc**) to cause (damage or chaos, etc) on a disastrous scale. **2** to take (vengeance) ruthlessly (on someone).

wreath n **1** a ring-shaped garland of flowers and foliage placed on a grave or memorial as a tribute. **2** a similar garland hung up as a decoration, eg at Christmas. **3** (usu **wreaths**) a ring, curl or spiral of smoke, mist, etc.

wreathe vb **1** to hang or encircle (something) with flowers, etc. **2** of smoke, mist, etc: to cover or surround (something). ♦ **wreathed in smiles** smiling broadly.

wreck n **1** the destruction, esp accidental, of a ship at sea. **2** a hopelessly damaged sunken or grounded ship. **3** a crashed aircraft or a ruined vehicle. **4** colloq someone in a pitiful state of fitness or mental health. ➢ vb **1** to break or destroy (something). **2** to spoil (plans, hopes, a holiday, relationship, etc). **3** to cause the wreck of (a ship, etc).

wreckage n the remains of things that have been wrecked.

wrecker n **1** someone or something that wrecks. **2** someone who criminally ruins anything. **3** hist someone who deliberately causes a wreck in order to plunder the wreckage. **4** N Am a person or business whose job is to demolish buildings or vehicles, etc. **5** N Am a breakdown vehicle.

Wren n **1** a member of the Women's Royal Naval Service. **2** (**the Wrens**) the service itself.

wren n a very small songbird with short wings and a short erect tail.

wrench vb **1** (often **wrench off** or **out**) to pull or twist (something) violently. **2** to sprain (an ankle, etc). **3** to twist or distort (a meaning). ➢ n **1** an act or instance of wrenching. **2** a violent pull or twist. **3** an adjustable tool for gripping and turning nuts and bolts, etc. **4** N Am a spanner. **5** a painful parting or separation.

wrest vb **1** to turn or twist (something). **2** to pull or wrench (something) away, esp from someone else's grasp or possession. **3** to extract (a statement or promise, etc) with difficulty.

wrestle vb **1** tr & intr **a** to fight by trying to grip, throw and pinion one's opponent; **b** to force (someone) into some position in this way; **c** to do this as a sport. **2** (usu **wrestle with**) to struggle to deal with (a problem). ○ **wrestler** n.

wrestling n the sport or exercise, governed by certain fixed rules, in which two people WRESTLE (verb sense 1).

wretch n **1** a miserable, unfortunate and pitiful person. **2** a worthless and despicable person.

wretched adj **1** pitiable. **2** miserable, unhappy, distressed or distraught. **3** inferior or poor; humble or lowly. **4** infuriating. ○ **wretchedly** adv. ○ **wretchedness** n.

wriggle vb, tr & intr **1** to twist to and fro. **2** to make (one's way) by this means. **3** to make (one's way) deviously. **4** (**wriggle out of sth**) to manage cleverly to evade or escape from (a disagreeable situation, etc). ➢ n a wriggling action or motion.

wring vb (**wrung**) **1** (also **wring out**) to force liquid from (something) by twisting or squeezing. **2** to force (information or a consent, etc) from someone. **3** to break (the neck) of a bird, etc by twisting. **4** to keep clasping and twisting (one's hands) in distress or agitation. **5** to crush (someone's hand) in one's own, by way of greeting. **6** to tear at (the heart or emotions). ♦ **wringing wet** soaking wet.

wringer n, hist a machine with two rollers for squeezing water out of wet clothes.

wrinkle n **1** a crease or line in the skin, esp of the face, appearing with advancing age. **2** a slight crease or ridge in any surface. **3** a minor problem or difficulty to be smoothed out. ➢ vb, tr & intr to develop or make (something) develop wrinkles. ○ **wrinkly** adj.

wrist n **1** anat the joint between the forearm and the hand. **2** the part of a sleeve that covers this.

writ n a legal document by which someone is summoned, or required to do or refrain from doing something.

write vb (past tense **wrote**, past participle **written**) **1** tr & intr (also **write sth down**) to mark or produce (letters, symbols, numbers, words, etc) on a surface, esp paper, usu using a pen or pencil. **2 a** to compose or create (a book, music, etc) in manuscript, typescript or on computer, etc; **b** to be the author or composer of (a book or music, etc). **3** intr to compose novels or contribute articles to newspapers, etc, esp as a living. **4** to make or fill in (a document or form, etc). **5** *tr & intr* to compose (a letter, etc): *I must write to him.* **6** to say or express in a letter, article or book, etc. **7** to underwrite (an insurance policy). **8** to fill (pages or sheets, etc) with writing. **9** to display clearly: *Guilt was written all over his face.* **10** *comput* to transfer (data) to a memory or storage device. ◊ **write off** to write and send a letter of request: *I wrote off for a catalogue.* **write sth off 1** to damage (a vehicle in a crash) beyond repair. **2** to cancel (a debt). **3** to discontinue (a project, etc) because it is likely to fail. **4** to dismiss (something) as being of no importance. **write sth out 1** to write it in full; to copy or transcribe it. **2** to remove a character or scene from a film or serial, etc. **write sth up 1** to write or rewrite it in a final form. **2** to bring (a diary or accounts, etc) up to date. **3** to write about it or review it, esp approvingly.

write-off *n* something written off, esp a motor vehicle involved in an accident.

writer *n* **1** someone who writes, esp as a living; an author. **2** someone who has written a particular thing.

write-up *n* an written or published account, esp a review in a newspaper or magazine, etc.

writhe *vb, intr* **1** to twist violently, esp in pain or discomfort; to squirm. **2** *colloq* to feel painfully embarrassed or humiliated. ➤ *n* the action of writhing; a twist or contortion.

writing *n* **1** written or printed words. **2** handwriting. **3 a** a literary composition; **b** the art or activity of literary composition. **4** (*usu* **writings**) literary work. **5** a form of script: *Chinese writing.* ♦ **in writing** of a promise or other commitment: in written form, esp as being firm proof of intention, etc.

written *adj* expressed in writing, and so undeniable: *written consent.* ➤ *vb, past participle of* WRITE.

wrong *adj* **1** not correct. **2** mistaken. **3** not appropriate or suitable. **4** not good or sensible; unjustifiable. **5** morally bad; wicked. **6** defective or faulty. **7** amiss; causing trouble, pain, etc. **8** of one side of a fabric or garment, etc: intended as the inner or unseen side. ➤ *adv* **1** incorrectly. **2** improperly; badly. ➤ *n* **1** whatever is not right or just. **2** any injury done to

someone else. ➤ *vb* **1** to treat (someone) unjustly; to do wrong to (someone). **2** to judge unfairly. **3** to deprive (someone) of some right; to defraud. ◦ **wrongly** *adv.* ♦ **don't get me wrong** *colloq* don't misinterpret or misunderstand me. **get out of bed on the wrong side** to get up in the morning in a bad mood. **get sth wrong 1** to give the incorrect answer to it, or do it incorrectly. **2** to misunderstand it. **go wrong 1** of plans, etc: to fail to go as intended. **2** to make an error. **3** of a mechanical device: to stop functioning properly. **in the wrong** guilty of an error or injustice.

wrongdoing *n* evil or wicked action or behaviour. ◦ **wrongdoer** *n*.

wrongfoot *vb* **1** *tennis, etc* to catch (one's opponent) off balance by making an unpredictable shot, etc to a point away from the direction in which they are moving or preparing to move. **2** to contrive to place (an opponent in a dispute, etc) at a tactical or moral disadvantage; to disconcert them.

wrongful *adj* unlawful; unjust. ◦ **wrongfully** *adv.*

wrong-headed *adj* obstinate and stubborn, adhering wilfully to wrong principles and/or policy.

wroth *adj, old use* angry.

wrought /rɔːt/ *adj* of metal: beaten into shape with tools.

wrought iron *n* a malleable form of iron with a very low carbon content.

wry *adj* **1** eg of a smile: slightly mocking or bitter; ironic. **2** of a facial expression: with the features distorted or twisted into a grimace, in reaction to a bitter taste, etc. **3** of humour: dry. ◦ **wryly** *adv.* ◦ **wryness** *n*.

wuss /wʊs/ or **wussy** *n* (**wusses** or **wussies**) *slang* a weakling; a feeble person.

WWW or (*in Web addresses*) **www** *abbrev* World Wide Web.

wych-elm or **witch elm** *n* a tree of the elm family, native to N Europe and Asia.

WYSIWYG or **wysiwyg** /ˈwɪzɪwɪg/ *abbrev, comput* what you see is what you get, indicating that the type and characters appearing on screen are as they will appear on the printout.

X¹ or **x** *n* (**Xs**, **X's** or **x's**) **1** the twenty-fourth letter of the English alphabet. **2** an unknown or un-named person.

X² *symbol* **1** *math* (*usu* **x**) an unknown quantity; the first of a pair or group of unknown quantities. Compare Y³, Z². **2** the Roman numeral for 10. **3** a film classified as suitable for people over the age of 17 (in the USA) or 18 (in the UK; now replaced by '18'). **4** a mark used: **a** to symbolize

a kiss; **b** to indicate an error; **c** as the signature of an illiterate person, etc.

X-chromosome *n, biol* the sex chromosome that when present as one half of an identical pair determines the female sex in most animals, including humans.

Xe *symbol, chem* xenon.

xenon /ˈzɛnɒn, ˈziːnɒn/ *n, chem* an element, a colourless odourless inert gas used in fluorescent lamps, photographic flash tubes, and lasers.

xenophobia *n* intense fear or dislike of foreigners or strangers. ○ **xenophobe** *n*. ○ **xenophobic** *adj*.

xerography /zɪə'rɒgrəfi/ *n* an electrostatic printing process used to make photocopies of printed documents or illustrations. ○ **xerographic** *adj*.

Xerox /'zɪərɒks/ *n*, *trademark* **1** a type of xerographic process. **2** a copying-machine using this process. **3** a photocopy made by such a process. ➤ *vb* (*usu* **xerox**) to photocopy something using this process.

Xmas /'ɛksməs, 'krɪsməs/ *n*, *colloq* Christmas.

X-ray *n* **1** an electromagnetic ray which can pass through many substances that are opaque to light, producing on photographic film an image of the object passed through. **2** a photograph taken using X-rays. **3** a medical examination using X-rays. ➤ *vb* to take a photograph of something using X-rays.

X-ray diffraction *n*, *chem* the characteristic interference pattern produced when X-rays are passed through a crystal, often used to determine the arrangement of atoms within crystals.

xylem /'zaɪləm/ *n*, *bot* the woody tissue that transports water and mineral nutrients from the roots to all other parts of a plant.

xylene /'zaɪliːn/ or **xylol** /'zaɪlɒl/ *n*, *chem* a colourless liquid hydrocarbon obtained from coal tar, etc, and used as a solvent and in the manufacture of organic chemical compounds.

xylophone /'zaɪloʊfoʊn/ *n* a musical instrument consisting of a series of bars of different lengths, played by being struck with wooden hammers. ○ **xylophonist** /zaɪ'lɒfənɪst/ *n*.

Yy

Y¹ or **y** *n* (**Ys**, **Y's** or **y's**) the twenty-fifth letter of the English alphabet.

Y² *abbrev* yen.

Y³ *symbol* **1** *chem* yttrium. **2** *math* (*usu* **y**) the second of two or three unknown quantities. Compare X^2, Z^2.

yacht /jɒt/ *n* a boat or small ship, usu with sails and often with an engine, built for racing or cruising. ○ **yachting** *n*, *adj*.

yachtsman or **yachtswoman** *n* a person who sails a yacht.

yack or **yak** *derog slang*, *vb* (**yacked, yacking; yakked, yakking**) *intr* to talk at length and often foolishly or annoyingly. ➤ *n* persistent, foolish or annoying chatter.

yah *exclam* **1** expressing scorn or contempt. **2** *colloq* often attributed to an upper-class speaker: yes.

yahoo¹ /jɑː'huː/ *n* a lout or ruffian.

yahoo² /jɑː'huː, jə'huː/ *exclam* expressing happiness, excitement, etc.

yak¹ *n* (**yaks** or **yak**) a large ox-like Tibetan mammal with a thick shaggy black coat.

yak² see YACK

yakked or **yakking** see under YACK

Yale lock *n*, *trademark* a type of lock operated by a flat key with a notched upper edge (a **Yale key**).

yam *n* **1** a climbing plant cultivated in tropical regions for its edible tubers. **2** the thick starchy tuber of this plant. **3** *N Am* a sweet potato.

yammer *vb* **1** *intr* to complain whiningly. **2** *intr* to talk loudly and at length. **3** to say something, esp as a complaint, loudly and at length. ➤ *n* the act or sound of yammering.

yang see under YIN

Yank *n*, *colloq* a person from the US.

yank *colloq*, *n* a sudden sharp pull. ➤ *vb*, *tr & intr* to pull suddenly and sharply.

Yankee *n* **1** *Brit colloq* a person from the US. **2** *N Am* a person from New England or from any of the northern states of America.

yap *vb* (**yapped, yapping**) *intr* **1** eg, of a small dog: to give a high-pitched bark. **2** *derog, colloq* of a person: to talk continually in a shrill voice, often about trivial matters. ➤ *n* a short high-pitched bark. ○ **yappy** *adj* (**-ier, -iest**)

yard¹ *n* **1** in the imperial system: a unit of length equal to 3 feet (0.9144m). **2** *naut* a long beam hung on a mast, from which to hang a sail.

yard² *n* **1** *often in compounds* an area of enclosed ground associated with a building. **2** an area of enclosed ground used for a special industrial purpose. **3** *N Am* a garden.

yardarm *n*, *naut* either of the tapering end-sections of a YARD¹ (sense 2).

yardstick *n* **1** a standard for comparison. **2** a stick exactly one yard long, used for measuring.

yarmulka or **yarmulke** /'jɑːməlkə/ *n* a skull-cap worn by Jewish men.

yarn *n* **1** thread spun from wool, cotton, etc. **2** a story or tale, often a lengthy and incredible one. **3** *colloq* a lie.

yarrow *n* a creeping plant with finely divided aromatic leaves and white or pink flower heads.

yashmak *n* a veil worn by Muslim women that covers the face below the eyes.

yaw *vb*, *intr* **1** of a ship: to move temporarily from, or fail to keep to, the direct line of its course. **2** of an aircraft: to deviate horizontally from the direct line of its course. ➤ *n* an act of yawing.

yawl *n* **1** a type of small sailing-boat, esp one with two masts. **2** a ship's small boat.

yawn *vb, intr* **1** to open one's mouth wide and take a deep involuntary breath when tired or bored. **2** of a hole, gap, etc: to be or become wide open. ➤ *n* **1** an act or an instance of yawning. **2** *colloq* a boring or tiresome event, person, etc.

yaws *sing n, pathol* an infectious skin disease of tropical countries, characterized by red ulcerating sores.

Yb *symbol, chem* ytterbium.

Y-chromosome *n, biol* the smaller of the two sex chromosomes, whose presence determines the male sex in most animals.

yd *abbrev* yard.

ye¹ *pron, archaic or dialect* you (pl).

ye² *definite article, old or affected use* the: *Ye Olde Englishe Tea Shoppe.*

yea /jeɪ/ *formal or old use, exclam* yes. ➤ *n* a positive reply or vote.

yeah /jɛ, jɛə/ *exclam, colloq* yes.

year *n* **1 a** the period of time the Earth takes to go once round the Sun, about 365¼ days; **b** the equivalent time for any other planet. **2** (*also* **calendar year**) the period between 1 January and 31 December, 365 days in a normal year, 366 days in a leap year. **3** any period of twelve months. **4** a period of less than 12 months during which some activity is carried on: *an academic year.* **5** a period of study at school, college, etc over an academic year: *She's in her third year now.* **6** students at a particular stage in their studies, considered as a group: *She had a meeting with the third year this morning.* ♦ **year in, year out** happening, done, etc every year, with tedious regularity.

yearbook *n* a book of information updated and published every year.

yearling *n* an animal which is a year old.

yearly *adj* **1** happening, etc every year. **2** valid for one year. ➤ *adv* every year.

yearn *vb, intr* **1** (**yearn for** or **after sth** or **to do sth**) to feel a great desire for it. **2** to feel compassion. ○ **yearning** *n, adj.*

years *pl n* **1** age: *He is wise for his years.* **2** *colloq* a very long time: *She's been coming for years.* **3** some period of time in the past or future: *in years gone by.*

yeast *n* any of various single-celled fungi that are capable of fermenting carbohydrates, widely used in the brewing and baking industries.

yell *n* a loud shout or cry. ➤ *vb, tr & intr* to shout or cry out.

yellow *adj* **1** of the colour of gold, butter, egg-yolk, a lemon, etc. **2** *derog, colloq* cowardly. **3** *often offensive* when used as a term of racial description: having a yellow or yellowish skin. ➤ *n* **1** any shade of the colour of gold, butter, egg-yolk, etc. **2** something, eg material or paint, that is yellow in colour. ➤ *vb, tr & intr* to make or become yellow. ○ **yellowness** *n.* ○ **yellowy** *adj.*

yellow-belly *slang, n* a coward. ○ **yellow-bellied** *adj.*

yellow card *n, football* a yellow-coloured card shown by the referee as a warning to a player being cautioned for a serious violation of the rules.

yellow fever *n, pathol* an acute viral disease, transmitted by the bite of a mosquito and causing high fever, jaundice and haemorrhaging.

yellowhammer *n* a large brightly-coloured bunting with a yellow head and underparts.

Yellow Pages *pl n, trademark* a telephone directory, or a section of one, printed on yellow paper, in which entries are classified according to the nature of the trade or profession of the individuals or companies listed.

yelp *vb, intr* of a dog, etc: to give a sharp sudden cry. ➤ *n* such a cry.

yen¹ *n* (*pl* **yen**) the standard unit of currency of Japan.

yen² *colloq, n* a desire. ➤ *vb* (**yenned, yenning**) *intr* (*usu* **yen for sth**) to feel a longing or craving for it.

yeoman /ˈjoʊmən/ *n* (**yeomen**) **1** *hist* a farmer who owned and worked his own land. **2** *mil* a member of the YEOMANRY (sense 2).

yeoman of the guard *n* a member of the oldest corps of the British sovereign's personal bodyguard.

yeomanry /ˈjoʊmənrɪ/ *n* (*-ies*) **1** *hist* the class of land-owning farmers. **2** a former volunteer cavalry force formed in the 18c.

yep *exclam, colloq* yes.

yes *exclam* used to express agreement or consent. ➤ *n* (**yesses**) an expression of agreement or consent.

yes-man *n, derog* someone who always agrees with the opinions and follows the suggestions of a superior, employer, etc.

yesterday *n* **1** the day before today. **2** *often in pl* the recent past. ➤ *adv* **1** on the day before today. **2** in the recent past.

yesteryear *n, literary* **1** the past in general. **2** last year.

yet *adv* **1** (*also* **as yet**) up till now or then; by now or by that time: *He had not yet arrived.* **2** at this time; now: *You can't leave yet.* **3** at some time in the future; before the matter is finished: *She may yet make a success of it.* **4** even; still: *yet another mistake.* ➤ *conj* however; nevertheless. ♦ **yet again** once more.

yeti *n* an ape-like creature supposed to live in the Himalayas. Also called **abominable snowman.**

yew *n* **1** a cone-bearing evergreen tree with reddish-brown flaky bark and narrow leaves. **2** the hard close-grained reddish-brown wood of this tree.

Y-fronts *pl n* men's or boys' underpants with a Y-shaped front seam.

Yid or **yid** *n, offensive* a Jew.

Yiddish *n* a language spoken by many Jews, based on medieval German, with elements from HEBREW and other languages. ➤ *adj* consisting of, or spoken or written in, this language.

yield vb **1** to produce (an animal product such as meat or milk, or a crop). **2** finance to give or produce (interest, etc). **3** to produce (a specified quantity of a natural or financial product). **4** tr & intr to give up or give in; to surrender. **5** intr to break or give way under force or pressure. ➤ n **1** the amount produced. **2** the total amount of a product produced by an animal or plant, or harvested from a certain area of cultivated land. **3** finance the return from an investment or tax.

yielding adj **1** submissive. **2** flexible. **3** able or tending to give way.

yin n in traditional Chinese philosophy, religion, medicine, etc: one of the two opposing and complementary principles, being the negative, feminine, dark, cold and passive element or force (as opposed to the positive, masculine, light, warm and active **yang**).

yippee exclam, colloq expressing excitement, delight, etc.

YMCA abbrev Young Men's Christian Association, a charity providing accommodation and other services, orig for young men and boys, but increasingly now for both sexes. Compare YWCA. ➤ n a hostel run by the YMCA.

yo exclam **1** used to call someone's attention. **2** used as a greeting. **3** esp US used in answer to a call: present; here.

yob or **yobbo** n, slang a bad-mannered aggressive young person (usu male). ○ **yobbish** adj. ○ **yobbishness** n.

yodel vb (**yodelled, yodelling**) tr & intr to sing (a melody, etc), changing frequently from a normal to a falsetto voice and back again. ➤ n an act of yodelling. ○ **yodeller** n. ○ **yodelling** n.

yoga n **1** a system of Hindu philosophy showing how to free the soul from reincarnation and reunite it with God. **2** any of several systems of physical and mental discipline based on this, esp (in Western countries) a particular system of physical exercises. ○ **yogic** adj.

yoghurt, yogurt or **yoghourt** n a type of semi-liquid food made from fermented milk, often flavoured with fruit.

yogi n a person who practises the philosophy of YOGA.

yoke n **1** a wooden frame placed over the necks of oxen to hold them together when they are pulling a plough, cart, etc. **2** a frame placed across a person's shoulders, for carrying buckets. **3** something oppressive; a great burden: the yoke of slavery. **4** dressmaking, etc the part of a garment that fits over the shoulders and round the neck. **5** a pair of animals, esp oxen. ➤ vb (always **yoke sth to sth else** or **yoke two things together**) **1** to join them under or with a YOKE (sense 1). **2** to join or unite them.

> **yoke, yolk** These words are sometimes confused with each other.

yokel n, derog an unsophisticated country-dweller.

yolk n **1** in the eggs of birds and some reptiles: the yellow spherical mass of nutritive material. **2** cookery, etc this yellow part of an egg, as distinct from the WHITE (sense 4).

Yom Kippur n an annual Jewish religious festival devoted to repentance for past sins, and celebrated with fasting and prayer. Also called **Day of Atonement**.

yonder adv in or at that place over there. ➤ adj situated over there.

yonks n, colloq a long time.

yoo-hoo exclam, colloq used to attract someone's attention.

yore n, literary or archaic times past or long ago.

yorker n, cricket a ball aimed to pitch directly under the bat.

Yorkist hist, n a supporter of the House of York in the Wars of the Roses. Compare LANCASTRIAN. ➤ adj relating to the House of York.

Yorkshire pudding n a baked pudding of unsweetened batter, traditionally served with roast beef.

you pron **1** the person or people, etc spoken or written to, with or without emphasis: When are you all coming to visit us? **2** any or every person: You don't often see that nowadays.

you'd contraction **1** you would. **2** you had.

you'll contraction **1** you will. **2** you shall.

young adj **1** in the first part of life, growth, development, etc; not old. **2** in the early stages: The night is young.

youngster n, colloq a young person.

your adj belonging to you.

you're contraction you are.

yours pron **1** something belonging to you. **2** (also **yours faithfully, sincerely** or **truly**) conventional expressions written before a signature at the end of a letter.

yourself pron (pl **yourselves**) **1** the reflexive form of YOU. **2** used for emphasis: Are you coming yourself? **3** your normal self: You don't seem yourself this morning. **4** (also **by yourself**) alone; without help.

yours truly pron, colloq used to refer to oneself, esp with irony or affected condescension: Yours had to fetch it.

youth sing n **1** the state, quality or fact of being young. **2** the early part of life, often specifically that between childhood and adulthood. **3** the enthusiasm, rashness, etc associated with people in this period of life. **4** (**youths**) a boy or young man. **5** (sing or pl noun) young people in general: the youth of today.

youth club n a place or organization providing leisure activities for young people.

youthful adj **1** young, esp in manner or appearance. **2** of someone who is not young: young-looking, or having the energy, enthusiasm, etc of a young person. ○ **youthfulness** n.

youth hostel n a hostel providing simple and

inexpensive overnight accommodation.

you've *contraction* you have.

yowl *vb, intr* esp of an animal: to howl or cry sadly. ➤ *n* such a howl.

yo-yo *n* a toy consisting of a pair of wooden, metal or plastic discs joined at their centre, and with a piece of string attached, the toy being repeatedly made to unwind from the string by the force of its weight and rewind by its momentum. ➤ *vb* (**yo-yoed**) *intr* to fluctuate repeatedly in any way.

yr *abbrev* **1** year. **2** younger. **3** your.

yrs *abbrev* years.

ytterbium /ɪˈtɜːbɪəm/ *n, chem* a soft silvery lustrous metallic element used in lasers, and for making steel and other alloys.

yttrium /ˈɪtrɪəm/ *n, chem* a silvery-grey metallic element used in alloys to make superconductors and strong permanent magnets.

yuan /juˈɑːn/ *n* (*pl* **yuan**) the standard unit of currency of the People's Republic of China.

yucca *n* a tropical and subtropical American plant with a short thick trunk, stiff narrow sword-shaped leaves and waxy white bell-shaped flowers.

yuck or **yuk** *colloq, n* a disgusting mess; filth. ➤ *exclam* expressing disgust or distaste. ○ **yucky** or **yukky** *adj* (*-ier, -iest*).

Yule *n, old, literary & dialect* Christmas.

yummy *adj* (*-ier, -iest*) *colloq* delicious.

yum-yum *exclam* expressing delight at or appreciative anticipation of something, esp delicious food.

yuppie or **yuppy** *n* (*-ies*) *derog, colloq* an ambitious young professional person.

YWCA *abbrev* Young Women's Christian Association. Compare YMCA. ➤ *n* a hostel run by the YWCA.

Zz

Z¹ or **z** *n* (**Zs, Z's** or **z's**) the twenty-sixth and last letter of the English alphabet.

Z² *symbol, maths* (*usu* **z**) the third of three unknown quantities. Compare X^2, Y^3.

Z³ *symbol,* **1** *chem* atomic number. **2** *physics* impedance.

zabaglione /zabalˈjoʊnɪ/ *n, cookery* a dessert made from egg-yolks, sugar and wine, whisked together over a gentle heat.

zany /ˈzeɪnɪ/ *adj* (*-ier, -iest*) amusingly crazy.

zap *vb* (**zapped, zapping**) *colloq* **1** to hit, destroy or shoot something, esp suddenly. **2** *comput* to delete all the data in (a file) or from (the main memory of a computer). **3** *intr* to change TV channels frequently using a remote-control device. **4** *tr & intr* to move quickly or suddenly.

zeal *n* great, and sometimes excessive, enthusiasm.

zealot /ˈzɛlət/ *n often derog* a single-minded and determined supporter of a cause. ○ **zealotry** *n*.

zealous /ˈzɛləs/ *adj* enthusiastic; keen. ○ **zealously** *adv.* ○ **zealousness** *n*.

zebra *n* (**zebras** or **zebra**) a stocky black-and-white striped African mammal with a stubby mane, related to the horse.

zebra crossing *n, Brit* a pedestrian crossing marked by black and white stripes on the road.

zed *n, Brit* **1** the name of the letter Z. **2** (**zeds**) *slang* sleep.

zee *n, N Am* the name of the letter Z.

Zeitgeist /ˈzaɪtgaɪst/ *n* (*also* **zeitgeist**) the spirit of the age; the attitudes of a specific period.

Zen or **Zen Buddhism** *n* a school of Buddhism which stresses the personal experience of enlightenment based on a simple way of life,

close to nature, and simple methods of meditation.

zenith *n* **1** *astron* the point on the celestial sphere directly above the observer. **2** the highest point.

zephyr /ˈzɛfə(r)/ *n, literary* a light gentle breeze.

zeppelin or **Zeppelin** *n* a cigar-shaped airship.

zero *n* **1** the number, figure or symbol 0. **2** the point on a scale which is taken as the base from which measurements may be made: *5 degrees below zero.* ➤ *adj* **1** being of no measurable size. **2** *colloq* not any; no: *She has zero confidence.* ➤ *vb* (**zeroes, zeroed**) to set or adjust something to zero. ◊ **zero in on sth** to aim for it; to move towards it.

zero hour *n* the exact time fixed for something to happen.

zest *n* **1** keen enjoyment; enthusiasm. **2** something that adds to one's enjoyment of something. **3** *cookery* the coloured outer layer of the peel of an orange or lemon, or the oil contained in it, used for flavouring. **4** piquancy; agreeably sharp flavour. ○ **zestful** *adj*.

zigzag *n* **1** (*usu* **zigzags**) two or more sharp bends to alternate sides in a path, etc. **2** a path, road, etc with a number of such bends. ➤ *adj* **1** having sharp bends to alternate sides. **2** bent from side to side alternately. ➤ *vb* (**zigzagged, zigzagging**) *intr* to move in a zigzag direction. ➤ *adv* in a zigzag direction or manner.

zilch *n, slang* nothing.

zillion *n, colloq* a very large but unspecified number.

Zimmer or **Zimmer frame** *n, trademark* a

tubular metal frame, used as a support for walking by the disabled or infirm.

zinc *n, chem* a brittle bluish-white metallic element used in dry batteries and various alloys, and as a corrosion-resistant coating to galvanize steel.

zinc oxide *n* a white crystalline solid, widely used as an antiseptic and astringent in skin ointments, and as a pigment in paints, plastics and ceramics.

zing *n* **1** a short high-pitched humming sound, eg that made by a bullet or vibrating string. **2** *colloq* zest or vitality. ➤ *vb, intr* to move very quickly, esp while making a high-pitched hum.

zinnia *n* a plant, native to Mexico and S America, with brightly coloured daisy-like flower heads.

Zionism *n* the movement which worked for the establishment of a national homeland in Palestine for Jews and now supports the state of Israel. ○ **Zionist** *n, adj*.

zip[1] *n* **1** a ZIP FASTENER. **2** *colloq* energy; vitality. ➤ *vb* (*zipped, zipping*) **1** *tr & intr* (*also zip up*) to fasten, or be fastened, with a zip fastener. **2** *intr* to make, or move with, a whizzing sound. **3** *comput* to convert (a file, etc) into a compressed form in order to save storage space.

zip[2] *n, US slang* zero; nothing.

zip code *n* in the US: a postal code.

zip fastener *n* a device for fastening clothes, etc, in which two rows of metal or nylon teeth are made to fit into each other when a sliding tab is pulled along them.

zipper *N Am, n* a zip fastener. ➤ *vb* to fasten with a zipper.

zippy *adj* (*-ier, -iest*) *colloq* lively; quick.

zircon *n, geol* a hard mineral form of zirconium silicate, which is the main ore of zirconium.

zirconium *n, chem* a silvery-grey metallic element that is resistant to corrosion.

zit *n, slang* a pimple.

zither *n* a musical instrument consisting of a flat wooden box, one section of which has frets on it, over which strings are stretched.

zloty /ˈzlɒtɪ/ *n* (*zloty* or *zlotys*) the standard unit of currency of Poland.

Zn *symbol, chem* zinc.

zodiac *n* **1** (**the zodiac**) *astron* the band of sky that extends 8° on either side of the Sun's ECLIPTIC, divided into 12 equal parts, each of which once contained one of the zodiacal constellations, though some no longer do. **2** *astrol* a chart or diagram (usu a circular one), representing this band of sky and the **signs of the zodiac** contained within it. ○ **zodiacal** /zəʊ-ˈdaɪəkəl/ *adj*.

zombie or **zombi** *n* (*zombies* or *zombis*) **1** *derog, colloq* a slow-moving, stupid, unresponsive or apathetic person. **2** a corpse brought to life again by magic.

zone *n* **1** an area or region of a country, town, etc, esp one marked out for a special purpose or by a particular feature. **2** *geog* any of the five horizontal bands into which the Earth's surface is divided by the Arctic Circle, the Tropic of Cancer, the Tropic of Capricorn and the Antarctic Circle. ➤ *vb* **1** (*also* **zone sth off**) to divide it into zones; to mark it as a zone. **2** to assign to a particular zone. ○ **zonal** *adj*.

zonk *vb, colloq* to hit with a sharp or firm impact. ◊ **zonk out** *tr & intr* to collapse or make someone collapse into unconsciousness or in exhaustion.

zoo *n* a garden or park where wild animals are kept for the purpose of study, breeding of rare species for conservation, etc, and where they are usually on show to the public.

zoological garden *n, formal* a ZOO.

zoology /zʊˈɒlədʒɪ, zəʊ-/ *n* the scientific study of animals, including their structure, function, behaviour, ecology, evolution and classification. ○ **zoological** *adj*. ○ **zoologist** *n*.

zoom *vb* **1** *tr & intr* (*often* **zoom over, past,** *etc*) to move or cause something to move very quickly, making a loud low-pitched buzzing noise. **2** *intr* (*usu* **zoom off,** *etc*) to move very quickly. ◊ **zoom in on sb** or **sth** of a camera or its operator: to close up on somebody or something using a zoom lens.

zoom lens *n* a type of camera lens which can be used to make a distant object appear gradually closer or further away without the camera being moved.

zoophyte /ˈzəʊəfaɪt/ *n, zool* any of various invertebrate animals which resemble plants, such as sponges, corals and sea anemones.

Zoroastrianism *n* an ancient religion of Persian origin founded or reformed by Zoroaster (c.630–c.553BC), which teaches the existence of two continuously opposed divine beings, one good and the other evil. ○ **Zoroastrian** *n, adj*.

Zr *symbol* zirconium.

zucchini /zʊˈkiːnɪ/ *n* (*zucchini* or *zucchinis*) *esp N Am & Aust* a courgette.

Zulu *n* (*Zulu* or *Zulus*) **1** a Bantu people of S Africa. **2** an individual belonging to this people. **3** their language. ➤ *adj* belonging or relating to this people or their language.

zygote *n, biol* the cell that is formed as a result of the fertilization of a female gamete by a male gamete. ○ **zygotic** *adj*.

Some interesting word histories

alphabet From *alpha* and *beta*, the first two Greek letters

arena From a Latin word meaning 'sand', after the sand-covered areas in which Roman gladiators fought

armadillo From a Spanish word meaning 'armed man', because of the animal's weapon-like plates

assassin From an Arabic word meaning 'hashish eater', after an Islamic sect during the Crusades who took the drug before assassinating Christians

atlas After a mythological giant called *Atlas*, who was pictured on early books of maps supporting the heavens on his shoulders

balaclava After the battle of *Balaklava* in 1854, during the Crimean War, when such headgear was first worn

barbecue From a Haitian creole term for a wooden grid or frame

bedlam After St Mary of *Bethlehem* Hospital, a former mental asylum in London

bikini Named after the atomic test site of *Bikini* Atoll in the Pacific Ocean, because of the swimming costume's supposedly 'explosive' effect on men

boffin Said to come from a scientist who gave his colleagues nicknames from characters in the novels of Charles Dickens. Mr Boffin is a character in *Our Mutual Friend*

boycott After Charles *Boycott*, a British estate manager ostracized by the Irish Land League in the 19th century

budget Originally a small bag; the parliamentary sense of *budget* stems from an insult directed at Robert Walpole implying he was a quack or pedlar

bumf Originally short for 'bum-fodder', *ie* toilet paper

bunkum From *Buncombe* county in North Carolina, whose representative once gave a rambling speech in Congress

bureau A French word which comes from *burel*, a type of coarse cloth which was used as a cover for writing tables

calculate Based on a Latin word meaning 'stone', from the use of stones as an aid in mathematics

calico Originally *Calicut cloth*, after the port in SW India from where it was exported

candidate From a Latin word meaning 'dressed in white', because of the white togas worn by electoral candidates in ancient Rome

canter Originally *Canterbury gallop*, referring to the pace at which medieval pilgrims rode to the town

caprice Originally meaning 'horror', from an Italian word which translates as 'hedgehog head'

cardigan Named after the 19th-century Earl of *Cardigan*, who advocated the use of buttonable woollen jackets

castanets From a Spanish word for 'chestnuts', because of their shape

caterpillar Based on a Latin phrase which translates as 'hairy cat'

chauvinism After Nicolas *Chauvin*, a French soldier and keen patriot during the time of Napoleon

chopsticks Literally 'quick sticks', from Pidgin English *chop* for 'quick'

cockney Literally 'cock's egg', an old word for a misshapen egg, which was later applied to an effeminate person, and so to a soft-living city-dweller

coconut Based on a Portuguese word meaning 'grimace', because of the resemblance of the three holes on the base of the fruit to a human face

cravat From a French word for 'Croat', because of the linen neckbands worn by 17th-century Croatian soldiers

criss-cross Based on the phrase *Christ's cross*

dahlia Named after Anders *Dahl*, an 18th-century Swedish botanist

daisy Literally 'day's eye', so called because of its opening during the day

dandelion From the French phrase *dent de lion*, meaning 'lion's tooth'

deadline Originally a line in a military prison. The penalty for crossing it was death

decimate Literally meaning 'reduce by a tenth'

delta From the fourth letter of the Greek alphabet, which was triangular in shape

denim From the French phrase *de Nîmes*, meaning 'from Nîmes', the town in the south of France where the fabric was first manufactured

denouement From a French word literally meaning 'untying' or 'unravelling'

dinosaur Coined in the 19th century, from Greek words which translate as 'terrible lizard'

diploma From a Greek word meaning a letter folded double

dismal Based on a Latin phrase *dies mali*, meaning 'evil days', referring to two days each month which were believed to be unusually unlucky

doily Originally a light summer fabric, named after *Doily*'s drapery shop in 17th-century London

doldrums The *doldrums* take their name from an area of the ocean about the equator famous for calms and variable winds

dollar From a shortened form of *Joachimsthaler*, the name of a silver coin produced at Joachimsthal in what is now the Czech Republic

dunce Originally a term of abuse applied to followers of the medieval Scottish philosopher, John *Duns Scotus*

éclair From a French word meaning literally 'lightning', perhaps because it is eaten quickly

equator From a Latin word meaning literally 'something that makes equal', because night and day are of equal length there

ermine From *Armenia*, because the ermine was known to the Romans as the 'Armenian mouse'

exchequer From the chequered cloth formerly used on the tables of tax offices, and on which accounts were recorded

farce Based on a French word meaning 'stuffing', after humorous scenes which were performed in between the acts of a play

fascism From the *fasces*, a bundle of rods with an axe in the middle, carried before magistrates in ancient Rome to symbolize their power to inflict punishment

fez Named after the city of *Fez* in Morocco, where such hats were made

fiasco Based on an Italian phrase *far fiasco*, literally 'make a bottle', meaning to forget your lines on stage

foolscap Referring to the original watermark used on this size of paper, showing a jester's cap and bells

freelance Originally referring to a medieval knight who would fight for anyone who paid him

Frisbee® Based on the name of the *Frisbie* bakery in Connecticut, whose lightweight pie tins inspired the invention

galore Based on an Irish Gaelic phrase *go leor*, meaning 'sufficient'

gamut From the name of a medieval 6-note musical scale, two notes of which were *gamma* and *ut*

garble Originally meaning 'sift', which gradually developed into the sense of confusing by leaving out too much

gargantuan After *Gargantua*, a giant with an enormous appetite in a 16th-century French novel by Rabelais

gerrymander After US governor, Elbridge *Gerry*, who rearranged the map of Massachusetts in 1811 to a shape resembling that of a sala*mander*

gorilla The *Gorillai* were a tribe of hairy women in ancient times

grenade From a French word for 'pomegranate', because of its shape

groggy Originally meaning 'drunk', from *grog*, a mixture of rum and water

guillotine Named after Joseph *Guillotin*, a French doctor who recommended its use for executions during the French Revolution

gung-ho Based on a Chinese phrase meaning 'work together'

gymkhana From a Hindi expression *gend-khana*, meaning 'racket-court'

Gypsy Based on *Egyptian*, because of the belief that the Romany people came originally from Egypt

haggard Originally a falconer's term for an untamed hawk

halcyon From the Greek word for 'kingfisher' in the phrase 'kingfisher days', a period of calm weather in mid-winter

handicap Originally a gambling game in which wagers were drawn by *hand* from a *cap*

helicopter A coinage based on Greek words meaning 'spiral wing'

hippopotamus Based on a Greek word which translates as 'river horse'

hobby Originally *hobby-horse*, a horse used in morris dances and therefore for amusement or pleasure

hoi polloi Taken from a Greek phrase for 'the people'

hubbub Originally meaning 'battle' or 'war cry', based on an Irish Gaelic word

hysteria Based on a Greek word for 'womb', because hysteria was originally thought to be caused by a disorder of the womb

insulin Based on the Latin word for 'island', because insulin is secreted by cells called the *islets* of Langerhans

intoxicate Literally, to affect with arrow-poison

jeopardy Originally a gambling term, based on the French *jeu parti* meaning 'even chance'

jodhpurs Named after *Jodhpur* in India

jubilee From a Hebrew word for 'ram's horn', which was blown to announce the start of a celebratory Jewish year

juggernaut From a Hindi word for a large wagon used to carry the image of the god Krishna in religious processions

ketchup Originally spelt *catsup*, as it still is in US English; based on a Chinese word for 'fish brine'

khaki From an Urdu word meaning 'dusty'

knickerbockers Named after Diedrich *Knickerbocker*, a fictional Dutchman invented by US author Washington Irving in the 19th century

kowtow Based on a Chinese phrase meaning to prostrate yourself before the emperor

lemur From a Latin word meaning 'ghost', because the animal has a thin, pale face and appears at night

leotard After Jules *Léotard*, a French trapeze artist who popularized it

lieutenant From a French word meaning literally 'holding a place'

limerick After *Limerick* in Ireland, the name of which was repeated in nonsense songs in an old Victorian parlour game

limousine Named after a type of cloak worn in *Limousin* in France, because the car's roof was supposedly similar in shape

Luddite Originally a group of protesters against the Industrial Revolution in the early 19th century, who based their name on Ned *Ludd*, an earlier opponent of machines for weaving stockings

lynch Named after William *Lynch*, a 19th-century Virginian planter who organized unofficial trials of suspected criminals

magpie Originally *maggot pie*, meaning 'pied Margaret'

mah-jong A Chinese expression literally meaning 'sparrows', thought to refer to the chattering sound which the little bricks make while the game is being played

malaria From an Italian phrase meaning 'bad air', malarial fever being originally thought to be caused by poisonous marsh gases

marathon After the distance run by a Greek soldier from *Marathon* to Athens with news of the victory over the Persians

masochism After Leopold von Sacher-*Masoch*, a 19th-century Austrian novelist

maudlin From Mary *Magdalene*, who was frequently depicted crying in religious paintings

maverick After Samuel *Maverick*, a Texas rancher who never branded his cattle

meander After the winding *Maeander* river in Turkey

mentor After *Mentor*, who guides Telemachus in his search for his father in Homer's poem *The Odyssey*

mesmerize An earlier term than *hypnotize*, the word comes from the name of the 18th-century Austrian doctor, Franz Anton *Mesmer*, who claimed to be able to cure disease through the influence of his will on patients

mews Originally a cage for hawks, *mews* took on its present meaning after royal stables were built in the 17th century on a site formerly used to house the king's hawks

money The Roman goddess Juno was known in ancient times as Juno *Moneta*, and it was in her temple in Rome that money was coined. This resulted in the word *moneta* being used first to mean 'a mint', and then the money which was made there

nemesis After *Nemesis*, who was the goddess of revenge in Greek mythology

nicotine Named after Jean *Nicot*, a 16th-century French ambassador who sent tobacco samples back from Portugal

nightmare The *-mare* ending comes from an old English word meaning 'evil spirit', nightmares being thought to be caused by an evil spirit pressing on the body

oboe From a French word *hautbois*, meaning literally 'high wood'

ombudsman From a Swedish word meaning 'administration man', introduced into English in the 1960s

omnibus A Latin word meaning 'for all', originally adopted in English to refer to a vehicle which could seat a large number of people

orang-utan Based on a Malay phrase which translates as 'wild man'

oscillate From the Latin *oscillum*, literally 'small face', referring to a mask of the god Bacchus which hung in Roman vineyards and swung to and fro in the wind

ostracize Based on *ostrakon*, a piece of pottery used in ancient Greece to cast votes to decide if someone was to be exiled

palace From the *Palatine* Hill in Rome, where the Roman emperors lived

panache Literally meaning 'a plume', from the use of feathers in flamboyant headgear

pandemonium The name of the capital of Hell in John Milton's poem *Paradise Lost* (1667)

pander After *Pandarus*, who acts as a go-between in the story of Troilus and Cressida

panic From a Greek word meaning 'fear of the god Pan'. Pan was said to roam about the woodland and scare people and animals

paparazzo After the name of a photographer in Federico Fellini's film *La Dolce Vita*

paraphernalia Originally a woman's property which was not part of her dowry, and which therefore remained her own after marriage

pariah Originally a member of a low caste in southern India

parole From French *parole* meaning 'word', because prisoners are released on their word of honour

pasteurize Named after Louis *Pasteur*, the 19th-century French chemist who invented the process

pedigree Literally 'crane's foot', because the lines of a family tree were thought to resemble the forked feet of the bird

piano A shortened form of *pianoforte*, which was formed from the Italian words for 'soft' and 'loud'

pidgin A distorted form of the word 'business', originally used in Chinese

posh Probably from a Romany word meaning 'a smart person', although many people think it stands for *Port Out, Starboard Home*, which represented the most desirable position of cabins for European passengers on ships travelling to Asia and back

psephology Based on a Greek word for 'pebble', because pebbles were used in ancient Greece to cast votes

quintessence Literally 'fifth essence', sought after by medieval alchemists as the highest essence or ether

regatta From the name of a gondola race held on the Grand Canal in Venice

rigmarole Originally *ragman roll*, a Scots term for a long list or catalogue

robot A word invented by Karl Capek, a Czech playwright, based on a Czech word meaning 'work'

rubric From a Latin word for red ink, originally an entry in a Biblical text written in red ink

rugby Named after *Rugby* School in Warwickshire, where the game was supposedly invented

sabotage From a French word meaning 'clog', popularly supposed to refer to a form of protest in which workers put their clogs into machines in order to stop them working

sadism Invented to describe the particular type of sexual cruelty which the 18th-century French author Marquis de *Sade* wrote about in his novels

salary Based on a Latin word for 'salt', from the money given to

Roman soldiers to buy salt

sandwich After the 18th-century Earl of *Sandwich*, said to have invented it to allow him to gamble without interruption for meals

saxophone After Adolfe *Sax*, who invented it in the 19th century

scapegoat Literally 'escape goat', after an ancient Jewish ritual of transferring the people's sins to a goat which was afterwards let free in the wilderness

serendipity After a fairy story called *The Three Princes of Serendip*, in which the heroes were always making lucky discoveries. Serendip was an old name for Sri Lanka

shambles Originally meaning a place where animals were slaughtered

shrapnel After Henry *Shrapnel*, 18th-century British general who invented the shell

silhouette After the 18th-century French finance minister, Etienne de *Silhouette*, although the precise reason is uncertain

slapstick After the name of a theatrical device which made a loud noise when an actor was hit with it

snob Originally a slang term for 'shoemaker' which changed its meaning to someone of low social class, and later to someone who enjoys showing off their wealth and social standing

spa After the town of *Spa* in Belgium, which was famous for its healthy spring water

stationer In Medieval Latin, a *stationarius* was a tradesman, usually a bookseller, who did not travel from place to place, but had a regular station or a permanent shop

sterling So called after the image of a small star that was impressed on medieval silver pennies

stymie Originally a golfing term for an opponent's ball in the way of your own

supercilious Based on a Latin word meaning 'eyebrow', from the habit of raising the eyebrows to show scorn or superiority

sushi A Japanese word meaning literally 'it is sour'

tabloid Originally a trademark for a medicine in tablet form, and then, by association, the name for a small-sized newspaper giving information in concentrated form

tangerine Originally meaning 'from Tangiers', the port in Morocco from where the fruit was exported in the 19th century

tattoo From a Dutch term meaning to shut off beer taps at closing time, later applied to a military drumbeat at the end of the day

taunt Originally a phrase *taunt for taunt*, based on the French *tant pour tant* meaning 'tit for tat'

tawdry From *St Audrey's lace*, once used to make cheap lace neckties. The lace was sold at fairs held on the feast of St Audrey on 17 October

teddy bear Named after the American President *Teddy* Roosevelt, who was well-known as a bear hunter

thespian Named after *Thespis*, the reputed founder of ancient Greek tragedy

thyroid Based on a Greek word meaning 'door-shaped', because of the shape of the cartilage in the front of the throat

Tory Originally one of a group of Irish Catholics thrown off their land who waged guerrilla war on British settlers, later applied to any royalist supporter

trilby So called because a hat of this shape was worn by an actress in the original stage version of George du Maurier's novel, *Trilby* (1894)

tulip Based on a Persian word for 'turban', because of the similarity in shape

turquoise Literally 'Turkish stone', because first found in Turkestan

tycoon Based on a Japanese title for a warlord

ukulele A Hawaiian word meaning literally 'jumping flea'

umbrella Literally 'little shadow' and originally used to refer to a sunshade

umpteen Originally *umpty*, a signaller's slang term for a dash in Morse code

urchin Originally meaning 'hedgehog', the prickly sense of which survives in *sea urchin*

utopia Literally 'no place', coined by Thomas More for his fictional book *Utopia* (1516)

vandal After the *Vandals*, a German tribe who invaded and destroyed Rome in the 5th century

ventriloquist Literally 'stomach speaker' and originally meaning someone possessed by a talking evil spirit

veto Latin for 'I forbid', a phrase originally used by people's tribunes in ancient Rome when objecting to proposals

volcano Named after *Vulcan*, the Roman god of fire

walrus A Dutch word meaning literally 'whale horse'

whisky Based on Scottish Gaelic *uisge beatha*, meaning 'water of life'

Yank or **Yankee** Originally a nickname for Dutch settlers in New England in the 18th century, possibly because of the Dutch forename *Jan*

zany After the name of a clownish character in Italian comic drama

zodiac From Greek, meaning literally 'circle of animals'